CANADA

ESOTA
ESABI RANGE
Duluth
Isle Royale
Lake Superior
MAINE
Augusta
Lake Champlain
Montpelier
Portland

WISCONSIN
MICHIGAN
Lake Huron
ADIRONDACK MTS.
VT.
N.H.
Concord
Manchester

Minneapolis
St. Paul
Madison
Milwaukee
Grand Rapids
Lansing
Flint
Detroit
Lake Ontario
Buffalo
Rochester
Albany
MASS.
Springfield
Boston
Providence
Cape Cod

OWA
Cedar Rapids
Chicago
Toledo
Cleveland
Lake Erie
NEW YORK
Finger Lakes
Hartford
CONN.
R.I.
Long Island Sound
Long Island

PENNSYLVANIA
Harrisburg
Pittsburgh
Newark
New York City
Trenton
N.J.

Peoria
ILLINOIS
Springfield
INDIANA
Indianapolis
OHIO
Columbus
Cincinnati
Philadelphia
DELAWARE
Dover

St. Louis
Jefferson City
Louisville
Frankfort
Lexington
WEST VIRGINIA
Charleston
Baltimore
MD.
Annapolis
Washington, DC
Delaware Bay

PLAINS
MISSOURI
Lake of the Ozarks
PLATEAU
KENTUCKY
VIRGINIA
Richmond
James River
Norfolk
Chesapeake Bay

Lake Barkley
Kentucky Lake
Nashville
Knoxville
Cumberland River
CUMBERLAND PLATEAU
GREAT SMOKY MTS.
Roanoke River
Pamlico Sound
Cape Hatteras

ARKANSAS
ITA
Little Rock
Memphis
TENNESSEE
Chattanooga
Tennessee River
Winston-Salem
Raleigh
NORTH CAROLINA
Charlotte
SOUTH CAROLINA
Columbia

White River
MISSISSIPPI
Birmingham
ALABAMA
Montgomery
Atlanta
Macon
GEORGIA
Savannah
Charleston
Sea Islands

Shreveport
Jackson
Alabama R.
Chattahoochee River
Savannah River
Okefenokee Swamp

COASTAL
PLAIN
LOUISIANA
Baton Rouge
New Orleans
Chandeleur Islands
Mobile
Pensacola
Tallahassee
Jacksonville
FLORIDA

Mississippi Delta
Cape Canaveral

Gulf of Mexico
Tampa
St. Petersburg
Orlando
FLORIDA PENINSULA
Lake Okeechobee

Miami
THE BAHAMAS

The Everglades
Cape Sable
Florida Keys
Straits of Florida

ATLANTIC OCEAN

ATLANTIC COASTAL PLAIN

APPALACHIAN MOUNTAINS

St. Lawrence River
St. John River
45° N

⊛ National capital
★ State capital
• Other city

SCALE
0   250   500 Miles
0   250   500 Kilometers

CUBA

THE AMERICAN EXPERIMENT

A HISTORY OF THE UNITED STATES

Steven M. Gillon ★ **Cathy D. Matson**

University of Oklahoma *University of Delaware*

HOUGHTON MIFFLIN COMPANY ★ BOSTON NEW YORK

Editor-in-Chief: Jean Woy
Sponsoring Editor: Jeffrey Greene
Senior Development Editor: Jennifer E. Sutherland
Editorial Associate: Michael A. Kerns
Senior Project Editor: Rosemary R. Jaffe
Senior Production/Design Coordinator: Jill Haber
Senior Manufacturing Coordinator: Marie Barnes
Senior Marketing Manager: Sandra McGuire

Cover design: Martin Yeeles
Cover image: Torchlight Parade in Denver, Colorado, November 12, 1888, for the Benjamin Harrison Election, by R. Smellie. (Colorado Historical Society.)

Printed in the U.S.A.

Library of Congress Catalog Card Number: 00-133862

ISBN: 0-395-67751-3

1 2 3 4 5 6 7 8 9-DOC-05 04 03 02 01

Brief Contents

1 Out of Old Worlds, New Worlds   1

2 The First Experiments, 1540–1680   40

3 Imperial Connections, 1660–1748   82

4 Colonial Maturation and Conflict, 1680–1754   121

5 Forging the American Experiment, 1754–1775   161

6 Winning Independence, 1775–1783   199

7 The Federal Experiment, 1783–1800   242

8 Striving for Nationhood, 1800–1824   285

9 An Emerging Capitalist Nation, 1790–1820   322

10 Transforming the Political Culture, 1820–1840   363

11 Industry and Reform in the North, 1820–1850   404

12 Slavery and Plantation Culture, 1820–1850   445

13 The Westward Experiment, 1820–1850   485

14 The Sectional Challenge, 1848–1860   525

15 Transforming the Experiment: The Civil War, 1861–1865   563

16 Reconstruction and the New South, 1865–1900   607

17 Conquering the New West, 1862–1900   653

18 The Industrial Experiment, 1865–1900   693

19 The New Urban Nation, 1865–1900   727

20 State and Society, 1877–1900   764

21 The Progressive Era, 1889–1916   804

22 The Experiment in American Empire, 1865–1917   845

23 Making the World Safe for Democracy: America And World War I, 1914–1920   886

24 The New Era, 1920–1928   927

25 "Fear Itself": Crash, Depression, and the New Deal, 1929–1938   967

26 War and Society, 1933–1945   1008

27 The Cold War, 1945–1952   1050

28 The Consumer Society, 1945–1960   1091

29 Consensus and Confrontation, 1960–1968   1133

30 The Politics of Polarization, 1969–1979   1177

31 The Reagan Experiment, 1979–1988   1219

32 America After the Cold War, 1988–2000   1259

iii

Contents

Preface   xxiv

1 ⭐ **Out of Old Worlds, New Worlds**   1

The First Americans, to 1500   4
    Earliest North Americans   4
    North American Cultures   5
    Mesoamerican and South American Cultures   9

Old World Peoples in Africa and Europe, 1400–1600   12
    West African Cultures and Kingdoms   12
    Traditional European Societies   14

Europe's Internal Transformation, 1400–1600   17
    Agriculture and Commerce   17
    The Nation-State and the Renaissance, 1400–1600   20
    The Reformation, 1517–1563   22

Taking to the Seas, 1420–1600   24
    Portuguese Exploration and African Slavery   25
    Christopher Columbus   27
    The Spanish Century   29
    The Effects of Contact   31

CONCLUSION   34

Competing Voices: Interpreting the Cultures of Strangers   37

2 ⭐ **The First Experiments, 1540–1680**   40

Struggles for New World Dominion, 1540–1680   42
    Governing Spain's Empire   42
    French Toeholds   46
    Dutch Republican Colonies   48
    Early English Exploration and Settlement   50

England's Southern Plantings, 1607–1680   53
    Virginia's Beginnings   53
    Founding Maryland   56
    Life and Labor in the Chesapeake, 1640–1680   58
    Sugar and Slavery in the Caribbean   59
    Tobacco and Slavery in the Chesapeake   61

The New England Colonies, 1620–1680   62
    Separatists at Plymouth   62
    The City upon a Hill   64

Dissent and Compromise   67
Daily Life in New England   69
Colonists and Indians: Coexistence and Conflict, 1630–1680   72
Cultural Contrasts   72
Early Tensions in the North   73
New England Erupts   74
Southern Conflicts   76

CONCLUSION   77

Competing Voices: Race, Land, and Political Rights on the Frontier   79

3 ★ Imperial Connections, 1660–1748   82
The Restoration Colonies, 1660–1685   84
The Carolinas   84
New York and New Jersey   88
Pennsylvania and Penn's Delaware   89
Shaping Imperial Commerce   92
Mercantilism and the Colonies   92
The Maturing Atlantic System   94
Crises at Home and Abroad, 1685–1700   97
The Dominion of New England, 1686–1689   97
The Glorious Revolution, 1688–1689   98
Colonial Political Revolts, 1689–1691   99
Little Parliaments   100
Witches   102
Politics and Culture in the New Century, 1700–1748   104
Renewed Imperial Warfare   104
Challenging Imperial Arrangements   106
Midcentury Warfare   109
Transatlantic Cultural Influences   111

CONCLUSION   115

Competing Voices: Colonial and Imperial Views of the Assemblies   118

4 ★ Colonial Maturation and Conflict, 1680–1754   121
Growth and Diversity in the Colonies   123
New Immigrants   123
Families and Servants   126
Varieties of Life in the North   129
The Atlantic Economy   129
Cities and Market Towns   131
New England   136
The Mid-Atlantic   138
Varieties of Life in the South   139
The Chesapeake Colonies   139
Slavery and the Chesapeake   141

The Carolinas   143
Georgia   144
Slave Work and Culture   144
Maturity Brings Conflict, 1739–1754   148
Slave Resistance and Rebellion   148
The Great Awakening   149
Land in Trouble   152
CONCLUSION   154
Competing Voices: Two Views About Transatlantic Slave Trading   158

5 ★ Forging the American Experiment, 1754–1775   161
The Great War for Empire, 1754–1763   164
Onset of War, 1754–1760   164
Global War   166
Tensions on the Frontier   169
Rethinking Empire, 1763–1765   172
Markets and Goods   173
Legislating Obedience   175
Deepening Commitment, Rising Violence, 1765–1770   178
The Stamp Act Crisis   178
The Sons of Liberty   179
The Townshend Duties Crisis   182
Toward Independence, 1770–1773   185
The Boston Massacre   185
The Problem with Tea   187
Forging a Political Community, 1774–1775   190
The First Continental Congress   191
Lexington and Concord   192
CONCLUSION   194
Competing Voices: The Southern Frontier Erupts   196

6 ★ Winning Independence, 1775–1783   199
The Decision for Independence, 1775–1776   202
The Second Continental Congress   202
Common Sense   205
Declaring Independence   207
The Revolution in Earnest, 1776–1778   208
A Year of Exuberance   208
Philadelphia, Saratoga, and Valley Forge   211
The French Alliance   213
The Character of War   214
Armies and Taxes   214
Prices and Wages   217
Loyalists   219
Spies, Prisoners, and Evaders   222

The New Republican Order   224
   From Colonies to States   225
   The Articles of Confederation   228
Winning the War, 1778–1783   230
   The War in the West   230
   The War in the South   231
   Victory at Last   234

CONCLUSION   236

Competing Voices: Two Views of the Imperial Crisis   239

7 ★ **The Federal Experiment, 1783–1800   242**
The New Nation's Culture   244
   Religion   244
   Servitude and Slavery   246
   Republican Womanhood   248
The Precarious Peace, 1783–1786   251
   Soldiers and Loyalists   251
   Commercial Decline and Recovery   252
   Debtor Relief and Shays's Rebellion   253
   Shaping the West   255
The Constitutional Convention, 1787   259
   Thinking Continentally   259
   At Philadelphia   260
   The Public Debate   263
A New Political Nation, 1789–1791   267
   The First Congress   267
   Hamilton's Plans   268
From Factions to Parties   270
   Hamiltonians versus Republicans   271
   Rifts Widen   272
   The Frontier Besieged   274
Parties and Interests   276
   The Idea of Political Parties   276
   Toward a Party System   277

CONCLUSION   280

Competing Voices: Subduing the Old Northwest   283

8 ★ **Striving for Nationhood, 1800–1824   285**
Democratic-Republicans in Power   286
   Simplifying Government   287
   The Judiciary and the Common Law   288
   Defining Politics and American Identity   291
Expansion and the Agrarian Republic   294
   Lands of Promise   295
   The Louisiana Purchase   297

Lewis and Clark   299
Indian Relations   301
International Relations, 1800–1815   305
Spain in North America   305
The Atlantic Community   306
The War of 1812   309
Postwar Political Culture, 1815–1824   311
New Frontiers   311
Government and Development   312
The Panic of 1819   313
The Missouri Crisis   315
The Monroe Doctrine   316

CONCLUSION   317

Competing Voices: The Government's Role in Building
Institutions   319

9 ★ **An Emerging Capitalist Nation, 1790–1820**   **322**
Improvement and Invention   323
Roads and Turnpikes   325
Steamboats and Canals   327
Mills and Manufactures   332
Samuel Slater and Family Mills   336
Distinctive Lives and Lifestyles   337
The Binding Ties of Commerce   338
Northern Agriculture   341
The Old Northwest   343
King Cotton Emerges   344
Republican Cultural Patterns   347
Immigration and Cities   347
Republican Women and Families   350
Emotional and Rational Awakenings   353

CONCLUSION   356

Competing Images: Houses in the Early Republic   360

10 ★ **Transforming the Political Culture, 1820–1840**   **363**
Popular Politics, 1820–1828   365
Extending the Right to Vote   366
Popular Participation   369
An Old Order Passes   370
The Jacksonian Persuasion   373
Gathering Momentum   373
Storming Washington   375
Patronage, Democracy, Equality   377
The Experiment in Action, 1829–1836   379
Indian Removal   379
Tariffs   382

Banks 384
Changing Legal Doctrines 387
Dissenting Strains, 1832–1840 388
The Whig Persuasion 388
Workingmen's Parties 391
The Panic of 1837 395
The Election of 1840 396

CONCLUSION 398

Competing Voices: Cherokee Removal 401

11 ★ **Industry and Reform in the North, 1820–1850** **404**
Immigration and Urbanization 406
Old Cities and New 406
Frontier Cities 409
Rich and Poor 410
Order and Disorder 413
The Accelerating Industrial Experiment 414
Coastal and Frontier Farming 415
Transportation, Communication, Invention 416
Northern Labor 420
The Lowell Experiment 423
Varieties of Social Reform 427
Individualism and Improvement 427
Temperance 428
Asylums and Prisons 429
Family Roles and Education 431
Women's Rights 433
Intellectual Currents 434

CONCLUSION 439

Competing Voices: Equality and Opportunity in the Cities 442

12 ★ **Slavery and Plantation Culture, 1820–1850** **445**
Abolition and Antislavery Movements 446
Gradual Emancipation and Colonization 447
Immediate Emancipation and Rebellion 448
American Anti-Slavery Society 449
Women and Emancipation 451
Southern Society 453
A Distinctive Economy 453
Expansion 456
The Slave Trade 456
African-American Culture 458
Family and Community 458
Slave Men and Women at Work 461
Resistance and Rebellion 463
Free African-Americans 466

Planters and Yeomen   470
   Planters   470
   Yeomen and Tenants   472
   Defending Slavery   475

CONCLUSION   479

Competing Voices: Southern White Views of Slavery   482

13 ★ **The Westward Experiment, 1820–1850   485**
   A Great Transfer of Peoples   488
      Manifest Destiny   489
      Sponsors and Entrepreneurs   490
      The Westward Impulse   491
      Making the Trip   494
      The Indian Territory   497
   Destinations and Encounters   498
      Mexico and Its Territories   499
      The Alamo and the Republic of Texas   501
      Oregon   503
      California   505
   Expansion and Sectionalism, 1840–1848   506
      Annexation and the Election of 1844   506
      The Mexican-American War   509
      Internal Tensions   510
      The Wilmot Proviso   513
      The Election of 1848   515
      Gold!   516

CONCLUSION   519

Competing Voices: The Passage West   522

14 ★ **The Sectional Challenge, 1848–1860   525**
   Territory and Politics   528
      Political Ambiguities   528
      The Compromise of 1850   530
      The Fugitive Slave Act   534
      The Election of 1852   536
      Renewed Foreign Expansionism   537
   A New Party System Emerges   538
      The Kansas-Nebraska Act   538
      Bleeding Kansas   541
      Nativism   542
      The Republican Party   545
   The Slide into War, 1856–1859   546
      Southern Stridency   546
      Dred Scott   547
      The Lecompton Constitution   549
      Panic and Depression   550

Lincoln and the Union, 1856–1860   551
  Lincoln's Rise   551
  Forging Principles   553
  The Election of 1860   555
  Disunion   556
CONCLUSION   558
Competing Voices: The Lincoln-Douglas Debates   560

15 ★ Transforming the Experiment: The Civil War, 1861–1865   563
The War Begins, 1861   564
  The Search for Compromise   566
  The Attack on Fort Sumter   566
  The Battle for the Border States   568
  The Balance of Power   570
Stalemate on the Battlefield, 1861–1862   571
  The First Battle of Bull Run   572
  The Peninsular Campaign   573
  Fighting in the West   574
  The Naval War   575
  The *Trent* Affair and European Neutrality   576
  Antietam   577
Mobilizing for War, 1861–1863   578
  Raising an Army   579
  Financing the War   580
  Presidential Leadership   581
  Lincoln and Civil Liberties   583
War and Society, 1861–1865   584
  The Soldier's War   584
  Economic Consequences of the War   586
  Women and the War   588
The Decisive Year, 1863   589
  Emancipation Transforms the War   589
  Gettysburg   591
  Vicksburg and Chattanooga   593
A New Experiment in Warfare, 1864–1865   594
  Waging Total War   594
  The Election of 1864   596
  Sherman's March to the Sea   597
  The Collapse of the Confederacy   598
CONCLUSION   600
Competing Voices: Civil War Songs   604

16 ★ Reconstruction and the New South, 1865–1900   607
Presidential Reconstruction: The First Experiment, 1864–1866   610
  The Legacy of Battle   610
  Lincoln's Plan for Union   612

Restoration Under Johnson   614
The President versus Congress   616
Congressional Reconstruction: The Radical Experiment, 1866–1870   617
Citizenship, Equal Protection, and the Franchise   617
Reconstruction and Women's Suffrage   621
The Impeachment of a President   622
The Radical Experiment in the South   623
The Southern Republicans   623
The Republican Program   624
The Meaning of Freedom   626
Sharecropping   627
President Grant and the Divided North, 1868–1876   629
Ulysses Grant and the "Spoilsmen"   630
The Liberal Revolt   631
The Money Question   632
The Failure of Reconstruction, 1870–1877   633
The South Redeemed   633
The Republican Retreat   635
The Compromise of 1877   637
The New South, 1870–1900   638
Visions of Industry   639
King Cotton and the Crop-Lien System   640
The Culture of the New South   641
The Triumph of White Supremacy   642

CONCLUSION   645

Competing Voices: The Boundaries of Congressional
Reconstruction   650

17 ★ **Conquering the New West, 1862–1900**   653
The Westward Experiment   656
The New Migrants   657
The Homestead Act of 1862   658
The Railroad and Western Expansion   661
The Assault on Native American Cultures   661
The Plains Indians   662
The Indian Wars   664
"Reforming" the Indians   667
Experiments in Resource Exploitation   670
The Mining Frontier   670
Cattle Kingdom   672
Cultivating the Land   674
Timber and the Origins of Conservation   675
Society in the West: Experiment and Imitation   677
Life in Western Towns   677
The Hardships of Farm Life   679

Racism in the West: The Chinese   680
The Hispanic Heritage in the Southwest   681
The West and the American Imagination   683
"The Myth of the Garden"   683
The End of the Frontier   684

CONCLUSION   686

Competing Voices: Native Americans, Whites, and the Land   690

18 ★ **The Industrial Experiment, 1865–1900   693**

The Setting for Industrial Expansion   696
Technological Innovation   696
Thomas Edison and the "Invention Business"   696
The Railroads   698
The New Consumer Society   700
The New Industrial Order   702
A Business Culture   702
The Gospel of Success and Its Critics   703
Managing the New Industrial Empire   704
Titans of Industry: Carnegie, Rockefeller, and Morgan   705
Regulating the Trusts   707
The Changing World of Work   709
The Factory System   709
Dreams of Social Mobility   711
Working People   712
The House of Labor   715
The Origins of Industrial Unionism   715
The Knights of Labor   717
The American Federation of Labor (AFL)   719

CONCLUSION   719

Competing Voices: Organized Labor   724

19 ★ **The New Urban Nation, 1865–1900   727**

The Birth of the Modern City   728
City People: Migrants and Immigrants   728
Immigrant Communities   732
The Transportation Revolution   734
City Neighborhoods   737
The Urban Environment   739
City Politics   741
New Experiments in Culture   743
A Democracy of Amusement   743
Spectator Sports   744
The Metropolitan Press   746
Literature and the Arts   747
Challenging Domesticity   748

The Persistence of Piety   750
    Defending "American" Culture   750
    The Purity Crusades   753
    Public Education   754
CONCLUSION   756
Competing Voices: The Threat of the City   761

20 ★ State and Society, 1877–1900   764
The Politics of Stalemate   765
    The Failure of Politics   766
    The Limits of National Government   770
    The Issues: Patronage, Money, and Tariffs   771
National Politics from Hayes to Harrison, 1877–1890   773
    Republicans in Power: Hayes, Garfield, Arthur   774
    The Election of 1884   776
    Grover Cleveland: A Democrat in the White House   779
    The Election of 1888   779
    Harrison and the Billion Dollar Majority   780
Agrarian Revolt, 1880–1892   781
    The Farmers' Discontent   781
    The Alliance Movement of the 1880s   784
    The Populist Party, 1892   786
The Crisis of the 1890s   788
    The Depression of 1893   788
    Social Unrest: Coxey's Army and the Pullman Strike   789
    Depression Politics   792
The Republican Triumph: The Election of 1896   793
    Democrats and Populists   793
    The Election of 1896   795
    The McKinley Presidency   797
CONCLUSION   798
Competing Voices: Populism and Its Critics   801

21 ★ The Progressive Era, 1889–1916   804
The Rise of Progressivism   806
    The Challenge to Social Darwinism   806
    Women and Social Justice   809
    The Muckrakers   811
    The New Professions   812
    The Appeal of Progressivism   813
Political Reform   814
    Reforming the City   814
    Reform in the States   816
    Women's Suffrage   819
    Controlling the Masses   820

Social Tensions in an Age of Reform   823
    African-American Activism in the Progressive Era   823
    Radical Reformers   825
    Feminism   827
The Progressive Presidents   827
    TR   828
    Taft and the Divided Republicans   832
    Whose Progressivism? The Presidential Campaign of 1912   833
    Woodrow Wilson and the New Freedom   836

CONCLUSION   839

Competing Voices: Managing Modern Society   842

22 ★ **The Experiment in American Empire, 1865–1917   845**
Roots of Expansion, 1865–1898   848
    Gilded Age Diplomacy, 1865–1889   848
    The New Manifest Destiny   849
    Seeds of Empire   852
    Hawaii and Samoa   854
War and World Responsibilities, 1898–1901   856
    Origins of the Spanish-American War   857
    "A Splendid Little War"   860
    Managing the New American Empire   863
    The Open Door to China   866
Theodore Roosevelt and the "Big Stick," 1901–1912   867
    "I Took the Canal"   868
    The Roosevelt Corollary   869
    The Far East   870
    Dollar Diplomacy   871
The New Freedom Abroad   874
    Woodrow Wilson and World Power   874
    The Far East   875
    Central America and the Caribbean   876
    The Mexican Revolution   876

CONCLUSION   879

Competing Voices: American Imperialism   883

23 ★ **Making the World Safe for Democracy: America and World War I, 1914–1920   886**
The Road to War, 1914–1917   888
    American Neutrality   888
    Peace, Preparedness, and the 1916 Election   892
    "Peace Without Victory"   894
War, Mobilization, and Progressive Reform, 1916–1919   896
    Creating an Army   896
    Regulating the Economy   899

Workers and the War   901
The Search for National Unity   903
Prohibition and Suffrage   906
Making War and Peace, 1917–1919   908
"Days of Hell"   908
Negotiating the Peace Treaty   911
The Fight over Ratification   913
An Uncertain Peace, 1919–1920   915
Unsettled Times   916
The Red Scare   918
The Election of 1920   919

CONCLUSION   920

Competing Voices: National Security versus Individual Liberty   924

24 ★ **The New Era, 1920–1928   927**
The Modern Age   928
The New Economy   929
Mass Communications and Mass Culture   933
Spectator Sports and the Cult of Individualism   934
The Limits of Prosperity   936
The Culture of Dissent   939
The New Morality and the New Woman   939
Discontent of the Intellectuals   942
New Visions in Black America   943
The Guardians   945
The Revival of Nativism   946
The "New" Klan   947
Fundamentalism   948
The Unintended Consequences of Prohibition   950
Republicans in Power   951
Republican Ascendancy   952
Divided Democrats   955
Commercial Diplomacy   957
Al Smith and the 1928 Election   959

CONCLUSION   961

Competing Voices: The Church and State   964

25 ★ **"Fear Itself": Crash, Depression, and the New Deal, 1929–1938   967**
The Great Depression   968
The Crash   970
Hard Times   971
The Ordeal of Herbert Hoover   976
The New Deal Experiment, 1933–1938   977
FDR and the 1932 Election   977
The First Hundred Days   979

Attacks from the Left and Right   984
The Second New Deal   986
The 1936 Election   988
The Decline of the New Deal   989
Depression Culture, 1929–1938   991
   Social Realism and Social Escape During the 1930s   991
   Entertaining the Masses   992
   The Golden Age of Radio   994
The New Deal and Society, 1933–1938   995
   The Rise of Organized Labor   995
   A New Deal for Minorities?   997
   Women During the 1930s   999
   New Deal Legacies   1001

CONCLUSION   1002

Competing Voices: Government and the New Deal   1005

26 ★ War and Society, 1933–1945   1008
America and the World Crisis, 1933–1941   1009
   The Gathering Storm   1010
   The Failure of Neutrality   1013
   The 1940 Election Campaign   1015
   To the Brink   1017
   "This Is War"   1018
Fighting a Global War, 1941–1945   1019
   The Arsenal of Democracy   1019
   The Battle for Europe   1023
   "D-Day"   1025
   Wartime Politics   1028
   The Yalta Conference   1029
War and National Culture, 1941–1945   1032
   Propaganda and Popular Culture   1032
   Japanese Internment   1033
   The Breakdown of Provincialism   1034
   Rosie the Riveter   1035
   The War for Racial Equality   1037
Victory, 1942–1945   1040
   War in the Pacific   1040
   The Bomb   1042
   The Legacy of War   1042

CONCLUSION   1044

Competing Voices: The Dropping of the Bomb   1047

27 ★ The Cold War, 1945–1952   1050
From World War to Cold War, 1945–1949   1052
   Roots of the Cold War   1052
   Harry Truman Takes Charge   1056

The Iron Curtain Falls   1057
Containing Communism: The Truman Doctrine and the
Marshall Plan   1059
Mounting Tensions, Precarious Solutions   1061
In the Shadow of FDR, 1945–1948   1064
The Economic Shock of Rapid Reconversion   1065
Harry Truman and the Divided Democrats   1066
The 1948 Election   1069
Trying for a Fair Deal   1072
The Cold War Heats Up, 1950–1952   1072
The Cold War Spreads to Asia   1073
The Korean War: From Invasion to Stalemate   1074
The Truman-MacArthur Bout and the Trials of Containment   1077
Consequences of Korea   1077
The Politics of Fear, 1945–1952   1078
The Second Red Scare   1078
Joseph McCarthy   1082
CONCLUSION   1084

Competing Voices: America's Role in the World   1088

28 ★ The Consumer Society, 1945–1960   1091
The Consumer Revolution   1092
The "Baby Boom" and the Rise of Mass Consumption   1094
The Rise of the Suburbs   1096
The Changing World of Work   1097
Shaping National Culture, 1945–1960   1099
The Share Images of Television   1099
The Car Culture   1100
Religious Revival   1102
The Rise of Rock and Roll   1102
Mass Culture and Its Critics   1104
The Politics of Moderation, 1952–1956   1105
"I Like Ike": The Election of 1952   1105
"Dynamic Conservatism" at Home   1107
The "New Look" Abroad   1109
Rhetoric and Reality of Liberation   1111
The Threat of Third World Nationalism   1113
American Ideals and Social Realities, 1950–1960   1115
Intellectuals and the Celebration of Consensus   1115
The New Poverty   1116
Women During the 1950s   1117
The Struggle for Black Equality   1118
The Montgomery Bus Boycott   1120
The Quest for National Purpose, 1957–1960   1121
Atomic Anxieties   1122
Political and Economic Uncertainties   1123
Kennedy and the 1960 Presidential Election   1124

CONCLUSION   1127

Competing Voices: The Politics of Race   1130

29 ★ Consensus and Confrontation, 1960–1968   1133

The Kennedy Presidency, 1960–1963   1136
 JFK and the "New Frontier"   1136
 New Frontiers Abroad   1138
 Escalating Tensions: Cuba and Berlin   1139
 The Cuban Missile Crisis   1139
 JFK and Vietnam   1141

The New Liberal Experiment, 1963–1966   1142
 Lyndon Johnson and the War on Poverty   1143
 The 1964 Election and the Great Society   1146
 The Reforms of the Warren Court   1148

The Struggle for Racial Equality   1149
 The Movement Spreads   1149
 The Civil Rights Act of 1964   1151
 Gaining Political Power   1153
 Black Power, White Backlash   1155

Vietnam: Containment and Tragedy,
1964–1968   1156
 The Decision to Escalate   1156
 America's War   1158
 The Soldier's War   1160

Challenging the Consensus, 1960–1967   1162
 The Youth Culture   1162
 New Left, New Right   1163
 The Antiwar Movement   1164

The Watershed Year, 1968   1165
 Johnson Under Assault   1165
 The Democratic Convention   1167
 The Center Holds: The Election of 1968   1169

CONCLUSION   1170

Competing Voices: Martin Luther King, Jr., and
Malcolm X   1174

30 ★ The Politics of Polarization, 1969–1979   1177

Experiments in Peacemaking, 1969–1974   1178
 Nixon's War   1180
 Peace With Honor?   1183
 Détente   1184
 The Limits of Realism   1185

Richard Nixon and the Two Americas, 1969–1974   1187
 The Search for Stability at Home   1187
 Mobilizing the "Silent Majority"   1188
 The 1972 Election   1190
 The Watergate Crisis   1191

Old Values, New Realities, 1970–1979   1194
  African-Americans: Action Without Affirmation   1195
  Voices of Protest: Hispanics, Native Americans,
  and Homosexuals   1197
  Women's Liberation   1199
  Cultural Crosscurrents   1202
The Age of Limits, 1974–1979   1203
  Congressional Resurgence and Public Mistrust   1203
  The Troubled Economy   1205
  The Environmental Movement   1207
  Gerald Ford and the 1976 Presidential Campaign   1208
  Jimmy Carter and the "Crisis of Confidence"   1209

CONCLUSION   1212

Competing Voices: The Politics of Gender   1216

31 ★ **The Reagan Experiment, 1979–1988   1219**
The Conservative Revival, 1979–1980   1220
  The Rise of the Religious Right   1221
  The Tax Revolt   1222
  The New Right   1224
  The 1980 Presidential Campaign   1225
The Culture Wars, 1980–1988   1227
  The Politics of Family Values   1227
  Abortion   1228
  Gay Rights and the AIDS Crisis   1229
  AIDS: The Worldwide Impact   1230
  American Identities   1231
The Reagan Presidency, 1980–1988   1234
  The Reagan Agenda   1234
  Attacking the Liberal State   1236
  Reagan Justice   1238
  The 1984 Presidential Campaign   1238
Reagan and the Cold War, 1980–1988   1240
  Fighting the "Evil Empire"   1240
  The Escalating Arms Race   1241
  Central America   1242
  Fighting Terrorism   1244
  The Iran-Contra Scandal   1245
Wealth and Poverty in Reagan's America, 1980–1988   1246
  The Money Culture   1246
  The MTV Generation   1247
  The Hourglass Society   1248
  The New Economy   1250
  The Reagan Legacy   1251

CONCLUSION   1253

Competing Voices: Debating the Environment   1256

32 ⋆ America After the Cold War, 1988–2000   1259

    The Post–Cold War Experiment, 1988–1992   1262
        The Search for Reagan's Successor   1262
        1989: "The Year of Miracles"   1263
        The New World Order   1266
        War with Iraq   1267
        Problems on the Home Front   1269
        The 1992 Presidential Campaign   1272

    The Clinton Administration, 1992–2000   1274
        The Clinton Agenda   1274
        Moving to the Center   1276
        Winning a Second Term: The 1996 Campaign   1277
        The New Internationalism   1277
        Trouble Spots: Iraq and Yugoslavia   1279
        Impeachment   1281

    The New Prosperity, 1992–2000   1282
        The Information Society   1282
        Wall Street Boom and the Politics of Prosperity   1285
        The 2000 Presidential Election   1287
        An Age of Leisure?   1288

    Social Tensions in the Nineties   1290
        Sex, Violence, and the Debate over Popular Culture   1290
        Race and American Justice   1291
        Terrorism American Style   1292

    CONCLUSION   1294

    Competing Voices: Congress Debates War or Peace   1297

Declaration of Independence   A-1

Constitution of the United States of America and Amendments   A-3

A Statistical Profile of America   A-18
        Population of the United States   A-18
        Immigrants to the United States   A-19
        The American Worker   A-20
        The American Economy   A-21

Presidential Elections   A-22

Presidents and Vice Presidents   A-27

Text Credits   A-30

Index   A-31

Maps and Graphs

North American Culture Areas Before European Contact   5
Africa in 1500   13
Extent of the Spanish Empire in the 1500s   44
European Settlement and Indian Cultures of Eastern North America, 1650   57
Sudbury, Massachusetts, c. 1650   71
The Restoration Colonies   86
Immigration and Migration in the 1700s   125
European Claims in North America, 1754 and 1763   166
War in the North   206
War in the West   224
War in the South   232
Cession of Western Land, 1782–1802   256
The Northwest Ordinance, 1785   258
Early National Expansion   297
The Lewis and Clark Expedition and the Louisiana Purchase   300
The Missouri Compromise   315
Rivers, Canals, and Roads to 1820   326
Universal White Male Suffrage   367
Indian Removal in the 1830s   381
Slavery and Agricultural Expansion, 1820–1860   455
Western Trails, 1820 to 1850   495
The Mexican-American War, 1846–1848   511
The Compromise of 1850   533
Railroads in the 1850s   540
The Election of 1860   556
Major Military Offenses of the Civil War   573
The Battle of Gettysburg   593
Grant's Campaign in Virginia, 1864–1865   595
Military Reconstruction Districts   619
Sharecropping in the South by County, 1880   629
The Election of 1876   638
From Public Land to Homesteads   660
Western Indian Wars and Reservations, 1860–1890   666
Cattle Trails   673
Railroads and Railroad Land Grants, 1870–1920   699
Vertical and Horizontal Integration of the Petroleum Industry   706
Rural and Urban Population, 1860–1920   730
Immigration, 1860–1930   732
Voter Turnout in Presidential Elections, 1868–1920   770

Voting in Presidential Elections of 1880, 1884, 1888   775
Consumer Prices and Farm Product Prices, 1865–1910   782
The Election of 1892, by County   787
The Election of 1896   797
Women's Suffrage Before the Nineteenth Amendment   821
The Election of 1912   837
Imports and Exports, 1865–1915   851
U.S. Expansion, 1865–1900   853
U.S. Presence in Latin America, 1895–1945   873
The Election of 1916   894
World War I, the Western Front   909
The Election of 1920   921
The Automobile Age   931
The Election of 1924   956
The Election of 1928   960
The Election of 1932   980
Labor Union Membership   996
The Election of 1940   1016
World War II in Europe and Africa   1024
The Election of 1944   1030
World War II in the Pacific   1041
Cold War Europe   1061
The Election of 1948   1071
Korean War, 1950–1953   1076
Gross National Product   1094
American Birthrate   1095
The Election of 1952   1107
The Election of 1956   1110
The Election of 1960   1126
The Election of 1964   1147
Vietnam, to 1968   1158
American Troop Levels in Vietnam   1160
The Election of 1968   1170
The Election of 1972   1191
Discomfort Index   1205
The Election of 1976   1210
The Election of 1980   1226
Growth of Hispanic Population in the 1980s   1232
The Election of 1984   1239
The National Debt, 1930–2000   1252
The Election of 1988   1264
The Gulf War   1268
The Election of 1992   1274
The Economic Boom of the 1990s   1286

Preface

America's written history began more than five hundred years ago with the encounters of Native Americans, Europeans, and Africans who struggled to bend nature to their needs and understand or overwhelm each other in countless ways. As this richly textured history unfolded, scholars also created many twists and turns in our understanding of this past. During the last quarter of the nineteenth century, historians in the United States emphasized the roles of political and intellectual leaders, elections and diplomacy, and national institutions. "History is past politics and politics are present history," declared Henry B. Adams, a founding member of the American Historical Association (AHA), in 1884.

Challenges to this perspective arose by the turn of the twentieth century, as when Carl Becker, in his own presidential address to the AHA, referred to "everyman" in the widest possible terms as "his own historian." But not until the 1960s did scholars pioneer fresh methods in writing a more democratic history. The "New History" emphasized telling history "from the bottom up;" it found "patterns of intimate personal behavior" that revealed the lives of people who had remained hidden from our understanding of the past. The New History represented a dramatic turn away from the traditional ways of representing our political and cultural past. It forced scholars to expand and deepen our understanding of what is political and what is cultural for far greater numbers of people over time.

Recent work in political and cultural history extends these boundaries even farther by seeking common ground between traditional approaches and the pathbreaking ones of the New History. This work expands the definitions of politics beyond the realm of elite actors and powerful institutions to include the far wider arenas of public and private culture, and it incorporates an appreciation of how race, class, and gender have shaped our past. Recent work also recognizes the need for synthesis in historical writing, but without neglecting the threads of individual experiences in the larger fabric of American history.

Approach

Drawing on the best of these new directions in political and cultural history, this book narrates the broad contours of change at the imperial or national level, and, at the same time, explains the lives of people in diverse communities who lived sometimes ordinary, sometimes extraordinary, lives. We believe that it is equally important to study how institutions emerged, rulers ruled, and economies developed, as it is to explain everyday work, family life, and different customs.

We have chosen the title, *The American Experiment,* to underscore our belief that North America's past can be best understood as an ongoing struggle of various competing ideals regarding individuals, communities, and nations. These ideals were contested and continually reshaped for almost two centuries in the crucibles of Native American villages, European settlements, and African-American communities. The American Revolution tested and extended these ideals during struggles for what was perceived to be liberty and equality. But in those years, as well as in the subsequent decades of the early republic, ideals coexisted uneasily with social realities. For most of their history, Americans have struggled to reconcile their broad belief in individual liberty and equality with the reality of racism, class conflict, and gender inequality. This book uses the prism of politics and culture to explore this unfolding American experiment.

Themes

This book's four central themes highlight these ideals and realities on many levels. The first theme focuses on competing views of the proper role of government. For generations, colonists, then independent Americans, debated just what degree of control a central government should have over their everyday lives, what kinds of powers should be given to the government, and what kinds of leaders should rule. But when scholars recount this story, too often they focus primarily on charting the growth in the size and scope of the national government and the achievements of its political and intellectual leaders. This kind of narrative cannot fully explain the dynamics of American politics. We believe that American politics has been characterized by competing views of the proper role of government, including but not limited to the persistence of conservative attitudes about limited government, self-help, and individualism in the face of the growth of national government.

A second theme addresses issues of identity. What qualities do Americans believe define them best? The answers, we believe, change over time. Our history has been defined by the shifting struggles among ethnic, religious, regional, class, and racial groups to shape both a multiplicity of particular identities and a sequence of unifying images about being "American." Being "colonists" suggested to thousands of settlers that they were politically subordinate, as well as culturally and economically dependent, on the imperial center. But settlers often paid more attention to religious backgrounds, local social status, or their identity as residents of one locale. Post-Revolutionary Americans embarked on an intense struggle to make—or make over—their identity. They often spoke and wrote about "the nation," but the term meant different things to different parts of the population. For most of our history, American identity has been defined in racial terms, as African-Americans underwent the unsettling transformations of slavery, fought for emancipation, and later demanded the rights of citizenship. But especially in recent years, it has included the attempts of other disenfranchised groups—Hispanics, Asians, women, and homosexuals—to challenge the dominant structure and force a reluctant acceptance of their unique identities and their contributions to American society.

Third, the book explores the evolution of culture, both national mass culture and the variety of regional, ethnic, religious, and racial subcultures. From the start, colonists sometimes willingly, sometimes unwittingly blended characteristics of European and African cultures with the Indian cultures and natural environments in which they settled. Long before the American Revolution, the continent's amazingly heterogeneous population was undergoing rapid changes, continually negotiating accommodation of its internal cultural differences, and sometimes facing bloody conflicts over them. By the beginning of the twentieth century, new instruments of mass culture produced intense conflict between local cultures and a dominant national culture. Through this cultural evolution, we ask, has a distinctive *American* culture emerged? If so, when and how? If not, how shall we understand a plurality of cultures under the umbrella of a nation called America?

Finally, our book examines America's ambivalent attitude toward the outside world. Enormous changes in the structure of relations among world nations have occurred as we evolved from a knot of English colonies into a world superpower. But as with our attitude toward government and our resistance to cultural change, Americans have not completely abandoned the isolationist streak that has been so much a part of our past. Indeed, even during the period of America's rise to world power, our leaders were driven more by a desire to remake the world in our image than by a need to join the international community of nations. In the pages that follow, we have asked how Americans explained their place in this world of nations at various turning points in their own national evolution.

Features

The focus on themes and the use of "experiment" as a motif for understanding the American past structure our narrative and give students an organizing framework. We make the narrative accessible to students with generous use of revealing quotes and anecdotes. The book also contains a number of special features to enhance the narrative and to reinforce the themes.

Each chapter begins with a colorful vignette that highlights one or more of its central themes and provides focus questions to guide reading of its chapter. In addition to a chronology and a brief conclusion, every chapter contains a primary-source feature, "Competing Voices." This feature provides students with the opportunity to examine primary sources. It includes two sources that represent differing viewpoints about a common issue along with headnotes that place the sources in context for the student. Students are introduced to the tools of working historians and the enduring evidence of ongoing tensions in American life.

Study and Teaching Aids

The American Experiment is supported by an extensive supplements package including print, online, and CD-ROM resources.

@*history*, Houghton Mifflin's CD-ROM that features nearly one thousand primary sources, including video, audio, illustrations, and text, is available in a version specifically keyed to the chapters in *The American Experiment*. Available in both instructor and student versions, *@history* is an interactive multimedia tool that can improve the analytical skills of students and introduce them to historical sources.

GeoQuest: United States is a CD-ROM designed to improve students' geographical literacy. The program consists of thirty interactive historical maps, each of which provides background information and a series of self-correcting quizzes so that students can master the information on their own.

The American Experiment web site has resources for both instructors and students. The instructor site includes the online *Instructor's Resource Manual*, primary sources with teaching hints, full-color maps, outline maps, and annotated links to other history sites. The student site includes ACE practice tests, primary sources, an annotated guide to the top historical research web sites, and research activities that can be used by instructors for assignments.

The online *Study Guide*, prepared by D. Antonio Cantu of Ball State University, includes learning objectives, chapter outlines with web links, identification terms, journal questions with Internet links, ACE practice tests, a multimedia scrapbook (an electronic exhibit of multimedia primary and secondary sources), and map activities. This *Study Guide* is free to students and may be found at www.college.hmco.com/history.

An online *Instructor's Resource Manual*, written by J. Kent McGaughy of Houston Community College–Northwest, is downloadable from Houghton Mifflin's U.S. history web site. It contains learning objectives, chapter summaries, chapter outlines, lecture strategies, topics for class discussion, historical perspectives, comparative chronologies, and map activities.

A printed *Test Bank*, also prepared by D. Antonio Cantu, provides over 1,200 multiple choice questions, and over 200 essay questions. These questions are also available in a *Computerized Test Bank* for both Windows and Macintosh platforms.

A set of *American History Map Transparencies* is also available to instructors upon adoption of the text.

Acknowledgments

At Houghton Mifflin, we would like to thank Sean Wakely and Beth Welch who skillfully guided the book through its early years, and Jan Fitter and Jennifer Sutherland who led us across the finish line. Most of all, we want to thank Jeff Greene, a patient but demanding editor who lifted our spirits at a difficult time, and Jean Woy who supervised the project from beginning to end. Finally, we appreciate all the hard work of Rosemary Jaffe, senior project editor; Jill Haber, senior production/design coordinator; Michael Kerns, editorial associate; Charlotte Miller, art editor; Pembroke Herbert and Sandi Rygiel, photo researchers; Cia Boynton, designer; Kathryn Daniel, copyeditor; Mary Dalton Hoffman, permissions editor; and Marie Barnes, senior manufacturing coordinator, who pulled it all together.

Steve Gillon also thanks his research assistants, Holly Furr and Heather Clemmer for all their help.

Writing a new textbook for U.S. history is an enormous task and one that couldn't have been done without the invaluable help of our colleagues who reviewed the manuscript at every stage. We thank:

Kathryn Abbott, *Western Kentucky University*
Timothy Allen, *Trocaire College*
Michael Barnhart, *SUNY, Stony Brook*
Lori Bogle, *University of Arkansas*
Kevin Boyle, *University of Massachusetts, Amherst*
John Buenker, *University of Wisconsin, Parkside*
William Byrd, *Chattahoochee Valley Community College*
D. Antonio Cantu, *Ball State University*
William Cario, *Concordia University, Wisconsin*
Victor Chen, *Chabot College*
Peter Coclanis, *University of North Carolina, Chapel Hill*
Bill Corbett, *Northeastern State University*
Dallas Cothrum, *University of Texas, Tyler*
Robert Cottrell, *California State University at Chico*
Bruce Dierenfield, *Canisius College*
William Dionisio, *Sacramento City College*
Richard Ellis, *SUNY, Buffalo*
James Farmer, *University of South Carolina, Aiken*
Mark Fernandez, *Loyola University of Louisiana*
Mark Grandstaff, *Brigham Young University*
L. Edward Hicks, *Faulkner University*
Christopher Kimball, *Augsburg College*
Kenneth L. Kitchen, *Trident Technological College*
Kevin Kragenbrink, *California State University, San Bernardino*
Alan Lehmann, *Blinn College*
Kenneth Marcus, *California State Polytechnic University at Pomona*
Robert Mathis, *Stephen F. Austin State University*
Carl Moneyhon, *University of Arkansas, Little Rock*
Benjamin Newcomb, *Texas Tech University*
Sherry Smith, *University of Texas, El Paso*
June Sochen, *Northeastern Illinois University*
David Stebenne, *The Ohio State University*
Richard Straw, *Radford University*
Tyrone Tillery, *University of Houston*
William Wagnon, *Washburn University*
Patricia Wallace, *Baylor University*
James Woods, *Georgia Southern University*

Steven M. Gillon
Cathy D. Matson

1

Out of Old Worlds, New Worlds

"*T*he earth," according to the Cherokee myth of creation, "is a great island floating in a sea of water, and suspended at each of the four [main compass] points by a cord hanging down from the sky vault, which is of solid rock." The earth's creation began when little Water Beetle, tired of being crowded in the sky with all the other animals, dove below the water to find a new place to live. Water Beetle "came up with some soft mud, which began to grow and spread on every side until it became the island which we call the earth." As the mud was drying, Great Buzzard flew about, and "wherever his wings struck the earth there was a valley, and where they turned up again there was a mountain." And so the Cherokee country was full of mountains and valleys.

Eventually other animals arrived, carried by the streams that flowed out of the mountains, and they commanded a sun to cross the sky each day. The animals were divided according to their needs and abilities, and "plants and people were made, we do not know by whom." "At first there were only a brother and sister until he struck her with a fish and told her to multiply, and so it was. In seven days a child was born to her, and thereafter every seven days another, and they increased very fast until there was danger that the world could not keep them. Then it was made that a woman should have only one child in a year, and it has been so ever since." But all Cherokee know, and fear, that "when the world grows old and worn out, the people will die and the cords will break and let the earth sink down into the ocean, and all will be water again." The Cherokee were afraid of this.

People everywhere tell stories to explain their origins. Sometimes the stories seem fantastical or heretical. Often, as in the Cherokee myth of creation, certain themes sound familiar to listeners or readers because different cultures share certain views of the world. Most of these myths are not historical accounts of migrations, lives of kings, or daily affairs. But they are more than mere fictions intended to entertain people, for each myth contains core beliefs and values of the people who create it. Over the centuries the Cherokee retold and reshaped the details of their creation myth, putting in order the component parts of the world and giving words to physical and psychological phenomena as they understood them. The evolving myth gave names and causes to what they experienced in their everyday lives and collective expression to what each person might imagine as his or her reason for existence.

For centuries before roughly A.D. 1400, the Western Hemisphere was populated by hundreds of different Native American cultures. Their myths of creation varied from one region to another, just as their environments, family lives, religions, and political structures also varied. But incredible transformations—political, social, economic, and cultural—were taking place in Europe and Africa at that time, too, that would put these populations on a collision course. Soon many North American Indians would experience the arrival of Europeans and Africans, whose cultures thrust additional distinctions into the mix.

African slaves who were forcibly introduced into North America brought new ways of farming and cooking, new family and religious traditions, and much more that set them apart from Indians. Europeans experienced even sharper cultural contrasts with North American Indians. Frequently, they dismissed Indian myths as fireside stories or, worse, the false legends of "uncivilized savages." Europeans tended to hold the rise of printing and books in privileged esteem, even though very few Europeans were themselves literate at the time they came to the Americas, and strong oral traditions still prevailed on every continent. In addition, the early Spanish, French, English, and Dutch colonizers found remarkable, and sometimes objectionable, contrasts among African, Indian, and European values and customs. Not only did most Indians not share the Biblical narration of creation, they also cared little for European Christian values. Furthermore, Europeans readily noted the natives' peculiar ways of working, structuring families, reckoning property, telling time, recognizing political authority, and many other cultural givens. Africans brought to North America were also placed (usually at the bottom) in this cultural and political hierarchy that Europeans developed in their minds, laws, and social behavior. Differences in appearance and behavior quickly became a basis for social and legal distinctions governing use of the land and its resources. The juncture in history of these cultures—indigenous American, African, and European— could be nothing other than transformative for all three.

What were the cultural backgrounds and historical experiences of the many different peoples who lived in the Americas and who came from other continents to this part of the world?

Chronology

30,000–10,000 B.C.	Ancient peoples cross Beringia
7000 B.C.	Cultivation of crops begins in the Mexican plains
3000–2000 B.C.	Cultivation of crops begins north of the Rio Grande
1000 B.C.–A.D. 500	Adena and Hopewell societies flourish in the Ohio Valley
500–1200	Anasazi flourish in southwest North America
600–1600	Rise of West African states
1000	Pueblo culture emerges in the Southwest
	Vikings reach North America
1400–1500	Maturing of the African kingdoms of Ghana, Mali, and Songhai
1420s	Portuguese explore west coast of Africa
1450	Iroquois form the Great League of Peace
1492	Columbus reaches the Caribbean
	Spain expels Moors and Jews
1515–1521	Spanish explore Florida
	Cortés conquers Aztecs
	Epidemics of smallpox ravage Caribbean and South American Indians
1517	Protestant Reformation begins
1533	Pizarro conquers the Inca
1534–1542	Cartier, De Soto, and Coronado explore areas of North America

▌ How did their first contacts affect these peoples from fundamentally different cultures? In what ways did they cooperate, and in what ways did they clash?

▌ What was the role of each culture in the destructive wars and devastating diseases that altered life for everyone? How did varieties of Indians, Europeans, and Africans share aspects of their cultures and blend their backgrounds into new cultures?

This chapter will address these questions.

The First Americans, to 1500

Indian creation myths often asserted that their particular people *always* lived in North America. Some myths also privileged one language group or tribe over its surrounding environment or elevated one group to a higher level of cultural accomplishment than neighboring groups. Scholars can show, however, that such claims could not have been true. Long migrations and numerous environmental adaptations marked the earliest known rising civilizations. Over centuries, hundreds of Indian cultures and languages developed (see map). A handful of great civilizations emerged and dominated different regions in the Western Hemisphere long before European and African presence.

Earliest North Americans

Migrations of people from other parts of the world into the Western Hemisphere probably began about 30,000 years ago. Many of the earliest migrants to North and South America shared their ancestry with Asians, and probably crossed a land bridge at the Bering Strait—also called Beringia—during the final Ice Age, which lasted from about 50,000 years ago until about 10,000 years ago. Enduring bitter cold, the earliest migrants into North America probably came in small hunting groups that followed large mammals such as the mastodon, bison, woolly rhinoceros, and a kind of antelope over long distances. Small hunter-gather bands of Paleo-Indians thrived on these animals as rich sources of meat for sustenance, dung for fuel, and bones for tools. Their populations grew rapidly and, by about 12,500 years ago, had spread overland from Montana to the southern tip of South America, called Tierra del Fuego, and throughout the eastern and southeastern portions of North America.

Another stream of migrants lived not on large animals as hunters, but rather on fish and small plants along the Pacific coastline of both continents. Ancient sites from about 12,000 years ago in Chile and Peru predate most of the earliest North American hunters, showing a possible second source of migration from some other part of the world than across Beringia. These South American populations were probably established by peoples who were semisedentary, or settled in camps only part of the year, and who migrated northward along the coast of South America from the southern tip of the continent.

Then about 10,000 years ago, the hemispheric climate warmed, and the large animals either became extinct or drifted far from human populations. In North America, Indian ancestors were forced to hunt smaller and scarcer supplies of game, and harsher conditions resulted in a decline in their numbers. Over time, dispersed populations adapted their societies to the deserts of the Great Basin, or turned to the resources of the forests around the Great Lakes, or pressed south and southeast to woodlands and plateaus.

As they became more sedentary, or more settled in semipermanent villages, these ancestors of modern Indians also began to cultivate certain plants. In central Mexico, the most important innovation was the cultivation of maize, or corn, along with beans, squash, sunflowers, and herbal grasses. The requirements of attending to these crops, and their abundant yields, stimulated a more highly organized polit-

North American Culture Areas Before European Contact   This map shows both the large regions of Native American populations across the continent and names many of the cultures living within those regions in about 1500. In all, there were as many as 800 language groups in North America at that time.

ical system and village culture, which permitted populations to grow in size and complexity beginning about 3,000 to 2,500 years ago. From place to place, gender divisions of labor became more clearly differentiated, with men and women performing more specialized and defined tasks. They developed political systems that elevated some community members to positions of leisure or prestige. By about 500 B.C., several regions showed significant distinctions between powerful centers of population and the tributary villages surrounding them.

North American Cultures

We can understand aspects of long dispersed or dead Native American peoples, not only from the knowledge locked in their myths, but also from their stone tools and carvings, architectural remains, fragments of textiles, shards of pottery, and their alterations to the land itself. Assembling this archaeological evidence has not given us a complete portrait of the Western Hemisphere over time, but it does allow us to reconstruct snapshots of a remarkably diverse number of peoples, whose many cultures and systems of government underwent constant changes well before a European presence overwhelmed them. Estimates of Indian population vary widely, mainly because scholars will never be able to judge accurately how many people could be supported in ancient ecosystems and technologies. But many agree that by about 1450, or shortly before the first European wave, as many as 80 to 100 million people could have been living in the Western Hemisphere (compared with about 70 million people in Europe at that time); between 4 and 10 million lived north of the Rio Grande, the river that today forms part of the border between Texas and Mexico. Up to 25 million lived in the complex societies of Mexico and Peru. Between six and eight hundred different languages were spoken throughout the Americas (see map), pointing to more extensive cultural diversity than Europeans had ever experienced or could anticipate. Remarkably diverse cultural groups arose in different North American regions.

The eastern interior regions around the Ohio and Mississippi Rivers supported great peoples known as the Woodland cultures. From at least three thousand years ago, hunting and gathering peoples began cultivating certain crops—tobacco and maize among them—along with their regular foraging activities. Along the upper banks of the Ohio River, the Adena culture flourished until at least the second century A.D. The Adena were probably the first of the sedentary and complex societies of mound builders in North America, named for the great burial mounds that survive as a testament to this society's sophisticated organization of labor and hierarchical culture.

As Adena reached its peak and then began to decline, the Hopewell culture rose throughout the Mississippi–Ohio Valley, where its people also built enormous mounds presumably for burials and other ceremonies. Artifacts discovered in and near the mounds suggest a trade network that brought these mound builders into contact with peoples far away in the Rocky Mountains, along the Gulf and Atlantic coastlines, and around Lake Superior in the first centuries A.D.

Some time later, between 950 and 1400 A.D., another mound-building culture arose along the Mississippi River near present-day St. Louis, Missouri. The main center of this culture, Cahokia, supported an urban center of perhaps forty thousand people, more than any North American city contained until well after the American Revolution. Such density of population was probably possible because these early Indians adopted prolific varieties of maize from sedentary populations to their south, used relatively sturdy planting tools such as the flint hoe, developed a vast trade network, and subjugated subsidiary peoples. It is possible that Cahokia served as a ceremonial and distribution center for population sites around it and that a centralized political authority emerged by sustained warfare over generations. Certainly Cahokia supported pottery, metalworking, and tool making. At its center stood a ceremonial earthen temple that rose nearly one hundred feet high and covered a base of about fifteen acres, from the heights of which a commanding elite could issue decrees and receive tribute. Cahokia collapsed suddenly in the early 1400s, perhaps because its concentrated population strained available natural and cultivated resources. It is also possible that diseases introduced by European explorers who landed briefly on shorelines hundreds of miles away had devastating effects far to the interior of the continent where Cahokia lay. To the south of Cahokia, the Natchez people preserved Mississippian culture for many more generations.

In the semiarid southwest of North America, the Hohokam, the Anasazi, and the Pueblo cultures also attained great complexity. The Hohokam (of present-day Arizona) built hundreds of miles of irrigation canals before 100 A.D., which enabled them to produce two yields of grains and cotton a year. They cultivated crops with hoes, and their use of combs and looms allowed them to wear woven cotton clothing instead of animal skins, as many Indians of forested areas did. Their intricately designed pottery was traded extensively deep into the central plains of Mexico.

The Anasazi of the Chaco Canyon in New Mexico built spacious apartments and recessed religious meeting halls, and developed seasonal calendars, sophisticated pottery, roadways, and extensive irrigation systems. Overcome by extensive drought and the onslaught of enemy peoples, the Anasazi were reduced greatly in number during the late 1200s. During the 1300s, Athapaskans, seminomadic migrants from much colder climates to the north, began to raid the farmlands of Anasazi and forced them to flee south.

The Pueblo, descended from the Anasazi in subsequent centuries, settled along the Rio Grande in present-day New Mexico. Theirs was a rich culture of several languages, elaborate matrilineal clans, and religious societies. Pueblo agricultural techniques permitted the cultivation of plentiful crops in extremely arid conditions.

Cliff Palace, Mesa Verde
The Anasazi constructed elaborate communities in the faces of dramatically steep mountainsides in the Southwest. Cliff Palace, in modern-day Arizona, had over 220 rooms and 23 ceremonial kivas. *(Photo Researchers. Photo by Werner Foreman.)*

They were living in over fifty large settlements when the Spanish came to that area in the 1500s. Some of the Pueblo towns contain the oldest continuously used dwellings in America. These "cliff dwellers" also built underground chambers called kivas for men's political and religious meetings. Some Athapaskan people gradually settled down around the Pueblo towns and turned to the farming methods Pueblos taught them. These became known as the Navajo.

Far to the east, descendants of the Adena–Hopewell peoples settled in the temperate and relatively wet climates stretching from the Great Lakes and Appalachian Mountains to the Atlantic coastline. Mainly comprised of small villages, clustered as tribes, and based on shared kinship, rising cultures extended from today's Florida through New England, across the southern piedmont and tidewater regions, and up into the valleys of the Hudson and Connecticut Rivers.

After the 1300s, the Chesapeake region proved to be hospitable for migrating Algonquian peoples, and by the late 1500s, about twenty thousand had settled in the area. Many of them formed a confederacy under the powerful leader, Powhatan. Toward the interior, the confederacies of Creek, Catawba, Choctaw, Chickasaw, and Cherokee also took shape. These Eastern Woodland cultures were very different from the highly structured and centralized peoples of the Southwest and Ohio Valley. Eastern peoples shared a combination of clan-based kinship lineage and villages sustained by pragmatic concerns about work, defense, integrating captives, and marriage alliances. They changed leaders frequently and allowed tribal members widespread participation in decision making. They also had minimal bureaucracies, little specialization of jobs and services, and frequent travel and game playing among clans.

The agriculture of these southeastern cultures would amaze Europeans. Although they were settled in villages most of the time, they did not till the soil in ways familiar to Europeans. Having chosen a section of forest to cultivate, young Indian men and women burned off the underbrush, and then mixed the ashes with decaying leaves to make a rich soil for planting. Often men and women also "girdled" trees by slashing off a swath of bark and wood around the circumference of the trunk; in subsequent seasons, the tree trunks remained standing but in the absence of shady leaf cover, Indians cultivated plants in the nutritious forest soil. Eastern peoples also kept their soil rich in nutrients, and increased their crop yields, by interplanting crops of maize and beans together. Sometimes they added dead fish to the soil as fertilizer. All of these practices were startlingly new to Europeans.

Native Americans of the eastern coastal plain rarely wasted any products that could be derived from trees. Houses were made of sapling poles, covered with layers of bark or leafy branches. Skilled Indian craftsmen devised needles for sewing clothing and household goods, eating utensils and bowls, weapons, baskets, even boats. In 1590 the English artist-turned-explorer Thomas Harriot would remark of the Algonquian in the southeastern woodlands, "the manner of makinge their boates . . . is verye wonderfull. For whereas they want [i.e., lack] Instruments of yron, yet they knowe howe to make them as handsomlye . . . as ours." Indeed, Native American cultures did not mine mineral ores such as copper, tin, lead, and iron—which might have led to the production of kettles, knives, axes, and plows.

Europeans frequently identified this shortcoming as the source of Native American inferiority. However, what Europeans presumed to be "advances," or evidence of their own superiority, also had at least one critical advantage for Native American cultures: by not mining ores, it had not become necessary to devastate their forests for fuel to run forges and mills, or to change the contours of the land to extract ores, or to reorganize their families and villages to provide labor for dramatically different kinds of labor in metal work. Native American alterations of the landscape were of a slower pace and a different quality than in the European experience.

Along the eastern coastline and north of the St. Lawrence River, Algonquian-speaking peoples of over fifty different cultures formed semisedentary or nomadic bands that hunted and fished on seasonal territories. The Cree, Micmac, Chippewa, Montagnais, and others of northerly climates remained thinly populated and spread out over expansive hunting grounds. A chain of Algonquian-speaking peoples also inhabited virtually the entire Atlantic coastline, where they adopted agriculture in their seasonal productive cycles; the hoe and fishing spear became important tools for the Narragansett, Pequot, Delaware, and others.

Between these two Algonquian-speaking regions lay the territory of the other large language group of the Northeast, the Iroquoian-speaking peoples who had settled into sedentary cultivation beginning about 4,500 years previously. As elsewhere in the Western Hemisphere, success in growing corn, beans, and other edible plants led to rapid population growth. So dense were the various Iroquois settlements by the 1400s that fifty to sixty "longhouses," often sheltering dozens of families each, spread out along the rivers of present-day western New York. By the 1570s, the five great "nations" of the Iroquois centered in what would become western New York—the Mohawk, Onondaga, Oneida, Cayuga, and Seneca—created a confederacy called the "Great League of Peace" for commercial and religious reasons, and probably to subdue enemy tribes around them. According to legend, the great orator Hiawatha carried the invitation to join the League from village to village, promising that even as all five nations claimed common descent from the same maternal line and spoke the same Iroquoian language, each nation could also continue to enjoy its separate clan identity. Their goal, professed Hiawatha, was peace within the League and unified war against enemies such as the Erie and Huron.

Mesoamerican and South American Cultures

In Mesoamerica and South America, a variety of cultures of varying sophistication—including the Olmec, Maya, Toltec, Aztec, Inca, and others—combined under powerful leaders. Unlike in North America, bands of hunter-gatherers (seminomadic groups who combined hunting and agriculture) and sedentary peoples organized into chiefdoms tended to come under the domination of imperial heads of elaborate state societies that grew into mighty empires. As in North America, the cultivation of new food crops supported much larger populations, which in turn required more complicated social structures. By about 2000 B.C., great temples and pyramids, bureaucracies dedicated to sustaining both living rulers and demanding gods, and religious castes that enjoyed tremendous luxury existed in Mesoamerica.

Each successive rising empire developed vast processing and craft enterprises that made tools, textiles, pottery, and weapons. And in order to sustain such unparalleled prosperity and extend their societies, each empire engaged in diplomacy and waged regular warfare that brought great areas of the countryside under centralized urban control in order to feed thousands of people at a time.

The primary culture in central Mexico to attain such cultural sophistication was the Olmec people, who settled a dense population on the highlands of what would become Mexico City between 1000 B.C. and about A.D. 650. The powerful Olmec religious and political elite dominated the production of thousands of weavers, stone masons, potters, and other craftsmen, and they gathered tribute from a great trading region that extended across the dry lands to the north into present-day Arizona. The majestic Pyramids of the Sun and the Moon stand even today as evidence of the masses of laborers subjugated by the Olmec Empire for temple building.

Around 900 A.D., the Toltec swept down from present-day Mexico City to conquer regions around the central places of Monte Albán and Teotihuacán—which may have grown to over 250,000 by then—and to overwhelm the Maya people of the Yucatan peninsula. Since about 300 A.D., the Maya had enjoyed a sophisticated agricultural culture, which supported a leisured class, jewelry of gold and silver, hieroglyphic writing, a mathematical system with the number zero, and calendars more accurate than anything Europeans would know for centuries.

Then, around 1200 A.D., the Toltec mysteriously retreated from the edges of their empire and drew in around the central highlands. Over the next century, the Aztec people migrated into this area from drier northern climes, consolidating their control over central Mexico. By 1325, they had founded Tenochtitlán (now Mexico City). By the time the Spanish approached this capital city in 1519, its population was about 300,000, making it one of the largest concentrations of people in the world. (London contained only 75,000 people in 1500.) Tenochtitlán supported thousands of craftsmen engaged in producing both necessary and luxury goods. Massive pyramids to the sun and moon gods stood at the center of the metropolis; there, high priests regularly sacrificed captives of war and virgins to their sun god. They constructed wide and deep causeways from outlying regions into the heart of the city, which carried resources and tribute from conquered peoples in outlying regions. An irrigation system brought fresh drinking water to the city; skilled craftsmen and important bureaucrats filled the streets, and everywhere markets filled with foods and household wares provisioned townspeople and traders. The Aztec rulers had subjugated well over 5 million people, from whom they collected not only agricultural tribute but also unfortunate captives who were regularly offered in sacrifice to the sun god, Huitzilopochtli, at bloody public rituals.

Stretching along the Andes Mountains in present-day Peru, another agricultural culture flourished between 900 and 200 B.C. At amazing heights of over ten thousand feet, Andean peoples irrigated their rich soil and produced yields of potatoes that the most modern farming techniques cannot match. Like the Aztecs, this Chavín mountain culture built great temples and developed a sophisticated bureaucracy until a prolonged drought decimated them around 300 A.D. In the next centuries, two new

The Great Temple at Tenochtitlán   At the height of Aztec-Toltec civilization in central Mexico, which coincided with the arrival of Cortés and his Spanish soldiers in 1519, this capital city—built on marshy lowlands and linked to the mainland by broad causeways—had a dense population of over 300,000, more than any European city. Its great public works and Pyramids to the Sun and Moon were connected by an elaborate irrigation system. From this metropolis, priests, warriors, and rulers held absolute authority over hundreds of thousands of people in the countryside.   *(American Museum of Natural History #32659.)*

empires arose in Peru: the Mochicans of the north developed fine pottery and fabulous pyramids, and the Tiwanaku farther to the south adapted crops such as cotton, potatoes, and the ever-present maize to elaborate terracing and irrigation systems. Both cultures, however, failed to survive the return of drought conditions.

Between roughly 1200 and 1400 A.D., the Inca (Quechua) peoples rose out of many warring farm populations to take control of the southern Andean highlands. In an epic battle in 1438, a young warrior leader who took the name Pachakuti subdued enemies to the north and reorganized the surrounding dense population into a centralized state. In their myth of creation, Andean peoples explained that their ancestors had come from nature and, upon death, had returned to the rocks, lakes, and trees. It was fitting, then, to honor and respect the land with many rituals, to take from nature only what was necessary. At the same time, Inca rulers aggressively extended the empire's influence over two thousand miles to the north and south of their Peruvian capital, Cuzco, a city of 250,000 people by the end of the 1400s. The trained warrior class was even fiercer than that of the Aztec, and a refined system of roads communicated edicts and routed massive tribute of grain from far-flung peoples. Imperial leaders also drove their subjects relentlessly to mine silver and gold in tremendous quantities. Whereas North Americans had no large domesticated animals, the Andean people used the llama extensively for heavy hauling, their wool for textile production, their dung for fuel, and their meat for protein. Neither the Aztec nor the Inca used wheels, but an elaborate accounting system that used knotted colored cords, or *quipu,* aided Inca couriers who spread news throughout the great expanse of the empire. By 1500 A.D., the Inca Empire embraced between 8 and 12 million people.

 ## Old World Peoples in Africa and Europe, 1400–1600

Across the Atlantic Ocean, other diverse societies developed on the west coast of Africa and in western Europe from roughly 500 B.C. to A.D. 1500. As Native American societies in the Western Hemisphere became dense and complicated settlements, many African cultures likewise rose to powerful stature or fell to the domination of neighboring peoples. African systems of hunting, fishing, and agriculture became highly productive by the time of the Inca Empire in the 1400s, and the population of sub-Saharan Africa reached as many as 20 million by then. Many African nations interacted with Muslim Arab traders crossing the Sahara, and soon West African peoples would also encounter Portuguese captains landing along the Ivory and Gold Coasts from yet another rapidly changing region of the world.

West African Cultures and Kingdoms

West Africa was peopled by many cultures speaking many languages, linked by various kinship structures, and following assorted economic systems. But from Cape Verde to Angola, most groups shared a few fundamental qualities (see map). Before 3000 B.C., people of the savanna, an open grassland straddling the equator between the Sahara Desert and the tropical rainforest, developed productive agricultural and herding practices that changed very little until the modern era. Rice, millet, sorghum, root crops, and various vegetables were grown by the same slash-and-burn technique used by North American coastal Indians. After clearing the land by burning away the brush, men and women worked the ash into the ground, cultivated small fields until they depleted the land of its nutrients, and then moved on to clear new lands.

Extended families were the basic source of individual and community identity for most West African societies. Families were often matrilineal, or structured along the female kinship line, so that property and political authority over others descended through a person's mother and aunts. Most West African cultures also based important decisions on complex family relationships: what crops to produce, how to distribute goods and services, and how to punish lawbreakers. Most of these cultures also believed, as North American Indians did, that spirits dwelt in all of nature, that a transcendent continuity linked human beings with the natural environment , and that ancestors of the living regularly intervened in worldly affairs. Consequently, a woman should cultivate the soil with respect and a man thank a hunted beast for the meat and hide it provided a village. Doing so honored departed ancestors and invited their guardianship of the harvest and hunt. Like some advancing societies on every continent at that time, certain African peoples organized themselves hierarchically, conferring different rights and obligations on individuals of different stature and at times creating mighty states.

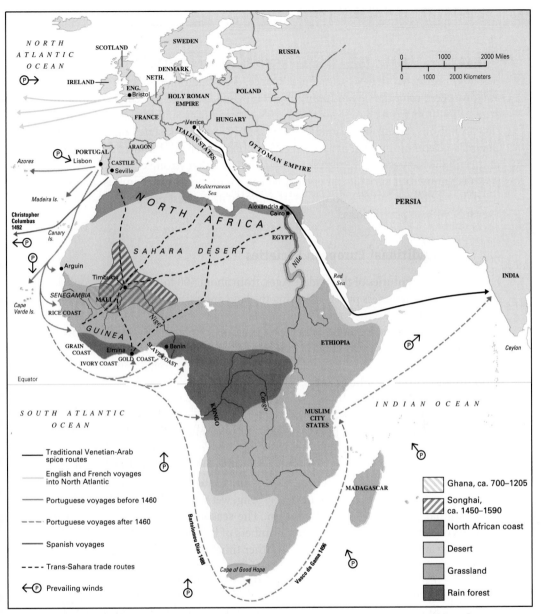

Africa in 1500   The great nation-states of Songhai and Ghana covered much of the western African territory soon to be in regular contact with European traders and slavers. Many cultures of western Africa were already familiar with the slave trade to their own interiors; after 1500 Europeans would also discover that the area was rich in resources.

From the sixth to the eleventh centuries, the powerful kingdom of Ghana developed on these agricultural and kinship foundations. Spanning the Sahara, to the Gulf of Guinea and the Atlantic Ocean, to the Niger River of the interior, Ghanaian rulers orchestrated the building of trading towns, training of skilled craftsmen, and caravan trading with far-flung Arab peoples. Ghanaians extended their influence over neighboring peoples by developing superior pottery and household crafts, iron tools, trade in salt and gold, and hierarchical social structures marked by tribute-gathering elites and great armies.

Invading northern African peoples, primarily Muslims, defeated the Ghana Empire after protracted struggles. In Ghana's place, the kingdom of Songhai (Mali) rose and prospered until the fifteenth century. Its religious and trading center, Timbuktu, attracted visitors from all over northern and western Africa, and even from Mediterranean nations. South of Songhai, in the sophisticated city-states of Congo and Benin, large communities of artisans, legal experts, and religious leaders congregated in thriving urban centers. Europeans noted with awe that strong elites were able to vanquish numerous agricultural villages within a large area. As Columbus sailed toward the Caribbean in 1492, Songhai was enjoying its greatest prosperity and power over subordinate populations.

Traditional European Societies

During the first centuries of the Middle Ages, from about 500 to 1100, most people in Europe lived in changeless poverty farming the land and raising livestock. Depending on where they lived and their relationship to the nobility or gentry, who owned most European lands, people might be called serfs, peasants, or tenants. Together, the overwhelming majority of the population experienced regular droughts, steep taxes, low crop yields, and the insular social relations of people who traveled and traded very short distances from their birthplaces.

Most peasant families labored long and hard merely to survive on land they could never expect to own. They worked with fragile wooden plows, only occasionally aided by draft animals, to break resisting soil. Neighbors shared the sickles they used to cut grain stalks by hand. Farming was task-oriented: men, women, and children performed their arduous duties according to the seasonal rhythms of the weather and the Catholic Church calendar, punctuated by occasional great fires sweeping across forests and fields, or overly long, wet winters that could tip a family's marginal existence toward starvation. The seasons were even related to the numbers of Europeans born, for greater numbers of babies entered the world in the early spring and early fall months than at other times of the year. Similarly, greater numbers of medieval Europeans died in the bitter months of January and February, and in disease-ridden August, than in other months. Infants and childbearing mothers lived a bit more precariously than most people did, but no one was spared undernourishment, disease, unemployment, and violence. Life was, as Thomas Hobbes put it in the early seventeenth century, "nasty, brutish, and short."

Across western Europe one-third of all children died before their fifth birthday, and only half of the young survivors endured the hardships of life until their twenty-second year. By the 1300s, regular crop failures resulted in famines that spread across the central and northern European countryside in swaths of starvation. The devastation reached unimaginable depths when the Black Death, or bubonic plague, wiped out one-third of Europe's population in the few years between 1347 and 1353.

Europeans developed a dramatically different relationship to the land than the Native Americans of the Western Hemisphere. They cleared the land of trees and other "encumbrances." They burned trees for fuel, chopped up logs for house construction, and overhunted their woodlands. They cultivated acreage by turning over the same soil year after year, or alternating tillage with fallow—or vacant—portions.

They planted in rows, marked their lands with fences, and valued attachment to the land over migration to new places. They herded livestock, which they kept in shelters and prized highly for the labor, manure, and food they yielded a farm family. And they worked long days and months in the same small fields to scratch out a subsistence, and maybe a little extra. The requirements of wood for housing, fuel, and mining and smelting industries led to widespread deforestation. In all of these ways, Europeans were dramatically different from Native Americans.

Moreover, European lands were owned exclusively by the sovereign, the church, or the nobility. Local peasants worked the land and craftsmen provided goods and services. Wealthy households also kept many retainers to attend to the needs of noble families. Their walled estates, castles, and monasteries created a stark reminder of wealth and power in contrast to the countryside's impoverished peasants and few scattered freehold farmers.

European laws and social customs often ensured that only men owned and inherited property, that women remained subordinate, and that children learned strict obedience and hard work under disciplining eyes—practices that stood in sharp distinction to Native American and African cultures. Boys of seven or eight years old were regularly sent to learn a trade and girls "farmed out" to learn housekeeping and perhaps supplement the family income. Such situations were not always happy ones; many children became lonely or suffered abuse in their adopted households, and anxious young adults often expressed an unfulfilled desire for personal independence. Among both the middling and well-to-do, marriage was not a matter of love and choice, but an arrangement by the parents to preserve lands and cement family relationships. In England, the oldest son might not marry until he was about thirty years old because he needed to wait until he could inherit a portion of his father's land or trade.

European Peasants at Work   This contemporary drawing shows peasants using a shared community draught horse to harrow their field in the spring. They also would have used hand flails to thresh grain in the early fall. Following the rhythms of the sun and the seasons, they worked hardest in the fields from March to August, but the chores of repairing wooden tools, threshing and grinding grain into flour, and attending to numerous other farm tasks by hand occupied peasants year round.   *(By permission of the British Library.)*

Peasants rarely had the opportunity to plan their children's work and marriages. Indeed, more often than not, they lived on the edge of survival. During the late Middle Ages, after 1100, some regions began to benefit from using more oxen and horses to cultivate fields, experimenting with crop rotation, introducing iron plows, improving milling, and taming wastelands and bogs for new fields. However, even though peasants enjoyed increased amounts of food, there was little improvement in general nutrition or longer lives. For one thing, most of the increase in food came from expanding cereal crops. Vegetables were still seasonal and scarce, and most peasants consumed fish or meat only occasionally. For another thing, increased agricultural production was often not enough to feed a family or village, especially when landlords or marauders took much of a crop by law or treachery. Then, too, many peasants faced dispossession—being thrown off the land by its owners—usually a sentence of early death. Roving bands of the landless became thieves and beggars along rural roads everywhere in Europe during the 1200s and 1300s.

While millions of peasants endured wrenching poverty, their rulers, the nobility, and church leaders led lives of comfort and privilege. The church and state levied endless taxes on their struggling peasant populations. Compounding the misery of the poor were the wars that broke out repeatedly among European princes and nobles. Eventually, the combination of tensions erupted into open peasant revolts in many parts of England and Europe. For example, Flemish peasants in northern Europe rose up against an oppressive Church and merciless landlords in the 1320s, demanding food and lower rents. Over the next seventy years, rebellion spread to other areas. By 1381, a peasant revolt spread over much of England's countryside in the largest lower-class rebellion in that island's history.

It also took many centuries for England and Europe to emerge as commercial powers on the high seas. For much of the Middle Ages, Viking warriors from northern Europe terrorized the coastal peoples of the British Isles and France. Eventually their streamlined boats mastered the forceful currents of the northern Atlantic; they first occupied Iceland to the west in the late 800s, and in the late 900s Erik the Red, an outlaw on the run, moved his bands of Norsemen on to Greenland. There Erik established contact with the Inuit (Eskimo) Indians, while his son, Leif, sailed along the coast of North America just after the year 1000 A.D. Although Leif Erikson left a few sailors at the short-lived colony called Vinland (in what is now Newfoundland), the Norsemen visited the area of present-day Maine only occasionally, to gather wood for fuel and to trade with Native Americans. Further voyages in later centuries by fishing vessels continued to whet the appetites of Europeans for dominion and resources in the Western Hemisphere. But the process of fanning out commercially and imperially was slow. Begun when Columbus arrived in the Caribbean, European expansion was still in its infancy when English settlers decided to stay permanently along the North American coast over one hundred years later.

One important catalyst of this commercial transformation was the growing number of merchants in England and Europe who had been expanding their trade and fortunes for some time. The Catholic Church and western European states sponsored two centuries of crusades (1095–1270) against Muslim "infidels" in the eastern Mediterranean countries. Despite the horrors of medieval warfare, contact with Muslim and other merchants throughout the Arab world promoted European trade with new lands, and consequently introduced nobles, professionals, and merchants to exotic material comforts.

Gradually, Italian merchants took control of the spice and silk trades. They led European efforts to bring back from China implements to measure earthquakes and locate direction (the compass), chairs, gunpowder, and skilled craft techniques. The introduction of these goods and ideas into Europe prompted more sophisticated merchant connections in banking and transportation routes, and more regularized fairs and marketplaces to trade. The young Venetian trader, Marco Polo (1254?–1324?) is the best known of these travelers to far eastern Asian kingdoms. By 1477, his journals had been published on European presses that owed much to the invention of moveable type in China, and his impressions of the Far East sparked great expectations about the benefits to Europeans of trade with China.

Europe's Internal Transformation, 1400–1600

From about 1050 to 1250, as faraway Cahokia and Ghana were achieving their greatest accomplishments, Europe entered a phase of dynamic internal transformation that would culminate in aggressive external expansion and colonization. On the land, powerful forces of change altered traditional agriculture and the population rose quickly. Across the seas, although China and the Islamic world would continue to be commercial giants, peoples of the eastern Mediterranean, Middle East, and northern Africa gradually yielded their dominant positions in trade and culture to Europeans.

Agriculture and Commerce

By the 1400s, England and Europe were undergoing profound transformations. In England, for example, until the 1400s cottagers, peasants, and laborers made up about three-fourths of the population. They typically lived in very small dwellings, kept vegetable gardens, and supplemented their needs with fish from local streams and game from nearby forests. Most of this population counted on having rights to use plots, or long strips of land, from the landlord's large open fields beyond their villages, on which they grew rye, wheat, barley, or oats. Together, villagers shared access to these plots, agreeing on communal rights and obligations in using and maintaining them.

During the 1400s, these traditions were noticeably giving way in England and on the Continent to new social relations in the countryside. New economic forces bound together farmers, merchants, and distant buyers to an extent never known before in Europe. Also during the 1400s, plagues, grinding scarcities of food, and peasant revolts seemed to ebb. Although half of the world's children still died before reaching the age of five, farmers were producing more to eat and the population began to grow slowly in fortunate regions of Europe. The terrible cycles of mass death subsided, and by the early 1500s, people began to comment on the rise of local populations, longer life spans, and more work to go around. For decades, even with more people available to produce food and clothing, old farming strategies could not keep up with growing needs. In northern Europe and England, inefficient strip farming kept crop yields very low. To make matters worse, more people were squeezed onto the same meager plots that had been used for centuries. The pastures and forests of many commons, which were used collectively by eligible members of the village, became crowded with livestock and depleted of game and timber.

Two other developments accelerated these changes. Once ships began to cross the Atlantic Ocean to search for land and wealth, the lifestyles of Europeans became tied to discoveries in their distant colonies. Most important, the great influx of New World silver into Europe and England led to inflation that drove up the price of consumer goods, and drove down the price of farmers' grain. Everywhere, it cost much more of a family's income to buy necessities. Even well-to-do yeomen—independent landowners—sometimes could not afford to hire necessary labor at harvest time. Second, England's prosperity was tightly bound up with the foreign markets for its raw wool and woolen cloth. Great amounts of merchants' capital and skilled labor supported this enterprise, which was in turn linked to the Dutch businesses in Antwerp that sent English woolens into markets of northern and eastern Europe. But when the Antwerp firms announced they had more wool than they could sell, and changes in the currency standards hurt merchants with outstanding foreign debts, England's economy entered a downturn. England's merchants and manufacturers argued that the country had to have new markets. Landlords in the countryside, wanting to take advantage of expanding urban and foreign markets, grew increasingly impatient with the inefficiencies of patchwork quilt strips farmed by dozens of peasants. Especially in England, landlords who wished to increase yields teamed up with woolen manufacturers who wished to take over land for sheep grazing. Powerful landowners turned to England's national government, Parliament, to secure laws for "enclosing" the open fields of traditional village communities. Under Parliament's Enclosure Acts, written titles were required in order to retain control over landed property; not surprisingly, these titles were issued to powerful individuals who consolidated holdings for cultivation or put up fences for sheep pastures.

Relations in the countryside underwent dramatic changes as a consequence of the Enclosure Acts. Among the winners were landlords in the English gentry who now owned enclosed lands. Yeomen sometimes hung on to their lands and benefited from the inflation during the 1500s by selling their surpluses to city consumers at rising prices. But the nobles who collected fixed rents from their tenants received payments declining in value. Shrinking income, combined with steeply rising prices for luxuries, crimped their aristocratic lifestyles and political prestige. And for the three-quarters of the population who were nontenant peasants and hired field laborers, enclosures created a tenuous existence, indeed. Peasants without titles to the land they worked were thrown off the soil.

A new set of social and legal arrangements, based on private access to the land and protection of contracts that gave title to landholdings, began to displace centuries of collective land use on the commons. Without a commons, the landless peasant had no place to graze a cow, gather firewood, or net a fish. Thousands of families lost their status as relatively autonomous farmers and became wage earners for new landlords or cottage spinners of wool. By 1600, sheep outnumbered people three to one in England, and malnourishment was rampant. As Sir Thomas More pointed out in his famous plaint, *Utopia* (1516), the loss of farm lands had destroyed a way of life, so that "your sheep . . . eat up men."

Eventually, thousands upon thousands of dispossessed farmers, servants, and craftspeople looked elsewhere in England for scarce employment. Many of them migrated to London from their now-enclosed lands or came as farmers' children seeking jobs as laborers, servants, and apprentices. Manufacturers and master artisans set up shops in cities because they knew the labor supply would be cheap and plentiful, and that workers would also be consumers of foods and finished goods. Ambitious professionals and merchants found that their fortunes were tied to the resources of cities, too.

But the influx of people from the countryside also created tremendous suffering in the cities. Migrating rural people competed for limited housing and jobs, and the prices of daily necessities skyrocketed. Huge numbers of destitute souls in the port towns and London plummeted into squalor. Urban society and culture also shocked newcomers to the cities. In London—as in Amsterdam, Lisbon, or Paris—the customary relations of rural villages, where people knew the rules of social decorum and where prices and rhythms of agricultural life hardly changed over a lifetime, were breaking down. Instead of weighing justice between buyers and sellers in village markets, or preserving the relatively unchanging values of goods and services, people seemed to be driven by the unabashed pursuit of private profit. Instead of changeless levels of rural poverty or maybe modest comfort, cities offered prospects for personal improvement—although they just as often produced bewildering amounts of failure.

Commerce changed in England, too. For centuries, most merchants had formed intimate partnerships with family and trusted personal friends in order to protect their investments from unscrupulous competitors and shelter themselves from excessive risks. Some merchants won specific government privileges as monopolied trading companies. But during the late 1400s, the view already circulating in thousands of small workshops and food stalls that profit seeking was acceptable—even good—permeated groups of merchant investors who sank their capital into urban projects, war expeditions, and "ventures" to foreign lands. Perhaps, many writers reasoned, it would be good for business and of great benefit to the nation to do away with these monopolies and their protected privileges. Then, individuals would be freer to bargain among themselves for the best prices, and to dispatch ships to richer markets, without regard for stultifying government restrictions.

Most English merchants did not adopt this way of thinking until production of commodities increased sufficiently for export to foreign buyers. But some of the most prominent merchants became champions of the Enclosure Acts when they discovered that landless country folk could be mobilized to receive raw materials from merchants and, in their homes, manufacture textiles, shoes, and small implements. In this "putting out" system, merchants focused on the production of woolen cloth; they directed women and children to wash and comb wool, which was then spun into yarn, which men in turn wove into cloth. Merchant dealers collected the cloth in the countryside for fulling and dying at city manufacturers' establishments. Of course, a strong market existed not far from producers' doorsteps, for every English

Merchants of Luxury Wares   In contrast to rural peasants, wealthy urban merchants in the 1400s and 1500s dealt with manufactured goods from a variety of regions and nations and, as this image shows, provided city dwellers with loans and credit to stretch their abilities to buy necessary and luxury wares.   *(Giraudon/Art Resource, NY.)*

household needed to replenish its woolen cloth and clothing from time to time, and few households could produce enough on their own. But merchants concentrated on exporting a steady supply of cloth to distant lands, and the government aided them with bounties, or cash incentives, to subsidize this exporting. Slowly, then, evolving rural and urban relations gave rise to interlocking dependencies among rural producers, merchants, and the government. Soon some of the people disaffected by these new social relations would make daring voyages across thousands of miles of ocean in order to make a fresh start in North America.

The Nation-State and the Renaissance, 1400–1600

The system of local lords constantly warring against their nominal rulers, and one another, came to a gradual end in the 1400s. First in Portugal, then in France, Spain, and England, new monarchs asserted their control over splintered factions and regions. Rising monarchs professed to be above the petty quarrels of fiefdoms, estates, or factions, and promised to unify feuding regions into nations, not unlike the imperial rulers of centralized states in the Americas might have promised. To do this, European monarchs raised great armies and created royal bureaucracies, paying for them with loans from wealthy merchants who benefited from crown protection of their interests on the seas and in foreign countries, and with taxes on the citizens who were promised protection from preying local lords.

This process of forming unified nation-states began in Portugal when John I consolidated fractured nobilities in the 1380s. In Spain, Ferdinand of Aragon married Isabella of Castile in 1469, uniting the two most important Spanish kingdoms. In order to create the social unity they needed for absolute rule, Ferdinand and Isabella then proceeded to crush the nobles of many regions of Spain, to support the Church's Inquisition, whose torture chambers tested the wills of all subjects suspected of disloyalty, and to expel Muslims (called Moors) from Grenada and then the entire country in 1492. Unconverted Jews were given six months to become Christians or be expelled, too, which prompted many Jews to migrate to more tolerant countries such as Holland and Ottoman-ruled Bosnia.

In France, Louis XI began to unite noble armies under his crown in the 1460s, which permitted general peace to return after nearly one hundred years of persistent warfare. In England, long-feuding noble households clashed in the War of the Roses in 1455. For the next thirty years, the Yorks and Lancasters battered each other, and only when Henry VII defeated the last Yorkist king in 1485 did peace return. For the next hundred years or so, English kings would rely, not on the nobles, but on the representative institution of Parliament to bolster their power.

The interests of merchants and monarchs often corresponded. For example, merchants used the new royal navies to protect their commerce from marauding pirates on the open seas. A few companies of merchants also enjoyed royal contracts, or monopolies, for exclusive commercial privileges. Groups of protected merchants in Constantinople, Genoa, or Antioch, for example, took the surpluses of small farmers living throughout the interior of foreign lands to markets at unimaginable distances. The same merchants returned to their homelands with ships full of exotic wares: salt and pepper, wines, spices, silk and tapestries, gunpowder, drawings and descriptions of technical inventions, and new books. Merchants promised to fill royal coffers with part of their commercial profits—especially the silver and gold they sought in foreign lands. In time, this alliance of politics and commerce, of crown and merchants, became indispensable for the migration of great numbers of European people to the Western Hemisphere.

These efforts during the 1400s to unify many different peoples into nation-states and to support the prosperity of merchants in international trade coincided with a sweeping cultural revival: the Renaissance. Across Europe beginning in the 1300s, many wealthy commercial families began to invest portions of their fortunes in an unparalleled burst of building, painting, mapping, printing, and traveling. Together, merchants, statesmen, and intellectuals renewed their interest in the Greek and Roman classics, in secular learning, and in nature and scientific inquiry. The leaders of countries, armies, churches, universities, and municipalities sought to validate or elevate their authority by enlisting the aid of inventors and artists in creating great public works. Painters sought to reconcile the intense Christianity of the era with both ancient philosophy and secular discoveries about nature and the heavens. Michelangelo (1475–1564) turned his artistic focus from mystical representation of divine subjects to studying the human body.

The Renaissance also spurred change in science, literature, law, and politics. Merchants hired Renaissance astronomers and cartographers to explore and map unknown lands to the south and east of Europe, and they promoted more efficient shipbuilding techniques. Entrepreneurs experimented with new navigational instruments such as the compass, the Arab astrolabe, which permitted accurate calculation of north–south distances (latitude), and the sextant, which measured the degree of altitude of celestial bodies. Galileo Galilei (1564–1642) challenged the teachings of the Roman Church when he turned his telescope from contemplating the "perfect" movement of heavenly bodies toward the craters and other imperfections of the Moon's surface. William Shakespeare (1564–1616) warned theatergoers about the disruption caused by corrupt heads of state, famines, and plagues; only wise rulers, a stolid social hierarchy, and satisfaction of people's essential needs could guarantee the security of the nation. Legal experts examined the sources of stability and order in societies. Niccolo Machiavelli (1469–1527), who wrote *The Prince* in 1513, rejected the tradition of investing politics with religious themes; instead, he wrote more personal, realistic, and sometimes scathing portraits of political rulers and their lust for power.

The Reformation, 1517–1563

The great religious revolt that developed alongside the agricultural, commercial, cultural, and political transformations shaking Europe is known as the Reformation. For centuries, the Catholic Church vied with traditional folk beliefs for spiritual power over European people. By the 1400s, it claimed the authority to sell "indulgences," or dispensations from punishments still due in earthly life and in purgatory (a station after life before the soul advances to heaven) even after sins were sacramentally absolved. Although indulgences had been granted in the 1000s to encourage men to fight in the crusades, by the 1400s, popes sold them to raise much-needed funds for building cathedrals and hospitals. Anxious masses of heaven-hungry people readily adopted the innovation, and dug deep into their pockets to help make the Church wealthy.

The German monk Martin Luther (1483–1546) recoiled from this practice of selling spiritual benefits. Even more, he rejected what he saw as the Catholic Church's teaching of a "theology of works." Since the 1100s, followers of church leader St. Thomas Aquinas believed that priests could help sinners improve their chances of salvation by administering the sacraments and forgiving sins. Luther wanted a return to the teachings of St. Augustine of Hippo who, around A.D. 400, professed the doctrine of predestination, or the belief that God alone determined who was saved and who was damned for eternity, without any regard to the conduct of people in this life. But Luther went a step further in the early 1500s, rejecting the idea of a vengeful God who dispensed justice and salvation capriciously and embracing the Biblical principle that sinful mortals could be sanctified through faith. Luther emphasized that eternal salvation was a gift from God, ensured only by faith in Christ and not something sinners, repentant or otherwise, could win by good works.

In 1517 Luther posted ninety-five theses on the door of the castle church in Wittenberg that criticized many practices of the Catholic Church. He encouraged lay people to turn to the Bible for authority and to query the wisdom of ordained priests. Although he did not set out to start a revolution, Luther's actions ignited smoldering discontents into a dissenting movement that would shake the foundations of European society. A church investigation of Luther's beliefs led to his excommunication, or expulsion, in 1521. But his teachings spread widely and an organized rival church emerged in the German states over the coming years. The emerging Lutheran Church retained only two of the seven sacraments (baptism and holy communion); discarded the practices of fasts, pilgrimages, and veneration of relics; and abolished the requirement of celibacy for priests.

What had begun as an internal church matter soon became a catalyst for political change. In his own country, Luther attracted the support of German princes who wished for greater autonomy from Rome. In the much larger Holy Roman Empire, Lutherans confronted the mighty opposition of the grandson of Ferdinand and Isabella, Charles V. The printing press, invented shortly before Luther was born, became a powerful instrument for the movement to spread its arguments against the Catholic Church, as well as Holy Scripture. Soon Lutheranism attracted massive numbers of European people willing to fight great religious wars that overlapped with the process of nation making over the next century.

In France, the state harshly persecuted the "Protestants" who embraced Luther's teachings. One such Protestant, the lawyer John Calvin (1509–1564), fled to Geneva, Switzerland, where he created a model Protestant community with even stricter rules than Lutherans advocated. Calvin extended the doctrines of Luther to include "predestination," or the belief that God had chosen a few "elect" citizens for salvation and had relegated the great majority to eternal damnation. Calvinists became vigilant of their every public and private action, watchful for the signs that they might be among the elect. Moreover, they tried to enhance their standing in the community and their personal material success in a "calling" so as to highlight the signs of election if they were present. As a result, Calvinists believed that thrift, hard work, sobriety, and providing strong role models to all citizens would join material success and spiritual commitment. Even if the appropriate moral behavior were not itself proof of election, an immoral life would surely indicate one's place among the "unregenerate," or the unsaved.

Calvinists energetically cultivated their beliefs beyond Geneva. Dutch and German Reformed churches grew quickly, and in Scotland, John Knox set up the Presbyterian Church. French Calvinists drew strength from merchants, rising middle classes, and nobles who tried unsuccessfully in 1560 to seize power and then suffered forty years of persecution by the French Catholic state. In the St. Bartholomew's Day Massacre of August 24, 1572, royal armies slaughtered thousands of believers, and only when Henry IV, who had been raised as a Protestant, ascended to the throne in 1589 did dissenters regain hope. Henry issued the Edict of Nantes in 1598, granting freedom of worship, but the majority of the population remained Catholic and Henry himself converted to Catholicism. Many French Protestants, called Huguenots, migrated out of the country, as many Lutherans had left Germany earlier, and soon the Catholic Church initiated a Counter-Reformation that promoted the teaching and missionary movement of Jesuits, who revitalized Catholicism in Europe and aided later efforts to expand abroad.

The Reformation followed a different path in England. Shortly after the Tudor family took the throne, King Henry VIII (ruled 1509–1547) asked the pope to annul his marriage to Catharine of Aragon, daughter of Ferdinand and Isabella, because she failed to bear a son to inherit the crown. When the pope denied Henry's request in 1531, the latter forced the annulment by co-opting the church's power in England and forcing a convocation of the clergy to recognize Henry as the supreme head of a new Church of England, which was also called the Anglican Church. Henry hand-picked a new Archbishop of Canterbury, Thomas Cranmer, who readily approved the king's annulment. Further, Henry took steps toward enhancing the prestige of his Anglican Church by selling extensive monastic landholdings to his political favorites.

But in the view of many English people influenced by the strong tide of reform ideas on the continent, the new church retained far too many Catholic beliefs and rituals. Henry's daughter Mary (ruled 1553–1558) briefly restored Catholicism, but the definitive settlement of the Anglican faith came during the reign of Henry's second daughter, Elizabeth I (ruled 1558–1603). By the time Elizabeth ascended the throne, a great number of English people were willing to embrace the Reformation, but not everyone agreed about just what that meant. On the one hand, the monarch emphasized the importance of English-language Bibles and an English-language liturgy, although she retained many of the ceremonies of the Anglican Church and its episcopal hierarchy. On the other hand, Calvinists demanded a wholesale "purification" of all traces of Catholicism and denounced the rituals of Mass; many withdrew from public worship and promoted private reading of the Bible.

These Puritans included aristocrats, gentry, intellectuals, some clergymen, and merchants, as well as middling artisans and farmers. In addition to Puritan experiences of religious repression, a brewing economic crisis during the late 1500s caused some of England's great Puritan gentlemen to lose their lands. Monopolied trading companies prevented many rising Puritan merchants from entering new routes of commerce. Chronic underemployment drove many impoverished artisans, especially in the textile trades, into the Puritan fold, along with hundreds of dispossessed farmers.

In England and in Europe, the Reformation also gave rise to smaller groups who criticized the "worldliness" of Calvinists. The Anabaptists, for example, appealed strongly to women and poor people who had been excluded from playing a role in the new dissenting churches and favored a stricter separation of church and state. Anabaptists were persecuted by traditional churches and Calvinists alike, as were other dissenting denominations that arose out of the era's religious fervor, including the Mennonites, Amish, Baptists, and Quakers (see Chapter 3). In time, many dissenters would join the large numbers of Puritans who exited England to share in the transformation of North America.

Taking to the Seas, 1420–1600

The transformations in Europe during the 1400s did not immediately spur the "discovery" of lands and peoples in the Western Hemisphere. Decades of consolidating innovations and institutions in Europe, of false starts and failures getting out of Europe, and of disappointing encounters with new peoples and new lands, preceded the permanent settlements that we often identify with European success.

In addition, not all European nations explored the "New World" at the same time or the same pace. Just as important, the various cultures of Africa and North America were at different stages of their own internal developments at the time scholars often associate with the encounters of Europeans with the New World. During the 1400s, Portugal dominated European exploration and was relatively unchallenged in the African slave trade. But in the next century, Portuguese influence over new lands and peoples was eclipsed by Spanish colonization.

Portuguese Exploration and African Slavery

African people were not strangers to the condition of slavery. Indeed, through human history slavery has existed in a bewildering number of societies for many different purposes. Slavery has been known in vast ancient empires and small agricultural kingdoms; Mediterranean, Chinese, Russian lands; warring and peaceful peoples. The reasons why people have been forced into slavery have also varied, from the need for labor to a desire for specialized craftsmen, warriors, concubines, artists, or victims for sacrifice. As Ghana rose in power, slavery grew in Europe and England; Slavs (from which peoples the term *slavery* is derived) taken in repeated wars were sold in large numbers to English masters, and in parts of Europe it was perfectly acceptable for parents to sell their children into slavery. When European attention turned to exploration of West Africa after 1400, slavery was already well known there. Arab traders and powerful coastal kingdoms frequently held African individuals in bondage for payment of debts or as an exchange for food during famines. Muslim caravans sold Africans as "chattel"—a kind of human property—to remote places.

The Slave Trade in Africa   Slavery was widespread in Africa long before Portuguese traders starting landing along the continent's western coastline. But for centuries, African slaves were primarily debtors, criminals, or captives of wars, and often slavery was a temporary condition. Once Europeans came, slaves were removed from Africa, permanently, and almost always for lifelong slavery. Europeans who landed at the Gold Coast, or what became known as the "Slave Coast," reached farther and farther into the interior to take larger numbers of Africans into bondage.   *(Paris, Bibliothèque nationale de France, photo © B.n.F.)*

By the early 1400s, the Portuguese became the first European nation systematically to explore West Africa and exploit its people and resources. Although the small country had never distinguished itself as a wealthy or a commercial nation, it was located strategically at the intersection of the coveted Mediterranean Sea and the mysterious Atlantic Ocean. Adventurers already knew about coastal Guinea's vast stores of gold, as well as Benin's renowned iron craftsmen. But it was not until the 1420s that Portugal's Prince Henry "the Navigator" (1394–1460) contributed church revenues to numerous expeditions that attempted to map and explore Atlantic islands and Africa's west coast. At home, Portuguese scholars promoted new sailing and shipbuilding techniques that they had learned from Ottomans and Arabs.

In short order the Portuguese set out to break the hold of Moorish (North African) and Turkish traders on the long-distance trade in goods and slaves. Establishing valuable connections to Madeira after 1418, and the Azores after 1427, where forced labor produced sugar and wine for ready European markets, Portuguese traders extended their reach. Crews of Portuguese sailors seized dozens of Africans in the 1440s and returned with them to Lisbon. In the following decade, the raiders paid Africans to capture neighboring people in exchange for coconuts, citrus fruit, swine, and small trinkets. Soon, the Portuguese built offshore "factories" on islands near Cape Blanco and Cape Verde, and from there conducted a lucrative slave trade. Although the Portuguese failed to subdue powerful African kingdoms to the interior, they exploited rivalries among the weaker small states and built outposts such as Elmina, on the Gold Coast of West Africa, in the 1480s. There, Africans of many languages and cultures could trade slaves for European goods, or the Portuguese could trade slaves for African gold. By 1487, Bartholomeu Dias had extended Portuguese influence in Africa below the Sahara all the way to the Cape of Good Hope. In 1497 Vasco da Gama rounded the Cape of Good Hope and journeyed up to India. Along the way he took slaves, spices, and valuable handicrafts that whet the appetites of the Portuguese elite for more of this trade.

Europeans had long associated slavery with the production of sugar. During the 1300s, Italians had taken sugar cane out of West Asia and set up plantations on Mediterranean islands that used slave labor. The Portuguese slave trade expanded rapidly once planters started sugar production on the island of Madeira in the 1470s, where their constant need for new supplies of West Africans was fueled by their policy of working slaves to death. Soon, Portuguese merchants extended slavery to the Canary Islands, and although Columbus failed to enslave native people of the Caribbean, voyagers who followed in his footsteps to Hispaniola carried African slaves to work the sugar mills constructed there in about 1510. To ensure a steady supply of African labor, Spain granted Portugal a monopoly of the carrying trade in 1518. They then teamed up with Dutch bankers to begin vast sugar enterprises in northeastern Brazil that were supported through the 1500s with shipload after shipload of African slaves.

The slavery Europeans developed after 1400 was quite different from their previous experiences of the institution. Although slavery was already well-entrenched in Africa, the forms known by most tribes were neither permanent nor heritable. Moreover, most African slaves in Africa became slaves as captives of war or intertribal conflict rather than based on race, and even in bondage they retained certain personal rights. When Europeans became involved in African slavery, however, they systematically exploited dense populations, removed native peoples from their soil to distant places, and put them and their descendents in permanent bondage.

Christopher Columbus

After Ferdinand and Isabella united Spain, they shifted their focus toward circumventing the Muslim traders who dominated the Mediterranean and northern African land routes to China and India. By the late 1400s, sailors, geographers, and merchants had long accepted that the world was round, but they mistakenly believed that Europe, Africa, and Asia covered more than half the world's surface and that the Atlantic Ocean was but a narrow ribbon of water. So, few people thought about how long a ship's voyage across the Atlantic might be. Of course, word spread quickly that Portuguese ships were already claiming the riches and power to be gained from finding a new route to the East. The Spanish monarchs also knew that the king of Portugal had refused to support the bold proposal of a young Genoese sea captain, Christopher Columbus (1451–1506), to find this route by sailing west. Heads of state in France and England had been even quicker to dismiss the preposterous bid. At first too concerned about national unification to pay much attention to Columbus, Isabella was later convinced by his persistence, as well as by Spain's desire to consolidate an empire of its own, to outfit a westward voyage.

Columbus set out from Palos, Spain, on August 3, 1492 with some ninety eager but mostly inexperienced young mariners on three small vessels. He had little formal education himself, but years of practical experience on the high seas. Nevertheless, the sailors' confidence in Columbus's dream of sailing west soon turned to fear and near mutiny. About three thousand miles out to sea, the crews demanded to go home. Columbus managed to quell this discontent for two more days, when on October 12 the island he would name San Salvador (now Samana Cay) appeared on the horizon. Believing that the Caribbean islands were a gateway to a vast stretch of China that lay just beyond their sight, he named his "discoveries" the West Indies and called the Arawak people of the island "Indians."

In a short time, Columbus and his crews sailed on to Cuba (which he mistook for Cipangu, or Japan), and then to Hispaniola. There, he encountered the great numbers of Taino living on the region's islands. Columbus was at first amazed at the physical perfection of the Taino, who were "very well built, with very handsome bodies and very good faces." Yet he also presumed Taino inferiority: "It appeared to me that these people were very poor in everything. . . . They bear no arms, nor are they acquainted with them, for I showed them swords and they grasped them by the blade and cut themselves through ignorance." Shortly, Columbus and others would conclude that differences of dress and physical appearance that were judged to be "uncivilized" suited Native Americans "to be good servants" of the Spanish (see Competing Voices, page 37).

In December 1492, Columbus, a number of Taino Indians, and a portion of his crews caught the westerly trade winds and sailed home. They arrived to the acclaim of the Spanish crown and publicists alike, and in the next years Columbus, now dubbed the Admiral of the Ocean Sea, received funding for three more expeditions. Although Columbus announced to his benefactors that "all the inhabitants" of the islands he had explored "could be made slaves," his political and financial backers kept their eyes on the material, not the human, riches he claimed to have found. Based on the gold jewelry he saw native people wearing, Columbus had left about forty of his mariners behind on the north coast of Hispaniola with orders to locate the gold mines he was certain were there.

Before they discovered how badly mistaken Columbus was about the gold, the Spanish monarchs appealed to the pope for support in declaring their right to rule over the places in which Columbus had staked their flag. Ferdinand and Isabella asked for nothing less than a division between Portugal and Spain of all as-yet-undiscovered lands to the west. In 1494 Spain and Portugal negotiated the Treaty of Tordesillas, drawing a line from north to south about 1,100 miles west of the Cape Verde Islands. All undiscovered lands to the west of the line would belong to Spain; to the east, to Portugal. The terms of this treaty made two matters clearer than ever: Portugal's preeminent imperial position would henceforth be challenged, and Spain's imperial authorities would be determined to conquer what Caribbean islands they could, and all lands that lay beyond them.

In late 1493, the Spanish crown had dispatched a convoy of seventeen ships laden with more than twelve hundred to colonize the Caribbean. However, when the fleet arrived at Hispaniola, nothing was left of the Spanish fort or the men planted there earlier, for their raids against Taino villages had brought retaliation that laid waste the Spanish settlement. In months to come, Columbus's failure to find gold and his brutal treatment of native peoples alienated him from both settlers on the islands and the Spanish monarchs at home. When on his third voyage in 1498 Columbus continued to exaggerate about his own leadership, and to mistreat Spanish sailors and Native Americans alike, the crown ordered him home in leg irons.

On a fourth, and final, voyage to the Caribbean from 1502 to 1504, Columbus engaged in now-familiar disregard of native peoples and their lands, this time along the coast of Central America. Everywhere Columbus had landed, disease, destruction of fields and settlements, and the introduction of slavery had transformed Indian ways of life. Even on his deathbed in debtor's prison in 1506, Columbus misguidedly insisted that the lands he discovered lay in the Far East. By then the Treaty of Tordesillas was a mere parchment pact, for France, Holland, and England would soon enter the contest for settlements in the Western Hemisphere despite Spain's imperial claims. As a final irony, it was not Columbus's name that was assigned to the two continents of the "New World," but that of Amerigo Vespucci (1451–1512), a Florentine merchant who sailed for Spain in 1499 near the South American coastline. By the early 1500s, a few Europeans had begun to understand that the large area of land across the Atlantic was not connected to Asia at all. Then in 1507 the German cartographer Martin Waldseemüller produced a world map that showed large land masses, "the new lands" of the Western Hemisphere, as a separate continent. He named it "America," in honor of Vespucci, and the name endured.

The Spanish Century

Spain's ascendancy among the European empire builders held firm during most of the 1500s. Its growing army of *conquistadors* accepted the invasion of the Western Hemisphere as a new crusade. Fame, personal wealth, and glory for their nation motivated scores of adventurers to undertake conquering missions, first in the Caribbean, and then into the North American interior. Spanish raids through the islands were especially cruel because the populations of native peoples lacked the means to fend off European attackers and succumbed quickly to the fiery weapons and devastating germs of their invaders. Spanish marauders subjugated the populations in the Bahamas, Hispaniola, Puerto Rico, Jamaica, and Cuba, forcing native islanders to work as slaves in intensive agriculture or brutal mining camps. As native populations declined rapidly in the early 1500s from disease and harsh labor conditions, Europeans were already clearing Caribbean land and importing African slaves to work the plantation estates that transformed life on the islands.

In 1511 Spaniards began making plans to explore the mainland to the west. Within two years, Vasco Nuñez de Balboa crossed the narrow Isthmus of Panama to the Pacific Ocean, and by 1519, Hernán Cortés (1485–1547) and his army of about four hundred men, a dozen horses, and some cannon, landed at the site of Vera Cruz. In the next months they marched two hundred miles to Tenochtitlán at the heart of the mighty Aztec empire of the Mexican interior (see page 11). Cortés's troops marveled at the splendors of this magnificent city, and at the works of the Aztec master-engineers whose thousands of drafted laborers put up the massive pyramids and numerous public buildings that dominated the city's life.

The thirty-four-year-old Cortés advanced quickly against local populations with superior arms made of steel, dogs trained to kill on command, and a steady supply of Spanish horses whose presence alone stunned thousands of native peoples into submission. He also had at his side an Aztec woman named Ala Malinche, who translated the Nahuatl language for Cortés as the conquest proceeded. The Spaniards also exploited discontent among portions of the subjugated countryside against the imperial Aztec rulers in a "divide-and-conquer" strategy; tribute-poor villages were willing to join in a revolt against their mighty overlord Moctezuma. Some of the peoples living on agricultural sites between the coast and Tenochtitlán may have believed that Cortés was the Toltec god Quetzalcoatl, returning to free them from the Aztec. Locals who chose not to fight alongside Cortés fled the central plains to remote mountains or the arid north, inadvertently hastening the conquest of Tenochtitlán and its surrounding area.

Once they invaded Tenochtitlán, Spanish *conquistadors* easily plundered the mountainous coffers of tribute lying in public storehouses, no small amount of which made its way back to the Spanish crown. Cortés and his relatively small entourage captured Moctezuma, the Aztec ruler, which further weakened the heart of the Aztec empire. Although the dwindling numbers of Aztec rallied to drive out the Spanish in 1520, smallpox continued to weaken them, and a reconquest of the capital city in 1521 ended Aztec resistance. Indeed, European diseases, primarily smallpox, reduced the Aztec Empire from nearly 25 million inhabitants to about 2.5 million in fifty years.

For some time to come, the Spanish faced serious difficulties sustaining permanent settlements in Mexico and ruling them effectively. But the lure of gold and glory outweighed the risks of failure, and *conquistadors* continued to answer its call in large numbers. In the 1520s, Francisco Pizarro (1470–1541) began a bloody march through the expansive Inca Empire with fewer than two hundred soldiers. He seized Cuzco, the capital city, in 1533 and mercilessly executed Inca chief Atahualpa. European diseases had reached the Inca long before they laid eyes on the foreigners, and by the time of Pizarro's arrival, virtually half the Inca population had already perished from his assault. Pizarro declared Spanish sovereignty over all the Inca with very little Indian resistance. In the next decades, Spanish explorers' discovery of rich silver mines through the Americas ensured that their monarchs would continue to support devastating invasion strategies.

Spanish *conquistadors* had less success conquering and settling the Gulf Coast region and the interior to the southwest. Juan Ponce de León (1460–1521) landed on the southern Atlantic coast in 1513, naming it after the Easter holiday, *pascua florida,* or Florida. Over the next years, Ponce de León made several unsuccessful attempts to take slaves from the nearby Indian villages, but in 1521 his efforts resulted in his own death at the hands of hostile warriors. In 1528 Panfilo de Narvaez and a small group of Spanish mariners began wandering along the Gulf Coast and into the dry Southwest. The significant legacy of this expedition was the amazing journal of Alvar Nuñez Cabeza de Vaca (1490–1557?), whose sometimes fantastical stories included an account of an opulent empire he called Cibola. There, Cabeza de Vaca had seen "cities of gold"—possibly misinterpreting vistas of the yellow sand and rock in the brilliant sun. Illusory or not, his claims prompted other Spaniards to trek into the North American interior, across what would one day become Texas.

Hernando de Soto (1496?–1542) landed in Florida in 1539 with an army of over seven hundred men and over three thousand hogs and cattle. De Soto pressed into the interior, forced Mississippian Indians into labor, and plundered food from villages as needed. As he despaired of finding an empire to conquer, preferably one mightier than the Aztec, De Soto was attacked first by the powerful Alibamu of present-day Alabama, and then by the enraged ancestors of the Chickasaw. His forces depleted, De Soto marched farther west across the Mississippi River, but died shortly after turning back in 1542. The next year his surviving soldiers reached other Spaniards in Mexico, where they reported the fierceness of the Indians they had encountered. What they could not report, however, was how severely the diseases they had carried with them on their exploits had reduced mighty chiefdoms to small, interdependent tribal groups.

In 1540 the Spanish officials in Mexico launched another attempt to find Cibola. Francisco Vasquez de Coronado (1510–1554) took three hundred men and horses, and over seven hundred Indian carters, along ancient Indian trading paths into North America. On the way, they passed the Pima settlements, and then the Pueblo Indians along the Rio Grande, whom Coronado attacked without apparent reason and scorned for what he thought was the rude simplicity of their culture. His expedition pressed into the western Great Plains and there spied great herds of buffalo. But there was no Cibola, no gold, and no glory for Coronado. He returned to Mexico in disappointment.

Spaniards concluded from these efforts that the great riches they had pillaged from the Aztec and Inca Empires were not duplicated in the lands north of the Mexican plains. Nevertheless, during the 1500s *conquistadors* and the settlers who followed them made an indelible imprint on the Western Hemisphere. For an entire century, the Spanish model gave other European nations a powerful example of how—and how not—to conquer regions of the New World.

The Effects of Contact

Overlapping the economic, religious, and political transformations occurring among the cultures that collided in the Western Hemisphere in the 1500s was a profound transfer of goods, foods, ideas, social organization, and diseases. Called the "Columbian Exchange," this transfer eradicated the centuries of separation between the hemispheres and started the process of regular communication among many different cultures. Few Europeans knew what to expect from their first encounters with Africans or Indians, but peoples of all three world regions continually adjusted to one another. Some of these adjustments were incremental and only slowly affected daily activities; others were jarring, violent, or even devastating.

Peoples who had developed very different ways of exploiting their environments and meeting their material needs shared the excitement of exchanging new items of comfort or necessity. Animals and plants were part of this trading phenomenon. Livestock came on the earliest ships to newly conquered cultures. Even on Columbus's first voyage, cargoes of cattle and horses ensured not only a supply of meat for Spanish consumption, but also animal power for cartage and construction. For Indians who had no experience of such animals, the scale of work and ease of transport made possible with European cattle and horses changed village life immeasurably. Grazing cattle, as well as foraging goats and swine, changed the ecology of many Caribbean islands. In Mexico, the cattle brought from Spain provided raw hides for export. Horses escaped from Mexico and migrated northward, where they made a tremendous impact on the lives of Pueblo, Yaqui, and other large populations of the Southwest. In time, the Arapaho, Sioux, and other peoples of the Great Plains also adopted horses. Besides livestock, the Spanish introduced barley, wheat, oats, rice, rye, melons, dandelions, olives, coffee, and other foods. Europeans also brought firearms and cannons, the "great fire trumpets" that terrified Mexican emperors and subjects alike.

Sugar was also among the items introduced from the Old World to the New. Already in the 1400s, Portuguese traders knew about the value of sugar grown in the Azores, and during the 1500s, the cultivation and consumption of sugar quickly surpassed animal hides to become the second-greatest export from the New World (next to silver). When the Portuguese took Brazil in the early 1500s, they relocated Native American populations to lands hundreds of miles away from familiar rivers and fields, and introduced African slaves to produce sugar for European markets. Dozens of merchants scurried to invest in growing Brazilian and Caribbean sugar, which became popular immediately in Europe and England despite its doubtful nutritional and medicinal worth. Quickly following the merchants were thousands of Spanish, Dutch, and French colonizers who aspired to make fortunes on this increasingly fashionable commodity.

In order to satisfy the constant demand for killing work in the cane fields, the now-entrenched slave trade provided the answer. By the end of the 1500s, over 90 percent of the Africans forcibly removed from their homelands to become slaves in the Western Hemisphere went to the West Indies, Brazil, and the Spanish borderlands. During the 1500s, about 250,000 African people came on slave ships to the New World. Another 200,000 were brought in chains in the brief period from 1600 to 1621. Such a massive scale of transplanting people for their labor had never been known in Africa or Europe. Moreover, the atrocious treatment slaves experienced on the "midpassage" across the ocean and the ruthless requirements of plantation labor were nothing like the predominantly domestic servitude of ancient and medieval slavery in Europe. Finally, in contrast with the many different ethnic and national peoples of Europe subjected to slavery as war captives or orphans during earlier centuries, slavery in the Western Hemisphere after 1500 became based almost entirely on race.

Europeans adopted many new foods found in the New World, including maize from Mexico, which was adopted as a staple of families everywhere, especially in the Mediterranean, and used as a food crop for livestock in other places. About three generations after maize had been cultivated in France, the Englishman John Locke marveled that it "serves poor people for bread . . . [and] is good nourishment for their cattle." Beans, squash, and various root crops also were transported back to Europe, where their ease of cultivation and high calorie content made them welcome dietary additions. Peru contributed the potato to northern European populations, and tomatoes entered the southern European diet. Tobacco, a New World crop at first believed to be a valuable medicine, was grown widely in Europe after 1550 because of the rage for chewing and smoking it. Vanilla, cotton, peanuts, and chocolate became standard fare in Europe by 1600, too.

The most important commodity that European people extracted from the New World was silver. Once they had subjected tens of thousands of Native Americans to forced labor in the mines, conquerors of the Inca and Aztec Empires helped themselves to vast quantities of gold and silver. Skilled craftsmen turned much of this wealth into jewelry and statuary, while merchants introduced great quantities of ingots and bullion into European trade. Between 1520 and 1600 shipload after shipload of silver returned to Spain. After the crown skimmed its Royal Fifth of the value of each delivery, merchant families spent other portions of it on lavish luxuries. In a short time, New World silver began to trickle into commerce with Spain's trading partners. With so much new wealth circulating in Europe, wars became more costly and more deadly, prices of daily necessities rose due to an inflationary spiral, and the standard of living for most Europeans declined dramatically. The wages craftsmen received for their work stayed the same, but the money bought less because of inflation. And the rents collected by aristocrats from their tenants were worth less in real value once inflation penetrated the countryside.

But the Indians of the New World experienced a far greater disaster: the rapid dying of great numbers of Indians from European diseases. When Columbus came to the Caribbean, the Taino probably numbered hundreds of thousands in Hispaniola, but by the 1520s, no more than a few hundred remained, and soon almost every trace of that culture had vanished. At about the time the Taino almost disappeared,

"Indio con Virguelas"
[Indian with Smallpox]
Smallpox was the greatest killer of Native Americans in the Western Hemisphere following the arrival of Europeans. In only two years, an epidemic that began with the Spanish invasion had swept through the plains of Mexico and ravaged the Aztec population; the grim scenario would be repeated among other peoples in generations to come. Not until the 1720s was inoculation against smallpox possible.   *(Trujillo Del Peru, v.2 by Martinez Camanon.)*

the Aztec of the Mexican highlands also were declining rapidly. Warfare, starvation, relocation and the resulting decline of Indian family life, and demoralization that reportedly led to widespread infanticide and suicide, claimed huge numbers of peoples who came under Spanish influence. European diseases claimed the most lives in these waves of decimation. Smallpox, influenza, typhus, malaria, measles, and pneumonia were the major causes of the worst demographic disaster in world history. By about 1520, one Indian reported from Peru that the smallpox "spread over the people as great destruction. . . . Very many died of it, they could not stir; they could not change position, nor lie down on one side, nor face down, nor on their backs. And if they stirred, much did they cry out."

How could the devastation of most Native American peoples have occurred so quickly? The answer lies in how diseases spread. Europeans had developed immunities to these invisible viruses, having been exposed to them repeatedly, but the New World populations had never before experienced them. The viruses brought by Europeans were even more mysterious when epidemics spread to Indian villages ahead of European contact, as it did in the American Southeast. And the fact that so many Indians died while few Europeans seemed to be affected confirmed some Native Americans' beliefs that arriving ships carried either great gods or invincible new human rulers. Much evidence also shows that Native Americans, in a kind of perverse revenge, gave syphilis to their European conquerors, probably beginning with Columbus's voyages, although it is also possible that milder strains of syphilis existed in Europe earlier.

CONCLUSION

The spread of agriculture over many centuries wrought profound changes in ancient Indian cultures. By the time Europeans encountered them, most peoples of the Caribbean and the coastal mainland lived in sedentary villages or semi-permanent encampments. They had organized themselves into clusters of families and hierarchical communities that were recognizable to Europeans, and they identified among themselves leaders, servants, and specialists of many kinds. With the notable exceptions of the Aztec and Inca, the Native American cultures that experienced the most contact with first Europeans were sometimes closer to the strangers from across the Atlantic Ocean than they were to nomads or hunter-gatherers who lived in high northern latitudes or remote regions of their own North American interior.

When the Portuguese and Spanish explorers pushed aside Islamic supremacy in commerce with a burst of energy in the 1400s, and went on to conquer islands and empires stretching over thousands of miles in the New World, they did not simply introduce new cultures to Africans and Native Americans, who then willingly adopted them. As we have seen, by 1450 the pace of change reached incredible heights in all three world areas. Some medieval technological, agricultural, and commercial innovations changed living conditions dramatically within Europe, while religious and political turmoil uprooted huge numbers of Europeans; together, these upheavals were preconditions for explorations and contact in the generations to come. Surely some of the fluctuating fortunes of city-states and villages in the Americas also set the terms of Indian responses to Europeans. And the rich and fluctuating heritages of African peoples not only affected the patterns of their forcible removal from that continent, but also set certain parameters for their mixing with other cultures in the New World.

Initial dreams of glory and gold gave way quickly to the reality of difference, disappointment, and sharpening tensions among strangers. The first toeholds of Europeans in the Americas contrasted sharply with the extinct and existing great Native American city-states of Mound Builders, Aztec, Inca, and southwestern peoples. And yet, within only a short period of time, the demographic tables reversed. While life was no doubt difficult for European colonizers, who experienced starvation, death, and disease in the first years of each settlement, millions of Indians and Africans throughout the Americas perished by the steel weapons, harsh work regimens, oppressive political authority, and especially the diseases of migrating European strangers. As Spain extracted shiploads of hides and precious metals from new lands, smallpox, cholera, measles, and other deadly diseases took a greater toll on Native Americans than Europeans had ever experienced in the bloodiest of wars. At the same time, Spanish explorers and settlers required greater and greater replenishment of slaves from Africa who, by the early 1500s, performed an array of tasks as forced labor.

The Cherokee myth of creation does not disclose what happened when the pressure of European and other Indian encroachments became unbearable. However, it does reveal much about the Cherokee respect for—and awe of—nature and the place of humans in a spectrum of living things. It is intriguing to wonder whether the myth's familiar explanations of creation eased introductions between the Cherokee and new Europeans, or whether its starkly different view of Cherokee homelands and social order contributed to alienation between the two cultures.

For thousands of years the Americas were separated from Europe and Africa. Long before peoples of different continents mixed, thousands of different North American cultures rose, flourished, and profoundly changed—sometimes repeatedly—in dynamic interaction with each other. Peoples of Africa and Europe, too, underwent significant changes that laid the foundations for both cultural sharing and cultural conflicts when they did finally meet.

SUGGESTED READINGS

Brian M. Fagan's *The Great Journey: The Peopling of Ancient America* (1987) is one of the most authoritative interpretations of early human history in the Western Hemisphere. Among the best work on North America before European contact, see the collection of essays in Thomas E. Emerson and R. Barry Lewis, eds., *Cahokia and the Hinterlands: Middle Mississippian Cultures of the Midwest* (1991); Bruce Smith, *The Mississippian Emergence* (1990); Frederick Katz, *The Ancient American Civilizations* (1972); William F. Keegan, ed., *Emergent Horticultural Economies of the Eastern Woodlands* (1987); and Philip Kopper, *The Smithsonian Book of North American Indians Before the Coming of the Europeans* (1986). Alvin M. Josephy, Jr., ed., *America in 1492* (1992), contains important essays by key scholars of many North American areas on the eve of European contact.

Studies that focus on Indian culture in interaction with Europeans in North America are numerous, but see James Axtell, ed., *The Indian Peoples of Eastern America: A Documentary History of the Sexes* (1981). For the Eastern Woodlands peoples, see Alfred Goldsworthy Bailey, *The Conflict of European and Eastern Algonquian Cultures, 1504–1700* (1969); and the fascinating and readable ecological study by William Cronon, *Changes in the Land: Indians, Colonists, and the Ecology of New England* (1983). Also, D. W. Meinig, *The Shaping of America,* Vol. 1: *Atlantic America, 1492–1800* (1986), is the best cultural view of European settlement in relation to the Indians; and Neal Salisbury, *Manitou and Providence: Indians, Europeans and the Making of New England, 1500–1643* (1982), is a signal contribution to the ethnohistory of the Northeast with a strong cultural emphasis. For the Southeast, see Charles Hudson, *The Southeastern Indians* (1976).

The indispensable and path-breaking work of Alfred Crosby, Jr., shows in detail how Indian and European cultures influenced each other extensively; see his *The Columbian Exchange: Biological and Cultural Consequences of 1492* (1972) and *Ecological Imperialism: The Biological Expansion of Europe, 900–1900* (1986).

For demographic patterns, see Russell Thornton, *American Indian Holocaust and Survival: A Population History Since 1492* (1987). For a wide variety of maps showing the locations and migrations of many Native American groups, and a comprehensive bibliography, see Carl Waldman, *Atlas of the North American Indian* (1985).

Three studies are excellent starting points for the African background: Paul Bohanan and Philip Curtin, *Africa and the Africans* (2nd ed., 1971); Basil Davidson, *The African Genius* (1969); and J. D. Fage, *A History of West Africa* (4th ed., 1969). Also see Richard Olaniyan, *African History and Culture* (1982). Recently, the magisterial study by John Thornton, *Africa and Africans in the Making of the Modern World, 1400–1680* (1992), makes fascinating connections between African life and slave trading patterns. A valuable look at how the slave trade affected Africans is in Paul E. Lovejoy, "The Impact of the African Slave Trade on Africa: A Review of the Literature," *Journal of African History,* 30 (1989): 365–94.

For overviews of the great changes overtaking European people and western European nation states, see Ralph Davis, *The Rise of Atlantic Economies* (1973); J. H. Parry, *The Establishment of the European Hegemony: Trade and Expansion in the Age of the Renaissance* (1966); Kenneth R. Andrews, *Trade, Plunder, and Settlement: Maritime Enterprise and the Genesis of the British Empire, 1480–1630* (1984); and David B. Quinn, *England and the Discovery of America, 1481–1620* (1974).

For work on European exploration and conquest before Columbus, see the detailed overview by Samuel Eliot Morison, *The European Discovery of America: The Northern Voyages, A.D. 500–1600* (1971); and for changes within Europe, Carlo M. Cipolla's *Guns, Sails, and Empire: Technological Innovation and the Early Phases of European Expansion 1400–1700* (1975) contains fascinating detail and important analysis. Kirkpatrick Sale, *The Conquest of Paradise: Christopher Columbus and the Columbian Legacy* (1990), though one of the most critical appraisals of Columbus, also offers a provocative perspective for discussions.

For the Portuguese, see Charles Boxer, *The Portuguese Seaborne Empire: 1415–1825* (1969) and *The Dutch Seaborne Empire, 1600–1800* (1965). For the earliest French settlement in the New World, see Olive P. Dickason, *The Myth of the Savage and the Beginnings of French Colonization in the Americas* (1982).

For Spain's long century of imperial domination in the Western Hemisphere, start with Charles Gibson, *Spain in America* (1966). Also see James Lang, *Conquest and Commerce: Spain and England in the Americas* (1975), and Hugh Thomas, *Conquest: Montezuma, Cortés, and the Fall of Old Mexico* (1993). For the French presence, see Marcel Trudel, *The Beginnings of New France, 1524–1663* (1973).

Important perspectives on European motives and influences during the early phases of colonization are offered by Simon Schama, *The Embarrassment of Riches: An Interpretation of Dutch Culture in the Golden Age* (1987), and Eric Wolf, *Europe and the People Without History* (1983).

Interpreting the Cultures of Strangers

Columbus Describes the Taino

In letters to the Spanish monarchs, Christopher Columbus offered some of the first written impressions of the New World made by a European. Although he was perplexed about the Taino Indians' political organization and ways of working, Columbus was clearly astonished at the natural bounty of the islands and physical beauty of the people. The following passage is dated February 15, 1493.

I found very many islands peopled with inhabitants beyond number. And, of them all, I have taken possession for their Highnesses, with proclamation and the royal standard displayed; and I was not gainsaid . . . I followed [the] coast [of the island Juana] westwardly and found it so large that I thought it might be the mainland province of Cathay. And as I did not thus find any towns and villages on the sea-coast, save small hamlets with the people whereof I could not get speech, because they all fled away forthwith, I went on further in the same direction, thinking I should not miss of great cities of towns. . . . I sent two men into the country to learn if there were a king, or any great cities. They traveled for three days, and found interminable small villages and a numberless population, but nought of ruling authority; . . . The lands thereof are high, and in it are very many ranges of hills, and most lofty mountains incomparably beyond the Island of [Tenerife]; all most beautiful in a thousand shapes, and all accessible, and full of trees of a thousand kinds, so lofty that they seem to reach the sky. And I am assured that they never lose their foliage; as may be imagined, since I saw them as green and as beautiful as they are in Spain. . . . And the nightingale was singing, and other birds of a thousand sorts. . . . There are palm trees of six or eight species, wondrous to see for their beautiful variety; but so are the other trees, and fruits, and plants therein . . . there is honey, and . . . in the earth there are many mines of metals; and there is a population of incalculable number. . . . In [La Spanola], there are many spiceries, and great mines of gold and other metals. The people of this island, and of all the others that I have found and seen, or not seen, all go naked, men and women, just as their mothers bring them forth; . . . and of fair stature, but that they are most wondrously timorous. . . . It is true that since they have become more assured, and are losing that terror, they are artless and generous with what they have, to such a degree as no one would believe but him who had seen it. Of anything they have, if it be asked for, they never say no, but do rather invite the person to accept it, and show as much lovingness as though they would give their hearts. And whether it be a thing of value, or one of little worth, they are straightways content with whatsoever trifle of whatsoever kind may be given them in return for it . . . they all believe that power and goodness are in the sky, and they believed very firmly that I, with these ships and crew, came from the sky; and in such opinion, they received me at every place where I landed, after they had lost their terror. And this comes not because they are ignorant; on the contrary, they are men of very subtle wit, who navigate all those seas, and who give a marvelously good account of everything . . . they never saw men wearing clothes nor the like of our ships. . . . It seems to me that in all those islands, the men are all content with a single wife; and to their chief or king they give as many as twenty. The women, it appears to me, do more work than the men. Nor have I been able to learn whether they held personal property, for it seemed to me that whatever one had, they all took share of, especially of eatable things. Down to the present, I have not found in those islands any monstrous men, as many expected, but on the contrary all the people are very comely. . . . Since thus our Redeemer has given to our most illustrious King and Queen, and to their famous kingdoms, this victory in so high a matter, Christendom should take gladness therein and make great festivals, and give solemn thanks to the Holy Trinity for the great exaltation they shall have by the conversion of so many peoples to our holy faith; and next for the temporal benefit which will bring hither refreshment and profit, not only to Spain, but to all Christians.

Las Casas Reveals the "Villainies of the Spanish"

Opponents of the *conquistadors* and Spanish crown policies gave voice to their concerns starting very early in the conquests. One of them was Bartolomé de Las Casas (1474–1566), a Spanish Catholic friar and later bishop of the Indies. Las Casas protested that Indians were not granted equal legal status under Spanish law. In 1540, the churchman brought together a mountain of chilling evidence about Spanish violations of Indian rights in *Brevisima relación de la destrucción de las Indias,* which he sent as a report to King Charles V.

There were ten kingdoms as large as the kingdom of Spain. . . . Of all this the inhumane and abominable villainies of the Spanish have made a wilderness, for though it was formerly occupied by vast and infinite numbers of men, it has been stripped of all people . . . over twelve million souls innocently perished, women and children being included in the sad and fatal list. . . .

As for those that came out of Spain, boasting themselves to be Christians, they had two ways of extirpating the Indian nation from the face of the earth: the first was by making bloody, unjust, and cruel wars against them; and the second was by killing all those that so much as sought to recover their liberty, as some of the braver sort did. And as for the women and children that were left alive, the Spaniards let so heavy and grievous a yoke of servitude upon them that the condition of beasts was much more tolerable. . . .

What led the Spanish to these unsanctified impieties was the desire for gold to make themselves suddenly rich, in order to obtain dignities and honors that were in no way fit for them. . . . The Spanish so despised the Indians . . . that they used them not like beasts, for that would have been tolerable, but looked upon them as if they had been the dung and filth of the earth, and so little did they regard the health of their souls that they permitted the great multitude to die without the least light of religion. . . .

From which time forward the Indians began to think of ways that they might take to expel the Spaniards from their country. And when the Spanish saw this they came with their horsemen well armed with swords and lances, making a cruel havoc and slaughter among them, overrunning cities and towns and sparing neither sex nor age. Nor did their cruelty take pity on women with children, whose bellies they ripped up, taking out the infants to hew them to pieces. They would often lay wagers as to who could cleave or cut a man through the middle with the most dexterity, or who could cut off his head at one blow. The children they would take by the feet and dash their innocent heads against the rocks. . . . They erected a kind of gallows broad and low enough so that the tormented creatures might touch the ground with their feet, and upon each one of these they strung thirteen persons, blasphemously affirming that they did it in honor of our Redeemer and his apostles. ▮

These contrasting views existed side by side for generations of European conquest in the Western Hemisphere. Flattering accounts of beautiful Indian physical features and material generosity persisted until they became codified into a "noble savage" perspective and inspired thousands of enthusiastic colonizers to join in the migrations to the "new world." This view almost always anticipated that Europeans' "civilized" religion and culture would prevail over cultures that seemed to be less mature, less endowed with prosperity and comfort, or more vulnerable to the environment and human enemies. Some views proposed—or assumed—that Indians could provide valuable sources of forced labor.

Critical accounts by writers such as Las Casas were intended to arouse public outrage and promote crown reforms of newly conquered areas. Las Casas wished to end the harsh system of Spanish tribute-taking begun by the *encomenderos,* or great landlords, of South America. But the rulers who rose to power in the New World refused to abide by reforms passed in distant Spain, and it was not until the 1570s that the depredations against Indians diminished somewhat.

In the hands of rival European nations, which were becoming increasingly Protestant and intent on creating empires of their own, Las Casas's writings were useful as scandal sheets that brought shame to Spanish colonizers. A Dutch artist named Theodore de Bry, who had never been to the colonies, depicted Spaniards wantonly exterminating defenseless Indians. To the semiliterate populations of Europe who saw De Bry's illustrations, Las Casas seemed to offer definitive proof of Catholic depravity and to support a somehow superior Protestant view of New World peoples. This *Leyenda Negra,* or Black Legend, fueled the propaganda machines of northern European states, although in light of modern studies that show unparalleled demographic disaster wherever Spain claimed dominion, the legend carried a ring of truth.

Questions for Analysis

1. What human and natural characteristics of the Taino does Columbus find amazing? Why?

2. What assumptions does Columbus make about the future of the Taino?

3. What major indictments does Las Casas bring against Spanish colonizers?

4. Reading historical documents involves distinguishing between verifiable facts and individual perceptions; facts are reliably true, whereas perceptions might be distorted. What is probably true in each of these accounts, and what is open to question? Which statements are observations, and which are judgments?

5. Are there any similarities between Columbus's and Las Casas's views?

2

The First Experiments, 1540–1680

"*B*e pleased to bring me home, with all due haste," wrote Mary, a young servant in Maryland, to a relative in London. "For I have been ill used in this country, worked at all manner of tasks both inside the house and out, and made the object of ridicule for each and sundry small error in keeping this wretched house." "The fire went out today," she wrote on March 3, 1668, "which brought wrath from master's oldest [son], and master used [beat] me sorely when he found the cider gone sour, though it be Amos [the master's slave] who left it in the sun." On another occasion, Mary pleaded for money to pay for a return trip to England, noting her frequent hunger and persistent headaches. Although she had been tempted to run away, Mary chose instead to deceive her master by stretching out her household chores so they took up most of the day, "else I must get to the [tobacco] field and bend my back til it ache."

Mary was thirteen years old when she came from London to the marshy shore of Maryland to be an indentured servant. Her ship captain noted that she was "good at house keeping and numbers" and that her new master had cleared land somewhere "in the tobacco country." Her story is typical of the experiences of many, many thousands of young men and women who came to Virginia, Maryland, Antigua, and Barbados during the early 1600s. Roughly 85 percent of the British who migrated to the colonies in the early seventeenth century came as indentured servants, or bound laborers, to masters who needed their labor to clear land, keep house, plant and tend tobacco fields, market goods, or care for motherless children.

Mary's new life must have been lonely: she was almost completely cut off from communication to England and, because her master did not live in a village, had only infrequent connections to other households scattered about the countryside. In addition, Mary's field and house labor was very different from traditional European women's work. For one thing, her tasks overlapped with men's chores, and for another, the household was often comprised of both kin and non-kin. Although Mary probably had been accustomed to poor living conditions in England, the ones she encountered in her master's home were even worse. A single-room house with a dirt or plank floor, almost no furniture, straw pallets for sleeping, and a stifling dimly lit interior without windows—these were Mary's daily surroundings. She had "one set of coarse linen clothing" to wear most of the year and a few articles of outerwear for the colder months. Most servants were glad to acquire shoes and elated to eat a meal of more than corn and a piece of meat, dried or in a soup. Mary was quite aware that the shortage of women in Maryland made it possible for her to have her pick of unmarried men. But she lamented that "not one of them be young as I, and none a likely father of my babes, most being advanced in years and disagreeable in manners." Yet it was unthinkable for a young woman to remain single in Mary's world, so she would have to choose one of the eligible, if less-than-satisfactory, men to provide her with the tentative securities of marriage and a roof over her head.

Mary's story ends abruptly in the historical record, but the few details we have about her experiences conform to the sketchy lives of many other early settlers in North America. Thousands of servants accepted harsh conditions because they hoped to rise above the poverty that was their lot in Britain or Europe. Few, however, expected the rough treatment and poor health they encountered, or the cultural adjustments they were forced to make. Thousands of others would come to North America in the early 1600s in families, with tools for farming or skills for making necessary goods. People of diverse national, religious, ethnic, and racial backgrounds struggled in numerous wilderness locations to begin their lives over again in dramatically different surroundings than they had ever known. Some early settlements failed, and some flourished. Like Mary's, their collective experiences raise important questions.

▌ What was the range of experiences of colonists coming from Spain, France, Holland, and England?

▌ Given the hardships they faced, why did so many thousands of settlers come to North America year after year?

▌ What did the early colonists hope to accomplish by starting life over on the other side of an ocean, and what immediate obstacles did they have to overcome?

▌ What political and cultural differences emerged as the earliest North American colonies took hold?

This chapter will address these questions.

Struggles for New World Dominion, 1540–1680

During the 1500s, Portugal and Spain sent out tens of thousands of adventurers, farmers, and servants to colonize its vast claims. Spain's conquest of the Western Hemisphere remained relatively unrivaled until the early 1600s. France, Holland, and England had a variety of plans for transplanting people during the 1500s, and a variety of motivations spurred small groups of individuals to migrate, but the great waves of migration from those nations came decades later. Dutch colonists in North America experienced frustrations, disasters, and near failure at their small settlements, while French migrants were sparsely dispersed across northern territories for generations. Although England's rising imperial power eventually would replace Spain's, the island nation established only a few small villages that hugged the North American coastline until the early 1600s. Moreover, European peoples' adaptations to new environments, conflicts with Native Americans, encounters with people from other European nations or ethnic origins, and growing reliance on the labor of African and Caribbean slaves introduced numerous unresolved cultural tensions.

Governing Spain's Empire

By the mid-1500s, many of Spain's missionaries and government officials in Florida and New Mexico viewed the Native Americans around them as potential allies in creating a buffer zone against Dutch, English, and French settlers. St. Augustine, established in 1565, served first as a Spanish outpost to spy on enemy ships sailing nearby, as well as a beacon to potential colonists of Spain's intentions to stay in North America (see map).

The Spanish Empire was officially the private property of monarchs in the home country, who tried to impose uniform control over their colonies by appointing *viceroys* to rule over new territories and hear local disputes. However, because Spain's American empire was vast and discontinuous—a collection of islands in the Caribbean, the Mexican highlands, and portions of South America—it was not the viceroys but the *conquistadors* and petty Spanish officials who lived in the scattered colonies amid Native Americans who held the empire together. *Conquistadors* and local officials organized the *encomienda* system, under which the Spanish forced local populations to work in mines and fields. Spaniards who became lords over large populations lived in high style on the tribute in goods and specie (gold and silver) they extracted from native residents.

At the New World's greatest mine at Potosí (meaning "to thunder," or "to burst") in Bolivia, thousands of Indian workers extracted silver in fourteen-hour shifts at altitudes Europeans could not endure. Starting in 1545, merchants sent its rich stores of silver on galleons to Spain, where runaway inflation resulted from introducing huge quantities of the precious metal (see page 18). By the 1570s, Potosí's population was over 120,000, making it larger than Seville, Madrid, Rome, or Paris.

Whether Europeans praised or scorned the Spanish conquest, few doubted that the lives of native peoples were changed dramatically by the encounter. Once the devastation of disease and warfare somewhat subsided, remnants of Native American populations came together to form new societies that melded attributes of

Chronology

1560s–1580s	England overruns Ireland
1565	Spanish found St. Augustine, Florida
1578	Gilbert receives patent for "Newe Founde Land"
	Drake reaches California
1584–1587	Roanoke settlement
1588	England defeats Spanish Armada
1603	Champlain begins colonization of New France
1607	Jamestown founded
1609	Hudson explores North America for Holland
1610	Santa Fe founded
1619	First Africans brought to Virginia
1620	Plymouth founded
1626	Dutch buy Manhattan Island
1630	Massachusetts Bay founded
1634	Maryland founded
1635–1637	Pequot War
1636	Williams founds Rhode Island
	Harvard College founded
1637	Hutchinson banished from Massachusetts
1643	New Sweden founded
1662	Halfway Covenant
1675–1676	Bacon's Rebellion
1675–1677	Metacomet's (King Philip's) War
1680	Pueblo Revolt in New Mexico

many peoples. Migrants from Spain constructed the cities of Quito, Mexico City, Havana, San Juan, and Santo Domingo on the ruins of Native American cities and temples. By the 1590s, over 200,000 Europeans, mostly Spanish, had crossed the Atlantic, and over 125,000 Africans had been forcibly brought to Brazil and Caribbean islands to work for Portuguese and Spanish plantation lords. Few European women came on the colonizing ships (10 percent of the total at most), but in time communities of mixed *mestizo* (Indian-European) and *mulatto* (African-European) peoples populated Spain's extensive empire.

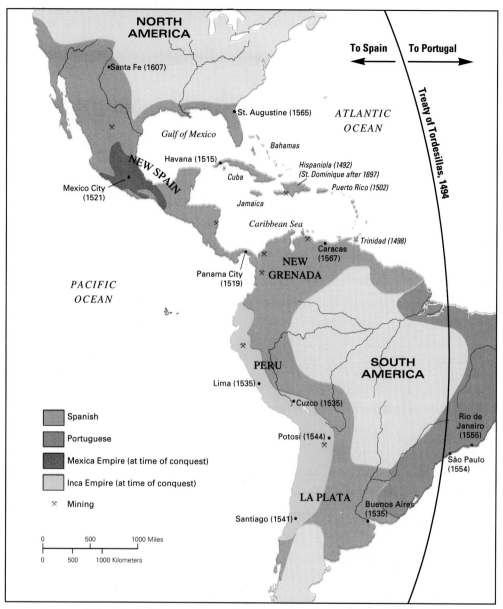

Extent of the Spanish Empire in the 1500s Spanish authorities governed vast amounts of the Western Hemisphere within a very short period of time after the first conquests. The Aztec and Inca empires, and numerous cultures through the Caribbean, Central America, and South America strenuously opposed the advance of Spanish troops and then settlers, but eventually succumbed. For over a century, no other European power claimed so much dominion outside its own nation-state, or held it for so long, as Spain in the Western Hemisphere.

Spain's religious objectives in its foreign colonies also led to policies that had unintended consequences. In 1573 Philip II decreed it illegal to enslave Indians or extract tribute from them forcibly. Thereafter, Spain's goal would be to convert Native Americans to Catholicism and create a *creole,* or mixed Spanish and Indian, culture that incorporated Spanish customs. The king's ban on Indian slavery was never effectively enforced, but his promotion of Native American conversion spurred renewed interest in mission activity abroad. Franciscan monks claimed to have converted thousands of Florida's Indians north of Mexico by about 1650, but few monks learned Indian languages, and few Indians mastered Spanish. Both cultures retained their clothing styles, food preparation methods, and sexual mores. The monks established over thirty missions in Florida, but once diseases ravaged surrounding populations, local farmers, weavers, cooks, and others refused to provide the labor that missions needed to survive.

Spanish soldiers and Franciscan missionaries also fanned out to Santa Fe, New Mexico (founded in 1610), 1,500 miles north of Mexico City. There they encountered the village complexes and irrigated farms of the Pueblo. The Franciscans took Native American wives and, together, built missions to protect and educate the new converts among the Pueblo villages. The first governor of New Mexico, captain-general Juan de Oñate, joined them with his wife Isabel Tolosa Cortés, the granddaughter of Mexico's conqueror and great-granddaughter of Moctezuma. Oñate's goal was to establish the five hundred Spanish who had accompanied him out of Mexico, including ten Franciscan monks, on a series of *encomiendas* in New Mexico. However, the Indians defiantly resisted. In 1598 at Acoma, numerous Pueblo villages banded together to oust the Spanish forces but lost about eight hundred men, women, and children to the weapons and brutal tactics of the Spanish. In years to come, Oñate's excessively cruel behavior drove many of the Spanish settlers off the *encomiendas* and into Santa Fe, and stiffened the resistance of Apache and Navajo people in the countryside to conversion efforts.

Spanish authorities in Mexico recalled Oñate in 1606, but tensions in New Mexico continued. By about 1630, almost 100,000 Pueblo, Apache, and Navajo people had been baptized, a much higher number of converts than New England Puritans could claim in years to come. But few Indians chose to live in the diminished *encomiendas,* and when a long period of drought set in, the Pueblo began to blame the Spanish for their troubles.

Finally, in August 1680, Pueblo villages revolted against the Spanish missionaries. Instigated by orders of Hopi chiefs, especially the charismatic leader Popé, Native Americans burned priests at the stake, and whole villages rose up against Spanish-speaking colonists who lived north of Santa Fe. Over 400 lay dead in the countryside, and some 2,000 took refuge in government buildings, while Pueblo warriors demanded that the Spanish release their peoples from forced labor, contrived intermarriages, and Christian practices. After a five-day siege, everyone affiliated with the Spanish missionaries fled to the south. Leaders of Pueblo villages then formed a strong confederacy dedicated to wiping out all trace of the Spanish, who retreated to El Paso.

A certain portion of the Pueblo population did not hold the Spanish in such contempt. After all, the Spanish had introduced sheep, wheat, fruit trees, and horses. And they had protected the Pueblo from the nomadic Apache and Navajo who routinely attacked their villages. Moreover, many villagers did not accept the new Pueblo confederacy leadership any more than they wished for a Spanish reconquest of New Mexico. The long-term solution, only slowly adopted, was a mixture of Pueblo and Catholic cultures after 1692.

French Toeholds

France's territories in North America remained far more sparsely settled than Spain's. One deterrent to settlement was manpower: France's perpetual need to send armies elsewhere in Europe skimmed off the poor, restless, and young male population that might have gone to the New World. In 1562 the Huguenot Jean Ribault helped bring nearly 150 religious dissenters to Parris Island (later Beaufort, South Carolina), where he left them to build a fort and shelters while he returned to France for supplies. But religious wars at home consumed Ribault, and the starving colonists resorted to cannibalism until a passing English pirate ship helped them escape their desperate situation. Two years later, another French expedition established a toehold on St. Johns River (later Jacksonville, Florida), where colonists put up Fort Caroline. They were at first well received by the Timucua Indians nearby, who in return for food and clothing asked for French help in warding off the Spanish. But in 1565 the Spanish captain-general, Don Pedro Menéndez de Avilés built a rival fort at St. Augustine, Florida, and marched his troops north through the swamps to Fort Caroline to slaughter over five hundred French colonists.

Far to the north along the coastlines of Newfoundland, Labrador, and Nova Scotia, fishermen and trappers established a tenuous presence. By 1500, the cod-rich Grand Banks was a regular stopping place for English, Dutch, Flemish, and Portuguese fishermen. When King Francis I sent out Giovanni da Verrazzano in 1524 to explore the region stretching from the Carolinas to Nova Scotia, he relied on fishermen to show him the way. Between 1534 and 1543, Jacques Cartier made three voyages along the St. Lawrence River in hopes of securing great wealth for the French king, each time accompanied by skilled fishermen. Cartier also looked for a route to the East Indies through the terrain that Waldseemüller's map (see page 28) now called America. Although he failed to find such an avenue to riches, Cartier did explore the maritime areas that Iroquoian-language Indians called Canada (probably meaning "village").

The fur trade quickly came to define the French presence in North America. In contrast to the great state systems of South American Indians, Canada's Micmac and Montagnais Indians were hunter-gatherers who lived in small family-based groups and had no permanent cities (see map of North American culture areas, p. 5). Nevertheless, enthusiastic about trading their furs for European iron wares, cloth, and glass trinkets, they welcomed Cartier's first trading post in 1541. By the late 1500s, the French government sponsored more aggressive exploration in Canada. Starting in 1604, Samuel de Champlain, a French cartographer and gentleman, began a series of eleven voyages to Canada. The Montagnais and Algonquian soon learned that Champlain was a fair dealer and readily agreed to trading terms. In addition, Champlain wanted to create a religious haven for Catholics and Huguenots who were beleaguered by the religious wars in France. Between 1604 and 1606, he was instrumental in planting Acadia (Nova Scotia) with mainly Huguenots, most of them impoverished refugees from their homeland. In 1608 he settled more of his countrymen in Quebec City, which would soon be a continental crossroads for the fur trade.

But amicable relations among cultures and religions deteriorated quickly in the next years. If the fur trade introduced welcome new technologies (such as guns) and tools (such as knives) to Indians, it also stimulated wars and long migrations of peoples in quest of precious peltry. By the early 1600s, members of the Micmac, Huron, Erie, and other cultures killed one another more efficiently and neglected the hunting and agricultural activities that had sustained their way of life. Champlain aided Algonquian raids against Mohawk villages on Lake Champlain, which initiated a long era of tensions. By 1615, the French traders reached Huronia, an area of dense settlements that wished to trade directly with the French and thereby undermine agreements with intermediate tribes to the east. European diseases also brought familiar demographic devastation, and weakened Indian communities became prey for their traditional enemies who now wished to corner the fur trade.

In addition, Huguenots and Catholics in Acadia argued fiercely over theology and civic responsibilities. In 1625 the French government declared Catholicism to be the religion of its territory in North America and in 1627 banned Protestants from New France, thereby deepening disagreements among French colonists. On the frontiers, Jesuit missionaries who lived among the Huron and Montagnais, attempting to convert natives to Catholicism, raised suspicions about their true intensions: when a smallpox epidemic broke out in 1644, the Huron believed it was part of missionaries' efforts to sabotage Indian control of the fur trade. Nevertheless, the fur trade continued to attract trappers known as *coureurs des bois* (forest runners) who extracted

A Northern Indian's Knife, 1600s
As the fur trade developed, Indians acquired many luxury and necessary goods from Europeans, including knives such as this one, which was decorated with a tracery of beads that showed the personal or tribal name of the owner. Knives were used not only in hunting but in many different household chores as well and became important articles of exchange. (*Musée de l'Homme.*)

valuable pelts and introduced European goods and economic ways. Far from the restraining laws of government or traditional institutions, these fur traders also married and lived with Algonquians of New France. To the scorn of Jesuit missionaries, trappers adopted many Indian customs and declined to teach Indians "civilized" French ways.

In all, no more than two thousand French settlers came to New France before 1663. But thereafter, the French government took over direct control of New France, planted a military-style leadership in the major cities of Montreal, Quebec, and Three Rivers, and then made arrangements to transport hundreds of women, most of them orphans and widows of European warfare, into the colony to become wives and servants of landowning farmers. By the 1690s, *seigneurs,* or landed gentry, accumulated vast stretches of land along the St. Lawrence River and imposed various taxes on local settlers, although they never consolidated political power enough in the colony to act like true aristocrats.

Meanwhile, some intrepid souls migrated down the Mississippi River, naming new settlements after renowned trappers such as Louis Jolliet or missionaries such as Jacques Marquette, and transplanting their wheat-based economies to the fertile valleys near the former Cahokia. René-Robert Cavelier, Sieur de La Salle, took parties of settlers to the Gulf of Mexico, seeking the elusive "northwest passage" to the Pacific Ocean. In 1682 La Salle claimed for France virtually all of the interior of North America, calling it Louisiana in honor of his king, Louis XIV. However, two years later La Salle returned by sea to the mouth of the Gulf of Mexico with about 280 soldiers and colonists, intending to use thousands of Natchez and Creek allies to raid Spanish forts and silver mines to the south. Instead he ended up in Texas, where he was murdered by his own recruits in 1685. For decades to come, French Louisiana was little more than a dumping ground for undesirable criminals and desperately poor Frenchmen, cross-hatched by fur trading trails and a few wretched forts, while most French migrants went to the warm and prosperous Caribbean islands of Martinique, Guadaloupe, and St. Dominique (taken from Spain in 1697).

Dutch Republican Colonies

During the late 1500s, the Netherlands, consisting of present-day Holland in the north and Belgium in the south, became the most prosperous country in Europe, and Amsterdam, the commercial capital of the Atlantic world. In 1602 city merchants, known as *burghers,* established the Dutch East India Company, which used the advanced shipping and financial services of their country to take over Portugal's role in Asian and African trade. In 1609 the different political districts of the Netherlands were united into the Dutch Republic, further boosting the efforts of Dutch planters to finance large Caribbean sugar plantations, search for exotic spices in Indonesia, secure grain and timber from Baltic peoples, and enter the New World fur trade.

North America was never a major target of conquest and colonization for the Netherlands, but its trappers and fishermen competed with French adventurers to find a passage to the East Indies. In 1609 the East India Company hired sea captain Henry Hudson to find this route; instead, he found the abundant river valley that was named for him and encountered the Iroquois who would become European trading partners. Once a few intrepid Dutch adventurers founded Fort Nassau near present-day Albany in 1614, Amsterdam merchants grew hopeful that the settlers could trade with Native Americans for huge amounts of beaver, martin, deer, otter, and other furs. The enterprising merchants funded a new Dutch West India Company (WIC) and secured a government charter for its business in 1621. This charter set up a joint stock company, an enterprise that sold shares of stock to investors in order to underwrite expensive ventures abroad while spreading the risk of investment. It also authorized Pierre Minuit to purchase the island of Manhattan from Native Americans for the equivalent of a dozen beaver hides in 1626. Minuit assumed leadership of the struggling settlement and began to recruit refugee Protestant families to the town of New Amsterdam.

But the fledgling colony of New Netherland got off to a slow start. Minuit complained that the Company's "servants" did not work enough and that "scrapings of all sorts of nationalities" coming to the island—including Germans, Scots, Scandinavians, French, free and slave Angolans, and Brazilians—harmed rather than helped settlement of the colony. Directors in Amsterdam were also dismayed about reports of Jewish families arriving, as well as "Papists, Mennonites and Lutherans . . . many Puritans . . . atheists and various other servants of Baal."

To make matters worse, trappers spent their time north of the settlement, and few people wanted to leave commerce for farming in New Netherland during these early years. Even when the Company began to grant *patronen*—or important landholders—huge tracts of land on which they were expected to settle at least fifty immigrant families as tenants within four years, the landscape seemed to remain empty. Only Kiliaen van Rensselaer set up a thriving patroonship upriver. Most immigrants chose instead to claim *bouweries*—small grants of free land to heads of households—in New Amsterdam or nearby on Staten Island and Long Island.

New Amsterdam was situated in the center of dense Algonquian village life. Following Minuit's rule, Governor Willem Kieft promised to protect Algonquians fleeing their Indian enemies in return for a close trading relationship. But overcome with greed for Algonquian land, Kieft instead launched a war against the vulnerable Indian settlements. From 1639 to 1645, attack followed attack, with Algonquians fleeing west across the Hudson River away from the "unnatural, barbarous, unnecessary, unjust, and disgraceful" assaults of the Dutch. Hundreds of Dutch settlers fearful of retaliation relocated to Caribbean islands. Over two hundred Europeans perished in the bloody massacres of those years; a thousand Indians may have died. To the interior, Dutch efforts to ally with their Iroquois fur trading partners heightened tensions with the French and Huron. As beaver hunting grounds receded from Dutch settlements, all sides used European guns to engage in bloody conflicts over furs. Almost constantly at war, the Iroquois became ever more dependent on imported Dutch goods that they previously made among themselves. By 1650, New Netherland had grown to only 1,500 souls.

In the meantime, Minuit returned to North America and in 1638 initiated a settlement of about four hundred Swedish Protestants around Fort Christina (near today's Wilmington, Delaware). The population at the fort and its surrounding farms,

Early New Amsterdam   Compared to its parent city, Amsterdam, this small colonial port had only a few homes crowding the tip of the island during the early 1600s. However, New Amsterdam became an important strategic location for Dutch trading. A few of the mother country's largest ships brought colonists much-needed goods each year, while colonial merchants waited anxiously to exchange furs and timber.   *(Library of Congress.)*

called New Sweden, was small; nevertheless, its settlers put up sturdy log cabins and traded successfully in the interior for furs the WIC wanted. In 1651 the Company and the ambitious governor at New Amsterdam, Pieter Stuyvesant (governed 1647–1664) agreed to lead a military expedition against New Sweden, which surrendered peacefully and accepted the WIC's authority. Soon, however, greater threats to New Netherland would come from English colonists in the Chesapeake and New England, as well as from "Yankee" English settlers moving onto farmland east of the Hudson River and on Long Island.

Early English Exploration and Settlement

Numerous English fishing and trapping parties made efforts to establish profitable stations in the North Atlantic during the 1400s, but it was not until 1497 that England established extensive claims over this territory. That year, Henry VII hired a young Genoese sailor named John Cabot to cross the ocean. Fishing crews guided Cabot to what might have been "newe founde lande" (Newfoundland) or Cape Breton Island, which he claimed for England. For the next half-century, English leaders did little to advance Cabot's slim inroad into North America. But while a few Englishmen voyaged each year to fish the Grand Banks, momentum gathered in England for colonization abroad. As people displaced by enclosures in the countryside (see page 18) surged into London, the population exploded from 55,000 in 1550 to 200,000 in 1600. Overwhelmed by the crime, health hazards, and demands on institutions to accommodate such huge numbers, public officials yearned to rid the city of its unwanted. When a sustained internal economic crisis added to England's difficulties, manufacturers and merchants also aggressively sought markets abroad.

Queen Elizabeth's rivalries with foreign powers, combined with her support for the Reformation, provided sparks for England's initial efforts at exploring the Western Hemisphere. The so-called Sea Dogs—Sir Francis Drake, Sir John Hawkins, Sir Humphrey Gilbert, and Sir Walter Ralegh—convinced Elizabeth to support their ambitions to build an overseas empire based on conquest, raiding for slaves, and piracy. In turn, Elizabeth relied on these brazen adventurers to provide her with aid to Protestant allies in the Netherlands and to groups of French Huguenots. Secretly, she encouraged English merchants to pool their capital for North American ventures.

In 1577 Drake set out from England with four tiny ships—one of them his famous *Golden Hind*—and 164 crew members on what was publicly billed as a voyage of trade and exploration. Unofficially, however, the queen had given Drake permission to prey on Spanish Caribbean ports and to sail to the Isthmus of Panama to capture Spanish gold and silver mined from Peru and Mexico. Drake's stupendously successful privateering richly rewarded his backers and whetted English appetites for dominion abroad. Elizabeth dubbed Drake a knight.

Meanwhile, English troops under the command of Drake and Gilbert relentlessly drove Irish Catholic clansmen out of their towns and fields in a kind of guerrilla warfare for decades in the 1500s, inflicting starvation and razing homes. English publicists contributed to the brutality with propaganda; Irish "savages," they wrote, deserved to be utterly wiped out because they resisted advancing English "civilization." The victors established a "plantation" system by granting Irish lands to English and Protestant Scottish freeholders. Having set a precedent for conquest over, and intolerance of, different cultures, Gilbert convinced Elizabeth in 1578 to grant him a charter to take settlers to lands previously claimed by Cabot. Although in 1583 he finally took three shiploads of settlers across the Atlantic to Newfoundland, most of them returned to their homelands. On the third voyage out to stock new settlements, Gilbert and his ship were lost at sea.

After Gilbert's disappearance, his half-brother, Sir Walter Ralegh, eagerly assumed the rights of the royal charter for exploring North America. Assured by a fisherman that "very handsome and goodly people" lived to the south, Ralegh began to recruit investors and colonists. In 1584 the gentry promoter Richard Hakluyt wrote *Discourse of Western Planting*, which professed that on American lands "great numbers [of English poor] may be set to work," "to the unburdening of the realm . . . at home." American settlements would stimulate the languishing English shipbuilding industry and put an end to Spanish domination of heathen peoples. Merchants also hoped that successful colonies abroad would provide them with markets for English manufactures.

Ralegh's first commissioned ship of settlers sailed in late 1584, past the West Indies, and to the Outer Banks of present-day North Carolina, where Roanoke Island lay. After a dire winter of scarcities and deaths, the few remaining settlers seemed to have made a beginning for themselves. Their chosen site lay where numerous Algonquian villages quarreled among themselves. Those closest to the coast, under the leadership of Wingina, hoped that Ralegh's people would ally with them against enemy Indians. But soon these Indian villages grew suspicious that the English had come only to steal from them and eventually overpower them.

Indian fears were justified, for no sooner had Ralegh named the region Virginia (after the virgin queen, Elizabeth I) than he ordered soldiers to force Indians to trap furs for export and turn over food to the English colonists. If they resisted, instructed Ralegh, "bring them all in subjection to civility." Settlers quarreled with the Indians, stopped farming their small clearings, and attacked Roanoke Indian villages in early 1586. When the pirate Francis Drake stopped at the settlement briefly and warned of possible Spanish raids along their coastline, many Virginians returned to England. The Indians slaughtered a second, small party of new settlers, and when the commander of a third ship arrived, only to find a vacant settlement, he left a few soldiers to garrison the meager fort while he returned to England for reinforcements.

Ralegh attempted to settle Roanoke and "civilize the heathens" again in 1587 on a fourth venture of 117 colonizers. This time the settlers included a more mixed group of women and children, craftsmen and farmers, and a governor and talented artist named John White. It was White's daughter, Virginia Dare, who may have been the first English child born in the Western Hemisphere. But their collective fate was firmly tied to events back in England in 1588, and success at Roanoke eluded this group, too.

Secoton, A Village in [North] Carolina in about 1585
John White, who accompanied the Roanoke settlers, created an extensive visual record of life among the villages of the Powhatan confederacy. In this picture of daily life, people gather around sacred fires to pray (lower left) and dance around a circle of posts (lower right), while women in the central aisle prepare food. Well-ordered fields of corn add to the sense of harmony and give a settled feel to the village. Well-thatched roofs over houses were intended to convey the "civilized"—as opposed to "savage" or nomadic—lifestyles of the Indians around Roanoke. *(Miriam and Ira D. Wallach Division of Art, Prints and Photographs, New York Public Library. Astor, Lenox and Tilden Foundations.)*

When John White returned to England for supplies, Elizabeth detained his ship for her navy. King Philip II of Spain had grown angry about Elizabeth's support for the Dutch Protestants who sought to dethrone him, and was furious at the success of Drake's Sea Dogs against his Spanish treasure fleet. With Mary Stuart, Queen of Scots, Philip conspired to overthrow the English government. When Elizabeth had Mary beheaded in 1587, an undaunted Philip stepped up plans to crush the Netherlands and invade England with his great Armada, a fleet of 130 ships, 2,400 pieces of artillery, and over 30,000 men. Under the command of Drake, however, English ships battled the Armada in the English Channel for nine days in 1588. Drake's small fire ships raged against Philip's impressive fleet and finally drove it away with the help of a strong "Protestant Wind."

Elizabeth was now able to proclaim England's naval supremacy, but for the suffering settlers in Roanoke, this was hardly inspiring news. When White returned to Roanoke in 1590, he found a "Lost Colony," empty of inhabitants. The houses had been "taken down" and household goods "spoiled and scattered about." White believed that hostile Indians attacked and killed the English soldiers and settlers. Modern scholars have also proposed that perhaps Spain struck a fatal blow from the south, and a third possibility is that the settlers, in order to survive, assimilated into the Indian villages nearby or to the north in the Chesapeake Bay. Whatever their fate, the only trace of the former colony was a single word carved into a doorpost—"Croatoan," the name of an Indian tribe near present-day Ocracoke that had befriended English settlers.

 ## England's Southern Plantings, 1607–1680

Elizabeth's successor, King James I, renewed crown interest in colonizing North America at the opening of the new century, and the economic crisis in his kingdom spurred groups of adventurers and settlers to begin anew across the Atlantic. Seeking riches, resources, and trading opportunities, hundreds of people came to Virginia and Maryland. These settlements quickly departed from the customs and cultures that people knew in their homelands, and distinctive communities arose in frontier conditions. In time, many Chesapeake settlers would achieve relative stability, and some would enjoy phenomenal economic success. In the early years, however, numerous Indian wars, widespread servitude and slavery, and increasingly unequal land ownership strained the small societies forming in that region.

Virginia's Beginnings

Disappointed with his Roanoke failure, Ralegh transferred his rights to settle in North America to a group of London merchants, who recruited additional investors and in 1606 accepted a charter from King James I (reigned 1603–1625) for the Virginia Company. Two groups were set up within the Company. One of them, the Virginia Company of Plymouth, attempted a settlement of about a hundred men on the Kennebec River at Sagadahoc in present-day Maine. But disease, Indian attacks, and a bitterly cold winter without sufficient supplies convinced the settlers to abandon their camps.

The other group, the Virginia Company of London, settled much farther south. Three ships left England in late 1606 with 144 men who were expected to find riches in the New World quickly. A midwinter Atlantic crossing made the expedition arduous, but 105 hardy colonists survived. The next April they reached the mouth of the James River in present-day Virginia, where they set about putting up meager thatched huts and a protective fort.

Over the next three years, about four-fifths of the colonizers died from starvation and disease. The river was a perpetual source of typhus and dysentery, and few of the earliest migrants knew how to fish and farm. They might have completely perished if the Indians nearby had not helped by bringing food. Powhatan, recognized as a chief over about twenty-two area tribes, quickly grew wary of the Englishmen but hoped that, in return for food, colonists would help him subdue enemy villages beyond his current area of influence.

Food was not the only problem; the settlers also failed to find rich stores of silver and gold to send their investors back home. In 1609 the Company formed a joint stock company, which drew in life-saving funds for the colony, established a plan for granting land to would-be settlers, and appointed a resident governing council. They honored their king by naming the permanent settlement James Town.

Still, colonists quarreled incessantly—about sharing work and supplies, about allotments of land for houses and fields, about access to arms and ammunition, and just about everything else. In 1608 John Smith, an experienced military commander, joined James Town's governing council and gradually imposed his authority over the settlement and set colonists to work. "He that will not work," he declared, "shall not eat." With the blessings of Company directors in England, Smith negotiated with the Indians for peace and food and set up land surveys to determine boundaries of private and government holdings.

Troubles were not over, however. In early 1609 an interim governor, Sir Thomas Gates, set out from England with about five hundred additional settlers. Although the ships were blown off course and spent some weeks in Bermuda (a journey immortalized in Shakespeare's *The Tempest*), many settlers arrived in James Town eventually. Of these newcomers, many could not, and others would not, work the mosquito-infested fields around the fort. Some of them preferred to steal corn and other necessities from Powhatan's tribes. Powhatan lamented the cruelties of the English: "Why will you take by force what you may obtain by love? Why will you destroy us who supply you with food? What can you get by war?" In the midst of natural bounty, colonists destroyed Indian resources and chose to starve; they burned their shelters for fuel, they ate every last animal, and sent home alarming reports of cannibalism. When the horrid winter of 1609–1610 was over, only about sixty of the five hundred residents were still alive.

Just when the remaining few had decided to leave, a new fleet of three hundred men, including Gates's replacement Governor Thomas West, Baron De la Warr, arrived and ordered the starving Virginians to stay, share the supplies his ships brought, and reset land boundaries. In 1612, a legal code of *Laws, Divine, Morall, and Martiall* stipulated the requirements of work for every inhabitant, on both common and private projects, as well as their duties of military defense. The struggling band of settlers began to send a few commodities back to the English investors by 1614, including furs, timber products, silk grass, a crude kind of iron, and local herbs.

But De la Warr also inherited ongoing tensions between settlers and Indians of the region. For many months, Powhatan's warriors had been killing individuals who wandered from James Town, to which the English responded by slaughtering whole villages. By 1614, Powhatan, whose villages were worn out by disease and warfare, sent his English-speaking daughter Pocahontas to James Town for peace negotiations. Pocahontas did more than negotiate: she stayed, converted to Christianity, and married John Rolfe.

Desperate to turn a profit for their English investors, the Company directors in London resorted to three measures. First, they permitted Rolfe to introduce "oronoco," or West Indian tobacco, into English markets in 1614. Until then, King James I and much English public sentiment protested the cultivation and use of the commodity. Smoking, said James, was "a custom loathsome to the eye, hateful to the nose, harmful to the brain, dangerous to the lungs, and in the black stinking fumes thereof, the nearest resembling the horrible smoke of the pit that is bottomless." But even James had to admit that import duties imposed on the popular "weed" brought the crown much-needed revenue. By 1618, Virginians were sending regular shipments of tobacco to eager London buyers; by 1620, the colony turned almost exclusively to producing tobacco. Until 1629, prices soared to undreamed-of heights.

Second, in order to lure able workers to Virginia's tobacco fields, the Company put Edwyn Sandys in charge of the colony in 1618. Two years before that, the Company introduced a new system for distributing land, known as the headright system: each head of household would receive 50 acres of land for himself and 50 acres more for each immediate family member and servant he brought to the colony. The Company was at first hopeful that this plan would stimulate migration. But in the process of making claims, unforeseen distortions in the headright system began to develop. Surveying and patenting land was so complicated and costly that many newcomers to Virginia sold their claims to land brokers who could survey or dispose of individuals' lands at profit. In addition, some colonists consolidated large holdings by pooling family claims or by buying those of newcomers. Soon, "plantations" (a term that at first meant simply a farm but in the Virginia context came to imply a great estate) filled the fertile river ways around James Town, although most large land claims remained uncultivated for some time.

Third, in 1619 the Virginia Company granted settlers the first representative assembly in North America, called the House of Burgesses. The governor and councilors, who were chosen based on their land claims, swore to make and interpret laws "as the home Parliament doe." But the new government system had barely begun when disaster struck in 1622. Long-suffering local Indians had been deprived of their lands, forced into labor, and nearly starved themselves by feeding their crops to Englishmen. In March, Powhatan's brother, Opechancanough, sent warriors to attack several defenseless farms along the James River. They killed at least 347 settlers and prompted many others to flee from the countryside and demand to return to England. The shocked and besieged colonists became demoralized and nearly starved that winter.

A royal investigation of the troubles resulted in King James revoking the Company's charter and declaring Virginia a royal colony in 1624. The king now appointed the governors, and although the burgesses still initiated colonial laws, the crown rather than the Company now approved them in England. In addition, the crown extended the right to vote for burgesses from certain landed men in the colony to all free adult men.

Tobacco exports, rising immigration, and more stable government in Virginia provided settlers with a formula for becoming a permanent colony. But these measures did not bring immediate calm. By the mid-1620s, the nearly 6,000 colonizers who came to Virginia under the Sandys government had been reduced to less than 1,200. For the next ten years, colonists fought with Opechancanough and the villages he controlled, and they still lacked sufficient farming tools, ate meagerly, and witnessed an appalling number of their infants die. When the population did begin to rise by the 1630s, tensions grew again with the Indian villages adjacent to their frontier plantations. In 1644 Opechancanough led a last desperate attack, slaying over five hundred colonists. The English settlers struck back with a vengeance, crushing whole villages and killing Opechancanough. Finally in late 1646 the remaining Powhatan confederacy members recognized their dependence on the crown of England, and both sides agreed on territorial boundaries.

Meanwhile, Virginia's government assumed the structure it would keep for the rest of the colonial era. In 1634 the assembly created counties, each with a justice of the peace presiding over local affairs. Each county also had a court, usually comprised of the most prestigious landowners. Each county also overlapped as an Anglican parish, with a church and a vestry—often the justices—who chose ministers. By the 1640s, justices also served frequently in the legislature, so that prosperous planters could hope to attain high status and serve in important offices. Almost all key leaders in Virginia's county and provincial governments were appointed by the governor, and political positions quickly became a means to acquire land or commercial privileges. Through shrewd marriage arrangements, council and assembly members created interlocking kinship networks that inherited wealth and power for generations to come.

Founding Maryland

George Calvert, Lord Baltimore, did not sponsor colonization in order to make profits in the New World, but rather to provide persecuted English and Irish Catholics a new start. In 1632 King Charles I gave Baltimore a charter for a proprietary colony, one that conferred great powers—not unlike a medieval lord's—to organize use of the land and defend it against outsiders. Soon known as Maryland, its proprietor Lord Baltimore was tantamount to king over the 6.5 million acres given to him. But he died before he could assume such honors, and his son Cecilius succeeded him both as Lord Baltimore and proprietor of Maryland.

The first migrants to Maryland in 1634 founded the tiny settlement of St. Mary's City. But the colony grew very slowly. Baltimore's plan assumed that Catholic gentlemen would claim titles to vast estates in the colony, just as manor lords of a bygone

European Settlement and Indian Cultures of Eastern North America, 1650 Numerous towns and settlements dotted the Atlantic coastline by midcentury, while Indian populations disappeared or dispersed toward the interior of the continent.

English era, and on these estates they would settle Protestant servants who were expected to honor the authority of quasi-feudal courts. But few Catholics migrated to Maryland during Charles I's relatively tolerant reign (1625–1649), while the large number of Protestants who came as servants to work the colony's tobacco fields built a majority quickly.

When the Civil War broke out in England in 1642, Protestants overthrew Lord Baltimore. To regain his colony, Baltimore had to concede a bicameral legislature that gave Protestants a majority in the elective assembly. He also granted toleration to all Christians (though not to the small Jewish community) in the colony. By 1660, when religious and political rebellion ended, Maryland had a system of courts like Virginia's and an Assembly capable of thwarting the will of any remaining Catholic lords.

Life and Labor in the Chesapeake, 1640–1680

Once they overcame the worst of their "starving times," Chesapeake settlers set about stabilizing their fragile societies. Although religion remained a major difference between white Virginians (primarily Anglican) and white Marylanders (mixed Anglican, Catholic, and Puritan), both colonies developed similar labor systems and family structures. Both colonies quickly turned to tobacco as their most lucrative export crop, and both turned to their homeland's young and poor for labor. Indentured servants, migrants such as Mary, who agreed to work for a master for a set number of years (usually from four to seven) in return for passage to the colony, came to the Chesapeake in large numbers by the 1620s. Contracts signed in England usually stipulated that servants to Virginia were to receive "freedom dues"—a modest amount of clothing, and some food—at the end of their terms. In Maryland, freedom dues usually consisted of a hoe or an ax, a suit of clothes, and the right to claim 50 acres of their own land beyond established settlements.

Many servants brought useful agricultural skills, and three-fourths of the arriving servants during the seventeenth century were men, most of them under twenty-five years old. But the opportunity to start life over with freedom dues at the end of service was more often a dream than reality. Grueling work and abusive masters often spurred servants to run away before the end of their terms. Two-fifths of Chesapeake's seventeenth-century servants died before they fulfilled their contracts. Those who survived years of servitude watched tobacco prices fall and stay low after 1630, while land prices rose and a few great planters accumulated most of the good riverbank sites. By the 1660s, many planters simply refused to grant servants their freedom dues and instead rented land to them as tenants. Remigration to England increased, and frontier life became dangerous and uncertain for runaways and landless poor ex-servants.

Family life in the Chesapeake before the 1680s departed dramatically from patterns in the home country. Life expectancy remained below the English average: at age twenty, a man in Virginia could expect to live to forty-five, with 70 percent dead by age fifty. Although women who lived to age eighteen in England could expect to live to about age forty-five, the same women in the Chesapeake were likely to die in their thirties from complications of childbirth and lowered resistance to typhus and dysentery during pregnancy. In the first years, Chesapeake men outnumbered women five to one, and even when live births finally began to outnumber deaths in the colony, this stark imbalance of genders persisted. As a result, beginning a family was difficult, and about 70 percent of men never married or produced heirs. Since women had to finish their terms of service before marrying, many of them bore their first child well into their twenties. One-fifth of women in the seventeenth-century Chesapeake had illegitimate children, and about one-third were pregnant at their weddings. Men who married in their thirties or later often left widows and hungry children behind. Although many widows remarried quickly, half the children in parts of the Chesapeake had lost at least one parent by age twelve; one-third of the children could expect to lose both parents before they reached adulthood.

Family loyalties, patterns of inheritance, and emotional bonds were seriously affected by these developments. Servants were at first little more than strangers to most masters, yet they had to live in his household or on his property. Orphans became a financial burden for the county courts or were divided among distant relatives, who were obliged to care for them and make important life decisions for them. Stepparents and stepsiblings made claims on property that deprived children of their anticipated inheritances. When fathers died young, traditions of hierarchical household roles began to break down. Many English customs and laws about paternal authority gave way to colonial innovations. For example, because men anticipated the possible early death of their sons, many Chesapeake husbands named a wife as the executrix of their wills, thereby increasing the authority of women over family land. Other husbands left land to their widows in order to enhance their chances of remarriage.

Creating a farm in the Chesapeake wilderness was arduous work for both men and women. While new settlers broke ground to plant food crops and tobacco, they often lived in lean-to huts because felling trees and planing boards was very time-consuming. Even when time permitted building a sturdy dwelling, planters tended to build modest one-room houses averaging 18 by 22 feet so they could put more labor into tending their tobacco fields and gardens. Since there were few gristmills in the countryside, farm women and girls pounded corn for two or three hours a day to produce the family's regular subsistence. Women were constantly busy tending garden vegetables, making cider or beer, preserving meat, baking, plucking chickens, or laboring at some other endless daily chore. In addition, women turned sheep's wool and flax into fiber for spinning, weaving, and fulling cloth, which was then cut, sewn, and mended until it wore out. Straw mattresses, hand-made wooden tools and bowls, perhaps a rough-hewn table and sitting bench, and a cherished carving knife were among the most important household items in the early years. Visitors rarely saw chairs, curtains, eating utensils, or storage chests. Even at the end of the 1600s, most Chesapeake farmers washed their few articles of clothing very infrequently and stood around the table to eat. The most well-to-do Chesapeake planters had not yet begun to acquire the clocks, wine glasses, or imported silks that elite English families enjoyed.

Sugar and Slavery in the Caribbean

By 1600, hundreds of thousands of people from four continents had transformed the Caribbean islands into profitable plantations based on slave labor (see page 29). Seventeen tiny English settlements were founded between 1624 and 1641. Although many of them did not survive, after the 1620s Barbados, St. Kitts, Antigua, Nevis, and Montserrat attracted large numbers of settlers from England who purchased tracts of fertile land. For a while, tobacco cultivation guaranteed prosperity; when its price plummeted after 1630, planters in Antigua and Barbados turned to a new staple export: sugar.

Dutch traders, who seized Brazil in 1630, began a marketing campaign to turn sugar and its byproducts, molasses and rum, from luxury commodities into items of mass consumption in Europe. They introduced Brazilian methods of growing and processing sugar cane to English planters at Barbados and transported sugar to Europe for the fledgling English colony. Barbadian and Antiguan planters were readily attracted to the higher profits from sugar production than from tobacco, but only a few of them could afford the equipment needed to cut, boil, refine, and package sugar. Those few consolidated huge estates, relegating the majority of farmers to tiny holdings. With England's acquisition of Jamaica in the 1650s, another island began to produce "white gold."

Planting, harvesting, and processing sugar cane was unrelenting work and required a reliable and constantly replenished labor supply. The blistering tropical climate, miserable food quality, and inadequate clothing dissuaded many potential indentured servants from coming to the islands. By the early 1660s, planters complained regularly that unruly servants "knew not their place in the order" of social relations or ran away. So when Dutch merchants offered to bring slaves from Africa to Barbados, planters rejoiced. Already they had enslaved Indians since 1627, but their population was declining rapidly. Soon planters discovered that African slaves were genetically protected from the deadly malaria that afflicted New World settlements in recurring waves, and that the Dutch could bring a steady supply of slaves.

A Female Caribbean Slave
Although this image of a woman weighted down by slavery was created in 1795, the conditions of endless toil, the shame of being deprived of clothing and personal modesty, and the cruelty of being chained like a criminal to the plantation system were all present in the early 1600s Caribbean plantations. *(Tozzer Library, Harvard University.)*

A Female Negro Slave, with a Weight chained to her Ancle.

London, Published Dec.* 1.* 1793, by J. Johnson, St Paul's Church Yard.

Caribbean laws tell the tale of the rapid rise of slavery. By 1636, every black person brought to Barbados became a slave for life, and over the next years, additional laws gave masters extensive rights to their slaves' labor and leisure time. By the 1660s, these slave codes excluded slaves from testifying against free people in courts of law and mandated brutal physical punishments for food theft or practice of African religious rituals. Other Caribbean islands adopted slavery and slave codes similar to the Barbadian example.

By the 1660s, unfree blacks in the Caribbean outnumbered whites, despite an astoundingly high mortality rate on sugar plantations. By the 1670s, when slavery was just beginning to gain a foothold in the Chesapeake, some 30,000 slaves toiled on Barbados alone. At least half of all children born into Caribbean slavery died before the age of five, and adults brought from Africa to the islands rarely survived more than ten years of incessant plantation work. Most Caribbean landlords and masters chose to live a leisured lifestyle in London, while their hired overseers managed the cultivation of crops and disciplining of slaves on the islands.

Tobacco and Slavery in the Chesapeake

Planters in both the Caribbean and the Chesapeake regions grew dependent on international markets, and together they experienced withering tobacco prices in glutted foreign markets after 1630, which forced them to find new economic strategies. But unlike Caribbean growers, Chesapeake planters continued to grow tobacco as their primary export. Typically, they cultivated a smaller tract of land than in the Caribbean and worked as many hours as their indentured servants did each day. And although the Chesapeake adopted slavery, its rise differed from Caribbean slavery.

In 1619 John Rolfe purchased Virginia's first blacks from a Dutch shipper. More Africans soon followed, but for decades Africans and black Caribbeans introduced into Virginia and Maryland had an ambiguous status. Through the 1650s, it was unclear how the Virginia courts should treat slave or mulatto women who sued white men for abuse. Nor did the courts have a consistent stance toward white men who defended the black "servants" of other white men (the word *slave* was not yet regularly applied to African-Americans) against charges of running away. England's repression of the Irish had demonstrated clearly that language, customs, and religion were sufficient reasons for sustained acts of violent prejudice. But in the Chesapeake, early official documents did not automatically associate people of dark skin color with the status of servant or slave. Indeed, a few Africans owned land and worked alongside their white servants. Anthony Johnson, for example, came to Virginia as an indentured servant in 1621 but eventually achieved his freedom and owned a tract of 250 acres on the eastern shore. Johnson employed not only white servants but also a black man whom he claimed was his "Negro for his life."

Only gradually did planters begin to describe people of African origins as slaves and declare their offspring to be slaves. They were aided in this transformation by a few important factors. First, European settlers came from cultures that accepted degrees of freedom and unfreedom in every layer of society. Force and violence, absolute rights to a person's contracted labor, and harsh legal punishments for infractions of laws were familiar to settlers. Further, physical differences and "heathen" religions were long held in scorn by most Europeans.

Second, indentured servants became a less reliable source of labor over time. Third, by the 1650s, the Caribbean example of slave plantations provided a legal model for creating a permanent supply of human labor, a supply that steadily increased. Beginning in the 1640s, legislators of Virginia and Maryland began to institutionalize slavery, passing a series of laws forbidding Africans to own guns, join the militia, make labor contracts with servants, or travel without permission. In 1661 a Maryland statute defined black people as slaves for life; Virginia laws did the same in 1670.

Over the next thirty years, Chesapeake lawmakers stipulated that a slave's Christianity would not qualify the person for manumission. They defined the status of black laborers as "chattel slaves," or human property, and denied them most of the civic and legal privileges of white society. In a radical departure from the historical examples of slavery in the Mediterranean and Africa, Chesapeake planters declared that the children of female slaves would be born into lifelong slavery. In 1705 the Virginia Assembly declared that no master could whip a white servant without his or her permission, but the law was silent about how masters might punish slaves. Courts affirmed that white servants could bring suits about property, but slaves could not acquire land or contest its ownership.

Even so, the number of slaves in the Chesapeake rose only gradually. In 1640 only 150 blacks were reported in Virginia, not all of them slaves. In 1680 the number had climbed to only about 4,000 slaves, but shortly thereafter the demand for labor on maturing mainland plantations grew significantly and the price of slaves began to fall noticeably, initiating a period of much greater slave importations.

 # The New England Colonies, 1620–1680

Starting two hundred miles north of the Chesapeake, climate and geography made it impossible to produce staple crops for export. The earliest settlers to that region extracted furs and timber and established a mixed economy that included livestock grazing, diverse craft production, and trades-related commerce. The first English migrants into the northern colonies were a relatively diverse people, often coming as families, and they agreed that they should live in tightly knit villages centered around strong civic and religious institutions. Many came as Protestant religious dissenters who were committed to establishing utopias in the wilderness. A steady and substantial flow of migrants each year, as well as the large families they produced, visibly reinforced the prosperity of Plymouth, Massachusetts Bay, Connecticut, and Rhode Island—the northern English colonies founded by 1660 and known as New England.

Separatists at Plymouth

After the Virginia Company of Plymouth failed to establish an outpost at Sagadahoc (see page 53), the directors decided to renew exploration in this northern part of their patent a few years later. In 1614 they hired Captain John Smith, who had helped stabilize Virginia, to explore the area. Smith gave "this most excellent place" the name New England in 1616, and the site of his encampment in the Company patent—a former Pawtuxet village—he called Plymouth. A horrendous epidemic wiped out many coastal Indian villages that year, convincing Smith that "Providence" had created a "vacant lande" for English settlement. In 1620 the Company directors in London created a separate Council for New England and announced that they would make grants of land in Plymouth.

However, some of the English investors in the Virginia Company rejected the Council for New England. Instead, they approved the plan of a London merchant named Thomas Weston to form a joint stock company and deliver a group of colonizers to the northern patent. In return for passage and supplies, settlers agreed to send back fish, furs, and timber products for seven years, after which time their debt to the Company would be cleared. Weston signed up 102 colonists—35 from Leyden, Netherlands, and the others from around London—who crammed themselves into a tiny wine carrier called the *Mayflower.*

The Leyden migrants were Separatists, a subgroup of Protestant Puritans who had fled Scrooby, England, in 1609. As Puritans, they denounced vestiges of Catholicism in the Church of England and rejected modernization, including the corrupting influences of troubled commercial cities and the armies of poor people displaced by enclosures. They supported the stern poor laws and labor guilds that regulated social and economic behavior. Eventually their beliefs compelled these Separatists to leave the Church of England, and since denunciation of the state church could result in a death penalty, they left England. But in the Netherlands they again encountered materialism that interfered with their religious zeal, so they appointed William Bradford to arrange with Weston for passage to America.

The Separatists who embarked on the *Mayflower* in September 1620 became known as the Pilgrims. From the beginning, these "saints" were a minority among "strangers" outside their religion. Moreover, when the settlers realized that their crowded and leaky vessel had come ashore outside of their Company grant, forty-one Separatists agreed "to covenant and combine together into a civil body politic" that had only nominal attachment to the sovereignty of King James I. On November 21 they asked all adult male Separatists and "strangers" alike to sign this document, the Mayflower Compact.

The Mayflower Compact would remain only a parchment commitment until settlers could assure their survival. During their first winter, women and children, along with seriously weakened men, slept aboard the *Mayflower.* Disease, compounded by bitter cold and few supplies, carried away half of the settlers during this initial "starving time." Had it not been for the Wampanoag Indians, more would have perished. Massasoit, the Wampanoag leader, offered food and taught the newcomers how to plant maize; in return, the Pilgrims promised to protect the Indians if they were attacked by the Narragansett. Squanto, a Wampanoag who already spoke both Spanish and English, became a valued agricultural adviser to the Pilgrims. An Abenaki from Maine named Samoset also befriended the newcomers.

Despite a good first harvest and the famous first Thanksgiving feast in the fall of 1621, settlers' relations with the Indians around them grew strained. The first governor, William Bradford, believed the Indians were "savage and brutish men," little more than "wild beasts." When word of the Virginia massacre of 1622 reached Plymouth, Miles Standish, a Non-Separatist professional soldier, insisted on arming men in the settlement and barring Indians from entering Plymouth—behavior unbecoming an ally. Meanwhile, Pilgrim cattle were ranging freely on Wampanoag hunting grounds, and settlers took over homes in Indian villages that had been abandoned in the wake of European diseases. When Standish ferociously raided Indian enemies, and then put the head of a Narragansett Indian on a stake at the village entrance, Massasoit realized that the settlers wanted more than to extract furs peacefully and defend the region together against external enemies.

When new ships came, carrying scores of non-Separatists, the original Pilgrim goals of living compactly in mutually dependent relations rapidly broke down. Hard work, shared resources, a community granary, and equally shared land became utopian dreams as colonists turned to other activities. For example, settlers at Mount Wollaston (renamed Merry Mount in 1628) cavorted around a maypole and enticed Indians into their camp with a promise of alcohol and guns. Bradford sent Miles Standish to arrest and remove the instigator, Thomas Morton. Also, in 1624 Bradford and his closest advisers gave up their communal goals and made each family responsible for a private holding. Settlement became decentralized, and many colonists turned from securing furs and timber products for the Company to herding cattle and planting fields for themselves. By the 1650s, the colony comprised eleven town centers surrounded by individual family farms and grazing tracts.

These social problems were aggravated by the absence of a crown charter in Plymouth that could have stipulated government structure and procedures. Instead, the religious goals of the settlement became tied closely to the activities of government. To be a "freeman" with the right to hold land and serve in the representative assembly (established in 1639) required membership in a Separatist church. However, the Non-Separatist majority resented having to pay taxes while being excluded from the political life of the colony. Numerous challenges to the colony's laws arose by the 1660s. In addition, few Plymouth colonists wanted to conform to English trade regulations during the 1600s; instead, they exchanged their surpluses of food and hides with Protestant neighbors in the Massachusetts Bay colony to the north and quarreled with English investors about what returns they should send back to the mother country. By 1692, Plymouth was far surpassed in strength and prosperity by its neighbor Massachusetts Bay.

The City upon a Hill

Most of the first settlers at Massachusetts Bay were also Puritans from England. But unlike the Pilgrims, Massachusetts Puritans did not separate from the Church of England, but rather wished to reform it from within. In addition, these Puritans did not reject the modernizing processes in England outright, but sought to shape social change by altering the corruptions of government and making individuals accountable through hard work and moral virtue. From hundreds of pulpits and many seats in Parliament, Puritans challenged the monarch's claim to rule by divine right and denounced the Church of England's similarities with the Catholic Church. When Charles I adjourned Parliament in 1629 and set loose the Bishop of London, William Laud, to persecute Puritans, they began to plan their migration to a safe haven abroad. This decision was made urgent by the economic depression that threw numerous Puritan spinners and weavers out of work in the English midlands.

Under the formidable leadership of John Winthrop, a member of the English gentry who had attended Cambridge and practiced law, a group of Puritans obtained a land patent from the Virginia Company's Council for New England, as well as a joint stock company charter from Charles I. Within a short time, the directors and most stockholders of the Massachusetts Bay Company were Puritans. At a meeting in Cambridge, England, they secretly elected Winthrop their governor in North America and pledged to take the charter with them, leaving them free to govern themselves.

Aboard the ship *Arbella* in 1630, Winthrop implored the first colonists to remember that "we shall be as a City upon a Hill." Success of the first generation would ensure that others would follow, for "the eyes of all people are upon us." The first step toward that success was the large number of Puritans who came to Massachusetts. The first four hundred settlers established Salem, and a few months later nearly seven hundred more migrants—about half of them Puritans—left England on eleven ships and came to the Boston area.

Predictably, however, the first winter was difficult. "We built us our wigwam, or house," wrote one settler. "It had no frame, but was without form or fashion, only a few poles set together, and covered with our boat's sails." Others burrowed into caves and hillsides. Over 200 died of exposure, undernourishment, and disease, while some 100 gave up and returned to England. But by the end of spring, six new towns had been "planted"; by the fall, another 1,500 settlers arrived. Nearly 18,000 more colonists came to Massachusetts Bay in the next twelve years in this "Great Migration," thus ensuring the colony's survival.

Additional reasons accounted for early success in Massachusetts. The first generation of Puritan Massachusetts came not as soldiers of fortune, or single young male servants, but largely as families with skills as artisans, farmers, and household producers. Most heads of households had been freeholders, or landowners and taxpayers, in England. They came to the New World not primarily to seek personal fortune—though many hoped to prosper in their callings—but to establish communities in which distinctions between the rich and poor were smaller than in English society. Massachusetts colonists also had well-educated leaders, many of them clergymen, who were experienced in local government.

Although many settlers did not come to Massachusetts out of religious zeal, Puritans held Calvinist beliefs in predestination and the election of "saints" to salvation (see page 63), which had a powerful impact on the colony's development. The Puritan conversion experience—an intensely individual moment of realizing one's own unworthiness and receiving God's redeeming grace that came only at the end of prolonged self-examination, self-doubt, and self-discipline aimed at an impeccable moral record—helped give intellectual and spiritual coherence to the colony. So did the training of an erudite ministry, which was able to attend Harvard College after its founding in 1636 and to lead congregations of Puritans for generations in Massachusetts.

Puritans also set a high standard of diligence and justice in their daily living with non-Puritans through the doctrine of the "calling," or work at some employment or public service endeavor that contributed to secular and spiritual improvement. Work for survival and worldly gain thus became dignified as a moral contribution to society. Learning to read, too, was a means to recognize God's grace in the writings of the Bible, as well as an invaluable aid in business.

Decentralized self-governance, through local churches and town meetings, also strengthened rather than fragmented their experiment in its early years. Minister John Cotton insisted that each congregation, or local group of worshipers, have control over its own membership and sit as one enclave in church. Only those presumed to be male saints would choose ministers for each congregation, keep the church finances, and admit other saints to their group, and only saints would enjoy the sacraments of baptism and communion.

Soon Winthrop and a close group of supporters institutionalized these political trends by transforming the colony's charter into the Massachusetts General Court, a body that combined the governor and a unicameral legislature of Assistants chosen by the "freemen," or the small portion of all males in the colony who were both shareholders in the Company and members of the Puritan Church. The General Court enjoyed extensive governing powers over both freemen and all other residents of the colony. Its laws, for example, limited the right to vote and hold office to adult male members of Puritan congregations, even though they were never a majority. By 1634, Assistants also sought more authority to tax the entire population of colonial residents.

But Assistants also expanded the political and legal powers of the towns, which somewhat dispersed authority outward from the colonial leadership. Over Winthrop's objections, the Assistants decreed that each town would elect two deputies to represent townspeople in the legislature. In 1641 Assistants passed a "Body of Liberties" that defined crimes against property and citizens; rights to vote and hold office would be based on sainthood rather than property, which included much of the population in the first generations. In England, where landholding was the basis of the franchise, few adult men could vote. Also, Massachusetts freemen elected their local officials and determined their duties; in England, crown appointees held considerable powers over local citizens.

The Massachusetts government further refined itself when, in 1644, Goody Sherman sued a wealthy merchant named Robert Keayne for the return of one of her sows, which she claimed the merchant had taken and penned on his land. Although the Assistants sided with Keayne, representatives of the towns and general public opinion favored Goody Sherman and ruled in her favor. The decision stood, but just to make sure that the town representatives would not override them in the future, the Assistants separated the two wings of the General Court and required that both houses approve all legislative measures with a majority vote. Thus was created a bicameral legislature intended to balance the rights of local townspeople and the emerging colonial elite.

Dissent and Compromise

In Winthrop's utopia, mutual dependencies were supposed to knit colonists together. The rich would help provide for the needy, and the middling and poor would work hard and respect the authority of their betters. Distinctions of class and status would not tear the colony apart because Puritans' faith united them in a higher truth. But the same Puritans who had been a dissenting, partly underground movement in England refused to tolerate religious and intellectual differences in New England. For example, when Roger Williams, minister of the church in Salem, Massachusetts, protested that spiritual matters had been unjustly blended with the duties of government, leaders around Winthrop grew alarmed. When Williams opposed the government's policy of seizing Indian lands without payment, he further infuriated the General Court, which banished Williams from the colony in 1635. Williams took a number of followers to a spot they named Providence and, true to his beliefs about Indian lands, bought a tract from the Narragansett. Portsmouth and Newport rose quickly, and in 1644 the towns acquired a charter from Parliament to set up self-rule as the colony of Rhode Island.

Differences also arose in Massachusetts over the activities of Anne Hutchinson, a mother of seven living children and a well-respected, skilled midwife. Hutchinson was an intellectual and social leader in Boston, a woman "of a nimble wit and active spirit," who held weekly prayer meetings in her home primarily for women

The Trial of Mrs. Hutchinson
Despite her long ordeal of being questioned by Massachusetts clergy and political leaders, Anne Hutchinson showed stamina, wit, and almost perfect consistency in her stated beliefs throughout her trial.
(Miriam and Ira D. Wallach Division of Art, Prints and Photographs, New York Public Library. Astor, Lenox and Tilden Foundations.)

of the neighborhood. Salvation, Hutchinson reminded her listeners week after week, came through the "covenant of grace" and direct revelation by God of one's election. In order for Puritans to discover their election, they needed to reject all worldly interference and to submit only to the saintliest and most inspired ministers. Perhaps, some colonists whispered, their ministers in Massachusetts were not saints at all.

Hutchinson was a threat to Puritan clergymen not only because of what she said, but also because she was a woman. Just as women did not vote in their communities or hold church and political offices, they were not supposed to preach to congregants. In addition, Hutchinson was popular. Her devoutness drew a wide following of merchants who scorned commercial regulations imposed by the General Court, craftsmen who resented restrictions on their wages, young people who tired of firm control by their elders, and women who attended Hutchinson's meetings.

Hutchinson was brought to trial in 1637 for the heresy of *antinomianism,* or asserting that inner grace was sufficient to achieve salvation and that church rules and ministers were unnecessary for that goal. She stood for three days before Winthrop and an array of other powerful men, explaining that her meetings were merely open discussions and that her beliefs accorded with Calvinism and Scripture. But she was found guilty of eighty-two offenses against the church and government, especially her claim to have a direct relationship with God. Banished, she and her children followed Roger Williams into Rhode Island. She moved later to Westchester County, New York, where she was killed in an Indian attack.

Other dissenters also appeared in Massachusetts. Baptists, who insisted that not infants but only adults who had been properly instructed and lived a godly life should be baptized, were run out of the colony. Quakers, who abolished baptism and communion entirely and taught that everyone could find salvation through an Inner Light, were denounced as Antinomians. Four Quakers, including Hutchinson's disciple Mary Dyer, were hanged for their views. Even within the Puritan fold, baptized infants growing up in holy households were not experiencing conversion. Such "declension," or sliding away from the Puritan mission, had serious consequences for the future of the colony, since those unconverted inhabitants would not be able to present children for baptism and church membership in the future.

The hunger for land and the steady increase in population led to further "hiving off" of settlers in new directions away from the original core of settlements. For example, Thomas Hooker migrated out of the colony in 1630 because he feared leaders were too restrictive about landholdings. His group settled the town of Hartford, and other groups of land-seekers founded Windsor and Wethersfield; together these settlements became a self-governing colony in 1639 called Connecticut. In time they accepted the protection of a single charter over the entire province, which mostly replicated Massachusetts Bay's charter but also gave most male property owners—not just church members—the right to vote. Families in the fishing and fur trades settled additional towns, including the prosperous and rigorously Puritan ones in the colony of New Haven, founded in 1643, and the frontier communities of Maine and New Hampshire.

Rising religious dissent, fewer conversions, and the scattering of settlers, gave Massachusetts ministers strong reasons for concern that the non-Puritan majority would destroy their experiment utterly. Events in England intensified these concerns when in 1642 thousands of Puritans joined Scots Presbyterians in a civil war against Charles I. Puritans in Parliament and in peoples' armies were finally victorious in 1646. Under Oliver Cromwell, God's rule on earth seemed assured, for in 1649 Parliament executed Charles and installed a republican commonwealth. Encouraged by rising Puritan power in England, Massachusetts ministers met in 1648 and formulated a reply to quell their own internal discord. Their Cambridge Platform decreed that each church would have additional local powers: to choose its ministers and dismiss them, refine matters of doctrine, and examine its own applicants for membership.

But then in the 1650s spirits sank in New England as Cromwell's government turned dictatorial. Charles II, son of the recent king, restored monarchical government in 1660 and dashed Puritan expectations of the millennium. Moreover, in New England the intense zeal of the first generation continued to wane among children of the next generation. In 1662 ministers adopted the Halfway Covenant in an effort to regenerate their congregations. All baptized parents could henceforth present their children for baptism, even though they themselves claimed no conversion experience. Baptism, and not conversion, became the route to a "halfway" membership in the church, a step that drew in thousands of new members.

Daily Life in New England

The first institution established in every Massachusetts locale was the congregation and its meetinghouse, the site of both church services and local government affairs. But the formation of "townships," or systems of land owning and use, rapidly followed. In Massachusetts Bay and Connecticut, provincial leaders made township grants of roughly 36 to 50 square miles to certain heads of households known as "proprietors." These men parceled out some of the land among themselves and dispensed other plots to arriving heads of households in "fee simple," or free of obligations to landlords or the government. These freeholders were able to use the land as they chose, to rent or sell it as they pleased—the antithesis of the manorial system that England had known for centuries, and of the obligations of tenancy and social hierarchies of plantations in the Chesapeake.

In practice, the tight-knit communities envisioned by the first immigrants were hard to create and harder to sustain. In the towns, all male heads of households could attend town meetings at which they chose "selectmen" to govern them and passed a host of legal ordinances to see that fences were maintained, wolves run off town lands, petty disputes among inhabitants settled, and affairs among townspeople regulated. But many town meetings became raucous occasions for airing all manner of personal quarrels. In addition, many early Massachusetts towns tried to reproduce an open-field system of agriculture that emphasized clustering around a town center and sharing common fields for grazing, cutting timber, or orchards. But colonists soon divided their open fields into permanently owned family lots, and the tradition of sharing land faded quickly as settlers turned all the land in their grants into private holdings.

Landholdings became more unequal, too. As townships multiplied rapidly, proprietors granted themselves parcels of land repeatedly while newcomers got smaller single tracts (see diagram). Large landholdings reinforced social status and political authority of some proprietors in the towns. Further, the practice of "partible inheritance," by which fathers bequeathed their estate in portions to all of their male children, or all male and female children, accentuated differences among colonists. By the end of the third generation, the holdings of some family heirs were too small to support a sizeable family or to be handed down to the even more numerous next generation.

Yields of crops in New England did not rise as quickly as many farmers hoped they would because of rocky soil and limiting traditional technology. But many farmers prospered by diversifying their activities. Inhabitants processed agricultural goods and manufactured small crafts at home that could be sold in villages or distant towns. Cheese, feathers, tar, straw hats, and other items that even children could be set to making, filled up the corners of wagons going to coastal towns loaded with grain and vegetables. Timber provided containers, tools, vessels for inland and transatlantic trade, houses and barns, fences, and cider presses. Diligent farm families used potash produced from burning underbrush and worn wooden objects to make soap and finish homemade cloth; many supplemented agricultural activities with fishing or cattle herding. By the 1640s, when migration slowed, colonists were exporting small surpluses of agricultural products to the West Indies and Chesapeake settlements; by the 1660s, many families hired out their children occasionally to neighbors who needed extra hands for harvests, plantings, weaving, smithing, or pressing cider. By the end of the 1600s, over one-fifth of New Englanders made a primary living from lumbering, fishing, or producing crafts.

In the midst of this emerging prosperity, traditions of social and family structure altered noticeably. Compared with the Chesapeake, New Englanders saw less disease and enjoyed better diets. As a result, New Englanders lived longer, bore healthier babies, and raised more children to adulthood than their neighbors to the south. Life expectancy for men was sixty-five, and for women sixty-two. Most children not only survived infancy, but thanks to the relatively even gender ratio, they also married young and reared large families. It was not at all unusual for families to boast eight to thirteen children, though five or six living into their teenage years was the norm. Such relatively large New England families did not often require many indentured servants or slaves to perform fieldwork. The male head of household ensured that fields were planted and livestock tended, while his wife took care of the vegetable garden, swine and chickens, supply of wood fuel, dairy house, and local exchanges. Growing daughters watched the youngest children and helped with tedious chores. Some children were sent to work as apprentices in nearby towns or seasonal laborers on neighbors' farms. But most stayed at home where they were needed for planting, hoeing, harvesting, mending, washing, cooking, chopping, and all manner of other tasks. Nobody should

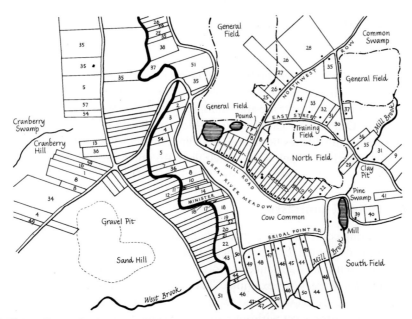

Sudbury, Massachusetts, c. 1650   Although many English towns had been laid out with large areas that were shared by inhabitants and preserved for generations as common land, most New England settlers experienced rapid development of townships based on private landholding. The buying and selling of land led to clusters of "home lots" for original settlers at the center of town with many additional plots added to family holdings over time.   ("Figure 9: Sudbury, Massachusetts: The Village Center" from Sumner Chilton Powell's *Puritan Village: The Formation of a New England Town* © 1963 by Wesleyan University, by permission of University Press of New England.)

live alone, intoned Puritan leaders; individuals needed to be members of families, congregations, and towns, in which rights and obligations were clearly known, and survival could be ensured.

Gradually, this productive family unit underwent further change. Numerous individuals—some of them merchants and fishermen, some widows or sons who left home—did not belong to congregations or participate regularly in town affairs by the third generation. In addition, quarreling between neighbors and within families was on the rise. For example, children and young servants, who were expected to be obedient and cheerful, were being disciplined by New England courts more frequently by the mid-1660s. Violence between fathers and sons, and between men and their female servants, was another reason for legal intervention. Sometimes wives who failed to "keepe the household tranquilitye," or servants who talked back once too often, became subjects of official rebuke or discipline. But overall, wives were legally handicapped in the same ways their female English forebears had been. Common law traditions did not allow a woman to own property independently of her husband, unless he wrote a will or marriage agreement entitling her to a share. A law in England, duplicated in most New England colonies, reserved for the wife a "widow's third," or use of a third of her husband's property when he died.

Colonists and Indians: Coexistence and Conflict, 1630–1680

Colonists struggled to establish families and farms in their first coastal settlements. In addition to this challenge, every new colony in North America faced the difficulties of maintaining peaceful trade and diplomacy with Native Americans throughout the frontier. Often, peace gave way to conflict. By the late 1600s, cultural, political, and economic differences between Europeans and Native Americans could not be negotiated effectively. Open warfare marked both northern and southern frontiers in 1675.

Cultural Contrasts

Europeans, having come from countries where forests had been reduced dramatically, game animals hunted to near extinction, and wild fruits and nuts endangered, marveled at the natural abundance of North America. They had never seen such sizes and varieties of trees, for example. "The soil is most fruitful," wrote the first James Town settlers, "laden with good Oake, Ashe, Walnut trees, Poplar, Pine, sweet woods, Cedar, and others yet without names." It seemed incredible to Europeans that Native Americans did not exploit the forests for profit.

Further, Indian forms of worship and spiritual beliefs scandalized many Europeans because they seemed similar to the horrors of the Catholic Inquisition or even witchcraft. Although many Native American tribes organized their religions around deities and priest-like leaders, and practiced regular rituals and feasts, Europeans failed to see any similarities to Christian practices. English, French, and Spanish writers could not understand why Indians believed in a continuity of kinship between humans and animals, as well as polytheism—the belief in many gods or spirits. It did not take long for Europeans to begin using the labels of "savage," "heathen," and "barbarian" to characterize Indian religions.

Most Woodlands Indians had a keen attachment to the land around them, but they neither owned land nor formulated laws about inheriting it, and buying and selling land was unheard of. In contrast, Europeans believed that the Old Testament had enjoined them to take dominion over the earth, to transform nature for their use, and to observe a strict separation between humankind and the environment. Private possession of land for a man's profit and his heirs' enjoyment seemed fitting. So did fences, protective legal codes, and rules of family inheritance. When Indians failed to tame the wilderness with fields and fences, argued settlers, they lost their rights over it.

Few Native Americans strove to own goods the way Europeans did. Most eastern Indians stressed the community's access to important resources; they shared food, shelter, medicine, and fuel roughly equally during times of need. Although most Indians welcomed the opportunity to trade, they prized strength, bravery, and sound judgment more than items of private wealth. As one European observer noted, "They love not to bee encumbered with many utensils." Most eastern Indians traded goods because it brought prestige to individuals and peace to communities. Scholars use the word *reciprocity* to explain how many Woodlands peoples sustained a network of interdependent villagers and clansmen who shared goods in ongoing exchanges as a way to soften differences between rich and poor, or to redistribute the bounty of fortunate families among those whose resources ran low. Europeans accumulated goods for quite different reasons, including advancing personal comfort or enhancing individual reputation.

Few Native American rulers inherited their positions or held their authority over villages or clans permanently. Men or women earned a temporary right to lead in battle or make important community decisions based on their prowess or generosity. Through the European lens of understanding, however, Indian politics was "primitive" because it typically lacked supreme rulers with permanent, absolute authority over all members of a geographical nation.

Europeans admired the way Native American families nurtured and educated children for many years in tight kinship and village groups. But they puzzled over the weakness of marriage ties and the strong voice of Indian wives in important matters. French, Spanish, and English settlers all noted with horror the frequency of premarital sex and the practice among some Indian men of taking more than one wife. In addition, Europeans often regarded Indian men as lazy because they rested at home for long periods between hunting and warring expeditions, whereas women appeared to work harder because they daily tended both fields and households.

Europeans often thought that Native Americans did not know how to keep records and, some said, even lacked a recorded history. In fact, most Indian cultures recorded information with beads, paintings, or pictograms, and they recounted their histories orally. Although few Europeans could write, and even fewer owned books, they were surrounded by written records such as economic accounts, land deeds, legal agreements, letters, and diaries that affirmed relations between people. For generations, treaties signed between Indians and Europeans carried various meanings for the different parties, sometimes leading to deep misunderstandings.

Early Tensions in the North

Cultural differences between Europeans and Native Americans underlay many of the tensions that persisted after the first years of contact. Tensions arising from conflicting perceptions about the land erupted in 1637 when Pequot warriors attacked Puritan farmsteads in the Connecticut River valley that were impinging on their hunting grounds. The Massachusetts General Court called out militiamen from the townships to lead assaults on the Pequot. In short order, Puritans had leveled a central village of some five hundred Pequot, tracked down survivors, and sold some into Caribbean slavery. Native Americans' "sinful" and socially alien ways, declared Cotton Mather and other Puritan ministers, had been the "the Devil's owne work."

In 1643 leaders of Massachusetts Bay, Plymouth, New Haven, and Connecticut formed a New England Confederation to defend themselves against the threat of further Indian attack and to deflect Indians' anger against them by setting the tribes against one another. Other colonists attempted to Christianize friendly Native Americans by setting up special mission towns for "praying Indians" and introducing John Eliot's translation of the Bible into Algonquian. But their successes were few; the spread of the gospel was often dampened by the spread of disease into

Indian villages. Moreover, Algonquian villagers acquired alcohol and guns, which drastically altered their customs of ritual and war.

English colonizers greedily sought the animal hides they knew would be valuable for hats, coat and glove linings, and home furnishings. Indians in turn were pleased to acquire strouds (large pieces of rough cloth), iron implements and pots, and small household amenities. But the effects of this trade far surpassed anyone's expectations. Native Americans quickly became dependent on Europeans for tools and clothing, hunting their western reserves more intensely in order to satisfy European demand for furs. In the uncontrolled search for beaver and deer, Native Americans exhausted the sources of their own nourishment and shelter, which unbalanced their ecology in numerous unforeseen ways. Once beaver were hunted to depletion in an area, their dams no longer controlled the flow of creeks; with deer and other small game gone, valuable clearing of underbrush ceased. When the supply of game sank so low that it did not reproduce itself enough to feed Micmac, Algonquian, and other tribes, they believed their entire religious cosmology was in crisis. "We have displeased the spirits of the beaver," noted one village elder, and "the beaver will now displease us" by bringing deep hunger, long winters, and internal quarreling.

European settlers knew that without peaceful diplomacy, the fur trade would deteriorate and frontier settlers would be endangered. But it was difficult to determine how, and with which tribes, to form agreements. By the 1660s, intense competition among Iroquois villages was exacerbated by increased warfare against the Huron and Erie villages near the Great Lakes and by the persistent migration of Europeans from the east. The French averted serious warfare in their advance south along the Mississippi River by negotiating trading terms with the Natchez, Choctaw, Chickasaw, Illinois, and other tribes. In the northeast, Dutch and English settlers along the Hudson River invited Iroquois hunters to bring pelts to their forts to conduct trade. Although this policy introduced inconveniences between trading parties, it avoided the terrible open conflicts that would erupt elsewhere when some English settlers insisted on pressing relentlessly into the interior for land and resources.

New England Erupts

The white population of New England grew to about 55,000 by the 1670s, while the Indian population steadily declined from over 100,000 on the eve of European settlement to a few thousand inhabitants in the 1670s. Hungry for land, colonists in Plymouth and Rhode Island encroached on Wampanoag and Narragansett hunting grounds. For years Metacomet, the son of Wampanoag chief Massasoit, had listened to appeals from his people to stop the Europeans. In 1671 the Wampanoag were forced to surrender their guns and agree to be ruled by Plymouth's English law. Tensions grew over the next years, and Indians murdered a number of English settlers in western towns, for which Massachusetts authorities ordered the hanging of three Wampanoags. In July Metacomet (or, as the English named him, King Philip) led large bands of warriors against the English towns on the western fringe. By the fall, Narragansett and Nipmuck had joined Metacomet's men, and raids against the English spread to the Connecticut River valley.

Portrait of Metacomet, or King Philip

This ennobling portrait of the New England Wampanoag leader shows a mixture of adaptations to English trappings—note his gun, powder horn, regal cape, and bejeweled crown—along with traditional Indian attire. Metacomet tried repeatedly to accommodate the wishes of New England settlers but, in the end, fought to preserve his authority among his confederacy and to prevent excessive settler claims on Indian land by driving the newcomers "into the Sea." Metacomet's people lost, and their leader's head was displayed on a post. (*Courtesy of the Haffenreffer Museum of Anthropology, Brown University.*)

Colonists at first thought they would win a quick victory. But Metacomet's men had secreted away hundreds of guns over years of trading and had learned how to repair them. His warriors ambushed Europeans trampling noisily through the woods. In early 1676, they attacked Plymouth and Providence. One-tenth of all the men in Massachusetts were killed or taken captive, and at least eighteen New England towns were flattened. Almost 1,200 homes were ruined and 8,000 cattle—critical to Plymouth's economy—were slaughtered. King Philip's warriors got within twenty miles of Boston, and on the frontier they held shivering captives in their tents. Mary Rowlandson, a minister's wife from a small western town, spent over eleven weeks in 1675 as a captive assigned to work as a servant of a warrior and his three wives. Although Rowlandson was released unharmed, others were less fortunate. Atrocities were reported on both sides.

In the summer of 1676, Massachusetts settlers rallied to the common defense and began to retaliate in what became New England's bloodiest war against Native Americans. New Englanders asked Mohawk from New York to stage ambushes against the Narragansett and persuaded the converted "praying Indians" to spy on Narragansett villages. With the murder of King Philip, and subsequent food shortages, the Native American alliance fell apart. King Philip's head was displayed on a stake in Plymouth, and New Englanders sold dozens of war captives into slavery in the West Indies. Metacomet's War exacted enormous casualties on both sides, and it took years to replant colonists' fields and replenish the brush that harbored Indians' game. Fear reached even into New York, where Iroquois leaders and colonists met at Albany in 1677 to form an alliance called the Covenant Chain, which sought to protect the fur trade for everyone and insulate the Iroquois against their enemies to the east and west. But for generations, colonists recounted the horrors of frontier conditions and retold Mary Rowlandson's captivity story.

Southern Conflicts

By the second generation of settlement, Virginia had become a colony of remarkable contrasts. While a few great planters consolidated estates in the coastal region stretching from Delaware to Albemarle Sound and prospered from tobacco production there, many colonists failed to attain the benefits of good land, marriage and family, and marketable surplus crops. By then, planters were exploiting the labor of many indentured servants, some of whom were denied the freedom dues stipulated in their contracts. Though servants continued to come to the Chesapeake, slavery also took hold. And with each new ship came a few optimistic planters who disembarked hoping to attain a great plantation and gentry status.

Nathaniel Bacon, one of these would-be great planters, acquired considerable grants of land and political privileges through his kinship with Governor William Berkeley. Bacon arrived in Virginia in 1674, just as western settlers had begun turning selective acts of violence into full scale raids against the Doeg and Susquehannock (see "Competing Voices" page 79). Berkeley implored "poor, indebted, discontented, and armed" settlers to cease their hostilities. But some of the Virginia militia, led by an ancestor of George Washington, ignored Berkeley's urgings and joined with forces from Maryland to attack Susquehannock encampments. Before Virginians could claim any decisive victory, Doeg and Susquehannock Indians slaughtered over thirty settlers in January 1676, sending the entire colony into panic demanding immediate retaliation.

Governor Berkeley responded with orders to construct forts above the Virginia fall line, a natural divide between eastern settlements and frontier Indian villages. Further, he restricted the fur trade to a few carefully licensed colonists. Both measures angered frontiersmen, who demanded freedom to hunt as they chose. In addition, growing numbers of ex-servants, migrating new settlers, and runaway slaves grew land-hungry and, frustrated with Berkeley's cautious land-granting policies, joined in the protests. In Maryland, small planters agreed to ride with Bacon into the frontier and issued their own stern protests against their colony's high taxes, low tobacco prices, and seemingly arbitrary government.

Bacon, whose plantation lay east of the fall line near brewing troubles, believed he had been denied the political privileges due to a man of his inherited status. Seeing his chance to gain preferment, he organized disgruntled frontiersmen against Doeg villages with demands on the governor to push Native Americans farther back from expanding planters, ex-servants, and squatters. At first Bacon convinced the colonial assembly to confer authority on his ragged band of malcontents to overrun the frontier and turn Indians into slaves. But in the early summer of 1676, Berkeley expressed opposition to this policy, dismissed Bacon from the council, and denounced the militia's depredations on the frontier. Bacon in turn won election to the House of Burgesses and, from the frontier, marched scores of agitators against James Town. There, the rebels tried to burn the capital to the ground while Bacon exhorted slaves to leave their masters. Although Berkeley fled the city, and the county militia refused to fire against their hero Bacon, he never effectively took over government. By the fall, Bacon had died in jail of swamp fever, and the rebellion soon wound down.

Although Bacon's Rebellion was the largest internal colonial uprising before Lexington and Concord in 1774, poor and discontented southern frontiersmen joined in protests elsewhere during the 1670s. For example, in the more sparsely settled Carolina region, mutinous small planters under the leadership of John Culpepper and George Durant demanded lower duties on tobacco exports and better tracts of interior land. Piggy-backing on Virginia events, they ran the governor out of office at Albemarle and briefly controlled the provincial government. Near still-tiny Charles Town (later, Charleston), planters encouraged Cherokee, Yamasee, Creek, and Chickasaw warriors to capture their Indian enemies and sell them as slaves to both English planters and Spanish missions to the south. Intermittent warfare sparked by fur traders and exporting merchants intensified tensions on the Carolina frontier and put government elites on notice about the region's instability.

CONCLUSION

For over a century, Spain was the primary European power in the New World, holding dominion over Mexico and the Caribbean, and expanding into the Floridas and New Mexico. While *conquistadors* marched across the lands, pillaging and extracting great riches from the conquered lands, English propagandists struggled to arouse interest in exploration in their country, and the Dutch and French added a small presence to the mixture of peoples in North America.

In the early 1600s, England's colonists established two regions of settlement, reflecting two ways of life. Lagging behind the Caribbean colonies, Virginians slowly overcame their starving times when they turned to growing staple crops for export and adopted servants and slaves to perform the work on their plantations. The first New Englanders often brought dissenting religious convictions and usually came as families able to develop a diversified economy. Within both regions, a few hardy settlements included a bewildering array of people from European backgrounds who went through a daily grind of chores, adapting to local conditions, prior inhabitants, labor needs, and religious impulses in particular ways.

From the beginning cultural strains complicated the colonizing process, and most European settlements soon reached a point of intense competition with Indians and other Europeans for furs, fish, or some other resources. Cloth, metal weapons, and cooking pots transformed the lifestyles of Iroquois, Catawba, Cherokee, Creek, and other tribes, as well as the Algonquian peoples along the coast who survived early wars and epidemics, and then endured the introduction of guns and alcohol. By the 1670s, northern and southern regions erupted into large-scale warfare that transformed relations among all cultures on the landscape.

By 1680, there was much success to celebrate and many obstacles yet to confront. Although some colonists gained a degree of material prosperity, religious toleration, and political liberty, not everyone in the colonies shared a good life. Three times more people, including thousands of servants such as Mary who pleaded to go home at the opening of this chapter, migrated into the Chesapeake during the seventeenth century than into the northern colonies. Yet the Chesapeake population remained smaller than New England's for years. The gap between rich and poor, skilled and unskilled, protected and vulnerable, entitled and oppressed, grew wider in each colony over the years. Slavery also became more institutionalized, putting a stain on colonists' belief that their settlements might revitalize or liberate human potential. Despite these mixed results, a few North American colonies had been planted and would endure.

SUGGESTED READINGS

For the Spanish presence, David Weber's *The Spanish Frontier in North America* (1992) is a model of comprehensive coverage and judicious argument, covering Spanish settlement and governance from Florida to California. For French colonization of Canada, the best work is W. J. Eccles, *The Canadian Frontier, 1534–1760* (rev. 1983). The background to English colonization is treated best in Nicholas P. Canny, *Kingdom and Colony: Ireland in the Atlantic World, 1560–1800* (1988), and David B. Quinn, *Raleigh and the British Empire* (1947). Karen Ordahl Kupperman, *Roanoke: The Abandoned Colony* (1984), is a fascinating account of the "Lost Colony."

Peter Wood et al., eds., *Powhatan's Mantle: Indians in the Colonial Southeast* (1989), is the best collection of essays about early European and Indian contact in the Southeast. For the development of the Chesapeake during the 1600s, see T. H. Breen and Stephen Innes, "*Myne Owne Ground*": *Race and Freedom on Virginia's Eastern Shore, 1640–1676* (1980); Lois Green Carr, Russell R. Menard, and Lorena S. Walsh, *Robert Cole's World: Agriculture and Society in Early Maryland* (1991); Wesley Frank Craven, *White, Red, and Black: The Seventeenth Century Virginian* (1971); James Horn, *Adapting to a New World: English Society in the Seventeenth Century Chesapeake* (1994); and Gloria L. Main, *Tobacco Colony: Life in Early Maryland, 1650–1720* (1982).

For Caribbean sugar and slavery, Richard Dunn's *Sugar and Slaves: The Rise of the Planter Class in the English West Indies, 1624–1713* (1972) is the most authoritative account. Philip D. Curtin, *Africa Remembered: Narratives of West Africans from the Era of the Slave Trade* (1967), offers valuable first hand accounts, while Winthrop D. Jordan, *White over Black: American Attitudes Toward the Negro, 1550–1812* (1968) offers the best and most comprehensive interpretation of attitudes and values about race. Daniel P. Mannix and Malcolm Cowley, *Black Cargoes: A History of the Atlantic Slave Trade* (1962) focuses on the capture and transport of African slaves; see also James A. Rawley, *The Transatlantic Slave Trade* (1981).

Edmund Morgan makes two short but influential contributions to understanding Puritan settlement in *The Puritan Dilemma: The Story of John Winthrop* (1958) and *The Puritan Family* (1966). For the Separatists, see John Demos, *A Little Commonwealth* (1970). For understanding why settlers came to New England, what ideas and institutions they transported with them, and the cultural ways they developed in the 1600s, see David Grayson Allen, *In English Ways: The Movement of Societies and the Transferal of English Local Law and Custom* (1981); David Cressy, *Coming Over: Migration and Communication Between England and New England in the Seventeenth Century* (1987); and David Hall, *Worlds of Wonder, Days of Judgment* (1989). Hall's study makes the argument that popular religious beliefs endured alongside stabilizing Puritan ones. Neal Salisbury, *Manitou and Providence: Indians, Europeans, and the Making of New England, 1500–1643* (1982), explains cultural encounters in the first years.

The best starting point for understanding Metacomet's War is Russell Bourne, *The Red King's Rebellion: Racial Politics in New England, 1675–1678* (1991). Two opposing views of the governor and Nathaniel Bacon are offered in Wilcomb E. Washburn, *The Governor and the Rebel: A History of Bacon's Rebellion in Virginia* (1957), and Thomas Jefferson Wertenbaker, *Torchbearer of the Revolution: The Story of Bacon's Rebellion and Its Leader* (1940).

"Manifesto Concerning the Troubles in Virginia"

By autumn 1675, Doeg and Susquehannock Indians in western Virginia had begun to ambush and murder settlers who refused to stop fencing in frontier land for their private use. Friction erupted into the warfare of Bacon's Rebellion that brought poor servants, runaway slaves, recent immigrants, and land-hungry planters together against the Indians. Nathaniel Bacon rallied supporters to arms and defended their actions with a stirring rationale for revolt.

If virtue be a sin, if Piety be guilt, all the Principles of morality goodness and Justice be perverted, We must confess That those who are now called Rebels may be in danger of those high imputations, Those loud and several Bulls would affright Innocents and render the defence of our Brethren and the enquiry into our sad and heavy opressions, Treason. But if there be as sure there is, a just God to appeal to, if Religion and Justice be a sanctuary here, If to plead the cause of the oppressed, . . . If after the loss of a great part of his Majesty's Colony deserted and dispeopled, freely with our lives and estates to endeavor to save the remainders, be Treason, God Almighty Judge and let guilty die . . . but let us trace these men in Authority and Favour to whose hands the dispensation of the Countries' wealth has been committed; let us observe the sudden Rise of their Estates compared with the Quality in which they first entered this Country . . . let us consider their sudden advancement and let us also consider whither any Public work for our safety and defence or for the Advancement and propagation of Trade, liberal Arts or sciences is here . . . adequate to our vast charge, . . . and see what sponges have sucked up the Public Treasure and . . . juggling Parasites whose tottering Fortunes have been repaired and supported at the Public charge. . . .

Another main article of our Guilt is our Design not only to ruin and extirpate all Indians in General but all Manner of Trade and Commerce with them, . . . [but] Although Plantations be deserted, the blood of our dear Brethren Spilt, on all Sides our complaints, continually Murder upon Murder renewed upon us, [there are the Governor's licensed traders] at the Heads of the Rivers . . . [who] buy and sell our blood, and do still notwithstanding the late Act made to the contrary, admit Indians painted [for warfare] and continue to Commerce, although these things can be proved yet who dare be so guilty as to do it.

Another Article of our Guilt is To Assert all those neighbour Indians . . . to be outlawed, wholly unqualified for the benefit and Protection of the law. . . . [For] since the Indians cannot according to the tenure and form of any law to us known be prosecuted, Seized or Complained against, Their Persons being difficulty distinguished or known, Their many nations' languages, and their subterfuges such as makes them incapable to make us Restitution or satisfaction would it not be very guilty to say They have been unjustly defended and protected these many years.

"Virginia's Deplored Condition"

Many eastern planters sympathized with the grievances raised by frontier settlers, but few endorsed the methods used by Bacon and his followers. Bacon not only defied the governor's orders respecting arms and violence, but attacked the central authority of a fragile and self-conscious elite. At stake was the law of the frontier and the social hierarchy white Virginians had inherited from English tradition. William Sherwood, an eastern planter, voiced the establishment's condemnation of Bacon. It's original subtitle—An Impartial Narrative of the Murders Committed by the Indians There, and of the Sufferings of His Majesty's Loyal Subjects Under the Rebellious Outrages of Mr. Nathaniel Bacon—was anything but impartial.

... [E]very one endeavours to get great tracts of Land, and many turn Land lopers, some take up 2000 acres, some 3000 Acres, others ten thousand Acres ... and never cultivate any part of it, only set up a hog house to ... prevent others seating, so that too many rather than to be Tenants, seat upon the remote barren Land, whereby contentions arise between them and the Indians ... turning their Cattle and hogs on [the Indians' lands] and if by Vermin or otherwise any be lost, then they exclaim against the Indians, beat & abuse them ... for it is the opinion of too many there, (and especially of their General Mr. Bacon) that faith is not to be kept with the heathens. ...

[Bacon, not content with the Governor's pardon of his initial depredations on the frontier] gets the discontented rabble together, and with them resolved to put himself, once more on the stage, and on the 21st day of June [1676] he entered James Towne, with 400 foot, & 120 horse, set guards at the state house, kept the Governour, Council and Burgesses prisoners, and would suffer none to pass in or out of Town, and having drawn up all his forces to the very door & windows of the state house, he demanded a Commission to be General of all the forces that should be raised during the Indian War, he and all his soldiers crying out No Levies, No Levies. The Assembly acquainted him they had taken all possible care for carrying on the Indian War at the easiest charge that could be, that they had redressed all their Complaints, and desired that for satisfaction of the people, what they had done might be publicly read, Mr. Bacon answered there should be no Laws read there, that he would not admit of any delays, that he came for a Commission, and would immediately have it, thereupon sending his soldiers into the State house, where the Governour, Council & Burgesses were sitting and threatening them with fire and sword if it was not granted, his soldiers mounting their Guns ready to fire ... so that Order was given for such a Commission as Mr. Bacon would have himself. ... The next morning ... now Mr. Bacon having a Commission, shows himself in his colours, and hangs out his flag of defiance (that is) Imprisoning several loyal Gentlemen and his rabble used reproachful words of the Governour ... it was imagined he & his soldiers would march out of Town, yet they continued drinking and domineering, the frontier Counties being left with very little force, and the next day came the sad news that the Indians had that morning killed Eight people within thirty Miles of town, in the families of some of them that were with Mr. Bacon, yet they hastened not away, but the next day having forced an Act of Indemnity, and the Assembly being at the Burgesses' request dissolved, Mr. Bacon after four days' stay, marched out of Town. ...

During Mr. Bacon's thus Lording it, and seizing the estates of such as he terms Traitors to the Commonality ... The Indians taking advantage of these civil commotions, have committed may horrid murders, ... not only in the frontier Counties, but in the inward Counties. ...

Thus is that Country by the rashness of a perverse man exposed to ruin, and is in a most calamitous & confused condition, lying open to the cruelty of the savage Indians. ... God in mercy divert the Issues of War which much threateneth the Country, by the Indians & the rabbles killing up, & destroying the stocks of Cattle, pulling down the Corn field fences, turning their horses in, and such like Outrages, so that unless his sacred Majesty do speedily send a considerable supply of men, Arms, Ammunition, & provision, there is great cause to fear the loss of that once hopeful Country, which is not able long to resist the cruelty of the Indians or rebellion of the Vulgar. ▮

Although Bacon's rebels marched into Jamestown, they could not hold the capital for long. Nor did they take over the frontier. Indeed, on Governor Berkeley's orders, soldiers hanged twenty-three rebels after Bacon died in jail. But the rebellion was widespread, and it showed how frustrated many indentured servants and poor farmers had become, and the extent to which Indians had become a scapegoat for white settlers' land hunger. Colonists needed land to grow crops, create an inheritance for their children, and claim many civil rights in Virginia. That need was now overlaid with perceptions about the nature of the frontier and racial tensions among different peoples. Frontier settlers' fear and loathing of Indians rarely abated but only grew in the years to come. Moreover, the great eastern planters and royal officials who deplored the violence on the western frontier had no abiding concern for the welfare of the Indian peoples. Rather, they feared the threats to their own elite rule and property that arose during the prolonged violence of Bacon's Rebellion.

Questions for Analysis

1. What were Bacon's grievances with regard to the frontier and political authority in Virginia?

2. What defense did Berkeley's supporters make of their efforts to suppress Bacon? Which reasons for opposing Bacon are vitally important, and which are secondary?

3. What racial attitudes are expressed in these passages?

4. Are there any areas of agreement between the disputants?

5. Do Bacon and Sherwood exaggerate the truth? If so, for what purpose?

3

Imperial Connections, 1660–1748

*L*ate in 1731, Parliament's House of Commons summoned retired ship captain Fayer Hall to testify before the members about his years of experience living and trading in the West Indies. For months, the politicians had been conducting hearings on the state of the Caribbean trade. Angry planters and merchants from the islands were demanding that Parliament "end the wretched habits of the illicit trade" between French, Spanish, and Dutch foreigners in the islands and the British North American colonists. Foreigners, they lamented, paid well for colonial goods and sold their sugar, molasses, and rum at far lower prices than the British did, so colonists were attracted to the foreign islands for trade. It was foreign sugar, they insisted, that ended up on the tables of British citizens, which not only diminished planters' and merchants' profits but, worse, undermined the moral fiber of the British Empire.

This "sugar interest" of absentee landowners, slave traders, Jamaica and Barbados merchants, and London sugar refiners blamed colonists for trading more between "the bays of Boston to the bays of Spain's Havana" than within the British Empire. And they promoted sweeping legislation to keep North American colonists away from foreign islands. Now Fayer Hall, an inveterate smuggler hated by this "sugar interest," stood before some of the most prestigious men in the empire and delivered advice that Parliament did not want to hear.

"'Tis the best known secret," Hall reminded Parliament, "that our illicit trade to foreign parts does bring us a greater benefit than the legal runs of goods." Hall would know. He had hauled goods from one place to another in the Atlantic world for many years. He had traded in peace and war, to mainland and island colonies, legally and illegally. Widely respected for "fair dealing with goods of any nation," Hall insisted that whatever legislation Parliament passed to please planters and merchants of the "sugar interest" would be useless and possibly detrimental to Britain's interests.

In truth, said Hall, "our home ports [in England] will never take in much of the bounty rising from colonial soil," and "there is not sufficient trade in the English parts of the [Caribbean] to keep the New England merchants happy." Colonists who shipped their surpluses of farm and forest goods to the West Indies never found sufficient markets at the English islands, and so they traveled "around and about the foreign ports" to trade. "Colonials need the foreign stops," he insisted, in order to sell all of the goods they carry. In addition, it was the "illegal profits from the French and Dutch" trade that enabled colonists to pay English merchants for the cloth, tools, metal wares, and many household necessities they imported. As Hall put it, "The French and Netherlanders [in the Caribbean] want the colonial wheat, and will give a higher price than our own [English] islands will offer. In consequence, the risk of being caught running into foreign ports, though considerable, is generally thought to be productive of greater [profits] than the legal trade."

The island planters and merchants carried tremendous weight in British politics, more so than a retired captain who spoke for colonists on the other side of the Atlantic Ocean. The House of Commons listened respectfully to Hall's defense of colonial interests and his plea that Parliament "leave the trade of our empire free and clear" of restrictions "in all of its ports," and promptly disregarded his counsel. The Molasses Act of 1733 established higher duties on sugar, rum, and molasses, and detailed the principle of keeping Britain's trade in the British Empire. From a diplomatic point of view, Parliament argued, the empire had to protect itself from foreign competition and show the world its strength as a closed imperial system. In addition, the Molasses Act, if enforced properly, would force colonists to submit to the will of the mother country.

Colonial North American merchants greeted news of the Molasses Act's new taxes and crackdown on smuggling with anxiety. As Fayer Hall had reasoned before Parliament, it was "but natural and of practical Sense" for merchants to "follow their own Interest" by finding buyers and sellers wherever they were conveniently located. Parliament's new law seemed "selfish." And as Hall predicted, merchants systematically evaded the act, while royal officials seldom enforced its provisions.

These discussions about sugar—an immensely popular but nutritionally unnecessary commodity—symbolized two important developments in the English Empire. First, as the initial colonies took root, the political, economic, and cultural connections between colonists and the imperial center matured and deepened. Colonists had many reasons to be optimistic about opportunities for expanding onto their frontiers and trading across many national and geographical boundaries. But second, British subjects in both worlds became increasingly aware of the problems of ruling a large empire. As the empire matured, as its network of social relations became more complex, the different interests within the empire expressed uncertainty about how to cultivate, regulate, or restrict their particular interests. Even as North Americans became more aware of their Englishness, they also noted the differences between the home country and colonies, as well as the differences marking colonists from one region, religion, occupation, or race to another. The coexistence of both optimism and tensions raises important questions about British North America in the century after 1660.

- As the process of founding and developing colonies proceeded, what distinctive features characterized the new colonies in North America after 1660?

- How did English authorities try to organize the trade, politics, defense, and cultures of their colonies? How did colonists respond?

- How did colonists participate in developing their political, economic, and cultural opportunities in light of their positions both within North America and within the British Empire?

- How did the colonists reconcile their continuing expansion and maturing societies with the numerous wars and social tensions that persisted in North America?

This chapter will address these questions.

 ## The Restoration Colonies, 1660–1685

The first settlements in North America had been grounded on the religious convictions of individuals and the initiatives of private companies. These experiments took root, flourished as agricultural communities or staple-exporting colonies, and began to expand onto new frontiers. Clusters of crown officials and local representative assemblies ran the settlements. After 1660, new streams of settlers from various countries began migrating to other parts of North America. In England, Charles II (reigned 1660–1685) restored the Stuart monarchy. The colonies' expanding populations and England's need to manage and defend its interests in the New World prompted Charles to take firm control of governing the empire.

Colonies formed during the Restoration would be different from the earlier ones (see table page 91). Charles II took an active interest in sponsoring two new regions of settlement. One, between New England and Virginia (see map page 86), became known as the mid-Atlantic region and included New York, New Jersey, Pennsylvania, and Delaware. The other, south of the James River to Spanish Florida, was known as "the Carolinas" (later divided into South and North Carolina). In each case, Charles chose proprietors from among his political inner circle, men who could be counted on to support the crown's commercial goals, the Anglican Church, and the divine right of kings. Detesting the rising power of the colonial assemblies in the original colonies, Charles appointed colonial governors who were committed to utter royal control and experienced in military, rather than civilian, affairs.

The Carolinas

Few Europeans had come ashore between Virginia and Spanish Florida before 1660. A handful of Puritans and West Indian planters had tested the land but failed to at-

Chronology

1642–1649	Civil War in England
1649–1660	Cromwellians rule England
1651	First Navigation Act
1660	Restoration of Charles II
1663	Carolina proprietorship established
1664	English conquer New Netherland
1681	Pennsylvania founded
1683	New York assembly established
1685	James II becomes King of England
1685–1689	Dominion of New England
1688	Glorious Revolution
1689	Leisler's Rebellion
	Andros ousted from Massachusetts
	Maryland rebellion
1689–1697	King William's War
1692	Salem witch trials
1702–1713	Queen Anne's War
1715	Yamasee War
1718	New Orleans founded
1720–1742	Walpole serves as prime minister in England
1720s–1740s	Land bank experiments
1728	Benjamin Franklin begins *Pennsylvania Gazette*
1733	Molasses Act
1740–1748	War of Jenkins's Ear (War of the Austrian Succession)

tract a large flow of colonizers. In 1663 Charles II gave a group of eight proprietors extensive personal rights over this region, known as "the Carolinas," permitting them to shape the destinies of their territories in North America. As aristocrats, most of them wished to establish strictly hierarchical societies, with inherited land ownership.

In 1669 one of the proprietors, Anthony Ashley Cooper, hired rising scholar and publicist John Locke to create a plan for settlement. In subsequent years, Locke would become associated with political upheavals that paved the way for property-tied individualism and representative government. But during the founding of the Carolinas, he believed in a conventional, hierarchical form of social organization.

The Restoration Colonies

During the 1660s two large regions were added to England's empire in North America. One, which emerged following the conquest of the Dutch in 1664, was the mid-Atlantic area that became New York, East Jersey, West Jersey, Pennsylvania, and Delaware. The other, stretching from Virginia to Spain's claims at the Savannah River, was Carolina, or as colonists called it "the Carolinas."

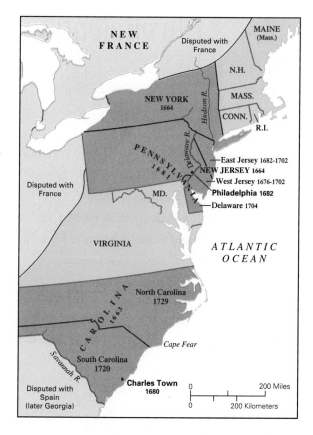

His *Fundamental Constitutions of Carolina* called for a nearly feudal form of landownership, complete with nobles, yeomen, and serfs. The plan was impressive on paper but impossible to implement in the New World environment, and little true government developed until the 1720s.

Instead, over two hundred planters from Barbados immediately staked out private plantations and introduced "seasoned," or acclimated, African slaves to herd cattle and do field labor. A few English servants and farmers, as well as some French Huguenot refugees, settled where the Ashley and Cooper Rivers met near what became Charles Town. Residents around the small trading post also ignored the proprietors' wishes when they started a thriving fur trade with Native Americans and began to capture slaves from enemy Indian camps. The quest for fur and slaves set planters and small farmers in the Carolinas on a course of prolonged frontier violence that lasted to the 1720s. In 1715 frontier tensions erupted into a devastating war of trappers, small farmers, and aspiring planters against the Yamasee people.

Meanwhile, planters sought a cash crop that could turn a profit as great, or greater, than the tobacco grown by Virginia planters to their north. By the early 1690s, Carolinians had found it: rice. Long a staple in the diet of West Africans, rice was brought to North America by slaves and slave traders. Slaves probably taught Carolina planters how to transform the marshy coastal lowlands into rice fields. Within the first generation of settlement, rice planters' profits far outstripped those of their Virginia neighbors. By 1720, the countryside around Charles Town supported a dense population of slaves growing and processing rice. The "rice belt" stretched from Cape Fear (now North Carolina) to the edge of Spanish dominion on the Savannah River.

Success depended on the steady importation of slaves. When seasoned Caribbean slaves proved insufficient in numbers, planters stepped up importation of African slaves, who had the advantage of resistance to malaria. This disease, transmitted from Africa by the same ships that brought slaves, was often deadly to Europeans but far less threatening to Africans. Just after 1700, within the lifetime of the first planters, the number of slaves surpassed the number of whites in the colony. By 1720, almost two-thirds of the colony's population was African slaves, subject to the severe slave code treatment that Barbadian planters had perfected (see page 61). And, with little toleration themselves for the mosquito-infested swamps, planters left cultivation to their slaves and overseers and lived in the comforts of Charles Town. In all these respects, Carolina differed from the Chesapeake colonies and resembled the Caribbean island societies.

In the northern parts of the Carolinas, a few settlers ventured into the Albemarle Sound region during the 1660s and 1670s. They were cut off from the Chesapeake planters to their north by the shallow inlets of the Dismal Swamp, which prevented even ships from approaching. Poor families came to the sound from Virginia, raising tobacco and corn, and ignoring the proprietors' demands for quit-rents. In 1664 William Drummond arrived from England to govern the settlers around the sound,

Mulberry Plantation   In 1708 Thomas Broughton began to acquire hundreds of acres for his rice and indigo plantation near Charles Town on the Santee River. In the foreground of this painting stand the slave quarters, built in African style and housing multiple slaves. During the Yamasee War of 1715, the Broughton mansion in the background was fortified against assault from Indians.   *(The Gibbes Museum of Art, Carolina Art Association.)*

but he, too, discovered the hostility of the independent farmers. In 1677 farmers seethed with discontent about the cost of rents and export taxes on their tobacco. John Culpepper, a leading Albemarle Sound planter, spearheaded the ouster of Drummond and frightened the proprietors into leaving settlers' land alone.

In 1704 the colonists around the sound finally established their first town, Bath. By then, the frontier was home not only to farmers, but to ranchers, miners, and lumbermen as well. Although the land was too dry for rice cultivation, it was heavily forested with pines, which provided sources of naval stores such as tar, pitch, turpentine, and ship masts. Subsidies from the English government after 1705 for producing naval stores failed to attract large numbers of migrants, however, and the Albemarle area remained sparsely settled in the 1700s. In 1719 royal authorities separated South Carolina from lands to its north and made it a royal colony. The proprietors' families retained North Carolina until 1729, when it too became a royal colony.

New York and New Jersey

Just before the Second Anglo–Dutch War (1665–1667), Dutch settlers at New Netherland surrendered peaceably to a small British fleet in its harbor in 1664. From the Dutch point of view, the colony had never been profitable; from the English point of view, it lay within the original Virginia charter of 1606 and had been wrongfully occupied by the Dutch. Charles II gave his brother James, duke of York and Albany, proprietary rights over a vast stretch of land north of the small port. Already lord high admiral and a leader in the African slave trade, James eagerly appointed his first governor, Colonel Richard Nicolls, and pledged religious toleration and property protection for all residents of New York.

Like the eight proprietors of the Carolinas, the duke of York held almost unlimited power over his colony. Although he never set foot in New York, he tried to rule personally from afar by appointing government officials, making laws regulating public affairs and commerce, and overseeing the courts. Often he appointed inept or corrupt royal governors; nevertheless, the colony gained stability from the influx of energetic farming peoples after the 1670s. English immigrants lived relatively quietly alongside Dutch residents, and the colony gained a reputation for toleration of diverse languages and religions. A few well-connected merchants built strong links to English commerce during the late 1600s, but commerce with Amsterdam continued as well. Although English residents followed their traditions of inheritance and social institutions, strong elements of Dutch custom and law prevailed among the original families. For example, though churches abounded in the colony, no Anglican parishes appeared until the 1690s.

Nicolls tried to rule New York without a representative assembly. For a while, he governed with the advice of a handpicked council, and colonists took legal disputes to an appointive court of assizes firmly under Nicolls's control. But this arrangement fell apart when in 1665 the duke of York gave a portion of his grant between the Hudson and Delaware Rivers to two friends, Sir George Carteret and Lord John Berkeley (brother of the Virginia governor), thus creating New Jersey. Carteret and Berkeley gave New Jerseyans the right to elect an assembly, which helped attract more immigrants to that colony than to New York. As unsettling as this was, James was even more unnerved when leading Dutch families failed to support his efforts to defend English settlers in the Delaware River Valley and on Manhattan or Long Island during the third Anglo–Dutch War (1672–1674). In New York City, former Dutch civic and political leaders, who were still the leading figures of the Dutch community, refused to aid English military efforts. In 1673, the port city became Dutch again for fifteen months. After the restoration of English rule, a few prominent Dutch merchants refused to swear allegiance to England, giving in only after the new governor, Edmund Andros, threatened to confiscate their property. Other wealthy Dutch families coped with shifting political alignments by marrying into, or socializing with, English families.

With the coming of peace, many Dutch settlers resented their wealthy countrymen, who "became more English by the day." For their part, English colonists began to resent Andros's accommodation to Dutch trade. Especially irksome were his refusal to curtail trade with Amsterdam and his decision not to renew commercial revenue laws that favored their trade through England. When Andros returned to England in 1680, English leaders in the colony refused to pay import duties until the colony was guaranteed a representative assembly. In 1683 the duke of York finally yielded to this demand.

Nearby, the two proprietors of New Jersey soon found out that a number of Puritans and Dutch Protestants had settled in their dominion already. Resisting rule and taxation by Restorationists, these religious dissenters created a dilemma for the proprietors. In 1674 Berkeley decided to sell his lands to two Quakers, but they soon fell to quarreling over the management of the colony. In the next decade they turned the grant over to three trustees, one of whom was the influential Quaker William Penn (see below).

In 1676 the province was divided into West and East Jersey, the latter going to Carteret, who in turn sold his share in 1682 to yet another group of proprietors, one of whom was Penn. In order to attract capital and make the colony solvent, Penn brought in even more proprietors over the next years, until twenty-four owner–rulers headed the divided colony. Here and there in the east and west portions of the colony, settlers of diverse backgrounds clustered into towns. An influential population of Quakers emerged in many towns and farms along the Delaware River. By 1702, however, proprietors and citizens alike grew weary of their constant fragmentation. They agreed to unite the two portions and become one royal colony of New Jersey.

Pennsylvania and Penn's Delaware

Pennsylvania also began as a gift from the crown to a proprietor. In 1681 Charles II awarded a great tract of land to William Penn, primarily to pay off a debt the crown owed to Penn's father. The northern boundary stretched far into the unknown west. To the south, Penn's grant overlapped Maryland claims, which were finally settled in 1767 when Charles Mason and Jeremiah Dixon surveyed a line between the two colonies.

In his early twenties, Penn had left behind a life of privilege and wealth to join the relatively new dissenting Protestants in the Society of Friends, or Quakers. By his mid-thirties, Penn had published fifty books and pamphlets about Quaker beliefs. His grant of land, which he named Pennsylvania, became a refuge for fellow Friends. Quakers were a radical sect within the Protestant fold, but they were not Calvinists. As their founders George Fox and Margaret Fell taught, salvation was available to all believers because each person carried an "inner light" of grace. This idea was not much different from the notion of individual reason that liberal philosophers were beginning to popularize in the broad movement called the Enlightenment (see page 111). Quakers gathered in weekly meetings, but unlike Puritan services, their worship was not led by a pastor or centered on a sermon. Rather, anyone could speak out at meetings about their experiences of inner light. Pious and principled, Quakers were nevertheless persecuted because they refused to fight in the army, pay taxes to support the Church of England, or conform to gestures of cultural deference such as tipping one's hat to "betters."

Penn's colony also differed from established ones in secular matters. Colonists did not have to fight for the creation of an assembly because Penn's charter required him to convene one. His Frame of Government of 1681 provided that Christians of all denominations could vote and hold office and that no taxes could be used to support a church. In the legislature, both upper and lower houses were to be elected by the enfranchised male property holders. The governor was to have no veto, and there was to be no established church. Penn insisted, however, that the structure of government was less important than the men who ran it. "Governments rather depend upon men than men upon governments. Let men be good, and the government can't be bad."

Such toleration of personal and religious beliefs encouraged rapid settlement in Pennsylvania. In the early years, great numbers of Quaker immigrants from England, Ireland, and Wales flocked to the new colony, outdone only by Puritan New England immigration in its first generation. Although this population was diverse in its skills, material endowments, and origins, Pennsylvania nevertheless bore a strong imprint of Quaker ideals. Elsewhere in North America, Quakers' antipathy to prevailing social hierarchies, wars, and conventional dress brought ridicule and persecution. The Quaker belief that women in their churches were as capable as men of leading their followers stirred up much opposition outside Quaker communities in Pennsylvania.

Land, declared Penn, would not be free, but neither could any person accumulate vast estates. Instead, it would be available at a low cost and widely distributed. In just over a decade, thousands of people came from northern England and Germany, settling the fertile lands close to good waterways and the carefully planned port city of Philadelphia, meaning "brotherly love." As Quakers spread away from the coastline, relations with Indians remained peaceful thanks to the settlers' religious convictions about generosity and love, and Penn's firm policy of friendliness and purchasing titles for Indian lands. The Lenni Lenape (or Delaware) Indians were especially open to forming an alliance with Penn's settlers because it implied protection against their long-time enemy, the Iroquois.

ENGLISH COLONIES IN NORTH AMERICA

Name	Founded by	Founded	Charter	Made Royal	Type of Colony in 1775
Virginia	London Co.	1607	1606 1609 1612	1624	Royal (under the Crown)
Plymouth	Separatists	1620	None		(Merged with Mass., 1691)
Maine	F. Gorges	1623	1639		(Bought by Mass., 1677)
New Hampshire	John Mason and others	1623	1679	1679	Royal (absorbed by Mass., 1641–1679)
Massachusetts	Puritans	c. 1628	1629	1691	Royal
Maryland	Lord Baltimore	1634	1632	———	Proprietary
Connecticut	Mass. emigrants	1635	1662	———	Self-governing
Rhode Island	R. Williams	1636	1644 1663	———	Self-governing
New Haven	Mass. emigrants	1638	None		(Merged with Conn., 1662)
N. Carolina	Virginians	1653	1663	1729	Royal (separated informally from S.C., 1691)
New York	Dutch	c. 1613			
	Duke of York	1664	1664	1685	Royal
New Jersey	Berkeley and Carteret	1664	None	1702	Royal
Carolina	Eight nobles	1670	1663	1729	Royal (separated formally from N.C., 1712)
Pennsylvania	William Penn	1681	1681	———	Proprietary
Delaware	Swedes	1638	None	———	Proprietary (merged with Pa., 1682; same governor, but separate assembly, granted 1704)
Georgia	Oglethorpe and others	1733	1732	1752	Royal

Penn also held that government should enforce religious morality. At first Quakers affirmed their determination that "lying, profane talking, drunkenness, drink of healths [toasts], obscene words, incest, sodomy, rapes, whoredom, fornication, and other uncleanness . . . all prizes, stage plays, cards, dice, May games, gamesters, masques, revels, bull-baitings, cock-fightings, bear-baitings, and the like . . . [and all] rudeness, cruelty, looseness, and irreligion, shall be . . . discouraged and severely punished." Although the frequent restatement of these and other Quaker guidelines for orderly lives set a lasting tone for Philadelphia society, the increasing size of the city and its densely settled surroundings made enforcement of such laws very difficult.

In 1682 Penn inherited the mixed Swedish and Dutch settlement of Delaware (see page 49), which had become English at the time of the conquest of New Netherland in 1664. Unwilling to rule the small colony, James, the duke of York, handed it over to Penn, who in turn called it the Lower Three Counties because it was perceived as merely an appendage of Pennsylvania. However, the strategic and commercial significance of Delaware, whose entire eastern shore lay along a bay and river way leading to Philadelphia, was not lost on future generations. In 1701 Delawareans were granted their own representative assembly, though they continued to share Pennsylvania's governor. That same year, Pennsylvanians got a new Charter of Privileges that increased the assembly's powers to make laws, especially those concerning taxes, by effectively abolishing the upper house and creating a single, or unicameral, legislature—the first one in any English colony. In 1704 Penn granted Delawareans status as a separate government.

 ## Shaping Imperial Commerce

As European nations began to spread their influence throughout the Western Hemisphere, they developed policies to organize and govern their colonies. Some policies addressed the interests of manufacturers, shipbuilders, and merchants; some aided conquering armies; and some defined the ways colonists were to develop the economies and political life of their new environments. Underlying those policies were fundamental ideas about how people throughout the empire should live together and prosper.

Mercantilism and the Colonies

Spain, the preeminent colonial power in the 1500s, set the model for imperial economic policy that other nations would follow. Spanish rulers actively protected shipbuilding and the transport of goods and people. One group of investors, the Casa de Contratación, held a monopoly of ships, merchants, and goods crossing the Atlantic Ocean, including the navy convoys that escorted merchant vessels through dangerous waters. Dutch and English merchants and manufacturers pressured their governments to create monopolies as well. Directors in the Dutch East India Company (1602) and the Dutch West India Company (1621) obtained exclusive privileges to transport goods and people to the vast areas of the Far East and the Western Hemisphere. The English East India Company (1600) and the Royal African Company (1672) enjoyed immense power as the sole legal carriers of British goods and people among many continents.

Support for monopolies began to decline, however, when new manufacturing and colonizing interests rose in these countries. In England, the government nurtured new economic and political interests that opposed the old commercial monopolies. Monopolies, they reasoned, privileged only a few traders and prevented competition or expansion of trade. If England wished to take its place alongside powerful nations, the new interests argued, it would have to encourage home production, export goods of greater value than it imported, and protect the moral character of its inhabitants by prohibiting the importation of certain "superfluities," or luxury goods. English traders would also have to defeat the formidable commerce of the Netherlands, whose power monopolies were giving way to open competition among shippers. But whereas Dutch merchants enjoyed benefits from the commercial principle that "free ships make free goods," English merchants sought extensive government intervention in the economy to protect now one, and now another, rising economic interest. Their thinking and policies later became known (and criticized) as *mercantilism,* the term used in 1776 by the famous Scottish political economist, Adam Smith.

In the 1600s, most mercantilists believed that, given the chance, people would serve their own self-interests and compete for personal gain. They also believed that the world contained only a finite amount of wealth and that wars against competing nations were the primary way to increase their own nation's share. As the philosopher and scientist Francis Bacon put it in the mid-1600s, in order to prosper you had to "beggar thy neighbour." Within the nation, mercantilists said, inhabitants needed a wise government to harness production, to curb the greedy and destructive tendencies of competition, and to promote and channel the exchange of goods through regulation.

By the late 1600s, many mercantilists believed that wealth was not necessarily finite, but that expanding commerce with far-flung peoples helped create strong empires. A commercial empire, they wrote, should have one center from which flowed finished goods and many widely distributed satellites that consumed the center's manufactures and sent back raw materials for additional production in the "home country." Eventually, argued optimists, the English Empire would become independent of all foreign ports of call. And since, shipload for shipload, finished goods cost more than raw materials, the home country would benefit the most.

In the early 1600s, the tobacco and sugar plantations in the West Indies were the primary basis for England's rise to world power. But through the century, the North American colonies became increasingly important suppliers to the West Indies of food, work horses, lumber products, and agricultural surpluses. In payment for these goods, West Indies merchants and planters provided North Americans with credit notes and specie, or silver and gold, which were then sent to England and Europe to pay bills for manufactured goods.

This pattern of dependencies stayed in place for generations to come. But in these early years, England did not fully appreciate their West Indies colonies, and the Dutch took over much of the Caribbean and North American carrying trade. In 1651 one observer noted that "nine of ten shippes that doe departe from our island possessions [in the West Indies] land at Amsterdam" with tobacco and sugar. That year, Cromwell's Commonwealth Parliament passed the first extensive code of mercantile regulations, called Acts of Trade and Navigation, which established England's right to all of its colonies' trade. All goods were to be carried on English or colonial ships, manned by crews that were at least half English or colonial, and return to England before touching at any foreign ports. English sailors were forbidden from serving on Dutch ships, and foreign ships were barred from trading between colonial English ports.

With little enforcement machinery in place to ensure compliance, colonists largely ignored the first Navigation Act. Sugar and tobacco merchants who used Dutch carriers protested against the Navigation Act. In the northern colonies, some leading Protestants were also dismayed that Cromwell's government would pass such regulations. And from the southern colonies, planters wrote to London demanding to "continue our free trade with the Netherlanders" and other nations.

The Restoration government of Charles II (1660–1685) ignored colonial protests. In 1660 Parliament increased the proportion of English crewmen to three-fourths on every ship. It also "enumerated," or listed, colonial products that could be traded only within the empire and had to be shipped first to England to pay duties. All of the critical staple goods—tobacco, sugar, indigo, molasses, dyewoods (used to color fabric), cotton, furs, pitch, tar, masts, resin—were listed, along with a few products New Englanders exported. The duties on enumerated commodities would add revenues to English coffers, while the channeling of all colonial goods to England would undermine Holland's commercial supremacy.

Future navigation acts elaborated on the principles of protection, raising revenue, and self-sufficiency in the empire. The Staple Act of 1663 required merchants to carry all tobacco, sugar, and indigo to England, pay duties there, and only then have the freedom to re-export the goods to other ports. All European goods intended for colonists also had to stop in England first and pay duties. A Duty Act of 1673 required captains of colonial ships to post bond that guaranteed they would deliver all enumerated goods to England or else pay a "plantation duty" before sailing.

Other acts implemented the mercantilist principle that colonies should not manufacture goods that competed with English products. The Wool Act of 1699 prohibited colonial exportation of finished woolens and imposed duties on English woolen imports. A bevy of customs collectors was sent to the colonies to enforce the act in the vain hope that smuggling would cease. In 1696 Parliament established a system of admiralty courts to hear maritime cases and mete out justice without juries. London also created a Board of Trade to watch over governors and customs officials. Comprised of merchants, politicians, and economic writers, the board became a powerful advisory bureaucracy.

The Maturing Atlantic System

The three Anglo–Dutch imperial wars that ended in 1674 officially broke the Dutch hold over New Netherland, the Delaware River, and much of the African slave trade. The peace that followed, along with the Acts of Trade, gave English and colonial merchants more freedom to develop their own commerce. In 1600 English exports consisted almost entirely of woolen cloth. By 1690, English merchants were exporting ships, textiles, and many necessary goods to colonial ports, and re-exporting great quantities of sugar and tobacco to European ports. England's most important markets were now in the New World. Mercantile policies stimulated productivity, brought rising incomes to many English people who found employment in commercial trades, made the seas safer for commerce, and raised revenue for the government's treasury.

The defeat of the Dutch and their monopoly of the African slave trade brought important benefits to England and its North American colonies. The slave trade and slave labor allowed many English merchants and island planters to amass huge fortunes. By the late 1600s, commodities produced by slaves in the Western Hemisphere accounted for the overwhelming value of goods sent to England. In addition, many North American colonists benefited from providing insurance, wharfage, and storage services; sailors, clerks, and carpenters found their services in demand; and retailers stocked their stores with goods from distant places. Consumers throughout the colonies became accustomed to such goods as sugar, tea, wine, and numerous household amenities.

By the early 1700s, islands and continents were linked by numerous interdependent relationships. Some arose and survived because particular mercantile regulations protected and promoted them. For example, sugar, coffee, and rum were shipped to England, and in return the West Indies planters received credit or gold and silver from London merchants. Planters and island merchants paid out the credit or cash to slave traders from Africa and northern merchants who supplied foodstuffs and timber products. Northern colonists used profits from this West Indies trade to purchase English manufactured goods.

Other dependencies developed between the northern colonies and West Indies islands. By the 1690s, nearly half of Boston's entering goods came from the West Indies. In the next decades, Boston captains regularly stopped on their return trips for Carolina rice or Chesapeake tobacco, both of which were re-exported out of northern colonial ports to Europe. The West Indies trade permitted colonists to earn the specie and credit to pay for goods coming from England. But planters needed North American colonists, too, because of their strong focus on slavery and staples production. Up and down the coastline colonists gristed grain into flour, salted fish and packed it into barrels, and fashioned timber into containers. The West Indies trade promoted more shipbuilding and shipping services, as well as the employment of hundreds of fishermen, millers, and craftsmen in cities such as Boston, New York, Philadelphia, Baltimore, Salem, and Newport. Some colonists processed Caribbean goods for local use. Household consumers snapped up refined sugar, and their demand for rum made from West Indies molasses rose rapidly after 1690. A few venturesome manufacturers turned cocoa beans into chocolate that some felt was superior to the best Dutch chocolate.

It is impossible to know whether these activities expanded because of England's commercial regulations, or in spite of them. No doubt, certain markets developed because English laws made them a better risk than other available options. A rising merchant in Connecticut, for example, told his partner in London that he "would

London's Docks By the 1690s, the West Indies trade had become a vital part of England's overseas commerce. At this time, more than a dozen oceangoing ships were likely to be docked in London, unloading their cargoes of sugar, tobacco, and other Caribbean products. Within a few years, an entire section of the London docks sheltered scores of Caribbean-bound vessels at one time.   *(West India Committee Archives.)*

just as soon get potash from a hundred farmers here, and have a ready sale in the home country, as venture with some other product of great value but no bounties [cash incentives paid from England]." But it is also true that some exports never covered by mercantile laws became a vital part of colonial commerce. Among these were grain and flour, fish, lumber, livestock, dairy products, and small agricultural surpluses from all the northern colonies.

As Captain Hall's testimony to Parliament revealed, another portion of colonists' trade also fell outside of mercantile laws: the smuggling network. Colonial merchants regularly visited foreign ports in the West Indies, illegally trading food and shoes for French sugar, or flour and barrel staves for Spanish molasses. For over a century, smuggling had steadily risen throughout the English Empire. Port officials could be bribed to falsify customs papers and allow goods to enter the colonies duty-free. Petty colonial traders helped the great transatlantic merchants by stashing away containers of forbidden items that eventually made it into retail shops throughout the country.

By the 1720s, sugar, rum, and tea were high on the list of desirable illicit goods. Smugglers themselves were popular heroes in colonial ports because they brought welcome foreign goods and sold them cheaply. The same smugglers often were legal traders, too, for they carried colonial wheat and flour, cheese and butter, and other untaxed necessities to consumers throughout the Atlantic world.

Rulers in England and the colonies worried constantly about the growth of illegal trade. No matter whether it was Dutch, French, Spanish, or English, an empire required unifying policies to channel people and goods, give institutional character to imperial goals abroad, protect and support its colonizers, and shape the beliefs and behaviors of its inhabitants. Imperial writers incessantly reminded colonists that their interests were subordinate to those of the home country. But officials were helpless to halt most illegal trade, and their complaints became empty pleas against what they saw as serious dangers to the orderly rise of the empire.

In all, despite colonists' complaints that the Acts of Trade inhibited their commercial growth, much of their economy was left unregulated and much of their trade went through illegal channels that imperial authorities did not—or could not—block. The colonists prospered both because some mercantile laws existed, and because some potential restrictions did not exist. Indeed, colonists enjoyed exclusive control over a wide range of economic activities. Before long they would associate these expansive productive activities with the political rights associated with self-government.

Crises at Home and Abroad, 1685–1700

Mercantile regulations and Restoration politics annoyed many colonists who wanted to secure opportunities for commercial advancement or political preferment. Designing men at the center of the empire, men who knew little about the practical side of colonial life, seemed to be snatching away those opportunities. Economic restrictions interfered with "the natural course of our traffic," complained New Englanders, and the stipulations of the Massachusetts charter conflicted with the many new mercantile laws. Charles II's hopes for aristocratic rule and domination of the Church of England in religious affairs in the Carolinas and New Jersey also sent alarming signals to Protestants. Thus, when Charles's Catholic successor, James II, assaulted long-held liberties, the colonists resisted, sometimes with violence.

The Dominion of New England, 1686–1689

In 1684, incensed that Massachusetts had systematically violated the Acts of Trade and denied Anglicans the right to vote, the crown revoked the colony's charter, a cornerstone of Puritan claims to legitimacy since the 1630s. On Charles II's death in 1685, his brother and successor James II set plans in motion to ensure that other colonies did not expand their assemblies' privileges. Most colonial assemblies, or lower houses of bicameral legislatures, had been increasing their powers over governors, crown-appointed judges, and royal officials. Assemblies had begun to realize the value of having representative government, in which trusted local leaders served as counterweights to imperial authority.

In 1686 James II abolished New York's assembly and turned over the government to a royal governor. James then appointed Sir Edmund Andros, a former governor of New York, to the now-royal Massachusetts government, which had been renamed the Dominion of New England. Next, James canceled the founding charters of New York and New Jersey and the corporate charters of Connecticut and Rhode Island, and combined all of the charterless colonies, along with New Hampshire and Plymouth, into the Dominion. Finally, the king attacked many colonial rights in Massachusetts: he abolished the assembly, declared the Church of England the only legitimate religion in the colony, vowed stringent enforcement of the Acts of Trade and Navigation, and revoked many privileges to which township and county governments had become accustomed.

In addition to this political restructuring, James and Andros favored a handful of loyal merchants with Royal Navy protection of their commerce in return for cooperation with royal measures. Merchants outside this charmed circle were outraged when Andros consistently waived port regulations for his favorites. Andros also raised taxes in the Dominion and challenged all existing titles to land granted under the original colonial charter of Massachusetts—a step that naturally infuriated town leaders. As Puritan minister Cotton Mather wrote, "The fox has been made master of the hen house." Soon Andros would find that he had gone too far in destroying the liberties and institutions that had evolved for three generations.

The Glorious Revolution, 1688–1689

James II converted to Catholicism in 1676 and during the next decade made many efforts to bring Catholics into high political offices in England. He favored closer trade and diplomatic relations with predominantly Catholic France, where Protestant Huguenots were still persecuted (see page 46). Fearing that irreversible trends had been initiated, Parliament plotted to replace James with his Protestant daughter Mary, who had married the Dutch head of state and a Protestant, William of Orange. In 1688, at the head of a small army and with widespread popular support, William and Mary assumed the crown from a fleeing James in what became known as the Glorious Revolution.

The new monarchs agreed to accept a Bill of Rights, which set limits on their authority, as well as on the powers of the judiciary. No longer could the crown make or suspend laws, levy taxes, or keep standing armies without the consent of Parliament. Moreover, Parliament gained the right to control the expenditure of tax money. In turn, Parliament was to have frequent meetings, free elections, and open debate of issues. In law courts, every person was guaranteed trial by jury. William and Mary promised to restore traditional civil liberties and to act as "limited monarchs" who could no longer claim to rule by "divine right."

The Glorious Revolution spurred a reexamination of many central political beliefs. Long hoping to enhance the authority of Parliament at the expense of the monarchy, a dissenting group of politicians known as Whigs—including the earl of Shaftesbury and his secretary John Locke, who had been instrumental in the founding of Carolina—put themselves in the service of the new regime. In his *Two Treatises on Government*, published in 1689–1690, Locke eloquently justified the Glorious Revolution. He began by stating that each individual has inalienable rights, including life, liberty, and property. Governments are necessary because inequalities naturally develop over time and the strong prey on the weak. But governments are voluntary agreements between the people and their rulers, and governments derive their rights from the consent of the people. This radical notion became a cornerstone of representative government. Governments have the responsibility to protect their citizens, and the only just taxes are those that the people—either directly or through their elected representatives—agree to grant the government. James II had so systematically violated the contract between rulers and ruled that the Glorious Revolution had been right and necessary.

Locke's political writings were read widely in North America. Consent of the governed and the right to be represented in government were ideas that gave legitimacy to colonists' assemblies, or "little parliaments," and inspired direct action against the governors James II had appointed.

Colonial Political Revolts, 1689–1691

In Boston, news of the Glorious Revolution turned frustrated and angry colonists against hated magistrates and port officials. In April 1689, the local militia overthrew Andros's regime. Although he tried to flee dressed as a woman, one wary colonist noticed a man's heavy boots under his skirts. Andros was arrested and deported to England. Ministers, intellectuals, artisans, and the poor dismantled the existing government. For three years the colony was run outside of the Dominion of New England framework, without a charter, but with a form of representative self-government.

For a time, the colony's elite feared that great numbers of disgruntled people might rise up against duly constituted authority. However, nothing came of lower-class disorder in the streets, and the elite were consoled when William and Mary refused to grant Massachusetts voters the right to elect their own governor in the new royal charter of 1691. In other respects, the elite and average Massachusetts citizens grew disappointed together. This happened most notably when the crown insisted that voting rights be based on property ownership rather than church membership, and that Anglicans be granted full citizenship with Puritans. These political changes were applied not only to Massachusetts, but also to Plymouth, too, which was united with Massachusetts in 1692.

In New York, word that Andros had been deposed in Boston set off long-smoldering tensions in that colony, where about 60 percent of the inhabitants still claimed Dutch heritage. When news arrived that William and Mary had assumed the throne in England, the New York City militia overran Fort James and renamed it Fort William. When the governor fled to England, rebellious colonists took over the colony. The core of the rebellion was made up of Dutch settlers; their leader was the German-born Jacob Leisler, who traded extensively with Dutch merchants. The movement that emerged in New York was comprised mainly of "a middling sort" of Dutch, German, and French citizens and "the rising traders of this fair city." Long Islanders, farmers along the Hudson River, and middling residents in New York City may have defined themselves differently, but they were united in their loathing of the "papist" governor and James II.

In the next thirteen months, Leisler focused the attention of the insurrectionists on two goals. One was to defend the colony from hostile French and English actions. This required constant pleading with small landowners, Albany fur traders, and working people in the port city for revenue to buy military supplies. Leisler's second goal was to keep order within the colony. After freeing debtors from jail and admitting artisans and petty traders into city government, Leisler turned toward repressing his enemies. He denied many English colonists legal and social rights and imprisoned many merchant opponents for months without a trial. He even sent the representative assembly home when its actions displeased him.

At first city merchants and wealthy landowners hoped to benefit from Leisler's takeover. But when his government struck down legislation that had protected city privileges, including its monopoly on sifting and grading the colony's grain and flour exports, defections mounted. In 1690 King William sent English troops and a new governor to restore calm, and royal authority, to the colony. The governor appointed anti-Leislerians to his council and called for the coup leader's arrest. In 1691 Leisler and his son-in-law, Jacob Milbourne, were hanged and decapitated for high treason. But Leisler was so popular that few New Yorkers attended the hanging, even though in England hangings were among the most popular public entertainments. For years to come, New York's artisans and housewives told stories about their briefly popular leader.

In Maryland, a Protestant rural protest against the Catholic Lord Baltimore erupted in 1681. Tensions remained high for years. When word reached the colony in 1689 that William and Mary had replaced James, John Coode and Josias Fendall led a Protestant Association to depose Baltimore. Coode and Fendall were seasoned rebels, for both had supported Nathaniel Bacon in Virginia fourteen years earlier. The Association seized control of the government in July 1689 and pledged to cut taxes and fees paid by planters, reform the customs agencies that annoyed exporters, and expand the rights of the largely Protestant Assembly. The new Maryland rulers implemented most of these measures, and in 1691 William and Mary made the colony royal. The crown also established the Church of England and deprived Catholics of the right to vote and worship publicly. When the fourth Lord Baltimore converted to the Church of England in 1715, the colony became a proprietary holding once again.

Little Parliaments

In the wake of the Glorious Revolution, much remained the same about how colonists were governed. They were, after all, inheritors of English political ideas and institutions, lived under English charters and appointed governors, and abided by English common law traditions. But much would change, too. During the 1690s, the crown took firm control over the appointment of governors and granted them extensive powers. Governors decided when the assemblies sat in session, exercised veto power over the assemblies' choices of speaker, commanded their handpicked councils (upper houses of legislature) to initiate desirable legislation, and appointed justices to virtually all colonial courts. Governors also had tremendous economic power because of their ability to grant landholdings and dispense provincial revenue. Most governors saw their position as a stepping stone to higher office in England; some were corrupt or contemptuous of the people they ruled.

Other, and eventually far more significant, changes occurred beneath the level of governors' authority. For example, the Glorious Revolution inspired the colonial assemblies to be vigilant for signs of imperial encroachments or arbitrary royal rule in the colonies, as republican theory had taught. The seething discontent of certain religious, ethnic, and occupational groups added to challenges against repressive royal officials, and many interest groups developed a political distance from the governing elite. The assemblies became important vehicles for colonists to develop a political identity separate from their imperial one. The 1689–1691 rebellions made it possible for assembly representatives to claim a much greater degree of self-government in provincial affairs than they enjoyed just a generation earlier. Although they had not yet read John Locke's treatise about individual liberties and consent of the governed, many colonists were expressing disagreement with the crown's claim to have absolute authority over subjects who lived a thousand miles from the mother country. (See Competing Voices, page 118.)

Colonial assemblies nurtured both political innovations that stemmed from the Glorious Revolution and republican ideas about balanced government, liberty, and corruption. Citizens demanded, and got, annual elections in many colonies after 1689. Assemblies wrested control from governors of certain revenues. Although they were not permitted to print money without Parliament's approval, some assemblymen led efforts to gain a greater hold over assessing and collecting taxes and spending the revenue they raised. This power of the purse gave assemblymen important leverage in negotiating with governors, as when they withheld revenue for military expeditions or governors' salaries, or attached provisions to new tax bills that favored the interests of their rural or middling urban constituents. Assemblies also began to experiment with printing their own paper money as a way to promote economic development and help rural people and debtors meet their obligations.

As the assemblies grew stronger, especially relative to the governors, many colonists also began to think about the qualities that should be required of good rulers. Elites in most colonies were still politically and culturally weak. They lacked the uncontestable stature of high birth, landed inheritance, and continuous cultural recognition that distinguished the English gentry. After the Glorious Revolution, however, individuals in the emerging elites had to negotiate carefully their authority over colonists. Although "great citizens" of many colonies feared that the colonial assemblies would become parochial discussion clubs concerned only with mundane local duties, they dared not dismiss the growing authority of the assemblies to strip "high-standing families" of their customary privileges.

These fears diminished as colonial elites became more stable. Provincial leaders made powerful family alliances through shrewd marriages or networks of commercial and professional ties in New England, Virginia, and New York. These families in turn sought and won many provincial political positions. In Virginia, the Lees, Byrds, Randolphs, and Carters headed most important committees. In New Jersey, a small coterie of families ran the assembly year after year. The Lees, Carters, Adamses, Livingstons, DeLanceys, and other families used their influence and official positions to protect their interests against imperial trade and tax policies. For example, elite assemblymen frequently responded to popular outcries against imperial prohibitions on certain exports by nullifying specific trade laws. Or they might refuse to authorize higher taxes to support imperial military campaigns.

In order for colonial elites to succeed, they needed the support of middling colonists. Because events surrounding the Glorious Revolution created greater sensitivity about the rights of individual citizens in the political process, colonial representatives listened more carefully to the demands of ordinary people. For example, after Bacon's Rebellion, the Virginia elite knew that yeomen farmers would not hesitate to rise again if the burdens of taxes and debt became too great. The assembly therefore lowered poll taxes and property taxes in Virginia during the eighteenth century and minimized the property requirement for voting despite royal wishes to raise it. Some of the northern colonies also lowered their property requirements for voting. Almost universally, colonists accepted the premise that land should define the electoral process, although sometimes they added the requirement of membership in the established churches. In seven colonies a man had to be at least sixteen years old and own a "freehold" of roughly fifty acres, or show proof of working a farmstead, in order to vote. Given the wide availability of land in the early generations, the electorate expanded to nearly 60 percent of colonial free white adult men during the 1700s. The remaining 40 percent were single sons living at home, indentured servants, or landless individuals.

Comparatively few men could hold provincial office, however, since colonies typically required ownership of a thousand acres or more for officeholding. Even freeholders who owned enough land or property to vote often faced obstacles to the ballot. Generally, when voting took place at county seats or coastal cities, participation diminished as distance from the polling place grew. In New York, Virginia, or New Jersey, where colonists often cast their votes *viva voce* (by stating a preference out loud), the fear of reprisals for publicly choosing the "wrong" candidate kept many voters away from the polls. Furthermore, some towns or regions were reluctant to send representatives to distant government halls because they would lose their services in the local community. In addition, the free choice of candidates was diminished when candidates plied voters with liberal servings of alcohol in a practice known as "passing the sack" or "swilling the bumbo." Very few colonists objected to this kind of personal appeal for votes, and the practice underscored expectations that members of the elite would hold all significant colonial offices because they were the "natural betters" of the people and would rule in everyone's best interests.

Witches

While the crises involving the Dominion of New England and responses to the Glorious Revolution brewed, the conditions leading to the greatest outbreak of witchcraft in colonial America also unfolded. Belief in supernatural causes for everyday events had remained strong in the colonies, as in Europe, and colonists were periodically accused of being possessed by Satan or witches. Even the most educated and devout Puritans believed God sent them signs of his pleasure and wrath through nature. Newborn infants were searched for deformities that might indicate a mother's or baby's corruption by the forces of evil. Astrological charts were a common means of determining when to plant crops.

Although many New England colonists, especially leading merchants and ministers, no longer held these traditional beliefs, a significant portion of all local populations did. Some of them joined other vigilant colonists in ferreting out supposed witches for public trials, often recalling the biblical passage, "Thou shalt not suffer a witch to live." Occasionally, civil authorities in Massachusetts or Connecticut agreed to hang people, primarily outspoken older women, single women, or town gossips and nuisances. In addition, colonists harbored suspicions about women who were not able to have healthy children, widows who wished to be economically independent, and the elderly.

The causes of the events in Salem Village and Town during 1691 and 1692 may never be entirely clear. Certainly, some factors can be traced to the revocation of Massachusetts's charter in 1684 and the subsequent overthrow of Andros. Over a longer period of time, rivalries among local families over landholding, jealousies over farming success, and a contentious new minister's arrival also created tensions in the community. Poor farmers of Salem Village resented the rising status of the commercial and trading families of Salem Town. Some of the young women of the Village worked as servants in the homes of mature women who may have made no secret of these resentments. The servants may in turn have felt anxious about their potential for successful marriage and homemaking. When the epidemic of accusations began, some of the targets of witchcraft accusations were married women who had ordered the "afflicted" girls to perform "endless" chores.

At first, the daughter and niece of Village minister Samuel Parris simply played at voodoo and dancing they had learned from the household's West Indies slave, Tituba. When the girls extended their play to having fits, gesturing wildly, and "speaking in tongues," the village elders stepped in to extract a confession from Tituba. To rid themselves of suspicion, the girls further accused an elderly pauper woman and a homeless village widow of tormenting them. As events unfolded,

The Salem Witch Trials
These images of punishments of witches portray events in early England. The Massachusetts hangings during the summer of 1692 probably resembled the top drawing. *(Folger Shakespeare Library, Washington, D.C.)*

other girls from the Village accused certain wealthier church members from Salem Town of witchcraft. Afflicted, supposedly tormented accusers turned on members of their community with charges of having used "cunning," conjuring, spells, and consorting with the Devil to win over the young girls to witchcraft.

Within a few weeks, not just peripheral elderly women but some of the most respected successful "good wives" of the community were accused and sent to jail to await trial. Over a hundred suspected witches, including a four-year-old child who was kept in chains for nine months, filled the jails. But without a charter or royal governor, trials could not proceed. Finally, in May 1692, when Governor William Phips arrived, a special court was set up to hear testimony. Dozens of community folk who had been caught up in the vortex of accusation, deceit, and doubtful evidence set neighbors against one another. Of the twenty-seven people who came to trial, nineteen were condemned and hanged; when Giles Cory refused to enter a plea, he was pressed under stones until he died.

Events in Salem highlighted tensions that had been smoldering for decades. Similar conditions could be found in many other places, sometimes giving rise to fears of impending social chaos. But the episode in Salem was not repeated elsewhere, possibly because nowhere else were the particular combination of personal and social tensions duplicated. Within a few months of the executions, word had spread about the hysteria, and a popular outcry against the Salem excesses helped quell its spread. Moreover, some colonial leaders, including prominent Boston ministers, scoffed at the pagan heritage that explained unforeseen events as the workings of the devil or witches.

Politics and Culture in the New Century, 1700–1748

By 1700, colonists had made a number of painful political and cultural adjustments, but their settlements had matured and begun to prosper noticeably. As the new century began, however, colonists entered a prolonged period of reassessing their place in the empire, in both war and peace. As colonists expanded onto new frontiers of North America and traded more widely with distant peoples, they became more aware of their own independent opportunities to prosper. Moreover, they were increasingly "refined" and "improved," they said, by the new goods and new intellectual trends they encountered by mingling with people in numerous places outside the imperial settlements. At the same time, British rulers were redefining the political, cultural, and economic interests of the whole empire, and involving colonists in struggles to secure and defend those interests. Thus wars, too, became transforming experiences.

Renewed Imperial Warfare

The Protestant monarchs, William and Mary, initiated a new era of warfare. After a generation of warring against Europe's commercial titan, the Netherlands, English rulers, merchants, and soldiers turned against rising imperial France after the Glorious Revolution. In 1689 war broke out with France over James II's claim to the English crown. King William's War (known in Europe as the War of the League of Augsburg) sparked conflicts along the frontiers with New France for eight years. Following a flurry of skirmishes against fur trading forts around Montreal and New York's northern waterways, Iroquois and English forces attacked French, Huron, and Erie forces, eventually taking Port Royal in Acadia (later known as Nova Scotia). The French repeatedly attacked frontier settlers in Maine, New Hampshire, and New York, destroying Schenectady in 1690. In the Caribbean, French troops took over the sugar island of Santo Domingo in 1697 and renamed it St. Dominique. Overall, however, neither nation won much territory, and colonial militiamen came home to New York and New England resentful of their treatment by British officers, the near-starvation rations they endured, and the devastating effects of smallpox on their troops.

The greatest losers in this war were the Iroquois. Their fur trade lay in shambles as hostilities had drawn every warrior, young and old, into battle. Hundreds of women, children, and aging Mohawk and Oneida people fled to French forts seeking shelter from Indian enemies in the Ohio Valley. Even after the Treaty of Ryswick in 1697, France's Indian allies kept attacking Iroquois villages, until finally in 1701 the Iroquois agreed to remain neutral in future European conflicts and forgo future raids and blood feuding against the pro-French Indians. Long into the eighteenth century, the Iroquois remained wary of both English and French traders and diplomats, fine-tuning their own methods of negotiation and defending the land between French Canada and English America for the remnants of their confederacy.

European powers were at peace only briefly. By 1702, England was at war again, this time fighting both France and Spain in Queen Anne's War (called the War of the Spanish Succession in Europe). French troops and their Abenaki allies burned several frontier settlements in Maine. In 1704 Abenaki and Mohawk Indians attacked settlers in Deerfield, Massachusetts, burning fields, looting homes and stores, and killing 48 residents; another 112 were taken captive. English soldiers were able to hold Newfoundland and, in 1710, recapture Port Royal in the northern periphery, partly because the Iroquois did not want to fight in this war and chose to protect their fur trade instead. But when the British tried to take the city of Quebec in 1711, they suffered a costly defeat.

Because Spain and France were allies, Queen Anne's War also drew in southern planters and Indians. Very early in the war, English forces burned much of the Spanish settlement of St. Augustine. Then in 1704 Carolinians mobilized thousands of Creek warriors to march into Florida, where they razed Pensacola and Apalachee villages near Spanish fields. In response, Spanish soldiers invaded from the south, crossing into the vulnerable plantations around Charles Town and nearly overrunning the city in 1706.

Queen Anne's War was a contest among Europe's empire builders for territory and peoples around the world. By the Treaty of Utrecht in 1713, which brought it to a close, England gained all of Newfoundland, Acadia, and the icy lands of Hudson Bay. It also acquired Gibraltar and negotiated trading rights with portions of Spanish South America. In anticipation of renewed hostilities, the three imperial powers fortified North American frontiers adjacent to their older settlements, as well as the major cities of St. Augustine, Havana, and Louisiana. Spain, fearing English expansion into the Floridas and the land around its valuable silver mines, put up permanent settlements in Texas starting in 1718. Over the next few years, hundreds of Spanish soldiers, missionaries, and ranchers moved into the region. The Caddo people fought in vain to ward off Spanish and Mexican efforts to settle in their "Kingdom of Téjas." In the years to come, Caddo villages were able to trade goods with both French missionaries and Spanish farmers. Nevertheless, the Caddo people were gradually edged farther into the interior. All that would remain of their legacy was the name Texas.

Postwar tensions also developed between English frontier settlements and their Indian neighbors. Sparsely settled Carolinians lived in fear of Indian attacks from remnants of the Yamasee villages that Europeans had tried to devastate during the early years of the fur trade and Queen Anne's War. In New York, the Iroquois had developed a refined diplomacy before the war that gave them a great deal of control over the fur trade. By negotiating arrangements to trade with both the French and English, they also built a Covenant Chain of many treaties that held their Huron and other western Indian enemies at bay. After Queen Anne's War, the Iroquois resumed these trade and diplomatic relations. But English colonists did not recover as easily: the war had strained resources and exacted a death toll that left a tragic imprint on their farming communities.

Colonists also learned important lessons about their ability to sustain long and costly wars. The colonial militia was difficult to mobilize and move quickly to points of conflict. Colonists were consistently stingy about supplying food and blankets, and loathed paying their taxes. Merchants, retailers, and women consumers throughout the colonies had been made painfully aware of the crushing difficulties inflicted by war on their commercial economy. The few fortunes made by privateers hardly compensated for the misery coastal towns faced long after treaties were signed. Dependent on the crown for commercial protection and military defense, and impoverished by wars that had lasted nearly twenty years, colonists were sorely ready for peace.

Challenging Imperial Arrangements

During the reign of George I (1714–1727) and the early years of George II (1727–1760), England was mostly at peace. Its statesmen focused less attention on internal colonial activities than in the period between 1685 and 1713, and more attention on strengthening the political and economic life of the mother country. The leading politician for many of these years was Sir Robert Walpole, the king's closest minister and adviser from 1720 to 1742. Walpole enjoyed the support of Whig manufacturers and merchants who favored aggressive economic expansion, and he developed a new style of politics based on patronage and favoritism. In addition, Walpoleans expanded the government bureaucracy and promoted more widespread banking and financial services.

The rise of this "court" party—so named because of its identification with urban, commercial, and banking interests—alarmed many Britons. The Glorious Revolution had helped "true born Englishmen" become suspicious of powerful central government. Now, Walpole had initiated a practice of doling out important government and military positions to men who promised to support particular crown measures. Appointments to important posts, inside information about business deals, and outright bribery were all in Walpole's arsenal of favoritism. His critics in England—known as the "country" faction—feared that Walpolean bureaucracy and patronage would destroy Parliament's hard-won independence from the crown. Corruption of political leaders would ensue, they charged, with the inevitable result of harming the very character of the English people. Critics believed that unstable new groups of merchants, investors, bankers, and office seekers in the court faction had replaced the proper leadership of the country faction, or landed gentlemen. Walpole's administration had created a permanent national debt and a standing army, both of which were additional perils to the English people.

The "country" arguments offered colonists strong reasons to be suspicious of incompetent or malicious government officials who might rule against the wider interests of the colonists, just at the time that the colonial assemblies began asserting new powers. Governors, wrote some colonists in their budding newspapers, too often had gained their posts by marrying daughters of influential politicians. Once in office, they asked the assemblies to allocate precious colonial tax revenues for their exorbitant salaries or unnecessary military fortifications. Some crown appointees tried to curb the powers of the assemblies, but usually to their regret after 1730. Others simply neglected to direct colonial affairs firmly, thereby creating habits of "assembly governance." For example, when Governor George Clinton of New York quietly decided not to impose certain crown directives on the colonists in 1744, including new taxes on goods they consumed, assembly representatives debated how to raise revenues and conduct internal trade according to their own perceptions of the colony's welfare.

In other colonies, assembly representatives defied imperial wisdom and printed colonial paper money. For decades, colonists complained that their merchants shipped most coin and paper credits to England to pay for imported goods, leaving scant amounts of money in the colonies for use in daily transactions. Some assemblies had approved modest printings of paper money to help fund military expeditions or ease the burdens of rising taxes. Now, during years of relative peace in the 1720s to 1740s, eleven colonies printed paper money that would circulate in domestic exchanges and would be drawn out of circulation regularly by making the money valid for paying colonial taxes. Some colonies also issued paper money widely to internal settlements and based repayment of the paper notes on the mortgages of farmers' land. By most colonial reports, these "land banks" helped ease payments of local debts and stretched the buying power of thousands of colonists. Opposition came, however, from merchants on both sides of the Atlantic when some colonies kept printing more and more paper money without providing for its withdrawal through taxation. In Rhode Island and Massachusetts, paper money had so depreciated by the 1740s that storekeepers began to grumble that their debtors were offering "worthless scraps of paper."

International traders who needed silver, gold, or bills of exchange for their business abroad also protested against paper money. Parliament responded to their complaints of "a deteriorating medium of exchange" by passing a Currency Act in

1751 that disallowed the New England colonies from creating land banks or accepting paper money as legal tender. The crown advisers on the Board of Trade also bristled against the colonial currency practices. Colonists, argued board member Charles Townshend, had grossly violated the "natural order" of colonial subordination to crown authority by printing their own money.

Walpolean Whig policies on economic development and international commerce also irritated colonists. Numerous Acts of Trade passed in the late 1600s affirmed the mercantilist belief that colonists should not be manufacturing goods that competed with production in the home country, and that they should conduct their trade only within the empire. Through Queen Anne's War, additional legislation restated the theoretical limitations of colonial economies. But few of these laws entirely suppressed colonial production or exchange of the goods they regulated. Indeed, growing trade with the West Indies islands—British and foreign—proved to be the linchpin of colonial growth. Shortly after Queen Anne's War, colonists noted that the British sugar islands were unable to buy all the flour, grain, fish, and timber products of the mainland colonies. American ships began to call at French, Dutch, and eventually Spanish islands, where merchants paid in cash.

British observers grew alarmed that this trade would undermine the power of the empire, especially when it became illegal smuggling during wars. For one thing, colonists preferred French over English molasses, which was used to distill rum (especially in New England). This trade deprived English merchants of carrying the raw material in their ships to English rum manufacturers, whose business also declined. For another, colonists sent larger and larger portions of their grain, flour, and timber products to the French islands, and then carried away French sugar to mainland colonists or to European ports. Indeed, when a serious international recession hit world trade during the 1720s, many English sugar planters feared the collapse of their island enterprises.

In the wake of a heated public and Parliamentary discussion about the future of the British West Indies and role of northern American colonies, island planters won the Molasses Act of 1733. In order to make English prices for sugar and molasses more competitive, colonists were henceforth expected to pay a relatively high duty (6 pence per gallon) on French molasses purchased for their colonial distilling enterprises. In addition, it was hoped that by making prices of English island goods acceptable, colonists would take more of their provisions to them.

Colonists disagreed with both the reasoning and the tax. All of the West Indies islands, and not just a few English ones, were the "sinew and blood" of colonial trade, argued northern merchants. Without open markets for their goods at any islands they chose, farmers would suffer and captains would fail to bring back the cash and credit that was vital for paying colonial debts for English manufactured imports. The whole triangle of dependent commercial relations would vanish. Parliament, however, turned its back on colonial pleas. And even when sugar prices rose in England and Europe by the mid-1730s, colonists persisted in smuggling, bribing port officials, and collecting foreign coin to "grease the trade of our humble [colonial] peoples."

Once again, however, mercantile legislation was powerless to hold back colonial production or trade with the West Indies. Colonial merchants' ships, although smaller than the oceangoing vessels of England, were becoming so numerous that

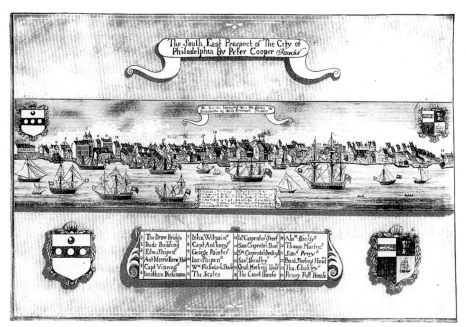

Southeast Prospect of the City of Philadelphia, 1720   Although settled much later than Boston, Jamestown, and New York, Philadelphia became the premier city of North America by midcentury. The scale of ships, warehouses, and brick homes is dwarfed by any view of a great European port at this time, but the artist is clearly trying to show the rising prosperity of this colonial port.   *(Library Company of Philadelphia.)*

by 1750 captains from Boston, Philadelphia, and New York City brought over 80 percent of colonists' exportable goods to the West Indies. By then, colonial merchants also handled and shipped well over half of the imports North Americans purchased from England. In addition, colonial production of textiles multiplied despite the Wool Act of 1699; their production and exchange of fur hats continued despite the Hat Act of 1732; and their manufacture of raw iron and iron goods grew rapidly despite the Iron Act of 1750.

Midcentury Warfare

The end of Queen Anne's War in 1713 initiated a generation of peaceful commerce—though not continuous prosperity—that was interrupted with renewed warfare in 1738 when the War of Jenkins's Ear began (in Europe, the War of the Austrian Succession, 1740–1748). Robert Jenkins, a popular English smuggler who was trading illegally at Spanish Caribbean islands, drew colonists abruptly into war when Spanish *guarda costas* captured Jenkins and tortured him. The incident gave George II sufficient pretext to order England into war.

At first, an expedition against Porto Bello in Panama went very badly for the thousands of southern colonists who volunteered to fight the Spanish; hundreds died in battle and of yellow fever. In addition to Virginia and Carolina troops, the new colony of Georgia became a buffer against the mainland Spanish settlements, and General James Oglethorpe raised Georgia troops to raid St. Augustine on behalf of British interests. By 1744, France had entered the war to aid Spain, and border raids began along the northern colonial frontier. Governors mustered troops from Massachusetts and Maine, first to hold Port Royal in Nova Scotia, and then in 1745 to seize French Louisbourg on Cape Breton Island and raise the British flag over this French stronghold in North America.

Although southern British settlements seemed to be secure, and much northern French territory under British control, the war began to take a terrible toll on mainland colonists. Massachusetts soldiers began to die of diseases in Canadian camps, Indians and French attacked many spots on the northern English frontier, taxes in New England rose to unbearable levels, and naval press gangs yanked young New England men out of their homes and job sites to serve in the Royal Navy. In 1748 the war ended in relative stalemate, for in the Treaty of Aix-la-Chapelle England exchanged Louisbourg for Madras in India, which had fallen to the French during the European phase of the war.

Colonial Americans greeted news of the peace treaty with dismay. The return of hard-won Louisbourg proved especially disappointing. Suddenly, too, the impulses to expand onto the frontier seemed stymied. Fur traders from Pennsylvania, New York, and Virginia who had extended British influence into the Ohio Valley looked forward to dominating the trade around the Great Lakes and to the Mississippi River. But the French still stood in their way.

Thousands of French migrants had settled in the lower Mississippi River basin early in the 1700s, especially at Biloxi and Mobile, despite violent opposition from the Natchez Indians. After a devastating war between the French and Indians in 1729, remaining colonizers congregated around the budding port of New Orleans. With aid from the Choctaw and the introduction of slavery, the French began producing indigo and rice. Aggressively pursuing trade with Indian tribes around them, the French drew great quantities of deer skins, tobacco, and grains into New Orleans. The small French settlements thrived and grew—to the consternation of English colonial planters who wished to expand westward.

British colonial land speculators also formed companies to occupy the Ohio Valley and beyond. Aided by ambiguous wording in their original charters, which stipulated no definite western boundaries, some southern colonial governments backed the grand plans of the land companies. For example, the Virginia legislature created the Ohio Company of speculators in 1749, and the crown promised 500,000 acres of land north of the Ohio River. Naturally, news of the company's plans for expansion, and rumors about the formation of even more land companies, was met with alarm in French settlements. Along with their Indian allies around the Great Lakes, French authorities expressed grave fears about the encroachments of trappers and speculators in the disputed Ohio Valley.

Fears grew, too, in the frontier British settlements, where hundreds of unprotected colonists were staking new claims and building towns. And along the coastline, townspeople also became dismayed to learn that English merchants regularly traded at Spanish and French ports in the Caribbean. While not technically illegal during times of peace, such open business relations with long-standing foreign rivals flew in the face of efforts by English policymakers to subordinate colonial

Many Peoples in Louisiana By the early 1700s, French missionaries and traders had encountered many different Indian peoples near the mouth of the Mississippi River. The Illinois people (on the left) became important fur trade partners with the French and Spanish; here they display a hunting bow, fishing spear, various plants, and cured skins. Some Indians, including the man standing at the far right, became slaves on European farms and worked alongside the African slaves introduced by Europeans to the region by the early 1700s. *(Peabody Museum, Harvard University.)*

interests to those of the imperial center with new commercial regulations during the 1730s and 1740s. Together, territorial and commercial issues at midcentury caused many colonists to become anxious about relations with their own colonial elites, as well as rulers in the mother country.

Transatlantic Cultural Influences

By the late 1600s, the rise of mercantilism and the new emphasis on representative governments were producing profound cultural changes throughout Britain's empire. Throughout England and the Continent, a "scientific revolution" had been challenging folk, pagan, and traditional views about the natural and intellectual world. Simultaneously, a "commercial revolution" embodied the efforts of emerging European empires to take over foreign lands, make ships and shipping more competitive, and increase the wealth of nation-states by expansive trade. As these two revolutions continued, an intellectual movement known as the Enlightenment extended and deepened the cultural refinement and interconnectedness of European peoples throughout the transatlantic empires.

Enlightenment writers questioned cherished traditions or invited experimentation in daring new realms of science and nature, religion, civil law, and even universal truths. In 1687 English mathematician and astronomer Sir Isaac Newton published

Principia, or Mathematical Principles of Natural Philosophy. In it, Newton explained that all physical objects obeyed not God's particular commands, but unchanging scientific laws, such as gravity and the laws of motion. God, according to this Newtonian view of the world, did not have to intervene in every little event but could stand back and watch his creations operate as designed. In turn, human beings could measure, predict, and even manipulate nature to their needs and wants. Indeed, any right-reasoning individual could discover the underlying causes and effects of all natural phenomena.

John Locke's *Essay Concerning Human Understanding,* printed in 1690, rejected the long-standing belief that individuals are born with innate traits and are prefabricated to think and act in given ways. The mind at birth is, in his famous phrase, a *tabula rasa,* a blank slate, on which the person's senses and his or her ongoing experiences write the stuff of life. According to Locke, reason, environment, and experience shape character; education, actions guided with regard for others in the community, and the exercise of universal natural rights in the political arena are the proper focus of human efforts.

These Enlightenment ideas, which gradually diminished the direct role of God in everyday events, emphasized individual reasoning and the limitless potential for human intervention in shaping the forces of nature. But Puritan leaders and northern governors often embraced ideas from the Enlightenment without abandoning their religious convictions. John Winthrop, Jr., the governor of Connecticut for many years, owned a telescope and corresponded with members of the Royal Society of London, the most renowned group of English philosophers and scientists. Microscopes made minutia accessible for detailed study, and telescopes brought the heavens close to Earth. Detailed reports, attention to methodologies, claims to having found proofs, dissemination of findings to broad audiences, and critical debates that demanded even more investigation—all marked a burgeoning interest in making science a field of study with regular laws and accessible to people across national and language barriers. In commerce, too, writers claimed to be finding the "laws of trade" that might render human behavior in markets more predictable. Harvard, an early training ground for colonial ministers, soon added astronomy, chemistry, geology, and other "lawful sciences" to its curriculum.

By the early 1700s Enlightenment writers tended to undermine beliefs in witches, supernatural events, and philosophies based on the world's essentially chaotic character. The world, they insisted, had been created in an orderly fashion, and human beings, through reasoning, had the capacity to investigate and understand it. Each person had the power to comprehend the natural laws of the universe by careful study. Some colonists, convinced by Enlightenment notions, became deists who looked for God's plan in nature rather than in the Bible, and who tended to blend science and reason with God's laws for human action. And many Enlightenment writers used provocative and alluring language to convince many people of their correctness. They were aided by the growing number of printing presses in major cities that disseminated new ideas through public print.

Nobody epitomized the Enlightenment's impact in the colonies as fully as Benjamin Franklin (1706–1790). As the son of a Boston soap- and candle-maker, he came from a humble background. But when at age seventeen he ran away from his brother's shop, where he was apprenticed to learn printing, Franklin began a rapid rise in Philadelphia. At age twenty-three he owned his own print shop, where he edited and published the *Pennsylvania Gazette,* a journal he printed continuously until his death. At age twenty-seven he finished the first *Poor Richard's Almanac,* a periodic publication that offered advice, reflected on the weather, reported new inventions, and reminded readers about the best routes to personal happiness and success. By age forty-two, Franklin stood at the center of Philadelphia's educated and scientific community. He had founded the Library Company; established a fire company; began the academy from which the University of Pennsylvania would emerge; and organized a "semblance of the Royal Society of London," which soon became the American Philosophical Society. Then Franklin retired from business and devoted himself to scientific inventions such as the Franklin stove, the lightning rod, treatises on geology and astronomy, experiments in surgery and medicine, and improvements in ship designs. Just as significant, by the 1740s, Franklin had entered politics. His views on immigration, paper money, land speculation, and colonists' role in the empire made him a national figure. Franklin repeatedly served as a representative to pan-colonial meetings, as a colonial agent in London, and as the American ambassador to France after the Revolution. Franklin served as the oldest member of the Constitutional Convention as well.

Benjamin Franklin   This Charles Willson Peale portrait of the famous colonial politician, philosopher, scientist, and cultural leader was done late in Franklin's life, but it shows him at the height of refined American dress and stately composure. Paper, ink, and pen convey Franklin's extensive participation in the intellectual life of the empire, and the bolt of lightning in the background is grounded by a rod, invented by Franklin.   *(Historical Society of Pennsylvania.)*

It is hard to evaluate the precise effect of the intellectual elite's labors on a semi-literate public accustomed to speaking and listening in a much different way. But certain Enlightenment influences permeated the colonies by the early 1700s. For example, here and there, planter and merchant families began to shift their strategies of child rearing. Some backed away from traditional wisdom that held that infants were born with evil wills that had to be broken, and proposed instead that children were "but blanks or voids upon whom the kind glances and firm direction" of the parent could inscribe wisdom conducive to social good.

Some leading urban colonists also initiated new societies that brought middling and elite people together, including debate clubs to discuss philosophical issues; "improvement societies" to promote literacy, sobriety, and civic-mindedness; and "invention societies" to "promote useful knowledge." Presumably, great numbers of colonists could afford the time and money these learning and leisure organizations entailed. Judging by the membership lists, however, it was clusters of gentlemen and rising merchants in the major cities who sustained the Subscription Library Society and the Moot Club of New York, or Franklin's Union Fire Company and American Philosophical Society of Philadelphia.

Wealthy Quaker and Anglican merchants also undertook a variety of social reform efforts. The Hospital for the Sick Poor was built in Philadelphia in 1751 and the Bettering House for the elderly and feeble in 1767. The able-bodied poor, widows, and orphans were housed in "spinning schools," where they were required to produce goods that the institutions' merchant–owners could sell, thereby reducing taxes the wealthy paid for poor relief and reimbursing the owners for their investment. Critics charged that the wealthy were attempting to control the lives of colonists who preferred to live and work independently. Indeed, hospitals and poorhouses looked like imposing jails.

Enlightenment thinking also changed the way colonists thought about doctors and lawyers, and paved the way for acceptance of both professions. Before the 1720s, colonial lawyers were trained in England, some to be Anglican clergymen, and some to be philosophers. As a result, many colonial lawyers could recite the works of Locke and other political philosophers but knew little about the great legal theorists of their era. Southern lawyers in particular were prone to write poetry and editorials while they practiced law, in part because their services were infrequently needed, and in part because their education had neglected training in the law. To many colonists, lawyers simply awaited opportunities to accept cases in which they argued pretentiously and "fooled the entire courtroom into some desired outcome." In addition, lawyers seemed to charge outlandish fees for their services. But the Enlightenment's emphasis on reason and empirical knowledge encouraged literate colonists to read widely, and many of the books available for them to import were legal treatises. Harvard and Yale began to offer courses in the law, although a training period with a practicing lawyer was of greater help in learning practical aspects of the profession.

Physicians, especially those trained in Edinburgh's medical school, drew public criticism as well. For generations colonists had believed in treating injuries and diseases with a minimum of intervention; most colonists had never met a person who had experienced surgery. Dissecting human cadavers and lecturing on anatomy and chemistry were considered to be intolerable breaks with the course of nature. Eventually, however, enlightened medicine gained respectability. Some New England ministers, for example, found room within their spiritual teachings to support new wisdom about halting the spread of certain diseases. In the early 1720s, a few Massachusetts preachers were in the forefront of those who supported inoculating Bostonians against smallpox with injections of a less virulent strain of the virus.

Boston boasted a printing house as early as 1674; William Bradford printed works in Philadelphia in the 1680s, and then moved on to New York in 1693. Their minor print-runs of religious texts, however, reached small audiences. But in 1704, the *Boston News-Letter* began to appear, and by the 1720s, New York City and Philadelphia had weekly publications as well. Charles Town residents could read the *South Carolina Gazette* by 1732, and even Williamsburg printed the *Virginia Gazette* after 1735. In New York, John Peter Zenger's *New York Weekly Journal,* launched in 1733, became a mouthpiece for criticizing the governor. Zenger was tried for sedition—spreading antigovernment sentiments—in 1735 and won a significant victory for freedom of the press when the jury acquitted him. Most of the newspapers changed hands frequently (Franklin's *Pennsylvania Gazette* was an exception) and reprinted stories about European and English events. But some papers also lifted excerpts or printed wholesale the essays of English publicists who were close to the Enlightenment. Richard Steele's *The Spectator* and Joseph Addison's *The Tatler* delighted readers in Boston during the 1720s. Week after week, readers could find reprints of John Trenchard and Thomas Gordon's polemical essays against religious bigotry and financial corruption in government, published under the pseudonym Cato during 1720–1723 and compiled as *Cato's Letters.* Caustic, humorous, and always up-to-date about political intrigues and scandals, these essays helped colonists understand and adopt messages of the Enlightenment as they were filtered through the oppositionist political discussions of England.

The ideas and cultural experiments that began in elite circles had two profound effects on ordinary citizens during later colonial decades. First, formal education had the intended result of reinforcing distinctions among different social layers of colonial society. Few poor or middling colonists took courses in geometry, cartography, astronomy, anatomy, or fine arts at college. Second, it had the unforeseen result of popularizing notions about the duty of rulers to conform to the public will, as John Locke had espoused in his *Second Treatise of Government,* and about the capacity of individuals to overcome the adversities of birth and station through hard work, Benjamin Franklin's theme.On the one hand, the Enlightenment seemed to separate the elite from the majority of colonists; on the other hand, it seemed to promote a greater degree of social equality and natural ability among all white males.

CONCLUSION

Migrants who built farms and cities in the Restoration colonies after 1660 did not have to struggle for a toehold in North America as hard or long as the earlier waves of migrants did. And by the 1680s, they enjoyed unmistakable signs of stability and prosperity. Expanding commerce and colonial settlement spurred colonists' optimism about attaining ever-higher levels of material comfort, institutional maturity, and cultural refinement. To a great extent, policymakers in England aided these colonial developments by creating commercial bureaucracies, trade and manufacturing regulations, and laws against foreign connections. Together, mercantile policies imposed a rudimentary system of governance and commerce over the colonies.

However, it was one thing for policymakers to design an empire in London, and quite another for colonists to live by that design. The crown exercised greater control over its dominion after the Restoration, and carefully picked governors to enforce royal authority. But the Glorious Revolution reinforced colonists' habits of expecting certain political "rights" through their representative assemblies. And decades of practicing local lawmaking and community building taught colonists to cherish self-government.

Similar tensions arose concerning colonists' commerce. If trade was, on the one hand, the sinews connecting all parts of the empire into a great power to compete against foreign empires, it was also, on the other hand, the means by which colonists pursued new opportunities to grow—often outside the watchful gaze of imperial officials, or blatantly defying that gaze. And the new imported commodities, which made life a little better for great numbers of middling white colonists, also set apart and helped consolidate the authority of a few elite officeholders, merchants, and planters.

The expanding theaters of international warfare, and the persistent possibility that it could erupt again, underscored the fragility of political leadership in the British colonies and the need to be watchful for commercial opportunities and setbacks. Wars proved to be long and costly affairs, and they failed to give one empire or another definitive claims over contested areas of North America. Moreover, war proved to be a mixture of commercial or political opportunity for some colonists, and dire hardship for others.

As the eighteenth century progressed, colonists continued to appreciate the political, institutional, and cultural benefits of life in the English Empire. But where the empire's influence did not extend, or where imperial authority was easily ignored, opportunities for colonial distinctiveness arose and set the stage for rising tensions between the imperial center and its colonies in years to come.

SUGGESTED READINGS

For the rise of English commerce and mercantilism, good starting places are Kenneth R. Andrews, *Trade, Plunder, and Settlement: Maritime Enterprise and the Genesis of the British Empire* (1984); Thomas Barrow, *Trade and Empire* (1967); Ralph Davis, *The Rise of Atlantic Economies* (1973); and Michael Kammen, *Empire and Interest: The American Colonies and the Politics of Mercantilism* (1970). For opposition to mercantilism, see Joyce Appleby, *Economic Thought and Ideology in Seventeenth Century England* (1978). Ian K. Steele, *The Politics of Colonial Policy* (1968), is the most readable introduction to European imperial efforts at shaping Atlantic and frontier policies simultaneously.

For the impact of mercantilism on the colonies, see Paul G. E. Clemens, *The Atlantic Economy and Colonial Maryland's Eastern Shore: From Tobacco to Grain* (1980); Curtis Nettels, "British Mercantilism and the Economic Development of the Thirteen Colonies," *Journal of Economic History, XII* (1952): 105–14; Marcus Rediker, *Between the Devil and the Deep Blue Sea: Merchant Seamen, Pirates, and the Anglo-American Maritime World, 1700–1750*

(1987); and James F. Shepherd and Gary M. Walton, *The Economic Rise of Early America* (1979). The maturing Atlantic system of commerce is covered perceptively in Richard Pares, *Yankees and Creoles: The Trade Between North America and the West Indies Before the American Revolution* (1956), and important comparative perspectives on colonies, staple crops, and slavery are presented in Richard B. Sheridan, *Sugar and Slavery: An Economic History of the West Indies* (1973).

Development of the North American colonies established after 1660 may be followed in Kenneth Coleman, *Colonial Georgia* (1976); Thomas Condon, *New York Beginnings* (1968); Mary Maples Dunn, *William Penn: Politics and Conscience* (1967); H. T. Merrens, *Colonial North Carolina* (1964); Oliver Rink, *Holland on the Hudson: An Economic and Social History of Dutch New York* (1986); and Robert M. Weir, *Colonial South Carolina* (1983).

The most useful starting point for events in North America during the Glorious Revolution is David S. Lovejoy, *The Glorious Revolution in America* (1972). The impact of the Glorious Revolution on the colonies is also covered admirably in Richard R. Johnson, *Adjustment to Empire: The New England Colonies, 1675–1715* (1981); D. W. Jordan, *Maryland's Revolution of Government, 1689–1692* (1974); and Jack M. Sosin, *English America and the Restoration Monarchy of Charles II* (1982).

Witchcraft is one of the most popular topics of colonial scholarship. For the English background, see Keith Thomas, *Religion and the Decline of Magic: Studies in Popular Beliefs in Sixteenth- and Seventeenth-Century England* (1973). For a multilayered approach, turn to John Demos, *Entertaining Satan: Witchcraft and the Culture of Early New England* (1982). For the view that witchcraft arose out of tensions created by rapidly growing New England communities, see Paul Boyer and Stephen Nissenbaum, *Salem Possessed* (1974); and for a fascinating account of the gender and inheritance aspects of witchcraft, see Carol F. Karlsen, *The Devil in the Shape of a Woman: Witchcraft in Colonial New England* (1987).

Provincial political development, as it departed from English traditions of legislative process and state power, is the subject of Bernard Bailyn, *The Origins of American Politics* (1986). For a focus on the ideological differences between England and America, see Robert M. Calhoon, *Dominion and Liberty: Ideology in the Anglo-American World, 1660–1801* (1994); Edmund Morgan, *Inventing the People: The Rise of Popular Sovereignty in England and America* (1988); Jack M. Sosin, *English America and the Revolution of 1688: Royal Administration and the Structure of Provincial Government* (1982); and Kammen, *Empire and Interest,* cited above. The more local, and particularly American, aspects of political development may be followed in Bruce Daniels, *Town and Country: Essays on the Structure of Local Government in the American Colonies* (1978); Jack P. Greene, *Peripheries and Center: Constitutional Development in the Extended Politics of the British Empire and the United Sates, 1607–1788* (1986); and Kenneth Lockridge, *Settlement and Unsettlement in Early America: Political Legitimacy Before the Revolution* (1981). Alan Tully, *Forming American Politics* (1994), shows the connections between inherited ideas and rising political institutions in Pennsylvania and New York.

Colonial wars are admirably covered in Howard Peckham, *The Colonial Wars, 1689–1762* (1964). For aspects of cultural development, whether related to European Enlightenment or distinctive American developments, see Jean-Christophe Agnew, *Worlds Apart: The Market and the Theater in Anglo-American Thought, 1550–1750* (1986); Richard D. Brown, *Knowledge Is Power: The Diffusion of Information in Early America, 1700–1865* (1989); Charles E. Clark, *The Public Print: The Newspaper in Anglo-American Culture, 1665–1740* (1994); Ronald W. Clark, *Benjamin Franklin* (1983); David Conroy, *In Public Houses: Drink and the Revolution of Authority in Colonial Massachusetts* (1995); Richard Beale Davis, *Intellectual Life in the Colonial South* (2 vols., 1978); Brooke Hindle, *The Pursuit of Science in Revolutionary America, 1735–1789* (1956); Kenneth Lockridge, *Literacy in Colonial New England* (1974); Irving Lowens, *Music and Musicians in Early America* (1964); Hugh Rankin, *The Theatre in Colonial America* (1965); and A. G. Roeber, *Faithful Magistrates and Republican Lawyers: Creators of the Virginia Legal Culture, 1680–1810* (1981).

Colonial and Imperial Views of the Assemblies

Charter of Privileges, October 28, 1701

Contests developed in many colonies over the proper balance of power between assemblies and governors. In Pennsylvania, founder William Penn was committed to the principle of political participation by the governed, and the colony's charter reflected that principle. Then, in 1692, just ten years after the colony's founding, Parliament placed Pennsylvania under the royal governor of New York. As the crown-appointed rulers tried to restrict the assembly's privileges, assemblymen responded by enlarging their powers and reducing those of the governor's council of advisers. In 1701 the assembly, under Penn's leadership, printed a plan of government that reinstated basic civic freedoms and the assembly's authority.

I the said William Penn do declare, grant and confirm, unto all the Freemen, Planters and Adventurers, and other Inhabitants of this Province and Territories, these following Liberties, Franchises and Privileges. . . .

First

Because no People can be truly happy, though under the greatest Enjoyment of Civil Liberties, if abridged of the freedom of their Consciences, as to their Religious Profession and Worship . . . I do hereby grant and declare, That no Person or Persons, inhabiting in this province or Territories, who shall confess and acknowledge *One* almighty God . . . shall be in any Case molested or prejudiced . . . nor be compelled to frequent or maintain any religious Worship, Place or Ministry, contrary to his or their Mind. . . .

And that all Persons who also profess to believe in *Jesus Christ,* the Saviour of the World, shall be capable . . . to serve this Government in any Capacity, both legislatively and executively. . . .

For the well government of this Province and Territories, there shall be an Assembly yearly chosen, by the Freemen thereof, to consist of Four Persons out of each County, of most Note for Virtue, Wisdom and Ability . . . Which Assembly shall have Power to chuse a Speaker and other their Officers; and shall be Judges of the Qualifications and Elections of their own Members; sit upon their own Adjournments; appoint Committees; prepare Bills in order to pass into Laws; impeach [indict] Criminals, and redress Grievances; and shall have all other Powers and Privileges of an Assembly, according to the Rights of the free-born Subjects of *England* and as is usual in any of the King's Plantations in *America.* . . .

That the Freemen in each respective County . . . may . . . chuse . . . sheriffs and Corners . . . And that the Justices of the respective Counties shall or may nominate and present to the Governor *Three* Persons, to serve for Clerk of the Peace for the said County. . . .

That the Laws of this Government shall be in the Stile, viz. *By the Governor, with the Consent and Approbation of the Freemen in General Assembly met.*

William Shirley to George Clinton, August 13, 1748

New York was a more tightly controlled royal colony than Pennsylvania. For nearly a century after the English conquest in 1664, its ruling families were tied closely to English affairs, and New York's governors maintained a powerful hold over law-making, the dispensation of justice, and revenue collection and spending. But by the 1740s, assemblymen had accumulated one small power after another. By the time Governor George Clinton took office, clearly defined political interests existed in the assembly and those interests often were at odds with the crown's instructions to Clinton. Clinton looked to William Shirley for guidance on how to stem the New York assembly's "usurpations" of power. Shirley had spent many years as a judge of the admiralty courts, governor of Massachusetts, commander of Anglo-American forces in imperial wars, and then governor of the Bahamas. His assessment of the situation and advice to Clinton show that he was deeply loyal to the crown and de-termined to enforce its authority in North America.

Sir, . . . I have informed myself of the state of His Majesty's government within this Colony [of New York] and find that several late innovations have been introduced by the Assembly into it, and incroachments made upon His Majesty's prerogative greatly tending to weaken his government. . . .

It appears by the Acts of Assembly that . . . for about twenty eight years past, . . . the [financial] support of His Majesty's Government were made for the term of five years, and no application of any part of the money . . . was made in these Acts; but there was only one general appropriation in them, vizt. *For the support of His Majesty's government* . . . all monies levied by Acts of Assembly were during that time drawn out of the Treasury by warrant from the Governor and Council.

And I find that during that time all publick warlike stores for the defence of the Colony were lodged in the King's Magazine with the Store Keeper and issued by order of the Governour in whose sole disposal they were.

And it does not appear that within this time the Assembly assumed to them-selves the appointment of such officers, as it appertain'd to the Governour to appoint. . . .

BUT I find that in the year 1743 . . . the Assembly instead of making the . . . support of His Majesty's Government for the term of five years, pass'd an Act . . . [that stipulated] the granting salaries for the support of the governours and other officers from year to year only . . . tending to create an intire dependency of the Governour and other Officers upon the Assembly, and to weaken His Majesty's Government in this Colony . . . and in cast the Governour or any of those officers dye . . . there is no provision for the support [of government.]

It appears by the Minutes of the Assembly's proceedings that the Acts thus made for your Excellency's annual support are pass'd the last of the Sessions, and . . . that unless you pass the others which are lay'd before [by the Assembly] for your Consent, the Act [to pay your annual salary] will not be passed.

It appears likewise that since the year 1743 considerable advances have been made by the Assembly towards usurping the nomination of Officers which it ap-pertains to the Governor to appoint, and the power of turning such as are actu-ally appointed by him, our of their posts. . . .

The Assembly have likewise taken the custody and disposal of the gunpowder provided for the use of the King's garrison and defence of the Colony, out of your Excellency's hands into their own. . . .

And I find likewise they have taken from your Excellency the passing of the Muster Rolls of all the troops raised for the defence of the Colony . . . and issuing the pay for them and their officers. . . . I find also that since 1743, they have assumed the power of erecting, by Acts of Assembly, fortifications. . . .

The Assembly seems to have left scarcely any part of His Majesty's prerogative untouched, and they have gone great lengths towards getting the government, military as well as civil, into their hands. . . . I think no time should be lost for letting the Assembly know you expect that for the future they should provide for the support of His Majesty's government in the same manner which former Assemblies used to do it.

Neither Clinton nor his successors were able to reverse the New York assembly's gains during the coming years. Elsewhere in North America, other colonial assemblies were also expanding their authority over the daily lives of colonists and sometimes openly defying the crown's principle that colonies were always subordinate to the interests of the imperial center. But after the Glorious Revolution, colonial assemblies grew more vigilant about their "liberties," refining their definitions of them in the context of conflicts with imperial authorities. Although colonists often referred to these liberties as the freedoms of all "true born Englishmen," they were usually clear that this was not the same thing as "the English system of rule," in which liberty was reliant on deference, patronage, and elite privilege.

Questions for Analysis

1. What privileges does the Pennsylvania charter spell out? Why are they so important to colonists, and so likely to cause alarm in English government?

2. What are Shirley's main objections regarding the "incroachments" of colonial assemblies on royal power? Why does he believe these privileges are dangerous in the hands of colonial assemblymen?

3. What were the implications of colonial claims to greater self-government?

4. How might growing assembly powers in many colonies have contributed to the growing sense of a separate identity?

4

Colonial Maturation and Conflict, 1680–1754

A s William Morison traveled north from Maryland in 1744, he gave some people the impression of being "a very rough spun, forward, clownish blade, much addicted to swearing." During his stay at "Curtis's [inn] at the sign of the Indian King" in New Castle, Delaware, Morison grew "much affronted with the landlady . . . who, seeing him in a greasy jacket and breeches and a dirty worsted cap . . . took him for some ploughman or carman and so presented him with some scraps of cold veal for breakfast." Agitated, Morison cried, " . . . if it wa'n't out of respect to the gentleman [sitting with me]," he would throw the food "out the window and break her table all to pieces should it cost him 100 pounds for dammages."

The gentleman who traveled northward with Morison that spring—and the recorder of these events—was the well-respected Maryland physician Alexander Hamilton. Hamilton was careful to write in his journal that Morison was not the ruffian he seemed to be, but a fun-loving man of the "middling sort." Morison did not have inherited status in the gentry or an important crown appointment. Next to Hamilton, debonair in green velvet coat and lace-trimmed shirt, Morison "seemed to be but a plain, homely fellow." "Yet," continued Hamilton, "he would have us know that he was able to afford better than many that went finer." At the conclusion of his outburst against the landlady, Morison took "off his worsted night cap, [and] pulled a linnen one out of his pocket and clapped it upon his head," declaring, "Now, . . . I'm upon the borders of Pensylvania and must look like a gentleman." As the men rode away, Morison also insisted that "he had good linnen in his bags, a pair of silver buckles, silver clasps, and gold sleeve buttons, two Holland shirts, and some neat night caps; and that his little woman at home drank tea twice a day."

These material possessions certainly did not put Morison close to the wealth of true gentlemen who displayed far more refined clothing, manners, and speech. But neither was he poor. Just days before meeting Morison, Hamilton had dined with the family of a Susquehanna ferryman, who ate their meal from "a dirty, deep, wooden dish which they evacuated with their hands, cramming down skins, scales, and all. They used neither knife, fork, spoon, plate, or napkin because, I suppose, they had none to use."

Morison was one of thousands of colonists who enjoyed modest prosperity from work on their landholdings and at small trades that produced household and personal goods. Life for most colonists by midcentury was better than it could have been in England or Europe. In addition, Morison, and so many others of this "middling" station who sought material comfort and public recognition, did not overtly challenge the authority of their "betters," at least not often. In their optimism, the "middling sort" praised the openness of colonial society, the many different geographical regions, cultural origins, high wages, and job opportunities for people willing to work. Indeed, by the 1750s free white inhabitants of the North American colonies enjoyed the fastest-rising living standards in the world.

Some colonists, however, were shocked at the rapid rise of this new wealth among their neighbors, and especially that it had begun to replace inheritance of property and family name in creating status. Left unchecked, they believed, the trend would cause the decline of colonial elites in the near future, while others predicted threats to imperial rule itself. Still other colonists pitted the relative security of middling colonists to the growing number of poor. In every region, the gap was widening between those who became successful or even privileged, and those who, despite struggle, experienced downturns, bad luck, devastating illness, and daily hunger. In Northern cities the extremes of rich and poor became distressingly evident by the 1720s. The frontier remained a questionable terrain for making a fortune. In the Chesapeake region, the stratified social organization was becoming more hierarchical, more uneven. And the South was witnessing the apparent paradox of opening up political institutions to more white citizens *and* tightening the reins of slavery. Some of these disparities foreshadowed the midcentury conflicts within the colonies that accompanied their maturation.

▌ What kinds of social and cultural distinctions developed among colonists during the 1700s?

▌ What groups of immigrants continued to stream into the colonies, why did they come, and where did they settle?

▌ How did the political and cultural maturation of rural settlements differ from those of cities and villages on the coast?

▌ What kinds of tensions marked the colonies during the 1700s, and why did some of them erupt into significant conflicts?

This chapter will address these questions.

Chronology

1689–1697	King William's War
1702–1713	Queen Anne's War
1705	Rice no longer enumerated
1711–1713	Tuscarora War in the Carolinas
1712	Slave uprising in New York City
1720s	Scots-Irish immigration increases
	Germans settle mid-Atlantic colonies
1730s	Virginia tobacco inspection laws
1732	Georgia colony chartered
1739	Stono Rebellion
1739	Great Awakening begins
1741	Second slave uprising in New York City
1740–1748	King George's War
1747	Ohio Company of land speculators formed
1754	Disputes with French and Indians in Ohio country grow

 ## Growth and Diversity in the Colonies

Sooner or later, every colony overcame the initial scarcities of supplies, difficulties of defense, and losses due to illness and demoralization during the "starving times." Stable, then growing population developed in New England first, then the mid-Atlantic, and finally the South by the early 1700s. In each region, people in the white population began to marry younger and live longer. Then, the trickle of immigrants to North America in the later 1600s became a flood in the last colonial decades. Indeed, more people came per year from the Old World to the New in the last portion of the colonial era than in any other time of settlement. Some of these newcomers stayed near coastal settlements where they benefited from existing social networks, resources, and institutions. But most of them headed to the frontier.

New Immigrants

In 1700 about 250,000 people of European and African descent lived in the North American colonies. In the next generation that number more than doubled, and by the eve of the American Revolution, 2.5 million people resided in the thirteen colonies. Immigration accounted for a significant proportion of this rising population. Over 4,500 people arrived each year from 1700 to 1760; in the next fifteen years an amazing average of about 15,000 individuals arrived per year. Between

1700 and 1770, nearly 275,000 African slaves were brought into North America, and about 50,000 English convicts came, primarily to Maryland and Virginia, bound to many years' labor. In that same time, about 210,000 free whites came into the mainland colonies, including many more women and children than had come on the transatlantic ships during the founding decades of settlement. Whether white or black, colonists were surrounded by the very young and the aging. In 1775 half of the colonial population were under sixteen years old, and many children had the novel experience of getting to know their grandparents.

This unprecedented growth introduced cultural changes that colonists only began to grasp before the mid-1700s. White women in most settlements could marry early in their twenties and hope to raise a number of children to adulthood; a majority of them bore five to ten children. Most families in the north, and wealthy families in the south, lived in environments of greater abundance than in Europe, and they enjoyed a comparatively better diet than Europeans. This healthier and longer-lived population, said some observers, would make colonists ever-more powerful members of the empire. Benjamin Franklin noted in a 1751 pamphlet that England's overall population of nearly 7 million was greater than white North America's for the time being, but colonists were doubling their numbers every twenty-five years, a rate of growth much faster than England's. Soon, warned Franklin, the colonial population would overtake England's in size and tip the balance of cultural and political power toward the colonies.

Immigration also rose to new heights during the mid-1700s. Conditions of travel across the ocean remained difficult—over 15 percent of migrants died on the middle passage from Europe or shortly after their arrival—and even in the final colonial years, when would-be servants flocked into North America, traders bought and sold human labor "as they do their horses." Still, ships bringing scores of white indentured servants seeking land and employment came to the northern ports of Boston, New York, and Philadelphia more frequently than to the Chesapeake—where slavery increasingly replaced white labor.

Great numbers of people surged onto the far frontiers by the 1740s, searching for fertile land in the Appalachian foothills and along the river ways of the interior (see map). Unprecedented numbers of non-English people came in these late colonial years. One group, the Scots-Irish, descendants of Presbyterian Scots whom the British government had forced to settle in northern Ireland during the 1600s, flocked through Philadelphia to seek farm land and greater religious freedom. At least 100,000 and maybe 150,000 came before 1760, and another 55,000 came in the last fifteen colonial years. When they found that land was not simply there for the taking, hundreds of Scots-Irish became squatters on Native American lands on the western frontiers of Pennsylvania, Maryland, Virginia, and North Carolina. The Tuscarora and Yamasee had been weakened by disease, and during the 1730s the Cherokee and Catawba suffered from smallpox on the Carolina piedmont. While these reduced populations struggled to rebuild their strength or moved temporarily to new hunting locations, immigrating Europeans assumed the land was vacant. By the late 1730s, Scots-Irish had filled the Shenandoah Valley of Virginia; in the 1740s they headed over the piedmont plateau into North Carolina; by the end of the colonial period, they were streaming into the frontiers of South Carolina, where they raised grain, livestock, and tobacco without slaves.

Other groups of immigrants also arrived during the 1700s. About 80,000 Irish poured into the Delaware Valley over the century. A smaller number of Scots—probably about 40,000—came toward the end of the colonial period. Most of them were Jacobites, supporters of the Catholic Stuart monarchs, forced to migrate after the failure of rebellions in 1715 and 1745. In 1746 the defeated Jacobites were loaded onto departing vessels and put down in North Carolina, where a hard-scrabble life awaited them.

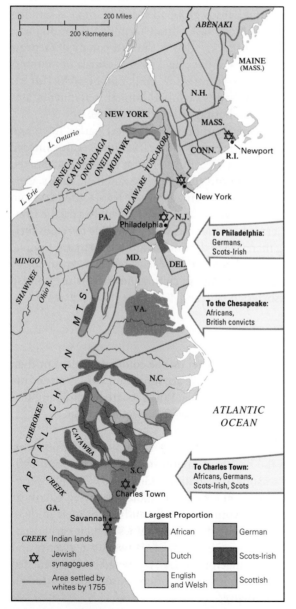

Immigration and Migration in the 1700s After 1720 both slave importation and European immigration increased dramatically in many colonies. At the same time, colonists were expanding onto western frontier lands 200 miles beyond the first ribbon of colonial settlement. Thousands of newcomers were German, Scots-Irish, and Scottish in the last colonial decades.

Over 90,000 Germans also arrived after 1720, most of them from the severely depressed Rhineland. Most, too, endured a grueling voyage of about fifteen weeks fraught with filth, hunger, disease, and harsh treatment by the crew. Germans who came to the mid-Atlantic region often became redemptioners, voluntary servants who stayed together as families and bound themselves to masters for a set period of time. Unlike indentured servants, redemptioners found their own masters. Following the pathways of earlier frontier migrants, these *Deutsche* (later, Pennsylvania Dutch) settled rich soil just beyond the fringe of settlement, twenty to one hundred miles west of the Delaware River. Later, they fanned out toward the foothills of the Appalachian Mountains in the Cumberland and Shenandoah Valleys. Lutherans, Moravians, Mennonites, and smaller religious groups tended to come as families and began with grave earnestness the difficult task of transforming the countryside. To the south, a sizeable group of Salzburgers settled in the new colony of Georgia (see page 144). To some colonists of British heritage, these German newcomers sometimes added a startling dimension to frontier life. Benjamin Franklin, for example, complained that German "aliens" had "swarm[ed] into our settlements" until they outnumbered colonists of English heritage in certain regions.

Small numbers of Huguenots fled persecution in France to Charles Town and New York City during the 1700s, where their French cultural identity became melded with the polyglot populations around them. In contrast, Jewish families that entered northern cities made distinctive contributions to commerce and handicrafts. Germans and Scots, far more numerous than either Huguenots or Jews, settled far from the "melting influences" of cities, preserving their culture and identities on the frontier. In the mid-Atlantic region, German immigrants were often able to retain their language and tradition by rejecting marriage to the English around them. In Virginia, where white planters and small farmers shared a fear of slave rebellion, the colony's elite cherished its Anglican background and English cultural heritage, while Scottish frontiersmen maintained their Presbyterian faith and distinctive cultural ways.

Families and Servants

The burgeoning birth rate had even more impact on the colonial headcount than rising immigration. Growth from natural increase accounted for two-thirds of the new population born after 1700 in North America. While women in England had about five live births and fifteen grandchildren, white colonial women averaged eight births and forty-two grandchildren.

Such phenomenal growth, which fundamentally altered traditional family ways, had two general causes. One was the healthier environment for parents and children. More plentiful foods, fewer seasons of scarcities, and less crowded living conditions permitted local populations to fight off diseases more effectively. Colonists were also marrying earlier. In England women typically married in their mid- to late-twenties; in the colonies many married and began families in their early twenties. Since pregnancy and childbirth happened regularly between age twenty and forty-five for many women, and was a dangerous ordeal, wives and mothers created elaborate networks of support in local communities, often coordinated by the talents and ceaseless energies of town midwives.

In European society the family had long been seen as "a little commonwealth," with clear roles prescribed for fathers, mothers, and children. Colonial families of European origin inherited this model and applied it to their settlements. The male head of the household represented the family in public affairs, voting in local elections and serving as an elder of the church. He also wielded nearly unqualified authority over his wife, children, servants, occasional laborers, and slaves.

On farms, men built homesteads, barns, and other outbuildings, planted and cultivated the fields, mended fences, and herded and butchered livestock. Harvests were especially difficult episodes for families short of children and servants. Daily toil was relieved briefly with trips to markets with surpluses of farm goods or to stores to buy sugar, tea, sewing notions, or nails. A visit to the miller brought with it welcome conversation and a drink with friends. Over 90 percent of colonial families organized their lives around farming, but men also regularly shared skills such as carpentry, blacksmithing, milling, and butchering with neighbors. Some of these activities afforded men more contact with people outside the family and immediate neighborhood than women had.

Throughout the colonies, white children were the subordinates of their fathers, who assigned their household tasks, meted out discipline, and decided whether they should be sent to a neighbor or town craftsman as a servant or apprentice. Parents frequently expected unquestioning obedience from their children, and because children's contributions were essential to the household economy, only elite parents—who had servants or slaves to perform the menial tasks typically assigned to children—could afford to indulge their sons and daughters.

Almost all colonists of European origin agreed that women were naturally subordinate to men. In the earliest New England settlements, the Puritan minister John Winthrop had declared that a woman's husband "is her lord, and she is subjected to him, yet in a way of liberty, not of bondage; and a true wife accounts her subjection her honor and freedom." Modesty, chastity, deference, and quiet diligence in household tasks were among the qualities expected in women. Most spent their lives under the firm rule of fathers, husbands, and perhaps male relatives. In many colonies, laws permitted husbands to "correct" their wives' behavior with verbal chastisement and physical punishment.

Most women accepted the limitations and demands of marriage, although slowly over the 1700s women gained modest privileges, such as the ability to help choose their husbands. Few widows stayed unmarried for long, for their homemaking skills and their children's labor were highly prized. Of course, not all marriages proved to be good ones. In New England it was possible, if difficult, to end a poor union; outside of New England, laws permitted only men to initiate divorce proceedings.

According to English law, widows and unmarried women could own property, run businesses, and be heard in court. But once married, a woman became subject to her husband under the law of *coverture* and could no longer make contracts to start a business, for example, or sail a ship, hire a servant, sell a farm, or write a will. Her property became that of her husband upon marriage, and her husband was entitled to all her wages. Only in the case of her husband's prolonged absence or sudden death could a woman act in her husband's name to handle business obligations.

Daily Life in the Colonies

Almost every young woman spent hours every week spinning wool or cotton yarn that went into making bed linens, garments, and fabrics used for sifting flour or making sails. Not every household had a spinning wheel, but one was always nearby at a neighbor's or relative's house. Once spun, yarn was woven into fabric by men in some areas, by women in others. *(American Textile History Museum.)*

Indentured servant women often were treated worse than women of middling families. Well into the 1700s, young female servants wrote to English relatives about "toiling almost day and night" with "scarce any thing but Indian corn and salt [pork] to eat" or little clothing against cold weather. Many were forbidden to marry during their contracts because masters feared they would run away or neglect their duties. Servants who became pregnant risked having their services lengthened if masters believed they took too much time off to have and nurture infants. At the end of her service, perhaps in poor health and well advanced into her child-bearing years, a female servant often had difficulty finding a man willing to marry her.

However, both servants and married free women could gain some recognition of their worth through their work. The relentless rhythms of gardening and laundering, procuring and processing foods, cooking and baking, consumed many hours each day. Intermittently, smoking meat, dairying, pressing cider, tending chickens, and transforming wool and flax into usable clothing occupied another large portion of time. Homemakers counted themselves fortunate when their daughters were old enough to help with chores or tend smaller children. Most farm wives also could break away—although only temporarily—from their prescribed domestic roles when they helped in the fields during planting and harvesting times, or when they made trips to local shops to exchange small surpluses or acquire imported goods. As a woman aged, she instructed younger people, gained expertise in managing complex household enterprises, and exercised significant moral influence on community decisions. And among women, the birthing of a child provided a forum not only for helping a neighbor but for sharing news and arranging community events that brought additional recognition to the vital roles women played in the colonial experience everywhere.

Varieties of Life in the North

As the seventeenth century ended, many northern colonists hoped that the tribulations of the Glorious Revolution, witchcraft trials, frontier and international wars, and settling the wilderness would be put behind them. Well-ordered townships and families, many colonists agreed, should continue to provide a foundation for social order and future prosperity. A stratified society in which colonists understood their obligations to rulers, wives and children deferred to the will of their husbands and fathers, and servants and slaves labored obediently for their masters, continued to dominate thinking about proper social organization. However, these beliefs continued to be challenged in many ways after 1700.

The Atlantic Economy

The overwhelming majority of colonists farmed or engaged in activities related to farming. Still, many of them would have agreed with one New York farmer who regularly shipped flour to urban residents: "Commerce is the sinews that link us to each other, and all of us to the greater world of empires." The risks of trading goods in long-distance markets continued to perplex merchants everywhere in the 1700s, but most colonists welcomed the new imported goods that increased their daily comfort. English merchants continued to satisfy much of the colonial demand for clothing, agricultural implements, earthenware goods for households, medicines and seeds, glassware and paper products, and other "dry goods." In fact, colonists collectively were debtors to English firms for most of the 1700s. By the late colonial years, debts for imported goods from England had risen, said some American merchants, to "alarming heights."

But colonists continued to import more and more desired goods, such as manufactured tools and dish wares, and by the 1720s English goods were reaching even the remotest corners of the colonies. On the other side of the Atlantic Ocean, however, English firms did not increase their demand for northern colonial products. So, in order to pay what they owed English merchants and manufacturers, colonial businessmen aggressively sought other markets that might have goods to carry into England and Europe, or that would pay gold, silver, or bills of exchange for colonial products. By the late 1600s, merchants at southern European islands (the Canaries, Madeira, the Azores), plus those at Caribbean ports of call, received the salted fish, barrel staves, shingles, cheese, and work horses that New Englanders traded for slaves, molasses, dried fruit, and other tropical commodities colonists craved, or for cash that could be sent to English creditors. Most northern merchants agreed that without the West Indies markets, they "might have collapsed under the dual weight of debt to the mother country and too many goods from our own producers" which England would not buy. The West Indies markets, both English and foreign, became the nerve center of northern merchants' trade by the 1720s. Merchants in New England and the mid-Atlantic regions also increasingly carried southern tobacco, indigo, and rice directly to English markets. In fact, this coastal trade, which consisted of a series of linkages among colonial ports, grew by leaps and bounds during the 1700s—to nearly half of northern colonial cities' trade by 1750.

International trade involved more than the exchange of goods among far-flung nations. It also brought colonists into contact with one another across long distances and forged new kinds of social relations among them. Coastal cities and market towns became focal points for the exchange of goods and information among all layers of colonists. Craftsmen and manufacturers distributed goods such as shoes and straw hats through middlemen, while retailers collected many small supplies of cheese, feathers, beeswax, flaxseed, and other goods from rural households for later transport to urban exporters. In the larger towns, distillers turned West Indian molasses into rum and then marketed it throughout the north and via the African slave trade. Boston, New York, and Philadelphia merchants invested in enterprises to produce glassware and simple iron house wares, refine sugar and make chocolate, or process tobacco into snuff and timber waste into potash (used to make soap and glass). Ironworks dotted the countryside not far from New York and Philadelphia, and by the end of the colonial period, merchant-manufacturers operated some 80 furnaces and 175 forges near mines, timber, and employable townspeople, which in turn supplied colonists with kettles, implements, and gun parts.

International commerce also drew merchants, middlemen, sailors, workers, and clerks into new kinds of employment. Fishing and lumbering became more complicated enterprises that served worldwide demand. Young men whose family land had become unproductive turned to whaling. Shipbuilding and shipping services flourished in Boston; Newport, Rhode Island; and New Haven, Connecticut. Colonists there benefited from collecting fees from carrying goods, as well as sales of ships to merchants in distant ports, thereby helping to offset the ever-present debts to English merchants. By the 1730s, northern colonists built most of the vessels that carried goods into the West Indies and developed intricate webs of exchange with ports along the Atlantic and in the Caribbean. New England ships dominated this American traffic, though New York City and Philadelphia merchants aggressively competed in shipbuilding. Their city docks teemed with several hundred oceangoing vessels, many of them now produced and owned by colonists.

Ancient lore told of pirates roaming the Mediterranean Sea and Indian Ocean, looting and burning merchant ships. The Spanish discovery of great wealth in Mexico and Peru had attracted hundreds of pirates to the Western Hemisphere, and by the end of the seventeenth century they felt comfortable docking at Port Royal, New York City, and numerous Caribbean islands. During the 1690s, New York City became an especially hospitable New World rest stop for pirates fresh from harassing the sea lanes out of West African and Red Sea ports. Governors welcomed the money and loot enriching some city stores and homes. Only in 1699 did the new Whig governor, the earl of Bellomont, move to end the colony's piracy by arresting the notorious ringleader, Captain William Kidd, and sending him to England for a highly publicized trial. After Kidd was hanged in spring, 1701, Parliament issued a series of new laws to enable colonial governors and admiralty courts to round up pirates.

After this, piracy in North America declined. In its place, smuggling gained larger appeal at every colonial port. Despite certain protections and incentives that the Acts of Trade guaranteed, the acts for the most part irritated colonists, particularly when they forced goods into certain markets or required payment of port duties. By 1700, mercantilist policymakers in England knew very well that colonists systematically ignored the Acts of Trade provisions that limited their commercial opportunities. Merchants became outspoken critics of laws that channeled staples such as sugar and tobacco to England, foreclosing the possibility of seeking better markets elsewhere on their own. And numerous northern merchants simply resorted to lawbreaking: regularly entering ports "under cover of night," bribing port officials, and trading with the enemy during the many wars of the colonial era.

Cities and Market Towns

Coastal cities and towns were the vital connections between rural settlements and transatlantic peoples. As much as 25 percent of a city's jobs were in trades affiliated with commerce, including rope and sail making, shipbuilding, carting, insurance services, and warehousing. Colonial cities were also the primary centers of politics, culture, and material growth. Royal officials and key colonial authorities resided in cities and port towns. Changing fashions and cultural innovations filtered through cities from distant places.

These civic and cultural nerve centers were relatively small. Boston had peaked at about 16,500 inhabitants in the mid-1700s and was slowly declining. New York City rose to about 22,000 near the time of the Revolution; Philadelphia reached nearly 30,000 by then. Charles Town and Newport boasted about 10,000 souls each by 1750. Numbers such as these fell far short of the populations of London, Paris, or Amsterdam, but for the typical colonist the quality of life in colonial cities and towns was decidedly different from life in the countryside. People of many cultural backgrounds mingled in crowded public spaces during market or election days. City residents built homes close together, many at dockside where the coming and going of ships attracted finely dressed merchants, sailors from distant places, immigrants, and British port officials. Although city residents still depended on country producers for many foods, they enjoyed a wider range of available crafts and services than farm families did.

Although only 5 percent of colonists lived in cities during the 1700s, they shared an undisputed importance in linking all colonists to the outside world. The European Enlightenment had its most direct influence on urban people (see page 112). And the "traffick and mercantile business" of myriad shops and marketplaces in Philadelphia, Boston, and New York City supplied people with goods from unheard-of places. Boston was "furnished with many fair shops; their materials are brick, stone, lime, handsomely contrived . . . and a townhouse built upon pillars where the merchants may confer. . . . Their streets are many and large, paved with pebble stone, and the south-side adorned with gardens and orchards. The town is very rich and populous." In 1725 a writer complained in the *Boston News-Letter* that personal prosperity had reached such proportions that he "could hardly hear the minister's first prayer for the rustling of silk gowns and petticoats."

At the apex of the urban social structure were a small number of families, most of whom owed their status to royal appointments and commerce. Merchants who enjoyed the advantages of a family inheritance or a shrewd marriage could expect to sustain commercial success during their adult lives, and to do far better than middling colonists. In Philadelphia, well over half the trade of the city was controlled by about a hundred families, the very richest of whom were Quakers. In Boston and New York City, the wealthiest inhabitants owned ships that sailed beyond the West Indies and Europe to the Red Sea, West Africa, and Honduras.

In their public and private lives, the elite emulated the English gentry. Great brick mansions, with columned porticoes, lofty balconies, and rooftop gardens, were the pride of New York City's well-to-do. A number of rising citizens also boasted townhouses that colonists rarely saw in the northern countryside. Brightly colored wallpaper adorned the Walton, Beekman, Cruger, and Roosevelt homes in New York, and female gentility was hardly complete without expensive silver and china to host teas. Festive turtle barbecues drew important families together every spring. Coaches, great parlor clocks, and writing tables became signs of economic success, although most elite homes were still sparsely adorned compared with English gentry estates.

Daring commercial families who wished to expand their influence beyond shipping invested in real estate, rented properties to tenants, provided insurance and banking services to neighbors, and started small manufacturing enterprises. Their agents operated transportation into the interior to buy up farmers' surpluses for export. The "better sort" also filled top public offices and shared command of colonial troops with royal officers.

In all, though, elite families in the colonies were few. Urban communities contained a much larger number of middling families—many of them rising artisans and shopkeepers, or enterprising merchants. Artisans produced glassware, stoneware, paper, nails, guns, locks, cabinets and chests, and numerous other household and farm goods. Along with retailers and waged workers, they built shops, made goods in them, and tended to their sales and distribution throughout the city. They baked bread, butchered meat, constructed cabinets, built churches, tailored clothing, and hauled all manner of goods to and from the surrounding countryside. Even small crossroads towns such as Baltimore grew in the mid-1700s because its merchants and artisans exported great quantities of wheat and flour to the West Indies, which in turn gave employment to many coopers, blacksmiths, carters, and sailors.

Some of the "middling sort" prospered more than others. Men who had weathered the difficulties of establishing a business or setting up a successful shop after completing an apprenticeship could expect to acquire a few amenities—chairs might replace crude benches, knives and forks complement the spoons of earlier generations, wooden storage chests provide for clothing, extra tools aid householders, firkins hold cheese and pickles. Middling colonists who prevailed against debt and disease could expect to have windowpanes and bedspreads by the 1750s, and perhaps extra clothing for special occasions.

Still, even city producers who owned their houses, tools, and personal items were far less affluent than the great merchants. A hard-working artisan might become prosperous enough to pay his debts and expand his shop's business by hiring apprentices and occasional laborers. But most artisans were content to pass on the

THE COOPER.

Urban Craftsmen Coopers were one of the most common and necessary kinds of craftsmen in colonial America. They supplied merchants, storekeepers, and householders with all manner of containers for storage and shipment. This view of a cooper's shop shows the simple tools and unharried, close working conditions that these skilled men experienced. *(Courtesy, American Antiquarian Society.)*

"secrets of the trade" to their children and to earn a "competency," or a modest income that provided a few comforts for their families.

At the bottom of northern colonial society were domestic servants, day laborers, recent immigrants, cartmen, unemployed veterans, orphans, and sailors. The many unskilled laborers and recent immigrants who gravitated to the cities were likely to experience extended periods of poverty. Male laborers rarely secured enough weeks of work per year, or enough pay, to support a growing family. Wives and children often supplemented the family income as domestic servants, wood haulers, hemp combers, or washerwomen. Freed slaves and indentured servants filled about half of the laborers' jobs of Philadelphia during the later 1700s.

When wars or recessions disrupted international commerce, people near the bottom of the social ladder became even more vulnerable to hunger and poor health. Although this "lower sort" were less numerous than the middling, colonial cities did not always have sufficient essential resources, or have them at affordable prices, for their poor. Hundreds of people in the major coastal cities lived in crowded rented houses where they subsisted on a bare minimum of food and fuel.

Rarely could a family accumulate enough food and fuel to tide them over during the inevitable illnesses, accidents, confinements after childbirth, or fluctuating employment conditions.

Sometimes poverty struck a family or an individual for a short period of time, as when illness prevented a young man from working, or infirmities of old age forced a person to rely on the kindnesses of family and neighbors. Sometimes, too, a family overcame the temporary setbacks of migrating or going bankrupt and went on to live in greater security as the years passed. But more and more often, northern cities could not adequately provide for their homeless, unemployed, widowed, and orphaned. Rural women who had lost their husbands and had little prospect of remarrying in the countryside came to the cities in ever larger numbers after 1720, where some hoped to open a shop or help run a boarding house. Many of them resorted to domestic servitude or prostitution.

The primary means by which a city could act charitably toward the poor was by raising taxes. But the wealthy strenuously resisted this remedy, and payments to the needy remained woefully small. Poorhouses, workhouses, and orphans' asylums provided a little temporary help, but they were chronically overcrowded. As conditions worsened during King George's War (1740–1748), Bostonian rioters attacked several institutions and demanded that authorities remove the homeless, prostitutes, and infirm from the city altogether.

The Boston riots stemmed from deep concerns of many colonists about the growing number of destitute or helpless residents in the cities. Some feared that poverty would bring increased crime against property or higher taxes for prosecuting and punishing criminals. By the early 1700s, many families and small communities in the North were less willing, and often less able, to provide jobs and shelter individually for the poor. Instead, they began to argue that government officials—who were usually middling and wealthy colonists—ought to shoulder the responsibility.

These discussions about poverty were related to changing cultural attitudes about wealth. Many of the "better sort" and middling colonists were beginning to shed their anxieties about seeking profits and to praise rather than scorn those who prospered. Looking out for oneself began to replace the older rule of cooperating for the community's welfare and setting fair prices and wages. In previous times most colonists had expected merchants to provide for local needs first, before exporting foods. During the 1700s, merchants argued that selling goods abroad, where rapidly rising prices might bring great profits, would increase the wealth of the colonies overall.

Traditional beliefs about the community's welfare lingered on in colonial life, and sometimes erupted in anger when consumers and small producers thought principles of market fairness had been violated. Impoverished colonists with hungry families occasionally protested the departure of a ship full of colonial grain. And from time to time, poor and middling inhabitants of many towns and cities fiercely opposed higher prices for food and necessities. Often their efforts resulted in temporary local legislation to fix certain prices, but no overall remedies materialized.

Periodic wars left deep scars on colonial cities. By the end of Queen Anne's War in 1713, widows, orphans, and disabled veterans were an inescapable presence in all northern cities. After a generation of peace, King George's War gave a few merchants opportunities to make immense profits from contracts to supply troops and privateer against enemies, but average citizens felt the sting of soaring taxes and shortages of necessary goods. The expedition against Louisbourg in 1744 left unprecedented numbers of Boston widows and orphans reliant on public relief, while the end of the war in 1748 brought high unemployment in shipbuilding and provisioning trades. Almost 20 percent of the Boston population was deemed too poor to pay taxes, and the workhouse and almshouse overflowed. In New York, over six hundred widows and orphans depended on the city government for subsistence and the bottom half of taxable citizens owned only about 4 percent of urban wealth.

Since the North's temperate climate did not support sugar and rice agriculture, slavery was never as significant there as it was in the South. Still, slaves were present in every northern port. By the 1740s, Philadelphia's population was about 9 percent slave; New York City's, about 18 percent. New Jersey and Pennsylvania together had about 14,000 slaves by the end of the colonial period, Delaware about 2,000, and New England about 15,000. New Yorkers owned 19,000 slaves by the late colonial period, some 3,000 of whom worked in the homes, stables, and busy docks of New York City's elite. Newport, Rhode Island, merchants had the dubious distinction of being more involved in the slave trade than any other northern port, as they supplied interior settlements with much-needed labor. Northern slaves were widely dispersed, no more than a few in any given household or farm. Many served as liverymen who worked with horses or as boatmen who ferried goods between country estates and the city.

Urban slaves had more opportunities to learn skills and hire themselves out for wages than rural slaves. But racial tensions also flared more intensely in cities than on farms. In 1712 twenty-three slaves in New York City took an oath of secrecy and vowed to avenge the poor treatment they endured from their masters. Armed with hatchets, homemade knives, and pikes, they set fire to a barn and killed at least nine white colonists. During the subsequent investigation, dozens of slaves were questioned, some tortured, and twenty-one executed; some committed suicide when they learned they would be hanged for treason, and some were burned at the stake. In 1741 a more elaborate "conspiracy," probably involving dozens of slaves, free African-Americans, and white servants, came to light. An informer divulged to authorities that plans were underway to raze the city, set free its three thousand slaves, and flee to the countryside. A series of suspicious fires erupted around the waterfront, damaging merchants' warehouses, and the spreading blaze destroyed part of Fort George at the entrance to Manhattan. In the following months, testimony in the courts dragged on. A sixteen-year-old Irish servant woman was offered her freedom in exchange for fingering some free blacks and slaves in the city, while numerous free blacks gave contradictory and confusing statements about the alleged arson plot. By the early fall, fearing that the Spanish—whom they were then fighting in King George's War—would send spies into the city to conspire with the slaves against them, colonists hastened to judgment. Eighteen slaves and four whites were hanged, thirteen slaves burned at the stake, and about seventy banished to the West Indies.

A few colonists questioned the social and moral rightness of slavery. In 1754 Philadelphia Quaker writer John Woolman insisted that human beings had a single original source of creation, and that the inferior level of intelligence and moral

Urban Slavery   Colonial cities were home to hundreds, or even thousands, of slaves by the mid-1700s. City slaves often learned specialized skills for serving in a master's business or household. But cities also became the ports of entry for new slaves put on auction. Slaves from many nations and languages, as well as different stages of "seasoning," mingled in northern colonial cities.   *(Nantes, Musée du Château des ducs de Bretagne, photo © Ville de Nantes-A.G.)*

refinement attributed to slaves was not inborn but the result of degrading treatment by their masters. Since, reasoned Woolman, white labor had not undergone generations of treatment similar to that of African labor, "Should we, in that case, be less abject than they now are?" But overall, Woolman's view was an exception, and not until the Revolution did colonists question slavery more widely.

New England

By 1720, New England's population reached 100,000, most of it native born. This was far too many people to enjoy the earlier traditions of partible inheritance, by which fathers bequeathed a sizeable farmstead or lands to all or most of their offspring (see page 70). Already, lands had been divided repeatedly, and overpopulated towns pressed hard on the resources available for local subsistence. As a result, increasing numbers of men and women approached their late twenties or early thirties waiting for their fathers to bequeath a marginal tract to them. Buying a distant parcel was costly, especially because young people who had lived at home for years rarely had savings. Moving away from local, familiar relationships was also a daunting prospect for many colonists. Even when colonists could claim a landed inheritance, it was often too small or too "worn out" and infertile to yield a subsistence by the eighteenth century. As many New Englanders put it, their settlements had become "crowded."

Increasingly, young people in New England looked for ways to make a living while they waited for a landed inheritance, or uprooted themselves from kin and neighbors to make a life elsewhere. One solution to crowding on the land was for young people to leave the towns of their births and migrate to cities in search of jobs. Unfortunately, such efforts ended in adding rural migrants to the growing pool of underemployed and poor. Another solution was to resettle on the frontiers of western New York, Nova Scotia, the southern piedmont, or what eventually became New Hampshire and Maine.

A more promising solution was for young men from crowded farms and towns to hire themselves out to other farmers in the area in return for some cash payment, room, and board for a contracted period of time. Alternatively, rural men could apply themselves at part-time work in "by-employments," or trades related to farming such as carpentry, barrel making, trapping, fishing, beekeeping, cider pressing, and fence mending. By-employments helped bring in cash that could be set aside for purchasing land later on. Moreover, demand for these skills increased after 1700 because migration into New England slowed and fewer tools and household items arrived on in-coming ships. As a consequence, colonists had to produce more of these items themselves and find different ways to exchange their meager farm surpluses for manufactured imports. Fishing, whaling, shipbuilding, and carrying other colonies' goods provided a partial safety valve for some New Englanders. Many young people from Connecticut and Massachusetts turned away from farming entirely and tried their luck at blacksmithing, seafaring, carpentry, or storekeeping. Salem and Marblehead fishermen sold their plentiful catches of cod and mackerel to feed Caribbean slaves and southern Europeans. By the 1750s, over 4,500 men were employed in the coastal fishing industry.

After acquiring his own land, a farmer might continue enhancing his income with by-employments, especially in remote communities where land had to be cleared and shelters built. Men with special skills were valuable not only to their families, but to the community as a whole. After toiling at ceaseless rounds of daily chores, wives and daughters earned cash or "store-bought" goods by selling cheese, bags of feathers, garden vegetables, small pieces of fabric, and the like for trade with other households. A family of six or eight would not only struggle mightily to bring in agricultural crops, but also be consumed between seasons and in evenings improving or repairing the farm and equipment. Sometimes this work could be done by a farmer and his sons, but often it required the special skills of a neighbor who would expect a "payment" of cash, time, or equivalent skill in return. In all of these ways, many New Englanders in the countryside adjusted to the "crowding" that early prosperity brought.

Sometimes colonists were unable to adjust to adversity. For example, New Englanders faced a serious commercial downturn after Queen Anne's War ended in 1713. Large numbers of men had gone off to distant fronts in that war—in some New England locales, up to one-third of the adult male population—and many did not return. As a consequence, far fewer colonists engaged in farming, fishing, construction, and many small trades. When combined with the declining quality of eastern New England soil, merchants had much less fish, lumber, and flour to export between 1715 and 1727 than in prewar years. Coastal and West Indies traders were thus forced to import more grain and flour from the mid-Atlantic. To pay for it they carried more sugar, molasses, coffee, and slaves from West Indies ports. In addition to earning profits from these new arrangements, merchants stimulated colonial consumption of the goods they carried, as well as greater production of rum, especially in Massachusetts.

The Mid-Atlantic

New Jersey, Pennsylvania, Delaware, and parts of New York comprised another region. Farmers, artisans, and merchants in this mid-Atlantic area shared many social and cultural characteristics with New Englanders, but their opportunities to prosper were more widespread and sustained. Wartime expeditions did not require as many men and such high taxes as in New England. In southeastern Pennsylvania, a dense population of farmers blessed with rich soil, a long growing season, and intricate markets for surplus foodstuffs steadily increased the prosperity of commercial farm families. Farmers and merchants of New York, Pennsylvania, and New Jersey were poised by the 1730s not only to help feed Caribbean islanders and southern European people, but also to support growing populations of craftsmen and retailers in colonial towns. When King George's War struck, demand rose for the foodstuffs that mid-Atlantic colonists could supply, and few men were pulled away from rural production for military duties. After the war, poor harvests in eastern Europe forced England and southern Europe to import large amounts of grain and flour from Philadelphia and New York merchants, while West Indies demand also revived quickly. As the contrasts between the mid-Atlantic region and New England during the late 1730s and 1740s became widely known, ever more immigrants shunned Boston and Newport in favor of mid-Atlantic ports, especially Philadelphia.

By midcentury, the Hudson and Delaware River valleys had become colonial bread baskets. But the two areas developed differently. In New York, great estates had been granted to governors' favorites at the end of the seventeenth century, and the interior filled more slowly with fewer freeholders than the lands spreading west of Philadelphia. In New York, many tenants and small farmers rented farmland from the manor lords, who often imposed rules for what was grown, how tenants could market their goods, and what obligations they owed the landlords. These obligations probably did not thwart the ambitions of either landlords or tenants, both of whom wished to forward their agricultural exports to the growing port at the base of the Hudson River. But in time the perception of widening inequalities, and of missed opportunities for freeholders, grew into open conflict in the hinterlands of New York.

Although Pennsylvania was settled long after other northern areas already flourished, it developed quickly because it became a magnet for immigrants and the government readily granted freeholds to colonists. By midcentury, the land beyond Philadelphia was the fastest-growing region in North America. The maturing hinterlands produced beef and pork, wheat and flour, cheese and other farm surpluses for export, which in turn supported a coastal merchant community. Wheat produced in southeastern Pennsylvania and northern Delaware was renowned in the West Indies and southern Europe; and Philadelphia's construction of new ships surpassed New York's in quality and number by the 1750s. Merchants sent great quantities of English and European goods into the interior, while wagoners and boatmen traveled throughout the settled areas of Pennsylvania, Delaware, and eastern Maryland collecting bushels of wheat and barrels of flour. These activities spurred the production of conveyances and containers, employment at mills and taverns, and elaborate networks of buying and selling at small shops throughout the region. Farmers were often able to perfect craft skills alongside their rural enterprises or expand into shopkeeping. Western New Jersey and northern Delaware farmers were natural satellites in these maturing relationships between country and city, as were the rising numbers of itinerant or semiresident farm laborers throughout the entire mid-Atlantic region. Although many single men and families failed to become freeholders after the 1720s and were thus obliged to rent cottages and acreage as tenants, the generalized poverty of England's countryside was unknown in the colonial mid-Atlantic.

 ## Varieties of Life in the South

From the eastern shore of Maryland, through Virginia, the Carolinas, Georgia, and down to the Spanish borderlands, the southern colonies shared characteristics that set them apart from their northern neighbors. It was not just the presence of slaves and reliance on agriculture that created southern distinctiveness. Rather the key difference was southern planters' deep dependence on the labor of slaves and the export of staples to prosper. The plantation system did not spur city development, for its people were more dispersed. The white population was also sharply divided between the few great planters and the majority of struggling tenants and small farmers. Together, the "slave colonies," as merchants referred to southern settlements, produced about 95 percent of the value in goods that England bought from its mainland colonies during the 1700s. Still, there was no single "South," but rather many distinctive regions, founded at different times by settlers with varied cultural backgrounds and political goals.

The Chesapeake Colonies

By 1700, the poverty of Virginia's and Maryland's early years had given way to relative prosperity of cleared farms and generally rising tobacco export levels, widespread use of slave labor, and defined social and political groups. Indentured servants continued to migrate into the upper Chesapeake, but fewer came to the region after 1700. Instead, planters imported slaves whose labor created greater profits and greater material comfort for increasing numbers of white settlers, and slaves produced by far the greatest value of goods that flowed into Britain. In addition, a middling population of farmers—maybe 30 percent of white families in the region—owned land and slaves. By clearing farms a few miles from inlets and swamps, these new settlers avoided the diseased conditions of coastal areas. As larger numbers of white women arrived, the gender ratio began to even out. Better health and the greater probability of marriage made stable families possible, including more living children, and eventually kinship networks extended over counties in tight webs of sharing, indebtedness, and inheritance.

As Chesapeake society continued to mature, social relations more closely resembled European traditions emphasizing men's authority over women. By 1700, the Chesapeake was home to fewer widows because both men and women lived longer and married at more nearly equal ages than they did in the early years. But simultaneously, women who did become widows lost power over their husbands' estates and their children's futures because patriarchal norms stipulated that collateral male kin—uncles, brothers-in-law, fathers-in-law—should control property and offspring. At all levels of Chesapeake society, men exercised ever-more power over younger kin, servants, and slaves as communities settled into familiar European family patterns.

Men's greater authority at home went hand in hand with the creation of more stable elites among the so-called first families of the Chesapeake. Whereas in the founding years, planter-businessmen busily invested in land, supervised their labor, and struggled to develop strong commercial ties, by the 1720s the elite boasted fortunes that bought luxury goods to adorn their home. A few Chesapeake planters had become wealthy tobacco plantation owners who used their economic stature to exert political and cultural control over other colonists.

The elite expected deference from lesser white property owners, just as they expected obedience from their slaves. Sometimes this deference took the form of coercing the "lesser sort" to conform to the elite's rules of behavior. But usually deference to the colonial elite took more subtle forms. For example, in the Virginia tidewater region, roads were so poor and the demands of farm work so continuous that social visiting was rare; only very special events such as weddings, court days, or funerals brought people together. Under these conditions, meetings among colonists took on pointed, sometimes ritualistic, significance. Court days, barn raisings, and holiday church services became the occasions for prolonged contact between the elite and small farmers of the Chesapeake, times when personal and economic business could be transacted. In the process, deference could be ratified by institutional rituals. Drinking, hunting, gambling, horseracing, and dancing together underscored that all white men observed common traditions and civil laws. At the same time, differences of dress, speech, kinship connection, or political office affirmed that elite men would best display and protect those traditions and laws. Public feast days, especially those honoring military victories or celebrating elections, brought colonists of all social levels together. Militia musters, for instance, required all men between sixteen and sixty of particular neighborhoods to gather in central locations. On these occasions, white colonists bonded across the social hierarchy, while the elite reinforced its superiority to poor white colonists. For the first families, public events became times for soliciting votes to public offices, which few begrudged them. Most colonists agreed that the great propertied planters would understand how to secure the political interests of small farmers and establish "natural government" controlled by society's "better sort."

Within a few years, the distance between the elite and the rest of Chesapeake society grew measurably. Wealthy planters focused ever more on emulating, or imitating the manners and lifestyles of the English gentry. They began to build larger houses, wear finer clothes, sponsor grand balls and election day parties, narrow the circle of intermarrying, and tout their educations in cultural refinement and classical scholarship. Expensive attire, important public offices, and cultivation of gentrified manners were important avenues for this elitism. For girls, music, dancing, and reading the Bible were often the extent of their formal educations. For boys, private tutoring in classical texts and languages, as well as accounting, could be a stepping-stone to higher social status.

Slavery and the Chesapeake

By the 1690s in the Chesapeake, greater and greater numbers of slaves were becoming essential for the success of planters' agriculture. Southern gentry families and northern merchants alike benefited from the production and transport of staple crops, the slave trade, and the constant shipbuilding, barrel making, warehousing, insurance brokerage, and middlemen's enterprises required by Chesapeake (and other southern) agriculture.

Once the Dutch monopoly of slave transport ended in the 1690s, British merchants began to carry first thousands, then hundreds of thousands, of slaves from Africa and the Caribbean to southern plantations (see Competing Voices, page 158). About 6 million Africans were forced into slavery by the English and French during the 1700s, most of whom were carried to the West Indies and Brazil. By 1750, the

Eleanor Darnall (1704–1796)
Though not yet a teenager in this painting, Darnall is dressed in the fine clothing of Chesapeake elite families and has the facial and body composure of a much older woman. Surrounded by the domestic comforts of a pet and flowers, and standing before a lavish estate she will one day inherit, Eleanor is an example of refinement and distinction that most colonial young women would never share. *(Maryland Historical Society.)*

single island of Jamaica had nearly seven hundred sugar plantations worked by over 100,000 slaves. Shippers brought between 260,000 and 320,000 slaves into the mainland colonies, 90 percent of them to the South, from 1700 to 1760.

The Chesapeake tobacco planters participated actively in this great forced migration. From 1700 to 1770, they acquired as many as 80,000 Africans, and by the 1730s, they could also count on steady natural increase of "country-born" slaves—those born in the colonies. In 1704 Virginia had a white population of 75,600 and roughly 10,000 slaves. Maryland's slave population was also about 10,000 by then.

The transition in the Chesapeake from a society in which many white farmers labored alongside indentured servants and a few black slaves to one in which slaves provided almost all the field labor in tobacco occurred at the end of the 1600s. Fewer indentured servants chose to migrate into the Chesapeake by then, for a variety of reasons. At the same time, planters turned more systematically to the labor of slaves and solidified the separation of races by strict slave codes (see page 61).

By the 1730s, tobacco prices had recovered and remained high for a number of years. Virginia legislators passed effective inspection laws in 1730, and Maryland followed with similar legislation in 1747, which regularized packaging and raised the quality of leaves sent to market. An agreement written in England to supply France with great amounts of southern tobacco also renewed planters' interest in producing "the weed." They responded quickly to both the higher prices and the additional French demand by working slaves harder, encouraging the birthing of more slaves, and cultivating more extensive plots of tobacco throughout the tidewater stretching from Delaware, through Maryland, Virginia, and North Carolina's Albemarle Sound. Since the Chesapeake's tobacco agriculture required regular, but not excessively demanding, attention from slaves, planters did not have to work their slaves with the reckless disregard for health and welfare shown in the Caribbean. Moreover, many colonial tobacco planters realized the importance of encouraging slaves to develop families and produce children. Many Virginia planters grew solicitous of slave children's health, and some permitted pregnant female slaves to reduce their work regimens. As a result of these "considerations," by the 1750s, American-born slaves outnumbered Africans in the Chesapeake.

During these same years, planters became better entrepreneurs as well. Growers extended tobacco planting into the region beyond the fall line, a sharp break in the landscape that marked the end of the tidewater and beginning of the piedmont. The most successful tobacco planters had become creditors or local bankers for less prosperous farmers. Elite planters became middlemen and marketers for their lesser neighbors' tobacco as well, and received substantial fees for their work.

This era of agricultural and commercial expansion, as well as uncontested business leadership in the Chesapeake, did not last. "Factors," or representatives, came from Scotland to buy tobacco directly from Chesapeake growers and transport it to Glasgow firms. At first, Scottish factors provided the large planters with valuable services and credit, and they helped small tobacco farmers wrest their economic independence from the local elite. In time, however, colonists would lament their loss of control over their commerce to foreigners.

In addition, environmental and commercial conditions spurred many planters in Maryland and northern Virginia to convert some of their investments from tobacco to wheat. By the late 1740s, when the price of grain and flour in Europe was rising rapidly, some planters began to reason that wheat would be a good crop to sell abroad, especially given tobacco prices' unnerving fluctuations. Moreover, wheat, unlike tobacco, gave rise to new jobs and more complicated markets. Middlemen gathered up small surpluses, millers set up impressive buildings to grist flour, coopers made waterproof barrels, and a host of shipbuilders and shipping firms welcomed wheat and flour exporting. Greater economic diversity in turn boosted the growth of towns such as Baltimore and Norfolk, which were as populous as many northern coastal cities by the 1770s, boasting nearly 10,000 people each and a host of new services and retail shops. Tobacco remained the most important export for Chesapeake farmers, but grain cultivation brought important changes to the region.

The Carolinas

For a half century after 1660, the Carolina region was more heavily populated by Native Americans than by European immigrants. Indeed, European settlers reported such frequent and hostile Indian raids against them that only a few daring cattle ranchers and fur traders came to stay at first. Seasoned Caribbean and West African slaves—present from the beginning of Carolina settlement—taught planters herding and trapping techniques. By the 1700s, North Carolinians extracted lumber products and processed tar and pitch—vital to shipbuilding—for sale to English merchants. South Carolina merchants sent deer hides to England and carried Caribbean sugar to many ports. By the 1740s, Eliza Lucas Pinckney, who had grown up on a South Carolina plantation, developed ways to grow and process indigo, a plant that thrived in dry soil unfit for other crops, and produced a dark blue dye used in textile manufacturing. An English bounty, or cash incentive, to produce more indigo also spurred production and export of that crop.

But one commodity above all others characterized the agriculture and labor of the colonial Carolinas: rice. Rice was not an obvious choice for production in the low country, for European peoples had rarely consumed rice before the 1700s. It was Africans who provided the labor, the field skills, and knowledge about tools, such as heavy mortars and pestles, used to separate the husks from the grain. Thus, even though the Chesapeake planters got an earlier start with their slaveholding and tobacco agriculture, Carolina planters surpassed them quickly in the value of their exports, numbers of their slaves, and profits lining their pockets by the 1730s. After 1705, rice was no longer enumerated by Parliament's Acts of Trade, and in 1730 the crown permitted planters to ship rice directly to southern Europe, where demand grew rapidly. Following King George's War, planters and merchants diverted supplies to additional markets in northern Europe. Slaves already made up about 70 percent of Carolina's population, and by the 1760s they represented about 80 percent of coastal people throughout the South. At the same time, thanks to the labor of thousands of slaves, a handful of rice planters were the richest men in North America.

In many respects, the Carolinas had more in common with Caribbean plantations than with Chesapeake settlements. In the Caribbean, a few absentee planters held immense wealth made from the slave trade and sugar production on the islands; Carolina planters also tended to leave their slaves and fields in the hands of overseers. Sugar and rice production both altered the ecologies in which they were produced and required such thorough transformations of the landscape that Native American societies were devastated. Slaves brought from Africa or the Caribbean islands—as opposed to those born on the plantations—continued to be a large proportion of South Carolina's and the Caribbean's laborers. For planters, the brutal toil of slaves on the sugar and rice plantations produced unimaginable wealth. Although Chesapeake tobacco would play a major role in filling the imperial treasury, sugar and rice became even more significant for England's shipbuilding, commercial employment, refining enterprises, and rapidly expanding personal wealth even at the end of the colonial era.

Georgia

Georgia, named for King George II (ruled 1727–1760), was founded in 1732. The colony was given three herculean tasks to accomplish for imperial rulers in England: provide an environment for England's poor to work as silk and wine farmers; defend the perimeter of the empire by regular militia drilling; and be a model of how a colony could grow and remain virtuous without alcohol or slavery. James Oglethorpe, John Percival (later, the earl of Egmont), and trustees who also held Parliamentary seats joined together to acquire a charter, at first raising capital for the enterprise from wealthy Anglicans. But when the Georgia promoters came forward with their lofty goals, Parliament for the first time invested funds in a colonial scheme.

The enlightened founders of Georgia sent out nearly three thousand settlers in the first two years, but the majority were not English and only a fraction of them stayed very long. Most early Georgians were Protestant dissenting Salzburgers who had been expelled from Germany, Moravians who wished to leave their homelands in Bohemia and Moravia, French Huguenots who had grown weary of intolerance, and Scottish Highlanders. Soon, pacifist Moravians left for North Carolina because they did not wish to fight Native Americans and Spaniards in Georgia. Then Scots who failed to secure decent landholdings left in disgust for South Carolina. Others complained that inspired leaders had foolishly laid out Savannah as an impracticable grid on a sandy and marshy topography, and that settlers received far too little land to support their families.

Between 1750 and 1752, trustees of Georgia recognized they were failing. Twenty years after the founding there were fewer people in the colony than at the time of the first ships. Colonial leaders dropped the ban on alcohol, allowed the importation of slaves, gave up on silk and wine production, and permitted enterprising rice and indigo growers to step in. Georgians surrendered their charter in 1752 and became a royal colony. Within a few years, the coastal settlements took on the distinctive characteristics that already marked South Carolina: a slave majority, a small resident planter elite, and staple crop agriculture.

Slave Work and Culture

Africans forcibly removed from their native villages and homelands were packed by the hundreds into the holds of cargo vessels for the "middle passage" to the Western Hemisphere. It is difficult to grasp the pain and despair Africans faced when they were captured and coerced onto ships that would remove them from homelands forever. Terrified by the appearance of white Europeans and dismayed at their inability to communicate, many Africans taken into bondage rebelled and were killed before they even boarded vessels. Others were branded and then faced horrors on board the hellish ships. Chained immobility, inadequate nutrition, fear, lice, dysentery, suicide, and contagious diseases claimed the lives of over 15 percent of Africans headed for Brazil, the West Indies, or North America.

On arrival in the West Indies or mainland low country, the crises of relocation did not abate. Completely severed from kin, local communities, familiar food and language, and adequate sleep, slaves were forced into a new life of relentless toil. Epidemics of yellow fever, smallpox, measles, and intestinal diseases took many more lives. But work itself was the most brutal killer.

In the British West Indies, the price of sugar remained high and the cost of slaves declined during the 1700s. As a result, masters worked slaves as hard as possible in the cane fields in order to satisfy the rapidly expanding demand for sugar. For example, Barbados planters imported over 80,000 slaves in the first three decades of the eighteenth century, but the black population rose only about 4,000. Moreover, because many more male slaves were brought to the Caribbean than females, and because poor nutrition and harsh treatment significantly reduced the number of children that women bore, the African population in the West Indies did not grow naturally until after emancipation in the 1800s.

North American slave communities differed from those of the Caribbean. Peoples of many nations mingled in the Carolinas and Chesapeake, constantly negotiating particular cultural and labor conditions. Country-born slaves did not always share cultural traits with recently arrived Africans. Among African arrivals, Angolans and Ibo had difficulty communicating with each other. "Seasoned," or acclimated, slaves from the West Indies had little in common with a Philadelphia

A Tobacco Plantation   While a planter smokes a pipe and confers with his overseer, slaves on this Chesapeake plantation perform all of the tasks related to planting, cultivating, harvesting, sorting, packaging, and delivering the profitable tobacco. Slaves also fashioned the tools for coopering and made barrels for transporting hogsheads of "the weed." Ships in the background navigate right up to the edge of the plantation lands.   *(Library of Congress.)*

house slave. Yet the condition of enslavement itself, and the preservation or compromising of cultural ways forged in the labor conditions imposed on slaves, resulted in distinctive slave communities.

In the Chesapeake, most farms remained relatively small or were parceled into a number of sections. But tobacco required constant attention. Slaves transplanted young seedlings; scoured the plants for bugs and worms; nurtured the leaves along; picked and hung the leaves at harvest; sorted and barreled them; and kept racks, hoes, and sheds in repair. Slaves in the Chesapeake generally worked in "gangs," which were supervised closely and devoted to repetitive field work from sunup to sundown. When slaves were concentrated in larger numbers on Chesapeake plantations, they had the opportunity to specialize in particular skills. Planters who wished to produce much of their necessary food, building materials, clothing, and tools encouraged slaves to learn the required skills. African-American midwives attended white and black women giving birth; African-American men made nails, fine cabinets, and riding gear. On the expansive Virginia plantation of George Mason, for example, slaves labored as coopers, sawyers, carpenters, tanners, cord-wainers, spinners and weavers, curriers and farriers, and all manner of food preservers.

In South Carolina the work regimen on rice plantations more closely resembled life in the West Indies than in the Chesapeake. Carolina planters imported slaves at a faster rate, and brought more of them directly from Africa, than their counterparts in colonies to their north. Most Carolina slaves worked in rice fields, where disease and relentless irrigating or planting in marshy areas took a heavy toll and made pregnancy and childbirth arduous. In rice country, mortality was high and, even with new shiploads of Africans, males outnumbered females significantly. During hot seasons in South Carolina, when malaria and yellow fever were nearly a certainty, planters fled to Charles Town. In their place, black overseers organized and disciplined working slaves into teams for the monotonous and isolated chores of rice cultivation. Although a large number of slaves might work together on a plantation, the close supervision of work and the swampy terrain of lowland Carolina made it difficult for slaves to create extended kinship networks or communicate with neighboring plantations.

Still, many South Carolina slaves acquired personal property under the region's "task system." Unlike the gang labor system of the Chesapeake, tasking involved completing a stipulated amount and kind of work. Once slaves finished their allotted task on a rice or indigo field, they were free to grow and sell vegetables, row boats for local white people, or raise chickens or fish for extra protein. Time away from tasking could amount to half a working day. The tiny bit of autonomy permitted by the task system did not mitigate the harshness at the core of slavery, but it helped slaves invent survival tactics and lent a modicum of dignity to their daily existence.

Whether in the Chesapeake or newer colonies to the south, most slaves lived in quarters, clusters of small cottages set apart from the master's house. In the Chesapeake, large tobacco estates were divided into a few quarters, each organized by an overseer or the planter himself. When the day's fieldwork was declared finished, slaves retreated to quarters, a community within a community, to build support networks, share food, and transmit valued medical advice. Although masters often did not recognize slave marriages and could sell individual slaves away from their plantations and partners at any time, slaves created parent and spouse roles within the extended black community. Existing families adopted children who had been sold away from their mothers on other plantations. And slaves in the quarters fostered both practical and emotional ties across family lines; for example, a shawl that provided a young woman's sole added adornment at weddings might be passed from one house to another for years. Members of the entire quarters drew comfort and resources from one another. African terms for *brother* or *sister, uncle* or *aunt,* were readily applied beyond the boundaries of kinship. Given the precariousness of slave life and nuclear families, extended kinship networks were far more important for slaves than for whites.

Slaves from Africa brought a great range of customs to the colonies and spoke a variety of languages. In South Carolina's lowlands, for example, a majority of African-born slaves understood a Gullah dialect that incorporated words from English and several African tongues. In the Chesapeake, where many slaves chose to adopt English as a common language, extended and nuclear families developed their own surnames and long-standing kinship traditions, which they passed on from one generation to the next. In both regions, slaves retained many of their customs and languages in work songs, agricultural technology, ceremonies, and religious practices. On quarters, they often built houses in familiar African styles and constituted families based on African marriage, coming-of-age, and funeral customs.

Despite pressures from masters to adopt Christian ways, many slaves preserved basic African religious traditions or combined African and Christian religious ways, especially in their music and dance. Planters often protested against slave adoption of Christianity, though, because they feared that preaching love, equality, and universal brotherhood might lead slaves to question their condition. But over time, and especially during the Great Awakening of the 1740s (see page 149), some slaves adopted and altered Christian messages about inner freedom and the value of community, reshaping them to suit the rhythms and regimens of their new lives.

Masters generally forbade or ignored slave marriages, and they always retained the power to break up families by sales of adults or children. But they could not stop the frequent informal weddings and baptisms in slave quarters. Further, masters who denied the connections of family and community in slave quarters risked the longer-term consequences of fewer slave children being born and poor work performance. Compared with the extremely harsh conditions of the West Indies, mainland masters better clothed, fed, and cared for the health of their slaves.

Although many slave families and communities were resilient and endured for generations, relationships in the slave system overall were, by definition, subordinate to the desires and laws of masters. For example, white male sexual exploitation of vulnerable female slaves created a sizeable mulatto population in South Carolina by the late 1700s, making it all the harder to constitute stable slave relationships. Slave women, of course, did not share even the most minimal personal and civil rights that free or servant white women enjoyed. The slave work regimen prevented accumulation of many worldly goods and sufficient leisure time for formal education and the arts. Endless work sapped energy and opportunity for the "refinement" that many white Europeans anticipated their own work would bring. Moreover, white European values and laws usually were hierarchical and violent. In the English culture, laws punished numerous petty crimes by death, riots occurred over personal insults, and nations went to war over religious beliefs. It was a small step for Britons to extend violent power over slaves in the colonial south. Southern planters often believed that branding, castration, tearing apart families, public whippings, and shameful disfigurement were extensions of white European values, reinforced by long-standing views about racial inferiority.

 ## Maturity Brings Conflict, 1739–1754

Everywhere in British North America by 1750, maturing settlements showed unmistakable signs of having achieved many colonial and imperial goals. Yet along with their successful production and reproduction, colonists were beginning to note that cities and older coastal farmlands were growing "crowded." And they often tempered their exhilaration about taming the wilderness with fears about social conflicts on the frontiers. Cutting across both northern and southern coastal and frontier regions, colonists also began to understand that the blessings of rapid natural increase, great influx of immigrants, and established slavery also heightened class, family, and racial tensions.

Slave Resistance and Rebellion

Many masters reasoned that slaves had a barbarous, savage nature that had to be constantly checked. Indeed, slavery was premised on the use of force and the prevalence of fear among both masters and slaves. Yet slaves throughout the colonies developed ways to accommodate or resist daily degradation. Building separate cultural and economic spheres was one way to reinforce personal dignity and perhaps gain a small increment of food or clothing. Some slaves worked odd jobs for planters or hired themselves out during slow weeks of the agricultural seasons in order to acquire cooking utensils or shoes.

More daring slaves resisted work by slowing down, breaking tools, or stealing from their master's household bit by bit. Some took the incredible risk of poisoning a beloved pet in the master's household, sassing the overseer, or sneaking out at night to visit neighboring slaves. Brutal punishments awaited those who were caught running away.

Open rebellion by groups of slaves was rare in colonial North America because the likelihood of being caught was so great, and the consequences so severe. The widespread assumption that Africans and African-Americans were slaves based on skin color made hiding from white society almost impossible. Moreover, in every colony but South Carolina, the white population was sufficiently large and dispersed to deter slaves from forming independent runaway slave societies such as those that appeared in Brazil or the mountains of Jamaica. A few mainland slaves "took their freedom" and escaped to the homes of free blacks in Philadelphia, New

York, Newport, or Williamsburg during the colonial era. Even then, their safety was never assured.

The most violent colonial slave revolt occurred in late 1739 near Charleston, South Carolina. Since 1699, governors of Spanish Florida, who wished to set up a buffer zone between their settlements and the English, had been inviting Carolina slaves to run away to Spanish territory with promises of freedom and land. As a result, scores of runaway slaves formed small communities in the countryside around St. Augustine, the largest of which was America's first free black community at Gracia Real de Santa Teresa de Mose (Mose, for short), which was led by an educated former slave, Francisco Menéndez, in the 1730s.

Then, in September 1739, South Carolina newspapers rumored that nearly seventy slaves had run away recently to an area near Spanish St. Augustine. The trickle of runaways, feared planters, was turning into a flood that would sweep huge numbers of "rice slaves" out of South Carolina. When the opening conflicts of King George's War (called the War of Jenkins's Ear) broke out between Spanish and English people in the West Indies later that year, fears became reality. Near the Stono River, at least seventy-five newly arrived Africans and a few more seasoned slaves who spoke Gullah began a march toward Spanish Florida, hoping to convince hundreds more to join them. Along the way, the runaways broke into white storekeepers' shops and killed a number of whites who they feared would spread word of their location to plantation masters.

At first it seemed that a great number of Carolina slaves had successfully escaped their monotonous field routines and masters' random brutalities. In a clearing along the way, they chanted joyfully about their new "liberty." But the runaways stayed too long in the marshes and lit campfires that attracted the colonial militia, who caught and killed two-thirds of the runaways. Planters executed another sixty fugitives in the coming months. Despite this outcome, revolts took place the next year elsewhere in South Carolina and in Georgia, possibly inspired by the Stono Rebellion and almost certainly sustained by the great stream of African slaves brought into the southern colonies during the 1730s.

The Great Awakening

During the mid-1730s, clergymen and itinerant preachers began to remind colonists about the dangers of material success, rising incidence of both luxury and poverty, and the apparent waning of religious fervor. Concerned ministers blamed the "cold formality" of church services for declining membership in congregations, and they set out to inspire renewed piety and faith with preaching that appealed more to the heart than the head. A "Great Awakening," as scholars often call it, swept through settled North America, exhilarating people of all statuses, occupations, levels of education, and regions. Its leading ministers exhorted colonists to abandon their trust in reason to resolve the era's anxieties and to rely on the heart instead. Not through books and newspapers, but through the preached word—in dramatic, huge, public encounters—ministers counseled ordinary colonists to reject the emptiness of material goods. Revivalists insisted that listeners admit their utter personal depravity and prophesied the divine wrath to be unleashed on unrepentant populations. Waves of cholera, diphtheria, and influenza seemed to be signs of God's displeasure. Crop failures resulting from hail, locusts, and wheat rust provided sufficient warnings about impending greater doom should the masses not repent immediately.

Jonathan Edwards, a Congregationalist minister in Northampton, Massachusetts, preached stingingly to his flock in 1735: "The God that holds you over the pit of Hell, much as one holds a spider or other loathsome insect over the fire, abhors you. His wrath toward you burns like fire; He looks upon you as worth of nothing else but to be cast into the fire." In rural New Jersey and Pennsylvania Presbyterian minister William Tennent called on sinners to have a spiritual rebirth, claiming that his own son had been raised from the dead by God's wonderful powers. Dutch Reformed leaders such as Theodore Frelinghuysen also led large public prayer meetings during the mid-1730s.

Then, in 1739 an English Anglican clergyman named George Whitefield came to the colonies and inspired thousands upon thousands of colonists to listen to messages of sin and salvation even more fervently. Newspapers printed reports of his revival meetings in England and the colonies, spreading anticipation of his visits. Whitefield came to the American colonies seven times, and during the mid-1740s stayed for three years, enthralling thousands with his traditional biblical messages and appeals for renewal of faith. Whitefield walked and rode on horseback through the colonies, drawing out converts to the new waves of "enthusiasm." His message was simple: individuals had allowed intellectual influences to crowd out the purity of religious feeling that flowed from the heart, and established clergymen had used Enlightenment rationalism to justify their elite styles and to distance themselves from their congregations.

Thousands of young adults joined churches for the first time during the Great Awakening. Thousands more were "born again" and helped split off portions of their existing congregations in order to form new churches. William Tennent's son, Gilbert, denounced Boston Congregational clergymen and built a huge following among the poor and single females of the city. In Southold, New York, James Davenport led hundreds of converts out of Congregationalist churches to form "New Light" churches. By 1742, New Light ministers and followers existed up and down the coast.

Old Lights, or leaders of the original Presbyterian, Congregational, and Anglican churches, lashed out in protest. In the South, the rising number of converted slaves was especially disturbing to planters, who banned their slaves from joining white churches. Converted African-Americans along the Savannah River were even able to call black preachers before the end of the colonial period. Baptists, at first strong only in New England, continued to grow in number in Virginia through the 1750s and 1760s. Old Lights insisted that the "wildness," the "quakings and tremblings" of revival followers were little more than provocations by untrustworthy—and outsider—clergymen. But splits in the colonial Protestant denominations endured for years. Presbyterians did not agree to reunite until 1758, and then the criticisms of New Lights were incorporated into church procedures and liturgy. Anglicans lost

George Whitefield (1714–1770)
A tireless itinerant through towns and rural crossroads from Georgia to Massachusetts, Whitefield came from England to the colonies to spread the Great Awakening message to thousands of listeners, who responded in droves and in turn questioned both spiritual and political authority. Whitefield and a few other dissenting preachers spearheaded a grassroots movement that led to new religious denominations, and revivals of the old, at midcentury. *(Trustees of the Boston Public Library.)*

untold numbers to the Presbyterians and Baptists—permanently. In Massachusetts and Connecticut, Old Lights tried to punish dissenters by forcing them to pay taxes to the original churches and banishing many New Lights from political office. But the swell of influence continued to grow until New Lights won control of the Connecticut assembly in 1759.

Indeed, although the Great Awakening reached a peak in 1742, it continued to have a strong impact on colonists' public and personal religious character. Quakers, who did not really participate in the revivals, waned in numbers thereafter. Anglican and Congregational churches declined as well, whereas Presbyterians and Baptists rose in influence over the coming years. Great Awakening leaders shuddered that humanistic Enlightenment teachings had permeated existing Old Light schools. In 1746 New Light Presbyterians, dissatisfied with Harvard, formed the College of New Jersey (later Princeton University). In 1754 the Baptists followed with the formation of the College of Rhode Island (later Brown University), the Dutch Reformed with Queen's College (later Rutgers University) in 1766, and the Congregationalists with Dartmouth in 1769. Even earlier, in the 1740s, a new denomination—the Methodists—was splitting from Anglican ranks as well. Although Methodists did not form a separate church until 1800, individuals believed that the Anglican ministers were preaching abstractions and appealing mostly to wealthy southerners for membership. Partly in response to criticisms of Methodists and others, Anglicans created new institutions in the 1750s to reinforce their heritage: the College of Philadelphia (later University of Pennsylvania) and King's College in New York City (later Columbia University).

Amid all the splintering of old denominations and the proliferation of new religious persuasions, most New Light preachers emphasized to their converted masses the importance of emotion over doctrine, and the need to seek an experience of God's grace rather than submit blindly to any particular clergyman. New Light ministers were receptive not only to the poor, young, and anxious white population. Free and slave blacks were accepted into many of the new Protestant churches, and at times encouraged to form their own meetinghouses. Furthermore, although New Lights never put forth an explicit political program for secular society, they did give colonists a vehicle for developing a critical posture toward figures and institutions of authority in politics, religion, and the law. This would be important by the final colonial decades, when critical religious sensibilities that had brewed for over twenty years helped give voice to the emerging American identity at the time of the Revolution.

Land in Trouble

Colonists often regarded their frontiers with fear, as places that harbored hostile Native Americans, strange ethnic groups, and runaway servants and slaves. Many frontiers bordered on the dominion of foreign nations, such as French territory along the Great Lakes or the southern Spanish borderlands. These areas often had permeable or uncertain boundaries across which people of different nations sought freedom from bondage, markets for goods, or perhaps just a plot of land for cultivation or herding.

In the British South, almost continuous settlement existed from the coastal plains to the Appalachian Mountains by about the 1740s. But in the piedmont and foothills, colonists sometimes were not certain about ownership of tracts, which in turn fueled clashes among different groups of Europeans and with Native Americans. For example, Virginia speculators, whom Indians called "long knives," organized the Ohio Company in 1747 and attempted to survey a large land claim near what later became Pittsburgh. While Native Americans sent war parties against the intruders, the young surveyor George Washington learned that his job measuring uncleared terrain required Indian-fighting skills as well. Further to the south, settlers were spreading westward out of South Carolina into Cherokee lands, provoking minor clashes that would soon erupt into warfare during 1760 (see Chapter 5).

The southern frontier also became contested terrain by the 1750s. The Great Awakening was still flourishing in the South's western regions, where new Baptist churches threw up serious challenges to the gentry's religious and cultural authority. At the same time, many frontier settlers began to grow weary of making peaceful appeals for political representation or lower taxes for frontier inhabitants, and to mobilize for more forceful changes. These frontier "Regulators" lived along the entire Carolina fringe of settlement. In South Carolina, backcountry farmers, mostly recent Scots-Irish immigrants, formed vigilante bands for local protection during the 1760s and condemned the eastern establishment for failing to enforce its own laws in the west. Further, threatened the Regulators, if frontiersmen did not gain representation in the colonial government, they would take responsibility themselves for the protection of their homes and fields from Indian raids, bandits, and speculators. In 1769 the colonial assembly granted six new courts in the west and reduced taxes, but they denied the western counties representation.

In North Carolina, Regulators demanded not more government but less. Taxes, they cried, were collected in the west but benefited only easterners. In any event, frontiersmen were unable to pay them. Farmers demanded paper money and an end to suits against them for debts, mortgages, and nonpayment of taxes. So deeply felt were the Regulators' grievances that in 1771 they fought bitterly against eastern militiamen at the Battle of Alamance. Governor William Tryon's 1,200 militiamen rode out to the heart of Regulator territory to defeat some 2,000 men in armed uprising. Only a few died on each side, but in months to come the uneasy eastern establishment forced frontier settlers to swear allegiance to the crown government.

In the northern colonies, western and rural conflicts tended to erupt not over political rights but over ownership of land. During the 1740s, for example, farmers in eastern New Jersey angrily defended land that had been granted to them by New York governors when the two colonies were connected imperial jurisdictions. Once New Jersey gained independent colonial status, its proprietors sent wealthy agents into the countryside to claim rights over some lands that the farmers held, provoking fierce rioting from 1745 to 1755.

Property rights also sparked tensions along New York's Hudson River, where tenants of the Livingston and other landed families refused for a number of years to pay their rents. In 1753 anti-rent riots broke out. Then during 1765 and 1766, the Hudson River valley was turned upside down. Three generations previously, the New York governor had awarded huge tracts of land to favored colonial families. Although much of the disputed land lay completely undeveloped, some heads of these families rented out hundreds of small parcels to poor immigrant tenants, many of them German or Dutch. By midcentury, New Englanders who were spreading west expected to take up portions of the great landlords' estates, either by buying them outright or simply squatting and tilling the soil. When the landlords attempted to evict the squatters with court orders, and then to forcibly remove them, riots broke out. For months squatters ranged through the countryside, burning buildings and threatening tenants who remained loyal to the landlords. They clashed openly with county jail keepers and sheriffs until royal officials ordered British troops sent from New York City to quell the riots.

Farther to the west in New York, speculators tried to take Mohawk lands that lay outside Albany after 1753, only to have Chief Hendrick announce to the governor that henceforth the Iroquois would not honor the Covenant Chain between them. In the early 1760s, farmers moving out of New England with titles from New Hampshire to settle new lands just to the west (which would become Vermont later), clashed with speculators who held titles from New York. By staunchly defending lands that were technically claimed by New York, Ethan Allen's "Green Mountain Boys" created a de facto state of Vermont by 1777.

Beyond the land settled by British subjects were vast areas inhabited by Native Americans and claimed by rival Spanish and French. The Spanish were making important strides toward colonizing the Floridas, the Southwest, and California through the final decades of British rule in North America (see Chapter 5). The French also extended their influence over North American Indians, squatters, and land companies. During the 1740s, the French began to refortify their positions along the St. Lawrence River and to establish a military presence in the Ohio River valley. Colonists, especially Pennsylvanians who had been sent out by their government to create habitable trading posts and farms, and the Virginians whose settlements lay closest to new French forts, bristled. In 1753 Virginia sent George Washington on another mission into the wilderness, this time to warn the French under Marquis Duquesne to leave the area. Washington, now a commander of the Virginia militia, was not willing to negotiate terms with the Delaware, Mingo, and Shawnee who lived in the territory. Furthermore, Duquesne rebuffed him. The French proceeded to take over the Virginia encampment and scatter the colonial militia. In the spring of 1754, Washington returned to the Ohio country. This time he simply ordered his men to open fire on the first French patrol they encountered, which happened about fifty miles from Great Meadows where the Allegheny and Monongahela Rivers meet. This attack started the bloodiest colonial war.

CONCLUSION

By the end of the colonial era, a steady line of settlement stretched from Georgia to Maine, from the Atlantic coastline to the Appalachian ridge. Tentacles of settlement reached from cosmopolitan cities where shops displayed fineries from Europe, into the wilderness where colonists lived with the barest of essential goods. Colonists were linked by commerce to foreign places that previous generations of settlers had never heard about, and the level of their material comfort was rising steadily. Great numbers of middling people were overcoming rude lifestyles, periodic unemployment, and political exclusion.

Although colonists typically still thought of themselves as inhabitants of separate provinces, or as "true born Englishmen," they were beginning to recognize a new identity: their shared Americanness. Expansion, immigration, and maturation contributed to new colonial thinking about being Americans. Communication among the colonies also drew people together as never before. The life-sustaining activities of commerce invited many colonists to think not so much about their immediate surroundings as about the fluctuations of international markets and effects of wars. South Carolina rice planters, for example, communicated more frequently with New York City merchants than with neighboring planters in Virginia. Rivalry with Native Americans, resistance of slaves, and continuing claims by France and Spain to both West Indies islands and North American borderlands also spurred colonists to think about their cultural distinctiveness from other peoples.

At the same time, distinctions among the social ranks of colonists grew more noticeable, and ethnic diversity, distinctive family patterns, different labor systems, and many cultural factors all made it hard to imagine how colonists might be united. Regional differences were also becoming pronounced, for in many respects New England culture and community ways were growing more remote than ever from Virginia's, and both were increasingly distinct from the West Indies or Mississippi frontier. Even at the end of the colonial era, there was no single American character, but rather a rich diversity of ethnic, religious, economic, and regional circumstances. To say that despite their differences, colonists were unified in their attachment to an empire defined as "English" stretches reality, for much of colonial life was not "English." South Carolina's slave majority was an obvious reminder to colonists that they were far from London. So was continuing contact between Native Americans and colonists, and the violence of huge, and advancing, frontiers. Colonists underscored their differences when they called Scottish frontiersmen "Jacobites" long after the English episode that had earned them the label as dangerous political dissenters. Quakers and Catholics were never welcome in colonial Massachusetts. Women of elite households often were as resentful of widows and orphans draining tax revenues for their upkeep as male politicians were. Farmers along the Hudson River scorned efforts by merchants in New York City to set the prices and terms of grain sales. Visitors from England mocked efforts by some of the southern gentry to emulate the lifestyles of gentlemen in London.

Indeed, colonists never shared a common condition, or a common set of aspirations for the future. Rather, they shared a willingness to criticize the heightened intervention of imperial authorities in their everyday lives. And eventually they shared general views about constitutional and political crises developing in the empire after 1763. These shared views enabled colonists to create a temporary political community in order to transcend other differences and separate from the empire during the Revolution.

SUGGESTED READINGS

Bernard Bailyn, *The Peopling of British North America* (1986), is a short but grand overview of immigration into the colonies. Exciting new scholarship has explored aspects of frontier change due to immigration and migration, with respect to ethnicity, religion, and race. See, for example, Donald Chipman, *Spanish Texas, 1519–1821* (1992); Gregory Evans Dowd, *A Spirited Resistance: The North American Indian Struggle for Unity, 1745–1815* (1992); Tom Hatley, *The Dividing Paths: Cherokees and South Carolinians Through the Era of Revolution* (1993); Rachel N. Klein, *Unification of a Slave State: The Lives of the Planters in the South Carolina Backcountry, 1760–1808* (1990); Robert D. Mitchell, *Appalachian Frontiers: Settlement, Society, and Development in the Preindustrial Era* (1991); Timothy Silver, *A New Face on the Countryside: Indians, Colonists, and Slaves in South Atlantic Forests, 1500–1800* (1987); Daniel B. Thorp, *The Moravian Community in Colonial North Carolina: Pluralism on the Southern Frontier* (1989); Albert H. Tillson, *Gentry and Common Folk: Political Culture on a Virginia Frontier, 1740–1789* (1991); and Daniel Usner, Jr., *Indians, Settlers, and Slaves in a Frontier Exchange Economy: The Lower Mississippi Valley before 1783* (1992).

For the cultural maturation see Richard Bushman, *The Refinement of America: People Houses, Cities* (1992); and for political and institutional maturation see Jack P. Greene, *Pursuits of Happiness* (1988). For work and home life, including material culture, see James A. Henretta and Gregory H. Nobles, *Evolution and Revolution: American Society, 1600–1820* (1987); Ronald Hoffman, Cary Carson, and Peter J. Albert, eds., *Of Consuming Interests: The Style of Life in the Eighteenth Century* (Charlottesville, 1994); Stephen Innes, ed., *Work and Labor in Early America* (1988); and Stephanie Grauman Wolf, *As Various as Their Land: The Everyday Lives of Eighteenth-Century Americans* (1993).

For family life in colonial America, see Karin Calvert, *Children in the House: The Material Culture of Early Childhood, 1600–1800* (1992); Philip Greven, *Four Generations* (1970); Edmund Morgan, *The Puritan Family* (1966); David Narrett, *Inheritance and Family Life in*

Colonial New York City (1992); Mary Beth Norton, "The Evolution of White Women's Experience in Early America," *American Historical Review, LXXXIX,* 593–619; Daniel Blake Smith, *Inside the Great House: Planter Family Life in Eighteenth-Century Chesapeake Society* (1980); Laurel T. Ulrich, *Good Wives: Image and Reality in the Lives of Women in Northern New England, 1650–1750* (1982); and Helena M. Wall, *Fierce Communion: Family and Community in Early America* (1990).

On the centrality of commerce, see Marc Egnal, "The Economic Development of the Thirteen Continental Colonies, 1720–1775," *William and Mary Quarterly, XXXII,* 1975, 191–218; Thomas M. Doerflinger, *A Vigorous Spirit of Enterprise: Merchants and Economic Development in Revolutionary Philadelphia* (1986); James H. Levitt, *For Want of Trade: Shipping and the New Jersey Ports, 1680–1783* (1981); Nancy F. Koehn, *The Power of Commerce: Economy and Government in the First British Empire* (1994); John McCusker and Russell Menard, *The Economy of British America, 1607–1789* (rev. ed., 1991); and Cathy Matson, *Merchants and Empire: Trading in Colonial New York* (1998). The most important contribution for northern cities is Gary Nash, *The Urban Crucible* (1979); but see also Billy Smith, *The "Lower Sort": Philadelphia's Laboring People, 1750–1800* (1990); and G. B. Warden, *Boston, 1689–1776* (1970). For slavery in the northern cities, see Thomas J. Davis, *A Rumor of Revolt: The "Great Negro Plot" in Colonial New York* (1985); and Jean R. Soderlund, *Quakers and Slavery: A Divided Spirit* (1985).

No single study has covered the North comprehensively, but regional aspects and comparative perspectives are offered in many important works. See, for example, Richard Bushman, *From Puritan to Yankee: Character and the Social Order in Connecticut, 1690–1765* (1967); Barry Levy, *Quakers and the American Family* (1988); James T. Lemon, *The Best Poor Man's Country* (1972); Kenneth Lockridge, *A New England Town: The First Hundred Years, Dedham, Massachusetts, 1636–1736* (1970); Paul R. Lucas, *Valley of Discord: Church and Society Along the Connecticut River, 1636–1725* (1976); Jackson T. Main, *Society and Economy in Colonial Connecticut* (1985); Peter C. Mancall, *Valley of Opportunity: Economic Culture Along the Upper Susquehanna, 1700–1800* (1991); and Stephanie Grauman Wolf, *Urban Village: Population, Community, and Family Structure in Germantown, Pennsylvania, 1683–1800* (1976). Sharon V. Salinger, *"To Serve Well and Faithfully": Labor and Indentured Servitude in Pennsylvania, 1682–1800* (1987), is the most meticulous analysis of indentured servants in the mid-Atlantic region.

Two important new works synthesize the extensive scholarship on slavery, plantations, commerce, and culture of the colonial south: Ira Berlin, *Many Thousands Gone: The First Two Centuries of Slavery in North America* (1998), and Philip D. Morgan, *Slave Counterpoint: Black Culture in the Eighteenth-Century Chesapeake and Lowcountry* (1998). Aspects of slavery and plantation life in the Chesapeake are also perceptively captured in T. H. Breen, *Tobacco Culture: The Mentality of the Great Tidewater Planters on the Eve of the Revolution* (1985); and Mechal Sobel, *The World They Made Together: Black and White Values in Eighteenth-Century Virginia* (1987). The classic study that explains slavery's origins and rise in the context of labor needs and the southern qualities of agriculture is Edmund Morgan, *American Slavery, American Freedom: The Ordeal of Colonial Virginia* (1975). For the low country, see Betty Wood, *Slavery in Colonial Georgia, 1730–1775* (1984), and Peter Wood, *Black Majority* (1974). An important comparative study is Philip Curtin, *The Rise and Fall of the Plantation Complex: Essays in Atlantic History* (1990). For work on the early development of slave communities within the southern agricultural system see Gwendolyn Midlo Hall, *Africans in Colonial Louisiana: The Development of Afro-Creole Culture in the Eighteenth Century* (1922), and A. Leon Higginbotham, Jr., *In the Matter of Color: Race and the American Legal Process in the Colonial Period* (1978).

Much work remains to be done on the life of small farmers in the Chesapeake and low country, but see the admirable study by Gregory A. Stiverson, *Poverty in a Land of Plenty: Tenancy in Eighteenth-Century Maryland* (1977). For smaller regions within the South, see Paul G. E. Clemens, *The Atlantic Economy and Colonial Maryland's Eastern Shore* (1980); E. Roger Ekirch, *Poor Carolina: Politics and Society in Colonial North Carolina, 1729–1776* (1981); Harry Roy Merrens, *Colonial North Carolina in the Eighteenth Century* (1964); and Robert Weir, *Colonial South Carolina: A History* (1983). For Georgia's emergence, see Kenneth Coleman, *Colonial Georgia* (1976), and Betty Wood, *Women's Work, Men's Work: The Informal Slave Economies of Lowcountry Georgia* (1995).

Two important works link the Great Awakening to the American Revolution: Patricia Bonomi, *Under the Cope of Heaven: Religion, Society, and Politics in Colonial America* (1986), and Alan Heimert, *Religion and the American Mind* (1966). A pathbreaking study that applied anthropological methodologies to master–slave relations and to the religious revivals of the era in Virginia is Rhys Isaac, *The Transformation of Virginia, 1740–1790* (1982). Outstanding biographies of leading New Light preachers include Frank Lambert, *"Pedlar of Divinity": George Whitefield and the Transatlantic Revivals* (1994); Perry Miller, *Jonathan Edwards* (1949); and Patricia Tracy, *Jonathan Edwards, Pastor: Religion and Society in Eighteenth-Century Northampton* (1979).

Two Views About Transatlantic Slave Trading

The Horrors of the Middle Passage

Every person transported from Africa to the Western Hemisphere as a slave experienced the wrenching terrors of the transatlantic voyage known as the "middle passage." Many did not survive, and nobody survived unscathed. Olaudah Equiano, whose recollections are excerpted below, was a slave in three places: Africa, Barbados, and Virginia. He bought his freedom after years of service to various masters and on the eve of the American Revolution fled to London. There, he published his memoirs in 1789.

One day [in Africa], when all our people were gone out to their works as usual and only I and my dear sister were left to mind the house, two men and a woman got over our walls, and in a moment seized us both, and without giving us time to cry out or make resistance they stopped our mouths and ran off with us into the nearest wood. I was left in a state of distraction not to be described. I cried and grieved continually, and for several days I did not eat anything but what they forced into my mouth. At length, after many days' travelling, during which I had often changed masters, I got into the hands of a chieftain in a very pleasant country. This man had two wives and some children. . . . This first master of mine, as I may call him, was a smith, and my principal employment was working his bellows.

I was again sold and carried through a number of places till . . . at the end of six or seven months after I had been kidnapped I arrived at the sea coast. The first object which saluted my eyes when I arrived on the coast was the sea, and a slave ship, which was then riding at anchor, and waiting for its cargo. These filled me with astonishment, which was soon converted into terror, when I was carried on board. I was immediately handled, and tossed up, to see if I were sound, by some of the crew; and I was now persuaded that I had got into a world of bad spirits, and that they were going to kill me. . . .

When I looked round the ship too and saw a large furnace or copper boiling, and a multitude of black people of every description chained together, every one of their countenances expressing dejection and sorrow, I no longer doubted of my fate; and, quite overpowered with horror and anguish, I fell motionless on the deck and fainted. When I recovered a little I found some black people about me, who I believed were some of those who had brought me on board, and had been receiving their pay; they talked to me in order to cheer me, but all in vain. . . . I now saw myself deprived of all chance of returning to my native country, or even the least glimpse of hope of gaining the shore, which I now considered as friendly; and I even wished for my former slavery in preference to my present situation, which was filled with horrors of every kind, still heightened by my ignorance of what I was to undergo. I was not long suffered to indulge my grief; I was soon put down under the decks, and there I received such a salutation in my nostrils as I had never experienced in my life; so that with the loathsomeness of the stench, and crying to-gether, I became so sick and low that I was not able to eat.

. . . Two of the white men offered me eatables; and on my refusing to eat, one of them held me fast by the hands, and laid me across, I think the windlass, and tied my feet, while the other flogged me severely. I had never experienced any thing of this kind before; and, although not being used to the water, I naturally feared that element the first time I saw it, yet, nevertheless, could I have got over the nettings, I would have jumped over the side, but I could not; and besides, the crew used to watch us very closely. . . .

At last we came in sight of the island of Barbados; the white people got some old slaves from the land to pacify us. They told us we were not to be eaten but to work, and were soon to go on land where we should see many of our country people. This report eased us much; and sure enough soon after we were landed there came to us Africans of all languages. . . .

On a signal given (as the beat of a drum) the buyers rush at once into the yard where the slaves are confined, and make choice of that parcel they like best. The noise and clamour with which this is attended, and the eagerness visible in the countenances of the buyers, serve not a little to increase the apprehension of terrified Africans, who may well be supposed to consider them as the ministers of the destruc-tion to which they think themselves devoted. In this manner, without scruple, are relations and friends separated, most of them never to see each other again. ▋

Justifying the Slave Trade

By the mid-1700s planters did not have to prove the profitability of the slave trade to representatives in Parliament. Nevertheless, when English policymakers needed to promote a new war or planters wished to compete effectively with foreigners, they justified the slave trade anew with newspaper articles and pamphlets. The following passage was penned in 1745, by a British writer who tried to link the economic ad-vantages with an intellectual rationale for the slave trade.

But is it not notorious to the whole World, that the Business of Planting in our British Colonies, as well as in the French, is carried on by the Labour of Negroes, imported thither from Africa? Are we not indebted to that valuable People, the Africans, for our Sugars, Tobaccoes, Rice, Rum, and all other Planta-tions Produce? And the greater the Number of Negroes imported into our Colonies, from Africa, will not the Exportation of British Manufactures among the Africans be in Proportion; they being paid for in such Commodities only? The more likewise our Plantations abound in Negroes, will not more Land become cultivated, and both better and greater Variety of Plantation Commodities be pro-duced? As those Trades are subservient to the Well Being and Prosperity of each other; so the more either flourishes or declines, the other must be necessarily affected; and the general Trade and Navigation of their Mother Country will be proportionately benefited. . . .

. . . that the general NAVIGATION of Great Britain owes all its Encrease and Splendor to the commerce of its American and African Colonies; and that it cannot be maintained and enlarged otherwise than from the constant Prosperity of both those Branches, whose Interests are mutual and inseparable?

Whatever other Causes may have conspired to enable the French to beat us out of all the Markets in Europe in the Sugar and Indigo Trades, etc. the great and extraordinary Care they have taken to cherish and encourage their African Company, to the End that their Plantation might be cheaply and plentifully stocked with Negroe Husbandmen, is amply sufficient of itself to account for the Effect; for this Policy, they wisely judged, would enable them to produce those Commodities cheaper than we, who have suffered the British Interest to decline in Africa, as that of the French has advanced; and when they could produce the Commodities cheaper, is it at all to be admired that they have undersold us at all the foreign Markets in Europe, and hereby got that most beneficial Part of our Trade into their own Hands? . . .

As Negroe Labor hitherto has, so that only can support our British Colonies, as it has done those of other Nations. It is that also will keep them in due Subserviency to the Interest of their Mother Country; for while our Plantations depend only on Planting by Negroes, and that of such Produce as interferes only with the Interests of our Rivals not of their Mother-Country, our Colonies can never prove injurious to British Manufactures, never become independent of these Kingdoms, but remain a perpetual Support to our European Interest, by preserving to us a Superiority of Trade and Naval Power.

Masters and slaves existed together in a world of stark contrasts between them. Slaves struggled to prevail against conditions that stripped them of their heritage and dignity—or simply to survive the conditions of work—while British officials and colonial planters put the requirements of building an empire and personal fortunes above moral concerns. The slave trade occupied a prominent place in the British commercial system covering many continents and many peoples. Often the imperatives of competing with rival nations for the lands and resources of the New World gave the slave trade, and the labor of slaves on plantations, first priority in the minds of policymakers. Certainly, the profits to be made in the slave trade and in the products of slave labor were unsurpassed in all of imperial commerce. But the costs for the millions of people who were forcibly made a part of this profitable system were tremendous.

Questions for Analysis

1. Olaudah Equiano exemplifies many different reasons to condemn the slave trade. Find passages that address psychology, family, quality of life, and general physical conditions. Which complaints seem to be most compelling?

2. What criticisms of the slave trade are directed at conditions in the New World, and what ones stem from West African experiences? How are Equiano's two experiences different?

3. What specific points are made in defense of the slave trade? What general attitudes about race and slavery are revealed in the specific points?

4. Is there a tension between economic motivations for the slave trade and its moral justification? Can the two views be reconciled?

5. How might slave trading have differed in the many European nations involved in the practice?

5

Forging the American Experiment, 1754–1775

*T*oward the end of 1768, well-to-do southern planter William Drayton grew alarmed about the turn of events in South Carolina. The year before, Parliament had enacted the Townshend Duties, back-breaking taxes on a long list of colonial imports and an elaborate enforcement system. Now, men of "scant education" and "dearth of public service" had entered the political limelight in South Carolina to lead protests against the act. Small retailers, butchers, carpenters, shoemakers, and others "of modest means" had formed committees to cease importing goods from England, hoping to pressure English merchants into supporting colonists' pleas for repeal.

Drayton was not opposed to such a "nonimportation movement" in principle. Three years earlier, planters and merchants had led a similar boycott to win repeal of the Stamp Act. What annoyed Drayton was that "gentlemen of property and standing" were suddenly sharing public life with men of little political experience, men who might provoke riotous behavior. "Nature never intended that such men should be profound politicians or able statesmen," sneered Drayton. Traditionally, men with Drayton's high stature in the colonial assembly, secure wealth and family name, and close connections to English commerce and culture had assumed the leadership of political protests.

But by October 1769, "middling" men led South Carolina's nonimportation movement, declaring that they would no longer "stoickally submit to all the illegal encroachments that may be made on [their] property, by an ill-designing and badly-informed ministry" in England. Nor would they wait for genteel leaders such as Mr. Drayton to formulate their political response to Parliament. They, the middling colonists, had been "in some degree useful to society"; their hard work earned "a decency suitable to their stations in life." Furthermore, these upstarts argued, they represented "ninety-nine out of every hundred . . . *of all North-America*," and had "as equal a measure of *common sense* as any men." What did Drayton represent? Nothing, said the artisans, except an inherited fortune. He had never worked "by the labour of either his head or his hands."

Such bold challenges to authority—against both colonial and imperial leaders—arose more frequently after 1750. A prolonged war fought in North America from 1754 to 1763 raised anxieties about the character and future of the empire. Following the war, a parliamentary discussion about how the North American colonies should grow and prosper led to numerous laws to shape the empire's future. With each passing year, colonists formulated replies to real and imagined parliamentary aims. At the same time, colonists grew anxious about the future of their frontiers and commerce. They began rethinking both their place in the empire and their relationships to one another in North America. Along the way, they tested many kinds of responses to Parliament's offensive new laws. Some of their actions came from calm consideration of grievances; some came from frustration and growing habits of violence.

During the long process of thinking, writing, and rioting from 1764 to 1775, many colonists also changed their minds about their place in the empire and in the colonies. William Drayton was one of them. In 1775 he wrote that he had erred in his earlier disapproval of actions by "the people of my good province." Perhaps Drayton had cynically calculated that he could hold political office only if he followed popular opposition to Parliament, for he knew he was a "servant of the public." Perhaps he genuinely believed Parliament had overstepped its authority. In any event, Drayton joined thousands of colonists in the third and final nonimportation movement initiated by a Continental Congress of delegates from all the colonies.

▮ What kind of war did colonists fight in between 1754 and 1763, and how did that war affect the rising tensions in the English Empire?

▮ What kind of goals did colonists formulate for their own futures as they repeatedly protested the actions of Parliament?

▮ How did protests lead to new colonial political authority, extralegal committees, and outright mob actions?

▮ What shared cultural identity helped colonists forge unified actions? What differences hampered cooperation among them?

This chapter will address these questions.

Chronology

1754	Albany Congress
1755	Braddock defeated by French and Indians
	Acadian removal begins
1756	Seven Years' War begins in Europe
1760	George III takes the throne
1763	Treaty of Paris
	Pontiac's Rebellion
	Proclamation Line determined
	Massacre of the Paxton Boys
1764	Sugar (or Revenue) Act
	Currency Act
1765	Stamp Act
	Sons of Liberty formed
	First Quartering Act
	First nonimportation agreement
1766	Declaratory Act
1767	Townshend Duties
1768	Incident with Hancock's sloop, *Liberty*
	British troops arrive in Boston
1770	Boston Massacre
1771	Tryon defeats Regulators at Battle of Alamance
1772	First Committee of Correspondence
	Gaspée incident
1773	Tea Act and tea parties
1774	Coercive (or Intolerable) Acts
	First Continental Congress and Association Agreement
1775	Battle of Lexington and Concord

The Great War for Empire, 1754–1763

King George's War, which ended in 1748, had exacted a heavy toll on colonial lives and morale. In addition to the burdens of higher taxes, disrupted farming, and loss of lives, the British had handed back their main acquisition, Louisbourg. Worse, French expansion into the heart of North America continued to worry English colonists beginning to settle in the vast lands west of Virginia in the Ohio Valley. In 1754 French troops and the Virginia militia clashed near the Ohio River. One year later, the frontier erupted into the greatest war for empire in colonial experience. In a short time, the conflict spread throughout Europe. Its major theaters of action, though, lay in this vast expanse of contested land, still largely unknown to Europeans, but for centuries home to great numbers of Native Americans.

Onset of War, 1754–1760

The first clashes of what would become a global contest among European nations for the dominion of North America began in the forests of the Ohio Valley. In 1749 Parliament granted the Ohio Company of Virginia rights over land that was already settled by a mixture of many Native American groups, French trappers and squatters, and migrating British colonists. Raiding parties of Canadians and Ottawa Indians struck at both colonial settlers and the Miami, Shawnee, Seneca, and Delaware Indians of the region through 1753.

In early 1754, a young militia captain and surveyor named George Washington was sent into the contested area with a Virginia contingent to repel the French who had moved south from Canada. As tensions grew and skirmishes led to deaths in an undeclared war, Washington built Fort Necessity at a southern fork of the Ohio River. French soldiers attacked colonists and set up Fort Duquesne nearby. Washington responded in May with a retaliatory raid from his encampment up the Monongahela River, killing all but one of a French reconnaissance party. Responding in turn, the French attacked Washington and his troops at Fort Necessity on July 3. Washington, overmatched, surrendered at Great Meadows the next day, and as the Virginia militiamen retreated, French troops forged an alliance with nearby Delaware and Shawnee Indians.

Even before news of this defeat reached London, British officials had requested that colonists come together, along with members of the Iroquois Confederacy, to plan a common defense. At first, some colonists cheered this opportunity to conquer "popish slavery" in French Canada and defend "British libertie" in the Ohio Valley. Benjamin Franklin drew up the Plan of Union in early spring 1754. The plan proposed formation of a grand council of representatives from the colonial assemblies and a chief negotiator appointed by the crown. This council would discuss and settle on terms of mutual interest to Indians and colonists regarding frontier defense, trade, and land occupation. The masthead of Franklin's *Pennsylvania Gazette* carried a cartoon of a segmented snake, broken into pieces representing the British mainland colonies and bearing the injunction that colonists "Unite or Die."

In June 1754, representatives from the New England colonies, New York, Maryland, and Pennsylvania met in Albany, New York, to develop a plan for dealing with the threat of French troops on the frontier and to negotiate alliances with the Iroquois. However, the Albany Congress foundered and failed. For one thing, Iroquois chiefs had grown weary of repeated land grabs by New York colonists and angrily broke off relations. Instead of cooperating, the Iroquois villages north and northeast of English settlements threatened to redirect their fur trade and diplomacy to New France.

For another thing, colonial legislators were not willing to combine their militias, finances, and political authority. They jealously guarded their separate colonial identities as competitors for western land. Moreover, even as the official meetings were in session, land and fur trade agents from various colonies flocked to Albany to make secret deals with individual Iroquois leaders. The Iroquois delegates grew furious that individual colonists would try to undermine efforts of their official negotiators, who were presumably working for the mutual interests of everyone. In the face of such conflicting colonial actions, the Iroquois broke off talks and refused all proposed alliances with the British.

The Albany plan's failure and Washington's surrender to French troops at Virginia's back door were evidence to British policymakers that the colonists could not defend themselves or the interests of the empire. Focusing their concerns on the strategic Ohio Valley and fishing and whaling communities of Newfoundland, including the fortified outpost of Louisbourg, and on the farming families of Nova Scotia, the British government discussed ways to eliminate the French presence. French troops continued to live in Newfoundland after King George's War, and French fishermen harvested huge quantities of cod from the northern waters. Anticipating that hostilities would spread to this region, British officials ordered troops and settlers to found the city of Halifax, Nova Scotia, in 1749.

By mid-1754, tensions in both the Ohio Valley and Canada built to the breaking point. In 1755 Major General Edward Braddock, the British commander-in-chief in North America, met with governors from eight colonies to plan the eviction of the French from North America. They initiated a multipronged attack on the Ohio Valley, the Mohawk Valley, and French Acadia (see map). Braddock set out against France's Fort Duquesne in the Ohio Valley himself, where he encountered formidable opposition from enemy troops. Brushing off offers of aid from the western Delaware Indians, and hampered by lack of experience in the wilderness, Braddock ordered his troops to slice a road through the dense forests. His baggage train included luxuries suited to a gentlemanly lifestyle, a typical entourage in more formal English warfare. As Braddock swaggered to within ten miles of Fort Duquesne, 1,500 French foot soldiers and Indians surrounded and annihilated both the redcoats and Braddock. The disaster was the worst defeat of British forces in North America to that time.

The British had one important success in 1755: they were able to expel the French from Acadia. About a thousand French settlers had remained in Acadia (present-day Nova Scotia) when Britain assumed control of the area in 1713. By 1750, their numbers had grown to about ten thousand. When representatives of Acadian villages refused to swear oaths of allegiance to England, Nova Scotia's British governor ordered the expulsion of the entire Acadian community. In August 1755, British troops marched in and began the forcible removal of civilians, looting

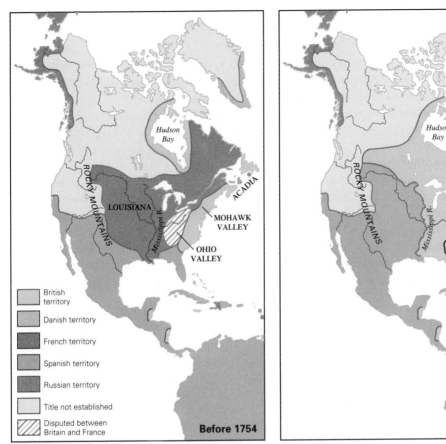

British territory	
Danish territory	
French territory	
Spanish territory	
Russian territory	
Title not established	
Disputed between Britain and France	

Before 1754

In 1763

Proclamation Line of 1763

European Claims in North America, 1754 and 1763 The French and Indian War was truly a conflict for dominion of North America. By the Peace of Paris in 1763, the disputed Ohio Valley and northern fisheries had become British territory, as had the entire French claim throughout the continent and Spanish Florida.

and burning farms. Land-hungry New Englanders flocked into the area and bought farms at drastically reduced prices, while hundreds of Acadians dispersed into the countryside to the west and down the St. Lawrence River with few possessions and little to sustain themselves in hostile territories. Eventually, a few hundred out of the ten thousand Acadians settled near multiethnic New Orleans, where they contributed much, including the name "Cajun," to the local culture.

Global War

In 1756 France and Britain formally declared war on each other, and the conflicts that began in the North American forests spread to colonial possessions in the Caribbean, the Pacific, and India. As this French and Indian War widened and spread into Europe as well, it became known as the Seven Years' War, or the Great War for Empire. Braddock's replacement, Lord Loudoun, arrived in North America in 1756. Initially, he fared just as poorly as his predecessor. The French fought with guerilla war tactics in the dense forests, mustering a combination of poorly trained Canadian and European soldiers, Indian allies from the dispersed smaller tribes around the southern Great Lakes, and Irish conscripts who had fled British rule. Thousands of Americans fled from western Pennsylvania and New York to the safety of eastern settlements. To the southeast, Cherokees and Choctaws tried in vain to remain officially neutral. But in the confusion of frontier fighting and traditions of intertribal rivalries, many village leaders exploited British and French hostilities and made no consistent efforts to defend frontier settlers. Overall, colonists soon realized this war was broader than any previous encounter between European empires in North America. Its goals involved capturing complete dominion over North America and the costs to do this—human and financial— were immense.

British and colonial ways of fighting and attitudes toward warfare couldn't have been more different. Loudoun favored highly organized campaigns with soldiers trained to fight in formation, as well as to set up camp, build shelters, and perform numerous menial tasks on command. For even small infractions of discipline, soldiers in this "standing army" submitted to brutal floggings or reduced food rations. The colonists, in contrast, were accustomed to service in local or colonial militias, as volunteers for a single campaign or short stay. Few militiamen knew how to drill, and fewer still were accustomed to following orders unconditionally. Most had learned to find cover and aim from behind trees rather than to march in formation or advance in bayonet charges. Colonial militia usually served under captains whom they knew, and they resented the British officers who declared militia units to be "the dirtiest, most contemptible, cowardly dogs that you can conceive." Many colonial volunteers resisted British command altogether.

To make matters worse, civilians grew ambivalent about rising colonial taxes that their assemblies passed in order to support the war. Legislators themselves protested Loudoun's requisitions of supplies from coastal populations and the endless need for tax money to underwrite campaigns that butchered their citizens. The forests, they also charged, were no place for gentlemen's wardrobes and tea services. For his part, Loudoun grew increasingly disgusted with colonists whom he believed "have assumed to themselves, what they call Rights and Privileges, totally unknown in the Mother Country. . . . They will give you, not one Shilling, to carry on the War; they will give you not one thing, but for double the Money it ought to cost."

Loudoun's French counterpart was Marquis Louis-Joseph de Montcalm, a veteran of European warfare. In 1756 Montcalm initiated measures to professionalize the French forces in North America, including stringent drilling practice and attacking in formation. At first, the strategy proved successful when the French took Oswego, New York. But in 1757 Montcalm's European standards of conduct backfired tragically. When he took Fort William Henry, Montcalm offered the British soldiers and camp followers the opportunity to return home in return for their promise not to fight against the French again. But his Erie and Huron allies refused to conform to French rules of war. They proceeded to take prisoners, murder, and scalp New Englanders as they left the fort. In the days to come, they also indiscriminately massacred neutral Indians and New York citizens.

On the other side of the Atlantic, new parliamentary leaders and policies changed the course of the war. William Pitt became secretary of state in late 1757 and remained responsible for directing the war effort until its virtual end in 1761. Pitt understood the gravity of the colonists' claim that they bore huge financial burdens for a war over which they had little control. Pitt offered colonists a compromise they could not refuse: in return for colonial commitment and obedience in the field, he promised reimbursements to the assemblies in proportion to their contributions, more decentralized command of the colonial militia, and the removal of Loudoun. Colonial morale began to revive in early 1758, and Pitt further boosted provincial spirits by sending thousands of fresh British troops to serve alongside the militia.

In 1758 the British again took Louisbourg, the premier symbol of French military strength in North America. Shortly thereafter, George Washington happily commanded the lead battalion that captured Fort Duquesne, renaming it Fort Pitt (later, Pittsburgh). Then the last of the French outposts on the New York frontier fell to the British. Within months, Montcalm retreated to Quebec, where on September 13, 1759, he met the British forces under General James Wolfe at the Battle of Quebec on the Plains of Abraham. In a great European-style formal battle, both European commanders lost their lives, and each army lost over two thousand soldiers. But the British won the day. In the following year, the British cut off supply movements from southern France and moved against Montreal. By forging an alliance with the Iroquois and cornering a few last French forces at Montreal, the British finally forced the enemy's surrender on September 8, 1760.

Fighting raged on elsewhere in the world for another three years. In the Caribbean, most French possessions fell to the British, and in the Philippines, Manila surrendered to the British in late 1762. Finally, the Treaty of Paris brought the Great War for Empire to an end in early 1763 (see map page 166). Under its terms, France regained its precious sugar islands of Martinique and Guadaloupe in the Caribbean. But it lost all claim to land east of the Mississippi River and gave to Spain (its ally at the end of the war) all French lands to the west of the river, plus the city of New Orleans, the "gateway to North America." Spain also reclaimed the Philippines and Cuba, but it lost the Floridas to Britain in 1763. For decades, Spanish authorities had tried to consolidate their empire's rule in North America over native and migrating populations of Mexico, California, Texas, and New Mexico. The loss of St. Augustine in Florida and the lack of population growth in Louisiana would create serious setbacks to Spain's imperial goals.

Britain, however, gained dominion over vast lands stretching from Hudson Bay to the Caribbean Sea, and from the Atlantic Ocean westward to the Mississippi River. In England, raucous parades and public gatherings celebrated victory against the country's archenemies, Spain and France, both of which were financially crippled and almost completely expelled from North America. In the colonies, the lands stretching to the north and west of older settlements offered tremendous prospects for expansion. In addition, colonists anticipated rapid commercial recovery because their vital connections to West Indies islands and British ports could be resumed. It seemed like a joyous time to identify with the British Empire.

The Death of General Wolfe   The British capture of Quebec in 1759 was a turning point in the Seven Years' War. The heroic death of Britain's leading commander, here surrounded by concerned officers and Native American allies on the Plains of Abraham, was elevated to mythic proportions by Benjamin West's painting years later. The painting rallied patriotic fervor in London just as Americans were recovering from the shock of the Boston Massacre.   *(National Gallery of Canada, Ottawa.)*

Tensions on the Frontier

The Treaty of Paris gave the British Empire unparalleled claims over new land. But those claims spurred numerous disputes within North America. For example, New Yorkers and New Hampshire residents clashed over the soil that lay east of Lake Champlain. During the 1760s and 1770s Ethan Allen, his Green Mountain Boys, and a rising tide of migrants into this area endured years of conflict with outsiders until they became a new state, Vermont, in 1777. In the 1760s, Pittsburgh and Wheeling became small frontier villages surrounded by quarrelling speculators, officials, and farm families. And farther south, dozens of families settled in remote North Carolina along the Watauga River, where they jostled over land rights for years.

These disputes overlapped with the tensions between Europeans and Native Americans in the land negotiated by the peace treaty. For decades it had been clear that Native Americans did not have the same frontier objectives as Europeans. Throughout the war, alliances between Indians and Europeans also proved elusive and frustrating. For example, in late fall 1759, between three and four thousand Cherokee responded to the persistent wartime violence on their hunting grounds by renouncing their long-term trading alliance with South Carolinians and attacking backcountry colonists. Repeatedly assailed by the Cherokee and their allies, frontier settlers relocated closer to the coastline. When Cherokee bands continued the attacks, British regular troops retaliated by destroying Native American towns along the Appalachian foothills. In 1761 the Cherokee farther west also threatened to overrun Virginia until they, too, were subdued temporarily by British troops. However, for years to come, Cherokee villages sporadically raided backcountry settlers, who in turn demanded more protection from the South Carolina government.

The greatest Indian uprising of all came in the region around the Great Lakes, where Native American grievances had been building ever since the British took possession of the French forts there at the end of 1760. British traders had defrauded tribal members in sales of rum, blankets, and fishing tools, while British soldiers occupied forts on tribal lands, recklessly overhunting and overfishing the resources on which neutral villages depended. Worst of all, the British general Jeffery Amherst abandoned the conventional courtesy of giving "gifts" of kettles, gunpowder, and provisions to secure friendly relations with the Indians. Amherst declared that the midwestern tribes must learn to live "without our charity." As a consequence of this measure, the inhabitants of many villages that depended on British guns and ammunition for hunting nearly starved.

Spurred by these frustrations, a number of young tribal warriors and rising chiefs adopted the teachings of the Algonquian-speaking visionary Neolin. Convinced that Native Americans had been corrupted by European goods, Neolin called for a pan-Indian alliance to drive Europeans from their lands and return to traditional ways. As the alliance grew during 1760–1761, it elevated strong cultural leaders who could motivate large numbers of their people. One of these leaders, the Ottawa chief Pontiac, brought together tribes from Michigan to western New York in May 1763 and led them against the British garrisons west of Fort Niagara. Then thousands of Native Americans proceeded to attack Fort Michilimackinac in upper Michigan and to massacre over two thousand white settlers in the area.

An enraged General Amherst vowed revenge against Pontiac's Rebellion. In a flurry of letters to commanders at western forts reviling the Indians as "vermin" and "ignorant savages," Amherst proposed that the British should spread smallpox through the tribes by offering "gifts" of infected blankets from the Fort Pitt hospital. Captains at Fort Pitt were happy to comply. The resulting epidemic laid waste Delaware, Shawnee, southern Creek, Chickasaw, and Choctaw throughout the southeast.

Ultimately, Pontiac's Rebellion ended with the return of British prisoners, the surrender of some Indian leaders to British courts of justice, and acknowledgment of British political control over the region. Determined to prevent future conflicts, the British ministry also drew a line on maps of the frontier intended to define the limit of European expansion. The Proclamation Line of 1763 (see map page 166) extended from the farthest northern tip of Maine to the southernmost parts of Georgia. Land to the west of the line was off-limits to European settlement or speculation.

Indians along the Appalachian ridge expressed their satisfaction with the terms of the Proclamation Line, but colonists seethed. The war, they fumed, had been won by their long and costly sacrifices, and now the West should be cleared for their use. In Pennsylvania anger rose to a fever pitch, when in December 1763 a group of fifty-seven vigilantes known as the Paxton Boys—predominantly Scots-Irish Presbyterians—marched against Indians at Conestoga, in Lancaster County. Under the mistaken belief that these Indians had been part of Pontiac's Rebellion, the Paxton Boys massacred six of them. Two weeks later, they slaughtered another group of Conestoga Indians who had been offered protection in a public workhouse. In their boldest move, the Paxton Boys ignored their Quaker rulers' pleas that the violence cease and pursued the Moravian Indians near Bethlehem. When the Indians took refuge in Philadelphia, at least six hundred frontier rebels marched into the city, where only Benjamin Franklin's promise to defend frontier land claims against the Indians calmed the disturbance.

Meanwhile, thousands of colonists moved west, unaware that they approached—and then crossed—the Proclamation Line. New Englanders crossed into the northern Green Mountains; New Yorkers poured into Mohawk country; hunters and poor families reached the foothills of Appalachia in Virginia and North Carolina; and hundreds of immigrants began clearing the land that would become Tennessee and West Virginia. Streams of families and individuals looking for farms and grazing lands formed the front guard of this migration. Hard on their heels came the surveyors of influential land companies formed by ambitious speculators in groups such as the Ohio Company. Anticipating that this region would became a great heartland, these companies made claims on millions of acres they hoped to turn into huge profits.

Given the surge of settlement that violated the Proclamation Line's protection of Native Americans, British authorities adjusted their policies. Frontier negotiators began to press the Iroquois and Cherokee to cede lands permanently to the British. The Treaty of Hard Labor, signed in 1768, granted large numbers of European settlers the right to stay on Cherokee lands along the upper Tennessee River. The Treaty of Fort Stanwix later that year determined that the Iroquois would retreat from the Ohio Valley and remain on homelands farther northeast.

In the southern backcountry, formal treaties meant very little. Tensions throughout the 1760s encompassed not only enduring strife between colonists and Indians, but scuffles among colonists as well. In South Carolina, the French and Indian War and the Cherokee struggle left a legacy of violence. Planters and yeomen denounced the raids of highway bandits, runaway slaves, horse thieves, and angry Native Americans against their property. Lacking "proper sheriffs and law," frontier planters organized themselves in 1763 into groups known as the Regulators and took justice into their own hands. Claiming that they had lived for years without political representation, paying high taxes to an eastern establishment that ignored them, the Regulators periodically whipped or taunted outlaws on the fringes of South Carolina society whom they suspected of theft, arson, or simple "vagrancy." In 1769 the colonial legislature set up six new circuit courts in the backcountry. Assemblymen also lowered frontier taxes. But to the end of the colonial era, Regulators in the western counties argued that their representation in the Assembly was inadequate and their safety under constant threat.

North Carolinians asked not for more, but less, government (see Competing Voices, page 196). After 1740, their frontier was increasingly dotted with storekeepers who imported textiles, agricultural implements, and small household items for ambitious small farmers who offered hides, tobacco, corn, tallow, or feathers in exchange. Even so, economic security eluded many farmers. Hundreds of new families built up enough credit to buy slaves and establish tobacco plantations out west, but when tobacco prices plummeted after 1763, storekeepers began to dun farmers for unpaid debts, and eastern authorities raised property taxes to help pay war debts. For struggling and cash-poor farmers, these were frightening times. The situation worsened when sheriffs refused to take country goods as payment for taxes, the colonial government refused to issue sufficient paper money, and frontier farms were seized during 1768 for nonpayment of taxes.

In response, western North Carolinians organized their own Regulator movement and attempted repeatedly to close the county courts that heard cases against debtors. Taxes, argued Regulators, should be levied in proportion to what the land could grow, not according to number of acres a farmer owned. In addition, farmers should be allowed to pay taxes in the goods they produced from the forests and soil. After all, they had little else. In 1769 the North Carolina assembly passed the Johnston Bill, which declared such protests "unlawful rioting" and possibly treasonous against the crown. In 1770 Governor William Tryon raised a large company of eastern militia to march west against the Regulators. In early 1771, over 2,000 Regulators met Tryon and his men at the Battle of Alamance. When the smoke cleared, 29 men were dead and over 150 others wounded. One Regulator was executed on the spot; twelve others were tried later for treason—of whom eight eventually "swung from ropes." But as the treason trials proceeded in the east, violence continued to brew out west on the piedmont. Tryon's petty officials, trying to extract oaths of allegiance to the crown from the nearly seven thousand western North Carolinian families, reported miserable failures.

In the final colonial years, Shawnee Indians north of the Ohio River exerted claims over their historical lands, but Lord Dunmore, the last colonial Virginia governor, sent two expeditions against the Shawnee in 1774. In the melée that is now called Dunmore's War, the Shawnee surrendered their claims to Virginia. But very quickly, two neighboring colonies attempted to grab the Shawnee land now in Virginia's possession. Aggressive Pennsylvanians moved to, and rebuilt, abandoned Harrodsburg, while speculating North Carolinians organized the Transylvania Company in order to occupy land between the Cumberland and Kentucky Rivers. Meanwhile, a prominent planter-judge, Richard Henderson of North Carolina, hired the strapping Daniel Boone to oversee the construction of the first major western roadway, through the Cumberland Gap to the Kentucky River. This Wilderness Road cut a swath through valleys and forests from eastern settlements in North Carolina to the remote posts of Boonesborough and Harrodsburg. This road fueled speculators' efforts to organize a government for the proposed colony of Transylvania, which was to cover most of today's Kentucky. But by 1775, events in the East had taken a turn toward crisis, and colonists turned their attention across the Atlantic more intently than ever.

 ## Rethinking Empire, 1763–1765

After the French and Indian War, the British Empire entered an unprecedented upswing of commercial development that put its people into successful competition with the Dutch, Spanish, and then the French for dominion and resources on four continents. The war also extended British influence across thousands of square miles of new terrain in North America. Soon, England would become the first western nation to enter the Industrial Revolution. This amazing confluence of rising commerce, new dominion, and early industrialization provoked a transatlantic discussion about the role of colonies in the empire: What benefits did colonists enjoy because they were in the empire, and how fully would they share in England's prosperity? To what extent should colonists help defray the costs of the French and Indian War, and help defend frontiers from Spanish and French interests in the future? Following 1763, inhabitants of the British Empire were propelled into an unforeseen, deeply consequential period of discussion about these issues, a period known as the Imperial Crisis.

Markets and Goods

The French and Indian War had a mixed impact on colonists. While some experienced economic opportunities, others encountered one difficulty after another. The war heightened demand in the colonies and England for iron, wood, and textiles, and brought new people into production of war supplies. Before the war's end, new

Iron Foundry of Peter Curtenius Despite Parliament's efforts to regulate colonial production of finished iron goods in 1750, mining and manufacturing developed at a rapid pace in the colonies. In 1767 Peter Curtenius took advantage of colonial demand and nearby sources of timber for fuel and iron ore to build a successful foundry outside New York City. At first, Curtenius's factory focused on making agricultural and household items; by 1775, the enterprise was poised to produce bayonets and small cannon balls for patriots. (© *Collection of the New-York Historical Society.*)

ways to harness water and steam power, new tools to fashion goods, and newly organized factories began to replace traditional small-shop production in England. These changes in turn encouraged new work and consumption habits throughout the empire. Innovative rules changed the ways colonists used their labor and leisure time and separated their workplaces more distinctly from home. New work arrangements in turn made possible the importation and production of more goods, and of higher quality.

After the war colonists imported more household goods—dishware, textiles, cabinets, notions, and the like—from abroad than ever before. By 1765, English merchants were sending about 20 percent of the country's exported manufactures to colonists, who enjoyed greater buying power and rising levels of comfort. Shopkeepers' inventories expanded, newspapers advertised imports from all over the world, and probate records of the deceased listed a startling array of fabrics, trinkets, tools, and furniture.

How did colonists pay for these wants and needs? The answer depends on the colonial region, and the strata of buyers and sellers. In most locales, agricultural exports provided the backbone of credits earned abroad. For a few years after the French and Indian War, western small farmers experienced a devastating decline of tobacco prices. By the final colonial years, tobacco prices recovered and production through the tidewater and frontier counties surged. Scottish investors subsidized the planting of new land in Virginia and Maryland, granted year-long credit to migrating small farmers, and set up stores that provided imported goods and accepted farmers' firkins of cheese, buckets of tar, and bags of feathers, which the storekeeper transported to the coast. Some South Carolina planters rose far above middling means to enjoy lavish lifestyles based on slave labor. Just as Parliament initiated a discussion that reshaped imperial policy toward the colonies, South Carolina planters aggressively marketed larger exports of indigo to England and rice to southern Europe.

The mid-Atlantic breadbasket benefited from a combination of rich soil, ambitious farmers, and a maturing infrastructure of crafts and local markets. Ship after ship departed the northern Chesapeake Bay or Delaware River laden with flour and wheat for the West Indies and southern Europe. After 1765, eastern European production of wheat fell, and England imported large amounts of flour and grain from Philadelphia and New York City. High demand abroad assured colonial farmers and merchants of rising prices, which in turn generated greater efforts to produce for export. The resulting prosperity of the Connecticut, Hudson, and Delaware valleys became obvious to foreign visitors, who marveled at the expansive cultivated fields and the comforts of commercial farming homes. Families pressing onto the frontier of Virginia and Maryland cleared lands to grow not only the ever-present tobacco but also wheat. "We are certain to find markets for our flour in the [Caribbean] islands, and to sell all but our wagon wheels to the merchants," boasted a Maryland miller.

New England producers were more diversified than mid-Atlantic colonists. The northern fisheries employed over four thousand men and over four hundred small craft in harvesting and drying cod and haddock for southern Europeans. New England merchants, sailors, and shipbuilders involved in the West Indies trade supplemented wheat and flour shipments with leather and shoes, shingles and wooden containers, and an array of crafts from Boston, Newport, Providence, Hartford, and Salem. Like New Yorkers, New Englanders invested portions of their fortunes in processing West Indies goods at sugar refineries, rum distilleries, and chocolate "manufactories." New Englanders also carried over half a million gallons of locally distilled rum to foreign buyers after the French and Indian War.

Indeed, colonists seemed to be recovering quickly from the French and Indian War and realizing unheard-of commercial and farming opportunities. Colonial and English writers noticed that items formerly treated as "luxuries," and accessible only to the wealthy, were becoming available to great numbers of middling consumers in America who had a "natural taste to refine their living" after the war. Together, accelerated production, falling prices, and aggressive marketing added up to what many scholars call the "consumer revolution" of the late 1700s.

Not all colonists experienced such rapid recovery after the French and Indian War. Indeed, large numbers of colonists felt the aftershocks of war for years. British troops stationed on the postwar frontier needed food and other necessities that colonists often withheld. Despite Pitt's promises to reimburse colonial war expenses, he authorized less than half of the standing army's continuing costs during the 1760s, which left soldiers with little means for paying their bills. In the cities, artisans and shopkeepers had struggled to fill orders for military goods, often on the promise of payment some time in the future. But after the war, some of them joined the "starving poor with naught but a will to live to sustain them" as they wandered from town to town. Thousands of young sailors lost their lives at sea on privateering vessels, and thousands of fathers and sons did not return home from western fronts. In New York City, Boston, and Philadelphia, the charity dispensed to widows and orphans depleted meager government resources. Small producers complained about shortages of raw materials—wood, leather, and farm by-products—which stymied their work. Consumers complained that wartime prices had soared and then not declined in the peace that followed. Colonists began to realize that although the French and Indian War opened up a huge western space for their future development, it also bequeathed a thick web of debts, unemployment, and uncertain commercial revival.

Individual merchants had made direct loans to colonial governments from their own fortunes, and by 1763, they clamored for repayment. And although some merchants had profited handsomely from raiding enemy ships or smuggling to Cuba, Martinique, or the coastline of Honduras, many had risked their ships and goods and lost everything. Among the merchants who tried to meet colonists' huge demand for imported goods after the war, many fell deeply into debt to English creditors. English creditors usually required silver, gold, or bills of exchange as forms of payment, but colonial merchants often did not have enough of these after the war and frequently failed to make their payments. In 1765 a few of the most reputable merchants of New York and Philadelphia went bankrupt, sending shivers through urban populations and calling forth renewed warnings against consuming "luxuries and superfluities."

Legislating Obedience

The Great War for Empire was a crushing burden to the English treasury. By 1763, the country's debt to soldiers who had been quartered in the colonies, and to creditors who had loaned the government huge sums, approached an unprecedented £130 million. How would such a debt be paid? British officials such as William Pitt, Charles Townshend, and Thomas Pownall—who rose in power along with the progress of the recent war—blamed the North American colonists for the problem. Colonists, they argued in Parliament, had refused to raise sufficient taxes for the war effort. Worse, they had systematically evaded the Acts of Trade and Navigation, elevating smuggling with French possessions to an art. Now, they continued, the empire's prosperity and power depended on enforcing colonial economic obedience and political subordination.

Parliament began to implement its harsher perspective in 1761. It urged colonial governors to clamp down on the illegal entry of foreign goods and end the widespread practice of bribing officials to overlook customs duties. Beginning in Massachusetts, the governor issued documents called Writs of Assistance, which permitted port collectors to inspect the holds of ships and merchants' warehouses for illegal goods. James Otis, a prominent lawyer from a highly reputable family, assailed the writs as an invasion of private property. In a famous argument before the Massachusetts Supreme Court in 1761, Otis insisted that protection of a citizen's private property must be held in higher regard than a parliamentary statute. The writs, Otis argued, violated "the [unwritten] English Constitution," which in turn guarded "customary practice" or "fundamental law"—that is, the basic natural rights of all citizens. But Otis lost his case. Most legal experts at that time did not share Otis's point of view. Instead, they still believed that parliamentary law and custom had equal weight. In addition, the Writs of Assistance case bore on merchants' business, but it did not touch most people's daily affairs directly and so did not attract widespread attention.

The British government continued to pass stringent legislation intended to make colonists subordinate to the interests of the crown and Parliament. In 1761 Lord Bute had been appointed secretary of state and first lord of the treasury by the young King George III (reigned 1760–1820). In 1762, as a step toward halting the illegal trade between colonists and the foreign Caribbean islands, Bute steered the Revenue Act through Parliament. The act prohibited crown-appointed customs officials from subcontracting their jobs to other men, who depended on bribes from merchants to pay the appointed officials for the privilege of holding such positions. The act also authorized royal navy ship captains to seize all British vessels trading at French islands. Bread, shoes, and timber had been "flowing in profitable channels to the popish merchants of the [French] islands," lamented a British soldier, "while our regulars starve in their naked feet" on the American frontier.

Bute resigned in 1763, and the task of shoring up British finances fell to George Grenville. Early in his short term, Grenville became widely unpopular in England because he attempted to arrest a popular parliamentary representative, John Wilkes, for seditious libel against the crown. Although the radical Wilkes fled safely to France, Grenville's actions led to rising public demands for freedom of the press. When Grenville attempted to raise land taxes, wealthy English landowners dug in their heels and refused additional taxes on their estates. In addition, a recession in England made it hard to squeeze middling and lower-rung consumers with higher excise and luxury taxes. The average English consumer or small producer sometimes paid as much as one-third of her or his income to sheriffs and county tax collectors.

By contrast, colonists paid very little, most no more than 5 percent of their incomes, on taxes to local and provincial government; and they seemed to be ordering huge quantities of goods from English merchants following pent-up wartime demand. Indeed, British policymakers believed that colonists were in a better position to help pay the debts of the French and Indian War than were the people of England. But Grenville knew that colonists would resist higher taxes and opposed Parliament's proposal to raise them. The legislation that Parliament passed ensured that colonists would not be asked to defray the British national debt, but only to help offset the cost of keeping ten thousand troops in North America.

But to colonists, Grenville's revenue proposals did not seem mild at all. They already associated him with enforcement of the Proclamation Line and vilification of popular colonial smugglers and privateers. Now, making colonists pay for regiments of the standing army during peacetime seemed authoritarian and unjust. Postwar ministries had vowed they would govern by persuasion and compromise, but Grenville was spouting hard-line mercantilist reasoning that reduced the colonies to minor satellites of the glorious imperial center in London.

In 1764 the Grenville ministry's Sugar Act extended the terms of the Revenue Act. It combined the battle against smuggling with the search for revenue. Crown officials in residence at colonial posts now had to extract huge amounts of paperwork from captains and merchants. Failure to have the proper papers made illicit traders more vulnerable to capture after 1764, and quick prosecution of naval laws in the crown's vice-admiralty courts kept violators away from "democraticall" colonial juries and assemblies.

Colonists loudly protested the Sugar Act's duty of three-pence per gallon on molasses. Since passage of the Molasses Act in 1733 (see page 108), foreign sugar, molasses, and rum had been taxed at higher levels than equivalent British goods in hopes of making British commodities more competitive. But crown officials barely enforced the Molasses Act, so New England merchants bought cheap French and Spanish molasses for their expanding rum distilling enterprises. In this trade, colonial merchants also sold large amounts of farm produce, timber, and flour. As payment, in addition to molasses and sugar, they received silver and paper credit that was used to offset debts to English merchants for the manufactured goods colonists imported. This web of trade was absolutely necessary for the survival of the empire, argued colonial merchants.

Nevertheless, the Sugar Act created conditions that had long-term repercussions for relations between the colonies and England. Unlike earlier mercantilist legislation, the Sugar Act combined explicit revenue-raising provisions with enforcement machinery. The act affirmed the right of royal government to tax the property of colonial merchants and exact their obedience.

Colonists reacted to the Sugar Act swiftly but moderately. The colonial assemblies petitioned for its repeal, but raised no serious challenge to the right of Parliament to regulate and tax them. Only a few voices insisted that "all Taxes ought to originate with the people." Some traders simply evaded the law and continued smuggling with impunity. Others corresponded with fellow merchants, expressing their irritation with the increased number of surprise searches. In New York and Boston, merchants called on urban artisans and shopkeepers to support a movement to halt imports from England until Parliament repealed the Sugar Act. This first attempt to organize a generalized boycott (see page 161) did not win widespread support, however, because the act had little direct impact on most colonists. In a short time, colonists resumed trade as usual.

Shortly thereafter, Parliament sent the Currency Act to the colonies. This measure prohibited colonists from printing any more paper money (see pages 107–108) and ordered the withdrawal of existing colonial currency from circulation by 1769. Merchants in London objected that colonial paper currency reduced the value of British goods when Americans converted their local monies for international exchange. Colonial paper money also violated a central maxim of that era: that all "artificial" currency had to be backed by sufficient "funds" of truly valuable gold and silver. Colonists simply let their currency "float on the crest of public trust," which could collapse at any time under the weight of public and private debt.

Grenville added the Quartering Act in early 1765, which authorized army commanders in the colonies to requisition supplies from assemblies and build barracks for troops or quarter them in public buildings and taverns. Although the act forbid the army from taking over private homes and warehouses—actions that had outraged many Americans when Lord Loudoun commanded French and Indian War forces—soldiers seemed to swarm through northern colonial cities. Already overcrowded and coping with great postwar poverty and joblessness, cities became quite unfriendly places to house redcoats, as we shall see.

Deepening Commitment, Rising Violence, 1765–1770

Until 1765, colonists believed that Parliament's new laws were misguided but justifiable attempts to create commercial and legal order for the mutual benefit of all imperial inhabitants. But subsequent laws seemed to betray different parliamentary intentions and different colonial consequences. Beginning in 1765, new policies disrupted widespread colonial habits of consumption, challenged cherished assembly privileges, and undermined the principle of reciprocal benefits throughout the empire by insisting on colonial subordination to the sovereignty of Parliament. As they experienced the Stamp Act, the Townshend Duties, the Boston Massacre, and the Tea Act, colonists began to see a deliberate design to deprive them of natural liberties.

The Stamp Act Crisis

To house and supply the British troops in the colonies in 1765, the Grenville ministry turned to a common English source of revenue: a stamp tax. Since 1694, fees collected from stamping certain documents or taxing particular commodities had been an important source of revenue in the home country. Even some of the colonies had experimented with stamp taxes from time to time. Why, then, did colonists raise a storm of protest when they received word of Parliament's Stamp Act, due to take effect in 1765?

In part, the sweep of the act was alarming to colonists. The measure levied taxes on court documents, contracts, playing cards, land titles, newspapers, and most other printed items. Even more important, Parliament had imposed a tax on "internal commerce," colonists' daily exchanges of necessary goods and services. Previously, colonists had legislated most of their own domestic tax needs, while Parliament had taxed external affairs, especially international commerce. The Stamp Act shattered this tradition.

Eight colonial assemblies discussed openly the extent of Parliament's authority over them. Although most assemblymen admitted Parliament's right to tax, they differed over whether that authority was absolute or limited. If limited with respect to taxation, then in what other ways might Parliament's power be limited? If absolute, then what was the nature of colonial assembly jurisdiction over revenue? Many voices insisted that although Parliament had sole authority to tax and regulate international commerce, only the provincial assemblies could levy taxes on colonists' internal business and property. For decades, colonists called internal taxes a "gift of the people," delegated to their duly elected representatives, by their free consent. Colonists had gradually conferred on their "little parliaments" in each colony sole authority to initiate money bills, allocate funds for public projects, and set levels of taxation. Even Grenville admitted that colonists should be taxed "only with their own Consent."

Colonists raised still another question: How could they give or withhold consent for parliamentary legislation when they did not have representatives in that body? British leaders countered that parliamentary legislators "virtually" represented everyone in the empire, but this argument did not convince many colonists. Benjamin Franklin proposed that "if you chuse to tax us, give us Members in your Legislature [Parliament], and let us be one People." But officials in England rejected Franklin's idea. Colonists lived too far away to be incorporated into Parliament. In any event, theory and policy held that colonists had to remain subordinate members of the empire.

In May 1765, young Patrick Henry rose in the Virginia assembly to give a radical interpretation of events. Virginians, he stated, enjoyed all the privileges of British citizens in the empire, including the right of self-taxation. No laws that originated outside their colony required Virginians' obedience. The Virginia assembly voted down the Henry plan, but newspapers published his *Virginia Resolves* widely, alongside the many newspaper protests appearing by mid-1765. By then, the Stamp Act had begun to touch the lives of colonists in all economic strata, from city to country, from New England to Georgia. Critics denounced not only the pocketbook effect that the act would have on average citizens, but also its unconstitutional nature.

The Sons of Liberty

Protests against the Stamp Act spread beyond representative assemblies, into the shops, inns, and streets of towns throughout the colonies. In August 1765, a group of merchants, artisans, and shopkeepers in Boston called the Loyal Nine organized

Patrick Henry The young Virginia lawyer and colonial assemblyman was one of the first, and most radical, southerners to become an ardent patriot. Beginning with his authorship of the Virginia Stamp Act Resolution in 1765, and continuing through the stormy final months of the Continental Congress in 1775, Henry never wavered in his zeal for individual rights and popular liberty. *(Colonial Williamsburg Foundation.)*

a mass demonstration of city inhabitants, which marched through the streets and hung an effigy of Andrew Oliver, the colony's stamp distributor. Through the night, bonfires lit up the city and protesters cried for Oliver's resignation. Although Oliver pledged not to enforce the Stamp Act, the crowd's actions continued until the night of August 26, when a mob pulled down the wealthy Lieutenant Governor Thomas Hutchinson's house.

Meanwhile, in New York City, merchants and tradesmen joined together to form the Sons of Liberty, a coalition of urban dissenters who sought to join citizens throughout North America together against the Stamp Act. Sons of Liberty groups formed quickly in every colonial city from Portsmouth, New Hampshire, to Charles Town, South Carolina. Middling colonists joined the Sons in order to play a greater role in politics "out of doors"; some members of the elite joined in hopes of controlling angry mobs. Even the most radical members of the elite, including Christopher Gadsden of Charles Town and Samuel Adams of Boston, worried that the Sons of Liberty would discredit the protest movement by engaging in excessive violence.

Hundreds of colonists joined leaders of the Sons of Liberty at a pan-colonial Stamp Act Congress in New York in October 1765. Delegates from nine colonies formulated a bold "Declaration of Rights and Grievances" that set forth their view of the proper limits of British rule in the colonies. Parliament, the declaration stated, did not have the right to tax colonists without their legislative consent. The delegates demanded repeal of the Stamp and Sugar Acts because they infringed on American "rights and liberties." Merchants, rising smaller traders, and artisan entrepreneurs at the Congress also protested the Stamp Act's undermining of regular trading relations. In October, about two hundred merchants in New York City and Albany called for a nonimportation movement. Several women called "she merchants" joined the protest, and hundreds of consumers in New York agreed that halting merchants' orders for goods would help bring Parliament to its knees. Shortly thereafter, their Boston and Philadelphia compatriots also agreed to suspend orders for English goods. Hundreds of urban merchants, artisans, and consumers signed agreements to boycott British imports and produce more of their own "necessities."

Even with this organized resistance underway, crowds continued more violent activities "out of doors" in 1765. Reports of tarring and feathering officials who supported the Stamp Act appeared up and down the coastline. Peter Oliver, a loyalist to British rule in America, described unruly colonists heating "Tar untill it is thin, & and pour[ing] it upon the naked Flesh . . . After which, sprinkl[ing] decently upon the Tar . . . as many Feathers as will stick to it, Then hold[ing] a lighted Candle to the Feathers."

"Respectable" colonists criticized these activities as the deeds of a "rabble" and a "reptilian mob" that could lead the colonies into "anarchy." But few colonists acted spontaneously or randomly, and most protest actions involved little more than ridicule and ostracism as means of punishing their enemies. Even at times of violence, the Sons of Liberty carefully chose their targets before crowds entered the streets, and the targets tended to be property, not persons. Andrew Oliver and Thomas Hutchinson went unharmed amid mob actions. Jared Ingersoll, a prominent resident of Connecticut, at first opposed the Stamp Act but then volunteered to collect provincial taxes under the law's auspices. Confronted by an angry mob that demanded his resignation, Ingersoll capitulated and returned home peacefully. In November 1765, about three thousand citizens raged through New York's streets crying "Liberty!" and advanced on the homes of British regimental officers; but no harm befell them. That same day, a large crowd threw bricks at New York's Fort George, where a humbled and unharmed Lieutenant Governor Cadwallader Colden agreed to hand over the tax stamps.

This kind of urban crowd behavior had a long tradition in England and its colonies. For generations, Britons had formed mob protests against Catholics and Jews, "usurious" merchants and greedy millers, or prostitutes and excisemen. Every November 5, zealous Protestants burned the pope in effigy and celebrated Catholic Guy Fawkes's failure to destroy English government in 1605. Fishermen, artisans, and laborers in every colonial port had, from time to time, rioted against being forced into the royal navy. In 1765 Stamp Act rioters drew on this varied tradition of joining poor and middling citizens together to protect economic self-interest, jobs, and businesses, and to voice deep-seated fears that crown authority could become overblown and tyrannical. Their arguments and the nature of their popular resistance were not new. However, they occurred more frequently than in the past and contributed to a generalized breakdown of deference toward crown authority.

The frequent cry of "Liberty!" during the Imperial Crisis also sounded familiar to most colonists, for it was the term used for centuries to invoke the individual's birthright to be shielded from governments that tried to usurp life and property. Liberty guaranteed personal rights to acquire and enjoy property, exercise civil responsibilities in society, and defend fellow citizens from internal and external threats to liberty.

Colonists were also familiar with writings that warned them to be vigilant over the delicate balance between good government and power-hungry interests that could corrupt the public good. These republican writings insisted that it was the duty of Parliament to check the crown's tendency to grasp at power, especially in the form of excessive taxes and expensive war chests. In order to detect infringements of liberty, republican representatives had to be selfless and public-spirited, "virtuous" to a fault. In 1765, when colonists raised the cry "Liberty and Property!" they believed Parliament was not protecting their liberties. To the contrary, Parliament had brushed aside colonial consent, denied them direct representation, and passed a series of unjust laws against colonists' property. They rushed into protests, invoking their republican heritage. But at that time, most colonists hoped for repeal of bad laws and a return to normal. Very few of them challenged the authority of Parliament and crown to govern.

By the time the Stamp Act Congress's declaration reached Parliament late in 1765, the king had replaced Grenville with Lord Rockingham, a "softer mind" who viewed America as a continent of vast productive potential and commercial markets for English manufactures. Rockingham agreed with London merchants that colonial nonimportation was seriously harming imperial commercial interests. Along with Old Whigs who favored compromise with colonists, he agreed to work for repeal of the Stamp Act. But hard-liners in Parliament held a majority, and they were incensed at reports of violence against port officials in America. In March 1766, Rockingham and the Old Whigs compromised with the hard-liners: Parliament repealed the Stamp Act but added the Declaratory Act, a strong restatement of its sovereign power to "bind the colonies and people of America in all cases whatsoever."

Colonists greeted news of the Stamp Act's repeal with a mixture of celebration and suspicion. Some believed that the nonimportation movement had forced Parliament to back off. Others pointed to measures that still irritated colonists. The New York assembly, for example, refused to comply with the 1765 Quartering Act. Only in 1767, when Parliament passed a Restraining Act suspending the assembly's activities until it supplied the resident army regiments, did New Yorkers reluctantly obey the law to quarter redcoats.

The Townshend Duties Crisis

Rockingham's ministry collapsed following the repeal of the Stamp Act, and the king appointed William Pitt, the hero of the French and Indian War, as prime minister. Pitt, chronically ill with gout, handed over the ministry to the Chancellor of the Exchequer, Charles Townshend, in 1767. Townshend had served for many years on the Board of Trade, the crown-appointed body that oversaw commercial affairs, and he supported parliamentary hard-liners who wished to tax colonists more. However, Townshend shifted the focus of colonial taxation in two ways. First, instead of using taxes to pay war debts and billet British soldiers in America, he proposed to use them to pay salaries of governors, customs officials, and judges, thereby freeing them from dependence on colonial legislatures. Colonial assemblies stood to lose their hard-won "power of the purse-strings" as political leverage against salaried crown appointees. Second, Townshend diverted revenue collection from internal to external trade, hoping to address colonial complaints about their rights and win their compliance.

However the duties passed by Parliament in 1767 aroused colonial resentments once again. The extensive list of items Townshend proposed to tax—imports such as paper, paint, lead, glass, and tea—would translate into huge financial sacrifices for colonists. Moreover, Parliament established a Board of Customs Commissioners to enforce the Townshend Duties and assigned a number of new customs officials to American ports. Four vice-admiralty courts were set up in Halifax, Boston, Philadelphia, and Charles Town to hear cases of trade violations.

Resistance to the Townshend Duties arose quickly in the colonies. Captains and merchant ship owners became enraged for two reasons. For many of them, smuggling had become a regular part of their trade with the West Indies. Customs officials played directly into their illicit activities by holding out their palms for bribes. Now, the Board of Commissioners would enforce their authority to take one-third the value of every captured smuggling ship and its cargo, and the new vice-admiralty court justices would prosecute captures, earning them little more than colonial wrath. Sailors on board oceangoing ships also harbored deep anger when the new laws went into effect. For generations, crews on merchant ships had been permitted to buy and sell goods "on their own accounts" at ports of call. Merchants and captains accepted this activity as a harmless means of adding to sailors' meager wages. But imperial law now prohibited the sale of any goods that were not written on the official ship's manifest. Although the violence that erupted between sailors and port officials at many colonial ports during 1768 and 1769 may not have been directly related to the Townshend Duties, the new parliamentary laws probably cemented many resentments along the waterfronts.

When port officials entrapped Henry Laurens, a prominent South Carolina exporter, on a minor technicality regarding a ship's entry and recording of cargo, colonists buzzed with indignation. When officials boarded John Hancock's sloop *Liberty* in Boston in June 1768, and subsequently seized it on the grounds that he held undeclared (and thus untaxed) imports in the hold of the vessel, townspeople reacted openly. An angry crowd gathered on the docks, threw the offending agents into the water, and marched to the customhouse to recover stores of goods held there. Hancock, one of North America's wealthiest merchants and a popular wine, paper, tea, and silk smuggler, eventually went to a vice-admiralty court for trial. The conditions under which he was tried outraged Bostonians. No jury heard his case, surly justices employed "judge-made law," prosecution witnesses gave perjured statements, and defense lawyers were denied certain rights in the "crown's court." As word about these conditions spread, the court was forced to drop the case. If such an exalted citizen's property and civil rights could be invaded so easily, asked many Bostonians, how secure could the rights of other "true born Englishmen" be?

The Townshend Duties also prompted colonists to consider whether they should allow any distinction between internal and external taxes. Perhaps, argued some, Parliament's authority over them did not extend to taxation at all. John Dickinson lashed out at the Townshend Act's external duties in his 1768 *Letters from a*

Farmer in Pennsylvania, twelve spicy pieces intended to arouse colonists to resistance once again. Dickinson believed that Parliament was almost always justified in regulating what colonists could trade, and where. On the other hand, it was *never* justified in legislating taxes to raise revenue on their trade without obtaining colonists' consent. Such laws, Dickinson argued, violated colonists' constitutional authority over taxation. Although he used strong words, Dickinson favored petitions and legislative responses to the Townshend Duties rather than violence.

While Dickinson argued about constitutionality, the Sons of Liberty led a new round of street actions in northern cities during 1768, and radical leaders appealed for a more far-reaching reaction to Parliament's new laws. Samuel Adams sent a "circular letter" to all the colonial assemblies in North America, proposing a united plea for repeal of the Townshend Duties and another pan-colonial congress. The Massachusetts assembly approved Adams's document, and the Virginia assembly replied enthusiastically. However, a copy reached the king's close advisers on the Privy Council, which ordered colonial governors to suspend the assemblies in the event of any organized challenge to the Townshend Duties. Meanwhile, Lord Hillsborough, the British secretary of state for the colonies, demanded that Massachusetts governor Francis Bernard force the assembly to rescind its approval of the circular letter. But Hillsborough timed his order poorly: ninety-two Massachusetts representatives affirmed the demand for repeal (only seventeen remained loyal to the crown) in June 1768, just as Hancock's trial proceeded. In both assembly and courts, said colonists, Parliament was assaulting "the cause of liberty," and "92" became a symbol throughout the colonies of resistance to arbitrary rule.

Colonists also organized another nonimportation movement in response to the Townshend Duties. In fall 1768, boycotters from Charles Town and Williamsburg in the South, to Philadelphia, New York, and Boston in the North, coordinated pledges to halt importation. Once again, merchants hoped to reduce the glut of goods in their warehouses. In addition, hundreds of shopkeepers, artisans, and housewives pledged to abstain from buying British goods for one year beginning January 1, 1769. Local newspapers printed the names of merchants who continued to import goods, and men and women vandalized stores in which retailers sold recently arrived British wares. Broadsides posted around Boston praised small producers and women for rejecting the corrupting influence of British "luxury and dissipation" and the goods "dumped on them, draining their very Livlihoods." During 1769, colonial imports fell by about 40 percent.

Unlike the first nonimportation movement, the second one brought together colonists of every social layer, in all regions, and in very large numbers. The boycott drew in consumers and small producers who never paid port duties or wrote orders to London merchants, but who dreaded the rising prices for items covered under the new acts. Daughters of Liberty, women of elite and middling means, denounced tea consumption in 1769. By early 1770, numerous rural women joined them and pledged to drink only "rye coffee" sweetened with maple syrup from their own woodlots. In Boston in early 1770, over three hundred "ladies of patriotic leanings" vowed to forgo imported sugar, tea, coffee, molasses, and "other superfluities." Women in New York City issued statements of solidarity to merchants, noting that their boycott of British imports was crucial to the movement's victory. In Providence, Rhode Island, women met regularly in public places to spin, while rural women in other northern locales announced their intentions to learn "the arts of weaving," a trade traditionally associated with men. Indeed, cloth making became more than a household task: when whole townships encouraged production of "homespun" and kept track of their collective progress, spinning and weaving became political activities. By denying their households the use of certain imports and supporting community textile production, hundreds of women were brought into public political participation. In all, thousands of colonists took another step toward translating their economic potential into a confident political community. Moreover, they began to associate the different roles of various colonists with a unified movement. For the first time, a number of colonists also identified people who joined nonimportation as "patriots," or defenders of longstanding political liberties against tyrannical encroachments from Parliament.

 ## Toward Independence, 1770–1773

While the responses to the Townshend Duties gained momentum, merchants and policymakers in England grew ever more concerned about how to restore imperial political authority. Together, colonial protest movements and the crisis of imperial rule created mounting fears on both sides of the Atlantic. Added to the organized protests and official policies, however, was the increasing level of tension leading to persistent scuffles in the streets, bitter dialogues in the newspapers, and unforeseen bloodshed years before colonists declared political independence.

The Boston Massacre

Lord North became prime minister in 1769. Although he was a firm believer in Parliament's absolute sovereignty over the colonies, North was also aware that nonimportation was creating serious commercial and political difficulties throughout the empire. On March 5, 1770, North stood before Parliament to seek partial repeal of the Townshend Duties. An ocean away on the same day, British troops killed five civilians in Boston.

Circumstances had been building toward the Boston Massacre for some time. Since October 1768, Bostonians had tolerated some 1,700 British troops living and mustering within their town of about 18,000 people. Citizens walking to and from jobs, markets, and taverns constantly encountered armed sentries and off-duty redcoats. Townspeople resented that rank-and-file soldiers were permitted to compete for scarce jobs and accepted wages lower than desperate local laborers needed for survival. Children, many of them war orphans, wiled away hours taunting redcoats; tippling soldiers picked fights at night in alleys. It did not help that Samuel Adams fueled bad tempers by circulating his own inflammatory printed versions of incidents, or that crown officials deliberately strolled on the commons with off-duty soldiers in their scarlet uniforms.

Word reached Bostonians in January 1770 that violence had erupted in New York City. Laborers, artisans, and young orphans had turned to violence against redcoats garrisoned there. British troops answered by tearing down the city's Liberty Pole, the rallying point in many colonial towns for planning protest activities, sharing information, and posting notices of general political importance. A week of clashes between citizens and soldiers ensued in what historians call the Golden Hill riots.

On February 22, 1770, Boston events heated up, too. Several children pelted the home of a townsman known to have informed against smugglers. The informer leaned out of a second story window and fired his gun into the crowd, killing a young boy. A mammoth funeral procession, organized by the tireless Sam Adams, channeled the public outrage temporarily. But on March 2, local rope makers and carpenters harassed, then beat, three soldiers seeking work at John Hancock's wharf. The number of mobbing laborers and soldiers grew quickly until a commanding officer intervened and took his men back to their barracks.

Then after a weekend of relative calm, citizens and soldiers collided violently. The evening of March 5 was moonless and especially frigid. Despite the cold, a large crowd began to congregate near the customhouse—long a symbol of hated taxes and crown authority—where a lone sentry stood at his post. Children threw snowballs and shouted insults at him, as they had on previous occasions. But this night, the crowd grew to alarming proportions, and the sentry called for help from a barracks nearby. Captain Preston and seven soldiers arrived shortly, positioned themselves in front of the sentry, and held their firearms in a half-cocked position. Although Preston appealed to a number of Boston gentlemen to help disperse the crowd, his men grew restless as heckling youngsters dared them to shoot. At a certain point, someone shouted "Fire!" and as one soldier tripped over a chunk of ice, his gun went off. The other soldiers also fired, though without any order to do so. When the smoke cleared, eleven citizens had been hit. Five of them died, including a sailor of mixed Indian and African-American descent named Crispus Attucks.

No British soldier could fire on civilians without an order from a civil magistrate, even in self-defense, under penalty of hanging. As a military commander, Preston lacked the authority to give such a command. So who could have shouted "Fire!" on that bloody night? Perhaps one of the boys unintentionally pushed an overwrought soldier over the edge. Perhaps Sam Adams used the opportunity to escalate city tensions to a breaking point. In any event, the soldiers retreated to Castle William in the city's harbor. In the months to come, colonial lawyers John Adams and Josiah Quincy, Jr., defended Captain Preston and six of his men against murder charges. The court acquitted all but two of the soldiers; these two received "benefit of clergy," or a branding on their thumbs, and were released.

The Boston Massacre shook colonists everywhere. Where, asked inhabitants as far away as Georgia, would the standing army's potential for tyranny over innocent civilians lead next? Were these murders, asked frontier people at Fort Pitt, the inevitable outcome of Parliament's ill-conceived designs and laws against colonists? James Bowdoin, a future Massachusetts governor, penned *A Short Narrative of the Horrid Massacre in Boston* to circulate the view that British soldiers had planned the assault for some time. Engraver Paul Revere did his part, too, to produce an exaggerated version of the massacre. He illustrated a popular broadside showing the soldiers firing point-blank, together, into a defenseless crowd. Sam Adams organized yet another funeral attended by thousands of Bostonians.

The Boston Massacre As this reproduction of Paul Revere's engraving of the event shows, the soldiers and citizens were crowded into a small commons as tempers flared the night of March 5. The accuracy of this depiction of the massacre is questionable, however, since written depositions at the trial indicate the soldiers did not fire in unison and no command to fire was issued formally by an officer such as the one in this image. *(Library of Congress.)*

The Problem with Tea

At Lord North's urging, Parliament repealed all the Townshend Duties except the one on tea in April 1770. The tea tax would remind colonists of Parliament's sovereignty. Most colonial merchants sighed with relief, since repeal meant they could claim nonimportation a victory and place orders for goods from English firms to restore their depleted inventories. The Sons of Liberty, supported by many artisans, requested that nonimportation continue until Parliament repealed all legislation passed after 1763, but consumers wished to purchase imports again, and the movement declined by late summer 1770. When the Quartering Act expired and Parliament repealed portions of the Currency Act during late 1770, colonists took little notice and instead returned to business as usual.

Then, in 1772, tensions between spheres of the empire arose again. Early in the year, the British schooner *Gaspée* ran aground near Providence, Rhode Island.

Already the vessel's crew had earned notoriety in New England because they had arrested colonists who violated the Sugar Act, plundered unwary colonial vessels at sea, demanded bribes at port entrances, and preyed on coastal villages for supplies and shelter. Exasperated local populations could not resist going out, under cover of night, to burn the *Gaspée* to the waterline. British authorities dispatched a commission to round up suspects and take them to England for an admiralty trial—a blatant violation of colonists' right to a trial by civil jury.

While the residents of Providence made sure that the commissioners found no suspects, the local "Committee of Correspondence" warned neighboring colonies about the incidents. The Providence committee was one of many being formed by 1772 in New England towns, and eventually in all of the colonies, to spread information and tie colonists of the interior to leaders in coastal towns. Resistance leaders sitting in colonial assemblies used the committees as conduits of propaganda to tens of thousands of widely scattered farmers and craftsmen. Once people were linked in this way, they also began to take sides on important issues and commit themselves to a broadening resistance movement. In March 1773, Thomas Jefferson, Richard Henry Lee, and Patrick Henry urged Committees of Correspondence to report regularly "to all parts of the mainland."

Then, in May 1773, Parliament's Tea Act shattered colonists' hope for repeal of the odious duty and restoration of constitutional equilibrium in the empire. The British East India Company, one of the two largest corporations in the world at that time and holding a monopoly on English tea importation from the East Indies, hovered on the brink of bankruptcy due to financial mismanagement at home and misguided military engagements in India. Since some Parliamentary representatives held many shares in the company, they were keen to save it from ruin. As a result, company directors and key spokesmen in Parliament together agreed that colonists must cease their extensive smuggling and buy more company tea. Lord North, convinced that the East India Company was a pillar of England's international commerce and defender of the nation's interests in India, accepted this reasoning. Americans, North insisted, must buy tea only from the company, and port officials must suppress all smuggling into the colonies from the Dutch and French. To these ends, Parliament passed the Tea Act, which waived the company's obligation to pay import duties at English ports and permitted the company to sell tea directly to colonists without colonial middlemen interfering. How, asked American merchants, could they possibly compete against such blatant favoritism and the Company's resulting low tea prices?

North and his supporters in Parliament expected colonists eagerly to choose the cheaper East India Company tea. But in the heightened ideological climate of 1773, a far different dynamic resulted. The committees of correspondence quickly spread news of the Tea Act. Parliament's new offense, said committee literature and newspapers, was no less than a conspiracy to abolish the economic and political rights of colonists. The Tea Act, argued writers from Boston to Charles Town, took away colonists' right to consent to all legislative acts. Their response should be a complete boycott of East India Company tea and intercolonial agreement to turn around all East India Company ships headed to their shores. In New York City and Philadelphia, merchants gained promises from harbor pilots not to admit tea ships. In Philadelphia and Newport, broadsides posted on trees and taverns warned of "warm pots of tarr and feathers" for selling tea. Uneasy company agents wisely resigned their commissions.

In late November 1773, an East India Company ship named the *Dartmouth* entered Boston harbor with 114 chests of tea. Customs officers inspected the vessel and announced that the owners and captain had twenty days to pay the required Townshend Duty taxes on their tea, just as all legal colonial importers did. If they failed to pay, the cargo would be seized and sold at auction. Two more ships with another 128 chests of East India Company tea entered the port. A New England Quaker merchant owned one of them. Rather than violate the patriots' agreement to resist the Tea Act, he announced his intention to return his ship, and the offending goods, to England. Boston leaders John Hancock and Sam Adams, who feared that disgruntled citizens would take matters into their own hands, pleaded with Lieutenant Governor Hutchinson to release the Quaker merchant's ship.

Hutchinson, however, was determined to enforce the Tea Act. Already, Stamp Act rioters had destroyed his house; the Sons of Liberty had stolen his private correspondence in 1768 and smeared his reputation; and the legislature regularly threatened to withhold his salary. So he was not surprised when, on December 16, just hours before the twenty-day deadline, thousands of Bostonians gathered at a public meeting to denounce him. About fifty men from the crowd dressed as Mohawk Indians and headed for the wharf, followed by huge numbers of others. In the next few minutes, a few of the disguised colonists boarded the *Dartmouth* and hacked forty-five tons of tea out of their wooden crates. Authorities later estimated the value of the tea dumped into the harbor at a staggering £10,000. When the Boston Tea Party ended, people simply returned to their homes.

"The Bostonians Paying the Excise-Man" This London cartoonist's view of disorderly conduct was intended to arouse British opposition to colonial demands. Here, under the symbolic Liberty Tree, on which the Stamp Act is nailed upside-down, colonists of various classes tar and feather a tax collector and force tea down his throat. In the background, a tea party is under way. *(Library of Congress.)*

Tea parties took place in Annapolis, Maryland; Perth Amboy, New Jersey; New York City; and other coastal ports. Shocked when he heard the news, George III warned Lord North that the issue was whether "we have, or have not, any authority in that country." "Concessions," stormed the king, "have made matters worse." In the spring of 1774, Parliament responded with four Coercive Acts—colonists called them the Intolerable Acts. On April 1 the Port Bill closed Boston's harbor until colonists paid for the ruined tea, a measure Parliament knew would throw the city into economic distress. The Government Act annulled the colonial charter, made upper house delegates subject to the governor's appointment rather than election, and restricted town meetings to one a year under the governor's supervision. A new Quartering Act ordered the colony to garrison soldiers in barracks or private homes. The Administration of Justice Act (colonists called it the Murder Act) permitted crown officials who had been accused of serious crimes to be tried in courts outside the mainland colonies.

The crown hoped to make Massachusetts an example to the other colonies with this combination of acts, which attacked almost every cherished political and legal ideal in North America. But the plan backfired. A new round of violence ensued in northern cities. In Boston, John Malcolm, a port collector notorious for extorting money from importers, experienced "how well he appeared in black tarr and coop feathers" in fall 1774. George Washington, in Virginia, responded to news of the Coercive Acts much as many others did: "The cause of Boston . . . is . . . the cause of America." The New York assembly declared the acts a "hostile invasion" and agreed to send food to besieged Boston. From many regions, Massachusetts citizens received words of support and wagonloads of supplies.

Quickly on the heels of these acts, Parliament passed the Quebec Act of 1774. Although the Proclamation of 1763 stipulated that French people in Quebec would have a governor and elected assembly similar to most British colonies, the Quebec Act granted Canadians freedom of religion, restored old French civil law, allowed Canadians to hold crown appointed offices, and extended the jurisdiction of Quebec's governor into the Ohio Valley. American colonists' anger flared not only because the act encouraged the spread of "papacy" close to their own borders, but also because it permitted Canadian expansion into the area closed to Americans by the Proclamation of 1763. Virginia and Pennsylvania land speculators who had long coveted the rich Ohio lands for colonists worried that they would not be able to renegotiate the terms of the Proclamation Line. In addition, land covered by the Quebec Act fell within Virginia's charter privileges to expand "from sea to sea." Virginians immediately declared the Quebec Act "utter despotism," clear proof of Parliament's plot to deprive Americans of their "true English liberties."

Forging a Political Community, 1774–1775

By 1774, many colonists had joined repeatedly in protests against the actions of Parliament or local royal officials. Many regularly participated in committees that gave increasingly coherent expression to colonists' grievances. A significant minority of colonists moved steadily closer to understanding that their time in the

British Empire was probably limited. But in 1774 political relations in the empire reached a qualitatively new stage when Parliament passed a comprehensive set of laws to assert its sovereignty. A congress of colonial delegates met and replied to this new level of parliamentary "tyranny" with joint statements and pan-colonial organizations. When dozens of soldiers and citizens shed blood at Lexington and Concord in 1775, colonists were already much closer to forging a political community separate from their imperial inheritance.

The First Continental Congress

In September 1774, the First Continental Congress convened in Philadelphia. In the first intercolonial meeting since the Stamp Act Congress of 1765, fifty-five elected delegates from twelve colonies (excepting Georgia, Florida, Quebec, and Nova Scotia) met to discuss the Coercive Acts. The delegates agreed on their solemn purpose: suffering alike from Parliament's "tyranny laid against our liberties," they needed to formulate a common response. They readily acknowledged their differences of religious persuasion, territorial claims, professional training, sectional economic interests, and political beliefs. These differences had produced petty jealousies and conflicting perspectives in the past and could render the Congress totally ineffective. While each delegate risked losing the confidence of people who had sent him to these 1774 deliberations if he did not satisfy their local interests, each of them also understood the need to identify a unifying cause.

Delegates first established that each colony would have one vote, ensuring a basic equality among all the provinces. They then discussed a bold document brought by the Massachusetts delegates. These "Suffolk Resolves" declared colonial resistance to the Coercive Acts and announced preparations for a military defense against British tyranny. Delegates from New York, Pennsylvania, and Delaware did not yet wish for such far-reaching rejecting of Parliament's authority over them. Pennsylvania's moderate Joseph Galloway proposed instead a "Grand Council" that combined colonial and imperial authority for governing and taxing throughout the empire. John Adams spoke for a more radical point of view: the time for shared rule had passed, he asserted, and the Galloway plan was a vain hope for reconciliation. In October, Virginia delegate Patrick Henry voiced an emerging belief in a new identity that opposed British rule when he declared, "I am not a Virginian, but an American."

Delegates compromised these points of view in preparing a Declaration of Rights that condemned the actions of Parliament while still recognizing the king's sovereignty over them. In the declaration, the Continental Congress underscored that all colonists enjoyed certain rights, which were secured by "the immutable laws of nature, the principles of the English constitution, and the several charters" originally granted to the colonies. While Parliament had the right to regulate imperial commerce, efforts to destroy colonial systems of justice with new admiralty courts, to decree internal taxes, to close their assemblies, or to revoke crown charters were unmistakable signs of Parliament's utter corruption. Colonists had rehearsed these ideas many times in the preceding years, but in 1774 their unified voice in a delegated Congress added significant weight to the charges.

Without waiting for the king's reply, Congress initiated a third economic boycott in early 1774. A broad intercolonial Association Agreement urged colonists to halt importation of British goods after December 1, cease exportation of colonial commodities to England after September 1, 1775, and pledge themselves to nonconsumption of English goods. The association urged colonists to "encourage frugality, economy, and industry, and promote agriculture, arts and the manufactures of this country." Further, delegates "discountenance[d] and discourage[d] every species of extravagance and dissipation," including many of the gentry's public entertainments, and they called on all "virtuous countrymen" to "break off all dealings" with violators.

Congress's declaration and association were important new steps beyond local and colonial Committees of Correspondence and toward shaping a national political community. The delegates' endlessly busy committees laid the basis for much wider public deliberation that spilled over into pamphlets and newspapers that circulated across colonial boundaries. Hundreds of Daughters of Liberty made homespun wool and produced substitutes for imported goods. Women in areas committed to the association eagerly enforced its provisions. For example, in October 1774, fifty-one North Carolina women declared their "sincere adherence" to the association by abstaining from drinking tea and affirming their "duty" to do "everything as far as lies in our power" to uphold the "publick good." Even after official nonimportation ended, women from dozens of small towns urged their neighbors to continue with modest forms of dress, scaled-down funerals, and less ornate holiday celebrations as signs of patriotic support.

When the crown dismantled provincial governments beginning in 1775, thereby severing relations between governors and the people, the habit of working through independent committees became stronger than ever. Thousands of colonists helped forge a new intercolonial identity by joining these committees, declaring beliefs openly, and punishing those who wavered or disagreed. In order to enforce the association and convene special courts to hear cases of infractions, Congress authorized Committees of Observation and Safety. These same organizations called out local and colonial militia companies from time to time, and they became important testing grounds for the new language of *nation, America,* and *states.* Large numbers of colonists still had not chosen between remaining in the empire or declaring political independence. Nevertheless, they took a significant step toward independence in early 1775 when various colonies formed "provincial congresses," or new legislatures, which established a dual authority alongside the governments still run by royal governors.

Lexington and Concord

Although many colonists concluded during 1774 that they could no longer live happily in the British Empire, when did large numbers of them relinquish their identity as British subjects and call themselves Americans? The answer varies, depending on the colonists' region, political and religious persuasion, and social and economic condition. Many continued to hope that the Association Agreement and Declaration of Rights would restore harmony in the empire, and long after 1775, indecision and shifting commitments marked colonial politics. But certainly in the early months of 1775, the patriotic cause gained large numbers of firm supporters.

"A Society of Patriotic Ladies at Edenton in North Carolina"
The British scorned women's involvement in public patriotic activities, as this London caricature makes clear. Here women are portrayed in many unflattering or scandalous poses, neglecting their children, mixing with slaves, and drinking heavily while they put their signatures to the Continental Congress's Association Agreement. *(Library of Congress.)*

Parliament once again discussed whether to punish the colonies or to seek a compromise. Hard-liners favored sending more troops to rein in the "unruliness of our children in America," and in early 1775 they pushed through legislation to restrict commerce to and from the colonies. William Pitt tried to soften these measures, but Parliament voted him down. In March, Edmund Burke, a parliamentary representative from Bristol and long a friend of merchants and great landed families in the colonies, eloquently appealed for conciliation. Further coercion, he insisted, would only alienate colonists from imperial authority. When authorities replace dialogue with military force, Burke reminded Parliament, "the cement is gone, the cohesion is loosened, and everything hastens to decay and dissolution." Far away in Virginia, assemblyman Patrick Henry made another impassioned speech at almost the same moment. "Is life so dear or peace so sweet as to be purchased at the price of chains and slavery? Forbid it, Almighty God! I know not what course others may take, but as for me, give me liberty or give me death!"

In Massachusetts, local militia members drilled frequently and towns stockpiled arms. The Committee of Safety, organized by the rebel provincial government, ordered the militia to be prepared to "rise up in a minute's alarm," hence the name minutemen. From Boston, Governor Thomas Gage responded to a rumor that activities had centered a few miles to the west in Concord. On April 18, 1775, he ordered about seven hundred British troops to seize supplies there. Riding quickly "to sound the alarm," Paul Revere and William Dawes warned colonists in towns along the road out of Boston that the British were approaching. At Lexington, about seventy minutemen met the redcoats, and after an inconclusive few rounds, eight colonists lay dead and one redcoat wounded. The British soldiers marched on to Concord, where they torched supplies and leveled a Liberty Pole. The smoke alarmed neighboring farmsteads, and soon great numbers of people flocked toward Concord. Over the next few hours, hundreds of minutemen and other citizens fired their muskets on the British redcoats. Refusing to fight in European-style formation, the minutemen used the camouflage of trees and stone walls, hid in barns, and popped out of farm buildings to fire repeatedly at the retreating regulars. By the end of the day, 73 redcoats lay dead along the sixteen miles of road back to Boston, and over 200 were wounded or missing; of the nearly 4,000 militiamen, 95 died. On the following day, thousands of Bostonians and country inhabitants came together to seize the British garrison. British troops and officials began evacuating the city by sea. Clearly, colonists had entered a new phase of resistance. But would it become a movement for independence?

CONCLUSION

In the wake of the French and Indian War, a series of events unfolded in mainland North America that at first seemed unrelated. Frontier violence erupted into the Cherokee War, the Paxton Boys' march on Philadelphia, the Regulator movements, and tenants' riots in many colonies. Urban tensions rose, too, some of them due to the usual postwar difficulties of reconstructing the economy, and others to the particularly heavy strains of this last imperial war in North America. Seen individually, or from a significant distance, any particular event could be viewed as one of the growing pains of an expanding and prospering people. Besides, asked many colonists, what did the affairs of a shoemaker have to do with those of an indigo planter? What did the troubles of Rhode Island have to do with those of South Carolina? At the end of the French and Indian War, colonists shared new lessons about paying for expensive imperial wars and the differences between their colonial militia and the British standing army. But within North America, their political and cultural identities remained separate.

Slowly, however, colonists began to perceive patterns in Parliament's thinking and actions toward them, and to experience patterns in their own responses to the tightening reins of political control over them. During the Imperial Crisis, Parliament moved beyond former disconnected policies to create a more deliberate plan for ruling the colonies. Its postwar legislation came in quicker succession than previous ones; its policies invaded colonial property and rights more thoroughly than previous laws. From the mid-1760s to the mid-1770s, colonists detected an intentional effort to suppress their liberties, and as their fears of tyranny grew, their protests intensified.

During the Imperial Crisis, transatlantic legislation and debate fueled profound political and cultural changes in colonial identity. At first, colonists relied on traditional forms of resistance: petitions, verbal appeals, pressure on neighbors and shopkeepers. As the frustrations of the Imperial Crisis continued, however, colonists added new forms of resistance, or intensified familiar ones: the Sons of Liberty, nonimportation boycotts, networks of committees, mob intimidation, personal violence. Public political activities also incorporated greater numbers of women of all classes, artisans, and servants. These would provide the seeds of a new, American, identity. Yet even in 1775, colonists remained fragmented in important ways. It was not yet clear that enough citizens wanted independence to declare a separation from the empire, nor did colonists envision what kind of society and governing structure might replace the British system. And most colonists did not yet think of themselves as "Americans."

SUGGESTED READINGS

Fred Anderson, *The Crucible of War: The Seven Years' War and the Fate of Empire in British North America, 1754–1766* (1999), is the most recent reappraisal of the immensely important events of those years. Another social look at the ranks is in Sylvia R. Frey, *The British Soldier in America: A Social History of Military Life in the Colonial Period* (1981). For political and social aspects of the French and Indian War, compare the important contributions of Naomi Griffiths, *The Contexts of Acadian History, 1686–1784* (1992); Francis Jennings, *Empire of Fortune: Crowns, Colonies, and Tribes in the Seven Years' War in America* (1988); and Howard Peckham, *Pontiac and the Indian Uprising* (1947).

For colonial discord on the frontier in the 1760s, see Richard M. Brown, *The South Carolina Regulators* (1963); Richard Beeman, *The Evolution of the Southern Backcountry* (1984); David Corkran, *The Cherokee Frontier: Conflict and Survival, 1740–1762* (1966); Bernard Bailyn, *Voyagers to the West: A Passage in the Peopling of America on the Eve of the Revolution* (1986); and Michael McConnell, *A Country Between: The Upper Ohio Valley and its People, 1724–1774* (1992).

Parliament's reassessment of the role of colonies is covered admirably in Thomas C. Barrow, *Trade and Empire: The British Customs Service in Colonial America* (1967); John Brewer, *Party Ideology and Popular Politics at the Accession of George III* (1976); W. A. Speck, *Stability and Strife: England, 1714–1760* (1977); and Robert Calhoon, *Dominion and Liberty: Ideology in the Anglo-American World* (1994).

For a readable account of the first legislation of the Imperial Crisis, and colonial responses, see Edmund Morgan and Helen Morgan, *The Stamp Act Crisis* (1965), and Ian Christie, *Crisis of Empire* (1966). For the Sons of Liberty, see especially Peter Shaw, *American Patriots and the Rituals of Revolution* (1981). For the deepening crisis in the late 1760s, see especially Michael Kammen, *Empire and Interest: The American Colonies and the Politics of Mercantilism* (1970), and for the increasingly violent 1770s see Hiller B. Zobel, *The Boston Massacre* (1970); Benjamin W. Labaree, *The Boston Tea Party* (1974); and Stephen E. Lucas, *Portents of Rebellion: Rhetoric and Revolution in Philadelphia, 1765–1776* (1976).

The process of coalescing colonial patriots and weeding out loyalists is covered in Ian Christie and Benjamin Labaree, *Empire or Independence, 1760–1776* (1976); David Ammerman, *In the Common Cause: American Response to the Coercive Acts of 1774* (1974); Richard D. Brown, *Revolutionary Politics in Massachusetts: The Boston Committees of Correspondence and the Towns, 1772–1774* (1970); David Conroy, *In Public Houses: Drink and the Revolution of Authority in Colonial Massachusetts* (1995); and Janice Potter, *The Liberty We Seek: Loyalist Ideology in Colonial New York and Massachusetts* (1983).

For the last phases of radicalization, see John Shy, *Toward Lexington: The Role of the British Army in the Coming of the American Revolution* (1965); Robert Gross, *The Minutemen and their World* (1976); and T. H. Breen, *Tobacco Culture: The Mentality of the Great Tidewater Planters on the Eve of the American Revolution* (1985). On the limits of radicalization, see Jay Fliegelman, *Prodigals and Pilgrims: The American Revolution Against Patriarchal Authority, 1750–1800* (1982), and A. Roger Ekirch, *"Poor Carolina": Politics and Society in North Carolina, 1729–1776* (1981).

The Southern Frontier Erupts

Regulators Explain Their Grievances, 1769

Repeated clashes with Native Americans west of the colonial lines of settlement became an integral part of the Imperial Crisis. On the southern frontier, Regulator movements of discontented frontier settlers grew strong in South Carolina and North Carolina by the late 1760s. Regulators demanded representation in the colonial government, regular legislative and legal government, and recognition of their expansionist land claims against Native Americans. In North Carolina, these grievances combined with hatred of coastal planters. Finally, in January 1771, rural rioters were declared guilty of treason by the colonial assembly, and in May at the Battle of Alamance, vigilante violence escalated into war. North Carolina Regulators from the town of Salisbury justified their protests in an open letter to the colony.

To the Inhabitants of the Province of North-Carolina
Dear Brethren,

Nothing is more common than for Persons who look upon themselves to be injured than to resent and complain. . . . Excess in any Matter breeds Contempt; whereas strict Propriety obtains the Suffrage of every Class. The Oppression of inferior Individuals must only demand Tutelage of superiors; and in civil Matters our Cries should reach the authoritative Ear. . . .

The late Commotions and crying Dissatisfactions among the common People of this Province, is not unknown nor unfelt by any thinking Person. No Person among you could be at a Loss to find out the true Cause. I dare venture to assert you [are] all advised to the Application of the Public Money; these you saw misapplied to the enriching of Individuals, or at least embezzled in some way without defraying the publick Expenses. Have not your Purses been pillaged by the exorbitant and unlawful Fees taken by Officers, Clerks, etc. . . . Have you not been grieved to find the Power of our County Courts so curtailed, that scarce the Shadow of Power is left[?] . . . In Consequence . . . very small Sums drags us to Superior Courts . . . many at the Distance of 150 Miles. Add to this a double Fee to all Officers. . . .

For what End was the Jurisdiction of the Courts reduced to such narrow Limits? Is it not to fill the Superior Houses with Business?. . . Is it not evident, that this was calculated for the Emolument of Lawyers, Clerks, &ct. What other Reason can be assigned for this amazing Scheme? none Brethren, none! . . .

Exorbitant, not to say unlawful fees, required and assumed by Officers, the unnecessary, not to say destructive Abridgement of a Court's Jurisdiction, the enormous Encrease of the provincial tax unnecessary; these are Evils of which no Person can be insensible. . . .

But whence received they this Power? Is not their Power delegated from the Populace? . . . we have chosen Persons to represent us to make Laws, etc. whose former Conduct and Circumstance might have given us the highest Reason to expect they would sacrifice the true Interest of their Country to Avarice, or Ambition, or both. . . . [But] is it not evident their own private Interest is, designed in the whole train of our Laws? . . . What can be expected from those whose . . . highest Study is the Promotion of their Wealth? . . .

. . . [As] you have now a fit Opportunity, choose for your Representatives or Burgesses such Men as have given you the strongest Reason to believe they are truly honest: Such as are disinterested, publick spirited, who will not allow their private Advantage once to stand in Competition with the publick Good . . . let them be such as enjoy no Places of Benefit under the Government; such as do not depend upon Favour for their Living, nor do derive Profit or Advantage from the intricate Perplexity of the Law.

Are you not sensible, Brethren, that we have too long groaned in Secret under the Weight of these crushing Mischiefs? How long will ye in this servile Manner subject yourselves to Slavery? Now shew yourselves to be Freemen, and for once assert your Liberty and maintain your Rights. . . .

Have they not monopolized your Properties; and what is wanting but Time to draw from you the last Farthing? Who that has the Spirit of a Man could endure this? Who that has the least Spark of Love to his Country or to himself would bear the Delusion?

In a special Manner then, let us, at this Election, rose all our Powers to act like free publick spirited Men. . . .

Address of the Inhabitants of Anson County to Governor Martin. 1776

Just six years after Regulators of western North Carolina deluged the colonial assembly with such petitions, hundreds of the same colonists signed petitions expressing their "loyal support of his Majesty in America." Following the Battle of Alamance, many backcountry residents continued to seethe with discontent because coastal leaders still ignored their demands. Their western discontent against eastern leaders easily turned into their loyalist opposition to the patriot planters in 1776, as the following outline of Regulator grievances explains.

Most Excellent Governor:

Permit us, in behalf of ourselves, and many others of His Majesty's most dutiful and loyal subjects within the County of Anson, to take the earliest opportunity of addressing your Excellency, and expressing our abomination of the many outrageous attempts now forming on this side of the Atlantick, against the peace and tranquility His Majesty's Dominions in North America, and to witness to your Excellency, by this our Protest, a disapprobation and abhorence of the many lawless combinations and unwarrantable practices actually carrying on by a gross tribe of infatuated anti-Monarchists in the several Colonies in these Dominions; the baneful consequence of whose audacious contrivance can, in fine, only tend to extirpate the fundamental principles of all Government, and illegally to shake off their obedience to, and dependence upon, the imperial Crown and Parliament of Great Britain; the infection of whose pernicious example being already extended to this particular County. . . .

We see in all public places and papers disagreeable votes, speeches and resolutions, said to be entered into by our sister Colonies, in the highest contempt and derogation of the superintending power of the legislative authority of Great Britain. . . .

We are truly sensible that those invaluable blessings which we have hitherto enjoyed under His Majesty's auspicious Government, can only be secured to us by the stability of his Throne, supported and defended by the British Parliament. . . .

Duty and affection oblige us further to express our grateful acknowledgements for the inestimate blessings flowing from such a Constitution. And we do assure your excellency that we are determined, by the assistance of Almighty God, . . . to contribute all in our power for the preservation of the publick peace . . . and to see a misled people turn again from their atrocious offences to a proper exercise of their obedience and duty. . . .

The North Carolina Regulators represented many, though not all, of the settlers and migrants into the backcountry in the last colonial years. The content of their grievances may have sounded strange to foreign visitors, and certainly East Coast leaders believed that the elite had a clear right to determine the rights and privileges of everyone in their jurisdiction regardless of changing circumstances or unique conditions. But from the Regulators' point of view, westerners were asking only for the rights and privileges to which all members of the empire were entitled. Regulator petitions used familiar language to ask for the extension of familiar institutions into their settlements. Still, neither side resolved these tensions before the Imperial Crisis ended.

Questions for Analysis

1. What specific grievances do the Regulators express in the first document? Are these likely to arise elsewhere in North America? Why or why not?

2. What kind of people do the Regulators project themselves to be? Do you believe the image is accurate? What would you add about their social status, lifestyles, and ambitions?

3. Explain why violent regulators in 1769 "abhorred" violence in 1776? Are there different kinds of violence? different purposes that activate violence?

4. Why do the Anson County petitioners pledge support to the crown in 1776?

5. What impact would Regulator beliefs have on forging a unified American identity during the period to come?

6

Winning Independence, 1775–1783

ighteen miles north of Philadelphia in late December 1777, Albigense Waldo, a surgeon in the Continental Army's Connecticut Line, watched exhausted patriot soldiers dine on "loathsome firecake," a pasty mash of flour and water. Of the dwindling army provisions, wrote Waldo, no more than twenty-five barrels of flour remained, and no meat, no fish, no salt at all. General George Washington's "ragamuffins" had just straggled into their winter quarters at Valley Forge, exhausted from fighting at Germantown, Pennsylvania, when they heard about the food shortages. To the cries of "No meat! No meat!" the troops added desperate pleas for something better to eat than the firecake that "turned their gutts to pasteboard."

Washington was ill prepared for the dilemmas that faced him that winter, and Waldo's reports offered the commander little solace. Officers had chosen to camp the roughly twelve-thousand-man army at Valley Forge because it lay on rolling high ground that could be defended from British attack and yet afforded a view of the British occupying Philadelphia. Washington also reckoned that Valley Forge was remote enough from the refugees fleeing Philadelphia to avoid depleting resources—food, fuel, and fodder—that would never be sufficient for both the army and the civilian population. Washington thought his troops could probably survive on the goodwill of local farmers and the abundance of nearby forests.

Instead, Washington recorded that his soldiers at Valley Forge endured "unmentionable distress" that winter. Even flour ran out by January, and foraging parties scoured the woodlands for small game. Soldiers lacked the most basic necessities of army life, including shoes and socks, jackets and shirts, soap, and utensils. They had lived for weeks virtually in the open and, now that the weather had turned cold, could not find craftsmen to build barracks. Washington ordered the men still fit for duty—about 8,200—to put up wooden huts fourteen feet square and sealed with clay from the rain-soaked ground. Each hut became home for at least twelve men; most had no straw for mattresses and slept on the frozen ground. Soldiers and camp followers crawled into the huts for days on end, emerging only to ransack nearby fields for corn stalks to boil. Over three thousand people died in camp that horrible winter, and hundreds of horses perished.

In their misery, the soldiers began to refocus their attention from fighting the British to finding scapegoats for their anguish. Many of them at first blamed the local farmers for withholding food and fuel. It quickly became obvious that troops, refugees, and civilians had "utterly scoured and laid waste" the region around Valley Forge. But supplies were not coming in from the outside, either. Licensed civilian storekeepers and merchant suppliers charged exorbitant prices to the troops for necessities. Wagoners embezzled supplies and sold them elsewhere or hired their vehicles to anyone who could pay cash. Rumors that farmers and millers were sending flour to New England almost provoked a general mutiny among Washington's men.

Then, too, some blamed the military suppliers, who offered "an endless stream of excuses" for failing to deliver essential goods. The army's Commissary of Purchases and Quartermaster General's department were devilishly unreliable. They had turned up precious little food, fuel, and fodder to send to Valley Forge, and yet they had "laid upon Congress very great charges for flour and pork never tasted" in the camp. Government contractors cut up blankets into four pieces and sold each one as a whole blanket; they adulterated flour with pebbles and weeds; and they transported wet gunpowder to the wrong places.

Despite the many examples of such "peculation" among both citizens and suppliers, few Americans knew that the primary sources of the widespread shortages were the transformation of an agricultural society into a war machine and the British blockades of their vital international commerce. By February 6, 1778, Washington wrote that his troops were starving and that "a general famine ravages the countryside" with "sickness threatening to carry us all away." The seven hundred women camp followers at Valley Forge busied themselves caring for the wounded, scavenging for scraps of fuel, and burying the dead. Still, even when soldiers began to desert the army altogether and to die in frightening numbers at Valley Forge, Washington forbid his troops from seizing civilian goods. Taking what was not given or sold to them, insisted Washington, would "corrode the moral fiber" of the Revolution. When American soldiers acted out of "selfish private interests" and "beyond the force of laws," their behavior was "unrepublican" and suited only the British regulars.

Chronology

1775	Second Continental Congress
	Washington appointed commander of Continental Army
	Battle of Bunker Hill
1776	Paine's *Common Sense* published
	Declaration of Independence adopted
	Cherokee attack North Carolina frontier
1777	Battle of Saratoga
	Howe captures Philadelphia
	Soldiers encamp at Valley Forge
1778	France enters the war
	Brant leads Iroquois in western Pennsylvania and New York
1779	Spain enters the war
	Philadelphia food riots
1780	Cornwallis invades North Carolina
	Dutch loans help the war
1781	Robert Morris becomes superintendent of finance
	Articles of Confederation ratified
	Cornwallis surrenders at Yorktown

Although the Continental Army at Valley Forge marched into battle six months later "in fraternity and brotherhood," their horrible winter highlighted important issues that Americans would confront as they sustained their war for independence and built a new system of government. Some of these issues concerned the character of a republican citizenry, especially when it tried to sustain a long revolution that did not succumb to the arbitrary authority of the English army and government. Others issues concerned the balance between political authority and individual rights. Even in the midst of their Revolution, Americans entered a discussion about what kind of government they wished to create and the character of the people who would live under that government's laws. They learned much in that discussion about their own frailties and contradictions—in particular, that no shared cultural, political, or racial identity yet made them one nation. Moreover, their discussion would continue for years after the Revolution.

▌ What ideas and experiences account for a large part of the diverse colonial population making the decision for independence, and these colonists' ability to stay committed at each turn of the war?

▌ Who joined the American patriots in the Revolution, who actively opposed independence, and who remained neutral?

▌ As the war progressed, what kinds of social divisions, shortages, and sacrifices did revolutionaries endure? How did revolutionaries win the war?

▌ To what extent were patriots motivated by republican values about individual character and the proper role of governments? by the desire for economic success and political self-government?

This chapter will address these questions.

 # The Decision for Independence, 1775–1776

It was one thing to petition for repeal of revolting legislation and burn stamp masters in effigy. These activities were typical methods of popular dissent in western Europe. It was quite another to set up a new government and raise an army against the imperial might of England. Yet that is what people in thirteen North American colonies did starting in 1775, even though few of them understood where such unprecedented opposition would lead them.

The Second Continental Congress

Colonial minutemen and citizens marched back from Concord to Boston in April 1775 and put the city under siege for the next two months. Governor Thomas Gage declared their activity treasonous but offered pardons to all colonists who turned in their arms and took an oath of allegiance to the crown. Very few did. Instead, thousands of patriots fortified Breed's Hill on the north side of Boston near Charles Town on June 16. The next day, General William Howe ordered his redcoats to assault the colonists hunkered down on the hill (and next to it, on Bunker Hill) in three reckless charges up the slope. The battle left more than 1,000 redcoats killed and wounded, including 92 officers, and nearly 450 colonists killed and wounded, most of them during their scattered withdrawal once they ran out of ammunition. The battle, known ever since as the Battle of Bunker Hill, was thus a British victory—although an extremely costly one—and enabled the British to hold Boston nine more months. At the same time, the battle convinced many northern farmers that—though untrained and poorly supplied—they could nevertheless effectively fortify a hill from which to combat the formal lines of the British standing army.

Elsewhere in 1775, royal governments collapsed as crown officials fled to safe havens or left the colonies altogether. Patriot leaders in the deteriorating provincial governments retreated into the countryside, where they created new sources of rep-

"Don't Tread on Me" A significant change from Franklin's segmented snake, which symbolized the divided colonies at the time of the Albany Congress (see pages 164–165), this image of the coiled rattlesnake on the flag of the Continental Navy became common after 1775. Army, militia, and naval flags abounded during the Revolution. *(National Archives.)*

DONT TREAD ON ME

resentative political authority. The first acts of these new governments including activating the Committees of Correspondence and arousing their militia to begin taking over "loyalist nests." In May 1775, Vermont's Green Mountain Boys under Ethan Allan, Connecticut's militia led by Captain Benedict Arnold, and the now-famous Massachusetts militia surprised and captured the British garrison at Fort Ticonderoga on Lake Champlain, New York. Other patriot militia occupied the fort at Crown Point eight miles farther north.

As this undeclared war dragged on, delegates convened a Second Continental Congress of "Confederated Colonies" in Philadelphia in May 1775. Like the first Congress, the second one was a voluntary meeting of representatives chosen by colonial assemblies to deliberate about matters of mutual concern to all Americans. At first, Georgia did not send delegates, stating that the colony was preoccupied with Creek attacks and slave resistance. But by September, backcountry settlers and Savannah merchants agreed to join other southern colonies that had entrusted Congress with their protection. The arrival of the Georgia delegation brought the number of colonies represented to thirteen.

Knowing that British officials would try to use Quebec as a staging area to strike at northern American provinces, the Continental Congress made appeals to Canadians in late 1774 and early 1775 to join its cause. Some colonists were certain that Nova Scotia would take up arms with them because of the large influx of New England migrants there. But Halifax became a tightly controlled British outpost during 1775, and one of the main cities to attract "loyalists"—colonists whose support for the crown endangered their lives. Similarly, the British military kept tight control of the multiethnic, multiracial population in East and West Florida. Assemblies of the British Caribbean possessions of Grenada, Jamaica, and Barbados opted to join the American independence movement, but the crown's military forces on the islands overwhelmed the rebels before they could arm themselves. In the future, these islands would also attract many fleeing loyalists.

So the thirteen colonies deliberated on their own. As a first step, the delegates resolved that "we must put ourselves in an armed condition" against the war in progress. Thomas Jefferson, a Virginia planter and lawyer who had steeped himself in Enlightenment ideas, noted the "frenzy of revenge" coursing through delegates' discussions. Colonists, wrote Jefferson, had a desire to raise "resistance in every corner of the continent."

But what kind of military force should Congress create? Most delegates reflected the general public's distrust of standing armies, especially since the French and Indian War, and asserted that they had no authority to create a centralized national institution. Perhaps the colonial militias would be adequate. Other delegates pointed out that the resistance movement "engaged a continent," which required a trained and centrally commanded force. Militiamen served short terms of enlistment; their loyalty often stemmed from serving under officers of their choosing and from their locales; and they balked at training or military discipline. A revolutionary war required very different terms of service. Furthermore, although militiamen proved time and again to be intrepid fighters, few went into battle with knowledge of sustained bloodshed and few understood that returning home between battles could be interpreted as desertion.

In June 1775, George Washington and John Adams presented a plan that addressed the objections to a standing army. Congress should raise a Continental Army of ten companies of riflemen from "among the best frontier marksmen" (rifled muskets had a much longer range of fire than conventional muskets) to supplement the Massachusetts militia now on the outskirts of British-held Boston. The next day, delegates voted unanimously to place the forty-three-year-old Virginian, Brigadier George Washington, at the head of the new Continental forces and dispatched them to the Boston area. A few days later, Congress gave Washington a staff of major generals and voted to issue $2 million in paper currency to fund the troops.

Congress had been able to create an army, a commander, a military staff, and an intercolonial currency without great public resistance because the crisis in Massachusetts demanded such measures in 1775. But the delegates did not constitute a central government. The Second Continental Congress had no authority to coerce colonies or citizens to support independence, nor had it defined the longer-range political goals of all "confederated colonies in congress." Some delegates favored an immediate call for political independence from the British Empire. Others openly denounced the gathering momentum toward such a split. Still others proposed a compromise. On July 5, 1775, John Dickinson of Pennsylvania presented the Olive Branch Petition to Congress, a document delegates voted to send to George III affirming colonial loyalty to the monarch, asking that British army hostilities cease, and proposing a sincere discussion of differences.

Although some leading colonists argued for compromise with the British government, many others sponsored stronger statements of colonial liberties. Dickinson himself helped Thomas Jefferson draft a Declaration of the Causes and Necessities of Taking Up Arms the day after Congress sent the Olive Branch Petition to the king. The Declaration of Causes denounced the actions of Parliament since 1763 and declared Congress's intention to defend the colonists' traditional English liberties with arms. In early August, a few congressional delegates began negotiations with Indians in the mid-Atlantic region, especially the Iroquois, to win their support, or at least their promise of neutrality. Congress appointed Benjamin Franklin as postmaster general in charge of coordinating intercolonial communication.

George III was still raging about British losses at Bunker Hill when he received the Olive Branch Petition in August. Lambasting the colonists as "traitors," "enemies of the Britons," he refused to read it. Congress now had little choice but to entrench itself deeper in war. In fall 1775, two regiments of the green Continental Army marched into Canada to secure support from citizens for the American cause before the British did so. General Richard Montgomery seized Montreal in November; Colonel Benedict Arnold trudged through Maine and reached Quebec in December. Montgomery joined Arnold beneath the walls of Quebec. Acting on rumors that their troops would leave when enlistment terms expired that month, the commanders attacked the city desperately on December 31. But redcoats killed, wounded, and captured hundreds of Americans. Montgomery died in battle and Arnold was wounded. Americans failed to take the city, and after holding their position outside the citadel for a few desperate months, the American forces retreated out of Canada.

As the Continentals marched north in late 1775, southern patriot militia forces engaged with loyalists, who took up arms in the countryside and in cities where redcoats had been stationed. In Virginia, the former Governor Dunmore organized slave regiments (see page 221) that defended crown interests bravely, but the colonial militia defeated loyalists, redcoats, and armed slaves by fall 1775. In retaliation, Dunmore's troops bombarded and scorched Norfolk, Virginia, on the last days of 1775, further alienating planters and small farmers from the crown's cause. Southern patriot merchants began honoring the conditions of Congress's Association Agreement, which stipulated a halt to all trade with Britain (see page 192). In retaliation, Parliament passed the Prohibitory Act outlawing all English trade with the colonies after December 1775. The stage was thus set for a long war in the South.

Common Sense

Although fighting had erupted during 1775, colonists did not rush to declare their independence from England. It was not until early 1776 that Thomas Paine, a recent English immigrant to Philadelphia, helped put into words the meaning of colonists' grievances and spurred deeper commitment to independence. While still

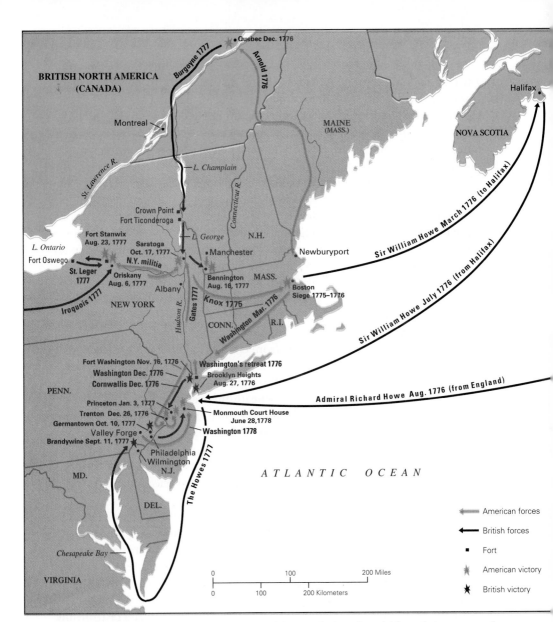

War in the North   During the first months of the Revolution, the British made important advances against Boston and Philadelphia. By early 1776, British troops began invading New York and New Jersey.

in England working as a corset maker and then a petty tax collector, Paine wrote occasionally against crown policies. But he did not express any special interest in American affairs until he befriended Benjamin Franklin in London, and only when he reached Philadelphia in 1774 did his popular literary talents emerge. Paine took a job with the *Pennsylvania Magazine* in 1775 and became friendly with congressional delegates who frequented the public houses. Soon Paine agreed to take up his pen for the patriots' cause (see Competing Voices, page 239).

Common Sense, Paine's masterpiece, appeared in January 1776. In it, Paine used language of "common sense" to wipe away "ancient prejudices"; his metaphors came from familiar evangelical and republican traditions. He restated long-held beliefs about natural law and justice in colorful imagery that colonists could, and did, quote widely. And he put ambivalent and tentative thoughts into bold formulations about right and wrong. Most consequential in 1776, Paine shattered patriots' last vestiges of loyalty to the monarchy. "There is something exceedingly ridiculous in the composition of monarchy," wrote Paine, especially government under the "crowned ruffian," the "hard hearted sullen Pharaoh of England" who "hath little more to do than to make war and give away [political] places."

Colonists devoured *Common Sense.* They purchased over a hundred thousand copies before midyear. More colonists heard portions of the pamphlet, or read reprinted excerpts in newspapers, than any other statement of political and cultural beliefs during the era. They read it aloud in public coffee houses, passed it around in neighborhoods and ladies' teas, and posted selections on church doors. Shunning the details of this or that objection to public resistance, Paine's argument became a ringing call to arms.

Declaring Independence

The reconstituted colonial governments in New England, Virginia, and the Carolinas created committees and built popular support for independence through 1775. Colonists in the mid-Atlantic region, however, hesitated to go this far. Instead, they looked for ways to compromise with their traditional assemblies and governors. But these assemblies had increasingly become the last official bastions of loyalist control. When patriots finally drove them from the continent during mid-1776, some rebel governments "declare[d] the United Colonies free and independent states."

In Congress, Virginia delegates put forward a resolution on June 7, 1776, "That these United Colonies are, and of right ought to be, free and independent States . . . and that all political connection between them and the State of Great Britain is, and ought to be, totally dissolved." Moderates from New York, Delaware, and New Jersey stalled significant discussion of the proposal until July. A committee that included Franklin, Jefferson, John Adams, and two others began preparing a longer document elaborating on the Virginia resolution.

On July 1, Congress took a first vote on the redrafted resolution. Four colonies cast negative or inconclusive votes: Pennsylvania, South Carolina, Delaware, and New York. July 2 brought better results. After an entire night of deliberations, Pennsylvania and South Carolina switched their votes, and Caesar Rodney of Delaware raced on horseback through drenching rain to weigh in for independence. For the next two days, delegates combed through Jefferson's draft, and finally on July 4 twelve colonies approved the revised draft of the Declaration of Independence. Dickinson did not sign the final version, and delegates from New York held out.

What Paine had implored the general population to do, Congress now made official: a final break with the crown. The preamble of the document, one of the most stirring passages in American letters, established the fundamental republican principles on which patriots rested their actions. There were, wrote Jefferson, "self-evident truths" embodying the "inalienable rights" of citizens, rights each citizen enjoyed from birth that could not be taken away by any ruling authority. Governments obtained their "just powers from the consent of the governed" and, as John Locke had taught during the Glorious Revolution of 1688 (see page 98), could be overthrown if they violated the trust and consent of the people.

But congressional delegates did not spend much time discussing the preamble—after all, some said, matters that are "self-evident" and apply to "all men" do not require debate—and moved on to the body of the Declaration. There, the document listed numerous ways that the crown had violated the public trust and foisted unjust and unconstitutional acts on colonists; in sum, the king was "unfit to be the ruler of a free people." After this "long train of abuses," Congress had little choice but to dissolve the bonds of empire and vest political authority in the people as a whole. For years to come, Americans struggled to shape this new collective authority, "the people," into workable governments.

Delegates signed one official copy of the Declaration and hid it. Copies that did not include the signers' names—after all, they had committed treason and feared reprisals from loyalists—rolled off the press immediately, and an eager public finally knew what Congress had accomplished. The American experiment had been launched.

The Revolution in Earnest, 1776–1778

While Paine's pamphlet was galvanizing public sentiment and Congress was inching toward the Declaration, the North Carolina militia had defeated a loyalist Highland Scots force at Moore's Creek Bridge on February 27, 1776. Washington's new army fortified Dorchester Heights near Boston and pummeled the British until they evacuated the city on March 17. Colonists successfully defended Charles Town from British attacks in June. Many Americans believed they had virtually expelled the British from the rebellious thirteen colonies by then. But had they? Hopes for a short war were dashed as delegates put their names to the Declaration of Independence: a massive British flotilla of men and materials approached Staten Island, New York. As the war ground on and on, the level of sacrifice demanded from citizens and soldiers grew to unimagined proportions, almost impossible to sustain. By the third year of the war, political doubts, vulnerable governments, persistent scarcities, and mounting deaths threw the War for Independence into the balance.

A Year of Exuberance

Britain's professional standing army ranked among the best in the world, and the royal navy was indisputably the best. But by 1776, half its naval ships needed repairs, desertion and mutiny had drastically reduced the number of sailors, and mostly very young and very old men remained enlisted in the British fighting force for the duration of the war. Over thirty thousand German Hessian mercenaries joined English, Scottish, and Irish rank and filers, and over fifty thousand Americans became active supporters of the crown during the Revolution. Supplying such forces would be a constant difficulty. American privateers mobilized every available craft to prey on British supply ships. In fact, so many British vessels carried basic supplies that not many remained available for blockading American ports. To pay for these shipments, British citizens bore the steepest taxes in memory.

Americans enjoyed the benefits of fighting on home soil, where the civilian population provisioned them more easily and the "rage for libertye" in 1776 buoyed men marching off to war. About 220,000 men from sixteen to forty-five—a very high proportion of patriot adult males—served for some length of time as citizen-soldiers in the militia or enlistees in the Continental Army. During the opening months of fighting, the militia used effective guerrilla-like tactics, familiarity with the terrain, and ability to identify and intimidate loyalist neighbors to build support. Militiamen, many Americans noticed, did not give up on the patriotic cause in appreciable numbers because they made frequent trips home and had contact with kin and neighbors during battles.

In contrast, the Continental Army marched far from home, and men served fixed terms of longer duration than the militia. In 1776 Washington projected that he needed twenty thousand men to create an effective striking force; during the following months, about thirteen thousand men enlisted. To fill the gap, Congress assigned troop quotas to each provincial assembly, which in turn ordered local communities to supply specified numbers of soldiers. Committees of Public Safety helped enlist servants, the unemployed, and unmarried farm laborers, along with male heads of households.

Although freedmen served in northern militia units from the beginning of the war, Congress initially barred slaves and free African-Americans from serving in the Continental Army. As the war dragged on, the New England governments permitted free black enlistments in the hundreds and allowed slaves to enroll if their masters approved. Southern patriot governments avoided enlisting free African-Americans, but masters permitted hundreds of slaves in the Chesapeake region to serve as their own replacements. In all, probably five thousand black men served under patriot command, often in separate units.

Despite such enthusiasm, Washington often noted the failings of his men. Troops had little conception of sanitation, cleanliness, or sobriety, he lamented, and when soldiers' leaves came up, they departed from camps and battlefields regardless of the military circumstances. Lack of deference to commanding officers and fraternization among the ranks of soldiers plagued efforts to conduct campaigns. Overall, the army was relatively untrained and poorly armed. These problems loomed larger when the British focused on taking coastal American cities beginning in July 1776.

That month, General William Howe landed 10,000 troops in New York, intending to take the city, move up the Hudson Valley, and cut off New England from the rest of the rebellion. In the next weeks, over 8,000 Hessians and thousands more British troops arrived, along with a steady stream of supplies and large forces under the command of Admiral Richard Howe. The British won a stinging victory over the Continentals in the Battle of Long Island on August 27, 1776. Over 1,500 Americans lay dead or wounded, a huge loss given the army's small ranks. Washington had little choice but to pull his remaining troops, a ragged lot of what he called "scum," first out of Brooklyn Heights, and then back to Harlem Heights.

As huge numbers of well-armed British soldiers poured onto Manhattan Island, a poor woman taking shelter in a cellar full of gunpowder torched the city. Fires raged for days, gutting a quarter of New York. Another woman, the wealthy Quaker wife of merchant Robert Murray, detained General Howe long enough to help Washington evacuate his troops to White Plains, up the Hudson. But Howe had just taken Fort Lee, New Jersey, in November, and moved against Washington's troops at Fort Washington, New York, as patriot troops settled in. Howe took nearly three thousand patriot prisoners. Washington fled with his weary men and camp followers into Pennsylvania, anticipating relocation far to the interior. Fearful as the British front line crept closer, Congress abandoned Philadelphia and fled to Baltimore.

But before reaching a suitable location for encampment, Washington received reports about British positions that altered his plans. On Christmas night 1776, Washington crossed the Delaware River with about 2,500 men to surprise and rout celebrating Hessians stationed at Trenton, New Jersey. A second victory at Princeton on January 3 forced the British evacuation of New Jersey. Washington set up camp at Morristown, and Congress returned to Philadelphia. But political leaders began to worry out loud that British commanders planned to keep New York City, take Philadelphia for good, and, with the middle ground secured, turn north and

New York City Ablaze, 1776 Although the accuracy of this image has been challenged because it shows fires starting in multiple locations and suggests that the British were the instigators, the New York fire did level a large portion of the city. Wooden structures near the waterfront were ravaged within hours, and in another portion of the city, destroyed structures became home for hundreds of runaway slaves who took refuge in the city. *(Museum of the City of New York.)*

south toward the more difficult areas of New England and Virginia. Congress's assessment of this divide-and-conquer strategy proved to be correct.

War in the North could have ended very badly for the Americans in this first year if both sides had accepted all-out warfare. But British and American armies both avoided frontal assaults; each hoped to press the opponent into surrender and to avoid decimating whole regiments. British troops normally did not fight during the winter. Moreover, commanders had been indoctrinated to put down rebel governments, not to destroy whole peoples and their ways of life. Besides, taking Washington's army would require compliance with the rules of treason and war: trials of officers, hangings of resisters, whippings, maybe deportations of thousands of citizens, with the inevitable alienation of whole regions from the crown's authority. Of course, the British troops committed arson, confiscated property, and looted storehouses, but they hardly ravaged populations and towns. Howe's men ranged through New Jersey, extracting oaths of allegiance to the crown, living off the land, and imprisoning a few selected officers.

Indeed, both sides remained relatively cautious during the first year of war. Washington tried to draw the British into the countryside, away from supply lines and civilian populations, and permitted his troops to make a few stabs against the enemy to bolster their morale. British troops along the coastline and in cities made little effort to take over the hinterlands. But it turned out that such caution on both sides probably prolonged the war. The retreat into the countryside certainly aggravated the difficulties of supply movement and troop recruitment.

Philadelphia, Saratoga, and Valley Forge

General Howe believed that once he had New York City, the next step, and perhaps the winning maneuver, would be to capture Philadelphia. England's minister of war ordered a three-pronged attack. General "Johnnie" Burgoyne would march south from Canada; Sir Henry Clinton would hold New York City; and Colonel Barry St. Leger would advance east from Oswego in upstate New York. Together they would reinforce Howe's Philadelphia campaign. But Howe rejected the plan as too dispersed and undermanned; he decided to attack Philadelphia by sea. In June 1777, Howe sailed with thirteen thousand men from New Jersey to the Delaware Bay, where Americans fired fiercely on redcoats and prevented river pilots from guiding Howe's forces into Philadelphia. So the British fleet proceeded to Head of Elk, Maryland, landing on August 24. Hessian and British troops marched toward Philadelphia across the upper Chesapeake and southeastern Pennsylvania, scorching the countryside as they proceeded. In the Brandywine Valley of northern Delaware, Howe's troops inflicted heavy losses on Washington's forces on September 11. Two weeks later, Howe occupied Philadelphia. Congress fled once again, this time to Lancaster. Washington attempted to quash the redcoats at Germantown, but failed and retreated to Valley Forge.

Earlier that month, Burgoyne had taken Fort Ticonderoga. St. Leger's nearly 1,800 soldiers and Iroquois besieged Fort Schuyler in August but retreated when Benedict Arnold marched 1,000 American militiamen and Continentals against the fort. Burgoyne's nearly 7,800 troops began a march from Fort Ticonderoga toward Albany. However, American general Horatio Gates ordered his men to impede Burgoyne's advance by laying hundreds of trees across the trails, thereby starving the British troops now stymied in the backcountry near Saratoga, New York. When Burgoyne tried to resupply his forces by sending about 700 men into the nearby forests, John Stark's New Hampshire militia, about 2,600 strong, routed the British completely. Although Burgoyne's 650 Hessians made a final attempt to take Albany, militiamen from Massachusetts, New Hampshire, and New York poured in to support Gates and decimate the British. On October 17 the patriot militias and army surrounded and overwhelmed the weary British troops, capturing about 5,000 of them and securing their munitions. Burgoyne surrendered at nearby Saratoga.

Victory at Saratoga proved to be a turning point in the war because it demonstrated that colonial militia and the Continental Army could rout the British forces. Securing such huge portions of the interior boosted public patriot morale immeasurably at the end of 1777, just as soldiers withdrew to winter camps. Yet events at Saratoga contrasted sharply with what the military and civilian populations experienced in the next phase of the war. After the first year of fighting, army recruits tended to come from the most desperate ranks of society, many of whom enlisted for three years in order to collect a small cash enlistment bounty and a signed promise of 100 acres at the end of the war. Henry and John Laurens, South Carolina planter-merchants and ardent patriots, promoted a plan to enlist about 3,000 slaves in the army with the offer of freedom at war's end, but they failed to garner enough support. Morale sagged seriously in the North and South when the currencies issued by individual governments declined rapidly in value. By early 1778, the value of enlistment bounties shrank to almost nothing. Also, many recruits wearied of life in the field, most of them never having been far from home before, let alone gone off to prolonged war. Some panicked in the face of heavy fighting, and thousands walked away from battle.

The wretched winter of 1777–1778 at Valley Forge strained all of the problems related to recruiting and sustaining the army to the breaking point. Indeed, the troops' winter at Valley Forge has become notorious as a severe test of military endurance and civilian support, as well as a defining moment of the American commitment to political independence and their republican character. Alexander Hamilton, a young recent immigrant from the West Indies who served during the Revolution as Washington's aide-de-camp, thought that all republican virtue had vanished and, with it, the foundation for a new nation.

Helpless to enlarge his army and secure its necessary supplies, Washington appealed to Congress for measures to stem its total demise from desertion and demoralization. However, Congress at first replied that a number of stiff regulations already existed for treating drunkenness, insubordination, taking multiple bounty payments, desertion, and other infractions of military laws. Eventually, Congress enacted stiffer penalties—usually physical punishments—but Washington and his officers could not uniformly and consistently whip or imprison every delinquent soldier—there were simply too many. Repeated attempts by a soldier to desert were supposed to result in the death penalty, but Washington rarely ordered it because an execution produced even greater demoralization among the troops. He preferred to offer soldiers incentives to return to camp. Congress also devised incentives, including bonuses to soldiers who enlisted for three years and larger land bounties for those who stayed for the duration of the war.

Training in field tactics and the use of arms probably improved conditions in the army after the winter of 1778-1779 more than stiffer rules of conduct. Help came from the timely intervention of a few experienced foreigners. Baron von Steuben, a Prussian officer committed to the American cause, trained Continental troops in field duty and distributed a drill manual to intermediate officers that helped prepare the rank and file for more efficient fighting. Two others, the French Marquis de Lafayette and the German Johann Baron de Kalb, joined Washington at Valley Forge during that terrible winter. The Poles Thaddeus Kosciuszko and Casimir Count Pulaski also helped create an increasingly professional Continental Army.

The French Alliance

The victory at Saratoga not only boosted American morale but also convinced the French government to ally with the independence movement. Eighteen months earlier, before the Declaration of Independence had been drafted, the French firm of Roderique Hortalez et Compagnie had begun to receive large sums from the French government to smuggle gunpowder, clothing, and military supplies to Americans through the pitifully weak British blockade. In December 1776, Benjamin Franklin arrived in Paris as an unofficial liaison for Congress, winning the hearts and minds of the French people and working secretly with the courtier, Pierre Augustin Caron de Beaumarchais, to secure French supplies and privateering vessels. Then, once Philadelphia fell to Howe, King Louis XVI (reigned 1774–1792) agreed that Americans desperately needed French aid; Saratoga convinced him that Americans deserved it. The French foreign minister, the Comte de Vergennes, and Franklin worked out two agreements in February 1778. One granted Americans open trade with all French possessions. The other recognized American independence, committed French forces to fight in North America, and relinquished all French territorial claims on the continent (though American diplomats recognized France's claims on any West Indies conquests it might make).

British leaders grew desperate to prevent France's entry into the war. William Pitt stormed in Parliament that an American victory would crush the British Empire, and then collapsed into an illness that killed him a month later. George III fumed that if the Americans won their war, the West Indies and Ireland would be next to rebel. Lord North, the hard-liner who had so enraged Americans during the Imperial Crisis, wrote a plan for conciliation that he attempted to deliver to Congress in June 1778. But Congress, hoping for a quick end to the war now, rejected North's overtures. On May 4, 1778, Congress voted unanimously to ratify both treaties with France, thereby creating America's first alliance with a foreign nation.

North's ministry in turn declared war on France and ordered General Henry Clinton to pull out of Philadelphia in order to concentrate his forces in New York City. Washington's more highly trained forces met Clinton's retreating redcoats at the Battle of Monmouth Court House in New Jersey. There, a number of women joined the Continentals in battle, including the renowned Mary Ludwig Hays, "Molly Pitcher," who took her husband's place behind a cannon when he fell. The British won the battle but retreated to New York City knowing they would encounter formidable Continental forces from that time onward. Attempting to consolidate their strength, the British evacuated Newport during 1778, used New York City as a supply depot and prisoner camp, and ordered supporters of the crown to abandon the countryside for the greater safety of the city. Indeed, except for a few minor skirmishes, the war had ended in the North.

The Character of War

The Revolutionary War was much more than formal battles. In thousands of parlors and kitchens, women, servants, and children made persistent sacrifices. In local committees, experienced politicians and inexperienced new officeholders grappled with the tasks of raising troops and mediating disagreements among civilians about a range of issues, including taxation. And in the halls of Congress, American leaders argued over policies for arming, feeding, relocating, and punishing patriots. These arenas of discourse and decision making profoundly affected the future character of American life.

Armies and Taxes

As good republicans, patriots saw the British standing army as a threat to peace and a drain on public resources. As a consequence, Congress's creation of a Continental Army evoked ambivalent, sometimes hostile reactions. Citizens who had sacrificed year after year for the public good grew disgusted when Continentals ravaged the "neutral ground" between army fronts for forage, wood fuel, and food from their gardens. In May 1779, a Connecticut man wrote that "this whole part of the Country are Starving for want of bread, they have been drove to the necessity of Grinding Flaxseed & oats together for bread." Yet the "armed soldiery somehow believe we hide our bread, and tear down our barns to find it." Washington's troops at Valley Forge tore up fence posts to burn; Hessians on Long Island did likewise, so that "the cattle stray[ed] away."

Many citizens struggled mightily to be "true republicans." Stretching meager supplies and turning used goods into valuable army wares became synonymous with patriotism. Women organized war aid societies that mobilized scattered resources into substantial contributions. In 1776 almost four thousand Philadelphia women pledged to produce "soldier cloth" in their homes. Volunteer organizations such as the Ladies Association of Philadelphia, founded by Esther DeBerdt Reed and continued after her death by Sarah Franklin Bache (Ben Franklin's daughter), solicited door to door for money to purchase linen to make over 2,200 soldiers' shirts. Townswomen in Northboro, Massachusetts, spun 2,600 miles of woolen yarn, which they subsequently used to make uniforms. Baltimore women outfitted Lafayette's soldiers in new uniforms before their march into Virginia in 1781.

Women everywhere turned metal plates and pots into bullets and hemp into rope; households gave every firkin, wheel, sheet, and dried onion they could spare. Women managed farms and stores while men fought far away. Young people delayed marriages and schooling in order to contribute their energies to the war effort in whatever way they could.

Nearly twenty thousand women became "camp followers" who marched along with troops as cooks, washerwomen, and nurses. Generals' wives, including Martha Washington, Catherine Greene, Lucy Knox, Deborah Putnam, Molly Stark, and Kitty Stirling, traveled with the moving troops from time to time, too. Women became indispensable workers, spending hours every day toting heavy pots, small children, and baggage through rough terrain. At times, women and children traveled with troops—British and American—because they would have endured worse conditions at home. Hannah Winthrop identified with the plight of the British prisoners captured at Saratoga who were marched through Cambridge, Massachusetts, in November 1777. Along with the soldiers, there marched "a sordid set of creatures in human Figure . . . great numbers of women, who seemed to be the beasts of burthen, having a bushel basket on their back, by which they were bent double—the contents seemed to be Pots and Kettles, various sorts of Furniture—children peeping thro' gridirons

Nancy Hart A legendary frontierswoman from Georgia, Hart wielded a rifled musket against six Tories who invaded her homestead when her husband was gone to a neighbor's farm. When the Tories ordered her to cook a family turkey, she killed not the turkey but one of them and wounded at least one other soldier. The remaining soldiers were hanged by Hart's husband on his return. Hundreds of patriot women remained alone on remote farms for months at a time during the war. *(Library of Congress.)*

and other utensils, some very young Infants who were born on the road; the women bare feet, cloathd in dirty raggs, such effluvia filld the air while they were passing . . . ." Prostitutes followed both armies as well, and although officials frowned on "consorting," they could not eradicate it. A military court, for example, charged officer Adam Stephen with "taking snuff out of the Boxes of strumpets" in 1777, but the court returned him to his command without further ado.

Although most American patriots agreed to sacrifice comforts, or even necessities, for the revolutionary cause, few of them expected the deprivations to last long. Most people comforted themselves with the prospect that "our sacrifices at this moment will set the terms for our great plenty" once independence had been secured. For some time before the war, New England and mid-Atlantic farmers and craftsmen had developed a thickening web of market exchanges that stretched far beyond their immediate neighborhoods. During the nonimportation movements of the 1760s and 1770s, colonists argued that their exports were vitally important to the growing populations of England, the West Indies, and Europe, and that by halting importation from England, they could bring its merchants to their knees. The success of nonimportation had been predicated on colonists' frugality, albeit only temporary. But colonists also professed that nonimportation would spur their own manufacturing and lay the foundation for greater self-sufficiency as a people. In the face of constant difficulties plaguing all layers of society, this hope in America's future prosperity made the rigors of the war bearable.

Despite this underlying current of confidence, the war sometimes seemed to utterly sap the energy and will of citizens. No matter how many sacrifices they made, Americans heard constant pleas from every political and military corner for still more. Above all, Congress needed huge sums of money to keep troops in the field. But it faced formidable obstacles to raising funds because provincial governments had their own wartime burdens and their citizens abhorred taxation from any quarter. Furthermore, Congress had no accepted authority to lay taxes on Americans, and it quickly depleted the funds that wealthy patriots loaned to the revolutionary cause.

In order to create the circulating funds necessary to fight the war, Congress resorted in 1775 to the familiar strategy of printing paper money—$6 million at first, but quickly growing to $200 million by the time it stopped the presses in 1780. And to surmount its lack of power to force the circulation of this money, Congress distributed it to the individual provincial governments and required them to pass the laws that would permit Americans to pay their taxes with this "continental currency." Congress hoped that each of the thirteen governments would withdraw its quota of paper money through these taxes, thereby keeping the amount of circulating currency low and public trust high.

But the continental currency system instead created a crisis of public trust. By 1779, so little of the money had been withdrawn that depreciation became serious. At the end of that year, it took forty-two "continentals" to buy one specie dollar worth of goods. In March 1780, Congress tried to withdraw continentals from circulation and issue new ones, but with little success. By December, one hundred continentals had the value of one specie dollar. Making matters worse, reports of widespread counterfeiting of paper currency reached Congress.

Even with the printing presses running night and day, Congress required ever more currency. One important addition to the circulating money was Congress's certificates to wealthy individual Americans, which held their value because Congress secured them with part of a $6 million loan from France. Other French loans, and then Dutch ones, increased the acceptability of these certificates, as well as the paper money still in circulation. However, foreign loans, though they represented important diplomatic alliances, amounted to only a drop in Congress's leaky financial bucket.

Congress's circulating currency was also supplemented by its Loan Offices, whose appointed officers issued interest-bearing bonds in large denominations to wealthy Americans and made them redeemable by the states. The certificates carried first 4 percent interest, and then 6 percent interest after February 1777—neither rate as attractive as the 10 to 18 percent private loans made during the war. And, like paper money, the Loan Office certificates depreciated quickly until Congress closed Loan Office operations in 1781.

Each state also issued its own paper money, a total of over $209 million during the war. But only Delaware and Georgia required a "fund"—collateral—of real estate to back the currency with something of widely accepted value. Elsewhere, the states tried to redeem the currency in future taxes (hence their name "tax anticipation notes"), but the need for funds rose much faster than legislative tax laws could meet. Various taxes on goods, land, houses, licenses to operate businesses, and even crops were not unusual. But their burden became unbearable to many citizens, and by early 1779, petitions flooded state legislatures for relief from both the tax laws and the jail sentences imposed on those who could not, or would not, abide by them.

Prices and Wages

When farmers marched off to war and abandoned their fields, and when British blockades began to cut off necessary imports, prices skyrocketed. During 1778, some coastal towns reported over 1,000 percent price increases in daily necessities. Salt in Maryland and Virginia that sold for $1 a bag in 1776 went for over $3,500 by 1779—when it could be found. In April 1779, George Washington wrote that "a wagon load of money will scarcely purchase a wagon load of provisions."

Congress and the states responded by trying to regulate the flow of goods and their prices. Early in the war, Congress implored citizens to sell goods "at reasonable prices," and repeated this call over and over. Some farmers and small producers discovered they could hoard goods and take them to market when prices rose steeply. Others, when approached by military suppliers with government certificates to pay for goods, supported "open prices" that they could negotiate to their own advantage. In the cities, merchants complained that price controls thwarted "the nature of commerce," which they believed should "be as free as air."

Artisans, shopkeepers, and "citizen consumers" agitated for price regulations on food and fuel brought from the countryside. Popular committees tried to fix prices among townspeople by general agreement—and sometimes by force—but they met with only partial success. Congressional calls for delegated conventions to determine fixed prices also faltered or failed. A convention of New England delegates met in 1776 in Providence to establish a list of wages and prices for every conceivable job and commodity, but its measures "fell into dissipation" before the end of 1777. Elsewhere, regional coalitions of new states made similar unsuccessful efforts to regulate prices and wages.

Instead, governments representing new states tried to address alarming inflation and scarcities by imposing embargoes that would keep necessities at home. New England states also passed "land embargo" laws that prohibited sales across state lines of necessary goods such as cider, wood, linen, and fodder. Most of the new states also tried to douse farmers' temptations to hold back goods in order to force prices up by decreeing that dairy, meat, grain, and vegetable products must be given up for immediate sale to needy populations. Massachusetts wrote a model law in 1779 to prevent "monopoly and forestalling" in the countryside that permitted only bakers to keep on hand more staples than one family needed to get through a season. The law also created county committees to search for hoarded goods and arrest violators.

But regulations did not prevent frequent outbursts of violence over scarcities or price hikes, often under female leadership. Shopkeepers and housewives from two western Virginia counties stormed Richmond warehouses to "set free" supplies of salt in 1776. Women of Beverly, Massachusetts, and a few dozen citizens of East Hartford, Connecticut, seized hogsheads of sugar from merchants in 1777 and forced the offenders to agree to sell at a fair price in the future. Boston women descended on Thomas Boylston's store in 1777 demanding that he sell coffee at a fair price. As Abigail Adams later recounted, "a number of females, some say a hundred or more, . . . marched down to the warehouse and demanded the keys, which [Boylston] refused to deliver. Upon which, one of them seized him by the neck and tossed him into a cart," while other women "opened the warehouse, hoisted out the coffee themselves, put it in to the truck and drove off."

In many instances, "republican townspeople" who insisted that governments set prices with "more justice in them" resorted to prolonged violence. In Philadelphia, mobs demanding lower food prices were joined by sailors and artisans demanding higher wages; together, they stormed the streets for days in January 1779. When daily necessities became so costly that the poor faced starvation, broadsides wailed that "in the midst of money we are in poverty, . . . You that have money, and you that have none, down with your prices, or down with your selves. . . . We have turned out against the enemy and we will not be eaten up by monopolizers and forestallers."

For a while, Philadelphia authorities regulated the public markets and tried to impose fair prices. But new rioting broke out during April and May. Housewives and youth gangs taunted flour merchants whom they perceived to have caused artificial shortages so they could raise prices. "Men with clubbs etc. have been to several Stores, obliging the people to lower their prises," wrote the elite lady Elizabeth Drinker in her diary. But such "popular regulation" seldom lasted long before merchants returned to "open markets" of unregulated sales.

On October 4, some two hundred Philadelphia militiamen rose up against price increases and marched on the house of James Wilson, a lawyer who publicly supported the offending merchants. Lawyers, merchants, and army friends joined

Wilson at his house, and Captain Campbell of the Continental Army opened fire on the protesters. In the mêlée known as the Fort Wilson riot that followed, militiamen killed Campbell and five other men. After hours of conflict, public authorities arrested and fined fifteen of the militiamen, and in the next days they distributed food to the poor.

Protests about wages and prices occurred because many Americans perceived that the Revolutionary War challenged two cherished ideals. One was the belief that republican citizens should always put the "common good" before individual gain. Farmers who withheld food in the countryside and merchants who sent it to distant markets violated the common good, and the people had a right to protest the breach in customs. Second, many patriots believed that governments should be responsive to public need, especially regarding food, fuel, and clothing. But regardless of principle, Congress had no spare funds to relieve the poor, and Washington refused to share his meager army budget with the general citizenry. Some county governments in Virginia and Connecticut dispensed small amounts of relief to needy families, usually in the form of bushels of grain or sides of pork. But elsewhere, provincial and local governments, unable to solve the dire problem of poverty, encouraged the families of wounded and dead soldiers to seek private handouts. Indeed, patriots learned over and over that the "common good" and government accountability were very difficult to attain.

Loyalists

A great number of colonists made no enduring commitment to support or oppose the Revolution, but instead changed sides as circumstances suited them. But a significant portion of the population declared their allegiance to the crown. In 1775 and early 1776, thousands of loyalists rushed out of North America with a few of their household goods and financial assets. Most believed they would return after a short absence. Probably one-fifth of the white population in the thirteen colonies actively fought for the crown after 1775, and probably another fifth did not take up arms for the crown but continued to believe in its authority over the colonies. This was the core of the loyalist population. As many as fifty thousand of them joined makeshift militias, informal vigilante groups, and the British Army. More than eighty thousand left their homes to resettle in Canada, the West Indies, or England.

Loyalists shared a belief in the legitimacy of British rule in North America. This legitimacy derived not only from England's time-honored right to rule over the parts of its empire, but also from the benefits conferred by England's protection of colonial frontiers and commerce. But beyond this common ground, loyalists comprised a varied cross-section of colonial society.

Governors and their close supporters stood at the top of the list of loyalists, especially Lord Dunmore in Virginia, Benning Wentworth in New Hampshire, and Thomas Hutchinson in Massachusetts. Clergy of the Church of England and lawyers of established reputations joined loyalists ranks by 1774 and 1775, too, denouncing separation from the empire as illegal and unconstitutional. Even after the Continental Congress declared in June 1775 that support for recent parliamentary laws constituted treason, loyalists used the pulpit, tavern, and courthouse steps to win wider support for the crown. Some leading loyalists funded the publication of inspired broadsides that combined impassioned political rhetoric and shocking stories of their mistreatment by patriots.

Many wealthy merchants, great landlords, and substantial slave owners joined the patriots, but far more of them could not imagine breaking from the empire. For them, aristocracy, monarchy, and social stability itself hung in the balance. Deference, the fragile cultural foundation of political power over local populations in many areas, could dissolve without the bonds of empire to support it. Property, institutional stability, and cultural traditions depended on the imperial trading system, they argued. As the Sons of Liberty and hundreds of local committees gained their own voices, which challenged the status quo to its roots, families "of reputation and property" grew anxious about the "democratic mob" they saw rising throughout North America.

Large numbers of loyalists came from the middling and lower strata of colonists. They also came from all occupations, as well as all age and ethnic groups. Sometimes a colonist's loyalism stemmed not from support for the crown, but from opposition to patriots who owned the estates on which they lived. This was certainly the case for hundreds of tenants along the Hudson River. Throughout New Jersey, hundreds of small farmers, the majority of Dutch descent, joined the pro-British New Jersey Volunteers. On the eastern shore of Maryland, many struggling farmers became loyalists when the landed and slave-owning gentry became patriots. The Regulators of North Carolina tended to join loyalist regiments because of their deep-seated distrust of the patriot coastal gentry.

Religion and ethnicity motivated some colonists to become loyalists. French Canadians, almost always Catholic, affirmed their loyalty to the crown by the hundreds and called for protection from frontier patriots under the terms of the 1774 Quebec Act. German groups, especially recent immigrants who had moved quickly onto the far frontiers, believed their religious freedom depended on British rule. Highland Scots in the Carolinas organized fierce resistance to the patriot militia, largely because they still identified with their British heritage and worried that future waves of newcomers to the frontier would take their land and challenge their religious freedom. And the thousands of British soldiers stationed in hostile cities or the lonely backcountry often welcomed the chance to prove their loyalty to the mother country.

At least fifty thousand slaves ran away to British lines or British territories, most of them from regions south of Richmond. Thousands of slaves "took their freedom" and escaped to Canada or northern colonial cities, especially New York City. Hoping to find a refuge in Indian villages, many Virginia and South Carolina slaves fled into the wilderness. Large numbers also tried to pass as freed persons in Florida or northern cities. In 1775 hundreds of runaway slaves made it to Sullivan's Island, South Carolina, but patriot forces overran this refuge in December and returned most of the escapees to their masters. Over the ensuing years, however, hundreds of slaves drifted back to the island for shorter or longer periods of time. In New York City, runaway slaves from patriot-held areas took shelter in the homes of resident slaves and their masters to form a "slave city."

Hundreds of slaves accepted the offer to enlist in loyalist regiments in exchange for their freedom. In Virginia, as news of Lexington and Concord spread, Governor Dunmore announced he would arm all slaves who defended the crown and free them at the end of hostilities. In November 1775, he made this promise an official decree, under which some eight hundred slaves applied to fill British army ranks within a couple of months. Most of them were relegated to noncombat roles such as keeping camp, constructing bridges, foraging, and repairing wagons. In addition, smallpox and cholera ravaged the "tent cities" where slaves encamped separately. Still, as many as twenty thousand slaves enlisted in the private brigades of British commanders or in the ranks of the British army, and thousands more aided the loyalists indirectly as the fighting shifted into the South. Once the Revolutionary War erupted, these practical rehearsals for freedom turned into a surge of African-Americans joining the military fray—on both sides.

Aside from the Catawba in South Carolina and Oneida of New York, most Native Americans became loyalists, if they chose a side at all. The Iroquois, long torn between opposing imperial forces on the frontier, had grown fearful about westward migration. As the Revolution neared, the Mohawk leader Joseph Brant sought reassurances from the British that settlers' land grabbing would cease. In return, Brant guaranteed that most Iroquois villages would support the British.

Loyalists who remained in civilian areas during the war became vulnerable to patriot humiliations, seizures of goods, confiscation of estates, house arrests, and

Joseph Brant, Chief of the Mohawks (1742–1807)
Also called Thayendanegea, Brant became a commissioned officer of the British Army and fought against patriots near Canada for much of the Revolution. Before 1776, Brant had been befriended by Sir William Johnson, Indian superintendent in New York, and served against the French at the Battle of Crown Point in the Seven Years' War. Brant's accomplishments were not confined to warring: he learned numerous European languages in Connecticut schools, traveled to London in 1775, and translated the New Testament and Anglican prayer book into Mohawk. (*National Gallery of Canada.*)

suspension of their civil rights. Patriots hurled the epithet "Tory"—a term that once identified die-hard defenders of absolute monarchy, but came to designate all supporters of British rule in North America—at loyalists in all ranks of society. Tories in New York City and Philadelphia were forced to "ride the rails," a painful trip through the streets astride a fence rail, and in many places tarring and feathering continued for the duration of the war. Patriots hung a few particularly recalcitrant loyalists by their wrists. New treason laws made it a crime to speak or write against the patriot cause. Patriots also used existing British laws, especially bills of attainder, to seize loyalist presses and lands. And they tended to regard women according to English common law, as "under the care and authority" of their fathers and husbands, enabling them to disregard even sincere declarations of neutrality and confiscate family businesses and farms from the women left to tend them.

Spies, Prisoners, and Evaders

Secretive communications and interpersonal betrayals marked revolutionary activity from the beginning. As early as 1776, Washington issued orders to patriot agents to establish a spy base and "secret correspondence for the purpose of conveying intelligence of the Enemy's movements and designs." Washington also regularly received information from refugee loyalists and British army deserters. Both sides used fraudulent reports and disguised infiltrators. Farmers and businessmen who crossed combat lines to make deliveries made excellent spies. Washington, for example, relied on the resourceful John Honeyman, a New Jersey butcher and weaver who plied his trades within British lines. Honeyman persuaded Hessian commanders that Washington did not intend to recross the Delaware River and collected essential information for the patriot attack on Trenton, December 26, 1776.

On the other side, the Boston physician Benjamin Church became a member of the Massachusetts Provincial Congress, but he also supplied General Thomas Gage with information on Lexington and Concord before the British raid and alerted the British about fortifications at Bunker Hill. Patriots discovered Church's treachery in 1777, but not before he had become Director General of American army hospitals and chief military physician. Church spent the rest of the war years confined in a Connecticut jail.

One of the most notorious loyalist spies was Benedict Arnold, a hero of the Continental campaigns in Canada and Saratoga. But in 1779 he turned against the patriots' cause and became a paid informer for General Henry Clinton, the head of British forces in occupied New York City. In 1780 Arnold used his post at West Point to betray patriot movements, and then fled behind British lines when patriots uncovered the plot to deliver the stronghold to the enemy. Major John André, a promising young officer in the British army, had worked closely with Arnold at West Point until patriots captured him in the "neutral ground" of northern New York and sent him to the gallows on October 2, 1780. In subsequent months, Arnold led raids against his home state of Connecticut, and then Virginia. He retired with a handsome pension in England, where he heard a running stream of news about the deep hatred that Americans bore against him.

Each side held thousands of prisoners of war. Generally, the British soldiers fared better than Americans did, largely because patriots took captives to the countryside and gave them food and outdoor work. Lancaster, Pennsylvania, became a major place of confinement, though the neighboring towns of York, Carlisle, Reading, Lebanon, and Hebron hired out thousands of captives as farm servants and iron foundry workers. British officers, on the other hand, often moved about freely, buying extra food and clothing when it was available. Although the southern gentry and northern urban elite enjoyed the intellectual and social company of cultivated European officers and their families, local people often greeted the enemy with hostility. For example, when Baroness Riedesel, wife of the Hessian commanding general, arrived in Virginia with her two children, one householder refused the baroness extra food: "The corn we need for our slaves because they work for us, but you come here to kill us."

Many American prisoners endured horrid conditions in New York City prisons and British hospital ships anchored offshore, and great numbers of them did not survive the ordeal. The British deprived patriots of rations, fuel, and sanitation. Fewer than 800 of the 4,500 prisoners taken in the siege of New York and the flight to White Plains survived to be exchanged later in the war. Typhus, called "jail fever," claimed hundreds of lives, and starvation carried off hundreds more. The British also executed nearly 300 of the men taken in these early campaigns. Living conditions in the floating jails moored in New York and Charles Town harbors were abominable. Prisoners spent days below deck retching, ate meat and biscuits full of worms, and slept standing up. Guards treated complaints with beatings and shackles. In the New York jails alone, between 8,000 and 11,500 rebels died, more than all the men killed in military action during the Revolution. And neither side offered an effective form of prisoner exchange until very late in the war.

Patriots raised evasion of service to a high art by 1777. Congress and the states had two ways to recruit soldiers, both of them fraught with difficulties. One was to promise or directly pay cash bounties for enlistment. But congressional and state recruiters both tried to fill assigned quotas, and their competition for men bid up the bounties to such tempting amounts that unscrupulous citizens enlisted several times. By 1779, multiple enlistments were common in every state. In the second method of recruitment, state governments ordered local conscription officers to draft quotas of men. Officials accepted substitutes for drafted men—as European armies had for generations—and soon the practice of hiring substitutes to fight was a regular practice. In the South, masters tried to pass off their slaves into service, and in many cities, artisans hired handicapped or mentally unfit persons to report to camp, knowing that "the ringers" would be sent home and everyone would escape conscription. Dissenters such as the Quakers, Mennonites, and Amish made legitimate claims to be exempted on the basis of religious beliefs or pacifism, although some were fined heavily as a consequence. Moravians of North Carolina stated that "we Brethren do not bear arms," but they willingly gave financial and

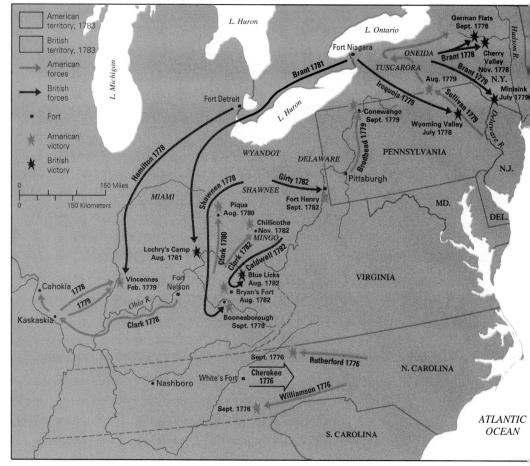

War in the West Although patriots won important victories in the Hudson and Mohawk river valleys during 1777, the Ohio and Pennsylvania frontiers remained vulnerable to British attacks.

material aid to patriots and worked in military hospitals. The result of all these factors was a fighting force of increasingly poor, propertyless men of doubtful commitment to the cause.

The New Republican Order

As the war dragged on, with its dire need for manpower, indecisive battles, low morale, and a crumbling economy, revolutionaries discussed what kind of political structures were suited to their republican character. When delegates approved the Declaration of Independence, they stepped out of the empire, but they did not replace their former colonial governments with new ones right away. Shunning aristocracy and monarchy, in their place the patriots created a weak central government during the Revolution. They also agreed to distribute most political authority separately to the thirteen former colonies. And it was in these jurisdictions that revolutionaries groped toward redefining what their particular republican rights and privileges would be. Although most patriots still believed that pure democracies were an unreliable form of authority, they readily dropped their identity as "subjects" of the empire and began to call one another "citizen."

From Colonies to States

Patriot leaders knew they were embarking on a great experiment. Their experiences expanding the power of the colonial assemblies, creating committees and congresses during the imperial crisis, and sustaining a war for independence focused many discussions on a single critical issue: how to refine the rights and obligations of citizens and their rulers. Often, they turned to classical and republican writers to express their ideas about good government. As Tom Paine had reminded Americans, "The word *republic,* means the *public good,* or the good of the whole." Benjamin Rush's words to Americans intoned that virtue, the opposite of corruption, came from deep within individuals: "Every man in a republic is public property. His time and talents—his youth—his manhood—his old age—nay more, life, all belong to his country." Rush, and thousands of Americans who put pen to paper in these years, believed that every patriot should exhibit republican virtue. But the day-to-day circumstances of the war revealed that virtue was fragile, and the wisdom of the ages taught that any government constituted on a republican basis could not endure. Moreover, opponents reminded revolutionary leaders that the English monarchy had already lasted for about a thousand years, whereas every republic had become corrupted and declined in a short time.

In order to make the ideal of republicanism a more practical reality, revolutionary leaders insisted on certain innovations. First of all, a virtuous citizenry required written constitutions comprised of explicit principles. The unwritten British constitution, made up of many centuries' worth of customs and precedents, could not be studied, known, and altered by a great number of citizens participating in politics. Further, written documents would be based on popular sovereignty—the principle that governments derive "their just powers from the consent of the governed," or "the people," as the Declaration of Independence set forth. Still, the Declaration did not prescribe what form of government should follow from this axiom. Nevertheless, during the Revolution, each former colony created distinct but compatible written republican constitutions that embodied popular sovereignty.

Second, Americans writing new constitutions believed that the most durable and just republics were small ones. The Baron de Montesquieu's *Spirit of the Laws,* a widely read treatise on different forms of government, cautioned that rulers should regularly consult the interests of the ruled. To do this, rulers should be physically near the people. Governments deliberating too far from the people could not enact wise policies. Distant governments out of touch with "the circumstances of their domain" eventually became sources of tyranny.

Numerous writers grappled with how to create new governments along these lines. In New Hampshire in 1776, an anonymous pamphleteer proposed in *The People the Best Governors* that all power should reside in one elected body, without property qualifications for any official position, and with universal adult male suffrage. Furthermore, the judicial branch also should be elected; most legislation should emanate from town meetings at the local level; and taxes should be raised and used in the towns or counties. Paine's *Common Sense* proposed a similarly democratic form of government, with no property qualifications for voting or holding office, and no upper council of wealthy lawmakers. Paine substituted a unicameral, or one-house, legislature instead, and he proposed to eliminate imprisonment for debt, protect small producers and commercial farmers, and educate all citizens. Pennsylvania's 1776 constitution incorporated many of these radical measures; Georgia's and Vermont's constitutions provided for unicameral legislatures.

John Adams proposed a different form of state government, one adopted by Virginia and then other states. Adams thought Paine's plan was far too democratic and too simplistic. He set out his own ideas in *Thoughts on Government* (1777), as a direct reply to Paine. Americans should abandon the "mixed government" of the unwritten British constitution, Adams wrote, under which three different social orders—king, lords, and commons—acted together. Instead, the powers of government should be divided among three separate branches—executive, judicial, and legislative. The legislature should have two houses, neither of which would base officeholding on social rank. Adams agreed with many radical patriots that governments should rest on republican virtue, the sacrifice of self-interest for the common good. Republics could not rule by force, but rather by talent, wisdom, and the consent of the governed. Government, he wrote in a famous metaphor, should mirror the diversity of society. But, Adams continued, the popular multitudes ought not to have whimsical authority over all officials. Justices should be appointed, not elected, and governors should have the power to veto legislation.

State delegations tended to write more democratic constitutions early in the war than they did later on. Some, as in Virginia and Georgia, started by defining individual, or civil, rights before proceeding to form their representative governments. They assumed that "the people" had to carve out the boundaries of their rights before they surrendered some of them to governing bodies. Among these rights were protection of property and life, abolition of hereditary privileges, frequent elections and short terms of office, trial by jury, religious toleration, and an extended franchise. Most of the early state governments also gave state legislatures sovereignty over all other parts of government. In 1776 Virginia created a legislature elected by qualified voters annually; the legislature was to appoint the governor, his council, and most state justices. Virginians denied their governor a veto power and strictly limited his powers to the area of appointing officials.

The differences between upper and lower houses of the early and more democratic state governments were minor. Candidates for the upper house did not need great property holdings to be elected, and three states permitted the lower house to elect the upper, which further restricted the rise of political privilege. In addition, these states created larger lower houses and began to create counties in their western regions that gained representation in government. As a result, men of modest means often held legislative seats. The early, more democratic states also created executive branches made up of committees, implemented voting by secret ballot, opened their legislative sessions to the public, and published proposed bills prior to voting on laws.

Some of the first new states not only unseated the wealthy, but turned out entire ruling factions. In Pennsylvania, for example, middling artisans, retailers, and professionals, many of them recent German and Scottish immigrants, asked why "men of great property" always led citizens when "men of modest means" were equally qualified? These groups formed an alliance that swept away the dominating Quaker elite and proprietary party. The new Constitutionalist party formulated many elements in the radical state constitution of 1776. Then, under the pressures of mobilizing the militia, taxing and regulating the economy of starving citizens, and quelling disorders on the frontier, the Constitutionalists found themselves in the unexpected position of resorting to force against their opponents, including many pacifist Quakers whom they disfranchised. Although many Scots-Irish and Germans played an important role in the Constitutionalist party after 1777, more experienced leaders could easily brush them aside during wartime.

Indeed, from 1777 on, new state constitutions began to reflect the more conservative reasoning of Adams's *Thoughts on Government.* New York established a bicameral legislature with the lower house determined by population, a governor with a strong veto power, an appointed judiciary, and property qualifications that restricted voting to only 40 percent of adult white men. South Carolina's constitution of 1778 required governors to have a debt-free estate of at least £10, 000, and other officials to own property as well. About 10 percent of the white male population were qualified to hold office, and only a small minority of men even qualified for voting. Maryland's 1777 constitution, the most conservative of all, adopted voting and electing requirements similar to those in South Carolina, but added that judges and high executive officers should sit for life.

Serious internal divisions in some states prevented easy resolution of their differences from the onset of constitutional discussions. In Massachusetts the divisions between east and west, older towns and newer settlements, established political privileges and rising ambitions, persisted for over four years. In the fall of 1776, the provincial government asked the towns for authorization to draft a constitution. In the past this request would have been granted without question. But by now, some of the towns had grown distrustful of central authority and wished to have newly created powers emanate directly from them. The government got just enough support to proceed, but when the delegates sent the constitution to the towns for ratification two years later, it was overwhelmingly rejected.

Massachusetts citizens had various opinions about the particular rights and obligations outlined in the proposed state constitution. But they generally agreed that a special convention should be assembled to discuss matters and draft a satisfactory document. Following John Locke's reasoning, some town leaders argued that the Declaration of Independence had torn down former governments, leaving citizens in a "state of nature," and that they now needed collectively to create a government from scratch.

In December 1779, state leaders did, indeed, organize a special convention in Boston, at which delegates wrote a draft constitution to be submitted to all free adult males for ratification. The resulting document stipulated annual elections for both houses of the legislature, the lower one chosen by the free adult voters of the towns and the upper one by counties according to property holdings rather than population. The constitution permitted the governor a veto, albeit a limited one. It narrowed the franchise to citizens worth £50 in real estate or £100 in personal property; officeholders had to meet higher property qualifications. Voters approved the Massachusetts constitution in spring 1780, and it became the most popular model for states formed in the next years. Despite its apparent bias toward elite officeholding, the Massachusetts constitution had been drafted in a special convention at which political discussion was open to middling citizens. The wider public discussions and deliberations in turn spurred leaders at the national level to consider the importance of this popular sovereignty for their political reforms.

Despite the differences in the various state constitutions, and despite the elitist qualities of some, American political culture became more democratic during the Revolution. Most new states reduced the authority of their executive branches. Most lower houses apportioned seats according to population, which gave all regions of the states an opportunity to send representatives to legislatures. Eight of the state constitutions incorporated statements of individual rights that followed from the premise that "all men are created equal." Furthermore, there was widespread discussion in every state about important issues such as the frequency of elections, the extent of suffrage, and the duties of officeholders. This open forum emboldened "men not quite so well dressed, nor so politely educated, nor so highly born" to become active in the affairs of their new states, and at times even to hold office. In their thinking, revolutionary Americans rejected "democracy" because they believed it inclined too easily toward mob rule and licentiousness. Instead, they chose the identity of "republicans" who entrusted government to men of superior genius and talent. But in practice, many more artisans and commercial farmers were serving in the lower houses by 1785. In a short time, large numbers of Americans who had never played a direct role in determining legislation or returning their "betters" to office would begin to identify their political interests with like-minded people and move onto the public stage of electioneering and party life.

The Articles of Confederation

As the Revolutionary War proceeded, the Continental Congress initiated a discussion about what powers a national government should have. Given that colonists had declared their independence from the coercive authority of one great empire, they wished above all to avoid another highly centralized government. As a consequence, the proposed Articles of Confederation set strict limits on the powers of Congress. Strong traditions of local governance within all the colonies reinforced this commitment to weak central power. The Articles stipulated that each province would have one vote in a national assembly, which would be one body without separate "chambers," and that the Articles be approved unanimously by all thirteen provinces in order to have effect. Once the Articles were approved, each province could send two to seven delegates to the new Confederation Congress, each delegate serving no more than three out of six years. Congress would determine most matters by a simple majority; important issues would require the approval of at least nine provinces. Congress could declare war and make peace, coin or print money, raise loans for public uses, regulate Indian trade, decide disputes between states and territories, run the postal system, and establish a system of weights and measures. But it could not tax citizens directly; rather, it had to request money or supplies from the thirteen provinces.

In November 1777, Congress submitted its draft of the Articles of Confederation to the thirteen rebelling former colonies for their collective ratification. By mid-1778, eight of the newly created states had ratified the Articles, but to take effect, all thirteen had to approve the document. Four more new states ratified in the next year, but Maryland held out. During deliberations in Congress about what rights a national government should have, one important privilege stayed in the hands of states and individuals: control over western lands. Now during the ratification process, Maryland's leaders demanded that Congress have more control over these lands. Otherwise, the eight large states with extensive land claims in the West would use occupation and sale of land to expand their political power to an inordinate degree. Marylanders did not wish to strengthen Congress, but rather to weaken the large states. Maryland's legislators demanded that large states "cede" portions of their western territories to Congress, creating a "national domain" outside of individual states' control. Speculators who held shares in western land companies went along, hoping to make special deals with Congress. Eventually, New York and Virginia ceded portions of their western claims to Congress "for the good of the public." Mollified, in March 1781, Maryland signed the Articles of Confederation.

By the time the Articles became law, most of the war had been fought. Indeed, certain members of Congress, known as the "nationalists," attributed the sorry state of the army and civilian living conditions during the war to the absence of an effective central governing power. Once the individual provinces approved the Articles, nationalists quickly proposed remedies for pressing problems. Most important, Robert Morris, possibly the wealthiest merchant in America, became the superintendent of finance in May 1781. By that time, Congress's currency was "not worth a continental" and ceased to circulate. Morris stepped in with a masterful plan to turn around Congress's dire financial condition. First he persuaded Congress to charter the first private commercial bank in America, the Bank of North America (BNA). In it Morris deposited the silver, gold, and bills of exchange loaned to America by Holland and France, as well as large sums of his own money. Morris then asked Congress to authorize a printing of new certificates, to circulate freely with the backing of BNA funds and to earn interest. In mid-1781 Morris initiated a new means to supply the army, a bidding system for supply contracts. Both the bank-backed certificates and the army contracts operated with "the full credit and name of Congress."

Morris wanted to do still more. With the support of his fellow nationalists in and out of Congress, he proposed amending the Articles of Confederation to allow him to create a national revenue based on taxes. Although citizens expressed widespread opposition to granting Congress authority to tax, twelve states approved the proposed duty on commercial imports, or "impost," by fall 1782. Only Rhode Island, or "Rogue's Island" to impatient nationalists, refused, but without this tiny state's vote, the duty—America's first proposed tariff—failed. Later that year, New York rescinded its support for the impost as well. Over 1782–1784, some provinces also began paying the interest on war debts and certificates directly to their citizens, bypassing Congress. In this way, Pennsylvania, New York, New Jersey, and Maryland took over, or "assumed," about one-third of their national debt by 1786, thereby undermining the authority Morris had so carefully crafted.

Given the significance of debt and taxes to the creation of central governing authority, nationalists grew fearful about state assumption. They began to perceive a profound division of interests between Congress and the thirteen provinces. Even as the war wound down and negotiators went to the peace talks in Paris, nationalists began to discuss ways to bolster the central taxing authority of Congress. They also knew they would have to revisit another issue: the disposition of western lands.

 Winning the War, 1778–1783

Congress rejoiced over the French alliance of 1778, which secured money, soldiers, and guns for the patriot cause. But military victory was far from assured. Tensions in the West heated up until they erupted into unconventional forms of fighting involving Indians, Spanish, and frontier settlers of different political persuasions. In addition, Lord North commenced a brutal southern campaign that left Americans wondering, again, whether their virtue and sacrifice would lead to independence after all. In the end, while the British army floundered in an alien military environment, it was Americans' ability to withstand the bitter final struggles in the southern states that pulled them through.

The War in the West

In 1778, a year after France forged its alliance with Americans, Spain also declared war on Britain. Although Spain had not committed itself directly to the American cause, its armed strikes against Britain in various parts of the world indirectly aided the patriots. Spain tried to retake Gibraltar, but failed. Next, it tried to overrun British West Florida, and succeeded. Then, setting its sites farther west, Spain aimed to protect the Louisiana territory, which it had received as a gift from France by the Treaty of Paris in 1763. Spain had slowly built up trade and Indian diplomacy to prosperous levels around San Diego and San Francisco, California, and immigrants from the Canary Islands, Acadia, and French trading posts created viable towns with strong Spanish identities along the Mississippi River.

Elsewhere in the West, most Indians remained neutral unless their own immediate interests favored an expedient alliance with the British to defend their homelands. Only the Catawba, deep in the South, favored the American rebels during the Revolution. The Choctaw, Creek, Cherokee, and Chickasaw waged fierce war against the patriot backcountry in the South. The Cherokee, in particular, suffered from warfare on their lands, first in 1760 (see page 167) and again in 1776. By the end of the Revolution, Cherokee and Shawnee villages had been rebuilt far into the West.

Out in Ohio country, beyond the Appalachian ridge, the Revolution assumed characteristics that few Britons anticipated in 1776. Already the Iroquois and Cherokee had sold their claims to this vast area, and the Shawnee continued to regard Virginians with hostility even after surrendering their claims in the valley. Continued American expansion into the Ohio country revitalized Indian hatreds and enhanced tribal support for an alliance with the British. Indian allies of the British torched the American settlements at Boonesborough in 1778 and terrorized Americans by taking scalps in return for British bounties. From 1778 to 1781, Iroquois rampaged across the Wyoming Valley of east central Pennsylvania, joined by the Great Lakes Indians to fend off hostile settlers in the Ohio Valley.

George Rogers Clark, an inveterate Indian fighter still just twenty-six years old, led a combined force of American and French frontiersmen from Kaskaskia, Illinois, and militiamen from Virginia against an alliance of Creek and Ohio Indians during the winter of 1779. Clark's "Long Knives" held Vincennes, deep in the American interior, for some months before the Native Americans drove them out in 1781. But by then, Clark had taken the last of the British forts and established firm American claims over the entire region north of the Ohio River. Other battles, far from the diplomatic centers of the Revolution, engaged hundreds of Americans who died defending the wilderness from Indian, British, and French belligerents. For generations to come, these hostilities seethed. Frontier "buckskins" and American troops continued to shield the advancing line of European settlement, even when doing so required atrocities.

In the North, the Iroquois divided. Mohawk chief Joseph Brant, in alliance with the Seneca, helped loyalists and British troops raid patriot villages on the Pennsylvania and New York frontier. But in retaliation, patriots combined with friendly Oneida and Tuscarora to attack villages allied with Brant. The mighty confederacy of Iroquois nations almost disintegrated during 1779.

The War in the South

In late 1778, the British navy took Savannah, Georgia. From there, royal commander General Henry Clinton planned to launch an assault on Charles Town, South Carolina, and wage a pacification campaign in the southern countryside. Clinton would leave Lord Cornwallis in charge of southern forces while he returned to the north to attack Washington's army in New Jersey. This effort, Clinton knew, required full mobilization of redcoats and the aid of thousands of loyalists.

The first part of Clinton's plan worked with unprecedented success. Cornwallis took Charles Town from Benjamin Lincoln and his five thousand Continentals in May 1780, making it the single greatest surrender of the war. By July, Cornwallis had evicted patriots from the city, established military control of the state, and purged rebels from government. His forces organized rice production and export, and forced loyalty oaths (including promises to take up arms for the crown) on all able-bodied Carolinians. Cornwallis enjoyed the support of marauder loyalists under Banastre Tarleton, who chased about 350 patriots toward the North Carolina border during June, slaughtering all who stood in his way and then murdering those who surrendered. British officer Patrick Ferguson led another group of armed vigilantes against patriot settlements along the Santee River.

South Carolina patriots also mobilized vigilante raiders, whose unconventional methods of fighting became normal in the final Revolutionary campaigns. Under Thomas Sumter, a planter-merchant, eight hundred mounted raiders stormed Hanging Rock on August 6. Their target was not British soldiers but nearly five hundred loyalist settlers scattered in dozens of new homesteads. Sumter's riders overran the largely defenseless loyalists and then succumbed to looting and drinking. Meanwhile, commander Horatio Gates moved his wing of Continentals from

War in the South   After the British invaded Georgia in 1778, their strategy was to move deep into the Carolina interior, where numerous battles tested the morale and endurance of both sides until the decisive patriot victory at Yorktown in October 1781.

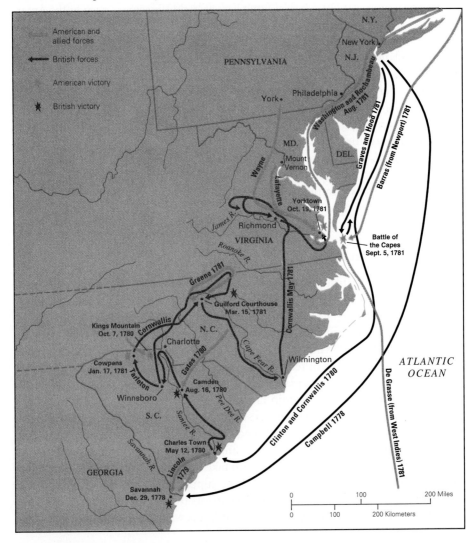

Maryland and Delaware into the South, where two thousand Virginia and North Carolina militia joined them. But at Camden, South Carolina, on August 16, Cornwallis leveled the combined patriot force. Two days later, Tarleton's bandits raided Sumter's camp at Fishing Creek, where they killed over two hundred and wounded up to three hundred patriots. Violence was common in colonial life, especially on the frontiers, but the massacres at Hanging Rock and Fishing Creek escalated partisan animosities to unheard-of levels. From then on, both sides threw themselves into a backcountry civil war that bore little resemblance to what regular armies or militiamen had been trained to do. Patriot leader Gates remained dumbfounded at the "murders and devastations" all around him.

With British now in control of South Carolina, many patriots feared reprisals from the thousands of slaves who had flocked to the British side. Unlike their counterparts anywhere in the North, southern loyalists not only professed their allegiance to the crown boldly, but also organized large fighting units that turned viciously against the rebels.

But the tide began to turn against Cornwallis in 1780. France dispatched five thousand troops under General Comte de Rochambeau. They arrived in Newport, Rhode Island, in July and August, and awaited orders to march against either Clinton's troops in New York City or Cornwallis's in South Carolina. In addition, patriots redoubled their efforts to defend the southern backcountry. Cornwallis had embarked on a plan to plunder any portions of the North Carolina frontier that did not join the British. In response, patriot riflemen from across the Blue Ridge descended on Patrick Ferguson's loyalists in early fall 1780. The bloody encounters that ensued involved mostly civilians on both sides. Finally, in a battle at King's Mountain, patriot woodsmen prevailed and captured about six hundred of Ferguson's men; in October they hanged a few loyalists and shot many prisoners. Local communities were quick to point out that patriot tactics were no less brutish than Tarleton's. Meanwhile, Cornwallis's advance into North Carolina ended.

Washington also replaced Gates with General Nathanael Greene, who entered South Carolina by land with a small number of Continentals in October 1780. At about that time, "the Swamp Fox," Francis Marion, recruited hundreds of patriot backcountry settlers from remote origins. Heeding Marion's advice that he divide his troops into small spearheads, Greene sent 300 men with Marion and another 300 riflemen with Daniel Morgan to encircle Cornwallis's troops. Morgan picked up about 700 militia as he crossed the countryside and set up camp with his back to the river at Cowpens, South Carolina. When Tarleton attacked on January 17, 1781, Morgan deployed first his militia sharpshooters, then the Continentals, and finally an armed cavalry, in a bewildering array of choreographed moves that decimated Tarleton's army.

Although Cornwallis held his ground at the Guilford Court House on March 15, 1781, it was a shallow victory because he had exhausted his troops by chasing Greene deeper and deeper into terrain that British cannon and wagons could not manage. Cornwallis confessed that he did not know where to go next. The British had almost no connection to coastal supply lines, while bases of support "plentifully fed" patriot troops in Virginia.

The Battle of King's Mountain   This painting by Robert Windsor Wilson of the 1780 struggle between the "over mountain men" and redcoats depicts the close contact of soldiers. Toward the end of the Revolution, when most battles had shifted into the South, more frontier patriots banded together, often foraging in the backcountry woods and sleeping in the open for weeks. Many patriots from western counties of South Carolina hoped they would get more responsive government and internal development from the Revolution, as had the Regulators before them. *(Collection of the State of South Carolina.)*

Cornwallis decided to keep marching north, into Virginia. He set up camp at Yorktown in late August 1781. And there he and his 8,000 men waited while American and French forces regrouped and converged on them. Rochambeau and his 5,000 French troops were still fresh and ready in Newport, Rhode Island. When Washington found out that French commanders had steered their Caribbean fleet toward the Chesapeake, he asked Rochambeau to provide reinforcement in the bay outside Yorktown. Lafayette moved down the interior of Virginia's eastern shore to join them and French Admiral Count de Barras approached from the north by sea. From the water, American and French forces bombarded the British for nearly a month until mid-October, when Cornwallis realized he would not be reinforced by Clinton and his own supplies gave out. After two days of negotiations, he sent out from the trenches his second-in-command, General Charles O'Hara, to surrender. On October 19, 1781, the British admitted defeat to the "bloody colonials," whom they had regarded with contempt as inferiors for generations.

Victory at Last

The reasons for the American victory are not straightforward, but certain factors were critical. For one thing, the Continental Army matured over time and learned discipline and formal battle routines they needed when facing the redcoats in open battle. For another, American civilians, for all of their failings of virtue, sacrificed enormously over seven long years of warfare, from Lexington to Yorktown. Once they dismantled British government in most areas, Americans worked together to create new government structures and sustain the war. In addition, French troops, arms, and silver aided patriots considerably, and the Spanish navy provided well-timed modest support as well.

For their part, the British faced formidable difficulties supplying their forces in the interior of North America, especially when a recession developed in England and its subjects grew openly war weary. Britain also fought this costly and long war without European allies. Commanders Howe and Clinton usually chose cautious maneuvers and clung to the official rules of eighteenth-century warfare when Americans readily and regularly adapted to terrain and local circumstances. Nor did the British use their loyalist strength effectively: in the north, loyalists operated relatively autonomously from the redcoats at crucial moments, and in the south, loyalists formed vicious vigilante groups that drove large numbers of back-country people into the arms of patriots. Finally, the Continental Congress, Continental Army, state governments, and civilian committees all provided vehicles for patriots to affirm and extend republican political authority throughout the countryside that was fundamentally at odds with monarchy. The British reason for continuing to fight in North America—restoring Americans to royal rule—became unrealistic.

The war need not have ended with the fall of Yorktown. After all, Clinton still held New York City. But when Lord North sensed that his own career had been dashed, he resigned in November 1781. In March 1782, King George accepted the new Rockingham administration's proposal to recognize American independence. The Continental Congress's representatives, Benjamin Franklin, John Adams, and John Jay, discussed the terms of peace with British and French officials for months. Eventually it became clear to the Americans that their French allies did not have the same objectives. The French wanted to divide up the colonies and give England rule over New York, Georgia, and the Carolinas. The American negotiators could not accept this; they claimed not only all thirteen independent provinces but Canada as well.

In November 1782, all the parties set their names to the Treaty of Paris, which recognized the United States to be "free Sovereign and independent States." Canada remained British, but the United States would extend to the Mississippi. In a separate treaty between Britain and Spain, Florida became Spanish once again. The Treaty of Paris permitted creditors to collect pre-war and wartime debts, in sterling, which in time created hardship for southerners. And Congress agreed to ask the states to consider returning all confiscated property to loyalists—which the states eventually declined to do. Finally, Britain agreed to withdraw its troops on the frontier—a provision that also went unfulfilled for many years. The Treaty of Paris was signed on September 2, 1783. It was followed by the exodus of thousands of British troops and loyalists, who left New York, Charles Town, and Savannah to begin again in St. Augustine, Nova Scotia, West Indies islands, and London.

CONCLUSION

The Revolution was the longest war in American history until Vietnam. Perhaps as many as one in ten of the available population served under arms. During its eight years, communities divided deeply and endured dire economic and social duress. And going into the war, few patriots expressed an identity as "Americans." For the majority of rebels, local attachments were the strongest ones. The war itself offered further challenges to soldiers and citizens concerning taxes, army recruitment and supply, and civilian survival.

But the struggle for independence did, indeed, prevail. Patriots committed to the movement for political independence believed that the existing imperial political and social system had become unbearable. As they advanced from declaring independence toward forming a new republican order, they began to formulate their alternative to life in the empire. A significant number of patriots must have been convinced—though to different degrees—that their victory would make their lives better in political, cultural, and economic terms. Although, for the most part, their plans did not include women or people of color, the ideal of republican citizenship for male heads of households underlay patriots' efforts to define the powers granted to Congress and new state governments. The need for alliances and material support from foreign nations also forced leading patriots to begin formulating the rebellious North Americans' relationship to existing nations.

Beyond this, the expanse over which patriots fought the war, and their many internal divisions, did not permit a singular vision of the future or a unified identity as Americans. The war taught as much about the limits of individual sacrifice as it did about the virtues of the revolutionary cause. The creation of new governments did little to settle questions about who should run them and who should benefit from their actions. At war's end, citizens of the new states were more divided than ever.

After 1781, people throughout the separate states faced the awesome tasks of demobilizing an army and reconstructing society. Many Indians and slaves felt entitled to land and freedom in return for their sacrifices during the Revolution. Thousands of relocated loyalists left homes and estates that needed to be disposed of; thousands more wished to stay in the new republic, but it was not clear how to reintegrate them. The Continental Congress had been too busy raising an army and financing a war to clarify much about its relationship to citizens or state governments. Republican rhetoric asked revolutionaries to sacrifice their private interests for the public good, but continual internal discord was the norm. Now that they had won the war, survivors would have to secure the peace among themselves.

SUGGESTED READINGS

There are some valuable general works on the American Revolution, each with a different perspective. For social portraits, see Edward Countryman, *The American Revolution* (1985); Steven Rosswurm, *Arms, Country, and Class: The Philadelphia Militia and the "Lower Sort" During the American Revolution* (1987); Alfred Young, ed., *The American Revolution: Explorations in the History of American Radicalism* (1976), and the older but invaluable Merrill Jensen, *The Founding of a Nation: A History of the American Revolution, 1763–1776* (1968).

For the political culture of the era, Jack P. Greene, ed., *The American Revolution: Its Character and Limits* (1987) is the best starting point. The most recent effort to synthesize historical scholarship is Gordon Wood, *The Radicalism of the American Revolution* (1992). For a series of detailed vignettes about ideas, political processes, and military events, see Jack P. Greene and J. R. Pole, eds., *The Blackwell Encyclopedia of the American Revolution* (1998).

For contrasting perspectives about the last efforts at compromise and the forging of oppositional currents, see John Brooke, *King George III* (1972). The biography by Philip Lawson, *George Grenville: A Political Life* (1984), represents an effort to show scholarly balance and fractured communication during the era.

For the Continental Congress's work and the Declaration of Independence, see Jack Rakove, *The Beginnings of National Politics: An Interpretive History of the Continental Congress* (1979); Pauline Maier, *American Scripture: Making the Declaration of Independence* (1997); Richard Ryerson, *The Revolution Is Now Begun* (1978); and Peter Shaw, *The Character of John Adams* (1976). The best single study of Paine and the urban scenario of Philadelphia is Eric Foner, *Tom Paine and Revolutionary America* (1976).

The exuberance of the first year is captured in Charles Royster, *A Revolutionary People at War: The Continental Army and American Character* (1980).

The social aspects of the war, on the field and off, provide some of the most fascinating reading about the Revolution. The best places to start are Robert Gross, *The Minutemen and Their World* (1976); Dirk Hoerder, *Crowd Action in Revolutionary Massachusetts, 1765–1780* (1977); Ronald Hoffman, *A Spirit of Dissension: Economics, Politics, and the Revolution in Maryland* (1973); and Michael Belleisles, *Revolutionary Outlaw: Ethan Allen and the Struggle for Independence on the Early American Frontier* (1993).

For frontier warfare, see Colin G. Calloway, *The American Revolution in Indian Country: Crisis and Diversity in Native American Communities* (1995); Barbara Graymont, *The Iroquois in the American Revolution* (1972); James H. O'Donnel III, *Southern Indians in the American Revolution* (1973); Alan Taylor, *Liberty Men and Great Proprietors: The Revolutionary Settlement on the Maine Frontier, 1760–1820* (1990); and Richard White, *The Middle Ground: Indians, Empires, and Republics in the Great Lakes Region, 1650–1815* (1991).

The best study about the corruption, doubts, and deceits of the Revolutionary War, especially related to the army supplying, is E. Wayne Carp, *To Starve the Army at Pleasure: Continental Army Administration and American Political Culture, 1775–1783* (1984). On the loyalists: Wallace Brown, *The Good Americans: The Loyalists in the American Revolution* (1969), and Robert Calhoon, Timothy Barnes, and George Rawlyk, eds., *Loyalists and Community in North America* (1994).

On army and militia life in the field, see the very engaging work of James Kirby Martin and Edward Mark Lender, *A Respectable Army: The Military Origins of the Republic, 1763–1789* (1982), and Holly Mayer, *Belonging to the Army: Camp Followers and Community During the American Revolution* (1966). For a more ideological study, which also explains many political twists and turns during the war, see Don Higginbotham, *The War of American Independence: Military Attitudes, Policies, and Practice, 1763–1789* (1983).

For the struggles over public commitment to the patriotic effort, many insights about daily local life are offered in Richard Buel and Joy Day Buel, *The Way of Duty: A Woman and Her Family in Revolutionary America* (1984).

The best book about forging new state governments is Gordon Wood, *The Creation of the American Republic* (1969). But Jack Rakove adds important dimensions to the state-level discussion about rights, property, and sovereignty in his new work, *Original Meanings: Politics and Ideas in the Making of the Constitution* (1996); and the older volume by Jackson T. Main, *The Sovereign States, 1775–1783* (1973), is still a valuable source on this subject.

Work on the southern campaigns often overlaps with portrayals of the frontier and Native Americans. See the indispensable studies, Jeffrey Crow and Larry Tise, eds., *The Southern*

Experience in the American Revolution (1978), and Ronald Hoffman and Thad W. Tate, eds., *An Uncivil War: The Southern Backcountry During the American Revolution* (1985). In addition, the final months of struggle are covered well in James O'Donnell, *Southern Indians in the American Revolution* (1973); John Pancake, *The Destructive War: The British Campaign in the Carolinas, 1780–1782* (1985); and Russell Weigley, *The Partisan War: The South Carolina Campaign of 1780–1782* (1970).

Important work assessing what patriots gained during the Revolution are Ira Berlin and Ronald Hoffman, *Slavery and Freedom in the Age of the American Revolution* (1983); John Ferling, ed., *The World Turned Upside Down: The American Victory in the War of Independence* (1988); and John C. Dann, ed., *The Revolution Remembered: Eyewitness Accounts of the War for Independence* (1980). All of these works illuminate, through local studies and personal portraits, the role of different social constituencies. The matter of new rights and obligations for women is treated admirably in Linda Kerber, *Women of the Republic: Intellect and Ideology in Revolutionary America* (1980), and Mary Beth Norton, *Liberty's Daughters: The Revolutionary Experience of American Women, 1750–1800* (1980); but also see the social framework of women's rural life in Joan Jensen, *Loosening the Bonds: Mid-Atlantic Farm Women, 1750–1850* (1986).

Slavery is treated in many of the studies listed above. For separate treatments that focus on slaves and free African-Americans, see Jeffrey Crow, *The Black Experience in Revolutionary North Carolina* (1977); Sylvia Frey, *Water from the Rock: Black Resistance in a Revolutionary Age* (1991); Gary Nash, *Forging Freedom: The Formation of Philadelphia's Black Community, 1720–1840* (1988); and Gary A Puckrein, *The Black Regiment in the American Revolution* (1978).

Daniel Leonard Condemns Rebellion, 1775

When events heated up in 1775, Daniel Leonard, a lawyer from an elite Massachusetts family, was forced to flee from his country home and take shelter in British-
occupied Boston until he could escape, first to Halifax and then to Bermuda.
Leonard wrote seventeen eloquent appeals to fellow colonists to remain loyal to the
British crown. The selection that follows appeared in the *Boston Gazette* two weeks
before Lexington and Concord.

We have been so long advancing to our present state, and by such grada-
tions, that perhaps many of us are insensible of our true state and real danger. Should you be told that acts of high treason are flagrant through the country,
that a great part of the province is in actual rebellion, would you believe it true?
Should you not deem the person asserting it an enemy to the province? Nay,
should you not spurn him from you with indignation? Be calm, my friends, it is
necessary to know the worst of a disease, to enable us to provide an effectual remedy. Are not the bands of society cut asunder, and the sanctions that hold man to
man trampled upon? Can any of us recover a debt, or obtain compensation for
an injury, by law? Are not many persons, whom once we respected and revered,
driven from their homes and families, and forced to fly to the army for protection, for no other reason but their having accepted commissions under our King?
Is not civil government dissolved? . . . [Is it not wrong and treasonous] for a body
of men to assemble without being called by authority, and to pass governmental
acts, or for a number of people to take the militia out of the hands of the King's
representative, or to form a new militia, or to raise men and appoint offices for a
public purpose, without the order or permission of the King or his representative;
or for a number of men to take to their arms, and march with a professed design
of opposing the King's troops . . . ?

. . . We already feel the effects of anarchy; mutual confidence, affection and
tranquility, those sweeteners of human life, are succeeded by distrust, hatred and
wild uproars; the useful arts of agriculture and commerce are neglected for ca-
balling, mobbing this or the other man, because he acts, speaks or is suspected of
thinking different from the prevailing sentiments of the times, in purchasing arms
and forming a militia; O height of madness! . . . Let us consider this matter: However closely we may hug ourselves in the opinion that the Parliament has no right
to tax or legislate for us, the people of England hold the contrary opinion as
firmly; they tell us we are a part of the British empire; that every state from the
nature of government must have a supreme uncontrollable power coextensive
with the empire itself; and that, that power is vested in Parliament. It is as unpopular to deny this doctrine in Great-Britain as it is to assert it in the colonies. . . .

Thomas Paine Urges Independence, 1776

Tom Paine had only recently come to Philadelphia in 1774, penniless and unemployed. But he quickly entered the circles of political discussion and became fast friends with the city's most important intellectual and political leaders. At their behest, Paine wrote a pamphlet that was intended to portray the Imperial Crisis in the sharpest relief and raise the level of commitment in America to the patriot cause. *Common Sense* did exactly that.

Some writers have so confounded society with government, as to leave little or no distinction between them; whereas they are not only different, but have different origins. Society is produced by our wants, and government by our wickedness; the former promotes our happiness *positively* by united our affections, the latter *negatively* by restraining our vices. . . . Society in every state is a blessing, but government even in its best state is but a necessary evil; in its worst state an intolerable one. . . . Government, like dress, is the badge of lost innocence; the palaces of kings are built on the ruins of the bowers of paradise. For were the impulses of conscience clear, uniform, and irresistibly obeyed, man would need no other lawgiver; but that not being the case, he finds it necessary to surrender up a part of his property to furnish means for the protection of the rest; and this he is induced to do by the same prudence which in every other case advises him out of two evils to choose the least.

. . . But there is another and greater distinction for which no truly natural or religious reason can be assigned, and that is, the distinction of men into Kings and Subjects. Male and female are the distinctions of nature, good and bad the distinctions of heaven; but how a race of men came into the world so exalted above the rest, and distinguished like some new species, is worth enquiring into, and whether they are the means of happiness or of misery to mankind. . . .

In England a k— hath little more to do than to make war and give away places; which in plain terms, is to impoverish the nation and set it together by the ears. A pretty business indeed for a man to be allowed eight hundred thousand sterling a year for, and worshipped into the bargain! Of more worth is one honest man to society, and in the sight of God, than all the crowned ruffians that ever lived. . . .

. . . America would have flourished as much, and probably much more, had no European power had any thing to do with her. The commerce by which she hath enriched herself are the necessaries of life, and will always have a market while eating is the custom of Europe. . . . Besides, what have we to do with setting the world at defiance? Our plan is commerce, and that, well attended to, will secure us the peace and friendship of all Europe. . . .

It is repugnant to reason, to the universal order of things, to all examples from the former ages, to suppose, that this continent can longer remain subject to any external power. . . . Small islands not capable of protecting themselves, are the proper objects for kingdoms to take under their care; but there is something very absurd, in supposing a continent to be perpetually governed by an island. In no instance hath nature made the satellite larger than its primary planet, and as England and America, with respect to each other, reverses the common order of nature, it is evident they belong to different systems: England to Europe, America to itself. . . .

> O ye that love mankind! Ye that dare oppose, not only the tyranny, but the tyrant, stand forth! Every spot of the old world is over-run with oppression. Freedom hath been hunted round the globe. Asia, and Africa, have long expelled her. —Europe regards her like a stranger, and England hath given her warning to depart. O! receive the fugitive, and prepare in time an asylum for mankind. ▌

Generations after the Revolution, it became possible to explain the sequence of events leading up to colonists' declaration of political independence. But during the Imperial Crisis, the colonists were not necessarily clear about what was happening in the empire. Even in 1775, most colonists who protested parliamentary laws or chafed under the monarchy did not consider leaving the empire. A large number of people who would eventually become loyalists agreed with protesters that Parliament acted at least hastily against the colonists, and perhaps unjustly. The lines of distinction between patriot and loyalist were drawn slowly, haltingly.

Leonard, a member of the colonial elite, believed that the colonial majority should defer to the wisdom and experience of their rulers. He feared that colonists would destroy the best features of the traditional social and political order, and insisted that all rebellion was "the most atrocious offense" against civility and good government. The colonial independence movement had developed so gradually, Leonard observed, that few colonists realized how the "demagogues of a minority" had led many to "ill-founded views" and, by 1775, were prepared to take over governance of America from the traditional elite.

Paine had no fear of changing the old order. Indeed, he pleaded with colonists to realize that their critique of Parliament and colonial governors was just the first—not the last—step toward realizing their own tremendous potential as a separate people. More than any other writer in the last months before the rebellion, Paine measured the gap between the hesitating and loyal part of the population and the energized and organized revolutionary part—and declared it unbridgeable. Committees of Correspondence, regular public acts of violence, the Sons of Liberty, nonimportation movements, and constant public discussion of differences—all of these, Paine knew, were the prelude to taking a final step toward declaring independence. It was that final step that he now implored colonists to take.

Questions for Analysis

1. What does Daniel Leonard believe are the boundaries of legitimate protest, and in what ways have colonists crossed those boundaries?

2. Compare each writer's view of what is troubling the empire. Who is to blame for the troubles, and what is the implied or stated remedy?

3. What does Paine believe is happening to America? What does he believe *should* happen?

4. Each writer has a view of "the people" and their rights. Find passages in each selection that capture those views.

5. How do Leonard and Paine define legitimate political authority? Identify passages that demonstrate their contrasting views.

7

The Federal Experiment, 1783–1800

*I*n the first years of peace after the Revolution, Mercy Otis Warren confided fearful thoughts in her diary and in letters to friends. The Revolution's accomplishments seemed to be buckling under too many pressures—might it be in danger of ruin? As one of the most educated women of her generation, Mercy had put herself at the head of patriot women during the Revolution. Indeed, her famous family of lawyers and politicians had nurtured Mercy to be an enlightened public citizen. As a young adult, Mercy married Charles Warren, a prominent Boston patriot who encouraged her to develop her talents and revolutionary commitment to their fullest extent. "Having accepted my personal and political liberty," Mercy wrote, "I strained every nerve of my female constitution" to participate in the vibrant, sometimes stormy, public debates about the republican experiment that the patriots had undertaken.

But during the first years of peace, Mercy expressed worry in her diary and in letters to close friends that "all soon shall be lost." After all their sacrifices during the Revolutionary War, Americans were suddenly turning to self-indulgence, luxury, and greed. "A most remarkable depravity of manners pervade[s] the cities of the United States," she moaned. It was bad enough that wealthy people wished to restore "their dissipated habits" of dress and public entertainments so that "every principle of that republican spirit which requires patience, probity, industry, and self-denial" might vanish. But even worse, "multitudes of people" were buying more foreign goods than they could afford. Republican governments could never recover social order and reconstruct war-torn areas in the face of such pervasive, and perverse, popular indulgence. Moreover, observed Warren, even political leaders had become demagogues. But they could no longer point to British politicians as the source of moral and political corruption, for these qualities now characterized American political life.

How, she wondered, had such a remarkable reversal occurred? Mercy Otis Warren wrestled mightily in her writings to understand why Americans, in the postwar years, seemed to have lost their republican virtue. Her answers, some of them published, gave solace to other anxious observers of American political and cultural life. Warren insisted that the growing incidence of rowdy public behavior, disrespectful political discussions, and wanton purchasing and indebtedness were not inherent characteristics of Americans. No, Warren reassured her readers. At fault was the war. The Revolution had brought out citizens' best patriotic efforts, but it had also tempted them into dangerous behavior. Warren blamed the persistent "state of war; a relaxation of government; the sudden acquisition of fortune; a depreciating currency; and a new intercourse with foreign nations" for the chaos of the 1780s. The true identity of independent American citizens would emerge when they recognized their depravity and restored social order. Until then, Warren was not at all certain that Americans' republican experiment would turn out well.

But the problem did not stop there. Warren also feared that the remedies proposed in the federal Constitution of 1787 "overly corrected the dangers of licentious" political and cultural life by threatening to undermine "the people's liberties" that revolutionaries fought so hard to win. The new federal experiment could "unhinge" the so-called Spirit of '76. In the years to come, Warren felt compelled to part ways with the revolutionary leaders, many of whom she had admired, and to join opponents of the Constitution.

Ambivalence about the future of the republic transcended class and gender. Thousands of men and women shared Warren's anxieties about the uncertain, shifting conditions of the 1780s. The Revolution had introduced many changes—desired by some, dreaded by others—and more would follow that no one could have anticipated. While many people welcomed opportunities to alter social relations and develop a national identity according to a new vision of themselves, many others longed to restore public order and slow the pace of cultural and economic change during the 1780s and 1790s. The intense public debate that developed in these years divided Americans in many ways, and yet also inched them closer to a new national identity.

■ Who participated in the widespread postwar discussion about American political and cultural identity?

■ How would the new republic recover from the Revolution and extend the liberties that had been promised to Americans?

■ What powers should the new states enjoy after the Revolution, and would they be adequate to protect Americans from both external threats and internal discord?

■ Given the spectrum of social conditions in so large a nation, how would the great natural abundance of America be divided among citizens?

This chapter will address these questions.

The New Nation's Culture

The Revolution initiated a number of important transformations in American life. Despite their scorn for the British standing army, Americans created the Continental Army and sustained it through many years of warfare. Americans had also eagerly begun to discuss what forms of political organization might be appropriate for them and had created new republican states. Even so, in the years after Yorktown, issues of personal and institutional freedom remained largely unsettled and continued to concern Americans. But the independent republic was still, as one war veteran put it, "unsecured from the clutches of our own internal skemes [schemes] . . . and the claws of foreign powers." How, asked many Americans during the 1780s, would their new governments protect their liberties and extend their opportunities? For some time to come, they found no clear answers.

Religion

The Declaration of Independence made it impossible for King George III to reign over religious matters in his former colonies. Indeed, the Revolution initiated a widespread reorganization of North American religious denominations and numerous efforts to give churches a distinctive American identity. During the Revolution, many Anglican clergy retained their right to collect taxes for the established church and to sanction members' marriages. But slowly, new denominations such as the Methodists and Baptists, especially in the southern states, began to gain members. Religious dissenters rejoiced that political independence paved the way for official recognition of new denominations. In 1786 Thomas Jefferson submitted Virginia's Statute of Religious Freedom, which swept away many Anglican privileges and decreed that church attendance and financial support of clerical leaders would henceforth be voluntary. In 1789 a convention of bishops and clergy in Philadelphia recreated the Anglican Church's identity by establishing the Protestant Episcopal Church of the United States.

Religious freedom emerged by degrees in other areas of the new republic. In northern states, where the Congregational Church was strong and in some cases the established religion, legislatures continued to raise taxes for that denomination's support but permitted new ones—especially the Baptists—to earmark taxes paid by their members for their own clergy. Officially, most American states still stipulated that offices be held by Christians, or even Protestants, but many people agreed that they must not otherwise curtail freedom of conscience. For example, new Catholic and Jewish places of worship gained tolerance during the 1780s, and in predominantly Anglican strongholds, Presbyterians and Quakers began to spread. In 1774 colonists had registered loud protests against the crown's "papist" Quebec Act; less than a quarter-century later, in 1790, John Carroll of Maryland became the first Roman Catholic bishop in America.

While established denominations changed, new ones grew by leaps and bounds after the Revolution. On the frontiers, settlers without churches welcomed itinerant Baptist and Methodist ministers. Circuit riders reached out to new converts, invit-

Chronology

1783	Treaty of Paris
	British evacuate New York
1784	Treaty of Fort Stanwix
	Economic depression begins
	Spain closes New Orleans to American trade
1785	Shays's Rebellion
1786	Annapolis Convention
1787	Constitutional Convention
	Northwest Ordinance
	Publication of *The Federalist*
1789	French Revolution begins
1790	Judiciary Act
	Indian Intercourse Act
	Hamilton's funding and assumption plan
1791	Bank of the United States chartered by Congress
	Bill of Rights ratified
	Whiskey Tax passed in Congress
	Hamilton's Report on Manufactures
1791–1796	Slave revolts in Saint Dominique
1793	Congress passes Neutrality Proclamation regarding England and France
1794	Battle of Fallen Timbers
	Whiskey Rebellion
1795	Treaty of Greenville
	Jay's Treaty
1796	Adams elected president
1797	XYZ Affair
1798	Alien and Sedition Acts
	Virginia and Kentucky Resolutions
1799	Fries's Rebellion in Pennsylvania
1800	Jefferson elected president

ing the "awakened" to rousing camp meetings. At Cain Ridge, Kentucky, for example, thousands gathered for five days of gospel preaching under tents and in the open air, reveling in their distance from genteel religious traditions and their newfound emotional spirituality. No more learned clergy and rigid church hierarchies, they agreed. Revivalists urged their audiences to find personal religious self-reliance and independence from established institutions. In a few short years, these postrevolutionary changes would swell into what historians call the Second Great Awakening (discussed further in Chapter 9).

Servitude and Slavery

The Revolution's language of freedom and equality challenged many of the social dependencies and distinctions that existed in colonial society. New laws and social norms in the 1780s began to reform the degrees of legal nonfreedom that defined indentured servants, apprenticed youth, and certain religious and ethnic groups. White men, in particular, found it increasingly odious to bear any dependent status, including temporary servitude, because it was "contrary to . . . the idea of liberty" that all citizens now embraced. In a very short time, indentured servitude shrank to negligible proportions of the laborers in Philadelphia and New York. The term "servant" dropped from use in many areas. Instead, many immigrants who worked in urban households referred to themselves simply as "the help" and negotiated a range of privileges, including "freedoms to come and go as we please" once they completed their chores.

The condition of slaves and free African-Americans was dramatically different in the new republic. True, the calls for patriotic "liberty" raised hundreds of individual claims for manumission and spurred thousands of slaves to "take their freedom" by running away during the Revolution. In addition, tens of thousands of slaves, mostly in the Chesapeake and southern states, gained freedom during the fighting. The British army freed a majority of Georgia's slaves by sweeping them into its regiments during the second half of the war; the northern patriotic governments accepted hundreds of African-American volunteers, too. As many as one-fourth of South Carolina's black majority obtained their freedom from the advancing British troops. As the British fled Charleston and Savannah at the end, fleeing masters took thousands of slaves to the West Indies, Canada, and West Africa.

Some of the northern states abolished slavery during the war, though unevenly and for varied reasons. When Vermont became a state in 1777, its constitution abolished slavery. The 1781 state Bill of Rights in Massachusetts allowed some slaves to sue for their freedom in state courts on the grounds that they had been "born free and equal." Thousands of northern slaves in Massachusetts and New Hampshire simply walked away from the shops, forges, stables, and farms of their masters over the next years.

To ease the transition for white masters, Pennsylvania, Connecticut, and Rhode Island legislators provided for gradual emancipation. In 1780 Pennsylvania declared that all offspring born to slaves from that time forward could claim their freedom at age twenty-eight. In New York and New Jersey, where slaves accounted

Elizabeth Mumbet Freeman
This painting, done in 1811 by Susan A. Livingston Ridley Sedgwick, is of a Massachusetts former slave who sued her master for her freedom in 1781. In her court hearing, Freeman told the justices that she believed the "rights of man" should be accorded to all women as well, slave and free. She won, and became a domestic servant earning wages. *(Massachusetts Historical Society. Gift of Maria Banyer Sedwick, 1884.)*

for more than 10 percent of the population, gradual emancipation came even later. Only in 1799 did the New York legislature yield partially to demands from white abolitionists and black leaders by granting freedom to slave children when they reached age twenty-five. In 1804 New Jersey became the last northern state to grant gradual emancipation. Still, a decade into the new century, in 1810, more than 25,000 African-Americans remained enslaved in the North. In addition to those slaves who had not yet come of age for emancipation, hundreds were sold by their northern masters into the southern states before the deadline for emancipation. Masters also lied about the ages of their slaves in order to retain their labor.

Even when free, African-Americans voted only occasionally and almost never attempted to hold local or state office. In Delaware free blacks outnumbered slaves three to one by 1800, but new laws excluded them from full civil and political rights. By 1810, many northern free African-Americans believed "life is no whit better" day to day in northern cities, and "maybe just one whit better" without "master's heel on our backs."

Some free blacks prevailed against social prejudice and adverse laws to develop their talents, build community institutions, or become outstanding leaders. White and black philanthropists formed the Abolition Society of Pennsylvania during the 1790s to protect former slaves and ease the transition to freedom. The Quaker Anthony Benezet funded a school for free African-Americans, and the black Reverend

Absalom Jones established a huge congregation in Philadelphia known as St. Thomas's African Episcopal Church. Although freeholding, political rights, and property ownership remained the preserve of white society, free black churches, clubs, and schools sprang up in every northern city. By the 1790s, thousands of free African-Americans in the North and in the Upper South created the Baptist Association, Williamsburg African Church, African Marine Fund in New York, and numerous African Free Schools. A distinctive African-American voice appeared in Jupiter Hammon's writings about the failed promises of the Revolution and in Phillis Wheatley's poems describing her own mixed African and American heritages. "Every human breast," wrote Wheatley, "is impatient of oppression, and pants for deliverance."

In the southern states from Virginia to Georgia, social and economic advancement for free African-Americans was far more difficult than in northern states. Although many new congregations of Methodists and Baptists supported abolition during the early 1780s, the next decades witnessed their retreat from such positions. Methodist leadership carefully laid out new rules for church organization and membership prohibiting both freed and slave African-Americans from acquiring equal stature in congregations with white members. Virginia and Maryland permitted individual masters to manumit slaves beginning in 1782, and by 1810 they had freed about one-fifth of Maryland's slaves. Masters in Virginia freed a smaller proportion of their slave population, probably about 10,000 of the state's 300,000 slaves by 1790. Then, a 1792 law made manumission harder to achieve, sparking more instances of resistance and open revolt against masters' authority. In 1800 the freeman Gabriel Prosser attempted to lead a slave uprising in Virginia, but authorities quickly suppressed the revolt and hanged nearly forty slaves with Prosser (discussed further in Chapter 12).

Below the Chesapeake, slavery laws and daily treatment of bound labor tightened even more. In North Carolina the state government negated individual Quaker manumissions as early as 1776 and confirmed the right of masters to re-enslave African-Americans who had been set free during the Revolution in 1788. New North Carolina laws also stiffened penalties for runaway slaves headed toward the North. After 1800, expanding cotton cultivation created a huge demand for slave labor in South Carolina and Georgia, where planters dug new furrows to raise "white gold" and dug in their heels against efforts to free valuable slave labor. Because most slaveholders were also state and national political leaders, they were in a position to preserve the institution. For over twenty years after the end of the Revolution, these states imported slaves by the thousands. The number of southern slaves grew roughly from 400,000 in 1770, to 700,000 in 1790, and to 1.2 million in 1810.

Republican Womanhood

Many women accepted new roles during the Revolutionary War as heads of households, active business partners, spies, or producers for the army. As the war progressed, some women demanded more permanent authority over household decisions, while others decided to stay in retail businesses that male kin had established before the war. When women throughout the northern countryside sporadically pooled resources of textiles or food for needy soldiers, they learned important public economic and political roles. For example, women of the Philadelphia Ladies Association made shirts and coats for Continental soldiers and nursed the wounded taking refuge in the city. Many women also readily crossed military lines to supply troops, risks that sometimes brought valuable news, goods, and cash into their communities and families.

After the war, many circumstances thwarted these experiences of economic and political empowerment. For instance, farms did not recover uniformly once the troops were gone, which kept household purchasing power low and prolonged dire necessity for imported goods. The postwar recession also challenged the wits of women in cities and country villages faced with running a household. Women and children worked hard just to produce enough to survive. Continuing high prices provoked many community outbursts of rage. Women who had participated in riots to "liberate" goods from rapacious storekeepers' shops during the 1770s once again entered public arenas: driven by necessity, they forced millers to free up supplies of flour, fishermen to distribute their catches at discount prices, and urban retailers to unlock hoarded goods.

Despite reverses, many women persevered in their efforts to extend their new economic and political roles. Some demanded more equality within marriage and greater respect from the men in their lives. One target was the common law tradition of coverture, which denied wives legal personalities. Some women pleaded successfully with state legislatures to be allowed to keep the property of departed loyalist husbands, since it was their sole source of income. Others demanded to be treated equally in marriage, as when Lucy Knox wrote during the war that "there is such a thing as equal command" at home even if it did not obtain on the battlefield. Parents of middling and elite families began to shed traditions of arranging marriages and careers for their children, and to recognize the right of their children to choose their own spouses. Revised property and inheritance laws in some states gave women more authority over their own and their children's futures. Most states wrote new laws that broke the tradition of recognizing inheritance through the male line of kinship, and moved toward favoring the descent of property within married couples. Pre-Revolution laws allowing widows only the "use" of one-third of their deceased husbands' estates gave way to new laws favoring their outright ownership of that portion. Moreover, the northern states began to recognize not just the eldest son's privilege, but all sons' and daughters' roughly equal status in inheritance disputes. Every state except South Carolina liberalized its divorce laws soon after the Revolution.

The same Enlightenment and republican ideals that shaped the independence movement in general also inspired new thinking about women's education and family roles. By the 1780s, a few writers were suggesting that women were morally superior to men and enjoyed a greater facility with reading and writing. These idealized qualities equipped women to be "republican wives" and "republican mothers" who not only gained higher stature within middle-class and elite families, but who also bore most of the moral responsibility to nurture husbands and sons in these qualities. Republican wives would soften the aggressive entrepreneurial pursuits of men with profound patriotism toward civic affairs. Republican mothers would shelter their children from the temptations of immoral behavior and selfish materialism by providing a proper moral education at home.

While writers, artists, and politicians began to shape these ideal family and nurturing roles, some outspoken individual women began to demand more personal independence. The most outspoken advocate of women's education, Judith Sargent Murray, insisted that women "should be taught to depend on their own efforts, for the procurement of an establishment in life." Although many clergymen and politicians ridiculed such views as coming from "women of masculine minds" and "masculine manners," Murray stated confidently that she stood on the brink of "a new era in female history." Many male educators agreed with Murray, but they usually coupled the benefits of female education with women's inherent duties to nurture republican husbands and children. Benjamin Rush, for example, believed women "ought to have suitable education, to concur in instructing their sons in the principles of liberty and government." That is, women should not seek education for their own enrichment, but to produce a better citizenry of publicly minded men.

Liberty Displaying the Arts and Sciences   America's republican virtue is portrayed as a refined woman who shares music, literature, and worldly wisdom with free African-Americans, whom she invites to become full members of the nation. She holds a pole with the cap of liberty perched on top, and a bountiful countryside fills the background.   *(Courtesy, Winterthur Museum.)*

In fact, even though many women enjoyed a privileged moral role in their homes and widening opportunities in education, many legal and political rights remained closed to them. Legislators who relied on common law traditions to shape legal rights in the new states withheld certain fundamental privileges from women, or granted them partially. The New Jersey constitution of 1777 conceded to propertied widows the right to vote, but then revoked the privilege in 1807. Elsewhere, republican traditions and the common law together limited women's civic participation. For example, the requirement of property ownership for the franchise, long a treasured precept of the common law and republicanism, linked property to political commitment and independent political judgment and prevented women from voting altogether.

 ## The Precarious Peace, 1783–1786

At first, congressmen and negotiators thought the Treaty of Paris (see page 235) was the best agreement Americans could have hoped to sign. In territorial terms, the new nation's frontiers provided tremendous potential for expansion. In commercial terms, Americans looked forward to rapid recovery and expansion into new, distant markets. But soon after diplomats John Jay, Benjamin Franklin, and John Adams returned from Paris, they realized this "parchment agreement" provided very little guarantee of peace or grounds for development. For years, pressing issues demanded congressional and state attention. Soldiers and loyalists, widows and rural debtors, merchants and army suppliers, among others, emerged from the war's stresses and strains with high expectations and many disappointments. These years, known later as the "Critical Period," tested the revolutionary experiment on numerous fronts.

Soldiers and Loyalists

As Americans waited from 1781 to 1783 for the war to end officially, Continental soldiers and officers grew restless in their camp at Newburgh, New York, just north of West Point. Over ten thousand men and about a thousand women demanded back pay and the bounties of land Congress owed them. Congress had promised to give life pensions at half-pay to officers who enlisted for the duration of the war; but Congress had made no payments. If the army disbanded once negotiators signed a peace treaty, officers believed they might never see that pay. So, in January 1783, a group of prominent officers petitioned Congress to commute their pensions into a single payment of five years' full pay.

Congressional delegates divided deeply over the officers' demand. While some delegates favored appeasing the Newburgh petition, a majority rejected it. Officers at Newburgh also disagreed among themselves. General Horatio Gates led a faction calling for a meeting to force Congress's hand; General George Washington countered with a meeting of his own on March 15, 1783. He appeared before his men knowing full well that if he could not calm the officers quickly, a military coup might shatter the tenuous Revolutionary victory before the peace treaty was even signed. In an emotionally charged speech, Washington acknowledged the officers' years of selfless sacrifices and then pleaded with them to retract their thoughts of coercing Congress and the American people to satisfy their demands. It worked. Within a week, the officers informed Congress they would not take action, and a relieved Congress granted the five-year bonus.

Washington needed more than personal charisma to calm the troops in those early months of 1783. Fortunately, he had firmly established military subordination to congressional authority. When he resigned in December, he was both a military and a civilian hero. Meanwhile, in late 1783, Congress permitted soldiers to begin returning home, some of them still short of pay and some with the assurance of getting cash or land bonuses soon. By early 1784, the Continental Army had become a shell of its former self.

While the army disbanded, large numbers of former loyalists sought the right to return home or to recover their abandoned belongings. Alexander Hamilton was one leading patriot who believed that these exiled "valuable citizens" should be welcomed back and restored to their property. He cited the Treaty of Paris provision that loyalists had twelve months to return and settle their personal or business affairs. Gradually, former loyalists resurfaced in colleges, churches, and even local political offices in major northern cities. Some states, including radical Pennsylvania, repealed anti-Tory legislation such as the test oaths administered during the Revolution. Connecticut legislators explicitly invited loyalists to share their commercial, inventive, and political genius in reconstructing the new state. Hamilton himself defended legal claims of loyalists who sued New Yorkers for restoration of their prewar property. Although many Americans feared that the "stain of loyalism" would mar the new republic's fragile identity, thousands of former loyalists quietly reintegrated themselves into a rapidly changing American society.

Commercial Decline and Recovery

Despite high hopes for recovery after 1783, Americans entered a prolonged commercial depression. For a few years the reduction in urban population and scarcities of building materials caused by the war hampered the ability of urban centers to recover. Even when the population of the original thirteen states began to grow again from natural increase and immigration, per capita exports did not keep up over the 1780s, for overall American households did not yet produce as much as they had before the war. Lowered levels of production meant fewer purchases of consumer goods—especially imports. In the South, tobacco exports recovered slowly because of ravaged fields and low European demand, which meant that southerners did not earn credits for necessary imports of manufactured goods. Virginia and Maryland farmers already had begun a significant shift from producing tobacco for export toward growing grain for export and local consumption. Overall, imports from England fell nearly 70 percent below pre-Revolution levels in southern states by 1787.

Although Americans had less money to spend during the depression, British firms continued to flood city stores with goods priced lower than American-made ones. In response to demands from artisans to protect their trades, some state governments placed high import taxes on imported manufactures. But merchants still needed to repay debts to English and other foreign creditors, and so gold and silver "flew like lightning bolts" from the country. To make matters worse, in 1784 Parliament passed a series of written decrees that closed off the West Indies ports to American ships, thereby stifling the long-standing trade between northern cities and Caribbean ports and upsetting the entire balance of commerce for the new states.

During the 1780s, American merchants began to cultivate new trading partners to substitute for their reliance on England. Trade with southern France and the French Caribbean provided some relief but not nearly enough long-term credit and, according to some Americans, far too many "luxuries" such as French brandy and silk. In 1784 a consortium of merchants sailed the *Empress of China* to new markets in the East, but it would take years to find the right products in sufficient quantities, and to build enough seaworthy vessels, to make many voyages to East Asia.

Debtor Relief and Shays's Rebellion

Most states owed large sums to private citizens for their loans of money or sales of goods and services during the war. Some legislatures raised average citizens' taxes steeply in order to acquire the revenue to extinguish these debts, mostly held by merchants and landowners. In an attempt to relieve their citizens of the burden imposed by higher taxes, many states tried two remedies: One, familiar to former colonists, was to print huge quantities of paper money in order to facilitate business and tax payments. The other was to pass "stay laws" that postponed repayment of debts that citizens owed to one another. However, so much paper currency entered circulation that its value declined rapidly, and stay laws increased the anxieties of merchants whose foreign creditors were kept waiting "because we have so little payment coming in from the countryside."

In Maryland, landowners in the legislature proposed staving off debtor discontent by replacing the poll tax, which had been a hardship for the poor for generations, with a property tax on lands. However, more conservative state leaders rejected the measure in 1785. In South Carolina, farmers gained a little relief when a new law permitted them to repay creditors in installments, thereby avoiding seizure of their land and goods. In Rhode Island, a large coalition of rural candidates won control of the state government in 1786 and proceeded to issue huge amounts of paper money. New laws declared the currency legal tender for all personal and public debts, which meant that creditors would have to accept the money regardless of its market value. Additional laws decreed that debtors could deposit partial payments of their debts with county judges if creditors refused to accept the legal tender. Merchant creditors expressed alarm that debts, which had always been defined as sacred personal contracts, could be wiped out by such "licentious and unchristian injustice" of "farmer laws." But so long as debtors controlled the state government, creditors had no recourse.

In Massachusetts, farmers did not gain a majority in the legislature and failed to get debtor relief legislation. Moreover, eastern merchant and creditor groups consistently rebuffed petitions from the countryside for paper money and approved of laws that kept raising taxes. By 1785, when many farmers and small producers in the western counties defaulted on their taxes or their mortgages, merchants, landlords, and sheriffs dragged them into court and repossessed their farms. As tensions grew during 1786, farmers in Springfield and Worcester began to hold meetings, what James Madison called "conventions of their own making," to protest high taxes and mistreatment by sheriffs and lawyers. In some areas, angry farmers closed the courts by force or set free their jailed neighbors.

By early fall, hundreds of western and central Massachusetts citizens had organized an extralegal army of "regulators" under Captain Daniel Shays, a local hero and Continental Army veteran. The "Shaysites" demanded lower taxes, restoration of homes to their former owners, and more political representation of western areas in the state government.

On January 25, 1787, Shays marched 1,500 men toward the Springfield arsenal to capture its 450 tons of military stores. The state militia, defending the arsenal, opened heavy artillery fire on the Shaysites, killing four and wounding twenty. At about the same time, the state legislature passed a Riot Act outlawing all unauthorized assemblies and inviting eastern merchants and lawyers to finance a special army to restore order in the western counties. With Governor James Bowdoin's help, a private army of 4,400 men marched west, caught up with the retreating cold and hungry Shaysites, and captured 150 of the rebels. The legislature subsequently voted acquittals for all but Shays and his coleader Luke Day. However, they did not vote tax reductions, and skirmishes between local authorities and tax resisters continued in western counties. In the next election, disgruntled farmers and artisans turned Bowdoin out of office.

In New York, Pennsylvania, Connecticut, and New Hampshire—and in the independent republic of Vermont—other debtors' rebellions arose. In South Carolina,

Country Politics in the 1780s
During the uncertain decade after the Revolution, western counties of many states were filled with indebted small producers and farmers who began to play a more vocal role in local affairs and to hold local offices. However, taxes remained high, and wealthy men in state legislatures resisted the demands of overburdened debtors for relief. Here, an angry artisan throws a wealthy officeholder into the mill creek as sympathetic townspeople look on. *(Library of Congress.)*

North Carolina, Georgia, and western portions of Virginia, debtors sent petitions demanding changes in taxation policies, meanwhile resisting the collection efforts of their local sheriffs. From Canada and London, as well as their military posts in the West, British officials gloated that the "disunited States" verged on collapse, while in America urban elites and former revolutionary leaders lamented the "Anarchy and public Convulsion" in the states. Rural regulators, cried one Massachusetts gentleman in February 1787, seemed to be making "a declaration of war against the United States!" The stability and future of the Confederation, warned some, was in doubt.

Shaping the West

The Articles of Confederation of 1781 and the Treaty of Paris of 1783 (see page 235) established Congress's control over extensive new land beyond the former colonies. However, as Congress began efforts to settle, develop, and sell portions of this "national domain," some western claimants challenged Congress's jurisdiction, including new states, Native Americans, and independent settlers, known as squatters, who would occupy thousands of land parcels without legitimate titles. One early step toward resolving these overlapping claims came when New York, Virginia, and Massachusetts ceded land north of the Ohio River to Congress between 1781 and 1786. In future years, Connecticut ceded land in the Western Reserve south of Lake Erie, and New Hampshire and New York gave up claims to Vermont in 1791. These lands became known as the Northwest Territory. South of the Ohio River, Virginia, North Carolina, South Carolina, and Georgia ceded additional lands to the nation between 1792 and 1802 (see map).

Congress outlined tentative efforts to assert its authority over the West. In 1784 Thomas Jefferson drafted a land ordinance designed to divide the area into ten territories and to guarantee settlers self-rule—a constitution and government of their own choosing. Once a territory achieved population equal to the smallest of the revolutionary states, it could petition to become a state in the Confederation. Congress defeated Jefferson's plan because too many delegates feared it would shift political power to newly populated areas and create a frontier in which settlers would live "willy nilly" without orderly settlement and "fall to the level of the savages." Partly to satisfy these objections, Jefferson submitted an additional Land Ordinance in 1785 that provided for land surveys. Based on the old New England system of settlement, the revised ordinance divided land into townships of thirty-six sections, one square mile (or 640 acres) each (see map). The ordinance reserved one section for a local school, and four sections for future public use. Sections were to sell for $1 per acre, giving Congress sorely needed revenues and attracting thousands of small farm families to orderly communities.

However, most small farmers could not afford the $640 needed to buy a section, so sales under the congressional act were largely to wealthy investors. In 1785 Congress allowed the Ohio Company, a group of aggressive speculators, to purchase 1.5 million acres for $1 million dollars. Military veterans under the leadership of Manassah Cutler from Massachusetts, and ambitious investors such as William Duer from New York City, combined forces to underwrite this tremendous land grab.

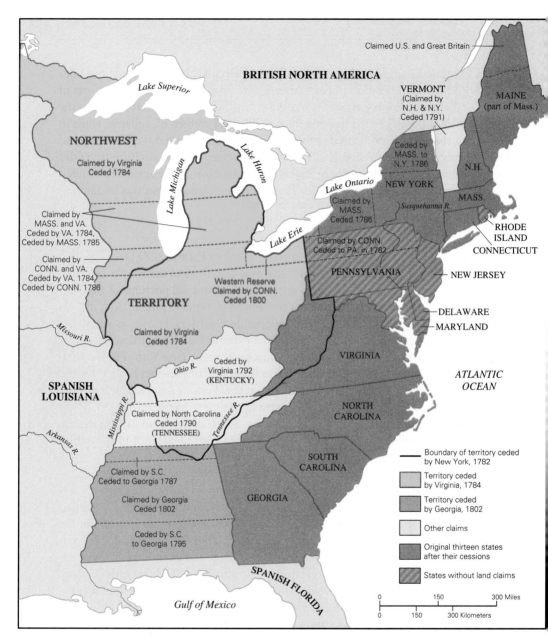

Cession of Western Land, 1782–1802 By the end of the Revolution, most of the new thirteen states claimed large areas of the western territory. Overlapping claims, based on the original colonial charters, as well as new waves of settlers fighting over titles to tracts of land, led to violence on the frontier and political confusion in Congress. A series of compromises among the states and federal government eventually resolved most disputes.

These "mushroom companies" paid for territorial land in revolutionary paper money and securities that its investors had purchased at drastically depreciated prices from thousands of farmers and small-time army suppliers.

Another threat to the Jeffersonian vision for orderly western settlement was the continuing presence of British troops on the frontier. In 1784 Congress appointed John Jay to negotiate with the British for the removal of these troops, but Jay failed.

Settlers attributed the diplomatic setback to Congress's indecision. Some Ohio settlements even threatened to leave the Confederation and seek protection from the British, while others decided to live without any government's authority. Acting on rumors of western discontent, Spanish officials hired Americans George Rogers Clark and General James Wilkinson to gather information from the "Kentucky wilderness" to see whether those Americans could be persuaded to live under Spanish rule. Wilkinson briefly tried to organize western Pennsylvanians into an independent state under the protection of the Spanish government. In another example of this "separation tendency," when Congress refused to let Vermont gain independence from New York during the early 1780s, the Green Mountain Boys negotiated temporarily with London for readmission to the empire as a colonial province.

Related difficulties unfolded in the South. Spain still claimed rights to the Mississippi River, but Americans in the Northwest Territory needed the river passage for exporting goods to southern and eastern markets quickly and cheaply. Hauling goods overland was a far more costly and dangerous undertaking for small producers in the Ohio Valley and Indiana country. When Spain disallowed American river transport from New Orleans southward after 1784, settlers in the Northwest and southern politicians promoting expansion fumed. John Jay stepped in again, attempting to persuade the Spanish minister, Don Diego de Gardoqui, to accept American sovereignty over the river, promising that Spain would enjoy equally "free transit" as Americans. When that proposal was rejected, he offered to recognize Spanish sovereignty over the waterway if Americans could trade freely at all Spanish ports on the river. Although the northern states would have been happy with this compromise, congressmen from the southern states blocked passage of Jay's plan.

Trouble with Native Americans also plagued efforts to settle the Northwest Territory. Many Americans assumed that, since European powers had recognized American dominion as far as the Mississippi River when they signed the Treaty of Paris, that dominion included a right of conquest over all peoples within those lands. But many Ohio Valley Indian tribes and New York Iroquois villages thought differently. With encouragement from British troops stationed just north of the Ohio River, Native Americans throughout the valley defended their homelands against advancing American settlement. Although Congress did not recognize any need to forge treaties with Indians in the territory, it nevertheless saw the diplomatic wisdom of trying to secure the frontier from continuous multisided warfare among Americans, British, and various Indian peoples.

But negotiation of treaties often dissolved into land grabs or the use of force against Indians. In the Treaty of Fort Stanwix in 1784, Congress's first agreement with an Indian tribe, the Iroquois ceded great areas of land to the United States, literally at gunpoint, and agreed to relocate to Canada or live on small reservations. In the Treaty of Fort McIntosh in 1785, Congress further secured national interests over the Ohio Valley, and the Wyandot, Delaware, Ottawa, and Chippewa villages succumbed to the rush of white settlers. Nevertheless, government surveyors worked quickly to measure and sell lands taken by treaty. By 1786, congressional efforts to "clear the savage forces" from the Great Lakes down to the Gulf of Mexico encompassed many Native American peoples, including the Creek, Shawnee, and

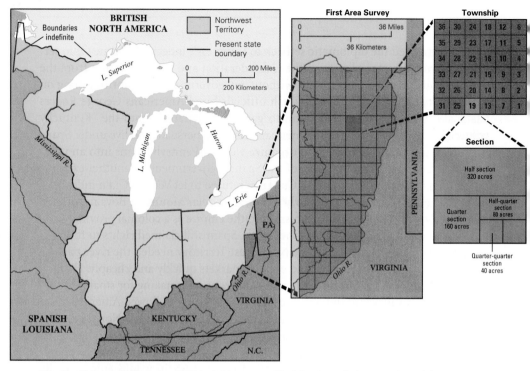

The Northwest Ordinance, 1785 This act provided for the orderly surveying of the extensive lands now under American jurisdiction following the Revolution. The Ordinance divided the land into townships of thirty-six sections of one square mile each. Although many Americans could not afford to purchase such large tracts of land, settlers continued to migrate westward in great numbers. The Northwest Ordinance of 1785 was later modified in 1787 to divide the area into three to five territories, give a structured government, and prohibit slavery in these new lands.

Miami nations. Because Americans had extracted these agreements by force, however, some Indians repudiated the measures and attempted to reclaim their sovereignty over their lands. For example, Mohawk chief Joseph Brant declared that the Iroquois were "equally free" as any Americans to claim rights over land.

Land companies, Indians, and government surveyors all complained about yet another "evil force at work against peace and order" in the West: the thousands of squatters who moved into areas ahead of surveys and heedless of Native American treaties. During the Revolution, hundreds of settlers had crossed the Appalachian Mountains into the fertile Ohio Valley. By 1785, over 30,000 farmers and traders occupied Kentucky territory (admitted as a state in 1792), and by the end of the decade, its population stood at over 74,000. The Tennessee territory (admitted as a state in 1794) held 36,000 people by 1790. From 1784 to 1788, settlers streamed from North Carolina into what is now eastern Tennessee, where they set up a quasi-government and called themselves the State of Franklin. Though they petitioned Congress repeatedly for statehood, national leaders feared the Franklin settlers would choose not to join the union and so refused the petitions.

Congressmen admitted that they needed a "strong toned government" to bring order out of the chaos of territorial settlement. So their last important act was to pass a modified Northwest Ordinance in 1787. It provided for the creation of three to five states in the huge Northwest Territory (future Ohio, Indiana, Michigan, Wisconsin, and Illinois), to be "admitted on an equal footing with the original states." In place of self-government, Congress decided that appointed judges and governors would provide greater stability in the West. Once a territory's population reached five thousand citizens, inhabitants would choose an assembly modeled on those of existing states. The governor would have an absolute veto over all legislation until the territory achieved statehood. Of great future significance, slavery was prohibited in the territories.

The Northwest Ordinance established principles for orderly occupation of the land, as well as the peaceful transfer of citizenship and government to new areas. It helped Americans view the different parts of the new nation as a coherent whole and deterred secessionist movements by giving settlers a means to become states and identify with national development. At the same time, the Ordinance established national claims against the Indians, Spanish, and French peoples in the West, claims that would be applied to the trans-Mississippi frontier in the future, and would in turn provoke fierce reactions from the Indians who occupied that land.

 ## The Constitutional Convention, 1787

By 1786, Congress's credibility was fading fast. Its instability and lack of authority, insisted some critics, had become symbolically clear in its repeated relocations: from Philadelphia, to Princeton, New York City, Trenton, and Annapolis. Critics overlooked the substantial gains made by individual states in recovering from the Revolution. They also dismissed the very great contributions of the Land Ordinances, noting—correctly or not—that settlers would amass in the new region regardless of political provisions for survey, protection, and government. Instead, nay-sayers focused on the numerous difficulties facing the new nation and hinted that Americans were in danger of losing the entire republican experiment. What voices would rise above this din of fears and criticism—some of it founded, some of it fabricated—to organize effective political responses? What new social alignments did Americans need, and what new institutional forms?

Thinking Continentally

Advocates of a stronger central government had been prominent in American politics for some time. Earlier identified as "nationalists," or "men who think continentally," they began to call themselves "Federalists" in 1786. This cadre of national leaders included men whose views had been nurtured in long years of revolutionary struggle: Washington, Hamilton, Madison, Jay, Adams, Knox. To most Federalists, republicanism implied preservation of elite rule, an aristocracy of talent, the security of private property, and a hierarchical social order—conditions that many new state constitutions had begun to eliminate. Federalists believed that state governments had reached too far beyond the Revolution's goals, that they invited "democratic disruptions" by elevating "base layers of unpropertied citizens" above their rightful political and social stations. Just as colonists had successfully defended their liberty from British tyranny, now Americans had to guard against creating too much liberty.

Federalists were appalled by the violence of agrarian Shaysites in the backcountries of many states. But they knew that such violent challenges to the social order would end only when Congress found long-term remedies for the problems of the Critical Period. Since the Confederation's creation in 1781, argued Federalists, the states had focused on paying their own private and public debts, while neglecting to provide for the national debt. Moreover, the states were unable to reopen West Indies and Mississippi River trade that had been closed to American merchants by foreigners. Instead, they passed discriminatory legislation against one another, thereby fragmenting their potential for a great national commerce. Further, the states individually could not secure peace and orderly settlement in the national domain. It would take a strong national government to correct these, and other, ills.

The first step came in 1785, when George Washington invited representatives of Maryland and Virginia to a small conference at his Virginia home, Mount Vernon, to settle a dispute over use of the Potomac River. James Madison, perceiving that this agreement made a good beginning toward interstate cooperation, persuaded the Virginia legislature to call on all the states to meet at Annapolis, Maryland, to discuss additional commercial improvements. On September 5, 1786, delegates arrived at Annapolis from four mid-Atlantic states and Virginia, and New Yorker Alexander Hamilton immediately presented a report on international trade.

Hamilton, born in the Leeward Islands, where his mother taught him bookkeeping skills and introduced him to powerful merchant firms, rose to prominence quickly in New York's post-Revolution commercial and political life. His service in Washington's army, his defense of returning loyalists, and his efforts to raise national revenues during the 1780s exposed him to both the grandeur and the petty jealousies and corruption of public life. When the Annapolis Convention failed to correct the "anarchy of these disunited states," Hamilton urged fellow nationalists to call on Congress to hold a convention that might "render the constitution of the Federal Government adequate to the exigencies of the Union." The following February, Congress agreed to organize a convention, to be held in Philadelphia. Twelve states—all but Rhode Island—said they would participate.

At Philadelphia

In all, 55 delegates attended the Philadelphia convention at one time or another from mid-May to mid-September 1787. The average daily attendance, however, was about 35 men. Twenty-nine delegates had college degrees; 34 had practiced law; 24 had served in the Confederation Congress; and 21 had been officers during the Revolution. Many called themselves merchants and slave owners, but no artisans, small farmers, or free African-Americans came to Philadelphia to deliberate. Washington, Franklin, Hamilton, Robert Morris, and numerous other men identified with political, military, and legal leadership of the Revolution participated in the important convention deliberations. Because of his position at the head of the Continental Army, Washington was the obvious choice to preside over the convention. Madison rose hundreds of times to speak on the convention floor and tirelessly recorded summaries of delegates' speeches. His notes are the only relatively continuous record of those proceedings, which broke from previous practices and took place behind closed doors. Some leading patriots did not appear at the convention: Thomas Jefferson still served as minister to France, John Adams represented America in England, and Patrick Henry refused to participate in any design to reduce the powers of the states.

Most delegates came to the convention to revise the Articles. But an outspoken core of leaders was determined to achieve more far-reaching changes in the structure and functioning of the American republic. Accordingly, they asked the convention delegates to consider a plan that would replace, not revise, the Articles of Confederation.

Madison for the most part had drafted this initial plan, which Edmund Randolph of Virginia presented to delegates on May 29. It proposed a strong national government with one central "consolidated authority" over "the aggregate interests of the community" of all citizens. This "Virginia Plan" proposed a bicameral legislature with representation in both houses apportioned according to population. The legislature would choose the national executive and national judiciary, and it would have all the powers currently held by Congress plus the power to settle disputes between state governments. Congress would have the authority to veto state laws that contradicted the laws of Congress but it would not be able to tax citizens or regulate interstate and international trade.

After only two weeks of debate, the delegates agreed to some of the provisions of the Virginia Plan, including that representatives of a lower house would serve for three years and those of an upper house for seven years, and that a single elected person would hold executive power for seven years.

But the key issue of representation was a sticking point. Delegates from the smaller states argued that basing representation on population would naturally shift power to the most populous states. In June they countered this so-called large-state plan with their own small-state plan. Introduced by William Paterson of New Jersey, the small-state, or "New Jersey Plan," proposed to preserve as much of the existing Confederation structures as possible. It would have granted Congress new powers to tax domestic trade and goods, tax imports, regulate commerce, and demand state requisitions of money and goods. Most important, each state would have one vote in a unicameral Congress, which would guard against excessive influence of very populous states, in particular Virginia, Pennsylvania, and Massachusetts.

In addition to these two plans now on the floor for discussion and refinement, some delegates proposed extravagantly impractical measures. Hamilton, for example, put forward the idea that members of the executive and upper house of government hold offices for life—a proposal inspired by Britain's model of the monarch and peerage. When Hamilton's proposal met vigorous opposition in late June, he went home to New York for a month. Luther Martin of Maryland presented a plan almost the mirror opposite of Hamilton's: Martin insisted that the convention rigorously respect the integrity of the states and eradicate "all smell of aristocracy." When delegates soundly rebuffed him, Martin retreated to his home state to prepare for the long battle to defeat whatever plan emerged from Philadelphia. However, because the delegates knew what the voters would accept and what would best unite their range of views, most of these extreme ideas faded quickly from the convention floor.

In the oppressive heat of June and July, debate was often acrimonious. Gunning Bedford of Delaware threatened that if the large states insisted on proportional representation, "the small ones will find some foreign ally" to turn to. The large-state delegates were equally frightened that their entire republican experiment would fail if Shaysites, or dissenters anywhere, overran the fragile new state governments. As the convention deliberated during July, Secretary of War Henry Knox warned delegates that "a general confederacy has been formed of nearly all the Indians to the Northward of the Ohio" and was "preparing an insurgency against the republic." A compromise of their various interests was now of the utmost urgency.

The deadlock was broken starting on July 12 when Roger Sherman of Connecticut proposed what became known as the Connecticut Compromise, or the Great Compromise. Sherman's plan accepted proportional representation for the lower house of Congress, but gave each state one vote—or equal state representation—in the upper house. Terms of office were shortened to two years for the lower house (House of Representatives), six years for the upper house (Senate), and four years for the executive. An electoral college comprised of all representatives and senators would choose the executive.

The Great Compromise also established the principle of *federalism,* or the sharing of power between the states and central government. Delegates agreed that the central government should have certain powers to create particular supreme laws, enforceable on all individuals of the republic. Further, they gave Congress the authority to levy and collect taxes, settle disputes among the states, negotiate with foreign nations, and set the standards for citizenship. Congress would have veto power over state laws only in cases involving "the supreme law of the land," but it would set the terms of interstate commerce and frontier diplomacy, including enforcement of existing treaties with Indians and protection of citizens by the federal government, not the states. Finally, in addition to the specific powers reserved to central government, Article 1, Sections 8 and 10, of the final draft included a "necessary and proper clause" available for Congress's use in cases delegates could not foresee or immediately decide on. This so-called elastic clause provoked many disputes in years to come: some praised it as a green light for expansive government action, whereas others condemned it as a gift of excessive authority to national rulers.

The Great Compromise also addressed sectional interests between North and South. Southern delegates argued that although slaves were not citizens, they should be counted toward political representation. Northern delegates retorted that slaves should be counted for representation only if they were also counted for purposes of direct taxation. Few delegates wished to argue for the abolition of slavery although Gouverneur Morris stormed that slavery was "a nefarious institution." Most northern delegates believed that the provision in Article 4, Section 2, for the capture and return of runaway slaves was only a small concession to southern interests, especially because delegates at the Confederation Congress had recently agreed to prohibit slavery in the Northwest Territory. The dispute was resolved by what became known as the "three-fifths compromise": representation in the lower house of Congress would be determined by each state's free population plus three-fifths of "all other persons," namely slaves. In addition, southerners won a guarantee that the slave trade would continue—"the migration or importation of such persons as any of the states now existing shall think proper to admit," as it was termed in the final document—for the next twenty years.

Before delegates finished their business, they agreed to present the document to special ratifying conventions in each state for consideration. In this way, delegates hoped there would be a wider public discussion of the tremendous changes being proposed, while at the same time less opportunity for special interests to oppose the constitution from within the existing state governments. To avoid long delays and ensure passage of their controversial document, the delegates also stipulated that the Constitution would become law as soon as nine states had approved it.

On the last day of the convention, September 17, forty-two men remained in session. Three refused to sign the Constitution, and some indicated their reluctance to promote it publicly. Thirty-nine signers, however, put aside whatever misgivings they had and formally added their names to the document, knowing that they would have to argue strenuously for its acceptance. Their deliberations had been utterly secret, and their new document brushed aside the existing Confederation's written basis for a central government. But they believed they had devised the best alternative to the crises of the 1780s. Although delegates conferred popular sovereignty only on propertied white males in America, they hoped that widespread public discussion and special conventions would win over a more expansive "will of the people." Failing that, the republican experiment itself could fail.

The Public Debate

Once the states received copies of the Constitution, Americans began an intense discussion about whether to ratify the radical changes it proposed. They expressed a great spectrum of opinions about different provisions within the document, and they used the press, pulpit, and public podiums to spread their views into every social layer of society. Sometimes differences hinged on great political principles, and sometimes they derived from petty personal quarrels. Before long, however, the many issues at stake in this discussion polarized into two constituencies: Federalist supporters of the Constitution and Antifederalist opponents.

Both Federalists and Antifederalists appealed to the republican ideals of the Revolution to determine what kind of government and society was best suited to Americans' identity. But there were also significant differences between Federalists and Antifederalists. Federalists argued that government should have "majesty" and a significant degree of power over the lives of Americans. Too often, state and local governments succumbed to the "mischief of petty interests" that refused to compromise for the greater good. Citizens needed an "energetic" government to coordinate and develop the nation's great potential. Federalists also believed that both branches of the legislature should be filled with men of property, education, wealth, and "reputation."

Federalists published scores of newspaper essays and separate pamphlets, but their most influential writing appeared in *The Federalist,* a series of pathbreaking essays by the eminently influential trio of Madison, Hamilton, and Jay. *The Federalist* systematically defended central measures in the Constitution and depicted for its readers a bold new vision of federal power and government structure. During the months before the Constitutional Convention, Madison had studied the histories and constitutions of Western governments from ancient Greek to recent European times. Now, in *The Federalist,* he marshaled the wisdom of those classical works, and the practical experience of the convention itself, to argue for building the "energy" of government and expanding the territory of the country.

Madison's famous *Federalist* No. 10 took as its starting point a widely shared idea that political factions or parties were wrong because they represented only "partial interests" and were likely to arouse violent differences rather than protect the general welfare of a people. However, argued Madison, factions would arise inevitably in any republic, especially in one as large and dynamic as America. Furthermore, most people would not put public virtue first, but would serve their self-interests, which grew out of their individual liberty, above all else. Therefore, a strong republic would seek not to destroy but to regulate the natural interests that gave rise to factions. Such reasoning was a bold departure from traditional belief that governments and economies should seek to preserve themselves rather than to expand. Madison also reasoned that conflicts and negotiations in a dynamically expanding republic were natural and could be channeled creatively. Federalists generally argued that expansive commerce and westward settlement were important guarantees of a secure "republican empire." Madison, among others, thus turned America's great size, and its diverse, self-interested population, into virtues. And the federal government proposed by the Constitution would give institutional structure to the new nation.

Antifederalists arose in every locale and social strata of America. Some longtime state leaders, including George Clinton of New York and Patrick Henry of Virginia, provided their strongest voices. Clinton and Henry argued that the Constitution would create an overly centralized federal authority that would strip state governments of many legitimate powers. During the Imperial Crisis, republican rhetoric taught Americans that selfish interests of men in political power easily corrupted governments. Now, during the ratification controversy, Antifederalists reminded citizens that Federalists were proposing to create an equally dangerous, overly "energetic" national government, and to overturn the revolutionary goal of building effective states. Indeed, many states were recovering admirably from postwar crises under effective state leaders.

Other Antifederalists expressed more truly democratic sentiments. They warned against the "monied interests" and distant authority that would be created by the Constitution. Local governments, they contended, would be much more responsive to people's immediate needs. A few, such as New Yorker Melancthon Smith, believed that by concentrating political power in the hands of a wealthy minority, the Constitution would introduce dangerous class divisions. Many Antifederalists agreed with Mercy Otis Warren, who admitted that government needed more "dignity" and strength, but insisted that Americans had "struggled for liberty" and "the rights of man" too hard simply to hand them over to a few politicians deliberating in isolation from the "true interests of the people." Other Antifederalists cited the French Enlightenment political philosopher Montesquieu, who taught that republics should be small and roughly homogeneous in their "manners" or social composition. In such circumstances, contentious political factions and special interests would not corrupt public virtue. Governments should reflect their citizenry, and rulers should be responsive to public needs.

In the fall of 1787, elections were held for the state ratifying conventions. Only about 20 percent of Americans voted for delegates to these conventions, and some conventions—Delaware, New Jersey, New York, and Georgia—saw meager attendance. Predictably, public support for the Federalists came from coastal and urban areas; merchants, artisans, rising entrepreneurs, and shopkeepers all favored the Constitution in great numbers. But large numbers of laborers also supported the Federalist promise of commercial recovery and manufacturing protection. In the mid-Atlantic region, commercial farmers and southern planters enjoyed the benefits of an economic revival. Frontier Georgians found the Federalist promises of Indian defense and central political power appealing, given their weak position. And even though people in the unorganized territories did not vote on the Constitution, support tipped toward the Federalists in many frontier settlements.

Still, judging from the records of town meetings, petitions reprinted in the newspapers, state legislative discussions, and many personal memories, most Americans probably opposed the Constitution or were indifferent. Antifederalists dominated large portions of rural New England, western New York, central Pennsylvania, piedmont and southern Virginia, and large portions of the Carolinas. Average or poor farmers who were not well connected to the export economies of the coastal areas tended to agree with Antifederalist messages about the need for local control over politics. Few of these people expressed concern about shaping a great American nation, except to protest that such a goal would consume the resources of the states and raise taxes again.

Delaware, Pennsylvania, and New Jersey ratified in December 1787. Georgia and Connecticut followed suit in January 1788. Massachusetts weighed in sixth, but only after deep controversy. The state's Federalists slowly won over the strong Antifederalist majority by promising to include a list of amendments to the Constitution—something the drafters had rejected in Philadelphia—as a condition of ratifying. Then, once Maryland and South Carolina approved the Constitution with strong majorities, the approval of only one more state would secure ratification of the document.

On June 21 the New Hampshire convention squeaked out a slim majority and became the ninth state to ratify. But New York and Virginia, two of the most populous states and home to many leading Federalists, still had not acted. In the next days, brilliant and sustained Federalist oratory, as well as massive propaganda campaigns, secured ratification in both states—with winning margins of just ten votes in each convention. Then, once the matter was settled, a tremendous outpouring of public support followed. Thousands of New Yorkers marched in the streets in the summer of 1788 to celebrate ratification—lawyers and merchants headed the processions; craftsmen were arrayed next, according to the unspoken hierarchy of their various trades; and last came laborers. In contrast, North Carolina did not ratify until November 1789, and always-contentious Rhode Island bowed to the inevitable in May 1790—months after the first federal government was in operation.

How did Federalists win, given such great and protracted opposition? Certainly, the special ratifying conventions aided in their victory because they bypassed the likely political explosions in the state legislatures. Also, Federalists controlled much of the public press and marshaled much of the collective wisdom and experience gained from the revolutionary years. Many Federalist leaders had hammered away for years at the need to recast the Articles of Confederation. By 1787, many Americans believed that the multiplying problems of the new nation could not be solved by the states alone, which were the centerpiece of all Antifederalist alternatives. Although many Americans protested that the Constitution prolonged the existence of slavery, they agreed with Madison that "great as the evil is, a dismemberment of the union would be worse." Other Federalists asked, "If not this, then what?" Antifederalists, though eloquent defenders of revolutionary republicanism, had no coherent answer for the crises at hand.

"The Good Ship *Hamilton*"   Ratification of the Constitution was celebrated with elaborate parades in major cities. Here, in New York, a float of the "ship of state" rolls past George Washington and members of Congress and fires a thirteen-gun salute. Despite the great opposition to changes proposed by Congress in the 1780s, and fears of federal government still lingering in 1788, the public expressed relief and joy that the "Critical Period" was over.   *(Miriam and Ira D. Wallach Division of Art, Prints and Photographs, The New York Public Library. Astor, Lenox and Tilden Foundations.)*

A New Political Nation, 1789–1791

Citizens throughout the nation had many reasons to be jubilant about the ratification of the Constitution. At last, sighed Federalists, there was a governmental structure suited to both the responsibilities of a rising nation and what some founders called "the genius of a people." But the controversy over ratification of the Constitution did not end when the document was narrowly approved. In the very first federal Congress, Federalists themselves began to quarrel over the appropriate taxation, commercial, defense, and other policies. Soon differences among Federalists became irreconcilable, and permanent political factions emerged. Outside Congress, too, the identity of the new nation was far from clear. Indeed, many Americans wondered whether they could become one nation.

The First Congress

Americans voted in the first federal election in November 1788, and the men they elected took their seats in the first federal Congress in late spring 1789. Of the ninety-one Congressmen, forty-four had either attended the Constitutional Convention or strongly favored ratification; only eight Antifederalists served in the first House session. Electors agreed quickly on Washington as president and John Adams as vice president, both of them strong Federalists.

Federalists knew that Americans followed every action of the new government with anticipation. The first federal administration not only would make laws but also would define the culture of national leadership. Some Federalists believed that the people wished to look with awe on the majesty of their rulers, as when John Adams proposed the title, "His Highness the President." Others, thinking that citizens should be reminded regularly of the government's great power, proposed to stamp coins with a "regal view of the president" and to adorn public buildings with busts and paintings of leaders "in majestic garb." Most Congressmen, however, rejected such "artificial chimera." Virtuous republican leaders, they insisted, should look and act like their constituents—the American people—not like the corrupt officials of the British Empire.

As president, Washington was aloof from the general population. He rode a carriage pulled by six horses and attended by liverymen, and he entertained members of the urban elite "in the grand style." Washington also conducted foreign affairs face to face and addressed Congress personally, according to the customs of royalty in Europe. But he also stemmed his use of the executive veto power and created a cabinet of department heads reflecting various points of view. He included Thomas Jefferson as secretary of state, Alexander Hamilton as treasurer, Henry Knox as secretary of war, and Edmund Randolph as the head of the justice department, or attorney general.

Congress's first major step was passage of the Judiciary Act in 1789, which established a six-justice Supreme Court, thirteen district courts, and three circuit courts that would hear cases appealed from the states. However, the apparent power given to these courts was actually quite limited because federal judges did not preside over a uniform national code of civil and criminal justice, but rather over the many bodies of state law. Differences between federal and state judicial interpretations thus began with the creation of the federal government.

Another of Congress's early actions was to pass the constitutional amendments known as the Bill of Rights. The Philadelphia convention delegates had determined that special provisions to protect individual rights and popular sovereignty were unnecessary elaborations of the federal government's powers. But Antifederalists revived pressure to amend the Constitution with guarantees of "essential rights." Madison reluctantly accepted the chore of collating over two hundred specific demands from state ratifying conventions and shaping them into a workable set of amendments. In June 1789, Congress considered Madison's list of twelve amendments and submitted them to the states; the ten provisions approved by the states became the Bill of Rights in 1791. Many of the amendments further restricted Congress's authority over citizens: they prohibited established (government-supported) religion; guaranteed freedom of speech, press, assembly, and petition; limited the quartering of troops in private homes, unreasonable searches of citizens and their property, and breaches of the common law; and secured many individual legal rights, including due process of law and the right of citizens to refuse to testify against themselves.

Hamilton's Plans

The first important signs of division in Congress came with efforts to repay Revolutionary War debts still outstanding. Most legislators agreed that the best source of government income was not direct taxes on property or private incomes, but import duties on commerce. Hence, the Tariff Act of 1789, which taxed tonnage of foreign ships coming to American ports and all imported goods, but at low enough levels to encourage merchants to expand business. Over the next thirty years, revenue from commerce provided 90 percent of the national government's income.

With a stable source of income guaranteed, it was finally possible to tackle the problem of federal debts. Hamilton submitted a "Report on the Public Credit" to Congress in January 1790. The report outlined three kinds of debts Hamilton believed Congress should repay: approximately $12 million owed to foreign countries, over $30 million owed to private American citizens, and another $25 million that the states had not repaid to private citizens. By consolidating all state and national debts into one fund, and repaying them from the national treasury, at an annual interest rate of 4 percent, the federal government would assure the world at large, as well as America's creditors, that the new nation could honor its obligations.

Congress readily agreed that foreign debts should be paid quickly and fully, since the political reputation of the country rested on its good credit abroad. But a prolonged discussion ensued about how, and how much, to pay private American creditors of the states and Congress. During the Revolution, congressional notes had depreciated from their face value to near worthlessness. Out of necessity, many soldiers and farmers sold off "continentals" at low market value in order to get cash.

But debate surrounding Hamilton's report—and possibly information he floated to insiders—fueled speculators' hopes that Congress would repay its debts at face values much higher than the market values, which in turn spurred a frenzy among speculators to acquire as much of the depreciated currency as possible. Hamilton's assistant secretary of the treasury, William Duer, formed a syndicate of speculators in the North; by the time Hamilton's report reached Congress, a few northern businessmen, merchants, and brokers controlled most of the national paper debt.

Hamilton's proposal also included provisions for "assuming" outstanding state debts and repaying them at face value. Since all of the southern states except South Carolina had already paid off most of their debts during the 1780s, neither those state governments nor their speculators stood to gain much by federal assumption. In the North, however, state debts were largely unpaid and became the objects of energetic speculation when Hamilton unveiled his plan. The sectional benefit to the North was not lost on southern congressmen.

Hamilton urged Congress to look beyond the private benefits for a few speculators and to contemplate the greater public welfare that his report set forth. Assumption and funding of the debts would enlarge America's reputation in a "world of watching nations" and secure the support of the country's wealthiest citizens to the goals of the federal government. The national debt, Hamilton argued, would become a "national blessing."

In his next report to Congress, in December 1790, Hamilton underscored this reasoning even more. Using the Bank of England as his model, his "Report on the Bank of the United States" proposed that Congress charter a central bank, which would then sell stock in the amount of $10 million to both private investors and the government. From these funds, the Bank would make loans to merchants, warehouse government revenues, and issue notes to investors. Did Congress have the constitutional authority to create such an institution? Hamilton thought so, pointing to the "necessary and proper clause" of the Constitution, an interpretation that became known as "loose construction."

Although acrimonious discussion challenged Hamilton's reasoning, President Washington approved the Bank's opening in Philadelphia in 1791 under a twenty-year charter. The Bank of the United States provided merchants with an international circulating credit, and many Americans benefited from Bank notes in ordinary business transactions for many years to come. Revenues from commercial tariffs poured into the government coffers, some of which was channeled into the Bank's backing fund. In April 1791, Hamilton convinced Congress to approve additional excise taxes on the consumption of wine, tea, coffee, and distilled spirits, the last of which also included a tax on whiskey produced in the frontier. The Bank quickly established eight branches around the country, and state governments had begun to specially charter their own banks.

With his plans for public credit and banking in place, Hamilton submitted his last proposal in December 1791, the "Report on Manufactures." It was an ambitious plan for using government resources to promote development. Certain that the British mercantile model was the best in modern Western times, Hamilton pored over the reports about American manufacturing conditions that Assistant Secretary

Alexander Hamilton, 1792
By modern standards, Hamilton was still a young man of thirty-seven when John Trumbull painted this portrait. By then, the great statesman and economic visionary had seen many of his plans to alter the American political economy come to fruition. (*Yale University Art Gallery, Trumbull Collection.*)

of the Treasury Tench Coxe laid before him. Hamilton also undertook an extensive refutation of the views popularized by Adam Smith. Smith, a Scottish Enlightenment figure whose 1776 tome, *The Wealth of Nations,* had captured widespread attention, urged policymakers and philosophers to abandon their faith in government regulation of trade and domestic production. Smith repudiated the subsidies, discriminatory tariffs, prohibitions, and embargoes that mercantilists often supported. Let demand for goods and services determine the level of production and prices, wrote Smith, and trust that the negotiations of buyers and sellers would create the best environment for market exchanges.

On the contrary, Hamilton believed government should protect "infant industries." His report was clear that inventions of new machinery, more skilled labor, and new technologies still lay in the future, and that investment capital was in short supply throughout America. But he believed that federal bounties for experiments in production, as well as higher import duties on foreign goods, would stimulate growth.

However, Congress consigned Hamilton's Report on Manufactures to rapid defeat. Entrepreneurs and artisans in the cities sputtered that Hamilton did not want to give them protective tariffs to keep out foreign competition. Farmers and southern planters slammed the Report as biased in favor of cities and the "money interest" in them. Merchants—otherwise important allies of Hamilton—were more concerned about shipbuilding and commerce than manufacturing. When word spread in late 1791 that Hamilton had encouraged a handful of prominent speculators to invest their "flimsy paper credit" in the transformation of Paterson, New Jersey, into a manufacturing entrepôt, the congressional report collapsed. Only in the next American generation would manufacturing gain effective government support.

Nevertheless, when judged by the enduring impact of the principles and institutions he promoted, Hamilton possibly influenced the framing of early national government and economy more than any other individual. The financial health of the country improved dramatically within a short time; foreign confidence in America revived, and foreign investment in government securities increased; commerce recovered and grew.

From Factions to Parties

The constitutional founders believed that Americans would live in a one-party nation whose federal structure of government would prevent factions from disrupting peace and derailing development. But even in the first Congress, debates about the national debt, banks, and manufactures revealed important differences emerging in that one party. Madison and Jefferson soon began to voice serious objections to Hamilton's plans, and their opposition became the basis for congressional divisions on important policies during 1791 and 1792. Hamilton's opponents believed that nothing less than the future of the revolutionary experiment was at stake. Their arguments generated a renewed public discussion about Americans' national identity. Soon, factional divisions in Congress spread throughout the republic. During the 1790s, these divisions coalesced into the first political parties in the nation.

Hamiltonians Versus Republicans

Madison readily admitted the wisdom of a national tariff in 1789, and he took the lead in shaping the Bill of Rights. But as soon as Hamilton presented his assumption and funding plans, Madison loudly voiced his fears that fellow Federalists in Congress were falling behind a scheme to favor a northern "monied interest" that presented grave danger to republican citizens. He recoiled from the "immorality" of speculators who bought depreciated wartime currencies from soldiers, widows, and descendants of wartime farmers and artisans with the calculated intention of redeeming them at face value if Congress passed Hamilton's plans. As an alternative to assumption of creditors' debts at face value, Madison proposed that Congress give the current holders only a prevailing market value for their securities—which would be far below their face value—and to return remaining amounts up to face value to the original holders of the money. This was high moral ground, but the House of Representatives rejected Madison's plan as utterly impractical, for it would be nearly impossible to find the original holders of revolutionary debts. Besides, many congressmen held securities and thus stood to profit from government's funding of private debts.

Madison rose again to protest another aspect of Hamilton's report on public credit, the federal assumption and funding of the state debts. Since southern states had repaid most or all of their revolutionary obligations, they stood to benefit very little by Hamilton's plan. Madison objected to the "injustice" of discriminating against an entire section of the country. So, in order to gain southern support, Hamiltonians agreed to place the federal capital on the Potomac River, a location that Madison believed reflected the "majesty" of an agrarian republican countryside that had not fallen under the "baneful influences" of urban corruption. As in 1787, political compromise temporarily calmed sectional animosities.

Four months later, Hamilton's plan for the Bank of the United States passed in Congress, but before President Washington signed the Bank bill into law, opponents exploded with objections. Jefferson raged against the creation of a national bank that would "enrich a monied power." The Bank, he charged, would benefit wealthy merchants and investors by granting them loans and paying them interest on their deposits, but would enable only a few to prosper from a fund created by huge numbers of average citizens. Such an institution was blatantly unfair. Moreover, there was a "decidedly unrepublican" blending of political and economic interests, according to Jefferson: thirty Congressmen owned stock in the national Bank, and "great numbers" of them owned some part of the government debt. But most important, Jefferson and Madison insisted that the Constitution did not give Congress the power to charter a bank as part of its "necessary and proper" functions, and to do so would exercise unwarranted central authority against the rights of the American people. Jefferson pleaded for a more narrow interpretation, or "strict construction," of constitutional powers. However, Washington was persuaded that the Bank would be a beneficial institution, and the act became law.

Rifts Widen

Madison and Jefferson did not have to marshal strenuous arguments against Hamilton's 1791 Report on Manufactures to sink it because both Congress and the American public rejected it outright. But by mid-1792, both opponents had concluded that Hamiltonians had set out to overturn the republic and establish a monarchy in America. Reaching out to state legislatures, public organizations, the press, and popular opinion in general, opponents of Federalist "designs and corruptions" began to organize outside Congress. Modeling themselves on the Sons of Liberty (see page 180), citizens formed "constitutional societies" and "rights watches" to "fully inform our neighbors far and wide of [Federalist] governmental encroachments." By the end of the year, dozens of "Democratic-Republican," or "Republican," societies simmered with dissent.

These clubs and public meetings often started with discussions of the Hamiltonian programs, but quickly included other issues. Thousands of miles away in 1789, the French people had initiated their own revolution that assaulted all remnants of feudalism, instituted a constitutional monarchy, and promised to build a republican society in time. Many Americans applauded the French Revolution's egalitarianism as a new stage in the development of republicanism and adopted the French term "citizen" as a democratic form of address. Many also associated the French Revolution with greater possibilities for open commerce among many nations and world peace—an attractive antidote to the stifling restrictions imposed in the British trade.

Federalists scoffed at this Jeffersonian optimism. By late 1792, France was at war with the monarchies of Prussia and Austria; internally, revolutionaries began to execute thousands of leaders in the church, aristocracy, and monarchical resistance in the Reign of Terror. Wealthy, deeply religious, and Hamiltonian Americans were repulsed when French revolutionaries beheaded Louis XVI in 1793, and even more when the French republic declared war against England. Federalist merchants in the northern states feared losing their British trading partners. Even if they appreciated the French experiment in republicanism, they needed English imports.

Washington tried to avoid American involvement in the wars that grew out of the French Revolution. In early 1793, he urged Congress to declare American neutrality. In response, Congress passed the Neutrality Act, which barred the ships of fighting nations from American ports and suspended America's obligations under the treaty of 1778 to defend France in any war with Britain.

The American public responded enthusiastically to the declaration of neutrality. Merchants interpreted the move as an invitation to trade openly with both French and British West Indies colonies. Commercial farmers in the Chesapeake and mid-Atlantic regions stepped up grain production because it seemed as though warring European countries would now become eager buyers. And port cities generally welcomed the prospects of high employment in trades related to shipping. Property values skyrocketed and urban people watched in awe as the nation's first building boom transformed coastal cities.

However, neutrality on the high seas did not tame political factionalism at home. Tensions rose again in April 1793 when Jeffersonians enthusiastically linked the activities of their Democratic-Republican clubs to the visit of French diplomat Edmond Genêt. "Citizen" Genêt spoke to huge crowds of pro-French Americans, who generously donated funds to support their fellow revolutionaries abroad. Young men signed up by the thousands to privateer against British and Spanish ships in the Caribbean. In mid-1793, Genêt challenged Washington's Congress to a debate about the neutrality policy, hoping to persuade it to declare war on Britain. Federalists assailed Genêt as an agent provocateur, and many Jeffersonians, or Republicans, despised his ill-disguised attempts to lure America into war. There was a collective sigh of relief when Washington demanded his recall in August 1793.

Although many Democratic-Republicans distanced themselves from the Genêt affair, their local and state opposition to the Federalists grew stronger than ever. More Democratic-Republican societies formed from Georgia to Maine, claiming the heritage of republicanism, decrying the presence of British troops on the frontier, and demanding removal of the Spanish from the Mississippi River. Federalists, they charged by 1794, ignored the urgent problems of the frontier as they defended monarchy, special privilege, and measures that sucked the life out of local government. For their part, Federalists replied that Democratic-Republican opposition was "self-created," or outside the authority of official institutions or constitutions. "Without the force of law," complained Federalists, "the lowest orders of mechanics, laborers and draymen" had nullified "the respectability we seek in statesmen."

By fall 1793, international neutrality on the high seas began to crumble. Britain declared a blockade against France, and the British began to seize American ships trading with the French West Indies and southern France. Within six months, British naval commanders had taken over 250 American vessels, forced thousands of American men to serve under them, and stolen sugar and indigo of incalculable value. American merchants failed to win compensation for lost property from British admiralty courts. In an effort to end this "piracy" against American shippers, Washington sent Chief Justice John Jay to London in spring 1794 with orders to negotiate a resolution.

Jay returned to America that fall with a more comprehensive document than Americans anticipated, but no direct resolution of their problems. In the first place, Jay's Treaty proposed that Americans make "full and complete compensation" to British firms for all debts outstanding at the onset of the American Revolution twenty years before. The treaty also permitted Britain to take French property from neutral—that is, American—ships for the duration of the European war, thereby erasing the tradition that "free ships make free goods." British arbitration panels would hear American claims for commercial compensation, but most West Indies ports remained closed to American shipping. The British agreed to withdraw their troops from six forts on the American frontier.

Democratic-Republicans proclaimed Jay's Treaty a fiasco. Jay had returned without provisions to compensate masters for slaves who fled to the British side during the Revolution; nor had he secured terms for peaceful trade between France and America; nor were there guarantees that British troops would leave the frontier. With some exaggeration, Jay said he could travel across the American continent at night by the light of fires burning him in effigy. Congress deadlocked in a debate about the treaty for months.

Then in 1795 Congress learned that Spain wished to negotiate an end to hostilities on the Mississippi. Envoy Thomas Pinckney, a southerner who supported open trade and American expansion into the Southeast, worked out an agreement with Spain to set its claims at the thirty-first parallel and open the Mississippi (plus New Orleans) to American shipping. Congressmen compromised factional and sectional interests by tying the Pinckney and Jay treaties together. The Senate then ratified Jay's Treaty in June 1795 with the required two-thirds majority.

The Frontier Besieged

In 1787 the Northwest Ordinance had recognized the independence of Native Americans from national government, and in 1790 the first federal administration reinforced this view with the Indian Intercourse Act. The act stipulated that only the federal government could negotiate the terms of travel and trade on Indian lands; created a federal licensing system and regulated prices of frontier trade; asserted that only the federal government, not individuals could acquire Indian lands; and instituted a treaty-making process.

Frontier people regularly abused the act, however. Traders cheated and cajoled Native Americans into unfavorable relationships; government agents used force to obtain Indian land by sham treaties; and American citizens carried on "private expeditions against the Indians" to obtain fertile land along the Ohio River. In 1790 chief Little Turtle led the Shawnee, Delaware, and Miami in a bloody victory against the American army forces. A year later the same confederacy of Native Americans attacked settlers in the Northwest Territory under Governor-General Arthur St. Clair. Over nine hundred Americans died in the days-long siege. Fighting continued for three years until Americans under the command of General Anthony Wayne defeated Little Turtle and his pan-Indian army in the Battle of Fallen Timbers on August 20, 1794. The following year, in the Treaty of Greenville, twelve Indian nations ceded the land that would become Ohio and Indiana.

At the same time, Spain was consolidating its territorial claims around the Gulf Coast from the Floridas to New Orleans, in California, and in the Caribbean. Most frightening for Americans, the Spanish tried to block American expansion through the Southeast by courting close friendships with populations of runaway slaves, Acadian refugees, and Native American peoples, as well as by closing off the lower Mississippi to American ships. Farmers from the Ohio country and planters in South Carolina and Georgia grew increasingly anxious about their ability to export goods and expand territorially.

In the 1790s, the Spanish Floridas flourished as a multiethnic, multiracial crossroads, laced with waterways that no authorities could effectively develop or police. Italians, Greeks, and Minorcans came by the hundreds, most of them Roman Catholic, and lived alongside the Seminole and black settlements created during the revolutionary era. In contrast to the southern American plantations to the north, a large free Creole population born in Spanish and French colonies of the Caribbean and South America thrived in Florida, as did hundreds of African and country-born runaways after the British evacuation in 1783. Remnants of Lord Dunmore's "Ethiopians" had formed maroon communities along the Savannah River, where they fought against a joint force of Catawba Indians and South Carolina and Georgia militias. Spain did not always encourage these maroon societies to settle in its empire, but runaway communities on the mainland were magnets for rebellious slaves fleeing Saint Dominique in 1796. St. Augustine's population reached nearly 50 percent free and slave black people by about 1800.

Washington confided to close advisers in 1794 his belief that persistent violence on the frontier put the entire republic in peril. At about that time, westerners began to inundate the administration with petitions decrying "the burden of great taxes for the support of government." They singled out Hamilton's excise tax as the most "unreasonable and unjust of all" because it fell hardest on "industrious citizens" farming in western Pennsylvania, North Carolina, and Kentucky. Because they risked the loss or spoilage of corn crops during transport on open flatboats down river—turbulent waters could capsize crops, and rains could wipe out a season's labor in a few hours—farmers converted corn into whiskey. For farmers still living in mud shacks, deeply in debt for their tools and land, producing spirits promised sure profits.

Western farmers had rallied in 1792 against sheriffs who attempted to collect the whiskey tax, and court officials who tried to fine and arrest violators. The Whiskey Rebellion broke out in 1794 when the local militia marched against tax collectors in

Mingo Creek, Pennsylvania (near Pittsburgh). Their cries were the familiar ones of the Stamp Act riots, Shays's Rebellion, and the French Revolution: "Liberty, Fraternity, and Equality, and no Excise." Farmers and distillers burned local sheriffs in effigy and broke open the courts here and there on the frontier. Angry protesters cried that the government had taxed westerners without their consent and imposed unjustified force against "a free people." Washington responded decisively to this threat against the new republic. He reasoned that if Americans successfully thwarted their government, Spanish, British, and Indians would follow. The president ordered an army of thirteen thousand federal troops, commanded by Hamilton and led by the commander-in-chief himself for part of the march, to suppress the rebels at once (see Competing Voices, page 283).

Parties and Interests

As he prepared to leave office in 1796, an exhausted sixty-four-year-old President Washington pleaded with Americans to avoid the "baneful effects of the spirit of party." Most of his listeners would have agreed; all healthy republics avoided party politics. Americans, Washington stated, should be actively "extending our commercial relations" around the world, seeking "peace and prosperity" in the exchange of goods and peoples. But they should have "as little political connection as possible" with foreign nations—otherwise, they would inevitably be drawn into costly and debilitating wars. Federalists and Democratic-Republicans shared this political philosophy. But in the world of practical affairs and fallible human beings, could they achieve peace and prosperity without political conflict?

The Idea of Political Parties

For generations, colonial and revolutionary Americans had believed in deference, social hierarchies, and rule by one's "natural betters." Of course, colonial assembly representatives had often divided into factions; but they usually based alliances on kinship, marriage, crown patronage, or rifts within the elite over land, commerce, or religion. During the revolutionary years, factions remained shifting and temporary alliances, and no state constitutions provided for permanent political divisions. Most Americans still expected that the "better sort" should naturally assume rule over all others and that only the crassly self-interested actively campaigned for offices. During the 1790s, Washington and Jefferson grew apart politically but shared scorn for parties. Even Madison's frank vision in *Federalist* No. 10 of factions arising in the republic did not portray such coalitions as permanent.

But these views slowly changed. The Revolution had nurtured belief in "the people," and new state legislatures had experimented with more democratic forms of rule. Although the Federalists had begun to create strong institutions and central political authority, they also stimulated opponents to speak out for more personal liberty and limited government. As a result, during the 1780s and 1790s, a great public debate considered the role of citizens in a republic, the nature of a standing army marching against the likes of the Whiskey Rebels, and America's status among nations. These political issues became more and more poignant in the cultural atmosphere of changing family and gender roles, shifting religion and educational life, new consumer goods and western lands.

In the fall elections of 1794, Democratic-Republicans showed rising strength in national congressional debates, local political societies, and state contests for offices. By 1796, conflicts over Hamiltonian programs, taxes, foreign affairs, and America's frontiers propelled citizens another step away from their colonial past and toward an uncharted political culture. By then, grass-roots contests between Federalists and Democratic-Republicans encompassed national issues. The presidential election thus became the occasion for a full-blown national contest, with candidates vying for citizens' votes at all levels of society and identifying with party-based policies. For the first time, parties held caucus meetings to choose candidates for office and determine how to reach voters with their messages. Newspapers spread the idea that two political "parties" were emerging: Federalists who supported "order," elite rule, and the Washington administration; and Democratic-Republicans (or just Republicans) who stood for the revolutionary heritage, democratic tendencies, a Bill of Rights, and "free government."

Toward a Party System

Thomas Jefferson resigned as secretary of state at the end of 1793 and joined Madison's opposition to the Federalists during Washington's second administration. Their efforts at first targeted Hamilton's programs, but they soon developed a separate view of the proper role of government that reached deeply into every aspect of American society. As a man of the Enlightenment, Jefferson was widely educated in science, agriculture, diplomacy, natural history, architecture, and political theory. He worked steadfastly toward religious toleration, broader educational opportunities, social refinement, and westward expansion. As a southern gentleman planter and slaveholder in the eighteenth century, Jefferson did not profess equality of the races. He believed in "moral improvement" for whites through the vehicle of agricultural, not urban, life, and he defined *personal independence* as the ownership of a parcel of land and *social independence* as continual westward expansion. On the other hand, a dependent people, such as England's city dwellers, could be known by their wage labor, factories, and luxury consumption. Jefferson had set out these ideas in the Land Ordinances of the 1780s, and they shaped his vision of America for years to come.

The nationwide appeal of Jefferson's vision became clear in the national election of 1796. The Federalists still had enough prestige, wealth, and experience in public life to win a majority in Congress and the electoral college. The latter chose Washington's vice president John Adams to succeed him as president. After rejecting the avid southern expansionist Thomas Pinckney for vice president, the electors turned to Thomas Jefferson to fill that office.

John Adams, a New Englander, had sparred with Jefferson on almost every important issue of the 1790s. As president, Adams upheld a pro-British foreign policy and grew increasingly irritated with continuing French seizures of American sailors, ships, and goods on the high seas. Following moderate Federalist policy, Adams attempted to negotiate compensation for losses and a more lasting peace with the French. But an American delegation sent to Paris discovered that three of the French prince Talleyrand's agents assigned to "treat with" them demanded a bribe before they would begin talks.

Although Adams fumed at the insult to American honor, he shrewdly turned the affair to his advantage. When Democratic-Republicans in Congress demanded proof of the French insults, Adams divulged secret correspondence, with the French agents' names changed to *X, Y,* and *Z.* As planned, the XYZ Affair aroused anti-French sentiment throughout America. The slogan "Millions for defense, but not one cent for tribute!" rang through the country. Congress passed an embargo act that stopped trade against France and authorized privateering against French ships. In May 1798, Congress allocated funds for a large naval buildup to defend the American coast against French attack. In July Congress repealed the entire treaty of 1778 and approved the recruitment of ten thousand army troops. From 1798 to 1800, the Adams administration in effect fought an "undeclared war" against the French republic.

As it became clear that the XYZ Affair would not cow Democratic-Republicans, Adams determined to repress political dissent in the country. Fearing that foreign subversives would flock to American shores, the Federalist Congress passed an Alien Act during the summer of 1798. The act permitted the president to order the imprisonment or deportation of noncitizens. Strictly speaking, Congress had been granted such a power to regulate immigration and naturalization of citizens under Article 1, Section 8, of the Constitution. The Alien Act's special targets included the Irish and Scottish dissenters with pro-French sympathies who publicly denounced the government's pro-British policies. To allay growing public fears of "foreign meddling" in policymaking, Congress also passed the Naturalization Act, which raised the residency requirement for citizenship from five to fourteen years. And as a capstone to Federalists' fears, Congress passed the Sedition Act, which prohibited exaggerated, ill-intentioned, or untruthful written attacks on Congress or the president. But the main Federalist mouthpiece, the *Gazette of the United States,* bordered on excessive silencing of the party's opponents when it raged that no opposition to the Federalists would be tolerated. "All who are against us are at war," stormed the *Gazette.*

In the next months, government officials arrested almost two dozen Republican editors and legislators for sedition. Matthew Lyon, who had come to America in 1764 as an Irish indentured servant, was one of them. Lyon had risen quickly in revolutionary years by profiting as a supplier to the patriot militia, acquiring confiscated loyalist estates, and ambitiously seeking political office in the new state of Vermont. In February 1798, the "scrapper Lyon," a Democratic-Republican from Vermont, spit at Connecticut House Federalist Roger Griswold. Griswold struck Lyon with his cane, and Lyon returned the blows with a pair of fire tongs. Because few Americans accepted the legitimacy of political parties and loyal opposition in those years, it seemed to many Federalists that Lyon had attacked the majesty of the republic itself. Under the terms of the Sedition Act, Lyon's subsequent accusations of Adams as full of "ridiculous pomp, foolish adulation, and selfish avarice," caused Lyon to serve four months in a Vermont prison. Independent-minded Vermonters, however, voted him into Congress that same year.

Today, silenced writers and politicians could turn to the courts for a ruling on provisions in the Bills of Rights, including freedoms of speech, press, and assembly. But in 1798, most Republicans viewed courts as bastions of Federalism. Few people knew what powers the courts had over citizens and legislation. Instead, Americans looked to their state governments as counterweights to the authority of the national government, and that is exactly how Madison and Jefferson mobilized sentiment against the Alien and Sedition acts. Prodded by Jefferson, the Kentucky legislature passed a resolution making the offensive congressional laws "void and of no force" and asserting the absolute authority of each state to "judge by itself" which federal laws to follow. A similar resolution in Virginia went even further, asserting that states had the right to nullify any powers exercised by the federal government that were not explicitly granted in the Constitution. The Virginia and Kentucky Resolutions of 1798 thus argued for a strict construction of the Constitution. In 1787 Madison had pressed for extensive national powers; now he was insisting that the states should use their powers to guard public virtue.

By 1798, Democratic-Republicans and Federalists were regularly airing their political differences in public, and both parties used fiery rhetoric to denounce opponents. Federalists portrayed Democratic-Republicans as "handmaids of the irreligious French devil" and "without scruple for our foreign reputation." Though they were somewhat fearful of the social consequences of tensions building between European nations, they continued to favor England's war against France. Federalists hoped to calm internal discord, too. But they formulated policies that added to citizens' burdens and led to new eruptions of violence, as when the Direct Tax of 1798 led to Jacob Fries's Rebellion in eastern Pennsylvania in 1799.

For their part, Democratic-Republicans took advantage of Americans' war weariness and called for an end to the shrill newspaper feuds, less government intrusion in citizens' lives, westward expansion, and commercial revival "on terms of equal freedom among all nations." Voters fed up with belligerence on the oceans and high taxes turned away from the Federalists. In the 1799 state elections, Pennsylvania and New York went over to the Democratic-Republicans, joining the Jeffersonians in southern and new western states.

Then, in 1800, electors handed Jefferson and Aaron Burr, both Democratic-Republicans, a majority of seventy-three votes each for executive office. It fell to the House of Representatives to decide who would become president. In a desperate attempt to prevent Jefferson's ascendancy, the Federalist-controlled House blocked ballot after ballot. Then, after thirty-five ballots, Hamilton begged his fellow Federalists to turn away from Burr—the "embryo Caesar" who, Hamilton argued, would stop at nothing to destroy federal authority and raise up contentious local interests—and accept Jefferson. At least Jefferson would preserve the federal union and the Constitution, even if on Democratic-Republican terms. And so the House ratified the "bloodless Revolution" that transferred power peacefully, but definitively, to a new party. It seemed to many observers that the American experiment might be preserved after all.

Mad Tom in a Rage, 1790 For years, Tom Paine was identified as a spokesman for the American revolutionary cause and a supporter of the new federal government. But when the French Revolution began, his support for the extension of American ideals of liberty to that foreign country drew scorn from Federalists, who thought Paine wanted to destroy America's strong central government. In this Federalist cartoon, Paine tries to dismantle the national government with the help of a familiar symbol of disloyal political opposition. Only after 1800, with Jefferson firmly in power, did many Americans accept the legitimacy of political factions or parties. *(Library of Congress.)*

CONCLUSION

Mercy Otis Warren agreed with a majority of Americans during the 1780s that the new states were handling the post-revolutionary recovery well, and that the Federalists exaggerated the problems of the Critical Period. She also agreed with many Americans that the Constitution of 1787 introduced dangerous tendencies to centralize political authority and stifle the creative energies of people in their locales. Like other Antifederalists, Warren was somewhat reconciled to the new national government by passage of the Bill of Rights, but she refused, ever, to accept Hamilton's plans. In her declining years, Warren hailed Jefferson's 1800 victory as a second chance for the republican experiment of the Revolution to succeed.

Jefferson himself called his triumphant election the "Revolution of 1800," but many other Americans understood that the Democratic-Republican ascendancy had come from below. Bitter partisan battles, originating in the differences between Federalists and Antifederalists, had shaped their political identity and their place among other nations. In the years between independence and the election of 1800,

Americans decisively shifted from support for a republic of stable and like-minded citizens to support for boisterous and factional politics that invited widespread public participation.

But if a new political era dawned, few Americans at the time understood its profound social, economic, and cultural significance. New England still harbored large numbers of Federalists, while the South nurtured leading Democratic-Republicans and the mid-Atlantic region defied clear political tendencies. Federalists drew much of their support from merchants, manufacturers, and commercial farmers, whereas Democratic-Republicans boasted the solid backing of wage earners, artisans, shopkeepers, new immigrants, religious minorities, southern exporting planters, and small farmers throughout the interior. While Federalists imagined the benefits of a "natural aristocracy," Democratic-Republicans dreamed of making a "decent living within the reach of the better part of mankind." Yet women, Indians, and African-Americans continued to be excluded from the franchise—and from the vision of both parties.

SUGGESTED READINGS

Religious issues during the revolutionary generation are presented best in Ruth H. Bloch, *Visionary Republic: Millennial Themes in American Thought, 1756–1800* (1985), and Nathan Hatch, *The Democratization of American Christianity* (1989). An assessment of slavery is made by the contributors in Ira Berlin and Ronald Hoffman, eds., *Slavery and Freedom in the Age of the American Revolution* (1983). The most compelling case study of emancipation in the North is Gary Nash and Jean Soderlund, *Freedom by Degrees: Emancipation in Pennsylvania and Its Aftermath* (1991).

Most studies about women's gains during the revolutionary generation draw guarded conclusions. See especially Jay Fliegelman, *Prodigals and Pilgrims: The American Revolution Against Patriarchal Authority, 1750–1800* (1982); Linda Kerber, *Women of the Republic: Intellect and Ideology in Revolutionary America* (1980); and Jan Lewis, *The Pursuit of Happiness: Family and Values in Jeffersonian Virginia* (1983).

An excellent recent study of the problems faced in commercial relations after the Revolution is John E. Crowley, *The Privileges of Independence: Neomercantilism and the American Revolution* (1993). The tremendous problems related to repaying the war debts owed by Congress and the states are clarified in E. James Ferguson, *The Power of the Purse: A History of American Public Finance: 1776–1790* (1967).

For Shays's Rebellion, start with the stimulating collection of essays in Robert A. Gross, ed., *In Debt to Shays: The Bicentennial of an Agrarian Rebellion* (1993), and the major work of David P. Szatmary, *Shays's Rebellion: The Making of an Agrarian Insurrection* (1980).

For the relationship of difficulties during the 1780s and the promise of prosperity and opportunity, see Merrill Jensen, *The New Nation: A History of the United States During the Confederation* (1950); Ronald Hoffman et al., eds., *The Economy of Early America: The Revolutionary Period, 1763–1790* (1988); and Cathy Matson and Peter Onuf, *A Union of Interests: Political and Economic Thought in Revolutionary America* (1990).

For the background to the Constitutional Convention, important starting points are Lance Banning, *The Sacred Fire of Liberty: James Madison and the Founding of the Federal Republic* (1995); Gordon S. Wood, *The Creation of the American Republic, 1776–1787* (1969); and Richard Beeman et al., eds., *Beyond Confederation: Origins of the Constitution and American National Identity* (1987). For the intellectual discussions embedded in the political struggles at Philadelphia, see Richard Bernstein and Kym Rice, *Are We to Be a Nation? The Making of the Constitution* (1987). For the ideas that shaped public discussions, see Donald

Lutz, *Popular Consent and Popular Control: Whig Political Theory in the Early State Constitutions* (1980); Staughton Lynd, *Class Conflict, Slavery, and the United States Constitution* (1967); and the Pulitzer Prize–winning contribution by Jack Rakove, *Original Meanings: Politics and Ideas in the Making of the Constitution* (1996). Richard B. Morris has composed short biographical sketches of the leading constitutional framers in *Witnesses at the Creation: Hamilton, Madison, Jay, and the Constitution* (1985).

Aspects of ratification of the Constitution are covered best in Steven Boyd, *The Politics of Opposition: Antifederalists and the Acceptance of the Constitution* (1979), a detailed account of the range of Antifederalist opposition to the Constitution during the late 1780s. See also the fine articles in Michael Gillespie and Michael Leinesch, eds., *Ratifying the Constitution* (1989), and the intellectual history by Michael Kammen, *A Machine That Would Go of Itself: The Constitution in American Culture* (1986). Two outstanding earlier studies that remain required reading on this topic are Jackson T. Main, *The Antifederalists: Critics of the Constitution, 1781–1788* (1961), and Robert Rutland, *The Ordeal of the Constitution: The Antifederalists and the Ratification Struggle of 1787–1788* (1966).

The first federal government is treated in Kenneth Bowling, *Politics in the First Congress, 1789–1791* (1990), and Stanley Elkins and Eric McKitrick, *The Federalist Era* (1993). Hamilton's plans are judiciously presented in the biography by Jacob E. Cooke, *Alexander Hamilton* (1982), and in John R. Nelson's excellent *Liberty and Property: Political Economy and Policymaking in the New Nation, 1789–1812* (1987).

The entangling web of foreign diplomacy, commerce, internal development, and political factionalism are presented in Ralph Ketcham, *Presidents Above Party: The First American Presidency, 1789–1829* (1984); Richard Buel, *Securing the Revolution: Ideology in American Politics, 1789–1815* (1972); and Daniel Lang, *Foreign Policy in the Early Republic* (1985). An older study that encompasses the Federalists' rise and fall at the national level is John C. Miller, *The Federalist Era, 1789–1800* (1960). For Federalist repression at the end of the century, see James Morton Smith, *Freedom's Fetters: The Alien and Sedition Laws and American Civil Liberties* (rev. ed., 1966).

Recently, historians have returned their attention to Federalists' opponents to understand the roots of Jefferson's appeal. See, for example, Joyce Appleby, *Capitalism and a New Social Order* (1984); Michael Durey, *Transatlantic Radicals and the Early American Republic* (1997); Alfred Young, *The Democratic Republicans of New York* (1967); and Richard Twomey, *Jacobins and Jeffersonians: Anglo-American Radicalism in the United States, 1790–1820* (1989).

For contentions on the frontier, see Stephen Aron, *How the West Was Lost: Kentucky from Daniel Boone to Henry Clay* (1966); Andrew Cayton and Frederika Teute, eds., *Contact Points: American Frontiers from the Mohawk Valley to the Mississippi, 1750–1830* (1998); Gregory Dowd, *A Spirited Resistance: The North American Indian Struggle for Unity, 1745–1815* (1992); Reginald Horsman, *The Frontier in the Formative Years, 1783–1815* (1970); and J. Leitch Wright, *Britain and the American Frontier, 1783–1815* (1975). On the Whiskey Rebellion, see Thomas P. Slaughter, *The Whiskey Rebellion: Frontier Epilogue to the American Revolution* (1986).

The rift that grew between Federalists and Antifederalists, then Democratic-Republicans, and finally the party of Jefferson, is analyzed in Joseph J. Ellis, *American Sphinx: The Character of Thomas Jefferson* (1996); Noble Cunningham, *The Jeffersonian Republicans: The Formation of Party Organization, 1789–1801* (1957); and Lance Banning, *The Jeffersonian Persuasion: Evolution of a Party Ideology* (1978). The ideas that supported political choices and policies are thoroughly covered in Buel, *Securing the Revolution,* cited above. For explanations of the ideology and structures of political parties as they first emerged, see both John F. Hoadley, *Origins of American Political Parties, 1789–1803* (1986), and the classic study by Richard Hofstadter, *The Idea of a Party System: The Rise of Legitimate Opposition in the United States, 1780–1840* (1969).

Subduing the Old Northwest

Competing Voices

Hamilton Denounces Frontier Scofflaws

Alexander Hamilton was furious with the open defiance of the 1791 Whiskey Tax on the frontier—so furious that he urged Washington to raise troops to crush the so-called Whiskey Boys. As the troops gathered for their march westward, Hamilton defended their mission with an article in a Federalist newspaper.

Shall the majority govern or be governed? Shall the nation rule or be ruled? Shall the general will prevail, or the will of a faction? Shall there be government or no government? It is impossible to deny that this is the true and the whole question. No art, no sophistry can involve it in the least obscurity.

The Constitution *you* have ordained for yourselves and your posterity contains this express clause: "The Congress shall have power to lay and collect taxes, duties, imposts, and excises, to pay the debts, and provide for the common defense and general welfare of the United States." You have, then, by a solemn and deliberate act, the most important and sacred that a nation can perform, pronounced and decreed that your representatives in Congress shall have power to lay excises. You have done nothing since to reverse or impair that decree.

Your representatives in Congress, pursuant to the commission derived from you, and with a full knowledge of the public exigencies, have laid an excise. . . . But the four western counties of Pennsylvania undertake to rejudge and reverse your decrees. You have said, . . . "An excise on distilled spirits shall be collected." They say, "It shall not be collected. We will punish, expel, and banish the officers who shall attempt the collection. We will do the same by every other person who shall dare to comply with your decree expressed in the constitutional charter, and with that of your representatives expressed in the laws. The sovereignty shall not reside with you, but with us. If you presume to dispute the point by force, we are ready to measure swords with you, and if unequal ourselves to the contest we will call in the aid of a foreign nation [British or Spanish frontier troops]. We will league ourselves with a foreign power."

Jefferson Condemns Excessive Force

Jefferson was astounded that thirteen thousand troops were sent against the distillers and farmers of western Pennsylvania. He saw the suppression of the rebels as an excessive use of force deployed to increase the prestige and power of the national government. In the following account, Jefferson writes to his friend James Madison (both living in Virginia at the time) lamenting the raid's potential to damage, rather than bolster, the public's image of its new national government.

The excise law is an infernal one. The first error was to admit it by the Constitution; the second, to act on that admission; the third and last will be to make it the instrument of dismembering the Union, and setting us all afloat to choose which part of it we will adhere to.

The information of our militia, returned from the westward, is uniform, that though the people there let them pass quietly, they were objects of their laughter, not of their fear; that a thousand men could have cut off their whole force in a thousand places of the Alleghany; that their detestation of the excise law is universal, and has now associated to it a detestation of the government; and that separation, which perhaps was a very distant and problematical event, is now near, and certain, and determined in the mind of every man.

I expected to have seen justification of arming one part of the society against another; of declaring a civil war the moment before the meeting of that body [Congress] which has the sole right of declaring war; of being so patient of the kicks and scoffs of our [British and Spanish] enemies, and rising at a feather against our friends; of adding a million to the public debts and deriding us with recommendations to pay it if we can, etc. etc.

The Whiskey Tax that Secretary of the Treasury Alexander Hamilton proposed, and Congress passed, in 1791 was especially damaging for the livelihoods of frontier farmers. With poor and costly transportation, they paid dearly to cart their surplus rye and corn to markets. Most of them chose to convert grain into the distilled beverages that a large consuming public on the East Coast readily purchased. Under the provisions of the bill, farmers who operated stills and refused to pay taxes on the transport of whiskey would be sued by the government. Trials would be held far from their frontier homes, under the jurisdiction of unfamiliar judges, and before juries certain to be prejudiced against the "ruffians of the west." Like western Regulators before the Revolution, the whiskey producers of Kentucky and western Pennsylvania were keenly aware that they lacked good government in their settlements. When the Whiskey Boys encountered sheriffs and government tax collectors, they were likely to tar and feather them, beat them, or burn their homes—in self-defense, they would say, and to protect their frontier enterprises from heavy taxation and unjustified assaults.

Questions for Analysis

1. How does Hamilton use the Constitution to support his argument?

2. On what grounds does Jefferson oppose the excise tax?

3. How do Hamilton's and Jefferson's views of the proper role of governments differ? How does each explain the limits of federal authority and the rights of citizens?

4. How does each author describe the activities of the army? of the western settlers? What do their characterizations reveal about their opinions of these people?

8

Striving for Nationhood, 1800–1824

Shortly before noon on March 4, 1801, Thomas Jefferson, the Democratic-Republican president-elect, walked from his lodgings at a Washington, D.C., boarding house through the muddy streets to the half-finished Capitol building. The city contained fewer than four hundred dwellings, most of them "small miserable huts" surrounding the seat of national government. The capital's first inaugural was likewise humble, a far cry from the grand procession of "carriages and lace cuffs" that heralded Washington's administration. Jefferson dressed as "a plain citizen, without any distinctive badge of office." His Federalist predecessor, John Adams, was not present when Jefferson stood quietly before Chief Justice John Marshall to take the oath of office. In his inaugural address, Jefferson announced his intentions to create a government more suitable for a republican people, to purge the government of lingering Federalist influences, and to respect the individual states.

Jefferson called his electoral victory the "Revolution of 1800," indicating that profound political and cultural change in the republic could occur without bloodshed. The electoral revolution, said Jeffersonians, represented a peaceful transition from the nation's founding political party, the Federalists, to a new party organization, the Democratic-Republicans. It also seemed to signal the decline of political processes based on deference and privilege, and the rise of new social interests, more economic opportunity, and greater democracy in government. As Jefferson said in his inaugural address, "We are all republicans, we are all federalists."

Bitterness among political opponents still lingered after the contentious election in 1800, but Jefferson's speech to Congress voiced hope that Americans could move forward peacefully. In contrast to the bellowing speeches of congressmen in years to come, Jefferson spoke barely above a whisper, insisting that his powers as president were strictly limited and that the great tasks of shaping the nation's growth and expansion required citizens to "unite in common efforts for the common good." He reminded listeners that the revolutionary experiment, the accomplishment of his own generation, was a work in progress. In addition to the victory of a war for independence, the American people now had to complete the "revolution in the principles of our government."

Hogs ran through Washington's streets, and Jefferson never expressed urgency about "citifying" the rural crossroads of Washington, D.C., or finishing the construction of government buildings. But to many Democratic-Republicans, the unrefined and unfinished nature of Washington suited the proper roles of national government: to be small in size and modest in its guardianship over the people. Over the next three decades, wide constituencies of Americans continued to believe that they could escape the dangerous tendencies of growth and rapid pace of development that could lead them to the brink of wars and breed internal cultural corruption. Public discussion and local political policymaking reflected Americans' yearnings for a republican citizenry. But expansion into new frontiers, the growing use of national government to create opportunities and divide resources, and continuing international controversies all threatened to annihilate the republican ideals that framed American political culture.

- How did the Jeffersonian Democratic-Republicans attempt to calm the bitterness of political factionalism, keep government small, and promote substantial development?

- What contributions did Hamiltonians make to shaping American institutions, internal development, and international commerce?

- How did America's expansion into new frontiers—in North America and abroad—affect other nations' interests?

- In what ways were Jeffersonians forced to alter their vision for America as the great public effort to define, secure, and develop the new American republic unfolded?

This chapter will address these questions.

Democratic-Republicans in Power

Democratic-Republicans founded their party on the ideals of republican citizenship and a responsive, local, and lean government. Their ideals emerged when America was still small in territory and population, and close to agricultural and craft pro-

Chronology

1801	Jefferson inaugurated as president
1803	Louisiana Purchase
	Marbury v. *Madison*
1804–1806	Lewis and Clark expedition
1807	Embargo Act
1808	James Madison elected president
1809	Tecumseh forms Indian alliance in territories
1811	Battle of Tippecanoe
1812	War of 1812 begins
1814	Hartford Convention
	Treaty of Ghent
1815	Battle of New Orleans
1816	Congress charters Second Bank of the United States
1818	Jackson invades Florida
1819–1820	Panic of 1819
	Missouri Crisis and Compromise
1819	Adams-Onís Treaty
1823	Monroe Doctrine pronounced in Congress

duction. For many Democratic-Republicans, Federalist policies seemed to be harmful, especially Hamilton's financial plans. But as the years went by, Democratic-Republicans—in office and in the public at large—witnessed the republic expanding and developing in unforeseen ways. Their notions about the ideal republican citizen and a virtuous republic required regular adjustments as the years passed. Changing Democratic-Republican policies reflected this adjusted thinking.

Simplifying Government

Jeffersonians had pledged themselves to creating a new political era of "simplicity and frugality." In practical terms, this meant bolstering the integrity of the states, "the surest bulwarks against anti-republican tendencies"; reducing government spending and repaying the public debt; restraining military buildup; and guarding the freedoms enumerated in the Bills of Rights. As the government paid off its debts, Democratic-Republicans would struggle mightily not to incur new ones and, in doing so, would wipe out the need for Hamilton's fiscal state. A small government, argued Jeffersonians, ruling over an expanding agricultural and commercial people, suited republican Americans the most.

In some respects, Jefferson's plan did suit the early republic, for the national government did not play a significant role in the daily lives of citizens at that time. The states still fulfilled many important functions related to education, law enforcement, promotion of the economy, and building roads. The national government had a small budget and very few employees. Washington, D.C., itself had the appearance of a country town during Jefferson's administration, and it did not grow nearly as rapidly as Cincinnati, Baltimore, New Orleans, and Wilmington.

Government expenditures, though never high in Washington's years, diminished even more in Jefferson's first administration. The fledgling navy almost disappeared; Jefferson cut military spending dramatically and kept only a few troops on the western frontier after 1803. Jefferson did not fire all Federalists from their positions, although he did reduce the number of clerks, post office employees, military officials, and diplomats, especially those whom corruption, incompetence, and reported scandal had touched. Nor did Jefferson hand-pick replacements with wild revolutionary ideas, as Federalists feared he would. Rather, he drew to Washington Democratic-Republican gentlemen of the highest social standing. He also used patronage, as Federalists before him had, to appoint loyal Democratic-Republicans to offices in New England, where Federalists had held majorities in many local and state offices for many years. However, Jefferson also reserved three key cabinet positions for Federalists.

Congress, acting on Jefferson's plea, abolished the Federalist excise taxes and Direct Tax of 1798, and allowed the Alien and Sedition Acts to expire. The national debt, which stood at about $80 million when Jefferson took office, declined to a little more than half that amount when happy voters went to the polls in 1804, and stood at about $43 million when he left office. Although major Hamiltonian institutions, including the Bank of the United States, continued to exist, Jeffersonians did not expand their operations or rely on them for the success of their goals.

The Judiciary and the Common Law

Jefferson promised "equal and exact justice to all" in his inaugural address, but many of his supporters in Congress believed that two obstacles stood in the way of achieving this promise. One was the Federalist Judiciary Act of 1801, which created many new circuit courts and added additional federal marshals and regional judges. The other was President Adams's numerous "midnight appointments" of loyal Federalists to these new posts just before he left office. Many Democratic-Republicans believed that Federalists would not apply their common law traditions properly. Although the common law blended precedents—decisions made in previous cases—with an intellectual tradition that embodied natural law and reason, in practice it had emerged during the regimes of monarchs, aristocrats, and great landlords whose interests often were upheld by Federalists and were opposed by Jeffersonians. Federalist court officials had supported wealthy landowners against settlers in the West who needed protection of their claims. Federalists also had upheld the monopoly privileges of old families against the energy and capital of new developers across the nation.

Throughout the 1790s, Federalists had insisted that Americans needed an independent judiciary, secure against attacks from political enemies or "mob democracy." They continued to support old, or prior, economic privileges against the encroachments of new wealth and enterprise. For example, Federalist courts often ordered new mills to cease operations when they diverted water for their use from the farms that lay nearby. These new enterprises, the judges repeatedly ruled, interfered with prior owners and "the established will of the community."

Many Jeffersonians challenged this long-standing legal wisdom. As products of radical intellectual changes during the revolutionary generation, they believed the law should change as American circumstances and people changed. Laws emerged, they held, from contentious interests and political negotiation, as a "positive law . . . which is the will of THE PEOPLE." Popular sovereignty, they insisted, should permeate the judicial process just as it should the legislative and executive. Jeffersonians also feared the "excessive interference" of Federalist courts in matters they felt should be left to Congress or state legislatures.

Now, in the early 1800s, Jeffersonians countered that the courts ought not to nullify legislation initiated by the people's representatives, nor should it hold back new development. In February 1802, Congress—overwhelmingly comprised of Democratic-Republicans—repealed the Judiciary Act, eliminating all the new courts and offices it had created. The following year, it began impeachment proceedings against select Federalist judges for their "dangerous opinions" that could "work the destruction of the Union." Congress then brought impeachment charges against Samuel Chase, a justice of the Supreme Court, for "intemperate and inflammatory political harangues" that threatened "to excite the fears and resentment of the . . . people . . . against the Government." This time, Jeffersonians had overstepped themselves, and the Senate acquitted Chase.

By the early 1800s, Jeffersonian thinking about the law began to reorient many court decisions and to have a profound effect on economic development. New interests demanded, and won, the right to take private property from prior users when their improvements brought "progress for great numbers" of citizens. The owners of new mills and small factories were permitted to flood farmlands, and ruined farmers had to accept reasonable compensation. By 1815, legislatures were granting private turnpike and canal companies the authority to cut through rural land holdings, and the courts upheld the "creative privilege" of these ambitious new interests.

But tensions between elected government representatives and justices remained strained during the Jefferson presidency. John Marshall, chief justice of the United States Supreme Court in 1801, was a strong Federalist. Appointed by John Adams, Marshall dominated the Court until his death in 1835. One of his major goals was to establish the principle that came to be known as judicial review, by which the Supreme Court had the power to strike down acts of Congress, a power granted to it by the Judiciary Act. In *Marbury* v. *Madison* (1803), Marshall established this principle of judicial review. William Marbury, who had been nominated a justice of the peace by Adams but then did not receive his commission when Jefferson took office, sued the government. Under the terms of the Judiciary Act, the court had the power to demand that James Madison, the secretary of state, hand over Marbury's commission. Marshall agreed that "it is emphatically the province and duty of the judicial department to say what the law is." However, he also declared that it was impolitic and illogical for the Court to force the executive branch to put Marbury in a position that was almost over by the time the case reached the court. Although at first this second part of his decision seemed to ally Marshall with the Jeffersonians, it was his firm stance on judicial review that became a hallmark of Marshall's entire tenure in office. In addition, Marshall's decisions invariably favored strong federal government over state government.

In *McCulloch* v. *Maryland* (1819), Marshall asserted Federalist principles and the implied nationalist powers of the Constitution even more clearly. When Congress chartered the Second Bank of the United States in 1816 (see below), it assumed the authority to deal not only with national funds but also with deposits to its branch banks made by the states as well. In turn, the branches of the Bank issued notes that circulated widely in the business community. Leading Maryland politicians grew unhappy with this arrangement, charging the Bank with excessive powers, and imposed a tax on the Bank's operations. Other states, disturbed over the national Bank's assumption of superiority over state banks, leaned toward following Maryland's example. A large group of Maryland depositors and lawyers insisted that the Second Bank of the United States was as unconstitutional as the first one

"John Marshall (1755–1835)," by Charles-Balthazar Julien Févret de Saint-Mémin, 1801 Marshall, who served as chief justice of the United States from 1801 to 1835, sat for this portrait his first year on the Court. A strong Federalist, he rendered many decisions favoring both the political and economic the power of the national government and gave the Court a major role to play in shaping the destiny of the early federal republic. *(Duke University Archives.)*

had been, and that any state had the right to tax institutions within its own boundaries. Marshall's Court took the Federalist approach to interpreting the Constitution, ruling that the Bank was "necessary and proper" for the functioning of national government. In addition, the court disallowed the Maryland tax, arguing that "the power to tax involves the power to destroy"—in this case, to destroy the national Bank (see Competing Voices, page 319).

In order to establish judicial review, Marshall sometimes took decisions out of state control and made them federal cases. In *Fletcher* v. *Peck* (1810), Marshall upheld that matters of constitutional interpretation should be heard in the highest courts in the land and, in this case, the principle that states could not impair "the obligation of contracts" between governments and individuals. *Fletcher* involved the Georgia legislature's grants of land to the Yazoo Land Company. When a newly elected state government tried to nullify the company's claims on the grounds of speculation and corruption in acquiring them, Marshall insisted that, regardless of company wrongdoing, the contract between Yazoo claimants and the state of Georgia must be honored.

In *Dartmouth College* v. *Woodward* (1819), Marshall interfered with the intentions of a state government in order to uphold older corporate claims of individuals. The trustees of Dartmouth had been fighting off efforts by the New Hampshire legislature to convert the college into a public institution, which, in true republican terms, would "serve the greater number" of citizens. They hired Daniel Webster, a formidable Federalist Massachusetts lawyer, to argue their case, which hinged on the original "corporate rights and privileges" inherent in the college's charter before the Revolution. Webster insisted that such institutional charters were contracts, and according to the Constitution such contracts must be held sacred. Despite strong opposition from some colleagues on the bench, Marshall's majority opinion supported Webster. In years to come, the nation's entrepreneurs benefited immeasurably from the reasoning about contracts articulated in the Dartmouth case, and creditors would find it easier to pursue their debtors in countless cases brought before courts. Even today, many courts respect the fundamentally Federalist principles of constitutional law established in the *Fletcher* and *Dartmouth* cases.

Defining Politics and American Identity

For generations, colonial Americans accepted a political process premised on deference toward elites, which required that most citizens remained aloof from the affairs of political decision making. In the postrevolutionary years, many new families moved into positions of political power, but they tended to perpetuate elite control of offices, and to exclude Indians, women, and (in most new states) unpropertied white men such as shopkeepers, carpenters, teamsters, seamen, and commercial farmers from governing the new nation.

During the 1790s, political discussion had become a noisy, participatory activity. Vote getting and office holding required close attention to an increasingly demanding citizenry. Using the language of republicanism, many Americans challenged hierarchical authority and called for more legal (though not social and economic) equality for free white men. John Adams had said Americans created a "government of laws, not of men," in which there would be no aristocracies of birth. Thousands of voters took his reasoning a step further and declared that in practice office seekers who wore powdered wigs and silver buckles would now have to share public offices with the middling, unadorned, citizens of the country.

As the public sphere of politics grew, many state governments expanded the franchise. After 1789, the very small percentage of adult white males who could vote slowly, but surely, grew. Four states created universal manhood suffrage in 1800; other states gradually reduced property requirements and restrictions on religious affiliation for voting or holding office. Connecticut and New York abolished property qualifications in the early 1800s. The new states of Indiana (1816), Illinois (1818), and Alabama (1819) permitted universal suffrage to free white men. These measures set the stage for more and more Americans to enter public political participation during the coming three generations. In the original New England states, 70 to 90 percent of eligible voters went to the polls during local and state elections by 1820. But over the years, as middling white men gained more political rights, the diminished place of women and African-Americans also became clearer—and eventually less tolerable.

The vibrant public political discussion of the early national years stimulated new forms of communication. On the eve of the Revolution, 37 journals, most of them weeklies, nourished the colonists' need for news. By 1789, printers put out 92, including 8 daily publications, and by 1810, Americans read 376 different papers, some weeklies and some biweeklies, with combined circulations of over 22 million. This was an amazing publishing effort, given that the population had reached only 8 million people by 1810, half of them under age sixteen and one-fifth of them slaves whom the law forbade to read. Post offices, libraries, taverns and public houses, and even street corners provided public venues for the constant buzz of exchanging news.

During the rising political factionalism of the 1790s, newspapers were not only the eyes, ears, and mouths of Federalists and Democratic-Republicans, they were also the focus of discussions about rights guaranteed by the Bill of Rights, especially freedom of expression. With the demise of the Sedition Act, Jefferson was able to assure Americans in 1801 that "error of opinion [would] be tolerated, where reason is left free to combat it."

In the next decades, the proliferating number of bookstores and book peddlers in the countryside attested to Americans' hunger for the printed word. Literacy rates in the coastal states rose rapidly, and literary societies sprang up in many locales. In New England the Connecticut Wits charmed readers with their biting commentary; in Philadelphia erudite circles of intellectuals and entrepreneurs joined the American Philosophical Society; and New York City's Tontine Society attracted the native and immigrant intellectuals of property. Combining the activities of newspaper printing, public speaking, book collecting and library subscription clubs, and organized distribution of printed tracts, some intellectual circles also drew urban artisans into their membership.

In their articles and novels, American writers reflected on the rapid changes of American life and sought to define a distinctive identity for the country. Frontiersmen in Kentucky, "unmannered and uncivilized" hunters in Georgia, the so-called new man rising from poverty to comfort, or the self-made servant who roamed from place to place working for entrepreneurs and tinkers—these kinds of characters fired the imaginations of early national readers. Simultaneously, some writers began to write histories of the colonies and the American Revolution, including Mercy Otis Warren's erudite 1805 account of the Revolution from a republican point of view. Michel-Guillaume Jean de Crèvecoeur's reflections on the postrevolutionary American character in *Letters from an American Farmer* (1782) and Parson Weems's laudatory and sometimes fabricated *Life of Washington* (1800) are examples of a new genre of moral and introspective writings that appealed to Americans widely. Crèvecoeur proposed that the "new man" of America was a blending of many cultures and represented the strongest characteristics of each one. Romantic fiction, initiated by William Hill Brown in the first American novel, *The*

Noah Webster's *American Spelling Book*   This text created a sensation when it first appeared in 1789, and its popularity prompted many reprintings in the next years. Webster's efforts to create distinctive spellings of many commonly used words and expressions, and to teach basic literacy to the first generation of children after the Revolution, were significant contributions to an American national identity.   *(Courtesy, American Antiquarian Society.)*

Thomas and *Andrews's FIRST* EDITION.

THE

AMERICAN

𝕾𝖕𝖊𝖑𝖑𝖎𝖓𝖌 𝕭𝖔𝖔𝖐 :

CONTAINING AN EASY

STANDARD of PRONUNCIATION,

BEING THE

FIRST PART

OF A

GRAMMATICAL INSTITUTE

OF THE

ENGLISH LANGUAGE.

BY NOAH WEBSTER, JUN. ESQUIRE.
AUTHOR of " DISSERTATIONS on the ENGLISH LANGUAGE."

Thomas and *Andrews's* FIRST EDITION.
With additional LESSONS, corrected by the AUTHOR.

PRINTED AT *BOSTON*,
BY ISAIAH THOMAS AND EBENEZER T. ANDREWS.
Sold, Wholefale and Retail, at their Bookftore, No. 45, NEWBURY
STREET, and by faid THOMAS at his Bookftore in *Worcefter.*
MDCCLXXXIX.

Power of Sympathy (1789), also sold well, especially to the widening reading audience of women. Susanna Haswell Rowson's *Charlotte Temple,* published in 1791, provided a racy tale of seduction and abandonment, levened with moral cautions about the dangers of emotional entanglements.

Americans also purchased or borrowed copies of Noah Webster's *American Spelling Book.* First published in 1783, Webster's compilation of words and examples of their usage became the number one best-seller of secular texts by 1810. In 1828 Webster astonished Americans again by publishing the *American Dictionary of the English Language,* which attempted to replace "the King's English" with "more common sensical" spellings, such as *odor* instead of *odour,* and added many new technical terms.

As Americans strove to define their popular political life with the expanded suffrage and greater discussion of political issues in a growing press, they also developed a distinctive American cultural identity. Indeed, print culture and popular public involvement with the political process became intertwined. As America grew by leaps and bounds, Jeffersonian political culture enveloped settlers of the new states and waves of people in older regions who acquired new political rights. At the same time, Federalists became more and more associated with a worn-out, even irrelevant, approach to governing at both the national and local levels.

Expansion and the Agrarian Republic

While Jeffersonians limited the role of government in the civil and legal affairs of American citizens, and reduced the size and expense of government, they promoted energetic use of state and federal governments for internal improvements (discussed in Chapter 9) and westward expansion. This improvement and expansion, argued Jeffersonians, corresponded with republican ideals about what constituted a good citizenry and would cement people's political liberty under conditions of relative social equality and broad popular use of the land. Without relatively widespread ownership of modest parcels of land, argued Jeffersonians, Americans risked developing the crime-infested, immoral urban centers such as in Europe, falling into habits of luxury, and thereby creating the conditions for political despotism or monarchy. Horrifying European examples of great cities, overgrown central governments, excessive commercial wealth, and degrading manufactures had "destroyed the manners and morals" of whole nations. For Jefferson, the pinnacle of republicanism was the yeoman farmer becoming an independent landowner earning a comfortable living from the soil. It followed that the government ought to acquire "an empire of the west" and organize its settlement and use by a "virtuous, expansive people." Beside, argued many Jeffersonians, settlement of new western lands would establish America's claim over a great expanse of territory that might otherwise be "overrun by foreign foe" such as the Spanish, French, and British. And although Jefferson promised that western lands would remain cheap enough for yeomen farmers to afford, their sale would nevertheless provide government with additional revenue. However, as Americans expanded across abundant lands and integrated new settlements into the Democratic-Republican political culture of the nation, they also encountered numerous tests of their republicanism.

Lands of Promise

In 1800 the population of the United States stood at only 5.3 million, but already it was growing at the astounding rate of 3 percent per year. Greater numbers of people moved from place to place, occupying new lands or migrating from town to town, than ever before or since in American history. Much of this migration flowed in a westerly direction. In one stream, New England "Yankees" moved into Vermont and Maine, western New York, or even all the way to Pittsburgh, and then down the Ohio River. Since the late colonial period, dozens of small towns had become overcrowded. Younger sons and daughters, having run out of eligible spouses and employment opportunities, gambled on their future prosperity by packing up a few belongings and heading for the uncultivated fertile river valleys in unfamiliar terrain.

From 1790 to 1820, New York's population more than quadrupled; the newly settled western counties alone boasted over 800,000 inhabitants. About 400,000 more Americans splayed out into the Ohio Valley beyond. Some of these people bought their land from established land companies, including the Genesee investment group of British investors and the Holland Land Company of mainly Dutch speculators. The members of entire Congregational churches sometimes resolved to move together into New Hampshire or western New York. Other times, extended kin networks pooled resources for the long journey and difficult first years on new soil. Alongside these communities, a handful of American investors grabbed huge tracts of land at cheap prices and offered tenants attractive rental conditions. Most New England farmers preferred rent-to-buy conditions, by which they could be assured that their payments to landlords would eventually win them a freehold; few, however, realized this dream. Those who could not afford the rising cost of real estate out west simply squatted on available tracts of land.

Farmers left behind in New England adjusted to the loss of laborers and consumers by developing strategies to get higher yields of crops and better marketing of surpluses. Potatoes, turnips, and other vegetables "trucked," or taken by wagon to towns, became valuable additions to New England diets by the 1820s, while almost every farmer from Massachusetts to Virginia planted at least a little grain. New Jersey and Pennsylvania farmers practiced more crop rotation, fertilization, and deeper plowing, all of which increased farm yields and permitted more diverse cultivation. Better tools compensated somewhat for the sons who left their fathers' farms.

From the Chesapeake region, white tenant farmers and impoverished freeholders headed by the thousands into Kentucky and Tennessee (see map page 297). Meanwhile, planters in Virginia and Maryland lamented the loss of population in the older settlements. Whole counties that had once been full of valuable taxpayers and free laborers seemed now to be deserted. By 1800, a steady stream of families were moving through the Cumberland Gap (see map), lugging their belongings into the forbidding mountains and cutting trails with the crude agricultural implements they would need to clear land in years to come. Few Kentuckians held prior claims to lots; virtually all of them simply squatted on the land. They counted on "ancient traditions" to confirm their rights to the soil: settlers earned title to their lands by occupying them and building "improvements" of fences and homes in what was otherwise the "savage wilderness."

Squatters' rights remained a compelling reason why many farm families and small entrepreneurs risked much to move into the Northwest Territory or across the Southeast during the early 1800s. But squatters encountered solid opposition from speculators and land companies that held deeds to vast tracts of this land, courtesy of state legislatures that bowed to the demands of powerful investment collectives. In addition, many politicians in state legislatures agreed with land company agents that a more orderly occupation of the West was desirable, and only land companies could produce revenues from land sales that could be shared between investors and governments. In the scramble for occupation, title, and development of the Northwest Territory, squatters often lost their struggles for homesteads, or fought violently to defend their claims against encroaching land companies. Many of them became poor tenants scratching out a living, no better off on the cotton and hemp farms west of the Appalachian Mountains than they were before migration.

Not all migrants came from the Northeast and mid-Atlantic regions. Beginning in the 1790s, southerners pressed toward the Mississippi River, through Alabama and Mississippi, and then into territory west of the river. Some of the new settlements filled with small farmers and former Chesapeake tenants who were able to get a freehold. More migrants, however, were planters who reproduced the slave and export agriculture system of the older South. When Chesapeake area planters converted from tobacco cultivation to wheat, they sold off many of their slaves to migrating planters in the new southern territories (see Chapter 9), where the harshening realities of cotton and sugar cultivation required large amounts of labor. In addition, down to 1808, when the Constitution's ban on the transatlantic slave trade became effective, Georgia and South Carolina planters imported nearly 250,000 new slaves, about as many as they had brought in during the entire colonial period, to help make their expansive agriculture a success. Tidewater region planters who migrated into Kentucky and Tennessee also took large numbers of slaves with them. In all, by 1820, nearly 250,000 slaves were sold from the older plantation regions into the new cotton and sugar South, and almost 50,000 were relocated into the trans-Appalachian region. Indeed, the hope of the Constitution's framers that slavery would "fade from our national life" now seemed naïve.

These strands of migration, in which eastern and southern peoples carried their distinctive identities into the new western territories, slowed the rise of national identity. German-speaking communities could be found in 1820 in Lancaster, Pennsylvania, near Savannah, Georgia, and in Ohio country. People of Scots-Irish heritage rarely mingled and intermarried with those of New England Congregational backgrounds. Although newspapers enlarged the political participation of urban Americans and began to bring rural people closer to coastal events, only members of professions and economic elites participated in a national culture regularly. Even as the franchise widened, most people expressed political demands and obligations of citizenship in local and regional terms.

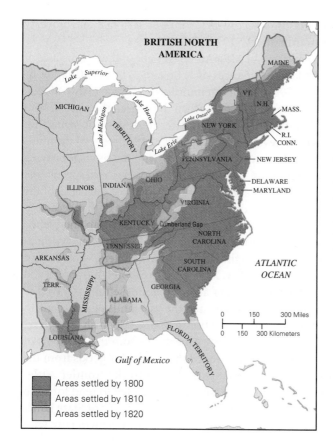

Early National Expansion
In the decades after the Revolution, waves of immigrants and migrating Americans spilled over the Appalachian Mountains. By 1820 a quarter of the nation's people lived in this trans-Applachian frontier. (Source: Adapted from *Out of Many: A History of the American People,* Combined Edition, Third Edition, by Faragher/Buhle/Czitrom/Armitage, 1997, Prentice-Hall, Inc., Upper Saddle River, N.J.)

The Louisiana Purchase

In 1893 historian Frederick Jackson Turner wrote a highly influential essay, "The Significance of the Frontier in American History." Turner believed that Americans had developed a unique national identity as a result of their experience of the West. The West of the early 1800s differed from the frontiers that colonial settlers had experienced. This new West had been defined as a national domain, much of it acquired through international treaties. Sectional contests, the presence of Indians, the "rudeness of nature," and other characteristics of the West imparted to American settlers a particular character: democratic, pragmatic, forward-looking, and individualistic. Of course, Americans adapted a great deal to frontier conditions in the early 1800s. New kinds of soil, distance from markets, and the difficulties of starting farms and stores required skills that settlers had not used in their former locales.

But Turner grossly underestimated the power of regional heritage, kinship, and cultural traditions that people brought with them into the frontier. And he virtually overlooked evidence that frontier settlers aimed to reproduce the institutions, relationships, and culture of their coastal homes. Moreover, success came slowly to most migrants. Democracy and capitalism did not naturally, or always, travel with migrants out onto the frontier. On the contrary, years of struggle and poverty marked the lives of most westward settlers.

Jefferson shared the deep convictions of most Americans about the significance of new land for settlement, as the land ordinances of 1785 and 1787 (see Chapter 6) demonstrated. In the Land Act of 1796, Federalists enunciated different goals—of raising great sums from sales of the national domain—when they raised the price of land to a minimum of $2 per acre in lots of 640 acres. Such terms of sale put ownership outside the typical family's reach, however. A new Land Act of 1801 reduced the minimum lot to 320 acres and permitted incremental payments, with discounts for paying in cash. Within the next eighteen months, families, land companies, and speculators purchased nearly 500,000 acres—more than the government had sold during all of the 1790s. The government sold over 500,000 acres each year for the rest of that decade.

Despite these efforts to provide yeomen farming families with cheap and plentiful tracts of land, security often eluded settlers. Speculators and greedy land companies continued to create a jurisdictional nightmare for many settlers, while Indian resistance continued to plague the Ohio Valley. The presence of foreign trappers and troops along important rivers added to migrants' anxieties about settling the West.

In 1800 Spain signed a secret treaty that returned the vast lands of Louisiana to France, though its local government and population remained Spanish. Two years later, Spanish officials in Louisiana began barring Americans from the vital port of New Orleans, a serious blow to farmers who needed that outlet for goods from the trans-Appalachian territories and to merchants trading with the frontier settlements. Meanwhile, word reached America that Napoleon intended to send forces to crush the slave rebellion of Toussaint L'Ouverture in Haiti. Secretary of State James Madison raised the possibility of American merchants trading beneficially with Toussaint's new government.

Wishing to avoid open conflict with France, Jefferson instructed the American minister in Paris, Robert R. Livingston, to buy New Orleans. To Livingston's surprise, in April 1803 Napoleon agreed to sell not only the port, but also the entire territory of Louisiana. By then, Napoleon's plan to retake Haiti had failed because rampant yellow fever and persistent slave resistance made landing impossible. And without Caribbean stations, Napoleon was also unable to launch efforts to subdue the vast Louisiana. Once the hope of securing Haiti faded, it made less sense to hold on to Louisiana, whose main purpose would have been to grow food for the slave islands. Napoleon also feared that if Britain followed through on its threat to invade French-dominated Europe, Americans would seize the opportunity to invade Louisiana.

Napoleon offered some 830,000 square miles to America for a mere $15 million. Jefferson quickly set aside arguments, many of them from his Democratic-Republican party allies, that making such a purchase violated the letter of the Constitution and was not "necessary and proper" for the running of the government. However, faced with the possibility of expanding the "empire for liberty," Jefferson waived these objections and used the treaty-making power of the executive branch to seal the deal with France.

More serious opposition came from Federalists, especially in New England, who feared that this new western land would "drain" people from the East and dilute the "civilized character" of the American people. Worse, westward migration would tip the balance in Congress toward an alliance of the West and South as new territories became states. Some Federalists in New York and New England circulated rumors of secession. As a first step toward forming a northern confederacy separate from the United States, they supported the candidacy of Aaron Burr, a disgruntled Democratic-Republican leader, for governor of New York in 1804.

Hearing of these threats to divide the country, Hamilton bristled with indignation, and Burr challenged him to a duel—formerly a means for aristocrats to settle disputes, but now illegal in most northern states. In July 1804 the two men drew arms in New Jersey, and Burr's gunshot wounded Hamilton fatally. Burr was promptly indicted for murder, but he fled west once his term of office was completed. There he plotted with the Louisiana military governor, General James Wilkinson, to seize the territory and perhaps portions of northern Mexico. The plan failed, and John Marshall, in his capacity as circuit court judge, tried Burr for treason. Marshall refused to interpret Burr's duel and western escapades as treason, and the court acquitted Burr. Further talk of a separate northern confederacy ceased, but the entire ordeal illustrated deep sectional divisions in the American political culture.

Lewis and Clark

Despite party factionalism and regional sectionalism, the public cheered news of the Louisiana Purchase, and land offices reported soaring sales of tracts on either side of the Mississippi River. Jefferson wanted detailed information about this "great unknown wilderness." Even in the 1790s, he had believed a convenient waterway might be found traversing North America to the Pacific Ocean. Earlier than that, fur traders had reckoned that the Columbia and Missouri Rivers might provide the best way through Indian territories and around Spanish settlements in California, Nevada, and Utah. In 1783 William Clark—a Virginian who had fought in the Revolutionary War in Ohio—declined Jefferson's offer to head an expedition into the trans-Mississippi West. Twenty years later, with the Louisiana Purchase completed, Jefferson had a more convincing argument. America, he pleaded with Congress, had a duty to displace all foreign nations remaining in the West and to make the Purchase secure for westward migration. By that time, Jefferson's view was supported widely by Americans, who viewed Louisiana as an expanse of land so large that it could provide hundreds of thousands of yeomen settlers with sizeable estates, and perhaps room to resettle Indians from east of the Mississippi River without disturbing white migration.

Jefferson asked Congress for money to send out an expedition and appointed Meriwether Lewis, his private secretary, to head the team. Lewis began in Pittsburgh in August 1803 with a keelboat and a Corps of Discovery crew that included seven soldiers, three young men eager to travel, and a pilot. Clark, now enthusiastic, joined the party two months later, at Clarksville, Indiana, with a handful of Kentucky woodsmen and hunters. Together they went down the Ohio River, to St. Louis; wintered over at Camp Dubois; and headed up the Missouri River from May 1804 through the summer and early fall (see map).

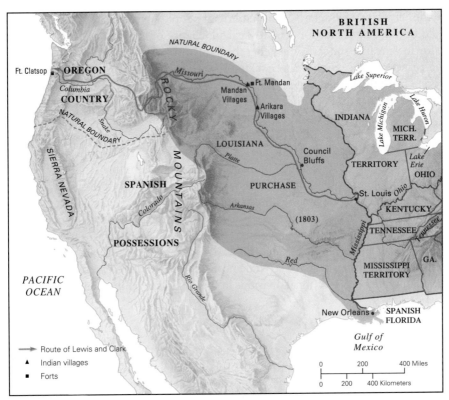

The Lewis and Clark Expedition and the Louisiana Purchase   Acquisition of the vast Louisiana territory in 1803 made American dreams of westward expansion and Jefferson's "Empire for Liberty" seem possible to fulfill. Within a year, Lewis and Clark led an expedition into the farthest section of the territory and beyond. The explorers brought back from the Pacific coast news and artifacts that ignited widespread popular excitement about the West.

Word of the expedition spread through Indian villages ahead of the eastern strangers' arrival. By October 1804 the Mandan villages of the upper Missouri River teemed with excitement at the prospects of new trade and military support against their enemy, the Sioux. Chief Black Cat welcomed the Americans and informed them of their dire need for assistance. In previous years, "the smallpox destroyed the greater part of the nation," the chief told Clark. At one time, the Mandan had been numerous and "all the nations before this malady [were] afraid of them." But weakened by disease and hunger, the Mandan were frequent victims of the warring Sioux.

Lewis and Clark arrived at Fort Mandan with a full complement of twenty-nine men. They informed the Mandan leadership that President Jefferson expected them to forge bonds of friendship and trade, and that the Indians would in return pledge their loyalty to the American government of the East. Over the next months, Lewis and Clark's party gathered great amounts of valuable information about the culture of the Mandan and the environment of the region. In early spring 1805, the Americans hired several French-Canadian fur trappers and traders who lived in the Mandan villages part of the year to translate for them and accompany them on the remaining westward journey. In addition, they added the young Shoshone pathfinder, Sacagawea, to their expedition. Sacagawea, the wife of a French trapper, carried her baby through the rest of the trek, providing the Corps of Discovery with a signal to other Native American villages that they came in peace. In April they left with canoes and dugouts to navigate the Lemhi River, Salmon River, and the Lolo Trail to the Bitterroot Mountains. The Nez Percé helped guide the weary explorers through rough terrain, until they could descend to the Snake and Columbia Rivers. They reached the Pacific coast in November 1805 and wintered over near the mouth of the Columbia.

Lewis and Clark not only saw dramatically different terrain from their eastern homelands, they also encountered remarkable new cultures. Americans had only a vague knowledge of the Plains Indians, who lived on grasslands and hunted the great herds of buffalo. The explorers observed with amazement how the Indians shared the environment with the buffalo, their main source of food, shelter, and spiritual life. The buffalo's pathways determined Indian patterns of migration, the nature of their hunting, and the relationships with other Indian nations. North of the Plains, exploring parties met the Mandan and Minitari, who lived in numerous small groups in colder climates and river valleys in sedentary villages. Leading Mandan already served as middlemen for French and British fur traders when Lewis and Clark met them.

The expedition returned rapidly, by September 1806, because Lewis and Clark were eager to report their findings of friendly Indians, rich and varied landscapes, and the success of European traders and settlers in the far Northwest. Their reports, which were published soon after their return and distributed widely to an eager public, spurred settlement in the northern part of the Purchase. Americans took possession of the trans-Mississippi West for the first time, naming it, settling it, and transforming its landscape with great enthusiasm.

While Lewis and Clark were on their way back to Washington, D. C., Lieutenant Zebulon Pike set out in other directions. First he explored the Mississippi River from St. Louis to its source in northern Minnesota. Then he trekked across the southern half of the Purchase to Colorado, where he named one of the Rocky Mountain summits Pike's Peak. Continuing deep into territory held by the Spanish, Pike's party crossed the Rio Grande, passed into the Mexican desert, turned north and moved through San Antonio. Like Lewis and Clark's account, Pike's reports about the expedition prompted numerous plans for American settlement in those directions as well.

Indian Relations

Most people who settled west of the Mississippi River in the early 1800s did not plan to farm. Instead, this new area of American migration attracted speculators, fur traders, French and Spanish wanderers and bandits, confidence men waiting to lure travelers into uncharted areas, and a few adventurers from Kentucky and Ohio country picking their way west. These sparsely dispersed Americans encountered great numbers of Indians of varied cultures. In the Ohio Valley, north of the famed river, a loose confederation of Delaware, Miami, Shawnee, Potawatomi, and numerous villages of mixed populations fended off early American expansion. South of the river, the so-called Five Civilized Tribes of Cherokee, Choctaw, Creek, Chickasaw, and Seminole grew familiar with the imperial policies of both Spanish and Americans. Long before 1800, the tools and guns of Europeans had reached the Mandan, Hidatsa, Cheyenne, Arapaho, and others far to the West. After 1800, the relentless westward expansion of American people changed the Indian frontier decisively and devastatingly.

Most Americans generalized that all Indians were "savages" of inferior character, unsuited for republican citizenship. A few shrill voices demanded that Native Americans simply be pushed west, ahead of the tide and out of settlers' way. Many Americans, however, believed that large numbers of Indians could eventually be assimilated into white culture. Baptist, Moravian, and Quaker missionaries launched efforts to convert "the heathen" of western New York and Pennsylvania. The Society for the Propagation of the Gospel (1787) undertook to christianize and educate Native Americans in the Northwest Territory, though with only modest success.

The Indian Intercourse Act of 1790 stipulated that the government had to secure Indian lands by treaty, not by conquest or seizure. But this policy quickly became interpreted as the federal government's right to aggressively take Indian land, and the law did little to prevent the surge of westward white migration in advance of official surveys and treaty negotiations. Time and again, land-hungry Americans combined with state militias or the national army to crush Indian resistance to white territorial advances. Jefferson deplored the violence on the western and southeastern frontiers. His solution, hardly an adequate one, was to ask Indians to cede their lands peacefully in return for instruction in the agricultural ways of yeomen and "the culture of a more civilized nation."

Already in disarray because of internal wars, many tribes west of the Appalachians had become defenseless against white migration by 1810. Some served as interpreters and middlemen in the fur trade that extended around the Great Lakes and, in the case of John Jacob Astor's American Fur Company, to the far Northwest. This trade brought Native Americans useful goods such as blankets, iron pots, and hoes. It also brought harmful patterns of economic dependence, smallpox, and depletion of game on their hunting grounds. Other Indians fled west, and then fled again as wagons and sod houses spread out over the prairies.

Ultimately, Native Americans who assimilated into "civilized" American ways only accelerated their disorientation and fragmentation. But when villages chose to migrate farther west, they often met equally difficult conditions trying to share the same environments with Native Americans already present in an area. In either case, few villages survived the waves of American migration intact. Between 1790 and 1820, most Indians between the Appalachian ridge and the Plains beyond the Mississippi experienced some degree of disease, economic dependence on the East, cultural transformation, bitter political splits, or demoralizing accommodation—any or all of which accelerated changes in tribal life and introduced unforeseen trauma.

Of the Indians who chose extensive adaptation to white culture, the most successful were the Cherokee. In 1800 they still controlled vast acreage in western North Carolina, eastern Tennessee, and backcountry Georgia. But villages quickly succumbed to disease and warfare, and fleeing remnants of clans consolidated with villages far from ancestral soil. Meanwhile, settlers created new counties that encompassed Cherokee lands and imposed American law and economic institutions on reluctant individuals. Within the Cherokee nation, a bitter feud developed between families who wished to fight back against the southern state governments versus the accommodationist families who feared a destructive war with white armies if they resisted. John Ross, a leader of the "peace" group, helped accommodationists win internally and then create their own Cherokee National Council in 1808. The council organized dispersed villages under one governing body, wrote a code of law, and encouraged their people to become literate. One of their greatest scholars, Sequoyah, devised a Cherokee alphabet, and a few enterprising individuals printed a Cherokee newspaper. Most villages accepted a system of boarding schools run by missionaries, and many Cherokee set up their own stores, gristmills, and blacksmith shops.

Accommodation produced mixed results. Most Cherokee no longer lived as hunters but rather as sedentary farmers, seldom rising above poverty. A few prospered and acquired African-American slaves to work large tracts modeled on white cotton plantations. By 1827, the council oversaw distribution of a constitution, modeled on those of the southern states, which declared Cherokee status as an independent nation with sovereignty over tribal lands in Georgia, Alabama, North Carolina, and Tennessee. In 1829 the council made it an offense against the entire Cherokee people for any individual to sell land to a white settler. But accommodation eroded quickly when relentless white expansion raised the prospect of Cherokee removal far to the West (see Chapter 10).

The Shawnee of the Ohio Valley resisted the advancing line of white settlers until their decisive defeat at Fallen Timbers in 1794. Of the remaining population, many accepted the efforts of Quaker and Moravian missionaries to convert them and settle them on farms. Others chose to move west but found that a life of constant removal and hunting further weakened their diminishing numbers. Tecumseh, a young Shawnee warrior, led some of his people into the Indiana Territory around 1805, where the governor, William Henry Harrison, had been pressuring Delaware, Miami, and other tribes to sign treaties that carved out a series of reservations. That same year, Tecumseh's brother, Tenskwatawa, began sharing his spiritual visions with other Shawnee, visions in which the revitalization of Indians would occur once they rejected American culture, goods, and settlers. Tenskwatawa, also known as The Prophet, preached that turning away from American influences would restore the health, peace, and prosperity of the Shawnee.

Tecumseh drew on Tenskwatawa's powerful spiritual message to create a military confederation of many different tribes in the Michigan, Illinois, and Indiana region. After 1807, the British realized it suited their interest to send arms and food to this pan-Indian movement. By 1809, Tecumseh aroused the movement to active resistance against further white migration into their hunting lands: "the mere presence of the white men," he insisted, "is a source of evil." That year, Harrison presided over the signing of the Treaty of Fort Wayne, by which the Delaware and Potawatomi ceded nearly 3 million acres of land in Indiana. Tecumseh vowed defiance. He insisted that all Indians held this land in common, that no single Indian tribe could cede it forever, and that his alliance would defend such collectively used Indian lands "in a war of extermination against the paleface."

On November 7, 1811, Harrison advanced about 1,000 troops to the village of Tippecanoe, where in a pitched battle about 150 from each side died. Harrison claimed a victory, but in truth, the hundreds of Indians expelled from the area made war against vulnerable settlers throughout the interior of Michigan and Indiana territories. Tecumseh forged an official alliance with the British, while the word spread eastward that the frontier harbored more dangers than ever.

To the south, a young militia commander named Andrew Jackson urged President Jefferson to authorize a campaign against the Creek "Red Sticks" who refused to be removed from northern Georgia and Alabama. A planter from Tennessee who supported slavery, Jackson declared himself an ardent Indian fighter. But from 1808 to 1813, Washington politicians ignored his petition to exterminate the Creek. Finally, however, Creek atrocities against settlers became unbearable, and Jackson began a march with thousands of Kentucky and Tennessee militia into the heart of Creek lands. David Crockett accompanied him to the battle at Horseshoe Bend in early 1814, where over eight hundred Indians died—the heaviest losses in one battle in the entire history of U.S.–Indian warfare. Jackson, however, determined to subdue the Creek "completely." In the next months, he scorched the surrounding

Tecumseh (1768–1813) This Shawnee military leader had led Indian resistance to expansion into the northwest area of the trans-Appalachian region for many years by the 1780s. In that decade, as American settlement progressed rapidly into Kentucky, Tecumseh formed an alliance of midwestern tribes that engaged in numerous rebellions. Hoping to blend the support of the British and the fierce resistance of Indian peoples on the far side of the Appalachians, Tecumseh ultimately failed when an overwhelming American military force ended the uprisings. Tecumseh died at the Battle of the Thames in 1813. *(Field Museum of Natural History FMNH Neg #A993851.)*

region, constructed Fort Jackson at the center of the Creek nation, and declared American sovereignty over 22 million acres of traditional Creek soil.

 ## International Relations, 1800–1815

George Washington had left office with the plea for "no entangling alliances," and into the early 1800s, many Democratic-Republicans accepted this wisdom. For many years they had recoiled from making English connections, but increasingly the French had also become suspect. Americans, insisted Jeffersonians, needed to blend their bounteous agriculture with overseas commerce to prosper: farmers could produce the foods that Europeans needed, and merchants could bring home the finished manufactures of more advanced nations. For Jeffersonians, these mutual relations shielded Americans from the dangerous concentration of wealth, corrupt cities, and degraded lives of wage workers that marked Europe. But Napoleonic designs on the Western Hemisphere endangered this view of trade and peace.

Spain in North America

After a long era of relative indifference, Spain began to grow uneasy about its dominion in North America. From the 1760s to 1783, Spain's King Carlos III maintained a keen interest in securing the vast lands north of New Spain that lay loosely within his empire: the Floridas, Louisiana, much of present-day Texas, and portions of present-day Arizona and California. Following the French example, Spanish viceroys throughout these borderlands pursued a policy of divide and conquer. Spanish officials forced Native American peoples who refused to sign treaties of submission into dependent trade relations or extermination. The Apache and Comanche of Texas entered years of fierce warfare, while the Pima, Pueblo, Navajo, and other peoples in Arizona and California succumbed to forced labor, liquor, and disease.

Spain's power in North America reached its highest point in the 1790s. Its hegemony stretched from East Florida across the Gulf Coast and beyond, through Texas and New Mexico. In California, Spanish landed estate holders and merchants ruled over numbers of Native American peoples and a rich environment. For several decades, the government sent missionaries and soldiers north from Mexico to set up missions and *presidios* from San Diego to San Francisco. Father Junipero Serra, a leading Franciscan priest, set up a series of missions that soon dominated California's lush valleys. Serra and his mission staff put thousands of Indians to work on the missions, sometimes by conversion, sometimes by force. Just before the American Revolution, a number of southern California mission Indians rose up against their Spanish rulers, the deplorable conditions of work, and rampant disease and death. They burned the mission at San Diego and organized rebellions throughout the countryside during the 1770s. But with their numbers reduced significantly by then, the southern California Indians were unable to reestablish their former village lifestyles.

Even as Spain subdued these outlying areas of its New World empire, its rule was being threatened in its eastern holdings. Pinckney's Treaty of 1795 had given Americans access to the Mississippi River and voided Spanish claims in the Ohio Valley. Then Spain tried to forge a strong alliance with France by giving up Louisiana in 1800, only to see France sell the region to America in 1803.

In 1808 Napoleon installed his younger brother Joseph on the Spanish throne. In Mexico *mestizos* (people of mixed Spanish and Indian heritage) and Indians rose up against royalist rule and declared their social and economic rights. In 1810 and 1812, revolts led by Father Miguel Hidalgo and Father Jose Maria Morelos demanded Mexican independence but were easily crushed by the Spanish authorities. In Texas, a few American settler-invaders, supported by the Mexican republican leader Bernardo Gutierrez, declared the province a republic in 1812, but they, too, fell into the hands of royalists who warred against American rebels, Mexican republicans, and homesteaders.

In 1810 American adventurers also occupied Spanish West Florida, claiming territorial rights that included several important rivers that drained to the Gulf of Mexico. Americans demanded annexation to the United States, which Congress granted in May 1812. During the War of 1812 (see below), American troops occupied Spanish West Florida and incited citizens to overthrow the Spanish governor. In 1817 Andrew Jackson marched into East Florida, where he seized Spanish citizens and forts under the pretense that Seminole Indians and Spanish troops had raided American settlements nearby. John Quincy Adams, the secretary of state under President James Monroe, took advantage of these open conflicts—though he disagreed with Jackson's methods—to force Spain into signing the Adams-Onís Treaty in 1819. Spain, facing rebellions in Mexico and throughout its South American colonies, was in no position to bargain.

Under the treaty, the United States annexed East Florida, took responsibility for paying the claims of its citizens against Spanish who had destroyed their property in the borderlands, and set a boundary between Louisiana and New Spain. In 1818 Adams had signed a separate treaty with England that secured the boundary between Louisiana and British Canada. Once British troops cleared out of the Ohio Valley, as they did in the years following the Rush-Bagot Treaty of 1817, Americans could rejoice in their undisputed possession of all territory west of the Appalachian ridge and south of the forty-ninth parallel as far as the Rocky Mountains.

The Atlantic Community

Jeffersonian leaders dreamed of building a lasting international peace, but they experienced a different reality when Americans encountered trouble abroad or when foreigners threatened American interests in North America. For example, between 1801 and 1806, naval vessels brought numerous reports that the Barbary states of Algiers, Morocco, Tripoli, and Tunis had launched raids against American trade vessels in the Mediterranean Sea. On many occasions, Jefferson and naval officials ordered armed ships into hostile waters to escort merchant ships, and they continued to express diplomatic concerns about the attacks against Americans in that part of the world.

The hope that the tensions of the undeclared war with France in 1798–1799 would not grow into open war also became strained once Napoleon came to power.

As Napoleon sent his armies across Europe from 1803 to 1814, Jeffersonian out-pouring of support for the French Revolution diminished noticeably. Federalists and Democratic-Republicans agreed that Americans needed trade with both England and France. American ships carried food, cotton, and semiprocessed goods to both England and France, and foreign West Indies islands provided vital markets for American agricultural exports and goods for reexport to Europe. Yet after 1792, these ships became targets for French and British frigates, and by the end of the decade, the policy of neutrality was difficult for either political party to support.

By 1805, Napoleon's armies had overrun most of continental Europe, while Britain retained mastery of the high seas and had effectively blockaded France's international commerce. Democratic-Republicans and Federalists alike wished for neutrality in this new round of foreign belligerence, especially because non-alignment would keep trade with both France and England open. The government's official declaration of neutrality at first brought great profits for American grain and staples exporters; from 1803 to 1807, exports rose over 40 percent. And merchants who imported foreign goods from the Caribbean, transferred them to American ships at U.S. ports, and shipped them to Europe saw their trade rise over 400 percent.

Neutrality lost its luster after early 1805. Although Napoleon continued to rule on the continent, England's Royal Navy, under Lord Nelson, destroyed French and Spanish fleets at the Battle of Trafalgar (near the Straits of Gibraltar), and the English government passed the Essex decision, which stipulated that European countries could not open up their national and colonial trade to neutral nations during war if they normally prohibited that trade during peace. In effect, the decree attacked the most important sector of American trade, its reexport of French and Spanish West Indies goods through American ports to European buyers across the Atlantic. At the same time, Britain stepped up seizures of American vessels in the Caribbean and attempted to recapture thousands of British sailors who had deserted to American ships for higher wages and kinder commanders.

These incidents infuriated American merchants, especially in the New England states, which relied on the reexport trade as the "sinews of the republic." Jefferson agreed, and added that the British had delivered a serious blow to international protocols respecting neutrality. But he knew that Congress and the nation would not willingly enter another war, especially because Jeffersonians had reduced the navy to an insignificant force against the British fleet, the world's strongest. Hoping to secure a more enduring peace, Jefferson and his close supporters convinced Congress to pass a Non-Importation Act in 1806, modeled on the boycotts of the revolutionary crisis. But this time, the boycott of British imports failed to bring manufacturers and merchants in England to their knees because it was neither thorough enough to shut down trade nor fully supported by northern American merchants.

Meanwhile, British naval officials tried to recover their losses of sailors by capturing Americans. From 1803 to 1811, the British navy illegally impressed, or forced into service, some six thousand American sailors. In 1807 tensions erupted into open confrontation when the *Leopard,* a British ship, stopped the American

Chesapeake in American waters in order to apprehend deserters from the Royal Navy. When the *Chesapeake*'s captain refused to hand over any seamen, the *Leopard* fired its cannon, killing three men and wounding eighteen others; the British then took four men who may have been Americans.

As it became clear that nonimportation was a failure, Jefferson tried a different policy. He asked Congress for an Embargo Act in December 1807. Unlike the embargoes of the colonial years, which had halted either imports to, or exports from, certain ports, Jefferson's proposal barred American ships from sailing to *any* foreign port. He intended not only to cut off American markets for British finished goods but also to deprive British manufacturers of raw materials. This last-ditch effort to "peaceably coerce" the British resulted in disaster. As exports dropped during 1807–1808 to one-fifth their pre-embargo levels, the nation fell into a deep depression. Cities in the Northeast entered a phase of scarcities and gloom. Smuggling compensated for some loss of commerce and satisfied some consumer demand in northern cities. Coastal traders falsified documents or simply showed up at foreign ports not specified on their bills of lading. But these illicit tactics did not revive commerce. In the meantime, British shippers rejoiced in the lack of American competition and cultivated new markets in South America and the Far East.

Federalists could not bear to watch commerce languish, "for our trade is our civilizing influence." Hundreds of leading New England Federalists simply defied Jefferson's embargo. Their anger reached a fever pitch when the Democratic-Republican Congress passed a Force Act in 1808 to curtail American smuggling into Canada and the West Indies. The act, argued New Englanders, was another instance of Jeffersonians using excessive federal power, and this time it harmed American trade more than European. At one point, Jefferson ordered federal troops to Lake Champlain, New York, to arrest smugglers, but the local population defied national authority by burning goods on federal revenue vessels and retaking seized cargoes. Ironically, a few loud voices proclaimed that "rights belonging to the states" had been violated by federal officials who proclaimed to be Jeffersonians and yet "wear the mantle of our former foe," the Federalists.

Jefferson left office despondent about America's future. James Madison, also of Virginia and a good friend of Jefferson, assumed the executive office in March 1809 at a difficult moment. Almost immediately, Congress repealed the embargo, replacing it with the Non-Intercourse Act, which reopened America's trade with all nations except France and England. But Americans desperately needed these two highly important trading partners. So, in 1810 Congress added Macon's Bill No. 2, which tentatively opened trade with France and England but at the same time stipulated that the president might reimpose the Non-Intercourse Act on one nation if the other lifted its restrictions against American commerce. In September Napoleon's foreign minister in America announced that France would rescind the Berlin and Milan decrees and reopen trade with America, thereby putting Madison in the position of declaring hostility toward England. Madison gave England three months to follow France's lead, after which time he promised to reimpose the Non-Intercourse Act. England called his bluff: British officials refused to

"Ograbme, or, The American Snapping-Turtle," by Alexander Anderson, 1807   Congress passed the Embargo Act in 1807 in an effort to stop both English and French warring navies from harassing American shippers and sailors on the high seas. But the halt of exportation had disastrous effects on American commerce and did little to change foreign nations' policies. Few foreign merchants wanted to send goods to American ports if they could not secure exports for their return voyages. In addition, numerous mid-Atlantic American merchants smuggled flour and other goods out of their ports in violation of the embargo, as indicated by the "superfine" stamped on the bottom of the barrel. Jefferson has unleashed his snapping turtle, the Force Act of 1808, to catch smugglers and bring them to justice ("Ograbme" is "embargo" spelled backward). (*© Collection of The New-York Historical Society.*)

revoke their commercial restrictions and told Madison to withdraw the Non-Intercourse Act until France repealed every last measure against British trade. Madison faced a dilemma: either submit to the imperial authority of the former mother country or go to war.

The War of 1812

In November 1811, Congress voted to begin a military buildup in preparation for war with Britain, and in the following year the country entered what some scholars call the "second war for independence." War Hawks in Congress—a loose coalition of some Democratic-Republicans—believed the war was necessary to defend American citizens at sea and recover shipping and sailors from belligerent foreigners. War, declared the faction's congressional leaders Henry Clay and John C. Calhoun, would also defend western and southern land claims against Indians and

Spanish Florida. While most Federalists, now concentrated in New England and the northern mid-Atlantic region, feared the loss of commerce, War Hawks who stood behind Madison declared a war to defend America's maritime and territorial rights. The war vote in June 1812 clearly reflected this partisan and sectional alignment: all thirty Federalists and most northeastern Democratic-Republicans in Congress opposed a declaration of war against Britain, whereas the southern and western Democratic-Republican majority supported war.

Despite predictions that the war would end quickly, initial campaigns in Canada proved inconclusive and costly. At first, General William Hull's midwestern troops fell under fierce attack by Tecumseh during early 1812. But Commodore Oliver Hazard Perry's naval forces kept the region south of Lake Erie from falling into British hands, while General William Henry Harrison redoubled attacks against Tecumseh's forces and the British regiments that fell back from Detroit. Tecumseh died at the Battle of the Thames in October 1813, just as an American naval squadron burned and looted Toronto (then York).

Before Americans could claim victory over much of Canada, New England states withdrew both troops and financial support from any further invasions of "foreign British soil" at the end of 1813. Federalists in Congress tried to block national appropriations of funds and to roll back tariffs. Northerner Daniel Webster led their efforts to discourage enlistment in the American army and to prohibit recruitment of local militiamen into national forces. Democratic-Republicans appeared to many sectors of the country to have become the War Hawks, while Federalists shrank the military budget and sought renewed peaceful commerce.

But British warships stymied commerce along the American coastline, blocking trade and menacing civilian fishermen. In 1814, the Royal Navy rushed the shoreline of the Chesapeake Bay, overran coastal towns, and sacked the area around the capitol in Washington. The presidential house, still unfinished and cluttered with materials, was burned along with government buildings; Madison's household fled. Then, as the British troops headed toward Baltimore, Americans were able to turn them back at Fort McHenry, but fears of weak defenses gripped the South. In another couple of months, the British nearly took New York at the Battle of Lake Champlain, and by December 1814, it looked as if the British might cut off access to the sea through New Orleans.

Word arrived late in 1814 that Britain and its allies had defeated Napoleon. English negotiators now anxiously sought peace in order to lower taxes in England and reopen trade lines with America. But American enthusiasm was not universal. New England Federalists, whose loyalty had been lukewarm throughout the war, met in Hartford, Connecticut, to discuss reform of the Constitution or even secession from the union. Federalists, especially those in New England, wished to end the Democratic-Republican policies that had strangled their trade. The Hartford Convention called for a one-term limit on the presidency, restrictions on the length of national embargoes, and diminished presidential powers over foreign policymaking, the creation of new states, and trade restrictions. Although Federalist authority had declined too much to win these changes, their convention heightened anxieties brewing during "Madison's Little War."

The commissioners negotiating an end to the conflict finally recognized that they had deadlocked. Britain would not give up large portions of Canada and Florida, and America refused to set aside a large land reserve for the Native American allies of the British. On December 24, 1814, the Treaty of Ghent fixed the prewar boundaries as the grounds for peace. But how could the Democratic-Republicans sell the lack of territorial gains to the American public after three long years of war? Spirits sagged everywhere during late 1814, until word reached eastern newspaper offices and pulpits—before word of the treaty did—that General Andrew Jackson and his ragtag army of multiethnic, multiracial troops had decimated the British forces at the Battle of New Orleans on January 8, 1815.

Jackson's victory boosted morale immeasurably throughout the nation and elevated his own stature as a symbol of rugged individualism and frontier determination. The immense loss of life on the British side—some 700 dead and 10,000 wounded or imprisoned—contrasted sharply with America's mere 13 dead and 58 wounded. This lopsided victory, said some, proved the "RISING GLORY OF THE AMERICAN REPUBLIC." It also helped preserve Democratic-Republican political authority and consigned the Federalists to further obscurity. However, Monroe's subsequent two terms as president also proved to be years of deepening tensions and a fragmenting Democratic-Republican party system, which laid the groundwork for a new political party that war hero Jackson eventually led.

 ## Postwar Political Culture, 1815–1824

Following the War of 1812, Americans welcomed a period of relative quiet in national political life and international relations. The Democratic-Republicans—now called simply Republicans or sometimes National Republicans—continued to dominate national policymaking, despite the crises of the two previous decades. In the postwar years, politicians of James Madison's and James Monroe's presidencies formulated bold new definitions of America's place in the world. Some would call the years from 1815 to 1824 an Era of Good Feelings. But was it? Seething crises in western development, Indian wars, and a shattering economic panic in 1819 reminded Americans everywhere that they still lived in a fragile republic.

New Frontiers

In 1790 only 5 percent of the American population lived west of the Appalachian ridge; by 1820, 25 percent did. The trickle of prerevolutionary migration into frontier lands beyond coastal settlement had become a river of people, wagons, and goods flowing into the Old Northwest territories and the southwestern area covering western Georgia, Alabama, Mississippi, and Louisiana. Who were these people? Almost 2.5 million native-born Americans, most of them in farm families, chose to leave the increasingly crowded towns and worn-out lands of the northeastern coast or Chesapeake regions. The end of the War of 1812 brought news that Indians had been defeated or removed and that British troops finally had cleared out. Then, too, Congress had slowly reduced the price of western land from its high of $2 an acre under revenue-hungry Federalists. The Land Act of 1820 reduced the price of land to $1.25 an acre, the minimum lot size to eighty acres, and down payments to only $100 cash. In addition, the act gave squatters the right to "preempt" Congress's terms and buy land even more cheaply when they made "improvements"—homes, fences, mills, and stores—to their plot. Of course, speculators continued to plague the "sturdy yeomen's" efforts to settle fertile expanses in the West. Overlapping claims and open violence among squatters, speculators, and trappers on the frontier made something of a mess out of Jefferson's landed ideal for the continent. But liberal land policies made the prospect of westward movement more attractive to hundreds of thousands of average Americans.

Migrants poured across western New York, through Utica and Syracuse, toward the new settlement on Lake Erie called Buffalo; across the turnpike connecting Philadelphia to Pittsburgh; out of Baltimore, itself a fresh new port city, toward new trading towns in the Ohio Valley; and down the Wilderness Road along the Appalachian ridge, through the Cumberland Gap, and into Kentucky. They clustered in settlements widely spread out on the frontier, along the fall line and rivers that provided milling power and transportation.

Each new frontier region reproduced parts of its migrants' former culture, while adapting to new frontier conditions as well. From New England came emigrants who were young, for the most part, and anxious to be released from the crowded towns and depleted soil of their home counties. They came, too, as families, often with foreknowledge about a particular spot where kin or neighbors had begun a settlement. But once they arrived at these promising locations, over half of the East's migrants moved on again within a few years. Rumors and newspaper accounts of even richer land still farther west kept pulling them into areas "just beyond the next rise or even to the horizon." People who stayed behind in the new territorial towns more often than not rose to political and economic prominence as boosters, developers, bankers, real estate agents, and merchants amid the constantly fluctuating population of newcomers. Southern planters favored the rich soil around Natchez, Mississippi, and brought large numbers of slaves to labor for them. They soon understood the rapidly rising value of cotton—"white gold"—and turned toward New Orleans for exporting it to Britain. A well-developed system of labor and agriculture was thus transplanted into unknown lands. Through market calculation and adaptation to new conditions, a few planters grew immensely rich in this delta region and drew planters from Virginia, the Carolinas, and Georgia to the new cotton belt after 1815. Still, some migrants from the South and East moved into the Northwest Territory and looked to a life on free soil without slavery.

Government and Development

By 1815, Republicans were often promoting policies that at one time only hard-line Federalists had advocated. By then, the early Jeffersonian vision of self-reliance had receded far from view. President James Monroe continued the "Virginia Dynasty" of Republican presidents, but he filled his cabinet with men from all regions and both parties. John Quincy Adams, with his New England Federalist pedigree, became secretary of state; John C. Calhoun, a southern War Hawk and emerging states' rights champion, became secretary of war. From the start, Monroe also identified closely with westerners such as Henry Clay, who advocated a stepped-up program of internal improvements.

Already in 1815, Madison had enunciated support for what contemporaries then, and historians since, call the American System. It included the promotion and funding by government of a Second Bank of the United States, protective tariffs, and a network of roads and canals. In the past, Jefferson and his close supporters had denounced such improvements as a plan to usurp power from local and state control. By Madison and Monroe's administrations, however, proponents of government-sponsored development had become more vocal in the press, and in Congress. Early advocates of the American System premised its benefits on a vision of America's mixed commercial and agricultural economy. More and more Republicans hoped for additional government aid to transportation and financial institutions that helped developers, but they hardly foresaw the elaborate networks of capital flows, factory systems, and wage labor that lay ahead.

In 1816 Monroe kicked off the American System with two important federal measures. Congress chartered the Second Bank of the United States for another twenty years, thereby explicitly promoting a strong national currency and large funds of capital for the rapidly growing economy. Despite continuing protests from agrarian-minded Americans, some "nationally-minded Republicans" joined Federalists in support of the Bank. Monroe's 1816 message to Congress also implemented the first truly protective tariff in American history, largely in response to the flood of manufactured goods that the British dumped at American ports once the eight long years of boycotts and battles came to an end. American craftsmen and small entrepreneurs grew outraged with the competition from England's cheaper goods. The tariff imposed higher duties on woolens, cottons, leather, fur hats, paper, sugar and candy, and iron products. For the time being, the Bank and higher tariffs answered the immediate needs of America's commercial and "infant" manufacturing interests. Later, however, they would be the subjects of profound disagreement among Americans of various economic and political persuasions.

The American System also encompassed energetic promotion of roads and canals under Madison and Monroe. However, as Republicans, both presidents believed the Constitution prohibited the use of federal funds for such projects because, they reasoned, most roads and canals would cut through portions of states, or benefit only two or three states. For the time being, development originated primarily in the minds and pocketbooks of state governments and private citizens (discussed further in Chapter 9).

The Panic of 1819

In the early 1800s, most Americans worked directly on the land or in small shops at crafts and retailing. Here and there entrepreneurs started small businesses, mechanized their mills, or hired wage labor, but few investors yet envisioned a true factory system. Indeed, the economy had many familiar characteristics until long after the

War of 1812. Merchants renewed their commerce with England and Europe after the war, importing finished goods and sending southern agricultural goods to foreign ports. English ships were beginning to sail east for cotton, but southern planters still did not grow much of that commodity. In addition, the English Corn Laws after the War of 1812 prohibited imports of American grain and flour, which diminished American sales abroad and forced shippers to begin looking for new markets.

At first, it seemed to many Americans that although the export economy did not recover and grow according to their postwar expectations, they could turn west for prosperity. Land offices opened up in the new states formed out of the Northwest Territory, and planters snatched up cotton-growing land in the Southeast all the way to the Mississippi River. Proliferating local banks offered easy credit to eager settlers who wished to purchase land, and eastern speculators teamed up, not for the first time, with directors in the Second Bank of the United States to promote the land-grabbing frenzy. Prices for agricultural goods rose rapidly, which fueled even more land hunger.

However, when the national Bank needed funds to make a last foreign payment for the Louisiana Purchase, it turned to local banks for a supply of specie. These local banks had been built on overextended credit to eager farmers and entrepreneurs, and although required to cover their loans with a specie fund, few of them provided that safeguard. In 1819 the national Bank's unmet needs drew attention to the inflated credit of the local banks, with the result of demolishing public confidence, then private credit. The subsequent failure of numerous banks meant that thousands of farmhouses and herds of livestock went up for auction, while recently purchased slaves went up for sale.

Once panic set in, a stream of bankruptcies followed and unemployment rose to alarming heights. Laborers by the thousands lost jobs, employers sliced wages to a small fraction of wartime levels, and farmers experienced foreclosures. In southern states, rapidly falling cotton and tobacco prices forced many planters to switch to grain production before they lost all hope of economic survival. The courts were jammed with lawsuits, families lost houses and farms, and young people despaired of setting up businesses of their own.

A wave of dislocation washed over every class, region, and occupation in America. Nearly half a million workers lost their jobs when city businesses failed. Homeless families roamed the streets of northern cities, and soup kitchens could not meet the growing demand for food. Moreover, the Panic of 1819 revitalized images of the famous credit and banking "bubbles" that had burst in previous centuries, including the specter of financial and institutional ruin brought on by unscrupulous individuals. Many supporters of Maryland's case against the Second Bank of the United States (see *McCulloch* v. *Maryland*, page 290) were motivated by such traditional considerations. But as the panic wore on, some Americans began to interpret economic trauma in different terms. Perhaps it was not deceitful individuals or poor judgment of risk, some observers mused, but structural problems with state and federal institutions, or political policies, that lay at the root of so much human misery. When the next panic occurred in 1837, Americans still had not abandoned their traditional view of banks and business failure, but they were increasingly prone to blame government officials—especially at the national level—for their hardships.

The Missouri Crisis

As economic panic gripped the country, the issue of slavery in the western states and territories riveted congressional attention. Since the Constitutional Convention and the Northwest Ordinance, political leaders had negotiated the expansion of slavery with great caution. With each new acquisition of land, with each surge of population into the West, the specter of slavery threatened to break the fragile terms of agreement among political and regional interests. With each territory's application for statehood, politicians cobbled together a fragile new consensus on the boundaries of slavery.

When Missouri applied for admission to the United States in 1819, Congress had not yet made provisions to allow or disallow slavery in the region west of the Mississippi River. Immediately, Missouri became the subject of sectional divisions between different parts of the country. Senator Rufus King of New York proposed that Missourians prohibit slavery while still a territory and enter the nation as a free state. Predictably, southerners wanted to transport their way of life and their system of labor into the new western lands. People in each section feared that a victory for

The Missouri Compromise   After years of bitter Congressional debate, Maine was admitted as a free state, while Missouri became a slave state, in 1820. Although north of 36°30′ would remain free territory, a number of policymakers anticipated opportunities to create slave territories as the nation expanded.

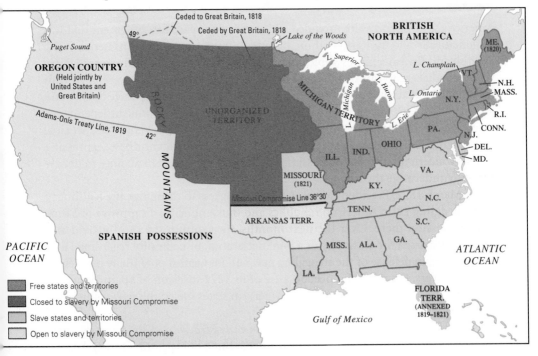

the other would shatter a delicate political and economic balance in the nation. If Missouri became a free state, argued southerners, the North would control Congress and its opposition to slavery would be imposed—by law and by force—on the southern way of life. Over recent years, insisted southern Old Republicans, an amalgamation of western and northeastern citizens had formed under the umbrella of "new-style" Republicans who wanted to channel resources for development and settlement to northern citizens. King's proposal intensified these fears, especially because northern public opinion favored it strongly.

During the months-long congressional debate about Missouri statehood, latent sectional arguments were laid bare. Many northern social reformers worried that unless the entire West was made free territory, "the future character of our nation" would deteriorate. Jefferson, from the more contemplative vantage of his home at Monticello, believed that the sectional divisions over slave and free territory were "like a fire-bell in the night, [that] awakened and filled me with terror." Fortunately for the southern slave owners' viewpoint, Maine had applied for statehood as this debate unfolded, which allowed Congress to work out what became known as the Missouri Compromise. Missouri would come into the nation as a slave state, Maine as a free state. Congress also extended Missouri's southern border of 36°30′ latitude to the Rocky Mountains (see map). For years to come, planters understood that they could spread slavery onto land south of the line, while they also negotiated strenuously to redraw that line farther to the north.

 ## The Monroe Doctrine

America's sprawling empire provided a gigantic open space for settlement that was diplomatically and militarily—though not culturally—free of the influence of the Spanish and British empires. Optimism about westward migration increased every year. But adjacent to this frontier, in Latin America, the early 1800s were filled with instability. Liberation movements grew strong enough first to challenge Spain's and Portugal's rule over their colonies and then, by 1822, bring about independence from Old World hegemony in four important nations: Chile, Venezuela, Mexico, and Brazil. American newspapers responded in anxious watchfulness, expressing serious concern that France or Russia—far stronger nations than Spain—might attempt to undermine the new republics.

In March 1822, President Monroe urged Congress to recognize the legitimacy of the fledgling Latin American republics and thus implicitly disapprove of European aggression there. Over the next months, foreign ministers to England and America discussed the feasibility of a joint declaration of neutrality regarding Latin America and in defense of the struggling new nations against potentially belligerent foreign powers. Fears that France, because of its 1822 invasion of Spain, would be the first nation to attack the new Latin American states fueled the sense of urgency among American policymakers.

At first Monroe believed that the joint declaration would be America's best course of action; Madison and Jefferson agreed. But a bolder John Quincy Adams, who was less interested in protecting young republics in Latin American than in holding back the power of European nations in the Western Hemisphere, convinced the president not to ally with Britain on this issue. Instead, Monroe agreed to use his annual message to Congress in December 1823 to warn Spain and all other European powers to abandon all designs on the Western Hemisphere, especially the regions in Mexico and Latin America declaring themselves independent republics. In his speech, written by Adams, Monroe declared that "the American continents, by the free and independent conditions that they have assumed and maintained, are henceforth not to be considered as subjects for future colonization by any European power." This Monroe Doctrine, as it came to be known, pledged the American government to keeping unwanted European presence out of the Western Hemisphere. But it did not commit the United States to noninterference in Latin American affairs. For the time being, America's expansionist concerns turned westward, across the North American continent, but Latin American leaders remained wary about the United States' ultimate intentions.

CONCLUSION

The Revolution of 1800 that brought Jefferson into the presidency proved to Americans that their nation could withstand bitter political factionalism and witness a peaceful transfer of federal power. It also ushered in the long rule of the Republicans. The Louisiana Purchase added so much new territory that the republican ideal of an expanding agricultural yeomanry seemed to be secure for generations to come. The "second war for independence," from 1812 to 1815, demonstrated decisively that the new republic was strong enough to resist Britain's attempt to turn them into colonists again.

Jeffersonian political policies often reinforced the emerging national identity. They significantly reduced the presence of government, while also invoking federal powers to expand the "empire of liberty" and safeguard the country from foreign and Indian nations. Jefferson could rejoice during his retirement at Monticello that he had helped to restore toleration for different opinions in political life; that direct taxes on American property had been repealed; that the national debt had been reduced and would no longer be used to create stronger national power; and that the franchise had become more inclusive.

But the party that rose to national office on a platform of local control and international peace in fact tolerated Hamiltonian institutions to a significant degree and occasionally wielded federal power over citizens in Hamiltonian fashion. Moreover, sectionalism and regional contentions grew, rather than shrank, during the so-called Era of Good Feelings that followed the War of 1812. The Panic of 1819 shattered two decades of commercial growth, the Missouri Compromise brought to the forefront political disagreements rooted in deep moral differences among citizens, and the frontier continued to be a dangerous place filled with hostile Europeans, runaway slaves, and recalcitrant Indians. By 1824, Americans were poised to undertake a new experiment in rapid and transformative growth, while at the same time entering a new era of political strife.

SUGGESTED READINGS

The best studies of Jefferson's first years in the presidency include Lance Banning, *The Jeffersonian Persuasion: Evolution of a Party Ideology* (1978); Noble E. Cunningham, *The Jeffersonian Republicans and Power: Party Operations, 1801–1809* (1963); and Drew McCoy, *The Elusive Republic* (1980) and *The Last of the Fathers: James Madison and the Republican Legacy* (1989). A recent collection, Peter Onuf, ed., *Jeffersonian Legacies* (1993), offers fresh interpretations of the political and cultural Jefferson. For Jefferson's relationship to popular politics see Merrill Peterson, *Thomas Jefferson and the New Nation: A Biography* (1970); and for his relationship to Federalists, see Stanley Elkins and Eric McKitrick, *The Age of Federalism: The Early American Republic, 1788–1800* (1993). The political life in the national capital is effectively captured in James S. Young, *The Washington Community: 1800–1828* (1966). For the role of the courts in this era, especially the Supreme Court, see G. Edward White, *The Marshall Court and Cultural Change, 1815–1835* (1991).

Westward expansion in the early 1800s is best covered in Stephen Aron, *How the West Was Lost: Kentucky from Daniel Boone to Henry Clay* (1966). For aspects of settlement and conflict on the Old Northwest frontier, see Andrew Cayton, *The Frontier Republic: Ideology and Politics in the Ohio Country, 1780–1825* (1986); Robert Mitchell, ed., *Appalachian Frontier: Settlement, Society, and Development in the Preindustrial Era* (1991); and Thomas Slaughter, *The Whiskey Rebellion: Frontier Epilogue to the American Revolution* (1986).

Stephen Ambrose's *Undaunted Courage, Meriwether Lewis, Thomas Jefferson, and the Opening of the American West* (1996) is a spellbinding account of the Lewis and Clark expedition. For Native American relations with settlers going west, the best accounts are in Richard White, *The Middle Ground: Indians, Empires, and Republics in the Great Lakes Region, 1650–1815* (1991); Colin G. Calloway, *Crown and Calumet: British-Indian Relations, 1783–1815* (1987); and R. David Edmunds, *Tecumseh and the Quest for Indian Leadership* (1984), and *The Shawnee Prophet* (1983).

The best studies of the diplomacy and political policies related to commerce are Doron Ben-Atar, *The Origins of Jeffersonian Commercial Policy and Diplomacy* (1993); Roger H. Brown, *The Republic in Peril* (1964); Lawrence Kaplan, *"Entangling Alliances with None": American Foreign Policy in the Age of Jefferson* (1987); Bradford Perkins, *Prologue to War: England and the United States, 1805–1812* (1961); and Peter Onuf and Nicholas Onuf, *Federal Union, Modern World: The Law of Nations in an Age of Revolution, 1776–1814* (1993).

Two of the most informative studies of the War of 1812 remain Harry L. Coles, *The War of 1812* (1965), and Reginald Horsman, *The Causes of the War of 1812* (1962). A more recent work explains the political culture of public opinion and internal regional developments related to the war: Steven Watts, *The Republic Reborn: War and the Making of Liberal America, 1790–1820* (1987). The best biographies of Madison during these testy years are by Robert Rutland: *James Madison, The Founding Father* (1987) and *The Presidency of James Madison* (1990). For the Canadian perspective, see Pierre Berton, *The Invasion of Canada* (1980).

The political crisis of postwar America is treated admirably in Harry Ammon, Jr., *James Monroe: The Quest for National Identity* (1971), and James Banner, *To the Hartford Convention: The Federalists and the Origins of Party Politics in the Early Republic, 1789–1815* (1967). Recently, historians have returned to the topic of emerging American national identity. See first the older work by George Dangerfield, *The Awakening of American Nationalism, 1815–1828* (1965). Then look at the more cultural approach of David Waldstreicher, *In the Midst of Perpetual Fetes: The Making of American Nationalism* (1997).

The Missouri Crisis is explained in rich detail in Glover Moore, *The Missouri Compromise, 1819–1821* (1953). And for the Monroe Doctrine, the best treatments are Ernest R. May, *The Making of the Monroe Doctrine* (1975), and Dexter Perkins, *The Monroe Doctrine, 1823–1826* (1927).

McCulloch v. *Maryland* (1819) and the National Bank

The Second Bank of the United States, chartered by Congress in 1816, evoked both intense public criticism and hearty applause. Among the Bank's supporters was Chief Justice John Marshall, whose Supreme Court heard a momentous case in 1819 that challenged its constitutionality. The Court unanimously rejected the challenge, and Marshall's opinion would stand as a landmark statement affirming the authority of the government to create powerful national institutions.

We [justices of the Supreme Court] admit, as all must admit, that the powers of the government are limited, and that its limits are not to be transcended. But we think the sound construction of the constitution must allow to the national legislature that discretion, with respect to the means by which the powers it confers are to be carried into execution, which will enable that body to perform the high duties assigned to it, in the manner most beneficial to the people. Let the end be legitimate, let it be within the scope of the constitution, and all means which are appropriate, . . . are constitutional.

That the power of taxation is one of vital importance; that it is retained by the states; that it is not abridged by the grant of a similar power to the government of the Union; that it is to be concurrently exercised by the two governments—are truths which have never been denied. . . . The states are expressly forbidden to lay any duties on imports or exports, except what may be absolutely necessary for executing their inspection laws. . . . The same paramount character would seem to restrain . . . a state from such other exercise of this power as is in its nature incompatible with, and repugnant to, the constitutional laws of the Union. A law absolutely repugnant to another, as entirely repeals that other as if express terms of repeal were used.

On this ground the counsel for the Bank place its claim to be exempted from the peer of a state to tax its operations. There is no express provision for the case, but the claim has been sustained on a principle which so entirely pervades the Constitution, is so intermixed with the materials which compose it, so interwoven with its web, so blended with its texture, as to be incapable of being separated from it without rending it into shreds.

This great principle is that the Constitution, and laws made in pursuance thereof, are supreme; that they control the constitutions and laws of the respective states, and cannot be controlled by them. From this, . . . other propositions are deduced as corollaries. . . . These are: 1. That a power to create implies a power to preserve. 2. That a power to destroy, if wielded by a different hand, is hostile to, and incompatible with, these powers to create and preserve. 3. That where this repugnancy exists, that authority which is supreme must control, not yield to that over which it is supreme. . . .

That the power to tax involves the power to destroy; that the power to destroy may defeat and render useless the power to create; that there is a plain repugnance in conferring on one government a power to control the constitutional measures of another . . . are propositions not to be denied.

If we apply the principle for which the state of Maryland contends, to the Constitution generally, we shall find it capable of changing totally the character of that instrument. We shall find it capable of arresting all the measures of the government, and of prostrating it at the foot of the states. The American people have declared their Constitution, and the laws made in pursuance thereof, to be supreme; and this principle would transfer the supremacy, in fact, to the states.

If the states may tax one instrument employed by the government in the execution of its powers, they may tax any and every other instrument . . . the mail . . . the mint . . . patent rights . . . papers of the custom-house . . . judicial process . . . to an excess which would defeat all the ends of government. This was not intended by the American people. They did not design to make their government dependent on the states. . . .

The question is, in truth, a question of supremacy. And if the right of the states to tax the means employed by the general government be conceded, the declaration that the Constitution, and the laws made in pursuance thereof, shall be the supreme law of the land, is empty and unmeaning declamation.

Niles's Weekly Register Denounces the Decision

The Court may have been unanimous in its judgment, but the people were not. Hezekiah Niles, the Baltimore editor of America's most influential weekly newspaper, wrote a scathing refutation of the Supreme Court decision. Not only had Congress exceeded its authority in 1791 when it established a federal bank, but it now tampered with the powers inherent in each state government. Following is an excerpt from *Niles's Weekly Register* in 1819.

. . . A deadly blow has been struck at the sovereignty of the states, and from a quarter so far removed from the people as to be hardly accessible to public opinion. . . . We are yet unacquainted with the grounds of this alarming decision, but of this are resolved—that nothing but the tongue of an angel can convince us of its compatibility with the Constitution of the United States, in which a power to grant acts of incorporation is not delegated [to the federal government], and all powers not delegated are retained.

Far be it from us to be thought as speaking disrespectfully of the Supreme Court, or to subject ourselves to the suspicion of a "contempt" of it. We do not impute corruption to the judges, or intimate that they have been influenced by improper feelings. They are great and learned men; but still, only men. And, feeling as we do—as if the very stones would cry out if we did not speak on this subject—we will exercise our right to do it, and declare that, if the Supreme Court is not mistaken in its construction of the Constitution . . . their sovereignty is at the mercy of their creature—Congress. It is not on account of the Bank of the United States that we speak thus . . . it is but a drop in the bucket compared with the principles established by the decision, which appear to us to be these:

1. That Congress has an unlimited right to grant acts of incorporation!

2. That a company incorporated by Congress is exempted from the common operation of the laws of the state in which it may be located!

... Our sentiments are on record that we did not wish the destruction of that institution but, fearing the enormous power of the corporation, we were zealous that an authority to arrest its deleterious influence might be vested in responsible hands, for it has not got any soul. Yet this solitary institution may *not* subvert the liberties of our country, and command every one to bow down to it as Baal. It is the principle of it that alarms us, as operating against the unresigned rights of the states.   ▌

In 1791 Jefferson and Hamilton sharply disagreed about the constitutionality of the First Bank of the United States. Three decades later, Democratic-Republicans and Federalists were still debating whether the federal government had the power to establish such a strong central institution. Jeffersonians had struggled to diminish federal powers, especially in cases in which Bank directors had used the institution's funds to speculate in real estate and public improvements projects. Thus, the views expressed by opponents such as Niles remained strong and would challenge the Bank—as well as other institutions and developments associated with Federalists— repeatedly during the coming years. In Maryland, state legislators responded to the public outcry against such abuse of public banking powers by putting a high tax on that state's branch of the Bank and causing it to fold operations.

Federalists argued that the Bank, and many other institutions and improvements supported by the national government, were responsible for securing the republic's very existence. Chief Justice John Marshall, who steadfastly maintained his Federalist posture even when the party faded from prominence, also declared in *McCulloch* v. *Maryland* that the Second Bank of the United States was perfectly constitutional and stood above the Maryland tax law. He was therefore protecting the interests that favored a strong national bank and its functions in helping to promote the national economy. Further, Marshall's decisions in a series of cases challenging federal powers firmly held that the government had a constitutional right to establish national institutions "necessary and proper" for the running of the country and that no state had the authority to destroy them by taxation.

Questions for Analysis

1. What are the central points of Marshall's argument? What does the chief justice mean when he writes that "the power to tax is the power to destroy"?

2. Is Niles more concerned about the power of the Bank of the United States over Maryland citizens or about federal encroachments on the rights of the states?

3. What language in Niles's article would appeal to Jeffersonians in any section of the country?

4. Which parts of each argument speak to the particular issues raised by this case in 1819, and which speak to much larger issues concerning federal and state powers that arose frequently in early American history?

5. What would you say are some of the benefits of banks—whether state or national institutions—during this period of time, and what are some of their drawbacks?

9

An Emerging Capitalist Nation, 1790–1820

*I*n September 1811, Nicholas Roosevelt boarded his steamboat *New Orleans* at the Pittsburgh docks and waived enthusiastically to friends and family who stood gawking on shore. Months before this, they had "united in endeavoring to dissuade" Roosevelt "from what they regarded as utter folly, if not absolute madness." It seemed to them that Roosevelt had joined the endless parade of visionaries, tinkerers, and deluded developers who kept trying to "tame" nature and "civilize" newly settled regions. In these early years of the new republic, many of these efforts failed. But a few of them succeeded spectacularly, and these in turn spurred new efforts to transform the landscape with human entrepreneurship.

Despite the misgivings of skeptics, Nicholas Roosevelt stuck by his plan to navigate the Ohio River by steamboat, thereby joining the many other Americans making internal improvements that reshaped the early republic. His hired craftsmen labored diligently under Roosevelt's watchful eye at the shipyard, until the morning when he turned to the crowds, shrugged off public doubts and private fears, climbed onto the *New Orleans,* and began a daring voyage past many budding Ohio River towns. Two days later, as the "grand lady" chugged downriver at eight miles per hour, curious onlookers flocked to Cincinnati's docks to deliver their own advice. One local merchant shouted, "Your boat may go *down* the river; but, as to coming *up* it, the very idea is an absurd one." Crowds at Louisville repeated the refrain of doubt, but the determined Roosevelt ordered his crew to take the *New Orleans* upstream a bit, which he hoped would convince townspeople how his investment could "make good headway *up* the river."

But having begun to replace scorn and cynicism with "universal incredulity" about the magnificent steamboat, Roosevelt then encountered "days of horror." Four days into the trip, the vessel met low water at the falls of the Ohio River. Once the water rose sufficiently, Roosevelt ordered full speed to descend through the falls. "The safety valve shrieked; the wheels revolved faster than they had ever done before, and the vessel . . . fairly flew away from the crowds on shore." Shortly thereafter, the captain recorded fire on board, then an earthquake that shook "the length of the Mississippi," and then numerous uncharted patches of sandbars that confounded the steamboat's pilot. Sparks from the steam engine's chimney lit clothes on fire, and smoke backed up into sleeping chambers more than once on the fourteen-day trip. No wonder the Chickasaw Indians who followed briefly in their small craft called the *New Orleans* a "fire canoe." But the steamboat survived the mishaps and finally reached New Orleans, achieving acclaim for a "voyage which changed the relations of the West—which may almost be said to have changed its destiny."

After the War of 1812, steamboats did not immediately replace the familiar keelboats and flatboats coursing down major rivers, but their powerful engines and greater carrying capacity became more and more familiar on the country's inland waterways. By 1820, at least a dozen steamboats made daily trips between New York City and Albany. Other "transportation wonders"—graded roads, canals, and eventually railroads—were also part of an incredibly rapid transformation of the American landscape.

New experiments shaped not only the landscape during the early 1800s, but urban and frontier life also underwent far-reaching change, and the cultural arenas of work, religion, and family were likewise deeply altered. Some observers marveled that Americans had become "a breathless people." But few Americans understood the consequences of the sweeping changes they experienced. Historians today still debate the nature and meanings of change in the early republic.

▌ How did new machines and technologies change commerce in the early republic? Who sought change, and who benefited from it?

▌ How did the far-reaching material innovations knit frontiers and settled areas together into one nation? How did they enhance differences from region to region?

▌ How did Americans react to economic and social change in the early republic? How did their reactions affect the cultural institutions of family and religion?

This chapter will address these questions.

Improvement and Invention

In some important respects, American life in 1790 continued much as it had in prerevolutionary years. Local attachments to family and neighbors, nearby markets, poor transportation and communication, hand tools and customary methods of

Chronology

1790	Slater opens first mill
	Federal patent law validates Evans's milling equipment
1793	Whitney invents cotton gin
1801	Cane Ridge, Kentucky, revival
1807	Livingston and Fulton send *Clermont* up the Hudson River
1807–1808	Jeffersonian embargo of American commerce
1810	First steamboats ply the Ohio River
1816	First protective tariff
1817	Erie Canal begun
1818	National Road finished to Wheeling, Ohio
1824	*Gibbons* v. *Ogden* puts interstate travel under federal authority
	Hall introduces the American System of Manufactures

farming, small farms with depleted soil in older regions and uncleared fields on the frontier, all were familiar to Americans. In the next thirty years, however, the pace of economic and cultural change accelerated. Farmers, entrepreneurs, and shippers swamped their state legislatures with requests for special laws to promote particular projects. New terms such as *development, expansion, improvement, refinement,* and *invention* began to be heard, and older concerns about protection, persistence, deference, and neighborliness faded. Many Americans tried actively to harness nature, inventing the belching, lurching contraptions that increasingly occupied the landscape after 1800. Edward Everett, a leading political orator, distinguished editor, and Harvard graduate, exulted that Americans had "the means of private comfort by the inventions, discoveries, and improvements" they made. They stood poised to transform their culture and take "first place in the world." Aided by "wise laws" and political security, experiments in internal improvement of the countryside and in manufacturing would flourish.

It followed that federal and state governments had a duty to grant funds and special privileges to build the infrastructure that connected peoples across great distances. That duty, wrote many Americans, rose to special importance in the early republic because people's demands for new roads, canals, and time-saving machines outstripped their ability to pay for them privately. The need for governments to fund improvements generously also derived from what many people believed to be the American experiment's mission to expand across the continent.

Roads and Turnpikes

In the 1790s, people who lived along the major eastern rivers benefited from their natural accessibility, easily exchanging imported goods or coastal manufactures for frontier timber and furs. But migrants into the Genesee and Mohawk frontiers of western New York, or into certain mountainous areas of Pennsylvania, lacked access to continuous riverways that led to the east, and their overland travel remained arduous. Even along the coastline, a coach ride from New York City to Philadelphia in 1800 took two days, and a journey to Boston four days. When George Washington died in Virginia in 1799, Kentucky inhabitants first heard the news nearly a month later. By 1820, travel by land was faster, but it still took a week to get from New York to Pittsburgh.

Frontier settlers found that the hardships of clearing land and starting farms in their new environment became even more difficult because of their isolation from goods, news, and kin. But if local barter and neighborhood self-sufficiency marked settlers' meager existence at first, they gradually overcame these conditions by looking to government. Their demands for the national government to provide roads, canals, military protection, and political representation equivalent to what easterners enjoyed were loud and long.

State and national political leaders were not deaf to these demands. While Jefferson attended to his controversial embargoes in 1807 (see page 308), his secretary of the treasury, Albert Gallatin, implored Congress to extend earlier efforts at "opening roads and making canals" throughout America. Since the 1780s local and state governments had occasionally poured resources into roads and canals they believed would make the citizenry "one and indivisible." But pressing political reasons persuaded Congress to fund even more of these projects, over longer distances. For one thing, the new states of Kentucky, Ohio, and Tennessee had enlarged the republic to daunting proportions, but they were still not a connected and secure part of the nation. Spanish, French, and British traders and wilderness settlers spread word to their governments that Americans in these new landlocked states might be willing to form new national allegiances with foreign powers. Frontier settlers often complained of their distance from the advantages of coastal cities and international commerce. When groups of them started speaking about forming republics under a British or Spanish flag, the American Congress and public opinion readily agreed about the urgency of Gallatin's message.

But unifying the country's parts was a formidable task. Traveling more than a hundred miles was likely to involve a combination of horses, wagons, flatboats, small sailing vessels, barges, or canoes. In 1800 most American roads were suitable for little more than foot traffic, and those that were designed for wagons easily turned to muddy swamps or became overgrown with brush. Even on the country's best roads, a traveler needed ten 16-hour days to get from Boston to Washington, much of it by walking.

Roads to the west of the Appalachian Mountains were so treacherous that in the autumn, after crops had been harvested, communities banded together to organize trains of pack animals to carry produce to Baltimore or Pittsburgh or Cincinnati. These trains afforded westerners a small amount of mutual protection and support

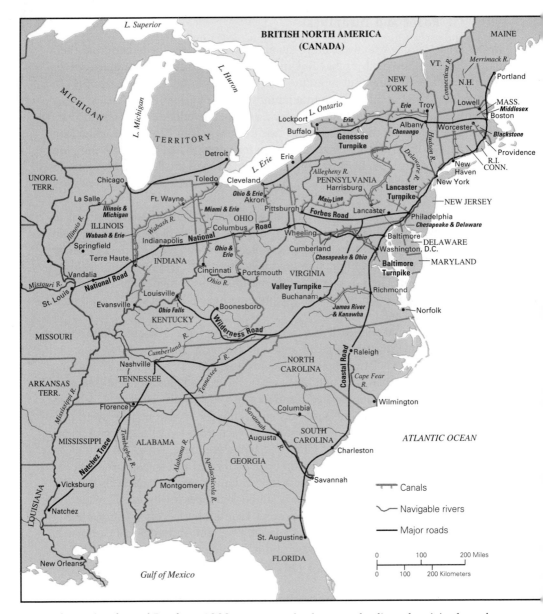

Rivers, Canals, and Roads to 1820 Migrants, developers, and policymakers joined together to create a dense transportation network in the early republic. These links were both the result of, and further spur to the rapid development of the nation's interior.

on a journey that was dangerous and lonely. Paths leading through valleys, over precipices, and into thick underbrush carried goods slowly, each animal carrying maybe two hundred pounds of goods. Needless to say, this method of transport made sense for farmers only if their crops brought prices high enough to cover the cost of transportation and provide a small profit. Although men and boys could drive hogs from Kentucky to Baltimore "on the hoof" and thus avoid most transportation costs, wheat was too heavy and too perishable to be shipped east profitably during the early 1800s, so many farmers converted it into distilled spirits (see the Whiskey Rebellion, Chapter 7). Farmers in Lancaster, Pennsylvania, were outraged that it cost as much to cart goods overland to Philadelphia as it did to ship them from Philadelphia to London.

Transporting goods by river and stream tended to lower costs and reduce time getting to markets, but water travel had perils of its own. Beavers clogged small waterways with their dams, flooding or freezing hindered traffic at certain times of the year, and mills often diverted the flow of water on once-navigable rivers. If a farmer got his wheat, ginseng, and maple syrup overland from, for example, western New York to Albany, he might have to wait months for the Hudson River to thaw and float his goods to New York City—if they did not rot or spoil in the meantime. Meanwhile, he paid fees for storage.

At the center of Gallatin's proposed system of internal transportation was a "great turnpike road, from Maine to Georgia, along the whole extent of the Atlantic sea coast," and "four first rate turnpike roads" to join the four main rivers flowing from the Appalachians into the Atlantic Ocean (see map at left). Already by 1807, some of the northern states had actively promoted new turnpikes by granting to private companies liberal charters that stipulated extensive land grants, rights to sell stock to the public, and provisions for taking tolls. One successful chartered company project, the Lancaster Turnpike, was "a masterpiece of its kind . . . paved with stone the whole way, and overlaid with gravel."

The War of 1812 prompted even more heightened interest in road construction when British blockades cut off most coastal shipping and forced coastal populations to rely more on inland producers for necessary goods. After the war, the momentum of public interest rose as more and more interests pressed for construction of roads to link east and west in "a system of internal improvements." Legislators in Pennsylvania and Massachusetts granted scores of special charters to private turnpike companies, while private investors sponsored numerous roads connecting settlers of the Ohio Valley to Detroit, St. Louis, and New Orleans.

The height of these efforts came when the federal government committed funds to build the National Road. In 1815 construction of a turnpike that was intended to lead from Cumberland in western Maryland, through southwestern Pennsylvania, to Wheeling, on the Ohio, was initiated. By 1818, this leg of the National Road was completed; by 1833, additional government allocations extended the road to Columbus, Ohio; and by 1850, the turnpike reached nearly to the Mississippi River at Vandalia, Illinois. Gradually, roads linked America's borderlands to the heartlands of the Northwest Territory and from there, to the oldest parts of the country. One New Yorker saw the trend as more than lines on a map: "The roads that connect trading interests and laws across the great spaces between us, have a tendency to mingle various manners, dress, and habits of people otherwise separated."

Steamboats and Canals

Comparing his early life before the American Revolution to his old age in the early 1800s, one New Jerseyan reflected that goods and people "flowed through our riverways as blood flows through arteries, the same in my declining years as in my youth." Americans had added the Ohio and Mississippi Rivers to their important "arteries," but they transported goods much the same way. Once inland transports reached points such as Pittsburgh or Wheeling, arduous overland trails gave way to relatively faster river travel by flatboats that could carry tons of bagged grain or a few head of livestock, downstream to Cincinnati, the mouth of the Wabash River, or even far down the Mississippi. Long into the 1800s, flatboats moved bulky goods more cheaply, more quickly—and often more safely—than Conestoga wagons could on the National Road.

But ambitious commercial farmers teamed up with entrepreneur-inventors to create even faster ways to get crops and people from one place to another, and to break down the distinctions that marked the different regions. "We wish," wrote a retailer in eastern Tennessee, "not to continue in the present rude condition in which you see us but to advance in our trades, and hence in our civilizing tendencies." The major problem they identified was getting their flatboats and canoes to go as easily upstream, against the current, as they could go down.

The answer was the steamboat. Harnessing steam power to drive watercraft was one of the early republic's great achievements, and the initiative to do so came from the same pragmatic considerations as the road and canal boom of the era. The first efforts to launch steam-powered boats came in the 1780s on the Delaware River between Trenton and Philadelphia, but technical difficulties led to failure. Then Robert Fulton, a long-time advocate of "energetically fund[ing] the unifying ties of internal commerce," teamed up with New Yorker Robert R. Livingston, who had acquired a twenty-year monopoly on all steam transportation along the Hudson River. In 1807 they sent the *Clermont* up the Hudson River to Albany. By then, Fulton and Nicholas Roosevelt had introduced innovations to improve steam adaptation to the centuries-old method of harnessing water power with wooden paddlewheels. Though builders continued to use white pine for the bodies of steamboats, as they had for almost two hundred years of shipbuilding, a sheet of metal covering the hull helped protect the "belching whales" from being torn apart from below or catching fire from stray sparks. Although many steamboats did catch fire, snag on tree trunks and sink, or explode, the benefits of faster travel soon outweighed initial fears of Fulton's "sea monster." It was the team of Fulton, Livingston, and Roosevelt that made the risky 1811 *New Orleans* project possible. By the end of the War of 1812, steamboats began making the unprecedented journey from New Orleans to the Ohio River and its tributaries. Soon after, steamboats regularly puffed up the Missouri River.

Enthusiastic witnesses felt certain that steamboats were an essential ingredient in realizing Jefferson's western "empire for liberty." "Our new steamboats," remarked an eastern traveler to Cincinnati, "take with all due speed the spirits [whiskey], candles, [corn]meal, barreled meats, and sundry barrels of country production, to the remotest points which few fellows can imagine in their life times; and they return with the refinements of a life their fathers left behind [in the east] long ago."

Steamboats introduced their share of trauma, including long mechanical delays at unfriendly trading posts, fires, choking engines, and bursting boilers in the "smoke-belching machines." Then, too, when steamboat enterprises proliferated, private in-

Fulton's Sketch of His Steamboat, 1809 Harnessing steam engines to furnace-heated boilers, and attaching both to wooden boats, transformed river travel and laid the basis for steam technology on the railroads decades later. Transport became faster and cheaper when steamboats could go against river currents and link people and markets more directly than in the past. Robert Fulton sent his first steamboat up the Hudson in 1807 and made this sketch to accompany his 1809 patent application. The idyllic setting he created fails to represent the horrifying fires and boiler explosions that occurred on a regular basis throughout the steamboat era. (*American Society of Mechanical Engineers.*)

vestors competed for rights to waterways and customers. In the absence of state and federal government regulations, it was only a matter of time before competitors wound up in court. In 1824 the Supreme Court, still under John Marshall's leadership, ruled in *Gibbons* v. *Ogden* that travel on the Hudson River passed through two or more states and was thus a form of interstate traffic under federal control. Any state monopoly issued in New York, the Court decided, unfairly hindered development and competition of new enterprises in other states. The ruling cleared the way for new enterprises to create even better transport of goods and passengers in years to come.

During these same years private interests and local governments initiated efforts to cut short watercourses through land to join busy river systems. Modest projects were begun in the 1780s and 1790s in eastern portions of Virginia, Massachusetts, and South Carolina. Soon these efforts developed into a canal-building craze. By the 1790s, every major coastal city had plans to cut canals into the interior. Some established lotteries to fund the projects with public money, while others allocated municipal and state funds to underwrite construction. Philadelphia immigrants and urban semiskilled laborers signed up by the thousands to dig the ditches connecting area waterways.

Then, in the early 1800s, wealthy investors teamed up with a few skilled mechanics to initiate greater engineering projects. Canals, they agreed, could follow natural highways of water that required only a little alteration to float heavier traffic. Barges could pass easily into the interior with only four feet of water, and mules trudging along towpaths could pull great loads. Sleighs, reasoned many early writers, could glide along the same waterways when canals froze over. At that time, engineers knew little of how to dig and line deep trenches, or how to make dam locks that would not burst under the force of sudden rushes of water. But they learned important skills from millwrights, surveyors, and shipbuilders.

Although engineering troubles or insufficient funds doomed many state canal projects to failure, Pennsylvania, Maryland, and New Jersey promoted some very successful systems that linked their agricultural hinterlands with coastal cities. One of these was the Schuylkill Canal, which linked Pennsylvanians for 108 miles when it was completed in 1826. By then, however, another state canal attracted far more attention because, upon completion, it profoundly transformed the lives of thousands of farmers and eastern peoples throughout the mid-Atlantic and New England regions.

This was the Erie Canal, an "artificial river" that was cut through portions of New York's Mohawk Valley wilderness, where no single river linked west to east, and where trappers and traders trekked by canoe and foot. Since the revolutionary era, public promoters felt certain that the region could become an abundant breadbasket if only transportation were improved. Hence the plan for the Erie Canal to slice across the region for 363 miles from the Hudson River to Lake Erie, thereby opening a continuous water route from New York City to Chicago.

In early 1817, Governor De Witt Clinton urged the state legislature to issue bonds to the public—in effect, to get loans from New Yorkers which the state would repay—to construct the canal. Over the coming years a work force of nearly four thousand unskilled laborers, many of them recent Irish immigrants, pulled stumps, cut stone, blasted cliffs, hauled rubble, mixed cement, tended the dozens of horses used to supplement human muscle power, and built over 300 bridges and 83 locks. Lack of prior experience in such work made the project a major outdoor school of engineering.

Early on, skeptics insisted on calling the project "Clinton's Folly" because of its unheard-of scale and exorbitant costs. But by the time it was completed in late 1825, the Erie Canal was a colossal success. Toll money poured in as the locks and towpaths teemed with drivers shouting at mules and oxen pulling freight-laden barges at about four miles per hour. Within five years, Erie Canal barges hauled over fifty thousand people a year to western territories. Syracuse, Rochester, Buffalo, and Erie became boomtowns that attracted migrants from cities and abroad to western lands and transported imported textiles, New England shoes, eastern cabinets and chairs, and numerous other items from seaboard cities into the frontiers. Foodstuffs, hogs, whiskey, hemp, and other farm goods meanwhile made their way east to eager urban consumers. Many New York City merchants pivoted their attention from financial markets in Amsterdam and dry goods purchases from London to the exploding demand from Buffalo and points west.

Between 1816 and 1840, other states cut nearly 3,400 miles of "ditches" linking towns of the interior to one another, and to vital people and supplies of the coastal cities. Canals extended like deep veins from Toledo to Cincinnati, Richmond to Lynchburg, or Philadelphia to Pittsburgh. They brought daily necessities to migrating people, took rich lodes of coal out of the Allegheny Mountains, and delivered farm products from the interior of the Old Northwest to river towns along the Ohio and Mississippi Rivers. Small trading posts such as Cleveland and Dayton in Ohio and Harrisburg in Pennsylvania became significant manufacturing and residential cities. By 1828, Cincinnati boomed with commerce that flowed from eastern cities along the Erie Canal, through the Great Lakes, down from Toledo, and out of Cincinnati along the Ohio to the Mississippi River and points south. Cincinnati had become not only a significant trading center, but also the Old Northwest's largest producer of steamboats.

Canals had a profound effect on the livelihoods and households of untold thousands of Americans by the 1820s. For one thing, the cost and time of transporting goods fell dramatically. Freight handlers and wholesale agents reported that a ton of grain could be shipped and hauled from Buffalo to New York City for about $100 in 1820; just five years later, this transaction cost only $9. By 1830, it cost fifty to seventy

Construction of the Erie Canal   Thousands of workers and engineers, and hundreds of horse-powered cranes, labored to haul away rock and dirt, build stone locks, and reinforce the banks of the Erie Canal. Many of the workers were recent Irish immigrants who spent weeks at this hazardous work digging "Clinton's Ditch" and then stayed as farmers and townspeople on the frontiers transformed by the canal.   *(Miriam and Ira D. Wallach Division of Art, Prints and Photographs, The New York Public Library. Astor, Lenox and Tilden Foundations.)*

times more to haul by wagon than it did to pay canal rates. When the costs of transport fell, so did prices that consumers paid for wheat and bread, salt and coal.

Canal towns continued to draw young men from sleepy eastern mill towns and rural villages, as well as from immigrant ships, into the countryside. Most hoped to find jobs and eventually set up farms near the conveniences and culture of growing river towns. By the 1820s, it had become clear that this migration would not merely transport the traditional ways of eastern families into the wilderness. New social and work relations developed as distances between producers and consumers grew. For example, international commerce had already spurred many mid-Atlantic and eastern rural families to give up local exchange of household products such as textiles, flour, barrels, or candles. Instead, they made clothing and bedding from "store-bought" fabric and bought more of their tools, while certain family members worked for cash incomes. One hundred miles and more into the interior, wives and daughters also made less of the cloth for family linens and clothing, and purchased more textiles from a local retailer. At the same time, many young women on the frontier continued to spin yarn at home on an "outwork" basis, which they sold for a little cash to agents of eastern manufacturers and merchants.

Mills and Manufactures

In 1791, when Hamilton proposed his Report on Manufactures (see page 269), Americans did not yet work in factories where many workers congregated under one roof, reported to work by shrill whistles, and stood before clanging machines all day. Fewer than one in ten adult white men "manufactured" items, and traditional hand tools were the norm. The workplace was often a home or a small shop, where diverse activities were performed by two or three craftsmen. At the same time, farmers did carpentry on the side, barrel makers shaved shingles when work was slow, millers ran small retail shops on the side, and most adults exchanged labor time with neighbors. Women from farms near major towns produced and sold large quantities of butter and cheese to eager consumers. Peddlers who rode about the countryside hawked the handcrafted goods of farmers, blacksmiths, and artisans. Bustling production often took place not in major cities, but in rural saw and gristmills, cider works, village smith shops, glassworks, and paper mills dotting the countryside.

The pace of handicraft work in the early republic had not changed noticeably since prerevolutionary decades. It was slow and irregular when demand was off, slow and regular when neighbors needed items. Artisans and skilled farmboys made yokes, shoes, baskets, and all manner of agricultural implements by hand. The rhythms of work fluctuated according to supplies of raw materials, as well as family and community demands on time.

But despite the defeat of Hamilton's bold plan for manufacturing and the persistence of traditional production, change was in the air by the end of the 1790s. Would-be manufacturers applauded the scurry of people to new western lands and the unprecedented energy people unleashed everywhere to "improve" their household income and comfort. They did not immediately introduce huge machines or build large factories, but instead entrepreneurs adapted new kinds of ownership and work to the existing forms of shop and home manufacturing. Some rising cabinetmakers, barrel makers, sail makers, silversmiths, and other skilled craftsmen who weathered the crises of the 1780s and 1790s (see Chapter 7) opened up their own shops, hired apprentices or wage laborers, and joined the civic enthusiasm to invest some of their profits in canals, real estate, or shipping services.

As western land prices and transportation costs fell, and as foreign demand for eastern ships and western agricultural goods rose in the early 1800s, many Americans experimented with more efficient ways of performing work and with perfecting or inventing labor-saving tools. For example, during the 1790s, a few tinkerers, working independently, began to improve the woodsman's axe, the farmer's iron plow, and the homemaker's kettle. Despite the federal Patent Law of 1790, few inventions brought profits or exclusive recognition to their developers, for local blacksmiths and clever farmers ignored the law and adapted innovations to their personal needs. Such was the "inventive spirit" that gripped Americans.

While some new products—cast-iron plows, for example—were too expensive for many individual farm families to purchase, other innovations were adopted by just a few individuals and had far-reaching consequences. Those of Oliver Evans must be included in the latter category. Between the fall of Yorktown in 1781 and the Constitution, Evans had progressed from an "improving farmer" and storekeeper in northern Delaware to the architect of a great flour mill that incorporated new mechanical devices to move, grind, cool, sort, and bag flour with top-notch efficiency. Ships pulled up next to Evans's redesigned mill without unloading, hauling overland, and then lifting grain to the grinding stones. A few workers unloaded grain directly onto conveyor belts, and Evans's mechanization made it possible to operate mills almost entirely "without the aid of manual labor," which in turn cut millers' costs tremendously. Evans substituted leather buckets and pulleys, conveyor belts, and revolving rakes for the men and boys whom millers normally hired.

Despite receiving only the third registered patent under the 1790 law, which gave him the sole right to make and market his milling inventions, Evans faced skeptical millers and contended with blacksmiths and wheelwrights who copied his inventions and undermined his potential profits. Nevertheless, Evans's buckets and pulleys transformed milling, one of the key industries in the early republic. Old mills in the mid-Atlantic region were converted and enlarged to accommodate Evans's machinery, and new mills were almost always built according to his plans. Between 1800 and his death in 1819, Evans also put steam engines into his mills, introduced steam-powered shovels for dredging canals near Philadelphia, and introduced large steam flour mills to far western towns such as Lexington and Pittsburgh. By 1840, nearly twenty thousand new mills incorporated some or all of Evans's ingenious ideas; between 1810 and 1860, the value of flour produced in such mills rose nearly 200 percent. And just as Evans had wished, flour became America's number one industry, while the number of artisans and laborers employed in milling declined dramatically.

A second innovation preceded, and paved the way for, America's factories: precision-made interchangeable parts. For centuries, craftsmen made their parts and assembled and repaired items in a single shop, creating each commodity from start to

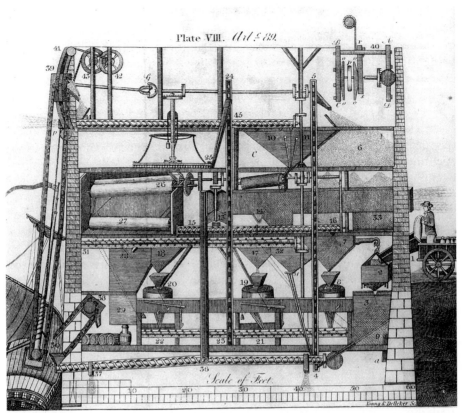

Oliver Evans's Mill Until Oliver Evans introduced a series of innovations in flour milling during the 1780s, the typical mill was far smaller than the one shown here and employed a number of local artisans. This etching from "The Young Mill-wright and Miller's Guide" (1795) emphasizes the greater scale of production and the absence of all but one worker at the more technologically efficient mills adopting Evans's equipment in the mid-Atlantic region. (*The Young Mill-wright and Miller's Guide, 1795.*)

finish. In the case of complicated machinery—such as guns and clocks—worn-out or malfunctioning parts had to be made by hand to fit the particular item. But in a couple of workshops, tinkerers strove to make milling machines that could grind each part to exact and uniform measurements. Then Simeon North, John Hall, and Eli Whitney each independently proposed that the separate parts of any product might be made from molds of standard sizes and assembled by semiskilled mechanics or, when one part broke or malfunctioned, purchased and repaired by the consumer.

In 1798 Whitney responded to the federal government's call for a steady supply of firearms "produced with . . . expedition, uniformity, and exactness" in America. Until then, both the government and consumers purchased expensive handcrafted firearms from artisans or imported French muskets that were available in large numbers, but were unreliable and costly. Whitney won a contract to supply ten thousand American-made rifles within a matter of months by implementing the principle of interchangeable parts. Whitney pretty much failed in his endeavor, however, and it was left to Simeon North, a Connecticut gunsmith, to fill the demand for weapons. By 1816, North had created milling machines to make many copies of each gun part. Within a short time John Hall was also using interchangeable parts to make rifles at the national armory at Harpers Ferry, Virginia. A Springfield, Massachusetts, armory was soon using the process as well.

These men participated in what is called the American System of Manufactures (not to be confused with the political program called the American System, discussed in Chapter 8). Their inventions did not transform manufacturing overnight, for many artisans continued to craft goods in their small shops. But larger machine shops appeared in coastal cities soon after the War of 1812, some of them owned by artisan-entrepreneurs who hired wage workers to produce the parts or build the engines used in more mechanized enterprises. Workers were taught specialized skills representing just one part of manufacturing pumps, power looms, grindstones, or nately lathed furniture wood, or smooth-bore gun barrels, and then reproduced the standardized parts over and over. By the 1820s, Eli Terry, Seth Thomas, and Chauncey Jerome mass-produced clocks for the homes of many middling families. In time, too, the American System of Manufactures encouraged farmers, lumberjacks, and miners to provide more raw materials to productive shops, while more consumers enjoyed these manufactured products because their prices fell.

A third innovation that preceded full-scale manufacturing involved the application of merchants' capital and credit to the traditional "putting out" system (see Chapter 7). Given the growing number of unattached and underemployed semi-rural people in New England and the mid-Atlantic, merchants had little difficulty encouraging some of them to transport raw materials such as cotton, leather, timber, or flax to central locations. Merchants then distributed these supplies to homes and small shops to be processed into the next stages of manufactured goods. Women and children welcomed the chance to earn a little extra cash by spinning yarn for merchants. Men and women who had looms could earn even more by weaving the yarn into cloth. The rough cloth was taken to mill sites owned by merchants and middlemen to be "fulled" by wetting, pounding, and smoothing it.

Putting out transformed work around Lynn, Massachusetts, where thousands of women and children earned low "piecework" wages by sewing together the sections of shoe leather that had been cut to patterns in central shops. After gathering the upper portions, merchants sent them out again to other workshops employing men who attached the soles. Farm families welcomed the piecework because it could be done between regular chores without responsibility for investing in materials or marketing finished goods. Some skilled artisans were able to endure the transition from traditional craft production to wage work by becoming manufacturers. However, most skilled artisans in Lynn who used to make whole shoes lost control over the process of shoemaking and the direct relationship with their customers. Some became shop foremen, but gradually most of them became workers who earned wages in large shops run by "bosses."

The cultural consequences of these gradual changes in Lynn were profound. As farm families did more tasks away from their land, they hired more occasional or contract laborers to work fields while they produced items for sale. Since Lynn artisans needed leather for shoemaking, some farmers in the region enthusiastically gave up plowing grain fields and turned to grazing cattle. As elsewhere, people in the coastal mid-Atlantic and northeast regions used more cash than ever before, which in turn stimulated purchases of food and textiles from storekeepers. Young girls who pricked their fingers with needles as they sewed leather uppers were glad to have "a modest contribution toward a new petticoat." Only later, when factories took young people further away from household chores, did they lament the impersonal drudgery that these changes introduced.

Samuel Slater and Family Mills

Inventions, interchangeable parts, available investment capital, and greater division of labor in the work force, all set the stage for industrialization in America. A further step toward industrialization was the appearance of so-called manufactories employing a dozen or more people. Although a few colonial and revolutionary Americans proposed factories for more efficient production or employment of the poor, none succeeded until the 1790s. Samuel Slater introduced one of the first.

In 1789 Slater defied English prohibitions on skilled mechanics leaving that country. Trained as a technician and manager of textile factories, Slater came to New York with the design in his head for Richard Arkwright's advanced cotton spinning machinery and water-powered loom. Beginning in 1790, Slater teamed up with Rhode Island merchant investors Moses Brown and Richard Almay to put together a highly efficient—for the time—factory system on the Blackstone River. Slater built and maintained the equipment of the factory and supervised the daily production of cotton cloth. Merchants Almay and Brown supplied the raw cotton. Women and young children spun yarn in the main mill, while handloom weavers—men and women—turned the yarn into cloth in nearby homes. Merchants took up the finished product to sell. In this first American textile factory, the skills of a mechanic and manager merged with the capital and commercial connections of merchants. The conditions of factory production mixed well with remnants of the putting out system.

Slater's factory had its problems, of course. Merchants from whom he bought imported equipment and southern cotton wished to be paid more promptly than traditional arrangements had taught him, leaving Slater often scrambling for cash to satisfy merchant creditors. Workers required their wages regularly, even when depleted supplies of cotton, lubricating oils, and timber for repairs caused work stoppages. Like most mills of its day, Slater's operations were set on a river because of the water wheel, but far from skilled repairmen and commercial linkages. In time, Slater grew exasperated with doubts and demands. He left this first business arrangement and went on to build about fifteen of his own textile mills during the early 1800s.

These mills generally employed thirty to eighty people, most of them children from seven to twelve years old who could be assigned tasks that required climbing onto equipment or crawling around amid moving parts. Slater started out employing the children of struggling local farmers, but after a few years he hired children from orphanages and the workhouses built to employ destitute families. Slater was not alone in hiring youths. By 1820, nearly half of Connecticut's wage labor force, and over half of Rhode Island's, were children. Up and down the East Coast, children worked in these earliest dismal, chilly factories for seventy-two to eighty-four hours a week.

During the 1820s, Slater looked for alternatives to child labor because state law required him to pay the children's parents an apprenticeship fee and to provide his young workers with a rudimentary education, which he deemed too costly. So he began to bring entire families to his mills, built houses for workers to rent, supplied looms for skilled weavers, and stocked local stores with daily household necessities. These arrangements seemed to be an efficient solution to the difficulties of getting and paying for labor. However, the families working for Slater were not always happy attending the church of his choice and shopping at stores he built and provisioned.

By the 1820s, many other rural mills dotted the countryside along with Slater's experiments. Most of them produced flour or textiles, spurred by the demand in cities during the embargoes of 1807–1808, the subsequent blockades, and the War of 1812. After the war, state and federal governments entered a long period of imposing tariffs on cotton cloth imports. By the 1820s, tariffs were high enough to protect America's "infant manufactures" of textiles using southern cotton and northern factories. That same decade, manufacturers began to cut their costs by hiring immigrant workers at wages lower than what Slater's rural American residents demanded. By his death in 1835, dozens of other cotton mills and nearly one hundred woolen mills had improved on Slater's plans.

Distinctive Lives and Lifestyles

The inventions and improvements of the 1790s to 1820s accelerated the transition from a life that had much in common with colonial times to one that resembled the industrial era to come. Most white Americans never traveled far from home, and most still relied primarily on face-to-face communication with one another. They worked and worshiped in very small communities, with neighbors ironing out their mutual concerns by personal negotiations. One traveler through the mid-Atlantic put it well: when a farmer or small businessman assessed whether his condition had improved over time, "he took his measure from the status of his neighbors—or at most, his travels to market."

Other observers remarked that commerce, transportation networks, maturing credit and banking institutions, and a flourishing inventive genius prepared citizens for unparalleled material prosperity and expansion westward in Jefferson's "empire for liberty." A postal service, newspapers, and celebrations of national holidays helped give restless Americans unifying experiences. Families who moved far from familiar surroundings enthusiastically melded their traditional ethnic and regional customs with those of their new neighbors.

Americans did not agree about the consequences of this experiment in growth. Did it unify them as a nation? Or did it underscore their ethnic, regional, and cultural differences? To many, it seemed that Americans were *both* more integrated and more separated. For all the changes wrought by the proliferation of new machines and the closing of great distances, there were still "Yorkers" in New York, "Yankees" making the most of rugged New England, "buckskins" in the western counties of southern states, and "cavaliers" on the large coastal plantations.

The Binding Ties of Commerce

Although commercial recovery from the Revolutionary War years was well under way by the 1790s, Americans still looked forward to breaking the ties of foreign dependence and discovering new markets of their own. Merchants did not anticipate that they could reach these goals by changing the way they conducted commerce. Relations, in fact, remained much the same in the early 1800s as they had been in the early 1700s. Merchants still tended to form limited, temporary partnerships and hired perhaps two or three clerks. Their transatlantic ships entered and cleared ports two or three times a year (though West Indies traders darted in and out of ports more frequently). And they relied on their personal reputations to find buyers and sellers in distant markets.

But two other important conditions gave northern merchants confidence after 1791 that America might become an important commercial nation. One of these

"Tontine Coffee House," by Francis Guy   By 1792, daytime street life in New York City's commercial district had become a bustling mixture of merchants conducting business, artisans making containers and hardware related to shipping, and cartmen transporting goods. A wall of ship masts provides the backdrop to the shops and warehouses shown here, conveying the commercial optimism of the decade.   (© *Collection of the New-York Historical Society.*)

was the creation of concrete government institutions that extended businessmen's capacity for commerce. Alexander Hamilton's plans to fund the national debt, assume the state debts, initiate the Bank of the United States, and develop a national taxing system (Chapter 7) allied important merchants and foreign investors with the Federalist government. The credit of the nation was, according to many commentators, tied intimately to the collective credit of its merchants. When state legislatures realized that banks provided the valuable services of making loans and warehousing capital for merchants, they chartered more and more of them. Soon farmers, artisans, and small entrepreneurs joined merchants in clamoring for more ready credit. By the War of 1812, nearly 200 state-chartered banks were dispensing loans and enjoying rising public support; by 1830, the number had grown to 330.

In addition to chartering banks, states granted many other kinds of corporate charters that protected would-be investors in risky ventures by stipulating their privileges—usually, the exclusive rights enjoyed by the corporation, its years of operation, and its exemptions from certain taxes or public claims. Corporations could also sell stock to their supporters and thus raise capital for projects such as roads, canals, and small manufactories. Once merchants began to prosper by the turn of the century, chartered corporations became an alluring form of investment for merchants' commercial earnings. State laws aided merchant investments by creating "limited liability"—or liability only up to the amount of an individual's original investment—when corporations failed and creditors came forward with unpaid claims. Before 1820, the states chartered over eighteen hundred corporations with limited liability.

The other important ingredient of America's commercial prosperity was the prolonged period of war (from 1792 to 1815) between England and France. War in Europe, though it confronted American merchants with dangers on the high seas, also offered them the chance for windfall profits. Both England and France desperately needed American grain, flour, timber products, and whatever foodstuffs were available. As demand rose, so did the prices foreigners were willing to pay American merchants, who in turn clamored for farmers and artisans to send goods from the countryside to their wharves for export. The structure of commercial relations did not, in itself, change during these years, but the sheer quantities of goods moving through American cities to foreign destinations was unprecedented.

Robert Oliver, probably America's first millionaire, began as a young agent for Irish merchants in the small town of Baltimore in 1783. For years, he studied America's trade with the Caribbean and South America as he performed his duties for the men who paid his commissions from Ireland, and as he formed safe partnerships with American merchants. By the 1790s, Oliver was ready to trade "on his own account," not only to West Indies markets for coffee and sugar, but to British and Spanish possessions in many parts of the world for exotic spices and silver. Oliver wrote that his success came from "calculated boldness," a combination of careful prediction, ambitious investments, and, he confessed, "good luck."

Stephen Girard shared many of Oliver's qualities. Girard migrated from France to Philadelphia in 1776, a man in debt to creditors in Bordeaux and without capital or connections to acquire a position in commerce. The Revolution pointed Girard toward many opportunities, but they failed one after another when the British seized his ships, debtors refused to pay up, and privateers preyed on his goods. After the Revolution, Girard expanded his links to the Caribbean, including a smuggling business with Haiti and Saint Dominique merchants that flourished. Over the 1780s, Girard fed starving Frenchmen with American flour, surviving the postwar depression and finally boasting about his great fortune by 1790. Admirers and critics alike called Girard "a walking tyrant" who "chewed up" ship captains and tenants, and who rejected the comforts of a grand lifestyle and the pleasures of close friendships. Yet Girard also improved his reputation by giving generously of his time and money to set up a hospital for yellow fever victims during the horrible August of 1793. "A rich man, such as I wish to be and shall be," he wrote, "must yet assure the public that he will not only take great risks to get his ships back and forth with goods in demand, but that he will be useful to citizens in general in times of crisis." Over the next years, Girard invested heavily in local enterprises such as coal mines, canals, and early railroads around Philadelphia.

War in Europe also provoked American merchants to experiment with new markets. A spectacularly bold venture by wealthy investors in Philadelphia and New York sent the *Empress of China* to Canton, China, with a cargo of ginseng in 1784. Upon its return the next year with silks, porcelain wares, and eastern teas, the sponsors pulled in an incredible profit of 30 percent. During the next few years, other combinations of merchants sent their ships to other uncharted Pacific destinations. Bostonian Robert Gray sailed around Cape Horn at the southern tip of Argentina, and up to the frigid waters of Nootka Sound west of Vancouver Island, where the Chinook Indians sold his dealers thousands of sea otter skins. Gray ventured across the ocean to China, sold the furs at unbelievably steep prices, and returned to Boston with eastern teas. In a few short years, fur traders would be sending shiploads of pelts back to the eastern states.

Financial institutions, European wars, and successful ventures on new shores revived coastal cities from roughly 1791 through 1807. Shipbuilding employed every available hand, ports buzzed with people moving goods in and out, and consumers welcomed cargoes from distant lands. Thousands of Americans invested small sums in the insurance companies, brokerage and real estate firms, and lending agencies connected to international trade. Ropewalks produced the cordage all commercial enterprise needed; coopers made endless wooden containers for shipping goods; carpenters built and repaired ships; sail makers kept busy; and metal tradesmen provided the small parts, hoops, chains, and bolts that held the wood and cloth together. Although many new firms did not survive the risks of business life in these years, many others prospered beyond their dreams.

The commercial revival of the early republic, and the resulting urban boom, spurred farmers to bring more wagonloads of goods to coastal markets. Burgeoning population growth in Europe created demand for foods such as flour, wheat, and rice, as well as woodcrafts such as chairs, barrels, and shingles. New towns and growing cities of the East Coast created additional demand for food and fuel from western counties.

Jefferson's Embargo of 1807 (see page 308) abruptly ended this commercial heyday. With prohibitions on exporting, most merchants would not take the risk of being caught on the high seas with illicit cargoes. A hardy core of traders kept smuggling during the embargo, but the majority of port merchants looked for ways to make a living within America. Moses Brown and his son-in-law William Almay of Providence, for example, had traded for years to far-flung international markets, but at the onset of the embargo, they linked up with ambitious small-scale entrepreneurs to start a textile manufacturing business. Dozens of merchants in New York City invested commercial capital in city real estate or western land companies during the embargo. Some commercial leaders in other port cities bought out craft shops or took control of supplying raw materials to them. In time, these merchant-manufacturers were able to monopolize production and markets for, say, iron kettles, birch brooms, or maple candy.

After a brief commercial revival when the embargoes ended, the War of 1812 put another damper on commerce. Foreign blockades and renewed (although more limited) American embargoes curtailed trade for four more years. After the war, Parliament passed so-called Corn Laws to keep shipments of grain and flour from America's mid-Atlantic region out of England. To make matters worse, England's cheap manufactured goods flooded American stores after 1815, undercutting new manufacturers. Then the Panic of 1819 put a halt to business everywhere (see Chapter 8). Merchants struggled to put their idle ships out to sea and groaned over bloated inventories of unsold goods, defaulting debtors, and a collapse of the real estate markets. Only a few would withstand the shocks of this period and return to commerce; instead, many turned their ambition to manufacturing. When commerce revived in the mid-1820s, new faces crowded the docks and coffeehouses where merchants organized their commerce.

Northern Agriculture

In 1790 nearly 90 percent of Americans worked primarily at cultivating the soil or raising livestock. Even in 1820, nearly 80 percent of America's labor force worked on farms. Indeed, land remained America's most valuable resource. In the Northeast and mid-Atlantic states, rural families still relied on neighbors and kin to help put up barns, thresh grain crops, lend tools, and share the endless tasks of maintaining and expanding farm production. No family could be entirely self-sufficient, and many signs pointed toward generalized interdependence throughout the settled parts of northern states, which extended inland roughly fifty to seventy miles from the coastline. Governed by the changes of weather, the soil, the tools to be had, available family and neighborhood labor, and good personal judgment, a rural head of household faced built-in limitations on his ambitions for prosperity.

Fathers passed on knowledge about farming to their sons by an informal apprenticeship, working side by side for years. The range of knowledge was very broad, for most families in the North still made and repaired their essential tools and household items. Because members of farm families made particular commodities that neighbors regularly needed, informal barter, borrowing, and sharing could somewhat compensate for—and stretch the benefits of—the intense personal labor each farm family applied to clearing land, planting crops, making basic clothing, and living day to day. In this sense, northern farms intertwined family life and work, the shared tasks of men and women, and household chores and public marketing.

In farm households in the 1790s, many young women performed the same tasks their mothers had, and their grandmothers as well. From December through May, girls and unmarried older sisters spent much of their time spinning and weaving. Elizabeth Fuller, a teenager in the 1790s, spent January and February spinning, and March through May weaving. On June 1 she pronounced, "Welcome sweet Liberty," and put down her tools to take up other household and garden duties. In one season she had produced 176 yards of cloth, enough for a year's worth of sheeting, underclothes, and children's outfits for a small family. Somehow, she would have to find time to cut and sew the cloth into usable items.

A few women confronted this seasonal and annual sameness, the lack of noticeable gain from revolutionary years, directly. Ruth Belknap, for example, knew very well that her condition in Dover, New Hampshire, was somewhere between the poverty she had seen in the cities and the rising prosperity of her genteel sisters. In a poem written in 1782, "The Pleasures of Country Life," Belknap poked fun at women who did not have to "toil and sweat," the "starch'd up folks that live in town, / That lounge upon your beds till noon, / That never tire yourselves with work, / Unless with handling knife & fork."

But the dream of sustaining a large family farm was becoming elusive for large numbers of northerners. Partible inheritance (see page 136) shrank farms to averages of 100–200 acres through many old areas of the Northeast. A few large holdings dotted prosperous counties in any state, but many families barely made it from year to year on small surpluses. Southeastern Pennsylvania, long held to be a prosperous "best poor man's country" was, by the early 1800s, stretched to the limit of its resources.

Under these conditions, many young men chose to migrate to western New York, Ohio, or Kentucky (see pages 295–297). People who stayed behind in New England often entered their adult years as tenants or struggling farm hands. Even freeholders with farms of their own had to adjust to the loss of so many young people to the western frontiers. One adjustment involved new agricultural techniques. To make up for natural disadvantages of the soil and loss of human labor power, farmers began to adopt "scientific" farming methods and to diversify crops. Potatoes caught on in New England, and orchards flourished in the mid-Atlantic states. Experimental crops such as oats and rye, when alternated with wheat, increased the fertility of the soil, while hay and Indian corn provided food for livestock. More and more farm families produced a variety of vegetables, fruits, and animal by-products for their own use. Retailers began to carry cast-iron plows, which dug deeper furrows with less effort than the brittle wooden or metal-tipped plows colonists had used. Agricultural improvement societies and newspaper articles informed the "scientific farmer" how to fertilize with manure and occasional crops of clover or rye and how to rotate crops, try new strains, hybridize plants, breed sheep, and graft seedlings. In some areas of Pennsylvania, Delaware, and Maryland, average yields of wheat rose from fifteen to twenty-five bushels per acre, which in turn provided millers with greater surpluses to grind for export. Many rural people in New England, New Jersey, Pennsylvania, and Maryland began to raise sheep for wool and cattle for meat, tallow, and hides for local markets. Industrious women and children made woolens and dairy products for neighbors and townsfolk.

In time, these experiments and adaptations by New England farm families also gave rise to new social relations in the countryside. More country storekeepers and increasingly familiar itinerant peddlers collected country surpluses for transport to markets far away, and also met rural demand for new American or imported goods. Along the riverways of Massachusetts, Connecticut, New York, New Jersey, and Pennsylvania, towns attracted enterprising capitalists who agreed to receive farm goods, arrange for their transport to major cities, advance credit and goods to rural families, and order new store goods from urban merchants. In addition, by the early 1800s, a number of the many landless young men in northern communities were willing to work for wages on other men's farms. To the extent that prosperous commercial farmers could afford their labor, some of these willing hands worked on a day-to-day or week-to-week basis during plantings or harvests.

By several measures, northern freeholders were modestly successful in the early republic. But they gauged their success according to conditions of their own times. Privacy was rare in most homes, given the size of families and the few small rooms they occupied (see Competing Images, page 360). Even when there was tea and a china service, families might lack fuel to boil the water; homemakers might revel that their house had window holes, even if it lacked windowpanes. But newspapers were replete with reports of land purchases, high yields of grain, investments in new farm buildings, and successful markets abroad. Visitors to the Brandywine River in northern Delaware remarked that its huge three-story mills "afford perhaps the best flour in the world." Estate inventories taken on the death of a household head show increasing quantities of store-bought clothes and furniture, mirrors, chinaware, playing cards, and other amenities. From Lancaster County, Pennsylvania, to Albany, New York, bustling communities boasted a considerable "refinement of manners."

The Old Northwest

The Jeffersonian vision taught that, in contrast to England and Europe, America had endless stretches of available land, offering equally endless opportunity for self-improvement. In the early republic, government policies made it cheaper and easier for New England farm families to acquire frontier land. Thousands marched westward out of New England, into New Hampshire and Vermont, then western New York, and into the Ohio valley. Other families moved out of Pennsylvania into Kentucky, joining the steady wave of migrants who clamored for private investors and federal government to provide "the amenities of bridges, roads, postal stops" to existing settlers and "incentives for a well-put sort of people" to move west. Above the Ohio River, agriculture developed mostly as an extension of New England and Pennsylvania ways of farming; south of the river, cotton and slavery took hold in Kentucky and Tennessee.

By the early 1800s, new western settlements produced enough not only for local exchange, but also for very distant markets that set the terms of sale and prices for their farm goods. Cheaper land, taken in huge amounts from Native Americans, lured struggling easterners far away from families of birth, while rising southern planters continued their restless search for rich soil. Thousands began to cross the Alleghenies, and by the 1820s, the West had its own communities of bankers, land speculators, developers, and "infant manufacturing" nestled along riverways.

Much of the Kentucky and Tennessee frontier during the 1780s to 1810s was first acquired by speculators with connections to state and federal legislatures, and with commercial or banking capital to invest. Robert Morris, the financier of the Revolution, snagged about 1.3 million acres in central New York for about 6 cents an acre at a time when the going federal rate for the small freeholder was $2 an acre. Morris sold much of his holding to British investors, who set up land offices in New York City and sold small parcels—often overlapping with other speculators' claims—to thousands of farm families moving west. Dutch investors in the Holland Land Company did likewise and added an important incentive for would-be migrant yeomen: in exchange for improving the land, the company offered short-term leases with the option to buy tracts, thereby attracting settlers who could not afford full payment up front. But the high interest rates on start-up loans, and the steep transportation fees farmers paid to get surplus crops to market, created frontiers of debt rather than new waves of independent yeomen. Within a few years, many migrants turned into long-term tenants paying rents to eastern landlords.

Frontier land clearing was backbreaking work, often lasting from sunup to sundown in the first seasons of setting up a farm. Poor populations occupied the fringes of existing Maine, Tennessee, and Louisiana towns, and gradually dotted the deeper interior. But frontier poverty was different from its urban counterpart: people on the frontiers tended to accept their poverty as a temporary condition of new settlements. As the first trickles of eastern and immigrant families risked hostile Indian encounters and greedy itinerant traders, they turned hardships into myths of heroic "injun fightin'" and spread stories about the bigger-than-life characters who were reputed to eat alligators raw or fist-fight their way through Indiana trading posts.

The Shenandoah, Mohawk, and Ohio Valleys changed markedly before the 1820s. The rough life of early settlers rapidly transformed into complicated networks of exchange. People of the growing river towns advanced from subsistence to modest comfort and, for some, to a fashionable life on the frontier. Farmers traded their log cabins for sided houses or even two-story frame structures. "We have within ourselves," remarked one 1819 newspaper editorial in Kentucky, "every improvement that will give us the appearance of Boston."

King Cotton Emerges

Since the early 1700s many observers believed that sectional differences between the North and the South surpassed all other regional distinctions. Northern free labor and wide ownership of property contrasted sharply with southern slavery, plantations, struggling poor farms, and enduring paternalism. Even the casual observer would readily identify the different uses of the land and kinds of labor systems. Diversified agriculture marked the northern countryside, whereas staple crop production dominated southern life. Free labor and slave labor contrasted sharply as work regimens, systems of discipline and reward, and ways of thinking. The North was full of talk about advancement, ambition, attainment. In the South, those who did not own slaves regarded prosperity and social status as out of reach, often permanently. Foreign travelers noted how the "great middle" of "generally educated and hard working" people in New England contrasted to both the "rude manners and easy solace in whiskey" of poor southerners and "passion for games of chance and courting rituals" among the planter elite.

The South was undergoing an important transition by 1800. Tobacco had always been a risky crop for Chesapeake planters. Prices depended on fluctuating international markets, and then the Revolution disrupted planting and shattered many planters' commercial connections in tobacco. Even before the Revolution, many Chesapeake growers had turned away from tobacco and toward grain crops, especially wheat. Afterward, agriculture in the region continued to diversify, as did the artisan crafts, milling, and transport services related to grain-based economies. Overseers taught slaves many new skills as barrel makers, smiths, and boatmen. But because grain required fewer intensive days of labor in a season than tobacco did, planters did not need as many slaves.

The result was a "surplus" of slaves in the Chesapeake during the early 1800s. Chesapeake slave families and communities grew rapidly during the first decades of the early republic. The slave population increased from about half a million in 1776 to nearly 2 million by the early 1820s. Compounding the surplus, the Constitution guaranteed the slave trade's existence until 1808, so planters continued importing—over 250,000 new slaves came into the country before the deadline. Fears rose among planters that their slave property would decline in value and idle slaves would become a burden to care for.

Planters responded to their dilemma in different ways. Some sent slaves to cities such as Baltimore or Wilmington to become "servants" to employers who paid the owner, not the worker. Under those conditions, slaves experienced life in the two worlds of plantation and city. Some of them never returned to the plantation, a small number eventually bought their freedom, and many tried to "take their freedom" by running away to Philadelphia or New York City for asylum in the growing African-American neighborhoods there. Emancipation, however, was not an option.

Increasingly, planters also responded to the "surplus" of slaves by separating large numbers of slaves from their families and selling them out of the Chesapeake into newly settled frontiers beyond South Carolina and Georgia. There, the lure of great profits from a new commodity—cotton—was building the demand for slave labor. In the area that would become known as the Black Belt, breaking new soil, establishing plantations, and bringing in harvests of "white gold" required a large labor force.

Cotton, known for centuries on other continents, was not a crop of choice in the American South until after the Revolution. Sea Island, or long staple, cotton grew well in the warm, moist tidewater area, but it did not thrive in the upcountry areas of new expansion. Short staple cotton was a hardier variety that gave large yields to upcountry planters, but it required long hours of labor to pick the seeds from the cotton fiber. Some planters reported that it took a slave all day to pluck seeds from a mere pound of cotton.

It did not take long for planters to begin calling for a solution to this dilemma—some kind of tool or mechanical device that would speed cotton production. In 1792 Eli Whitney became the first to create such a device. During his childhood on a Massachusetts farm, Whitney had repeatedly shown an aptitude for making labor-saving gadgets. At age sixteen, he turned away from farming to supply the Continental Army with nails made at his own forge. After the Revolution, Whitney paid his own way through Yale, but upon graduating, instead of becoming a lawyer, he resolved to pay off his heavy tuition debts by teaching plantation children in the South. On the way to South Carolina, Whitney stopped to visit his friend Phineas Miller, an overseer at the Mulberry Hill, Georgia, plantation of a Revolutionary War widow. There, Catherine Greene challenged Whitney to invent a machine that could separate the seed from the fibers of the recently introduced short staple cotton. Within ten days, Whitney came up with a small contraption he called a "cotton gin" (*gin* was short for *engine*). His small, hand-cranked box, in which a rotating cylinder fixed with teeth combed the seeds from the cotton, "made the labor fifty times less" for southern farmers readying cotton for market.

Eli Whitney's "Cotton Engine"
The cotton gin, a simple mechanical innovation that planters adopted widely during the 1790s, made it possible to process cotton for English—then American—textile manufacturing at incredibly faster rates than the former method of picking seeds from the raw cotton by hand. The gin spurred agricultural expansion, international trade in cotton, textile production, and the demand for both slave field hands and free factory workers. *(Eli Whitney Papers, Manuscript and Archives, Yale University Library.)*

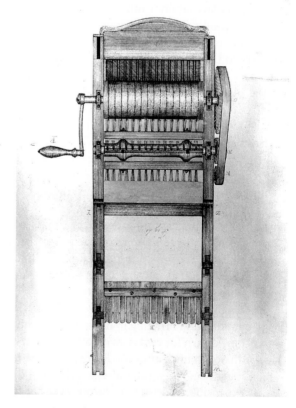

As the War of 1812 came to a close, England's accelerating industrial revolution stepped up mechanized spinning and weaving, and consequently consumed endless supplies of raw cotton. New England merchants eagerly sought southern staples to transport, as well as markets for finished goods coming out of northern states. New southern settlements—stretching from the fringe of South Carolina and Georgia into recently taken Cherokee and Creek lands, and farther westward into the territories of Alabama, Mississippi, eastern Tennessee, Louisiana, and Arkansas—drew planters from more crowded areas of the Chesapeake tidewater and Carolina low country. On these new lands, slaves who were experts in agriculture and planters who were well-connected to eager markets labored to produce short staple cotton.

The simplicity of Whitney's gin made it easy to copy, and thus cost him his opportunity to profit handsomely. The device was adopted rapidly and changed southern life almost overnight. A relatively insignificant experimental crop in the 1780s, cotton provided nearly 40 percent of American exports by 1810. By the 1820s, cotton represented over half the total value of exports. Only a comparatively few southern planters grew rich, but many thousands of small farmers and storekeepers benefited from rising production by providing cotton plantations with foodstuffs, leather goods, wooden tools and containers, and—paradoxically—textiles. Many northern merchants prospered from opportunities to ship cotton to England's and, eventually, New England's mills, and in turn to ship manufactures to southern states. Many of them invested the capital earned in southern commerce into New England's first manufacturing enterprises. In this way, the rise of the "Cotton Kingdom" boosted northern shipbuilding and commerce as well.

 ## Republican Cultural Patterns

For Americans who lived through both the pre- and postrevolutionary period, the country seemed to be undergoing alarming change. The largest coastal cities were still commercial and administrative centers, but they were also becoming the entry point for numerous immigrating foreign peoples and rising numbers of poor and unskilled people, whose lives were strained to the edge of endurance. An emerging middle class also became visible in cities and towns during these years. These middling families with established reputations, often headed by entrepreneurs rising in fortune, had only just begun to define their place in American culture. This new middle class would begin to define its character and roles through the changing American family, and also in the wave of religious fervor initiated by the Second Great Awakening. Soon, cultural and religious change would sweep through middle-class households and congregations, into the remotest corners of western frontiers, and into the homes and hearts of the poorest Americans.

Immigration and Cities

Before the Revolution, North America's few thriving cities were intimate places in which rich and poor lived almost side by side. Merchants lived above or next door to their warehouses or stores; artisans worked in shops that fronted their family homes. The "lower orders" of poor, unemployed, and recent immigrants did not yet live in separate neighborhoods, but rather lived alongside the craftsmen and laborers of Philadelphia, New York, and Boston. Only the very wealthiest men of northern port cities shared political offices, which dispensed broad privileges to citizens or restricted their activities. Small clusters of wealthy families set prices for important commodities, regulated markets, licensed taverns and cultural events, and organized relief for the poor.

After the Revolution, the social intimacy of the cities changed dramatically. For one thing, cities grew rapidly and became far more crowded, receiving immigrants from abroad and migrants from the countryside in numbers that put a strain on urban housing and services. During the revolutionary generation, immigration had almost ceased, but then the devastating Napoleonic Wars displaced millions of Europeans from their homes, and some of them made it all the way to America. In the early 1790s, upheaval in the major Caribbean islands triggered a major exodus to safer conditions, including American cities. Overall, from 1783 to 1820, about seven thousand people arrived per year, most of them free Scots and Germans.

Free African-Americans, too, added to the ranks of city dwellers. Although freeing slaves in northern cities was a gradual, not a sudden and complete, process, communities of free African-Americans flourished in every major northern coastal city by the 1790s. Philadelphia's free African-American population swelled into the thousands as refugees of both the American and Haitian Revolutions flocked to the city, and as merchants and Quakers manumitted their slaves. More than half of New York City's 6,300 African-Americans were free.

In 1820 only five cities in the United States had populations over 25,000; New York City was growing the fastest, topping 150,000 by the 1820s. By then, over a third of Britain's people lived in large cities, but only about 7 percent of America's did. Nevertheless, the quality of America's urban life was changing quickly. For one thing, cities were becoming seats of manufacturing as well as commerce. Workshops and open-air work sites were being consolidated into "industries" under one roof. Milling and processing, often of the goods being imported to nearby docks, flourished. Increased production of shoes, textiles, hats, chocolate, flour, and many other items strengthened early manufacturing enterprises, too. By the 1820s, the country's largest coastal cities were poised to look both out over Atlantic ocean commerce and inward to their own productive energies.

Gaps between the rich and the poor had always been more pronounced in North American cities than in rural towns and villages. But the gap between these groups grew noticeably during the early 1800s. Most shocking to many observers was the glaring discrepancy between an upper-level citizenry that accumulated unprecedented amounts of household goods, real estate, and paper investments, and a down-and-out citizenry that multiplied in numbers but gained very little. A few merchant families at the pinnacle of society after 1800 controlled more real estate, dock space, and stores than the wealthiest prerevolutionary families and lived in far greater luxury. Although these families were few, their prosperity was conspicuous, especially compared with the economic hardships, epidemics, and twists and turns of wars that affected the lives of other city inhabitants.

During these early years of the century, the "middling sort" grew in numbers and social importance, especially in cities. Many lawyers, ministers, doctors, shopkeepers, tavern keepers, and ambitious entrepreneurs never attained great stature and wealth, but they shared a degree of comfort and occupational success, and they made an important mark on growing cities. Sometimes artisans advanced to become independent manufacturers, as was the case with Duncan Phyfe, a New York cabinetmaker "of exquisite taste and unparalleled skill," according to a prominent merchant. Then, too, there were expanding professions such as managers, stock agents, insurance brokers, and printers whose services rarely led to fortunes but did link these middling city residents to urban elites and distant places. But these links were at first tenuous, and the people entering the middling sort had much to prove. By the 1820s, the middling sort was striving to uphold cultural standards that would set it apart from the lower orders and emulate characteristics of the elite. Close observers insisted that the middling should be known by their habits of sobriety, hard work, family order and modest comfort, lack of indebtedness, obedient children, and civic involvement.

At the same time, more and more wage workers and unskilled laborers were pushed to deplorably low levels of subsistence. Eighty percent of an unskilled

"Family Group in a New York Interior," by Francois Joseph   This painting from 1807 shows an ideal middle-class family at home in the North. The fine clothing, printed rug, mirror, silver tea set, writing desk, and other household items convey a level of comfort to which many Americans aspired. The division of men's and women's activities is also underscored here, especially men's literacy and women's nurturing role.   *(Warner Collection of Gulf States Paper Corporation.)*

worker's wages was spent on clothing, shelter, and food for a family of four or more. City dwellers depended on farmers to come to them with most of their meats and vegetables. Prices could be high, and country producers did not always have sufficient surpluses to satisfy urban demand. Fuel, so plentiful in country woods, was expensive and scarce in cities during the early republic.

The poor made up 60 to 70 percent of urban populations by the 1820s. Their hardscrabble lives showed the strains of surviving in a very young economy that offered only unskilled work and few urban amenities. Those who lived to the age of twenty might expect to live on to the age of forty-five, but not much longer—a pattern that persisted for the next hundred years in America's crowded cities. Difficult hours and conditions of work, undernourishment, and misguided medical practices, all combined to shorten the lives of many poor people. Infant mortality was high and the rigors of childbirth often fatal to mother, child, or both. Families sometimes sent out their children to scavenge for bare necessities for hours each day.

Cities periodically became death traps: one-third of all city children died from cholera, yellow fever, measles, smallpox, and diphtheria during the early 1800s. Few people could afford the care of a physician, resorting instead to dangerous home remedies and self-diagnoses. Those who did turn to professional care might be treated to extensive bleeding, blistering, or purging. Even worse, cities could not yet provide clean water to neighborhoods. Philadelphia's water system required fee payments that the poor could not afford, and other large cities did not initiate running water systems until the 1840s. No wonder, then, that Philadelphians suffered regular epidemics in the 1790s. In early 1793, an outbreak of cholera created panic in the "better sections" of the city, from which the wealthy fled, while the poor died in terrifying numbers. Within months, 10 percent of the city's population had been buried, mainly by the free African-Americans who offered to stay behind and care for the ill. Little was known about disease prevention, and there was no cure for cholera. Efforts to quarantine people in their homes, to dispose of dead bodies quickly, and to clean up the filthy streets all gave minimal relief. Epidemics returned with a vengeance again in 1796 and 1797.

Republican Women and Families

While some northern states abolished slavery after the Revolution, few legislatures in the nation restructured women's rights or opportunities in the republic. Nevertheless, gender roles and family life changed markedly in the two generations following the Revolution. The country's astounding population growth was a major factor. Both high birthrates and stepped-up immigration during the early 1800s added to the boom. By 1820, America was a far more youthful place than in prerevolutionary years. Over half of the population was under twenty years old, and during that decade the country was the youngest it has ever been. And according to some contemporary writers, the rapidly rising number of young Americans fueled other centrifugal forces gripping the country. As one commentator put it, when "a nation becomes crowded," for so it felt in certain New England and mid-Atlantic communities, "its people move more frequently, its families depart from the warmth of kith and kin" to spread out across new frontiers. Sons and daughters, the pundit continued, reject the care and discipline of parents "at a tender age." Meanwhile, shrinking farms in New England and the mid-Atlantic continued to push sons westward where land was relatively cheap. Or, complained fathers, maturing sons left farming altogether for careers as craftsmen or seafarers.

In response to the sudden youthfulness of the country, many writers began to offer advice on child rearing and mothering. Some writers called on politicians to create unique ordinances addressing children's circumstances. Guidebooks implored parents to honor the individual personalities of their offspring and to avoid excessive punishment for small infractions of family rules. Orphans became the special objects of public attention, and during the 1820s, concerted efforts began to build workhouses and private orphan homes.

Another cause behind changes in gender roles and family life was the turmoil of the revolutionary years. Political independence heightened many women's expectations for personal economic independence and social justice, and during the next generation, those expectations challenged a lot of thinking about family roles. Some writers questioned whether husbands had the right to demand unquestioned obedience from wives; others spoke out stridently for women's legal control over their dowries and inheritances. After all, hadn't many women run households, acted on behalf of their husbands at stores and public markets, and protected family properties in the absence of husbands during the war? Hadn't many women sacrificed on battlefields for the patriot effort? Deborah Sampson Gannett, who had dressed as a man and served for seventeen months in the Continental Army, was proud that she had "burst the tyrant bands, which held my sex in awe."

In the early republic many widows continued a husband's business when he died; worked as servants, laundresses, or nannies; ran shops; or even migrated to frontiers to set up trading posts. Even when they traveled to find a spouse or to remarry quickly after the death of one, many postrevolutionary women lived on their own for certain periods of their lives. In marriage, awareness about spousal abuse grew, as did sensitivity about the vital tasks women performed within households. Young women increasingly shirked the fixed hierarchical roles of an earlier era, including their parents' choices of potential husbands. As they rejected arrangements of economic convenience, which might have brought them increased wealth or land holdings, they demanded marriages based on love and physical attraction. Together, middle-class men and women also began explaining that their marriages should be based on companionship.

Still, law and custom limited these changes. First of all, most of women's gains after the Revolution could be measured in emotional and domestic terms. When it came to property or public life, women still did not have equality within the marriage relationship. Husbands of the early republic retained legal, economic, and ideological authority over their wives. For example, few states granted women equal title to family estates during the marriage, and no state granted women clear and uncontested title to estates upon the death of a spouse. In the republican political culture, only propertied white men had legitimate authority.

Evangelical leaders also supported the divisions between men's and women's roles. They urged men to step into political controversies where they might exercise their civic rights, and at the same time recommended that women provide a stronger nurturing and spiritual role at home. In their "domestic sphere," women had unique abilities to sustain the moral life of the republic, including the rearing of children into valuable citizens. The older view that women were by nature intellectually inferior and sexually loose began to fade. A newer view proposed that, in their virtuous republican capacities, women were models of modesty, piety, and nurturing motherhood.

This new view of women applied largely to the elite and middle classes. Elite women became the arbiters of taste in manners and customs, while middling women accepted the weighty task of educating sons about "the principles of liberty and government" that they would take into public life. In rearing their children, republican mothers were required not only to teach the "practical arts" of housekeeping to their daughters, but also to instruct girls and boys in moral beliefs, personal habits, and social manners desirable in "children of means." Increasing divisions between public and private life, between work and home, also defined the role of middle-class women. As their fathers and husbands focused more attention on their public political and occupational roles, middle-class women took on more responsibility for managing households that were both a refuge from fast-paced public life and models of virtuous child rearing. Their homes would be "an elysium to which [a husband] can flee and find rest from the stormy strife of a selfish world."

Many poor Americans would have found it difficult to follow republican prescriptions for gender roles and family life. Often, they rented living space, indentured or contracted out their children, took in hours of outwork a day, or toiled at jobs away from home for barely living wages. Little time was left over for attending public lectures about child rearing, and little spare family income to buy copies of popular ladies' magazines such as *Mother's Monthly Journal*. For families who needed every hand gainfully employed, enrolling a child in school was unthinkable.

As widespread public discussions more firmly defined the roles of virtuous married mothers and wives—at least in the elite and middle layers—they also began to address America's unprecedented population growth. Back in the 1750s, New England women commonly bore eight to ten children; by 1800, more infants survived the first months of life, but the number of births was declining toward six to seven per woman. Over the next five decades that number fell to five. Thus, the population growth in that region, although still rapid, began to slow.

A number of factors account for reduced family size in the Northeast. As farm sizes shrank in older areas and young men migrated westward, the women remaining in older areas did not find spouses easily. As a result, they tended to marry later, which reduced a woman's fertile years during a marriage. In addition, scholars find much evidence showing that urban middle-class couples sometimes deliberately limited the size of their households—usually by abstaining from sexual intercourse—in order to provide a full education and an inheritance for each of their "tender republican citizens." The poor in cities did not necessarily limit family size deliberately, especially because a larger family of workers could produce a greater income. But when the rundown neighborhoods of the poor were struck by ravaging diseases, the young and the very old died in huge numbers. Parents in such vulnerable urban households could be left with only one or two children as women neared the end of their childbearing years.

Emotional and Rational Awakenings

The First Great Awakening of the 1740s arose out of quarrels in local communities and within existing congregations (see pages 149–152). In its wake, new evangelical denominations arose over the next three decades, including the Baptists and Methodists, and congregations of older denominations split in the tense conflicts. A second wave of revivalism from the 1790s to the 1820s had more diverse roots and spread into the newly settled western frontiers very rapidly. Moreover, it transcended regional differences and eventually doubled church membership in the nation. This Second Great Awakening fed on the discussions about equality of opportunity that permeated the new republic, and it unleashed a deluge of religious fervor based on widespread belief in the potential for universal salvation.

Early leaders of the Second Great Awakening believed the Catholic and Episcopal Churches were enclaves of privilege, wealth, and ritual control. Newer denominations of Protestants created alternatives that became magnets for people who were discontented with the older churches or who were drawn to the excitement of newly created Protestant churches. Presbyterians, in particular, attacked the top-down hierarchy of power in many Congregational and Anglican Churches and replaced it with a bottom-up election of laymen to church offices. Beginning as early as 1797, revivals spread from the Congregational churches of New England far into the countryside. Women left behind when marriageable men migrated westward, and facing the prospects of a bleak life of late marriage or no marriage at all, turned desperately to the awakening's preachers for consolation and hope. Some young women joined church missionary societies or charities that organized the urban poor and educated children on very distant frontiers. Indeed, in New England, women composed 70 to 80 percent of new members in Presbyterian and Baptist churches.

In the mid-Atlantic, Methodists began to decrease emphasis on the church's internal hierarchy and discipline, and to encourage widespread emotional participation of lay members, along with music, outdoor gatherings, and active recruitment from the lower ranks of cities and towns. By 1800, Quakers and Baptists, too, caught the fire of the Second Great Awakening, attracting thousands of converts to a more democratized religion in a republic devoted to promoting economic and political opportunity. Not until the 1820s, when more politicized and secular reform movements attracted the energies of anxious Americans, did evangelical fervor subside.

Around 1800, the tone and theology of revivalism also spawned a few religious sects that remained smaller in numbers than the great revival denominations, but that had an influence on religious and cultural life in America far beyond their numbers. In northern New England, for example, Universalists rejected the strict Calvinism of older days that still lingered in the Baptist and Shaker traditions. Instead, they preached that predestination was far too selective, that salvation could be universal among all declared believers.

The southern and western frontiers gave rise to even more inclusive and noisy proclamations of universal salvation for all believers. Spurred by eastern clergy who worried about "sin, vile sin, and lack of preparation for the coming of Christ," western missionary movements grew after 1800. Itinerant preachers "rode circuit" through newly settled areas or counties full of Germans or Scots-Irish immigrants. Presbyterian missionaries organized camp revival meetings throughout western South Carolina and portions of Ohio, Kentucky, and Tennessee. Earnestness, exhortation, and a hearty dose of exaggeration in the sermons of revival preachers could transport listeners for hours. Physical displays of religious conversion—trembling and quaking, calling out, "rattling" with uncontrollable "transportation to some other place beyond the ground we stood on"—infected masses of frontier people at a time. The burgeoning Methodist and Baptist churches appealed to deep emotional aspects of conversion. At Cane Ridge, Kentucky, Presbyterians, Baptists, and Methodists came together in 1801 for a days-long open-air revival that attracted some twenty thousand settlers. Throughout the new cotton belt in the Southwest, Baptist and Methodist preachers also drew African-American slaves into their churches, while in northern cities free African-Americans built independent churches of their own.

Other groups of Americans in the early 1800s also rejected the strict teachings of Calvinists, especially the insistence on declaring one's depravity before being saved. In place of Reformation-based sources for their religious convictions, certain ministers adopted the Enlightenment's message of reason, understanding, and individual free will. In New England, highly educated commercial and professional families drifted toward Unitarianism—the rejection of the Holy Trinity and its replacement with a single, indivisible God. Recoiling from the overly emotional aspects of camp revivals, Unitarians insisted that not the heart, but the head could comprehend "the idea of God." William Ellery Channing's Unitarian sermons drew directly from Enlightenment texts.

Moderate forms of rational religion also arose. Many Congregationalists resisted the intense fire of evangelicalism in favor of important reforms proposed by Methodists and Baptists. The prominent Congregationalist minister Lyman Beecher, for example, preached against predestination to his New England churchgoers. He accepted that although all humans had a natural tendency toward sinful ways, they could also choose righteousness through individual will. Samuel Hopkins, who as a young man had been inspired by the First Great Awakening's Jonathan Edwards, enjoined his congregants to find personal salvation first, and then reach out to the poor and unemployed with "disinterested virtue and generous pockets." Hopkins—and other dissenting pastors—connected public charity and work relief for the indigent to the inner joys of spiritual redemption.

Rational religion spread beyond the older regions into new settlements, too. Lane Theological Seminary in Ohio and the Andover Theological Seminary in

"A Camp Meeting at Eastham, Massachusetts, 1851"   Religious revivals, often away from major population centers, immersed large numbers of people in prolonged searches for grace and redemption. At this New England camp meeting, typical of the Second Great Awakening, a number of repentant converts renewed church ties with enthusiasm and probably also became involved in social reforms such as temperance, asylums, education, and the abolitionist crusade. *(Gleason's Pictorial Magazine, 1851, Boston Athenaeum.)*

Massachusetts drew together the ministers, educators, and lay church leaders of Protestant denominations throughout eastern and western areas. Such gatherings provided a forum for discussing issues that touched many churches at once and became the basis for homogenizing matters of liturgy, recruitment policies, and missionary efforts. The American Sunday School Union (begun in 1824) was just one of the interdenominational societies formed as a result of these coordinating efforts. It served as a network for the transmission of cultural and political values, as well as a forum for extending the influence of Protestantism.

Whether in new churches or old, evangelical or rationalist, the new religious climate gave women unprecedented opportunities to take their rising moral stature as "republican mothers" out of the parlor and into the church, where they could join charitable agencies, mission societies, and moral educational experiments. In both old and new Christian denominations, religious leaders adapted republican thinking about the special virtues of women to church goals. Quaker women in Philadelphia and evangelicals in New York City set up relief agencies for the poor. Methodist and Baptist women in New England states organized special prayer meetings, some of which became vehicles for mass "conversion of souls." Magazines and broadsides advised young couples throughout the nation about Christian courting and "Christian child rearing." Seminaries and academies that combined classical and moral training opened their doors to young, middle-class women starting in the early 1800s. By the early 1820s, female missionary schoolteachers entered frontier towns as far away as Maine, Ohio, and Louisiana to extend the messages of the Second Great Awakening, as well as their own job opportunities.

One of the "leading lights of the awakened" was Charles Grandison Finney, an inspired young preacher who brought religious revival messages to the waves of new immigrants flowing into New York's frontier along the path of the Erie Canal. Life in western New York, where the canal transformed frontier life in a twinkling, exposed Finney to both the material prosperity introduced by canal commerce and the unsavory culture of drinking, gambling, prostitution, and "bald usury" that colored the boomtowns. In 1821 Finney was struck with "a wave of electricity going through and through me," which he "knew could be no other than God's pure love." Finney turned his own sudden personal awakening on the teeming populations of Rochester, Rome, and Utica, where he insisted that prosperous business families were obliged to reach out to immigrants and poor laborers with benevolence. During 1824–1826, middle-class women urged their families to attend Finney's meetings, and then reached out with evangelical zeal to help perfect the blacksmiths, millers, tanners, and other "lost" workers in western New York's canal towns. In 1832 Finney moved to New York City and carefully applied the drama and rhetorical flourishes that were used by politicians to his massive First Presbyterian congregation. "Vote for Lord Jesus!" cried Finney. Thousands did, and in 1836 Finney's "electorate" of church members funded the Broadway Tabernacle, a huge arena modeled on the theaters just down the street that had begun to draw hundreds of citizens to "godless" plays.

CONCLUSION

By 1800, commercial separation from England and increasing migration into the West carried the promise of change. Canals, mills, inventive technology, and new ways of doing work deeply affected lives everywhere. In this setting, citizens strove for the revolutionary ideal of the equal worth of all citizens in a republic, regardless of wealth and family name. Promoting vast economic experimentation, more Americans wrote about, and agitated legislatures for, the realization of economic opportunity. *Development, expansion, refinement, improvement, invention*—these terms filled the vocabulary of ambitious people in every nook and cranny. By 1800, profits in foreign trade and cotton sales not only recovered, but endowed thousands of people with new money to finance their dreams: to start up a store or blacksmith shop, invest in a new gadget, buy supplies for a frontier settlement, send a cargo to the West Indies, buy a slave, or launch a son in business. Large numbers of Americans plunged into enterprises, some recklessly and some with careful calculation.

Commerce and agriculture had only started to show more modern characteristics in the early 1800s, and so most social relations remained familiar. International commerce still lay at the vortex of economic recovery and progress, and important cultural differences persisted from area to area. Often a rural frontier community had more in common with another rural frontier community hundreds of miles away than it had with a nearby coastal city. Travelers remarked about the separate regional patterns of speech, dress, manners, ethnic concentrations, and even business practices.

Northern and midwestern agriculture was only slowly and sporadically becoming more diverse and productive, and the most crowded or land-hungry communities continued to witness a drain of young men toward western soil. Most of the North's farmers did their chores as generations before them had. In the South during this era, staple agriculture and slavery continued to dominate social relations and the nature of economic development. The spread of cotton cultivation became a harbinger of increasing differences between the South and America's other populous regions, the Old Northwest, the mid-Atlantic, and the Northeast.

But in many respects Americans still shared traditional lives, regarding the pace and character of change with ambivalence and anxiety. People in all regions still relied on the ties of neighbors and family to satisfy wants and needs. "Manufactures" were still performed more at home than in workshops and factories. Only a minority of Americans worked regularly for wages. Urban populations also coped with a bewildering array of class, ethnic, and cultural differences, aided by only a few of the institutions and services that rapidly growing cities required.

But the early 1800s saw the dawning of a great discussion that preoccupied Americans for generations to come: did they belong to a nation as Americans, or did they retain membership in a local community, an immigrant group, a church, an occupational skill, or a class? Migrating peoples of many kinds strove to "civilize" landscapes to their west, but it was not clear if they were making those lands suitable for many different peoples coming from settled coastal areas, or for one homogenized populace. Easterners celebrated their efforts to become a prosperous people, but they had not yet examined the political and cultural consequences of rapid change and competition. By the 1820s, it was becoming clear that attending to the community's welfare and the neighbors' needs were rapidly fading traditions. "Everyone knows," said a farmer near Norfolk, Virginia, "that the only job worth doing is one that brings rewards." During the next decades, open ambition, self-interest, and individualism grew. Soon it would infuse partisan political discussions as well. Americans would ask themselves more and more frequently whether their political and cultural experiment could simultaneously unfetter the individual liberties of Americans and build a republican nation.

SUGGESTED READINGS

A number of studies about early national development admirably weave together social policy and technology. See the path-breaking work, George R. Taylor, *The Transportation Revolution, 1815–1860* (1951), and the still valuable study by Carter Goodrich, *Government Promotion of American Canals and Railroads* (1960). The importance of water transport is treated in Erik F. Haites, James Mak, and Gary M. Walton, *Western River Transportation: The Era of Early Internal Development, 1800–1860* (1975). The best works on canal development are Nathan Miller, *Enterprise of a Free People: Aspects of Economic Development in New York State During the Canal Period, 1792–1838* (1962); Harry N. Scheiber, *The Ohio Canal Era: A Case Study of Government and the Economy, 1820–1861* (1969); Ronald E. Shaw, *Canals for a Nation: Canal Era in the United States, 1790–1860* (1990); and Carol Sheriff, *The Artificial River* (1996). For a more general study about changing technology in agriculture and manufactures, try Brooke Hindle, *Emulation and Invention* (1981).

The best overview of the era's manufacturing is Stuart Bruchey, *The Roots of American Economic Growth* (1965). Robert Dalzell, Jr.'s, *Enterprising Elite: The Boston Associates and the World They Made* (1987) looks at manufacturing from the vantage of the capitalists who initiated factories. Alan Dawley, *Class and Community: The Industrial Revolution in Lynn* (1976), examines the changing social relations of craftsmen and townspeople in one New England town. Thomas Dublin, *Women at Work: The Transformation of Work and Community in Lowell, Massachusetts* (1979), studies the effects of factory production on women. For the emergence of new awareness about work outside the home, see Bruce Laurie, *Working People of Philadelphia, 1800–1850* (1980).

During recent years, exciting work has been done on the relationship of society to new machines and industrial processes, including Brooke Hindle and Steven Lubar, *Engines of Change: The American Industrial Revolution, 1790–1860* (1986); David Jeremy, *Transatlantic Industrial Revolution: The Diffusion of Textile Technologies Between Britain and America, 1790–1830* (1981); and Judith McGaw, *Most Wonderful Machine: Mechanization and Social Change in Berkshire Paper Making, 1815–1885* (1987).

For the American System and family modes of early manufacturing, see Otto Mayr and Robert Post, eds., *Yankee Enterprise: The Rise of the American System of Manufactures* (1981); Merrit Roe Smith, *Harpers Ferry Armory and the New Technology* (1977); and Barbara Tucker, *Samuel Slater and the Origins of the American Textile Industry, 1790–1860* (1984). The organization of manufacturing and its effects on communities are thoroughly covered in Jonathan Prude, *The Coming of Industrial Order* (1983), and Philip Scranton, *Proprietary Capitalism* (1983).

Some of the best work on the nature of international commerce and the early republic includes somewhat older studies of particular port cities or merchant families. See, for example, Robert G. Albion, *Rise of New York Port, 1815–1860* (1939); Stuart Bruchey, *Robert Oliver: Merchant of Baltimore, 1783–1819* (1956); Edwin Dodd, *American Business Corporations Until 1860* (1954); David Gilchrist, ed., *The Growth of the Seaport Cities, 1790–1825* (1967); Freeman Hunt, *Lives of American Merchants* (5 vols., 1856–1858); and John B. McMaster, *The Life and Times of Stephen Girard, Mariner and Merchant* (2 vols., 1918). More recently, scholars have been examining the relationship of commerce to policymaking and shifting structures of the American market: among the most noteworthy contributions are Glen Porter and Harold C. Livesay, *Merchants and Manufacturers: Studies in the Changing Structure of Nineteenth-Century Marketing* (1971); Burton Spivak, *Jefferson's English Crisis: Commerce, Embargo, and the Republican Revolution* (1979); and Jeffrey S. Adler, *Yankee Merchants and the Making of the Urban West* (1991).

Manufactures, commerce, and agriculture took shape during the rise of many new institutions in the early republic, including courts and legal training. On the relationship of the law to development, Leonard Baker, *John Marshall: A Life in Law* (1974), Jonathan Glickstein, *Concepts of Free Labor in Antebellum America* (1991), and Morton J. Horowitz, *The Transformation of American Law, 1780–1860* (1977), are highly recommended.

The most important overviews of early expansion beyond the Ohio and Mississippi Rivers include Paul W. Gates, *The Farmer's Age: Agriculture, 1815–1860* (1960), and Malcolm Rohrbough, *The Land Office Business: The Settlement and Administration of American Public Lands, 1789–1837* (1968). Eugene Genovese's *The Political Economy of Slavery* (1965) offers an interpretation of distinctive southern development that departed from all previous interpretations and paved the way for intense scholarly debate. For additional views of southern agricultural society, see Stephanie McCurry, *Masters of Small Worlds* (1995), and John H. Moore, *The Emergence of the Cotton Kingdom in the Old Southwest* (1988).

The changing character of northern urban life, especially with respect to its immigrant and free African-American populations, is treated best in Leonard P. Curry, *The Free Black in Urban America, 1800–1850* (1981), and Christine Stansell, *City of Women: Sex and Class in New York, 1789–1860* (1986). For the development of neighborhoods and conditions of working people, see especially Elizabeth Blackmar, *Manhattan for Rent, 1785–1850* (1989); Paul Gilje, ed., *Wages of Independence: Capitalism in the Early American Republic* (1997); Howard B. Rock, *Artisans of the New Republic: The Tradesmen of New York City in the Age of Jefferson* (1979); Billy Smith, *The Lower Sort: Philadelphia's Laboring People, 1750–1800* (1990); and Ronald Schultz, *The Republic of Labor: Philadelphia Artisans and the Politics of Class, 1720–1830* (1993). Sean Wilentz, *Chants Democratic: New York City and the Rise of the American Working Class, 1788–1850* (1983), analyzes "artisan republicanism," and Edward Pessen, *Riches, Class and Power Before the Civil War* (1973), covers the gaps between rich and poor.

A unique study of one woman's domestic and community networks of meaning is offered by Laurel T. Ulrich in *A Midwife's Tale: The Life of Martha Ballard, Based on Her Diary, 1785–1812* (1990). For northern women's work in the early republic, see Jeanne Boydston, *Home and Work: Housework, Wages, and the Ideology of Labor in the Early Republic* (1990), and for exciting treatments of rural farm labor, Joan Jensen, *Loosening the Bonds: Mid-Atlantic Farm Women, 1750–1850* (1986), and Mary Ryan, *Cradle of the Middle Class: The Family in Oneida County, New York, 1790–1865* (1981). For southern women's lives, see Jan Lewis, *The Pursuit of Happiness: Family and Values in Jefferson's Virginia* (1983); Suzanne Lebsock, *Free Women of Petersburg: Status and Culture in a Southern Town, 1784–1860* (1984); and Kathryn K. Sklar, *Catharine Beecher: A Study in American Domesticity* (1973), which explores the extent and limits of women's southern lives.

Although dated, Whitney Cross's *The Burned Over District* (1950) is still a valuable study about the relationship of migration, expansion, and religion. Paul John, *A Shopkeeper's Millennium* (1979), is also helpful. For details about the revival movement of the early republic, see John Boles, *The Great Revival, 1787–1805* (1972), and Paul Conkin, *The Uneasy Center* (1995). An older but nevertheless useful cultural study of religion during the period is Timothy Smith, *Revivalism and Social Reform* (1957).

Houses in the Early Republic

Slave House   *(© Collection of the New-York Historical Society.)*

One way to gain valuable insights into the variety of people living in America during the early republic, as well as their cultural views of themselves and one another, is to study their homes. Where people lived in relation to one another and the kinds of houses they built provide valuable clues about their identity, as these illustrations show.

Slaves' houses came in all varieties of styles, some African in origin and some adopted from European architectures. All known dwellings were one-story frame or thatch buildings with two rooms. Often the rooms were, in fact, closed off from each other, sharing a chimney between them and having two exterior doors. This suggests that two families, or two separate groups of slaves, lived in these dwellings. A single room could be shared by six to twenty-four slaves on Virginia plantations. However, some slaves lived as separate families with a two-room house of their own, usually about twelve by eight feet in size. On occasion, a skilled slave might have his own private dwelling. Most slave quarters had

Modest Farmhouse   *(State Historical Society of North Dakota.)*

no windows or, at best, small holes cut by the slaves after construction. Slaves were often expected to add their own shelves and make benches for sitting and trunks for storage. Some dug root cellars in the interior floors or made smoke houses away from the dwellings. Masters might provide a blanket, cooking pot, and bed—or not.

Poor and middling white farm families tended to pass through stages of home ownership. Most started out with a bare-bones lean-to, often similar to slave houses, to get through the first seasons of planting or herding. Slowly, they accumulated the timber for a sturdier—though still impermanent—dwelling and a few household goods. Small clapboard dwellings in the countryside were often uncomfortable, especially as families grew. On the frontiers, the traditional log cabin or lean-to was usually a telltale sign that settlements were just beginning. Begun by the Swedes in Delaware, the log cabin was adopted by Pennsylvania settlers and spread into the West. One-room log cabins went up more quickly than frame houses did, and they did not require time-consuming planing, joining, sawing, nailing, and finishing, for which settlers often lacked the tools. In time, log cabins also became symbols of American myths of rugged individualism, frontier simplicity, and family self-sufficiency.

Working people of northern cities also lived in cramped quarters. The very high cost of shelter—rents rose over 200 percent in cities during the Revolution—prohibited most families from occupying much space. Single-story dwellings in Philadelphia measured eleven by fourteen feet, to perhaps twelve by eighteen feet. Many families took in boarders to help with living expenses and rents; few had separate kitchens and instead cooked

Frontier Cabin
(The Oakland Museum.)

Urban Working-Class Rental *(Philadelphia Historical Commission #40232.)*

Mount Vernon *(Mount Vernon Ladies' Association.)*

meals where they gathered to warm themselves, at the fireplace. On the outskirts of growing cities, immigrant and poor families flocked to tenement housing or makeshift lodgings. To create additional space for increasingly crowded neighborhoods, landlords rented out subdivided basements, cellars, attics, and even sheds behind dwellings.

By the early 1800s, successful master artisans were able to separate their living and working spaces. In many cases, their hired journeymen no longer lived with them but instead found their own poor lodgings in declining neighborhoods or emerging suburbs. Middle-class masters, in contrast, moved into single-family federal-style row housing that was both newer and more spacious. Grocers, printers, craftsmen in the luxury trades, and other high-end middle-class producers distanced themselves from the activities of markets and shops. Small manufacturers and professionals tried to live as close to the homes of wealthy merchants and rich retailers as they could afford.

Affluent urban families lived in two- or three-story homes, often made of brick. The houses tended to be narrow across their fronts, like working people's homes, but far deeper from front to back. Wealthy Americans usually had servants who performed their many tasks in outbuildings such as kitchens, stables, and wash-houses. Southern planters' lavish mansions stood in the landscape as stark contrasts to the housing of most white tenants and homeowners, and all slaves. Members of America's elite, whether great planters in Virginia or wealthy merchants in New York City, embellished their status by displaying their wealth in expensive architecture.

Questions for Analysis

1. As your eyes move from one picture to the next, how would you describe the differences in types of homes? Think not only about size, comfort, and protection, but also about family activities, privacy, and status.

2. Is the housing of poor white farmers and craftsmen, especially on the frontier, very different from slave quarters? In what ways would living conditions be different on the frontier, compared with slave quarters, even if the houses themselves are the same?

3. How should we compare the living spaces surrounding rural houses to their urban counterparts?

4. How might space have been organized in urban middle-class homes? Where were businesses located? servants' quarters? kitchens? entertainment areas?

5. Why do you think planters built such large mansions, especially compared with modest white farmers' households? What were the different purposes of spaces in planters' mansions?

10

Transforming the Political Culture, 1820–1840

agon wheels stuck in the muddy ruts of Washington, D.C., streets on March 4, 1829. Taverns and inns teemed with throngs of country people, many of whom had traveled hundreds of miles to attend the presidential inauguration of General Andrew Jackson. Jackson's own trip to Washington had seemed to ratify his commitment to "the common man" and the "civilizing" transformation of the West, for he had traveled down the Cumberland River and up the Ohio to Pittsburgh by steamboat, and finished his journey on a new turnpike. Jackson entered the nation's capital with great dignity, barely acknowledging the masses who wished to view him because, as he later divulged, he wished to impress on his constituents the gravity of the political transformation they were about to experience.

But Jackson was helpless to suppress the multitude's excitement over the Democratic Party victory in the 1828 national election. On inauguration day, thousands of people packed the street in front of the Capitol building and held their breath, rapt, as Jackson read a speech of no more than ten minutes. Most of the "monstrous crowd of people" could not have heard Jackson's exact words, but they did not need to. They were certain, wrote the doubtful Daniel Webster, "that the Country is rescued from some dreadful danger." Another observer wrote that this "free people, collected in their might," was "an imposing and majestic spectacle, . . . without distinction of rank, collected in an immense mass around the Capitol." Then, when Jackson completed the oath of office, they broke into roaring huzzah's and strode with Jackson to his new home in the White House.

But if this day demonstrated unprecedented popular support for a new president and the victory of a new "Democratic" Party, the scenes that followed also introduced Americans to "this new animal, this mob Democracy" that had been unleashed by fundamental changes in the country's political culture. The crowds followed Jackson right into the White House for the traditional reception, where they shed all gentility. "A rabble, a mob, scrambling, fighting, romping" pressed in through doors and windows. "Cut glass and bone china to the amount of several thousand dollars had been broken in the struggle to get refreshments," according to Mrs. Margaret Bayard Smith, whose husband was president of the Bank of the United States branch in the city. The "country farmers" shredded draperies and put their filthy boots up on stately furniture.

In the jostling that soon consumed Jackson's hard-drinking well-wishers, "ladies fainted, men were seen with bloody noses and such a scene of confusion took place as is impossible to describe." Supreme Court Justice Joseph Story decried "the reign of King 'Mob,'" the excesses that, unfortunately, had to be expected from a democracy of ordinary citizens. High society gentlemen in attendance at Jackson's reception demanded that "the hoards" be thrown out onto the White House lawn, "with the bowl of punch."

The disruptions at the White House were frightening to an older breed of politicians and social elite. They believed that order had given way to destruction of property, that respect for elite rule had yielded to a dangerous popular democracy. "Old Hickory," as campaign organizers called Jackson, had little in common with either the Virginia dynasty of previous presidents or the New England gentility of the Adams family. Instead, Jackson had steadily gained widespread popularity during the 1820s as a leading representative of "the common man" in American life, and he had pledged to launch a new political experiment grounded on the needs and interests of this kind of American.

▌ What conditions and values gave rise to the new political culture called "the era of the common man"?

▌ How did Jacksonian democracy depart from the traditional republican political culture of the postrevolutionary period?

▌ What did Jacksonians do in office, and how did their politics and policies represent the values and aspirations of most Americans?

▌ In what ways did Jacksonians reflect what it meant to be an "American" politically and culturally? How did other groups of people interact with Jacksonians to create important new meanings of "Americanness"?

This chapter will address these questions.

Chronology

1821	Van Buren's Bucktails win in New York, broaden franchise
1823	Monroe Doctrine pronounced
1824	J. Q. Adams elected president
1828	Tariff of Abominations passed
	Jackson elected president
1829	New York Working Men's Party formed
1830	Jackson vetoes Maysville Road Bill
	Indian Removal Act
1832	Nullification crisis begins
	Jackson vetoes Second Bank charter
1834	Whig Party organized
1836	Van Buren elected president
1837	Panic of 1837
	Charles River Bridge v. *Warren Bridge*
1838	Trail of Tears begins
1840	Harrison elected president
	Independent Treasury Act
1841	Harrison dies; Tyler becomes president

Popular Politics, 1820–1828

Following the War of 1812, local and state elections began to turn away some of the men whom John Jay, a Federalist and former Supreme Court justice, identified as "those who own the country." Politicians boasting great wealth, landholdings, and powerful family dynasties watched in amazement as the old deferential order gave way to men of modest means but powerful ambition and political aspirations. The criteria of personal disinterest and leisure time to rule eroded, and in their place Americans praised self-interested men on the make.

The word *democracy* appeared in the American vocabulary with greater frequency. Even before the war, preacher Elias Smith sang out praises of democracy: "The government adopted here is a DEMOCRACY. It is well for us to understand this word, so much ridiculed by the international enemies of our beloved country.

The word DEMOCRACY is formed of two Greek words, one signifies *the people,* and the other the *government* which is in the people. . . . Let us never be ashamed of DEMOCRACY!" This was in 1809; by the 1820s, others also praised "the common man" and declared that America had entered the "age of the self-made man." Privilege and elite rule were being replaced, rapidly, by middling white men who gained rights at the voting polls and in the public political life of the nation. But even as this boisterous new political culture took shape, few of its supporters or critics understood the profound changes it would bring in American life.

Extending the Right to Vote

Most of the state constitutions written during the revolutionary years restricted political rights because Americans believed that very few people had enough republican virtue to make public decisions wisely. Republicans of the revolutionary years believed that their liberty was safeguarded by a government run by "the better sort," or men who held the required amounts of property—often stipulated as land—to govern with personal disinterest and wisdom. Thus the first generation of political leaders were men who enjoyed the benefits of wealth and education.

For many years after the Revolution, most people thought that what was needed to govern a republic—the virtues of property, wealth, and education—rested in a few great men, but not in political parties. Parties, or factions, were self-interested and scheming by definition. And democracy, or the direct rule by the mass of people, would be as disastrous as tyranny; democracies in large geographical areas were inherently unstable, contentious, and changeable. Although historians give the name First Party System to the quarrels that took shape during the 1790s and the contested years of Alexander Hamilton and Thomas Jefferson, no true parties existed at that time. Politicians did not recognize the claims of factions or permanent interest groups, only of individuals. Hamiltonian Federalists and Jeffersonian Republicans locked horns in important factional conflicts over policies and principles after the Revolution, but most of them continued to believe that politics ought *not* to be based on contests for the right to rule.

Slowly, Americans began to recognize that factions were becoming a part of their political culture. Starting in the 1790s, discussions about equality, liberty, and virtue challenged the basis for the old republican view of elites ruling. Voices rose against property qualifications for holding office, the small number of men in government, and the restrictions on male citizens' right to vote. The throngs of Americans living in new states west of the Appalachian Mountains demanded political participation in the republic. One of their strongest demands involved expanding the suffrage, or the right to vote, to at least portions of this western population. In 1792 Kentucky entered the Union with provisions to let every adult male vote. In 1796 Tennessee became a state and required males over twenty-one to pay only very low taxes in order to vote. Ohio followed Tennessee's lead when it gained statehood in 1803. Constitutions written for the new states of Indiana (1816), Illinois (1818), and Alabama (1819) included provisions for a broad male franchise.

Older states in the East expanded the right to vote, too. Maryland and New Jersey eased property qualifications for voting early in the 1800s, in hopes of keeping farmers from moving West. Sometimes factional infighting among the elites of coastal states resulted in a wider franchise for middling citizens, granted in efforts to win popular votes for one faction or another. This was the case in Connecticut where, by 1817, all men who paid taxes or served in the state militia could vote. Many small farmers there turned their backs on Federalist rulers and voted for the Republican candidates who claimed to have won them the ballot. Western counties in South Carolina put up fierce fights to achieve the franchise and won it in 1810. In New York, Republicans promised to give most white men the right to vote, which in turn helped the party gain more state government seats in 1821; the state legislature made good on its promise that same year. In fact, most of the older states followed the precedents of the frontier by dropping qualifications for voting. By 1825, all white men could vote in every state except Rhode Island, Virginia, and Louisiana; by 1840, nearly 90 percent of adult white males in America could vote for their local, state, and national leaders (see map).

Universal White Male Suffrage As a comparison of these maps shows, most new states admitted to the Union during the early republic did not require voters to own property. In addition, many older eastern states liberalized voting requirements during these years. However, this increasing democratization of white men's voting rights did not extend to women and was increasingly taken away from free African-Americans in various states. (Source: Adapted from *Out of Many: A History of the American People*, Combined Edition, Third Edition, by Faragher/Buhle/Czitrom/Armitage, 1997, Prentice-Hall, Inc., Upper Saddle River, N.J.)

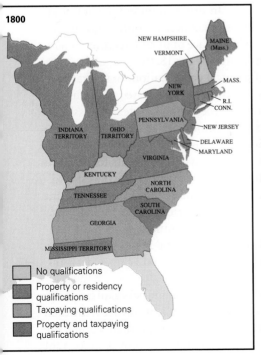

1800

1830

No qualifications

Property or residency qualifications

Taxpaying qualifications

Property and taxpaying qualifications

This process of expanding the franchise had a tremendous impact on political life in the nation. The visiting gentleman Benjamin Latrobe was astounded by the transformation in American political life. The extended suffrage, he declared, "planted a germ which has gradually evolved, and has spread actual and practical democracy and political equality over the whole union." When all can vote, he continued, distinctions of class and reputation begin to disappear. Men of modest means and moderate education are more trusted, said Latrobe, than men of great wealth and superior professional training. Americans had "what may be called an unlettered majority" governing at all levels. By the 1820s, others also called this phenomenon a "democracy," and extended its meaning beyond merely "majority rule" to encompass the political culture of ordinary white men deliberating together regardless of family name, occupation, or wealth.

As politics became more democratic, men who had never dreamed of attaining prestige and power stepped into important positions. But it was not always easy for farmers, migrants, and middling craftsmen to attain local and state offices. On the western frontier, for example, small farmers and town traders looked forward excitedly to electing men like themselves, or men who would be responsive to their demands for cheaper land, "squatters' rights," abolition of debtors' prisons, lower taxes, and protection from Native Americans. But more often than not, the new men who took office in state legislatures were businessmen and land speculators who helped steer funds for pet projects or important legal privileges to their supporters. Entrepreneurs poured money into buying legislative support and lobbying for roads, bridges, and right-of-way privileges that suited ambitious group interests. Bankers demanded more charters for local banks, and speculators demanded statutes to evict small landholders or squatters. In order to serve their interests, these men mobilized average voters into more or less coherent political groupings. "Factions" and "parties" had shed their stigma in the face of pragmatism, and membership in all kinds of political organizations soared by the 1820s.

Not all Americans gained these rights of political participation. In several mid-Atlantic states, legislators who formulated new voting laws neglected to discuss the half-million free African-Americans who resided there. Some states expressly denied African-Americans the vote, even as they democratized requirements for white citizens. In 1821, at the same time they were loosening the requirements for white men, New York lawmakers set very high property requirements for African-Americans wishing to vote. Despite the optimistic promise of the Northwest Ordinance, which prohibited slavery in the territories north of the Ohio River, some new states were among those that forbade African-Americans from voting. Only gradually did a few New England states grant free African-American men the franchise before the Civil War. And in the southern states, old and new, the harsh daily reality of slavery underscored the denial of the franchise to African-Americans, free and unfree.

Women were forming an unprecedented number of voluntary organizations in which they could express independent views and wield public influence. However, none of the first state constitutions of the revolutionary years granted women the right to vote (although New Jersey legislators made a temporary provision to grant white women this privilege, they revoked it in 1807). Moreover, across the nation, official policy and rhetoric increasingly defined participation at the polls as "manhood suffrage," which reinforced the exclusion of women from the polls and political party life. In addition, the formal disfranchisement of women echoed the trends that set women apart socially and culturally in a "separate sphere" (see Chapter 9).

Popular Participation

By the 1820s, American politics was not just a matter of voting in periodic elections, nor was it limited to forming constituencies to instruct candidates and watch their behavior in office. Politics had become an ongoing discussion of attitudes and expectations for the early republic's future. Through politics, Americans negotiated access to the nation's abundant natural benefits.

Huge numbers of Americans participated directly in this public political culture. One gauge of this was the great number of public meetings that involved expansive audiences. Sometimes artisans and small retailers feared that these huge public gatherings would become forums in which the outmoded elite could claim popular support for the right to rule. Sometimes members of the elite grew just as fearful that popular politics would get out of hand and "democracy will indeed take the form of mobocracy." "Do we see there the solid, substantial, moral and reflecting yeomanry of the country?" asked one critic of a large rally. "No. They comprise a large portion of the dissolute, the noisy, the discontented, and designing of society." Organizers of public gatherings, however, were overjoyed that they included not only a cross-section of the electorate but also many others who lent valuable collective support even when they could not vote in the 1820s.

Another measure of expanding public political participation was the rapidly growing demand for newspapers and other printed materials, a sign not only of expanding literacy but also of widespread desire to absorb news from many sources and to be connected more deeply to people and goods who were great distances away. By 1826, printers were adopting steam-powered presses and the public was clamoring for printed material. For example, the moral reformers of the American Tract Society invested in one of the new presses and churned out millions of religious pamphlets. At the same time, newspapers were undergoing dramatic change. Printers not only churned out thousands of copies of each issue before the news was old, they also reduced the price of newspapers so that dailies, covering regular news from a spectrum of political viewpoints, reached millions of Americans by the early 1830s. By 1835, publishers produced about nine hundred newspapers, sixty-five of them urban dailies.

In 1833 New York printed the first "penny press," which came out in a smaller format and contained a new kind of content. Instead of the commercial news that merchants sought, or the lists of retailers' goods and land auctions that traditionally filled many columns of colonial newspapers, the new press at first publicized workers' demands for a ten-hour day and better wages and connected artisan needs to the activities of the existing political parties. The penny press flourished, and soon included even more popular news about scandals and tragedies of the moment, as well as local social and political gossip, stories of murder, fallen morality, racial violence, and Indian frontier wars. By 1836, the penny press of Philadelphia, Boston, New York, and

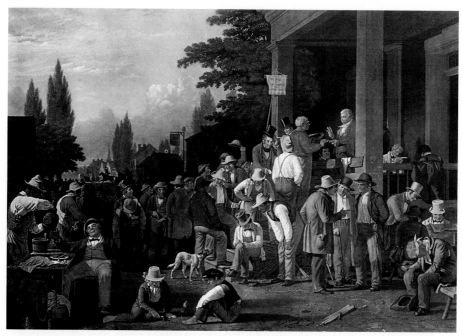

"The County Election," by Caleb Bingham (1854)   The political culture of the era involved white men of all social strata in the activities surrounding elections. Even on election day, as this image shows, gentlemen appealed to farmers and artisans for their votes, while neighbors gossiped, traded horses, or passed the time with heavy drinking. Near the humble men climbing the stairs to be sworn in for voting—symbolizing the "common man"—is a banner that proclaims "The Will of the People The Supreme Law."   *(Private Collection.)*

Baltimore carried regular news about local and regional political affairs alongside the latest scandals.

Another vehicle of popular politics was the expanding public entertainments available to Americans of this bustling era. For a small admission fee, hundreds of townspeople could attend traveling stage productions and lectures, dramatic readings of plays and poetry, or demonstrations of medical breakthroughs. Unlike previous generations, who had shunned such spectacles, Americans of the 1830s and 1840s flocked to open-air shows and indoor auditoriums for performances. Actors continued to produce Shakespearean comedies and tragedies, mixing these performances with popular melodramas and blackface minstrel shows, in which white performers blackened their faces and parodied masterpieces of literature or music in racial stereotypes. It did not take long before local politicians—and soon, national candidates—realized that these shows provided important opportunities for promoting political issues and stumping for votes.

An Old Order Passes

In the early 1800s, leading Republicans had hoped to end the nation's political factionalism. They sought to achieve compromise among sectional interests and welcomed into their fold the remaining Federalists. They praised the one-party system. After the War of 1812, President Monroe strove for an "Era of Good Feelings" to wash away the contentious spirit of party politics. Factional wrangling did not disappear, and local interest groups continued to fight over access to precious resources, but Americans widely shared the desire to trade the strife of the constitutional era and the war for "the calm that ensues when all political interest dissolves." President Monroe was certain in 1816 that "the existence of parties is not necessary to free government."

But then the Panic of 1819 hit, and the Missouri Crisis reminded Americans that they did not agree about how to shape the West. By 1824, the good feelings had dissolved into renewed political disputes. The War of 1812 had convinced some Republicans that a strong government was necessary. Congressional Republicans began to discuss the merit of a national bank, higher tariffs, and federal support for development. Young Henry Clay from Kentucky and South Carolina's influential John C. Calhoun hailed from the Republicans but became advocates for important measures formerly associated with Federalists. Opposing them were representatives clustered around Republican Presidents Madison and Monroe who favored strict construction of the Constitution and modest use of national government for development.

The new style of popular politics was making the Republicans who held state and local offices appear old-fashioned. Traditionally, politics was conducted through personal and factional channels, and groupings of politicians were merely temporary expedients. But by the 1820s, thinking about parties was changing rapidly. A new breed of politicians and the rise of countless voluntary organizations that brought people together publicly gave credibility to the idea that political parties were good, not simply necessary evils. Parties, the new view held, provided an arena in which contentious interests could negotiate their differences, which in turn would produce harmony and stability in the republic. To perform such a valuable service not only to elites but to all American citizens, parties should become permanent and establish their own rules for party loyalty and electoral strategies for putting party candidates into offices.

These new views took root in state legislatures gradually. In South Carolina small planters and farmers catapulted John C. Calhoun into power after 1800. A Richmond Junto took control of Virginia's state politics after the War of 1812, and in Tennessee new men rose quickly to take over the state by 1822. In New York, voters were willing to overlook Governor De Witt Clinton's origins from "old money" and "aristocratic privilege" because he promoted aggressive state development, especially the Erie Canal. But they criticized his habit of giving out political favors to loyal family and friends. This was, the popular press insisted, too reminiscent of the political patronage used in colonial days.

A rising middling layer of political activists in New York and other states resented the persistent power of old families such as Clinton's in the Republican fold. Martin Van Buren represented this disgruntled group, a new breed of citizens active in politics. Thousands of other local political leaders were also ambitious in business, excited about the fast pace of American life, and fed up with the privilege that came from long family lineages and inherited wealth. Van Buren, whose political savvy earned him the nickname "Little Magician," took the lead in New York. He rose to prominence from within the party by denouncing lingering tendencies to rule by dispensing personal favors. Political leaders, Van Buren insisted, ought to be "guided by higher and steadier considerations" than their own individual power and influence.

While Clinton served as New York's governor and Irishmen dug the Erie Canal, Van Buren worked steadily after 1819 with other disaffected Republicans to form a faction known as the Bucktails (because of the deer tails they pinned to their hats). The upstart Bucktails won two-thirds of the seats to an 1821 convention for ratifying a new state constitution. At the gathering, Van Buren's supporters won provisions to limit the use of political patronage, streamline the structure of party politics, and redefine manhood suffrage to include thousands more voters. Henceforth, argued the Bucktails, their party should represent the collective will and interests of its members in the state and nation; its policies should reflect the constituencies that conferred authority on elected officials.

When the new constitution took effect—adding to the electorate men who paid taxes, served in the militia, or entered the employ of the state to work on its roads—more than four-fifths of New York's adult males enjoyed the right to vote. In the years to come, family dynasties built on the fortunes of commerce began to cede political authority to rising professionals, entrepreneurs, and manufacturers who expressed new political interests. Men who held offices pledged to heed the demands of constituents, to adhere to majority rule, and to give up seeking personal influence.

Van Buren's Bucktails also thought hard about how political parties could assess the popular will and how parties could create internal loyalty. In addition to setting up a party press to disseminate the party stance on current issues, Van Buren spearheaded the formation of a legislative caucus. The caucus would function as a subgroup that would meet to decide on party positions and to map out strategies for persuading members to support these positions. Van Buren and his swelling body of supporters insisted that masses of ordinary people were willing and able to form a political community that was not built on influence, fortune, or great reputation. In the new-style political party, declared Van Buren's supporters, "individual partialities and local attachments" had little place compared with the "INTERESTS AND PERMANENCY OF THE REPUBLICAN PARTY" itself. Loyalty to the party dissolved all other distinctions between individual citizens and became the sole criterion of a person's political identity. Officeholders would not be chosen by virtue of their family ties and name, their personal attachments to men of wealth and fame, or even their accomplishments in business and culture. Party membership could not be secured by gentlemanly letters of introduction or personal friendships. Only loyalty to the party machine and party rules merited consideration for membership. It followed, said many Van Buren Republicans, that patriotism would never bind citizens so completely to the republic as patronage could. Love of country and virtuous behavior "are not half so strong as personal interests and private influence." For the next twenty years, the transformed New York Republicans, called the Albany Regency, ran state politics and provided a model of the new politics for other states—and eventually for the national government.

The Jacksonian Persuasion

As state leaders were shaping new party politics, Van Buren joined a group of ambitious first-term senators packing off to serve in Washington. For years Van Buren worked hard to transform his vision for party loyalty and patronage into a national Democratic Party. It was fitting that a new kind of politician would advance his goals. Andrew Jackson, a military hero of the War of 1812 and a rising politician out of the West, stood ready to challenge the old Republicans. During the 1820s, the popular press called Jackson "Old Hickory" in honor of his humble backcountry origins. Under Jackson's leadership, however, the Democratic Party itself was never humble; rather, it helped shape the swelling political culture that professed the grand ideals of equality, democracy, and unfettered opportunity.

Gathering Momentum

In 1824 the long-dominant Republicans fractured irreparably into five factions, each presenting a candidate for president. John Quincy Adams of Massachusetts and Henry Clay of Kentucky distanced themselves from the party's Jeffersonian heritage and argued for strong nationalism and government intervention to promote economic development. John C. Calhoun began to speak loudly now for a states' rights position he would develop more in years to come (see pages 382–383), drawing his support almost entirely from the Lower South. Andrew Jackson stood for traditional Jeffersonian ideals in 1824, including limited government and an agricultural foundation. Finally, William Crawford, the most traditional Jeffersonian of all and drawing from a more southern constituency than Jackson, became too ill to pursue the campaign to its end. Overriding the issues, however, was the fact that electors who had the job of casting votes for presidential candidates tended to adhere to local and regional loyalties. This had the effect of splitting the electoral college votes so that no candidate received a majority; Calhoun dropped out of the race in order to accept the vice-presidential nomination, leaving Jackson to receive 99 electoral votes, Adams 84, Crawford 41, and Clay 37. So once again (as in 1800), the House of Representatives decided the presidency.

Congressman Clay, who believed Adams would promote his beloved American System (see Chapter 8) and make him secretary of state, mobilized New England and Ohio Valley representatives to throw their support to Adams, who won the office. But Jackson rightly fumed that he had the greatest number of electoral votes and charged the House with sealing a "corrupt bargain." The southern voice of John C. Calhoun chimed in that the Adams-Clay alliance was "the most dangerous stab, which the liberty of this country has yet received." Both Jackson and Calhoun felt personally slighted; but even more, they feared an alliance of northern and western states against southern interests.

These fears were partially justified. Once the portion of Clay's American System related to internal improvements came up for discussion in Congress, it became clear that Adams favored the entrepreneurs and developers of the Northeast, as well as the commercial farmers of new western states. Southerners knew they would fall behind developmentally if left to raise most of their capital for improvement from state revenues while other sections enjoyed federal favor. Politically, southern congressional power would weaken if other sections developed rapidly and grew in population. Joining these southern opponents were many small family farmers in recently settled areas who feared the vigorous national government that Adams and his coalition promoted with the American System. Everywhere in America, voices insisted that the state legislatures, not Washington, should continue to shape development.

Opposition proved stronger than support for the Adams-Clay proposals, which largely went down to defeat in Congress and ended up in the laps of state legislatures once again. There, the clamor for improvements created the grounds for more "mixed enterprise" funded by states, counties, and eager private interests. In addition, states became the main authority to grant special charters for the expanding banking system.

Sectionalism intensified surrounding the Adams administration's higher tariff policies, too. Southern leaders as different as Thomas Jefferson and John C. Calhoun denounced rising import duties that would fall heavily on their states. In 1824 Adams's administration imposed a 35 percent protective tax on imported manufactures, including the vital imports of woolen and cotton cloth and iron goods. Mid-Atlantic politicians and voters from rural areas expressed dismay over the duties, since they still imported large quantities of the covered goods. Rising manufacturers who understood the benefits of high protective duties were still a small group, but New Englanders in crafts and manufacturing, especially in coastal areas, approved of the Adams tariffs as well.

Van Buren and other opponents of Adams were eager to use sectional tensions over tariffs to build support for a new party. Disregarding the long-term benefits of higher tariffs, and the immediate benefits of protectionism for manufacturers and small producers in America, Van Burenites simply wished to meld together as much voter support as possible for the 1828 election. They struck a bargain between southern and mid-Atlantic voters that was probably as consequential as the Adams-Clay deal in 1824. In the first place, Van Buren's coalition proposed to help small producers of New York, Pennsylvania, Kentucky, Ohio, and Tennessee (and thereby win their votes) by imposing higher import duties on certain unfinished goods: flax, hemp, lead, molasses, iron, and raw wool. Secondly, the coalition agreed to support northeastern manufacturers' demands for an import duty of nearly 50 percent on all imported British cloth. This 1828 "Tariff of Abominations" enraged the South. Southerners complained that since they had to import so many manufactured goods that they, as a planting agricultural society, did not make, they would suffer disproportionately from both the high duties on foreign imports and the high prices of American alternatives.

Southerners also feared that the huge federal revenue collected from the rising import tariffs would be funneled primarily into the northern states. Blind to the benefits of protection and revenue for all areas of the nation, they blasted a haughty, paternalistic, and "north-loving" President Adams for sanctioning tariffs that undermined the southern way of life.

Southern Congressmen also blocked Adams's efforts to forge diplomatic agreements with South American leaders in these years. In the wake of successful liberation movements, which threw off powerful imperial authorities and moved slave populations closer to freedom, Adams wanted to establish mutually beneficial hemispheric ties. But many leading southern planters insisted that this would send the wrong signals to their slaves and backcountry yeomen, even to the point of risking "the contagion of revolt" among their own slaves.

In short, the hopes Adams entertained about healing sectional rifts within the nation proved to be a mirage. As the next presidential election drew near, sectional controversy about tariffs continued to seethe. When voters turned Adams out of office in 1828, a new political party and a new presidential agenda inherited these "lamentations on taxes." Van Buren's coalition now had to join this southern opposition to its constituents of other regions.

Storming Washington

By 1828, Senator Van Buren led an awesome political machine poised to sweep Andrew Jackson into the presidency. Jackson's would be the first modern campaign in which ambitious new office seekers would be encouraged to "run" for office instead of "stand" for election. It was the first national campaign that promised to reward prominent supporters with offices and that built political coalitions on the grounds of loyalty to party members and programs.

In the North, Van Burenites mobilized the press and appealed for support from prominent voluntary societies and artisan clubs. In the South, they claimed the memories of Jefferson, Madison, and Monroe. They also drew in the planter elite by tapping Calhoun to run for vice president with Jackson. From the Old Southwest, especially Tennessee, Jackson could count on many supporters because of his frontier roots and his long record of promoting federal and state aid to the region.

Jackson was born in 1767 to a poor Scots-Irish family in the Carolina backcountry, where he came of political age following the American Revolution. By the time he was a teenager, he had been a prisoner of the British during the Revolution and had lost parents and brothers to the era's epidemics of cholera and smallpox. But his fortunes improved when he settled down to study law in North Carolina. He moved to Nashville to acquire land and slaves as he earned his reputation at the bar and married into an elite local family. Jackson also earned a reputation for fighting and dueling, but despite his rough public persona, the new state of Tennessee sent him as a representative to Congress in 1796.

In a few years Jackson's ambitious, forceful frontier personality caught national attention when he led a bloody series of raids against the Creek Indians in the South in 1813–1814. His victory at the head of a multiracial band of troops at the Battle of New Orleans in 1815 catapulted Jackson to national heroism. His escapades against the Seminole Indians in Spanish Florida in 1817–1818 enhanced his fame among a public that overwhelmingly favored his strategy of "clearing the frontier for the advance of civilization."

Jackson's presidential campaign drew in not only every region, but also many types of Americans. "Equality among the people" was one of his most appealing

Andrew Jackson, by Ralph Earl (1833) Jackson rose to political prominence based on his bold command of troops at the Battle of New Orleans in 1815 and his readiness to use force against Indians on the southeastern frontier. *(Memphis Brooks Museum of Art.)*

phrases, one that encapsulated widespread hostility to privilege, great wealth, and special interests in law and business. Immigrants and traditional artisans who did not directly benefit from new manufacturing enterprise applauded Jackson's verbal attack against rising tariffs of the American System; to them, lower tariffs implied that merchants would have fewer costs to pass on to consumers for imported items. When Congress passed the Tariff of Abominations, Jackson won support from the South by distancing himself from what he called the tariff's "great excesses." Yet at the same time he took credit for helping mid-Atlantic farmers gain higher duties protecting goods they produced, thereby shielding farmers from foreign competition. Small producers and squatters of the Old Northwest shared Jackson's hostility to Native Americans. In general, Jackson suited the restlessness of the nation, the entrepreneurial spirit gripping every region, and the rapid pace of a market revolution that was sweeping away old social elites and making room for ambitious rising interests.

Jackson swept the electoral votes in 1828 and became Americans' first president from the West. That year more than a million voters came out to choose a presidential candidate, and the popular vote would continue to rise through the 1830s. The wider franchise, the expanding arenas of public political activity, the unabashed development of "interests" and "opinions" allied with political parties, and the consolidation of party loyalty—all of these propelled Americans toward the Jackson coalition. And although universal male suffrage was still a novelty, voters overwhelmingly chose "the Jackson party."

Patronage, Democracy, Equality

Eventually, voters adopted the name Democratic Party to identify the coalition of interests formed around Andrew Jackson. Scholars have never agreed about who rallied to the Democratic Party banner, or exactly why. However, certain Americans were more likely than others to support the Jacksonian persuasion. Men in cities whose wealth was new, men of small means and large dreams about internal development, and men whose entry into the professions came by way of apprenticeships rather than a college degree—these provided fuel for the Democratic Party revolution. So, too, did obscure men without social position or recognized family names; and the great numbers of foreign immigrants coming into the cities and frontiers flocked to Jacksonian meetings. Even without the right to vote, large numbers of working women, as well as midwestern and southern farm women, favored Jackson's promises to help their families get ahead.

Jacksonians in Washington gained the reputation of being loyal but "lacking in fame or distinction," and the president filled federal offices with them. As he put it, "In a country where offices are created solely for the benefit of the people, no one man has any more intrinsic right to official station than another." Traditional concern for honor, dignity, leisure, and expensive appearances faded quickly. In their place, voting Americans assumed officeholders should be very much like them, that they would come from the same constituencies, have the same party loyalty, and formulate policies that reflected the interests of Democratic Party members.

Out of an intensely loyal party leadership, Jackson chose an informal group of advisers, called his "kitchen cabinet," which included rising newspaper editor Francis Preston Blair, speechwriter Amos Kendall, attorney Roger B. Taney, and the president's ever-present campaign manager and political engineer, Secretary of State Van Buren. Beyond this, Jackson also expanded the long-standing system of patronage in government, whereby loyal supporters and trusted confidants were rewarded with government positions.

With the Democratic Party securely established, and Van Buren's brainchild of disciplined party loyalty becoming a reliable feature of the Democrats, it was a small step for Jackson to rotate officeholders into and out of positions, according to their devotion to building the party. Leading Democrats reasoned that frequent and regular rotation of officeholders had the advantage of extending access to political positions to greater numbers of average party members. Moreover, nobody would hold any one office long enough to create insidious factions built on personal interest.

But Jackson's methods were soon known as the "spoils system," for as one senator put it, the Democrats popularized the view that there was "nothing wrong in the rule that to the victor belong the spoils of the enemy." In the spoils system, Jacksonians did not flinch at ousting political opponents from post offices, surveying offices, military supply posts, and other positions of government appointment. What was at first an egalitarian appeal to rotating officials slowly became a system of selective rewards. Jackson and his party loyalists justified such measures as the legitimate creation of "influence" that cemented the country together against frightening fast-paced changes in the era.

Apart from political offices, Democrats also attached central importance to the rank-and-file membership of the party. The emerging Democratic Party took hold of the expanding male franchise and the rise of popular political activity and channeled those trends into the party's goals. The Democratic Party's leaders proclaimed it to be a party of mass participation that would unite Americans across geographic barriers into one grand organization. Democrats, insisted the party newspapers, would knock down the walls that divided southern gentry from white voting yeomen, northern merchant princes from artisans, educated professionals from commercial farmers. This would not be a party of particular private interests or rival elites, but rather inclusive and attentive to public opinion. This would be a party of "the common man."

At the same time, many Americans argued that the Democratic Party would provide an umbrella over the great variety of voluntary societies and contending voices rising from the unleashed energies of the early republic. The Democratic Party would give Americans a unifying voice, with a national structure. In place of the horrifying prospect that huge numbers of separate interest groups would clash, and eventually self-destruct, in their aggressive selfishness, the Democratic Party would coordinate equality of opportunity.

Slowly, deference toward a would-be American elite gave way to a boisterous political culture based on representative government by "the common people." Admitting that equal wealth and equal reputations among people were impossible in so diverse and vast a country, many writers nevertheless insisted that the legal and civil rights conferred by representative government should fall equally on all citizens. William Findley had heralded this attitude in the 1780s when he said "no man has a greater claim of special privilege for his £100,000 than I have for my £5." From Connecticut, Abraham Bishop wrote that ordinary people had too long felt the "humiliation" of "wealth and power . . . a leading cause of all the slavery on earth." Rule by the traditional gentry could not endure, he believed, for Americans were progressively shedding their "fear and awe" of the elite, the "delusions" of the past which made the majority into fawning sheep of the "well fed, well dressed, chariot rolling, caucus keeping" elite of his New England. Once upon a time, Americans had believed in rule by "the better sort of people." But now, this notion was "thoroughly contemptible and odious," for "the people rule themselves."

Bishop, like so many enthusiastic optimists of his era, exaggerated. To opponents, Jacksonian patronage was a form of political favoritism; the rhetoric of mass participation did not guarantee any particular mandate for policymaking; and talk of democracy and equality all too often turned out to be more like wishful thinking than social reality. Still, Jacksonian rhetoric and the Democratic Party gave meaning and hope to huge numbers of Americans who wanted to participate and prosper in the early republic.

The Experiment in Action, 1829–1836

The Democratic Party developed a mass organization that prided itself on supporting democratic ideals of widespread suffrage and political participation, as well as greater economic and social opportunity for new and ambitious interests. In addition, many Americans believed it was essential to expand the country's territorial influence and increase its economic development. But Americans had still not worked out how much power the government should have to fulfill those goals. Once in office, Jackson had few misgivings about exercising extensive executive power to achieve the conditions he believed appropriate to those ideals. Jackson boldly relocated whole peoples, destroyed central national institutions, and attacked major components of the American System.

Indian Removal

Removing Indians from their homelands to distant places was not new; it had been going on for generations of European settlement in North America. Following the American Revolution, land-hungry settlers applied intense pressure on Native Americans in the Ohio and Mohawk Valleys. Treaties repeatedly attempted to set boundaries between peoples and to establish political and territorial rights that distinguished between Americans and "foreign nations" of Indians. Giving up land for a limited degree of sovereignty suited many Native Americans because the exchange tended to avert further destructive wars. But they paid an extremely high price for accepting the lesser evil of treaties: relocation to reservations—land with fixed boundaries that was often distant from their original homelands—and the shrinking size of their "nations."

During the War of 1812, Andrew Jackson began a phase of systematic violation of the foreign nations theory. Instead of negotiating treaties, he insisted that Indians were the "subjects" of the United States and led expeditions against the Creek who lived in Tennessee, Georgia, and Alabama, taking millions of acres of new land. John Quincy Adams tried to support the rights of Native Americans in southern states during his presidency. But popular and planter pressure to take ever more land thwarted his efforts. So, too, did missionaries who believed that establishing separate reservations neglected the responsibility of Americans to assimilate and "civilize" Native Americans. With Congress's support, starting in 1819, missionaries gained huge public funds and the government's blessing to teach in Indian schools, convert villages, and train the native people west of the Ohio River in "settled agricultural ways."

By the 1820s, then, competing views vied for favor and put the future of Native Americans in jeopardy. Few experts could answer the recurring question: What kind of political, legal, and social relationship would American citizens have with the quarter-million Indians resident on land claimed by both peoples? The answer was easy for southern planters who wanted to expand cotton production onto Indian lands, and elsewhere a widespread commitment to racial inequality and popular demand for "opening the West" bolstered their view. Jackson readily accepted the intricate web of economic development, westward expansion, white male democracy, Indian dispossession, and slavery.

Policies and beliefs reached a new stage when, in 1825, national officials and a group of Creek Indians signed a treaty to cede extensive land to the state of Georgia. When the Creek National Council repudiated the deal made by only a small number of their members and vowed not to move from their lands, Georgia's Governor George M. Troup appealed to Congress to enforce the treaty. He blamed the Creek resistance on Adams's earlier desire to be an "unblushing ally of the savages." Soon Congress extinguished all Creek land claims, based on the 1825 treaty, and state troops removed reluctant Creek to new homes farther west.

This pattern of disputed claims and eventual forcible removal of Native Americans would be repeated over and over for years to come. By the late 1820s, white westerners clamored for extensive resettlement of Native Americans to lands far west of the Mississippi River. Some advocates of removal wished simply to clear the land of "heathens," often coupling their demands with racist intonations to white Americans' "civilizing" influences. Others, including President Jackson, believed that the only humanitarian response to the "inevitable march of American empire," which was the American republic's right and proper goal, was to help relocate Native Americans for their own protection.

In 1827 the Cherokee, whose land covered portions of Tennessee, Georgia, Mississippi, and Alabama, met in council and adopted a constitution inspired by American representative government. They then proceeded to declare themselves a separate nation within the boundaries of the United States. The Georgia legislature, already practiced in removing the Creek, would have none of this "independency" and retorted that the Cherokee lived as the guests of the state, protected by federal troops at Americans' expense. When Cherokee leaders appealed to Jackson for support, he stated flatly that any state of the American union was "sovereign over the people within its borders." To underscore the rights of individual states, he also recalled federal troops that had been protecting the Cherokee, and in 1830 he urged Congress to hurry passage of an Indian Removal Act, which offered Native Americans new lands west of the Mississippi River in return for abandoning their ancient claims in the southeastern states (see map).

A small group of Cherokee accepted the terms of this offer, exchanging about 100 million acres of eastern land for $68 million and about 32 million acres of land "with clear title forever" in the West. Other Cherokee, however, stood firm. The following year, leaders of many villages defended their claim to be recognized by the federal government as a separate nation according to provisions in the U.S. Constitution; their case, *Cherokee Nation* v. *Georgia,* reached the Supreme Court in 1831. There, Chief Justice John Marshall struck down the Cherokee definition of their status and declared all Indians within the United States to be "domestic dependent nations" that could not enjoy full recognition as separate foreign governments. So far, Jackson and northern Democrats were satisfied that the court denied Cherokee claims.

But in an appeal case, *Worcester* v. *Georgia* (1832), Marshall went on to rule with the majority of the Court that the state of Georgia could not exert its state law

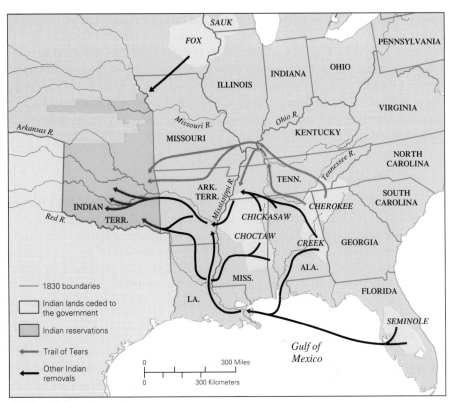

Indian Removal in the 1830s Jacksonian policies established a large Indian reserve west of the Mississippi River, which became the new residence of numerous eastern peoples. The Cherokee called their forced migration to this reservation the Trail of Tears.

against the Cherokee, for they had "territorial boundaries, within which their authority is exclusive" and protected by the laws of the federal government. This time, the decision to place the destiny of the Cherokee in federal hands quickly drew Jackson's wrath. "John Marshall has made his decision," Jackson supposedly fumed; "now let him enforce it."

Jackson tested the Indian Removal Act in 1832 when he ordered federal troops into western Illinois to forcibly remove Chief Black Hawk and the Sauk and Fox peoples following him. For years, tensions had been seething between these Native American people and the rising tide of new settlers. Now, when Jackson increased pressure on Native Americans by applying the federal law and sending troops onto that frontier, Black Hawk refused to be removed to lands across the Mississippi. He fled with whole villages, including about 1,000 warriors, into Wisconsin Territory, and on August 3 lost nearly 850 Indians in a brutal daylong massacre at Bad Axe.

Farther south, the Cherokee and Seminole peoples resisted the same strategy of forcible removal by federal troops. In Florida the Seminole recruited runaway slaves, fur trappers, and Spanish allies to fight federal troops and the state militia in a guerrilla war that lasted nearly a decade. Although about 2,000 Cherokee began to leave their ancestral lands under the terms of the earlier treaty signed by a minority of their people, over 17,000 Cherokee remained to resist General Winfield Scott's army beginning in early summer 1838. Scott's troops forced about 14,000 Cherokee to begin a brutal march that covered over 1,200 miles. Three thousand Indians, mostly the aging and very young, starved or died of exposure (see Competing Voices, page 401). The designated "Indian Territory," in today's Oklahoma, became home to a few thousand remaining demoralized Cherokee. Their miserable march is remembered as the "Trail of Tears."

Tariffs

Jacksonians often proclaimed that the national government should have diminished power over citizens. President Jackson understood this to be a mandate for cutting back, and maybe ending, federal support for internal improvements under the American System. His most direct means for doing this was to use the executive veto power to reject congressional proposals for aid. In fact, Jackson used his executive veto power more than all presidents before him combined.

In 1830, for example, he vetoed the Maysville Road bill, a favored project of Henry Clay's that would have used congressional money to expand the National Road through the Cumberland Gap. Advocates from the West proposed tapping federal funds to extend the road from Maysville, Ohio, to Lexington, Kentucky. But Jacksonian voices insisted such improvements should stay in the hands of states. Using federal funds for projects that Jackson believed would benefit particular state interests and were not a clear national interest not only drained the government of precious revenue, but also gave new meaning to the pre-Revolutionary Republican fears of corruption. Jacksonians further feared that to generate federal funds for projects associated with the American System, politicians clustered around Clay would seek higher and higher federal taxes on commerce. "Republican principles," declared Jackson, required a reduction of taxes and abolition of the national debt. Most important, states and their citizens, and not the national government, should decide how to invest their money.

Following the Maysville veto, Jacksonians set out to dismantle other parts of the American System, including protective tariffs and national banking. Jacksonians inherited Congress's 1828 Tariff of Abominations. During the campaign, Jackson had denounced aspects of the tariff (although he had supported some measures of the law), gaining many votes for the Democrats as a result. But once he was president, Jackson could not ignore the sectional tensions created by rising import duties. South Carolina was particularly anxious that northern and western interests had combined to harm southern interests. Living in perpetual fear of slave revolts and lurching international prices for their staples, southern planters nevertheless focused the blame for their precarious situation on the import duties that had been rising with each new national tariff law.

Calhoun returned to his state of South Carolina after the election to organize protest against the new Tariff of Abominations. He authored a pamphlet (anonymously, since he was then vice president), *The South Carolina Exposition and*

Protest, which condemned the tariff and pronounced the doctrine of nullification. The doctrine had a long theoretical pedigree, dating at least from Antifederalist opposition to the creation of a strong national government in the 1780s, and involving no lesser men than Jefferson and Madison when they had objected strongly to the use of national power in the Alien and Sedition Acts of 1798 (see page 288). For decades, in fact, dissenting interests had argued against the unjust and unconstitutional creation of national powers that annihilated states' rights. Now, in 1828, Calhoun declared that the national government rested its authority on the false claim that somehow it embodied "the will of the people," or the sovereignty of all Americans collectively. Such sovereignty could not exist, according to Calhoun, because the states were prior to, and continued to hold more authority than, the national government. As a consequence, true sovereignty could reside only in the people acting through their state governments. States were thus perfectly justified in forming special conventions to decide whether to support or nullify—to make void within that state—any national law. Even if the weight of most other states were brought to bear against a particular state's nullification, the latter's actions were, insisted Calhoun, perfectly constitutional. In addition, the dissenting state always held the right to secede from the republic.

Despite his resolve to decrease the authority of the national government and correct the upward rise of tariffs, Jackson opposed South Carolinian efforts to nullify an act of Congress in the name of states' rights. In early 1830, Jackson and Calhoun sat in on a congressional debate over the issue. Senator Robert Hayne of South Carolina rose to defend nullification, expressing fears that the North represented only one part of the nation's people and goods. Indeed, he continued, the North wished to crush other regions of the nation, especially the South, under the weight of oppressive tariffs. Senator Daniel Webster replied in a speech lasting nearly two days. The republic, he declared, was not a compact of states but of all citizens. Webster posed the horrible specter of Americans drenched in blood if states started to separate from the republic. Personal and collective liberty could not be secured with each state acting on its own, Webster insisted. In defense of a national perspective, and congressional policies, Webster demanded "liberty *and* Union, now and forever, one and inseparable."

Calhoun and Jackson listened intently to this Webster–Hayne debate, which had extended the issue of tariffs to the much weightier matter of states' rights, which in turn developed into a sectional argument about federal powers over western lands and slavery. Fearing that the web of interrelated issues could divide the Union, Jackson quickly announced his reply about the tariffs and the impending nullification crisis: "Our Union. It must be preserved!"

But in 1832, Congress exacerbated southern fears by passing yet another tariff that increased duties on imported cloth and iron goods, and although the new law removed some of the "abominations" of the 1828 tariff, it did not significantly lower rates. South Carolina's governor and legislature immediately contested the measure as an assault against the southern way of life. In November 1832, a convention of businessmen and planters in the state adopted an Ordinance of Nullification, which declared the tariffs of both 1828 and 1832 null and void. The ordinance further declared that port officials would not collect those duties in South Carolina after February 1, 1833.

Jackson's reply was swift and firm. South Carolina's ordinance, Jackson intoned, broke with the principles of the federal Constitution and was "unauthorized by its spirit, inconsistent with every principle on which it is founded, and destructive of the great object for which it was formed." In January 1833, he asked Congress for a Force Act to use the army and navy against southern violators and threatened to invade South Carolina to enforce national law, if necessary.

At the same time, Jackson agreed to help Congress move in the direction of reducing tariffs, thereby permitting South Carolina to save face, rescind its nullification ordinance, and keep peace in the union. Calhoun, disturbed by the turn of events toward physical confrontation, resigned as vice president, got himself elected to the U.S. Senate, and worked with Henry Clay to create a plan of reduced duties for the Tariff of 1833. When their compromise tariff passed in March in Congress, sectional interests quieted temporarily.

Banks

While disputes over tariffs built toward the nullification crisis, Jackson and his supporters became embroiled in equally divisive disputes over the national bank. Since 1816, the Second Bank of the United States had operated with a twenty-year charter from Congress; the government owned 20 percent of the stock. Many supporters of the national Bank agreed that it helped control the flow of money in the country and that it checked the tendency of state banks to issue too much paper money. The Bank did this by periodically calling in state loans and requiring the state banks to have a sufficient supply of specie, or gold and silver, on hand to cover their financial obligations to depositors and the national bank.

Through the 1820s, the Bank was successful in these functions. However, by the end of the decade the land- and credit-hungry settlers of the Midwest were demanding more credit from their infant local banks than the institutions could support. When the national Bank began to call in large amounts of the paper credit issued by these local midwestern banks, farmers and shopkeepers on the frontier suddenly felt pinched to repay loans for real estate and businesses. Longer-term development, and their immediate survival, they complained, was being stymied by "eastern monopolies" with control over their purse-strings.

Settlers' hostility to the Bank had deep roots in the past, even before the American Revolution, and had been nurtured through the subsequent decades of conflict between central and local institutions. By the late 1820s, western fears of being controlled by bankers and brokers hundreds of miles away grew volatile. Few Americans truly understood the regulatory functions of the Bank. They usually simply feared its authority to close the local institutions that gave them credit for purchases of land and farm supplies. Without that credit, another panic, like the one of 1819 and its ensuing depression, would be the inevitable result.

Another group of Bank opponents included wealthy easterners and leaders of chartered banks in the Midwest, who wished to create powerful competing state institutions over which they could wield control. It was not large banking per se, but the Bank of the United States and its president, Nicholas Biddle, in particular, that drew their angry protests. As friends of Jackson, they appealed to the national government to reallocate banking power to the states.

The charter of the Bank would expire in 1836, but in 1832 Biddle's supporters, including Henry Clay and Daniel Webster in Congress, sought an early recharter of the Bank of the United States. In moving early, they anticipated they represented a majority point of view. Banks were springing up everywhere that businesses operated and settlers arrived in America. They dispersed paper money, gave liberal credit, and expanded public confidence in bold development projects. Bank loans "knitted people together as tightly as roads and canals," observed one traveler to Ohio. They helped unleash more of the burgeoning energy of myriad Americans who had a lot of imagination but very little capital. And at the center of it all, the national Bank helped build confidence that central government existed in partnership with citizens.

However, when Congress framed a new charter for the Bank of the United States in July 1832, Jackson and his supporters rejected the bill with a thundering NO. Jackson vetoed the proposal for recharter, despite predictions that such an action could cost him the popular support he needed for the next presidential election. Further, he sealed his veto with a stinging public pronouncement of his views about the Bank. In a veto message that summarized the Jacksonian insistence on restricting the scope of federal institutions, Jackson invoked both constitutional principles and popular mythology about the Bank. Following Jefferson's strict construction of the Constitution, Jackson insisted that Congress lacked the authority to charter a national bank at all. Pointing to foreign investments in the Bank, Jackson evoked strong nationalist fervor favoring only "purely American" institutions. Borrowing from the anti-Bank rhetoric of previous generations, Jackson also convinced his audience that national banks were "subversive of the rights of the States" and "dangerous to the liberties of the people" because they embodied special privileges and shut out "the farmers, mechanics, and laborers" of the republic. When the Senate failed to override Jackson's veto, the proposal to recharter the Bank went down to defeat.

Jackson's veto message, as well as his firm stance against the unfolding crisis with South Carolina, electrified the political process during the presidential election of 1832. Jacksonians built an emotional appeal and carried it directly to voters. For the first time in American history, parties developed platforms and used party conventions to nominate candidates. Henry Clay's National Republican (forerunners of the Whig Party) ticket won only 49 electoral votes, while Jackson's Democratic slate tallied 219. It was clear to most observers that the Democrats swept up the support of northeastern working men, western farmers, rising entrepreneurs, shopkeepers, and ambitious professionals who favored Jacksonian attacks against privilege and Jacksonian promises of economic opportunity.

Riding on this crest of electoral support, Jackson moved boldly in 1833 to squelch the existing Bank before its charter expired. Declaring that his electoral victory was a mandate to "kill the Bank," and not waiting for congressional approval, Jackson appointed his friend and adviser, Roger B. Taney, as secretary of the treasury

"The Race Over Uncle Sam's Course," by David Claypool (1833) In this pro-Whig cartoon, Henry Clay and his American System are winning the race for national excellence and political control of the White House. Jackson stumbles over the ruins of the national Bank he has destroyed with the presidential veto, while Martin Van Buren, not a "Little Magician" but rather a monkey, faces toward the past and clings to the tail of the Democratic Party. Notice Jackson's Napoleonic cap and feather, representing his military dignity earned in the war of 1812, are flying off his head. *(Trustees of the Boston Public Library.)*

and instructed him to remove the government's gold and silver reserves from the Bank. This had the effect of removing the secure backing for printed money and threw banking into disarray. Taney ordered the specie to be deposited in selected state banks, soon known as Jackson's "pet banks."

Nicholas Biddle, director of the Bank, was outraged over these measures and set out to use the Bank to puncture Jackson's popularity. In very early 1834, Biddle called in bank loans to merchants and developers in the Northeast, hoping to tighten credit and make business leaders angry with Jackson. Biddle's maneuver succeeded in turning business leaders against Jackson, but it also threw the country into a sharp recession when credit networks collapsed near the end of the year.

While Biddle acted through the Bank, Jackson's congressional opponents introduced a resolution to censure the president. In March, Henry Clay, the resolution's author, sternly warned that the Bank crisis was "a war." "We are in the midst of a revolution, hitherto bloodless, but rapidly descending towards a total change of the pure republican character of the Government, and the concentration of all power in the hands of one man." Bank opponents, however, could not hold back Jackson's plan to destroy "the monster institution." By 1836, Jackson and his supporters had transformed the Bank's headquarters in Philadelphia into a state bank, thus symbolically affirming that Jacksonians had accomplished one of their major objectives.

Changing Legal Doctrines

Related to Jackson's goal of annihilating a "monster institution" such as the Bank was his intent to create power and privilege for new economic interests emerging throughout the nation by the 1820s, some of which were still fragile. The courts proved to be a useful vehicle for this "creative destruction" of "ancient rights," especially in one important Supreme Court case.

In 1785 the Massachusetts legislature had given to a corporation called the Proprietors of the Charles River Bridge the right to put up a bridge linking Charlestown to Boston. For years the proprietors enjoyed exclusive privileges to channel citizens across their bridge and to collect tolls for its maintenance. But then in 1828, the state government permitted a consortium of Boston merchants to build a rival Warren Bridge. The proprietors of the first bridge sued the new corporation, charging that their original contract gave them permanent exclusive privileges according to the U.S. Constitution's "necessary and proper" provisions in Article I, section 10 (see page 291).

Daniel Webster agreed that the Charles River Bridge Proprietors had an "original vested property right" in the bridge and argued their case. In 1837 the case made it all the way to the U.S. Supreme Court, where Justice Joseph Story wrote the minority opinion supporting Webster's reasoning about the Proprietors. As Story insisted, when the exclusive privileges granted by one legislature could be taken away by a subsequent one, there was "no surer plan to arrest all public improvements founded on private capital and enterprise." Projects that protected and furthered the public welfare, he went on, were far more important than the whims of changeable political bodies. Even when men made personal profits by investing their capital, they most likely promoted the public welfare and deserved the court's support. "There must be some pledge that the property will be safe," Story argued. These words seemed to echo what the Federalist and nationalist Chief Justice John Marshall might have argued had he not died in 1835.

However, in *Charles River Bridge* v. *Warren Bridge*, the majority of the Supreme Court did not share this older view of contracts and private property. Instead, the forceful reasoning of Roger B. Taney swayed a majority of the justices to knock down the old charter. Taney, hand-picked by his close friend Andrew Jackson to be the new chief justice, scoffed at the notion of protecting old property rights against the creative impact of new ones. It was the duty of courts to set aside outmoded contracts and thereby promote development. Unless the courts could use such a power, "we shall be thrown back to the improvements of the last century," Taney reasoned, "and obliged to stand still." New bridges, turnpikes, and canals "are now adding to the wealth and prosperity, and the convenience and comfort" precisely because new interest groups can hope to gain their own charters for development projects. This argument for dynamic growth, or "creative destruction" of exclusive property rights, would have far-reaching consequences for businesses, technologies, and railroads in the years to come.

The Taney Court championed other decisions that paved the way for the state governments to charter new privileges or waive legal obligations for fragile new enterprises. In *Briscoe* v. *Bank of Kentucky* (1837), for example, the Court ruled that despite constitutional prohibitions against the states issuing their own currencies, a state-chartered bank could issue notes and regulate their circulation. In addition, the Court supported movements in many of the states to chip away at chartered monopolies, contractual arrangements, and legislative statutes formulated for powerful groups of citizens. In so doing, the Court applauded efforts to allow more business risk and let individuals enjoy, and profit from, more "democracy of the market place."

 ## Dissenting Strains, 1832–1840

Jacksonian democracy did not shape every aspect of the new American self and society. It faced competing ideals in the popular culture, in some religions, and among economic interests. In politics, dissent from Jacksonian policies did not at first take shape as a rival party, but by 1832, opponents of Jackson and the Democratic Party began to rally together in significant numbers. At first they clustered around aspects of the American System, affirming that the government should have a strong role in economic development. In Congress, some outspoken critics adopted the name Whigs to symbolize a return to the spirit of late-colonial opposition to the arbitrary power of Parliament and the crown. Eventually a widespread Whig persuasion focused political discourse on all aspects of political, economic, and cultural development. Outside the Whig fold, but also unhappy with the Democrats, labor radicals stepped forward with their own criticisms of the increasingly unequal social relations in the rapidly changing republic. And just as dissenting strains of thought and action began to coalesce around viable new political organizations, another financial panic spun Americans into renewed depression.

The Whig Persuasion

As a political party, the Whigs took shape gradually. Daniel Webster of Massachusetts, Henry Clay of Kentucky, and John C. Calhoun of South Carolina, senators whose sectional interests otherwise put them at odds with one another, shared an opposition to Jacksonian policies over the period 1828 to 1834. In the election of 1832, these congressional leaders were still identified with the fading National Republican Party and campaigned in the old-fashioned way: seeking support from influential people in high places while ignoring most of the electorate. But when Jackson's raucous parades, picnics, and rallies that year gave him a landslide victory, his opponents adopted the ways of the political party system set in place by Van Buren, with its mass appeals to public opinion. Starting in 1834, Jackson's opposition began calling themselves Whigs and soon formed coalitions that, by 1835, were taking shape as a new political party. Between 1834 and the national election of 1836, Whigs aimed to take control of national politics from the Democrats, holding regular party meetings, nominating candidates, and formulating a political platform just as Democrats did.

Clay was the most charismatic Whig leader, and the most ambitious. Five times Clay tried—and failed—to become president. At age twenty-nine he had become a U.S. senator, and at thirty-three he was Speaker of the House of Representatives. In the next years "Harry of the West" wielded immense power in Washington, eventually serving twenty years in the Senate. In some respects, Clay shared characteristics with Jackson. Both were slave owners; both came from a southern heritage and lived in the new West. Both believed deeply in the ideal of the self-made man and exhibited inexhaustible ambition. But as the foremost architect of the American System, Clay became identified with the national institutions and developmental plans that required strong government intervention in the economy, which Jacksonians had attacked for years.

Like Jacksonians, Whigs were a coalition of interests from all sections of the country. But important political, cultural, and economic issues set them apart from their opponents. Many Americans were drawn to the Whig Party because they believed that Jackson violated his own rhetoric and took too much power from local and state levels of government, using it to enhance his own strength as president. Like abusive monarchs of the past, "King Andrew" had not put the running of government into the hands of the American people. Instead, he had used strong presidential authority to dramatically alter the direction of the country on behalf of "the people." Many Whigs criticized the Democrats' blatant peddling of patronage and influence, which horrified significant numbers of Americans. When, as president, Jackson ousted officeholders and replaced them with Democratic loyalists, critics lambasted his rash of appointments as a "monarchical tendency."

Oddly enough, many Whigs who feared Jackson's strong use of personal executive power also feared the rise of "the common man" Jacksonians adored. Many Whigs charged Democrats with wooing immigrants and Catholics while ignoring the justified claims of rising middle-class, entrepreneurial, and Protestant interests. Numerous people in the 1820s and 1830s recoiled in alarm and anger at what America was becoming. Men on the make and eager land-grabbers were symptomatic of growing evils. It was also becoming impossible to ignore the harsh realities of poverty, unemployment, and shabby living conditions in the cities. Social critics of the 1820s and 1830s pointed to northern urban centers that seemed to be growing more and more like the dangerous, crime-ridden European cities that Jefferson warned them never to emulate.

The intellectual Whig leaders responded to these observations by reviving the argument that a natural hierarchy of ability existed in all developed societies, and that it would of course produce natural inequalities of wealth. But it was misguided to believe that although "the common element" grew in numbers, it should rightfully rule the country. Whig leaders in the states worried that inexperienced, ambitious, and "unrefined" men were governing as Democrats. Philip Hone, a gentleman-politician and conservative leader of the Whigs said in 1834 that Democrats intended to "bring down the property, the talents, the industry, the steady habits of that class which constituted the real strength of the Commonwealth, to the common level of the idle, the worthless, and the unenlightened" who flocked to the Democrats.

Throughout the northern and mid-Atlantic regions, the Whig Party attracted many business leaders in manufacturing and traditional commercial families. The party also appealed to small businessmen and professionals, who believed that Whigs would actively promote Clay's American System. They favored an active role for the federal government respecting internal improvements, protective tariffs, federal subsidies to help the states with regional projects, and banks at national and state levels. Although many Jacksonians and Whigs shared enthusiasm for successful enterprise and energetic mobilization of resources, Whigs expressed deep concern about Jacksonian efforts to dismantle government regulations and central institutions such as the Bank. In addition, rising businessmen, textile and iron manufacturers, and skilled workers in the North hoped for Whig protective tariffs.

In the western and mid-Atlantic states, people found the promise of federal aid for development very appealing. Commercial farmers, rising country merchants, skilled craftsmen of small towns, and the entrepreneurs of the fast-growing towns in the Ohio Valley and Great Lakes regions wanted active governments to invest in canals, bridges, and banks. Clay assured midwestern farmers that the Whig Party would support grants of funds and land subsidies for these internal improvements.

Whigs were a loose enough coalition to include certain important southern voices, too. Some southern Whigs were not keen about rising tariffs and internal improvements that seemed always to benefit northern interests. Planters defended

Henry Clay Even after defeat in the presidential election, Henry Clay continued to command tremendous respect from political leaders and citizens alike. He also continued to be a tireless advocate of internal improvements, American manufactures, and government sponsorship of growth in general. *(Metropolitan Museum of Art, Gift of I.N. Phelps Stokes, Edward S. Hawes, Alice Mary Hawes, Marion Augusta Hawes, 1937.)*

slavery as superior to a working class; they promoted large-scale paternal landholding as opposed to the rootlessness of urban and rural northerners who owned no property. Southern Democrats who controlled state offices often supported these same positions, but they also represented traditional planter authority. New southern Whigs made a bid to break with the patriarchy of the past and create a more energetic planter elite that was attached to commerce, banking, internal improvements and—by extension—interests in the northern states. These entrepreneurial planters, joined by coastal merchants and urban bankers, mobilized support from many nonslaveholding white farmers on the frontier who had chafed under elite state rule since the Regulator days of the 1760s (see page 152).

The Whig Party was able to attract such widespread support for its candidates in 1836 and 1840 because it combined both economic individualism and moral reform. The latter drew not only great numbers of voting men but also many nonvoting women to the Whig persuasion. Party leaders formulated high moral standards that became a model by which to conduct their own lives, as well as to judge the failings of certain other Americans. "Reform" and "improvement" would be available only to Americans of moral superiority which Whig middle-class reformers tended to link to their efforts at eradicating poverty, disease, excessive consumption of liquor, ignorance, and slavery during the 1820s–1840s. Sometimes, these Whig political reform efforts translated into an echo of traditional elite rule and suggested Whigs' suspicions of lower class whites. Many middle-class Whigs also linked their claim of moral superiority to the republican family ideal, which set "true Whigs" apart from large numbers of poor, working-class, and immigrant families.

By 1834, the Whigs had coalesced strength sufficiently in their individual states to win a majority of the seats in the House of Representatives. In the 1836 national election, the Whigs took 49 percent of the popular vote and seriously undermined the Democratic Party's strength in every geographical and social sector of the country. However, the Whigs lost the electoral vote by a landslide to Martin Van Buren, master builder of the Democratic Party and modern elections.

Workingmen's Parties

The rapidly changing political and cultural structure of America altered workingmen's lives dramatically during this era. Artisans in northern cities joined together more frequently during these years to protest that immigrants and migrating rural people degraded their skills and social stature. Ambitious entrepreneurs, they charged, were hiring low-paid semiskilled laborers to build toll bridges and canals. Some found the causes of their declining standard of living in the poor immigrants and female workers in outwork shops. In cities, prices for everyday necessities rose quickly after 1820, so that stagnating wages could not be stretched as far to pay a family's rent and fuel bills.

At first, workers formed mutual aid societies to provide benefits to families when a head of household became incapacitated or died. Although these organizations created important social and cultural links among working people, they were never adequate. And working people still lacked viable public institutions for relief and reform. Eventually, many urban workers would be attracted to the Democratic Party and would vote for its candidates. But during the 1820s, the issues of economic opportunity and political democracy were often discussed outside mainstream party developments, and sometimes in opposition to them.

Among the ardent critics of Democrats and emerging capitalism in the 1820s, Thomas Skidmore stands out. Like so many other young men of his generation, Skidmore began life in a poor New England family but as a teenager began to travel and work odd jobs. In his early twenties, Skidmore settled in Wilmington, Delaware, and conducted numerous experiments on machines and scientific instruments. Skidmore moved on to New York in 1819 as a machinist, just when the city entered a phase of tremendous commercial and manufacturing growth. During the next decade, countless artisans and wage workers were displaced from traditional skills and edged into low-paying putting-out systems or piecework arrangements. Skidmore was among them when they began to raise independent voices of protest.

For years, artisans and machinists in coastal cities had eagerly played roles in the literary, educational, and inventing movements of the early republic. Many of them just as eagerly read and wrote for the newspapers and broadsides that gave expression to workingmen's own popular culture. Public speeches, as well as evening meetings of educational academies and philosophical societies, brought together large congregations of workers regularly, while enthusiastic urban parades reinforced the spoken word.

Republican ideas helped workers understand and criticize this bewildering era. They taught that property conferred a "stake in society" and therefore white citizens should own it widely and in roughly similar amounts. Independent urban artisans believed this property was not just of the landed kind—as traditional republicans proposed—but also their hard won skills and their entitlement to enjoy the fruits of their labor as workers and citizens. These beliefs sharpened many artisans' understanding about how their work was changing during these years, and they offered elements of a critique against harsh aspects of capitalism. This "artisan republicanism" mixed the largely political character of Jacksonian democracy with an economic assessment of labor's conditions more generally.

Artisan republicanism's message about work quickly became the basis for organized political action. Between 1827 and 1837, Skidmore and others rose to become leaders among urban artisans, intellectuals, and immigrants who organized workingmen's parties in opposition to the Democratic and Whig Parties. In 1829 various strands of unrest came together in the New York Working Men's Party. Its first activity was to organize protests against bosses who tried to lengthen the working day from ten to eleven hours. In the coming years the "Workies" also demanded banking that was accessible to all laboring people, abolition of corporate monopolies, taxation based on wealth, and better education for their children. Starting in the fall of 1829, committees began to write a new political program and to select candidates for election to the state legislature.

Skidmore's formulations about the problems artisans and urban workers faced lay at the heart of the subsequent campaigns. The current social system, Skidmore argued, was more like slavery than freedom for most working people, for it took away most of their entitlements to hold land and enjoy their property, and put most people in a condition of want. Skidmore's solution involved abolishing the legal and property structure, as well as the political system, that characterized capitalism in early national America, and substituting for them a more equal ownership of land for everyone. A new political party of the poor and workers, he was sure, could achieve more equitable redistribution of property and citizens' rights.

A meeting of over five thousand people hailed Skidmore's plan in October 1829 and carried it as their standard into the political fray. Two weeks later, the Working Men won about one-third of the votes cast in New York City for candidates to the state legislature and put one of their members in office. But the elation over such a stunning success at the polls soon evaporated, for within a few short weeks, other political and social persuasions invaded the Working Men. Just then, Democrats were offering powerful new alternatives in northern local areas to old political elites. Urban social reformers siphoned off some working-class discontent into temperance and evangelical movements, where laboring people's voices were stifled by the stronger ones of middle-class leaders or manufacturers who had different economic interests. Calls for property redistribution were overwhelmed by the worthy, but less radical, demands for state-funded education and development projects.

Still, for decades to come, alternative working-class parties would arise out of the same rapidly altering master–artisan relations that characterized towns and cities throughout the North. Many of them shared the Working Men's point of view and drew strength from the ways that Skidmore and others had built a viable protest movement based on their republican heritage. Some new organizations grew out of economic grievances, while others stressed the need to extend political rights when exiting parties failed them. For example, in 1831 New York City's female seamstresses faced a cut in their already-low wages and piecework rates. In response to their grinding poverty, crowded tenement living, long hours of work, and little hope of change for their children, 1,600 women organized the United Tailoresses Society and demanded decent pay at mass strike meetings. But without help from organized and unorganized male journeyman, who generally scorned women laboring outside the home, the strikes were doomed to fail.

In the mid-1830s, newspaper editor William Leggett became a leader of New York's Equal Rights Party (called Locofocos by critics), which believed that Democrats should have extended their opposition to the national Bank to state bank charters as well. Only hard money and private transactions were legitimate. In addition, Locofocos attacked Democratic and Whig quarrels over special government legislation to regulate this or that aspect of the national economy. Only absolute freedom of individual opportunity in the market place could create economic justice. All people, Leggett wrote, should enjoy "the free exercise of their talents and industry." The Equal Rights Party was one of many crusades for entrepreneurial equal rights, a laissez-faire approach to development that arose against fears of "monopolistic privilege" that dissenters detected in both of the established parties.

By the 1830s, huge numbers of urban people were attracted to radical political alternatives, while these alternatives in turn drew opposition from the two major

Labor Organizes Politically

The symbol of the arm and hammer and its caption, "By Hammer and Hand All Arts Do Stand," appeared for the first time in 1836 in the newsletter of the General Trades' Union in New York City, which called for all working people in the city to support the tailors brought to trial on charges of "conspiring" against employers for higher wages and better conditions. The broadside, printed the following year, announced another general meeting of city workers. It was common to compare the struggles of unionists in the 1830s to the revolutionary struggle for liberty half a century earlier. *(Top: "The Union," July 14, 1836; New York Public Library, Rare Books; bottom: "New York City Labor Troubles, 1837," Library of Congress.)*

Working Men, Attention!!

Globe Office
Saturday, November 20. 1837

It is your imperious duty to drop your *Hammers and Sledges*! one and all, to your post repair, **THIS AFTERNOON**, at *FIVE* o'clock **P. M.** and attend the

GREAT MEETING

called by the papers of this morning, to be held at the **CITY HALL**, then and there to co-operate with such as have the **GREAT GOOD OF ALL THEIR** *FELLOW CITIZENS at Heart.* Your liberty! yea, your *LABOUR!!* is the subject of the call: who that values the services of **HEROES** of the *Revolution* whose blood achieved our Independence as a Nation, will for a moment doubt he owes a few hours this afternoon to his wife and children?

HANCOCK.

parties, the courts, and powerful employers. But working people's organizations met their greatest obstacles with onset of the Panic of 1837 and the ensuing depression. Many labor radicals returned to the northern Democratic Party. Labor leaders gave up mass meetings to arouse support for social reform and concentrated their battles at the workplace. Efforts to organize unions, primarily of the unskilled, and to put decent wages into workers' pocketbooks became more prevalent than electoral struggles in the late 1830s.

The Panic of 1837

Although Jackson had tried to reduce the power of the national Bank and stem a rising tide of overextended credit by creating "pet banks" around the country, Americans continued to clamor for loans and credit to buy land and start businesses. The chartered state banks were able to respond to this public demand because large quantities of Mexican silver flowed into America from foreign trade and were dispersed into the state banks, thus creating new backup funds of "real and natural value." In the rush to get loans, citizens hardly noticed that their demand for ready cash outstripped the supply of silver, resulting in inflation. The newspapers noted only a few complaints when prices of real estate, food, and basic services rose rapidly by 1835. Southern planters paid little attention to the rising interest rates they paid on loans to purchase land and slaves. Speculators grabbed millions of acres of western land in 1835 and early 1836 with little more than flimsy pieces of bank paper.

Jackson did notice the inflation, however, and ordered legislation to restrict its feverish rise. In 1836 the Treasury Department issued a Specie Circular, which stipulated that land could be purchased only with gold or silver. Bankers in the Midwest and South curtailed loans in response to the order and called in outstanding debts. Struggling farmers and small planters began to feel pinched.

The impending disaster also had foreign causes. For years foreign—primarily British—investors had been pouring capital into northern transportation improvements and southern cotton expansion. But when the British economy fell on hard times by 1833, and its textile mills cut back on southern cotton imports, the international economy began to break down. Cotton prices fell and planters could not repay debts to state banks; the banks in turn faltered in their obligations to English creditors. Many southern banks closed their doors in early 1837.

In March, Van Buren took office. A month later, public fears about the country's financial stability spread to the northern states. Soon the panic set in. Merchants in New York and Philadelphia witnessed declining commerce; many declared bankruptcy. Average consumers and small investors flooded to the banks and demanded withdrawals of their savings in silver and gold, but the banks could not cover such demands and suspended specie payments. Eventually, the international and banking credit crisis reached small businesses, infant manufacturing, and farmers throughout the northern countryside. People could not pay their taxes, and cash was in such short supply that stores and toll ways closed. Public panic reached new heights when state governments announced that they could not finance bonds earmarked for canal building or their debts to private enterprises. British investors responded to the snowballing crisis by halting the flow of foreign credit into the American North.

The depression that overtook the country was worse than in any living American's memory. Prices rose steeply, store goods became scarce, unemployment skyrocketed in the cities, and farmers despaired of selling their surpluses to impoverished townspeople at any price. With little hope of recovery coming soon, the infant labor movement lost leverage with employers. Hysterical mobs of citizens banged on the closed doors of banks to recover their savings—to no avail. "The volcano has burst and overwhelmed New York," wrote Philip Hone, a wealthy Whig whose son lost a thriving business in 1837; then, there was a "dead calm . . . all is still as death. No business is transacted, no bargains made, no negotiations entered into . . . all is wrapped up in uncertainty."

These were bleak years for Americans everywhere. As businesses failed and eight hundred banks closed, thousands of city dwellers lived off their wits in the streets, and mobs broke open grocers' shops and flour mills to get food. Into the 1840s, Democrats charged Whigs with rushing into development and supporting dangerous speculation. Whigs charged Democrats with recklessly destroying the national Bank and the money system of the nation. The federal and state governments did little to help Americans, partly because government resources in those years were utterly inadequate to the great tasks of economic recovery, and partly because the nation lacked institutions to aid the bank directors, investors, and unemployed workers who had fallen into the doldrums.

The Election of 1840

The depression, which lasted until 1843, had a profound impact on politics. The Democratic Party won back the support of many workers, now unemployed, who left their fragile radical labor organizations and returned to the Jacksonians seeking protection of their declining living standards. At the same time, though, the party's "hard money" policies and attacks on national banking alienated other constituents during the deep crisis after 1837. Farmers in the Midwest and mid-Atlantic regions, and consumers everywhere, blamed "tight-fisted" Jacksonians for the foreclosures and shortages of goods. Others insisted that destroying the Second Bank of the United States had crushed important new internal improvements projects, and the Specie Circular's requirement of gold and silver to pay for land undermined the great republican promise to make western settlement possible for the average citizen. Whig politicians pointed out that Democrats had affirmed their commitment to less government involvement in people's lives just when it was most needed to lift them out of the depression.

Democratic president Martin Van Buren heightened public fears that shortages of money and goods might lead to a total collapse of the republic. In 1837, he proposed an Independent Treasury Act. As a long-time opponent of Jackson's "pet banks," which had held the redistributed government reserves of gold and silver in various states since 1833, Van Buren used his executive authority to call in all the federal government money in those banks. He then put it in a central treasury,

Election Scene in Cincinnati   During the 1840 election campaign, mass public meetings occurred across the country in support of the Democratic, Whig, and Liberty Parties. In Cincinnati, shown here in a local etching, Whigs put up a "triumphal arch" emblazoned with a banner
blending calls for universal white male suffrage and territorial expansion. Flags proclaimed "Protection to Industry, A Sound Currency, A Protective Tariff."   *(Cincinnati Museum Center.)*

where it was to sit unused. The act, though delayed, was finally passed in 1840 at the
end of Van Buren's presidency.

This was far from the kind of national banking that Whigs such as Clay and
Webster favored, and it became fuel for the presidential campaign that year. More-
over, "Van Ruin," as the Whig press called him, did nothing to protect citizens, as
the tariffs, improvements, and federal investments that Whigs promised with their
American System would have done. In 1840 the Whigs passed over the ambitious
Clay and nominated William Henry Harrison, a military hero of the Battle of
Tippecanoe and the War of 1812, who hailed from the heartland of Ohio. Virginian
John Tyler joined him on the ticket. With little substantial platform of his own,
Harrison nevertheless eagerly accepted his party's leadership. He also adopted the
Democratic style of appealing to popular culture to transmit political ideas. Using
mass outdoor meetings and popularizing fictitious images of Harrison living in a
simple log cabin, Whigs stumped enthusiastically across the nation. Thousands of
women, though unable to vote, flocked to meetings to hear the moral intonations

of Harrison's Whig supporters and organized political fundraising through their churches and benevolent societies. Whigs borrowed the language of the Democrats to reach "the common man" and concocted snappy slogans of their own, especially "Tippecanoe and Tyler Too."

The 1840 national election marked the first time in American history when two organized political parties appealed for the votes of a mass electorate. Although scholars have called the earlier rivalries between Federalists and Republicans the "First Party System," the leaders of those groupings neither recognized each other as permanent parties nor admitted to organizing campaigns to win over the electorate. By 1840, the electorate was far larger—a full 80.2 percent of adult white males voted that year—and the reading public far more eager to know what each party promised. Large crowds turned out to hear Whig and Democratic candidates, and a new conception of "constituencies" made the parties sensitive to demands of ordinary citizens. Through the years of controversy between Democrats and their opponents, eventually coalesced into the Whigs, a "Second Party System" had emerged.

Although the Whigs gained a majority in Congress as well as the White House, Harrison died of pneumonia within a month of his inauguration. His successor, John Tyler, was a former Democrat who supported states' rights and split from that party during the nullification crisis. As president, Tyler was only nominally a Whig, for he was critical of the American System's economic nationalism. He vetoed measures intended to create a Third Bank of the United States and raise tariffs, which prompted his own Whig Party to pass a congressional resolution that effectively expelled him from the party organization. Undaunted, Tyler went on to reject Whig proposals to raise the price of western land in order to generate national revenue. Instead, he supported Congress's Preemption Act of 1841, which permitted settlers to claim up to 160 acres freely and purchase it later at the low price of $1.25 an acre. Whig leaders in Congress and the northern states grew exasperated in the next couple of years when Tyler's western expansionist goals grew to include the annexation of Texas to the union. Few politicians disagreed with the assessment that Tyler acted more like a Democrat than a Whig.

CONCLUSION

The jostling crowds that cheered President Andrew Jackson's inauguration were rapidly leaving the world of Jefferson and Hamilton behind. Political parties had become acceptable vehicles for negotiating differences and policy reform. White men's right to vote, an inclusive political culture, and the nation's territory were all expanding. An emerging American identity celebrated ambitious, entrepreneurial, and individualistic activity. Jackson entered Washington with a solid popular mandate to democratize American political life, extend opportunities for development and prosperity, diminish the American System, and put more control of institutions in state and local hands. The Jacksonian experiment made important strides toward accomplishing these goals between 1829 and 1840. Even after 1840, Democrats continued to make room in their party for Irish and German immigrants in northern cities, poor farmers in the North and Midwest, small planters in the South, and

skilled and unskilled workers in cities and towns everywhere. And Democrats continued making their claims to be the party of expansive opportunity for white
males, of states' rights, and of an enlarged republic.

The social costs of these accomplishments were great, as the tensions over Indian
removal, tariffs and nullification, and banks attest. Moreover, the ideal of releasing
people from restraints and regulations had varied results. On one hand, it shrank the
government's authority over Americans' lives and paved the way for tremendous entrepreneurial activity. But on the other hand, it increased the gap separating privileged Americans from the vulnerable "common man," and from Indians and slaves.
Numerous dissenting working-class organizations and reform efforts arose to seek
redress of these growing inequalities. But few of them could withstand the panic and
depression that swept across the country for years starting in 1837.

For their part, the Whigs also contributed immensely to the American identity
emerging during these decades. Whigs reminded Americans that their ambitions
and fast-paced growth required checks; it needed control, order, regulation, and
morality. For decades after the Whig Party faded out of sight, what it stood for—
active federal support for internal development, protective tariffs, sales of national
lands to create federal revenues, and moral and social control of the disadvantaged
by the middle class—would be embodied in one or another major party. Clay's
American System lived on in new guises, overlaid with Jackson's praise for democracy, white men's territorial expansion, and occupational mobility. Years after the
Whigs' departure, Abraham Lincoln unabashedly identified with their political
goals. "The legitimate object of government," wrote Lincoln, "is 'to do for the people what needs to be done, but which they can not, by individual effort, do at all, or
do so well, for themselves.'"

SUGGESTED READINGS

Assessing the role of popular opinion and participation on the development of parties has
enjoyed a revival of interest in recent years. See especially Jean Baker, *Affairs of Party: The Political Culture of Northern Democrats in the Mid-Nineteenth Century* (1983); Kenneth Cmiel,
Democratic Eloquence: The Fight over Popular Speech in Nineteenth-Century America (1990);
and Harry Watson, *Jacksonian Politics and Community Conflict* (1981). Two somewhat older
works that tied the Second Party System closely to public sentiment and support are Ronald
Formisano, *The Birth of Mass Political Parties, 1827–1861* (1971), and Marvin Meyers, *The
Jacksonian Persuasion: Politics and Belief* (1957). A still older and, in its time path-breaking,
view of Jacksonians as rising entrepreneurs and urban artisans is Arthur Schlesinger, Jr., *The
Age of Jackson* (1945). Myers would later link Jacksonians to rural agrarian values.

For leadership and the party system, the best places to start are Merrill D. Peterson, *The
Great Triumvirate: Webster, Clay and Calhoun* (1987); Donald Cole, *The Presidency of Andrew Jackson* (1993); Richard Latner, *The Presidency of Andrew Jackson: White House Politics,
1829–1837* (1979); and Richard P. McCormick, *The Second American Party System* (1966).

Scholarship about Indian removal and reservation policies during this era is voluminous.
One of the older works that provides a useful overview is Grant Foreman, *Indian Removal:
The Emigration of the Five Civilized Tribes of Indians* (1953). For work that is strongly critical
of Jacksonian policies, see Robert Berkhofer, Jr., *The White Man's Indian: Images of the American Indian from Columbus to the Present* (1979); Angie Debo, *And Still the Waters Run: The*

Betrayal of the Five Civilized Tribes (1972); Michael Paul Rogin, *Fathers and Children: Andrew Jackson and the Subjugation of the American Indian* (1975); and Anthony F. C. Wallace, *The Long, Bitter Trail: Andrew Jackson and the Indians* (1993). Robert Remini's *Andrew Jackson and the Course of American Empire* (1977) is more sympathetic to the Democratic Party's western policies. J. Leitch Wright, Jr., in *Creeks and Seminoles* (1986), gives a wide-angled view of Indian life overall.

The best work on nullification is William Freehling, *Prelude to Civil War* (1966). For the bank wars of the Jacksonian years, see the following three works: John McFaul, *The Politics of Jacksonian Finance* (1972); James Roger Sharp, *The Jacksonians Versus the Banks: Politics in the United States After the Panic of 1837* (1970); and Peter Temin, *The Jacksonian Economy* (1965).

Rising alongside the Jacksonian persuasion was the Whig culture and party development, and this is treated most evenhandedly by both Maurice Baxter, *Henry Clay and the American System* (1995), and Daniel Walker Howe, *The Political Culture of the American Whigs* (1980). For cultural life during the Jacksonian years, start with the readable and engaging work by Paul Johnson, *A Shopkeeper's Millennium: Society and Revivals in Rochester, New York, 1815–1837* (1978); John F. Kasson, *Rudeness and Civility: Manners in Nineteenth-Century America* (1990); and Keith Melder, *Beginnings of Sisterhood: The American Women's Rights Movement, 1800–1850* (1977). On workingmen's parties and the urban economy, the best case study is Sean Wilentz, *Chants Democratic: New York City and the Rise of the American Working Class, 1788–1850* (1983). And the best one-volume sweeping synthesis of the era is Charles Sellers's *The Market Revolution: Jacksonian America, 1815–1846* (1991).

The Cherokee Nation Opposes Removal, 1830

Understandably, Native Americans often resisted removal from their homelands. In 1829, when the federal government approved policies to forcibly relocate the Cherokee from the Southeast to reservations west of the Mississippi River, tribal leaders delivered well-rehearsed speeches against such injustices. Following is one of their most forceful replies.

We are aware, that some persons suppose it will be for our advantage to remove beyond the Mississippi. We think otherwise. . . . Not an adult person can be found, who has not an opinion on the subject, and if the people were to understand distinctly, that they could be protected against the laws of the neighboring states, there is probably not an adult person in the nation, who would think it best to remove; though possibly a few might emigrate individually. There are doubtless many, who would flee to an unknown country, however beset with dangers, privation and sufferings, rather than be sentenced to spend six years in a Georgia prison for advising one of their neighbors not to betray his country. And there are others who could not think of living as outlaws in their native land, exposed to numberless vexations, and excluded from being parties or witnesses in a court of justice. . . . We are not willing to remove; and if we could be brought to this extremity, it would be not by argument, not because our judgment was satisfied, not because our condition will be improved; but only because we cannot endure to be deprived of our national and individual rights and subjected to a process of intolerable oppression.

We wish to remain on the land of our fathers. We have a perfect and original right to remain without interruption or molestation. The treaties with us, and laws of the United States made in pursuance of treaties, guaranty our residence and our privileges, and secure us against intruders. Our only request is, that these treaties may be fulfilled, and these laws executed.

But if we are compelled to leave our country, we see nothing but ruin before us. The country west of the Arkansas territory is unknown to us. . . . All the inviting parts of it, as we believe, are preoccupied by various Indian nations, to which it has been assigned. They would regard us as intruders, and look upon us with an evil eye. The far greater part of that region is, beyond all controversy, badly supplied with wood and water; and no Indian tribe can live as agriculturalists without these articles. All our neighbors, in case of our removal, though crowded into our near vicinity, would speak a language totally different from ours, and practice different customs. The original possessors of that region . . . have always been at war, and would be easily tempted to turn their arms against peaceful emigrants. Were the country to which we are urged much better than it is represented to be, and were it free from the objections which we have made to it, still it is not the land of our birth, nor of our affections. It contains neither the scenes of our childhood, nor the graves of our fathers. . . .

Andrew Jackson's Second Annual Message to Congress, 1830

Although in 1829 and 1830 many Americans raised strong voices against Jackson's calls for Indian removal, the president's annual address to Congress in December 1830 turned a deaf ear to such protests.

■■■ It gives me pleasure to announce to Congress that the benevolent policy of the Government, steadily pursued for nearly thirty years, in relation to the removal of the Indians beyond the white settlement is approaching to a happy consummation. Two important tribes [Choctaw and Chickasaw] have accepted the provision made for their removal at the last session of Congress, and it is believed that their example will induce the remaining tribes also to seek the same obvious advantages.

The consequences of a speedy removal will be important to the United States, to individual States, and to the Indians themselves. . . . It puts an end to all possible danger of collision between the authorities of the . . . governments on account of the Indians. It will place a dense and civilized population in large tracts of country now occupied by a few savage hunters. . . . [I]t will incalculably strengthen the southwestern frontier and render the adjacent States strong enough to repel future invasions without remote aid. . . . It will separate the Indians from immediate contact with settlements of whites; free them from the power of the States; enable them to pursue happiness in their own way and under their own rude institutions; will retard the progress of decay, which is lessening their numbers, and perhaps cause them gradually, under the protections of the Government and through the influence of good counsels, to cast off their savage habits and become an interesting, civilized, and Christian community. . . .

. . . I have endeavored to impress upon them my own solemn convictions of the duties and powers of the General Government in relation to the state authorities. For the justice of the laws passed by the states within the scope of their reserved powers they [the states] are not responsible to this government [the federal one]. As individuals we may entertain and express our opinions of their acts, but as a Government we have as little right to control them as we have to prescribe laws for other nations.

With a full understanding of the subject, the Choctaw and the Chickasaw tribes have with great unanimity determined to avail themselves of the liberal offers presented by the act of Congress, and have agreed to remove beyond the Mississippi River. Treaties have been made with them . . . and they have preferred maintaining their independence in the Western forests to submitting to the laws of the states in which they now reside. These treaties . . . give the Indians a liberal sum in consideration of their removal, and comfortable subsistence on their arrival at their new homes. . . .

Humanity has often wept over the fate of the aborigines of this country, and Philanthropy has been long busily employed in devising means to avert it, but . . . one by one have many powerful tribes disappeared from the earth. . . . [T]rue Philanthropy reconciles the mind to these vicissitudes as it does to the extinction of one generation to make room for another. . . . Philanthropy could not wish to see this continent restored to the condition in which it was found by our forefathers. What good man would prefer a country covered with forests and ranged by a few thousand savages to our extensive Republic, studded with cities, towns, and prosperous farms, embellished with all the improvements which art can devise or industry execute . . . ?

. . . The waves of population and civilization are rolling to the westward, and we now propose to acquire the countries occupied by the red men of the south and west by a fair exchange, and, at the expense of the United States, to send them to a land where their existence may be prolonged and perhaps made perpetual. . . . To better their condition in an unknown land *our* forefathers left all that was dear in earthly objects. Our children by thousands yearly leave the land of their birth to seek new homes in distant regions. . . . These remove hundreds and almost thousands of miles at their own expense, purchase the lands they occupy, and support themselves at their new homes from the moment of their arrival. . . .

And is it supposed that the wandering savage has a stronger attachment to his home than the settled, civilized Christian? Is it more afflicting to him to leave the graves of his fathers than it is to our brothers and children? Rightly considered, the policy of the General Government toward the red man is not only liberal, but generous. He is unwilling to submit to the laws of the States and mingle with their population. To save him from this alternative, or perhaps utter annihilation, the General Government kindly offers him a new home, and proposes to pay the whole expense of his removal and settlement.

Wholesale removal of peoples was not new in the 1830s. The earliest settlers had "removed" Indians to "reservations," and the British "removed" Acadians from their homeland during the turmoil of the Seven Years' War in the 1750s, some as far away as Louisiana. Jefferson, along with many statesmen and policymakers in the early republic, advocated removal of Native Americans on the grounds that the savage, dangerous frontier needed to be made safe for westward movement.

A few bold voices kept up the opposition to removal, including Protestant missionaries on the frontiers and Ralph Waldo Emerson, the transcendentalist philosopher and essayist. Emerson's speeches would arouse thousands of New Englanders against slavery in years to come. In 1830 his published letters to President Martin Van Buren reminded readers of the moral and legal wrongs of removal.

At the same time, the Seminole resisted encroachments on their lands violently. The Cherokee chose to use American courts to challenge alien political policies and lost their court battles. Once the reservation lands called the Indian Territory had been set aside across the Mississippi River, voices of protest faded. More and more Indian peoples were placed within its boundaries during the 1830s and 1840s.

Questions for Analysis

1. What words and phrases do the Cherokee people use to express opposition to removal? Is the language reminiscent of other contexts?

2. Review in this textbook other examples of people who had been removed from their homelands and compare the Cherokee, and the condition of removal, with these other groups.

3. Describe the national context in which removal took place. Why did Indian removal become such a pressing issue during the 1820s and 1830s?

4. Trace the Trail of Tears on the map on page 381, and speculate as to what the great distance from home and different geography might have meant to the Cherokee.

5. According to Jackson, how will removal be good for Indians? for Americans?

11

Industry and Reform in the North, 1820–1850

*I*n the spring of 1836, a "Horrid Murder" shook New York City. A twenty-three-year-old prostitute, Helen Jewett, was found axed to death in her bed; to hide the crime, her killer had set the room on fire. Educated, beautiful, and cultured, Jewett was well-known as a fun-loving "exceedingly fair and highly accomplished" courtesan who mingled with scores of the city's best-placed men of commerce and politics.

Richard Robinson, a young merchant's clerk who had come to New York from an upstanding Connecticut political family, had been seen frequently with Jewett at cultural events in the city. Because of his association with the prostitute, Robinson gained instant notoriety as the prime suspect in this "deed of darkness." Officers in the city's newly created police force arrested Robinson, questioned him, and escorted him to the dim and dank Bridewell prison. There were no other suspects.

Newspapers up and down the coastline, many only recently transformed from genteel weeklies into popular "penny press" dailies that battled for the attention of an eager public, carried the Jewett story for weeks into the summer of 1836. In fact, New York's *Sun, Transcript,* and *Herald* not only raced to typesetters day after day with each new breaking detail but became the arbiters of public opinion about this sensational crime.

At first New Yorkers were certain that Jewett had been brutally victimized. Friends told reporters that she mingled with respectable people, attended plays and public entertainments in the finest of imported clothing, and was "set apart" from the other women of waterfront brothels. But as the summer of 1836 wore on, reports in the popular press shifted from sympathy for Helen's plight to her supposed nature as a seductress. Some writers suggested that perhaps New York City was not a morally healthy place for so upstanding a citizen as Mr. Robinson. Perhaps, some reporters insisted, only "depraved minds" could revel in the details of so lurid a crime and conclude that a man of Robinson's stature was capable of an ax murder. Jewett, others began to write, was a "panderer of vice," a "dangerous" woman because of the very nature of her trade. Her character was suspect because of the public places she frequented. Hundreds of men each night were "beguiled" by the "winning smiles" of "ladies of the night," including Jewett.

Weeks of investigation revealed no new facts; no new public evidence pointed toward Robinson's actual innocence or guilt. But during 1836, the popular press mobilized a court of public opinion that subtly redirected guilt from Robinson to Jewett, and eventually a court acquitted Robinson. These were violent times, as the press kept reminding readers. Jewett's trade was one form of flagrant disregard for social propriety that major cities experienced regularly by the 1830s. In addition, gangs roamed freely in New York streets after dark; heavy drinking in public places led to frequent brawls; and the many laborers, sailors, and migrants passing through the city created an atmosphere of suspicion and tension.

Very uncommon things happened in this "Era of the Common Man" during which Helen Jewett met her fiery end. Both Jewett and Robinson reminded readers about the temptations and dangers of cities for the unfortunate poor and the unwary outsider. The pace of American life was not only quickening, it was also manifesting qualitative changes introduced by new technology, institutions, consumer goods, and relations in workplaces. As Americans crowded into coastal cities and spread into distant frontiers in unprecedented numbers, they were simultaneously exhilarated with feelings of opportunity and abundance, and disquieted with fears about deep and rapid change.

- How was northern life transformed during the 1820s to 1850s? Who welcomed new cultural and economic opportunities, and who resisted them?

- As industrialization unfolded in the North and upset social relations, how did the democratization of institutions and political culture continue to grow, and how did tensions among ethnic groups and social classes intensify?

- Who stepped forward to address the imperfections and unevenly distributed benefits of this developing northern society, and what kinds of reforms did they propose? What did these popular reform movements have in common with elite intellectual currents?

- In what ways was a distinctively American culture beginning to develop, despite regional, ethnic, class, and other differences?

This chapter will address these questions.

Immigration and Urbanization

Contests between Jacksonian and Whig persuasions grew out of fast-paced and deep-running changes in American life. From the 1820s to the 1840s, people in the North continued to experience those changes in sometimes unsettling ways. Politically and socially, they wrestled with how to address rapidly changing circumstances with institutional experiments. Immigration of new national groups introduced additional ethnic and religious distinctiveness throughout the older settled areas of the region, accompanied by tensions that both Jacksonians and Whigs needed to address. In addition, cities underwent an exciting—and sometimes frightening—degree of transformation in these same years. They not only made room for the cultures of new immigrants, but also became the centers of government and business institutions built by northern elites. At the same time, cities became laboratories of restructured working conditions in which the new material comforts of a rising middle-class arose beside unimagined crowding and poverty.

Old Cities and New

From the 1820s through the 1850s, New York City became America's largest metropolitan collection of people, and its most productive manufacturing city. At first glance, this claim seems far-fetched, for the city had few sources of fast-running water to power mills. Moreover, although the city had increasingly crowded living conditions, it did not have many large factories producing manufactured goods in massive quantities. New Yorkers had risen to prominence through commerce and for generations had imported cheap manufactures of daily goods from abroad.

Along with New York, Philadelphia, Boston, and Baltimore also grew by leaps and bounds during this era. More than a third of the people in the New England and mid-Atlantic regions lived in cities, the highest degree of urbanization in the country. Sustained by commerce and bolstered by milling and transportation services, these cities continued to expand. They became the nation's premier centers of credit and banking, importing and retailing, booming real estate development, and immigrant ghettoes. Although they were not yet centers of industrialization, these showcase cities nevertheless developed institutions and cultural life to complement their unprecedented economic vitality during these years.

One development that propelled coastal northern cities forward during these decades was the rapid rate of population growth in and around them. By the 1830s, huge influxes of immigrants arrived from England, Germany, and Ireland, along with a steady flow of rural people looking for a better chance after the disruptions of American and European revolutions and wars. Whereas fewer than 9,000 newcomers landed at American ports in 1820, about 23,000 came in 1830, and 84,000 in 1840. During the decade of the 1820s, about 129,000 people arrived from foreign countries; during the 1850s, the incoming tide rose to over 2.8 million newcomers (see graph page 408).

Chronology

1820s	Slater mill system spreads
1823	Boston Associates open Lowell mills
1826	American Society for the Promotion of Temperance founded
1827	Working Men's Party founded in Philadelphia
	Public schools movement emerges in Massachusetts
1830	Charles Grandison Finney preaches in Rochester
1833	The *New York Sun,* first penny paper, begins publication
1834	National Trades Union formed
	Female Moral Reform Society founded
1837	Panic begins
1841	Beecher publishes *Treatise on Domestic Economy*
1844	Mormon leader Joseph Smith killed
1847	New Hampshire passes first ten-hour-workday law
1848	Seneca Falls Convention for women's rights
	Oneida founded
1854	Thoreau publishes *Walden*

The influx of English continued throughout this era, especially during years of epidemic diseases and crippling crop failures. But by the 1830s, large numbers of Irish had also become conspicuous in northern American states as they fled unemployment and destitute poverty throughout their overpopulated country. In the next decade, this immigration into America swelled enormously when a blight struck three out of every four acres of Ireland's staple crops of potatoes, producing a famine that drove massive numbers of people out of the countryside. From 1847 to 1854, between 100,000 and 220,000 Irish entered America per year. Most came from tenant farming conditions, but few had the resources to buy even the cheapest land out West. As a result, the Irish crowded into tenement housing or, in the case of young men who migrated ahead of their families or came seeking their personal fortunes, followed the canal and railroad projects that cut into the countryside. Thousands of young Irish men stayed in eastern cities to work on the waterfronts or at unskilled labor, while young women sought work as domestic servants and seamstresses. Most were able to get only the worst-paying jobs, often unskilled and temporary. As Catholics and outsiders, the Irish overwhelmingly gravitated to the political umbrella of Jacksonian Democrats. In Boston, this political choice contrasted sharply with the Whig control of many city institutions and reinforced Irish

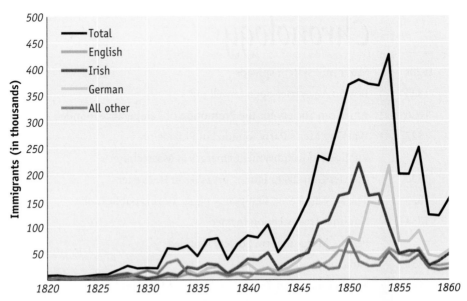

Immigration During the 1820s to 1850s Although large numbers of British and European peoples continued to come to America during the 1820s and 1830s, their numbers increased manifold by the mid-1840s due to political upheavals and economic hardships in many nations. Only with the return of relatively better times in the 1850s did immigration subside temporarily.   (Source: *Historical Statistics of the United States*, 1975 edition)

distinctiveness. In Boston, the Irish "East Enders" created a lively community, sustaining their separate religion and distinctive cultural ways. Their neighborhood raised funds to marry and bury residents who were penniless; nuns and priests of the Catholic Church attended to the health and educational needs of Irish families.

German immigration into America differed markedly from the Irish experience. For generations there had been a sizeable German population in Pennsylvania. By the 1830s, when difficult European conditions promoted a new wave of German immigration to America, established German-speaking communities were already in place. But most Germans during the 1830s and 1840s came on the return voyages of southern cotton and tobacco ships, and were thus dropped at the ports of New Orleans and Baltimore. From those places, many Germans ventured up the Mississippi River to St. Louis and points east along the Ohio River. A large number of Germans crossed into Texas, where they obtained a land grant from Mexico. Unlike the Irish coming at the same time, Germans arrived with money or valuables needed to set up farms and shops. In addition, German families carried numerous skills into their new lives in the midwestern settlements. In and around St. Louis, Cincinnati, San Antonio, Chicago, and Milwaukee, Germans made a considerable mark on cuisine and culture. Thousands of German families took advantage of declining land prices to acquire prosperous farms.

Sustained heavy immigration contrasted starkly with the declining birthrate of older resident American families. By the 1820s, most American-born women bore fewer than the formerly typical eight children. By the 1850s, they bore on average only five, while at the same time over 300,000 people came to America per year until the Civil War impeded the flow temporarily during the 1860s. By then, Americans noticed two salient characteristics of these trends: a great proportion of the American population was foreign-born—nearly 20 percent—and the immigrant and native populations together were incredibly young. In the crowded urban centers of New York and Philadelphia, 50 percent of the population were under sixteen.

Some visitors to American coastal cities felt overwhelmed by the crowded confusion of burgeoning populations that clamored for goods and services. Others joined the more optimistic observers who sought ways to harness the energy of growing populations (see Competing Voices, page 442). Hard work, proliferating new businesses, and rising consumer demand for basic necessities would avert the entrenched poverty and periodic famines of Europe. Bakers, builders, tailors, leather workers, toolmakers, and many other trade groups both hired the new population and satisfied its demand for goods.

Frontier Cities

Beyond America's oldest settled areas, Great Lakes cities such as Rochester, Buffalo, and Chicago, and river cities such as Cincinnati, St. Louis, and Columbus, became the focal points of booming manufacturing and transportation services for America's vast rural population of grain and meat producers. Ambitious people in coastal areas took advantage of their prize locations near superb waterways and deep bays, as well as their connections to consumers and merchant exporters, to expand their ties to the interior. Although Illinois had been remote from Americans' imagination and development plans during the century's early decades, Chicago became the greatest midwestern city by the late 1850s. Not industrial development, but rather distribution and transportation services, turned that old Indian trading town into an overnight wonder. Farmers and ranchers came to Chicago's markets and stores from hundreds of miles away; railroad workers settled down near Chicago when they were laid off at this western terminus; insurance brokers and shopkeepers enjoyed steadily rising business in this booming region.

Out on the Ohio River, Cincinnati (see page 328) continued to bustle and boom, becoming the country's third-largest industrial center by 1840. Key to the city's rapid rise were its varieties of opportunity for manufacturing and the adaptability of its entrepreneurs to many kinds of work. Through midcentury, most young people in Cincinnati still labored in small shops using tools that would have been familiar to colonial artisans in metal trades and food processing. But blacksmiths, for example, while still providing horseshoes and chains, also added machine parts and huge carriage wheels to their regular product lines. And about one-fifth of Cincinnati's working population, which was increasingly German and Irish, made their primary living by work in factories. Skilled craftsmen in the furniture business, for example, still finished chairs and sofas, but machines increasingly helped them cut, bore, and plane the wood frames. Too, entrepreneurs began to reorganize factories so that skilled craftsmen no longer handled the entire production process, but instead specialized as upholsterers, carpenters, or finishers.

In both cases—adapting to machine technology or retooling as specialists—craftsmen earned decent pay. The same was not always true for Cincinnati's unskilled recent migrants, who were taken into the meatpacking and sewing industries for periods of time, given low wages, and turned out of employment when business slowed. In their households, wives and daughters supplemented family incomes by taking outwork making "men's rough clothes." They were paid by the piece, earning barely enough to put another meal on the table after hours bent over a needle.

Rich and Poor

Who enjoyed the new goods and services cities offered? This Era of the Common Man was, in fact, one of widening distinctions among Americans. Nowhere was this clearer than in northern cities, where in 1830 the top 1 percent of New Yorkers held 40 percent of the total wealth; the top 4 percent held 75 percent. Boston and Philadelphia approximated these figures, too. Each northern city had its few families who rose "from rags to riches," from modest means as wage earners or from distressed immigrant status to eminent stature in the elite. The complex of mill operations at Waltham, Massachusetts, depended on the investments of a few tightly knit families whose fortunes came from shipping services. Anson Phelps, whose ships carried cotton for southern exporters during the 1820s and 1830s, invested a commercial fortune in iron mines, forges, and rolling mills in Pennsylvania and Connecticut. John Jacob Astor arrived in New York from Germany in 1784 with little in his pockets; by exploiting the western fur trade and city real estate markets, he had become the wealthiest man in America by the time he died in 1848.

These fortunes, however, represented a tiny proportion of northern Americans. Far more numerous by the 1840s were the "middling sort" of somewhat less affluent businessmen, merchants, artisans, and successful immigrants who benefited from opportunities for advancement during the era. Most had adapted quickly to the depression conditions of the late 1830s, or had never invested wildly to begin with. This growing section of the population included new managers, tellers, brokers, insurance agents, and medical and legal "experts." Hundreds of former artisans in every northern city put on white collars to go to work each day by the 1840s, and their numbers grew steadily. Meanwhile, the elite of major cities remained committed to marrying and forming business alliances among themselves, in efforts to protect "dilution [of their class] by the rising shopkeepers."

The homes of wealthy and middle-class people in cities changed dramatically between the 1790s and 1840s. By the latter decade, families of modest incomes could enjoy iron cook stoves, rugs and window coverings that gave warmth and comfort, tubs in which to bathe with plenty of soap, and oil lamps and cheap candles for illumination. The increasing manufacture of textiles, soap, bread, and other necessities outside the home enhanced the household mistress's role as a consumer rather than a producer. By the 1820s to 1840s, middling housewives also aspired to hire domestic servants to take over the routine sweeping, scrubbing, polishing, sewing, cooking, and other chores of their households. According to popular advice manuals, the "perfect home" would be a bustling scene of servants working under the supervision of a "truly republican" middle-class household mistress.

By midcentury, the sewing machine was beginning to change one of women's ceaseless forms of toil: producing family clothing and linens. Sewing machines, invented by Elias Howe and Isaac Singer, not only reduced the amount of time it took to make necessary items, they also spread interest in fashion, which began to change more frequently. Although most homemakers did not themselves own sewing machines before the late 1800s, ready-made clothing fell in price as it came closer to being mass-produced. First imports, then American-manufactured outerwear, became cheap enough for most families to have a few outfits. Quilts became more decorative and elaborate in design, whether made at home or purchased. However, the sewing machine became a curse for many young women and spinsters who earned a living finishing textiles manufactures. Manufacturers preferred to set up the machines in shops, where work discipline replaced the sociability and convenience of outwork at home.

Most urban residents were poor. Despite the flow of people to the frontier and job opportunities provided by proliferating development projects, large numbers of people remained in cities who did not fare well. Travelers at the end of the colonial

Woman with Singer Sewing Machine   The Singer sewing machine, patented in 1851, dramatically changed the way women produced clothing and fabric household items. The machine's continuous and rapid stitching was first adapted to factory production of ready-made clothing for men and women, but soon it became a highly desirable commodity in middle-class households.   *(Private Collection.)*

era had marveled at the relative absence of persistent poverty and the apparently small gap in wealth between rich and poor. By the 1840s, however, visitors to northeastern cities gasped at the poverty of waterfront and tenement areas. Modern scholars estimate that by 1840, the top 5 percent of the population in large cities owned about two-thirds of all the wealth, with about 15 percent of artisans attaining somewhat prestigious positions as shop owners, small importers, or mill managers. But 50 to 70 percent of artisans and immigrants could barely make ends meet.

The urban poor usually lived in the rapidly rising new tenements of old urban neighborhoods. In contrast to the wealthy, who were relocating to the nation's first true suburbs, most city residents could not afford to pay to have water pumped from local rivers through the city's wooden pipe system. Water for drinking, cooking, bathing, and cleaning was only one essential item that proved difficult and costly to obtain. Most of the poor in the city also foraged outside their neighborhoods for fuel and daily food. Owning a home was beyond the means of most workingmen's families, and beyond the housing supply of most cities. About two-thirds of the average laborer's wages went to feed his family. If he was unfortunate enough to lose a job, or worked only occasionally, his wages would not even stretch far enough to provide food. In those cases, other family members took jobs carrying dirt and stones, hauling lumber, or mucking out horse stalls; some sold vegetables from small family gardens or scavenged through the alleys. Winters often forced families into charity shelters or workhouses.

While elite neighborhoods became elaborate arenas for carriage drives, flowering gardens, and grand parties, the tenement districts of northern cities decayed alarmingly. Many tenements, lacking running water and seldom heated, crammed ten or more people into each one-room apartment. Tiny shacks filled alleys behind shops, and large families squeezed into the basements or garrets of already-full tenements. Public officials hired to investigate the conditions of New York City's Corlaers Hook neighborhood found "hideous squalour and deadly effluvia, the dim, undrained courts oozing with pollution, the dark, narrow stairways, decayed with age, reeking with filth, overrun, with vermin; the rotted floors, ceilings begrimed and often too low to permit you to stand upright; the windows stuffed with rags . . . gaunt, shivering forms and wild ghastly faces, in these black and beetling abodes."

Large communities of free African-Americans rooted themselves in northern cities, but their living conditions often were difficult. Philadelphia had the largest free African-American community, about 22,000, by the 1820s, but all cities attracted families and individuals looking for education and job opportunities. Although in terms of wages and lifestyles, few free African-Americans ever attained the comforts of urban middle-class whites, notable achievements marked the 1820s to 1840s, including thriving networks of black newspapers and circular bulletins, lending libraries, and Baptist and African Methodist Episcopal (AME) churches. Black communities developed intricate social means of absorbing runaway slaves and recently manumitted freedmen into the strangeness of urban freedom.

But the law did not recognize equal rights and citizenship for freedmen. In addition to suffering disenfranchisement (see page 368), free African-Americans who excelled at an occupation often were victimized by resentful white workers. And the generalized view of African-American inferiority proved an insurmountable obstacle for many struggling families. Often denied access to jobs, white schools, and the protection of civil institutions, African-Americans reinforced neighborhood and kinship networks of self-help and protection. For blacks, segregated housing and exclusion from public buildings became the norm in northern cities.

Order and Disorder

The pace of change and the obvious inequalities in the North's urban environment erupted into violence of many kinds during the mid-1800s. Fathers, whether they suffered from job stress, status anxiety, or alcohol abuse, did not always live up to the era's expectations for an affectionate, well-ordered family. Mothers at home sometimes cracked under the pressure of both working for wages and managing all the household chores in cramped living quarters. Even women who enjoyed the labor of servants sometimes could not withstand the accompanying pressure to exhibit republican moral perfection.

Domestic violence and the chaos of crowded tenement life spilled out onto the streets with growing frequency, too. By the late 1820s, theatergoers noticed a marked increase in outbursts of violence during and after performances, and within a few years the "respectable crowds" of middle- and upper-class attendees established separate theaters from those of the rowdy lower class. Raucous amusements on the waterfronts or in lower class-neighborhoods—including circuses sporting exotic animals, feats performed on horseback, wrestling, and wild dancing—frequently became sites of crime. Taverns that served as places to congregate for gossip and sociability saw their share of commotion as the night wore on. Orphan gangs and young men's clubs in rough neighborhoods fought over space to play sports or simply linger. Groups of single males, and sometimes of females, banded together temporarily to lash out at targeted officials or institutions. The popular press fed a growing public hunger for lurid details about "horrid murders," labor strikes, sailors' brawls on the docks, and "shocking drunken rages." Only a few writers pointed out that elite members of society also resorted to violence at times, as when congressmen engaged in fistfights in the revered halls of government. More commonly, observers were preoccupied with the activities of the "dangerous classes" at the bottom of the social ladder.

Racial and ethnic differences fueled the tensions in northern cities. In the late 1820s, Boston erupted frequently in nightlong rioting between immigrant Irish and American-born populations, or between white working-class youths and African-Americans. In 1829 in Cincinnati, white rioters, in response to rumors of generalized southern emancipation, descended on free African-Americans who owned homes and shops and drove the majority of them out of town. The Cincinnati riots reflected the atmosphere in most new states west of the Alleghenies. White westerners, eager to overturn the prohibitions in the Northwest Ordinance against slavery (see pages 258–259), also talked about removing all African-American people from those states. Perhaps because of its large African-American community, Philadelphia became the worst center of race rioting. Almost yearly, mobs attacked some part of the black community, and repeated acts of personal violence marked city life from 1820 to 1850. A violent race riot involving hundreds of Philadelphians convulsed the city in "fiendish brutality" for nearly a week in 1834. The mounted state militia restored order only with difficulty. In the ensuing investigations, arrested rioters vented their resentment against African-Americans who competed for scarce jobs, a common grievance in northern ports. Remarkably, in 1835 white and African-American workers protested together for shorter working hours in Philadelphia and New York City.

Only in the 1830s did the middle class of northern cities begin to establish a few of the professional institutions associated with keeping public order. The colonial system of rotating responsibility for the night watch among citizens, or occasionally appointing constables, could not deal adequately with these explosions of violence. Without systems of law enforcement, cities of the early republic had little or no means to investigate crime. In New York City, citizens who volunteered to keep order chose only to aid the infirm and give street directions to strangers, fleeing at the hint of unruliness. In some quieter coastal towns, constables gradually took on the duty of inspecting suspicious situations and entering buildings to arrest criminals or deliver court orders. In 1833 the city of Philadelphia hired a few policemen to patrol the streets, but in the face of angry mobs, they were helpless.

When New York authorities called out armed militia to suppress disorder, mobs often broke down the authority of such a volunteer force by winning over militiamen who had neighbors or relatives in the crowd. The result, all too often, was chaos in the streets, escalated violence, and more deaths. Starting in 1845, New York's city government finally created a professional police force that held itself more aloof from the grievances of people in the street. A paid, trained, and uniformed presence reinforced the distance of policemen from ordinary people. By the 1850s, most city governments had created police forces of their own.

The Accelerating Industrial Experiment

At an 1833 "Exhibition of American Manufactures," rural storekeepers and laboring Philadelphians ogled at more than seven hundred articles of every conceivable kind, a cross-section of the manufacturing that was flourishing in the Northeast after 1820. Along with textiles in an array of textures and patterns, there were fine-fashioned tea sets, porcelains, cabinets and chairs, and clocks. New power machinery demonstrated how, in the corridor stretching from New England to Maryland, entrepreneurs processed wheat, timber, and leather into useful commodities. Exhibits showcased goods from paper mills that sprang up all around Philadelphia, and from the iron and metalware foundries that clustered around mining and transportation networks in New Jersey, Maryland, and Pennsylvania.

Northern Americans were poised to begin their industrial revolution during these decades. Industrial experiments would begin in both coastal cities and the agricultural hinterlands. Ambitious entrepreneurs everywhere used the familiar ingredients of water, wood, and human muscle to build and power new laborsaving machines, inventing contraptions that brought together new groups of laborers or created the need for new skills. Many observers marveled at the increasing pace of goods moving through the countryside, coaches roaring through city streets, and mail traveling to distant correspondents. Wonderful new goods lined storekeepers' shelves. Others, however, noticed that along with early industrialization came considerable upheaval in the ways Americans worked and lived together.

Coastal and Frontier Farming

From the 1820s to the 1850s, the majority of working men still labored hard on the soil as heads of rural households. But New England's poor soil and diminishing farm size continued to encourage migration westward. By the 1830s, more and more families journeyed farther and farther west to settle land that offered greater yields. "The grass out here [in Michigan]," wrote one young man to his mother back in Vermont, "is greener, higher, and makes the cattle all grow bigger."

Families who chose to stay in New England, New York, and Pennsylvania accelerated changes in farming technologies and cultivation strategies that began in a previous generation. By the 1840s, farm families fertilized and rotated crops more than ever. They plowed deeper in order to churn up rich new soil, and they gave up their traditional scythes for more efficient cradles to harvest grains. New journals taught them how to be "scientific farmers," while skilled woodworkers and blacksmiths sold their skills for wages at neighbors' farms, sometimes for a season and sometimes under contract for a year. These "by-employments" provided important supplemental cash income for struggling families.

Northern farm families also continued to produce more and more for growing local markets in nearby cities and towns. A shipment of milk, eggs, and fruits on the Erie Canal might prove stale when it reached city consumers, but deliveries from farms just five miles out of town provided variety and freshness. Consumers in Philadelphia counted on the produce of adjacent Lancaster and Chester Counties, as well as of New Castle County in Delaware; farmers' wagons crushed together on city streets during market mornings. Likewise, Long Island and Hudson River valley farmers delivered hundreds of loads of food to New York City weekly. Once railroads created fast transportation between East and West, distant farmers shipped durable fruits and vegetables to cities: peaches from Delaware, apples from western New York, onions and greens from the mid-Atlantic.

The lives of northern farm women did not change as quickly as the lives of urban and immigrant women who worked for wages in other people's homes and shops. Farm wives and daughters still spun wool, churned butter, prepared meals and preserved foods for the future, tended gardens and helped press cider, threshed wheat, and collected fuel wood. But in areas that lay near roads and canals, or within rapidly growing eastern counties, change became apparent. Once cheaper imports of cloth and household implements became available, women could devote more time to making marketable goods that brought in household cash, including butter and cheese for sale in town markets. Young women around Pittsburgh took homemade butter to storekeepers who stocked bolts of cloth, sugar, iron kettles, and other desirable goods. When the storekeeper's barrels filled with butter, he hauled them to Philadelphia markets, where an array of imported clocks and mirrors, as well as local craftsmen's cabinets and shoes, enticed "country buyers" thinking of their female customers back home. Indeed, these marketing trips drew women into active public exchanges on a scale that had been discouraged by supporters of women's "separate sphere."

Farming on the frontiers of the Old Northwest Territory, beyond the Appalachian ridge, took on its own distinctive characteristics as the area became heavily settled between the 1820s and 1850s. Families along the Ohio River specialized in corn and pork production by the 1820s and developed links to southern plantation buyers. In the next two decades, new waves of migrants flooded into Ohio, Indiana, and Illinois. They tended to follow the transportation improvements that tied them to more easterly markets, which demanded more wheat than corn and pork. On the heels of a third wave of migration during the 1840s, farmers on the frontier of southern Wisconsin, eastern Iowa, and southern Michigan provided huge quantities of wheat to hungry city dwellers.

An important attraction luring pioneers into these new frontiers was the availability of land and its declining price. In 1836 public land sales reached an all-time high of nearly 20 million acres, much of it acquired in the Old Northwest Territory. Settlers could purchase eighty acres of government land for about a hundred dollars. Thousands of young men borrowed from fathers, kinsmen, and banks to acquire their "stake." If they did not have cash left over for tools, household goods, seed, and animals, farmers could rent from well-endowed landowners. Tenancy, after all, had long been the best stepping-stone toward improvement and possibly even independent farm ownership. Hired itinerant laborers soon became another regular feature of western settlements. In fact, scholars estimate that tenants and itinerant laborers made up at least 25 percent of the western rural population. This proportion roughly equaled that in the Northeast. However, in the older states, landless men tended to experience downward mobility, whereas landless men on the new midwestern frontier could still hope to succeed.

Although such prosperity came to some frontier families, many trans-Appalachian migrants persevered through years of hardship. Crop failures and bankruptcies took their toll, as did lack of medicine in the unhealthy spring thaws or enough warm clothing in the brutal mid-Western winters. But slowly, second-generation frontier families improved their lots. Log cabins with a single room in which to eat, cook, sleep, and produce family necessities in time gave way to slightly larger and more comfortable clapboard dwellings. Gradually, with traditional hand tools and weary animals that were shared by whole neighborhoods, settlers cleared lots from the woods. Fences—building them and repairing them—occupied even more time than they had in colonial years, but eventually pioneers could hold the wolves at bay.

Transportation, Communication, Invention

America was still very much a commercial nation in the 1820s and 1830s. In addition to intricate coastal and Caribbean networks of importing and exporting, merchants plied the Atlantic highway with cargo ships, and numerous new packet lines carried passengers great distances. The Black Ball Line between New York City and Liverpool, for example, moved thousands of travelers and their belongings each year. By 1845, fifty-two trans-Atlantic packets offered similar services. "Square-riggers" ran on regular schedules from New York; others touched at Savannah, New Orleans, Charleston, and St. Augustine. That same year, the first clipper ship, *Rainbow,* took to the seas with its long, narrow hull and great spans of sail. For two decades, clippers moved people and goods faster than ever imagined, on both the Atlantic and the Pacific, and captured the imaginations of journalists and novelists worldwide. Only after the Civil War would Americans give up the glamour of the clipper ship for the greater cargo space and durability at sea of the steamship. A joint venture in 1838 of the British and American Steamship Navigation Company tried to traverse the Atlantic by steam navigation, but into the 1850s transatlantic steamships retained their sails as a backup.

In addition to international commerce, many Americans also attached the word *commerce* to the energetic transformation of the countryside. The transportation revolution (discussed in Chapter 9) was moving people and goods at unprecedented speeds, simultaneously linking and segmenting regions of the nation. By the 1820s, some writers even put internal commerce above foreign trade, as when a Pennsylvania governor insisted that "foreign commerce is a good" undertaking, "but of a secondary nature, [for] happiness and prosperity must be sought for within the limits of our own country." Americans shifted their focus not only from

Clipper Ship Card: *W. B. Dinsmore* With its sleek hull and legions of sails, the swift clipper ship commanded much of the passenger and cargo travel along the East Coast, into the West Indies, and as this advertisement boasts, to San Francisco during the 1840s. Faster and safer than most long-distance overland travel (the express package carriage in this view was also common in America during the era), clippers also "outran" steam vessels and became the fastest mode of transport to the West Coast during the Gold Rush. *(Museum of the City of New York.)*

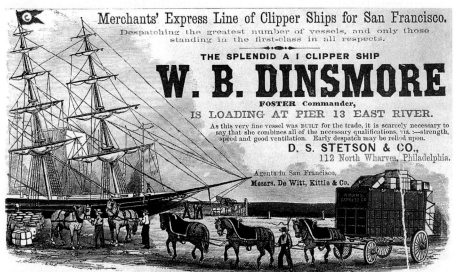

external to internal commerce, but also from skepticism about the effects of commerce to a celebration of its transformative powers. Even the ardent southerner John C. Calhoun had exulted in 1817 that commerce would "bind the republic together," and indeed by the 1820s, hundreds of canal ditches and turnpikes threaded through the American countryside. On rivers, goods and people could move against downstream currents at unimaginable speeds of 10 to 20 miles per hour.

In the momentum building toward industrialization, developers and inventors strengthened their partnership with local, state, and national governments to accomplish projects that had widespread consequences. For example, Samuel F. B. Morse spent years tinkering with devices to send coded messages over long distances. But until he received federal government funds as capital for equipment and workers' wages, Morse was unable to prove his vision. When, in 1844, Morse completed the first telegraph line and sent a message over wire from Washington to Baltimore, the public marveled at such "instantaneous communication." In the past, it had taken days to send commercial reports from New York merchants to Charleston shippers, or to let folks in Boston know the outcome of policy deliberations in Washington. The telegraph transmitted such news at once, allowing it to reach millions of Americans. Within a few months, plans unfolded for connecting the Northeast to other regions with Morse code.

Improvement and invention—supported by government funds, eager manufacturers, and ready consumers everywhere—often began in the North and spread quickly to other regions. Manufacturers in Boston and New York adapted French food preserving techniques to airtight "tin cans" that began to replace glass containers in the 1820s. Northern retailers carried Gail Borden's condensed milk in cans by the late 1830s. The John Deere steel plow, which made its appearance in 1837, speeded the cultivation of new land. Down in Virginia, Cyrus Hall McCormick perfected his "grain cutter," or reaper, a horse-drawn machine that enabled a farmer to harvest ten times more wheat per day. As soon as he patented the reaper in 1834, northern manufacturers began to market it. By the late 1840s, Midwestern wheat farmers were buying McCormick's reapers as quickly as they could be produced. The cast iron stove replaced fireplace cooking and changed northern middle-class women's daily routines forever.

"We live in a most extraordinary age," wrote Daniel Webster in 1825. "Events so various and so important that might crowd and distinguish centuries, are, in our times, compressed within the compass of a single life." As another observer put it, "Every man seems born with some steam engine within him, driving him into an incessant and restless activity of body and mind." Each person, he wrote, seems to be involved with "a thousand projects, and only one holiday—the 4th of July—working from morning till night with the most intense industry."

The railroad captured Americans' relentless pursuit of improvement more than any other innovation during this era. During the 1820s, engineers and politicians in the East set out to "tame and transform" the countryside and tie coastal cities to backcountry regions without reliable waterways. In 1828 the Baltimore and Ohio Railroad laid 13 miles of track; by the end of 1831, the entire country boasted just 73 miles. But in the early 1830s, Charleston merchants funded a plan to link their business to Hamburg, Georgia. Other lines were spreading out from Boston. By 1840, 3,000 miles of track stretched most of the length of the Northeast, and another 5,000 miles linked internal settlements to the coastline during the 1840s. By 1860, Americans traveled on 30,000 miles of railroad bed, much of it forming a spider web of connections linking New England and New York to the Old Northwest; rail lines linked Boston, Albany, Buffalo, Philadelphia, Wheeling, St. Louis, and Pittsburgh.

Until the late 1850s, canals continued to carry more goods—and more safely—through northern and midwestern regions than railroads did. Most rail lines serviced local areas for short distances and ran on their own gauges (the width between the rails). Varied gauges meant that goods and people had to be transferred from one train to another if the distance to be covered spanned more than one line, which proved expensive for shippers and consumers alike. In addition to this inconvenience, the iron straps holding down wooden rails often snapped loose and shot up through the thin floors of passenger cars. Fires that started in wood-burning engines or from stray hot coals caused much shrieking when clothing and luggage ignited.

Still, railroads stimulated iron companies to produce rails and employed craftsmen to provide skilled wood and metal work. Immigrants quarried the stone for rail beds and moved with construction crews to lay new rail or to transport supplies to frontier work sites. Indeed, by the 1850s, there was no mistaking the cultural and economic impact of the "iron horse." Not the Erie Canal, but the railroad boosted Chicago from a sleepy village to a boomtown during that decade. Many thriving river towns faded from prominence as flatboat transportation was replaced by the roar and smoke of trains that joined newer settlements elsewhere. Wealthy Americans who had made fortunes in commerce, lending, or real estate poured their capital into railroad development, and eager foreign investors purchased nearly 25 percent of the bonds that funded U.S. railroad construction.

Exciting Trial of Speed   As this view of the locomotive "Tom Thumb" shows, one of the first steps toward developing railroads involved attaching a tiny soot-belching brass steam engine to a passenger carriage, which sped down the rails at a full eighteen miles per hour. Not everyone would hail the demise of horse-drawn transportation in 1830 when Tom Thumb appeared, but in the next three decades, governments and private entrepreneurs together funded construction of thousands of miles of railroad track.   *(Museum of the City of New York.)*

Before the Civil War, local and state governments throughout the North and Old Northwest also provided a major stimulus for railroad construction. Politician-businessmen enthusiastically aided railroad development, just as they had promoted canals and turnpikes in the previous generation, by favoring special laws of incorporation, loopholes in tax legislation, and incentives to underwrite development bonds, or by giving direct loans to groups of developers. State and federal governments gave valuable land bounties that totaled nearly 20 million acres by the eve of the Civil War and many millions more in years thereafter.

Northern Labor

Until the early 1800s, most Americans believed that regular labor was reserved for society's middle class and "lower sort." Gentlemen aspired not to work. But the growing political culture and the rapidly changing social structure in America evoked new thinking: working at a useful occupation became a requirement for virtue and goodness in a person. Inventors and developers received public acclaim, and politicians seeking high offices in the North shed their associations with leisure and gentlemanly status, donning the mantle of "an honest working man." Happiness, argued clergymen and politicians, came from industriousness. Speeches and outpourings in newspaper articles insisted that the future belonged not to the "idle wealthy" but rather to the "industrious laboring people," which would include laborers, craftsmen, professionals, intellectuals, and often merchants.

No doubt, some independently wealthy gentlemen claimed to be hard-working only to gain the hearts and minds of voters. But the new attitude nevertheless supported dramatically changing structures of work in the North from the 1820s through the 1850s. At the beginning of this era, over two-thirds of the clothing and shoes, blankets and linens, and processed foods consumed in the North still came from households relatively nearby. In the next decades, however, new technologies, new forms of business organization, and new ways of doing work accelerated and expanded processes that had only begun in the early years of the century. Rising entrepreneurs and ambitious investors began to reorganize the traditional craft shops that dotted the rural landscape. A new breed of "mechanics," or semiskilled workers with extensive practical knowledge, entered every niche of bustling northern life. Tinkerers, improvers, and gentlemen changed this or that small part of a work process, slowly altering old ways of producing after many little experiments with primarily wooden materials.

Most Americans still believed that the ideal setting for these transformations was the countryside. As Jeffersonians had warned for years, cities brought crowding, poor health, and temptations to do evil; manufacturing in cities would only exacerbate these tendencies. Most commentators regarded factories with suspicion, not as places of exciting opportunity. Even workers in the early factories tended to think of themselves as temporary wage earners who would soon leave. In addition, entrepreneurs required moving water to power machinery and transport goods, as well as timber for fuel and construction, both of which were plentiful in myriad rural locations. And since these early "manufactories" remained small handicraft shops with five to ten workers, owners did not yet have to be concerned about recruiting great pools of labor from urban immigrant neighborhoods.

Even in the largest northern cities, factories were still rare before the 1840s. More often, the rapidly growing immigrant neighborhoods became the source of workers in the putting-out system (see page 335). Working for a pittance in garret shops, basements, unlit apartments, and even on rooftops, immigrants and poor native-born Americans accepted pieces of cut fabric from "bosses," who subdivided the work into "bits and parts" throughout the neighborhood. While they watched children, mothers sewed pieces of precut cotton fabric into shirts or petticoats. Girls and boys sat for hours stitching the leather uppers of shoes and then delivered them back to shops where men pieced the tops onto soles. In growing northern cities, this putting-out system eroded workers' ability to see unshaped materials slowly become a useful article.

Entrepreneurs in this system controlled the raw materials, made decisions about how to break down the work, and determined the piecework pay rates. Although bosses touted the convenience for women of working in their homes at traditional needle arts, piece-rates were always appallingly low, and bosses could withhold work when markets were slow or dump inhuman amounts of sewing on young people. In addition, putting out this piecework undermined artisan shops and hastened the demise of the apprenticeship system in northern cities, a trend foretold in Lynn, Massachusetts. Traditional skilled craftsmen who made an entire pair of shoes, a range of iron products for farming, or complete wooden tools and butter churns relinquished work to entrepreneurs who subdivided their trades among women and children in homes. Masters who once worked side by side with apprentices had to adapt or close shop. Between 1820 and 1850, weavers, silversmiths, cabinetmakers, shoemakers, tailors, shirt makers, and other craftsmen in northern cities watched helplessly as their old ways of life faded.

Disruption of the apprenticeship system contributed to the second very consequential development for workers in this era: the breakdown of paternalistic social relations in traditional crafts. In their place, the widespread introduction of wages marked a shift toward "free labor" social relations. Wage workers had the right to seek work wherever they could find it and to leave a job without breaking obligations to a master. Employers stipulated a wage at the time of hire, in addition to work rules and hours; in time, they took less responsibility for the living arrangements and moral conduct of workers. At first, these changes seemed to offer men, women, and even children a measure of the independence that all republican citizens deserved, and to clarify the value of a worker's time and skills applied to a job. Moreover, free labor implied the antithesis of the coercion inherent in slavery. Republican thought held that all white male citizens had a right to decent employment. Free labor was the mutual commitment by employers and workers, which, as one prominent labor leader explained, "decency required should be a living wage" from the employer in return for "faithful execution of the

Shoemakers, 1850s Daguerreotype Perhaps surmising that their small craftsman's shops would be eclipsed by factories and large businesses before long, these shoemakers proudly evoke the era rapidly fading from view. Their clothing—although probably cleaner and in better condition than during regular work—places them among humble working people, as do their tools and finished leather products. *(Library of Congress.)*

tasks" of a job by workers. Claims to freedom could have meaning only because they were morally binding.

It was a small step to extend the meaning of free labor from personal mobility and individual rights to include significant social values. Northerners who lionized the honest workingman celebrated the value of hard work, self-discipline, abstinence from drinking, and the absence of personal debt or obligations to others. Attaining these personal virtues, many argued, was the first step toward upward mobility and possibly the proprietorship of a business and a middle-class lifestyle. From that platform, in turn, the free citizen could begin to promote the upward mobility of still other virtuous workers.

However, this optimism about free labor was counterbalanced by important limitations in the new wage relations. Now, employers could fire workers at will, terminate a company without further obligation to workers, and eradicate the benefits and paternalistic protection that many artisans enjoyed in the past. And free labor ideas often obstructed workers' collective efforts to protect jobs or create community networks for their mutual protection and benefit. Occasionally, when wages were depressed during the 1830s, hungry workers tried petitions, slowdowns, and strikes to persuade employers to meet their perceived moral commitments.

Efforts to form trade unions revived after the worst of the Panic of 1837 had passed. But employers often blacklisted—or refused to hire—workers who became visible and vocal organizers. In New York, Connecticut, and Pennsylvania, employers in the clothing and shoe making trades went even further. They claimed sole power to hire and fire any worker, and fought vigorously against "closed shops," or businesses that required all workers to belong to a particular union. Carrying their argument to the state supreme courts, employers argued that they had a "sovereign right" to control their work forces, and that most union contracts represented "conspiracies" against the superior authority of employers to control the conditions of work. Time and again, in state after state, the courts agreed that each worker should bargain separately with the employer for the best hours and wages, and that employers must have control over working conditions and the fate of "the boss's goods." By and large, then, courts agreed with employers that free labor could not be construed as a collective ideal. Wage work was a matter of individual choice, individual competition for pay and advancement, individual attainment or failure.

The Lowell Experiment

America's first factories were small places. Usually, a few entrepreneurs pooled capital, introduced familiar technology or simple new machines, and hired wage labor from the neighboring countryside. Rapid population growth at home and rising demand abroad spurred early mechanization of milling and refining sites in the countryside. The mechanical improvements of Oliver Evans's mills and the simple cotton gin of Eli Whitney "answered our needs expertly," and Samuel Slater's first family mills suited an agricultural lifestyle (see Chapter 9). Boot and shoe manufacturing was more centralized in the countryside, too, as were papermaking and tanning, once small handicrafts associated with the forests and rural herds of livestock.

By the 1820s, entrepreneurs in New England and mid-Atlantic states began to bring together capital and labor along waterways to form larger factories that further consolidated and mechanized textile production. In Dudley and Oxford, Massachusetts, Slater added to his putting out enterprises with a series of complex mill sites that brought workers away from their homes. However, he had to contend with local farmers who feared that he would divert the flow of streams to run his mills and objected to transitory workers who would use roads and schools without paying taxes. Slater's workers, charged local journalists, were transient and antisocial, an "unsettled bunch" that contrasted with the "settled citizenry." By 1831, Slater petitioned the state government to form a separate mill town of Webster, which subsequently adopted independent ordinances about factory sites and mill workers' lives.

Factory conditions such as these did not arise overnight. The most famous complex of great red brick structures, built at Lowell, Massachusetts, arose out of decades of incremental change that set the stage for the town's system of manufacturing. Beginning in the 1780s, many farmers supplemented their work on poor New England soil with cattle herding, lumber milling, orchards, and woodworking. In time, some skilled craftsmen and jacks-of-all-trades prospered and invested in roads, canals, banking, and distilling.

In Waltham, Massachusetts, prosperity from this diversification laid the foundations for new elite families without connection to old colonial networks. The new local elite around Waltham were mostly merchant shippers who carried cotton, the "white gold" grown and picked by southern slave labor. Some prosperous merchants reinvested their profits in cotton shipping, while a few others bought up the water rights along Massachusetts rivers, where they set up foundries and mills that added to their fortunes. During the War of 1812, they began to put spinning machinery into shops and to hire young women to process raw cotton into thread. This was the "Waltham system."

In the 1820s a third group of investors, some of them new to the area, took control of textile production from Waltham's new elite and consolidated operations in small factories. By 1823, they had moved operations to the town named for the merchant and investor Francis Cabot Lowell, and from that location they sent agents out into the countryside to recruit women from struggling farm families. So successful was this complex of people and production that it attracted the attention of prominent merchant businessmen in Boston, who in 1830 took over a large portion of Lowell's operations. These Boston Associates, linked by birth and marriage, owned shares in numerous banking, insurance, and canal projects. Many of them had made fortunes in the China and India trades, and kept a close eye on possibilities for transporting southern cotton exports in their ships.

Soon the Associates introduced copies of the famous English power looms used for weaving thread into cloth. Unlike Slater's method of dispersing spinning and weaving tasks to different places, the Lowell system integrated all aspects of textile manufacturing in one place. Raw cotton entered one end of the mill complex of six buildings, and finished cloth emerged from the other. The Lowell mills were four stories high, with almost all the machinery hooked up to a huge central water wheel by shafts and belts.

Very early on, the Lowell factory was converted to a limited liability corporation, which allowed the owners to pool their individual resources but limit their individual risk: in the event of failure, only company assets could be used to pay outstanding debts. Backers thus gained confidence in the long-run possibilities of the Lowell system, which attracted more capital. Indeed, by 1835, Lowell was a complex of fifty-two mills employing more than twelve thousand people at the juncture of the Merrimack and Concord Rivers.

Unconventionally, Lowell's owners initially chose a work force of young women who did not bring mechanical skills from the countryside. Most of them had lived and worked on typical New England farms all their lives, but during the 1820s, they came by the dozens to sign contracts promising to stay in the mills at least a year and obey all mill rules. In the early Lowell years, the idea of single, unmarried ladies leaving home for months to work for strangers shocked observers. But the Lowell owners assured skeptics that their "operatives" would be well cared for under the work rules, religious training, and moral rectitude enforced on their premises. Pleasant dorm-like living quarters in wooden frame buildings, encircled with white picket fences, gave the visual impression that Lowell was a home away from home.

"Lowell girls" often reinforced arguments about the benefits of their new factory life in these first years. In letters to their families and friends, as well as in private diaries, they wrote about why they chose to enter the factory: it added cash to the family income; it gave them a chance to escape the drudgery of farm life; and it put them in touch with fashion, education, and the wider New England culture. The three dollars a week in wages was also a strong incentive. Mill work was a "freer life" for eleven-year-old Lucy Larcom, who wrote fondly about Lowell in her old age. Boardinghouse supervisors and factory overseers gave glowing reports about the productivity and happiness of the operatives.

But within a few years the operatives began to voice discontent. Air in the mills was hot and filled with cotton lint, and the machines were dreadfully noisy. The work—hour after hour, six days a week—was tedious. Far away from home, and from male company, gulping down monotonous meals, and subject to the whims of the company managers on the work floors, the young women argued for relief from the constraints imposed on them in their twelve-hour workday. But the company replied by tightening rules of behavior in the mills and imposing harsh penalties for infractions. Living by a regimented schedule marked by the peal of bells—awakening to bells, reporting to work by bells, going to lunch and returning again by the same bells—grated on workers' nerves. Within a few years, the work itself was degraded by giving each Lowell girl an unskilled or semiskilled task, for which she was paid a meager wage; the title of operative was reduced to "hands." Viewed by the mid-1830s as less than a whole person, as an extension of the machines, many a Lowell hand had little but her wages to look forward to.

Even leisure time was regimented at Lowell, including time spent in sleeping quarters and on Sundays. In defiance of rules for reporting to dorm rooms at night, one young female worker wrote, "I now make my own wage, and I shall make my own private time too." After regular working hours, the young women increasingly insisted, the Lowell Company had no right to control their living conditions and leisure pleasures. Operatives' complaints were seconded by a number of outside observers who drew bleak pictures of the young girls working away from home. Seth Luther, a carpenter who helped construct some of New England's early textile factories, wrote indignantly about the deplorable conditions of farm girls at Lowell and immigrant children hired at neighboring factories. Long hours, severe punishments in "whipping rooms," and the absence of fresh air and time to play, all contributed to the dour, short lives of factory hands. Women worked "like slaves for thirteen or fourteen hours every day" in the "prisons in New England called cotton mills." "Cotton mills where cruelties are practiced, excessive labor required, education neglected" had become "palaces of the poor."

In the 1830s, verbal discontent grew to open violations of mill rules and printed protests in the mill hands' paper, *The Lowell Offering.* Then in the years preceding the Panic of 1837 (see Chapter 10), falling credit and cotton markets compelled mill owners to squeeze more productivity from their workers or cut wages—or both. When the Lowell owners imposed wage cuts because of competition from textile producers elsewhere and deteriorating economic conditions, Lowell girls "turned out" in strikes. Starting in 1834, nearly eight hundred hands turned out when their wages were summarily cut about 25 percent. The cut pushed the value of their labor as "daughters of freemen" "below decency." But wages continued to fall. Again in 1836 owners reduced wages and the mill girls struck; when they failed for a

New England Spinning Mill Interior, c. 1850   Compared with the modern American factory, the relatively simple machinery, small shop floor, and exposed leather bands attached to power equipment shown here seem truly to be from an earlier era. Compared with the small craft shops still prevalent during the 1840s, however, this early New England textile mill would have been a startling environment in which to work. The women mill operatives probably came from the farms in the surrounding countryside. Their conditions of work would have been notably different from those of the shoemakers on page 422.   *(George Eastman House.)*

second time, many young women lost hope that the mills could offer them decent opportunities, and they returned to the countryside.

For those who stayed in the mills, conditions worsened. In fact, female hands were gradually replaced by impoverished Irish male immigrants desperate for jobs. Nevertheless, spokesmen such as Luther, and their ardent pleas for regulation, led the state of Massachusetts to pass the country's first child labor law in 1842, one that prohibited children under twelve from working more than ten hours a day. Elsewhere in the country, male skilled workers were demanding a ten-hour workday, which inspired the New England Female Labor Reform Association of Lowell and its surrounding mills to petition the Massachusetts government for similar reform. The ten-hour proposal they sent in 1845 fell on deaf legislative ears, as did one in 1846 supported by ten thousand signatures. Only in 1847, when women workers in Nashua, New Hampshire, refused to stay on the job after sunset, did their state pass a ten-hour-day law; other states reluctantly followed with similar laws in the coming years.

Varieties of Social Reform

Immigration, urbanization, and industrialization called forth many critics and reformers from the 1820s to the 1850s. Some of them expressed their beliefs through literature and the fine arts. Others, fueled by the moral fervor of the Second Great Awakening and the perceived duty of emerging middle-class families to be models of virtue, set out to identify and uplift idle, sinful, criminal, intemperate, and impoverished citizens. They implored "unrefined and unmannered" American-born and immigrant people to follow their example of upstanding behavior. Some reformers started institutions to control or rehabilitate individuals deemed "deviant" from reformers' middle-class ideals. Others founded movements for profound moral and social reform across American society. By the 1840s, an array of organizations promoted individual self-improvement—especially the avoidance of drinking and gambling—and benevolent agencies strove to put the idle to work and to reform the criminal and insane. As the reform momentum built, organizations grew and their efforts took a qualitative leap into political struggles to secure rights for women and freedom for slaves.

Individualism and Improvement

Through the 1820s, important voices continued to associate America's territorial expansion and growing social complexity with political democracy and economic opportunity. The articulate French observer Alexis de Tocqueville traveled widely in old and new regions of the nation during the late 1820s. Tocqueville believed that restlessness with their current condition was the most salient characteristic of the nation's citizens. Its results were, in part, the widest spread of democracy anywhere in the world. Ceaseless climbing from one rung of the social ladder to another, an "innumerable crowd of those striving to escape from their original social condition," marked American life. Few adhered to traditions of accepting their "station"; few now wished to be ruled passively by their "betters."

But by 1820, it was clear to many others that northern prosperity was not universal. Since the early 1800s, boom alternated with bust; spells of bountiful harvests seesawed with stark years of scarcity; floods of imported "necessaries and superfluities" dried up during seasons in which few ships docked at urban ports. Jobs came and went, wages rose and fell, apparently in little correlation with skills or personal diligence. The Panic of 1837 blew like a frigid chill through the country, and the subsequent depression from 1837 to 1843 froze hundreds of thousands of Americans in icy unemployment and debt.

Journalists, intellectuals, businessmen, and farmers all tried to understand this fluctuation of good and bad times. Few of them identified structural or institutional causes for crises. But individualism, often promoted as the basis for collective prosperity in America, seemed to backfire all too often and without apparent cause. How could so many ambitious and virtuous individuals fail to achieve success?

By the time Tocqueville was writing, voices of optimism were being drowned out by misgivings about individualism and free market forces. For example, merchant

Samuel Mitchell in New York lamented that too many Americans wanted not only their independence from England, but "to be equally independent of each other." And when "every man is for himself alone and has no regard for any person farther than he can make him subservient to his own views," then lawlessness and "savagery" lay around the corner. Skeptics pointed toward the fearful rise in murder, suicide, theft, prostitution, and children's gangs. Under the guise of middle-class respectability, some entrepreneurs were enticing unwary consumers with underhanded deals and price gouging. At the same time, upstanding middle-class people recoiled from the dirty children and their haggard mothers living in urban hovels. Too many people, regardless of class or national origin, seemed to have lost their self-discipline and resorted to the liquor bottle when poverty or business failures overcame them. Too many people had lost all respect for civic responsibility, social manners, and public order. It seemed all too clear that some Americans could not handle their new republican liberties of political democracy and free labor.

What could be done? Some observers in the North proposed that the growing number of disadvantaged people required external help to attain "their true promise" as improved individuals. At first, a few intellectuals broke away from mainstream churches and literary circles and proposed that "perfection" would occur not within society, but within the individual. A few people dedicated to moral self-improvement and the regeneration of virtue in America, they proposed, would initiate small self-contained societies; in time, these societies would grow and prevail over the corrupted elements of American life. From the 1830s to 1850s, however, these separatist efforts were gradually eclipsed by larger movements that sought to reform American life with direct action. Women's rights activists, for example, protested the hypocrisy of advocating universal personal improvement, and then denying fully half of the population the opportunity for such fulfillment. Religious reformers such as Charles Grandison Finney confronted the powerful appeal of individualism with the equally powerful attraction of social harmony, what he boldly called "the complete reformation of the whole world." And, as detailed in Chapter 12, a growing number of abolitionists contended that individualism, political democracy, and free labor were thriving at great cost: the perpetual enslavement of an entire race.

Temperance

Temperance reformers had a big job on their hands. By 1830, Americans drank more than five gallons of distilled spirits per person each year, or more than any European nation admitted and over three times more than Americans consume today. Whiskey, rum, and hard cider were regular features of the working day, and of leisure time. A thousand distilleries operated in New York City during the 1820s, and the cost of distilled beverages sold by the glass in dram shops declined to easy affordability over the coming years.

However, concerns about public order and private health were also growing. Reformers linked excessive drinking to domestic violence, loss of valuable family income, loss of time on the job, and public rowdiness. But the root of the problem, most of them insisted, was the tradition of drinking throughout the day both on the job and after hours. The developing middle class deplored this habit. Businessmen began to forbid their work crews from drinking on the job; some urged workers to give up alcoholic beverages for good. Within a few years, a large movement to enact temperance legislation had formed, spearheaded by middle-class clergymen, entrepreneurs, and Whig politicians in the North.

In terms of the sheer number of members, the American Society for the Promotion of Temperance, founded in 1826 by evangelical reformers intent on leading drinkers toward prayer and personal conversion, was the largest reform organization of the era. Connecticut evangelical minister Lyman Beecher was the movement's early leader. Beecher, echoed by hundreds of local temperance chapters of the Society, warned that drinking inevitably led to poverty, adultery, social crime, and brutalities against family members. By 1834, millions of Americans had met in public gatherings, confessed their "fall into the sin of drink," and taken "the pledge" to stop drinking altogether. In 1836 the newly organized American Temperance Union moved beyond individual reform and brought its full weight to legislative halls, where it demanded laws to shut down dram shops and to license taverns more strictly. As that legislative crusade continued, the Panic of 1837 and its ensuing depression led skilled artisans and rising manufacturers to give up a drinking lifestyle they could no longer afford. People flocked to join temperance societies that required stern pledges of abstinence. Great numbers of women—the wives, mothers, and sweethearts of working, and drinking, men—found the combination of familiar republican language and stirring evangelical influences a powerful force against the "evils of drink." Women's groups, some called the Martha Washington Societies, worked for temperance legislation despite their inability to vote. Finally, the legislative crusade against liquor scored a success in 1851 when Maine became the first state to go dry by banning the sale or manufacture of any alcoholic beverages. Over the next years, other states would pass "Maine laws" as well.

Asylums and Prisons

Like the temperance movement, efforts to address so-called deviant behavior led individual reformers to propose government legislation. Those efforts also linked popular evangelicalism with middle-class presumptions about molding a moral society. Helen Jewett, for example, was a "fallen woman" in the eyes of this middle class; she had resisted the "cleansing power of prayer" and had spurned decent employment and marriage. The Female Moral Reform Society, founded in 1834 by middle-class women in the North's burgeoning evangelical movement, avoided ridiculing prostitutes and instead targeted the poverty that drove most women into prostitution. The society organized charity, work, and soup kitchens for them. At about the time of Jewett's murder, these reformers were also seeking legislation to enact penalties for clients as well as prostitutes brought to court. Although those efforts largely failed during the 1830s, the Moral Reform Society earned public acclaim for identifying the male clients of prostitutes in New York City and publishing their names. In this way, the burden of prostitution shifted somewhat away from individual women who seemed to have no other economic choice, and onto the shoulders of government and its institutions.

Reformers also stepped into the lives of people defined as criminal or insane. For generations, colonists and early national Americans did not distinguish clearly between these two kinds of people. Individuals who could not cope with the demands of social laws and moral standards—whether out of willful criminality or unwitting insanity—had been entrusted to their families or given temporary relief in tiny public institutions. But by the early 1830s, reformers in major cities protested that a maturing and crowded America required a more systematic approach. They demanded not only larger institutions, but also more enlightened responses to those who had been born into physically or mentally challenging situations or who had fallen on hard times. The criminal and insane, noted reformers with disgust, had been thrown together into dank and filthy rooms where they were neglected or subjected to unjustified cruelties. Every individual, they insisted,

The Stepping Mill, 1823 Reformers who grew concerned about the growing number of vagrants in already-crowded northern cities began to build establishments for putting the idle and poor to work in the 1820s and 1830s. Treated virtually as prisoners put to hard labor for six months at a time, vagrants made rope, paved city streets, or, as this illustration shows, worked the treadmill, or "stepping wheel." Bellevue (New York) Hospital's wheel was a twenty-foot-long cylinder attached to millstones; it was turned by sixteen "inmates" for eight minutes at a time. The city's mayor hoped the mill would induce forced workers to find meaningful employment. (© *Collection of the New-York Historical Society.*)

could be personally improved if given the proper environmental and educational conditions.

A leading proponent of this view was Dorothea Dix, who during the 1830s spent years investigating the treatment of insane women. In 1843 she reported to the Massachusetts legislature her horror at finding "the mixing of impoverished and ravaged" poor women with hardened criminals in the same cells. No efforts, she found, had been made to bring hundreds of women—"degraded, beaten, naked, and chained"—back into society; instead, they were locked up and "utterly ignored." Traveling thousands of miles for dozens of speaking engagements, Dix was able to awaken lawmakers to the need for more humane treatment for the insane. By the late 1850s, most states had created separate institutions for criminals and the insane. During the same decade, other reformers joined forces in northern states to move away from random private charity for orphans and the poor, toward the creation of public orphanages, hospitals, shelters, and immigrant aid societies.

Zealous reformers also hoped that by building "model prisons" in rural settings "away from the rigors of our cities," they could create conditions for teaching self-discipline and an orderly personal lifestyle—the first steps toward reintegrating criminals back into civil society. But these hopes failed. Even in new prisons, inmates' daily lives became regimented; guards watched, directed, and some said "herded" them. Absolute silence was imposed for long periods of time, prescribed Bible readings assigned. Separated from one another in individual cells, prisoners experienced isolation to the point of widespread depression and suicide in the early years of these experiments. The model prisons of Auburn and Ossining ("Sing Sing") in New York became focal points for journalists' outrage.

Family Roles and Education

During the early 1800s, wealthy and middle-class Americans idealized their families as moral institutions that nurtured republican virtue. Women in these families owed their first allegiance to their homes, where they raised and educated their children to become patriotic adults and comforted husbands who "retreated each day from the rigors of business and politics" to the haven of the family domicile. But by the 1820s, many middle-class women were taking their "female" responsibilities outside the home in very important ways. Urban voluntary associations distributed religious pamphlets, instructed children of orphanages in moral character, or taught in Sunday schools, which were activities suited to the presumed moral character of women. Women who attended evening lyceum lectures or enrolled in extensive instruction from clergymen sometimes stepped out of their prescribed female roles to join political activists in the abolitionist movement. Catharine Beecher, a writer and speaker as talented as her father Lyman, traveled widely to deliver public lectures on numerous subjects. Beecher, who authored a much-read *Treatise on Domestic Economy,* provided an inspirational model of a woman "building the moral government of God," promoting temperance, and tirelessly supporting educational and health institutions.

These activities also drew attention to the place of children in American families. Middle-class children enjoyed a diversity of entertainments and educational opportunities by the 1840s. They were schooled in academic subjects, dance and the arts, and etiquette. Novels and newspaper stories provided strong moral messages for children, instructed parents in childrearing, and became workbooks for household education of "young republicans." But children in working-class and immigrant families lived very differently. They often made vital contributions to household incomes by sewing for wages, earning pennies a week at shipyard jobs, or tending the small gardens alongside rundown homes. Poor children sometimes spent hours a day scavenging for food and fuel. Formal education was obviously out of the question.

Although few observers suggested that these growing social differences among children might be remedied by the wholesale reform of the American economy, many middle-class reformers fought for far-reaching educational reforms that would affect children of all social layers. Women active in their churches were among the first to stress childen's natural innocence and openness to moral instruction, rebutting colonial views of children as inherently sinful (see page 114). And for republican women who strove to nurture their children to be good republican citizens, it was a short step to believe that long-term, institutional education would benefit all children and strengthen the moral fabric of America. Before the Civil War, a variety of private and public schools appeared.

Northern states started public schools during the period from 1790 to 1820, most of them meeting in a room at the teacher's house or at church. By the 1820s, girls and boys attended in about equal numbers, and they came out of the schools with solid foundations in reading and accounting. Private academies also took root in the North and proved especially important for women who sought a frontier missionary career or the polish to rise in middle-class society.

In 1827 Massachusetts passed the first law to support public schools with taxes, thanks to the efforts of Horace Mann, the first secretary of the state Board of Education. Within a few years, white children from age five to nineteen could obtain a free education in numerous subjects. States throughout the North began to train female teachers in free "normal schools" and to monitor curriculum to include basic skills. By the late 1830s, school buildings were a regular feature of most northern and western towns (the South was slower to reform education). Oberlin College, founded in Ohio by leading religious and abolitionist activists from the East, was the first school of higher education to admit women, beginning in 1837. Oberlin also admitted African-Americans. Meanwhile, Mann crusaded during the 1840s to have all schools separate children by age, in order to encourage children with peer reinforcement, and then by ability within their age groups, in order to pace children's learning according to ability.

Teacher-training programs helped prepare some young women to take positions in the new schools, but most teachers relied on their background in religious and classical private education to give them a grounding as educators. By the mid-1820s, single young women left the security and comfort of eastern families by the dozens to take up positions in schoolhouses on the distant frontiers of Maine, Wisconsin, or

Indiana. Many young ladies were such welcome members of struggling frontier communities that they were asked to give advice on household accounting, land surveying, or the feasibility of building this or that manufactory. Families named their newborn children after the teachers who brought "so generous a portion of the mental life" to lonely settlers. But frontier teachers expressed their own lonely sentiments in letters to family members, lamenting the rapid onset of homesickness, depressingly low pay, and absence of eligible marriage partners. Teaching was still not a viable career for most young women.

Despite the increasing availability of public education, not all children went to school very long. Urban boys often attended sporadically and then left at age fourteen to begin a job as a retailer's clerk or a grocer's errand boy, thereby providing a necessary addition to their family's income. Rural children attended school for two or three months a year, depending on when their families could release them from work.

Women's Rights

Middle-class women who identified with republican ideals of home and motherhood entered every reform movement of the era, believing that women could make important contributions to changing the lives of wayward or unfortunate people around them. They also generally continued to accept the duties of their separate sphere. But a few outspoken and ambitious women sought more: to create conditions of legal, social, and emotional equality among men and women. In 1848 Elizabeth Cady Stanton and Lucretia Mott organized a convention in Seneca Falls, New York, to discuss these goals in an organized manner. Like many other women's rights advocates, Stanton and Mott had already been active in the growing movement to end slavery, and from that experience they appealed to the republican ideals of the Declaration of Independence for their women's rights platform. All men and women, their founding document proclaimed, "are endowed by the Creator with certain inalienable rights." To spark public awareness and action, delegates resolved to "employ agents, circulate tracts, petition the State and national legislatures, and endeavor to enlist the pulpit and the press on our behalf." Separate spheres of public and private activities for the genders, the convention concluded, perpetuated women's inequality.

Susan B. Anthony joined Stanton and Mott in 1851 and became one of the movement's powerful organizers. Hailing from a Quaker family in Massachusetts, Anthony had already begun her reform career in the temperance, moral reform, and antislavery movements in previous years. She left the teaching profession after experiencing repeated gender discrimination there, resolved that women had to organize and lead their own reform efforts. Anthony developed networks of female "captains" who could mobilize hundreds of women throughout New York to muster thousands of petition signatures on short notice. She trained women to speak before legislatures and to lobby energetically for the right to bring suit in courts, to retain all property they brought into marriage if the union dissolved, and to keep their own wages when they worked. Northern local groups expanded Anthony's teachings to include struggles for women's custody of children when they lost husbands, and guarantees of women's entry into places of higher education and seminaries. They made some modest legislative gains. For instance, between 1848 and 1858, women in some northern states were guaranteed protection of family property on the death of a husband, a measure that indirectly helped wealthy women because it ensured that their husband's property remained a family inheritance and did not pass into the clutches of creditors. A more radical demand was for the right to vote. Reformers declared "we do not seek to protect woman, but rather to place her in a position to protect herself," which the right to vote would aid. This more sweeping demand for female suffrage would, of course, remain unmet for decades to come. However, able leaders of the wider women's rights movement had laid a foundation of leadership and experience by the Civil War. This early women's rights movement set important precedents for women writing and speaking on behalf of their gender.

Intellectual Currents

The printed and spoken word traveled much faster after 1820, but its effects were varied and sometimes ambiguous. On the one hand, ideas and stories in newspapers, information about goods and their prices, and itinerant amusements brought people of many backgrounds closer together, especially in the political culture. On the other hand, popular culture and intellectual life in this era also illuminated differences, just as occupations, origins, and social status divided Americans into different groups.

Susan B. Anthony, 1852
Anthony was one of the most tireless female reformers of the era. Along with Elizabeth Cady Stanton, Anthony founded the Women's State Temperance Society in New York in 1852, and together they were active abolitionists and female labor reformers. Later, Anthony was an outspoken suffragist as well. (*Susan B. Anthony House.*)

Clergymen continued to be important intellectual leaders of communities. During the 1820s, for example, Lyman Beecher led efforts to prevent businesses from operating on Sundays. Throughout the North, church members galvanized behind political lobbying and neighborhood petitioning in support of the era's many moral reforms. Religious institutions drew in hundreds of thousands of members, provided instruction and inspiration to involve members in active reform, and then linked them back to public educational, temperance, and other reform movements.

Some religious groups gave up trying to reform society around them and opted instead for escape into isolated communities. Members left churches of both the older Protestant denominations and the newer evangelical churches to found "utterly purified" sects. In 1830 Joseph Smith came forward to announce that he had received the Book of Mormon teachings from an angel in a vision, leading him to found the Church of Jesus Christ of Latter-Day Saints. Members of the new religion, known as the Mormons, developed strong communal discipline and very quickly became economically successful wherever the church had members. But their success in living self-sufficiently and apart bred jealousy in non-Mormon neighboring communities, whose hostility drove Smith's followers from place to place. Harassed in New York, they moved on to the frontier of Ohio, then across Indiana and Illinois, into Missouri. From 1839 to 1844, Mormons thought they had found the perfect location for their growing number of believers in Nauvoo, Illinois. But once again, intolerant neighbors besieged them. This time, local authorities arrested Joseph Smith and his brother, claiming their crime was the Mormon practice of polygamy, or marriage between one man and many wives. Once in jail, a mob attacked and killed the two men. A new leader, Brigham Young, relocated the Mormons in 1846–1847 to Salt Lake City, far from the all-too-familiar persecution. There, in the unfamiliar challenging western environment, the struggling community eventually thrived.

Some eastern evangelicals developed exaggerated fears of imminent disaster, perhaps an apocalypse, and promoted extreme responses to the era's rapid change and economic turmoil. William Miller, a New England Baptist preacher prophesied that the Second Coming of Christ would happen on October 22, 1843. Until then, conditions would deteriorate throughout the nation. Rejecting the spirit of reform during the era, Millerites sold their worldly goods, bid farewell to family and neighbors, and prepared for their ascension to heaven on the Day of Judgment. When the anticipated Coming did not arrive, Millerites revised the date and continued to wait.

Other radical sects believed that their perfection did not require a Second Coming and entry into the next world; rather, they could achieve "heaven on earth" in their own ideal communities. Over a hundred of these communitarian—or utopian—societies were generated between the Revolution and the Civil War, although the greatest number of them existed during the 1840s. One influential group was the Shakers, founded in 1744 when Mother Ann Lee left the Quakers to establish a community of equal brothers and sisters that would replace the traditional family. The Shakers also practiced celibacy. During the 1830s they settled in communities established on the fringe of existing towns totaling about six thousand members in eight states.

Another kind of utopian society, radical free-love advocates, gathered at Oneida, New York. Founded by John Humphrey Noyes in 1848, Oneidans agreed to form one family in "complex marriage," in which any "saved" man or woman could have intercourse with any other, but in which only certain males were selected to father children, who were in turn raised communally. Shocked outsiders viewed Oneida as scandalous, but the community survived for many years as a successful economic enterprise, producing first animal traps and then flatware.

Socialist utopians formed New Harmony, Indiana, in 1825 under the leadership of the Scottish intellectual-industrialist Robert Owen. Owen believed that private property lay at the root of unemployment and poverty, so his community adopted carefully planned work regimens and an ethic of group sharing. But New Harmony's goals were too lofty, and the community folded within a few years. From the start, it was overcrowded, so inclusive as to invite constant infighting, and so bookish that residents neglected agricultural production.

Also scattered through the midwestern states were the "phalanxes," or huge social complexes designed by the French intellectual Charles Fourier. Fourierism purported to divide work tasks "rationally" according to suppositions about personality, age, gender, and physical stature. Fourierists rejected the creed of individualism and competition, substituting communal ownership.

Some utopian experiments functioned as retreats for reformers who sought intellectual and emotional closeness. In Massachusetts, Brook Farm in West Roxbury and Hopedale in Milford allowed temperance, women's rights, educational, and antislavery reformers to talk and write together, and to sustain themselves with farm labor. Fruitlands, a communitarian experiment near Concord, Massachusetts, that attracted radical intellectuals, set out to farm productively but foundered when members spent too much time studying and writing. All in all, cooperative and socialist communities sprang up in dozens of spots across the northern states. Although they proposed important intellectual and social alternatives to mainstream American life, their numbers always remained modest compared with the many thousands of members joining the middle-class voluntary associations during these years.

In another small but influential trend, elite institutions promoting intellectual pursuits flourished in the northern states by the 1820s. After its modest beginnings before 1800, modeled on the Royal Society of London, Philadelphia's American Philosophical Society (APS) gained a reputation for entertaining statesmen and scientists of note. APS members heard scientific papers presented by members and invited guests, and shared ideas about how to promote Philadelphia's growth. The Boston Athenaeum began lending books in 1807, and New Yorkers revived a subscription library that had begun in colonial years. Both brought together gentlemen and interested middle-class citizens to attend lectures or share reading material. Starting before the War of 1812, Boston's *North American Review* regularly published information about European intellectual trends, thereby bringing the professional, business, and political elite of New England more directly into world affairs.

Out beyond the major towns, however, intellectual life was a mixture of influences carried from the East and those arising from new conditions in the West. In large river towns such as Lexington and Cincinnati, settlers enjoyed regular traffic with eastern cities, which allowed both printed and word-of-mouth exchange of news. Their civic leaders and local merchants who wished to influence distant politicians or promote local improvements held meetings that sometimes became a form of public entertainment. But many settlers in Ohio country found little to read except the omnipresent religious tracts of the Society for the Propagation of the Gospel or the Methodists. Almanacs and collections of tall tales sold much better than literary magazines to new populations just settling in.

Even in the more cultured East, the gap widened between the fine arts embraced by the elite and the maturing popular culture of urban middle and working classes. Middle-class women began to crave the American-authored sentimental novels that became immensely popular starting in the 1820s. Recoiling from the rapid pace of change and the rank individualism rising all around them, sentimental authors appealed to inner feeling, family security, and social sincerity. Sentimentalists warned against dangerous eastern cities and Mississippi River boomtowns that were filled with untrustworthy predators. Prostitutes, confidence men, frauds, and cheats would subvert, without a shred of remorse, any virtuous young woman who failed to tread a moral path. Most of these stories adhered to a moral formula that idealized middle-class republican motherhood and the sheltering home. Heroic women cheerfully met the most trying of circumstances and prevailed against a cruel world to create lovingly nurtured families. Along the way, many of these "republican novels" reinforced the ideology of separate spheres and the rewards of nurturing virtuous republican citizens. Sentimental works also taught women how to behave in public, how to entertain at home "in the genteel manner,'" and even how to dress for various ritual occasions. Ironically, women wrote most of these novels and journalistic pieces, thereby breaking into public professional circles that were typically closed to them.

Eastern writers who appealed to a popular audience—though one still bound by literacy and the ability to buy printed volumes—often chose themes drawn from the frontier experience. Daniel Boone, the hearty individualist of mythical proportions, provided the model for Natty Bumppo in James Fenimore Cooper's *Leatherstocking Tales*. One of these epics, *The Last of the Mohicans* (1826), portrays the march of civilizing tendencies across the Old Northwest and the tragedies of wiping out Iroquois villages. A few years before that, Washington Irving mesmerized middle-class readers with his stories about Rip Van Winkle and the Headless Horseman, both of whom were characters set in rural simplicity. Other writers populated their work with realistic details drawn from everyday life and elevated them to romantic national icons. Authors praised the mundane chores of farmers, the Saturday night impromptu dances of Irish immigrants, the meticulous jottings in a retailer's account book, and the frontier "school marm."

Paralleling these new literary styles, many artists also tried to capture on canvas what it was to be an American. Thomas Cole founded the Hudson River school of painting that romanticized the landscapes of New York's Catskill and Adirondack Mountains in frankly nationalistic tones. Karl Bodmer and George Catlin captured the dramatic scenery of the West on canvas during the early 1830s and thus helped impart to eastern and southern viewers a sympathy for the vast expanses of land and the Indians being displaced from it. Naturalists also put into watercolors and oils the birds, mammals, and varied flora of places few Americans would ever visit. Yet great numbers of Americans embraced these printed and painted scenes of unknown frontiers as a part of their national identity.

A small but influential group of intellectuals known as transcendentalists arose during the 1830s. Professing that the material world was inferior to the spiritual and intellectual life of individuals, a core of New England radicals abandoned their urban and industrial communities and went to live at Brook Farm. Many of them were Unitarian ministers and scholars of German and English romanticism, a movement that stressed emotion, imagination, and freedom from social conventions. Foremost among the transcendentalists, Ralph Waldo Emerson articulated the philosophy that there existed an ideal reality, the Universal Being, which transcended ordinary life. Each person, insisted Emerson, could intuit this reality quite apart from government, churches, or social clubs. As he wrote in one famous essay, "Nature," in 1836, individual existence is best perfected directly in the natural world, where "standing on the bare ground—my head bathed by the blithe air, and uplifted into infinite space—all mean egotism vanishes . . . the currents of the Universal Being circulate through me." On the lecture circuit, Emerson spoke to packed rooms around the country about the virtues of America's cultural separation from Europe. Ironically, Emerson probably did not intend to inspire young people to achieve business and professional success, but his praise for individualism had that effect. Like Finney's mystically converted Christian and Cooper's self-reliant Natty Bumppo, Emerson's morally perfected individual was beyond the reach of corrupted civil society. As most transcendentalists did, Emerson vehemently opposed slavery and expressed horror to his huge audiences when, in 1850, Congress passed the Fugitive Slave Act, which guaranteed the return of runaway slaves to masters.

"Niagara Falls," by Frederic Edwin Church (1857)   Church's painting of Niagara Falls captured the grand scale and magnificent beauty of nature that landscape artists of the Hudson River School were depicting during the era. In addition to being one of the highly idealized subjects of art, Niagara Falls was quickly becoming a popular resort area for visitors who took guided tours of this sublime attraction.   *(The Corcoran Gallery of Art.)*

Henry David Thoreau, a friend of Emerson's, took the transcendentalist message about individualism further. Thoreau left the Massachusetts communities around him and, for a short time, opted for a hermit's life in the woods at Walden Pond (near Concord). *Walden, Or Life in the Woods* (1854), his most famous work, stingingly rebuked the "get-ahead generation" who sought lives of rank materialism and ended up leading "lives of quiet desperation." Another transcendentalist, Margaret Fuller, toured widely in the 1840s and wrote about the great social and intellectual potential of women, if only they could be released from the constraints of conventional norms. And Walt Whitman, whose *Leaves of Grass* (1855) exploded poetical traditions, tried to capture Emerson's call to have an "original relation" with nature. Each person, Whitman insisted, could reach a state of equality with "divine nature" and thereby reach equality with all "souls of our democracy."

Some contemporaries denounced the transcendentalists in New England as dangerous radicals. Thoreau and Fuller, feared clergymen and journalists, would bring down the exciting transformations and opportunities of life in the 1830s–1840s, and either return Americans to rustic simplicity or create the appalling spectre of women's equality. Traveling through the transcendentalist circle briefly, novelist Nathaniel Hawthorne has his adulterous couple in *The Scarlet Letter* (1850) rejected by their community for violating the norms established for orderly living. Their individual redemption can occur only outside the community, in the next world. In Herman Melville's *Moby Dick* (1851), the obsessively self-reliant Captain Ahab cannot hope to capture the great white whale that took off his leg unless he commands the cooperation of a large crew. In the end both individualism and cooperation fail against the forces of nature. Despite these and many other works critical of Emerson's celebrations of individualism, his message was more in keeping with emerging middle-class values and remained an important validation of the era's middle-class reforms.

CONCLUSION

From the 1820s to the 1850s, many Americans in northern society enjoyed unparalleled opportunities to acquire new land, become manufacturers or entrepreneurs, fill their homes with new goods, and offer their children education and cultural enrichment. But during this era, the republic also confronted waves of impoverished new immigrants who crowded into cities that rarely had adequate resources and jobs. The Panic of 1837 and its subsequent depression left huge numbers of people destitute, and changing patterns of work shook social relations between bosses and workers, and within families, to their very foundations.

Americans responded in varying ways to the rapid economic and social change of the era. Many celebrated the unleashed material prosperity that a rising urban middle class enjoyed. Others shuddered at the apparently hastening moral decline, increasing social and economic inequality, and entrenched indifference toward abolition of slavery and women's rights. As Americans framed it in those years, the greatest challenge was simultaneously to enjoy the marvelous changes around them, elevate individual opportunities for advancement, and yet also give the nation institutional and moral coherence. Reformers tried to meet that challenge. Their experiments brought mixed, sometimes modest, results. But the scope and zeal of reform movements, and the range of their efforts to reform Americans, was as unprecedented as the depth of the problems they addressed.

SUGGESTED READINGS

The immigrant group more studied than any other in this era is the Irish. Oscar Handlin's, *Boston's Immigrants* (rev. ed., 1959), was a path-breaking work that looked at especially the Irish adaptation to life in the American city. See also Hasia Diner, *Erin's Daughters in America* (1983). For studies that integrate immigrant groups into their views of urban growth, politics, culture, and services see Thomas Bender, *Toward an Urban Vision* (1975); Elizabeth Blackmar, *Manhattan for Rent, 1785–1850* (1989); and Stuart Blumin, *The Urban Threshold: Growth and Change in a Nineteenth-Century American Community* (1976). Sean Wilentz, *Chants Democratic* (1983), is a fascinating case study of the social history of artisan republicans in New York City before the Civil War.

The starting place for understanding the sweeping changes occurring throughout the North is Norman Ware, *The Industrial Worker, 1840–1860* (1964). The best recent studies of northern industrial change highlight social tensions of emerging classes, as well as the struggles of households to confront altering labor and cultural conditions. Among them are Mary Blewett, *Men, Women, and Work: Class, Gender, and Protest in the New England Shoe Industry, 1780–1910* (1988); Jeanne Boydston, *Home and Work: Housework, Wages, and the Ideology of Labor in the Early Republic* (1990); Alan Dawley, *Class and Community: The Industrial Revolution in Lynn* (1976); and Thomas Dublin, *Women at Work: The Transformation of Work and Community in Lowell, Massachusetts, 1826–1880* (1979). An especially enlightening look at gender during early industrialization is Sylvia Hoffert's *When Hens Crow: The Women's Rights Movement in Antebellum America* (1995).

For "rural industrialization," the best work to date is Anthony F. C. Wallace, *Rockdale: The Growth of an American Village* (1977). Steven J. Ross's study of a midwestern city in *Workers on the Edge: Work, Leisure, and Politics in Industrializing Cincinnati, 1788–1890* (1985) is highly recommended.

An important, though dated, overview of the reform movements of this era is Carol Bode's *The Anatomy of American Popular Culture, 1840–1861* (1959). Ronald Walters's *American Reformers, 1815–1860* (1978) offers one of the first comprehensive treatments of reform movements. Steven Mintz, *Moralists and Modernizers: America's Pre–Civil War Reformers* (1995), is a more recent survey of all major reform movements, with an emphasis on the ideas and beliefs that motivated reformers.

For arguments about the centrality of women in antebellum reform, start with Lois Banner, *Elizabeth Cady Stanton* (1980); Ann Douglas, *The Feminization of American Culture* (1977); and Lori Ginzberg, *Women and the Work of Benevolence* (1990). The overlapping, mutually influential roles of religion, gender, temperance, and medicine are sorted out in Barbara Epstein, *The Politics of Domesticity: Women, Evangelism, and Temperance in Nineteenth-Century America* (1981). Also see the enduring valuable work by Charles Rosenberg, *The Cholera Years: The United States in 1832, 1849, 1866* (1962). Contemporary medical theory and medical practice are best presented in David Rothman, *The Discovery of the Asylum* (1971); Paul Starr, *The Social Transformation of American Medicine* (1982); and Ian Tyrrel, *Sobering Up: From Temperance to Prohibition in Antebellum America* (1979).

Keith J. Hardman, *Charles Grandison Finney, 1792–1875* (1987), is a highly readable account of the reform revival movement in the North. For educational reforms, see Carl F. Kaestle, *Pillars of the Republic: Common Schools and American Society, 1780–1860* (1983);

and for intellectual currents, start with Cathy Davidson, *Revolution and the Word* (1986). New work emphasizes that what once passed as "highbrow" culture may have been more pervasive in American society; see especially Richard John, *Spreading the News: The American Postal System from Franklin to Morse* (1996); David Reynolds, *Walt Whitman's America* (1995); and Bryan J. Wolf, *Romantic Re-Vision: Culture and Consciousness in Nineteenth-Century American Painting and Literature* (1982).

For popular culture generally, the most representative studies include Ann Fabian, *Card Sharps, Dream Books, and Bucket Shops: Gambling in Nineteenth Century America* (1990); David Grimsted, *Melodrama Unveiled: American Theater and Culture, 1800–1850* (1968); Peter Dobkin Hall, *The Organization of American Culture, 1700–1900* (1982); and Karen Halttunen, *Confidence Men and Painted Women: A Study in Middle-Class Culture in America, 1830–1870* (1982), which surveys sentimentalism and the new middle class of the North. A useful survey is Jack Larkin's *Reshaping Everyday Life, 1790–1849* (1988).

The more far-reaching plans of utopian reformers are surveyed in Lawrence Foster, *Women, Family, and Utopia* (1991), and Carl Guarneri, *Utopian Alternative: Fourierism in Nineteenth-Century America* (1991).

Equality and Opportunity in the Cities

From "The Sanitary Condition of the Laboring Population of New York"

John H. Griscom mercilessly criticized the daily life of certain New York City neighborhoods during the early 1840s. Few residents, he insisted, owned enough real or personal property to do more than scrape and survive, and Griscom's contemporaries and modern research have validated this claim. As a doctor and an active social reformer, Griscom appealed to middle-class residents' sensitivities—as well as their pocketbooks—to make changes on behalf of the poor. His graphic portrayals of urban poverty evoked widespread response from reformers.

It may well be questioned, whether improvement in the physical condition of the lower stratum of society, is not a necessary precedent, in order that education of the mind may exercise its full and proper influence over the general well-being. . . . But without sound bodies, when surrounded with dirt, foul air, and all manner of filthy associations, it is vain to expect even the child of education, to be better than his ignorant companions . . . .

The system of tenantage to which large numbers of the poor are subject, I think, must be regarded as one of the principal causes, of the helpless and noisome manner in which they live. . . . The tenements, in order to admit a greater number of families, are divided into small apartments, as numerous as decency will admit. Regard to comfort, convenience, and health, is the last motive. . . . These closets, for they deserve no other name, are then rented to the poor, from week to week, or month to month, the rent being almost invariably required in advance, at least for the first few terms. . . .

Very often, perhaps in a majority of the cases in the class of which I now speak, no cleaning other than washing the floor, is ever attempted, and that but seldom. Whitewashing, cleaning of furniture, of bedding, or persons, in many cases is *never* attempted. Some have old pieces of carpet, which are never shaken, (they would not bear it,) and are used to hide the filth on the floor. Every corner of the room, of the cupboards, of the entries and stairways, is piled up with dirt. The walls and ceilings, with the plaster broken off in many places, exposing the lath and beams, and leaving openings for the escape from within of the effluvia of vermin, dead and alive, are smeared with the blood of unmentionable insects, and dirt of all indescribably colours. The low rooms are diminished in their areas by the necessary encroachments of the roof, or the stairs leading to the rooms above; and behind and under them is a hole, into which the light of day never enters, and where a small bed is often pushed in, upon which the luckless and degraded tenants pass their nights, weary and comfortless. . . . The almost entire absence of household conveniences, contributes much to the prostration of comfort and self-respect of these wretched people. The deficiency of water, and the want of a convenient place for washing, with no other place for drying clothes than the common sitting and bed room, are very serious impediments in the way of their improvement. . . .

The subject of *sewerage* is destined to be one, which of necessity must ere long occupy the attention of the people and the government . . . the rain water cisterns [are] useless, the bottoms of them have in many instances been taken out, and they have been converted into cesspools, into which the refuse matter of the houses is thrown. . . . [A]n immense mass of offensive material, will thus be soon collected, its decomposition polluting the air, in the immediate precincts of our chambers and sitting rooms, and generating an amount of miasmatic effluvia, incalculably great and injurious. Discharge all the contents of our sinks and cesspools, through sewers into the rivers, and we will avoid two of the most powerful causes of sickness and early death. . . .

From "Society, Manners, and Politics in the United States"

Michael Chevalier, French ambassador to America during the early 1830s, took note that the franchise was very widespread in the North and most free urban male residents lived without fear of expressing their political and cultural beliefs. Indeed, Chevalier concluded that, in contrast to most of Europe, in America the "commoners" ruled. America, he wrote, was a dynamic and youthful country, and relatively middle class throughout, as the following passage shows.

There is one thing in the United States that strikes a stranger on stepping ashore . . . it is the appearance of general ease in the condition of the people of this country. While European communities are more or less cankered with the sore of pauperism, for which their ablest statesmen have as yet been able to find no healing balm, there are here no paupers, at least not in the Northern and Western States, which have protected themselves from the leprosy of slavery. If a few individuals are seen, they are only an imperceptible minority of dissolute or improvident persons, commonly people of colour, or some newly landed emigrants, who have not been able to adopt industrious habits. Nothing is more easy than to live and to live well by labour. Objects of the first necessity, bread, meat, sugar, tea, coffee, fuel, are in general cheaper here than in France, and wages are double or triple. . . . The term *democrat,* which elsewhere would fill even the republicans with terror, is here greeted with acclamations . . . .

The architectural appearance of Cincinnati is very nearly the same with that of the new quarters of the English towns. The houses are generally of brick, most commonly three stories high, with the windows shining with cleanliness, calculated each for a single family, and regularly placed along well paved and spacious streets, sixty feet in width. Here and there the prevailing uniformity is interrupted by some more imposing edifice, and there are some houses of hewn stone in very good taste, real palaces in miniature, with neat porticoes . . . and several very pretty mansions surrounded with gardens and terraces. . . .

The appearance of Cincinnati as it is approached from the water, is imposing, and it is still more so when it is viewed from one of the neighbouring hills. The eye takes in the windings of the Ohio and the course of the Licking [Rivers], which enters the former at right angles, the steamboats that fill the port, the basin of the Miami canal, with the warehouses that line it and the locks that connect it with the river, the white-washed spinning works of Newport and Covington with their tall chimneys, the Federal arsenal, above which floats the starry banner, and the numerous wooden spires that crown the churches. . . . The population . . . lives in the midst of plenty; it is industrious, sober, frugal, thirsting after knowledge, and if . . . it is entirely a stranger to the delicate pleasures and elegant manners of the refined society of our European capitals, it is equally ignorant of its vices, dissipation, and follies.

Bustling with enterprise, teeming with both newcomers and resident elites, and rapidly reproducing the institutions associated with modern urban life, northern cities drew the close attention of many writers. The pace of life, the variety of goods and entertainments, and the frightening crush of people in such relatively small spaces gave many cities the appearance of European cities, and separated them starkly from the majority of rural Americans.

But observers could not agree about the meaning of urbanization, or even its true characteristics. Critics were biased against many urban developments, usually because they were believed to harbor numerous threats to the virtue and stability of republican citizens. Admirers, however, thrilled at the pace of change and the excitement of cultural diversity and urban conveniences. Critics tended to record the dangers, filth, and immorality of city life. Supporters reveled in the ceaseless, restless ambition of citizens who took advantage of opportunities for real economic gains.

Arguably, both critics and supporters of the nation's urbanization drew attention to conditions that demanded many different kinds of responses. By the 1830s, a triumvirate of interests—courts, lawmakers, and investors—was beginning to initiate reforms to regulate, control, investigate, and simply understand this amazing social change. Often, they relied on the writings of astute observers such as Griscom or Chevalier to shape their proposals. Just as importantly, however, these writings became important printed vehicles for shaping public opinion about cities. In time, many observers would shift from recording primarily the material conditions of urban life to making more poignant judgments about the ethnic, religious, and class components of cities.

Questions for Analysis

1. Find details in each account of urban life that have drawn the attention of the writers. What sights, sounds, and smells do they record with displeasure or distaste? What pleases them?

2. What underlying judgments do you detect about city dwellers in each piece? Are their concerns about material conditions colored with any ethnic or class biases?

3. What, if anything, do older cities like New York have in common with newer cities like Cincinnati?

4. What cultural and economic differences arose between Americans who settled in the eastern seaboard cities and those who settled in America's interior?

5. Can we attribute some of these different characteristics to ethnic origins, others to social class, and still others to environment? Explain.

12

Slavery and Plantation Culture, 1820–1850

*T*homas Garrett of Wilmington, Delaware, did not suspect how different the spring of 1845 would be from the ones that had preceded it. For twenty-five years, since 1820, this Quaker iron merchant had devoted his fortune and risked his physical safety to run a "station" of the Underground Railroad from his home. That spring he agreed to assist an African-American family of eight, along with four additional Maryland slaves, in their joint escape to freedom. Sam Hawkins was a freed man but his wife, six children, and traveling companions were slaves. Earlier in the year they had "gone missing" from their Maryland plantation, and their master had chased them right into Middletown, Delaware, where the slaves were captured and jailed. Garrett convinced the judge to release all of the slaves, based on a legal technicality. But when he then tried to take the group to Wilmington, the same court trumped up a new charge, this time also implicating Garrett: the court said he was now harboring fugitives. They fled, night and day, on foot and in hired wagons, until they reached deep into Pennsylvania. Still fuming, however, the slave owner sued Garrett and all who had assisted him for the value of his missing property.

By 1845, "Conductor" Garrett had provided over two thousand slaves with safe havens on their journeys from slavery to freedom. His "station stop" in Delaware, a border state, was strategically important for runaways. This made the suit against Garrett all the more significant to citizens of both Delaware and Maryland, and in 1848, when the case was tried at the New Castle

Courthouse, with U.S. Supreme Court Justice Roger Taney presiding, hundreds of people followed the proceedings closely. Taney read out a guilty verdict and ordered Garrett to pay a fine of $4,500, the sum total of his remaining fortune.

As Garrett left the courthouse, stamped by the press as a lawbreaker and now facing poverty, he paused on the steps to address Taney. "Thou hast left me without a dollar," Garrett reminded the harsh court. But he then assured Delawareans that he would continue in his moral choice to take slaves out of the southern states to freedom. "If anyone knows a fugitive who wants shelter," he challenged Taney and state authorities, "send him to Thomas Garrett and he will befriend him."

Thomas Garrett, born the year Delaware's delegates signed the Constitution, sacrificed his fortune and risked his personal safety time and again for slaves he did not know. When the Thirteenth Amendment to the Constitution guaranteed freedom to slaves, African-Americans praised Garrett as their Moses. He was one of hundreds of whites and free African-Americans who operated the Underground Railroad in every state, and who struggled mightily to end slavery in the South.

As this struggle unfolded, free African-Americans endured difficulties that often made the pursuit of freedom seem indistinguishable from the condition of slavery. Despite the formal rights of citizenship for all men, runaway slaves who blended into northern society and manumitted ex-slaves experienced constant discrimination on the job, in the streets, and in churches. Slaves in the South suffered even more direct legal, physical, and emotional affronts as the southern plantation system spread territorially and "King Cotton" ruled the southern economy. Still, as southern planters sharpened arguments justifying their way of life, two other developments qualified their domination in the South. One was the rapid growth of the small farming yeomanry, many of whom had little expectation of owning slaves or becoming prosperous, and great numbers of landless tenants who did not even own land. The other was the continuing efforts by slaves to preserve African ways and adapt African cultural inheritances to Euro-American culture. To varying degrees, slave communities throughout the South created distinctive identities within the dominant planter culture.

- What was the range of attitudes about slavery in the North? in the South?

- What made southern culture and economy distinctive from the cultures and economies of the North and West?

- How did slaves create separate cultural ways from their masters and other white people within the South?

- What tensions developed between planters and slaves? between small farmers and great planters?

This chapter will address these questions.

 ## Abolition and Antislavery Movements

Runaway slaves, freedmen in northern states, and Underground Railroad activists appealed persistently for a more widespread assault on slavery. By 1820, Americans had nurtured their republican beliefs about personal independence for decades,

Chronology

1800	Gabriel's rebellion
1808	External slave trade legally ends
1816–1819	Boom in cotton prices
1817	American Colonization Society founded
1822	Vesey's rebellion
1827	First African-American newspaper, *Freedom's Journal*
1829	Dew's defense of slavery appears
1831	Garrison begins publishing *The Liberator*
	Nat Turner's rebellion
1833	American Anti-Slavery Society founded
1837	Lovejoy killed
1852	Stowe publishes *Uncle Tom's Cabin*
1854	Fitzhugh's *Sociology for the South* appears
1857	Helper releases *The Impending Crisis*

and the antislavery movements in England and the Caribbean inspired some Americans to think similarly. In 1808 Congress outlawed the importation of slaves into America, just as the Constitution had mandated; and in 1820 the Missouri Compromise prohibited slavery in much of the vast Louisiana Purchase. But for a growing number of white and black Americans, these were only first steps against the blot of slavery.

Gradual Emancipation and Colonization

The American Colonization Society, founded in 1817, urged masters to manumit, or set free, their slaves in return for compensation and worked to transplant freed slaves to Africa. The society established a West African colony called Liberia. Many colonization advocates, including Thomas Jefferson, believed that although slavery was a moral wrong, blacks themselves composed a "separate nation" that would never be able to mix in white American society. Members of the society in New England and New York agreed that even employed free blacks in their cities were failing to "civilize in both their mental and spiritual capacities." Several states denied or restricted African-American suffrage (see Chapter 10).

The colonization movement also attracted southern developers from Virginia, Maryland, and North Carolina who believed that abolishing slavery would be the South's first step toward the economic and social development that northerners enjoyed. Like Thomas Jefferson, many of them argued that emancipation without colonization could trigger a race war. As he promoted aspects of his American System, Henry Clay repeated this view. Other southerners opposed emancipation altogether but supported the Colonization Society because it could help remove free African-Americans from their region and thus make it safer for slavery.

One of the era's most radical utopians, Frances Wright, established a community based on the principles of gradual emancipation and colonization. Wright came from a wealthy Scottish commercial family, but at a very young age she dreamed of living in America and pursuing her ideal of becoming a social reformer. In 1824 she arrived with the celebrated French hero of the American Revolution, the Marquis de Lafayette, and stayed as a guest at Thomas Jefferson's Monticello. Jefferson encouraged Wright to found a utopian community of whites and freed blacks who would live together in full equality. In 1825 Wright gathered over thirty freed adult slaves in Nashoba, in western Tennessee, a settlement that eventually grew to over two thousand acres. Settlers were to earn their emancipation by clearing and planting the land, while their children were to receive an education suited to their eventual cultural and civic entry into American society. By 1828, however, Nashoba had failed to prosper agriculturally or to attract many additional recruits. Wright migrated to New York with Robert Dale Owen, the son of utopian Robert Owen (see page 436). There, she lectured widely to mixed audiences of men and women on the evils of capitalism and the benefits of universal compulsory education and women's rights. By the 1830s, Wright's early advocacy of gradual emancipation seemed very tame compared with her bold crusading for the northern working class.

Immediate Emancipation and Rebellion

Most free African-Americans rejected colonization because it denied them rights that, as Philadelphia's Bethel Church members said in 1817, "the Constitution and the laws allow to all." Thousands of African-Americans had already established themselves in the North after the Revolution. Independent churches, schools, and benevolent organizations were beginning to knit a community of African-Americans recently freed and born free, runaways, and urban African-American servants and slaves. Colonization directly jeopardized these efforts and denied these communities the opportunity to develop in confident freedom.

A growing number of free African-Americans believed that inadequate progress toward ending slavery justified open rebellion. David Walker, who had come from North Carolina to Boston in the 1820s, was familiar with slave conspiracies to take over southern plantations and cities. He sponsored the first African-American newspaper, *Freedom's Journal,* in 1827 to arouse northerners to help slave resisters. But two years later, fed up with the reluctance of white northern society to compel southern slave owners to free their slaves, Walker wrote *Appeal . . . to the Colored Citizens.* Walker's appeal warned that slaves would rise up in arms and take their freedom by force from masters in the South, with or without northern help.

Frederick Douglass, son of a white father and Maryland slave mother, escaped to the North as a young man. Douglass was a rare individual who had learned to read and write when he was a slave, and despite the physical and psychological brutalities of a harsh "slave breaker" to whom he had been sold, became a skilled ship caulker. By the mid-1830s, Douglass became the foremost African-American abolitionist in the North, although for years his white audiences bristled at his eloquent speeches on behalf of emancipation.

American Anti-Slavery Society

Frederick Douglass, Harriet Tubman, and Sojourner Truth were leaders in the black abolitionist movement that demanded an immediate end to slavery, but the thousands of free African-Americans who joined over fifty abolitionist societies fanned out far beyond the leaders. By the 1830s, a number of white opponents of slavery identified more closely with slaves who resisted and rebelled than with arguments for colonization. With moral urgency, evangelical ministers and women's rights organizations insisted on the sinfulness of slavery and masters' debilitation of slaves' inherent moral goodness. Theodore Dwight Weld, for example, was the son of a Congregationalist minister and had listened raptly to Charles Finney's sermons in New York State. Weld decided to take similar messages of moral reform on tour through New York and into Ohio, where he reached out to temperance and educational reform societies before he focused his greatest talents on abolition. In 1834 Weld convinced some of the students at Lane Theological Seminary in Cincinnati to form an antislavery society. When seminary president Lyman Beecher objected to this extension of the seminary's work beyond academic instruction, the antislavery

Frederick Douglass, 1848
Ten years after he escaped from slavery in Maryland, Douglass became a highly regarded orator for the abolitionist cause and equal rights for women. Although he lectured tirelessly to white, as well as mixed white and black, audiences during the 1840s, Douglass became weary of waiting for legislators to emancipate slaves and came to regard violence as necessary for abolition of the institution. *(Chester County Historical Society.)*

supporters moved to Oberlin College, where they were encouraged to study the relationship between religion and universal freedom.

Secular northern reformers joined religious leaders to rebuke merchants involved in the slave trade and organize lectures to raise public consciousness about the southern institution. William Lloyd Garrison was among the most tireless opponents of gradual and compensated emancipation. During the 1820s, he collaborated with Quakers in Baltimore to put out the *Genius of Universal Emancipation,* a serial that ardently promoted immediate emancipation. In 1830 Garrison spent a few weeks in jail for writing against a slave trader, his fine paid by Arthur Tappan, a prominent wealthy merchant from New York who was at the time affiliated with Oberlin College. Not to be silenced, Garrison in 1831 started *The Liberator,* a major voice for immediate emancipation that condemned the American Colonization Society. Even the Constitution, wrote Garrison, was "a covenant with death, an agreement with Hell" because it failed to abolish the institution of slavery.

Garrison and *The Liberator* became a magnet for radical abolitionists during the 1830s. In 1832 they joined to form the New England Anti-Slavery Society, which in 1833 was recast as the American Anti-Slavery Society. Weld, Garrison, Tappan and his brother Lewis, along with about sixty other white and free African-American abolitionists, developed a program that they hoped would attract massive numbers of middle-class Americans. Although some delegates to the society's first meetings called for "direct action" against slave owners in the South, the majority adopted the strategy of "moral suasion." This more moderate stance proved effective in attracting members: over the 1830s some 250,000 northerners joined the Anti-Slavery Society.

The society had two approaches. One was to reach out to great numbers of uncommitted Americans. Using the organizing method of evangelicals, abolitionists sponsored huge, hours-long public gatherings and arranged home visits in immigrant neighborhoods. And with financial donations from wealthy members, they kept antislavery printing presses churning day and night. In 1835 more than a million pieces of literature rolled off the presses and into the hands of northerners. That same year, the society flooded the fledgling post office with hundreds of thousands of antislavery pamphlets.

The second strategy of the American Anti-Slavery Society was to agitate for specific legislation from state and federal governments. Prominent merchants, transcendentalists such as Emerson and Thoreau, and some state-level Whig politicians pressed for congressional action. In the mid-1840s Thoreau would link together northern urban violence, a brewing war with Mexico, and southern slavery in stinging writings. In 1848 he published anonymously his famous essay, "Civil Disobedience," which advocated individual resistance to government wrongs and professed his belief in a moral law higher than man-made statutes.

As rank-and-file abolitionists stuffed envelopes for the post office to deliver in 1835, the movement mobilized supporters to circulate hundreds of petitions calling on Congress to stop admitting slave states into the Union, remove the "three-fifths compromise" from the Constitution (see page 263), abolish slavery in the nation's capital, and end the slave trade within America. Over the next three years, Congress received almost 500,000 petitions; more than half the signers were women.

Women and Emancipation

Few women stepped forward to speak against slavery in mixed male and female audiences in the early 1830s. But their numbers grew in the following years, especially as women's rights organizations took form and evangelicals coalesced moral outrage against slavery. The Philadelphia Female Anti-Slavery Society, founded by Lucretia Mott in 1833, and the Boston Female Anti-Slavery Society, founded by Maria W. Chapman in 1835, formed the core of growing female abolitionist networks that raised funds, operated printing presses, organized speaking engagements, taught free African-American children, and helped run the Underground Railroad.

Angelina and Sarah Grimké left their father's South Carolina plantation to join abolitionists in Philadelphia, where beginning in 1836 they lectured frequently to men and women. When challenged by clergymen and politicians for their bold entry, as women, into this highly charged reform movement, Angelina retorted, "It is a woman's right to have a voice in all the laws and regulations by which she is governed." In 1838 Angelina married Theodore Weld, and together with Sarah they compiled one of the era's best-selling books, *American Slavery as It Is: Testimony of a Thousand Witnesses* (1839). Culling excerpts from southern newspapers, the authors put together thousands of accounts of physical punishments, dehumanizing descriptions of runaways, and cold testimonials of masters.

For years, the Grimké sisters insisted that the treatment of women and slaves had many points in common, and by 1840, they associated women's traditional position in society with "domestic slavery." At the Anti-Slavery Society convention of 1840, Garrison agreed that women should have an equal right to participate in the abolitionist movement, a measure that prompted many middle-class northerners to leave the Society and found the all-male American and Foreign Anti-Slavery Society. Along with Garrison, Abby Kelley, Lucy Stone, Lucretia Mott, and Elizabeth Cady Stanton continued to combine abolitionist struggles with the reform of women's lives. Sojourner Truth, one of many African-American women to speak out during the 1830s and 1840s in public forums, linked women's rights in the North directly to women's rights under slavery. In her stinging rebuke of the treatment women received under slavery, Truth asked, "I have ploughed and planted and gathered into barns, and no man could head me—and ar'n't I a woman? I have borne thirteen children, and seen most of 'em sold into slavery, and when I cried out with my mother's grief, none but Jesus heard me—and ar'n't I a woman?"

Although Harriet Beecher Stowe never joined an antislavery organization, her famous 1852 novel, *Uncle Tom's Cabin,* found its way into more homes, and hearts, than any antislavery pamphlet did. Daughter of minister Lyman Beecher and sister of Catharine Beecher, Stowe advanced moral reform as a central message in her writing. The title character, Uncle Tom, endures abuses and agonies

Sojourner Truth She gained her freedom from slavery in 1827 and became one of the earliest participants in the women's rights and abolitionist movements. Excluded from a discussion of women's rights at an Akron, Ohio, convention in 1851, Truth rose to her full six feet height and demanded of the white women around her, "Ar'n't I a woman?" Already, she was widely known for her chilling lectures about the cruelties and indignities of slavery. In her lap, Truth has the daguerrotype of Frederick Douglass shown on page 449. *(Massachusetts Historical Society.)*

familiar to many slaves, including runaways who described their personal stories in detail to Stowe and then became incorporated into her book. Other characters also deeply touched northern Americans who read about Tom's sale and separation from his children: Eliza Harris, who risks running away and carries her son across the icy Ohio River to freedom, and little Eva, who dies in the midst of the system's cruelties.

Stowe believed that family life lay at the foundation of all moral authority, and that mothers in their spheres were indispensable for halting the political crises of the Union in the 1850s as sectionalism intensified. Joining a growing list of female reform authors, Stowe articulated slavery's degradation of families and women: slave women, unlike white women, had no separate sphere, and not many slaves were granted the basic right to nurture their own children in families. *Uncle Tom's Cabin* sold over 350,000 copies quickly after publication and continued to be America's most celebrated novel for years. It was tremendously popular abroad, too, and its wide acclaim would influence English attitudes toward the South for years to come.

Southern Society

It was obvious to Frenchman Alexis de Tocqueville, touring America in the late 1820s, that the nation was divided sectionally. The root cause was also obvious. "Almost all the differences which may be noticed between the character of the Americans in the Southern and Northern states," he wrote in 1831, "have originated in slavery." Slavery and the production of exportable agricultural crops had long dominated the southern way of life. Planters who turned to cotton in the early 1800s renewed their commitment to slavery and plantation agriculture, and to the acquisition of ever more land. The distinctive sectional characteristics that set the South apart from the North did not erode, as some Americans had predicted after the American Revolution, but instead deepened.

A Distinctive Economy

Production of the staple crops tobacco, sugar, hemp, rice, and cotton was based on certain conditions found exclusively in the South. For example, soil conditions and climate were better in the South than in the North for growing tobacco; cotton requires long warm seasons and abundant spring rains, conditions that characterized large areas of the coastal South from Virginia to Texas. In addition, English textile manufacturing created seemingly endless demand for all the cotton southerners could produce, and Whitney's cotton gin aided planters in meeting that demand. In addition, territorial expansion and declining government prices for western land beckoned southerners into unsettled areas that they believed were suited to cotton production.

As the older sections of the Chesapeake turned to cultivating more cereals, especially wheat, the production of tobacco moved west, mainly into Tennessee and Kentucky, during the 1820s to 1850s. In this same region, hundreds of farmers also began to plant hemp, a product used to make rope and coarse cloth. Although hemp was protected during the 1820s and 1830s by a steep tariff on foreign imports, the market was modest and fortunes were few.

On the other hand, along the ribbon of tidewater land through North and South Carolina and along the coastline of Georgia, rice planters prospered. To prepare rice marshes and maintain the canals and floodgates, great numbers of slaves populated the rice districts. For the planter who could invest heavily in slaves and land, rice often generated huge profits through these decades. So did sugar, a product that had made many Caribbean planters wealthy and drove hundreds of thousands of Caribbean slaves to early deaths. Although sugar grew well only in tropical climates, a few bold Louisiana planters won protective tariffs covering New Orleans and proceeded to grow rich on newly settled American soil by driving thousands of slaves mercilessly. Like rice, sugar required heavy capital investment, both in slaves and in machinery for grinding and boiling the cane. Sugar harvests were the most demanding of all slave work regimens: crews had to work fast and often through the night to cut the ripened cane, haul it to the sugar mills, tend the milling machines that ground the cane, and then boil cane in vats.

King Cotton, however, would surpass all other staple crops in the amount of land it covered and the number of slaves it consumed (see maps). In 1830 southern states produced about 720,000 bales of cotton; in 1850, nearly 3 million bales; and in 1860, almost 5 million—about 60 percent of the value of all American exports. Cotton exporting was thus unquestionably profitable for many planters—despite periodically rising prices paid for slaves and fluctuating prices received for crops—and it supported the livelihoods of numerous northern merchants who carried the raw cotton to industrial destinations in England, traded slaves to southerners, and returned from abroad with textiles for American buyers. Northern investors, such as the Boston Associates who financed the Lowell mills, planned for the day when they themselves would be able to process southern cotton into finished American textiles.

Southerners' emphasis on plantation agriculture tied them intimately to the credit, services, and goods provided by northerners, and precluded channeling many resources into other ways of developing their region. For one thing, a much smaller proportion of southerners lived in cities before the Civil War than northerners; nine-tenths of southerners lived in rural areas. Although New Orleans, Mobile, and Charleston attracted many immigrants, a large proportion of them continued migrating to northern cities. Charleston and Savannah grew far more slowly than New York City or Boston before 1860, and many southern states had no significant port city. The two exceptions were Baltimore and New Orleans. Baltimore grew to over two hundred thousand people by 1860, capitalizing on its position as a primary port for the Chesapeake region's agricultural exports of grain and flour, hides, and cotton. New Orleans, at the mouth of the Mississippi River, was a major crossroads between western settlements, the Ohio Valley, and southern plantations.

Travelers who headed inland from southern ports were immediately struck that the South had far fewer canals than the North. Antebellum (before the Civil War) newspaper editors often noted that the South had only about 30 percent of the country's railroads and no more than 15 percent of the country's factories. Some of these factories were impressive works, including the large iron foundries and rolling mills in Richmond, Virginia, and an armory at Harpers Ferry in northern Virginia. In addition, some of the largest gristing mills in America dotted the Maryland and Virginia countryside. William Gregg used his promotional skills and personal capital to construct the Graniteville, Georgia, cotton mill in 1846. He then put up a model village not unlike Lowell in design, including homes, a school and church, a library, a hospital, and a massive stone factory that became a marvel to Georgians and a workplace for many of them. The Tredegar Iron Works in Richmond hired skilled slaves from area planters to produce the military goods, boilers, steam engines, axes, saws, and other iron products shipped widely outside the South. In addition, southern state governments joined with private investors to create banks that gave generous credit for development projects and new railroad lines from 1830 to 1850, which in turn speeded up expansion of the plantation system into Louisiana, east Texas, and what would become Oklahoma.

Nevertheless, southerners invested far less of their collective capital in industry, education, and transportation before midcentury than northerners did. Planters created more wealth by investing in slaves and land than by building factories and schools. Consequently southern development lagged further and further behind

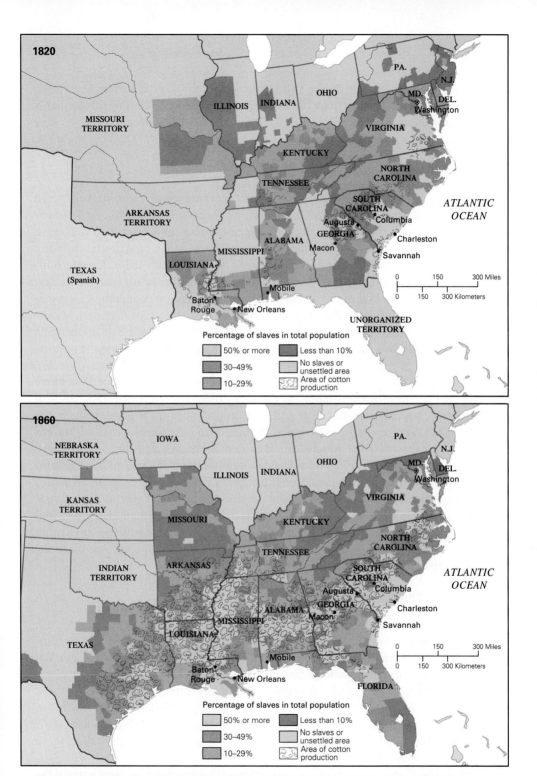

Slavery and Agricultural Expansion, 1820–1860 Although Americans were migrating westward in great numbers for many reasons by the 1820s, the expansion of plantation agriculture determined the spreading influence of slavery more than any other factor. By the 1850s, over 50 percent of all southern slaves worked in cotton fields, increasingly those of new western states. Rice, hemp, and sugar accounted for about 15 percent of slave work.

rapidly growing northern trade and industry. Moreover, no southern state instituted a public school system before midcentury. As long as cotton remained highly profitable, most planters concluded that internal improvements and factories were unwise and risky business ventures.

Expansion

Jefferson's vision of filling the West with hard-working white freeholders collapsed quickly south and west of the Ohio River, where cotton agriculture and slavery spread. Although the Panic of 1819 (see page 313) produced a dramatic decline in cotton and land prices, and thousands of new planters failed, even greater numbers of planters and slaves undertook the westward trek by the late 1820s. Already, hundreds of planters had settled in Kentucky, Tennessee, and Missouri. Georgia planters demanded the removal of Indians in order to expand cotton production. Unprecedented expansion during the 1820s and 1830s into new lands of Alabama, Mississippi, and Louisiana—what would become the southern "Black Belt"—and then during the 1840s into Texas set the framework for King Cotton's rise and the removal of entire Indian populations (discussed in Chapter 10).

Forced to move with their masters, or sold from older eastern plantations where they had become "surplus labor" as tobacco production declined, thousands of slaves were wrenched from family and community roots in the Chesapeake in the early 1800s. Setting out from Virginia, Maryland, and the Carolinas, slaves walked for days or weeks across rough terrain to east Tennessee and the new southern states. Having been separated from loved ones, from the pride and material benefits of working at diverse skills, and from customary negotiated arrangements with a master, relocated slaves then began the backbreaking work of starting new farms. Auctions and sales of slaves, and the forced marches to new plantations, spread slavery's influence remarkably quickly. By the 1830s, planters carried slaves and cotton production across the Mississippi River into Texas, as well as southward into the former Spanish territory of Florida.

The Slave Trade

The Constitution stipulated that American involvement in the international slave trade should cease in 1808, and during the twenty years after the American Revolution, the northern states had discussed and passed laws providing for gradual emancipation or manumissions. Successful revolts in Haiti during the early 1790s, and rumblings of additional independence movements in the Caribbean, produced enough fear in southern states that their legislators prohibited all importation of foreign slaves. England's Parliament abolished the international slave trade in 1807, and there was much talk of moving forward with general emancipation of slaves in the Caribbean during the next years.

But King Cotton was becoming so profitable that southern planters entered the smuggling business energetically during the 1790s and clamored for reopening the foreign slave trade, which South Carolina did in 1804. Slave auctions flourished: over forty thousand Africans were imported into Charleston alone before 1808 when the constitutional prohibition became national law. With King Cotton's even more rapid expansion following the War of 1812, middling and large planters saw slavery as their only way to remain prosperous. Because the Constitution prohibited future slave importation, their prosperity had to be based on the rising birthrate and internal buying and selling of slaves. Planters in Maryland, Delaware, Virginia, and Tennessee who had converted to grain production required fewer slaves for labor and offered hundreds of thousands of slaves for sale into the new southern states after 1820. Some scholars estimate that about half of the slaves in the Upper South were sold "down the [Mississippi] river" or to masters in the Black Belt states. The new states along the Gulf Coast accounted for one-third of the South's slaves by 1860.

The transplanting of slaves from one region to another was fraught with hardship and marred by violence. The breakup of families was common. Although relocating

Slave Trade, Watercolor by Lewis Miller   The internal slave trade, primarily from the Chesapeake to the new areas of cotton expansion, broke up the families and settled lives of thousands of slaves. Sales of "surplus" slaves profited white planters in the older states, while also helping populate the new plantations beyond the Appalachian Mountains and in the emerging Black Belt. Usually, the slaves were "driven" by foot, chained together in coffles. (*Colonial Williamsburg Foundation.*)

planters sometimes took all of their slaves to new states, planters who stayed behind often sold individual slaves to middlemen who transported them to new masters far away. Many bankers and merchants—both northern and southern—served as brokers for the internal slave trade. With private capital, they bought slaves, hired white middlemen to escort them to their destinations, and received payments from auctioneers in Black Belt cities. Richmond and Charleston had "slave pens" for collecting groups of slaves before sending them by ship to booming auctions at cities such as Natchez, Mobile, or New Orleans. Slaves herded overland to internal plantations usually wore chains; drivers linked slaves together in "coffles."

African-American Culture

The widespread dislocation of slave communities and the demands of plantation labor introduced new challenges to slave culture, family life, and even survival. But during the decades before the Civil War, slaves continued to build communities within the plantation system, as they had throughout the eighteenth century. As they accommodated to plantation regimens of relentless work and masters' ultimate power over their lives, slaves combined their own African-American values and attitudes with selected European ones to form a distinctive slave culture within the dominant planter culture. This culture provided many slaves with the means to endure, and at times to resist, the inherent cruelties of the South's "peculiar institution."

Family and Community

Living conditions for slaves varied widely, depending on the size of the plantation, the "settledness" of the region, and the individual planter. Generally, small planters gave their slaves sleeping space in their houses or barns. Sometimes they shared the same food, though often they ate their meals separately. The great planters typically constructed separate slave quarters that consisted of cabins with dirt floors. The cabins might house ten to fifteen slaves, which could represent two or three families; thus they lacked privacy and sometimes even enough room for everyone to sleep indoors. As one observer noted, "More disease and loss of time [at work] on plantations was engendered from crowded negro cabins than from almost any other cause." Travelers to southern states noticed that American slaves lived more comfortably than European peasants; ornaments, brooms, cupboards, fences, handheld mirrors, and other amenities captured outsiders' attention. Separate quarters also offered a place for rest and the evening meal apart from white people, a place to gather around a fire for stories, or a vegetable garden to supplement the typical diet of salted pork and corn. Masters supplied clothing, usually consisting of a homespun cloth shirt or two, two pairs of pants, and a pair of shoes for a man, and a few yards of homespun cloth for women to make their own and their children's smocks for a year. Some slaves were permitted blankets and coats, but many slaves complained that they were hardly adequate in the cold winter months.

Laws barred slaves from forming contracts, so whites did not legally recognize slave marriages. Indeed, the great planters in the Black Belt often forced unrelated mixed groups of slaves to live together under one roof, although slaves shunned unions with cousins and often identified strongly with families of birth and joined in what passed as marriage in the slave community. Farther to the north, in longer-settled regions of the Carolinas and tidewater Chesapeake, slaves more successfully established ties of romance, obligation, and kinship than in the new cotton region. The end of legal slave importation in 1808 slowed the introduction of new slaves from abroad and increased the proportion of African-Americans born and raised on Chesapeake or Carolina soil. Plantation agricultural work was arduous in these old regions, but it did not kill slaves at nearly the same rate as Louisiana and Caribbean sugar "factories" did. As a result, in the Chesapeake and North Carolina regions, slaves could develop the cultural habits and emotional links that grew out of familiar long-term relationships. By the early 1800s, families of three or more generations of slaves, with both parents playing a role in child rearing, became regular features on Virginia plantations.

Slave families and kin groups solidified their bonds with many cultural practices. One was to give newborns African names, a simple but meaningful way to cement lineages and reaffirm origins. In Virginia and Maryland, however, slaves often took names of English derivation and then passed on the names into the next generations, naming sons after fathers, uncles, or grandfathers, or daughters after grandmothers. Repeating names through the generations linked kin to kin and established patterns that evoked order in an otherwise cruel and arbitrary existence. In addition, slaves used kinship terms for nonrelatives, which helped knit together extended households and communities. Children, for example, often addressed all older women as Auntie or Granny.

Although state laws did not recognize slave marriage, some masters encouraged slave parents to wed and live together because they believed stable relationships led slave women to have more children, a future source of profit for planters. For their part, slaves sought marriage as a sanction of their intimacy and bonds of love or to avoid the shame their traditional cultures associated with unwed motherhood. But unlike male-dominated white marriages, which limited women to restricted public and private roles, slaves grounded marriage on greater equality. The fact that men and women often shared the same fieldwork and the same degraded powerlessness over their condition supported such an attitude. Married couples also helped sustain oral memories of kinship and could work together to teach survival skills and provide comfort and protection to young people. Yet masters who encouraged slave marriages also could separate slaves from each other, especially in the internal slave trade. Some 10 to 15 percent of slave marriages ended when one partner was sold away, and a similar proportion of children experienced the breakup of their families.

Fears and uncertainties created by these conditions made it important for slaves to forge bonds in the wider slave community. Mothering was shared throughout the slave quarters on large plantations, with most or all women cooperating to provide for children's daily needs. When slave women died in childbirth or were sold away, children could count on the maternal care of the wider community. Slave children who lost parents might be "adopted" by the family who shared the same cabin. On very large plantations a slave who worked in the master's house could assume the care of a few children if necessary. Over time, bonds strengthened between unrelated women and children, so that on some large plantations masters and overseers could not identify slaves by their families of birth.

Under slavery, African-Americans often retained traditional symbols, songs, art forms, and rituals from their countries of origin, although masters tried to prevent slaves from practicing their African traditions openly. Religion also offered many slaves opportunities for personal and internal solace in a harsh and potentially uprooted life, although planters interpreted many aspects of African religions as superstitions, pagan folk beliefs, or even witchcraft. Many masters tried to control whether and how slaves adopted Christianity. Fearing that slaves would take the biblical messages of equality and individual responsibility for spiritual regeneration too literally—and rebel against their condition as a result—masters hoped to transform slaves into docile, obedient workers by stipulating what elements of Christianity slaves might share with whites. Some of them forbade slaves to gather in African-American churches and insisted that they attend white church services where masters could control religious experiences. Pulpits became forums for preaching obedience and justifying the inequalities of slavery with Scripture.

Despite such interference, slaves adapted elements of Christianity to their daily needs and their traditional religions. As one ex-slave put it, "Dey law us out of Church, but dey couldn't law 'way Christ." Slaves attended frequent prayer meetings and impromptu religious gatherings. Many West African peoples traditionally believed in a Supreme God above all others in the pantheon of gods, which brought them closer to Protestant beliefs. Both West African religions and Protestant Christianity emphasized benevolence, forgiveness, and the promise of eternal life in some form. Additional beliefs in reincarnation and elements of ancestor worship divided some West Africans from European Christians, but in the tidewater, slaves often merged Anglican worship with African religious customs. Closer to the Mississippi River, many slaves brought Catholic influences into folk traditions after 1800. When the Second Great Awakening swept through the slave communities after 1790, Baptists and Methodists welcomed African-American preaching and separate slave churches.

Aside from attendance at white churches on Sundays, slaves in the Old Southeast observed many African religious traditions from day to day. They preferred to honor their own dead at night funerals and bury slaves at places of their own choosing. Native African languages, music, and dances persisted long into the 1800s throughout Louisiana and Mississippi. African "call and response," as well as group singing, endured in most areas of the slave South. Often, slaves adapted song lyrics to plantation work:

> We raise de wheat, Dey gib us de corn;
> We bake de bread, Dey gib us de crust;
> We sif' de meal, Dey gib us de huss;
> We peel de meat, Dey gib us de skin;
> And dat's de way, Dey take us in . . . .

Spirituals such as "Steal Away" and "Go Down, Moses" joined slaves emotionally and reminded them of the promise of deliverance in the afterlife and the hope of freedom in this life. Slaves often rejected teachings about original sin, and many who turned to Christianity openly shunned Calvinism's predestination. African-American preachers emphasized not internal conversion experiences but an externalized mission to mobilize the chosen people of God to liberate humanity. Nevertheless, slave religion did not lead toward mass rebellion because such a move would have been suicidal. Rather, slave Christianity imparted personal dignity and serenity, as well as group affirmation that slaves could transcend their shared hardships spiritually. Thus, whether African-Americans stressed their African heritage in their American environment or adapted English culture to their African legacy, distinctive communities emerged. These communities not only gave order and meaning to slave lives; they also helped slave men, women, and children create strategies for resisting the worst abuses of masters and southern laws.

Slave Men and Women at Work

The kind of work slaves did, and the treatment they endured, varied depending on the size of the plantation and its main activities. Over half of the South's slave owners had only one to five slaves and depended on the diverse skills of these individuals to accomplish many farm tasks. Moreover, regional differences between Delaware and east Tennessee, for example, and South Carolina or Georgia required drastically different work regimens. The cotton economy did not develop on Delaware soil in the same way, or to the same extent, as it did farther south. This, and strong antislavery sentiment (despite its officially remaining a slave state), accounts for the shrinking proportion of slaves and their special positions in Delaware. By 1860, when the number of slaves had shrunk to 2 percent of the state's population, many slaves had purchased their freedom and lived in daily contact with white commercial farmers and entrepreneurs.

In contrast, by the 1850s, 75 percent of slaves in the South lived on large plantations where freedom was a remote dream. Laboring from sunup to sundown, or longer at harvest times, distinguished field hand conditions on staples plantations from urban or small-farm lifestyles. Large planters were less likely to pay attention directly to the health of slaves than yeomen who lived in closer contact with the African-Americans they owned. In either case, however, few white planters understood much about basic nutrition, adequate housing, sanitation, and medical treatment. As a result, mortality rates for slave infants and children up to age five were double the rates for white children. Work regimens often denied pregnant slave women sufficient rest, which put their newborns immediately at risk. Malaria, yellow fever, and cholera claimed many babies and children, as well as undernourished adults. The harsh work on sugar plantations and in lumber camps along the Gulf of Mexico coastline of Mississippi and Louisiana created unusually high rates of chronic dysentery and cholera that killed many slaves within months of their arrival from the distant Chesapeake.

The "gang" and "task" systems of labor continued to divide slaves in different regions, depending on which staple crops they cultivated (see Chapter 4). In the rice and indigo fields of the Carolinas, tasking slaves were permitted a wide range of independent activities once they completed their stipulated tasks. Although slaves in rice fields stood knee-deep in water for hours, and their work regimens shortened life, they nevertheless had some means to negotiate with their masters certain modifications of rules about length of time at tasks and the quality of the finished jobs. This bargaining led to "the custom of the place," or the arrangements negotiated between slaves and masters. As a result, many slaves in the rice fields of South Carolina won periods of time to work in their own vegetable patches, trade with neighbors, find jobs off the plantation that earned food or household amenities, or simply rest.

Gang labor continued to apply in the Chesapeake, where tobacco plants had to be tended continually and slaves worked under the watchful eye of the master. As planters switched to wheat production, they easily modified gang labor to suit the intensive physical needs of planting and harvesting seasons. In tobacco and grain country, gang work lasted from sunup to sundown, often under the supervision of black drivers, or hired white overseers, and the system offered little incentive to work quickly. Chesapeake planters observed that "nothing can be conceived more inert than a slave . . . he moves not if he can avoid it; if the eyes of the overseer be off him, he sleeps." But gang labor was ideal for spreading King Cotton. Planters moving into the Georgia upcountry by the early 1800s brought the gang system to their new cotton plantations. Over time, they extended it to Alabama and Mississippi. Cotton growing required intensive plowing and planting, constant weeding with a heavy hoe, and painful separation of the ripe cotton from bolls that pricked slaves' stiff fingers. Each of these jobs was performed by large gangs that worked at the fastest pace a driver could squeeze from the slaves—the harshest might demand a grueling 150 pounds of cotton a day. Gangs in Chesapeake tobacco and wheat country were unable to negotiate working conditions as liberally as tasking slaves, although sometimes they effectively prevented the sales of particular members of their quarters or acquired additional clothing by agreeing to higher quotas or longer workdays.

It was not unusual for slave women to work in the fields with black men at tasks considered by white society to be too difficult for or unsuited to white females. While aging slave "grannies" cared for their children, many slave women worked with men to cut down trees, clear land for cultivation, and haul logs by leather straps attached around their chests. Slave women plowed cotton with mules and hoed fields to prepare them for planting; they helped build roads and repair wagons. A white observer at a Mississippi cotton plantation in 1852 remarked about slave women's stamina under extreme adversity: "Twenty of them were plowing together, with double teams and heavy plows. They were superintended by a male negro driver, who carried a whip, which he frequently cracked at them, permitting no dawdling or delay." On some plantations men did most of the heavy hauling and women sorted cotton lint and graded it, but this kind of separation was by no means universal, or even typical. As one fugitive slave insisted, "Women who do outdoor work are used as bad as men."

In addition to the unfailing duties of fieldwork, slave women worked at a variety of other tasks. They tended the slave and white children, who often mixed freely until age seven or eight, when slave children went to work. Other slave children began working at an early age doing light chores around the blacksmith shop, running errands to neighbors, or cleaning in the master's house. All were forbidden by law to learn reading and writing. Adult female slaves chosen to work in the "big house" cleaned, cooked, nursed, laundered, and sewed for the master's family. Some young women undertook weaving for masters and slaves on the plantation. Although this work was physically less demanding than the rigors of hoeing and picking cotton, it required long days (and sometimes nights) away from family members. It also involved the constant supervision of white people issuing orders and corrections. House slaves, unlike field hands, usually had to show subservience and respect or face severe punishments, especially when the "big house" filled with guests. When they returned to slave quarters, women often had to grind corn into meal or hominy, cook for their own families, and tend to the many chores of providing for others.

The rigors of field- and housework were sometimes broken up by opportunities for travel or group activities. Slave women with special skills, including seamstresses, cooks, and midwives, might travel to neighboring plantations and local towns as hired-out labor. Midwives were perhaps the most well-traveled of all slaves, since their services were needed in masters' families, neighboring slave quarters, and yeomen farmers' homes. Many masters relied on the medical knowledge of slave women to heal their slaves, which brought these specialists into contact with slaves and white people across a wide area. At the end of the week, Saturday afternoons might become occasions for group laundering or quilting. Sometimes slave women even slipped away to hold their own prayer meetings.

Skilled slave gardeners, blacksmiths, carpenters, tanners, and mechanics often worked in the master's house. Although such assignments brought slaves certain privileges, especially relief from fieldwork, being skilled could increase their chances of being sold away from their families or hired out to harsher masters. For example, on the docks of Natchez slaves worked as carpenters, chandlers, teamsters, sail makers, rope makers, and general deckhands alongside free African-Americans. Other slaves were hired out as miners, ship or dock hands, lumber camp workers, or forge men at iron mills. But for slaves hired out to the sugar mills of Louisiana planters, the backbreaking work of cutting and boiling cane was hardly a welcome relief from house labor.

Resistance and Rebellion

Slaves endured hard work, whippings, the sexual advances of masters, verbal abuse, and daily degradations of many forms. One ex-slave, recollecting her childhood spent with an unrelentingly cruel master on a small farm, said "that cowhide . . . would cut the blood out of you with every lick." Another, Harriet Jacobs, was rarely whipped or punished, and had more material comforts than "the torrent of Irish crowding our cities." But Jacobs was the victim of repeated sexual abuse by her "unprincipled master" and tormented verbally by her "jealous mistress," for whom "no terms were too vile for her to bestow upon me." Once pregnant, her master denied his role, and Jacobs's only close relative, her grandmother, turned her away for a few agonizing days. They reconciled, however, and in time Jacobs went into hiding in an attic for seven years until she could escape to New York City and Boston.

Slaves' resistance to abuses took many forms. Some tactics were subtle, as when slaves appeared to accommodate work orders but in reality set their own limitations to work or poked fun at drivers and masters. Other forms of resistance were riskier, such as pilfering supplies, slowing down completion of a task, sabotaging crop production, damaging tools, or using effusive apologies and praise of the master in order to avert suspicion and punishment for misdeeds. Frederick Douglass repeatedly told his white audiences about the use of deceit and guile among slaves: "As the master studies to keep the slave ignorant, the slave is cunning enough to make the master think he succeeds."

Leaving a plantation or factory without authorization was a more dangerous step for slaves to take. Some slaves who left work without permission simply intended to "go visitin'" family members or kinfolk on a nearby plantation, though the punishments for such travel and neglect of work duties could be serious indeed. Others wished to "disappear" temporarily just to show the master that escape was possible. Still others attempted to run away permanently and find their way to freedom. In Georgia and the new Black Belt states, running away was far more perilous than in the older states. To begin with, few slaves knew a safe haven to run to, especially once Spain ceded the Floridas to America in 1819. In addition, harsh work weakened slaves' ability to run far enough to attain freedom or thwarted their will to try. And rumors spread quickly that the forests and creeks of the Old Southwest were filled with hostile Native Americans and bounty hunters. Sometimes African traditional beliefs warned about vile creatures in swamps, forests, and mountains. By the 1840s, planters in Louisiana and Mississippi regularly hired slave catchers and their trained attack dogs to track fugitives.

Still, despite the odds, over a thousand slaves "took their freedom" by running away each year during the 1840s and 1850s. Most of the runaways were men between sixteen and thirty-five; many had work skills and could read and write. Women were much less likely to run away, perhaps because of their attachments to nurturing children. A network of white and black antislavery activists aided escapees with passage on the Underground Railroad. Both the law and slave catchers fought efforts to conduct slaves to freedom, posing a grave risk to everyone concerned in the enterprise. Many brave white abolitionists, including the Quaker merchant Thomas Garrett, sacrificed their time, money, and sometimes their reputations, to such efforts nevertheless. But the most valuable source of support came from free African-Americans in cities such as Richmond, Charleston, New Orleans, Baltimore, and Wilmington. In these communities, runaway slaves could find temporary refuge on their way north, secure food and new clothing, perhaps find a sponsor or escort to a safer region, or simply merge their identities with the free African-Americans around them. Some runaways, rather than moving on, devoted themselves to helping others escape. Harriet Tubman, an escaped slave and prominent abolitionist lecturer, worked tirelessly on the Underground Railroad. Tubman returned to the South nineteen times despite the danger of being re-enslaved or murdered each time she organized a trip to bring out slaves.

Open and organized group resistance to overseers and cruel masters was not frequent. It was most likely to occur where free African-Americans and slaves came in contact with one another or where runaways knew that a safe haven might harbor them. One intended revolt, in 1800, involved the plan of Gabriel Prosser, a liter-

Torture Mask The laws of southern states had long stipulated that masters could use whatever means they deemed necessary to prevent slave runaways and insolence. In the early 1800s, some planters adopted this so-called restraining mask to punish slaves. *(Library of Congress.)*

ate blacksmith, to take over Richmond. With about a thousand slaves from the area, and the expectation that recently freed black people from Haiti would join them, Prosser declared "Death or Liberty." Although the rebellion was quashed at the last minute, and planters assented to the hanging of nearly forty slaves as examples to potential future resisters, Richmond residents had been seriously shaken.

Then, in 1822, Denmark Vesey's Charleston plot unfolded. Vesey, a free African-American, had the double distinction of owning his own carpentry shop and having an outstanding reputation in the city for eloquent speaking. Moreover, he had recently become a preacher. Many southern white leaders at the time were still proclaiming that the Missouri Compromise (see page 315) had given them the right to extend slavery into the trans-Mississippi West. Vesey shared his disgust over this interpretation of the compromise with his congregation. Gullah Jack, a folk medicine man from the South Carolina low country who spent time in Charleston, grew close to Vesey and together they connived to take the city. The conspirators planned to steal guns from the Charleston arsenal and horses from private stables, and then rally the support of widely dispersed house slaves to murder whites in their homes. Eventually the slaves would reach the docks and sail to freedom in Haiti.

Vesey and Gullah Jack convinced about eighty city and country slaves to join them, including the house slaves at the governor's mansion in Charleston. But two weeks before the appointed insurrection day, a reluctant recruit informed the authorities about the plot. When confronted, the leading insurgents denied the charges and deterred officials, but when the charge was raised once more by another house slave, Charleston authorities did not wait for proof. For days, slaves were grabbed up, thirty-four hanged alongside the swinging corpse of Vesey, and thirty-seven sold down the river to new masters. But not all the conspirators were caught, and the Charleston elite lived on for years in fear that a new revolt might be brewing. Leading citizens even appealed to the local government to close off the city to visitors. White citizens destroyed Vesey's church, and in late 1822, the South Carolina legislature enacted a law requiring that all black sailors be confined in local jails while their ships were in port, an attempt to limit contact between Charleston's slaves and free African-Americans who might have dangerous ideas.

In 1831 the violence that David Walker predicted shook the Chesapeake region. Nat Turner was a slave from Southampton County, Virginia, a self-taught, widely respected leader among the region's African-Americans, and something of a religious visionary. He had been promised his freedom, but a second master refused to grant it, while a third master separated Turner from his wife. Despite the kindly treatment of his current master, Joseph Travis, Turner became embittered. He professed to have experienced a religious vision of whites and blacks "engaged in battle," where "blood flowed in streams." Following a conversion experience, Turner believed he was destined to direct his inner rage at slave masters. Along with five others, Turner killed Travis on August 20, 1831, and then ran from plantation to plantation killing the white people they encountered and offering freedom to the slaves. Fifty-five whites died, but when a group of mounted and armed planters rounded up the nearly sixty runaway slaves, action came to a halt. Vengeful militiamen rampaged through the countryside and armed cavalry murdered dozens of slaves, hoisting fifteen of their heads on poles to send clear signals of their intentions. Trials of about fifty slaves resulted in twenty hangings. Eventually Turner himself was caught and met the same end. Although no other serious slave revolts broke out before emancipation, southern whites shuddered collectively for years as successful runaways provided constant reminders about discontents.

Free African-Americans

The American Revolution's language of political independence, and both patriot and British offers of freedom to slaves who aided their causes, inspired many slaves to break away from their bondage. After the Revolution, gradual emancipation provisions in northern states increased the numbers of free African-Americans, and private manumissions or self-purchases gained freedom for some former slaves. George Washington, for example, provided in his will for the manumission of his slaves. But increasingly, southern planters limited these opportunities for freedom, especially after Nat Turner's bloody revolt. Slaves turned to the more desperate measure of running away to cities where they could blend anonymously with free African-Americans.

Some slaves worked long years to buy freedom for themselves and their families. James L. Bradley "made collars for horses, out of plaited husks," according to his memoirs. With a little money from this work, Bradley bought a pig and tended a small plot of corn for feed; in time, he bred a large number of hogs, which he sold, along with small amounts of tobacco. After five years, Bradley bought time from his master to work odd jobs "morn and night," until he purchased himself for $700. In 1849 John H. Hammond told fellow South Carolinians that "whenever a slave is made a mechanic he is more than half freed." For many whites, including Hammond, this was reason enough to limit such opportunities for slaves. For other whites, slaves were a valuable addition to the labor force, as when railroad owners in Lynchburg, Virginia, or Nashville, Tennessee, hired slaves, or when the tobacco and hemp factory owners in Virginia and Kentucky did likewise. Scholars estimate that in the 1840s and 1850s between 5 and 10 percent of southern workers were hired slaves, some for a few days and some for a year at a time.

By the time of the Civil War, 500,000 African-Americans were free, about half of them living in southern states. Most free African-Americans, whether southern or northern, were landless rural laborers or tenants of white landowners. In North Carolina and Arkansas, the majority of the free black population continued to work for white planters or remained indebted to the white business class. But large numbers of free blacks migrated into southern cities such as Savannah, Charleston, Memphis, and Natchez, alarming white populations. In Washington, D.C., 30 percent of the population remained enslaved in the 1830s and 1840s, but fears among the white population grew as many slaves gained the right to live apart from masters in wooden shantytowns where they mingled with free slaves and all too often slipped from the grip of their masters.

In both the South and the North, African-Americans hardly enjoyed the unmitigated blessings of free society. Indeed, they usually lived somewhere between freedom and slavery. Courts, businesses, and schools frequently denied free African-Americans formal legal rights in practice. Immigrant Irish, German, and other peoples forced African-Americans out of jobs as horse tenders, domestic workers, barbers, and tailors in cities such as Richmond, Charleston, New Orleans, and Mobile. In St. Louis the black population became increasingly more rural, edged out of the city by immigrating unskilled workers from Europe. Most free African-Americans survived on meager wages at dreary jobs as carters, laundresses, horse handlers, barbers, carpenters, quarrymen, and road crewmen. A few former slave women in each city landed employment as nannies and housekeepers, their paltry wages sometimes the sole income for their families. Free black men hired themselves out in large numbers to sugar plantations in Louisiana by the 1850s, and to small shops as coopers, carters, and carpenters in Virginia and Maryland.

Nor was freedom for ex-slaves always secure. For example, slave traders such as James H. Birch of Washington, D.C., built a network of kidnappers and tricksters who abducted free African-Americans from northern homes and sold them into slavery in Louisiana, Mississippi, and Texas during the 1840s. In Washington, D.C., white citizens feared the rapid influx of free African-Americans, possibly because the city also had become an important location for large slave auctions and a crossroads for slaves being shipped from the Chesapeake to Georgia and South Carolina. The nation's capital enacted Black Codes in 1808 to control the liberties of freed slaves migrating into the city. These new laws imposed fines and whippings for public gatherings after 10 P.M., for "tippling" in local taverns, and for "nightly and disorderly meetings"—the latter measure outlawing virtually all social and religious gatherings of the city's African-Americans. In the wake of Nat Turner's rebellion in Virginia, Washington's Black Codes became even harsher; for example, a black person who struck a white person could have his ears cut off.

A few free African-Americans in Washington, D.C., reached middle-class status, owning property and serving in benevolent and religious organizations. George Fisher, for example, ran a blacksmith shop on East Capitol Street; Spencer Johnson made shoes to order at Pennsylvania Avenue and Twenty-first Street. The Reverend John Cook ran the Union Seminary, a private high school for free men of color, started in 1834, as well as the Young Men's Moral and Literary Society. By the 1850s, nearly 10 percent of blacks in Washington, D.C., owned property. Although the city boasted almost thirty schools for white girls, journalists widely noted that African-American girls got a far better education at their one female academy.

Washington, D.C., did not have the most stringent Black Codes. An 1806 Virginia law required newly manumitted ex-slaves to leave the state within a year or face re-enslavement; Maryland followed with a similar law of its own. Chesapeake laws also took away free African-Americans' rights to sue or serve in courts, and by 1830, it was nearly impossible to gain manumission. Throughout the South, free black people were forbidden to carry firearms or gather in meetings; were systematically denied the right to file lawsuits or to be tried by juries in criminal cases; and were required to carry "freedom papers" proving they were not slaves. Ex-slaves were not permitted to vote, hold office, or serve in the militia. In verdicts requiring punishments, laws stipulated that all black people—slave and free—would receive the penalties reserved for slaves.

Even the southern cities that had permitted all residents to own property and run businesses began to curtail the activities and opinions of free blacks in the 1840s and 1850s. Free black tradesmen in Charleston had to carry identification papers and wear badges attesting to their legitimate employment. The white community of Natchez deported numbers of poor free blacks during the 1840s under the pretense that they were "incendiaries" and "abolitionists."

Some free African-Americans overcame great adversity to achieve distinction. A few, often through self-education, attained public recognition and wealth, such as the surveyor and architect Benjamin Bannaker and the merchant Robert Sheridan. The nearly one thousand free African-Americans of Natchez who lived in abject poverty regarded with scorn the few ex-slaves who became prominent businessmen in the city, some of whom owned slaves and cultivated cultural relations with the white community. In Charleston, elite free black people offered goods and services to a white clientele who also permitted free blacks to educate their children in separate schools and to move about the city freely. Free African-Americans ran hotels, stables, and mills in and around Charleston. Urban ex-slaves who had advanced up the economic ladder considerably in the early 1800s often lived in white neighborhoods; some even acquired slaves to work in their shops.

Free African-Americans in Philadelphia at first joined the churches of white citizens (though they sat in separate sections), but in 1794 Reverend Absalom Jones

Free African-American Poet Frances Watkins Although freedom eluded all but a small proportion of slaves before the Civil War, those who gained freedom often prevailed against difficult conditions to become outstanding intellectuals. Frances Ellen Watkins Harper used her talents as a poet and lecturer to champion the antislavery cause. She became the first woman faculty member at Union Seminary in Ohio in 1850 and then moved to Pennsylvania in order to help with the Underground Railroad. (*Library Company of Philadelphia.*)

founded the first African-American Baptist church. Nearby in the same city, Reverend Richard Allen began the first Methodist congregation of African-Americans. Allen was born a slave in Philadelphia in 1760 but, as a teenager, had been sold with his family to a farmer in Delaware, where the fires of Methodism inspired Allen's master to let him buy his freedom. After the Revolution, Allen first became an itinerant Methodist speaker and then a minister who gained high esteem in Philadelphia's abolitionist and Methodist circles. But after witnessing years of discrimination, including separated pews for worship in churches and separate burial grounds, Allen decided to answer the burning desire of free African-Americans to control their worship. Allen was equally dissatisfied with proposals for gradual emancipation and colonization. In 1816 Allen brought together a number of breakaway African-American church members to found the African Methodist Episcopal (AME) Church, America's first independent black denomination.

Bringing talents together into new organizations often gave additional strength and autonomy to free African-Americans living in the North. Groups of freedmen founded societies for mutual aid, separate medical care, or dissenting religious worship. Numerous African-American women participated in efforts to found schools in northern communities. Freedmen's organizations also overlapped with the membership and activities of antislavery organizations. Sojourner Truth, David Walker, and Frederick Douglass helped build bridges that strengthened both African-American churches and abolitionist societies. In the South, AME churches gave slaves a degree of temporary autonomy from white religion and the slave institution. Denmark Vesey, the fiery speaker who inspired his congregation to the point of revolt, was an AME preacher.

 ## Planters and Yeomen

Great plantation mansions rose out of the southern landscape here and there, as if to remind all viewers that the profits of slave labor would concentrate in the hands of a very few wealthy families. But very few southern landowners had twenty or more slaves on their plantations. The great majority of white planters occupied land between and around the great plantations stretching from Virginia and Tennessee to Louisiana and Texas. From poor tenants and itinerant white laborers, to middling white farmers—some of whom owned one to five slaves—this numerical majority enjoyed few of the cultural, economic, and political privileges that elite planters did. The planter's paternal identity vis-à-vis his slaves contrasted sharply with middling and poor white southerners' anxieties over slave competition for jobs and challenges to their belief in free white labor. Nevertheless, landowning yeomen and landless tenants constantly interacted with great planters and experienced the effects of the slave system daily.

Planters

In the 1850s only one-third of southern white people owned slaves—18 percent owned fewer than five, 16 percent owned five to twenty, and only about 2.5 percent owned more than twenty. As late as the eve of the Civil War, only about 46,000 planters in the South owned twenty or more slaves; fewer than three thousand white men owned over one hundred. But slave owners, especially the elite among them, shaped much of the culture, politics, and economy of the South, and they fiercely defended their interests against encroachments from small farmers in the region and against all critics outside the region. Some planters' mansions commanded awe and conferred authority by their opulence. The estate became a site for displays of elegance, grace, and constant expensive entertainment.

Tidewater and low country plantations that rose before the Revolution represented enduring property and power in the hands of a few men. After 1800, planter expansion into Kentucky, Louisiana, and Mississippi added a layer of new elite families. New Orleans and Natchez planters sometimes boasted hundreds of slaves and hundreds of thousands of acres producing cotton for ready shippers at the docks.

Some planters also enjoyed many hours a week of leisure reading, horseback riding, or "gaming" with neighbors. Most planters, though, were businessmen who attended carefully to surveying crops, reviewing slaves' work and planning work regimens, keeping account books and notations, and scouring the newspapers for pricing trends and commercial conditions. Many planters tried to furnish all of their own food and supplies and trained slaves to be carpenters, blacksmiths, weavers, and coopers. Even among planters who owned many slaves, mansions were rare until the 1850s. More typically a home of a few rooms stood amid outbuildings for cooking, tanning, dairying, and other chores related to provisioning a household.

Whether cultivating great wealth or sustaining a more modest productive enterprise, southern planters relied on the ideology of paternalism to maintain their supremacy over both slaves and wives. Paternalism taught that the complex social network of a plantation was a family, with the planter acting as the master and father of both his white household and his slaves. His wife and children, as well as his slaves, all fit along a continuum of roles. The master had to provide the basic needs of everyone in this "family" and was expected to treat both white and black members humanely. Wives, in return, would obey according to what their roles dictated, as would the master's children, as would slaves. Paternalism offered the ideal of constituting all plantation relations into "a harmonious whole." Masters had not only plentiful privileges and absolute control over the lives under their authority, but also the duty to provide necessities and protection for grateful family members and obedient slaves.

Masters in the Chesapeake region and parts of the new Black Belt supervised their plantations personally as businessmen. This put them in direct daily and personal contact with slaves, giving masters many opportunities to enforce their authority when necessary, but also requiring them to maintain a delicate balance of respect and solicitation of the welfare of slaves. Also, since the importation of slaves nearly ceased after 1808, any expansion of the master's slave labor force would have to come from domestic sales and natural increase. Thus, to encourage safe and regular childbearing, masters had to ensure at least a minimum of care for the physical and emotional well-being of slaves. Again, this afforded slaves at least some opportunity to negotiate conditions of work and leisure and to obtain small items of sustenance or comfort. Planters slowly gave up the most severe forms of punishment, including castration, branding, and physical mutilation. Still, these small measures did not indicate so much a master's moral or emotional conscience as his attention to profits. Supervisory methods constantly reaffirmed the status of slaves as inferior and "childlike," and the use of coercion—including whipping and withholding food, for example—was always a potential threat.

Paternalism gave the plantation mistress especially difficult burdens. In addition to cultivating all of the virtues that women everywhere were supposed to share—obedience, chastity, purity, and piety—the planter's wife and daughters managed the household slaves, spun and wove, cared for sick family members and slaves, arranged hospitality for visitors, and did the countless daily tasks that large households entailed. But overlaying this arduous routine, southern women bore the additional burdens of paternalistic ideology, which created an image of southern plantation mistresses at odds with their daily lives. Although plantation mistresses bustled ceaselessly about their homes, they were expected to refrain from "drudge work" and to delegate as many responsibilities as possible to master-husbands. Ideal southern mistresses were supposed to have very little real control over important domestic decisions, and thus to have far less authority in their "sphere" than northern women claimed. Ideal southern master-husbands, unlike northern men, were supposed to have extensive control over their households and to dominate all work and social affairs as they did in their plantation fields.

Plantation mistresses differed from northern female homemakers in another sense: southern ladies were strictly prohibited from entering public activities, and thus were shut off from important arenas of social reform. The isolation of rural plantations reinforced the social and emotional distance of white women from friends and kin, too. Although they often were surrounded by slave women of all ages, the chasm of differences between the races could not be easily bridged. The scholarly record shows some remarkable efforts by plantation mistresses to befriend or defend female slaves. Some softened the harshness of cruel masters by defending a slave's version of misdeeds, by handing out apples or molasses at slave quarters, and by helping at the birth of slave babies. Many pleaded on behalf of slaves who came to masters with minor requests for favors. And there are numerous stories of mistresses who entrusted slaves with arranging secret meetings with suitors or delivering love letters. Annie Broidrick, a white woman raised on a Mississippi plantation, recounted late in her life that "many a romantic tale was confided by mistress and maid to each other during the hours the hair was being brushed." But in the final analysis, as most of these recollections note, the more dominant note was one of great social and emotional distance between the races of women in plantation households.

Yeomen and Tenants

By the 1850s, when the slave population reached its zenith before emancipation, fully 65 percent of southern white heads of households did not own slaves. But few

Varieties of Racial Family Roles Although voluntary racial mixing had been scorned by much of American society for generations, white and black people actually lived in many different family and community arrangements. African-American women were nannies and nurses, field hands and washerwomen, mothers and lovers, indispensable to many planters' households as well as to their own in slave quarters. Although most African-American women remained the most subordinate members of southern society, this young lady enjoyed a special relationship to the white infant, who was probably in her care. *(J. Paul Getty Museum.)*

landowning yeomen or landless tenants challenged the appropriateness of elite planter domination and slavery in the South. After all, many of them admired wealthy planters and hoped to rise into a better condition themselves through the acquisition of slaves and cultivation of fertile soil. The republican ideal, so acclaimed by Thomas Jefferson, taught that a piece of independently held land was the starting point for true citizenship and a virtuous personal life.

Yeomen—independent landowning farmers—in the older tidewater areas produced food for their own families and sometimes for the plantations nearby. Upcountry Georgia farmers who lived on land once held by Cherokee Indians added livestock grazing to their agriculture and sometimes earned small amounts of cash from sales of a bale or two of cotton after each harvest. Occasionally, an upcountry yeoman fared better than his neighbors and was then able to buy more land, or even to become a slave owner. Those who moved farther into the interior found that the rich soil of the Shenandoah, Ohio, and other river systems yielded large crops of corn and wheat or provided extensive grazing for herds of cattle and sheep.

Southern yeomen clung to the Democratic Party's promise to expand America's western empire on behalf of the common man during the 1830s. For some this implied opportunities to rise into the ranks of the slave-owning political leadership, while for others the promise held out hope for the more modest acquisition of a small landholding and perhaps a couple of slaves—enough to secure "freedom" from domination by great planters or wealthy developers. In addition, landownership and its association with white male suffrage created a common bond of white racial superiority over blacks. And yeomen also cherished the ideal of self-sufficiency or modest comfort that could distance them from both the northern industrialization many southerners feared and the indebtedness of landless poor southern white families around them.

These beliefs tended to obscure the widening cultural and economic gap between yeomen and the great planters. Economically, most yeomen could not expect to grow wealthy, for their production of one to six 400-pound bales of cotton per year could not compare with the hundreds of bales that a great planter might produce. In addition, the small amounts of cotton sent to market put the farmer in touch with the distribution and pricing mechanisms that great planters controlled. Many yeomen needed the services of local millers and blacksmiths, who might be connected closely to the functions of the great plantations. In those cases, elaborate arrangements among many parties got the yeoman's grain gristed on the plantation mill in return for leather hides, barreled pork, or some other farm product. If he wished to get cotton to port cities, a yeoman needed help from well-connected planters. If he acquired slaves, a yeoman might hire them out to needy planters. If he needed workers, he might rent slaves from a planter. Sometimes the ledgers of farmers show detailed exchanges of labor time between farms and large plantations. But most yeomen, struggling just to squeeze a decent crop from their 150 to 200 acres, depended on regular cooperation among white neighbors to get in the harvests. Indeed, slaves themselves expressed a preference for being owned by a great planter rather than a yeoman, for the wealthy master tended to have greater economic security, which in turn offered the prospect of more enduring ties in slave quarters and perhaps family life. Although some yeomen prospered enough for modest comfort, many of them, as one ex-slave told it, "lived by scanty means, at the edge of their survival and mine."

Just as the spectrum of landowning yeomen included successful farm families that might have slaves and struggling farmers who barely survived from one year to the next, so there was a spectrum of landless southern whites throughout the South. Away from the tidewater and lowlands of plantation slavery, where hills and then mountains rose out of the countryside, the soil was less hospitable for growing cotton, and many would-be yeomen found it impossible to attain the ideal of owning a self-sufficient farm. Tilling the worst land, often far from waterways leading to markets, poor hill-country whites often fell outside the definition of republican yeomen citizens. Many of these poor whites focused on production for household consumption and local exchange, raising hogs, sheep, and cattle along with food crops. Neighbors borrowed tools, seed, and household goods from one another; they traded at small country stores for notions, salt, and yard goods; and they bartered with friends for food, tool repairs, midwifery services, and harvesting. Unlike plantation mistresses and rising yeomen, upcountry farmers' wives did household chores with their daughters and worked in the fields as well.

With little hope of acquiring land, many poor whites became the tenants of yeomen or planters, or moved from job to job in search of stability or survival. One-third of Georgia's upcountry farmers were tenants on other men's land. In the far western parts of North Carolina, South Carolina, and Virginia, from 40 to 50 percent of white people owned no land. The lowlands of Alabama and the pine barrens along the Atlantic coast were also home to large numbers of struggling poor whites. Throughout these areas by the 1830s, thousands of laborers, tenants, and occasional wage workers lived in utter poverty, surviving on minimal food of poor quality and enduring long bouts with debilitating diseases such as pellagra, hookworm, and anemia. And as King Cotton took over more and more of the best soil in new states, and the price of land skyrocketed, the yeoman ideal receded further and further beyond their reach. During agricultural harvests and in factories, poor whites and black slaves—both hired temporarily—might work side by side. Some landless poor whites rented land from planters hoping someday to repay their debts and save enough to buy a small tract.

The relationships between poor whites and slaves were filled with tension, for while most landless tenants and occasional laborers shared the yeoman's ideal of becoming independent landowners, in reality they had much in common with slaves and free African-Americans. Some sympathetic whites helped slaves escape and hide in obscure places. Some entered petty business deals to deliver liquor or extra food to slaves who were forbidden these items by planters. Planters often accommodated this trade by lowering the prices of flour, salt pork, or fabric that they sold to slaves in hopes of undermining trade outside their plantations. But, as one planter in Mississippi noted, there were "poor whites within a few miles who would always sell liquor to the negroes, and encourage them to steal, to obtain the means to buy it of them." In this way, the lines between free whites and slaves were often temporarily blurred.

Defending Slavery

For generations, presses, politicians, and pulpits had justified slavery to southerners. Historical examples of slavery in the Bible and in Classical Greece and Rome had bolstered arguments by colonists in the 1600s that for some people to be in permanent bondage to others was "the natural condition" (see Chapter 2). In the early 1800s, writers deemed slavery an evil developed by colonial ancestors and a burden borne by southern planters. Jeffersonians had dared to imagine the South without slaves, through discussion about "civilizing the dark races" and colonization of slaves in communities outside America.

Once the southern cotton boom was under way in the early 1800s, it became increasingly difficult for planters to contemplate emancipation of individual slaves. Some began to argue that the entire economic system of the South required slavery. Thomas Jefferson and a few others had proposed that slow individual manumission and colonization might be a viable response to slavery, but they also feared the mixing of the races and defended slavery as a "necessary evil" in national life. As Jefferson put it, "We have the wolf by the ears; and we can neither hold him nor safely let him go. Justice is in one scale, and self-preservation in the other."

Indeed, the nation did not move toward individual or general emancipation. Southern slave codes passed during the early national years ensured slavery's continuing existence. Northern and western states explicitly limited the rights of free African-Americans, some by imposing a property requirement for voting, some by prohibiting African-Americans from serving on juries or testifying against whites in courts, and some by closing public services, transport, land offices, and schools to African-Americans. The Constitution itself provided that seats in the House of Representatives would be determined by a count of the whole white population and three-fifths of the black population; runaway slaves would be returned to their masters; and the international slave trade could continue for twenty more years, until 1808. Moreover, a federal Fugitive Slave Act in 1793 encouraged kidnappers and bounty hunters to seize free African-Americans from northern neighborhoods and sell them into slavery.

But by the 1820s, disquieting ambiguities troubled southern planters. Although the Missouri Compromise of 1820 opened the door for expanding slavery west of the Mississippi River, the same act granted free African-Americans the right to vote in Maine, thereby heightening sectional fears between North and South. Some southerners believed that creating a free state, Maine, transcended a simple balance of political representation; it encouraged "convulsive and destructive" northern antislavery sentiment to grow.

And antislavery sentiment *did* grow. In one of their more spectacular efforts, abolitionists conducted a massive petition drive to flood Congress with requests to abolish slavery and the slave trade in Washington, D.C. But Congress was swayed by strong southern opposition to the petitions, and by prodding from President Andrew Jackson, to pass a gag rule in 1836 that prohibited discussion of the petitions in the House or Senate. Already, southerners had acted forcefully against the presence of petitions in their states, as well as use of the federal postal system to circulate them. In 1835 a proslavery mob broke into a Charleston post office and confiscated batches of antislavery petition forms and literature, which they proceeded to burn. Now, with support from Congress to stifle national discussion about slavery, planters became more arrogant in their defense of the institution.

By the early 1830s, Southern defensiveness about slavery was entering a new phase. As one far-seeing southerner put it in 1833, "So interwoven is it [slavery] with our interest, our manners, our climate and our very being, that no change can ever possibly be effected without a civil commotion." Although he added that "the heart of a patriot must turn with horror" from such national violence, the coercion inherent in slavery, the potential and real violence between the races, and the sheer numbers of black people in southern states had both entrenched the slave system and aroused opposition to it.

In their majority, southern legislators, printers, and clergymen defended their culture, including slavery, paternalism, and planter domination. In addition to passing laws that tightened their grip on slaves, southern leaders also articulated arguments in their press and pulpits that solidified their commitment to the so-called peculiar institution. For example, the constitutions of Louisiana, Alabama, and Mississippi included language permitting slavery. By 1835, every southern state passed additional laws to restrain the movement of slaves and to monitor or restrict public gatherings, dances, and African-American church services. With the exception of Kentucky, Tennessee, and Maryland, all southern states forbade slaves from learning how to read, and many outlawed manumissions. Slave patrols—vigilante groups of poor white men who whipped and tortured slaves caught without passes after curfew—became a regular feature of country roads and southern cities.

The violence based on racial attitudes associated with southern slavery spread through northern and midwestern communities in the 1830s to 1850s. For example, Irish immigrants mobbed antislavery activists in New York and Boston because the immigrants feared cutthroat competition for jobs should southern slaves be emancipated and move north. Free labor beliefs taught American-born and immigrant workers that slaves shared their aspirations for cheap land and decent wages.

Violence spilled out into the territories and new western states, too. In the Old Northwest, an area guaranteed by Jefferson's 1787 ordinance to remain free soil, "black laws" attempted to exclude or expel free African-Americans, and these were in turn enforced by self-appointed groups of white "slave police." In border states, white violence against blacks on plantations carried over into factories where slaves had been hired out by masters, and it threatened to break out whenever both races gathered together publicly, as at revival meetings or July 4 celebrations. In Alton, Illinois, the abolitionist editor Elijah P. Lovejoy endured the destruction of his printing press by angry mobs not once, but four times, before he was killed in 1837 by "border ruffians" who wished to spread slavery into Kansas.

In settled border states and Chesapeake-area cities, too, violence reached new levels by the 1830s. Northern abolitionists charged slave traders with "stealing" free African-Americans and selling them into slavery far from their homes. The New England Anti-Slavery Society called the traders "inland pirates" who had little concern for the true status of their "human cargo." In cities, racial tensions also grew between whites and blacks working in households and small shops, and occasionally individual confrontations took place. After Nat Turner's Rebellion in 1831, Chesapeake region planters advocated more stringent Black Codes. But codes did not satisfy everyone, and the animosity of white mobs toward free and slave African-Americans turned ugly. For example, in Washington, D.C., in 1835 a slave desperate for his freedom tried to murder the widow of the U.S. Capitol architect, Mrs. William Thornton, which provoked white retaliation. Angry young whites banded together for days in what was later called the "Snow Storm" and rampaged through the city's streets destroying black homes and businesses. For years, mob violence was periodically incited with the cry of "Avenge Mrs. Thornton!"

In addition to racial violence, legal restrictions, and increased abolitionist activities by the 1830s, some of slavery's southern supporters developed their justifications for the South's "peculiar institution" further. James Henry Hammond, a South Carolina planter who became a legislator in the 1830s, wrote that slavery was neither evil nor immoral because "civilized gentlemen" had organized the system rationally and efficiently. If slaves' privileges had been withdrawn and their punishments had grown harsh, it was the fault of abolitionist agitators who aroused slaves to disobedience. William Harper, a distinguished South Carolina jurist and advocate of nullification, insisted that evidence pointed to "some form of slavery in all ages and countries," and thus planters were unexceptional in that regard. Moreover, since slaves' "nature tended to the immoral," and prominent passages of both the Old and New Testaments of the Bible could be interpreted to dictate the permanent inequality of the races, masters simply followed the principles of benevolence when they subjected African-Americans to slavery.

Thomas R. Dew, a Virginia apologist for slavery, expanded the arguments of some southerners who found fault with John Locke's teachings about natural rights (see Competing Voices, page 482). All individuals, argued Dew, do not have inherent, God-given equality of rights within societies. Moreover, Locke was wrong in positing that at one time individuals came out of their "state of nature," or primitive competitive condition, to join in societies with rules and governments. Instead, Dew argued that the social order had evolved slowly over time, that it was suited for stability rather than legal changes or revolutions, and that it was an organic whole of mutually dependent people, not a set of "artificial" markets and institutions. Humans, insisted Dew, had strikingly different capacities from birth and could function only in pyramidal relationships of authority, especially across racial lines. People organize themselves, said Dew, more around their duties than around their rights. It was the duty of white masters to shelter, feed, protect, and permanently own black people.

During the 1850s, George Fitzhugh took the proslavery argument another step. In his influential books, *Sociology for the South; or, The Failure of a Free Society*

(1854), and *Cannibals All! Or, Slaves Without Masters* (1857), Fitzhugh argued that southern slaves actually lived in a condition of greater freedom than northern "wage slaves"; black slaves were tended by paternalistic masters in a "community of interests" from cradle to grave, whereas northern workers were hired, paid less than a decent wage, used up, and turned out into the world again if illness or old age made them useless to the employer. Fitzhugh was a respected Virginia lawyer and planter, and when he expressed the belief that northern industrial life had succumbed to impersonal market forces, in which profits were the sole aim of factory owners and wages the sole aim of workers, southerners nodded in agreement. Masters, wrote Fitzhugh, established cultural examples for poor whites and slaves to emulate. They lived a refined life that not only reflected their profits from the labor of slaves but also set a tone of civility and public virtue in the South that slaves grew to respect. Many years before this, John C. Calhoun had argued that slavery made it possible for the master race to perfect itself culturally and intellectually.

No matter how convoluted these intellectual arguments for slavery became, most of them rested on the assumption of African-Americans' racial inferiority. Those who accepted such a premise could then argue that force, restrictions, and of course slavery naturally followed. Slavery was not only a fitting condition for all people of African descent; it was the best framework for raising up, or "civilizing," African-Americans. Dew felt certain that "slaves of a good master are his warmest, most constant, and most devoted friends." Yet even the poorest whites did not need such paternalistic "friendship" because they supposedly were not racial underlings.

Not all southerners defended slavery, and a few of them turned against the institution. In the mid-1830s, the Grimké sisters left South Carolina and became outspoken abolitionists; the Kentucky antislavery spokesman James G. Birney became the abolitionist candidate for the Liberty Party in 1840. In 1832 Virginia's backcountry small farmers struck out against the great planters of the coastline when, fearing more rebellions like Nat Turner's, they forced the state government to discuss the feasibility of gradual manumission. By the 1840s, some yeomen complained about the difficulties of purchasing land and slaves, both of which were becoming more expensive, and their consequent inability to enter the ranks of slave owners.

Other small farmer whites fiercely resisted the encroachments of banks, railroads, and creditors reaching from coastal regions into the backcountry. These people did not aspire to become slave owners, but rather to sustain their republican independence against the southern system of slavery with its political and economic elite. They were no less racist than northern white people who feared the economic competition and cultural presence of African-Americans in their communities, nor than their southern counterparts who owned great landed estates. Hinton Helper, a North Carolinian who left the South to join northern abolitionists, wrote *The Impending Crisis of the South* (1857), in which he argued that unlike northern free labor's plentiful opportunities for economic advancement, southern slavery held non–slave owning whites in thrall to the dominant plantation and labor system. The true victims of the slave and plantation system were nonslaveholding whites. Although Helper intended to stimulate poor white sentiment in the South against both African-Americans and the institution of slavery, yeomen demands in southern politics continued to be subordinated to planters' elite power over all of southern political life.

CONCLUSION

Both northerners and southerners agreed that slavery was the basis for understanding the South. Slavery was the linchpin of southern rural and urban life, white and black culture, economy and politics. Despite the small number of large plantations compared with yeoman farmsteads and tenant tracts, it was staples agriculture and the slave labor system supporting it that set the South apart from the North most fundamentally.

Slavery unquestionably grew during this era, both numerically and territorially. Despite the official end to slave importation, the institution grew tremendously from the 1820s to 1850s. From fewer than 700,000 in 1790, the slave population in the South mushroomed to nearly 4 million by 1860. As slavery officially ended in the Caribbean, the numbers of "country-born" slaves in the American South rose dramatically. In 1860, 95 percent of America's blacks lived in southern states from Delaware to Texas, accounting for 25 percent of the southern population.

The "peculiar institution" spread to numerous new states in those years, too, and its defenders looked forward to its continuing expansion far beyond the Mississippi River. The Missouri Compromise gave southern expansionists hope that the southern way of life—its slavery, plantation agriculture, and planter paternalism—might defeat the ideals of free labor and independent family farming that northerners propounded. Despite the great disparity of social and economic conditions between rich planters and impoverished yeomen and tenants in the South, most white people agreed that slavery was necessary for their mutual survival.

But the southern way of life was fraught with inherent instabilities. Slaves built resilient communities within the great plantations and benefited from ongoing exchanges with yeomen for small household comforts. They mitigated the daily drudgery and brutality of work with song, sabotage, slowdowns, and other small acts of defiance that affirmed slaves' dignity to everyone who took notice. And they ran away in ever-increasing numbers during the 1830s and 1840s, to hiding places in the South and free cities of the North.

Faced with the volatile nature of master–slave relations, the growing movements of moral reformers and abolitionists, and the persistent political and cultural tensions of westward expansion, southern slave owners defended slavery more and more anxiously as the 1840s unfolded. By the 1850s, southern fears about the consequences of northerners transplanting their culture and economy into new territories became shrill. As slavery, King Cotton, and the southern way of life continued to expand over these years, so did the routes of the Underground Railroad and the number of eager northerners moving into the West. Indeed, Abraham Lincoln grew up in a heartland of racial tensions that stretched at first across the Allegheny Mountains, then to the Mississippi River, and then beyond.

SUGGESTED READINGS

David B. Davis, who wrote *The Problem of Slavery in the Age of Revolution, 1770–1823* (1975), was among the first scholars to place American antislavery activities into world perspective. Influential studies of the northern abolitionists include Lawrence Freidman, *Gregarious Saints* (1982); Gilbert Barnes, *The Anti-Slavery Impulse* (1933); and Ronald G. Walters, *The Antislavery Appeal: American Abolitionists After 1830* (1976). A fine biography of the movement's most important African-American leader is William McFeely, *Frederick Douglass* (1991). For the backlash against the abolitionist minority, see Leonard Richards, *"Gentlemen of Property and Standing": Anti-Abolition Mobs in Jacksonian America* (1970).

For an overview of southern social and economic life, see the highly informative work by David Roller and Robert Twyman, eds., *The Encyclopedia of Southern History* (1979). For views about the extent of southern economic and social development before the Civil War, see Fred Bateman and Thomas Weiss, *A Deplorable Society: The Failure of Industrialization in the Slave Economy* (1981); John Boles, *The South Through Time: A History of an American Region* (1995); and Ronald L. Lewis, *Coal, Iron, and Slaves: Industrial Slavery in Maryland and Virginia, 1715–1865* (1979). Kenneth M. Stampp's *The Peculiar Institution* (1956) turned the tide of most earlier scholarship by arguing that slavery was both immensely profitable and, from the slave's vantage point, socially horrible. In 1965 Eugene Genovese's work, *The Political Economy of Slavery,* proposed a dramatically new interpretation that questioned profitability arguments by introducing a distinctive southern mindset and regional departures from the rest of the nation. Since Genovese, many new lines of inquiry have developed. For example, Robert W. Fogel and Stanley L. Engerman, *Time on the Cross: The Economics of American Negro Slavery* (1974), argues for the profitability, though not the long-term viability, of slavery; Herbert G. Gutman, ed., *Slavery and the Numbers Game* (1973), challenges this view. James Oakes, in *The Ruling Race: A History of American Slaveholders* (1982), agrees slavery was profitable, but does so from the vantage of the small slave owners; Oakes argues that the South was capitalist. Fogel reexamines his own and others' work about slave productivity and well-being in *Without Consent or Contract* (1988). Michael Tadman, *Speculators and Slaves: Masters, Traders, and Slaves in the Old South* (1989), offers one of the finest studies of the internal slave trade of the South.

The most influential work on slave culture in the Old South is Eugene Genovese's *Roll, Jordan, Roll: The World the Slaves Made* (1974), which argues for great variety of slave experiences and paternalism of masters. Important objections are made to Genovese's contentions in Oakes, *The Ruling Race.* For rich details about slave culture also see George Rawick, *From Sundown to Sunup* (1972); Stampp, *The Peculiar Institution;* John Blassingame, *The Slave Community: Plantation Life in the Antebellum South* (1979); John Boles, *Black Southerners, 1619–1869* (1983); and Charles Joyner, *Down by the Riverside: A South Carolina Slave Community* (1984). To add details about the legal, demographic, and general social condition of slaves in every part of America, see the recent overview of scholarship by Peter Kolchin, in *American Slavery, 1619–1877* (1993). For an intellectual history of slave culture, the most important contribution is Lawrence Levine, *Black Culture and Black Consciousness* (1977).

Engaging portraits of free African-Americans abound in Ira Berlin's *Slaves Without Masters* (1974); urban and factory slavery are covered in the highly readable Robert Starobin, *Industrial Slavery in the Old South* (1970). For women's experiences as free African-Americans and slaves, start with the comprehensive overview by Jacqueline Jones, *Labor of Love, Labor of Sorrow* (1985); the biography by Melton McLaurin, *Celia, A Slave* (1991); and Deborah G. White, *Ar'n't I a Woman? Female Slaves in the Plantation South* (1985). Slave revolts have been reassessed recently in the work of Douglas Egerton, *Gabriel's Rebellion: The Virginia Slave Conspiracies of 1800 and 1802* (1993), and Stephen B. Oates, *The Fires of Jubilee: Nat Turner's Fierce Rebellion* (1975).

For the ideology of southern white planters, see standard overviews by Wilbur Cash, *The Mind of the South* (1941); Randolph Campbell and Richard Lowe, *Wealth and Power in Antebellum Texas* (1977); Bruce Collins, *White Society in the Antebellum South* (1985); and Clement Eaton, *The Growth of Southern Civilization, 1790–1860* (1961). A biography with deep insights into the southern mind is Drew G. Faust, *James Henry Hammond and the Old South* (1982). Still very important is George Fredrickson, *The Black Image in the White Mind: The Debate on Afro-American Character and Destiny, 1817–1914* (1971). For ways in which planter, small farmer, and slave experiences overlapped, see Donald G. Mathews's *Religion in the Old South* (1977).

The best works about plantation mistresses are Catherine Clinton, *The Plantation Mistress: Woman's World in the Old South* (1982), and the long but rewarding Elizabeth Fox-Genovese, *Within the Plantation Household* (1988). Recent scholarship on southern society often focuses on yeomen, tenants, and upcountry poor folks. See the very influential work by Lacy Ford, Jr., *Origins of Southern Radicalism: The South Carolina Upcountry, 1800–1860* (1988), and J. William Harris, *Plain Folk and Gentry in a Slave Society* (1985). To these, the interested reader should add Robert Kenser, *Kinship and Neighborhood in a Southern Community* (1987), and Stephanie McCurry, *Masters of Small Worlds* (1995).

The literature about southern planters' defense of slavery is prodigious and often includes valuable collections of documents to supplement scholarly opinion. Start with the comprehensive work of Larry Tise, *Proslavery: A History of the Defense of Slavery in America, 1701–1840* (1987), and the introduction and readings in Drew Gilpin Faust, ed., *The Ideology of Slavery: Proslavery Thought in the Antebellum South, 1830–1860* (1981). For a provocative and influential interpretation of the southern mentality, see Bertram Wyatt-Brown's *Southern Honor* (1982).

*Southern White Views
of Slavery*

Dew on the Virtues of Slavery, 1831

Thomas R. Dew, a wealthy planter and slave owner, was also president of the College of William and Mary when he wrote *The Virtues of Slavery, The Impossibility of Emancipation* in 1831. As a stalwart defender of slavery, Dew objected to a debate about the feasibility of slave emancipation that had taken place that year in the Virginia legislature. It was one of the last times southerners openly and genuinely debated emancipation, and Dew's point of view would become overwhelmingly prevalent in the coming years.

We have now, we think, proved our position, that slave labor, in an economical point of view, is far superior to free negro labor; and have no doubt that if an immediate emancipation of negroes were to take place, the whole southern country would be visited with an immediate general famine, from which the productive resources of all the other States of the Union could not deliver them.

It is now easy for us to demonstrate the second point in our argument—that the slave is not only *economically* but *morally* unfit for freedom. And first, idleness and consequent want are, of themselves, sufficient to generate a catalogue of vices of the most mischievous and destructive character. . . .

The great evil, however, of these schemes of emancipation, remains yet to be told. . . . Two totally different races, as we have before seen, cannot easily harmonize together, . . . and even when [the black person] is free, . . . idleness will produce want and worthlessness, and his very worthlessness and degradation will stimulate him to deeds of rapine and vengeance. . . . [L]iberate [our] slaves, and every year you would hear of insurrections and plots, and every day would perhaps record a murder. . . .

[Thomas Jefferson] has supposed the master in a continual passion—in the constant exercise of the most odious tyranny, and the child, a creature of imitation, looking on and learning. But is not this master sometimes kind and indulgent to his slaves? . . . We may rest assured, in this intercourse between a good master and his servant, more good than evil may be taught the child; the exalted principles of morality and religion may thereby be sometimes indelibly inculcated upon his mind. . . . Look to the slaveholding population of our country, and you every where find them characterized by noble and elevated sentiments, by humane and virtuous feelings. . . .

Let us now look a moment to the slave, and contemplate his position. Mr. Jefferson has described him as hating, rather than loving his master. . . . We assert again, that Mr. Jefferson is not borne out by the fact. . . . We have no hesitation in affirming, that throughout the whole slaveholding country, the slaves of a good master are his warmest, most constant, and most devoted friends; they have been accustomed to look up to him as their supporter, director and defender. Everyone acquainted with southern states, knows that the slave rejoices in the elevation and prosperity of his master; and the heart of no one is more gladdened at the successful debut of young master or miss on the great theatre of the world, than that of either the young slave who has grown up with them, and shared in all their sports, and even partaken of all their delicacies—or the aged one who has looked on and watched them from birth to manhood, with the kindest and most affectionate solicitude, and has ever met from them all the kind treatment and generous sympathies of feeling.

Helper on the Impending Crisis, 1857

Hinton Helper was a middle-class non–slave owner from North Carolina who moved north to gain advanced education and write professionally. During the 1840s and 1850s, he joined his voice to many others in advocating more southern manufacturing, transportation, and education to overcome decades of dependence on the outside world. Helper also concluded that slavery denied nonslaveholding white southerners the opportunities for advancement that free white northerners enjoyed. In 1857 he put these views together in *The Impending Crisis of the South: How to Meet It.*

Our theme is a city—a great Southern importing, exporting, and manufacturing city, to be located at some point or port on the coast of the Carolinas, Georgia or Virginia, where we can carry on active commerce, buy, sell, fabricate, receive the profits which accrue from the exchange of our own commodities, open facilities for direct communication with foreign countries, and establish all those collateral sources of wealth, utility, and adornment, which are the usual concomitants of a metropolis, and which add so very materially to the interest and importance of a nation. Without a city of this kind, the South can never develop her commercial resources nor attain to that eminent position to which those vast resources would otherwise exalt her. . . .

Whether Southern merchants ever think of the numerous ways in which they contribute to the aggrandizement of the North, while, at the same time, they enervate and dishonor the South, has, for many years, with us, been a matter of more than ordinary conjecture. . . . Let them scrutinize the workings of Southern money after it passes north of Mason and Dixon's line. Let them consider how much they pay to Northern railroads and hotels, how much to Northern merchants and shop-keepers, how much to Northern shippers and insurers, how much to Northern theatres, newspapers, and periodicals. Let them also consider what disposition is made of it after it is lodged in the hands of the North. Is not the greater part of it paid out to Northern manufacturers, mechanics, and laborers, for the very articles which are purchased at the North. . . . They have shown their wisdom in growing great at our expense, and we have shown our folly in allowing them to do so. Southern merchants, slaveholders, and slave-breeders, should be the objects of our censure; they have desolated and impoverished the South; they are now making merchandize of the vitals of their country. . . .

What about Southern Commerce? Is it not almost entirely tributary to the commerce of the North? Are we not dependent on New York, Philadelphia,

Boston, and Cincinnati, for nearly every article of merchandise, whether foreign or domestic? Where are our ships, our mariners, our naval architects? Alas! Echo answers, where? . . .

We are all spendthrifts; some of us should become financiers. We must learn to take care of our money; we should withhold it from the North, and open avenues for its circulation at home. We should not run to New York, to Philadelphia, to Boston, to Cincinnati, or to any other Northern city, every time we want a shoe-string or a bedstead, a fish-hood or a handsaw, a tooth-pick or a cotton-gin. In ease and luxury we have been lolling long enough; we should now bestir ourselves, and keep pace with the progress of the age. We must expand our energies, and ac-quire habits of enterprise and industry; we should arouse ourselves from the couch of lassitude, and inure our minds to thought and our bodies to action. ∎

For generations, Americans in every state and every walk of life debated whether slavery should exist. In the early 1800s, many outspoken southern planters and in-tellectuals argued that slaves should be emancipated. Their views usually held that slavery ran against the moral and economic interests of the region. But they wres-tled with the question of where and how freed slaves should live, since even people who opposed slavery believed blacks inferior to whites. Gradually, even this quali-fied support for emancipation began to fade in the South. Political differences with the North became shriller, expansion into the West became a more aggressive en-terprise that involved national and international negotiation, and southern poor whites and yeomen bolstered the need for a more rigid defense of slavery. Indeed, Dew joined many other voices in defense of slavery; he was impervious to compro-mise in national politics and closed to an alternative lifestyle and labor system.

As Helper learned from having lived in the North, active opposition to slavery grew slowly and advocates of complete, immediate emancipation were a minority of citizens in that section of the country. Nevertheless, their numbers and influence grew after 1830. Alongside abolitionist organizations, the budding Whig Party of-ten attracted citizens of northern and western areas who believed that an end to slavery should somehow be sought. When Helper published his work in New York at an especially difficult moment in sectional tensions, his views about the growing gap between between slave owners and non–slave owners within southern white so-ciety helped galvanize northern views.

Questions for Analysis

1. What are the main differences between these two writers' views? Do they share any common ground? Explain.

2. According to Dew, why should slavery not only exist but expand?

3. How might opponents have responded to Dew's defense of slavery?

4. According to Helper, what are the causes of southern "backwardness"? Does he point mainly to personal characteristics of southern people, or to the entire social system and economy of the South? How legitimate do you find his arguments?

5. What kind of conversation might Helper have had with a northern abolitionist?

13

The Westward Experiment, 1820–1850

S ome time during 1845, brothers Jacob and George Donner, prosperous farmers in Illinois, caught the "emigration fever" and decided to head west to California. They sold their land, houses, farm equipment, and most of their household belongings. They talked their friend James Reed into moving his family west with theirs, and together they bought oxen, cattle, bagged and barreled food, and heavy Murphy wagons. Advice books instructed them to hire teamsters who could guide them through rough terrain and across forbidding rivers that stretched out beyond Independence, Missouri, for two thousand miles.

The plan was daring but not unusual. Already thousands of Americans had left behind land, jobs, and culture to move west. But from the start, the Donners and Reeds met with more than their share of disappointments, failures, and setbacks. The Donner and Reed men were already in their sixties; each had remarried, and together they had sixteen children, some of them infants. On arriving at Independence in May 1846, they learned that most of the twelve hundred westbound wagons that spring had already left with their guides and would soon cut north for Oregon. In a week or so, they took heart when they caught up with a group of fifty California-bound wagons. But even being surrounded by other migrants provided little comfort during the days and weeks of trekking from the Missouri River to the Rocky Mountains, over land believed to be "almost wholly unfit for cultivation." Dust storms, thunderstorms, mud, stinging alkali dust, stubborn mules, and bad water strained their tempers. Anger rose easily among the women by the end of May, and George Donner flinched in disgust at the sight of some migrants beating their weary cattle and dogs to keep them stumbling forward. Word of conflict with Mexico raised the nagging possibility of a war in progress at their California destination.

During a welcome rest at Fort Laramie, the Donner and Reed men pored over a map showing what was called a "shortcut" around the southern edge of Salt Lake City that would take them into California more quickly. A couple of California trappers who overheard them warned about the dangers of taking a large number of wagons, animals, and people through the shortcut, adding that the route had never been attempted by wagon trains. The map, insisted the trappers, was little more than "the plan of that madman and speculator, Lansford Hastings," who hoped to lure settlers away from the well-trodden path into Oregon and set up his own independent republic in northern California. At that very moment, in fact, Hastings was rounding up a private army in California to replace the Mexican–Spanish settlements with the "Pacific Republic."

But knowing that they had to reach the far side of the mountains before snow began to fall, the Donners and Reeds decided to lead about twenty of their party's seventy wagons toward the Continental Divide and the shortcut that skirted around the southern edge of the Mormon settlement at Salt Lake City (see page 435). By July, the mountains loomed before them, higher than they had ever imagined. As they traveled through the Rockies—one or two exhausting, plodding miles a day—they glimpsed a searing desert that promised to test them severely during the days ahead. As oxen tired, families threw out precious household goods; some abandoned their wagons and carried what they could, while others quarreled bitterly over meager supplies of food. Hostile Paiute Indians killed cattle and dogs, and a few members of the party died from exhaustion. The Donner brothers realized when they reached the Humboldt River that the "shortcut" had saved no time at all.

On September 30 the Sierra Nevada faced them. A trapper along the way insisted that all the seasoned "mountain men" up ahead believed snow would be late that winter and thus would not block passage for the wagon train. But it did start to snow, and as the weary migrants trudged up the first rising eastern slopes, the weather worsened. Several of the worn-out travelers decided to wait out the storm at an abandoned cabin they spotted at the base of the foothills. Another group totaling about sixty men, women, and children continued through the foothills of the Sierra Nevada but then fell back to the cabin, where they put up four poor huts and crammed themselves in. A third party, including the Donners and some of the Reeds, pressed on. When they became trapped in the thickening drifts they huddled together under hides.

As hunger gnawed, the ill-fated Donner–Reed party of fifteen first caught a scrawny coyote and a single owl, then ate their dogs, oxen, and horses. Foraging parties failed to find anything more, except grass and moss. After nine days and nights out in the cold, they saw another blizzard darken the skies and two men, then two children, died. Their corpses became food for the starving survivors. Four more of the party died over the next twenty-three days out on the mountainside. Back at the

Chronology

1821	Mexico gains independence from Spain
	Santa Fe Trail opened to Americans
	Austin settles Texas
1830	Indian Removal Act
1834	Mission movement in Oregon Territory begins
1835	Texas revolts against Mexico
1836	Battles of the Alamo and San Jacinto
	Texas Republic founded
1841	Oregon Trail wagon trains begin
1843	Frémont initiates California migration
1844	Polk elected president
1845	Texas annexed as a slave state
	O'Sullivan popularizes "manifest destiny"
1846	War with Mexico begins
	Bear Flag Revolt in California begins
	Wilmot Proviso
1847	Notion of "popular sovereignty" announced
	Mormons begin migration to Salt Lake, Utah
1848	Treaty of Guadalupe Hidalgo
	Free-Soil electoral gains in the North
	Taylor elected president
1849	California gold rush begins
1851	Government reservations policy for far western tribes begins

encampment, thirty-seven of the sixty migrants perished in the grueling struggle for life. When the blizzard broke, seven of the Donner–Reed group made it out and reached the safety of Sutter's Fort, where they organized a rescue party to bring back a few more of the stranded survivors.

The Donner–Reed tribulations were remarkable only because so many people in that wagon train died, but many others perished as they moved west on the overland trails. The trek always brought difficulties, as young and old alike made their way through blistering deserts and across forbidding mountains, testing their endurance and will every mile. But the promise of land—plentiful and fertile—lured hundreds, then thousands, of Americans into the Far West from the 1820s to 1850s. Indeed, just a few months after the terrible Donner–Reed disaster, thousands more migrants set out in their footsteps on the strenuous trip to California and Oregon. Within a year, a handful of settlers near Sutter's Fort, California, would discover flakes of shiny yellow and initiate a massive rush for gold in the same deadly foothills.

Many easterners believed the "American imagination" had riveted completely toward Oregon, California, Texas, and other trans-Mississippi territories. They watched in amazement as extended families and whole towns uprooted themselves and carried their identities and culture into what was then an unknown wilderness. Others observed that, especially during the 1840s, the political agendas of existing state governments and federal officials were driven more by the West—how to acquire its lands, how to shape its future—than any other issue. What seemed equally remarkable to many Americans was how quickly far western frontier communities established familiar institutions and laws.

- What hardships did Americans face on their trek into the West? What experiences might have been exhilarating or inspiring? What kinds of communities did they build in the strange new lands beyond the Mississippi?

- What ideas did westward migrants share about their right to occupy the West, the kind of culture that should develop there, and the government's role in supporting the daunting tasks of transforming the western landscape and defining legal rights?

- What tensions arose between native inhabitants and western settlers, and between native inhabitants and new migrants from the North and South?

- What were the U.S. government's goals in the Mexican War, and why did so many Americans come to oppose the war?

This chapter will address these questions.

 ## A Great Transfer of Peoples

By the 1820s, Americans had spilled over the Allegheny Mountains and into the farthest corners of the Northwest Territory. Settlements dotted the Midwest as far as the Mississippi River. Beyond the river, however, only the heartiest individuals explored, mapped, trapped furs, and undertook religious missions. But those conditions were about to change. In the next four decades, a swelling number of Americans turned their attention to the trans-Mississippi West, lured by the hope of attaining a large tract of productive soil or beginning over after the Panic of 1837 and its subsequent depression. Promoters and publishers told exciting stories about the lush environment out west. Guides offered advice about what goods to take and how to navigate the overland trails through varied landscapes. By the 1840s, the West was fixed firmly in Americans' national imagination; it had become their manifest destiny to "conquer space" beyond the Mississippi—whether by unflagging settlement or by irresistible force. Migrants streamed west by the thousands every spring, but few of them were sufficiently prepared for the dangers and hardships of the trail, and few succeeded quickly and to the degree they imagined possible at their far western destinations. Americans truly knew the promises and perils of moving west only after they arrived there.

Manifest Destiny

The trans-Mississippi West captured intense public interest by the 1820s. The budding popular print culture brought curious readers exotic details about scenery and peoples in that remote region, while landscape artists and naturalists added a visual dimension to people's knowledge. Grand depictions of the West in newspapers, novels, and painting suited the efforts of both southern planters and northern entrepreneurs who wished to expand into and develop the West. By the 1840s, these words and images—often exaggerated and romanticized—fueled a sense of urgency spreading through much of the population to join the swelling trans-Mississippi migration.

These optimistic perceptions of the West overlapped with darker, more aggressive notions stemming from widespread beliefs about race and political rights. In 1845 Democratic newspaper editor John O'Sullivan helped focus these other ideas about the West when he declared it an urgent necessity for Americans to carry their influences into the West, to "civilize" Indians and Mexicans with American culture and Christianity, and if necessary forcibly eject Spanish, French, and British people from the continent. In a December 1845 article, O'Sullivan gave these impulses a term that soon became popular: it was, he wrote, "our manifest destiny to overspread the continent and to possess the whole of the continent which Providence has given us for the development of the great experiment of liberty and federated self-government entrusted to us."

O'Sullivan's bold statement of manifest destiny came just as Americans recovered from the devastating depression that followed the Panic of 1837. Expansion seemed to offer new, perhaps unlimited, arenas for markets and resources. Senator Thomas Hart Benton of Missouri urged Congress to support taking control of the Pacific Coast's harbors from Mexico, which would provide launching points for transoceanic trade. The God-given right to expand also dovetailed with the great revivalist movements sweeping over the East, which in turn spawned numerous missionary efforts to transform the Indian peoples of the West. Moreover, by the 1840s, the West offered an escape from the fearful pace of industrialization and urbanization, a chance to return to the imagined Jeffersonian ideals of an agricultural people spreading out over space. Manifest destiny infused these ideals with justifications for preparing that space to receive migrating Americans—clearing it of other peoples, by force if necessary.

In reality, westward migration was not as full of opportunities as settlers believed it would be. Nor did the great spaces of the West ensure that social and political relations would be harmonious. Often, as settlers shaped new lands with old tools—customs and institutions long familiar in the East or South—they put equality and justice to severe tests. People from many different regions and backgrounds frequently clashed openly over what kind of life to build in the West. Many endured rude poverty for years; others succumbed to despair or returned home.

Sponsors and Entrepreneurs

Intrepid individual explorers, wilderness entrepreneurs, and active government intervention shaped many aspects of western development. For example, the fur trade represented both an economic incentive to explore the open wilderness everywhere in North America, and the energetic first forays into coveted lands for future settlers. John Jacob Astor began amassing the fortune that catapulted this poor immigrant to the topmost elite of New York City by diligently extracting furs from the far Northwest along the Pacific in the early 1800s. Simultaneously, the Hudson's Bay Company of fur traders and shippers accumulated great riches from the fur trade north of Astor's claims in Canada. By the 1820s, ambitious American newcomers competed with the Hudson's Bay Company and quickly upset its domination. They accomplished this by reorganizing the purchase and transport of furs into a highly efficient system. For generations, western trappers had pieced together a system of trapping, skinning, and transporting hides through informal trade and personal connections. Now easterners, led by the Rocky Mountain Fur Company of merchants and bankers, sent agents to certain central locations at designated times of the year to purchase hides. The trade fairs in this "rendezvous system" allowed trappers to bring their bundles of furs to closer points for trade, and to buy or trade for necessary supplies without traveling to St. Louis or other supply terminals hundreds of miles to the east.

Trade fairs were already a regular part of Indian life in the Far West. Mandan villagers, whom Lewis and Clark had met early in the century (see page 300), gathered once a year to trade, gossip, conduct business, and play games. Once Americans joined the trade fairs system, Indian culture changed rapidly. For one thing, the flow of manufactured goods from east to west grew steadily, and the fairs became crossroads of peoples and goods that blended elements of the western wilderness and eastern cities. For another thing, some easterners came to live permanently in the West. "Mountain men" who spent most of their mature lives trapping deep in the Rocky Mountains often married Indian women and learned many dialects of Indian languages. Sometimes the encounters between mountain men and long-time Indian residents of an area produced fear and conflict; but typically, Indians tolerated trappers or even cooperated in fishing and hunting efforts during nomadic winter seasons. One of these men, Jedediah Smith, made a career of fur trapping along the Platte River, across the Rockies, and throughout the northern parts of Mexico's western possessions. Smith's reputation for fair dealing in the beaver trade stretched from Independence, Missouri, to San Francisco, California.

By the 1840s, trappers had all but depleted the beaver supply of the far western frontier. Settlers, too, had begun to implement the familiar pattern of wearing down forests, interfering with Indian activities, and introducing their own diverse cultural ways into the West. Reflecting on environmental strains, one trapper lamented that "lizards grow poor, and wolves lean against the sand banks to howl." At the same time, the first wave of adventurers into the West bequeathed well-trodden trails for the permanent settlers who came in the next generations, as well as reports of people and sights, and maps of western geography that gave confidence to untold numbers of families. Many mountain men hired themselves out as guides for the first families coming to Oregon and California during the 1840s. Others related stories about their exploits to eastern journalists, who in turn embellished and romanticized the lives of mountain men and gave their excited readers somewhat false hopes about the tempting possibilities for personal success in the West.

Government help for western development came indirectly and directly. When Congress granted legal rights-of-way across federal land or timber rights along proposed routes, government indirectly helped private companies fund new railroads. Furthermore, railroad companies aided in the collection of knowledge about the Far West when they sponsored exploration and mapping for their own business purposes. Most ambitious of the railroad company efforts was the Northern Pacific Railroad's surveys during the 1850s for a potential transcontinental route. In this case, the government granted company investors unprecedented privileges to exploit land in the public domain.

Direct government support for westward migration had begun at the federal level when Jefferson boldly purchased the Louisiana Territory in 1803. Subsequent federal funds for scientific exploration that began with Lewis and Clark (discussed in Chapter 8) was extended to efforts at mapping, exploring, and then exploiting other parts of the trans-Mississippi West. Zebulon Pike led expeditions in 1806 and 1807, with government forces, to the Rocky Mountains in Colorado. Although the Spanish captured him in their territory and took him into Mexico, Pike took advantage of confrontation to record his observations about the region that one day would become Texas. After the War of 1812, the government became an active partner in transforming the West, providing land bounties to veterans of the war, funding troops to remove Indians year after year, and erecting forts to house soldiers whose job was to enforce treaties between America and Indian nations. In 1819–1820, the government dispatched Major Stephen Long to try to remove British fur trappers on the Great Plains. Long returned with maps and journals documenting aspects of "arid and forbidding" life there. During 1843–1844, John C. Frémont, who had much to do with the founding of California and the decline of Mexican power in the West, mapped the overland trails to Oregon and California.

The Westward Impulse

Development in the trans-Mississippi West was thus spearheaded by a combination of adventurous entrepreneurs, corporate enterprise, and government activity. But thousands upon thousands of families and small groups of settlers proved equally influential in transforming the western landscape in the years before the Civil War. The diaries and letters of people who went west after 1820 often expressed optimism about what lay ahead. "Each advanced step of the slow, plodding cattle," wrote one woman on her way to Oregon, "carried us farther and farther from civilization into a desolate, barbarous country. . . . But our new home lay beyond all this and was a shining beacon that beckoned us on, inspiring our hearts with hope and courage." By the 1840s and 1850s, the "shining beacon" sometimes represented the West's role as a new religious homeland. Just as often it heralded the republican promise of acquiring a family freehold or a planter's desire to relocate slaves and staple crop cultivation.

The rising tide of migrating families blended their belief in their "manifest destiny" to conquer the West with their belief in the need to build democratic institutions. The West, said many observers, had leveling tendencies. That is, migrants to new lands could abolish the irksome effects of rule by "ancient families" and rebuild institutions to suit their democratic aspirations. According to many optimists, so much mobility, so much mingling of people from various backgrounds, so much mutual reliance for life's necessities must surely impart a democratic spirit in frontier people. At a minimum, moving west promised a fresh start. Indeed, the popular belief in the power of the West to transform American sectional and national identity endured throughout the 1800s, until it was codified into Frederick Jackson Turner's powerful essay of 1893 (see page 297).

Numbers seemed to confirm these beliefs. By the 1820s, the Old Northwest Territory had been converted into states and was on its way to being integrated into the nation's development. Thousands of small farmers who had streamed out of Virginia and Maryland were sending large quantities of corn and pork products to hungry easterners. By 1820, nearly 25 percent of the American population lived west of the Appalachian Mountains. In the next decade, another large swath of settlers moved out of New England, through Vermont and New Hampshire, and then into Michigan, Iowa, and Wisconsin, where wheat farms and stock grazing dominated. Unlike in the crowded East, farms in the new midwestern states were large. The stubborn sod required that cast iron plows be traded in for more durable steel plows, and scythes for more efficient self-raking reapers that harvested much larger yields of cereal crops after the 1830s. A new tier of southern states—Alabama, Mississippi, and Louisiana—attracted thousands of planter families to field and forests that once were home to Creek Indians. Planters in North Carolina noted an "Alabama fever" which "has carried off vast numbers of our Citizens" and slaves to the far Southwest. By the late 1830s, more than a third of the American population lived west and south of the original thirteen states, spreading up to the Mississippi River. By 1860, over half of the nation's people lived west of the Appalachian Mountains.

Land out west also got easier to claim and cheaper to buy. The Land Act of 1820 had established a minimum price of $1.25 an acre, and a minimum purchase of eighty acres (compared with the 640-acre minimum set in the Northwest Ordinance of 1785), with a down payment of $100. Although thousands of families claimed farmsteads in western New York and Pennsylvania, and then in Ohio, the prevalent mode of land acquisition remained speculation in the 1820s. Congress's Preemption Acts of 1830 and 1841 allowed squatters—people living on land for which they had not paid and did not own a survey map and title—to stake out up to 160 acres and pay for it later at $1.25 an acre, provided that the claimants had built a house and "improved" the land. The purpose of preemption was to give small farmers a better chance to make a start in the trans-Mississippi West, and to undermine speculators' efforts to grab the most desirable lands. To some extent, the law worked. By the Graduation Act of 1854, the government stipulated that land not sold quickly would go down in price over time, the lowest price being 12½ cents an acre thirty years after the first offering.

Transportation improvements encouraged more rapid migration across natural barriers, and hastened the integration of different regions. Already the roads and canals of the American System linked the new states to coastal populations. By the 1850s, another mode of transportation—the railroads—made it possible to envision the movement of people and goods over even greater distances, at far more rapid speeds and much lower costs. As prices for transport of goods fell dramatically, western lifestyles were enriched by a variety of foods, clothing, tools, and household comforts. Rapidly growing cities such as Louisville, St. Louis, Detroit, and Milwaukee developed complicated social and cultural linkages between older eastern centers and trans-Mississippi settlements. Mills, packing plants, food

Cincinnati in 1843   One of America's fastest growing western cities by the 1820s, Cincinnati had a booming dockyard jammed with steamboats and flatboats, as well as expanding neighborhoods filled with a blend of eastern and southern settlers, slaves and free African-Americans, and foreign born immigrants who provided diverse labor skills and a cultural richness equal to that of coastal cities.   *(Rare Books & Special Collections, Cincinnati Public Library.)*

processing industries, shipbuilding, tool making, and numerous other enterprises attracted thousands of immigrants and semiskilled eastern workers to the new urban centers of the West, which became the steppingstones for movement into the far western frontiers.

Making the Trip

Not all people who moved West remained optimistic about the opportunities and benefits of leaving home. Although many families relocated their homes and businesses more frequently in the 1800s than we do today, it may have been a more traumatic experience then than now. Migrants who entered the Susquehanna, Mohawk, and Ohio Valleys in the first part of the century severed their familiar roots and encountered strange, sometimes fearful, environments and peoples. Some left family and friends behind forever. Abraham Lincoln's family, for example, moved to five different locations, leapfrogging from Virginia, to Kentucky, to Indiana, to southern Illinois, and finally to Springfield, Illinois. Still, these early migrants traveled far shorter distances than the pioneers who ventured along the great trails leading westward from the Mississippi River toward the Rockies and the Pacific Ocean.

Westward-bound migrants usually launched their journey from Independence, Missouri, which was already far from their eastern and southeastern homes. From this point they pressed on for another grueling two thousand miles to Oregon or California (see map). Travel was slow and perilous. The walk was tedious and lonely for many people on the trails, and often utterly exhausting. The famous Murphy wagons, called the "clipper ships of the West," were three by sixteen feet in dimension, barely large enough to contain a family's worldly belongings and the necessary supplies for the trip, and rarely allowing room for sleeping or riding. A full Murphy wagon required ten or twelve mules to pull it, but even then, the five-foot-high iron-rimmed wheels creaked over dry Plains soil, stuck in muddy ruts, and broke from their axles on steep mountain climbs.

The trip to Oregon cost more than most families had on hand, so before starting out, a farm family usually sold most of their tools, land, household goods, and livestock. With the proceeds, they purchased oxen and wagons, extra clothing, seed to get themselves through the first phase of settlement, and a minimum of implements for housekeeping and land clearing. Families then banded together for mutual support in wagon trains. They came from all settled areas east of the Mississippi River—from midwestern farms, from the upcountry of the southern interior, from small towns and cities everywhere. Most migrants could not have been truly poor, given the high cost of outfitting a wagon, buying oxen and supplies, and paying a guide. The typical head of a wagon train family was a man who wanted a larger farm, a better-stocked and prosperous retail store, or a career as an independent provider of insurance, banking services, or some craft skill.

All but the most feeble walked alongside animals and wagons, and everyone helped guide precious livestock and goods through difficult terrain or across swift rivers, often on rafts. At Independence or some other embarkation point east of the

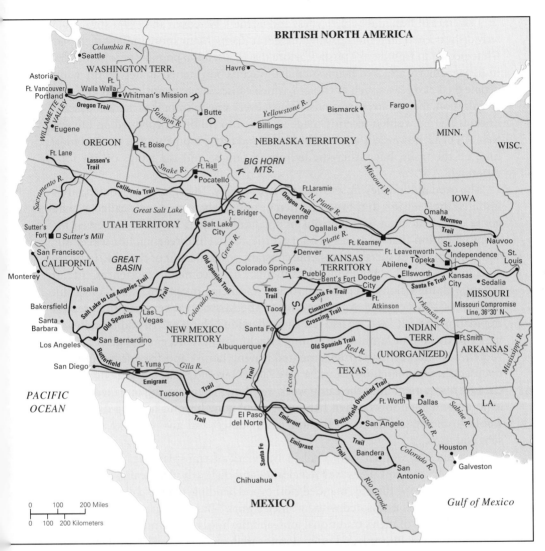

Western Trails, 1820 to 1850 As the United States acquired territories west of the Mississippi River and organized new western settlements and governments, citizens carved out trails through vast stretches of prairie, mountains, and lush forests. Oregon and California attracted huge numbers of migrants before Nebraska and Kansas territories did.

Mississippi, migrants often hired a guide to keep them on the unfamiliar trails west of that river. Trains started out in the spring once the grasses of the Plains began to turn green enough to feed the livestock, and they covered about twelve to fifteen miles a day through the rugged grasslands, dusty prairies, mountains, and mud pits. Long periods of travel without water alternated with broad rivers that drenched or even drowned the trekking parties. Then, once across the Columbia River leading to Oregon, or the Platte River on the way to California, formidable mountains loomed ahead. The typical trip took about six months.

Extremes of heat and cold, dryness and wetness, boredom and exhaustion regularly disheartened migrants crossing the Great Plains. Many more Indians died than white people in frontier skirmishes before the 1850s, but a popular perception that Indians regularly attacked helpless circled wagons heightened anxiety. More white people died of diseases such as cholera, which causes severe vomiting, diarrhea, and dehydration, than of arrow wounds. Almost every wagon train that made it past the Rockies carried women recently made widows and children orphaned on the way west. All in all, however, it was not the heroic and tragic moments that marked most time on the trails, but rather the tedium of fatigue and the pangs of low food rationing.

The overland journey upset women's lives deeply. To begin with, women rarely initiated the decision to move and often opposed what one diarist called a "wild goose chase" of "men with notions of splendor in their heads." Also, given the reigning notion that women's primary duties were child rearing, housekeeping, and "cultivating the social virtues," the constant physical labor of the trail, in open-air camps, required tremendous adjustments. Often women's experiences did not square with the vision of republican society advancing intact across the continent. Margaret Chambers, for example, crossed the Missouri River with the greatest trepidation and felt "as if we had left all civilization behind us." In addition, loneliness and the loss of familiar sustaining attachments caused endless grief for uprooted women. Lavinia Porter lamented leaving family and friends behind and doubted she was marching toward a new Zion: "I would make a brave effort to be cheerful and patient until the camp work was done. Then starting out ahead of the team and my men folks, when I thought I had gone beyond hearing distance, I would throw myself down on the unfriendly desert and give way like a child to sobs and tears."

Nevertheless, women were vital in the work of transplanting thousands of Americans to new soil. They washed clothes and dishes, boiled beans, picked and prepared fruit along the way, mended clothes and bedding, tended children, and did many other chores associated with "women's work." But women moving west also performed many of men's traditional jobs, and the line between men's and women's "spheres" of work blurred, and often disappeared, on the trail. They gathered buffalo chips for fuel, helped drive cattle and dogs through rough country, built rafts and repaired bridges, and took over leading the entire family through all kinds of terrain when their husbands fell ill with cholera or mountain fever. When Eliza Farnham's husband collapsed "under the tremendous sufferings of that terrible journey," she "yoked and unyoked the oxen, gathered fuel, cooked their food, drove the team, hunted wood and water . . . and for months performed all the coarser offices that properly belong to the other sex." Most women banished thoughts of socializing—at least regularly—with other women or sharing childcare responsibilities, since each family worked incessantly on the trail to sustain only itself. When trekkers had to discard belongings to lighten the wagons or consolidate loads if oxen died, they threw out mirrors, clocks, tea services, and other amenities of a "comfortable home," further demoralizing many women. Indeed, what woman of that era could identify the dilapidated, cramped Murphy wagon as a true home?

Life on the Trail   Although the passage from east to west was fraught with muddy trails, steep ravines, ice-cold rivers, and in the case of these two migrants, no visible passage across seemingly endless prairie or meadow, it also offered the minor pleasures of a trailside meal and conversation. Although most westward migrants would not have had the tinned fruit and meats this later image shows, the landscape and the wagons did not change much over the years.   *(Kansas State Historical Society.)*

Even if these conditions were temporary, some roles and beliefs about the proper social places of men and women were subtly, but permanently, changed on the overland trails.

The Indian Territory

Popular opinions about the Far West often distorted or ignored the reality of the Native American presence. The romantic view of Indian life captured in the art and literature of the 1820s–1850s usually excluded the reality of removal and warfare on the western frontier. By the 1830s, many Indian peoples had been removed from their homelands to a region across the Mississippi designated by Congress in 1830 as the Indian Territory. Covering today's Oklahoma, Kansas, and Nebraska, and bordering on the grasslands of the Great Plains, the Indian Territory became home to numerous peoples from east of the Mississippi. From the Old Southwest, Chickasaw, Choctaw, Creek, and Seminole joined the Cherokee in the southern portion of the territory. Together, these were known as the Five Civilized Tribes when the U.S. government planned for their removal to the Indian Territory. From the Old Northwest, Fox, Shawnee, Delaware, Wyandot, and numerous others were resettled in the northerly portion of the territory.

The purpose of establishing this reserve stemmed from the same reasoning that Thomas Jefferson enunciated years before: that until Indian peoples became "civilized," they would not be able to coexist with those of European origin. At first policymakers in eastern states and Congress believed that the Indian Territory lay far enough beyond the advancing white frontier to avoid racial mixing and conflict; the "civilizing process" could safely begin at arm's length But white people moved west much faster than predicted, and by the 1830s, they were following the Santa Fe trail into and through the Indian Territory. In the next years, the overland trails to Utah, Oregon, and California encroached even more on Native American lands. Many newly removed Indians had few means to resist dependency on unscrupulous migrants, peddlers, and speculators for goods and services because the land was unfamiliar and they had moved with few belongings. Others remained more aloof. In the area that is now Oklahoma, the Cherokee, Chickasaw, Creek, Seminole, and Choctaw established thriving new communities under very trying conditions. Despite efforts by overland trail traders and eastern merchants to make these tribes economically dependent, the Indians set up their own systems of law, education, and religious worship. Within the southern Indian Territory, an elite even arose that used slaves to cultivate cotton for shipment to New Orleans.

Removal policies and direct confrontations with federal troops did not weaken the resolve of many Native American peoples to resist the advancing line of land-hungry speculators and frontier families. In some places in the West, Indian resistance became more desperate as the flow of migrating settlers and the government forces sent to protect them became stronger. But Indian resistance had little impact on determined waves of migrants and major federal policies. For example, a number of recently settled Indian tribes in the northern part of the Indian Territory gained permanent reservation lands in 1851, only to lose them three years later when the federal government established the Kansas and Nebraska Territories and opened them up to white migration. Immediately, three overlapping tensions erupted into open conflict. In the first place, would-be white settlers, already steeped in sectional conflict over slavery's expansion, had little patience for the claims of Indian residents on the land. Second, Indians tried unsuccessfully to adjust old ways of agriculture and hunting to the requirements of farming on the arid land of the new territory. Third, in addition to migrating white people, the Sioux, Arapaho, Comanche, Cheyenne, and Kiowa from the Great Plains encroached, sometimes in huge numbers, on the eastern tribes who settled in the Indian Territory. As a result, the entire region remained inhospitable for years to come.

Destinations and Encounters

Americans' convictions about manifest destiny were a powerful influence not only on the northern and Great Plains migrations, but also on developments in the southwestern territories. While eastern and midwestern migrants set their sights on the Oregon territory during the 1830s, Texas was the logical place for southern planters to expand in that decade. But Mexico controlled Texas, as well as the great stretches of land west to California and east to Florida. As American migration and settlement grew in all of these areas during the 1840s, tensions with Native Americans and foreign nations also raised questions about what kind of people would live there and what kinds of political structures and cultures would develop.

Mexico and Its Territories

For three centuries, explorers and rulers attempted to extend Spain's jurisdiction throughout the North American borderlands. Through the 1700s, pockets of mission labor developed from San Francisco to San Diego, while internal trade was linked to coastal commerce at Santa Fe, New Orleans, along the Gulf Coast to the Floridas and St. Augustine. Multiracial crossroads dotted Spanish jurisdictions, which were otherwise thinly settled because of forbidding environments, few immigrants, and hostile and dense nations of Native Americans. *Presidios,* originally forts built to protect Spanish and Mexican interests in the new territories and to confer political authority over local populations, soon became the central sites for exacting tribute and forced labor from Indian populations. In California, thousands of Indians experienced the profound cultural, political, and religious shock of giving up semisedentary ways for the rigid work rules and settled cultivation introduced by Mexican and Spanish settlers.

Bit by bit, however, Spain relinquished its hold on the borderlands. In 1795 Pinckney's Treaty gave access to the lower Mississippi River and trade at New Orleans to Americans. In 1800 Napoleon forced Spain to return vast and ungovernable Louisiana to France. Then, in 1811 and 1813 Spain ceded portions of West Florida to the United States. By the terms of the Adams-Onís Treaty, written in 1819 and ratified by Congress in 1821, East Florida also became United States territory.

But Spanish and Mexican cultural influences remained strong across these lands. Many settlers of Spanish and Mexican descent inhabited the territory north of the Rio Grande River and the Southwest. During the early 1800s, Spanish traders maintained a strong presence in Santa Fe, preventing American merchants from dominating the southwestern trails and overland commerce. Spanish officials treated overland migrants and explorers harshly when they wandered into Mexico. Businessmen and merchants of Spanish descent continued to protect runaway slaves who made it to New Orleans and St. Augustine early in the 1800s, hiring skilled African-Americans and tolerating their distinct cultural and religious practices.

Conditions in the borderlands began to change significantly in 1810 when the Mexican Revolution erupted into war against Spanish royalists. While popular leaders led masses of people in an independence movement in Mexico, a combination of Mexican and American settlers declared the Republic of Texas in 1812. Although the Republic could not resist Spanish royalist troops' onslaughts, Mexico gained its independence from Spain in 1821. Immediately, the new rulers in Mexico invited American merchants to send agents through the forbidding deserts and Comanche lands to trade at the forts and trading posts hugging the Arkansas River's banks and the Santa Fe Trail winding through the Southwest. Around the city of Santa Fe, people of Indian, Hispanic, and European descent began agricultural settlements to supplement the commercial activities in town.

To the east of Santa Fe in Tejas, or Texas, another mixed population emerged. Over two thousand Spanish-speaking residents, or *tejanos,* clustered around missions and *presidios,* as Mexican-Spanish settlers had done in southern California, and also settled in the surrounding countryside on large ranches. There, legendary skilled *vaqueros,* or cowboys, herded cattle and poor laborers worked as agricultural tenants on the difficult Texas soil.

For generations, Spanish administrators regarded the *tejanos* as very distant from the center of imperial rule in the New World. Still, settlements at San Antonio, Nacogdoches, and Goliad provided outlying buffers against hostile Indians and French encroachments, much as settlements on the fringe of Spanish Florida had guarded against British expansion for generations. But the nomadic Comanche and Apache thundered through the outlying *tejano* settlements on regular raids. The Comanche consistently resisted efforts to incorporate their people into settled villages, choosing instead to follow the buffalo herds in their traditional way of life. Following independence, the new government attempted to reinforce the policy of building the outlying settlements of mixed Spanish and Mexican peoples. But the towns and ranches remained weak, and the Mexican government remained concerned about its ability to govern its extensive territories. Having correctly anticipated that American settlers would flow into Louisiana, and then into Texas, the Mexican government offered certain conditions to migrating Americans instead of trying to eject them. To the Germans who began entering the trans-Mississippi region in the early 1820s, and then the southern cotton planters who expanded across the river, Mexican officials offered protection against hostile Indians in exchange for their becoming Mexican citizens and Catholics. In return, Mexican officials looked forward to collecting much-needed tax revenue from Americans and transforming the area into prosperous ranches and agricultural settlements.

The first person to accept this offer was Moses Austin, who in 1821 received a grant of eighteen thousand square miles inside Texas, supposedly unencumbered by any Indian or foreign title. The possibility of acquiring free land in Texas without even a survey amazed Americans moving west. Moreover, Mexico permitted the American land agents for Texas to give out stupendous grants of 4,605 acres to each applying family, more than enough land to mitigate the requirement to relinquish American citizenship for Mexican and become nominally Roman Catholic.

Some two dozen additional settlements quickly began along the Sabine, Brazos, and Colorado Rivers. A few early parties of immigrants adopted the *tejano* ways of cattle herding. But since the Mexican government ignored the presence of slavery in Texas, even when Mexican law forbade it, most of the new settlers turned quickly to growing cotton for export through New Orleans. Indeed, Austin's son, Stephen, welcomed southern Americans who treated Texas as a convenient steppingstone in the spread of plantation life westward. Few planters actually became Mexican citizens, and most refused to adopt the Catholic religion once they lived in Texas. When Mexican officials denied Americans the right to establish local governments modeled on their experiences east of the Mississippi, Americans nominally pledged their support to Santa Anna, the head of the Mexican government, but in reality simply rejected Mexican government and laws and lived as they wished. By 1835,

27,000 white settlers and about 3,000 slaves had moved into Texas, greatly outnumbering the 3,500 *tejanos* in the region.

The Alamo and the Republic of Texas

From the Mexican authorities' point of view, their northern province of Texas had become unmanageable by 1830. The government announced its intention to bring Texans more closely in line with the laws and customs of Mexico. New legislation restricted the flow of Americans, outlawed slavery, regulated trade of Texans with foreign powers, and prohibited Texan taxes of many kinds. Americans in eastern Texas wrote to family and contacts across the Mississippi that they were being treated like the British had treated "the American colonists of old." Some believed the appropriate response was to "rebel against the injustice," just as American revolutionaries had. Adding to Americans' belligerence was their association of many Mexicans' swarthy complexions with the skin color of southern slaves. Given southern racism's close ties to skin color, its introduction into Texas helped sharpen white Americans' opposition to Mexican laws.

In 1833 Texans petitioned Mexico's president and commander of the army, Antonio Lopez de Santa Anna, for an independent state of Texas. Stephen Austin went to Mexico City that July. For months, the Mexican government ignored Austin, prompting him to write impatient letters to fellow Texans to the north. Finally Santa Anna granted not independent statehood, but full protection from Indian attacks and other rights afforded to Mexican citizens. However, as Austin started back to Texas with the heartening news, Mexican officials arrested and jailed him for his earlier letters against their government. Moreover, while Austin sat in jail for about eighteen months, Santa Anna transformed his power structure in Mexico virtually into a dictatorship. By mid-1835, when Austin finally rode home, the border between the two countries had become a staging ground for intermittent bloody skirmishes and widespread Texan fears of Santa Anna's unruly troops.

In the fall of 1835, revolutionary fervor spilled over into open warfare. Stephen Austin led a joint force of American Texans and *tejanos* in taking San Antonio and Goliad from the Mexicans. In November 1835, a small group of Texas town representatives met and organized a provisional government. On March 2, 1836, Americans meeting at a convention proclaimed Texas an independent republic and, under Austin's leadership, established a constitution that legalized slavery. Four days later, Santa Anna led a massive attack to retake San Antonio. A small garrison of Americans and *tejanos* made a stand behind the adobe walls of the Alamo, a former mission in the city. Their small numbers were no match for Santa Anna's four thousand troops. Davy Crockett, a frontiersman who joined Americans defending the fort, and Jim Bowie, known for the sturdy hunting knife he perfected, were among the 187 who died in the siege. Moving on to Goliad, Santa Anna rounded up and executed 371 American rebels and declared victory over two major Texan strongholds on March 27.

The American press began to spread news about the rebellion—and the massacres—within days, and an outpouring of nationalistic support for Texas

Siege of the Alamo   This contemporary woodcut conveys well the direct assault made by Mexican and Spanish troops who scaled the walls of the mission.   *(Texas State Library & Archives Commission.)*

mushroomed. Perhaps, argued many northern journalists and southern observers alike, a great influx of Americans into Texas would help resolve the conflict. After all, Monroe had enunciated stern warnings against Spain's imperial goals in the Western Hemisphere in his famous Monroe Doctrine speech to Congress in 1823 (see page 317). Many publicists now insisted in 1836 that the same warning should apply to Mexico's influence in North America. Almost overnight, packet boats from New York City set sail with thousands of young men, and sometimes whole families, who believed that in exchange for their help in a few brief skirmishes against the "papal scourge of Mexicans" they would be granted huge land bounties by the federal government.

Santa Anna thus pursued a growing force of combined American and *tejano* rebels, who were commanded by General Sam Houston. Houston was a seasoned military leader and former Tennessee governor who had served in battle under Andrew Jackson. On April 21, 1836, Houston's nearly 800 men voted to attack Santa Anna's resting troops at the San Jacinto River in east Texas. Raising the cry "Remember the Alamo!" they overwhelmed the greater number of nearly 1,300 Mexicans. Nine Texans died at the river, and 34 more were wounded; on the other side,

63 Mexicans fell, and 730 were taken prisoner. Among those captured was Santa Anna, who quickly agreed to grant independence to the new Republic of Texas north of the Rio Grande River. Citizens of the Republic granted Sam Houston its presidency.

However, when Santa Anna returned to Mexico City in 1836, his own congress refused to accept the terms of the peace treaty. In the coming months, the Mexican congress also rejected President Andrew Jackson's offer to buy the northern province, largely out of fear that Americans also coveted the New Mexico province adjacent to Texas. Meanwhile, Texans petitioned the American Congress in 1837 for annexation of their territory to the United States, which alarmed many Americans. Northern congressional representatives, led by the former president John Quincy Adams, joined Whig leaders throughout the North and Midwest to oppose admission of a fourteenth slave state when the application came before Congress. Southern Democrats, however, favored annexation and the prospects of extending slavery across the Mississippi into a new state. Jackson remained ambivalent about annexation, but in March 1837, he met Democrats halfway with a measure to grant diplomatic recognition to Texas, which implied that American military aid could be used against future Mexican belligerence. Many proslavery Texans—as well as many angry northern abolitionists—interpreted the measure as a first step toward annexation.

Meanwhile, American settlers in the Republic struggled mightily from 1836 to 1842 to impose more of their culture and political ways on the *tejanos,* first by depriving them of their property in outlying areas, and then by taking over their businesses in towns. Many *tejanos* fled to Mexico, leaving behind their land claims for Americans to seize. Although most towns in Texas remained more Mexican than American in cultural terms, they were becoming magnets attracting a growing immigrant population that had been living under the customs and laws of American society. In this environment, ethnocentrism flourished, as well as the conviction that "Mexico and the United States are peopled by two distinct and utterly unhomogeneous races." Texan Americans thus justified their continued appeals for annexation to the United States during the presidencies of Democrat Martin Van Buren and Whig John Tyler.

Oregon

Oregon, the destination of choice for most Americans who crossed the continent in the 1820s and 1830s, encompassed present-day Oregon, Washington, Idaho, small sections of Montana and Wyoming, and a portion of Canada. The United States and Britain held the territory according to a joint occupation treaty signed by the nations in 1818. At first, most of the early settlers who ventured so far were either mountain men who hunted beaver and other small game, or skippers who stopped along the coast for trade. Britain's Hudson's Bay Company kept a fort at Vancouver that attracted local Chinook Indians, French and American trappers, and traders from Hawaii. Races and nations mixed behind the walls of the British company's garrison in a multicultural environment on the far northwestern frontier.

By the 1830s, a few permanent American and French Canadian settlements took root in Oregon's Willamette Valley, also known as French Prairie. Eliza Farnham, just married in western New York, set out in February 1836 with a small party that made its way first by wagon to Pittsburgh, then by riverboat to Liberty, Missouri, and then by horseback to Fort Walla Walla on the Columbia River. On July 4, 1836, Eliza became the first white woman to cross the Continental Divide through the Rockies. A number of female missionaries from both Protestant and Catholic societies soon followed, many of them joining the migrations of family and village groups from the Midwest.

But it was not until 1842 that midwestern farmers began to arrive in Oregon. As the Panic of 1837 dragged on into a long depression that racked both urban and rural communities in the Midwest and East, hundreds of families made plans to leave after the spring rains and arrive on the far side of the Rockies before the winter snow. Few were concerned about arriving too late to clear land and plant their first crops, since news about the natural abundance and lush forests of Oregon's Willamette Valley seemed to promise plenty of alternatives to cultivation that first year in the new land. In addition, Hudson's Bay Company stores extended generous credit to newcomers. About five thousand settlers had followed the Snake and Columbia Rivers into Oregon by 1845. Among them were several Presbyterian and Methodist missionaries who made largely futile attempts to assimilate local populations of semi-nomadic Oregon Indians into American and Canadian religious and cultural ways.

Others soon followed in response to promoters' guarantees of autonomous local self-government and "free land," although the latter had been taken without treaties between the newcomers and local Indians, and without resolution of land rights between British and American claimants to the region. "Oregon Societies" and "Western Emigration Societies" published exaggerated reports of the riches beyond the Rockies. The Oregon fever began to take hold of midwesterners who had been hit hard by the depression following the Panic of 1837, and during 1843 and 1844, a rash of newspaper articles advised what to take and what routes to follow toward the Rockies. No need for heavy steel plows in Oregon, said journalists; leave them with the tough sod of the prairies, and bring only "your wooden plow, your scythe, and gentle oxen."

Some pessimistic voices continued to decry the dangers of the Great American Desert east of the Rockies and moan about the impossibility of getting wagons and livestock through the South Pass in what is now western Wyoming. Horace Greeley, the editor whose urgent appeals to "Go West! Young Men, Go West!" peppered his *New York Daily Tribune* before trans-Mississippi migration was truly underway, was by 1843 urging readers to "not . . . move one foot" beyond St. Louis. "It is," insisted Greeley, "palpable homicide to tempt or send women and children over this thousand miles of precipice and volcanic sterility to Oregon."

By 1846, Oregonians from many eastern areas wrote a constitution that legally prohibited slavery and defined liberal rules for voting and officeholding among the white population. "Oregon Conventions" convened in the new towns, pledging residents to shed "the lawlessness of the trail" and the "singleness of each family's survival." Instead, townspeople assembled under elected officials, adopted constitutions familiar in eastern counties and states, and instituted particular rules "for the purpose of keeping good order and promoting civil and military discipline" in their new homeland. The scattered farmsteaders of Oregon created networks of kinship and barter for goods and services until they could establish links to the East. Many homes regularly accepted boarders just arriving from the Midwest, exchanging shelter and food for the labor of newcomers during the fall harvests.

California

In 1821, when Mexico gained independence from Spain, the California territory was a crossroads of cultures. Nearly 200,000 Native Americans of many languages and cultures occupied the varied landscape. Over 22,000 labored under the control of Mexican and Spanish descendants in the *presidio* system that had been implemented generations previously. About 8,000 descendants of Mexican and Spanish settlers also lived at California's *presidios*. Some of them had intermarried with the local *mestizos* of Spanish-Indian heritage, while other Mexicans formed an elite of *californios* who remained separate from the "mixed bloods."

No more than a handful of Americans lived in California during the 1820s, most of them having entered Oregon first and then traveled into the Sacramento Valley searching for farmland or trapping furs. However, American and Russian ships cruised the coastline of California regularly. Their captains traded manufactured goods and provisions for sea otter and cattle hides, meat and tallow. *Californios* controlled most of this maritime commerce with the outside world, especially the very lucrative business with the Russian American Fur Company, headquartered in Alaska, which contracted for huge quantities of hides in exchange for textiles and iron tools. *Californios* also supplied Russian trappers and company employees with provisions when their ships lay over at coastal harbors.

The *presidio* and foreign trade systems changed dramatically after Mexican independence. Authorities opened California trade to ships of all nations, and in 1832 the Mexican government freed Indians from the *presidios*. Two consequences resulted. First, foreign merchants sent agents to live permanently in coastal California towns, where they competed for business with *Californios*. In time, many American settlers intermarried with this resident elite and became Mexican citizens, but they introduced many new cultural ways and often depended on America's eastern commercial establishment for credit and trade. The changing business climate was less accommodating to Russian fur traders, who all but abandoned trade with California by the 1840s.

Second, the Indians freed from life in the *presidios* left a vacuum of labor, which in turn contributed to the rapid breakdown of Indian agricultural production. In its place, Americans introduced new arrangements on the land. At first, because population was sparse, it seemed that new settlers might reinstate forced labor. When Johan Augustus Sutter came from Switzerland to California in 1839, he became a Mexican citizen and obtained a lush tract of land in the Sacramento Valley. To tend his vast cattle ranch and work his sawmills and mines, Sutter brought in forced Indian labor and built a walled compound to protect his supplies and provide living quarters for himself and his laborers. When a few Americans began to trickle into California by the early 1840s, Sutter's Fort provided valuable supplies to newcomers.

These venturesome Americans had a keen desire to establish independent farms in California valleys and be free of *californio,* Mexican, and Indian influences. Shortly, they would join the struggle to wrest California from Mexican control altogether.

 ## Expansion and Sectionalism, 1840–1848

The widespread belief in America's manifest destiny and the growing tide of westward movement had momentous political consequences during the 1840s. Negotiations with the Indian tribes in the western areas and with the foreign nations vying to settle the West required skillful diplomacy. The American public had unquestionably riveted its attention beyond the Mississippi, but its attitudes alternated between optimism and belligerence, leaving politicians struggling over the appropriate policies to shape America's future in the West. One thing became certain to attentive Americans by the 1840s: their manifest destiny could not be secured peacefully. Events in Texas, Oregon, and California proved that. While settlement and diplomacy gave way to aggression and warfare, however, a strong opposition to both forceful acquisition of western land and the expansion of slavery also emerged in the 1840s.

Annexation and the Election of 1844

Americans in the Republic of Texas relentlessly pursued annexation to the United States after the battles at the Alamo, Goliad, and the San Jacinto River in 1836. Annexation became more and more appealing to southern Americans, especially as a means to prevent a rumored possible alliance between Texas and England, which would surely deprive the South of room to expand King Cotton. In political terms, the extension of slavery under the terms of the 1820 Missouri Compromise threatened to deepen sectional differences, but many southerners and midwesterners agreed that perhaps new states in the West might "add leavening" to politics and "balance the ship of state." Despite the spread of slavery, argued many close observers, most governments of the nine new western states between 1800 and 1840 also expanded white male suffrage.

In fact, optimism about balancing political and cultural interests in the West was miscalculated. Westerners, it turned out, raised many new demands for state and federal resources for defense, Indian treaties, viable government, and internal improvements. Each request for resources provoked an intense political battle among congressional factions. Throughout older portions of America, the press, pulpit, and American street corner persistently turned images of western opportunity and abundance into discussions about how to serve one or another sectional or partisan interest.

By 1844, Texans were again engaged in bloody skirmishes with neighboring American immigrants, Mexicans, and Native Americans. Some Texans fled the border area. Annexation had become a deeply divisive issue in American politics, especially because many Americans—whether for or against the annexation of Texas—believed that the very survival of the Republic was at stake. A huge shift in

American public opinion had been taking place in the early 1840s, from fear of another international war to support for annexation even if it required Americans going to war to win Texas. Many voices proposed that England's and America's joint occupation of Oregon equally stood in the way of resolving conflicts with western Indians and setting up orderly government for new settlers in the Oregon territory. Swept up in the public discussion about America's manifest destiny to expand against all opposing cultures and political systems, and riveting their attention on the westward migration to Texas and Oregon territories, great numbers of Americans accepted war as a viable means to secure the West.

The election of 1844 concentrated the political focus of the nation on these issues. President John Tyler hoped to gain popular support for his reelection by announcing his desire to annex the Republic, even though this position departed from a large portion of his Whig Party constituents in the North. But his political expectations were dashed when Secretary of State John C. Calhoun, a Democrat and a strong voice of the slave owners, introduced an annexation treaty to Congress in June 1843 before Tyler could announce his own intentions. Then Tyler's own Whig Party censured him and turned to the ever steady Henry Clay as its presidential nominee in 1844. As usual, Clay represented a compromise position: he was not opposed to Texas annexation, but he refused to promote it actively out of concern that he might alienate sectors of the Whig Party.

In contrast, the Democrats pulled out every stop for manifest destiny and annexation. Party leaders rejected the northern stalwart, Martin Van Buren, and chose an ardent expansionist from Tennessee, James K. Polk. During his campaign in 1844, Polk swept up the strength of southern and midwestern expansionists by making the annexation of Texas and the acquisition of other trans-Mississippi lands part of the United States. Although some Democrats were at first skeptical about supporting this "dark horse" candidate, Polk assured southerners that he would not only annex Texas but also support using federal funds for southern development. In addition, Polk earned midwestern support when he gave them hope that the federal government would subsidize removal, and possibly wars against, Native Americans.

Texas was not the only trans-Mississippi territory that preoccupied the American public and policymakers in 1844. Polk also pledged to bring the huge territories of Oregon, New Mexico, and California into the American republic if he should win the presidency. These promises appealed not only to the thousands of migrants by now setting out for the West each year, but also to the American people generally. Fear that Mexico would reincorporate Texas into its customs and laws, and fear that England and France had developed interests in coastal trade with Texas and California, churned up more ardent cries for manifest destiny at any cost. Although many fears were exaggerated, Polk believed he had a mandate to negotiate for, or go to war for, Texas, Oregon, and California territories. And although England probably had no intention of wresting California from American interests, many high-ranking officials imagined the worst. The American minister in Mexico said it "will be worth a war of twenty years" to keep England out of California.

Polk's slogan, "Fifty-Four Forty or Fight," reflected the growing commitment to defend manifest destiny. Instead of dividing the Oregon territory with England, the

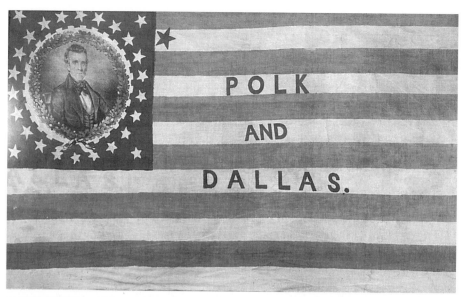

Polk and Dallas This campaign flag clearly illustrates Polk's support for Texas annexation during the 1844 presidential race. While the existing twenty-six states are represented by stars ringing Polk's portrait, the "Lone Star" of Texas is still outside the Union. *(Collection of Janice L. and David J. Frent.)*

Democratic Party ran on a platform of keeping all of it for American expansion. Though the electoral college vote favored Polk widely over Clay in 1844, Polk's popular vote margin was narrow. Clay's middle-of-the-road stance on annexation and southern development was widely appealing to many sectors of the American people, but his ability to capture enough electoral votes to win in 1844 was hampered by a split in Clay's Whig Party. Antislavery Whigs deserted Clay and ran their own candidate, James G. Birney, under the Liberty Party banner. Formed in 1840 to oppose slavery, the Liberty Party ran the first antislavery campaign at the national level in 1844. Its 62,000 supporters at the polls could not unseat either major political party, but they made Clay's defeat more certain.

In any event, Polk and leaders from all major parties interpreted his victory as a mandate to annex Texas and acquire all of Oregon and California. But public opinion in the nation remained deeply divided in early 1845. What turned many northern congressmen toward support for Texas annexation was repeated news that England, France, and Mexico were negotiating how to serve their mutual international interests by keeping Texas independent and not annexed to the United States. Persistent fears of foreign dangers swayed enough northern votes to favor annexation, and in March 1845 the resolution passed in Congress. In December, Florida and Texas became the fourteenth and fifteenth slave states. By June, after months of holding firm on his commitment to end the joint occupation of Oregon, Polk signed an agreement with English officials to make the territory American soil from the forty-second to the forty-ninth parallel. That same month, John Frémont, an explorer who may have hoped to gain great power in California, joined his small force with a larger group of California rebels who wished to oust Mexicans. Together the Americans declared the Bear Flag Republic. But before the meaning of this declaration could be sorted out by Americans west and east of the Mississippi, the disputes in Texas, Oregon, and California had merged with a far wider war to win the entire Southwest.

The Mexican-American War

By early 1845, settlers between the Nueces and Rio Grande Rivers were involved in bloody border skirmishes once again. President Polk had sent General Zachary Taylor to the Nueces River with about 3,500 men and orders to defend Texas, which officially only lay north of the Rio Grande, if Mexico invaded. The area between the Nueces and Rio Grande continued to be disputed by Texans and Mexicans. At the same time, Polk ordered Pacific naval forces to seize California's ports if Mexico initiated a war, and he spread word to diplomats in the region that he would not suppress internal rebellions by Americans who attempted to take California. He singled out the Bear Flag Republic for special praise. In November 1845, Polk further pressed his goals by sending a secret envoy, John Slidell, to Mexico with orders to offer up to $40 million to Mexico's President Herrera to set the Rio Grande as the Texan border and to grant the United States the western Mexican provinces of New Mexico and California. The Mexican government could not give Slidell an audience without precipitating internal discord. Just as Congress was voting to make Texas a new state, without Mexican approval, Polk responded to the Mexican rebuff of Slidell with an order to General Taylor to advance his forces south to the Rio Grande. Americans everywhere knew that Mexico still claimed this soil.

Mexico ended diplomatic relations with America as soon as Texas gained statehood and then ordered all non-Mexican armed parties to leave California, including John C. Frémont and the men in his hire. Frémont went to Oregon temporarily, but returned when he learned that a small group of Americans in Sonoma were about to declare California free of Mexican rule. Lansford Hastings had been luring migrants off the overland trails that led to Oregon and onto "shortcuts" across dangerous terrain into California in order to build support for his own independent republic; it had been Hastings who influenced the Donner–Reed party's disastrous decision to alter its route in 1845. Now in early 1846, Frémont feared for the safety of the misguided settlers and the diplomatic reputation of the United States, not to mention his own future as a statesman in the West. In an effort to strengthen and guide the emerging revolt, Frémont returned to California and joined his forces with groups of rebels seeking to defend their land claims against Mexico, as well as to remove all Mexicans from the territory. In June 1846, California's new settlers followed the earlier Texas example and declared its separation from Mexico as the Bear Flag Republic. For the next two years, rebels fought to win California from the resident Mexicans and to secure statehood from the American federal government.

Meanwhile, American and Mexican troops collided briefly along the Rio Grande in April 1846—precisely what Polk needed to take a war message to Congress:

"Mexico has passed the boundary of the United States, has invaded our territory and shed American blood upon American soil." Despite strong hesitation in many American quarters, as well as Mexican authorities' desire to end hostilities if possible, Polk seized the moment to add, "War exists, and, notwithstanding all our efforts to avoid it, exists by the act of Mexico herself." Congress responded with a declaration of war on May 13, 1846 (see map).

Polk sent General Taylor into northeastern Mexico to capture the cities of Palo Alto in May and Monterrey in September 1846. At the same time, Colonel Stephen Kearny marched hundreds of midwestern volunteers across forbidding dry lands to Santa Fe, where they accepted the city's surrender. Kearny's force then proceeded to southern California, where he occupied the region with the help of American naval forces and Frémont's irregulars.

Although it appeared that American forces had secured a vast stretch of southwestern lands, Mexico refused to negotiate peace and instead chose to keep fighting. In February 1847, Santa Anna, who was once again at the head of Mexico's troops, attacked Taylor's forces at Buena Vista but was repulsed by the Americans. Within a month General Winfield Scott attacked the coastal city of Vera Cruz with an amphibious force and crushed its resistance. But it took until September for Scott to lead his forces to Mexico City and put an end to the country's resistance. Along the way, brutal battles took a heavy toll on Mexican and American troops, and both sides reacted to battle casualties by retaliating with rape, robbery, and banditry.

But once Mexico City fell to the American forces, the war was over. The chief clerk of the State Department, Nicholas P. Trist, carried papers into Mexico City that outlined Polk's terms for peace, and on February 2, 1848, both sides signed the Treaty of Guadalupe Hidalgo. Mexico ceded California and all land in Texas north of the Rio Grande River. In addition, Mexico ceded the vast territory of New Mexico (today's Nevada, Arizona, Utah, and part of Colorado). The United States agreed to pay Mexico $15 million in settlement and to assume about $2 million in claims by American citizens for war damages. In all, the United States was enlarged by about 1.2 million square miles and acquired jurisdiction over hundreds of rebel Americans in the territories and nearly eighty thousand Spanish-speaking people.

Internal Tensions

At first, the Mexican-American War was immensely popular in certain regions of the country. Expansionist leaders in Congress, including Stephen A. Douglas, a young Democratic senator from Illinois, championed the war. To many midwesterners, gaining the New Mexico and California territories seemed to be the logical next step in America's manifest destiny to expand to the Pacific Ocean. To many in the South, the press was correct to declare that "every dollar spent there, but insures the acquisition of territory which must widen the field of Southern enterprise and power in the future." The burgeoning penny press also whipped up public enthusiasm for the war, especially the newspapers closely allied with the Democratic Party. By the 1840s, reporters following the troops in Mexico could use the recently invented telegraph

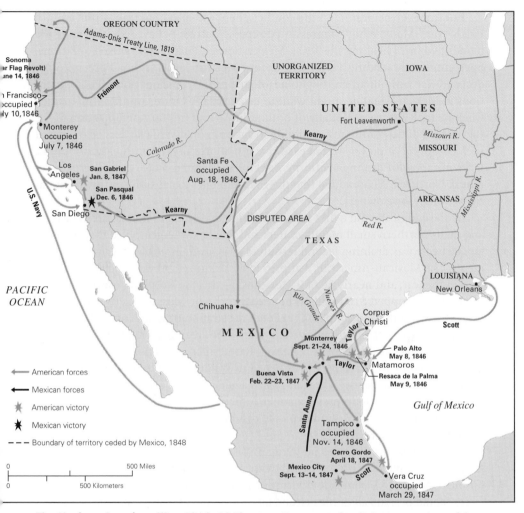

The Mexican-American War, 1846–1848 American troops fought in many regions of the Southwest and Mexico during this war. After claiming the disputed area shown here, the army took land to the Rio Grande, then New Mexico and Alta California. Later on, all of California fell to American naval control. General Winfield Scott finally invaded Mexico at Vera Cruz, and occupied Mexico City in the final major confrontation of the war.

to relay up-to-date information to their editors in eastern cities, who in turn printed stories for an eager public about "war atrocities" in Mexico. Reports straight from the battlefield were read out on street corners and in local gathering places, making it a more immediate, emotional experience than a war on foreign soil would otherwise have evoked. Taylor's and Scott's victories in early 1847 were cause for widespread celebration throughout the South and Midwest, largely because the news arrived quickly and directly from the scene. In May 1847, New York City organized perhaps its largest parade to that time; observers estimated that over 400,000 people took to the city's streets to glory in Scott's successful landing at Vera Cruz.

But from the beginning of the conflict, there was also loud opposition to "Mr. Polk's War." Many Whig congressional representatives believed that, despite the blood shed in 1845 along the Texas-Mexico border, Polk had provoked additional open conflict by sending Taylor deeper into Mexican lands and had precipitously declared war without attempting to negotiate peace. Suspicions about Polk's intentions in Mexico—that he might want to take over the entire country—intensified when he took charge personally of both political and military organization of the war instead of delegating responsibility to subordinates. Whig leaders charged that such co-opting of power was an excessive use of presidential authority, not unlike Jackson's forceful dealings with the Bank of the United States and Cherokee removal. Northern Whigs added that the goals of Polk's expansionism suited primarily southern slave owners.

By the end of the war's first year, opposition expanded to northeastern farmers and many northern small manufacturers and retailers who grumbled that the military struggle was draining federal resources away from essential internal improvements. The Mexican-American War proved costly indeed. About 13,000 Americans died in the war, and nearly 50,000 Mexicans. Taxes rose steeply in every state, and war expenses topped $100 million before its end. The Massachusetts state legislature passed a resolution condemning Polk's declaration of war as unconstitutional. In that state, essayist-philosopher Henry David Thoreau objected to rising taxes to pay for what he considered an unjust war. Rather than pay, Thoreau chose to go to jail (though only for a night) and returned to Walden Pond to pen the much-read essay, "Civil Disobedience." Thoreau gained a wide hearing for his view that when a government acted in an immoral manner, individuals had a right—in fact, a duty—to resist it. Since then, his model of civil disobedience has inspired many leaders, including Martin Luther King, Jr.

Political tensions were also building in Washington by war's end. When Trist returned to Washington with the signed treaty between America and Mexico, Polk was furious. Given Scott's tremendous victories, Polk believed by late 1847 that American forces should overrun all of Mexico and take much more territory than he had at first told Trist to negotiate for. To Polk, Trist had foolishly ignored the opportunity to win all of Mexico in the treaty's final terms. However, this hyperaggressive expansionism contrasted with widespread war-weariness by early 1848. Whig congressional and state leaders, as well as popular intellectual leaders such as Ralph Waldo Emerson, cried out that Americans had enough war and high taxes. Even some southern War Hawks believed that taking Mexico invited political disaster for Americans. Senator John C. Calhoun, for example, articulated a widespread racist argument that it was sufficient to take the "nearly vacant" lands of Mexico's former northern provinces, but that to take into America "the colored and mixed-breed" Mexicans who lived south of the Rio Grande would "taint" American politics and culture immeasurably.

Polk relented and accepted the treaty with Mexico. In fact, in the short span of three years, he had attained most of his political goals, including the acquisition of 1.2 million square miles of new territory—Texas, Oregon, California, and the huge New Mexico territory—increasing the size of the United States by some 70 percent. Still, many statesmen and citizens continued to question the means by which Polk and his circle took such vast lands, and to doubt the necessity of the Mexican-American War. Abraham Lincoln, for example, reflected many years later, "The act of sending an armed force among the Mexicans was unnecessary, inasmuch as Mexico was in no way molesting or menacing the United States or the people thereof; and . . . it was unconstitutional, because the power of levying war is vested in Congress, and not in the President."

The Wilmot Proviso

The war with Mexico drew Americans everywhere into a protracted political discussion, often very heated, about the meaning of the West and how it would be shaped by settlement and policies. Many important issues were subsumed in support for, or opposition to, manifest destiny in the West. Among them were concerns about pursuing diplomacy and relations with foreign nations, protecting settlers already in the western frontiers, heeding the demands for government and statehood that poured from the West regularly during the 1840s, and spreading the "civilizing tendencies" of American culture into the "untamed" West. But no issue was more divisive in American political and cultural discussions about the West than slavery.

When, for example, Daniel Webster intoned in 1846, "We want no extension of territory; we want no accession of new states. The country is already large enough," he went on to clarify that if America grew any larger, southern slave interests would rush into the new territories. Webster's view did not win many adherents during the war's early months of feverish patriotism, but slowly this view gained support in Congress. David Wilmot, a Democrat from Pennsylvania, rose during a congressional discussion about appropriations for the Mexican-American War to propose that slavery be banned in any territory acquired from Mexico. The South could keep slavery as it existed, he conceded, but under no circumstances should it be carried into the new territories.

Wilmot's Proviso of August 1846 provoked congressional representatives and state leaders to make an important decision about slavery in the territories. The result was jarring to every political interest in the nation: southern Whigs joined southern Democrats against the proviso, while northerners of both parties supported it. Party loyalty, which had been so strong since Jackson's early days in office, broke down over this all-important issue, and sectional loyalty replaced it. In the coming years, both parties would remain unable to pull their northern and southern wings together over matters related to slavery and the admission of new territories to statehood. Any decisive stance on these issues would only drive deeper wedges between members of either party, based on sectional interests. Once again, the American political culture was in crisis.

More lay behind Wilmot's proposal than strong feelings about slavery. Like many fellow Democrats, Wilmot feared the rising influence of abolitionists in the North and Midwest. The Liberty Party had been growing steadily since 1840, and its nearly 62,000 northern votes in the 1844 election had come from both Whigs and Democrats. The Liberty Party proposed to unseat all senators who held slaves, which would have decimated the southern states' power in that body. The party also proposed to keep out of the Union any territories that held slaves when they applied for statehood, to end slavery in the District of Columbia, and to crush the interstate slave trade.

The founders of the Liberty Party had first become politically active in the abolitionist movement during the 1830s. Voters who sided with the party in 1844 realized that its platform of strong antislavery positions could win only in the North, and that a Liberty Party victory would split the Union. Their votes nevertheless showed that thousands of Americans wished to express opposition to slavery in an official way. Outside the Liberty Party, the majority of northern citizens did not wish to abolish slavery in the South but hoped to secure expansion in the new states exclusively for white people. This majority coalesced into the free-soil movement after the 1844 election. To free-soilers, slavery was not necessarily immoral; it was an economic and political threat to the manifest destiny of white male expansion in free territories. Free-soilers supported a strong Union, even if that meant allowing slavery to continue to exist in the southern states. But the northern values of individualism, political liberty, and small free farms could be achieved in the unorganized territories and new western states only if slavery was prohibited there.

During the mid-1840s, free-soil support swelled among northerners and midwesterners who wished to halt the spread of slavery into the new territories. Reasoning in pragmatic terms, free-soilers argued that the southern plantation system would compete directly with white farm families moving into the Ohio Valley, and in all other regions across the Mississippi. Many free-soilers took cues from the labor movement of the 1830s and 1840s, which often promoted the values of free labor: hard work, personal independence, and the sanctity of individual property. Southern slavery was antithetical to these values, argued free-soilers. Some of them also believed that southern poor whites, by virtue of choosing to live in the South, did not hold the values of free labor either.

By 1848, these views coalesced into concrete political action. When Secretary of State James Buchanan proposed to extend the Missouri Compromise line to the Pacific Ocean—thereby admitting slavery into most of today's New Mexico, Arizona, and southern California—free-soilers attracted to their banner great numbers of Americans who wished to shape the West in the political and cultural image of the free labor North. The Free-Soil Party was born.

While many Free-Soilers came out of abolitionist backgrounds, and many party members believed free white and free African-American people could live well together in all of the free states, a constituency in the party adamantly opposed any mixing of races. As northern political radicals pointed out, only a few outspoken abolitionists sought true social and economic equality among the races of North America, and they tended to join radical abolitionist organizations. The majority of people in the North regarded African-Americans, whether slave or free, as inferior to whites. Moreover, African-Americans would compete for economic opportunity and employment in newly settled areas just as they did in the eastern states. Thus that a constituency of Free-Soilers reflected this majority and wished to cleanse the new territories of all African-American people came as no surprise to William

Lloyd Garrison, or to Sarah and Angelina Grimké. Already Indiana, Illinois, Iowa, and Oregon had enacted laws prohibiting African-Americans within their boundaries, though officials were unable to enforce the laws consistently.

The Election of 1848

By the time male citizens turned out to vote in 1848, the Treaty of Guadalupe Hidalgo had stretched America's boundaries around vast new lands. Streams of new settlers were beginning to determine the character of territorial life. But in 1848 American policymakers and citizens had still not resolved the central issue of the Wilmot Proviso: whether slavery would exist in the new territories.

Nor did the campaign for the presidency in 1848 give voters decisive choices. All three national party candidates declined to take a stand on the principled questions of freedom or slavery. Instead they developed their positions based on pragmatic political considerations. The Democratic Party candidate, Lewis Cass of Michigan, risked losing northern voters if he spoke out directly for slavery in the territories, and he risked losing southern voters if he said nothing at all about slavery. He chose the most ambiguous middle course available: the government should adopt a policy of popular sovereignty. This doctrine would leave the decision about slavery versus freedom to the citizens of each territory. It sounded very democratic since it would put decisions about the character of the territories in the hands of locally elected bodies of the Jeffersonian and Jacksonian "common man." In reality, Cass and other leading Democrats knew that popular sovereignty was no solution to sectional divisions at all. For one thing, every territorial and state government would be made up of the same political parties that argued about slavery at the national level. Divisions along party lines in the new territories would probably develop as mirror images of party disputes in older areas. For another, Cass's proposal for popular sovereignty also failed to say when and how a territory would choose its slave or free status, leaving it up to the various party factions and sectional interests of older regions to influence territorial outcomes.

The Whig Party also contributed its share of sectional and political confusion to the campaign of 1848. Instead of choosing the ever-willing Henry Clay to run, the party picked General Zachary Taylor, who was far from being a typical Whig. Taylor was, in the first place, not from a strong Whig center in the North or Chesapeake, but from Louisiana. Furthermore, as a slaveholder, he could not appeal to abolitionists, as so many leaders of his party could. In addition, where many of his party had opposed the Mexican-American War, Taylor had catapulted to heroic stature because of his military role in the war. Whigs hoped that Taylor would attract the votes of party members in every national region, including southern and midwestern Democrats who applauded Taylor's slaveholding and expansionist stance. To have such broad appeal, Taylor avoided taking a clear position on the issue of slavery in the territories.

The third national force in the election, the growing Free-Soil Party, scooped up the votes of northern Democrats who opposed the Mexican War's benefits for southerners, Whigs who did not thrill to Taylor's background and qualifications, and Whigs who had already associated themselves with the principled position of the Liberty Party and now wanted to vote their convictions in 1848. With the former Democrat Martin Van Buren as their presidential candidate, third-party supporters backed the slogan, "Free Soil, Free Labor, Free Men."

The Free-Soil Party gained 291,263 votes, or 10.1 percent of the popular vote. Almost all of the party's support was in the Northeast and Midwest, especially among small farmers and urban workers who wanted to improve working conditions and halt the extension of slavery. Although the Free-Soil Party did not officially endorse abolitionism, many free African-American leaders, including Frederick Douglass, welcomed the party's campaign as a good start in the much larger effort to end slavery everywhere. The Free-Soil turnout was enough to divide the Democrats (electoral votes of the powerful states of New York and Pennsylvania went to Van Buren) and to dampen the Whig victory. Taylor won the presidency with only 47.4 percent of the popular vote, as the candidate of a party he hardly seemed to fit, and without addressing the most serious issues dividing the country.

Gold!

One month before Mexico ceded California and New Mexico to the United States, James Marshall, an employee at one of Sutter's mills, found flakes of gold about as large as dimes in the millrace. Soon, all hands around the mills and mines on Sutter's land dropped their usual work to pan for gold. Within six weeks the news had spread, and men began to leave jobs from as far away as Monterey and San Francisco to join others who were reporting modest finds of gold from streams. By June 1848, "gold fever" was epidemic in California, and by September, ships returning to Boston and Philadelphia, as well as wagons returning to Independence, Missouri, reported that a few people had struck it rich.

When a couple of miners produced actual gold nuggets and little bags of gold dust, the news spread like wildfire and the initial California rush became a torrent of prospectors. Until 1849, only about fifteen thousand Americans had traveled overland to California; in 1849 alone, some eighty thousand men, women, and children left their farms and urban jobs in the East and Midwest to race to the western foothills of the Sierra Nevada Mountains. Later called the "forty-niners" because of the year most of them went west, gold seekers crossed the plains on the Overland Trail or took ships to San Francisco. Prospectors came from every walk of life, from every state and territory, from Mexico, Europe, and China, to stake claims in California. Within a year, they transformed California from a ranching and mining outback into a chaotic mixture of peoples from all around the world.

Chinese immigrants arrived by the hundreds during 1849 and 1850 to mine for gold, most with the expectation of returning home quickly. The first waves of Chinese were primarily men, and they often lived apart from American camps in their own "Chinatowns." Their success in extracting gold from the hillsides added to the intense economic competition of the gold rush, and resentment and racial stereotypes of Chinese appearances and customs developed quickly. When over twenty thousand more Chinese came to San Francisco in 1852, they seemed to whites to flood the port with a "foreign danger," and open racism became a regular feature of life in the city.

San Francisco had become a boomtown overnight, thanks to the discovery of gold. In little more than a year, it grew from 1,000 to 35,000 people, all of whom needed housing, food, mining supplies, and work animals. Tents rose out of the mud, as the swelling population burst the seams of makeshift city neighborhoods over and over. Saloons sprang up randomly. Fortunes, said many small entrepreneurs, were easier to make from needy prospectors and land agents than from hunting for gold. Agents of eastern merchants flocked to the city to sell shiploads of sugar, coffee, tea, rum, iron tools, pots and kettles, guns, and other necessities of frontier life. One ambitious entrepreneur was Levi-Strauss, a German Jew who brought his tough canvas material to San Francisco with the hope of manufacturing tents. But the sturdy cloth proved more useful in the form of men's pants. Miners soon learned from advice manuals that in addition to "your mule, your lamp and your pan," every miner would be grateful to carry along "a pair of well-sewn Levi pants."

Out in the mining camps and foothills where the prospectors worked, people survived with minimal comforts and many hardships. Amid the stench of people living together with little concern for public sanitation or personal hygiene, careless

The Bar of a Gambling Saloon   By 1855, the California gold rush had attracted a variety of people, for a variety of purposes, to mining country and had converted small trading posts to thriving cities. Against the ornate background of this drinking establishment in San Francisco, men from many continents made business deals, discussed commercial and political news, and shared the same cultural space.   *(© Collection of The New-York Historical Society.)*

campers often polluted water, and diseases took their toll as a consequence. Nor was the camp diet healthy; most miners lived on the boring fare of stale bread, beans, and salt pork. Few took the time to hunt or fish—which may have required going far from the camps overnight—and many neglected to build decent shelters for the rainy winter months.

Mining camps attracted people willing to provide services, usually at excessive cost. Because few miners were willing to take the time to do everyday chores, those who had money or small bits of gold would pay others to do the chores for them. Cooks, tailors, and laundresses made decent money in the camps, if they survived the ravages of disease, theft, and absconding employers. Saloonkeepers, prostitutes, and boarding house owners often met early deaths because of violence, venereal disease, or drug or alcohol abuse, although a few made fortunes and returned to the East.

Violence was a regular feature of this camp life. "Claim jumpers"—men who robbed successful miners of their gold or stole their claim papers—hung about in most mining camps, ready to engage in all manner of mayhem. Chinese, African-American, and Mexican miners endured especially harsh racist attacks; many minority miners were driven from their claims, taunted into leaving, or beaten brutally. Although Americans had entered California before 1848 as "foreigners," the wave of Americans entering the new republic assumed it was their right to dominate the territory and designated other groups of people as foreigners. Americans subjected the Chinese, in particular, to demeaning mining taxes.

Few of the forty-niners found any gold at all. And once the quest had depleted their savings and hopes, it was difficult to return to their former homes. Large numbers of them went to work for mining companies for wages. Where individual miners with their pans or picks could tap only the surface of potential deposits, organized mining companies pooled large amounts of capital to buy expensive machinery and probe deep for gold. In fact, after the first rush of independent prospectors into the foothills of the Sierra Nevada, it was wage workers who mined most of the California "Mother Lode" that stretched over one hundred miles southward from Sutter's Mill.

By the mid-1850s, individuals and companies had extracted more than $10 million in gold from California's mountainsides, and the gold rush was all but over. In its wake a multicultural population, some of it made affluent by the boom and some of it left desperately poor, made another transition to settled agricultural and commercial life in California. All of the undercurrents of tension among different races remained, especially in blatant forms of racism against the growing Chinese population. In addition, the California Indians who had lived in large numbers in the central valleys fled or died when waves of eastern migrants took over the environment. New settlers cultivated orchards and vineyards and vegetable fields that disrupted the ecological balance of Indian hunting grounds. To the south and west, along the coastline, Americans forced *californios* off their lands and legally annulled their former Mexican grants, compelling them to become another minority component of unstable communities in post–gold rush California. By 1860, the scramble for valuable mineral wealth had moved into Arizona and New Mexico. At first, copper mines yielded new fortunes; soon, silver was discovered at the Comstock Lode in Nevada. By the end of the Civil War, nearly $300 million in silver had been added to the world supply of precious metals.

CONCLUSION

By 1848, it seemed that Americans were fulfilling their "manifest destiny" to win and transform great stretches of land beyond the Mississippi River. The American government had secured over a million square miles in three years, by treaty and by war. The American people were moving onto that land with enthusiasm despite the tremendous hardships of life on the trails. Advancing over the Louisiana Purchase, Florida, Texas, the huge territories of New Mexico, California, and Oregon, Americans were occupying the landscape in successive frontier communities at an unprecedented pace. By 1860, nearly 350,000 people attempted the trek from Independence, Missouri, to Oregon and California.

Migrants carried many experiences from their former lives into the West. At the same time, many of them also tried to forge distinctive new communities in their adopted western homes. In either case, the processes for "civilizing space" in the West were not as easy and peaceful as promoters and publicists told Americans they would be. Almost 34,000 trans-Mississippi migrants before the Civil War died of exposure, disease, accidents, or hunger and fatigue before their wagons rolled across grasses and along the deep ruts that are visible even today. The majority of sojourners into the West also adjusted their expectations and endured hardships beyond the imagination of even the most accurate newspaper reporters of the era. Most settlers in the 1840s and 1850s did not replicate, or better, their farming efforts in the East. Most did not set up family farms as Jefferson and so many others envisioned for "the empire of the West," but instead trapped and hunted, mined, lumbered, constructed new towns and roads, provided services to newcomers, carried merchandize and the mail, fought Indians, and defended military claims. Their wives faced life-altering hardships on the overland trails, and then set up their new homes in communities fraught with scarcity, sometimes with violence, and almost always with lonely remoteness from the domestic culture they left back in the East.

Wars, especially the Mexican-American War, played an important role in gaining trans-Mississippi territory for Americans' goals. A powerful combination of ideas about their manifest destiny, their sectional quarrels over slavery and free soil, their anxieties about foreign alliances against America, and their restless migration into the West, all guided large numbers of Americans toward the conviction that a war with Mexico was necessary. As Americans in Texas continued to petition for annexation, as Americans in Oregon pleaded for orderly government and government aid, and as Americans in California declared their republic and sought annexation, a groundswell of sentiment rose favoring the tremendously costly war with Mexico. However, as the costs in lives and tax monies sapped the nation, public support for the war declined during its later months.

The West also focused Americans' deepening sectionalism and political divisions. The reformers and developers who shaped eastern and midwestern political culture from the 1820s to early 1840s turned their attention more and more to shaping the future of new territories. Discussion about the future of slavery could not be separated from territorial acquisition. Every political candidate for major office feared confronting the issue squarely, and yet all compromise positions failed to glue the rapidly shifting political forces into a viable national party. The election of 1848, one of America's most divisive, put a Whig in office who had southern identity and sentiments. It came at a time when territorial acquisitions made America a continental nation, but also when sectional tensions over the identity of the West and the existence of slavery rose to new heights.

SUGGESTED READINGS

Clyde Milner et al., eds., *The Oxford History of the American West* (1994), contains numerous essays that summarize old and new scholarship about many relevant topics. Patricia Limerick, Clyde Milner, and Charles Rankin, eds., *Trails: Toward a New Western History* (1991), brings together new work that stresses the role of the federal government in shaping the West and the multicultural character of frontier life.

Important starting places for understanding manifest destiny and expansionist ideology in nineteenth-century America include the standard work, Frederick Merk, *Manifest Destiny and Mission in American History: A Reinterpretation* (1963), which explains the sense of mission carried into frontier development; and Henry Nash Smith, *Virgin Land: The American West as Symbol and Myth* (1950), which analyzes the images of the West that inspired migration. See also Thomas Hietala, *Manifest Design: Anxious Aggrandizement in Late Jacksonian America* (1985), and Reginald Horsman, *Race and Manifest Destiny: The Origins of American Racial Anglo-Saxonism* (1981).

Early 1800s promotion of migration and exploration can be traced in Jennifer S. H. Brown, *Strangers in Blood: Fur Trade Company Families in Indian Country* (1980); James P. Ronda, *Astoria and Empire* (1990); Theodore J. Karaminski, *Fur Trade and Exploration: Opening of the Far Northwest, 1821–1852* (1983); and Dale Morgan, *Jedediah Smith and the Opening of the West* (1982). For the earliest experiences of migrants on the trails, see the engaging studies by Richard Bartlett, *The New Country: A Social History of the American Frontier, 1776–1890* (1974), and Sandra Myres, *Westering Women and the Frontier Experience, 1800–1915* (1982).

Indian experiences with Americans in the trans-Mississippi West before the Civil War are covered in the lively work of Robert Utley, *The Indian Frontier of the American West, 1846–1890* (1984), and Richard White, *"It's Your Misfortune and None of My Own": A New History of the American West* (1991), which is also a cultural and environmental study of the always-changing frontier and the many peoples who shaped it.

Ray Allen Billington's *The Far Western Frontier, 1830–1860* (1956) remains the best overview of the overlapping destinies of Texas, California, and Oregon in this era. For more detailed accounts of the Lone Star Republic and its struggle for annexation, see Gene Brack, *Mexico Views Manifest Destiny, 1821–1846* (1975), and Arnaldo DeLeon, *The Tejano Community, 1836–1900* (1982). David Weber, *The Mexican Frontier, 1821–1846* (1982), is one of the finest studies of the borderlands before American settlement transformed the region. The stories of Americans on the overland trails to Oregon and California are legion, but the best summaries include Leonard J. Arrington and Davis Bitton, *The Mormon Experience* (1979); William Bowen, *The Willamette Valley: Migration and Settlement on the Oregon Frontier* (1978); Malcolm Clark Jr., *Eden Seekers: The Settlement of Oregon* (1981); and John Mack Faragher, *Women and Men on the Overland Trail* (1979).

The best accounts of Texas and annexation, in addition to Billington's standard account, are Frederick Merk, *Slavery and the Annexation of Texas* (1972); David Montejano, *Anglos and Mexicans in the Making of Texas, 1836–1986* (1987); and David M. Pletcher, *The Diplomacy of Annexation: Texas, Oregon, and the Mexican War* (1973). For the progress of the war, Jack Bauer's *The Mexican War, 1846–1848* (1974) and Robert Johannsen's *To the Halls of the Montezumas: The Mexican War in the American Imagination* (1985) provide thorough coverage. The nature of Polk's actions regarding Texas and America's role in the war are treated with balance in Paul H. Bergeron, *The Presidency of James K. Polk* (1987), and portions of William Freehling, *The Road to Disunion* (1990), give valuable insights about tensions within the South regarding expansion, slavery, and the war.

Following the Mexican-American War, the years of political turmoil are engagingly related in Chaplain W. Morrison, *Democratic Politics and Sectionalism: The Wilmot Proviso Controvery* (1967), and Joseph Raybeck, *Free Soil: The Election of 1848* (1970). The best study of political party changes in the 1840s is Joel Silbey's *The Shrine of Party: Congressional Voting Behaviour, 1841–1852* (1967).

For the California gold rush and that territory's rapidly changing character, see John W. Caughey, *The California Gold Rush* (1975); William Greever, *Bonanza West: The Story of the Western Mining Rushes, 1848–1900* (1963); and Neal Harlow, *California Conquered: The Annexation of a Mexican Province, 1846–1850* (1982). For the consequences of multicultural contact in California, the most important studies include Robert H. Jackson and Edward Castillo, *Indians, Franciscans, and Spanish Colonization: The Impact of the Mission System on California Indians* (1995); Charles McClain, *In Search of Equality: The Chinese Struggle Against Discrimination in Nineteenth-Century America* (1994); and Leonard Pitt, *The Decline of the Californios: A Social History of the Spanish-Speaking Californians, 1846–1890* (1970).

The Passage West

The Hope of a New Zion

Mrs. Priscilla Evans was a Mormon pioneer who walked the thousand miles from Iowa City to Salt Lake City in 1856. Not all westward trekkers were from eastern towns and midwestern farms: Priscilla was a recent immigrant from Wales, and among her fellow travelers were newcomers from Germany, Denmark, Sweden, and Holland. Together, they pulled handcarts filled with their belongings for five months of muddy spring rains and scorching summer heat. Unlike many less fortunate settlers who perished from exposure and hunger on the arduous journey, the pregnant Priscilla arrived at her destination, healthy and ready to create a new home with her husband.

We took a tug from Penbroke [England] to Liverpool. . . . I was sick all the way. We landed in Boston . . . then travelled in cattle cars . . . to Iowa City . . . [where] my husband was offered ten dollars a day to work at his trade of Iron Roller, but money was no inducement to us, for we were anxious to get to Zion. We learned afterwards that many who stayed there apostatized [fell from religious grace] or died of cholera.

When the carts were ready we started on a three-hundred-mile walk to Winter quarters on the Missouri River. There were a great many who made fun of us as we walked, pulling our carts, but the weather was fine and the roads were excellent. . . .

We began our journey of one thousand miles [from the Missouri River] on foot with a handcart for each family. . . . There were five mule teams to haul the tents and surplus flour. Each handcart had one hundred pounds of flour, that was to be divided and [more got] from the wagons as required. At first we had a little coffee and bacon, but that was soon gone and we had no use for any cooking utensils but a frying pan. The flour was self-raising and we took water and baked a little cake; that was all we had to eat.

After months of travelling we were put on half rations and at one time, before help came, we were out of flour for two days. We washed out the flour sacks to make a little gravy.

There were in our tent my husband with one leg, two blind men . . . a man with one arm, and a widow with five children. . . . The tent was our covering, and the overcoat spread on the bare ground with the shawl over us was our bed. My feather bed, and the bedding, pillows, all our good clothing, my husband's church books, which he had collected through six years of missionary work, . . . all had to be left in a storehouse. We were promised that they would come to us with the next emigration in the spring, but we never did receive them. . . .

No one rode in the wagons. Strong men would help the weaker ones, until they themselves were worn out, and some died from the struggle and want of food, and were buried along the wayside. It was heart rending for parents to move on and leave their loved ones to such a fate, as they were so helpless, and had no material for coffins. Children and young folks, too, had to move on and leave father or mother or both.

Sometimes a bunch of buffaloes would come and the carts would stop until they passed. Had we been prepared with guns and ammunition, like people who came in wagons, we might have had meat, and would not have come to near starving. . . . We were much more fortunate than those who came later, as they had snow and freezing weather. Many lost limbs, and many froze to death . . . they got started too late. My husband, in walking from twenty to twenty-five miles per day [had pain] where the knee rested on the pad: the friction caused it to gather and break and was most painful. But he had to endure it, or remain behind, as he was never asked to ride in a wagon. . . .

The Lure of California Gold

In January 1848, when the first news leaked out that sawmill carpenters near Sacramento had found gold nuggets in the millrace, most people just laughed. But James H. Carson, a loner and adventurer, had few attachments to hold him in the East. "Just a little of the golden stuff would fix me fine," he wrote to relatives. Carson reached northern California where a few early prospectors were already panning the streams, hopeful of becoming rich if they survived camp conditions.

. . . I was knee deep in water, with my wash-basin full of dirt. . . After washing some fifty pans of dirt, I found I had realised about four bits' worth of gold. Reader, do you know how an *hombre* feels when the gold fever heat has suddenly fallen to about zero? I do. Kelsey's and the old dry diggings had just been opened, and to them I next set out. . . . I saw Indians giving handsful of gold for a cotton handkerchief or a shirt—and so great was the income of the Captain's trading houses that he was daily sending out mules packed with gold. . . . The population then there (exclusive of Indians) consisted of about three hundred—old pioneers, native Californians, deserters from the Army, Navy, and Colonel Stevenson's volunteers. . . . Every one had plenty of dust. From three ounces to five pounds was the income per day to those who would work. The gulches and ravines were opened about two feet wide and one foot in depth along their centres, and the gold picked out from amongst the dirt with a knife. . . .

Honesty (of which we now know so little) was the ruling passion amongst the miners of '48. Old debts were paid up; heavy bags of gold dust were carelessly left laying in their brush homes; mining tools, though scarce, were left in their places of work for days at a time, and not one theft or robbery was committed. . . .

We lived on beef and beans—beef dried, fried, roasted, boiled and broiled, morning, noon and night; as much as every man wanted, without money or price; and with a change, at times, to elk, venison and bear steak. . . . The discovery of gold raised the price of stock in proportion with everything else. Horses and mules in the mines were worth from two to four hundred dollars; cattle from one to two hundred dollars per head. I have seen men . . . ride them from one digging to another—take their saddles off, and set the animals loose (never looking for them again), remarking that "it was easier to dig out the price of another, than to hunt up the one astray."

The morals of the miners of '48 should here be noticed. No person worked on Sunday . . . [they] spent it in playing at poker, with lumps of gold for checks; others, collected in groups, might be seen under the shades of neighboring trees, singing songs, playing at "old sledge" and drinking whisky. . . . We had ministers of the gospel amongst us, but they never preached. Religion had been forgotten, even by its ministers, and instead . . . they might have been seen with pick-axe and pan, travelling untrodden ways in search of "filthy lucre" & treasure that "fadeth away," or drinking good health and prosperity with friends.

Americans of the early republic only glimpsed the possibilities for westward movement into Jefferson's "empire for liberty," but by the 1840s, waves of settlers crossed the Great Plains into Oregon Territory. Some turned south into California, which became a state by 1850. This conquest of space did not happen overnight, and it did not happen easily. Many bloody battles with Indians and Mexican-Spanish residents, and disputes with people of European nations, took place as Americans followed their manifest destiny. At the same time, Americans debated whether they would extend free labor or slavery into the new lands they took over.

The result was a succession of frontiers filled not only with sturdy yeomen and successful entrepreneurs, but also with speculators, bankers, squatters, poor immigrants, failed gold-diggers, tenant farmers, and widows and orphans. A great number of migrants satisfied their deepest longings for modest success in a new life, and a few of them got rich. Priscilla Evans and her husband gradually prevailed against harsh Utah conditions. She bore twelve children and lived to know some of her grandchildren. James H. Carson led an altogether different life, but one equally representative of the thousands of single men and women who left trades or farms behind in order to begin a life anew on the far western frontiers.

Questions for Analysis

1. In what ways are these two accounts similar and in what ways different? Are these two individuals drawn to the West for the same reasons?

2. How do you think frontier life affected families, especially women and children? How was traveling west different for single men than for married men?

3. In what ways do each of these accounts emphasize the successes of frontier life? What are some of the difficulties migrants faced?

4. What do you think the journey and resettlement might have been like for less inspired farm families than the Evanses, or for less successful miners than Carson? Could you rewrite these accounts in other ways?

5. What do these accounts tell us about the variety of experiences and lifestyles on the far western frontier? What details strike you as uniquely far western, as opposed to southern or eastern?

14

The Sectional Challenge, 1848–1860

ohn Brown's leather tanning businesses in Ohio and northwestern Pennsylvania during the 1830s and 1840s had been sadly unsuccessful. His try at sheep ranching in Massachusetts flopped. Year after year, Brown endured not only business failures, but also the tragedies of his first wife's death, unrelenting hunger and disease among his children, the death of four beloved infants, the mental illness of more than one growing son, and the persistent poor health of his second wife. Unbowed, he tried to teach his sons to seek virtue in backbreaking farm labor and to take solace in family Bible readings. Somehow, his family grew and some of his children survived.

John Brown called all of his family's hardships and losses "small things" in comparison to the "one great thing" that sustained his passion and anger over the years: the existence of slavery. Although Brown failed in worldly occupations, he very successfully raised his children to be obedient, both to God's laws and to their father's will, and to struggle against slavery with every fiber of their beings. As a young man, Brown concealed many fugitive slaves who had crossed the Ohio River seeking freedom in the North. He befriended leading abolitionists in the Northeast and worked on a plan to raid the South, destroying planters' property and convincing slaves to run away. Deeper and deeper into the South, explained Brown, the "forces of Christian liberty" would march, until "floods of our bound brethren . . . flowed into northern freedom."

Brown moved his family to North Elba, New York, to farm an estate donated to him by the prominent abolitionist Gerritt Smith. There, Brown and his growing sons continued to ferry runaway slaves along the Underground Railroad to points farther north.

Once the government opened the Kansas Territory for settlement, Brown began to send his sons, one after another, into the West to farm. But soon they wrote home that "border ruffians" from Missouri and southern slave states were crossing into Kansas bent on establishing large slave plantations. John Brown the abolitionist could not sit idly by. He planned his own relocation to Kansas, leaving his wife and youngest children in New York, and raised funds for hundreds of Sharps rifles. By 1856, Brown was ready to do battle in "the inevitable war against that prime of all evils," slavery.

Naive? Visionary? Insane? Brown's plan was all of these. In May 1856, Brown gathered his living sons and sons-in-law in the Kansas Territory and led them in the massacre of five proslavery men and their sons on the Pottawatomie Creek. Even after his son Frederick was killed on a subsequent raid, Brown insisted that "the holy war" against slavery had to continue. Back east in October 1859, he decided the moment had arrived to enable southern slaves to "take their freedom" and force slave owners to die defending their odious system. With thousands of dollars from northern antislavery supporters, Brown purchased cases of weapons. He led eighteen heavily armed veterans of the battles in Kansas to the federal arsenal at Harpers Ferry, Virginia. There, "God's angry man" and his liberators seized the arsenal, killed a number of local citizens, and waited for a massive slave rebellion to catch fire.

But not many southern slaves even knew about Brown's plan, and no uprising occurred. The local militia, armed planters, and a detachment of U.S. Marines commanded by Colonel Robert E. Lee descended on the arsenal where Brown's men held out. A number of Brown's "antislavery warriors" died within hours, and the military took Brown prisoner. Virginia state authorities charged Brown with treason and ordered him to be executed on December 2, 1859. His hanging provoked some of the largest mourning parades the North had ever witnessed. The entire sequence of events sent shock waves through the South.

Public opinion about Brown's raid on Harpers Ferry was divided. A Richmond newspaper reflected that "the Harpers Ferry invasion has advanced the cause of disunion more than any other event that has happened since the formation of [the] government." In the North, members of the new Republican Party, which stood opposed to slavery in the territories, kept their distance from Brown's scheme. Republican Abraham Lincoln believed the martyr was little more than "an enthusiast" who "fancie[d] himself commissioned by Heaven to liberate" slaves. "He ventures the attempt, which ends in little else than his own execution." Stephen A. Douglas, the prominent Democratic senator who was in the forefront of discussions about the future of the western territories, used the Harpers Ferry episode to berate abolitionists and radical Republicans. Brown's raid, he charged, was "a natural, logical, inevitable result of the doctrines and teachings of the Republican party." Democrats elsewhere used correspondence between Brown and his northern abolitionist friends to fuel southern animosity.

Chronology

1848	Taylor elected president
1850	Compromise of 1850
	California admitted as a free state
	Know-Nothing Party formed
1851	Stowe publishes *Uncle Tom's Cabin*
1852	Pierce elected president
1853	Gadsden Purchase
1854	Kansas-Nebraska Act
	Indian Territory reorganized
	Republican Party formed and Whigs dissolve
1855	Bleeding Kansas
1856	Pottawatomie massacre
	Brooks assaults Sumner in the Senate
1857	*Dred Scott* decision
	Lecompton Constitution
	Lincoln-Douglas debates
1858	Brown's raid on Harpers Ferry
1859	Lincoln elected president
1860	South Carolina secedes

But numerous abolitionists and Unitarian ministers, including Thomas Wentworth Higginson and Theodore Parker, stepped forward to praise Brown as "the Christian martyr of a mighty cause." Henry David Thoreau called Brown "an angel of light" on a very dark issue, a principled individual in a "sea of murky indecision." Undoubtedly, many Americans interpreted Brown's violence as the logical consequence of the tensions that racked the territories and the sectional disputes that worsened with each passing month in 1859. But like his opponents, Brown's supporters were not raising controversial issues, or confronting violence over the matter of slavery, for the first time. Indeed, during the stormy decade of the 1850s, numerous Americans strove desperately to produce compromises that might repair or repress the deep divisions that split them. Their repeated failures raise significant questions about those last years before the Civil War:

▌ What was the role of western frontier development in the long-term sectional divisions between northern and southern Americans?

▌ What kinds of compromises did political and cultural leaders attempt to forge in these contentious years?

▌ Who spoke out for each section, each major interest, and what arguments did they give for their political proposals and personal beliefs? What was the role of new political party alignments?

▌ Why did compromise ultimately fail?

This chapter will address these questions.

 ## Territory and Politics

If Alexis de Tocqueville had returned to America a generation after his first visit, he would have seen a dramatically altered nation. Over 2 million acres had been added to the geography, and the weight of America's population was shifting steadily westward. The Old Northwest and the Old Southwest had been organized into states. Each region had already passed through its rudimentary frontier stages and acquired many of the signs of maturity that marked the coastal states. But farther west, great new land acquisitions beckoned citizens to cross the Mississippi. Northerners and southerners divided over how to settle these new lands, with people in each section believing they were entitled to transplant their own, incompatible, social and cultural systems. How would the federal government resolve the sectional and territorial disputes that emerged as people began to settle in these new lands?

Political Ambiguities

When Whig Zachary Taylor won the presidency in 1848 with less than half the popular vote, the deep divisions in American political life became evident. Neither Democrats nor Whigs could sustain party unity across sectional lines. Issues and loyalties that had previously molded party identities across regional lines were rapidly dissolving into purely sectional alignments. Many northern Whigs who supported the Wilmot Proviso voted for Taylor, but a large number of northern and midwestern voters abandoned both parties to vote for the Free-Soil Party's candidate. Northern Democrats who were expansionists but did not want slavery in all of the new territories were helplessly divided from southern Democrats who demanded slavery's extension. With all eyes focused on the trans-Mississippi territories, each party seemed irreparably torn on the greatest question of all: freedom or slavery in the West?

From a southern point of view, Texas continued to be a logical place for planters' expansion, and the Wilmot Proviso's proposed denial of slavery in huge amounts of the West would unfairly limit southern expansion. John C. Calhoun reiterated his states' rights doctrine, insisting that the territories were jointly owned by the existing states and any citizen of any state had the right to carry his property (including slaves) into newly acquired lands. Congress, he argued, had no constitutional au-

Harpers Ferry Arsenal, 1859   John Brown and his band of supporters entered this national arsenal with the intention of laying hold of its munitions and using the site as a staging point for a general slave uprising out of the South. Although the buildings shown here were fortified, the arsenal site as a whole was easily surrounded and taken by federal and state troops.   *(National Archives.)*

thority to regulate or exclude slavery in the territories. Other southern Democrats, more pragmatic than Calhoun, were willing to negotiate some extension of slavery into the territories without arguing for the principle of slavery on all new American soil. Still other Democrats, especially in the Midwest, adhered to popular sovereignty, which postponed national decisions about slavery in the territories and put all future decisions about statehood in the hands of "the people."

During the 1850s, support for popular sovereignty grew in states north of the Ohio River and in new territories west of the Mississippi River. But few Americans understood how and when such popular sovereignty should be exercised. Should it be determined at the time settlers organized the territory, or at the time they applied for statehood? And should it be granted by a constituted legislature, by delegated convention, or by a general vote of all white citizens? The question was put to the test soon enough. California continued to grow even after the gold rush frenzy subsided. Early settlers had sent back word to families in the East that the environment was lush and farms would "instantly prosper, should you only take the risk and come NOW." Miners and farmers alike wished to have California organized as a territory and to elect "a regular representative government."

Here was a chance to test popular sovereignty. Few planters had migrated into California to that time, so the convention that wrote a constitution and applied for statehood during 1849 heard few proslavery voices raised. In addition, Democrats in California tended to be Irish and poor southern migrants who were hostile toward African-Americans, slave or free, on racist grounds. The application sent to Congress expressed the California majority's desire to be admitted as a free state.

But President Taylor had his own political goals that did not accord with popular sovereignty or having California settlers vote independently on the issue. He responded to California settlers' demands for statehood as soon as he took office in March 1849, advising that they apply immediately, skipping the phase of territorial jurisdiction. Taylor's goals were threefold. In the first place, he hoped his call to bring California into the Union quickly would give members of the national Whig Party a unifying cause. Second, he hoped admitting California as a free state would attract Free-Soil Party members, as well as northern and midwestern Democrats, to the Whigs. Third, he wished to bring California into the Union as a free state without challenging the slave South directly, and without testing the political efficacy of popular sovereignty.

But southerners were stunned when, at the end of that year, Taylor simultaneously presented Californians' application for free statehood and recommended that New Mexico also be admitted as a free state. In addition to thwarting southern planters' expansionist aims, two more free states would upset the political balance in the Senate. In 1845 the admission of Texas and Florida as slave states had given the South a political edge of fifteen slave states, to thirteen free. The admission of Iowa (1846) and Wisconsin (1848) as free states restored parity to the Senate. Now the California–New Mexico proposal threatened southern interests again. Some southerners additionally feared that California's admission as a free state would encourage Free-Soilers and Whigs to unite forces long enough to carve up the remaining land between the Mississippi and California into many more free states. For the rest of 1849, Congress remained deadlocked.

The Compromise of 1850

Congressmen openly recognized that the future of slavery, and the rights of southerners to compete against northerners for each section's way of life in the territories, were on the line in early 1850. Voices for and against slavery were becoming shriller each year, and sectional interests seemed more divided with each occasion for making political harangues or casting controversial votes.

Neither northerners nor southerners would give up their territorial imperatives, their desire to expand. Each section believed in manifest destiny, though on different terms. Each argued for the correctness of its position based on "fundamental rights": many northerners appealed to the virtues of republican free labor and the rights of individual white male citizens, whereas many southerners defended states' rights and the sanctity of personal property, including slaves. Just as it was impossible to negotiate freedom or slavery, it was impossible to reconcile "rights" as sectional interests defined them.

By 1850, it also seemed clear to spokespeople from both North and South that two antithetical cultures and economies were facing off. Southern writers defended cotton and slavery as the "resources of great wealth" in their section, the basis for "cementing the most consequential of alliances with our brethren of other nations." Cotton, southerners pointed out, continued to be America's principal export and the source of a few tremendous fortunes, of southern planters' expansion across the Mississippi River, and of a population of about 4 million slaves by the 1850s. To this, some added the argument that slavery was a blessing for African-Americans who otherwise would not survive in a bitter, racially divided country (see Chapter 12). The North, in contrast, had established a form of "wage slavery" that hired and fired at will, refusing to care for workers in sickness and old age.

But northerners were correct to retort that although cotton production and slave labor had made a few southern planters fabulously wealthy, the southern way of life was not the source of America's economic vitality. The interdependent relations of manufacturing in the North and farming in the Midwest, linked by canals and railroads, created more dynamic development than occurred in the South. The North also had a far greater share of the country's cultural institutions, intellectual energy, and newspaper and communications systems. Northerners, in turn, accused planters of willfully declining to "improve" southern poor and middling white farmers, and of largely turning their backs on mining, manufacturing, and transportation development.

These arguments, delivered in the fog of political frustration and fractured party politics of the early 1850s, exaggerated the real differences between North and South. But they represented opposed values and moral systems that lay deeply embedded in the political reality of the decade.

With the California–New Mexico proposal before them, Congressmen confronted the difficulty of reconciling their varied goals. As they were discussing California, Utah applied for statehood as well, and the slave state of Texas was virtually at war with settlers in New Mexico who wished to form a free state. Antislavery forces from northern states were also loudly demanding that Congress abolish slavery in the District of Columbia, while southern planters bemoaned the rising number of slave runaways and clamored for their return. Accusations flung at northerners of harboring southerners' property raised the issue of their violating federal law.

In early 1850, Congress began an eight-month-long debate encompassing all of these touchy issues. Three veteran congressmen, representing the three major settled sections of the country, struggled mightily during those months to achieve a political compromise. It was the last time each would try to impose his imprint on policies that addressed the most pressing matters facing the nation.

Henry Clay, the Kentuckian present at the debates over the Missouri Compromise and a long-time advocate for development in the Old Northwest, gave a brilliant speech despite a "burning fever" that sent him from the Senate floor immediately afterward. The "Great Pacificator" urged that both North and South make some concessions for the sake of averting national political disaster and possibly the breakup of the Union. If necessary, he implored northern congressmen, they should agree to a fugitive slave law that would appease southern complaints.

Calhoun, at the brink of death from tuberculosis at the age of sixty-eight, sat and listened to a colleague read the speech he had prepared. Predictably, he repeated the southern states' rights position and now added that the North must leave slavery alone and keep the Senate balance of slave and free states. Calhoun asserted once again the South's right to secede from the Union to preserve its way of life.

Massachusetts senator Daniel Webster was also sixty-eight and ailing. Though a northerner, Webster did not support abolitionism during the debate. Indeed, he appealed to abolitionists to compromise to prevent the South's secession. "I speak today," he said, "for the preservation of the Union." Why, he reasoned to the overflowing chambers, should Congress legislate at all about slavery in the territories; the South would never extend slavery into the West because cotton would not grow there (a point about which Webster was quite wrong).

Antislavery congressmen, though a minority, were by 1850 skeptical that any compromise was possible. William Henry Seward, a New York Whig, wished to contain slavery within its existing boundaries and eventually exterminate it. In reply to Calhoun, Seward invoked "a higher law than the Constitution, which regulates our authority over the domain . . . the common heritage of mankind." Salmon P. Chase, an Ohio lawyer, then U.S. senator, and later governor of Ohio and chief justice of the U.S. Supreme Court, was well known for defending fugitive slaves. In response to southern frustrations over escapees, Chase argued for termination of all fugitive slave acts.

The president had intended to address the Senate himself and insist that southern representatives relinquish some of their demands. But he died suddenly on July 9, 1850, and Millard Fillmore assumed the task of moderating the Senate's deep divisions. Fillmore was not as keen as Taylor had been to force southerners to give ground. Already Clay had composed an elaborate plan for compromise, a puzzle with all the pieces of sectional interests laid out in neat order. Fillmore, however, passed on the job of presenting and motivating the compromise to rising, ambitious younger senators. Stephen A. Douglas of Illinois, just thirty-seven years old, was one of Fillmore's chosen spokesmen. Douglas won acclaim for ushering the Compromise of 1850 through Congress.

The Compromise of 1850 had four central tenets when it finally became a package plan in September. First, southerners won a new Fugitive Slave Law that replaced the 1793 law and now required federal officials to aid planters seeking runaway slaves in free states. The law denied slaves caught outside the slave states a right to testify on their own behalf or to have a jury trial over flight from their masters. Second, the compromise admitted California as a free state and created the territories of New Mexico and Utah, which were to be admitted on the basis of popular sovereignty. Third, it set the western boundary of Texas farther to the east than Texans wished, thus giving more land to New Mexico. In compensation to Texans, Congress assumed $10 million in debts still unpaid to citizens who suffered losses in the conflicts with Mexico before Texas statehood. Fourth, the act abolished the slave trade in the District of Columbia, although it permitted slavery's continued existence.

For now, most southerners pulled back from their threat of secession, and thousands of northerners demanded printed copies of Webster's moving appeal for compromise. Clay traveled through the country delivering over seventy speeches to

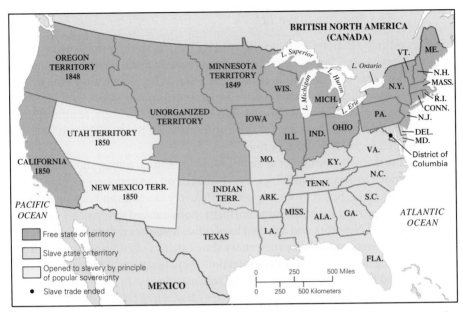

The Compromise of 1850 By the time Congress negotiated a new territorial arrangement for the trans-Mississippi West, America was a continental nation. By the terms of the compromise, California was admitted as a free state, the borders of Texas were fixed, and in the region covered by Utah and New Mexico territories, popular sovereignty would decide future status.

the public, pleading for conciliation. But hidden behind the votes that passed the Compromise of 1850 were ominous signs of continuing discord. Most important, in Congress it was moderate northern Democrats and moderate southern Whigs who favored compromise most. But some congressmen also expressed extreme views. Antislavery leaders such as Seward opposed the package, as did ardent proslavery leaders such as Jefferson Davis, both of whom argued fiercely in the Senate against the compromise.

In the southern states, proslavery Democrats lamented the loss of Calhoun, who died soon after his statement to the Senate, and regrouped around strong new leaders, making clear their intention to break with southern Whigs in order to defend slavery. These "fire-eaters" urged fellow southerners to boycott northern goods and shipping services, though the years of cotton and slavery prosperity made such appeals hopeless.

In the northern states after 1850, many Whigs who favored direct prohibition of slavery in the territories broke with their party leader and president, Fillmore, to denounce his advocacy of popular sovereignty. As Salmon Chase wrote from Ohio, "The question of slavery in the territories has been avoided. It has not been settled." Poet John Greenleaf Whittier and numerous outspoken clergymen gave harsher judgments. Ralph Waldo Emerson, the prominent philosopher, transcendentalist, and abolitionist, denounced Webster's call for compromise: "The word *liberty* in the mouth of Mr. Webster sounds like the word *love* in the mouth of a courtesan."

The Fugitive Slave Act

Scholars estimate that, by 1850, southern slave owners were losing about a thousand runaways a year. Some planters placed the estimate much higher, no doubt because of their fear that the Underground Railroad, "a freedom train to the cellars and closets of abolitionists," had become a widespread success. Now, with the Fugitive Slave Act, called the "Bloodhound Bill" by angry northerners, southern slave owners could demand the return of slave runaways and the punishment of those who harbored fugitives with heavy fines.

Many northerners saw the act as an affront to legislators, courts, and human dignity. Moderate Democrats and Whigs, who had been on the periphery of slavery discussions to this time, began to attend public antislavery meetings and donate funds to help the Underground Railroad. Some northern mobs jumped slave catchers who entered Boston and New York and attacked local officials who tried to enforce the act.

Slaves who were captured by mercenary slave catchers often were removed from the reach of legal support and court protection. Sometimes free African-Americans were abducted from their communities and sold into slavery. In *Twelve Years a Slave*, Solomon Northrup recounted his harrowing ordeal: a free black, he had been kidnapped in Washington, D.C., and served various masters for years before he could get word to friends to bring legal proof of his status. Stories such as Northrup's, published in 1853, spurred abolitionists to seek sterner measures to circumvent the Fugitive Slave Act. In response to previous fugitive slave laws, some states had passed "personal liberty laws" that made enforcement difficult by prohibiting the use of local jails for federal purposes.

Once the federal act went into effect in 1850, abolitionists added extralegal actions to their arsenal of resistance. More than once, angry mobs broke into courtrooms, seized runaways being tried for escape, and secreted them to upstate New York or Canada. In Syracuse, New York, one-third of the townspeople poured in through the doors and windows of the courthouse in 1851 to rescue a runaway slave and then helped him hide until state authorities stopped investigating. In the so-called Border States of Maryland and Delaware, Quakers who had long been active on the Underground Railroad helped large numbers of slaves evade the catchers from South Carolina and Georgia, risking steep fines and federal imprisonment for their efforts. While Daniel Webster lamented these actions, and President Fillmore declared them "mob rule," wider community sympathy with the abolitionists grew by the month. Antislavery societies organized mass meetings more regularly. Prominent abolitionist William Lloyd Garrison spoke to throngs of outraged city folk in 1851, declaring of the Fugitive Slave Act, "We execrate it, we spit upon it, we trample it under our feet."

Between 1851 and 1854, federal troops mobilized repeatedly to protect court proceedings against African-Americans and to give slave catchers safe passage back to the South. Armed abolitionists, led by the Unitarian minister Thomas Wentworth Higginson, stormed the Boston federal courthouse in 1854 to snatch back Anthony Burns, a runaway slave who was being sued by hired slave catchers. Although the mob failed to secure Burns's freedom, the president was fearful enough to send in artillery, marines, cavalry brigades, and a convoyed federal vessel to transport Burns back to the South. Even when members of the Boston abolitionist societies raised large sums to buy Burns's freedom, the president ordered the federal attorney on the case to deny the purchase. As Burns was walked in irons toward the dock, Bostonians lined the streets, standing in silence, dressed in black funeral garb, to show solidarity with the fugitive slave.

Although many attempts to free runaway slaves from the clutches of southern planters' paid hirelings failed, public sentiment grew stronger against slavery and against the government's Fugitive Slave Act. Abolitionists grew bolder, and some began to speak out in favor of violent resistance. Frederick Douglass, already a respected abolitionist leader in the North (see Chapter 12), called on citizens to resist "the bloodhound kidnappers" with the same force perpetrated against runaways. Increasing numbers of northerners believed that the new federal law had not helped compromise between the sections at all. Instead, it "brought the notion of slavery into our northern cities, it made all people of a particular color slaves, whether that be true or no." Not many northerners granted African-Americans true racial equality, but many now called the institution of slavery wrong. For Harriet Beecher Stowe (see page 451), the Fugitive Slave Act was an unforgivable assault on the dignity of both African-Americans and the moral integrity of families, white and black, everywhere.

"Practical Illustration of the Fugitive Slave Law"   Many northerners, including some who opposed slave emancipation, found laws requiring the capture and return of runaways to be demeaning and impractical. In this cartoon the southern slave owner sits astride Daniel Webster, who voted for the act, while abolitionist William Lloyd Garrison takes aim in defense of runaways.   *(Library of Congress.)*

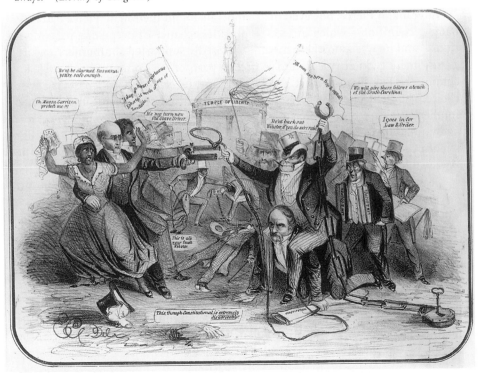

The Election of 1852

Because President Fillmore supported popular sovereignty and had enforced the Fugitive Slave Act, Whigs rejected his candidacy in 1852. Clay and Webster had died. Seward, the New York antislavery spokesman, had become party head unofficially and put forward General Winfield Scott for nomination. Scott, another military hero candidate, was at first rejected by southern Whigs, but after many ballots, the northern wing of the party achieved his nomination. The 1852 convention, however, proved to most Whig leaders that their days as a national party were numbered. Southern Whigs had become increasingly disaffected, and many now left the party rather than support Scott. Northern abolitionist Whigs expressed disappointment that their party did not take a firmer official stand against slavery. Though individual Whigs continued to win national offices and maintained a strong presence in the government, the Whigs never ran a presidential candidate again.

Democrats did not have a clearer program or stronger unity than the Whigs in 1852, but they accommodated their sectional divisions enough to win the election. Large numbers of northern Democrats had made it clear they would support neither the extension of slavery nor popular sovereignty. So party leaders quickly rejected nominations for candidates who held southerner Calhoun's radical position that planters had a right to carry their property anywhere in the Union. After some debate, they also spurned potential nominees who supported popular sovereignty, even party stalwarts such as Lewis Cass, Stephen A. Douglas, and James Buchanan.

In Franklin Pierce, however, the Democrats found their man. Pierce had little name recognition—which in 1852 implied less chance of deepening party divisions—and he was a northerner who supposedly supported southerners' expansionist interests. Pierce pledged to enforce all parts of the Compromise of 1850, including the Fugitive Slave Act. At election time, it seemed that Pierce was a wise choice. The Democrats won a resounding popular majority, scooping up disaffected southern Whigs and sustaining a strong northern Democratic vote among workers and immigrants. Many Free-Soil voters left their party happy with Pierce's pledge to enforce the Fugitive Slave Act. Some of them hoped popular sovereignty in the West would lead to free states, as in California.

Scott won a significant popular vote in 1852, larger than Taylor's in 1848, but he carried only four of the thirty-one states. Even more, deep sectional differences would not go away. Popular sovereignty was widely appealing to Americans of many persuasions for it seemed to straddle sectional disputes with a viable democratic solution to territorial expansion. Californians' decision to enter the Union as a free state reassured northerners that popular sovereignty might be a panacea. But many leading southerners still favored the Calhoun position, and many leading northerners still touted an abolitionist stance. Pierce's response to these sectional extremes was not to seek compromise between the sides, but rather to ignore them. Like his predecessor Polk, Pierce diverted American attention to foreign expansion.

Renewed Foreign Expansionism

The 1848 revolutions in Europe seemed to bolster beliefs that manifest destiny made possible the spread of democracy and "civilizing tendencies" outside America. Ardent expansionists even suggested that their successes with manifest destiny had inspired the transformative liberal bourgeois revolutions in France, Germany, Italy, and Hungary. And they cheered again when President Franklin Pierce's envoy to Japan, Commodore Matthew C. Perry, returned with a path-breaking commercial treaty. Manifest destiny, according to some Democratic newspapers, would meld "the advanced peoples" of the world together "in peaceful markets" and among ever-expanding chosen peoples.

Over the 1840s, northern American merchants had actively pursued new markets in the Far East. Trade with China had declined markedly, but at first other trans-Pacific nations were reluctant to initiate commercial relations with America. Between 1846 and 1852, federal negotiations with Japan began to open doors for American merchants, and in 1854 Perry obtained a first treaty with Japan to begin modest mutual trading. President Pierce declined Perry's offer to use his squadron to take possessions in the area, primarily Formosa. But Pierce did extend Perry's commercial treaty and sought closer diplomatic relations with Japan. In 1854 he sent Townshend Harris to obtain these goals. It took numerous negotiating sessions with Japanese officials, at which Harris used his long experience trading in that part of the world to invoke traditional Japanese fears about the power of China, Russia, and Europe—fears Americans promised to help allay. Finally, in 1858 Japan signed a sweeping commercial treaty with American diplomats in Edo (later Tokyo) Bay. In the future, this treaty would bear important cultural and political fruits for both nations.

Pierce's support for expansionism extended within the Western Hemisphere as well, to Cuba, Mexico, and Nicaragua. Since the Mexican-American War a number of southern Democrats had pressed for an invasion of Mexico to secure additional territory. Polk had rebuffed this demand gently but remained interested in buying Cuba from Spain. A growing "Young America" movement within the Democratic Party coalesced around the ideas of a broader manifest destiny encompassing even more hemispheric territory, all earmarked for the southern plantation economy. Young Americans supported stirring up an anti-monarchy revolution in Cuba, which they hoped might lead to the island's becoming an American slave state. They secretly funded three expeditions to invade the island, called filibusters (from the Spanish word *filibustero*, or "piratical adventure"), led by the Cuban exile General Narciso Lopez.

On one of these filibusters in 1854, Spanish officials in Cuba confiscated an American ship in violation of international port regulations. Pierce demanded the release of the *Black Warrior* and its cargo, and turned to Congress for sanction to seek redress and apologies from Cubans and Spain. Secretary of State William L. Marcy threw his weight behind negotiations for indemnity and the return of the *Black Warrior*. But when northern Democrats balked at the possibility of going to war to establish a new slave state, Pierce had no choice but to accept lesser terms from Spain. Pierce also agreed to end the filibusters. He issued a proclamation that the federal government expected all private forces to cease their activities and abide by international neutrality laws.

But other interests still worked against Pierce. Once efforts to purchase Cuba from Spain for $130 million failed later in 1854, Marcy instructed Pierre Soule, the American minister in Spain, to meet with the British minister, James Buchanan, and the French minister, John Y. Mason, to set up an alternative plan to pressure Spain into giving up Cuba. In October they sent Pierce a message, now known as the Ostend Manifesto (the ministers met in Ostend, Belgium). "If we possess the power," it said, Americans were justified "by every law, human and Divine" in taking Cuba by force. When, two weeks later, administration insiders leaked the manifesto to the press, northerners raged against "the dirty plot" and forced Pierce to give up efforts to acquire Cuba.

But that was not the end of the filibusters. William Walker invaded Nicaragua four times, setting himself up as ruler of the country first in 1855 and inviting southerners to take up great landholdings from displaced local farmers. In 1856, after Walker declared the reintroduction of slavery in Nicaragua, he was happy to receive both Pierce's commendation for setting up an independent "republic" and the Democratic Party's endorsement of his rule. Neighboring Hondurans, however, drove Walker out of power in 1857, and he met his fate in front of a firing squad in Honduras in 1860.

A New Party System Emerges

Events in Cuba and Nicaragua showed Americans who did not already believe it that extending manifest destiny forcefully into other countries could fail. It showed Democrats that such efforts—especially when they ended in failure—could not build party unity. In 1854 Democrats, in an effort to survive as a national party, pinned their hopes once again on popular sovereignty and the expansion of slavery.

The Kansas-Nebraska Act

While the Young Americans pressed for imperialist expansion abroad, others revisited the matter of territorial expansion at home. Following the Mexican-American War, many Americans immediately turned their attention to settling California and Oregon. Politicians feared that the new western territories would break away from the Union if the existing states did not quickly integrate them into eastern life. Entrepreneurs saw the new lands as opportunities for development. But getting people and their trappings to the West presented challenges (see Chapter 13). Going by sea, across the isthmus of Panama or around South America, cost too much and took too long.

The only feasible way to link East and West was by railroad. Promoters hoping for government aid and huge fortunes put forward numerous plans for transcontinental lines, but it soon became clear that the government would subsidize only one line. Immediately, sectional interests came into the fray, since the favored proposal for a rail line would not only confer riches on the developers but also increase population and trade in the entire area that the line traversed.

Southerners proposed the Southern Pacific Railroad, which would run through Houston, Texas, all the way to Los Angeles, California. But the best route would have to cut through a portion of land in northern Mexico, where the mountains gave way to lower plains. A few leading southern expansionists, including Secretary of War Jefferson Davis, pushed for additional negotiations to acquire a swath of land for the railroad. Davis arranged for James Gadsden, a South Carolina railroad promoter, to be appointed minister to Mexico and commissioned to work with Santa Anna to acquire about thirty thousand square miles for $10 million.

Northerners protested this "wasteful use of public monies to buy a desert." But southerners retorted that the Gadsden Purchase would enable developers to cut a Southern Pacific route through completely American soil and, compared with other proposed lines, across fairly gentle terrain. The Senate approved the Gadsden Purchase in 1853.

Together, northern entrepreneurs and politicians realized that their success in getting a northern railroad line approved by Congress might depend on routing it through organized territory. Until 1854, however, a vast expanse separated the northern free states and the new possessions of California and Oregon. The Nebraska territory was still unorganized. However, overland trails had cut through the area for many years, and land-hungry migrants were pressing from the East.

In 1854 Stephen A. Douglas pounced on the opportunity to simultaneously organize this huge northern area for settlement and make a northern railroad possible, thereby counterbalancing southern goals. Douglas introduced the Kansas-Nebraska Act, which would open up the lands inside the northern part of the Indian Territory to migrating Americans, who would then set up a government and seek statehood for two territories—Kansas and Nebraska—according to popular sovereignty. Douglas's measure thus proposed to ignore treaties with Indians in Kansas and displace the many tribes living in that portion of the Indian Territory, there in the first place by the process of removal. The measure's popular sovereignty provisions also reopened the question of slavery in the territories.

Douglas had another goal, too. As a prominent railroad promoter, and a senator from Illinois, he wished to bring the much-discussed transcontinental railroad line through Chicago instead of the more southerly St. Louis, or the very distant New Orleans. In order to win congressional approval, not to mention funds and land grants to build such a line, land west of Iowa and the Minnesota Territory had to be organized into territories, and eventually new states. Southerners, quite predictably, resisted the formation of Kansas and Nebraska unless they were open to slavery. Northerners viewed the region as a contiguous part of free-soil states.

Douglas believed his solution to a potential congressional deadlock was popular sovereignty. As he and many other Democrats reasoned, northerners would get the railroad line and the possibility of excluding slavery with a future popular vote. Southerners would get explicit erasure of the Missouri Compromise line and the possibility of bringing slavery into the north with a future popular vote. Even before the act became law, however, the simmering sectional tensions over

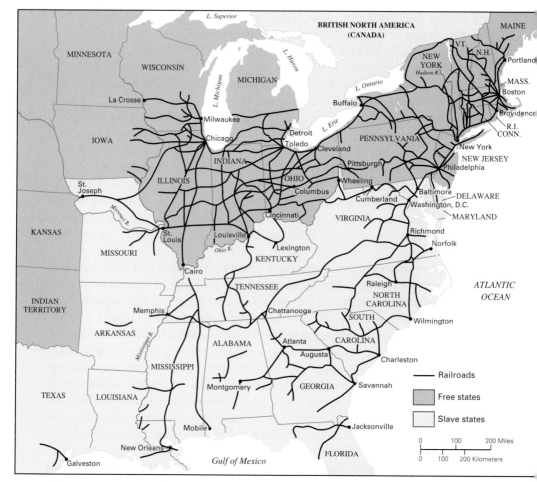

Railroads in the 1850s   Only some of the northern and midwestern lines are shown in this map, but those regions constructed a thick network of rail transportation through a combination of private and public funding. Although the South had numerous railroad lines by 1860, many remained unconnected to each other, and in states of incomplete construction and varied track widths.

Kansas-Nebraska began to boil. Southern Democrats and Whigs now joined in support of the act, whereas northern Whigs opposed it loudly as a violation of the free-soil principle. The public debate and congressional vote on the act made clear that the Whigs were now irreconcilably split. Although northern Whigs kept a strong presence in the government, the party could never again run a presidential candidate. As for the Democrats, southern political leaders who supported the act—and slavery's extension—rose on a crest of southern popular acclaim and took many new seats in Congress in the 1854 midterm elections. Northern Democrats, squeezed between their southern party spokesmen and Whig popularity in the North, lost two-thirds of their seats.

Sectional views about railroads, land, and slavery thus played out in the congressional elections. Douglas's dreams of becoming a presidential candidate in 1856 were dashed. Many northern Whigs blamed him for writing "a dastardly plan that fell sweetly into the laps of southern slavers." Rallies in numerous northern cities denounced Douglas and the Democratic Party. In calmer but deeply worried tones, the wealthy bankers, merchants, and manufacturers who were tied to southern cotton, and thus called "Cotton Whigs," feared that the Kansas-Nebraska Act would arouse violent antislavery sentiment and tear the Union apart. Cotton Whigs urged southerners to vote against the act "out of our own mutual self-preservation." But southern Democrats felt too confident about the possibility of extending slavery to heed Whig warnings.

Bleeding Kansas

As soon as Congress passed the Kansas-Nebraska Act in 1854, a rush of events occupied Americans of every political persuasion. Government agents quickly proceeded with extracting treaties from the many Indian tribes in the newly designated territories. The Cheyenne and Sioux moved into the western part of Kansas for a few years. The Kickapoo, Shawnee, Sauk, and Fox agreed to live on reduced reservations. The Wea, Delaware, Iowa, and other small tribes sold their grants to American land companies.

And then the rush of American settlers began. Missourians, led by their own state senator, David Atchison, set up proslavery towns such as Atchison, Leavenworth, and Kickapoo, and staked out the lands around them. When the time came to elect territorial officials, the proslavery settlers not only encouraged people to vote more than once, but brought in a rowdy crew of "border ruffians" to pose as legitimate residents of Kansas. Kansas proslavery agitators dared Missourians to "enter every election district in Kansas . . . and vote at the point of a Bowie knife or revolver." In the coming months and years, the border ruffians also served as willing recruits in an open war to make Kansas a slave state. Identified by their "stinkin', ragged, drunken appearance," they wanted no part of a settled farming or ranching life on the frontier, only the cash bounties their fraudulent votes might bring.

Northerners organized a free-soil response. Right away in 1854, the wealthy Massachusetts manufacturer Amos Lawrence donated large funds to send out antislavery settlers from New England. Their first town, named Lawrence, Kansas, attracted over a thousand people from the summer to winter of 1854. Eli Thayer founded the New England Emigrant Aid Society and continued to channel more free-soilers into Lawrence and Topeka, Kansas. Many of those who agreed to start their lives over in what proved to be a hostile environment were already active in temperance and educational reform organizations, and most had been committed abolitionists back in New England.

Americans soon learned that popular sovereignty would be achieved not by calm deliberation and the ballot, but by bloody conflict. Border ruffians, already supplied with Bowie knives, revolvers, and Kentucky rifles, raided free-soil camps and rustled cattle. Abolitionists happily received crate after crate marked "Bibles" that were actually full of Sharps repeating rifles sent from the East. During 1855 and early 1856, armed slavery defenders arrived from Mississippi and Alabama, and free-soil ranks grew with migrants from Iowa, Illinois, and Indiana.

In the spring of 1856, heavily armed proslavery raiders burned most of Lawrence to the ground, stole their cattle and hogs, and scattered women and children who had watched men slaughter one another. Under cover of night, a small band of abolitionists retaliated by invading five farmsteads on Pottawatomie Creek and murdering the men living there. The murderers were the stalwart, uncompromising abolitionist John Brown, his sons and a son-in-law. But no marshals or sheriffs arrested Brown's bandits. They, and many others, continued to maraud through the countryside in months to come. Few peaceful farming settlers remained on the land by the end of 1856; most fled to military forts for protection. John Brown and his sons tainted the free-soil efforts in Kansas and Nebraska, and proslavery vigilantes in the territories alienated many of their politically active brethren in the southern states. "Kansas bleeds," wrote the northern press. Sectional interests had erupted into a territorial civil war.

The same week that Kansas erupted in violence, Congressman Preston Brooks of South Carolina attacked Senator Charles Sumner as he sat at his desk on the floor of the Senate. Brooks repeatedly struck Sumner, even on the head, with blows so hard that his cane broke. In his speech a few days earlier, "The crime against Kansas," Sumner had insulted Senator Andrew Butler, also of South Carolina and Brooks's uncle, by accusing him of sleeping with "the harlot, slavery." Bound by the traditional southern code of honor, Brooks had no choice but to seek revenge, just as Sumner had felt obliged to express abolitionist principles.

Nativism

Americans' fears of foreign immigrants—their religions, their customs, their need for jobs and material support—was strong by the 1830s and grew in proportion to rising immigration levels. During the 1850s, the American population was still multiplying as rapidly as Benjamin Franklin had noted a century previously, doubling about every twenty-five years. In 1790 only two cities, Philadelphia and New York, had populations over 20,000, but by 1860, forty-three did, and many others approached that size. Each of them experienced the growing pains of providing adequate housing and sanitation services, coping with poverty and ethnic conflict, and meeting the crises of periodic epidemics or shortages. In the countryside, farming populations in midwestern states began to grow rapidly, and family size rose after three decades of steady migration from Chesapeake and northeastern states. By 1840, large numbers of frontier people in the Midwest also were foreign-born.

As in previous eras, more population growth came from natural increase than from immigration. But unprecedented numbers of immigrants did enter America during the 1840s and 1850s. Over 1.7 million people arrived during the 1840s, and over 2.6 million in the 1850s. The immigration rate of about 60,000 per year during the 1830s suddenly tripled in the 1840s, and then quadrupled in the 1850s. Fleeing political and religious intolerance, over a million Germans chose to start over in

Free State Battery, Topeka, 1856   The slave state of Missouri opposed the entry of anti-slavery advocates for years and, by the 1850s, actively tried to prevent their migration through Missouri on the way to Kansas. "Free-staters" organized migration through Iowa instead, often bringing with them arms. This small cannon, left over from the Mexican War, helped create "Bleeding Kansas." *(Kansas State Historical Society.)*

America. Struggling against famine and utter economic ruin, a million and a half Irish came between 1840 and the Civil War. Both groups of people would continue to stream into America in later decades, too. There were also new immigrant groups, including the nearly 35,500 Chinese who came, primarily to California, by 1860. By that date, more than one-eighth of the U.S. population was foreign-born.

Starving and desperate Irish potato farmers arrived in eastern cities, mainly Boston and New York, with few industrial skills and no cash to move west. In order to make ends meet, everyone in the family worked at something: women washed and cooked in Protestant homes, men heaved loads on city docks or followed construction opportunities with railroads and canals, and children did piecework in sweatshops or scavenged in city alleys for food and fuel. Vibrant and interdependent community relationships developed in the Irish neighborhoods, but beyond the ghetto borders, ethnic and religious prejudice awaited, as did the lowest-paying urban jobs.

Although many Germans came to America for economic opportunity, a significant number of liberal political leaders chose to leave their country when repressive armies defeated the bourgeois revolutions of 1848 and thus ended the experiment in democracy there. Many of the German immigrants carried money and property with them, came in family groups, and brought skills and years of education. And they preferred to move quickly through port cities out to the breadbasket of the Midwest, including Wisconsin, Illinois, and Iowa. Germans usually shunned areas where slavery flourished.

In 1834 Lyman Beecher preached numerous anti-Catholic sermons in Boston, which fueled mob angers and instigated the burning of Ursuline Convent in Charleston, Massachusetts. Samuel F. B. Morse, the inventor of the telegraph, ran for mayor of New York City in 1836 based on his strong anti-immigrant views and fears that "Catholic corruption" would destroy the republican fiber of "true" American culture. And in Philadelphia, Whig reformers and Democratic entrepreneurs and craftsmen heaped scorn on German and Irish newcomers through the 1830s until, in 1844, open religious clashes produced twenty deaths and about a hundred injuries.

Various American interests stigmatized Irish immigrants as poor, Catholic, crammed into urban hovels, and frequent tipplers. Huge numbers of Bostonian Irish were attracted to the political machines that organized party voting and promised charity, drink, and neighborhood development in return for their vote. Despite their unpropertied status, in New York over half of the city's voters were foreign-born in the 1850s, which made them important objects of the emerging political machine at Tammany Hall. Already in the 1780s, the Tammany Society of artisans and mechanics began organizing the working-class vote and cementing neighborhood alliances in New York City. During the 1830s, Tammany was closely affiliated with the Democratic Party and helped sponsor party picnics, parades, publications, and—of course—the vote. During times of economic hardship, ethnic immigrants and American-born workers had few means to correct the capitalist system's inequities. But they did have strength in their numbers and could turn out local and state votes that won important reforms.

While the political machines organized immigrants in their taverns and poor neighborhoods, evangelical and temperance reformers, often Whigs, tried to change immigrants' lives in other ways. Overall, however, they were not as successful. But out of their efforts, a minority of these reformers developed strong nativist, or anti-immigrant, feelings during the 1830s to 1850s. These feelings intensified when Irish immigrants expressed openly their antiblack prejudices and competed violently with free African-Americans for unskilled jobs. In addition, Whigs accused the Irish as a group of being too easily persuaded to vote the way Democratic machine politicians told them to. Immigrants, charged nativists, were responsible for rising levels of urban crime, as well as rising taxes to pay for poor relief.

In 1837 anti-immigrant activists started the Native American Association in Washington, D.C. By 1850, secret societies had formed to oppose "the Catholic presence in our Union" and coalesced as the Order of the Star-Spangled Banner and Native American Clubs. These organizations usually held secret meetings that were open only to Protestants born in America, drawing into their membership white professional and skilled men in northern cities and farmers who feared a declining way of life. In 1851 these nativists formed the American Party, also called the "Know-Nothings" because they refused to divulge information about themselves to the public. Their political program included ending poor relief to noncitizens who did not pay taxes and instituting literacy tests for voting (which they believed would disfranchise many immigrants). They demanded that no foreigners hold offices and called for laws to extend the period before naturalization into citizenship from five to twenty-one years. American Party leaders teamed up with female missionaries and educational reformers to proselytize in immigrant communities about American democracy and the virtues of "women's sphere."

In the 1854 state elections, Know-Nothings won nearly 40 percent of the vote in Pennsylvania and took control of the legislature in Massachusetts. The American Party also garnered large wins in Maryland and New York. Free-soilers with an eye on the West, racists who feared losing jobs and community security as free African-Americans moved nearby, and antislavery advocates who watched the Whig Party decline tended to accept the American Party's nativism. In the eyes of many northerners, the Democratic Party's associations with slavery and Catholic immigrants—"slavery, rum, and Romanism"—were an obvious assault on "freedom, temperance, and Protestantism."

The Republican Party

In 1854 northern Whigs no longer could claim a national party, and many northern Democrats despised Douglas's compromise over Kansas with the South. Many members of these two displaced and disgruntled groups joined with Free-Soilers and the American Party in 1854 to elect many local officials. Within a few months of the election, however, these forces began forming a new political party. Resurrecting the old Jeffersonian term *Republican,* the party's organizers drew together many different strands of the fragmented political culture.

Many political views comfortably coexisted within the Republican Party. Some Republicans were former northern Whig abolitionists; some were former Free-Soil or northern Democratic voters who agreed that slavery should be kept out of the territories but allowed to persist in the South; and some were reformers who focused on temperance, religion, education, and immigration in their home states. Northern and western merchants and manufacturers drifted to the Republican Party, too, because it promised to use a strong national government to promote commerce and internal improvements. Northern and western farmers also liked the Republican Party's commitment to cheap land.

But one demand above all others linked all of these strands to the Republican Party: no slavery in the new territories. Many Republicans loathed and feared the southern way of life. Masters represented force, inhumanity, and absolute power within plantation society, qualities that would be even more dangerous when planters exported them into territories where free white families also lived. Planters, in the minds of many northerners, also deliberately shunned entrepreneurship and hard work, which were qualities valued by Americans who embraced free labor and industrialization. Abraham Lincoln, an early member of the Republican Party, championed northern values of social mobility and a strong work ethic. Like most other Republicans, Lincoln joined in celebrating individualism, even though the

North was, in reality, more class-divided and economically unstable than ever during the mid-1850s.

By 1856, the Republican Party had catapulted to the forefront of national politics. In the presidential election that year, Democrats turned at first to their outstanding national leaders, Stephen A. Douglas and President Franklin Pierce. But both men had promoted the Kansas-Nebraska Act and were identified with the slave South as a result. In 1856, the election of either man would split the party sectionally and cost it the votes of northern Democrats. So the Democratic Party chose to run Pennsylvanian James Buchanan, who had been out of the country during the Kansas-Nebraska deliberations.

The Republicans ran John C. Frémont, the California explorer, for president. But Frémont's name appeared on the ballot in only four southern states, where he won almost no votes anyway. Instead, the southern states really pitted Buchanan against the American Party candidate, former president Millard Fillmore. Fillmore gained strong support from former southern Whigs and took a large percentage of the popular vote in most southern states. But the electoral vote was sectional: Buchanan mopped up the electoral vote of all southern states, while Frémont carried the electoral vote of eleven northern states.

Buchanan gained enough of the popular vote—45.3 percent—to win the election nationally. He had taken hold of the southern vote and scraped together enough support in the North to put a Democrat in the presidential office. But Republicans knew that if they had carried just two more northern states, in particular Pennsylvania and New Jersey, they might have won. Furthermore, Republicans had displaced the American Party as a viable national organization. The election of 1856, sectional as it was, drew out 78.9 percent of eligible voters, one of the highest turnouts in American history. The waning influence of the American Party during the campaign also showed that northerners cared less about the "immigrant problem" than about the extension of slavery into the West. Indeed, a Third Party System had emerged from the contests of 1854 and 1856, one based on deepening sectional differences.

 ## The Slide into War, 1856–1859

The election of 1856 demonstrated many political surprises to wary Americans, but one truth stood out above all the ambiguities: that on the issue of slavery, the North and South had become more entrenched in their positions. Would President Buchanan show the South that his federal office would protect slavery? Or, would he focus on weakening Republicans by negotiating on the matter of free soil?

Southern Stridency

Since the early 1830s, a number of southerners rejected any proposals for gradual emancipation of slaves and turned a deaf ear to northern antislavery appeals. Writers such as Calhoun and Thomas R. Dew (see page 477) were among many who argued for the natural inferiority of African-Americans and the need for slave labor to sustain a southern way of life. By the mid-1840s, in response to the Republican Party's claim on free soil, social mobility, economic advancement, and individualism, southern writers became shrill defenders of the slave system.

By the 1850s, a number of southern writers referred to northern free labor as "wage slavery," including the poet William Grayson from Charleston. Among the most authoritative southern writers, George Fitzhugh codified the southern fears of northern industrialization in two important books: *Sociology for the South; or, The Failure of a Free Society* (1854) and *Cannibals All! or, Slaves Without Masters* (1857). A respected Virginia lawyer and planter, Fitzhugh argued that northern life had succumbed to impersonal market forces. Talk about the freedom of workers was a thin veneer over the reality of treating human laborers as mere commodities, bought and sold according to market values out of any employer's or worker's control. Under the free labor system, profits were the only goal of employers and wages the only goal of workers. Therefore, northerners put almost no focus on personal needs, argued Fitzhugh; they gave each other almost no mutual support and comfort to soften the ambition that drove every individual. The old and weak were unemployable, the very young not yet paid for their work, and all of these northerners together were vulnerable to the "freedom" of poverty, hunger, homelessness, and loneliness.

Fitzhugh insisted that slavery was a more humane kind of labor and more benign social system. Masters were more than employers; they were responsible for housing, medical and old-age care, meals, and most other aspects of slaves' lives. Masters established cultural examples for poor whites and slaves to emulate; they lived a refined life that not only reflected their profits from the labor of slaves but also set a tone of civility and public virtue in the South that slaves grew to respect. Fitzhugh and others writing during the 1840s and 1850s took the southern defense of slavery much further than Jefferson's generation, when many writers still believed in the possibility of "civilizing the dark races" and colonization. By the 1840s writers more frequently justified slavery as a positive good, comparatively more humane and "progressive" than northern industrialization. Slavery, argued Calhoun, made it possible for the master race to perfect itself culturally and intellectually.

Dred Scott

In the mid-1850s, the prevailing view of northerners toward slavery remained rooted in the free-soil position. The prevailing view of southerners was summed up by Calhoun—that the Constitution guaranteed slavery's right to exist in the territories. Time and again, elections and political policies had faced this sectional division. But how would the Supreme Court address it?

The moment to find out came in 1857 when the Court handed down its decision in the famous *Dred Scott* v. *Sandford* case. Dred Scott had been born into slavery and, as an adult, owned by a Missouri army surgeon, John Emerson. Emerson took Scott with him during the 1830s to Illinois, a free state, and then to Wisconsin, a free territory because it lay north of the Missouri Compromise line. While in free land, Scott married another slave, Harriet; their daughter Eliza was born in free territory. In 1846 Emerson returned to Missouri with the Scotts, where Dred Scott sued for his freedom on the grounds of having established residence on free soil.

It took eleven years for the case to climb through the legal system to the Supreme Court. Then, two days after Buchanan assumed office, the Court announced its decision. Northerners had not been hopeful about the pending decision since the Court had been southern-dominated for years and Chief Justice Taney had not given any signs of disappointing the South now. In 1857 northern fears were realized. All of the southern members of the Court supported Taney in a decision that bolstered slavery. The bloc was joined by a northern justice whom Buchanan pressured (all other northern justices dissented).

In the majority opinion, Taney made momentous statements from that exalted bench. He announced that the Missouri Compromise was unconstitutional because the federal government had no right to interfere with the free movement of property throughout the territories, as Calhoun had enunciated for many years. Taney further announced that the entire *Dred Scott* case would be dismissed summarily, on the grounds that only citizens could bring suits in courts of law, and all African-Americans were by birth slaves and not citizens—a pronouncement that threatened the quarter million free African-Americans in the South.

Dred Scott After suing for his liberty in the Missouri courts, Scott found himself caught up in legal and political quarreling that landed his case in the Supreme Court, where justices ruled against him. This painting was done in 1881, years after general slave emancipation had been declared. *(Missouri Historical Society.)*

The northern press denounced *Dred Scott* immediately and loudly. Not only was the Court's decision immoral, wrote many newspaper editorials; justices had also declared their decision "the law of the land," thereby thwarting congressional and state laws. President Buchanan's clear support for the *Dred Scott* decision fanned sectional flames even more. By overturning the Missouri Compromise, the *Dred Scott* decision wiped out one of the cornerstones of the Republican Party's program. Abraham Lincoln grew indignant: he accused Buchanan of conspiring with the southern justices on the Court to tear down the American political system and substitute judge-made law. Lincoln rhetorically, but alarmingly, posed the possibility that the same Court might next try to legalize slavery in the free states.

The Lecompton Constitution

While Taney wrote his *Dred Scott* decision, President Buchanan openly sided with the proslavery settlers in Kansas. Open conflicts between free-soilers and proslave settlers had continued without letup since 1855, and a rigged election that year—huge numbers of Missouri border ruffians voted illegally in the territory—put proslavery forces in charge of the territorial legislature in Lecompton, Kansas. Free-soilers repudiated the Lecompton government as illegitimate and set up their own in Topeka. They also stayed home in June when proslavery leaders called a constitutional convention. The Lecompton Constitution reflected the proslavery majority that did attend and, predictably, endorsed slavery in the future state. Then, despite a clear majority for free-soilers in an October election for new territorial officials, President Buchanan urged Congress to support the Lecompton Constitution and bring Kansas into the Union. If Kansas entered as a slave state, a new parity in the Senate of sixteen free and sixteen slave states would be achieved.

Stephen A. Douglas stepped into the fray once again. Knowing that a proslavery vote on Kansas would alienate the northern Democrats, he separated himself from his party's leader and his president to protest Buchanan's position. Furthermore, Douglas insisted that true popular sovereignty had to be exercised by all the voters in Kansas, and in fair elections. His arguments swayed Congress, which in April 1858 denied Kansas admission to the Union on the basis of the Lecompton Constitution. Back in Kansas a popular referendum also resoundingly rejected the constitution, and in 1859 the territory held a new convention that was dominated this time by Republican Party members. In January 1861, a new proposal—that Kansas come into the Union as a free state—passed in Congress. But by then, many southern representatives were no longer active in national government.

This final vote on Kansas did not resolve deeper tensions. For one thing, the Democratic Party was clearly no longer a united national party. Buchanan and Douglas represented two opposing positions within the same party, each dominated by sectional concerns. Southern Democrats seethed that Douglas had betrayed them, and Buchanan himself had taken a blatantly pro-southern stance. Secondly, Kansas was still bleeding. Daily violence racked the territory, and occasionally mass killings sent new shock waves through the unstable tent towns of the open plains. Constitutions, said one demoralized free-soiler, "are mere parchment with ink, and none wish to take time for reading out here."

Panic and Depression

Americans were familiar with periodic economic crises. Panics in 1792, 1819, and 1837 had started with the ruin of a few financial speculators and turned into full-scale downturns. Years of widespread commercial and manufacturing stalemate, accompanied by unemployment and deepening urban poverty, followed each panic. And in 1857, another panic demonstrated to Americans that they still lacked the institutional and regulatory safeguards to prevent widespread misery. The signs of impending crisis loomed when gold kept pouring in from the West, which inflated currency across the nation. War abroad stimulated the production of grain and flour for export, and westward migration put pressure on banks and creditors to speculate with land and railroad stock.

When exports from the Midwest and South fell off sharply in late 1856 and early 1857, creditors began to call in farmers' loans before cash "dried up." In addition, railroad investors in the Midwest had overextended themselves; in 1857 new construction halted and layoffs began. Soon, credits and debts stopped flowing in other sectors. At first, a relatively small Ohio credit agency and investment firm collapsed in August 1857, and then others followed. Before long, the word was out: newspaper editors rushed to print, and telegraph offices hummed all the way to Wall Street with details about Ohio's misfortunes. Investors on the East Coast rushed to sell stocks and bonds, and to pull assets from banks. Within a month, businesses were failing and thousands of workers lost their jobs. Until 1861, unemployment in the North and along the Ohio River remained at about 10 percent.

Expecting that the depression, like its predecessors, would be long, Republicans in Congress believed that they should raise tariffs to protect manufacturers hurting from the crisis. Many northern Democrats and all southern representatives disagreed and easily outvoted the proposal. Their cotton exports were not suffering and economic dislocation in the South was minimal. Although import-dependent southerners had been opposing tariffs for decades, in 1857 their stance seemed to be still more proof to northerners that the "slave power" intended to divide the Union along sectional lines. Wage workers in the North who lost their jobs in the depression readily believed that stubborn southern sectionalism—rather than excessive midwestern land and railroad speculation—lay at the heart of their misery. As for southerners, continuing relative economic well-being prompted the widespread view that the South was a more stable and prosperous region. This, it turned out, was one of the delusions that made compromise with the North harder in the four years to come.

Depression in the North and Midwest spurred the demand for free land in the national public domain. As a relief to the ruinous poverty of many northern cities, as well as a reward for the risks of migrating, reformers advocated that the government give free 160-acre homesteads to all applicant families. But these hopes met with stiff opposition from two directions. Northern manufacturers believed that free farms would "drain away the best of our hands" for factory work. Southerners feared that small homesteads would fill with free-soilers and deny planters a chance to expand. For two years Congress deliberated on the free land proposal. Only in 1860 did the government finally approve a plan to grant land at 25 cents an acre. President Buchanan, however, vetoed the proposal, and it languished until the Civil War was well under way. Finally in 1863, people everywhere in the existing states applauded the Homestead Act's becoming law.

Southerners also believed they had been successful in lowering tariffs over the early 1850s. In fact, tariffs had been reduced to their lowest point since the War of 1812. Then, when the Panic of 1857 set in, the public coffers emptied quickly and the need for public revenues became acute. Moreover, northern manufacturers clamored for protectionism during the stormy seasons of commercial crisis that followed the panic. Tariffs inched up again, but not as much as these manufacturers wished. By 1859, world prices for cotton rose slowly again, and southern exporters proclaimed the centrality of southern agriculture to the world economy. The South's more rapid recovery seemed to validate Fitzhugh's premise that southern slave plantations were a superior economic form to northern free labor.

Lincoln and the Union, 1856–1860

By 1859, sectionalism had taken a tremendous toll on national political parties and the American political culture. The Whigs had collapsed. The Democrats hovered near break-up. The Republicans were rising but uncertain about how to compromise the strands of difference in the party. Crises in the territories and Border States throughout 1857 and 1858 threatened not to subside, but to spread. More and more Americans began to doubt that there was a political solution to these crises, and to forecast a disastrous social collision of sectional interests.

Lincoln's Rise

Abraham Lincoln's early life and political career were intertwined with the most important cultural and political issues of his generation. Born in 1809 into one of the thousands of farm families moving in a westward direction early in the 1800s, Lincoln was also exposed to the era's fast-paced, ambitious energies of Americans on the make. His family moved from Kentucky, to Indiana, and then to Illinois. Lincoln contributed to the meager family income by ferrying goods on flatboats down the Mississippi River to New Orleans in 1828 and 1831. Then Lincoln decided to leave farming life and became a store clerk in New Salem, in central Illinois.

Lincoln was popular with the rising middle class and the town rowdies alike. His schooling was minimal, except for the kind attentions of a local schoolmaster and a few friends who loaned him books. But he loved to participate in public debates and was a regular client at the local tavern. The first year of his business, local townsmen appointed him to head their company of volunteers for the Black Hawk War.

These experiences shaped Lincoln not for the relative isolation of farm life or the relative calm of an intellectual career. Instead, he threw himself into politics. In 1832 Lincoln ran for the Illinois state legislature with a program Henry Clay would have smiled at, favoring internal improvements and education. Lincoln lost this first race, but he accepted a position as postmaster and deputy county surveyor. And he attached his future to a prominent Whig lawyer and state legislator, and began to study law. In two years, he ran for state office again, and this time he won.

With a panic and depression setting in by mid-1837, Lincoln nevertheless passed his law exams. In 1842 he married Mary Todd, the daughter of a prominent businessman and slave owner from Kentucky. From 1834 through 1840, he continued for four terms in the state legislature's lower house. Here, Lincoln adhered to general Whig measures such as state-chartered banking, more canals and roads, and protectionism. In 1844 he eagerly grabbed at the opportunity to support Henry Clay, the political figure Lincoln admired above all others, in his presidential campaign. By 1846, Lincoln was ready to run for a congressional seat; and he won.

Suddenly, Lincoln was immersed in sectionalism, slavery, and the Mexican-American War, matters that had seemed so remote from his life in Illinois but were consuming the attention of men in Washington. Lincoln had already decided that slavery had caused many injustices in the Midwest. In 1838 he had denounced the mob that attacked and killed the printer Elijah Lovejoy in Alton, Illinois. But Lincoln had just as ardently rejected the violence of abolitionists who tried to deny southern migrants a place in the West. As a midwestern Whig, he knew that abolitionists leaned toward the Liberty Party in 1844, which harmed his hero Henry Clay. And as a student of the Constitution, Lincoln doubted whether the federal government could deprive citizens in the slave states of their property.

These beliefs were not easy to blend and sustain consistently. Lincoln tried to take the high moral road when he went to Congress in 1847. Already the war with Mexico was underway, and when Polk demanded appropriations to support the troops, Lincoln could not in good conscience abandon American men in a foreign war. But he also spoke strongly against Polk's war policies; plainly, he insisted, the war was unconstitutional. Lincoln also voted for the Wilmot Proviso and introduced the first resolution for gradual abolitionism in Washington, D.C.

Thus, Lincoln staked out a moderate position compatible with Whig beliefs and friendly to free-soilers. He opposed slavery's extension, and he supported gradual emancipation and colonization in Africa. But by the end of the 1848 presidential campaign, Lincoln understood that moderation could be costly in the real world of politics. Because of his support for gradualism, northern abolitionists denounced him as a friend to slave owners. Because of his opposition to the immensely popular Mexican-American War, he lost the good will of voters in Illinois. For about five years, Lincoln retreated into his law practice, serving railroad and manufacturing interests in the Midwest, and witnessing the Whig Party crumble in the intensifying sectional controversies of the early 1850s.

Above all, Lincoln feared the demise of moderation in politics. Abolitionists and southern extremists both threatened the Union, he wrote often in the early 1850s. But when Stephen Douglas introduced the Kansas-Nebraska Act and touted its provisions for popular sovereignty, Lincoln decided it was time to return to political life. Popular sovereignty, he believed, was a dangerous opening for the extension of slavery. Denouncing both Douglas and his act as the "gravest mischief to the Union," Lincoln ran for both the state legislature and the national congress in 1854. "Love of justice" required that slavery be confined to the states where it already existed. Already Lincoln was speaking strongly in support of what would become the central planks in the Republican platform later: moral opposition to slavery, the need to use the federal government to keep the territories free, and the hope that the southern slave owners would emancipate their slaves state by state.

Forging Principles

For the next two years, Lincoln worked hard to bring together remnants of the Whigs, free-soilers, abolitionists, Know-Nothings, and Democrats who could be persuaded to reject Douglas's program. By May 1856, he assumed the head of the new Republican Party in Illinois. Following the *Dred Scott* decision, which Lincoln scorned publicly, he ran another vigorous campaign in 1858 against Douglas for the U.S. Senate seat. In that campaign, he iterated some of the most frequently quoted words in American history:

> A house divided against itself cannot stand. . . . I believe this government cannot endure permanently half *slave* and half *free*. I do not expect the Union to be dissolved— I do not expect the house to *fall*—but I do expect it will cease to be divided. It will become *all* one thing, or *all* the other.

The dispute between Douglas and Buchanan over popular sovereignty, Lincoln insisted, paled next to the far greater issue that lay before the nation: slavery or freedom.

As the Senate campaign commenced, Lincoln challenged Douglas to a series of seven debates in Illinois. Thousands of people attended each debate and newspapers buzzed with reports about them. Douglas, long associated with railroad promotion in the state, was a high-profile candidate. Everywhere he went, Douglas raised his proposal for a transcontinental line through Chicago. By then, railroads were booming: the 9,021 miles of rail in 1850 tripled to 30,627 miles in 1860. But the issue of where to put a transcontinental line, and how to fund it, overlapped with the sectionally divisive matters of slavery, free labor, and party politics.

Lincoln was less well known than Douglas in 1858, and had much to prove to his listeners. But at each of the three-hour debates, Lincoln shone as an orator and staked out important ground on which Republicans would stand for years to come (see Competing Voices, page 560). He did not believe that "the various races" in America were socially equal, but he did believe that slavery was a moral wrong. "I, as well as Judge Douglas, am in favor of the race to which I belong, having the superior position." But slavery, he insisted, denied African-Americans the natural rights and liberties outlined in the Declaration of Independence. In so doing, the institution undermined equal opportunity. Black men and white men alike had the right to "labor in the soil" and "eat the bread, without leave of anybody else, which his own hand earns." Time and again, Lincoln also underscored, Democrats had collaborated with the "slave power": in the Kansas-Nebraska Act, in *Dred Scott*, in favoring the Lecompton Constitution, and in defeating improvement and tariff proposals brought to Congress.

Douglas responded with what scholars call the Freeport Doctrine (because he introduced it in Freeport, Illinois), which modified the popular sovereignty position. Settlers, Douglas patiently explained, could keep slavery out of their territories in practice by using their collective local authority against the Supreme Court's decision. In territories that did not prohibit slavery (and thus admitted it), local governing bodies could simply refuse to adopt legislation to protect slavery. By their numbers and their different lifestyles, settlers could, in practice, overwhelm and neutralize efforts to bring in slavery.

Although Douglas narrowly won the Illinois election in 1858, he modified his popular sovereignty position so much that most of his proslavery support evaporated. In response to the Freeport Doctrine, southern Democrats demanded that their party reaffirm its commitment to protecting slavery in the South and permitting its extension. Democrats in the Midwest wished to return to the original popular sovereignty position. But the most brazen spokesmen in the cotton South stepped forward to demand slave codes in the territories, reintroduction of the international slave trade, and meetings to discuss secession from the Union. These "fire-eaters" put fellow party members on notice that not only the defense of slavery where it existed, but its future extension, were nonnegotiable.

The Lincoln-Douglas Debates   In their hours-long debates before huge crowds of Illinois voters, Abraham Lincoln and Stephen Douglas took the opportunity to expound not only on state issues but also on the extent of federal authority, definitions of national character, and the blight of slavery. Such open-air speeches, often exercises in eloquent oratory, were crucial vehicles of political opinion-making during the early nineteenth century.   *(Corbis-Bettmann.)*

Only a small number of southerners were fire-eaters, and only a small number of northerners were ardent abolitionists. But at certain important moments, each extreme influenced public sentiments beyond the weight of its numbers. John Brown was a violent abolitionist whose actions sent the nation reeling closer to the precipice of national civil war in 1859.

The Election of 1860

By 1859, Republicans were well positioned to win the presidency. William H. Seward of New York, a highly visible senator, wished to be nominated. For years he had been identified as an antislavery spokesman, and some months previously he had warned that an "irrepressible conflict" was building between North and South. But he was not popular among nativists in the North, or among moderate Republicans. The majority of party leaders looked around and found in Abraham Lincoln a more moderate candidate who could surely carry the midwestern states.

The Republican Party had numerous issues inclining in its favor. The Panic of 1857 and ensuing depression gave the party an opportunity to appear the "saving force of the Union's downcast" by promoting free land in the West and protection for ailing craft production. Republicans thus promised a homestead act and a transcontinental railroad. Republicans, by their pledges to raise tariffs, also gained the support of manufacturers. And throughout the Union, voters could choose Lincoln as an opponent of slavery in the territories, but equally an opponent of racial equality.

The election also proved that the Democrats were near break-up. The party held its nominating convention in Charleston, South Carolina, the heart of the "solid south." For days of rancorous discussion, delegates could not decide on a candidate. Stephen A. Douglas could not please enough delegates of both sections to win the necessary two-thirds support for nomination. On the one hand, his long-standing commitment to popular sovereignty made it impossible to accept the southern demand for a slave code that would guarantee slavery's protection in the territories. On the other hand, northerners insisted that support for popular sovereignty was essential for the party candidate's campaign. Deadlocked, the convention adjourned.

When delegates met a second time, in Baltimore, it became clear that the Democratic Party was irrevocably split. Southerners bolted and held their own convention, at which they nominated John C. Breckinridge of Kentucky, a staunch supporter of slavery's extension into the territories. Northern Democrats went ahead and nominated Douglas. Then, with the party split and running two candidates, southern Whigs and Border State nativists formed a third party, the Constitutional Union Party. John Bell of Tennessee represented them at the polls.

A split Democratic Party and a dissenting third party reinforced the near certainty of a Republican Party victory. Breckinridge carried only southern states, and Bell snared some support that might have fallen to Breckinridge and Douglas. Douglas knew he had only a slim chance of winning. In fact, although his popular vote was considerable, he received only twelve electoral votes. Still, he stumped to "save the Union" and traveled through both northern and southern states tirelessly warning against dissolution of the nation.

"Honest Abe," whose name did not even appear on ballots below the southern boundaries of Virginia, Kentucky, and Missouri, ran a race primarily against Douglas in the North. Lincoln and his Republican campaigners buoyed northern optimism for union and "victory against the slave interest." Mass meetings, parades, and nightly speeches absorbed the public in a frenzy of political activity. Meanwhile, the race in deep southern states was primarily between Bell and Breckinridge.

Voter turnout in 1860 was tremendous: a higher percentage of people voted than in any other election to that time and turnout has been topped in American history only once since then, in 1876. But the election was thoroughly sectional in its results. Breckinridge lost southern votes because of Bell's campaign, but Lincoln carried all eighteen of the northern free states (except for a split vote in New Jersey) despite Douglas's energetic stumping. Lincoln's electoral vote overwhelmed the other three candidates combined, and he took 54 percent of the northern states' popular vote. Yet ten southern states did not even put Lincoln's name on their ballots, underscoring even more dramatically the sectional nature of the election.

Disunion

After John Brown's raid, vigilance committees in the interior areas of some southern states kept a watchful eye open for slave revolts. Southerners' fears of growing abolitionist sentiment, and anger about ineffective enforcement of the Fugitive Slave Law, also grew during 1859. Even during the 1860 campaign, some state leaders in the South began to talk of secession. When election results came in, talk turned to shock, and then to horror that the South might forever be overwhelmed

The Election of 1860
The division of the existing states proved a deep sectional division in American politics. Lincoln won no electoral votes in the South, Breckenridge won none in the North. States such as California, Illinois, and Pennsylvania shifted to Republican Party support between 1856 and 1860. What this electoral vote map cannot show, however, is the great number of northern Democrats who still opposed Lincoln.

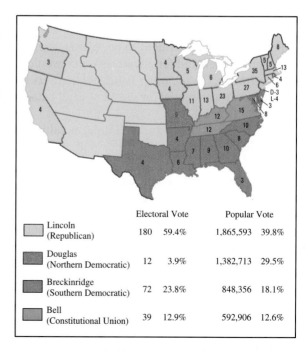

	Electoral Vote		Popular Vote	
Lincoln (Republican)	180	59.4%	1,865,593	39.8%
Douglas (Northern Democratic)	12	3.9%	1,382,713	29.5%
Breckinridge (Southern Democratic)	72	23.8%	848,356	18.1%
Bell (Constitutional Union)	39	12.9%	592,906	12.6%

by "free-state enthusiasts." Outspoken planters feared the imminent end of life as they had known it, and Lincoln's election "by and for the north" gave them the opportunity to take some decisive action.

Vigilance committees began to form armed militia units in the Upper South. Alabama, Mississippi, and South Carolina issued calls for special state conventions to discuss their next steps, including secession from the Union. Dissenters who hoped for reconciliation with the North were silenced by proslavery voices, as well as by the rush of events between Lincoln's election and December 20, 1860. On that date, South Carolina seceded from the Union. Buchanan did nothing. Over the next weeks, six more states—Mississippi, Florida, Georgia, Alabama, Louisiana, and Texas—also seceded, with near-unanimous votes in their respective special conventions. Still the president watched and waited.

In South Carolina marching bands and fireworks brought on the dissolution of the Union with grand public excitement. In other seceding states, fanfare also marked declarations of leaving the nation, with little regard for the other eight southern states that had not made any decisions yet. Indeed, southern secessionists believed that their declarations were drastic measures, but ones that would "bring the northern states to their senses" and let "our slavery solution follow its own course." Buchanan's inaction seemed to indicate northern acceptance of the South's peaceful departure from the Union. In fact, this was hardly the case.

Between the fall, when Lincoln was elected, and March, when he took office, proposals for compromise flew about Washington. Most of them involved some concessions to southern interests. But Lincoln refused them all, reaffirming his commitment to no slavery in the territories, and thus alienating potential support for compromise from Border States and southern moderates. Lincoln hoped to prevent the remaining eight southern states from seceding and to promote solutions from within the South itself. For a while this strategy seemed to be working.

But on another matter—whether to let the seceding states remain outside the Union—Lincoln was unyielding. As he put it, no "minority have the right to break up the government whenever they choose." Democracy, he insisted, "would not endure on such a principle." In addition, he could not allow seceded southern states to take over federal military forts and federal customshouses. But should he force seceded states back into the Union with federal troops? Lincoln hesitated, trying to avoid military confrontation.

In February 1861, before Lincoln took the oath of office, the seven seceded states created the Confederate States of America in Montgomery, Alabama. They chose Jefferson Davis as president, and Alexander Stephens of Georgia as vice president. Both men were moderates, not fire-eaters, which offered hope that seceded states might win support from undecided states and convince wavering citizens that secession was peaceful, moral, and legal. After all, argued Davis, if consent of the government is a central principle of American government, and southerners freely consented to leave the Union, then there was no cause for alarm or force to change that decision. The American Revolution itself had been based on the right of the governed to modify their systems of rule when they became outmoded or unjust. But when Confederates also adopted the United States Constitution for their new government, they incorporated two crucial changes: the principles of states' rights rather than federalism, and unambiguous support for slavery's continuation. The Confederacy, then, established the inseparable privilege of white over black, and states over federal authority.

What would Lincoln do once inaugurated? The entire North waited with bated breath to find out. On his ride from Springfield, Illinois, to the White House, Lincoln was careful not to provoke southern sensitivities. Nor did he assuage northern anxieties. His public began to demand some kind of response to the progress of southern events. At his inauguration, March 4, 1861, Lincoln reminded Americans that despite recent events and sectional divisions, they were still one nation of people. "Though passion may have strained, it must not break our bonds of affection. The mystic chords of memory, stretching from every battlefield, and patriot grave, to every living heart and hearthstone, all over this broad land, will yet swell the chorus of the Union, when again touched, as surely they will be, by the better angels of our nature." The crowd murmured, wondering when these "better angels" might appear.

CONCLUSION

After the Mexican-American War, northerners and southerners focused their attention on sectional differences and tied their destinies closely to territorial expansion. In efforts to calm sectional tensions, Congress renegotiated the Missouri Compromise line and framed a Compromise of 1850. Already, shifting interests were reconstituting the political party system. But the violence of the 1850s dashed most hopes that compromises would hold the political party system together.

A number of crises hastened the slide toward the Civil War. The Fugitive Slave Act presented northern antislavery reformers with a direct challenge to their beliefs. "Bleeding Kansas" seemed to prove that popular sovereignty could not peacefully organize the territories. The *Dred Scott* decision drove a deeper wedge between constituencies of the Democratic Party and aligned the Supreme Court with proslavery forces. When President Buchanan offered support for Kansas's Lecompton Constitution, Democrats and Whigs from the North and Midwest flocked to the Republican Party. Southern proslavery voices more stridently defended the "peculiar institution." John Brown's seizure of the Harpers Ferry arsenal was just another step in the escalating tensions.

A number of political and intellectual leaders recalled that in 1858 Senator William H. Seward had called these tensions an "irrepressible conflict." Lincoln's election did nothing to prevent secession of many southern states, and in the months that followed, Lincoln himself could not staunch the flow of blood that soon would flow.

SUGGESTED READINGS

For detailed studies of sectional tensions during the 1850s and the efforts to resolve political differences, start with Michael Holt, *Political Parties and American Political Development from the Age of Jackson to the Age of Lincoln* (1992); Richard H. Abbott, *Cotton and Capital: Boston Businessmen and Antislavery Reform, 1854–1868* (1991); Eric Foner, *Politics and Ideol-*

ogy in the Age of the Civil War (1980) and *Free Soil, Free Labor, Free Men: The Ideology of the Republican Party Before the Civil War* (1970); William E. Gienapp, *The Origins of the Republican Party, 1852–1856* (1987); William Freehling, *The Road to Disunion* (1990); and the older, but very readable, Holman Hamilton, *Prologue to Conflict: The Crisis and Compromise of 1850* (1964). David M. Potter, *The Impending Crisis, 1848–1861* (1976), is the most detailed account of the slide into Civil War, especially the political events. For a more specialized account of politics in the South, see Mark Stegmaier, *Texas, New Mexico, and the Compromise of 1850* (1996).

The reflections of literary circles, both northern and southern, are covered well in Thomas Gossett, *Uncle Tom's Cabin and American Culture* (1985). For the southern attitudes about development and economic competition with the North, see Vicki V. Johnson, *The Men and the Vision of the Southern Commercial Conventions, 1845–1871* (1992), but also see Thomas H. O'Connor, *Lords of the Loom: The Cotton Whigs and the Coming of the Civil War* (1968). The best study of women's roles in the 1850s across the nation is Wendy Hamand Venet, *Neither Ballots nor Bullets: Women Abolitionists and the Civil War* (1991).

Studies that tie the problems of development, slavery, and Native Americans together often focus on the trans-Mississippi West. Among the most helpful are Robert Dykstra, *Bright Radical Start: Black Freedom and White Supremacy on the Hawkeye Frontier* (1993); Joseph Herring, *The Enduring Indians of Kansas: A Century and a Half of Acculturation* (1990); and James A. Rawley, *Race and Politics: "Bleeding Kansas" and the Coming of the Civil War* (1969). Studies that focus on the politics and economics of railroads include Albert Fishlow's *American Railroads and the Transformation of the Ante-Bellum Economy* (1965) and John F. Stover's *The Life and Decline of the American Railroad* (1970) and *Iron Road to the West: American Railroads in the 1850s* (1978). The fine study by James Huston, *The Panic of 1857 and the Coming of the Civil War* (1987), analyzes the economy of the 1850s.

The best overview of the final moments before southern secession is Kenneth Stampp, *American in 1857: A Nation on the Brink* (1990). The increasing extremism of sectional and national politics during the 1850s is covered admirably in Tyler Anbinder, *Nativism and Slavery: The Northern Know Nothings and the Politics of the 1850s* (1991); Stanley Campbell, *The Slave Catchers: Enforcement of the Fugitive Slave Law, 1850–1860* (1970); Thomas P. Slaughter, *Bloody Dawn: The Cristiana Riot and Racial Violence in the Antebellum North* (1991); and Don Fehrenbacher, *The Dred Scott Case: Its Significance in American Law and Politics* (1978). The best collection of scholarly views about the complicated character of John Brown is Paul Finkelman, ed., *His Soul Goes Marching On: Responses to John Brown and the Harpers Ferry Raid* (1995), but see the distinctive view of Stephen B. Oates, *To Purge This Land with Blood: A Biography of John Brown* (1970), as well.

For the Republican Party's rise and growing importance, two works by Don Fehrenbacher—*Prelude to Greatness: Lincoln in the 1850s* (1962) and *The South and Three Sectional Crises* (1980)—are good starting points. See also the 1857 debates covered in Robert Johannsen, *Stephen A. Douglas* (1973) and *The Lincoln-Douglas Debates* (1965). For the Republican Party's national rise and Lincoln's place in the secessionist crisis, see William L. Barney, *The Road to Secession* (1972); Steven A. Channing, *Crisis of Fear: Secession in South Carolina* (1970); and David Herbert Donald, *Lincoln* (1995). Older, but readable and highly informative, is Kenneth Stampp, *And the War Came: The North and the Secession Crisis, 1860–1861* (1960).

Competing Voices

The Lincoln-Douglas Debates

Lincoln Clarifies His Position on the Equality of the Races

Abraham Lincoln, an Illinois lawyer who had served in his state Congress during the 1840s, wished to take a seat in the national Senate in 1858. Boldly, "Honest Abe" challenged his opponent, Stephen A. Douglas of the Democratic Party, to a series of seven debates on current affairs. The first soundoff was on Saturday, August 21, 1858, in Ottawa, Illinois, where nearly twelve thousand people participated in hours-long open-air exchanges. In this excerpt, Lincoln takes up the charge from Douglas that he and his fellow Republicans believed in the perfect natural equality of African-Americans with whites.

My Fellow Citizens: When a man hears himself somewhat misrepresented, it provokes him—at least, I find it so with myself. But when the misrepresentation becomes very gross and palpable, it is more apt to amuse him. (laughter)

... Anything that argues me into his [Douglas's] idea of perfect social and political equality with the Negro is but a specious and fantastic arrangement of words, by which a man can prove a horse chestnut to be a chestnut horse. (laughter)

I will say here, while upon this subject, that I have no purpose directly or indirectly to interfere with the institution of slavery in the states where it exists. I believe I have no lawful right to do so, and I have no inclination to do so. I have no purpose to introduce political and social equality between the white and the black races. There is a physical difference between the two, which in my judgment will probably forever forbid their living together upon the footing of perfect equality, and inasmuch as it becomes a necessity that there must be a difference, I, as well as Judge Douglas, am in favor of the race to which I belong having the superior position.

I have never said anything to the contrary, but I hold that, notwithstanding all this, there is no reason in the world why the Negro is not entitled to all the natural rights enumerated in the declaration of Independence, the right to life, liberty, and the pursuit of happiness. (loud cheers) I hold that he is as much entitled to these as the white man. I agree with Judge Douglas he is not my equal in many respects—certainly not in color, perhaps not in moral or intellectual endowment. But in the right to eat the bread, without leave of anybody else, which his own hand earns, *he is my equal and the equal of Judge Douglas, and the equal of every living man.* (great applause)

Douglas Advocates for Popular Sovereignty

Douglas, the incumbent Democratic Party senator from Illinois in 1858, side-stepped the matter of slavery's morality and focused on the more practical political view that no federal court or distant national government should have the final word on the existence of slavery in the territories. In the following passage, Douglas enunciates this reasoning in what has become known as the Freeport Doctrine.

First, he [Lincoln] desires to know if the people of Kansas shall form a constitution by means entirely proper and unobjectionable and ask admission into the Union as a state, before they have the requisite population for a member of Congress, whether I will vote for that admission. . . . I hold it to be a sound rule of universal application to require a territory to contain the requisite population for a member of Congress, before it is admitted as a state into the Union. . . .

The next question propounded to me by Mr. Lincoln is, can the people of a territory in any lawful way against the wishes of any citizen of the United States[,] exclude slavery from their limits prior to the formation of a state constitution? I answer emphatically, as Mr. Lincoln has heard me answer a hundred times from every stump in Illinois, that in my opinion the people of a territory can, by lawful means, exclude slavery from their limits prior to the formation of a state constitution. . . . It matters not what way the Supreme Court may hereafter decide as to the abstract question whether slavery may or may not go into a territory under the Constitution, the people have the lawful means to introduce it or exclude it as they please, for the reason that slavery cannot exist a day or an hour anywhere, unless it is supported by local police regulations. . . . Those police regulations can only be established by the local legislature, and if the people are opposed to slavery they will elect representatives to that body who will by unfriendly legislation effectually prevent the introduction of it into their midst. . . . [T]he right of the people to make a slave territory or a free territory is perfect and complete under the Nebraska Bill. . . .

The third question which Mr. Lincoln presented is, if the Supreme Court of the United States shall decide that a state of this Union cannot exclude slavery from its own limits will I submit to it? I am amazed that Lincoln should ask such a question. . . . He knows that there never was but one man in America [Roger B. Taney, the chief justice], claiming any degree of intelligence or decency, who even for a moment pretended such a thing. . . .

The Black Republican creed lays it down expressly, that under no circumstances shall we acquire any more territory unless slavery is first prohibited in the country. I ask Mr. Lincoln whether he is in favor of that proposition. Are you opposed to the acquisition of any more territory, under any circumstances, unless slavery is prohibited in it? That he does not like to answer. When I ask him whether he stands up to that article in the platform of his party, he turns, Yankee-fashion, and without answering it, asks me whether I am in favor of acquiring territory without regard to how it may affect the Union on the slavery question. . . . I answer that whenever it becomes necessary, in our growth and progress to acquire more territory, that I am in favor of it, without reference to the question of slavery, and when we have acquired it, I will leave the people free to do as they please, either to make it slave or free territory, as they prefer. . . .

Political life during the 1850s was still more local than national in scope, but in the cases of Lincoln and Douglas, the spectacle of their seven debates underscored and furthered their eminent reputations. Douglas had played a prominent role in formulating the Compromise of 1850 and the Kansas-Nebraska Act. Moreover, voters in the Midwest and Northeast identified Douglas as a founding spokesman for popular sovereignty, as well as a foremost advocate of a northern route for a transcontinental railroad. In each role, Douglas seemed to be a moderate politician in a decade of extremes and violence. In light of the *Dred Scott* decision in 1857, in which the Supreme Court made sweeping pronouncements about the nature of the territories and the status of slaves, it became harder to promote the idea that citizens in a given territory might decide for themselves whether to become a slave or free state. But Douglas tried to do just that in his Freeport, Illinois, speech. When he ran for reelection to state office in 1858, he won easily against the newcomer, Abraham Lincoln. For all of these reasons, Douglas also was favored to win the 1860 presidential election.

However, Lincoln's political star was rising. His high-pitched voice held the Ottawa, Illinois, audience in thrall for hours during the first debate with Douglas. At the end of the day, thousands of Republican Party supporters at the debate bore him off in triumph from the platform. In less than two years, Lincoln would accept the Republican Party's nomination for the presidential campaign of 1860. Also known for his moderation, Lincoln never joined the antislavery Liberty or Free-Soil parties, remaining in the Whig Party until it was no longer a viable organization. Although Lincoln believed African-Americans had certain economic rights—to satisfy basic needs and to strive in their labor as whites did—he never wished or assumed that in the free states African-Americans would be socially and culturally the equals of whites. Still, Lincoln's firm moral opposition to slavery in the debates of 1858 made Douglas appear to be a greater defender of slavery than he in fact was. Thus, two prominent men who occupied places toward the center of the intellectual and political spectrum in America in 1858, rather than at either extreme, could articulate deep and consequential differences.

Questions for Analysis

1. What passages demonstrate that Abraham Lincoln was a moderate Republican in 1858?

2. What did Lincoln say that might have angered northern abolitionists? What statements would have been offensive to southerners?

3. Summarize what popular sovereignty means, and compare it with the conditions established by the *Dred Scott* decision.

4. What differences between those two doctrines does Douglas emphasize? How do you think Lincoln would have responded to Douglas?

5. What parts of each speaker's arguments express his core beliefs and party positions, and what parts are just rhetorical flourishes?

6. In an era before radio and television, and in a part of the country not yet saturated by newspapers and telegraph, what do you think was the role of such speeches in molding public opinion? in shaping the views that defined the sections of the country?

15

Transforming the Experiment: The Civil War, 1861–1865

*B*ecause of the epic proportions of the Battle of Gettysburg it seemed only fitting that the dead should be honored with a proper ceremony. Officials set aside seventeen acres and announced a date—November 19, 1863. Organizers invited the noted orator Edward Everett to dedicate the new graveyard. As an afterthought, they sent an invitation to President Abraham Lincoln to deliver a "few appropriate remarks." The casual invitation was not meant as an insult: burying war dead was a state responsibility, and no one expected the head of the federal government to play a significant role. Lincoln accepted the invitation, hoping to use the opportunity to mend political fences in Pennsylvania and to redefine the purpose of the war.

It rained in the early morning of the nineteenth, but the sky soon cleared and the sun shone brilliantly on the rolling countryside. Over fifteen thousand people had flooded the small college town bordering the battlefield, most of them relatives of slain soldiers, "who had come from distant parts to look at and weep over the remains of their fallen kindred," a reporter said. Flags flew at half-mast. At ten o'clock, a procession led by Lincoln on horseback crawled to the top of Cemetery Hill, which had anchored the northern end of the Union line. The president, wearing his customary black suit and stovepipe hat, took his seat on the temporary wooden speakers' platform.

From his vantage point on the top of Cemetery Hill, Lincoln had a clear view of the battlefield that had claimed 51,000 casualties in a bloody three-day orgy of violence. Looking to the South, Lincoln could see long rows of coffins waiting for burial—a visual reminder of the cost of civil war—as he sat patiently through Everett's two-hour oration. Near the end of the speech, the president took his manuscript from his coat pocket and put on his steel-rimmed glasses. When Everett sat down, Lincoln stepped to the front of the platform and recited in "a sharp, unmusical treble voice" his hymn to the dead.

"Four score and seven years ago our fathers brought forth on this continent, a new nation, conceived in Liberty, and dedicated to the proposition that all men are created equal." The Civil War, he argued, tested "whether that nation, or any nation so conceived and so dedicated, can long endure." Lincoln called on those gathered to devote themselves to "the unfinished work which they who fought here have thus far so nobly advanced." That work, was nothing short of the preservation of the nation: "That this nation, under God, shall have a new birth of freedom—and that government of the people, by the people, for the people, shall not perish from the earth."

Lincoln's Gettysburg Address took three minutes to deliver, and consisted of only 272 words, but it articulated what the war had come to mean. From the beginning of the Civil War, both North and South fought more over ideas and rights than over land. The Confederates emphasized the founders' commitment to individualism and states' rights. Lincoln at Gettysburg offered a much different view that recognized the power of the national government to define and enforce liberty and that made equality—the "proposition that all men are created equal"—the central concept of American political culture. The conflict was between two societies that had carried the American experiment in different directions. The Gettysburg Address made poignantly clear that the military battles between the Blue and the Grey would also represent a clash between two different ideas of what it meant to be an American.

▌ How did the Northern and Southern war strategies reflect each society's view of its strength and resources?

▌ How did culture and institutions influence how each side mobilized for battle?

▌ What impact did the war have on both societies?

▌ How did emancipation transform the war?

This chapter will address these questions.

 ## The War Begins, 1861

"War is not merely an act of policy," noted the famous nineteenth-century Prussian military strategist Carl von Clausewitz, "but a true political instrument, a continuation of political intercourse, carried on with other means." Unable to resolve their differences by political compromise, North and South turned to war to achieve their objectives. While battling for control of neutral Border States, Union and Confederate leaders took stock of their assets and liabilities and developed a military strategy

Chronology

1860	Lincoln elected president
	Secession begins
1861	Fort Sumter attacked
	Lincoln institutes martial law in the Border States
	First Battle of Bull Run
	Trent Affair
1862	Peninsular Campaign
	Battle of Shiloh
	Union navy seizes Memphis and New Orleans
	Battle of Antietam
	Battle of Fredricksburg
	Confederate conscription act
	Homestead Act
	Morrill Land Grant Act
1863	Emancipation Proclamation
	Union army enrolls black enlistees
	Federal conscription act
	New York City draft riot
	Battle of Chancellorsville
	Battle of Gettysburg
	Vicksburg falls
1864	Grant made commander of all Union forces
	Grant's Wilderness Campaign
	Lincoln reelected President
	Grant lays siege to Petersburg
	Sherman takes Atlanta and begins his march to the sea
1865	Confederacy enlists black troops
	Petersburg and Richmond fall
	Lee and Johnston surrender

designed to achieve victory. Passions ran high on both sides as North and South defined the purpose of the war.

The Search for Compromise

When Lincoln won election in November 1860, there were thirty-three states in the Union. By the time he took the oath of office in March 1861, only twenty-seven remained. Many secessionists, especially large slave owners, viewed Lincoln and the Republicans as revolutionaries determined to destroy the slaveholding system. Lincoln's election, declared a Southern newspaper, "shows that the North [intends] to free the negroes and force amalgamation between them and the children of the poor men of the South." In fact, Lincoln's approach to the slavery issue was far from revolutionary, and he struggled to reassure the South that he wished only to prevent slavery's spread, not to abolish it. "Do the people of the South really entertain fears that a Republican administration would, directly or indirectly, interfere with their slaves, or with them, about their slaves?" Lincoln asked shortly after his election. "If they do, I wish to assure you . . . that there is no cause for such fears." But even attempts to limit slavery's expansion badly frightened Southern slaveholders, who believed that their peculiar institution needed to grow in order to survive.

While Southern leaders struggled to set up a new government, many moderates in the North searched for compromise. The tired and discredited President Buchanan was in no position to offer decisive leadership, so any resolution of the secession crisis would have to come out of Congress. No compromise could arrest secession unless the Republicans strongly favored it, and initially they showed little interest. But Republican businessmen with close economic ties to the South soon joined Northern Democrats in pressuring congressional Republicans to offer a compromise.

Many moderates rallied around a proposal offered by Kentucky Senator John J. Crittenden. The Crittenden Compromise suggested that Congress extend the Missouri Compromise line of 36°30′ to California as the dividing line between slavery and free soil, forbid federal interference with the internal slave trade, and provide compensation for any slaveholder prevented from recovering escaped slaves in the North.

Abolitionists and free blacks in the North opposed the compromise efforts. Said Frederick Douglass, "If the Union can only be maintained by new concessions to the slaveholders, if it can only be stuck together and held together by a new drain on the negro's blood, then . . . let the Union perish." Lincoln and other party leaders feared that accepting the compromise would doom the Republican Party, which had made opposition to the spread of slavery its core message. Lincoln made it clear that the party had to stand firm. "Entertain no proposition for a compromise in regard to the extension of slavery," he instructed key congressmen. Taking their cue from Lincoln, Republicans in Congress thwarted the Crittenden measures. Compromise was no longer possible.

The Attack on Fort Sumter

In March 1861, an assassination threat forced Lincoln to abandon his plans for a triumphant march into Washington to take the oath of office. Instead, the president, accompanied only by a railroad detective and a close friend, slipped into Washington anonymously on a night train—"like a thief in the night," he said. In a carefully worded inaugural address, delivered on March 4 from the steps of the unfinished Capitol building, the new president was both firm and conciliatory. He promised not to interfere with slavery where it already existed but also denied that any state had the right to secede from the Union and promised to "hold, occupy, and possess" all federal installations in the South. He concluded on a note of reconciliation, reminding white Southerners of the common heritage they shared as Americans. "The mystic chords of memory, stretching from every battlefield, and patriot grave, to every living heart and hearthstone, all over this broad land, will yet swell the chorus of the Union, when again touched, as surely they will be, by the better angels of our nature." The South, however, was in no mood for reconciliation, and profound ideological differences rendered moot Lincoln's eloquent appeal for union.

On setting up their own state governments, the secessionists had seized federal property and installations throughout the Lower South. One of the few still under federal control was a modest garrison of eighty-three men at Fort Sumter in Charleston Harbor, South Carolina. Fort Sumter, under the command of Major Robert Anderson, was no serious military threat to the Confederacy, but Confederate leaders viewed its presence in Charleston, the heart of the secession movement, as an insult to Southern pride. President Jefferson Davis, heeding the calls of his more militant advisers, demanded that the Union withdraw Anderson and his men.

The Confederacy's tough line forced a confrontation with Lincoln. Though he still hoped to avoid war, Lincoln concluded that withdrawal from Fort Sumter would feed Confederate hopes and demoralize the North. On April 6, he decided to send food and other essential nonmilitary supplies to the Fort. Lincoln did not want the North to fire the first shot in the war with the South. His decision forced Davis to choose between war and peace.

Word of Lincoln's decision reached Montgomery on April 8. The next day, the Confederate Congress instructed General P. G. T. Beauregard, the Confederate commander at Charleston, to demand an immediate surrender of Fort Sumter. On April 12, Beauregard, supported by 6,000 eager South Carolina militiamen, sent an ultimatum to Anderson: surrender by 4 A.M. or face attack. Anderson, a career soldier and former slave owner whose devotion to the Union was unshakable, refused to surrender. Confederate artillery shells opened fire on Fort Sumter at 4:30 A.M. For thirty-two hours, Anderson maintained the unequal contest. Then, on the afternoon of Saturday, April 13, with the fort in flames, he surrendered. As he was escorted away, Anderson carried with him the tattered American flag that had flown so proudly over the fort.

The American Civil War had begun. The news of Fort Sumter electrified both the North and the South. Writer Ralph Waldo Emerson noted that "the attack on Fort Sumter crystallized the North into a unit, and the hope of mankind was saved." On the other side, Mary Chesnut, the wife of a former South Carolina senator, observed, "The war spirit is waking us all up." On April 15, Lincoln called on the states

Fort Sumter A Confederate flag waves over the first battleground of the Civil War on April 14, 1861. The Confederate forces under General Beauregard bombarded the fort for two days before Major Robert Anderson surrendered. *(National Archives.)*

for 75,000 militiamen to quell the "insurrection." On May 6, the Confederate Congress countered by formally declaring that a state of war existed.

The Battle for the Border States

The first battles of the Civil War were over control of the Border States. Eight of the fifteen slave states did not send delegates to the Montgomery Convention and hoped to remain neutral in the conflict. Following Fort Sumter, neutrality was no longer possible.

The Union cause had little support in those states that shared close cultural and economic ties to the South. "The militia of Virginia will not be furnished to the powers at Washington," the governor wrote Lincoln. "Your object is to subjugate the Southern States. . . . You have chosen to inaugurate civil war."

When Virginia left the Union, its largest city, Richmond, became the new capital of the Confederacy. The rest of the Upper South quickly followed Virginia out of the Union. Arkansas left on May 6. On May 20, the North Carolina convention, under pressure from pro-Confederate newspapers to withdraw from the "vile, rotten, infidelic, puritanic, negro-worshipping, negro-stealing, negro-equality . . . Yankee-Union," unanimously adopted a secession ordinance. Tennessee seceded on June 8.

The support of the Upper South states was crucial if the South was going to have any chance of winning the war. These states almost doubled the population of the Confederacy, giving it eleven states to stand against the Union's twenty-three. Just as important, they provided the South with natural resources and skilled artisans that it needed to create weapons and feed and clothe an army. Most important of all was the Tredegar Iron Works in Richmond, which provided the Confederacy with its only factory capable of producing heavy ordnance. Virginia put one frontier of the new nation within shouting distance of the Union's capital at Washington. Arkansas and Tennessee extended Confederate control of the vital Mississippi River corridor.

At the same time, the Confederacy struggled to win over the so-called Border States—Delaware, Missouri, Kentucky, and Maryland—whose secession would seriously weaken the Union's military position. While Delaware remained solidly in Union control, the other three states would have increased the South's military manpower by 45 percent and its manufacturing capability by 80 percent. If Maryland seceded, for example, the capital at Washington would have been surrounded by enemy territory. Confederate control of Kentucky would imperil river transportation along the Ohio, which was vital to the Northern economy. The secession of Missouri would further extend Southern control of the Mississippi.

Securing control over Maryland was Lincoln's most pressing strategic goal in late April. Although slavery was of declining importance in Maryland, and Unionist sentiment predominated, Southern sympathizers maintained some strength in Baltimore and along the Eastern Shore. On April 19, a prosecession mob in Baltimore attacked the Sixth Massachusetts Regiment passing through on its way to Washington. Rebel supporters destroyed railroad bridges and telegraph lines north of Baltimore. Since all rail traffic into Washington had to pass through Baltimore, Washington was cut off from communication with the free states.

By the time the Maryland legislature met on April 29 to consider secession, Lincoln was prepared to use whatever means necessary to guarantee a Union victory. He ordered Winfield Scott, the general-in-chief of the Union army, "to adopt the most prompt and efficient means to counteract [secession], even, if necessary, to the bombardment of their cities." Lincoln, instituted martial law in the state, sent federal troops to occupy Baltimore, and suspended the writ of *habeas corpus*, allowing the military to imprison pro-Confederates without formal charges by a grand jury. Union soldiers arrested numerous pro-Southern citizens in Maryland, including the mayor and police chief of Baltimore and thirty-one members of the state legislature, and threw them in prison for months without trial, and in a few cases for more than a year. The intimidation tactics worked. The legislature rejected secession by a vote of 53–13, ending the threat of secession in Maryland.

Lincoln invested an enormous amount of time trying to maintain the neutrality of his home state of Kentucky. While reassuring residents that he "intended to make no attack, direct or indirect, upon the institution or property of any State," Lincoln worked closely with Unionist forces to frustrate Confederate plans to capture the state. Lincoln was not as adroit in his handling of Missouri, where Union rebels—called Jayhawkers—fought a bloody guerrilla war against Confederate agitators—called Bushwhackers. Over the next three years, warfare devastated the countryside and pitted neighbor against neighbor. "The prairies are ablaze," a Kansas paper reported. "There is nothing talked about here except war." In the end, Missouri stayed in the Union.

Divisions in Virginia led to the creation of a new pro-Union border state. Appalachian Virginia, the one-third of the state west of the Allegheny Mountains, and populated overwhelmingly by nonslaveholders and small farmers, was anti-Confederate from the very beginning. After a series of complex, irregular, and probably illegal maneuvers, West Virginia declared its independence and was admitted into the Union in June 1863.

Farther to the west, the Confederate government sent agents to enlist the support of the so-called Five Civilized Tribes (see page 497), which had settled in Indian Country (later to become the state of Oklahoma). The Choctaw and Chickasaw embraced the Confederate cause, but the other tribes split. Many Indian leaders favored neutrality, fearing that the war would aggravate internal tensions and shatter the delicate peace among the tribes. "I am—the Cherokees are—your friends," Principal Chief John Ross told the Confederate representatives, "but we do not wish to be brought into the feuds between yourselves and your northern brethren. Our wish is for peace." But peace and neutrality were no longer possible, and eventually most tribes sided with the Confederacy. Over the next few years, they fought against Union troops in the western theater and against the handful of pro-Union tribes in a bitter internal civil war.

The Balance of Power

Even with alignment of the Border States unsettled, both sides went into the Civil War with considerable advantages and liabilities. The North's chief asset was its enormous size and its thriving industrial economy. There were nearly 21 million people in the North, just 9 million in the Confederacy, 3.5 million of whom were slaves. The North had more than twice as many miles of railroad track as the South. Most of the nation's heavy industry was concentrated in the North. In 1860 Union states produced 97 percent of the nation's firearms, 94 percent of its cloth, and 90 percent of its boots and shoes. One state, New York, produced four times as many manufactured goods as the entire South. The North in 1860 built fourteen out of every fifteen railroad locomotives manufactured in the United States. The Union navy floated ninety ships; the Confederacy had to build a navy from scratch.

Its superior resources and powerful navy shaped the North's military strategy. Five days after the surrender of Fort Sumter, Lincoln announced a blockade of all Confederate ports. "Whereas an insurrection against the Government of the United States has broken out in the States of South Carolina, Georgia, Alabama, Florida, Mississippi, Louisiana, and Texas," he declared, it was "advisable to set on foot a blockade." Lincoln and his generals believed they could achieve victory by squeezing the Confederacy, applying a naval blockade of Southern ports and seizing control of the Mississippi River. The Union reasoned that frustrated Confederates, cut off from essential trade, would gradually lose their will to fight. This so-called Anaconda Plan, named after a giant snake that wraps around and suffocates its prey, assumed a bloodless triumph for the North.

The Rebel states were not intimidated by the Union's advantages in human resources and industrial might. Confederate leaders had the psychological advantage that their people were fighting to preserve their own territory. "Lincoln may bring his 75,000 troops against us," said Vice President Alexander Stephens. "We fight for our homes, our fathers and mothers, our wives, brothers, sisters, sons and daughters!" For decades, Southerners had dominated the nation's military academies and officers' corps, and Confederates could count on experienced military men defecting from the North to lead their army. Also, although the South had only 40 percent as many people as the North, the availability of slaves freed a much larger proportion of whites for military service.

With the obvious example of the American Revolution in mind, Southerners believed that a determined nation could successfully win or maintain its independence against invaders with larger armies and more material resources. George W. Randolph, the Confederate secretary of war in the fall of 1861, confidently stated, "There is no instance in history of a people as numerous as we are inhabiting a country so extensive as ours being subjected if true to themselves." Like George Washington's forces during the American Revolution, Southerners could lose most of the battles and still win the war, but only if they could convince their opponent that victory was too costly. Union armies had to penetrate deep into enemy territory, gain control of it, and eventually break the Confederate will to resist the reestablishment of federal power. This offensive strategy required larger numbers of troops than the defensive operation employed by the Confederacy.

Finally, while drawing parallels between themselves and the American revolutionaries, the Confederates looked for support from an unlikely ally: Great Britain. The Confederacy hoped that Britain, which imported 80 percent of its cotton supply from the South in the 1850s, would rush to its defense once the flow of cotton was cut off by the combined effects of the Union blockade and a voluntary embargo in the South on cotton exports. The North, on the other hand, anticipated that a powerful antislavery sentiment in Britain and France would compel their leaders to oppose the slaveholding South.

Despite their differences, both sides called upon a common history and a shared language to justify the war. People living in the North and South believed they were the true heirs of the American Revolution. The Confederates used the language of individual freedom and liberty to justify their support of slavery and explain their break with the Union. Initially, Lincoln used similar language to explain his hostility toward slavery and his desire to preserve the Union. The contradiction between liberty and slavery built into the foundation of the republic had torn an irreparable breach in the American experiment.

Each side also widely believed that the war would be short and relatively bloodless. Most young men who marched off to battle in early 1861 held a romanticized image of war and glory. The harsh reality of war and death would soon shatter that illusion.

Stalemate on the Battlefield, 1861–1862

The early battles of the war dashed any hope of quick victory for either side. The North scored some victories in the West and gained the upper hand on the sea, but the Army of the Potomac was bogged down in the East, where Confederate forces scored a series of victories in defense of their capital at Richmond. However, when the Confederate army tried to build on their success by invading Maryland, Union forces turned them back in a shockingly bloody battle. Neither side gained a strategic advantage, but both suffered a tremendous loss of human life that was unimaginable when the war began.

The First Battle of Bull Run

While sparring continued for control of the Border States, popular attention in 1861 focused on northern Virginia. Pushed by public pressure for a quick, decisive victory that would demoralize the South, Lincoln ordered Union troops into Virginia. The hundred-mile stretch between the two capitals of Washington and Richmond was destined to become the most bitterly contested military terrain of the war. More than half the Union soldiers who died on the battlefield fell on this bloody ground.

In the summer of 1861, Union General Irvin McDowell had 35,000 troops at Washington. They were disorganized and undisciplined, but their term of enlistment, set for three months, was about to expire. With the public clamoring for a quick end to the war, Lincoln ordered McDowell's "grand army" of recruits to march toward Richmond. It took them two and a half days to march twenty-five miles, a stretch that seasoned troops would have covered in half the time. Newspaper reporters and crowds of spectators accompanied the army. Some brought binoculars, picnic baskets, even bottles of champagne, expecting to see a fight that would crush the rebellion in a single blow.

On July 21, McDowell met General Joseph E. Johnston's Confederate force of 22,000 at Manassas Junction, a little town on a creek called Bull Run, about twenty-five miles southwest of Washington. The North gained the offensive and eager soldiers shouted, "The war is over!" But holding the hill at the center of the Southern line was General Thomas "Stonewall" Jackson, whose troops stood firm long enough for Confederate reinforcements to arrive. The sight of fresh Rebel forces demoralized the Union men, most of whom had now been marching and fighting in brutal heat without food or water for fourteen hours. When the Confederates counterattacked, the Union army retreated.

The Battle of Bull Run gave Americans their first taste of the carnage that lay ahead. Some 4,500 men were killed, wounded, or captured on both sides in the battle that the North, which named battles after the landmark nearest to the fighting, called Bull Run and the South, which chose the town that served as its base, called Manassas (see map).

The defeat at Bull Run sobered the North. "Today will be known as BLACK MONDAY," wrote attorney George Templeton Strong when the bad news reached New York. "We are utterly and disgracefully routed, beaten, whipped by secessionists." Though shaken by the defeat, Lincoln did not panic, and the next day called for the enlistment of 500,000 additional troops to serve for three years. Tens of thousands of volunteers rushed to join the Army of the Potomac, while exhilarated Southerners strengthened fortifications around Richmond.

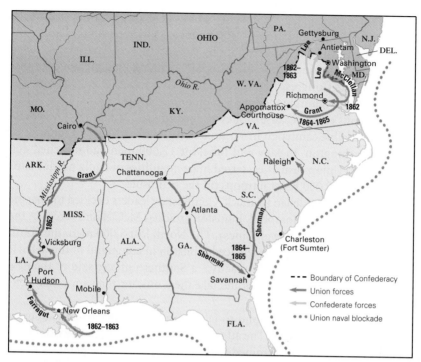

Major Military Offenses of the Civil War   While the Confederacy began the war with a strategy of defense, the Union went on the offensive in both the western and eastern theaters in 1862. While Farragut and Grant made slow progress in the West, Confederate forces in the East forced McClellan off the Virginia Peninsula and led the way to Robert E. Lee's first offensive into the North—Antietam. Lee's second offensive into the North at Gettysburg in the summer of 1863 proved to be his last as Grant and Sherman, transferred to the eastern theater, began their attacks on the heart of the South.

The Peninsular Campaign

Following the defeat at Bull Run, Lincoln selected General George McClellan to take charge of the Union forces at Washington. A vain and powerful man who was said to be able to bend a quarter with his fingers and lift a 250-pound man over his head, McClellan was a hero of the Mexican War and the author of manuals on military tactics. "The true course in conducting military operations," McClellan declared, "is to make no movement until the preparations are complete." True to his philosophy, McClellan spent most of the fall and winter in camp, training his new troops for future battles. Congress and the president grew impatient as McClellan delayed. "If General McClellan does not want to use the Army," the frustrated president said, "I would like to borrow it for a time."

In January the president ordered McClellan to move toward Richmond by February 22. Rather than drive through a powerful Confederate force at Manassas Junction, McClellan proposed to circumvent it by floating his vast army to the tip of the York–James Peninsula by sea, then fight west to Richmond. It took three weeks to ferry the Army of the Potomac to Fortress Monroe on the peninsula: 121,500 men, 14,592 horses and mules, 1,150 wagons, 44 batteries of artillery.

Progress up the peninsula was slow, but by the end of May, McClellan's stood poised just five miles outside Richmond. The Confederate capital prepared for disaster. The Confederate Congress fled town. But McClellan hesitated, pleading for reinforcements before beginning the final assault on the city's defenses.

No reinforcements came because Stonewall Jackson had tied down two Federal divisions in a remarkable campaign in Virginia's Shenandoah Valley to the west of Richmond and Washington. In May and June, his 17,000 men had marched 400 miles, inflicted 7,000 Union casualties, seized huge quantities of badly needed supplies, and kept almost 40,000 Federal troops off the peninsula.

Rather than wait for McClellan to attack, Confederate leaders decided to take the offensive. On Friday, May 31, Joseph E. Johnston attacked McClellan's forces in the indecisive battle of Fair Oaks (Seven Pines). The North lost 5,000 men, the South 6,000. After Fair Oaks, Robert E. Lee replaced Johnston in command of the defense of Richmond. "His name might be 'Audacity,'" a Southern officer said of the new commander. "He will take more chances and take them quicker, than any other General in this country, North or South."

Determined not to allow Richmond to fall, Lee attacked McClellan's superior forces on June 26 at Mechanicsville. The attack cost Lee 1,500 men, but he would not let up. He continued forward, determined to drive McClellan off the peninsula. The Union forces won most of the individual battles, but the ever-cautious McClellan fell back steadily. By July 3, McClellan's retreating army had reached the bank of the James River within the protection of Federal gunboats. The Peninsular Campaign was at an end. In just one week, Lee had forced McClellan's huge army to retreat over ground it had spent three months taking, creating fear in Washington and celebrations in Richmond.

Fighting in the West

While most of the nation focused on the battles around Richmond, Union troops were having more success in the West. In 1861 General Ulysses S. Grant seized Paducah, Kentucky, which controlled access to the Tennessee and Cumberland Rivers. In 1862 he led an assault against two Confederate forts protecting the Kentucky–Tennessee border: Fort Henry on the Tennessee River and Fort Donelson on the Cumberland.

Fort Henry quickly fell on February 6, but Fort Donelson resisted longer. In February, with the Union force closing in on the Rebel defenders, the Confederate commander asked for surrender terms. Grant responded: "No terms except an unconditional and immediate surrender can be accepted. I propose to move immediately upon your works." Shortly afterward, the garrison's commander and his 15,000 troops surrendered. The Tennessee and Cumberland Rivers were now in Union hands, and the North celebrated its first major military victory. "Chicago reeled mad with joy," declared the *Chicago Tribune*.

In April, Grant moved south along the Tennessee River to continue his penetration of the Middle South. On a Sunday morning, April 6, 1862, Confederates commanded by Albert Sidney Johnston charged into Grant's camps in a surprise attack that began the bloodiest battle of the war to that point. The fighting, which took place around a small white church called Shiloh, a Hebrew word meaning "place of peace," raged for two days. On the first day, waves of Confederate soldiers pushed the Union army back almost into the river at Pittsburg Landing. However, Union General Don Carlos Buell arrived that night with 25,000 fresh troops, and the next day, the Federal force, now 50,000 strong, counterattacked successfully, forcing the Confederate troops to retreat. When the fighting was over, corpses littered the battlefield so thickly in some places, Grant remembered, that "it would have been possible to walk across the clearing in any direction stepping on dead bodies without a foot touching the ground." One hundred thousand men fought at Shiloh. Nearly one in four was a casualty. Three thousand four hundred and seventy-seven men died in those two days—more than all the Americans who had fallen in the Revolutionary War, the War of 1812, and the Mexican War together.

The Naval War

Grant was working on the Tennessee–Cumberland drainage because it was a link to the Mississippi, but to cut transport and communications more completely, the big river itself had to be controlled. In the spring of 1862, Union fleets attacked Southern strongholds on the river. On June 6, Union ships subdued Memphis. At the same time, another Union fleet of twenty-four ships, commanded by Admiral David G. Farragut, was ordered to sail up the river and seize New Orleans, the South's largest city and busiest port. As they approached New Orleans, a makeshift Confederate squadron of eight ships sailed out to meet them. Farragut sank six of them, and the city surrendered without firing a shot. In what the *New York Tribune* called "A Deluge of Victories," Union forces had conquered 50,000 square miles of land, gained control of 1,000 miles of navigable rivers, and captured the South's prime seaport.

Control of the Mississippi was key to the Union campaign of blockading the South, a strategy made possible because of its superior navy. When the war began, one-quarter of the navy's regular officers had defected to the South. Secretary of the Navy Gideon Welles had just forty-one vessels in commission—half of them officially obsolete. Over the next few years, the Union navy built, bought, or fitted out with guns scores of ships—sailboats, yachts, ferryboats, and tugs. By 1862, Union naval forces had established footholds at key Southern installations, and 427 federal ships rode at anchor off Southern ports to support the blockade. The Union navy controlled or had blocked every major Atlantic Coast harbor, except Charleston and Wilmington, North Carolina.

The Confederacy began the war without a single ship in its navy. Under the innovative leadership of Secretary of the Navy Stephen R. Mallory, the South decided that it could not build a navy as large as the North's. Instead, it would concentrate on a few specialized tasks that would minimize the North's advantage. He authorized the development of mines that were planted at the mouths of harbors and rivers. By the end of the war, mines had sunk or damaged forty-three Union ships. Mallory encouraged the construction of the world's first combat submarine, the C.S.S. *Hunley.* He also built a small number of ironclad ships that could outfight the Union's wooden fleet and punch holes in the blockade. Despite shortages of iron and a lack of rolling mills, the Confederacy developed a surprising number of these vessels. The most famous of the Confederate ironclads was the *Virginia,* originally the United States warship *Merrimack,* which Union forces had intentionally sunk when they abandoned the Norfolk navy yard in Virginia at the beginning of the war.

Raised and refitted, the *Virginia* had its superstructure covered with four-inch iron plate, ten guns, and a cast-iron ram on its bow. On March 8, 1862, just as Mc-Clellan began his campaign on the peninsula, the *Virginia* emerged from Norfolk into Hampton Roads and began attacking the wooden vessels of the Union fleet supporting McClellan's forces. The *Virginia* sank the U.S.S. *Cumberland,* the most powerful conventional ship in the Federal navy. In the words of an observer, the *Cumberland*'s cannon fire "struck and glanced off" the iron hull of the *Virginia,* "having no more effect than peas from a pop-gun." The *Virginia,* firing red-hot shot, then set the U.S.S. *Congress* aflame. A low tide forced the *Virginia* to return to her moorings in Norfolk. The worst day in the eighty-six year history of the U.S. Navy had ended, but the *Virginia* planned to return the next day to continue the destruction.

The next morning, however, the *Virginia* was confronted with a new, more powerful, opponent. After learning of the Confederate ironclad's construction, the North had responded by building its own ironclad—the U.S.S. *Monitor.* Armed with two 11-inch guns, the *Monitor* put herself between the *Virginia* and the wooden ships, and a spectacular duel took place. The two ships hammered away at each other, fighting at such close range that five times the vessels collided as the men inside loaded and fired. The battle between the *Virginia* and the *Monitor* ended in a draw, but the Confederate ship had to return to Norfolk to repair its defective engines. Two days later, when forced to abandon Norfolk, the Southerners ran the *Virginia* ashore and burned the vessel to prevent its capture.

Mallory was equally prompt in purchasing or commissioning conventional vessels for the Confederate navy. These ships were designed not to combat Union warships, but rather to harass the United States merchant marine. The most successful of these vessels was the *Alabama,* built in Liverpool, England. Between 1862 and 1864, the *Alabama* patrolled the Atlantic, Indian, and Pacific Oceans, hunting down and destroying sixty-nine Union merchantmen, valued at more than $6 million. Not until nearly the end of the war could the Union navy corner and sink the raider.

The *Trent* Affair and European Neutrality

While waging a battle for control over the seas, both North and South continued to hope for decisive European intervention in the conflict. The British, however, had little desire to get involved in the conflict. "For God's sake," the British foreign minister exclaimed in May 1861, "let us if possible keep out of it." Both sides in the conflict had overestimated their leverage on European decision makers. The South discovered that cotton was *not* king as European manufacturers turned to other suppliers to meet their demands. Antislavery sentiment ran strong in Europe, but the North had not yet made emancipation a war aim. In the end, national self-interest, and the preservation of a delicate balance of power in Europe, dictated a hands-off approach to the American conflict. On May 14, 1861, the British government issued a proclamation of neutrality, which recognized the Confederacy's legal right to engage in war, but also acknowledged the legality of the Union blockade, ensuring that British ships would not challenge it.

Since the South needed British aid more than the North, the neutrality policy favored the Union. Before the end of the year, however, the North had placed its advantage at risk. In November 1861, Union captain Charles Wilkes learned that President Davis was sending permanent envoys to replace the temporary commissioners he had sent to France and Britain. Envoys John Slidell and James M. Mason traveled on a British ship, the *Trent*. On November 8, Wilkes, commanding the U.S.S. *San Jacinto*, stopped the *Trent* on the high seas with two shots across her bow. Then Wilkes forcibly removed Mason and Slidell and brought them back to New York. The two commissioners were later sent as prisoners to Fort Warren in Boston harbor.

Wilkes's action was a clear violation of international law. When news of the incident reached Britain, hostility toward the Union government flared up. "You may stand for this," Prime Minister Lord (Henry) Palmerston told his cabinet, "but damned if I will!" The British foreign minister drafted a stiff letter demanding the immediate release of the envoys. The angry British government at once sent eleven thousand of its best troops to Canada. Largely a symbolic gesture, it was nevertheless a clear warning. After conferring with cabinet members and senators, the president decided on Christmas Day to release the Southern envoys. "One war at a time," Lincoln said, explaining his reasons for backing down to the British threats.

Antietam

As Union advances ground to a halt by midsummer 1862, the Confederates planned a grand offensive of their own. In the West, two Southern armies under Generals Braxton Bragg and Edmund Kirby-Smith swept through eastern Tennessee in August; by September, they were operating in Kentucky. The early phases of their offensive were brilliantly successful, but the campaign as a whole was fruitless because of a lack of coordination between the two Southern armies and because of Bragg's indecisiveness. After a bloody battle at Perryville (October 8), the Confederate forces withdrew toward Chattanooga.

The more daring part of the Confederate offensive unfolded in the East. While McClellan's army was slowly being withdrawn from the peninsula, Lee turned quickly on the Union forces under General John Pope that had remained in Virginia to guard Washington. Concentrating his entire strength on this segment of the Union army, Lee scored a brilliant victory in the Second Battle of Bull Run (August 29–30). In September, with the enemy "weakened and demoralized," Lee led 40,000 soldiers across the Potomac into Maryland. A decisive victory on Union soil, Lee reasoned, would bolster the chances of European intervention, dishearten Northerners, and erode support for the Lincoln administration. He showed little regard for McClellan. "He is a very able general but a very cautious one," Lee told an officer.

On this occasion, however, McClellan had a clear advantage. A Union soldier discovered an envelope containing Lee's orders to his troops. "I have all the plans of

Confederate Dead at Antietam This photograph of corpses awaiting burial was one of ninety-five taken by Matthew Brady and his assistants of the Antietam battlefield, the bloodiest single day of the war. It was the first time Americans had seen war depicted so realistically. When Brady's photographs went on display in New York in 1862, throngs of people waited in line to view their horror. *(Library of Congress.)*

the rebels and will catch them in their own trap if my men are equal to the emergency," McClellan telegraphed Lincoln. On September 15, Lee's army took up positions along the crest of a three-mile ridge just east of the town of Sharpsburg, Maryland. In front ran a little creek called Antietam. By September 16, McClellan had amassed a force of nearly 95,000 men on the other side. Once again McClellan delayed, giving Lee the chance to reinforce his position.

At dawn on September 17, the Union forces attacked. By the end of the day, the armies had suffered more than 25,000 casualties, with at least 5,000 dead. The next day an eyewitness noted "the most appalling sights upon the battlefield . . . the ground strewn with the bodies of the dead and the dying . . . the cries and groans of the wounded . . . the piles of dead men, in attitudes which show the writhing agony in which they died—faces distorted . . . begrimed and covered with clotted blood, arms and legs torn from the body or the body itself torn asunder."

Still, for all the carnage, the Union commander could finally claim a victory. Lee's invasion had been stopped. Lincoln wanted the Union forces to pursue Lee and destroy his outnumbered army. "God bless you and all with you," Lincoln wired his commander. "Destroy the rebel army if possible." But McClellan did not attack, and on the eighteenth, the Confederate army slipped back south across the Potomac, defeated but intact.

Mobilizing for War, 1861–1863

The need to deploy massive armies, raise large sums of money, and produce weapons and material for the war presented both North and South with an unprecedented challenge. Neither side was prepared for the organizational demands imposed by war. As late as 1830, Washington counted only 352 federal employees.

"We have more of the brute force of persistent obstinacy in Northern blood than the South has," Frederick Law Olmstead wrote, "if only we can get it in play. . . ." To get it "in play," Lincoln concentrated an enormous amount of power in the hands of his central government. Davis too was forced to press for government power, but secessionist states' rights ideology hampered his efforts. Lincoln also had to contend with serious opposition but proved more effective in forging consensus, inspiring the people, and, when necessary, using an iron fist to crush dissent. In the end, Lincoln's experiment in centralization marshaled the North's power and contributed to the reach of government after the war.

Raising an Army

By the end of the war, over 2 million men had served in the Union army and 800,000 in the Confederate army. As the war wore on into its second year, the initial zeal for volunteering abated, and both presidents moved, in 1862, to take a more active role in recruiting troops. On April 16, 1862, the Southern Congress passed the first conscription law in American history. The act made every able-bodied white male between the ages of eighteen and thirty-five subject to military service. But the Southern Congress included numerous exemptions, among them a rule allowing people to purchase substitutes and a so-called 20-Negro law, which exempted from service an owner of twenty or more slaves.

Critics condemned the conscription act as a violation of the same states' rights principles that had been invoked to justify secession in the first place. One of the strongest critics, Governor Joseph E. Brown of Georgia, attempted to block implementation of the act. "The Conscription Act, at one fell swoop, strikes down the sovereignty of the States, tramples upon the constitutional rights and personal liberty of the citizens, and arms the President with imperial power." Other critics complained that conscription was class legislation that benefited the educated and the wealthy at the expense of the poor. Opposition to the draft grew rapidly, especially among nonslaveholders, who increasingly described the Civil War as "a rich man's war and a poor man's fight."

In the North, too, conscription evoked bitter criticism. Congress passed the first Northern draft act in March 1863, declaring all able-bodied males between the ages of twenty and forty-five liable for military service. But it promptly contradicted itself by permitting those who could afford to do so to hire substitutes. It also permitted young men to purchase an outright exemption from military service for $300. The fee was too high for most unskilled workers, who were lucky to earn $300 in an entire year. "[This law] is a rich man's bill," Congressman Thaddeus Stevens charged, "made for him who can raise his $300, and against him who cannot raise that sum."

Opposition to the draft was strongest among Irish and German Catholics, and poor midwestern farmers. In Wisconsin, Kentucky, and Pennsylvania, in Troy, Newark, and Albany, there was outright resistance to the enrolling officers, and in several instances federal troops had to be brought in to quell the uprisings. But none of these outbreaks neared the scope or ferocity of the one that rocked New

York City, with its large Irish population and powerful Democratic machine. The drawing of the first draftees' names triggered a three-day riot (July 13–15, 1863) by a mob of predominantly Irish workingmen. The rampaging mob ransacked draft offices, attacked federal buildings, looted stores, and burned homes of the wealthy. Desperately fearful that a Union victory in the war would bring ex-slaves streaming north to take away their jobs, the Irish workers unleashed most of their fury on blacks. After burning the Colored Orphan Asylum, they hunted down any luckless black found on the streets. The violence ended only when troops were rushed back from the front to put down the riot by force.

Financing the War

As in recruiting their massive armies, both sides faced a formidable and unprecedented task in paying for the war. In antebellum America, the national government had only modest responsibilities and limited sources of revenue. This was especially true of the South, which had few public services, no mechanism for levying internal taxes, and no tradition of paying them. The North raised most of its revenue from tariffs and from the sale of public land. As spending on the war increased, both governments needed to look to new ways of raising money.

In the Union, the federal budget mushroomed from $63 million in 1860 to nearly $1.3 billion in 1865. Treasury Secretary Salmon P. Chase used a number of new methods to meet the repeated government shortfalls. First, he sold bonds to the public, which could be redeemed with interest at a later date. Nearly a million Americans, or roughly one in four Northern families, bought the bonds, which funded about two-thirds of the North's military bills.

Taxes were the second weapon in the Union Treasury arsenal to fight the budget gap. In August 1861, Congress passed a 3 percent tax on incomes of more than $800. The following year, Congress passed the Internal Revenue Act, which levied a 3 percent tax on incomes between $600 and $10,000, and 5 percent on incomes over $10,000. Ultimately these taxes brought in about 21 percent of the total wartime expenditures of the Union government.

Finally, the North resorted to printing paper money to finance the war. Early in 1862, Lincoln signed into law the Legal Tender Act, which authorized $150 million in paper money, called greenbacks. Union officials made the greenbacks legal tender, meaning people could use them to pay their bills. But the greenbacks were fiat money—that is, paper money that was not backed by any explicit promise of redemption in gold or silver specie. The move created a storm of protest. Critics denounced it as unsound and immoral. Most Americans believed that gold or silver could provide the only sound currency; thus paper money nonredeemable in specie was inherently dishonest because it represented no real value. Greenbacks also represented the first time the federal government had moved to create a uniform national currency. The Republicans were able to push through the greenback legislation only because of the pressing need to meet the unprecedented costs of the war.

The Confederacy faced a similar financial situation but with far fewer tools. When the war began, the Rebels owned only 30 percent of the nation's wealth and 21 percent of its banking assets. Southern planters found themselves with little money to invest in the war effort, so bond drives raised only 35 to 40 percent of the cost. In 1861 the Southern Congress passed a small tariff and a modest tax on real and personal property. Most states, charged with collecting the revenues, ignored the legislation. In desperation, the Congress adopted a comprehensive tax measure in April 1863 that included an income tax and occupational and license taxes. The law included a "produce loan," which compelled producers of wheat, corn, oats, potatoes, sugar, cotton, tobacco, and other farm products to pay one-tenth of their crop each year to the government. All told, the Confederacy raised only about 5 percent of its income from taxes.

With taxation and bond sales unable to meet the price of the war, the Confederacy came to rely on what Treasury Secretary Christopher Memminger called "the most dangerous of all methods of raising money"—printing paper money. By the end of the war, the Confederate Congress had printed $1.5 billion in notes. These notes financed about 60 percent of the war effort. As Confederate greenbacks flooded the economy, inflation spiraled out of control.

Presidential Leadership

The North had a clear advantage in the leadership of Abraham Lincoln. A masterful politician, sensitive to public opinion, and skilled at balancing competing interests, Lincoln knew when to stand firm and when to compromise. As an admiring Republican noted, "He always moves in conjunction with propitious circumstances, not waiting to be dragged by the force of events or wasting strength in premature struggles with them." The hallmark of Lincoln leadership was the ability to elicit broad public support for his policies. Throughout the war Lincoln generally remained on good terms with his party's vying factions. The most troublesome group were the so-called Radicals, who pushed for Lincoln to prosecute the war more aggressively and to expand Union goals to include emancipation. On the other side were the conservatives, who hoped for the end of slavery but wanted to see it accomplished by voluntary action. Lincoln identified with the moderates, who opposed slavery but feared the consequences of emancipation. By linking the conflict to the deepest values of Northern society, Lincoln managed these internal party differences and inspired popular support for the war. At the outset, he described the war as a struggle that "presents to the whole family of man, the question, whether a constitutional republic, or a democracy" could survive.

A two-party system in the North, which disciplined and channeled political activity, aided Lincoln's effort to maintain public morale. Republicans disagreed among themselves but were united in their opposition to the Democrats, who, though often divided among themselves, opposed the expansion of federal power while clinging to the goal of reunion through peaceful negotiation and opposing any plan to free the slaves. "The Constitution as it is; the Union as it was," they

Lincoln at Sharpsburg, October 1862 Very much the commander-in-chief, President Lincoln visited Union forces on the battlefield on several occasions and was deeply involved in every aspect of the war's prosecution. Although his only military experience before taking office consisted of brief service in the Black Hawk War, Lincoln's abilities as a military strategist far exceeded that of most of his generals. Here he stands behind Union lines at Antietam with Allan Pinkerton, the detective who provided the Union army with intelligence information, and General John McClernand, who often accompanied the president in his travels. (*Library of Congress.*)

proclaimed. With the Democrats in opposition, the Republican Party became the means for mobilizing war resources, raising taxes, and enacting conscription. The parties drew clear lines and allowed the public to register their support or disapproval at the polls.

Jefferson Davis had a more difficult time establishing a firm grip on the Confederate government. For one thing, Davis had to struggle with a rift at the heart of the Confederate ideology. He was trying to win a war while forging a nation out of states that were ferociously protective of their prerogatives and deeply suspicious of centralized government. The governor of South Carolina, for example, expressed outrage because officers from outside his state occasionally commanded local troops. The governor of Georgia threatened to secede from the Confederacy. "If the Confederacy falls," Jefferson Davis said, "there should be written on its tombstone: Died of a Theory."

Davis, unlike Lincoln, did not have the advantage of a political party to help forge consensus. As a demonstration of unity, the South rejected rival parties, but the show of solidarity actually encouraged disunity. Without parties to impose discipline on congressmen or governors, Davis's government was plagued by rival, and frequently, personal factions. "They sat with closed doors," Vice President Stephens said of the Confederate Congress. "It was well they did, and so kept from the public some of the most disgraceful scenes ever enacted by a legislative body."

Davis's leadership style compounded his institutional problems. Aloof, stubborn, and humorless, he lacked both Lincoln's common touch and his flexibility and proved far less successful at instilling a sense of unified purpose in his people. "If anyone disagrees with Mr. Davis he resents it and ascribes the difference to the perversity of his opponent," his wife remarked. High turnover plagued the administration. Davis had to contend with three secretaries of state and six secretaries of war. Supremely confident in his own military judgment, Davis frequently quarreled with his commanders. One historian has suggested that the differences between Davis and Lincoln were so great, if the North and South had exchanged presidents, the South would have won the war.

Lincoln and Civil Liberties

Lincoln used tact and skill with rivals in his party but was far less tolerant of dissenters who opposed the war. Lincoln dealt with antiwar obstructionists mainly by military arrest and imprisonment without trial. His early actions in Maryland set the tone. Many critics objected to Lincoln's harsh treatment of dissenters and, in particular, to the suspension of *habeas corpus*. The Constitution (Article I, Section 9) ambiguously declares that *habeas corpus* shall not be suspended "unless when in cases of rebellion or invasion the public safety may require it." But the Constitution does not say who has the power to order such a suspension.

Lincoln eventually extended the military's authority to suspend *habeas corpus* to the whole country. Most of those arrested had in fact engaged in activities with military significance, such as attacking Union soldiers, burning bridges, blowing up supply dumps, and spying. But some men were arrested for merely speaking or writing in favor of peace with the Confederacy or against the war policies of the Union government. No one knows precisely how many Americans were seized and held without trial during the war, but the total was well above 13,500.

One of the most notorious wartime violations of civil liberties occurred in Ohio, where a military court convicted Democratic gubernatorial candidate Clement L. Vallandigham "of having expressed sympathy" for the enemy and having uttered "disloyal sentiments and opinions." The Vallandigham case raised a serious constitutional question: Did the military have the right to impose martial law in an area removed from the battlefield where the civil courts were functioning? Lincoln, who learned of Vallandigham's arrest by reading the papers, attempted to minimize the political damage by commuting his sentence from imprisonment to banishment. In another celebrated case, Lambdin P. Milligan, an Indiana civilian, was convicted of treason by a military court in 1864 for aiding Confederate agents trying to foment an uprising in the North. The Supreme Court, in *Ex parte Milligan* (1866), overturned Milligan's conviction, ruling that civilians cannot be tried by military courts in a region where the regularly established courts of the land are functioning. Constitutional historians consider the Milligan decision to be a landmark in the defense of civil liberties, but the ruling came after the war was over.

War and Society, 1861–1865

"This is essentially a people's contest," Lincoln told Congress in 1861. The Civil War was more than a clash of armies; it was a battle between two societies. No groups escaped the consequences of the war. The millions of men who served as soldiers in the Union and Confederate armies paid the greatest price for the conflict. But their loved ones on the home front also suffered. Women assumed the responsibility for looking after the family, and many found opportunities to help in the war effort. The terrible consequences of war took their toll, especially in the South. "Is anything worth it?" asked Mary Chesnut. "This fearful sacrifice, this awful penalty we pay for war?"

The Soldier's War

The average age of a soldier in either army was twenty-five. Law set the minimum age for enlistment at eighteen, but recruiters frequently ignored it. As many as 800,000 underage soldiers signed up to fight. Charles E. King, believed to be the youngest soldier in the war, was twelve when he enlisted in the Pennsylvania Volunteers. He was barely a teenager when he died at Antietam.

Ordinarily a volunteer enlisted in one of the regiments being raised in his community. In the initial enthusiasm for war, whole towns rushed to sign up. The Tenth Michigan Volunteers was comprised entirely of Flint men; their commander was the mayor. When a regiment had filled its ranks, the town invariably held a farewell ceremony. As they went off to fight, thousands of soldiers posed for *cartes de visite*, small photographic portraits mounted on cards.

The Union army was the best equipped in history to that point. The story was far different in the South where Union invasions, a poor transportation system, the Union blockade, and an economy based on growing cotton and tobacco made it difficult to supply troops with essential supplies. Many solders went into battle in ragged uniforms, even without shoes. A Georgia major reported after Manassas that he "carried into the fight over one hundred men who were barefoot, many of whom left bloody foot-prints among the thorns and briars through which they rushed." Food was often scarce. "I came nearer to starving than I ever did before," noted a Rebel soldier in Virginia.

Even a well-supplied soldier's diet was not very appealing. Union troops were issued beans, bacon, pickled beef—called "salt horse" by the men—"desiccated compressed mixed vegetables," and a dried cake that yielded a thin soup when crumbled into boiling water. But the staple was hardtack—square flour-and-water biscuits so hard, some said, they could stop bullets. In the Southern army, men favored something called "sloosh," cornmeal swirled in bacon grease, then wrapped around a ramrod and cooked over the campfire. Coffee was the preferred drink of both armies. Union troops crushed the beans with their rifle butts, drank four pints of brew a day ("strong enough to float an iron wedge"), and when they could not build a fire, were content to chew the grounds. Southerners often made do with substitutes brewed from peanuts, potatoes, or chicory.

Men of the First Texas Brigade Camp life on both sides of the lines included routine chores, such as washing clothes and cooking. These Confederate troops pose in front of their quarters at Camp Quantico, Virginia, in 1861. Their log cabin was an unusual dwelling for soldiers—most lived in tents during both winter and summer months. Conditions on the field were extremely harsh, and more men died of disease and malnutrition than of battle wounds. *(Austin History Center, Austin Public Library #03674.)*

The Civil War coincided with new technology of warfare that made the battlefield a much more dangerous place. The most important single innovation was a new bullet. For centuries infantry had been equipped with smoothbore muskets that required a solider to ram a bullet down the barrel of the rifle after each firing. In the 1850s, an American adoption of a French invention produced the "minie ball," a bullet sufficiently smaller than the rifle barrel to permit relatively rapid loading and reloading. The new bullet expanded into a gun barrel's rifled grooves and spun at great speed from the muzzle. The minie ball from a rifled barrel could kill at half a mile and was accurate at four hundred yards—five times as far as any earlier one-man weapon.

The traditional infantry charge remained a standard tactic, however. The result was mass slaughter. Frontal assaults in compact formations were suicidal in the face of accurate, long-distance rifle fire. It was not uncommon for regiments to experience battlefield casualties in excess of 50 percent in a single engagement. More than 90 percent of battle wounds came by bullets. Faced with the high probability of death, many soldiers wrote out their own "identification tags" before going into battle, pinning scraps of paper to their uniforms with their names, next of kin, and civilian address. If killed, they hoped to be returned to loved ones for burial near home.

Nevertheless, disease proved a greater adversary than enemy soldiers. "There is more dies by sickness than gets killed," complained a recruit from New York in 1861. His assessment was accurate. Two soldiers died of disease for every one killed in battle. The most common killers were scurvy, dysentery, typhoid, diphtheria, and pneumonia. In one year, 995 of every 1,000 men in the Union army contracted diarrhea and dysentery. Their opponents suffered as badly. "All complainants were asked the same question," a Confederate physician remembered. "How are your bowels? If they were open, I administered a plug of opium; if they were shut, I gave a plug of blue mass."

Medical assistance was usually primitive. One commentator described military hospitals in the war's early years as "dirty dens of butchery and horror." The war was fought, the Union surgeon general remembered, "at the end of the medical middle ages." Physicians knew nothing of what caused the diseases they treated, nor did they understand the need for good sanitation and nutrition. Since scientists were only beginning to comprehend the germ theory of disease, wounds frequently led to gangrene or tetanus. Amputation was the usual remedy. "We operated in old, blood-stained and often pus-stained coats," a surgeon recalled. " . . . We used undisinfected instruments from undisinfected plush-lined cases." Federal medical officials responded to most complaints by handing out generous quantities of opium-based painkillers. By some estimates, they distributed 10 million opium pills and 2.8 million ounces of opium-related medicines, resulting in widespread addiction.

Conditions for troops on the battlefield were horrible, but they were worse for captured soldiers. The Civil War was the first war in which a large number of Americans were held in military prisons. Both sides had more prisoners than they could handle. Nearly 50,000 men died in these prisons, including 13,000 Union soldiers at Andersonville in southwestern Georgia. Opened in 1864 and meant to hold a maximum of 10,000 Federal prisoners, Andersonville held 33,000 by August 1864, more than the fifth-largest city in the Confederacy. In that month, 3,000 prisoners died; on one day, they died at a rate of a man every eleven minutes. At Belle Isle, 90 percent of the survivors weighed less than one hundred pounds. "Can those be men?" asked the poet Walt Whitman.

The imposition of the draft, the realization after Shiloh that the battlefield was a slaughterhouse, wretched provisions, and spreading economic misery on the home front, especially in the South, produced widespread desertions. Union General Joseph Hooker reported that one in four soldiers under his command were absent. The problem was more severe for the South. At Antietam, Lee estimated that one-third to one-half of his soldiers were "straggling"—that is, absent without leave. At the start of 1863, unauthorized absences averaged 30 percent in the Southern armies.

Economic Consequences of the War

Overall, the war produced widespread prosperity in the North. Nourished by government contracts, the profits of industry boomed. Chicago, the country's railroad and livestock capital, experienced unprecedented growth in population, construction, banking, and manufacturing. Coal mining and iron production boomed in

Pennsylvania. Dismal crop harvests in Europe opened up new markets for Northern agriculture, which thrived during the war. Numerous Americans who would take the lead in reshaping the nation's postwar economy created or consolidated their fortunes during the Civil War, among them Andrew Carnegie, John D. Rockefeller, Jay Gould, J. P. Morgan, and Philip Armour. These and other future "captains of industry" managed to escape military service, some by hiring substitutes.

At the same time, Congress adopted policies that promoted further economic expansion. With clear majorities in both Houses, the Republicans in Congress passed the Pacific Railroad Act of 1862, which provided for the development of a transcontinental railroad. The Homestead Act, passed in 1862, granted 160 acres of public land to settlers after five years of residence on the land. By 1865, twenty thousand homesteaders occupied new land in the West under the act. In 1862, Republicans passed the Morrill Land Grant Act to make higher education available to common people. By giving proceeds from the sale of public lands to the states, the act spurred the growth of large state universities, mainly in the Midwest and West.

Perhaps the federal government's most significant long-term contribution to business development was the creation of a national currency and a national banking system. Before the Civil War, private banks (chartered by the states) issued their own banknotes, which were used in most economic transactions; the federal government paid all of its expenses in gold or silver. In 1863, Congress passed the National Bank Act, providing for the chartering of federal banks. This legislation, amended and strengthened in 1864, meant, among other things, that a uniform national currency began to replace the dozens of issues by local banks.

Not all groups in the North benefited from the war. As greenbacks flooded the economy and as consumer goods fell into short supply, prices climbed rapidly— about 20 percent faster than wages. Skilled workers, whose labor was in high demand, might be able to keep up. But unskilled workers were hit hard by inflation. "We are unable to sustain life for the prices offered by contractors, who fatten on their contracts by grinding immense profits out of the labor of their operatives," wrote a group of Cincinnati seamstresses to President Lincoln in 1864.

Inflation, combined with scarcity, crippled the Southern economy and produced widespread suffering. In 1862 prices increased by 300 percent while wages for skilled and unskilled workers grew by only 55 percent. In January 1864, it took twenty-seven Confederate dollars to buy what one dollar had bought in April 1861—an inflation rate of 2,600 percent in less than three years! The average family food bill rose from $6.65 per month before Fort Sumter to $68 by mid-1863. Southern urban workers could not keep up with this kind of inflation. In April 1863, a bread riot broke out in Richmond; over a thousand women, infuriated by soaring prices, stormed through downtown shops, smashing windows and gathering up armfuls of food and clothing. "Bread! Bread!" they shouted. "Our children are starving while the rich roll in wealth." Similar incidents took place in Augusta, Columbus, Milledgeville, Mobile, and a half-dozen other towns. The riots were touched off by working-class housewives protesting not so much food shortages as the exorbitant price of what was available. They simply could not afford to feed their families when industrial wages came nowhere near meeting the tenfold increase in the price of food during the first two years of the war.

State governments experimented with novel ways to address the suffering. As early as the fall of 1861, state governments passed laws preventing the collection of soldiers' debts and providing some financial assistance to the indigent through special county taxes. These measures proved insufficient, and by 1863, the states were distributing food to the poor and spending millions on direct relief. Toward the end of the war, 20 to 40 percent of Confederate white civilians were on some form of public relief. Over half of Georgia's budget in 1864 was devoted to relief, and the funds for this aid to soldiers' families came from stiff progressive taxes that shifted the fiscal burden of the war onto the rich. Ironically, in the battle for individual liberty, many Southern governors presided over a dramatic centralization of the power to collect and distribute revenues in their states.

Women and the War

The writer Louisa May Alcott summarized the feeling of most women on both sides of the conflict when she declared, "As I can't fight, I will content myself with working for those who can." Though officially barred from combat, as many as four hundred women donned men's clothing and volunteered for the armies disguised as men.

Women Volunteer Units The majority of Southern white men served in the Confederate army during the war, leaving their wives and daughters to assume their roles at home. Southern women ran plantations, managed slaves, and even took up arms to defend themselves against any possible danger, such as a slave uprising or the encroaching Union army. The women in this photograph have banded together in a women's defense unit. *(National Archives.)*

Most, however, found other ways to contribute to the war effort. Hundreds of thousands of women took part in organizations that gathered medical and other supplies for soldiers. The largest of these agencies, the U.S. Sanitary Commission, coordinated relief activities throughout the North, shipping large quantities of clothing, food, and medical supplies to troops on the front lines.

Along with aiding the war effort, women filled jobs on the home front left vacant by men gone to war. More than 100,000 jobs opened up during the war. For the first time, the federal government hired women as clerks and copyists. By 1864, women held 33 percent of all manufacturing jobs, up nearly 10 percent since the start of the war. In most cases, companies paid women less than the men they replaced, and they were forced out of their positions once the war ended.

Not all the advances were temporary, however. In some areas, such as the nursing profession, women made permanent inroads. Most army doctors resisted having women in the wards, claiming they were too weak and refined. In addition, they charged that women were incapable of dealing with the bodies of strange men. Women, who stressed their traditional roles as caretakers, won the debate. In 1862 the Confederate Congress passed a law allowing civilian nurses to work in army hospitals, "giving preference in all cases to females where their services may best subserve the purpose." That same year the Union issued an order requiring at least one-third of army nurses to be women. Union nurses were more organized than their Confederate counterparts, thanks to the pioneering work of Dorothea Dix, a fifty-nine-year-old crusader for the mentally ill who assumed the title of Superintendent of Female Nurses in 1861. Referred to as "Dragon Dix" by her fellow nurses because of her autocratic style, Dix barred any applicant she thought interested only in romantic ventures. "All nurses are required to be very plain-looking women. Their dresses must be brown or black, with no bows, no curls, no jewelry and no hoop skirts."

 ## The Decisive Year, 1863

In 1863 a number of decisive moves on the battlefield broke the military stalemate. Lincoln, realizing that bold initiatives were needed to break the logjam, began the year by issuing the Emancipation Proclamation, which redefined the purpose of the war and infused the Union cause with moral purpose. The war, initiated over the issue of limiting the spread of slavery, had been transformed into a moral crusade to free the slaves. The emancipation experiment assigned new power and a new duty to the national government. "The character of the war will be changed," Lincoln observed. "It will be one of subjugation." Later that summer, Union victories at Gettysburg, Vicksburg, and Chattanooga turned the tide of the war.

Emancipation Transforms the War

As the fear of Border State secession receded and Union manpower needs increased, pressure mounted on Lincoln to free the slaves. The very success of Confederate resistance in what Northerners had assumed would be a short, victorious war was converting more and more whites to what had been the abolitionist position from the beginning of the conflict. Containing slavery would never be enough. Northern public opinion was slowly but inexorably turning toward emancipation. Most influential in changing Lincoln's mind was his grim recognition that after eighteen months of combat, the war could not be ended by traditional means. Yet he wanted a victory that would build support at home and abroad for a bold step. Antietam gave him the opportunity for which he had been waiting. On September 22—five days after the battle—the president issued his Emancipation Proclamation, saying it would take effect in one hundred days. On January 1, 1863, Lincoln signed the proclamation. "If my name ever goes into history," he said, "it was for this act."

As of this day, the document declared, the 3 million slaves in the rebellious states "shall be then, henceforth forever free." Lincoln was careful to limit the immediate impact of the proclamation to those slaves living in the rebellious states, or in parts thereof not under Union control. Excluded from the provisions were slaves living in the Border States that remained in the Union—Delaware, Kentucky, Maryland, and Missouri—as well as those living in Union-controlled areas of Tennessee, Louisiana, and Virginia. "The Government liberates the enemy's slaves as it would the enemy's cattle," blustered the *London Spectator,* "simply to weaken them in the coming conflict. . . . The principle asserted is not that a human being cannot justly own another, but that he cannot own him unless he is loyal to the United States."

Despite its limitations, the proclamation set off wild rejoicing among white and black abolitionists. For the first time, the government had committed itself to freeing slaves. Firing the Northern effort with moral purpose, emancipation transformed a war of armies into a conflict over beliefs over what America stood for (see Competing Voices, page 604). "We shout for joy," wrote Frederick Douglass, "that we live to record this righteous decree." In Washington, D.C., a crowd of blacks gathered in front of the White House to cheer the president, who appeared at the window. To Charlotte Forten, a young black woman living in South Carolina, "it all seemed . . . like a brilliant dream." There was even jubilation among the slaves in loyal Border States who were exempted from the proclamation's provisions.

The Emancipation Proclamation officially authorized the enrollment of black troops in the Union army, but in that, it simply recognized changes that were already taking place on the front lines. In 1862 Congress had passed the Militia Act, which called for enrolling blacks in "any military or naval service for which they may be found competent." In areas they controlled, Union forces used blacks labor for physically demanding tasks: chopping wood, hauling supplies, and building fortifications. Congress sanctioned this work by passing confiscation acts declaring that the slaves of any person who supported the rebellion would be free if they fell into Union hands.

Many blacks welcomed the chance to fight for their freedom and for that of their families. As Solomon Bradley of South Carolina put it, "In Such times I used to pray the Lord for this opportunity to be released from bondage and to fight for

African-American Union Soldier Almost 200,000 African-Americans fought for the Union. These soldiers served in racially segregated units under white officers and were assigned the most menial tasks. Nonetheless, they fought bravely when given the chance, helping to elevate the pride of other African-Americans and dispel myths of their inferiority. Their presence also enraged Confederates, who threatened to execute any captured black soldier in Union uniform. *(Chicago Historical Society.)*

my liberty, and I could not feel right so long as I was not in the regiment." Constituting less than 1 percent of the North's population, blacks would make up nearly one-tenth of the Northern army by the end of the war. Although large numbers of free Northern blacks joined the Union army, more than 80 percent of black soldiers had been recruited in the slave states.

Still, opportunities were limited for African-Americans in the Union army. Union generals used black troops primarily for garrison and rearguard duty, freeing whites for combat service. In many cases, they were stationed in areas where white troops had been decimated by yellow fever and malaria. The combination of poor condition and inferior medical treatment produced a black mortality rate that was 40 percent higher than that of white Union soldiers. Black troops earned $10 a month whereas their white counterparts received $13 plus a clothing allowance of $3.50. If captured by Confederates, blacks ran the risk of being executed under Southern laws for inciting slave insurrections. Realizing that their wartime service gave them a powerful claim to full equality and citizenship at the end of the war, African-Americans endured these indignities and served with distinction.

Gettysburg

The outcome at Antietam gave Lincoln the Northern victory he needed to issue the Emancipation Proclamation and begin the active enlistment of black soldiers. It did not, however, mark an overall change in the North's fortunes on the battlefield. Convinced by Antietam that McClellan was not bold enough to destroy Lee's army, Lincoln replaced him with General Ambrose Burnside. Lee, having regrouped in

Virginia, dug his troops in on the hills overlooking Fredericksburg. In December 1862, Burnside sent his superior force of 120,000 men on a reckless frontal assault of Lee's well-fortified position. A Union officer said the troops seemed to "melt . . . like snow coming down on warm ground." The Rebels beat back fourteen assaults, and over 9,000 Union soldiers died before Burnside decided the hills could not be taken. "It can hardly be in human nature for men to show more valor," a reporter wrote, "or generals to manifest less judgment."

The defeat at Fredericksburg shook Washington. "If there is a worse place than Hell," Lincoln remarked, "I am in it." In March 1863, amid bitter recrimination among congressional Republicans about the faltering war effort, Lincoln replaced Burnside with General Joseph Hooker, a Massachusetts soldier who had demonstrated his tenacious courage on the peninsula and at Antietam. On April 27, Hooker began moving toward Chancellorsville, ten miles west of Fredericksburg. Lee was again outnumbered nearly 2 to 1, but again he scored a decisive victory. On May 6, Hooker retreated, having lost 17,000 men. Chancellorsville was another terrible blow to Northern morale. "My God! My God!" Lincoln cried hearing the news. "What will the country say?" He replaced Hooker with General George G. Meade in late June.

Lee's victories set the stage for another Confederate thrust north, this time reaching into Pennsylvania. Meade shadowed Lee's movements, keeping a defensive wall between the Confederate troops and populated Union cities such as Washington, Baltimore, and Philadelphia. By the morning of July 2, 1863, 150,000 Union and Confederate troops had converged on the tiny town of Gettysburg, Pennsylvania. After chaotic initial clashes, the Southerners occupied a line west along Seminary Ridge. The Union men waited along Cemetery Ridge—a slightly more elevated crest that ran south toward two hills, Big and Little Round Top. In its shape, the Union line resembled the mirror image of a question mark.

For the next two days, the Confederate army assaulted Union positions on a series of hills mostly south of Gettysburg. On July 3, Lee made his last desperate bid for victory by sending three divisions of 15,000 infantrymen, under the leadership of Major General George E. Pickett, across open ground to break the center of the Union line. A Union soldier saw "an overwhelming resistless tide of an ocean of armed men sweeping upon us! . . . on they move, as with one soul, in perfect order. . . ." The battle noise was "strange and terrible, a sound that came from thousands of human throats . . . like a vast mournful roar." Fearsome though the charge was, Union artillery struck with deadly accuracy while a hail of gunfire from the Federal batteries decimated the Confederate troops (see map).

Pickett's charge had failed, and more than 25,000 Confederate soldiers, nearly one-third of Lee's army, had been wounded or had died at Gettysburg, the bloodiest battle of the war. Gettysburg and nearby towns were flooded with the wounded. A Quaker nurse summarized the carnage: "There are no words in the English language to express the sufferings I witnessed today."

The South could not afford such losses. Gettysburg was Lee's last offensive campaign. During a pouring rain on the evening of July 4, the shattered remnant of the Confederate army began its last retreat to the Potomac. Despite Lincoln's pleas to

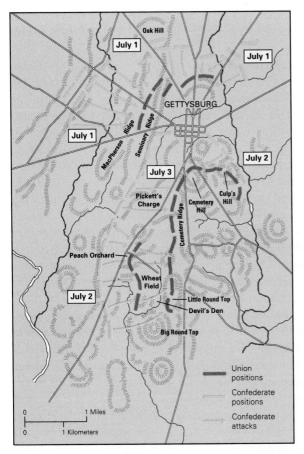

The Battle of Gettysburg

Attempting to relieve pressure on Vicksburg, Lee decided to create a diversion by moving his troops northward through Maryland and into southern Pennsylvania. On June 30, a Confederate scavenging party entered the city of Gettysburg looking for shoes and instead found several Union calvary units. The main forces on both sides quickly converged on the site and on July 1, Confederates attacked the Union position at Seminary Ridge and forced them to pull back south of town to a more defendable position at Cemetery Ridge. For the next two days, Lee was on the offensive, trying to pry the Union army from the ridge—first trying from the flanks (Battle of Little Round Top), and then from the center (Pickett's Charge). Lee's casualties in the three days of battle forced him to retreat south back into Virginia.

follow up victory with an all-out attack that might finish off Lee's army, Meade's forces were too exhausted to pursue the retreating Rebels.

Vicksburg and Chattanooga

On the same day, General John C. Pemberton surrendered the great stronghold of Vicksburg on the Mississippi River to Grant. In May, Grant had moved down the river and crossed into Mississippi to get at Vicksburg from the rear in one of the riskiest military maneuvers of the war. Plunging into enemy territory without any secure base of supplies, Grant surprised the Confederates and laid siege to the city. With the inhabitants on the brink of starvation, Pemberton surrendered. The capture of Vicksburg represented the North's most important strategic victory of the war, justifying Grant's later assertion that "the fate of the Confederacy was sealed when Vicksburg fell." Along with the city, Pemberton gave up 170 cannon, 50,000 small arms, and 30,000 men. Four days later, Port Hudson, Louisiana, fell to a Union expedition led by General Nathaniel P. Banks. Showing boldness and tenacity, Grant had realized one of the key war aims of the Union—control of the

Mississippi. After Grant's triumph at Vicksburg, Lincoln gave him command of all Union armies in the West. "Grant is my man," the president declared, "and I am his the rest of the war."

The year ended on yet another dismal note for the Confederacy with the defeat of Rebel forces poised to retake Chattanooga, Tennessee, an important railroad junction linking the eastern and western parts of the Confederacy. After capturing the city in September, Union forces under General William Rosecrans had pursued the retreating Confederate troops into Georgia. Under General Braxton Bragg, bolstered by reinforcements, the Confederates dug in along the Chickamauga River. On September 19, the two armies clashed in the bloodiest two-day battle of the war—one of the few in which the Confederate troops had a numerical advantage. Casualties totaled over 34,000, and 18,000 were Confederates. Although Bragg won, he had lost 30 percent of the troops he threw into the battle.

The battered Union forces retreated back to Chattanooga. Confederate troops surrounded the city, seizing the hills and cutting off rail and water supply routes. Rosecrans's army was in danger of being starved out, and the Confederates were poised for a much needed victory when, in November, Grant arrived with reinforcements to take charge of the Union forces. On November 24, the Union troops fought their way out of the city, pushing the Confederates back into Georgia.

In a decisive year of battles, the Confederates had surrendered an entire army at Vicksburg, had nearly been bled white at Gettysburg, and had been humiliated at Chattanooga. News of the Confederate defeats dashed lingering hopes of European intervention. "It is now conceded that all idea of intervention is at an end," Henry Adams wrote from London. The South also suffered enormous losses in manpower and morale. In the last half of the year, absentee rates rose from 35 to 40 percent, as families pleaded for their loved ones to return home. "The women write to their husbands to leave the army and come home," Julia Gwyn of North Carolina noted in 1863, "and that's the reason that so many of them are deserting." The end of the war was in sight.

A New Experiment in Warfare, 1864–1865

In 1864, the last full year of the war, Lincoln finally found in Ulysses S. Grant a general who would take advantage of the Union's superior resources. "That man," observed a Confederate officer, "will fight us every day and every hour until the end of this war." Lincoln had transformed the purpose of the war with the Emancipation Proclamation, now it was Grant's turn to mold a new, more aggressive military strategy to achieve victory. While Grant attacked Lee's army in the East, General Sherman invaded Georgia from the West. Amid the changing military fortunes, Lincoln faced an uncertain election in 1864, while Lee and his forces fought on, clinging to life.

Waging Total War

In March 1864, Lincoln appointed Grant to the specially created rank of lieutenant general, last held by George Washington. In that post, Grant held command of all

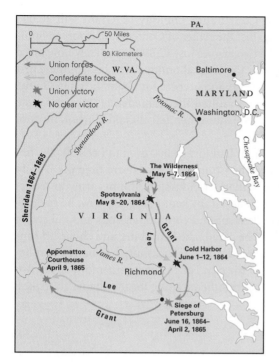

Grant's Campaign in Virginia, 1864–1865 Ulysses S. Grant became general-in-chief of the Union army in March 1864 and by May had begun his campaign in Virginia. Unlike earlier Union generals, Grant did not retreat despite suffering heavy casualties at the Battle of the Wilderness and Cold Harbor. Instead, Grant continued to move his men to the left, advancing slowly southward as Lee, suffering from his own growing casualties and running out of replacements, was forced to follow. Meanwhile, Philip Sheridan's cavalry descended on the Shenandoah Valley, cutting Lee off from his main source of food. Reaching the end of his supplies and manpower, Lee retreated from Petersburg in April 1865 with Grant in hot pursuit. With his escape route blocked by Sheridan, Lee was forced to surrender at Appomattox Courthouse.

the armies of the United States, 533,000 armed men. Grant's all-out and largely successful approach to battle had won the confidence of a president who had been dissatisfied with his more cautious generals. "I wish to express my entire satisfaction with what you have done up to this time," Lincoln said. "The particulars of your plans I neither know nor seek to know."

Grant's strategy was to wage total war. He planned a coordinated movement of federal armies in the East and West so as to apply simultaneous pressure all along the Confederate line. By fighting a coordinated war on all fronts Grant hoped to exploit the North's advantage in numbers and resources. He recognized that victory would result not from winning individual battles but from destroying the resources and morale of the Confederacy. Ultimately, the capacity of Confederate armies to wage war depended on the economic and psychological support they received from the civilian population. To win its war of conquest, the Union under Grant would target civilians as well as Confederate armies. In the East, Grant planned to keep sustained pressure on Lee's army while ordering William T. Sherman to attack the Rebel army in Georgia (see map).

On the night of May 3, 1864, Grant's army crossed the Rapidan River in northern Virginia and began to fight its way through the wilderness west of Fredericksburg. In the first two days of battle, Grant lost 17,000 men. That night in his tent, Grant wept. The next morning, he ordered his men to attack again. "Whatever happens," Grant assured Lincoln, "we will not retreat." Instead, he attempted to move southward around Lee's army, rather than directly toward Richmond. Lee positioned his army to stop him at Spotsylvania Courthouse. On May 12, Grant sent 20,000 men under Winfield Scott Hancock against the center of Confederate troops at Spotsylvania. The Confederates held as the two armies lost 12,000 men. They now raced for a crossroads called Cold Harbor, near the Chickahominy River. Lee got there first and ordered his men to entrench themselves and prepare for Grant's assault. On the morning of June 3, 60,000 Union men assaulted the Confederate lines and were again repulsed. Between 5,600 and 7,000 Union men fell at Cold Harbor, most of them in the first eight minutes.

In thirty days of battle with Lee, Grant had lost 55,000 men to Lee's 30,000, but Grant knew that such losses weakened the Confederacy far more than the Union. Unlike his predecessors, this Union commander did not permit his army to retreat when repulsed, or to rest when victorious. Grant kept going. By now, he had decided to bypass Richmond and target Petersburg, a communications and rail center just south of the Confederate capital. If he could take Petersburg and choke off supplies, Richmond would be forced to surrender, just as Vicksburg had been a year before. In June, Grant dug in for a siege of the city. For the next nine months, the two armies alternately glared at and fought each other, waiting for the chance to strike a decisive blow.

The Election of 1864

Four days after the slaughter at Cold Harbor, Republicans gathered to renominate President Lincoln. "I am going to be beaten," Lincoln said, "and unless some great change takes place, badly beaten." He had reason to feel pessimistic about his chances. Grant was stalled at Petersburg. Sherman was halted near Atlanta. Northern opinion was shocked by the heavy casualties reported from the battlefields. History seemed to be conspiring against Lincoln as well. No other nation had ever held an election during a civil war. Neither party had renominated an incumbent for president since 1840. The last president to win a second term was Andrew Jackson, over three decades earlier.

The Republicans formed a coalition with Democrats supporting the war. The name "Union Party" was substituted for "Republican." To help win the votes of Democrats, party leaders chose the Tennessee war-Democrat, Andrew Johnson, former senator and military governor of his home state, to run for the vice presidency. The Republican platform committed the party to the indivisibility of the Union, the defeat of the rebellion, the avoidance of any compromise with the Confederacy, and the "utter and complete extirpation of slavery" through a constitutional amendment.

Republicans were hardly inspired by Lincoln, and in May a small band of Radical Republicans broke with the president. "Mr. Lincoln is already beaten," cried Horace Greeley, Republican editor of the *New York Tribune*. "He cannot be elected. And we must have another ticket to save *us* from utter overthrow." The Radicals blamed Lincoln for the reverses on the battlefield and feared that he favored a "soft" policy on the South after the war. They selected John C. Frémont, the 1856 Republican nominee, to run for president on a platform that endorsed "the one-term policy for the Presidency." They chose the name Radical Democracy for their party.

The Democratic Party met in Chicago in August, proclaimed the war a failure, demanded an immediate cessation of hostilities, and called for the restoration of the Union by means of a negotiated peace. They nominated the former head of the Army of the Potomac, General George McClellan. Many in the South rejoiced at McClellan's nomination—"the first ray of real light," said Vice President Stephens, "since the war began."

Democrats, early in the campaign at least, hoped to capitalize on the war weariness that was sweeping across the North. They made much of Lincoln's arbitrary use of executive power and the infringement of civil liberties. They objected to the unfairness of the draft. They accused the Republican Congress of rewarding northeastern businessmen at the expense of midwestern farmers by enacting protective tariffs, handing out railroad subsidies, and creating a national banking system. The Democrats endlessly harped on the antiblack theme, protesting that the Lincoln administration had changed the war for union into a war for emancipation. If Lincoln was reelected, they charged, Republicans were planning to amalgamate the black and white races. The word *miscegenation* (race mixing) made its first appearance in an 1864 campaign document.

By the fall, however, the military situation in Georgia had improved, and Republicans united behind Lincoln. On election day, the president scored a decisive victory. Lincoln was reelected in November by a vote of 212 to 21 in the electoral college, carrying all states except New Jersey, Delaware, and Kentucky. His popular vote was less sweeping 2,206,938 (55 percent) to 1,803,787 (45 percent)—400,000 more than McClellan's in a total of 4 million votes cast.

Sherman's March to the Sea

Lincoln's success in the election owed much to Sherman's success in Georgia. While Grant dug in at Petersburg, Sherman was on the move. The first and most important objective was to seize Atlanta, the "Gate City of the South" and the second-most-important manufacturing center in the Confederacy. On September 1, the Confederates evacuated Atlanta. Sherman's troops marched into the city the next day. "Atlanta is gone," wrote Mary Chesnut.

After burning Atlanta, Sherman led his army into the heart of Georgia. On November 16, 1864, he set out with his 62,000 men marching in two vast columns. Their supply train stretched twenty-five miles. A slave watched part of this mighty host stream past and wondered if anybody was left in the north.

Confederate General John Bell Hood promised to fight Sherman to the death. "Better to die a thousand deaths than submit to live under you . . . and your negro allies," he said. The Confederate general's left arm had been crippled at Gettysburg and only a stump remained of his right leg, amputated at Chickamauga. After evacuating Atlanta, Hood, strapped in the saddle, set off to retake Tennessee and his native

Kentucky, hoping Sherman would leave Georgia to chase him. Sherman dispatched a force to follow Hood, but remained with the bulk of his army in Georgia. After a valiant but futile attempt to defeat the Union forces at Franklin, Tennessee, on November 30, Hood's army disintegrated in the battle of Nashville on December 5.

Sherman, meanwhile, swept across Georgia toward Savannah on the coast. He had planned the march with grim determination to make Georgia "an example to rebels": his troops burned public buildings, depots, and machine shops; destroyed stores of cotton; and confiscated ten thousand horses and mules. Grant had ordered Union troops to strip the valley so thoroughly that "crows flying over it for the balance of the season will have to carry their provender." In short, he shattered the military potential of the area and left its civilians struggling to supply their daily needs. Sherman, on Christmas Day, sent a telegram to Lincoln that announced, "as a Christmas gift, the city of Savannah, with 150 heavy guns, plenty of ammunition and about 25,000 bales of cotton." The president was thrilled. "Grant has the bear by the hind leg," he quipped, "while Sherman takes off its hide."

The Collapse of the Confederacy

By early 1865, the Confederacy was desperate. Desertions became even more frequent, food increasingly scarce. A single stick of firewood cost $5 in Richmond. The price of a barrel of flour had risen to $425. "The surgeons and matrons," wrote a hospitalized Confederate soldier, "ate rats and said they were as good as squirrels, but, having seen the rats in the morgue running over the bodies of the dead soldiers, I had no relish for them."

Having seized Savannah, Sherman turned north into South Carolina on January 17. His army laid waste to much of the state where the rebellion began and reached its capital, Columbia, in less than a month. Like Atlanta, Columbia went up in flames. In April Sherman's army, faced by Confederates under the command of Joseph E. Johnston, stood outside the North Carolina capital of Raleigh.

As Union armies moved across the Confederate heartland, President Davis announced his support for proposals calling for the impressment of slaves for service with the army. In February 1865, the scheme received the backing of General Lee, who wrote that employing blacks as soldiers was "not only expedient but necessary" and announced plainly that slaves who served should be given their freedom. The next month, by a very close vote, the Confederate Congress passed an act calling for 300,000 more soldiers, irrespective of color. Promptly the recruiting of black troops began, and some black companies were raised in Richmond and other towns. By this time, however, the end was near, and none of the black Confederate soldiers ever saw military service.

As Sherman continued to advance and Lee remained unable to break the siege at Petersburg, leaders in Richmond increasingly realized that further resistance was useless. A delegation headed by Vice President Stephens met Lincoln onboard a ship at Hampton Roads, Virginia, on February 3, 1865, to discuss terms of surrender. Lincoln insisted on two points: the restoration of the Union and the abolition

Lee After Appomattox
After opposing secession, General Robert E. Lee accepted a commission in the Confederate army and commanded the Army of Northern Virginia for most of the war. Photographer Matthew Brady took this picture of Lee (center), his son Major General G. W. C. Lee (left), and his aide Colonel Walter Taylor (right) eight days after Lee's surrender to General Grant. The forlorn expression on the general's face vividly demonstrates the agony of defeat. *(Library of Congress.)*

of slavery. The Southerners rejected these terms as "unconditional submission to the mercy of conquerors," and the conference broke up. "I can have no common country with the Yankees," declared Davis. Lee also advised continuation of the war, hoping to fight on long enough to win more favorable terms.

The war's last awful battle took place in Virginia. By the spring of 1865, the lines at Petersburg ran for 55 miles. The efficient Union army kept its men fed, supplied, and reinforced. The Confederate army—ill fed, ill clothed, and hopelessly outnumbered—steadily melted away as desertions increased. Lee knew he could no longer defend Richmond. In one of the war's most dramatic moments, seasoned African-American troops under Grant's command led the final assault on the city; black soldiers were among the first Union troops to enter the capital of the Confederacy. They marched in carrying the Stars and Stripes and singing an anthem to John Brown, much to the amazement of Richmond's citizenry, black and white.

Now nearly surrounded, Lee left his trenches at Petersburg on April 2, 1865. He led his army westward in a desperate quest for food and to join forces with Johnston, still fighting Sherman in North Carolina. Grant's huge force eagerly followed and soon blocked Lee's escape route. On April 7, Grant wrote to Lee, "General, the result of the last week must convince you of the hopelessness of further resistance." Seeing no way to save his exhausted and hungry army, Lee consented to discuss Grant's terms of surrender.

The two great generals met in a farmhouse at Appomattox Courthouse on April 9. After a few minutes of friendly conversation, during which they recalled their comradeship in the Mexican War, Grant wrote out the terms of surrender. They were extraordinarily generous. Officers and men could go home without fear of prosecution for treason, and soldiers who owned horses were able to keep them. Lee immediately signed the terms. The agreement served as a model for the surrender of other Confederate armies. Johnston surrendered his army of 37,000 men to Sherman near Durham, North Carolina, on April 26; Generals Richard Taylor in Alabama and Edmund Kirby-Smith in Arkansas surrendered their armies to the Union commanders in the Southwest. All told, some 174,000 Confederate troops laid down their arms. Jefferson Davis was captured on May 10 at Irwinsville, Georgia, and imprisoned for two years. After his release, he lived quietly in the South until his death on December 6, 1889.

CONCLUSION

Both sides approached the war confident of victory. The North planned to use its superior economic resources and powerful navy to strangle the South. Hoping for a decisive victory, Lincoln ordered an assault on Confederate forces in Virginia. The South, confident of its military skill and convinced the North would quickly tire of the conflict, assumed a defensive military posture, forcing the North to secure and control large areas of land. The South also hoped for foreign intervention, believing that a cotton embargo would force the British to support its cause. Leaders on both sides of the conflict expected a short, largely bloodless conflict. The Union defeat at the First Battle of Bull Run shattered that illusion, and the Battle of Shiloh foretold the incredible slaughter that would follow.

The war placed extraordinary demands on both the Union and Confederate governments, leading both to experiment with methods to raise armies and finance the war. Both sides resorted to conscription to recruit soldiers. The North, which had more experience with national government, developed a number of methods to pay for the effort, including higher taxes, bond sales, and the printing of paper money. The Confederacy depended largely on printing paper money, which in turn, produced rampant inflation. On numerous issues related to the war effort, Southern leaders were torn between their ideological commitment to states' rights and their practical need to develop a coordinated national strategy.

The war exacted a terrible toll on the nation. Nearly 3 million men served in the Union and Confederate armies. For many soldiers, new technology and old battlefield strategies were a lethal combination. A new bullet made rifles more accurate from long ranges, but military tactics called for frontal assaults on fortified positions. If not felled by enemy bullets, soldiers often fell victim to poor diet and primitive medical care. Soldiers on the front lines were not the only ones to suffer. In the South, inflation and scarcity produced widespread suffering.

It was a different story in the North, where the war produced a boom in many industries, though most unskilled workers found their wages failed to keep up with inflation. The war also provided new opportunities for women, who filled temporary jobs in wartime industry and created permanent inroads in the nursing profession. At the same time, Republicans used their large majorities in Congress to dramatically increase federal power, creating a national currency and a national banking system.

After eighteen months of indecisive battles, Lincoln altered both the goals and strategy of the war by issuing the Emancipation Proclamation. What began as a conflict over the spread of slavery was now transformed into a war to free the slaves. "This government cannot much longer play a game in which it stakes all, and its enemies stake nothing," Lincoln observed. The president turned to General Ulysses S. Grant to execute the new strategy of "total war" that would defeat and devastate the South. With Lee's surrender at Appomattox, the American experiment entered a new period in a new form.

SUGGESTED READINGS

The best brief treatments of the Civil War can be found in Brooks Simpson, *America's Civil War* (1996); William L. Barney, *Battleground for the Union: The Era of Civil War and Reconstruction, 1848–1877* (1990); and Allen C. Guelzo, *The Crisis of the American Republic: A History of the Civil War and Reconstruction Era* (1995). Geoffrey C. Ward's *The Civil War: An Illustrated History* provides a lucid and colorful account of the war and its consequences. The most comprehensive general treatment of the war is Allan Nevins's four-volume study *The War for the Union* (1959–1971). Other good overviews are two works by James McPherson, *Battle Cry of Freedom: The Civil War Era* (1988) and *Ordeal by Fire: The Civil War and Reconstruction* (1982).

The most thorough military history from the Confederate viewpoint is Shelby Foote's three-volume work *The Civil War: A Narrative* (1958–1974). For a Northern perspective, *How the North Won: A Military History of the Civil War* (1983) by Herman Hattaway and Archer Jones treats all aspects of the Northern war effort. Bruce Catton's three-volume *The Centennial History of the Civil War* (1961–1965) provides a balanced treatment. *Civil War Command and Strategy: The Process of Victory and Defeat* (1992) by Archer Jones is a good overview of Civil War tactics and their place in the larger history of warfare. Charles Royster's *The Destructive War: William Tecumseh Sherman, Stonewall Jackson and the Americans* (1991) explores the relationship between the vicious military tactics used in the war and the American psyche. Howard P. Nash's *A Naval History of the Civil War* (1972) is a good overview of the war on the seas.

Each battle/campaign has its own studies. A few of the best are Joseph Glatthaar, *The March to the Sea and Beyond: Sherman's Troops in the Savannah and Carolinas Campaign* (1985); Stephen W. Sears, *Landscape Turned Red: The Battle of Antietam* (1983); Richard Sommers, *Richmond Redeemed: The Siege of Petersburg* (1981); and James Lee McDonough, *Shiloh: In Hell Before Night* (1977). Michael Shaara's *Killer Angels* (1974) is a brilliant fictionalized account of Gettysburg. Michael Fellman's *Inside War: The Guerilla Conflict in Missouri During the American Civil War* (1989) provides a fascinating look at a lesser-known side of the military war.

The experience of the common soldier is explored in Bell Wiley's classics, *The Life of Johnny Reb* (1943) and *The Life of Billy Yank* (1952). More recent studies include Reid Mitchell, *Civil War Soldiers: Their Expectations and Their Experiences* (1988), James I. Robertson, *Soldiers Blue and Grey* (1988), and Michael Barton, *Goodmen: The Character of Civil War Soldiers* (1981). Each of these works explores the similarities and differences between the cultures, characters, and causes of Northern and Southern troops. Gerald Lindman explores the chasm between the soldier's disillusioning combat experience and the civilian's sustained idealism in *Embattled Courage: The Experience of Combat in the American Civil War* (1988).

Some of the best studies of the war concern the war's impact on Northern and Southern societies. Concerning the North, Philip Shaw Paludan's *"A People's Contest": The Union and Civil War, 1861–1865* (1988) is an excellent examination of how the war fueled the ongoing processes of modernization and industrialization to transform the lives of the American people. George Fredrickson offers a probing look at the war's intellectual impact in *The Inner Civil War: Northern Intellectuals and the Crisis of the Union* (1965). Iver Bernstein's *New York City Draft Riots: Their Significance for American Society and Politics in the Age of the Civil War* (1990) demonstrates how the war magnified and exacerbated the problems of race, class, and power in the rapidly growing American city. In *The Fate of Liberty: Abraham Lincoln and Civil Liberties* (1991), Mark Neely examines Lincoln's ambiguous record on civil liberties through the personal experiences of those arrested by the military during the suspension of the writ of *habeas corpus*. J. Matthew Gallman provides a good overview of the Union home front in *The North Fights the Civil War: The Home Front* (1994).

Several books have been written recently on Southern society, and in particular Southern nationalism during the war. Emory Thomas, in *The Confederate Nation, 1861–1865* (1979), explores the crumbling of Southern identity under the strain of war as it necessitated the abandonment of Southern practices and values, such as decentralized government. Paul Escott examines Jefferson Davis's role in this disintegration in *After Secession: Jefferson Davis and the Failure of Southern Nationalism* (1978), arguing that policies such as the 20-slave law created disunity and hampered the growth of southern nationalism. Wayne Durrill presents a local study of the war's detrimental effect on Southern society in *War of Another Kind: A Southern Community in the Great Rebellion* (1990). Finally, Drew Gilpin Faust looks at failed Southern efforts to create a unified culture through appeals to religion, protest against inflation, and the reform of slavery in *The Creation of Confederate Nationalism: Ideology and Identity in the Civil War South* (1988).

There has recently been an explosion of scholarship on women's war experience. Concerning Southern women, Drew Gilpin Faust's *Mothers of Invention: Women of the Slaveholding South in the American Civil War* (1996) is an engaging look at how elite planter women "invented new selves" in the atmosphere of war and the destruction of slavery. George C. Rable, author of *Civil Wars: Women and the Crisis of Southern Nationalism* (1989), explores Southern women's changing opinions on the war, their loyalty to their class and race, and their participation in the reconstruction of old gender roles at the war's conclusion. A fascinating first-hand account of the war from a Southern woman's perspective is *Mary Chesnut's Civil War*, edited by C. Van Woodward (1981).

Elizabeth Leonard's *Yankee Women: Gender Battles in the Civil War* (1994) offers insight into women's war work, the male opposition they encountered, and the extent to which the Civil War was a watershed in women's progress toward equality. Stephen Oates's excellent biography of Clara Barton, *A Woman of Valor* (1994), is also informative on the subject of women's contribution to the Civil War. Most recently, Jeanie Attie examines the war as a testing ground for women's entrance into the body politic in *Patriotic Toil: Northern Women and the Civil War* (1998). Catherine Clinton and Nina Silber are editors of an impressive collection of essays on the meanings of the war for both men and women, Northern and Southern, *Divided Houses: Gender and the Civil War* (1992).

The politics of the Emancipation Proclamation are addressed in two studies, LaWanda Cox's *Lincoln and Black Freedom: A Study in Presidential Leadership* (1981) and Robert Durden's *The Gray and the Black: The Confederate Debate on Emancipation* (1972). The former dispels the notion on Lincoln as a "reluctant emancipator" and examines the political considerations he was forced to deal with in issuing his proclamation. Durden's book uncovers the surprising support among Southerners, including Jefferson Davis, for some sort of emancipation, but concludes their motives were not humanitarian but strategic.

Several wonderful studies have been done on the black transition from slavery to freedom. Leon Litwack's masterful *Been in the Storm So Long* (1979) is perhaps the most comprehensive. He identifies the ambivalent attitude the former slaves had toward their new situation. Willie Lee Rose's *Rehearsal for Reconstruction* (1964) is a local study of the ex-slaves of the South Sea Islands and the Northern reformers who came down to aid their adjustment. David Blight examines the reaction to emancipation of one of America's greatest black thinkers in *Frederick Douglass's Civil War: Keeping Faith in Jubilee* (1989). Ira Berlin et al. (eds.), *Freedom: A Documentary History* (1982), and C. Peter Ripley (ed.), *Witness for Freedom: African American Voices on Race, Slavery, and Emancipation* (1993), are collections of primary sources documenting the African-American reaction to the war and emancipation.

Dudley Cornish's *The Sable Arm: Black Troops in the Union Army, 1861–1865* (1956) was one of the first studies of black soldiers and is still a useful source. More recently, Joseph T. Glatthaar takes up the subject in *Forged in Battle: The Civil War Alliance of Black Soldiers and White Officers* (1990). Both works account the opposition and discrimination black troops underwent as well as their heroics in battle. Glatthaar's work portrays the complex and evolving relationship they had with their white officers, and the difficult postwar adjustments of both groups. Edwin S. Redkey's (ed.) *A Grand Army of Black Men: Letters from African-American Soldiers in the Union Army, 1861–1865* (1992) presents the black soldier's experience in his own words.

Competing Voices

Civil War Songs

"The Bonnie Blue Flag"

After "Dixie," "The Bonnie Blue Flag" was the most popular Confederate song, both with the army and the public. It was first sung in New Orleans in 1861 by Marion Macarthy, sister of the song's author, Harry Macarthy, a noted Southern author and performer. The words tell the story of secession.

We are a band of brothers, And native to the soil,
Fighting for our Liberty, With treasure, blood, and toil;
And when our rights were threaten'd, The cry rose near and far,
Hurrah for the Bonnie Blue Flag, that bears a Single Star!

Hurrah! Hurrah! For Southern rights hurrah!
Hurrah! Hurrah! For the Bonnie Blue Flag that bears a Single Star.

As long as the Union was faithful to her trust,
Like friends and brethren kind were we, and just;
But now, when Northern treachery attempts our rights to mar,
We hoist on high the Bonnie Blue Flag that bears a single star.

First gallant South Carolina nobly made the stand,
Then came Alabama and took her by the hand;
Next, quickly Mississippi, Georgia, and Florida,
All raised on high the Bonnie Blue Flag that bears a single star.

Ye men of valor gather round the banner of the right,
Texas and fair Louisiana join us in the fight;
With Davis, our loved President, and Stephens, statesmen rare,
We'll rally round the Bonnie Blue Flag that bears the single star.

And here's to brave Virginia, the Old Dominion State,
With the young Confederacy at length has linked her fate;
Impelled by her example, now other States prepare
To hoist on high the Bonnie Blue Flag that bears a single star.

Then cheer, boys, cheer, raise a joyous shout
For Arkansas and North Carolina now have both gone out,
And let another rousing cheer for Tennessee be given,
The single star of the Bonnie Blue Flag has grown to be eleven.

Then here's to our Confederacy, strong we are and brave,
Like patriots of old we'll fight, our heritage to save;
And rather than submit to shame, to die we would prefer,
So cheer for the Bonnie Blue Flag that bears a single star.

"The Stripes and Stars"

Sung to the same tune as the Confederate song, the Union version was written by Colonel J. L. Geddes of the Eighth Iowa Infantry. He wrote it to respond to the "distortions" of the Confederate version.

We're fighting for our Union, we're fighting for our trust,
We're fighting for that happy land where sleeps our Father's dust.
It cannot be dissever'd, tho' it cost us bloody wars.
We never can give up the land where float the Stripes and Stars.

Hurrah! Hurrah! For equal rights hurrah!
Hurrah! For the brave old flag that bears the Stripes and Stars.

We treated you as brothers until you drew the sword,
With impious hands at Sumter you cut the silver cord,
So now you hear our bugles; we come the sons of Mars,
We rally round that brave old flag which bears the Stripes and Stars.

We do not want your cotton, we care not for your slaves,
But rather than divide this land, we'll fill your southern graves.
With Lincoln for our Chieftain, we'll wear our country's scars.
We rally round that brave old flag that bears the Stripes and Stars!

We deem our cause most holy, we know we're in the right,
And twenty millions of freemen stand ready for the fight.
Our bride is fair Columbia, no stain her beauty mars.
O'er her we'll raise that brave old flag which bears the Stripes and Stars.

And when this war is over, we'll each resume our home
And treat you still as brothers where ever you may roam.
We'll pledge the hand of friendship, and think no more of wars,
But dwell in peace beneath the flag that bears the Stripes and Stars!

Although each side shared a commitment to "freedom" and the Constitution, North and South divided over the meaning of those ideals. For the South, freedom was for white men only; Southerners saw no contradiction between their support for individual freedom and their support for the institution of slavery. For white Southerners, freedom meant independence from the national government. The majority of Southerners who did not own slaves supported the war because they believed that encroaching federal power threatened their way of life. They viewed the Constitution as a nonbinding pact between the states and the federal government. If a state did not feel properly represented, or believed the federal government had misused its powers, it could simply withdraw from the Union. "Ours is not a revolution," Jefferson Davis claimed. "Our struggle is for inherited rights. [We seceded] to save ourselves from a revolution" that threatened the cornerstone of the Southern economy and culture—slavery.

At the beginning of the war, most Northerners shared the belief that freedom should be limited to white men. While they did not support the abolition of slavery in the South, most Northerners opposed its expansion into new territories. Freedom meant the chance for the individual to move up in society through hard work. A society that included slaves hampered the freedom of everyone—white and black—by reducing the opportunity for wage labor. In time, many Northerners would expand their definition of freedom to include African-Americans and embrace Lincoln's call for emancipation. Initially, it was the desire to preserve the Union, and not a commitment to expand freedom, that convinced most in the North to take up arms. They viewed the Union as a sacred bond, ordained by God, one that could not be broken at will. Revolution against government was only justified in the case of repressive government, which was certainly not the case in the United States.

These differing motivations of North and South are displayed quite vividly in the music of the era. Southern songs such as "Dixie" and "The Bonnie Blue Flag" usually invoked the defense of home, family, the land, and "Southern rights." Northern songs spoke of liberty and Union and in some cases, as with "The Battle Hymn of the Republic," employed religious imagery to signify the epic proportions of their cause.

Questions for Analysis

1. What lines in "The Bonnie Blue Flag" capture the Southern defense of rebellion?

2. How does the song illustrate the Southern concept of the Union?

3. Why do you think the song does not mention slavery, even though the issue was so central to the war?

4. What lines in "The Stripes and Stars" highlight why Northerners fought?

5. To what concept of rights does the lyric "For equal rights hurrah" refer?

6. What does this song say about the Northern concept of the Union?

7. Contrast the last stanza with the third stanza. What does the change in tone say about the Union attitude toward the South?

16

Reconstruction and the New South, 1864–1900

*T*he opening act of the play *Our American Cousin* had already begun when the president's carriage pulled up on April 14, 1865, to Ford's Theater in Washington. At 8:25 P.M. President Lincoln, accompanied by his wife Mary and a young couple, Major Henry Rathbone and Clara Harris, quietly made his way to the presidential box, which overlooked the stage. But someone in the theater spotted Lincoln, and within minutes the packed crowd of 1,675 were on their feet giving the president an enthusiastic ovation. The actors paused and joined in the demonstration while the band struck up "Hail to the Chief."

Lincoln settled into his black walnut rocking chair; Mrs. Lincoln sat on his right. The guard who had been sitting outside the door leading to the president's box had decided to go across the street to meet some friends. It proved to be a fatal mistake. During the third act, John Wilkes Booth, a deranged actor and Confederate sympathizer, dashed into the president's box, pulled a small pistol from his pocket, and placed it within six inches of Lincoln's head. As he cried out "Sic semper tyrannus!" ("Thus be it ever to tyrants!"), Booth pulled the trigger. The president slumped forward in his chair. Booth jumped out of the haze of blue gun smoke brandishing a dagger. While Mary embraced her husband, Major Rathbone wrestled with the attacker. Booth escaped Rathbone's grasp by slashing his arm to the bone. Then he leaped from the box, only to catch his spur on a flag adorning its rail and crash to the stage.

The president lay mortally wounded. The bullet had struck behind his left ear, tunneled through his brain, and lodged behind his right eye. Four soldiers and two doctors carried him to a small privately owned house across the street. An observer recorded the scene in his diary: "The quaint sufferer lay extended diagonally across the bed, which was not long enough for him. . . . His slow, full respiration lifted the [bed] clothes with each breath he took. His features were calm and striking." The physicians gathered around Lincoln's bed knew that he could not survive his wound. Mary, overcome with grief, refused to accept his fate. "Love, live but one moment to speak to me once—to speak to our children," she cried. Lincoln never spoke again. The following morning, April 15, at 7:22 A.M. Abraham Lincoln, the sixteenth president of the United States, took his last breath. "Now he belongs to the ages," whispered Secretary of War Edwin Stanton.

Union troops engaged in a massive manhunt to find Lincoln's killer. They tracked him down in a barn in Virginia and killed him in a blaze of gunfire. His last words were: "Tell mother I die for my country. I thought I did for the best." Investigators quickly discovered that Booth had not acted alone. On the same night that Booth shot Lincoln, his accomplices planned attacks on Vice President Andrew Johnson and Secretary of State William Seward. Johnson escaped unharmed, but Seward suffered severe stab wounds. A military tribunal convicted eight people of conspiracy to kill the president. Despite often flimsy evidence, four were hanged.

The bullet that killed Lincoln also changed the direction of Reconstruction, the government policy toward the defeated South. Lincoln's death removed from the scene a masterful politician, emboldened those seeking to impose a punitive peace on the South, and elevated to the presidency a man unprepared for the bitter political debates that followed. The experiments of the Reconstruction Era (1863–1877) brought intense struggles between groups with competing notions of government power, individual rights, and race relations. President Johnson, believing he was following Lincoln's plan for a quick "restoration" of the Union, rigidly supported states' rights, leniency toward the former rebels, and noninterference to protect the rights of the freed people. Radical Republicans, who included former abolitionists and freed slaves, challenged Johnson's program and were able to seize control of Reconstruction policy in 1866. Wielding the power of national government, they hoped to punish unrepentant planters, ensure the political and economic rights of the former slaves, and solidify the Republican Party's control of the South.

African-Americans were central players in the Republican effort to "reconstruct" southern society. Freed from the bonds of slavery, they moved to strengthen old institutions such as the family and church, to create new political institutions, and to secure economic independence. Despite important gains, black experiments in freedom were soon frustrated by white Democrats who clamored for the "redemption" of the defeated South. Using violence and intimidation, "Redeemers" successfully fought to recreate the white-dominated social order that had existed before the war. In the face of determined southern Democrats and internal divisions in the North, the Republicans backed away from their commitment to Reconstruction, leaving the experiment incomplete. The "New South" that emerged from war and Reconstruction had changed in significant ways, but for many African-Americans it bore striking similarities to the South of old.

Chronology

1863	Lincoln issues Proclamation of Amnesty and Reconstruction
1864	Radical Republicans pass Wade-Davis Bill
1865	Lincoln assassinated; Johnson becomes president
	Freedmen's Bureau created
	Southern states pass "Black Codes"
	House forms the Joint Committee on Reconstruction
	Thirteenth Amendment passed and ratified; prohibits slavery
1866	Fourteenth Amendment passed; establishes citizenship for blacks
	Fifteenth Amendment passed; gives black males the vote
	Republicans sweep off-year elections
1867	First Reconstruction Act
	Tenure of Office Act
1868	Johnson impeached and acquitted
	Fourteenth Amendment ratified
	Grant elected president
1869	National Woman Suffrage Association and American Woman Suffrage Association founded
1870	Fifteenth Amendment ratified
	Ku Klux Klan launches terrorist campaign
	First Enforcement Act
1871	Last of southern states rejoin the Union
	Ku Klux Klan Act
1872	Liberal Republicans nominate Greeley for president
	Grant reelected president
	Crédit Mobilier, "salary grab," and Whiskey Ring scandals uncovered
	General Amnesty Act
1873	Panic of 1873 begins
	Colfax Massacre
1875	Civil Rights Act of 1875
1876	Presidential election is disputed
1877	Compromise of 1877; Hayes becomes president
1880	Harris publishes *Uncle Remus*
1884	Twains publishes *The Adventures of Huckleberry Finn*
1895	Washington's "Atlanta Compromise"
1896	*Plessy* v. *Ferguson* establishes "separate-but-equal" doctrine

- Why did President Johnson and congressional Republicans divide over Reconstruction policy?

- What did the Radical Republicans hope to accomplish, and what role did government play in their methods?

- How did African-Americans respond to freedom and political participation? How did southern whites react to black participation?

- Why has Reconstruction been called "America's unfinished revolution"?

- How did the New South reflect the failure of Reconstruction? How different was it from the Old South?

This chapter will address these questions.

Presidential Reconstruction: The First Experiment, 1864–1866

The North's victory had ended the Civil War, but the battle for the peace had just begun. The battleground switched to Washington, where congressional Republicans and the White House clashed even before the war ended over a central question: How much authority did the federal government have to impose conditions on the defeated states of the South? Lincoln had experimented with a lenient plan for returning the rebel states to the Union, but his assassination strengthened Republican support for harsher measures. The difficult task of formulating a new policy fell to Vice President Andrew Johnson, a man ill equipped for the difficult challenges ahead.

The Legacy of Battle

The war had devastated southern society. The countryside, said one observer, "looked for many miles like a broad black streak of ruin and desolation." Most major cities were gutted by fire. A northern visitor called Charleston a place of "vacant houses, of widowed women, of rotting wharves, of deserted warehouses, of weed-wild gardens, of miles of grass-grown streets, of acres of pitiful and voiceless barrenness."

More than just razing cities, the Civil War shattered an entire generation of young men in the South. In Alabama, 29 percent of the 122,000 men who bore arms died. One-third of Florida's 15,000 soldiers failed to return. An estimated 23 percent of South Carolina's white male population of arms-bearing age were killed or wounded. Many of those who survived were maimed in battle. In 1866 the state of Mississippi spent a fifth of its revenues on artificial arms and legs for Confederate veterans.

The war ruined the South's economic life. The region's best agricultural lands lay barren. It would take more than a decade for the staples of the southern economy—cotton, tobacco, and sugar—to recover from the wartime devastation. Most factories were dismantled or destroyed, and long stretches of railroad were torn up. According to some estimates, the South's per capita wealth in 1865 was only about half what it had been in 1860. The defeat of the South had also made all Confederate money

The Ruins of Richmond   Burned-out shells of buildings were all that remained of the Richmond business district in April 1865. Confederate troops, not wanting supplies to fall into the hands of the Union army, had actually set many of the fires as they fled. The ruins are indicative of the total devastation of the South at the war's end. The massive rebuilding effort was just one of the monumental tasks facing the nation during Reconstruction.   *(Library of Congress.)*

worthless. But most unsettling of all the changes the war had brought was the end of slavery. Slave property, which was estimated at over $2 billion in 1860, disappeared.

In contrast, the North emerged from battle with new prosperity and power. The Republicans who dominated the wartime Congress enacted a uniform system of banking and a transcontinental railroad. They also fueled the North's economy through generous appropriations for internal improvements. Railroads thrived by carrying troops and supplies; the meatpacking and textile industries soared in response to demands from troops for food and clothing. The per capita wealth of the North doubled between 1860 and 1870. The number of manufactures increased by 80 percent, and property values increased from $10 billion to over $25 billion. In 1870 the per capita wealth of New York State was more than twice that of all eleven ex-Confederate states.

The war also ravaged the political landscape in America. War-born hostility shaped the competition between the two parties long after the war had ended. Republicans depended on hatred of southern rebels to cement their biracial coalition. "The Democratic party," proclaimed Indiana governor Oliver P. Morton, "may be described as a common sewer and loathsome receptacle, into which is emptied every element of treason, North and South." Democrats appealed to their natural constituency of former slave owners by charging that Republicans were the defenders of economic privilege and political centralization, and a threat to individual liberty. Stressing the potent message of white supremacy also drove an ideological wedge between freed slaves and poor whites.

The war had a long-term impact on the sectional balance of power in the nation. Before 1861, the slave states had achieved an extraordinary degree of power in the national government. In 1861 the United States had lived under the Constitution for seventy-two years. During forty-nine of those years, the country's president had been a southerner—and a slaveholder. After the Civil War, a century passed before another resident of the Deep South was elected president.

The war gave birth to the modern American state, dominated by a national government far more powerful than anything the nation had known previously. The federal budget for 1865 exceeded $1 billion (twenty times the budget for 1860), and with its new army of clerks, tax collectors, and other officials, the federal government became the nation's largest employer. The change in the size and scope of government found expression in language, as northerners replaced references to the country as a "union" of separate states with a new emphasis on a singular, consolidated "nation."

The presence of nearly 3.5 million former slaves represented the most dramatic legacy of the war. The black abolitionist Frederick Douglass observed that the former slave "was turned loose, naked, hungry, and destitute to the open sky." The new challenges that freedom presented forced experimentation by black and white. What labor system would replace slavery? Was freedom enough, or would blacks obtain the right to vote?

Lincoln's Plan for Union

Though not committed to any single plan for Reconstruction, Lincoln favored a lenient and conciliatory policy toward the South, as he made clear in 1863. Lincoln hoped that a charitable approach would produce defections from the southern cause and hasten the war's end. Beyond outlawing slavery, he offered no protection for freed slaves. He also insisted that ultimate authority for Reconstruction of the states rested with the president, not Congress. Since the Union was "constitutionally indestructible," Lincoln argued that the southern states had never officially left the Union but had merely engaged in military rebellion. Therefore, Lincoln's power as commander-in-chief gave him control over the defeated states in the South.

In December 1863, Lincoln issued a Proclamation of Amnesty and Reconstruction declaring that southern states could organize new governments after 10 percent of those who had voted in 1860 declared their loyalty to the Union and accepted the Union's wartime acts outlawing slavery. Each state would then convene a constitutional convention and elect new representatives to Congress. Lincoln offered a general amnesty to all Confederate citizens except high-ranking civil and military officials. His plan did not extend the right to vote to freed people. Carrying out his policy, the president recognized reconstituted civil governments in Louisiana and Arkansas in 1864, and in Tennessee in February 1865.

Many congressional Republicans argued that by declaring war on the Union, the Confederate states had broken their constitutional ties and were "conquered provinces" subject to the authority of Congress. The most strenuous criticism came from a group of Radical Republicans. Most Radicals believed that it was the national government's responsibility to guarantee political rights and economic opportunity to the freed people in the South. Led by Senator Charles Sumner of Massachusetts and Representative Thaddeus Stevens of Pennsylvania, the Radicals wanted the North to impose a more punitive peace settlement. The Radicals planned to reshape southern society by confiscating southern plantations and redistributing the land to freed slaves and white southerners who had remained loyal to the Union. The North must, Stevens contended, "revolutionize Southern institutions, habits, and manners . . . or all our blood and treasure have been spent in vain."

In 1864 the Radicals challenged Lincoln by passing their own, more stringent peace plan. The Wade-Davis Bill, sponsored by Senator Benjamin Wade of Ohio and Representative Henry Winter Davis of Maryland, required that 50 percent of white male citizens had to declare their allegiance before a state could be readmitted to the Union. Moreover, only those southerners who pledged—through the so-called ironclad oath—that they had never voluntarily borne arms against the Union could vote or serve in the state constitutional conventions. The bill required the state conventions to abolish slavery and exclude from political rights high-ranking civil and military officers of the Confederacy.

Lincoln killed the bill with a pocket veto, meaning he "pocketed" it and did not sign it within the required ten days after the adjournment of Congress. The authors of the bill denounced Lincoln's action in the Wade-Davis Manifesto. Lincoln had to understand, they warned, that "the authority of Congress is paramount and must be respected." Flexing its muscle, Congress refused to seat the delegates from states that applied for readmission under Lincoln's plan.

The vast majority of Republicans fell somewhere between Lincoln and the Radicals. Like the president, these so-called moderates wanted a quick end to the war and a speedy restoration of the Union. They showed little interest in the Radical plans for social and economic Reconstruction. Many wanted to keep former Confederate leaders from returning to power and hoped to provide a minimum of political rights for freed people. The former slave, argued Lyman Trumbull, will "be tyrannized over, abused, and virtually reenslaved without some legislation by the nation for his protection." But the critical question was, how much protection? What all Republicans shared was a determination to solidify their party's power in the North and extend their influence in the South. Hostility toward former rebels and political expediency, more than reformist zeal, shaped their approach to the South.

Behind the scenes, Lincoln was working to find common ground among his fellow Republicans. In March 1865, the president and Congress agreed on the creation of the Bureau of Refugees, Freedmen, and Abandoned Lands (Freedmen's Bureau) to provide "such issues of provisions, clothing, and fuel" as might be needed to relieve "destitute and suffering refugees and freedmen and their wives and children." Over the next few years, the bureau built schools, paid teachers, and established a network of courts that allowed freed people to file suit against white people.

Lincoln, a masterful politician, might have maintained a congressional majority behind a fairly moderate program. In the last speech he ever delivered, three days before his death, Lincoln suggested that he might support freedmen's suffrage, beginning with those who had served in the Union army. Whether Lincoln and his party could have forged a unified approach to Reconstruction is one of the great unanswered questions of American history.

Restoration Under Johnson

A few hours after Lincoln's death, Vice President Andrew Johnson of Tennessee was sworn in as president. Johnson rose from humble origins. His father, a porter and janitor, died when Andrew was three. Working as a tailor's apprentice at the age of ten, Johnson taught himself how to read and eventually started his own tailor shop. After prospering in business, he decided to enter politics. A Democrat, Johnson modeled himself after his hero, Andrew Jackson, who had fought for "common people" against powerful interests. "I am for the people," he declared as he rose from state assemblyman to U.S. senator. During the war, Johnson refused to support secession and, after Federal forces captured Nashville, Lincoln appointed him as Tennessee's military governor. Many Republicans believed that Johnson, a southern Democrat who had remained loyal to the Union, could help unify the nation. In 1864 party leaders nominated him to serve as Lincoln's vice president.

Once in office, Johnson tried to continue Lincoln's lenient policy while also appeasing the radicals. Like Lincoln, he insisted that the president held authority over Reconstruction policy, and he was more interested in "restoring" the Union than in "reconstructing" southern society. Unlike Lincoln, however, Johnson was a vain man consumed by deep suspicions and insecurities. He was ill suited for the delicate compromising and negotiating that would be necessary to maintain the Republican coalition. Moreover, Johnson, a states' rights activist, was openly hostile to former slaves and deeply skeptical of Radical plans to provide the freedman with political rights. "This is a country for white men," the president said in 1865, "and by God, as long as I am President, it shall be a government for white men."

Initially, he kept Radicals off balance with his strong denunciations of Confederate leaders. "Treason is a crime and crime must be punished. Treason must be made infamous and traitors must be impoverished," he declared. The president's rhetoric resulted from his populist hostility toward powerful southern planters, but Radicals interpreted it as support for their agenda. "Johnson, we have faith in you," Radical leader Ben Wade of Ohio remarked after visiting the new president. "By the gods, there will be no trouble now in running the government."

During the summer of 1865, Johnson executed his own plan of restoration. He appointed a provisional governor for each of the former Confederate states (except those states that had begun Reconstruction under Lincoln) and instructed the governors to convene constitutional conventions. The president insisted that the new constitutions revoke their ordinances of secession, repudiate the Confederate debt, and ratify the Thirteenth Amendment, which declared that "neither slavery nor involuntary servitude, except as punishment for crime . . . , shall exist within the United States."

Johnson also took a lenient approach to former rebels. He offered "amnesty and pardon, with restoration of all rights of property" to almost all southerners who took an oath of allegiance to the Constitution and the Union. Those ex-Confederates who were excluded from amnesty could petition Johnson personally for a pardon. The president approved nearly 90 percent of the petitions. By October 1865, ten of the eleven rebel states claimed to have passed Johnson's test for readmission to the Union. The Thirteenth Amendment was ratified in December. Satisfied with the South's progress, Johnson told Congress in December that the "restoration" of the Union was virtually complete.

Initially, most Republicans supported the outlines of Johnson's policy. Moderates wanted to strengthen some provisions but agreed that the federal government could not guarantee suffrage or civil rights for African-Americans. Radicals, though calling for stronger protections for blacks, hoped southern leaders would respond favorably to the president's policy and offer the vote to some African-Americans. Over the next few months, however, Republican support for the president's policy faded as evidence mounted of both southern defiance and increasing discrimination against the freed people.

Southern leaders were in no mood for compromise or conciliation; they were committed to restoring the old racial order. The delegates who met to form the new governments in the South showed contempt for northern Reconstruction plans, rejecting even Johnson's benign policy. In fact, the "restoration" government

Taking the Oath of Allegiance   President Johnson's Reconstruction plan included amnesty, pardon, and the restoration of property rights to all southerners who would swear allegiance to the Union. The plan, although it expedited the process of readmitting southern states, proved too lenient. The new state constitutions did not protect the freed slaves' civil rights, and southern voters returned several former Confederate leaders, including Confederate Vice President Alexander Stephens, to elected office.   (*The South: A Tour of its Battle-Fields and Ruined Cities* by John Trowbridge, 1866.)

looked much like the old Confederate government. Many of the conventions approved of constitutions that limited suffrage to whites. The 1865 Louisiana Democratic platform declared, "There can in no event nor under any circumstances be any equality between the white and other Races." The provisional governor of Alabama declared that "the State affairs of Alabama must be guided and controlled by the superior intelligence of the white man." Southern voters defiantly elected to Congress the former vice president of the Confederacy, Georgia's Alexander Stephens, four Confederate generals, eight colonels, six cabinet members, and a host of other rebels.

All of the newly constituted state governments passed a series of stringent laws, called "Black Codes." The codes varied from state to state, but all were designed to restrict the freedom of the black workers and keep the freed people in a subordinate position. All included economic restrictions that would prevent former slaves from leaving plantations. Some states tried to prevent African-Americans from owning land. Other laws excluded African-Americans from juries and prohibited interracial marriages. Edmund Rhett of South Carolina summed up the purpose of the Black Codes: "The general interest both of the white man and of the negroes requires that he should be kept as near to the condition of slavery as possible, and as far from the condition of the white man as is practicable."

The President versus Congress

Southern resistance angered Radicals and many moderates in Congress. When the Thirty-ninth Congress convened in December 1865, moderates and Radicals refused to allow the newly elected representatives from former Confederate states to take their seats. Immediately after the House of Representatives turned the southerners away, Thaddeus Stevens called for the appointment of a special Joint Committee of Fifteen on Reconstruction "to inquire into the conditions of the States which formed the so-called Confederate States of America." The Joint Committee, consisting of nine House members and six senators, was headed by a moderate, Senator William Pitt Fessenden, but Radicals quickly seized control.

After public hearings that revealed evidence of violence against freed slaves, the committee recommended congressional passage of new legislation to protect them. In January 1866, Congress voted to extend the life of the Freedmen's Bureau and enlarge its powers. In February, Johnson issued a stinging veto message. The following month, Congress passed a civil rights bill that extended the authority of federal courts to protect blacks. Again, Johnson angrily vetoed the measure.

Why did Johnson assume such a confrontational posture? There is no doubt that he sincerely believed both bills to be unconstitutional. The civil rights bill, he declared in his veto message, represented a stride "toward centralization and the concentration of all legislative power in the National Government." Political considerations, however, were just as important. Johnson hoped that by forcing a confrontation he could isolate the Radicals from moderate Republicans. He refused to believe that moderates would break with him over the issue of freed people's rights. Ultimately, he hoped to build a new coalition that would include Democrats in the North and South, and a small number of moderate and conservative Republicans in the North.

But Johnson seriously miscalculated the lines of division within the party. In the words of the *New York Herald*, the president's actions were "a windfall, a godsend. He [Johnson] gave them Johnson to fight instead of fighting among themselves." The Senate vote to override his veto of the Freedmen's Bureau bill should have given him pause. Though the vote fell two votes short, thirty of thirty-eight Republicans voted in favor. In April, moderates joined with the Radicals to override the presidential veto and enacted the Civil Rights Act of 1866. Despite all of their differences, Radicals and moderates now shared a common disdain for the president and his Reconstruction policies, which rewarded rebels and made disaffection respectable in the South. "I have tried hard to save Johnson," observed moderate William Fessenden, "but I am afraid he is beyond hope."

A number of violent incidents in the South strengthened the Radicals' resolve to protect the rights of the freed people. In May, a mob composed of white policemen and firemen invaded a black neighborhood in South Memphis, Tennessee. Before the riot ended, forty-eight people, all but two black, were dead; five black women had been raped; and hundreds of homes, churches, and schools had been torched. Three months later, in New Orleans opponents of Radical Reconstruction went on a violent rampage, killing thirty-four blacks and three white Radicals. "It was not a riot," declared the military commander of the region. "It was an absolute massacre by the police." Radicals blamed Johnson's lenient policies for the outbreak. "Witness Memphis, witness Orleans," cried Sumner. "Who can doubt that the President is the author of these tragedies?"

Most people did not go as far as Sumner in blaming the president for the riots, but the violence undermined Johnson's claim that southern blacks did not need federal protection. In July, Radicals and moderates joined forces again to pass the Freedmen's Bureau bill over a second veto. By overriding two presidential vetoes, Congress asserted its control over Reconstruction.

Congressional Reconstruction: The Radical Experiment, 1866–1870

Commanding a clear majority in Congress, Radicals sent to the states the Fourteenth and Fifteenth Amendments to the Constitution. Believing the federal government should be the protector of individual rights, they designed the amendments to protect the rights of freed people and to strengthen the Republican Party's position in the South. Given the prevailing gender assumptions of the time, Radicals specifically excluded women from the protections of either amendment, angering women's suffrage supporters and creating deep divisions within the movement. Republican efforts to safeguard their gains by limiting the president's power resulted in the nation's first impeachment trial.

Citizenship, Equal Protection, and the Franchise

In June 1866, the coalition of moderates and Radicals passed the Fourteenth Amendment to the Constitution. The amendment was the first national effort to define

American citizenship. It declared that "all persons born or naturalized in the United States" were "citizens of the United States and of the state wherein they reside" and were guaranteed "equal protection" and "due process" under the law. The amendment reflected the growing consensus among Republicans that national legislation was necessary to force the South to deal fairly with blacks. By asserting that the national government played a role in guaranteeing individual rights, the amendment established an important foundation for future challenges to the states' rights doctrine.

The amendment was a compromise measure designed to enhance the Republican Party's power. At the insistence of many moderates, it stopped short of enfranchising black men. But radicals added a provision requiring a reduction in the representation in Congress of any state that denied adult males the vote. Either way the Republicans gained. Southern states would either extend the franchise to black voters, thus increasing the number of likely Republicans, or they would lose seats in Congress. The amendment also included a Radical demand that former Confederate leaders be prevented from holding federal or state offices; but moderates added a clause giving Congress the authority to override the disqualification in individual cases.

To take effect, the amendment had to be ratified by three-quarters of the states, and it became the central campaign issue during the fall 1866 congressional elections. Johnson denounced the amendment and urged southern states not to ratify it. Interpreting the elections as a referendum on the Fourteenth Amendment and his Reconstruction policy, the president planned an unprecedented campaign tour—called "a swing around the circle"—that took him from Washington to Chicago and St. Louis and back. He hoped the trip would exploit public sentiment against extending political rights to blacks and focus anger on Republican leaders. Instead it further eroded support for presidential Reconstruction within his own party. At a number of stops, the president exchanged hot-tempered insults with hecklers. He alienated many moderate Republicans with his description of Radicals as "factious, domineering, tyrannical" men. "Why not hang Thad Stevens and Wendell Phillips?" he shouted to an audience in Cleveland.

Republicans skillfully focused the campaign on Johnson's support for the disloyal South. They successfully employed the tactic of "waving the bloody shirt" to remind northern voters of the thousands of family members and friends who died at the hands of southern armies. Viewing themselves as the defenders of the Union, Republicans held Johnson and the South responsible for thwarting Reconstruction.

On election night the voters appeared to repudiate the president. The Republicans won a three-to-one majority in Congress (margins of 42 to 11 in the Senate, and 143 to 49 in the House) and gained control of the governorship and legislature in every northern state, as well as West Virginia, Missouri, and Tennessee. "This is the most decisive and emphatic victory ever seen in American politics," exclaimed the Radical journal, *The Nation.*

The moderate Republicans interpreted the election results as a clear call for Radical Reconstruction. Congress moved rapidly and, on March 2, 1867, adopted the First Reconstruction Act; supplementary acts followed in 1867 and 1868. These acts reversed presidential restoration and established new requirements for southern states to gain entry into the Union.

The First Reconstruction Act declared that "no legal government" existed in the South. It divided the South (with the exception of Tennessee, which had ratified the Fourteenth Amendment) into five military districts, each under the command of a Union general. To be considered reconstructed, the law required southern states to call new constitutional conventions in which all male citizens were eligible to vote. The convention delegates then had to draft and approve state constitutions that guaranteed black suffrage. Finally, after the newly elected legislatures ratified the Fourteenth Amendment, the states would be accepted into the Union. During 1868, six states—North Carolina, South Carolina, Florida, Alabama, Louisiana, and Arkansas—met the requirements and were readmitted (see map).

The new plan was far tougher than Johnson's policy, but many Radicals wanted to go further. They pressed for federal support for black schools and the disfranchisement of ex-Confederate leaders. A few Radicals called for the distribution of land to former slaves. Thaddeus Stevens advocated confiscating millions of acres of land from the "chief rebels" in the South, and giving forty acres to every adult male freedman. "How can republican institutions, free schools, free churches, free social

Military Reconstruction Districts With the Reconstruction Act of 1867, Congress took control of Reconstruction in the South, dividing the states that had seceded into five military districts. In each district, Union generals assumed control until state constitutional conventions ratified the Fourteenth Amendment and created new constitutions that guaranteed freedmen the right to vote. Only Tennessee was exempt from this Act, having ratified the Fourteenth Amendment in 1866.

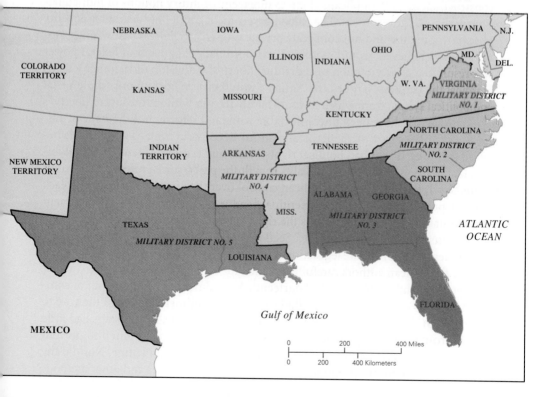

intercourse exist," he asked, in a "community" of wealthy planters and "serfs"? (See Competing Voices, page 650.)

Stevens was right in recognizing that without large-scale redistribution of land, blacks had little hope of achieving economic independence. But the Republicans failed to develop a systematic land distribution program. At the end of the war, as Union armies occupied parts of the South, Union commanders had developed a variety of plans for dealing with confiscated lands. General William T. Sherman set aside the Sea Islands off the Georgia coast and large tracts of land in South Carolina for African-American refugees who burdened his army. Each family received forty acres of land and the loan of army mules. By the summer of 1865, some forty thousand freed people had settled on "Sherman's land." In October, however, Johnson ordered the head of the Freedmen's Bureau to tell Sea Island blacks that they would have to work out arrangements with the legal owners of the land. Angry blacks protested: "Why do you take away our lands? You take them from Us who have always been true, always true to the Government! You give them to our all-time enemies! That is not right!" When some of the Sea Islanders refused to deal with the white owners, Union soldiers forced them to leave or work for their old masters.

In 1866 Republicans tried to address the land problem by passing the Southern Homestead Act, which set aside 44 million acres of land for freedmen and loyal whites. But most freed people, and many whites, lacked the resources to buy the land or purchase the tools needed to work it. For Republicans, even many Radicals, the idea of land reform was too extreme. Despite their support for federally imposed Reconstruction, most Republicans clung to nineteenth-century notions of individualism and limited government. The federal government could only guarantee equality of opportunity; it could not confiscate private property to redress past wrongs. Doing so, most believed, would require an extraordinary expansion of federal power and result in a clear violation of individual liberty. "A division of rich men's lands amongst the landless," argued the *Nation*, "would give a shock to our whole social and political system from which it would hardly recover without the loss of liberty."

Radicals may have been uncomfortable with land reform, but the issue of suffrage was at the heart of the Radical plan for Reconstruction. Most Radicals believed that once blacks had political rights, social and economic benefits would follow. Black enfranchisement would also benefit the party, since grateful black voters in the South could solidify Republican control over the region. To safeguard black votes, Republicans framed the Fifteenth Amendment. Section 1 of the amendment forbade states to deny their citizens the right to vote on the grounds of "race, color, or previous condition of servitude." Section 2 gave Congress power to enforce the amendment by appropriate legislation.

The Republican authors carefully designed the Fifteenth Amendment to further their political ambitions. Like the Fourteenth Amendment, it was the result of compromises between moderates and Radicals. The amendment extended the vote to blacks, but it did not guarantee universal manhood suffrage. Republicans had little to gain from supporting universal male suffrage. Republicans wanted to prevent former Confederates—most of whom were Democrats—from voting. Nor did the amendment, as Radicals proposed, prohibit the use of poll taxes and other methods to restrict black voting. Mainstream Republicans wanted to preserve voting restrictions against immigrants in the North. Massachusetts and Connecticut used literacy tests to deny the vote to recent European immigrants. California used them to prevent Chinese immigrants from voting.

Ratification of the amendment in March 1870 produced widespread Republican jubilation. Frederick Douglass announced that blacks now would "breathe a new atmosphere, have a new earth beneath, and a new sky above." White and black men marched in a large parade through Washington, D.C., waving banners that read "The Nation's second birth" and "the fifteenth amendment, Uncle Sam's bleaching powder."

Reconstruction and Women's Suffrage

The debates over the Fourteenth and Fifteenth Amendments represented a turning point in the struggle for women's suffrage. Nineteenth-century feminists had been closely tied to the antislavery cause, and many male abolitionists had been active in the movement for women's rights. During the war, feminists had put aside the suffrage issue to support the Union cause in abolishing slavery. Once the war ended, however, feminist leaders hoped to refocus public attention on the question of women's suffrage.

Potential allies, however, saw little political reward in extending the franchise to women. Most Republicans believed that black male votes were the key to gaining control of the southern states. Former abolitionists who had supported women's suffrage in the past worried that pushing the issue now would distract attention from the most important question: political and economic rights for former slaves. As Wendell Phillips admonished women leaders, "One question at a time. This hour belongs to the Negro."

Instead of supporting their former suffragist allies, Republicans sanctioned the denial of suffrage. The Fourteenth Amendment, in fact, wrote the term *male* into the Constitution for the first time. Disappointed feminists accepted defeat at the federal level and focused on the reform of state constitutions. In 1866 Elizabeth Cady Stanton, Susan B. Anthony, and Lucy Stone created the Equal Rights Association to lobby and petition for the removal of racial and sexual restrictions on the state level. Not only were their efforts unsuccessful, they also provoked bitter divisions within the suffrage movement, eventually resulting in an open break between Radicals supporting Stanton and Anthony and more moderate followers of Stone. As Republican men withdrew funding and support, many feminist leaders felt betrayed, convinced, as Stanton declared, that woman "must not put her trust in man" in seeking her own rights. "Standing alone, we learned our power," Stanton and Anthony wrote later. "Woman must lead the way to her own enfranchisement and work out her own salvation."

Angry with their former allies, Stanton and Anthony campaigned against ratification of the Fifteenth Amendment. Ratification, Anthony charged, would create an "aristocracy of sex." They employed racist and elitist arguments in opposing the new amendment. Stanton argued that black men should not be elevated over "women of wealth, education, virtue, and refinement." In 1869 she urged her followers to support women's suffrage "if you do not wish the lower orders of Chinese, Africans, Germans and Irish, with the low ideas of womanhood to make laws for you and your daughters." That same year, these radicals formed the all-female National Woman Suffrage Association (NWSA).

Another group of feminists led by Lucy Stone broke with Stanton and supported the amendment, conceding that this was "the Negro's hour." Women, they contended, could afford to wait for the vote. Their goal was to maintain an alliance with Republicans and to support the Fifteenth Amendment. They believed that this was the best way to enlist Republican support for women's suffrage after Reconstruction issues had been settled. To advance their cause, they formed the moderate American Woman Suffrage Association (AWSA), which focused on achieving suffrage at the state level. This disagreement over strategy would divide the women's movement for a generation to come.

The Impeachment of a President

Fearing that Johnson would subvert its plans for the South, Congress passed several laws in March 1867 aimed at limiting his presidential power. The Tenure of Office Act, the most important of the new restrictions, required the president to seek Senate approval before removing any officeholder who had been previously approved by the Senate. In this way, congressional leaders could protect Republican appointees, such as Lincoln appointee Secretary of War Edwin M. Stanton, who opposed the president's Reconstruction policy and was openly collaborating with the Radicals. In August 1867, Johnson suspended Stanton and, as required by the Tenure in Office Act, asked for Senate approval. When the Senate refused, Johnson had Stanton physically expelled from his office and appointed Union General Ulysses S. Grant interim secretary of war.

On February 24, the House of Representatives, seizing on Johnson's violation of the Tenure of Office Act, voted to impeach the president. It charged him with eleven counts of "high crimes and misdemeanors." Of the eleven articles of impeachment, the first eight related to Johnson's attempt to violate the Tenure of Office Act by his "illegal" dismissal of Stanton. Article X accused Johnson of bringing Congress into disgrace by "inflammatory and scandalous harangues" and of degrading his office "to the great scandal of all good citizens."

The trial in the Senate, which the Constitution empowers to act as a court in impeachment cases, opened on March 5, 1868, and continued until May 26, with Chief Justice Salmon P. Chase presiding. To remove the president from office, two-thirds of the Senate, 36 of 54 Senators, needed to vote for impeachment. On the first day of the trial, Radical Benjamin Butler of Massachusetts presented the charges against the president. "This man by murder most foul succeeded to the Presidency, and is the elect of an assassin to that high office, and not of the people," he charged. "We are about to remove him from the office he has disgraced by the sure, safe, and constitutional means of impeachment."

The president's attorney, Henry Stanbery, argued that Stanton was not protected by the Tenure in Office Act because he had been appointed by Lincoln. And in any case, Johnson's removal of Stanton was not a criminal act but a test of the legality of a law that was probably unconstitutional.

As the case came to an end, it was obvious that the vote would be close. "It hangs in almost an even balance," Representative James Garfield wrote two hours before the vote. "There is an intensity of anxiety here, greater than I ever saw during the war." At the last moment, seven moderate Republicans broke ranks, voting for acquittal along with twelve Democrats. The impeachment failed by one vote. The moderates agreed that Johnson had broken the law, but they believed the violation did not warrant removal from office, fearing such a move would establish a dangerous precedent and weaken the presidency.

The Radical Experiment in the South, 1865–1872

With a majority of Democrats and former Confederates prevented from participating in the political life of the South, the Republican Party emerged as the dominant force in southern politics. It controlled the state conventions, wrote the new constitutions, and controlled the new governments. At the same time, millions of African-Americans took advantage of their freedom to strengthen traditional institutions, especially the family and the church. But their hopes for economic independence were frustrated by a new labor system that trapped them between freedom and slavery. Despite political domination, the white South struggled to maintain its own social structure and cultural identity, including distinctions of class and race.

The Southern Republicans

The southern Republican Party was an uneasy coalition of three distinct groups. African-Americans formed the largest group of the Republican rank and file. In five states—Alabama, Florida, South Carolina, Mississippi, and Louisiana—blacks constituted a majority of registered voters. In three others—Georgia, Virginia, and North Carolina—they accounted for nearly half the registered voters. In 1865 and 1866, African-Americans throughout the South organized scores of mass meetings, parades, and petitions that demanded civil equality and the right to vote. Hundreds of African-American delegates, selected by local meetings or churches, attended statewide conventions.

The number of African-Americans who held office during Reconstruction never reflected their share of the electorate. No state elected a black governor; only a few selected black judges. In only one state—South Carolina—did blacks have a majority in the legislature. But blacks did win a number of important political positions throughout the South. Over six hundred blacks, many of them former slaves, served in state legislatures during Republican rule. Sixteen African-Americans served in the

U.S. House of Representatives in the Reconstruction era. In 1870, Mississippi's Hiram Revels became the first African-American member of the United States Senate.

A second group of Republicans were a diverse lot whom critics called "carpetbaggers," suggesting that they came South with all their belongings packed into a single carpet-covered traveling bag. In 1871 a Democratic congressman described a carpetbagger as an "office seeker from the North who came here seeking office by the negroes, by arraying their political passions and prejudices against the white people of the community." In fact, carpetbaggers were a diverse group that included northern businessmen, former Freedmen Bureau agents who had invested money in the region, and Union army veterans who stayed in the South after the war. Most combined a desire for personal gain with a commitment to reform the South by introducing northern ideas and institutions. They made up only a sixth of the delegates to the state conventions, but carpetbaggers held more than half the Republican governorships in the South and almost half its seats in Congress.

The third group consisted of white southerners who resented the planter elite and believed that Republican policies would favor them over the wealthy landowners. They included southern Unionists, small town merchants, and rural farmers. Democrats called them "scalawags," an ancient Scots-Irish term for small, worthless animals. To Democrats, a scalawag was "the local leper of the community," even more hated than the carpetbagger. "We can appreciate a man who lived north, and . . . even fought against us," declared a former North Carolina governor, "but a traitor to his own home cannot be trusted or respected."

It was a fragile coalition. Class differences divided the business-minded carpetbaggers and poor scalawags. With a more limited vision of state power, scalawags opposed high taxes to fund the reformist social programs carpetbaggers endorsed. But race remained the issue with the greatest potential for shattering the Republican coalition in the South. Black demands for political rights and economic independence clashed with the deeply held racial attitudes of most scalawags. "[O]ur people are more radical against rebels than in favor of negroes," declared a scalawag leader.

The Republican Program

Although fragile, this coalition of southern Republicans had a profound impact on public life in the South. Under Republican rule, all the southern states rejoined the Union between 1868 and 1871. In states where the Republican coalition remained unified—South Carolina, Louisiana, and Florida—Reconstruction governments remained in power for as many as nine years. In other states, such as Virginia, they ruled for only a few months. Republicans hoped to remake southern society in the free-labor image of the North.

The new Republican regimes expanded democracy. They repealed Black Codes, modernized state constitutions, extended the right to vote, and made more offices elective. The "fundamental theme" of the South Carolina constitution was "a raceless and classless democracy." Arkansas's document committed the state to "the political and civil equality of all men." Reconstruction administrations guaranteed the political and civil rights of African-American men. They could now serve on juries, school boards, and city councils; hold public office; or work as police officers. To ensure these rights were not violated, many state legislatures passed tough antidiscrimination laws. A South Carolina law, for example, levied a fine of $1,000 or a year's imprisonment for owners of businesses that practiced discrimination.

Believing that education was the foundation for a democracy, many Republican governments established public school systems for the first time. An 1869 Louisiana law prescribed universal free schooling "without distinction of race, color, or previous condition." In theory, public schools were open to both races, but in practice, whites stayed away from schools that admitted blacks. When the Reconstruction government forced the University of South Carolina to admit African-Americans in 1873, nearly all the whites withdrew. Two years later the university was 90 percent black. Few African-Americans objected to the segregation. For now, they agreed with the abolitionist Frederick Douglass, who accepted that separate schools were "infinitely superior" to no schools at all.

African-Americans eagerly embraced the expanded educational opportunities. Throughout the South, African-Americans raised money to build schoolhouses and pay teachers. A Mississippi farmer vowed, "If I never does do nothing more, I shall give my children a chance to go to school, for I consider education next best thing to liberty." By 1869 the Freedmen's Bureau was supervising nearly three thousand schools serving over 150,000 students throughout the South. Over half the roughly 3,300 teachers in these schools were African-Americans. Between 1865 and 1867, northern philanthropists founded Howard, Atlanta, Fisk, Morehouse, and other black universities in the South.

In most cases, however, the efforts to improve education were overwhelmed by crowded facilities and limited resources. Often African-American and poor white children had to skip school so they could help their family by working in the fields. Between 1865 and 1870, only 5 percent of black children in Georgia attended school regularly; for whites, the figure was 20 percent.

The new Republican governments embarked on ambitious programs to rebuild and expand the South's infrastructure, which had been destroyed during the war. They paved new roads and subsidized investment in manufacturing. Believing that transportation was the key to southern industrial development, Republicans poured enormous energy into rebuilding the region's railroad system. Between 1868 and 1872, the South added over three thousand new miles of track. State governments also spent more money than ever before on public institutions such as orphanages and asylums.

Paying for the task of rebuilding the devastated South proved troublesome. Like their northern counterparts, southern states used general property taxes to pay for the expanded services. By levying taxes on personal property as well as real estate, the states hoped to force wealthy planters to bear much of the burden. But despite higher taxes, spending outpaced revenues, producing large deficits. During the 1860s, the southern tax burden rose 400 percent. Between 1868 and 1872, the deficits of Louisiana and South Carolina almost doubled, and between 1868 and 1874, that of Alabama tripled.

Students at Hampton Institute, c. 1870 Education was a top priority for the freed slaves. At first, northern missionary societies funded and staffed most schools and colleges for African-Americans. The American Missionary Association, with the help of the Freedmen's Bureau, founded Hampton Institute in 1868 to provide "industrial training" and teacher training for former slaves. Over time, African-Americans preferred to run their own schools, institutions that became centers of the black community. *(Hampton University Archives.)*

Corruption compounded the revenue problem. In South Carolina, for example, the state maintained a restaurant and barroom for the legislators at a cost of $125,000 for one session. White southerners pounced on the stories of corruption in Republican governments, claiming it proved their charge that blacks were incapable of self-government. Corruption during this period, though widespread, was not limited to one race, one party, or one region. Southern black officials were no more corrupt than their white counterparts, and the Democratic urban machines in the North probably stole more public money than the Republican regimes in the South. Critics ignored the evidence because they were not really concerned with corruption. What they objected to was African-Americans gaining and exercising political power.

The Meaning of Freedom

A black Baptist minister, Henry M. Turner, stressed that freedom meant the enjoyment of "our rights in common with other men." The newly freed slaves sought countless ways to challenge the authority whites had exercised over their lives. Freedmen acquired belongings—dogs, guns, and liquor—that had been forbidden under slavery, and they abandoned the old expressions of humility—tipping a hat, stepping aside, casting eyes low. They dressed as they pleased. As slaves, they often had no surname. Freedom provided them with the opportunity to assume the last name of a prominent person. Free to travel for the first time, many former slaves packed their meager belongings and left the plantation.

For many former slaves, freedom provided the cherished opportunity to reunite with family members. "In their eyes," wrote a Freedmen's Bureau agent, "the work of emancipation was incomplete until the families which had been dispersed by slavery were reunited." Parents reunited with each other and with children who had been taken in by planters and overseers. Thousands of African-American couples who had lived together under slavery flocked to churches to have their relationships sanctioned by marriage. By 1870, the majority of African-Americans lived in two-parent families.

Freedom changed gender relations within the black family. Slavery had imposed a rough equality on men and women: both were forced to work long hours in the fields. But freedom allowed them to define separate spheres. Initially, men continued to work in the fields, while many women wanted to stay at home and attend to the family. Some wives, however, asserted their independence by opening individual bank accounts, refusing to pay off their husbands' debts, and filing complaints of abuse. In most cases, however, economic necessity ended the hopes of independence or domesticity by forcing women back into the fields. According to one former slave, women "do double duty, a man's share in the field, and a woman's part at home. They do any kind of field work, even ploughing, and at home the cooking, washing, milking, and gardening."

African-Americans pooled their resources to buy land and build their own churches. During slavery, southern Protestant churches had relegated blacks to second-class status, forcing them to sit in the back rows and preventing them from participating in many church functions. By 1877, the great majority of black southerners had withdrawn from white-dominated congregations and founded, then filled, their own churches. The new churches, and the ministers who led them, played key roles in the social, political, and religious lives of the parishioners.

Sharecropping

For many African-Americans, economic independence was the most powerful expression of freedom. "All I want is to get to own four or five acres of land, that I can build me a little house on and call my home," a Mississippi black said. Without large-scale redistribution of land, however, few former slaves realized their dream of land ownership. Instead, they were forced to hire out as farm laborers. At first, most freedmen signed contracts with white landowners and worked in gangs, laboring long hours under white supervisors, much as they had in slavery. What the freed people wanted, a Georgia planter observed, was "to get away from all overseers, to hire or purchase land, and work for themselves." The desire to gain a degree of autonomy led many freed people to abandon the contract labor system in favor of tenant farming. As a South Carolina freedman put it, "If a man got to go

Abyssinian Baptist Church

African-Americans demonstrated their preference for autonomy in religious matters by founding their own churches. Their withdrawal from mixed congregations of every denomination was in part a response to the poor treatment they received from white church members. Seating was segregated, and black members were usually barred from church government. Religion had historically been crucial to African-American identity, and these independent churches soon became the most important institutions in their communities. *(Library of Congress.)*

cross the river, and he can't get a boat, he take a log. If I can't own the land, I'll hire or lease land, but I won't contract."

The most widely used form of tenant farming was known as sharecropping. Under this scheme, former plantation owners subdivided their land into farms of 30 to 50 acres, which they leased to workers. The tenants were given seed, fertilizer, farm implements, and food and clothing to take care of their families and grow a cash crop, usually cotton. In return, the landlord took a share of the crop (hence "sharecropping") at harvest time. At first, freed people were enthusiastic about sharecropping. The system provided workers with a sense of freedom and many saw it as a first step toward independence. It allowed families to work the fields together and the reward, usually a half-share of the crop, exceeded the small wages they had received under the old system. While thousands of poor white farmers became sharecroppers, the vast majority were black (see map).

Rather than being a step toward independence, however, sharecropping trapped many African-Americans in a new system of labor that was neither slave nor free. Because of a chronic shortage of capital and banking institutions, sharecroppers turned to local merchants for credit. The merchants, who were often also the landowners, advanced loans to sharecroppers and tenant farmers in exchange for a lien, or claim, on the year's cotton crop. As the only available creditors, merchants and planters could charge usurious interest rates and mark up prices. "It's owed before it's growed," complained many tenant farmers. With half their crop owed to the landowner and half, or often more, owed to the merchant, sharecroppers fell into debt they could not escape.

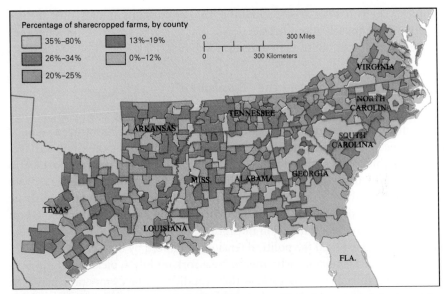

Sharecropping in the South by County, 1880 As a result of the war and the depression of the 1870s, increasing numbers of southerners worked land that they did not own. Without any other economic opportunities, poor whites and blacks alike found themselves tied to the land through sharecropping, an endless cycle of cotton production and perennial debt. The areas with the heaviest concentration of sharecropping were located where cotton remained king—from South Carolina to eastern Texas.   (Source: U. S. Census Office, Tenth Census, 1880, *Report of the Production of Agriculture*. Washington, D. C.: Government Printing Office, 1883, Table 5).

In effect, an informal system of debt peonage replaced the formal structure of slavery. A black laborer described his unenviable condition. "I signed a contract— that is, I made my mark for one year. The Captain was to give me $3.50 a week, and furnish me a little house on the plantation. . . ." A year later, he found himself in debt to the planter, and so he signed another contract, this one for ten years. During this time, he was "compelled" to buy his food, clothing, and other supplies from the plantation store." At the end of his contract, he tried to leave the plantation but was told he owed $165 and consequently found himself reduced to a "lifetime slave."

President Grant and the Divided North, 1868–1876

In 1868 Republicans looked to Civil War hero Ulysses Grant to lead the party. But Grant proved a weak leader and soon reports of scandals eroded support for his administration. The revolt of "Liberal Republicans" in 1872 revealed the depth of disaffection with Grant and the growing divisions among Republicans in the North. Concerned by the intrusive federal role in Reconstruction, Northern liberals hoped to end the government's interventionist experiment in the South. The president won reelection, but his second term was dominated by continuing revelations of corruption. The persistent debate about the "money question" underscored the uncertainty Americans felt about federal power and began to set battle lines between the eastern business establishment and rural America.

Ulysses Grant and the "Spoilsmen"

By the time of the Republican national convention in 1868, the most popular man in the country was General Ulysses S. Grant, whose troops had destroyed General Robert E. Lee's Confederate army in Virginia, effectively ending the Civil War. Despite the terrible losses suffered by Grant's army, long lines of veterans formed to shake his hand wherever he went. Months before the election, Republicans were forming Grant clubs. "No man ever had a better chance to be a great magistrate than he," noted an observer. It was no surprise that Republicans nominated Grant on the first ballot at their convention in Chicago.

The campaign exposed the political tensions produced by the Civil War and Reconstruction. The Democrats, who met in New York on July 4, picked Horatio Seymour, former governor of New York, as their candidate. The Democratic platform blasted the Republicans for subjecting the nation, "in time of profound peace, to military despotism and negro supremacy." The Republicans once again reminded voters that they had saved the Union and charged that Democrats were the party of rebellion.

Grant carried the Republicans to victory on election day, winning 214 electoral votes to Seymour's 80 and carrying twenty-six states to Seymour's eight. The popular vote did not match his resounding victory in the electoral college. He won by only 306,592 votes (3,013,421 to 2,706,829). In fact, Grant's victory was made possible by the 450,000 votes cast by the freed people in the southern states under military occupation. In Congress, the Democrats picked up a few seats, but Republicans retained their large majorities in both the House and Senate.

Grant's success on the battlefield did not translate into effectiveness in the White House. The growth in federal power, and the close relationship between government and business, provided elected officials with ample opportunity for personal gain. With a few exceptions, Grant appointed greedy men who could not resist the temptation for personal gain. These "spoilsmen" tainted the Grant administration with scandal. In 1869 the president's brother-in-law gave into the temptation by joining the crafty financier Jay Gould in an effort to corner the gold market. In 1872 a congressional committee confirmed newspaper reports of widespread bribery of high government officials by the Union Pacific Railroad. The railroad promoters created a phony construction company, called Crédit Mobilier, so they could divert profits into their own pockets. While the Union Pacific floundered, the Crédit Mobilier flourished, awarding its stockholders a single-year dividend of 348 percent. Fearful that Congress might intervene and expose the corrupt arrangement, the directors gave stock to a number of prominent Republicans.

In that same year, greedy congressmen pushed through a bill doubling the president's salary and increasing by 50 percent the salary of Congressmen. The congressional increases were made retroactive for two years, thus granting each member $5,000 in back salary. The press vehemently protested the "salary grab," and public indignation forced Congress to repeal the law in 1874.

The most dramatic scandal, which reached into the White House itself, involved the so-called Whiskey Ring, a network of large whiskey distillers and Treasury agents who defrauded the Internal Revenue Service of $4 million in taxes. The ringleader was a former Union general, John A. McDonald, whom Grant had appointed to the post of supervisor of internal revenue in St. Louis. Worst of all, Grant's private secretary, Orville E. Babcock, was involved in the duplicity. There is no evidence that Grant knew about the fraud, but his poor choice of associates earned him widespread public censure.

The Liberal Revolt

As early as 1870, a small but vocal group of distinguished Republicans had become disaffected with Grant's administration. These self-proclaimed "Liberal Republicans" were a mixed lot, though most were educated, middle-class reformers who believed in limited government and rule by an enlightened elite. The Liberals wanted people like themselves to replace the party hacks who dominated the Grant administration. As a result, they made the creation of a civil service system, based on merit rather than political appointments, the centerpiece of their campaign.

In keeping with their belief in limited government, the Liberal Republicans also supported amnesty for all former Confederates and removal of troops from the South. Many saw the "southern question" as a distraction that enabled party spoilsmen to retain the allegiance of voters by "waving the bloody shirt," while avoiding more important issues: civil service reform and effective government. Reconstruction seemed to exemplify the worst consequences of state activism. Reformers had abolished slavery, the Liberals argued; now it was up to African-Americans themselves to make the most of their new opportunities.

In 1872 the Liberal Republicans organized a national convention that produced a platform criticizing the parent party's southern policy and advocating civil service reform. For president they nominated Horace Greeley, the eccentric editor of the *New York Tribune* and a longtime champion of reform. The choice stunned many veteran political observers, who believed that Greeley had little chance of beating Grant. One reporter gibed that there had been "too much brains and not enough whiskey" at the convention.

A month after Greeley's nomination, the regular Republicans met in Philadelphia, choosing Grant for reelection on the first ballot. Despite his declining popularity and new revelations of scandal, Grant was still a powerful political force, enjoying support from southern Republicans, business interests, and Radicals. Above all, he still evoked the glory of his Civil War victory at Appomattox. The Republicans adopted a platform paying lip service to civil service reform and waffling on the tariff issue, but taking a strong stand in favor of political and civil rights for all citizens in every part of the country.

Democrats realized they had a lot to gain by joining forces with the disaffected Liberal Republicans. "Anything to Beat Grant" became their slogan. That meant that Democrats had to support Greeley, who had been a severe critic of the Democratic Party. The choice between Grant and Greeley, moaned Georgia's Alexander Stephens, was a choice between "hemlock and strychnine." At their convention in Baltimore, Democrats overlooked their differences and nominated Greeley.

The campaign degenerated into what the *New York Sun* called "a shower of mud." Greeley campaigned for a "New Departure," declaring that his administration would provide equal rights for black and white, offer universal amnesty to Confederate officers, and establish thrift and honesty in government. Cartoonist Thomas Nast portrayed Greeley as an assassin, shaking hands with John Wilkes Booth over Lincoln's grave.

In the election of 1872, Grant won 56 percent of the popular vote, a larger percentage than in 1868. Grant carried thirty-one states and took 286 of the 349 electoral votes. His popular vote margin (3,596,745 to 2,843,446) was the highest since Andrew Jackson's in 1828. But the election also revealed the extent of southern disaffection with Radical Reconstruction. In the South, the Republicans could muster only 50.1 percent of the popular vote.

The Money Question

Continuing revelations of corruption and persistent arguments about "the money question"—referring to federal monetary policy—dominated Grant's second term in office. To help finance the Civil War, Congress had issued almost $450 million in greenbacks—paper currency that was not backed by either gold or silver. The inflation of the money supply led to a steep increase in prices and shook public faith in the government. When the war ended, the government proposed to call in "greenbacks" for payment in gold or silver.

In general, restricting the money supply hurt debtors and helped creditors. People who had borrowed money when the currency was inflated would have to repay loans when fewer dollars were in circulation. Conversely, creditors who had loaned inflated dollars would receive payment in more valuable currency. The debate, however, was never that simple, since not everyone viewed the issue in terms of economic self-interest. Eastern business interests tended to see the debate over paper currency in religious terms. Government had a moral obligation to back its currency in gold; failure to do so was sinful. In addition to fear over falling farm prices, hatred of the eastern establishment—the "money power"—drove many farmers to favor inflated money.

The conflicting and complicated views on the currency cut across party lines. Despite disagreement within his own party, Grant sided with the advocates of hard money, endorsing payment of the national debt in gold as a point of national honor. The president's support for hard money could not have come at a worse time. In 1873 the bankruptcy of the Northern Pacific Railroad set off the "Panic of 1873"—a steep economic depression that lasted for six years. By 1876, eighteen thousand businesses were bankrupt, and nearly 15 percent of the labor force was unemployed. In 1878 alone, more than ten thousand businesses failed. Those who managed to hold on to their jobs suffered painful wage cuts.

Many people, believing that Grant's tight money policy contributed to the depression, increased their calls to print more greenbacks. In 1874 the Democrats and a handful of Republicans succeeded in passing a bill that increased the number of greenbacks in circulation, but Grant vetoed it. The following year, Republicans passed the Specie Resumption Act, which called for redeeming all greenbacks in circulation by 1879 and replacing them with certificates backed by gold. The legislation satisfied creditors, but it failed to calm the fears of small farmers and debtors who worried that any money standard tied to gold would be too restrictive. As the nation emerged from depression in 1879, the clamor for "easy money" subsided. It would resurface more persistently in the 1890s.

 ## The Failure of Reconstruction, 1870–1877

By the mid-1870s, a number of forces conspired to produce the downfall of Radical Reconstruction. In the South, the persistent tradition of individual rights and local control, combined with a belief in white supremacy, allowed the Democrats to topple a number of Republican state governments. A host of influences—disillusionment with government corruption, fears of a Democratic resurgence, economic strains, and general weariness—convinced northerners it was time to abandon their experiment. In a series of decisions, the Supreme Court signaled the North's retreat. The "Compromise of 1877," which resolved a disputed presidential election, marked the end of Reconstruction.

The South Redeemed

Former large slave owners were the bitterest opponents of the Republican program in the South. The Republican effort to expand political and economic opportunities for African-Americans threatened their vested interest in controlling agricultural labor and their power and status in southern society. In response, they staged a massive counterrevolution to "redeem" the South by regaining control of southern state governments.

Initially, some Democrats tried to woo black voters away from the Republicans with moderate appeals on racial and economic questions. When their appeals fell on deaf ears, they launched an ideological attack designed to unify southern whites and stir up fear and uncertainty among blacks and their allies.

In making their case against Republican rule, the Redeemers tapped into values that had deep roots in American political culture. They claimed that the Republican Party favored centralized power and special privilege over local rule and individual rights. "The principle of the Union is no longer justice, but force," declared a prominent white southerner. Most of all, however, the Redeemer appeal rested on the South's social and cultural foundation of racism and white supremacy. Alabama's State Conservative Committee designated January 30, 1868, a day of fasting and prayer to deliver the people of the state "from the horrors of negro domination." Mississippi Democrats in 1868 condemned the black members of the state's Radical constitutional convention as "destitute alike of the moral and intellectual qualifications required of electors in all civilized communities."

For Democrats, playing "the race card" served two purposes. First, the appeal to racial pride lured poor whites away from the Republicans and prevented the formation of a class-based, biracial coalition. "I may be poor and my manners may be crude, but I am a white man," declared a disgruntled scalawag. "That I am poor is not as important as that I am a white man; and no Negro is ever going to forget that he is not a white man."

Second, Democrats hoped to frighten blacks and Republican whites into avoiding voting and other political action. Throughout the Deep South, planters and their supporters organized secret societies to terrorize blacks and Republicans. The Ku Klux Klan emerged as the most powerful of the new terrorist groups. In 1865 a social circle of young men in Pulaski, Tennessee, organized themselves as the "Invisible Empire of the South." New chapters of the secret lodge quickly formed in other states. Klan members, who included poor farmers as well as middle-class professionals, donned ghostly white robes and indulged in ghoulish rituals. Their intention was to frighten their victims into thinking they were the avenging ghosts of the Confederate dead.

After 1870 the Ku Klux Klan fought an ongoing terrorist campaign against Reconstruction governments and local leaders. Acting as a guerrilla army for those who sought the restoration of white supremacy, Klansmen whipped and killed Republican politicians, burned black schools and churches, and attacked Republican Party gatherings. In some communities, Klan members paraded through the streets carrying coffins bearing the names of prominent Radicals and labeled "Dead, damned and delivered." In the bloodiest episode of violence, Klan members murdered nearly one hundred African-Americans in Colfax, Louisiana, on Easter Sunday 1873.

In response to the racial terrorism, Congress passed three Enforcement Acts in 1870 and 1871. The first act prohibited state officials from interfering with a citizen's right to vote. A second created federal election marshals to oversee congressional elections. In April 1871, Congress passed the Ku Klux Klan Act, which outlawed the Klan and any other conspiratorial group that sought to deprive individuals of their rights under the Constitution. It also empowered the president to suspend *habeas corpus* and to use federal troops to suppress "armed combinations."

The legislation restricted Klan activities, but it could not stem the Democratic resurgence in the South. Democrats redeemed Virginia, North Carolina, and Georgia from Radical rule between 1869 and 1871; Texas followed in 1873, and Arkansas in 1874. In 1875 a notorious campaign of terror and intimidation against black voters allowed the Democrats to seize control of Mississippi. The Democratic slogan became: "Carry the election peaceably if we can, forcibly if we must." Republicans

The Colfax Massacre, 1873 Throughout the Reconstruction period, freed slaves faced the threat of violence from whites who resented any alteration of the social order. The killing of one hundred blacks in Colfax, Louisiana, was the bloodiest incident during Reconstruction. Although three whites were convicted of Colfax crimes by the federal government, the Supreme Court overturned the verdicts in *U.S. v. Cruikshank*. The Court argued that under the Fourteenth Amendment, the federal government could prosecute only states, not individuals, for civil rights violations. *(Frank and Marie Therese Wood Print Collections, Alexandria, Va.)*

fearful of violence stayed away from the polls. "The Republicans are paralyzed through fear and will not act," the anguished carpetbag governor of Mississippi wrote to his wife. "Why should I fight a hopeless battle . . . when no possible good to the Negro or anybody else would result?"

The Republican Retreat

At the national level, too, a number of forces were pushing the Republican Party to abandon its Reconstruction experiment. First, the idealism that had once informed Republican efforts had long since faded. The Liberal Republican revolt in the 1872 elections revealed the changing sentiment in the party. Many party leaders felt that "waving the bloody shirt" was counterproductive. Republicans now sought reconciliation, not confrontation, with the South. In May 1872, Congress passed a General Amnesty Act that, with some exceptions, allowed Confederate leaders to vote and to hold public office.

Second, Republicans realized they were paying a heavy political price for their southern policies and receiving little benefit from it. Divided among themselves, Republicans watched their congressional majorities dwindle in the wake of a dramatic Democratic resurgence. In 1874 the Democrats gained a majority in the House of Representatives for the first time since 1856. "The election is not merely a victory but a revolution," declared a New York newspaper.

The Panic of 1873 outweighed Reconstruction as a factor in the Republican defeat, but the election's implications for Reconstruction policy were clear. Northern voters were tired of dealing with the "southern question" and the "Negro question." "The truth is our people are tired out with the worn out cry of 'Southern outrages'!!" a weary Republican cried. "Hard times and heavy taxes make them wish the 'ever lasting nigger' were in hell or Africa."

Third, northerners increasingly accepted the southern view of African-Americans as people inferior in intelligence and morality who required the paternal protection of the superior white race. Negative stereotypes in northern newspapers depicted blacks as ignorant, lazy, and dishonest, incapable of exercising the same rights as whites. "They [blacks] plunder, and glory in it," one northern journalist summed up; "they steal, and defy you to prove it." Even loyal administration supporters were convinced that Reconstruction was organized theft. The *New York Times* called the South Carolina legislature "a gang of thieves," its government "a sort of grand orgie."

Fourth, serious strains emerged within Republican ranks in the South. Race played a central role in fracturing the always fragile southern Republican Party. Poor whites were never willing to concede political equality to blacks. Republicans found it difficult to satisfy their black constituents' demands for equality without alienating whites. White Republicans were also divided among themselves. Scalawags resented carpetbaggers who they believed had seized offices that should have gone to native whites. Meanwhile, in state after state, Democrats skillfully exploited deepening fiscal problems by blaming Republicans for excessive spending and sharp tax increases.

These pressures proved too much for most Republicans. With support for Reconstruction unraveling, Radical pleas for new measures to protect the political and civil rights of African-Americans fell on deaf ears. The one exception was the Civil Rights Act of 1875, passed in the closing hours of the Republican-controlled Congress. The law guaranteed persons of every race "the full and equal treatment" of all public facilities such as hotels, theaters, and railroads.

However, several Supreme Court decisions involving the Fourteenth and Fifteenth Amendments undermined protection of black rights. In the so-called *Slaughterhouse Cases* of 1873, the Court offered a narrow definition of the Fourteenth Amendment by distinguishing between national and state citizenship. The amendment, the justices declared, guaranteed only those rights dependent on national citizenship. What were those rights? Most were of little concern to freed people: access to courts and navigable waterways, the ability to run for federal office, travel to the seat of government, and be protected on the high seas and abroad. By giving the states primary authority over citizens' rights, the courts weakened civil rights enforcement. In 1876 the court decided, in *United States* v. *Cruikshank*, that a mob attack on blacks trying to vote did not violate the Fourteenth Amendment. In 1883 the Court reaffirmed its limited view of the Constitution in *United States* v. *Harris,* which argued that the lynching of four black prisoners did not represent an infringement of their Fourteenth Amendment rights.

The Compromise of 1877

Republican leaders approached the 1876 presidential campaign with foreboding. "My God, it is ruin!" exclaimed Republican James G. Blaine. In an effort to distance themselves from the scandals of the Grant administration, party leaders turned to Ohio governor Rutherford B. Hayes. Not only did Hayes hail from an electoral-vote–rich state, but he had earned a reputation for honesty, possessed an honorable Civil War record, and supported civil service reform. He also had articulated a moderate stance on Reconstruction, which Republicans hoped would appeal to conservative Republicans and moderate Democrats.

Signaling that they planned to make the Grant scandals a central theme of their campaign to gain the presidency, the Democrats nominated Governor Samuel J. Tilden of New York, a well-known fighter of corruption. At their June convention in St. Louis, gleeful Democrats chanted "Tilden and Reform" and passed a platform promising to save the nation from "a corrupt centralism which has honeycombed the offices of the Federal government itself with incapacity, waste, and fraud."

On election night, it appeared that the Democrats had regained the White House for the first time since before the Civil War. Tilden received 51 percent of the popular vote (4,284,020) to Hayes's 48 percent (4,036,572). But Republicans charged that Democrats won the elections in three southern states—Louisiana, South Carolina, and Florida—by fraud and intimidation. Both sides claimed the electoral votes in those states (see map).

When Congress reconvened in January it confronted an unprecedented situation: three states with two different sets of electoral votes. If Congress accepted all the Republican votes, Hayes would have a one-vote electoral majority. The Constitution did not cover such a scenario, and as weeks passed without a solution, people feared that the impasse could escalate into a major national crisis.

On January 29, 1877, Congress set up a Joint Electoral Commission to resolve the dispute. The committee was made up of eight Democrats and eight Republicans, with the swing vote going to an independent member of the Supreme Court, Justice David Davis. But Davis withdrew from the Court and declared himself ineligible for the commission. Since there were no independents or Democrats on the Court, a Republican named Joseph P. Bradley took Davis's seat on the commission. The Republicans now controlled nine seats on the commission, the Democrats eight. Not surprisingly, the commission voted along straight partisan lines and gave the election to Hayes.

But Congress still had to approve the results, and the Democrats were threatening to filibuster. On February 26, 1877, prominent Ohio Republicans and powerful southern Democrats met at the Wormley House hotel in Washington, where they

The Election of 1876

Without any clear issues in 1876, Democrats and their presidential nominee Samuel J. Tilden emphasized the corruption that had hampered Grant's administration, while Republican nominee Rutherford B. Hayes linked the Democratic Party to the Confederacy. When the electoral votes were counted, Republicans and Democrats disputed the results in Louisiana, Florida, and South Carolina. Congress made the final decision, selecting Hayes despite the fact that he had trailed Tilden in the uncontested electoral votes.

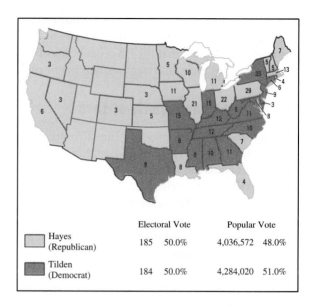

	Electoral Vote		Popular Vote	
Hayes (Republican)	185	50.0%	4,036,572	48.0%
Tilden (Democrat)	184	50.0%	4,284,020	51.0%

reached an informal agreement, later called the Compromise of 1877. The Republicans promised that Hayes would withdraw the last federal troops from Louisiana, Florida, and South Carolina, include at least one southerner in his cabinet, and give conservatives control of political patronage. In return, the Democrats promised to support Hayes's election, to accept the Reconstruction amendments, and to refrain from partisan attacks against Republicans in the South. On March 2, 1877, only two days before the scheduled inauguration, the House voted to accept the report and declared Hayes elected by an electoral vote of 185 to 184.

Hayes's election signaled the formal end of the Reconstruction era. In his first month in office, the new president appointed a southern Democrat to his cabinet and withdrew the last of the federal troops from the South. In a speech in Atlanta in the fall of 1877, Hayes told former slaves that their "rights and interests would be safer" if southern whites were "let alone by the general government."

The New South, 1870–1900

At the end of Reconstruction, southern propagandists filled the newspapers with calls for economic experimentation to create a "New South." They wanted the South to abandon its old agrarian ways and transform itself into a bustling center of commerce and industry. Despite the development of new factories and the rise of a few large cities, southern society, steeped in white supremacy, remained economically dependent on cheap labor and king cotton. This burden prevented the South from making major gains. Culturally, southerners remained deeply tied to the past at the same time that they experimented with new forms of artistic expression. For many African-Americans, the New South looked much like the old. Southern leaders developed a number of ingenious methods to limit black voting, and they imposed a rigid system of segregation.

Visions of Industry

In the early 1880s, boosters of the New South told everyone who would listen about the profound changes transforming the region. Led by Henry Grady, editor of the *Atlanta Constitution,* propagandists promised to remake the southern economy in the image of the North, claiming that a society of machines and factories was needed to replace the old agrarian order. Henry Watterson, a Louisville editor and orator, urged that "the ambition of the South is to out-Yankee the Yankee." The first step, however, was to convince southerners of the need for change. "Beyond all question," insisted a Richmond journal, "we have been on the wrong track and should take a new departure."

The clearest evidence of change was the rise of cities. People from every level of rural society left the countryside for towns. "The towns are being recruited by those too poor to be able to live in the country, as well as by those too rich to be willing to live there," observed a reporter. Atlanta, which had only 14,000 residents at the close of the Civil War, had a population close to 40,000 in 1880 and 90,000 two decades later. Birmingham, Alabama, saw its population grow from 3,000 in 1880 to 38,000 in 1900.

The spirit of the New South penetrated the halls of statehouses and governors' mansions. Many state legislatures tried luring northern bankers and capitalists with attractive investment opportunities. William H. Harrison, Jr., a prominent New South spokesman, maintained that no foreign country offered "such tempting inducements to the capitalist for profitable investments" as did the New South. In 1877 five southern states repealed laws reserving land for private homebuilders so that they might entice investors to exploit their coal, iron, and timber resources.

With the aid of new investment, southern industries such as textiles, iron, and lumber experienced a boom. The South's textile mills boasted the latest and most sophisticated machinery. By 1890, textile spindles, which doubled the output per worker, appeared in 90 percent of southern mills compared with only 70 percent of New England mills. Jefferson County, the home of Birmingham, had only twenty-two factories in 1870; thirty years later, it had five hundred. By the late 1880s, southern pig iron production had surpassed the total output of the entire country in 1860. By 1910, the South was producing almost half of all lumber produced in the United States. The lumber industry claimed one in five southern manufacturing workers. "Never before has the lumber business been so active," a paper proudly reported in 1882.

To make their new factories accessible to northern markets, many states built new railroad tracks. Between 1880 and 1890, track mileage more than doubled, from 16,605 to 39,108. The South integrated its railroads with the North by adopting a standard gauge, or track. On May 30, 1886, work crews throughout the South pushed thousands of miles of track three inches closer to create a uniform

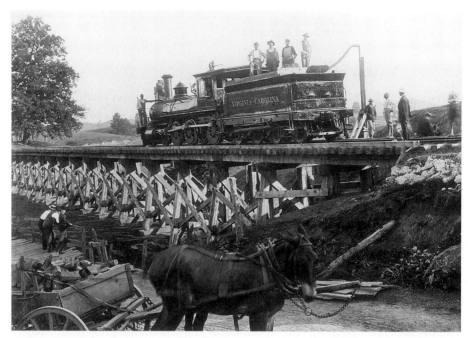

Virginia Coalfields After the war, the South lagged far behind the North in economic development. Closing the gap became a major goal of Reconstruction. The discovery of coalfields in Virginia in 1873 provided a major impetus for railroad construction and buoyed the region's economy. Although the South made great strides toward industrialization during Reconstruction, southern industry still accounted for only 10 percent of the United States' industrial capacity by 1900. (*Virginia Historical Society.*)

national railroad system. The change helped railroads to expand the development of land-locked mineral resources of the South, particularly the iron mines of Tennessee, Virginia, and Alabama. By 1898, Birmingham was the largest shipping point for pig iron in the country and the third largest in the world.

King Cotton and the Crop-Lien System

Proponents of the New South exaggerated the amount of change that had actually taken place. Despite the growth of cities and the increase in manufacturing, most people in the South continued to live in rural areas. The 1890 census showed that only 3.9 percent of North Carolinians and 5.9 percent of Alabamans were considered urban. By 1900, the South was still the most rural and agrarian section in the settled portions of the country. Although new industries and signs of progress abounded, the South continued to lag far behind the prosperous North. In 1860 the South housed 17 percent of the country's manufacturing; by 1904 it had only 15 percent.

The economy of the postwar South remained tied to agriculture. The spread of the crop-lien system as the South's main form of agricultural credit forced more and more farmers, both white and black, into growing cash crops—crops that could earn the most money on the open market. Cotton, which yielded more value per acre than any other crop, became the crop of choice. By 1880, nearly three-quarters of the African-American farmers and about one-third of the white farmers in the cotton states were sharecroppers or tenants. The number of cotton mills in the South rose from 161 in 1880 to 400 in 1900. In 1880 there were 45 mills in the United States producing 7 million gallons of cottonseed oil annually for export; by 1900, there were 357, all but 4 in the South.

The South's dependence on a single crop had many unforeseen consequences. For one thing, it made the South less self-sufficient, since many farmers plowed over land that had been used to grow food and replaced it with cotton. By 1880, the South was not growing enough food to feed its people. The near total dominance of "King Cotton" also inhibited economic growth across the region. As more and more farmers turned to cotton growing as the fastest way to obtain credit, expanding production depressed prices. Competition from new cotton centers in the world market, notably Egypt and India, furthered the downward spiral. The decline in cotton prices dragged the rest of the southern economy down with it. By the 1890s, per capita wealth in the South equaled only one-third that of the East, Midwest, or Far West.

Declining cotton prices produced a grim desperation in the South and only increased suspicion and hostility toward the North. In 1879 the *New York Tribune* showed little sympathy: "Fifteen years have gone over the South and she still sits crushed, wretched, busy displaying and bemoaning her wounds."

The Culture of the New South

Paralleling the contrast between industrial boosterism and continued dependence on agriculture, cultural trends pulled the South in different directions. On the one hand, a wave of nostalgia swept across the South as whites honored Civil War soldiers. The movement began as a defense of the "Lost Cause" in the 1860s, then evolved into a nostalgic celebration of old soldiers. Caught up in the "cult of the Confederacy," many white southerners joined the United Confederate Veterans and the United Daughters of the Confederacy, which raised funds for the erection of new monuments. Nine thousand whites of all ages dragged a new statue of Robert E. Lee to its site in Richmond in 1890. Over a hundred thousand people attended the unveiling three weeks later. The region's natives revered Decoration Day, when they carried spring flowers to the graves of the soldiers killed during the war.

At the same time that many white southerners were celebrating the past, southern fiction writers were questioning the relevance of the values and customs that had shaped their society. These writers attempted to explain their region to northern readers at the same time that they challenged prevailing notions of race and gender. In *Uncle Remus: His Songs and Sayings* (1880), Joel Chandler Harris allowed a black slave to tell stories in which the weak could outwit the strong. The success of Harris's book convinced Mark Twain, America's most visible and successful man of letters, to take another look at the South. In 1881 Twain took a boat trip down the Mississippi to reacquaint himself with a region he had explored earlier in his book *Tom Sawyer* (1876). He was shocked by what he witnessed. The New South,

Twain declared, was "a solemn, depressing, pathetic spectacle." His impressions created the backdrop for his greatest work, *The Adventures of Huckleberry Finn*, published in 1884. Among other things, the book explored the enormous distance between the South's perception of itself as a bastion of civilization and its real status as an impoverished and violent place.

Women writers played a prominent role in shaping the literature of the New South. Ruth McEnery Stuart's short stories about white women in fictional "Simpkinsville" portrayed females as active agents and men as ineffectual and absent. Kate Chopin juxtaposed what she saw as more honest and healthier European standards of sexual behavior with the conventions of Protestant America. Her book *The Awakening*, published in 1899, created such an outcry that it was pulled from library and bookstore shelves. The leading woman writer of the New South was Ellen Glasgow. Her most famous novel, *The Deliverance*, became the second best-selling book in America in 1904. It told the story of young people of the South achieving success, but only after overcoming the suffocating burden of southern customs.

Music emerged as the most powerful force for cultural innovation in the New South. Music appealed to people of every description. Musical instruments were among the first mass-produced commodities southerners bought. Cheap banjos were mass-produced in the 1880s, guitars in the 1890s. Students of both races were eager to learn formal music. Instructors taught classical music and voice throughout the towns and cities of the South. Bouncy popular music filled parlors, stages, tents, and streets. Every town of any size had an "opera house" that hosted traveling performers. In 1891 a band tournament in Troy, Alabama, drew four thousand visitors and ten brass bands from nearby towns.

In every other aspect of southern society racial distinctions were hardening, but culturally the line between white and black music was blurring. In southern cities throughout the South, the polyrhythms and improvisation of African music blended with traditional European styles. Much of the experimentation took place in New Orleans, which contained the largest concentration of musicians in the South. The city attracted black and white musicians who trained together, played in the same bands and nightclubs, exchanged ideas, and borrowed styles.

The Triumph of White Supremacy

The Redeemers who gained power in the South ousted, state by state, the carpetbag rule of the Reconstruction era. Some Redeemers gained power by compromising with their opponents; others conquered by brute force. They were a mixed group that included the scions of the old planter class as well as new business leaders. They were united by what they opposed: biracial coalitions and the use of state power as an agent of change.

Free from interference from the North, the Redeemer governments in the South waged an aggressive assault on African-Americans. Democrats regained control of state governments and imposed sweeping changes, slashing social programs, lowering taxes, and placing a premium on restoring social stability. Education programs were especially hard hit. Public schools closed in some parts of Maryland in 1871.

In 1872 only a third of Tennessee's counties levied school taxes; only about 28 percent of the state's children attended school. "Schools are not a necessity," declared the governor of Virginia.

Most important, the Democrats manipulated the law to ensure a stable black work force. Local ordinances in heavily black counties restricted leisure activities—such as hunting, fishing, and gun carrying—that would distract blacks from their work. States passed tough laws against trespassing and theft.

All former Confederate states changed their constitutions to create methods by which they could exclude the black vote. The Mississippi constitution of 1890 set the pattern. It required a poll tax of $2 from prospective voters at registration. Men who intended to vote at elections had to present their receipt at the polls. Anyone who mislaid his receipt forfeited his vote. Other states included literacy tests that required prospective voters to be "able to read the Constitution, or to understand the Constitution when read." Since white Democratic registrars interpreted the ability to read or understand, officials could use these ordinances to discriminate in favor of poor illiterate whites and against black citizens, literate or not. Louisiana adopted the "grandfather clause," which limited the franchise to anyone who had a grandfather on the electoral roll in 1867. Since the grandfathers of most blacks had been slaves, and unable to vote, the measure effectively barred them from voting.

The results of these various efforts to eliminate the black vote were dramatic. Louisiana, for example, contained 130,334 registered black voters in 1896. Eight years later, there were only 1,342. In Alabama 181,000 black voters were registered in 1890; in 1900, 3,000. In the South as a whole, black voter participation fell by 62 percent. In 1900 Ben ("Pitchfork") Tillman of South Carolina boasted on the floor of the Senate, "We have done our best. We have scratched our heads to find out how we could eliminate the last one of them. We stuffed ballot boxes. We shot them. We are not ashamed of it."

Along with disfranchising blacks, southern lawmakers gave informal segregation in public facilities the force of law. Until the 1880s, the South had established a system of segregation by custom. Schools, hospitals, parks, courthouses, hotels, and restaurants were separated by race. Social custom reinforced the distance between the races. Whites never addressed black men they did not know as "mister," but rather as "boy," "Jack," or "George." Black women were never called "Mrs." but rather "aunt" or by their first name. According to custom, the two races did not shake hands, walk together, or fraternize in public. Black men removed their hats in public places reserved for whites, whereas whites did not remove their hats even in black homes.

While some blacks resisted the exclusion from white-owned hotels and restaurants, they could usually find accommodations in black-run businesses. Travel was a different story, for members of both races had no choice but to use the same railroads. When middle-class blacks carrying first-class tickets refused to be consigned to second-class seating, southern whites developed "separate but equal" railcars. These new restrictions—called "Jim Crow laws" after a minstrel song of 1830 that presented blacks as childlike and inferior—made it impossible for blacks and whites to mingle. The laws were soon extended to libraries, hotels, restaurants, hospitals, prisons, theaters, parks, and playgrounds. Blacks and whites used separate bathrooms, separate toilets, and were even buried in separate cemeteries.

The Supreme Court, which had already made discrimination by individuals and businesses legal, now allowed state governments to make segregation a part of the fabric of American life. In *Plessy* v. *Ferguson* (1896), the Court upheld, by a 7 to 1 majority, a Louisiana law that required railroads to provide "equal but separate accommodations for the white and colored races." The Court ruled that the Fourteenth Amendment applied only to political rights and did not extend to "social equality." Legislatures were thus free to pass laws that maintained "the customs and traditions of the people." Justice Henry B. Brown of Michigan, speaking for the majority, ruled with racist candor, "If one race be inferior to the other socially, the Constitution of the United States cannot put them upon the same plane." A year later, the judges endorsed segregated public schools as a means to prevent "commingling of the two races upon terms unsatisfactory to either." The justices also upheld the poll tax and literacy tests, which were used by state officials to disfranchise blacks.

Growing Democratic power emboldened whites to resort to violence, without fear of reprisal. Between 1889 and 1898, blacks suffered 187 lynchings a year in the United States, four-fifths of which were in the South. Lynchings flourished where whites were surrounded by what they called "strange niggers"—blacks who were unknown in the area and had no white person to vouch for them. Most were accused of raping white women. Southern newspapers reported the hangings in graphic detail to stimulate and attract readers and to intimidate blacks.

Democratic restoration also led to the expansion of the convict lease system. In 1876 three Georgia companies contracted to lease the state's convicts for twenty years, in return for a $25,000 annual payment. The convicts were assigned to labor camps in which brutal and degrading conditions prevailed, and overseers forced them to toil from sunrise to sunset, disciplined by the rod and whip.

Southern blacks struggled to persuade whites to stop the persecution. The most prominent voice belonged to Booker T. Washington. Born in 1856 to a slave woman and her white master, whose identity he never knew, Washington later attended the Hampton Institute in Virginia, a black school established and run by northern whites. In 1881 Washington helped organize the Tuskegee Institute, a state vocational school for blacks. He gained national prominence in 1895 when white organizers invited him to speak at Atlanta's Cotton States and International Exposition—the first time in southern history that a black man had been asked to address whites at such an important event.

Washington's speech, which became known as the "Atlanta Compromise," suggested that African-Americans trade political activity and integration for black economic progress. Blacks, he told his segregated audience, should put aside their ambitions for political power and social equality and instead focus on developing useful vocational skills. "It is at the bottom of life we must begin, and not at the top," he said. Political and social equality would proceed naturally once blacks had proven their economic value. "Dignify and glorify common labor," he urged. "Agitation of questions of racial equality is the extremist folly." To both races, he advised cooperation and mutual respect. "In all things that are purely social we can be as separate as the

Lynching Victims After federal troops pulled out of the South in 1876, racial violence gradually reached epidemic proportions, with white southerners lynching thousands of African-Americans before the century's end. The victims, deemed "uppity" by whites, were usually singled out for being too assertive or successful, or for refusing to show the proper deference to whites. These four Kentucky sharecroppers were guilty of being sympathetic toward a black man who had killed his white employer in self-defense. One of the bodies bears the message, "Let white people alone or you will go the same way." (*Gilman Paper Company Collection.*)

fingers, yet one as the hand in all things essential to mutual progress." Washington's message of accommodation was almost universally popular with whites. Blacks were more ambivalent. Southern blacks who favored gradual nonconfrontational change embraced his philosophy, but some northern black leaders complained that Washington had compromised too much.

For the freed people, whose aspirations had been raised by Republican rule, the impact of "redemption" was demoralizing. No one could deny the enormous changes that had transformed American society over the previous two decades: slavery had been abolished and a framework of legal rights had been enshrined in the Constitution. African-Americans created political and social institutions that had not existed before Reconstruction. But as the African-American leader W. E. B. Du Bois observed, "The slave went free; stood a brief moment in the sun; then moved back again toward slavery." Reconstruction had failed to provide blacks with either economic independence or political rights. For many African-Americans, the long road to freedom had just begun.

CONCLUSION

The question of how to deal with the defeated South divided the North at the end of the war. Radicals, who passionately opposed slavery, took an expansive view of federal power, believing that the national government had the right to reshape southern society by breaking up the old plantation system and guaranteeing political and economic rights to the freed people. President Johnson, on the other hand, was a strong supporter of states' rights, opposed the expansion of federal power, and favored a lenient policy toward the former Confederate states. Politics also played a role in the conflicting experiments. Radicals hoped that former slaves would form the foundation of a powerful Republican Party in the South. Johnson, on the other hand, planned to use opposition to Reconstruction to build a new national coalition of moderate Democrats and Republicans.

The president's disdain for compromise and negotiation complicated his relationship with Congress and allowed the Radicals to seize control of Reconstruction policy in 1866. Once in power, the Radicals passed the Fourteenth and Fifteenth Amendments to the Constitution. Republican regimes in the South expanded democracy, built biracial public schools, and embarked on an ambitious public works program. The Radical experiment, however, quickly unraveled, confronted by a rejuvenated Democratic Party in the South that was willing to use violence and intimidation to regain power. At the same time, a steep depression, widespread charges of corruption, and concerns about government power divided the northern Republican Party. The Compromise of 1877 signaled the Republicans' retreat from Reconstruction. The Republicans had destroyed the slave system, but their experiment in securing basic economic and political rights for African-Americans remained incomplete.

African-Americans played a central role in defining the new meaning of freedom in the South. Their experiments cast aside old forms of deference to whites, built up community institutions, and restored ties among family members separated by slavery. Economic independence, however, remained elusive for most African-Americans. By 1880, nearly 75 percent of black southerners were working as sharecroppers.

Propagandists of the New South hoped to remake the southern economy in the image of the North, but southern realities limited economic experimentation. The region remained predominately rural and agricultural, tied to a single crop—cotton. Culturally, many whites celebrated the past at the same time that others questioned the underpinnings of southern society. No ambiguity, however, obscured the way the white South exercised power. The white "Redeemer" governments moved aggressively to limit the rights of African-Americans, prevented them from voting, and imposed a formal system of segregation that would dominate southern life well into the next century.

SUGGESTED READINGS

Eric Foner's *Reconstruction: America's Unfinished Revolution, 1863–1877* (1988) is an impressive synthesis of recent scholarship on all aspects of Reconstruction, with the experience of the freedmen as the central theme. *The Era of Reconstruction, 1865–1877* (1965) by Kenneth Stampp is the classic revisionist work on the period, dismissing the idea of Reconstruction as harsh and corrupt. James McPherson's *Ordeal by Fire: The Civil War and Reconstruction* (1967) includes a basic overview of the events and politics of the time.

Reconstruction under Lincoln's tenure is treated by Peyton McCrary in *Abraham Lincoln and Reconstruction: The Louisiana Experiment* (1978). He argues that Lincoln's primary aim was to restore the South to the Union as expediently as possible. His plan included little in the way of social reform because those in charge erroneously assumed that this would slow down the process. Louis Gerteis demonstrates the haphazard nature of wartime Reconstruction through an examination of the government's dealings with the former slaves in *From Contraband to Freedman: Federal Policy Toward Southern Blacks, 1861–1865* (1973).

Historians generally agree that Lincoln's plan is difficult to assess because it was largely unformed at the time of his death. They therefore have a better grasp on the policies of his successor, Andrew Johnson. Eric McKitrick leads off the barrage of criticism historians have heaped on Johnson with *Andrew Johnson and Reconstruction* (1966). He demonstrates how the president bungled the opportunity to create a moderate coalition through his insistence on a strict interpretation of the Constitution and on personal control. *Andrew Johnson and the Uses of Constitutional Power* (1980) by James Sefton places Johnson's rigid behavior on Reconstruction issues in the larger context of his life and personality. Hans Trefousse examines the impact of Johnson's impeachment on Reconstruction politics in *Impeachment of a President: Andrew Johnson and Reconstruction* (1975). He argues that the failure to remove Johnson forced the president into reckless opposition to Congress, putting limits on congressional attempts at reform.

The rise of the Radical Republicans is discussed by several historians. Edward L. Gambill's *Conservative Ordeal: Northern Democrats and Reconstruction, 1865–1868* (1981) demonstrates how factionalism within the Democratic Party destroyed its chances to mount serious opposition to the Radicals. Michael Les Benedict, in *A Compromise of Principle: Congressional Republicans and Reconstruction* (1974), looks at the inner workings of the Republican Party and finds that the split between moderates and Radicals was not over principles but over their political expediency. In *An American Crisis: Congress and Reconstruction, 1865–1867* (1963), W. R. Brock maintains that Radicals had early and widespread popular support, based primarily on their commitment to economic expansion and equal opportunity.

The collapse of congressional Reconstruction is the subject of William Gillette in *Retreat from Reconstruction, 1869–1879* (1979), a survey of national politics during the time that blames the Republican Party's lack of commitment to racial equality for Reconstruction's short life. In *The Radical Republicans and Reform in New York During Reconstruction* (1973), James Mohr examines Radical Republicans' substantial reform record in New York, which he claims foreshadowed progressivism there, and its destruction in the fight over black suffrage within the Republican Party. David Montgomery, author of *Beyond Equality: Labor and the Radical Republicans, 1862–1872* (1967), argues that the Radicals foundered on the issue of class, not race, dividing over labor policy. Ian Polakoff discusses the official end of Reconstruction in *The Politics of Inertia: The Election of 1876 and the End of Reconstruction* (1973). He argues that the high level of popular participation and factionalism in the parties left them without effective leadership to deal constructively with the disputed election of 1876.

The constitutional aspects of Reconstruction is treated by Harold Hyman in *A More Perfect Union: The Impact of the Civil War and Reconstruction on the Constitution* (1973), in which he demonstrates how the crises of war and reunion transformed the Constitution into a more dynamic document. Stanley Kutler examines the Supreme Court during this period in *The Judicial Power and Reconstruction Politics* (1968), countering the image of the Court as a foe of congressional Reconstruction. In *Emancipation and Equal Rights: Politics and Constitutionalism in the Civil War Era* (1978), Herman Belz evaluates Reconstruction from a constitutional perspective and judges it a success.

For discussion of northern political life in general during congressional Reconstruction, *The Press Gang: Newspapers and Politics, 1865–1878* (1994) by Mark Wahlgren Summers is an entertaining and insightful read. Brooks Simpson examines Grant's stance toward Reconstruction and his transition from soldier to politician in *Let Us Have Peace: Ulysses S. Grant and the Politics of War and Reconstruction, 1861–1868* (1991).

Willie Lee Rose's *Rehearsal for Reconstruction: The Port Royal Experiment* (1964) is perhaps the best examination of wartime Reconstruction in action. She focuses particularly on the experience of blacks and their relationship to white northerners trying to guide them into freedom. Leon Litwack's *Been in the Storm So Long: The Aftermath of Slavery* (1979) and Joel Williamson's *After Slavery: The Negro in South Carolina During Reconstruction* (1966) also discuss the former slaves' response to emancipation.

Examinations of Johnson's plan in the South further a negative view of the president. In *Reunion Without Compromise: The South and Reconstruction, 1865–1868* (1973), Michael Perman contends that Johnson and Congress encouraged southern defiance by giving the South too much choice and that it was this stubbornness that ultimately doomed presidential Reconstruction. Donald Nieman, in *To Set the Law in Motion: The Freedmen's Bureau and the Legal Rights of Blacks, 1865–1868* (1979), examines Johnson's role in the failure of the Freedmen's Bureau to defend adequately the rights of blacks. Dan Carter's *When the War Was Over: The Failure of Self-Reconstruction in the South, 1865–1867* (1985) contrasts with most of these works, portraying the southern white leaders during presidential Reconstruction not as reactionary ardent secessionists but as cautious conservatives.

Numerous studies have been done on the South during congressional Reconstruction. *The Road to Redemption: Southern Politics, 1869–1879* (1984), Michael Perman shows how division within each party in the South led to a merger of moderate factions by the end of Reconstruction. Steven Hahn examines the Reconstruction origins of southern populism in the transition of southern yeomen from subsistence to capitalist farming in *The Roots of Southern Populism: Yeoman Farmers and the Transformation of the Georgia Upcountry, 1850–1890* (1983). James Roark studies the impact of emancipation and Reconstruction on the former slaveholders in *Masters Without Slaves: Southern Planters in the Civil War and Reconstruction* (1977).

The African-American experience during congressional Reconstruction is covered by W. E. B. Du Bois's still classic *Black Reconstruction in America* (1935). More recently, Thomas Holt's *Black Over White: Negro Political Leadership in South Carolina During Reconstruction* (1977) and Edmund L. Drago's *Black Politicians and Reconstruction in Georgia* (1982) examine the experience of blacks in Reconstruction governments.

The role of southern violence in the demise of Reconstruction is discussed in *White Terror: The Ku Klux Klan Conspiracy and Southern Reconstruction* (1967) by Allen Trelease and *But There Was No Peace: The Role of Violence in the Politics of Reconstruction* (1984) by George Rable. Both books argue that the Republican Party died in the South as a result of a vigorous campaign of intimidation and murder on the part of southern whites.

C. Van Woodward's classic *Origins of the New South, 1877–1913* (1951) is still a valuable treatment, focusing on the rise of a business-oriented middle class in the South after the Civil War. Jonathan Weiner offers a different take in *Social Origins of the New South, 1860–1885* (1978). He argues that the New South evolved from the planter elite's rigid control over unskilled labor during the modernization process. Edward Ayers offers an insightful analysis in *The Promise of the New South: Life After Reconstruction* (1992). On the Lost Cause, see Gaines Foster's *The Ghosts of the Confederacy* (1989). Robert Kenzer examines the role of blacks in the economy of the urban South in *Enterprising Southerners* (1997).

The rise of Jim Crow is also discussed by C. Van Woodward in another classic, *The Strange Career of Jim Crow* (1955). He argues that the South only capitulated to racism once the forces of northern liberalism, southern conservatism, and southern radicalism declined in their efficacy in checking racial discrimination. Leon Litwack's *Trouble in Mind: Black Southerners in the Age of Jim Crow* (1998) is a comprehensive and moving account of the trials of African-Americans in the post-Reconstruction South. The perpetuation of black poverty after slavery is the subject of Jay Mandle's *Not Slave, Not Free: The African American Economic Experience Since the Civil War* (1992). He argues that the southern plantation system, responsible for the black economic condition, was simply revised after the war, becoming the equally enslaving sharecropping system.

The Boundaries of Congressional Reconstruction

A Southern Critique of the Reconstruction Acts

Benjamin H. Hill, a former Confederate senator, gave this speech on July 16, 1867, in Atlanta. He was responding to the passage in March of the Reconstruction Acts, which eliminated the southern governments established under presidential Reconstruction and imposed military rule across the former Confederacy. His seething anger is directed at Congress, which he believed had overstepped its legal boundaries with its ambitious plan for transforming the South.

The people of the North honestly love the Constitution, but the leaders there hate it and intend to destroy it. . . .

By carrying out these measures you disfranchise your own people. Suppose we concede, for argument, that it is right to enfranchise all the negroes; if this be right, by what principle of law or morals do we disfranchise the white people? . . . In the face of the fact that a republican government can rest upon and be perpetuated only by the virtue and intelligence of the people, you propose to exclude the most intelligent from participating in the government forever! . . .

But you say that you are in favor of going into the Union, because if you do not your property will be confiscated. . . . I am ashamed to talk or use arguments about confiscation in time of peace! It is a war power, not known to international law except as a war power, to be used only in time of war, upon an enemy's goods! Confiscation in time of peace is neither more nor less than robbery! . . .

These bills propose at every step to abrogate the Constitution—trample upon the State and its laws—to blot out every hope—to perjure every man who accepts them, with every principle of honor, justice, and safety disregarded, trampled upon, and despised—all to perpetuate the power of their wicked authors. . . . That which is now proposed is *force*. It is proposed by men who do not live in this State, and whose agents do not live here; and it is sought to be accomplished by military power, but under the pretense of your sanction—not to please yourselves, but them. . . .

This whole scheme is in violation of all the issues of the war . . . and all the terms of surrender. More than a hundred thousand men abandoned Lee's army because they were assured that if they laid down their arms they would be in the Union again with all their rights as before. . . . The people—the soldiers of the United States—were then willing to fulfill the obligation; but the politicians intended to deceive you. . . .

My colored friends, will you receive a word of admonition? Of all the people, you will most need the protection of the law. . . . Do you believe that the man who is faithless to the Constitution will be faithful to you? . . . They promise you lands, and teach you to hate the Southern people, whom you have known always and who never deceived you. Are you foolish enough to believe you can get another man's land for nothing, and that the white people will give up their land without resistance?

If you get up strife between your race and the white race, do you not know you must perish? . . . You can have no safety in the Constitution and no peace except by cultivating relations of kindness with those who are fixed here, who need your services, and who are willing to protect you. . . .

Thaddeus Stevens Proposes Land Reform

Pennsylvania congressman Thaddeus Stevens was perhaps the most Radical of the Republicans. In his view, the Reconstruction Acts did not go far enough. He envisioned a complete overhaul of southern institutions and real political and economic opportunity for the freed slaves. In the midst of the debate over the Reconstruction Acts, on March 19, 1867, he introduced a land reform bill that would have given each freedman household forty acres of land. The bill was defeated.

. . . The cause of the war was slavery. We have liberated the slaves. It is our duty to protect them, and provide for them while they are unable to provide for themselves. . . .

Have we not a right, if we chose to go to that extent, to indemnify ourselves for the expenses and damaged caused by the war? We might make the property of the enemy pay the $4,000,000,000 which we have expended, as well as the damages inflicted on loyal men by confiscation and invasion, which might reach $1,000,000,000 more. This bill is merciful, asking less than one tenth of our just claims. . . .

The first section orders the confiscation of all the property belonging to the State governments, and the national government which made war upon us, and which we have conquered. . . .

The fourth section provides first that out of the lands thus confiscated each liberated slave who is a male adult, or the head of a family, shall have assigned to him a homestead of forty acres of land (with $100 to build a dwelling), which shall be held for them by trustees during their pupilage. Let us consider whether this is a just and politic provision.

Whatever may be the fate of the rest of the bill I must earnestly pray that this may not be defeated. On its success, in my judgment, depends not only the happiness and respectability of the colored race, but their very existence. Homesteads to them are far more valuable than the immediate right of suffrage, though both are their due.

Four million persons have just been freed from a condition of dependence, wholly unacquainted with business transactions, kept systematically in ignorance of all their rights and of the common elements of education, without which none of any race are competent to earn an honest living, to guard against the frauds which will always be practiced on the ignorant, or to judge of the most judicious manner of applying their labor. But few of them are mechanics, and none of them skilled manufacturers. They must necessarily, therefore, be the servants and the victims of others unless they are made in some measure independent of their wiser neighbors. . . .

Make them independent of the old masters so that they may not be compelled to work for them upon unfair terms, which can only be done by giving them a small tract of land to cultivate for themselves, and you remove all this danger. You also elevate the character of the freedman. Nothing is so likely to make a man a good citizen as to make him a freeholder. Nothing will so multiply the productions of the South as to divide it into small farms. Nothing will make men so industrious and moral as to let them feel that they are above want and are the owners of the soil which they till. . . .

I do not speak of their fidelity and services in this bloody war. I put it on the mere score of lawful earnings. They and their ancestors have toiled, not for years, but for ages, without one farthing of recompense. They have earned for their masters this very land and much more. . . .

Congress is dictating the terms of peace. . . . This bill is very merciful toward a cruel, outlawed belligerent, who, when their armies were dispersed, would gladly have compromised if their lives were saved. . . .

Thaddeus Stevens, long an advocate for African-American rights, was a leader among both the Radical Republicans and the House of Representatives as a whole, admired even by those who were enraged by his strident style and unorthodox views. He and his fellow Radical Republicans saw in Reconstruction a "golden moment" not only to ensure the equality of blacks under the law, but to foment real change in the South through the destruction of the plantation system and the transformation of the freed slaves into small farmers, self-sufficient and upwardly mobile. On more than one occasion, Stevens introduced plans for the redistribution of southern land, at one time going as far as advocating the seizure of wealthy southerners' property by the federal government. Stevens' plans exemplified innovative social and political thinking, which not only included economic opportunity for the former slaves and the restructuring of southern society, but also envisioned using the federal government in unprecedented ways to accomplish these ends.

Stevens's ambitious ideas challenged existing views of federal power, which suggested that government could ensure legal, but not economic, equality of all its citizens. Even the Reconstruction Acts, which did pass into law, pressed the boundaries of federal power, as southerners were quick to point out. White southerners protested against the federal government's occupation of southern soil, its imposition of martial law, and its insistence on setting the terms of the states' readmission to the Union. After declaring they could secede from the Union, the white South now claimed it had never left and should not be treated as a conquered nation. The South felt it should be able to form new governments quickly, with little federal interference, and with minimal impact on southern institutions and traditions.

Questions for Analysis

1. Why does Hill call congressional Reconstruction unconstitutional? Do his claims have any merit? Explain.

2. Whom does he blame for this alleged assault on the Constitution?

3. What is Hill's advice to the freed slaves? Do you think he is sincere?

4. What are the provisions of Stevens's bill?

5. Why does Stevens believe Congress has the right to pass such a bill?

6. What reasons does he give to support the necessity of land reform?

7. How do you think our society might be different today had Reconstruction gone further? How would it be the same?

17

Conquering the West, 1862–1900

ate in 1888 in western Nevada, a Paiute Indian named Wovoka had a vision of the future that predicted a return to the past—to a time before the white man had stolen the Indians' lands, forced them onto reservations, and slaughtered the buffalo that sustained them. "My brothers, I bring to you the promise of a day," he preached, "when the red men of the prairie will rule the world." To hasten the day of salvation, he taught, Indians must dance in a large circle. If their faith was strong enough, the old world of their ancestors would return and the white man would vanish. Word quickly spread across the Plains and the Great Basin about the messiah and his "ghost dance."

The new ritual terrified many whites. Missionaries condemned the "heathen" Native American religious practice, claiming it kept Indians from becoming "civilized." The press, always hungry for a sensational news story, began writing about "hostile" Sioux. Army officials worried that the mysterious dancing would lead to unrest. "Indians are dancing in the snow and are wild and crazy," a nervous agent at Pine Ridge Reservation in South Dakota wired to Washington. "We need protection and we need it now."

The War Department responded by dispatching army troops to the Indian reservation to arrest the Ghost Dance "fomenters of disturbances." The army was convinced that Sioux chief Sitting Bull was the "high priest and leading apostle of this latest absurdity." On the morning of December 15, 1890,

U.S.-trained Indian policemen at the Sioux's Standing Rock Reservation in South Dakota burst into Sitting Bull's house to arrest him. A group of the chief's armed and angry supporters confronted the policemen. One of them, Bear That Catches, pulled a gun from under his blanket and shot one of the officials. A hail of bullets followed, leaving Sitting Bull, eight of his followers, and six policemen dead.

The news of Sitting Bull's murder alarmed Big Foot, the aging chief of another band of Sioux, who fled with his people into the wilderness. On December 28, five days after starting south to Pine Ridge to join other chiefs for a meeting, Big Foot surrendered to the Seventh Cavalry. The soldiers escorted Big Foot, along with the 120 men and 230 women and children traveling with him, to a camp near a frozen creek called Wounded Knee, where they pitched their tepees in a low hollow. The soldiers—a total of about 500—camped on a rise just to the north.

"The following morning there was a bugle call," remembered an Indian named Dewey Beard. Surrounded by mounted soldiers, the Indians were ordered to assemble at the center of camp and turn over their weapons. Big Foot advised his men to

Wounded Knee, South Dakota   Over 150 Sioux Indians, including many women and children, were killed by U.S. cavalrymen at Wounded Knee. A Sioux may have fired the first shot, but the Indians were badly outmanned by the machine-gun wielding horse soldiers. Although the incident was very much a one-sided massacre, journalists who flocked to the scene characterized the tragedy as a "battle" won by the U.S. forces. This type of distortion was extremely common in the Indian wars of the late nineteenth century and partly accounted for the dearth of sympathy for Native Americans among the American public.   *(Chicago Historical Society.)*

Chronology

1851	Treaty of Fort Laramie
1862	Pacific Railroad Act
	Homestead Act
1864	Massacre at Sand Creek
1866	Fetterman massacre
1867	Treaty of Medicine Lodge Creek
	Abilene established as major cattle depot
1868	Battle of the Washita
	Second Treaty of Fort Laramie
1869	Transcontinental Railroad completed
1872	Yellowstone National Park founded
1873	Timber Culture Act
1874	Red River War
	Women's National Indian Association founded
	Glidden invents barbed wire
1876	Battle of Little Bighorn
1877	Desert Land Act
1878	Timber and Stone Act
1879	Exodusters migrate to Kansas
1881	Jackson publishes *A Century of Dishonor*
1882	Congress prohibits Chinese immigration
1887	Dawes Act
1890	Wounded Knee massacre
1891	Forest Reserve Act
1892	Miners' strike at Coeur d'Alene
	Sierra Club founded
1893	Turner's frontier thesis
1903	*The Great Train Robbery*

give up old, damaged guns but to hide the good ones. Realizing the deception, the cavalry commander intensified his search, ordering his men to move from tepee to tepee. As the tension built, the medicine man, Yellow Bird, began dancing and chanting Ghost Dance songs, urging the young braves to be firm. "Do not fear," he shouted, "but let your hearts be strong." Suddenly, one Indian, Black Coyote, pulled a rifle from under his blanket and held it over his head. Two soldiers grabbed him and struggled for the gun. It went off, firing overhead. Several braves grabbed rifles and aimed at the cavalry. "By God, they have broken!" an officer shouted. The Indians fired, and at about the same moment came the command "Fire! Fire on them!"

The cavalry's superior firepower quickly overwhelmed the Indians. "We tried to run, but they shot us like we were buffalo," said Louise Weasel Bear. The actual fighting lasted only a few minutes, but it killed 250 Native Americans. "Dead and wounded women and children and little babies were scattered all along there where they had been trying to run away," Black Elk reported. "The soldiers had followed them along the gulch, as they ran, and murdered them in there."

The massacre at Wounded Knee represented the end of the most violent phase of America's westward expansion—Indian suppression. For the previous three decades, with the help of a generous government land policy, millions of people—native-born, foreign immigrants, and Mexicans—had flooded into the West. Some mined for gold, some raised cattle, and still others turned to farming. Despite their differences, those who settled in the West shared a thirst for new opportunity and a reckless attitude toward the land and its native inhabitants.

Americans in the West undertook social and economic experiments in keeping with the nation's traditions. By the end of the century, the West had taken on some of the characteristics of the industrial East. Large business interests dominated the economic landscape; mining camps and temporary cow towns had grown into thriving communities. As the frontier disappeared, Americans transformed the idea of the West into a national mirror that reflected their view of themselves as a nation of rugged individuals who had tamed a savage empire.

- What role did the federal government play in settling the West?

- Why did westward expansion devastate Native American society and culture?

- How did migrants to the West approach the environment and its resources? In what ways did western enterprise reflect that in the East?

- What cultural attitudes and racial stereotypes did the settlers bring with them, and how did these assumptions shape the societies they created in the West?

- Why did Americans transform the West into a cultural symbol of rugged individualism?

This chapter will address these questions.

 ## The Westward Experiment

The generation after the Civil War witnessed the most extensive movement of population in American history. This migration included immigrants from China and Europe, African-Americans from the South, Hispanics from the Southwest, and small farmers from the East. Despite their diverse backgrounds, millions who experimented with relocation searched for the same thing: opportunity. Promoting their quests were a government eager to give public lands to private developers and railroad executives hungry to attract business. The combination created a recipe for expansion.

The New Migrants

"The wagons are going in our direction by the hundreds," observed Uriah Wesley Oblinger in 1872. A former Union army veteran and farmer from Indiana, Oblinger had grown tired of working for other people and decided to establish a homestead of his own in Nebraska. "We meet a good many coming east that have been out and located and are going to move permanent in the spring," he observed. Oblinger was part of one of the greatest migrations in history. During the last four decades of the nineteenth century, more than 2 million people flooded into the American West. Together, they added 190 million acres of cultivated lands to the country's inventory, an area equal to Great Britain and France combined.

Before the 1850s, most settlers had skipped over the center of the nation and headed directly to California or Oregon. Most of the new migrants, however, settled on the Great Plains, the semiarid, mostly treeless region that extended from Montana and the Dakotas south to Texas. This vast area made up one-fifth of the United States. Rainfall averaged less than fifteen inches per year, and the soil produced few trees to harvest for lumber to build homes. Farther west were the rough High Plains—including present-day Montana, Wyoming, Colorado, New Mexico, and Arizona—which rolled into the Rocky Mountains. Sandwiched between the Rockies to the east and the Cascade and Sierra Nevada Mountains to the west was the Great Basin of Idaho and Utah. In other words, what people referred to as "the West" was a diverse region containing many discrete locations and unique features.

Who took part in the migration? A very large minority of western migrants were born outside the United States. In Nebraska, 25 percent of the 123,000 people living in the new state in 1870 were foreign-born. Immigrants made up between 20 and 30 percent of the populations of South Dakota, Montana, Wyoming, and Colorado. In 1890 in North Dakota the figure was 45 percent, higher than any other state in the country. In the northern Plains states, large numbers of Norwegians, Swedes, Germans, Irish, and Canadians set up communities. Between 1876 and 1890, more than 200,000 Chinese arrived at West Coast ports on steamships. The Chinese migrants were mostly men, planning to work away from home temporarily. They were illiterate or had very little schooling, but they dreamed of new possibilities inspired by stories of the "Golden Mountain."

Far to the south, a frontier of Hispanic settlers in New Mexico spread throughout the Southwest and as far north as Colorado. They were aided by the U.S. Army, which subdued the Navajo and Apache Indians who had prevented Hispanic expansion in the region. Peasants and tradesmen looking for new trading opportunities pioneered the new settlements. By 1900, as many as 100,000 Mexican immigrants were living in southern Texas, Arizona, New Mexico, and southern California.

The vast majority of new migrants, however, were native-born. Between 1870 and 1900, over 2.5 million native-born Americans moved from east to west. Among these settlers were a small number of African-Americans. In 1879, following brutal murders and general repression of blacks during the election campaigns of 1878 in the South, African-Americans known as the Exodusters left their homes in Louisiana, Mississippi, and Texas to establish new and freer lives in Kansas. As many as 26,000 may have left the South for Kansas and Kansas City, Missouri, in 1879–1880.

Native-born migrants to the West shared a number of characteristics. First, those who planned to establish farms believed their seeds and farm animals would adapt best if they moved horizontally, staying on the same latitude as their home state. Settlers from Mississippi, for example, were likely to move to Texas, while those from Illinois settled in Nebraska. Second, since it cost money to move and establish a farm, most of the new migrants were relatively prosperous farmers, merchants, and professionals. Third, migrants who moved to work in mines, cut timber, or raise livestock tended to be overwhelmingly male, while family settlements predominated in farm communities. Fourth, the stream ebbed and flowed depending on fluctuations in the economy, increasing during boom times and decreasing in times of depression. Finally, the settlers tended to be restless people who moved more than once.

For all new migrants, both foreign and native, the West offered the promise of a better life. "Hardly anything else was talked about," observed writer Hamlin Garland about his Iowa neighbors. "Every man who could sell out had gone west or was going." A popular saying had arisen: "If hell lay to the west, Americans would cross heaven to get there." It was a sentiment shared by Americans and immigrants, by whites, blacks, Europeans, Mexicans, and Chinese. "All I know," a Chinese immigrant later recalled, "was that [travelers to the Golden Mountain] who came back were always rich." When asked his motives for coming, a black migrant to Kansas in the 1870s answered: opportunity. "That's what white men go to new countries for isn't it? You do not tell them to stay back because they are poor."

Railroad companies, young western states, and land speculators encouraged migration to the West because settlement drove up land prices and created a population of potential consumers. New states, needing the revenue from the sale of land to fund schools, hired promotional bureaus to lure new settlers. Land speculators advertised their western holdings with handbills, pamphlets, and newspaper stories. Promoters often exaggerated the fertility of the West, claiming that development had transformed the environment. A succession of unusually wet years in the 1870s and 1880s convinced many people that "rain follows the plow."

Personal contact with western family members or neighbors who returned for visits often provided another incentive to go west. Ephraim G. Fairchild, a resident of Jones County, Iowa, in 1857 wrote to a relative, "I think that I can plough and harrow out hear without being nocked and jerked about with the stones as I allways have been in Jersey . . . if father and Mother and the rest of the family was out here . . . they would make a living easier than they can in Jersey."

The Homestead Act of 1862

Except during the Civil War, the federal government rarely touched the lives of most Americans during the nineteenth century. That was not the case in the West, however, where the national government shaped every aspect of settlement. In 1862 Congress launched one of its boldest attempts to lure migrants west by passing the Homestead Act. The new law allowed any citizen (or any immigrant who had taken the first step toward becoming a citizen) to claim 160 acres of land simply by paying a fee of $10. If he "lived upon or cultivated" the land for five years, the land became his, free and forever. If the homesteader did not want to wait five years, he could pay for the land at $1.25 an acre and own it outright after six months.

The Republican architects of the Homestead Act believed that free land in the West would help ordinary white Americans achieve independence, keeping the United States free of the dependent relations of either an industrial society such as Europe's or a slave society as the South had been. Proponents, who called the act "the greatest democratic measure of all history," believed that it would create a class of prosperous farmers who would form the economic and political backbone of the nation. The *New York Tribune* claimed the legislation would diminish "the number of paupers and idlers and increase the proportion of working, independent, self-subsisting farmers in the land evermore."

Though it played an important role in the settlement of the West, the Homestead Act fell short of its framers' intention of awarding most western land to small farmers. Instead, the legislation allowed wealthy speculators to obtain immense tracts of land. They hired men to stake out claims and then deed the land over to their employers. Few prospective homesteaders could afford to compete with the speculators because they lacked the money to pack up their belongings, travel west, and buy the machinery necessary to start a farm. In addition, eastern lawmakers with little understanding of the unique conditions in the West had designed the legislation. A 160-acre parcel was ideal for a farm in the East, but in the West it was too small for grazing or dry farming and too large for irrigated farming. Despite these problems, many individual families did establish homesteads in the West. By the end of 1895, for example, over 430,000 settlers filed homesteads in Kansas, Nebraska, and the Dakotas.

Over the next few years, Congress passed a number of other measures to encourage movement west. In each case, though, instead of helping struggling young farmers, the legislation aided land speculators who used the poorly written laws to seize large holdings. In 1873 came the Timber Culture Act, which allowed a homesteader (or a rancher or speculator) to claim an additional 160 acres if he would plant trees on 40 of the acres. In 1877 Congress passed the Desert Land Act, which allowed an individual to claim 640 acres of land if he would begin irrigation. In most cases, no water existed and nearly 95 percent of the claims were estimated to be fraudulent. Under the Timber and Stone Act of 1878, any citizen or immigrant could purchase up to 160 acres of western forest for $2.50 an acre. This measure enabled lumber companies to obtain thousands of acres by hiring dummy applicants whom they marched in gangs to the land offices, paying them a few dollars for their time after they had signed over their claims.

The national government exercised a direct and powerful influence in the region. As new areas of the West opened, they were organized as territories under the control of Congress and the president. In 1860 almost one-third of the area of the

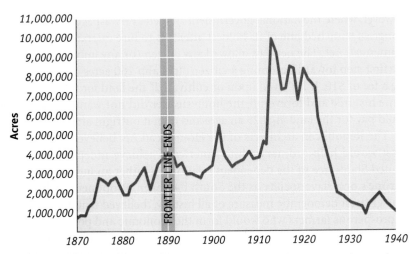

From Public Land to Homesteads   Despite the end of the frontier line in 1890, the number of homesteads carved from public lands continued to rise well into the twentieth century. Note the dramatic jump during the 1910s when America provided food for Europe during World War I and the precipitous decline as agriculture prices dropped in the 1920s, bottoming out just as the rest of the nation entered the Great Depression.

United States was divided into territories. The president selected the governor and judges in each territory. Congress set budgets and oversaw the activities of territorial governments. Political connections were often more important than qualifications when it came to making appointments. "You pledged us that we should have good men and good lawyers sent to us as judges, and we get to constitute our Supreme Court an ass, a knave, and a drunkard," a Dakota resident complained to the U.S. attorney general.

While it avoided active involvement in the affairs of local territories, Congress was occasionally capable of forceful intervention. Its attacks on the Mormon practice of polygamy (having more than one wife) were a good example. Following a Supreme Court decision in 1878 ruling the practice illegal (*United States v. Reynolds*), Congress passed legislation imposing heavy fines and imprisonment against anyone convicted of practicing polygamy. In 1887 Washington increased the pressure by directly attacking the Mormon Church: Congress passed legislation forbidding it from holding assets over $50,000. Four days after the Supreme Court ruled the law constitutional, the president of the Mormon Church announced that by divine revelation he had been instructed to ban polygamy.

Congress also established the procedures for statehood. After residents of a territory signed a petition, Congress established the boundaries and authorized an election of delegates to a state constitutional convention. After the constitution had been ratified by popular vote, the territory officially applied for statehood. Kansas used these procedures to enter the Union in 1861, and it was soon followed by Nevada (1864), Nebraska (1867), and Colorado (1876). Then partisan struggles between Democrats and Republicans blocked the admission of new states until 1889, when North

Dakota, South Dakota, Montana, and Washington gained statehood. After Utah banned polygamy, Congress approved the territory's statehood petition in 1896. The process of establishing states in the West was completed early in the next century when Oklahoma (1907) and Arizona and New Mexico (1912) joined the Union.

The Railroad and Western Expansion

The federal government was not alone in its effort to lure migrants to the West. In 1862 Congress passed the Pacific Railroad Act, which pledged the nation to building a train link between East and West. The Central Pacific started building eastward from San Francisco in 1864 while the Union Pacific laid track westward from Omaha, Nebraska. In May 1869, after only five years of construction, the two work gangs met at Promontory Point, Utah, just east of the Great Salt Lake. The Union Pacific's "Engine No. 119" and the Central Pacific's "Jupiter" "kissed amid a shower of champagne," joining the nation, east to west, across a "desert" that an earlier generation had believed would never be settled.

Only five days after the linking of the rails came the announcement that the first transcontinental railroad was beginning regular service. Whereas the wagon trip to Oregon along the Overland Trail had taken six to eight weeks, the rail journey took one week. Once a day, the Pacific Express would head west from Omaha for Sacramento. And once a day, eastbound passengers would board the Atlantic Express in Sacramento for a run of about two thousand miles to Omaha. During the next fifteen years, three more routes were opened across the Rockies.

The railroads launched a massive campaign to attract settlers to live along their tracks and provide business for their freight trains. "You can lay track to the Garden of Eden," said a railroad executive, "but what good is it if the only inhabitants are Adam and Eve?" Railroad land departments organized excursions for newspapermen, sent agents abroad to attract immigrants, and distributed handbills describing the fertile lands available for purchase. In 1874 an office set up by Union Pacific promoter General Grenville Dodge spent $105,000 to advertise its lands in 2,311 newspapers and magazines. As added incentive, the railroads provided credit terms and special passenger rates for prospective settlers. The Burlington and Missouri River Railroad Company advertised "millions of acres" for sale—on ten years' time, at 6 percent interest, and with the cost of a land excursion ticket to be deducted from the first payment if the purchase was made within thirty days. The promotional efforts brought dramatic results: the 1870 population of Kansas had been 364,000; in 1887 more than a million and a half people lived there.

 ## The Assault on Native American Cultures

The new migrants showed little regard for the Native American communities that existed in the West. Believing Native Americans to be racially inferior, the settlers subdued, sometimes brutally, Indians who blocked their path to the region's rich natural resources. Many Indians, their societies dependent on resources that white incursion disrupted or destroyed, struggled to preserve their communities and their lifestyles. But by the end of the century, their experiment in resistance had failed. The new migrants had established their hold over the land and overwhelmed the rich native cultures of the West.

The Plains Indians

In 1865 approximately a quarter of a million Native Americans lived in the western half of the country. Some were eastern tribes, such as the Cherokee, Creek, and Shawnee, who had been forced west by the federal government. In the Southwest were the Pueblo Indians, sophisticated farmers who lived in huge apartment complexes of adobe or stone. The Ute, Shoshone, and Nez Percé settled throughout the central and northern Rocky Mountains. Nearly two-thirds of the Native Americans, however, lived on the Great Plains. Included among the Plains tribes to the northwest were the Blackfoot of Idaho and Montana. The central Plains were home to the Cheyenne, Crow, and Arapaho, while the Kiowa, Apache, and Comanche roamed the land of present-day Texas and New Mexico. The Sioux of present-day Minnesota and North and South Dakota were the dominant power on the northern Great Plains.

Plains Indians Numerous Native American tribes, including the Sioux, Cheyenne, Arapaho, and Nez Percé, inhabited the western Great Plains in the latter half of the nineteenth century. Most of these tribes lived a nomadic lifestyle, following the buffalo herds on which they depended for food, clothing, and shelter. Tepees such as this beautifully painted one were ideal homes because they could be easily transported from place to place. *(Library of Congress.)*

The Plains Indians were a diverse group, and simple generalizations are not easy. Tribes spoke different languages. Some practiced sedentary farming, while others were seminomadic hunters. Most tribes, which sometimes boasted populations in the thousands, were subdivided into smaller bands of three to five hundred men and women. Each band had a governing council, though most members participated in decision making. In most tribes, the men hunted, traded, and supervised the bands' religious life. Women were responsible for raising children, preparing meals, and growing and gathering vegetables and wild fruits, though there were exceptions to these generalizations.

Native American views of the environment were strikingly different from those of the white settlers. Although Indian beliefs varied, they tended to imbue the nonhuman world with a spiritual dimension, wherein plants and animals were conscious beings endowed with symbolic and religious meaning. No Indian thought of himself as owning a piece of the land. He might own his horses, his weapons, his tepee, but the land itself was the "property" of the whole tribe, to be used communally and protected from other tribes. Whites, on the other hand, believed that God had created the land and its resources for human domination and development. They thought that progress depended on individual ownership of land and mastery over its resources. Indians were mystified by the white man's emphasis on individualism and private property. "The White man knows how to make everything," said the Sioux leader Sitting Bull, "but he does not know how to distribute it" (see Competing Voices, page 690).

The proliferation of horses from the Spanish Southwest in the sixteenth century transformed Indian life on the Plains. Until the arrival of the horse, Indian tribes depended on dogs to carry supplies. The Indian work dog could carry about 50 pounds on its back and pull another 75 pounds. A horse, by comparison, could carry 200 pounds and pull another 300 pounds for ten to twelve miles a day. Trained from an early age to ride horses, Indians became effective hunters and fighters. "A Comanche on his feet is out of his element," observed western explorer George Catlin, "but the moment he lays his hands upon his horse . . . he gracefully flies away like a different being."

The horse aided the Plains Indians in the activity that became central to their survival and their culture: hunting buffalo. Before the horse, Indians had stalked buffalo on foot—a slow process that limited the number of animals they could kill. On horseback, however, braves could surround and kill dozens of buffalo in a few minutes. Before the arrival of horses, Indians organized extended hunting trips to kill buffalo for the village. With the horse, many tribes such as the Cheyenne abandoned farming and became nomadic, roaming the land in pursuit of buffalo herds.

In the early nineteenth century, nearly 30 million buffalo roamed the Great Plains. The buffalo provided Indians with food, clothing, and shelter. "Everything the Kiowas had came from the buffalo," a Native American woman recalled. "The buffalo were the life of the Kiowas." Indians dried the meat in the hot air. They used the skin to make tepees, blankets, and robes. They carved buffalo bones into knives and stretched their tendons into bowstrings. Even buffalo manure did not go to waste; the Indians burned it for fuel.

By the 1850s, however, a combination of overhunting, drought, and disease threatened the herds. Then in the 1860s, the coming of the railroads sounded the death knell for the buffalo. Eastern manufacturers had learned to turn stiff buffalo hides into soft leather for shoes, cushions, and belts, and the railroads provided the means of transporting the product to eastern markets. Not content to be freight carriers, the railroads offered buffalo excursions for professional hunters and church groups, allowing them to blast away from the windows of the train. Between 1872 and 1874, commercial and sport hunters killed over 4 million buffalo. The slaughter of more than 13 million buffalo by 1883 represented a crushing victory in the white man's war on the Plains Indians.

The Indian Wars

Before the 1850s, Americans named the land west of the Mississippi "Indian Country," relocated eastern tribes to the region, and prohibited white settlement. The idea of a permanent Indian country fell victim to American expansionism. As steamboats churned up the Missouri and Conestoga wagons rolled across the Plains, whites killed livestock and destroyed Indian crops. Many Indians resented the encroachments on their land. The incidence of violence rose, and major confrontations threatened.

In 1851, fearing that Indian antipathy toward the intruders might burst into open warfare, the Department of Indian Affairs decided to divide Indian lands into small, well-defined tribal territories, or reservations. In the Treaty of Fort Laramie, representatives of the northern Plains tribes agreed to stay within a defined territory and vowed not to harass wagons traveling designated paths. In return, the government offered $50,000 worth of supplies every year for fifty years, plus the promise of quick punishment of any white who trespassed on Indian lands. Two years later, the government negotiated a similar treaty with the southern Plains Indians, securing safe passage for migrants on the Santa Fe Trail. Together the treaties created northern and southern "Indian colonies" divided by an American corridor.

The treaties failed to resolve the conflict. For one thing, the boundaries proved difficult to enforce. White settlers continued to usurp Indian lands, and many Indians refused to accept the new boundaries. In the late 1850s and early 1860s, miners and other settlers moved into Colorado, creating a stage line running across Cheyenne hunting grounds. In 1864, after a series of violent clashes, Cheyenne and Apache warriors accepted the invitation of the territorial governor to gather at Sand Creek in southeastern Colorado. Promised safe passage by the governor, Chief Black Kettle led his community of seven hundred followers to the site.

Early on the morning of November 29, 1864, a group of Colorado militia led by Colonel John M. Chivington surrounded Black Kettle's people. "Kill and scalp all, big and little," Chivington told his men. Black Kettle tried to convince the soldiers of his peaceful intent by raising a white flag, but Chivington ignored the gesture. In the slaughter that followed, ninety-eight Cheyenne women and children and a handful of older men died. Chivington's soldiers scalped and mutilated the Indian corpses, gathering grisly trophies to take back to Denver. The white public applauded the slaughter at Sand Creek. The *Rocky Mountain News* called it a "brilliant feat of arms." The army, however, was appalled by Chivington's slaughter of unarmed women and children. General Nelson A. Miles called the massacre the "foulest and most unjustified crime in the annals of America."

Following the attack, the central Plains exploded into war. Cheyenne runners carried war pipes to the Lakota, Arapaho, and Cheyenne camps. "We have now raised the battle ax until death," declared one chief. By early 1865, Sioux, Cheyenne, and Arapaho bands had retaliated for Chivington's attack by burning stagecoaches, pulling down telegraph wires, and looting ranches along the South Platte River. In 1866 the Teton Sioux ambushed Captain William J. Fetterman and his seventy-nine soldiers in Wyoming. "All this country is ruined," concluded an army major. "There can be no such thing as peace in the future."

The army cried out for vengeance against the Indians after the Fetterman massacre. "We must act with vindictive earnestness against the Sioux, even to their extermination, men, women, and children," declared Civil War hero William T. Sherman, who now commanded the army in the war against the Indians. But officials in the Interior Department, who remained in control of Indian policy, had a different idea. In 1867 they formed a peace delegation to end the war with the tribes by pursuing "the hitherto untried policy of conquering with kindness."

The result of the peace overture was the Treaty of Medicine Lodge Creek (1867). According to the agreement, the southern Plains tribes—Cheyenne, Arapaho, Kiowa, and Comanche—agreed to relocate away from white settlement and onto reservations in western Oklahoma. In return, the government promised to provide food and supplies for thirty years and establish schools. The following year, a handful of northern tribes signed a second Treaty of Fort Laramie, agreeing to remain on a reservation that encompassed all of present-day South Dakota, including the Black Hills, which many Sioux regarded as a sacred dwelling place of spirits. For its part, the government recognized the Sioux's right to buffalo outside the reservation "so long as buffalo may range there in numbers sufficient to justify the chase." Many Indian chiefs, however, refused to move to the new reservations. "I don't want to settle," declared a Kiowa chief. "I love to roam over the prairies."

It took the concerted effort of the army to coerce the Indians onto the reservations. On November 27, 1868, Lieutenant Colonel George Custer commanded a surprise attack on a Cheyenne village led by Chief Black Kettle. In this "battle of the Washita," Custer and his men killed over one hundred Cheyenne, including Black Kettle. Still, bands of Kiowa, Comanche, and southern Cheyenne continued to leave the reservation to hunt and conduct raids into Texas. In 1874 the "Red River War" erupted after southern Plains Indians attacked a trading outpost in the Texas panhandle. The army forced the Indians back onto their reservations and, in 1875, sent many of their leaders to prison in Florida. Only then did conflict on the southern Plains subside (see map).

White expansion remained the chief obstacle to lasting peace. In 1874 reports that the Black Hills were rich in gold began to circulate. By the middle of 1875, thousands of white prospectors were illegally digging and panning in the area. The Sioux protested the invasion of their territory and the violation of its sacred ground. The

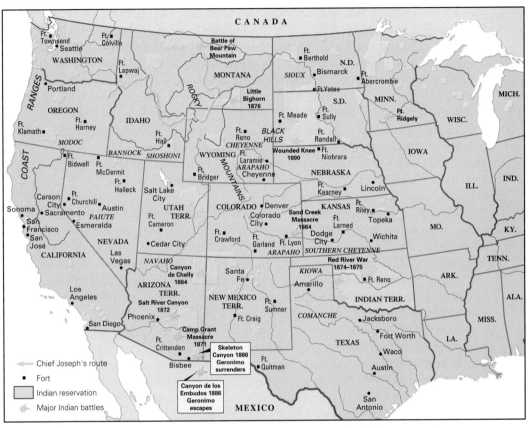

Western Indian Wars and Reservations, 1860–1890 From the time of the Civil War, American soldiers fought to round up Native American tribes and transplant them to reservations to make way for white settlement. Though many tribes evaded capture for a time, such as the Nez Percé led by Chief Joseph and the Chiricahua Apache led by Geronimo, all were eventually settled on reservations. The massacre at Wounded Knee in 1890 proved to be the last major act of resistance.

government offered to lease the Black Hills or to pay $6 million if the Indians were willing to sell the land. "You should bow to the wishes of the Government which supports you," an official told the chiefs. "Gold is useless to you, and there will be fighting unless you give it up." When the tribes refused, the government imposed what it considered a fair price for the land and ordered Indians to move. In the spring of 1876, the army developed a plan to remove the Indians from the Back Hills and force them onto the reservation.

Sitting Bull, leader of the Hunkpapa Sioux, prepared to meet the white troops. "We must stand together or they will kill us separately," he said. "These soldiers have come shooting; they want war. All right, we'll give it to them." He sent couriers to every Sioux, Cheyenne, and Arapaho camp, summoning them to a rendezvous on the Little Big Horn River. In June, more than three thousand Indians joined Sitting Bull in defiance of the government's orders to cede the Black Hills. "There were more Indians. . . ," a Cheyenne woman named Kate Big Head noted, "than I ever saw anywhere together."

The U.S. Army's Seventh Cavalry, led by Colonel George Custer, was not far behind. Custer, a West Point graduate who finished thirty-fourth in a class of thirty-four, was a superb horseman with a commanding presence and a flair for the dramatic. He also burned with ambition and was determined to make his mark. On June 25, 1876, Custer recklessly advanced on what he thought was a minor Indian encampment. Instead, it turned out to be the main Sioux force of warriors. They surrounded and slaughtered Custer and his men, including several Indian scouts, in the greatest Native American victory of the Plains wars.

If Little Bighorn was a disaster for the army, it also sealed the fate of the Indians. After the deaths of Custer and his soldiers, the national mood hardened. "Who slew Custer?" asked the *New York Herald*. "The celebrated peace policy . . . which feeds, clothes, and takes care of their noncombatant force while men are killing our troops." The army sent fresh troops to crush Indian resistance once and for all. Companies of cavalry were expanded from sixty-four to one hundred men each, and recruits hurried to join up as "Custer's Avengers." That winter, soldiers swept across Sioux lands without mercy, slaying warriors, destroying villages, burning food supplies, and leaving women and children homeless in terrible cold. Though fighting flared periodically for fifteen years between the army and the Native American tribes, there was never again a real war, nor a battle on the scale of the Little Bighorn.

Why did Indian resistance fail? First, the army had many technological advantages over the Indians. Telegraph communications and railroads enabled the troops to be quickly concentrated and deployed. Second, the soldiers were better armed. In 1873 the frontier forces received their first standardized arms issue, the single-action Colt revolver and the new Springfield rifle and carbine—all employing powerful .45-caliber ammunition. The Springfields were single-shot weapons, but they were less prone to misfires and had greater accuracy than older rifles; their maximum range was 3,500 yards. The Springfields' range on many occasions kept Indians at distances that rendered their less powerful repeating weapons or bows and arrows useless. Third, in addition to advantages in communications and firepower, the army skillfully exploited tribal rivalries to prevent the Indians from concentrating their united power against a common enemy. By capitalizing on animosities between tribes, the army found it easy to recruit Plains warriors as scouts. Indians from pacified nations—Pawnee, Crow, and Arikara—welcomed the chance to seek revenge against their perpetual, powerful enemies, the Sioux and Cheyenne.

"Reforming" the Indians

"This civilization may not be the best possible," declared a government official in 1889 about the white world, "but it is the best the Indians can get. They cannot escape it, and must either conform to it or be crushed by it." Already demoralized by their confinement on reservations, Indians confronted a wholesale assault on their culture and community organization in the 1880s. Dictated by government policy, this assault was an experiment in converting the Indians to white civilization—to make them "walk the white man's road," as Sitting Bull put it.

Ethnocentric reformers led the assault on Native American cultures. Clergymen, social workers, and government officials were committed to assimilating Indians into American culture. Indian reformers capitalized on the outrage provoked by best-selling books such as Helen Hunt Jackson's *Century of Dishonor* (1881), which exposed American duplicity and corruption in dealing with the Indians. The reform spirit energized organizations such as the Women's National Indian Association (WNIA), founded in 1874, and the Indian Rights Association, an offshoot of WNIA. Indian children as young as five were taken from their families and sent to

"Seven Little Indians in Four Different Stages of Civilization" After the Civil War, white philanthropists, believing that white civilization would destroy the Indian if it did not include him, began a concerted effort to assimilate Native Americans into white culture and society. Educating Indian children at boarding schools, completely cut off from Native American society, was one means to this end. White teachers gave students Christian names, dressed them in "proper" clothing, and inculcated them with white Protestant values. These seven children, probably students at such a school, have been outfitted to demonstrate the progressive stages of the "civilization" process. Ironically, these reformers did as much as Indian removal itself to destroy Native American culture. *(The Photography Collection, Carpenter Center for the Visual Arts at Harvard University.)*

Seven little Indians in four different stages of civilization.

boarding schools where they were taught to abandon old ways and become members of a "new social order." In the schools and on the reservations, reform programs forced Indians to abandon their language, their customs, and their faith. The goal, declared a reformer, was to "kill the Indian and save the man."

Land reform was the centerpiece of the reformers' effort. They believed that the key to civilizing Indians was to convert them into individual landowners. As long as Indians owned their lands in common, Massachusetts senator Henry Dawes contended, they would lack "selfishness," which was "at the bottom of civilization." To break the Indians' old communal concept of land, the reformers proposed that reservations be divided into lots and given to the Indians in "severalty"; that is, the Indians were to be treated as "several" or separate individuals. According to a reformer, with the breakup of the reservations and the sale of "surplus" lands to whites, Indians would learn the "habits of thrift and industry" and the pride of proprietorship. "The aggressive and enterprising Anglo-Saxons" would set up their farms "side by side" with Indian farms, and "in a little while contact alone" would lead Indians to emulate the work ethic of their white neighbors.

This view became policy in 1887 when Congress passed the Dawes General Allotment Act, which supporters claimed would serve as "a mighty pulverizing engine for breaking up the tribal mass." The law provided varying amounts of land for all tribal members with the maximum amount, 160 acres of farmland or 320 of grazing land, being allotted to a head of a family. Once each family had received its allotment, the government would sell the remaining land as "surplus," which could be purchased by white homesteaders. "The Indian may now become a free man," noted a partisan, "free from the thraldom of the tribe; free from the domination of the reservation system; free to enter into the body of our citizens."

This conversion of Indians into individual landowners was marked at "last-arrow" pageants. On these occasions, the Indians were ordered by the government to attend a large assembly on the reservation. Dressed in traditional tribal costume and carrying a bow and arrow, each Indian was individually summoned from a tepee and told to shoot an arrow. He then retreated to the tepee and reemerged wearing "civilized" clothing, symbolizing a crossing from the savage to the civilized world. Standing before a plow, a white official sealed the transition: "Take the handle of this plow, this act means that you have chosen to live the life of the white man—and the white man lives by work." At the close of the ceremony, each allottee was given an American flag and a purse with the instruction, "This purse will always say to you that the money you gain from your labor must be wisely kept."

The reformers failed to achieve their goals, and their good intentions forced Native Americans to pay a heavy price. White grafters moved in quickly; Indians were persuaded to adopt white "guardians" for their tracts, and these guardians would rob them of their land. U.S. agents, who supervised the allotment procedure, were sympathetic to western economic interests and settlers. In most cases, they assigned the most arid acreage to Indians and sold the best land as surplus. In 1881 Indians held 155 million acres of land. By 1890, this figure had declined to 104 million, and by 1900, it had dwindled to 77 million acres.

Experiments in Resource Exploitation

The migrants who traveled in search of wealth viewed the West and its resources as limitless. Over the next few decades, they aggressively extracted minerals from mountains, rounded up cattle for slaughter, harvested crops for the market, and cut trees for production. Few of the hardy individualists who discovered the gold, herded the cattle, or staked out the farms reaped great wealth from their ventures. In time, large investors muscled out the small entrepreneurs and captured most of the profit. And by the end of the century, a small group of critics had begun challenging the notion that the West had limitless resources. The West, it turned out, was not as different from the East as many people had believed.

The Mining Frontier

Mining was a powerful magnet attracting people to the West. The discovery of gold in the foothills of the Sierra Nevada Mountains had triggered the California gold rush of 1848. By the mid-1850s, as opportunity for making a quick fortune in California declined, prospectors spread across the West. For decades, mining represented the largest nonagricultural source of jobs in the region. The lure of gold and other precious metals drew large numbers of foreign immigrants to the West. In most mining camps, between one-quarter and one-half of the population were foreign-born.

In 1859 news of fresh strikes near Pike's Peak in Colorado and in the Carson River valley of Nevada set off wild migrations—one hundred thousand miners had arrived in Pike's Peak country by June 1859, many in covered wagons inscribed with "Pike's Peak or Bust!" While prospectors were gathering around Pike's Peak, a couple of adventurous miners discovered the Comstock Lode on the slopes of Mount Davidson, near Gold Hill, Nevada. Thousands of miners climbed the Sierra Nevada in the summer of 1859. Comstock became the great success story of western mining. The biggest strike came in 1873 when a team of miners hit a seam of gold and silver more than 54 feet wide, the richest discovery in the history of mining. Between 1859 and 1879, miners extracted $306 million worth of gold and silver from the Comstock Lode.

During the 1860s and 1870s, veins of gold brought thousands of miners to Washington, Idaho, Colorado, Montana, and the Dakotas. To collect the gold, the prospectors used a simple process called placer mining—washing the dirt from a stream in a pan or sluice. The water carried off the lighter silt and pebbles, leaving the heavy grains of gold in the bottom. Prospectors occasionally found as much as eight thousand dollars worth of gold in a day, but the initial discoveries played out quickly.

As the placers gave out, a great deal of gold remained, but it was locked in quartz or buried deep in the earth. Mining became an expensive business, far beyond the reach of independent prospectors. Tapping veins of gold or silver required powerful machinery to move vast quantities of dirt and sand and huge mills to crush the ore. Hydraulic mining, which depended on large-scale reservoirs and elaborate flumes delivering massive volumes of water at high pressure, devastated streambeds and created mountains of rubble.

Hydraulic Mining The discovery of vast quantities of natural resources lured prospectors to the West. These miners are using pressurized water jets to mine gold. Such techniques, aimed at fast profit, devastated the environment. Hydraulic mining clogged rivers and streams with residue, resulting in flooding and mudslides that ruined countless acres of farmland. *(Collection of Matthew Isenburg.)*

As hard-rock mining supplanted placer operations, more miners became laborers paid by the day or week to work in gangs underground. Work in the mines was difficult and dangerous. By 1880, a census showed 2,770 men working below ground at the Comstock Lode. They suffered in underground temperatures that sometimes soared above 100 degrees. Poor ventilation often led to headaches and dizziness, while long term exposure to quartz dust and lead produced fatal diseases of the lungs. Miners had to contend with misfired dynamite, cave-ins, and fires. For a time, so many accidents occurred that a worker died every week. In the late 1870s, accidents disabled 1 of 30 miners and killed 1 of 80. Overall, as many as 7,500 men died digging out silver and gold on the western mining frontier, and perhaps 20,000 more were maimed.

The threatening working conditions in the mines produced angry, and frequently violent, confrontations between workers and mine owners. In many cases, the mining corporations and their managers inspired the rise of trade unionism by refusing even to discuss basic issues with their employees and by importing "scabs" to replace striking workers, calling for the National Guard to suppress strikers, and seeking injunctions to terminate strikes. The tactics did not prevent the union movement from spreading. In 1892 miners struck at Coeur d'Alene, Idaho, demanding recognition for their union. When angry miners destroyed mill property, the governor declared marshal law, sent in six companies of the Idaho National Guard, and crushed the strike. Such powerful allies gave mine owners the upper hand in labor disputes.

Cattle Kingdom

The grasslands of the West offered another way to get rich: cattle ranching. Early in the sixteenth century, the Spanish began importing European cattle into America. Over the years the cattle multiplied. Some escaped and became wild, especially in southern Texas, where they bred with cattle brought by American settlers. The result was the Texas longhorn, a breed that multiplied rapidly and lived easily on the land, until nearly 5 million were roaming the Plains by the mid-nineteenth century.

After the Civil War, the supply of meat increased and so did the demand. The federal government purchased more than fifty thousand head of western cattle every year to feed Indian tribes living on reservations. The invention of refrigerated train cars allowed cattle ranchers to ship their beef to cities in the East and Midwest. In New York City, a three-year-old steer brought eighty dollars; in Illinois, a steer brought forty dollars. This rising demand combined with plentiful supply in the West offered great opportunity for enterprising cattle ranchers. There was one small problem: a tick, barely the size of a pinhead, rode along on Texas cattle. The tick carried the Texas fever which, though it had no effect on cattle, killed most other forms of livestock, causing fearful farmers in Missouri to block Texas cattlemen from bringing their herds north.

In 1867 an Illinois entrepreneur named Joseph G. McCoy came up with a solution to the problem: he would lead his cattle up the Chisholm Trail through Oklahoma, a westerly route that avoided farm lands. He established a shipping point for cattle at the small town of Abilene, Kansas, located where the Kansas Pacific Railroad crossed Mud Creek. When he first visited Abilene in 1867, McCoy described it as a "small, dead place, consisting of about one dozen log huts." He paid $2,400 for a town site and its 480 acres. McCoy quickly began to develop his purchase. Within sixty days he had transformed the village of Abilene into a well-equipped cattle town, with a shipping yard to accommodate three thousand head, a barn, an office, and "a good three story hotel."

The first train carrying longhorn cattle to Chicago left Abilene in September 1867. By 1870, drovers were driving thousands of cattle northward, sometimes for distances as long as 1,500 miles. By 1880, more than 6 million cattle had been driven to the rails. The cow towns and the trails followed as the railroads moved west. In Kansas new towns sprouted up in Ellsworth, Wichita, Caldwell, and Dodge City. As homesteaders filled the southern and central Plains or as ranching depleted grazing, cattle drivers sought the unexploited grasslands further north in Ogallala, Nebraska; Cheyenne, Wyoming; and Miles City, Montana (see map).

The long drives north from Texas to the cow towns marked the heyday of the American cowboy. The number of cowboys who rode the cattle trails across the

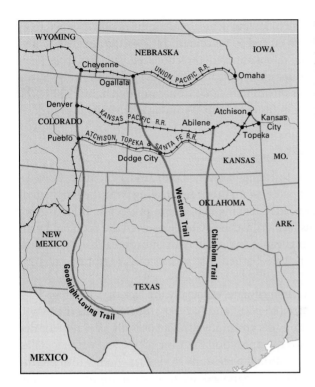

Cattle Trails As the railroad and farming settlements moved west, so did the great cattle trails. Starting their journey in southern Texas, cowboys drove their herds through sparsely populated territories to meet up with the ever-expanding railroad system. Towns that emerged along the rail line, like Dodge City and Cheyenne, became centers for the livestock industry and provided entertainment and lodging for restless cowboys.

Great Plains totaled no more than forty thousand. They were surprisingly young—their average age was only twenty-four. About one in every six or seven was Mexican. In fact, it was Mexicans and not Americans who had been the first cowboys. They originated almost all of the tools of the cowboy's trade, from big hats and kerchiefs to tooled leather saddles and boots. African-Americans, many of whom had learned how to ride and rope while serving as slaves on Texas ranches, made up a similar proportion of cowboys.

By the mid-1880s, cattle represented by far the biggest business in the Old West—with perhaps no more than three dozen people controlling more than 20 million acres of U.S. soil. Attracted by the prospect of huge profits, eastern investors included the varied likes of William Rockefeller, William K. Vanderbilt, and a wealthy New Yorker and future president named Theodore Roosevelt. Along with the eastern investors came a host of money-heavy Scots, Englishmen, and other Europeans who had learned of huge profits to be made in cattle. They bought large tracts of land and mass-produced cattle for eastern consumers. The most impressive operation was the XIT Ranch in the panhandle country of Texas. Extending for two hundred miles, the ranch occupied parts of ten counties and employed as many as 150 cowboys who rode 1,000 horses, herded 150,000 head of cattle, and branded 35,000 calves a year.

The boom, however, was short-lived. Overgrazing destroyed the grass cattle needed for grazing. Severe weather on the southern ranges in the winter of 1885 killed nearly 85 percent of the herd. The following winter, temperatures that dropped to 45 degrees below zero killed between 40 and 50 percent of cattle on the northern Plains. The cattle business recovered, but it took different directions. Outside capital, so plentiful in the boom years, dried up. Many ranchers turned to sheep raising. Sheep needed less water and grazed on shrubs that cattle would not touch. By 1900, sheep had replaced cattle as the leading industry in both Wyoming and Montana.

Cultivating the Land

With migration into the Plains bringing vast new lands under the plow between 1870 and 1900, farmers developed new methods for dealing with the harsh environment. For one thing, they needed fencing material to protect their lands from herds of cattle. In 1874 Illinois farmer Joseph F. Glidden solved the problem by inventing barbed wire, which was cheaper and could cover more area than traditional methods of fencing. Within ten years, barbed wire was a standard feature on farms across the country.

A second problem was the harsh climate, especially the lack of rainfall, and the punishing physical labor required to plant and harvest crops. Some farmers used windmills to pump water from underground wells. Farmers also developed "dry farming" techniques, which slowed evaporation by covering the soil with a blanket of dust. Many experimented with drought-resistant crops that could withstand the severe Plains winters. As the century progressed, technological improvements cut the amount of labor required to plant and harvest. Between 1850 and 1900, farm machinery reduced the cost of producing leading crops by about half.

In a brief period of time, the small farmer, like the enterprising individual miner and cattle rancher, was replaced by large business interests. By the late nineteenth century, huge bonanza farms dominated the nation's agricultural landscape, underscoring the increasing influence of corporations. The growth of agribusiness was most visible in California. In 1871 reformer Henry George described California as "not a country of farms but a country of plantations and estates." Statistics supported his observations. By 1900, nearly two-thirds of the state's farms covered a thousand acres or more. California was not alone. By 1900, the average farm in the Dakotas measured seven thousand acres.

During the 1880s, worldwide overproduction combined with bad weather to produce a dramatic fall in crop prices, wiping out thousands of farmers on the western Plains. Many small farmers remained on their homesteads, but they were increasingly frustrated with their failing economic prospects. A Minnesota girl described her family's plight to the state governor: "We have no money now nothing to sell to get any more clothes with as the grasshoppers destroyed all of our crops what few we had for we have not much land broke yet. . . . We . . . almost perish here sometimes with the cold."

Poor harvests and falling prices failed to dampen the enthusiasm for new farm settlements. Following the Civil War, land speculators began lobbying Congress to open up Indian Territory in present-day Oklahoma to white settlement. In 1889 Congress sided with the speculators, over the heated objections of the fifty-five tribes

The New Agriculture   With the advent of new technologies, Plains farming became a big business. Steam-powered tractors and threshers, like the one pictured on the right, allowed those farmers who could afford them to sow enormous tracts of land, sometimes up to fifteen thousand acres. These so-called bonanza farms made it difficult for small farmers to compete effectively and forced many of them into tenancy or off the land altogether. Aggressive commercial farming also had a negative impact on the environment, exhausting the topsoil and stripping the Plains of their protective grass covering.   *(Minnesota Historical Society.)*

that called the area home. The government officially opened the land to the rush of would-be owners at noon on April 22, 1889, but many settlers—called "sooners"— had illegally entered the territory beforehand and established claims on the best land. By nightfall, hopeful homesteaders had laid claim to 1.2 million acres of land.

Despite the hardships of Plains farming, the region became the breadbasket of America in the decades after the Civil War. Farm output more than tripled between 1860 and 1900. California sent fruit, wine, and wheat to eastern markets. Vast wheat fields stretched across Minnesota, the Dakotas, Montana, and eastern Colorado. By 1890, American farmers were exporting large amounts of wheat and other crops. To an Austrian observer, the surplus produced seemed "the greatest event of modern times."

Timber and the Origins of Conservation

The demand for lumber and timber needed by the mining industry and growing towns and cities in California led to the opening of forestry operations in the West. Between 1850 and 1860, California's population soared from 93,000 to 379,000. San Francisco, which saw its population explode from 2,000 to 55,000 between 1849 and 1855, was at the heart of the demand. Six times in the space of eighteen months between December 1849 and June 1851, the boom town burned to the ground; each time it was rebuilt, a process that consumed millions of trees.

The great forests of the Northwest covered thousands of square miles and contained a host of majestic trees. The Douglas fir, which ranged southward from British Columbia to western Oregon, reached heights of 250 feet and 10 feet in diameter. The coastal redwood, which extended from Oregon south to Monterey, California, towered 350 feet and had a diameter of 15 feet. The redwood's inland cousin, the Sierra redwood, contained enough wood to build 40 five-room houses. Entrepreneurs from other timber-producing states such as Maine, Michigan, and Wisconsin marveled at the size of the trees and recognized the potential profit from harvesting the timber. The development of railroads opened the area to timber operators, allowing them to ship lumber to markets in the East. In 1900 Frederick Weyerhaeuser inaugurated the era of lumber giants when he bought nine hundred thousand acres of prime land in the Pacific Northwest.

The firms recruited "homeless, womenless" lumberjacks from New England and the Midwest to work in the forest and mills. The work proved hard and dangerous. An average of one logger died every day from 1870 to 1910—a total of 7,500 according to one estimate. The greatest threat to both loggers and the industry came from fire. In 1902 fires raged from Canada to California for seven days. The flames destroyed almost three-quarters of a million acres—an area as big as Yellowstone National Park.

The Lumber Industry   In the Pacific Northwest, the lumber industry was the way to make a quick buck. Like mining and commercial farming, it too had devastating environmental consequences, as no regulations were yet in place to protect what should have been a renewable resource. In this photograph, a team of oxen hauls logs out of a forest in Washington State. (*Whatcom Museum Archive.*)

The depletion of the nation's forests by loggers led a few critics to question the popular view of the West as an area of limitless resources. In 1879, in his widely read *Progress and Poverty,* the reformer Henry George challenged the government's policy of giving away publicly owned natural resources to individuals or corporations seeking to enrich themselves. People have a right to what they produce themselves, he wrote, "but man has another right, declared by the fact of his existence—the right to use so much of the free gifts of nature as may be necessary to supply all the wants of that existence, and which he may use without interfering with the equal rights of anyone else; and to this he has a title as against all the world."

By the 1870s, some government officials were beginning to exhibit concern over the consequences of indiscriminate land use and resource exploitation. In 1872 Congress set aside the first major reservation of federal land when it created the 2-million-acre Yellowstone National Park to be a "pleasuring ground for the people" in perpetuity. But at the time, creating Yellowstone Park was an isolated event rather than a reversal of the practice of giving away federal resources to private interests.

Concern about the environment inspired a small but dedicated group of activists. John Muir, a bearded, mystical Scotsman, emerged as the most eloquent and effective voice for protecting the environment. People, he argued, should honor and safeguard the wilderness. "Climb the mountains and get their good tidings," he wrote. "Nature's peace will flow into you as the sunshine into the trees. The winds will blow their freshness into you, and the storms their energy, while cares will drop off like autumn leaves." Muir was a driving force behind the Forest Reserve Act of 1891, which gave the president authority to set aside portions of the federal domain. The government quickly withdrew from potential sale 13 million acres to set up fifteen forest reserves. Six years later, President Grover Cleveland created another thirteen reserves totaling over 21 million acres. In 1892 Muir helped found the Sierra Club, which devoted itself to "preserving the forests and other natural features of the Sierra Nevada Mountains."

Society in the West: Experiment and Imitation

Many people who traveled west planned to start a new life amid the boundless opportunity they expected. In most cases, however, they struggled to recreate a society they had known before they migrated. Settlers from the eastern United States and Europe not only brought familiar institutions and old values to their experiments in community building, they also incorporated racial attitudes that dismissed minority cultures as inferior. The Indians were the greatest victims of these racial attitudes, but other minority groups in the West, most notably those of Chinese and Hispanic heritage, suffered as well.

Life in Western Towns

Few new western towns were lucky enough to attract the full array of skills and talents that contributed to the convenience and comfort of life in the East. There were few qualified doctors or schoolteachers. Still, any community that hoped to grow beyond infancy needed a range of services. Typically, one of the first citizens of any community was the editor of the local newspaper, hired by the town's promoters. His function was not so much to report on local events as to sing the praises of his community for the benefit of any prospective settlers. A hotel—to accommodate future townspeople as well as transients—was generally among the first structures in new towns. Saloonkeepers were particularly numerous in towns whose prime visitors were cowboys or miners. Abilene, Kansas, boasted eleven saloons to welcome the trail-parched cowboys who rode into town. No town was complete without a blacksmith, whose services were needed to shoe horses and oxen, sharpen plows, and repair wagons. Perhaps the most indispensable townsman of all was the merchant who ran the cornerstone of a new town's commercial life—the general store.

Western towns offered an impressive slate of entertainment to tired and lonely residents. Local tastes differed, but certain types of entertainment were popular virtually everywhere. When John Robinson's Great World Exposition rolled into western communities, all hearts thrilled to its triumphant parade of "31 Chariots, 4 Steam Organs, 60 Cages, 8 Bands and 2 Calliopes." Boxing matches, usually held in saloons, were popular. An 1867 prizefight in Cheyenne between John Hardey and John Shannessy for a purse of $1,000 ran 126 rounds. Each round lasted until one man was knocked down, at which point the boxers rested for thirty seconds.

Gambling was the frontier's favorite pastime. To assuage the rigors, loneliness, and boredom of life, people bet not only on poker and dice but also on a dozen other games of chance. If anyone tired of these diversions, it was easy to find wagers at a dog or cock fight, a battle between bulls and bears, a horse race or a boxing match. In San Francisco, nearly a thousand gambling halls sprouted within a few years of the discovery of gold at Sutter's Mill in 1848. Inside the gilded walls of one of these sumptuous palaces, wrote British diarist J. D. Bortwick, "Nothing was heard but a slight hum of voices, and the constant clinking of money."

Along with gambling and drinking, prostitution was central to the early social life of largely male camps and towns. In 1860, 2,306 men and only 30 women—mostly prostitutes—were living in the Comstock Lode towns of Gold Hill and Virginia City. A decade later, when the population was more gender balanced, at least one in twelve women was a prostitute. A Seattle writer expressed the common western attitude that while eastern vice was "silent, muffle-footed, velvet-gloved, masqued-faced," the western variety went about "openly, unclad, unpolished, open-handed."

Western towns were frequently rough and violent places. "I have seen many fast towns," one seasoned cowboy declared, "but Abilene beat them all." A local merchant characterized the town as a "seething, roaring, flaming hell." In cow towns, drunkenness and fistfights were common, but strict gun control laws kept the killing to a minimum. Many cattle towns outlawed the carrying of handguns within the city limits and established police forces to patrol the streets and enforce the ordinances. No cattle town ever buried more than five murder victims during a single year despite the presence, on both sides of the law, of gunfighters like Doc Holliday, John Wesley Hardin, Bat Masterson, and Wyatt Earp. The mining camps were rougher and rowdier than the cattle towns. Fistfights escalated into gunfights far more often in mining towns because few passed gun control laws. The mining town of Bodie, California, was a good example. During its boom years, Bodie had 29 killings, which converted to an annual homicide rate of 116 per 100,000 population. No eastern city in the 1880s had a crime rate remotely close to Bodie's.

Middle-class women led the effort to "civilize" the boisterous cattle and mining towns by creating the institutions—schools, churches, and charity associations— that often checked male-inspired disorder and created family-oriented communities. The white women who left their homes to live in the West carried with them prevailing notions of domesticity, which suggested that women represented the moral foundation of the family and society. An honorable woman "is a missionary of virtue, morality, happiness and peace to a circle of careworn, troubled, and often, alas, demoralized men," Eliza Farnham noted in her influential 1856 book *California, Indoors and Out.* As expected, white women living in western towns led the efforts for moral reform, attacking prostitution, liquor, gambling, and crime.

Joining women reformers in their efforts were Protestant missionaries who saw the salvation of the West as part of their patriotic and Christian duty. Many people welcomed churches in their towns as a sign of civility and stability, even if they rejected the message preached from the pulpit. A church, editorialized the *Albuquerque Morning Democrat* in 1893, "does as much to build up a town as a school, a railroad, or a fair." In mining towns and cattle towns, ministers tried to pass laws promoting temperance, limiting public activities on Sundays, and restricting gambling. Most of the measures failed, but by focusing public attention on the problems, ministers and their allies gradually succeeded in confining prostitution and gambling to specific areas of town.

The Hardships of Farm Life

Since trees were in short supply on the Plains, the log cabin that had been the usual first home of settlers in earlier periods to the east yielded to the sod house and dugout in the West. These dim dwellings allowed little light or air to enter. Unless they were walled and plastered, they were also damp and dirty places. As one Nebraska girl put it, "There was running water in our sod house. It ran through the roof." Settlers shared their homes with mice, centipedes, spiders, and snakes that crawled out of the walls. One such dugout in Nickolls County, Nebraska, had a single room nine feet by twelve feet, housing six family members as well as a bed, a stove, a table, and several boxes. In 1876 nine-tenths of the settlers of Butler County, Nebraska, lived in houses made of dirt.

Climate presented a new challenge for western settlers. In addition to being dry, the interior West was hotter in the summer, colder in the winter, and windier at virtually any time than the eastern states. Glendive, Montana, in 1893 recorded a 164-degree range in temperatures from a summer high of 117 degrees to a winter low of 47 degrees below zero. The winters brought blizzards, sometimes lasting for days, and east of the Rockies, the summers brought tornados.

And then there were the grasshoppers. In a bad year, such as 1874, grasshoppers swarmed onto the northern prairies in such numbers that farmers mistook them for storm clouds massing on the horizon. When the insects arrived, they fell from the skies like hail until they lay four to six inches deep on the ground. A Wichita newspaper reported in 1878 that the grasshoppers devoured "everything green, stripping the foliage off the bark and from the tender twigs of the fruit trees, destroying every plant that is good for food or pleasant to the eyes, that man has planted."

The grueling conditions were especially difficult for farm women. Unmarried women might find jobs as teachers, seamstresses, and domestic servants, but for most married women work revolved around the family: cooking meals, taking care of children, and maintaining the house. Girls and women occasionally helped on the farm, but the gender boundaries between male and female work remained clear. "I could help the boys with the plowing or trapping," recalled Susie Crockett of Oklahoma, but "they would never help me with the sewing." Men socialized with other farm or ranch workers, but women were often isolated at home. At times the isolation and loneliness could overwhelm with thoughts of desolation: "I was alone all the daylight hours with the cattle, and all around me the prairie was dying. The sound of death was in the wind that never stopped blowing across the whitening grass, or rustling the dead weeds at the edges of the fields," wrote Grace Snyder, a farmer's wife in Custer County, Missouri. "As long as I live I'll never see such a lonely country," a woman said of the Texas plains; and a Nebraska woman sighed, "These unbounded prairies have such an air of desolation, and the stillness is very oppressive."

Farm women also had to contend with extra burdens. As late as the 1920s, a typical farm wife could expect to devote nine hours a day to such chores as cleaning, sewing, laundering, and preparing food. An additional two hours a day were spent cleaning the barn and chicken coop, milking the cows, caring for poultry, and gardening. Childbirth was perhaps the greatest trial of all, since it often took place without either a midwife or a doctor in attendance. One woman remarked that farm wives were "not much better than slaves. It is a weary, monotonous round of cooking and washing and mending and as a result the insane asylum is ⅓d filled with wives of farmers."

Racism in the West: The Chinese

During the 1860s, twenty-four thousand Chinese, two-thirds of the Chinese population in America, worked in the California mines. Mining profits had already begun to decrease in California, however, and the Chinese were leaving the gold fields. Thousands of them joined other Chinese migrants to work on the transcontinental railroad. Then, after the completion of the Central Pacific line in 1869, many Chinese workers flocked to cities. By 1900, nearly half the Chinese population of California lived in urban areas, with San Francisco's Chinese neighborhood emerging as the largest community.

In 1868 an observer noted that San Francisco's Chinatown was a thriving and colorful community "made up of stores catering to the Chinese only," where residents strolled the streets "in their native costumes, with queues down their backs." In addition, Chinatown boasted a host of organizations and associations. Locals established temples for worship and formed district associations to find shelter and jobs for new arrivals. Other groups settled disputes among community members and provided educational and health services. For recreation, residents attended the local theater, which featured an all-Chinese cast and orchestra.

Though successful in creating flourishing communities, the Chinese found their lives circumscribed in many ways. Only Native Americans suffered more racial violence than the Chinese. Most whites tolerated Chinese workers when jobs were plentiful, or when they took the arduous and unappealing task of building railroads. When they moved into the cities, however, they competed against white workers for desirable positions. Anti-coolie clubs, which began springing up in California during the late 1860s and blossomed in the 1870s, sought laws against employing Chinese workers and organized economic boycotts of Chinese-made goods. Their protests soon became violent as economic depression led to anti-Chinese riots by unemployed white workers throughout California. Racial unrest spread across the region. In Rock Springs, Wyoming, whites murdered twenty-eight Chinese. In Seattle, angry whites rounded up Chinese, placed them in boats, and forced them out to sea.

Thus by the early 1870s, anti-Chinese agitation had become an almost irresistible way for politicians to attract the votes of white workers. The new California constitution of 1879 denied the vote to the Chinese and forbade their employment on any state or local public works project. In 1882 Congress suspended Chinese immigration for ten years. Later legislation extended the ban. Such discrimination and immigration restriction served to reduce drastically the total Chinese population in the United States. Many migrants returned to China, and new migrants could not enter to replace them. The Chinese population of California fell by at least one-third between 1890 and 1900.

Those Chinese who remained found themselves concentrated in low-wage jobs, segregated within individual industries, and paid less than white workers—if they could find work at all. Many were forced into self-employment. By 1890, there were 6,400 Chinese laundry workers in California, representing 69 percent of the state's launderers. In 1900 one out of four employed Chinese men worked in a laundry.

The Hispanic Heritage in the Southwest

The wave of white settlement transformed Hispanic communities scattered across Texas, New Mexico, Arizona, and California. While a small group of Hispanic elite, the *Ricos,* profited by aligning themselves with the encroaching Anglos, most Hispanics suffered.

Throughout the Southwest, white settlers, lawyers, and politicians cheated Hispanics out of their lands. In 1848 the U.S. government had promised *Californios* (Hispanic residents of California) U.S. citizenship and the "free enjoyment of their liberty and property." Despite the promise, *Californios* working in the Gold Rush mines were forced to pay a Foreign Miners Tax. As white immigrants flooded into California, they squatted on large Hispanic ranches, killing livestock and laying claim to the land. The government eventually upheld most Hispanic land claims, but not before long and expensive litigation had drained them penniless. Hispanics, "who at one time had been the richest landowners," a group of *Californio* ranchers complained in 1859, "today find themselves without a foot of ground, living as objects of charity." The story was similar in New Mexico, where businessmen and politicians swindled over 2 million acres of land from the original residents. An observer noted that "by 1860 the Anglos had gotten control, by fair means or foul, of nearly every ranch worth having north of the Nueces."

The coming of the railroads created a new national trading system that destroyed the local markets and independent farms that had formed the backbone of the Southwest's economy. Hispanics found themselves, along with migrants from Mexico, thrust into a racially divided labor system. On Texas cattle ranches, for example, the managers were Anglo while the cowhands were Mexican. In New Mexico gold mines, Mexicans executed the dangerous manual work while Anglo workers operated the machines. In Los Angeles, 75 percent of Mexican workers were employed in unskilled and low-paying jobs, compared with 30 percent of the Anglos. Even when Mexicans did the same work as Anglos, they were paid less than their counterparts. "The differences in the wages paid Mexicans and the native-born and north Europeans employed as general laborers," a congressional investigation reported, ". . . are largely accounted for by discrimination against the Mexicans in payment of wages."

In many areas, Hispanics fought to preserve control of their societies. In New Mexico, the only territory where Spanish-speaking residents represented a clear majority, angry *Hispanos* (as they were called in New Mexico) organized themselves

Mexican-American Mine Workers, Southwest, 1890s   The southwestern United States, part of Mexico before 1848, had always had a large Hispanic population. But the growth of economic enterprise—mining, ranching, farming—in the late nineteenth century instigated a new wave of Mexican immigration before 1900. Whereas the earlier Hispanic community of the Southwest was well established and included a small aristocracy, the new immigrants who came looking for work mostly found low wages and racial discrimination by white employers. *(Wyoming Division of Cultural Resources.)*

as a masked night-riding outfit known from their costume as *Las Gorras Blancas* (the White Caps). With perhaps seven hundred men joining the raids, in 1889 and 1890 they cut Anglos' fences, burned their haystacks, and, occasionally, torched their barns and houses. In most areas, however, the tide of Anglo migrants simply overran Hispanic communities. In 1845 only seven thousand Anglos lived in California; by 1900 their numbers had swelled to nearly 1.5 million.

The influx of Anglos eroded Hispanic political influence. In Los Angeles, for example, the Spanish-surnamed part of the city's population fell from more than three-fourths of the city's population in 1850 to 19 percent in 1880. Santa Barbara's experience illustrated the process. For years the most important center of Spanish and Mexican culture in California, Santa Barbara had a class of vigorous and well-to-do ranchero families who were accustomed to ruling themselves. As late as 1867, Spanish-surnamed voters composed nearly 63 percent of the electorate in the city and nearly as much in the county. By 1873, the proportion of Spanish-surnamed voters had shrunk to about 34 percent in the city and county.

The West and the American Imagination

Americans came to view the disappearing frontier as a proving ground for the American experiment. By the end of the nineteenth century, the West had assumed many of the characteristics of the East. Yet in the popular imagination, the West emerged as a symbol of traditional American values of rugged individualism, limited government, and social progress.

"The Myth of the Garden"

As the frontier faded in the face of technology and change, twentieth-century Americans clung to what historian Henry Nash Smith described as "The Myth of the Garden." According to this notion, the West was an agrarian Eden where free land and honest toil produced virtuous citizens. The myth served a clear purpose: it transformed the West into a symbol of American character. "All the associations called up by the spoken word, the West," wrote novelist Hamlin Garland in 1891, "were fabulous, mythic, hopeful." The myth reinforced America's perception of itself as a land of rugged individuals, as a civilization with a mission to remake the world—or in this case the continent—in its own image, and as a society unencumbered by oppressive government.

The myth found its fullest expression in popular culture. The first "westerns" appeared in the form of dime novels, which by the 1860s were selling in editions of fifty thousand or more. In 1887 Edward L. Wheeler created the most memorable western hero: Deadwood Dick. Young and handsome, Dick used his daring horsemanship and finely tuned shooting skills to fight against powerful villains. Such a hero, observed a historian, "confirmed Americans in the traditional belief that obstacles were to be overcome by the courageous, virile, and determined stand of the individual as an individual."

Other popular writers joined in the celebration of the West. In the 1880s, in his widely read, multivolume *The Winning of the West*, a young Theodore Roosevelt described the West as a land of strong, virtuous, hardworking people who were extending civilization into "barbarian" territory. The conquering of the West by English-speaking people, he wrote, was "the great, epic feat in the history of our race." The West embodied all of the qualities that Roosevelt admired in America. "No man can really understand our country, and appreciate what it really is and what it promised," he wrote, "unless he has the fullest and closest sympathy with the ideals and aspirations of the West."

For the American public, nothing brought the mythic West more directly into their lives than the Wild West shows. From among fifty or more traveling shows, the one to popularize the American West most successfully was Buffalo Bill's "Wild West and Congress of Rough Riders." By the time Buffalo Bill got around to opening his "Wild West, Rocky Mountain, and Prairie Exhibition" in 1883, he already enjoyed wide fame as a western personality. A well-known scout for the frontier army, Cody assumed celebrity stature during the 1870s thanks to the literary vision of Edward Zane Carroll Judson, who used the pen name Ned Buntline.

Cody's shows accommodated twenty thousand people and presented "actual scenes, genuine characters" from the West. Native Americans in flowing headdress and carrying elegantly feathered sticks rode bareback into the arena on stunning painted horses. The Sioux leader Sitting Bull joined the show as a living, breathing exhibit, riding around the arena on horseback to a serenade of boos and catcalls. The cowboys, who wore spotless ten-gallon hats and furry chaps, bore little resemblance to typical sweat-stained ranch hands. Cody brought Americans the perfect frontierswoman in the person of Annie Oakley. Her remarkable marksmanship skills set her apart from effête eastern ladies, but her genteel appearance and stylish costumes revealed her to be a "true" woman.

One of the most popular performances reenacted "Custer's Massacre," culminating with Cody standing head bowed in a spotlight on the darkened battlefield. Mark Twain was delighted: "Genuine . . . down to its smallest details." The show made $100,000 in 1885 and did far better the following season, when it drew a million people during its run on New York's Staten Island and another million during a winter stand in the city's Madison Square Garden.

The End of the Frontier

In 1893 historian Frederick Jackson Turner added a scholarly dimension to the popularization of the western myth. A few years earlier, the superintendent of the census noted that he could no longer locate a continuous frontier line beyond which population thinned out to fewer than two per square mile. "Up to and including 1880," he reported, "the country had a frontier of settlement, but at present the unsettled area has been so broken into by isolated bodies of settlement that there can hardly be said to be a frontier line." The report provided the inspiration for Turner's provocative frontier thesis, which he first presented in a paper titled, "The Significance of the Frontier in American History." Turner argued that, more than anything else, the frontier concept had shaped the American character. "The existence of an area of free land," Turner wrote, "its continuous recession, and the advance of American settlement westward, explain American development." The frontier, he argued, separated America from Europe because it allowed individualism and democracy to develop. Turner concluded, "Four centuries from the discovery of America, at the end of a hundred years under the Constitution, the frontier has gone and with its going has closed the first period of American history."

Scholars criticized Turner for ignoring European influences on American culture and for espousing a crude form of environmental determinism, but his writing reflected a widespread concern about the fading frontier. The same worries inspired popular artists and writers to romanticize the Old West. Publications such as *Cosmopolitan, Ladies' Home Journal, Collier's Red Book,* and the *Saturday Evening Post* depended on a dozen or more western illustrators for the art accompanying western fiction pieces. One of the most notable, William H. D. Koerner, turned out more than twenty-four hundred illustrations, approximately six hundred of which depicted western themes. He, like other artists, depicted westerners as individuals of character, refinement, and integrity.

For most of the twentieth century, movies and, later, television played the central role in perpetuating the myth of the West. Beginning with *The Great Train Robbery* (1903), a trailblazer in cinematic storytelling that ran for a full nine minutes, movie producers transformed the western into a set formula for movies and television. The key ingredient was a noble cowboy, usually a youthful bachelor who, against great odds, made up his mind to right a wrong. Along the way he was forced to fight villainous characters: desperate Indians, corrupt cattle ranchers, or heartless outlaws.

Thus a diverse group of writers, artists, and scholars presented Americans with an engaging but distorted view of the past. The celebration of rugged individualism failed to acknowledge the role the government had played in every step of western development. The view of the frontier as the westward-moving source of America's democratic politics exaggerated the homogenizing effect of the frontier environment and failed to account for the persistence of racial, class, and gender differences. In most of these scenarios, Native Americans appeared as noble savages whose disappearance documented the cultural superiority of white society. Hispanics were depicted as docile peasants, ferocious bandits, or sensual fandango dancers. The contributions of African-Americans, Asians, and women were ignored altogether.

The popular portrayals of the West may have failed to capture the diversity and complexity of the region, but they offered powerful reinforcement to America's perception of itself as a land of individual freedom and unbounded opportunity—beliefs that would be sorely tested in the years ahead.

CONCLUSION

Following the Civil War, new migrants traveled west in search of a better life, and the federal government played a central role in making that experiment possible. Washington passed laws that offered Americans an economic incentive to settle the West and to develop its resources. The Homestead Act, and others like it, succeeded in attracting hundreds of thousands of settlers, but contrary to the intentions of its authors, the law tended to benefit land speculators more than independent farmers. The federal government's presence in the region went beyond passing laws: it organized each territory, selected the governor and judges, set budgets, and established procedures for statehood.

The forceful removal of Native Americans represented the most visible demonstration of federal power in the West. The new immigrants to the region came from diverse backgrounds, but they shared a desire to possess and harness the West's natural resources. They disregarded existing treaties guaranteeing Indian land rights and ignored Native American cultural traditions, which rejected private ownership of land and imbued nature with symbolic and religious meaning. When the new and old cultures clashed, the national government used its superior technology and firepower to suppress the Indians. Having defeated the Indians in battle, the government continued the experiment in suppression by joining with reformers to destroy their culture. The Dawes Act forced Indians to adopt "Western" notions of land management, while reformers worked to "civilize" the Indians, forcing them to abandon their culture, language, and traditions.

With the Indians out of the way, farmers, miners, and ranchers moved aggressively to exploit the region's natural resources. In each case, however, large industries replaced small ventures, imposing on the region an industrial order similar to that which existed in the East. Conservationists such as John Muir challenged the widespread idea that the West was a land of limitless resources, but theirs were often lonely voices.

Like the economy, the new society that emerged in the West also replicated older cultural values. Reflecting traditional notions of domesticity, middle-class women often led the effort to civilize tough mining and cattle towns. Along with spearheading crusades for moral reform, they founded schools, churches, and charity associations designed to foster a family-centered environment. Racial stereotypes and discrimination migrated to the region with the majority of settlers. Chinese immigrants who sought opportunity in the West were often victims of racial violence. In 1882 Congress responded to the violence by eliminating the target: banning Chinese immigration. In California and New Mexico, wealthy Hispanic landowners found themselves defrauded of millions of acres of land. At the same time, the Anglo majority relegated working-class Hispanics to the lowest-paying jobs.

Ironically, Americans transformed the West into a powerful symbol of individualism and self-help, a place where the American experiment could achieve its full potential. Dime novels, popular Wild West shows, and later, motion pictures, reaffirmed America's view of itself as a nation of rugged individuals who conquered the

Indians and civilized a rugged continent. The portrayals often ignored the role that government played in settling the region and usually neglected the contributions of women, African-Americans, Hispanics, and Asians. But the popular view of the West revealed the power of myth, and the persistence of Americans' deeply held attitudes about themselves and the world around them.

SUGGESTED READINGS

The history of the American West has received considerable attention in the last two decades, as evidenced in the number of general surveys and essay compilations published. A good overview of the shift that occurred in the late nineteenth century, as the pioneer became tied to the industrialized economy, can be found in Rodman W. Paul's *The Far West and the Great Plains in Transition, 1859–1908* (rev. ed., 1998). Other historians have taken a topical approach to the history of the West, as seen in Robert V. Hine's *The American West* (2nd ed., 1984), which includes the early conquest of the region by the Spanish, as well as the history of western racial conflict. A comprehensive examination of the western experience is found in the twenty-three essays compiled by Clyde A. Milner II, Carol A. O'Connor, and Martha A. Sandweiss, eds., *The Oxford History of the American West* (1994). This work covers a variety of issues, from the West's unique heritage to its current role in American culture. Another collection of essays, *Historians and the American West* (1983), edited by Michael P. Malone, reflects the diversity of the western peoples from the prehistoric Indians to the metropolis of the twentieth century. An excellent survey of the American West that has stood the test of time, and five editions, is R. A. Billington and Martin Ridge's *Westward Expansion: A History of the American Frontier* (5th ed., 1982). Billington, a student of Frederick Jackson Turner, traces the various frontier experiences and the impact of the West on its inhabitants.

The last two decades have seen a number of historians reject Turner's frontier thesis, a move toward what many are calling the "New Western History." Leading this attack against the past is Patricia Nelson Limerick in her book *The Legacy of Conquest: The Unbroken Past of the American West* (1987). Limerick argues for replacing Turner's thesis with a description of the West that takes into account the ongoing competition for property and profit that led to the conquest and domination of numerous minority groups. In *"It's Your Misfortune and None of My Own": A New History of the American West* (1990), Richard White continues this theme of conquest as he examines the interaction between different racial and ethnic groups as they, and the federal government, sought to prosper from the region's natural resources. Rejecting another aspect of Turner's thesis, the image of the isolated frontier, serves as the foundation for William Cronon's *Nature's Metropolis: Chicago and the Great West* (1991). For Cronon, the frontier did not begin out on the Plains but in the city of Chicago. Cronon traces the importance of the expanding urban economy and its influence on the rural West that supplied the city's needs. Cronon, along with George Miles and Jay Gitlin, edited *Under an Open Sky: Rethinking America's Western Past* (1992), which explores the role of the West in American history through such issues as the environment, race relations, and regional identity.

Historians have produced numerous works concerning the role of women in the West, and good examples of the progress being made in this area are two books edited by Susan Armitage and Elizabeth Jameson. The first, *The Women's West* (1987), provides twenty-one essays, covering three centuries, that examine the lives of women as they constructed their place in a male-dominated society. Armitage and Jameson's second collection, *Writing the Range: Race, Class, and Culture in the Women's West* (1997), adds further dimensions to the history of women as twenty-nine historians explore the diversity of western peoples who came into contact with one another as they sought to create their own identities. Other works have provided detailed descriptions of particular aspects of women's lives and occupations in the West.

Glenda Riley examines the work of women on the Great Plains as they contributed to society both inside and outside their homes in *the Female Frontier: A Comparative View of Women on the Prairie and Plains* (1988). Several books focus on the western woman living in the emerging towns of the region. Anne Butler explains the reasons women became prostitutes in western cities in *Daughters of Joy, Sisters of Misery* (1985). Butler analyzes their interaction with other prostitutes, their families, and the community at large. Another study of women's occupations in western communities is Paula Petrik's *No Step Backward: Women and Family on the Rocky Mountain Mining Frontier, 1865–1900* (1987), in which she traces the transformation of women as they sought to advance their economic opportunities and social equality. In other western towns, women joined forces in the home mission movement to improve conditions for women no matter their race, class, or ethnicity, as addressed in Peggy Pascoe's work, *Relations of Rescue: The Search for Female Moral Authority in the American West, 1874–1939* (1990).

The impact made by African-Americans in the West has also slowly become the focus of historical analysis. William L. Katz's breakthrough work, *The Black West* (3rd ed., 1987), tells the history of blacks who, despite their omission from most historical accounts, participated in every stage of frontier development—from fur trapper to cowboy. The role of black soldiers in the West after the Civil War is the focus of Monroe L. Billington's *New Mexico's Buffalo Soldiers, 1866–1900* (1991). Despite civilian and military discrimination, these soldiers served in campaigns against hostile Indians, protected reservations, and kept the peace. The migration of freedmen from the South serves as the backdrop for Nell Irvin Painter's *Exodusters: Black Migration to Kansas After Reconstruction* (1992). She describes why these families chose to move out onto the Plains, as well as what they found in this alleged Promised Land.

The Hispanic community in the West has also found a voice in a number of works, illustrating their position as original landholders and recently conquered peoples. In *Chicanos in a Changing Society: From Mexican Pueblos to American Barrios in Santa Barbara and Southern California, 1848–1930,* Albert Camarillo traces the loss of power urban Mexican-Americans faced as whites moved onto their land and attempted to exploit or remove the native population. Sarah Deutsch has also depicted the transformation of Hispanic life in her work *No Separate Refuge: Culture, Class, and Gender on the Anglo-Hispanic Frontier in the Overland Trail* (1979). Deutsch combines women's history with Hispanic and labor history to fully illustrate the development and decline of the unique Spanish-speaking communities in New Mexico and Colorado.

Native Americans suffered from the same exploitation that plagued Hispanics as whites spread across the continent. Wilcomb E. Washburn's *The Indian in America* (1975) serves as a good introduction to the struggles between Indians and whites from the colonial period through the 1970s. Robert Utley, a prominent Native American historian, has written a number of works on the issue of Indian–white relations, and his book *The Indian Frontier of the American West, 1846–1890* (1984) provides a synthesis of the hostilities created as Native Americans fought the reservation system that the government imposed on western tribes. The images of Indians held by white Americans certainly affected interracial relations and government policy, as seen in Robert Berkhofer's *The White Man's Indian: Images of the American Indian from Columbus to the Present* (1978). Francis Paul Prucha also examines the government's image of Indians as childlike dependents as he traces Indian policy from the Revolution to 1980 in *The Great Father: The United States Government and the American Indians* (1984).

The impact of federal policy on Indians in the West has proven a fertile topic among historians. Richard White's *The Roots of Dependency: Subsistence, Environment, and Social Change Among the Choctaws, Pawnees, and Navajos* (1983) compares the experiences of three tribes over several centuries as whites forced them to abandon independence and economic self-sufficiency. Frederick E. Hoxie describes how white politicians, anthropologists, and reformers attempted to remake the Native American in their own images through government land policies, education, and citizenship. In *The Dispossession of the American Indian, 1887–1934* (1991), Janet A. McDonnell argues that these government projects proved disastrous to the Native Americans because the government, while acting as benevolent father, failed to protect Indian ownership of land from insatiable white land speculators.

Whether they experienced it first-hand or through others' detailed accounts, Americans throughout the nineteenth century held particular images of the West. Henry Nash Smith was the first to analyze a number of American beliefs about the West in his work *Virgin Land: The American West as Symbol and Myth* (1950). While Smith emphasizes the literature of the day, William H. Goetzmann and William N. Goetzmann examined the impact of visual images of the West on Americans in *The West of the Imagination* (1986). They argue that artwork might have had a greater impact on the western myth than the written ones. In *Wilderness and the American Mind* (1973), Roderick Nash traces the history of American's preoccupation with nature from the Puritan wilderness to the ecological conflicts between preservationists and conservationists in the twentieth century. The image of the West as a garden ultimately led to the creation of national parks, the focus of Albert Runte's *National Parks: The American Experience* (1979).

Competing Voices

Native Americans, Whites, and the Land

"Marvels of the New West"

In this article written in 1887, W. M. Thayer sings the praises of the potential of western lands. When he views the land, he sees great wealth and opportunity through agriculture.

■ Who has not heard of the cornfields of Kansas and the wheatfields of Dakota? Not that all the mammoth fields of corn and wheat are found in these localities; for the New West, clear to the Pacific coast, challenges the world to survey its empire of golden grain. . . .

The wildest dream has become reality. . . . Nothing is too large for belief. Twenty and even thirty thousand acre farms, and a hundred bushels to the acre, is not an extravagant story now. Corn eighteen feet high, with ears long and heavy enough for a policeman's club, is not questioned now even by the uninitiated. Harvests like an army with banners, waving their golden plumes above the house which the farmer occupies, require no stretch of the imagination to realize. . . .

A farm of twenty or thirty thousand acres . . . is divided into sections, with superintendent and army of employees for each section, who go to work with military precision and order. The . . . workers . . . [sweep] forward like a column of cavalry, turning over a hundred acres of soil in an incredible brief period of time. . . . Under this arrangement the earth is easily conquered by this mighty army of ploughers, who move forward to the music of rattling machines and the tramp of horses. It is an inspiring spectacle—the almost boundless prairie farm and the cohorts of hopeful tillers marching over it in triumph. Steam also reinforces the battalions of workers on many bonanza farms, largely multiplying the amount of labor performed. . . .

"Necessity is the mother of invention"; and so the wheat-raisers found a way of harvesting their enormous crops. . . . A machine of cutting, binding, and placing the bundles in an upright position met the needs of the hour. The problem of harvesting the largest fields of grain was solved by this invention. . . . These machines move before the horses—from twenty to twenty-four horses to each machine—cut and thresh and stack the grain, and leave the sacks in piles. Four men work them, and cut and thresh from twenty-five to forty acres a day. . . .

The New West . . . is a veritable "Wonderland" as crowned with OPPORTUNITIES as it is with marvels. Men live rapidly here—a whole month in one day, a whole year in a month. Some have lived a hundred years in the twenty-five or thirty they have spent here. They have seen an empire rise and grow rich and powerful in that time. . . . It seems as if God had concentrated his wisdom and power upon this part of our country, to make it His crowning work of modern civilization on this Western Continent. For history is Providence illustrated—God in the affairs of men to exhibit the grandeur of human enterprise and the glory of human achievement. . . . ■

Native Americans and Land Ownership

In these two selections, Chief Joseph of the Nez Percé and a group of Hopi chiefs try to explain their people's attitude toward and usage of their land, in hopes of averting more governmental interference. The Hopi were addressing specifically the Dawes Act of 1887, which subdivided Indian lands into individual titles, a concept foreign both to the Hopi traditional land tenure system and to their concept of farming. Chief Joseph speaks eight years after peacefully resisting an illegal treaty to cede Nez Percé land. In 1877 his people were finally captured and forced on to a reservation.

(Chief Joseph, 1871) The Earth was created by the assistance of the sun, and it should be left as it was. . . . The country was made without lines of demarcation, and it is no man's business to divide it. . . . I see whites all over the country gaining wealth, and see their desire to give us lands which are worthless. . . . The earth and myself are of one mind. The measure of the land and the measure of our bodies are the same. Say to us if you can say it, that you were sent by the Creative Power to talk to us. Perhaps you think the Creator sent you here to dispose of us as you see fit. If I thought you were sent by the Creator I might be induced to think you had a right to dispose of me. Do not misunderstand me, but understand me fully with reference to my affection for the land. I never said the land was mine to do with as I chose. The one who has the right to dispose of it is the one who has created it. I claim a right to live on my land, and accord you the privilege to live on yours.

(Hopi Petition, 1894) According to the number of children a woman has, fields for them are assigned to her, from some of the lands of her family group, and her husband takes care of them. Hence our fields are numerous but small, and several belonging to the same family may be close together, or they may be miles apart, because arable localities are not continuous. There are other reasons for the irregularity in size and situation of our family lands, as interrupted sequence of inheritance cause by extinction of families, but chiefly owing to the following condition, and to which we especially invite your attention.

In the Spring and Summer there usually comes from the Southwest a succession of gales, oftentimes strong enough to blow away the sandy soil from the face of some of our fields, and to expose the underlying clay, which is hard, and sour, and barren; and as the sand is the only fertile land, when it moves, the planters must follow it, and other fields must be provided in place of those which have been devastated. Sometimes generations pass away and these barren spots remain, while in other instances, after a few years, the winds have again restored the desirable sand upon them. In such event its fertility is disclosed by the nature of the grass and shrubs that grow upon it. If these are promising, a number of us united to clear off the land and make it again fit for planting, when it may be given back to its former owner, or if a long time has elapsed, to other heirs, or it may be given to some person of the same family group, more in need of a planting place. . . .

The American is our elder brother, and in everything he can teach us, except in the method of growing corn in these waterless sand valleys, and in that we are sure we can teach him. . . .

Historically, white culture has viewed its environment as a commodity, believing God created nature for human use and that humanity's right and duty was to develop and control it. Most white settlers viewed the Great Plains as an endless source of economic opportunity, whether in mining, ranching, or farming. Despite warnings from scientists such as John Wesley Powell that the climate was too hot and dry for growing cash crops, thousands of families moved west, encouraged by the promise of free land and profit and lured by railroad companies and land speculators eager to develop the area and make a buck themselves.

Indian use of the land was far different from that of whites because of the cultural significance they gave to their environment. Although each tribe's culture was unique, all Native American cultures gave the land a spiritual significance. They tried to live in harmony with the land, believing that the human world and the natural world shared a larger consciousness. While the Indians also manipulated their environments, using burning to discourage certain species and cultivate others, their cultural beliefs placed limits on the use of nature. For whites, the market culture encouraged competition between individuals, disrespect of the land, and extensive and intensive farming. Indian culture produced a more communal economy, conservative hunting practices, and subsistence and migratory farming practices that protected the soil from overuse and erosion.

Instead of considering that Indians might have something to teach whites about the limits of their environment, the U.S. government sought to eradicate Indian culture in order to make way for white destiny. The decimation of the buffalo, the restriction of Indians to small reservations, and finally the attempted conversion of Indians into commercial farmers through the Dawes Act, all ultimately opened more land for white use. White use was often abuse, as white Plains farmers employed techniques such as deep plowing and irrigation in an effort to counter the natural tendencies of the local environment. The result was soil erosion, cycles of drought, and general ecological instability that culminated in the great Dust Bowl of the 1930s.

Questions for Analysis

1. What phrases reveal Thayer's attitude toward western lands?

2. How does he see new technology as unleashing and enhancing the West's potential?

3. What do you think he means when he says, "Men live rapidly here"?

4. What difference does Chief Joseph see in the white and Indian relationships with the land?

5. Does Chief Joseph claim ownership of the land? Why or why not?

6. Why does the traditional Hopi land system not include permanent, continuous farms?

7. In what ways is Hopi farming and landholding communal rather than individualistic?

8. How is the balance between progress and respect for the environment being handled today?

18

The Industrial Experiment, 1865–1900

*T*he day was May 10, 1876, and not even the spring showers that had turned the Philadelphia fairgrounds into a muddy quagmire could dampen the spirits of the thousands of people who stood waiting for the opening of an exhibition honoring the nation's one-hundredth birthday. With memories of a bloody Civil War still fresh in public memory, many people hoped the centennial would demonstrate a new unity that Americans longed for and symbolize the nation's optimism about the future.

The celebration opened with the blast of steam whistles, a hundred-gun salute, and the voices of a choir singing Handel's "Hallelujah Chorus." The centennial exhibition covered 236 acres in downtown Philadelphia, filling 167 buildings with over 30,000 exhibits. The Main Exhibition Building measured 1,800 feet long and 464 feet wide, the largest building in the world at the time. Four other great halls—Machinery Hall, Agricultural Hall, Horticultural Hall, and Memorial Hall—dominated the landscape. By all accounts, the fair was a smashing success. Between May and November, more than 10 million visitors attended the extravaganza. Never had any single attraction brought together such large, enthusiastic crowds from across the nation. One happy visitor called it "the most stupendous and successful competitive exhibition that the world ever saw."

The centennial observance revealed a great deal about America's hope for the future. The vast majority of the exhibits celebrated the industrial and mechanical transformation of American life. "One thinks only of the glorious triumphs of skill and invention," admitted one visitor. The federal Patent Office displayed over five thousand patent models. Alexander Graham Bell personally demonstrated his brand-new electric telephone (1876); nearby, Thomas Edison explained his latest brainchild, the automatic telegraph (1874). The mammoth Corliss engine, the largest steam engine in the world, gained most of the attention. Rising more than forty feet, the engine generated 2,500 horsepower and ran eight thousand assorted gadgets simultaneously.

The exhibit also revealed the continuing tensions of race, class, and gender in American life. Organizers refused to hire African-Americans and failed to include an exhibit marking their place in American society. Planners filled the Women's Pavilion with devices to lighten domestic labor: a hand-operated washing machine, a self-fitting dress pattern, a manual dishwasher. Hoping to limit the corrupting influence of poor immigrants, organizers banned popular amusements and closed the exhibition on Sundays—the one day when workers might be free to attend. They could do nothing, however, about the unofficial "Centennial City" that sprang up directly across the street, which entertained people who could not afford admission to the Exposition grounds.

In its first one hundred years, the United States had evolved from a confederation of thirteen colonies to a nation of 40 million citizens and thirty-eight states. Little in its past, however, had prepared it for the enormous economic experimentation that would transform American life in the last half of the nineteenth century. The rise of big business, the emergence of a national economy, and the changing nature of work fundamentally altered the way Americans earned a living. The wrenching impact of industrialization led to new experiments in regulating business and organizing unions to protect workers' interests. Whether or not they favored the changes taking place around them, most Americans would have agreed with the observation of Harvard historian Henry Adams. "My country in 1900," he wrote, "is something totally different from my own country in 1860. I am wholly a stranger in it. Neither I, nor anyone else, understands it."

▌ How did advances in technology, marketing, and transportation—particularly the railroads—spur industrial expansion after the Civil War?

▌ How did American cultural values sanction competition? What methods did business managers use to limit competition, and how did government respond?

▌ Who were the working people of industrializing America, and what conditions did they encounter?

▌ How did organized labor respond to the new environment? Why weren't organizing efforts more successful?

This chapter will address these questions.

Chronology

1859	Darwin publishes *The Origin of Species*
1866	National Labor Union created
1867	Invention of the typewriter
	Introduction of Pullman Sleeping Car
1869	First transcontinental rail line completed
	Great Atlantic and Pacific Tea Company (A&P) opened
	African-Americans form the Colored National Labor Union
	Knights of Labor organized
1872	Ward starts first successful mail-order business
1873	Financial panic leads to depression
1876	Centennial Exposition held in Philadelphia
	Bell patents the telephone
1877	Great Railway Strike sweeps nation
	Edison invents the phonograph
1879	Invention of the cash register
	Edison successfully tests his electric light bulb
	George publishes *Progress and Poverty*
1881	Standard Oil Trust formed
1884	Knights win victory against Union Pacific Railroad
1886	Westinghouse develops first alternating current system
	Sears, Roebuck, and Company founded
	Haymarket Square bombing
	American Federation of Labor formed
1887	Interstate Commerce Act
1888	Bellamy publishes *Looking Backward*
1889	Carnegie publishes "The Gospel of Wealth"
1890	Sherman Antitrust Act
1901	United States Steel Corporation organized

The Setting for Industrial Expansion, 1865–1889

In 1889 economist David A. Wells announced, "An almost total revolution has taken place, and is yet in progress, in every branch and in every relation of the world's industrial and commercial system." Some essential components of the industrial revolution Wells observed were America's growing population; large deposits of natural resources such as coal, iron, timber, and petroleum; the development of new inventions that raised productivity and lowered costs; the expansion of the railroads; and the emergence of a national marketplace that kindled consumer demand. This favorable environment invited entrepreneurs and government to launch ambitious experiments in harnessing the nation's industrial potential.

Technological Innovation

A writer looking back in 1896 insisted that the period after the Civil War was "an epoch of invention and progress unique in the history of the world. . . . It has been," he noted, "a gigantic tidal wave of human ingenuity and resource, so stupendous in its magnitude, so complex in its diversity, so profound in its thought, so fruitful in its wealth, so beneficent in its results, that the mind is strained and embarrassed in its effort to expand to a full appreciation of it." There was certainly much to crow about: between 1790 and 1860, the U.S. Patent Office recorded 36,000 patents; during the 1890s alone, it registered 234,956.

After the Civil War, in every branch of industry and manufacturing, new inventions raised productivity and lowered the cost of finished products. Specialized machines gradually replaced hand operations in textile manufacturing, shoemaking, and metalworking operations. The invention of the typewriter (1867), the cash register (1879), and the adding machine (1891) allowed businesspeople to work more efficiently.

Among the most enduring inventions were those that enhanced the quality of life in America. The flush toilet, invented in England in the 1870s, appeared in America during the 1880s. The tin can also altered American life by allowing producers to preserve food for long periods of time. For the first time, people could eat vegetables and fruits out of season and store meat and milk conveniently in the home. Railroad refrigeration cars enabled growers to ship their produce long distances. By the end of the century, the urban middle class could eat fresh lettuce, strawberries, and grapes, as well as beef and pork, shipped from the South and West.

Innovations in communication allowed organizations to operate on a national scale. Expansion and improvements in the use of the telegraph allowed for the instant transmission of information from one coast to the other. By 1880, Western Union, which controlled 80 percent of the country's telegraph lines, operated nearly 200,000 miles of telegraph routes. After Bell transmitted the first words over wire in March 1876, demand for the modern telephone grew quickly. By 1880, fifty thousand telephones were in use in the United States, including one in the White House, and fifty-five cities had local service. In 1885 the Bell interests organized the American Telephone and Telegraph Company, and by 1900, the number of telephones had increased to 1.5 million.

From the standpoint of industrial output, perhaps the most significant breakthrough took place in the production of steel. Manufacturers and builders preferred steel over iron because of its increased strength and durability. But making steel in large quantities required a furnace that could produce enough heat to melt wrought iron. After the Civil War, two new processes—the Bessemer and the open hearth—revolutionized the production of steel, stimulating a phenomenal expansion in that industry. In 1860 the United States produced 13,000 tons of steel. By 1879, American furnaces were turning out over a million tons a year. By 1910, the United States was making over 28 million tons and was by far the number one producer of steel in the world. Like the railroads, steel companies grew larger and larger. In 1880, only nine companies could produce more than 100,000 tons a year. By the early 1890s, several companies exceeded 250,000 tons, and two produced over 1 million tons a year.

Thomas Edison and the "Invention Business"

Leading the advances in technology were a group of independent inventors such as Thomas Edison (incandescent lamp, phonograph, and motion picture system), William Stanley (electric light and power transmission), and Wilbur and Orville Wright (internal-combustion engine airplane). Free from organizational entanglements, they worked in small labs with a handful of assistants on problems of their own choosing. In the absence of adequate theory, they resorted to experimentation. "No experiments are useless," Edison snapped when told he carried out too many. While their passion lay in creation, the inventors often formed alliances with capitalists to create companies to manufacture and sell their patented inventions, but they distanced themselves from day-to-day managerial responsibilities. Edison, for example, founded Edison General Electric, a family of manufacturing firms designed to implement his lighting system.

Edison, in fact, was the most prolific inventor of his day. During his lifetime he registered 1,328 patents, and a host of new industries grew from his innovations. In 1876 Edison, who was not yet thirty years old, set up shop in Menlo Park, New Jersey, a railroad stop halfway between New York and Philadelphia, and went full-time into the "invention business." Before settling into his new lab, Edison proposed as a goal "a minor invention every ten days and a big thing every six months or so." Over the next few years, "the Wizard of Menlo Park," produced a stream of new creations including the phonograph, dictaphone, mimeograph, dynamo, and methods to extend electric transmission. His discovery of the phonograph sparked the idea for motion pictures. "It should be possible," he wrote in his notebook, "to devise an apparatus to do for the eye what the phonograph was designed to do for the ear."

Edison's most noteworthy breakthrough came in 1879 when he successfully tested the first incandescent electric light bulb. In the hunt for an ideal filament, Edison claimed to have tested "no fewer than 6,000 vegetable growths" before stumbling on a strip of tungsten. With considerable fanfare, Edison unveiled his new creation on New Year's Eve 1880, when he illuminated Menlo Park with forty incandescent

Edison with His Phonograph
Thomas Edison, the most prolific inventor of the post–Civil War era, and his invention "factories" patented hundreds of creations, including the phonograph, the light bulb, and the motion picture. He had enormous appeal for Americans, not only because he gave them incredible new devices, but because he proved that the power of individual genius still had significance in the age of the corporation. *(Library of Congress.)*

bulbs. In 1882 the Edison Electric Illuminating Company began to supply current to four hundred lights servicing eighty-five customers in New York City.

Because he used direct current, Edison's lighting system was limited to a radius of about two miles. In 1886 George Westinghouse, who founded the Westinghouse Electric Company, developed the first alternating current system, which allowed transmission of electricity over longer distances. Two years later, Nikola Tesla, a Croatian immigrant, discovered a way to convert alternating current into power that could drive machines and, together with Ohio engineer Charles Brush, enabled factories to use electrical power.

The Railroads

Railroads played a crucial role in America's industrial revolution both by consuming industrial output and by helping to develop a powerful national economy. By 1890, railroads criss-crossed the nation, linking consumers with producers. The completion of the transcontinental line in 1869 (see page 661), combined with the construction of a complex web of railroad systems in the Midwest and Northeast, connected raw materials in the West to factories and markets in the East. The nation was laced with 35,000 miles of railroad in 1865; by 1900, 200,000 miles were in operation—more railroad mileage than in all of Europe. The surge in railroad construction spurred the expansion of the other industries, especially steel, stone, and lumber. In 1882, for example, the railroads purchased nearly 90 percent of all steel produced in the United States (see map).

At the same time, technological improvements—the invention of the air brake (1869) and the automatic car coupler (1873), and the introduction of the Pullman Sleeping Car (1867)—made rail travel safer and more comfortable. Between 1877 and 1890, the volume of railroad freight rose from 231 million tons to 691 million, and passenger traffic swelled from 180 million to 520 million miles.

Railroad expansion required huge investments of capital. Government—federal, state, and local—provided cash loans totaling over $150 million. State and local governments also granted the railroads tax exemptions. In addition, the federal government contributed 134 million acres of public land, and states added another 48.9 million acres. Together the gifts of public lands, comprising an area larger than the United Kingdom, Spain, and Belgium combined, was valued at between $130 million and $500 million. The demands for extraordinary amounts of private capital to finance the railroads led to the centralization of America's money and investment markets on Wall Street. Railroads listed their stocks and bonds on the New York Stock Exchange to attract investors from across the country and from Europe. The modern investment house grew up to handle the selling of the new securities.

Railroads and Railroad Land Grants, 1870–1920   Setting a national precedent, the Pacific Railroad Bill of 1862 provided federal land grants to railroad companies in order to facilitate improved transportation. After the Civil War, railroad expansion soared, promoting a national economy and encouraging the growth of heavy industry.

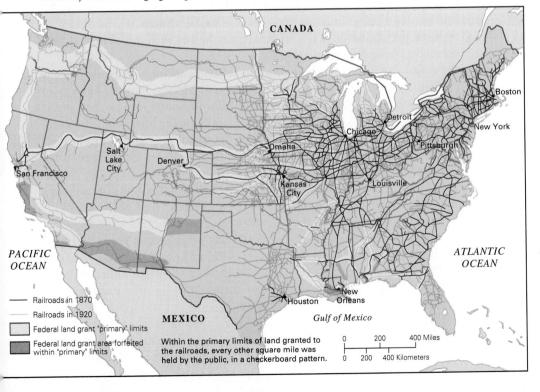

In size and complexity, the railroads dwarfed all other enterprises, both private and public. In 1891 the Pennsylvania Railroad alone employed more workers than the largest government agency (the Post Office). Since the railroads extended over thousands of miles, and involved a complicated system of planning and coordination, executives pioneered the development of new managerial methods that would spread to other industries. Railroads were the first to develop a central controller's office to handle financial transactions and modern accounting practices to measure performance and set rates. Accountants filled out and tabulated "cost sheets" that detailed statistics about every aspect of production. Timekeepers monitored the workers' hours on their jobs. Time-study engineers calculated the most efficient system for doing a particular job. Quality-control inspectors reviewed the finished work. To keep track of the burgeoning white-collar empire of managers and supervisors, railroads produced the first organizational chart.

The New Consumer Society

Improved transportation contributed to major changes in American shopping habits. In the early nineteenth century, when most Americans lived in villages and on farms, they bought items they needed from general stores, which sold almost everything, from silk ribbon to gunpowder to pickled fish. By the late nineteenth century, large department stores and chain stores were eclipsing the general store, especially in larger towns and in cities. Bypassing middlemen, they bought directly from manufacturers and, since they purchased large quantities of goods, negotiated volume discounts that they passed on to their customers in the form of low prices. Department stores also made service their hallmark. Unlike general stores or smaller shops, they delivered goods to consumers' homes, guaranteed quality, and accepted returns from dissatisfied customers.

Every major city had one or more leading department stores. Shoppers in New York strolled down the aisles of A. T. Stewart and Macy's. Bargain hunters in Philadelphia flocked to Wanamaker's and Gimbel's. In Boston, people shopped at Jordan Marsh and Filene's. Chicagoans spent many Saturday afternoons browsing at Marshall Field's and Carson, Price, Scott. By the end of the century, most urban department stores featured restrooms, lunch counters, nurseries for children, complaint and credit counters, and post offices.

The chain store complemented the department store in the transformation of shopping. The first chain was the Great Atlantic and Pacific Tea Company (A&P), which opened the same year that the first transcontinental railroad was completed, in 1869. By 1876, A&P boasted a network of sixty-seven stores. Frank Winfield Woolworth opened his first "five-and ten-cent store" in Lancaster, Pennsylvania, in 1879. By 1910, he was operating over a thousand stores nationwide. Other chains—Grand Union (1870s), Kroger, and Jewel Tea—changed the way Americans shopped for groceries.

The expanding consumer culture reached rural areas through mail-order catalogs, which offered a host of consumer products, from clothing to cutlery. Aaron Montgomery Ward established the first successful mail-order business in 1872.

Macy's Department Store, 1902   Technological innovation and the revolution in transportation in the late nineteenth century permitted the mass-marketing of goods in settings such as the department store. This photograph of the Macy's food section displays an abundance and variety of goods that lured in the consumer. The department store was more than a convenience; it was a wonder that turned shopping into an adventure, particularly for American women, who increasingly became the target demographic for retailers. Women, like this Macy's clerk, were also a strong presence behind the counter at department stores.   *(Museum of the City of New York.)*

Sears, Roebuck, and Company, founded in 1886, offered stiff competition with its lavishly illustrated catalog. When asked by his Sunday School teacher where the Ten Commandments came from, a boy from rural Idaho replied, "From Sears, Roebuck, where else?" From the Sears catalog, consumers could order everything from watches to stoves to thimbles. By the 1890s, the Ward's catalog contained ten thousand products.

Retailers turned to professional advertisers to reach a vast pool of ready customers. By 1900, American advertisers spent $95 million a year, which marked a tenfold increase over the amount spent in 1865. "Goods suitable for the millionaire at prices in reach of the millions," Macy's boasted to potential buyers. In addition to traditional formats—handbills, circulars, and posters—advertisers took special advantage of the growth of urban newspapers. Department stores bought full-page advertisements in the metropolitan dailies and promoted featured merchandise in Sunday supplements. Rather than simply informing customers of products, advertisers tried to persuade people they needed to purchase a particular brand. Outdoor advertising also assumed a new scale. In every city, by the turn of the century, mammoth electric signs glowed aside and atop buildings.

 ## The New Industrial Order

America's industrial empire rested on a cultural foundation that glorified competition, limited government, and individual achievement. These ideas, popularized by writers such as Andrew Carnegie and Horatio Alger, fostered a "Gospel of Success." A new generation of industrial experimenters, including Carnegie, John D. Rockefeller, and J. Pierpont Morgan, devised new methods for managing the new industrial order. While these industrial titans praised competition as bringing the fittest to the fore, their efforts to control prices and corral competition raised new questions about the role that government should play in regulating industry.

A Business Culture

Social thought in the last quarter of the nineteenth century reinforced deeply ingrained American faith in Jeffersonian concepts of individual liberty and limited government. The convergence of three different streams of thought—*laissez-faire*, Social Darwinism, and the gospel of success—created a powerful incentive for growth.

The eighteenth-century Scottish thinker Adam Smith, a professor of logic and moral philosophy at the University of Glasgow, was the father of the doctrine of laissez-faire. In 1776 Smith published his monumental work on political economy, *The Wealth of Nations*, which argued that the free market, guided by a self-correcting "Invisible Hand" and unencumbered by government regulation, would guarantee economic growth. Smith considered self-interest the prime motivation for human behavior and the free market the most efficient method for realizing that self-interest. The public interest, he reasoned, would be served through the widespread private pursuit of self-interest.

Nearly a century later, Smith's ideas found support from an unlikely source: naturalist Charles Darwin. After a four-year voyage around the world observing flora and fauna, Darwin developed a radical new theory of evolution. In a ground-breaking book, *The Origin of Species* (1859), Darwin concluded that plant and animal species had evolved over thousands of years. Species that evolved and adapted to changing environments survived; species that did not successfully adapt became extinct. Nature, he argued, had established clear rules that guided the competition among and within species, allowing for the survival of the fittest.

Many people tried to extend Darwin's findings to human development, and their speculations led to what has been called Social Darwinism. The free enterprise system, as they conceived it, gave everyone an equal chance for survival and riches. William Graham Sumner, a professor of political economy at Yale, emerged as the most influential Social Darwinist in America. Just as natural laws governed the working of the universe, he believed, so did natural laws determine man's social and economic behavior. It was foolish for governments to attempt to change or ameliorate these forces. To take power or money away from millionaires, Sumner scoffed, was "like killing off our generals in war." It was "absurd," he wrote, to pass laws permitting society's "worst members" to survive or to "sit down with a slate and pencil to plan out a new social world."

The Gospel of Success and Its Critics

The gospel of success had always been an important part of American culture. The Puritans had preached that the possession of worldly goods was a sign of grace, and writers such as Benjamin Franklin made a virtue of wealth. In the late nineteenth century, however, Americans seemed preoccupied with the secrets of material success. Periodicals and success manuals, many of them written by Protestant clergy, emphasized that financial gain was not incompatible with Christian teaching, and that hard work and thrift were essential for both earthly success and eternal salvation. "Work has sometimes been called worship, and the dusty, smoky workshop a temple," observed a popular writer, "because there man glorifies the great Architect by imitating him in providing for the wants of his creatures." Two writers—Andrew Carnegie and Horatio Alger—added new force to this appealing belief.

In 1889 industrialist Andrew Carnegie wrote a widely circulated article, "The Gospel of Wealth," which celebrated the benefits of better goods and lower prices that resulted from competition. Carnegie argued that "our wonderful material development" outweighed the harsh costs of competition. The concentration of wealth in the hands of a few leading industrialists, he concluded, was "not only beneficial but essential to the future of the race." Those most fit would bring order and efficiency out of the chaos of rapid industrialization. Unlike most other industrialists, Carnegie also insisted that the rich were obligated to spend some of their wealth to benefit their "poorer brethren."

By far the most popular writer of success stories was Horatio Alger. His novelettes, which bore such titles as *Work and Win, Strive and Succeed, Do and Dare, Sink or Swim, Risen from the Ranks,* and *Facing the World,* sold 20 million copies by the end of the century. Book after book was the tale of rags to riches, from poverty to fame and fortune. Alger's typical hero was a boy of about fifteen who possessed the predictable virtues of honesty, sobriety, and a commitment to work hard. These qualities were instrumental in each success story, but many of Alger's heroes also achieved their goals by accident or chance. Not everyone accepted the new business culture. In 1888 Edward Bellamy, the son of a Baptist minister in Chicopee Falls, Massachusetts, published his best-selling *Looking Backward,* which envisioned a utopian socialist society. In Bellamy's utopia, the government owned the means of production and distributed wealth equally among all citizens. Since government provided for all its citizens, competition was irrelevant. He denounced "the imbecility of the system of private enterprise," and the callousness of industrialists, who "maim and slaughter [their] workers by thousands." Though *Looking Backward* inspired the creation of Bellamy clubs, which met periodically to discuss the social implications of utopian socialism, it never translated its condemnation of capitalist society into a successful reform movement.

In his book *Progress and Poverty* (1879), Henry George joined Bellamy in offering a biting critique of the emerging industrial order. George objected to the crass materialism and growing disparity between rich and poor, which he believed resulted from inflated land prices. Wealth in the industrial era, he argued, was created not by productive labor, but by speculation. He proposed a simple solution to the problem: a "single tax" of 100 percent on the profits from selling land. "It is not necessary to confiscate land," he wrote; "it is only necessary to confiscate rent [the difference between the buying and selling price of land]." *Progress and Poverty* sold over 3 million copies and sparked the formation of Land and Labor Clubs to promote the single tax idea.

Both George and Bellamy criticized the emerging business culture, but neither challenged deeply held American notions about limited government. Their radical rhetoric reflected their loyalty to traditional values and their indignation that the promise of American life was not being fulfilled. George believed that the single tax would result in a smaller government that was closer to "the ideal of Jeffersonian democracy." He opposed the creation of a large, centralized federal government, claiming that the state should "clear the ways, and then let things alone." He embraced capitalism, opposed income taxes, and viewed labor unions as a temporary evil. Bellamy believed that irrational competition, not the nature of capitalism itself, was to blame for most social problems. Citizens of his utopian state would experience "far less interference of any sort with personal liberty."

Managing the New Industrial Empire

To coordinate their vast industrial empires, business leaders created the modern corporation. A number of features distinguished the modern corporation from older forms of business organization. The first differences concerned the nature of ownership. Traditional business enterprises had been owned by one individual or a small number of people bound by ties of kinship and marriage. The owners also managed the business, making key decisions, and overseeing the day-to-day operations. In contrast, ownership of the modern corporation was spread over a large number of stockholders who, in turn, hired professional managers to run the business.

The law gave legal sanction to this new arrangement. In the 1880s a number of states adopted incorporation laws to encourage commerce and industry. Under these laws stockholders could share in the profits of the company, but their risk would be limited to the amount of money they invested. The Supreme Court gave corporations broad protection under the Fourteenth Amendment, claiming that states could not deny corporations equal protection under the law nor deprive them of their rights without due process.

Over time, corporations developed new management techniques to streamline their operations and maximize their efficiency. Most business leaders followed the example of the railroads, which had developed methods for coordinating hundreds of workers across thousands of miles. Corporations created layers of managers to implement long-range plans and to oversee the day-to-day affairs of their far-flung operations. Managers created formalized procedures to govern the selection of qualified workers and to oversee the production and distribution processes. They devised organizational charts, with clearly defined lines of authority to guarantee the smooth running of the corporation. One by-product of these changes was that relations between owners and workers, and even among managers, became distant and impersonal.

Along with producing a clear organizational structure, corporations devised new ways to consolidate their control over the market. One method was vertical integration, whereby a company attempted to control the entire production and distribution process for its products, from extracting raw materials, to creating the product, to transporting the finished product to retailers. Gustavus Swift used vertical integration to establish dominance over the meatpacking industry. By the 1890s, the Chicago-based Swift and Company had integrated forward, moving closer to consumers, by purchasing refrigerated railcars to ship the meat to markets in the East and hiring wagons to deliver the goods to butcher shops. At the same time, the company integrated backward, closer to the raw materials, by raising its own cattle.

A second method of seizing control of the market was horizontal integration, which took place when firms engaged in similar activities collaborated to limit competition (see figure, page 706). The railroads pioneered the use of "pools" to establish control over the market. To avoid cutthroat competition, railroad executives entered into voluntary agreements to divide traffic and artificially inflate rates. Since they were not legally enforceable, the agreements rarely worked for long, but that did not stop other industries eager to limit competition and guarantee profits from following suit.

Titans of Industry: Carnegie, Rockefeller, and Morgan

During the 1880s and 1890s, Andrew Carnegie applied the idea of vertical integration to dominate the steel industry. Born in Scotland, Carnegie emigrated to the United States with his impoverished parents in 1848. Over the next thirty years, he gradually climbed the American industrial pyramid, starting out as a messenger boy in a Pittsburgh telegraph office. In 1873, at the age of thirty-eight, he used money earned from investments to build the giant J. Edgar Thomson Steel Works in Pittsburgh. Mingling the Puritan doctrine of stewardship with newer ideas of Social Darwinism and ruthless business practices, Carnegie managed to keep his prices low and drive competitors out of business. Steel was made from pig iron, which often fluctuated in price and supply. To guarantee adequate pig iron supplies for his steel mills, Carnegie acquired sources of iron ore, and of the coke and coal that fired the furnaces, and developed a fleet of steamships and a railroad for transporting them directly to his mills. "From the moment these crude stuffs were dug out of the earth until they flowed in a stream of liquid steel in the ladles," noted a contemporary, "there was never a price, profit, or royalty paid to an outsider."

While Carnegie championed the benefits of vertical integration, a young merchant from Cleveland, John D. Rockefeller, used horizontal integration to build the Standard Oil Company into one of the titans of corporate business. Born in 1839 in upstate New York, Rockefeller settled in Ohio and invested in an oil refinery during the Civil War. Over the next decade, he consolidated his control over the oil industry. He managed to reduce costs and drive the competition out of business by keeping wages low, paying meticulous attention to detail, and negotiating secret deals with the

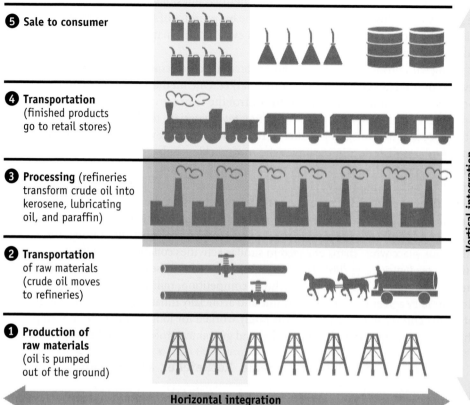

5 Sale to consumer

4 Transportation
(finished products
go to retail stores)

3 Processing (refineries
transform crude oil into
kerosene, lubricating
oil, and paraffin)

2 Transportation
of raw materials
(crude oil moves
to refineries)

1 Production of
raw materials
(oil is pumped
out of the ground)

Vertical integration

Horizontal integration

● Steps in petroleum production/distribution

Vertical and Horizontal Integration of the Petroleum Industry   Prior to the dominance of Standard Oil Company, many different companies were involved in the specialized steps within petroleum production, from producing the raw materials to transporting products to merchants to sell to consumers. John D. Rockefeller entered the business by building a refinery and then expanded his company to include other refineries (horizontal integration as indicated by the gray band). Rockefeller gradually extended the reach of Standard Oil vertically, acquiring oil leases, oil wells, and pipelines, and setting up advantageous contracts with railroads, and retail stores (as indicated by the yellow band).

railroads. In 1871, for example, he joined with other refiners to form a secret pool, called the South Improvement Company, which negotiated massive rebates with railroad agents. Rebates were secret agreements in which the railroad reduced freight rates in return for the privileged customer's promise to ship large volumes. The pool existed for only a few months before it was exposed, but during that time Standard bought 21 of the 26 refineries in Cleveland. Like Carnegie, Rockefeller also practiced vertical integration, making his own barrels, building his own storage warehouses, and manufacturing his own chemicals. Rockefeller's success was staggering. In 1870 he had controlled 10 percent of the refined petroleum produced in the country; by the end of the decade, he produced 90 percent.

Confronted with the need to coordinate his far-flung financial empire, and to regulate production levels and prices to assure steady profits, Rockefeller created a novel business organization, the trust. Ohio law prohibited corporations from owning plants in other states or from owning stock in out-of-state corporations. In 1881 Rockefeller used a loophole in the law to establish the Standard Oil Trust, which consisted of nine trustees empowered "to hold, control, and manage" Standard's numerous assets. The new arrangement allowed company stockholders to exchange their stock for trust certificates. The trust allowed Rockefeller to exert greater control over the business, centralize the management and decision-making process, and adjust quickly to changing circumstances. During the 1890s, with trusts under attack from Congress and the courts, Rockefeller developed another ingenious method of industrial consolidation, the holding company. In these large-scale mergers, holding companies bought the stock of member companies and therefore established direct, formal control over their operations.

Rockefeller's example inspired other manufacturers to follow his lead. Between 1880 and 1904, the nation experienced 318 mergers affecting four-fifths of the nation's manufacturing industries. By 1904, the two thousand largest business firms in the United States made up less than 1 percent of the nation's businesses but controlled 40 percent of the economy. By 1900, James Buchanan Duke's American Tobacco Company was producing half the smoking tobacco, 62 percent of the chewing tobacco, and 93 percent of cigarettes made in the United States. Henry O. Havemeyer's "Sugar Trust" employed 25,000 of the 30,000 refinery workers in the country. The United States Steel Corporation, organized in 1901 as the first billion-dollar corporation, controlled 60 percent of the industry. A congressional committee reported in 1888 that "the number of combinations and trusts formed and forming in this country is . . . very large. . . . New ones are constantly forming and . . . old ones are constantly extending their relations."

The merger movement gave birth to a new type of businessman, the broker who raised the money to permit business expansion. In the late nineteenth century, many American corporations wanted to grow but lacked the money to purchase new equipment and expand production. They searched for investors who, for a share of the profits, would loan them money for expansion. J. Pierpont Morgan emerged as the most famous investment banker of his age. By channeling European capital into the United States, Morgan facilitated the union between finance and industry. He successfully managed the reorganization of several railroads and raised the necessary money for the creation of the U.S. Steel Corporation in 1901. A congressional committee in 1912 reported that the House of Morgan held 341 directorships in 112 corporations, which controlled over $22 billion in assets, more than the assessed value of all property in the twenty-two states and territories west of the Mississippi River.

Regulating the Trusts

Public reaction to the consolidation of American business was confused and uncertain. Americans enjoyed the benefits of the rising industrial order—new products were flooding the market, prices for most items were actually declining, and most of the vast combines, from telephone and telegraph to meatpacking, were providing the services promised. Though often exaggerated, the "rags to riches" stories of industrialists such as Andrew Carnegie struck many Americans as proof that anyone could achieve the American Dream of success. Critics, however, complained that the trusts destroyed competition, stifled individual opportunity, and undermined the foundation of the free enterprise system. "If the tendency to combination is irresistible, control of it is imperative," warned Henry Demarest Lloyd, a Chicago lawyer, journalist, and author.

Struggling with these contradictory attitudes, the public moved to address some of the abuses committed by big business. Not surprisingly, they turned first to the railroads. By 1875, many states established regulatory commissions to supervise railroads within their borders. The courts, however, often took a conservative view of state regulation, and most of the commissions proved ineffective. By the mid-1880s, Congress was being pushed to regulate by groups who felt discriminated against by the railroads' high rural rates and preferential treatment of powerful customers: farm organizations and oilmen in the Pennsylvania fields. In January 1887, Congress passed the Interstate Commerce Act. Attacking both the monopolistic and the competitive evils connected with the railroads and declaring that rates must be "reasonable and just," the act created a five-man commission empowered to use the federal courts to enforce decisions.

Public outcry against the trusts continued to swell. The 1888 Republican platform declared "opposition to all combinations of capital, organized in trusts or otherwise, to control arbitrarily the conditions of trade among our citizens." The Democrats attacked "trusts and combinations . . . which . . . rob the body of our citizens by depriving them of the benefits of natural competition." Congress responded to the pressure in 1890 by passing, with only one dissenting voice in either house, the Sherman Antitrust Act. The law declared illegal "every contract, combination in the form of trust or otherwise, or conspiracy, in restraint of trade or commerce among the several States, or with foreign nations." Any individual who was "injured in his business or property" by corporations violating the act was authorized to sue for triple damages.

Neither the Interstate Commerce Commission nor the Sherman Antitrust Act had any measurable impact on the trend toward consolidation. The laws were poorly drafted, reflecting the divided loyalties of most lawmakers, who opposed government interference in the marketplace but wanted to be responsive to public sentiment. In the end, the two measures turned enforcement over to the courts, which looked skeptically on government power. Both laws, however, established an important precedent for federal regulation of industry, and both would become powerful weapons in the hands of an activist government in the next century.

In many ways, the trust represented a rational adjustment to the challenge of production and distribution in an expanding national market. Despite their many abuses, trusts provided central coordination over the specialized functions of the new industrial organizations. Business consolidation was part of a larger social trend of consolidation and coordination that shaped every aspect of American society. As the leader of an organized charity movement observed: "We live in an atmosphere of organization. . . . Men are learning the disadvantages of isolated action. Whether or

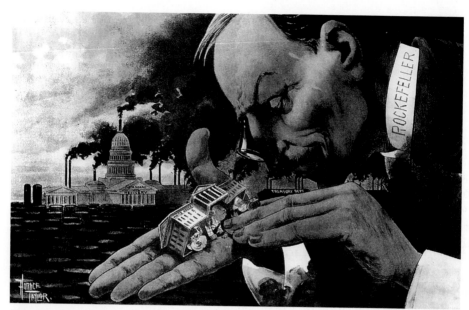

"The Verdict," 1900   This cartoon shows John Rockefeller holding the White House in the palm of his hand, while Congress and the Treasury Department have become refineries of his Standard Oil Company. By the late nineteenth century, many Americans believed that large corporations not only corrupted the free enterprise system, but also undermined the American democratic process itself. This fear generated a movement away from strict laissez-faire government and eventually fed into the huge impulse for reform after the turn of the century. *(Library of Congress.)*

not we approve of trusts and trades-unions and similar combinations, and whatever their motives, they rest on a foundation which is sound alike from the business and religious standpoint: namely, the principle of union and co-operation."

 ## The Changing World of Work, 1870–1900

The industrial revolution fundamentally altered the nature of work in America. Laboring in large factories forced workers to discard an older style of work and adjust to the monotony of repeating their task over and over. Along with the nature of work, the composition of the work force changed as well. Immigrants, women, and children held most of the new jobs in America's manufacturing centers.

The Factory System

Before the Civil War the United States was an overwhelmingly agricultural nation. About 60 percent of all workers toiled on a farm versus about 30 percent involved in nonagricultural pursuits. By the end of the century, those numbers had reversed. The manufacturing work force, centered in the nation's growing urban areas, quadrupled, from 1.5 million workers in 1860 to nearly 6 million in 1900.

Workers not only moved from agriculture to manufacturing, they labored in large factories rather than small shops. The factory became an ever-present urban institution, dominating the lives of its workers. "Of the nearly three millions of people employed in the mechanical industries of this country, at least four-fifths are working under the factory system," a statistician estimated in 1880. Between 1870 and 1900, the average work force in cotton mills and tobacco factories doubled. The Cambria Iron Works in Johnstown, Pennsylvania, employed 1,000 workers in 1860; by the end of the century, that number had swelled to nearly 10,000. In many cities, huge factories employing thousands of workers became commonplace. By 1910, General Electric employed 15,000 workers at its plant in Schenectady, New York. In Chicago, both the Pullman Car Company and International Harvester likewise counted 15,000 employees.

Finally, workers who had been self-employed now depended on someone else to pay their wages. In 1860 as many people were self-employed as earned wages. By 1900, two of every three Americans relied on wages. The transformation from small shop production to factory wage earner robbed many workers of their sense of independence. "They no longer carried the keys of the workshop, for workshops, tools and keys belonged not to them, but to their master," observed union leader Terence Powderly.

Managers searching for new ways to organize and control the workplace placed their faith in so-called scientific management. Pioneered by an engineer named Frederick W. Taylor, scientific management imposed a new level of regimentation on factory life. Taylor suggested that companies could lower costs and increase profits by subdividing manufacturing into small tasks. Taylor used a stopwatch to dissect the "millions of different operations" that workers performed. With these time-motion studies, he was able to determine the simplest, and cheapest, way of performing each job.

Taylor's system of scientific management eventually resulted in the standardization of work procedures that made many factory tasks painfully monotonous. "The different branches of the trade are divided and subdivided so that one man may make just a particular part of a machine and may not know anything whatever about another part of the same machine," machinist John Morrison told a Senate committee in 1883. At a Boston meeting of working women in 1869, Aurora Phelps described the consequences for working women:

> When I was younger girls were taught full trades. They made pants, coats, overcoats, and then they learned to cut. Now one stitches the seam, another makes the buttonholes, and another puts the buttons on, and when the poor girl stitches up the seams and finds her work slack she goes from shop to shop, perhaps for weeks, before she can find the same kind of work.

The factory system also burdened workers with a tighter system of discipline. Employers often forbade singing, drinking, joking, smoking, or conversation on the job. Foremen imposed fines for even minor infractions. Many companies denied immigrant workers time to celebrate their national holidays and holy days. Companies enamored of the rigors of scientific management abolished older work patterns, which saw periods of heavy work followed by leisurely breaks, and institutionalized a continual pace of work synchronized with machines. "In the factory there is no chance to read," explained one man, "and the noise and hum of machinery prevent general conversation, even when the rules and discipline do not positively forbid it."

Dreams of Social Mobility

There is conflicting evidence on whether workers experienced a higher standard of living during these years. Industrialization and the development of a national consumer marketplace actually led to a measurable drop in wholesale prices for most goods. The biggest plunge came in the price of food. A cut of meat that cost $1.00 in 1870 sold for only 78 cents in 1880. As a result, between 1880 and 1914, real wages of the average worker rose about $7 a year. But figures showing a rising standard of living can be deceptive. The earnings of skilled workers—machinists, engineers, carpenters, printers—improved much more than did those of unskilled workers. The average annual wage for manufacturing workers in 1900 was only $435, or $8.37 a week. Unskilled workers were paid ten cents an hour on average, about $5.50 a week. Regional variations were also pronounced. In 1880 workers in the South earned about 30 percent less than their counterparts in the East and Midwest.

Despite some general figures showing progress, large numbers of workers remained desperately poor. An 1883 study of working conditions in Illinois estimated that 25 percent of the state's workers, both skilled and unskilled, "fail to make a living." Job insecurity plagued most workers. Periodic depressions ravaged the American worker in 1873–1878, 1883–1885, and 1893–1897. In his book *Poverty* (1904), social scientist Robert Hunter claimed that unemployment was the most common cause of poverty in America. "The annual wages of more than one workman in every four," he observed, "suffered considerable decrease by reason of a period of enforced idleness, extending in some cases over several months."

The harsh reality of the new industrial order clashed with popular image of rags-to-riches social mobility. "A man here may be a common laborer," a business leader expounded in typical fashion in 1883, "but if he has the right material in him there is no reason why he should not occupy the best place in the nation." The fragmentary evidence from the period, however, suggests otherwise. A handful of unskilled workers managed to join the ranks of the semiskilled, but few reached middle-class status. The poor improved their condition over time, but often by putting the entire family to work. With a few exceptions, the leaders of industry came from established families of old American stock.

Not surprisingly, contemporary accounts of worker attitudes are filled with expressions of resentment toward the new industrial system. Workers resisted many of the new work restrictions and requirements by forming cooperative alliances and organizing wildcat strikes. But most felt helpless against the onslaught of industrialization. "That a deep-rooted feeling of discontent pervades the masses, none can deny," Terence Powderly wrote in 1885. Two years later, after surveying working-class opinion in his state, a government official in Connecticut commented on "the feeling of bitterness which so frequently manifests itself in their utterances," their "distrust of employers," and their palpable "discontent and unrest."

Working People

Changes in the composition of the work force were just as dramatic as the changes in the nature of work. Immigrants eager for work filled many of the new factory jobs. "Not every foreigner is a workingman," a Chicago clergyman observed, "but in the cities, at least, it may almost be said that every workingman is a foreigner." In 1870 nearly one-third of all workers in manufacturing jobs were foreign-born. Native workers often resented the new migrants, fearing they would depress wages by agreeing to work for less money. An iron worker in Wisconsin complained, "Immigrants work for almost nothing and seem to be able to live on wind—something which I can not do." Another worker charged that immigrants bring "wages down below the breadline."

The new factory system also pulled a greater number of women into the workplace. Between 1870 and 1900, the number of women working outside the home nearly tripled. By the turn of the century, 5 million American women were earning wages, nearly a quarter through manufacturing jobs. Three of four women workers were under twenty-five, most of them were either recent immigrants or the daughters of immigrant parents. Most saw work as a means of supporting their families, not as an act of personal liberation. The head of the Massachusetts Bureau of Labor reported in 1882 that "a family of workers can always live well, but the man with a family of small children to support, unless his wife works also, has a small chance of living properly."

When employed in factories, women tended to occupy jobs that were viewed as natural extensions of household activity. About half worked in the garment industry, making gloves, hats, and stockings. A government study in the 1880s found that the average weekly wage for a working woman in a major city was $5.24, but weekly expenses for a self-supporting woman were about $5.51. Women were excluded from skilled work and from the professions. Only 5 of the nation's 40,736 lawyers, 67 of 43,874 clergy, and 525 of 62,383 doctors were women in 1870.

The dominant view was that a woman did not require a "living wage" because, as one investigator reported, "it is expected that she has men to support her." The vast majority of Americans firmly believed that a woman's place was in the home, "queen of a little house—no matter how humble—where there are children rolling on the floor." Since many employers assumed that women entered the work force for "pin money" "to decorate themselves beyond their needs and station," they assumed they could pay them less money than they paid men. Unions were often hostile to female workers. "Wherever she goes," a labor official declared in 1900, "she is reducing [man's] wages, and wherever large numbers of women are employed in any occupation, the point will be reached where women get as much as a man by making man's wages as low as a woman's."

Women Typesetters, 1883   The new economy expanded the number of unskilled jobs, thus facilitating the entrance of a greater number of women into the work force. While working-class women worked in factories, educated middle-class women, usually while they were still unmarried, found employment in more white-collar settings. These women, working at a press in Kansas, are most likely this latter type of female labor. Though their working environment was more pleasant than that of their working-class sisters, white-collar women's salaries were similarly low, and they were expected to quit their jobs once they married.   *(Kansas State Historical Society.)*

The fastest-growing sector of women's employment was in clerical positions as typists, bookkeepers, and sales clerks. In 1870 women made up only 3 percent of office workers; twenty years later, they held 17 percent of clerical jobs in the United States. These working "girls" tended to be native-born, white, young, single women, eighteen to twenty-four years old. Corporations and the federal government led the way in hiring women to fill clerical positions, primarily as stenographers and typists. "No invention has opened for women so broad and easy an avenue to profitable and suitable employment as the Type-Writer," E. Remington and Sons, a major manufacturer of the machines, declared in 1875. Department stores also hired women as sales clerks. In 1870 "saleswomen" were too few to be counted in census records. By 1900, they numbered over 142,000.

The era witnessed another addition to the industrial work force: children. Not only did children work for less pay than adults, but they could work inside delicate machinery that was inaccessible to adults. The number of working children in nonagricultural positions tripled between 1870 and 1900. In 1900 one out of every ten girls and one out of every five boys between the ages of ten and fifteen held jobs.

In the South, children provided a pool of cheap labor for the region's cotton and woolen mills. In Paterson, New Jersey, about half of all boys and girls aged eleven to fourteen had jobs. In a Chicago candy factory, children worked eighty-two hours a week during the Christmas season. "Poor, puny, weak little children," complained a female spinner in one of Rhode Island's mills, "are kept at work the entire year without intermission of even a month for schooling. The overseers are to them not over kind and sometimes do not hesitate to make them perform more work than the miserable little wretched beings possibly can."

Throughout this period, African-Americans continued to labor on the fringes of the industrial work force in menial occupations. Nearly 75 percent of African-Americans lived in the South and were engaged in agricultural work, but the handful who found jobs in the manufacturing sector earned less than other workers at almost every level of skill. In 1870 Atlanta blacks held over three-fourths of their city's unskilled jobs. Whites moved into comparatively well-paid jobs in cotton mills, while blacks marched off to work in flour mills and tobacco factories. "In this city it is the negroes who do the hard work," admitted a man from Nashville. Even when working at the same job, blacks received lower wages than whites. In 1870 white hands at the Atlanta Rolling Mill earned three dollars a day while blacks received one dollar.

The Hazards of Child Labor

The working-class family usually required several of its members' labor in order to make ends meet. Over half a million children under the age of sixteen worked long hours and in dangerous conditions in factories around the nation. Children's poorer coordination and more exuberant natures made them particularly susceptible to injury on the job. This fourteen-year-old in Cincinnati lost his arm to a veneering saw in a box factory. (*University of Maryland Baltimore County.*)

The House of Labor

Wendell Phillips, an abolitionist and labor reformer from Massachusetts, enumerated in an 1871 address entitled "The Foundation of the Labor Movement" what the workers of America wanted: "short hours, better education, cooperation in the end and, in the meantime, a political movement that will concentrate the thought of the country on this thing." Despite the painful adjustment to factory work and its difficult conditions, organized labor achieved only limited success in focusing the attention of the nation on "this thing." Organizers needed to unite a work force that was deeply divided by geography, race, level of skill, and gender. Initially, labor attempted to challenge the foundation of the industrial order. The rise of the American Federation of Labor (AFL), however, signaled a new experiment in accommodating the industrial system and working within it to achieve incremental reforms.

The Origins of Industrial Unionism

In seeking to form national unions, nineteenth-century labor leaders faced a number of obstacles. First, business leaders opposed unions so vehemently that they were willing to use force to prevent their formation, and they could depend on the courts to favor capital against labor. Second, faith in social mobility and individualism had limited the development of class solidarity among workers in America. After surveying textile workers, officials with the Massachusetts Bureau of the Statistics of Labor reported that most laborers supported unions "in the abstract," but considered local organizations "simply vehicles for the fomentation of incipient riots and disorderly conduct." Finally, the diversity of the work force militated against feelings of labor solidarity. The high proportion of immigrants created divisions by language, ethnic origin, and religion, and both native-born and immigrant laborers refused to associate with blacks. These differences made it easy for employers to play one group off against the other.

The new industrial order, however, provided workers with powerful incentives to unionize. Struggles with employers over wages and working conditions, and especially over reducing the workday to eight hours, inspired union organization in a number of trades. Workers drew on a rich ideological tradition to justify their efforts. Native-born workers tapped into the egalitarian ideals of the American Revolution to support their claim for equal treatment. At the same time, many immigrants, especially those from Germany, Ireland, and Britain, brought with them more radical notions of class solidarity. The International Workingmen's Association, founded by German immigrants in 1868, set as its goal "the abolition of all class rule."

In 1866 workers took the first steps toward forming a national labor organization when several craft unions and reform groups met in Baltimore to create the National Labor Union (NLU). Claiming three hundred thousand members by the early 1870s, the organization supported a range of causes including temperance, women's rights, and the establishment of cooperatives to bring the "wealth of the land" into "the hands of those who produce it," thus ending "wage slavery." Its central demand, however, was the adoption of a national eight-hour-day law for all workers.

Seeking wide labor support, many NLU leaders supported admitting African-Americans and women. If "workingmen of the white race do not conciliate the blacks, the black vote will be cast against them," observed NLU founder William Sylvis. But most of the member unions refused to admit blacks, and in 1869 African-American workers, calling their exclusion "an insult to God and injury to us, and disgrace to humanity," formed the separate Colored National Labor Union (CNLU). Most male workers also opposed admission of women to the NLU, claiming they did not belong in the workplace and their presence depressed male wages.

The depression that began with the panic of 1873 and continued for more than five consecutive years decimated the NLU. Thousands of workers lost their jobs, and unemployment in cities such as New York ran as high as 33 percent. "The sufferings of the working classes are daily increasing," wrote a harried worker. "Famine has broken into the home of many of us, and is at the door of all." Caught in an unprecedented economic squeeze amid massive unemployment, industrial workers were more concerned with survival and relief than with passage of an eight-hour law. Workers abandoned their newly formed unions in droves. In New York City, for example, union membership plummeted from 45,000 in 1873 to 5,000 in 1877.

Union membership declined, but industrial activism increased. The Panic of 1873 ushered in a period of labor strife and turmoil in which a wave of railroad strikes swept the nation. The most dramatic confrontation took place in March 1877, after the heads of the nation's four largest railroads announced a 10-percent cut in worker salaries. "The great principle upon which we joined to act was to earn more and to spend less," they declared. In the first national strike in American history, angry workers in cities and towns across the country rose up in protest. In July, when workers in Martinsburg, West Virginia, seized trains and other railroad property, President Rutherford Hayes ordered federal troops into the region to quell the "insurrection."

The decision to use federal force in a domestic labor dispute outraged most workers and precipitated wider protests. In Baltimore police shot and killed nine strikers before President Hayes sent in federal troops to impose order. In Pittsburgh, rioters burned freight cars, looted stores, and exchanged gunfire with troops. When the mayhem was over, twenty protesters lay dead, including a woman and three small children. The strike fever spread as far as Galveston, Texas, and San Francisco. "The country was in a feverish state of excitement from Boston to San Francisco, from the Lakes to the Gulf," observed a St. Louis newspaper. Before the unrest ended two weeks later, over a hundred people were dead and property damaged had soared into the millions.

The "Great Railway Strike" produced mixed results. In the short run, labor suffered a humiliating defeat: management refused to accept their demands, many demonstrators ended up in jail, and public opinion turned decidedly hostile to the increasingly violent protests. But the confrontation also focused national attention on the legitimate concerns of workers. Determined to avoid future confrontations, railroad executives devoted more time and resources to labor relations. Workers also learned a valuable lesson from the strikes: labor's position was strengthened by organizing on an industry-wide basis rather than by specific crafts.

The Knights of Labor

The Noble Order of the Knights of Labor, a trade union of Philadelphia garment cutters, seized the faltering banner of national unionism. After the strikes of 1877, union leader Uriah S. Stephens promised to organize workers into one "great brotherhood." Trade unions, he complained, were "too narrow in their ideas and too circumscribed in their field of operations." In 1879 the Knights chose Terence V. Powderly as their "Grand Master Workman." Under Powderly's leadership, the Knights called for an eight-hour workday and opened their ranks to unskilled workers, blacks, immigrants, and women. The Knights demanded the eight-hour day, equal pay for women, and the abolition of child labor, but they rejected the notion that workers constituted a permanent class, or that the interests of labor and capital were incompatible. Unwilling to accept the new economic order, they opposed strikes as "acts of private warfare" and instead emphasized cooperation between labor and management.

With the Knights leading the charge, the labor movement gained new ground. An economic depression in the early 1880s, and the drastic wage cuts accompanying it, gave the labor movement its greatest impetus for growth. In 1884 militant local unions affiliated with the Knights struck and won a victory against the Union Pacific Railroad. The following year they scored a greater triumph against Southwestern Railroad. Powderly opposed both strikes, but in the wake of the victories, fought against two of the most powerful corporations in America, workers across the country jumped on the bandwagon. By 1886, the Noble Order boasted 15,000 local assemblies representing between 700,000 and 1 million members. Nearly 10 percent of the country's nonagricultural work force claimed membership.

Among the workers joining the Knights were large numbers of African-Americans and women. "The colored people of the South are flocking to us," a Knights organizer bragged in the 1880s. In Alabama, West Virginia, and Tennessee, African-American coal miners formed the backbone of the Knights. In 1884, after some initial hesitation, Powderly declared that "women should be admitted on equality with men." By the end of the decade, women made up nearly 10 percent of Knights membership. The organization took a very different approach, however, to Chinese immigrants. Reflecting the prejudice of many white workers, the Knights barred Chinese workers from joining and lobbied for passage of legislation prohibiting Chinese immigration. On the West Coast, which had the country's largest Chinese community, the Knights placed a "white" label on union products.

In 1886 the powerful Knights faced perhaps their greatest challenge when the giant McCormick reaper works locked out its employees in February and reopened the following month with nonunion labor. When police killed two unionists in a May 3 rally, a group of anarchists, who preached the violent overthrow of the capitalist system, called a meeting for the following day "to denounce the latest atrocious act of the police." They chose to meet at the cavernous Haymarket Square—a plaza near downtown Chicago. Rain kept the crowd small—it peaked at perhaps 1,200—and only 330 remained near the end of the rally when a force of 180 policemen arrived and ordered the protesters to disperse. As the police moved in, someone threw a bomb. After the explosion, the police regrouped and charged the crowd, firing guns and swinging clubs. When it ended, one policeman lay dead and sixty people were injured. A local reporter described the scene at Haymarket as one of "wild carnage."

Overnight the shock waves of the Haymarket bombing swept across the country. An outraged middle-class public denounced the anarchist workers as "vipers" and "curs," "hyenas" and "serpents." "The only good anarchist is a dead anarchist," a Cincinnati newspaper judged. Eventually, eight men were tried for the bombing. Despite flimsy evidence, all were convicted. Four men were hanged; one committed suicide in jail. In 1893 Illinois governor Peter Altgeld pardoned the three surviving anarchists, claiming that prosecutors never produced evidence of guilt and that the trial had been unfair.

Haymarket broke the force of direct labor resistance to the new industrial order for nearly a decade. Though the Knights repudiated the anarchists and had not been involved in the Haymarket incident, a business propaganda campaign linked trade unionism with anarchy. "The explosion of the bomb on the Haymarket square abruptly ended [the movement]," a government official in Illinois reported.

Haymarket Scene from the Cover of Frank Leslie's Illustrated Newspaper
The bloody incident in Haymarket Square was devastating for labor's public image. Though the protest was initially a peaceful one and the origins of the bomb remain a mystery, the press portrayed the event as a one-sided attack on police. Notice that the crowd on the left side of the top frame is shown fleeing the scene heavily armed with swords. For middle-class Americans, the popularized version of the events was a disturbing commentary on the radical and violent potential of organized labor. *(Library of Congress.)*

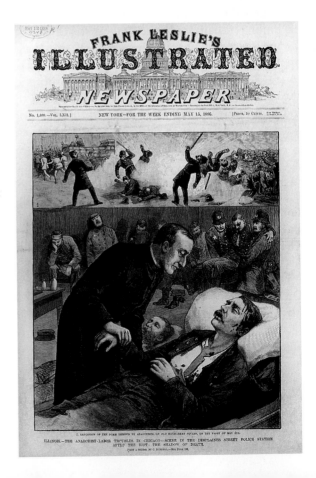

In the second half of 1886, employers locked out some 100,000 workers. The Knights, helpless to protect their members, lost them in droves. From a peak of 1 million supporters in 1886, membership slipped to 500,000 the following year.

The American Federation of Labor (AFL)

The Haymarket incident lent momentum to more conservative trade unionists who objected to the Knights' ambitious social agenda. They believed that the Knights expended too much energy talking about brotherhood and cooperation and not enough fighting for tangible benefits for working people (see Competing Voices, page 724). In December 1886, trade union representatives met in Columbus, Ohio, and organized the American Federation of Labor. As its name implied, the AFL was a loose federation of skilled trades—cigar makers, iron workers, carpenters, and others—linked through an executive council to lobby for prolabor national legislation and to offer assistance during strikes.

The new organization reflected the philosophy of Samuel Gompers, who served as president from 1886 until his death in 1924. Born in London in 1850, Gompers emigrated to the United States in 1863 and rose through the ranks of the cigar makers' union. He believed in "pure and simple" unionism, which rejected sweeping assaults on the existing economic system and concentrated on winning concrete benefits: higher wages, shorter hours, and better working conditions. By rejecting the more ambitious political agenda of the Knights, and by focusing on bread-and-butter issues of immediate concern to workers, Gompers signaled labor's acceptance of the new wage-labor system and organizers' desire to work within that system. He claimed that his philosophy could be summed up in one word: "More."

Under Gompers's leadership, AFL membership swelled from 140,000 in 1886 to nearly 1 million by 1900. Consisting largely of workers in skilled trades, it made little effort to recruit among semiskilled workers in mass-production industries. After a brief and half-hearted attempt, the AFL abandoned its efforts to unionize women. The AFL denied that women needed to work and argued that their real job was at home raising children and taking care of their husbands. "In our time, and at least in our country, generally speaking," Gompers said in 1905, "there is no necessity of the wife contributing to the support of the family by working." The AFL believed that "the man is the provider" and that working women "bring forth weak children."

Despite the success of the AFL, only a small fraction of American workers belonged to unions. In 1900 only about 1 million of 27.6 million workers were unionized. Most workers were concerned with getting and keeping a job, not with union organizing. The growing power of big business would continue to test the resolve of American workers, exposing the strengths and limitations of the AFL's brand of unionism.

CONCLUSION

Following the Civil War, the United States began an experiment in industrialization that in a few decades would transform America's economy and society. Economic and technological innovation created a climate in which the nation's vast resources could be harnessed for their industrial potential.

The railroads served as a powerful engine driving America's industrial revolution. Construction of thousands of miles of new track linked manufacturers with both resources and consumers, forging a national marketplace and leading to new methods of stimulating and satisfying consumer demand. Other industries expanded operations to meet the insatiable demands of the railroads for steel, lumber, and other materials needed to build track and assemble cars. Finally, railroad managers pioneered the use of new methods for coordinating large organizations. The railroads hired accountants, timekeepers, and comptrollers—positions that were to become common features of modern business bureaucracies.

The American tradition of individual liberty and limited government meshed easily with economic and social doctrines that emphasized competition and individual achievement. In this cultural climate, many Americans accepted the idea that wealth was the just reward for successful competition. Andrew Carnegie extended this idea, arguing that the concentration of wealth and industry among a few proven industrial leaders would benefit society as a whole.

At the same time that they lionized competition, industrialists took measures to control it. Railroads were the first to experiment with practices designed to limit competition and to ensure profits. Their methods of organizing "pools," based on voluntary agreements among industry representatives, seemed primitive compared to the trusts and holding companies that John D. Rockefeller created to seize control of the oil industry. Rockefeller was so successful that dozens of other industrialists followed his example. The result was a wave of mergers and a consolidation of the market as a handful of powerful business leaders gained greater control of whole industries.

The consolidation experiment confronted the federal government with new questions, and new challenges. After some initial hesitation, Washington decided that government had a role to play in limiting the power of trusts and protecting competition in the marketplace. The federal government took its first tentative steps toward regulation with passage of the Interstate Commerce Commission (1887), which regulated the railroads, and the Sherman Antitrust Act (1890), which declared trusts illegal. In the short run, neither law had much impact. In the long run, however, these early experiments provided the legal and administrative scaffolding for government regulation in the twentieth century.

American workers experienced the full force of industrialization's impact. Before the industrial revolution, most workers either labored on farms or in small, independently owned shops. By the end of the century, the majority of American workers earned wages by toiling in immense, impersonal factories. Management's fascination with principles of scientific management, the standardization of work procedures, and tougher discipline, contributed to a workplace that was often tedious, repetitive, and dangerous. Many of the new industrial workers were immigrants, and differences in backgrounds often created tension among working people. Families' needs to make a living also forced women and children to join the work force in large numbers. In most cases, they labored under difficult conditions for lower wages than their adult male counterparts.

Workers resisted the hardship of industrialization by forming cooperative alliances, organizing wildcat strikes, and joining unions. In these early years of the labor movement, union organizers faced two central questions: (1) Should working people form alliances with other reform groups to challenge the foundation of the new industrial order, or should they focus solely on labor issues? And (2) should unions attempt to organize all workers, or concentrate on those skilled workers who possessed the most power? Both the National Labor Union and the Knights of Labor espoused similar answers to these questions: they hoped to build a broad-based reform movement, made up of skilled and unskilled workers, that would challenge the foundation of the industrial order. The American Federation of Labor (AFL), which emerged in 1886 after the decline of the Knights, took a very different approach. Under the leadership of Samuel Gompers, the AFL focused its attention on the bread-and-butter issues that were of most concern to its skilled membership. By the end of the century, the AFL and its brand of national unionism had emerged as the dominant force in American labor.

Most American workers, however, remained unorganized. Unionizing efforts confronted resistance from business, the courts, and most non–working-class Americans. Workers themselves remained divided by ethnic differences and thought less about joining unions than about their own day-to-day well-being in the new industrial society.

SUGGESTED READINGS

The best recent survey concerning the economic transformations occurring in the late nineteenth century United States is Walter Licht's *Industrializing America* (1995). *Scale and Scope: The Dynamics of Industrial Capitalism* (1990), by Alfred D. Chandler, Jr., also examines the changes in technology, marketing, and management vital to the growth of industrialization. Maury Klein's *The Flowering of the Third America* (1992) provides a general overview of inventions, the factory system, communication, and the growing inequality of classes. For an older economic history of the last decades of the nineteenth century, from the formation of trusts to the training of more efficient workers, see Edward C. Kirkland's *Industry Comes of Age* (1961).

The social impact of technology and the role of culture as an impetus to innovation are the focus of a number of works. Alan I. Marcus and Howard P. Segal's *Technology in America* (1989) traces the impact of American culture on new technology from the earliest settlers in Jamestown to the present. Carolyn Marvin in *When Old Technologies Were New* (1988), on the invention of the telephone and the light bulb, shows how technology reshaped social relations and altered Americans' perception of the world. Focusing on the city of Chicago, Harold L. Platt's *The Electric City* (1991) examines how electricity changed the city itself and how its inhabitants adapted to new machines. Emphasizing the dynamic technological and social changes wrought by steel, Thomas J. Misa traces its production and use in *A Nation of Steel* (1995).

Arguably America's greatest inventor, Thomas Edison is the topic of a number of historical works. Neil Baldwin provides an excellent biography of Edison, as well as vivid descriptions and drawings of his inventions, in *Edison: Inventing the Century* (1995). As David E. Nye describes the social and cultural impact of electrification, he argues in *Electrifying America* (1990) that Edison's greatest invention was in the production, distribution, and marketing of electricity. Andre Millard's *Edison and the Business of Innovation* (1990) examines the relationship between business and new technology as seen in Edison's career and the unique way in which the inventor laid the foundation for new industries.

A number of books address the importance of the railroad industry in shaping continued economic growth in the late nineteenth century. The history of the American railroad, from wooden tracks to modern technological advances, is the basis of *The North American Railroad* (1995) by James E. Vance, Jr. Albro Martin's *Railroads Triumphant* (1992) examines the rise of railroad companies, the role of the railroad in the growth of the United States economy, and the railroad's impact on industrial and urban development. The unique relationship between the railroads and urbanization is the focus of John R. Stilgoe's *Metropolitan Corridor* (1983). Stilgoe argues that the American urban environment emerged along the railroad track and helped to create urban industrial districts, as well as commuter suburbs. For the life cycle of the railroad worker, from recruitment to retirement, see Walter Licht's *Working for the Railroad* (1983).

Editors T. J. Jackson Lears and Richard W. Fox chronicle the rise of America's consumer culture in a series of essays on advertising, mass market techniques, politics, and the use of space entitled *The Culture of Consumption* (1983). The essays define consumer culture, as well as describe how America became immersed in consumerism. The history of American department stores and the relationship between saleswomen, managers, and customers are the themes of Susan Porter Benson's *Counter Cultures* (1986). Stephen Fox's *The Mirror Makers* (1984) looks at the societal changes responsible for the evolution of advertising and business marketing. Daniel Pope focuses on the development of advertising agencies and the changing styles they used to appeal to consumers in his book *The Making of Modern Advertising* (1983). The role of businessmen who helped advertisers create mass markets in order to appeal to consumers and amass profits is the subject of Susan Strasser's *Satisfaction Guaranteed: The Making of the American Mass Market* (1989). The impact of the mass market, as well as technological innovations, changed the diets of most Americans, according to *Revolution at the Table* (1988) by Harvey A. Levenstein.

The modern business culture that emerged in the last half of the nineteenth century is a topic touched upon by a number of historians. In *Power and Morality* (1980), Saul Engelbourg traces businessmen's changing standards of conduct and argues that business ethics improved as a result of publicity and regulation. The ways in which corporate organizations reshaped American culture are analyzed in Alan Trachtenberg's *The Incorporation of America* (1982). Conflicting versions of America's work ethic serve as the foundation of Daniel T. Rodgers's look at labor conditions and the morality of work in *The Work Ethic in Industrial America* (1978). A number of prominent individuals who rejected the changes in business and work ethics are examined in John L. Thomas's *Alternative America: Henry George, Edward Bellamy, Henry Demarest Lloyd and the Adversary Tradition* (1983).

The management systems developed to operate the new industrial empires are examined in works such as Alfred D. Chandler's *The Visible Hand* (1977), in which the author traces the history of industrial management from small household firms to corporate giants. The reasons for business consolidation and the economic impact of these mergers form the framework for Naomi R. Lamoreaux's *The Great Merger Movement in American Business* (1985). Joanne Yates examines how managers took control of companies as businesses grew and how they implemented new ideas in her work *Control Through Communication* (1989). Oliver Zunz's *Making America Corporate* (1990) analyzes the relationship between middle-class professionals and the new work culture they created.

Historians have written numerous biographies of the intriguing men behind the rise of big business. Ron Chernow's *The House of Morgan* (1990) examines the creative ways in which the Morgan family made its money. One of the best biographies on John D. Rockefeller, Sr., that seeks to depict the complexities of the oil giant's life rather than presenting the familiar one-dimensional robber baron image, is Ron Chernow's *Titan* (1998). Focusing on Andrew Carnegie's business contributions is Harold Livesay's *Andrew Carnegie and the Rise of Big Business* (1975).

The changing nature of work and the culture surrounding work are the focus of David Montgomery's *The Fall of the House of Labor* (1987). Montgomery traces labor management from the early codes of conduct created by the common laborers themselves to the adoption of management styles designed to weaken labor unionism. The changing relationship between employees and employers, intensified by the efficient managerial practices of Frederick W. Taylor, is the topic of Daniel Nelson's *Managers and Workers* (1979). Herbert G. Gutman's *Work, Culture, and Society in Industrializing America* (1976) examines the social and cultural values that industrial employees brought to the factory that shaped the nature of their work.

The impact of industrialization on the working class, especially on women, is a common subject for labor and social historians. For essays on working women's views on industrial and domestic labor, see Sarah Eisenstein's *Give Us Bread, Give Us Roses* (1983). Alice Kessler-Harris's *Out to Work* (1982) surveys the transformation in women's paid and domestic work from the colonial period to the present. The growing number of women in office jobs is the theme of Margery Davies's *Woman's Place Is at the Typewriter* (1982). Susan E. Kennedy's *If All We Did Was to Weep at Home* (1979) looks at the temporary nature of women's work outside the home and working-class attempts to mirror the middle-class cult of domesticity. For a more recent study of working-class men and women and their division and unity within the work force, see the essays in *Work Engendered: Toward a New History of American Labor* (1991), edited by Ava Baron.

Other works have examined the life of the working class, both inside the factory and within the home. Herbert Gutman's *Power and Culture* (1987) presents essays concerning nineteenth-century wage earners, immigrants, and freed slaves. In *The Shadow of the Mills* (1989), S. J. Kleinberg describes the familial and individual costs of industrialization on workers in Pittsburgh. Peter R. Shergold compares the living standards of workers in Pittsburgh and Birmingham, England, in *Working Class Life* (1982) and discovers that the standard of living for American laborers did not exceed that of English laborers until the twentieth century, and only then at a substantial cost to their health.

Numerous works deal with the formation of unions to combat the worst aspects of industrialization. Several focus on the rise and fall of the Knights of Labor, among them Robert E. Weir's *Beyond Labor's Veil* (1996). Kim Voss's *The Making of American Exceptionalism* (1993) analyzes the Knights of Labor in the context of union radicalism and its decline as a result of employer counteroffenses. The differences between the Knights of Labor and the American Federation of Labor are explored in Gerald N. Grob's *Workers and Utopia* (1961). A balanced study of Samuel Gompers and his role in shaping the American Federation of Labor is Harold Livesay's *Samuel Gompers and Organized Labor in America* (1978). Attempts by women to unionize are examined in Barbara Mayer Wertheimer's *We Were There* (1977) and Susan Levine's *Labor's True Woman* (1984). The relationship between black factory workers and the unions is described in William H. Harris's *The Harder We Run: Black Workers Since the Civil War* (1982).

Competing Voices

Organized Labor

The Constitution of the Knights of Labor

The Knights of Labor, under the leadership of Terence Powderly, adopted its constitution at its 1878 convention in Reading, Pennsylvania. The document expresses the Knights' broad vision for organizing all workers and reforming society as a whole.

The recent alarming development and aggression of aggregated wealth which, unless checked, will invariably lead to the pauperization and hopeless degradation of the toiling masses, render it imperative, if we desire to enjoy the blessings of life, that a check should be placed upon its power and upon unjust accumulation, and a system adopted which will secure to the laborer the fruits of his toil; and as this much-desired object can only be accomplished by the thorough unification of labor, and the united efforts of those who obey the divine injunction that "In the sweat of thy brow shalt thou eat bread," we have formed the [Knights of Labor] with a view of securing the organization and direction, by cooperative effort, of the power of the industrial classes; and we submit to the world the objects sought to be accomplished by our organization, calling upon all who believe in securing "the greatest good to the greatest number" to aid and assist us:—

I. To bring within the folds of organization every department of productive industry, making knowledge a standpoint for action, and industrial and moral worth, not wealth, the true standard of individual and national greatness.

II. To secure to the toilers a proper share of the wealth that they create; more of the leisure that rightfully belongs to them; more societary advantages; more of the benefits, privileges, and emoluments of the world. . . .

IV. The establishment of cooperative institutions, productive and distributive.

V. The reserving of the public lands—the heritage of the people—for the actual settler; —not another acre for railroads or speculators.

VI. The abrogation of all laws that do not bear equally upon capital and labor. . . .

X. The substitution of arbitration for strikes, whenever and wherever employers and employes [sic] are willing to meet on equitable grounds.

XI. The prohibition of employment of children in workshops, mines and factories before attaining their fourteenth year. . . .

XIII. To secure for both sexes equal pay for equal work.

XIV. The reduction of the hours of labor to eight per day. . . .

XV. To prevail upon governments to establish a purely national circulating medium. . . .

It is intended by the Knights of Labor to supersede the wage system by a system of industrial cooperation, productive and distributive.

Samuel Gompers on the American Federation of Labor

In the first selection, Gompers, a founding member of the AFL and its first president, recounts the formation of the organization out of the conflicting aims of the

724

Knights of Labor and the trade unions. The second selection is from Gompers's testimony before the Senate Education and Labor Committee in August 1883. He explains why he supports strikes and believes that arbitration will not succeed until workers achieve economic and organizational power.

After my initiation of the [Knights of Labor] in the seventies, I heard of it now and then but never as a substitute for trade unions. With the eighties, when it abandoned complete secrecy, it grew much more rapidly. . . .

[F]riction [soon began] developing over K. of L. encroachments on trade union functions. The two movements were inherently different. Trade unions endeavored to organize for collective responsibility persons with common trade problems. They sought economic betterment in order to place in the hands of wage-earners the means to wider opportunities. The Knights of Labor was a social or fraternal organization. It was based upon a principle of cooperation and its purpose was reform. . . .

The struggle between the trade unions and the K. of L. was at high tide when I assumed the task of making the American Federation of Labor something more than a paper organization. . . .

My earliest official efforts were concentrated in promoting stability of labor organizations. This had to be done by making the idea an inseparable part of the thought and habits of trade unionists by establishing a business basis for unionism and then driving home the fallacy of low dues. Cheap unionism cannot maintain effective economic activity. Sustained office work and paid union officials for administrative work have become the general practice since the Federation was organized. A big service of the Federation has been in crystallizing and unifying labor thought and practice. . . .

Economic betterment—today, tomorrow, home and shop—was the foundation upon which trade unions have been built. Economic power is the basis upon which may be developed power in other fields. It is the foundation of organized society. Whoever or whatever controls economic power directs and shapes development for the group or the nation. Because I early grasped this fundamental truth, I was never deluded or led astray by rosy theory or fascinating plan that did not square with my fundamental.

While I am in the labor movement and take a stand opposed to strikes whenever they can be avoided, I have no sympathy with, nor can I endorse or echo, the statement of many men who are too ready to condemn strikes. Strikes have their evils but they have their good points also, and with proper management, with proper organization, strikes do generally result to the advantage of labor, and in very few instances do they result in injury to the workingmen, whether organized or unorganized. . . .

Strikes ought to be, and in well-organized trades unions they are, the last means which workingmen resort to to protect themselves against the almost never satisfied greed of the employers. Besides this, the strike is, in many instances, the only remedy within our reach as long as legislation is entirely indifferent to the interests of labor. . . .

By the late 1870s, industrialization had drawn clear battle lines between labor and capital, and the former seemed to be losing the war. An economic depression had settled over the country, hitting those at the bottom of the socioeconomic ladder the hardest and eroding what little force workers possessed in the face of increasing corporate power. As the independent artisan gave way to the assembly line, workers increasingly felt like cogs in the industrial machine, stripped of their autonomy.

The apparent solution to the dilemma of the industrial worker was to confront organized capital with organized labor. The Knights of Labor was the first relatively successful attempt at assembling workers in a national body. But under Terence Powderly, the Knights became a reform movement that sought to bind all the "productive classes"—workers and farmers, regardless of skill, sex or race, and even some employers—together to build a society that embodied economic cooperation, equality of opportunity, and the virtues of hard work. The K. of L. worked not just for broad economic change; it pressed government for political and moral reforms, such as women's suffrage and the prohibition of alcohol.

Samuel Gompers found the Knights' high ideals and pursuit of broad reform impractical. Whereas Powderly glossed over class conflict, Gompers insisted that workers and their employers had fundamentally different interests. Unless wage workers organized separately and defended themselves, they would be exploited. While the Knights disapproved of strikes, Gompers believed that until workers could improve their overall economic position, strikes were often "the only means whereby the rightful demands of labor can be secured." He accepted that the industrial order was here to stay; workers must now fight for what they might realistically achieve, the "bread and butter" issues instead of sweeping reform. He also more clearly understood that only a tightly controlled organization of skilled workers could challenge corporate power. Progress for a select group of laborers was better than none at all.

The Knights of Labor and the American Federation of Labor represented two different conceptions of modern America. One remained optimistic that the industrial order could be reconciled to traditional values and molded into a cooperative society; the other recognized that industrialization had divided the parties into opposing camps in a cutthroat battle for economic gain. The AFL achieved its goals by limiting them, and the Knights died out with the last vestiges of an older America.

Questions for Analysis

1. What are the aims of the Knights of Labor?

2. What primary methods does their constitution propose for achieving them?

3. What does the slogan "the greatest good to the greatest number" say about the Knights' values?

4. What are the aims of the AFL?

5. What are the methods Gompers proposes?

6. What does Gompers's endorsement of striking say about his view of American society?

7. Can you think of any recent issues over which idealists and pragmatists divided in seeking similar goals?

19

The New Urban Nation, 1865–1910

*L*ike the millions of other immigrants who left their homelands and traveled to America around the turn-of-the-century, Anzia Yezierska longed for a better life in her new country. "From the other end of the earth from where I came," she recalled, "America was a land of living hope, woven of dreams, aflame with longing and desire." Born in Poland in the 1880s, Yezierska traveled to America with her poor parents and eight siblings, arriving in New York sometime in the early 1890s. Like many other Jews from eastern Europe, she and her family settled into a crowded tenement apartment on Manhattan's Lower East Side.

Over the next few years, Yezierska survived by working long hours in a local sweatshop. "While the morning was still dark I walked into a dark basement," she remembered. "And darkness met me when I turned out of the basement." In addition to the challenge of making enough money to pay rent and buy food, Yezierska struggled to assimilate to American society. She enrolled in English classes and joined a local women's association, but she still felt estranged from America. "Between my soul and the American soul were worlds of difference that no words could bridge over," she reflected. But one day she had a revelation: "I saw that it was the glory of America that it was not yet finished," she realized. "And I, the last comer, had her share to give, small or great, to the making of America."

Newcomers such as Yezierska, who flooded American cities at the end of the nineteenth century, presented the nation with new challenges and great opportunities. Since most immigrants crowded into a handful of cities, local governments were overwhelmed by a host of new problems: crowded living arrangements, poor sanitation, intense poverty. When established institutions proved unresponsive, many immigrants turned to neighborhood social institutions and powerful political machines to help ease the transition to their new lives. The presence of so many new migrants, combined with innovations in transportation, altered the size and shape of American cities. Immigrants also created a dynamic urban culture, a "democracy of amusement," that would transform the cultural landscape in America. Not everyone welcomed urbanization and its social experiments. The last quarter of the nineteenth century witnessed a potent backlash against immigrants and the emerging urban culture.

▍ What impact did the flood of new immigrants have on urban life in the last quarter of the nineteenth century?

▍ How did changes in transportation and improvements in technology influence the geography of the city?

▍ How did urban life influence American culture?

▍ Why did many middle-class Protestants find the city threatening, and what did they do about it?

This chapter will address these questions.

 ## The Birth of the Modern City

"We live in the age of great cities," the Reverend Samuel Lane Loomis informed his seminary students in 1886. "Each successive year finds a stronger and more irresistible current sweeping in toward the centres of life." Among the most powerful currents that Loomis identified were a huge surge in population, which dramatically altered the social landscape, and technological improvements, especially the development of mass transit and the elevator, which allowed cities to grow both upward and outward. But "the age of great cities" also produced unprecedented problems of congestion, sanitation, crime, and vice, which vexed public officials. Urban political bosses undertook some public safety and sanitation measures while lining their own pockets, but improvements seldom reached the working-class bulk of city populations.

City People: Migrants and Immigrants

The number of people living in the United States tripled between 1860 and 1920, from 31 million to over 105 million. During that same period, however, the number of people living in American cities increased ninefold, from 6 to 54 million. By 1900, almost 40 percent of Americans lived in cities. In 1860 only three cities—New York, Philadelphia, and Brooklyn—had more than 250,000 residents. By 1890,

Chronology

1862	Morrill Act gives land to states for colleges
1868	First women's club, Sorosis, established
1869	Boss Tweed gains control of New York's political machine
1871	The Great Chicago Fire
1873	First cable cars operate in San Francisco
1874	Women's Christian Temperance Union (WCTU) organized
	Chautauqua education program launched
1876	National League of Professional Baseball Clubs organized
1880	Salvation Army begins work in New York
1882	Chinese Exclusion Act
1883	Pulitzer buys *New York World*
1884	Twain publishes *The Adventures of Huckleberry Finn*
1885	Safety bicycle invented
1887	Members of the St. Louis Browns refuse to play an all-black baseball club
	American Protection Association founded
1888	First electric trolley line completed in Richmond, Virginia
1891	Basketball invented
1895	Anti-Saloon League formed
	Coney Island amusement park opens in Brooklyn
1896	First motion picture shown in New York's Koster and Bial Theatre
1897	First subway constructed in Boston
1900	Proportion of Americans living in cities nears 40 percent
1902	Macy's opens in New York
1913	Woolworth Building completed in New York

eleven cities had surpassed that size. By 1920, the census showed that for the first time more than half the U.S. population lived in cities. "We cannot all live in cities," a newspaper commented, "yet nearly all seem determined to do so." Some of the figures are astonishing: Between 1860 and 1920, New York saw its population explode from 800,000 to 5.5 million; Chicago, the second-most-populous city, grew from

100,000 to 2.7 million. A flood of migrants transformed Los Angeles from a sleepy town of 5,700 in 1870 to a thriving metropolis of over 600,000 by 1920.

Many new city residents were rural laborers pushed off the land by economic hardship and drawn to the city by the prospect of jobs and a better life. Mechanization not only reduced the number of people necessary to harvest crops, it flooded the market with surplus product, which led, in turn, to lower prices and a declining quality of life for many farmers. A less tangible but important lure for migrants was the glitter of city life. Many farmers were overwhelmed by the social isolation of rural life, the long lonely days working in the fields, the great distances between neighbors, and the lack of social and cultural institutions. Rural people were dazzled by the excitement of urban life, its shops, theaters, restaurants, churches, department stores. Kansas City, noted a rural migrant, was a "gilded metropolis" filled with "marvels," a veritable "round of joy." As a result, between 1870 and 1920, 11 million Americans left the farm for the city (see graph).

Rural southern blacks also fed the migratory stream into northern industrial cities. Between 1900 and 1920, nearly 750,000 African-Americans fled the discrimination and terrorism of the South and traveled north in search of greater freedom and new economic opportunities. In 1900 thirty-two cities reported more than ten thousand African-American inhabitants. By 1920, almost 85 percent of blacks living outside the South lived in urban areas. The black population in a handful of cities—New York, Philadelphia, and Chicago—surpassed 100,000, while a number of smaller cities such as Denver, Oklahoma City, and Los Angeles witnessed a surge in African-American residents.

Joining the migrants from rural America were a flood of immigrants from Europe. Cheaper and better transportation made the great tide of immigration possi-

Rural and Urban Population, 1860–1920 In the second half of the nineteenth century and in the early twentieth century the American population continued to grow, thanks to natural increase and immigration. Better transportation, increasing job opportunities, and a rising immigrant population resulted in a more rapid population increase in urban areas than in rural areas. By 1920, more Americans lived in areas that the census considered "urban" than in rural regions. (Source: *Historical Statistics of the United States.*)

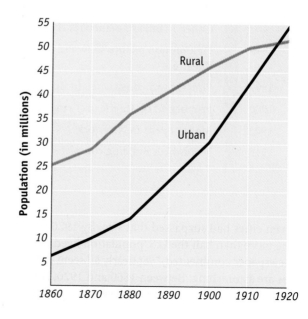

ble, but dissatisfaction with conditions at home, plus expectations of better opportunity in America, sparked most decisions to leave. Overpopulation, unemployment, famine, and chronic and epidemic diseases drove many from their homelands. In other cases, new agricultural techniques led landlords to consolidate their lands and farming operations, thereby evicting long-time tenants. Government policies pushed others to leave. In eastern Europe, especially in Russia, the official persecution of minorities led millions of Jewish families to emigrate. While they were pushed by many different forces, nearly all the new immigrants were pulled by the demand for unskilled labor. America's emerging industrial empire required a large pool of cheap labor to keep its factories and mines functioning at full capacity. Speculators and steamship lines eager to promote business advertised exaggerated tales of an America whose streets were "paved with gold."

Immigration figures were staggering. During the forty years before the Civil War, 5 million immigrants poured into the United States to seek their fortunes. From 1860 to 1900, almost 14 million arrived. In one year alone, 1882, nearly 789,000 people came. By 1890, about 15 percent of the population, 9 million people, were foreign-born. In the first decade of the new century, almost 6.3 million immigrants entered the United States—more than 1.3 million in 1907 alone. "The magnitude of immigration to America is unmatched in the history of mankind," noted an economist.

The first wave of immigrants came ashore in the mid-1800s and hailed from Britain and Ireland, Germany, and Scandinavia. Irish and Germans were the largest groups. Also, between 1850 and 1882, more than three hundred thousand Chinese entered the United States, settling mostly in the West. Then the pattern slowly began to change. By 1890, Irish, English, Germans, and Scandinavians made up only 60 percent of all immigrants, while "new immigrants" from southern and eastern Europe (Italy, Poland, Russia, Austria, Hungary, Greece, Turkey, and Syria) made up most of the rest. Italian Catholics, followed by Slavs and eastern European Jews, were the most numerous. Between 1876 and 1930, more than 5 million Italians and 2 million Jews settled in the United States. The Slavic groups—which included Russians, Ukrainians, Slovaks, Slovenes, Poles, Croatians, Serbs, and Bulgarians—accounted for about 4 million new arrivals (see graph, page 732).

Except in the South, immigrants dominated the population of the nation's major cities. Most of the new urban residents settled in the nation's industrial core, which stretched from Massachusetts south to Maryland, and westward to Illinois, southern Wisconsin, and eastern Missouri. By 1920, this region claimed 16 of the 25 largest cities, and 9 of the top 10. In 1920 more than 80 percent of all Irish, Russian, Italian, and Polish immigrants lived in cities, and nearly two-thirds of all immigrants resided in urban areas. Nearly 90 percent of Chicagoans were first- or second-generation immigrants by 1880. In New York, Milwaukee, Detroit, and St. Louis, the figure was about 80 percent. New York City, where most immigrants arrived and many stayed, was home to more Italians than lived in Naples, more Germans than lived in Hamburg, and twice as many Irish as lived in Dublin. In 1916, 72 percent of people living in San Francisco spoke a foreign language.

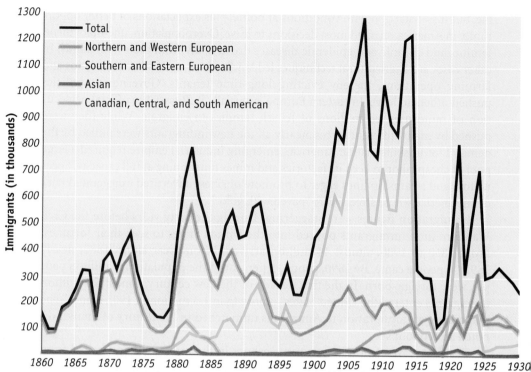

Immigration, 1860–1930 In the 1880s, America experienced its first sharp increase in immigration since the Civil War as a result of increased industrialization in the United States and unsatisfactory conditions in Europe. In the last decades of the nineteenth century the United States also saw a shift in the national origin of immigrants as the number of people from southern and eastern Europe climbed, surpassing the number of northern and western European immigrants after 1895. Also note the impact of World War I on immigration and the effects of the Immigration Act of 1924. (Source: *Historical Statistics of the United States.*)

Immigrant Communities

Ethnic groups frequently traveled to the United States as part of a larger migratory chain that was made up of relatives and friends, often from the same neighborhood or village in the old country. Relatives and friends who had emigrated sent back instructions on where to make steamship and railroad connections, advice on where to live and work, and money for the passage to America. More than half of the Italians who settled in Cleveland before World War I, for example, came from a handful of villages in southern Italy.

Once in America, immigrants tried to recreate an older sense of community, forming urban enclaves with a wide range of support institutions and associations. New York's Lower East Side, Boston's North End, Chicago's West Side, and Los Angeles's East Side *barrio* were home to close-knit concentrations of immigrants. These domains provided newcomers with a supportive community and familiar customs as they adjusted to the strangeness of American urban society. Journalist Jacob Riis claimed that a map of New York City in 1890 "coloured to designate nationality, would show more stripes than on the skin of a zebra, and more colours than any rainbow." Czech immigrants living in the Pilsen district on Chicago's West Side attended church services conducted in Czech, ate at Czech restaurants, and read Czech-language newspapers. Not far away, near the corner of Halsted and Maxwell Streets, more than 90 percent of the residents were Jewish, as evidenced by the forty Orthodox synagogues clustered in the neighborhood. Just north of Halsted Street, Yiddish gave way to Italian and, a few blocks later, Greek. Here, according to a visitor, "practically all stores bear signs in both Greek and English, coffee houses flourish on every corner, in dark little grocery stores one sees black olives, dried ink-fish, tomato paste, and all the queer, nameless roots and condiments which are so familiar in Greece."

Since they depended on ties of kinship and friendship, new arrivals not only clustered in the same neighborhoods, they often concentrated in similar occupations. The Slavic groups were heavily represented in Chicago's slaughterhouses and Pennsylvania's steel mills, as well as in mining and industrial regions in western Pennsylvania, Ohio, and Illinois. Many Greeks opened small businesses. A reporter noted in 1904 that "practically every busy corner in Chicago is occupied by a Greek candy store." Italians, who accounted for the largest number of common laborers of any ethnic group, also dominated the fruit business in New York City. By 1916, nearly 70 percent of the garment workers in New York City were Jews.

For many immigrants, the family provided a bulwark against the challenges of urban life. The strains of adapting to a strange environment and the need to earn a living forced family members to mute differences and stress cooperation. The nuclear family remained the model for most immigrants. In 1905 about 95 percent of Jews and Italians in New York City were members of intact families. Parents exercised considerable power over the career paths of their children, often forcing boys and girls to leave school early to work in a mill or a family business. Among unskilled German immigrants in Detroit, 66 percent of young men and 43 percent of teenage girls worked outside the home. Girls faced the added responsibility of performing household chores and caring for younger siblings. "When you work, you understand, you used to bring your pay home and give it to your parents," recalled an immigrant. "And whatever they feel they want to give you, they decide. There was no disagreement." While children worked outside the home, married women focused their attention on their roles as wives, mothers, and homemakers. A survey of immigrant families in Chicago in 1900 revealed that only 2 percent of wives worked outside the home.

For many newcomers, the church served as the critical link to the Old World. The traditions and rituals of religion provided immigrants with a cultural connection to the past. Immigrants who may never have attended services in the old country joined churches and synagogues for social as well as spiritual support. Churches celebrated important events—births, deaths, and weddings—and fellow church members offered assistance during times of unemployment. Many churches established social services such as welfare organizations, hospitals, and orphanages. In many communities, ethnic groups fought against established church authorities, insisting that priests conduct services in their parishoners' native language and that churches honor distinctive cultural practices and local patron saints of their former villages. German, Polish, and Irish Catholics, for example, organized their own parishes and built separate church buildings. Jewish immigrants from eastern Europe, who objected to the more liberal American Reformed Judaism, formed their own synagogues.

In addition to family and church, most newcomers created mutual aid societies to provide financial security and cultural autonomy. Usually organized by men from the same town in the old country, the societies collected modest dues from their members to bankroll a fund for aiding needy families. By 1910, seven thousand such aid societies were serving nearly two-thirds of Polish immigrants in America. Though founded to provide social insurance, societies often evolved into male social clubs. Many immigrant groups set up loan societies to help budding entrepreneurs. Jews founded thousands of free-loan societies, while Chinese communities aided small businesses through the *woi*, a family loan society.

The saloon also played a central role for immigrants in the modern city. A 1900 survey of Chicago found over five hundred saloons serving the 120,000 working-class residents of the Stockyard district. The nearby middle-class neighborhood of Hyde Park contained only twenty-one drinking establishments for its 65,000 residents. Saloons provided the services of a neighborhood center, a place where men could relax and enjoy a break from the harsh demands of everyday life. Patrons played cards, discussed politics, exchanged tips on jobs, and held union or fraternal meetings. Saloons provided the only free public toilets in the city, and many offered their customers free lunch and newspapers. Many times, saloonkeepers also cashed checks and loaned money to regulars.

The Transportation Revolution

The influx of new immigrants coincided with dramatic changes in transportation. Before 1825, no city in America possessed a mass-transit system, so the physical expansion of the city was limited to walking distances, usually about two miles from the city center. As a result, the "walking city" was compact and congested. All the city's inhabitants—African-Americans, immigrants, and native-born white workers—clustered near the waterfront in houses and tenements. Wealthy people established separate neighborhoods, but they too lived in the city center close to their places of business. Owners, managers, and workers not only lived near one another, they all set up residence close to their common place of work.

Innovations in urban mass transit revolutionized the nature of the walking city. In the 1830s many cities began experimenting with the horse-drawn omnibus. The omnibus, which traveled over a fixed route and charged between 6 and 12 cents for a daily fare, became a standard feature in large cities by the 1850s. In 1853 New York operated 700 omnibuses, which transported 120,000 passengers a day. The carriages were often crowded and the ride was noisy and bumpy. "Modern martyrdom may be succinctly defined as riding in a New York omnibus," the *New York Herald* complained in 1864. While omnibuses were appearing on city streets, steam-powered commuter railroads were shortening the distances between cities. At the same time, many cities switched to the horse railway, in which omnibuses rolled on rails. By the mid-1880s, more than 300 cities were operating 525 horse-car lines, which offered a faster and smoother ride than the older omnibus. In 1873 San Francisco introduced the cable car, which was pulled by an underground chain and was especially useful in hilly cities. By the mid-1890s, residents of over twenty American cities rolled along some 626 miles of cable car track. More than 86 miles of track criss-crossed Chicago alone, which claimed the largest cable car system in the country.

The electrification of the street railways, however, represented the most significant innovation in urban transportation in the nineteenth century. Electric streetcars, or trolleys, were faster, more reliable, and covered greater distances than either horse-cars or cable car systems. By 1900, most cities had replaced their horse-powered cars with new electric streetcars. In one year alone, 1902, trolleys carried more than 2 billion urban passengers on 22,000 miles of electrified track. In 1890, for example, Pittsburgh had 13 miles of electrified track carrying 46.3 million passengers. By 1902, the steel city boasted 470 miles of track that transported 168.6 million riders. Electrification also allowed engineers to develop mass-transit systems above and below the ground. In the 1880s, Brooklyn, Boston, Philadelphia, Kansas City, and Chicago built elevated lines. In 1897, Boston became the first city to construct a subway system, with New York (1904) and Philadelphia (1908) not far behind.

Mass transit fundamentally altered the social and economic fabric of American metropolitan areas. The omnibus, horse railways, commuter trains, and especially the electric trolley extended the outer reach of urban settlement. In 1850 Boston extended about two miles outward from city hall. By 1900, it had spread more than six miles. Initially streetcar lines were built to existing areas on the fringe of the city, which allowed small towns to develop into large communities. In 1886 President Grover Cleveland purchased a house in the underdeveloped outskirts northwest of Georgetown. Within a few years, however, a trolley line transformed the area into the thriving community of Cleveland Park. In city after city, the homeowners moved along the trolley tracks.

For the white middle class, the suburbs offered the best of both worlds: easy access to the business district but safe distance from the congestion, dirt, and crime of downtown. Advertisers and land developers played to both concerns. "Those who wish to secure a quiet home sufficiently remote from the city to be out of its turbulence and yet within a convenient business distance had better seek out North New York," claimed a suburban advertisement. The appeals seemed to work. Between 1900 and 1915, the population of Manhattan increased by 16 percent, but the population of the suburb of Queens surged 160 percent. During the same period, Boston saw its population climb by 9 percent, while the surrounding neighborhood of Dorchester soared 52 percent.

As mass transit made the suburbs accessible to the middle class, new construction techniques made single homes affordable. The balloon-frame house, which

Electric Cars of New Orleans   In nineteenth-century urban transportation, nothing compared with the significant role played by electric streetcars. Rail lines extended from downtown centers to the urban fringe, uniting people and services, giving residents more mobility, and expanding the reach of American cities. This transportation explosion affected cities across the country, including New Orleans, as seen in this picture of Canal Street in 1890.   *(Library of Congress.)*

used an inexpensive interior wood frame joined by nails, made private homes affordable to middle-income families. A carpenter named Augustine Deodat Taylor constructed the first balloon-frame building in Chicago in 1833, and by the end of the decade the structures sprouted up in small towns and old cities across the nation. Taylor's formula required fewer workers and simpler tools than older homes, which used exterior masonry walls or complicated joints. The new structure put single-unit homes within financial reach of the middle class and fueled the exodus to the suburbs.

Historian Kenneth Jackson claimed that the rise of suburbs "represented the most fundamental realignment of urban structure in the 4,500-year past of cities on this planet." As the wealthy and the middle class abandoned the central district of the city as a place of residence, they left behind the poor and racial minorities. The process of suburbanization, which would intensify later in the century, led to a widening physical and social gap between rich and poor and a hardening of racial division in America.

City Neighborhoods

With the physical expansion of the city and the rise of suburbs, urban areas developed distinctive identities. The "downtown" business and shopping districts provided the economic nucleus of the modern city. To attract a largely middle-class female clientele, retailers clustered together large department stores designed to make shopping both convenient and pleasant. Manhattan located its finest stores along Broadway and Fifth and Sixth Avenues. In Chicago shoppers and tourists could wander up and down State Street, peering in the windows at the cornucopia of consumer goods. New York's Macy's store, offering twenty-three and a half acres of consumer goods, a restaurant, and elaborate floor displays, opened its doors in 1902. Five years later, Marshall Field's built a similar shopping emporium in Chicago. Luxury hotels sprouted up to accommodate business travelers and wealthy shoppers. A newspaper noted in 1897 that guests at New York City's Astoria Hotel "will be lodged and fed amid surroundings as gorgeous as those of king's palaces."

Demand for more space for managing, marketing, and financing the new industrial corporations and their products combined with technological innovation to push cities upward as well as outward. The church spire had dominated the skyline of preindustrial cities, but after the 1850s, the invention of the elevator and the use of iron, rather than masonry, for structural support enabled the construction of buildings more than a few stories in height. By the early twentieth century, the skyscraper, or "cloudscraper" as contemporaries sometimes called it, had altered the urban skyline. Skyscrapers turned streets in New York into caverns. The Woolworth Building, completed in 1913, stood fifty-five stories high, soared 760 feet into the air, and ranked as the tallest building in the world until surpassed by the Chrysler Building (1929) and then the Empire State Building (1931).

A cluster of diverse neighborhoods ringed the central business district. The jewel in every city's crown was the area of large mansions that housed its wealthiest citizens. In New York the barons of American industry—Astors, Goulds, Fricks, Whitneys, and Carnegies—lined Fifth Avenue. Boston's economic elite preferred Back Bay, while Philadelphia's most prominent families chose Rittenhouse Square. Mining magnate William Clark's New York mansion contained 130 rooms, and the Whitney residence, just a few blocks away, included a seventeenth-century ballroom and eleven marble bathtubs.

Although opulent mansions were out of their reach, the new urban middle class earned enough money to purchase a house or rent a comfortable apartment. The industrial revolution had swelled the ranks of the middle class, which now included a variety of managerial, technical, clerical, and public service workers, in addition to the traditional professionals and businesspeople. The number of white-collar workers increased from 374,433 in 1870 to 3.2 million in 1910. Since they needed to get to work every day, middle-class residents sought areas of owner-occupied, single-family homes in the suburbs.

Living conditions were not as comfortable for the city's poor and working-class residents. In 1890 in New York, 1 million people, two-thirds of the population, were packed into 32,000 tenement buildings. Conditions were particularly bad on the Lower East Side, that section of Manhattan east of Third Avenue and south of Fourteenth Street. As historian Kenneth Jackson has noted, the Lower East Side at the turn of the century had "the highest recorded density of population in world history." The problem, however, was not confined to New York. Some parts of Chicago had three times as many people as the most crowded parts of Tokyo and Calcutta.

Urban tenement houses were generally congested and filthy. The first tenement house of record was erected on Water Street in New York City in 1833. By 1867, more than 18,000 shabby tenements had sprung up in the city, only to run down. Built on long but narrow lots of 15 by 100 feet, most tenements were four to six stories in height, with four separate apartments on each floor. The tenement, Lewis Mumford wrote in *Sticks and Stones* (1924), "raised bad housing into an art." Each six-story building was designed as close quarters for up to twenty-four families, but since many tenants shared apartments, a single building would often house as many as 150 people. Residents crammed into tiny rooms barely 8 feet wide, with poor ventilation and no heat, bathrooms, or kitchens. A New York housing inspector investigating odors emanating from a tenement found the "entire cellar floor covered with a putrid slime; imbedded therein were various kinds of organic matter in every stage of decomposition, together with dead cats, dead rats, and the skeleton remains of several small animals."

Most cities also contained vice districts and skid row neighborhoods, which served as home to prostitutes, gamblers, pimps, and society's outcasts. Most of Chicago's gambling houses, dance halls, pawnshops, and brothels were concentrated in the Levee. New York's Tenderloin, San Francisco's Barbary Coast, and New Orleans's Storyville were among the best known red-light districts. Within a few miles of the gilded quarters of the wealthy, the city's poorest residents lived in cheap lodging-house slums, home of five-cent-a-night flophouses. A middle-class observer who spent a night in Chicago's skid row claimed that "the animalism and despicable foulness and filth made one almost despair of mankind." Chicago estimated its transient down-and-out population at thirty thousand, and every major city counted thousands who endured similar hardship.

Still, the makeup of urban neighborhoods changed constantly. In a ten-year period between 1905 and 1915, nearly two-thirds of the Jews living on New York's Lower East Side left, migrating to other less-congested parts of the city. In urban neighborhoods across the country, Italians were giving way to Greeks, Irish to Poles, and Germans to Czechs. In most cities, however, racism prevented African-Americans from participating in this ritual of residential mobility. In 1908 the white residents of Chicago's fashionable Hyde Park organized to prevent blacks from moving into their neighborhood. "The districts which are now white must remain white," pronounced a local leader. Within a few years, a number of cities—

Chicago Tenement Scene   Tenements housed many families in crowded and deteriorating conditions. Residents slept, ate, cooked, cleaned, and sometimes worked in a few small, cramped rooms they shared with their extended families, and even boarders. This picture of a mother and two of her children suggests the multitude of tasks performed in a single room as well as the conditions in which the working class lived.   *(Chicago Historical Society.)*

Baltimore, Louisville, Atlanta, Richmond, Dallas, and New Orleans—passed laws making it illegal for blacks to move into white neighborhoods. In 1917 the Supreme Court declared residential segregation ordinances unconstitutional, but most cities found informal methods to achieve the same end.

The Urban Environment

Urban residents were assaulted daily by the stench of human and animal waste and the noise of clattering cable cars and trolleys. Journalist H. L. Mencken recalled that his hometown of Baltimore smelled "like a billion polecats." One reason was horse manure. In a city such as Milwaukee, a horse population of 12,500 deposited up to 133 tons of manure every day. In 1900 health officials in Rochester, New York, estimated that if they stacked all the manure produced by the city's 15,000 horses in a single day, it would rise 175 feet in the air, cover an acre of land, and breed 16 billion flies.

Another source of odor was the privy, "a single one of which," noted a city health official, "may render life in a whole neighborhood almost unendurable in the summer." In 1877 Philadelphia had 82,000 cesspools. The census of 1880 reported that the soil of New Orleans was saturated "very largely with the oozings of foul privy vaults." A middle-class visitor to a city slum wrote, "Look up, look down, turn this way, turn that—there is no prospect but the unkempt and the disorderly, the slovenly and the grim; filth everywhere, trampled on the sidewalks, lying in windows, collected in the eddies of doorsteps."

Most cities simply dumped what little waste they collected in the nearest body of water. New York, Boston, and Chicago installed underground sewers to carry wastes into nearby oceans or lakes. By 1916, New York City was dumping nearly 500 million gallons of raw sewage a day into the Hudson and East Rivers. In most cases, the polluted waters also served as the main source for the city's drinking water. In 1870 no city had a filtration system, and by 1900, only 6 percent of the urban population received filtered water. Pittsburgh waited until its death rate from typhoid fever reached four times the national average before constructing a public filter system.

Other infectious diseases, too, found breeding grounds in squalid city neighborhoods. In Philadelphia, a scarlet fever epidemic killed 1,755 people in 1869–1870 and left hundreds more with chronic heath problems. Two thousand Philadelphians died from a smallpox epidemic in 1870. Other cities, including Chicago, Boston, Baltimore, and Washington, suffered similar epidemics. The problem was especially acute in southern cities, which could not depend on the winter chill to kill vermin and retard the putrefaction of garbage. In just one year, 1873, Memphis suffered three major epidemics—yellow fever, smallpox, and cholera—which infected one-fourth of the city's population and killed thousands. "The deaths grew daily more numerous," claimed a witness; "funerals blocked the way."

Since most cities lacked building codes or professional fire departments, the threat of fire was as great as the risk of fever. Successive fires in the 1870s took enormous tolls of life and property. Fire swept through Boston's business district in 1872 and destroyed hundreds of buildings. Chicago survived the most spectacular fire of the century. In 1871 an inferno destroyed over 17,000 buildings and left 150,000 people homeless. Personal ads appeared in the paper as people tried to find loved ones: "Henry Schneider, baby, in blue poland waist, red skirt, has white hair. Lost."

The influx of millions of immigrants combined with intense poverty to produce soaring crime rates. "Crime was never so bold, so frequent, and so safe as it is this winter," complained a frustrated New Yorker in 1870. "We breathe an atmosphere of highway robbery, burglary, and murder. Few criminals are caught, and fewer punished." The nation's homicide rate nearly tripled in the 1880s, much of the increase coming in the cities. Gangs of urban youths roamed the streets. The Hayes Valley gang terrorized residents of San Francisco, while the Baxter Street Dudes, the Daybreak Boys, and the Alley Gang menaced New Yorkers. In 1900 the *Chicago Tribune* estimated that murders and homicides nationally had climbed from 1,266 in 1881 to 7,340 in 1898, or from about 25 per million people to over 107 per million.

Many cities responded to the new problems by creating housing commissions, professional firefighting and police forces, and regulatory codes designed to improve the quality of urban life. In the 1880s and 1890s, the widespread recognition of the germ theory of disease led many state and municipal boards to enact new measures to protect public health. Building codes required firewalls and professional firefighting departments. City governments purchased steam engines and pumping machinery to battle blazes. Despite the notable progress, a strong tradition of privatism and a reluctance to assert municipal authority limited the effort to respond to the growing public need for a clean, safe environment. In most cities, landlords who wanted sewer and water in their buildings, for example, had to pay for the connections from the street, passing the costs onto already hard-pressed residents. Occupants of crowded buildings in poor neighborhoods who needed better sanitation the most were the least likely to be able to afford it.

City Politics

The growth of the American city presented unprecedented problems for urban government, which remained weak and fragmented. *Harper's Weekly* noted in 1857 that New York City had become "a huge semi-barbarous metropolis . . . not well-governed and not ill-governed, but simply not governed at all." State legislators viewed cities as a source of patronage, not real power. Most mayors were figureheads. To fill the vacuum in urban government, a new political phenomenon arose: the urban machine.

The machine bosses served an important function in urban life. The machine provided urban residents with jobs, legal assistance, food, and welfare. They greeted immigrants as they arrived at the docks, helped workers who had lost their jobs, and intervened with the police when their constituents ran afoul of the law. If a family's breadwinner was injured or died, the bosses donated food and clothing. During cold winters they made sure families had coal to heat their tenement apartments. They organized picnics for poor children and donated money to hospitals and orphanages. "There's got to be in every ward somebody that any bloke can come to—no matter what he's done—and get help," said a Boston ward leader. "Help, you understand; none of your law and justice, but help." Bosses won the favor of city businessmen by selecting local firms to build streets and sewers, granting franchises for operating utilities, and choosing printers, banks, and other small firms to receive municipal contracts. Businessmen paid kickbacks to the boss for the privilege of receiving city business.

In return, the bosses expected, and usually received, the votes of those benefiting from their efforts. Leaving nothing to chance, however, the local machine developed numerous techniques for cheating at the polls. These included padding the registration lists with phony names and addresses. In Philadelphia the list of voters once included a boy of four and his dog. One politician boasted that the signers of the Declaration of Independence still voted in Philadelphia. Machines employed gangs of men whose motto was "vote early and often." In any election, several precincts might record more votes cast than there were residents. One voter who claimed to be an Episcopal bishop, William Croswell Doane, had an argument at the polls. "Come off," scolded an election official. "You're not Bishop Doane." The man retorted, "The hell I ain't, you bastard!"

Who Stole the People's Money?   As city populations inflated, the power and responsibilities of city leaders likewise increased. With this growth came political corruption and the rise of political machines. This 1871 Thomas Nast cartoon shows corruption in New York City running much deeper than a few machine bosses. No one wants to take the blame for corruption, but all are implicated—from government officials, to business owners, right down to every "Tom, Dick, and Harry." *(Harper's Weekly, 1871.)*

William M. Tweed, head of the famed Tweed Ring in New York, may have been the most famous of the bosses. Tweed rose through the ranks of New York's dominant Tammany Hall political machine, serving in turn as city alderman, member of Congress, and New York State assemblyman. By 1867, Tweed held seventeen different city offices simultaneously and controlled twelve thousand patronage jobs. During a reign of barely a dozen years, Tweed milked New York City out of millions of dollars. In 1870 the city spent more than $12 million on a new courthouse, including $7,500 for thermostats and $41,190 for brooms. A similar courthouse in Brooklyn cost only $800,000. A small portion of the ring's graft trickled down to the poor, helping struggling families and supporting local institutions, but most of the money ended up in the pockets of party officials. By 1871, Tweed, worth $12 million, owned an expansive apartment on Fifth Avenue and an estate in Connecticut. Tweed's empire collapsed that same year when he was arrested and convicted of 104 counts of fraud and bribery. He died in prison a few years later.

Tweed may have been the most notorious of the political bosses, but many other local political leaders used similar methods. In Washington, D.C., in the 1870s, Alexander R. Shepherd embarked on an ambitious $20 million public works program, laying sewers, paving streets, and building bridges. The initiatives improved urban life, but it also provided an opportunity for extensive corruption that made Boss Shepherd a wealthy man. While cities such as Washington, D.C., New Orleans, Baltimore, and Cincinnati followed the Tweed model by concentrating power in the hands of a single boss, Chicago and Boston followed a more decentralized design in which individual ward leaders carved out their own empires, refusing to relinquish power to a city-wide leader.

 ## New Experiments in Culture

The concentration of millions of people from different backgrounds into a relatively small space produced a dynamic new urban culture. In their search for shared experiences, city people turned to a new "democracy of amusement." Spectator sports, vaudeville, and theater helped foster a sense of community for urban residents. The democracy of amusement, however, remained an exclusively white experiment, since African-Americans were systematically excluded from participating. The new culture also found expression in the arts, as writers and artists displayed a new emphasis on realism. Amid the cultural experimentation, many women, taking advantage of new opportunities, challenged traditional notions of womanhood.

A Democracy of Amusement

At just the time when the city was becoming more sharply divided by race and class, a new democracy of amusement emerged to blur some of the lines. The enormous expansion of cities, the growing demand for leisure time activities among workers, and the widespread use of electricity provided the foundation for a new world of "public" amusement, which brought people of diverse backgrounds together in a shared culture.

The vaudeville house was the most popular of the new forms of entertainment. "The vaudeville theatre," wrote actor Edwin Milton Royle in *Scribner's Magazine* in 1899, "is an American invention. There is nothing like it anywhere else in the world." During its heyday, about one in seven Americans attended a show at least once a week. At one time New York had thirty-seven vaudeville houses, Philadelphia thirty, and Chicago twenty-two.

Because the theater was open six days a week, from noon to midnight, and charged only ten cents for admission, vaudeville operators had to design programs that appealed to as many people as possible. A 1911 survey of "public recreation" in San Francisco reported vaudeville audiences were neither "predominantly 'rich' or 'poor'," but "fair-to-do" and "struggling." The shows typically opened with a trained animal routine or a dance number. Comic skits followed, ridiculing the trials of urban life. After further musical numbers and acts by ventriloquists, jugglers, strongmen, and magicians, the curtain came down following a "flash" finale such as flying trapeze artists.

According to *Theatre Magazine*, vaudeville's popularity revealed that city residents were taking their "amusement seriously." But more serious theater also drew crowds. Middle-class Americans flocked to live theater for drama, musical comedy, and revues of every kind. New York captured the lead in theatrical excellence early in the nineteenth century with houses in the Bowery, Astor Place, and Union Square. Between 1890 and 1900, the combined seating capacity of New York City's theaters more than doubled. By the turn of the century, New York had more theaters than any city in the world. A British visitor in 1912 was astonished to find "nearly twice as many first-class theaters in New York as in London." Other major cities—Chicago, Boston, San Francisco, New Orleans—built lavish theaters. New York was the site of the first motion picture show, which opened at the Koster and Bial Theatre in New York on April 27, 1896.

Millions of Americans traveled to amusement parks to escape the rigors of everyday urban life. In 1870 amusement parks were unheard of in America; by 1900, they were a standard feature in every major city. The most famous was New York's Coney Island, where for only a few dollars a family could enjoy the exciting mechanical rides such as the roller coaster in Steeplechase Park. Most parks offered a complement of mechanized rides, dance halls, pavilions, and ballrooms where men and women could mingle. "The men like it because it gives them a chance to hug the girls," observed the owner of a Coney Island fun house, and "the girls like it because it gives them a chance to get hugged."

African-Americans were systematically excluded from participating in the new democracy of entertainment. One black vaudeville performer recalled that "colored people could buy seats only in the peanut gallery." American entertainment helped build a sense of community among white urbanites by highlighting their differences from blacks. Entertainers used humor and insult to reinforce the wall that separated the races. Building on the tradition of blackface minstrelsy popular before the Civil War, white songwriters, illustrators, promoters, and performers produced a flood of "darky shows" and "coon songs." More than six hundred "coon songs" were published during the 1890s; one, titled "If the Man in the Moon Were a Coon," sold upward of 3 million copies.

Spectator Sports

City dwellers, confined to monotonous work in factories or sedentary work in offices and stores, craved new forms of physical recreation. Cycling and roller skating crazes swept the country, and new sports such as golf, lawn tennis, and ice hockey were introduced. Basketball, which required little equipment and could be played on urban playgrounds, emerged as the preferred sport of working-class communities.

But while many Americans participated in sports new and old, far more people joined in as spectators at elite and professional events. Boxing attracted large city crowds. During the 1880s, John L. Sullivan, the "Boston Strong Boy," traveled around the country offering to pay opponents who could go four rounds with him. In 1892 Sullivan lost to James J. Corbett in the first championship bout in which the fighters were required to wear padded gloves. While working-class communities embraced basketball and boxing, the middle and upper middle classes adopted football as their sport. The annual Thanksgiving Day game between Princeton and Yale—the two best college teams in the nation—marked the beginning of New

York's winter social season. Wealthy patrons paid up to $150 for box seats to watch the matchup.

Baseball emerged as the most popular new urban sport. Baseball in its modern form had appeared during the 1840s when a group of wealthy New Yorkers organized the Knickerbocker Club. In 1862 in Brooklyn, William H. Cammeyer built the first enclosed baseball field in the country, but it was not until 1869 that teams began to charge admission and pay players. In 1876 eight teams—New York, Philadelphia, Hartford, Boston, Chicago, Louisville, Cincinnati, and St. Louis—came together to form the National League of Professional Baseball Clubs. By the late 1880s, annual attendance at the National League games had reached 8 million a year. Men and boys tried to emulate the professionals in vacant lots and on empty streets.

Choosing Sides   Americans increasingly turned to sports to fill their leisure time. Whether active participants or interested spectators, people were especially drawn to baseball. The first professional league was founded in 1876, but community baseball clubs had begun years before. Besides organized baseball games, neighborhood children often met in vacant lots to play, as in this picture of boys selecting team members.   *(National Baseball Hall of Fame.)*

Baseball grabbed America's imagination. "As an amusement enterprise, baseball today is scarcely second to theater," a fan noted in 1910. The game imposed rules and created a sense of order on chaotic urban society, while the expanse of greenery appeared to bring the countryside into the metropolis. Many people believed that the shared cultural experience at the ballpark would erode class differences. Reformer Jane Addams wrote of the "outburst of kindly feeling" after a home run in a ballpark and asked, "Does not this contain a suggestion of the undoubted power of a public recreation to bring together all classes of a community in the modern city unhappily so full of devices for keeping men apart?"

Baseball may have blurred class distinctions in the city but it reinforced racial differences in America. Integrated teams were fairly common in the north in the late 1870s, and by the middle of the next decade blacks were playing with whites at the highest levels of organized baseball—the major and minor leagues. But then in 1887, all but two members of the St. Louis Browns refused to play an exhibition game against an all-black club. Rather than face a full-scale revolt, the major league owners shook hands on a "gentleman's agreement" to sign no more blacks. The minor leagues followed suit, formally declaring that black players would no longer be welcome. From the mid-1880s to the 1940s, no black ballplayer, other than those who passed for Indian or Cuban, played in the major or minor leagues. African-Americans who came to the ballpark as spectators suffered similar indignities. Even in ballparks where "Negro" teams played against one another, seating was segregated. The vast majority of black fans stayed away from the major and minor leagues.

The Metropolitan Press

Technological innovations in printing and manufacturing of newspapers combined with a growing public need for information to create a new form of journalism—a journalism of exposure. The invention of the steam press and the use of paper made of wood and pulp, rather than more expensive cloth, allowed printers to produce more copy at lower cost. For most of the nineteenth century, newspapers had limited circulation, were often mouthpieces for political parties, and ignored local events, preferring instead to focus on national or state issues. After the Civil War, newspapers attracted readers with human interest stories and investigative articles that exposed the scandals and injustices of contemporary society. The new style of journalism filled a pressing need as city residents tried to make sense of the bewildering events around them. Ambitious publishers, such as Joseph Pulitzer, who acquired the *New York World* in 1883, and William Randolph Hearst, who purchased the *San Francisco Call* in 1887, were eager to tap into the growing urban market.

Newspapers expanded coverage of urban affairs, increased in size, and added special features. Papers adopted a new format, with separate sections for sports, financial news, book notices, and theater reviews. Publishers also tried to reach out to non–English-speaking immigrants by publishing cartoons and comic strips. Since advertisers believed women exercised control over family income, newspapers scrambled to attract female readers. The *World* added stories on fashion and etiquette, along with advice on attaining beauty. In 1883 the paper expanded its coverage to include "advice letters" on family issues. At the end of the decade, the *Philadelphia Inquirer* devoted a section of its Sunday edition to "women's topics," which included a series on "The Art of Dressing." Readers seemed to enjoy the changes. In 1840 readers could choose from 138 daily and 1,141 weekly newspapers in the United States. By 1900, publishers were turning out 2,190 dailies and more than 15,813 weeklies. The United States published more newspapers than the rest of the world combined.

In addition to the changes in mass-circulation newspapers, many immigrant communities issued their own foreign-language papers, which allowed newcomers to adjust to life in America while simultaneously asserting their cultural autonomy. By 1917, there were 1,323 foreign-language newspapers in the United States, including 522 in German, 103 in Italian, 84 in Spanish, and 17 in Japanese. The Yiddish-language *Jewish Daily Forward* was the most popular immigrant newspaper in the country, selling 175,000 copies daily.

Literature and the Arts

The new social environment of an industrialized society influenced artistic developments in America. In contrast to the midcentury artists and writers who had celebrated a romanticized view of America's landscape and people, late-century works highlighted the darker aspects of American life. "Let fiction cease to lie about life," William Dean Howells wrote; "let it portray men and women as they are." Howells applied this new realism in a number of works, including his popular novels *The Rise of Silas Lapham* (1885) and *A Hazard of New Fortunes* (1890), both of which deal with characters forced to contend with the corrupting influences of money and power.

Mark Twain, the pen name of Samuel Langhorne Clemens, gave a distinctive and very American style to realism in fiction. The first major American author to be born west of the Mississippi, Clemens added local color to his writings by drawing on his experiences as a river pilot and a newspaper reporter in the Mississippi Valley region. His most famous book, *The Adventures of Huckleberry Finn*, provided a critical examination of the existing social order in America. Floating down the Mississippi on a raft, Huck and his black friend Jim try to outrun what Twain contemptuously called "sivilization": a society filled with corruption, petty materialism, and hypocrisy. After witnessing a mob tar and feather a local con man, Huck concluded, "It was enough to make a body ashamed of the human race. . . . I never seen anything so disgusting."

Other writers, deeply influenced by Social Darwinism, developed a style of literary naturalism. Like the realists, these writers preached fidelity to the details of contemporary life, but they informed their novels with a tone of pessimistic determinism. Writers such as Frank Norris, Theodore Dreiser, and Stephen Crane viewed life as a relentless struggle in which powerful social forces determined an individual's fate. In *The Octopus* (1901) Norris wrote about a predatory railroad that destroyed wheat growers in the nation's heartland. Dreiser's powerful novel *Sister Carrie* (1900) traces the downward journey of an innocent country girl who, corrupted by urban pleasures, becomes a prostitute.

The same fascination with urban realism influenced artists who tried to capture the frenetic pace of city life. The key figure in this new artistic realism was Robert Henri, who used his position as head of the Pennsylvania Academy of Fine Arts to train an entire generation of artists, later to be dubbed the Ashcan school. Henri believed that artists had an obligation to capture the harsh reality of modern life. Heeding Henri's call for "making pictures from life," his students searched for authenticity in everyday events and people. George Luks used the backdrop of crowded tenements and shops on New York's Lower East Side for his depiction of *Hester Street* (1905). George Bellows celebrated the raw energy of urban life in *Cliff Dwellers* (1913), a depiction of slum life in crowded Manhattan.

Challenging Domesticity

The growing independence of middle-class women was one of the most noticeable expressions of the new urban culture. The nineteenth-century "cult of domesticity" stressed that a woman's proper place was in the home, where she provided for the moral, spiritual, and physical well-being of her family. During the last half of the nineteenth century, a number of changes provided American women with the opportunity to challenge traditional notions of gender roles.

Many women tried to redefine their relationship with men. In 1800 the average white woman had seven children; by 1900, the figure had fallen to less than four. The reduced birthrate resulted from women beginning to attain control over their sex lives. "Woman must have the courage to assert the right to her own body as the instrument of reason and conscience," observed feminist Lucinda Chandler. Another very tangible indicator of women's changing relationship to men was the substantial rise in the divorce rate between 1880 and 1900. In 1880 one in every twenty-one marriages ended in divorce. By 1900, the rate had climbed to one in twelve.

Since they spent less time caring for children, middle-class white women had more options to receive an education, seek professional employment, or join same-sex organizations. Between 1870 and 1900, eighteen thousand women received college degrees. Nationally, the percentage of colleges admitting women jumped from 30 percent to 71 percent. A number of all-women's colleges opened their doors—Vassar, Bryn Mawr, Smith, and Wellesley—to name four. At these schools, noted the president of Bryn Mawr, "everything exists for women students and is theirs by right not by favor." Education gave many women the self-confidence to break with the Victorian ideal of passive womanhood and allowed them to make gains in the professions. In 1890 women made up only 17 percent of the work force, but they held 36 percent of all "professional" positions. However, traditional male professions such as law, medicine, and the ministry resisted woman entrants, and colleges steered women toward a handful of occupations, such as teaching, nursing, library science, and social work.

Career women argued that their maternal skills and sensibilities made them especially well-suited for addressing certain important public issues—schooling the young, tending to the poor, and improving the health of women and children. "The home does not stop at the street door," noted the dean of women at the University of Chicago in 1911. "It is as wide as the world into which the individual steps forth. The determination of the character of that world and the preservation of those interests which she has safeguarded in the home, constitute the real duty resting upon women."

Educated, middle-class white women created female-dominated institutions that provided a base for mutual support, allowing women to learn from one another and work toward common goals. The women's club movement began in 1868 with the formation of Sorosis, established by journalists and other career women. The club described itself as "an order which shall render the female sex helpful to each other and actively benevolent in the world." By 1892, the General Federation of Women's Clubs, an umbrella organization established that year, boasted 495 affiliates and a hundred thousand members. By 1900, women's clubs' rosters had swelled to 160,000. One woman writer declared: "We have art clubs, book clubs, dramatic clubs, poetry clubs. We have sewing circles, philanthropic organizations, scientific, literary, religious, athletic, musical, and decorative art societies." Devoted

Nannie Helen Burroughs   Nannie Burroughs, holding the banner, exemplified the reformist spirit of her age as an activist for women and African-Americans. Burroughs founded the Women's Industrial Club and was the first president of the National Training School for Women and Girls in Washington, D.C. Both organizations sought to educate young women in the domestic sciences and in technical skills. She also supported efforts to encourage racial pride and black history, advocated equal rights for women, and cofounded the Women's Convention, an auxiliary of the National Baptist Convention, U.S.A., sponsor of this picture.   *(Library of Congress.)*

to "self-culture," women's clubs often read and reported on "great literature" and organized cultural events. In their own way, they were important training grounds for public activity. Club women learned to speak in public, to prepare and present reports, to raise and manage money.

African-American women, barred from participation in the white clubs, formed their own associations. Like their white counterparts, members ran day nurseries, reading programs, and welfare projects, but they also concerned themselves with race-specific issues such as antilynching campaigns. Josephine Ruffin, who formed Boston's New Era Club for black women, described her mission as "the moral education of the race with which we are identified." She set out to improve "home training" of children, provide racial leadership, and demonstrate that black women could forge "an army of organized women for purity and mental worth."

Victorian constraints on women were further loosened at the end of the century when a bicycling vogue swept urban America. Men and women joined in the craze and were pedaling over 10 million bicycles by 1900. To ride a bike, women had to wear divided skirts and simple undergarments. Over time, the bicycle contributed to a new image of women as physically active and independent. The "Gibson Girl," the creation of magazine illustrator Dana Gibson, became the popular icon of the new woman. Pictures showed the self-sufficient Gibson Girl relishing her freedom, playing tennis, swinging a golf club, or riding a bicycle.

 ## The Persistence of Piety

The new urban culture seemed threatening to many middle-class Protestant Americans, who feared the erosion of their traditional values. Many members of the American middle class, their ranks expanded by the growing number of salaried employees working in new industrial clerical and management positions, organized to defend the dominant values rooted in the nation's rural past. Reformers preached about the need for cultural refinement, created private societies, and tried to convert urban residents to Protestantism. When persuasion and preaching failed, they turned to coercion. They enacted obscenity laws, banned entertainment on Sundays, and boarded up saloons. But while some focused on such reformist experiments, other Americans, fearful of the waves of poor foreigners washing up on America's shores, fought to limit immigration.

Defending "American" Culture

Most of the cultural and political battles of the late nineteenth century pitted native-born Protestant values against the culture of the immigrant city. Often, native-born white Americans viewed the urban masses in menacing terms. City residents, a New Jersey educator declared in 1879, knew "little, or positively nothing . . . of moral duties, or of any higher pleasures than beer-drinking and spirit-drinking, and the grossest sensual indulgence. . . . [T]hey eat, drink, breed, work, and die."

White Protestants frequently expressed fear that millions of foreigners would dilute the native American racial stock. "It is scarcely probable that by taking the dregs of Europe," social scientist Richard Mayo Smith wrote in 1890, "we shall produce a people of high social intelligence and morality." Newspaper editorials assailed the "invasion of venomous reptiles" and "long-haired, wild-eyed, bad-smelling, atheistic, reckless foreign wretches, who never did an honest hour's work in their lives." Others saw immigrants as direct threats to their jobs.

No one articulated the nativist position more forcefully than the Reverend Josiah Strong (see Competing Voices, page 761). In his popular and influential book, *Our Country: Its Possible Future and Its Present Crisis* (1885), Strong stated flatly that "the typical immigrant is a European peasant, whose horizon has been narrow, whose moral and religious training has been meager or false, and whose ideas of life are low." Immigration, he added, "not only furnishes the greater portion of our criminals, it is also seriously affecting the morals of the native population." In ominous tones Strong concluded that "immigration complicates our moral and political problems by swelling our dangerous classes."

Many people worried that immigrant women would have more children than native-born Protestants, allowing "the ignorant, the low-lived and the alien" to take over the country by sheer numbers. To encourage population growth among the American-born, reformers opposed birth control and divorce. Between 1860 and 1890, forty states and territories enacted anti-abortion statutes. At the same time, they tightened divorce statutes to discourage marital separation. In most states, divorce laws were rewritten around the concept of "fault" or moral wrongdoing. To obtain a divorce, it had to be shown that one party had transgressed seriously against the other.

The middle-class reaction to the new urban culture took many forms. On one front, prominent spokesmen tried to instill a code of manners that would model respectable values. Good manners, including proper etiquette in all social occasions, especially dining and entertaining, became an important badge of status. Americans published more than 150 etiquette manuals between 1830 and 1910. Etiquette writers taught Americans who wished to be respectable and successful how to observe the dictates of decorum, including frequent bathing and conventional grooming. They expressed a persistent concern with instituting an American code of manners that would tame the excesses of democracy. "Brutes feed. The best barbarian only eats. Only the cultured man can dine."

On a larger scale, reformers founded museums, art galleries, libraries, and other institutions designed to inculcate appreciation for the respectable arts. In the 1870s, New York, Boston, Chicago, and Philadelphia constructed museums of fine arts. In the 1890s, workers completed construction of the Boston Public Library, the New York Public Library, and the Library of Congress. By 1900, more than 9,000 public libraries enlightened the country.

A broader effect on urban geography came from public parks built to serve as a green oasis in the midst of the city, where urban dwellers could escape to a more natural, more "American" landscape. The rise of the city represented a profound crisis in American life. It challenged the deeply ingrained Jeffersonian vision of independent farmers living on and occupying the land. "The life of great cities," Henry George warned in 1898, "is not the natural life of man." To remedy the problem, architects such as Frederick Law Olmsted envisioned large public parks as a way to bring rural beauty to the modern city, to create a psychological sense of freedom, and to provide moral uplift to urban life. In the 1850s, Olmstead helped design New York's Central Park, the first major public park in the United States. "No one who has closely observed the conduct of the people who visit [Central] Park," Olmsted declared in 1870, "can doubt that it exercises a distinctly harmonizing and refining influence upon the most unfortunate and most lawless classes of the city,—an influence favorable to courtesy, self-control, and temperance." By 1870, as many as one hundred thousand people visited the park daily.

Looking inward as well as outward, middle-class spokesmen organized private meeting places to escape the pressures of everyday life and reinvigorate their faith. In 1874 John Vincent, a Methodist clergyman, and Lewis Miller, an Ohio businessman, started a summer program at Lake Chautauqua in New York's scenic Allegheny Mountains to train Sunday School teachers. The Chautauqua Literary and Scientific Circle promoted "habits of reading and study in nature, art, science, and in secular and sacred literature, in connection with the routine of daily life." In addition to instruction, the assembly offered recreation on the lake and lectures on topics other than religious themes. Chautauqua grew to be one of Victorian America's most popular middle-class resorts. By the 1890s, more than two hundred thousand people participated in similar programs organized around the country.

Finally, American Protestants engaged in an aggressive campaign to recruit new members. The swelling numbers of Catholics and Jews in the nation's cities convinced many church leaders of the need to extend their influence in urban areas. A number of Protestant denominations founded missions, which combined lively preaching with charity work. The Salvation Army, founded in England by Methodist minister William Booth and established in New York in 1880, proved the most successful of the Protestant initiatives to reach the urban masses. By 1900, the Salvation Army claimed seven hundred branches in cities across the United States. Another familiar technique for reaching urban residents was the revival. In 1875 Dwight L. Moody conducted highly publicized Protestant revivals in Brooklyn, Philadelphia, New York, Chicago, and other cities. With financial support from wealthy supporters, and a mesmerizing speaking style, Moody drew thousands of middle-class followers to his rallies, where he preached the "three R's" of the gospel: "Ruin by sin, Redemption by Christ, and Regeneration by the Holy Ghost." The efforts of Protestant preachers produced a dramatic increase in church membership—from 4.5 million in 1860 to 12.5 million in 1890.

Not all Protestant reformers chose to work through the church. Many middle-class Americans turned to the charity organization movement, an ostensibly "secular" initiative designed to improve the "moral character" of urban residents. Participants in the charity movement believed that poverty and vice resulted from individual failing, not from a lack of opportunity. "Misery and suffering," chided an organization handbook, "are the inevitable results of idleness, filth, and vice." In most cases, poverty's roots lay in "the characters of the poor themselves." The solution called for "the moral elevation of the poor." The key, argued a movement leader, was to promote "the personal intercourse of the wealthier citizens with the poor at the homes," by sending a "friendly visitor"—usually a middle-class woman—to meet with slum families each week. The visitor's purpose was to use "the moral support of true friendship" to embed in the poor a "new desire to live rightly."

The Purity Crusades

Initially, then, reformers established clubs and agencies to help immigrants adopt middle-class values of temperance and domesticity. Voluntary efforts, however, soon evolved into legislative coercion. The purity movement, which included Protestant clergy, former abolitionists, and women's rights activists, launched an assault on the vice districts common to cities, which they viewed as seedbeds for prostitution. They pressured city officials to form special commissions to investigate the vice problem. A Chicago commission called prostitution "the greatest curse which today rests upon mankind." By 1913, city police had shut down the entire red-light districts in forty-seven cities. Suppression, noted a Minneapolis reformer, represented "the only sane and safe method of correcting the depraved passions of the human heart."

By the mid-1880s, the attack on prostitution had evolved into a broad crusade for social purity. Reformers took aim at the many manifestations of urban culture—vaudeville, theaters, college football, dance halls, and amusement parks. One reformer who visited a dance hall later reported with alarm, "I saw one of the women smoking cigarettes, most of the younger couples were hugging and kissing, [and] there was a general mingling of men and women at the different tables." Many American cities and towns passed ordinances that promoted religious observations on Sunday by banning all business activities. Between 1886 and 1895, the social purity campaign succeeded in raising the age of consent for sex from as low as ten years in some states to between fourteen and eighteen in twenty-nine states.

Many reformers believed that any attempt to purify the social environment required the legal suppression of unwholesome influences. Anthony Comstock, the founder of the New York Society for the Suppression of Vice, emerged as the most powerful spokesman for censorship. In 1873 he wrote and helped steer through Congress the so-called Comstock Law, which banned from the mails any matter "designed to incite lust." As special agent to the postmaster general, he saw to it that the law was rigorously enforced and was quick to halt distribution of any publication containing advertisements for contraceptives. In a single decade, Comstock confiscated an estimated fourteen tons of books and about one and a half million circulars, poems, and pictures.

No reform, however, attracted more middle-class support than the assault on that bastion of male working-class culture, the saloon. Reformers had long been concerned with temperance, but before the Civil War they had attacked drinking primarily as an individual rather than a social problem. Most of their activities focused on reforming individual drinkers, not on eliminating alcohol altogether through institutional change. By 1870, however, Protestant middle-class women, working through the Women's Christian Temperance Union (1874) and the Anti-Saloon League (1895), organized a national crusade against alcohol, which culminated in the 1920s with passage of a constitutional amendment banning the sale of alcohol.

All efforts to "improve" or "better" urban residents and their culture reflected opposition to immigrants and their cultural and religious practices. Many Americans, however, felt the answer rested not in reforming immigrants, but in restricting their numbers and their rights. Private groups opposed to immigrants often took direct action against them. The American Protection Association (APA), a secret organization founded in 1887, led the anti-immigrant campaign. The APA attracted support from workers threatened by competition from Irish laborers, and from native-born Americans worried about Catholic conspiracies. Its members pledged "to strike the shackles and chains of blind obedience to the Roman Catholic church from the hampered and bound consciences of a priest-ridden and church-oppressed people." The APA intimidated Catholic political candidates with hints of violence. In 1894 a group of Boston patricians formed the Immigration Restriction League, a tenacious political lobbying group that advocated literacy tests for all immigrants in an effort to drastically limit the number allowed into the country.

The Chinese suffered the sharpest nativist attacks. Starting in the 1850s, businessmen lured thousands of Chinese to fill jobs in western mines and railroad construction, and by 1880, more than 75,000 Chinese lived in California, making up about 9 percent of the state's population. As nonwhites and non-Christians, Chinese immigrants frightened Americans. Steadily growing discrimination and prosecution culminated in the Chinese Exclusion Act of 1882, by which Congress suspended Chinese immigration (see page 681).

Public Education

By 1890, most cities and states with large immigrant populations mandated compulsory schooling between certain ages (usually eight to fourteen). As a result, attendance in public schools increased from 6.9 million in 1870 to 17.8 million in 1910, and the number of public schools mushroomed from five hundred to ten thousand. Many cities created kindergarten programs for preschool children and expanded high school from three to four years. City schools also initiated night school programs to help older immigrants learn English and vocational skills. By 1900, nearly a dozen states required schools to provide students with free textbooks.

Supporters argued that public schools would help immigrants to abandon old ways and assimilate into American society. The superintendent of New York's system claimed that a school should be "a melting pot which converts the children of the immigrants of all races and languages into sturdy, independent American citizens." In 1903 a writer noted that kindergartens presented the "earliest opportunity to catch the little Russian, the little Italian, the little German, Pole, Syrian, and the rest and begin to make good American citizens of them." Along with Americanizing the immigrants, advocates of public education saw schools as a vehicle for maintaining social order. In addition to the traditional curriculum, students learned about the value of good citizenship, patriotism, and respect for authority.

Immigrant communities usually embraced the opportunity to receive free education. In 1914 nearly all elementary-age Jewish children in New York City attended public schools. Families often chose to violate compulsory attendance laws, however, because they depended on the earnings of their school-aged children. In New York, fewer than 33 percent of German children and only 25 percent of Italians attended high school, compared with 60 percent of native-born white children. In Chicago less than 10 percent of Italian and Polish children advanced beyond the sixth grade in 1910.

Many immigrants, worried that public schools threatened their cultural traditions or their religious values, established private or church schools or pressured public officials to offer special classes. By 1900, nearly a million children were attending

Americanization Class As immigration to the United States rose, various sectors of the American population called for better public schools. Education would provide immigrants with the skills needed to improve their conditions, and teachers could use the opportunity to promote American history, culture, and values. Educators worked just as diligently on adult studies as they did on the schooling of children. Day and night classes, like this one, brought various nationalities together for the purpose of learning the English language and deciphering the complexities of America's governmental structure. *(Library of Congress.)*

Catholic elementary schools. In cities with large Catholic populations, between 20 and 40 percent of school-age children were enrolled in parochial schools. By 1914, California's Japanese community had established thirty-one schools to teach the Japanese language. German immigrants took a different approach, pressuring public schools themselves to teach German. By 1900, nearly 25 percent of public high school students in the United States studied German. School districts in St. Louis and Buffalo, both with large German populations, offered bilingual instruction in German and English.

The increasing numbers of Americans attending secondary school produced greater demand for higher education. In 1862 Congress passed the Morrill Act, which provided generous federal grants to the states for the establishment of colleges to teach "agriculture and the mechanic arts." By the end of the century, all but a handful of states had founded land-grant colleges. At the same time, large donations from wealthy industrialists led to the creation of Vanderbilt (1873), Johns Hopkins at Baltimore (1876), Drexel Institute at Philadelphia (1891), and Stanford (1893). In 1892 John D. Rockefeller revived the faltering University of Chicago with a $34 million gift. By 1900, five hundred colleges and universities served 232,000 undergraduates and 5,700 graduate students.

Leading universities experimented with curriculum changes, adding new subjects such as economics, political science, and modern languages to the standard offering of Latin, Greek, mathematics, rhetoric, and theology. Private and public universities created graduate programs in numerous scholarly disciplines and added professional schools in medicine, law, architecture, engineering, business, and education. While academic quality and standards varied greatly, a British observer noted approvingly in 1888 that the United States possessed "not less than fifteen and perhaps even twenty seats of learning fit to be ranked beside the universities of Germany, France and England."

CONCLUSION

In the last quarter of the nineteenth century, millions of migrants from Europe, and from rural areas in the North and South, transformed American cities. The diversity of newcomers and their experiments in adaptation contributed to the multicultural flavor of urban life. In an effort to maintain an older sense of community, they formed ethnic enclaves and created a variety of support institutions and associations. Cities became collections of distinct neighborhoods, each with its own dialect, cuisine, and religious institutions. In most cities the demands for public services—decent housing, clean water, sanitation, fire protection—overwhelmed local officials. Human and animal waste, polluted water, epidemics, destructive fires, high crime rates, and incessant noise became standard features of the new urban environment. When established institutions failed to address their needs, many immigrants turned to representatives of powerful local political machines such as Boss Tweed's Tammany Hall in New York.

While immigrants transformed the city's environment, a revolution in transportation helped recast the urban landscape. A series of advances in mass transit, beginning with the horse-drawn omnibus and culminating with the electric street trolley, expanded the distance that people could live from the city center and still commute to work. As people spread out from the city core, urban space became more specialized and more segregated. The downtown emerged as a center for shopping and business, the city's wealthiest citizens clustered in one neighborhood, the poor and working class in another, and the middle class began moving to the suburbs.

Ironically, while mass transit was pushing city residents apart, a new urban culture was pulling them together. Public amusements—vaudeville shows, theater performances, and amusement parks—created a social environment in which the city's diverse population could share a common experience. City dwellers embraced spectator sports and came together in huge numbers to watch basketball, football, and baseball. The new "public" culture was for whites only, however. African-Americans were barred from participation in major sporting events and forced to enter vaudeville houses through the back door. In an effort to reach the mass of city residents, newspapers expanded their coverage of local affairs and included special features to attract readers. Writers and artists, often using the city as a backdrop, developed new methods and styles to capture the harsh reality of industrializing America. Middle-class women challenged older notions of domesticity and gained more control over their sex lives. Increasing numbers attended college and entered professions such as teaching, nursing, and social work.

Not everyone welcomed the changes swirling around them. Many middle-class Protestants feared that immigrants were intellectually and morally inferior to native-born white Americans and viewed cities as breeding grounds for vice, corruption, and poverty. Protestant reformers tried to uplift the new urban culture by teaching cultural refinement and by building libraries, museums, and public parks. Church members organized rallies to convert the largely Catholic and Jewish newcomers, while "secular" reformers embraced charity work. When persuasion failed, reformers resorted to coercion, using state power to forbid prostitution, censor sexually explicit materials, and ban alcohol. Some private nativist groups took direct action to limit immigrants' political rights and lobbied for immigration restriction. Many states adopted mandatory school attendance laws, hoping that public education could hasten the assimilation process.

The emotional cultural debates pitting native-born Protestants against immigrants dashed the expectations of Americans who hoped for a peaceful period of unity following the Civil War. Americans who looked to their political leaders for experiments to address the pressing problems of industrialism or to ameliorate the intense social conflicts were sorely disappointed.

SUGGESTED READINGS

Several surveys on urban history trace the growth of American cities in the late nineteenth century, as seen in Raymond A. Mohl's *The New City: Urban America in the Industrial Age, 1860–1920* (1985). Other books, including Howard P. Chudacoff's *The Evolution of American*

Urban Society (rev. ed., 1994) and Eric H. Monkkonen's *America Becomes Urban* (1988), examine the transformation of American cities from their early formation in the colonial period to the modern day, emphasizing the dynamic mobility of people and the impact of changing government services and transportation on the urban community. In *The Other Bostonians: Poverty and Progress in the American Metropolis, 1880–1970* (1973), Stephan Thernstrom studies the persistent mobility of Boston's residents as each generation slowly bettered its socioeconomic situation. Howard P. Chudacoff explores urban mobility in *Mobile Americans: Residential and Social Mobility in Omaha, 1880–1920* (1972) and the development of the urban bachelor life in *The Age of the Bachelor* (1999).

Migrants from rural parts of the United States included an increasing number of southern blacks in the late nineteenth century. William H. Harris's *The Harder We Run* (1982) analyzes the racism African-Americans faced in northern industries and their efforts to adapt to an urban way of life. In *Black Migration and Poverty* (1979), Elizabeth Pleck discusses the limited opportunities open to African-Americans in Boston during the late nineteenth century and the subsequent impact on black families, religion, politics, and the community as a whole. James Borchert's *Alley Life in Washington* (1980) examines the black community and argues there was far more stability and continuity in the lives of these urban dwellers than has been previously assumed.

Numerous historians have focused their attention on the rising flood of immigrants into American cities—for example, Ala M. Kraut in *The Huddled Masses* (1982). Walter T. K. Nugent's *Crossings: The Great Transatlantic Migrations* (1992) analyzes the reasons people decided to leave Europe, focusing on the growing populations and declining opportunities in their homelands. *The Transplanted* (1985) by John Bodnar describes how immigrants adapted to their new surroundings in American cities and attempted to maintain control of their lives.

Many more historians narrow their work to include only certain groups of immigrants. Josef F. Barton's *Peasants and Strangers* (1975) compares the adjustments made to life in Cleveland by the city's Italian, Rumanian, and Slovak population. In *The World of Our Fathers* (1976), Irving Howe tells the story of eastern European Jews who migrated to the United States and the culture they brought with them. Placing the Italian experience in Chicago into a larger context of urbanization, Humbert S. Nelli's *Italians in Chicago* (1970) describes the desire for better living conditions and the impact of ethnic divisions between northern and southern Italians. Ronald Takaki's *Strangers From a Different Shore* (1989) investigates the adaptations of Asian migrants to life in the United States and their unique and varied reactions to discrimination. Essays compiled by Sucheng Chan in *Entry Denied* (1991) look at the racial tension Chinese immigrants encountered and the ways in which these new migrants handled social and legal exclusion.

The nativist backlash to immigration is best analyzed in an older work by John Higham. *Strangers in the Land* (1955) attempts to explain the political, social, economic, and institutional pressures that influenced nativists and their opinions concerning new immigrants. David Ward's *Poverty, Ethnicity, and the American City* (1989) analyzes native-born Americans' fear of immigrants and the application of scientific principles to combat what they perceived as the immorality of these ethnic groups. Leonard Dinnerstein and David M. Reimers examine the impact of nativist pressure on the deterioration of immigrants' native heritage in *Ethnic Americans* (1982).

A number of works describe the expansion of the city and the impact of the transportation revolution on an urban population. The evolution of transportation in the nineteenth century, as evidenced in the changes to public transportation in New York, Boston, and Philadelphia, is recorded in Charles W. Cheape's *Moving the Masses* (1980). From the horse car to the subway, Cheape traces developments in technology, management techniques, and government regulation. The improvements in transportation influenced residential patterns and the decentralization of the city, as depicted in Kenneth T. Jackson's *Crabgrass Frontier* (1985).

The problems facing the urban environment and the responses of city residents have caught the attention of recent historians. Eric H. Monkkonen's *Police in Urban America* (1981) covers the history of America's police force from the adoption of uniformed agencies to the establishment of well-defined crime control and adversarial tactics. Alan M. Kraut's *Silent Travelers: Germs, Genes, and the "Immigrant Menace"* (1994) examines Americans' fear of diseases brought by foreigners and the innovations made in public health care and government initiative to stave off this threat. Health concerns and the desire to better conditions for all residents led to the emergence of sanitary engineers, as described in Martin V. Melosi's *Garbage in the Cities* (1981). Stanley K. Schultz's *Constructing Urban Culture* (1989) discusses the work of not only sanitary engineers, but judges, architects, and novelists whose ideas concerning better urban living sparked the rise of city planning.

A general study of city politics is a work edited by Alexander B. Callow, *The City Boss in America* (1976). An interesting study of five big city bosses is John M. Allswang's *Bosses, Machines, and Urban Voters* (rev. ed., 1986). Allswang finds that key to the longevity of these five political machines was their ability to gain, and maintain, a broad base of electoral support. Despite the corruption in urban politics, Jon C. Teaford argues in *The Unheralded Triumph* (1984) that city governments provided numerous benefits through public services, if only to those who could afford them.

The rise in urban entertainment and its connection to the working class are the focus of several works. Kathy Peiss's *Cheap Amusements* (1986) looks at working women's attempts to escape from domestic restraints through the dance halls, parks, and clubs they visited. The voice of the working class could also be found in vaudeville shows, as described by Robert V. Snyder in *The Voice of the City: Vaudeville and Popular Culture in New York City* (1989). Class struggle is evident in Roy Rosenzweig's *Eight Hours for What We Will* (1983), in which he examines the ethnic, reform, and commercial forces that shaped working-class leisure activities. Despite class tensions portrayed in other works, Gunther P. Barth finds that some city institutions promoted commonalities among all citizens in *City People: The Rise of Modern City Culture in Nineteenth Century America* (1980).

The emergence of professional and collegiate sports in the late nineteenth century is well documented. Stephan A. Riess's *City Games* (1989) examines the relationship between the rise of the modern city and the growth of modern sports. A broader survey of the history of sports in America, from pre-Columbian games to modern athletic events, is Allen Guttmann's *A Whole New Ball Game* (1988). The adaptation of professional sports to the college model and the role of Harvard and Yale in setting the pace of collegiate sports are examined in Ronald A. Smith's *Sports and Freedom* (1988).

The changing image of women and the rising independence of the New Woman are the themes of Martha Banta's *Imaging American Women* (1987), which studies the ideals society imposed on women and how changes in those ideals reflected changing times. Sheila M. Rothman's *Woman's Proper Place* (1978) describes the changes in technology and education that helped alter women's activities and social roles. Linda W. Rosenzweig's *The Anchor of My Life* (1993) explores the relationship between Victorian mothers and their New Women daughters and the generational tensions created by shifting images of womanhood.

The attempt of upper-class reformers to control the lives of all city residents in order to quell their own fears of social and moral disorder is the subject of Paul Boyer's *Urban Masses and Moral Order in America* (1978). John F. Kasson's *Rudeness and Civility* (1990) looks at the evolution of manners as the cruder colonial times gave way to structured rules of behavior and dress. In *The New Urban Landscape* (1986), David Schuyler describes the upper classes' vision of a more pastoral urban environment and their application of professional planning to upgrade the city.

Efforts to reform society's working class by controlling their social and sexual behavior are the focus of David J. Pivar's *Purity Crusade* (1973). Nicola Kay Beisel's *Imperiled Innocents: Anthony Comstock and Family Reproduction in Victorian America* (1997) looks at Comstock's work as part of larger effort of upper classes not only to impose their beliefs on others, but also to improve socioeconomic opportunities for their children. The work of women in these moral reform movements and their growing desire for the vote as a means to social control are the subjects of Lori Ginzberg's *Women and the Work of Benevolence* (1991).

The education of native-born and foreign-born city dwellers is the subject of several works, such as David B. Tyack's *The One Best System* (1974), which looks at the power relationships and ethnic blocs that lay at the heart of urban education. Lawrence A. Cremin's *American Education: The Metropolitan Experience* (1988) looks at education as a variety of institutions, from schools to cinemas, transmitting knowledge, values, attitudes, and skills to the young. As societal values teetered between egalitarianism and social hierarchy in the late nineteenth century, so did the education received by urban youths, according to David Nasaw in *Schooled to Order* (1979). The higher education of the upper class produced our modern emphasis on professionalism, as seen in Burton J. Bledstein's *The Culture of Professionalism: The Middle Class and the Development of Higher Education in America* (1976).

The Threat of the City

Josiah Strong Warns of the City's Dangers

For many Americans, urbanization was a terrifying process. Josiah Strong, an Ohio minister and reformer, was one such anxious American. This selection from Strong's best-selling book, *Our Country: Its Possible Future and Present Crisis* (1885), describes a dramatic confrontation between city and country. The future of America, he believes, rides on the outcome of the battle.

The city has become a serious menace to our civilization. . . . It has a peculiar attraction for the immigrant. . . . While a little less than one-third of the population of the United States is foreign by birth or parentage, sixty-two per cent of the population of Cincinnati are foreign, eighty-three per cent of Cleveland, sixty-three per cent of Boston, eighty-eight per cent of New York, and ninety-one per cent of Chicago.

Because our cities are so largely foreign, Romanism finds in them its chief strength.

For the same reason the saloon, together with the intemperance and the liquor power it represents, is multiplied in the city. . . . Of course the demoralizing and pauperizing power of the saloons and their debauching influence in politics increase with their numerical strength.

. . . The rich are richer, and the poor are poorer, in the city than elsewhere; and, as a rule, the greater the city, the greater are the riches of the rich and the poverty of the poor. . . .

Socialism not only centers in the city, but is almost confined to it; and the materials of its growth are multiplied with the growth of the city. Here is heaped social dynamite; here . . . lawless and desperate men or all sorts congregate; . . . here gather foreigners and wage-workers; here skepticism and irreligion abound; here inequality is the greatest and most obvious . . . ; here is suffering the sorest. . . . Under such conditions smolder the volcanic fires of a deep discontent. . . .

Do we find conservative forces of society equally numerous and strong? . . . The city, where the forces of evil are massed, and where the need of Christian influence is peculiarly great, is from one-third to one-fifth as well supplied with churches as the nation at large. . . .

What of city government? . . . As a rule, our largest cities are the worst governed. It is natural, therefore, to infer that, as our cities grow larger and more dangerous, the government will become more corrupt, and control will pass more completely into the hands of those who themselves most need to be controlled. . . .

As civilization advances, and society becomes more highly organized, commercial transactions will be more complex and immense. As a result, all business relations and industries will be more sensitive. Commercial distress in any great business center will the more surely create widespread disaster. . . . When such a commercial crisis has closed the factories by the ten thousand, and wage-workers have been thrown out of employment by the million; when the public lands, which hitherto at such times have afforded relief, are all exhausted; when our urban population has been multiplied several fold; . . . when class antipathies are deepened; when socialistic organizations, armed and drilled, are in every city . . . ; when the corruption of city governments is grown apace; when crops fail . . . ; . . . THEN will come the real test of our institutions, then will appear whether we are capable of self-government.

F. J. Kingsbury Defends the City

Critics denounced the city for its myriad problems and its apparent assault on traditional, rural-based values. But not everyone was frightened by its rise. Kingsbury, the president of the American Social Science Association, gave this address in 1895 in which he views steady urbanization as inevitable. Although he was under no illusions about the down side of city life, he also was confident that the city could enrich American culture.

. . . Aside from all the questions of mutual defence and protection and mutual helpfulness in various ways, and industrial convenience, doubtless one of the very strongest forces in the building of the city is the human instinct of gregariousness. . . . There is always a craving to get where there are more people. . . . Poor food, and little of it, dirt and discomfort, heat and cold, —all count as nothing in competition with this passion of gregariousness and desire for human society. . . .

Doubtless one of the most potent forces in the modern growth of the cities has been the immense improvement in the facilities for travel. . . . Facilities for travel make it as easy to get from city to country as from country to city; but the tide, except for temporary purposes, all sets one way. . . .

All modern industrial life tends to concentration as a matter of economy. It has long been remarked that the best place to establish or carry on . . . business is where that business is already being done. For that reason we see different kinds of manufactures grouping themselves together. . . . Then every kind of business is partly dependent on several other kinds. . . . Where there is a large business of any kind, . . . subsidiary trades that are supported by it naturally flock around it; whereas in an isolated situation the central establishment must support all these trades itself or go a considerable distance when it needs their assistance. Fifty or sixty years ago small manufacturing establishments in isolated situations and on small streams were scattered all through the Eastern States. The condition of trade at that time rendered this possible. Now they are almost wholly disappeared, driven out by economic necessity; and their successors are in the cities and large towns. . . .

Our great Civil War compelled us to find out some way in which to replace the productive power of a million men sent into the field and suddenly changed from producers to consumers. . . . A hundred thousand of these places . . . were filled by women; and the deficit left by the remainder of the million was supplied by newly invented machinery. . . . The result was that, when the war was over, a million men, or as many as came back, found their places filled. . . . In all rural occupations this was especially the case; and, being driven out of the country by want of work, they flocked to the city as the most likely place to find it. . . .

We must remember, too, that cities as places of human habitation have vastly improved within half a century. About fifty years ago neither New York nor Boston had public water, and very few of our cities had either water or gas, and horse railroads had not been thought of. When we stop to think what this really means in sanitary matters, it seems to me that the increase of cities is no longer a matter of surprise. . . .

In the years after the Civil War, America's cities exploded, some doubling and even tripling their populations. Along with this growth came concern over urbanization's influence on the American social order. The extremes of the city—great wealth and high culture next to abject poverty and vulgarity—prompted a vigorous debate over its merits. For everyone, the city was a symbol of a changing America. Within the debate over the city lay larger cultural issues concerning the definition of the American character. Rural Americans now had to compete with urbanites for cultural dominance. Their America was one of self-contained and self-centered small towns, filled with people who mostly shared the same religion (Protestant), ethnic background (white Anglo-Saxon), and—to some degree—social class (roughly middle class). Rural folk and their many urban middle-class soulmates held on to traditional American values, believing that government should be small, directed by the people, and uninvolved in their economic lives; that hard work was honorable and should produce something tangible that benefited society; that a man could ascend if he were industrious, thrifty, and temperate; and that America would be a prosperous and good nation only if its citizens remained virtuous and in charge of their own lives.

The city offered a competing version of American life, one that was multicultural, hedonistic, self-interested, and class-stratified. Instead of seeing rich cultural diversity, rural Americans knew only that urban immigrants held foreign values that threatened social stability. The great disparity of wealth also alarmed them: the poor challenged the view of America as the "land of opportunity," while the idle rich undermined the notion of productive, hard work, and thrift. Corrupt city governments abused democracy. But the most disturbing aspect of urban America was that it was gaining ground. Its culture, transported around the country, enticed small-town youth to see for themselves; its megabusinesses gobbled up small farms and stores. America was becoming the city writ large, and Americans steeped in rural tradition felt powerless to erase it.

Questions for Analysis

1. How does Josiah Strong feel about the city? What specifically disturbs him? Does he see any merits in the city?

2. What do his positions reveal about his own religious, ethnic, and class bias?

3. What are Strong's predictions for the future?

4. What is F. J. Kingsbury's attitude toward urbanization?

5. What reasons does he give for the growth of the city?

6. What advantages does Kingsbury see in city life and in the influences of the city on American culture?

20

State and Society, 1877–1900

*T*he twenty thousand people packed into the sweltering convention hall were restless. All were Democrats, gathered at the Chicago Coliseum, the largest exhibition building in the world, to select a candidate to lead them in the 1896 presidential campaign, and now eagerly awaiting the arrival of William Jennings Bryan. The delegates were a contentious group, deeply divided over national policy. Desperate farmers from the South and West favored an inflationary policy of "free silver," which would allow the use of plentiful silver for money. Conservative interests in the East wanted to assure business leaders by maintaining support for the gold standard.

At the young age of thirty-six, Bryan had already developed a reputation as the most powerful orator of his time. His magnetic voice and evangelical style earned him numerous titles: the "Nebraska Cyclone," "Knight of the West," the "Boy Orator of the Platte," and the "Silver-tongued Orator." Born in a small farming town in southern Illinois, Bryan moved to Lincoln, Nebraska, and won election to Congress in 1890. A tall, powerfully built man with a thick mane of black hair, Bryan viewed politics through a moral prism as a proving ground on which the forces of good and evil did battle. He possessed unbounded faith in the wisdom of common people, steadfastly opposed privilege and monopoly, and longed to return the nation to its Jeffersonian roots.

Bryan felt faint in the minutes before he ascended the podium, but once he took the stage, the jitters passed. For the next forty minutes he mesmerized the audience. "His wonderful voice filled the auditorium," recalled a delegate. The money issue "was not a contest between persons," Bryan said, but "a question of principle." It represented a clash between "the common people" and "the encroachments of organized wealth." Bryan posed the fundamental question of the campaign: "Upon which side will the Democratic party fight; upon the side of 'the idle holders of capital' or upon the side of 'the struggling masses'?" As his captive audience sat in stunned silence, Bryan moved to his dramatic close. In response to those who advocated a gold standard, Bryan vowed, "You shall not press down upon the brow of labor this crown of thorns, you shall not crucify mankind upon a cross of gold." To add dramatic effect to his metaphor, Bryan stretched out his arms and tilted his head as if he were hanging from a cross.

Bryan's speech electrified the convention hall. For nearly an hour, delegates carried him on their shoulders. Many supporters were so moved by Bryan's eloquence that they slumped in their seats and wept. One reporter called Bryan "a young David with his sling, who had come to slay the giants that oppressed the people." The following day delegates nominated Bryan for president.

The 1896 presidential campaign, which pitted Bryan against the Republican William McKinley, was one of the most exciting elections in American history. It also marked a turning point in American politics. The previous twenty years had been characterized by a stubborn stalemate that produced mediocre leaders and meager legislation. Fearful of offending potential voters, neither party strayed far from the political center. But in 1896, for the first time since the Civil War, serious issues divided the parties. A crippling economic depression combined with the rise of a powerful agrarian protest movement in the 1880s and 1890s, which provided the backbone of Bryan's campaign, upset the political balance and led many to demand new experiments in national politics. The Populists offered a compelling vision of government that contrasted sharply with prevailing views of either party. In nominating the controversial Bryan, the Democrats abandoned an incumbent president, Grover Cleveland, and embraced an inflationary monetary policy. In nominating McKinley and championing the conservative "gold standard," Republicans set up the election as a contest over national policy. The 1896 election would mark the end of the Gilded Age and its inconclusive national politics.

▌ What failings and limitations characterized the national government during the Gilded Age?

▌ What were the roots of the farmers' discontent?

▌ How did different groups of Americans view the crisis of the 1890s?

▌ What attitudes toward government were at odds in the 1896 election?

This chapter will address these questions.

 ## The Politics of Stalemate

In 1873 Mark Twain and Charles Dudley Warner created an enduring label for politics in post-Reconstruction America when they wrote a novel entitled *The Gilded Age*. Like the book's fictitious characters, American politicians during this period seemed more interested in gaining office than in addressing issues or experimenting to solve problems. Locked in political stalemate and reluctant to alienate potential voters in close elections, they nominated similar candidates and avoided controversial questions. During the Gilded Age, heated debates over tariffs, patronage, and money replaced the passionate clashes over slavery and states' rights of the Civil War era.

The Failure of Politics

The two decades following Reconstruction represent one of the least memorable periods in American political history. Between Lincoln and Theodore Roosevelt, the United States produced no memorable leaders. How often do we hear the name of a single president between 1877 and 1901? Southern writer Thomas Wolfe referred to the Gilded Age presidents as "the lost Americans: their gravely vacant and bewhiskered faces mixed, melted, swam together. . . . Which had the whiskers, which had the burnsides: which was which?"

Even contemporaries poked fun at the inferior and uninspiring efforts of men who occupied public life during these years. "The period," complained the Harvard historian Henry Adams, "was poor in purpose and barren in results." He went further, suggesting, "One might search the whole list of Congress, Judiciary, and Executive during the twenty-five years and find little but damaged reputations."

Why was the period so lackluster in political style and content? For one thing, Americans emerging from the turmoil of Civil War and Reconstruction had grown weary of the heated debates over emotional issues. Assaulted by the forces of industrialization, immigration, and urbanization, Americans searched for stability and order in their politics, not idealism and passion. But stability required politicians to avoid great issues and divisive debates and to focus instead on building powerful organizations. Patronage replaced ideology as the glue that bonded the parties together. British observer James Bryce said the two major parties "were like two bottles. Each bore a label denoting the kind of liquor it contained, but each was empty."

Equilibrium stemmed from another unique feature of Gilded Age politics: the parties were evenly balanced in numbers with neither able to gain the upper hand. Henry Adams observed that though "no real principle divides us, . . . some queer mechanical balance holds the two parties even." In the years between 1872 and 1896, no president won a majority of the popular vote. In the presidential contest of 1880, the Republicans won 48.5 percent of the popular vote, the Democrats 48.1 percent. After that election, the Congress had 147 Republicans and 135 Democrats in the House. Each party had 37 representatives in the Senate. As a consequence of the divided electorate, no president between 1877 and 1897 served with a majority of his party in control of both houses of Congress for a full term.

Because of the tight competition, party leaders searched for bland candidates who would not alienate powerful voting blocs. Both parties vied for control of a handful of "swing" states—Connecticut, New Jersey, New York, Indiana, Ohio, and Illinois—whose electoral votes would determine election outcomes. The ideal presidential candidate during the Gilded Age resided in a critical state, had fought for the Union during the Civil War, and had avoided taking controversial positions.

Chronology

1873	Twain and Warner publish *The Gilded Age*
	Congress demonetizes silver
1877	Hayes becomes president
	Great Railway Strike
	Munn v. *Illinois* affirms state regulation of railroads
1880	Garfield elected president
1881	Garfield assassinated; Arthur becomes president
1883	Pendleton Civil Service Act
1884	Cleveland elected president
1886	National Alliance Exchange system established
1888	Harrison elected president
1890	"Billion Dollar Congress"
	Sherman Antitrust Act passed
	McKinley Tariff passed
	Sherman Silver Purchase Act passed
1892	Populist Party wins over a million votes
	Homestead strike
	Cleveland elected president
1893	Panic of 1893
1894	Coxey's Army invades Washington
	Pullman strike
	Congress repeals Sherman Silver Purchase Act
1895	*Pollock* v. *Farmers Loan and Trust* strikes down income tax
1896	McKinley elected president
	Populists "fuse" with Democrats
1897	Dingley Tariff
1900	Gold Standard Act

There were real differences between Democrats and Republicans, but internal divisions often obscured ideological divisions, preventing either party from speaking with a unified voice. The Republican Party, referred to as the Grand Old Party (GOP) after 1880, reflected the continuing loyalties that grew out of the Civil War. Based in the Northeast and Midwest, it celebrated its legacy as the party of Lincoln, which had freed the slaves and saved the Union. More willing than Democrats to advocate federal activism, Republicans promoted economic growth through land grants, subsidies to railroads, and protective tariffs. In the North, Republicans "waved the bloody shirt," symbolically invoking the memory of fallen Union soldiers by labeling Democrats the "party of treason," responsible for the war between the states and unworthy of governing. "Not every Democrat was a Rebel," they reminded voters, "but every rebel was a Democrat." The appeal was especially persuasive with the 1 million surviving veterans of the Civil War, organized into a powerful lobby called the Grand Army of the Republic (GAR), which urged its members to "vote as you shot." An 1880 poll of Civil War veterans in Indiana showed that 69 percent voted Republican. Not surprisingly, Republicans nominated a Union veteran as president in eight of nine presidential contests between 1868 and 1900. With grateful memories of emancipation and Reconstruction, African-Americans too voted for the party of Lincoln.

As was often the case during this period, Republicans were divided among themselves, often unable to present a united front. The most pronounced divisions among Republicans were between "Half-Breeds" and "Stalwarts." The *Cincinnati Commercial* observed, "The Republican party in Congress is composed of factions in such deadly antagonism to each other that the hate among them is more intense than that given the Democrats." The Stalwarts were led by state bosses such as Senator Roscoe Conkling of New York, who was known for his arrogant manner, flair for fine clothes, and passion for political intrigue. Politics "is a rotten business," he declared. "Nothing counts except to win." Having built a powerful political machine in New York on the back of political patronage, Conkling opposed reform efforts that would diminish his fiefdom. He summed up his political philosophy in a sentence: "I do not know how to belong to a party a little." James G. Blaine of Maine, leader of the Half-Breeds, emerged as Conkling's chief challenger for control of the party. A consummate politician, Blaine, whom his supporters called "the plumed knight from Maine," never forgot a name or a face and was capable of arousing the party faithful with his inspiring oratory. The Half-Breeds believed their appeal rested on issues, not patronage. They wanted to build a coalition based on calls for economic nationalism and political reform.

Like the Republicans, the Democrats were divided into rival camps. In the South, Democrats waved their own bloody shirt to maintain the support of the provincial Protestant farmers who viewed northern Republicans as the real traitors. A second wing of the Democratic Party consisted of urban political machines and their loyal immigrant constituency. What united the disparate factions was a common commitment to the antimonopoly rhetoric that had begun with Andrew Jackson in the 1820s. Democrats promoted states' rights and a decentralized, limited government. "Local self-government," the party's 1872 platform declared, "will guard the rights of all citizens more securely than any centralized power." Democrats also shared a belief in white supremacy. In the South their racial views translated into efforts to disfranchise blacks; in parts of the West they fought to deny citizenship to Chinese immigrants.

Important issues divided the parties, but a new generation of political leaders was determined to soften their ideological identities. Republicans often muted their support for centralized government in an effort to appeal to more conservative voters. The Kansas Republican Party platform declared that "the powers of the general government having been stretched to an unhealthy extent, to meet the crisis of civil war and reconstruction, [they] should now be restored to their normal action." For their part, Democrats tried to win over key swing voters by downplaying their Civil War support for slavery and states' rights. In Ohio, the Democratic platform proposed a "New Departure," calling on the party to "accept the material and legitimate results of the war."

Many people, dismayed with both the Democrats and Republicans, turned to third parties. Though they advocated different causes and appealed to different voters, all third-party challengers drew scores of supporters from both mainline parties. A national Prohibition candidate ran for president in every election after 1872. Anti-monopoly parties sprang up in eleven states during the mid-seventies. In 1878 the Greenback Party, which called for an expansion of the currency, won more than a million votes. In 1892 angry farmers in the West and South created the Populist Party.

However, ethnic and religious issues, not questions of economic policy, frequently determined election outcomes. In the North and West, Republicans wooed Protestants of British descent or established American stock by promising to maintain high moral standards, which usually meant support for Sunday-closing laws, English-only public schools, and prohibition of alcohol. The Republican message attracted the support of "pietistic" religious groups—Methodist, Baptist, Congregational, and Presbyterian—who defined sin broadly and felt obliged to impose those standards widely. Outside the South, Democrats captured the allegiance of Irish Catholics and other urban immigrants by opposing such moral and ethnic controls. They appealed to "liturgical" religious faiths—Catholics, German Lutherans, and Episcopalians—who defined sin narrowly and opposed using government power to enforce proper behavior. As one Chicago Democrat explained, "A Republican is a man who wants you to go to church every Sunday. A Democrat says if a man wants to have a glass of beer on Sunday he can have it."

Ironically, despite the mediocre candidates and dull debates, parties played a central role in the political life of Gilded Age Americans, providing a sense of national attachment and group identity. Election campaigns were elaborate and festive affairs, filled with colorful parades and mass rallies. Novelist Brand Whitlock described a typical parade—"the smell of saltpeter, the snorts of horses, the shouts of men, the red and white ripple of the flags that went careering by in smoke and flame." If the spirited rallies were not enough to motivate voters, the parties provided other more tangible incentives. Before the 1890s, the parties controlled the voting process. Voters filled out distinctive "slip tickets" in full view of party officials before depositing their votes in the ballot box. The system encouraged straight-ticket voting and widespread corruption. Parties hired operatives to get people to the polls and then paid them for their votes. The standard rate for a Pennsylvania congressional race was said to be $30 plus room and board.

The combination of passion and organization produced the highest percentages of voter turnout in American history (see graph). In some states outside the South it soared above 80 percent. In 1876, for example, Ohio registered a 94 percent turnout, Indiana 95 percent. Iowa, where 99 percent of voters went to the polls, set an all-time U.S. record. Of course, the universe of eligible voters remained small. Women could not vote. Whites in many areas in the South were experimenting successfully with new methods such as the poll tax to restrict black suffrage (see page 643). Their counterparts in the North used similar methods to discourage recent immigrants from voting. Despite these restrictions, the United States had more legal voters than any other democracy—11 million in 1880. About 1.8 million males of voting age—14 percent of the total—could not vote. In comparison, 40 percent of the adult male population were denied the ballot in Britain.

The Limits of National Government

With the exception of Reconstruction and western land development, the federal government remained largely invisible to most citizens. "An American may," James Bryce observed, "through a long life, never be reminded of the federal government,

Voter Turnout in Presidential Elections, 1868–1920   The average proportion of eligible voters in presidential elections, indicated by the bar, remained around 80 percent during the post–Civil War era, beginning a gradual decline in 1896. While the gap between the state with the highest average voter turnout (shown above the bar) and the lowest average voter turnout (shown below the bar) varied, it is interesting to note the impact of Mississippi's constitution of 1890 and of the efforts of other former Confederate states to exclude black voters (see page 643).

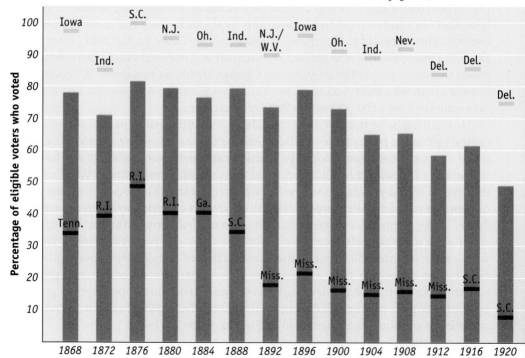

except when he votes at presidential and congressional elections, lodges a complaint against the post-office, and opens his trunks for a custom-house official on the pier at New York when he returns from a tour in Europe." Despite its growth during the Civil War, the national government was relatively small, employing only nine thousand nonmilitary personnel, of whom six thousand were stationed in Washington. The federal budget, which in the last year of the Civil War had ballooned to $1.3 billion, dropped to $242 million by 1886. With the exception of the Post Office, which accounted for half of all civilian federal employees, and the Pension Office, which disbursed benefits to Union veterans and their families, the federal government had little direct impact on the daily lives of most Americans.

In Washington, the Congress replaced the president as the focus of political power. The impeachment of Andrew Johnson (see page 622) had shifted the balance of power away from the chief executive. Grant had deferred to Congress in making appointments and in developing legislation, and subsequent presidents tended to follow suit. The prevailing wisdom was that the president should execute the laws, not propose new legislation. Senator John Sherman of Ohio framed the situation clearly: "The executive department of a republic like ours should be subordinate to the legislative department." In any case, no Gilded Age president could command majorities in Congress to push through innovative legislation.

Congress gained new power, but it lacked the will or the resources to govern effectively. An unruly institution, Congress was constrained by rules that, in the words of one congressman, were designed "to disturb legislators and obstruct legislation." The Senate, which was known as the Millionaire's Club, became the home of powerful party leaders who felt little loyalty to the institution or to the president. Since senators were still elected by state legislatures, it was easy for wealthy men to "buy" a Senate seat. Each senator, observed one member, "kept his own orbit and shone in his sphere, within which he tolerated no intrusion from the President or from anybody else."

It was the states and counties, not the federal government, that did most of the governing. Most states funded schools and prisons and provided homes for disabled Civil War veterans. By the 1880s, many states had created commissions to oversee railroads and to regulate social and economic activities—chartering corporations, granting divorces, licensing saloons. Most state constitutions specified that the legislature should be in session only a few months a year. As a result, most people looked to local authorities for nearly all their government services. City and town governments built and maintained roads, established boards to manage the public schools, and collected property taxes.

The Issues: Patronage, Money, and Tariffs

In previous decades, Americans had debated the momentous issues of freedom and slavery; in the Gilded Age, elections frequently turned on questions of patronage. Beginning in the 1830s, winning candidates for national office instituted the spoils system, rewarding supporters and contributors with government jobs. The spoils system made party loyalty, not qualifications and competence, the chief criterion for public office. President William Henry Harrison estimated that during the first eighteen months of his term he had spent four to six hours a day dealing with job seekers. Throughout the period, party leaders, who expected to be able to fill party posts and other positions with loyal followers regardless of their qualifications, battled with reformers, who charged that patronage bred corruption and wasted money.

The second issue that animated political discussions concerned the money supply. During the Civil War the government had issued $450 million in "greenbacks"—paper money not backed by gold or silver. For the next two decades, Americans debated whether to print more paper money or to remove it from circulation entirely. The dispute raged through the 1870s and led to the formation of the Greenback Party. Just as the battle over greenbacks began to subside, a new fight erupted over silver-backed money. Since 1837, the nation's money supply had been tied to the value of gold and silver. Congress had set the ratio at 16:1, meaning that one ounce of gold was worth sixteen ounces of silver. By 1870, so little silver remained in circulation that Congress stopped coining it. But the resulting contraction of the money supply led to a steep economic slide and provoked renewed calls for some form of silver coinage.

"A Presidential Conjurer"　Although he built his political career on patronage, including a lucrative position as New York's customs collector, Chester A. Arthur spent his years as president working for civil service reform. Despite Arthur's personal convictions, many people believed that the president would have to bow to pressures within his Republican Party to maintain the spoils system. In this cartoon by Joseph Keppler, Arthur is the magician, pulling political appointments out of his hat in order to satisfy politicians, while reserving a table full of "tricks" for his own future use.　(Puck, *October 12, 1881, University of California at Berkeley, Bancroft Library.*)

On one side of the divide were debt-ridden farmers in the South and West. They believed that the amount of money in circulation determined the level of activity in the economy. The more paper money the government printed, the more business activity and the more prosperity for everyone. An expanded money supply allowed farmers to charge higher prices for their products and to pay back loans with inflated dollars. On the other side, bankers and businessmen, who held loans and owned property that would decline in value if the money supply expanded, wanted to maintain the status quo. They developed great reverence for the gold standard, whereby all money printed had to be backed by gold reserves, which unlike silver were limited and stable. Business interests often found unlikely allies in urban workers who feared higher prices for food and other essentials. Over the next twenty years, as the two sides struggled over this contentious issue, the mundane question of the money supply took on moral implications that went beyond simple economics. For many people, support for an expanded money supply translated to rural interests over urban, a power shift from the industrial bankers of the Northeast to the yeoman farmers of the South and West.

Finally, Americans debated the wisdom of maintaining high tariffs on imported products. The tariff issue was as old as the republic, but it assumed a new importance following the Civil War. During the war, the government raised tariff rates to protect American industry, which paid heavy taxes to support the war effort, from competition from foreign companies. At the end of the war, the government dropped the taxes but kept the tariff, giving American producers a protected market in which to sell their goods. Since they faced little competition, America's expanding and industrializing manufacturers raised their prices and amassed record profits. At the same time, the Treasury Department was building a sizable bank account from tariff revenues. During the 1880s, the Treasury surplus averaged over $100 million a year. This surplus stood as a continual temptation to legislators, who wanted to spend it on pork-barrel projects in their home districts. Businessmen, who gravitated toward the Republican Party, strongly supported continued high tariffs. Over time, Democrats, responding to the pleas of western farmers, called for reduced tariff rates.

National Politics from Hayes to Harrison, 1877–1890

Questions of patronage and civil service dominated the Republican administrations of Rutherford Hayes, James Garfield, and Chester Arthur. In 1884, the Democrats regained the White House. Although the new president, Grover Cleveland, differed little from his Republican predecessors on most issues, his bruising battles over pension benefits, patronage, and the tariff left him vulnerable to Republican attacks. Late in his presidency he made tariff reduction the central issue of the 1888 campaign. Benjamin Harrison, the Republican candidate, took advantage of Cleveland's liabilities to win election. High tariffs remained safe in the hands of Harrison, but the "Billion Dollar Congress" during his term depleted the Treasury with its reckless spending.

Republicans in Power: Hayes, Garfield, and Arthur

Rutherford B. Hayes tried to bring a new integrity to the White House in the wake of the corruption that had marred the Grant administration. His wife, known derisively as Lemonade Lucy, added to the new tone by refusing to serve alcohol in the White House. Visitors accustomed to free drinks complained that in the Hayes White House "the water flowed like wine."

His tainted election victory in 1876 (see page 638) prevented Hayes from becoming a strong president. Democrats controlled the House throughout his administration and the Senate for the last two years. House Democrats, who called him the "de facto President" and "His Fraudulence," seized every opportunity to embarrass the chief executive.

The president's limited view of executive power contributed to his ineffectiveness. He proposed little legislation designed to deal with pressing economic and social problems. When an economic slump occurred in 1873, he insisted that a return to the gold standard was the only remedy. "Let it be understood that during the coming year the business of the country will be undisturbed by governmental interference with the laws affecting it." Hayes also had no policy for dealing with the first great industrial conflict in American history—the railway strike that began on the Baltimore and Ohio Railroads in July 1877 (see page 716). At the request of four state governors, Hayes sent federal troops to intervene in the strike and restore order. He angered labor further when he vetoed a bill in 1879 to restrict Chinese immigration. Labor unions on the West Coast had pushed for the restrictions, claiming that Chinese "coolie" immigrants were stealing jobs from American workers.

Hayes did make a systematic effort to attack one controversial issue: patronage and corruption in government. He called for civil service reform in his inaugural address, and in June 1877, the president challenged Conkling's New York machine by issuing an executive order forbidding federal officeholders "to take part in the management of political organizations, caucuses, conventions, or election campaigns." Conkling dismissed the effort toward "snivel service reform." In October, after Congress was in recess, Hayes fired two leading members of Conkling's machine—customs collector Chester A. Arthur and naval officer Alonzo Cornell—after an investigation accused them of fraud. An irate Conkling fired back, blocking Senate confirmation of the president's replacements for the two officials. Eventually Hayes won the battle of wills. Congress approved the new replacements, thus underscoring that the president, not party leaders, controlled the most important federal appointments.

Since Hayes had announced at the start of his term that he would not seek reelection, Republicans scrambled to find a new candidate to head the ticket in 1880. Each of the party's factions pushed its candidate: Stalwarts rallied around a third term for Grant. Half-Breeds supported Blaine. Independents favored John Sherman. When it became clear that none of the rivals would receive enough votes for nomination, delegates turned to a compromise candidate: James A. Garfield. A former president of Hiram College in Ohio, Garfield turned to politics in 1859, when he won election to the Ohio Senate. He rose quickly through the party ranks and emerged as one of the leading members of Congress. A self-taught scholar, Garfield could speak both German and French and write Latin with one hand and Greek with the other at the same time. To appease the Stalwarts, delegates offered the vice presidency to Chester A. Arthur—the New York customs official and Conkling henchman whom Hayes had dismissed from office!

The Democrats tried a new tactic by adopting the Republican strategy of nominating a Civil War hero: General Winfield Scott Hancock. In keeping with the tone of Gilded Age politics, both candidates ignored important issues and focused on personalities. The Republicans emphasized Garfield's log-cabin roots and mocked Hancock for his lack of political experience. Republicans published a book entitled *Record of the Statesmanship and Achievements of General Winfield Scott Hancock.* The book was filled with blank pages. The Democrats responded by tying Garfield to the Crédit Mobilier scandal (see page 630).

On election day Garfield eked out a narrow victory. Only 39,213 votes out of the 9 million cast separated winner and loser (4,453,295 to 4,414,082). Garfield's margin in the electoral college was more commanding: 214–155. Though the campaign was uninspiring, 79.4 percent of eligible voters turned out on election day (see map).

Battles over patronage consumed the early months of Garfield's administration. Conkling had helped the Republicans win New York, and now he expected his reward: control over all patronage positions in the state. Garfield rejected Conkling's

Voting in Presidential Elections of 1880, 1884, 1888 The impact of the Civil War was still evident in the partisan politics of the 1880s. Though a few scattered states shifted allegiances, most states that fought for the Union remained consistently behind the Republican Party. In the South, the Democratic Party held firm and gained support from the Border States. (Reprinted by permission of Harlan Davidson, Inc. from *American Politics in the Gilded Age, 1868–1900,* by Robert W. Cherny, copyright © 1997 by Harlan Davidson, Inc.)

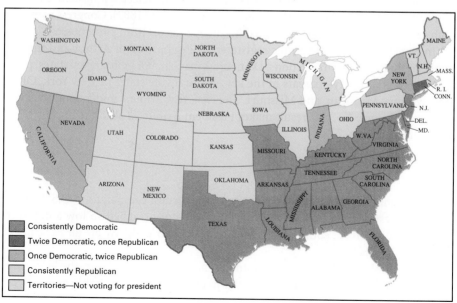

- Consistently Democratic
- Twice Democratic, once Republican
- Once Democratic, twice Republican
- Consistently Republican
- Territories—Not voting for president

claim and forced the issue by withdrawing all appointments from the Senate until Conkling backed down. When his fellow senators abandoned him, Conkling resigned his seat. The president did not have much time to savor his victory. On July 2, 1881, just four months after taking the oath of office, President Garfield was shot and killed by a deranged office seeker named Charles Guiteau. "I am a Stalwart and Arthur is President now," Guiteau shouted as he pulled the trigger. Garfield lingered incapacitated for two months before dying on September 19.

Garfield's death elevated Stalwart leader Chester Arthur to the presidency. "Chet Arthur, President of the United States?" one of his friends exclaimed. "Good God!" To everyone's surprise, however, Arthur sided with advocates of civil service and tariff reform, and against his old Stalwart ally Roscoe Conkling. He skillfully used public sentiment, aroused by the Garfield assassination, to encourage congressional efforts to enact the first national civil service law. The Pendleton Civil Service Act, passed in January 1883, set up an independent three-member Civil Service Commission to provide "open competitive examinations for testing the fitness of applications for the public service now classified or to be classified." The law listed only 14 percent of federal jobs as "classified services," but it gave the president the power to enlarge the classified services at his discretion. By 1901, the law covered 44 percent of all federal employees and served as a model for most state and local governments. In 1882 Arthur supported the recommendation of a congressional commission to reduce the tariff, but House Republicans watered down the proposal, and the bill Arthur eventually signed—dismissed as the "Mongrel Tariff"—provided for only a small reduction in rates.

Arthur accomplished more than anyone would have predicted, but he won few friends. His vigorous prosecution of the so-called Star Route Frauds, a scheme to win contracts for postal routes, angered old political cronies who hoped to profit from the plot. Arthur's liberal use of the presidential veto angered many groups that hoped to benefit from government spending. In 1882 he rejected a wasteful $18 million river and harbors bill and the Chinese Exclusion Act (1882). Congress overrode both vetoes, but Arthur had established his independence from party bosses.

In November 1882, the public registered its disapproval of Arthur and the Republicans in the midterm elections. Democrats made major gains in key states, picking up a total of thirty-six seats in the key electoral vote states of New York, Ohio, Pennsylvania, Michigan, and Missouri. The *New York Tribune* understood the election's significance: ". . . this result makes President Arthur an absolute impossibility as a future candidate."

The Election of 1884

The presidential election of 1884 was one of the dirtiest campaigns in U.S. history. "Party contests," cried the *Nation*, "have never before reached so low a depth of degradation in this . . . country." Henry Adams told a friend, "We are all swearing at each other like demons."

The Republicans dumped Arthur and turned to James G. Blaine, the long-time leader of the Half-Breeds and one of the Republicans' most capable and experienced leaders. Though popular with party regulars, Blaine was shadowed by suggestions that he once profited from shady deals with the Union Pacific. The questions about Blaine's role were nearly a decade old and had been investigated by a congressional committee. No proof emerged that Blaine had broken the law, but highly suggestive questions lingered. The controversy gained new life on September 15 when the *Boston Journal* released letters Blaine had written in 1876 to a railroad attorney. In a cover letter, Blaine pleaded with the attorney to sign a statement clearing him of any misdeeds. Blaine signed off with a warning: "Burn this letter!" The correspondence revived an old issue and cast doubt on Blaine's integrity.

High-minded reformers in the Republican Party refused to support a Blaine-headed ticket. The *Nation*'s editor, E. L. Godkin, remarked that Blaine had "wallowed in spoils like a rhinoceros in an African pool." The editor of the *New York Sun* labeled Godkin and his fellow reformers Mugwumps, ironically adapting an Algonquian word meaning a great chieftain, to ridicule a reformer as a political fence-sitter whose "mug" was on one side of the fence and his "wump" on the other. The Mugwumps cultivated a style of independence and moral rectitude that disdained the ordinary demands of partisan politics. Most were old-stock Americans, educated at elite universities, who rejected the crass political gamesmanship of partisan politics. Since many were prominent educators and journalists, they used their positions to influence public opinion. But their contempt for the general public prevented them from building a mass political movement. "Whoever is right," Henry Adams commented to his brother on the Mugwumps' attitude, "the majority is wrong."

The presence of the Mugwumps on the political scene convinced the Democrats that they could seize the moral high ground by nominating a principled opponent. For that role they selected New York governor Grover Cleveland, who had attracted national attention for battling graft and corruption as mayor of Buffalo, New York. In 1882 the Democrats ran him for governor, and he won. Over the next two years, his attacks on New York's Tammany Hall organization (see page 742) earned him the nickname "Grover the Good."

Cleveland, too, was forced to defend himself against withering assaults on his character. On July 21 the *Buffalo Evening Telegraph* published a piece headlined "A Terrible Tale: A Dark Chapter in a Public Man's History." The story revealed that Cleveland had, some ten years earlier, fathered an illegitimate child. Though disappointed by the blemish on his private life, the Mugwumps threw their support behind Cleveland. As one of them put it, "We should elect Mr. Cleveland to the public office which he is so admirably qualified to fill and remand Mr. Blaine to the private life which he is so eminently fitted to adorn."

The scandals, both personal and public, produced some of the most colorful campaign slogans in American politics. "Blaine, Blaine, James G. Blaine, the continental liar from the state of Maine," Democrats chanted. Republicans countered with "Ma, ma, where's my pa?" To which Democrats responded, "Gone to the White House, ha, ha, ha!"

The race appeared to be a dead heat going into the final weeks. As with most of the elections during this period, the outcome hinged on New York, with its thirty-six

The 1884 Presidential Campaign   The fight for the White House between James G. Blaine and Grover Cleveland focused more on the personal integrity of the two nominees than on any political issue. Democrats repeatedly accused Blaine of corrupt dealings with big business. While appearing more politically credible, Cleveland faced allegations that he was the father of an illegitimate son born to a Buffalo widow. Republicans' main tactic was to attack Cleveland for this impropriety, as seen in this cartoon.   *(Granger Collection.)*

electoral votes. Blaine had made inroads into the powerful Irish-American community and threatened to carry the state. Then on October 29, Blaine's "Black Wednesday," the candidate made a serious mistake that probably cost him the election. When Blaine attended a morning meeting of Protestant ministers, a preacher welcomed him with a reference to Democrats as the party of "Rum, Romanism, and Rebellion." Blaine, perhaps failing to catch the implied insult to Catholics, let the slur pass without objection. Within hours Democrats flooded the city with handbills repeating the remark.

The episode undoubtedly helped Cleveland win a narrow victory because Blaine lost New York by only a little more than 1,100 votes, and the votes of that state proved to be decisive in the electoral college, where the margin was 37 votes (Cleveland's 219 versus Blaine's 182). Nationally, only about 29,000 votes of the 10 million cast separated Cleveland and Blaine (4,879,507 to 4,850,293).

Grover Cleveland: A Democrat in the White House

Cleveland became the first Democrat to occupy the White House since the Civil War, but the change in power did not signal a change in governing strategy. Cleveland embraced the prevailing belief that the federal government should refrain from meddling in people's lives or in the economy. The proper role for the president, he believed, should be to restrain Congress from granting special privileges to some groups at the expense of others. "Though the people support the government the government should not support the people," Cleveland asserted. In his inaugural address, which he recited from memory, he promised to adhere to "business principles," and his cabinet consisted of conservatives and business-minded Democrats from the East and South.

Cleveland's fiscal conservatism led to a number of costly political confrontations. Believing that "public office is a public trust," Cleveland vetoed pork-barrel bills for rivers and harbors, and he ejected ranchers and railroad companies from public lands. In 1887 he vetoed a general pension bill for Civil War veterans, claiming that it was unnecessary and wasteful. The decision may have reflected sound economic policy, but as a Democrat without a war record, Cleveland was vulnerable to partisan charges that he was pro-South and unpatriotic. The Grand Army of the Republic blistered Cleveland for his decision, and the intense public reaction that followed forced the president to retreat. By the end of his term, Cleveland had vetoed three times as many bills as all his predecessors combined.

The president's record on the civil service was mixed enough to alienate both reformers and spoilsmen. He filled three-quarters of nonclassified federal offices with Democrats, including all internal revenue collectors and nearly all the heads of customhouses. But at the same time Cleveland increased by two-thirds the number of jobs classified as civil service.

Cleveland's vocal opposition to high tariffs angered many businessmen. In 1887 he devoted his annual message to Congress entirely to arguments for tariff reduction. Calling tariffs "vicious, inequitable, and illogical," he predicted "financial convulsion and widespread disaster" if the high rates continued. The president claimed that the existing tariff presented two problems: it created a large federal budget surplus that tempted Congress to spend money on wasteful projects, and it encouraged monopoly by eliminating competition to domestic manufacturers. Noting that the surplus had transformed the Treasury into "a hoarding place for money needlessly withdrawn from trade and the people's use," the president advocated lowering tariffs to cut the federal surplus, reduce prices, and slow the development of trusts. Given his views of presidential power, however, Cleveland exercised little leadership, leaving it to Congress to develop legislation. In the end, Senate Republicans blocked Democratic efforts to adjust the tariff.

The Election of 1888

Cleveland had made many enemies during his four years as president, but the Democrats renominated him to head the ticket in 1888. Republican kingmakers searched for a candidate who would not offend voters and would allow the campaign to target Cleveland's record. They found their man on the seventh ballot when they nominated former senator and outspoken protectionist Benjamin Harrison of Indiana, grandson of former president William Henry Harrison. A man of intelligence and integrity, Harrison lacked personal warmth and charm. "Harrison sweats ice water," declared a critic. Harrison promised to conduct a high-minded campaign focused on issues, not personalities. "We have joined now a contest of great principles," he declared. The Republican platform accepted the protective tariff as the chief "great principle" and also promised generous pensions to veterans. For all their professions of principle, Republicans were not above using dirty tricks in the campaign. Cleveland spent much of his time battling false rumors, including one that he had beaten his wife.

A last-minute campaign trick left Cleveland on the defensive. A Republican, posing as an English immigrant and using the false name "Charles F. Murchison," had written to a British minister asking advice on how to vote. The minister took the bait and suggested that he should vote for Cleveland. "Would you do England a service by voting for Cleveland and against the Republican system of tariff," he wrote. Gleeful Republicans published the letter on October 24. As planned, the minister's reply provoked a storm of protest against foreign intervention on the president's behalf.

With Cleveland in the White House fending off groundless rumors, Harrison and the Republicans raised over $4 million—the largest campaign fund to date—from business leaders worried about falling tariff rates. John Wanamaker, a Philadelphia merchant and chief Republican fundraiser, sent a letter putting matters bluntly to leading businessmen: "We want money and we want it quick." Campaign leaders used the contributions to purchase millions of pamphlets, flyers, and handbills, and to pay speakers to travel around the country drumming up support for Harrison.

Despite the Republicans' vigorous efforts and Cleveland's troubles, the outcome was very close. Cleveland won the popular vote by a margin of nearly 100,000: 5,537,857 to 5,447,129. But Harrison, victorious in the key states of Indiana and New York, carried the electoral college by 233 to 168. When his campaign manager arrived in Indianapolis to congratulate Harrison on his victory, the president-elect exclaimed, "Providence has given us the victory." The cynical adviser was stunned that the pious Harrison gave God more credit than his operatives. "Think of the man!" he ranted to a journalist. "He ought to know that Providence hadn't a damn thing to do with it." Harrison would never know, he charged, "how close a number of men were compelled to approach the gates of the penitentiary to make him president."

Harrison and the Billion Dollar Majority

Not only had Republicans laid claim to the White House in 1888, they also secured majorities in the House and the Senate. Taking advantage of the opportunity, they passed some of the most significant legislation enacted in the entire period. The Sherman Silver Purchase Act, passed to mollify the western wing of the party, increased the amount of silver to be purchased by the Treasury to 4.5 million ounces a month. The McKinley Tariff raised duties to their highest level. Not all Republican initiatives succeeded, however. House Republicans tried to pass a federal election bill that would have guaranteed the voting rights of blacks in the South. Democrats, who condemned the legislation as a "force bill" to restore "Negro rule," succeeded in filibustering it to death.

Of the pieces of legislation to emerge from the Republican Congress, the Sherman Antitrust Act eventually proved one of the most important. The first attempt to regulate big business, it imposed stiff penalties on "every contract, combination in the form of trust or otherwise, or conspiracy, in restraint of trade or commerce." The Senate approved the act by 52–1, and the House passed it without a dissenting vote (see page 708).

Harrison and the Republicans did not stop at legislative initiatives. They also rewarded their supporters by raiding the Treasury surplus. To serve as commissioner of pensions, the president appointed a past GAR commander who, soon after taking office, exulted, "God help the surplus!" The Congress assisted his efforts to provide "an appropriation for every old comrade who needs it" by passing the Dependent Pension Act of 1890. Within five years, the number of pensioners grew from 676,000 to nearly a million, and federal pension expenditures ballooned from $80 million to $159 million. Rivers and harbors expenditures also reached new highs, and the Republicans returned federal taxes paid by northern states during the Civil War. Such lavish spending quite properly earned the label "Billion Dollar Congress" for the 1890 session.

Voters punished the extravagant Republicans in the midterm election of 1890, rewarding the Democrats with sixty-six congressional seats and control of the House of Representatives. This voter response represented more than just a stinging rebuke of the Billion Dollar Congress. In many key states, religious and ethnic groups revolted against the Republican Party's affection for restrictive social legislation such as prohibition. Most of all, the election revealed the growing political activism of farmers in the South and West.

Agrarian Revolt, 1880–1892

Few groups suffered more in the new industrial system than America's farmers. Frustrated with falling prices and high costs, farmers fought back. By the 1880s, they had formed a powerful new movement of Farmers' Alliances in the West and South. Realizing that most of the farmers' needs were beyond the power of the state governments, Alliance members developed a national program seeking new forms of federal intervention. The Alliance platform stressed a number of bold proposals, including the free minting of silver, and the experiment in political activism created a new sense of solidarity among farmers. In 1892, after scoring impressive victories in the 1890 election, Alliance members formed the Populist Party.

The Farmers' Discontent

Since the early days of the republic, the American farmer had symbolized independence and self-sufficiency in a society that revered these qualities. "Those who labor in the earth," Thomas Jefferson once wrote, "are the chosen people of God." Farmers, however, confronted a paradox: though an emblem of self-reliance, they prospered or struggled at the whim of uncontrollable forces. Foremost among those forces was the weather, but the new industrial order, which integrated farmers into an international market, introduced a host of other factors. Farmers suddenly found themselves depending on an impersonal system that they could not understand, let alone control.

American farmers now had to contend with competition from abroad as countries such as Russia and Argentina expanded their wheat production to capture a part of the U.S. market. Most of all, farmers became victims of their own success. They produced such an overabundance of wheat and cotton that supply outpaced demand, producing lower prices. The average price of American wheat fell from $1.05 per bushel in 1866, to 67 cents in 1895. Corn dropped from 43.1 to 29.7 cents a bushel, and cotton from 15.1 to 5.8 cents a pound. The price of corn dropped so low that farmers in Kansas burned it in place of coal. Ironically, as commodity prices dropped, farmers had to cultivate more wheat or cotton to try to raise the same amount of money. The result was a vicious cycle of surpluses, price declines, and debt (see graph).

Frustration increased in the heartland as farmers watched everyone else benefit from their labors—railroad and grain storage operators who charged exorbitant rates, consumers who bought their product at low costs, machinery salesmen who sold new equipment at tariff-protected prices. Farmers, on the other hand, saw a dramatic decline in their quality of life. As one exasperated speaker put it, "The farmer fed all other men and lived himself upon scraps."

Consumer Prices and Farm Product Prices, 1865–1910   Farm prices, on a steady decline after the Civil War, remained above consumer expenditures until the late 1870s. As consumer prices began to level in the 1880s, farm prices continued their downward trend, leading farmers to spend more on consumer products than they made.

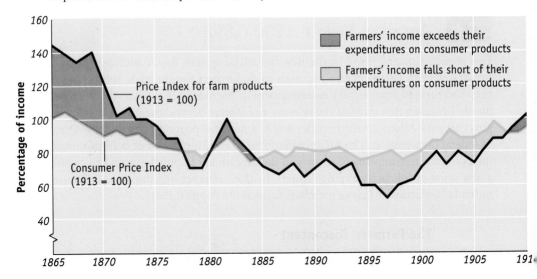

Farmers searching for an explanation for their plight saw the railroads as the chief villain. Farmers felt victimized by the high railroad rates that prevailed in farm regions having no alternative forms of transportation. On long hauls, the rates were low because of competition; on local hauls, for which there was no competition, the rates were disproportionately high. It cost Minnesota farmers more to ship their grain to St. Paul or Minneapolis than to New York. The railroads also favored the big shipper, who had leverage to negotiate lower prices, over the small shipper.

A second target of farmers' complaints were grain elevator operators. The elevators were giant storage bins located next to railroad tracks, from which grain was loaded onto trains. Western railroads forced farmers to sell their grain to local elevator operators or use their services for a fee. The operators were supposed to pay for the grain according to market rates. However, especially in the remote West, unscrupulous operators exploited farmers by offering less than the standard price. Since the elevator operators had a monopoly on access to the railroad and no other suitable transportation was available, farmers could not negotiate a better price or sell their crops to another bidder.

Already by the mid-1860s, some farmers had begun to organize to share their grievances and pool their resources. In 1867 Oliver Hudson Kelley, a clerk in the Department of Agriculture, founded the National Grange of the Patrons of Husbandry. Initially, the Granges functioned as social groups, sponsoring picnics, dances, lectures—anything to break up the loneliness of farm life. By 1875, Granges had attracted 800,000 members in 20,000 locals throughout the Midwest, South, and Southwest, and had become more activist. The Granges tried to lower the cost of consumer goods by appointing agents to negotiate directly with manufacturers, cutting out middlemen. In 1872 Montgomery Ward, the first company to sell goods by catalog, was founded specifically to do business with Grangers. The Granges also founded or acquired mills, elevators, and plants for production, and insurance companies and banks for finance.

To deal with their chief adversary—the railroads—Grange members focused on state regulation, seeking and obtaining laws to establish the maximum rates that railroads and elevators could charge. When states did pass new regulations, business groups often resisted, and many of the cases ended up before the Supreme Court. In *Munn* v. *Illinois* (1877), the most important, the justices upheld the right of Illinois to regulate private property so long as it was "devoted to a public use." But it was not the victory it seemed. The Court ruled that state commissions had the power to regulate local rates, but not long-haul rates. Railroads responded by raising the long-distance rates to compensate for the lost revenue on local rates. Later decisions limited regulation of railroads by ruling that states did not have the power to determine rates of carriers that crossed state lines.

The Grange movement ran out of steam at the end of the 1870s. In some states, their victory in the *Munn* case convinced farmers that the battle with monopolies had been won. In other states, the railroads used fear and intimidation to discourage farmers from organizing. Everywhere inexperience and mismanagement plagued Grange efforts to develop into a powerful economic force.

The Alliance Movement of the 1880s

At the end of the 1880s, amid another slump in prices for farm products, a host of organizations blended into the national Alliance Movement. Initially, the movement developed distinct branches in the South and Midwest. In the Plains, many Grange members formed the Northwestern Alliance. In the South, farmers organized in Texas to form the Southern Alliance. A Colored Farmers' Alliance for blacks grew up alongside the Southern Alliance, which was a whites-only organization. Most estimates place its membership at about 250,000—a remarkable accomplishment when white violence was a common response to blacks' attempt to organize in any way. In 1886 Dr. Charles W. Macune, an energetic and inspiring leader, expanded the southern network of local chapters, or suballiances, into a national system of state Alliance Exchanges.

The Alliances established an elaborate system for reaching farmers in isolated areas. Each created its own press supported by hundreds of local papers that reached millions of readers each week. Between 1887 and 1891, the Alliances sent

General Richard Manning Humphrey A Confederate veteran and Baptist preacher, this South Carolinian spent the postwar years farming and preaching in East Texas before becoming involved in agrarian politics. While other whites around him joined the Farmers' Alliance, General Humphrey turned to the organization of black farmers. The Colored Farmers' Alliance emerged parallel to the whites-only group, but blacks could not count on white farmers' support. When Humphrey organized a work stoppage of cotton pickers in Arkansas in 1891, white farmers killed at least fifteen strikers. The growing power of segregation and violence often frustrated the efforts of people such as Humphrey who attempted to promote black activism. The Colored Farmers' Alliance disintegrated in the 1890s. *(Torreyson Library, University of Central Arkansas.)*

lecturers into forty-three states and territories to recruit members and encourage cooperation. The farm movement's vibrant leaders excited audiences. In Kansas, Mary Elizabeth Lease captured the popular imagination by telling audiences of farmers "to raise less corn and more hell." An Irish-American raised in Pennsylvania, Lease had lost her father and two brothers in the Civil War. After the war she moved to Kansas and became one of the state's first female lawyers; from that foundation she advanced to leadership in the Alliance.

Lease's high profile underscored the Alliance effort to expand its coalition to include women, working people, and African-Americans. Novelist Hamlin Garland observed, "No other movement in history—not even the anti-slavery cause—appealed to the woman like this movement here in Kansas." Not all Alliance groups allowed women to assume leadership roles, but overall the movement expanded the opportunities available for women. Hoping to build a partnership of the "producing classes," the Alliances also advocated the eight-hour workday and government support of labor unions' right to bargain collectively. At the same time, Georgia's Tom Watson, one of the most respected of the Southern Alliance leaders, appealed to black tenant farmers and sharecroppers to join with their white counterparts in ousting the white political elite. "You are made to hate each other," he informed black and white farmers, "because upon that hatred is rested the keystone of this arch of financial despotism which enslaves you both."

In 1889 the Alliances met in St. Louis to develop a national program. Their platform called for breaking up the concentrated power of railroads, grain buyers, and banks. "The fruits of the toil of millions are boldly stolen to build up colossal fortunes for a few, unprecedented in the history of mankind," they complained. Their solution was to call for government ownership of the railroads and banks. "We believe the time has come," the Populists proclaimed in 1892, "when the railroad companies will either own the people or the people must own the railroads." Their platform called for inflation of the money supply, by either printing more greenbacks or minting silver, or both. In addition, they advocated structural changes to make government more responsive to the public: the initiative and referendum (which permitted voters to propose legislation through petitions and void laws passed by the legislature), secret ballot, and popular election of United States senators.

The centerpiece of their program was Macune's subtreasury plan, which called for the creation of federal subtreasury offices near warehouses or elevators into which farmers could deposit their nonperishable crops. Subtreasuries would guarantee 80 percent of the value of the stored commodities. This arrangement would allow farmers to market their produce at any time of the year, providing the leverage they needed to bargain for the highest price for their crops.

Members of the Farmers' Alliance tapped into deep currents in American culture to articulate a powerful critique of the emerging industrial order. Evangelical Protestantism inspired the soul of the agrarian protest movement. Alliance members viewed themselves as missionaries restoring the message of Christianity to American life. Their rhetoric was laden with religious imagery, and their rallies resembled religious camp meetings. "The battle is between God's people and the worshippers of the golden calf," proclaimed a Kansas farmer. Deeply rooted fears of concentrated wealth and power fed into the farmers' protest. Alliance supporters, soon to be called Populists, combined two powerful—and often conflicting—strands in American political thought. Like many Democrats since the days of Andrew Jackson, Populists identified themselves with the interests of the "common man" in their struggle against the power brokers of the new industrial order. On the other hand, like the Republicans of their time, they believed that a powerful federal government should play a role in protecting the public welfare. To these existing ideas they added a commitment to increased public participation in the decision-making process and a disdain for traditional political parties.

In 1890 Alliance members decided to enter national politics. Farmers in the Midwest clamored for a third party to challenge both the Democrats and the Republicans. In the South, farmers tried to capture control of the powerful Democratic Party. Though the midwestern and southern strategies varied, the results were the same: farm candidates scored impressive victories. The Plains farm movement, organized as the People's Party in Kansas, won control of the state legislature, elected five congressmen, and filled a Senate seat. In Nebraska, Populists took two of the three congressional seats and seized control of both houses of the legislature. The Southern Alliance, which worked to elect sympathetic Democratic candidates, elected four pro-Alliance governors, captured the legislature in seven states, and sent forty-four congressmen and several senators to Washington.

The Populist Party, 1892

Inspired by their victories, Alliance leaders laid the groundwork for a national third party to challenge the Democrats and Republicans. The People's Party of America opened its convention on July 4, 1892, in Omaha, Nebraska. "It was a religious revival," reported one observer, "a crusade, a pentecost of politics in which a tongue of flame sat upon every man, and each spoke as the spirit gave him utterance." The Populists presented a long list of reforms, including the popular election of senators, a graduated income tax, antitrust legislation, and public ownership of the railroads. The central issue was a proposal to increase the amount of money in circulation by adopting the free and unlimited coinage of silver at a ratio of sixteen ounces of silver to one ounce of gold.

For president the Populists nominated General James Baird Weaver, a former Union general and Greenback Party candidate in 1884. Large and enthusiastic crowds responded to Weaver's Populist message in the Midwest. At many campaign stops the forceful Mary Lease joined Weaver and stirred up crowds, claiming that the government "is no longer a government of the people, by the people, and for the people, but a government of Wall Street, by Wall Street, and for Wall Street." It was a different story in the South, where many white farmers opposed the Populists' racial egalitarianism and remained wedded to the Democratic Party. Lease said that on one southern campaign stop so many people threw eggs at Weaver that he looked like "a regular walking omelet."

While Weaver and the Populists struggled to build a new party, the Democrats and Republicans offered a replay of the 1888 election. Republicans nominated Harrison on the first ballot and approved a platform that attributed "the prosperous conditions of our country" to the "wise revenue legislation" of their party, exemplified by the McKinley Tariff. The Democrats selected former President Grover Cleveland and passed a platform denouncing "Republican protection as a fraud, a robbery, of the great majority of the American people for the benefit of the few."

The new Populist Party made an impressive debut on election day, but it was not substantial enough to derail the major parties. Weaver earned 1,029,846 votes and 22 electoral votes, and Populist candidates won five Senate seats, eleven congressional races, and three governorships. Nationally, nearly 1,500 Populist candidates won election in 1892. Capitalizing on the disenchantment with Republicans that voters had expressed in the 1890 midterm elections, Cleveland achieved a decisive victory, winning 277 electoral votes to Harrison's 145. He drew about 373,000 more popular votes than his Republican challenger (5,555,426 to 5,182,690). For the first time since the Civil War, the Democrats won a majority in both Houses of Congress (see map).

The Election of 1892, by County Despite limited success in the electoral college, the People's Party candidate, James B. Weaver of Iowa, received over one million votes. While most of Weaver's votes were from the farmers of the West, the People's Party made inroads into the Democratic dominated South as shown by the number of counties that voted for Weaver.

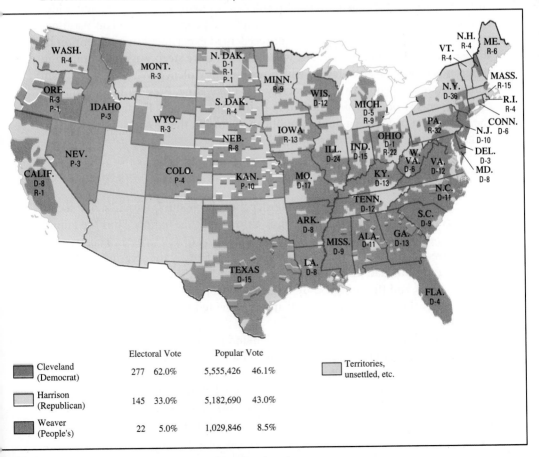

	Electoral Vote		Popular Vote	
Cleveland (Democrat)	277	62.0%	5,555,426	46.1%
Harrison (Republican)	145	33.0%	5,182,690	43.0%
Weaver (People's)	22	5.0%	1,029,846	8.5%

Territories, unsettled, etc.

Despite the Populists' impressive showing in the election, troubling signs clouded the future of the Populist Party. Believing their party could not win the presidency without southern votes, southern Democrats indulged in bribery, stuffing ballot boxes, and fraudulent counting to maintain party loyalty and thwart Populist candidates. Fraud and intimidation peaked in Georgia where the popular Tom Watson, seeking reelection to Congress, made a special effort to bring black tenant farmers into the Populist Party. "Watson ought to be killed and it ought to have been done long ago," the Democratic governor dared declare. Democratic operatives murdered as many as fifteen African-Americans. They shipped more cooperative blacks across state lines to swell Democratic vote totals. The vote recorded in Watson's home district was double the number of legal voters. The tactics succeeded; Watson lost the election.

 ## The Crisis of the 1890s

Leaving office in 1893, President Harrison boasted, "There has never been a time in our history when work was so abundant, or when wages were so high." Yet within a few months the United States plunged into a deep depression. The economic downturn that the recently inaugurated President Cleveland inherited created widespread fears of social unrest. Armies of unemployed people descended on Washington in search of relief, asking for an unprecedented experiment in intervention by the national government. Workers, who had to endure steep wage cuts, joined in thousands of strikes, not a few of which resulted in violence. While such activism convinced many people that U.S. society was unraveling, President Cleveland focused his energy on returning the nation to the gold standard. His failure to reverse the depression produced a huge Republican victory in the 1894 midterm election and set the stage for the 1896 presidential election.

The Depression of 1893

The new industrial order created an interdependent economy: a crisis in one sector of the economy sent shock waves rippling throughout the nation. Thus the failure of the Philadelphia and Reading Railroad in the spring of 1893 started a chain reaction that resulted in the deepest depression to that date. By the summer, a number of other railroads had also failed, including the Erie, the Northern Pacific, the Union Pacific, and the Santa Fe. By August, a quarter of all U.S. railroads, which covered forty thousand miles of track and represented $2.5 billion in capital, were bankrupt.

As railroad construction ceased, the demand for steel dropped, forcing dozens of companies out of business. Overextended banks failed—nearly five hundred in 1893. Cash-poor banks called in their loans, and those individuals and firms who could not repay went bankrupt. The wave of bank failures flooded Wall Street with panic selling as stock prices reached all-time lows. On May 5, 1893—"Industrial Black Friday"—the market suffered its most severe drop ever. At the same time, the demand for gold produced a dangerous drain on Treasury reserves, which sank below the $100 million mark. A business journal noted in August that "never before has there been such a sudden and striking cessation of industrial activity."

The depression, which lingered for four years, created widespread suffering. As companies folded, the numbers of laid-off workers multiplied. By 1894, nearly 3 million workers were idle. By the end of the year, at least one worker in five was out of work. "Men died like flies under the strain," Henry Adams observed, "and Boston grew suddenly old, haggard, and thin."

Since most people believed that assisting the poor was a private matter, the burden of relief fell heaviest on local charities, benevolent societies, churches, labor unions, and ward bosses. But these groups were overwhelmed by the demand for services. Over 100,000 homeless people roamed the streets of Chicago. "Famine is in our midst," declared the head of the city's relief efforts. At one point Chicago saloons were handing out free lunches to an estimated 60,000 people a day. A Washington, D.C., newspaper reported "a vast army of unemployed, and men pleading for food who have never before been compelled to seek aid."

Fear of social unrest gripped the entire country. "We are on the eve of a very dark night," a writer warned President Cleveland, "unless a return of commercial prosperity relieves popular discontent." Industrialist James J. Hill wrote the president, "Business is at a standstill and the people are becoming thoroughly aroused. Their feeling is finding expression about as it did during the War of the Rebellion." The editors of *Railway Age* shared the fear of social turmoil. "It is probably safe to say, that in no civilized country in this century," they wrote, "has society been so disorganized as it was in the United States during the first half of 1894."

Social Unrest: Coxey's Army and The Pullman Strike

For a brief period Americans seemed to have lost faith in democracy. In the spring of 1894, masses of unemployed formed small "armies" that threatened to "invade" Washington to secure relief from the depression. It was the first time that so many protesters had called on the federal government to provide jobs for the unemployed. Altogether seventeen industrial armies marched on Washington, scaring the administration into thinking that they represented incipient rebellion across the country. The most famous march was led by "General" Jacob Coxey, a wealthy quarry owner from Ohio. Starting on Easter Sunday 1894, Coxey, accompanied by his wife and infant son, Legal Tender Coxey, led five hundred unemployed men, women, and children from Ohio to Washington. Coxey and his followers planned to present government leaders with "a petition with boots on," in support of a public works program of road building. The press covered the march as if it were a foreign invasion. "For every two sloggers in Coxey's ranks there was at least one reporter," recalled a journalist. When Coxey entered the Capitol grounds, a hundred mounted police routed the demonstrators and arrested him for trespassing on the grass.

Violent labor strikes contributed to a growing fear of revolution. Even before the depression, rumblings of unrest rolled across the land. The Great Railway

Coxey's Army The depression of 1893 caused tremendous economic turmoil, and by 1894, hundreds of disgruntled unemployed laborers decided to protest their plight by confronting politicians in Washington, D.C. Led by Jacob Coxey, men from across the country marched on the capital. Coxey's Army, seen in this photo, impressed spectators with its size and enthusiasm, and stirred fears of further labor unrest. *(Library of Congress.)*

Strike of 1877 had ignited nearly two decades of labor violence (see page 716). In 1892 labor disputes shook Andrew Carnegie's steel plant in Homestead, Pennsylvania. When workers objected to the company plan to reduce wages, manager Henry Clay Frick ordered a lockout, hired three hundred strikebreakers from the Pinkerton National Detective Agency, and built a barbed-wire fence around the plant to keep out workers.

Early on the morning of July 6, the strikebreakers tried to sneak into the plant on barges sailing down the Monongahela River from Youngstown. Workers, who had set up a twenty-four-hour watch, greeted their replacements with rocks, sticks, and gunfire. After an all-day battle, the Pinkertons surrendered. Three Pinkertons and ten strikers died in the fighting. The strike dragged on through the summer. By October, with the help of eight thousand state militia troops, Frick had hired new workers and forced the strikers to accept a harsh new settlement. The strike left a legacy of bitterness and ended effective organizing in the steel industry for a half-century.

After 1893, discontent mounted as wages were cut, employees laid off, and factories closed. During the first year of the depression, 1,400 strikes sent more than half a million workers from their jobs. The worst walkout idled 170,000 coal miners in Pennsylvania and the Midwest, where strikers bombed mine shafts, dynamited coal trains, and fought state militia. For nearly two weeks in June 1894, fighting rocked coalfields in Illinois, Ohio, and Indiana.

While Coxey's Army was calling for government aid to the unemployed, the Pullman Palace Car Company was laying off a large portion of its workers. The number of employees fell from 5,500 in July 1893 to 3,300 in May 1894. Many of those who kept their jobs saw their wages reduced as much as 25 percent. The company did not, however, reduce the rent it charged workers in the model factory town where most employees lived. In May 1894, workers went on strike when the company refused their requests for lower rents or higher wages. In June the American Railway Union (ARU) came to the assistance of the Pullman workers by voting to boycott all Pullman cars, which were pulled by the trains of most railroads. Until the ARU was created in 1893, railroad workers were represented by separate unions of engineers, firemen, switchmen, and conductors. Under the dynamic leadership of Eugene Debs, an official of the locomotive firemen's union, the ARU forged a powerful alliance of all railroad workers, making it the largest single union in the nation with more than 150,000 members. As a result of this solidarity, the strike spread rapidly and resulted in delaying the mail and tying up railroad traffic in the Chicago area.

The Chicago press reacted violently to the strike. The *Herald* openly supported the railroads, declaring, "If they yield one point it will show fatal weakness." The *Tribune* ran a series of stories branding Debs as a drunken tyrant whose "reckless" actions had endangered "the lives of thousands of Chicago citizens." No one opposed the strike more than U.S. Attorney General Richard Olney. He wired the federal attorney in Chicago: "I feel that the true way of dealing with the matter is by a force which is overwhelming and prevents any attempt at resistance." Under pressure from the business community and urging from Olney, President Cleveland decided to put an end to the boycott. When the strikers ignored a court injunction, Cleveland exploded. "If it takes the entire army and navy to deliver a postcard in Chicago, that card will be delivered," he swore, and promptly dispatched two thousand troops to Chicago to "restore law and order."

The arrival of the troops on July 4 incited widespread protest and violence. Angry strikers burned railroad cars, and reports estimated the damage to railroad property at $340,000. A *Chicago Evening Post* headline screamed, "Frenzied Mob Still Bent on Death and Destruction." After a few days, the federal troops restored order and helped crush the strike. At the same time Debs and other union leaders were arrested for violating the injunction and sentenced to six months in jail.

Most people supported Cleveland's tactics, but a few critics complained. Ohio governor John Peter Altgeld protested the president's use of federal troops without a request from the state, calling the order a "violation of a basic principle of our institutions." The government's decision to imprison Debs without a jury trial or conviction worried many people, even conservatives. However, with the fear of social unrest raised to a fever pitch, most people applauded Cleveland's use of force. Future president Theodore Roosevelt, then serving as a civil service commissioner, advised his fellow citizens that such radical sentiment could only be suppressed "by taking ten or a dozen of their leaders out, standing them against a wall and shooting them dead."

Depression Politics

Despite the army of unemployed and clear signs of social unrest, Cleveland clung to his conservative faith that government had no responsibility to assist those in distress. "While the people should patriotically and cheerfully support their Government," President Cleveland had explained at his inauguration, "its functions do not include the support of the people."

The causes of the depression may have been complex, but Cleveland was certain he had discovered the culprit: the collapse of the international monetary system. Equally convinced of the solution, he committed all the powers of his office to balancing the budget and returning the United States to the gold standard. In August, he called Congress into special session to repeal the Sherman Silver Purchase Act. Western interests responded with a bill calling for free coinage of silver. After a passionate, sometimes brilliant debate, Cleveland's forces carried the day. The voting revealed the sectional differences over the issue. Nearly all the votes in favor of the White House proposal came from the East; almost all the votes in support of the free silver proposal came from the West.

Cleveland's action precipitated a run on gold reserves as people flooded into banks to redeem their silver certificates. Worried that the government would not have enough gold to support all the certificates, Cleveland turned to J. P. Morgan and a group of Wall Street bankers to provide backing for new government bonds. The syndicate bought the bonds at a discount and then sold them to the public for a hefty profit. The move did little to stop the drain on gold reserves but it aroused public ire. It seemed to ordinary people that this was another tightfisted bargain in which wicked capitalists had profited. Critics complained that Cleveland was "now fastened by golden cords to a combination of the worst men in the world." Not until 1896, when the Treasury issued $100 million in bonds supported by public subscription, did the crisis pass.

Cleveland's depression policies angered millions of Americans; and his efforts to lower tariffs particularly alienated many of his business supporters. Shortly after assuming office, Cleveland endorsed congressional efforts to reduce tariffs. Senate Republicans, however, succeeded in adding nearly six hundred amendments to the original bill, which actually increased tariffs on many items even as it placed numerous raw materials on the "free" list. On August 28, 1894 the Wilson-Gorman Act became law. Cleveland, who refused to sign the law, declared that "the livery of Democratic tariff reform has been stolen and worn in the service of Republican protection."

The most significant feature of the legislation had nothing to do with tariffs, however; it was a controversial federal income tax. Congress included the tax—a modest 2 percent on all incomes over $4,000—to cover the lost revenue. Americans had experimented with the income tax during the Civil War, but outraged critics viewed the imposition of a permanent peacetime tax as a threat to American liberty. Senator John Sherman of Ohio called it an "attempt to array the rich against the poor." A divided Supreme Court agreed, and in *Pollock* v. *Farmers Loan and Trust* (1895), the Court struck down the tax. Speaking for the majority, Justice Stephen Field warned, "It will be but the stepping stone to others, larger and more sweeping, 'til our political contests will become a war of the poor against the rich; a war constantly growing in intensity and bitterness."

The public registered its dissatisfaction with Cleveland's response to the depression in the 1894 midterm elections. The Democratic Party suffered the greatest defeat in congressional history, losing 113 House seats. "The truth is," said one senator, "there was hardly an oasis left in the Democratic desert."

Despite the massive display of discontent with the Democrats, internal squabbling, combined with resistance from the major parties, kept Populist gains in the election to a minimum. Nationally, the Populists elected only four senators and four congressmen. In Kansas, Republicans held a mock funeral to mark the death of the Populist challenge. With the Democrats confined to the South and the Populist advance fizzling, the Republicans reigned supreme. They had every reason to feel confident about the upcoming 1896 presidential election.

The Republican Triumph: The Election of 1896

The Democrats abandoned the beleaguered Cleveland in 1896, nominated the dynamic William Jennings Bryan, and championed the "free silver" cause. The Democrats' change of heart left the Populists in a quandary: should they nominate their own candidate or form a coalition with the Democrats? After a bruising fight, they decided to endorse Bryan but select their own candidate, Georgia's Tom Watson, for vice president. When the Republicans nominated Ohio's William McKinley, the 1896 campaign became a sectional clash over the "money question" and the national government's economic policy role. The outcome would end the political stalemate of the previous twenty years.

Democrats and Populists

Cleveland's decision to return to the gold standard produced serious strains in the Democratic Party between midwestern farmers who clamored for silver and eastern business interests who favored gold. The contending factions descended on the Democratic convention in Chicago to battle for the party's soul. "You ask us to endorse Cleveland's fidelity," "Pitchfork" Ben Tillman, the Democratic governor of South Carolina, shouted to Cleveland's supporters in the platform debate; "I say he has been faithful unto death, the death of the Democratic party."

The key moment in the proceedings came on the second day of debate when Nebraska's William Jennings Bryan gave his famous "Cross of Gold" speech. Aroused by Bryan's passionate address, the pro-silver insurgents took control of the platform hearing. The party's platform, which adopted all of the insurgents' agenda, condemned "trafficking with banking syndicates"; demanded free and unlimited coinage of both silver and gold at the legal ratio of 16 to 1; attacked the protective tariff; and denounced the Supreme Court for invalidating the income tax.

The next day, Democrats nominated Bryan for president. To balance the ticket and calm the fears of conservative Democrats, the convention selected as his running mate Arthur Sewall, a multimillionaire banker and shipbuilder from Maine. Gold Democrats, determined not to be crucified on a cross of silver, bolted the party and nominated Senator John M. Palmer of Illinois. The *New York World* observed, "The sceptre of political power has passed from the strong certain hands of the East to the feverish, headstrong mob of the West and South."

In embracing the silver issue, the Democratic Party had commandeered the centerpiece of the Populist program. As they gathered in St. Louis for their convention, Populist Party leaders debated how to respond to the changing political situation. Many midwestern Populist leaders believed they would be most effective if they joined forces with the Democrats. They wanted to endorse Bryan—in other words, create a "fusion" ticket. Congressman Jerry Simpson cautioned that if the Populists did not endorse Bryan, the party "would not contain a corporal's guard in November." Another party leader, rationalizing that Bryan was "more of a Populist than a Democrat," proclaimed "there was nothing left of the Democratic party at Chicago but the name."

Advocates for fusion ran into tough opposition. Southern Populists, who had fought a bitter war against an entrenched Democratic Party in their home states, rejected the idea of a fusion ticket. Tom Watson complained that merging with the Democrats would mean "we play minnow while they play trout; we play June bug while they play duck; we play Jonah while they play the whale." In the Midwest, memories of the Democratic Party's support for slavery and disunion dimmed hope for a fusion ticket. Kansas's Mary Elizabeth Lease angrily declared, "My father and brothers died on the field of battle defending the flag and the Union that the Democratic party, represented by Bryan . . . sought to destroy." Joining Watson and Lease were urban radicals who viewed the Populist Party as a vehicle for more radical changes in the industrial order. Free silver, they believed, was a diversion from the main task of building a new reform party. Predicted Minnesota's Ignatius Donnelly, "Narrow Populism to free silver alone and it will disappear in a rat hole."

After a long and rancorous debate, the convention adopted the fusionist strategy. The Populist Party endorsed Bryan as its presidential candidate but, in an effort to retain its separate identity, nominated its own candidate for vice president, Georgia's Tom Watson. The fusionist strategy ultimately demoralized and destroyed the party. Ignatius Donnelly complained afterward that "the Democrats raped our convention while our leaders held the struggling victim." By the time the campaign was over in the South, Thomas Watson admitted, "Our party, as a party, does not exist any more. Fusion has well nigh killed it. The sentiment is still there, but the confidence is gone."

The Election of 1896

The Republican convention lacked the excitement and drama that characterized both the Democratic and Populist gatherings. "There is no life in it," William Allen White wrote. "The applause is hollow; the enthusiasm dreary and the delegates sit like hogs in a car and know nothing about anything." The party regulars nominated William McKinley of Ohio for president and Garret A. Hobart, a corporation lawyer, as vice president.

McKinley had served in the Union army during the Civil War before winning a seat in Congress in 1876. After losing his congressional seat in 1890, he served two terms as Ohio's governor. A calm, affable man, McKinley had earned a reputation as a political moderate who understood the need for compromise. "He was a small-town man with considerable sophistication," observed historian H. Wayne Morgan, "and a political success who never let power or fame turn his head." During his years in Congress, McKinley angered traditional Republicans by occasionally supporting silver measures. By 1896, however, McKinley had recanted his silver votes, and that shift, along with his strong support for high tariffs, had made him the favorite of party regulars.

The famous attorney Clarence Darrow described the 1896 presidential campaign as "the greatest battle of modern times." Between August and November, Bryan traveled eighteen thousand miles by train, visited twenty-six states and more than 250 cities, and communed with millions of Americans—most of them struggling farmers and "common people" who traveled hundreds of miles to hear him speak. Bryan personified the spirit of democratic insurgency. Countless citizens who felt excluded from the new industrial order, especially struggling farmers, looked to Bryan for hope and inspiration. Novelist Willa Cather noted how "rugged, ragged men of the soil weep like children" when listening to Bryan. Another observer noted that after his speeches hundreds of "the poor, the weak, the humble, the aged, the infirm" reached out "hard and wrinkled hands with crooked fingers and cracked knuckles to the young great orator, as if he were in very truth their promised redeemer from bondage." When he arrived in North Carolina, his followers ignited tar barrels along the tracks from Asheville to Raleigh to light his way.

In obvious contrast to Bryan, McKinley stayed at home in Canton, Ohio, speaking to groups of supporters from his front porch. When urged to challenge Bryan on the campaign trail, McKinley replied, "I might just as well put up a trapeze on my front lawn and compete with some professional athlete as go out speaking against Bryan." Strengthening McKinley's campaign, however, was a new breed of political boss. Under the watchful eye of Cleveland businessman Mark Hanna, the Republicans pioneered new methods of campaigning that would set the tone of political campaigns for the next century. They began by raising large sums of money. The Republican National Committee pulled in and paid out over $4 million—the

The 1896 Presidential Campaign The election of 1896 pitted two very different politicians and personalities against each other. Republican nominee William McKinley conducted a front-porch campaign, receiving supporters at his home in Canton, Ohio, where he gave only well-rehearsed speeches. Carefully selected reporters in the crowd then circulated his speeches in newspapers across the country. William Jennings Bryan, the Democratic and Populist candidate, chose to run a more active campaign. Bryan's whistle-stop tour led him around the country by railroad. At each stop, Bryan gave impromptu speeches to the people of the community, often using the railcar platform as his podium. *(Nebraska State Historical Society.)*

most ever spent on a political campaign and ten times more than the opposition. Standard Oil alone spent $300,000 on the campaign—almost matching the entire Democratic war chest. Hanna sent speakers to support local candidates, mobilized professional party workers, and hired scholars and public relations experts to write pamphlets that addressed the concerns of specific groups. McKinley supporters unveiled a new campaign weapon—buttons with a pin attached to the back. As McKinley observed, "This is a year for press and pen."

While Bryan's silver crusade appealed to the Democrats' traditional base of struggling farmers and big city machines, McKinley used his considerable resources to craft a broader message. Bryan's emphasis on higher crop prices and cheaper money proved unattractive to many urban workers, who desired low food prices and a stable currency that would preserve the real value of their wages. AFL president Samuel Gompers complained that Bryan showed little concern for the economic well-being of "the merchants and laborers of the industrial centres." The Republicans successfully portrayed Bryan as a radical whose agenda would destroy capitalism, at the same time that they stressed McKinley's support for the protective tariff and the gold standard as keys to economic recovery. The *New York Tribune* denounced Bryan as a "wretched rattle-pated boy, posing in vapid vanity and mouthing resounding rottenness." The *Louisville Courier Journal* slammed the smooth-talking Democrat as "a dishonest dodger . . . a daring adventurer . . . a political faker."

The election produced tremendous public interest, with four of every five voters going to the polls. Voter turnout in closely contested midwestern states reached as high as 95 percent. So many people cast ballots that Bryan received more votes than any previous presidential candidate in history and still lost the election! McKinley reaped the benefits of his campaign strategy, winning 7,102,246 popular votes to Bryan's 6,492,559. In the electoral college he collected 271 votes to Bryan's 176 (see map).

The election accentuated the continuing sectional differences in America. Bryan, who carried twenty-one states, did not take one outside the South or east of the Mississippi. The twenty-two great industrial states of the North and East, plus Oregon, voted decisively for McKinley. Many urban voters, alienated by Bryan's evangelical Protestantism and worried about his economic agenda, turned to the Republicans. For his part, McKinley downplayed potentially divisive moral issues and emphasized his support for the protective tariff and the gold standard, both of which were popular with workers. The appeal worked: of the eighty-two cities with a population of at least 45,000, only a dozen supported Bryan, and seven of these were in the Solid South and two in the silver states. As a Kansas Republican noted, "McKinley won because the Republicans had persuaded the middle class, almost to a man, that a threat to the gold standard was a threat to their prosperity."

The McKinley Presidency

The 1896 election produced the first undisputed majority since 1872. It shattered the stalemate that had mired the parties since the Civil War. McKinley took advantage of the opportunity, pushing through Congress key parts of the Republican agenda. In 1897 Congress passed the Dingley Tariff, which, along with reducing the number of items on the "free" list, raised rates to the highest level in American history. The Republicans passed the Gold Standard Act of 1900, which set the gold dollar as the sole standard of currency. To appease western interests, the act allowed

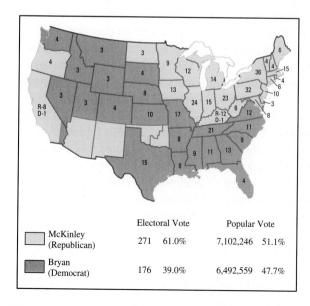

	Electoral Vote		Popular Vote	
McKinley (Republican)	271	61.0%	7,102,246	51.1%
Bryan (Democrat)	176	39.0%	6,492,559	47.7%

The Election of 1896 With the People's Party endorsement, Democratic nominee William Jennings Bryan used his campaign time to tour the country, promoting his free silver platform like a moral crusade. Meanwhile, his opponent, William McKinley, conducted a "front porch" campaign, promising prosperity for all from his home in Canton, Ohio. Bryan's strong support in the West and South was not enough, however, to defeat McKinley's majority in the electoral college.

for the creation of national banks in small towns, granting them authority to issue paper money. On both the tariff and gold issues, Republicans displayed remarkable party unity—97 percent voted for the tariff and 100 percent for the gold act.

The reform spirit that drove the Populist crusade lost much of its steam after 1896. The Republican triumph left many farmers demoralized, while the gradual return of prosperity eased social tensions. As a result, McKinley felt little need to respond to the wide-ranging Populist agenda for regulation of industry and direct democracy. The dawn of the new century, however, would produce a new generation of progressive reformers determined to revitalize the Populist agenda.

CONCLUSION

During the Gilded Age, a new politics of stalemate replaced the experiments in activist Republican government of the Civil War and Reconstruction eras. With the bitter debates over slavery and federalism fading, Americans longed for a period of political stability. The political parties, torn by internal rifts and vying for votes in a handful of key states, were unable to forge governing coalitions. In addition, the presidency lost much of its power following the impeachment trial of Andrew Johnson, and an unruly Congress was incapable of filling the vacuum. People remained passionate about politics, voting in unprecedented numbers, but presidential campaigns often revolved around personalities and scandal, while avoiding discussion of important issues. The result was a string of mediocre presidents and a host of unresolved national issues.

One of the most pressing "unresolved" issues concerned the plight of farmers in the South and Midwest. Increased production brought a dramatic decrease in prices for farm products and a declining standard of living for many farmers. Convinced that greedy railroad and grain elevator operators were at fault, farmers created the Grange movement in the 1860s. By the 1880s, Granges gave way to the formidable Farmers' Alliance, which articulated an ambitious program, including government ownership of the railroads, an inflated money supply, and direct democracy measures. When the major parties failed to respond to their agenda, farmers moved into electoral politics by forming the Populist Party. In 1892 the high point of the agrarian experiment, the Populist presidential candidate scored twenty-two electoral votes, and the party won a number of Senate and congressional seats.

Beginning in 1893, a severe economic depression provided momentum to the Populist challenge. With more than 3 million workers unemployed, many Americans feared widespread social unrest. Those fears seemed confirmed when "armies" of the unemployed marched on Washington calling for federal assistance, and when violent labor disputes shook Andrew Carnegie's steel plant in Homestead, Pennsylvania, and the Pullman Palace Car Company in Chicago.

Many of the social tensions of the decade found expression in the 1896 presidential election, which mirrored the continuing sectional divisions in America. The Democrats co-opted the Populist platform and nominated William Jennings Bryan as their nominee. The Republicans selected William McKinley, who stood firmly on the gold standard. Bryan's message of reform resonated with struggling farmers in the

Midwest and South, while McKinley's steadfast support for the gold standard endeared him to business interests in the East and Midwest. The decisive Republican triumph ended the politics of stalemate and inaugurated a new era of Republican dominance. The Populist challenge had failed, but the Republican administrations to come would open a new round of experimentation in national government.

SUGGESTED READINGS

Several excellent overviews of the Gilded Age discuss the period's politics and political culture. Sean Dennis Cashman's *America and the Gilded Age: From the Death of Lincoln to the Rise of Theodore Roosevelt* (1984) and Mark Wahlgren Summers's *The Gilded Age: or, The Hazard of New Functions* (1997) are both highly readable surveys. *The Gilded Age: Essays on the Origins of Modern America* (1996), edited by Charles Calhoun, is a collection of essays on a wide range of topics, from partisan politics to the experience of African-Americans to science and technology. For more thesis-driven studies, Samuel Hays's *The Response to Industrialism, 1885–1914* (1957) and Robert Wiebe's *The Search for Order, 1877–1920* (1967) are insightful. Both see changes in political culture as part of a larger shift in values in response to rapid industrialization after the Civil War.

H. Wayne Morgan's *From Hayes to McKinley: National Party Politics, 1877–1896* (1969) is a good overview that corrects previous interpretations of Gilded Age politics as devoid of real issues or party differences. R. Hal Williams's *Years of Decision: American Politics in the 1890s* (1978) agrees with this assessment and argues that the Republican Party eventually won out in the 1890s because its activist vision was better suited to the needs of an industrial society. David J. Rothman's *Politics and Power: The United States Senate, 1869–1901* (1966) views the emergence of modern politics in the Gilded Age through the lens of the Senate. A synthesis of the pivotal election of 1896 is provided in Paul Glad's *McKinley, Bryan and the People* (1964).

Good political biographies of the major political figures of the period include Lewis Gould's *The Presidency of William McKinley* (1980), Ari Hoogenboom's *Rutherford B. Hayes: Warrior and President* (1995), Justus D. Doenecke's *The Presidencies of James A. Garfield and Chester A. Arthur* (1981), Richard E. Welch's *The Presidencies of Grover Cleveland* (1988), and Louis W. Koenig's *Bryan: A Political Biography of William Jennings Bryan* (1971). Gerald W. McFarland follows the careers of a group of Mugwump reformers into the Progressive Era in *Mugwumps, Morals and Politics, 1884–1920* (1975).

Several studies have tackled the major issues of the Gilded Age. Civil service reform is covered by John G. Sproat in *"The Best Men": Liberal Reformers in the Gilded Age* (1968). Tom Terrill examines the tariff issue in *The Tariff, Politics, and American Foreign Policy, 1874–1901* (1973). He argues that the two parties initially divided over the domestic issues underlying the tariff debate but eventually found consensus concerning the manipulation of the tariff to expand U.S. foreign markets. The currency issue is treated by Irwin Unger in *The Greenback Era: A Social and Political History of American Finance, 1865–1879* (1964) and Walter Nugent in *Money and American Society, 1865–1880* (1968). Both examine the larger political and social issues involved; Nugent also puts the issue in international context.

In the past thirty years, historians have uncovered a fascinating and vibrant political culture in the Gilded Age. Robert Cherny provides a synthesis of recent interpretations in *American Politics in the Gilded Age, 1868–1900* (1997). Morton Keller's *Affairs of State: Public Life in Late Nineteenth Century America* (1977) is a comprehensive study, covering national, state, and local politics and examining a wide range of issues, from government regulation to public schools, and their relation to the political culture of the time. In *The Third Electoral System, 1853–1892: Parties, Voters and Political Cultures* (1979), Paul Kleppner studies

American voting behavior and concludes that the differences between the major parties were rooted in antagonisms between social groups within the electorate. Michael McGerr, in *The Decline of Popular Politics* (1986), argues that even while popular participation reached its zenith during this time, political reform had already begun eroding it with measures that reduced the communal nature of partisan politics.

More specific aspects of the political culture are covered by several commendable works. Rebecca Edwards offers a fascinating look at the gender dimension of political culture during this time in *Angels in the Machinery: Gender in American Party Politics from the Civil War to the Progressive Era* (1997). Robert Kelley's *The Transatlantic Persuasion* (1969) puts Gilded Age political culture in international perspective, finding similarities among the liberal democracies in England, Canada, and the United States. Richard Jensen and Paul Kleppner have written ethnocultural studies of midwestern politics. In *Cross of Culture: A Social Analysis of Midwestern Politics, 1850–1900* (1970), Kleppner finds that ethnicity and religion matter more than class in party affiliation. Jensen comes to a similar conclusion in *The Winning of the Midwest: Social and Political Conflict, 1888–1896* (1971). He finds that the Republicans' pluralistic appeal eventually gave them a stronghold in the Midwest.

The economics behind the Panic of 1893 are examined by Charles Hoffman in *The Depression of the Nineties: An Economic History* (1970). He concludes that, contrary to the prevailing opinion of the time, the amount of currency in circulation had little impact on the health of the economy. Samuel McSeveney examines the political ramifications of the depression in *The Politics of Depression: Political Behavior in the Northeast, 1893–1896* (1972). He argues that the panic upset ethnic and cultural alignments and put economic issues at center stage, giving the Republican Party the opportunity to break the political deadlock of the previous fifteen years.

Several excellent books have been written on the social unrest that accompanied the depression. Carlos Schwantes's *Coxey's Army: An American Odyssey* (1985) is a highly readable narrative that follows the experiences of the men who marched on Washington. Paul Krause examines the larger issues involved in the Homestead strike in *The Battle for Homestead, 1880–1892: Politics, Culture and Steel*. He argues that the conflict was about more than economic security; it was also the workers' attempt to defend a way of life that placed value on a worker's skill. Stanley Buder offers a wonderful examination of the Pullman strike in *Pullman: An Experiment in Industrial Order and Community Planning* (1967). He places the strike in the historical context of the town's founding and life as a model community.

Richard Hofstadter's major work *The Age of Reform* (1955) focused on the reactionary aspect of the Populist movement. Since the fifties, this perception has been challenged by a number of works, most notably Lawrence Goodwyn in *Democratic Promise: The Populist Movement in America* (1976). Goodwyn's thorough study of the Populist movement from the inside portrays it as a careful critique of the American political economy. Gene Clanton also stresses the genuine reform content of the movement in *Populism: The Humane Preference in America* (1991), arguing that the Populists' central tenet was the belief that government should serve human rights instead of property rights. In *The Populist Response to Industrial America* (1962), Norman Pollack likewise views Populism as a broad "social gospel" movement, until the currency issue superseded all others and killed the movement. Robert Durden offers a contrasting interpretation in *The Climax of Populism: The Election of 1896* (1965). He minimizes the Populist commitment to ideology, maintaining that the Populist Party, like the major parties, was primarily concerned with organization. In *American Populism: A Social History, 1877–1898* (1993), Robert McMath takes a grass-roots approach to the movement, examining rural protest organizations from the 1870s through the 1890s, especially their roots in the social and economic networks of rural communities.

The Populist Party Platform

On July 4, 1892, the People's Party unveiled its platform at its first national convention in Omaha, Nebraska. The preamble, written by Minnesota Populist leader Ignatius Donnelly, crystallized the basic ideals and discontents of the Populist movement, including its demand for the coinage of silver.

The conditions which surround us best justify our co-operation; we meet in the midst of a nation brought to the verge of moral, political, and material ruin. Corruption dominates the ballot-box, the Legislatures, the Congress, and touches even the ermine of the bench. The people are demoralized. . . . The newspapers are largely subsidized or muzzled, public opinion silenced, business prostrated, homes covered with mortgages, labor impoverished, and the land concentrating in the hands of capitalists. . . . The fruits of the toil of the millions are boldly stolen to build up the colossal fortunes of the few, unprecedented in the history of mankind; and the possessors of these, in turn, despise the Republic and endanger liberty. From the same prolific womb of governmental injustice we breed the two great classes—tramps and millionaires.

The national power to create money is appropriated to enrich bond-holders; a vast public debt payable in legal-tender currency has been funded into gold-bearing bonds, thereby adding millions to the burdens of the people.

Silver, which has been accepted as coin since the dawn of history, has been demonetized to add to the purchasing power of gold by decreasing the value of all forms of property as well as human labor, and the supply of currency is purposely abridged to fatten usurers, bankrupt enterprise, and enslave industry. A vast conspiracy against mankind has been organized on two continents, and it is rapidly taking possession of the world. If not met and overthrown at once, it forebodes terrible social convulsions, the destruction of civilization, or the establishment of an absolute despotism.

We have witnessed for more than a quarter of a century the struggles of the two great political parties for power and plunder, while grievous wrongs have been inflicted upon the suffering people. . . . Neither do they now promise us any substantial reform. . . . They propose to drown the outcries of a plundered people with the uproar of a sham battle over the tariff, so that capitalists, corporations, national banks, rings, trusts, watered stock, the demonetization of silver and the oppressions of the usurers may all be lost sight of. . . .

We seek to restore the government of the Republic to the hands of the "plain people," with which class it originated. We assert our purposes to be identical with the purposes of the National Constitution. . . .

Our country finds itself confronted by conditions for which there is no precedent in the history of the world; our annual agricultural productions amount to billions of dollars in value, which must, within a few weeks or months, be exchanged for billions of dollars' worth of commodities consumed in their production; the existing currency supply is wholly inadequate to make the exchange; the results are falling prices, the formation of combines and rings, the impoverishment of the producing class. We pledge ourselves that if given power we will labor to correct these evils by wise and reasonable legislation, in accordance with the terms of our platform.

We believe the powers of the government—in other words, of the people—should be expanded . . . as rapidly and as far as the good sense of intelligent people and the teachings of experience shall justify, to the end that oppression, injustice, and poverty shall eventually cease in the land. . . .

William Allen White Criticizes the Kansas Populists

Not everyone shared the Populist enthusiasm for reform. In 1896 William Allen White, the editor of a small Kansas newspaper, the *Emporia Gazette*, wrote a scathing critique of populism and its impact on his home state. The essay, which was published during the heat of the 1896 presidential campaign, was widely reprinted in Republican newspapers.

If there had been a high brick wall around the state eight years ago, and not a soul had been admitted or permitted to leave, Kansas would be half a million souls better off than she is today. . . . In five years ten million people have been added to the national population, yet instead of gaining a share of this—say, half a million—Kansas has apparently been a plague spot and, in the very garden of the world, has lost population by ten thousands every year.

Not only has she lost population, but she has lost money. Every moneyed man in the state who could get out without loss has gone. Every month in every community sees someone who has a little money pack up and leave the state. This has been going on for eight years. Money has been drained out all the time. In towns where ten years ago there were three or four or half a dozen money-lending concerns, stimulating industry by furnishing capital, there is now none, or one or two that are looking after the interest and principal already outstanding. . . .

Go east and you hear them laugh at Kansas; go west and they sneer at her; go south and they "cuss" her; go north and they have forgotten her. Go into any crowd of intelligent people gathered anywhere on the globe, and you will find the Kansas man on the defensive. The newspaper columns and magazines once devoted to praise of her, to boastful facts and startling figures concerning her resources, are now filled with cartoons. . . .

"There are two ideas of government," said our noble [William Jennings] Bryan at Chicago. "There are those who believe that if you legislate to make the well-to-do prosperous, this prosperity will leak through on those below. The Democratic idea has been that if you legislate to make the masses prosperous, their prosperity will find its way up through every class and rest upon them."

That's the stuff! Give the prosperous man the dickens! Legislate the thriftless man into ease, whack the stuffing out of the creditors and tell the debtors who borrowed the money five years ago when money "per capita" was greater than it is now, that the contraction of currency gives him a right to repudiate.

Whoop it up for the ragged trousers; put the lazy, greasy fizzle, who can't pay his debts on the altar, and bow down and worship him. Let the state ideal be high. What we need is not the respect of our fellow men, but the chance to get something for nothing.

Oh, yes, Kansas is a great state. Here are people fleeing from it by the score every day, capital going out of the state by the hundreds of dollars; and every industry but farming paralyzed, and that crippled, because its products have to go across the ocean before they can find a laboring man at work who can afford to buy them. Let's don't stop this year. Let's drive all the decent, self-respecting men out of the state. Let's keep the old clodhoppers who know it all.

The Populist Party grew out of widespread rural discontent over falling farm product prices, rising costs due to high tariffs, high rates for rail contracts and grain elevators, and exorbitant credit terms. Gradually, farmers' complaints evolved into a broader critique of American society and the financial underpinnings of the new industrial order. Tapping into a rich rhetorical tradition, which pitted the noble aspiration of the "common man" against greedy concerns of the elite, the Populists charged that a cabal of eastern capitalists had manipulated the money supply and cheated the "producing class" out of their fair share. They looked to the federal government for assistance, proposing a host of solutions, including greater democracy, regulation of the railroads, easier credit, and an expanded currency through the coinage of silver. For many struggling farmers, free coinage of silver emerged as a panacea for all the ills of the new industrial order. Expanding the currency would allow farmers to pay off debts with inflated money and raise the price of farm products.

Not everyone accepted the Populists' critique of current conditions, or their ambitious program for reform. Many middle-class and business groups complained that the Populist commitment to silver, seething hostility to business, and unquestioned faith in the "common man" would lead to economic calamity. Urban workers, who shared the Populist anger toward big business and were equally frustrated with the established political parties, feared that expanding the currency would produce rampant inflation and lower living standards. Populists may have possessed good intentions, these critics charged, but their efforts to use government power to help the poor would strangle business and choke off prosperity. White viewed the economic crisis in Kansas as evidence that the siren call of Populism would lead to disastrous consequences. Republicans successfully used these arguments against William Jennings Bryan in the 1896 presidential campaign.

Questions for Analysis

1. Whom do the Populists blame for the nation's moral and economic crisis?

2. Why is the silver issue so significant for the Populists?

3. Why do they see a need for a third party?

4. What are their views of government?

5. What is White's grievance with the Populists, and why does he blame them for Kansas's economic misery? Is his judgment fair?

6. How does his view of government differ from the Populist view?

21

The Progressive Era, 1889–1916

*O*n September 18, 1889, Jane Addams, the thirty-year-old daughter of a prosperous Quaker from Cedarville, Illinois, and a college friend, Ellen Gates Starr, rented a rundown mansion at the corner of Halsted and Polk Streets on Chicago's West Side and began the first settlement house, or neighborhood center, in the Midwest. "Probably no young matron ever placed her own things in her own house with more pleasure than that with which we first furnished Hull House," Addams reflected.

Like a growing number of other educated, middle-class women, Addams was dissatisfied with the traditional options available for women. For most of the previous decade she had searched for a constructive outlet for her humanitarian instincts. The idea of creating a settlement house came to her when she visited Toynbee Hall in London, the world's first settlement house, which had been founded by students from Oxford University. "It is so free of 'professional doing good,' so unaffectedly sincere and so productive of good results in its classes and libraries so that it seems perfectly ideal," she wrote.

Addams returned to America determined to start her own Toynbee Hall. She would need determination, and more, to overcome many daunting obstacles. Chicago, the second-largest city in the country, was bursting at the seams with new immigrants from Europe. The area surrounding Hull House was one of the city's dirtiest and poorest neighborhoods. Most immigrants lived in crowded tenements with raw sewage flowing through the foul smelling streets outside. Tuberculosis and smallpox ran rampant. Well-fed rats patrolled the neighborhood. Journalist Lincoln Steffens described the neighborhood as "first in violence, deepest in dirt, loud, lawless, unlovely, ill-smelling, criminally wide open, commercially brazen, socially thoughtless and raw."

Addams wanted to help her new neighbors but she lacked a detailed blueprint of how to accomplish that goal. "We had no definite idea what we were there to do," she recalled. "But we hoped, by living among the people, to learn what was needed and to help out." She started by establishing a nursery for the children of working women, then expanded to include a kindergarten and a boys club for older youths. By the turn of the century, the settlement covered an entire city block, included a gymnasium, auditorium, and library, and offered a wide range of services: a health clinic, vocational training, English classes, and music and art education. The "social experiment on Halsted Street" evolved into a workshop for urban progressivism—a collection of reform movements that focused on using government to tame the excesses of industrialization and urbanization.

Like many other progressive reformers who grew up in comfortable middle-class, Protestant families, Addams believed that urban problems such as crime and poverty resulted not from individual failures, but from an unhealthy environment. Addams also shared contemporary fears that the massive influx of immigrants, combined with the evils of industrialization, would widen class and cultural differences in America. For solutions to many of the problems plaguing America's cities, Addams and other progressive reformers looked to government. She believed that only government could provide the services and the regulation that were necessary for future progress. To convince officials to take action, Hull House residents made elaborate studies of child labor, tenement conditions, and wage rates in the neighborhood. They joined coalitions with other progressive groups for protective labor legislation for working women and children. They led the way in enacting legislation to regulate the sale of narcotics and initiated an investigation into the city's impure milk supply that helped lower the infant mortality rate.

Jane Addams represented just one part of a new reform spirit that gathered momentum in the last decade of the nineteenth century and began to affect nearly every aspect of American life between 1900 and 1916. People living at the time felt the sense of excitement in the air. One reformer declared in 1913 that "one of the most inspiring movements in human history is now in progress." Millions of people called themselves progressives. They did not always agree on the proper pace or the critical focus of reform. While social justice advocates like Jane Addams sought to make society more compassionate, other progressives concentrated on making it more efficient. Still others focused on improving social morality, which they hoped to do by prohibiting the sale of alcohol, outlawing prostitution, and limiting immigration.

For all of their differences, progressives spoke a common language of discontent, which emphasized the dangers of monopoly power, stressed the importance of community, and articulated a passion for social efficiency. In addition, progressives borrowed some of this language, and many of their ideas, from thinkers in Europe who were confronting many of the same social problems. Finally, when they agreed on an issue, progressives formed alliances with other groups. But the coalitions were usually short-lived, and allies one day might be opponents the next. All of the activity made the progressive period one of the most confusing in American history, but also one of the most exciting eras of experimentation in local and federal government.

▌ What was progressivism, and what groups in society tended to join in progressive reform movements?

▌ What was the progressive agenda, and what new roles did progressives expect government to play in correcting America's problems?

▌ What was the difference between radicals and progressives?

▌ How was progressivism manifest in national politics and in actions by the federal government?

This chapter will address these questions.

 ## The Rise of Progressivism

A number of groups played an important role in laying the foundation of the progressive movement. By 1900, intellectuals were challenging the assumptions of Social Darwinists, who argued that immutable laws of nature had shaped society. While intellectuals chipped away at the pillars of Social Darwinism, many middle-class women contributed to the reform spirit by campaigning for social justice. A new breed of investigative journalists, called muckrakers, aroused public anger with their graphic depictions of corruption in America. The new middle class, fascinated with social efficiency and scientific management, searched for ways to create a more orderly society. These various reform elements were united by a common desire to use activist government to limit the power of corporations and improve society.

The Challenge to Social Darwinism

Gilded Age intellectuals like William Graham Sumner had argued that Charles Darwin's theories of evolution could be applied to contemporary society. Reform was unnecessary, even counterproductive, they argued, because nature dictated the rules of the game and guaranteed the "survival of the fittest" (see pages 850–851). By 1900, a number of intellectuals had initiated a spirited assault on Sumner's ideas. In the process, they laid the intellectual foundation for the Progressive Era.

The new intellectuals showed less interest in how society was supposed to function than in how it really did. They differed widely in their views, but they shared the basic belief that man could improve society through reason and intelligence. Psychologist William James, older brother of novelist Henry James, laid the groundwork for much progressive social thought in his seminal book, *Principles of Psychology* (1890). James challenged the determinism and pessimism of Social Darwinism by arguing that human beings could control the process of their own evolution. His philosophy of pragmatism argued that modern society must rely for guidance less on old ideals and moral principles and more on the test of scientific

Chronology

1889	Addams founds Hull House
1892	Wells-Barnett begins antilynching campaign
1895	Anti-Saloon League founded
1901	Roosevelt becomes president after McKinley's assassination
1902	TR intervenes in the coal strike
1903	Holmes appointed to Supreme Court
1904	TR elected president
	Northern Securities Company dissolved as a railroad trust
1905	Industrial Workers of the World founded
	Pure Food and Drug Act passed
1906	Hepburn Act passed
	Sinclair publishes *The Jungle*
1908	Taft elected president
	Staunton, VA, hires U.S.'s first city manager
1910	NAACP founded
1911	Triangle Shirtwaist fire
1912	TR bolts Republican Party
	Wilson elected president
1913	Seventeenth Amendment (direct election of senators) ratified
	Federal Reserve Act passed
	Underwood-Simmons Tarriff lowered overall average duty on imports
1914	Sanger indicted for obscenity
	Clayton Anti-Trust Act passed
1916	Brandeis appointed to Supreme Court
1919	Eighteenth Amendment (Prohibition) ratified
1920	Nineteenth Amendment (women's suffrage) ratified

inquiry. No idea was valid, he claimed, unless it worked. "Pragmatism," he wrote, "is willing to take anything, to follow either logic or the senses, and to count the humblest and most personal experiences."

An expanding network of social scientists brought this same concern for scientific inquiry into other areas of thought. Lester Frank Ward, a Brown University sociologist, argued that human intelligence allowed people to plan and to order their worlds as they saw fit. In his book *Dynamic Sociology* (1883), Ward argued that the Social Darwinists had underestimated the capability of human intelligence to alter the environment and improve society. Economist Thorstein Veblen added his influential voice to the chorus of social critics in two important books, *A Theory of the Leisure Class* (1899) and *The Theory of Business Enterprise* (1904). Veblen poked fun at the industrial tycoons of the late nineteenth century to show that greed, not natural laws, governed economic relations in America. As an antidote to laissez-faire, he called for a new class of government experts to develop policies for managing the economy. In his book *Economic Interpretation of the Constitution* (1913), the progressive historian Charles A. Beard set out to show that greed and self-interest, not divine inspiration, had influenced the creation of the Constitution. It was, he argued, a human document that could be changed to address new circumstances.

Others called for the new faith in scientific reasoning to be applied to education. In books such as *The School and Society* (1902) and *Democracy and Education* (1916), philosopher-educator John Dewey emphasized the value of a creative, flexible approach to education that would enable students to acquire practical knowledge. Dewey rejected the rote memorization of traditional education and instead tried to "make each one of our schools an embryonic community life, active with the types of occupations that reflect the life of the larger society." The scientific method, he believed, would be the governing principle of this new, "instrumental" education.

Progressive legal thinkers such as Oliver Wendell Holmes, Jr., who was appointed to the Supreme Court in 1903, and Louis D. Brandeis, appointed in 1916, hoped to transform the law from a bulwark of the status quo into a vehicle for change. Although the two justices would not always line up on the same side of an issue, Holmes and Brandeis shared a similar conception of the relationship of law to society. "The life of the law has not been logic; it has been experience," Holmes argued in *The Common Law* (1881). Brandeis agreed, writing that the law must "guide by the light of reason." As a lawyer, Brandeis used mounds of statistical evidence showing that long working hours contributed to poor health to convince the courts to accept legislation establishing a ten-hour workday for women (*Muller* v. *Oregon* 1908). The law, he argued, must consider actual working conditions and not just legal precedent. It was a rare victory: Holmes and Brandeis seldom convinced a majority on the court, but their views influenced a generation of legal thinkers.

Church workers challenged the prevailing belief in Social Darwinism by appealing to religious conviction. Proponents of the Social Gospel argued that the main teachings of Christianity—social justice and sacrifice—should form the foundation of modern society. In his popular book *In His Steps* (1896), Charles Sheldon urged readers to ask, "What would Jesus do?" as they made choices in their daily lives. Walter Rauschenbusch, a Protestant theologian from Rochester, New York, was the leading proponent of this new Social Gospel, a theology rooted in his own grim experience: this first assignment, in 1886, led him to New York's Hell's Kitchen, where he encountered the harsh realities of poverty and misery. In his most important works, *Christianity and the Social Crisis* (1907) and *Christianity and the Social Order* (1915), Rauschenbusch argued that all people should work toward creating the Kingdom of God on earth.

The growing presence of the Salvation Army in many cities was the most visible sign of the desire to proclaim the message of Christian social responsibility to an industrial society. The Salvation Army, founded by William Booth in London in 1873, boasted a corps of three thousand officers and twenty thousand privates by 1900. Along with ministering to spiritual needs, the Salvation Army provided material aid—food pantries, employment bureaus, and daycare centers—to the urban poor.

Women and Social Justice

Excluded from formal participation in politics, and from most male-dominated trade unions and fraternal organizations, women created separate organizations to shape legislation and protect their interests. Middle-class reformers expanded the nineteenth-century cult of domesticity—which held that a woman's proper place was in the home—to support their expanding role in influencing public policy. "Woman's place is in the Home," wrote the suffragist Rheta Childe Dorr in 1910, "but Home is not contained within the four walls of an individual home. Home is the community." Reformers broadened the dominant belief in the moral superiority of women, and their special responsibility for dealing with the family and protecting children, into a "maternalist" vision of gender-specific reform.

To realize that vision, women reformers created a host of voluntary associations. The Woman's Christian Temperance Union (WCTU), founded in 1874, organized women in campaigns to enforce sobriety and defend the home. The National Congress of Mothers (1897), which promoted "all those characteristics which shall elevate and ennoble," sponsored playgrounds and kindergartens in a number of cities. The Women's Trade Union League (1903) attempted to organize women workers. The Young Women's Christian Association played an active role in local communities.

African-American women, barred from white clubs, organized their own groups to improve community life. The Women's Convention of the Black Baptist Church raised money for black women to attend college. In 1896 members of three dozen black clubs came together to create the National Association of Colored Women (NACW). Led by Mary Church Terrell, a graduate of the old abolitionist stronghold Oberlin College, the NACW offered self-help classes, homes for the elderly and for working girls, and public health information.

Paralleling the settlement house movement, female reformers used their voluntary associations to develop social welfare programs for working-class women and their children. One of the most successful advocates of social legislation was Florence Kelley. Born into a wealthy Philadelphia family, Kelly graduated from Cornell University in 1882. Refused admittance to the University of Pennsylvania for graduate studies because she was a woman, Kelley traveled to Switzerland. There she attended school, married, and gave birth to three children. In 1886, after her marriage fell apart, she returned to the states and became a resident at Hull House. Over the next few years she emerged as an outspoken and tireless champion for legislation to protect children and women. She published numerous studies documenting the ill effects of long hours on women and children, and in 1893 convinced the Illinois legislature to pass an eight-hour workday law for women. When the state supreme

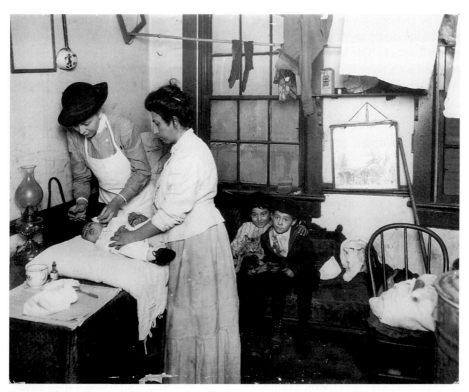

Nurses Visit a Tenement   Progressive reformers were greatly concerned about the poor conditions in which the urban working classes lived. Social workers and nurses, like the one attending the baby in this photograph, went door to door in tenement buildings, assessing the living conditions, teaching residents better sanitation and home economics, and administering medication. Most of these visiting professionals were educated, middle-class women; the work gave them a respectable outlet for their talents. Although their motives were sincere, social workers often condescended to their clients, showed a lack of understanding of their values and situation, and tried to impose their own domestic ideals on them.   *(Chicago Historical Society.)*

court invalidated the legislation, Kelley took her cause to Washington. In 1899 she became the secretary of the National Consumers League, which attempted to mobilize public opinion in favor of new social legislation. After her death in 1932, Supreme Court justice Felix Frankfurter wrote that Kelley "had probably the largest single share in shaping the social history of the United States during the first thirty years of this century."

More militant members of the social justice movement looked to class action. Among these were young female labor organizers who challenged the craft unionism of the AFL by trying to organize unskilled workers. In November 1909, the New York Women's Trade Union League and a local of the International Ladies Garment Workers Union held a massive and emotional rally in New York City's Cooper Union. After listening to impassioned speeches emphasizing their common struggle as exploited working women, thousands of garment workers voted to strike, demanding union recognition, higher wages, and better working conditions. Raising their right hands high in the air, the women sealed their commitment to strike with an oath. "If I turn traitor to the cause I now pledge, may this hand wither from the arm I now raise."

Over the next three months the strikers were arrested by police and beaten by thugs. But their spirits remained high. As one observer noted, "Neither the police, nor the hooligan hirelings of the bosses nor the biting frost and chilling snow of December and January damped their willingness to picket the shops from early morn till late at night." The strikers returned to work without union recognition, but their efforts had forced major concessions from management, including a fifty-hour workweek, wage increases, and preferential hiring for union members.

Some of the strikers worked at the Triangle Shirtwaist Company in downtown New York City. On March 25, 1911, a fire exploded in the building. As the flames spread through the top three floors of the ten-story building, many workers, mostly young Jewish women, found themselves trapped by exit doors that had been locked from the outside to prevent workers from slipping out for breaks. Forty-seven women leaped to their deaths attempting to escape the flames. "They hit the pavement just like hail," reported a fireman. "We could hear the thuds faster than we could [see] the bodies fall." Another ninety-nine victims were consumed by flames and smoke. The tragedy led to the creation of the New York State Factory Commission, which recommended laws for improving working conditions and regulating hours and wages for women and children.

The Muckrakers

A small army of investigative reporters contributed importantly to the progressive reform spirit's sense of moral indignation and idealistic purpose. Theodore Roosevelt branded these new journalists "muckrakers," after the "Man with the Muckrake" in John Bunyan's *Pilgrim's Progress,* "the man who could look no way but downward with the muckrake in his hands." Muckrakers combined factual reporting with heavy moralizing to expose dishonesty, greed, and corruption in American society, and to arouse the indignation of middle-class readers.

Technological innovations allowed the muckrakers to reach a wider readership. Inexpensive popular newspapers and eye-catching specialty magazines proliferated thanks to new developments in printing. To sell more magazines, publishers began to replace political prose with news and feature articles. In 1902, *McClure's* ran a series of articles by Ida Tarbell, which described the unfair business practices of John D. Rockefeller's Standard Oil trust. She described Standard Oil as "a big hand [that] reached out from nobody knew where, to steal" the oil entrepreneurs' accomplishments "and throttle their future." In another series, Lincoln Steffens described municipal corruption in several large eastern and midwestern cities. Other journalists jumped on the muckraking bandwagon. Ray Standard Baker exposed the brutal labor practices of railroad and mine owners. David Graham Phillip depicted the U.S. Senate as a playground for rich and powerful interests. These stories, often published later as books, reached millions of Americans. The most famous muckraker was a young radical novelist, Upton Sinclair, whose realistic novel *The Jungle* (1906) presented all-too-vivid descriptions of filth and confusion in "Packingtown" as beleaguered workers processed tainted and sometimes spoiled meat for public consumption.

The New Professions

Industrial society created a new layer of middle-class workers who kept it running smoothly and efficiently at the same time that the growth of scientific knowledge increased the power and prestige of physicians, lawyers, and others with advanced education. The new middle class, and the interest groups they formed, created a powerful force for reform during the Progressive Era.

Many members of the new middle class shared a fear of social disorder and a passion for efficiency. The middle class was at the vanguard of a bureaucratic revolution that valued scientific procedures, centralized management, and social planning. "There are two gospels I always want to preach to reformers," Theodore Roosevelt said. "The first is the gospel of morality, the next is the gospel of efficiency." Like most people, Roosevelt believed that American society had become too chaotic and confused. As an example of how to remedy the problem of disorder, many progressives pointed to the modern corporation, which, for all its faults, offered a model of organization and efficiency that could be extended to the larger society. "The trust," remarked Jane Addams, "is the educator of us all." Addams did not like trusts, and she certainly did not want to see their power expanded, but she, like most progressives, admired their efficiency.

Not surprisingly, the new middle class created a host of professional organizations both to protect their interests and to implement their ideas of social order. By 1916, lawyers had established professional bar associations in all forty-eight states. Teachers created the National Education Association in 1905. Social workers formed the National Federation of Settlements (1911). Business groups gave rise to some of the most powerful and effective organizations, including the National Association of Manufacturers (1895) and the United States Chamber of Commerce (1912). The most successful and influential new professional association emerged in medicine. In 1901, doctors reorganized the American Medical Association (AMA) into a modern organization that established strict standards of admission to the profession. In 1901, only 8,400 doctors were members of the AMA. Ten years later the AMA claimed over 70,000 members, nearly 50 percent of the nation's physicians. The AMA orchestrated a concerted effort to organize the nation's doctors to upgrade standards and restrict the number of new physicians. Increased scrutiny forced many less rigorous medical schools to close their doors and slashed the number of new physicians entering practice.

As the political parties began to lose their grip on voter loyalties, these interest groups exercised greater political clout. Civil service reform during the 1870s and 1880s, combined with the widespread use of the secret ballot in the 1890s, weakened the power of party bosses and provided voters with more freedom to choose candidates. The new middle-class interest groups moved to fill the political void, encouraging voters to split their tickets and support reform candidates.

The Appeal of Progressivism

"Slowly as the new century came into its first decade I saw the Great Light," observed Kansas editor William Allen White. The "Great Light" brightening the horizon was progressivism—the collective effort of various reformers to tame the consequences of industrialism and urbanization. Their goals were different, sometimes even contradictory. Labor wanted better wages and hours; female reformers wanted the alleviation of poverty and better public education; temperance workers demanded laws to protect the family against saloons; farmers wanted debt relief and lower railroad rates. Ironically, many businessmen jumped on the progressive bandwagon, hoping heightened government involvement might stabilize the economy and restore competition.

For all their differences, progressives shared a common belief that government could be used as a powerful tool for social betterment. The depression of the mid-1890s added urgency to calls for activist government. By aggravating the festering social problems in the nation's cities and accelerating the trend toward corporate consolidation, the depression pushed the questions of how to regulate trusts and maintain social order to the top of the political agenda.

The progressives' temperament and agenda borrowed heavily from the Populist wave of the 1880s and 1890s, although the two movements were hardly identical. Progressives tended to be educated and middle-class, based largely in the eastern and midwestern states. Populists, on the other hand, were largely uneducated farmers living in the South and West. But the Populists ceded to their urbane cousins both a moralistic world-view, which saw political issues as a clash between right and wrong, and an agenda for using government to rein in the trusts and empower the people. William White observed that the progressives "caught the Populists in swimming and stole all of their clothing except the frayed underdrawers of free silver."

In addition to a shared desire to expand government, progressives articulated a common social philosophy. First, they believed that people were essentially rational, and when confronted by evidence of corruption and inefficiency, they would respond by demanding changes to make government more responsive to the public will. Second, whether they were attacking the trusts or advocating for municipal ownership of utilities, progressives tapped into a deep-seated fear of monopoly power. "It is funny how we have all found the octopus," noted William White. Third, they challenged the notion that in a modern industrialized society individuals could live independently of one another. Progressives hoped to purge society of its individualistic excesses by stressing cooperation and emphasizing social responsibility. Finally, progressives shared a passion for social efficiency. Certain that most social problems resulted from a poor environment, progressives planned to employ experts and professionals to alter social conditions and improve society. "Those who have studied the causes of poverty and social evils have discovered that nine-tenths of the world's misery is preventable," said a reform-minded mayor. "Science has countless treasures yet to be revealed."

American progressives joined with reformers in Europe and Australia, who were struggling with many of the same social problems, to form a remarkable international conversation that focused on the central issue of the time: How to use government power to address the unwanted consequences of urbanization and industrialization. "America no longer teaches democracy to an expectant world," Walter Weyl observed in *The New Democracy* (1912), "but herself goes to school to Europe and Australia." Through travel and study abroad, international seminars, and professional journals, American progressives joined forces with like-minded reformers in England, Germany, and France to develop strategies for using public power to tame the excesses of industrialization. Convinced of their own righteousness and confident in their solutions, progressives looked for the opportunity to implement their new ideas, both in local communities and in the nation at large.

 Political Reform

The progressive faith in reform through government intervention first found expression at the local level where reformers mobilized to restructure city governments and pass new social justice measures. After conquering city hall, they carried their agenda to the statehouse where, inspired by Robert La Follette's "Wisconsin Idea," progressives enacted a number of structural reforms to give voters a greater voice in policymaking. These reforms reduced the power of political parties and helped interest groups such as the prohibitionist Anti-Saloon League make their influence felt. Tapping into the reform spirit, suffragists pushed for enactment of a constitutional amendment granting women the right to vote. There was, however, a darker side to reform as many progressives used government power to regulate morality as they saw it.

Reforming the City

American cities continued to experience spectacular growth in the Progressive Era. Between 1900 and 1920, New York's population exploded from 3.4 million to 5.6 million; Chicago's from 1.7 million to 2.7 million. Immigrants made up 40 percent of New York's population in 1910. Including American-born children of immigrants, the figure soared to 80 percent! The influx of millions of immigrants strained the city's ability to provide adequate housing, transportation, and municipal services (see pages 728–731).

Many native-born Americans viewed the cities as threats to American democracy. In their view, local bosses built powerful political machines by preying on the ignorance of new immigrants. "Saloons and gambling houses and brothels," one Baltimore reformer charged, "are the nurseries of urban statesmen." Many reformers, ignoring the inherent difficulties of managing the exploding urban growth, blamed machine politicians and poor administration for urban problems such as unpaved streets, poor sanitation, corruption, and mismanagement. Using the corporation as a model, they promised to make government more efficient, honest, and responsive to the public interest.

During the 1890s reformers built a broad-based coalition to demand structural reform and policy changes in city government. Muckrakers aroused public indignation with their exposés of municipal corruption to help reformers seize control of city halls. Once in power, progressives pushed for initiatives designed to undermine the power of urban bosses. To dilute the power of local immigrant machines, they switched from ward to citywide elections, in which candidates needed to appeal to a broad spectrum of voters, not just to those in the neighborhoods they represented.

Some cities experimented with a commission form of government. This new method of urban management developed as an emergency measure. On a hot summer night in 1900, a giant tidal wave killed one out of every six people in Galveston, Texas. The tidal wave also overwhelmed the local government, which proved incapable of dealing with the massive destruction. To meet the crisis, reformers replaced the old system with a special commission of five men to run the government. Rather than dividing executive and legislative authority between a mayor and city council, the new system vested all power in a handful of commissioners, each of whom headed a particular city department. Galveston began to recover, and within a few years, Houston, Dallas, and Austin had adopted the commission form of government. By 1911, nineteen states had granted their cities authority to establish commission government, and within five years, the idea had spread to more than four hundred municipalities.

A third approach involved hiring a city manager to take charge of local government. In 1908 Staunton, Virginia, became the first municipality to hire a city manager—a professional, nonelected administrator who ran the government under the direction of the elected city council and mayor. Five years later, Dayton, Ohio, attracted wider attention to the scheme when it adopted the new system after a major flood. Borrowed directly from the corporate model, the city manager served as the chief executive officer of the city. The ideal city, observed a Dayton reformer, was "a great business enterprise whose stockholders are the people."

The commission and city manager systems appealed to the business community and to the middle class, who valued efficiency and who resented the patronage power of big city bosses and their immigrant machines. The new system replaced the older, decentralized system of city services, which benefited the working class, with a more centralized government controlled by the new professionals. Urban areas that adopted citywide elections, for example, saw a dramatic decrease in working-class and minority representatives. In Los Angeles, the change prevented blacks and Hispanics from winning election to the city council. In Pittsburgh, the reform allowed upper-class businessmen and professionals to gain control of the city council and the school committee.

The most successful efforts at urban reform came from reform mayors who won election calling for an end to corruption and advocating an ambitious agenda for social reform. By 1900, progressive mayors had won election in New York, Chicago, Baltimore, and many other cities. The first was Hazen Pingree, mayor of Detroit from 1889 to 1896, who won election with the support of the city's conservative business community. Once in office, however, he implemented a program of administrative efficiency and broad social justice. He reduced the cost of utilities, slashing streetcar fares and gas rates, and exposed corruption in city government. During the depression of the 1890s he started work-relief programs for Detroit's unemployed, built schools and parks, and required the wealthy to pay higher taxes to finance the programs. In time he brought his reform agenda to the state level after winning election as governor in 1896.

Ohio produced two of the most famous reform mayors. In Toledo, Samuel Jones, who served as mayor from 1897 to 1903, earned the nickname "Golden Rule" because he gave city workers an eight-hour workday, provided paid vacations, and barred child labor. Tom Johnson, mayor of Cleveland from 1901 to 1909, lowered fares on local trains, improved the police force, and provided free bathhouses and recreational facilities. His administration, he often bragged, was staffed by men who combined "efficiency and a belief in the fundamental principles of democracy." He outraged business interests by advocating city ownership of utilities. "Only through municipal ownership," he argued, "can the gulf which divides the community into a small dominant class on one side and the unorganized people on the other be bridged."

Though they succeeded in capturing city hall, the reformers failed to fulfill many of the expectations they had raised. In most cases, they helped make the cities cleaner and healthier, but they were more successful at arousing indignation than at creating responsive government. Efficient administration and modest social justice measures were no match for the enormous problems created by the flood of new immigrants and the consequences of industrialization.

Reform in the States

Progressives discovered that the road to reforming the city led inevitably to the state-house. The states wrote the charters that spelled out city government powers. "Whenever we try to do anything, we run up against the charter," complained the progressive mayor of Schenectady, New York. "It is an oak charter, fixed and immovable." States also set the requirements for suffrage and voting procedures, regulated business and labor conditions, and legislated to enforce morality. Progressives discovered that city governments did not have a monopoly on corruption and intransigence. "The legislature met biennially," William Allen White wrote of Missouri in a 1903 issue of *McClure's*, "and enacted such laws as the corporations paid for, and such others as were necessary to fool the people, and only such laws were enforced as party expediency demanded."

The most successful progressive reformer on the state level was Wisconsin governor Robert M. La Follette. Born in Primrose, Wisconsin, in meager circumstances, La Follette worked his way through the University of Wisconsin law school before deciding to enter politics. He won a seat in Congress before his thirtieth birthday and then earned election as governor in 1900. A superb orator with a combative style, who vowed "never to know defeat in a good cause," La Follette emerged as a national symbol of progressivism. During his two terms as governor—he won election to the Senate in 1906—"Battling Bob" modernized the state government through what came to be known as the "Wisconsin Idea." La Follette turned Wisconsin into what reformers across the nation praised as a "laboratory of democracy." His state reform program included laws to establish a direct primary—which allowed voters a voice in the process of selecting a party nominee—to improve the civil service, to create a graduated state income tax. He cracked down on corporations, forcing them to pay higher taxes and to face tougher regulation. "Selfish interests," he proclaimed, "may resist every inch of ground, may threaten, malign and corrupt, [but] they cannot escape the final issues. That which is so plain, so simple, and so just will surely triumph."

The "Wisconsin Idea" quickly spread to other states. In New York, attorney Charles Evans Hughes, elected Republican governor in 1906, established stricter supervision of insurance companies and created a state public service commission to regulate utilities. In New Jersey, former Princeton University president Woodrow Wilson initiated a program of progressive reforms following his election as governor in 1910. In California, attorney Hiram Johnson campaigned against the Southern Pacific Railroad and its dominance of state government and entered the governor's mansion in 1911 with a slate of reforms.

What was the progressive agenda for the states? Rhetorically, the progressives promoted democracy as the antidote to corruption. "The voice of the people,"

"Battling Bob" La Follette   Wisconsin governor Robert La Follette (1900–1906) became famous for his progressive reforms, such as the direct primary, the regulation of railroads, and the use of statistics to research problems and draw up legislation. Other states and cities soon imitated the "Wisconsin Idea," and eventually it became a model for reforms on the national level. In 1906 La Follette was elected to the U.S. Senate, where he continued to work on the forefront of the progressive crusade.   *(Library of Congress.)*

proclaimed White, "is indeed the will of God." But before enacting their agendas, progressives "purged" the electorate of voters they considered unqualified. In the South, this meant disfranchising blacks. In the North, it meant eliminating newly arrived immigrant voters through increased residency requirements, thereby restricting suffrage to native-born or fully naturalized citizens.

After removing what they viewed as undesirable elements from the election rolls, progressives enacted a number of "direct democracy" measures. These measures represented an assault on the power of political parties, which reformers believed had become captive to powerful corporate interests. "The people have come to see," editorialized the *Saturday Evening Post* in 1905, "that parties are to a great extent the tools of the unscrupulous who make of politics a profession." Progressives proposed a number of measures designed to transfer power from organized parties to the people. The initiative allowed reformers to bypass legislatures by petitioning to submit legislation directly to the voters, who could then vote directly on the proposed legislation in a referendum. In 1902, Oregon became the first state to enact such reforms. By 1918, nineteen other states had followed. To improve the quality and responsiveness of elected officials, progressives created the direct primary and the recall. The recall allowed voters to call a special election to remove an elected official. Progressive reformers achieved a major political victory in 1913 when the states ratified the Seventeenth Amendment, which provided for direct election of senators. Before 1913, senators had been elected by state legislators.

Progressives argued that the democratic reforms gave "to the people direct and continuous control over all the branches of government," so that they could "direct their attention more profitably to the problems connected with the prevention and relief of social and economic distress." Their efforts were aided by an influential group of college-educated female social workers such as Hull House residents Jane Addams, Grace Abbott, and Florence Kelley, who used their positions as members of state boards of charity and local welfare agencies to create the scaffolding of the modern welfare state. Women reformers lobbied state legislatures for passage of laws providing a monthly stipend to single mothers. In 1911 Illinois enacted the first statewide measure. By 1919, thirty-nine states had enacted mothers' pensions.

Progressive women were responsible for a host of other important social legislation as well. Drawing on their experience at settlement houses such as Hull House, reformers helped establish juvenile courts with probation officers, secured laws establishing an age limit on the employment of children, and led the drive for workmen's compensation for laborers injured on the job. By 1916, every state had laws protecting children and nearly two-thirds had established workmen's compensation.

Progressives also placed great hope in the power of independent commissions, such as the New York Factory Commission, to regulate business. They created state commissions to regulate railroads, utilities, and insurance companies. Progressives viewed the commissions as a moderate alternative to unrestrained competition on one hand or government ownership of industry on the other. The commissions were empowered to examine corporate records, hold public hearings, and establish prices and rates. In practice, however, they often lacked a clear sense of the public interest and lacked the authority to compel powerful groups to accept their demands. In many cases, the commissions were dominated by the very interests they were created to regulate.

Women's Suffrage

The abolitionists' insistence on equal rights for all Americans served as the intellectual springboard for the modern drive for women's suffrage. Women's rights advocates had supported the drive to free the slaves, hoping that their male colleagues in the abolitionist cause would in turn support their struggle for suffrage. But their old allies proved fickle friends: after the war they dismissed women's claims to suffrage (see page 621).

Still, suffrage supporters slowly gained ground. They received a boost when Carrie Chapman Catt took over the leadership of the National American Woman Suffrage Association in 1900. A shrewd political strategist, Catt developed a grass-roots campaign at the state level that she called "the winning plan." She found many allies among middle-class women and the nexus of voluntary associations they had created. By 1910, nine states, all of them in the West, had granted women the vote. Fearing that the Supreme Court would invalidate their gains, suffrage supporters pressed for passage of a constitutional amendment granting women the right to vote.

Suffrage advocates refined and extended their arguments to win over reluctant male legislators. To appeal to other reformers, they argued that women would expand the universe of middle-class, educated voters and battle against corrupt party politicians. Suffragists toned down appeals for equal rights and justice and instead emphasized the positive qualities that women would bring to politics from their "separate sphere" (see pages 352, 369). Tragedies such as the Triangle Shirtwaist fire convinced many women that they needed the vote to protect their interests as mothers and as workers. They argued that the vote would allow them to carry out their traditional role in the family. How could a mother teach her children about citizenship, they asked, if she was unable to exercise those rights herself?

Like other progressive reformers, supporters of women's suffrage sometimes based their appeal on nativism and racism. Suffragists from the South opposed voting by blacks. Many of these women favored the imposition of a literacy test to "abolish the ignorant vote." The southern suffragist Belle Kearney boldly predicted in 1903: "The enfranchisement of women would insure immediate and durable white supremacy, honestly attained." In the North, many advocates of women's suffrage suggested that middle-class Protestant women would dilute the immigrant vote in large cities. "Cut off the vote of the slums and give it to women," advised Carrie Chapman Catt.

Opponents turned the suffragist appeals to separate spheres on its head, charging that suffrage would in fact undermine traditional gender roles by blurring the line separating the male and female realms. A woman's place was in the home; men were responsible for the affairs of state. Giving women the right to vote, complained a congressman, "would disrupt the family, which is the unit of society, and when you disrupt the family, you destroy the home, which is the foundation of the republic." Indeed, a senator charged their "milder, gentler nature" made women unprepared "for the turmoil and battle of public life."

Suffragettes in New York City, 1912 Women had been agitating for the right to vote for over half a century, but during the Progressive Era, they finally seemed to be making progress. In 1915 Carrie Chapman Catt reorganized the efforts of the National American Woman Suffrage Association, integrating state campaigns with the Washington headquarters, compiling information on every congressman and senator, and launching crusades in every electoral district. Although these strategies produced the Nineteenth Amendment (1919), the feminist movement stalled. As this photograph seems to indicate, most American women, including the suffragettes themselves, would maintain a traditional, family-centered outlook. *(Library of Congress.)*

When, before the presidential election of 1912, the Progressive Party splintered from the Republican Party, it endorsed the cause of women's suffrage. To signify its support, party leaders invited Jane Addams to make a major seconding speech for nominee Theodore Roosevelt. When the Progressive Party dissolved after the election, Republican and Democratic politicians began promoting the suffrage cause in hopes of gathering former members to their side. The sense of shared sacrifice during World War I aided the cause. By 1919, thirty-nine states had granted women the right to vote in at least some elections; fifteen had allowed them full participation (see map). That same year, the Senate adopted the Nineteenth Amendment with barely a two-thirds majority. It was ratified by its passage in the Tennessee legislature on August 21, 1920.

Controlling the Masses

Many progressive reformers were determined not only to improve institutions, but also to improve human behavior. To mold an America that reflected their values, they set out to purge society of drinking and prostitution and to cut off the influx of new immigrants.

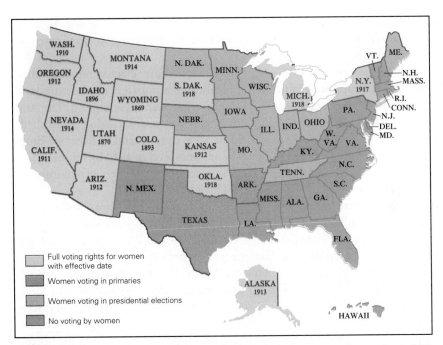

Women's Suffrage Before the Nineteenth Amendment   As Americans migrated West after the Civil War, the issue of women's suffrage traveled with them, finding fertile ground in the West where women had full voting rights. Other states further east provided limited suffrage in presidential elections, but women in the South and in New England would have to wait for the passage of the Nineteenth Amendment before being granted the right to vote in any elections.

By 1900, prohibitionists battling to outlaw alcohol consumption won support from many progressives who viewed the urban saloon as the most striking symbol of urban dissipation and disorder. The Reverend Mark Matthews, pastor of the largest Presbyterian congregation in the world, called the saloon, "the most fiendish, corrupt and hell-soaked institution that ever crawled out of the slime of the eternal pit." Prohibitionists denounced liquor interests for polluting the political system, ruining families, eroding worker efficiency, and foisting new poorhouses and prisons onto taxpayers' shoulders. To members of the new urban middle class, the elimination of alcohol from American life was a necessary step in the task of restoring order to society.

As late as 1900, the issue of prohibition was too hot for either political party to handle. Democrats were reluctant to pursue the issue because they depended heavily on Catholic immigrants; Republicans also counted many urban voters in their coalition. With the parties deadlocked, unwilling to alienate an important constituency group, prohibition supporters were forced to create an independent political pressure group—the Anti-Saloon League. Founded in Ohio in the 1890s, the league started on the local level by supporting "local option" laws, which allowed citizens in local communities to vote on whether to license saloons. Through this method reformers were able to isolate "wet" areas. In 1900, only 18 million of the nation's 76 million people were living in saloon-free cities and towns. By 1906, about 35 million, or 40 percent of the population, were living in "dry" territory, most of them under local option.

The league then moved to the state level. Since many elected representatives were unwilling to support prohibition, prohibition supporters used a number of measures of direct democracy—especially the initiative and referendum. The strategy worked. Between 1906 and 1909, a dozen states went dry. Having established a strong foothold in many local areas with the local option, and in over two dozen states, the Anti-Saloon League moved to the national level in 1913 by lobbying for a constitutional amendment to prohibit the "sale, manufacture for sale and importation for sale of beverages containing alcohol."

In 1917 progressive advocates of prohibition finally steered through Congress a constitutional amendment embodying their demands. Two years later, after ratification by every state in the nation, except Connecticut and Rhode Island, the Eighteenth Amendment became law, to take effect in January 1920.

Crusades against the saloons often spread to prostitution. Muckrakers exposed the operations of "white slavery" rings that kidnapped young women and forced them into prostitution. Between 1910 and 1915, at least thirty-five cities and states conducted major studies of prostitution. Besides the tools of investigation and publicity, anti-vice crusaders held marches and outdoor prayer meetings in the heart of red-light districts. Convinced that poor living and working conditions were at the root of prostitution, reformers supported such progressive reforms as wage-and-hour laws and factory safety legislation. "Is it any wonder," asked the Chicago Vice Commission, "that a tempted girl who receives only six dollars per week working with her hands sells her body for twenty-five dollars per week when she learns there is a demand for it and men are willing to pay the price?" In 1910, Congress enacted the Mann Act, which prohibited transporting women across state lines "for immoral purposes." By 1915, every state had outlawed brothels and the public solicitation of sex.

Many progressives also pushed for legislation limiting immigration. Support came from many quarters. Rural Protestants wanted to dry up the cities' source of new voters. Labor leaders saw how employers exploited ethnic tensions to prevent effective union drives. Others based their appeal on simple prejudice. Sociologist Edward A. Ross painted new immigrants as "beaten members of beaten breeds" with "sugar loaf heads, moon faces, and goose-bill noses," who "lack the ancestral foundations of American character." Twice Congress passed laws imposing restrictions on immigration. Both times the president, Taft in 1913 and Wilson in 1915, vetoed the legislation. In 1917 though, following America's entry into World War I, Congress overrode Wilson's second veto.

Some of the bitterest battles over immigration were fought on the state level. Many progressives in California crusaded against Japanese immigrants. Between 1901 and 1908, more than 125,000 Japanese immigrants came to the United States to work on the railroads, in mines, and in logging camps. After 1900 a wave of anti-Japanese hysteria swept through the state. Labor organizations and patriotic societies charged that Japanese immigrants lowered America's standard of living, refused to assimilate into American culture, and represented a threat to American security. Newspaper headlines blared warnings about the Japanese threat: "Brown Man an Evil in the Public Schools" and "The Yellow Peril—How the Japanese Crowd Out the White Race."

In 1906 the San Francisco School Board began segregating Japanese school-children. When the Japanese government protested the decision, President Roosevelt intervened, forcing the school board to rescind the order. Two years later, Roosevelt negotiated an agreement with Japan—the Gentlemen's Agreement of 1908—limiting Japanese immigration to the United States. The agreement could not stem the tide of anti-Japanese feeling. The California Senate approved by a wide margin a 1913 bill denying Japanese immigrants the right to buy land. Over the next few years, twelve other states passed similar laws.

 ## Social Tensions in an Age of Reform

The spirit of reform was not confined to the white middle class; in fact, some of those advocating change proposed social and governmental reforms that challenged the traditional values of most progressives and most Americans. The progressive period witnessed growing activism among African-Americans who found creative ways to protest injustice. Though excluded from most progressive organizations, blacks were invited to join the Socialist Party and militant labor groups, both of which gathered momentum during the period and called for radical changes in American society. The Progressive Era also witnessed the emergence of an articulate feminist movement, which looked beyond suffrage to challenge the prevailing gender assumptions of the time.

African-American Activism in the Progressive Era

Most progressives were blind to the contradiction between their rhetoric about helping ordinary Americans and their conscious discrimination against racial minorities. Beginning in the 1890s, southern whites, fearful of a developing interracial alliance under populism, began the systematic disfranchisement of blacks and poor whites. Progressives continued the process. Progressive governors such as James K. Vardaman of Mississippi saw little conflict between their support for social reform and their vicious racism. While championing a number of progressive measures, including increased spending for education and tougher regulations of railroads, banks, and insurance companies, Vardaman denied that blacks had the right to vote. The African-American, he sneered, was "a lazy, lying, lustful animal which no conceivable amount of training can transform into a tolerable citizen."

Not all progressives endorsed discrimination against African-Americans. In 1910 a handful of white progressives joined with the black Niagara Movement to form the National Association for the Advancement of Colored People (NAACP). The new organization committed its energy and resources toward ending racial segregation, guaranteeing equal education, and extending the franchise to all African-Americans. Over the next decade, NAACP attorneys scored significant legal victories. In *Guinn* v. *United States* (1915), the Supreme Court ruled that Maryland and

Oklahoma laws excluding blacks from voting were unconstitutional. Two years later, in *Buchanan* v. *Worley,* the justices struck down a Louisville, Kentucky, ordinance that required blacks and whites to live in separate communities.

Though black Americans were largely excluded from the progressive movement, they found creative ways to organize and to improve their lot. One way they did so was to "vote with their feet." Between 1890 and 1920, over half a million black southerners moved to northern cities in search of better wages and freedom from the oppressive racial code of the South. Blacks not only went north; they also traveled west, establishing predominately black towns.

Those blacks who remained in the South did not passively endure segregation. In 1891, when Georgia passed a law allowing segregation on streetcars, blacks launched a massive boycott that crippled transportation companies in Atlanta, Savannah, and Augusta. Southern blacks also boycotted segregated banks and steamship lines. Black industrial workers, most of whom lived in the South, unionized. When barred from white unions, as was often the case, blacks formed their own. Black workers who did not belong to unions found informal ways to protest, usually by switching jobs or by slowing the pace of work.

Sometimes white racism led to violence. During the 1890s and 1900s, major race riots broke out in a number of cities, including Memphis, Mississippi and Atlanta. In the 1906 Atlanta riot, African-Americans opened fire when a violent white mob, incited by a newspaper story accusing black men of raping white women, invaded their town.

For African-Americans education symbolized freedom and autonomy, so when southern states withheld funds for black schools, they found alternative ways to educate their children. A black woman in South Carolina recalled that "there was no school for ten miles in no direction," so her father constructed a "small log house" and used it as a school. By 1915, blacks in Georgia had established 1,544 schools serving more than 11,500 students. Local Alabama communities joined forces with northern philanthropist Julius Rosenwald to create 92 schools between 1914 and 1916.

Black activists fought racial prejudice in the North as well. Ida Wells-Barnett, one of the most famous black activists of this period, began a massive antilynching campaign in 1892 after white vandals destroyed the office of her Memphis paper, *Free Speech.* Forced to flee to the North, she founded black women's clubs, such as the Women's Loyal Union in New York, and taught racial improvement and self-help. The club's motto, "Lifting as We Climb," expressed a hopeful spirit of racial progress and solidarity.

Southern educator Booker T. Washington remained the most prominent spokesman for African-Americans during the Progressive Era (see page 644). The black intellectual W. E. B. Du Bois disagreed with Washington's cautious message. The first African-American to earn a Ph.D. at Harvard, Du Bois taught at Atlanta University from 1897 to 1910, and articulated his views in a book, *Souls of Black Folks* (1903). In a direct attack on the accommodationist philosophy of Washington's Atlanta Compromise, Du Bois said that blacks could not sit in "courteous and dumb self-forgetting silence" until whites chose to rescue them. Du Bois based his hopes for change on what he called the "Talented Tenth" of black leaders who would lead the struggle for civil rights. In 1910 Du Bois joined like-minded reformers, both black and white, to organize the National Association for the Advancement of Colored People (NAACP), which would play a major role in the struggle for civil rights.

Du Bois demonstrated the limits of Washington's strategy of accommodation, but his approach, too, was ineffective. His faith in a "Talented Tenth" had little impact on the vast majority of African-Americans who lacked basic social and political rights. "This faith in a black elite," observed one historian, "failed to recognize that there were few blacks as well educated as he, few white liberals who could be counted upon, and few judges who were willing to challenge white attitudes."

Radical Reformers

The enormous changes occurring in the United States in the late nineteenth century provided a breeding ground for radicalism. Like progressive reformers, radicals were troubled by the immense disparity of wealth, the deplorable condition of the urban poor, and the increasing power of huge corporations. Unlike reformers, however, radicals believed altering society on the surface was not enough, and instead called for fundamental changes—public ownership of industry, for example—in the structure of American society. The leading proponents of radical reform during the progressive era were the Socialist Party and the Industrial Workers of the World (IWW).

Rev. and Mrs. Reverdy Ranson, c. 1900 Although the concerns of African-Americans were generally ignored by white progressives, some blacks took an active role in the reforms of the day. Rev. Ranson, pastor of the Bethel A.M.E. Church, established the Institutional Church and Social Settlement in Chicago, the first settlement house for African-Americans in the city. Like its white-run counterparts, Ranson's settlement offered a wide variety of social services—a kindergarten, a mother's club, home economics courses, and an employment bureau. *(Chicago Historical Society.)*

Though deeply divided by rival factions, the Socialist Party emerged as a significant political force after 1900. It held special appeal for urban workers, intellectuals, migrant laborers, and tenant farmers of the southern plains who felt displaced in the new industrial order. While socialists of every stripe agreed on the inherent inequities of capitalism, they were too divided ideologically to agree on a common agenda. They were united, however, in their passionate support for one man: Eugene Debs. A fiery and flamboyant speaker who had little patience for the ideological hairsplitting that consumed most Socialists, Debs spoke passionately about the needs of society's outcasts. "While there is a lower class I am of it, while there is a criminal class I am of it, while there is a soul in prison I am not free." In 1904 Debs received just over 400,000 votes as the party's presidential candidate, and almost 1 million when he ran eight years later.

Debs's national support was not enough to win elections, but local support put many socialists in office. By 1912, the party held 1,200 public offices in 340 cities, including seventy-nine mayors in twenty-four states. Once in office, these radicals pursued a moderate agenda, building coalitions with progressive reformers on social justice and direct democracy measures, but opposing progressives on prohibition, immigration restriction, and other issues.

The most radical group during this period was the Industrial Workers of the World (IWW), or "Wobblies," as they were often called. Founded in Chicago in 1905 by a zealous partnership of radical unionists and political leaders, and led by the dynamic William (Big Bill) Haywood, the IWW envisioned a utopian state run by workers. "The final aim is revolution," said a Wobbly organizer. Unlike progressives who looked for common ground between workers and industry, the IWW sided exclusively with labor. "The working class and the employing class have nothing in common," Haywood declared. While the more conservative American Federation of Labor (AFL) denied membership to African-Americans and favored immigration restrictions, the Wobblies embraced society's outcasts, welcoming blacks, immigrants, and women into their ranks.

The Wobblies achieved a few significant victories, but overall, their influence was marginal. In 1912 they joined forces with progressives to win higher wages for textile workers in Lawrence, Massachusetts. Progressives also fought to protect the IWW's right to free speech when police in California used force to prevent them from speaking on street corners. For the most part, however, the Wobblies' small membership—never exceeding 100,000—and their uncompromising radical stance, prevented them from building broad-based coalitions with other reform-minded groups. Most Americans, including workers, rejected the emphasis on class warfare. Whereas Debs and his party obtained respectability from middle-class Americans, the IWW earned only their suspicion.

Ultimately, both the IWW and the Socialist Party suffered from the incompatibility of their twin goals: seeking both immediate gains for workers and the long-term overhaul of society. The former necessitated working within the very system the latter sought to destroy. The Socialists were more successful because they focused on immediate reforms, but in doing so, they compromised their role as a revolutionary organization. The Wobblies never compromised their radical principles, but as a result, they failed to achieve the mass support of American workers, who were more concerned with improving their daily existence than with overthrowing the industrial order.

Feminism

While suffragists gathered momentum by adapting their arguments to traditional gender notions, a new generation of feminists called for liberation from all forms of sexual discrimination and demanded the freedom that men took for granted. Most were unmarried, college educated, self-supporting, and eager to challenge the restraints of women's "separate sphere." "All feminists are suffragists," said one advocate, "but not all suffragists are feminists."

Among the outspoken leaders of this new feminist perspective was Emma Goldman, a Russian Jewish immigrant who fled to America in 1885. Goldman advocated sexual liberation. Voicing her views in the journal *Mother Earth*, Goldman attacked the "conventional lie" of marriage and woman's role as "sex commodity." Women, she said, "must no longer keep their mouths shut and their wombs open." Frequently jailed for her radical activities in support of women and workers' rights, she was ultimately deported to Russia in 1919.

Feminists fought for both economic and sexual independence. Charlotte Perkins Gilman, in *Women and Economics* (1898), challenged the satisfactions of domesticity: "Only as we live, think, feel, and work outside the home," she wrote, "do we become humanly developed, civilized, and socialized." Gilman argued that women must have the same opportunities as men to find freedom and satisfaction through meaningful work. Gilman crusaded for a form of communalism featuring large housing units, day nurseries, central kitchens, and maid service to relieve women of domestic chores. Margaret Sanger, a visiting nurse in New York's East Side, hoped to give women greater control over their lives by distributing information about contraception. Her advocacy of birth control aroused the wrath of traditionalists who viewed the movement as a threat to family and morality. In 1914 the government indicted Sanger on nine counts of obscenity. The charges were later dropped, and in 1918 the courts permitted doctors to distribute birth control information.

 ## The Progressive Presidents

In 1901 the progressive reform agenda moved to the national level when Theodore Roosevelt assumed the presidency. Viewing the presidency as a "bully pulpit," Roosevelt expanded the regulatory power of the national government and supported a wide range of progressive reforms. The public responded enthusiastically to the style and substance of his leadership. Progressives, however, rarely spoke with a single voice and, following the failure of his handpicked successor, William Howard Taft, Roosevelt had to contend with the growing popularity of New Jersey governor Woodrow Wilson. The 1912 presidential campaign displayed two competing progressive reform agendas. Roosevelt's "New Nationalism" insisted that only a powerful federal government power could regulate the economy and guarantee social justice. Wilson, on the other hand, appealed to traditional public distrust of centralized power by calling for a "New Freedom." This tension, between the public's desire to use government to solve social problems and its deep-seated fear of ceding too much power to Washington, which Roosevelt and Wilson so eloquently articulated in 1912, would remain a dominate theme in American political discourse for the rest of the century.

TR

On September 6, 1901, President McKinley was shot in Buffalo, New York, by a lone anarchist, Leon Czolgosz. McKinley lingered for eight days before dying from internal bleeding and infection. At his death, Vice President Theodore Roosevelt, only forty-two years old, became the youngest man ever to assume the office of chief executive.

Born into a distinguished New York family, Roosevelt had plunged into New York politics in 1880, winning election as a Republican state assemblyman after his graduation from Harvard. However, a profound personal tragedy struck in 1884 when his wife and mother died on the same day. Roosevelt sought refuge in the Dakota Badlands where he worked as a rancher before returning to New York and resuming his climb up the political ladder. In 1889 he became a member of the Civil Service Commission, and in 1895 president of the New York City Police Board. In 1897 President McKinley appointed him assistant secretary of the navy. He resigned his office to fight in the Spanish-American War. As commander of a volunteer regiment known as the "Rough Riders," the young officer led a heroic charge that helped secure strategic San Juan Hill. "The only trouble" with the conflict, he said later, "was that there was not enough war to go around." In 1898 he returned from that war a hero and was elected governor of New York. In his spare time, Roosevelt managed to read voraciously and to write ten books, including five works of history.

Campaigning as a war hero, Roosevelt chose a conventional route to political power, but he was anything but a conventional politician. While police commissioner, he went on nighttime journeys through New York's slums to get a firsthand view of crime. He impressed settlement workers with his compassion for the poor and his willingness to learn new ideas. His youthful exuberance and dynamic personality impressed nearly everyone he met. "You go into Roosevelt's presence," a journalist wrote, "you feel his eyes upon you, you listen to him, and you go home and wring the personality out of your clothes."

During his two years as governor, Roosevelt angered party bosses with his public criticism of powerful trusts and his strong support of land conservation. In 1900, hoping to remove him from the limelight, Republican leaders nominated the upstart to be McKinley's running mate. It was a risky strategy, as Republican power broker Mark Hanna understood when he wrote McKinley that "your duty to the Country is to live for four years from next March." Roosevelt complained that he would "a great deal rather be anything, say professor of history, than Vice-President." Despite his reservations, he accepted the offer.

McKinley's assassination upset the plans of party leaders. Hanna regretted bitterly that "that damned cowboy" had become president. Roosevelt assured worried

Republicans that he would continue McKinley's policies, but it was only a matter of time before he made his mark on the office. He understood the power of the presidency to mold public opinion. Calling the office a "bully pulpit," he cultivated the press to enhance his popularity and to gather support for his policies. He maintained public interest by feeding reporters a steady diet of colorful antics. He became the first president to ride in an automobile, fly in an airplane, or be submerged in a submarine. On one occasion he went swimming naked in the Potomac River. The public responded to Roosevelt's exuberance. People called him "Teddy," and when a toy manufacturer heard the story of the president protecting a bear cub, he named a stuffed bear (the Teddy bear) after him.

Roosevelt brought more than just a sense of style to the presidency; he carried with him a well-developed political philosophy. Fearing both the excessive power of corporate wealth and the dangers of working-class radicalism, Roosevelt planned to use the presidency to mediate disputes and uphold the public interest. "The unscrupulous rich man who seeks to exploit and oppress those who are less well off is in spirit not opposed to, but identical with, the unscrupulous poor man who desires to plunder and oppress those who are better off," he said.

His approach revealed itself in dealing with one of the central questions of the time: How should government deal with the trusts? The process of corporate consolidation, which began in the late nineteenth century, picked up steam in the early

Theodore Roosevelt Making Use of his "Bully Pulpit"

A vigorous public speaker, Roosevelt fascinated the press and garnered widespread popularity with the American people. His exploits took him on numerous hunting trips, to Panama to view the construction of the canal, and on one occasion, skinny-dipping in the Potomac River with a foreign diplomat. His exuberance for life translated into an active presidency that permanently expanded the powers and expectations of the executive branch. He reorganized the army, built up the navy, modernized the diplomatic corps, and generally made the federal government more efficient and energetic. (*© Collection of the New-York Historical Society.*)

twentieth century. By 1904, 1 percent of American companies produced 38 percent of all manufactured goods. A few corporate giants dominated the industrial landscape. J. P. Morgan's U.S. Steel controlled 80 percent of the market, while his International Harvester Company monopolized 85 percent of the farm-equipment business.

Roosevelt regarded centralization as a fact of modern economic life. "This is an age of combination," he said in 1905. However, he made the distinction between "good" trusts—those that did not abuse their power and contributed to economic growth—and "bad" trusts—those few companies that used their market leverage to raise prices and exploit consumers. He earned a reputation as a "trustbuster" largely because of his prosecution of J. P. Morgan's Northern Securities Company, which controlled nearly all the long-distance railroads west of Chicago, eliminated competition, and created the threat of higher rates. Morgan tried to bargain, telling the president to "send your man to my man and they can fix it up." Roosevelt resisted, and in 1904 the Supreme Court, siding with the president, ordered the combination dissolved. During his administration the president used the Sherman Anti-Trust Act twenty-five times, prosecuting some of the country's largest corporations, including Standard Oil of New Jersey and the American Tobacco Company.

Imbued with the progressive faith in scientific management, and committed to enlarging presidential power, Roosevelt sponsored legislation that expanded the administrative power of the federal government. In 1903 Congress passed the Expedition Act, which required courts to give higher priority to antitrust suits. The same year, Congress created the Department of Commerce and Labor, which included a Bureau of Corporations to investigate firms involved in interstate commerce. Finally, the Elkins Act (also 1903) made it illegal for the railroads to give, or shippers to receive, rebates.

A similar faith in the regulatory power of the federal government shaped Roosevelt's approach to labor. In 1902 the president intervened with much fanfare to support Pennsylvania coal miners who went on strike to demand a 20 percent wage increase, an eight-hour day, and recognition of their union. Roosevelt spoke out publicly in support of the miners and summoned both sides to the White House, where he asked them to accept impartial federal arbitration. When the mine owners refused to compromise, Roosevelt lashed out at their "arrogant stupidity" and threatened to send in 10,000 federal troops to seize the mines and resume coal production. The operators finally relented. Arbitrators awarded the strikers a 10 percent wage increase and reduced the workday to nine hours, but they refused to grant recognition to the union. Afterward, Roosevelt boasted that he had offered both sides a "square deal." The phrase stuck and became a familiar label for his policies as president.

Roosevelt's colorful style and progressive policies made him the most popular president since Andrew Jackson. He easily won his party's nomination in 1904. The Democrats passed over two-time loser William Jennings Bryan and selected a lackluster New York judge, Alton B. Parker, as their nominee. On election day, Roosevelt won 7,628,461 popular votes (57.4 percent) to Parker's 5,084,223 (37.6 percent) and carried thirty-three of the forty-five states. His 336 electoral votes were the most ever won by a candidate up to that time. All of his opponent's 140 electoral votes came from a handful of southern states. The breadth of TR's victory stunned even his supporters. "What are we going to do with our victory," asked a Republican senator?

Roosevelt had no doubts about the significance of the election. "Tomorrow," he cried the day before his inauguration, "I shall come into my office in my own right. Then watch out for me." With public desire for bolder federal action increasing, Roosevelt announced his support for an ambitious social agenda including regulation of the railroads, increased federal power to regulate commerce, and passage of a range of legislation to improve working conditions. In 1906 he pushed through Congress the Hepburn Railroad Regulation Act, which authorized the Interstate Commerce Commission to set aside railroad rates on the complaint of a shipper and to establish lower rates. With Roosevelt's support Congress passed the Pure Food and Drug Act of 1905. The legislation made it a crime to sell adulterated foods or medicines and provided for correct and complete labeling of ingredients. Capitalizing on publication of Upton Sinclair's powerful novel *The Jungle* (1906), Roosevelt won passage of the Meat Inspection Act, which led to more effective supervision of meat processing.

Roosevelt's agenda on behalf of ordinary Americans produced mixed results for African-Americans. TR made a number of symbolic gestures toward blacks, including meeting with Booker T. Washington at the White House. But he shared the prevailing view that blacks were intellectually inferior. "[A]s a race and in the mass," he declared, "they are altogether inferior to the whites." In 1906, angered by unsubstantiated reports that black soldiers had killed a man in Brownsville, Texas, he discharged 160 blacks from the army, including six Medal of Honor recipients. It took more than sixty years for the army to rectify Roosevelt's unjust punishment. In 1972 the secretary of the army granted the men, many of whom were by then dead, honorable discharges.

As president, Roosevelt was committed to using his office to bolster the American conservation movement. While western business interests advocated unrestrained exploitation of the nation's natural resources, the growth of congested cities and the closing of the frontier raised public concern about the environment. Essayist John Muir, the founder of the modern environmental movement, emerged as the most passionate and forceful proponent of the inherent value of the modern wilderness. In 1892 he helped create the Sierra Club, which fought to protect the pristine beauty of Yellowstone National Park.

By temperament Roosevelt sided with Muir and the preservationists, but he understood the political power of western business interests and their representatives in Congress. Blending idealism and self-interest, he claimed that sound conservation and management were necessary for future development and for preserving America's natural heritage for future generations. A democratic tone echoed in his credo that natural resources should be reserved for all citizens, not just "for the very rich who can control private reserves." He was not a strict preservationist, but he sought to balance the needs of economic development with the desire to preserve the nation's wilderness heritage.

To carry out his policies, Roosevelt appointed Gifford Pinchot to head the new U.S. Forest Service. Like Roosevelt, Pinchot championed a "wise use" philosophy of public management. Following Pinchot's recommendation, Roosevelt used his executive authority to add 150 million acres of western virgin forest lands to the national forests and to preserve vast areas of water and coal from private development. The president also provided federal funds for the construction of huge dams, reservoirs, and canals in the West. By 1915, the government had invested $80 million in twenty-five projects to open new lands for cultivation and provide cheap electric power. It also strengthened the national park system. By 1916, the government had designated thirteen national parks, which the writer Wallace Stegner called the nation's "crown jewels."

Taft and the Divided Republicans

Having promised in 1904 not to seek reelection, Roosevelt decided to back his good friend and political ally William Howard Taft as his successor. Now secretary of war, Taft had been a restrained and moderate jurist, the solicitor general of the United States, a federal circuit court judge, and governor of the Philippines. Roosevelt was confident that Taft would continue his reform efforts. "Things will be all right," he had assured people when he took vacations from Pennsylvania Avenue. "I have left Taft sitting on the lid."

The Democrats nominated William Jennings Bryan for the third time. Bryan adopted a broad progressive platform that embraced strict antitrust policy, railroad regulation, and a host of social justice measures. "Shall the people rule?" he asked, framing the election as a choice between a government devoted to people's rights and a government by privilege. Taft counterattacked, charging that Bryan's economic views would produce "a paralysis of business." With the support of both Roosevelt and much of the Republican Old Guard, Taft easily won the election of 1908, although his popular margin was smaller than Roosevelt's in 1904. Taft took 51.6 percent (7,675,320) of the votes to 43.1 percent (6,412,294) for Bryan. His electoral margin was a comfortable 321 to 162.

In style and temperament William Howard Taft was a much different man than Roosevelt. Physically, Roosevelt was dynamic and charismatic; Taft was lazy and ponderous. Politically, Roosevelt had taken an expansive view of presidential power; Taft was more cautious, insisting that the president must observe the strict letter of the law. Taft was, in journalist Mark Sullivan's words, "a placid man in a restless time."

A major rift soon developed between Taft and progressive Republicans that would eventually destroy his presidency. On March 15, 1909, just eleven days after his inauguration, Taft called Congress into special session to lower tariff rates. A bill favored by progressives sailed quickly through the House but ran into tough opposition from Senate conservatives headed by Nelson W. Aldrich. For weeks, a spirited battle raged on the Senate floor. Fearful of a party split, Taft retreated and threw his support behind the conservatives who succeeded in gutting the House bill and passing the Payne-Aldrich Tariff, which actually raised tariffs on many important imports. Progressives, led by Robert La Follette, felt betrayed by the president. Their tempers boiled over when Taft described the new law as "the best tariff the Republican Party ever passed."

The wedge between Taft and the Republican progressives was driven deeper by the president's role in efforts to reform the House of Representatives. Initially Taft supported progressive efforts to diminish the almost dictatorial power of House Speaker Joseph Cannon, a sixty-five-year-old tyrant who used his power to frustrate reform efforts. "I am god-damned tired," Cannon said, "of listening to all this babble for reform." However, when Taft realized that he needed Cannon's support to pass tariff reform in the House, the president backed off and support for the rebellion fell short. The following year, progressives succeeded in stripping the Speakership of its power to make committee assignments. But once again they felt betrayed by a president who had raised their hopes and failed to deliver.

Taft also alienated progressive conservationists. This struggle stemmed from charges by chief forester Gifford Pinchot that Richard Ballinger, Taft's secretary of the interior, had conspired to turn over Alaska coalfields to a group of wealthy businessmen. Taft examined the charges and concluded that Ballinger had done nothing wrong. When Pinchot continued his attack, Taft fired him for insubordination. Taft was certainly no enemy of conservation. He had used his executive power to remove more public land from private use than Roosevelt had done in a comparable period of time. But progressives viewed Pinchot's dismissal as an ominous sign that Taft was betraying the conservationist cause. In fact, the issues were not so clear-cut.

During most of Taft's first year in office, Theodore Roosevelt was far from the political fray. He embarked on a long hunting safari in Africa. When he returned to New York in 1910, Roosevelt claimed he would stay out of internal party squabbling, but within a month he announced that he would embark on a national speaking tour. He lashed out at Taft, complaining that the president had "completely twisted around the policies I advocated and acted upon."

A final break between Taft and Roosevelt occurred in October 1911, when the president ordered an antitrust suit against U.S. Steel, forcing the giant company to sell off its Tennessee Company. Roosevelt, who had approved U.S. Steel's acquisition in 1907 of the Tennessee Coal and Iron Company, feared that Taft's action would create a panic on Wall Street. "To attempt to meet the whole problem by a succession of lawsuits," Roosevelt snapped, "is hopeless." Taft disagreed with TR's regulatory approach, arguing that the Sherman Act was a "good law that ought to be enforced, and I propose to enforce it." As a result, Taft filed more antitrust suits in four years than Roosevelt had in seven and a half.

Whose Progressivism? The Presidential Campaign of 1912

For Roosevelt the antitrust suit against U.S. Steel was the final straw. In February 1912 he announced that he would challenge Taft for the Republican nomination. "My hat is in the ring!" he declared with typical exuberance. "The fight is on and I am stripped to the buff!" Though Taft was a bigger trustbuster than Roosevelt, his compromise on the tariff had alienated progressives who remained solidly in Roosevelt's corner. The campaign for the Republican nomination had now become a battle between Roosevelt, the champion of the progressives, and Taft, the candidate of the conservatives. In the months that followed, Roosevelt, clearly the favorite of the rank and file, scored overwhelming victories in the direct presidential primaries now held in thirteen states. Nevertheless, Taft controlled the party machinery, which chose most of the delegates at the convention, and secured renomination, narrowly, on the first ballot.

Roosevelt, outraged by the back-room methods Taft employed to deny him the party nomination, decided to run for president as the head of a third-party organization. On August 6 in Chicago, ten thousand frenzied supporters singing "Onward Christian Soldiers" formed the Progressive Party and nominated Theodore Roosevelt as its presidential candidate. In his acceptance speech, Roosevelt, pronouncing himself "as strong as a bull moose," delivered a spirited "Confession of Faith" in which he criticized Democrats and Republicans for protecting "the interests of the rich few."

In his speech, Roosevelt gave the fullest accounting of his political philosophy, which he called the New Nationalism (see Competing Voices, pages 842). TR argued that progressives needed to recognize that true freedom and democracy could be achieved only through a powerful central government. Only a strong federal government, Roosevelt asserted, could protect the public's interest. Democracy was not incompatible with increased government; indeed, only government could guarantee true democracy. Rather than breaking up the great corporations, Roosevelt wanted to increase the power of government to regulate industry. In many ways, TR envisioned the modern broker state that his cousin, Franklin D. Roosevelt, would create with his New Deal programs in the 1930s. In keeping with the New National-

The Arrival of the "Bull Moose" This cartoon from the 1912 presidential campaign depicts a bewildered Democratic donkey and Republican elephant observing a strange new creature, the Progressive Party Bull Moose (so called because as he accepted the nomination, TR exclaimed he felt "as strong as a bull moose"). TR bolted the Republican Party after it failed to give him its nomination over President Taft. The campaign proved to be one of the more interesting in American history, with TR, the third-party candidate, coming in second. Roosevelt ran an energetic campaign, even completing a speaking engagement after being shot by a crazed man in Milwaukee. (New York Herald, *July 1912, Culver Pictures.*)

THE LATEST ARRIVAL AT THE POLITICAL ZOO

DRAWN BY E. W. KEMBLE

ism philosophy, the Progressive Party platform, called a "Covenant with the People," advocated a bold list of new reforms including strict regulation of corporations, a national presidential primary, the elimination of child labor, a minimum wage, and universal women's suffrage.

With the Republicans divided, the Democrats were confident of victory. They nominated New Jersey governor Woodrow Wilson to lead the party. Born in Virginia and raised in Confederate Georgia, Wilson graduated from Princeton in 1879, studied law at the University of Virginia, and earned a Ph.D. in political science at the Johns Hopkins University in 1886. He then taught at the elite colleges Bryn Mawr and Wesleyan before returning to Princeton in 1890. Twelve years later Princeton named him president. In 1910, after a bruising battle with the dean of the graduate school, Wilson left the Ivy League to run a successful campaign for governor of New Jersey. The Democratic machine thought Wilson would be a "safe" candidate who would not pursue radical change, but over the next two years the "scholar turned statesman" compiled an impressive record of progressive legislation that earned him a national reputation.

Like Roosevelt, Wilson possessed a strong intellect, a commitment to expansive presidential leadership, and a penchant for moralizing. A brilliant speaker, and a shrewd political tactician, Wilson possessed an uncanny ability to sway an audience and a keen sense of public opinion. Tall, lean, and stiff, he could be aloof and self-righteous, intolerant of opposing points of view. A devoutly religious man, Wilson was certain that he had been placed on earth to do God's work. One politician noted that Wilson "said something to me, and I didn't know whether God or him was talking." Sometimes, Wilson himself had trouble telling the difference. Medical historians speculate that health problems, including a possible stroke in 1906, may have affected his personality, accentuating his intolerance of opposition.

Wilson responded to Roosevelt's call for a New Nationalism by developing his own reform program, which he called the "New Freedom." Wilson's program borrowed heavily from the brilliant progressive lawyer Louis Brandeis, who believed that concentrations of economic power threatened liberty and foreclosed economic opportunity. Echoing Brandeis's ideas, Wilson warned that regulatory agencies would become captive to the industries they were designed to control. He spoke in evangelical tones of the need to emancipate the American economy from the power of the trusts. "What this country needs above everything else," he said, "is a body of laws which will look after the men who are on the make rather than the men who are already made." Where Roosevelt envisioned a powerful federal government using its powers to regulate large corporations, Wilson wanted Washington to use its limited powers to break up large concentrations and promote free competition.

The duel between "nationalism" and "freedom" that the 1912 campaign slogans touted was more than a contest between Roosevelt and Wilson; it was part of a dilemma that American society would continue to face for the remainder of the century. Wilson, firmly rooted in the Jeffersonian tradition of individualism and limited government, believed it was government's responsibility to allow independent individuals to prosper free from either large corporations or a powerful government. Roosevelt, persuaded that concentration of power was inevitable, believed

Americans should discard their outworn faith in rugged individualism and adjust to the realities of an industrialized nation. Though Roosevelt recognized the inevitability of big government he failed to appreciate how deeply wedded Americans were to their Jeffersonian roots.

From another perspective, newspaper editor William Allen White dismissed the differences between the two men: "Between the New Nationalism and the New Freedom was that fantastic imaginary gulf that always had existed between Tweedle-dum and Tweedle-dee." Many people agreed with White, and they turned to a more radical alternative—Socialist Party candidate Eugene Debs, who told audiences that workers had created the Socialist Party "as a means of wrestling control of government and industry from the capitalists and making the working class the ruling class of the nation and the world."

The campaign soon developed into a two-way contest between the moralizing Wilson and the crusading Roosevelt. Realizing he had little chance of winning, Taft refused to campaign. "I think I might as well give up so far as being a candidate is concerned," he wrote his wife in July. "There are so many people in the country who don't like me." Wilson held the lead as the campaign entered its final months. Roosevelt, who loved the thrill of battle, continued his crusade. Nothing, not even a would-be assassin's bullet could stop him from campaigning. On October 14, as he entered an automobile in Milwaukee, a lone attacker fired a single bullet into Roosevelt's chest. It fractured a rib and lodged below his right lung. Roosevelt first ordered the crowd not to harm his assailant, then insisted on attending a previously scheduled rally, where he spoke to a stunned crowd for more than an hour. "It takes more than that to kill a Bull Moose," he told them.

The Republican split allowed Wilson to win the election. Though he won only 41.9 percent of the popular vote, he captured forty states and 435 electoral votes—beating TR's 1904 record. Roosevelt got 27.4 percent of the popular vote, carrying six states with 88 electoral votes. Taft finished a distant third with 23.2 percent of the vote and 8 electoral votes. Socialist Debs received nearly 1 million ballots, about 6 percent of the total (see map). The Democrats also won control of both houses of Congress, and the new president planned to use his position as party leader to secure passage of his New Freedom legislation.

Woodrow Wilson and the New Freedom

Only the second Democrat to occupy the White House since the Civil War (the other, Cleveland, had been elected twice), Wilson continued the expansion of presidential power that had begun under Roosevelt. Using every device at his disposal to corral supporters, he conferred regularly with legislative leaders and enforced party discipline by dispensing patronage. He cultivated the press, holding weekly press conferences during his first two years in office. Wilson became the first president since Jefferson to deliver in person his annual State of the Union messages before joint sessions of Congress.

The president's tactics worked. Within a year and a half of Wilson's inauguration, Congress had passed a number of new initiatives. The Underwood Tariff Act (1913) reduced import taxes on most goods and levied a graduated income tax to

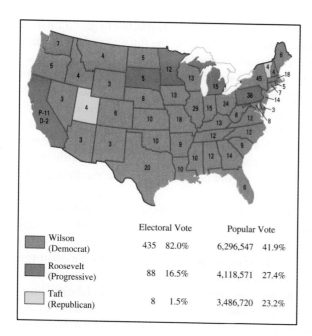

The Election of 1912 The Republican nomination went to President Taft, but Theodore Roosevelt was undeterred, and formed the Bull Moose Party. Despite being wounded early in the campaign, Roosevelt's calls for a "New Nationalism" drew Republican supporters to him and away from Taft, who failed to win outside Utah and New Hampshire. However, the split within the Republican Party was enough to give the election to Woodrow Wilson.

	Electoral Vote		Popular Vote	
Wilson (Democrat)	435	82.0%	6,296,547	41.9%
Roosevelt (Progressive)	88	16.5%	4,118,571	27.4%
Taft (Republican)	8	1.5%	3,486,720	23.2%

replace the lost income, an option made possible by the recent ratification of the Sixteenth Amendment. Incomes under $4,000 per year were excluded, which exempted over 90 percent of American families in 1914, the first year the tax was in effect.

Wilson kept Congress in session through the summer to pass the most important progressive measure of his presidency—the Federal Reserve Act of 1913. The law created the nation's first centralized banking system since Andrew Jackson had destroyed the Second Bank of the United States in the 1830s. Brokering a compromise between the interests of eastern conservatives, who argued for a privately owned central bank, and southern and western farming interests, who wanted the government to control the bank, the legislation reflected the progressive desire to regulate the economy by creating twelve regional banks to hold the cash reserves of member banks throughout the nation. These district banks had authority to lend money to member banks at low rates of interest called the discount rate. By adjusting this rate, the regional banks could adjust the amount of money a bank could borrow and thereby increase or decrease the amount of money in circulation.

Wilson, influenced by Brandeis, was also the guiding force behind two initiatives that increased the government's power to regulate powerful trusts. In September 1914 Congress created the Federal Trade Commission with authority to investigate corporate operations and outlaw unfair practices. Three weeks later, Congress passed the Clayton Anti-Trust Act (1914), which amended the Sherman Anti-Trust Act by outlawing monopolistic practices. The Clayton Act exempted trade unions and agricultural organizations from antitrust laws, and it curtailed the use of court injunctions during strikes. Future court decisions weakened the legislation, but at the time it promised a new age in labor–management relations. AFL head Samuel Gompers called it the "Magna Carta of Labor."

Convinced that reform had gone far enough, Wilson wanted to go no further. The New Freedom was complete, he wrote in late 1914, the future would be a "time of healing." Two years later, political circumstances forced Wilson to reassess his position. Democrats fared poorly in the 1914 midterm elections, losing two dozen seats in the House and giving up the governorships of New York, New Jersey, Illinois, and Pennsylvania. Wilson realized that to win reelection he needed to reach out to the progressives who had supported Roosevelt in 1912. As a first step, he nominated Louis D. Brandeis, an outspoken critic of big business, to the Supreme Court. The nomination thrilled progressives, who waged a successful battle in the Senate to confirm Brandeis's elevation to the bench. He became the first Jewish member of the Court.

To make further inroads in Roosevelt's old constituency, Wilson advocated several measures he had resisted during his first two years in the White House. He supported passage of the Federal Farm Loan Act, which created banks to lend money at low interest rates to farmers. Faced with a railroad strike, he signed the Adamson Act, establishing an eight-hour workday for railway workers and guaranteeing them time-and-a-half overtime pay. The Keating-Owen Act outlawed child labor in businesses engaged in interstate commerce. The Workman's Compensation Act established an insurance program for federal workers. The president endorsed, and Congress passed, the Federal Highway Act of 1916, which appropriated $5 million to the states for road construction.

However, to African-Americans looking for support from Washington in their struggle for civil rights, Wilson was a bitter disappointment. A product of the segregated South, Wilson sanctioned the spread of discrimination against blacks in the government bureaucracy. In Georgia, a federal official announced, "There are no government positions for Negroes in the South. A Negro's place is in the cornfield." The NAACP complained that federal agencies, such as the U.S. Post Office and the Treasury Department, had separate shops, offices, and lunchrooms for their black employees. But Wilson was unconcerned: "I sincerely believe it to be in their [the blacks'] best interests."

Wilson, who came to the presidency promising to restore an older version of democracy, wound up continuing the trend toward greater concentration of power in Washington. By the end of his first term in office, Wilson had for all intents and purposes abandoned the New Freedom and embraced the New Nationalism. In 1901 there were 239,000 government employees. By the end of Wilson's first term in office, the number had grown to 349,000. The federal budget, which totaled $587,685,000 when Roosevelt became president, had swollen to $782,535,000. Together, Roosevelt and Wilson dramatically increased the stature and power of the president. All future presidents would build on their example.

Wilson, like Roosevelt, contributed to and reflected an important shift in public attitudes toward government. During the progressive period the American people, viewing the government as a positive force for social change, created laws and regulatory agencies that established the government's responsibility to protect the public interest. The change in attitudes toward government should not be exaggerated, however. Progressives may have enlarged the capacity of government, but they did not shed deeply held notions of individualism, limited government, and self-help.

CONCLUSION

A number of reform streams flowed together in the first years of the twentieth century to create the progressive period. Intellectuals challenged the nineteenth-century notion that immutable rules of nature governed society. Middle-class women such as Jane Addams campaigned for social justice while a new breed of investigative reporters reminded people of the problems that needed to be addressed. The middle class, fearful of the social disorder provoked by urbanization and industrialization—and infatuated by social efficiency and scientific management—joined the chorus calling for change. The various groups did not campaign for the same causes. Some people worked to improve the quality of life for working people, especially women and children; others concerned themselves with making society more efficient; and still others wanted to uplift the nation's soul through moral reform. Despite the different agendas, these disparate reform efforts were united in their belief that government at all levels—local, state, and federal—needed to limit the power of large corporations and improve social conditions in the nation's urban areas. They were also committed to gradual change, working through the established institutions of government. Progressives were reformers, not revolutionaries.

Initially, progressives focused their efforts on the cities, where they believed the combination of explosive population growth and political corruption threatened social order. Reformers experimented with new forms of city government, including the commissioner and city manager models. Progressives modeled their reforms at the state level on the "Wisconsin Idea" of Robert La Follette, which included initiatives designed to make government more responsive to the public will. Progressive reform also possessed a dark side. When in power, progressives systematically disfranchised many segments of the population, particularly blacks in the South and immigrants in the North. In their drive to improve human behavior along with human institutions, progressives tried to outlaw the consumption of alcohol and succeeded in many states and counties.

Not all activists accepted the progressive faith that change should occur gradually and in cooperation with established institutions. African-Americans, who were largely excluded from mainstream political life in the South, developed alternative ways to improve their lives, including boycotts and protests. Socialists and the Wobblies struggled to build a class-based reform movement that challenged the very foundation of capitalism. Feminists, meanwhile, advocated an end to all forms of sexual discrimination.

The progressive movement moved to a national stage when Theodore Roosevelt assumed the presidency in 1901. Roosevelt helped expand the power of the federal government. He regulated some trusts and broke up others; occasionally sided with the labor movement in its battles with management; and allied himself with the fledgling conservation movement. William Howard Taft, Roosevelt's handpicked successor, succeeded him, but Roosevelt quickly became dissatisfied with what he saw as Taft's half-hearted commitment to reform. In 1912 TR bolted the Republican Party and ran as a third-party candidate. Roosevelt's was not the only articulate voice for reform on the national stage. The 1912 presidential contest witnessed two competing visions of progressivism: Roosevelt's New Nationalism and former New Jersey governor Woodrow Wilson's New Freedom. Wilson won the election, calling for smaller government and less regulation, but over the next few years he implemented many of the ideas of the New Nationalism.

The progressive impulse had rested on an optimistic view of human nature and a faith in the possibilities of reform. By 1916, a brutal conflict in Europe threatened those assumptions. America's entrance into World War I in 1917 would twist the progressive agenda in ways that most reformers never imagined.

SUGGESTED READINGS

The Progressive Era has one of the most robust bodies of literature on any period in American history. Richard Hofstadter's *Age of Reform* (1955) remains one of the classic surveys of the progressive movement. Robert Wiebe provided the seminal study of the new, professional middle class and its response to industrialization and urbanization in *The Search for Order, 1877–1920* (1967). *A Very Different Age* (1998) by Steven J. Diner is a recent synthesis that includes social and political topics. Alan Dawley's *Struggles for Justice* (1991) is another recent survey of the era, with particular emphasis on the origins of the new activist state.

Several scholars have tried to highlight the various distinct strains of thought that fed into the progressive movement. Robert Crunden examines the religious and moral traditions of the middle-class Protestants in the movement in *Ministers of Reform* (1982). In his *New Radicalism in America* (1965), Christopher Lasch portrays progressivism as a cultural revolt. The intellectual supports of progressive reform are outlined in Morton White's crucial work, *Social Thought in America: The Revolt Against Formalism* (1975). Charles Forcey focuses on the political thought of these intellectuals in *The Crossroads of Liberalism* (1961). James Kloppenberg's *Uncertain Victory* (1986) and Daniel Rodgers's *Atlantic Crossings* (1998) examine the growth of progressive thought from a transatlantic perspective.

The women reformers in the movement are the subjects of Nancy Woloch's *Women and the American Experience* (1984), while Allen F. Davis's *Spearheads of Reform* (1967) focuses on the settlement houses. Davis also published a thoughtful biography of Jane Addams, *American Heroine* (1973). More recently, Mina Carson's *Settlement Folk* (1990) and Ruth Hutchinson Crocker's *Social Work and Social Order* (1992) examine the settlement house movement. Robyn Muncy in *Creating a Female Dominion in American Reform, 1890–1935* (1991) argues that women during this period created a network of reform institutions that thrived into the 1930s. A good starting point for work on women in the labor movement is Susan Glenn's *Daughters of the Shtetl* (1990); Nancy Dye's *As Equals and Sisters* (1980) examines the connection between working-class women reformers and upper-class women progressives.

Fewer works have focused on the rising middle class, but John Buenker's *Urban Liberalism and Progressive Reform* (1973) covers the basics. Oliver Zunz's *Making America Corporate* (1990) shows how white-collar employees established a corporate work environment. James Weinstein explains the appeal of progressivism's "efficiency" in *The Corporate Ideal in the Liberal State* (1969). David Chalmers's *The Social and Political Ideas of the Muckrakers* (1964) is a useful introduction to the muckrakers.

John Teaford's *City and Suburb* (1979) offers a broad survey of urban reform efforts. Bradley Rice critiques the rise of the commission government in *Progressive Cities* (1972). Jack Tager evaluates the impact of the elite intrusion into municipal government in *The In-*

tellectual as Urban Reformer (1968). Kenneth Finegold's *Experts and Politicians* (1995) examines the reform challenge to machine politics. Camilla Stivers's *Bureau Men, Settlement Women* (2000) also explores municipal reform, with an emphasis on the issue of gender.

For reform in the states, Wisconsin is the natural starting point. The premiere study of the state is David Thelen's *The New Citizenship* (1972). A more recent biography of La Follette is Carl Burgchardt's *Robert M. La Follette, Sr.: The Voice of Conscience* (1992). Other insightful examinations of progressivism on the state level include Thomas Pegram's *Partisans and Progressives* (1992) on Illinois, David Thelen's *Paths of Resistance* (1986) on Missouri, and William Link's *The Paradox of Southern Progressivism* (1992).

The women's suffrage movement is studied in Aileen Kraditor's *The Ideas of the Woman Suffrage Movement* (1965). For feminism in the Progressive Era, Rosalind Rosenberg's *Beyond Separate Spheres* (1982) is essential. For works on progressivism as social control, see Paul Boyer's *Urban Masses and Moral Order in America* (1978). The world of prostitution in the Progressive Era is examined from both sides in Ruth Rosen's *The Lost Sisterhood* (1982). Norman Clark's *Deliver Us from Evil* (1976) covers the Prohibition reform movement, as does a recent synthesis on the movement, *Battling Demon Rum* (1998) by Thomas Pegram. The nativist movement is the subject of John Higham's *Strangers in the Land* (1955). Several books explore the relationship between government and business during this time, including Louis Galambos and James Pratt's *The Rise of the Corporate Commonwealth* (1988) and Martin Sklar's *The Corporate Reconstruction of American Capitalism* (1992). Two books by Morton Keller, *Regulating a New Society* (1994) and *Regulating a New Economy* (1990), are essential for understanding progressive public policy.

Two of the best introductions to African-American activism in this period are Louis Harlan's *Booker T. Washington* (1983) and Stephen R. Fox's *The Guardian of Boston: William Monroe Trotter* (1971), which emphasizes the revival of black protest. Also see August Meier's *Negro Thought in America* (1963) for the intellectual underpinnings of black activism in this period. A valuable book on the Great Migration is James Grossman's *Land of Hope* (1989), in which he portrays the migration as a grass-roots effort for greater freedom. William Cohen's *At Freedom's Edge* (1991) examines the issue of black mobility as a whole and southern efforts to contain it.

The material available on the socialists and other radicals of this area is immense; James R. Green's *The World of the Worker* (1980) provides a thorough introductory overview. Melvyn Dubofsky's *We Shall Be All* (1969) is the best history of the Wobblies, while Nick Salvatore's *Eugene V. Debs* (1982) is the most acclaimed biography of that important socialist leader.

Two of the most readable accounts of the progressive presidents were both written by John Morton Blum: *The Republican Roosevelt* (1954) and *Woodrow Wilson and the Politics of Morality* (1956). John Milton Cooper's *The Warrior and the Priest* (1983) is an excellent comparative biography of Wilson and Roosevelt. Arthur Link's *Woodrow Wilson and the Progressive Era* (1954) is still a good choice. A recent survey of politics in this time period is Sean Dennis Cashman's *America Ascendent: From Theodore Roosevelt to FDR* (1998).

Managing Modern Society

The New Nationalism, 1910

On August 31, 1910, Theodore Roosevelt launched his campaign to return to the White House in a speech before a group of Civil War veterans in Osawatomie, Kansas. Calling for a "New Nationalism," Roosevelt argued that the national government retained the right to regulate the use of property "to whatever degree the public welfare may require."

I stand for the square deal. But when I say that I am for the square deal, I mean not merely that I stand for fair play under the present rules of the game, but that I stand for having those rules changed so as to work for a more substantial equality of opportunity and of reward for equally good service.

. . . The citizens of the United States must effectively control the mighty commercial forces which they have themselves called into being. There can be no effective control of corporations while their political activity remains. To put an end to it will be neither a short nor an easy task, but it can be done.

Combinations [trusts] in industry are the result of an imperative economic law which cannot be repealed by political legislation. The effort at prohibiting all combination has substantially failed. The way out lies, not in attempting to prevent such combinations, but in completely controlling them in the interest of the public welfare. . . .

The absence of effective State, and especially national, restraint upon unfair money-getting has tended to create a small class of enormously wealthy and economically powerful men . . . we should permit [such fortunes] only so long as the gaining represents benefit to the community. This, I know, implies a policy of a far more active government interference with social and economic conditions in this country than we have yet had, but I think we have got to face the fact that such an increase in governmental control is now necessary.

The man who wrongly holds that every human right is secondary to his profit must now give way to the advocate of human welfare, who rightly maintains that every man holds his property subject to the general right of the community to regulate its use to whatever degree the public welfare may require it.

The New Nationalism puts the national need before sectional or personal advantage. It is impatient of the utter confusion that results from local legislatures attempting to treat national issues as local issues. This New Nationalism regards the executive power as the steward of the public welfare.

The New Freedom, 1912

Roosevelt's speech on the New Nationalism had set the terms of the 1912 presidential campaign; in the final months of the race, Democratic candidate Woodrow Wilson laid out an alternative vision of the role of government in modern society. In a series of speeches during October 1912, he called for a "New Freedom," through which Americans could live free of interference from both large corporations *and* big government.

▋▋▋ Gentlemen have been saying for a long time that trusts are inevitable. . . . [T]hey say that the particular kind of combinations that are now controlling our economic development came into existence naturally and were inevitable; and that, therefore, we have to accept them as unavoidable and administer our development through them. They say that the only thing we can do, and the only thing we ought to attempt to do, is to accept them as inevitable arrangements and make the best out of it that we can by regulation.

I answer that this attitude rests upon a confusion of thought. Big business is no doubt to a large extent necessary and natural. But that is a very different matter from the development of trusts, because the trusts have not grown. They have been artificially created; they have been put together, not by natural processes, but by the will of men who were more powerful than their neighbors in the business world, and who wished to make their power secure against competition.

I am not willing to be under the patronage of the trusts, no matter how providential a government presides over the process of their control of my life. My thought about both Mr. Taft and Mr. Roosevelt is that of entire respect, but these gentlemen have been so intimately associated with the powers that have been determining the policy of this government . . . [that] their thought is in close, habitual association with those who have framed the policies of the country during all our lifetime. Those men have coordinated and ordered all the great economic forces of this country in such a way that nothing but an outside force breaking in can disturb their domination and control.

The hands that are being stretched out to monopolize our forests, to prevent the use of our great power-producing streams—the hands that are being stretched into the bowels of the earth to take possession of the great riches that lie hidden [there] . . . are the hands of monopoly. Are these men to continue to stand at the elbow of government and tell us how we are going to save ourselves—from themselves? You can not settle the question while monopoly is close to the ears of those who govern.

I take my stand absolutely, where every progressive ought to take his stand, on the proposition that private monopoly is indefensible and intolerable. And there I will fight my battle. ▋

Theodore Roosevelt and Woodrow Wilson couched the 1912 election in terms of "the struggle of free men to gain and hold the right of self-government as against the special interests." They had in mind a specific group of free men—working people and small businessmen—and a specific group of special interests—modern industrial corporations. Yet in their competing visions of how government could help those free men "to gain and hold" those rights, Roosevelt and Wilson struggled with a question that is as old as the federal government itself. When is it right for government to intervene in society to protect some private individuals from the depredations of others?

The founders of the Republic had not initially worried about this question. They were concerned with limiting the *abusive* power of government, and to that end they tried to limit its activities as much as possible. Within a few years, however, politicians had begun to take sides over which government actions were abusive. On one side were Alexander Hamilton and his allies, who argued that government had a responsibility to encourage industry and protect the financiers who provided the capital for economic growth. On the other side stood Jefferson and his supporters, who saw Hamilton's policies as favoritism to the rich and called for a limited government that allowed the common man—ideally, the "yeoman farmer"—to prosper.

Though the players changed over the years—as Federalists begat Whigs and Republicans, and the Democratic-Republicans spawned the Democrats and Populists—the terms of the argument did not. The two options available in the political mainstream were a powerful government that supported the holders of wealth and capital versus a limited government that, in a pinch, sided with the working people or the *petite bourgeoisie*. The election of 1912 was important because in that election, Theodore Roosevelt *changed the terms of the debate*. He brought a new argument from the fringes to the mainstream of political thought: a strong, activist government was a good thing, *provided it worked for the weak as well as the strong*. In his 1910 speech on the New Nationalism, he claimed that the old division between Hamilton and Jefferson was irrelevant to a modern, industrial society. Americans should develop a new concept of government, one that borrowed the strengths of both of the old arguments.

The idea that society had fundamentally changed—that traditional ideas of government and individualism were inappropriate for modern society—was essential to Roosevelt's argument. Woodrow Wilson attempted to refute this idea during the campaign. He called for a New Freedom in his later campaign speeches, arguing that the old Jeffersonian ideals of free competition and individual liberty were still relevant in the modern world. Unlike Roosevelt, who was willing to accept large concentrations of wealth and power and wanted to regulate them for the common good, Wilson wanted to dismantle the trusts, which would ultimately require less government intervention in society.

Though Wilson's ideas won the campaign, Roosevelt's seemed to win the war. During his two terms in office, Wilson came to enact many of the reforms that Roosevelt had proposed. In the new age of activist government, though, Wilson's "conversion" did not amount to the betrayal it might have been had it occurred in the nineteenth century. For the activist government of the twentieth century held out promises to both sides of the old debate: government could both encourage industry and protect the common man.

Questions for Analysis

1. What are the "present rules of the game" that Roosevelt refers to in his opening?

2. How does Roosevelt propose to employ an activist government?

3. What makes him think trusts are inevitable?

4. According to Wilson, why is Roosevelt wrong to claim that trusts are inevitable?

5. Why does Wilson distrust the Republican and Progressive reformers?

6. How does Wilson propose to deal with trusts?

7. Are the New Nationalism and the New Freedom incompatible? Why or why not?

8. Are Roosevelt's and Wilson's ideas still applicable to today's society? If so, which candidate would you choose in an election? Why?

22

The Experiment in American Empire, 1865–1917

O n November 9, 1906, President Theodore Roosevelt set sail on the new 16,000-ton *Louisiana*, the largest battleship in the growing U.S. Navy. The first president ever to leave the country during his term in office, Roosevelt was headed for Panama to examine progress on the construction of a new U.S. canal—the most daring and ambitious engineering marvel of the time. Convinced that the United States needed a gateway between the Atlantic and Pacific Oceans, Roosevelt had maneuvered to purchase the rights to the canal from Panama in 1904. Not even the fierce rainstorm that greeted Roosevelt's arrival on November 15 could dampen his enthusiasm for the project. Over the next two days, the president leaped into ditches, inspected the complicated gears used to operate the great locks, and steered the gigantic steam shovel that moved mountains of earth and rock. Afterward, Roosevelt wrote to his son that the canal was "the greatest engineering feat of the ages. . . . I went over everything that I could possibly go over."

The canal was made possible by the marriage of imagination with industrial might and technological know-how. Engineers slashed through mountains, carved out ditches, fabricated locks wide enough to float the world's biggest ships, and constructed the largest dam ever built. "Everything is on a colossal scale," noted *Scientific American*. How colossal? Manufacturers poured millions of tons of concrete to erect the mammoth canal walls—enough concrete to build a wall 8 feet thick,

12 feet high, and 133 miles long. American factories churned out the hardware—special bearings, gears, wheels, and struts—that opened and closed the immense locks. Ironically, the greatest threat to success came from the tiniest of enemies, the mosquito. Carriers of malaria and yellow fever, mosquitoes had helped doom an earlier French effort to build a canal, wiping out more than twenty thousand workers. U.S. Army doctors, however, developed effective countermeasures, destroyed the mosquito population, and reduced the incidence of disease.

The U.S. government had never undertaken a project as big, complex, and expensive as the Panama Canal. It took the U.S. Army Corps of Engineers eight years to finish the 50-mile-long canal, which a British observer called "the greatest liberty Man has ever taken with Nature." When opened in August 1914, the canal shortened the distance between New York and San Francisco by boat from 15,615 miles to 5,300 miles. U.S. merchants and warships now moved easily between the Atlantic and Pacific Oceans.

The experiment in canal building was an outgrowth of America's growing global ambitions, its desire to quicken the pace of commerce and to project military power abroad. In the two decades following the Civil War, Americans remained too absorbed in westward expansion and industrialization to devote serious attention to foreign policy. By the end of the century, however, a new spirit of imperialism gripped the nation. In 1898 the United States went to war with Spain to assert its influence in the Western Hemisphere. It also extended its power in the Pacific by annexing the Hawaiian Islands and establishing a protectorate over the Philippines.

Despite their differences, the Progressive Era presidents—Roosevelt, Taft, and Wilson—shared an expansive view of the nation's global interests and showed a new willingness to flex U.S. military muscle. Projecting the reform impulse outward, they sought to extend American values through the experiment in empire building. Theodore Roosevelt established American dominance in the Caribbean and worked to maintain open markets in China. His decision to build the Panama Canal was the most dramatic expression of America's muscular foreign policy. Woodrow Wilson came to office promising a foreign policy based on morality, not self-interest. But his active intervention in the Caribbean, especially Mexico, demonstrated that his policies differed little from the militaristic Roosevelt's.

■ Why did America abandon its traditional isolationism at the end of the nineteenth century?

■ In what way was the war with Spain a critical turning point in U.S. foreign policy?

■ What was Theodore Roosevelt's view of America's world role, and how successful was he in implementing it?

■ How did Wilson's foreign policy differ from Roosevelt's? What did their policies have in common?

This chapter will address these questions.

Chronology

1867	Seward purchases Alaska
1872	*Alabama* claims settled
1889	U.S. enters tripartite protectorate over Samoan Islands
1890	Naval Act passed
1895	Venezuelan border dispute
1896	McKinley elected president
1898	Spanish-American War begins and ends
	Hawaii becomes a U.S. territory
	U.S. annexes part of Samoa and Wake Island
	Anti-Imperialist League formed
1899	U.S. sovereignty established over the Philippines and Puerto Rico
	Philippine insurrection begins
	Hay's Open Door notes
	Boxer Rebellion in China
1901	Roosevelt becomes president
1904	Senate approves Panama Canal treaty
	Roosevelt Corollary
1905	Portsmouth peace conference
1907	Great White Fleet sails around the world
1908	Root-Takahira Agreement
	Taft elected president
1909	Taft unveils dollar diplomacy
1912	Marines invade Nicaragua
	Lodge Corollary
	Wilson elected president
1914	World War I begins in Europe
	Panama Canal opens
	American troops invade Mexico
1915	Marines invade Haiti

The Roots of Expansion, 1865–1898

Except for a handful of expansionist thinkers such as Secretary of State William Seward, few Americans expressed interest in foreign policy in the years following the Civil War. By the end of the nineteenth century, however, a number of forces—the search for new markets, the popularity of Social Darwinism, social anxieties bred by the end of the frontier, and the emergence of influential advocates of expansion—were pushing the United States to experiment with a more aggressive role in the world. America's involvement in Hawaii and Samoa revealed a growing interest in distant markets and lands.

Gilded Age Diplomacy, 1865–1889

During the 1860s and 1870s few Americans cared about foreign policy. Isolationists dominated Congress, and public sentiment favored internal improvement and development westward over external expansion. The *Chicago Tribune* noted soon after the Civil War that "we already have more territory than we can people in fifty years."

Americans lacked any sense of imminent threat from abroad. Geographical distance continued to protect America from what Jefferson had called "the broils of Europe." Moreover, a stable balance of power had preserved international peace in Europe for most of the nineteenth century after Napoleon's defeat. But social peace was another matter. The waves of new immigrants seeking opportunity on the nation's shores reaffirmed Americans' fears about the corruption of the "Old World" and reinforced the desire to avoid entangling alliances with European powers. Even if Americans had wanted to get involved in world affairs, they lacked the means to do so. The State Department consisted of only sixty full-time staff members. In the 1880s the United States was represented abroad by twenty-five ministers, but no ambassadors. In 1883 the U.S. Navy was a pitiful collection of 90 woeful ships, 58 made of wood. Representative John D. Long of Massachusetts described it as "an alphabet of floating washtubs." Foreign policy was impulsive rather than systematic. American leaders responded to individual crises but lacked a global strategy or a coordinated vision of America's role in the world.

During these years the United States nevertheless made its first steps toward world power. Leading the charge were bold expansionists, in particular Secretary of State William H. Seward (served 1861–1869). Seward's belief that the United States should hold a "commanding sway in the world" foreshadowed American foreign policy in the next century. Believing that "empire has, for the last three hundred years . . . made its way constantly westward," Seward wanted the United States to establish its dominance over Latin America and extend its reach into Asian markets, especially China, which he called "the chief theatre of events in the world's great hereafter."

Acting on his expansionist impulses, Seward negotiated a treaty with Nicaragua in 1867 giving the United States rights to build a canal from the Atlantic to the Pacific at a later date. Two months later he annexed the Midway Islands west of Hawaii, which opened up a commercial route to Korea, Japan, and China. The Senate, however, which was consumed by the impeachment of President Andrew Johnson, rejected Seward's efforts to buy the Virgin Islands, St. Thomas and St. John in the Caribbean, from Denmark for $7.5 million.

In his most significant, and controversial, acquisition, Seward purchased Alaska from Russia in March 1867. Critics, who called the deal "Seward's Folly," complained that the United States had little need for "a barren, worthless, God-forsaken region." Supporters emphasized Alaska's rich mineral resources and suggested that acquiring Alaska would lead to the possible annexation of Canada. Although the Senate approved the purchase on April 6, Congress did not appropriate the purchase money of $7.5 million until 1870, and then only after the Russian minister had spent some of it in advance to bribe influential congressmen. Seward thus added 586,000 square miles, or an area more than twice the size of Texas, to the Union.

In 1869 newly elected President Grant appointed Hamilton Fish to replace Seward as secretary of state. Like Seward, Fish struggled against strong isolationist forces. The administration's attempt to annex Santo Domingo for $1.5 million aroused a storm of public protest. In June 1870, the Senate fell ten votes short of ratification and the treaty died. Americans were opposed to annexing more territory in the Caribbean, but they were willing to go to war to defend America's national honor. A major crisis arose in 1875, when a Spanish gunboat seized the *Virginius,* a Cuban-owned ship in international waters that was carrying weapons to rebels on its home island. The crew, which included eight Americans, were later tried and executed. Cries went up in the United States for revenge. Fish, after discovering that the ship was not legally registered in the United States, negotiated an agreement by which Spain agreed to pay $80,000 for the lives of the crew members.

More pressing than acquiring additional territory was settling disputes with Great Britain left over from the Civil War. Many in the North wanted the British to pay reparations for the damage inflicted on the Union by English-built Confederate ships. Most controversial of all were the *Alabama* claims, stemming from the destruction wrought by a single British-based raider. Charles Sumner, chairman of the Senate Foreign Relations Committee, claiming that such ships had prolonged the war by two years, demanded that Britain bear half the total cost of the war. His bill totaled $2.1 billion, but Sumner suggested that the United States would be happy to accept Canada instead of cash. After protracted negotiations, a joint Anglo-American–appointed judicial commission ruled that Britain had been negligent in allowing the *Alabama* and the other cruisers to participate in the war. In September 1872, it awarded the United States $15.5 million in compensation.

The New Manifest Destiny

As the last quarter of the nineteenth century unfolded, a number of forces were pushing the United States to assume a more aggressive posture toward the world. Developments in transportation and communication produced a shrinking world economically and militarily. Steam-powered ships made travel between nations easier. In 1886 an underwater transatlantic cable linked the United States and Europe, cutting the transmission time for messages from weeks to hours. The U.S. telegraph system allowed direct communication with Brazil and Chile. "Commerce follows the cables," Henry Cabot Lodge observed in 1898, pointing out the link between communications and business. After devoting a generation to conquering the West and creating an industrial giant, many Americans turned their attention to new opportunities beyond the border.

Among the leading proponents of expansion were businessmen who believed that continued economic growth required tapping new markets abroad. Business did not speak with a single voice on the issue of overseas markets, however. Many business leaders, fearing that economic ties would inevitably entangle the United States in costly political struggles abroad, emphasized the importance of cultivating markets at home. Other businessmen saw the possibility of unlimited profits in untapped markets in Asia and Latin America. These regions also offered abundant raw materials such as sugar, coffee, oil, rubber, and minerals. In 1896 the newly formed National Association of Manufacturers declared "that the trade centres of Central and South America are natural markets for American products."

The decline in domestic consumption during the depression helped spread the conviction that the United States needed to aggressively cultivate markets abroad. "A policy of isolation did well enough when we were an embryo nation, but today things are different," Senator Orville Platt of Connecticut said in 1893. "We are sixty-five million of people, the most advanced and powerful on earth, and regard to our future welfare demands an abandonment of the doctrines of isolation."

Regardless of the debate over foreign markets, the last quarter of the nineteenth century witnessed an explosion of American economic involvement in the world. Between 1865 and 1898, the values of American exports jumped from $281 million to $1.3 billion, while imports rose from $259 million to $616 million. The young iron and steel industry exported 15 percent of its goods by the turn of the century. Almost 50 percent of copper mined in the United States was sold abroad. The Singer Company sold as many of its sewing machines overseas as it did at home. Over half of the petroleum refined in the United States ended up in Europe. Though most of the products flowed to Europe and Canada, American producers were also reaching into other areas. U.S. exports to Latin American, for example, increased from $50 million in the 1870s to over $120 million in 1900. Exports represented a small percentage of the gross national product (GNP)—between 6 and 7 percent—but Americans were looking more and more to foreign markets for future growth (see graph.)

Many expansionists argued that it was America's destiny to expand, not only to promote prosperity at home, but also to extend American blessings of liberty and democracy to the rest of the world. Americans had always believed they possessed a special mission to reshape the world in their own image. Senator Albert Beveridge of Indiana explained in 1900 that God "has marked the American people as his chosen nation to lead in the regeneration of the world."" Josiah Strong, a Congregational minister and author of the influential book *Our Country* (1885), promised that God was "preparing mankind to receive our impress." The United States, he charged, was "divinely commissioned" to spread Protestant Christianity and civilized values to the rest of the world. "As America goes, so goes the world."

The growing popularity of Social Darwinism (see page 806) added force to the notion of an expansionist mission. Extending the notion that only the "fit" survive

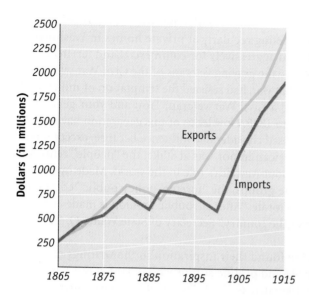

Imports and Exports, 1865–1915 The rapid expansion of American industry after the Civil War also spurred America's involvement in the international economy. While America maintained a favorable balance of trade for most of this period, the rise in imported goods paralleled the advancements made in the export market. (Source: Paterson, Thomas G., J. Garry Clifford, and Kenneth J. Hagan, *American Foreign Relations: A History,* Fourth Edition. Copyright © 1995 by D.C. Heath and Company. Reprinted with permission of Houghton Mifflin Company.)

to nations and societies, some expansionists argued that the United States needed to compete vigorously with other nations, or perish. "The rule of the survival of the fittest applies to nations as well as to the animal kingdom," an American diplomat noted in 1898.

The idea of natural selection also engendered a clear sense of racial hierarchy. New pseudoscientific studies suggested that people of Anglo-Saxon origin, namely Britons, Germans, Scandinavians, and Americans of those heritages, were superior to members of other races. By all standards of measure according to these theorists—industrial progress, military might, wealth, and influence—Anglo-Saxons were clearly at the pinnacle of the racial pyramid. This conviction of racial superiority encouraged a belief that the United States had an obligation to take part in instructing the world's less developed peoples in the superior ways of Anglo-Saxon civilization, but it also raised fears of racial mixing that would dilute the "pure" Anglo-Saxon stock.

Social anxieties born of the shrinkage in open land and opportunity in the West fed the expansionist appetite. For most of their history Americans had entertained the comforting belief that the constant movement westward acted as an escape valve for social tension. In 1893 a young University of Wisconsin historian, Frederick Jackson Turner, pronounced the frontier closed. Never again, he argued, would the frontier provide "a gate of escape from the bondage of the past." With the West settled, many people believed that Americans needed to find new outlets to absorb their dynamic energy. Turner observed that the frontier's disappearance created "demands for a vigorous foreign policy ... and for the extension of American influence to outlying islands and adjoining countries."

Finally, in the mid-1890s, a small group of influential men challenged traditional isolationist sentiment and advocated an expansionist foreign policy. Led by Assistant Secretary of the Navy Theodore Roosevelt and Republican senator Henry

Cabot Lodge of Massachusetts, these intensely nationalistic young men formed a close-knit circle of influence. Meeting regularly at private homes in Washington, they developed plans and lobbied aggressively for commercial and territorial expansion. They promised to replace the graying veterans of the Civil War who, chastened by their suffering during that war, had resisted the temptation of military adventure. As Teddy Roosevelt told a Civil War veteran, "You and your generation have had your chance from 1861 to 1865. Now let us of this generation have ours!"

This foreign policy elite exercised considerable influence because, except on occasions when they believed American honor was at stake, the "people" remained largely disinterested in debates about America's role in the world. Made up of educated upper- and middle-income groups, the "foreign-policy public" comprised about 10 to 20 percent of the electorate. "After all, public opinion is made and controlled by the thoughtful men of the country," Secretary of State Walter Q. Gresham noted in 1893.

The new foreign policy elite found their inspiration in the writings of Alfred Thayer Mahan, a naval strategist and prolific author who taught at the Naval War College. Mahan insisted in books such as *The Influence of Sea Power upon History* (1890) that control over international communications was the key to success in modern war. Believing that national power depended on sea power, Mahan supported U.S. colonies in both the Caribbean and the Pacific, linked by a canal built across Central America. In a Darwinian world, powerful nations had an obligation to dominate weak ones. If the United States was to be a great power, he argued, it must have a navy capable of carrying the battle to the enemy and not just defending the coastline (see map).

Mahan's followers lobbied Congress to build a new fleet of ships outfitted with the most modern weapons. A nation without a navy, they warned, could make little headway in world affairs in an age of sea power. "The sea will be the future seat of empire," observed Secretary of the Navy Benjamin F. Tracy. "And we shall rule it as certainly as the sun doth rise." The appeal found broad support in Congress, which set about repairing and improving the navy. In 1883 the legislature commissioned three steel-hulled, steam-powered cruisers, and in 1886 two battleships, the *Maine* and the *Texas*. The Naval Act of 1890 authorized the building of "three sea-going coastline battleships designed to carry the heaviest armor and most powerful ordnance." In 1880 the American navy was ranked the twelfth most powerful in the world. By 1900, it was third, with seventeen battleships and six armored cruisers.

Seeds of Empire

In diplomatic policy, the new expansionism was evident in the administration of Benjamin Harrison, who came into office in March 1889. His secretary of state James G. Blaine, the "Plumed Knight from Maine" (see page 776) said the goal of foreign policy must be to bring peace and trade to Latin America. "Our great demand is expansion," he stated. "I mean expansion of trade with countries where we can find profitable exchanges." Apprehensive about European influence in Latin America, he called the First International American Conference in 1889 and invited

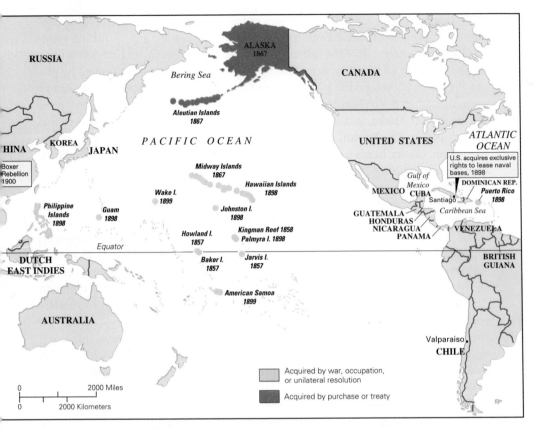

U.S. Expansion, 1865–1900 As America's trade with Asia grew, so did cries for expansion into the Pacific Ocean. A massive wave of acquisitions occurred in the last decade of the nineteenth century as the United States used its economic and military strength to expand its sphere of influence.

delegates from seventeen Latin American nations to discuss the creation of an inter-American common market. The conference failed to achieve that lofty goal, but it did lead to the building of the first Pan-American Highway system. The following year Congress passed a new "reciprocity" tariff that allowed certain Latin American products (especially coffee, hides, and sugar) to enter the United States freely as long as the nations that produced them allowed U.S. exports into their countries equally free from tariff restrictions. Under the 1890 reciprocity treaties, trade immediately boomed with Cuba and Brazil, among others.

The goodwill generated by the conference was short lived, however. In October 1891 more than a hundred drunken American sailors on shore leave from the U.S.S. *Baltimore* fought with anti-American Chileans in the port town of Valparaiso, Chile. Two sailors were killed, seventeen badly hurt. President Harrison insisted on a "prompt and full reparation," but the Chilean government scorned the demand. Harrison threatened war, and in January a new Chilean government apologized for the incident and paid a $75,000 indemnity.

While extending American influence in Latin America, the United States' continuing tensions with Great Britain centered on the question of U.S. fishing rights in Canadian waters. By 1886, after a number of attempts to reach a settlement, Canadians were seizing American fishing vessels, and Congress responded by giving President Cleveland the power to ban Canadian ships from American waters. Soon thereafter, the United States began seizing Canadian ships hunting seals in the Bering Sea off Alaska, and in 1889 Congress declared the Bering Sea closed to foreign shipping. The British, refusing to accept America's claim, sent warships into the region. Cooler heads prevailed, however, and both nations agreed to submit the case to international arbitration, which eventually ruled against the United States and ordered the government to pay damages to Canada.

Less easily resolved was a fifty-year-old dispute over the boundary between Venezuela and British Guiana. Tensions between the two countries flared in 1895 when prospectors discovered gold in the disputed area. When Venezuela suspended diplomatic relations with Britain, the United States offered to arbitrate. But neither side was prepared to settle, and the dispute lingered on. In an effort to force an end to the conflict, President Cleveland instructed his secretary of state, Richard L. Olney, to draft a note that invoked the Monroe Doctrine to warn the British against interference in the Western Hemisphere. "Today, the United States is practically sovereign on this continent, and its fiat is law upon the subjects to which it confines its interposition . . . because, in addition to all other grounds, its infinite resources combined with its isolated position render it master of the situation and practically invulnerable as against any or all other powers."

Britain rejected both the American offer for arbitration and Olney's broad and pompous expression of the Monroe Doctrine. "The disputed frontier of Venezuela has nothing to do with any of the questions dealt with by President Monroe," declared the prime minister. Cleveland, who pronounced himself "mad clear through," made it plain in a message of December 17, 1895, that if Britain would not accept arbitration, he would impose a settlement. The British, distracted by a new crisis with Germany and fearing a conflict with the United States, agreed in the Treaty of Washington to accept arbitration by an independent commission. On October 3, 1899, the commission upheld most of the British claims. The peaceful resolution of the border dispute foreshadowed a new spirit of cooperation and goodwill that would characterize Anglo-American relations in the next century.

Hawaii and Samoa

By the 1870s, the growing U.S. interest in Hawaii and Samoa revealed how American attitudes toward the world were changing. The Hawaiian (or Sandwich) Islands lay 2,300 miles southwest of California and served as the "Crossroads of the Pacific." After 1820, American missionaries arrived on the islands; by 1840, the capital, Honolulu, was an established port of call for American merchant ships and whalers.

In 1875 the United States and Hawaii signed a reciprocal trade agreement that allowed Hawaiian sugar to enter the United States duty-free and prevented the island monarchy from making treaties with other powers. With the rich U.S. market at their disposal, white planters forced a new constitution, which gave them dominance over the islands' economic and political life. Between 1876 and 1885, they raised their sugar production from 26 million pounds to 171 million pounds. Both sides renewed the reciprocal trade treaty in 1887, adding a provision giving the United States exclusive rights to a naval base at Pearl Harbor. In 1890, 99 percent of Hawaiian sugar exports went to the United States. Secretary of State James Blaine called the islands "a part of the productive and commercial system of the American states."

Not everyone on the islands welcomed the growing American presence. Native Hawaiians believed that increasing American involvement would end in annexation. In 1890 the McKinley Tariff Act ended the special status for Hawaii sugar. The new law sent the Hawaiian economy into a tailspin; unemployment rose and property values plummeted, along with the planters' profits. The following year a strong-minded nationalist, Queen Liliuokalani, assumed the throne. Tapping into deep resentment against the white minority, she abolished the constitution— the "Bayonet Constitution," she called it—and increased the power of native Hawaiians.

Seeing the Hawaiian nationalists as a threat to their predominance, the white plantation owners fought back, turning to the United States for help. They found a ready ally in John L. Stevens, the American minister in Honolulu. "They were lying in wait," Queen Liliuokalani remembered. In 1893 plantation owners launched an armed revolt to unseat the Hawaiian government, and Stevens, acting on his own

Queen Liliuokalani (1838–1917) Though Hawaiians had resented the growing influence of American sugar planters since the 1870s, not until Queen Liliuokalani assumed the throne in 1891 did they actively resist American imperialism. The indomitable monarch scrapped the Hawaiian constitution, drafted under the pressure of white planters, and declared "Hawaii for the Hawaiians." Her efforts, however, were no match for U.S. military might, which supported a planter coup in 1893. Hawaii was formally annexed to the United States in 1898. (*Hawaii State Archives.*)

authority, ordered 150 marines from the offshore U.S.S. *Boston* to guard locations in Honolulu. After three days of fighting, Queen Liliuokalani surrendered and the white minority established a provisional government. Stevens declared an American protectorate over Hawaii and raised the U.S. flag. "The Hawaiian pear is now fully ripe, and this is the golden hour for the United States to pluck it," he wrote. In February a committee for the new government signed a treaty of annexation with the United States.

By the time the Senate began considering the treaty, the Harrison administration, which favored annexation but had been voted out of office the preceding November, was over. The new president, Grover Cleveland, withdrew the treaty and dispatched a special commissioner, James H. Blount, to Hawaii. In July 1893, Blount reported that the "undoubted sentiment of the people is for the Queen, against the provisional Government and against annexation." Cleveland proposed restoring the queen to the throne, but the new government refused. In August Cleveland reluctantly recognized the independent Republic of Hawaii. The debate over annexation, however, continued through the 1890s.

Hawaii was not the only island in the Pacific that piqued American interest. The secretary of state during Cleveland's first term, Thomas F. Bayard, saw Samoa, a group of fourteen volcanic islands located 4,100 miles from the coast of California, as a valuable strategic asset in the South Pacific. On January 17, 1878, the Senate approved a treaty establishing U.S. trading rights and authorizing construction of a coaling station at Pago Pago on the island of Tutuila. Over the next few years the United States, Great Britain, and Germany jockeyed for power in the island chain. German Foreign Office officials angrily muttered that Bayard was extending the principles of "the Monroe Doctrine as though the Pacific Ocean were to be treated as an American lake."

Negotiations eventually eased tensions, and on June 14, 1889, the United States entered into a tripartite protectorate with Britain and Germany over the Samoan Islands, ratified by the Senate on February 4, 1890. Secretary of State Walter Q. Gresham (served 1893–1895) observed later that the treaty represented "the first departure from our traditional and well-established policy of avoiding entangling alliances with foreign powers in relation to objects remote from this hemisphere."

War and World Responsibilities, 1898–1901

The United States had been experimenting haphazardly with greater world involvement, but a series of events was about to propel the nation into the position of world power. In 1898 the United States found itself involved in a simmering revolt against Spanish policy in Cuba. The American public, aroused by sensationalized reports in mass-circulation newspapers, sided with the Cuban rebels in their fight for independence. In April 1898, smarting from perceived provocations, the United States declared war on Spain. The war lasted only a few months, but the United States reaped great benefits from victory, including new territories in the Caribbean and the western Pacific. For the first time Americans debated questions of empire and its role in the American experiment. While trying to quell an insurrection in the Philippines and establish stable governments in Cuba and Puerto Rico, the United States struggled to open new markets in China through a series of "Open Door" notes.

Origins of the Spanish-American War

For most of the previous quarter-century, Cubans had been revolting against Spanish colonialism. In February 1895, a new insurrection threatened Spanish rule on the island. Rebels established a provisional government and waged a guerrilla war against Spain. Both sides kept a cautious eye on the United States, which had investments totaling more than $50 million and depended on the island for its sugar exports. "The sugar industry of Cuba is as vital to our people as are the wheat and cotton of India and Egypt to Great Britain," declared the American minister to Spain.

The Spanish dispatched 150,000 soldiers who, under the command of General Valeriano Weyler, known as "the Butcher," tried to destroy the rebels' base of popular support by instituting the brutal *reconcentration* program. Weyler's soldiers forced peasants into armed camps and then turned the Cuban countryside into a desert, burning crops, killing animals, and poisoning wells. About four hundred thousand *reconcentrados*, nearly a quarter of the Cuban population, perished in the camps. The revolution nevertheless continued to spread, and the insurgents responded with a scorched-earth strategy of their own, burning cane fields, blowing up mills, and disrupting railroads in an effort to make Cuba an economic liability to Spain. "The chains of Cuba have been forged by her own richness," declared the rebel leader.

Events in Cuba attracted the attention of the American press, which played on strong American sentiment in favor of the rebels. William Randolph Hearst's *New York Journal* and Joseph Pulitzer's *New York World* were locked in a battle for readers. Fiercely competitive, they experimented with new methods to attract readers, including using bold print that covered the front page and adding illustrations and an expanded Sunday edition with color comics. They fed the public a steady diet of titillating articles such as "Strange Things Women Do for Love." Both papers also carried a cartoon character, "The Yellow Kid," and became known as "yellow journals." Pulitzer and Hearst sent correspondents to Cuba to cover the grim story of the revolt. They sent back ghastly reports, often exaggerated, that inflamed the passions of Americans already inclined to view the Cuban insurrection in light of their own revolution against England.

Public and business pressure for action mounted. The combination of altruism and self-interest provided a powerful argument for intervention. Outraged Americans held public meetings in major cities to protest Spain's actions. Congress responded to the pressure in April 1896, passing resolutions endorsing recognition of Cuban rebels and urging the president to support Cuban independence. President Cleveland, however, resisted public pressure and insisted on maintaining a policy of neutrality toward the conflict. The president believed the Cubans incapable of self-government and supported Spanish control, but he urged Spain to initiate modest political reforms to appease some of the rebels and neutralize the rebellion.

William McKinley came to office in early 1897 calling for a strong navy and demanding "the eventual withdrawal of the European powers from this hemisphere." But McKinley had little enthusiasm for war. As an eighteen-year-old volunteer, he had fought in the Civil War's bloodiest battles. "I have been through one war," he told a friend. "I have seen the dead piled up, and I do not want to see another." For now, McKinley tried to walk a fine line between preserving American honor and avoiding armed intervention in Cuba.

Immediately after assuming office in March, he sent an aide to investigate conditions in Cuba. The aide returned with a horrifying account of Spanish atrocities that had wrapped Cuba "in the stillness of death and the silence of desolation." In June 1897, McKinley demanded an end to the "uncivilized and inhumane conduct" of the Spanish. He pressed Spain to end the fighting and to grant reforms, indicating that otherwise the United States might intervene. A new government in Madrid offered a few concessions, removing "Butcher" Weyler, suspending its reconcentration camps, and offering the first steps toward Cuban autonomy.

Spain's action produced a temporary lull in the crisis, but two unpredictable events pushed the nations closer to war. On February 9 Hearst's *New York Journal* published a private letter from Spain's minister in Washington, Enrique Dupuy de Lôme, to a senior Spanish politician touring Cuba. The letter poked fun at McKinley, calling him "weak," a "bidder for the admiration of the crowd," and a "would-be politician." Along with the insults of McKinley, the letter suggested that the promised Cuban reforms were not being carried out in good faith. The *Journal*, in a screaming headline, called the letter the "Worst Insult to the United States in History!" The little trust that Americans had in the Spanish evaporated.

Six days later, on February 15, an explosion destroyed the *Maine*, one of the U.S. Navy's most modern and imposing battleships, while it sat in Cuba's Havana harbor. The United States lost 260 sailors in the explosion. Though the cause of the explosion remained uncertain, Americans blamed Spain. Headlines clamored for vengeance. The *New York World* roared: "Remember the *Maine!* To hell with Spain!" Assistant Secretary of the Navy Theodore Roosevelt called the sinking "an act of dirty treachery on the part of the Spaniards."

After the *Maine*'s destruction, McKinley asked Congress for $50 million to begin mobilization for war. On March 9, Congress granted his request. "It seemed as though a hundred Fourths of July had been let loose in the House," a clerk noted. On March 17, Republican senator Redfield Proctor of Vermont, widely recognized as a sober and judicious man, stood on the Senate floor and delivered a powerful speech denouncing Spain's policy in Cuba. "That speech means war," a fellow senator declared; "that speech will stir the people of the United States from Maine to California, and no power on earth can longer keep them back."

But McKinley still hoped for peace. Between March 20 and 28, he sent a series of demands to Spain. The Spanish would have to pay an indemnity for the *Maine,* promise not to use the reconcentration camps, declare a truce in fighting with the rebels, and negotiate for Cuban independence, through U.S. mediation if necessary. The Spanish government, hoping to avoid a confrontation with the United States, surrendered to all the demands except the last.

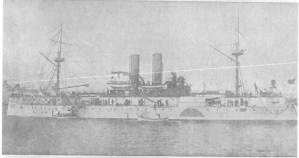

Remembering the *Maine*
The combination of an explosion on the U.S.S. *Maine* and an exploitative press created a public clamor for war so loud it forced a reluctant McKinley ever closer to war. The explosion that sent the ship to the bottom of Havana harbor on February 15, 1898, was never investigated, and the press immediately accused Spain for orchestrating the tragedy, even though Spain was actually doing everything possible to avoid war with the United States. This sheet of music demonstrates how the event became a propaganda tool, as Americans demanded their government "avenge" the impugning of American honor. *(Courtesy of the John Carter Brown Library at Brown University.)*

McKinley's peace overtures, however, incurred the wrath of a nation intent on war. The *Journal* declared that the "whole country thrills with the war fever." The *World* commented on "the warlike spirit of the multitude." Theodore Roosevelt, banging his war drums, called McKinley "a white-livered cur." "The President," Roosevelt jeered, "has no more backbone than a chocolate eclair." The taunts and abuse took their toll on McKinley who, according to a friend, "broke down and cried like a boy of thirteen."

Reluctantly, McKinley prepared his war message. On April 11, 1898, in a long, tempered address, the president declared that the three-year struggle on the island had caused "very serious injury to the commerce, trade, and business of our people, and the wanton destruction of property." McKinley's war message triggered a spirited debate in Congress. Administration allies fought off attempts to include recognition of Cuban independence as part of the war declaration. Congress did, however, include the Teller Amendment, which disclaimed "any disposition or intention to exercise sovereignty, jurisdiction, or control over" Cuba and announced American intent "to leave the government and control of the island to its people." On April 21, Spain severed diplomatic relations with the United States. The following day, American ships blockaded Cuba. On April 24 Spain declared war. The next day, Congress declared that a state of war had existed since April 21.

A variety of motives pushed the nation into war. Moralism inspired many religious leaders to march in the war parade. Lyman Abbott, pastor of Plymouth Church in Brooklyn, thought war the "answer to America to the question of its own conscience: Am I my brother's keeper?" Emotional nationalism, infused with notions of American superiority, played a role. The de Lôme and *Maine* incidents, combined with the sensationalized accounts of Spanish atrocities, provoked widespread anger and convinced many Americans that intervention was both right and just. "At last, God's hour has struck. The American people go forth in a warfare holier than liberty—holy as humanity," noted a partisan. Business leaders, who had originally feared that conflict would disrupt commerce and endanger U.S. investment in the island, now saw war as a way to open trade doors by eliminating a colonial power from the hemisphere. Imperialists rallied around the prospect of the war's extending America's empire and serving as justification for an enlarged navy. Even many Americans who opposed empire hoped the war would halt the killing and restore order to a troubled nation.

"A Splendid Little War"

The United States army was ill-prepared for battle. The regular army consisted of only 28,000 officers and men, scattered in small detachments around the country. The only officers with experience commanding troops in battle were aging veterans of the Civil War and Indian conflicts. The president called into service 200,000 volunteers, who flocked to army camps in Tampa, Florida, the base for the Cuban expedition. The army owned no accurate maps of Cuba. Essential equipment was in short supply. Ultimately soldiers would be sent off to fight in a tropical climate with uniforms made of heavy wool, flannel, and cowhide. The food supplies sent with them rotted in the tropical heat. One food that did not, canned beef, contained so many chemical preservatives that soldiers called it "embalmed beef."

Among the units ordered to Florida were four African-American army regiments that had been serving in the northern Plains and on the Mexican border. These black soldiers eventually made up almost one-fourth of the invasion force that sailed for Cuba. As they moved eastward by train, they were greeted by cheering crowds. "All the way from northwest Nebraska this regiment was greeted with cheers and hurrahs," observed a black chaplain. The cheering stopped when the trains entered the South. Sergeant Frank W. Pullen wrote, "We were 'niggers' as they called us and treated us with contempt." Once they arrived in Florida, black soldiers stationed near segregated towns endured constant indignities. In one town a sign read, "Dogs and niggers not allowed." At times tensions exploded into violence. In Tampa, a confrontation led to a night of rioting in which three whites and twenty-seven black soldiers were wounded. A black chaplain asked, "Talk about fighting and freeing poor Cuba and of Spain's brutality; of Cuba's murdered thousands, and starving *reconcentrados*. Is America any better than Spain?"

Even before the declaration of war, Assistant Secretary of the Navy Theodore Roosevelt had been plotting American strategy. Believing that U.S. naval forces could cripple the Spanish fleet with a surprise attack in the Pacific, he had ordered Commodore George Dewey to head for Spain's colony in the Philippines and be ready to engage the Spanish there in case of war. On April 30, just one week after war was declared, Dewey arrived in Manila with four cruisers and two gunboats. After four hours of cannon fire, the Spanish fleet lay in ruins, having lost almost four hundred men. No U.S. ship was badly hit, and only eight sailors were wounded. Every American ship in Manila harbor, declared Connecticut senator Orville Platt, was "a new *Mayflower* . . . the harbinger and agent of a new civilization." After defeating the Spanish fleet, Dewey waited for reinforcements before leading a land assault. On August 13, the strengthened U.S. force, with the help of Filipino rebels, gained control of Manila and accepted Spain's surrender of the Philippines.

While Dewey gained control of the Philippines, a force of marines seized Cuba's Guantanamo Bay. On June 21, the main American invasion party of seventeen thousand men landed at Daiquiri in southeastern Cuba. The first major battle took place on July 1 when American troops, joined by experienced Cuban rebels, captured the fortified town of El Caney and drove the Spanish from San Juan Hill.

At the same time, Theodore Roosevelt led a smaller unit in supporting an assault on nearby Kettle Hill. Hoping to get "in on the fun," Roosevelt had quit his position in the Navy Department and volunteered for service in Cuba. Determined to fight in style, he ordered a custom-fitted uniform from Brooks Brothers and organized a volunteer regiment that he called the "Rough Riders." Wanting his regiment to represent the best elements in American life, Roosevelt recruited other wealthy and educated men from Ivy League schools. But it was the cowboys he had met while living in the West who made up the backbone of the regiment. No one was more eager for battle than Roosevelt. Mounted and exuberant, he charged directly at the Spanish guns. "I waved my hat and we went up the hill with a rush," he recalled in his autobiography. The Rough Riders stormed the slope, joined by black troopers from the Ninth and Tenth Cavalry. After a day of fierce fighting, the Spanish troops withdrew, but only after inflicting heavy casualties on the Americans.

Victory gave the Americans control of the strategic high ground overlooking the city of Santiago, where a fleet of Spanish ships was bottled up by an American blockade. As U.S. troops moved into Santiago by land, the Spanish ships in the harbor tried to escape. On the morning of July 3, the Spanish squadron ran directly into the path of twelve American vessels waiting in ambush. As the Americans engaged in what amounted to target practice, one U.S. officer felt moved to shout the order, "Don't cheer, men! Those poor devils are dying." On July 17, the Spanish in Santiago surrendered. The following week an American force seized control of Spanish-held Puerto Rico.

On August 12 representatives from the United States and Spain met at the White House to sign an armistice. The war had lasted four months. According to the terms of the treaty, Spain gave up control of Cuba, and the United States

Two Faces of War

Never were image and reality so starkly contrasted as during the Spanish-American War. In the public mind, it was a "splendid little war," short, painless, and heroic. The bombastic Teddy Roosevelt and his masculine band of Rough Riders taking San Juan Hill (shown above in a lithograph by W. G. Read) was the enduring image of the conflict. The reality included disease, disorganization, and death. William Glackens, an artist employed by *McClure's*, made the sketch at right at the Guamas River, where Spanish snipers killed and wounded hundreds of American soldiers. (*Library of Congress.*)

annexed Puerto Rico and occupied Manila until the two nations reached a final agreement on the Philippines. It all seemed so easy. At the cost of 2,900 lives (all but 400 the victims of disease, not enemy gunfire) and only $250 million, the United States became a great world power. John Hay, a future secretary of state, wrote his friend Theodore Roosevelt: "It has been a splendid little war; begun with the highest motives, carried on with magnificent intelligence and spirit, favored by that fortune which loves the brave."

The war with Spain marked a critical turning point in America's role in world affairs. For the first time, the United States acquired overseas land and entertained hopes of creating its own empire. The nation had moved "from a position of comparative freedom from entanglements into the position of what is commonly called a world power," Assistant Secretary of State John Bassett Moore observed. "Where formerly we had only commercial interests, we now have territorial and political interests as well."

Managing the New American Empire

For many Americans the euphoria of victory spawned dreams of empire. Much attention focused on the Philippines—more than seven thousand islands and 7 million people, stretched over 115,000 square miles. Businessmen saw commercial possibilities in the islands. The San Francisco Chamber of Commerce asked the president to keep the islands "with a view to strengthening our trade relations with the orient." Most Americans, reflecting prevailing racial attitudes, believed that the Filipinos were incapable of self-government. The United States, they maintained, had an obligation to teach Spain's former subjects the wonders of democracy.

America's control of the Philippines raised new interest in Hawaii, which provided a base for ships headed to Manila. Two days after learning of Dewey's victory in Manila, McKinley asked the Senate for Hawaiian annexation, declaring, "We need Hawaii just as much and a good deal more than we did California. It is manifest destiny." "To maintain our flag in the Philippines," the *New York Sun* editorialized, "we must raise our flag in Hawaii." McKinley still did not have the two-thirds vote needed for Senate ratification, so he resorted to the device of annexation through joint resolution of the House and Senate. The majorities needed for passing the joint resolution were easily secured in both houses, and on August 12, 1898, Hawaii became a U.S. territory. The United States also reached an agreement with Germany that each would annex part of the Samoan Islands. In 1898 the United States laid claim to Wake Island, located between Guam and the Hawaiian Islands.

Not everyone agreed with the new territorial ambitions. An anti-imperialist movement had grown rapidly during 1898 to oppose McKinley's policy on the Philippines (see Competing Voices, page 883). To build public support for their position, they formed the Anti-Imperialist League in November 1898. The league organized mass meetings and published pamphlets calling on those "who believe in the republic against Empire." Within a few months the organization boasted nearly half a million members, including former presidents Grover Cleveland and Benjamin Harrison, reformer Jane Addams, labor leader Samuel Gompers, and industrialist Andrew Carnegie.

The anti-imperialists' powerful arguments against empire would echo through the next century. Many took racial attitudes of the time a step further than the imperialists, arguing that dark-skinned peoples were incapable of participating in a self-governing democracy. A South Carolina senator warned against "the incorporation of a mongrel and semi-barbarous population into our body politic." Others feared that imperialism abroad would erode freedom at home—that the acquisition of new lands would burden the United States, requiring a large defense buildup to protect far-flung, vulnerable possessions. Besides, they argued, the Constitution did not give the federal government the power to acquire foreign territory. "The power to conquer alien people and hold them in subjugation is nowhere expressly granted" to Washington by the Constitution, and "is nowhere implied," noted Senator George Hoar.

Above all, anti-imperialists argued, an aggressive foreign policy was incompatible with American liberty. Charles Sumner predicted ominously that "adventurous policies of conquest or ambition" would transform the American experiment in democracy into "another empire just after the fashion of all the old ones." Empire, he charged, would enlarge the power of the state, concentrate power in Washington, and produce factions that would vie for state favors.

McKinley, bent to annexation pressures, demanded U.S. sovereignty over the Philippines and Puerto Rico. Spain relinquished to all the American demands and, in return, the United States offered a payment of $20 million. On December 10, 1898, the two nations signed the Treaty of Paris. Senate ratification provoked a bitter clash between imperialists and anti-imperialists. On February 6, 1899, the Senate voted in favor of the treaty after engaging in what Senator Lodge described as the "closest, most bitter, and most exciting struggle I have ever known, or ever expect to see in the Senate."

Filipinos were outraged by the treaty. The rebel forces that had fought alongside American troops to defeat the Spanish now began fighting the better-armed American troops. "War without quarter to the false Americans who have deceived us!" the rebel leader Emilio Aguinaldo ordered his troops. "Either independence or death!" During the first days of fighting, U.S. troops overwhelmed Aguinaldo's poorly equipped army of eighty thousand men. Shooting Filipinos, an American solider wrote, was "more fun than a turkey shoot." U.S. troops drove the insurrectionists into the hills, burned villages, and confined villagers in reconcentration camps similar to those used by the Spanish in Cuba. "We are destroying down to the root every germ of a healthy national life in these unfortunate people," admonished philosopher William James.

Unable to defeat the Americans using conventional tactics, the rebels turned to guerrilla warfare to frustrate American hopes of a quick victory. They raided supply lines, cut communications, and ambushed small detachments. After massacring an American regiment, Filipinos stuffed the corpses with molasses to attract ants. In

March 1901, American soldiers penetrated a rebel camp and captured Aguinaldo. On April 19 he asked his troops to stop fighting. "There has been enough blood, enough tears, enough desolation," he said. The resistance soon faded. It had taken American troops three years to quell the rebellion. More than 5,000 Americans and 200,000 Filipinos died. Nearly 130,000 U.S. troops served in the war, which cost the United States at least $160 million.

On July 4, 1901, the United States transferred authority on the island from the military to a new civilian governor, William Howard Taft, then a prominent Ohio judge. His mission, he lectured the Filipinos, was to create a government "which shall teach those people individual liberty, which shall lift them up to a point of civilization . . . , and which shall make them rise to call the name of the United States blessed." Over the next few years Taft jailed dissenters and suppressed calls for independence at the same time that he expanded educational opportunities, built bridges and roads, and restructured the tax system. Not until July 4, 1946, however, would the United States grant the Philippines their independence.

As events in the Philippines unfolded, the United States also debated the future of the other nations it had liberated from Spain—Cuba and Puerto Rico. Should Cuba be granted independence or annexed by the United States? Most American leaders considered the Cubans incapable of independence. Asked when Cuban self-government might be possible, a U.S. general responded, "Why those people are no more fit for self-government than gun-powder is for hell." But McKinley, fearful of racial mixing, also ruled out annexation. Instead he opted for a middle ground. Because Cuba was so close to U.S. shores, he argued, the United States could control it without having to annex it. He appointed General Leonard Wood as military commander of the island, telling Wood, "I want you to go down there to get the people ready for a republican form of government."

Wood established a democratic procedure for the election of delegates to a Cuban constitutional convention. The convention adopted a new constitution modeled after the American Constitution. Under intense pressure from Wood, the delegates, by a vote of 15 to 11, also accepted the conditions set forth in the Platt Amendment. Passed by Congress in 1901, the Platt Amendment gave the United States the right to intervene in Cuban affairs, required the Cuban government to limit its debt with European nations, and prohibited the Cuban government from negotiating a treaty with a foreign power. The amendment also gave the United States a ninety-nine year lease on the naval base at the island's Guantanamo Bay. The Platt Amendment continued to be the basis of U.S. policy in Cuba until 1934.

Puerto Rico also raised fundamental questions about how America would govern its distant territories. Shortly after conquering the country, the U.S. military commander announced that the United States intended to give Puerto Ricans "the immunities and blessings of the liberal institutions of our government." But instead of granting such blessings, Congress passed the Foraker Act of 1900, which made Puerto Rico an "unincorporated territory" subject to the laws of Congress but governed by the War Department. Residents could elect a Lower House, but the U.S. president would appoint the governor, the heads of executive departments, and

"CIVILIZATION BEGINS AT HOME."

The Anti-Imperialist Opposition   The annexation of the Philippines and other territories after the Spanish-American War provoked intense criticism from many prominent Americans with a variety of motivations. Though some opponents of annexation acted out of racism, most believed imperialism contrary to fundamental American values. Others felt it was hypocritical to attempt to export those values when they had not yet been perfected at home. This cartoon of Lady Justice uncovering America's own problems with liberty reflects the latter sentiment and focuses attention, rare for the time, on the issue of racism in the United States.   (*Literary Digest*, *November 26, 1889.*)

members of the Upper House. Critics challenged the premise of the Foraker Act, asserting that "the Constitution followed the flag." Nevertheless, in a series of decisions known as the *Insular* cases, the U.S. Supreme Court upheld the procedure. The justices ruled that the United States could annex an area, make it an "unincorporated" territory, and refuse to grant its people citizenship.

The Open Door to China

Americans debated questions of empire amid growing national and international attention toward China. American attitudes toward China were shaped by a mix of paternalism and profit. For years missionaries had enthralled Americans with stories of their work in the Far East, creating deep sympathy for the Chinese people.

China accounted for only 2 percent of U.S. foreign trade, but American businessmen had high hopes for the vast Asian market. An astute Secretary of State John Hay noted in 1900 that whoever understood China "has the key to world politics for the next five centuries." A group of New York businessmen agreed with Hay and in 1896 formed the American Asiatic Association to promote trade and development.

Many U.S. business interests feared being squeezed out of the China market. By the late 1890s, Japan, Russia, Germany, France, and England had already carved out spheres of influence in China, which had been rendered helpless following its defeat in the Sino-Japanese War. "The various powers," observed a Chinese leader, "cast upon us looks of tiger-like voracity, hustling each other in their endeavors to be the first to seize upon our inner-most territories." Hay responded to this threatening situation by sending a series of notes to America's rivals in China. In these "Open Door" notes, Hay asked the other powers to guarantee that ports would remain open to all nations and to avoid offering special privileges to any group. The other nations sent ambiguous replies, but Hay announced agreement of all powers as "final and definitive."

Just as Hay was declaring victory, a new, more ominous threat to American interests emerged in China. In 1899 a radical antiforeign and militaristic society, the "Righteous and Harmonious Fists" (called "Boxers" by journalists), began murdering foreigners. By June, Boxers controlled the capital and were besieging areas where most foreigners lived. In 1900 the United States sent 2,500 troops to join an international delegation to lift the siege. In addition, Hay dispatched a second series of notes in which he asked all powers to preserve "Chinese territorial and administrative integrity." Russia, Japan, Germany, and Britain accepted Hay's second Open Door notes.

This second round extended America's involvement in the Far East. Not only did the United States endorse and demand open commercial dealings in China, it now obligated itself to maintaining the political integrity of an endangered empire. But although Hay committed the nation to defending China, he knew that the United States lacked the will and the military might to abide by that commitment. The United States, Hay wrote, was "not prepared . . . to enforce these views on the east by any demonstration which could present a character of hostility to any other power." It was not until the 1930s, when an aggressive Japan threatened the balance of power in the region, that the United States would invoke the Open Door notes.

Theodore Roosevelt and the "Big Stick," 1901–1912

No one was more eager to assume the responsibilities of world power than Theodore Roosevelt, who became president in 1901 (see page 827). Roosevelt asserted that only the president could conduct foreign policy. "Occasionally great national crises arise which call for immediate and vigorous executive action," he said. He came to the presidency with strong convictions about America's role in the world. A student of the writings of Captain Alfred Thayer Mahan, he was committed to establishing American control in the Western Hemisphere and opening new trade routes to Asia. He oversaw the building of the Panama Canal and he established the Roosevelt Corollary to the Monroe Doctrine. His successor, William Howard Taft, who lacked Roosevelt's skill or vision in foreign policy, failed in his effort to flex American economic might.

"I Took the Canal"

Roosevelt hoped to use American influence to ensure order and stability in the hemisphere. When diplomacy would not achieve that result, Roosevelt was willing to use force. "There is a homely adage that runs 'speak softly and carry a big stick; you will go far,'" he noted in 1901. Although he could be forceful in dealing with other nations, Roosevelt was careful not to overextend American commitments, and his diplomatic experiments were characterized by restraint and by a firm grasp of the realities of international power politics.

Roosevelt believed that the emergence of new powers, especially Germany, Russia, and Japan, threatened the stability of the nineteenth-century world order. He was also motivated by a belief that the "civilized" nations had the obligation to uplift people in less developed countries. "More and more," he lectured Congress in 1902, "the increasing interdependence and complexity of international political and economic relations render it incumbent on all civilized and orderly powers to insist on the proper policing of the world." He urged Americans to take an active role in foreign affairs. "If we shrink from the hard contests," he warned, "then the bolder and stronger people will pass us by. . . . Let us therefore boldly face the life of strife." To prepare America for the challenge of world responsibility, Roosevelt centralized foreign policy decision making in the White House, doubled the size of the navy, reorganized the army and National Guard, and established several army war colleges to train new officers.

In keeping with the tenets Mahan espoused, Roosevelt's top priority was to build an American-controlled canal in the Caribbean. An initial obstacle was the 1850 Clayton-Bulwer Treaty with the British, which required joint Anglo-American control of any Central American canal. By November 1901, however, Secretary of State Hay and the British ambassador to Washington had negotiated the Hay-Pauncefote Treaty, which allowed the United States to build and control a canal of its own.

Now the United States needed to decide where to build the canal. Panama, a province of Colombia, offered one possibility. An isthmus of only 50 miles separated the Atlantic and Pacific Oceans along this route. But the New Panama Canal Company, a French-chartered firm that held the canal rights, was asking for an inflated sum of $109 million to sell its holdings. Another possible route crossed Nicaragua. It was 200 miles long, but it would be an easier challenge because it traversed Lake Nicaragua and other natural waterways. In 1902 Congress authorized a canal through Nicaragua, citing cost as the chief reason. After the decision, the New Panama Canal Company's American lawyer, William Nelson Cromwell, agreed to drop his price and began an intense lobbying campaign to get the decision reversed. On January 22, 1903, Hay negotiated a treaty with Thomas Herran, the Colombian chargé d'affaires. By its terms, the United States received a ninety-nine-year lease on a 6-mile-wide zone across the isthmus of Panama; in return the United States granted an initial payment of $10 million to Colombia and $250,000 annual rental.

But on August 12, 1903, the Colombian senate unanimously rejected the Hay-Herran treaty because the senators wanted more money and because the agreement, which severely infringed on Colombian sovereignty, was unpopular with the Colombian people. The senators demanded an initial payment of $15 million from the United States, and they also tried to extract $10 million from the New Panama Canal Company.

Further negotiations could have achieved an agreement with the Colombians, who were eager to have the United States build the canal. Instead, the imperious president lashed out at "those contemptible little creatures in Bogotá." Roosevelt complained that "you could no more make an agreement with the Colombian rulers than you could nail currant jelly to the wall." The president planted stories in the press that he would not be displeased if Panama revolted against Colombia. The Panamanians, whose strong nationalist movement had repeatedly organized uprisings, needed little encouragement.

With American warships within view to prevent Colombian troops from interfering, the Panamanians again revolted in November 1903. "The Americans are against us. What can we do against the American Navy?" asked a Colombian diplomat. Roosevelt recognized the new nation two days after the rebellion started. He soon signed a treaty by which Panama accepted the original offer of $10 million plus $250,000 a year for U.S. rights to a 10-mile-wide strip that cut the country in half. The treaty granted the United States "power and authority" within the zone "in perpetuity" as "if it were the sovereign of the territory."

While the American public overwhelmingly approved the new treaty and the means required to achieve it, many major newspapers were critical of Roosevelt's actions. The "Panama foray is nefarious," thundered a Hearst newspaper. The *New York Times* declared that the United States had followed "the path of scandal, disgrace, and dishonor." Some Senate Democrats disapproved of the president's ruthless measures to gain control of the canal, but the complaints left Roosevelt unfazed. "I took the Canal Zone and let Congress debate," he bragged. On February 24, 1904, the U.S. Senate overwhelmingly approved the new treaty.

The Roosevelt Corollary

Now that the United States possessed the ability to project its military power in the region, securing the canal was but part of Roosevelt's broader vision for the Caribbean. He also wanted to exclude other powers from the area. In December 1902, when Venezuela refused payments on bonds held by European investors, Britain and Germany bombarded ports, seized ships, and imposed an economic blockade on Venezuela. Initially Roosevelt acquiesced to the action, but he soon began to worry that such limited military actions could lead to permanent occupation. "These wretched republics cause me a great deal of trouble," he complained. In January 1903, he ordered the navy to conduct maneuvers in the Caribbean to underscore his call for a quick end to the dispute. Both Britain and Germany immediately lifted the blockade and submitted their claims to the Permanent Court of World Justice at The Hague.

When a crisis threatened the stability of the Dominican Republic, Roosevelt announced a new American approach to the Caribbean. In 1904 the leaders of that financially strapped island pleaded with Roosevelt "to establish some kind of protectorate" to keep their European creditors from intervening. Roosevelt claimed to have as much interest in taking over the islands as "a gorged boa constrictor might have to swallow a porcupine wrong-end to." He did, however, want to prevent further European involvement in the Western Hemisphere. His new policy, which became known as the Roosevelt Corollary to the Monroe Doctrine, asserted that "chronic wrong-doing" or "impotence" by a nation of the Western Hemisphere could "force the United States, however reluctantly, in flagrant cases of such wrongdoing or impotence, to the exercise of an international police power." Roosevelt claimed that the ensuing American intervention would free the people of Santo Domingo "from the curse of interminable revolutionary disturbance" and give them "the same chance to move onward which we have already given the people of Cuba."

Roosevelt's corollary marked a historic break from Monroe's doctrine and shaped U.S. policy toward Central America for the rest of the twentieth century. The Monroe Doctrine had urged a policy of nonintervention in local revolutions in Latin America. Roosevelt, however, asserted America's right to intervene in any situation that threatened the order and stability of the region. Monroe believed that mutual economic ties, not U.S. military or economic power, would shape U.S. relations with Latin America. Roosevelt used the tools Monroe had shunned, U.S. economic and military might, to transform the Caribbean into an "American lake."

Roosevelt applied his new policy, taking charge of the Dominican Republic's revenue system, which, as in most small Caribbean countries, consisted primarily of customs revenues. Within two years Roosevelt had also established protectorates in Cuba and Panama. In 1905 the United States took over the customs and debt management of the Dominican Republic. The Roosevelt Corollary would guide American policy until the 1930s when Franklin Roosevelt instituted the "Good Neighbor Policy."

The Far East

Roosevelt was less successful in the Far East where American influence was limited. Roosevelt remained committed to the Open Door in China, but he recognized that the United States lacked the military muscle to enforce the treaty. The Open Door policy was "an excellent thing" on paper, he conceded, but it "completely disappears as soon as a powerful nation determines to disregard it, and is willing to run the risk of war." The United States had to be careful not to offend traditional Asian powers such as Japan because they could easily overrun the Philippines, which he called "our heel of Achilles." Lacking a strong military option, Roosevelt hoped to protect American commitments in Asia by maintaining a delicate balance of power among the other powers in the region.

Russian and Japanese ambitions in Manchuria threatened that balance. When Russia stationed 175,000 troops in Manchuria and demanded exclusive commercial rights over the region, Tokyo decided to launch a preemptive strike, destroying Russia's Asian fleet in a surprise attack in 1904. Initially, Roosevelt cheered the Japanese attack, claiming that the war would enhance American interests by destroying the potential for "either a yellow peril or a Slav peril." However, he grew concerned when Japan scored a series of resounding military successes that threatened to drive Russia out of the region. Roosevelt agreed that Japanese victory might signify a "real shifting of equilibrium as far as the white races are concerned." He then inaugurated a series of secret maneuvers that culminated in both Japan and Russia agreeing to attend a peace conference in Portsmouth, New Hampshire, in the summer of 1905. By that time both nations were exhausted by the conflict and receptive to Roosevelt's diplomacy. In the resulting settlement Japan received control over Korea and in return promised an open door in Manchuria for the United States and the other powers. The Japanese also obtained key Russian bases in Manchuria, vital parts of the Chinese Eastern Railway running through Manchuria, and the southern half of the strategic island of Sakhalin. For his efforts, Roosevelt became the first American to win the Nobel Peace Prize.

The promise of the Open Door, however, soon proved empty. Such major American exporters as Standard Oil, Swift and Company meatpacking, and the British-American Tobacco Company found themselves being driven out of Manchuria by Japan. Tokyo capped its policy in 1907 when Japan and Russia, bloody enemies just twenty-four months before, agreed to divide Manchuria, with the Japanese exploiting the south and the Russians the north.

A temporary calm set in, but TR knew that he was confronting an aggressive Japan. To show his resolve, he decided to send sixteen American battleships on a cruise to the western Pacific. They were, he said, "sixteen messengers of peace" on a "good will cruise" around the world. As Roosevelt expected, the visit of the Great White Fleet to Japan in 1907 impressed the Japanese and produced effusions of friendship on both sides, but it failed resoundingly to persuade Tokyo officials to retreat in Manchuria. In November 1908, the United States and Japan signed the Root-Takahira agreement, which affirmed the pledge to the Open Door but accepted Japan's control of South Manchuria. The agreement represented Roosevelt's attempt to balance America's ambition in East Asia with its real interests and its ability to defend them.

Dollar Diplomacy

William Howard Taft, Roosevelt's hand-picked successor (page 827), came to the presidency with extensive experience in foreign affairs. Not only had he served as the first civil governor of the Philippines, but as secretary of war he had conducted delicate negotiations with Japan and dealt successfully with Panama and Cuba. Pledging to continue Roosevelt's popular foreign policies, Taft chose Philander C. Knox, Roosevelt's attorney general, as his secretary of state. Unfortunately, Taft and Knox lacked the flexibility, energy, and forcefulness to adapt to a changing international environment.

Taft planned to add a new dimension to Roosevelt's policies. He described his approach as "substituting dollars for bullets." In 1910 Taft explained that he would engage in "active intervention to secure for our merchandise and our capitalists opportunity for profitable investment." America's burgeoning financial power, not

TR Reviews the "Great White Fleet" No one personified the new, activist American foreign policy better than Theodore Roosevelt. Roosevelt directed diplomacy more closely than any president before him, energetically maneuvering the United States into a strong position on the world stage. One of his methods was to build the American military, especially the navy, which he felt was the key to national power. In 1907, he sent sixteen battleships of the newly expanded American navy on a world tour to show off the United States' might. (*Theodore Roosevelt Birthplace, National Park Service.*)

armed troops, would be his main foreign policy instrument. To justify his policy, Taft pointed out that American overseas investments had increased from about $800 million in 1898 to more than $2.5 billion in 1909. Taft believed the United States could reorder the world by marketplace supremacy.

In the Caribbean, Taft believed the greatest threat to American security lay in the possibility that European powers would intervene to collect defaulted debts. To address the problem he moved to replace European loans with American money. Overall American investment in Central America increased from $41 million in 1908 to $93 million in 1914. In 1909 the president asked American bankers to assume the debt in Honduras to ward off European interest. A year later, he persuaded them to stabilize the finances of Haiti by investing in the National Bank of Haiti.

Taft used the marines to protect his new investments. When a new government in Nicaragua resisted American demands that it pay off long-standing claims to Great Britain by borrowing large sums from American bankers, the president withheld recognition and dispatched a warship to pressure the government into acceding to American demands. The Nicaraguans quickly signed the agreement. But the threat of intervention had lit the fires of Nicaraguan nationalism and imperiled the American-controlled government. In 1912 Taft, who vowed to maintain order in Central America even if he had to "knock their heads together," sent more than two thousand marines to protect American lives and property and to prevent European powers from intervening to shield the interests of their own citizens. The forces remained, reduced in number, until 1925, and then had to return in 1926 for another seven-year stay.

While the president dispatched troops to Central America, the United States Senate also tried to protect American interests in the area. In 1912 the Senate added the so-called Lodge Corollary to the Monroe Doctrine in reaction to the threat of a private Japanese company obtaining land in Mexico. The Lodge resolution stated that no "corporation or association which has such a relation to another government, not American" could obtain strategic areas in the hemisphere. This greatly extended the compass of the Monroe Doctrine, which had previously applied only to foreign governments, not companies. The State Department used the resolution during the next quarter-century to stop the transfer of lands, particularly in Mexico, to Japanese concerns (see map).

U.S. Presence in Latin America, 1895–1945 Basing their decisions on the Roosevelt Corollary and America's growing economic needs, government officials intervened in Latin America to promote capitalism and to protect American interests. The United States sent troops to suppress national opposition when they threatened America's goals in the region.

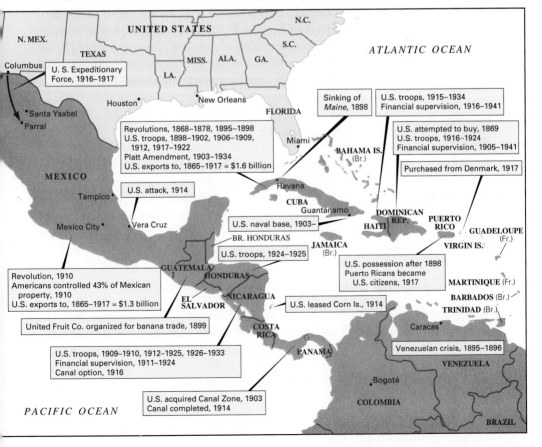

America's relations with its neighbor to the north, Canada, also suffered during Taft's administration. In 1911 the United States and Canada signed a reciprocity trade agreement. Canadian officials were initially pleased, believing that the pact opened the mammoth American market to their country's raw material producers. But the agreement also made these producers an integral part of the United States industrial complex. Careless U.S. politicians, who likened the move to "another Louisiana Purchase," raised fears north of the border that the new treaty would make Canada an American colony. Angry and frightened Canadian conservatives killed the agreement. A new government came to power, repudiated the reciprocity pact, and passed higher tariffs against United States goods.

In China, Taft reversed Roosevelt's policy of appeasing Japan. The president hoped that dollar diplomacy would strengthen Chinese nationalism, block Japanese aggression, and open new markets to American industry. "The more civilized they become, the more active their industries, the wealthier they become, and the better market they will become for us." His efforts to apply financial leverage failed. Waving the Open Door principle, the secretary of state proposed a "neutralization" scheme designed to break the Japanese-Russian hold on Manchuria. According to the plan, Americans and Europeans would pool their money to offer an international loan to China so it could buy back the key railroads in Manchuria from the Russians and Japanese. The Russians and Japanese were not receptive to the idea and moved closer together to fend off Knox. A Japanese official complained that the United States was "asking us to internationalize what is our property acquired by us at the cost of much treasure and many lives." On July 4, 1910, the two nations signed a fresh treaty of friendship. Seven weeks later, Japan formally annexed Korea.

 ## The New Freedom Abroad, 1912–1917

Woodrow Wilson came to the presidency promising a change from the imperial experimentation of Roosevelt and Taft. In practice, however, Wilson's approach differed little from that of his predecessors. In Asia, circumstances forced Wilson to abandon the principles of the Open Door and recognize Japan's predominance in the region. Wilson's response to the Mexican revolution highlighted the weaknesses of his new experiment in moralistic foreign policy.

Woodrow Wilson and World Power

When he took office in 1913, Woodrow Wilson knew little about foreign affairs. "It would be the irony of fate if my administration had to deal chiefly with foreign affairs," he told a friend in 1912. Though he possessed no expertise in foreign policy, Wilson was supremely confident in his ability to manage world affairs. Like Roosevelt, he took an expansive view of presidential power. "He *exercises* the power, and *we obey*," he once wrote.

Wilson shared contemporary views about the superiority of American values. Democracy, Wilson believed, offered the best possibility for stability and order.

"When properly directed, there is no people not fitted for self-government," he noted. The American experience also highlighted the importance of slow, gradual change, and, by contrast to the European example, exposed the dangers of revolution. He also assumed it necessary to search for new economic markets abroad. U.S. producers, Wilson told the Democratic national convention in 1912, "have expanded to such a point that they will burst their jackets if they cannot find a free outlet to the markets of the world. Our domestic markets no longer suffice. We need foreign markets." Taft's dollar diplomacy, declared an administration official, tried to "till the field of foreign investment with a pen knife; President Wilson intends to cultivate it with a spade."

The new president promised to usher in a new idealistic foreign policy based more on morality than self-interest. "We dare not turn from the principle that morality and not expediency is the thing that must guide us," he declared in 1913. To demonstrate his break with the policies of Roosevelt and Taft, Wilson appointed William Jennings Bryan, an outspoken opponent of imperialism and militarism, as his secretary of state. Bryan launched an aggressive effort to convince other nations to settle disputes through mediation, not war. He signed "cooling off" treaties with over two dozen leaders. The treaties required nations to subject all disputes to an international commission.

The new president undertook a number of other initiatives to signal his break with the past. He pledged the United States to withdraw from the Philippines "as soon as a stable government can be established." In 1914 Bryan negotiated a treaty with Colombia, which was still smarting from Roosevelt's peremptory actions in Panama. The United States expressed "sincere regret" for its actions and paid an indemnity of $25 million.

The Far East

In his first major diplomatic action, Wilson scrapped Taft's dollar diplomacy in Asia. Wilson wanted to go it alone in China, using growing U.S. economic power in an effort to build China to the point where Japan and Russia could no longer exploit it at will. The Chinese revolution, which erupted in 1911 against both the Manchu dynasty and foreign interests, made a shamble of his policies, and the approach collapsed completely when World War I began in August 1914. Suddenly the British, French, Germans, and Russians—who Wilson assumed would check each other and the Japanese in China—were absorbed in Europe.

Virtually unchallenged, Japan swiftly moved to seize German possessions, including the strategic Shantung Peninsula. "When there is a fire in a jeweller's shop," a Japanese diplomat explained, "the neighbours cannot be expected to refrain from helping themselves." In January 1915, Tokyo tried to impose the so-called "Twenty-one Demands" on the Chinese. If China had acquiesced, these demands would not only have consolidated the Japanese hold on Manchuria, but would also have given Japan a protectorate over all of China. Wilson strongly protested the demands, but it was British pressure and Chinese resistance, not Wilson's strong words, that finally forced the Japanese to withdraw them.

In November 1917, the secretary of state negotiated the Lansing-Ishii Agreement. The United States recognized that "territorial propinquity creates special relations between countries," meaning it accepted Japanese dominance in such areas as southern Manchuria. In return, the Japanese secretly promised that they would not take advantage of the world war to seek privileges in China that would abridge the rights or property of Americans and citizens of the Allied powers.

Central America and the Caribbean

In Latin America Wilson and Bryan pledged to replace Taft's emphasis on the "pursuit of material interest" with the pursuit of "human rights" and "national integrity." A few months after his inauguration, Wilson promised that the United States would "never again seek one additional foot of territory by conquest." In the end, however, he continued Roosevelt's nationalistic policies, intervening more than either Taft or Roosevelt and for essentially the same reasons. In 1916, when the Dominican Republic threatened to default on its debt, Wilson sent in the marines. The following year U.S. troops entered Cuba once again, remaining until 1921 in order to protect American-controlled sugar plantations, particularly from attacks by armed Cubans.

Wilson's most controversial intervention in the Caribbean came in Haiti. A small nation sharing the island of Hispaniola with the Dominican Republic, Haiti had become the world's first black republic in 1804 when its black, largely slave majority defeated the ruling French colonials. Until 1910 the United States had displayed relatively little interest in Haiti. But then the nation's central bank fell into the hands of New York City bankers. Soon afterward, political turmoil threatened to destabilize the bank. In 1915, when a mob brutally killed the Haitian president, Wilson ordered more than three hundred marines to the island. A new government signed a treaty in August 1915 that granted the United States control over the country's foreign and financial affairs. It also granted the United States the right to intervene whenever Washington officials thought it necessary. The marines remained for nineteen years.

The Mexican Revolution

Three weeks before Wilson took office in 1913, the forces of General Victoriano Huerta gained control of Mexico's government and murdered Francisco Madero, an idealistic reformer who had gained power in 1911. Wilson saw Mexico as an opportunity for moral instruction. "I am going to teach the South Americans to elect good men," he declared. In a break with the American tradition of recognizing established governments, Wilson announced: "I will not recognize a government of butchers." Denouncing Huerta as a "diverting brute! . . . seldom sober and always impossible," the president demanded that Mexico hold democratic elections and institute broad land reform, insisting that the Mexican government "be founded on a moral basis." Business interests clamored for the United States to recognize the new government, but Wilson claimed that he was "not the servant of those who wish to enhance the value of their Mexican investments." Morality, not economic self-interest, would guide American policy.

Wilson searched for the opportunity to intervene. He threw his support behind Venustiano Carranza, the rival leader of the "Constitutionalist" faction. The president tried to turn a minor clash between U.S. sailors and Mexican soldiers into a major international dispute and a justification for intervention. In April 1914, Huerta's agents arrested seven U.S. sailors who, while on shore leave, had strayed beyond the restricted area. Huerta quickly apologized and released the sailors, but he rejected Wilson's demands for concessions to satisfy American "honor," which included a twenty-one-gun salute to the United States flag. Two days later, Wilson asked Congress for the authority to use military force in Mexico "to obtain from General Huerta and his adherents the fullest recognition of the rights and dignity of the United States."

While Congress debated the president's request, Wilson learned that a German ship planned to unload arms for Huerta at Vera Cruz on Mexico's Caribbean coast. Wilson ordered the navy to land troops and occupy the port. The next day, on April 22, 1914, firing broke out that killed 19 Americans and over 126 Mexicans. Although the U.S. invasion was intended to overthrow General Huerta, it offended Mexicans of all political persuasions, who viewed the U.S. actions as an affront to their nationalism and a threat to their independence. A humbled Wilson avoided war when he accepted an offer of mediation from other Latin American countries.

During the summer of 1914, Carranza forces drove Huerta from power. Wilson hoped the new government would accede to his plans for Mexico. An ardent nationalist, Carranza refused to bargain with Wilson. Instead, he announced plans for agrarian reform and asserted Mexico's claim to all its subsoil mineral rights. The revolution had turned sharply to the left and threatened U.S. oil companies who had invested over $2 billion in oil exploration and production.

The frustrated president again withheld recognition and now turned to aiding anti-Carranza forces, including Francisco "Pancho" Villa. Wilson saw Villa as a Robin Hood who had spent "a not uneventful life in robbing the rich in order to give to the poor." This was a serious miscalculation, for Carranza's forces were too strong for Villa. In 1915, distracted by growing tensions in Europe and realizing that Villa had been all but defeated, Wilson abandoned his Mexican crusade and reluctantly recognized Carranza's government. "Carranza will somehow have to be digested," he said. Villa responded by terrorizing Americans, hoping to force Wilson into military retaliation that would undermine Carranza's popularity. On March 9, 1916, Villa led a force of fifteen hundred revolutionaries across the border to burn the town of Columbus, New Mexico. The bloody battle left seventeen Americans and more than a hundred Mexicans dead.

Outraged by the attack, Wilson dispatched a punitive expedition into Mexico under the command of General John J. Pershing. His mission was to capture Villa and bring him back to the United States to stand trial. But Villa's force, seeming to blend

Pancho Villa and His Men   The failure to capture General Francisco "Pancho" Villa was emblematic of President Wilson's chaotic policy toward Mexico. From 1911 to 1917, Wilson took sides in a series of Mexican power struggles, the last of which found the United States supporting Villa's opponent Venustiano Carranza. After Villa was defeated, he raided Columbus, New Mexico, for revenge. When the American army chased Villa three hundred miles into Mexico without success, even Carranza rebuked Wilson for his interference.   *(Corbis-Bettmann.)*

into the country's wooded ravines, eluded the Americans. In vain pursuit, Pershing expanded his army to 11,600 men and moved them more than 300 miles into central Mexico. Carranza, agitated at the growing size and scope of the American military operation, ordered Pershing to stop his advance. On June 21, Mexican troops loyal to Carranza clashed with the Americans near Carrizal. Twelve Americans were killed and another twenty-four were captured.

War with Mexico now seemed inevitable. At this point, however, American soldiers admitted they had started the Carrizal incident. Pacifists deluged Wilson with appeals for restraint, but an outraged public demanded a tough response. Carranza released the prisoners. Negotiations between the two countries then deadlocked over the sensitive issue of Pershing's troops, which Carranza demanded be withdrawn, and which Wilson, facing reelection, did not dare to remove. But with the election safely behind him, and the prospect of having to fight in Europe looming dead ahead, Wilson knew he had to retreat. In January 1917, he ordered the withdrawal to begin, and in March, almost three years after Carranza had taken power, Wilson finally offered him official recognition.

In early 1917 the last American troops left Mexico. Carranza issued a new constitution several months later. Wilson had utterly failed to control the Mexican revolution. His motives and methods were condescending and heavy-handed. Wilson tried to impose gradual, progressive reform on a society sharply divided by race and class. The chief legacy of Wilson's meddling would be lingering Mexican resentment and mistrust of the United States.

CONCLUSION

The last quarter of the nineteenth century witnessed a transformation in America's role in the world. A number of forces pushed the nation to experiment with an expansionist posture. A revolution in communications was bringing the world closer together. Many Americans believed that the closing of the frontier made foreign markets essential to ensuring future prosperity. A missionary zeal, combined with deeply ingrained racial attitudes, fed the belief that the United States had an obligation to spread American values and culture to "backward nations." Military strategists like Alfred Thayer Mahan argued that survival in a competitive world required a large navy and global possessions.

In the first decades after the Civil War, the United States took its first tentative steps toward world power. In 1867 the United States purchased Alaska from Russia. Next America extended its influence in Latin America, asserting its right to mediate a border dispute between Great Britain and Venezuela. In a clear break with tradition, the United States developed close economic ties in Asia and the Pacific, and debated whether to annex the Hawaiian Islands.

The war with Spain in 1898 represented an important turning point in America's role in the world. The war, fought to free Cuba from an oppressive Spanish rule, ended quickly and with few casualties. But the victory forced the United States to confront new responsibilities. What relationship should it have to the former Spanish colonies? While expansionists cried for the annexation of the Philippines, a vocal group of anti-imperialists argued against U.S. control. In the end, President McKinley sided with the expansionists. The result was a heated debate at home and a bloody struggle with independent-minded rebels in the Philippines. With the annexation of the Philippines, the acquisition of the Hawaiian Islands, and the declared commitment to an Open Door in China, the United States embarked on its experiment with the responsibilities of a world power.

For all of their differences in style and temperament, the progressive presidents—Roosevelt, Taft, and Wilson—shared a belief that the United States needed to play a major role on the world stage. Reflecting the general ethos of the Progressive Era, all three presidents wanted the federal government to shake off its isolationist inertia and begin to spread American values and institutions abroad. Just as reformers at home tried to assimilate immigrants, the progressive presidents hoped to Americanize other societies, teaching them the benefits of democracy and the rule of law.

Theodore Roosevelt proved the most skilled at the art of international diplomacy. Along with fulfilling his goal of constructing the Panama Canal, Roosevelt expanded U.S. control over Latin America while balancing America's global ambitions with its limited power in the Far East. Taft's foreign policy, which stressed the primacy of economics, floundered because of a lack of imagination and energy. Despite his professions of idealism and morality, Wilson used force more often than any of his predecessors. By 1916, the United States had assumed the mantle of world power. It was only a matter of time before America's global experiment would draw the nation into a growing conflict in Europe.

SUGGESTED READINGS

Robert Beisner provides a concise and helpful synthesis on this period in *From the Old Diplomacy to the New, 1865–1900* (2d ed., 1986). He employs a "paradigm shift" thesis in explaining the emergence of a more deliberate, active foreign policy in the 1890s. Walter LaFeber's *The New Empire: An Interpretation of American Expansion, 1860–1898* (1983) and *The American Age* (1989) serve as examples of the economic school of interpretation, arguing that the drive for foreign markets was behind the development of U.S. foreign policy. Thomas Paterson et al. provide a useful and readable synthesis in *American Foreign Relations: A History* (1995).

Most historians agree that the 1890s were pivotal years in the history of U.S. foreign policy. An excellent overview of these years is given in R. M. Abrams, "United States Intervention Abroad: The First Quarter Century" (*American Historical Review*, 79, 72–102). On the 1860s, Ernest Paolino's *Foundations of the American Empire: William Henry Seward and U.S. Foreign Policy* (1973) is informative, arguing that sustained U.S. intervention began in the 1860s, not the 1890s, and that Seward was the pioneer. Michael Hunt offers a provocative thesis about the roots of American expansion in *Ideology and U.S. Foreign Policy* (1987). David Pletcher examines the policies of Secretaries of State Blaine and Frelinghuysen in *The Awkward Years: American Foreign Policy under Garfield and Arthur* (1962). Like Paolino, he finds important innovations in the pre-1890 years, arguing that, while their diplomacy was often inept, Blaine and Frelinghuysen were early expansionists, forerunners of McKinley and Roosevelt. Several good studies have been done on specific events during the 1865–1890 period, including Adrian Cook's *The Alabama Claims: American Politics and Anglo-American Relations* (1975) and Richard Bradford's *The Virginius Affair* (1980).

For the intellectual roots of empire, Richard Hofstadter's *Social Darwinism in American Thought, 1860–1915* (1945) and Robert Bannister's *Social Darwinism: Science and Myth in Anglo-American Social Thought* (1979) are very informative. Milton Plesur also emphasizes intellectual forces over economic ones in the emergence of American world power in *America's Outward Thrust, 1865–1900* (1971).

The 1890s have received quite a bit of attention from historians. Ernest May examines changing European opinion of the United States in the 1890s and the "mass hysteria" that forced McKinley into war in *Imperial Democracy: The Emergence of America as a Great Power* (1961). David Healy's *U.S. Expansion: Imperialist Urge in the 1890's* (1970) covers a wide range of issues in the attempt to understand the "expansionist mystique." He revises the stereotype of imperialists as monolithic thinkers and finds them to be a very diverse group. Emily Rosenberg's *Spreading the American Dream: American Economic and Cultural Expansion, 1890–1945* (1982) and *Financial Missionaries to the World* (1999) demonstrate how business interests, missionaries, journalists, and others established in the 1890s a pattern of American cultural expansion that influenced foreign policy for decades to come.

Several regional studies shed light on American foreign policy in the 1890s. Michael Hunt's *The Making of a Special Relationship* (1983) is an essential overview of U.S. involvement with China. Also on China are Warren Cohen's *America's Response to China* (2d. ed., 1980), which looks at the background and impact of the Open Door notes, and Marilyn Young's *The Rhetoric of Empire: America's China Policy, 1893–1901* (1968), which sees the efforts of business interests and missionaries as causative in the new diplomatic focus on China in the 1890s. The debate over the annexation of Hawaii is the subject of Thomas Osborne's *"Empire Can Wait": American Opposition to Hawaiian Annexation, 1893–1898* (1981), which contends that the persistent and principled efforts of the anti-imperialists were the cause of the delay in annexation.

The central event of the 1890s, and what most historians see as the culmination of growing trends in foreign policy, was the Spanish-American War. Historians have offered quite differing views on the reasons behind the war and McKinley's role in it. John Dobson's *Reticent Expansionism: The Foreign Policy of William McKinley* (1988) portrays McKinley as following public opinion into war rather than his own particular vision. Lewis Gould comes to the exact opposite conclusion in *The Spanish American War and President McKinley* (1982). He argues that McKinley was a modern leader who used new modes of communication to guide public opinion and Congress. In *America's Road to Empire: The War with Spain and Overseas Expansion* (1965), H. Wayne Morgan agrees that McKinley was not pushed into war nor did he go impetuously, but that he was following the traditional U.S. policy toward the Spanish–Cuban relationship. John Offner offers a unique interpretation on the origins of the war in *An Unwanted War: The Diplomacy of the United States and Spain over Cuba, 1895–1898* (1981). He argues that while the war was inevitable because of the deep differences between Spain and Cuba, no one involved wanted war and the chief blame belongs to the inflexible Cuban rebels. Gerald Linderman's *The Mirror of War: American Society and the Spanish-American War* (1974) examines the rationale behind the American people's clamor for war; he sees the war as an attempt to retain preindustrial values amid the massive social upheaval surrounding industrialization.

On the war itself, David Trask's *The War with Spain in 1898* (1981) is the most comprehensive account. For a shorter version from the perspective of the ordinary soldier, see Frank Friedel's *The Splendid Little War* (1958). Friedel portrays the American military effort as mismanaged and chaotic. Philip Foner's two-volume *The Spanish-Cuban-American War and the Birth of American Imperialism, 1895–1902* (1972) agrees with this assessment and argues that the Cuban rebels neither needed nor wanted American help in defeating Spain. A fairly recent popular account of the war is G. J. A. O'Toole's *The Spanish War: An American Epic–1898* (1984).

Several impressive works have been written on American imperialism in the Philippines. Stuart Creighton Miller's *"Benevolent Assimilation": The American Conquest of the Philippines, 1899–1903* (1982) and Richard Welch's *Response to Imperialism: The United States and the Philippine-American War, 1899–1902* (1979) both examine McKinley's decision on annexation, the anti-imperialist protest, and the guerrilla war. Miller is particularly strong on the war itself, emphasizing the cruelty of the American army toward the Filipinos. Welch's main focus is on the anti-imperialists. Another helpful book on that subject is Robert Beisner's *Twelve Against Empire: The Anti-Imperialists, 1898–1900* (1975). He views them as a diverse group who agreed on little else besides the Philippine issue. Finally, a sweeping and engrossing examination of the entire history of American influence in the Philippines is Stanley Karnow's Pulitzer Prize–winning book *In Our Image: America's Empire in the Philippines* (1989).

Howard Beale's *Theodore Roosevelt and the Rise of America to World Power* (1956) portrays the president as gifted, but too heavily influenced by the distorted ideas of Kipling and Mahan. Frederick Marks II's *Velvet on Iron: The Diplomacy of Theodore Roosevelt* (1979) is more favorable, portraying Roosevelt as careful, patient, and sensitive to the views of the

American people and peoples around the world. Charles Neu also views Roosevelt as a skilled diplomat in his study, *An Uncertain Friendship: Theodore Roosevelt and Japan, 1906–1909* (1967). David McCullough's *The Path Between the Seas: The Creation of the Panama Canal, 1870–1914* (1977) views Roosevelt's actions with regard to the canal as part of a larger continuum of U.S. policy in Central America that was primarily guided by the Monroe Doctrine. William Tilcin's *Theodore Roosevelt and the British Empire* (1997) examines TR's approach to Europe. John Milton Cooper offers an insightful dual biography of Roosevelt and Wilson in *The Warrior and the Priest* (1983).

Arthur Link's *Woodrow Wilson and the Progressive Era* (1954) is a survey of all aspects of Wilson's presidency and has several informative chapters on his foreign policy. Frederick Calhoun's *Power and Principle: Armed Intervention in the Wilsonian Foreign Policy* (1986) argues that Wilson's use of force for idealistic and political ends led the war in the instrumentalist approach in American foreign policy. Robert Quirk's *An Affair with Honor: Woodrow Wilson and the Occupation of Vera Cruz* (1962) is less favorable toward the president, characterizing him as ignorant of other cultures and moralistic. P. Edward Haley looks at the differing responses of Taft and Wilson to unrest in Mexico in *Revolution and Intervention: The Diplomacy of Taft and Wilson with Mexico* (1970).

McKinley Justifies U.S. Acquisition of Spanish Territories

President McKinley was a devout Christian, committed to the idea that the United States needed to serve as a moral beacon to the rest of the world, promoting democracy and liberty around the world. In this speech given in Atlanta in December 1898, he seeks to reconcile this idealistic vision of America's virtuous role in the world with his support for the war with Spain and the acquisition of overseas territories that had belonged to Spain.

The peace we have won is not a selfish truce of arms, but one whose conditions presage good to humanity. The domains secured under the treaty yet to be acted upon by the Senate came to us not as the result of a crusade or conquest, but as the reward of temperate, faithful, and fearless response to the call of conscience, which could not be disregarded by a liberty-loving and Christian people....

... New conditions can be met only by new methods.... Without abandoning past limitations, traditions and principles, by meeting present opportunities and obligations, we shall show ourselves worthy of the great trusts which civilization has imposed upon us....

[B]efore Manila and Santiago our armies fought, not for gain or revenge, but for human rights. They contended for the freedom of the oppressed, for whose welfare the United States has never failed to lend a helping hand to establish and uphold ... the result will be incomplete and unworthy of us unless supplemented by civil victories, harder possibly to win, but in their way no less indispensable.

We will have our difficulties and embarrassments. They follow all victories and accompany all great responsibility.... But American capacity has triumphed over all in the past ... our own history shows that progress has come so naturally and steadily on the heels of the new and grave responsibilities that as we look back upon the acquisitions of territory by our fathers, we are filled with wonder that any doubt could have existed or any apprehension could have been felt....

Forever in the right, following the best impulses and clinging to high purposes, using properly and within right limits our power and opportunities, honorable reward must inevitable follow.... If we had blinded ourselves to the conditions so near our shores, and turned a deaf ear to our suffering neighbors, the issue of territorial expansion in the Antilles and the East Indies would not have been raised....

With less humanity and less courage on our part, the Spanish flag, instead of the Stars and Stripes, would still be floating in Cavite, at Ponce, and at Santiago, and a "chance in the race of life" would be wanting to millions of human beings who to-day call this nation noble, and who, I trust, will live to call it blessed.

Thus far we have done our supreme duty. Shall we now, when the victory won in war is written in the treaty of peace, and the civilized world applauds and waits in expectation, turn timidly away from the duties imposed upon the country by its own great deeds? . . .

Carl Schurz Opposes U.S. Expansion

Schurz was a German immigrant who became a brigadier general in the Union Army and later served a term as a U.S. senator and as secretary of interior under President Hayes. Here, in a convocation address at the University of Chicago in 1899, he vigorously opposes the U.S. acquisition of Spanish possessions.

According to the solemn proclamation of our government, the [Spanish-American] war had been undertaken solely for the liberation of Cuba, as a war of humanity and not of conquest. But our easy victories had put conquest within our reach, and when our arms occupied foreign territory, a loud demand arose that . . . the conquests should be kept. . . .

The advocates of annexation answer cheerily, that when they belong to us, we shall soon "Americanize" them. . . . This is a delusion of the first magnitude. We shall, indeed, be able, if we go honestly about it, to accomplish several salutary things in those countries. But one thing we cannot do. We cannot strip the tropical climate of those qualities which have at all times deterred men of the northern races, to which we belong, from migrating to such countries in mass, and to make their homes there, as they have migrated and are still migrating to countries in the temperate zone. . . .

If we [rule territories as subject provinces], then we shall, for the first time since the abolition of slavery, again have two kinds of Americans: Americans of the first class, who enjoy the privilege of taking part in the government in accordance with our old constitutional principles, and Americans of the second class, who are to be ruled in a substantially arbitrary fashion by the Americans of the first class. . . .

If we do, we shall transform the government of the people, for the people and by the people . . . into a government of one part of the people, the strong, over another part, the weak. Such an abandonment of a fundamental principle as a permanent policy may at first seem to bear only upon more or less distant dependencies, but it can hardly fail in its ultimate effect to disturb the rule of the same principle in the conduct of democratic government at home. . . .

Nothing could be more irrational than all the talk about losing commercial or other opportunities which "will never come back if we fail to grasp them now." Why, we are so rapidly growing in all the elements of power ahead of all other nations that, not many decades hence, unless we demoralize ourselves by a reckless policy of adventure, not one of them will be able to resist our will if we choose to enforce it. . . .

"But we must civilize those poor people!" Are we not ingenious and charitable enough to do much for their civilization without subjugating and ruling them by criminal aggression? . . .

. . .Whatever our duties to them may be, our duties to our own country and people stand first; and from this standpoint we have, as sane men and patriotic citizens, to regard our obligation to take care of the future of those islands and their people. . . .

Thus we shall be their best friends without being their foreign rulers. . . . However imperfect their own governments may still remain, they will at least be their own. . . .

If this democracy, after all the intoxication of triumph in war, conscientiously remembers its professions and pledges, and soberly reflects on its duties to itself and others, and then deliberately resists the temptation of conquest, it will achieve the grandest triumph of the democratic idea that history knows of. . . .

The United States entered the war against Spain with the battle cry, "Cuba Libre!" Fighting for Cuba's independence from Spain seemed consistent with American democratic ideals of promoting democracy and freedom; in addition, Cuba's proximity qualified it as part of the American sphere of influence under the Monroe Doctrine. Although the war had its critics, the case could be made that it had been both a noble mission and in the national interest.

But no sooner did the war conclude than the prospect of U.S. colonization reared its ugly head. American statesmen and intellectuals in the late nineteenth century subscribed to the ideas of Social Darwinism, a fanciful application of evolutionary biology to people and nations, which argued that strong countries would by nature dominate the weak. They were also influenced by Alfred T. Mahan, a historian who believed that the nations who controlled the seas ruled the world. With European powers already carving out places for themselves in world trade and establishing overseas colonies, many members of the "power elite" pushed for the United States to do the same. But the American public remained instinctively isolationist, unconvinced by lofty ideas and global strategy, and reluctant to involve the nation in foreign affairs. McKinley, who sincerely believed in American expansion, sought to convince his fellow citizens that foreign involvement, and the acquisition of new territory, were consistent with traditional American principles. He claimed the United States was actually doing the people of the Philippines and other territories a favor by exposing them to Protestant Christianity, democratic government, Western education, and American business.

But others saw deep contradictions in the American presence in the Philippines in particular, a concern heightened by a bloody resistance to U.S. rule that lasted from 1899 until 1902. Although many anti-imperialists were motivated by isolationism and racism, idealism also played a role, as seen in Carl Schurz's comments. As with many of the new phenomena of the emerging modern America, imperialism raised deep concerns over the safety of the traditional values that Americans held so dear.

Questions for Analysis

1. How does McKinley defend the Spanish-American War?
2. How does the president apply this defense to acquiring territory from Spain in its aftermath? What contradictions, if any, do you find in his rationale?
3. Why doesn't he mention the economic advantage that might come from U.S. colonies?
4. Why does Schurz so vehemently oppose overseas acquisitions?
5. What problems does he see in attempting to "Americanize" other cultures?
6. What comparisons does he make between American imperialism and slavery? What is his point?

23

Making the World Safe for Democracy: America and World War I, 1914–1920

A large crowd assembled at the White House on the rainy evening of April 2, 1917. Thousands more lined Pennsylvania Avenue. While waiting to get a glimpse of President Wilson as he made his way to the Capitol, they sang patriotic songs, including "The Star-Spangled Banner" and "Yankee Doodle." The city was decorated in red, white, and blue, and overflowing with nationalistic fervor. Shortly before 8:00 P.M. the president's car, flanked by motorcycle police and cavalry guards, left the White House.

At 8:30 the Speaker of the House announced the arrival of the president to a joint session of Congress. As Wilson walked down the center aisle to the Speaker's platform, members of Congress, both Democrats and Republicans, erupted in thunderous applause. For two minutes they stood waving their tiny American flags, clapping their hands, and shouting their support. Wilson waited for the ovation to die down. Then, holding his typed address firmly with both hands, the president began talking in a subdued, conversational tone, outlining German violations of American neutrality. The suspense increased as Wilson moved closer to the critical part of his address. "I advise," he declared in a stern voice, that Congress "formally accept the status of belligerent which has thus been thrust upon it; and that it take immediate steps not only to put the country in a more thorough state of defense but also to exert all its power and employ all its resources to bring the government of the German Empire to terms and end the war." Before he finished the sentence, the packed chamber erupted into wild cheering. Wilson continued, intending to ensure the world understood idealism, not selfish gain, had propelled America into war. "The world," he declared, "must be made safe for democracy."

As the president walked out of the hall, the audience stood in applause. Those who were carrying flags waved them high in the air. Those who had been wearing them in their lapels tore them off and waved with the rest. Only a few dared dissent from Wilson's noble vision. One of the president's most vocal critics, Senator Robert La Follette of Wisconsin (see page 816), stood motionless, his arms folded tight to register his disapproval.

Although some progressives opposed U.S. entry into the war, fearing that it would sap momentum from the reform effort, many others believed that by joining the Allies America could shape the peace and therefore create a new liberal world order. At home, the war would promote collective action, patriotic sacrifice, and national unity—all critical ingredients in the progressive formula for social progress. The editors of the liberal *New Republic* observed that the "extension of government power during wartime was an opportunity to secure that radical reconstruction of American society which had long been advocated."

In the end, however, these hopes would not be realized. The American military helped ensure an Allied victory, but Wilson failed to secure a just peace. The Allies rejected most of Wilson's peace plan and instead imposed a punitive treaty on the Germans. The belligerents agreed to create a League of Nations to mediate future disputes, but the United States Senate, in a stunning blow to Wilson's pride, rejected any experiment in internationalism and failed to approve America's participation in the new organization. At home, progressive hopes for the postwar world turned quickly to bitterness and strife. The drive for national unity produced labor strikes, social unrest, and a postwar Red Scare that resulted in widespread violations of civil liberties and civil rights. By 1920, Americans, disillusioned with the war and with Wilson, looked to the Republicans to restore order.

▮ What traditions and values made Americans reluctant to enter World War I, and what events overcame that reluctance?

▮ What impact did the war have on individual rights and social reform at home? How did the demands of war mobilization change the scope of government power?

▮ What were the key ingredients in Wilson's peace plan, and what obstacles did he face in "selling" it abroad and at home?

▮ What social and cultural tensions contributed to the civil unrest and the Red Scare at the end of World War I?

This chapter will address these questions.

The Road to War, 1914–1917

When fighting broke out in Europe in August 1914, Wilson pledged the United States would remain neutral. But genuine neutrality proved difficult to sustain. When German submarines attacked unarmed ships, killing Americans, Wilson announced a policy of "strict accountability." Reflecting traditional American attitudes toward the world, the public wanted to protect American honor but also to avoid getting entangled in European affairs. When Germany announced it would sink all neutral ships trading with England, Wilson felt he had no other recourse than war.

American Neutrality

On June 28, 1914, a Serbian youth assassinated Archduke Franz Ferdinand, heir to the throne of the Austro-Hungarian Empire. The assassination shattered the delicate balance of power that had maintained a fragile international peace in Europe since the early nineteenth century. Two alliance systems dominated Europe: the Central Powers of Germany, Turkey, Italy, and Austria-Hungary; and the Triple Entente (or Allied) powers of Great Britain, France, and Russia. When Austria threatened Serbia to avenge Franz Ferdinand's assassination, Russia rushed to Serbia's defense, setting off a chain reaction of military mobilization.

Over the next few weeks, the combination of intense nationalism, seething economic rivalries, and extraordinary ineptitude propelled Europe into war. Germany launched an offensive against the west, smashing through neutral Belgium and pushing to the outskirts of Paris, where French and British forces managed to gain back some ground. By September 1914, the Allied and Central Powers were locked in a deadly war of attrition—glaring at each other across trenches that stretched from the English Channel to the Alps. Both sides launched giant offensives, only to gain a few square miles of territory at the cost of tens of thousands of lives. In one failed offensive the Allies would suffer 1 million casualties.

When the war began, nearly all Americans assumed that the United States would never become involved. "I thank Heaven for many things—first the Atlantic Ocean," the American ambassador in London wrote the president, reflecting the popular belief that geography would isolate the United States from the conflict. On August 14, President Wilson urged Americans to "be neutral in fact as well as in name during these days that are to try men's souls. We must be impartial in thought as well as in action." Newspaper accounts, illustrated with battlefield photographs, of the miserable conditions of trench warfare reinforced America's desire to stay out of the conflict. The lyrics of a popular song expressed the feeling of most Americans: "Don't Take My Darling Boy Away."

However, genuine neutrality proved impossible. America's large immigrant population had roots on both sides of the conflict. While Irish and German immigrants were strongly anti-British, many Protestant Americans were tied to the Allies by cultural links and commercial contacts. British propagandists cleverly manipulated American support by swamping the United States with sensationalized stories of German soldiers mutilating children and raping women. Despite their professed

Chronology

1914	Archduke Franz Ferdinand of Austria assassinated
	World War I begins; President Wilson announces American neutrality
1915	British liner *Lusitania* sunk by German U-boat
	Bryan resigns and Lansing becomes secretary of state
	U-boat sinks *Arabic*
1916	Germany issues *Sussex* pledge
	Wilson reelected
1917	Germany resumes unrestricted U-boat warfare
	U.S. enters the war
	Selective Service Act sets up national draft
	Race riot in East St. Louis, Illinois
	National Civil Liberties Union founded
1918	Wilson outlines Fourteen Points for peace
	Debs imprisoned for speaking against the war
	Alien and Sedition Acts passed
	Armistice signed
1919	Peace treaty signed at Versailles
	May Day bombings help stimulate Red Scare
	Communist Party of the United States of America founded
	Versailles Treaty rejected by Senate
1920	Palmer raids organized by Justice Department
	American Civil Liberties Union created
	Harding elected president

desire not to choose sides, Wilson and nearly all his leading advisers believed that American interests and ideals would fare better in the postwar world if Britain prevailed over Germany. Wilson confessed at one point that a German victory "will be fatal to our form of Government and American ideals." Secretary of State William Jennings Bryan, who did not want the United States to enter the war on either side, was perhaps the only genuinely neutral member of the cabinet.

In fact, America's long-standing economic ties with the Allies made neutrality impossible. Even before the outbreak of hostilities, England was America's primary trading partner, and the war only intensified that relationship. In 1914 U.S. exports to the Allies totaled $753 million. By 1916 trade soared to nearly $3 billion. During that same period trade with Germany tumbled from $345 million to a paltry $29 million. Initially, the administration banned private banks from making loans to the cash-strapped Allies. Bryan protested that such loans, though legal, were "inconsistent with the true spirit of neutrality." In 1915 Wilson, worried that the prohibition would stifle profitable wartime trade, reversed course and lifted the ban, ending any pretense of financial neutrality. Bankers, who had close ties to England, immediately floated over $500 million. "Our firm had never for one moment been neutral," a Morgan partner recalled. "From the very start we did everything we could to contribute to the cause of the Allies." By 1917 America had loaned $2.2 billion to the Allies, but only $27 million to Germany.

America's relationship with the belligerents—the nations at war—was further complicated by British control of the ocean. To strangle Germany, Britain took liberties with international law, expanding the definition of *contraband* of war to include nearly every possible item, including food. The Royal Navy forced neutral ships into port for inspection and halted trade to Germany's neutral neighbors, Holland and Denmark. The British, observed a critic, "ruled the waves and waived the rules." The British navy frequently intercepted American ships, causing long delays, and confiscating some or all of their cargoes. When Wilson protested, the British government temporarily eased the blockade or offered to pay American companies for seized goods. Despite occasional complaints, Washington acquiesced to the British maritime system. Not only were Wilson's closest advisers partial to the British, but the United States feared antagonizing its chief trading partner. The British managed to sever American trade with the Central Powers without rupturing Anglo-American relations.

In an effort to challenge British control of the seas, the Germans launched a frightening new weapon, the U-boat (short for *Unterseeboot,* or "undersea boat"). On February 4, 1915, the German foreign minister announced that waters around Great Britain and Ireland would become a war zone in which German submarines would seek "to destroy every enemy merchant ship." "Neutrals," he continued, "are therefore warned against further entrusting crews, passengers, and wares to such ships." Not only did the German submarines threaten Allied shipping, they muddied the waters of international maritime law. The fragile U-boat, vulnerable to gunfire on the surface and dependent on the element of surprise, ignored laws requiring belligerent ships to allow civilian passengers and crew to disembark before attacking.

The German announcement set the stage for a major confrontation with the United States. Wilson told German leaders that if any American property or lives were lost in the war zone, Germany would be held to "strict accountability." His message amounted to an ultimatum, a threat of war if German attacks killed Americans. Because the Germans promised not to attack American ships in the war zone, the issue became the right of Americans to sail and work on the ships of belligerents.

The issue came to a head on May 7, off the southern Irish coast, when a German submarine torpedoed the British luxury liner *Lusitania*. The ship, whose cargo included 4.2 million rounds of rifle ammunition, sank in eighteen minutes, carrying

1,198 people to their deaths, 128 Americans among them. Most Americans were horrified by the attack. "The Torpedo which sank the *Lusitania*" *The Nation* editorialized, "also sank Germany in the opinion of mankind." Theodore Roosevelt, beating his war drums, called it "an act of piracy."

The sinking narrowed Wilson's options. In an attempt to calm public outrage, he declared that "There is such a thing as a man being too proud to fight. There is such a thing as a nation being so right that it does not need to convince others by force that it is right." At the same time, he sent the Germans stiff notes demanding the payment of reparations for injuries and a pledge to cease submarine attacks on passenger liners. Berlin did not want to antagonize America, but it was unwilling to abandon one of its most effective weapons against British control of the seas. Eventually, Germany expressed "regret" over the American deaths and agreed to pay an indemnity.

The sinking of the *Lusitania* incited a debate at home over Wilson's liberal application of neutrality law, which he claimed gave Americans the right to travel safely on the ships of belligerent nations. Critics of Wilson's "strict accountability" policy wanted the president to require American passengers who wished to traverse the war zone to travel on American ships. In February, Congress began debate on the Gore-McLemore resolutions, which warned American citizens not to travel on armed belligerent ships. The resolutions generated widespread public support, but

News of the *Lusitania*
Although Germany had issued warnings that the *Lusitania* was a legitimate target, Americans were outraged when a German U-boat sank the ship, killing 128 Americans. The morning papers brought news of the tragedy and of rumors that the incident might mean war for the United States. It would actually be two more years before the United States entered the conflict, but the *Lusitania* sinking was a turning point that rallied the American people against Germany. (© *The New York Times Company. Reprinted by permission.*)

Wilson opposed any compromise of American neutral rights and the resolutions went down to defeat. Clinging to a rigid definition of neutrality, Wilson refused to respond to the complications created by the submarine or to appreciate how his policy clearly benefited the British. To prevent American passage on ships, he declared, would produce national humiliation and the destruction of the "whole fine fabric of international law." The United States, he said, should not allow "any abridgement of the rights of American citizens in any respect." The British may have been violating U.S. commercial rights, he reasoned, but the Germans were violating human rights.

Wilson's strong stand on American neutrality rights led to the resignation of Secretary of State Bryan, who feared the president's policy would lead inevitably to war. "He is absolutely sincere," Bryan said of Wilson. "That is what makes him dangerous." Bryan's replacement, Robert Lansing, an international lawyer and conservative Democrat with pro-British leanings, supported Wilson's position. Years later, Lansing recalled that after the *Lusitania,* he was convinced "that we would ultimately become an ally of Great Britain."

Events in the summer of 1915 confirmed Lansing's prediction. On August 30, 1915, a German submarine torpedoed another British liner, the *Arabic,* killing two Americans. Lansing warned Germany that if it continued attacking passenger liners the United States, "would certainly declare war." Berlin responded with the so-called "*Arabic* pledge," promising never again to attack a passenger ship without warning. However, in March 1916, a German submarine attacked a French channel steamer, the *Sussex.* Four Americans were injured. The submarine claimed to have mistaken the *Sussex* for a minesweeper, but the attack was an overt violation of the "*Arabic* pledge." On April 18, 1916, an angry Wilson instructed the Germans that unless they abandoned their "present methods of submarine warfare against passenger and freight-carrying vessels," he would move to sever diplomatic relations. The Germans, unwilling to risk war with the United States, again promised (the "*Sussex* pledge") not to attack merchant ships without warning. Germany also pleaded with Washington to stop British violations of international law—a request that Wilson ignored.

Peace, Preparedness, and the 1916 Election

Issues of war and peace dominated the 1916 presidential campaign. Republicans charged that Wilson's "strict neutrality" policy failed to protect American interests. The Germans, one critic said, were "standing by their torpedoes, the British by their guns, and Wilson by strict accountability." Theodore Roosevelt, more militaristic than ever, called the president a "peace prattler," who had "done more to emasculate American manhood and weaken its fiber than anyone else I can think of."

Though many of these critics stopped short of advocating war, they called for an aggressive campaign to build up the military in case of war. Initially, Wilson opposed a preparedness campaign, but as tension mounted, he gradually switched positions. In the fall of 1915, he endorsed an ambitious proposal to increase the size of the armed forces. Calling for a "navy second to none" he supported the Naval Construction Act of 1916, which proposed an aggressive expansion of the navy, including the construction of ten battleships, ten cruisers, fifty destroyers, and one hundred submarines. The president also supported passage of the National Defense Act of 1916, which increased the size of the regular army from 90,000 to 223,000 and expanded the National Guard. During the winter of 1916, he went on a whirlwind two-week speaking tour to rally public support for the measures. Wilson's strong endorsement secured passage of both measures despite stiff opposition from peace advocates in Congress.

His outspoken support for preparedness damaged Wilson's relationship with progressive peace advocates. In 1915 feminists Jane Addams and Carrie Chapman Catt formed the Women's Peace Party. Their platform demanded that "as human beings and the mother half of humanity," they must have a say in national affairs. Peace sentiment was strong in the Plains states and the Midwest, which had weaker commercial and sentimental ties to the Allies and (in some cases) were home to relatively large numbers of German-Americans. Progressive Republican senators, such as Wisconsin's La Follette and George Norris of Nebraska, feared the abridgement of individual liberties and the growth of close government–business ties that would result from a war. The Socialist Party, and its leader Eugene Debs, condemned the war as "unjustifiable," fomented largely by big business.

In the 1916 presidential campaign, Republicans attempted to capitalize on Wilson's difficulties. By 1916, many of the insurgents who fled the party four years earlier to support Roosevelt's Progressive Party had returned to the fold. At their convention, united and confident, they nominated Supreme Court Justice Charles Evans Hughes, formerly a progressive governor of New York. Hughes tried unsuccessfully to focus public attention on the failure of Wilson's diplomacy while avoiding a clear stand that might divide elements of his own party. Unable to excite even traditional Republican audiences, he tried to play both sides of the fence on the peace issue. He told German-American audiences in the Midwest that he favored neutrality. When campaigning in the East, he criticized Wilson for not supporting the Allies more strongly. Teddy Roosevelt frustrated Hughes's effort to reach out to the peace groups by publicly pressuring him to take an unequivocal position in favor of a more aggressive pro-Allied policy.

While Hughes floundered, Wilson and the Democrats managed to harness the peace issue. The Democratic Party campaigned on the slogan "He kept us out of war." A Democratic handbill reminded voters, "You Are Working—Not Fighting! Alive and Happy—Not Cannon Fodder!" Even while campaigning on a peace platform, Wilson recognized a potential danger in his policy of strict accountability: it depended on German restraint. "I can't keep the country out of war," he observed privately. "Any little German lieutenant can put us into war at any time by some calculated outrage."

The election was too close to call as voters went to the polls on November 7. First returns, which showed Hughes winning in the Northeast and Midwest, suggested a big Republican victory. But results trickled in during the night showing Wilson scoring well in the West. Not until two days later, when votes from California were counted, was Wilson declared the winner. A difference of fewer than four thousand votes in California would have removed Wilson from the White House.

Final returns gave him 9,127,695 popular votes and 277 electoral votes from thirty states to Hughes's 8,533,507 and 254 from eighteen states. Wilson won with less than 50 percent of the popular vote—49.4 percent to 46.2 percent (see map). The Democratic strength continued to be based in the South and West. The Republican stronghold remained the Northeast and Midwest. The Democrats retained narrow majorities in the Senate and the House.

"Peace Without Victory"

Two months after the election, Germany announced that it would resume unrestricted submarine warfare on February 1, 1917. The German government warned that all ships, including unarmed American merchant ships, would be attacked on sight in the war zone. The Germans realized that this action would provoke the United States to enter the war, but they hoped to starve the Allies into defeat before American troops could be mobilized. "England will lie on the ground in six months, before a single American has set foot on the continent," boasted a German naval commander.

On January 22, 1917, in an eloquent speech before the Senate, the president called for "a peace without victory," in which nations would guarantee the fundamental rights of all people. He attacked the European balance of power, which had repeatedly failed to prevent war. "There must be not a balance of power, but a community of power; not organized rivalries, but an organized common peace." Such a peace, he insisted, needed to be based on self-determination for all nations, freedom of the seas, and an end to "entangling alliances." "These are American principles, American policies," he declared in a final effort to convince the combatants to abandon their destructive ways and embrace a more enlightened approach to the world.

The Election of 1916
Rejecting Theodore Roosevelt for his beliefs that Americans should take a more active stand on the war raging in Europe, the Republican Party turned to Charles Evans Hughes, a Supreme Court Justice since 1910. While Hughes managed to win eastern states with large electoral votes, Woodrow Wilson's pledge to keep America out of the war won him the West and the South—enough to win the election.

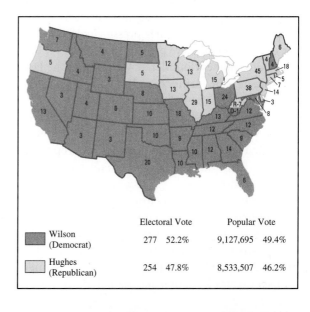

	Electoral Vote		Popular Vote	
Wilson (Democrat)	277	52.2%	9,127,695	49.4%
Hughes (Republican)	254	47.8%	8,533,507	46.2%

The speech scored well with Congress and the public, but it fell on deaf ears in Europe. A French writer compared Wilson's "peace without victory" to "bread without yeast, . . . love without quarrels, a camel without humps, night without moon, roof without smoke, town without brothel." Germany responded by fulfilling its pledge to initiate total submarine warfare on February 1. Two days later, Wilson broke diplomatic relations with Germany. It was, he told Congress, the only "alternative consistent with the dignity and honor of the United States."

Wilson still hoped to avoid war with Germany. Only "actual overt acts," he said, would convince him that Berlin intended to carry out its threats. On February 26, he asked Congress to grant him authority to arm merchant vessels. The bill passed the House but got bogged down in the Senate where a group of noninterventionist senators, led by Wisconsin's Robert La Follette, filibustered it to death. Furious, Wilson excoriated them as a "little group of willful men, representing no opinion but their own, who have rendered this great nation helpless and contemptible." After consulting with the attorney general, Wilson declared that his executive authority gave him the right to arm the ships without congressional consent.

Meanwhile, an unforeseen event had pushed America closer to war. On February 24, the British had given Wilson an intercepted telegram sent by Arthur Zimmermann, the German foreign secretary, to the Mexican government. The message, dated January 16, 1917, proposed a military alliance with Mexico if the United States entered the war against the Central Powers. In return, Germany promised Mexico the "lost territory in Texas, New Mexico, and Arizona." For millions of Americans the threat of Mexican involvement brought what had been a distant conflict desperately close to home.

Events were driving the United States from armed neutrality to war. On February 26, Germany provided the "overt act" that the president had been waiting for by sinking the American merchant ship *Laconia,* killing two Americans. Armed neutrality did little to protect American ships from German torpedoes. In March several more went down, and newspaper headlines screamed with the sinking of each. The assault on American shipping produced a wave of emotion in favor of war. Six hundred Republicans met at the Union League Club in New York to demand intervention. Aroused citizens held mass public rallies in New York, Philadelphia, Chicago, Boston, and Denver. The Russian Revolution of March 1917, which replaced Russia's totalitarian monarchy with a constitutional monarch and democracy, added to the momentum for war by making it easier for Americans to view the Allied cause as a democratic crusade.

Increasingly, Wilson felt he had no options other than war. German aggression had to be resisted and American neutrality defended. Moreover, the president believed that the United States would have more influence in shaping the peace if it entered the war. On March 20, his previously divided cabinet unanimously favored war with Germany. Wilson delivered his war message on the evening of April 2.

Over the next four days Congress debated the president's war resolution. Emotions ran high. Opposition to the war was strongest in the agricultural Midwest. Nebraska's populist senator George Norris denounced the resolution as a conspiracy engineered by Wall Street. "We are going into war upon the command of gold," he thundered. "We are about to put the dollar sign upon the American flag." Six senators and fifty representatives ultimately voted against American entry into the war, more than opposed any other war resolution in American history. "I want to stand by my country," declared Representative Jeannette Rankin, the first woman elected to Congress, "but I cannot vote for war." Opponents, however, were outnumbered in Congress, their voices drowned in a patriotic tidal wave. After the vote a newspaper headline screamed the battle cry: "The Yanks Are Coming!" For the first time in its history, the United States was to enter a war on another continent.

War, Mobilization, and Progressive Reform, 1916–1919

A few weeks after Wilson's war message, journalist Walter Lippmann declared that the nation stood "at the threshold of a collectivism which is greater than any as yet planned by the Socialist party." How would Americans balance the need for collective action with the respect for individual rights and small government? In facing the challenges of mobilization—creating an army, regulating the economy, forging a sense of national unity—the administration relied on a combination of patriotic appeals and government coercion. Often concern for individual rights fell by the wayside, sometimes a victim of ethnic prejudice. The war did, however, produce gains for many Americans. It also gave momentum to the drive to pass constitutional amendments to prevent the sale of alcohol and to grant women the right to vote.

Creating an Army

On April 1, 1917, the U.S. Army, which numbered only 5,791 officers and 121,797 enlisted men, ranked seventeenth in the world. In comparison, Germany had 200 divisions massed on the western front, and in the next two months the British army alone lost 177,000 men in a single offensive. The War Department still relied on a table of organization devised by John C. Calhoun in 1817. The military significance of the United States, scoffed a German official, was "zero, zero, zero."

To mobilize armed manpower as quickly as possible, Wilson proposed a draft requiring all men between the ages of twenty and thirty to register. The draft raised widespread fears in a nation that valued individual freedom and disliked distant and impersonal government. Memories of Civil War conscription, which had created offensive disparities and led to bloody rioting in New York City, soured many Americans on the idea. Some objected to the restriction of personal freedom. House Speaker Champ Clark declared that "there is precious little difference between a conscript and a convict."

The administration diffused these objections through a massive public relations campaign. The worst feature of the Civil War draft, declared one official, was that it "bared the teeth of the Federal Government in every home within the loyal states." Calling its program "selective service" rather than "conscription," the administration tried to remove the stigma of a distant and impersonal government by allowing local citizens to administer the draft through draft boards, which became "buffers between the individual citizen and the federal Government." The president reassured the nation, declaring that the draft was "in no sense a conscription of the unwilling," but rather "selection from a nation which has volunteered in mass."

Wilson had designated June 5, 1917, as the first day of national registration. Many people predicted violent protest, but the administration's use of patriotic appeals blunted any hint of rebellion. Local officials joined in massive celebrations of patriotic fervor to encourage men to register. The recruits were, according to an observer, "exhorted by their mayors, prayed for by their clergymen, and wept over by sundry females." By the end of the day, nearly 10 million Americans between the ages of 21 and 35 registered for the draft. (In 1918 the ages for draftees changed to between 18 and 45 years of age.)

By war's end 24 million men, or 44 percent of American males, had registered for the draft. Almost 5 million were drafted into the service, and 2 million had been sent to fight in France. More than 1.5 million Americans enlisted in the army. Another 520,000 signed up for service in the navy and the marines. Over 20,000 women served in the armed forces. Almost 5,000 went to France where they worked as army nurses, but most served as clerks and secretaries. The military awarded deferments to millions of draft-age men because they worked in war industries or had dependents. Over 340,000 men—11 percent of candidates—evaded the draft by refusing to register or not responding when called. Almost 65,000 declared themselves conscientious objectors, mostly based on religious beliefs.

Proponents of military training viewed the army as an ideal vehicle for forging a common sense of identity. "The military tent where they all sleep side by side," observed Teddy Roosevelt, "will rank next to the public schools among the great agents of democratization." In fact, the army reflected the divisions within American society. The armed forces remained rigidly segregated. The marines excluded blacks; the navy assigned them to mess duty. Blacks, relegated to separate areas in training camps, received inferior equipment and training. The War Department made no provision for commissioning or training black recruits as officers until protests by the NAACP led to the establishment of one officer candidate program in June 1917. Its graduates always worked under white supervision. "Under capable white officers and with sufficient training," declared John J. Pershing, "negro soldiers have always acquitted themselves creditably."

Blacks made up about 1 percent of the officer corps of an army with 13 percent black enlisted men. When the United States entered the war, the highest-ranking black officer was Colonel Charles Young of the Tenth Cavalry Division. The third black graduate of the United States Military Academy, Young had acquired a distinguished service record in the war with Spain, and later in fighting Pancho Villa's guerrillas in Mexico. Despite his record, a number of white officers refused to serve under him. Four of them complained to their senators, who then lobbied the secretary of war to remove Young from his command. Shortly afterward, the army forced Young to retire. Other black officers suffered similar indignities. An investigator reported that at one army camp, nearly 90 percent of the whites refused to salute black officers.

Given such attitudes, it is unsurprising that the armed forces were not exempt from the racial violence that plagued civilian society. In August 1917, black troops stationed at Houston, Texas, angered by the constant humiliation of that city's Jim Crow laws, exploded in violence. On the night of August 23, they shot to death seventeen white civilians. The army, under intense pressure from southern congressmen, dealt harshly with the troops. More than a hundred blacks, denied benefit of an appeal to the War Department, were court-martialed, and thirteen were executed. After the riot, the War Department dispersed black recruits throughout its camps, maintaining a 2-to-1 ratio of white to black trainees.

The draft and voluntary enlistments solved America's manpower needs. Now the army had to build camps to train the new recruits, provide them with arms, and transport them overseas. The army had to construct from scratch thirty-two training camps, each equipped to handle forty thousand men. According to one estimate, the army used enough wood in the construction to build a boardwalk 12 inches wide and 1 inch thick to the moon and halfway back! After creating the small cities, the military had to supply them with medical equipment, food, clothing, weapons, and ammunition. "The supply situation was," in the words of one official, "as nearly a perfect mess as can be imagined." Recruits frequently trained in civilian clothes for weeks before receiving uniforms. The army owned only three thousand transport trucks and six hundred thousand rifles. As of July 1917, the navy owned only seven troop and cargo ships. For most of the war effort, American troops used equipment furnished by Britain and France.

In staffing and assigning military personnel, the army made use of a new psychological tool—the intelligence quotient, or IQ test. The scientists who administered the test concluded that 31 percent of recruits were illiterate. Minorities and whites from rural regions scored especially low. Questions such as "Who wrote 'The Raven'?" (a poem by nineteenth-century author Edgar Allan Poe) revealed a great deal about the class backgrounds and cultural assumptions of the university-trained scientists who created the test but offered little insight into the ability of the enlistees who took it.

The army also initiated an ambitious program of sex education to limit the threat from sexually transmitted diseases. By 1917, over a million French troops had contracted either syphilis or gonorrhea. Because researchers had not yet developed antibiotics, these venereal diseases could sap the strength of fighting forces. The War Department established a Committee on Training Camp Activities (CTCA) to shut down red-light districts near its training camps. The CTCA turned out lurid films and issued pamphlets that taught trainees how to keep "fit to fight." The messages were often explicit. "You wouldn't use another fellow's toothbrush. Why use his whore?" The army even issued condoms to soldiers.

For many young men the war seemed to offer an exciting opportunity to go "Over There." Sustained by the belief that theirs was a noble cause, they embarked on what Theodore Roosevelt called the "Great Adventure." The harsh realities of mud, poison gas, and mangled bodies would soon dim many of these expectations. "How I wish the whole business was over," Lieutenant Frederick T. Edwards wrote his family in 1917, "and that we could pick up the things we did and dropped last Spring . . . for the war is like a Winter, chilling and freezing the soul."

Recruiting an Army   When President Wilson signed the Selective Service Act in May 1917, the U.S. armed forces consisted of less than 130,000 men. The ranks would swell to almost 5 million by the war's end. The enthusiasm shown by the soldiers in this photograph belies the reluctance of many men to enlist. To induce their cooperation, recruiting posters usually aroused young men's fears of having their manhood questioned if they did not participate.   *(Brown Brothers.)*

Regulating the Economy

The U.S. economy was wholly unprepared for war in April 1916. The government lacked any mechanism for coordinating the war effort, for making decisions about what the Allies would need and how to apportion material between military and civilian use. Transporting millions of troops and vast quantities of war supplies overwhelmed the nation's railroad system. At one point, railroad cars destined for the East Coast were backed up as far west as Chicago. Military demand for food and fuel produced shortages, raising the prospect of civilians going cold and hungry.

With the mobilization effort a shambles, Congress passed the Lever Food and Fuel Control Act in August 1917. The legislation, one of the most sweeping grants of executive power in American history, authorized the president to regulate the output, distribution, and price of food, and to control every product that was used in food production. Exercising his new powers, Wilson created a Fuel Administration and a Food Administration, charging the new agencies with expanding output and restricting civilian consumption. The head of the Food Administration, Herbert Hoover, rejected coercive rationing and price-fixing and instead depended on "the spirit of self-sacrifice." Hoover mobilized huge publicity campaigns to promote "wheatless Mondays," "meatless Tuesdays" and "porkless Thursdays and Saturdays." At the same time he encouraged increased production by arranging for the government to buy crops at high prices, enticing farmers to plant more. The Fuel Administration, headed by Williams College president Harry Garfield, following Hoover's example, instituted fuel "holidays." Garfield introduced daylight savings time to conserve energy and set high prices on coal so that even inefficient mines could make a profit.

In December 1917, the government moved to ease the transportation crisis by taking control of most of the country's railroads. The president created a Railroad Administration, naming Treasury Secretary William Gibbs McAdoo as its director-general. McAdoo quickly took charge of nearly four hundred thousand miles of track, including railroad terminals and warehouses. He suspended unessential traffic, poured in money to improve track conditions, consolidated ticket offices, and gave railroad workers a generous pay raise to improve morale. His actions showed immediate results: the logjam disappeared, trains ran more efficiently, and the railroad system benefited from the infusion of resources.

Along with running the nation's railway system, McAdoo had to deal with the daunting task of developing ways to finance the war. Before it entered the war, the federal government spent almost $1 billion a year. By 1920, annual expenditures had soared to $19 billion. How to pay for the war became a central question in the White House and on Capitol Hill. Conservatives called for higher taxes on consumer goods, which would be distributed broadly. Progressives wanted wealthy individuals and corporations to bear the heaviest burden. McAdoo recognized that higher taxes were inevitable, but he also believed that patriotic appeals could help the government to pay for the war. The administration launched a drive to solicit loans by selling so-called Liberty Bonds to the American people. "Every person who refuses to subscribe," McAdoo asserted, ". . . is a friend of Germany." By 1920, sales of liberty bonds produced $23 billion—far less than the $32 billion in expenses for the war. In the end, taxes paid for about one-third of the war expense.

Despite its modest nature, the tax program produced a fiscal revolution in America. In part, the revolution was psychological. The war introduced the principle of progression—the idea that the tax burden should fall on those most able to pay—into the nation's tax system. The 77.7 percent of taxpayers whose income was less than $3,000 paid less than 3.6 percent of all tax receipts; corporations and the wealthy paid the rest. The war also built on the foundation constructed by the income tax amendment of 1913 to dramatically enlarge the tax base. The number of tax returns filed jumped from 437,036 in 1916 to 3,472,890 in 1917 and then doubled again in 1920. "Never before," observed the historian Bruce D. Porter, "had federal taxation affected so many Americans so directly."

The keystone of the wartime mobilization effort was the War Industries Board (WIB), which coordinated the government's purchases of military supplies, helped convert plants to military production, and arranged for the construction of new factories. In March 1918, Wilson appointed Wall Street businessman Bernard Baruch to take control of the board. Assuming extraordinary new powers, Baruch set production schedules, mediated disputes between industries, and standardized procedures. Whenever possible, Baruch avoided using coercion. Instead, he used lucrative contracts to persuade manufacturers to shift to war goods and promised to cover all costs and guarantee a profit. Coercion remained an available method, however. When one executive refused WIB requests, Baruch threatened to turn public opinion against him and make him "such an object of contempt and scorn in your home town that you will not dare to show your face there." When auto companies refused to cut back on the production of passenger cars, Baruch threatened to cut off coal and steel supplies, with swift results.

Workers and the War

Samuel Gompers, the head of the AFL (see page 719), hoped to translate support for the war into tangible gains for organized labor. An intense labor shortage provided both government and business with a strong incentive to develop a partnership with organized labor. By July 1918, thirty-four states faced a serious shortage of unskilled workers. At the same time, strikes plagued a number of industries deemed essential to the war effort. In 1917 more than a million workers took part in 4,200 strikes in war-related industries.

In September 1917, Wilson established the Mediation Commission to further "the development of a better understanding between laborers and employers." The commission consisted of two business and two labor representatives. The group and its secretary, Harvard law school professor Felix Frankfurter, visited strike-plagued areas and made recommendations for improving labor–management relations.

In April 1918, the president established the National War Labor Board (WLB) as a kind of supreme court for labor controversies. When Gompers and the AFL executive committee offered a "no strike" pledge, Wilson instructed the board to protect the right of workers to organize and bargain collectively—the first time a federal agency had wielded a pro-labor policy. The administration backed up the pledge with muscle. When the management at Smith and Wesson arms plant in Springfield, Massachusetts, and the Western Union telegraph company violated WIB rules, Wilson sent federal agents to take over the plants. The board also attempted to guarantee all workers under their jurisdiction a "living wage"—an income sufficient to provide a minimum of health and decency—and it compelled the adoption of the eight-hour workday. Federal support for organizing efforts helped union membership rise from 2.7 million in 1916 to over 4 million in 1919.

The federal government also helped workers by building low-cost housing near war plants and shipyards. With the war consuming material needed to build new homes, the nation faced a severe housing shortage, especially in the areas around booming factories. Many workers who moved to take jobs in wartime plants found themselves without a place to live. To remedy the problem, the Labor Department formed the United States Housing Corporation (USHC) and the Emergency Fleet Corporation (EFC) in 1917. The USHC built accommodations for nearly six thousand families and over seven thousand individuals. In some cases, the government constructed model communities, such as Union Park Gardens in Wilmington, Delaware, which included schools, a playground, and a community center.

Wartime spending produced a tremendous economic boom. America's gross national product increased from $62.5 billion in 1916 to $73.6 billion in 1919. But the benefits were not equally distributed. Though labor's wages increased during the war, inflation eroded most of the gains. The great mass of workers saw their purchasing power drop by more than 20 percent between 1916 and 1919. Not surprisingly, business gained the most from the war. Corporate profits, even after higher taxes, jumped 30 percent between 1914 and 1920. The profits of U.S. Steel skyrocketed from $76 million to $478 million between 1914 and 1917.

Many women hoped the wartime need for labor would break down traditional barriers that had barred them from employment. "At last, after centuries of disabilities and discrimination," declared a feminist, "women are coming into the labor and festival of life on equal terms with men." To a limited extent, the optimism was warranted. About a million women joined the work force for the first time during the war. Many of the 8 million women who already worked in low-paying positions switched to higher-paying industrial jobs. Between 1910 and 1920, the number of female clerical workers more than doubled, while the number of female domestic servants declined. The number of female railroad workers tripled during the war. A survey of 690 plants in Cincinnati, Ohio, found a 22.7 percent increase in the number of females employed between 1917 and 1918.

For most women, the opportunities proved limited and brief, ending with the war. During the war, women were paid less than men for the same work. In milling companies in Cincinnati, men earned between $15 and $20 per week; women performing the same work averaged between $6 and $10. Trade unions remained hostile to women workers and assumed, like most people, that women would return to the home at the end of the war. A union official bluntly suggested that "the same patriotism which induced women to enter industry during the war should induce them to vacate their positions after the war." Most women, willingly or not, followed the advice.

The war also raised the expectations of African-Americans, who hoped both to prove their loyalty and to benefit from the labor shortage. W. E. B. Du Bois (see page 824) urged blacks "to seize the opportunity to emphasize their American citizenship" because "out of this war will rise, too, an American Negro with the right to live without insult." The search for better-paying jobs in war-related industries accelerated a massive migration of blacks from the rural South to the industrial Northeast and Midwest. Between 1910 and 1920, about 330,000 blacks fled poverty and oppression in the South, heading north for Detroit, Chicago, and New York City. The black population of Chicago swelled from 44,000 to 109,000; New York's grew from 92,000 to over 153,000.

Most found work in heavy industry—steel, auto, shipbuilding, meatpacking, and mining—where they were relegated to unskilled jobs at low wages. In some cases the increase in African-American employment was pronounced. The Westinghouse Company employed only 25 blacks in 1916; by 1918, it employed 1,500. The number of black shipyard workers rose from about 37,000 to over 100,000 in the same period. Black women also made advances during the war. Many moved from domestic work into factories. The number of African-American women in manufacturing rose from over 67,000 in 1910 to almost 105,000 in 1920.

The war offered African-Americans economic opportunity in the North, but it did not provide sanctuary from racism. Northerners, alarmed by the "invasion" of

1915–1919, retaliated by imposing discriminatory residential requirements that ghettoized the new migrants. Mobs beat blacks who strayed out of their neighborhoods and stoned black families who dared to move into white areas of the cities. Racial tensions erupted in riots in twenty-six cities during 1917, including one in East St. Louis that killed thirty-nine blacks and nine whites. Following the East St. Louis melée, the NAACP staged a protest in New York. One of the banners asked, "Mr. President, why not make America safe for Democracy?"

Southerners also viewed the migration to the North with alarm. "We must have the Negro in the South," declared the *Macon (Georgia) Telegraph.* "It is the only labor we have, it is the best we possibly could have—if we lose it, we go bankrupt!" Many whites in the South used violence and intimidation to stem the tide fleeing North. Lynching increased from thirty-four cases in 1917 to sixty in 1918, and to more than seventy in 1919.

In the Southwest, Mexicans benefited from the wartime labor shortage. Growers needing labor to run their farms pressured the government into relaxing immigration restriction and exempting Mexican workers from the draft. Between 1917 and 1920, 100,000 Mexicans migrated across the border into Texas, California, Arizona, and Colorado. Like African-Americans, Mexicans confronted segregated communities, schools, and restaurants. Although they found employment, Mexicans were paid less than Anglos who worked with them.

The Search for National Unity

Many progressives believed the war would promote national unity by ending class and ethnic divisions. The struggle would infuse the nation's citizens with a new sense of patriotism and thus undermine dangerous radicalism. A new moral purpose would replace selfish individualism. The war, they believed, could represent the culmination of decades of progressive efforts to forge a sense of social bonding.

In its search for public unity, the Wilson administration authorized a massive propaganda campaign. On April 14, 1917, eight days after the declaration of war, Wilson asked George Creel, a progressive journalist from Denver, to head the Committee on Public Information. Creel remarked that his goal was to mold Americans into "one white-hot mass . . . with fraternity, devotion, courage, and deathless determination." Before the war had ended he had mobilized 150,000 lecturers, writers, artists, actors, and scholars in what Creel called "the world's greatest adventure in advertising." Officially titled "Four-Minute Men," the volunteers appeared in front of movie screens and on stages at schools, lodges, and union halls to give brief speeches on topics such as "Why we are fighting" and "Maintaining morals and morale." The committee placed illustrated advertisements in magazines such as the *Saturday Evening Post,* exhorting readers to report to the Justice Department "the man who spreads pessimistic stories . . . , cries for peace, or belittles our efforts to win the war." It produced upbeat films such as *Pershing's Crusaders* and *The Beast of Berlin.* Fears of disloyalty among the foreign-born prompted the CPI to organize "Loyalty leagues" in ethnic communities.

When persuasion failed, the government resorted to coercion. The Espionage Act, enacted in June 1917, specified imprisonment and heavy fines for persons who

The Home Front   Women, such as these riveters in Puget Sound, Washington, filled in for men absent from the work force. The war offered new job opportunities and better wages for women, but these gains did not persist after the war's conclusion. Women's work greatly aided the war effort, as did their role as managers of the family economy.   *(National Archives.)*

engaged in spying or sabotage. But other repressed activities were less clearly criminal or treasonous. The act made illegal any public criticism that could be considered detrimental to the war effort. The Trading with the Enemy Act (1917) forbade trade with the enemy and empowered the postmaster general to deny use of the mails for any printed matter that, in his opinion, advocated treason, insurrection, or forcible resistance to the laws of the United States. The Alien Act (1918) gave the government broad power to deport noncitizen residents suspected of disloyalty. Finally, the Sedition Act, enacted in 1918, made it a crime to obstruct the sale of war bonds or to use "disloyal, profane, scurrilous, or abusive" language against the government, the Constitution, the flag, or military uniforms. It made almost any publicly voiced criticism of government policy or the war effort a crime punishable by fines, imprisonment, or both. Dissent, a protected right, had become a crime.

Postmaster General Albert Burleson and Attorney General Thomas W. Gregory made full use of their new arsenal of weapons to crush dissent. "May God have mercy on them," Gregory said of war opponents, "for they need expect none from an outraged people and an avenging government." Burleson used his new power to prevent the mailing of most socialist publications. Max Eastman, editor of a leading socialist journal, *The Masses,* ironically invoked the Bill of Rights guarantee of peaceful assembly when he complained, "You can't even collect your thoughts without being arrested for unlawful assembly."

While the post office tried to weed out literature critical of the war effort, law enforcement officials moved against suspected opponents of the war. Gregory's Justice Department initiated nearly 2,200 prosecutions and secured 1,055 convictions under the Espionage and Sedition Acts, and used threats to bully many more people into silence. Like Burleson, Gregory made socialists the main target of his assaults. Among socialist leaders prosecuted under the Espionage Act were Victor Berger of Milwaukee, who was twice denied his seat in Congress as a result of his conviction. The most famous victim of wartime repression was Eugene Debs, the Socialist Party leader who had received nearly 1 million votes for president in 1912 (see page 836). He was arrested and sentenced to ten years in federal prison for telling listeners, "You need to know that you are fit for something better than slavery and cannon fodder." The Justice Department took aim at other radical unionists who threatened to disrupt wartime production. In September 1917, federal agents arrested 133 leaders of the Industrial Workers of the World (Wobblies) for interfering with the war effort.

To help track down potential subversives, the Justice Department supported the creation of a quasi-vigilante organization called the American Protective League (APL). Carrying "Secret Service Division" cards, APL agents spied on, slandered, and arrested other Americans. They opened mail, intercepted telegrams, and organized raids against draft evaders. The APL was, according to one scholar, "a force for outrageous vigilantism blessed with the seal and sanction of the federal government." The government looked the other way when other ultra-patriotic groups—bearing such names as the American Defense Society, the Sedition Slammers, and the Boy Spies of America—engaged in similar illegal activities.

State and local authorities joined with the federal government to stifle antiwar attitudes. Nine states outlawed opposition to the war effort. Local communities created committees, often called a "council of defense," to help the federal government rouse patriotic feeling and fight dissent. By 1918, 184,000 local chapters policed opinion across the country. The councils encouraged Americans to spy on one another and to report evidence of disloyalty. In Washington a state-sponsored group called the "Minute Men" planted spies in schools and colleges to report on instructors who taught the German language. Council handbooks advised members to turn in family members who criticized the government. The *Tulsa (Oklahoma) Daily World* advised its readers, "Watch your neighbor. If he is not doing everything in his power to help the nation in this crisis, see that he is reported to the authorities."

Most of these groups hoped to use civic fervor to exclude aliens and immigrants and to preserve older ways of life. The *Saturday Evening Post* voiced their sentiments when it demanded the removal of "the scum of the melting pot." German-Americans were the most frequent targets, but anyone who questioned the war effort was a potential victim. In April 1918, a Missouri mob seized Robert Prager, a young man whose only crime was that he had been born in Germany. He was bound in an American flag, paraded through town, and then lynched. A jury acquitted his killers on the grounds they had acted in self-defense. By the summer of 1918, almost half the states forbade the teaching of German or church services conducted in German. Even everyday language was cleansed. Sauerkraut was renamed "liberty cabbage," and German measles, "liberty measles." Communities banned music that German giant Ludwig van Beethoven had composed a century before. A well-meaning motion picture producer was sentenced to ten years in jail for his movie *The Spirit of '76* because it allegedly aroused hostility to Britain, America's wartime ally. Perhaps the crowning blow of absurdity came when Cincinnati removed pretzels from saloon lunch counters.

In response to government repression, a young social worker named Roger Baldwin founded the National Civil Liberties Union in 1917. Raised in a wealthy Protestant family, Baldwin challenged both the government's refusal to grant conscientious objector status to opponents of the war and the increasing censorship. Critics dismissed Baldwin and his followers as a "little group of malcontents." "Jails are waiting for them," the *New York Times* warned. The organization increased in size and, in 1920, became the American Civil Liberties Union (ACLU).

In 1919 the Supreme Court catered to illiberal feelings by sustaining the wartime statutes. The Espionage Act, Justice Oliver Wendell Holmes held in *Schenck* v. *U.S.* (1919), was justified (see Competing Voices, page 924). "The question in every case," he ruled, "is whether the words are used in such circumstances and are of such a nature as to create a clear and present danger that they will bring about the substantial evils that Congress has a right to prevent." To illustrate his point, Holmes used the analogy of shouting "Fire!" in a crowded theater. Authorities could, he argued, restrict speech under such conditions of "clear and present danger."

Holmes later rethought his position on the First Amendment. In August 1918, the government arrested six anarchists protesting the deployment of U.S. troops in the new Soviet Union. "Workers, our reply to the barbaric intervention has to be a general strike!" read one of their leaflets. Charged with violating the Espionage Act, the group was convicted and given sentences of up to twenty years. By a 7–2 vote, the U.S. Supreme Court in *Abrams* v. *U.S.* upheld their convictions, with Holmes and Justice Louis Brandeis dissenting. Holmes's reversal stunned the legal community. Tightening the "clear and present danger" standard, Holmes argued that the government had to prove "imminent danger" to the war effort to justify curtailing free speech. Advocating resistance, he said, should have to mean urging "some forcible act of opposition to some proceeding of the United States in pursuance of the war." Although Holmes's argument failed to convince the Court in 1918, it would eventually form the foundation on which Supreme Court decisions favoring free speech would rest.

Prohibition and Suffrage

The war added a powerful new weapon to the prohibitionists' arsenal—patriotism. Since grain supplies were limited, Congress prohibited the use of grain for distilling and brewing. The Anti-Saloon League (see page 821) forced adoption of an amendment to the Selective Service Act of 1917 forbidding the sale of alcoholic beverages at or near army camps and naval bases. The league charged that brewers, most of whom had German names, were sabotaging the war effort: "The worst of all our German enemies, the most treacherous, the most menacing are Pabst, Schlitz, Baltz, and Miller."

Emboldened by their success, prohibitionists made the final push for a constitutional amendment to forbid the manufacture, sale, and consumption of alcoholic beverages. In December 1917, their appeals to patriotic idealism convinced Congress to approve the amendment and pass it on to the states for ratification. Since twenty-seven states were already dry, prohibitionists needed the additional support of only nine states to win. The thirty-sixth state ratified on January 14, 1919. Only New Jersey, Rhode Island, and Connecticut—all states with large immigrant populations—rejected the amendment. After the war, Congress passed the National Prohibition Act, called the Volstead Act, which established the enforcement procedures for the amendment.

The war also helped progressives win the battle for women's suffrage. By the time the United States entered the war, women had gained the vote in eleven states. By 1917, however, the suffrage engine seemed stalled. Suffragists revived the movement by wrapping themselves in the flag. They downplayed the earlier opposition of prominent feminists to American entry into the war and emphasized the incongruity of fighting a war for democracy while denying the vote to half the population. Before the war, suffrage advocates argued that the vote could help women reform American society; now they contended that enfranchised women would help America reform the world. The moderate National American Woman Suffrage Association, under the leadership of Carrie Chapman Catt, orchestrated an effective lobbying campaign on Capitol Hill and in state capitals. While appealing largely to principle, they were not above tapping into public prejudice. "Every slacker has a vote," Catt told audiences. "Every newly made citizen will have a vote. Every pro-German . . . will have a vote. . . . It is a risk, a danger to a country like ours to send 1,000,000 men out of the country who are loyal and not replace those men by the loyal votes of women they have left at home."

At the same time, more radical feminists, led by the Quaker activist Alice Paul, formed the National Woman's Party (NWP). In January 1917, the NWP began picketing outside the White House. Over the next eighteen months, thousands of women marched silently past the gates carrying banners that read, "How Long Must Women Wait for Liberty?" When police arrested the marchers, the protesters insisted on being treated as political prisoners and went on a hunger strike in jail. Wilson complained that the Women's Party seemed "bent on making their cause as obnoxious as possible." But the pressure worked. "My God," cried a New York politician, "we'd better do something to satisfy those hellions."

The combination of Paul's aggressive tactics, which generated a great deal of publicity, and Catt's lobbying, which won new converts, helped secure congressional approval of the amendment giving women the vote. The amendment sailed through the House in January 1918, but then languished in the Senate. During the summer of 1918, Wilson actively lobbied Senate Democrats, calling suffrage "an essential psychological element in the conduct of the war for democracy." In June 1919, the Senate narrowly passed the amendment. The following year, in August

1920, three-fourths of the states approved it. With the Nineteenth Amendment in place, women prepared to vote in a presidential election for the first time in 1920.

■■★ Making War and Peace, 1917–1919

While American soldiers helped secure victory on the battlefield, the president had a difficult time convincing either the Allies, or the U.S. Senate, to accept his liberal peace plan. At Versailles, Wilson had to contend with the conservative agenda of French and British leaders determined to preserve their empires and to impose a harsh peace on Germany, and with the growing attraction toward Russian communism that threatened his liberal program. At home, the bitter debate over U.S. entry into the League of Nations underscored the tension between internationalism and nationalism that shaped America's view of its role in the world.

"Days of Hell"

The belief that U.S. involvement would be brief and limited encouraged Americans' enthusiasm for the war. "They don't need more warriors," said the *New York Morning Telegraph* in April 1917; "they want money and food, and munitions of war." American leaders soon learned, however, that the plight of the Allies required a greater commitment. In April an Allied delegation to Washington outlined the desperate conditions. By 1917, Britain was on the verge of exhaustion. The Italian army was disintegrating. The Russians, who had suffered over 9 million casualties, appeared ready to quit the war effort.

In desperation the French and British asked Wilson to rush fresh troops to Europe to bolster Allied spirits and to demoralize the enemy. "We want men, men, men," French Marshall Joseph Joffre begged. Responding to the request, the American First Division departed for combat in June 1917. By December, 200,000 American soldiers were in Europe, stationed in "quiet" zones where they could train for future battles.

In March 1918, the Germans forced Russia out of the war, imposing a harsh peace in the Brest-Litovsk Treaty. In the south, the Italians suffered a disastrous defeat at Caporetto, a village in Yugoslavia. With its eastern front secure, Germany launched a major offensive against the west, smashing through Allied lines, driving the French back toward Paris. Shock and fear ran through the Allies, who pleaded for American troops to cut short their training and enter combat. Wilson directed General John J. Pershing, the leader of the American Expeditionary Force (AEF), to allow American troops to be used as replacements in British and French units until Americans arrived in sufficient numbers to form an independent force.

In May, Americans participated in a series of bloody battles at Belleau Wood to first blunt, and then repel, the German offensive. For twenty days, in what Private Hiram B. Pottinger called "days of hell," American marines stopped the German advance and slowly pushed the enemy back, all the time enduring withering machine-gun fire, exploding artillery shells, and deadly poison gas. In one day of fighting the Americans lost 1087 men. Of the eight thousand marines who participated in the battle to recapture Belleau Wood, over five thousand were killed or wounded. By July, the Germans were retreating, their offensive quashed. "On the Eighteenth, even the most optimistic among us knew that all was lost," observed the German chancellor.

The American troops had helped turn the tide, but the war was not over. Between September 12 and 16, the American First Army, grown to six hundred thousand troops and fighting in concert with French forces, retook a strategically important rail junction south of Verdun. In two days they captured fifteen thousand prisoners at a cost of fewer than eight thousand casualties. Two weeks later 1.2 million American soldiers drove into the Argonne Forest. In forty days and nights of heavy fighting, they fought their way through the forest and the formidable defenses of the Hindenburg Line. To the west French and British forces staged similar drives. On November 1 the Allies broke through the German center and raced forward (see map). As the western front crumbled, the German High Command pleaded for peace. "Open armistice negotiations as soon as possible," a general told Kaiser Wilhelm, the German monarch. The stalemate was over.

World War I, the Western Front   American troops were not deployed in large numbers before early 1918, but they would play a crucial role in the last year of the war. In the battles of Cantigny, Belleau Wood, and Chateau-Thierry, American soldiers showed their willingness to act and boosted Allied morale. Beginning with the Second Battle of the Marne, Americans and their allies began to push the Germans back, with the final offensive at Meuse-Argonne.

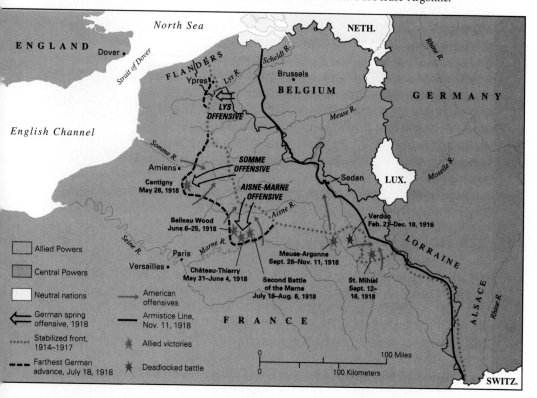

American soldiers on the front were unprepared for the hardships of battle. They were forced to spend weeks in water-soaked trenches surrounded by decaying bodies and body parts, and human and animal waste. Lice crawled on their bodies and rats patrolled the trenches, often nibbling on the toes and fingers of sleeping men. Many soldiers were traumatized by the sight of mangled, decaying bodies, the odors of poison gas and human excrement, and the cries of wounded comrades. Perhaps the most terrifying moments came with the prolonged head-splitting concussions of bombs. "To be shelled is the worst thing in the world," recalled a soldier. "There is a faraway moan that grows to a scream and then a roar like a train, followed by a ground-shaking smash and a diabolical red light."

How decisive was American involvement in World War I? In the nick of time, Winston Churchill later reflected, the Allies had gained "a new giant in the West to replace the dying titan of the East." The arrival of significant numbers of fresh American soldiers starting in mid-1918 tipped the balance decisively toward the Allies. On April 1, 1918, the Germans had a superiority of 324,000 infantrymen on the western front. By June, American reinforcements had given the Allies a manpower majority. And by November, the Allied preponderance was more than 600,000 men, enough to overwhelm the German defenses. "The American infantry in the Argonne [Forest] won the war," commented German Marshal Paul von Hindenburg.

Women at War Thousands of American women traveled to France to serve the men in uniform as nurses with the Red Cross, the YMCA, and other organizations. This woman, with the Salvation Army, writes a letter home for a wounded American soldier. *(National Archives.)*

Negotiating the Peace Treaty

Wilson led the nation into war promising that a stable peace and a renewed international commitment to democracy would follow. The postwar settlement, he had declared, should be based on moral principle not selfish interest. On January 8, 1918, Wilson had outlined his vision of the postwar settlement in his Fourteen Points Address to a joint session of Congress. Among his specific recommendations were calls for self-determination for all people, freedom of the seas, open covenants (an end to secret agreements) among nations, free trade, and reduced spending on the military. The final and, for Wilson, the most important point outlined "a general association of nations . . . [to guarantee] political independence and territorial integrity to great and small states alike."

An armistice that virtually disarmed Germany ended the fighting at the eleventh hour of the eleventh day of the eleventh month of 1918. The Americans had lost 48,909 men killed, with another 230,000 wounded. Losses to disease, mainly influenza, eventually ran the death total to over 112,000. The loss was small compared to the 1,700,000 Russians, 1,357,000 French, and 900,000 Britons who died.

In the final weeks of the war, Wilson lured the Germans into overthrowing the kaiser and surrendering by promising them a peace based on the Fourteen Points. He then pressured the Allies into accepting the Fourteen Points, somewhat modified, as the basis for conducting the impending peace conference that would shape international relations in the postwar world. Relishing his role as world leader, Wilson decided to head the American delegation to the treaty negotiations in Paris. On December 4, 1918, Wilson sailed from New York aboard the U.S.S. *George Washington*. Except for a few days in March 1919, he would remain abroad for almost six months. Enthusiastic crowds greeted the president and his call for a just peace when he arrived in Paris on December 13. "No one ever heard such cheers," observed a journalist.

The crowds loved him, but Wilson faced serious obstacles in his effort to create a new stable world order based on American values. First, support for his peace program had eroded at home, at least in Congress, owing to a number of political blunders. During the 1918 congressional campaign Wilson asked the voters to elect Democrats who would support him in his global mission. The voters, concerned with domestic issues, particularly inflation, promptly elected Republican majorities to both houses of Congress. The outcome of the 1918 elections meant that any treaty Wilson brought back from Paris would have to be ratified by a Republican-controlled Senate. Wilson compounded his error by not including a prominent Republican in the five-man peace delegation he brought to France.

Second, the European leaders who greeted him in Paris shared little enthusiasm for Wilson's plan. Twenty-seven nations assembled in Paris, but most matters were decided among the leaders of four nations—the United States, Britain, France, and Italy. The European leaders, determined to punish the Germans and committed to maintaining control of their colonies, had little patience with Wilson's pleas for a just peace and self-determination. Referring to Wilson's peace plan, French premier Georges Clemenceau said, "President Wilson and his Fourteen Points bore me. Even

God Almighty has only ten!" Prime Minister David Lloyd George of Britain and Clemenceau of France were immovable in their resolve to impose a harsh settlement on Germany, securing punitive economic and territorial aims that they had secretly mapped out early in the war. The Italian delegate, Prime Minister Vittorio Orlando, was concerned primarily with gaining disputed territory for his country. The Japanese exerted pressure for further concessions in East Asia.

The specter of Bolshevism, or communism, also haunted the conference. While battling with the conservative ambitions of his French and British allies who hoped to return Europe to its pre-1914 status—absent a powerful Germany—Wilson had to contend with the radical message of class revolution coming from the Soviet Union. In November 1917, V. I. Lenin led his Bolsheviks, or radical socialists, in toppling the Russian government. After seizing power, the Bolsheviks made peace with Germany, nationalized banks, placed factories under worker control, confiscated private property, and launched an attack on organized religion. Secretary of State Lansing observed that the Bolsheviks fundamentally challenged Western "political institutions as they now exist." The president feared that communism would appeal to millions of war-weary people around the globe, providing a radical alternative to his liberal agenda. "Bolshevism is gaining ground everywhere," a close White House advisor noted in his diary. "We are sitting upon an open powder magazine and some day a spark may ignite it."

The question facing the Allies was how to deal with the Soviet threat. Wilson's friend Ray Stannard Baker observed that "Paris cannot be understood without Moscow." France and Britain favored military force to overthrow Lenin. Wilson, who privately complained about the "poison of Bolshevism," suggested that the only way to deal with the Soviets was "to open all the doors to commerce." Only after repeated requests from the Allies did the president choose, however reluctantly, to send American forces to northern Russia in the summer of 1918 to guard Allied military supplies sent before Russia had pulled out of the war. Despite Wilson's stated desire to avoid mingling in Soviet internal affairs, the troops provided assistance to an unsuccessful effort to overthrow the Bolshevik regime. The western powers also imposed a strict economic blockade in an effort to cripple the Soviet government. The tactics ultimately backfired. After crushing their opposition, the Bolsheviks used the Allied intervention to arouse nationalist feelings in Russia.

The weight of the obstacles at home and abroad overwhelmed Wilson and prevented him from achieving the type of peace treaty he had envisioned. Throughout the long negotiating sessions, he compromised away parts of his Fourteen Points. He fought hard for decolonization and for self-determination, but he had to make many concessions to imperialism. The Versailles Treaty placed former German colonies in the Middle East and Africa in a mandate system that gave the French, British, and Japanese access to their resources. Japan assumed responsibility for Germany's holdings in China as well as many of its former Pacific island colonies. France occupied Germany's Rhineland, which abutted the French border. The treaty said nothing about freedom of the seas or the lowering of international economic barriers. The secret negotiating sessions at Versailles made a mockery of Wilson's call for "open covenants of peace openly arrived at." Most serious of all, the victors imposed a severe, vindictive penalty on Germany, forcing it to agree to pay reparations that would total $33 billion. The debates over reparations, noted American adviser Bernard Baruch, revealed the "blood-raw passions still pulsing through people's veins." By crippling the German economy, the treaty designed to end one great war planted the seeds of a second.

Wilson did not leave the conference empty-handed, however. The president achieved his central goal—with European agreement the treaty created a League of Nations for the postwar world. The heart of the League's covenant was Article X, the collective security provision. It provided for League members to "respect and preserve as against external aggression the territorial integrity and existing political independence" of all members. To enforce Article X, the delegates agreed to a collective security arrangement whereby all member nations were bound to defend each other against aggression.

The Fight over Ratification

While the peace conference was still in session, Republican Senator Henry Cabot Lodge of Massachusetts, a Harvard-educated patrician who chaired the Foreign Relations Committee, circulated a resolution signed by thirty-nine senators, more than enough votes to block ratification, stating that the League charter did not protect American national interests. Wilson responded by writing language into the League covenant that exempted the Monroe Doctrine (see pages 316) and U.S. internal matters from League jurisdiction. The additions failed to satisfy Lodge, who introduced fourteen reservations, modifications that he wanted made in the League charter, before he would approve the treaty. These reservations, designed to protect American sovereignty, included exempting U.S. immigration policy from League decisions and giving Congress the right to approve any League resolution that implemented Article X.

Wilson returned home with the flawed Versailles Treaty on July 8, 1919. Initially, the public responded favorably to the treaty. Thirty-two state legislatures and thirty-three governors endorsed the League, while a poll indicated that an overwhelming majority of the nation's newspapers held a similar opinion. Critics soon gained the upper hand, however. Many progressives attacked Wilson's betrayal of his Fourteen Points. "How in our consciences are we to square the results with the promises?" asked journalist Walter Lippmann. Senator La Follette said the treaty's provisions confirmed his view that World War I was nothing more than a struggle between rival imperialists. Isolationists feared Article X would obligate the United States to provide armed forces to preserve collective security in every corner of the postwar world.

Senate Republicans presented Wilson with his biggest obstacle. The forty-nine Republican senators who opposed the treaty formed two distinct factions. The first group earned the name "Irreconcilables" because they opposed the treaty in any form and were determined to oppose it with or without reservations. They were joined by a second group of "Reservationists," led by Lodge, who were willing to support the treaty if Wilson included the added amendments. Both groups were troubled by the same questions. As Lodge asked, "Are you willing to put your soldiers and your sailors at the disposition of other nations?" Republicans also asked whether the terms of the treaty would require the United States to intervene to repress democratic movements in the British and French empires. "I am opposed to American boys policing Europe and quelling riots in every new nation's back yard," explained California progressive Hiram Johnson.

Wilson began to realize that the situation was passing out of his control, and he decided on bold steps. In September he set out on a cross-country speaking tour to rally public support for the treaty. He traveled more than eight thousand miles

The Fate of the League of Nations This cartoon reflects on the short life of Wilsonian ideals. Although the Treaty of Versailles on the whole disappointed Wilson, it did include one major victory, the creation of the League of Nations. However, on Wilson's return home, the Republican-dominated Senate burst even that "bubble" by revising the treaty to weaken the United States' role in the League. Wilson refused to support the amended treaty, and it went down to defeat. *(National Archives.)*

through the Middle and Far West for three weeks in September and delivered some thirty-seven addresses. Yet the effects of strain began to take their toll on Wilson even before the tour was half over. He began to have blinding headaches and to show signs of exhaustion. Finally, after one of his longest and most important speeches at Pueblo, Colorado, on September 25, he collapsed. His physician then canceled the remaining speeches and ordered the presidential train to return to Washington. On October 2, Wilson suffered a stroke that paralyzed the left side of his face and body. For days his life hung in the balance.

In November 1919, shortly after Wilson suffered his stroke, Lodge reported out the treaty with fourteen reservations. Most Democratic supporters of the League seemed willing to accept Lodge's version. Most of the reservations made little difference, they pointed out, and even the modification of Article X was acceptable to the European powers. Had Wilson followed their advice, it is possible that the treaty would have passed. But Wilson, his concentration hampered and his stubbornness accentuated by the stroke, refused to compromise. Lodge's reservations, he insisted, removed America's all-important moral obligation. Before the votes were taken, the Senate Democratic floor leader, Gilbert Hitchcock, told the president that the treaty could not pass without reservations. He suggested that "It might be wise to compromise." Wilson responded curtly, "Let Lodge compromise!" Obstinately, he instructed his Democratic followers to hold firm, and on November 19 they joined the Irreconcilables in voting against the treaty with reservations, 55–39. In March 1920, the treaty came up for another vote. A number of Democrats broke ranks and supported the revised treaty, but the vote, 49 to 35, fell short of the necessary two-thirds majority needed for passage. "It is dead," Wilson told his cabinet.

The debate over American entry into the League exposed an old tension about America's role in the world. Wilson believed that America's long-term interests could best be protected through international collective security. Lodge and other opponents of the treaty tapped into both a strong sense of nationalism and a deep-seated American isolationism. Neither perspective, Wilson's nor Lodge's, offered the American people a realistic framework for understanding America's role in the twentieth century world. Wilson may have appreciated the need to join forces with other nations, but his vision was hopelessly naive and self-righteous. Lodge expounded on the dangers of collective security but failed to offer a realistic alternative for defining and protecting American national interests. That unresolved debate, between nationalism and internationalism, would remain at the core of American experiments in foreign policy for the rest of the century.

An Uncertain Peace, 1919–1920

The summer and fall of 1919 were a tense, anxious time for many Americans. Almost five million men had been drafted from familiar surroundings. Great numbers of women had left home to work in war industries. African-Americans had flocked to northern cities. During the war Americans sanctioned a degree of government control over the economy that deviated from traditional economic individualism. "Never did the crust of civilization seem so thin," reflected a disillusioned progressive. "There is so much unrest. So much unreason, so much violence; so little sense!" Shocked by seeming threats to their social and economic traditions, Americans reacted to the turmoil by searching for scapegoats. Fear of social unrest, combined with a growing concern about communist revolution, produced one of the most repressive periods in American history. By 1920, progressivism had run its course. Americans, tired of Wilsonian idealism and progressive reform, turned to the Republican Party, which promised a return to "normalcy."

Unsettled Times

During the winter of 1918–1919, Americans had to contend with a deadly influenza epidemic that had already swept through Europe, killing tens of thousands. About 20 million Americans fell ill; over half a million died. More American soldiers died from the flu than were killed by enemy bullets. The flu created fear and panic in American cities, where many people resorted to wearing surgical masks to avoid the germs. Public facilities that could spread the flu—dance halls, phone booths, theaters, even some churches—were closed.

The Invisible Enemy   Of the 112,000 American soldiers who died in World War I, half were casualties of disease. Influenza was a particularly deadly killer; epidemics in 1918 on both sides of the Atlantic and at sea killed thousands and afflicted even more. Though some believed the Germans had introduced the disease as a form of warfare, the 186,000 German victims of the virus indicate otherwise. Here Red Cross nurses make gauze masks for distribution in hopes of stopping the flu's fatal march.   *(Brown Brothers.)*

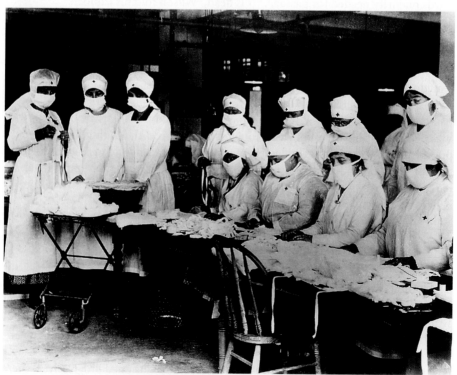

An epidemic of racial violence also infected the United States following the war. African-American soldiers returned to their homes in the South emboldened by their experience in Europe. The 200,000 African-Americans who served overseas had tasted an equality unknown in their native South. "I'm glad I went," declared a black veteran. "I done my part and I'm going to fight right here till Uncle Sam does his." Du Bois observed a "new, radical Negro spirit," among veterans. The attitude of the "New Negro," he said, was "I ain't looking for trouble, but if it comes my way I ain't dodging." NAACP membership reached ten thousand by 1918 and was over sixty-two thousand by 1919.

Southerners viewed the new activism with alarm and moved to crush it. Ten black veterans, several of them still in uniform, were lynched in 1919; fourteen blacks were burned at the stake. Southern white terrorism also found expression in the rapid spread of the newly revived Ku Klux Klan.

The clash between African-American pride and white hostility was explosive. Beginning in July 1919 the nation experienced an outbreak of the most fearful race riots in American history. The first riot began in Longview, Texas, and a week later violence erupted in the nation's capital, where mobs composed principally of white servicemen pillaged the black section. The worst riot broke out in Chicago after an altercation between whites and blacks on a Lake Michigan beach. Mobs roamed the slum areas of the city for thirteen days burning, pillaging, and killing. When it was all over, 15 whites and 23 blacks were dead; 178 whites and 342 blacks were injured; and more than 1,000 families were homeless. During the next two months, major riots broke out in Knoxville, Tennessee, Omaha, Nebraska, and Elaine, Arkansas. The final count by the end of 1919 revealed some twenty-five riots, with hundreds dead and injured and property damage running in the millions.

In addition to social and economic tensions, basic values seemed under assault. In September 1919, when the favored Chicago White Sox lost the World Series to the Cincinnati Reds, rumors circulated that Chicago players had thrown the game, taking payoffs from professional gamblers. A jury refused to convict them, but the commissioner of baseball banned the eight from the game for the rest of their lives. "Say it ain't so, Joe," a young fan pleaded with Chicago's star centerfielder "Shoeless Joe" Jackson. "Yes, kid, I'm afraid it is," Jackson replied.

The rising cost of living added to postwar anxiety. The war ended before the administration could devise a plan for reconversion to a peacetime economy. Wilson lifted all price controls as soon as the war ended, but with contracts for war orders running until 1920, the supply of goods fell far short of the demand among Americans freed from the need to conserve resources. Prices shot up as consumers scrambled for scarce products. In 1919 the consumer price index rose by 77 percent over the 1916 level. The *Washington Post* in August 1919 called rising prices, "the burning domestic issue."

Concern about inflation produced a series of paralyzing strikes that threatened to cripple the economy. Released from their no-strike pledges, labor leaders fought to make sure that wages kept up with the spiraling inflation. There were more strikes in 1919 than in any other year in American history: more than 4 million workers— about 20 percent of the industrial workforce—walked off their jobs in 2,665 strikes. In January 1919, shipyard workers in Seattle went on strike. When laborers in other trades joined them, it appeared for a few days that a general strike of 100,000 people might paralyze the region. The mayor denounced the general strike as an attempt "to duplicate the anarchy of Russia." Public reaction was hostile. "The strike is Marxian," cried the *Los Angeles Times.* The strike collapsed in nine days.

Fears of public disorder rose again in September 1919 when three-quarters of Boston's fifteen hundred policemen went on strike. Wilson called the walkout a "crime against civilization." For a few days, the streets of Boston belonged to rioters and looters. Boston newspapers branded the striking policemen as "agents of Lenin." The governor of Massachusetts, an obscure Republican politician named Calvin Coolidge, called out the Massachusetts National Guard, which restored order and broke the strike. "There is no right to strike against the public safety by anyone, anytime, any where," Coolidge declared.

The Red Scare

To many Americans, the greatest threat seemed to come from Russia, where the Bolsheviks had proclaimed their dedication to worldwide revolution. In 1919 the Soviets established the Comintern to promote world revolution and in that year radical socialists formed two Communist parties in the United States. Communist uprisings occurred and failed in Hungary and Germany. Nervous Americans, aware that a small, disciplined band of revolutionaries had come to power in Russia, worried that revolution might find a foothold in the United States.

Thus many Americans were certain revolution was at hand when more than thirty-six homemade bombs, timed to go off on May Day, were delivered to unsuspecting targets. Among the intended victims were John D. Rockefeller, Postmaster General Burleson, and Seattle's mayor Ole Hanson. "Reds Planned May Day Murders," headlines screamed. On June 2, bombs exploded in eight American cities at the same hour; one damaged the home of Attorney General A. Mitchell Palmer.

Although only a small number of radicals were involved in these plots, the bombing unnerved Americans, who responded by lashing out at potential enemies. Sensational newspaper reports magnified the events and stimulated widespread public alarm. In May 1919, an enraged sailor shot and killed a man for not standing during the playing of "The Star-Spangled Banner." According to press reports, "The crowd burst into cheering and handclapping" following the shooting. In February a jury in Hammond, Indiana, deliberated for two minutes before acquitting a man for killing an alien who had shouted, "To Hell with the United States." Some four hundred soldiers and sailors invaded the offices of the *New York Call*, a Socialist daily, and beat up several May Day celebrants. In other parts of New York, and in Boston and Cleveland, May Day paraders clashed with servicemen and police.

A. Mitchell Palmer, who had been appointed attorney general in March 1919, stepped forward to save America from Communist revolution. A former congressman from Pennsylvania with solid progressive credentials, Palmer had opposed wartime repression of civil liberties. But he also possessed a genuine fear of Bolshevism and planned to ride the red tide into the White House in 1920. Claiming America was in imminent peril of revolution, Palmer hired a young lawyer named

J. Edgar Hoover to direct a new Bureau of Investigation. Hoover placed thousands of people in many organizations under surveillance.

In November, Palmer, using information provided by Hoover, staged raids on radicals in twelve cities, where they seized files, broke up machines and furniture, and arrested 250 people. In December the government deported 249 aliens, including the veteran anarchist Emma Goldman (see page 827), to Russia. A month later Palmer's men arrested more than four thousand alleged Communists in one night of raids in thirty-three cities. Many of the suspects were held in filthy, overcrowded jail cells without food or water. They were prevented from talking with family or lawyers. The raids were justified, Palmer said, because the country was infested with the "moral perverts and hysterical neurasthenic women who abound in communism."

The Red Scare subsided almost as quickly as it had started. In April 1920, Palmer warned of a series of radical activities planned for the anniversary of the 1919 mail bombings. When the day passed without incident, newspapers ridiculed Palmer, dismissing him as a modern-day Chicken Little squawking that the sky was falling. By midsummer of 1920, most of the conditions that fed the fear of radicalism had dissipated. Labor agitation had been quashed and American radicals had split into warring factions of Socialists, Communists, and Communist Laborites. Most important, Americans relaxed as the threat of Bolshevism in Europe subsided. By September Americans refused to respond to Palmer's proclamation of impending revolution even after a wagonload of bombs exploded on Wall Street, killing 33 and injuring 200 more. Presidential candidate Warren Harding, no radical, pronounced the epitaph: "Too much has been said about Bolshevism in America."

The cruel and high-handed treatment of dissenters during 1919 and 1920 marked the most widespread peacetime attack on civil liberties in American history. And it profoundly discouraged people who might otherwise have worked for reform. Frederic Howe, the immigration commissioner who fought deportations, confessed that his faith in public power as an agent of reform had been misplaced. "My attitude toward the state," he wrote later, "was changed as a result of these experiences. I have never been able to bring it back. I became distrustful of the state."

The Election of 1920

The presidential campaign of 1920 revealed America's disenchantment with progressive reforms and with Wilsonian idealism. Over the previous eight years, Wilson had managed to alienate large groups of voters. Irish- and German-Americans resented his support of the British. Industrialists and businessmen rebelled against higher taxes and government regulation. Meanwhile, diehard reform-minded progressives were angry over the Palmer raids and the harsh peace treaty. "The country," said the *New York Tribune,* "was weary of Wilsonianism in all its manifestations."

With Wilson no longer a viable candidate, Democrats struggled over which new face should lead the party. At the convention, forces of Wilson's son-in-law and secretary of the treasury, William G. McAdoo, and Attorney General Palmer fought to a standstill for thirty-seven wearying ballots, before Ohio governor James M. Cox was nominated on the forty-fourth roll call on July 5. As his running mate, Cox chose the assistant secretary of the navy, and prominent Wilsonian, Franklin D. Roosevelt of New York. Wilson wanted his party to make the election a "solemn referendum" on the League of Nations. Party leaders, showing more sensitivity to public opinion, only reluctantly embraced the League.

The eager Republicans smelled victory in 1920. The front-runner, General Leonard Wood, inherited most of the following of Theodore Roosevelt, who had died in 1919. Other candidates were Governor Frank O. Lowden of Illinois, Senator Hiram W. Johnson of California, Herbert Hoover, and a number of favorite sons, including the nondescript Senator Warren G. Harding of Ohio. When the Wood and Lowden forces deadlocked at the Republican convention in June 1920, the party's Old Guard selected Harding. For vice president, the convention nominated Governor Calvin Coolidge of Massachusetts police strike fame. The platform roundly repudiated Wilsonianism. It condemned Wilson's League but approved membership in the World Court and international agreements to preserve peace. It promised a return to traditional GOP domestic policies—high tariffs and low taxes—and an end to further federal social legislation. Finally, it pledged to support restrictions on immigration and aid to farmers.

Harding captured the mood of the times when he told a Boston audience, "America's present need is not heroics, but healing; not nostrums, but normalcy; not revolution, but restoration; not agitation, but adjustment; not surgery, but serenity; not the dramatic, but the dispassionate; not experiment, but equipoise; not submergence in internationality, but sustainment in triumphant nationality." A critic sniped that Harding's speeches "left the impression of an army of pompous phrases moving over the landscape in search of an idea."

Harding's speeches may not have impressed critics, but his call for a "return to normalcy" struck a chord with voters. The result was a smashing electoral triumph. "It wasn't just a landslide," said a politician, "it was an earthquake." Harding received 16,143,407 popular votes, or 60.4 percent of the total; he won all the states outside the South, for an electoral vote of 404; and he even broke the Solid South by carrying Tennessee. Cox came away with only 9,130,328 popular and 127 electoral votes (see map). The Republicans' sweep in the senatorial and congressional contests gave them a commanding majority of 22 seats in the Senate and 167 in the House.

The election signaled an important shift in the public mood. The war disillusioned a generation of progressives who had shared Wilson's idealistic dream of "making the world safe for democracy." The war had exposed progressivism's vulnerability. In the words of William Allen White, Americans in 1920 were "tired of issues, sick at heart of ideals, and weary of being noble."

CONCLUSION

When war broke out in Europe in 1914, America still embraced its traditional isolationism, and many Americans hoped the country would remain neutral. Many progressives feared entry into the war would set back reform efforts, and Americans of German and Irish heritage felt little sympathy for Britain. Genuine neutrality, however, proved elusive. America had close cultural and commercial ties to the Allies, and

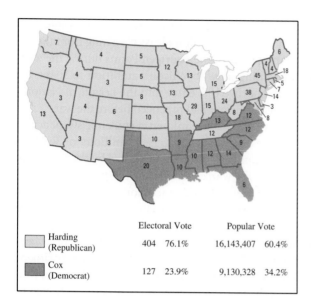

Electoral Vote · Popular Vote

	Electoral Vote		Popular Vote	
Harding (Republican)	404	76.1%	16,143,407	60.4%
Cox (Democrat)	127	23.9%	9,130,328	34.2%

The Election of 1920

With World War I and the fierce battle over the Treaty of Paris behind them, many Americans agreed with Republican candidate Warren G. Harding's call for a return to "normalcy." Republicans spent most of the campaign attacking the policies of Woodrow Wilson rather than attacking the platform of the Democratic candidate, James Cox, who failed to emerge from the ailing president's shadows.

a number of key members of the Wilson administration made clear they preferred a British victory. The British navy's domination of the seaways strangled U.S. trade with Germany, belying U.S. claims of neutrality. German use of a new undersea weapon, the U-boat, to attack civilian ships further tested the limits of American neutrality.

Through it all Wilson called for a policy of "strict neutrality," insisting that Americans had the right to travel safely on the passenger ships of belligerent nations. The president ignored critics who suggested that his policy would push the nation into the war. The critics were right. When Germany, convinced it could score a decisive blow against the Allies before the United States could mobilize, announced that it would begin unrestricted submarine warfare in the Atlantic, Wilson's policy left him no choice but to ask Congress for a declaration of war.

Once war was declared, Congress gave the president broad powers to regulate the economy and to restrict individual liberty. Washington seized control of the railroads, regulated the production and distribution of food, dramatically increased the tax base, and created the War Industries Board (WIB) to coordinate the conversion to military production. To forge a sense of national unity, the administration created the Committee on Public Information (CPI). When propaganda failed, Wilson resorted to coercive measures to compel loyalty. Armed with wartime legislation banning dissent, Postmaster General Albert Burleson led a crusade to identify and imprison suspected subversives. Patriotic appeals also helped progressives to achieve two major victories: passage of constitutional amendments to ban alcohol and to give women the right to vote. World War I succeeded, where the progressive experiment had failed, in broadening the scope of government.

Having entered the war to shape the peace, Wilson offered the world a liberal plan based on his Fourteen Points, which included self-determination for all people, open covenants among nations, free trade, demilitarization, and a League of

Nations. The president proposed his plan as an alternative both to the traditional European balance of power politics and to the new radical ideas emanating from the Soviet Union. Wilson had to compromise most of the Fourteen Points during the writing of the Versailles Treaty. In a stunning blow to Wilson's ambition to shape the postwar world, the Senate refused to approve U.S. entry into the League of Nations. The United States returned to the isolationism it had practiced before the war.

War's end found little peace at home. A massive influenza epidemic swept across the country. As the economy slowed and inflation soared, millions of workers struck for better labor conditions. African-Americans, encouraged by their employment gains and military service during the war, called for fair treatment—to which the white mainstream reacted with a series of bloody race riots. Fearful of the new "red" menace in the Soviet Union, government officials expanded the wartime restrictions on individual rights.

By 1920, many Americans were tired of the unrest and upheaval that had characterized the Wilson years. Disenchanted with social and international experimentation, the public gave a landslide victory to Republican Warren G. Harding, who called for a return to "normalcy." As the war experience faded, Americans hoped to find peace and stability through their traditional political and social values.

SUGGESTED READINGS

David M. Kennedy's *Over Here* (1980) is the most comprehensive one-volume study of the war's impact on domestic life. Ronald Schaffer argues in *America in the Great War* (1991) that America's involvement in World War I sparked the rise of the welfare state and promoted progressive reforms. Robert Ferrell's *Woodrow Wilson and World War I* (1985) provides a detailed survey of the war, at home and abroad, as well as of the war's impact on the immediate postwar years. Meirion and Susie Harries's *Last Days of Innocence* (1997) provides insight on the relationship between the war and American society. Neil A. Wynn's *From Progressivism to Prosperity* (1986) links the war years with currents from the Progressive Era and developments in the 1920s. Ellis W. Hawley argues that World War I was a turning point for modern societies in *The Great War and the Search for Modern Order* (1979).

Ernest R. May's *The World War and American Isolation* (1966) chronicles the shift from neutrality to intervention, emphasizing the role of Germany's U-boats. John Coogan examines the shift in popular attitudes toward intervention in *The End to Neutrality* (1981). In *Spreading the American Dream* (1982), Emily Rosenberg focused on the ideological support for American intervention. Ross Gregory's *The Origins of American Intervention in the First World War* (1971) is a detailed one-volume survey of the domestic and international forces pushing for intervention. C. Roland Marchand looks at the peace and antiwar movements of the period in *The American Peace Movement and Social Reform* (1973).

John Whiteclay Chambers, Jr., details the history of the draft in *To Raise an Army* (1987). Paul Chapman covers the rise of intellectual testing in *Schools as Sorters* (1988), while Allan Brandt describes the anti–venereal disease campaign in *No Magic Bullet* (1985). The work of the Commission on Training Camp Activities in providing wholesome recreation for conscripted troops is the focus of Nancy Bristow's *Making Men Moral* (1996).

Robert D. Cuff's *The War Industries Board* (1973) provides a representative study of war mobilization. Kathleen Burk studies the industrial cooperation between Great Britain and America in *Britain, America and the Sinews of War* (1985). Charles Gilbert provides a detailed study of the financiers behind the war in *American Financing of World War I* (1970).

Valerie Jean Conner explores the government's policies toward labor in *The National War Labor Board* (1983). The effects of World War I on publicists and journals that promoted the progressive movement is the theme of John A. Thompson's *Reformers and War* (1987).

Maurine W. Greenwald's *Women, War and Work* (1980) analyzes the war's impact on women in the economy. Barbara Steinson evaluates women's social and political contributions to the war effort in *American Women's Activism in World War I* (1982). The role of women in protesting the war is examined in Kathleen Kennedy's *Disloyal Mothers and Scurrilous Citizens* (1999). David Morgan studies the political tactics of the suffragist movement in *Suffragists and Democrats* (1972). Joe William Trotter, Jr., collects several essays on the African-American experience of World War I in *The Great Migration in Historical Perspective* (1991).

Stephen Vaughan examines the efforts to promote national unity in *Holding Fast the Inner Lines* (1980). Alfred E. Cornbise focuses on the "Four-Minute Men" in *War as Advertised* (1984). Michael Pearlman explores the vigilante preparedness committees in *To Make Democracy Safe for America* (1984). The plight of German-Americans during the war is covered in Frederick Luebke's *Bonds of Loyalty* (1974). The civil liberties issues raised by mobilization are examined in Paul L. Murphy's *World War I and the Origin of Civil Liberties* (1979).

Edward M. Coffman's *The War to End All Wars* (1968) is a solid overview of the World War I armed forces. Laurence Stallings focuses on the battlefront experience in *The Doughboys* (1963), which is also the foundation of Byron Farwell's *Over There* (1999). Mark Meigs's *Optimism at Armageddon* (1997) describes the war through the words of American soldiers and explains why they believed the United States had to fight. Dorothy Schneider and Carl J. Schneider document the work of American women who served in the war in *Into the Breach* (1991), while A. E. Barbeau and Florette Henri chronicle the experience of black soldiers in *The Unknown Soldiers* (1974).

N. Gordon Levin, Jr.'s *Woodrow Wilson and World Politics* (1968) documents Woodrow Wilson's reaction to the Bolshevik Revolution and his role at Versailles. Arthur Link's *Woodrow Wilson: Revolution, War, and Peace* (1979) and Arthur Walworth's *Wilson and His Peacemakers* (1986) describe Wilson's efforts to create world order around principles of self-determination and democracy. Charles M. Lee outlines the weaknesses of the Versailles Treaty in *The End of Order* (1980).

Ralph A. Stone provides a blow-by-blow account of the Senate fight over the League of Nations in *The Irreconcilables* (1970). Thomas Knock's *To End All Wars* (1992) emphasizes the role of ideology in Wilson's approach to peacemaking. A more recent work that studies the failure of the Senate to ratify the treaty is Herbert Margulies's *The Mild Reservationists and the League of Nations* (1989). The Russian intervention is covered in Peter Filene's *Americans and the Soviet Experiment* (1967) and George F. Kennan's *The Decision to Intervene* (1958).

William M. Tuttle, Jr.'s *Race Riot* (1970) offers a tragic account of the Chicago race riot of 1919. James R. Grossman's *Land of Hope* (1989) also has good material on postwar race relations. The strikes of 1919 and antilabor sentiment are the subjects of Burl Noggle's *Into the Twenties* (1974). Robert K. Murray's *Red Scare* (1955) is still the best study of the Bolshevik Revolution's impact on domestic politics.

*National Security versus
Individual Liberty*

Schenck v. U.S., 1919

In 1917 Charles Schenck, the general secretary of the Socialist Party, mailed fifteen thousand leaflets to conscription-age men urging them to resist the draft. Shortly thereafter, he was arrested and charged with obstructing the war effort in violation of the Espionage Act of 1917. Schenck appealed his conviction, arguing that the act violated the freedoms of speech and the press protected by the First Amendment. In a unanimous decision, the Court upheld both Schenck's conviction and the constitutionality of the Espionage and Sedition Acts. Writing the Court's decision, Justice Oliver Wendell Holmes outlined the "clear and present danger" clause: individual rights could be constrained, he argued, when their exercise posed a direct and unmistakable threat to national survival.

■■ . . . The document in question upon its first printed side recited the first
■■ section of the Thirteenth Amendment, said that the idea embodied in it was violated by the Conscription Act and that a conscript is little better than a convict. In impassioned language it intimated that conscription was despotism in its worse form and a monstrous wrong against humanity in the interest of Wall Street's chosen few. It said, "Do not submit to intimidation" but, in form at least, confined itself to peaceful measures such as a petition for the repeal of the act. The other and later-printed side of the sheet was headed "Assert Your Rights." It stated reasons for alleging that any one violated the Constitution when he refused to recognize "your right to assert your opposition to the draft." . . . Of course the document would not have been sent unless it had been intended to have some effect, and we do not see what effect it could be expected to have upon persons subject to the draft except to influence them to obstruct the carrying of it out. . . .

But it is said, suppose that that was the tendency of this circular, it is protected by the First Amendment to the Constitution. . . . We admit that in many places and in ordinary times the defendants in saying all that was said in the circular would have been within their constitutional rights. But the character of every act depends upon the circumstances in which it is done. . . . The most stringent protection of free speech would not protect a man in falsely shouting fire in a theatre and causing a panic. . . . The question in every case is whether the words used are used in such circumstances and are of such a nature as to create a clear and present danger that they will bring about the substantive evils that Congress has a right to prevent. It is a question of proximity and degree. When a nation is at war, many things that might be said in time of peace are such a hindrance to its effort that their utterance will not be endured so long as men fight and that no Court could regard them as protected by any constitutional right. . . . The statute of 1917 in §4 punishes conspiracies to obstruct as well as actual obstruction. If the act, . . . its tendency and the intent with which it is done are the same, we perceive no ground for saying that success alone warrants making the act a crime. . . . Judgments affirmed. ▮

Address to the Jury, 1917

On June 15, 1917, federal marshals raided the joint offices of Emma Goldman's *Mother Earth* magazine and Alexander Berkman's labor newspaper, *The Blast*. They were charged with conspiring to obstruct the conscription effort. After President Wilson signed the Draft Bill in May of 1917, Berkman and Goldman printed and distributed 100,000 copies of a No-Conscription Manifesto. Goldman and Berkman acted as their own attorneys during their trial. In her summation to the jury, Goldman pleaded with the jury to remember that speaking in opposition to the war effort did not by itself make one a conspirator.

Gentlemen of the jury, we respect your patriotism. . . . But may there not be different kinds of patriotism as there are different kinds of liberty? I for one cannot believe that love of one's country must consist in blindness to its social faults . . . neither can I believe that the mere accident of birth in a certain country or the mere scrap of a citizen's paper constitutes the love of country.

I know many people—I am one of them—who were not born here, nor have they applied for citizenship, and who yet love America with deeper passion and greater intensity than many natives whose patriotism manifests itself by pulling, kicking, and insulting those who do not rise when the national anthem is played. Our patriotism is that of the man who loves a woman with open eyes. He is enchanted by her beauty, yet he sees her faults. So we, too, who know America, love her beauty, her richness, her great possibilities—above all we love the people that have produced her wealth, her artists who have created beauty, her great apostles who dream and work for liberty—but with the same passionate emotion we hate her superficiality, her cant, her corruption, her mad, unscrupulous worship at the altar of the Golden Calf.

We say that if America has entered the war to make the world safe for democracy, she must first make democracy safe in America. How else is the world to take America seriously, when democracy at home is daily being outraged, free speech suppressed, peaceable assemblies broken up by overbearing and brutal gangsters in uniform; when free press is curtailed and every independent opinion gagged. Verily, poor as we are in democracy, how can we give of it to the world? . . .

The District Attorney has dragged in our Manifesto, and he has emphasized the passage, "Resist conscription." [A]dmitting that the Manifesto contains [that] expression . . . is there only *one kind* of resistance? Is there only the resistance which means the gun, the bayonet, the bomb or flying machine? Is there not another kind of resistance? May not the people simply fold their hands and declare, "We will not fight when we do not believe in the necessity of war"? May not the people who believe in the repeal of the Conscription law, because it is unconstitutional, express their opposition in word and by pen, in meetings and in other ways? . . . ▮

Total war was a new thing to America in 1917. Not even the Civil War had required the degree of mobilization that seemed necessary to fight in World War I. Americans had watched the fighting in Europe for three years and had seen the massive, intrusive government agencies that the combatants had made to oversee the war effort. The Wilson administration was determined not to create such an apparatus. Instead, Wilson decided to persuade Americans to voluntarily contribute work and money for the mobilization. Ironically, it was this effort to avoid government coercion that gave birth to World War I's massive violations of civil liberties.

Through the propaganda of the Committee on Public Information, the Wilson administration stressed the need for unity and national security. Yet because the system Wilson devised was noncoercive, it had no way to prevent the excesses of patriotic citizens. The federal government did not have to work hard to violate people's rights; in the mania that gripped the country during the war, private citizens were happy to do the violating themselves.

Justice Holmes's opinion in the *Schenck* case can be interpreted in light of these feelings. The "clear and present danger" clause Holmes outlined is not itself a threat to civil liberties. Its application to *Schenck*, however, was controversial. Was Schenck shouting "Fire!" in a crowded theater? Or was he rather standing outside a theater, telling people not to enter because of a fire inside? Such criticism, though, missed the more fundamental argument in Holmes's decision: the standard by which we judge threats to national security is different in war than in peacetime.

Emma Goldman never accepted Holmes's argument. Goldman questioned if total national unity was necessary even to fight a major war. The damage done by Wilson's repression to American democratic institutions, she argued, would be far greater than that done to the war effort. Was the United States willing to make that sacrifice?

National security and individual liberty are often opposed to each other, and usually exist in delicate balance. In 1917 Wilson upset the balance between these two values. The government restricted rights as though America's survival was threatened, but America had not been attacked. The Wilson administration treated skepticism and public dissent like threats to national safety.

While the Committee on Public Information demanded total unity, Emma Goldman and other thinkers developed a more nuanced conception of loyalty and love of country. She placed love of a people above loyalty to a government, and suggested that following government orders, if they were against the public interest, was foolish. In such a case, she said, it is one's patriotic duty to oppose the government.

Both Holmes's new, intensified conception of loyalty and Goldman's new, subtler defense of disloyalty have become features of American politics. Their clash of ideals presaged the Red Scares of the 1920s and the 1950s. The public hysteria of World War I offers a lesson about national emergencies: perception of a threat can be more important than actual danger in shaping public behavior.

Questions for Analysis

1. Why does Schenck cite the Thirteenth Amendment in his leaflet?
2. According to Holmes, why are Schenck's actions not protected under the First Amendment?
3. What constitutes a conspiracy for Holmes?
4. How does Goldman define love of country?
5. What does she find lacking in American democracy?
6. How does she propose to resist the government?
7. Goldman spoke almost two years before Holmes's decision. Did she anticipate any of his arguments?
8. Is Holmes justified in restricting rights in wartime? To what degree?

24

The New Era, 1920–1928

*O*n May 20, 1927, an early morning fog had settled over Long Island's Roosevelt Field, but the weather did little to dampen the spirits of the hundreds of spectators lining the runway, who had gathered in the predawn hours to witness aviation history. At 7:42 A.M. Charles Lindbergh, a twenty-five-year-old airmail pilot, climbed into his cramped, single-engine plane, the *Spirit of St. Louis.* Equipped with the latest in aviation technology and burdened with 450 gallons of gasoline, the plane lurched down the muddy runway. It hopped into the air only to bounce back to the ground. With only a few thousand feet of runway left, the plane finally climbed into the sky, clearing telephone wires at the end of the runway by a few feet. His destination: Paris.

Lindbergh would not be the first person to fly across the Atlantic, but his flight from New York to Paris would be four hundred miles greater than any before and, most important, he was doing it alone. Shortly after sunrise on the twenty-sixth hour of his flight he spotted a fishing boat. "Which way to Ireland?" he shouted to the men below. Next came the coast of England, and finally, France, "like an outstretched hand to meet me." It was ten o'clock at night in Paris when Lindbergh picked out the floodlights showing the edge of a runway at Le Bourget airport. After circling the Eiffel Tower, he set the *Spirit of St. Louis* down as an enthusiastic crowd of 100,000 rushed to greet him, thirty-three and a half hours after leaving New York.

America erupted in celebration on hearing the news that Lindbergh had safely completed the 3,610-mile journey. President

Coolidge decorated him with the Distinguished Flying Cross and awarded him the rank of colonel in the army reserves. Several days later in New York City more than 4 million people lined the streets to shower their hero with confetti and ticker tape. Advertisers offered him hundreds of thousands of dollars to endorse their new consumer products.

The outpouring of affection and adulation that Lindbergh's feat inspired highlighted the intense cultural conflict of the decade. Many Americans marveled at the benefits of a modern industrialized society that made transatlantic flights and other amazements possible, even as they clung tenaciously to the values of rugged individualism deeply rooted in the nation's agricultural past. Lindbergh was a product of the new machine age, but the plainspoken, clean-cut aviator also seemed to represent the image of a simpler America. Americans refused to see his flight as a triumph of technology. Rather it was a pioneering personal accomplishment, affirming the importance of traditional values—individualism, hard work, and self-sacrifice—that seemed suddenly vulnerable in a more complex and mechanized world. Charles Lindbergh, observed a contemporary, "has shown us that we are not rotten at the core, but morally sound and sweet and good."

The same confused reaction characterized America's response to other changes in the 1920s. Technological breakthroughs led to the production of a host of new products and the beginning of a consumer society. Many young urbanites rebelled against the older order of things. Young men and women challenged Victorian values. African-Americans trumpeted a sense of nationalism and pride in their heritage. Confronted by these extraordinary changes, many Americans tightened their grips on the past. The growth of the Ku Klux Klan, the rise of fundamentalism, and support for immigration restriction and prohibition revealed traditional America's desire to preserve the past against the onslaught of social experimentation.

▍ Why is the decade of the twenties called the "New Era"?

▍ What was at issue in the cultural clash that characterized the 1920s?

▍ Who were the contestants in the struggle?

▍ What trends in national politics reflected the era's tensions?

This chapter will address these questions.

 ## The Modern Age

People living during the 1920s marveled at the extraordinary changes they witnessed. Experimentation and drive led to advances in technology and the development of new consumer goods that fueled a growing economy, though not everyone shared equally in the prosperity. The communications revolution, which began breaking down regional and class barriers, helped erect the scaffolding of a national culture. Little wonder that contemporaries referred to the 1920s as the "New Era."

Chronology

1915	Ku Klux Klan revived
1917	Garvey founds Universal Negro Improvement Association
1920	KDKA covers presidential race in nation's first radio broadcast
	League of Women Voters organized
	Fitzgerald publishes *This Side of Paradise*
	Prohibition begins
	Harding elected president
1921	Farm bloc organized in Congress
	National Woman's Party founded
	Washington Conference on naval disarmament
1922	Lewis publishes *Babbitt*
1923	Harding dies; Coolidge becomes president
1924	Green becomes AFL president
	Johnson-Reed Immigration Act passed
	Coolidge elected president
	Dawes Plan rescues postwar Germany
1925	Scopes trial
1926	Hemingway publishes *The Sun Also Rises*
1927	Sacco and Vanzetti executed
1928	Kellogg-Briand Pact
	Hoover elected president

The New Economy

World War I had inspired a brief business boom, which was then followed by a recession that lasted until 1921, when the economy again began to heat up. Between 1922 and 1929, every index of economic growth measured impressive gains. Not even a mild recession in 1924 could stem the remarkable surge. The national income rose from $63.1 billion to $87.8 billion. The gross national product grew from $74.1 billion to $103.1 billion. The nation's manufacturing output increased by more than 60 percent. Unemployment remained below 4 percent while inflation never topped 1 percent. By the end of the decade, most Americans were working fewer hours, producing more goods, and earning fatter paychecks. Between 1920 and 1930, factory workers saw their hours decrease from 47.4 per week to 42.1, and their wages increase by about 11 percent.

A number of changes contributed to the new prosperity. Technological innovations improved manufacturing efficiency and yielded new products. Advances in technology allowed for the mass production of manufactured goods at reduced cost. In 1913 Henry Ford had opened the first moving assembly line for manufacturing his Model T automobile, known affectionately as the Tin Lizzie. In 1927 he perfected the assembly line at his River Rouge plant in Michigan. The assembly line, which succeeded by "taking the work to the men instead of the men to the work," emphasized uniformity, speed, and precision that produced high profits for manufacturers and low prices for consumers. The assembly line cut the amount of time it took Ford workers to build a car from twelve and a half hours to sixty seconds. Soon the assembly line became a standard feature in American factories and the key to American industrial supremacy.

Streamlined factories began to run on new power sources, and to produce new products. During the decade, the electric motor replaced the steam engine as the chief source of power. By the end of the decade almost half of the nation's manufacturing plants were powered by electricity. In 1912 only 16 percent of U.S. households had access to electricity; by 1927, that figure had soared to 63 percent. Electricity, in turn, opened up a vast market for home appliances. Americans were bombarded with new devices and gadgets that changed the daily habits of millions: refrigerators, radios, washing machines, automatic ovens, vacuum cleaners, electric toasters. The number of telephones doubled, to over 20 million between 1915 and 1929. "What an age," declared a journalist. "Machines that think. Lights that pierce fog. . . . Vending machines to replace salesmen. . . . The list of modern marvels is practically endless."

Los Angeles Suburb, 1924 This photograph of Whittier Boulevard demonstrates the interconnections in the new economy. Electricity allowed the cheap manufacture of cars and other consumer products, while the automobile fueled the construction of suburbs, and suburbs provided new markets and helped drive a new consumer culture. These advancements also changed the way Americans lived. Cars gave them mobility and freedom, while electricity filled suburban homes with new appliances and other conveniences. *(Seaver Center, Natural History Museum of Los Angeles.)*

It was the phenomenal growth of the automobile industry, however, that provided the keystone for the prosperity of the 1920s. The automobile's impact on the economy in the 1920s was similar to the railroad's impact in the late nineteenth century. By the end of the decade, more than half of all American families owned a car. New York City alone had more cars than the entire continent of Europe. One of every eight U.S. workers was employed in automobile-related jobs. According to one estimate, the industry was responsible for the employment of nearly 4 million workers in 1929. Fifteen percent of all steel and 80 percent of all rubber went into the production of automobiles. By 1925, local and state governments were spending over $1 billion on roads, parkways, bridges, and tunnels to handle the explosion in traffic—the second-highest public expenditure after education. When asked to explain the changes taking place in Muncie, Indiana, during the 1920s, an older resident responded, "I can tell you what's happening in just four letters: A-U-T-O!"

The car gave Americans new mobility, and highway development opened up new areas for settlement and business. Paved roads helped establish a wider sense of community, connecting small towns with larger cities, bringing people who had lived in geographic isolation in touch with a larger universe. By the end of the decade, about one-fifth of America's 3 million miles of roads were paved. Florida built the Tamiami Trail through the swampy Everglades, Arizona paved a road through the desert west of Phoenix, and Massachusetts carved the Mohawk Trail out of the Hoosac mountain range. By 1928, a driver could travel on hard-surfaced roads from New York to Kansas. The nation witnessed a number of "firsts" as the landscape changed to accommodate the new technology: the first "mo-tel" (in San

The Automobile Age   In the 1920s, mass production decreased the price of cars and enabled increasing numbers of Americans to purchase their own. The chart, which traces the tremendous rise of registered passenger cars in the United States, also suggests the growing significance of the automobile in Americans' daily lives.   (Sources: *Historical Statistics of the United States, Colonial Times to 1970.* Washington, D.C.: U.S. Government Printing Office, 1975, 716; *Statistical Abstract of the United States, 1994.* Washington, D.C.: U.S. Government Printing Office, 1994, 630.)

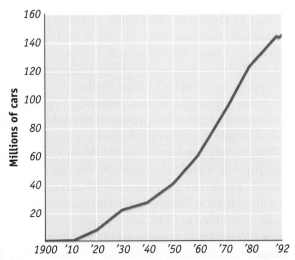

Luis Obispo, California, 1925), first traffic lights (New York City, 1922), first road atlas (1924), and the first parking garage (Detroit, 1929).

The automobile allowed people to escape crowded cities for the more spacious suburbs. For the first time, suburbs (defined as the residential area outside the core city but within the larger metropolitan region) grew at a faster pace than the nation's central cities. The borough of Queens, across the East River from New York City's business district on Manhattan Island, doubled its population in the 1920s. Suburbs surrounding Detroit and Chicago grew by over 700 percent in ten years. By 1930, nearly one in six Americans lived in the suburbs. Most Americans applauded the suburban trend, which made attractive neighborhoods available to ordinary citizens. Signs of future trouble, however, began to simmer: the suburbs drained talent and resources from the inner cities, intensified race and class divisions, and wreaked havoc on the local environment.

The suburban boom was part of an unprecedented demand for new housing that followed World War I as returning veterans swarmed to the cities. Between 1920 and 1930, the population of Miami, Florida, ballooned from 29,571 to 110,637. To accommodate the new demand, cities had to grow both vertically and horizontally. Architects used steel-skeleton construction to build skyscrapers. In 1931 workers completed New York's Empire State Building, which towered eighty-six stories in the sky, making it the tallest building in the world. Big cities were not the only ones building skyscrapers: Tulsa and Oklahoma City, Houston, Cleveland, and dozens of other medium-sized cities boasted skylines. Cities also spread outward, spilling over into the surrounding countryside. Los Angeles, a sprawling metropolis connected by multilane highways, saw its population increase from around 100,000 in 1900 to over 1 million by 1930.

Many corporations turned to advertising to stimulate consumer demand. Advertising income increased from $1.3 billion in 1915 to $3.4 billion in 1929. Advertising, Calvin Coolidge proclaimed in 1926, "is the most potent influence in adopting and changing the habits and modes of life, affecting what we eat, what we wear, and the work and play of the whole nation." The makers of Listerine mouthwash used fear of what their ads called halitosis (bad breath) to increase sales from $100,000 in 1920 to over $4 million in 1927. Public relations man Ivy Lee came up with the slogan "Breakfast of Champions" to sell Wheaties and created Betty Crocker as the symbol for General Mills products. Curtiss Candy Company promoted its Baby Ruth candy bar—"a center of caramel filled with peanuts enrobed in chocolate"—by dropping free samples from an airplane.

For the first time, many companies allowed customers to purchase products on credit. Time payment schemes, reported a special commission on social trends during the decade, allowed people "to telescope the future into the present." A family could purchase a $97.50 washing machine for just $5 down and $8 a month. "A dollar down and a dollar forever," a critic remarked. By the end of the 1920s, Americans were buying over 60 percent of their cars, and 80 percent of their radios and furniture, on the installment plan. Between 1925 and 1929, the amount of money Americans owed creditors doubled to $3 billion.

Paralleling the new techniques in manufacturing and marketing, corporations redesigned their management techniques to make them more effective and efficient.

The spread of "scientific management" (see page 710), pioneered by Frederick W. Taylor before the war, encouraged this trend. Corporations also increased their commitment to research and development and reorganized into divisions organized by function—sales, marketing, production—and created a top tier of management to oversee the entire operation. As corporations grew larger and their stock ownership became more diverse, professional business administrators began to appear in boardrooms. By the end of the decade, a "managerial revolution" had transformed the modern corporation as plant managers and corporate executives, rather than owners, made key decisions.

The businessman bathed in the warm glow of public adulation. A poll of college students early in the decade named Henry Ford the third-greatest figure of all time, trailing behind Jesus Christ and Napoleon. "The man who builds a factory builds a temple," President Coolidge declared. "The man who works there worships there." In a 1925 book entitled *The Man Nobody Knows,* advertising executive Bruce Barton claimed that Jesus Christ was the "founder of modern business." Jesus, he argued, was a great executive who "picked up twelve men from the bottom rank of business and forged them into an organization that conquered the world." The book became an instant bestseller. "Presumably," observed historian Michael Parish, "one served God not only by following a calling but also by taking advantage of the installment plan."

The reorganized corporations accomplished a consolidation of American business. By 1929, the leading two hundred corporations controlled 49 percent of all corporate wealth and received 43 percent of corporate income. Before 1910, two hundred firms had made cars, but by 1930, the Big Three—Ford, General Motors, and Chrysler—with 83 percent of sales, had established their control of the industry. Chain stores, with large inventories and low prices, took the place of smaller, less efficient stores. A&P, the most successful of the new chains, expanded from 400 grocery outlets in 1912 to 15,500 in 1932.

Mass Communications and Mass Culture

The proliferation of chain stores was part of a larger move toward greater standardization in American life. New advances in communications led the way, promoting many of the new consumer products at the same time that they nationalized standards of taste and style. For the first time, millions of Americans shared identical experiences: they watched the same newsreels and films, listened to the same radio broadcasts, and read similar style newspapers.

Movies emerged during the decade as the most popular form of public entertainment. By 1925, twenty thousand theaters dotted the nation. For 50 cents people could watch a silent movie along with a live stage show. In 1929 Chicago theaters had enough seats for half of the city's population to attend a movie each day. By 1930, the average weekly attendance was 90 million. Moviegoers in small towns and big cities flocked to see stars such as Douglas Fairbanks, Charlie Chaplin, Clara Bow, and Joan Crawford. Perhaps Hollywood's most famous silent-screen actor was Rudolph Valentino, an Italian gardener from Long Island, New York, who became the sex symbol of the decade after he abducted the swooning damsel in *The Sheik.* When he died suddenly in 1926, his funeral drew more than thirty thousand female mourners. The movies taught people how to dress, talk, and appear "sexy." Young women imitated Clara Bow's sexual gestures; men copied Valentino's baggy trousers.

Movies were not the only popular form of entertainment shaping a national culture. The growth and influence of radio were equally impressive. Pittsburgh-based Westinghouse station KDKA provided the nation's first public radio broadcast when it reported the presidential election of 1920. The first commercial radio station was licensed in 1921. Within a year 570 stations vied for air space, and hundreds of companies were manufacturing stylish new sets. Broadcasting created a national community of listeners. Early in the decade, local topics dominated the radio airwaves. In Chicago, radio broadcasters included a "Polish Hour," an "Irish Hour," and a "Chicago Federation of Labor Hour." By 1926, two radio giants began consolidating stations into nationwide networks—the National Broadcasting Company (NBC) and Columbia Broadcasting Systems (CBS). Network radio created a new phenomenon: the shared national experience. Millions of Americans, in big cities, small towns, and isolated farms, listened to *The Maxwell House Hour* and *The General Motors Family*.

Changes in print journalism contributed as well to the emergence of national culture. Though the literacy rate was rising rapidly during the 1920s, fewer and fewer sources of information were servicing larger and larger groups of people. The number of local newspapers was shrinking. Chicago boasted seven morning dailies at the beginning of the decade; by the end, only two. More than 600 newspapers died between 1914 and 1926. Many of those that survived were becoming parts of national chains. By 1927, fifty-five chains controlled 230 major newspapers. By the early 1930s, the massive Hearst organization owned one of every four Sunday papers sold in America.

Spectator Sports and the Cult of Individualism

Mass communications made possible another cultural phenomenon of the 1920s: the sports hero. The nineteenth century had admired its sporting heroes, but the mass media extended their reach, transforming local idols into national celebrities. A cultural dimension magnified the nation's fascination with athletic achievement. As society became more urban and collective, nostalgia for the free-spirited, untamed individual became more pronounced. Americans transformed the sports field into a new frontier and the athlete into a pioneer. In athletic competition, as on the frontier, men confronted physical obstacles and overcame them with talent and determination. Victory was the result of superior ability and courageous perseverance.

Millions of Americans crowded into halls to watch boxers, both professional and amateur, slug it out in the ring. No boxer received more adulation than Jack Dempsey, who embodied the nation's frontier past. Raised in Manassas, Colorado, he learned to fight in local bars against miners, cowboys, and anyone else foolish enough to challenge him. "Jack Dempsey hit like a sledgehammer and absorbed punishment like a sponge," wrote historian Michael Parrish. "He was not a boxer, but an earthquake that left blood, flesh, and bone scattered in its wake." During the twenties his two grueling championship bouts with Gene Tunney proved enormously popular. In 1926 Tunney defeated Dempsey in their first fight before a rain-soaked crowd in Philadelphia. While as many as 150,000 people paid to see their rematch the following year in Chicago, some 50 million listened to it on radio. The referee's famous "long count" may have cost Dempsey the second fight when he knocked Tunney to the canvas but failed to go immediately to a neutral corner.

Having gained momentum during the late nineteenth century (see page 745), baseball earned its reputation as the national pastime during the 1920s. Rooted in the nation's rural past, the game was now played in front of largely urban audiences. While talented players such as Lou Gehrig, Rogers Hornsby, Dazzy Vance, Walter Johnson, and Grover Alexander kept the myth of individualism alive, the game had become big business during the new corporate era of the 1920s.

No one did more for the game than "Bambino," Babe Ruth, who single-handedly transformed a contest of pitching and defense into a game of sluggers. Raised in an orphanage, Ruth showed that the American dream of rags to riches still existed in an industrial age. The New York Yankees, with Ruth clobbering home runs, won the American League pennant three consecutive years from 1926 to 1928, and the World Series twice. In 1927 he hit sixty home runs in a season of 154 games establishing one of sports' most enduring records. Three years later, the gate receipts having steadily mounted, the Yankees opened a grand new stadium in the Bronx, "the house that Ruth built." Ruth embraced his new role as celebrity. The first professional athlete to hire a press agent, Ruth used his star status to sell a host of new consumer products, everything from fishing equipment to alligator shoes.

Babe Ruth and His Fans   The rise of mass culture in the 1920s created national celebrities in sports and entertainment. The radio, the growth of leisure time, the automobile, and other aspects of modern culture made such fame possible. Here, Babe Ruth, the well-known and well-loved Yankee slugger, is seen in Syracuse, New York, engulfed by admirers, most of them young men and boys. *(Corbis-Bettmann.)*

Barred from segregated professional baseball, African-Americans developed the Negro League during the 1920s, which featured their own stars. In 1923 four hundred thousand black fans turned out to watch Negro league pitchers "Smokey Joe" Williams and "Bullet" Joe Rogan intimidate opposing hitters, or marvel at the speed and power of Oscar Charleston. While the mainstream media ignored black baseball players, they became popular figures in black communities across the United States.

The exploits of Ruth and Dempsey filled newspapers and airwaves but never exhausted the appetite of American consumers for sports heroes and heroines, who reaffirmed the value of individualism in a corporate, collectivized society. In his final college football season, Harold Edward "Red" Grange, the Galloping Ghost, rushed for over 360 yards against Pennsylvania. After college he signed with the Chicago Bears, who paid him the then astonishing sum of $12,000 a game. In addition to his successful football career, Grange had a lucrative business off the field endorsing products, selling chocolate bars, and even acting in a Hollywood movie. In 1923 seventeen-year-old Helen Wills won the women's singles title at the U.S. Open. That same year, Johnny Weissmuller swam the 200-yard freestyle in 1:59, then the fastest time in history. He won two gold medals in the 1924 Olympic games in Paris, and a third, four years later at Amsterdam. He went on to become a Hollywood star.

The Limits of Prosperity

Not everyone benefited from the extraordinary changes transforming American society. Some older industries, unable to satisfy changing consumer tastes, suffered during the decade. Railroads were unable to compete with the emerging trucking industry. Mine owners abandoned some coal fields, along with the mine workers, as more Americans used petroleum and electricity as sources of energy. The development of synthetic fibers for textiles turned New England cotton mill communities into ghost towns. Despite the postwar construction boom, lumber companies from Washington to Georgia showed only modest gains as builders turned to substitute materials such as concrete. While millions of Americans benefited from the booming economy, class barriers remained firmly entrenched. Sociologists Robert and Helen Lynd spent years studying the daily habits of residents of Muncie, Indiana. The "division into working class and business class" constituted "the outstanding cleavage" in the community noted the Lynds, determining everything from the schools people attended to the quality and variety of food they ate.

Small farmers suffered the most during the decade. During World War I, government purchases of farm products, combined with the devastation of European agriculture, had inflated prices for many crops. Between 1916 and 1919, net farm income more than doubled, from $4 billion to $10 billion. Convinced the prosperity would continue into the next decade, farmers took out loans to buy land and expand operations with new machinery. But the bubble burst in 1920 when the U.S. government stopped buying wheat and European farms recovered from the war. Prices plummeted as the market flooded with surplus crops. In just a few months in 1920, farmers watched as the price of a bushel of wheat plunged from $2.50 to less than $1. The value of cotton, hogs, and cattle suffered similar declines. Declining prices cut net farm income by 50 percent in one year. During the decade, both farm net income and real purchasing power fell by 25 percent. By the end of the decade, as they watched their share of the national income drop from 16 percent in 1919 to 8.8 percent, hundreds of thousands of farmers quit the land and looked for jobs in mills and factories.

In May 1921, a group of congressmen from agricultural states organized the farm bloc to fight for laws to aid beleaguered farmers. The new group managed to push through Congress a number of measures, but it was unable to address the basic problem of low farm prices. On four separate occasions Congress debated legislation that would have established federal price supports for agricultural products. Under the proposals, the government would purchase surplus crops according to "a fair exchange formula" that would protect farmers from wild fluctuations in the market. In the first two attempts the bills languished in Congress, but in 1926 and again in 1927 Congress managed to pass the legislation. Both times President Coolidge vetoed the experiment in government intervention.

Industrial workers fared better than farmers. Most workers saw their standard of living increase during the decade. Some workers benefited from a new paternalism among many employers, an experiment that came to be called "welfare capitalism." The term applied to a broad range of programs designed to inspire worker loyalty and to promote efficiency. "We must find ways and means to help our workers get their worries out of their minds, so they can get on the job rarin' to go," said E. K. Hall, president of American Telephone and Telegraph Company. A few of the country's largest corporations hoped to avoid labor disputes and limit the growth of unions by establishing grievance committees, group life insurance, old-age pensions, creating "employee representation" or company unions, and stock ownership plans. Henry Ford, for example, raised wages, shortened the workweek, and offered paid vacations.

Corporate paternalism failed to alter the gross inequities between labor and management, however. Most workers earned less than the $1,800 needed to maintain a decent standard of living. Welfare capitalism also affected only a small number of employees who happened to work in large corporations. It did nothing for teenage girls who worked long hours in cotton mills for 16 to 18 cents an hour, or for miners who enjoyed neither regular work nor basic civil liberties, such as freedom of speech. "We work in *his* mine," one complained. "We live in *his* house. Our children go to *his* school. On Sunday we're preached at by *his* preacher. When we die we're buried in *his* cemetery."

The combination of corporate assertiveness, political resistance, and labor timidity produced a decline in union membership from 5 million in 1920 to less than 3 million by 1929. In the wake of the reaction against suspected radicals during the Red Scare of 1919–1920, corporations exploited the fear of radicalism to push for open shop laws by which workers could choose *not* to join a local union. The National Association of Manufacturers called the open shop the "American Plan." The Supreme Court sanctioned many of the anti-union efforts, especially after the appointment of William Howard Taft as chief justice in 1921. Between 1921 and 1925, the Court issued a series of rulings that restricted the right to strike and limited the effectiveness of child labor and minimum wage laws.

Workers who tried fighting against the conservative tide by unionizing faced numerous obstacles during the decade. The Red Scare had marginalized radical labor leaders, giving added power to the conservative leadership of the American Federation of Labor (AFL), which concentrated its energy on working with business to maintain benefits for its skilled workers. Some people hoped that the death of cigar-chomping Samuel Gompers in 1924 would breathe new life into the AFL. But the new president, William Green of the United Mine Workers, did not alter the AFL's basic philosophy or tactics. Like Gompers, Green was more interested in maintaining the economic privileges of the craft unions' skilled members than in extending unionism to the 90 percent of the work force that remained unorganized. The AFL was also determined to convince the public that it was a respectable organization. Consequently, the number of strikes declined dramatically, from one hundred a year in 1919–1920, to only eighteen by the end of the decade.

Women found new opportunities as the business expansion increased the need for office clerks, typists, telephone operators, and salespeople. Two million women went to work during the decade, driving up the total to 10.8 million, a fivefold increase since 1914. The number of married women in the work force jumped from 15 percent of working women in 1900 to 29 percent in 1930. During that period, the number of women working in the professions increased by 50 percent. While impressive, the gains did little to challenge male domination of the workplace. Most working-class women clustered in the low-paying areas already defined as "women's work"—typing, stenography, bookkeeping, and sales. Three of four professional women entered areas such as education and social work, which had already been carved out and designated as "women's fields." The vast majority of working wives were African-Americans who were pushed by poverty into employment. "The woman," a reformer noted in 1929, "is nearly always the cheap or marginal worker, and . . . she is expected by the public and the employer to remain one."

The decade's prosperity also eluded the overwhelming majority of nonwhite Americans. Despite the movement of nearly 2.5 million blacks to northern cities by the end of the 1920s, most black Americans continued to labor in the South as tenant farmers, sharecroppers, and farm workers. In 1930 about 3 million blacks—25 percent of the nation's total black population—lived in the three Deep South states of Georgia, Mississippi, and Alabama, and 80 percent of these lived in rural poverty. Even in the North, blacks were systematically excluded from the work force, barred from joining most unions, and forced to live in segregated neighborhoods.

Mexicans, by far the largest minority group in the Southwest, suffered similar social and economic discrimination. According to the U.S. Immigration Service, an estimated 459,000 Mexicans entered the United States between 1921 and 1930. In the area from Texas, New Mexico, and Colorado to California, Mexicans provided much of the labor that transformed the desert landscape into rich agricultural farmland. Seventy-five percent of California's farm laborers, for example, were Mexican. Many Mexican-Americans gravitated toward the cities. By the end of the 1920s, Hispanics made up more than half the population of El Paso, slightly less than half of San Antonio, and one-fifth of Los Angeles.

The Culture of Dissent

In *Preface to Morals* (1929), journalist Walter Lippmann referred to the "acids of modernity" to describe the forces that were corroding the stability and certainty of contemporary life. Among the most corrosive acids were, first, a new morality that was eating away at Victorian notions of womanhood and, second, a chorus of intellectuals who questioned tradition and criticized the crass materialism of modern society. At the same time, African-Americans startled white America with new cultural and political institutions to articulate a sense of racial pride and to explore the dilemmas of race.

The New Morality and the New Woman

During the 1920s, many young women in large urban areas challenged traditional assumptions and experimented with new expressions of freedom. Teenage girls adopted the flapper image: The flapper wore cosmetics, cut her hair short, and hemmed her skirts above the knee. The flapper drank openly, played golf on public courses, and practiced the latest dances, which, according to one minister, brought "the bodies of men and women in unusual relations to each other." The liberated women of the 1920s considered cigarette smoking a symbol of emancipation. "Cigarette in hand, shimmying to the music of the masses, the New Woman and the New Morality have made their theatric debut upon the modern scene," observed a journalist.

The Ziegfield Follies Girls
One product of modernity was the "New Woman," characterized by her more overt sexuality and her greater personal freedom. The women performers of the Ziegfield Follies, seen here wearing skimpy bathing attire, exemplified the new female image. They are standing with the beaming Roscoe Turner, a famed air-racer, and another sign of modernity, his Sikorsky-29 airplane. *(W. P. Mayfield photograph, Marvin Christian Collection.)*

Changing sexual practices were among the most obvious manifestations of the "new morality." Middle-class girls led the way in replacing old courtship rules by which male suitors would "call" on them at home—under the watchful eye of a parent—with a new "dating" system in which a couple would go out unsupervised. The automobile, which replaced the front porch, contributed to the new dating ritual by providing young couples with an escape from their parents' scrutiny. Dating and the automobile contributed to another innovation in social ritual—petting. Traditionalists suggested that a woman not allow a man to kiss her unless he intended to marry her. One study of college youth during the 1920s found that 92 percent of coeds had engaged in kissing. A judge in Muncie declared that of thirty girls brought before his court for "sex crimes," nineteen had committed their crimes in a car.

The virtual legalization of birth control information and devices in many states permitted a substantial number of Americans to put into practice the radical idea that sex could be a source of pleasure detached from procreation. Birth control, wrote Walter Lippmann "is the most revolutionary practice in the history of sexual morals." It legitimized female sexuality, promoted sexual experimentation, and transformed marital ideals. Use of the diaphragm became commonplace among middle-class women. A survey in 1925 showed that 60 percent of women used contraceptives; for middle-class women, the figures were even higher. Family size declined accordingly during the 1920s as the birthrate fell from near 24 per thousand in 1920 to less than 19 per thousand in 1930.

By separating sex from procreation, birth control liberated women from "involuntary motherhood," raising expectations that marriage could be based on companionship and shared interest. Women now envisioned "sharing joys and sorrows with a mate who will be not merely a protector and provider but an all round companion." Sexuality was central to the marriage of the 1920s. In her manual *Happiness in Marriage*, birth control advocate Margaret Sanger wrote that both partners must realize "the importance of complete fulfillment of love through the expression of sex." The changed expectations may have contributed to a rising divorce rate. By 1928, one of every seven marriages ended in divorce.

To many Americans, recently publicized Freudian psychology seemed to support the new morality. Freud, the famous Viennese physician, had visited the United States briefly in 1909, but his theories about unconscious sexual urges failed to reach a larger audience until the 1920s. Webster's dictionary added the word *Freudian* to the language and terms such as *id* and *superego* became familiar. Numerous Americans became obsessed with Freud's psychosexual theories, but the public, misunderstanding the complexities of the irrational and the unconscious, grossly simplified them. Popular interpreters suggested that Freud called for abandoning all sexual inhibition and advocated unrestrained self-gratification. "Are you shackled by repressed desires?" asked an ad in a popular magazine. "Psychoanalysis, the new miracle science, proves that most people live only half-power lives because of repressed sex instincts."

Popular culture reinforced the emphasis on sex. People turned on the radio to hear songs with titles such as "Hot Lips," "I Need Lovin'," and "Burning Kisses." Popular movies included *Sinners in Silk*, *Women Who Give*, and *Rouged Lips*. Advertisers emphasized youth and beauty to sell their products. A clothing advertisement addressing a middle-aged woman acknowledged that "within this woman's soul burns still the flame of her desire for charm and beauty." Many women responded to the new sales pitch. The number of beauty shops expanded from five thousand to forty thousand during the decade. Between 1914 and 1925, sales of cosmetics exploded from $17 to $141 million. It was during the 1920s that the Miss America beauty contests became an annual ritual. The focus was exclusively on physical beauty. Contestants might have talent, noted one of the organizers, but "things would be better if they kept it to themselves."

The movement for sexual freedom was not as threatening to the family as many contemporaries feared. Despite their suggestive titles, most movies featured the wife returning to her husband and the young woman marrying the boy next door. Sexual liberation had little impact on the lives of working-class or minority women who struggled with the more mundane problems of earning a living and supporting a family. Even the liberated attitudes of young urbanites were wedded to old-fashioned aspirations. Few were willing to sacrifice marriage for career but hoped rather to attain "a richer and fuller life" with "an all round companion." Progressive women's colleges, such as Smith, Vassar, and Bryn Mawr, taught the value of domesticity. By the middle of the 1920s, Vassar offered courses in "Husband and Wife," "Motherhood," and the "Family as an Economic Unit." The college also founded a School of Euthenics whose purpose was to educate women "along the lines of their chief interest and responsibilities, motherhood and the home." Most of the Vassar women polled as early as 1923 believed that marriage was "the biggest of all careers."

The decade's preoccupation with private behavior prevented women from making significant gains in the public sphere. The achievement of suffrage removed the central issue that had given cohesion to the disparate forces of female reform activism. In the first few years of the decade, Congress responded to the possibility of an organized women's vote by passing the Sheppard-Towner Act of 1921. The first federal health care act, Sheppard-Towner provided states with matching federal funds to establish centers for mothers and children. Within a few years, however, much of the energy of the suffrage campaign had dissipated as young women showed little interest in organized feminism. "'Feminism' has become a term of opprobrium to the modern young woman," writer Dorothy Dunbar Bromley told the readers of *Harper's* in 1927.

Not only were young women less interested in the cause, but mainstream reformers split into rival camps at the end of the war. On one side stood the National American Woman Suffrage Association, which reorganized itself as the League of Women Voters (LWV) in 1920. About one-tenth of its former size, the league fought to democratize political parties, abolish child labor, and support protective legislation for women and children. On the other side of the debate, the National Woman's Party (NWP), founded in 1921, planned to fight for full legal and civil equality by working "to remove all the remaining forms of the subjection of women." In 1923 the NWP proposed a brief Equal Rights Amendment to the Constitution, which declared that "Men and women shall have equal rights throughout the United States and every place subject to its jurisdiction." Many social reformers complained that the NWP's agenda of outlawing legal discrimination ignored the concerns of working-class women, who were the chief beneficiaries of protective laws. "Women cannot be made men" by constitutional amendment, Florence Kelly charged. The conflict over equality and protection dominated women's politics during the decade, dividing the movement and decreasing its influence.

Discontent of the Intellectuals

The literature of the 1920s rebelled against the standardization of American life that resulted from mass production and large-scale industrialization. Disillusionment in the aftermath of World War I's seemingly senseless slaughter increased the tone of despair among young American writers, prompting Gertrude Stein to describe them as "a lost generation." Although a diverse group, these writers all explored the problems of life in an age of machines and mass culture, in a time of uncertainty and skepticism.

The theme of rootlessness and cynicism pervades the writing of the most famous writers of the Lost Generation. Ernest Hemingway, perhaps the most celebrated American writer of the twenties, captured the sense of loss following World War I. His characters are interested in simple pleasures, not lofty ideals. In *The Sun Also Rises* (1926) a hopelessly lost pack of friends travels from Paris to Pamplona in an alcoholic stupor, their adventures chronicled by Jake Barnes, whom the war left both physically and emotionally impotent. In his first novel of the decade, *This Side of Paradise* (1920), F. Scott Fitzgerald depicted a world occupied by a generation "grown up to find all Gods dead, all wars fought, all faith in man shaken."

While Hemingway and Fitzgerald focused on personal alienation, others launched a wider attack on the sterility of American culture, inveighing against the materialism and provincialism of contemporary life. In the pages of his magazines, first *The Smart Set* and later *The American Mercury,* Henry Louis Mencken ridiculed small-town and rural America. "Civilized life," he charged, was not "possible under a democracy" because it placed government in the hands of common people. Sinclair Lewis's *Main Street* (1920) described the complacency and narrow-mindedness that seemed to symbolize all small American communities. His most famous novel, *Babbitt* (1922), told the story of a small-town real-estate agent whose "symbols of truth and beauty" are mechanical contraptions. Lewis received wide acclaim for his penetrating portraits of national life and in 1930 became the first American to win a Nobel Prize in literature.

Many artists experimented with new modes of expression to capture the chaos of life in the machine age. Poets Hart Crane, e.e. cummings, and William Carlos Williams displayed new rhythms and challenged traditional lyric forms. Cummings, for example, underscored the irrationality of contemporary society by ignoring rules of capitalization and using inventive punctuation. In his powerful trilogy, *U.S.A.,* the novelist John Dos Passos used unconventional methods— "Newsreel" and "Camera Eye"—to break up the narrative and convey the fragmentation of modern life.

Intellectuals in other disciplines contributed to the critique of contemporary society. The Lynds' *Middletown: A Study in American Culture* emerged as the most influential sociological study of the decade. The authors exposed a wide gulf between the theory and practice of American democracy. Franz Boas, the father of modern anthropology, questioned traditional ideas about racial inferiority. He used the data from measurements of black skulls and brain cavities to help disprove the myth that low scores by blacks on intelligence tests were due to smaller, inferior brains. In a series of books beginning with *The Mind of Primitive Man* (1911), he demonstrated that environment, not heredity, played a major role in determining ability. Other anthropologists used similar scientific methods to question the superiority of Western culture. After studying Indian cultures in the Southwest, Ruth Benedict praised the uncompetitive and nonmaterialistic Zuñi tribe of Pueblo Indians. She published her findings in an influential book, *Patterns of Culture*.

New Visions in Black America

The northward migration of African-Americans stimulated by the war continued into the 1920s, when as many as 600,000 migrated from the South. By 1920, 2 million of the nation's 11 million blacks lived in the North. During the decade New York City's black population climbed from 152,000 to 328,000, Chicago's from 109,000 to 233,000. In New York's Harlem and Chicago's South Side, growing numbers of African-Americans crowded into grimy tenements. In 1927 a housing commission reported of Harlem that "the State would not allow cows to live in some of these apartments."

African-Americans faced rigid discrimination in employment. Most blacks could find jobs only as menial or unskilled workers, and even then took home less pay than their white counterparts. Most black men who found jobs worked as porters, waiters, or janitors; black women served as cooks, domestics, and washerwomen. There were two kinds of businesses in New York, the sociologist E. Franklin Frazier commented, "those that employ Negroes in menial positions, and those that employ no Negroes at all." Poverty produced chronic ill-health: the syphilis rate in Harlem was nine times higher than in white Manhattan; the tuberculosis rate was five times higher; and the pneumonia and typhoid rates were twice as high. The concentration of blacks in the industrial cities of the North increased racial tension that occasionally flared into violence. In the early 1920s, riots exploded in Knoxville, Tennessee, and Omaha, Nebraska.

These conditions made possible the spectacular success of Marcus Garvey. Born and raised in Jamaica, Garvey arrived in the United States in 1916 at the age of 28. In 1917 he established the United Negro Improvement Association (UNIA) in order to promote "the spirit of race pride and love." The following year he founded a weekly newspaper, *Negro World*, which exhorted blacks to build independent social and economic institutions and look toward Africa as a future homeland. He took as his colors red (for slave blood), black (for skin color), and green (for African fertility). "The world has made being black a crime," he said; "I hope to make it a virtue." His flamboyance, together with the pride in color that he evoked, gave his movement an unprecedented mass appeal in Harlem in the early 1920s. The UNIA claimed more than 700 branches in thirty-eight states while his newspaper had a weekly circulation of between 50,000 and 200,000.

Garvey tapped into a deep undercurrent of black nationalism, a desire to build and sustain African-American institutions. "We have a beautiful history," he declared,

UNIA Parade with Marcus Garvey   The black struggle for equality moved into a more militant phase in the 1920s. Marcus Garvey, the flamboyant founder of the United Negro Improvement Association, gained a huge following in the United States, particularly among lower-class blacks. His message of racial pride and self-help appealed to many African-Americans who had grown discouraged by the relentless racial discrimination they faced. But Garvey's movement faltered when the U.S. government deported him in 1927 for business fraud and mismanagement. (*© Donna Mussenden VanDerZee.*)

"and we shall create another one in the future." He established the Negro Factories Corporation, which operated grocery stores, restaurants, and a clothing factory. He sold stock to followers to create the Black Star Line, which owned three ships for transporting passengers between the United States, the West Indies, and Africa. All the employees—over one thousand at its peak—were black. "Girls who could only be washerwomen in your homes, we made clerks and stenographers," Garvey told white businessmen. There was, however, a darker side to Garvey's racial views. He championed the notion of "a pure black race" and opposed race mixing. He attacked moderate black leaders who tried to build alliances with white moderates.

Garvey's ideas were controversial among other black leaders. Many middle-class blacks rejected his separatist ideas, while the leaders of other activist groups complained that Garvey distracted people from the real battle for economic equality. A. Philip Randolph, a socialist and cofounder of the *Messenger* (subtitled the "Only Radical Negro Magazine in America"), was one of Garvey's toughest critics. Randolph tried to forge an interracial coalition of low-income people. In 1925 he started the Brotherhood of Sleeping Car Porters in an effort to develop working-class consciousness among African-Americans. Throughout the decade, he campaigned for interracial organization of workers and called for militant demonstrations aimed at breaking the power of corporate elites.

When Garvey's steamship line fell on hard financial times, many prominent black businessmen alerted J. Edgar Hoover, director of the Justice Department's general intelligence division who was about to become head of the FBI. Hoover's agents infiltrated the UNIA, combing through its records for incriminating evidence. Poor record keeping made an indictment easy, and in 1922 the government charged Garvey with using the mail to defraud investors. The following year he was convicted and sentenced to five years in prison. Late in 1927 President Coolidge commuted his sentence and the government deported him as an undesirable alien. He would spend the remaining twelve years of his life in exile in Jamaica and London.

The expressions of black nationalism were not confined to politics. The decade witnessed an extraordinary outburst of African-American writing, unprecedented both in the amount of poetry and fiction that it produced and in its racial assertiveness. The literary renaissance was based in New York's Harlem, which became a mecca for aspiring African-American artists during the 1920s. "We younger Negro artists," wrote Langston Hughes, the poet laureate of Harlem, "intend to express our individual dark-skinned selves without fear or shame." The person who did most to publicize the movement was Alaine Locke, a Phi Beta Kappa graduate of Harvard, and the first black awarded a prestigious Rhodes scholarship at England's Oxford University. "In Harlem," he wrote, "Negro life is seizing upon its first chances for group expression and self-determination."

Despite its intense poverty, Harlem emerged during the 1920s as a bubbling caldron of creativity. People gathered in small cafés and clubs to listen to the jazz musicians Louis Armstrong and Edward "Duke" Ellington. Painters such as Aaron Douglas and Archibald Motley, Jr., translated the jazz aesthetic onto canvas by using a new visual language of bold colors and improvised compositions. Singers such as Florence Mills and Ethel Waters performed in the growing circuit of black nightclubs, theaters, and vaudeville houses.

Many black artists who gathered in Harlem used their poetry, novels, and short stories to give expression to the pain of racism and to examine what it meant to be black in America. "I, too, sing America," Hughes wrote. "I am the darker brother. / They send me to eat in the kitchen / When the company comes, / But I laugh, / And eat well, / And grow strong." Questions of black identity were at the heart of much of the work produced in the Harlem Renaissance: What did it mean to be black in America during the 1920s? While some African-American artists emphasized the similarities between black and white cultures, most tried to build on the distinctiveness of the black experience in America.

The Guardians

Many of the New Era's instruments of mass culture—the automobile, the radio, and movies—forced a renewed confrontation between traditional Protestant values associated with the rural past and the new urban culture. "Americanism still has a mission to the world," declared Henry Ford's *Dearborn Independent,* but "we shall have to save ourselves before we can hope to save anyone else." Salvation, self-proclaimed guardians of American tradition believed, required an assault on foreign immigrants, a revival of fundamentalist Christianity, and the enforcement of prohibition.

The Revival of Nativism

World War I all but halted the influx of immigrants to the United States, but the flood resumed immediately afterward. In 1919, 110,000 immigrants arrived; in 1921 the figure shot up to 805,000, of whom two-thirds were from southern and eastern Europe. The new wave of immigration rekindled widespread concern that "inferior" immigrants from southern or eastern European stock, along with blacks and other undesirables, would overwhelm white, Protestant America. "The welfare of the United States demands that the door should be closed to immigrants for a time," observed an influential congressman in 1920. "We are being made a dumping-ground for the human wreckage of the [world] war." The fears were widespread: Journalists complained that in cities such as New York, where three out of every four persons were foreigners or the children of foreigners, immigrants were responsible for rising crime rates. Prominent scientists, infatuated by new theories of eugenics, claimed that recent immigrants from southern Europe and Asia possessed more "inborn socially inadequate qualities" and were therefore unable to assimilate. Business leaders fretted that the newcomers would swell the ranks of organized labor.

In 1924 Congress responded to these fears by passing the Johnson-Reed Immigration Act. Under the law, the government allocated visas to Eastern Hemisphere nations in ratios determined by the number of persons of each nationality in the United States in 1890. Not surprisingly, Europe consumed 98 percent of the quota, leaving only 2 percent for the rest of the world. Three countries—Ireland, Great Britain, and Germany—accounted for nearly 70 percent of the total. In addition to dramatically cutting immigration rates from southern Europe—Italians and Greeks were especially hard hit—the law almost completely excluded Asians. The quota did not apply to spouses or minor children of U.S. citizens or to residents of the Western Hemisphere, who could emigrate without restriction. In 1929 Congress legislated an even more draconian measure that set the yearly immigration quota at 150,000, with the proportion of entering nationals based on the 1920 census. Italy, for example, could send 6,000 immigrants under this law, although hundreds of thousands wished to enter.

Many intellectuals who opposed nativism viewed the sensational trial of two Italian immigrants, Nicola Sacco and Bartolomeo Vanzetti, as evidence of the decade's intolerance of foreigners. In 1920 Sacco and Vanzetti were arrested and charged with the murders of a paymaster and guard in South Braintree, Massachusetts. Both were convicted and sentenced to death after a trial marked by gross prejudice. Presiding Judge Webster Thayer, for example, referred to the defendants as "anarchistic bastards" and "damned dagos." Their cause won worldwide sympathy. Prominent writers such as John Dos Passos, liberal jurists such as Felix Frankfurter of the Harvard Law School, and Socialist Eugene Debs rallied around the convicted men. The verdict pleased some, such as evangelist Billy Sunday, who stormed: "Give 'em the juice. Burn them if they're guilty. That's the way to handle it. I'm tired of hearing these foreigners, these radicals, coming over here and telling us what we should do." On August 23, 1927, after years of protest and appeals, Sacco and Vanzetti died in the electric chair. After the executions, many in the funeral cortege wore armbands emblazoned, "Remember—Justice Crucified—August 23, 1927."

The "New" Klan

The revival of the Ku Klux Klan represented the most dramatic example of the rise of nativist and racist sentiment. In the years following the Civil War, white southerners had organized the Ku Klux Klan to terrorize blacks and prevent them from voting. This early organization passed away with the end of Reconstruction. The modern Klan was organized in 1915 by William J. Simmons, a onetime Methodist minister. On Stone Mountain, outside Atlanta, Georgia, before an American flag and a burning cross, the faithful swore allegiance to the new Klan. The ceremony coincided with the appearance in Atlanta of the popular motion picture *The Birth of a Nation,* which depicted heroic Klansmen redeeming the South from the grip of Radical Reconstruction. In the early 1920s millions of Americans joined the hooded order, although membership probably never exceeded 1.5 million at any one time.

The new Klan was not simply a reincarnation of the old. The Klan of the 1920s, although strong in the South, was stronger still in Indiana, Illinois, and Ohio. Perhaps three of every five members lived outside the South or Southwest. The new Klan also was not as heavily rural, but enlisted members in Chicago, Detroit, Atlanta, Denver, and other cities. One of every three Klansmen lived in a city with a population of over a hundred thousand. Finally, the Klan was no longer primarily a white supremacist group. The Invisible Empire gained legitimacy by fashioning itself as a middle-class Protestant populist movement crusading for social purity and against vice, crime, and deteriorating morality.

To symbolize its role as the inspired guardian of social and religious tradition, the Klan carried ritual, pageantry, and secrecy to the extreme. Klansmen met in a Klavern, held Klonklaves, carried on Klonversations, and even sang Klodes. They followed a Kalendar in which 1867 was the year 1. The white gowns and hoods they wore during ritualistic meetings stood for a purity of life now under siege from alien elements. To preserve that purity, the Klan resorted to threats, cross-burnings, beatings, kidnappings, mutilations, and murders.

In many states, women counted for nearly half of all Klan members. In Indiana, one-third of white native-born women in the state joined the Klan. What attracted so many women to the group? For many native-born white Protestant women, the Klan provided a social setting to celebrate their racial and religious privileges. Viewing the Klan as a powerful force for protecting their communities from corruption and immorality, Klanswomen mixed support for white Protestant women's rights with racist, anti-Semitic, and anti-Catholic politics. Women dramatically extended the reach of the Klan by orchestrating consumer boycotts through "whisper" campaigns, which encouraged people to avoid merchants who failed the test of whiteness and Protestantism.

The boycotts served as a powerful economic weapon, allowing the Klan to become a potent political force in California, Ohio, Indiana, and Oregon, as well as in the South. It showed considerable strength in northern cities, especially those to which blacks and immigrants had streamed during recent years. In Texas it helped elect a senator, held a majority in the state legislature for a time, and controlled the city government in Dallas, Fort Worth, and Wichita Falls. The Indiana Klan, under David Stephenson, built a machine that dominated state politics. In Denver a

KKK Women Marching in Washington   The revived Ku Klux Klan of the 1920s differed from its predecessor in its greater religious intolerance and its wider geographical spread. It also included large numbers of women for the first time. The presence of women was important to the Klan's claim to the role of guardian of traditional morality. The women who joined did so for the feeling of importance and power the Klan offered its members.   *(Library of Congress.)*

Klansman was named manager of public safety. On August 8, 1925, in a brazen demonstration of strength, more than fifty thousand Klan members marched down Pennsylvania Avenue in Washington, D.C.

After 1925, a series of internal power struggles and sordid scandals eroded support for the Klan. By 1930, the organization was in disarray. A fitting symbol of the organization's fall from grace occurred in Atlanta, where the Catholic Church took over the Klan's national offices and turned the building into the official residence of the archbishop.

Fundamentalism

Apparent disparities between modern science and religion became another focus for the cultural conflicts of the 1920s. The main dispute centered around Darwinism versus Biblical beliefs. Charles Darwin's *Origin of Species* (1859) posited a gradual evolution of species over a period of several million years, a theory at odds with God's seven-day creation of the world described in the biblical book of Genesis. Many modern Christians had reconciled the differences by accepting the Bible as divinely inspired but not literally true. Many others, however, rejected any compromise with Darwinism. These fundamentalists clung to the view that the truths of Scripture were absolute and all one needed to know. Fundamentalists were numerous during the 1920s, especially in the rural South. As the celebrated journalist H. L. Mencken noted, you could "heave an egg out of a Pullman and you will hit a Fundamentalist almost everywhere in the United States."

In the early 1920s fundamentalists crusaded for laws that would prohibit the teaching of Darwinism in public schools (see Competing Voices, page 964). More than twenty states debated such laws, but they became law in only five—Oklahoma, Florida, Tennessee, Mississippi, and Arkansas. The Tennessee bill barred the teaching of "any theory that denies the Story of the Divine Creation of Man as taught in the Bible, and [holds] instead that man has descended from a lower order of animals." In 1925 a group of citizens in Dayton, Tennessee, noticed an advertisement in a local newspaper by the American Civil Liberties Union (ACLU) offering support to any teacher who challenged the Tennessee law. Seeing an opportunity to draw much-needed attention (and business) to the sleepy town, they contacted part-time teacher John Scopes, who agreed to challenge the law, and a local official, who promised to prosecute.

The publicity stunt proved a dramatic success: press from around the world flooded into Dayton to cover "the trial of the century." The nation's foremost defense attorney, Clarence Darrow, agreed to defend Scopes. Former Democratic Party presidential nominee William Jennings Bryan joined the prosecution. The trial not only forged a dramatic confrontation between religion and science, it represented a clash between competing ideas of government. Bryan believed that the majority had the right to legislate whatever set of moral or ethical standards it desired. The ACLU and Darrow contended that anti-evolution laws violated freedom of religion by forcing the state to teach the biblical version of creation.

At the trial, Bryan defended the state's anti-evolution law by insisting that "it is better to trust in the Rock of Ages than to know the age of rocks; it is better for one to know that he is close to the Heavenly Father than to know how far the stars in the heavens are apart." But Bryan wilted under Darrow's intense cross-examination. He admitted that religious dogma was subject to more than one interpretation, and he conceded that the "day" of creation might mean a million years. For many members of the press, Bryan's poor performance on the witness stand symbolized the triumph of modernist scientific thinking over religious fundamentalism. The victory, however, was not so clear-cut. Not only was Scopes found guilty (his conviction was later overturned on a technicality), but anti-evolution laws remained on the books for forty-two more years. By 1930, 70 percent of high schools in the United States omitted any reference to evolution. Despite press ridicule of Bryan, who died two weeks after the trial ended, religious fundamentalism would remain a power in American life for decades to come.

Fundamentalism held the allegiance of millions of Americans thanks in part to the work of extraordinary revivalists who used fire-and-brimstone sermons to warn their followers of the evils of modern life. The athletic Billy Sunday strode back and forth across the stage, often stomping and jumping to emphasize his points. Perhaps the most popular evangelist was the Canadian-born Aimee Semple McPherson. The flamboyant McPherson, dressed in white satin robes, proclaimed the gospel from her huge lakefront temple outside Los Angeles. Preaching with the help of three bands, two orchestras, three choirs, and six quartets, she combined Hollywood showmanship, New York advertising, and old-fashioned religion to become the nation's most famous revivalist by the end of the decade. McPherson was as effective at raising money as she was at saving souls. A year after the temple was opened, Sister Aimee began broadcasting "The Sunshine Hour" every morning over Los Angeles radio station KFSG, which stood for Kalling Foursquare Gospel, the name of her church.

The Unintended Consequences of Prohibition

The progressive fascination with social efficiency and scientific management had helped secure passage of the Eighteenth Amendment banning the sale of alcohol. By the time it became law in 1920, however, prohibition became a rallying cry for those Americans who were fearful of the changes transforming the nation and hopeful of returning to a simpler past. At an emotional rally in Virginia on January 16, 1920, a zealous Billy Sunday captured the feeling of millions when he proclaimed that prohibition would cleanse the nation's soul. "Men will walk upright now, women will smile, and the children will laugh," he told the audience. "Hell will be forever for rent."

It quickly became evident that prohibition would not fulfill these expectations. The amendment did cut down on alcohol consumption. Rural areas went completely dry, and many working-class immigrants in the city, who could not afford the high prices of bootlegged beer, changed their drinking habits. But prohibition made drinking fashionable among the middle class, and alcohol easy to obtain. Bootleggers produced dozens of new concoctions. Their inviting names—Soda Pop Moon and Yack Yack Bourbon—were deceptive. Many of the drinks were poisonous. According to one story, a patron sent a sample of his ill-gotten alcohol to be analyzed by a chemist, who replied, "Dear Sir, your horse has diabetes."

Though intended to create a more orderly society, prohibition had the opposite effect. It stimulated organized crime, encouraging smuggling and bootlegging, and producing widespread disregard for the law. Illegal saloons, called "speakeasies" sprang up in most major cities. By the end of the decade, New Yorkers could choose from among 32,000, which was double the number of bars that had existed before Prohibition. In 1926 *Time* printed a recipe for making gin. A Prohibition agent conducted a survey to see how long it took to buy a drink in a number of cities: Atlanta, 17 minutes; Chicago, 21 minutes; in New Orleans, 35 seconds. In Washington, D.C., the agent searched for an hour before a policeman pointed him toward a local bootlegger.

Prohibition turned local mobsters into national celebrities. The tabloids were filled with the exploits of Al "Scarface" Capone, "Machine Gun" Jack McGurn, and George "Bugsy" Moran. "Prohibition is a business," Chicago gangster Al Capone insisted. "All I do is supply a public demand. I do it in the best and least harmful way I can." In fact, Capone presided over a vast criminal empire and was responsible for as many as three hundred murders. Most of the city's politicians and judges were on his payroll. In the age of the automobile he drove around in the biggest car of all—a seven-ton, armor-plated Cadillac, equipped with bulletproof glass and a special compartment for machine guns.

The "21" Club During Prohibition   Although the Eighteenth Amendment banned the sale of alcohol, the "speakeasies" in many cities in the 1920s outnumbered the saloons of the pre-Prohibition years. But unlike the old saloons, speakeasies were fashionable establishments, frequented by patrons with the means to pay for illegal spirits. "21" in New York, one of the most famous speakeasies of the decade, featured a restaurant, two bars, and a secret chute for disposing of liquor bottles in case of a raid. The social elite of New York—debutantes, stockbrokers, movie and Broadway stars—packed the club night after night for business dealings and socializing.   *(Courtesy "21" Club.)*

Despite evidence that the Prohibition experiment was a failure, many provincial, largely rural, Protestant Americans continued to defend it. In their minds, prohibition had always been about more than alcohol. It represented an effort to defend traditional American values against the growing influence of an urban, cosmopolitan culture. Throughout the decade, "wets" and "drys" battled to define America.

 ## Republicans in Power

The battles over the League of Nations and the social unrest that followed the end of World War I left many Americans longing for political stability during the 1920s. The Republicans controlled the White House and Congress by appealing to the tradition of smaller government and swearing off the preceding decade's experiments in centralization. They scaled back government regulations and promised to promote business expansion. Opening foreign markets and limiting the possibility of war dominated the Republican approach to the world. The demoralized Democrats, torn by divisive social issues that reflected the tensions of the era, failed to offer a compelling alternative during most of the decade. The party showed signs of recovery in 1928, however, when it nominated New York governor Al Smith for president.

Republican Ascendancy

Warren G. Harding won a landslide victory in the 1920 election. A senator from Ohio since 1914, Harding was the first man ever to move directly from the Senate to the White House. Reflecting the contemporary mood, Harding promised a return to "normalcy" (he meant to say *normality*).

Harding was a modest man who worked hard at the job of being president. "I am a man of limited talents from a small town," Harding confessed to friends. His personal style was always warm and gracious. He opened the White House every day so he could greet visitors and often stayed up late at night to answer routine mail from citizens. "It is," he lamented, "really the only fun I have." Despite his self-professed limitations, Harding tried to perform his responsibilities with distinction. He approved a new budget system, advocated a federal anti-lynching law, called for a Department of Public Welfare, intervened to end the twelve-hour workday in steel mills, and approved legislation assisting farm cooperatives and liberalizing farm credit. His tolerant approach to civil liberties brought Americans a necessary respite from postwar acrimony. Harding not only let Socialist Eugene Debs out of jail, he received him in the White House.

His chief defect was that he believed in rewarding old friends with federal jobs. He appointed many party hacks, members of the "Ohio Gang," to important offices. They gathered with Harding at the famous "Little Green House" on K Street, where they drank illegal alcohol (delivered courtesy of a corrupt Prohibition officer), played poker, and entertained attractive women. Many of them abused the president's trust by swindling the government. Charles R. Forbes, the director of the Veterans Bureau, stole nearly $250 million before fleeing the country to avoid arrest. Jesse Smith, a Justice Department official, accepted thousands of dollars in bribes for protecting criminals from prosecution. The attorney general resigned when charged with authorizing the sale of alcohol from government warehouses to bootleggers. The most infamous scandal centered around allegations that Harding's secretary of the interior, Albert Fall, had leased government oil reserves in Teapot Dome, Wyoming, to private owners in order to line his own pockets. Fall resigned in disgrace and later served a one-year prison sentence.

By the summer of 1923, Harding had learned of the corruption within his administration. "My God, this is a hell of a job," he lamented to a journalist. "I have no trouble with my enemies. . . . But my damned friends, my God-damned friends . . . they're the ones that keep me walking the floor nights!" That summer, tired and depressed, Harding traveled west to Seattle and San Francisco where, on August 2, he died of a massive heart attack.

Vice President Calvin Coolidge was in Vermont when he received word of Harding's death. His father, a local justice of the peace, administered the oath of office. In personality Coolidge and Harding could not have been more different. Harding was gregarious and warm; Coolidge was dour and cold. In the weeks following Harding's death, Coolidge held twice-weekly press conferences and regular radio addresses both to reassure the nation and to consolidate power.

A progressive Republican and supporter of Theodore Roosevelt's New Nationalism, Coolidge had won election as governor of Massachusetts in 1919 campaigning on a platform supporting women's suffrage, government regulation to protect the environment, and higher salaries for teachers and other public employees. Despite his early progressive record, Coolidge adopted a hands-off approach once in the White House. In an era of peace and prosperity, Coolidge felt little need to flex federal power. His outlook may well have been conditioned by the tragic loss early in his term of his sixteen-year-old son, who died when a blister he developed while playing tennis became infected. When Calvin Jr. died, Coolidge recalled, "the power and the glory of the Presidency went with him." Coolidge had always been a man of few words, but only after his son's death did he become "Silent Cal."

Americans' hostility toward federal power reflected long-held and deep-seated fears that became especially pronounced during the 1920s. During the war, the general public experienced the long arm of federal power: millions of young men were conscripted into the service; Washington's regulation of food and fuel touched every home; and government at every level restricted individual liberties. Before the war, progressives such as Jane Addams had argued that government power could expand individual opportunity by taming the excess of industrialism, but critics in the 1920s believed that intrusive federal power restricted individual freedom and local control. The "remorseless urge of centralization, the insatiable maw of bureaucracy," wrote a progressive senator, "are depriving more and more the people of all voice, all rights touching home and hearthstone, of family and neighbor."

Both Harding and Coolidge believed that Washington's primary goal was to foster business enterprise. This meant a hands-off policy in areas where businessmen wanted freedom of action and intervention in areas where they needed help. "Never before," observed the *Wall Street Journal*, "has a government been so completely fused with business." The emphasis on close business–government cooperation found expression in the regulatory commissions. Harding and Coolidge filled them with businessmen who believed their role was not to regulate but to assist business. Under Attorney General Harry Daugherty, the Justice Department refused to enforce antitrust statutes. "So long as I am Attorney General," Daugherty declared, "I am not going unnecessarily to harass men who have unwittingly run counter with the statutes." The Interstate Commerce Commission helped railroad companies to negotiate lucrative contracts with shippers. In 1925, when Coolidge appointed William Humphrey to head the Federal Trade Commission (FTC), big business seized control of the agency. Humphrey, who denounced the FTC as "an instrument of oppression" created to "spread socialistic propaganda," used the organization to help businessmen set prices and limit production costs.

THE CASH REGISTER CHORUS.

"The Cash Register Chorus"   The chief feature of the Harding and Coolidge administrations was a very favorable stance toward big business. Coolidge, who once said that "the business of America is business," believed that everyone benefited when business interests prospered, and government's chief function was to ensure that they did. This cartoon features a quartet of businessmen singing the president's praises, accompanied by a ringing cash register.   *(State Historical Society of Missouri.)*

Secretary of the Treasury Andrew Mellon, who resigned from the boards of directors of fifty-one corporations on assuming office, feared that if high taxes deprived the businessman of a fair share of his earnings, then "he will no longer exert himself and the country will be deprived of the energy on which its continued greatness depends." Mellon fought successfully to reduce taxes on inheritances, corporate profits, and the well to do. By 1926, Congress had cut the tax rate on an income of $1 million from 66 percent to 20 percent. These policies helped to widen the gulf between rich and poor and concentrate capital in relatively few hands.

Secretary of Commerce Herbert Hoover, who dominated the cabinets of Harding and Coolidge before becoming president himself in 1928, believed that enlightened businessmen should play an important role in government. He called for the creation of an "associative state" in which government and business would work together to promote the public interest. Government must refrain from using coercive power, he argued; its role should be limited to authorizing studies and collecting data. Implementing his philosophy of government as information gatherer, Hoover transformed the Bureau of Standards into a national research center that encouraged businesses to adopt common standards of production.

Divided Democrats

A divided and demoralized Democratic Party offered little opposition to the revitalized Republicans. For most of the previous quarter-century, the Democratic Party's roots had been firmly planted in the rural South and West. In recent years, however, many of the immigrants flooding the nation's cities had joined the party, often as part of powerful urban machines. During the 1920s the two factions fought for control of the party.

The tension between these two constituencies played out at the party's 1924 convention. The convention assembled on June 24 in New York City's Madison Square Garden. In the midst of a terrible heat wave, the delegates battled for seventeen days. The party's urban wing rallied behind New York governor Al Smith, whom Franklin Roosevelt called the "happy warrior of the political battlefield." Smith, a product of boss-led Tammany Hall, identified with the immigrant culture of the city. He wore the symbol of Tammany Hall—a brown derby hat set at a slight angle. A Catholic, and former altar boy, he hung a portrait of the pope in his office. He drank openly in defiance of prohibition, even earned the nickname "Alcohol Al." The rural, Protestant faction supported William Gibbs McAdoo of California, a strict prohibitionist, former secretary of the treasury, and son-in-law of Woodrow Wilson.

A fierce debate over a resolution to condemn the Klan exposed the deep cultural divide within the party and made futile any attempt to broker a compromise. The Smith forces hoped to embarrass McAdoo supporters by including a plank in the platform that condemned the Klan for its violations of civil liberties. William Jennings Bryan took the floor to oppose the amendment, which he claimed would tear the party apart. Smith delegates booed the former presidential nominee. During the balloting, delegates engaged in fistfights. The mayor called out an additional thousand policemen to patrol the convention floor. Finally, after hours of debate, the convention voted 542 to 541 not to mention the Klan by name.

The debate over the Klan polarized the convention. In ballot after ballot neither Smith nor McAdoo received the two-thirds vote needed for nomination. Finally, after 102 ballots, both candidates withdrew their names. The nomination went to the obscure John Davis—a West Virginian by birth and a Wall Street lawyer. In order to add geographic and political balance to the ticket, the convention chose Governor Charles W. Bryan of Nebraska—the younger brother of William Jennings Bryan—as its vice-presidential nominee.

The Republicans had little difficulty deciding on incumbent Calvin Coolidge. As his running mate they chose former budget director Charles Dawes. The Republican platform, reflecting Coolidge's conservative views, stressed limited government, immigration restriction, and support for prohibition.

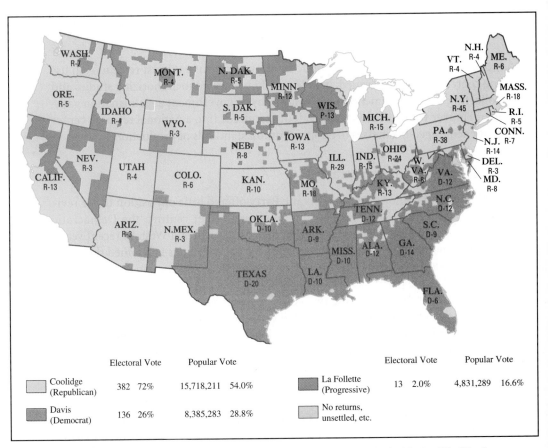

	Electoral Vote	Popular Vote		Electoral Vote	Popular Vote
Coolidge (Republican)	382 72%	15,718,211 54.0%	La Follette (Progressive)	13 2.0%	4,831,289 16.6%
Davis (Democrat)	136 26%	8,385,283 28.8%	No returns, unsettled, etc.		

The Election of 1924 The majority of Americans chose to "keep cool with Coolidge" in the 1924 election, but obvious signs of political discontent were present. Robert M. La Follette led a third party of farmers suffering from declining crop prices, but the party's platform failed to stir urban voters. Disaffection also plagued the Democratic Party, whose internal rifts prevented it from gaining many votes outside the rural South.

In July progressives, dissatisfied with both nominees, held their own convention in Cleveland to organize a farmer–labor party to "break the power of the private monopolistic system over the economic and political life of the American people." They called on sixty-nine-year-old Robert M. La Follette ("Battling Bob") of Wisconsin to head their ticket (see page 816). Opponents branded La Follette a dangerous radical, the candidate of "the Reds, the Pinks, the Blues, and the Yellows." The Progressives, moreover, faced many of the same obstacles that traditionally hamper third parties: lack of funds, absence of grass-roots organization, inability to get on the ballot in every state.

On election day, most voters decided to "Keep Cool with Coolidge." The Republican nominee won 54 percent of the popular vote, carried 35 states, and took 382 electoral votes. Davis received only 28.8 percent of the popular vote, 12 states, and 136 electoral votes. He carried only one state outside the South, Oklahoma. In four states—California, North Dakota, Wisconsin, and Minnesota—he carried less than 10 percent of the total vote. La Follette obtained 4.8 million votes—under 17 percent of the total—and captured only Wisconsin's thirteen electoral votes (see map). "In a fat and happy world, Coolidge is the man of the hour," observed William Allen White.

Commercial Diplomacy

The United States emerged from the war as a major power. During the 1920s, American diplomats tried to reconcile the nation's new status as an economic and military power with a persistent isolationist streak. The nation's approach to the world was characterized less by a strict isolationism than by an "independent internationalism." The goal was to limit the likelihood of future wars by emphasizing nonmilitary means—treaties, conferences, and disarmament—to achieve world stability, preserve the freedom to act independently to protect the national interest, and to extend American economic influence. The nation, observed a diplomat, championed a "commercial and non-military stabilization of the world."

Since neither Harding nor Coolidge had much interest in foreign policy, they delegated most of the responsibility to their secretaries of state. When a reporter asked Harding his views on Europe, the president responded, "I don't know anything about this European stuff." To run his foreign policy establishment Harding chose Charles Evans Hughes, a distinguished jurist, former governor of New York, and the 1916 Republican nominee for president. A patient and pragmatic diplomat, Hughes placed a premium on using international law and treaties to attain world order. The United States could not retreat from its world responsibilities. Instead, it must seek "to establish a *Pax Americana* maintained not by arms but by mutual respect and good will and the tranquilizing processes of reason." America, he maintained, needed to build a new international system, constructed and dominated by U.S. economic power.

That power was immense. After World War I the United States produced 70 percent of the world's petroleum and 40 percent of its coal. Between 1925 and 1929, it accounted for half of all industrial goods produced in the world. American private investment abroad grew fivefold, from $3.5 billion in 1914 to $17.2 billion in 1930. American culture also began its worldwide expansion as U.S. communications giants International Telephone and Telegraph (ITT), Radio Corporation of America (RCA), and Associated Press (AP) emerged as global giants. Hollywood as well extended its reach beyond the border. One critic observed that the sun "never sets on the British Empire and the American motion picture." The economic success fed the belief in the superiority of American values and the need to spread them to other nations. "There is only one first-class civilization in the world today, the *Ladies Home Journal* trumpeted. "It is right here in the United States."

The first step toward defusing international tensions was to stop growing military competition. The United States feared a new arms race with western Europe and Japan. Money spent on rifles was better invested in automobiles so standards of living could rise. The Far East remained a troubled spot. Policymakers worried that the alliance between Japan and a revitalized Britain would limit American influence and commerce in the region. In late 1921, Hughes invited eight leading powers (Britain, France, Italy, Japan, China, Belgium, the Netherlands, and Portugal) to Washington to discuss the naval arms race and competition in Asia.

In his opening speech at the Washington Conference, the bewhiskered Hughes startled the delegates by announcing that the United States would scrap thirty ships. He then turned to the British and Japanese delegates and challenged them to make similar cuts. "Secretary Hughes sank in 35 minutes more ships than all the admirals of the world have sunk in centuries," a British observer noted. Despite grumbling from naval officers, the diplomats successfully negotiated three agreements. In signing the Five-Power Treaty, the leading powers agreed to achieve real disarmament by scrapping existing naval vessels. They accepted ratios for tonnage of battleships, battle cruisers, and aircraft carriers (smaller vessels were not covered) of approximately 5 for the United States and Great Britain, to 3 for Japan, and 1.75 for France and Italy. The Four-Power Treaty (United States, Britain, France, and Japan) declared that each nation would respect the others' rights in the Pacific. Finally, the Nine-Power Treaty (signed by the four powers plus Italy, China, Belgium, the Netherlands, and Portugal) politely endorsed the ideals of the Open Door toward China.

Avoiding military entanglements with other nations became a preoccupation of American policymakers during the decade. In 1928, when the French foreign minister Aristide Briand pressed the United States to join an alliance against Germany, Secretary of State Frank Kellogg (who had replaced Hughes in 1925) transformed the request into an agreement to "condemn recourse to war for the solution of international controversies, and renounce it as an instrument of national policy." The Kellogg-Briand Pact, later laughed at as nothing more than an "international kiss," was signed by most nations in the world.

With the arms race under control, the Republican administrations focused their energy on the global economic system that was still reeling from the impact of World War I. The United States planned to use its economic might to create a new world economic order. "Our international problems tend to become mainly economic problems," Hughes proclaimed in 1922. In Europe, Germany remained the critical problem. "There can be no economic recuperation in Europe unless Germany recuperates," Hughes declared. But the German economy was in shambles. In 1922, burdened with a $33 billion bill for war reparations, uncontrolled inflation, and a crippled economy, the Germans defaulted on their loans. France and Belgium, hoping to keep the Germans in debt and therefore unable to threaten their neighbors, refused to abrogate the harsh terms. In 1923 the French sent troops into the rich Ruhr Valley to pressure the German government into maintaining its payments. With the European economic system threatened with catastrophe, Washington negotiated a new agreement called the Dawes Plan, after Chicago banker and, later, vice president of the United States, Charles G. Dawes. The plan reduced German reparations to $250 million annually and offered generous private loans to Germany.

The government aggressively flexed American economic muscle in Latin America. A 1924 survey revealed that of the twenty Latin American nations, only six were free of some kind of U.S. "management." During the 1920s, the United States relied on economic might and political subversion to maintain its control. U.S. investments in Latin America jumped from $1.26 billion in 1914 to $3.52 billion in 1929. American corporations such as United Fruit Company and ITT invested millions in the region, aided by the government programs that helped build highways, communications systems, and utilities needed to attract private capital. Nor did America reject all use of military force. In 1926, when political instability threatened U.S. investment in Nicaragua, President Coolidge sent in the marines to restore order. The following year, Washington negotiated the Peace of Tipitapa, which resulted in a U.S. supervised election in 1928.

Most Americans celebrated the economic and diplomatic achievements of the decade, but serious foreign policy problems remained. Nationalist leaders in Latin America resented U.S. dominance of the region. An Argentine writer called America the "new Rome," which enjoyed the "essentials of domination" without the "dead-weight of areas to administrate and multitudes to govern." Many of the treaties negotiated contained potentially fatal flaws. The Washington Naval Treaty did not limit submarines, destroyers, or cruisers. None of the armament treaties provided means for verification or enforcement. Since the major powers were trying to isolate the Bolsheviks, they excluded Russia from the conference. The Dawes Plan may have averted a crisis, but it created a rickety financial structure that depended on a vigorous expansion of world trade and a constant stream of American dollars flowing into Germany.

Al Smith and the 1928 Election

In August 1927, President Coolidge handed reporters a slip of paper containing a simple, twelve-word sentence: "I do not choose to run for President in nineteen twenty-eight." The announcement shocked the nation and forced Republican leaders to find a nominee. It did not take long. Nearly everyone agreed that Secretary of Commerce Herbert Hoover was the most qualified prospect. A skilled engineer, a successful administrator, and a shrewd businessman, he seemed the perfect candidate for the new corporate age. In accepting the party's nomination, Hoover said: "We in America today are nearer to the final triumph over poverty than ever before in the history of the land." Hoover stressed the American System of free enterprise as the source of prosperity, promising a "chicken in every pot and two cars in every garage."

The Democrats managed to avoid the turmoil that had marred their 1924 convention. The death of William Jennings Bryan, and William McAdoo's announcement that "in the interest of party unity" he would not run, left the rural faction of the party without a visible leader. It also left the nomination to Al Smith. To balance the ticket, Democrats selected Senator Joseph G. Robinson of Arkansas, a Protestant prohibitionist, to run for vice president. The platform avoided discussion of the social issues that had divided the party and instead took aim at Republican economic policies, which it charged had left the country with "its industry depressed, its agriculture prostrate."

Prosperity made a Republican victory almost certain, but social issues dominated the campaign. The two candidates highlighted the cultural clash of the decade. Smith opposed Prohibition; Hoover supported it. Smith hailed from the city; Hoover was from the country. Smith was Catholic; Hoover was Protestant. "If you vote for Al Smith," cried a preacher, "you're voting against Christ and you'll be damned." In radio broadcasts, one preacher equated Smith with the urban evils of "card playing, cocktail drinking, poodle dogs, divorces, novels, stuffy rooms, dancing, evolution, Clarence Darrow, overeating, nude art, prize-fighting, actors, greyhound racing, and modernism."

On November 6, Hoover rolled to an overwhelming victory. No Democrat could have defeated the Great Engineer in the fall of 1928. As Mencken observed ruefully, "I incline to believe that Hoover could have beaten Thomas Jefferson quite as decisively as he beat Al." He garnered 21.4 million popular votes (58.2 percent of those cast) to 15 million for Smith, and 330,725 for Socialist Norman Thomas and other minor party candidates. In the electoral college, Hoover's margin was even more crushing. He carried forty-two of the forty-eight states, including New York, for 444 votes to Smith's 87 (see map). For the first time since Reconstruction, the party of Lincoln broke the Democratic hold on the South, capturing Virginia, North Carolina, Texas, Florida, and Tennessee. The victor's coattails gave Republicans big majorities in both houses of Congress.

Though Smith lost the election, his candidacy had an important impact on the future of the Democratic Party. Smith brought millions of ethnics to the polls for the first time in a national election. He defeated Hoover by 2 to 1 in Boston. He won previously Republican cities such as New Haven, Albany, Scranton, and St. Louis. In 1920 Harding had carried all twenty-seven of the nation's major cities outside the South. In 1928 Smith captured eight of those and registered gains in all the rest. In 1924 Republicans carried the largest twelve cities by a plurality of 1.3 million. In 1928 the Democrats carried these same cities by 30,000 votes. As a result, the 1928

The Election of 1928   Herbert Hoover emphasized the Republican prosperity of the 1920s in his bid for the White House, while his opponent, Governor Alfred E. Smith of New York, had to combat his stereotyped image as an urbanite, a "wet," and a Catholic. In November, only the Deep South remained wedded to the Democratic Party.

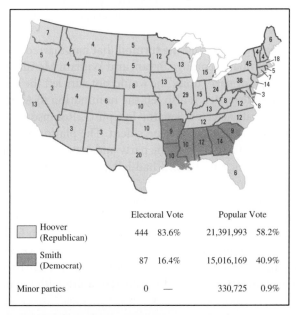

		Electoral Vote		Popular Vote	
	Hoover (Republican)	444	83.6%	21,391,993	58.2%
	Smith (Democrat)	87	16.4%	15,016,169	40.9%
	Minor parties	0	—	330,725	0.9%

election saw a dramatic increase in voter turnout, with many people voting for the first time. Almost 25 percent more people voted in 1928 than in the previous presidential election. In 1928 most people contented themselves with fulfilling the new president's promise of continued prosperity. Little did they realize that the world of the twenties was about to come crashing to an end.

CONCLUSION

Many trends and experiments from the previous decades—urbanization, industrialization, mechanization—combined to produce great social changes in American society during the 1920s. The innovations in industrial technology, corporate organization, and mass culture have earned the decade the moniker "the New Era." During this period, new technologies such as electricity and electrical appliances reached millions of homes. The automobile provided Americans with a new freedom of mobility, helping spawn the suburban boom that would radically transform living patterns and the natural landscape in the second half of the century. With the rise of advertising, consumer culture became an integral part of American life. Though the prosperity of the decade was by no means universal, many groups—such as industrial workers and the growing number of clerical workers—did see their standards of living improve.

The development of mass entertainment established the groundwork for a new national culture. For the first time, Americans in different parts of the country were watching the same movies, listening to the same radio stations, and reading the same popular magazines. Mass culture intensified the cultural conflict of the decade by bringing previously isolated groups into contact with one another. The "combatants" in this clash of cultures took several sides. One group consisted of those who embraced the New Era and its experiments: young women who chose to assert their sexuality and independence; young men who embraced the automobile and the freedom it provided; advertisers who worked to sell the modern age to consumers; urban workers who drank illegal liquor; jazz music *afficionados;* moviegoers; sports fans; and countless others. On the other side were people who distrusted modern society and disliked the new morality. This group included many white Protestants, prohibitionists, religious fundamentalists, Klansmen (and -women), and nativists. Disenchanted intellectuals formed a third group, one that criticized both the provincialism of the traditionalists and the crass materialism of the modern enthusiasts.

Amidst these cultural upheavals, politicians in the 1920s recoiled from the Progressive Era's reformist experimentation. Conservative Republican presidents Warren G. Harding and Calvin Coolidge focused on limiting government regulation, promoting business expansion, and opening foreign markets. In the wake of social agitation, reform, and war, the Republicans emphasized the theme of "normalcy." Abroad, they stressed free trade and commercial expansion, while working for international disarmament and trying to avoid military entanglements with foreign powers. An experiment in adapting traditional isolationism to its new global role, the "independent internationalism" allowed the United States to assume a prominent place in world affairs without fielding a large peacetime military.

National politics was not immune to the cultural conflicts of the decade, however. The clash of cultures played out at the 1924 Democratic convention, where the party's urban and rural factions battled to a standstill. Four years later the cultural conflict found expression in the presidential contest. The Democrats nominated New York governor Al Smith, a city-bred Catholic and outspoken critic of Prohibition. The Republicans chose Commerce Secretary Herbert Hoover, a Protestant from small-town Iowa and a supporter of Prohibition. Hoover soundly defeated Smith in the 1928 election, but Smith's campaign mobilized new voter groups—primarily immigrants and urban voters—and the Democrats captured the nation's large cities. This outcome presaged the alliance between the party's new urban wing and its traditional rural supporters that would become the New Deal coalition of the next decade.

SUGGESTED READINGS

Robert and Helen Lynd's *Middletown* (1929) provides a superb survey of American life and thought in the period. Frederick Lewis Allen's *Only Yesterday* (1931) appraises the so-called Roaring Twenties from the depths of the Great Depression. *Calvin Coolidge and the Coolidge Era* (1998), edited by John Earl Haynes, is a more recent collection of essays on a wide range of topics pertaining to the politics, diplomacy, economy, and culture of the period. Ellis Hawley examines the 1920s as a development of the First World War in *The Great War and the Search for a Modern Order* (1979). William Leuchtenburg's *The Perils of Prosperity* (1958) studies the economic weaknesses of the decade. Michael Parrish's *Anxious Decades* (1992) artfully connects the insecurities of the 1920s with the crises of the 1930s. Recent surveys of the social and political history of the 1920s are Lynn Dumenil's *The Modern Temper* (1995) and David Goldberg's *Discontented America* (1999). David Montgomery's *The Fall of the House of Labor* (1987) provides information on industrial workers and the decline of the labor movement in the decade.

Jim Potter's *The American Economy Between the Wars* (1974) offers an introduction to the new economy of the 1920s. The best history of the rise of the automobile is James Flink's *The Car Culture* (1975). The history of the suburbs is the focus of Kenneth Jackson's *Crabgrass Frontier* (1985), while John Teaford studies the cities in *The Twentieth-Century American City* (1986). The growth of the advertising industry is chronicled in Ronald Marchand's *Advertising the American Dream* (1985) and Daniel Pope's *The Making of Modern Advertising* (1983). Alfred Chandler, Jr.'s two works, *Strategy and Structure* (1962) and *The Visible Hand* (1977), cover the corporate revolution. James Gilbert's *Designing the Industrial State* (1972) examines the cooperation between business and government in the 1920s.

Daniel Boorstin traces the emergence of mass culture in *The Democratic Experience* (1973). The burgeoning movie industry is the subject of Robert Sklar's *Movie-Made America* (1976) and Neil Gabler's *An Empire of Their Own: How the Jews Invented Hollywood* (1988). Erik Barnouw studies the early development of radio in *A Tower of Babel* (1966). For sports in the 1920s, Elliott Gorn and Warren Goldstein's *A Brief History of American Sports* (1993) is a good starting point. Lizabeth Cohen's *Making a New Deal* (1990) describes how working people and immigrants adapted mass culture to fit their lives.

The "New Woman" and the new morality are the subjects of Sara Evans's *Born for Liberty* (1989). Beth Bailey studies the youth of the 1920s in *From Front Porch to Back Seat* (1988), while Susan Strasser examines middle-class women and popular culture in *Never Done* (1982). Angela Latham introduces women performers and the redefinition of sexual standards in *Posing A Threat* (2000). Alice Kessler-Harris focuses on wage-earning women in *Out to Work: A History of Wage-Earning Women in the United States* (1982). Sharon

Strom Hartman's *Beyond the Typewriter* (1992) explores the gender and class hierarchy of the office culture. The contradictions in organized feminism during the decade are outlined in Nancy Woloch's *Women and the American Experience* (1984). Also see Nancy Cott's *The Grounding of Modern Feminism* (1987). Kenneth Rose studies the role of women's groups in the campaigns for prohibition and repeal in *American Women and the Repeal of Prohibition* (1996).

For material on the Lost Generation, begin with Henry May's *The Discontent of the Intellectuals* (1963). Stanley Coben examines the role of intellectuals in the assault on traditional morality in *Rebellion Against Victorianism* (1992). Edmund Wilson's *The Twenties* (1975) also covers intellectuals during the 1920s, as does Roderick Nash's *The Nervous Generation* (1969). Paul Fussell analyzes the impact of World War I on these writers in *The Great War and Modern Memory* (1975). David Cronin's *Black Moses* (1962) is a helpful introduction to Marcus Garvey; Theodore Vincent's *Black Power and the Garvey Movement* (1970) places Garvey in the broader African-American struggle. The Harlem Renaissance has been the subject of many wonderful books; Nathan Huggins's *Harlem Renaissance* (1971) and Gloria Hull's *Color, Sex, and Poetry: Three Women Writers of the Harlem Renaissance* (1987) are two of the best.

Maldwyn Jones's *American Immigration* (1960) contains some excellent material on immigration restriction. Paul Avrich's *Sacco and Vanzetti: The Anarchist Background* (1991) is a cultural history of the immigrant world of the 1920s. For the "new Klan," Kenneth Jackson's *The Ku Klux Klan in the City* (1967) is classic; also see Richard Tucker's *The Dragon and the Cross: The Rise and Fall of the Ku Klux Klan in Middle America* (1991). Nancy MacLean's *Behind the Mask of Chivalry* (1994) studies the world-view of Klan members. Kathleen Blee's *Women of the Klan* (1991) explores the role women played in the group. Ray Ginger's *Six Days or Forever?* (1958) appraises fundamentalism in the 1920s, with an emphasis on the Scopes "monkey trial." Edward Larson's *Summer for the Gods* (1997) is an exhaustive study of the Scopes trial and places the debate in the larger context of the era. For the intellectual development of fundamentalism, see George Marsden's *Fundamentalism and American Culture* (1980). Prohibition has been studied at length; one thorough introduction is Andrew Sinclair's *Prohibition: The Era of Excess* (1962). Thomas Pegram's *Battling Demon Rum* (1998) is a survey of the entire temperance/prohibition movement, including repeal.

The Republican presidents of the 1920s were studied by John Hicks in *Republican Ascendancy* (1960) and by Robert Murray in *The Politics of Normalcy* (1973). Donald McCoy's *Calvin Coolidge* (1967) and David Burner's *Herbert Hoover* (1979) are two excellent biographies of the presidents. Robert Ferrell's *The Presidency of Calvin Coolidge* (1998) and *The Strange Deaths of President Harding* (1996) are recent assessments of the two presidencies. Emily Rosenberg studied the international expansion of American commerce and culture in *Spreading the American Dream* (1982). David Burner's *The Politics of Provincialism* (1967) is still the classic for the Democratic Party of the 1920s. Also see Oscar Handlin's *Al Smith and His America* (1958) and Kristi Andersen's *The Creation of a Democratic Majority, 1928–1936* (1979) for material on the Democrats and the 1928 campaign.

"For the Defense," 1925

Clarence Darrow was one of the country's most famous trial lawyers when he agreed to join John Thomas Scopes's legal team in 1925. He had won a reputation for fighting for progressive causes, defending the rights of labor, and opposing the death penalty. Since Scopes admitted he had violated the Tennessee law that prohibited teaching evolution in the state's public schools, Darrow could not free his client on a technicality. Instead, he argued that the law itself was unconstitutional because it violated the boundaries between church and state established by the Constitution of the State of Tennessee. The law required the teaching of religion, and because the people could not agree on one religion, the law was unenforceable and dangerous.

That is what was foisted on the people of this State . . . that it should be a crime in the State of Tennessee to teach any theory . . . except that contained in the divine account as recorded in the Bible.

But the State of Tennessee, under an honest and fair interpretation of the Constitution, has no more right to teach the Bible as the Divine Book than that the Koran is one, or the Book of Mormon, or the Book of Confucius, or the Buddha, or the Essays of Emerson. . . .

I know there are millions of people in the world who derive consolation in their times of distress from the Bible . . . but what is it? . . . The Bible is made up of sixty-six books written over a period of about 1,000 years, some of them very early and some of them comparatively late. It is a book primarily of religion and morals. It is not a book of science—never was and was never meant to be.

Who is the chief mogul that can tell us what the Bible means? . . . There are in America at least 500 different sects or churches, all of which quarrel with each other on the importance and non-importance of certain things or the construction of certain passages. All along the line they do not agree among themselves and cannot agree among themselves. They never have and they never will. . . . Who is it that can tell us that John Scopes taught certain theories that denied the . . . divine story of creation as recorded in the Bible? How did he know?

If today you can take a thing like evolution and make it a crime to teach it in the public schools, tomorrow you can make it a crime to teach it in the private schools . . . at the next session you may ban books and the newspapers. Soon you may set Catholic against Protestant, and Protestant against Protestant, and try to foist your own religion upon the minds of men.

"For the Prosecution," 1925

A celebrity also graced the ranks of the prosecution: William Jennings Bryan, the midwestern Populist who had three times been the Democratic nominee for president. Bryan was conservative on religious matters; a strict fundamentalist, he claimed to accept the Bible as literal truth. At the trial, Bryan argued for strict enforcement of the law. He contended that the people of Tennessee had a right to decide what to teach in their schools and that as a teacher Mr. Scopes had an obligation to comply with the people's will. The speech would be Bryan's swansong; he died only a few days after his famous cross-examination by Clarence Darrow.

Our position is that the statute is sufficient. The statute defines exactly what the people of Tennessee decided and intended and did declare unlawful, and it needs no interpretation.

The caption [of the statute] speaks of the evolutionary theory, and the statute specifically states that teachers are forbidden to teach in the schools supported by taxation in this State any theory of creation of man that denies the Divine record of man's creation as found in the Bible. . . .

. . . The people of this State knew what they were doing when they passed the law, and they knew the dangers of the doctrine that they did not want it taught to their children.

The question is, Can a minority in this State come in and compel a teacher to teach that the Bible is not true and make the parents of these children pay the expenses of the teacher to tell their children what these people believe is false and dangerous?

Has it come to a time when the minority can take charge of a state like Tennessee and compel the majority to pay their teachers while they take religion out of the heart of the children of the parents who pay the teachers? Shall we be detached from the throne of God and be compelled to link their ancestors with the jungle, —tell that to these children? This is the doctrine that they . . . would force upon the schools, that they will not let the Bible be read!

Your Honor, we believe that [the defense's] evidence is not competent. This is not a mock trial. This is not a convocation brought here to allow these men to come and stand for a time in the limelight and speak to the world. . . . The facts are simple, the case is plain, and if these gentlemen want to enter upon a larger field of educational work in the subject of evolution, let us get through with this case and then convene a mock court, or it will deserve the title of mock court if its purpose is to banish from the hearts of the people the Word of God as revealed.

It had all begun simply enough. In 1924 the State of Tennessee passed a statute prohibiting the teaching of evolution in the state's schools. The American Civil Liberties Union, who saw the statute as an unacceptable infringement on academic freedom, offered to pay the legal expenses of any teacher who was willing to challenge the statute in court. The ACLU knew that their challenge would produce a headline-grabbing trial, but they did not seem to realize how explosive such a case could be.

In Dayton, Tennessee, a group of townspeople read the ACLU's offer in the newspaper and decided that the trial could bring some much-needed publicity to their rundown steel town. They met with John Scopes, a math teacher and part-time football coach who had been teaching biology while the regular instructor was out sick. They explained that, by teaching evolution, he had been in violation of the new law. Then they asked: "John, would you be willing to stand for a test case?"

Everything seemed to be going according to the ACLU's plan. The plotters had failed to take into account, though, the larger debate that had been raging across the country. As Darwinian theory gained scientific credibility around the turn of the century, fundamentalist Christians began a campaign to keep the new scientific teachings out of the classroom. After several unsuccessful attempts in Kentucky and Georgia in 1921 and 1922, the anti-evolution crusade scored its first victory in Tennessee.

By the time of the ACLU test case in 1925, both sides of the debate were itching to fight over the issue. Champions for both sides volunteered quickly. William Jennings Bryan had personally campaigned for the Tennessee statute and offered to help prosecute Scopes. Clarence Darrow had been a critic of Christianity his entire life and jumped at the chance to match wits with Bryan in court. A narrow test of a new law's constitutionality had become a debate over evolution itself.

Yet the Scopes monkey trial was about more than just evolution. Many people were suspicious of where the decade's scientific "progress" was taking the country. If science and God had become incompatible, as Bryan argued, which should be retained? Many people also resented the Progressive Era's reliance on elites for reform. To many Tennesseans, the ACLU lawsuit was yet another example of self-appointed "experts" overriding the popular will in the name of the people's own good. This was what Bryan, a lifelong apostle of majority rule, argued. For the prosecution and their supporters, the teaching of evolution signified more than simply an assault on traditional beliefs; it symbolized the contempt the nation's educated elite had for the "common people."

Clarence Darrow did not question whether the majority of Tennesseans wanted evolution driven from the schools. He reminded the court of the harmful potential of majority rule. When the will of the majority interfered with the individual rights of the minority, he argued, the majority could and should be overridden. And when Tennesseans tried to enshrine religious dogma in the public biology classes, they were violating the individual rights of teachers, who would not be able to teach what they thought was the truth.

The Scopes monkey trial had been treated more as a showcase than a serious legal proceeding. Accordingly, the trial did not resolve this cultural conflict. If anything, it clearly defined the growing chasm between progress and traditional belief.

Questions for Analysis

1. Why does Darrow say the Tennessee statute requires the teaching of religion?

2. Why does he think teaching religion is impossible?

3. What dangerous consequences does Darrow see in the statute?

4. On what grounds does Bryan call the defense's case inappropriate?

5. According to Bryan, why is it just for Tennessee to pass such a statute?

6. Is Bryan's argument antidemocratic? Why or why not?

7. Is evolution really at the heart of this debate? If not, what is?

8. Why do you think religion and education have been at the heart of so many controversies in American history?

25

"Fear Itself": Crash, Depression, and the New Deal, 1929–1938

On March 4, 1933, in Washington, D.C., standing hatless and coatless on a dreary, windswept inauguration day, Franklin D. Roosevelt placed his hand on an old family Bible open at Paul's First Epistle to the Corinthians: "And now abideth faith, hope, charity, these three; but the greatest of these is charity." After reciting the oath of office, the new president turned to face the one hundred thousand spectators somberly gathered in front of the Capitol. Despite the festive music and waving flags, the faces that greeted him were lined with despair. A journalist had compared the preinaugural atmosphere in Washington to "that which might be found in a beleaguered capital in wartime." But in the winter of 1933, it was not war that threatened the American democratic experiment. It was a deep and relentless economic depression.

The four-month interval between Roosevelt's election in November 1932 and his inauguration in March 1933 proved to be the most painful winter of the Great Depression. One in four Americans were without a job. Each month, thousands of farmers and business owners went bankrupt. As people lost faith in the economy, they withdrew funds from local banks. By March 3, the day before Roosevelt took office, thirty-eight states had shut down all their banks, and the remaining ten states were moving to close theirs. Normal business and commerce ground to a halt. A Roosevelt adviser, Rexford Guy Tugwell, wrote in his diary, "Never in modern times, I should think, has there been so widespread unemployment and such moving distress from cold and hunger."

On inauguration day, as he glanced out from behind the Great Seal of the United States, Roosevelt knew that his first task as president was to restore a sense of hope in the future and confidence in government. "Let me first assert my firm belief that the only thing we have to fear is fear itself—nameless, unreasoning, unjustified terror which paralyzes needed efforts to convert retreat into advance." In a firm and confident voice, he promised to ask Congress for "broad executive power to wage a war against the emergency, as great as the power that would be given to me if we were invaded by a foreign foe." For twenty minutes Roosevelt held the audience under his spell. When he finished, the crowd responded with cheers and thunderous applause. A few days later, a man who had listened to the address on the radio, wrote a short note to the president that summed up the nation's reaction to the speech. "It seemed to give the people, as well as myself," he wrote, "a new hold upon life."

Roosevelt's words offered reassurance to a nation traumatized by the depression, but it would take more than words to ease the public's suffering. Beginning in 1933, the American people witnessed a frenzy of activity in Washington as Roosevelt launched a host of new programs and created a myriad of government agencies in the battle for recovery. The New Deal experiment built on the foundation of government activism laid during the Progressive Era to dramatically expand federal power. Despite the extraordinary changes, American social values and culture showed remarkable resilience. Most Americans endured the depression without losing faith in the capitalist system, or their belief in the traditional notions of individualism and self-help at the core of the American experiment.

▌ What factors contributed to the economic collapse of the early 1930s?

▌ What was the "New Deal" and how did it expand the role of government? How successful were New Deal programs at pulling the nation through the depression?

▌ How did American culture respond to the depression?

▌ What groups benefited the most from Roosevelt's policies? Why?

This chapter will address these questions.

The Great Depression

The prosperity of the twenties had been built on a foundation of quicksand. The stock market crash in October 1929 exposed those weaknesses and signaled a steep descent into depression. The economic collapse imposed extraordinary hardships on almost all Americans. Families struggled to maintain their homes and feed their children. Conventional wisdom and past practice suggested that Washington maintain a "hands-off" approach to the collapse. Only slowly and reluctantly did President Herbert Hoover try to use the federal government to pull the nation from depression; his modest efforts were too little, too late. By 1932, Americans looked desperately for new leadership and greater government involvement to guide them through the troubled times.

Chronology

1929	Stock market crashes
1930	New York's Bank of the United States closes
1931	Reconstruction Finance Corporation created
1932	Bonus Army and the "Battle of Anacostia Flats"
	F. D. Roosevelt elected president
1933	Emergency Banking Act
	First Fireside Chat
	Prohibition repealed
	Public Works Administration and Civil Works Administration established
	Agricultural Adjustment Act and National Industrial Recovery Act
	Tennessee Valley Authority created
	Disney produces *Three Little Pigs*
1934	Indian Reorganization Act
1935	National Labor Relations Act, or Wagner Act
	Social Security Act guarantees old-age pensions
	Works Progress Administration formed from Emergency Relief Appropriation
	Congress of Industrial Organization formed
	Schechter v. *U.S.*
1936	Roosevelt wins reelection
	Keynes publishes *The General Theory of Employment, Interest, and Money*
	Butler v. *U.S.*
1937	United Automobile Workers strike in Flint, Michigan
	Roosevelt attempts to "pack" the Supreme Court
	Economy slides into deep recession
1938	O. Wells broadcasts H. G. Wells's *The War of the Worlds*
1939	Steinbeck publishes *The Grapes of Wrath*

The Crash

The first signs that the fragile prosperity of the 1920s was about to shatter came on Wednesday, October 23, 1929. For the previous five years Wall Street investors had come to expect healthy profits as stock prices, in the words of a contemporary observer, "soared . . . into the blue and cloudless empyrean." The value of all stocks on the New York Stock Exchange almost doubled between 1925 and 1929, from $34 billion to $64 billion. The laws of economic gravity suggested that the market could not continue its upward spiral. No one, however, expected the fall to be so sudden or so steep. On October 23, however, a wave of panic selling gripped investors, who dumped more than $4 billion in stocks. By noon the next day, known as "Black Thursday," the market had lost another $9 billion.

Leading bankers assembled in an emergency meeting to develop a strategy to stem the collapse. They decided that all the nation needed was a show of confidence. "It's going to be all right," exclaimed the head of the nation's largest bank, who orchestrated a $20 million buying binge among leading investors. The reassuring words and the infusion of new money failed to slow the market's fall. The following Tuesday, October 29, in what the economist John Kenneth Galbraith called "the most devastating day in the history of the New York Stock Market," panicked investors sold more than 16.4 million shares—a record that would stand until 1968. By the end of the day, the market had lost $32 billion. An October 30 newspaper headline declared "Wall St. Lays an Egg." The slide continued for three more weeks. By the time it ended in mid-November, the stock market had lost nearly one-third of its value.

The market collapse had little direct impact on the overall economy. Only a handful of wealthy Americans—about 2.5 percent of the population—owned stock. No companies went bankrupt. Most economists, who blamed the crash on reckless speculation, saw the drop as a necessary correction and predicted a complete recovery. "The great task of the next few months," wrote the editors of the left-leaning *Nation*, "is the restoration of confidence—confidence in the fundamental strength of the financial structure . . . confidence in the essential soundness of legitimate industry and trade."

Had the economy been sound and healthy, public confidence could have been restored. But the economy was neither. The nation's haphazard banking system was the weakest link in the economic chain. Only one-third of the twenty-five thousand banks operating in 1929 were members of the Federal Reserve System, created by President Wilson in 1913 to bring financial stability and standardized practice to banks. Most were small, independent, and grossly undercapitalized. Beginning in 1930 depositors, worried about the economy and spooked by Wall Street, began withdrawing funds. Caught with huge outstanding liabilities and dwindling deposits, banks foreclosed mortgages, demanded repayment of loans, or went bankrupt, leaving investors empty-handed. Initially, the panic was confined to rural areas, but on December 11, 1930, it struck at the heart of the U.S. banking system, forcing New York's Bank of the United States, which held the savings of some four hundred thousand persons totaling nearly $286 million, to close its doors.

The combination of the stock market collapse and the bank failures killed any attempt to revive public confidence. Consumer spending, often on credit, had stoked the economic fires during the 1920s. In 1930, with many Americans shaken by the events on Wall Street and concerned about their jobs, consumer spending dropped by 10 percent, driving down the sales of new cars, homes, and household items.

By 1929, Americans' purchasing power was too feeble to keep the financial boat afloat in any case. Most of the decade's economic gains had gone to a handful of wealthy people whose spending habits could not sustain economic growth. By the end of the decade, the richest 1 percent of the population owned 60 percent of the nation's wealth. Industrial output had soared by 40 percent and corporate profits increased by 80 percent, but workers' wages grew by only 8 percent. Farmers, who had been plagued by falling prices for most of the decade (see page 936), had little money.

It also became clear by 1930 that the expansion rested on a flimsy framework of speculative buying and unregulated practices. There was no effective regulation of the securities market, and investment bankers, lawyers, and accountants allowed investors to borrow heavily and to purchase stock on margin, putting down as little as 10 percent of a stock's value. As long as the value of the stock increased, as it had for most of the decade, everyone was happy: investors made money and brokers reaped large commissions. The phantom prosperity evaporated when the market crashed. Brokers called in their loans, leaving individual investors with huge bills.

Finally, the frailties in the international economic system began to take their toll. World War I had left England and France heavily in debt to America. The Allies tried to fund repayment by squeezing Germany for reparations (see page 958). Until 1928, American investors helped prevent catastrophe by pouring loans into Germany, but the market crash choked off foreign loans. In addition, high U.S. tariffs stifled international trade, which fell by nearly $1.2 billion in 1930. Cut off from American credit and markets, Europe's economy crumbled. By September 1930, England was burdened with 25 percent unemployment. Rising joblessness in Europe, in turn, dried up markets for American goods and agricultural products. In the first three years of the depression, the value of American foreign trade fell from $9 billion to $3 billion. The precarious economic conditions caused an unprecedented decline in the national income, from $88 billion in 1929 to $40 billion four years later. In 1930, 26,000 businesses failed; the following year another 28,000 collapsed. Investment declined from $7 billion to less than $2 billion. Corporate profits fell from $10 billion to less than $1 billion. The gross national product dropped from $80 billion to $42 billion as the economy shrunk to half its former size. As one observer put it, "People felt the ground give way beneath their feet."

Hard Times

As the collapse constricted the economy, corporations cut production and slashed jobs and wages. Workers, who on average earned a weekly wage of $25 in 1929, received only $16.73 in 1933. And they were the lucky ones. Nearly a quarter of the work force were unemployed in 1933. In 1933 in Ohio, 50 percent of the labor force in Cleveland and 80 percent of workers in Toledo were without work. More than a million people were jobless in New York. Unemployed office workers sold apples on street corners, five cents apiece. *Fortune* magazine estimated that 27.5 million Americans had no regular income at all. Without paychecks, many Americans were unable to make mortgage payments on their homes. By 1933, nearly six hundred thousand homeowners had lost their property.

Unable to pay rents or mortgages, people and families without work either lived off the generosity of relatives or became part of the sea of homeless. By 1932, between 1 and 2 million people were homeless in America. In parts of Arkansas, families lived in caves; in Oakland, California, they sought refuge in sewer pipes. More than a million of the jobless roamed the country as hobos. The situation in Washington, D.C., was terrifying. "I come home from [Capitol] Hill every night filled with gloom," a newsman wrote. "I see on the streets filthy, ragged, desperate-looking men such as I have never seen before."

The growing waves of misery overwhelmed relief efforts, which existed only at the local level. Bread lines and soup kitchens staffed by local charities proliferated but failed to stem the tide of suffering. In the winter of 1931–1932, New York City families on relief got $2.39 per week. In Houston, city officials stopped processing relief applications from black and Hispanic families. Philadelphia, Detroit, and St. Louis dropped families from relief roles because of a lack of money. More than a hundred cities provided no relief at all. In 1932 total public and private expenditures on relief amounted to only $317 million, less than $27 for the entire year for each of the 12 million jobless.

For many people, finding food to eat became a daily struggle. One of five children attending school in New York City suffered from malnutrition. In depressed coal-mining areas of Illinois, Kentucky, Ohio, Pennsylvania, and West Virginia, more than 90 percent of children went hungry. In cities across the country, children and adults dug through garbage cans for rotten food. In Chicago, according to one report, after a trash truck dumped its cargo, a waiting crowd "started digging with sticks, some with their hands, grabbing bits of food and vegetables." When a teacher in West Virginia told a young girl to go home and eat, the child replied: "I can't. This is my sister's day to eat."

The majority of American families maintained at least some source of income during the depression, but it was often sharply reduced, and the average family struggled to adapt. Hard times curtailed family activity outside the home, forcing members to find support and comfort in one another. Many families tried to cut costs by sharing living space with other families. Young couples, worried about earning a living, delayed marriage. The year 1932 saw 250,000 fewer marriages than 1929. For the first time in American history, the birthrate dropped below the replacement level. Divorce rates also declined, a trend that inspired some observers to suggest that the depression strengthened families. A Muncie, Indiana, newspaper editorialized, "Many a family that has lost its car has found its soul."

This optimistic pronouncement did not take into account the tremendous strains the economic collapse imposed on families. Divorce declined, but desertion soared.

Hard Times   The bread line, like this one at a Chicago soup kitchen in 1931, was a familiar sight during the depths of the depression. In some cities, the ranks of the unemployed comprised 40 percent of the population, including many middle-class Americans who normally would have been too proud to accept charity. Such conditions to some degree broke the American spirit of individualism that had historically proved hostile to the idea of public assistance. *(National Archives.)*

By 1940, more than 1,500,000 married women lived apart from their husbands. The number of neglected or abandoned children placed in institutions increased by 50 percent during the first two years of the depression. More than two hundred thousand vagrant children, victims of broken families, roamed the nation's streets. The Children's Bureau reported that many children found themselves "going for days at a time without taking off their clothes to sleep at night, becoming dirty, unkempt, a host to vermin. They may go for days with nothing to eat but coffee, bread and beans."

The depression blurred gender roles within the family. Many men were overwhelmed by guilt because they could not support their loved ones. "I haven't had a steady job in more than two years," moaned one father. "Sometimes I feel like a murderer. What's wrong with me, that I can't protect my children?" The father's diminished role increased the mother's role as provider. Homemakers watched household budgets with a close eye. In towns and cities flowerbeds became vegetables gardens. Despite widespread hostility, many women entered the workplace. In most cases the opportunities were limited to traditional "women's work." But there were exceptions. In Mississippi, two-thirds of all female textile workers were married. In black families the economic contributions of married women were great. Forty percent of black women were in the labor force at any time, compared to 20 percent of white women. A government study, noting that nearly half of black women workers had lost their jobs, compared to three out of ten white women, concluded that the economic hardship of the depression had fallen "with double harshness upon Negro women."

In both the North and the South the depression pushed African-Americans deeper into poverty. In 1930 the majority of blacks still lived below the Mason-Dixon Line, most growing cotton as sharecroppers and tenant farmers. Their livelihoods crumpled even before the stock market: cotton prices had dropped sharply through the twenties from 18 cents per pound in 1919 to 6 cents in 1933. That year, two-thirds of the African-Americans cultivating cotton had no earnings after paying their debts. Moving to southern cities in search of work, blacks encountered angry unemployed whites shouting slogans such as "No Jobs for Niggers Until Every White Man Has a Job!" By 1931, more than 50 percent of blacks living in southern cities were unemployed.

Competition for scarce resources inflamed racial tensions, especially in the South. The Ku Klux Klan reported an upsurge in membership, and the number of lynchings tripled between 1932 and 1933. In 1935 alone, white mobs lynched nearly two dozen blacks. One of the most notorious cases of racial injustice revolved around the plight of the "Scottsboro boys." In 1931 authorities arrested nine black teenagers and charged them with raping two white women on a train bound for Scottsboro, Alabama. Twelve days after their arrest, an all-white jury sentenced them to the electric chair. The Supreme Court overturned the conviction the following year, claiming the young men had not received a proper defense. A second trial demolished the prosecution's case: there was no physical evidence of rape and one of the women recanted her testimony. Still another all-white jury found the youths guilty, only to have the Supreme Court once again reverse the decision, claiming the defendants had been denied due process. In 1935 state officials dropped charges against four of the "Scottsboro boys." The other five served long prison terms.

In northern cities, unemployment rates among blacks soared to levels similar to those in the South. In 1931 sociologist Kelley Miller described the black worker as "the surplus man, the last to be hired and the first to be fired." The statistics told the story of hardship and hunger. In a survey of 106 cities, the Urban League found that "with a few notable exceptions . . . the proportion of Negroes unemployed was from 30 to 60 percent greater than for whites." Discriminated against by both employers and unions, adult black males faced bleak alternatives.

Other ethnic minorities faced similar hardships. During the 1920s hundreds of thousands of Mexicans had moved to California and the Southwest. Mexican-Americans reacted to hard times by forming unions and engaging in strikes for better wages. The Immigration Service supported the efforts of powerful growers to break the strikes by deporting workers who joined unions. Aiding the growers was an influx of three hundred thousand white migrants who arrived in California's Central Valley desperate for work in the fields between 1935 and 1938. Growers were happy to hire them as strikebreakers and replacements for the Mexicans, many of whom were forcibly taken to Mexico or went voluntarily. An estimated five hundred thousand Hispanic workers, many of them legal residents or American citizens by birth, crossed into Mexico during the decade. By the late 1930s, poor whites made up 90 percent of the state's migrant farm workers. Most had come from the Great Plains states.

Residents of the Great Plains had to contend with the dual impact of depression and drought. Searing summer heat killed thousands of people, cattle, fish, and birds. By 1930, years of land mismanagement and below-normal rainfall were destroying whole communities on the Great Plains as the topsoil dried up and blew away. Between 1929 and 1933, scores of dust storms howled across the land each year. These black blizzards transformed western Kansas, eastern Colorado, western Oklahoma, the Texas Panhandle, and eastern New Mexico into an ecological wasteland. "This is the ultimate darkness," wrote a Kansas victim. A journalist traveling across the southern plains coined the phrase "Dust Bowl" to describe the tragic conditions he witnessed. "The impact is like a shovelful of fine sand flung against the face," reported an observer. "People caught in their own yards grope for the doorstep. Cars come to a standstill, for no light in the world can penetrate that swirling murk."

Millions of people fled the states of the stricken region. Nearly a million Dust Bowl refugees, collectively called Okies, took to the nation's highways and railroads. Railroad officials in Kansas City observed 1,500 transients a day hitching rides on freight trains. In 1936 seven counties in southeastern Colorado reported only 2,078 houses occupied; 2,811 houses were abandoned and another 1,522 homes had disappeared. Most of the migrants pushed their way to California where they hoped to find new opportunity. But in the words of one journalist, "To the vast majority of the refugees the promised land proved to be a place of new and cruel tragedy." A migrant family earned about $450 a year on average, less than

Life in the Dust Bowl   A mother and her child struggle to filter out the swirling dust with handkerchiefs as they pump water in Springfield, Colorado. Exploitative farming practices and overgrazing combined with natural phenomena to create the Dust Bowl, one of the worst ecological disasters in American history, affecting vast portions of the Great Plains. The dry and windy conditions sent literally hundreds of millions of tons of topsoil into the air, creating storms that snuffed out sunlight and swallowed streets, cars, and sometimes even small buildings when the dust finally settled. New Deal programs attempted relief and reform efforts but never addressed or corrected the fundamental environmental problems inherent in commercial farming. *(Wide World Photos, Inc.)*

half the subsistence level. One of the characters in John Steinbeck's novel chronicling a family's migration, *The Grapes of Wrath* (1939), lamented, "Oakie use' ta mean you was from Oklahoma. Now it means you're scum."

The Ordeal of Herbert Hoover

Few people were better prepared to confront the growing crisis than President Herbert Hoover. After saving Belgium and Russia from starvation as the head of the American Relief Administration at the end of World War I, Hoover spent eight years as commerce secretary. Along the way, he earned high marks for his progressive ideas and efficient administration. A journalist noted that Hoover "gave the effect of having thoroughly anticipated the debacle and mapped out the shortest road to recovery."

Most economists, and many leading politicians, argued that government should refrain from interfering with the market and allow the depression to run its course. The United States had experienced steep declines in the past, one as recently as 1921, and the economy had always rebounded without help from Washington. "You might just as well try to prevent the human race from having a disease as to prevent economic grief of this sort," advised Oklahoma's Democratic senator Thomas Gore.

Hoover, however, was unwilling to abide by the conventional wisdom. Like most Americans in 1929 and 1930, he assumed that the crash marked a temporary dip in the business cycle. "The fundamental business of the country is on a sound and prosperous basis," Hoover said the day after Black Thursday. But he also believed that the national government needed to take active steps to end the deflationary spiral and restore public confidence in business. In November 1929, during the Wall Street selloff, he summoned business leaders to the White House, pressuring them to agree to maintain wages and employment. He goaded the Federal Reserve System to ease credit by lowering its discount rate to member banks. In December, he asked Congress to appropriate $140 million for new public buildings.

The president's unprecedented response incurred the wrath of both the business community and many conservative Democrats and Republicans, but it failed to revive the economy. By the end of 1930, business failures reached 26,355, the gross national product had slumped more than 12 percent, and production in steel mills and automobile factories had dropped by 38 percent. When his efforts to revive domestic spending failed, Hoover turned his attention to stabilizing failing international economic markets. Claiming that "the major forces of the depression now lie outside of the United States," Hoover moved to balance the federal budget and raise taxes in 1931. A balanced budget, he contended, would reassure foreign investors, produce lower interest rates, and encourage business borrowing. In his boldest move, Hoover approved creation of the Reconstruction Finance Corporation (RFC), which lent money to financial institutions. By July, the RFC had pumped $1.2 billion into the economy. Later that year, he signed legislation allowing the RFC to lend money directly to state and local governments. He asked Congress to pass the Federal Home Loan Bank Act and to increase funding for federal land banks. The Glass-Steagall Act of February 1932 added $1 billion of gold to the money supply.

Hoover's experiments in economic intervention were far from timid, but nothing seemed to work. He, like the rest of the nation, was overwhelmed by the severity of the crisis. Critics, most of whom offered no viable alternatives to halting the suffering, pilloried the hapless Hoover, accusing him of being callous and indifferent to the despair around him. Democrats labeled the crisis the "Hoover Depression." The tarpaper-and-cardboard shacks housing the nation's homeless became "Hoovervilles." As public hostility increased, Hoover withdrew into himself, communicating with the American public through press releases. According to one story, Hoover asked Treasury Secretary Andrew Mellon, "Can you lend me a nickel to call a friend?" Mellon responded, "Here's a dime. Call all of them."

His reaction to the Bonus Army sealed Hoover's doom. The "army" was made up of veterans of World War I who descended on Washington to lobby for immediate payment of bonuses due them (in 1945) for their service. Many brought wives and children along. When the Senate rejected the bonus bill, most of the veterans left for home. About eight thousand, however, camped in ramshackle quarters on Anacostia Flats across the river from the Capitol, promising to squat there "until 1945" if necessary to receive their money. When a scuffle between some veterans and police resulted in gunfire, Hoover called in the army to maintain order. Army Chief of Staff General Douglas MacArthur, exceeding his orders, decided instead to forcibly remove the protesters. At dusk on July 28, 1932, MacArthur charged into the Flats with tanks and a column of infantry, tossing tear gas canisters into tents and plunging with bayonets drawn into crowds of men, women, and children. The image of armed soldiers routing citizens with tanks outraged many Americans. The so-called Battle of Anacostia Flats marked the low point of the Hoover presidency.

 ## The New Deal Experiment, 1933–1938

When Franklin Roosevelt assumed the presidency, a desperate public looked to him for action. "Yours is the first opportunity to carve a name in the halls of immortals beside Jesus," a citizen wrote in a letter to the White House. Roosevelt responded with a bold program of measures to provide relief for the unemployed and recovery for the economy. The unprecedented experiment called the New Deal did not end the depression or silence critics, but it did win the support of millions of Americans who now swore allegiance to the Democratic Party. It also earned him the lasting enmity of tradition-minded conservatives who opposed the New Deal's expansion of government size and influence. By 1938, the New Deal had lost momentum, but not before Roosevelt had dramatically altered the role of government and established himself as one of the most influential presidents in American history.

FDR and the 1932 Election

Franklin Delano Roosevelt was born on January 30, 1882, in Hyde Park, New York. His patrician family provided him with all the comforts of wealth. He received his early education from private tutors, learned to speak French and German, and enjoyed life on his family's 187-acre Hyde Park estate. In 1896 he enrolled in Groton,

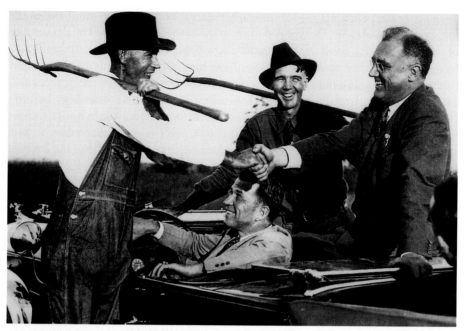

FDR, the Candidate Though he gave no specifics during the campaign, Roosevelt's promise of a "new deal for the American people" and the spirit of optimism he projected accounted for his enormous appeal in 1932. This photograph of Roosevelt greeting farmers in Georgia speaks to another of his assets, a common touch that belied his aristocratic background. Notice too that FDR is campaigning from his car; for most of his presidency, he managed to disguise the paralysis that confined him to a wheelchair. *(Hulton Getty/Liaison.)*

a distinguished prep school near Boston. Four years later he entered Harvard. While at Harvard he fell in love with his distant cousin Eleanor, who charmed him with her sincerity and intelligence. They were married in 1905. That same year Roosevelt enrolled in Columbia University Law School. Although he left without earning his degree, he passed the bar exam and entered a prestigious Wall Street law firm. But corporate law could never satisfy his ambition. He yearned for a larger arena and found it in politics.

Choosing the Democratic Party, Roosevelt began his political career in 1910 when he won election as a New York state senator. In 1913 he became Wilson's assistant secretary of the navy, and in 1920 he was the party's popular choice to run for vice president in the losing campaign of James Cox. The following year, Roosevelt's bright political life nearly ended when, at the age of 39, he was stricken with poliomyelitis. The disease left Roosevelt paralyzed from the waist down. Usually depending on a wheelchair, he managed to walk only with the aid of heavy steel braces and crutches. Roosevelt emerged from the ordeal with greater character, patience, and empathy for the less fortunate. He once told a friend that the hardest thing he ever tried to do was to wiggle his big toe after polio had destroyed his legs. After that struggle, he said, all else was easy.

In 1928 Roosevelt withstood the Republican landslide that swept Hoover into office and won election as the governor of New York. As governor he advanced many ideas that were to mark his early presidency—repeal of the Prohibition amendment, government regulation of electric utilities, unemployment insurance, and the use of public works to provide jobs. His political success made him a leading contender for president. Despite opposition from conservative Democrats, Roosevelt gained the party's nomination on the fourth ballot. To mollify the rural, southern wing of the party, he asked Speaker of the House John Nance Garner of Texas to join the ticket as the party's vice-presidential nominee.

The depression had crippled Hoover's presidency and made a Democratic victory almost certain. "All you have to do," Garner told FDR, "is to stay alive until election day." But Roosevelt responded by waging an energetic campaign, traveling by train on a 13,000-mile whistle-stop trip to the West Coast, giving nearly a hundred speeches along the way. His addresses failed to present the nation with a coherent agenda, and often his proposals for expanded public works seemed to contradict his pleas for lower taxes and reduced government spending. Though vague on specifics, Roosevelt managed to convey to most Americans that he planned to use the power of the federal government to lift the nation out of depression and aid those in need. In his acceptance speech at the Democratic convention, Roosevelt told the delegates, "I pledge you, I pledge myself, to a New Deal for the American people." He promised to look after the "forgotten men, the unorganized but indispensable units of economic power."

As expected, on election day the voters repudiated Hoover and the Republicans by decisive majorities. Roosevelt received almost 23 million votes to Hoover's almost 15.8 million. He carried 42 of 48 states and gained 472 electoral votes to Hoover's 59 (see map). The Democrats attained their largest majorities in both houses of Congress since before the Civil War, winning the House with 312 seats to 123 seats and the Senate with 59 seats to 37 seats.

The First Hundred Days

In the months between Roosevelt's election in November 1932 and his inauguration in March 1933, the nation slid deeper into the trough of the depression. "When we arrived in Washington on the night of March 2," wrote a Roosevelt adviser, "terror held the country in grip." How would the new president respond to the crisis?

The first order of business was to save the nation's banks, which had been bleeding money as panicked investors withdrew their life's savings. On March 5, Roosevelt proclaimed a nationwide "bank holiday" to last until he could push a recovery bill through Congress. With the banks closed, Roosevelt hurried through Congress the Emergency Banking Act, which provided expanded federal credit for banks and authorized the reopening of banks under strict new guidelines. The day before the banks were scheduled to reopen, Roosevelt addressed the nation in the first of his "Fireside Chats" over the radio (see Competing Voices, page 1005). In a commanding yet intimate voice, he reassured his 60 million listeners, explaining in

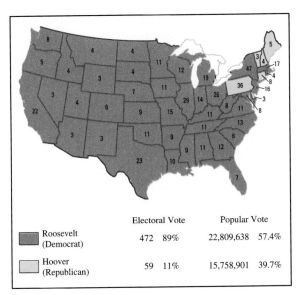

	Electoral Vote		Popular Vote	
Roosevelt (Democrat)	472	89%	22,809,638	57.4%
Hoover (Republican)	59	11%	15,758,901	39.7%

The Election of 1932 In 1932 Americans were looking for someone who could end the economic crisis, but few were willing to stray from the two major parties. Third parties such as the Socialists, who only polled 882,000 votes, were no match for the charismatic Franklin Roosevelt, whose confidence inspired voters.

simple terms "that it is safer to keep your money in a reopened bank than under the mattress." The public responded to Roosevelt's calming message. By March 15, deposits were exceeding withdrawals, and by the end of the month, nearly $1 billion had flowed back into the system. Later that spring, Congress passed a second Glass-Steagall Banking Act, which prevented commercial banks from engaging in risky investments and created the Federal Deposit Insurance Corporation (FDIC) to insure individual bank deposits up to $2,500.

On March 10, Roosevelt sent his second emergency proposal to Congress. The Economy Act fulfilled the president's pledge to reduce government spending, cutting $400 million from veterans' payments and $100 million from the salaries of federal employees. Congress approved the measure on March 20, and two days later passed the Beer-Wine Revenue Act, signaling an end to Prohibition. On April 7 beer was legally sold in America for the first time since 1919.

After the initial flurry of activity, the administration turned its attention to its two top priorities: relief for the millions of Americans left jobless by the collapse, and recovery for the ailing economy. The government offered relief to the unemployed by providing jobs in the new Civilian Conservation Corps (CCC). One of the most popular New Deal programs, the CCC provided jobs for more than 2 million men in army-style camps in national parks and forests. For $30 a month, they planted trees, cleared campsites, built bridges, constructed dams, and blazed fire trails. Congress appropriated $3.3 billion for a new Public Works Administration (PWA) to undertake an ambitious public construction program. The PWA's impact was limited by the cautious, penny-pinching ways of its head, Interior Secretary

Harold Ickes. "He still has to learn," complained one of his assistants, "that the Administrator of a $3 billion fund hasn't time to check every typewriter acquisition."

The Congress also approved creation of the Federal Emergency Relief Administration (FERA), headed by former social worker Harry Hopkins, to allocate $500 million to state and local governments to dispense to needy families. Half of the money went to the states on a matching basis of one federal for three state dollars. Hopkins had discretion to distribute the remaining $250 million on the basis of "need." In a flurry of executive action, Hopkins distributed over $5 million during his first two hours in office.

With FERA, the New Deal took its first tentative steps toward the welfare state. But FERA's brief history underscored the problems Roosevelt faced by challenging ingrained notions of self-help and limited government. Since FERA's staff was small, never numbering more than a few hundred people, Hopkins had to rely on state and county officials to screen applicants and distribute benefits. Even so, and even though most states had exhausted their own limited funds for dealing with the needy, many complained about federal intrusion into what had traditionally been a local function. More important, the whole idea of government relief ran counter to cherished American faith in self-sufficiency. A reporter noted that the state relief committee in North Dakota was dominated by officials who "think there is something wrong with a man who cannot make a living." Hopkins lamented that most relief administrators viewed applicants as "in some way morally deficient." The attitude was shared by the unemployed, who were reluctant and often embarrassed to seek relief. "I have seen thousands of these defeated, discouraged, hopeless men and

The Civilian Conservation Corps   The CCC, one of the most successful New Deal programs, put young men to work in the field of conservation. They planted trees, created reservoirs and irrigation systems, and built roads and campgrounds in national parks. These CCC workers are returning to camp after a hard day in Yosemite National Park.   *(National Archives.)*

women, cringing and fawning as they come to ask for public aid," said the mayor of Toledo, Ohio. "It is a spectacle of national degeneration."

By October 1933, Hopkins, having grown frustrated with the inherent problems of public relief, convinced Roosevelt to set up a temporary program that coupled relief with work, the Civil Works Administration (CWA). Within a month, Hopkins had put 2.6 million people on his payroll. CWA workers refurbished 500,000 miles of roads and 40,000 schools, and they built 150,000 outdoor privies throughout the South. Hopkins hired actors to give free shows and librarians to catalog archives. He even paid researchers to study the history of the safety pin. Jobs in the CWA gave hope and a sense of pride to the unemployed and the distressed. "When I got that [CWA] card it was the biggest day of my whole life," recalled a CWA participant. "At last I could say, 'I've got a job.'"

Developing programs to revive the economy proved more difficult. The administration realized that recovery would not be possible without an aggressive policy to aid the nation's ailing farmers. For most of the previous decade, farmers had produced more crops than the market could absorb. With supply outpacing demand, the prices farmers received for their commodities plummeted. A bushel of wheat that sold in Chicago for $2.94 in 1920 dropped to $1 by 1929 and 30 cents by 1932. To remedy the supply problem, Roosevelt pushed the Agricultural Adjustment Act (AAA) through Congress in May 1933. The law provided farmers with subsidies for letting acreage lie fallow or shifting its use to nonsurplus crops. Corn producers, for example, received 30 cents a bushel for corn not raised. The AAA also created a "commodity loan" program designed to keep crops that had already been harvested from reaching the market.

Secretary of Agriculture Henry A. Wallace was charged with the distasteful task of ordering farmers to plow up millions of acres of cotton, corn, and wheat, and to slaughter millions of baby hogs to be eligible for the subsidy payments. Over the next two years, farmers took more than 30 million acres out of production and received over $1.1 billion in government subsidies. These drastic actions, taken at a time when many Americans were starving, provoked angry disapproval. A critic noted that Roosevelt solved the paradox of want amid plenty by doing away with plenty. But the policies achieved their desired goals. The price of a bushel of wheat almost tripled between 1932 and 1936, and the price of hogs increased from $3.34 per hundredweight to $9.37. During the same period, farm income surged from $1.8 billion to $5 billion.

Not everyone benefited from the rising incomes. To make the AAA as democratic as possible, Roosevelt allowed local farmers to decide what lands to leave fallow. In most cases, large landowners cut the acreage of tenants and sharecroppers, or forced them off the land altogether. African-Americans, who made up the vast majority of sharecroppers, suffered the most. As many as two hundred thousand black tenant farmers were displaced from their land by the AAA. In 1934 ousted tenants and sharecroppers in Arkansas and Alabama organized unions to stem the evictions and increase their bargaining power. The landlords struck back, using violence to crush the union drive. Few blacks shed a tear when the Supreme Court, in *Butler* v. *U.S.* (1936), ruled the AAA unconstitutional.

A month after passing the AAA program for agriculture, Congress enacted a comprehensive program for industrial recovery called the National Industrial Recovery Act (NIRA), which set up a planning agency called the National Recovery Administration (NRA). Roosevelt called the NRA "the most important and far-reaching legislation ever passed by the American Congress." Under NRA supervision, competing businesses within a given industry met with union leaders and consumer groups to draft codes of fair competition that limited production and stabilized prices. Section 7(a) of NRA guaranteed workers' rights to join unions and to engage in collective bargaining. It also established minimum wages and maximum hours for workers. As a symbol of the program, the NRA adopted a blue eagle with the legend "We Do Our Part." Blue Eagle badges soon appeared on store windows, theater marquees, and delivery trucks.

From the beginning, the NRA ran into a host of problems that would ultimately erode public support and lead to its premature death. In many areas, especially steel and automobile manufacturing, the largest producers dominated the code-making bodies, generating cries of unfair treatment from small operators, labor, and consumer groups. In addition, developing codes for nearly every industry proved overwhelming. Almost overnight, NRA mushroomed into a bureaucratic giant. In its first two years, the NRA drafted thirteen thousand pages of codes and issued eleven thousand rulings. Even gravediggers and striptease artists had codes. Many businesses simply ignored or artfully evaded the codes. The public also turned against the Blue Eagle icon, which journalist Walter Lippmann now slammed as a symbol of "excessive centralization" and "the dictatorial spirit." The final blow came in May 1935 when the Supreme Court, in *Schechter* v. *U.S.*, ruled the NIRA unconstitutional.

Along with boosting farm prices and reviving industrial production, the New Deal embarked on a number of public electric power and water projects that both offered jobs to the unemployed and dramatically altered the environment to improve the quality of life in some rural areas. In 1935 the government completed work on the Boulder Dam, later called Hoover Dam, which was designed to harness the power of the Colorado River to generate electricity for Los Angeles and southern Arizona, and to provide drinking water for southern California. In 1938 it completed the 80-mile All-American Canal. Connecting the Colorado River to California's Imperial Valley, the canal opened up an additional 1 million acres of desert land. The West's largest power and irrigation project of all was the Grand Coulee Dam on the Columbia River northwest of Spokane, Washington. Completed in 1941, Grand Coulee was the largest concrete structure built up to that time. It towered 550 feet in the air and created a reservoir 150 miles wide. The construction of Grand Coulee, and a number of other smaller projects, successfully converted the power of the Columbia River into cheap electricity, irrigated previously uncultivated land, and stimulated the economic development of the Pacific Northwest. It also reduced the majestic Columbia River to a series of lakes.

In May 1933, Congress also created the Tennessee Valley Authority (TVA), one of the great achievements of the New Deal. The TVA spent billions in federal money constructing dams for flood control and to generate hydroelectric power for one of the poorest, most depressed areas of the nation. It provided power for farms and made possible the development of industry in the region. The dams were used in flood control, while other TVA projects reclaimed and reforested land and fought soil erosion. TVA also provided thousands of jobs for poor residents, both black and white, of the region. Critics condemned the TVA as "socialism," but it proved enormously popular among people living in the region.

No other New Deal measure improved the quality of rural life as much as the federally funded Rural Electrification Administration (REA). Until 1935 rural America lacked electrical power. Kerosene lamps illuminated homes after dark, and farms lacked washing machines, refrigerators, vacuum cleaners, and radios. In 1935 fewer than 10 percent of rural homes had electricity. By 1940, 40 percent were electrified, and by 1950, 90 percent.

Other significant early New Deal measures included the new Home Owners Loan Corporation (HOLC), which provided loans of up to $14,000 at 5 percent interest. By the end of Roosevelt's first term, the HOLC had made more than a million loans to homeowners totaling $3 billion. Roosevelt also took the nation off the international gold standard in order to inflate the currency to complement his efforts to raise domestic price levels through the AAA and the NRA.

Recovery remained elusive for most Americans, but they were grateful to Roosevelt for having done so much to help. Voters showed their appreciation in the 1934 elections, giving the Democrats an additional 13 seats in the House and 9 in the Senate. The party now enjoyed massive majorities in Congress, holding 322 seats in the House and 69 in the Senate. Forty-one of the forty-eight states elected Democratic governors. Confirming that the political balance of power in the party was migrating away from the rural South, and toward the industrial North and West, Democrats again scored well with urban voters, especially among Catholic and Jewish immigrants, and African-Americans living in the North. Arthur Krock of the *New York Times* exclaimed that the New Deal had won "the most overwhelming victory in the history of American politics."

Attacks from the Left and Right

Roosevelt's actions angered conservatives who charged that he was trying to assume dictatorial powers and extinguish individual rights. H. L. Mencken complained about the emerging welfare state, calling the Roosevelt administration "a milch cow with 125,000,000 teats." However, Roosevelt's greatest challenge came not from the right but from demagogues on the left who appealed to the dissatisfactions and frustrations of many Americans. Father Charles Coughlin, "the radio priest," developed a following of millions with his weekly radio program from the Shrine of the Little Flower. A masterful performer, Coughlin blamed the depression on wealthy bankers and rallied his large radio audience in support of Roosevelt's New Deal. By 1934, however, he turned against the president, denouncing him as a "liar," and a tool of the moneyed elite. He dismissed the New Deal, which he once referred to as "Christ's Deal," as a "Pagan Deal."

Dr. Francis E. Townsend, a retired dentist, proposed that all people over sixty receive $200 per month on the condition that they spend the money during the same month they got it. The money for the pensions would be raised by a "transaction tax," a sales tax levied each time goods were sold. He claimed his plan would both provide for the elderly and end the depression by pumping billions of dollars of purchasing power into the economy. Dr. Townsend's scheme attracted a huge following. He was offering seniors $200 a month at a time when only twenty-eight states provided old-age pensions, and those ranged from $8 to $30 a month. When a bill modeled after his plan was introduced in Congress in 1935, Coughlin secured 20 million signatures calling for its passage.

The most significant challenge to the New Deal came from Huey Long, a charismatic, ambitious, and shrewd politician. A gifted speaker, Long became governor of Louisiana in 1929 and U.S. senator in 1932. His program of imposing heavy taxes on big business to pay for public works earned him immense popularity among Louisiana's workers and farmers. On that foundation, he built a powerful political machine, dominated the legislature, and restricted the press.

At first, Long supported the New Deal, but he soon turned against Roosevelt. By 1935, fashioning himself as a modern-day Robin Hood, Long announced his "Share Our Wealth" plan, which promised to "soak" the rich and make "every man a king." The government, he insisted, must "limit the size of the big men's fortune and guarantee some minimum to the fortune and comfort of the little man's family." Share Our Wealth proposed using the government's tax power to confiscate all incomes over $1 million and all estates over $5 million. The money raised would go to farmers and industrial workers, furnishing each family with $5,000 for buying a farm or home, an annual income of $2,000, a free college education for their children, a radio, and other benefits. By 1935, 27,000 Share Our Wealth clubs claimed 4.7 million members eager to reverse their fortunes.

Long's scheme appealed to the aspirations of poor people during the depression, to their resentment of the rich, and to their disappointment with New Deal efforts. Like Coughlin, he tapped into a strong populist undercurrent by portraying politics as a struggle between the noble intentions of "the people" and the greedy interests of elites. The message had special appeal to middle-class Americans who had enjoyed a degree of independence and autonomy in the past, but who now felt threatened by the many changes around them. They lashed out at those groups—bankers, Jews, communists, and Washington bureaucrats—who they charged were responsible for the depression.

Roosevelt feared that a Long challenge in 1936 could siphon off needed support in key states. Polls showed Long running strong in a handful of states, and likely to garner about 12 percent of the popular vote. An assassin ended the threat of a Long candidacy in September 1935. Gerald L. K. Smith assumed control of the Share Our Wealth clubs, but without Long's charismatic leadership the movement quickly disintegrated.

Many other left-wing critics also railed against the New Deal. Both the Communist and Socialist Parties attacked it as too conservative. In California Socialist muckraker Upton Sinclair (see page 812) captured the 1934 Democratic Party gubernatorial nomination campaigning on a program he called End Poverty in California (EPIC). Although he lost to a conservative Republican, Sinclair attracted over eight hundred thousand votes. Minnesota governor Floyd Olson confessed, "I hope the present system of government goes right down to hell." Communism proved an attractive ideology for many. Membership in the Communist Party increased between 1928 and 1938 from 8,000 to 75,000. During the thirties the movement made inroads in labor and among intellectuals and leading Hollywood figures, but it never developed a mass following.

The Second New Deal

"I am fighting Communism, Huey Longism, Coughlinism, Townsendism," Roosevelt blustered in 1935. Attacks from the left, combined with growing resistance from business groups, convinced Roosevelt to move leftward. His rhetoric became bolder as he attacked the "unjust concentration of wealth and economic power," and his agenda more expansive as he declared that "social justice, no longer a distant ideal, has become a definite goal." His new agenda found expression in landmark legislation that would profoundly alter the relationship between the American people and the government: The National Labor Relations (or Wagner) Act, the Social Security Act, and the Emergency Relief Appropriation Act (ERA).

Roosevelt's fingerprints were all over the National Labor Relations Act (NLRA), which legislated the right of workers to unionize and to bargain collectively, reaffirming the guarantee in section 7(a) of the National Recovery Administration. Supporters called the NLRA "labor's Magna Carta." The brainchild of New York senator Robert Wagner, the NLRA created the National Labor Relations Board (NLRB) to supervise union elections and to issue "cease and desist" orders against companies that committed unfair labor practices. In the long term, the legislation made the federal government the arbitrator between labor and management.

In August 1935, after lengthy hearings and intense bargaining, Congress approved Roosevelt's ambitious plan for social security. Virtually alone among industrialized countries, the United States faced the depression without a national system to aid the unemployed and elderly. Nearly half of all Americans over 65 were on relief in 1935. The Social Security Act remedied that problem, promising to provide "security against the hazards and vicissitudes of life." The new law featured three forms of aid: pensions for people over sixty-five, unemployment compensation for people temporarily out of work, and "categorical assistance" for specific groups who could not qualify for WPA work or find other forms of employment, such as the blind, dependent children, and the disabled.

Compared with social insurance programs implemented by European nations, social security appeared skimpy. Because the old-age pensions did not extend to workers who held low-wage positions, the act excluded many minorities and women. Funding for the unemployment and categorical assistance programs depended on cooperation between the federal government and the states, and wide disparities emerged among states in funding and compensation levels. With all its faults, however, the social security law was a major step forward in assistance to the "forgotten man." As one social worker exulted, "During the years between 1929 and 1939 more progress was made in public welfare than in the hundred years after this country was founded."

In April 1935, Roosevelt proposed and Congress passed the Emergency Relief Appropriation Act (ERA). The ERA asked for the largest peacetime appropriation to date in American history—$4 billion in new funds to be used for work relief and public works construction. In explaining the bill to Congress, Roosevelt, learning from the experience with FERA, drew a sharp distinction between "relief" and "work relief." Doling out cash, he claimed, "induces a spiritual and moral disintegration fundamentally destructive to the national fibre." Work, on the other hand, nurtured "self-respect . . . self-reliance and courage and determination."

The most important program in the ERA was the Works Progress Administration (WPA). The WPA became the nation's biggest employer, hiring more than 3 million people in its first year, and during its eight years of operation, it created jobs for 8.5 million Americans at a cost of $11 billion. WPA workers built over 650,000 miles of roads, 125,000 public buildings, 8,000 parks, and hundreds of bridges. The WPA created New York City's La Guardia Airport, restored the St. Louis, Missouri's riverfront, excavated Indian burial grounds in New Mexico, and operated the bankrupt city of Key West, Florida.

Encouraged by Eleanor Roosevelt, the WPA established projects for thousands of artists, musicians, actors, and writers. "Hell, they've got to eat just like other people," WPA head Harry Hopkins told critics. Artists on WPA payrolls painted murals in post offices and other public buildings. The Federal Music and Theater Projects sponsored symphony orchestras and jazz groups, and brought dramas, comedies, and variety shows to cities and towns across the nation. Some young

WPA Artist at Work   The Works Progress Administration employed millions of Americans for a variety of construction projects, such as bridges and airports. In addition, the agency sponsored writers, artists, musicians, and actors. This Michigan artist sketches other WPA workers laboring on a construction project. The lasting results of the WPA include state guides, murals, and the Historical Records Survey. The agency also was a forerunner of the National Endowment for the Arts.   *(National Archives.)*

artists who acted and directed in the Theater Project, John Houseman and Orson Welles for example, would later achieve nationwide fame. At its height, the Federal Writers Project employed five thousand writers, including Richard Wright, John Steinbeck, and John Cheever, on a variety of programs. Most notably, it produced the American Guide Series, a popular set of guidebooks to each of the states, their major cities, and highway routes. The 150-volume *Life in America* series included valuable oral histories of former slaves, studies of ethnic cultures and Indians, and pioneering collections of American songs and folktales.

The 1936 Election

With public opinion polls taken in 1936 showing that his New Deal programs enjoyed broad popular support in all regions of the nation, Roosevelt turned his re-election campaign into a great nonpartisan liberal crusade, a clash between the "haves" and "have-nots." His opening speech attacked "economic royalists" who took "other people's money" to impose a "new industrial dictatorship." The forces of "organized money are unanimous in their hate for me," he told a cheering crowd in New York's Madison Square Garden, "and I welcome their hatred."

To oppose the popular president, the GOP turned to Alfred M. "Alf" Landon, a former follower of Theodore Roosevelt and then the progressive Republican governor of Kansas. Landon campaigned as a moderate, expressing support for New Deal goals but claiming he could achieve the same results more efficiently and with less bureaucracy.

Roosevelt and the Democrats swept to a landslide victory. Roosevelt received 27.8 million votes to Landon's 16.7 million. The Union Party, a third-party challenge made up of followers of Long, Coughlin, and Townsend, managed to draw only 882,479 votes. The president swept every state but Maine and Vermont, and carried with him into Congress unprecedented Democratic margins of 331 to 89 in the House and 76 to 16 in the Senate. Six million more people voted in 1936 than had cast ballots in 1932, and the bulk of these new voters voted for Roosevelt. Most were recruited from the ranks of the poor, people on relief, the unemployed, and the working classes, and these groups expressed their solidarity with the man who had created the New Deal.

By 1936, Roosevelt and the Democrats had forged a new political coalition firmly based on the mass of voters living in large northern cities. The ethnic groups and black voters in the cities had benefited from New Deal programs and were delighted at the attention New Dealers gave them. Hard times and New Deal programs had also attracted the votes of most farmers and of the elderly. Organized labor, as an integral part of the New Deal coalition, fused the interests of millions of workers, both skilled and unskilled, native-born and foreign-born, white and nonwhite, male and female. Many former Republican progressive middle-class voters and thousands of former Socialists also joined the Roosevelt coalition. By 1936, few besides conservative, old-stock Americans in small towns and cities, and business leaders, clung to the GOP.

The commanding personality of Franklin Roosevelt was the core of the new Democratic coalition. His smashing electoral victory confirmed his popularity and the political success of New Deal programs. "Every house I visited," a social worker reported after a tour in South Carolina, "had a picture of the President. These ranged from newspaper clippings (in destitute houses) to large colored prints, framed in gilt cardboard. The portrait holds the place of honor over the mantel;.I can only compare this to the peasant's Madonna."

The Decline of the New Deal

Uplifted by his electoral landslide, Roosevelt began his second term by raising hopes that new, perhaps even bolder, initiatives lay ahead. "I see one-third of a nation ill-housed, ill-clad, ill-nourished," the president declared in his second inaugural address. Instead of reform, however, Roosevelt's second term produced stalemate, and eventual retrenchment.

Two weeks after his inauguration, Roosevelt announced a misconceived plan to reform the Supreme Court. The plan called for the addition of a new judge to the Supreme Court whenever an incumbent refused to retire at the age of seventy. The Supreme Court, which then had six judges (of the nine total) over seventy, could be expanded to a maximum of fifteen. Publicly the president defended the change by suggesting that the Court had fallen behind in its work. In fact, as far as Roosevelt was concerned, the problem was that the Court was performing too efficiently. It had already overturned the NRA, the AAA, and the minimum wage. FDR worried that new initiatives, especially social security and the Wagner Act, would suffer similar fates unless he could add some supportive justices to the bench.

As expected, conservatives attacked the plan, accusing Roosevelt of trying to "pack" the Court. Much to the president's surprise, his reform plan also angered the public, which held the Court in high esteem and valued the independence of the judiciary. Many congressional Democrats, including the president's staunch liberal supporters, hotly denounced the plan.

Ironically, the Court itself undermined any support for the plan by suddenly reversing course. In two critical decisions, the justices sustained a minimum wage law and upheld the sweeping terms of the Wagner Act. The Court decided both decisions by a 5–4 margin with Justice Owen Roberts, until then a member of the conservative bloc, switching sides to give liberal justices the majority. The turnabout led one observer to suggest that "a switch in time saves Nine." Why Roberts switched is unclear, but his decision permitted Roosevelt to brag late in 1938, "We obtained 98 percent of all the objectives intended by the Court plan." What some scholars have called "The Constitutional Revolution of 1937," secured the New Deal's achievements and cleared the constitutional path for further reforms.

However, Roosevelt had expended a considerable amount of political capital on the Court fight, squandering the momentum from the 1936 election. The battle exposed deep wounds in the Democratic Party, and conservatives prepared to revolt against a weakened president. "What we have to do," North Carolina's Senator Josiah Bailey wrote, "is to preserve, if we can, the Democratic Party against his efforts to make it the Roosevelt party." The Court battle energized the conservative coalition of Republicans and southern Democrats into an organized legislative force determined to block future New Deal legislation. "The whole New Deal really went up in smoke as a result of the Supreme Court fight," reflected Henry Wallace.

A dramatic downturn in the economy further eroded Roosevelt's stature. Early in 1937, the economy seemed to be making steady progress toward recovery. Between 1933 and 1937, the gross national product grew at a yearly rate of 10 percent. Industrial output had increased and unemployment had declined. Believing the economy sound, and worried about the $4 billion budget deficit, Roosevelt reduced federal spending by cutting relief. But the president had overestimated the strength of the economy and underestimated the importance of continued government spending on the recovery. Roosevelt's actions precipitated a severe recession that lasted from the fall of 1937 to the spring of 1938. The rate of decline over the next ten months was sharper than in 1929. Nearly 4 million people lost their jobs, boosting total unemployment to 11.5 million. "We are headed right into another Depression," an adviser warned the president.

An intense battle erupted within the administration over how to respond to the crisis. White House advisers rehashed familiar debates between Theodore Roosevelt's New Nationalism and Woodrow Wilson's New Freedom. Should the president reassure business by cutting spending and limiting regulation? Or should he expand federal power through new regulations? Roosevelt equivocated for months, before cautiously siding with advisers who suggested a third direction: using consumer spending to lift the nation out of depression. This policy adopted the ideas of the British economist John Maynard Keynes, who in his book *The General Theory of Employment, Interest, and Money* (1936) proposed that government could spend its way out of depression. Keynes argued that during economic downturns, governments needed to abandon their faith in balanced budgets and pump money into the economy. In the spring of 1938, Roosevelt proposed a $3.75 billion package for public works and WPA programs. The spending eased the recession, but the pace of recovery remained slow.

People blamed Roosevelt and his party for the recession, and they expressed their anger toward the Democrats in the 1938 midterm elections. Roosevelt added to the Democrats' problems by announcing his plan to "purge" the party by campaigning in the primaries against conservatives who had opposed New Deal measures. The effort backfired. Most people resented the president's active involvement in local politics. Republicans, taking full advantage of the opportunity, picked up eighty-one seats in the House and eight seats in the Senate, and they gained thirteen governorships. Since all Democratic losses took place in the North and West, Southern conservatives emerged in a much stronger position. For the first time, Roosevelt could not form a majority in Congress without the help of some Republicans or southern Democrats. The mountain of political capital that Roosevelt had amassed in 1936 had been leveled in just two years.

By the end of 1939, the New Deal was for all practical purposes dead. A decidedly more conservative Congress abruptly cut off funds for the Federal Theater Project, repealed a New Deal tax measure, and refused to increase expenditures for public housing. Public attitudes had also shifted. Polls taken after 1937 indicated that a sizeable majority of people, including Democrats, wanted the Roosevelt administration to follow a more conservative course. Recognizing how far the pendulum had swung, Roosevelt became more cautious. He refused to endorse new legislation to strengthen social security or provide extended health care. Increasingly, foreign policy issues, especially events in Europe, occupied his attention.

Depression Culture, 1929–1938

The declining fortunes of Roosevelt's reform agenda at the end of the decade revealed the resiliency of conservative attitudes about government. American culture demonstrated a similar elasticity. The most striking feature of American culture during the depression was how quickly it adapted to crisis. Helen and Robert Lynd, the chroniclers of "Middletown," commented that "a Rip Van Winkle, fallen asleep in 1925 while addressing Rotary or the Central Labor Union, could have awakened in 1935 and gone right on with his interrupted address to the same people with much the same ideas." A few artists documented the pain and anguish of the "depression decade." Some, by suggesting that the economic collapse represented a failure of institutions, challenged traditional American individualistic values. Most Americans, however, searched for affirmation of older verities, or looked for an escape from the drudgery of daily life.

Social Realism and Social Escape During the 1930s

Novels of social realism, depicting a stark and unforgiving society, were popular with Americans trying to understand the depression. John Dos Passos's *Big Money* (1936), the concluding volume of his massive trilogy *U.S.A.,* describes the pernicious effect of materialism on characters cast as ordinary Americans. James T. Farrell's *Studs Lonigan* trilogy (1932–1938) depicts the harsh urban realities of his native Chicago. The trilogy ends when Lonigan, alone and unemployed, dies of tuberculosis. Richard Wright's *Native Son* (1940), set in Chicago's black belt, features the evils of racism and capitalism. Clifford Odets's *Waiting for Lefty* uses the struggle of a group of taxi drivers to highlight the limits of individualism and the need for collective action. William Faulkner's *As I Lay Dying* (1930) and *Light in August* (1932) paints vivid portraits of life in rural Mississippi. John Steinbeck's *The Grapes of Wrath* (1939) tells the story of an uprooted Dust Bowl family, the Joads, making their way along Route 66 to California. As Ma Joad says, "They ain't gonna wipe us out. Why, we're the people—we go on."

The influence of social realism was not limited to literature. Jacob Lawrence drew directly on his own experience growing up in Harlem in a series of sixty paintings entitled *The Migration of the Negro.* Together the paintings told the story of dispossessed blacks during the 1930s. Painters Reginald Marsh and Edward Hopper, members of the so-called Fourteenth Street School of New York, tried to capture the vitality of urban life on their canvases.

Many artists experimented with the camera to document the searing pain of the depression and to accentuate the valiant struggle of people fighting to preserve their dignity. Photography took on new vitality. "The image has become the queen of our age," noted a publisher. "We are no longer content to know, we must see." New photojournalism magazines, including *Life* (1936) and *Look* (1937), reflected the new documentary impulse. Poet-screenwriter James Agee and photographer Walker Evans documented the life of poor white tenant farmers in the South in *Let Us Now Praise Famous Men* (1941), capturing the tenants' transcendent sense of pride among their small wooden shacks and meager furnishings. Photojournalists such as Dorothea Lange and Marion Post Wolcott recorded the plight of migrant farm workers for the Farm Security Administration in a number of memorable images.

The best-selling books were not chronicles of contemporary pain and hardship but stories that offered readers a respite from the hardship of depression life. Margaret Mitchell's *Gone With the Wind* (1936) sold 178,000 copies within its first three weeks of publication. It remained on the best-seller lists for twenty-one consecutive months and sold 2 million copies. The panoramic love story paints a nostalgic picture of southern culture and white paternalism during the Civil War and Reconstruction.

Gone With the Wind revealed another depression trend in the arts: a renewed appreciation of small-town, rural ways of life. Because of hard times, some Americans romanticized the virtues of self-sufficient living close to the soil. Regionalist painters, led by John Steuart Curry, Grant Wood, and Thomas Hart Benton were among the most widely reproduced and popular artists of the decade. They revolted against European fashions in art and focused on pastoral scenes of the American Plains and Midwest. In 1930 a group of southern historians, novelists, and poets published *I'll Take My Stand*, which contrasted the harmony of life in the Old South (including slavery) with the impersonal and chaotic fate of modern society.

Entertaining the Masses

To cope with idleness, millions of unemployed Americans read more and took up stamp collecting, contract bridge, games, and fads. Dance marathons, roller derbies, six-day bicycle races, and flagpole-sitting contests became popular. The first All-American Soapbox Derby was held in Dayton, Ohio, in 1934. Millions of cash-strapped Americans tried to "make a killing" by accumulating make-believe fortunes in a new game called Monopoly.

Escapism and images of a better future scored well with the American public during the decade. Superman, who fought "a never-ending battle for truth, justice, and the American way," appeared in *Action Comics* in June 1938. Women's magazines, which claimed a readership of 13 million, offered a steady diet of love stories. *Reader's Digest*, the most popular periodical of the decade with a circulation of more than 7 million, carried upbeat articles about personal and business success. At the depth of the depression in 1933 and 1934, 20 million people marveled at the possibilities of science at the "Century of Progress" exposition in Chicago. In 1939 New York's World's Fair attracted nearly 50 million people who admired a 180-foot globe that symbolized "The World of Tomorrow."

Millions of Americans remained enthusiastic sports fans during the depression. The most popular sport continued to be baseball, the "national pastime." Each year millions of Americans clustered around their radios to listen to the World Series. In 1938 heavyweight boxing champ Joe Louis, "the Brown Bomber," pounded German Max Schmelling in New York's Madison Square Garden. The novelist Richard Wright wrote that in Louis's victory "blacks took strength, and in that moment all fear, all obstacles were wiped out, drowned." Another African-American athlete, sprinter Jesse Owens, "the Ebony Antelope," won four gold metals in the 1936 Olympic games held in Berlin. Despite the success of Louis and

Owens, black athletes faced many obstacles in competing in popular sports. Big Ten basketball barred black players. Hall-of-famers such as Satchel Paige and Josh Gibson played in the Negro baseball league of the 1930s, but few white Americans paid attention to the all-black Homestead Grays or Pittsburgh Crawfords.

In 1930 an estimated 110 million people attended movie theaters each week. Three years later, with the economy at rock bottom, 60 to 80 million managed to find the money for a 25-cent admission ticket. Over 60 percent of Americans attended one of the nation's 20,000 movie houses each week. Throughout the depression, the movie industry, fast becoming dominated by a small number of large studios, produced more than five hundred movies a year. The major studios tended to serve up escapist fare that steered clear of depression realities and avoided raising serious social issues. Horror pictures such as *Frankenstein* and gangster films such as *The Public Enemy,* both made in 1931, were popular. Outstanding comedians, among them W. C. Fields, Laurel and Hardy, Charlie Chaplin, Will Rogers, and the Marx Brothers, brought laughter to millions of Americans. Movie musicals offered plots that were usually upbeat, revolving around a story of rags to riches, or a poor chorus girl marrying a wealthy blueblood. But reality often intruded. *Gold Diggers* opened with Ginger Rogers and sixty showgirls singing "We're in the Money," but ended with local authorities closing down the show because the producer failed to pay his bills.

Hollywood Escapism   In difficult times, Americans looked to the entertainment industry to help them forget their troubles. The 1930s saw over 50 million Americans attending the movies every week. Films such as *Gold Diggers of 1933,* featured in this photograph, employed themes of wealth and optimism that starkly contrasted with the reality of the day. *Gold Diggers*' major musical number buoyantly declared, "We're in the money / We're in the money / We've got a lot of what / It takes to get along / We never see a headline/ About a breadline / Today." *(Photofest.)*

Walt Disney and Frank Capra emerged as the decade's most successful directors. Disney's *Three Little Pigs* (1933), featuring the hit song "Who's Afraid of the Big Bad Wolf?" reminded many people of Roosevelt's assertion that Americans had nothing to fear but fear itself. Capra's films reaffirmed faith in individual initiative and suggested that old-fashioned values of kindness, loyalty, and charity could solve most of the nation's ills. One observer noted in 1934 that "no medium has contributed more greatly than film to the maintenance of the national morale during a period featured by revolution, riot and political turmoil in other countries."

A few iconoclasts used movies to challenge conventional thinking. Perhaps no one was more successful at defying traditional values than the actress Mae West, whose liberated spirit and appetite for pleasure defied sexual mores. "Is that a gun in your pocket, big boy," she asked of her leading men, "or are you just glad to see me?" Traditionalists responded angrily to West's films and others viewed them as licentious. In 1933 the Catholic Church created the Legion of Decency and pressured Hollywood to establish strict guidelines of behavior on the screen. The new code banned kissing, nudity, and "sympathetic treatment of wrongdoing."

The Golden Age of Radio

Although many radio stations banned Mae West from the airwaves, film actors often took parts in radio dramas and variety programs. The 1930s became the golden age of radio. The number of Americans who owned radios increased from 10 million in 1929 to 27.5 million a decade later, at which time 90 percent of the nation's homes had at least one radio. Each radio, one survey found in 1937, was used for an average of 4¼ hours a day.

Music and variety shows dominated radio broadcasting during the decade. Millions gathered around their Philco or Stromberg-Carlson radios to hear the songs of Bing Crosby and Frank Sinatra, or the big band sounds Benny Goodman. Many others delighted in the wisecracks of Bob Hope and Jack Benny. Popular ongoing daytime stories were called soap operas because they were sponsored by soap companies. The plots were usually simple, appealing to the romantic fantasies of middle-class women. *Mary Noble, Backstage Wife*, was the story of "an Iowa stenographer who fell in love with and married Broadway matinee idol Larry Noble." In *The Romance of Helen Trent*, a woman learned "that romance can live in life at thirty-five and after."

Soaps about crime fighting were also popular with depression audiences searching for reassurance that the old rules of right and wrong still applied. In *The Shadow*, crime-fighter Lamont Cranston, reassured audiences: "Crime does not pay . . . the Shadow knows!" By 1939, *The Lone Ranger* was being heard three times a week on 140 stations. The hero, a mysterious masked man, aided by a faithful Indian companion, Tonto, brought justice to the Wild West. *The Green Hornet* sought to capture "public enemies that even the G-Men cannot catch."

By 1940, radio had supplanted newspapers as the public's primary source of information. Millions of Americans huddled next to the radio to listen to Roosevelt's Fireside Chats. In 1935 radio provided extensive coverage of the trial of Bruno Hauptmann, who stood accused of kidnapping and murdering Charles Lindbergh's infant son. In May 1937 Herb Morrison of Chicago's station WLS unexpectedly, and emotionally, covered the explosion of the *Hindenburg* passenger blimp as it attempted to dock in Lakehurst, New Jersey. Sometimes radio made it difficult to distinguish fact from fiction. A popular weekly news show, *The March of Time*, embellished news events with dramatization. In 1938 Orson Welles and his Mercury Theater broadcast H. G. Wells's classic science fiction tale, *The War of the Worlds.* "Ladies and gentlemen, this is the most terrifying thing I have ever witnessed . . . ," the "correspondent" sobbed as he described a Martian invasion of New Jersey. Hundreds of thousands of listeners believed every word. In New Jersey, terrified people jammed roads trying to avoid the advancing aliens.

The New Deal and Society, 1933–1938

The theme of continuity and change, which characterized the depression's impact on cultural values, also applies to the New Deal's influence on society. In many ways, the New Deal accepted and reinforced traditional divisions based on race, class, and gender. But in significant ways it challenged existing power structures, offering support to previously marginalized social groups. The New Deal enhanced the bargaining power of organized labor, which witnessed extraordinary gains during the decade. Minorities and women also received benefits from New Deal programs designed to help the poor and unemployed. On balance, New Deal reforms had a lasting impact on American society, but the New Deal experiment did not end the depression or threaten the basic tenets of capitalism.

The Rise of Organized Labor

Perhaps no group benefited more from the New Deal than organized labor, which made tremendous gains during the depression decade. Union membership jumped from 3.6 million in 1930 to nearly 10.5 million in 1941. Roosevelt's support for the Wagner Act, which created an atmosphere hospitable to labor, contributed to the growth. But it was the grass-roots activity of militant workers that produced the greatest gains. Many of these workers, who labored in large-scale, mass-production industries such as automobiles, steel, rubber, electrical goods, and textiles, engaged in a number of successful strikes. The number of workers involved in walkouts rose from 324,210 in 1932 to 1.6 million in 1933. In 1934 working class militancy reached new heights as violent industrial conflicts paralyzed cities in Ohio, California, and Minnesota. The strikes spurred increases in membership. The United Mine Workers grew from about 60,000 to over 500,000. The International Ladies' Garment Workers' Union (ILGWU) increased fourfold, and the United Textile Workers tripled its membership.

As in the twenties, the AFL continued to show little interest in organizing unskilled workers in mass-production industries other than coal mining and clothing. Following enactment of the Wagner Act, a group within the AFL, led by the forceful and articulate John L. Lewis of the United Mine Workers, demanded that the AFL commit itself to the "industrial organization of mass production workers." At its convention in 1935, AFL delegates, mostly from craft unions, rejected

Lewis's proposal. At the end of the convention an angry Lewis signaled his break with the AFL by punching carpenters head "Big Bill" Hutcheson, bloodying his face and leaving him to be carried from the platform. "With this historic punch," observed a labor historian, "Lewis signified the formal beginning of the industrial-union rebellion within the House of Labor and made himself the leading rebel."

Three weeks later, on November 10, 1935, Lewis and the heads of seven other AFL unions announced the formation of the Committee for Industrial Organization, later called the Congress of Industrial Organization (CIO). The CIO launched major organizing drives in mass-production industries in the late 1930s. In 1937 a total of 4.7 million workers were involved in 4,740 strikes that affected all of the nation's key industries—steel, coal, auto, rubber, and electricity (see graph).

In January 1937 in Flint, Michigan, the United Automobile Workers (UAW), a CIO affiliate, began a strike against General Motors, seeking union recognition. If Flint autoworkers could beat General Motors, the world's largest industrial corporation, their victory would galvanize workers in auto and other basic industries. Their grievances were common to auto plants of the 1930s: frequent layoffs, arbitrary management decisions, and poor working conditions. The strikers used a novel tactic, the "sit-down" strike, against the giant automaker. Participants refused to work but stayed in the factory to prevent nonunion workers from keeping the plants going.

The sit-down strike was highly controversial, but it worked. Company guards turned off the heat and barred strikers from bringing in food, but the strikers refused to budge. On January 11, sheriff's deputies and police stormed the plant. Strikers drove them back, deluging police with fire hoses and pelting them with car

Labor Union Membership The New Deal's inclusion of Section 7A in the National Labor Recovery Act and the 1935 Wagner Act opened the doorway to union membership by guaranteeing workers the right to organize. Leaders of the American Federation of Labor and the newly created Congress of Industrial Organizations worked diligently recruiting workers, and membership in both organizations soared.

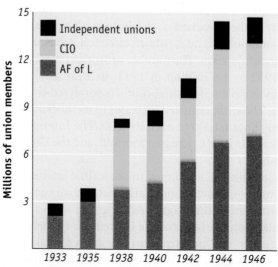

hinges, stones, and anything else they could get their hands on. Ten thousand people turned out the next day at UAW headquarters voicing support for the striking workers with the traditional union anthem "Solidarity Forever." During the first eight months of 1937, UAW membership increased from 88,000 to 400,000. Unable to dislodge the Flint strikers, the General Motors company, in February 1937, became the first major manufacturer to recognize the UAW. All the other auto manufacturers followed suit, except Ford, which held out until 1941.

CIO organizers soon moved against other industries. A few weeks after the settlement with General Motors, United States Steel agreed to recognize the CIO, increased wages by 10 percent, established a forty-hour week, and provided seniority rights and paid vacations. The lesser steel companies (known as "Little Steel") were far less ready to give in, however. On Memorial Day 1937 police attacked strikers picketing Republic Steel in Chicago, firing into a crowd, killing ten, and wounding dozens more. The "Memorial Day massacre" created widespread sympathy for the strikers, but Little Steel broke the strike and defeated the CIO's organizing effort. The companies did not officially recognize the steelworkers' union until 1941.

By the end of 1937, the new CIO unions claimed 4 million members. The number of women in CIO unions tripled to 800,000 in 1940. The AFL, revitalized by the CIO challenge, also experienced unprecedented membership gains. Still, the triumph of industrial unionism in the 1930s was far from complete. In 1939 the Supreme Court outlawed the sit-down strike. As late as 1940, American unions embraced only 28 percent of nonagricultural workers. Most of the unskilled remained unrepresented and relatively powerless.

A New Deal for Minorities?

Among the unorganized and powerless were millions of African-Americans, many of whom now looked to the White House for assistance. They were often disappointed. Unwilling to risk alienating southern whites and their conservative congressmen, Roosevelt never endorsed two key political initiatives of the 1930s: demands for a federal antilynching law and abolition of the poll tax. Neither effort succeeded.

African-Americans had other grievances against the administration. New Deal programs routinely accepted and practiced discrimination. The AAA forced thousands of black sharecroppers and farm laborers off the land in its effort to reduce acreage and production. It also offered white farmers and workers higher rates of support than their black counterparts. The National Recovery Administration failed to protect black workers from discrimination in employment and wages. Blacks denounced the NRA as "Negroes Ruined Again" and "Negro Removal Act" because the codes led many businesses to lay off black employees. The CCC was racially segregated, as was the TVA, which constructed all-white towns and confined black workers to low-paying job categories. Millions of African-Americans were excluded both from social security coverage and from the minimum wage provisions of the Fair Labor Standards Act. Relief agencies paid black clients less than whites. In Atlanta, African-Americans received $19.29 per month, compared with $32.66 for whites.

Yet blacks made some limited gains during the decade. By some estimates, nearly 30 percent of African-Americans received some form of New Deal assistance. In 1935 Roosevelt issued an executive order banning discrimination in WPA projects. Blacks, who accounted for 10 percent of the nation's population, held 18 percent of WPA jobs. The Public Works Administration employed black workers to construct a number of integrated housing complexes. The Farm Security Administration helped relocate 1,400 black families to "homesteads."

The New Deal also offered African-Americans a number of symbolic, but nevertheless significant, gains. Roosevelt invited many black visitors to the White House and appointed an unofficial "black cabinet" to advise him on issues important to African-Americans. At the 1936 convention, Democrats seated blacks for the first time as delegates and an African-American gave a seconding speech on behalf of the president. In 1937 Roosevelt appointed the first black judge to the federal bench, William Hastie. Two years later, in an effort to challenge discriminatory voting practices in the South, FDR encouraged the attorney general to create a Civil Rights Division in the Department of Justice.

Within the administration, Eleanor Roosevelt emerged as the most powerful voice for combating discrimination in New Deal programs and elsewhere. She visited black churches and colleges, and invited black leaders to the White House. She helped the NAACP raise money, and she added her name to fundraising ventures by other black groups. In 1939 the Daughters of the American Revolution denied renowned African-American opera singer Marian Anderson use of their Constitution Hall for a planned Easter Day concert. At Eleanor's urging, the Roosevelt administration suggested an alternative site: the steps of the Lincoln Memorial. On Easter Sunday 1939, more than seventy-five thousand people gathered to hear the recital. Seated in the front row with Eleanor Roosevelt were senators, congressmen, and Supreme Court justices.

Despite the shortcomings of the New Deal for African-Americans, they supported it enthusiastically. When black voters joined the Roosevelt coalition, they abandoned their historical allegiance to the Republicans—the party of Lincoln. "Go turn Lincoln's picture to the wall," said one writer. "That debt has been paid in full." Two-thirds of black voters had voted for Hoover in 1932. In 1936 two-thirds voted for Roosevelt. By 1938, Democratic candidates received 85 percent of the vote in African-American communities in New York's Harlem and Chicago's South Side.

Perhaps no minority group gained more from the New Deal than Native Americans. Ravaged by infant mortality, alcoholism and tuberculosis, and many other ailments, Indians suffered from the worst poverty of any group in the nation. In 1933 President Roosevelt appointed John Collier to reform the Bureau of Indian Affairs (BIA). Collier's greatest accomplishment was securing congressional passage, in 1934, of the Indian Reorganization Act. The "Indian New Deal" reversed the emphasis on assimilation that had been codified into law fifty years earlier by the Dawes Severalty Act (see page 669). In practice, the old land allotment system worked to transfer much Indian land to white ranchers, miners, and farmers. Since 1887, Indian landholdings had dropped from 138 million acres to 48 million. The Indian Reorganization Act restored lands to tribal ownership and protected Native American religious practices and traditional culture. It provided for Indian self-

Marian Anderson Performs at the Lincoln Memorial When the Daughters of the American Revolution barred Anderson from their stage, Eleanor Roosevelt resigned her membership, then helped organize the Lincoln Memorial concert. Mrs. Roosevelt's actions were typical of the Roosevelt administration's record on civil rights in two respects. First, FDR did not involve himself in the incident, instead leaving the matter to his wife and his subordinates; and second, the Anderson concert was largely a symbolic gesture. Although the importance of these gestures should not be underestimated, on the whole the New Deal did little to advance the economic and political rights of minorities. *(Thomas McAvoy/LIFE Magazine © Time, Inc.)*

government on reservations, new loans for economic development, and expanded medical and educational services. Many of the new tribal constitutions written under Collier's supervision promoted gender equality by giving women the right to vote in tribal elections and to hold office. Collier also made sure that the BIA offered native women training both in agriculture and animal husbandry and in nursing and secretarial work.

Women During the 1930s

The depression reinforced the belief that a woman's place was in the home, not in the work force. A Gallup poll revealed that 82 percent of Americans, including 75 percent of women, agreed that wives should not work if their husbands were employed. Federal regulations prohibited more than one member of a family from holding a civil service job. Three-quarters of those forced to resign were women. Most states passed laws excluding married women—whom one politician called "undeserving parasites"—from public employment. The AFL joined in the effort, claiming that married women with working husbands "should be discriminated against in the hiring of employees."

Family need, however, triumphed over traditional attitudes. The proportion of married women in the work force, often serving as temporary or part-time help, actually increased during the decade, from 11.7 to 15.3 percent. The overall female proportion of the work force rose from 22 to 25 percent. But discrimination still routinely forced women into low-paying and low-status jobs. Between 1930 and 1940, the percentage of women in the professions declined from 14.2 to

12.3 percent. Not surprisingly, the average woman worker earned about half of the yearly income of a working man—$525 compared with $1,027.

Women did benefit from many New Deal programs, however. In 1933 Harry Hopkins sent an order to all state FERA directors to "pay particular attention that women are employed whenever possible." By 1934, more than 300,000 women—more than half of those qualified for relief—were working on various CWA projects. The WPA hired nearly half a million women in 1936, nearly 15 percent of all its workers. Three-fourths of the NRA codes included provisions for equal pay to women workers. The National Youth Administration created programs to train young women and to give them work. Women wage earners, especially those employed in the garment industry and textile production, benefited from the New Deal's support of organized labor.

Women held a number of appointive positions in New Deal agencies. Concentrated in the Labor Department, the FERA and WPA, and the Social Security Board, they worked together to maximize their influence on government policy. FDR appointed Frances Perkins secretary of labor, the first woman cabinet member in U.S. history. Grace Abbott, a veteran of Hull House (see page 804), joined a handful of women reformers to write the welfare provisions of the Social Security Act. Eleanor Roosevelt was the central figure in the increase in women's political influence, working both in public and behind the scenes with a wide network of

Women Reporters with Eleanor Roosevelt Although the New Deal's record on women's issues was mixed, the Roosevelt administration appointed the first female cabinet member, Labor Secretary Frances Perkins, and the first women ambassadors and Appeals Court judge. Mrs. Roosevelt deserves a great deal of the credit for these advances. She not only influenced her husband, she worked with Perkins and others in the administration to study and address issues important to women. In addition, she held regular press conferences, to which she invited only female reporters. *(Stock Montage.)*

women professionals and reformers whom she had come to know in the l920s. Eleanor Roosevelt's closest political ally was Molly Dewson, who served as director of the Women's Division of the national Democratic Party. Under her leadership women became an important part of the Democratic Party machinery. "Those of us who worked to put together the New Deal," Frances Perkins reflected, "are bound by spiritual ties that no one else can understand."

New Deal Legacies

The New Deal transformed the relationship between the people and the federal government. First, it dramatically increased the size and scope of government. In 1932 there were 605,000 federal employees; by 1939, there were nearly a million. Before FDR, few Americans felt that Washington had, or should have had, much influence on their lives. During the New Deal era, the federal government became the focal point for civic life. People who had once turned to local and state governments now looked to Washington for solutions to problems. A British observer noted in 1939, "Just as in 1929 the whole country was 'Wall Street conscious,' now it is 'Washington conscious.'"

Second, the New Deal altered the distribution of political power. By empowering new groups—farmers, labor, and the urban working class—the New Deal political coalition forced business to share political power. The coalition, which would endure for a generation, offered tangible benefits to groups that had long been excluded from the mainstream of American political life.

The shift in political power produced a modest redistribution of wealth. In 1929 the top 5 percent of the population received 30 percent of national income. In 1938, at the end of the New Deal, the top 5 percent's share had dropped to 26 percent. The income did not travel far. Middle- and upper-middle-class families were the chief beneficiaries. They saw their share increase from 33 percent in 1929 to 36 percent in 1938. The income share going to the poorest families rose only slightly, from 13.2 percent to 13.7 percent.

The New Deal experiment failed to remedy the fundamental economic ill caused by the Great Depression. As the New Deal ended in 1938, over 10 million men and women were still without jobs; the unemployment rate hovered near 20 percent. New Dealers never solved the puzzle of unemployment. Underconsumption plagued efforts to boost production and sales. In 1929 new car sales totaled $6.5 billion. In 1938, at the end of the New Deal, the figure was $3.9 billion. Per capita national income did not regain 1929 levels until early 1940.

Still, by every measure, the New Deal had a profound and lasting impact on American society and politics. It preserved America's capitalistic system by rescuing it from collapse. Roosevelt "saved capitalism," declared author Gore Vidal. Though programs like the NRA and AAA faded into history, many of Roosevelt's reforms—social security, stock market regulation, minimum wage, insured bank deposits—became accepted features of American life. Apart from specific programs, Roosevelt reinterpreted the Constitution's pledge to "promote the general welfare," expanding it to give the federal government the right to intervene in all substantive aspects of the nation's economic life.

CONCLUSION

The economic prosperity that characterized the 1920s began to fall apart in October 1929. The crash on Wall Street—resulting from years of speculation and unsavory trade practices—was the first domino to fall. The banking system, which had always been unregulated and prone to failures, was next, depriving millions of their savings and eroding public confidence in the economy. The stock market crash and the banking failures exposed serious structural flaws in the economy—a decade-long weakness in the agricultural market, more recent industrial overproduction, and a continuing fragile international economic system. Herbert Hoover, who had been elected as a champion of prosperity in 1928, seemed unable to devise a solution for the nation's economic woes. In 1932 a frustrated nation turned to Democrat Franklin Roosevelt.

When Franklin Roosevelt assumed the presidency in March 1933, national and personal income had plummeted, and unemployment had soared to record levels. Unable to pay their bills or support themselves in these grim economic times, millions of families found themselves homeless and forced to look to private charity—which was itself quickly swamped by the demand. Even families who maintained some source of income found their standards of living sharply reduced.

In his first hundred days in office, Roosevelt proposed an ambitious federal experiment to revitalize the economy, aid the unemployed, and restore public faith. The New Deal dramatically extended the power of the federal government, creating a host of alphabet agencies that assumed responsibilities traditionally left to local government or private charity. The Civilian Conservation Corps (CCC) provided jobs to more than 2 million men, while the Federal Emergency Relief Administration (FERA) offered relief to needy families. Reviving the New Nationalism of his cousin Theodore, FDR created the Agricultural Adjustment Act (AAA) and the National Recovery Act (NRA) to help revive the struggling economy. With passage of the Social Security Act (1935), Roosevelt created the scaffolding of the modern welfare state. With its ambitious social agenda, the New Deal inaugurated the age of activist government.

Despite the broad popularity of Roosevelt and his reforms, the New Deal did not fundamentally change American values. Even as they took jobs in the new federal agencies and received aid money through programs such as social security, Americans still clung to their notions of individuality and self-support. American culture demonstrated a similar resiliency. While some artists, filmmakers, authors, and playwrights documented the pain and hardship suffered by Americans during the depression, most people sought refuge in more traditional entertainment and escapist fare that took them far from the drudgery of everyday life. Many people, disillusioned with contemporary life, looked back to idealized images of small towns and local solutions to problems.

The New Deal did, however, transform the American political landscape. Not everyone benefited; women, for example, were still largely confined to traditional, lower-wage occupations. Roosevelt also failed to take a bold stand on civil rights. Many poor farmers of all races were hurt by the New Deal's agricultural programs. By 1936, though, Roosevelt had dramatically expanded the traditional southern white base of the Democratic Party to include African-Americans, urban immigrants, and organized labor. This "Roosevelt coalition" would dominate American politics for the next thirty years, providing the political muscle for a more active federal government.

The Great Depression had confronted the United States with one of its most trying domestic challenges. By the end of the 1930s, however, a new and potentially more dangerous threat was rising in Europe, endangering the very existence of the American experiment.

SUGGESTED READINGS

Robert McElvaine's *The Great Depression* (1983) is an excellent one-volume survey of the 1930s; it has particularly strong material on the origins and early years of the depression. John Garraty's *The Great Depression* (1987) also offers a good overview, including an international perspective on the depression. David Kennedy's *Freedom from Fear* (1999) covers the entire period, paying extra attention to the later New Deal years and World War II. William E. Leuchtenburg's *Franklin D. Roosevelt and the New Deal, 1932–1940* (1963) is still the best single-volume study of the New Deal.

John K. Galbraith's *The Great Crash* (1955) is a landmark study of the stock market crash, its causes, and implications. Milton Friedman and Anna J. Schwartz offer an opposing explanation of the crash in *A Monetary History of the United States* (1965). Michael Bernstein supplies a more recent interpretation in *The Great Depression* (1989). Several oral histories about the privations of the depression years have been compiled. Studs Terkel's *Hard Times* (1970) is the most famous.

Among the several studies of Herbert Hoover and his response to the depression, George Nash's two-volume *The Life of Herbert Hoover* (1983, 1988) is the most extensive. Joan Hoff Wilson highlights Hoover's progressive roots in *Herbert Hoover: Forgotten Progressive* (1992). Martin Fausold's *The Presidency of Herbert C. Hoover* (1985) examines the complexities of the man, how the office of the president developed during his term, and the ways he attempted to handle the growing crisis.

For biographies on Roosevelt, the starting place is Kenneth Davis's encyclopedic three-volume collection, *FDR* (1985, 1986, 1993). Frank Freidel offers a detailed one-volume survey of Roosevelt in *Franklin Roosevelt: Rendezvous with Destiny* (1990). Arthur Schlesinger, Jr.'s *The Coming of the New Deal* (1959) is the definitive treatment of FDR's first hundred days. His *Politics of Upheaval* (1960) is a necessary accompaniment.

The literature on various New Deal reform measures is voluminous. Richard Polenberg offers a readable overview in *The Era of Franklin D. Roosevelt* (2000). Anthony Badger's *The New Deal* (1989) describes the extent of public need and Roosevelt's mixed attempt to address it. Jordan Schwarz argues in *The New Dealers* (1993) that the primary goal of agency leaders was the creation of self-sustaining regional economies, not relief measures. D. Clayton Brown's *Electricity for Rural America* (1980) is a fine study of the TVA. Linda Gordon gives readers a thoughtful study of gender and the origins of the welfare state in *Pitied but Not Entitled* (1995). Donald Worster studies the farm crisis in *Dust Bowl* (1979), as does Richard Lowitt in *The New Deal and the West* (1984). Janet Poppendieck examines the impact of food assistance on farmers and consumers in *Breadlines Knee-Deep in Wheat* (1986).

The premiere study of Father Coughlin and Huey Long is Alan Brinkley's *Voices of Protest* (1982), while Donald Warren's *Radio Priest* (1996) and William Hair's *The Kingfish and His Realm* (1991) deal with each protester individually. Mark Naison's *Communists in Harlem During the Depression* (1983) focuses on FDR's left-wing critics, as does Robin Kelley's *Hammer and Hoe* (1990). *Campaign of the Century* (1992) by Greg Mitchell looks at Upton Sinclair's gubernatorial race in California.

Roosevelt's second term has not been studied as intensely as his first, but James MacGregor Burns's *Roosevelt: The Lion and the Fox* (1956) contains an overview. Irving Bernstein's *Turbulent Years* (1969) has especially good material on the creation of the National Labor Relations Board. William Leuchtenburg's *The Supreme Court Reborn* (1995) chronicles the constitutional revolution in the Court during the 1930s. The opposition strategy pursued by the Republican Party is the focus of Clyde Weed's *The Nemesis of Reform* (1995). Alan Brinkley details the transformation and decline of the New Deal after the 1937 recession in *The End of Reform* (1996).

David Peeler's *Hope Among Us Yet* (1986) discusses the mixture of social criticism and spirit of hopefulness found in 1930s art. Richard Pells studies the growing radicalization of depression-era artists in *Radical Visions and American Dreams* (1973). Daniel Aaron's *Writers on the Left* (1961) is a good starting point for information on authors of the 1930s. *The Genius of the System* (1988) by Thomas Schatz examines how working within the new studio system made good studios great. Andrew Bergman's *We're in the Money* (1971) stresses the escapist tenor of most depression-era cinema. Nick Roddick's *A New Deal in Entertainment: Warner Brothers in the 1930s* (1983) shows how political developments influenced one movie studio, which in turn influenced popular culture.

Lizabeth Cohen's masterful synthesis, *Making a New Deal* (1990), highlights Roosevelt's impact on organized labor. David Milton's *The Politics of U.S. Labor* (1980) studies the reawakening of labor after 1929. Irving Bernstein traces the history of labor in the 1930s in *A Caring Society* (1985). Melvyn Dubofsky and Warren Van Tine's *John L. Lewis* (1977) portrays one of the most influential labor leaders of the decade, while Steven Fraser's *Labor Will Rule* (1991) looks at the CIO's cofounder Sidney Hillman. Alice and Staughton Lynd's *Rank and File* (1973) contains oral histories by many labor organizers from the period. Joseph Cohen's *When the Old Left Was Young* (1993) chronicles the fortunes of the American Student Union during the depression.

Harvard Sitkoff's *A New Deal for Blacks* (1978) examines the bitter fruits many African-Americans reaped from the New Deal. It should be read in concert with Nancy Weiss's *Farewell to the Party of Lincoln* (1983), since the two works offer conflicting interpretations of the black experience. John Kirby's *Black Americans in the Roosevelt Era: Liberalism and Race* (1980) studies FDR's muddied stand on civil rights. Dan Carter's *Scottsboro* (1969) is a moving account of this divisive case. It should be read along with James Goodman's *Stories of Scottsboro* (1995). Patricia Sullivan examines the relationship between the federal government, blacks, and whites in *Days of Hope* (1996). Laurence Kelly's *The Assault on Assimilation* (1983) is a detailed overview of the New Deal's impact on Native Americans. Abraham Hoffman's *Unwanted Mexican-Americans in the Great Depression* (1974) and Francisco Balerman's *In Defense of La Raza* (1982) evaluate the prejudices faced by Mexican-Americans during the depression.

Lois Scharf studies the movement of women into the 1930s work force in *To Work and to Wed* (1980). Susan Ware's *Holding Their Own* (1982) and *Beyond Suffrage* (1987) discuss the growing authority women assumed in many families during the depression. Blanche Wiesen Cook provides insight into the personality and influence of the First Lady in *Eleanor Roosevelt, 1884–1933* (1992) and *Eleanor Roosevelt, 1933–1938* (1999).

Roosevelt's Fireside Chat, 1934

In a series of radio broadcasts, which he called Fireside Chats, Franklin Roosevelt spoke directly to the people, explaining his policies and asking for their support. In this address, the president articulated why it was necessary to launch his sweeping and comprehensive New Deal reforms. The grave economic crisis, he argued, required bold experimentation, including an unprecedented expansion of government power.

I am happy to report that after years of uncertainty, culminating in the collapse of the spring of 1933, we are bringing order out of the old chaos with a greater certainty of the employment of labor at a reasonable wage and of more business at a fair profit. These governmental and industrial developments hold promise of new achievements for the Nation.

Men may differ as to the particular form of governmental activity with respect to industry and business, but nearly all are agreed that private enterprise in times such as these cannot be left without assistance and without reasonable safeguards lest it destroy not only itself but also our process of civilization. . . .

In our efforts for recovery we have avoided, on the one hand, the theory that business should and must be taken over into an all-embracing Government. We have avoided, on the other hand, the equally untenable theory that it is an interference with liberty to offer reasonable help when private enterprise is in need of help. The course we have followed fits the American practice of Government, a practice of taking action step by step, or regulating only to meet concrete needs, a practice of courageous recognition of change. I believe with Abraham Lincoln, that "The Legitimate object of Government is to do for a community of people whatever they need to have done but cannot do at all or cannot do so well for themselves in their separate and individual capacities."

In meeting the problems of industrial recovery the chief agency of the Government has been the National Recovery Administration [NRA]. Under its guidance, trades and industries covering 90 percent of all industrial employees have adopted codes of fair competition, which have been approved by the President. . . . Closely allied to the NRA is the program of public works provided for in the same Act and designed to put more men back to work, both directly on the public works themselves, and indirectly in the industries supplying the materials for these public works. To those who say that our expenditures for public works and other means for recovery are a waste that we cannot afford, I answer that no country, however rich, can afford the waste of its human resources. Demoralization caused by vast unemployment is our greatest extravagance. Morally, it is the greatest menace to our social order. . . .

I am not for a return to that definition of liberty under which for many years a free people were being gradually regimented into the service of the privileged few.

1005

I prefer and I am sure you prefer that broader definition of liberty under which we are moving forward to greater freedom, to greater security for the average man than he has ever known before in the history of America.

"This Threat to Our Liberty," 1936

Herbert Hoover had dabbled in many of the ideas later realized in the New Deal, though in a much more limited form, while he was president. Hoover never adopted a truly activist conception of government, however, and he drifted rightward during Roosevelt's first term in office. By 1936, he had emerged as one of the New Deal's harshest conservative critics. In this October 30 speech, Hoover leveled against the New Deal a classic conservative complaint: that government interference in the economy would lead to despotism. He claimed that government could create institutions that would stimulate the economy without interfering with the "economic liberty" of the individual citizen.

Through four years of experience this New Deal attack upon free institutions has emerged as the transcendent issue in America.

All the men who are seeking for mastery in the world today are using the same weapons. They sing the same songs. . . . But their philosophy is founded on the coercion and compulsory organization of men. True liberal government is founded upon the emancipation of men. This is the issue upon which men are imprisoned and dying in Europe right now. . . . Freedom does not die from frontal attack. It dies because men in power no longer believe in a system based on liberty. . . .

I gave the warning against this philosophy of government four years ago from a heart heavy with anxiety for the future of our country. It was born from many years' experience of the forces moving in the world which would weaken the vitality of American freedom. It grew in four years of battle as President to uphold the banner of free men.

And that warning was based on . . . my knowledge of the ideas that Mr. Roosevelt and his bosom colleagues had covertly embraced despite the Democratic platform. Those ideas were not new. Most of them had been urged upon me.

During my four years powerful groups thundered at the White House with these same ideas. Some were honest, some promising votes, most of them threatening reprisals, and all of them yelling "reactionary" at us. I rejected all these things because they would not only delay recovery but because I knew that in the end they would shackle free men.

The New Dealers say that all . . . that we propose is a worn-out system; that this machine age requires new measures for which we must sacrifice some part of the freedom of men. Men have lost their way with a confused idea that government should run machines.

Man-made machines cannot be of more worth than men themselves. Free men made these machines. Only free spirits can master them to their proper use. . . . Free government is the most difficult of all government. But it is everlastingly true that the plain people will make fewer mistakes than any group of men no matter how powerful. But free government implies vigilant thinking and courageous living and self-reliance in a people. Let me say to you that any measure which breaks our dikes of freedom will flood the land with misery.

Few events have shaken American society like the Great Depression. In the early 1930s the American economy seemed to be "broken." The failure of the economy to recover without government help forced Americans to confront deeply ingrained cultural notions. Though most Americans deeply valued self-reliance, millions were forced to seek relief aid; and though most people believed in private charity, the demands for aid quickly overwhelmed the capacity of private charity to respond. Where was an ill-paid, ill-fed, ill-housed nation to turn?

The idea that the federal government should marshal resources for public relief was not new. A number of groups including the Socialists, the Populists, and the progressives had argued that regulation of industry was necessary to protect the common people from the abuses of large businesses. They demanded a social safety net for those who were unable to provide for themselves. Franklin Roosevelt constructed his New Deal on the foundation created by previous generations of reformers. Only a democratically elected government, he argued, could protect the public welfare against the ravages of greed and industrial capitalism.

While his program won widespread popular support, skeptics on both sides attacked him for either doing too much, or not doing enough, to end the depression. Left-leaning critics such as Huey Long wanted the president to impose greater government controls on the economy by redistributing wealth from the rich to the poor. Conservatives such as Hoover argued that no crisis warranted the extent of government interference that Roosevelt proposed. FDR claimed to be searching for a middle ground between the extremism of the left and the right, reassuring the public that the New Deal's goal of providing the American people with security did not "indicate a change in values."

Ultimately, the debate between Roosevelt and Hoover revolved around competing notions of liberty. Roosevelt, always the political pragmatist, favored experimentation, arguing that the New Deal promoted liberty by freeing people from the shackles of poverty and depression. Hoover, reflecting America's deep-seated aversion to federal power, maintained that government coercion and individual liberty were incompatible. A powerful central government may be appropriate for European powers, he argued, but it clashed with the American faith in individualism and self-help.

Questions for Analysis

1. What does Roosevelt mean when he calls for "a practice of courageous recognition of change"?

2. Why do you think he quotes from Lincoln to justify his policies?

3. In his opening, ("All the men who are seeking...") Hoover compares Roosevelt to totalitarian dictators Hitler (Germany), Mussolini (Italy), and Stalin (the Soviet Union). Why does he draw that parallel?

4. What does Hoover see as the greatest threat to American democracy?

5. Are liberty and freedom synonymous?

6. Why are Americans so skeptical about government activism?

26

War and Society, 1933–1945

*A*t 7:55 A.M. on the morning of December 7, 1941, thirty-nine-year-old Japanese bomber pilot Mitsuo Fuchida, leader of a 353-plane armada, peered down at the 94 U.S. Navy ships, including 8 battleships and 29 destroyers, lined up at the U.S. naval base at Pearl Harbor, Hawaii. "To-to-to," the first syllable of the Japanese word for "charge," he shouted into his radio. That was followed by an even more significant transmission: "Tora, tora, tora," meaning "tiger," the message confirming that the attack was catching the Americans by surprise. The waves of Japanese bombers and fighters swooped down, dropped their deadly bombs on American ships and strafed planes parked wingtip-to-wingtip at nearby airbases. Fuchida set his sights on the U.S.S. *Arizona,* slamming a 1,000-pound, armor-piercing bomb against its hull. "I saw a huge explosion almost reaching the sky," he recalled. The ship split in half and quickly sank, entombing over a thousand sailors onboard. When the attack ended two hours later, twenty-four hundred Americans lay dead. Japanese pilots disabled or destroyed 18 ships—including all eight battleships, three light cruisers, three destroyers, four auxiliary craft—and 188 aircraft. The Japanese lost 29 planes and 96 men.

The next day, more than 60 million Americans huddled by their radios to hear President Roosevelt ask a joint session of Congress for a declaration of war against Japan, swearing to fight until total victory was won. December 7, 1941, he declared was "a date which will live in infamy." For two years the same

Congress had resisted the president's previous efforts to aid the Allies. Now it enthusiastically endorsed his call for war. The Senate approved a war resolution 89 to 0, the House 388 to 1. Congresswoman Jeanette Rankin of Montana, a pacifist and suffragist, was the lone dissenter. Three days later, Adolph Hitler declared war on the "half Judaized and the other half Negrified" American people.

The Japanese surprise attack on Pearl Harbor, and the declaration of war that followed, shattered the illusion that the United States could remain detached from world events. World War II converted the nation from isolationism to internationalism. It dramatically accelerated the preceding decade's growth in the size and scope of government, produced unprecedented economic expansion, and offered new opportunities to groups that had been excluded from the American mainstream. The conflict united the nation like no previous crisis, and helped to produce a national culture. These changes in the structure of American life did not, however, produce a rethinking of American values or attitudes toward government. In the face of new experiments in government power, Americans—as they had during the hardships of depression—remained deeply wedded to their faith in local democracy. The war-fueled economy offered new opportunities for minorities and women, but the United States remained a society deeply divided by race, class, and gender. The nation emerged from the struggle as the world's premier military and economic power. But despite the American experiment's now global proportions, most Americans were reluctant to accept the responsibility of power.

- How did isolationist sentiment shape American policy toward Europe and Asia during the 1930s?

- What was the Allied strategy for victory, and how did disagreements among the "Big Three" contribute to postwar tensions between the Soviets and the West?

- How did the war contribute to the development of a national culture? How did it contribute to social tensions?

- What impact did the war have on American attitudes toward government and world affairs?

This chapter will address these questions.

America and the World Crisis, 1933–1941

During the 1930s, leaders in Germany, Italy, and Japan decided to use the cover of depression to realize their expansionist goals. How would America respond to the growing threat in Europe and Asia? Amid advancing aggression, Franklin Roosevelt tried to navigate between a peace movement that wanted Washington to remain neutral, and a growing belief that the national interest required the United States to aid the Allies. Struggling with depression and conscious of the slaughter of World War I, Americans had little interest in international experimentation. As Hitler's army rampaged through Europe and Japan ransacked East Asia, Roosevelt nudged a reluctant nation closer to war.

The Gathering Storm

The first challenge to peace came in Asia, where Japan's army was on the march. Since the 1890s, Japanese leaders had coveted the Manchurian region in northern China. Comprising an area as large as France and Germany, Manchuria served as a defensive buffer against Russia. More important, it was rich in natural resources (coal, iron, timber, and soybeans) that the import-dependent Japanese desperately needed. In 1931 Tokyo seized Manchuria, established a puppet government, and dispatched colonists to settle the land. In 1937 Japan intensified and broadened its invasion, bombing Chinese cities, killing thousands of civilians. In Nanking, Japanese troops slaughtered one hundred thousand Chinese. In December, in the midst of a full-scale military attack against China, Japanese warplanes sank the American gunboat *Panay,* killing two American sailors and wounding thirty. Though Roosevelt privately considered responding with economic sanctions, he did nothing once Japan apologized.

While an emboldened Japan extended its reach into China, Italy attempted to realize its own territorial ambitions. Benito Mussolini, who had governed Italy since 1922, dreamed of creating an Italian empire in northern Africa. In October 1935, he tried to distract Italians from their economic woes at home by launching an invasion of the independent African state of Ethiopia. Within a year, he had gained control of the lightly armed country.

The greatest threat came not from Japan or Italy, but from a revitalized Germany. In January 1933, Adolf Hitler bulled his way to power as Germany's chancellor. A charismatic and demented leader, Hitler tapped into a deep well of resentment that Germans felt toward the West for imposing a punitive peace following World War I. He vowed to revive German economic and military power, to crush the Bolshevik threat, and to rid the German "race" of the "contamination" of Jewish influence, which he blamed for all of Germany's many severe problems. Once in office, Hitler took the title of *Fuhrer* ("leader") and outlawed political parties other than his own National Socialists, or Nazis. As the Nazis consolidated power at home, they also asserted it abroad. Hitler, repudiating the Versailles Treaty, withdrew from the League of Nations in 1933 and unilaterally announced that Germany would rearm. On March 7, 1936, Hitler ordered German troops into the Rhineland, the strategic buffer that lay between France and Germany.

Hitler accurately predicted that the West would respond feebly to his aggression. European powers, he said, would "never act. They'll just protest. And they will always be too late." Traumatized by their experience in World War I and consumed with economic problems at home, the European powers settled on a policy of "appeasement," hoping to satisfy Hitler's and Mussolini's limited goals in order to avoid another war. Britain acquiesced to German plans to rebuild its navy; France registered only mild protest when Germany advanced on the Rhineland. When Hitler's ally Mussolini annexed Ethiopia, the League of Nations imposed an embargo on the shipment of war-related goods to Italy but excluded the most important item—oil. The French and British were willing to sacrifice Ethiopia to prevent a general war in Europe.

Chronology

1931	Japan seizes Manchuria
1935	Italy invades Ethiopia
1936	Spanish Civil War begins
1937	Japan invades China
1938	Hitler forces the *Anschluss* and invades Sudetenland
	Munich Agreement
1939	Hitler invades Poland and war begins
1940	France surrenders to Germany
	Battle of Britain
	Roosevelt reelected
1941	Lend-Lease Act
	Pearl Harbor attacked
1942	Operation TORCH
	Battles of Coral Sea and Midway
1943	Allied invasion of Italy
1944	D-Day
	Roosevelt reelected
1945	Yalta Conference
	Roosevelt dies; Truman becomes president
	Germany surrenders
	Atomic bombs dropped; Japan surrenders

Encouraged by the timid response to their aggression, Hitler and Mussolini attempted to extend their influence in Europe by intervening in a civil war that broke out in Spain. In the summer of 1936, General Francisco Franco led an armed revolt against Spain's democratically elected government. While Germany and Italy fortified Franco's cause with military aid, the West hid behind the veil of neutrality. Most Americans were indifferent to the struggle, but a handful of impassioned idealists saw the struggle for Spain as a great moral confrontation between democracy and totalitarianism. American volunteers, many of them communist and calling themselves the Abraham Lincoln Battalion, went to Spain to fight for the republican cause. In early 1939, Franco prevailed, establishing an authoritarian government that lasted until his death in 1976.

American indifference to the Spanish Civil War seemed to confirm Hitler's belief that he had nothing to fear from the United States. America, he told an aide, "was incapable of conducting war." It was a "Jewish rubbish heap," incapacitated by depression and poor leadership. But Hitler underestimated Roosevelt's interest in world affairs. As a child, Roosevelt had traveled extensively throughout Europe, making his first trip at the age of three. While a student at the prestigious Groton School and later at Harvard, he debated international issues and gloated in his cousin Theodore's exploits. As undersecretary of the navy during the Wilson administration, Roosevelt became firmly convinced that a great power such as the United States should play an important role in world affairs.

As president, Roosevelt acted on his internationalist impulses. He chose as his secretary of state Cordell Hull, a former Tennessee judge and congressman, who believed that world trade was the key to international understanding. Under Hull's watchful eye, the president developed the Export-Import Bank (Ex-Im Bank), which helped U.S. businesspeople finance overseas sales, and the Reciprocal Trade Act (RTA), which gave the president new powers to bargain for foreign markets by automatically extending tariff preferences to favored nations. In November 1933, FDR overcame a decade of hostility and formally recognized the Soviet Union, hoping that diplomatic recognition would encourage the Soviets to pay their war debts and limit their propaganda in the United States. The Soviets also offered the United States a potentially lucrative trading partner—always a major consideration during the depression.

Along with recognizing the Soviets, Roosevelt moved to develop closer ties with other nations in the Western Hemisphere. In his inaugural address in 1933, Roosevelt announced a new "Good Neighbor" policy toward Latin America. At the Inter-American Conference at Montevideo, Uruguay, in 1933, the United States supported a declaration pledging nonintervention among Western Hemisphere states. The president underscored this policy by renouncing the Platt Amendment, which had given the United States the right to intervene in the affairs of Cuba. In a treaty with Panama in 1936, American negotiators relinquished similar privileges. The president withdrew marines from Haiti in 1934 and joined with representatives of twenty other governments in South America to ratify a Protocol of Non-Intervention at the Inter-American Conference in Buenos Aires, Argentina, in 1936. The following year, Mexico became the first country to test the U.S. commitment to nonintervention when it nationalized American oil companies. Despite heavy pressure from Hull to retaliate, Roosevelt refused to intervene.

A powerful wave of isolationism, however, limited Roosevelt's internationalist ambitions. Isolationist sentiment had deep roots in the American past. During the 1930s, disillusion with World War I and concern about jobs at home only intensified the hands-off attitude. Since the president's first priority was to resuscitate the American economy, international diplomacy necessarily took a back seat.

Popular writers, who claimed that selfish business interests conspired to lead the United States into World War I, whipped disenchantment with World War I into a frenzy. A thesis represented by books such as Walter Millis's *Road to War* (1935) argued that America mobilized in 1917 not to preserve democracy but to protect Wall

Street bankers. In 1934 a congressional committee headed by Gerald P. Nye of North Dakota added credibility to these charges. Despite flimsy evidence, the Nye Committee concluded that the bankers who had lent the Allies money, and the "merchants of death" who had sold them ammunition, had conspired with President Wilson to take the country to war. "For the sake of profits, for dollars to protect the loans of certain commercial interests in this country, 50,000 boys now lie buried in France," declared Senator Homer Bone of Washington. By 1937, 60 percent of Americans believed that U.S. involvement in World War I had been a mistake.

The combination of depression and disillusion produced a powerful peace movement. Led by women, clergy, and college students, the cause claimed 12 million members by the middle of the decade. On April 6, 1935, the eighteenth anniversary of American entry into the First World War, 50,000 veterans held a "march for peace" in Washington. Three days later, over 175,000 college students participated in a one-hour "strike for peace" on campuses across the country. "Schools, not battleships," they chanted. "Let us turn our eyes inward," exhorted a leading Democratic governor. "If the world is to become a wilderness of waste, hatred, and bitterness, let us all the more earnestly protect and preserve our own oasis of liberty."

Congress reflected the isolationist sentiment by passing restrictive neutrality legislation during the decade. As early as 1933, Congress refused to give Roosevelt discretionary power to apply arms embargoes against aggressor nations. It passed three major neutrality acts during the decade. In 1935 Congress imposed an automatic embargo on American arms and ammunition to all parties at war. The following year, Congress added a ban on loans to belligerents. In May 1937 Congress, still preoccupied with learning lessons from 1914–1917, banned American ships from war zones, prohibited Americans from traveling on belligerent ships, and extended the embargo to include not just armaments, but the oil, steel, and rubber needed for war machines. Foreign belligerents could buy such goods only if they paid for them in cash and carried them in their own ships. "With stout legal thread," observed historian David Kennedy, "Congress had spun a straitjacket that rendered the United States effectively powerless in the face of the global conflagration that was about to explode."

The Failure of Neutrality

Though alarmed by events in Europe and Asia, Roosevelt was distracted by the depression and restrained by the neutrality laws. In October 1937, he tested the depth of isolationist sentiment in a now famous speech in which he denounced the "reign of terror and international lawlessness" that threatened the peace. "When an epidemic of physical disease starts to spread, the community approves and joins in a quarantine of the patients in order to protect the health of the community." When public reaction proved mixed, Roosevelt backed away from the internationalist implications of his message. "It's a terrible thing," Roosevelt said, "to look over your shoulder when you are trying to lead—and find no one there."

In 1938, while America watched from the sidelines, Hitler pressed Europe to the brink of war, proclaiming the German nation's right to *lebensraum,* or living space. "Germany's problems could be solved only by means of force," he told his aides. In March he forced Austria into *Anschluss* (union) with Germany. In the fall Hitler threatened to invade Czechoslovakia when it refused to give him its Sudetenland, a mountainous region bordering Germany and inhabited mostly by ethnic Germans. British prime minister Neville Chamberlain and French premier Edouard Daladier hastily scheduled meetings with Hitler in Munich on September 29–30, 1938. Hitler reassured the Western leaders by promising, "This is the last territorial claim I have to make in Europe." Hoping to avoid confrontation, the West sacrificed the Sudetenland on the altar of appeasement, agreeing to a gradual transfer to German control. Denied outside support, the Czechs surrendered, demobilized their army, and allowed Germany to shear off the Sudetenland. Huge crowds filled the streets of London to celebrate Chamberlain's announcement that Munich had secured "peace in our time." Future prime minister Winston Churchill revealed a better grasp of the situation. "Britain and France had to choose between war and dishonor," he said. "They chose dishonor. They will have war."

Six months later German troops swept down on the rest of Czechoslovakia, smashing Western illusions that Hitler could be appeased. Within weeks, the British government reversed course, announcing that it was committed to the defense of Poland, Hitler's next possible target. The European situation grew more dangerous in August when the Germans and Russians concluded a nonaggression pact. Stalin was certain that Hitler would finish with Poland and invade the Soviet Union, and the Munich episode convinced him that the West would not come to his aid. His deal with Hitler would buy him time to rebuild his forces. The agreement provided for the partition of Poland and for Soviet absorption of the Baltic states, as well as territory in Finland and Bessarabia. With his eastern flank secured, Hitler unleashed his fire and steel on the Polish people on September 1, 1939. In a brilliant display of military skill and power, the Germans conducted a *Blitzkrieg* (lightning war), sending 1.5 million men pouring over the Polish border. "Close your hearts to pity," Hitler told his generals. "Act brutally." Two days later, honoring their commitments to Poland, Britain and France declared war on Germany. World War II in Europe had begun.

By late 1939, American sympathy was clearly with the Allies, but most people continued to believe that Britain and France could defend Europe without U.S. assistance. The British, who claimed the largest navy in the world, would strangle the German economy. Many military strategists believed France's 800,000-man standing army supporting the French Maginot Line of fortifications along the French-German border, could resist any invasion. The calm that settled over Europe during the winter of 1939–1940 added to the detachment. Isolationist Senator William Borah sniffed, "There's something phony about this war."

The lull complicated Roosevelt's task of educating the American people about the dangers posed by the European situation. Roosevelt hoped to avoid war by providing assistance to the Allies, but the Neutrality Acts tied his hands. "It is, of course, obvious that if the Neutrality Act remains in its present form, France and

England will be defeated rapidly," a diplomat informed the president. In November 1939, Roosevelt pressured Congress to pass a revised Neutrality Act that lifted the arms embargo against belligerents, but retained the cash-and-carry provision. The new law also forbade American merchant ships from entering a broad "danger zone" that included most of the major shipping lanes to Europe.

A German offensive in April 1940 shattered the false confidence that Hitler could be contained. On April 9, Hitler's *blitzkrieg* overran Denmark, and German troops swarmed over Norway, the Netherlands, Luxembourg, and Belgium, and on into France. In the chaos that followed the Allied retreat, Britain managed to rescue some 338,000 troops from the northern French port of Dunkirk, but the troops left behind ninety thousand rifles, seven thousand tons of ammunition, and 120,000 vehicles. On June 22, 1940, the French surrendered to Hitler in the same railcar in which the Germans had capitulated to the Allies in 1918. A reporter noted that Hitler was "afire with scorn, anger, hate, revenge, triumph." The Germans installed a puppet government in the town of Vichy. "The Battle of France is over," Churchill, who had become prime minister ten days earlier, told a somber Parliament. "I expect that the Battle of Britain is about to begin."

The fall of France changed the military calculus in Washington. Roosevelt had believed the combination of British sea and air power, French land forces, and American industrial might, would stymie Hitler's advance. The question now was: Could Britain survive alone against Hitler's military juggernaut? Beginning in the summer of 1940, Hitler hurled his *Luftwaffe* (air force) at the British. Soon frustrated by the resistance of the Royal Air Force (RAF), Hitler ordered the terror bombing of London. From September to November, during the Battle of Britain, nearly 250 German bombers dropped their deadly cargo over London every night. The British people, though badly battered, refused to break.

Following the fall of France, Roosevelt abandoned any pretense of neutrality by committing the United States to a policy of "all aid to the Allies short of war." The president offered the British fifty World War I–vintage destroyers in exchange for leases to eight British military bases. Congress also approved Roosevelt's request for $8 billion in additional funds to rearm the nation, and it authorized a one-year draft, the first peacetime conscription in American history.

The 1940 Election Campaign

Questions of war and peace dominated the 1940 campaign for the presidency. Growing concern about the deteriorating situation in Europe pushed the Republican Party to abandon its isolationist moorings and nominate little-known Wendell Willkie, a forty-eight-year-old Wall Street lawyer and utilities executive. Among the leading contenders for the Republican nomination were Ohio's Senator Robert Taft and Michigan's Senator Arthur Vandenberg, both identified with isolationism. Only Willkie had developed a clear anti-isolationist position on foreign policy.

Initially, Willkie expressed support for Roosevelt's defense policies and focused his attacks on the perceived failures of the New Deal. In August, trailing badly in the polls, Willkie shifted gears. Three days after publicly supporting Roosevelt's destroyers-for-bases deal, Willkie condemned the move as "the most arbitrary and dictatorial action ever taken by a President in the history of the United States." Over the next few months, he sharpened his attacks. Early in October, charging the president was leading the country into war, Willkie vowed that he would not send "one American boy into the shambles of another war."

Roosevelt, who was seeking an unprecedented third term, feared that the peace issue would catch fire. By mid-October, polls showed Willkie gaining ground in key states with large electoral votes, including Illinois, Indiana, and Michigan. The president decided to douse the flames with deception. In late October, in what became the most quoted statement of the campaign, Roosevelt told a crowd in Boston, "I have said this before, but I shall say it again and again and again: Your boys are not going to be sent into any foreign wars." By the fall of 1940, the president knew that his policies would likely lead the nation into war. Instead of engaging the American people in a thoughtful discussion of the issue, both Roosevelt and his internationalist-minded opponent told the American people what they most wanted to hear.

Roosevelt's reassurances worked. He fended off Willkie's late surge and won re-election handily. The president received 27 million votes to Willkie's 22 million. Roosevelt carried thirty-eight states and 449 electoral votes to Willkie's ten and 82 (see map). Willkie, who received 5 million more votes than Landon had in 1936, gave Roosevelt a tough challenge, but the New Deal coalition remained intact.

The Election of 1940 With war raging in Europe, Roosevelt spent most of the campaign season handling foreign affairs, while Republican candidate Wendell Willkie found Roosevelt's public support so strong that he was left with little besides his violation of the two-term presidential tradition to attack. The majority of Americans rejected the tradition and agreed with Roosevelt's slogan "Don't switch horses in the middle of the stream."

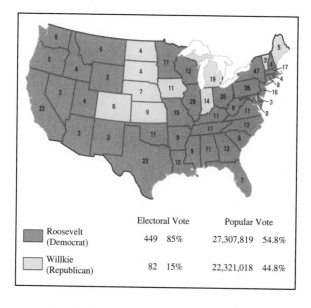

	Electoral Vote	Popular Vote
Roosevelt (Democrat)	449 85%	27,307,819 54.8%
Willkie (Republican)	82 15%	22,321,018 44.8%

To the Brink

The president interpreted the election as an endorsement of his policies. He moved quickly to push for more aid to Britain. Churchill privately warned Roosevelt that the war was draining money from the British Treasury and that the "moment approaches when we shall no longer be able to pay cash for shipping and other supplies." A few days after Christmas, Roosevelt responded by unveiling a "Lend-Lease" proposal, which would allow the United States to provide Britain with valuable war material. Roosevelt compared Lend-Lease to a garden hose one lends to a neighbor whose house is on fire—receiving it or a replacement when the fire is out. Aiding the British was the best way to keep America out of the war, he said, and urged the United States to "be the great arsenal of democracy."

Isolationists in Congress battled to defeat Lend-Lease. "Lending war equipment is a good deal like lending chewing gum," Senator Taft grumbled. Lend-Lease, its enemies cried, was a grim reaper's AAA that would "plow under every fourth American boy." Isolationists formed the America First Committee to organize opposition. Led by a diverse group that included Taft, aviator-hero Charles Lindbergh, and socialist Norman Thomas, committee members denied that Hitler posed a threat to American security.

However, the momentum of war was influencing American attitudes about the nation's role in the struggle for Europe. Polls showed over 60 percent of the American public supporting Lend-Lease. Internationalists organized the Committee to Defend America by Aiding the Allies, which called for unlimited aid to Britain. "Every time Hitler bombed London, we got a couple of votes," declared a supporter. The Lend-Lease proposal quickly passed in both the House and Senate.

As Roosevelt had hoped, Lend-Lease proved to be of vital assistance to the Allies. By 1945, it totaled some $50 billion, or four times the amount loaned to the Allies between 1917 and 1919. Passage of Lend-Lease marked a point of no return for America. The United States had committed itself to the survival of Great Britain with an economic aid program that amounted to a declaration of economic warfare on Germany. When Hitler turned on Stalin to launch a bold attack against the Soviet Union in June 1941, Roosevelt convinced Congress to include the Soviets in the Lend-Lease program.

Lend-Lease aggravated a growing controversy over escorts in the Atlantic. "The decision for 1941 lies upon the seas," Churchill warned Roosevelt. German U-boat (submarine) attacks were sinking British ships at nearly five times the rate at which new construction could replace them. British ships needed better protection, which only the United States could provide, but Lend-Lease specifically barred the U.S. Navy from providing convoys.

In August, Roosevelt and Churchill met at Placentia Bay in Newfoundland—the first of many conferences between the two leaders. The most famous product of the summit came in an eight-point statement of war aims—the Atlantic Charter. The two leaders pledged to honor the principles of self-determination, free trade, nonaggression, and freedom of the seas, promising a postwar world in which all people "may live out their lives in freedom from fear and want." More practical concerns were also addressed. Churchill pressed Roosevelt for a declaration of war against Germany. Roosevelt, believing that the public would not support such a bold move, promised "to wage war, but not declare it." He pledged the navy to protect British convoys as far east as Iceland while he looked for an "incident" to justify a more aggressive posture.

The president got his incident the following month. On September 4, 1941, a U-boat, after being chased for hours by a destroyer, U.S.S. *Greer,* turned and attacked the destroyer. The following month, a U-boat torpedoed the U.S. destroyer *Kearny,* killing eleven. "America has been attacked," Roosevelt blustered. On October 30, the *Reuben James* was hit with the loss of ninety-six men. In response, Roosevelt ordered all ships engaged in escort duty to "shoot on sight" any German submarines appearing in waters west of Iceland.

Public anger at the sinking of American ships provided Roosevelt with the support he needed to repeal the neutrality legislation. On November 13, 1941, Congress voted by a narrow margin to permit American ships to sail through war zones to British and Russian ports. The last remaining restrictions on American actions had been removed. The *New York Times* editorialized, "The Battle of the Atlantic is on."

"This Is War"

The story unfolded differently in the Pacific. Since 1931, the United States had criticized Japanese aggression in the Far East, refusing to recognize Tokyo's claim to territory in China. In reality, however, the United States lacked the power to challenge Japanese predominance in East Asia. The only effective weapon in the American arsenal was economic. Japan depended on the United States for a long list of strategic materials, especially oil. Throughout the decade, Roosevelt tried to use the economic leverage to tame Japanese aggression without triggering a confrontation that would distract attention and resources from the European theater. "I simply have not got enough Navy to go around—and every little episode in the Pacific means fewer ships in the Atlantic," Roosevelt complained.

Despite his worry, the logic of American policy moved the United States and Japan closer to confrontation. In 1939 Roosevelt threatened an economic embargo, hoping to shock the Japanese into tempering their action in the region. The threat did not deter the Japanese, who secured bases in Indochina on September 24. America responded immediately with an embargo on high quality scrap iron and steel. Japan's answer to the tightened sanctions was to announce the Tripartite Pact with Germany and Italy on September 27. The pact pledged its signatories to come to one another's help in the event of an attack "by a power not already engaged in war." The treaty clearly aimed to dissuade the United States from either joining the British against the Germans or directly opposing Japan's efforts to carve out an empire in China and Southeast Asia. When Japanese forces overran the rest of Indochina in July, the administration reacted by freezing Japanese assets in the United States and by ending all shipments of oil. Japan now faced a difficult choice: either it could submit to American demands or conquer new territory to secure oil for its war machine. Since peace with the United States now seemed impossible, Japan planned for war.

In October, the militant war minister Hideki Tojo, who opposed compromise with the United States, gained control of Japan's imperial government. On November 5, Tojo decided he would continue diplomatic efforts to relax the embargo for three more weeks. If no agreement were reached by November 26, Japan would go to war. He set the date for attack: December 7, 1941.

American officials learned of Japan's intentions by intercepting messages between Tokyo and its embassy in the U.S. capital, but they did not know where the attack would come. Military leaders warned all American military installations in the Pacific of possible attack. Most Americans expected Japan to attack British Malaya or the Philippines. On the evening of December 6, American intelligence decoded a long message from Tokyo to its ambassador in Washington. Its final section announced there was no chance of reaching a diplomatic settlement "because of American attitudes." Roosevelt, after reading the message, concluded, "This is war." On December 7, Washington sent another warning about a possible Japanese attack. The warning came too late. On the morning of December 7, Japanese planes launched their attack against Pearl Harbor. The next day, America entered World War II.

Fighting a Global War, 1941–1945

The declaration of war presented the administration with two monumental tasks. At home, it needed to refit the economy for wartime production; abroad, the challenge was to coordinate military strategy with Allied leaders to defeat Hitler's formidable army. The "Big Three"—Roosevelt, Churchill, and Stalin—shared the same goal, but they disagreed on strategy. The most important question was: When should the western allies launch a second front against Hitler to relieve pressure on Soviet troops battling in the east? Stalin insisted on an attack as early as 1942, but Churchill and Roosevelt stalled until 1944. The delay proved costly. It nurtured suspicion between Stalin and the West, making for a precarious peace at the end of the war.

The Arsenal of Democracy

The mobilization of the American economy for war was a staggering task full of confusion and chaos. It brought into conflict two competing forces: the need to coordinate a massive economy and build an army while preserving faith in volunteerism and local government. America's faith in democracy required that mobilization be conducted piecemeal. "If you are going to . . . go to war, . . . in a capitalist country," Secretary of War Henry L. Stimson observed, "you have got to let business make money out of the process." As much as possible, Roosevelt sought to elicit voluntary compliance from business, workers, farmers, and consumers.

Before the Japanese attack on Pearl Harbor, Roosevelt had rejected recommendations for a powerful administrator with government authority to limit supplies of important resources and force business to convert to war production. "I do not believe that there is an awful lot of Government action that is needed at the present time," Roosevelt said in May 1940. As a result of Roosevelt's indecision, the mobilization effort drifted. When in May 1940, Roosevelt issued a call for production of fifty thousand military aircraft, industry was capable of producing only half the needed aluminum. Steel shortages prevented the construction of ships needed to transport Lend-Lease supplies.

The mobilization effort shifted gears following Pearl Harbor. Congress granted the president extraordinary powers to reshuffle the domestic economy in any way necessary to guarantee the war effort. The president had to tackle four related but complicated issues: mobilizing industry to produce material for war; controlling wages and prices; financing the war; and raising an army.

In January 1942, Roosevelt created the War Production Board (WPB) to develop policies governing all aspects of production and to "exercise general responsibilities" over the nation's economy. To head the agency Roosevelt chose Donald Nelson, the former head of Sears, Roebuck and Company. Despite his broad mandate, Nelson took a limited view of his powers. He allowed "little czars" to retain considerable autonomy in dealing with petroleum, rubber, and labor, and he permitted both the army and the navy to maintain separate purchasing authority.

Perhaps most important, Nelson tried to gain the confidence of the business community by offering financial incentives. Government made war production attractive by underwriting the cost of expansion and by guaranteeing profits. Congress in 1940 allowed fast tax write-offs for capital diverted into defense use. The government granted generous "cost-plus" arrangements, promising repayment of all development and production costs as well as guaranteeing a percentage profit. The administration abandoned antitrust legislation, allowing large corporations to pool resources. Enticed by the incentives, business converted from domestic to wartime production. Manufacturers switched production from making shirts to mosquito netting, from cars to tanks.

The close government–business cooperation benefited large corporations that possessed the resources and workers to produce necessary materials. Two-thirds of military contracts went to one hundred firms. Almost half went to three dozen major corporations. With large firms controlling most of the market, competing for the leftovers pushed many small firms into bankruptcy. In 1940, 175,000 companies accounted for 70 percent of the nation's manufacturing output. By March 1943, that number had dwindled to just 100 companies. Corporate profits, after taxes, climbed from $6.4 billion in 1940 to $10.8 billion in 1944.

Despite the incentives, the mobilization effort remained plagued with problems. Industry scrambled to obtain scarce vital resources, producing bottlenecks in the production process. One of the biggest shortages was rubber. By early 1942, Japan had blocked off 90 percent of America's crude rubber supply in the Dutch East Indies and Malaya. Every armored tank used a ton of rubber. The president, sensitive to public fears of intrusive government, resisted calls for strict rationing and instead called for a voluntary scrap drive. On June 12 he appealed to the people to turn in "old tires, old rubber raincoats, old garden hoses, rubber shoes, bathing caps, gloves—whatever you have that is made of rubber." In less than four weeks, Americans donated 450,000 tons of scrap rubber. At the same time, the government spent $700 million to create a new synthetic rubber industry.

Mobilizing the People   Although the American people were of divided opinion before the United States' entry into the war, the attack on Pearl Harbor instantaneously unified and mobilized public opinion. "Remember Pearl Harbor" remained a rallying cry throughout the war. These workers at a factory in Minnesota celebrate the New Year just weeks after the attack. *(Myron Davis/Life Magazine © Time, Inc.)*

All of the problems could not obscure the obvious conclusion that conversion to wartime production had been a dramatic success. Between 1941 and 1943, America realized more than an 800 percent increase in military production. By then more than half of all world manufacturing was taking place in the United States. By the end of the war the United States had produced 86,000 tanks, 295,000 airplanes, 12,000 ships, 15 million rifles and machine guns, and 40 billion bullets. At its productive peak the United States built a ship a day and an airplane every five minutes.

The government worried that so much demand chasing so few products would produce spiraling inflation. In April 1940, in an effort to dampen inflation fears, Roosevelt created the Office of Price Administration and Civilian Supply (OPA) headed by Leon Henderson. The OPA established a system of rationing civilian purchases of tires, cars, gasoline, sugar, and later, shoes, oil, and coffee. "Use it up, wear it out, make it do or do without," became the OPA slogan. The agency also imposed a cap on most prices and rents. Political controversies overwhelmed the OPA. "Everyone admits that full conversion of the country to war makes sacrifices imperative," suggested Budget Director Harold D. Smith, "but each group tries to shift the sacrifices to others." Business lobbyists, farm bloc politicians, and union leaders waged unceasing "guerrilla warfare" against the OPA. Consumers chafed under rationing restrictions, particularly those on beef and gasoline.

To control inflation, the administration needed to regulate wage increases as well as prices. To carry out that task, Roosevelt created the National War Labor Board in January 1942. In July, the board adopted a formula that permitted wage increases in line with the 15 percent rise in the cost of living since January 1941. Organized labor objected to the check on their earning power and threatened to break the no-strike pledge they had given after Pearl Harbor. Work stoppages, though usually short-lived, increased from 2,968 in 1942 to 4,956 in 1944.

The most dramatic confrontation was a strike by four hundred thousand members of the United Mine Workers led by John L. Lewis in May 1943. "The coal miners of America are hungry," he charged. "They are ill-fed and undernourished." The president seized the coal mines and threatened to draft miners into the army. But in the end, he negotiated a settlement that offered the miners substantial new benefits. Congress, and the public, were less understanding. Lewis became the most hated man in America in 1943. In June 1943, Congress responded to labor arrogance by passing the Smith-Connolly bill (also known as the War Labor Disputes Act), which empowered the president to seize any vital war plant shut down by strikes. Not wanting to alienate an important ally, Roosevelt vetoed the bill. Congress, however, mustered the necessary votes to override the veto and enact the legislation into law.

To help pay for the government's prodigious wartime expenditures, Congress broadened and deepened the tax structure. The Revenue Acts of 1942 and 1943 created the modern federal income tax system. Most Americans had never filed an income tax return before World War II because the income tax, on the books since 1913, had been a small tax on upper-income families. Starting with 1942, anyone earning $600 or more annually had to file a return. Income tax withholding from paychecks went into effect in 1943. Income tax revenues rose from $5 billion in 1940 to $44 billion in 1945.

Still, Congress refused to ask Americans to pay the full cost of the war. Only 40 percent of the total came from taxes. To fill the gap, Congress tried to entice Americans to support the effort through voluntary loans. War bonds, peddled by movie stars and professional athletes, added $100 billion to the war coffers. But taxes and bonds fell far short of paying the bills. By war's end the national debt had climbed to $280 billion, up from $40 billion when it began.

The ultimate challenge of mobilization was to build, not ships and planes, but an army to fight the enemy. In the summer of 1940 the regular U.S. Army ranked eighteenth in the world, with barely 250,000 men, compared to Hitler's 6 million to 8 million. Following the Japanese attack on Pearl Harbor, Congress ordered the registration of all men between the ages of twenty (lowered to eighteen in 1942) and forty-four for war service. Recruits called themselves "GIs" because of the "Government Issue" stamp on their gear.

The nation committed itself to total war. "We must fight with everything we have," declared Herbert Hoover. Despite the commitment, the draft reflected the continuing strength of parochial interests. Reflecting America's faith in localism, the draft was administered by no fewer than 6,500 local draft boards. By 1944, the system had become a mess of special interests trying to avoid service despite the cries for total mobilization for total war. The farm lobby won deferments for farmers, including tobacco growers, whose crop Congress declared "essential." Despite all the deferments and disputes, the draft succeeded in achieving its original objective. During the war the nation peacefully registered 49 million men, selected 19 million, and inducted 10 million, twice the number who volunteered.

The Battle for Europe

The major Allied powers—Britain, Russia, the United States, and China—faced a bleak situation in 1942. The Axis powers—Germany, Italy, and Japan—possessed war-tested armies and the forced labor and resources of conquered peoples in Europe and Asia. On land, the German *Panzer* divisions mobilized firepower unequaled by the West. German "wolf pack" submarines controlled the oceans. In the first eleven months of 1942, they sank a total of 8 million tons of shipping. But although staggered by the opening onslaught, the Allies were not defenseless. They had clear numerical superiority, a unified command structure, and enormous industrial capacity.

Victory required that the Allies develop a unified military strategy, but from the very beginning of the war, clear differences emerged. The Soviets, fighting more than two hundred German divisions on the eastern front, desperately wanted Churchill and Roosevelt to relieve the pressure by opening a second front in western Europe. At first, the Americans responded favorably to the Russian request. But the British, who had lost a whole generation of young men through frontal attack in World War I, wanted to weaken the enemy by striking at the periphery of Axis power. They proposed instead Operation TORCH, a joint Anglo-American invasion of North Africa, where the British had been tied down in a struggle with Italian and German forces.

American military leaders vehemently disagreed with Churchill's plan, dismissing it as "strategically unsound." Roosevelt, however, felt he had little leverage in his discussions with Churchill since America had not fully mobilized and the British would be supplying most of the troops and ships. The decision to delay a second front infuriated Stalin and nourished the seeds of suspicion that would blossom in the postwar period. "I must state in the most emphatic manner," Stalin wrote Churchill, "that the Soviet Government cannot acquiesce in the postponement of a second front in Europe until 1943."

Anglo-American forces launched Operation TORCH on November 8, 1942. Under the command of General Dwight Eisenhower, they stormed ashore at points along the coasts of the French North African colonies of Morocco and French North Africa. At the same time, the British Eighth Army, under General Bernard Montgomery, pushed eastward from Egypt. After initial setbacks, the combined British-American forces trapped one of Hitler's best generals, Field Marshall Erwin Rommel (the "Desert Fox") in a giant pincer. On May 13, 1943, the Allied army captured a quarter of a million Axis troops, including 125,000 Germans (see map).

While the Allies were winning the North African campaign, the Soviets launched a winter offensive against the Germans. In less than a month, Hitler's troops had advanced more than three hundred miles into Soviet territory, but German soldiers lacked the clothing and equipment to sustain their attack through the harsh Russian winter. Stalin's army surrounded a large German force at Stalingrad. In February

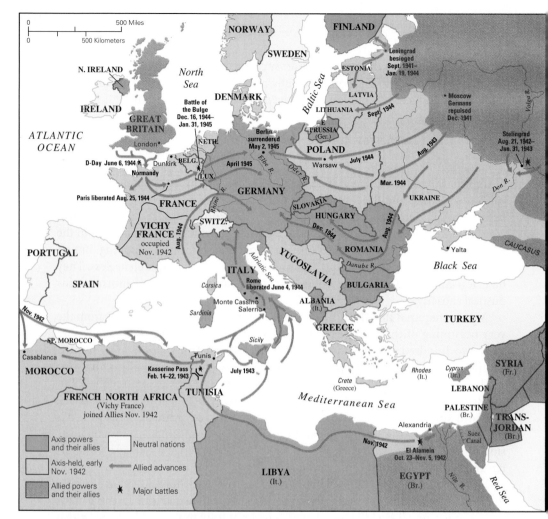

World War II in Europe and Africa   By 1942, the Axis powers had reached the furthest extent of their power in Europe. In 1943 the tide began turning in favor of the Allies in North Africa and in Russia. For the rest of the war, the Allies slowly strengthened their grip on the European continent, pushing and punishing Germany from all sides.

1943, after four months of intense fighting, the Germans at Stalingrad, having lost three hundred thousand men, surrendered.

In January, Roosevelt and Churchill met in the Moroccan city of Casablanca in northern Africa to discuss the next step in the European war. American military planners urged Roosevelt to push ahead with the second front, both to aid the Soviets and to strike at the heart of the German forces. Once again, Churchill held sway, calling instead for a continuation of the Mediterranean campaign with an invasion of Sicily.

In July, Allied troops assaulted the island. General George Patton sliced through weak Italian defenses and entered the city of Palermo on July 22. In the midst of the battle, Italy's King Victor Emmanuel II arrested and imprisoned Mussolini, and then surrendered to the Allies. Overnight, Italy was transformed from a German ally to a German occupied country as Hitler poured sixteen divisions into the peninsula. In September, three British and four American divisions glided onto the beaches of Salerno, beginning the long, bloody struggle for Italy.

In another major victory, by the end of 1943, scientific breakthroughs had given Allied naval power control of the Atlantic. Centimeter radar allowed aircraft to track enemy submarines, and sonobuoys, sound-detecting radio transmitters dropped by plane, allowed destroyers to home in on the noise from U-boat engines. Allied destroyers and planes unleashed a deadly array of new, more powerful anti-submarine rockets and depth charges. In May 1943, the Germans ordered all but a handful of U-boats out of the Atlantic. "We had lost the battle of the Atlantic," noted a German commander.

The Allies also gained control of the sky, launching B-17 bombers, popularly known as the "Flying Fortress," against strategic German targets: submarine yards, munitions factories, and railroad lines. The bombers flew their first missions in August 1942, shielded by a swarm of Royal Air Force (RAF) spitfire fighters. From 1943 to war's end, Allied planes dropped more than 2.5 million tons of explosives on occupied Europe and Germany. In one raid, on the city of Dresden in February 1945, the RAF dropped 2,660 tons of bombs, creating a firestorm that killed more than a hundred thousand civilians.

With the momentum of war shifting toward the Allies, Roosevelt traveled to Tehran, Iran to confer with Churchill and Stalin in late November 1943. The most pressing decision concerned the second front. Churchill continued to plead for delay, but this time he was overmatched by Roosevelt and Stalin. The three leaders formally approved an invasion across the English Channel, to be launched in the spring of 1944. During four days of meetings, the heads of state also discussed the future of the postwar world. Stalin demanded a buffer zone—Soviet control over eastern Europe—to protect against another invasion. Notwithstanding the Atlantic Charter's stated support for self-determination, Roosevelt reassured Stalin that the United States would not interfere, but he said that for political reasons he could not "publicly take part in any such arrangements at the present time." With the 1944 presidential campaign looming, Roosevelt feared alienating the millions of Americans of Polish and Lithuanian heritage who wanted self-determination in their former homelands. Roosevelt also explained that, as at the end of World War I, the persistent strength of isolationist sentiment would make a lasting American military force in Germany unlikely. After the Tehran conference, Roosevelt assured the American people in a radio address that "we are going to get along very well with [Stalin] and the Russian people—very well indeed."

"D-Day"

Reeling from the Soviet offensive in the east, the Germans prepared for an Anglo-American assault on the western flank. Knowing the invasion must come somewhere along the English Channel, Hitler reinforced heavily fortified bunkers on the French shoreline with three hundred thousand men. "The enemy must be annihilated before he reaches our main battlefield," General Rommel told his troops. "We must stop him in the water." While the Allies planned their assault for the French coast at Normandy, a complex deception operation, with fake radio signals, fooled the Germans into thinking the attack would come farther north at Pas de Calais. Hitler stationed his finest troops, including six *Panzer* divisions, to wait for the phantom army.

In the early morning hours of June 6, 1944, the designated day, or "D-Day," the Allies, under the supreme command of General Eisenhower, launched the long-delayed second front. Operation Overlord was the greatest amphibious assault in recorded history, employing over five thousand ships and eleven thousand airplanes. The first wave of landing craft carried American, Canadian, and British troops onto code-named beaches. The British and Canadian troops, who landed on the beaches Gold, Juno, and Sword, and the Americans who stormed Utah beach, encountered light resistance. The U.S. soldiers who assaulted Omaha beach were not so lucky. A wall of German gunfire and artillery pinned down fourteen thousand American soldiers. More than two thousand were killed or wounded in the first two hours of combat. "The surface of the water was covered with thousands and thousands of helmets floating upside down," recalled a participant. After three hours, a few GIs managed to climb the beach cliffs and destroy the German positions. By nightfall, the Allies controlled the five beaches, but not before losing 10,549 soldiers: 6,603 Americans, 3,000 British, and 946 Canadian.

In July, when General George Patton's Third Army broke through German defenses and moved inland through Brittany, Allied forces began their relentless

Hitting the Beach on D-Day   On June 6, 1944, the Allies launched the greatest amphibious invasion in military history, involving 175,000 men, over 5,000 sea craft, and 11,000 aircraft in the initial assault. The German army, fortified in the cliffs above the beaches, bombarded the Allied forces with artillery, and casualties in the first wave numbered in the thousands. Losses were particularly heavy on Omaha beach, where this American GI fights his way onto the shore. *(Robert Capa/Magnum Photos, Inc.)*

drive to Berlin. They streaked across France and liberated Paris on August 25. In December, as Allied troops massed on the German border, Hitler masterminded one final assault. In the Battle of the Bulge, German tanks crashed through weakly fortified Allied troops in Belgium. Before American air power blunted the assault, more than eight thousand American soldiers were killed, another twenty-one thousand captured or missing. But after the battle, the German war machine was in complete and final retreat.

As Allied armies liberated Poland and conquered Germany, they discovered the death camps that revealed the full horror of the Nazi regime. The sight of charred skeletons and living corpses shocked the Western world. "The smell of death overwhelmed us," recalled General Omar Bradley, who toured the concentration camp in Ohrdruf after Allied occupation. Throughout the 1930s, the Nazis persecuted Jews—organizing boycotts, limiting their civil rights, barring them from employment. In November 1938, after a Jewish man killed a German official, Nazi thugs had organized an orgy of arson and murder of Jews known as *Kristallnacht* (Crystal Night) for the pools of broken glass that littered German streets. A few days later, German officials confiscated all Jewish assets and shipped fifty thousand Jews to concentration camps. The brutal policy foreshadowed Hitler's "final solution" of the Jews. Beginning in 1941, German soldiers packed much of the Jewish population of eastern Europe and the Soviet Union into railroad freight cars and dumped them in death camps such as Buchenwald and Dachau. Another 3 million people— Poles and Russians, Slavs, gypsies, criminals, homosexuals, and resistance fighters— suffered the same fate.

Uncovering the Holocaust
Although the U.S. government had received classified information on the Nazis' extermination of European Jews as early as 1942, the world did not realize its full extent until Allied armies stumbled upon the death camps as they marched toward Germany. What they found horrified them—mass graves, gas chambers, starving inmates, including this one at an Austrian camp, and the personal effects of millions of victims. History has been critical toward the Roosevelt administration for doing so little to rescue Europe's Jews, 6 million of whom died at the hands of the Nazis, along with 4 million other civilians. *(National Archives.)*

The West failed to respond to the Holocaust. As the Nazis extended their reign of terror across Europe, Jews had flooded into immigration offices in an effort to escape persecution. Though outraged by Hitler's actions, Americans were unwilling to bend rigid immigration quotas to admit more European refugees—a view reinforced by anti-Semitism. Breckinridge Long, the State Department official responsible for refugee issues, blocked efforts to save Jews and later suppressed information about the death camps. In 1939 the U.S. government refused entry to 930 desperate Jewish refugees onboard the *St. Louis,* forcing the captain to return to Europe, where many of the refugees again suffered Nazi reprisals. "The cruise of the *St. Louis,*" editorialized the *New York Times,* "cries to high heaven of man's inhumanity to man."

Hitler tried to keep the death camps secret, but by 1942 the United States had reliable information about their existence. The reaction was indifference, and the State Department continued its policy of refusing visas to European refugees trying to enter the United States. "It takes months and months to grant a visa and then it usually applies to a corpse," a 1943 government study concluded. In response to the desperate appeals, Roosevelt created the War Refugee Board, which used private funds to establish refugee camps abroad. The board saved over two hundred thousand Jews, but for millions of refugees, it was too little, too late. Roosevelt's indifference to the Holocaust, concluded historian David Wyman, "emerges as the worst failure of his presidency."

Wartime Politics

At a press conference in 1943, President Roosevelt announced that "Dr. New Deal" had been replaced by "Dr. Win the War." During the 1940s Roosevelt backed away from liberal reform measures. Responding to new political realities, he agreed to drop several New Deal programs. The war and economic growth gave support to a growing conservative coalition in Congress, as people who were prosperous once more could afford to forget the assistance the Democrats had given them in the past. The resistance became clearly visible in 1942. With the war not yet going well militarily, Republicans made substantial inroads in the 1942 congressional elections. They gained 9 seats in the Senate and 44 in the House, giving them a total of 209 House seats—only 13 fewer than the Democrats' 222.

Compounding the effect of the Republican gains was the increased strength of conservative Democrats from the South. Democratic defeats in the North and Midwest continued to enhance southern influence. In the House, representatives from fifteen southern and border states claimed 120 of the 222 Democratic seats; in the Senate they held 29 of 57 seats. They also dominated the major committees. Thus, when Republicans and southern Democrats banded together, they constituted an insurmountable bloc.

The conservative coalition in Congress argued that the New Deal had gone too far. Conservatives wanted to cut back what they considered to be a bloated federal bureaucracy, to circumscribe the power of labor, and to end New Deal planning schemes that they contended impinged on free enterprise and individual initiative. They succeeded in virtually every sphere. Congress liquidated the Civilian Conservation Corps (CCC) and the Works Progress Administration (WPA). (Both faced declining enrollments in any case as better jobs became available in the massive war production effort.) In 1943 the National Youth Administration became another casualty. A whole range of other agencies suffered a similar fate.

Conservatives hoped to make further gains in the 1944 election, the first wartime presidential contest since 1864. The Republicans nominated New York governor Thomas Dewey, and chose John W. Bricker, the conservative governor of Ohio, as his running mate. Dewey accepted the broad outlines of Roosevelt's domestic and foreign policy. He supported social security, unemployment insurance, relief for the poor, and collective bargaining. But he attacked the bureaucratic inefficiency of the New Deal, complaining that the Democrats had "grown old in office," and had become "tired and quarrelsome."

Most of all, Republicans raised questions about Roosevelt's age and declining health. For most of the previous year, Roosevelt had been plagued with colds and bronchial problems. In March 1944, doctors learned that he suffered from heart disease and that his chronic high blood pressure had worsened, though they were careful to keep this information from the public. Reporters noted the president's haggard appearance—dark circles under the eyes, suits made baggy by excessive weight loss, a shaky hand—but they were unaware of the seriousness of his condition.

Roosevelt, always the practical politician, coasted with the political currents. At the Democratic convention he wooed conservatives by dumping his outspoken and liberal vice president Henry Wallace. At the request of party leaders, he asked Missouri Senator Harry S Truman to join the ticket. Truman had won national attention in the Senate as the head of a committee investigating corruption and graft in the defense program. Hailing from a border state, he was acceptable to party conservatives. As a protégé of party boss Tom Pendergast in Kansas City, he also had close ties to big city machines.

During most of the fall, Roosevelt paid little attention to either his opponent or Republican rhetoric. Then a month before the election, the president began to campaign energetically. Standing in drenching rain, riding in open-car motorcades, and speaking to huge crowds of supporters, FDR showed his stamina to rebut Republican charges that he was in poor health. Roosevelt could also count on the enthusiastic support of organized labor, which experienced remarkable growth during the war. Union membership increased from 9 million in 1940 to almost 15 million in 1945, a pace more rapid than at any time in American history. Organized labor spent over $2 million on FDR's 1944 campaign—nearly 30 percent of all party expenses. Many observers predicted a close election, but the 1944 results were nearly identical to 1940. The president carried thirty-six states and 432 electoral votes, and won over 3,500,000 more popular votes than Dewey: 25,606,585 to 22,014,745. The labor vote in the big cities made the crucial difference for Roosevelt. In cities with a population over one hundred thousand, Roosevelt received 60.7 percent of the vote. In many states, Roosevelt's plurality in urban areas overcame losses in suburban and rural areas (see map).

The Yalta Conference

In February 1945, flush from his electoral victory at home, Roosevelt traveled to Yalta, a resort on the Black Sea coast, to meet with Churchill and Stalin. The Big

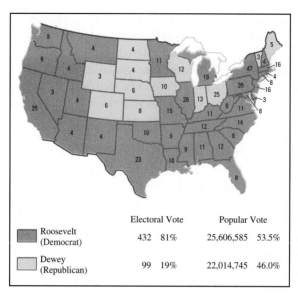

	Electoral Vote		Popular Vote	
Roosevelt (Democrat)	432	81%	25,606,585	53.5%
Dewey (Republican)	99	19%	22,014,745	46.0%

The Election of 1944   Unable to attack Roosevelt's popular domestic programs or his handling of the war effort, Thomas Dewey emphasized the need for new blood in the White House. Though Roosevelt at times showed signs of exhaustion, Americans remained strong supporters of the president and his new vice-presidential choice, Harry S Truman.

Three had to address a number of thorny questions: the occupation of Germany, the creation of the United Nations, and the status of eastern Europe. From the beginning, differences emerged between Stalin and his western Allies. The Soviets' vision of world stability differed greatly from what the English and Americans had in mind. Roosevelt, and to a lesser extent Churchill, subscribed to the principles of the Atlantic Charter, with its emphasis on free elections and self-determination, but Stalin insisted on maintaining a sphere of influence in eastern Europe.

The leaders reached compromises on many issues. Stalin promised to declare war on Japan within a few months of Germany's surrender. In return, Roosevelt accepted Soviet claims to the Kurile Islands in the Far East. Stalin dropped his demands for $20 billion in German reparations, agreeing to discuss the issue further. Roosevelt achieved one of his major diplomatic goals by gaining Stalin's support for the creation of the United Nations. All three leaders approved plans for a United Nations Conference in San Francisco in April 1945.

The postwar political status of Poland, which Churchill counted as "the most urgent reason for the Yalta Conference," caused the most controversy at the summit. Two Polish governments demanded recognition. The British and Americans supported the exiled government located in London. Stalin recognized a communist-led provisional government based in Lublin, Poland. To avoid letting arguments over Poland undermine conference harmony, the Allies worked out an agreement that papered over their significant differences with vague, elastic language. Stalin agreed to "free and unfettered elections" in Poland, but at a conveniently unspecified time in the future.

Roosevelt left Yalta convinced that he had laid the foundation for a peaceful postwar world. "We were absolutely certain that we had won the first great victory of the

The Big Three at Yalta   In February of 1945, Churchill, Roosevelt, and Stalin met amid the rubble in the Soviet city of Yalta to hammer out the details of peace. Bitter disagreements about Poland and war reparations led to a vaguely defined accord that only delayed a larger conflict between the Soviet Union and its Allies. Roosevelt, the one optimistic player, died a few weeks later, leaving a more suspicious Truman to make the peace.   *(National Archives.)*

peace," Harry Hopkins remarked. Years later, critics would charge Roosevelt with selling out to the Russians by acquiescing in Soviet domination of eastern Europe. But military and political realities weakened Roosevelt's bargaining position. By the time of the Yalta Conference, the powerful Red Army already dominated most of Poland, Czechoslovakia, and Hungary, and Roosevelt desperately wanted Russian assistance in defeating the Japanese. Knowing that most Americans wanted an end to the hostilities and a return of U.S. servicemen, the president had little choice but to accept Soviet control and focus on building trust between the two nations.

Roosevelt returned home from Yalta a very ill man. On March 1, the president told Congress that Yalta had been "a great success," and he asked the American people to support the agreements reached there. Soon afterward, Roosevelt retreated to his vacation home in Warm Springs, Georgia, to try and recoup his energy. Around noon on April 12, he slumped in his chair. "I have a terrific headache," he muttered. A few hours later, he died of a cerebral hemorrhage. Roosevelt's death left his successor, Harry S Truman, with the task of seeing the war to its end and resolving the complicated and confusing questions of postwar global security.

On April 25, the western Allied armies rolled up to the Elbe River, where they joined hands with the Russians who had been advancing from the east. A few days later, with Russian troops closing in on Berlin, Hitler married his mistress, Eva Braun, then killed her and himself in a suicide pact. On May 7, the new German government signed an unconditional surrender in Allied headquarters, and Eisenhower dictated his final note of World War II: "The mission of this Allied force was fulfilled 0241 local time, May 7, 1945."

War and National Culture, 1941–1945

Since nearly all Americans supported the war effort, Roosevelt did not employ the coercive methods against dissent that Wilson used during World War I. For the most part, the media exercised self-censorship and voluntarily joined the war propaganda effort. The treatment of Japanese-Americans was the one major exception to this record of restraint. By bringing together groups that had lived in isolation, the war blended ethnic and social differences and accelerated the development of a national culture. The war also offered new opportunities to groups that had been previously excluded, especially women and minorities, inspiring many to assert their rights in American society. Despite the enormous changes, traditional attitudes persisted, limiting the political and personal gains and undermining experiments with new social roles.

Propaganda and Popular Culture

World War II was the most popular war in American history. Five million young men volunteered for military service, and more than one hundred thousand nurses joined the WACS, WAVES, and SPARS—the women's branches of the army, navy, and coast guard. After Pearl Harbor, volunteers flooded into recruiting offices. Victory gardens sprouted everywhere. In 1943 gardeners grew more than 8 million tons of produce on 20 million individual plots.

In December 1941, Roosevelt created the Office of Censorship, which examined all letters going overseas and worked with publishers to suppress information that might be damaging to the war effort. But since the war was so popular, Roosevelt felt little need to resort to more coercive propaganda and restraint of dissent. An executive order of June 1942 created the Office of War Information (OWI), headed by Elmer Davis and staffed by advertising executives, which sold the war to the public.

The war poster became the most effective weapon in the OWI's arsenal. Posters were everywhere, pushing prowar activities and attitudes: Buy bonds. Enlist. Work Harder. Plant a Victory Garden. They were the "weapons on the wall" designed to arouse fear of the enemy and intense patriotism for the American cause. One poster shouted, "Stay on the job until every murdering Japanese is wiped out!" Another showed a dead GI slumped over a machine gun with the caption, "What did you do today . . . for freedom?"

Roosevelt's efforts were aided by the influence of the national media, which made Americans aware of their common culture and shared values. World War II was the first war given on-the-scene radio coverage. Millions of Americans sat by the family radio listening in suspenseful anticipation as newscasters Edward R. Murrow, Charles Collingwood, Howard K. Smith, and other pioneers of modern radio, described the march of German soldiers through Europe. Later they listened to morale-lifting programs such as "The Army Hour" and "Report to the Nation." The networks collaborated with the government to produce a 13-part series entitled *This Is War*.

The U.S. entertainment industry was an enthusiastic booster of the Allied cause. Washington understood the value of movies. OWI Director Elmer Davis said, "The easiest way to inject a propaganda idea into most people's minds is to let it go in through the medium of an entertainment picture when they do not realize that they are being propagandized." Hollywood released 1,500 films during the war; one-fourth were combat pictures. Box office receipts soared during the war from $735 million in 1940 to $1.4 billion in 1945. More than 60 million Americans attended movies weekly throughout the war. Moviegoers would have a complete war experience. An opening newsreel of war news, followed by a cartoon of Popeye fighting Japanese spies, ads for war bonds and enlistment, then a war movie. Afterward, patrons could visit a war-bond recruiting booth set up in the lobby.

Music makers also joined the war effort. Patriotic songs became enormously popular. Millions of Americans sat by their RCA Victrolas, playing their 78 rpm records of Kate Smith singing "God Bless America." Sentimental tunes, reflecting the loneliness of separations caused by the war, also topped the charts. The most-played recording composed during the war was Irving Berlin's 1942 "White Christmas," sung by Bing Crosby, which became the mantra of homesick soldiers. Other sentimental songs were also big hits, including 1944's "I'll Be Seeing You" and "I'll Be Home for Christmas."

Not even children's entertainment avoided military service. Comic-book hero Captain Midnight, who tracked down Nazi spies, asked children to recite a pledge "to save my country from the dire peril it faces or perish in the attempt." If enemy agents escaped the grasp of Captain Midnight, other super heroes, such as Superman or Jack Armstrong, stood ready to swing into action. (The government had granted Superman a deferment because he failed his induction physical for the army. When asked to read from an eye chart, his x-ray vision mistakenly read from a chart in the next room!)

Japanese Internment

The major exception to the administration's restraint in sedition control measures was the removal and incarceration of immigrant and American-born Japanese living on the West Coast. Shortly after Pearl Harbor, wild stories circulated about plots among Japanese residents to aid an enemy landing on the coast of California. The press, patriotic organizations, and powerful business groups joined in a chorus against Japanese-Americans. "Don't kid yourselves and don't let someone tell you there are good Japs," Representative Alfred Elliot of California declared in Congress in early 1942. "A good solution to the Jap problem," the governor of Idaho suggested, "would be to send them all back to Japan, then sink the island. They live like rats, breed like rats and act like rats."

On March 21, 1942, Roosevelt signed Executive Order 9066 authorizing the forced evacuation of Japanese residents on the West Coast. The order required more than one hundred thousand people, many of them American citizens, to dispose of their property and move to government "relocation centers" scattered throughout the West. "Truthfully," wrote an internee sent to the Arizona desert, "I must say this scorching Hell is a place beyond description and beyond tears." By December 1944, the government declared the emergency over and allowed residents to return home. By the time the Supreme Court ruled that same month (*Korematsu* v. *U.S.*) that the evacuation was constitutional, the camps had already begun to empty.

The treatment of the Japanese-Americans was the worst violation of civil liberties on the American side of the struggle. By one estimate they suffered nearly $400

Japanese Internment: Mother and Children   One of the darkest chapters in American history involved the wartime internment of over one hundred thousand Japanese-Americans in desolate camps. These Americans not only lived in stark conditions for months on end, they also lost their property, their jobs, and most of their personal belongings. The government claimed the action was in the interest of national security, and very few Americans raised any objections in the emotional climate after Pearl Harbor. As General John DeWitt, the West Coast military commander, claimed, "A Jap is a Jap. It makes no difference whether he is an American citizen or not."   (*Japanese American Citizens League.*)

million in property damage, not to mention the humiliation of being accused of disloyalty. Authorities invoked military necessity and national security to justify their actions. In 1982 a government commission reviewing the internment criticized the Roosevelt administration for "race prejudice, war hysteria, and a failure of political leadership." In 1988, agreeing with the commission's shameful findings, Congress compensated Japanese-Americans interned during the war.

The Breakdown of Provincialism

Increased geographic mobility added to the breakdown of regional differences in America. Fifteen million men and several hundred thousand women—one in nine Americans—moved because of military service. At least as many relocated to be near family members in the armed forces or to find new jobs in wartime industry. Lured by the surplus of wartime jobs, some 6 million people left farms to work in the cities. Nearly seven hundred thousand African-American civilians left the South during the war. By the end of the war, one in every five Americans had changed residence.

The development of war plants in the South and on the West Coast stimulated industrial development and reduced the economic uniqueness of both regions. Between 1941 and 1945, the federal government awarded more than $4 billion in war contracts to the South. By 1945, two-thirds of the nation's military bases and training camps were in a broad southern belt stretching from Washington, D.C., to El Paso, Texas. The influx of money and resources led to rapid urbanization in the region. Of forty-eight metropolitan areas in the South, thirty-nine experienced rapid war-related growth. Savannah grew by 29 percent between 1940 and 1950, Charleston by 37 percent, Norfolk by 57 percent, and Mobile by 61 percent.

The war had a similar impact on the West. Domestic mobilization diversified the western economy and made it more self-sufficient and independent. In four years a region almost entirely dependent on the extraction of raw materials transformed into one producing ships and airplanes, aluminum, magnesium, and steel. As in the South, the war spurred the pace of urbanization in the West, where it added to ethnic and racial diversity. San Diego doubled its population to 450,000. Los Angeles gained 30 percent in four years, as did San Francisco and Portland, Oregon. The state of California welcomed nearly 3 million new residents during the war, a 53 percent population growth.

The practical effect of the wartime experience enhanced national unity. Service in the armed forces constituted for millions of young men and women a common rite of passage that created a sense of shared values. People who had lived all their lives in small, provincial communities suddenly found themselves, because of new jobs or wartime responsibilities, in new and unfamiliar places, meeting new and unfamiliar people. The intermixing of cultures diminished the strong ethnic differences that had shaped American society for the previous generation. The foreign-language press lost ground. Between 1940 and 1945, more than two hundred ethnic-language newspapers failed. The whole range of ethnic theaters, language schools, political organizations, and lodges declined as well. Before World War II, "staying in America was something Italian-Americans did to make money. You didn't stay in America to lead a good life," explained an Italian-American veteran. "That happened after the war." Italian shops and basement wine cellars disappeared and Italians started speaking English to one another. 'We became respectable," he said.

While the war experience diminished ethnic identity, it increased the identity consciousness of other groups. Social mobility laid the foundation of the modern gay rights movement. "For many gay Americans," observed a historian, "World War II created something of a nationwide coming out experience." Hundreds of thousands of young men and women were given their first taste of freedom from parental supervision and from the social norms of their hometowns. After the war they migrated to large cities. In many large cities during the 1940s, exclusively gay bars appeared for the first time. The bars became seedbeds of collective consciousness that would flower in the 1960s.

Rosie the Riveter

On the eve of Pearl Harbor nearly 14 million American women (26 percent of the total work force) were employed as wage earners. Most were segregated into traditional women's work: teaching, nursing, social work, and the civil service. The vast majority of wage-earning black and Hispanic women were domestic servants. Young, unmarried women made up the bulk of the female work force. Almost half of all single women were employed in 1940, but only 15 percent of the larger pool of married women, and only 6 percent of women with children, worked outside the home.

With men being drafted for the service, employers looked to women to maintain the mobilization at home. "In some communities," Roosevelt said in 1942, "employers dislike to employ women. In others they are reluctant to hire Negroes. . . . We can no longer afford to indulge such prejudices or practices." The government encouraged women to work in steel plants, shipyards, and airplane factories. "Rosie the Riveter" who, according to a popular song of the time, was "making history working for victory," became the media symbol of the woman at work. She could do a man's job without compromising her feminine qualities. On the cover of the *Saturday Evening Post*, Norman Rockwell depicted a defiantly muscular Rosie. *Life* magazine hailed her as "the heroine of a new order."

Over the next four years, nearly 6 million women responded to the call. By the end of the war almost 19 million women (or 36 percent) were working, many at jobs from which they had previously been excluded. Nearly 2 million women— about 10 percent of female workers—took up jobs in defense plants. Almost

Women at War In the absence of so many American men, women enjoyed new job opportunities performing work that under normal circumstances would have been deemed inappropriate. These women are helping assemble an aircraft. But the gains proved temporary. As the war wound down, the government, which had conjured up "Rosie the Riveter" to vigorously recruit women workers at the war's start, urged women to resume more traditional roles. *(Lockheed-California Company.)*

500,000 worked in airplane industry; another 225,000 worked in shipbuilding. The percentage of black women who did paid housework declined from 69 to 35 percent, as many found work in industrial occupations.

Though Rosie the Riveter became a popular symbol of working women during the war, most women remained at home. In 1941 about 30 million women were homemakers. In 1944 seven of eight of these women were still engaged in homemaking. Polls showed that majorities of men and women disapproved of working wives, and most women of traditional childbearing age (20 to 34) remained at home. As a result, the war did little in the short run to challenge traditional notions that a woman's proper place was in the home raising the children. "The housewife, not the WAC or the riveter, was the model woman," observed historian D'Ann Campbell.

In the long run, however, the growth of female employment during the war widened the public sphere of women; the image of Rosie—strong and capable— challenged the older notions. As women ventured into the working world in ever-increasing numbers, they provided an economic and ideological underpinning to later movements for women's liberation. For many women, working in the factories represented "the first time we got a chance to show that we could do a lot of things that only men had done before."

The War for Racial Equality

W. E. B. Du Bois defined World War II as a struggle for "democracy not only for white folks but for yellow, brown, and black." The war forced Americans to look critically at racism at home. "A nation making an all-out effort . . . on the side of democracy," the *New York Times* editorialized, "must leave open the doors of opportunity to all, regardless of race."

For African-Americans, World War II offered economic opportunities marred by continuing discrimination. Twelve months after the bombing of Pearl Harbor in 1941, some half-million blacks had been inducted into a rigidly segregated Army. Military attitudes had changed little since a 1925 Army War College study reported that blacks possessed a "smaller cranium, lighter brain [and] cowardly and immoral character." In 1940 the army had just five African-American officers, and three of them were chaplains. Black soldiers had to watch the army segregate the blood plasma of whites and blacks. Regulations restricted blacks to their own barracks, movie houses, and commissaries. Traveling through the South to military camps, officers ordered them to pull down their train shades so as not to be shot at by local whites. In the navy, blacks were restricted to the minor roles of mess attendants or cooks. More than twenty riots or mutinies broke out on military bases, many of them ignited when northern blacks resisted the indignities of segregation.

Conditions on the home front were not much better. Management and labor joined forces to limit black access to the war boom. "We will not employ Negroes," declared the president of North American Aviation. "It is against company policy." Black migration from rural southern areas to the urban centers of war production caused terrible crowding and competition for scarce housing and schools in the cities. In 1942 a riot in Alexandria, Louisiana, left 28 African-Americans wounded and nearly 3,000 arrested. There were as many as 240 racial incidents in 47 cities in the summer of 1943. The worst riot erupted on a steamy June night in Detroit and left 34 people dead and more than 700 injured.

Faced with these conditions, black Americans launched a "double V" campaign: V for victory in the war against the dictators overseas and V for victory in their own struggle for fair treatment at home. In January 1941, A. Philip Randolph, head of the Brotherhood of Sleeping Car Porters, proposed a massive march on Washington to protest discrimination and segregation. FDR feared such a demonstration would tarnish the nation's image in the eyes of the world. How could America lead a crusade against Nazi atrocities when it practiced discrimination at home? Unable to convince Randolph to cancel the march, the president agreed to his demands. On June 25, 1941, President Roosevelt signed Executive Order 8802, which declared, "There shall be no discrimination in the employment of workers in defense industries or government because of race, creed, color, or national origin." The order established a President's Fair Employment Practices Committee (FEPC), which, though underfunded and understaffed, conducted a number of highly visible hearings that focused public attention on discrimination in government agencies.

Randolph's activism reflected a growing militancy among African-Americans. As one black newspaper noted, it "demonstrated to the Doubting Thomases among us that only mass action can pry open the doors that have been erected against America's black minority." Existing civil rights organizations witnessed dramatic growth during the war. NAACP membership soared from 50,000 in 1940 to over 450,000 in 1946. New civil rights groups appeared. In 1942 the Congress of

The Ninety-ninth Fighter Group Because of racial prejudice, only a handful of the hundreds of thousands of African-Americans who served in the armed forces during the war ever saw combat. Among those who did were the famed "Tuskegee Airmen," black fighter pilots trained at segregated facilities near the Tuskegee Institute in Alabama. These brave soldiers served their country with devotion and repeatedly distinguished themselves in battle. *(Gordon Parks.)*

Racial Equality (CORE), founded by a group of pacifists in Chicago, orchestrated sit-in demonstrations and picketing campaigns to desegregate public facilities. In 1944 picketers outside a segregated Washington, D.C., restaurant carried signs that read: "Are you for Hitler's Way or the American Way?" and "We Die Together, Let's Eat Together."

African-Americans also challenged employment discrimination by taking advantage of shortages in the labor market. Black employment rose by over 1 million during the war. The number of unemployed blacks dropped from 937,000 to 151,000. Union membership doubled. The number of African-American employees increased from 6,000 to 14,000 in shipyards and from zero to 5,000 in aircraft plants. Most African-Americans labored as janitors and custodians; few gained opportunities as craftsmen or foremen. Nevertheless, World War II constituted what one historian called "more industrial and occupational diversification for Negroes than had occurred in the seventy-five preceding years."

Like blacks, Hispanics faced opportunity tempered by discrimination during World War II. In 1940 about 1.5 million Spanish-speaking people lived in the United States, some in eastern cities, many more in the West and Southwest. The war caused an acute shortage of farm labor, and the federal government looked to Mexicans to help meet the need, importing contract laborers, or *braceros*. By the end of the war, over 120,000 workers were part of the program.

But the need for workers did not dispel discrimination. Anglos segregated Chicanos by skin color, frequently lumping them with African-Americans. "For Coloreds and Mexicans," read a sign outside a Texas church. Large growers forced *braceros* to work and live in dismal conditions, overlooked them for supervisory or skilled jobs, and paid them lower wages than white workers. Hispanics living in major cities faced a different form of discrimination. By 1943, Anglo anger focused on gang members called *pachucos,* or "zoot-suiters," because of their distinctive clothing. In the summer of 1943 in Los Angeles, following rumors that a gang of Mexican youths had assaulted a sailor, thousands of servicemen took to the streets, assaulting any youth wearing a zoot suit.

Labor shortages also shaped the war experience of Native Americans. By 1945, half of all Native Americans on the home front had left Indian reservations for war industries. Before the war only 5 percent of Native Americans lived in cities; by 1950, the figure had grown to 20 percent. For Indians, winning the war meant more than just defeating Hitler. "We want to win the war," an Indian said, "because victory will mean new hope for men and women who have no hope." The Commissioner of Indian Affairs reported that groups of Indians had shown up at his agency headquarters, "each man with his gun ready to register for Selective Service and to proceed immediately to the scene of the fighting." More than 25,000 Native Americans served in the armed forces, including 800 women. Among their contributions was the valuable service of using native languages such as Navajo to create unbreakable codes for American military communication.

Despite continuing discrimination at home the war offered African-Americans, Hispanics, and Native Americans a chance to "prove" their loyalty. "All we wanted," declared a Hispanic soldier, "was a chance to prove how loyal and American we were."

Victory, 1942–1945

Germany's surrender allowed the United States to focus its military might in the Pacific theater. After destroying the Japanese navy in two decisive contests, U.S. forces began advancing closer to the Japanese mainland in a series of bloody battles. Meanwhile American scientists created a powerful new atomic weapon. In an experiment that tested American values, President Truman had few reservations about using the bomb to bring about a quick end to the conflict. By the time it ended in August 1945, however, the war had transformed American society.

War in the Pacific

For six months after Pearl Harbor, the Japanese ruled the Pacific. The advancing Japanese army conquered Guam, Hong Kong, and Java. In February, they captured Singapore, the supposedly unconquerable "Gibraltar of the Pacific," forcing the surrender of eighty-five thousand British troops. As they pushed into the American-held Philippines, Roosevelt, knowing the islands were doomed, ordered General Douglas MacArthur to evacuate. "I shall return," MacArthur vowed. On May 6, more than 7,500 American and Filipino soldiers surrendered. Many of the prisoners died as their Japanese captors forced them to march, without water or food, sixty-five miles in the broiling heat to concentration camps.

The Japanese next turned their attention to Australia, sending a naval force to secure bases on the north coast. American military planners deciphered the Japanese code and rushed a task force to intercept them. At the Battle of the Coral Sea, the first naval battle fought exclusively by carrier-based aircraft, the U.S. blunted the offensive.

One month later, Japanese and American forces squared off again in the most important naval battle of the Pacific war—the Battle of Midway. Japan wanted control of the Midway Islands to launch air strikes against American installations in Hawaii. Knowing such a possibility would force the Americans to defend the islands, and hoping for a final decisive sea battle, Japan assigned four aircraft carriers, equipped with its best planes and pilots, to Midway. The American navy, still battered from Pearl Harbor, could muster only three carriers for the battle, including one, the *Yorktown*, that had sustained severe damage during the Battle of the Coral Sea. It appeared only a miracle could give the United States victory over vastly superior Japanese forces.

Once again, American code breakers scored an intelligence coup, if not a miracle, when they decoded a Japanese message that enabled them to learn the exact date, time, and place of the impending attack, and the composition of oncoming forces. Using this valuable information, Admiral Chester Nimitz, commander of the Pacific Fleet, was able to surprise the Japanese. Luck also played a part. On June 4, 1942, American fighter planes caught the Japanese carriers between launches of their aircraft, when they were most vulnerable. American dive-bombers sank all four Japanese aircraft carriers, destroying the heart of the enemy's mighty task force.

Following the victories in the Coral Sea and at Midway, American marines and army infantry began an "island-hopping" offensive in the South Pacific, inching closer to the Japanese mainland. After months of grueling combat in steamy jungles and rugged mountainous terrain, American troops gained control of the islands of

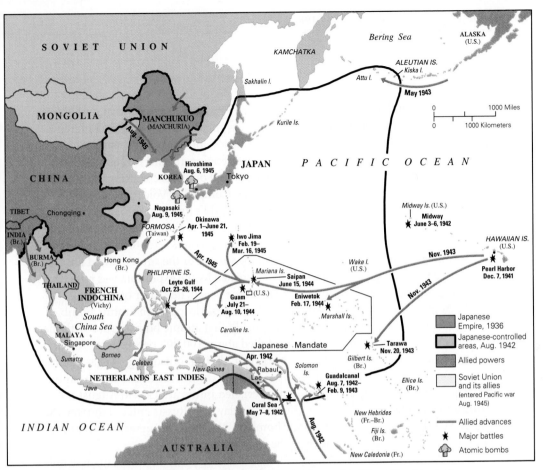

World War II in the Pacific   The Battles of the Coral Sea and Midway Island in the late spring of 1942 ended the Japanese expansion in the Pacific Ocean. The Allies then began a strategy of island hopping—cutting supply lines to Japanese strongholds before moving on to the next island chain, all the time inching closer to the Japanese mainland.

Guadalcanal, Saipan, and Guam. In August 1944, Roosevelt approved a massive air, land, and sea campaign to liberate the Philippines. Before regaining the islands, the U.S. met Japanese warships in the largest naval engagement in world history in the Battle of Leyte Gulf. The increasingly desperate Japanese for the first time used kamikazes, pilots trained to crash-dive their planes onto enemy aircraft carrier decks. Though they inflicted heavy losses on U.S. naval forces, kamikazes could not prevent a crushing Japanese defeat that secured U.S. naval control of the Pacific. As he had promised, General MacArthur then led U.S. troops in retaking the Philippines.

In February 1945, U.S. forces captured Iwo Jima, a speck of an island that cost 4,189 American lives. Two months later, 11,260 U.S. soldiers died in the successful assault on Okinawa. The fanatical resistance of Japanese defenders on Iwo Jima and Okinawa foretold that the inevitable invasion of their home islands would be a long, bloody campaign. War planners estimated the conquest of Japan, scheduled to begin on November 1, 1945, could take a year and could cost as many as 1 million American casualties.

The Bomb

An extraordinary new weapon radically altered the predicted scenario. In 1939 the noted scientist Dr. Albert Einstein had informed President Roosevelt that it might be possible to build "extremely powerful [atomic] bombs." Roosevelt, after conferences with scientific advisers, ordered work to begin to develop a nuclear weapon. Between 1941 and 1945, American and British scientists, engineers, and technicians, under the leadership of Dr. J. Robert Oppenheimer, labored on the secret, top-priority program, code-named the "Manhattan Project" (see Competing Voices, page 1047).

In July 1945, project scientists exploded the world's first atomic device at Alamogordo, New Mexico. The bomb weighed five tons. At its core was a package of uranium 235 about the size of a football. Within nine seconds after the explosion, the temperature at ground zero equaled that on the surface of the sun. An awed Dr. Oppenheimer, witnessing the enormous fireball created by the explosion, was reminded of a passage from Hindu scriptures, "I am become Death, destroyer of worlds."

On August 6, 1945, a B-29 named the *Enola Gay* dropped an atomic bomb on Hiroshima, Japan. The sky exploded: The world's first atomic bomb struck with the force of twelve thousand tons of TNT. It killed about 100,000 people instantly, and thousands more died later of burns, shock, or radiation poisoning. "What you remember most are the screams for water," recalled a survivor of the bomb. About 130,000 of the city's 250,000 inhabitants perished in the attack. On August 8 Red Army units invaded Manchuria and Korea. The day after Russia entered the war, the United States dropped a second atomic bomb on Nagasaki, incinerating forty thousand people and obliterating much of the city (see map).

Even after the atomic bombings and the Soviet entry into the war, Japanese military leaders wanted to fight on. Only the personal intercession of Emperor Hirohito induced them to surrender. On August 10 the Japanese offered to surrender if they could keep their emperor. Truman would accept only unconditional surrender, which came on August 14, although he did allow the Japanese to retain their emperor. Surrender ceremonies took place September 2.

The Legacy of War

The United States suffered fewer casualties during World War II than the other major warring nations. While just under four hundred thousand Americans lost their lives during the war, the struggle killed 2.8 million German soldiers. Combined military and civilian losses in Russia topped 20 million. Poland lost as much as 20 percent of its population. Throughout Europe the war's massive bombings left economies in ruins and millions homeless. Still, though U.S. cities were never bombed and civilian life continued with few interruptions, World War II served as a dramatic catalyst for change in American society.

The most obvious change was a dramatic increase in the size and scope of government power. The growing centralization of power in Washington, begun during the New Deal, accelerated during World War II. Between 1940 and 1945, the number of civilian employees in government posts rose from 1 million to 3.8 million. Federal expenditures from 1940 to 1945 rose from $9 billion to $98.4 billion. The final bill for the war came to more than $330 billion, a sum ten times larger than

The Remains of Hiroshima Strategists chose Hiroshima as the target for the first atomic bomb because the city's slight damage during the war made measuring the power of the bomb more accurate. Although scientists had tested an atomic bomb in the deserts of New Mexico, the destruction at Hiroshima stunned all involved. As seen in this photograph, the atomic bomb leveled a large area of the city, killing over 130,000 people. *(National Archives.)*

the direct expense of World War I and twice as large as the total of all government spending in the history of the United States to that point.

The dramatic increase in government spending produced prosperity that would have seemed unimaginable just a few years earlier. "The facts," Stuart Chase, a liberal economist, calculated, "show a better break for the common man than liberals in 1938 could have expected for a generation." National income jumped from $81 billion in 1940 to $181 billion five years later, or from $573 to $1,074 per capita. The war improved the distribution of income—an accomplishment that had eluded New Deal planners. The share of income owned by the richest 5 percent declined from 23.7 to 16.8 percent, while the average wages of workers employed full-time in manufacturing rose from $28 per week in 1940 to $48 in 1944. The enormous productivity of the war years fostered new confidence in government's ability to regulate the economy. Full employment was possible, liberal economists believed, and they now felt they knew how to use their tools to achieve that end.

America emerged from the struggle as the leading economic and military power in the world. Many leaders, including former isolationists, hoped to avoid the mistakes of the past. They argued that the United States needed to play a more active role in world affairs. "No more Munichs!" declared former isolationist leader Senator Arthur Vandenberg. "America must behave like the number one world power which she is." The rhetoric of economic internationalism echoed through the halls of government as well. Advocates argued that it was in the national interest to create new markets for American goods by rebuilding the economies of western Europe and Japan.

But older notions about the relationship between America and the rest of the world, deeply embedded in American culture, lived on beneath the surface of the new language of internationalism. Americans remained deeply skeptical about involvement in the affairs of other nations. The American people clamored for a quick return of servicemen abroad. They supported the creation of the United Nations, but only if the new organization did not impinge on American sovereignty.

On issues of both international diplomacy and domestic government, the people and Congress now looked to the president for leadership. The entire twelve years that Roosevelt spent in the White House were a time of crisis. Whether fighting the depression or rallying the nation to global war, Roosevelt made the presidency the focus of the public's hopes and expectations. Recognizing the growing power of the office, Congress delegated enormous power to the president, who in turn delegated it to the sprawling bureaucracy he controlled.

By raising expectations, the war laid the foundation for social changes that would occur in the 1950s and 1960s. "The war changed our whole idea of how we wanted to live when we came back," explained a veteran. Americans who fought in the war felt they deserved "a good job, a respectable life." War-bred opportunities whetted the appetite of women, who planned to build on those gains in the postwar period. Organized labor hoped to reap the benefits of the new prosperity. The aroused expectations exercised their most profound impact on African-Americans, who looked for continued improvement in their economic conditions and opportunities once the war ended. But when peace came in 1945, poet Maya Angelou saw black soldiers returning home, treated "like forgotten laundry left on a back yard fence."

CONCLUSION

During the 1930s, convinced that American participation in World War I had been a mistake and consumed by economic problems at home, most Americans believed they should remain aloof from the conflagration that was consuming Europe and Asia. Congress reflected the public mood by passing restrictive neutrality legislation that prevented the internationalist-minded Roosevelt from aiding the Allies. As German forces overran most of Europe in 1940, Roosevelt abandoned any pretense of neutrality, offering Britain military and financial aid. With the Japanese attack on Pearl Harbor in December 1941, America could not avoid joining the war.

The Big Three—Roosevelt, Churchill, and Stalin—clashed repeatedly over the proper military strategy to defeat Hitler's army. Stalin insisted on a second front in western Europe to relieve pressure on the Soviet army fighting Hitler in the east, while Churchill argued for delaying a cross-Channel attack and instead engaging German and Italian troops in North Africa and Italy. Roosevelt was sympathetic to Stalin but acquiesced to Churchill's plan to attack the Axis on the periphery. The Allies finally opened a second front in the D-Day invasion in June of 1944, but the nearly three-year delay had reinforced Stalin's suspicions of the West.

World War II was almost universally popular and war experiences contributed to the developing national culture. The home-front mobilization brought people of diverse backgrounds together, blurring the differences among social groups. The war industries also offered new employment opportunities for minorities and women. Millions of Americans—prompted by military service or employment opportunities—moved around the country during the war years. The creation of defense-related industries in the South and West, in particular, foreshadowed a long-term population shift away from the Northeast. Not everyone moved of their own free will: the government, fearing subversion, sent thousands of Japanese-Americans to internment camps. The internment, along with continuing racial discrimination and riots pitting whites against African-Americans and Chicanos, starkly highlighted the limitations of the new sense of national unity.

In the Pacific, the United States adopted a strategy of islandhopping. American forces steadily retook Japan's conquests and worked their way toward the Japanese home islands. Japan finally surrendered after the United States dropped atomic bombs on Hiroshima and Nagasaki.

The mobilization for total war and the growth of a national culture would have far-reaching consequences for American society. Ironically, at the same time that the war contributed to the growth of big government and the nationalization of culture, it reaffirmed Americans' faith in limited government and individualism. In all of the major initiatives of the war—building an army, mobilizing industry, controlling wages and prices—Americans experimented to balance the needs of war with the values of democracy. The brutality of Hitler's regime made Americans more skeptical of state power. In a war depicted as a struggle between good and evil, the victory over fascism seemed to confirm the continuing relevance of America's democratic experiment. Flush from victory, the United States prepared to launch a new crusade armed with enormous military might and confidence in the universality of American values.

SUGGESTED READINGS

John Morton Blum's *V Was for Victory* (1976) is a colorful analysis of American culture and society during World War II. Richard Polenberg's *War and Society* (1972) surveys the home front. Geoffrey Perrett's *Days of Sadness, Years of Triumph* (1973) studies both the domestic and military aspects of the war. John Keegan's *The Second World War* (1990) is the single best one-volume study of the military campaigns. William O'Neill's *A Democracy at War* (1993) is a fascinating look at the impact of American political ideology on mobilizing the country for war. Studs Terkel's *The Good War* (1984) is a powerful oral history of the war. *The Best War Ever* (1994) is a revisionist account by Michael Adams that dispels numerous myths about World War II, including the united home front and the enthusiastic soldier.

Robert Dalleck's *Franklin D. Roosevelt and American Foreign Policy, 1932–1945* (1995) remains the definitive account of FDR's approach to the world. Wayne S. Cole's *Roosevelt and the Isolationists* (1983) examines the battles over foreign policy in the 1930s and World War II. Robert Cohen discusses the peace movement of the 1930s in *When the Old Left Was Young* (1993). Patrick Heardon's *Roosevelt Confronts Hitler* (1987) focuses on the economic motivations for American entry into the war. The Atlantic Charter and the Anglo-American alliance is the subject of Theodore Wilson's *First Summit* (1991). Warren Kimball studies the Lend-Lease Act and its implications in *The Most Unsordid Act* (1969). Gordon Prange's *At Dawn We Slept* (1981) explores the events culminating in the U.S. entry.

Gordon Wright's *The Ordeal of Total War* (1968) is a standard account of America's military mobilization. George Q. Flynn's *The Mess in Washington* (1979) details the policy end of mobilizing, as does Bruce Catton's *War Lords of Washington* (1964). Nelson Lichtenstein covers the role of the CIO in fighting the war in *Labor's War at Home* (1983).

Gerald Linderman's *The World Within War* (1997) also examines the life of the average soldier, emphasizing the heavy psychological toll of the war. Stephen E. Ambrose's *The Supreme Commander* (1970) is a portrait of Dwight Eisenhower as a military coordinator. Mark A. Stoler explores the diplomatic wrangling among the Allies in *The Politics of the Second Front* (1977). John Keegan covers the D-Day invasion in his *Six Armies in Normandy* (1982), while John Toland's *The Last Hundred Days* (1966) details the end of the fighting in Europe. America's treatment of European Jews before and during the war is the subject of David S. Wyman's *The Abandonment of the Jews* (1984).

Warren Kimball's *Forged in War* (1997) examines the unique relationship between FDR and Churchill and their attempts to deal with Stalin. Stephen Ambrose's *Rise to Globalism* (1988) chronicles the United States' ascension to world power. Russell Buhite explores the ramifications of the Yalta Conference in *Decision at Yalta* (1986). John L. Gaddis locates the roots of the Cold War in World War II diplomacy in *The United States and the Origins of the Cold War* (1972).

Allan Winkler offers a valuable study of the Office of War Information in *The Politics of Propaganda* (1978). Holly Cowan Shulman studies the propaganda produced by the entertainment industries in *The Voice of America* (1991). Thomas Doherty's *Projections of War* (1999) demonstrates World War II's impact on the relationship between Hollywood and American culture.

Roger Daniels offers perhaps the definitive account of the Japanese internment in *Concentration Camps USA* (1981). Michi Weglyn's *Years of Infamy* (1976) has valuable primary source material on the internment. Gerald D. Nash explores the new mobility and the rise of the Sunbelt during the war in *The American West Transformed* (1985). John D'Emilio's *Sexual Politics, Sexual Communities* (1983) studies the impact of the war on gay Americans. Allan Berube's *Coming Out Under Fire* (1991) details the plight of gays on the home front and in the military.

Sherna Berger Gluck's *Rosie the Riveter Revisited* (1987) is a compelling oral history of women workers during World War II. Karen Anderson's *Wartime Women* (1981) examines the broad social transformations of women's roles during the war. Susan M. Hartmann's *The Home Front and Beyond* (1982) includes material on women at the battlefront. Molly Merryman's *Clipped Wings* (1998) is a history of the Women's Airforce Service Pilots.

Richard M. Dalfiume's *Desegregation of the U.S. Armed Forces* (1969) analyzes wartime race relations in the military. Albert Russell Buchanan's *Black Americans in World War II* (1977) is a moving account of the African-American struggle to challenge discrimination during the war. David Kryder's *Divided Arsenal* (2000) explores the government's dealings with the race issue as a whole. Mario T. Garcia's *Mexican-Americans* (1989) examines the Hispanic experience during the war. Kenneth Townsend addresses the impact of the war on Native Americans in *At the Crossroads* (2000). Dominic Capeci, Jr.'s *Race Relations in Wartime Detroit* (1984) and Mauricio Mazan's *The Zoot Suit Riots* (1984) explore the racial tensions of the period. Ronald Takaki's *Double Victory* (2000) is a general history of the wartime experiences of various segments of the American population.

The impact of the war and FDR's tenure on the presidency is the subject of Matthew Dickinson's *Bitter Harvest* (1997). James Atleson's *Labor and the Wartime State* (1998) argues that current policies toward and regulations of labor relations were formulated during World War II.

John Dower analyzes the racism among World War II Americans and Japanese in *War Without Mercy* (1986). Ronald H. Spector's *Eagle Against the Sun* (1984) is an in-depth account of the Pacific war. Akira Iriye studies the war from both sides in *Power and Culture: The Japanese-American War* (1981). Gordon Prange's *Miracle at Midway* (1982) chronicles this crucial battle.

There is extensive material on the atomic bomb. Gar Alperovitz studies the political aspects of the Manhattan Project in *Atomic Diplomacy* (1965). Herbert Feis's *The Atomic Bomb and the End of World War II* (1966) and Dennis D. Wainstock's *The Decision to Drop the Atomic Bomb* (1996) explore the development and decision to use the bomb on Japan. John Hersey's *Hiroshima* (2d ed., 1985) remains a powerful telling of the aftermath of the bombing. Paul Boyer's *By the Bomb's Early Light* (1985) investigates the intellectual culture behind the development of the bomb.

The Interim Committee, 1945

The Manhattan Project was so secret that not even Vice President Harry Truman had been informed of its existence. On April 25, 1945, thirteen days after Roosevelt's death, Secretary of War Henry Stimson briefed Truman on the bomb's development and the ongoing debate over whether to use it. Truman decided that he could not make such a decision by himself and appointed a committee of experts, drawn from the agencies working on the bomb, to advise him. Chaired by Office of War Mobilization Director James Byrnes, the so-called Interim Committee evaluated several scenarios for deploying the bomb. The following excerpts, describing the final deliberations before the committee decided to recommend using the bomb on a Japanese city, showcase the assumptions that dominated the decision-making process in the Truman administration.

On May 31, Secretary of War Stimson refuted arguments for a demonstration of the bomb and called for a surprise bombing. Arthur H. Compton, a scientist on the committee, later related the session:

> It was evident that everyone would suspect trickery. If a bomb were exploded in Japan with previous notice, the Japanese air power was still adequate to give serious interference. An atomic bomb was an intricate device, still in the development stage. . . . If during the final adjustments of the bomb the Japanese defenders should attack, a faulty move might easily result in some kind of failure. Such an end to an advertised demonstration of power would be much worse than if the attempt had not been made. It was now evident that when the time came for the bombs to be used we should have only one of them available, followed afterwards by others at all-too-long intervals. We could not afford the chance that one of them might be a dud. If the test were made on some neutral territory, it was hard to believe that Japan's determined and fanatical military men would be impressed. If such an open test were made first and failed to bring surrender, the chance would be gone to give the shock of surprise that proved so effective. On the contrary it would make the Japanese ready to interfere with the atomic attack if they could. Though the possibility of a demonstration that would not destroy human lives was attractive, no one could suggest a way in which it could be made so convincing that it would be likely to stop the war. . . .
>
> After much discussion concerning various types of targets and the effects to be produced, the Secretary expressed the conclusion, on which there was general agreement, that we could not give the Japanese any warning; that we could not concentrate on a civilian area; but that we should seek to make a profound psychological impression on as many of the inhabitants as possible.

The Franck Report, 1945

When James Franck brought his report to the White House on June 11, he was unaware Truman had already made the decision to drop the atomic bomb on a Japanese city. Franck, who chaired the Social and Political Implications Committee of the Metallurgical Laboratory at the University of Chicago, was among a handful of scientists who tried to convince the president not to drop the bomb on a civilian center. Like most of the scientists working on the Manhattan Project, Franck and his colleagues were not well briefed on the military situation in Japan. They focused on the longer-term strategic implications of the decision, and not on the moral or ethical ramifications of dropping the bomb.

The development of nuclear power not only constitutes an important addition to the technological and military power of the United States, but also creates grave political and economic problems for the future of this country.

Nuclear bombs cannot possibly remain a "secret weapon" at the exclusive disposal of this country for more than a few years. The scientific facts on which their construction is based are well known to scientists of other countries. Unless an effective international control of nuclear explosives is instituted, a race for nuclear armaments is certain to ensue following the first revelation of our possession of nuclear weapons to the world. Within ten years other countries may have nuclear bombs, each of which, weighing less than a ton, could destroy an urban area of more than ten square miles. In the war to which such an armaments race is likely to lead, the United States, with its agglomeration of population and industry in comparatively few metropolitan districts, will be at a disadvantage compared to nations whose population and industry are scattered over large areas.

We believe that these considerations make the use of nuclear bombs for an early, unannounced attack against Japan inadvisable. If the United States were to be the first to release this new means of indiscriminate destruction upon mankind, she would sacrifice public support throughout the world, precipitate the race for armaments, and prejudice the possibility of reaching an international agreement on the future control of such weapons.

Much more favorable conditions for the eventual achievement of such an agreement could be created if nuclear bombs were first revealed to the world by a demonstration in an appropriately selected uninhabited area.

In case chances for the establishment of an effective international control of nuclear weapons should have to be considered slight at the present time, then not only the use of these weapons against Japan, but even their early demonstration, may be contrary to the interests of this country. A postponement of such a demonstration will have in this case the advantage of delaying the beginning of the nuclear armaments race as long as possible.

If the government should decide in favor of an early demonstration of nuclear weapons, it will then have the possibility of taking into account the public opinion of this country and of the other nations before deciding whether these weapons should be used against Japan. In this way, other nations may assume a share of responsibility for such a fateful decision.

Most historians agree that Truman decided to use the bomb in order to save American lives. "Until newly found documents show otherwise, the available evidence points to the unremarkable conclusion that Truman approved using the bombs for the reason he said he did: to end a bloody war that would have become far bloodier had an invasion proved necessary," historian Robert Maddox wrote in 1995. Truman realized that if the public learned he had had a weapon that could have ended the war before an American invasion, they would be outraged.

Though the thesis that Truman dropped the bomb solely to intimidate the Soviets (historian Charles L. Mee, Jr., writing in this vein, called the bombings "wanton murder") has been largely discredited, political concerns certainly motivated Truman. In his analysis of the bombing, former Smithsonian director Martin Harwit cites Henry Stimson's numerous diary entries and State Department reports concerning, not the lives of GIs, but the Soviet Union. Stalin had pledged to enter the Pacific war within three months of the German surrender. Truman knew the Soviets were poised to dominate postwar developments in Manchuria and possibly Korea, and hoped the atomic bomb would force Japan to surrender before the Soviets could become involved there as well.

Several members of the Manhattan Project, though, had begun to have second thoughts about the bombing. Many of the scientists who helped develop the bomb had fled Europe and the Nazis. Certain that Germany was developing an atomic bomb, they thought the United States needed to counter this threat. When Germany surrendered in May 1945, some of those scientists were dismayed to learn the military planned to use the bomb on Japan.

"By the end of July 1945, if not before," historian David Wainstock has written, "Japan was militarily defeated. Fire raids had ravaged its major cities; its best troops were killed or missing in East Asia and the South Pacific, and many were still fighting in China. Twenty-two million Japanese were homeless, and the U.S. naval and air blockade had cut off imports of fuel, food, and raw materials." The men behind the Manhattan Project had begun to think beyond the present fighting to the postwar consequences of such a bombing. When Truman finally decided to use the bomb on the city of Hiroshima, he was motivated by calculations of international prestige and influence as much as by estimations of human lives.

Questions for Analysis

1. Why does the Interim Committee oppose giving Japan advance warning?

2. How does the Interim Committee picture the Japanese armed forces?

3. According to Franck why would the United States be at a disadvantage in a nuclear war?

4. Why do Franck and his colleagues want to delay using the bomb?

5. Were their predictions accurate?

6. How did assumptions about the world shape the strategic recommendations of the Interim Committee and the Franck Report?

7. How did the atomic bomb change America's international image?

27

The Cold War, 1945–1952

On February 22, 1946, the State Department's telex machine began clattering with a secret eight-thousand-word telegram from Moscow. The cable, written by George Frost Kennan, a forty-two-year-old Soviet specialist in the U.S. embassy, tried to explain Soviet aggression to puzzled officials in Washington. Since the end of World War II, U.S. policymakers had grown increasingly alarmed as the Soviets violated wartime agreements and tightened their military grip over Eastern Europe. Worried officials were all asking the same questions: What were Soviet intentions, and how should the United States respond to them? They turned to Kennan for the answers.

Kennan laid out a frightening picture of an aggressive Soviet Union intent on world domination. The Soviets, he wired, were driven by a "neurotic view of world affairs" that emerged from an "instinctive Russian sense of insecurity." They compensated for their insecurity by going on the attack "in patient but deadly struggle for total destruction of rival power, never in compacts and compromises with it." Moscow, he suggested, was "highly sensitive to logic of force. For this reason it can easily withdraw—and usually does—when strong resistance is encountered at any point." According to Kennan's analysis, the Soviets were solely to blame for international tensions; negotiations and compromise had reached an impasse; only military and economic pressure could tame the Russian bear.

Kennan's telegram caused a sensation in Washington. "Splendid analysis," exclaimed Secretary of State James Byrnes. "Magnificent . . . to those of us here struggling with the problem," said H. Freeman Matthews, the head of the State Department's Office of European Affairs. The following year, Kennan published an expanded public version of the telegram in an article written under the pseudonym "Mr. X." The Soviets, he argued, saw the world divided into hostile capitalist and communist camps between which there could be no peace. He recommended a U.S. foreign policy based on the "long-term, patient, but firm and vigilant containment of Russian expansive tendencies." From Kennan's essay a word emerged to characterize a new experiment in American foreign policy: *containment.*

The so-called Long Telegram and the Mr. X article provided the ideological justification for a new "get tough" approach with the Soviets. The strategy of containment fundamentally transformed American foreign policy. It ripped the United States from its isolationist roots, imposed new international obligations on the American people, and created a massive national security state.

At first, Harry Truman seemed ill prepared to lead the nation in its new international experiment and its return to a peacetime economy. But Truman managed to find his voice during the 1948 presidential campaign, unite the New Deal coalition, and score a surprising victory. Truman hoped his election would signal a revival of liberalism, but a public weary of New Deal–type experimentation, and a conservative coalition in Congress, frustrated most of his "Fair Deal" agenda. A series of foreign policy setbacks inflicted the most devastating blow to Truman's reform hopes. News that the Soviets had acquired atomic weapons, the communist victory in China, and, most of all, the communist North Korean invasion of South Korea in June 1950 eroded public trust in the administration.

Foreign policy setbacks abroad intensified fears of communist subversion at home. Critics charged that leftist sympathizers had aided the communist cause by passing atomic secrets to the Soviets. Charges of espionage and subversion gripped the nation. The anticommunist hysteria created a fertile breeding ground for demagogues who used fear of communism as a blunt weapon against dissent, real or imagined. Wisconsin senator Joseph McCarthy emerged as the leader of an unprecedented experiment in repression.

▮ What factors in the postwar period influenced Americans' attitudes toward government and reform? How did these attitudes affect Truman's domestic agenda?

▮ How did the Korean conflict manifest a new direction in foreign policy and military strategy?

▮ Why were Americans so fearful of communism, and how did that fear affect attitudes toward society and individual rights?

This chapter will address these questions.

From World War to Cold War, 1945–1949

During World War II, the need to sustain the Grand Alliance and defeat Nazi Germany forced the United States and the Soviet Union to downplay their differences. By the end of the war, however, serious questions had emerged about the future of the postwar world. As we saw in Chapter 26, Roosevelt at first tried to balance Soviet aims with American ambitions, but by 1945, Stalin's intransigence encouraged a tougher line with Moscow. Harry Truman picked up where Roosevelt left off. The Truman Doctrine and the Marshall Plan signaled a basic shift in American foreign policy that challenged isolationism and helped institutionalize the new hostility. Fear of mutual annihilation prevented the hostility from exploding into open warfare, but it gave birth to the precarious new peace that contemporaries titled the Cold War.

Roots of the Cold War

Who started the Cold War? The question has inspired passionate debate among historians. Some scholars place most of the blame on the Soviet Union, charging that its aggressive foreign policy was the logical outgrowth of an ideological commitment to world revolution. Other scholars contend that Russian aggression reflected a legitimate fear of American economic imperialism.

In recent years, historians studying the origins of the Cold War have emphasized that both nations shared responsibility for the conflict, though they differ greatly on how much responsibility to assign each side. Rather than seeing the Cold War as the product of conspiracies hatched in the Kremlin or in Washington, post–Cold War historians stress how history, ideology, and national interest created serious misperceptions, limited the range of options on both sides, and made confrontation nearly inevitable.

The Cold War between the Soviet Union and the United States had roots deep in the past. In 1917 relations between the two nations plummeted into the deep freeze when the Bolsheviks seized control of the Russian government. Under Lenin, the Soviets pulled out of World War I, leaving the West to fight the Central Powers alone. More important, the Soviets committed the new state to the goal of world revolution and the destruction of capitalism. Communism challenged the basic tenets of the American dream: it threatened democratic government, supported state power over individual freedom, cut off free markets, and eliminated religion altogether.

The brutality of the Soviet regime added to American hostility. Stalin, who seized control of the Soviet Union following Lenin's death in 1924, consolidated his power through a series of bloody purges that killed nearly 3 million citizens. He initiated a massive effort to collectivize agriculture that led to the deaths of 14 million peasants. In 1939, after Stalin signed the prewar nonaggression treaty with Hitler, he sent troops pouring into Finland, Estonia, Latvia, and Lithuania. By then most Americans agreed with the *Wall Street Journal* that "the principal difference between Mr. Hitler and Mr. Stalin is the size of their respective mustaches."

Chronology

1945	Yalta Conference
	FDR's death; Truman becomes president
	United Nations created
	Potsdam Conference
	US drops atomic bombs; World War II ends
1946	Kennan's "Long Telegram"
	Churchill's "iron curtain" speech
	Republicans win majority in both Houses
1947	Truman Doctrine and Marshall Plan announced
	Stalin creates Cominform
	President's Committee on Civil Rights established
	Taft-Hartley Act
	Federal Employee Loyalty Program established
	HUAC investigations of Hollywood
1948	Communist coup in Czechoslovakia
	Congress passes National Security Act
	Soviet blockade of Berlin begins
	Israel founded
	Truman elected president
	Truman moves to end discrimination in the military
1949	NATO approved by Senate
	China falls to Communists
	USSR explodes a nuclear weapon
	Hiss trial
	COMECON formed
1950	North Korea invades South Korea
	NSC-68
	China enters Korean War
	McCarthy announces communists in State Department
1951	General MacArthur fired
	Rosenbergs sentenced to death for espionage
1952	U.S. explodes first H-Bomb
1955	Warsaw Pact formed

The Soviets also had reason to distrust the United States. The rhetoric and actions of American policymakers lent credence to one of the principal teachings of Marxist-Leninist doctrine: the incompatibility of capitalism and communism. Western leaders, including President Wilson, made no secret of their contempt for Lenin or their desire to see him ousted. Wilson's decision to send American troops on a confused mission to Siberia in 1918 confirmed Soviet suspicion of a Western conspiracy to topple their government. The United States did not extend diplomatic relations to the Soviets until 1933—sixteen years after the new government came to power.

Hitler's invasion of Russia in 1941 forced the United States and the Soviet Union into a brief alliance to defeat Germany. Wartime cooperation greatly improved the Soviet Union's image in America. Confronted with evidence that the Russian people were willing to fight for their government, many Americans jumped to the conclusion that the Soviet Union had suddenly become a democracy. In the best-selling book *Mission to Moscow* (1943), Joseph E. Davies proclaimed that "the Russia of Lenin and Trotsky—the Russia of the Bolshevik Revolution—no longer exists." *Life* magazine in 1943 declared that Russians "look like Americans, dress like Americans and think like Americans."

The war may have softened American public opinion, but it did little to ease the mistrust between leaders. Roosevelt, though hopeful about a postwar settlement, recognized that "a dictatorship as absolute as any . . . in the world" ruled Moscow. At the same time, Roosevelt's agreement with Churchill in delaying a second front in Europe, and his refusal to share information about the development and testing of the atomic bomb, convinced Stalin that the Western allies could not be trusted.

As the war ground to an end, it became clear that the United States and the Soviet Union possessed fundamentally different visions of the postwar world. Since the early days of the republic, Americans believed in their mission to spread their revolutionary ideology of democracy, individual rights, and open markets, but they differed on how to fulfill that mission. Some Americans advocated a policy of active intervention in the affairs of other nations, while others suggested that America should keep to itself and lead by example. In the nineteenth century, America's sense of mission translated into a "manifest destiny" to expand to the Pacific and to civilize the Indians. During World War I, Woodrow Wilson expanded the notion to include spreading democracy and liberal capitalism around the globe. President Roosevelt extended that vision into the postwar world in the Atlantic Charter (1941), which affirmed the right of all peoples to choose their own form of government and assured all nations equal access to trade and raw materials.

America's vision of universal rights clashed with Stalin's insistence on maintaining a Soviet "sphere of influence" in eastern Europe. Since historians have just begun to examine the documents in Soviet archives (opened for research in the 1990s after the Soviet Union's collapse), it is hard to know Stalin's intentions at the end of the war. Most of the available evidence, however, suggests that the Soviets had one overriding goal: to secure their borders from foreign invaders. Twice in the twentieth century German armies had swept over Russia like hungry locusts. In the most recent assault by Hitler's Nazis, as many as 20 million Soviets died.

Six hundred thousand starved to death in the two-year battle and siege of Leningrad alone. Along with the millions of deaths, the war caused enormous physical destruction. The Soviets, determined to head off another attack, insisted on defensible borders and friendly regimes on their western flank. As early as December 1941, Stalin asked the British and Americans to accept Soviet influence in eastern Europe. "All we ask for," he told the British foreign minister, "is to restore our country to its former frontiers."

Europe emerged as the key battleground between these rival visions of the postwar world. The war had devastated Europe, weakened established powers, and created a power vacuum that the United States and the Soviets moved to fill. "The odor of death," recalled an American diplomat, "was everywhere." Fifty million people had perished. Great cities had been reduced to rubble. Tens of millions of people had no shelter. Everywhere farmlands had been despoiled, animals slaughtered. In Poland almost three-fourths of the horses and two-thirds of the cattle were gone.

The wretched conditions in Europe precipitated a historic shift in American foreign policy. The United States could not withdraw to its side of the Atlantic as it had after World War I. "We are for all time deisolated," wrote an observer. With the world's largest navy and air force, a monopoly on nuclear weapons, and a thriving economy, the United States seemed poised to fulfill its historic mission to spread the values of democracy and free enterprise to the rest of the world. "We are going forward to meet our destiny—which I think Almighty God intended us to have—and we are going to be the leaders," Harry Truman told his Missouri neighbors in 1945.

Yet despite its global military might, the United Sates was unable to control events in the Soviet "sphere of influence." In 1945, with its 10-million man Red Army in control of most of eastern Europe, the Soviets were in a position to impose their will by force. Within weeks of the Yalta Conference, at which he agreed to hold "free and unfettered elections," Stalin installed a pro-Soviet puppet government in Poland. With Poland firmly in his grasp, Stalin moved to strangle the rest of eastern Europe. He appointed a communist-led government in Rumania, and reoccupied Latvia, Estonia, and Lithuania.

American officials viewed Soviet actions as a real threat to U.S. interests. No policymaker worried about a direct Soviet assault on the United States, and few believed the Soviets could muster the resources—military, financial, or psychological—for an invasion of western Europe. The danger was that the Soviets would extend their influence politically by capitalizing on social and economic chaos in Europe, which created a fertile breeding ground for Soviet-dominated Communist Parties. In France, Italy, and Finland, 20 percent of the public voted Communist in elections after the war; in Belgium, Denmark, Norway, Holland, and Sweden, the figure was nearly 10 percent. If the trend continued, the Soviets could capture vital strategic resources and cut the United States off from potential markets.

By 1945, the battle lines were clearly drawn. Stalin interpreted U.S. calls for free elections and democratic reform in eastern Europe as part of a capitalist plot to surround the Soviet Union. The Americans viewed the Soviet Union's effort to consolidate its control over eastern Europe as the first step of a larger plan of global conquest. "We can't do business with Stalin," Roosevelt complained three weeks before his death. "He has broken every one of the promises he made at Yalta." Moscow and Washington became ensnarled in a "security dilemma": each step taken by one side to enhance its security appeared an act of provocation to the other.

Harry Truman Takes Charge

When he assumed the presidency in April 1945, Harry Truman knew little about Roosevelt's hardening line toward the Soviets. He learned quickly when he sought the recommendations of Roosevelt's advisers, most of whom favored a tougher policy toward the Soviets. "We had better have a showdown with them now than later," declared Secretary of the Navy James Forrestal.

A combative posture fit Truman's temperament. Impulsive and decisive, he lacked Roosevelt's talent for ambiguity and compromise. "When I say I'm going to do something, I do it," he once wrote. On his desk he displayed his credo in a sign: "The Buck Stops Here." Truman viewed the Yalta Accords as contracts between East and West. He was committed to seeing that Stalin honored the agreements.

The new president, emboldened by America's monopoly of atomic weaponry and eager to show critics and the nation that he was in charge, matched Stalin's inflexibility with calls for self-determination and free elections in eastern Europe. In office less than two weeks, he scolded Soviet foreign minister Vyacheslav Molotov for Soviet aggression in Poland. When Molotov protested, "I have never been talked to like that in my life," Truman retorted, "Carry out your agreements and you won't get talked to like that."

The Russians interpreted Truman's tongue-lashing as proof that the new administration had abandoned Roosevelt's policy of cooperation. When a bureaucratic blunder led to the abrupt termination of lend-lease shipments to the Soviets, a bitter Stalin complained that the United States was trying to use economic pressure to force political concessions. Despite reassurances that the decision resulted from a bureaucratic error, the incident likely reinforced the Kremlin's deep suspicion of the West. In May, former Undersecretary of State Sumner Welles charged, "Our Government now appears to the Russians as the spearhead of an apparent bloc of the western nations opposed to the Soviet Union."

Although Truman believed the United States needed to confront Soviet aggression, he also recognized that U.S.–Soviet cooperation was necessary to guarantee a lasting peace. In July 1945, Truman carried these conflicting goals to Potsdam, outside Berlin, for the final meeting of the Grand Alliance. Truman and Stalin squabbled over the sensitive issues of reparations and implementation of the Yalta Accords, but by the end of the meeting the leaders had reached tentative agreements. Russia would permit Anglo-American observers in eastern Europe to monitor free elections and would withdraw its troops from oil-rich Azerbaijan in Iran. In return, the West reluctantly accepted Soviet occupation of eastern Germany and approved Russian annexation of eastern Poland. On the key issue of reparations, the leaders agreed that each power would extract reparations from its own zone in occupied

Truman Tours Potsdam
The devastation of much of Germany was readily apparent when President Truman journeyed to Potsdam in July 1945 to meet with Stalin and Churchill. Here he views the ruins of the Reichschancellery, the scene of many of Hitler's public appearances. (Truman is seated on the far side of the car, wearing the white, bandless hat; next to him is Secretary of State James Byrnes.) The ravaged city hosted another epic battle during the conference itself, one of the opening rounds of the Cold War. Truman, less patient than Roosevelt had been, clashed with Stalin over the Polish border, German reparations, and other matters crucial for the shape of the postwar world. *(Harry S Truman Library.)*

Germany, and that the Western powers would transfer 15 percent of the capital equipment in their zones to Russia in return for food, coal, and other raw materials. Despite their obvious differences, Truman left Potsdam hopeful that he could develop a working relationship with Stalin. "I can deal with Stalin," he wrote in his diary. "He is honest—but smart as hell."

The Iron Curtain Falls

Truman's optimism proved unfounded. With the Red Army occupying half of Europe at the end of the war, Stalin moved decisively to establish his control over eastern Europe. Violating his pledge at Potsdam to allow free elections, Stalin tightened his grip over Poland, Bulgaria, Hungary, and Rumania. He denied Western observers access to eastern Europe and continued his occupation of Azerbaijan.

Soviet actions in Germany did little to ease U.S. suspicions about Soviet intentions. Yalta had divided Germany into four zones and Berlin into four sectors (U.S., USSR, British, and French). The Soviets, wanting to punish Germany for its aggression, planned to impose a harsh peace. By April 1946, the Soviets had stripped their zone of industry and started to make heavy demands for factories, power plants, and tools from the American and British zones. The Truman administration feared that the Soviets would cripple Germany, produce widespread famine, and require a massive infusion of American resources. Truman halted reparations for the Soviets in May 1946. In September Secretary of State James Byrnes stated that the U.S. would no longer seek agreement with the Soviets on the future of Germany.

Disputes over the control of nuclear technology further divided the former allies. In December 1945, the Big Three foreign ministers established an Atomic Energy Commission to deal with the question of nuclear weapons in the postwar world order. In June 1946, the Americans proposed a plan that allowed the United States to retain its nuclear monopoly while the United Nations implemented a system of international control. In its most controversial clause, the plan stipulated mandatory United Nations inspection of Soviet nuclear facilities—a condition the administration knew Stalin would never accept.

By the summer of 1946, neither Truman nor Stalin was interested in making a deal. Truman did not want to relinquish America's nuclear monopoly. We "should not under any circumstances," he declared, "throw away our guns until we are sure the rest of the world cannot arm against us." For his part, Stalin wanted no place in an international scheme that would prevent the Soviets from developing their own atomic bomb. Unable to reach agreement, the United States put aside plans for international cooperation. In 1946 Congress created the Atomic Energy Commission to control research and development of nuclear energy.

Both the Soviets and the Americans heightened tensions by engaging in a war of words. On February 9, 1946, Stalin delivered a rare public speech in which he explained the fundamental incompatibility of communism and capitalism. The American system, he stressed, needed war for raw materials and markets. The Second World War had been the most recent in a chain of conflicts that could be broken only when the world's economy made the transformation to communism. *Time* magazine concluded that the remarks were "the most warlike pronouncement uttered by any top-rank statesman" since the war had ended.

A few weeks later Winston Churchill returned the fire. Speaking in March 1946 in Fulton, Missouri, with Truman on the platform, the former prime minister declared of Europe that "from Stettin in the Baltic to Trieste in the Adriatic, an iron curtain has descended across the Continent." To counter the threat, he called for an association of English-speaking peoples to remain vigilant at all times.

Polls suggested that the American public agreed with Churchill's assessment. Shortly after the speech, a survey showed that 60 percent of the public believed that the United States was being "too soft" on the Russians. Soviet actions and hardening public attitudes pushed many isolationists into the internationalist camp. Most conservatives, distrusting European leaders and fearing that active involvement in world affairs would enlarge presidential power, had hoped to resurrect traditional isolationist sentiment after the war. By 1946, however, the threat of Soviet expansion forced many to reconsider their views. "I am more than ever convinced," said Senator Arthur Vandenberg, "that communism is on the march on a worldwide scale which only America can stop." For Vandenberg, fear of Soviet domination outweighed deeply held ideas about American self-reliance.

Americans supported a tougher line with the Soviets, but they remained deeply ambivalent about assuming the responsibility of world power. Many of the same people who feared Soviet aggression also clamored for the president to bring home American soldiers and to convert to a peacetime economy. Congress delivered the contradictory message directly to the president. Legislators eager to reestablish their control over foreign policy called on Truman "to get tough with Russia." Yet they also pushed for lower taxes and for a rapid demobilization of the armed forces. By mid-1946, the total number of American forces on active duty had dropped from 12 million to less than 3 million.

Containing Communism: The Truman Doctrine and the Marshall Plan

Reflecting his growing impatience with the Russians, Truman replaced his secretary of state, James Byrnes, with General George C. Marshall in January 1947. A distinguished military officer who had served as Army Chief of Staff during the war, Marshall had earned a well-deserved reputation for honesty and integrity. As secretary of state, Marshall presided over the process that transformed America's approach to the world.

For advice Marshall turned to two State Department professionals who had long harbored deep suspicions of the Soviets: Undersecretary of State Dean Acheson and Moscow diplomat George Kennan. An elegant and arrogant man, Acheson rejected suggestions that morality should drive American policy and instead stressed that American power was essential to peace. By 1946, Acheson urged Truman to employ the full range of American power—economic, military, and diplomatic—to tame the Soviet bear. "I think it is a mistake to believe that you can, at any time, sit down with the Russians and solve questions," he told the Senate in 1947, echoing many of the ideas Kennan espoused.

By 1947, a communist insurgency was battling the right-wing monarchy in Greece. Stalin was also pressuring Turkey to share control of the strategic Dardanelles strait, the waterway linking the Black Sea and the Mediterranean. In February 1947, the British ambassador informed the American State Department that his country could no longer afford to support Greece and Turkey with economic and military aid. The Truman administration, fearful that the Soviet-backed insurgents might gain the upper hand, wanted to fill the vacuum. First, it needed to overcome deep-seated American fears of getting involved in European affairs. Senator Vandenberg suggested that the administration build support by "scaring hell out of the country."

The administration accepted the challenge. On March 12, 1947, Truman stood before a joint session of Congress to make his case for American aid to Greece and Turkey. "I believe that it must be the policy of the United States to support free peoples who are resisting attempted subjugation by armed minorities or by outside pressures," he declared. The future of the "free world," he insisted, rested in America's hands. After setting the stage, Truman requested that Congress appropriate $400 million for Greek and Turkish military and economic aid. The American people rallied around the cause of freedom. Public opinion strongly supported the request, and Truman's poll ratings leaped ten points.

The Truman Doctrine represented a turning point in American foreign policy. By rooting America's response to a decidedly local conflict in traditional rhetoric of good and evil, free and unfree, Truman hoped to prepare the American people for their responsibility as a world power. Presidential aide Clark Clifford called it "the opening gun in a campaign to bring the people up to [the] realization that the war isn't over by any means."

The administration recognized that military assistance might deter the Soviets in Greece and Turkey, but it would not save war-torn western Europe from economic disaster. Europe, Churchill declared, had become "a rubble heap, a charnel house, a breeding ground of pestilence and hate." To challenge the strength of Communist Parties and Soviet influence, administration officials moved to shore up Europe's battered economy.

On June 5, 1947, Secretary of State George C. Marshall offered his prescription for recovery. He chose the Harvard University commencement ceremony to announce a bold new plan of economic assistance to Europe. Marshall explained that the aid program was "directed not against any country or doctrine but against hunger, poverty, desperation, and chaos." Marshall invited the participation of any country, including the Soviet Union, that was "willing to assist in the task of recovery." But Truman realized that Stalin would never accept a plan that required him to share vital economic information with the United States while Western leaders controlled how funds would be distributed. In December 1947, Truman submitted the plan to Congress, with a recommendation that the United States spend $17 billion over four years.

At first, congressional leaders were cool to the idea. Critics condemned the plan as a gigantic "international WPA," "a bold Socialist blueprint." Vandenberg led the bipartisan supporters, calling the plan a "calculated risk" to "help stop World War III before it starts." While Congress held hearings during the fall, Europe sank deeper into its economic abyss. England announced it was cutting individual meat rations to twenty cents worth per week.

Inadvertently, the Soviet Union provided the Marshall Plan with the boost it needed. During the summer of 1947, Stalin established the Communist Information Bureau (Cominform), which tightened his control in the Eastern bloc and within Russia. The Cominform also called upon communists in the underdeveloped world to accelerate "their struggle" for liberation. A U.S. diplomat called the creation of the Cominform "a declaration of political and economic war against the U.S. and everything the U.S. stands for in world affairs."

In February 1948, Communists staged a coup in Czechoslovakia, overthrowing a freely elected coalition government. Two weeks later, the popular Czech foreign minister Jan Masaryk died in a fall from a bathroom window. The Soviets said it was suicide; critics said he was murdered. Western leaders interpreted the coup as part of an aggressive Soviet plan to conquer Europe before it could be revived. According to Kennan, a "real war scare" swept Washington. Opposition to the Marshall Plan wilted in the heated atmosphere. On April 2, the House approved the plan by the lopsided vote of 318 to 75. The Senate roared its approval by an overwhelming voice vote. As a program to revitalize Europe's troubled economy, the Marshall Plan was a dramatic success. Thanks in part to its provisions, European industrial production increased 200 percent between 1948 and 1952. The British foreign secretary called the Marshall Plan "a lifeline to sinking men" (see map).

While debating the merits of the Marshall Plan, Congress institutionalized the Cold War with the passage of the National Security Act. The legislation created the skeleton of what would become an overpowering national security apparatus. The act expanded executive power by centralizing previously dispersed responsibilities in the White House. It established the Department of Defense to oversee all

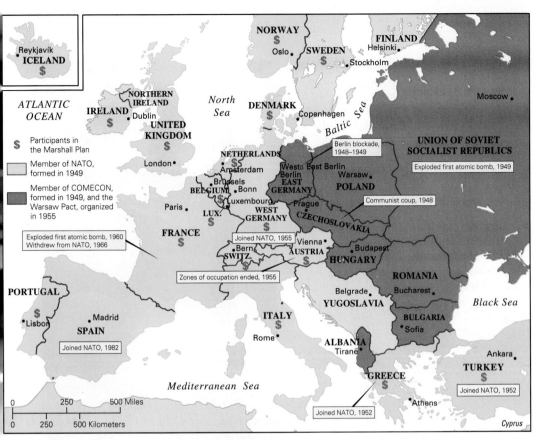

Cold War Europe With the end of World War II, political ideologies divided Europe. While Eastern Europe received its orders from the Soviet Union, the United States worked to maintain noncommunist governments in the West by means of the Marshall Plan and the North Atlantic Treaty Organization.

branches of the armed services and formed the Joint Chiefs of Staff, which included the generals of the three services and the marines. The act also created the National Security Council (NSC), a cabinet-level body to coordinate military and foreign policy for the president. Led by the president, the NSC included the head of the Joint Chiefs of Staff, the secretaries of state and defense, the vice president, and any other members the president chose to appoint. Finally, the legislation set up the Central Intelligence Agency (CIA), which carried out espionage operations directly under the authority of the National Security Council. Following the passage of the act, a journalist noted an ominous trend toward "militarization of [the] government and of the American state of mind." By blurring the line between peace and war, the Cold War led the government to adopt a constant state of readiness.

Mounting Tensions, Precarious Solutions

In June 1948, the West consolidated its hold on Germany. It fused the French zone with the British and American areas, creating "Trizonia," which contained Germany's richest industrial resources and a population of 50 million. The Western powers also invited the Germans to create a new government in West Germany and initiated financial reforms that produced a remarkable economic revival.

The Marshall Plan at Work in Austria

In the war's aftermath, the United States sent $17 billion to Europe in the form of money and supplies to bolster relief and rebuilding efforts. The European landscape and economy were devastated, creating a dangerous political and social vacuum that the United States feared the Soviet Union might exploit. Secretary of State George Marshall and other policymakers believed that massive aid would enable European nations to resist communism and would build loyalty to the United States among the European people. They certainly have won a friend in this little boy, who is obviously thrilled with his new shoes, brought by American planes and distributed by Red Cross workers. *(American Red Cross, Falls Church, Va.)*

The Russians retaliated on June 24 by clamping a tight blockade around West Berlin, which lay 110 miles within the Soviet occupation zone. The Western powers had failed to write clear arrangements for land access to Berlin into their agreement with the Soviets. Taking advantage of the legal confusion, the Soviets blocked all surface transportation into West Berlin, depriving some 2.5 million people of food and fuel.

The action forced Truman to respond. A retreat from Berlin, Marshall warned, meant the "failure of the rest of our European policy." But an effort to break the blockade might lead to armed confrontation, and Truman searched for a safer response that would demonstrate American resolve. His answer was a massive airlift operation. For the next 324 days, American and British planes dropped 2.5 million tons of provisions to sustain the 10,000 troops and the 2 million civilians in West Berlin. Truman threatened publicly to use "the bomb" if the Soviets shot down the relief planes. He wrote in his diary that "we are very close to war." On May 12, 1949, however, the Russians swallowed defeat and ended the blockade.

The Berlin crisis further catalyzed Western leaders to present a unified front to the Soviets. Already Great Britain, France, Belgium, the Netherlands, and Luxembourg had signed the Brussels Treaty (1948), which provided for collective self-defense. In January 1949, Truman proposed expanding the alliance by committing the United States to the defense of Europe. In April, he pledged American involvement

The Berlin Airlift Greeted by German Children   When the Soviet Union sealed off the city of Berlin in June 1948, the United States and Great Britain launched Operation Vittles, which involved sending hundreds of planes loaded with supplies to Berlin every day, month after month. As with the Marshall Plan, the airlift not only allowed West Berlin to remain free of Soviet domination, it created a psychological bond between West Germans and the United States. These children enthusiastically wave at an incoming plane. Notice they are standing on rubble, still plentiful in Europe three years after the war's end.   *(Corbis-Bettmann.)*

in the North Atlantic Treaty Organization (NATO), a mutual defense pact that bound twelve signatories to fight against aggression. Article 5 provided "that an armed attack against one or more . . . shall be considered an attack against them all."

The treaty still needed Senate approval, and Truman anticipated a heated debate. Since George Washington first warned against 'entangling alliances' with Europe, the United States had avoided peacetime involvement in collective security agreements with other countries. But NATO supporters, led by Vandenberg, argued that the Soviet threat required the country to develop a new approach to the world. On July 21, 1949, in a clear indication of the shift in American thinking from isolationism to internationalism, the Senate approved the NATO treaty by a wide 82–13 margin. In 1950 Truman appointed General Dwight D. Eisenhower to serve as NATO supreme commander and ordered four American divisions stationed in Europe.

While challenging the Soviets' claim to a "sphere of influence" in Europe, the United States consolidated its own sphere in the Western Hemisphere. In 1947 in the Rio Treaty, U.S. and Latin American signatories agreed that "any armed attack by any state against an American state shall be considered an attack against all the American states." The following year, North and Latin American countries created the Organization of American States (OAS). Despite these professions of unity, U.S. relations with Latin America were based on suspicion. Most Latin American countries remained politically unstable, suffering from wide gaps between rich and poor and governed by repressive military dictatorships. For now, American policymakers were more concerned about preventing Soviet military influence from creeping into the hemisphere than in offering economic assistance to needy neighbors.

The Cold War also shaped American policy in the Middle East. After World War II, many Jews who had survived Nazi concentration camps resettled in British-controlled Palestine. In 1947 the British, weakened by World War II, turned over control of Palestine to the United Nations, which voted to partition the region into separate Jewish and Arab states. The president's military advisers, including Secretary of State Marshall and Defense Secretary James V. Forrestal, feared that recognition of the Jewish state of Israel would anger Arab oil-producing nations. On an emotional level, however, the president empathized with the suffering of Jews during World War II. And as a practical matter, since Stalin had already announced his support for Israel, Truman worried about the possibility of a close Soviet-Israel relationship that would exclude the United States. Truman respected the political clout of Jewish voters at home. "In all of my political experience," Truman remarked during the campaign of 1948, "I don't ever recall the Arab vote swinging a close election." On May 14, 1948, Israel declared its independence. Within a few hours, the United States recognized the new state.

The Soviets matched the Western initiatives by intensifying their domination of Eastern Europe. In October 1949, Stalin created a separate government in East Germany, the German Democratic Republic. Moscow tightened its economic grip by sponsoring the Council for Mutual Economic Assistance or COMECON (1949), and its military clasp on Eastern Europe by forming the Warsaw Pact (1955). The Soviets poured massive aid into Poland, Czechoslovakia, and Bulgaria to accelerate industrialization and increase Soviet control. The only exception to Soviet domination was Yugoslavia, which stubbornly resisted Soviet influence and gradually managed to develop as an independent socialist state.

The adoption of the containment policy thrust onto the United States political and military responsibilities as a "world policeman" that went far beyond anything ever contemplated by the American people (see Competing Voices, page 1088). A few lonely voices questioned the containment policy. Journalist Walter Lippmann emerged as containment's most prominent critic. In a series of newspaper columns, later published in book form as *The Cold War*, Lippmann charged that containment would increase executive power at the expense of the other branches of government and divert energy and resources away from domestic needs. Worst of all, he argued that it would militarize American foreign policy and force it to support corrupt dictators, who only had to be anticommunist to be a U.S. friend. The policy, he wrote, "can be implemented only by recruiting, subsidizing and supporting a heterogeneous array of satellites, clients, dependents, and puppets." For now, however, few Americans wanted to consider the implications of their new internationalist experiment.

 ## In the Shadow of FDR, 1945–1948

Truman could not match his success in winning support for his Cold War policies abroad with similar achievements in domestic policy. Postwar prosperity, concern over the administration's anti-Soviet policies, and a divisive debate over civil rights exposed cracks in the Democratic coalition. Continuing currents of conservatism headed off Truman's liberal proposals. Truman managed to pull together the New Deal coalition to score a surprising victory in the 1948 election. But the Cold War drained reformist energy at home and prevented Truman from expanding Roosevelt's agenda.

The Economic Shock of Rapid Reconversion

At 7 P.M. on Tuesday, August 14, 1945, President Truman invited reporters to the Oval Office for a brief, informal press conference. For weeks rumors had circulated about an imminent Japanese surrender. As the horde of reporters rushed into the room, a solemn Truman rose from his desk to greet them. Reading from a prepared text, he announced that he had received a message of surrender from the Japanese government. "Arrangements are now being made," he said, "for the formal signing of surrender terms at the earliest possible moment." The president then smiled and sat down.

The nation exploded in celebration. Across the country, church bells rang, air raid sirens screeched, horns honked, and bands played. The celebrations were clouded, however, by doubts about America's ability to shift to a peacetime economy. "We are completely unprepared for a Japanese collapse," journalist I. F. Stone wrote a few weeks before the war ended, "and unless we act quickly and wisely [we] may face an economic collapse ourselves."

As Stone had predicted, the sudden end of the war sent shock waves through the American economy. Within a month, the government canceled $35 billion in war contracts and slashed war-related production by 60 percent. The cuts prompted massive layoffs. Within ten days of the Japanese surrender, 2.7 million men and women lost their jobs. Economists predicted that more than 10 million Americans would be thrown out of work by peace. At the same time, a flood of servicemen returned home looking for civilian jobs. The government released almost 7 million men and women from the armed forces by April 1946. The dislocations raised widespread fear that the nation was headed toward another depression.

Soaring inflation added to public anxiety. During the war, speculation had pushed property values and stock prices to new highs. Between 1941 and 1945, the national debt climbed from $61 billion to $253 billion; government spending rose from $9 billion to $98 billion. Savings accounts multiplied, increasing liquid assets of individuals and corporations to almost $200 billion. A postwar rush to spend the savings threatened to unleash a spiral of rising prices. In August 1945, Office of Price Administration (OPA) chief Chester Bowles said the nation was in "one of the most dangerous periods in our country's economic history."

Bowles, and many other liberals, wanted Truman to limit inflation damage by continuing wartime price controls. But a coalition of Republicans and conservative Democrats in Congress, eager to eliminate most wartime controls, slashed the OPA budget. Truman fought the effort but he lacked the votes in Congress to keep the OPA alive. The first week after controls ended in July 1946, prices increased 16 percent. Steak increased in price from fifty-five cents to one dollar a pound. Staples such as milk, butter, and vegetables all showed huge increases overnight. The public blamed the president, even though he personally opposed ending price controls. Truman's popularity fell from a peak of 87 percent to 32 percent in just a few months.

The combination of high prices and job losses squeezed organized labor. During the war labor unions had for the most part honored a voluntary no-strike pledge. With the war ended and prices rising, labor demanded steep wage increases. By October 1945, half a million workers went out on strike. In April 1946, John L. Lewis (see page 1022) led four hundred thousand coal miners out of the pits. For forty days the strike cut off the nation's supply of fuel and threatened European recovery. On May 21, Truman ordered government troops to take over the mines. "Let Truman dig coal with his bayonets," Lewis snarled.

Railway workers joined coal miners on the picket line, threatening to cut off an essential economic artery. Truman reacted angrily, telling the nation that "the crisis of Pearl Harbor was the result of action by a foreign enemy. The crisis tonight is caused by a group of men within our own country, who place their private interests above the welfare of the nation." On May 25, Truman went before Congress to ask for the authority to draft strikers into the army. The threat was effective: the strike ended after only a few days.

The Republicans, capitalizing on the pervasive dissatisfaction with rising prices, labor strikes, and Cold War anxieties, pounced on the hapless Democrats in the 1946 congressional elections. Their campaign slogan was as simple as it was effective: "Had enough?" The Republicans gained control of both Houses of Congress for the first time since 1930. Only 37 of the 77 liberal members of Congress were returned to office. Among the new members of the class of '46 were Representative Richard Nixon of California and Senator Joseph McCarthy of Wisconsin.

Harry Truman and the Divided Democrats

Truman's plummeting popularity and the Republican success in the 1946 election left liberals sour and disillusioned. Cold War with Russia and conservative resurgence at home frustrated their hopes for the postwar world. Most blamed Truman for their plight, agreeing with the *Nation*'s characterization of the president as a "weak, baffled, angry man." Columnists Joseph and Stewart Alsop, looking toward the 1948 election, predicted, "If Truman is nominated, he will be forced to wage the loneliest campaign in history."

Truman lacked the grace and magnetism liberals had come to expect from the White House. Born on May 8, 1884, in Lamar, Missouri, Truman spent most of his early years in the farm country of western Missouri. After high school, he moved to Kansas City, where he worked as a banker. In 1906 he returned to help with the family farm. Over the next eleven years, while keeping the farm afloat, Truman devoted considerable effort to courting Bess Wallace, whom he later married.

After a stint in the army during World War I, Truman set up a haberdashery and sold men's clothing in Kansas City until a steep recession in 1921 destroyed the business. A few years shy of his fortieth birthday, Truman confronted a bleak future: He had to contend with a failed business and the real threat of bankruptcy, and he had few career options. Then one day in the summer of 1921, a representative of the notorious Pendergast political machine, which dominated Kansas City politics, invited Truman to run for county judge. Truman won election in 1922 and served on the court for most of the next twelve years, fighting a constant struggle to satisfy his patron while also providing good government for his constituents.

In 1934 Truman won election to the United States Senate. Many people, including his fellow senators, treated him with contempt, dismissing him as the "Senator from Pendergast." Truman cast aside the criticism and threw himself into his work. With the nation mired in depression, Truman supported most of Franklin Roosevelt's New Deal agenda. It was during World War II, as head of a committee to investigate the national defense program, that Truman distinguished himself and caught the attention of party leaders. That exposure, along with his border-state background, helped gain him the vice-presidential nomination in 1944 when the Democrats were looking for a compromise choice.

"For a time," observed a journalist, "he walked in the long shadow of the dead President." Compared with his mythic predecessor's grace, dignity, and patrician vision, Truman seemed a provincial man who was incapable of transcending his modest roots. Compounding the problem, Truman frequently appointed to important government jobs his unremarkable political friends, who lacked the stature of the men who had served Roosevelt. The journalist I. F. Stone put it bluntly: "The Truman era was the era of the moocher. The place was full of Wimpys who could be had for a hamburger."

Unlike Roosevelt, Truman had to contend with a Republican Congress determined to reverse liberal gains achieved since the 1930s. The Republican Eightieth Congress frustrated most of Truman's domestic agenda, rejecting his appeals for public housing, federal aid to education, and relaxed immigration quotas. Fearing continued Democratic dominance of the White House, it passed a constitutional amendment limiting the president to two terms. In 1948, after failing twice to override Truman vetoes, Congress finally mustered enough votes to pass a large tax cut on personal income. Most significant, Congress passed, over Truman's veto, the Labor-Management Relations Act of 1947, better known as the Taft-Hartley Act. The measure outlawed the closed shop, which had required that all hiring be done through a union hall; permitted states to pass so-called right-to-work laws allowing nonunion members to work in unionized plants; empowered authorities to issue federal injunctions against strikes that jeopardized public health or safety; and gave the president power to stave off strikes by imposing "cooling-off" periods of up to eighty days. The legislation also required union leaders to swear that they were not communists. "We have got to break with the corrupting idea that we can legislate prosperity, legislate equality, legislate opportunity," declared Senator Robert Taft, the chief spokesman for economic conservatism.

These political setbacks further frustrated liberals, who were unanimous in their disaffection with Truman's domestic leadership but divided over how to respond to Cold War tensions. Many liberals, who called themselves Progressives, believed that continued American-Soviet cooperation was essential to the preservation of the wartime anti-fascist alliance. Believing that legitimate security needs inspired Stalin's actions in Eastern Europe, they opposed Truman's growing hard line with the Soviets. Many Progressives also hoped to rebuild the left-of-center Popular Front of the mid-1930s by forging a powerful coalition that would include labor, small farmers, intellectuals, communists, and socialists. Only by combining to fight the forces of re-action, they argued, could liberals retain power in the postwar period.

Progressives looked to former vice president Henry Wallace for leadership. In September 1946, Wallace, who served as secretary of commerce, criticized both U.S. and Soviet policy. Under pressure from Secretary of State James Byrnes and Repub-lican senator Arthur Vandenberg, Truman fired Wallace. In December 1947, Wal-lace announced that he would run for president on a third-party Progressive ticket. Few people believed Wallace could win the election, but many Democrats feared that he could siphon liberal votes away from Truman in key states.

By then, Stalin's repressive regime and Soviet aggression in Eastern Europe were making any coalition with communists at home less attractive to many liberals. In 1946 Walter Reuther purged communists from the United Auto Workers. Following his lead, in 1949 the CIO expelled nine unions, representing nine hundred thou-sand workers, for refusing to rid themselves of communist leaders. Similar house-cleaning occurred in Popular Front political organizations. In Minnesota the young mayor of Minneapolis, Hubert Humphrey, gained control of the Minnesota Farmer-Labor Party and weeded out communists from its ranks. In 1947 many leading anticommunist liberals met in Washington and created the Americans for Democratic Action (ADA).

Confronted by a revolt among liberals, Truman turned to his advisers Clark Clifford and James Rowe for advice on how to hold the party together. They pre-pared a brilliant campaign blueprint, a 43-page memorandum entitled "The Poli-tics of 1948." The memo argued that Truman should pursue a strategy of militant liberalism, which would undercut Wallace's support, and strident anticommunism. Running on a liberal platform would also allow the president to exploit the differ-ences within the Republican Party between the moderate national party, led by New York governor and likely nominee Thomas Dewey, and its conservative wing in Congress, led by Ohio senator Robert Taft.

Truman took the recommendations to heart. Over the next few months he championed an aggressive liberal reform agenda, calling for a far-reaching housing program, stronger rent control, a sweeping enlargement of social security coverage, and federal aid to education. Before Congress had a chance to act, he went on the offensive, blaming Republicans for not supporting his program. At the same time, the president highlighted his hard line with the Soviets to underscore his anticom-munist credentials.

Truman made support for civil rights a centerpiece of his fighting liberal pro-gram. In 1946 Truman had established the President's Committee on Civil Rights, the first presidential committee ever created to investigate race relations in Amer-ica. Later that year the committee released its report, *To Secure These Rights*, which called for an end to segregation and discrimination and advocated legislation to abolish lynching and the poll tax. In February 1948, Truman hailed the message as "an American charter of human freedom" and asked Congress to support the com-mittee's recommendations. In July Truman signed Executive Order 9981, which set up procedures for ending racial discrimination in the military. Though not imple-mented until the Korean War, the order symbolized Truman's commitment to civil rights. The *Chicago Defender*, a black newspaper, called the order "unprecedented since the time of Lincoln."

Truman's advocacy of civil rights in 1948 exposed the deep ideological and sectional strains in his party. His message diminished support for Wallace and nudged anticommunist liberals to his corner. After a failed attempt to draft war hero Dwight Eisenhower as a presidential candidate, the ADA reluctantly accepted the prospect of Truman's nomination. They made civil rights the litmus test of their support. Only if the president included a strong civil rights plank in the Democratic platform would they endorse the incumbent. Southern Democrats sent the president a much different message. Senator James Eastland of Mississippi warned that Truman's civil rights proposals "would destroy the last vestige of the South's social institutions and mongrelize her people." He and other southerners in Congress threatened to boycott the national convention if Truman's platform embraced civil rights.

In July, when Democrats assembled in sultry Philadelphia for their convention, Truman was feeling the southern heat on civil rights. Fearful of a revolt, he backtracked, endorsing a weak plank that made no mention of his own proposals. When Truman hedged, liberals took their fight to the floor. In a dramatic and emotional speech, Humphrey, who was seeking a Senate seat, called on the party to enact a "new emancipation proclamation." "The time has come," he declared, "to walk out of the shadow of states' rights and into the sunlight of human rights." Humphrey's emotional appeal carried the day. Convention delegates rejected Truman's compromise measure and approved a strong civil rights plank. Rejected by the national party, southern delegates stormed out of the convention, formed the States' Rights Democratic, or "Dixiecrat," Party and nominated J. Strom Thurmond, governor of South Carolina, for the presidency. "We stand for the segregation of the races and the racial integrity of each race," they proclaimed.

A few hours after the bitter civil rights fight, Truman accepted his party's nomination. As his running mate, Truman selected seventy-five-year-old Senator Alben Barkley of Kentucky. Truman gave a rousing acceptance speech, but he could do little to lift the spirits of Democratic leaders who feared that defections of Democratic voters to Wallace and Thurmond spelled doom in November. At a nearby convention hotel, a group of Democratic leaders called for room service. "Send up a bottle of embalming fluid," they moaned. "If we're going to hold a wake, we might as well do it right."

The 1948 Election

The Republicans, in contrast, were united and hopeful. With little fanfare and even less debate, they nominated New York governor Thomas E. Dewey, who had run a strong race against Roosevelt in 1944 and seemed certain to beat Truman. Their convention, which was the first ever televised, picked California governor Earl Warren for the second spot on the ticket and adopted a platform promising a foreign policy based on "friendly firmness which welcomes cooperation but spurns appeasement."

Confident of victory, Dewey spent much time campaigning for other Republican candidates in states that were not crucial to his own election. Ignoring Truman and avoiding specific issues, Dewey concentrated on convincing voters that he was an efficient administrator who could bring unity to the country and effectiveness to its foreign policy. According to one observer, Dewey sought the presidency "with the humorless calculation of a Certified Public Accountant in pursuit of the Holy Grail."

While Dewey tried to stay above the partisan fray, Truman waged a tough, bare-knuckled campaign. The president went on a whirlwind, transcontinental railroad trip in which he gave 351 speeches to an estimated 12 million people. He blamed the "do-nothing, good-for-nothing 80th Congress" for everything from high prices to poor health care. "If you send another Republican to Washington," he told audiences, "you're a bigger bunch of suckers than I think you are."

Truman tied himself to Roosevelt's legacy, reminding voters that the Democratic Party had led the nation through depression and world war. He peppered his speeches with references to "Republican gluttons of privilege," who had "stuck a pitch fork in the farmer's back" and "begun to nail the American consumer to the wall with spikes of greed." His speeches pictured politics as a struggle between the "people," represented by the Democrats, and the "special interests," represented by Republicans. Enthusiastic crowds shouted, "Give 'em hell, Harry!" Truman responded, "I don't give 'em hell. I just tell the truth and they think it's hell."

Despite his energetic campaign, Truman lagged behind Dewey in the polls. The day before the election, the Gallup poll gave Dewey 49.5 percent of the popular vote and Truman 44.5 percent. On election night, long before the votes were in, the *Chicago Tribune* ran its front-page announcement: "DEWEY DEFEATS TRUMAN."

Truman Triumphant   The 1948 presidential election was one of the closest in American history. Because the liberal Democratic vote was split three ways, Republicans and experts alike assumed the election would be an easy win for Thomas Dewey. But Truman, never one to shrink from a fight, launched an extensive rail tour, appearing to crowd after crowd from the back of his train car (sometimes in his pajamas), speaking off the cuff and castigating the "do-nothing" Republican Congress. His victory caught everyone by surprise, most embarrassingly the *Chicago Daily Tribune*. When Truman held up the paper's premature headline at a victory rally in St. Louis, he created the most enduring image of his presidency.   *(Wide World Photos, Inc.)*

Instead, Truman scored the most dramatic upset victory in the history of presidential elections, winning 24.1 million votes to Dewey's 22 million (see map). How did Truman pull off such a surprising victory? First, both Wallace and Thurmond were hurt by the public's reluctance to waste their votes on a third-party candidate with little chance of victory. At the same time, their campaigns actually helped Truman. With Wallace being openly supported by the communists, and with Truman denouncing him, the president was much less vulnerable than he might otherwise have been to charges of being "soft" on communism. The Dixiecrat rebellion against Truman's civil rights program encouraged the loyalty of liberals and most black voters, many of whom might otherwise have been attracted to Wallace or even to Dewey.

Second, Dewey's bland campaign failed to excite voters. Dewey was vague and unclear on the issues, and he ignited little grass-roots enthusiasm. Fewer Republicans came to the polls in 1948 than in either 1940 or 1944.

Finally, the election demonstrated the enduring appeal of the New Deal. "I talked about voting for Dewey all summer, but when the time came I just couldn't do it," confessed one farmer. "I remembered the depression and all the other things that had come to me under the Democrats." The Democrats, by picking up 9 seats in the Senate and 75 in the House, regained control of Congress. "[T]he party that Roosevelt formed has survived his death," Walter Lippmann observed, "and is without question the dominant force in American politics."

The Election of 1948   Thomas Dewey was the favorite in the polls, in large part due to the Dixiecrat split from the Democratic Party, but it was not enough to win him the election. "Give 'em hell, Harry" Truman made an impressive 31,000-mile whistle-stop tour of the country promoting the continuation of New Deal programs at home and support of democracy abroad. Such aggressive campaigning propelled him past his opponent with 50 percent of the popular vote.

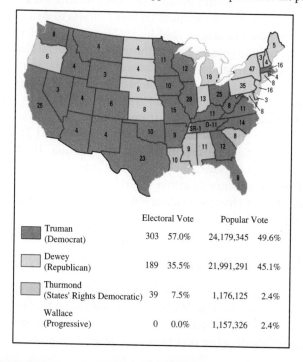

		Electoral Vote		Popular Vote	
■	Truman (Democrat)	303	57.0%	24,179,345	49.6%
□	Dewey (Republican)	189	35.5%	21,991,291	45.1%
□	Thurmond (States' Rights Democratic)	39	7.5%	1,176,125	2.4%
	Wallace (Progressive)	0	0.0%	1,157,326	2.4%

Trying for a Fair Deal

Although he won the election by a slim margin, Truman viewed his victory as a mandate for liberalism. The president outlined his ambitious social and economic program in his 1949 State of the Union message. "Every segment of our population and every individual," he declared, "has a right to expect from our Government a fair deal." Truman implored Congress to expand many New Deal programs, while launching new initiatives in civil rights, national health insurance, and federal aid to education. The liberal *New Republic* called Truman's Fair Deal "one of the boldest reform programs ever presented by an American President."

The Eighty-first Congress often complied with Truman's pleas to expand existing programs. In the most ambitious burst of reform since 1935, Congress increased the minimum wage from forty to seventy-five cents per hour, extended rent controls, and approved a displaced persons act admitting some four hundred thousand refugees to the United States. It passed the National Housing Act of 1949, which authorized the construction of 810,000 low-income housing units and provided funds for slum clearance and rural housing. In 1950 Congress increased social security benefits by an average of 80 percent, extending the system's coverage to an additional 10.5 million people.

Congress, however, showed little desire to support Truman's calls for new programs that moved beyond the New Deal. It rejected the president's proposals for federal aid to education, a crop subsidy system, and repeal of Taft-Hartley. When Truman proposed a system of national health insurance, the American Medical Association (AMA) hired an advertising agency to fight against the measure. "Would socialized medicine lead to socialization of other phases of American life?" asked an AMA leaflet. The answer: "Lenin thought so." Most Americans agreed and the bill died in Congress. Congress also stymied Truman's efforts to enact civil rights legislation. Truman proposed creating a Civil Rights Division in the Department of Justice to protect the right to vote, to abolish the poll tax in federal elections, and to establish a permanent Fair Employment Practices Committee. Southern Democrats and Republicans killed the bill before it reached the floor for debate.

To some extent, Truman's Fair Deal was a victim of the Cold War, which drained attention and resources away from domestic initiatives. The Cold War also strengthened the power of conservatives, whose support Truman needed to maintain his foreign and defense policies. At the same time, the promise of prosperity sapped public enthusiasm for government intervention. "Any illusion that the liberal Democrats dominate either the House or the Senate has been completely blasted," Hubert Humphrey observed. The 1948 election was "not so much a victory as a reprieve."

 ## The Cold War Heats Up, 1950–1952

Just as U.S.–Soviet tension stabilized in Europe with the creation of NATO in 1949, the Cold War expanded to Asia. With the "fall" of China to the Communists in 1949, American policymakers began rethinking U.S. defense priorities in Asia. The most dramatic policy decision occurred in June 1950, following the invasion of

South Korea by Communist North Korea. Viewing the attack as part of a larger Soviet design to challenge American interests around the globe, Truman reacted swiftly, sending American troops to repel the invasion. The U.S. response frustrated North Korean hopes of unifying the peninsula under communist rule. But a bitter dispute between Truman and General Douglas MacArthur raised troubling questions about America's containment experiment.

The Cold War Spreads to Asia

When World War II ended, China was torn between Jiang Jieshi's (Chiang Kai-shek's) Nationalists in the south and Mao Zedong's (Mao Tse-tung's) Communists in the North. At first the Nationalists had the upper hand, but Jiang's corrupt and incompetent government failed to inspire public support or stem the tide of Chinese communism. In 1945 and 1946, Truman, anxious to work out a peaceful settlement between Jiang and Mao, sent General George C. Marshall to China in a failed attempt to negotiate a compromise. U.S. efforts continued, but by 1949, Truman had grown weary of Jiang's refusals to undertake necessary reforms or attack corruption in his government. The president wrote in his diary that Jiang's government "was one of the most corrupt and inefficient that ever made an attempt to govern a country."

Deciding there was little the United States could do to salvage the noncommunist government, Truman stopped all aid to Jiang in 1949. Shortly afterward, Jiang's forces collapsed, sending the Nationalist leader scurrying to the offshore island of Formosa (Taiwan), where Nationalists set up an independent Republic of China. The Soviet Union consolidated its power in Asia by extending diplomatic recognition to Mao's Communist government and signing a "mutual assistance" agreement.

The Communist victory precipitated a firestorm of criticism at home against those responsible for "losing China." Friends of Jiang in the Republican Party complained that Democrats had let the Communists win. Led by publisher Henry Luce, the "China Lobby," an influential group that advocated U.S. intervention in China, wondered aloud why the Truman administration had stopped supplying weapons to Jiang after the Marshall mission of 1946. Years later, John F. Kennedy and Lyndon Johnson, remembering the bruising assault Truman endured for "losing China," would determine never to lose another inch to the communists.

The emotional reaction to the Communist triumph in China focused U.S. attention on Asia. At the end of World War II the United States occupied Japan and, under the leadership of General Douglas MacArthur, transformed the vanquished country into a model of Western democracy in which women could vote, trade unions were encouraged, and land redistributed among the peasants. Wanting to make sure that Japan would never reemerge as a military threat, the U.S. wrote a constitution, adopted in 1946, that renounced war, promising that "land, sea and air forces, as well as other war potential, will never be maintained." The growing communist threat in Asia, however, forced a dramatic shift in American policy. Now, viewing Japan as a potential military counterweight against China, policymakers negotiated a new treaty in 1951 that terminated the U.S. occupation and conceded to Japan "the inherent right of individual or collective self-defense."

The "fall" of China also transformed a local nationalist struggle against French rule in Indochina into a globally strategic battleground. During World War II, Roosevelt had expressed support for Vietnamese nationalist forces led by Ho Chi Minh, a communist educated in Paris and Moscow, and called for an end to French colonial rule. After Jiang's collapse, American policy shifted. Fearing that a communist "victory" in Indochina would become a sweep of Southeast Asia and tilt the global balance of power, the United States abandoned its pretense of neutrality and openly endorsed French policy in Asia. In 1950, when the Soviet Union and China extended diplomatic recognition to Ho's government, Truman supplied military aid to the French. America had taken its first step into the Vietnam quagmire.

While debating the consequences of the "fall" of China, Americans experienced another Cold War setback. On September 23, 1949, Truman issued a terse press release: "We have evidence that within recent weeks an atomic explosion occurred in the U.S.S.R." Though the administration publicly downplayed the significance of the Soviet breakthrough, it realized that, in Vandenberg's words, "This is now a different world." Since the United States could not match the Soviets in manpower, military planners had depended on "the bomb" to deter Soviet aggression.

Together the "fall" of China and the Soviet nuclear test forced American policymakers to rethink U.S. strategic doctrine. A fierce debate erupted in the administration over the development of a hydrogen bomb, potentially a thousand times more powerful than the atomic weapons that had destroyed Hiroshima and Nagasaki. J. Robert Oppenheimer, the "father" of the atomic bomb, questioned the morality of such a powerful weapon and feared the consequences of an escalating arms race. "We may be likened to two scorpions in a bottle," he wrote, "each capable of killing the other, but only at the risk of his own life." In January 1950, Truman sided with German-born physicist Edward Teller, who argued that the Soviets would eventually develop the weapon and use it to blackmail the United States.

In April 1950, after months of deliberation, the National Security Council recommended that the president initiate a massive rebuilding of the American military, both nuclear and conventional forces, to confront the new Soviet nuclear threat. The report, National Security Council Memorandum 68 (NSC-68), presented a frightening portrait of a Soviet system driven by "a new fanatic faith" that "seeks to impose its absolute authority over the rest of the world." To intimidate the Russians and inspire confidence in its allies, the report called for an extraordinary increase in the defense budget, from $13 to $50 billion a year.

On November 1, 1952, the United States exploded the first H-bomb, obliterating an uninhabited island in the Pacific. The bomb blast created a fireball five miles high and four miles wide and left a hole in the Pacific floor a mile long and 175 feet deep. The following year the Russians exploded their first hydrogen bomb. Britain and France soon joined the nuclear club. The arms race had entered a frightening new phase.

The Korean War: From Invasion to Stalemate

In January 1950, Secretary of State Dean Acheson omitted any mention of Korea when he outlined the "defensive perimeter" that the United States would protect in

Asia. At the end of the Second World War, the United States and the Soviets had temporarily divided the Korean peninsula, previously dominated by Japan, at the thirty-eighth parallel. Cold War tensions, however, ended any hope of unification. The Russians installed Kim Il Sung to lead the communist north while Syngman Rhee, a conservative nationalist, emerged as the American-sponsored ruler in the South. Korea was not a top American priority, however, and the U.S withdrew its troops from Korea in June 1949.

The scenario changed on June 25, 1950, when 110,000 North Korean soldiers crossed the thirty-eighth parallel and within hours overpowered South Korean forces. The circumstances surrounding the invasion remain unclear, but documents in Soviet archives, made available to historians at the end of the Cold War, suggest that the North Koreans, not the Soviets, pushed for the invasion. Truman viewed the situation in a dramatically different light. He interpreted the invasion as a Soviet-engineered assault, the opening salvo in a broader Soviet attack on America's global allies. With memories of Western appeasement of Hitler fresh in his mind, Truman immediately ordered American air and naval forces to support the South Koreans. "If this was allowed to go unchallenged," he wrote in his memoirs, "it would mean a third world war, just as similar incidents had brought on the second world war." Two days later, on Tuesday, June 27, 1950, Truman asked the United Nations Security Council to condemn North Korea as an aggressor and to send forces to South Korea. The resolution passed because the Soviet delegate, who could have used his veto to defeat the measure, was boycotting the meetings. The defense effort was theoretically a UN venture, but in the end the United States provided half the ground troops and most of the sea and air support.

In the first few weeks it appeared that the North Korean forces might win a decisive victory. Their troops pushed the South Koreans and the entire U.S. Eighth Army all the way to the peninsula's tip near the port city of Pusan. Then, on September 15, General Douglas MacArthur turned the war around with a daring amphibious invasion behind enemy lines at Inchon, near the South Korean capital of Seoul. At the same time the American and South Korean armies counterattacked in force at Pusan. The dual tactic fooled the North Koreans, who suffered heavy losses and quickly retreated beyond the thirty-eighth parallel. By the end of the month, American troops had liberated Seoul and reestablished Syngman Rhee's government in the South (see map).

The dramatic victory on the ground raised hopes that U.S. forces could advance beyond the thirty-eighth parallel, overthrow Kim Il Sung, and unite Korea under a noncommunist government. On September 27, Truman authorized MacArthur to cross into North Korea. Within a few weeks, MacArthur's forces had advanced within fifty miles of the Yalu River, the boundary between Korea and the Chinese province of Manchuria.

When the Communist Chinese condemned the U.S. invasion of North Korea and threatened retaliation, Truman began to have second thoughts about his strategy. In October, the president flew to Wake Island in the Pacific to consult with MacArthur. The general assured Truman that the Chinese Communists, despite their buildup of troops on the border and their loud warnings, would not intervene in the war, which MacArthur insisted was over. Acheson agreed with MacArthur's assessment. "I

The Korean War, 1950–1953

After the initial wave of North Korean troops swept through the South in the summer of 1950, United Nations' forces under General Douglas MacArthur countered at Inchon and Pusan. By November, UN troops occupied most of Korea, but Chinese troops quickly repulsed the advance and pushed MacArthur's men south of the thirty-eighth parallel. There the fighting remained until the armistice in 1953.

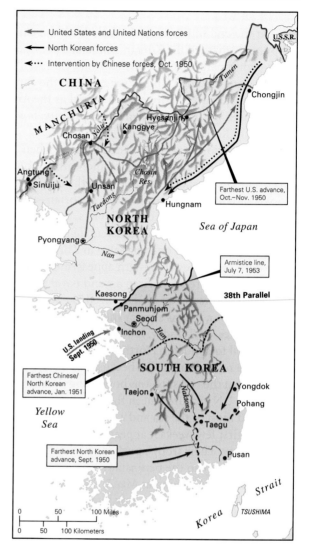

should think it would be sheer madness for the Chinese to intervene," he said. The president, uplifted by MacArthur's optimistic assessment and Acheson's unequivocal support, returned home confident that the war had been won.

MacArthur and Acheson were wrong. On November 27, 1950, a Chinese army of four hundred thousand men, armed with Soviet tanks and aircraft, attacked the American forces in North Korea. By Christmas, the massive wave of Chinese troops had pushed MacArthur south of the thirty-eighth parallel again. Shaken, the general pressured Truman for permission to attack Chinese military bases in the North. This time Truman rejected MacArthur's strategy, fearing that direct attack on Chinese installations would antagonize the Russians and precipitate a global conflict. In January 1951, the U.S. Eighth Army halted the communist advance and, by March, pushed back to the thirty-eighth parallel. The war then bogged down, with neither side able to gain the advantage.

The Truman-MacArthur Bout and the Trials of Containment

With the public growing weary of war and the threat of continued bloody fighting, Truman looked for a diplomatic solution to the conflict. MacArthur opposed a settlement and insisted U.S. forces must attack Chinese bases north of the thirty-eighth parallel. He criticized his civilian commander-in-chief in the press, sabotaged Truman's efforts to achieve a negotiated settlement, and sent long-winded telegrams to veterans' groups outlining his own personal foreign policy for Asia. In April he wrote a letter to Republican House minority leader Joseph J. Martin of Massachusetts denouncing the stalemate. As MacArthur hoped, Martin read the letter on the floor of the House. Truman, fed up with his general's insubordination, exploded. On April 11, 1951, he relieved MacArthur of his command.

Truman miscalculated the warrior's grip on the public imagination. Within twelve days the White House received over 27,000 angry letters of protest. MacArthur returned from Korea to a hero's welcome in San Francisco, and millions crowded downtown Manhattan for one of New York's largest-ever ticker-tape parades. Republican leaders clamored for a congressional investigation and threatened to impeach Truman. On April 19, MacArthur gave an impassioned farewell address to a joint session of Congress. He concluded by repeating a line from a West Point ballad: "Old soldiers never die, they just fade away." The words moved many congressmen to tears.

The general's appeal transcended mere sentimentality. The response to MacArthur's critique of Washington's handling of the Korean conflict revealed the frustration and confusion of a nation struggling to adjust to the idea of a limited war. Seventy years old when the Korean War started, MacArthur had been trained in the military doctrine of total war. His experience in two world wars taught him that "In war, there is no substitute for victory."

Truman and his advisers argued that the Cold War forced America to develop a new strategy suited to fighting limited wars. MacArthur, they argued, failed to recognize that the real enemy was not North Korea but the Soviet Union. The fighting in Korea was a strategic diversion, a Russian maneuver to draw American strength away from Europe. Larger strategic goals, namely containing Moscow, required the United States to avoid squandering its resources on the pursuit of "victory" in proxy wars in remote places.

The administration won the debate with MacArthur, but the questions raised by the confrontation would continue to haunt policymakers. Americans accustomed to waging total war and reaping the benefits of total victory never fully adjusted to the demands of limited war. Containment required Americans to settle for fighting limited, protracted wars, seeking diplomatic solutions rather than military victory, and enduring the tribulation of an uncertain peace.

Consequences of Korea

The stalemated fighting in Korea would drag on, amid cease-fire talks, for more than a year, ending soon after Truman left office. Despite its limited nature, the war resulted in 36,940 American deaths and left 103,284 American soldiers wounded. It also brought significant change within the United States. It produced a huge escalation of defense spending from approximately $14 billion in 1949 to $44 billion in 1953. As government spending created millions of new jobs, unemployment dropped to its lowest level in years. Federal expenditures, together with special tax incentives, encouraged industries to expand production. From 1950 to 1954, steel capacity increased by 24 percent, electrical generating capacity by 50 percent, and aluminum capacity by 100 percent.

The Korean War accelerated the desegregation of the armed services. By mid-1950, the navy and air force had taken strides toward desegregation, but the army still maintained separate black and white units. Critics had complained that segregation, besides being morally wrong, was also wasteful and inefficient. Korea exposed another problem with segregation: assigning African-Americans to noncombat duty led whites to suffer a disproportionate share of casualties. When white troops experienced heavy losses in the early days of the war, field commanders in Korea broke with existing policy and used black soldiers as replacements. In March 1951, the Pentagon announced the integration of all training facilities in the United States. By the end of the war, nearly all African-American soldiers were serving in integrated units.

The war continued the expansion of presidential power begun under Roosevelt. When North Korea invaded, Truman made a unilateral decision to intervene, acting with neither Congress's approval nor its declaration of war. Only after he had authorized American force did Truman meet with Congress to inform members about what he had done.

 ## The Politics of Fear, 1945–1952

The Korean War intensified suspicions of communist subversion at home. Americans viewed communism as a double threat. Ideologically, communist doctrine challenged basic American notions of private property and individual rights. Strategically, its chief supporter, the Soviet Union, was engaged in a global struggle against the United States. Rumors that Soviet spies had infiltrated the upper echelons of American society, especially government, ignited a wildfire of fear and suspicion. Anxious Americans rushed to prove their loyalty and to punish potential subversives, who seemed to be un-American. Ferreting out disloyalty became a duty of both the citizenry and the government. No one exploited these fears more effectively than Wisconsin senator Joseph McCarthy.

The Second Red Scare

In March 1945, government agents found numerous classified government documents in the Manhattan offices of the allegedly procommunist *Amerasia* magazine. A year later, a Canadian investigation led to the arrest of twenty-two men and women for passing classified U.S. documents to the Soviets. Together the cases proved that Soviet spies had gained access to secret government documents. "The disloyalty of American Communists is no longer a matter of conjecture," declared FBI head J. Edgar Hoover.

Americans cried out for protection against communist influence in government. In an attempt to quell public concern, President Truman, in March 1947, issued Executive Order 9835, which established the Federal Employee Loyalty Program. The Truman program allowed dismissal of any federal employee whenever "reasonable grounds exist for belief that the person involved is disloyal." The question of loyalty and disloyalty touched on a recurring issue in American history: What does it mean to be an American? Most loyalty review boards imposed a narrow definition of loyal citizenship, using the fear of communism to intimidate people who had different ideas. Civil rights activists came under intense scrutiny, and homosexuals were automatically dismissed as security threats. The head of one government loyalty board noted, "The fact that a person believes in racial equality doesn't prove he's a Communist, but it certainly makes you look twice, doesn't it?"

Truman also used a high-profile court case to convince the public that his administration was tough on communism. In July 1948, the administration charged eleven top communists with violating the Smith Act of 1940, which made it a crime to conspire to "advocate and teach" the violent overthrow of government. After ten months of trial and deliberation, a lower court declared the Smith Act constitutional and the communists guilty. The Supreme Court, in *Dennis* v. *U.S.* (1951), upheld the conviction, clearing the way for prosecution of other communist leaders.

In perhaps the most talked-about loyalty case, in August 1948 Whittaker Chambers, an editor at *Time* Magazine, accused Alger Hiss, who had served as a high-ranking aide to Franklin Roosevelt at Yalta, of having been a communist. Chambers claimed that in 1938 Hiss had given him microfilm of classified State Department documents. For many conservatives, Hiss was a symbol of the generation of young, idealistic, Ivy League liberals who had masterminded the New Deal. By attacking him, they hoped to undermine faith in the Democratic Party and remove some of the luster from Roosevelt's memory.

To prove his charges Chambers produced microfilm of supposedly secret documents taken from a hollowed-out pumpkin on his Maryland farm. (The documents, quickly labeled the "Pumpkin Papers," were later revealed to contain information on navy life rafts and fire extinguishers.) Testifying before a grand jury in New York, Hiss denied Chambers's charges. Since the statute of limitations on espionage had expired, Hiss was indicted for perjury. After one mistrial Hiss was found guilty in a second trial and sentenced to five years in jail. More than any other event, the Hiss trial convinced many Americans that the Roosevelt and Truman administrations had been oblivious to the dangers of communist espionage. California congressman Richard Nixon, among the most aggressive investigators of subversion, described the case as "the most treasonable conspiracy in American history."

Two weeks after Hiss's conviction, the British government announced the arrest of Klaus Fuchs, an atomic physicist who had worked at the Los Alamos atomic energy laboratory. Shortly afterward, the FBI arrested Julius and Ethel Rosenberg for conspiring with Fuchs to pass secrets to the Russians. The Rosenbergs denied the allegations, insisting they were the victims of anticommunist hysteria and anti-Semitism. In 1951, after a two-week trial, a jury pronounced them guilty of espionage. The presiding judge, Irving Kaufman, arguing their crime was "worse than murder" because it furthered the goal of "godless" communism, sentenced the Rosenbergs to death. In June 1953, despite personal pleas from the pope and worldwide protests, the husband and wife were executed.

Well before this time, actions against communists and their sympathizers had spread into American culture. In 1947 the House Committee on Un-American Activities (HUAC) opened a series of investigations into the Hollywood entertainment industry. "Large numbers of moving pictures that come out of Hollywood carry the Communist line," declared committee member John Rankin of Mississippi. In September, the committee subpoenaed forty-one witnesses. Most cooperated with the committee by offering names of suspected communists. A small group of screenwriters, the "Hollywood Ten," served prison terms for refusing to answer questions about their ties to the Communist Party. Shaken by the hearings, the studios initiated a policy of blacklisting writers, directors, technicians, and actors who refused to denounce communism. In 1950 two former FBI agents published *Red Channels: The Report of Communist Influence in Radio and Television,* which listed in alphabetical order 151 prominent communists in the industry. Many people listed had done nothing more subversive than support civil rights or combat censorship. Indiana required professional boxers and wrestlers to take a non-Communist oath before entering the ring. A small town in New York required residents to swear loyalty before getting a permit to fish in the local reservoir. The Cincinnati Reds baseball team proved its patriotism by changing its name to the Cincinnati Redlegs. On July 4, 1951, a reporter in Madison, Wisconsin, asked people to sign a petition that contained the words of the Declaration of Independence and the Bill of Rights. More than one hundred people read the petition. Only one signed it. The others dismissed it as communist propaganda.

The nation's schools and universities did not escape the ravages of the second Red Scare. In June 1948, the University of California required all of its four thousand faculty members to profess their loyalty to America. Some three hundred New York City schoolteachers were fired as security risks. Zealots forced libraries to purge their shelves of "subversive" works. A member of the Indiana State Textbook Commission tried unsuccessfully to ban from school libraries any reference to Robin Hood. The reason, he said, was that Robin Hood "robbed the rich and gave . . . to the poor. That's the Communist line. It's just a smearing of law and order."

Congress responded to the hysteria by passing the Internal Security Act of 1950. Among other restrictions, the act required communist and communist-front organizations to register with the government and to identify as communist all of their official mail and literature. The act's most severe provisions authorized the government to place all communists in concentration camps whenever a national emergency should occur. Truman vetoed the bill denouncing it as "the greatest danger to freedom of speech, press, and assembly, since the Alien and Sedition Laws of 1798." But Congress garnered enough votes to override the veto and enact the measure into law.

Was this fear of domestic communism justified? Previously secret American reports of decoded Soviet intelligence traffic during these years—called the Venona

Bogey and Bacall Attend the Hollywood Ten Trials   Anticommunist hysteria infiltrated all walks of American life, including the film industry, which the House Un-American Activities Committee (HUAC) began investigating in 1947. Actors, writers, and directors faced the difficult decision of cooperating with the investigation or risking their careers. When called before the committee, the Hollywood Ten refused to answer questions, claiming that, even if they were communists, the First Amendment gave them that right. Humphrey Bogart and Lauren Bacall, seen here going into the hearings, joined other stars to form the Committee for the First Amendment in support of those who refused to cooperate. However, most studio heads, fearing a public backlash against Hollywood, blacklisted the Ten and over two hundred others.   *(Corbis-Bettmann.)*

Intercepts—reveal that the Soviets had planted as many as one hundred spies in high-level government positions and offer incriminating evidence against Alger Hiss and Julius and Ethel Rosenberg. Declassified files from Soviet and eastern European archives support these conclusions while also suggesting that the Communist Party in America took its orders directly from Moscow. "Not every American communist was a spy," noted the historian Harvey Klehr, "but almost every spy was a communist."

While a handful worked as spies, most Communists, and their liberal sympathizers, did not threaten national security. The party was disintegrating in the wake of Cold War fears, evidence of Stalin's tyranny, and Truman's loyalty program. Party membership dropped from an estimated high of 80,000 in 1944 to only 40,000 in 1949. Ironically, it was the anticommunist crusaders who, in their reckless disregard for civil rights and liberties, posed a more serious threat to American society. "Whatever our mistakes," playwright and left-wing sympathizer Lillian Hellman wrote, "I do not believe we did our country any harm. And I think they [those who persecuted the Left] did."

Joseph McCarthy

Joseph McCarthy became the most feared demagogue of his time. Born in 1908 to poor Irish-American farmers in northeastern Wisconsin, McCarthy earned a degree in 1935 and entered politics in 1939, running successfully for circuit judge in Wisconsin's Tenth Circuit. With the outbreak of World War II, McCarthy decided to join the glamorous marines. For three years he served as an intelligence officer debriefing American pilots following raids over the Pacific. Not satisfied with his low-profile role but unwilling to risk injury in combat, McCarthy fabricated his military record for the folks back home. He bragged about his exploits as a tail gunner, flying dangerous missions, shooting down enemy planes. He claimed to have been injured when his plane crash-landed. During his Senate campaigns, he walked with a limp and complained about having "ten pounds of shrapnel" in his leg. In reality, he injured his leg not while flying on a dangerous mission, but during a hazing ceremony aboard a navy ship when he slipped as he was running a gauntlet of paddle-wielding sailors.

In 1946, armed with phony wartime press releases, McCarthy ran for the Senate. During his campaign to unseat sitting Republican Robert La Follette, Jr., McCarthy crisscrossed the state attacking the New Deal, criticizing wartime controls, and pleading with voters to send a "tail gunner" to the Senate. His energetic campaign style worked: McCarthy scored a surprising victory over La Follette in a GOP primary and went on to win easily against his Democratic opponent in the fall.

During his first few years in the Senate, McCarthy supported Truman's foreign policy initiatives but voted with the conservative wing of his party on domestic issues. He developed a close relationship with many corporate lobbyists. His efforts to end price controls on sugar earned him the nickname the "Pepsi-Cola kid." In Senate debates, McCarthy frequently distorted facts and manipulated evidence to prove his point. He reduced political issues to personal terms and turned Senate debates into angry brawls. "He can be the most affable man in the world," a fellow senator reflected, "and suddenly he will run the knife into you—particularly if the public is going to see it."

By 1950, McCarthy was searching for an issue that would grab the public's attention. He found it in Wheeling, West Virginia, where he had traveled to speak to the Republican Women's Club. His speech, standard Republican rhetoric of the time, charged that traitors and spies had infiltrated the State Department. What was different about the speech was McCarthy's claim to have proof. "I have here in my hand," he blustered, "a list of names that were known to the secretary of state and who nevertheless are still working and shaping the policy of the State Department." Though few people paid him much notice at first, he repeated, expanded, and varied his charges in succeeding speeches. By March he was front-page news across the country. McCarthy, observed a journalist, "was a political speculator who found his oil gusher in Communism."

Democrats tried to knock out McCarthy before he could do any damage to the president. Senate Democrats established a special committee to investigate McCarthy's charges and stacked it with administration loyalists. "Let me have him for three days in public hearings," boasted Maryland's powerful Millard Tydings, who chaired the committee, "and he'll never show his face in the Senate again." Tydings underestimated his opponent. McCarthy used the attention to make wild accusations. The hearings established to destroy McCarthy helped transform him into a towering national figure.

McCarthy shrewdly manipulated the press, which treated his sensational charges as page-one news. He held press conferences early in the morning to announce that he would soon release dramatic information on domestic spying. The nation's afternoon papers printed banner headlines, "McCarthy's New Revelations Expected Soon." When reporters hounded him for details, McCarthy announced that he would soon produce a key witness. Headlines the following day would read, "Delay in McCarthy Revelations: Mystery Witness Sought." McCarthy never produced the evidence to support his accusations. But his tactics gained him the publicity he needed and thus fueled his attacks.

By the fall of 1950, McCarthy was the most feared man in American politics. His face appeared on the cover of *Time* and *Newsweek*. Republican candidates begged him to make appearances on their behalf. By October, he had received more than two thousand speaking requests, more than were extended to all other senators combined. Though he campaigned around the country, McCarthy spent most of his time in Maryland where Millard Tydings faced a tough reelection challenge. "Joe was so preoccupied with Tydings," a friend recalled, "that he'd sit by the hour figuring ways to get revenge."

McCarthy and His Fans Senator Joseph McCarthy from Wisconsin went on a massive anti-communist witch-hunt in the early 1950s. His lists of suspects, which included people at all levels and in all branches of the government, terrified Americans. As this photograph indicates, McCarthy at first enjoyed widespread support from those who believed him to be a tireless crusader for national security. But when McCarthy launched televised investigations of top army officials, Americans saw firsthand how irrational and ruthless he was, and his popularity quickly evaporated. (*Wide World Photos, Inc.*)

Accusing his target of "protecting communists for political reasons," McCarthy distributed a widely reproduced photograph showing Tydings having a friendly conversation with deposed Communist Party head Earl Browder. The "conversation" never took place: McCarthy had combined two separate pictures. When Tydings lost the election, the media credited McCarthy with the victory. *Newsweek* spoke of the "political scalps dangling from his belt." Another journalist saw "a political landscape . . . littered with the wreckage of anti-McCarthy careers." A new word entered the language: McCarthyism.

Why did McCarthy have such appeal? Largely because of the way he capitalized on Cold War anxieties. McCarthy offered simple answers to the complex questions of the Cold War. Strong faith in the righteousness of their position left Americans ill prepared to comprehend the foreign policy setbacks of the immediate postwar years. McCarthy reassured a troubled nation that the string of bad news resulted from the traitorous actions of a few individuals, not from a flawed view of the world or the strength of communist opponents. China turned communist, he explained, because traitors in the State Department had sold out American interests, not because of the internal weakness of the Nationalist regime. The Soviets developed the atomic bomb because spies sold them America's secrets, not because they had talented scientists capable of developing their own bomb.

McCarthy's charges against the established elite tapped into a deep populist impulse in the American character. McCarthy called Dean Acheson a "pompous diplomat in striped pants, with a phony British accent." He denounced the "egg-sucking phony liberals" who defended "communists and queers." In focusing on liberal thinkers, homosexuals, and others who did not fit with Americans' traditional view of themselves, McCarthy exploited America's unease with its new international stature and its discomfort with alien ideas and lifestyles. In this sense, McCarthyism was part of a recurring pattern in American history. In 1798 Federalists had tried to silence critics by introducing the Alien and Sedition Acts, targeting dissenters as traitors. Waves of prejudice against foreigners swept the country during the 1850s and again in the 1870s. Following World War I, the U.S. tried to drown "radical" thoughts in a Red Scare wave of "100 percent Americanism."

Most of all, McCarthyism was the product of partisan politics at midcentury. McCarthy had the support of conservative Republicans, who saw him as a useful means to reassert their authority in the country. So long as McCarthy wielded his anticommunist club against Democrats, many Republicans were willing to overlook his offensive tactics. Many GOP members repeated the refrain: "I don't like some of McCarthy's methods but his goal is good."

CONCLUSION

The Cold War provided the dramatic backdrop for American politics and society at the end of World War II. The United States and the Soviet Union emerged from the war as the dominant military powers in the world. But the two nations, burdened by the weight of history and ideology, possessed fundamentally different visions of the postwar world. The Soviets, determined to prevent another invasion of their homeland, consolidated their control in eastern Europe. The United States, resolved to thwart potential aggression, insisted that the postwar structure must be based on universal principles of free elections and open markets. American policymakers interpreted Soviet actions as part of an aggressive plan to strangle markets and extinguish individual rights.

Cold War tensions forced the United States to take an active role in shaping the postwar peace. In assuming a prominent position in the peacetime affairs of Europe, policymakers abandoned a tradition of isolationism and signaled an important shift in U.S. foreign policy. The Truman administration adopted a policy of containment, using economic assistance and military might to deter Soviet aggression. The new policy found expression in three key initiatives: the Truman Doctrine, which extended U.S. military aid to Greece and Turkey; the Marshall Plan, which provided economic assistance to western Europe; and NSC-68, which dramatically expanded American defense capabilities.

The experiment in internationalism did not, however, mean that the United States had fundamentally altered the way it viewed the world. Most Americans interpreted the U.S. victory in World War II as an affirmation of their commitment to open markets and free elections. Since the founding days of the republic, Americans had believed fervently in their mission to remake the world in their own image. The Cold War added a new dimension to an old impulse. For the first time, the United States confronted a powerful enemy (the Soviet Union) that possessed an ideology (communism) to rival its own. Faced with the new challenge, American policymakers decided the nation needed to play an active role to fulfill its mission.

While building public support for his containment policy abroad, Truman struggled to build on the New Deal legacy at home. He encountered numerous obstacles: a conservative Congress, a public weary of government controls and regulation, and a party deeply divided over the Cold War and civil rights. Despite these problems, Truman managed to win a surprising victory in the 1948 presidential election. Emboldened by his triumph, Truman called for a Fair Deal—an ambitious program of reform that would extend and enhance the New Deal.

The president's reform agenda fell victim to hardening Cold War tensions and growing fears of communist subversion. The "fall" of China, the Soviet explosion of an atomic bomb, and most of all, the North Korean invasion of South Korea, sent global relations into a deep freeze. With U.S. soldiers engaged in a bloody conflict on the Korean peninsula, many Americans turned their attention to the covert battle against Soviet spies at home. Stories of Soviet spies—some real, some imagined—swept across the country, raising paranoiac fears that communists had infiltrated American institutions and were sowing the seeds of an alien ideology. The poisoned atmosphere provided a fertile environment for demagogues such as Senator Joseph McCarthy.

In many ways, America was a much different nation when Truman left office in 1952 from what it had been when he assumed the presidency in 1945. The Cold War had ripped the nation from its isolationist moorings and thrust it into a position of global leadership. But Americans had not completely abandoned the past. Nor had they lost confidence in the future. After fighting a world war and securing an uncertain peace, many Americans looked forward to celebrating the triumph of American values and enjoying the material benefits of the consumer society.

SUGGESTED READINGS

Walter LaFeber's *America, Russia, and the Cold War* (6th ed., 1990) provides a good overview of Cold War–era politics, while Stephen Ambrose's *Rise to Globalism* (8th ed., 1997) focuses on Cold War foreign policy. John Diggins surveys U.S. culture and politics in the 1940s and 1950s in *The Proud Decades* (1989). George Lipsitz studies popular culture during the era in *Class and Culture in Cold War America* (1981), as does Stephen J. Whitfield in *The Culture of the Cold War* (1996). Melvyn Leffler's *A Preponderance of Power* (1992) is the most comprehensive history of the early Cold War, with John L. Gaddis providing the most up-to-date synthesis in *We Now Know* (1997). The Cold War from the Soviet Union's perspective, using recently declassified materials, is *Inside the Kremlin's Cold War* (1996) by Vladislav Zubok and Constantine Pleshakov.

Bernard Weisberger's *Cold War, Cold Peace* (1984) is a solid standard account of the immediate postwar period. *The Devil We Knew* (1993) by H. W. Brands examines how the Cold War mentality developed and its affect on American society. Lloyd C. Garner's *Architects of Illusion* (1970) presents biographical vignettes of America's leading foreign policymakers and explores mistakes that contributed to the Cold War. Daniel Yergin's *Shattered Peace* (1977) demonstrates both the American and Soviet motives that contributed to the arms race.

Lawrence Wittner focuses on the Greek civil war in *American Intervention in Greece* (1982). Gregg Herken critiques U.S. leaders' reliance on the bomb in *The Winning Weapon* (1980), and Richard Rhodes's *Dark Sun* (1995) traces the development of the hydrogen bomb. Michael Hogan's *The Marshall Plan* (1987) is a thorough one-volume history of that ambitious initiative. Imanuel Wexler's *The Marshall Plan Revisited* (1983) offers a more critical analysis of the plan. Timothy P. Ireland examines the formation of NATO in *Creating the Entangling Alliance* (1981). Joyce and Gabriel Kolko's *The Limits of Power* (1972) discusses how the complexity of foreign affairs stymied American attempts to dictate world politics.

Bruce R. Kuniholm's *The Origins of the Cold War in the Near East* (1980) has interesting material on the formation of Israel, while the division of Germany is the foundation of Carolyn Eisenberg's *Drawing the Line* (1996). Richard Freeland's *The Truman Doctrine and the Origins of McCarthyism* (1972) links Truman's policies with the later Red Scare. George Kennan's *American Diplomacy, 1900–1950* (1952) and Dean Acheson's *Present at the Creation* (1970) offer intriguing insiders' accounts of the early Cold War, while John L. Harper compares these two men to FDR in *American Visions of Europe* (1994). Walter Isaacson and Evan Thomas's *The Wise Men* (1986) is a study of Truman's advisers' impact on American foreign policy.

Jack S. Ballard's *The Shock of Peace* (1983) recounts the economic trauma of demobilization at war's end. In *Beyond the New Deal* (1973), Alonzo L. Hamby assesses Truman's effort to preserve and expand the New Deal. Stephen K. Bailey chronicles the adoption of the Employment Act of 1946 in his *Congress Makes a Law* (1957). Robert J. Donovan captures the 1940s feeling of upheaval in *Tumultuous Years* (1982). Elaine T. May's *Homeward Bound* (1988) captures the impact of the Cold War on domestic life. David G. McCullough's *Truman* (1992) is a generally uncritical appraisal of Truman's life and policies. Alonzo Hamby provides the best biographical treatment of Truman in *Man of the People* (1995). Donald R. McCoy's *The Presidency of Harry S Truman* (1984) is more balanced.

The 1948 election is detailed in Zachary Karabell's *How Harry Truman Won the 1948 Election* (2000). William C. Berman's *The Politics of Civil Rights in the Truman Administration* (1970) covers the controversy within the Democratic Party. John C. Culver and John Hyde's *American Dreamer* (2000) traces the life of this controversial figure. Arthur Schlesinger, Jr., argues the virtues of Fair Deal liberalism in *The Vital Center* (1949). Susan Hartmann outlines Truman's first-term frustrations in *Truman and the 80th Congress* (1971). Monte S. Poen details the defeat of national health insurance in *Harry S Truman Versus the Medical Lobby* (1979).

Akira Iriye's *The Cold War in Asia* (1974) is a good introduction for developments on that continent. Russell D. Buhite's *Soviet-American Relations in Asia* (1982) details the superpowers' conflict over the region. Michael Schaller's *The American Occupation of Japan* (1985) and John Dower's *Embracing Defeat* (1999) both study the American role in postwar Japan. The fall of China and the domestic reaction is the subject of Kenneth Shewmaker's *Americans and the Chinese Communists* (1971), while the widening ideological gulf between the two nations is the subject of *Useful Adversaries* (1996) by Thomas J. Christensen.

Clay Blair's *The Forgotten War* (1988) offers a moving account of the first limited war and the people who fought it, while the best treatment of the causes and consequences of the conflict is William Stueck's *The Korean War* (1995). Rosemary Foot's *The Wrong War* (1985) explores America's unpreparedness to fight a war in Asia. Bruce Cummings's two-volume *Origins of the Korean War* (1981, 1990) is a detailed study of the politics around the conflict. For General MacArthur, William Manchester's *American Caesar* (1979) is the classic work; Michael Schaller's *Douglas MacArthur* (1989) is also helpful.

E. J. Kahn, Jr., covers the *Amerasia* controversy in *The China Hands* (1975). Allen Weinstein's *Perjury* (1978) explores the Hiss case. John E. Haynes and Harvey Klehr's *Venona* (1999) offers a new interpretation of the case, based on declassified Soviet documents. Walter and Miriam Schneir detail the Rosenberg trial in *Invitation to an Inquest* (1983). Victor S. Navasky surveys the world of informants and blacklists in *Naming Names* (1980). Larry Ceplair and Steven Englund's *The Inquisition in Hollywood* (1980) analyzes the Red Scare's impact on popular culture. Athan Theoharis and John S. Cox study the roles of J. Edgar Hoover and the FBI in the Red Scare in *The Boss* (1988)

Two of the most valuable studies of Joseph McCarthy are Richard Fried's *Nightmare in Red* (1990) and Stanley Kutler's *The American Inquisition* (1982). David M. Oshinsky's *A Conspiracy So Immense* (1983) portrays Joseph McCarthy as a product of the political conditions of the era. Ellen Schrecker's *The Age of McCarthyism* (1994) uses primary documents from the period to show how most politicians from both parties aided and abetted the Red Scare.

America's Role in the World

"Getting Tough with the Russians"

On July 12, 1946, while having drinks with a few aides in the White House, President Truman vented his frustrations with the Soviet Union. The president said that he was tired of being pushed around by the Russians, "here a little, there a little," and that it was time to stand up to Stalin. Why make new agreements, he asked, if the Kremlin refused to comply with the old ones? The president turned to Special Counsel Clark Clifford and asked him to produce a record of Soviet violations of international agreements.

Clifford and his assistant George Elsey decided to expand the scope of their project. In September 1946, Clifford sent President Truman a comprehensive statement on U.S.–Soviet relations. Written with the cooperation of senior administration officials, the report reflected America's growing hard line with the Soviet Union.

The most obvious Soviet threat to American security is the growing ability of the USSR to wage an offensive war against the United States. . . . Stalin has declared his intention of sparing no effort to build up the military strength of the Soviet Union. . . .

The primary objective of the United States policy toward the Soviet Union is to convince Soviet leaders that it is in their interest to participate in a system of world cooperation, that there are no fundamental causes for war between our two nations, and that the security and prosperity of the Soviet Union, and that of the rest of the world as well, are being jeopardized by the aggressive militaristic imperialism such as that in which the Soviet Union is now engaged.

However, these same leaders with whom we hope to achieve an understanding on the principles of international peace appear to believe that a war with the United States and the other leading capitalistic nations is inevitable. They are increasing their military power and the sphere of Soviet influence in preparation for the "inevitable" conflict, and they are trying to weaken and subvert their potential opponents by every means at their disposal. So long as these men adhere to these beliefs, it is highly dangerous to conclude that hope of international peace lies only in "accord," "mutual understanding," or "solidarity" with the Soviet Union.

Unless the United States is willing to sacrifice its future security for the sake of "accord" with the USSR now, this government must, as a first step toward world stabilization, seek to prevent additional Soviet aggression. . . .

The language of military power is the only language which disciples of power politics understand. The United States must use that language in order that Soviet leaders will realize that our government is determined to uphold the interests of its citizens and the rights of small nations. Compromise and concessions are considered, by the Soviets, to be evidences of weakness and they are encouraged by our "retreats" to make new and greater demands.

The main deterrent to Soviet attack on the United States, or to attack on areas of the world which are vital to our security, will be the military power of this country. It must be made apparent to the Soviet government that our strength will be sufficient to repel any attack and sufficient to defeat the USSR decisive if a war should start. The prospect of defeat is the only sure means of deterring the Soviet Union. ▌

"The Last Chance for Peace"

Escalating Cold War tensions troubled many liberals who hoped to continue Roosevelt's policy of wartime cooperation with Stalin. In July 1946, Secretary of Commerce Henry Wallace sent President Truman a twelve-page single-spaced letter asking him to reconsider his "get tough" policy.

▌▌▌ I should list the factors which make for Russian distrust of the United States and of the Western world as follows. The first is Russian history, which we must take into account because it is the setting in which Russians see all actions and policies of the rest of the world. Russian history for over a thousand years has been a succession of attempts, often unsuccessful, to resist invasion and conquest. . . . The Russians, therefore, obviously see themselves as fighting for their existence in a hostile world.

Second, it follows that to the Russians all of the defense and security measures of the Western powers seem to have an aggressive intent. Our actions to expand our military security system . . . appear to them as going far beyond the requirements of defense. I think we might feel the same if the United States were the only capitalistic country in the world, and the principal socialistic countries were creating a level of armed strength far exceeding anything in their previous history.

Finally, our resistance to her attempts to obtain warm-water ports and her own security system in the form of "friendly" neighboring states seems, from the Russian point of view, to clinch the case. After twenty-five years of isolation and after having achieved the status of a major power, Russia believes that she is entitled to recognition of her new status. Our interest in establishing democracy in Eastern Europe, where democracy by and large has never existed, seems to her an attempt to reestablish the encirclement of unfriendly neighbors which was created after the last war, and which might serve as a springboard of still another effort to destroy her.

If this analysis is correct, and there is ample evidence to support it, the action to improve the situation is clearly indicated. The fundamental objective of such action should be to allay any reasonable Russian grounds for fear, suspicion and distrust. . . .

We should make an effort to counteract the irrational fear of Russia which is being systematically built up in the American people by certain individuals and publications. The slogan that communism and capitalism, regimentation and democracy, cannot continue to exist in the same world is, from a historical point of view, pure propaganda. . . .

. . . We are by far the most powerful nation in the world, the only Allied nation which came out of the war without devastation and much stronger than before the war. Any talk on our part about the need for strengthening our defenses further is bound to appear hypocritical to other nations. . . . ▌

"We agreed that Kennan's Long Telegram was brilliant," Clifford recalled, "but he had confined himself to analysis." Clifford and Elsey decided "to fill the gap between Kennan's analysis and policy recommendations" by making concrete suggestions for the president to follow.

Clifford had not spoken with Secretary of Commerce Henry A. Wallace, the lone voice in high government circles for resisting Kennan's interpretation of Soviet behavior. Wallace, who had served as Roosevelt's vice president until being dumped from the ticket in 1944, believed that Russian friendship was essential to preserve international peace and security. The administration's most outspoken liberal, Wallace watched nervously as the administration, swayed by Kennan's Long Telegram, adopted a "get tough" approach to the Soviets.

Wallace's letter outlining his grievances with the administration's evolving hard line angered Truman, who wanted to fire the secretary but feared such a move would anger liberals. He complained to aides that Wallace was too idealistic and failed to understand the harsh realities of international power politics. "I do not understand a 'dreamer' like that," Truman wrote in his diary.

On September 12, Wallace delivered a major foreign policy speech at New York City's Madison Square Garden in which he repeated many of the points he had previously voiced in private. The press accurately reported Wallace's address as a stinging critique of administration policy. Secretary of State James Byrnes sent Truman an angry message threatening to resign if the president did not silence his commerce secretary. On September 20, Truman announced Wallace's resignation at a packed news conference. The last Cold War dissident had been forced out of the administration. After the reporters had left the room, Truman slumped into his chair, turned to his press secretary, and said, "Well, the die is cast."

Clifford's memorandum and Wallace's letter exposed a tension in the way Americans viewed their role in the postwar world. The struggle against fascism, and the emerging battle against communism, had convinced most Americans that the United States needed to play an active role in international affairs. But how would Americans define that role?

Questions for Analysis

1. Why does Clifford believe the Soviet Union is to blame for the Cold War?

2. What does Clifford mean by the "inevitable" conflict between the United States and the Soviet Union?

3. How does he propose the United States should respond?

4. On what grounds does Wallace reject Clifford's interpretation and recommendations?

5. What alternative explanation does he present to explain Soviet actions?

6. According to Wallace, how has the United States contributed to Cold War tensions?

7. Why did Truman consider Clifford a "realist" and Wallace an "idealist?"

8. If President Truman had asked you to analyze U.S.–Soviet relations, what would you have told him? What recommendations for action would you have made?

28

The Consumer Society, 1945–1960

s shocked journalists looked on, Vice President Richard Nixon and Soviet premier Nikita Khrushchev stood toe to toe in the hottest personal confrontation of the Cold War. The exchange took place in July 1959, as Nixon escorted the Soviet leader through the U.S. National Exhibition, a two-week exhibit in Moscow that celebrated American life. After playing with the new TV equipment and sipping soda from a bottle of Pepsi-Cola, they moved on to the most publicized display of American affluence: a six-room, model suburban ranch house filled with shining new furniture. "I want to show you this kitchen," Nixon said. "It is like those of our houses in California." "We have such things," Khrushchev retorted. But in the United States any worker could afford a $14,000 house, Nixon replied. When Nixon turned the topic to the new consumer devices making life easier in American homes, Khrushchev became enraged. "You Americans think that the Russian people will be astonished to see these things!" They were, he blustered, worthless gadgets.

Within minutes the conversation about television sets and washing machines escalated into an ideological clash between communism and capitalism. A defensive Khrushchev charged that the American military wanted to destroy the Soviet Union. Jamming his thumb into Nixon's chest to underscore his point, Khrushchev warned: "If you want to threaten, we will answer threat with threat." So as not to appear intimidated, Nixon brazenly waived his finger in Khrushchev's face and shot back that it was the Soviets, not the Americans, who threatened the world's peace. Later that evening at a state dinner, Nixon, still gloating over the display of American affluence, told his Soviet hosts that the United States had achieved "the ideal of prosperity for all in a classless society."

The "kitchen debate" captured the conflicting currents of the decade. Appropriately, the simulated kitchen of a suburban house hosted the Nixon–Khrushchev confrontation. During the 1950s, the United States experienced a "consumer revolution" as millions of Americans scrambled to buy a new home in the suburbs and to fill it with the latest consumer gadgets. Television, the most popular of the new products, reinforced the celebration of traditional values by offering Americans a steady diet of shared images. America's love affair with the material benefits of prosperity bred contentment, especially among the expanding white middle classes, and reinforced traditional American optimism about the future. For many of these people, President Dwight Eisenhower was a reassuring symbol. At home, he accepted the major outlines of the welfare state while promising to control its excesses. Abroad, despite some rhetorical excesses, caution guided his approach to the world.

But there was another side to the celebration of consumption during the 1950s. The decade was full of anxiety about the Cold War, fear of revolution in the Third World, and apprehension about the consequences of mass culture for American identity. It was a time when the celebration of family values limited opportunities for women, and when the signs of a booming economy obscured the growing gap between rich and poor. It was also a time when African-Americans established the foundation of a powerful social movement that would change forever the face of American society and the way Americans viewed one another.

▌ What were the roots of the "consumer revolution," and how did consumerism change American society?

▌ What were the manifestations of mass culture in the 1950s?

▌ How did American values shape Eisenhower's policies? What limitations constrained his approach at home and abroad?

▌ How did social realities in the 1950s differ from the ideals portrayed in mass culture?

▌ By 1960, what factors undercut Americans' sense of satisfaction and security?

This chapter will address these questions.

 ## The Consumer Revolution

The United States experienced an unprecedented economic boom following World War II. Between 1940 and 1960, the gross national product (GNP) more than doubled from $227 billion to $488 billion (see graph). The median family income rose from $3,083 to $5,657, and real wages rose by almost 30 percent. By 1960, a record

Chronology

1944	GI Bill
1947	First Levittown constructed on Long Island
1948	Kinsey's Sexual Behavior in the Human Male
1952	Eisenhower elected president
	Nixon's "Checkers" speech
1953	Korean War ends
	Stalin dies; Khrushchev comes to power
	Kinsey's Sexual Behavior in the Human Female
1954	Army–McCarthy hearings; Senate censures McCarthy
	Arbenz deposed in Guatemala
	Defeat of French forces at Dien Bien Phu
	Geneva Accords signed
	Brown v. Board of Education
1955	Ray Kroc establishes McDonald's chain
	Montgomery bus boycott
1956	Interstate Highway Act
	Elvis Presley hits it big with "Heartbreak Hotel"
	Eisenhower reelected; Democrats keep both Houses
	Nasser seizes Suez Canal; Israel invades Sinai Peninsula
1957	Eisenhower Doctrine
	Little Rock crisis
	USSR launches Sputnik
1958	Galbraith publishes The Affluent Society
	National Defense Education Act
1959	"Kitchen debate"
	Castro overthrows Batista regime
1960	Kennedy elected president
	U-2 incident

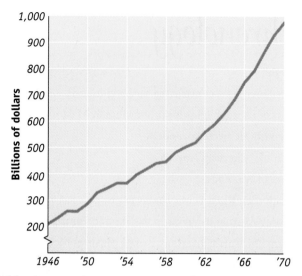

Gross National Product A number of factors, including pent-up consumer demands and profuse military spending, spurred the GNP upward after World War II. The climbing GNP figures reflect the prosperity of the 1950s and 1960s, with the numbers almost doubling from 1945 to 1960 and showing even more dramatic growth during the 1960s. (Source: Adapted from U.S. Bureau of the Census, *Historical Statistics of the United States, Colonial Times to 1970*, Bicentennial Edition, Washington, D.C.: U.S. Government Printing Office, 1975, 224.)

66.5 million Americans held jobs. And unlike in earlier boom times, runaway prices did not eat up rising income: inflation averaged only 1.5 percent annually in the 1950s. "Never had so many people, anywhere, been so well off," the editors of *U.S. News and World Report* concluded in 1957.

At the heart of the new prosperity was a dramatic increase in consumer spending. A postwar "baby boom" created enormous demand for new consumer goods that propelled the economy forward as Americans experimented with new ways of living and spending. To provide more room for growing families, millions of Americans moved to the new suburban communities sprouting up around major cities. The development of a consumer society produced important changes in the nature of work and confronted organized labor with new challenges.

The "Baby Boom" and the Rise of Mass Consumption

"It seems to me," observed a British visitor to America in 1958, "that every other young housewife I see is pregnant." Americans in the postwar period were marrying younger and having more children then ever before. Between 1940 and 1955, the United States experienced the largest population increase in its history—27 percent, from 130 million to 165 million. The so-called baby boom peaked in 1957, when 4.3 million babies were born, one every seven seconds (see graph).

Why the rush to have babies? Several reasons can be identified. First, young couples who had delayed getting married during World War II decided to make up for

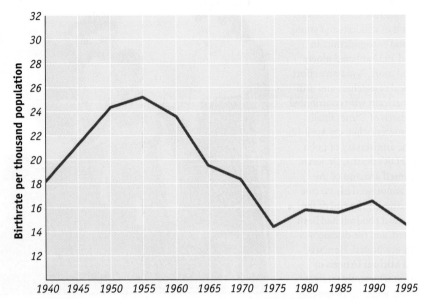

American Birthrate   The bulge in the birthrate from the end of World War II to the mid-1960s marks the height of the "baby boom." By their sheer numbers, the members of this generation could not help but shape every aspect of American culture for the rest of the twentieth century.   (Source: National Center for Health Statistics, U.S. Dept. of Health and Human Services, as reported in *Statistical Abstract of the U.S., 1997* and *World Almanac, 1998*.)

lost time. Then, as the decade progressed, the median age of those getting married hit historic lows—20.1 years for women and 22.5 for men. Young couples were starting families earlier and continuing to have children over a longer period of time.

Second, changing cultural attitudes toward sexuality and pregnancy created a "procreation ethic" that encouraged young couples to have children. Popular television shows and magazine stories celebrated the joys of pregnancy and motherhood, as did advertisers: "I'm Alice Cook," declared a suburban housewife in one aspirin commercial. "I have six children, and they come in all shapes and sizes. So do their colds."

Third, a general spirit of confidence about the future convinced young couples they could afford the demands of parenthood. Government policies played a key role in promoting the new optimism. The Serviceman's Readjustment Act, popularly known as the GI Bill, which Congress passed in 1944, pumped millions of dollars into the economy by providing veterans with unemployment compensation, medical benefits, business loans, and tuition reimbursements for continuing education.

Fourth, modern science contributed to the fertility euphoria by conquering diseases that had plagued human beings for centuries. Antibiotics and other new drugs subdued diseases such as tuberculosis, diphtheria, whooping cough, and measles. The most significant achievement was the victory over poliomyelitis (polio), most of whose victims were children. Between 1947 and 1951, this crippling disease struck an annual average of thirty-nine thousand Americans. In 1955, Dr. Jonas Salk of the

The End of Polio By the 1950s, polio had killed or disabled thousands of children and young adults, and two epidemics in 1950 and 1952 afflicted ninety thousand more. A massive effort by medical researchers and ordinary Americans who contributed to the March of Dimes finally yielded success when on April 12, 1955 (the anniversary of polio patient FDR's death), Dr. Jonas Salk, himself a victim of the disease, announced his vaccine was effective. By the end of the decade, most children had been inoculated, and the disease was virtually eradicated. Here six-year-old Michael Urnezis of San Diego reluctantly receives his vaccine while his twelve-year-old sister and polio survivor, Joanne, joyfully looks on. *(Corbis-Bettmann.)*

Pittsburgh Medical School developed the first effective vaccine against polio, and by 1960, vaccines had practically eliminated the disease in the United States.

The baby boom fueled the consumer revolution. In 1958 *Life* magazine called children the "Built-in Recession Cure," concluding that all babies were potential consumers who spearheaded "a brand-new market for food, clothing, and shelter."

Many people used credit cards to pay for their accumulating merchandise. The credit card business began in 1950 with the introduction of the Diner's Club card. Its enormous success spurred oil firms, motel and hotel chains, and many other companies to introduce credit cards in the 1950s as well. By the end of the decade Sears Roebuck, a large national department store, had more than 10 million charge accounts. *Newsweek* announced in 1953: "Never before have so many owed so much to so many." As a result, total private debts in the United States increased nearly 300 percent during the 1950s, from $73 billion to $196 billion.

The emergence of the credit card marked a fundamental change from an American tradition of independence and frugality to celebration of consumption and debt. The proliferation of new consumer goods and the emerging power of mass media encouraged Americans to buy now and pay later. "Thrift," one observer commented, "now is un-American."

The Rise of the Suburbs

Many urban Americans looked to the suburbs to provide the additional space needed for their growing families, while rural residents and farmers moved to the sprawling suburbs in search of better jobs and more opportunity. In New York City, 1.5 million people moved to the suburbs in the 1950s, while outside Los Angeles, Orange County more than tripled in population. Similar growth occurred around many other cities across the country, until by 1960 almost 60 million people, making up about one-third of the total population, resided in suburban areas.

Builders plowed under more than a million acres of farmland every year to make way for new communities. Of the 13 million homes built in the decade before 1958, 85 percent were built in the suburbs. Inexpensive housing in the suburbs led to a boom in home ownership, which by 1960 was double that of any other industrialized country in the world.

Builder William Levitt made the suburban dream a reality for millions of Americans. In 1949, Levitt bought four thousand acres of potato fields in Hempstead, Long Island. Using mass production methods he produced affordable suburban homes for young families. Every house was identical: one story high, with a twelve-by-sixteen-foot living room, a kitchen, two bedrooms, and a tiled bathroom. The price: $7,990, or $60 a month with no money down. Levitt produced as many as 150 homes a week. Builders throughout the country quickly followed his example.

Levitt built the houses, but government made the homes affordable for millions of young families. More than 3.75 million veterans bought homes under a Veterans Administration program that required only a token down payment and provided long-term, low-interest mortgages. The Federal Housing Administration financed 30 percent of all new houses in the 1950s.

The suburbs fed the consumer society's appetite for new products. The average suburban family earned 70 percent more income than the rest of the nation. "Suburbia," *Fortune* magazine observed in 1953, is "the cream of the market." But suburbanites were not the only Americans filling their homes with new furniture and the latest in electrical gadgetry. By 1960, 96 percent of the nation's families owned refrigerators, 87 percent their own TV sets, and 75 percent their own washing machines. The swimming pool, in the past affordable only by the rich, began to appear in the yards of more and more middle-class homeowners.

The Changing World of Work

Meeting the demands of the new consumer society produced enormous changes in the economy and the nature of work. The 1950s witnessed an acceleration of the trend toward concentration of power in the hands of fewer corporations. By the end of the decade some 600 corporations, which made up only half a percent of all U.S. companies, accounted for 53 percent of total corporate income. In the Cold War defense buildup, the government contributed to the growth of big business by awarding military contracts to a handful of large corporations. Industrial giants used their vast resources to gobble up smaller competitors. During the years 1950 through 1961, the 500 largest American corporations merged with or acquired 3,404 smaller companies.

Corporations not only merged, they extended their reach by establishing roots abroad. Boosted by government programs such as the Marshall Plan, U.S. corporate investment abroad increased by nearly 300 percent during the decade. After World War II, the most successful corporations developed new products and moved into new markets.

Expanding computer use represented the decade's most significant technological development. First developed to aid the defense effort during World War II, the original machines were massive: the Mark I, completed in 1944, stretched fifty feet in length and stood eight feet high. In 1946 engineers at the University of Pennsylvania marketed the first commercial computer. International Business Machines (IBM), already a leader in the office equipment industry, produced its first computer in 1953. The new technology was at the forefront of a wave of automation that promised to boost productivity and cut labor costs. By 1957, more than 1,250 computers were in use making airline reservations, forecasting elections, and helping banks process checks.

Important economic changes were also disrupting the lives of millions of Americans. From 1947 to 1957, the number of factory workers dropped 4 percent. Automation alone eliminated an estimated 1.5 million blue-collar workers, most of them union members, between 1953 and 1959. Those jobs were replaced by new service-sector positions. In 1956, for the first time in U.S. history, white-collar workers outnumbered blue-collar workers. In the two decades after 1950, 9 million jobs opened up for secondary school teachers, hospital support staff, and local government office workers. Consumer demand spurred the creation of new department stores and supermarkets staffed by 3 million additional employees.

The consumer economy presented organized labor with new challenges. At first glance, unions appeared to make tremendous gains during the decade. The number of union members in the United States climbed from 14.7 million in 1945 to 18 million in the mid-1950s. In 1955 the two most powerful labor organizations, the American Federation of Labor headed by George Meany and the Congress of Industrial Organizations led by Walter Reuther, merged into one great federation (AFL-CIO). But unions faced serious problems making inroads into the fastest growing segment of the work force: the white-collar employees. By 1960, unions had organized fewer than 184,000 of 5 million public employees, and only 200,000 of 8.5 million office workers.

During the 1950s, however, the significance of low white-collar unionization was not apparent. Labor–management relations became far less antagonistic than they had been in the 1930s, with few strikes or work stoppages. In 1950 General Motors and the United Automobile Workers signed a contract containing two provisions that would become standard in postwar contracts: (1) an automatic annual cost-of-living wage increase for workers, and (2) a guarantee that wages would rise with productivity. Critics charged that the new accord between labor and management bred contentment and stagnation as union leaders who joined the middle class lost touch with the problems plaguing the working class. "The young, class-conscious workingmen who had fought the battles of River Rouge and Flint in the 1930s," wrote historian William Leuchtenburg, "had become middle-aged, enbourgeoised members of the PTA."

Shaping National Culture, 1945–1960

Television emerged as the most visible symbol of the new consumer society. TV transformed the cultural landscape in America by bringing people from diverse backgrounds together in a shared experience. Along with the automobile, which broke down the geographical distance separating rural and urban, television helped promote a national culture. Popular music and religious revivalism added momentum to a homogenizing trend that worried many intellectuals. How would the experiment in fashioning a more uniform national culture affect what it meant to be an American?

The Shared Images of Television

Although television had been invented in the 1920s, it did not gain widespread acceptance until the 1950s. In 1946 about one of every 18,000 people owned a TV set. By 1960, nine out of every ten American homes had a TV. Its appeal was universal: designed for a mass audience, television did not honor race or class divisions. Most shows avoided controversy and celebrated traditional American values. Americans watched together as Milton Berle, Jackie Gleason, and Arthur Godfrey introduced a parade of entertainers on their live variety shows. Millions of families gathered around the television set each week to watch as Superman, a comic book hero turned television star, fought for "truth, justice, and the American way." Shows such as *Ozzie and Harriet, Father Knows Best,* and *Leave It to Beaver* presented a glossy image of middle-class suburban life. Supportive wives spent their days minding the household and the clean-cut kids while their husbands provided for the family and solved the family crisis of the day. Only a few shows, such as Jackie Gleason's *The Honeymooners,* which described life in a bleak urban apartment, hinted at the world beyond suburbia.

Late in the decade, television viewers tuned into quiz shows that offered excitement and instant success. The format, which frequently saw taxi drivers and bricklayers outwit doctors and lawyers for huge cash prizes, reaffirmed the rags-to-riches notion that anybody could strike it rich in America. Rumors and investigations of fraud on some shows did little to dampen enthusiasm for television.

Television transformed American social habits. Studies showed that the average household watched five hours of television a day. Most viewers confessed to reading fewer books and magazines after purchasing a TV set. Saturated by commercials, children recited the Pepsi-Cola theme song before they learned the national anthem and recognized the word *detergent* before they could read. As poet T. S. Eliot wryly observed, television provided a valuable shared experience, but it was "a medium of entertainment which permits millions of people to listen to the same joke at the same time, and yet remain lonesome."

Advertising executives discovered that television, because it was visual, could do what radio never could. "Show the product," one adman exclaimed, "and show it in use." Many advertisers did just that: a Remington razor shaved the fuzz off a peach and a Band-Aid lifted an egg with the same grip it applied to scraped knees. By promoting national brand names, advertising helped standardize purchasing decisions.

The combination of advertising, prosperity, and television produced overnight national fads. In 1954 the popular Disney show *Davy Crockett* produced the first fad of the decade. The King of the Wild Frontier became an instant hero among millions of children. Enterprising manufacturers flooded the market with Davy Crockett coonskin caps, knives, tents, bow and arrow sets, and records of the show's theme song, "The Ballad of Davy Crockett." Before the fad was over, more than $100 million worth of Crockett paraphernalia had been sold.

Professional sports flowered under the sympathetic eye of the camera. Television exposed more people to sports, making popular figures out of athletic heroes, and pouring money into team coffers. The leading spectator sport was baseball: in 1953, the sixteen major league teams drew 14.3 million into their parks, while millions more watched on television. Thanks to television, professional football became a new super sport, the first true rival to Major League Baseball for the nation's affection. Attendance at professional football games rose steadily for eight straight years, going from 1.9 million in 1950 to 2.9 million in 1957.

As television absorbed millions of dollars of advertising money, it squeezed out other entertainment sources. Radio suffered most, losing nearly half its audience between 1948 and 1956. Thousands of motion picture houses were forced to close their doors. "Why go to the movies," asked film executive Samuel Goldwyn in 1955, "when you can stay home and see nothing worse?" Many large-circulation magazines suffered a similar fate. General interest magazines such as *Life, Saturday Evening Post, Look,* and *Women's Home Companion* lost circulation and eventually ceased publication.

The Car Culture

Television nationalized culture by projecting a common set of images that Americans from coast to coast experienced in the comfort of their homes. At the same time, the dramatic increase in the number of automobiles and new highways narrowed the physical gap between rural and urban communities.

Manufacturers had halted the production of automobiles during World War II, but once the war was over, car sales boomed. Car registrations soared from 26 million in 1945 to 60 million in 1960. The number of two-car families doubled from 1951 to 1958. By 1956, an estimated 75 million cars and trucks sped along American roads, themselves expanded by the Interstate Highway Act of 1956. The largest public works project in American history, the Highway Act appropriated $32 billion to build 41,000 miles of highway.

The car had a profound impact on American life during the 1950s. By the end of the decade, the automobile was directly or indirectly responsible for one-sixth of the Gross National Product and millions of jobs. In turn the auto industry spurred production in related industries: petroleum, steel, tourism and travel, service stations, and highway construction and maintenance. The automobile also promoted the decline of metropolitan areas by accelerating the move to the suburbs, contributed to the decay of public transportation, and produced higher levels of air pollution.

Cars and new roads contributed to a massive population shift from the Northeast to the South and West. Florida's population boomed, fed by the tourist industry, the influx of retirees, and the rapid expansion of the fruit industry. The fastest growth occurred in California, which added 3.1 million residents and accounted for an astounding 20 percent of the nation's population growth in the fifties. By 1963, California had moved past New York as the nation's most populous state. By 1960, half of the people living in the West were living in a state different from the one in which they were born.

By opening the development of suburban retail commerce, the automobile also made the United States a more homogeneous nation. In metropolitan areas across the country, small mom-and-pop stores gave way to mammoth shopping malls housing national retail chains on the edges of the city. Interchangeable motels and fast-food chains materialized nearby. In 1955 an ambitious salesman, Ray Kroc, established a chain of burger joints called McDonald's, which would become the symbol of the fast-food industry.

The automobile boosted the travel industry and made possible new forms of entertainment. In July 1955, the vast Disneyland theme park opened in Southern California. The park attracted more than a million visitors in its first six months. Over 40 percent of the guests came from outside California, most of them by car. Inside the park, Main Street USA recalled America's small town past, Frontierland brought back the thrill of pioneer life, and Tomorrowland suggested the future frontier of space. While enjoying the thrill of Disneyland's amusements, visitors shared in the celebration of common cultural images that reaffirmed the nation's mythic past and its promising future.

Crossing the Moat at Disneyland
Disneyland, which cost $17 million to build, opened its doors in Anaheim, California, in 1955. Its accessibility to the ordinary American made it a contemptible emblem of the "mass society," whose packaged commercialism and mindless entertainment intellectuals despised. But for American families, who had more kids and more money than ever before, Disneyland was a modern marvel. Its combination of nostalgia for the past (Main Street) and excitement for the future (Tomorrowland) captured the mood of postwar culture. *(Wide World Photos, Inc.)*

Religious Revival

"Today in the U.S.," *Time* magazine claimed in 1954, "the Christian faith is back in the center of things." Considerable evidence existed to support the claim. Church membership skyrocketed from 64 million in 1940 to 114 million in 1960. Sales of Bibles reached an all-time high. In 1954 Congress added the phrase "under God" to the Pledge of Allegiance and the next year mandated "In God We Trust" on all U.S. currency. The return to religion found expression in religious songs such as "I Believe" and inspirational movies, among them *The Robe* and *The Ten Commandments*.

Television transformed religious preachers into overnight celebrities. The first clergyman to become a television star was the Most Reverend Fulton J. Sheen, who warned viewers that godless communism was infiltrating American institutions, especially government, and advised against making peace with the Soviets. At the height of his popularity, Sheen's *Life Is Worth Living* show played to a weekly audience of 10 million people.

Sheen competed for air time with ordained Methodist minister Norman Vincent Peale, who reached millions of people every week with his television and radio show and his own magazine. Peale preached a gospel of reassurance and comfort by mixing religion with traditional American ideas of success. Published in 1952 and selling for $2.95, his book, *The Power of Positive Thinking*, stayed at the top of the nonfiction bestseller list for 112 consecutive weeks. In 1954 it sold more copies than any other book except the Bible.

The most popular evangelist of the 1950s was undoubtedly Billy Graham. Handsome and dynamic, Graham used the mass media to reach millions of people. Like other popular preachers of the day, he downplayed doctrinal differences, emphasized the common link between Christian teachings and American values, and warned of the evils of communism, which he called "a great sinister anti-Christian movement masterminded by Satan."

Graham's ecumenical message helped transform Christianity into a national religion. Church membership and professions of faith became popular methods of affirming "the American way of life" during the Cold War. However, in an influential 1955 study, theologian Will Herberg complained that modern religion was "without serious commitment, without real inner conviction, without genuine existential decision." Polls showed that a majority of Americans could not distinguish the New Testament from the Old, or even name one of the gospels. Religion offered Americans what they needed most in the 1950s: a sense of belonging in a rapidly changing society and divine support for traditional American values in the battle with communism. As *The Christian Century* noted in 1954, it had become "un-American to be unreligious."

The Rise of Rock and Roll

The 1950s witnessed dramatic changes in musical tastes. At the beginning of the decade, a few popular singers such as Perry Como and Frank Sinatra held broad appeal, but most radio stations played to the musical tastes of a specific segment of the market. Educated whites tuned into classical stations; rural whites listened to country and western music; middle-class whites kept to pop; blacks to jazz or rhythm and blues. Teenagers played the key role in breaking down these self-imposed musical barriers.

During the 1950s, there were more young people in America than at any previous time in history. The word *teenager* entered the American language. Postwar prosperity provided America's 13 million teenagers with more money than ever before. In 1956 teenage income from allowances and part-time jobs reached $7 billion a year. The average teenager had a weekly income of $10.55.

Young adults changed musical taste in America by propelling rock and roll to the top of the charts. A mix of rhythm and blues, country, and white gospel music, rock and roll had gained enormous popularity among African-Americans in the late forties. Because of its association with blacks and its strong sexual overtones, most whites dismissed the new sound as "race music." At the beginning of the decade, it was being recorded only by small record companies and played only on African-American radio stations. In 1951 a white disc jockey named Alan Freed began playing "race music" on his popular Cleveland radio station, renaming it "rock and roll," an urban euphemism for dancing and sex. By bringing "race music" to a white teenage audience, Freed's "Moondog's Rock and Roll Party" shattered musical barriers and instigated a national music craze.

Initially, most white radio stations refused to play rock and roll music that was performed by black singers. Pressed by growing teenage demand, major record companies produced white versions of songs originally recorded by black singers. In 1955 twelve of the year's top fifty songs were rock and roll, including "Rock Around the Clock," written by two white songwriters and recorded by an all-white group, Bill Haley and the Comets.

The Comets' success opened the door for the most popular rock and roll star of the decade: Elvis Aaron Presley (1935–1977). A nineteen-year-old truck driver from Tupelo, Mississippi, Presley emerged in 1956 with his hit single "Heartbreak Hotel." The young entertainer adapted the powerful rhythms and raw sexual energy of "race music" to create his own unique style and sound. The new white star enthralled screaming audiences of white teens. Between 1956 and 1958, Presley had ten number one hit records, including "Heartbreak Hotel," "Hound Dog," "All Shook Up," and "Jailhouse Rock." Many parents were aghast at watching "Elvis the Pelvis" with his sensual pout and tight pants, swinging his hips while young female fans screamed in excitement.

By the end of the decade, white audiences were rushing to record stores to buy the original black versions of songs. *Billboard* magazine noted that "race music" was "no longer identified as the music of a specific group, but can now enjoy a healthy following among all people, regardless of race and color." Radio stations and record companies now featured black artists. Little Richard (born Richard Wayne Penniman) sang, shouted, danced, gyrated, and sweated profusely through "Tutti Frutti." Antoine "Fats" Domino, less threatening to whites than Little Richard, belted out songs such as "Blueberry Hill" (1956) and "Whole Lotta Loving" (1958). Chuck Berry, who developed a famous "duck walk" across the stage, hit the charts with "Roll Over Beethoven" (1956) and "Johnny B. Goode" (1957).

The emergence of rock and roll produced a boom in national record sales. In 1950 Americans purchased 189 million records; by the end of the decade, that number had soared to over 600 million. Teenagers accounted for nearly 70 percent of all record sales. In 1956 alone, Elvis Presley sold over 3.75 million albums.

Mass Culture and Its Critics

Many writers during the 1950s began to complain that mass culture promoted conformity and contributed to the homogenization of American society. The emphasis on consumerism had created a nation of ugly shopping strips, mindless entertainment, and rampant commercialization. In his popular book *The Lonely Crowd* (1950), sociologist David Riesman suggested that consumerism had moved America from an "inner-directed" culture in which people developed individualized goals to an "other-directed" society molded by peer-group pressures. Other critics took aim at the new service economy, which emphasized teamwork and frowned on mavericks. "When white-collar people get jobs, they sell not only their time and energy but their personalities as well," wrote sociologist C. Wright Mills in *White Collar* (1951).

Television received much of the blame for debasing American culture. Scores of articles and books suggested that television promoted violence, stifled communication in families, and suppressed intellectual creativity and independence of thought. In 1955 a bestselling book, *Why Johnny Can't Read*, blamed television for high rates of child illiteracy.

These critics pointed to the suburbs as evidence of the harmful impact of mass culture on contemporary society. Suburban communities, with their row after row of identical homes and well-manicured lawns, suggested a community that valued uniformity over individualism. Everyone in the suburbs, a hostile observer noted, "buys the right car, keeps his lawn like his neighbor's, eats crunchy breakfast cereal, and votes Republican."

While these critics were correct in highlighting the importance of mass culture, they frequently overplayed their hand. The public was not so passive, nor the dominant culture as monolithic, as they suggested. Despite dire warnings that television would overshadow other forms of information, Americans enjoyed a greater variety of cultural resources than at any time before. Book sales doubled during the decade. A dramatic increase in the number of specialized magazines such as *Sports Illustrated* and the *New Yorker* compensated for the decline of general readership publications. Innovative newspapers increased their circulations by playing to the changing taste of suburban readers.

It is also difficult to measure how viewers interpreted the images they saw on their TV screens. Americans tended to filter the "messages" of mass media through the prism of their own experiences. Italians in Boston's North End may have watched the same television show as African-Americans in rural Alabama, but they responded to the images in different ways. By depicting America as a satiated and affluent society, television may actually have served as an unwitting vehicle of social change. TV's nightly diet of product advertising whetted the appetite of groups excluded from the consumer cornucopia, namely the poor and minorities, and added momentum to their drive for inclusion.

Finally, suburbs, which appeared to some as manifestations of the growing conformity of modern life, were more diverse than critics recognized. Suburban communities included managers and assembly-line workers, Democrats and Republicans, as well as a variety of ethnic and religious groups.

The Politics of Moderation, 1952–1956

In style and manner President Dwight D. Eisenhower served as a political symbol of the age. As one historian commented, "If he sought not to arouse the people to new political challenges, he was suited to reassure them that their elemental convictions were safe from doubt and confusion." At home, Eisenhower's philosophy of "dynamic conservatism" was a policy experiment that attracted groups with differing views of government, reassuring conservatives at the same time that it consolidated New Deal programs. Abroad, despite Republican rhetoric about national "liberation," Eisenhower allowed caution to guide his policy. By the end of the decade, however, the rise of Third World nationalism exposed the limits of America's bipolar view of world affairs.

"I Like Ike": The Election of 1952

Eisenhower had not taken the typical route into politics. Born in Denison, Texas, on October 4, 1890, Eisenhower grew up in Abilene, Kansas, before becoming a career military officer. After leading the British-American military forces that defeated Germany in 1945, Eisenhower remained in the army as Chief of Staff until 1948, when he accepted the presidency of Columbia University. Three years later he was called back to serve as the first supreme commander of NATO forces in Europe.

Eisenhower's status as a war hero made him a popular choice to run for president in 1952. Bumper stickers across the country cheerily proclaimed "I Like Ike." At first, Eisenhower expressed little interest, but he feared that if he did not run, the Republican Party would nominate Ohio senator Robert Taft. Though Taft enjoyed a large following among the party's Old Guard his isolationist views and uninspiring manner dismayed Eisenhower and limited Taft's appeal to mainstream voters. When, in February 1952, Taft advocated bringing American troops home from Europe, Eisenhower decided to run. He resigned from NATO and entered his name for the Republican nomination.

After a bitter convention struggle, Eisenhower won the nomination. To appease the party's right wing he selected thirty-nine-year-old Senator Richard Nixon of California as his running mate. Besides hailing from an important western state, Nixon had close ties to party conservatives. He was also a ferocious, frequently unscrupulous campaigner who could keep the Democrats on the defensive while Eisenhower took the high road.

The Democrats faced a more difficult choice. In March a beleaguered President Harry Truman announced that he would not seek a second term. Recent investigations had linked appointees in Truman's administration to influence peddling and other corrupt practices. The scandals, added to the stalemate in Korea and McCarthy's persistent accusations that the administration was "soft on communism," drove Truman's popularity to an all-time low of 26 percent. With Truman out of the picture, many Democrats looked to popular Illinois governor Adlai Stevenson. Along with being an incumbent governor of a large and powerful state, Stevenson had endeared himself to party loyalists by taking strong positions on civil rights and civil liberties. Like Eisenhower, Stevenson expressed little interest in the nomination, but he bowed to party leaders' insistence. To balance the ticket, Stevenson selected a segregationist senator, John Sparkman of Alabama, to round out the ticket.

The candidates possessed strikingly different styles. Intellectuals and liberals found Stevenson's speeches eloquent and inspirational, but his aristocratic manner failed to arouse rank-and-file voters. Eisenhower, in contrast, endeared himself to the public. With a serene, confident manner and what one reporter called a "leaping and effortless smile," he seemed above partisan politics. Billboards in California challenged doubters: "Faith in God and Country; that's Eisenhower— how about you?"

Eisenhower became the first candidate to make effective use of television in a presidential campaign. To help craft his image, he turned to a New York advertising firm. The centerpiece of the strategy was a series of fifty 20-second commercials, called "spots," showing Eisenhower responding to questions from ordinary Americans. "What about the high cost of living?" asked one spot. "My wife, Mamie," Ike answered, "worries about the same thing. I tell her it's our job to change that on November fourth." Though simplistic and devoid of any substance, the ads carried Eisenhower's luminous smile into millions of living rooms. After 1952, spots would become a standard feature of American politics.

The GOP campaign correctly identified Korea, communism, and corruption as key issues. The Republicans complained of "plunder at home, blunder abroad" and promised to "clean up the mess in Washington." Nixon referred to "Adlai the Appeaser" who was a "Ph.D. graduate of Dean Acheson's cowardly College of Communist Containment." Eisenhower, just ten days before the election, declared, "I shall go to Korea." Though he did not say what he would do when he got there, his pledge was a masterful stroke. In a break with most presidential elections, which are decided primarily on domestic issues, more than half the electorate regarded the war as the country's single most important problem, and most people believed Eisenhower's military background made him the best candidate to end the conflict.

The Republicans did have to endure an embarrassing scandal of their own, however. In September, the *New York Post* revealed that a group of wealthy California businessmen had provided Nixon with an $18,000 private "slush fund" to pay for personal campaign expenses. On September 23, Nixon went on national television to defend himself, citing the emotional and material needs of his family, not personal ambition, as his reason for accepting the money. Near the end of the talk Nixon told the story of one special gift he had received—a "little cocker spaniel dog," which his daughter Tricia had named Checkers. He vowed his family would keep the dog "regardless of what they say about it." The address revealed the growing importance of television in politics. Over 9 million sets were tuned into Nixon's speech, and popular reaction was overwhelmingly favorable. Eisenhower, recognizing the positive response, assured Nixon, "You're my boy."

On election day, Eisenhower won 55.1 percent of the popular vote and carried thirty-nine states. Stevenson won 44.4 percent of the popular vote and carried nine states, all southern. Most significant, Eisenhower offset Democratic strength in major urban areas by scoring well in the growing suburbs (see map).

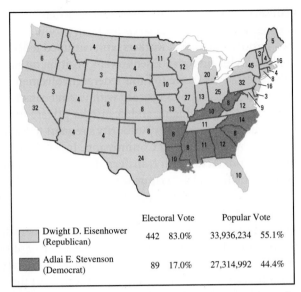

	Electoral Vote		Popular Vote	
Dwight D. Eisenhower (Republican)	442	83.0%	33,936,234	55.1%
Adlai E. Stevenson (Democrat)	89	17.0%	27,314,992	44.4%

The Election of 1952 Though a political novice, Dwight D. Eisenhower's persona as a war hero and man of the people gave him the edge over his more experienced, yet less-well-known opponent, Adlai Stevenson. Eisenhower's popularity and his promise to end the Korean War even swayed many southern Democrats to vote Republican for the first time.

"Dynamic Conservatism" at Home

Eisenhower called his political philosophy "dynamic conservatism," which he interpreted as "conservative when it comes to money and liberal when it comes to human beings." Like many conservatives, Eisenhower believed that the executive branch had grown too strong under Roosevelt and Truman. Government regulation had strangled business while the growth of executive power had disrupted the delicate constitutional balance among the branches of government. The solution, he argued, was to take a more restrained approach to the presidency. "I am not one of those desk-pounding types that likes to stick out his jaw and look like he is bossing the show," he said.

The new president was determined to reverse the direction taken by the New Deal and Fair Deal or, in his words, to remove "the Left-Wingish, pinkish influence in our life." To help carry out his program, Eisenhower selected a conservative cabinet and gave it wide discretion. "The White House will stay out of your hair," he said. Secretary of Agriculture Ezra Taft Benson vowed to get the government out of the business of supporting farm prices. Treasury chief George Humphrey, a former corporate executive and an old-fashioned fiscal conservative, considered it his job to reduce spending. Secretary of Defense Charles E. Wilson, former president of General Motors, expressed his economic philosophy: "What was good for our country was good for General Motors, and vice versa."

Acting on his conservative impulses, the president removed Truman's moderate wage and price controls, lowered price supports for farm products, cut the government payroll by two hundred thousand workers, and trimmed federal spending by 10 percent, or $6 billion, in his first year. Eisenhower's position on natural resource development clearly revealed his desire to limit federal involvement in the private sector. He reversed Truman's decision to proceed with federal construction of a hydroelectric plant in Hell's Canyon, Idaho, and licensed a private firm to complete the work. He opposed the Tennessee Valley Authority's request to build a new plant to furnish power for the Atomic Energy Commission. In May 1953, Eisenhower signed the Submerged Lands Act, which transferred control of about $40 billion worth of oil lands from the federal government to the states. The *New York Times* called it "one of the greatest and surely the most unjustified give-away programs in all the history of the United States."

Despite the hopes of many conservatives, and the fears of liberals, Eisenhower did not undermine the foundation of the modern welfare state. Political and economic realities prevented such a drastic step. Congressional Democrats, who recaptured control of both houses in 1954 and retained it throughout the remainder of Eisenhower's presidency, would have blocked any attempt to repeal established programs. Also, sharp recessions in 1954 and 1958 led the president to abandon his budget-balancing efforts and to accelerate government spending.

Indeed, in the end, Eisenhower's policies consolidated and strengthened the New Deal's economic and social programs. The president and Congress agreed in 1954, and again in 1956, to increase social security benefits and to broaden the federal system to include an estimated 10 million new workers. In 1955 Congress and Eisenhower compromised on a new minimum wage law that increased the minimum from seventy-five cents to $1 an hour. Between 1953 and 1961, the federal government spent some $1.3 billion for slum clearance and public housing. In health and medical welfare, Eisenhower also carried forward the programs begun by Roosevelt and Truman. On April 1, 1953, Eisenhower signed a bill that raised the Federal Security Agency to cabinet rank as the Department of Health, Education, and Welfare.

While consolidating the New Deal, Eisenhower outflanked his party's right wing by intensifying the campaign against internal subversion. Soon after taking office, he toughened the government loyalty program. Under his new guidelines, almost ten thousand federal employees resigned or were dismissed. The administration also supported the Communist Control Act. Passed by Congress in 1954, the law prohibited communists from running for public office.

Eisenhower hoped that his aggressive loyalty program would steal the limelight from Joseph McCarthy. But McCarthy had other ideas. In October 1953, McCarthy blasted the administration for conducting a foreign policy of "whiny, whimpering appeasement." At the same time his subcommittee conducted seventeen hearings, including ten that focused on current subversion in government.

Eisenhower had had enough. In March 1954, the president leaked to the press an army report that documented attempts by McCarthy and his staff to win preferential treatment for a former staff member drafted into the army. The Senate, embarrassed by the army's accusations, decided to hold investigative public hearings carried live on national television. Beginning on April 27, as many as 20 million Americans watched the proceedings for thirty-five days. Toward the end, McCarthy savagely attacked a lawyer for having once belonged to a left-wing organization. Outraged, attorney Joseph Welch berated McCarthy, concluding, "Have you no sense of decency, sir, at long last? Have you left no sense of decency?" After watching McCarthy on television, a majority of Americans were asking the same question. As his appeal ebbed, the Senate roused itself against McCarthy, voting in December 1954, 67 to 72 , to "condemn" him for bringing the Congress into disrepute. Three years later, at the age of forty-eight, Joseph McCarthy, once the most feared man in America, died of hepatitis and other health problems caused by alcoholism.

McCarthy's fall removed a major source of embarrassment and virtually guaranteed Eisenhower's reelection in 1956. Polls showed Ike leading all Democratic challengers by wide margins. The president's enormous popularity had as much to do with his style and personality as it did with his policies. Most people viewed Eisenhower as a strong leader and a likeable man who embodied traditional American values. He often spoke of old-fashioned virtues such as honor, duty, patriotism, and hard work. The White House seemed home to a traditional family, with First Lady Mamie Eisenhower playing the proper role of dutiful wife. "Ike took care of the office," she declared; "I ran the house."

Eisenhower used television not only when campaigning but also to build public support for his administration. Realizing that television allowed politicians to project themselves into the homes of millions of potential voters, Eisenhower hired movie star Robert Montgomery to help craft his media image. By 1955, Ike was so confident in his ability to perform for the cameras that he became the first president to allow television coverage of his press conferences.

After a spirited primary campaign, Democrats turned again to Adlai Stevenson to lead their party. Stevenson ran an energetic campaign for a "New America" where "poverty is abolished" and "freedom is made real for everybody." But he was no match for Eisenhower. On election day, Ike polled 35,590,472 popular votes and carried forty-one states to Stevenson's meager 26,022,752 votes and seven states. It was an endorsement, however, of Eisenhower—not of his party. The Democrats actually increased their majorities in Congress and their governorships (see map).

The "New Look" Abroad

Eisenhower came to the White House better prepared to handle foreign policy than any other twentieth-century president. He had toured the globe and served as supreme wartime commander of Allied forces and NATO. He came to office with a clear vision of America's role in world affairs. Like most Americans, Ike was convinced of the superiority of American values, committed to spreading the gospel of democracy and free enterprise around the globe, and determined to use American military might to limit Soviet expansion. But Eisenhower was also a practical man who appreciated the dangers of excessive idealism and understood the need for compromise in the international arena.

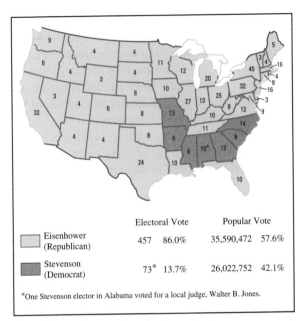

	Electoral Vote		Popular Vote	
Eisenhower (Republican)	457	86.0%	35,590,472	57.6%
Stevenson (Democrat)	73*	13.7%	26,022,752	42.1%

*One Stevenson elector in Alabama voted for a local judge, Walter B. Jones.

The Election of 1956 The 1956 election again pitted Dwight Eisenhower against Adlai Stevenson, and again Eisenhower won—by an even greater margin of victory than in 1952. This election also marked the first time that a state in the Deep South had voted Republican since Reconstruction.

Eisenhower delegated a great deal of authority to his secretary of state, John Foster Dulles, but he never relinquished control to him. A leading Republican spokesman on foreign policy, Dulles possessed supreme confidence, faith in the righteousness of his position, and a domineering personality. Dulles, people said, carried foreign policy under his hat. He possessed deeply held convictions about America's role in the world. He believed in a monolithic "world Communist movement," the "unholy alliance of Marx's communism and Russia's imperialism." He came into office denouncing Truman's containment policy. The Eisenhower administration, he vowed, was committed to "liberation" of nations under communist rule. He favored a policy of "brinkmanship"—pushing the Soviet Union to the brink of war before considering negotiations.

Though Dulles dominated the rhetoric during the decade, Eisenhower maintained control of policy. Eisenhower's fiscal conservatism shaped his views of American foreign policy. The Korean conflict taught him that the United States could not afford to fight local wars with conventional troops. America, he believed, should instead take advantage of its overwhelming superiority in nuclear weapons, attacking enemy forces with small nuclear weapons or even striking at the source of the aggression—Moscow or Beijing. Being cheaper than conventional forces, nuclear weapons offered "more bang for the buck." The administration called its defense strategy the "New Look."

A number of features distinguished Eisenhower's New Look strategy. First, to make credible the threat to use atomic arms, the administration dramatically increased the nation's nuclear arsenal. Between 1952 and 1959, the number of nuclear weapons in the American arsenal grew from around 1,500 to over 6,000. The navy introduced submarine-based intermediate-range Polaris missiles. The Strategic Air Command (SAC) replaced its aging propeller-driven B-36 bombers with jet-propelled B-47s that could fly six hundred miles an hour and hit targets in the Soviet heartland. Yet the New Look defense policy, coupled with the end of the Korean War, enabled Eisenhower to slash defense spending by some 20 percent in his first two years in office. Only the air force saw its budget rise from $15 billion to $19 billion between 1953 and 1959.

Second, in its efforts to surround the Soviet Union strategically, the Eisenhower administration negotiated a number of regional defense treaties. By the end of the 1950s, the United States had signed agreements to defend forty-three different nations against "communist aggression."

Third, the administration dramatically expanded the role of the Central Intelligence Agency (CIA), which provided an inexpensive method of protecting American interests abroad. Headed by Allen Dulles, the brother of the secretary of state, the CIA by 1955 employed almost fifteen thousand people, triple its 1950 staff. Among the employees were thousands of covert agents stationed in so-called trouble spots around the world. The CIA expanded its role beyond intelligence gathering to a wide range of political activities, including the overthrow of foreign governments.

Rhetoric and Reality of Liberation

Despite the tough language about brinkmanship and liberation, Eisenhower and Dulles discovered that the realities of international power and domestic politics prevented a radical departure from past practices. The first indication of the continuity in their approach to the world came in Korea, where Eisenhower was determined to end American involvement. But on what terms? Dulles and conservative Republicans objected to any peace proposal that left the communists in control of North Korea and divided the nation into two societies—one free, one communist. Eisenhower was more interested in ending the war and saving lives than in proving his fidelity to the Republican platform. As promised, he flew to Korea after the 1952 election to nudge the cease-fire talks. He also dropped hints to China that he was ready to use nuclear weapons in Korea. In July 1953, he agreed to terms that called for a division of Korea at approximately the same line that had marked the border in June 1950—the thirty-eighth parallel—with a demilitarized zone separating the two Koreas.

The president showed similar restraint in dealing with a potentially dangerous situation in China. During the fall of 1954, the Communist Chinese began to shell the offshore islands of Quemoy and Matsu, which were occupied by the Nationalist Chinese. Conservatives urged Eisenhower to respond forcefully, perhaps by bombing the mainland. Instead, Eisenhower signed a security agreement with the Nationalists that committed the United States to protect the strategically important island of Formosa (Taiwan), but left ambiguous America's commitment to Quemoy and Matsu. Again, he and Dulles issued public statements hinting at the possibility

We Like Ike   Dwight Eisenhower, with his illustrious military record and his jovial smile, enjoyed enormous popularity as president. Here he campaigns in Manhasset, New York, during the 1952 presidential race, surrounded by people of all ages and walks of life. Although "Ike" seemed to personify the blandness and simplicity of the decade, historians have since come to praise the president for his ability to work with the Democratic Congress behind the scenes, his ratification of the welfare state, and his caution in Cold War diplomacy.   *(Corbis-Bettmann.)*

of using nuclear weapons to stem communist attacks. Chinese leaders, uncertain whether Eisenhower was bluffing, stopped the bombardment.

Eisenhower also pursued a moderate course in his dealings with the Soviet Union. In March 1953, shortly after Eisenhower's election, Soviet leader Joseph Stalin died, raising hopes of a thaw in relations between the two countries. Nikita Khrushchev became Soviet premier and secretary of the Communist Party in March 1958. A shrewd politician, Khrushchev planned to ease Cold War tensions so that his country could spend less money on the military and more on consumer goods. He also hoped that lowering the heat of the Cold War would weaken ties between the United States and its Western allies.

Eisenhower approached the new regime cautiously. In a major speech on April 16, 1953, he invited the Soviets to end the arms race. In a dramatic address to the United Nations on December 8, he proposed that the major scientific nations of the world jointly contribute to a United Nations pool of atomic power to be used solely for peaceful purposes. "Let no one think," he said, "that the expenditure of vast sums for systems and weapons of defense can guarantee absolute safety."

The Soviets responded by settling their differences with Germany over war prisoners, by establishing diplomatic relations with Greece, Israel, and Yugoslavia, and by withdrawing troops from neutral Austria. These initiatives led to the first U.S.–Soviet summit meeting in a decade. In July 1955, Eisenhower and Khrushchev, with their British and French counterparts, met in Geneva for the first top-level conference of the wartime Allies since the 1945 meeting at Potsdam. "The United States will never take part in an aggressive war," Eisenhower told the Soviets. Eisenhower also won a propaganda victory with his "Open Skies" proposal, which called for aerial surveillance of both countries' nuclear facilities. The suggestion was neither as bold nor as innovative as many at the time thought. Since American skies were already open, Eisenhower was asking the Soviets to make a unilateral concession— something they refused to do. Ignoring advice from Dulles that he maintain an "austere countenance" in all photographs taken at Geneva, Ike flashed his famous grin while posing with his Soviet counterpart. The cordial atmosphere produced a brief thaw in superpower tensions, which the press labeled "the spirit of Geneva."

The friendly words and smiling faces of Geneva could not mask the serious differences between the two countries. The thaw ended on October 29, 1956, when 200,000 Soviet soldiers and hundreds of tanks swept into Hungary to repress a popular uprising demanding democratic reforms. The Soviet juggernaut killed 40,000 Hungarian freedom fighters and forced 150,000 refugees to flee the country. Conservatives expected the administration to intervene to support the rebels. The CIA recommended parachuting arms and supplies to the Hungarian freedom fighters. But Eisenhower understood the military risks of attempting to intervene in a country so close to the Soviet border. Hungary, he observed sadly, was "as inaccessible to us as Tibet."

The Threat of Third World Nationalism

Hungarians were not alone in striving for independence. Between 1945 and 1960, almost forty nations with 800 million people fought nationalist struggles against colonial rulers. The leaders of these countries tried to exploit superpower tensions to win concessions from both Washington and Moscow. These newly independent nations in Asia, the Middle East, Latin America, and Africa became the new battlegrounds of the Cold War. Henry Cabot Lodge, U.S. ambassador to the United Nations, first asked the question that plagued American policymakers in the years following World War II: "The U.S. can win wars," but, he asked, "can we win revolutions?"

The Middle East confronted the administration with its first serious nationalist challenge. In 1954 Egyptian leader Colonel Gamal Abdel Nasser increased trade with the Soviet bloc and officially recognized China. Two years later, Dulles, in an attempt to punish Egypt for its growing ties with communists, abruptly canceled American financing to build the Aswan Dam across the Nile. In response, Nasser seized control of the Suez Canal, the vital waterway between the Mediterranean and the Gulf of Suez, and used the revenue to complete the Aswan project. Arabs hailed Nasser as a hero for his bold stand against Western imperialism. The British, who had controlled the canal, and the French, angered by Nasser's aid to rebels defying French rule in Algeria, conspired to regain control of the canal and teach Nasser a lesson.

They got their chance on October 29, 1956, when, provoked by eight years of border attacks and fear of the Egyptian arms buildup, Israel invaded Egypt's Sinai Peninsula, advancing to within ten miles of the Suez Canal. In an attack carefully coordinated with the Israelis, the British and French bombed Egyptian military targets and seized the northern third of the canal.

The Anglo-French military action angered Eisenhower, who feared they would alienate nationalist elements in the Middle East and drive the entire Arab world, and its lucrative oil fields, closer to the Russians. The president publicly condemned the attacks on Egypt and worked with the Soviets through the United Nations for a cease-fire, and the creation of a special U.N. Emergency Force to supervise withdrawal of all outside forces from Egypt. By December 1956, the crisis was over, but the Suez affair had shaken the Western alliance to its foundations, provided the Russians with a foothold in the Middle East, and increased anti-Western sentiment in the region. In 1957 Eisenhower asked for, and both houses of Congress passed, a resolution that came to be called the Eisenhower Doctrine. The new plan provided the president with broad authority to provide economic and military assistance to defend any Middle East ally from "international communism."

The administration's foreign policy faced another test in Indochina, where Ho Chi Minh's nationalist movement controlled a part of northern Vietnam and continued to battle French colonial authority. Eisenhower, like Truman, viewed Ho as a communist puppet and believed that if southern Vietnam fell to the communists, all Southeast Asia would be at risk. He compared the nations of Southeast Asia to a row of dominoes: Knock one over and the rest would fall quickly. Eisenhower increased American military and economic aid to bolster the French, but in 1954 Vietnamese and Communist Chinese forces surrounded twelve thousand French troops at Dien Bien Phu, a remote jungle fortress. The French pleaded for direct American intervention to rescue their troops. For weeks the administration debated a course of action. Dulles wanted to take the nation to the "brink of war" by launching air strikes against the North Vietnamese. Vice President Nixon went further, advocating the use of tactical nuclear weapons. But once again, Eisenhower preferred caution. The president had little faith in the military capability of the French, whom he called "a hopeless, helpless mass of protoplasm." European allies, especially the British, opposed American intervention. At home leading Democrats, including Senators Lyndon Johnson and John F. Kennedy, warned against using American soldiers in Indochina. Eisenhower also worried about the moral implications of using tactical nuclear weapons in Asia. "You boys must be crazy," Eisenhower replied. "We can't use those awful things against Asians for the second time in ten years. My God." Without American support, the French garrison surrendered in May 1954.

In July the French government signed the Geneva Accords, which temporarily divided Indochina at the seventeenth parallel until the holding of free democratic elections in 1956. Realizing that the popular Ho Chi Minh would win in a free election, the administration installed as head of state in South Vietnam Ngo Dinh Diem, an ardent Vietnamese nationalist who hated the French. Diem was also a staunch anticommunist and devout Catholic. The United States poured economic and military aid into the South in hopes of making Diem a viable leader. In 1954, in an effort to stem Soviet and Chinese influence in the area, Dulles set up yet another anticommunist military alliance, the Southeast Asia Treaty Organization (SEATO). The treaty pledged the United States to defend Australia, New Zealand, Thailand, Pakistan, and the Philippines against communist aggression.

In other regions of the world, the administration relied on the CIA to quell nationalist uprisings that appeared to threaten American interests. In Iran, when the government of Mohammed Mossadegha nationalized the Anglo-Iranian Oil Company in 1953, the CIA planned, financed, and orchestrated a coup to overthrow him. To replace him, the CIA worked with Iranian army officers to consolidate power behind the pro-Western Shah Reza Pahlavi.

In 1954 the administration used the CIA to topple the leftist government of Jacob Arbenz Guzman in Guatemala. In 1953, the Arbenz government had launched an ambitious land-reform program, which included seizing more than two hundred thousand acres controlled by the American-owned United Fruit Company. Warning that the country could become an outpost for communism in the Western Hemisphere, the CIA organized and financed an anti-Arbenz coup. A new government, approved by the CIA, took power and restored the appropriated lands to United Fruit.

Eisenhower's experiments in intervention revealed the flaws in America's approach to nationalist revolutions. Viewing local struggles as part of the superpower competition and as threats to U.S. security, Americans confused indigenous nationalist movements with Soviet-inspired aggression. America's attitude revealed an arrogance of strength, a belief that U.S. power could and should shape the internal affairs of distant nations. In time, America would pay a heavy price for its miscalculations.

American Ideals and Social Realities, 1950–1960

Intellectuals, politicians, and a majority of Americans viewed postwar prosperity as a vindication of their faith in capitalism and individualism. Despite the popular belief that capitalism had eroded class differences, structural poverty remained a serious problem in the United States. A growing movement of women into the work force contradicted the popular veneration of traditional gender roles. Most striking of all was the continuing tension in the lives of African-Americans between the promise of equal opportunity and the reality of racial discrimination. In response, black leaders undertook new experiments in pursuit of civil rights.

Intellectuals and the Celebration of Consensus

Postwar prosperity, the lure of suburbia, the stifling effects of McCarthyism, and the oppressive atmosphere of the Cold War discouraged critical social analysis and muted vigorous political debate in 1950s America. Intellectuals gave their scholarly blessing to the self-satisfied images that pervaded mass culture. In 1956 *Time* magazine observed that the intellectual "found himself feeling at home" in America.

Historians, sociologists, and political scientists heralded an "age of consensus," a time when prosperity, social programs, and fear of communism rendered social protest obsolete. At the end of the decade, sociologist Daniel Bell declared all radical alternatives dead in *The End of Ideology* (1960). Historians such as Daniel Boorstin and Henry Steele Commager minimized the role of conflict and change in American history, and stressed the importance of continuity and consensus. Surveys showing that 75 percent of Americans considered themselves part of the middle class contributed to the growing sense that the nation was evolving toward a classless society.

Liberals joined in the celebration of consensus, abandoning or moderating their arguments during the Great Depression for sweeping changes in the nation's economic institutions. "American capitalism works," declared Harvard economist John Kenneth Galbraith early in the decade. Like earlier reformers, liberals in the 1950s believed that government needed to play a role in regulating the economy and guaranteeing social justice. But they also shared with many conservatives a reverence for the enormous potential of the free enterprise system and a fear of expansive federal power. Reflecting the broader consensus, liberals believed that sustained economic growth, with a minimum of government regulation, would eliminate class divisions, create opportunity for all citizens, and ensure a stable society.

The New Poverty

The fanfare over a "classless society" fizzled. In spite of the widening prosperity, the distribution of income remained uneven and utopian hopes proved unfounded. In 1960 the top 1 percent of the population held 33 percent of the national wealth, while the bottom 20 percent held only 5 percent. In 1959 a quarter of the population had no liquid assets; over half the population had no savings accounts. "If we made an income pyramid out of child's blocks, with each portraying $1,000 of income," economist Paul Samuelson explained, "the peak would be far higher than the Eiffel Tower, but almost all of us would be within a foot of the ground."

Although poverty had declined significantly since the Great Depression, about 40 million Americans representing 25 percent of the population were poor in 1960. The elderly, people over sixty-five, made up one-fourth of the poor. A fifth were people of color, including 45 percent of African-Americans. The majority of these poor people received little help from the meager welfare system. About half of America's poor families were not covered by social security in 1960. Only about 20 percent received assistance from the federal government. Money spent on them represented less than 1 percent of the gross national product.

What was new about poverty in the 1950s was that it had moved from the rural farm to the inner city. By 1960, some 55 percent of the poor lived in cities. African-Americans made up a majority of the new urban residents. Before World War II, 80 percent of African-Americans lived in the South. During the war, defense-related jobs lured almost 3 million southern workers to the nation's cities. In 1943 the mechanical cotton picker displaced perhaps 2.3 million family farm workers, many of whom traveled north looking for jobs. At one point in the 1950s, the black population of Chicago swelled by more than 2,200 new arrivals each week. By 1960, half of all African-Americans lived in central cities.

Other minority groups joined African-Americans in the cities. During the 1940s, the U.S. government encouraged the mechanization of Puerto Rico's sugar cane economy. As a consequence, rural employment plunged and a large Puerto Rican migration to the mainland began. Between 1940 and 1960, the Puerto Rican population of New York City increased from 70,000 to 613,000. In the West, between 1950 and 1960, the Mexican-American population of Los Angeles County doubled, from 300,000 to more than 600,000. By 1960, Hispanics made up 16 percent of California's population. Nearly 80 percent of Hispanic-Americans lived in urban centers.

Minorities flooded the nation's cities just as the white middle class, and many jobs, were fleeing to the suburbs. Discrimination prevented minorities from following the same route. Many private developers refused to sell homes to African-Americans. The Federal Housing Administration, which financed 30 percent of all new homes in the 1950s, endorsed "restrictive covenants" prohibiting sales to minorities. It also contributed to the declining quality of urban housing by supporting red-lining, the refusal to write mortgage loans to central city areas. At the same time, many cities adopted ambitious urban renewal projects, which demolished neighborhoods and displaced poor people in the name of progress. By 1963, urban renewal had uprooted 609,000 Americans, two-thirds of whom were minority group members. When planning the route of new superhighways to speed the commute between the suburbs and the central city, Los Angeles officials bypassed wealthy neighborhoods such as Beverly Hills and plowed through densely populated Chicano communities in East Los Angeles and Hollenbeck. In October 1957, the city displaced the Chicano community in Chavez Ravine to make room for the building of Dodger Stadium.

Women During the 1950s

A gap between popular perceptions and social realities also plagued women during the decade. In a special 1956 issue on American women, *Life* magazine concluded that the ideal modern woman married, cooked and cared for her family, and kept herself busy by joining the local Parent–Teachers Association and leading a troop of the Campfire Girls. She entertained guests in her family's suburban house and worked out on the trampoline "to keep her size 12 figure." Television shows reinforced this message.

However, the decade's celebration of family life failed to account for important changes in women's lives. Between 1940 and 1960, the number of women in the work force doubled. By 1952, 2 million more women were at work than during World War II. Many of the women who joined the work force were middle-aged wives looking for a second income to help their suburban families pay for their new consumer goods. By the early 1960s, one worker in three was a woman, and three of five women workers were married.

At the same time the expanding economy provided jobs for women, it also relegated them to low-paying positions. A greater portion of women's jobs than men's jobs were not covered by minimum wage or social security. In 1960 women represented only 3.5 percent of lawyers and 6.1 percent of physicians. But they made up 97 percent of nurses and 85 percent of the librarians. High school principals were 90 percent male, whereas elementary school teachers were 85 percent female.

Evidence of changing sexual behavior also challenged the celebration of traditional family life. Alfred Kinsey, an Indiana University zoologist who had previously

Life in Suburbia The domestic wife was an important component of the new suburban culture. She kept a tidy home and garden, cooked delicious meals, raised numerous children, all while looking beautiful, fit, and trim. In keeping with these trends, the fitness craze had its beginnings in postwar America. Here, suburban housewives exercise in front of another sign of the times, the television. *(Dan Weiner, Courtesy Sandra Weiner.)*

studied bees, decided to turn his attention to human sexuality. His studies on *Sexual Behavior in the Human Male* (1948) and *Sexual Behavior in the Human Female* (1953) concluded that premarital sex was common and that married couples frequently engaged in extramarital affairs. His finding that over a third of adult males had homosexual experiences shocked people, and his suggestion that women were as sexually active as men outraged traditionalists who liked to believe that women copulated only to give birth. *Life* magazine condemned Kinsey's results as an "assault on the family as a basic unit of society, a negation of moral law, and a celebration of licentiousness."

There was little desire to confront the contradictions in women's lives during the 1950s. When pollsters George Gallup and Evan Hill surveyed the views of "The American Woman" for the *Saturday Evening Post* in 1962, they had reason to conclude, after 2,300 interviews, that "few people are as happy as a housewife." Indeed, 96 percent of the women surveyed declared themselves extremely happy or very happy, though most wished that their daughters would marry later and get more education.

The Struggle for Black Equality

Nowhere was the contradiction between ideals and reality more striking than in the lives of African-Americans. The South's racially segregated schools formed only one piece in a vast mosaic of institutionalized racism. Wherever one looked in early postwar America, blacks were treated as second-class citizens.

Yet following World War II a combination of forces began undermining the pillars of racial segregation in the South. The war had dramatically changed the lives of many blacks, luring millions into armaments plants and labor unions in the North and West. Cold War concerns further eroded ingrained patterns of racism. The reality of racism proved embarrassing to a nation that denounced the Soviets for ignoring human rights and courted newly independent nations in Asia and Africa. It also became impossible to ignore when the mass media, especially television, revealed to the nation the violent white resistance that greeted civil rights activism in the South.

African-Americans led the assault on the system of segregation. For the previous half-century the National Association for the Advancement of Colored People (NAACP) had focused on fulfilling the constitutional promise of civil and political rights for African-Americans by doggedly pursuing test cases in the courts. Gradually, the Supreme Court began to chip away at the legal bases of segregation. In 1954 the Court overturned the legal justification for one of the linchpins of white supremacy—the separate-but-equal doctrine—in a unanimous decision popularly known as *Brown* v. *Board of Education of Topeka, Kansas* (see Competing Voices, page 1130). The *Brown* decision declared segregation in public schools to be illegal. A year later the Supreme Court instructed federal district courts to require local authorities to show "good faith" and to move with "all deliberate speed" toward desegregation of all public schools.

The historic decision triggered massive resistance to ending Jim Crow among state and local politicians in the South. They and newly formed White Citizens Councils employed legal maneuvers, economic reprisals, and outright defiance against blacks who challenged segregation. Senator James Eastland of Mississippi denounced the Court's "monstrous crime," which he warned would result in "the mongrelization of the white race." Nineteen southern senators and seventy-seven representatives signed a manifesto in 1956 that bound them to "use all lawful means to bring about a reversal of this decision which is contrary to the Court and to prevent the use of force in its implementation."

The first outright defiance of the federal courts occurred in Little Rock, Arkansas. Desegregation of Central High School was scheduled to begin in September 1957. But many whites wished to obstruct the plan, and the state's ambitious governor, Orville Faubus, believed that supporting desegregation would mean political suicide. Faubus called out the National Guard to prevent black students from entering Central High. The guardsmen, with bayonets drawn, tuned back the nine young African-American students, mainlining segregation for nearly three weeks until a federal judge ordered them removed. The students managed to enter the school, but only after a mob of unruly whites outside pelted and pushed the police who tried to protect the students. National television cameras recorded the ugly events. President Eisenhower, who privately deplored the *Brown* decision, responded by sending federal troops to uphold the court order. The president told a southern senator that "failure to act in such a case would be tantamount to acquiescence in anarchy and the dissolution of the union." For the first time since Radical Reconstruction, the federal government demonstrated that it would use military force to protect rights guaranteed to blacks by the Constitution. Troops patrolled the high school for months, but the controversy over desegregation convulsed the city for two more years.

The *Brown* decision and Eisenhower's forceful response in Little Rock offered hope that Washington had finally decided to join the black struggle for civil rights. African-Americans, however, were not going to wait for the federal government in their effort to end the daily humiliation of legal segregation. Even before *Brown*, African-Americans living in the South had laid the foundation of a powerful social movement that would challenge the edifice of white supremacy.

The Montgomery Bus Boycott

What would become one of the most dramatic symbols of the civil rights movement occurred in Mississippi in 1955. In September, Emmett Till, a fourteen-year-old black youth from Chicago visited relatives near Greenwood, Mississippi. After buying some candy at a rural store, Till allegedly said "Bye, baby" to the white female clerk. Three days later, after midnight, her husband and brother dragged Till from his home, shot him through the head, cut off his testicles, and dumped his body in the Tallahatchie River. Till's mother insisted on an open casket at the funeral so that, in her words, "All the world can see what they did to my boy." The image of Till's mutilated body, captured by television, seared itself into the consciousness of a generation of black leaders. Despite overwhelming evidence of guilt, an all-white, all-male jury found the two white suspects innocent of kidnapping.

The battered face of Emmett Till was fresh in people's minds when, on December 1, 1955, a forty-two-year-old black seamstress named Rosa Parks boarded a city bus in Montgomery, Alabama. When asked to give up her seat to a white person as required by Alabama law, Parks refused. "I felt it was just something I had to do," Parks said. Her simple act of courage became a challenge to the edifice of racial injustice in the south. After police arrested Parks for her defiance, black leaders decided to boycott the city bus system and sought the support of black ministers, the traditional leaders of African-American communities. Twenty-six-year-old Martin Luther King, Jr., pastor of the Dexter Baptist Church, agreed to head the Montgomery Improvement Association (MIA), created to promote and support the boycott. King had grown up in Atlanta, the son of a prosperous minister of one of the largest Baptist congregations in the country. After graduating from Atlanta's Morehouse College, he had attended Crozer Seminary in Pennsylvania and earned his doctorate at Boston University. King preached a philosophy of nonviolent resistance: "We must meet the forces of hate with the power of love; we must meet physical force with soul force."

To deal with their loss of public transportation, the bus boycotters organized a massive and complicated system of car pools that involved twenty-thousand people everyday. Some preferred to walk, as far as twelve miles a day, to underline their determination and hope. One elderly woman, known as Mother Pollard, vowed to King that she would walk until it was over. "But aren't your feet tired?" he asked. "Yes," she said, "my feets is tired, but my soul is rested."

The city tried intimidation tactics to break the will of blacks. Policemen stopped car-pool drivers, writing tickets for imaginary violations of the law. In January, the White Citizens Council drew ten thousand people to the Montgomery Coliseum for what was described as the largest segregation rally of the century. The Ku Klux Klan

Montgomery Bus Boycotters   In the 1950s, the civil rights movement moved into a new, more determined phase dominated by ordinary people, such as seamstress Rosa Parks, who sparked the Montgomery bus boycott in 1955 by refusing to give up her seat on a segregated bus. For months, African-Americans in the city refused to ride public buses, instead forming car pools and even walking miles to work each day. These black workers are waiting for their ride at a car-pool pickup site. Their sacrifices reduced the profits on city buses by 65 percent and produced a Supreme Court decision that declared segregation on city buses unconstitutional. *(Dan Weiner, Courtesy Sandra Weiner.)*

(KKK) marched in full garb through black neighborhoods in an attempt to terrorize residents. Local prosecutors began mass arrests of MIA leaders, including King, under a 1921 statute prohibiting boycotts "without just cause and legal excuse."

The relentless harassment failed. In June 1956, a panel of federal judges struck down Montgomery's segregation ordinances. The state appealed to the Supreme Court, which upheld the lower court decision. The Montgomery boycott demonstrated that intimidation, which had served for so long to repress black aspirations, would no longer work. In doing so, it laid the foundation for the civil rights struggle of the 1960s. It also established Martin Luther King as a persuasive and articulate spokesman for the movement.

The Quest for National Purpose, 1957–1960

As the 1950s drew to a close, many Americans began to question their view of themselves as a prosperous, satisfied, and secure society. The Soviets' successful launch of a satellite to orbit the earth shocked the American public's confidence in Eisenhower's

New Look. A combination of other events, at home and abroad, contributed to the sense that America had lost its way. America, many believed, had to muster a stronger resolve and dare a bolder experimentation to fulfill its mission. Echoing this conviction, the young senator from Massachusetts, John F. Kennedy made the issue of national purpose the centerpiece of his 1960 campaign for president.

Atomic Anxieties

On October 4, 1957, the Soviet Union launched a 184-pound space satellite called *Sputnik,* or "Little Traveler." One month later, it launched a second satellite carrying a small dog, the first living creature to leave Earth's atmosphere. The Soviets gloated, claiming the achievement demonstrated the superiority of their "socialist society." The Soviet success in space dealt a serious blow to American national pride and created a widespread and unfounded fear of a "missile gap" between the United States and the Soviet Union. Asked by reporters what Americans would find should they ever reach the moon, Edward Teller, father of the hydrogen bomb, replied: "Russians."

Sputnik brought to the surface America's underlying anxiety about atomic power. If the USSR had rockets powerful enough to launch satellites, it could also bombard the United States with nuclear weapons. Newspaper articles, books, and government studies reminded people they were vulnerable to Soviet nuclear bombs. A generation of schoolchildren learned to "duck and cover" in classroom drills for a nuclear attack. A 1959 congressional study concluded that 28 percent of the population likely would be killed by such an attack. Many wealthy Americans responded by building private bomb shelters.

Americans also feared the byproducts of the nuclear age, in particular, the health consequences of radioactive fallout from bomb tests. The United States exploded 217 nuclear weapons over the Pacific and in Nevada between 1946 and 1962. The Russians conducted 122 tests in the 1950s, the British at least 50. By the mid-1950s, Americans were growing increasingly alarmed by radioactive substances turning up in the soil and in food. The federal government downplayed the possible health consequences, reassuring Americans that ordinary citizens received more radiation from dental x-rays than from nuclear testing fallout. At the same time, however, military scientists used unsuspecting civilians as human guinea pigs in secret experiments on the consequences of prolonged exposure to radioactive substances.

The fears of atomic energy found creative outlet in popular culture. *Mad,* a favorite humor magazine among teens, fantasized that after a nuclear war, the "Hit Parade" would include songs that lovers would sing as they "walk down moonlit lanes arm in arm in arm." Hollywood produced a series of monster and mutant movies suggesting that nuclear tests had either dislodged prehistoric monsters or created new genetically altered creatures. Though universally panned for their cinematic quality, movies such as *The Creature from the Black Lagoon, The Blob,* and *Godzilla* played to public concern about life in the nuclear age.

Public sightings of unidentified flying objects (UFOs), or "flying saucers," also manifested America's atomic anxieties. The modern era of American UFO sightings began in 1947 when a pilot reported seeing nine aircraft resembling flying saucers moving across the sky at approximately twelve hundred miles an hour. In these anxious days of the Cold War, Americans speculated that the saucers had either come from outer space or were a new Soviet weapon. Whatever the explanation, the number of UFO sightings skyrocketed during the decade. More than a thousand people reported seeing flying saucers in 1952.

Political and Economic Uncertainties

Sputnik was only the first of a series of blows to Americans' pride and stature at the end of the decade. In May 1960, the Soviets shot down an American U-2 spy plane and its pilot, Gary Powers. Washington initially called the flight a weather-data–gathering mission that had strayed off course, but when the Soviets produced Powers and his espionage equipment, Eisenhower confessed responsibility for the U-2 flight. The incident took place two weeks before a scheduled summit meeting in Paris between Eisenhower and Khrushchev. An angry Khrushchev, who paraded the captured American pilot before the world media, canceled the summit and withdrew an invitation for Eisenhower to visit Moscow.

At home, a persistent recession contributed to the sense of unease. Unemployment, which had held steady at 4 percent from 1955 to 1957, jumped to 8 percent in 1959. Since fewer people were working and paying taxes, the floundering economy produced huge budget deficits.

Potentially the greatest threat to American pride occurred 90 miles off the coast of Florida on the small island of Cuba. On January 1, 1959, a young lawyer turned revolutionary, Fidel Castro, led a successful insurrection against the American-supported dictatorship of Fulgencio Batistia. American economic interests expressed concern when Castro began breaking up large cattle ranches and sugar plantations. When the United States threatened to cut off economic aid, Castro responded by declaring his support for communism and confiscating about $1 billion in U.S. property. In February 1960, the Cuban leader signed a trade agreement with the Soviet Union. In 1961 Eisenhower severed diplomatic relations with Cuba and authorized the CIA to train Cuban expatriates for an invasion of the island.

These blows to American pride spurred a debate over national purpose. The poet Carl Sandberg expressed contempt for America's "fat-dripping prosperity." In 1958, in his best-selling book *The Affluent Society,* Harvard economist John Kenneth Galbraith complained that the consumer culture had produced a materialistic society that valued private wealth over public needs. The National Goals Commission, created by President Eisenhower to develop national objectives, supported the opinion of social critics that rampant consumerism had weakened America's moral fiber. By calling for increased government support for education and scientific research, the commission rejected Eisenhower's "dynamic conservatism" and signaled the dawn of more activist government.

Many people blamed the educational system for allowing the Soviets to pass America in the development of space-age rockets. To remedy the situation, Congress passed the National Defense Education Act (NDEA) of 1958. The legislation provided loan funds for college students and fellowships for advanced study, and it promised more resources to strengthen the instruction in mathematics, the sciences, and foreign languages at the elementary and secondary school levels. Concern about Soviet missiles pushed Congress to accept the statehood applications of Alaska and Hawaii, areas positioned to provide an early warning system for potential Soviet rocket attacks.

Kennedy and the 1960 Presidential Election

Politically, Democrats planned to capitalize on the growing unease about national purpose. They sharpened their arguments in the 1958 congressional races, when they gained thirteen Senate seats and a massive majority in the House. Indicting a failure of leadership in Washington, Democratic congressional candidates won 56 percent of votes cast—the highest figure since 1936. They planned to continue the attack to capture the White House in 1960.

The Republicans, forced by the Twenty-second Amendment—which limited a president to two terms—to seek a new leader, turned to Vice President Richard Nixon to counter the Democratic offensive. "To your hands," President Eisenhower wrote to the GOP's new standard-bearer, "I pray that I shall pass the responsibility of the office of the Presidency." At Nixon's request, Henry Cabot Lodge, ambassador to the United Nations, was drafted as his running mate.

After a tough primary campaign, the Democrats turned to the youthful and attractive Kennedy. The forty-two-year-old senator was the first Catholic to contend for the presidency since Al Smith in 1928. "Jack" Kennedy grew up in a conservative Boston Irish family. After graduating from Harvard he enlisted in the navy during World War II. When a Japanese destroyer rammed his patrol boat, *PT-109*, Kennedy spent hours swimming in shark-infested waters trying to save his crew. He returned from the war a hero, ready to fulfill the ambitions of his father, Joseph P. Kennedy, a wealthy businessman who had served under Roosevelt as ambassador to Great Britain. "It was like being drafted," Kennedy reflected. "My father wanted his eldest son in politics. 'Wanted' isn't the right word. He demanded it." The political journey began in 1946 when Kennedy won a congressional seat. He served three terms in the House before winning election to the Senate in 1954. Six years later voters reelected him to the Senate by the widest popular margin in Massachusetts history.

Kennedy attracted considerable media attention. With the help of his talented group of advisers, he carefully cultivated the image of a youthful, robust leader, hero of *PT-109* and the brilliant author of the Pulitzer Prize–winning book *Profiles in Courage* (1956). In later years, historians would discover that Kennedy had manufactured much of the image. In reality, he suffered from various illnesses, including Addison's disease, which required regular injections of cortisone. A speechwriter had written most of *Profiles In Courage,* and his father's intervention had secured him the Pulitzer Prize. Many liberals also complained that Kennedy's failure to vote with other Democrats to censure Joseph McCarthy revealed that he was long on profile and short on courage.

Whatever his shortcomings, Kennedy possessed considerable political skill and broad popular appeal. He revealed his shrewd political instincts at the 1960 Democratic convention. Realizing he needed a running mate who could provide regional balance and help diminish criticism of his religion, Kennedy asked Texas senator Lyndon Johnson to join the ticket. The move startled the convention, especially liberals who felt the selection of a conservative southerner betrayed the party's New Deal heritage. In fact, Kennedy's decision represented a brilliant political stroke that revealed both his pragmatism and his moderation.

Few substantive differences separated Kennedy and Nixon. Both candidates reflected the widespread belief that American institutions were fundamentally sound, that economic growth had alleviated the need for social conflict, and that Soviet aggression presented the greatest threat to American security. Kennedy, however, understood better than Nixon the public's desire for dynamic leadership. Throughout the campaign he struck the right tone with his calls for positive leadership, public sacrifice, and a bold effort to "get America moving again." "I run for the Presidency because I do not want it said that in the years when our generation held political power . . . America began to slip," Kennedy declared with a crisp Boston accent.

Despite Kennedy's appeal, the election remained close. Nixon skillfully played to public concern about Kennedy's inexperience, especially in foreign affairs. Most of all, many Americans were reluctant to vote for a Catholic for president. In a bold stroke Kennedy appeared on September 12 before the Protestant Ministerial Association of Houston, Texas, to emphasize that he placed his oath to the Constitution

Kennedy Works a Crowd   The young and vibrant John F. Kennedy seemed to signify a new era in America. He challenged the country to reach higher, to refuse to be satisfied with the status quo. His charismatic presence, clearly visible in this photograph of the president in South Dakota, helped turn the tide of the 1960 presidential election in his favor. In the first televised debate in American politics, Kennedy emerged as the clear winner over the less exciting Richard Nixon. *(George Tames/NYT Pictures.)*

above the dictates of his church. "I am not the Catholic candidate for President," he said; "I am the Democratic Party's candidate for President who happens also to be a Catholic." Kennedy also energized the African-American community when he intervened to help secure Martin Luther King's release from a Montgomery jail.

The turning point in the campaign came in a series of four televised debates between September 26 and October 24. Kennedy used the debates—the first ever televised face-off between presidential contenders—to demolish the Republican charge that he was inexperienced and badly informed. And he succeeded far better than his opponent in communicating the qualities of boldness, imagination, and poise. Kennedy appeared alert, aggressive, and cool. Nixon, who perspired profusely, looked nervous and uncomfortable. Radio listeners divided evenly on who had won the debate. Television viewers, the overwhelming majority, gave Kennedy a decisive edge. The performance energized Kennedy's campaign, and the debates institutionalized television's role as a major force in American politics.

The momentum from the debate carried Kennedy to victory—though just barely. Of the nearly 68,500,000 popular votes cast, Kennedy won 34,226,731 and Nixon 34,108,157. Kennedy's popular majority of two-tenths of 1 percent was the smallest since 1880. His vote in the electoral college was only slightly more convincing, 303 to 219. Kennedy's victory signaled a desire for change, but the narrowness of his triumph reflected the caution with which Americans approached the challenges of the new decade (see map).

The Election of 1960 The 1960 election was not only the closest presidential race in the twentieth century, it also had the highest voter turnout (63 percent). Yet the discontent of white southerners over the issue of civil rights was evident as all of Mississippi's delegates and some of Alabama's rejected both parties and voted for prosegregationist Senator Harry Byrd of Virginia.

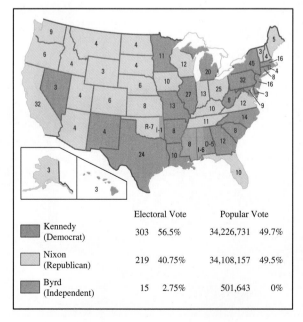

		Electoral Vote		Popular Vote	
	Kennedy (Democrat)	303	56.5%	34,226,731	49.7%
	Nixon (Republican)	219	40.75%	34,108,157	49.5%
	Byrd (Independent)	15	2.75%	501,643	0%

CONCLUSION

Although the 1950s are generally viewed as a time when Americans rejected social or political experimentation, America and its people underwent enormous change between 1950 and 1960. A consumer revolution transformed American society in the years after World War II. Driven by an unprecedented baby boom, a growing economy, and the seductive appeal of advertising, Americans rushed to fill their new suburban homes with the latest consumer products. The demand for new consumer goods rippled through society, altering the way Americans earned a living, conducted business, and spent their leisure time.

The pervasive influence of the consumer society also altered America's cultural landscape. Television, the most effective purveyor of mass culture during the decade, projected shared images into millions of living rooms across the country. At the same time, the boom in automobile sales and the construction of new highways broke down geographical barriers. The rise of rock and roll and the religious revivalism of the decade were further proof of the power of mass culture. While some commentators charged that mass culture eroded traditional values and stifled individualism, most intellectuals reinforced the consumer culture's upbeat message.

President Dwight Eisenhower emerged as the most convincing political symbol of the consumer society. Making effective use of television, Eisenhower convinced most voters that he was a strong but amicable leader, the embodiment of traditional American values. A political moderate, Ike struggled to tame liberals who called for a more activist government and to appease conservatives who hoped to dismantle the welfare state. In the end, the president consolidated and strengthened New Deal programs but refused to support new federal initiatives. The public rewarded his effort in 1956, returning him to office in a landslide.

In foreign policy, some rhetorical flourishes called for brinkmanship and liberation, and defense's New Look emphasized nuclear superiority, mutual assistance treaties, and covert intervention. But Eisenhower essentially continued his predecessor's containment policy. Like most Americans, the president believed the United States had a mission to make the world safe for democracy, and that international communism, spearheaded by the Soviet Union and China, represented the greatest threat to American security. But Eisenhower, the experienced soldier and diplomat, also understood that American idealism had to be tempered by political and military realities. He refused to intervene when Russian troops invaded Hungary in 1956 and attempted to lessen Cold War tensions by making peace overtures to the Soviets. The president's moderation did not extend to the Third World, where he unleashed the CIA to topple unfriendly governments and intervened in Indochina.

By portraying America as a prosperous and content society that had solved most of its pressing social and economic problems, the mass media blurred the line between American ideals and social realities. The pervasive image of prosperous white men and content suburban housewives disregarded that nearly 25 percent of the population lived below the poverty line; that sexual discrimination limited opportunities for women; and that African-Americans were denied the most basic political and civil rights.

The decade's placid public mood changed dramatically in October 1957 following the Soviets' successful launch of the space satellite *Sputnik*. Complacency yielded to anxiety as Americans fretted about the possibility of nuclear attack. A string of bad news—Soviet capture of an American spy, a communist revolution in Cuba, and a steep recession—led many Americans to believe that the nation had lost its sense of purpose. In the 1960 presidential campaign, Massachusetts senator John F. Kennedy tapped into the public mood with his calls to "get the nation moving again," and scored a narrow victory over his Republican rival, Vice President Richard Nixon. But the close election suggested that Americans were very cautious about any experimentation that might alter the status quo.

SUGGESTED READINGS

John Diggins's *The Proud Decades* (1988) is a good one-volume survey of America in the 1950s. William E. Leuchtenberg's *A Troubled Feast* (rev. ed., 1983) highlights the contradictions and anxieties of American society during the period, while James T. Patterson focuses on the role of prosperity and the baby boom in transforming postwar ambition in *Grand Expectations* (1996). David Halberstam's *The Fifties* (1993) traces the major events and anxieties of the decade. Gary W. Reichard's *Politics As Usual* (1988) surveys politics at midcentury. The transformation of America's self-image is the focus of Tom Englehardt's *The End of Victory Culture* (1995).

Richard Easterlin's *Birth and Future* (1980) provides a longitudinal study of the baby boomers and their impact on America. Landon Y. Jones tracks the largest generation through adolescence and early adulthood in *Great Expectations* (1980). Jane S. Smith recounts the development of the polio vaccine in *Patenting the Sun* (1990).

David P. Calleo's *The Imperious Economy* (1982) surveys the economic changes of the 1950s. John Kenneth Galbraith explores the postwar consumer culture in *The Affluent Society* (1958) and *The New Industrial State* (1971). Martin Campbell-Kelly and William Aspray study the rise of computers and automation in *Computer* (1996). Alfred D. Chandler chronicles the rise of the modern corporation in *The Visible Hand* (1977).

Kenneth T. Jackson's *Crabgrass Frontier* (1985) is a valuable survey of American suburbia. Dolores Hayden's *Redesigning the American Dream* (1984) discusses the social engineering behind the suburbs. Herbert Gans's *The Levittowners* (1967) is a nuanced study that focuses on the diversity of suburban communities. Tom Lewis's *Divided Highways* (1997) examines how the United States became an auto-oriented nation and describes the political support for highway projects.

Erik Barnouw's *Tube of Plenty* (1982) tracks the rise of television, with emphasis on its impact on American culture and politics. Lynn Spigel's *Make Room for TV* (1992) considers the transformation wrought by television on family life, as does Karal A. Marling's *As Seen on TV* (1994). Biographies of influential religious leaders include Carol George's *God's Salesman* (1994) about Norman Vincent Peale and William Martin's *A Prophet with Honor* (1991), which examines the ministry of Billy Graham. The history of rock and roll is examined in James Miller's *Flowers in the Dustbin* (1999), and the role of teens in the Cold War era is examined by Grace Palladino in *Teenagers* (1996).

Stephen E. Ambrose's *Eisenhower* (2 vols., 1983, 1984) is a comprehensive scholarly biography of the president, as is Chester Pach, Jr., and Elmo Richardson's *The Presidency of Dwight D. Eisenhower* (rev. ed., 1991). Fred I. Greenstein's *The Hidden-Hand Presidency* (1982) has interesting material on Eisenhower's campaigns against Adlai Stevenson. In *Reevaluating Eisenhower* (1986), Richard Melanson and David Mayers, eds., explore Eisenhower's relationship with New Deal programs. Nicol Rae's *The Decline and Fall of the Liberal*

Republicans (1989) chronicles the struggle between conservatives and moderates in the Republican Party.

In *Eisenhower and the Cold War* (1981), Robert Divine provides an excellent survey of U.S.–Soviet relations in the 1950s. Burton Kaufman's *The Arab Middle East and the United States* (1996) serves as an introduction to the American role in Middle East affairs. Stephen E. Ambrose's *Ike's Spies* (1981) details the rise of the American intelligence establishment, and the impact of a daring few in the CIA's early years is examined in Evan Thomas's *The Very Best Men* (1995). Richard Immerman provides a valuable case study of the CIA's actions in *The CIA in Guatemala* (1982). Andrew Rotter focuses on America's early Indochina policy in *The Path to Vietnam* (1987), as does David L. Anderson in *Trapped by Success* (1991).

Michael Harrington's *The Other America* (1962) is still a classic exposé of the 1950s have-nots. Thomas Sugrue's *The Origins of the Urban Crisis* (1996) focuses on how blacks were denied houses in the suburbs and confined to inner-city Detroit. Nicholas Lemann covers the postwar black migration in *The Promised Land* (1991). James T. Patterson's *America's Struggle Against Poverty* (1981) is a broad survey of the American underclass, as is Jacqueline Jones's tracing of interracial poverty in *The Dispossessed* (1992). Rodolfo Acuna's *Occupied America* (1988) has useful material on Hispanic poverty in the 1950s.

Glenna Matthews's *Just a Housewife* (1987) explores the world of 1950s homemakers, while Wini Brienes, in *Young, White, and Miserable* (1992), analyzes the conflicting sentiments of their daughters. Susan Strasser's *Never Done* (1982) paints a bleak picture of the demands placed on housewives. Betty Friedan's *The Feminine Mystique* (1963) is a critique of the affluent housewife, while the essays in Joanne Meyerwitz's *Not June Cleaver* (1994) examine women who did not fit the domestic stereotype. Elaine Tyler May's *Homeward Bound* (1988) is a valuable study of the American family during the Cold War. The unrealistic image of the ideal family is the theme of Stephanie Coontz's *The Way We Never Were* (1992).

Aldon D. Morris's *The Origins of the Civil Rights Movement* (1984) details the black community's organizing that presaged the upheaval of the 1960s. Mark Tushnet's *Making Civil Rights Law* (1994) examines the goals and legal work done by the NAACP. David Garrow provides a moving biography of Martin Luther King, Jr., in *Bearing the Cross* (1986). The death of Emmett Till and the subsequent trial and protest are the focus of Stephen Whitfield's *A Death in the Delta* (1991). Robert F. Burk evaluates Eisenhower's performance on race issues in *The Eisenhower Administration and Black Civil Rights* (1984).

Diane Ravitch describes the "crisis" in American education in *The Troubled Crusade* (1983). Robert Divine's *The Sputnik Challenge* (1993) examines Eisenhower's inability to suppress the American belief in a missile gap. Howard Ball's *Justice Downwind* (1986) studies the nuclear testing programs. Peter Wyden's *Bay of Pigs* (1980) details the American reaction to the Cuban Revolution, while Thomas Paterson's *Contesting Castro* (1994) examines U.S.–Cuba relations during Castro's uprising and successful revolution.

Competing Voices
The Politics of Race

Brown v. Board of Education, 1954

On May 17, 1954, Chief Justice Earl Warren read the Supreme Court's unanimous ruling in the case of *Brown* v. *Board of Education of Topeka*. The decision overturned the "separate-but-equal" doctrine established by the Court in 1896 in *Plessy* v. *Ferguson* (see page 644), which had provided the legal underpinning of the southern system of segregation.

... The plaintiffs contend that segregated public schools are not "equal" and cannot be made "equal," and that hence they are deprived of the equal protection of the laws. ...

In approaching this problem, we cannot turn the clock back to 1868 when the Amendment was adopted, or even to 1896 when *Plessy* was written. We must consider public education in light of its full development and its present place in American life throughout the Nation. Only in this way can it be determined if segregation in public schools deprives these plaintiffs of the equal protection of the laws. Today, education is perhaps the most important function of state and local governments. Compulsory school attendance laws and the great expenditures for education both demonstrate our recognition of the importance of education to our democratic society. ... In these days, it is doubtful that any child may reasonably be expected to succeed in life if he is denied the opportunity of an education. Such an opportunity, where the state has undertaken to provide it, is a right which must be made available to all on equal terms.

We come then to the question presented: Does segregation of children in public schools solely on the basis of race, even though the physical facilities and other "tangible" factors may be equal, deprive the children of the minority group of equal educational opportunities? We believe that it does. ...

To separate [children] from others of similar age and qualifications solely because of their race generates a feeling of inferiority as to their status in the community that may affect their hearts and minds in a way unlikely ever to be undone. The effect of this separation on their educational opportunities was well stated by a finding in the Kansas case by a court which nevertheless felt compelled to rule against the Negro plaintiffs: "Segregation of white and colored children in public schools has a detrimental effect upon the colored children. The impact is greater when it has the sanction of the law; for the policy of separating the races is usually interpreted as denoting the inferiority of the Negro group. ... Segregation with the sanction of law, therefore, has a tendency to retard the educational and mental development of Negro children and to deprive them of some of the benefits they would receive in a [racially] integrated school system." Whatever may have been the extent of psychological knowledge at the time of *Plessy* v. *Ferguson*, this finding is amply supported by modern authority. ...

We conclude that in the field of public education the doctrine of "separate but equal" has no place. Separate educational facilities are inherently unequal. ...

The Southern Manifesto, 1956

Angered by the *Brown* decision, many southern whites engaged in a campaign of massive resistance. Their defiance hardened after the Supreme Court ruled that local officials must move with "all deliberate speed" to implement desegregation. Prominent elected officials, such as Senator Harry Byrd of Virginia, helped orchestrate the resistance. Unable to secure the necessary votes for a congressional resolution denouncing *Brown,* Byrd issued the "Southern Manifesto" in March 1956. Signed by nineteen senators and eighty-two congressmen, the Manifesto sent a clear message of defiance to the rest of the nation.

We regard the decision of the Supreme Court in the school cases as clear abuse of judicial power. It climaxes a trend in the Federal judiciary undertaking to legislate, in derogation of the authority of Congress, and to encroach upon the reserved rights of the states and the people.

The original Constitution does not mention education. Neither does the Fourteenth Amendment nor any other amendment. The debates preceding the submission of the Fourteenth Amendment clearly show that there was no intent that it should affect the systems of education maintained by the states. . . .

When the amendment was adopted in 1868, there were thirty-seven states of the Union. Every one of the twenty-six states that had any substantial racial differences among its people either approved the operation of segregated schools already in existence or subsequently established such schools by action of the same law-making body which considered the Fourteenth Amendment. . . .

This unwarranted exercise of power by the court, contrary to the Constitution, is creating chaos and confusion in the states principally affected. It is destroying the amicable relations between the white and negro races that have been created through ninety years of patient effort by the good people of both races. It has planted hatred and suspicion where there has been heretofore friendship and understanding. . . .

With the gravest concern for the explosive and dangerous condition created by this decision and inflamed outside meddlers:

We reaffirm our reliance on the Constitution as the fundamental law of the land.

We decry the Supreme Court's encroachments on rights reserved to the states and to the people, contrary to established law and to the Constitution.

We commend the motives of those states which have declared the intention to resist forced integration by any lawful means.

We appeal to the states and people who are not directly affected by these decisions to consider the constitutional principles involved against the time when they too, on issues vital to them, may be the victims of judicial encroachments.

In 1951 the Reverend Oliver Brown tried to enroll his eight-year-old daughter, Linda, in an all-white elementary school in Topeka. School officials refused to admit her, citing a law in force in Kansas and sixteen other states requiring black children to attend segregated educational facilities. Instead of walking the four blocks to her neighborhood school, Linda had to board a bus every morning for the five-mile journey to an all-black school across town. With the help of a small team of skilled black lawyers from Howard University and the NAACP, led by Thurgood Marshall, the Reverend Brown took the case to court.

The suit claimed that refusal to admit Linda Brown violated the equal protection clause of the Fourteenth Amendment, according to which, "No State . . . shall deprive any person of life, liberty, or property, without due process of law; nor deny to any person within its jurisdiction the equal protection of the laws." The case quietly worked its way up the appeal system and reached the Supreme Court in 1954.

The Supreme Court's unanimous decision in the *Brown* case represented a historic affirmation of the egalitarian ideals of American society. These ideals found expression in the preamble of the Declaration of Independence, which proclaims that "all men are created equal." America's commitment to equality has often been tested, but never more so than on issues of race. The nation's founders sanctioned slavery in the Constitution. The Civil War brought about the abolition of slavery. But for most of the next one hundred years, hopes for true equality in race relations were frustrated by deeply imbedded racial attitudes, government indifference, and a pervasive system of racial segregation. In 1954 the Warren Court stepped into the moral void and resurrected the American ideal of equality in race relations.

Opponents of the *Brown* ruling were not without their own ideological resources. They could tap into a competing strain of American political thought that stressed individual liberty and fear of centralized government. The nation's founders believed that government power was antithetical to individual liberty, and the Constitution limited federal power by delegating broad authority to the individual states. The belief in liberty and states' rights found full expression in the Southern Manifesto.

The *Brown* decision struck a fatal blow to the system of public segregation in the South. It added legitimacy to the civil rights movement and quickened the pace of change. But it left many issues unresolved. Would abolishing legal segregation alone be enough to guarantee blacks equal opportunity? The *Brown* case dealt with schools that legally mandated segregation between the races. What about schools that were segregated because they were in all-black or all-white neighborhoods? Should the Court also force them to integrate? These questions would continue to perplex Americans as they struggled to find common ground between the competing values of liberty and equality.

Questions for Analysis

1. Why does the Court argue that segregated schools are "inherently unequal"?

2. Why is education regarded as fundamental to democratic society?

3. The *Chicago Defender*, a black newspaper, called *Brown* a "second emancipation proclamation." Is this assessment justified?

4. On what grounds does the Manifesto reject *Brown*?

5. Did the Court accept the NAACP's position, or did it find other reasons for overturning the doctrine of "separate but equal"?

6. How and why does the Manifesto's interpretation of the Fourteenth Amendment differ from the Supreme Court's?

7. What assumptions shape the Manifesto's view of race relations in the South? Does it recognize that a problem existed?

29

Consensus and Confrontation, 1960–1968

*I*n November 1963, President John F. Kennedy began laying the foundation for his 1964 reelection campaign by visiting the key state of Texas. Shortly after noon on the twenty-second, his entourage arrived at Dallas's Love Field airport. Kennedy, handsomely attired in a gray suit and pinstriped shirt, exited the plane with his wife, Jacqueline, who wore a strawberry-pink wool outfit and matching pill-box hat and cradled a bouquet of red roses. After shaking a few hands, the president, the First Lady, and Texas governor John Connally and his wife, Nellie, slid into the back of their open-top Lincoln limousine. Since it was a bright autumn day, Kennedy chose not to use the bulletproof bubble top.

Dense friendly crowds greeted the president's motorcade—eighteen cars and three buses. When the cars turned westward onto Main Street, people were everywhere, waving from office buildings, filling the streets, cheering. As they rolled slowly through the crowds, Mrs. Connally said, "Mr. President, you can't say Dallas doesn't love you." Kennedy answered, "That's obvious." The time was 12:30 P.M.

Suddenly the sound of gunfire ripped through the air. "Oh no!" Mrs. Kennedy cried. The president clutched his neck with both hands and slumped down in his seat. One bullet had passed through his throat; another had shattered his skull. Governor Connally had also been hit, seriously but not mortally. The driver pulled the limousine out of the motorcade line and sped to Parkland Hospital's emergency entrance, arriving at 12:36 P.M. A Secret Service agent lifted Kennedy from his wife's arms, placed him on a stretcher, and rushed him into Trauma Room 1. Doctors were shocked by the extent of his wounds. "I looked at the President's head," recalled one physician. "A considerable portion of the skull, of the brain, was gone." As a grieving Mrs. Kennedy looked on, doctors worked feverishly to revive her husband. Their efforts were in vain. The president was pronounced dead at 1 P.M.

On the presidential plane carrying the slain president's body back to Washington, Judge Sarah T. Hughes of the Northern District of Texas administered the oath of office to Lyndon Johnson. A stunned and blood-soaked Mrs. Kennedy stood to the left of the new president. Within hours of the assassination, Dallas police arrested Lee Harvey Oswald and charged him with assassinating the president. Two days later, Jack Ruby, a Dallas nightclub owner, shot and killed Oswald as police were transferring him to another prison.

The trauma, played over seventy-five straight hours on television, burned into the national consciousness. On Monday, November 25, more than 100 million people watched as a horse-drawn caisson, the same that had brought home Abraham Lincoln's body in 1865, carried Kennedy's remains from the White House to the Capitol. Television viewing reached the highest level ever recorded up to that time—93 percent of homes with a television were tuned in.

For a generation of Americans, Kennedy's assassination served as a symbolic marker separating the confident consensus that marked the 1950s from the period of social conflict and radical experimentation that followed. The president's death was only one of a series of shocks that challenged the illusion of consensus. Domestic turmoil exposed profound race and class divisions in America and the persistence of conflict over America's purpose and image. The bitter debates over the Vietnam War raised anew differences about America's role in the world.

Kennedy's death also helped inspire the nation to accept the most ambitious liberal experiment since the New Deal of the 1930s. After winning a landslide election in 1964, Johnson pushed through Congress legislation broadening the federal government's social role. Ironically, at the same time that events were eroding the foundation of consensus, Johnson was constructing a reform agenda based on its assumptions.

■ How did the liberal initiatives of Kennedy and Johnson underscore America's ambivalence toward larger government?

■ How did the American people attempt to reconcile the conflict between their support for individual rights and their devotion to equal opportunity?

■ What does the youth revolt suggest about social divisions in America?

■ What impact did the Vietnam War have on American attitudes toward world affairs?

■ Why did the liberal consensus prove illusory?

This chapter will address these questions.

Chronology

1960	JFK elected president
	Sit-ins begin
	SNCC and SDS founded
1961	Bay of Pigs invasion
	Berlin Wall constructed
	CORE Freedom Rides begin
1962	Cuban missile crisis
	Meredith enrolls in University of Mississippi
	The Port Huron Statement released
1963	Kennedy assassinated; Johnson becomes president
	Wallace stands in schoolhouse door
	March on Washington
1964	LBJ declares war on poverty
	LBJ elected president
	Civil Rights Act
	Freedom Summer in Mississippi
	Gulf of Tonkin Resolution passed
	Berkeley Free Speech Movement
1965	Medicare and Medicaid passed
	Voting Rights Act
	Watts riot
	Malcolm X assassinated
	Johnson commits American ground forces in Vietnam
1966	Carmichael coins phrase "Black Power"
1968	Tet Offensive
	LBJ drops out of presidential race
	King and Kennedy assassinated
	Democratic national convention erupts in violence
	Nixon elected president

The Kennedy Presidency, 1960–1963

Kennedy won election in 1960 by promising to "get the nation moving again." The new president's youthful style and soaring rhetoric inspired the nation, although his actions, especially on the home front, seemed timid by comparison. Reluctant to alienate conservatives, Kennedy chose to put off major experiments in government social reform. Abroad, Kennedy's get-tough policies produced some of the tensest moments of the Cold War as he asserted America's role as the world's guardian against communist aggression.

JFK and the "New Frontier"

At the age of forty-three, John F. Kennedy was the youngest man ever elected president and the first American president born in the twentieth century. Kennedy's inaugural address, delivered on a cloudless and cold January day in 1961, captivated the nation's imagination and captured the hope and expectations of the decade. Calling for "a struggle against the common enemies of man: tyranny, poverty, disease, and war," he promised a "New Frontier" of opportunity and challenge.

Kennedy's youth and charm suited him to the new medium of television. "Memories of the Kennedy days are memories of television," recalled a prominent television producer. With the help of a media-conscious staff, the administration

The King and Queen of Camelot   The Kennedys captivated the American people with their youth, style, and elegance. The First Lady in particular drew admiration; she served as the gracious hostess for lavish White House balls, wore beautiful designer gowns, worked tirelessly to restore the White House's interior, and of course took care of her young children, themselves favorites of Americans. The fresh breath the Kennedys brought to the presidency earned the administration the nickname "Camelot," after the mythic reign of King Arthur. Here they leave a performance at Ford's Theater looking every bit American royalty.   *(National Archives.)*

produced a constant flow of endearing Kennedy images. His sophisticated and glamorous wife, Jacqueline, and two handsome children, Caroline and John, added to the Kennedy mystique.

Kennedy surrounded himself with bright young men who shared his faith in activist government. Foreign relations counselor McGeorge Bundy, a former Harvard dean, and Dean Rusk, a Rhodes scholar and former diplomat, typified "the best and the brightest." Critics complained that the president's choice for attorney general—his younger brother Robert—lacked legal experience, but Kennedy trusted his shrewd political instincts, clear judgment, and firm support.

The "action intellectuals" who filled the White House shared the widely held belief that America had entered an age of consensus. Building on the ideas developed by liberal intellectuals during the 1950s, they argued that economic growth, when combined with prudent government social programs, would provide every American with a minimum standard of living and boundless opportunity for success. Prosperity offered the added benefit of rendering ideological conflict and social struggle obsolete. "Politics," Kennedy said in 1962, was to avoid "basic clashes of philosophy and ideology" and be directed to "ways and means of achieving goals." Proponents of consensus believed that international communism presented the greatest threat to American institutions and values. "The enemy," Kennedy declared with typical flourish, "is the Communist system itself—implacable, insatiable, increasing in its drive for world domination." Convinced that Eisenhower had failed to fight the Cold War with sufficient vigor, Kennedy moved to sharpen ideological differences and to increase military pressure on the Soviet Union.

Acting on the assumptions of the consensus, the new president focused much of his energy at home on revitalizing a stagnant economy. During the last two years of the Eisenhower administration, economic growth had slowed to about 2 percent and unemployment had started creeping upward. At Kennedy's request, Congress extended unemployment benefits, raised the minimum wage, broadened social security benefits, increased the defense budget by almost 20 percent, and approved over $4 billion in long-term spending on federally financed housing. It also approved the Area Redevelopment Act, which provided federal aid for poor regions, and the Manpower Retraining Bill, which appropriated $435 million for training workers. Kennedy prodded Congress to double the budget of the National Aeronautics and Space Administration (NASA) and approved a plan to put an American on the moon by 1970. Finally, Congress passed the Revenue Act of 1962, which granted $1 billion in tax breaks to business.

While using government spending to increase economic growth, Kennedy moved to keep the lid on price increases and control inflation by enlisting the aid of business leaders. When Roger Blough, the head of U.S. Steel, announced that he was raising prices $6 a ton in violation of a previous agreement with the White House, Kennedy complained about the "unjustifiable and irresponsible defiance of the public interest" by a "tiny handful of steel executives." After a well-orchestrated White House campaign, Blough retreated.

By 1963, a brief economic downturn convinced Kennedy that he needed to take bolder action. In January, the president proposed a tax reduction of $13.5 billion that he hoped would stimulate consumer spending, create new jobs, and generate economic growth. His support of a tax cut revealed Kennedy's willingness to experiment with unconventional ideas. Many liberals, who wanted higher government spending, not more tax cuts, opposed the plan. Conservatives blustered at the idea of intentionally running a budget deficit. Ignoring criticisms from left and right, Kennedy submitted his proposal to Congress.

Kennedy faced many obstacles in his effort to fulfill his campaign promise to "get the country moving again." His narrow victory denied him a clear mandate. He presided over a divided party. Democrats controlled Congress, but conservative southern Democrats who were unsympathetic to Kennedy's liberal proposals controlled key congressional committees. Congress enacted only seven of twenty-three bills that the president submitted in his early months in office, Among the bills defeated was an ambitious health care plan for the elderly and a proposal for federal aid to education.

New Frontiers Abroad

Frustrated by a stubborn Congress at home, Kennedy was freer to express his activist instincts in foreign affairs. The president believed that instability in the Third World presented the greatest danger to American security in the 1960s. He took seriously Khrushchev's warning that the Soviets would continue support for "wars of national liberation" in Asia, Africa, and Latin America. The president, and the men who surrounded him, believed that Eisenhower's approach of threatening massive retaliation prevented the United States from responding to communist insurgents trying to topple pro-American governments.

The administration called its new defense strategy "flexible response" because it expanded the options for fighting the communist threat. The new strategy had three components. First, it called for a dramatic increase in America's strategic and tactical nuclear capability. In 1961 Kennedy increased the defense budget by 15 percent. By 1963, the United States had 275 major bases in 31 nations; 65 countries hosted U.S. forces; and the American military trained soldiers in 72 countries. In 1961 the United States had 63 Intercontinental Ballistic Missiles (ICBMs); by 1963, 424. During the period 1961–1963, NATO's nuclear firepower increased 60 percent.

Second, it increased economic assistance in troubled parts of the Third World. The administration established the Agency for International Development (AID) to coordinate its foreign aid program. In 1962 the president created the Alliance for Progress, which called for a massive developmental program in Latin America. The most successful venture was the Peace Corps. Established by executive order in 1961, this volunteer group of mostly young Americans numbered 5,000 by early 1963 and 10,000 a year later. The volunteers went into developing nations as teachers, agricultural advisers, and technicians.

Finally, to deter aggression, the Pentagon and the CIA increased the training of paramilitary forces. The Pentagon established the Jungle Warfare School, which taught Latin American police squads how to infiltrate leftist groups. Kennedy personally elevated the status of the American Special Forces units, or "Green Berets," who were trained to fight unconventional wars.

Escalating Tensions: Cuba and Berlin

Kennedy's instinctive activism and strong anticommunism led him into the first blunder of his presidency. As president-elect, Kennedy learned of a secret plan, approved by Eisenhower in the spring of 1960, for the invasion of Cuba by anti-Castro refugees. A few aides expressed doubts about the plan, but the CIA and most military advisers assured Kennedy it was sound. Having criticized the Eisenhower administration for being soft on communism, Kennedy decided to support the plan.

The invasion on April 17, 1961, was a disaster. Castro's well-trained army anticipated the attack and lay wait for the sixteen hundred American-trained Cuban exiles who landed at *Bahia de Cochinos* (Bay of Pigs). After three days of intense fighting, the invaders surrendered.

"How could I have been so stupid to let them go ahead?" Kennedy asked. In retrospect, the invasion's poor planning became obvious. American officials had hoped that as news of the rebel landing swept across the island, the Cuban people would rise up in rebellion. Instead, the invasion aroused Cuban nationalist sentiment, strengthened Castro's control over the nation, and pushed him closer to the Soviet Union. The United States suffered widespread international condemnation and humiliating loss of prestige in Latin America.

The public rallied behind the president, but Kennedy remained deeply shaken by the Bay of Pigs fiasco. Hoping to prove himself a leader on the world stage, the president agreed to a summit meeting in Vienna with Soviet premier Khrushchev in June 1961. The meeting did little to boost Kennedy's spirits. Khrushchev was especially militant about Berlin (see pages 1057 and 1064), a divided city deep in Soviet controlled East Germany. The Soviet position in Germany had deteriorated in recent years. Thousands of skilled workers were pouring out of East Germany seeking refuge and jobs in the more prosperous West. Khrushchev was determined to stop the exodus. Yet Kennedy was just as committed to maintaining the autonomy of West Berlin. The American public seemed to support taking a hard line. A poll showed 57 percent of Americans believed Berlin "worth risking total war."

Khrushchev continued to heighten the tension over access to Berlin, and by July a war of words and nerves had developed. Kennedy decided to make Berlin, in the words of a speechwriter, "a question of direct Soviet–American confrontation over a shift in the balance of power." On July 25, Kennedy announced that he was increasing draft calls, extending enlistments, and mobilizing some National Guard units.

Before dawn on August 13, 1961, the Soviets responded by starting construction of a wall separating East and West Berlin. American and Soviet tanks stared at each other across the rising barricade. A false move or miscalculation could lead to fighting, perhaps escalating to a nuclear confrontation. The troops managed to avoid an incident, and Khrushchev backed down from his threat to block American supply routes. Tensions between the superpowers eased—but only temporarily.

The Cuban Missile Crisis

On October 14, 1962, an American U-2 spy plane discovered offensive nuclear missile sites in Cuba. Khrushchev "can't do that to me!" Kennedy declared. Two days later, Kennedy met with his top advisers to consider how to respond to this audacious strategic move. The military warned that the missiles would soon be operational and able to strike cities up and down the East Coast of the United States.

Kennedy initially supported an air strike to destroy the missile sites, but an air strike alone could not destroy all the targets. Attorney General Robert Kennedy, who played an important role in the discussions, warned that the Soviet response to a military action "could be so severe as to lead to general nuclear war." He also worried that it would diminish America's moral position in the world.

On October 22, Kennedy decided on a more moderate course of action: he would impose a naval quarantine of the island. A blockade would provide more time for each side to contemplate the costs of its actions and possibly provide the Russians with a graceful way to back out of the crisis. Later that evening, Kennedy delivered a nationwide television address to the American people. Declaring the Russian tactic in Cuba "deliberate, provocative, and unjustified," he insisted the United States must respond "if our courage and our commitments are ever again to be trusted by either friend or foe." Announcing establishment of a "strict quarantine of all offensive military equipment under shipment to Cuba," Kennedy asserted that the United States would demand "prompt dismantling and withdrawal" of all offensive missiles.

The nation, and the world, teetered on the edge of nuclear war. Tension mounted when Khrushchev denounced the blockade as "outright banditry" and accused Kennedy of driving the world to nuclear war. The crisis intensified as a dozen Soviet ships headed toward a possible confrontation with the U.S. Navy off the coast of Cuba. Raising the stakes, Kennedy ordered B-52 aircraft carrying nuclear weapons to stand ready and moved troops south to prepare for a possible invasion. Then he and his advisers waited for the Soviets' response.

Khrushchev believed Kennedy lacked the backbone to force a nuclear confrontation, but as the cargo ships pushed toward the American navy, his intelligence told him the Americans were holding firm. On October 28, Khrushchev retreated, ordering the Soviet ships to turn around. Secretary of State Rusk remarked, "We're eyeball to eyeball and I think the other fellow just blinked." Over the next few days the two superpowers hammered out an agreement to end the confrontation. The United States promised not to invade Cuba if the missiles were quickly withdrawn and if a number of Russian medium-range bombers were returned from Cuba to the USSR. Privately, Kennedy also agreed that American missiles in Turkey would be removed.

In the short run, the missile crisis set the stage for a gradual improvement in U.S.–Soviet relations. Both nations, traumatized by their close brush with nuclear war, appeared ready to lessen tensions. Taking the initiative in a speech at American University in June 1963, Kennedy called for a reexamination of American attitudes toward the Soviet Union and the Cold War. He proposed a joint Soviet–American expedition to the moon and approved the sale of $250 million worth of surplus wheat to Russia. The White House and the Kremlin agreed to install a "hot line" to establish direct communications between the leaders of the world's two superpowers. Perhaps the most tangible evidence of the new thaw in relations was the nuclear test ban treaty. The treaty, initialed on July 25, banned atmospheric and underwater nuclear testing.

JFK and Vietnam

Kennedy had less success in dealing with a deteriorating situation in Vietnam. Between 1955 and 1961, the United States had provided over $1 billion in aid to South Vietnam and sent more than fifteen hundred advisers to provide economic and military assistance. The American effort, however, focused on transforming Ngo Dinh Diem's government into an effective anticommunist fighting force, not on helping him to establish a firm base of public support.

Diem had inherited from the French a crippled economy, a poorly trained army, and a corrupt and incompetent government bureaucracy. Ho Chi Minh, the nationalist leader of the communist forces in North Vietnam, added to Diem's problems by creating the communist National Liberation Front (NLF), called Vietcong, in the South to fight a guerrilla war against the Diem government. Diem's aloof personality and authoritarian style contributed to his failure to win his people's support. Indifferent to the concerns of peasants living in the countryside, he ruthlessly suppressed dissenters, including powerful Buddhist groups.

Kennedy had once described Vietnam as the "cornerstone of the free world in Southeast Asia." During the 1950s he publicly supported the Eisenhower administration's decision to maintain a noncommunist South by funneling aid to the Diem government. Yet Kennedy also harbored doubts about whether Diem could unite the country, and he questioned the wisdom of using American ground forces in the jungles of Southeast Asia.

His advisers offered conflicting advice. In 1961 the Chairman of the Joint Chiefs of Staff, General Lyman L. Lemnitzer, urged Kennedy to "grind up the Vietcong with 40,000 American ground troops . . . grab 'em by the balls and their hearts and minds will follow." Undersecretary of State for Economic Affairs George Ball counseled caution, claiming that Vietnam was not a vital American interest. Caught in the middle, Kennedy initially tried taking a hard line with Diem, insisting that American aid was contingent on his willingness to reform his corrupt government and seek accommodation with dissident groups in South Vietnam. When Diem ignored the pressure, the administration backed down. Over the next three years, Kennedy increased both economic aid and the number of American military advisers.

The infusion of American support did little to stabilize the Diem regime. The North Vietnamese–supplied Vietcong established control over large portions of the countryside. At the same time, American officials watched helplessly as Diem gradually lost control. The situation reached a boiling point in the summer of 1963 when Diem ordered his troops to fire on Buddhist leaders holding banned religious celebrations. Anti-Diem forces immediately rallied to the Buddhists, and civil war threatened within the principal cities. Several Buddhists responded by publicly burning themselves to death, an act that Diem's government ridiculed as a "barbecue show." The deaths, flashed on the evening news in the United States, dramatized the growing opposition, and forced Kennedy's hand.

Confronted by the possibility of a massive revolt against the Diem government, Kennedy reconsidered his support of the beleaguered ally. When South Vietnamese generals approached Washington with plans for a coup, Kennedy reluctantly

Buddhist Monks Protest the Diem Government   From the beginning of American involvement in Vietnam, the United States found itself aiding less-than-democratic regimes in the South in order to thwart communism in the North. President Ngo Dinh Diem ruled autocratically, abolishing local elections, curbing the press, and harassing his enemies. By 1963, his actions literally drew fire from devout Buddhist priests, who set themselves ablaze to protest his administration. Photographs such as this one horrified the American public, who questioned why the United States supported a government that provoked this kind of defiance. President Kennedy, also disturbed, gave his tacit approval to a military coup that overthrew the hated government and assassinated the deposed Diem.   *(Wide World Photos, Inc.)*

agreed. On November 1, 1963, the generals seized key military and communications installations and demanded Diem's resignation. Later that day, Diem was captured and, despite American assurances of safe passage, murdered.

During Kennedy's years in office, the United States spent nearly $1 billion in South Vietnam, increased the number of American military advisers to more than sixteen thousand, and witnessed the deaths of 108 U.S. soldiers. But the Vietcong were stronger than ever. Two weeks after the coup, Kennedy ordered a "complete and very profound review of how we got into this country, what we thought we were doing, and what we now think we can do." Kennedy would never see the report.

 ## The New Liberal Experiment, 1963–1966

Lyndon Johnson's vision of a "Great Society" was an experiment built on a foundation of shared assumptions. The president, and many of his advisers, believed that a rising tide of prosperity would ease the inherent tensions in American life—between equality and individualism, local control and national power—by forging a national consensus in favor of economic growth, anticommunism, and activist government. Johnson used his masterful political skills to push through a long list of legislation designed to achieve his goals.

Lyndon Johnson and the War on Poverty

Within months of Kennedy's assassination, polls showed a majority of Americans questioning whether Lee Harvey Oswald had acted alone. To quell the doubts, President Johnson appointed Chief Justice Earl Warren to chair an investigative commission of seven prominent public figures. On September 24, 1964, the President's Commission on the Assassination of President Kennedy, popularly known as the Warren Commission, reported that there was no conspiracy, foreign or domestic: Lee Harvey Oswald had acted alone.

The Warren Commission's findings failed to convince skeptics. A *Newsweek* poll taken in 1983, on the twentieth anniversary of the assassination, showed that 74 percent of Americans believed that "others were involved." Critics charged that the Warren Commission ignored evidence and witnesses suggesting another shooter and implicating groups with a motive to shoot the president. But while critics have poked holes in the Warren Commission's findings, they have failed to undermine its final conclusion that Oswald acted alone or to develop a convincing alternative interpretation of events on November 22, 1963.

Kennedy's death brought to the White House a man with a strikingly different background and temperament. Lyndon Baines Johnson was born in 1908 in Stonewall, Texas, and raised in that depressed rural area of the Texas hill country. After completing his education at Southwest Texas State Teachers College in nearby San Marcos, Johnson taught school for a few years. In 1931 he traveled to Washington, where he worked as a clerk to a Texas congressman.

As a young man in Washington during the depression, Johnson developed deep admiration for Franklin Roosevelt, whom he described as "like a daddy to me." In 1937 he won election to Congress on a "Franklin D. and Lyndon B. ticket." He lost a Senate race in 1941, before serving as a lieutenant commander in the navy. In 1948 he earned the nickname "Landslide Lyndon" following his election to the Senate by a margin of 8 votes.

Once in the Senate Johnson impressed powerful Democrats with his energy and ambition. As minority leader and then as majority leader, he became a master of parliamentary maneuver and a skillful behind-the-scenes negotiator. A tall, physically imposing man, Johnson was not afraid to twist arms to bend recalcitrant senators to his will. Two journalists described this process as the Johnson treatment. "He moved in close, his face a scant millimeter from his target, his eyes widening and narrowing, his eyebrows rising and falling." In 1955 Johnson suffered a near-fatal heart attack but recovered to seek the Democratic nomination in 1960. Overshadowed by the charismatic Kennedy, he reluctantly accepted second place on the ticket.

The new president displayed a quiet dignity in the traumatic days following Kennedy's assassination. On November 26, he addressed Congress, committing himself to fulfilling the slain president's agenda. "We would be untrue to the trust

Signing a Piece of the Great Society into Law   Lyndon Johnson went further than any previous president to employ the federal government to meet people's needs and solve social problems. Key to his program was ensuring that every American child had an adequate education, from preschool through high school. Johnson, raised in poor, rural Texas, justified his generous education package by claiming that "education is the only valid passport from poverty." Here he signs the bill, accompanied by his first grade teacher at the site of the one-room schoolhouse he attended as a boy.   *(Wide World Photos, Inc.)*

he reposed in us," he told a joint session of Congress, "if we did not remain true to the tasks he relinquished when God summoned him." Johnson used his political talent to push Congress into enacting a number of Kennedy's initiatives. In February 1964, Congress passed the Kennedy tax package, reducing personal income taxes by more than $10 billion. Many economists believe the tax cut contributed to an economic boom that saw the nation's GNP rise from $591 billion in 1963 to $977 billion in 1970. Johnson also steered through Congress Kennedy's stalled housing and food stamp programs.

Johnson was not content merely to pass Kennedy's agenda. He sought to create a program that would bear his personal brand. In January 1964, in his first State of the Union message, Johnson declared "unconditional war on poverty.... [W]e shall not rest until that war is won. The richest Nation on earth can afford to win it. We cannot afford to lose it."

The war on poverty actually had its roots in the Kennedy administration. Like many Americans, Kennedy took office believing that economic growth alone would solve the problems of poverty. In 1962 social activist Michael Harrington passionately challenged that notion in a popular book entitled *The Other America.* Estimating the ranks of the poor at 40 to 50 million, or as much as 25 percent of the U.S. population, Harrington argued that poverty resulted from long-term structural problems, such as unemployment and low wages, which only the federal government could address. On November 19, 1963, just three days before his death, Kennedy asked Walter Heller, the chairman of the Council of Economic Advisors, to design a legislative proposal for fighting poverty. The day after the assassination, Johnson enthusiastically endorsed the council's solution.

The poverty legislation, called the Economic Opportunity Act, authorized almost a billion dollars for a wide range of antipoverty programs including Head Start for preschoolers and the Job Corps for inner-city youth. Volunteers in Service to America (VISTA), a domestic version of the Peace Corps, provided volunteers with the opportunity to work in poor urban areas and depressed rural communities. The law authorized creation of the Office of Economic Opportunity (OEO) to coordinate the antipoverty battle. Johnson chose Peace Corps director R. Sargent Shriver, a Kennedy brother-in-law, to administer the OEO.

The centerpiece of the economic package was the community action program (CAP). The initiative, intended to stimulate sustained involvement among the poor, called for the "maximum feasible participation" of local community members in shaping antipoverty programs. By 1967, however, local Democratic leaders complained that some community action programs had fallen into the hands of radicals. In response, Congress tightened the restrictions on allocating money, thus ending the brief experiment with "maximum feasible participation."

By some measures, the various programs that made up the war on poverty succeeded. The proportion of Americans below the federal poverty line fell from 20 percent in 1963 to 13 percent in 1968. For African-Americans, who faced the most desperate conditions, the statistics were even more impressive. The percentage of blacks living below the poverty line dropped from 40 percent to 20 percent between 1960 and 1968. However, a booming economy contributed to these statistics as much as did the antipoverty efforts.

The larger goal of eradicating poverty altogether remained elusive, especially in inner cities. It was naive to believe that educational opportunities, job training, and a climate of hope could untangle the thicket of social problems that produced chronic poverty. But it was not politically feasible, nor did Johnson ever intend, to challenge the nation's basic socioeconomic structure by redistributing wealth. Despite the ambitious scope of the antipoverty agenda, funding proved modest. Average annual expenditures were about $1.7 billion—a small sum to care for the 25 to 35 million Americans who fell below the poverty line. One writer called the war on poverty "a classic instance of the American habit of substituting good intentions for cold hard cash."

By raising expectations in the inner cities and then failing to follow through, the war on poverty left a legacy of bitterness and frustration. The gap between the promise and the performance generated a cycle of disillusion that undermined public confidence in the program. "The program," a critic wrote, "was carried out in such a way as to produce a minimum of the social change its sponsors desired, and to bring about a maximum increase in the opposition to such change."

The 1964 Election and the Great Society

While launching his war on poverty, Johnson was laying the foundation for the 1964 presidential election. At the party's Atlantic City convention, Johnson won the nomination by acclamation. As his running mate, he chose Minnesota senator Hubert Humphrey, a passionate proponent of civil rights and a leading liberal.

To oppose Johnson in November, the Republicans nominated Arizona senator Barry Goldwater. An outspoken critic of liberal reform, Goldwater hoped to rally millions of conservative voters in the South and West with his calls for smaller government and aggressive anticommunism.

Goldwater's extremism energized the party's vocal right wing but alienated Republican moderates and liberals. "Extremism in the defense of liberty is no vice," he orated. "Moderation in the pursuit of justice is no virtue." He suggested that nuclear weapons be used against Cuba, China, and North Vietnam if they failed to accede to American demands. "Our job, first and foremost," he wrote, "is to persuade the enemy that we would rather follow the world to Kingdom Come than consign it to Hell under communism." GOP campaign posters asserted: "In Your Heart You Know He's Right." (Democrats retorted, "In Your Guts You Know He's Nuts.")

By waging a campaign to court the right, Goldwater conceded the broad middle ground to Johnson, who brilliantly exploited the opportunity. He played the role of the fatherly figure committed to continuing the policies of the nation's fallen leader. Campaigning eighteen hours a day, he reminded voters of his party's past accomplishments and promised to carry the nation to new heights.

The election was never close. Johnson's percentage of the popular vote, 61.1 percent, matched Roosevelt's in 1936. Congressional Democrats coasted to victory on the president's coattails, providing the administration with large majorities in both houses: 68 to 32 in the Senate and 295 to 140 in the House (see map).

In the spring of 1964, Johnson coined a phrase meant to define his vision for the presidency, announcing that he hoped to build a "Great Society," "where men are more concerned with the quality of their goals than the quantity of their goods." At the heart of the Great Society was a belief that economic growth provided all Americans—rich and poor, urban blacks and rural whites, young and old—with the historic opportunity to forge a new national consensus.

Not surprisingly, many observers viewed the Great Society as a second New Deal. The comparisons pleased Johnson who, on the day after the election, declared, "I am a Roosevelt New Dealer."

Following his victory over Goldwater in November, Johnson and the massive new majorities in both houses launched his Great Society. The administration's top priorities were to rescue two staples of the Democratic agenda since the Fair Deal that had been held hostage by congressional conservatives: medical insurance for the elderly and education funding for the young. Johnson and his new allies in Congress overwhelmed the opposition. Along with providing medical assistance to people on social security (Medicare), the legislation included a Medicaid program that would pay the medical expenses of the poor, regardless of age. "No longer will older Americans be denied the healing miracle of modern medicine," a triumphant Johnson declared. The president also managed to quiet opponents of federal aid to

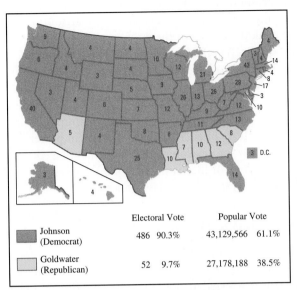

Electoral Vote | Popular Vote

		Electoral Vote		Popular Vote	
Johnson (Democrat)		486	90.3%	43,129,566	61.1%
Goldwater (Republican)		52	9.7%	27,178,188	38.5%

The Election of 1964   Republicans tried a new political strategy with their candidate Barry Goldwater, attacking the liberal domestic policies of Democratic presidents, including the New Deal and the war on poverty. Lyndon Johnson retaliated by campaigning to as wide an audience as possible and urged people at every point of the political spectrum to join him. This broad appeal led to a Johnson landslide.

education and convince Congress to pass his Elementary and Secondary Education Act of 1965. Its heart was Title I, which provided more than a billion dollars for textbooks, library materials, and special educational programs for poor children.

Mounting momentum enabled Johnson to push through a wide range of legislation. "The legislation rolled through the House and Senate in such profusion and so methodically," recalled one White House official, "that you seemed part of some vast, overpowering machinery, oiled to purr." Congress passed consumer protection acts and provided aid for mass transit, urban development, and slum clearance. The Immigration Act of 1965 eliminated discriminatory quotas and opened the door to an increased flow of immigrants from Asia and Latin America that would profoundly affect American life in the decades ahead.

Johnson made concern for the environment a central tenet of his Great Society. Prodded by the White House, Congress passed legislation mandating tougher regulation of water and air pollution. The Wilderness Act of 1964 set aside over 9 million acres of national forest to be preserved in their unspoiled state. A companion measure, the Wild and Scenic Rivers Act of 1968, similarly protected a number of rivers from the threat of development. The First Lady, Lady Bird Johnson, supported environmental awareness as an eloquent and effective leader of a campaign for national beautification.

Whether the Great Society programs were successful is a subject of heated scholarly debate. Supporters point out that programs such as Medicare and Medicaid provided essential medical benefits to the elderly and the poor. One scholar concluded that the combination of social insurance and public aid during the Great Society had a "highly egalitarian effect on income distribution." Critics, however, point out that the middle class, not the poor, were the chief beneficiaries of many Great Society programs. By refusing to impose restrictions on what doctors could charge patients, Medicare and Medicaid contributed to spiraling medical costs that benefited doctors. Medicare–Medicaid, observed the historian Alan Matusow, "primarily transferred income from middle-class taxpayers to middle-class health professionals." A similar complaint plagued Johnson's compensatory education program. To avoid raising fears of encroaching government power, Johnson gave local school districts authority for developing and implementing education programs. In a classic case of the "curse of localism," school officials skirted federal guidelines and redirected money toward middle class students.

The Reforms of the Warren Court

The same activist spirit that guided the president and Congress infused the third branch of government—the courts. Under the leadership of Chief Justice Earl Warren the Supreme Court asserted its right to review and declare unconstitutional legislation that it believed infringed on individual rights. A group of liberal judges—especially William O. Douglas, Hugo Black, and William J. Brennan, Jr.—formed a powerful coalition in favor of liberal ideas. Kennedy's 1962 appointment of Secretary of Labor Arthur Goldberg to the Court guaranteed a liberal majority. Acting on its philosophy, the court issued several landmark rulings.

On civil rights, liberal justices built on the foundation of *Brown* v. *Board of Education* (1954) by upholding the right of demonstrators to participate in public protests. The Court disallowed the use of the poll tax in state and local elections and in 1967 struck at the core of white supremacy doctrine by declaring laws prohibiting interracial marriages to be unconstitutional.

The Courts extended its definition of individual rights to other explosive social issues. In the early 1960s, twelve states required Bible reading in public schools. Children in New York State recited a nonsectarian Christian prayer: "Almighty God, we acknowledge our dependence upon Thee, and we beg Thy blessings upon us, our parents, our teachers and our country." The Supreme Court, in *Engel* v. *Vitale* (1962), ruled the New York prayer unconstitutional on the grounds that it was a religious activity that placed an "indirect coercive pressure upon religious minorities."

Nowhere did the Court break more decisively with the past than in the area of sexual freedom. In 1965, in *Griswold* v. *Connecticut*, the Court struck down a Connecticut statute banning the sale of contraceptives. In a ruling that would influence future debates about a woman's right to an abortion, Justice William O. Douglas wrote that the Constitution guaranteed "a right to privacy." In 1966 the Court ruled states could not ban sexually explicit material unless "it is found to be utterly without redeeming social value." Under that standard, nearly all restrictions on the right of an adult to obtain sexually explicit material vanished.

A number of decisions overruled local electoral practices that had prevented full participation in the political process. In 1964, in *Reynolds* v. *Sims*, the Court established the principle of "one man, one vote." Legislative districts, the Court ruled, had to be apportioned so that they represented equal numbers of people. "Legislators represent people, not acres or trees," Warren reminded the country.

Perhaps the Court's most controversial decisions concerned criminal justice. In *Gideon* v. *Wainwright* (1963), the Court ruled that a pauper accused in state courts of a felony must be provided an attorney at public expense. The following year, in *Escobedo* v. *Illinois*, it voided the murder confession of a man who had been denied permission to see his lawyer. In the most controversial criminal rights case, *Miranda* v. *Arizona* (1966), a divided court required police to inform suspected criminals of their right to remain silent and to have an attorney present during interrogation.

The expansion of judicial activism touched a raw nerve among Americans fearful of encroaching federal power. One congressman claimed the justices were "a greater threat to this Union than the entire confines of Soviet Russia." Rulings on pornography, school prayer, and contraception outraged Catholics, fundamentalists, and other religious groups. The court's involvement in apportionment offended traditionalists who charged that questions of representation were best handled by elected leaders. The Court's rulings on criminal rights irked white middle-class Americans worried about rising crime. A 1966 poll showed that 65 percent of Americans opposed recent criminal rights decisions.

The Struggle for Racial Equality

Racial tensions posed one of the gravest threats to Johnson's vision of a Great Society. By 1965, African-Americans' new, more confrontational strategy to challenge segregation in the South produced a number of notable achievements in securing blacks' rights as Americans. But the violence that ripped through many American cities after 1965, and the white backlash that followed, were powerful reminders of the limits of consensus and the persistence of racial divisions in America.

The Movement Spreads

Late in the afternoon on Monday, February 1, 1960, four well-dressed black students sat down at a segregated lunch counter at a Woolworth's department store in Greensboro, North Carolina, and ordered a cup of coffee. "I'm sorry," the waitress said, "we don't serve you here." By the end of the week, more than three hundred protesters occupied the Woolworth's lunch counter demanding service. As news of the sit-ins reached other cities, the protest spread "like a fever." By the end of 1960, over seventy thousand people in over 150 southern cities and towns had participated in sit-ins.

The sit-in movement represented an important change in the strategy of civil rights protesters. It revealed the growing frustration of many younger blacks who were impatient with the slow pace of change and convinced that more aggressive tactics could force the government to take bolder action to redress existing wrongs. In April 1960, these younger, more militant protesters formed the Student Nonviolent

Coordinating Committee (SNCC). The sit-ins also underscored the decentralized, grass-roots approach of the civil rights movement. The success of national figures such as Martin Luther King, Jr., rested on a foundation forged by the courage and commitment of ordinary local people such as Fannie Lou Hamer, Robert Moses, Amelia Boynton, and Fred Shuttlesworth.

In 1961 members of the Congress of Racial Equality (CORE) decided to challenge another pillar of racial segregation. By 1960, the Supreme Court had barred racial segregation in bus and train stations, airport terminals, and other facilities related to interstate transit. But southerners widely ignored these decisions. In May 1961, seven black and six white "Freedom Riders" left Washington on two buses headed for Alabama and Mississippi. "Our intention," declared CORE national director James Farmer, "was to provoke the southern authorities into arresting us and thereby prod the Justice Department into enforcing the law of the land." As the vehicles moved into the Deep South, white racists mobilized. At stops along the way, the Freedom Riders were assaulted by gangs of thugs brandishing baseball bats, lead pipes, and bicycle chains. A white mob in Birmingham, Alabama, beat the riders so badly that an FBI informant reported that he "couldn't see their faces through the blood." President Kennedy, fearful that the violence would undermine American prestige abroad, negotiated a compromise with southern authorities: if local officials would guarantee the safety of the riders, the federal government would not protest their arrest. Over the next few months over three hundred Freedom Riders were arrested. In September 1961, after hundreds had risked their lives, the Interstate Commerce Commission banned segregation in interstate terminals.

In the fall of 1961, SNCC chose Albany, Georgia, as the site of their next campaign. Attempting to rally opposition to continuing segregation in bus and train terminals, schools, libraries, and parks, local leaders called in Martin Luther King. But wily local authorities avoided the overt violence King needed to arouse national indignation. By the summer of 1962, King left town and the movement had suffered its first defeat.

The Albany campaign had failed, but it left an important legacy to the movement. It was here that African-American spiritual and cultural power found its fullest expression. The sounds of freedom songs, which traced their roots to slave music of the nineteenth century, rocked black churches in Albany, inspiring spiritual commitment to the cause. One slave spiritual—"We Shall Overcome"—became the anthem of the movement. When congregations rose to sing it, recalled one participant, "nobody knew what kept the top of the church on its four walls. It was as if everyone had been lifted up on high."

From Albany the movement moved to Oxford, Mississippi, where James Meredith, a twenty-eight-year-old black air force veteran, attempted to register at the all-white University of Mississippi. When Governor Ross Barnett, a demagogic segregationist, personally blocked Meredith's attempt to register on September 20, 1962, Attorney General Robert Kennedy sent five hundred federal marshals to the university campus. "The eyes of the nation and all the world are upon you and upon all of us," President Kennedy admonished Mississippians. The federal presence failed to intimidate Barnett and his supporters. On September 30 a white mob attacked the federal marshals, killing two and injuring 375. Outraged by the violence, the president ordered thirty thousand regular army troops and federalized national guardsmen to Oxford to restore order. The massive show of force worked: Barnett backed down, and Meredith enrolled.

In March 1963, the civil rights struggle focused on Birmingham, Alabama, perhaps the most segregated city in the South. White terrorists had blown up so many buildings there that some called the town "Bombingham." In March, King decided to violate a state court injunction against protest marches. He and fifty others were promptly arrested and thrown into jail. He spent his weeks behind bars responding to criticism from white Alabama clergy that his tactics were too militant. The result was King's powerful argument for civil disobedience, "Letter from Birmingham Jail" (see Competing Voices, page 1174). King's passionate defense of nonviolence galvanized the Birmingham movement. In May, after his release from jail, King organized a peaceful march to City Hall. Police assaulted the crowd with fire hoses, nightsticks, and police dogs.

Television coverage of the clubbings aroused the indignation of the nation. Kennedy went on national television calling upon the citizens of Birmingham to "maintain standards of responsible conduct that will make outside intervention unnecessary." Eventually, the business community, stung by the national publicity and a black boycott, broke with the city government and agreed to most of King's demands.

In June 1963, the stage shifted to Alabama where Governor George Wallace planned to fulfill his campaign promise to place himself in the doorway of any schoolhouse under court order to admit blacks. On the morning of June 11, under such a court order, two black students arrived to register at the Huntsville branch of the state university. With television cameras recording the drama, Wallace stood in the doorway, where a deputy attorney general confronted him. Having made his point, Wallace made a brief speech for the television cameras and then allowed the students to register.

The Civil Rights Act of 1964

That evening, Kennedy delivered one of the most eloquent, moving, and important speeches of his presidency. For the first time, he referred to civil rights as a moral issue, one that was, he said, "as old as the scriptures and as clear as the American constitution." Eight days later Kennedy sent his legislative proposals to Congress. He asked for laws to support voting rights, to provide assistance to school districts that were desegregating, to ban segregation of public facilities, and to empower the attorney general to initiate proceedings against the segregation of schools.

To build support for the legislation and to appeal to the conscience of the nation, black leaders organized a March on Washington for August 1963. On August 28, more than a quarter of a million people gathered under a cloudless sky at the Lincoln Memorial for the largest civil rights demonstration in the nation's history. The high point of the sweltering afternoon came when Martin Luther King took the speakers' podium. "Even though we face the difficulties of today and tomorrow," King intoned

The Birmingham Police Confront Marchers When civil rights demonstrators led by Martin Luther King, Jr., peacefully took to the streets of Birmingham in 1963, police met them with high-pressure fire hoses and trained attack dogs. In this photograph, a seventeen-year-old protester stoically marches ahead while a police dog viciously snaps at him. Images such as this one were displayed in newspapers and on television screens across the country, forcing all who saw them to rethink their positions on civil rights. One reader wrote in to his paper, "Never have I been so ashamed to be a member of the white race." *(Bill Hudson/Wide World Photos, Inc.)*

in his powerful cadence, "I still have a dream. It is a dream chiefly rooted in the American dream . . . . that my four little children will one day live in a nation where they will not be judged by the color of their skin but by the content of their character." For a brief moment the nation embraced King's vision of interracial brotherhood.

After Kennedy's death in November Lyndon Johnson, using the skills he had learned from years on the Hill, assumed personal control of the fight to pass the civil rights package. He told legislators that he would not accept any compromise. In the House, opponents of the legislation attempted to divide liberal forces by adding a provision that would bar employment discrimination against women as well as blacks. But the measure backfired when Congress adopted the amendment without controversy.

Still, for seventy-five days, opponents filibustered against the bill until, on June 10, Senate minority leader Everett Dirksen announced his support for allowing a vote. The next day, by a 73–27 tally, the Civil Rights Act of 1964 passed the Senate. Three weeks later the House followed suit.

The Civil Rights Act of 1964 was the most far-reaching law of its kind since Reconstruction. At its heart was a section guaranteeing equal access to public accommodations. It also strengthened existing machinery for preventing employment discrimination by government contractors and empowered the government to file school desegregation suits and cut off funds wherever racial discrimination was practiced in the application of federal programs.

Gaining Political Power

Many black leaders believed that racism would never be overcome until blacks exercised political power. In 1964 only 2 million of the South's 5 million voting-age blacks were registered to vote. In 1964 SNCC organized a voting rights campaign in Mississippi, where only 5 percent of blacks were registered to vote. The volunteer brigade working to help blacks register, which included many white college students, encountered fierce and sometimes fatal resistance. In June federal agents found the bodies of three workers who had been murdered.

Despite daily beatings and arrests, the volunteers expanded their program to challenge the state's lily-white Democratic organization. They formed their own Mississippi Freedom Democratic Party (MFDP) and elected a separate slate of delegates to the 1964 Democratic convention. When the regular all-white delegation threatened to walk out if the convention seated the protesters, Johnson offered the dissidents two at-large seats and agreed to bar from future conventions any state delegation that practiced discrimination. The Freedom Democrats rejected the compromise. "We didn't come all this way for no two seats," protested Fannie Lou Hamer, the daughter of sharecroppers who had lost her job and been evicted from her home because of her organizing efforts. In the end, however, Johnson, and his liberal allies prevailed and the convention voted to accept the compromise.

The compromise at Atlantic City angered many blacks who no longer felt they could achieve justice through the system. For others, however, it only intensified their efforts to gain the right to vote. In 1965 Martin Luther King chose Selma, Alabama, as the site of a renewed voting rights campaign. "We are not asking, we are demanding the ballot," he declared. Selma was home to 14,400 whites and 15,100 blacks, but its voting roles were 99 percent white and one percent black. SNCC workers had spent several frustrating months organizing local residents to vote. But their efforts had reaped few rewards. The chief obstacle was Sheriff Jim Clark, a bulldog-visaged segregationist who led a fearsome group of deputy volunteers, many of them KKK members.

Clark, however, fell prey to King's plan to provoke confrontation. The sheriff steadfastly turned away the waves of blacks who tried to register. During one week, more than three thousand protesters were arrested. As police patience wore thin, their actions became more violent. In February a mob of state troopers assaulted a group of blacks, shooting twenty-six-year-old Jimmie Lee Jackson as he tried to protect his mother and grandmother.

Jackson's death inspired black leaders to organize a fifty-four-mile march from Selma to Montgomery to petition Governor Wallace for protection of blacks registering to vote. On March 7, ignoring an order from the governor forbidding the march, 650 blacks and a few whites began walking through Selma. Conspicuously absent from the march was Martin Luther King who, after private pressure from the White House, returned to Atlanta.

On the other side of the Edmund Pettus Bridge, which crosses the Alabama River, a phalanx of sixty state policemen wearing helmets and gas masks awaited the marchers. After a few tense minutes, the patrolmen moved on the protesters, swinging bullwhips and rubber tubing wrapped in barbed wire. The marchers stumbled over each other in retreat. The images, shown on the evening news, horrified the nation and catalyzed the administration into action.

On March 15, Johnson went before Congress to make his case for a powerful new voting rights bill. Selma, he told the hushed chambers, marked a turning point in American history equal to Lexington and Concord. "Because it is not just Negroes, but really all of us who must overcome the crippling legacy of bigotry and injustice. And," he concluded, "we shall . . . overcome."

On August 6, 1965, after skillfully maneuvering the bill through Congress, Johnson signed into law the Voting Rights Act of 1965. The legislation authorized federal examiners to register voters, and it banned the use of literacy tests. The outcome permanently changed race relations in the South. The most dramatic result was in Mississippi. In 1965 just 28,500 blacks, a mere 7 percent of the voting age population, had been registered; three years later, 250,770 blacks were registered. In eleven southern states, black registration increased by 10 percent from 1964 to 1966, and by another 15 percent in the next four years.

A Former Slave Finally Gets the Vote Although the Fifteenth Amendment gave African-Americans the right to vote in 1869, that right was effectively withheld from them through loopholes and discriminatory state legislation. The Voting Rights Act of 1965 authorized the attorney general to suspend local and state regulations that interfered with voter registration. The act transformed southern politics in particular, admitting hundreds of thousands of citizens into the political process for the first time. One hundred years after he was freed from slavery, this 106-year-old Mississippi man registers to vote in Batesville. He is escorted by members of the Mississippi Freedom Democratic Party. *(Corbis-Bettmann.)*

Black Power, White Backlash

In August 1965, five days after Johnson signed the Voting Rights Act into law, the Watts section of Los Angeles exploded in violence. Before the rioting ended, thirty-four were dead, nearly four thousand arrested, and property damage had reached $45 million. Fourteen thousand national guardsmen and several thousand local police needed six days to stop the arson, looting, and sniping.

The Watts explosion marked the first of four successive "long hot summers." In the summer of 1966, thirty-eight disorders destroyed ghetto neighborhoods in cities from San Francisco to Providence, Rhode Island. The result was seven deaths, four hundred injuries, and $5 million in property damage. The following year, Newark erupted leaving twenty-five dead and some twelve hundred wounded. In Detroit forty-three were killed, and more than four thousand fires burned large portions of the city.

At the root of the riots were deeply ingrained social problems. Blacks living in northern cities confronted overcrowding, unemployment, crime, and discrimination. In 1966, 41.7 percent of nonwhites in urban America lived below the federal poverty line. President Johnson's National Advisory Commission on Civil Disorders, created to investigate the causes of the riots, speculated that despair, black militancy, and white racism combined to create a combustible situation. Ominously, the commission warned: "Our nation is moving toward two societies, one black, one white—separate and unequal."

The urban riots precipitated a crisis in black leadership. Martin Luther King's strategy of passive resistance seemed ill equipped to deal with the issues that fueled the new violence. SNCC leader Stokely Carmichael captured the anger of many urban blacks when he coined the phrase "Black Power." Instead of integration, which he called "a subterfuge for the maintenance of white supremacy," Carmichael said that blacks needed to develop their own cultural heritage and become self-dependent. "We don't need white liberals," Carmichael told supporters. "We have to make integration irrelevant." Rejecting nonviolence, Carmichael said, "Black people should and must fight back."

In developing his message of black power, Carmichael drew on the writings of Malcolm X. A spellbinding preacher and a charismatic leader, Malcolm X offered a compelling alternative vision to King (see Competing Voices, page 1175). In 1946, while in prison for robbery, Malcolm Little converted to the Nation of Islam, or Black Muslims. On joining, Little abandoned his "slave name" in favor of Malcolm X; the X stood for his lost African name. Dismissing the aspirations of white civil rights leaders, he said that black nationalists did not want "to integrate into this corrupt society, but to separate from it, to a land of our own, where we can reform ourselves, lift up our moral standards, and try to be godly." In 1963 Malcolm X broke with the Nation of Islam, and after a 1964 African pilgrimage to Mecca, his ethical position shifted. He rejected racism, spoke of the common bond linking humanity, and suggested that blacks build alliances with like-minded whites. But he emphasized the need for blacks to unify themselves before they reached out for help from whites and liberals. His evolution remained incomplete, however. In February 1965, he was gunned down at a Harlem rally, apparently by Black Muslim loyalists.

Most whites responded to the riots and the new militancy with fear and anger. Millions angrily turned away from the civil rights movement and its liberal defenders. In 1966 whites sought revenge against the Democrats at the polls. In California, second-rate movie actor Ronald Reagan won the governorship by blaming the Watts riot on liberal policymakers. Even his defeated opponent, liberal Pat Brown, declared in his concession speech that "whether we like it or not the people want separation of the races." The biggest change took place in Congress, where Republicans campaigning on a tough "law and order" platform gained forty-seven House seats and three in the Senate. The Democrats lost more seats in 1966 than they had won in 1964. After November 1966, there were 156 northern Democrats in the House, 62 short of a majority.

 ## Vietnam: Containment and Tragedy, 1964–1968

Like Kennedy, Johnson was torn between his commitment to preventing a communist victory in Vietnam and his reluctance to get pulled into a major confrontation in Southeast Asia. But his doubts did not prevent the president from dramatically enlarging America's involvement in the war. America's technological superiority and enormous firepower proved ineffective in the jungles of Southeast Asia. The young men who fought in Vietnam bore the brunt of a confused mission in an inhospitable environment, while Americans at home questioned the war's importance to U.S. global interests.

The Decision to Escalate

The president's key advisers, all leftovers from the Kennedy administration, urged a strong U.S. military response to the deteriorating situation in Saigon. In March 1964, North Vietnam sent twenty-three thousand fresh recruits south to join forces with the National Liberation Front, swelling the ranks of the Vietcong. North Vietnam improved and extended the Ho Chi Minh trail, a network of trails and roads on which supplies flowed south. The increased military pressure added to the political instability in the South. Desertions in South Vietnam's military, the Army of the Republic of Vietnam (ARVN), reached epidemic levels, exceeding six thousand a month in 1964. The CIA estimated that the Vietcong controlled up to 40 percent of the territory of South Vietnam and more than 50 percent of the people.

The president's military advisers believed the war could not be won without severing the flow of supplies from North Vietnam. They recommended a campaign of strategic bombing both to shore up the government in the South and to send a clear signal of U.S. resolve to the North. Only Undersecretary of State George Ball refused to support any bombing mission. "Once on the tiger's back," he observed, "we can not be sure of picking the place to dismount."

Like Kennedy, Johnson dreaded getting mired in a protracted ground war in Southeast Asia. A wider war, he feared, would distract attention from his Great Society programs and provide critics with ammunition to scale back domestic spending. He told biographer Doris Kearns "that bitch of a war" would destroy "the woman I really loved—the Great Society." At the same time, he remembered what a heavy political price Truman had paid for "losing China" (see page 1073), and he vowed not to become the president who "lost Vietnam." Like Kennedy, he accepted the major outlines of the containment policy: the United States had to maintain a strong presence in the world to thwart Soviet adventurism.

Despite his doubts, the president approved the recommendation of his military advisers calling for an incremental escalation in Vietnam. Before implementing the new tactics, Johnson wanted to neutralize potential critics by securing congressional support for a wider war. He needed a dramatic incident to convince the nation to support his plans. He did not have to wait long. On August 4, 1964, while operating in heavy seas about sixty miles off the North Vietnamese coast in the Tonkin Gulf, the U.S. destroyers *C. Turner Joy* and *Maddox* reported they were under attack by North Vietnamese torpedo boats. Neither saw any enemy vessels and afterward crew members speculated that poor weather conditions may have contributed to the confusion. Johnson expressed doubts. "For all I know, our navy might have been shooting at whales out there," he confided.

The reported attack nonetheless gave Johnson the opportunity he needed to establish congressional support for his actions in Vietnam. With little debate and strong public support, Congress overwhelmingly ratified the Tonkin Gulf Resolution, which authorized the president to take "all necessary measures to repel any armed attacks against the forces of the United States and to prevent further aggression." The resolution provided the legislative foundation for the Vietnam War. As Lyndon Johnson observed, it was "like Grandma's nightshirt, it covers everything."

Armed with congressional support for a wider war, Johnson launched "a carefully orchestrated bombing attack" against the North. The bombing accomplished neither of its objectives: the enemy intensified its efforts and the political situation in the South continued to deteriorate. In February 1965, the administration responded by launching operation Rolling Thunder, the sustained bombing of North Vietnam that would last until 1968. At first the president kept tight control of the bombing, claiming that the pilots "can't even bomb an outhouse without my approval." By spring he had loosened his control, authorized the use of napalm, and allowed pilots to drop their deadly cargos without prior approval.

Instead of intimidating the North Vietnamese, the bombing raids only stiffened their resolve; the flow of arms into the South actually increased. In 1964, for the first time, regular North Vietnamese troops moved south to join the indigenous Vietcong. By the spring of 1965, more than sixty-five hundred northern-born regular troops were fighting in the South. The South Vietnamese government, weakened by corruption and constant political intrigue, seemed incapable of stemming the communist advance.

The deteriorating military situation frustrated Johnson, who complained that a "raggedy-ass, fourth-rate country like North Vietnam [could] be causing so much trouble." The Joint Chiefs of Staff pressed the commander-in-chief for both unlimited bombing of the North and the aggressive use of American ground troops in the South. "You must take the fight to the enemy," declared the chairman of the Joint Chiefs. "No one ever won a battle sitting on his ass." In mid-July, Secretary of Defense Robert McNamara recommended sending 100,000 combat troops, more than doubling the number already there. Again Ball was the lone

Vietnam, to 1968 Despite the number of soldiers (see graph, page 1160): and military bases in South Vietnam and Thailand, American troops could not confine and fight an enemy as mobile as the North Vietnamese. With a constant supply line, known as the Ho Chi Minh trail, the North Vietnamese circumvented the border between the North and South, smuggling men and supplies through Laos and Cambodia to supporters in the South. The Tet Offensive of 1968 showed the effectiveness of the trail and perseverance of the North.

voice of dissent in the administration, telling the president he had "serious doubt that an army of westerners can successfully fight Orientals in an Asian jungle."

In July 1965, Johnson made the fateful decision to commit American ground forces to offensive operations in Vietnam. He scaled back McNamara's request for 100,000 troops to 50,000, though privately he assured the military that he would commit another 50,000 before the end of the year. Johnson made his decision without consulting Congress or the American people. Fearful of distracting attention from his Great Society programs, he refused to admit that he had dramatically increased America's involvement in Vietnam.

America's War

To lead the combat troops in Vietnam, Johnson chose General William Westmoreland, a veteran of World War II and former superintendent of West Point. Westmoreland planned to limit ground action to search-and-destroy missions launched from fortified bases in the countryside. Rather than confronting the enemy in large-scale ground assaults, he would depend on firepower from ground artillery, helicopter gunships, fighter aircraft, and B-52 bombers. "We'll just go on bleeding them," he said, "until Hanoi wakes up to the fact that they have bled their country to the point of national disaster for generations" (see map).

Westmoreland's optimism proved premature. The air war failed to sever the flow of supplies between North and South. Thousands of peasants worked daily to rebuild parts of the Ho Chi Minh trail damaged by American bombs. By 1967, some six thousand tons of supplies arriving daily in North Vietnam from China and the Soviet Union diluted the effects of the bombing. Since the North had an agricultural economy with few industries vital to the war effort, aerial sorties against cities in North Vietnam had little impact on supplies. The civilian toll, however, was heavy. All told, U.S. bombs killed an estimated one hundred thousand North Vietnamese civilians.

Unable to win the war from the air, the administration gradually increased the number of ground troops, from 184,000 in late 1965 to more than 500,000 in 1968 (see graph). The Viet Cong continued their guerilla tactics, avoiding fixed positions and striking from ambush. By the end of 1967, more than 16,000 U.S. soldiers had lost their lives, with more than 10,000 killed in the previous twelve months. Hanoi's strategy was to fight a war of attrition, confident that American public opinion would sour on an inconclusive war. As the U.S. death count mounted, predicted North Vietnamese General Giap, "their mothers will want to know why. The war will not long survive their questions."

On the Ground in Vietnam   For the "grunts" who faced the day-to-day reality of the Vietnam War, harrowing scenes such as this were all too common. These two GIs wait for a helicopter to carry them and their fallen friend out of the jungle in Long Khanh province. The guerrilla tactics of the Vietcong, their frequent use of ambush attacks, and the difficulty distinguishing enemy soldiers from civilians made the war experience particularly frightful for American troops. Almost sixty thousand U.S. soldiers were lost in the war, and those who made it home often faced lingering psychological effects and an unsupportive public.   *(National Archives.)*

American Troop Levels in Vietnam After Johnson's decision to send marines to Danang in 1965, the American presence in Vietnam skyrocketed. Not until the Tet Offensive in 1968, though, did Americans begin loudly to demand an end to the war. The outcry led to the election of a new president in 1968 and the de-escalation of American ground forces in Vietnam.

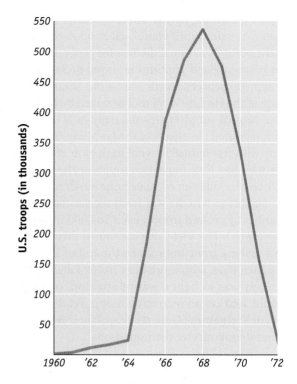

Along with trying to crush the enemy with its massive bombing and ground war, the United States launched a pacification and nation-building program in South Vietnam to build support for the noncommunist regime in Saigon. But the military effort directly undermined the political goals. By the end of 1968, almost 4 million South Vietnamese had lost their homes in aerial bombardments. Between 1965 and 1972, more than 1.4 million civilians died or were wounded by American forces. One American official observed, "It was as if we were trying to build a house with a bulldozer and wrecking crane."

The military's failure in Vietnam, despite its enormous advantages in firepower, underscored the fundamental problem with America's Vietnam policy. Blinded by a rigid anticommunism, American policymakers rejected the nationalist impulse behind the Vietnamese revolution. Insisting on viewing Ho as a puppet of Soviet and Chinese aggression, the United States aided in the transformation of a local struggle into a superpower conflict. "We both overestimated the effect of South Vietnam's loss on the security of the West and failed to adhere to the fundamental principle that, in the final analysis, if the South Vietnamese were to be saved, they had to win the war themselves," a contrite former secretary of defense Robert McNamara reflected in 1995.

The Soldier's War

Who fought in Vietnam? From 1964 to 1973, 2.2 million men were drafted, 8.7 million enlisted, and 16 million did not serve. The average age of American soldiers in

Vietnam was 19. In World War II, the average American solider was 26 years old. The estimated total of women who served in Vietnam, including those employed by private organizations such as the Red Cross, ranged from 33,000 to over 50,000.

The majority of the young men who fought in Vietnam came from either poor or working class backgrounds. Many youths from middle-class families used a liberal student deferment policy to avoid the draft. In 1969 *Newsday* traced the family backgrounds of four hundred men from Long Island who had been killed in Vietnam. "As a group," the newspaper concluded, "Long Island's war dead have been overwhelmingly white, working-class men. Their parents were typically blue collar or clerical workers, mailmen, factory workers, building tradesmen, and so on." Class was far more important than race in determining the overall social composition of American forces. Beginning in 1965, when African-Americans accounted for 24 percent of all army combat deaths, the Defense Department undertook a concerted campaign to reduce the minority share of the fighting. By 1970, blacks made up only 9 percent of combat troops in Vietnam.

For combat soldiers in the field, Vietnam could be hell. Climate and country imposed horrible conditions. Malaria, blackwater fever, and dysentery took their toll. "Our days were spent hacking through mountainous jungles," one marine remembered. "At night we squatted in muddy holes, picked off the leeches that sucked on our veins, and waited for an attack to come rushing at us from the blackness beyond the perimeter wire."

Combat involved constant patrolling, days and days of suspense waiting for an ambush or a booby trap, and then a short, intense firefight followed by more suspense. Units swept across the same area repeatedly, taking casualties each time, never seeming to achieve any lasting effect. One day they were trying to "win the hearts and minds" of local villagers; the next day they were ordered to destroy the village. A chopper pilot expressed typical bitterness: "Vietnam, man. Bomb 'em and feed 'em, bomb 'em and feed 'em."

In a war of attrition, the "body count" became the primary measure of success. It inflicted a terrible emotional toll on the nineteen-year-olds ordered to fight. "What am I doing here?" asked a young solider. "We don't take any land. We don't give it back. We just mutilate bodies." The tragic consequences of that policy played out in March 1968 when an American platoon led by Lieutenant William L. Calley descended on the tiny village of My Lai. Not a single shot was fired at them and almost no men of military age were present in the village. Nonetheless, the American soldiers slaughtered more than 450 people and burned the village to the ground.

In the final years of the war, as American troop withdrawals increased, many soldiers refused to risk their lives in what they believed was a futile effort. Who wanted to be, asked Lieutenant John Kerry, "the last man to die in Vietnam"? Desertion and absent-without-leave (AWOL) rates skyrocketed. Violence against officers multiplied. Drug abuse reached epidemic proportions. In 1969 the Pentagon estimated that nearly two-thirds of combat soldiers had used marijuana, while one-third had tried heroin. "What the hell is going on?" asked a bewildered general. "Is this a goddamned army or a mental hospital?"

Challenging the Consensus, 1960–1967

Vietnam became a catalyst in the debates that divided Americans in the late 1960s. Lyndon Johnson had built his vision of a Great Society on the belief that America had forged a new national consensus around shared goals of economic growth, anticommunism, and activist government. A generation of young people challenged the core of that belief and undertook political and social experiments that defied American cultural traditions.

The Youth Culture

Young Americans in the 1960s were not the first to speak against the injustice and hypocrisy of their elders, but social and demographic forces provided this generation with new clout. The postwar baby boom had dramatically increased the number of college-age students in America. In 1965, 41 percent of all Americans were under the age of twenty. College enrollments soared from 3.6 million in 1960 to almost 8 million in 1970. Because colleges contained the largest concentration of young people in the country, they became the seedbeds of youth protest.

In the 1950s, "Beat" poets and artists had begun to decry American materialism and complacency. Writer Jack Kerouac, author of the bestselling novel *On the Road* (1957), coined the term *beat* to express the "weariness with all the forms of the modern industrial state." Poet Allen Ginsberg in *Howl* (1955), railed against "Robot apartments! invincible suburbs! skeleton treasuries! blind capitals! demonic industries!" The Beats embraced open sexuality and free drug use as keys to spiritual liberation.

By the early 1960s the beat message, popularized in inexpensive paperback novels, television shows, and movies, had gained wide acceptance among young people and formed the backbone of the so-called counterculture movement. The movement lacked a coherent ideology but shared a core of attitudes and beliefs. In search of a "higher consciousness," the counterculture rejected the tenets of modern industrial society: materialism, self-denial, sexual repression, individualism, and the work ethic. To the alarm of many older Americans, counterculture fashion promoted long hair for men, Eastern symbols, and clothes purchased from the Salvation Army.

Drug use was part of the message. The prophet of the new drug culture was Timothy Leary, a Harvard psychologist who preached to his students (and anyone else who would listen) about the wonders of magic mushrooms and LSD. "Tune in, turn on, drop out," he advised the young. According to *Life* magazine, by 1966 over a million people had experimented with LSD. But the drug of choice for the young remained marijuana. By 1969, more than 30 percent of all college students in the United States had smoked pot.

The counterculture defined itself through music. Bob Dylan's rapid rise to fame was emblematic of the newly emerging cultural sensibility. Dylan, born Robert Zimmerman, emerged on the New York folk scene in 1961. His hugely successful second album, *The Freewheelin' Bob Dylan* (1963), which included calls to political and moral action in songs such as "*A Hard Rain's Gonna Fall,*" "*The Times They Are A-Changin',*" and "*Blowin' in the Wind,*" sold two hundred thousand copies in two months.

After 1964, Dylan had to compete with a host of new rock bands from England. The most popular, the Beatles, captured the hearts of teenage America following a TV appearance on the popular Ed Sullivan television show in 1964. Initially the Beatles, with ties, jackets, and well-kempt if long haircuts, hoped to reach a mass consumer market by avoiding a clear association with the counterculture. But their music, which seemed to mock the adult world, contained a message of freedom and excitement that belied their sometimes subdued lyrics. By 1967, however, with the release of *Sergeant Pepper's Lonely Hearts Club Band*, the Beatles were celebrating their new role as cultural antagonists. "When the Beatles told us to turn off our minds and float downstream," recalled one fan, "uncounted youngsters assumed that the key to this kind of mind-expansion could be found in a plant or a pill."

The Beatles changed their tune, in part, to keep ahead of other groups who were gaining widespread popularity by preaching a more potent message. In 1967 Mick Jagger, lead singer of the Rolling Stones, also a British import, was arousing young audiences with a mixture of anger and sexual prowess. During concerts Jagger would thrust the microphone between his legs and whip the floor with a leather belt in a deliberately ugly and blatantly erotic demonstration. "The Beatles want to hold your hand," said one critic, "the Stones want to burn your house."

New Left, New Right

Many young people found more conventional means of expressing their discontent. In 1960 two University of Michigan students founded the Students for a Democratic Society (SDS), which set forth its ideology in *The Port Huron Statement,* a founding text of the "New Left." While recognizing the need to address issues of poverty and racism, SDS suggested the crisis of modern life was primarily moral. "A new left," SDS proclaimed, "must give form to the feelings of helplessness and indifference, so that people may see the political, social, and economic source of their personal troubles and organize to change society."

In 1963, 125 SDS members, mostly middle-class white men and women, set up chapters to organize poor whites and blacks in nine American cities. Other members traveled to Mississippi in 1964 as part of the SNCC Freedom Summer. The direct exposure to the brutality of southern justice radicalized many of the students, who returned to campus the following fall searching for an outlet for their fear and fury.

In October 1964, the administration of the University of California at Berkeley provided one. President Clark Kerr decided to enforce campus regulations prohibiting political demonstrations at the entrance of campus—a traditional site for student political expression. In response, student groups organized a Free Speech Movement (FSM). The movement soon broadened its focus to protest the "multiversity machine." The revolt quickly spread to other campuses and championed many causes, from opposing dress codes to fighting tenure decisions.

While the public focused most of its attention on the Left, conservatives were healing old wounds and mobilizing new recruits. Until the 1950s, conservatives had been divided into rival camps of Libertarians, who opposed all limitations on individual freedom, and Moralists, who believed that maintaining moral standards was more important than defending individual rights. By the end of the decade, fear of communism and the growing threat from expanded government forced a fusion of the two strains of conservative thought. At the same time, conservatives abandoned their traditional isolationism and advocated an aggressive internationalism.

With their ideological rift healed, conservatives presented a compelling alternative to the mainstream consensus. Like the New Left, the New Right attacked the moral relativism that blurred the distinction between right and wrong. Unlike their counterparts in SDS, however, the new conservatives called for an aggressive foreign policy, dramatic increases in military spending, and an end to most social welfare programs. Their message struck a responsive chord. By 1964, the right-wing John Birch Society claimed about fifty thousand members and received more than $7 million a year in contributions. Between 1960 and 1964, the circulation of the conservative monthly magazine, *The National Review*, founded in 1955, tripled to ninety thousand. Noting the proliferation of conservative clubs on college campuses, one conservative proclaimed a "new wave" of campus revolt. These new collegiate conservatives, he predicted, would be the "opinion-makers—the people who in ten, fifteen, and twenty-five years will begin to assume positions of power in America."

The Antiwar Movement

President Johnson's decision to escalate the conflict in Vietnam fanned the flames of student discontent. On March 24, 1965, students at the University of Michigan organized the first anti-Vietnam teach-in. Organizers planned lectures and discussions about the war in the hope of "educating" students to the dangers of American involvement in Vietnam. The restrained and respectable form of protest spread quickly to other college campuses.

Student anger reached a new level when, in January 1966, Johnson ended automatic draft deferments for college students. The threat of the draft persuaded young people to join demonstrations in which protesters burned draft cards and an occasional American flag. By highlighting the angriest confrontations between students and police, television contributed to a widespread public impression that the nation's campuses had been overrun by radicals. In fact, antiwar protest was largely confined to elite private colleges and large state universities. One study concluded that between 1965 and 1968, only 20 percent of college students participated in antiwar demonstrations.

Antiwar spirits were bolstered by establishment figures who joined the cause. In 1966 Democratic senator J. W. Fulbright, the powerful chairman of the Senate Foreign Relations Committee, held nationally televised hearings on the war. The nation listened as George Kennan, the father of containment, complained that the administration's preoccupation with Vietnam was stretching America's power and prestige. In April 1967, Martin Luther King criticized the government for sending young black men "to guarantee liberties in Southeast Asia which they had not found in Southwest Georgia and East Harlem."

While the media publicized campus protests, it was not student ideology that turned the American public against the war. The student movement viewed the war as immoral, a reflection of fundamental problems in American society. To the great majority of Americans, however, the war was not immoral. It was a tragic mistake. They wanted to end the war because winning no longer seemed worth the price. Class resentment reinforced the ideological differences among war opponents. A large number of working-class Americans opposed the war, but they disliked privileged student protesters even more. "We can't understand," lamented a blue-collar worker, "how all those rich kids—the kids with the beads from the fancy suburbs—how they get off when my son has to go over there and maybe get his head shot off."

In the short run, the administration successfully exploited these divisions by appealing to ingrained habits of patriotism. As late as the summer of 1967 opinion surveys showed that a majority of Americans continued to support the president's Vietnam policy. In the long run, however, the antiwar protesters chipped away at one of the cornerstones of the postwar consensus: America's policy of global containment. Over time, the Vietnam tragedy raised widespread doubts about the nation's anticommunist obsession and forced a rethinking of America's role in the world.

The Watershed Year, 1968

All the conflicting currents of the decade converged during the 1968 presidential election year. The liberal consensus found itself under assault from every direction. Angry students protesting the administration's Vietnam policy flooded into the streets. Many working-class whites, frustrated with social protest and urban riots, turned against the Democrats. The assassination of two political leaders seemed to confirm the nation's descent into political and social violence. A close November election suggested that voters had not abandoned the tattered liberal consensus but hoped their new president would experiment with the consensus in new ways.

Johnson Under Assault

On January 31, 1968, communist troops launched an offensive during the lunar New Year, called Tet in Vietnam. The Vietcong invaded the U.S. embassy compound in Saigon and waged bloody battles in the capitals of most of South Vietnam's provinces. Sixty-seven thousand enemy troops invaded more than one hundred of South Vietnam's cities and towns. From a military perspective, the Tet Offensive was a failure for the North Vietnamese. They suffered heavy casualties and failed to gain new ground or incite a popular rebellion against the United States.

But if a military defeat for the North, Tet represented a striking psychological victory. The ferocity of the offensive belied the optimistic reports of General Westmoreland, who had proclaimed as recently as November 1967 that he had "never been more encouraged in my four years in Vietnam." Television pictures of marines defending the grounds of the American embassy in Saigon shocked the nation. "What the hell is going on?" blurted television news anchor Walter Cronkite, echoing many Americans. "I thought we were winning this war!"

The Tet Offensive dealt Johnson's credibility a crowning blow. At home, the chief political beneficiary was Senator Eugene McCarthy. The Minnesota senator had challenged Johnson in the New Hampshire primary, the first contest of the 1968 presidential campaign. The state's governor had predicted that Johnson would "murder" McCarthy in his state. Instead, McCarthy polled a stunning 42.2 percent of the Democratic vote to Johnson's 49.4 percent by galvanizing both "hawks" and "doves" who opposed Johnson's Vietnam policy. New Hampshire transformed McCarthy from a hopeless underdog into a serious challenger and demonstrated Johnson's vulnerability.

Four days after Johnson's embarrassment, Robert F. Kennedy, who had been a senator from New York since 1964, entered the race for the Democratic nomination. Many Democrats believed that Kennedy was the only politician in America who could pull together the fractured liberal coalition. On Vietnam, Kennedy, who had supported his brother's military escalation of the conflict, now called for a negotiated settlement. He focused most of his attention, however, on domestic issues. Kennedy believed that convincing poor people of all colors to pursue their shared class interests offered the only solution to the deep racial hostility that was tearing the nation apart. "We have to convince the Negroes and poor whites that they have common interests," Kennedy told a journalist. "If we can reconcile those two hostile groups, and then add the kids, you can really turn this country around."

Lyndon Johnson, meanwhile, seemed cornered by his own policies. Public support for his Vietnam policy dropped to 26 percent in the aftermath of Tet. His military advisers asked for an additional 206,000 troops, which would have brought the total to 750,000. His civilian advisers, led by veteran presidential consultant Clark Clifford recommended a negotiated settlement. "We seem to have a sinkhole"" Clifford said. Reluctantly, Johnson agreed.

On March 31 the president told a national television audience that he had ordered a temporary halt to the bombing and called for peace talks between the warring sides. At the end of the speech Johnson shocked the nation by announcing that he would not seek reelection. Three weeks later, Vice President Hubert Humphrey announced that he would run in Johnson's place.

While Kennedy and McCarthy battled in the Democratic primaries, another outspoken critic of the administration was raising his voice in protest. By 1968, Martin Luther King had abandoned his previous emphasis on dramatic confrontations and accepted the SNCC strategy of community organizing in an effort to build a class-based, grass-roots alliance among the poor. King spent most of the winter organizing a "poor people's march on Washington." Like Kennedy, King argued that America's racial problems could not be solved without addressing the issue of class. "We must recognize," he said in 1967, "that we can't solve our problems now until there is a radical redistribution of economic and political power." King now considered himself a revolutionary, not a reformer.

In March 1968, King supported striking garbage workers in Memphis, Tennessee, hoping a peaceful, successful walkout would further his new, more aggressive message of redistribution of power and his enduring commitment to nonviolence. While in Memphis in April to encourage the strikers, he reaffirmed his faith in the possibility of racial justice: "I may not get there with you. But we as a people will get to the promised land." The following day, April 4, King died, shot to death by assassin James Earl Ray, a white ex-convict.

King's death touched off an orgy of racial violence. Rioters burned twenty blocks in Chicago, where Mayor Daley ordered embattled police to "shoot to kill." The worst violence occurred in Washington, D.C., where seven hundred fires burned and nine people lost their lives. For the first time since the Civil War, armed soldiers guarded the steps to the Capitol. Nationally the death toll was forty-six. "Martin's memory is being desecrated," said one black leader.

With King dead, Kennedy became for many disaffected people, black and white, the only national leader who commanded respect and enthusiasm. Kennedy may have had the broadest base of support, but party leaders selected most convention delegates. A large majority of these delegates, remaining loyal to the administration, pledged their support to Humphrey. Kennedy's strategy was to sweep the remaining major primaries, showing such support at the polls that the convention delegates would have no choice but to nominate him.

Kennedy won a decisive victory over Humphrey and McCarthy in Indiana but lost in Oregon. The California primary on June 4 was critical, and Kennedy won. But that evening, after giving his victory speech, he was shot by Sirhan Sirhan, a Palestinian who opposed the senator's pro-Israel position. Twenty-five hours later, Robert Kennedy died, dimming Democrats' hopes of uniting their disparate coalition of blacks and whites, hawks and doves, young and old.

The Democratic Convention

Robert Kennedy's death assured Humphrey of the nomination on the first ballot. But in the months leading up to the Democratic convention in Chicago, he could not achieve a compromise on a Vietnam plank for the party platform that was acceptable to both the peace forces and the president, who said he would oppose any statement that implied criticism of his policy.

Johnson added just one combustible ingredient to the explosive atmosphere at the Chicago convention. Antiwar protesters contributed a second. The city's powerful mayor, Richard Daley, contributed the final ingredient. Determined to demonstrate that he was in control of the streets, Daley turned the city into a fortress. He surrounded the convention hall with barbed wire, mobilized 12,000 police, and placed 7,500 national guardsmen on alert.

The explosion took place on August 2, when police dispersed thousands of protesters from Lincoln Park. "The cops had one thing on their minds," one journalist said: "Club and then gas, club and then gas, club and then gas." The presence of television cameras and dozens of journalists from around the world did nothing to deter police violence. The police went berserk, a British journalist wrote; "the kids screamed and were beaten to the ground by cops who had completely lost their cool."

The next day the convention debated the Vietnam platform plank. At the end of nearly three hours of heated debate by the party's most distinguished leaders, the majority pro-administration plank won in a close vote. As the session ended,

Chicago, 1968 At the Democratic national convention, the tensions that had been building over the course of the decade came to a head. Twenty thousand armed police violently confronted demonstrators gathered to protest the nomination of Hubert Humphrey, while the demonstrators hurled insults at their assailants. The entire spectacle was broadcast on television before horrified Americans. Richard Nixon capitalized on the fears of the "silent majority" that American society was dissolving in chaos at the hands of people such as the "yippies" who "disrupted" the Democratic convention. *(Corbis-Bettmann.)*

supporters of the minority plank donned black armbands and remained in their seats, singing "We Shall Overcome." As dramatic as these events were, the real action was taking place outside the hall where the police assaulted a group of peaceful demonstrators seeking to march on the convention headquarters. With no attempt to distinguish bystanders and peaceful protesters from lawbreakers, the police smashed people through plate-glass windows, fired tear-gas canisters indiscriminately, and brutalized anyone who got in their way. "These are our children," *New York Times* columnist Tom Wicker cried out as the violence swirled around him.

Television crews filmed the melee as it occurred, and footage of the violence was shown during the nomination speeches. The dramatic scenes overshadowed Humphrey's nomination on the first ballot and his selection of Maine senator Edmund Muskie as his running mate.

The public's reaction to the police riot gave an indication of the American mood in 1968. Most Americans sympathized with the police. In a poll taken shortly after the Democratic convention, most blue-collar workers approved the way the

Chicago police had handled the protesters; some of them thought the police were "not tough enough" on them. Bumper stickers declaring "WE SUPPORT MAYOR DALEY AND HIS CHICAGO POLICE," blossomed across the country.

The Center Holds: The Election of 1968

Two candidates were vying for the allegiance of these angry voters. The most direct appeal came from American Independence Party candidate George Wallace, whose symbolic stance in a university doorway had made him a hero to southern whites. In 1968 Wallace's anti-establishment populism also appealed to many northern Democrats angry over the party's association with protest and integration. Wallace moved up in the polls by catering to the resentments of his followers: "If a demonstrator ever lays down in front of my car," Wallace told large and enthusiastic crowds, "it'll be the last car he'll ever lay down in front of." One survey showed that more than half of the nation shared Wallace's view that "liberals, intellectuals, and long-hairs have run the country for too long."

Joining Wallace in pursuit of the hearts and minds of America's angry white voters was the Republican nominee, Richard Nixon. In the years following Goldwater's defeat in 1964, Nixon had emerged as a centrist who could appeal to both the liberal and conservative wings of the Republican Party.

Nixon campaigned in 1968 as the candidate of unity, reflecting his belief that most Americans wanted an end to the civil discord. To capitalize on the yearning for tranquility, Nixon promised that he had a plan—never specified—to end the war in Vietnam. But his top priority, he declared, was the restoration of law and order. Nixon appealed to the "forgotten Americans," those whose values of patriotism and stability had been violated by student protesters, urban riots, and arrogant intellectuals. His strategy for the campaign was to stay above the fray. He refused to debate Humphrey, and he limited his public appearances to televised question-and-answer sessions before audiences of partisan Republicans.

Humphrey emerged from the debacle in Chicago a badly damaged candidate. Antiwar protesters blamed him for LBJ's Vietnam policies, while many working-class Democrats associated him with the violent protest and civil unrest of the convention. On September 30, Humphrey discovered his independent voice and announced that he would "stop the bombing of North Vietnam as an acceptable risk for peace." On October 31, less than a week before election day, Johnson helped Humphrey's cause by announcing a bombing pause in Vietnam.

The weekend before the election Humphrey pulled even with Nixon in many polls. But on election day, Nixon won by a razor-thin majority in the popular vote, receiving 31,785,480 votes compared with Humphrey's 31,275,166. Less than seven-tenths of 1 percent separated the two candidates. Nixon took only 43.4 percent of the popular vote, the smallest share earned by a winning candidate since Woodrow Wilson in 1912. He scored a more decisive triumph in the electoral college, amassing 301 votes to Humphrey's 191. Wallace carried five states, receiving 46 electoral votes and 13.5 percent of the popular vote—the best showing for a third-party candidate in forty-four years (see map).

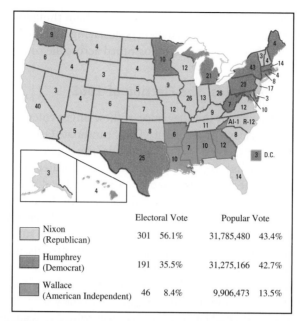

	Electoral Vote	Popular Vote
Nixon (Republican)	301 56.1%	31,785,480 43.4%
Humphrey (Democrat)	191 35.5%	31,275,166 42.7%
Wallace (American Independent)	46 8.4%	9,906,473 13.5%

The Election of 1968   With Johnson out of the race, both Richard Nixon and Hubert Humphrey pursued voters with promises to end the war in Vietnam. A third-party candidate, governor of Alabama George Wallace, won the Deep South with a segregationist platform, while Nixon carried all but four states west of the Mississippi. Vice President Humphrey, unable to shake his ties to Johnson, made inroads predominantly in the Northeast.

In a year that had witnessed almost unprecedented violence and turmoil, the voters produced a very conventional result. "Of all the extraordinary developments of 1968," observed one commentator, "perhaps least expected was the durability of characters and institutions in the face of defiant challenge." In a decade marked by challenges to established institutions, Americans looked to a familiar face and old values to guide them through the troubled days ahead.

CONCLUSION

In 1960 a common set of assumptions guided Americans into the new decade. Reflecting the broad outlines of the postwar consensus, most believed that economic growth, combined with finely tuned government programs, could solve most social problems, from poverty to civil rights. Abroad, Americans supported the continuing policy of global containment against a menacing Soviet Union.

No one captured the optimism of the consensus more eloquently than the new president, John F. Kennedy, who inspired the nation with his stirring rhetoric about national purpose. Restrained by a stubborn Congress from liberal experimentation at home, the young leader focused his energy on foreign policy, engaging in intense confrontations with the Soviets over Cuba and Berlin. Determined to prevent a Soviet advance in Southeast Asia, Kennedy increased support for America's beleaguered South Vietnamese ally.

Kennedy's death on November 22, 1963, stunned the nation, and his successor, Lyndon Johnson, invoked Kennedy's legacy and used his own political skills to advance an ambitious Great Society agenda. Under Johnson's watchful eye Congress passed the two most significant pieces of civil rights legislation since Reconstruction, banning segregation in public facilities and guaranteeing African-Americans the right to vote. The antipoverty programs, Medicare, and Medicaid expanded the social safety net and improved the quality of life for millions of Americans. Under Chief Justice Earl Warren the Supreme Court shared the activist temperament, issuing landmark rulings expanding individual rights and freedom of the press.

Yet despite these notable accomplishments, the 1960s also revealed the fissures in the liberal consensus. Popular fears of an intrusive national government limited the scope and effectiveness of Johnson's Great Society experiment. Antipoverty programs were plagued by modest funding and complicated administrative procedures that gave individual states control over funding. While many Americans supported legislation that banned segregation and provided African-Americans with basic political rights, they balked at more ambitious proposals for redressing economic inequality.

In many ways the much heralded consensus was an illusion. The black struggle for civil, political, and economic equality presented the most powerful challenge. In its early phase, moderate leaders like Martin Luther King, Jr., worked within the constraints of the consensus. King denounced violence, sought alliance with northern white liberals, and focused his efforts on banning segregation and achieving basic political rights. After 1965, however, the movement grew increasingly more radical as blacks pressed demands for economic as well as political equality. By 1966, King's experiment was overshadowed by militant calls for black nationalism. The urban riots that ripped through major cities between 1965 and 1968 underscored the deep racial divide in America.

While the civil rights movement exposed the limits of consensus at home, a costly war in Vietnam raised questions about America's policy of global containment. Confident in American power, Johnson escalated the conflict in Vietnam, transforming a local nationalist struggle into a superpower confrontation. Discontent and debate over the war exposed deep fault lines in American society, between hawk and dove, between young and old, and between working-class families and middle-class students.

Young people, too, organized a powerful challenge to consensus. College campuses became seedbeds of political activity as students mobilized to support the civil rights movement in the South and, later, to protest the war in Vietnam. Radicalized by divisive events, many middle-class college students complained that liberalism was too tepid, unwilling to advocate a massive redistribution of wealth and power in America. Not all young people became politically active. Many turned to music and other forms of cultural expression to vent their frustration with contemporary society. Over a million people followed Timothy Leary's advice to "tune in, turn on, drop out."

By 1968, protest and police violence outside the Democratic convention in Chicago drove home how badly the consensus had splintered. Conservatives moved to fill the power vacuum. Richard Nixon's shrewd calls for unity and patriotism appealed to white voters angry with the Democratic Party's support for civil rights, frustrated with the situation in Vietnam, and exasperated by student protesters.

This coalition of discontent gained control of the White House in 1968 and promised to flex its political muscle for years to come.

SUGGESTED READINGS

The 1960s were years conspicuous for the self-conscious commitment to social change they produced, a fact manifested in much of the gripping, often reflective writing produced by veterans of the period. Todd Gitlin, a former SDS President and war protester, combines memoir and critical analysis in his *The Sixties* (1987) to portray the social activism that gave the decade much of its dynamism and drama. Allen Matusow's *The Unraveling of America* (1984) offers a more distanced account of the decade that centers on the crisis of liberalism. John Blum's *Years of Discord* (1991) surveys the broad sweep of political strife that marked the Kennedy, Johnson, and Nixon administrations. David Burner captures the failed idealism of the decade in *Making Peace with the 60s* (1996).

John Kennedy's ability to grasp the reins of leadership sets the tone of Theodore White's classic on the art of modern campaigning, *The Making of the President, 1960* (1961). Arthur Schlesinger's epic *A Thousand Days* (1965) compounds the sympathy of a former Kennedy administration official with the perspective of an historian. With *JFK: The Presidency of John F. Kennedy* (1983), Herbert Parmet steps back from the ebullience of the Schlesinger generation to survey the major events of the Kennedy administration, balancing accomplishments against limitations. He is joined in that effort by James Giglio, *The Presidency of John F. Kennedy* (1991). Gary Wills's *The Kennedy Imprisonment* (1982) is a critical meditation on the troubling aspects of Kennedy's charismatic leadership. Thomas Brown casts a skeptical eye on the use of the media to create an aura surrounding the Kennedy image in his *JFK: The History of an Image* (1988).

Irving Bernstein's comprehensive *Guns or Butter* (1996) chronicles the many significant accomplishments of Johnson's Great Society and balances them against the compromises necessitated by the escalation of the Vietnam War. John A. Andrew offers a brief overview in *Lyndon Johnson and the Great Society* (1998). Robert Caro's critical biographies—*The Years of Lyndon Johnson: Path to Power* (1982) and *Means of Ascent* (1990)—need to be balanced with Robert Dalleck's masterful volumes, *Lone Star Rising* (1991) and *Flawed Giant* (1998). James Patterson's *America's Struggle Against Poverty, 1900–1994* (1995) analyzes the fateful consequences of the Great Society's "welfare explosion" from the longer-term perspective of modern poverty policy and its implementation. Michael Beschloss uses White House tape recordings to provide a rare glimpse inside the Johnson administration in *Taking Charge* (1997).

J. Harvie Wilkinson discusses the evolution of Supreme Court decisions concerning school integration in his instructive *From Brown to Bakke* (1979), underlining the increasingly expansive definition of the Court's role in national life. Alexander Bickel's collected lectures, *The Supreme Court and the Idea of Progress* (1970), critique the Court's "subjective" approach to jurisprudence, arguing that the judiciary had become overburdened in its attempt to redress social problems. In *Earl Warren* (1982), G. Edward White discusses the formative influences on Warren's progressive world-view and the ways they revealed themselves in public life. Anthony Lewis brings to life the personal stakes of judicial activism in his classic account of one man's extraordinary involvement in a landmark criminal rights decision, *Gideon's Trumpet* (1964).

In recent years historians have emphasized the grass-roots nature of the civil rights movement. John Dittmer's history of the civil rights movement in Mississippi, *Local People* (1994), reveals the commitment and grit of ordinary people that sustained an extraordinary social movement. Clayborne Carson's *In Struggle* (1981), a definitive history of SNCC, traces the evolution of black consciousness through the process of grass-roots mobilization and protest. Doug McAdam's *Freedom Summer* (1988) studies the impact of SNCC's watershed moment on a generation of activists. David Garrow, *Bearing the Cross* (1986), and

Taylor Branch, *Parting the Waters* (1988), take a more traditional look at the civil rights movement through the lens of King's leadership. Works on the violent side of civil rights include Robert Fogelson's *Violence as Protest* (1971) and Robert Conot's *Rivers of Blood* (1967). Important primary sources on civil rights include King's *Why We Can't Wait* (1964), James Baldwin's *The Fire Next Time* (1962), the Kerner Commission's *Report of the National Advisory Commission on Civil Disorders* (1968), and Stokely Carmichael and Charles Hamilton's *Black Power* (1967).

The literature on the conduct of the Vietnam War is immense. George Herring's *America's Longest War* (1986) and Stanley Karnow's *Vietnam* (1983) are good starting points.On the fateful decision to send troops, see Larry Berman's *Planning a Tragedy* (1982). Neil Sheehan captures the tragic dimensions of Americans' commitment to winning the war in his elegantly written *A Bright Shining Lie* (1988). David Halberstam, who made his name reporting from Vietnam, reveals in *The Best and the Brightest* (1972) the atmosphere of brash optimism and technocratic assurance that accompanied the U.S. commitment. *In Retrospect* (1995) offers Robert McNamara's reflections on mistakes made and lessons learned.

Godfrey Hodgson traces liberalism's cathartic passage through the 1960s, and the Cold War developments that necessitated the turmoil, in his masterful synthesis, *America in Our Time* (1976). Steve Gillon views the crisis within liberalism through the prism of the ADA in his *Politics and Vision* (1987). John Diggins, *The Rise and Fall of the American Left* (1992), discusses the culmination of the American Left's troubled legacy in the sixties. Maurice Isserman's *If I Had a Hammer* (1987) draws more sanguine connections between the Old Left and the New Left, although his account remains ambivalent. Jeff Shesol offers insight into the rivalry between Robert Kennedy and Lyndon Johnson in *Mutual Contempt* (1997). The political rift that dislocated liberalism in 1968, along with the collision of paradigms that caused it, is nicely encapsulated in David Farber's study of the Yippies, the antiwar protesters, and the Daley machine at the Democratic convention in *Chicago '68* (1988).

Much of the student activism that challenged centrist liberals in the 1960s was inspired by or patterned after the national prominent student movement described by W. J. Rorabaugh in *Berkeley at War* (1989). Kirkpatrick Sales's *SDS* (1973) places the equally influential student organization at the center of the cultural ferment of the sixties. Todd Gitlin unveils the opportunities and constraints the media posed for the New Left in *The Whole World Is Watching* (1980). Two especially good books on the antiwar movement are Charles DeBenedetti's *An American Ordeal* (1990) and Christian Appy's *Working-Class War* (1993). On Barry Goldwater and the rise of conservatism see Robert Alan Goldberg's *Barry Goldwater* (1995) and Mary C. Brennan *Turning Right in the Sixties* (1995).

The tendency to see the student protest movements as harbingers of a profound society-wide awakening of political activism and consciousness was influenced early on by two widely read essays, Theodore Roszak's *The Making of a Counter-Culture* (1969) and Charles Reich's *The Greening of America* (1971). Terry Anderson's *The Movement and the Sixties* (1995) looks closely at the underground sources to draw connections between the many protests of the period and see in them a much larger overall cultural shift toward activism. David Caute's *The Year of the Barricades* (1988) identifies 1968 as a moment of cultural epiphany when many discrete protests coalesced into something more significant than they had been separately. George Katsiaficas's *The Imagination of the New Left* (1987) views the protests of the 1960s as part of a world-historical movement. Martin Lee and Bruce Shlain emphasize the distance between the counterculture and establishment in *Acid Dreams: The CIA, LSD, and the Sixties Rebellion* (1985). For a gripping, dizzying journey into the lives of some pioneers of the counterculture, see Tom Wolfe's *The Electric Kool-Aid Acid Test* (1968).

Martin Luther King, Jr., and Malcolm X

Letter from Birmingham Jail

On Good Friday, April 16, 1963, Rev. Martin Luther King, Jr., was arrested and jailed for participating in a nonviolent protest in Birmingham, Alabama. While King sat imprisoned in a dark cell cut off from the demonstrations he had helped mastermind, eight Birmingham clergymen released a statement criticizing the protest and asking King to leave Birmingham. The plea, published in the local newspaper, called King "an outsider," attacked the demonstrations as "unwise and untimely," praised the police for keeping "order" and "preventing violence." King believed the comments could not go unanswered. His response, written on scraps of paper using a pen smuggled into his cell, explained the religious and philosophical underpinnings of King's strategy of nonviolence.

At first I was rather disappointed that fellow clergymen would see my nonviolent efforts as those of an extremist. I began thinking about the fact that I stand in the middle of two opposing forces in the Negro community. One is a force of complacency, made up in part of Negroes who, as a result of long years of oppression, are so drained of self-respect and a sense of "somebodiness" that they have adjusted to segregation; and in part of a few middle-class Negroes who, because of a degree of academic and economic security and because in some ways they profit by segregation, have become insensitive to the problems of the masses. The other force is one of bitterness and hatred, and it comes perilously close to advocating violence. It is expressed in the various black nationalist groups that are springing up across the nation, the largest and best-known being Elijah Muhammad's Muslim movement. Nourished by the Negro's frustration over the continued existence of racial discrimination, this movement is made up of people who have lost faith in America, who have absolutely repudiated Christianity, and who have concluded that the white man is an incorrigible "devil."

I have tried to stand between these two forces, saying that we need emulate neither the "do-nothingism" of the complacent nor the hatred and despair of the black nationalist. For there is the more excellent way of love and nonviolent protest. I am grateful to God that, through the influence of the Negro church, the way of nonviolence became an integral part of our struggle.

If this philosophy had not emerged, by now many streets of the South would, I am convinced, be flowing with blood. And I am further convinced that if our white brothers dismiss as "rabble-rousers" and "outside agitators" those of us who employ nonviolent direct action, and if they refuse to support our nonviolent efforts, millions of Negroes will, out of frustration and despair, seek solace and security in black-nationalist ideologies—a development that would inevitably lead to a frightening racial nightmare....

I had hoped that the white moderate would see this need. Perhaps I was too optimistic; perhaps I expected too much. I suppose I should have realized that few members of the oppressor race can understand the deep groans and passionate yearnings of the oppressed race, and still fewer have the vision to see that injustice must be rooted out by strong, persistent and determined action. . . .

. . . We will reach the goal of freedom in Birmingham and all over the nation, because the goal of America is freedom. Abused and scorned though we may be, our destiny is tied up with America's destiny. . . . We will win our freedom because the sacred heritage of our nation and the eternal will of God are embodied in our echoing demands.

The Autobiography of Malcolm X

King's message of integration and nonviolence appealed to the largely southern, middle-class African-Americans who dominated the leadership of the early phase of the civil rights movement. As the decade progressed, however, the movement shifted northward, where it was forced to address the seething anger of an urban underclass trapped in poverty. Malcolm X, a leader of the Black Muslims, emerged as the most forceful and charismatic spokesman of the new militancy of urban poor blacks. In his autobiography, published in 1964, Malcolm X questioned King's strategy of nonviolence and offered black nationalism as an alternative.

I don't go for non-violence if it also means a delayed solution. To me a delayed solution is a non-solution. Or I'll say it another way: If it must take violence to get the black man his human rights in this country, I'm *for* violence exactly as you know the Irish, Poles, or Jews would be if they were flagrantly discriminated against. I am just as they would be in that case, and they would be for violence—no matter what the consequences, no matter who was hurt by the violence.

White society *hates* to hear anybody, especially a black man, talk about the crime the white man has perpetrated on the black man. I have always understood that's why I have been so frequently called "a revolutionist." It sounds as if I have done some crime! Well, it may be the American black man does need to become involved in a *real* revolution. . . . So how does anybody sound talking about the Negro in America waging some "revolution"? Yes, he is condemning a system—but he's not trying to overturn the system, or to destroy it. The Negro's so-called "revolt" is merely an asking to be *accepted* into the existing system! A *true* Negro revolt might entail, for instance, fighting for separate black states within this country—which several groups and individuals have advocated, long before Elijah Muhammad came along.

Does white America have the capacity to repent—and to atone? Does the capacity to repent, to atone, exist in a majority, in one-half, in even one-third of American white society?

Many black men, the victims—in fact most black men—would like to be able to forgive, to forget, the crimes.

But most American white people seem not to have it in them to make any serious atonement—to do justice to the black man.

Indeed, how *can* white society atone for enslaving, for raping, for unmanning, for otherwise brutalizing millions of human beings, for centuries? What atonement would the God of Justice demand for the robbery of the black people's labor, their lives, their true identities, their culture, their history—and even their human dignity?

A desegregated cup of coffee, a theater, public toilets—the whole range of hypocritical "integration"—these are not atonement. . . .

I kept having all kinds of troubles trying to develop the kind of Black Nationalist organization I wanted to build for the American Negro. Why Black Nationalism? Well, in the competitive American society, how can there ever be any white–black solidarity before there is first some black solidarity?

. . . . I mean nothing against any sincere whites when I say that as members of black organizations, generally whites' very presence subtly renders the black organization automatically less effective. . . .

I tell sincere white people, "Work in conjunction with us—each of us working among our own kind." Let sincere white individuals find all other white people they can who feel as they do—and let them form their own all-white groups, to work trying to convert other white people who are thinking and acting as racist. Let sincere whites go and teach non-violence to white people! ▌

Nearly one hundred years after the Civil War, America remained a society deeply divided by race. The South enforced a rigid system of legal segregation by violence and intimidation. But the South did not have a monopoly on racism. In 1966, after spending months fighting for integrated housing in Chicago, an exasperated Martin Luther King exclaimed, "I have never seen such hate." In the North, racism relegated African-Americans to second-class citizenship, forcing them to live in communities plagued by crime, low employment, and poor public facilities.

Black leaders divided over the best strategy for confronting this racism and for improving the quality of life for most African-Americans. Like previous leaders, such as the educator W. E. B. Du Bois (1868–1963), King viewed confrontation as a means of achieving integration and equal rights. Conscious of their minority status, leaders such as Du Bois and King hoped to build coalitions with white liberals. The challenge, Du Bois wrote, was to find a way "to be both a Negro and an American." Malcolm X, on the other hand, shared more in common with leaders such as Marcus Garvey, who, during the 1920s, urged blacks to reject everything white and crusaded for black economic self-sufficiency.

It is interesting to note, however, that both King and Malcolm were evolving, their views converging. By 1964, Malcolm rejected racism and spoke of the common bonds that linked all humanity. King was growing more radical as he came to appreciate the need for fundamental economic reforms. Tragically, neither man had the opportunity to finish his spiritual and intellectual journey.

Questions for Analysis

1. Why was King confident about the ultimate success of the struggle for civil rights?

2. Why does Malcolm X oppose King's strategy of nonviolence?

3. What does he offer as an alternative?

4. What does King have to say about black nationalism?

5. How do King's and Malcolm's views of America differ?

6. In your opinion, which leader offered the best strategy for helping black America? Why?

30

The Politics of Polarization, 1969–1979

*A*t noon on Monday, May 4, 1970, students at Kent State University in Ohio organized for an antiwar rally on the Commons, a grassy campus gathering spot. For the previous three days the lush lawns and green elms and maple trees of this 790-acre campus had been the site of violent confrontation between students and police. What ignited the protest was President Nixon's announcement on April 30 of his decision to widen the war in Vietnam by sending American ground troops into neighboring Cambodia. The surprise announcement came as a shock to a nation lulled into complacency by troop withdrawals and declining body counts.

National Guard jeeps drove onto the Commons, and an officer ordered the crowd to disperse. A platoon of guardsmen, armed with M-1 rifles and tear-gas equipment, followed, moving methodically across the green and over the crest of a hill chasing the protesters. The crowd taunted the poorly trained guardsmen, chanting "Pigs Off Campus" and hurling stones and bricks. The troops, most of them local townspeople—accountants, bankers, barbers—responded by firing volleys of tear gas into the crowd.

Suddenly the crackle of gunfire cut through the tear-gas-laced air. A girl screamed, "My God, they're killing us!" Some students fled; others fell to the ground. The turmoil lasted only a few seconds, but by the time the shooting stopped, four students lay dead and another eleven were seriously wounded. None of those hit at Kent State had broken any law, and none was a campus radical; among them were two women who had never been part of the protest but were simply walking to class. An investigation by the Federal Bureau of Investigation agreed, calling the shootings "unnecessary, unwarranted, and inexcusable."

After the Kent State killings, in what Columbia University president William J. McGill called "the most disastrous month of May in the history of American higher education," over 400 colleges had to cancel some classes and 250 campuses were closed altogether as young people expressed their outrage. Not everyone was sympathetic to the students. One poll indicated that 58 percent of the public blamed the students for the Kent State deaths. A local resident told the town newspaper that the guardsmen "should have fired sooner and longer."

These responses reveal how divided Americans had become in their efforts to reconcile traditional beliefs and institutions with significant challenges to mainstream culture and politics. Abroad, the nation remained mired in a conflict it could neither win nor end. At home, minority demands for equal rights were met with growing resistance and anger from "middle America." Richard Nixon was elected on a promise to bring harmony to American politics. Despite his willingness to experiment in both foreign and domestic policy, his efforts to create a durable base of political support only clarified and hardened the divisions separating Americans.

Later in the decade, Americans were faced with a series of puzzling public problems that no one seemed able to solve. More than two decades of postwar economic growth came to a halt. Revelations of misconduct by high elected officials undermined public faith in political institutions. By the end of the decade an American president wondered at the cumulative effect of these shocks and warned the nation about its "crisis of confidence."

▌ How did the failure in Vietnam force Americans to reconsider their approach to the world?

▌ What was the "silent majority," and what accounted for its attitudes toward government and society?

▌ Why did so many groups mobilize to demand their "rights" during the 1970s?

▌ How did popular culture reflect the social conflicts of the decade? How did America's political institutions cope with the conflicting demands?

This chapter will address these questions.

Experiments in Peacemaking, 1969–1974

Nixon assumed the presidency confident in his ability to handle foreign affairs. He and his close aide Henry Kissinger believed that realism needed to replace the excessive moralism that often characterized American foreign policy. Consolidating enormous power in the White House, they launched aggressive experiments to secure "peace with honor" in Vietnam and to lessen tensions between the superpowers.

Chronology

1962	Chavez founds National Farm Workers Association
1966	NOW founded
1968	Nixon elected president
1969	Nixon announces Vietnamization
	Stonewall Inn riot
1970	Kent State massacre
	Nixon orders ground troops into Cambodia
	Clean Air and Water Acts
1971	*Pentagon Papers* published
	Environmental Protection Agency created
1972	Nixon goes to China and Soviet Union
	Watergate break-in
	Nixon reelected
	Congress passes ERA
1973	Paris Peace Accords signed
	Allende overthrown and killed in Chile
	Yom Kippur War begins; OPEC imposes oil embargo on U.S.
	Watergate hearings
	Wounded Knee occupied
	Roe v. *Wade*
	War Powers Act
1974	Nixon resigns; Ford becomes president
1976	Carter elected president
1977	Panama Canal treaties
1978	*Bakke* v. *University of California*
	U.S. recognizes China
	Camp David Accords
1979	Iran hostage crisis
	Soviets invade Afghanistan
	Nuclear accident at Three Mile Island

Nixon's War

The Vietnam War was the most pressing issue confronting the new administration. In developing his strategy for dealing with the conflict, Nixon relied heavily on his national security adviser, Henry Kissinger, who became secretary of state in October 1973. Born in Germany in 1923, Kissinger traveled to the United States in 1938. After serving in World War II, he attended Harvard, earned a Ph.D. in government, and joined the faculty.

Nixon and Kissinger shared both a personal style and a similar view of America's role in the world. They possessed a desire for power and a penchant for secrecy and intrigue. Together, they concentrated decision making in the White House and excluded even close aides from sensitive diplomatic initiatives. An observer suggested that Kissinger's aides were like mushrooms: "They're kept in the dark, get a lot of manure piled on them, and then get canned." For his part, Nixon, who took great pride in his knowledge of international relations, functioned as his own secretary of state. The man who actually occupied the position, William Rogers, had little foreign policy experience and no influence in the White House. Nixon and Kissinger also shared an essentially pessimistic view of the behavior of nations known as *Realpolitik*. Power, they believed, not ideals or moral suasion, counted in international affairs. Nations could be expected to act in their own narrowly defined interest.

Nixon understood that his administration's success hinged on diffusing the crisis in Vietnam. The president believed that by reducing the number of combat troops, which stood at 545,000 in 1969, he could cut the casualties that fueled

Nixon and Kissinger   In one of many private conversations, Richard Nixon discusses foreign affairs with special assistant for national security affairs, Henry Kissinger. Kissinger, a Harvard professor of international relations, served as Nixon's national security advisor until 1973 when he became secretary of state.   *(Camera Press/Retna Ltd.)*

home-front protest. In May 1969, he announced a new policy that he called Vietnamization: South Vietnamese forces would gradually be strengthened so that American troops could be withdrawn from the war. As promised, Nixon rapidly reduced the number of ground troops to thirty thousand by September 1972. In December 1969, Nixon announced a draft lottery system that eliminated many of the inequities of the older system. By 1973, troop withdrawals would allow him to end the draft and create an all-volunteer army.

This did not mean, however, that Nixon intended to give up in Vietnam. Like Johnson, Nixon was committed to preserving an independent, noncommunist South Vietnam. While official announcements focused on troop withdrawals, the president dramatically enlarged the bombing campaign. Nixon explained his approach as "the Madman Theory." "I want the North Vietnamese to believe I've reached the point where I might do anything to stop the war," he confided in 1968. In his first month in office Nixon authorized Operation Menu—the secret bombing of North Vietnamese bases and supply routes in Cambodia. Over the next fifteen months, American B-52 bombers served up a deadly diet of explosives. By 1971, the United States had dropped more bombs on Indochina than it had in all the European and Pacific theaters during World War II. "I refuse to believe that a little fourth-rate power like North Vietnam does not have a breaking point," Kissinger told his staff.

The bombings not only failed to intimidate the North Vietnamese, it did little to stem the losses on the ground in South Vietnam. The South's government was failing miserably in its efforts to win popular legitimacy and to build an effective military force. Its army suffered from massive desertions and poor, often corrupt and brutal, leadership. In 1970 a senior army official questioned whether the South Vietnamese army could develop "the offensive and aggressive spirit that will be necessary to counter either the VC or the NVA [North Vietnamese Army]."

American military officials believed the NVA, despite aerial bombing, was still using Cambodia as a staging ground for attacks on South Vietnam. In April 1970, Nixon ordered American ground troops into the neutral country. Claiming that an American defeat in Vietnam would unleash the forces of totalitarianism around the globe, he insisted that the invasion of Cambodia was a guarantee of American "credibility." "The most powerful nation in the world," he said, could not afford to act "like a pitiful helpless giant."

The raids achieved some of the short-term goals set by military planners. American units seized large caches of Vietnamese weapons and disrupted some North Vietnamese bases. But on the whole the invasion was a failure. The NVA survived intact, while the raids destabilized Cambodian society and undermined the Cambodian government. American bombing raids produced more than 1 million refugees, who fled the countryside and jammed already overcrowded cities. In this atmosphere of chaos a small group of dedicated communists—the Khmer Rouge— seized control of the country and began a deadly purge that killed millions more. At home, the invasion reinflamed antiwar sentiment and eroded support for Nixon's policy. Anger swept like wildfire across the nation and revived the fledgling peace movement, which had been lulled into complacency by news of troop withdrawals. Within days of the Kent State killings, about a fifth of the nation's college campuses were forced to cancel classes. More than one hundred thousand people gathered in Washington to protest the Cambodian invasion and the student deaths. In San Diego, a student holding a placard reading "In the name of God, end the war," doused himself with gasoline, then set himself on fire.

By the summer of 1971, over 70 percent questioned in one poll called American involvement in Vietnam a mistake, and only 31 percent approved of Nixon's handling of the war. Even in the heartland, people were turning against the war. "I don't think you could find a hawk around here if you combed the place and set traps," declared a small-town Kansas journalist.

Congress turned up the heat on the president. South Dakota's Democratic senator George McGovern censured his colleagues for their part in the war: "This chamber reeks of blood." The Senate Foreign Relations Committee denounced the "constitutionally unauthorized, Presidential war in Indochina." In June, Congress repealed the Tonkin Gulf Resolution of 1964 and considered amendments to cut off funds for all American military operations in Cambodia.

In public, Nixon appeared unconcerned about the growing signs of discontent with his policies. He made a point of telling reporters that he watched the Washington Redskins football game while one large demonstration clamored for attention outside the White House. In February 1971, to prove that he had not been intimidated by the protests, Nixon used American air cover in support of an invasion of neutral Laos. Once again the invasion produced no military advantage but resulted in thousands of civilian deaths and a sea of refugees.

Behind the confident façade, Nixon was growing increasingly isolated and embattled, paranoid that his enemies in the Congress, the press, and the antiwar movement were conspiring to destroy him. "Within the iron gates of the White House, quite unknowingly, a siege mentality was setting in," a Nixon aide recalled. "It was now 'us' against 'them.' Gradually, as we drew the circle closer around us, the ranks of 'them' began to swell."

The circle tightened in June 1971 when the *New York Times* began publishing *The Pentagon Papers*, a secret Defense Department study of American decision making in Vietnam before 1967. Leaked to the press by a former Pentagon official, Daniel Ellsberg, the report showed that Kennedy and Johnson had consistently misled the public about their intentions in Vietnam. Nixon tried to block further publication, claiming it would damage national security. The Supreme Court, by a vote of 6 to 3, ruled against the administration, citing the First Amendment freedoms of speech and the press. The decision enraged Nixon.

Nixon's Vietnam strategy also failed to intimidate the North Vietnamese. In March 1972, North Vietnam's forces launched a massive invasion of the South. In April the U.S. ambassador in Vietnam cabled Nixon: "ARVN forces are on the verge of collapse." Nixon, refusing to allow South Vietnam to fall, initiated a risky plan to use American airpower to give the North a "bloody nose." In May the president announced the most drastic escalation of the war since 1968: the mining of Haiphong harbor, a naval blockade of North Vietnam, and massive, sustained bombing attacks. Johnson lacked the will to launch such an aggressive operation, Nixon boasted. I "have the will in spades." By approving the campaign, code-named Linebacker, Nixon ran the risk of inflaming public opinion at home and jeopardizing a planned summit with the Russians. The gamble succeeded. The Soviets offered only tepid protest, and most Americans believed the North's invasion required a tough American response.

Peace With Honor?

The North Vietnamese invasion and Nixon's forceful counterthrust created an opportunity for negotiations. Both sides had reason to seek accommodation. The North Vietnamese wanted to end the punishing American bombings; the United States needed to end the war quickly. Since early in 1971, Kissinger had been holding private meetings in a suburb of Paris with his North Vietnamese counterpart, Le Duc Tho. The key stumbling block had been Tho's insistence that South Vietnam's president Nguyen Van Thieu be removed from power and that North Vietnamese troops be allowed to remain in the South. For a year neither side budged. The only thing they had agreed on was the shape of the negotiating table.

In September 1972, Kissinger made the first move by agreeing to allow North Vietnamese soldiers to remain in South Vietnam. Tho responded by dropping the long-standing demands that Thieu resign and a coalition government be created. A settlement appeared imminent, and Kissinger announced that "peace is at hand." He had not anticipated, however, the fierce opposition of President Thieu, who adamantly opposed North Vietnamese troops in the South. When Nixon supported Thieu, Kissinger returned to the negotiating table armed with new demands. Feeling betrayed, Tho suspended negotiations and returned to Hanoi.

Nixon decided that only a dramatic demonstration of American power could reassure the South Vietnamese and intimidate the North. On December 18, 1972, he ordered Operation Linebacker II, a massive, eleven-day bombing campaign over North Vietnam. "This is your chance to use military power to win this war," the president told the chairman of the Joint Chiefs of Staff, "and if you don't, I'll consider you responsible." The raids were directed at military targets, but inevitably bombs also fell on schools, hospitals, and prisoner-of-war camps. The American costs were also heavy: the loss of fifteen B-52 planes and the capture of ninety-eight American airmen. During the previous seven years, only one of these high-flying bombers had been downed.

The resumption of bombing, along with pressure from China and the Soviet Union, pushed North Vietnam back to the negotiating table. It did not, however, change the terms for peace. The stumbling block remained the same: Thieu refused to accept a settlement that would allow the North Vietnamese to keep troops in the South. With polls showing overwhelming public support for ending the war and with Congress threatening to cut off funding for the effort, Nixon needed an agreement. This time he privately warned Thieu of grave consequences if he rejected the agreement. He matched the threat with a promise to "respond with full force should the settlement be violated by North Vietnam."

The Paris Peace Accords, signed on January 27, 1973, officially ended U.S. involvement in the Vietnam War. The treaty required the United States to remove its remaining 23,700 troops and the North Vietnamese to return all American prisoners of war. As a face-saving measure for the United States, the accords also called for "free and democratic general elections" to choose a government for a unified Vietnam. More important, however, was the American and South Vietnamese concession that North Vietnamese troops could remain in the South.

Nixon told a national television audience that the United States had achieved "peace with honor." In fact, it had achieved neither peace nor honor. The North Vietnamese had no intention of abandoning their dream of unification. Kissinger hoped the treaty would provide only for a "decent interval" between the U.S. military withdrawal and the North's complete military conquest of the South. As Kissinger predicted, the North violated the cease-fire within a few months and continued its relentless drive South. Thieu appealed to the United States for help, but a war-weary Congress refused to provide assistance. By April 1975, when the North's troops captured the South Vietnamese capital of Saigon, America had already turned its attention away from the nation's longest war.

The battles had ended, but the war left deep scars. Among the dead were 57,000 Americans, 5,200 allied soldiers, 184,000 South Vietnamese, and perhaps as many as 925,000 North Vietnamese troops. Five times as many were wounded. The nations of Indochina were devastated by years of bloody battles and heavy bombing. Millions of civilians died in Vietnam, Cambodia, and Laos. American veterans returned home to a nation deeply divided by the war, and to a public that was indifferent to their suffering.

The war shattered the myth of American invincibility and rocked the foundation of postwar American foreign policy. "The United States entered the Vietnam War with the breezy self-confidence of a young warrior," remarked a journalist. "It limped away doubting itself and its powers." The broad consensus in favor of an activist, anticommunist foreign policy, which had shaped American foreign policy since the end of World War II, was replaced by acrimonious debates over the "lessons of Vietnam." Those on the left believed the war exposed the fallacy of containment and the limits of American power. "We should emerge from the tragedy of Vietnam with a clearer understanding of this nation's world role and a healthier realism about the limits of American power," declared Congressman Lee Hamilton of Indiana. Conservatives learned different lessons, charging that a failure of political will had led to America's defeat. According to this view, American Cold War assumptions were valid and the war winnable, but timid politicians, caving into pressure from a liberal media and a student rabble, imposed too many restrictions on the military. David Christin, a decorated veteran of the war declared, "If we had fought to win, we would have won the war." The "ghosts of Vietnam" would haunt the American psyche for years after the conflict ended.

Détente

For Nixon and Kissinger, achieving "peace with honor" in Vietnam represented only one piece in the larger puzzle of global politics. The key players, they argued, were the Soviet Union and China. Because they believed that the United States and the Soviet Union had reached a rough military parity, Nixon and Kissinger wanted to abandon the costly pursuit of weapons superiority and instead focus on peaceful economic competition. Nixon and Kissinger hoped that such a relationship, which they called *détente*, would lessen the threat of nuclear war, encourage the Soviets to pressure the North Vietnamese into a peace settlement, and diminish the possibility of another war like Vietnam beginning elsewhere in the Third World.

Détente was more than an abstract proposition. Circumstances had provided the administration both an urgent need and a historic opportunity to thaw the Cold War between the United States and the Soviet Union. The American public, weary of foreign involvement, seemed unwilling to provide the emotional or financial resources necessary to sustain the Cold War. The Soviets also had reasons to seek closer ties with the United States. Soviet leader Leonid Brezhnev presided over a struggling economy in desperate need of Western goods and capital. Like his American counterpart, he hoped to divert resources from the arms race to domestic use. The Soviets were also worried about the growing military power of China. Ancient animosities between the Russian and Chinese empires reached a new level of tension in 1964 when the Chinese exploded their first atomic bomb. In the spring of 1969, long-standing border disputes flared into skirmishes between Russian and Chinese regulars.

Shrewdly, Nixon and Kissinger began working to improve relations with Communist China, using the Sino–Soviet tension to America's strategic advantage. As an incentive Nixon offered the Chinese access to American technology, capital goods, and foodstuffs. With a solid groundwork established, Nixon made a historic trip to China in February 1972, becoming the first sitting American president to visit that nation and reversing more than twenty years of Sino–American hostility. At the end of the meeting, Nixon and China's Premier Zhou Enlai issued a joint communiqué calling for increased contacts between the two nations.

The Soviets watched nervously as anticommunist Richard Nixon embraced the world's largest communist country. Fearing closer ties between the United States and China, they pushed for their own deal with the Americans. Four months after his historic trip to China, Nixon boarded Air Force One for Moscow. "There must be room in this world for two great nations with different systems to live together and work together," Nixon declared. Nixon and Brezhnev signed trade and technology agreements, plus a statement of "Basic Principles" that called on both sides to avoid both military confrontations and "efforts to obtain unilateral advantage at the expense of the other."

More important, Nixon reached an agreement with the Soviets on the terms of the Strategic Arms Limitation Talks (SALT), an unprecedented breakthrough in Soviet–American relations. Thereafter, the aim of American nuclear doctrine shifted from achieving "superiority" to maintaining "sufficiency." The SALT I agreement limited the building of antiballistic missile systems (ABMs) and froze for five years the number of strategic offensive weapons in both arsenals, including intercontinental ballistic missiles (ICBMs) and submarine-launched missiles. And for the first time, improvements in spy satellites made it possible to monitor an arms limitation agreement.

The Limits of Realism

Because he believed that a communist victory anywhere in the world tipped the global balance of power away from the United States, Nixon supplied arms to a number of repressive regimes willing to oppose the regional interests of the Soviet Union. Among others, Nixon sent aid and approved arms sales to the shah of Iran, President Ferdinand Marcos in the Philippines, and Balthazar Vorster's white-supremacist government of South Africa. He also intervened more actively to douse potential hotspots. When a Marxist, Salvador Allende, won election as president of Chile, Nixon directed the CIA to support Allende's opponents. "I don't see why we need to stand by and watch a country go communist due to the irresponsibility of its own people," Kissinger declared. The president cut off economic aid and prevented private banks from granting loans to Chilean concerns. Convinced by Washington's actions that the United States would support them, Chilean military leaders staged a successful coup and killed Allende in September 1973. The new anticommunist regime, under General Augusto Pinochet, was one of the most repressive in the hemisphere, but it was quickly recognized by the United States and warmly supported.

The Nixon-Kissinger diplomacy faced a tough challenge in the Middle East. The region represented a tangle of competing interest: the United States supplied military and economic aid to ensure Israel's survival, but it was also heavily dependent on oil from the Arab states. Complicating the picture, the Mideast had become a Cold War battleground between Washington and Moscow. In 1967 Arab nations, which had never conceded Israel's right to exist, prepared to invade their neighbor. Forewarned, Israel attacked first, and in six days of fighting the Israeli army captured the Gaza Strip and Sinai Peninsula from Egypt, the West Bank and East Jerusalem from Jordan, and the Golan Heights from Syria. At a peace parley, Israel agreed to turn over the occupied lands in exchange for recognition and peace, but the Arab states refused to negotiate.

On October 6, 1973—the most sacred Jewish holy day, Yom Kippur—Syria and Egypt attacked Israel. At first the United States remained aloof from the struggle. In part, American indifference stemmed from confidence that the superior Israeli army would repel the invasion. The administration also hoped to shift American policy from its pro-Israeli leanings to a more neutral stance. Most of the Arab nations in the region were allied with the Soviet Union against the West, which troubled Nixon. He also feared Arab economic retaliation. Galvanized by humiliation in the 1967 war, a cartel of oil-rich Arab states had organized the Organization of Petroleum Exporting Countries (OPEC) to control the flow of oil—both to guarantee high profits and to wield as a diplomatic weapon if necessary. If the Yom Kippur War ended in a stalemate, America would offer its services to both sides as an impartial broker.

Circumstances confounded the administration's plans. In the first three days of fighting, Egyptian troops advanced into the Sinai crossed the Suez Canal while Syria's army in the North threatened to cut Israel in half by penetrating through the Golan Heights. With Israel's survival at stake, the United States ordered a massive supply of arms to its ally. The American aid proved decisive. Israel recovered and took the offensive before the fighting ended in late October. Over the next two years Kissinger pursued "shuttle diplomacy," traveling between capitals in the Middle East to promote peace. He met with limited success. He made progress with Egypt, but the other Arab states, bruised by America's pivotal intervention, imposed an oil embargo against the United States, Europe, and Japan. The embargo, which lasted from October 17, 1973, to March 18, 1974, produced dramatically higher energy costs. Thereafter, the OPEC nations continued to raise oil prices, which increased 400 percent in 1974 alone, with devastating consequences for the oil-dependent U.S. economy. Kissinger also found Israel reluctant at first to return territory gained in the 1967 war. The issue of "land for peace" would prove a source of continuing friction in the region.

Richard Nixon and the Two Americas, 1969–1974

Richard Nixon began his administration by extending an olive branch to his liberal critics, proposing innovative domestic programs and promising to bring the Vietnam War to a quick end. By 1970, Nixon abandoned his moderate tone and pursued an aggressive experiment in political power. Over the next few years, courting the "silent majority," he expanded the war, viciously attacked his opponents, and consolidated power in the White House. His strategy resulted in a landslide victory in the 1972 presidential election. But his paranoia precipitated his downfall and eventual resignation.

The Search for Stability at Home

By the time he took the oath of office in January 1969, Richard Nixon had been a part of American political life for more than twenty years. Born on January 9, 1913, in Yorba Linda, California, Nixon worked his way through Whittier College and Duke University Law School. In 1946 he won election to Congress, four years later moved to the Senate, and in 1952 became Dwight Eisenhower's vice president. In 1960 he ran for president and lost in a close election to John F. Kennedy.

Through it all, many people wondered who the real Richard Nixon was. He was a man of considerable intelligence and determination with an instinctive feel for public sentiment. At times he was capable of enormous acts of generosity. As a student at Duke Law School Nixon befriended a classmate crippled by polio. Every day he carried the student up the school's steep steps. As president, Nixon once wept while reading a Medal of Honor citation. Yet these insights into Nixon's inner self were rare. "His public self," wrote journalist Tom Wicker, "always has seemed palpably to be concealing a private self we do not know." What the public usually saw was a man who was haunted by self-doubt, poisoned by anger, and driven by ruthless ambition.

In the beginning of his administration, Nixon continued the message of unity that he had preached during the campaign. He told reporters that he planned to be a "consensus" president who would heal the deep wounds created during the 1960s. Acting on impulse, Nixon held a widely publicized meeting with his former rival Hubert Humphrey. He promised to do more for African-Americans than any other president in history. In his inaugural address he urged Americans to "speak quietly enough so that our words can be heard as well as our voices."

In his early years in office, Nixon adopted moderately progressive positions. As the first elected president since 1849 forced to work with a Congress controlled by the opposition party, he favored cooperation over confrontation. In addition to signing Democratic bills raising social security benefits, Nixon increased federal funds for low-income public housing and even expanded the Job Corps. His first term saw steady increases in spending on mandated social welfare programs, especially social security, Medicare, and Medicaid. His most novel and surprising proposal was the Family Assistance Plan (FAP), which provided a guaranteed minimum income of $1,600 to every U.S. family. Although the proposal died in the Senate, it revealed Nixon's capacity for domestic innovation. Michael Harrington, whose *The Other America* had helped inspire the war on poverty, called it "the most radical idea since the New Deal."

At the same time that he advocated his bold new Family Assistance Plan, Nixon placated conservatives by proposing to limit the size of the federal government and provide local communities with greater power. His plan, which he called the "New Federalism," was designed to "start resources and power flowing back from Washington to the people." In 1972 he pushed through Congress the State and Local Fiscal Assistance Act, a revenue-sharing plan that distributed $30 billion in federal money to the states.

Public morale received a big boost in July 1969 when *Apollo 11* astronaut Neil Armstrong lifted his left foot off the landing pad of his spacecraft and pressed it into the soft powdery surface of the moon's Sea of Tranquility. Over 1 billion people watched as Armstrong and fellow astronaut Buzz Aldrin planted an American flag and a plaque reading in part, "We came in peace for all mankind." The next day headlines around the world shouted the news: "MAN WALKS ON MOON."

For a brief time, Americans joined together to celebrate a triumph of the American spirit. The moon landing represented, glowed *Time* magazine, "a shining reaffirmation of the optimistic premise that whatever man imagines he can bring to pass." Many people hoped the sense of unity and accomplishment inspired by the moon landing would usher in a new decade of harmony and consensus. "For one priceless moment in the whole history of man," a hopeful Richard Nixon declared, "all the people of this earth are truly one."

Mobilizing the "Silent Majority"

Nixon shattered the delicate calm on April 30, 1970, when he announced the Cambodian invasion. Shocked by the public outcry, Nixon moved decidedly to the right, mobilizing the "silent majority" to build support for his policies. Nixon shrewdly played to the public's mood, which was growing increasingly hostile to protesters and reformers whose challenges often violated deeply held attitudes about patriotism and traditional values. Many began to worry about the fundamental stability of their society. "Everything is being attacked," declared a suburban housewife, "what you believe in, what you learned in school, in church, from your parents."

In the aftermath of the Kent State killings, the "silent majority" lashed out at the most visible symbol of the challenge to authority—student protesters. When New York's liberal mayor John Lindsay lowered the American flag in mourning for the Kent State dead, angry construction workers, chanting "All the way with the USA," waded into a pro-Lindsay crowd, swinging their tools and leaving seventy people wounded in their wake. "They went through those demonstrators like Sherman went through Atlanta," remarked one observer. Six days later, the leader of the local construction workers' union traveled to the White House to present Nixon with an honorary hard hat. Nixon accepted it as a "symbol, along with our great flag, for freedom and patriotism to our beloved country."

The "silent majority" viewed student protesters as part of a larger threat to social stability. Sensationalized stories of radical bombings, mass murders, and a rising crime rate added to fears that the social fabric was unraveling. Between September 1969 and May 1970, radical groups claimed responsibility for 250 bombings—an average of almost one per day. In February 1970, bombs ripped through the New York headquarters of corporate giants IBM, General Telephone and Electronics, and Socony Mobil. Far more threatening, however, was the growth in violent crime in communities, big and small, across the country. The Justice Department reported that the crime rate grew by 60 percent between 1960 and 1966, then leaped by another 83 percent between 1966 and 1971.

Political calculations were at the heart of Nixon's appeal to the "silent majority." Nixon believed that his political future depended on adding to his core supporters those people who had voted for George Wallace in 1968. Wallace had won 10 million votes, or about 13.5 percent of the total vote cast in 1968. Most of these voters were, in the words of two political scientists, "unyoung, unpoor, and unblack." "These are my people," Nixon boasted. "We speak the same language." His strategy was to play on public fear of urban violence and social disorder. The party of FDR, he told wavering Democrats, had been hijacked by antiwar protesters and New Left radicals.

Nixon and his advisers developed a four-pronged approach to tap into the frustrations of the "silent majority." First, he appealed to working-class whites by trying to block congressional approval of the Voting Rights Act and by ordering the Justice Department to delay implementing school desegregation cases. "For the first time since Woodrow Wilson," the head of the NAACP protested, "we have a national administration that can be rightly characterized as anti-Negro."

Second, he championed the cause of "law and order" and attacked the Supreme Court's liberal views on crime. The Nixon Justice Department pursued high-profile prosecutions of antiwar activists, including the so-called Chicago Eight for their antics at the 1968 Democratic convention. Promising to "get tough on crime" Nixon called for granting judges and police expanded powers to jail suspects and to search houses without a warrant. The president unleashed the full powers of government against potential "enemies" of his administration. Among other illegal moves, Nixon instructed the Internal Revenue Service to audit tax returns of critics, authorized the FBI to wiretap phones and infiltrate leftist groups, and told the Small Business Administration to deny loans to prominent antiwar or civil rights activists.

For the third prong, Nixon nominated conservative southern judges to fill Court vacancies. In 1969 he successfully nominated conservative Warren Burger to replace departing Chief Justice Earl Warren. Later that year, when another vacancy opened on the Court, Nixon turned to South Carolina judge Clement Haynsworth. Though no one questioned Haynsworth's legal credentials, his strong opposition to desegregation angered Senate liberals and worried many moderate Republicans. For the first time since the administration of Herbert Hoover, the Senate rejected a Supreme Court nominee. Nixon responded by nominating Judge G. Harrold Carswell, an undistinguished jurist who had once declared his belief in white supremacy. The Senate again refused to confirm the president's nominee. Nixon lost the battle but he won the political war by skillfully using the Senate rejection to score political points in the South. "I understand the bitterness of millions of Americans who live in the South," he said.

Finally, Nixon unleashed vice president Spiro Agnew, who traveled the country denouncing the media, radical professors, student protesters, and liberals. "Will America be led by a President elected by a majority of the American people," he demanded, "or will it be intimidated and blackmailed into following the path dictated by a disruptive radical and militant minority—the pampered prodigies of the radical liberals in the United States Senate?" Agnew called the Kent State murders "predictable and avoidable," and attacked the "elitists" who regarded the Bill of Rights as a protection "for psychotic and criminal elements in our society."

The 1972 Election

In 1972 the Democratic Party nominated as its presidential candidate Senator George McGovern, an outspoken liberal critic of the Vietnam War who sought to win election by directly challenging Nixon's interpretation of American politics and culture. McGovern and the delegates at the Democratic Party convention adopted an aggressively liberal platform. Among its more controversial points were a call for the immediate withdrawal of U.S. troops from Vietnam, amnesty for those who had fled the draft, busing to achieve integration in the schools, and the abolition of capital punishment. The platform also included a vaguely worded statement—"Americans should be free to make their own choices of lifestyles and private habits without being subject to discrimination"—which many people interpreted as an endorsement of drug use and homosexuality.

This platform, and McGovern's nomination, reflected important changes stirring in the Democratic Party. New rules governing the selection of delegates to the party's convention guaranteed added representation to more liberal groups—minorities, women, and the young—at the expense of more conservative Democratic Party constituencies. The Chicago delegation, for example, contained only three Polish-Americans and one Italian-American from the city that had been the greatest stronghold of ethnic Democrats. The delegation from Iowa did not have a single farmer. The delegation from New York included only three representatives of organized labor, although New York at that time had more union members than any other state. "There is too much hair, and not enough cigars at this convention," one labor leader declared.

The progressive Democrats who had fought for rules changes thought they were making the party more representative of America and therefore more likely to win in November. They believed that most Americans did not support the status quo and would embrace sweeping changes in the political system. It was in this spirit that George McGovern portrayed the campaign as "a fundamental struggle between the little people of America and the big rich of America, between the average workingman and woman and the powerful elite."

The Democrats badly misread the mood of the electorate. In 1972 Nixon's foreign policy pleased many voters. American casualties in Vietnam had declined steadily during Nixon's first term, and the president's assurance that America would achieve a peace with honor in Vietnam was closer to what voters wanted than McGovern's call for immediate withdrawal. When a would-be assassin shot and critically wounded George Wallace during the 1972 primaries, Nixon inherited many of his angry white supporters. Most were former Democrats who disapproved of their party's liberal position on domestic issues. They saw McGovern not as their champion but as the candidate of a liberal, intellectual, Northeast establishment.

On election day Nixon scored a resounding victory, winning 60.7 percent (47,169,911) of the popular vote. McGovern received only 29,170,383 votes, or 37.5 percent. Nixon carried every state except Massachusetts and the District of Columbia, for a margin in the electoral college of 521 to 17 (see map).

The Watergate Crisis

In the wake of this convincing victory, many expected that the second Nixon administration would consolidate its power and put its stamp on the nation. But a series of scandals almost immediately put the administration on the defensive. The

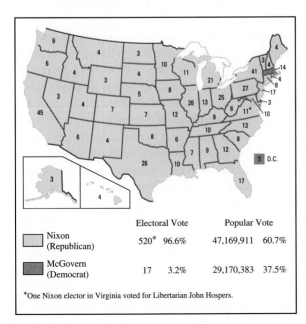

	Electoral Vote	Popular Vote
Nixon (Republican)	520* 96.6%	47,169,911 60.7%
McGovern (Democrat)	17 3.2%	29,170,383 37.5%

*One Nixon elector in Virginia voted for Libertarian John Hospers.

The Election of 1972 The assassination attempt on George Wallace and Edward Kennedy's personal crisis over Chappaquiddick removed two of the leading Democratic candidates for president, leaving Senator George McGovern of South Dakota to take the nomination. The apparent vacillations by McGovern on the campaign trail assisted Nixon in his reelection bid as he focused on his role as "global peacemaker." Nixon won by the largest majority of any Republican in American history.

trouble actually began before the election, on June 17, 1972, when a security guard foiled a break-in at the Democratic Party's national headquarters, in the Watergate complex. One of those apprehended, James McCord, was also security coordinator for the Committee to Re-elect the President (CREEP). The committee immediately fired McCord, and the president reassured the American public that no one in his administration had been involved in this "bizarre incident."

At the burglars' trial, McCord at first testified that he had acted alone, confirming the president's version of the break-in. But under intense pressure from federal judge John Sirica, McCord admitted that high White House officials had both approved the break-in and pressured the defendants "to plead guilty and remain silent." President Nixon praised Sirica's courage and pledged, "I will do everything in my power to ensure that the guilty are brought to justice."

It was the Senate, however, that made the next move, in February 1973, by creating a bipartisan select committee to probe further into the Watergate affair. Over the next months the committee, headed by North Carolina Democrat Sam Ervin, uncovered a trail of corruption leading to higher and higher levels of the White House staff. Investigators learned, for example, that Nixon fundraisers had coerced corporations into "donating" millions of dollars to the president's reelection campaign. Following the publication of the *Pentagon Papers*, Nixon used the money to form a Special Investigations Unit, nicknamed "the plumbers," to plug leaks of sensitive information and to harass and demoralize the administration's "enemies." The plumbers, witnesses testified, were also behind the break-in at the Watergate.

Armed with these and other troubling revelations, the Ervin committee began to televise its hearings on May 17, 1973. A parade of witnesses confessed to criminal acts ranging from bribery to blackmail. Then, on June 25, White House counsel John Dean told the committee that the president had known about efforts to cover up the Watergate operation by September 1972 and had spoken to him about paying "hush money." Dean's proximity to the president and the concrete details he offered in his 245-page testimony made him a compelling witness. Even before he offered his testimony, a large majority of Americans believed that Richard Nixon had either planned or helped cover up the break-in at the Watergate. By June 1973, only 17 percent in one survey believed that Nixon was telling the truth. Still, there was no physical evidence to prove the president's guilt, and Nixon continued categorically to deny any wrongdoing. Exasperated, many despaired of ever finding the truth.

At this moment of uncertainty, a witness revealed that Nixon had installed a secret taping system to record, "for posterity," his private conversations in the White House and Executive Office Building. Ervin demanded that his committee be given access to the tapes. The special prosecutor, Harvard law school professor Archibald Cox, asked the courts to order Nixon to release the tapes. Nixon refused. At issue, the president declared, was "the independence of the three branches of our Government." Ervin had a different definition of the question: "Whether the president is above the law."

When Cox persisted in his efforts to secure the tapes, Nixon ordered Attorney General Elliot Richardson to fire the special prosecutor. Richardson refused and was himself dismissed. His deputy, William Ruckelshaus, also refused, and he too was fired. On October 20, when Solicitor General Robert H. Bork finally carried out the president's order, a dramatic backlash ensued. The press referred to the firings as the "Saturday night massacre" and applauded Richardson and Ruckelshaus for their integrity. Members of Congress, citing an outraged public opinion, demanded appointment of a new special prosecutor and release of the tapes. Compelled by this unified opposition, Nixon yielded some of the tapes and named a new special prosecutor, Leon Jaworski of Texas. Once again he declared his innocence, this time on television. "I am not a crook," he insisted.

The Saturday night massacre came in the midst of a series of scandals that kept the administration and the American public reeling. Just ten days before, Vice President Spiro Agnew had pleaded no contest in federal court to charges of income tax evasion and admitted that he had accepted hundreds of thousands of dollars of bribes while governor of Maryland. Agnew resigned from the vice presidency, and Congress quickly confirmed Nixon's choice, Michigan Republican Gerald R. Ford, the House minority leader, to succeed Agnew under the terms of the Twenty-fifth Amendment. In late November, Judge Sirica informed the public that eighteen minutes had been erased from a critical June 20, 1972, tape of a meeting between Nixon and his chief of staff H. R. Haldeman. Nixon's secretary Rosemary Woods took responsibility, claiming that she had accidentally erased the tape while transcribing it. Experts testified, however, that the tapes had been deliberately tampered with by "manual" erasures. By December, Nixon's own personal finances had come under increasingly critical scrutiny. The IRS disclosed that the president owed more than $400,000 in back taxes and penalties.

The air of scandal and uncertainty continued to hang over the capital until July 24, 1974, when a unanimous Supreme Court ordered president Nixon to turn over all relevant tapes. Just as Dean had contended, the tapes revealed that Nixon had personally intervened to stifle an FBI investigation into the Watergate break-in and that he had authorized payments of more than $460,000 in hush money to keep the Watergate burglars from implicating higher-ups in the administration. On August 8, 1974, facing certain impeachment, a disgraced Richard Nixon became the first American president to resign from office. At noon the next day, Vice President Gerald Ford was sworn in as the country's new chief executive. "Our long national nightmare," he declared, "is over."

Many forces conspired to create America's "national nightmare." The extraordinary growth of presidential power during the Cold War, the social upheaval and intense partisan divisions of the 1960s and early 1970s, and the emergence of a skeptical and assertive media, all played important roles in Nixon's downfall. But it is impossible to understand Watergate without coming to terms with the ambitious, paranoid personality of Richard Nixon. Though he occupied the world's most powerful office, Nixon remained surprisingly insecure, fearful that his enemies in the establishment—liberals, media, and Congress—were out to destroy him. Since he equated his own political survival with the fate of the nation, Nixon felt justified in using whatever means necessary to destroy his opponents. "You were either for us or against us," recalled one aide, "and if you were against us, we were against you." In a chilling disregard for civil liberties, Nixon maintained that in curbing domestic dissent, "everything is valid, everything is possible." Perhaps

Nixon's Goodbye On August 8, 1974, Richard Nixon became the first American president to resign from office after fellow Republicans made it clear that Nixon would be impeached and removed from office for his role in the Watergate cover-up. Gerald Ford, the House minority leader who had replaced Spiro Agnew as vice president the year before, was then sworn in as president. In this picture, Nixon and his family are boarding the helicopter on the White House lawn for the last time. *(Nixon Presidential Materials Project, National Archives and Record Administration.)*

Nixon offered the most insight into his own downfall in his farewell speech to the White House staff. "[N]ever be petty," he said, and "always remember, others may hate you, but those who hate you don't win unless you hate them, and then you destroy yourself."

Old Values, New Realities, 1970–1979

Americans in the 1970s struggled to absorb the social and cultural aftershocks of the 1960s. The seventies left a mixed legacy of experimentation and inertia. On one level, many groups experienced unprecedented gains. Millions of African-Americans moved into the middle class, and black candidates won election to political offices. Other groups—women, gays, Hispanics, Native Americans—made important strides in their efforts to achieve equal rights. But the enormous material and political gains during the decade did little to eliminate race, class, and gender inequities in American society and culture. Many Americans, grown weary of the social struggles of the 1960s, turned inward in an attempt to make sense of the past and to find fulfillment in a confusing world.

African-Americans: Action Without Affirmation

As in the 1960s, racial relations continued to be the most divisive social issue with which Americans struggled. During the 1970s, African-Americans made significant advances in the workplace and in politics. Many took white-collar jobs and held union memberships for the first time, earning higher incomes and enjoying advances in job security. In the 1970s, the earnings of between 35 and 45 percent of African-American families rose to middle-class levels. By 1980, the University of Michigan's National Opinion Research Center concluded that American society had "a truly visible black middle class" for the first time in its history.

With vigorous enforcement of the Voting Rights Act of 1965, African-Americans also began voting in unprecedented numbers and dramatically increased their representation in Congress and in state houses and town halls across the nation. The most impressive gains took place on the local level. In 1964 only 70 elected black officials served at all levels of government; by 1980, there were 4,600, including more than 170 mayors.

The civil rights movement also achieved a major victory in the Supreme Court, winning the Court's vigorous support for the desegregation of schools. Ever since the 1954 *Brown* decision (see page 1119), the Supreme Court had called for the desegregation of educational institutions. But it declined to specify remedies or insist on deadlines for implementation, and little progress occurred. Local school boards fiercely resisted local court orders and pleas from activists and parents. In Greensboro, North Carolina, when parents of three black children won a court order allowing their children to attend a predominantly white school, the local school board transferred all white students out of the school. In Boston, school board officials began busing white and black students out of their neighborhoods in the 1960s to keep schools segregated. Faced with such determined resistance, liberals and civil rights activists petitioned the Supreme Court to take a more forceful stand on the issue. In two unanimous cases, *Alexander* v. *Holmes County Board of Education* (1969) and *Swann* v. *Charlotte-Mecklenburg Board of Education* (1971), the Supreme Court ordered a quick end to segregation, ruling that cities could be required to bus students if necessary to achieve integration. With the Supreme Court firmly behind busing as a remedy for school segregation, lower courts across the United States followed suit, ordering busing plans in numerous cities.

A divided Court also gave legal sanction to another controversial social policy: affirmative action programs that sought to achieve equality by reserving opportunities for minorities. In 1978 a white man, Allan Bakke, sued the University of California Medical School at Davis, claiming that the university had rejected him in favor of less-qualified minority candidates. A divided Supreme Court, in *Bakke* v. *University of California,* ruled that the university's absolute quota for minorities was illegal, but it also agreed that schools could consider race as a "plus factor" in admissions so as to foster "diversity" in the classes.

Unfortunately, legal and economic gains took place against a backdrop of increasing misery for many African-Americans. In the 1970s black America increasingly divided into a two-class society: while some black families rose to middle-class

Desegregating Schools Despite Nixon's insistence that integration of schools would take time, the Supreme Court under new Chief Justice Warren Burger, ordered the immediate end of segregation in Mississippi in *Alexander* v. *Holmes County Board of Education* (1969). *(Carl Mydans LIFE Magazine © Time, Inc.)*

income levels during the decade, about 30 percent slid deeper into poverty. African-Americans had long suffered disproportionately from poverty, but the impoverishment of the 1960s and 1970s was in many ways new, marked by a deeper isolation and hopelessness.

Tensions inherent in American political thought frustrated efforts to address racial injustice. Most whites supported racial equality as a general proposition. There was also broad support for African-American voting rights and the integration of public spaces. But minority leaders' and liberals' demands for affirmative action angered many whites. Such programs, many whites believed, elevated group remedies over individual rights and violated cherished notions of self-help. "Nobody ever gave me anything," said one frustrated man. "I worked hard to get a decent job to provide for my family. Now they want to change the rules and have everything given to them."

Many whites also resisted efforts to integrate schools and neighborhoods. By the 1970s, the enforcement of segregation by law or informal covenant was no longer legal, but the segregation of housing actually increased during the decade. Busing plans, which frequently encountered fierce opposition from whites, failed to integrate the nation's schools. Worse, the plans were deeply flawed. In its 1974 *Milliken*

v. *Bradley* decision, the Supreme Court prohibited the forced transfer of students between city and suburban schools. In many urban areas, the decision accelerated "white flight" to the suburbs, leaving urban schools more segregated than they had been before busing. Sixty-six percent of black students in the North and 50 percent in the South attended predominately black schools in 1979.

Voices of Protest: Hispanics, Native Americans, and Homosexuals

In the 1970s Hispanic-Americans—a diverse group including immigrants from Mexico, Puerto Rico, and Cuba—were the fastest growing minority group in the country. Between 1960 and 1970, the documented Hispanic population in the United States nearly tripled, from 3 to 9 million. During the 1970s the number of Hispanics increased to 14.6 million, about 6 percent of the total population.

Hispanics remained one of the poorest groups in America. Before the 1960s, nearly one-third of all Mexican-Americans worked long hours for low wages in the fields picking crops. In 1962 the United Farm Workers (UFW) began a successful effort to organize them. Cesar Chavez, the UFW's charismatic leader, was the key figure in the organization's success. Chavez, a Mexican-American farm worker, echoed the religious themes and nonviolence of the early civil rights movement, framing the struggle between workers and growers as one of an oppressed minority seeking justice and simple dignity. "We hope that the people of God will respond to our call and join us," he declared, "just as they did with our Negro brothers in Selma." Chavez's own religious faith and personal commitment inspired UFW members and supporters. By mid-1970, two-thirds of the grapes grown in California were harvested by workers under UFW contracts. The UFW also won passage of the 1975 California Agricultural Labor Relations Act, which gave farm workers the right to secret ballot union elections.

In the 1960s and 1970s, many younger Hispanics also challenged the value of assimilation, much as the black power movement did. Arguing that it was vital to preserve Hispanic traditions, they adopted the term Chicano to distinguish themselves from conservative Hispanics who wished to assimilate into Anglo culture. College courses in Hispanic culture were established in many universities. In 1968 Hispanic leaders and white liberals successfully lobbied the federal government to provide education in Spanish for children who had not yet learned English by the time they entered school. The government also recognized Hispanic Americans as a distinct group and extended minority protection to them. In 1975 an amendment to the Voting Rights Act of 1965 extended to Hispanics the same federal protection that the law afforded to blacks.

Similar themes of control and ethnic pride animated the "red power" movement among American Indians. After John Collier resigned as head of the Bureau of Indian Affairs in 1946, the federal government abandoned its New Deal era experiments with tribal self-determination and sought instead to force tribes off reservations into mainstream society. Fierce Indian resistance forced the government to cancel its plans.

The government's attempt to terminate federal protection for some tribes inspired Indians to take steps to improve conditions. In 1968 angry young Native

United Farm Workers on Strike Led by Cesar Chavez, Filipino farm workers in Delano, California protested the horrible conditions of migrant labor camps, the corrupt labor contracts, and the intense racism of the San Joaquin region in 1965. By 1970, protests and boycotts forced twenty-six grape growers to the bargaining table, improving conditions for migrant workers in the West. *(Matt Herron/Take Stock.)*

Americans founded the American Indian Movement (AIM). In December 1972, AIM members orchestrated the seizure of the headquarters of the Bureau of Indian Affairs in Washington, D.C., and held it for a week. In February 1973, when local whites who had murdered a Sioux were lightly punished, two hundred AIM members occupied the town of Wounded Knee, South Dakota. They held the area for over two months, demanding that the government honor hundreds of broken treaties and calling for major changes in reservation government.

Other Native Americans used more traditional tactics to win a series of legal actions that reinstated treaties and extended legal rights. Armed with copies of abrogated treaties, Native Americans marched into courts and won the return of land wrongly taken from them. They also won legal battles to block strip mining and to preserve rights to fishing and mineral resources on reservation land.

Despite impressive gains, Native Americans faced overwhelming obstacles. Reservations, shrunken by treaty violations and far from employment opportunities, were dismal places. In 1971 unemployment among reservation Indians ranged from 40 to 75 percent, and annual family incomes averaged about $1,500. Life expectancy was only forty-six years, compared with the national average of seventy. Infant mortality rates were the highest in the nation. Educational opportunities on reservations, according to a Harvard study, were "by every standard . . . the worst in the nation," and the dropout rate among Indian high school students was the highest of any ethnic group in the nation.

Homosexuals, too, challenged prevailing ideas about their place in society. The modern gay rights movement was born on Friday night, June 27, 1969, when a group of Manhattan police officers raided the Stonewall Inn, a gay bar in the heart of Greenwich Village. Such raids, and the police abuse that frequently followed, were routine affairs. Not this time. As one reporter noted, "Limp wrists were forgotten. Beer cans and bottles were heaved at the windows and a rain of coins descended on the cops."

The Stonewall Inn riot ignited a nationwide grass-roots "liberation" movement among gay men and women. Using confrontation tactics borrowed from the civil rights movement and the rhetoric of revolution employed by the New Left, the gay rights movement achieved a number of victories during the decade. The number of gay organizations in America grew from less than fifty to more than one thousand. In 1973 the American Psychiatric Association reversed a century-old policy and stopped listing homosexuality as a mental disorder. More than half the states repealed their sodomy laws, the Civil Service Commission eliminated its ban against employment of homosexuals, and a number of politicians declared their support of gay rights.

Women's Liberation

Each of these groups—African-Americans, Hispanics, American Indians, and homosexuals—initiated significant changes in American society during the 1970s. But it was the women's liberation movement that emerged as the largest and most powerful social movement of the decade. Many date its beginnings from the publication in 1963 of Betty Friedan's best-selling book, *The Feminine Mystique*, which had sold 1.3 million copies by 1967.

A Smith College graduate, Friedan described the painful contradictions that she and many other educated women experienced. According to the most respected ideas of womanhood—promoted by the media, teachers, businessmen, social workers, psychiatrists—women could find fulfillment only as wives and mothers and should leave careers for men. And yet, Friedan wrote, she and many of her peers found this life unsatisfying and confining. It gave them no chance to exercise their talents or develop their own identities. Suburbia was not the safe and secure haven they had been promised, but rather a "comfortable concentration camp" in which many felt trapped.

At the same time that *The Feminine Mystique* was released, the historic constituencies of American feminist movements—educated women and employed women—were growing dramatically. Although the percentage of women in American colleges had declined since the 1920s, the absolute number of women attending and graduating college had risen steadily. A booming economy attracted women to the work force in unprecedented numbers. Drawn by the desire for consumer goods, even many married women were working for pay for the first time—by 1968, 40 percent of married women with small children held at least a part-time job.

The women's movement took flight with two major wings. One group of feminists, led primarily by older professional women, sought to achieve change by working within the political system. The National Organization for Women (NOW) best exemplified this reform impulse. Formed in 1966 to lobby the government on behalf of issues of special concern to women, and modeled after the NAACP, NOW announced that its purpose was to "take action to bring women into full participation in the mainstream of American society now, exercising all the privileges and responsibilities thereof in truly equal partnership with men." NOW called for an Equal Rights Amendment (ERA) to the constitution, which they believed would help them win other benefits: equal employment, maternity leave, child care, and the right to choose abortion.

Younger feminist leaders by and large rejected NOW's moderate approach and advocated bolder measures. Many had worked with the Student Nonviolent Coordinating Committee (SNCC) during the Freedom Summer of 1964, or in one of the student protest movements, frontline crucibles in which their beliefs about politics and protest were shaped. Like others in the New Left, these women's liberationists, or radical feminists, distrusted establishment political tactics and instead sought ways to change American culture and to build a society based on participatory democracy. Irreverent and eager to challenge prevailing beliefs, they used the tactics of mass protest, direct action, and political theater characteristic of the civil rights struggles.

The feminist movement won a number of impressive victories in the courts and legislatures during the 1970s. In 1972 Congress passed Title IX of the Higher Education Act, which banned discrimination "on the basis of sex" in "any education program or activity receiving federal financial assistance." The legislation set the stage for an explosion in women's athletics later in the decade. Also in 1972 Congress passed and sent to the states a constitutional amendment banning discrimination on the basis of sex—the ERA. By the end of the year all fifty states had enacted legislation to prevent sex discrimination in employment. Federal and state laws protecting victims of domestic violence and rape were strengthened. Congresswoman Bella Abzug declared 1972 "a watershed year. We put sex discrimination provisions into everything." The following year, a divided Supreme Court ruled in *Roe* v. *Wade* that women had the right to choose abortion in the early stages of pregnancy.

There were also signs of change in American culture. At the grass roots, feminist organizations flourished: feminist bookstores, rape crisis and domestic violence centers, and chapters of NOW formed across the nation. A feminist magazine, *Ms.*, attracted a large national circulation. And the proportion of women entering professional and graduate schools rose substantially. By the 1980s, 25 percent of new graduates of law, medical, and business schools were women, up from only 5 percent in the late 1960s. Opinion surveys recorded new attitudes toward gender roles. "Women's liberation has changed the lives of many Americans and the ways they look at family, job and sexual equality," *Reader's Digest* concluded in 1976. Over two-thirds of college women the magazine questioned agreed that "the idea that a woman's place is in the home is nonsense."

Not everyone welcomed these changes in gender roles (see Competing Voices, page 1216). Traditionalists found a talented leader in Phyllis Schlafly, a conservative activist who campaigned tirelessly against the ERA. Tapping into traditional views of womanhood, she complained that feminists had abandoned their God-given roles of wife and mother, in favor of a radical political agenda that was "anti-family, anti-children, and

Dartmouth Tuck Graduates of 1970 The ideas that emerged from the feminist movement continued to influence women who demanded equal rights and opportunities. Growing numbers of women completed professional degrees in the late sixties and early seventies, including the woman in this photograph, Martha Frasson. In 1972, Congress passed the Educational Amendments Act, which required colleges to ensure equal opportunity for women like Ms. Frasson in the future. *(Courtesy, The Amos Tuck School of Business Administration Archives, Dartmouth College, Hanover, New Hampshire.)*

pro-abortion." The affirmation of traditional gender roles struck a responsive chord with conservative men, but it also appealed to many working-class women who felt estranged from the largely middle-class leadership of the feminist movement. Schlafly's charges that the ERA would promote lesbianism, require women to serve in combat roles in the military, and roll back protective legislation that housewives and female workers cherished, eroded public support and eventually killed the amendment.

Despite signs of progress, women still faced major discrimination in the workplace. In the 1970s, jobs were still typically classified as "men's" or "women's" work, and as a consequence over 80 percent of all women workers were clustered in 20 of the 420 occupations listed by the Census Bureau. "Women's" jobs—secretary, waitress, sales clerk—typically offered low pay, little security, and no chance for advancement. In those instances in which women did perform the same work as men, they received much lower wages. To compound these problems, unemployment rates among women consistently exceeded male averages by more than 20 percent.

This discrimination in the job market often had devastating consequences for women trying to live on their own. It was particularly hard on single women with children, who were increasingly numerous in the 1970s as divorce and out-of-wedlock births grew more common. During the 1970s, the number of women heading families with children increased by 72 percent. A large proportion of their households, as many as one third, fell below the poverty line. By 1980, 66 percent of all adults whom the government classified as poor were women. This new phenomenon, which sociologists called the "feminization of poverty," hit black women hardest of all. While the number of white families headed by women increased only marginally during the 1970s, the number of black families headed by women skyrocketed to 47 percent by 1980. One out of every three black children was born to a teenage mother, and 55 percent of all black babies were born out of wedlock. In inner-city ghettos, the figure often climbed above 70 percent, and two-thirds of all black families living in poverty were headed by women.

Cultural Crosscurrents

"In the '70s, hardly anybody was a hippie, because everybody was," declared one observer. Emblems of sixties protest, such as long hair and ultracasual dress, gained mainstream appeal during the 1970s. Natural food stores sprouted from coast to coast. National supermarkets carried bean curd. The use of recreational drugs, especially marijuana, was commonplace. The proportion of Americans favoring the full legalization of marijuana doubled from 12 to 25 percent. Attitudes toward sex underwent a similar change. In 1973, 53 percent of women saw nothing wrong with premarital sex, down from 74 percent just four years earlier.

Critics complained that these trends suggested that Americans had become more interested in personal pleasure than in social reform. One author called the 1970s the "Me Decade," and much evidence supported the unflattering label. The best-selling self-help book of the decade was *Looking Out for #1*. A health and fitness craze swept the nation as Americans by the millions started jogging. "If the emblem of the 60s was the angry banner of a protest marcher, the spirit of '79 was the jogger, absorbed in the sound of his own breathing—and wearing a smile button," observed *Newsweek*. Many Americans looked to Eastern religions "to get in touch with their feelings," taking up yoga, Zen Buddhism, and transcendental meditation (TM). The Korean missionary Sun Myung Moon, founder of the Unification Church, drew twenty thousand spectators to New York's Madison Square Garden. "I feel changed," exclaimed one convert. "I have much more of an inner peace."

Changing cultural fashions were most clearly evident in popular music. The protest songs of the 1960s were abandoned for the rhythmic beat of disco. This new musical craze, popularized by the hit movie *Saturday Night Fever* and by vocalists such as Donna Summer, mesmerized its audiences with glitzy dance halls and pulsating lights. By 1975, there were over ten thousand discos in North America—more than two hundred in New York City alone. The music moved millions of young people to dance, while the lyrics, which one critic described as "simple and repetitive to the point of absurdity," left their consciences unscathed.

The decade was not as shallow or as self-involved as critics suggested. The three major networks featured their share of mindless situation comedies, 1950s nostalgia, and sexual titillation. But the popular media also revealed the struggle of a culture attempting to reconcile new ideas with old realities. The popular ABC mini-series *Roots* (1976) provided audiences with a rich portrayal of the African-American experience. Norman Lear's popular sitcom *All in the Family* pitted Archie Bunker, who preferred an older, simpler America expressed in the theme song "Those Were the Days," against the progressive views of his liberal son-in-law, Michael. "Why fight it?" Michael asked Archie in the first episode. "The world's changing." But Archie, refusing to accept defeat, continued his fight against the forces of change, especially minorities, liberals, and radicals. "I'm against all the right things," Archie shouted: "welfare, busing, women's lib, and sex education."

A number of blockbuster movies also touched on sensitive issues and revealed the decade's conflicting social currents. In the 1976 Academy Award–winning film *Rocky*, filmwriter Sylvester Stallone played a streetwise white roughneck named Rocky Balboa, "the Italian Stallion," who challenged the outspoken and black Apollo Creed for the heavyweight championship of the world. Movie audiences cheered for the white ethnic underdog whom one movie critic called "the most romanticized Great White Hope in screen history." *Breaking Away* (1979), the story of blue-collar youth competing in a bicycle race in Bloomington, Indiana, offered a more nuanced and sensitive portrayal of working-class frustration.

Hollywood, and the nation, struggled during the decade to come to terms with Vietnam. The film *M*A*S*H* (1970), later made into a television sitcom, used the backdrop of an army field hospital in Korea to present a black comedy about Vietnam. In 1978 two Vietnam films, *Coming Home* and *The Deer Hunter*, swept the Oscars with their vivid portrayals of the war's traumatic impact on ordinary Americans. The message of *Coming Home,* which starred peace activist Jane Fonda, was solidly antiwar. *The Deer Hunter* was more ambiguous. In tracing the tragic journey of three friends from a steel-mill town in western Pennsylvania who volunteered for the war, director Michael Cimino showed the tremendous price, both physical and psychological, many Americans paid during the conflict. At the same time, critics charged that by depicting the Vietcong as "brutes and dolts" and the Americans as "innocents in a corrupt land," the movie took a subtle prowar position.

 ## The Age of Limits, 1974–1979

By the end of the decade, Americans had reason to question their optimistic faith in the future of the American experiment. Watergate eroded Americans' confidence in the nation's elected leaders and shook their faith in the nation's political institutions. Stagflation, a new and troubling combination of rising unemployment and soaring inflation, depressed the standard of living of millions of Americans and made them question whether they could pass on a better life to their children. Concern about limited resources also produced a broad-based environmental movement in the United States. Although a new president, Jimmy Carter, identified the malaise, neither he nor other public leaders offered convincing answers to the questions puzzling most Americans.

Congressional Resurgence and Public Mistrust

In the aftermath of Watergate and the Vietnam War, wrote Tom Wicker, many Americans had come to look on their government as "a fountain of lies." "All during Vietnam, the government lied to me," declared journalist Richard Cohen. "All the time.

Watergate didn't help matters any. More lies . . . I've been shaped, formed by lies." In response, the nation's political leaders undertook a series of political reforms, hoping to restore the public trust. Most of the effort was directed at limiting the power of the presidency. In 1973 Congress passed the War Powers Act over president Nixon's veto. The act required a president to "consult with Congress" within forty-eight hours of committing American troops abroad and ordered him to withdraw them within sixty days unless Congress approved the mission. The Congress also enjoined the president from undertaking any military action in Vietnam after August 15, 1973.

Next, Congress moved to increase its influence over domestic policy. The Budget and Impoundment Control Act in 1974 streamlined the budgeting process in Congress and created the Congressional Budget Office, which produces an independent analysis of the president's budget each year. Congress expanded the personal staffs of individual senators and House members and committee staffs in both houses, and added to the research service of the Library of Congress. These steps, though little noticed, represented a significant change in the relationship between the two branches. Congress acquired new capability to evaluate and challenge programs sought by presidents.

Recognizing the strength of popular support for reform, House leaders also agreed to changes in the House structure that greatly diffused authority. The chairs of the twenty-two standing committees in the House, a small group of senior legislators, had long been able to decide which bills would receive consideration in their committees and could organize support or opposition to a bill that was almost always decisive. In 1974 House Democrats adopted "the subcommittee bill of rights," which parceled out the power of the original 22 committees to 172 subcommittees. Many complained that this redistribution of power made it difficult to build coalitions that could pass legislation.

Hoping to prevent another Watergate, Congress moved to limit the influence of money in politics, but the effort backfired. The Federal Election Campaign Act of 1974 placed caps on the amount of money that individuals could donate to political campaigns and provided some public funding for presidential campaigns. But loopholes in the act allowed new mechanisms of fundraising and donation that actually led to an increase in the flow of private money into elections. Political parties developed direct mail techniques to solicit huge numbers of small donations, which they then funneled into important campaigns. Political action committees (PACs) proliferated and dispersed campaign funds. In 1974 there were only 608 PACs; by 1984 the number had soared to over 4,000. Critics charged that well-financed PACs gave powerful interests inordinate influence in Congress. "What is at stake," cautioned journalist Elizabeth Drew, "is the idea of representative government, the soul of this country."

As the nation prepared to celebrate its two hundredth birthday, polls showed that Americans had little confidence that their political leadership was dealing honestly with them. While faith in American political institutions remained firm, faith in Washington was languishing. A 1976 study revealed 69 percent of respondents felt that "over the last ten years, this country's leaders have consistently lied to the people." What Americans were saying, declared two social scientists, was that "the system" works but "it is not performing well because the people in charge are inept and untrustworthy."

The Troubled Economy

A host of statistics revealed that the American economy had stalled during the 1970s. During the long postwar boom from 1947 to the mid-1960s, the United States enjoyed average annual productivity increases of 3.2 percent. From 1965 to 1973, however, productivity growth averaged only 2.4 percent annually. By the end of the decade, productivity was declining in absolute terms. As inflation exploded to nearly 10 percent and unemployment crept upward, Americans found that their discretionary income declined by 18 percent between 1973 and 1980. The average price of a single-family house more than doubled during the 1970s (see graph).

The nation's economic difficulties had many causes. First, an inflationary trend began in the 1960s, when President Johnson and the Congress decided to expand defense and social spending without asking for higher taxes. Each year, high government expenditures stimulated the economy more than taxes slowed it down, creating upward pressure on prices.

Second, in the 1970s, America ran out of "easy oil," a serious challenge to the basic structures of the economy. The nation's expansion in the postwar era depended on the prodigious use of cheap energy. Americans living in sprawling suburban communities enjoyed driving powerful, energy-inefficient cars. Large single-family homes offered Americans more living space than people of any other country—but used a great deal of oil to heat in the winter and electricity to cool in summer. And as long as energy was cheap, American industry found it cost-efficient to use processes that were alarmingly wasteful.

In the early 1970s, political turmoil in the Middle East led to dramatically higher oil prices and undermined the bedrock of this system. Between 1972 and 1979, the price of oil quintupled. Higher energy costs rippled through the economy. Inflation, which never exceeded 5 percent between 1955 and 1972, and was often as low as 2 or 3 percent, suddenly exploded to nearly 10 percent by the end of 1973.

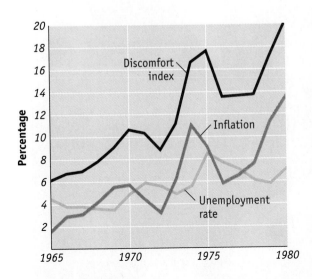

Discomfort Index   During the 1970s the United States experienced both rising inflation and increased unemployment. During the 1976 presidential campaign Democrats developed the "discomfort" or "misery" index to measure the public impact of this destructive combination, and to attack their Republican opponents for their poor management of the economy. In 1980, however, Republicans used the same index to highlight Jimmy Carter's economic mismanagement. (Sources: Washington, D.C.: U.S. Government Printing Office, 1981, pp. 238, 263; *Economic Report of the President, 1999; Statistical Abstract of the United States, 1996*)

A third cause for economic trouble lay abroad. For the first time since the end of World War II, American business faced stiff competition from other countries. The industrial economies of western Europe and Japan, finally recovered from the war, began to win an increasing share of international trade. The U.S. share of world trade declined by 16 percent between 1960 and 1970, and dropped another 25 percent during the 1970s. What was even more troubling was that foreign competitors were winning a large share of the rich American market. With exports declining and imports rising, the United States posted its first balance of trade deficit in almost a century. The surge in foreign competition offered consumers quality products at lower prices. But it also threatened jobs that had for years offered Americans high wages and dependable employment.

The decline of the American automobile industry provided a clear example of this trend. In the 1950s and 1960s, U.S. automakers had ruled the domestic market. In the 1970s, with gasoline prices soaring and buying power pinched by inflation, car buyers welcomed affordable, more fuel-efficient imports such as Japan's Toyota and Datsun. Detroit, geared toward producing bulky six-passenger sedans, failed to convert in time, and part of its market drifted away. By 1980, imports had grabbed 34 percent of the U.S. auto market. The United Stares now imported 3.2 million foreign cars annually, about 60 percent of them from Japan.

In the midst of these crises, political leaders seemed unable to find any solutions. Each presidential administration of the decade witnessed wild policy swings

Unemployed   During Gerald Ford's fifteen months as president, the United States slipped into its deepest recession since the Great Depression. Unemployment hit 9 percent in 1975, leaving millions of Americans with few options save filing for government relief. This was a choice few people, like this man at an unemployment agency in Cleveland, made easily.   (*Seattle/NYT Pictures.*)

as leaders and economists sought to understand the profound changes shaking the American economy. Many of the experiments were based on short-term thinking; none seemed to improve the nation's economy very much. In combination, they eroded the public's belief that the nation's leaders could manage the economy.

President Nixon, for example, began his administration by embracing the monetarist theories of Milton Friedman. The conservative Friedman claimed that prices could be lowered by reducing the quantity of money in the economy. If there were less money and it were more expensive to borrow, reasoned Friedman, economic activity would ease and prices would stabilize. In practice, a reduced money supply did slow economic growth, but it did not stop prices from rising. This new and troubling phenomenon, dubbed *stagflation,* haunted the economy for the rest of the decade.

Deeming monetarism a failure, Nixon tried other policies. In August 1971, faced with a combination of rising prices and high unemployment, Nixon shocked conservatives and delighted liberals by declaring, "I am now a Keynesian," (see page 990). Acting on his new faith, the president advocated traditionally liberal solutions, imposing wage and price controls, devaluing the dollar, and abandoning the gold standard. Fearing the political consequences of high unemployment in an election year, Nixon pressured the Federal Reserve Bank, the nation's central institution for setting interest rates and regulating the money supply, to turn on the money spigot. Commenting on Nixon's dramatic switch, a journalist quipped, "It's a little like a Christian crusader saying 'All things considered, I think Mohammed was right!'" Later that year, Nixon announced a "new economic policy" imposing a 10 percent surcharge on U.S. imports. "My basic approach," said Secretary of Treasury John Connally, "is that the foreigners are out to screw us. Our job is to screw them first." The policies realized their short-term political and economic goals. During the 1972 election year the GNP grew by 7.2 percent and the unemployment rate plunged from 6 percent to 5.1 percent. In the long run, however, Nixon's policies proved disastrous. By ignorning clear signs of inflation and intentionally expanding the economy he contributed to a cycle of spiraling inflation that would soon cripple the economy.

These reverses assaulted Americans' optimistic faith in progress. For most of their history, Americans had believed that hard work and talent would be rewarded with upward mobility and greater economic opportunity. More, they had faith that the ingenuity of the American people and the continent's rich resources would lead to an ever-increasing prosperity for all. Americans, Alexis de Tocqueville wrote as early as 1835, "consider society as a body in a state of improvement." By 1979, however, 55 percent of all Americans believed that "next year will be worse than this year." Nearly three out of four Americans polled agreed with the statement: "We are fast coming to a turning point in our history. The land of plenty is becoming the land of want."

The Environmental Movement

The obvious contribution of the oil shock to the nation's economic woes alerted many people to the possibility that their prosperity had been built on an unsustainable base and contributed to a groundswell of environmentalism. The birth of the modern environmental movement dated to the publication in 1962 of marine biologist Rachel Carson's book *Silent Spring,* which documented evidence that the widely used insecticide DDT was killing birds, fish, and other animals that ate insects. Sufficiently concentrated, DDT also posed significant health risks to humans. Chemical companies that manufactured DDT ridiculed Carson's book, but her eloquence and evidence won numerous allies. In 1972 the government banned the sale of DDT.

Highly publicized disasters fueled public concern about the costs of a technological society. When people living in the Love Canal housing development near Niagara Falls, New York, reported abnormally high rates of illness, miscarriages, and birth defects, investigators learned the community had been built on top of an underground chemical waste disposal site. In March 1979, a frightening accident at the Three Mile Island nuclear power plant in Pennsylvania heightened public concern about the safety of nuclear power and led to calls for tighter regulation of the industry.

The government responded with several pieces of legislation. In 1971 Congress created a cabinet-level position called the Environmental Protection Agency (EPA) to focus government efforts to protect the environment. Congress also passed legislation expanding the government's regulatory powers. The Water Quality Improvement Act and National Air Quality Standards Act strengthened controls against water and air pollution. The Resource Recovery Act provided $453 million for resource recovery and recycling systems. The National Environmental Policy Act required the government to consider in advance the impact of government programs on the environment.

Uneasiness about the state of the environment persisted and found expression in the popular culture of the 1970s. In best-selling books, such as Hal Lindsey's *Late Great Planet Earth*, scientists were heard to predict the end of global supplies of oil and other natural resources. A popular movie, *The China Syndrome*, portrayed a fictitious nuclear power plant in which incompetence and greed threatened to lead to a nuclear meltdown. Others, such as *Soylent Green*, envisioned a world in which technological development and overpopulation had exhausted the earth's natural resources. Providing clear evidence of the broad-based, diverse support for environmentalism was the success of the first annual Earth Day celebration on April 22, 1970. Twenty million people gathered in local events across the country to hear speeches and see exhibits and demonstrations promoting environmental awareness.

Gerald Ford and the 1976 Presidential Campaign

Faced with the delicate problem of succeeding Richard Nixon, Gerald Ford tried to present himself as a steady, sober leader whom the public could trust. With his friendly smile and reputation for honesty, Ford enjoyed wide respect. As he took the presidential oath of office on August 9, 1972, the sixty-two-year-old Ford announced his top priority was to heal "the nation's wounds" and to restore a sense of confidence in government. Within a month, however, Ford connected his administration to the Watergate scandal by granting Nixon "a full, free, and absolute pardon . . . for all his offenses against the United States." Overnight, Ford's approval ratings plunged from 71 to 50 percent.

Ford had a hard time overcoming this poor start. He fought constantly with Congress, vetoing more legislation than any president in history. Among the measures he rejected were popular programs such as federal aid to education and health care. Worse, Ford's efforts to solve the energy crisis and recession succeeded no better than did Nixon's. Hoping to choke off the inflation that followed Nixon's relaxation of price controls, Ford drove interest rates to all-time highs and vetoed a tax cut designed to give consumers more money to spend. Though this brought inflation down to 5 percent by 1976, it also produced a serious contraction in 1975 as unemployment reached a post-depression high of 9 percent.

During the 1976 Democratic primaries, one-term Georgia governor Jimmy Carter emerged from a crowded pack of contenders by convincing voters that only he, an outsider, could clean up the mess in Washington. Deciding that most people were more interested in leadership and integrity than in issues, Carter avoided taking positions on controversial questions. The main issues of the campaign, he claimed, were two: "Can government work? And can government be decent, honest, truthful, fair, compassionate, and as filled with love as our people are?" To a public still smarting from Watergate, Carter said, "I will never lie to you." To balance the ticket and appeal to mainstream Democrats, Carter selected Minnesota senator Walter F. Mondale, a protégé of Hubert Humphrey, as his running mate.

President Ford countered with a "Rose Garden strategy." Rather than campaigning around the country, he stayed close to the White House, where he could appear "presidential." Allowing the press to focus attention on the campaign of his overexposed challenger, Ford chided Carter for his vagueness on issues: "He wanders, he wavers, he waffles and he wiggles." Ford's strategy nearly worked: by early October, he had nearly eliminated Carter's once-formidable 33-point lead in the polls.

But the legacy of Watergate, continuing bad economic news, and his own lack of charisma were more than Ford could overcome. On election night the Democrats won a narrow victory. Less than 2 percentage points separated the candidates in the popular vote—Carter won 40.8 million votes to Ford's 39.1. In the electoral college, Carter defeated Ford 297 to 240. It was the narrowest electoral victory since 1916, when Woodrow Wilson defeated Charles Evans Hughes by 23 electoral votes. Judging from the turnout, it was also one of the least compelling. A smaller percentage of Americans voted in 1976 than in any election since 1948 (see map).

Jimmy Carter and the "Crisis of Confidence"

The new president faced enormous obstacles in his effort to build a national consensus. His narrow electoral victory provided a shaky foundation for bold proposals. He presided over a party still torn by divisions over Vietnam and civil rights. A resurgent Congress eager to reassert its authority after Watergate, and a public grown cynical about Washington and angry about rising unemployment and high inflation, compounded his difficulties.

Carter managed a few significant achievements in domestic policy. He appointed more African-Americans and women to positions in his administration than any previous president. He created new cabinet-level positions for the Departments of Energy and Education and he established a superfund to clean up chemical waste dumps. But much of Carter's presidency was marred by poor relations

The Election of 1976 Ford's failure to solve the nation's economic problems led to doubts within his own Republican party about his ability to lead the nation, while his opponent, Jimmy Carter of Georgia, emphasized the need for a moral president after years of political corruption unearthed by the Watergate investigations. Fallout from the Watergate era could also be seen in the low voter turnout for the election, as almost half of eligible voters, alienated by the scandal, failed to vote.

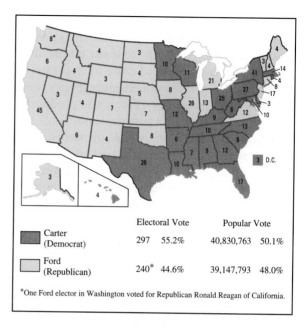

		Electoral Vote		Popular Vote	
■	Carter (Democrat)	297	55.2%	40,830,763	50.1%
□	Ford (Republican)	240*	44.6%	39,147,793	48.0%

*One Ford elector in Washington voted for Republican Ronald Reagan of California.

with Democratic congressional leaders, Speaker of the House Edward P. O'Neill and Senator Edward M. Kennedy. More liberal than Carter, they wanted him to support ambitious legislation to address the nation's economic problems and to overhaul the nation's health care system. Consummate insiders, they also often endured snubs by Carter, who frequently failed to do some of the hard work of coalition building and compromise required to pass bills in Congress. As a result, some of the administration's top legislative priorities were either gravely weakened or utterly abandoned.

Carter also had significant trouble managing the economy. He began his presidency by raising government spending in an effort to rein in the spiraling unemployment generated by Ford's fiscal and monetary restrictions. Unemployment did begin to come down, but only at the cost of another slow rise in inflation that ate into Americans' paychecks. Then, in 1979, OPEC announced another round of escalating oil prices that pushed inflation above 10 percent. Reversing course, Carter declared that inflation was the number one problem facing the economy. He cut back public spending and appointed leading conservative Paul Volcker to head the Federal Reserve Board. Volcker, determined to wring inflation out of the economy, instituted a severe tight money policy. In 1980 this policy had devastating effects: unemployment shot up to more than 7.5 percent, but inflation remained above 12 percent, and interest rates topped out at the incredible figure of 20 percent.

In foreign policy, the president achieved a couple of notable successes. In December 1978, Carter completed the process initiated by Richard Nixon by formally recognizing the People's Republic of China. In March 1979, his persistence and vision produced the most notable success of his administration—the signing of the Camp David Accords, a historic peace treaty between long-standing enemies Egypt and Israel. In the treaty, Egypt recognized Israel's right to exist as a sovereign state, and Israel agreed to return the Sinai Peninsula. President Carter also convinced the Senate, in a very close vote, to ratify a treaty that promised to turn over the Canal Zone to Panama by the year 2000.

For most of his four years in office, however, Carter struggled unsuccessfully to convince the American public that he could protect America's global interests from an aggressive Soviet Union. Carter came to power pledging to work for more amicable relations with the Soviet Union and to replace the Nixon-Kissinger commitment to realism with a concern for human rights. "We are now free of that inordinate fear of communism which once led us to embrace any dictator who joined us in our fear," Carter declared. He quickly opened a second round of arms limitations talks (SALT II) with the Soviet Union. But Carter was struggling to extend détente at a time when many Americans were questioning its benefits. Since Nixon and Kissinger had announced their aim of achieving détente, the Soviet Union had repeatedly made clear its continuing support for "liberation" struggles in the Third

Camp David Accords   Carter's greatest foreign policy achievement was his brokering of a historic peace between Israel and Egypt. In the Camp David Accords, signed by Egyptian president Anwar Sadat (left) and Israeli prime minister Menachem Begin, Israel promised to return all land in the Sinai in return for Egypt's recognition of the Israeli state. Though it did not solve the issue of Palestinian refugees, the Accords did lessen the tensions in the region.   *(Jimmy Carter Presidential Library.)*

World. It ordered Cuba to send troops to potential allies in Africa and worked to win influence among Arab nations sitting on the West's supply of oil.

At the end of 1979, a pair of disastrous foreign policy reverses fixed upon Carter a reputation for insufficient strength and clarity in foreign policy. Early in the year, revolutionaries had overthrown the pro-American regime of the shah of Iran, and Muslim fundamentalists loyal to religious leader Ayatollah Khomeini had gained control of the country. When Carter agreed to let the deposed shah come to the United States for cancer treatment, many Iranians took the act as a direct insult. In retribution, Iranian nationalists seized fifty-three American soldiers and diplomats and held them hostage in Tehran. With Carter unable to effect a release by threats or diplomacy, the hostages languished for week after week, then month after month. Evening news broadcasts began to announce each night the number of days that the hostages had been in captivity, and the litany became for many a daily and humiliating reminder of the limits of American power.

Only a few weeks later, in December 1979, the Soviets invaded neighboring Afghanistan to prop up a bumbling regime. Outraged, Carter called the invasion the "most serious threat to world peace since World War II." He moved decisively away from détente, forbade U.S. athletes from participating in the 1980 Moscow Olympics, put an end to the SALT II negotiations, and ordered an embargo on U.S. grain exports to the Soviet Union. In the context of other foreign policy events of his presidency, his response seemed to many Americans to be hollow and tardy gestures.

Battered by events, and searching for a way to understand the troubles that beset the nation and perhaps to save his presidency, Jimmy Carter spent a week at his Camp David retreat listening to the advice of religious leaders, historians, poets, and psychiatrists. Returning to Washington, Carter announced a presidential address. Most people were expecting to hear a fresh solution to the energy crisis. Instead they received a lecture about a "crisis of confidence," which the president claimed struck "at the very heart and soul and spirit of our national will." In the past, Carter declared, Americans had "believed in something called progress," characterized by "a faith that the days of our children will be better than our own." Now, he said, the country had lost its bearings: in a nation that "was proud of hard work, strong families, close knit communities and our faith in God, too many of us now tend to worship self-indulgence and consumption."

Carter had successfully diagnosed the deeper problems afflicting Americans in the 1980s, but he did not know what medicine to prescribe. The American defeat in Vietnam, the constitutional crisis of Watergate, the OPEC oil embargo, and the hostage fiasco deepened America's frustration and intensified the nation's effort to regain control of its future.

CONCLUSION

The aftershocks of the 1960s rumbled through the 1970s, producing angry recriminations, political polarization, and, eventually, stalemate. The decade witnessed a political and cultural clash between two powerful forces, each firmly rooted in American ideals, neither willing to compromise. On one side stood social reformers who, inspired by the struggles of the 1960s, mobilized to force national leaders to confront the contradiction between the reality of discrimination and the American ideal of equality.

On the other side stood the "angry white voters" who formed the backbone of Richard Nixon's "silent majority." Mobilized by a belief that student protests and racial riots threatened social stability, the silent majority organized an effective backlash against social reform. Like the advocates of social reform, the leaders of the silent majority appealed to American ideals, but their ideals were those of individual liberty and limited government. They viewed the demands for group remedy, preferential treatment, and activist government as a direct threat to traditional American values. Richard Nixon played to these concerns by emphasizing his commitment to law and order, by assailing his enemies as anti-American, and by stressing his commitment to small government. The silent majority rewarded him with a massive electoral landslide in the 1972 presidential election.

The two sides clashed repeatedly during the decade as they promoted conflicting experiments. Nixon's Cambodia incursion and the shootings at Kent State underscored the intense divisions generated by the Vietnam War. America's defeat in Vietnam shattered the postwar foreign policy consensus and raised troubling new questions about America's role in the world. Controversial issues such as busing and affirmative action highlighted racial differences.

The decade witnessed an unprecedented ferment of reform among various minority groups—homosexuals, Hispanics, Native Americans—as well as a powerful women's movement. The "rights revolution" raised public awareness, developed a greater sense of group identity and pride, and, especially in the case of women, achieved notable legislative successes. For the most part, however, results fell far short of expectations.

The conflicting currents of the decade found expression in popular culture. Trends from the 1960s—drug use, liberal sexual attitudes, long hair, and casual dress—continued and gained broader support during the 1970s. Popular media articulated Vietnam's lessons of cynicism and tragedy. At the same time, people cheered Sylvester Stallone's celebration of traditional values in the blockbuster movie *Rocky* and laughed at the antics of the angry and intolerant Archie Bunker in the hit television show *All in the Family*. Many Americans turned to jogging, Eastern religions, and disco music in an effort to escape the decade's swirling passions.

Both sides looked to the federal government to reconcile the competing visions of America, but the government was experiencing its own crisis of authority in the 1970s. The Watergate scandal, which resulted in the first forced resignation of an American president, shook the foundations of government and eroded public confidence in national institutions. Congress passed a number of reforms designed to rebuild public faith in government. But public mistrust swelled as national leaders failed to stem the tide of rising unemployment, higher prices, and declining real income. Concern about limited resources produced a broad-based environmental movement.

In 1976 Jimmy Carter recaptured the presidency for the Democrats by promising to restore America's faith in government, but instead his administration became a casualty of the "Age of Limits," unable to establish control over a divided party and an unruly Congress. The most severe blow to Carter's leadership came from abroad, where the hostage crisis in Iran and the Soviet invasion of Afghanistan seemed to symbolize American impotence. As the decade came to an end, Americans searched for experiments that might end the stalemate, restore confidence in their governing institutions, and reestablish their dominance in world affairs.

SUGGESTED READINGS

David Frum offers a critical assessment of the social and cultural changes of the decade in *How We Got Here* (2000). Peter Carroll's *It Seemed Like Nothing Happened* (1983) is a lively collection of anecdotes about the decade and its frustrations. James Reichley's *Conservatives in an Age of Change* (1981) details the changes in American politics during the Nixon and Ford Years.

Neil Sheehan's *A Bright Shining Lie* (1988) explores the government deception employed during the Vietnam War. George C. Herring's *America's Longest War* (1986) has good material on the legacy of the war. William Shawcross indignantly describes Nixon and Kissinger's Cambodia policy in *Sideshow* (1979). Melvin Small outlines the peace process in *Johnson, Nixon, and the Doves* (1988). Arnold Isaacs critiques Nixon's peace in *Without Honor* (1983). On the influence of the "Madman Theory" on Nixon's conduct of the Vietnam War, see Jeffrey Kimball's *Nixon's Vietnam* War (1998). Lewis Sorley offers a revisionist account of the final days of the war in *A Better War* (1999).

Robert S. Litwak's *Detente and the Nixon Doctrine* (1984) is a good introduction to Nixon's foreign policy. Tad Szulc's *The Illusion of Peace* (1978) contrasts Nixon's domestic message with his international actions. For Nixon's efforts toward disarmament, see Franz Schurmann's *The Foreign Policies of Richard Nixon* (1987). Edy Kaufman's *Crisis in Allende's Chile* (1988) details the events leading to the 1973 coup. Stephen Rabe covers the crises in the Middle East in *The Road to OPEC* (1982).

In *The Declining Significance of Race* (1980), William J. Wilson describes the economic polarization of African-American society. Douglas Glasgow's *The Black Underclass* (1980) describes the black economic decline of the 1970s. Nathan Glazer's *Affirmative Discrimination* (1975) details the controversy around affirmative action. Ronald Formisano explores the opposition to the busing movement in *Boston Against Busing* (1991). J. Anthony Lukas's *Common Ground* (1985) is a moving account of the Boston busing crisis through the eyes of three families.

Stan Steiner's *La Raza* (1970) describes the early Hispanic protest movement. Matt Meier and Feliciano Rivera explore the generational conflicts among Hispanics in *The Chicanos* (1972). Vine DeLoria, Jr.'s *Custer Died for Your Sins* (1969) is an early document of Native American activism. Helen Hertzberg's *The Search for an American Indian Movement* (1971) chronicles the rise of the Red Power movement. John D'Emilio's *Sexual Politics, Sexual Communities* (1983) explores the formation of gay identity in the postwar years. Martin Duberman's *Stonewall* (1993) describes the birth of the modern gay liberation movement.

Sara Evans describes how the women's liberation movement evolved from the civil rights struggle in *Personal Politics* (1979). Jo Freeman's *The Politics of Women's Liberation* (1979) and Judith Hole and Ellen Levine's *The Rebirth of Feminism* (1971) describe the rise of the women's movement. Gayle Graham Yates outlines the feminist ideology in *What Women Want* (1975). Alice Echols explores radical feminism in *Daring to Be Bad* (1989). Susan Hartmann's *From Margin to Mainstream* (1989) has good material on economic discrimination by sex. Joel F. Handler's *We the Poor People* (1997) explores the feminization of poverty.

Christopher Lasch's *The Culture of Narcissism* (1978) is an influential description of the "Me decade." Edwin Schur's *The Awareness Trap* (1976) describes the failure of social change and the rise of "awareness" movements.

Historians are still trying to come to terms with Richard Nixon and his presidency. For the best accounts see Melvin Small, *The Presidency of Richard Nixon* (1999); Joan Hoff, *Nixon Reconsidered* (1995); and Herbert Parmet *Richard Nixon and His America* (1990). Allen Matusow offers a critical appraisal of the president's economic policy in *Nixon's Economy* (1998). Kim McQuaid analyzes Nixon's mobilization of the "silent majority" in *The Anxious Years* (1989). Dan Carter examines George Wallace's impact on American politics and the Nixon administration in *The Politics of Rage* (1995). Thomas Edsall describes how Nixon helped mold public anger into a powerful conservative coalition in *Chain Reaction* (1992).

Stanley Kutler's *Abuse of Power* (1997) and *The Wars of Watergate* (1992) are essential reading for understanding Nixon's downfall. Bob Woodward and Carl Bernstein's *All the President's Men* (1974) and *The Final Days* (1976) are both captivating journalistic accounts; see also John Dean's *Blind Ambition* (1976), John Ehrlichman's *Witness to Power* (1982), and John Sirica's *To Set the Record Straight* (1979). For an insightful look at how Americans have remembered the events that led to Nixon's resignation, see Michael Schudson, *Watergate in American Memory* (1992). Athan Theoharis's *Spying on Americans* (1978) details the illegal actions of the Nixon White House against dissidents.

Arthur M. Schlesinger, Jr., studies the growth of executive power that presaged Watergate in *The Imperial Presidency* (1973). James I. Sundquist's *The Decline and Resurgence of Congress* (1981) tracks the changing balance of power between the branches of government. Robert Heilbroner and Lester Thurow diagnose the economic ills of the 1970s in *Five Economic Challenges* (1983). John P. Hoerr's tale of America's declining steel industry, *And the Wolf Finally Came* (1988), demonstrates the nation's industrial decline during the decade. Robert Heilbroner's *An Inquiry Into the Human Prospect* (1974) discusses the energy crisis. William Greider's *Secrets of the Temple* (1987) includes a detailed analysis of economic policy under Carter.

Rachel Carson's *Silent Spring* (1962) remains the eloquent first word of the environmental movement. Daniel F. Ford describes the nuclear power scare in *Three Mile Island* (1982), while Thomas Raymond Wellock looks at opposition to nuclear energy in California in *Critical Mass* (1998). Samuel P. Hays provides an overview of the movement in *Beauty, Health, and Permanence* (1987). Roderick Nash's *The Rights of Nature* (1989) outlines the environmentalist ethic.

John Robert Greene studies the Ford administration in *The Presidency of Gerald R. Ford* (1995). Jules Witcover's *Marathon* (1977) recounts the 1976 presidential campaign. On the Carter presidency see Charles Jones's *The Trusteeship Presidency* (1988); Burton Kaufman, *The Presidency of James Earl Carter, Jr.* (1993); and the collection of essays by Gary M. Fink and Hugh Davis Graham, *The Carter Presidency* (1998). Gaddis Smith's readable *Morality, Reason, and Power* (1987) provides the best overview of Carter's erratic foreign policy. William Quandt describes the Egypt-Israeli peace accord in *Camp David* (1986). Barry Rubin's *Paved with Good Intentions* (1983) covers America's relations with Iran.

Competing Voices | The Politics of Gender

The Feminist Perspective

A graduate of Smith College, Gloria Steinem was an aspiring journalist in the early 1960s, writing for popular journals such as *Esquire* and *Show* and the political satire magazine *Help!* Steinem established herself as an articulate and forceful proponent of a wide range of political causes—the peace movement, migrant farm workers, civil rights. In 1970 her name began to be linked with women's liberation when she outlined a vision of what the country might look like if only women had equal power—though she didn't have the power to keep *Time* magazine from shortening "women's liberation" to "women's lib."

... In Women's Lib Utopia, there will be free access to good jobs—and decent pay for the bad ones women have been performing all along, including housework. Increased skilled labor might lead to a four-hour workday, and higher wages would encourage further mechanization of repetitive jobs now kept alive by cheap labor.

With women as half the country's elected representatives, and a woman President once in a while, the country's *machismo* problems would be greatly reduced. The old-fashioned idea that manhood depends on violence and victory is, after all, an important part of our troubles in the streets, and in Vietnam. I'm not saying that women leaders would eliminate violence. We are not more moral than men; we are only uncorrupted by power so far.

Men will have to give up ruling-class privileges, but in return they will no longer be the only ones to support the family, get drafted, bear the strain of power and responsibility. Freud to the contrary, anatomy is not destiny, at least not for more than nine months at a time. In Israel, women are drafted, and some have gone to war. In England, more men type and run switchboards. In India and Israel, a woman rules. In Sweden, both parents take care of the children. In this country, come Utopia, men and women won't reverse roles; they will be free to choose according to individual talents and preferences.

Schools and universities will help to break down traditional sex roles, even when parents will not. Half the teachers will be men, a rarity now at preschool and elementary levels; girls will not necessarily serve cookies or boys hoist up the flag. Athletic teams will be picked only by strength and skill. Sexually segregated courses like auto mechanics and home economics will be taken by boys and girls together. New courses in sexual politics will explore female subjugation as the model for political oppression, and women's history will be an academic staple, along with black history, at least until the white-male-oriented textbooks are integrated and rewritten. ...

As for the American child's classic problem—too much mother, too little father—that would be cured by an equalization of parental responsibility. ...

Our marriage laws . . . are so reactionary that women's lib groups want couples to take a compulsory written exam on the law, as for a driver's license, before going through with the wedding. . . . [A] woman may lose so many of her civil rights that in the U.S. now, in important legal ways, she becomes a child again. . . .

Women's lib is not trying to destroy the American family. A look at the statistics on divorce—plus the way in which old people are farmed out with strangers and young people flee the home—shows the destruction that has already been done. Liberated women are just trying to point out the disaster, and build compassionate and practical alternatives from the ruins.

In Defense of Tradition

Steinem's chief antagonist was Phyllis Schlafly, a successful Illinois lawyer and an influential conservative activist in the Republican Party. After the Senate passed the Equal Rights Amendment in 1972, Schlafly entered the feminist fray. Called the "Sweetheart of the Silent Majority," Schlafly, the mother of six, accused feminists of being a radical fringe group out of touch with traditional values and intent on destroying the American family. In 1977 she published *The Power of the Positive Woman*, a forceful defense of traditional womanhood and a scathing attack on modern feminism.

If man is targeted as the enemy, and the ultimate goal of women's liberation is independence from men and the avoidance of pregnancy and its consequences, then lesbianism is logically the highest form in the ritual of women's liberation.

The Positive Woman will never travel that dead-end road. It is self-evident to the Positive Woman that the female body with its baby-producing organs was not designed by a conspiracy of men but by the Divine Architect of the human race. . . .

The Positive Woman looks upon her femaleness and her fertility as part of her purpose, her potential, and her power. She rejoices that she has a capability for creativity that men can never have. . . .

The women's liberationists are expending their time and energies erecting a make-believe world in which they hypothesize that *if* schooling were gender-free, and *if* the same money were spent on male and female sports programs, and *if* women were permitted to compete on equal terms, *then* they would prove themselves to be physically equal. Meanwhile, the Positive Woman has put the ineradicable physical differences into her mental computer, programmed her plan of action, and is already on the way to personal achievement. . . .

Despite the claims of the women's liberation movement, there are countless physical differences between men and women. . . . Males have a tendency to color blindness. Only 5 percent of persons who get gout are female. Boys are born bigger. Women live longer in most countries of the world, not only in the United States where we have a hard-driving competitive pace. Women excel in manual dexterity, verbal skills, and memory recall. . . .

The differences between men and women are also emotional and psychological. Without woman's innate maternal instinct, the human race would have died out centuries ago. . . . Even in the most primitive, uneducated societies, women have always cared for their newborn babies. . . .

Why? Because caring for a baby serves the natural maternal need of a woman. Although not nearly so total as the baby's need, the woman's need is nonetheless real. . . .

The woman's liberation movement complains that traditional stereotyped roles assume that women are "passive" and that men are "aggressive." The anomaly is that a woman's most fundamental emotional need is not passive at all, but active. A woman naturally seeks to love affirmatively and to show that love in an active way by caring for the object of her affections.

For most of American history, powerful cultural norms have established clear guidelines for male and female behavior. "The sum total of general belief of the most enlightened of both sexes," a speaker told the 1876 graduating class of Mount Holyoke College, "appears to be that there is a difference of kind in their natural endowments and that there is for each an appropriate field of development and action." Catharine Beecher, the author of a number of influential advice books in the 1860s and 1870s, urged women to gain the appropriate training for "her distinctive profession as housekeeper, nurse of infants and the sick, educator of childhood, trainer of servants and ministers of charities." ▮

Numerous changes transformed women's role in American society in the hundred years between Catharine Beecher and Gloria Steinem. Perhaps the most dramatic was the movement into the workplace. In 1940 only one-quarter of American women worked for wages; by 1974, 46 percent did so. These economic changes dramatically altered women's role in the home. As late as the 1950s, more than 70 percent of all American families consisted of a father who worked and a mother who stayed at home to take care of the children. By 1980, that description applied to only 15 percent of all families.

These economic changes, combined with the broader climate of protest during the 1970s, inspired feminists, like Steinem, to challenge the gap between America's professed faith in equal opportunity and the reality of gender discrimination. But Schlafly's successful campaign to defeat the ERA revealed that cultural values about gender roles proved more resilient to change. A poll taken in 1977 showed two-thirds of Americans thought that preschool children were likely to suffer if their mothers worked for wages, 62 percent thought married women should not hold jobs when jobs were scarce and their husbands could support them, and a majority thought it more important for a woman to advance her husband's career than to have one of her own.

Questions for Analysis

1. What does Steinem mean when she says "anatomy is not destiny"?

2. What changes would Steinem most like to see in her utopia?

3. What does she identify as the chief obstacle to her vision?

4. What qualities does Schlafly associate with being female? being male?

5. Why does she find women's liberation so threatening?

6. How are the women of Steinem's utopia different from Schlafly's "Positive Woman"?

7. Why have traditional values about gender roles proven so resistant to change?

8. Can you think of other times in American history when cultural values clashed with changing social realities?

31

The Reagan Experiment, 1979–1988

For almost three months before the opening of the 1984 Olympic games in Los Angeles, the Olympic flame wound its way across the country, through small towns and big cities, country roads and urban freeways. The appearance of the torch in many areas touched off something resembling an old-fashioned Fourth of July parade. The sight of the runner entering town set church bells ringing and fire sirens blaring. In many communities, people who had waited for hours to see the flame placed their right hands over their hearts and sang the national anthem. "When people see the torch, they relate it to patriotism," one runner observed. "There's a hunger for that in the land."

The torch ended its journey on July 28, when Gina Hemphill, granddaughter of Jesse Owens, the famed African-American sprinter who starred in the 1936 Berlin Olympics, sprinted into the Los Angeles Coliseum. She ran a lap and then, as the stadium shook with cheers, handed the torch to another African-American, Rafer Johnson, the 1960 decathlon gold medalist, who ran up two long flights of stairs and ignited the Olympic flame that would burn throughout the games. It was left to President Ronald Reagan to make the opening official: "Celebrating the 23rd Olympiad of the modern era, I declare open the Olympic Games of Los Angeles."

The Olympics represented an international celebration of sport, but hosting the games stirred an outpouring of national pride and patriotism among Americans that no one had anticipated. With the Soviet Union boycotting the event in protest against American foreign policy, American athletes collected a record eighty-three gold medals. At times the colors of red, white, and blue, seemed to overwhelm the main stadium as Americans waved flags and chanted, "U.S.A.! U.S.A.!"

The string of American victories thrilled an American audience in the grip of a resurgent nationalism that had swept the country since the election of Ronald Reagan. The new president came to office in 1981 riding a conservative wave of frustration with a stagnant economy, soaring inflation, high taxes, and the perception that America's international prestige was in decline. At issue was the role of government as it had been defined since the 1960s. Calling for a "New Beginning," Reagan enacted sweeping reforms to curtail "big" government, increase spending on the military, and cut taxes. Abroad, he asserted American power, engaging the Soviets in a tense confrontation and a renewed arms race. Two months after the Los Angeles Olympics, the public rewarded Reagan's experimentation with a resounding victory in the 1984 presidential campaign.

A rejuvenated economy fed the consumer society's appetite for money and wealth. Aging upper-middle-class baby boomers settling into their peak earning years seemed consumed with the pursuit of wealth, power, and status. But beneath the surface of prosperity and political good feeling, the American experiment was under stress. While much of the public debate focused on ways to obtain and display wealth, U.S. society suffered striking disparities between rich and poor, growing homelessness, and a stagnant middle class. At the same time, a powerful coalition of religious conservatives precipitated a cultural civil war over controversial social issues such as abortion, gay rights, and immigration.

▎ What were the roots of public anger with government that fueled the conservative reaction in the 1980s?

▎ Describe the culture wars of the decade. How did they represent a clash of competing views of what it meant to be an American?

▎ How did Ronald Reagan tap into public discontent, and why was he so successful?

▎ What attitudes shaped Reagan's view of the world, and how realistic was his approach?

▎ Why were many Americans so fascinated with wealth and status, and how evenly distributed were the benefits from the economic boom in the 1980s?

This chapter will address these questions.

 ## The Conservative Revival, 1979–1980

Numerous forces conspired during the 1970s to undermine public support for government and to feed the conservative revival. The old New Deal coalition unraveled as evangelical Christians, middle-class property owners, and business and neoconservative intellectual leaders revolted against what they viewed as the twin big-

Chronology

1978	California passes Proposition 13
1979	Falwell founds the Moral Majority
1980	Reagan elected president
1981	AIDS identified
	Attempted Reagan assassination
	O'Connor appointed to Supreme Court
	Economic Recovery Tax Act
1982	Reagan proposes Strategic Defense Initiative
	Contras infiltrate Nicaragua
1983	Marines invade Grenada
	U.S. barracks in Beirut bombed
1984	Reagan reelected
	Gorbachev comes to power in USSR
	Duarte elected in El Salvador
	Boland Amendment passed
	Newsweek's "Year of the Yuppie"
1985	Secret arms sales to Iran
1986	Terry founds Operation Rescue
	Immigration Reform and Control Act
	Rehnquist becomes chief justice
	Reykjavik Summit
	Iran-contra exposed
1987	Intermediate Nuclear Forces Treaty
1988	Pan Am 103 bombed over Lockerbie

government evils of social liberalism and high taxes. Promising a new experiment in conservative traditionalism, former California governor Ronald Reagan rode the wave of discontent into the White House in 1980.

The Rise of the Religious Right

After the Scopes monkey trial in 1926, journalist H. L. Mencken observed that conservative Christianity is a "fire still burning on a far-flung hill, and it may begin to roar again at any moment." That fire smoldered for nearly a half-century before roaring to life in the 1970s. The decade witnessed a dramatic increase in the number of self-identified evangelical Christians who had experienced a "born again" conversion, believed in a literal interpretation of the Bible, and accepted Jesus Christ as their personal Savior. The number of Americans who identified themselves as born again increased from 24 percent in 1963 to nearly 40 percent in 1978. More than 45 million—one of every five Americans—considered themselves fundamentalists by the end of the decade. While mainstream church membership dropped between 1965 and 1980, the number of Southern Baptists rose from 10.8 million to 13.6 million.

Many fundamentalists were converted by television preachers who used mass media to preach a return to traditional values. The three most successful "televangelists"—Jerry Falwell, Pat Robertson, and Jim Bakker—reached an estimated 100 million Americans each week with fire and brimstone sermons about the evils of contemporary life. Like traditional conservatives, the Religious Right believed in small government, low taxes, and free enterprise. Unlike the old Right, however, they viewed politics through the prism of morality. America, they preached, confronted a crisis of the spirit, brought on by the pervasive influence of "secular humanism," which stressed material well-being and personal gratification over religious conviction and devotion to traditional Christian values. In their mind, the federal government, and the liberals who staffed it, were responsible for America's moral decline. At the top of their agenda were overturning the 1962 Supreme Court's decision to ban prayer in the public schools *(Engel* v. *Vitale)* and the 1973 *Roe* v. *Wade* decision, which legalized abortion.

Religious Right ministers were as interested in swaying voters as they were in saving souls. Jerry Falwell, minister of the *Old-Time Gospel Hour,* claimed that God instructed him to bring together "the good people of America" in a Christian crusade against pornography, sex education, and abortion. To spread the word, Falwell combined old-time religion with the most sophisticated computer technology, targeting potential contributors and lobbying for political candidates who shared his conservative views. "Get them saved, baptized, and registered," Falwell advised his ministerial colleagues. In July 1979, he founded the Moral Majority, a group that lobbied on behalf of conservative causes, and within two years was claiming 4 million members.

The Tax Revolt

"You are the people," declared Howard Jarvis, a seventy-five-year-old curmudgeon who led the crusade for California's Proposition 13 in 1978, "and you will have to take control of the government again or else it is going to control you." Proposition 13, a referendum that voters approved by a 2–1 margin, reduced assessments, limited property taxes to 1 percent of full value, and prevented the easy passage of new taxes. "This isn't just a tax revolt," insisted President Carter's pollster, Pat Caddell. "It's a revolution against government." The success in California emboldened tax reformers in other parts of the country. A dozen states followed California's lead, though most chose more moderate measures. Only two states—Idaho and Nevada—passed Prop 13 look-alikes.

Jerry Falwell   In 1979, Reverend Jerry Falwell formed Moral Majority, Inc. to "promote morality in public life and to combat legislation that favors the legalization of immorality." Within two years of its founding, Falwell's organization had 4 million members.   *(Dennis Brack/Black Star.)*

Two powerful currents carried the tax revolt. First, between 1960 and 1980, federal, state, and local taxes increased from less than 24 percent to more than 30 percent of the gross national product. The burden often fell heaviest on traditional Democratic constituencies—working-class families and elderly people on fixed incomes. Second, while taxes kept rising, Americans were losing faith in government and the way it spent tax dollars. Poll after poll showed a majority of Americans believed that government was wasteful and inefficient. By the 1970s, many Democrats showed their anger by abandoning the party and joining forces with conservatives.

As the tax cut wildfire spread through the states, Prop 13's congressional cousin—the Kemp-Roth tax bill calling for a one-third slash in federal income taxes—gained converts in Washington. The idea was the brainchild of economist Arthur Laffer, who argued that hefty cuts in corporate and personal tax rates would stimulate investment and encourage production and consumption. Unlike the Keynesian principles that had guided policymakers since the 1930s (see page 990), Laffer's so-called supply-side theory argued that tax policy should reward the suppliers of wealth and not the consumers. By lowering taxes on the wealthiest

Americans, the government would provide an incentive for them to reinvest, creating new business and more jobs. Even though tax rates would be lower, revenues would actually increase because more people would be paying taxes.

Many economists challenged the underlying assumptions of supply-side theory, but the idea was politically seductive. When conservative Barry Goldwater campaigned for president in 1964 on a platform calling for reduced taxes, he felt compelled to announce what government programs he would eliminate to balance the books. Supply-side theory allowed conservatives to have the best of both worlds—they campaigned as tax reform crusaders but also claimed they would be able to protect popular government entitlements such as social security.

The New Right

For most of the 1960s and early 1970s, liberals were able to control the national agenda. During the 1970s, conservative intellectuals began to dominate the public debate, ensuring that conservative ideas would receive respect and attention. With funding from wealthy individuals and foundations, conservative "think tanks" produced mounds of studies advocating the need for smaller government and a return to traditional values. These new organizations provided an intellectual home to a number of prominent "neoconservatives," former liberals who had soured on government activism and who offered substantial intellectual ammunition to those seeking to reverse liberal "excesses." A neoconservative, observed social critic Irving Kristol, was a liberal who had been mugged by reality. Neoconservatives charged that many governmental programs of the sixties, designed to alleviate poverty and assist the working poor, had backfired. "Our efforts to deal with distress themselves increase distress," observed sociologist Nathan Glazer.

If neoconservatives provided the intellectual scaffolding for the conservative movement, corporate America provided the steel. During the 1970s, corporate America established a powerful lobbying presence in Washington to advance its agenda, which included not only antiregulatory goals but tax cuts as well. Many corporations and trade associations opened Washington offices, hired Capitol Hill law firms, and retained legions of political consultants to keep track of pending legislation and to develop strategies for promoting favorable policies and killing those considered antibusiness. By 1980, nearly 500 corporations had Washington offices, up from 250 in 1970, and the number of lobbyists had tripled. Trade associations opened national headquarters at a rate of one per week, increasing from 1,200 to 1,739 during the decade.

Corporate lobbyists took advantage of loopholes in the campaign finance system to fund incumbents and new candidates who supported their agenda. The proliferation of independent political action committees (PACs) allowed corporate interests to funnel millions of dollars to congressional candidates. When Congress passed campaign reform legislation in 1974, labor operated up to a third of existing PACs and accounted for half of all PAC spending. By 1982, business-related PACs were outspending labor in direct contributions to congressional campaigns by nearly 3 to 1.

The 1980 Presidential Campaign

By late 1979, President Carter's political stock hit rock bottom. During the summer, with inflation soaring into double digits, newly appointed Federal Reserve chairman Paul Volcker applied the monetary brakes. The nation's major banks responded by raising their prime interest rates, first to 13 percent and then to 14.5 percent. With the prime rate reaching all-time highs, the economy began its inevitable slowdown. In October, the Dow Jones index of industrial stocks lost nearly 100 points, auto sales dropped 23 percent compared with the previous year, while rising mortgage rates strangled the housing industry. Carter seemed helpless in the face of problems both at home and abroad. The menacing Soviet army that had invaded Afghanistan raised fears that its next move would be to capture valuable Middle East oil supplies. Iranian militants continued to "hold America hostage," threatening to put their American captives on trial.

Carter's own party was in open revolt. With polls showing him leading the president by a 3–1 margin, Senator Edward Kennedy, the youngest brother of President John Kennedy and Senator Robert Kennedy and the keeper of the flickering liberal flame, announced in the fall of 1979 that he would challenge Carter for the nomination. Portraying Carter as a weak and ineffective leader who had abandoned the party's liberal tradition, Kennedy confidently declared, "The only thing that paralyzes us today is the myth that we cannot move."

The American people, however, instinctively rallied around the president during a time of international crisis. Carter watched his job approval rating double to 61 percent in January—the sharpest one-month leap in forty-one years of polling. Capitalizing on his sudden surge of popularity, Carter played the role of national leader by standing above the partisan fray—and refusing to campaign. As Kennedy's campaign wilted in the patriotic afterglow, Carter secured his party's nomination on the first ballot.

Believing the president's rise in the polls would be temporary, a revived Republican Party rallied around former Hollywood movie actor turned politician Ronald Reagan, who cruised to victory in the primaries, besting five challengers. An effective speaker and master of the media, Reagan articulated a simple but compelling message: love of country, fear of communism, and scorn of government. Preaching what economist Herbert Stein called the "economics of joy," Reagan repudiated the traditional Republican economic doctrine of tight fiscal policy and balanced budgets, and instead preached the wonders of supply-side economics. Responding to fears that America's stature in the world was in decline, Reagan called for a muscular foreign policy, including huge increases in military spending. Reflecting the influence of the Religious Right, the GOP platform also adopted a plank opposing abortion and the Equal Rights Amendment (ERA). In an overture to moderate Republicans, Reagan selected the genial George Bush, a vanquished primary foe and former Central Intelligence Agency (CIA) head, as his running mate.

As the campaign moved into its final weeks, Carter and Reagan were deadlocked. Reagan's acting skills proved decisive in the lone debate held a week before the election. On debating points, the two candidates were evenly matched. But in his closing remarks, Reagan focused public attention on Carter's responsibility for double-digit inflation, the hostages in Iran, and Soviet troops in Afghanistan. "Are you better off than you were four years ago?" he asked. "Is America as respected throughout the world as it was?"

On election day, Reagan won 489 electoral votes to Carter's 49. In the popular vote, the Republican challenger received 43,904,153 million votes (50.7 percent) to Carter's 35,483,883 million (41 percent). Independent candidate John Anderson, a Republican congressman who bolted his party claiming that it had been hijacked by conservatives, won only 5,720,060 million popular votes (6.6 percent). The Democrats, moreover, lost 34 House seats and lost control of the Senate 53–47, as the Republicans gained 12 seats. Ominously, almost 48 percent of eligible voters did not cast ballots, the lowest voter turnout since 1948 (see map).

Most polling experts noted that the election represented "a strong call for moderate change." Though Reagan won a large margin in the electoral college, he captured only 51 percent of the voters, just 3 percent more than Ford had in losing in 1976. Reagan had assembled a disparate coalition joining traditional Republicans who wanted to shrink government with the Religious Right, which wanted to use federal power to enforce its moral agenda. This coalition snared two groups that had been important Democratic voting blocs since the New Deal: southern whites, still smarting from their party's support for civil rights, and working-class whites in the Northeast and Midwest who were angry about high taxes and the sluggish economy. In reality, these groups shared little in common other than frustration with the status quo. Yet because of his electoral college margin and his party's congres-

The Election of 1980 While Ronald Reagan won a landslide in the electoral college, the number of popular voters and non-voters provides a much more complex picture. Only 52.6 percent of eligible voters cast their ballots in the election, giving Reagan only 28 percent of the potential electorate and leading many to question why so many Americans chose not to vote.

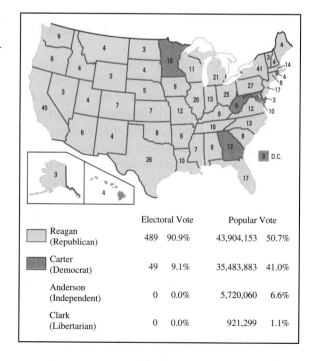

	Electoral Vote		Popular Vote	
Reagan (Republican)	489	90.9%	43,904,153	50.7%
Carter (Democrat)	49	9.1%	35,483,883	41.0%
Anderson (Independent)	0	0.0%	5,720,060	6.6%
Clark (Libertarian)	0	0.0%	921,299	1.1%

sional gains, many observers viewed Reagan's election as a mandate for conservatism. As Democratic senator Paul Tsongas oberved, "Basically, the New Deal died yesterday." Reagan's task was to transform appearance into reality.

 ## The Culture Wars, 1980–1988

Since the beginning of the republic, Americans have been torn between the belief in individual liberty, as expressed in the Declaration of Independence, and the quest to mold a morally righteous society, which found outlet in periodic religious "awakenings." That conflict intensified anew during the 1980s, as politically active fundamentalists and evangelical Christians fought against a host of challenges to their traditional values. They denounced especially a woman's right to choose an abortion and equal rights for homosexuals. The massive wave of immigrants that flooded American cities also raised new questions about American racial and ethnic identity. Ultimately, the conflict over values and culture represented a struggle over national identity—over the meaning of America.

The Politics of Family Values

The political influence of activist fundamentalists and evangelical Christians continued throughout the Reagan administration. By 1989, over 1,300 religious radio stations turned airwaves into pulpits, and more than 330 Christian ministries broadcast regularly on television. In addition to these enterprises, Christians boasted a billion-dollar book industry that offered instruction on how to be a better Christian, how to raise children, and how faith could cure an ailing nation.

Religious and New Right conservatives traced the roots of most of America's social problems to the decline of the traditional family. The problem was real: during the 1980s, a rising divorce rate accompanied the soaring numbers of illegitimate births, which doubled between 1975 and 1986. Conservatives blamed social liberalism and declining moral standards for the troubles plaguing the modern family. Paul Weyrich, a New Right political strategist, described the battle between the conservative pro-family forces and liberals as "the most significant battle of the age-old conflict between good and evil, between the forces of God and the forces against God, that we have seen in our country." In 1987 the Reagan administration released a "White House Task Force Report on the Family," alleging that family life had been "frayed by the abrasive experiments of two liberal decades." Calling for a return to "traditional values," the Religious Right organized in local communities to challenge the teaching of evolution, ban books that challenged religious teachings, oppose sex education, and reinstate school prayer.

Conservatives also criticized the pernicious influence of popular culture, which they said emphasized sexual intimacy outside of marriage, violence, and profanity. "Television," a preacher blustered, "is undermining the Judeo-Christian values you hold dear and work hard to teach your children." Conservatives waged war against the government-sponsored National Endowment for the Arts (NEA) for funding a controversial photographic exhibit by acclaimed artist Robert Mapplethorpe that included, among many others, a number of homoerotic photos. The American Family Association responded with full-page advertisements in newspapers asking, "Is this how you want your tax dollars spent?"

As the New Right pressed its case, liberals tried to redefine the debate over family values by focusing on economic issues—child care, tax credits for working families with children—that would lessen the burdens weighing on most Americans. They also touted individual rights and warned against unwarranted government intrusion into the lives of private citizens. In 1980 television producer Norman Lear founded the People for the American Way to provide a political counterweight to the New Right. "First and foremost among our shared values is a celebration of diversity and respect for the beliefs of others," he declared.

Abortion

The legalization of abortion following the Supreme Court's decision in *Roe* v. *Wade* (1973) created a new and highly focused setting for confrontation by opponents: the hundreds of abortion clinics scattered throughout the United States, in shopping centers, office buildings, and residential neighborhoods. Initially, "pro-life" organizers picketed and organized prayer vigils outside clinics. In January 1986, Randall Terry, thirty, a born again Christian, brought a more militant activism to the movement with his organization, Operation Rescue. Demonstrators passed themselves off as patients, then splashed paint in waiting rooms, dropped stink bombs, or chained themselves to examining tables. The number of bomb threats and actual bombings at clinics soared.

Opponents of abortion and birth control found an ally in the White House. Reagan persuaded Congress to bar most public funding for birth control and to stop Medicare from funding abortions for poor women. An administration measure provided funding for religiously oriented "chastity clinics" where counselors advised teenage girls and women to "just say no" to avoid pregnancy.

Among activists, the debate over abortion revolved around different conceptions of motherhood. Abortion opponents believed in traditional sex roles and saw motherhood as a woman's highest mission in life. Viewing the conflict as a clash between "nurturance" and "selfish individualism," they saw abortion as one more assault on the last bastion of human tenderness in a cold and uncaring world. "We've accepted abortion because we're a very materialistic society and there is less time for caring," observed an anti-abortion activist in Fargo, North Dakota.

The pro-choice activists, on the other hand, believed that motherhood was one of the many roles that women played. They argued that the best way to support families was to address gender inequalities that prevented women from competing equally against men. In the feminist strategy, the abortion option was indispensable: as the responsibility for children devolved to women, so must the choice as to when to bear them. Along with supporting a host of political and economic reforms—paid parental leave, flexible hours, child-care facilities—feminists trumpeted the value of individual liberty over government interference. Worried Planned Parenthood president Faye Wattleton, "The fundamental principles of individual privacy are under the most serious assault since the days of McCarthyism."

Debate over Abortion   As the Religious Right grew in political importance, so did the issue of a woman's right to an abortion, legalized by the 1973 Supreme Court decision in *Roe* v. *Wade.* Pro-life organizations held rallies and protested in front of abortion clinics, emphasizing that abortion was a form of infanticide. Though pro-choice advocates had the support of the courts, they continued to challenge the arguments made by pro-life advocates, pressing a woman's right to choose, as seen in this protest in Boston.   *(Evan Richman/The Boston Globe. Republished with permission of Globe Newspaper Company, Inc.)*

Activists on both sides represented a small proportion of opinions, however. Polls showed a public torn between the extremes of the abortion debate: overwhelming opposition to an absolute ban on abortion but discomfort with the absolute right to abortion. The public debate, however, obscured opportunity for consensus as both sides used powerful symbols to rally support for their cause. In 1984 anti-abortion activists produced a graphic videotape, *The Silent Scream*, which showed abortion "from the point of view of the unborn child." As their own symbols, pro-choice advocates often displayed coat hangers—grim reminders of the illegal and unsafe abortions that took place before the Supreme Court ruling.

Gay Rights and the AIDS Crisis

Perhaps with the exception of abortion, few issues during the 1980s generated more raw emotion than homosexuality. The gay rights movement, born at the Stonewall Inn in 1969, continued to gain momentum during the 1970s. During that decade, homosexuals flooded into cities such as San Francisco and New York, where they established a variety of support organizations. Between 1974 and 1978, more than twenty thousand homosexuals moved to San Francisco, many of them living in the city's Castro District. In response to the growing visibility of the gay community, a number of states repealed their sodomy statues, and a few enacted legislation preventing discrimination based on sexual orientation.

The movement took a tragic turn in 1981 when doctors in San Francisco and New York began reporting that young homosexual men were dying from rare diseases. As panic spread through the gay community, researchers at the Centers for Disease Control (CDC) discovered the villain: a deadly virus spread by bodily fluid that rendered the victim's immune system helpless against opportunistic infections. They named the mysterious disease Acquired Immune Deficiency Syndrome (AIDS).

Initially, the majority of AIDS victims were homosexual men infected through sexual contact. During the 1970s, many gay men associated freedom with sexual promiscuity. "The belief that was handed to me was that sex was liberating and more sex was more liberating," observed activist Michael Callen. "[Being gay] was tied to the right to have sex." As the death toll mounted, gay leaders organized to educate the public and to pressure government to find a cure. In New York, the Gay Men's Health Center spearheaded the effort, raising millions of dollars, offering services to the sick, and lobbying Washington. Gay writers, such as playwright Larry Kramer, *The Normal Heart* (1985), and journalist Randy Shilts, *And the Band Played On* (1987), raised public awareness about the disease and about gay life. At the same time, radical groups such as the AIDS Coalition to Unleash Power, or ACT UP, founded to protest a lack of commitment to finding a cure for AIDS, rattled politicians and drug companies with their colorful demonstrations. ACT UP's slogan, "Silence = Death," underscoring a pink triangle on black, became a trademark for late-1980s uncivil disobedience. In city after city, the gay community began exercising political muscle, demanding greater government support for AIDS research and protection against discrimination.

Conservatives reacted with horror, viewing gay rights as unnatural, contrary to God's will, and an assault on the traditional family. The gay rights movement represented "the most vicious attack on traditional family values that our society has seen in the history of our republic," declared a conservative congressman. White House adviser Pat Buchanan suggested that AIDS was God's revenge for violating natural law. "The poor homosexuals. They have declared war on nature and now nature is exacting an awful retribution."

AIDS: The Worldwide Impact

As long as the disease appeared confined to minority populations, the public remained largely apathetic. "If it spreads to the general public, it would be a medical crisis, demanding immediate government response," said one observer. Scientists, including Surgeon General Dr. C. Everett Koop, urged Reagan to endorse a "safe sex" program to combat AIDS. Koop described his remedy as "one, abstinence; two, monogamy; three, condoms." But the president, bowing to conservative pressure and personally uncomfortable dealing with questions of sexuality, shied away from personal involvement in the crisis. The administration barred the CDC from funding organizations that dealt explicitly with sex, homosexuality, or drug use. Not even the death from AIDS of movie star, and Reagan friend, Rock Hudson in 1985 inspired the administration to make combating the disease a top priority.

By the end of the 1980s, the AIDS epidemic had spread far beyond gay men. Thanks to grass-roots organizing and public education, the number of new AIDS cases among homosexuals had stabilized. In 1987, 50 percent of the deaths from AIDS in the United States were among intravenous drug users and their sexual partners, a group that was 90 percent African-American and Hispanic. Overall, blacks were three times more likely than whites to contract HIV, the precipitating virus. For Hispanics, the infection rate was twice as high. The disease was also spreading more rapidly among children than adults.

The World Health Organization (WHO) divided the AIDS epidemic into three distinct phases: the silent period (1970–1981), the initial discovery (1981–1985), and the worldwide mobilization (1985–). By 1992, HIV infected 12.9 million people worldwide, with most of its victims living in poorer nations that lacked the resources to mount effective campaigns to stem its spread. Sub-Saharan Africa, with 10 percent of the world's population, claimed 68 percent of the total HIV population (8.8 million). Scientists estimated that in urban areas as many as half of all adults, including 20 percent of pregnant women, were infected—the vast majority through heterosexual contact.

American Identities

According to the Census Bureau, the nation absorbed 8.9 million legal immigrants and, by most estimates, at least 2 million illegal ones, during the 1980s. In absolute numbers, the decade saw more immigrants (legal and illegal) than any other decade in U.S. history. By the early 1990s, over 1 million new legal immigrants were arriving in the U.S. every year, accounting for almost half of U.S. population growth. The vast majority of the new immigrants came from Asia and Latin America.

Most of these immigrants settled in large cities in a handful of states—New York, Illinois, and New Jersey, as well as Florida, Texas, and California. One of every three new immigrants entered the United States through California, making the nation's most populous state its unofficial Ellis Island. By 1990, the population of Los Angeles, the nation's second-largest city, was one-third foreign-born. Los Angeles was also home to the second-largest Spanish-speaking population (after Mexico City) on the North American continent. New York's foreign-born population, like Los Angeles's, also approached 35 percent of its total populace in 1990, a level the city had last reached in 1910.

Most Americans saw daily reminders of the cultural impact of the new waves of immigrants. Urban streets were a babble of foreign tongues. In Miami, three-quarters of residents spoke a language other than English at home; in New York City, the figure was four out of ten, and of these, half could not speak fluent English (see map). In kitchens across the country, salsa replaced ketchup as America's favorite condiment. In music, such Hispanic artists as Los Lobos, Lisa Lisa and Cult Jam, and the Miami

Sound Machine topped the billboards with hit songs. Many white artists tried assimilating new cultural impulses into their music. David Byrne injected Talking Heads music with African, Latin, and other rhythms. Peter Gabriel and Paul Simon found similar success with African rhythms.

The new diversity provided fertile ground for bigotry. "The more diversity and burgeoning minority groups we have," the National Conference of Christians and Jews observed, "the more prejudice we must overcome." Blacks, Hispanics, and Asians often felt as much animosity toward one another as they did toward whites. In Florida, Hispanics and blacks, who once considered themselves allies against the white power structure, battled each other for jobs and scarce resources. In many cities, African-Americans and Korean immigrants engaged in heated confrontations. At the root of the conflict, exacerbated by language and cultural differences, was resentment of Korean immigrants' success in running small businesses in economi-

Growth of Hispanic Population in the 1980s   For the first time in American history, the majority of immigrants came from countries outside of Europe. The Hispanic population claimed the largest percentage of new immigrants. This influx altered the social and cultural dynamics of cities and states across the nation, just as previous waves of immigration had done.

cally depressed black neighborhoods. In Spike Lee's movie, *Do the Right Thing*, set in Brooklyn, a Korean shopkeeper averts a confrontation with black residents of the neighborhood by shouting in desperation, "Me no white. Me no white. Me black."

Many white Americans complained that the new immigrants stole jobs from native workers, and many whites worried about the cohesiveness of American culture and its ability to absorb and assimilate so many different cultural influences. "Is it really wise to allow the immigration of people who find it so difficult and painful to assimilate into the American majority?" asked conservative journalist Peter Brimelow. In Miami, cryptic bumper stickers appeared: "Will the last American out of Miami please take the flag." After years of debate on how to control illegal immigration, Congress in 1986 passed the Immigration Reform and Control Act (IRCA). It offered legal status to undocumented aliens who had lived and worked in the United States for a specified period, but imposed fines on employers who hired new undocumented workers.

Fears about the swelling foreign-language populations produced a powerful "English-only" movement. "The language of American government is English," said a Connecticut Republican. "The language of American business is English. We are not a dual-language society." In 1986 California spearheaded the English-only drive by voting overwhelmingly for a referendum outlawing bilingualism and defending "English as a unifying force in the United States." Representatives of Hispanic groups condemned the movement as "fundamentally racist in character," but before the end of the decade, seventeen other states had joined California in passing English-only laws. "Language," the *Economist* noted, "symbolizes the United States' fear that the foreign body within its borders is growing too big ever to be digested."

A similar debate raged as colleges attempted to "increase sensitivity" to racial and cultural diversity in the university community. At Stanford, reformers fought to change the Western civilization curriculum, which they claimed presented a "male, Eurocentric" view of the world. Many universities accommodated the pressure to diversify by expanding the range of programs in disciplines such as women's studies, African-American studies, Hispanic studies, and gay studies. In 1987 Allan Bloom led the conservative counterattack on changes in American higher education with his book, *The Closing of the American Mind*. Subtitled "How Higher Education Has Failed Democracy and Impoverished the Souls of Today's Students," the book asserted the primacy of "the great books" of Western civilization. "You can't talk about Chaucer without someone saying 'What's the woman's perspective?', 'What about the Third World perspective?'" he lamented. Bloom's volume remained at the top of the *New York Times* best-seller list for seven weeks, selling more than a million copies.

Historical experience suggests that concerns about immigrants failing to assimilate were misplaced—similar fears about past waves of immigrants proved unfounded. The public has always looked favorably on past generations of immigrants and unfavorably on contemporary newcomers. In the nineteenth-century, Americans complained about the "lazy and hard-drinking Irish" who were "polluting" the cities; later waves of Italians and eastern Europeans confronted similarly hostile attitudes. Over time, however, those groups became acculturated and now swell the mainstream that fears the addition of new migrants from Mexico, Iran, and Haiti.

Increasingly strident affirmations of identity actually masked the waning of real ethnic differences—higher education, consumerism, movies and television, professional sports, and popular culture was working to make Americans more alike, whatever their ethnic origins. The rising rate of intermarriage between ethnic groups, especially Asian-Americans and non-Asians, also suggested that ethnic differences were softening over time. In the 1980s, more than one-half of all Japanese-Americans, and 40 percent of Chinese-Americans, married outside their ethnic groups.

 ## The Reagan Presidency, 1980–1988

The new president wasted little time in institutionalizing the new conservative creed. In 1981 he pushed his agenda of lower taxes and steep budget cuts through a reluctant Congress. At the same time, he appointed to his cabinet, and to the courts, conservatives who would carry out his vision of smaller government. Reagan's landslide in the 1984 presidential election underscored the political popularity of his conservative experiment. But the Reagan presidency exposed continuing tensions in American attitudes toward government. Americans applauded Reagan's rhetoric about reducing government power at the same time that they insisted on continuing, or in some cases expanding, popular federal programs.

The Reagan Agenda

At sixty-nine, Ronald Wilson Reagan was the oldest man ever elected president. Born in Dixon, Illinois, in 1911, Reagan graduated from Eureka College and worked briefly as a radio sports announcer before moving to California and signing a contract with Warner Brothers film studio in 1937. Over the next two decades he appeared in fifty-three movies but won little acclaim as an actor. The one exception was his role as George Gipp, Notre Dame's first All-American football player, in the 1940 classic *Knute Rockne, All American.* "Someday, when things are tough, maybe you can ask the boys to go in there and win just one for the Gipper," he pleads in a moving deathbed scene that brought tears to the eyes of millions.

Reagan made his political debut in 1964 when he delivered a moving tribute to Barry Goldwater. The speech established Reagan's conservative credentials and launched his successful bid for governor of California in 1966. After two successful terms, Reagan was ready for the national stage. With his telegenic features and extensive experience in front of a camera, Reagan was ideally suited for politics in a media age. Though intellectually unambitious and notoriously ignorant about the details of policies, Reagan brilliantly articulated the themes of patriotism, individualism, and limited government that resonated with countless Americans.

At the outset, the Reagan administration concentrated on reviving the slumping economy. The cost of living had increased by more than 12 percent in 1980, unemployment had risen to 7.4 percent, the prime lending rate was an astonishing 20 percent, and the government was facing a projected budget deficit of $56 billion. "In this present crisis," Reagan said in his inaugural address, "government is not the

Reagan and Nancy
A man who had spent the majority of his life in the eye of the camera, Reagan, pictured with his second wife Nancy, exuded grace, poise, and opulence, which Americans craved in a president during the materialistic eighties. *(Courtesy of Vanity Fair, June 1985/Conde Nast Publications, Inc. Photograph by Harry Benson.)*

solution to our problem; government *is* the problem." It was time, the new president declared, "to reawaken this industrial giant, to get government back within its means and to lighten our punitive tax burden."

The president's economic program consisted of three essential components. First, embracing the supply-side doctrine of the New Right, Reagan requested a 30 percent reduction in both personal and corporate income taxes over three years. Tax cuts, the administration reasoned, would stimulate the economy by providing incentives for individuals and businesses to work, save, and invest. Second, he planned to cut government spending for social programs by $41.4 billion in fiscal 1982. Reagan avoided trimming the politically sensitive, middle-class entitlement programs, social security and Medicare, and instead cut programs that directly benefited the poor, such as Food Stamps, Aid to Families with Dependent Children, school lunches, housing assistance, and Medicaid. Finally, he planned to use a tight monetary policy to squeeze inflation out of the economy.

But in late March 1981, before Reagan could implement his economic program, a would-be assassin shot and seriously wounded the elderly president. Through the ordeal, Reagan showed courage and spirit. As he was wheeled into the operating room, he quipped to his wife, Nancy, "Honey, I forgot to duck." Reagan's behavior in adversity magnified his popularity. "The bullet meant to kill him," observed a journalist, "made him a hero instead, floating above the contentions of politics and the vagaries of good news or bad." In the long run, however, the assassination drained precious energy from an already diminished president. Reagan lost more than half his blood as doctors engaged in a dramatic struggle to save his life. The president's authorized biographer called the operation "a chilling physiological insult from which he would never fully recover."

Reagan used his enhanced stature to sway Congress into supporting his radical economic plan. Casting the debate in stark ideological language, Reagan called on Democrats to support his program; those who did not would be defending the "failed policies of the past." In May dispirited Democrats joined Republicans in passing a budget resolution that called for deep cuts in many social programs and increased spending for the military. "The Great Society, built and consolidated over fifteen years, was shrunk to size in just 26 hours and 12 minutes of floor debate," observed *Newsweek*. In August Congress rubber-stamped the administration's massive tax cut, providing for across-the-board reductions of 5 percent the first year and an additional 10 percent in each of the succeeding two years.

It was an impressive legislative achievement that earned Reagan the begrudging respect of his critics, who compared his performance to FDR's. "Mr. Reagan has established his goals faster, communicated a greater sense of economic urgency and come forward with more comprehensive proposals than any new president since the first 100 days of Franklin D. Roosevelt," complimented the *New York Times*.

While the public gave the president credit for pushing his legislative program through Congress, it blamed him for the inevitable slowdown that resulted from his tight money policies. By limiting the amount of money in the economy, the Federal Reserve Board, with Reagan's implicit approval, incited a recession by making it difficult for businesses to borrow and expand. In 1982 and 1983, the "Reagan recession" forced some 10 million Americans out of work, and the 9.5 percent unemployment rate was the highest since 1941. The president urged Congress and the American people to "stay the course," predicting that the economy would rebound in 1983. He was right: the GNP increased an impressive 4.3 percent, and unemployment declined to 8 percent.

Attacking the Liberal State

As a presidential candidate, Ronald Reagan pledged to shrink the scope of federal government by returning greater authority and responsibility to the states. He appointed to his cabinet conservatives determined to loosen federal regulation. His secretary of energy, James Edwards, a dentist and an ex-governor of South Carolina who favored unregulated development of nuclear power, planned to eliminate his own department. Secretary of Labor Raymond Donovan was a private construction contractor with few links to organized labor and an advocate of the elimination of several of the labor movement's most cherished federal work-safety regulations.

The most controversial of Reagan's administrators was Secretary of the Interior James G. Watt. Under Watt's leadership, the Interior Department opened federal lands to coal and timber production, narrowed the scope of the wilderness preserves, and sought to make a million offshore acres with oil potential available for drilling. Watt believed that after twenty-five years of federal land management, it was time to return the use of government land to the public through the deregulation of natural resources. In his first official act as secretary, he opened up California's coastline to offshore oil drilling and called a halt to future acquisitions of land for national parks. He remarked to a group of park employees, "There are people who want to bring their motorcycles and snowmobiles right into the middle of Yellowstone National Park and our job is to make sure they can." Watt's policies and provocative public statements kept him in the middle of controversy until he finally resigned in 1983 (see Competing Voices, page 1256).

Paralleling the regulation phobia of agencies charged with protecting the environment, many government agencies created to protect the public welfare engaged in efforts to undermine safety standards. The National Highway Traffic Safety Administration decided to save automobile manufacturers money by permitting new cars to carry less substantial (and less safe) bumpers. The Department of Energy and the Nuclear Regulatory Commission ignored mounting evidence of unsafe conditions in the nuclear industry; civilian power plants were seldom penalized for safety violations. The Federal Communications Commission (FCC) cut public service broadcasting and increased the amount of time that television stations could air commercials. "Television is just another appliance," insisted FCC head Mark Fowler. "It's just a toaster with pictures."

The turbulent history of the savings and loan (S&L) industry during the 1980s exemplified the dangers of the Reagan passion for deregulation. Since the depression, S&Ls (called thrifts) had been restricted to using investors' money for low-risk mortgage lending, whereas banks could offer checking accounts, trust services, and commercial and consumer loans. When interest rates soared in the 1970s, money bled out of the S&Ls and into higher-yielding money market accounts. Conservatives, arguing that deregulation was the key to saving the S&Ls and reviving the banking industry, loosened the rules governing S&L investments at the same time that they increased federal insurance on S&L deposits from $20,000 to $100,000. "This bill is the most important legislation for financial institutions in the last 50 years," President Reagan said in a ceremony announcing the new rules. "All in all, I think we hit the jackpot," he added.

Flush with money from investors trying to turn a quick profit, many S&Ls made risky loans on malls, apartment complexes, office towers. Opportunists such as Charles Keating, owner of Lincoln Savings, turned their thrifts into giant casinos, using federally insured deposits to bet on high-risk corporate takeovers and junk bonds. It was a game of blackjack that only the consumers could lose. Instead of saving the S&Ls, the legislation produced a flood of bankruptcy by providing thrift owners with an incentive to engage in high-risk activity. Hundreds of thrifts folded, resulting in a $200 billion taxpayer-financed bailout that would cost $10 for every man, woman, and child in America.

Reagan Justice

As president, Reagan promised to appoint judges concerned with "protecting the rights of law-abiding citizens," defending "traditional values and the sanctity of human life," and maintaining "judicial restraint." Like many conservatives, he believed that government should relax its efforts to ensure justice and equal opportunity for African-Americans and other minority groups.

To achieve the latter goals, the Reagan administration cut funding for the Equal Employment Opportunity Commission and for the civil rights division of the Justice Department. In 1981 the Justice Department supported a case brought by Bob Jones University against the Treasury Department, which had refused it tax-exempt status on the grounds that the university discriminated against blacks. Though the Supreme Court by an 8–1 decision in 1983 upheld the Treasury Department, the administration's support for the university made it abundantly clear that Reagan hoped to turn back the clock on civil rights.

The New Right especially welcomed Reagan's efforts to realign the Supreme Court. In 1981 he appointed conservative Sandra Day O'Connor of Arizona as the first woman to serve on the High Court. When Chief Justice Warren Burger retired in 1986, Reagan elevated William Rehnquist, a strong advocate of law and order, to the chief justiceship. He offered the open seat to federal judge Antonin Scalia, a rigid advocate of executive power. In 1988 Reagan had sought to replace centrist Louis Powell with the conservative Robert Bork, but a coalition of civil rights and women's groups helped defeat the nomination. The seat was eventually filled by Anthony Kennedy, a federal appeals court judge from California.

The Reagan appointments yielded an aggressive conservative coalition of justices that took command of the court, issuing a series of decisions that reversed the direction of more than three decades of law on criminal procedures, individual liberties, and civil rights. Deciding most major cases by 5–4 margins, the Court ruled that under some circumstances police could submit as evidence confessions coerced from suspected criminals, and it curtailed the rights of immigrants to claim political asylum and limited the rights of death row prisoners to challenge the death penalty. In their most significant civil rights ruling (*Wards Cove* v. *Atonio,* 1989), the justices shifted the burden of proof from those accused of practicing discrimination to its victims. But the justices proved they were not always predictable. One surprise, much to conservatives' dismay, was the Court's decision that burning the American flag was political speech protected by the Constitution.

The 1984 Presidential Campaign

The improving economy of 1983–1984 revived Ronald Reagan's popularity. With polls showing the president enjoying a commanding lead against any potential Democratic opponent, many Republican strategists hoped for an electoral landslide that would herald Republican control of the White House for the rest of the century. The Reagan campaign strategy was simple: celebrate the president's identification with peace and prosperity, avoid a debate over specific issues, and identify his Democratic opponent with the "failed policies" of the Carter administration—high taxes, soaring inflation, and vacillating world leadership.

Reagan's challenger, former vice president Walter Mondale, had won his party's nomination after a bruising primary fight against civil rights activist Jesse Jackson and Colorado senator Gary Hart. Jackson, a former coworker of Martin Luther King, became the first African-American to win substantial support in his bid to receive a major party nomination. Mondale's challenge was to arouse the enthusiasm of the party's traditional constituencies—blacks, Jews, union members, urban residents—while reeling back into the party the "Reagan Democrats," the white middle class that had defected to the Republicans. As a first step in executing his strategy, Mondale tried to demonstrate that he was capable of bold leadership by selecting a woman vice presidential candidate, former congresswoman Geraldine Ferraro of New York City. A few weeks later, in his acceptance speech at the Democratic convention, Mondale tried to prove he was fiscally responsible by proposing to raise taxes to help reduce the deficit.

Riding a wave of personal and organizational confidence, Reagan exhorted voters "to make America great again and let the eagle soar." In his speeches and commercials, the president promoted themes of small government, patriotism, and family. "We see an America," he declared, "where every day is independence day, the Fourth of July." At Republican rallies smothered with balloons and music, the president repeatedly invoked a booming economy and a safer world as evidence of the nation's success under his leadership. "The essence of the Ronald Reagan campaign," ABC reporter Sam Donaldson observed, "is a never-ending string of spectacular picture stories created for television and designed to place the president in the midst of wildly cheering, patriotic Americans. . . . God, patriotism, and Ronald Reagan, that's the essence this campaign is trying to project."

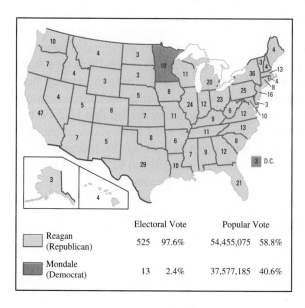

The Election of 1984 Basing his campaign on an improving economy and his tough stand against Communism, Reagan easily defeated his Democratic opponent, former vice president Walter Mondale.

	Electoral Vote		Popular Vote	
Reagan (Republican)	525	97.6%	54,455,075	58.8%
Mondale (Democrat)	13	2.4%	37,577,185	40.6%

On election day, voters returned Reagan to office with 58.8 percent (54,455,075) of the vote and the biggest electoral vote total in history—525. Mondale received 40.6 percent (37,577,185 popular votes) and 13 electoral votes. Reagan swept the entire nation except for Minnesota and the District of Columbia. The election, observed *Time* magazine, represented a collective "Thank You" to "a president who had made the country feel good about itself" (see map).

 ## Reagan and the Cold War, 1980–1988

Reinvigorating the traditional conviction that the United States had a divinely ordained mission to spread American values around the globe, the Reagan administration came to office determined to reassert American power. A classic Cold Warrior, Reagan saw the Soviets at the heart of every international dispute, from revolution in Central America to international terrorism in the Middle East. While the public applauded the president's tough rhetoric, it divided on the wisdom of his specific policy experiments. Like previous administrations, Reagan's White House discovered the limits of American power, but it also, inadvertently, presided over a defusing of U.S.–Soviet tensions.

Fighting the "Evil Empire"

After entering the White House, Reagan denounced the Soviet Union as "the focus of evil in the modern world." In a sermon-like address to evangelical Christians, he declared that the United States was "enjoined by Scripture and the Lord Jesus" to oppose the Soviet Union. Most of the president's national security and foreign policy advisers—Secretary of State Alexander Haig, his successor George Shultz, Secretary of Defense Caspar Weinberger, National Security Adviser Richard Allen, and Ambassador to the United Nations Jeanne Kirkpatrick—shared his exaggerated fear of Soviet power and his determination to assert American military might.

To thwart the Soviets, Reagan called for the largest and most expensive peacetime military buildup in American history. "Defense is not a budget item," Ronald Reagan told his staff. "You spend what you need." Along with accelerating the development of existing weapons systems—both nuclear and conventional—the administration reincarnated programs canceled under Carter, including the trouble-plagued B-1 bomber and the controversial neutron bomb. By 1985, the Pentagon was spending more than $28 million an hour—every hour, seven days a week. Excluding veterans' affairs, the defense budget surged from $157 billion in 1981 to $273 billion in 1986. Corrected for inflation, the increases averaged nearly 7 percent a year.

While strengthening America's strategic arsenal, Reagan declared that the United States stood ready to support anticommunist regimes anywhere in the world. In the Middle East, the Philippines, Chile, South Korea, and Angola, the Reagan administration supported repressive governments if they stood strongly against communism. This approach to world politics was especially clear with regard to South Africa, where the system of *apartheid,* which brutally excluded nonwhites from basic rights, threatened to provoke civil war. Committed to working with the South African whites-only government, the administration abandoned Carter's efforts to force change and adopted a policy known as "constructive engagement." Reagan resisted all calls by liberal and human rights groups to join other countries in coercing the government of South Africa into dismantling apartheid. South Africa, he believed, was a bulwark against the spread of communism. Congress repudiated his policy in 1986, demanding that Reagan take bold steps, including the imposition of economic sanctions, against the South African government.

The Escalating Arms Race

Reagan entered office with a deep-seated distaste for arms control, which he planned to subject to a period of "benign neglect" while the United States went about the business of "rearming." Thus he took a tough position in negotiations with the Soviets. As a goal for the Intermediate Nuclear Forces (INF) talks, initiated by the Carter administration to address the nuclear balance of power in Europe, Reagan embraced the "zero option" whereby the Soviets would agree to dismantle all intermediate range missiles in Europe and Asia while the United States would agree only to deploy no new medium-range missiles. In the separate Strategic Arms Reduction Talks (START), the president proposed a one-third cut in nuclear warheads. The reductions, however, were structured in such a manner that the Soviets would have had to destroy a disproportionate share of their heavy land-based missiles. The proposals angered the Soviets, who grew increasingly distrustful of Reagan and his leading advisers.

U.S.–Soviet relations were already tense when, in September 1983, a Soviet interceptor aircraft shot down a Korean Airlines plane, killing all 269 people on board, after the Boeing 747 strayed into Soviet air space on a flight from Anchorage to Seoul. American intelligence suggested the tragedy was the result of confusion and incompetence on the part of Soviet military officials who believed the civilian airliner was a spy plane, but Reagan used the incident to bolster his contention that the Soviets were an "evil empire." Moscow, angered by Reagan's moralistic condemnation and frustrated with the stalemate on arms control, walked out of the INF talks. "The international situation" declared Politburo member Grigory Romanov, "is white hot, thoroughly white hot." The walkout left the superpowers for the first time in fourteen years with no ongoing arms control talks. The United States responded by deploying new missiles in West Germany, Britain, and Italy. The Soviets moved new rockets into Czechoslovakia and East Germany. "The second cold war has begun," shrilled an Italian newspaper.

Not all Americans agreed with the administration's hard-line approach with the Soviets. A nationwide poll in the spring of 1982 showed that 57 percent of the respondents favored an immediate freeze on the testing, production, and deployment of nuclear weapons. A wide variety of religious and academic leaders were questioning the wisdom of the administration's policies. "Cease this madness," implored George Kennan, the father of containment. The American Catholic bishops issued a pastoral letter on the moral and theological dimensions of nuclear deterrence. The message of the letter was clear: "We must continually say no to the idea of nuclear war." In 1984 over 100 million people anxiously watched a docudrama, *The Day After,* which portrayed the effects of nuclear war on Kansas.

Reagan tried to defuse the growing calls for arms limitation by proposing, in 1982, a space-based defensive shield that used laser beams to destroy incoming missiles. The Strategic Defense Initiative (SDI), nicknamed "Star Wars" by the media, reflected the administration's belief that improbable technological solutions could solve complex political problems. The administration's top military scientist pointed out that unless it was coupled with an offensive arms control agreement, the defensive system could certainly be overcome by Soviet weapons. "With unconstrained proliferation" of Soviet warheads, he said, "no defensive system will work." Despite the criticism, the administration pushed forward, spending $17 billion on SDI between 1983 and 1989.

By 1984, however, a number of developments were pushing Moscow and Washington closer together. Concerned about a possible backlash against his policies in the upcoming presidential campaign, Reagan called for a "constructive working relationship" with the Kremlin. He claimed that the massive military buildup during his first three years in office allowed the United States to negotiate from a position of strength. At the same time, a new leader, who seemed readier than his predecessors to renew détente with the United States, assumed leadership in the Soviet Union. Mikhail Gorbachev, fifty-four, the youngest head of the Soviet Communist Party since Josef Stalin, came to power determined to reform Soviet society. At home he advocated *perestroika,* or restructuring to relax government economic and social control. Abroad he championed a new policy of *glasnost,* or openness. Hoping to avoid an expensive arms race, Gorbachev declared a moratorium on deployment of medium-range missiles in Europe and asked the United States to do the same.

The result of these developments was a series of four Reagan–Gorbachev summits. In 1986 the two leaders met at Reykjavik, Iceland, and agreed on a first step to cut strategic nuclear forces in half. Gorbachev wanted to go further, calling for the complete elimination of all nuclear weapons, but he insisted that the United States also abandon the SDI, something Reagan refused to do. The following year, the United States and the Soviet Union agreed to the Intermediate Nuclear Forces Treaty (INF), which, for the first time, called for the destruction of existing missiles and allowed for on-site inspections to verify compliance. In December Gorbachev traveled to Washington to sign the treaty in a warm ceremony with Reagan. While in the United States, the Soviet leader announced a unilateral reduction in Soviet military forces.

By the time Reagan left office, he and his counterpart in the Kremlin had toasted each other as "Ronnie and Mikhail." Opinion polls reported Americans feeling friendlier toward the Soviet Union than at any time since the end of World War II. When a reporter asked Reagan in 1987 if he still thought the Soviet Union was an evil empire, he responded, "No, I was talking about another time, another era."

Central America

Before and during *glasnost,* Reagan's Cold War views shaped his approach to radical insurgencies in Latin America. Ignoring the complex social and political conditions that fostered revolution in the region, Reagan believed Moscow was to blame for most of the trouble. "[L]et us not delude ourselves," he advised the American

Reagan in Moscow The thawing of Cold War tensions between the United States and the Soviet Union was evident in the signing of the Intermediate Nuclear Forces Treaty in December 1987, which eliminated intermediate-range nuclear missiles. This goodwill between the nations grew with Reagan's historic visit to Moscow in May 1988. Reagan and Mikhail Gorbachev toured Red Square and developed a cordial personal relationship. *(Wide World Photos, Inc.)*

people. "The Soviet Union underlies all the unrest that is going on. If they weren't engaged in this game of dominos, there wouldn't be any hot spots in the world." For Reagan and his advisers, any leftist victory in Latin America would threaten the possibility of another Cuba that could serve as a staging ground for Soviet expansion in the Western Hemisphere. Communist control of Nicaragua, White House communications director Patrick Buchanan warned, "would lead, as night follows day, to loss of Central America." His prophecy: "If Central America goes the way of Nicaragua, they will be in San Diego." The administration also worried that communist gains could produce a flood of political refugees who would pour over the U.S. border.

Since the administration viewed relations with Central America as an extension of the superpower conflict, it relied heavily on military aid and covert warfare to prop up friendly regimes and bring down unfriendly ones. In El Salvador, a poor country in which 2 percent of the people controlled nearly all of the wealth, a coalition of leftist guerrillas had been attempting to topple the government. Reagan, convinced that rebels against the established regime represented Soviet influence, spent nearly $5 billion providing military and economic aid to the government. The army used the arms to wage a fierce campaign of repression against civilians suspected of sympathizing with the rebels or agitating for social change. Between 1979 and 1985, army death squads killed as many as forty thousand peasants, teachers, union organizers, and church workers. On one day, December 11, 1981, troops systematically slaughtered nine hundred people in the town of El Mozote, raping women before shooting them and burning children alive. The Reagan administration, however, considered unfriendly communists more of a threat than friendly thugs. A few weeks after the attack, Reagan certified that El Salvador was making "a concerted and significant effort" to protect human rights. In 1984 the moderate José Napoleon Duarte won a popular election and opened talks with rebel leaders, but the bloody civil war continued.

In Nicaragua, Reagan committed the United States to overthrowing the Marxist-led Sandinistas, who had ousted repressive dictator Anastasio Somoza in 1979. Beginning in 1982, the CIA organized, trained, and financed the *contras,* a guerrilla army based in Honduras and Costa Rica. Infiltrating Nicaragua, the contras sabotaged bridges, oil facilities, and crops. The CIA offered them training in how to assassinate and kidnap political leaders. Reagan praised the contras as "the moral equivalent of our Founding Fathers," but the Congress, and the public, disagreed. In December 1982, Congress, fearful of getting the nation involved in "another Vietnam," halted military aid to the contras for one year. In October 1984, the House passed the Boland Amendment, which forbade any direct aid to the contras.

Meanwhile, Reagan's fear of communism in the Caribbean found an outlet in the tiny nation of Grenada, a 133-square-mile island whose principal export was medical students. In 1983, when a leftist government friendly with Cuba assumed power in Grenada, Reagan ordered six thousand marines to invade the island and install a pro-American government. The administration claimed the invasion was necessary to protect American students living on the island and to stop the construction of an airfield that would allegedly serve Cuban and Soviet interests. Critics asserted that the students were never in danger and the airfield was being built to boost the island's ailing tourist industry. World opinion condemned the invasion, but the first successful assertion of American military might since Vietnam renewed pride and confidence among millions of Americans.

Fighting Terrorism

The Reagan administration came to office convinced that during the 1970s, while Washington was seeking friendship and trade with Moscow, the Soviets were conspiring with terrorists of every stripe to disrupt or overthrow governments friendly to the United States. Secretary of State Haig accused the Soviets of "training, funding and equipping" the forces of worldwide terrorism.

The threat of terrorism was greatest in the Middle East where, despite the Israeli–Egyptian treaty (see page 1211), peace proved elusive. In 1983 Israeli forces attacked Palestine Liberation Organization (PLO) strongholds in southern Lebanon on Israel's northern border. The United States arranged for a withdrawal of both Israeli and PLO troops from Beirut, and sent two thousand marines into the region as part of an international peacekeeping force. In October 1983, a radical Shiite Muslim terrorist drove a truck loaded with explosives into the U.S. barracks near the Beirut airport. The explosion killed 241 marines. While insisting that the marines in Lebanon had been "central to our credibility on a global scale," Reagan quietly withdrew the remaining troops.

The bombing of the U.S. Marine barracks heralded a broader campaign of terror launched by radical Middle East groups. In 1985 terrorist attacks in the Middle East and Europe claimed the lives of more than 900 civilians, including 23 Americans. In June 1985, American television captured the ordeal of the 135 passengers aboard TWA flight 847. Hijacked over Greece, they endured seventeen nightmarish days of captivity before being released. A few months later, in October, PLO agents seized an Italian cruise ship, the *Achille Lauro,* and murdered a wheelchair-bound American passenger. "You can run but you can't hide," Reagan warned. In 1986, when Libyan agents were implicated in the bombing of a Berlin nightclub frequented by American soldiers, Reagan, calling Libya's president Muammar Qaddafi the "mad dog of the Middle East," ordered a retaliatory air attack. The raid killed an estimated 37 Libyans, including Qaddafi's infant daughter.

Americans applauded the flexing of U.S. military muscle, but the cycle of terrorism escalated. In December 1988, a Pan Am jet en route from London to New York crashed near Lockerbie, Scotland, killing all 259 aboard, including numerous Americans. Investigators found conclusive evidence that a bomb had been hidden in the baggage section.

The Iran-Contra Scandal

Reagan came into office in 1980 on a groundswell of public outrage over Iran's seizure of American hostages. Believing that the Iranians had released the hostages on the day he was inaugurated as president because they feared his tough-minded approach to the world, Reagan proudly emphasized that he would never negotiate with terrorists. "The United States gives terrorists no rewards," he said in June 1985. "We make no concessions. We make no deals." While talking tough, Reagan was negotiating behind the scenes with Iran to secure the release of American hostages taken in Beirut. A few months earlier, the president had approved a plan hatched by his national security adviser Robert McFarlane and CIA head William Casey. American agents would secretly try to curry favor with the radical regime in Iran by selling them high-tech U.S. arms, which they needed in their ongoing war against Iraq. The secretaries of defense and state had vigorously objected to the idea, dismissing it as "almost too absurd to comment on." The president, however, moved by the pleas of hostages' families to do something to bring their loved ones home, had approved the secret sale of state-of-the-art anti-tank missiles to Iran.

The plot had an added twist, U.S. operatives overcharged Iran for the weapons and diverted some of the profits to fund the contras in Nicaragua. The operation was carried out by National Security Council (NSC) aide Oliver North, who used various middlemen to funnel millions of dollars to the contras, and was in clear violation of the Boland Amendment, which expressly forbade aid to the contras. The flow of money continued through the early autumn of 1986 before a Lebanese news magazine exposed the scheme. At first, the administration denied that it had violated its own policy by offering incentives for the release of the hostages. Over the next few months, however, reporters exposed the sordid details of the arms sales and the funneling of money to the contras.

The scandal, which consumed Reagan's final two years in office, damaged the president's reputation as an effective leader. A congressional committee charged that the president had abdicated his "moral and legal responsibility to take care that the laws be faithfully executed," but stopped short of accusing him of intentionally breaking the law. Far more damaging was the report of independent counsel Lawrence E. Walsh, who concluded that the White House successfully constructed a "firewall" to protect the president, allowing lower-level officials—North along with two National Security Council officials, Robert McFarlane and John Poindexter—to take the blame for an illegal policy approved by the president. Walsh, however, never found conclusive evidence that linked Reagan directly to the illegal activities. And although troubled by the Iran-contra affair, the public, as with other scandals that plagued the Reagan administration, did not blame the president himself. Polls showed declining support for the administration, plus renewed questions about the president's casual leadership style, but Reagan remained immensely popular when he left office.

Wealth and Poverty in Reagan's America, 1980–1988

Reagan's attacks on the welfare state, his steep tax cuts, and his advocacy of small government struck a responsive chord with many young, affluent baby boomers who were entering their peak earning years. They helped lead the nation in a celebration of money-dominated American public life during the decade, but grimmer realities lay under the surface.

The Money Culture

Ronald and Nancy Reagan epitomized the new money culture of the 1980s. The public seemed fascinated by the air of unembarrassed extravagance that floated around the Reagans. The couple set the tone for the decade with an extravagant inaugural celebration that included two nights of show-business performances, an $800,000 fireworks display, and nine lavish inaugural balls. Once in the White House, First Lady Nancy Reagan unapologetically spent $209,508 for new White House china—a Lenox pattern with a raised gold presidential seal—while her husband was busy cutting welfare rolls.

The real nexus of the money culture, however, was Wall Street. Changes in the 1981 tax law, combined with the Reagan Justice Department's relaxed attitude toward enforcement of antitrust statutes, fueled a "merger mania" on Wall Street. Many of the nation's largest corporations, including R. J. Reynolds, Nabisco, Walt Disney, and Federated Department Stores, were the objects of leveraged buyouts. Between 1984 and 1987, Wall Street executed twenty-one mergers valued at over $1 billion each.

The money culture created lucrative opportunities for the battalions of bankers, investors, and venture capitalists who made money out of money. Among the very highest rollers was Ivan Boesky, who worked eighteen-hour days behind a three-hundred-line phone bank, lived like a feudal lord, and made $115 million in two huge petrocompany deals in 1984. "Greed is all right," he told a cheering University of California business school audience in 1985. "Everybody should be a little bit greedy." Greed, however soon landed Boesky in jail. In late 1986, he pleaded guilty to using confidential information about corporate takeovers to trade stocks illegally. In 1987 *Fortune* magazine named him "Crook of the Year." Boesky was far from the only lawbreaker. Between 1977 and 1989, Michael Milken raised more than $100 billion in funds for American business. In 1987 alone, he earned more than $550 million in commissions. He later confessed to defrauding investors and rigging the bond market.

The emphasis on making money was a manifestation of the maturing of the baby boom generation—the 76 million men and women born from 1946 through 1964 who were entering high-earning, high-spending adulthood at the start of the '80s. By mid-decade, observers had coined the acronym "Yuppie" to describe these ambitious, young, urban professionals. *Newsweek* magazine named 1984 "The Year of the Yuppie." Yuppies aspired to become investment bankers, not social workers. In 1985, for example, one-third of the graduating class at Yale applied for jobs as financial analysts at First Boston Corporation. When college freshmen were asked in the late 1960s about personal goals, roughly 80 percent listed to "develop a meaningful philosophy of life," and only about 40 percent listed being "well off financially." By 1985, 71 percent listed being well off financially, and only 43 percent mentioned a philosophy of life.

Popular culture reinforced the Reagan era infatuation with wealth and status. *Dallas,* the most successful prime-time soap opera of the decade, chronicled the business intrigues and torrid sex life of Texas oilman J. R. Ewing. Robin Leach's *Lifestyles of the Rich and Famous*, took viewers on shopping trips along exclusive Rodeo Drive and into the homes of the wealthy, before ending with Leach's trademark sign-off, "May you have caviar wishes and champagne dreams." In Oliver Stone's film *Wall Street,* Michael Douglas, playing Gordon Gekko, a ruthless corporate raider who relies on insider information to swing his deals, tells stockbrokers: "Greed, for lack of a better word, is good. Greed is right. Greed works."

The MTV Generation

As in other eras, technological changes during the eighties aided advertisers in their efforts to reach high-spending consumers. Over the decade, cable television grew from a flimsy presence in fewer than one in five homes to a favored place in 56.4 percent of television homes. By the end of the decade, the average television household received more than twenty-seven channels. As viewers' choices grew, and the three broadcast networks lost their automatic grip on the audience, the spoils went increasingly to the programmer who could cater to a special interest—and offer advertisers a small but well-targeted cluster of consumers.

At the cutting edge of this new TV environment, music television, known from the start as MTV, inspired a revolution in television broadcasting. "Ladies and Gentlemen," intoned a baritone voice at 12:01 A.M. on August 1, 1981, "Rock and roll!"

MTV showed music videos around the clock, broken only by ads and bits of connective patter from "veejays." From the beginning, MTV was designed to appeal to young adults with lots of disposable income. "It was meant to drive a 55-year-old person crazy," said chairman Tom Freston. But that was simply MTV's shrewd twist on the key selling strategy of the decade: "narrow casting," or niche marketing designed to "superserve" a narrowly defined viewer, or reader, or customer. In addition to MTV, networks pitched ads to children (Nickelodeon), to African-Americans (Black Entertainment Television), to news junkies (CNN), and to women between eighteen and forty-nine (Lifetime). Viewers willing to subscribe to premium services that charge an extra fee could choose all-sports, all-weather, all-movies, all-Spanish, all-sex, and more.

Television was only the most dramatic example of the culture's rearrangement into niches. Consumers could choose from hundreds of specialized magazines, among them 29 new automotive magazines, 25 devoted to computers, 9 food journals, 13 gay magazines, and 5 bridal magazines. The splintering of the media reinforced, and was fed by, a splintering of the consumer market. Retailing saw a proliferation of stores that sold only coffee, or only socks; within department stores, merchandise was increasingly fractured into miniature enclaves sorted according to designer.

The success of MTV and other forms of niche marketing contributed to the fragmentation of public culture. During the 1940s and 1950s, many technological changes helped create a sense of community and a more national culture. The advent of television, with just three networks, combined with the explosion in long-distance telephone service, the construction of interstate highways, and the expansion of air travel, helped shrink distances and bring people closer together. Until the explosion in cable television and the proliferation of new networks, most of the viewing public watched the same television shows. As recently as the 1970s, more than a third of U.S. homes tuned in weekly to watch *All in the Family*. "Television in the old days made it a smaller community," said producer Norman Lear. In the 1980s, technology was transforming the mass culture into endless niche cultures. With so many shows to choose from, the audience splintered into smaller subsets of viewers. Studies showed, for example, that blacks and whites watched completely different shows.

The Hourglass Society

The public focus on the money culture during the Reagan era obscured the social reality affecting most Americans. Society in the 1980s assumed the appearance of an hourglass: bulging on the extremes and thin in the middle. "There are more and more affluent people, and more and more poor people," said Martin Holler, a Methodist minister who ran a food bank in Wichita, Kansas, "more people who have much more than they have ever had, and more people with nothing."

The number of millionaires doubled during the decade. The net worth of the four hundred richest Americans nearly tripled. By the end of the decade, the top 1 percent of families owned 42 percent of the net wealth of all U.S. families, including 60 percent of all corporate stock and 80 percent of all family-owned trusts.

Stated another way, the richest 2.5 million people had nearly as much income as the 100 million Americans with the lowest incomes.

The flurry of business mergers and acquisitions gave a handful of corporations increasing control over decision making in the private economy. The largest two hundred industrial corporations controlled roughly 60 percent of the assets of all industrial corporations, up from less than 50 percent in the early 1950s. And despite the continuing celebrations of "people's capitalism," the percentage of American households owning at least one share of stock fell from 25 percent in 1977 to 19 percent in 1983, while the wealthiest 1 percent of all American households controlled nearly three-fifths of all corporate stock.

While the rich got richer, the poor got poorer. The government classified about 26.1 million people as poor in 1979, 11.7 percent of the total population. By 1990, the number of poor had reached 33.6 million, or 13.5 percent of the country. The aggregate numbers masked a major transformation in the nature of poverty. Government programs such as social security and Medicare had lifted most of the elderly and handicapped out of poverty, but they did little to alleviate the suffering of single mothers, young children, and young minority men, who made up the bulk of the poor population after 1980.

A marked jump in out-of-wedlock births, which doubled between 1975 and 1986, and in female-headed households, which did the same between 1970 and 1989, contributed to what analysts called the "feminization of poverty." By 1989, one of every four births in the United States was to an unwed woman. The feminization of poverty was also disproportionately black. By the early 1990s, 26 percent of all children under eighteen lived with a single parent, more than 60 percent of black children fell into that category. "With the exception of drugs and crime, the biggest crisis facing the black community today is the plight of the single mother," declared an NAACP publication.

By virtually any measure, the problems of society's poorest worsened during the 1980s. At any given time during the decade, between 250,000 and 400,000 Americans were homeless. "Get off the subway in any American city," said the head of the National Coalition for Low Income Housing, "and you are stepping over people who live on the streets." Most of the homeless were unskilled workers, the chronically mentally ill, and women fleeing abusive spouses. Most had already been living in poverty before becoming homeless. During the 1980s, high interest rates for construction coupled with tax law changes sharply cut commercial production of low-cost rental housing, leaving a shortage of affordable housing for low-income people. For many, the only choice was the streets. When Reagan's budget measures reduced funds available for homeless shelters, cities and states could not respond to the crisis.

As some of its members fell into poverty and others acquired wealth, the middle class shrank. According to some estimates, the middle class—families making between $20,000 and $60,000—dwindled from 53 percent of the nation in 1973 to 49 percent in 1985. After doubling between 1947 and 1973, median family income stagnated. In 1985 the average middle-class family earned less money than it did in 1973. Hardest hit were younger families, who feared the American Dream of rising prosperity would pass them by.

Homelessness During the 1980s the wealthiest 1 percent of the American population saw a dramatic rise in their average incomes, while the poorest segments of society saw a decline in income. Increasing numbers of families were reported to be homeless in America, along with former psychiatric patients and drug users. *(Wide World Photos, Inc.)*

The New Economy

A number of factors led to the growing disparity of wealth and poverty in America. First, most of the new jobs created during the decade were lower-paying service jobs. By 1985, more people were flipping hamburgers at McDonalds for minimum wage than were working in steel manufacturing—one of the cornerstones of America's industrial might. Between 1979 and 1984, six of ten jobs added to the U.S. labor market paid $7,000 a year or less. Most were in the service sector, as home health care attendants, sales clerks, food servers, janitors, or office clerks. Besides low pay, these jobs offered few pension or health care benefits, were often part-time or temporary, and held out few opportunities for promotion. As a result, real hourly wages declined 0.5 percent per year from 1982 to 1987.

Second, government welfare programs were cut back or abandoned during the Reagan era. By 1989, state and local welfare payments dropped by an average of 40 percent from their 1973 levels. Job training programs were also sharply curtailed, and inflation stripped the minimum wage (frozen by the Reagan administration at 1981 levels) of some 44 percent of its real value.

Third, organized labor lost more than 3 million members over the course of the decade. By 1990, unions represented only 16 percent of the nation's 100 million workers. Not only were unions underrepresented in the fast-growing service sector of the economy, but the Reagan administration dealt labor a major blow in 1981 when it fired striking members of the Professional Air Traffic Controllers Organization (PATCO). The president's actions emboldened management and dispirited workers.

Fourth, Reagan's tax cuts worsened the skew toward an hourglass social structure by offering the largest breaks to the wealthy. At the same time, social security taxes roughly tripled. The blow fell most heavily on the middle and lower classes, since the social security tax exempts the portion of wage and salary income above $45,000 a year and all income from interest, dividends, and rent. The result was that only the top 10 percent of the population received a significant net tax cut between 1977 and 1988; most of the other 90 percent paid a higher share of their incomes to Washington. At the extremes, the richest 1 percent got a net tax savings of 25 percent; the poorest tenth of workers saw 20 percent more of their incomes swallowed by taxes.

While conditions restricted the opportunity to make money for most people, expenses for basic necessities soared during the decade. A typical family home in 1984 absorbed 44 percent of the median family's yearly income, compared with 21 percent in 1973. Buying the average-priced car cost 23 weeks of pay in 1988. Ten years earlier it had cost 18 weeks of pay.

The Reagan Legacy

The Iran-contra scandal cast a dark shadow over the final years of the Reagan administration and intensified debate about the president's legacy. Supporters argue that Reagan's economic policies produced a remarkable period of sustained growth. Between 1983 and 1990, unemployment fell to 5.2 percent, the economy grew by a third and produced 19 million new jobs, while inflation remained stable at less than 4 percent. Abroad, Reagan's supporters contend his tough rhetoric and increased military spending not only pushed the Soviets to the bargaining table, but forced them to accept American terms. Reagan, they declared, was personally responsible for ending the Cold War.

The president's critics contend that his domestic policies imposed undue hardship on the poor and had little to do with the economic recovery. His income tax cut proved illusory for all except the wealthiest Americans. By the end of his administration, the average family was actually paying more in taxes than in 1980, thanks in large part to a sharp increase in social security taxes and hikes in state and local taxes to cover shortfalls from reduced federal outlays. Critics also challenge the notion that Reagan ended the Cold War: the Soviet Union they assert, collapsed under the weight of American's bipartisan policy of containment dating back to the Truman Doctrine and the Marshall Plan, and because of the inherent instability of communism.

It is difficult to reach conclusive answers on these questions. Until historians know more about the inner workings of Kremlin decision makers, it will be impossible to assess all the forces that contributed to Moscow's new openness to the West. Certainly Reagan's strident rhetoric and massive arms buildup intensified Cold War tensions, while many of his policies, especially those toward Latin America, overestimated Soviet influence and underplayed the role of local forces. Much to his credit, however, Reagan appreciated the need to soften his hard line with the Soviets, embracing Gorbachev and the new Soviet openness to the West.

On the home front, perhaps Reagan's chief legacy was a ballooning federal deficit. Reagan's inability to reconcile his tax-cutting policies with his spending priorities, especially the massive military increases, caused the federal deficit to soar. By the time Reagan left office, the federal government was spending $206 billion more per year than it was receiving in tax revenues. In just eight years, the national debt rose from $908.5 billion to nearly $2.7 trillion. The mountain of red ink may have inadvertently furthered Reagan's agenda, since it focused public attention on cutting spending and dashed liberal hopes of funding new social programs (see graph).

One Reagan legacy is little disputed, however. Reagan's skillful use of television transformed the style of presidential leadership. "Television in modern politics has been as revolutionary as the development of printing in the time of Gutenberg," journalist Teddy White observed. Television forced politicians to articulate themes that could appeal to a broad spectrum of the electorate at the same time that it personalized politics by allowing leaders to bypass parties and build a direct relationship with voters. President Reagan was a master craftsman of the new technology. Leaving the details of governing to aides, Reagan concentrated on the symbolic aspects of his presidency. Using television to emphasize resilient themes of self-help, individualism,

The National Debt, 1930–2000 Ending a trend of static or slightly rising national debt, the Reagan era saw the deficit more than triple from $908 billion in 1980 to $2.9 trillion at the end of 1989 as Congress and the president refused to raise taxes or cut popular programs. This trend continued into the nineties and beyond (the data for 1999–2000 are estimations). (Sources: *Historical Statistics of the United States* and *Statistical Abstract of the United States,* relevant years; *Economic Indicators,* Council of Economic Advisors; U.S. Government Printing Office, Washington, D.C., 1999.)

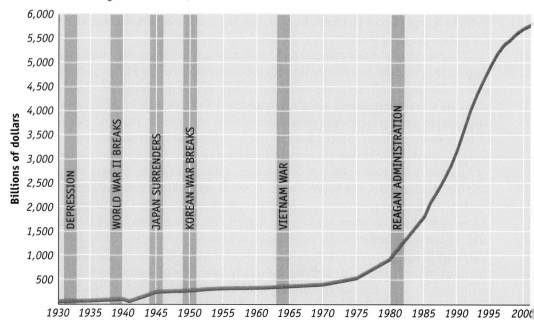

and limited government, he rarely discussed specific policies. The president's advisers carefully orchestrated the media coverage. By limiting access to Reagan, the staff minimized the president's penchant for verbal miscues, prevented the press from asking tough questions, and guaranteed that the public saw him in brief visuals that served to enhance his stature. These images, designed around a daily message, allowed the White House to focus public attention on Reagan's accomplishments while ignoring his numerous failures. "So far, he's proving Lincoln was right," observed a veteran reporter. "You can fool all of the people some of the time."

Reagan's media savvy helped boost his personal popularity to record levels. Polls showed his approval rating at 68 percent in his final month in office—the highest ever recorded for a departing president. Reagan's appeal rubbed off on the rest of Washington. In 1980 only 22 percent of people polled said they could trust government "most of the time." After eight years of Republican rule, the percentage had increased to 38 percent, and nearly half said they favored increased government spending. Perhaps the ultimate irony of Reagan's presidency was that he increased public faith in government at the same time that his massive deficits crippled Washington's ability to respond to demands for greater government services. It would be left to Reagan's successors to reconcile the contradiction.

CONCLUSION

Powerful conservative currents swept through American politics at the end of the 1970s. Religious conservatives mobilized to reverse what they considered the nation's moral decline; angry taxpayers revolted against an increased and often unequal tax burden; and conservative intellectuals launched an array of ideological missiles at the welfare state and government activism in general. The conservative currents flowed into the 1980 presidential contest, where the public, worried about soaring inflation, rising unemployment, and declining international prestige, rejected President Carter and elected former California governor Ronald Reagan. The former actor combined telegenic features and a simple but compelling message to win the election.

The rise of the Religious Right inspired an angry debate over social values during the decade. At the heart of the culture wars was a dispute about American identity. Both sides were convinced that their values were "American" and best served the nation's traditional experiment in liberty. Conservatives, with the help of the Reagan administration, launched an assault against "liberal permissiveness," which they blamed for the decline of the family. While the Left and Right battled over abortion and gay rights, a massive tide of immigrants was changing the face of America. But the new immigration touched off another heated controversy over how newcomers should be integrated into the mainstream, or if indeed they should be welcomed at all.

As president, Ronald Reagan launched an assault on the welfare state, pushing Congress to pass ambitious tax and spending cuts. He attempted to rein in Washington's power by appointing cabinet members and Supreme Court justices who shared his disdain for bureaucracy and his disaffection with state power. The public appreciated Reagan's leadership style and in 1984 rewarded him with a resounding victory over his Democratic opponent, Walter Mondale.

Reagan came to office determined to reassert American power and to tame the Soviet bear, which he believed was the instigator behind most trouble spots in the world. Convinced that the United States was losing its battle with the Soviet Union, the administration embarked on a massive armament program to build up the nation's stockpile of nuclear and conventional weapons. By 1986, the administration had retreated from its hard-line experiment with the Soviets. By the end of Reagan's second term, thanks in large part to new leadership in the Kremlin, the United States and the Soviets enjoyed the warmest relations since the end of World War II. That success was clouded by revelations that the White House had masterminded an illegal scheme to sell weapons to Iran and use the proceeds to fund anticommunist guerillas in Nicaragua.

Americans in the 1980s seemed consumed with wealth and status. A Wall Street "merger mania" produced new opportunities to make money, advertisers eager to sell their goods, and a popular culture that glorified the pursuit of wealth. The benefits of the booming economy were not evenly distributed. The decade witnessed a widening gap between haves and have-nots, aggravated by Reagan's policies and rising prices for basic necessities. Economically, Reagan's policy experiments left a mixed legacy, which included a huge federal deficit. His successor would confront the economic repercussions, as well as the diplomatic opportunities, that the Reagan era initiated.

SUGGESTED READINGS

The writing available on the 1980s is unusually polarized, but there are nonetheless some broad surveys of the period. Samuel Freedman's *The Inheritance* (1996) provides a good sense of the mood of many early Reagan voters. William Berman's *America's Right Turn* (1994) paints a broad picture of the rise of conservatism from Nixon to George Bush. Michael Schaller offers the first historical work on the 1980s in *Reckoning with Reagan* (1992).

Wiliam Martin's *With God on Our Side* (1996) describes the changing politics of the Religious Right. Clyde Wilcox studied the leaders of the Religious Right in *God's Warriors* (1992), while Burton Yale Pines looks at the cultural appeal of fundamentalism in *Back to Basics* (1982).

Robert Kuttner covers the tax revolt in the late 1970s in his definitive work *Revolt of the Haves* (1980). Sidney Blumenthal's *The Rise of the Counter-Establishment* (1986) chronicles the emergence of the neoconservatives. Michael Lind, a defector from the conservative camp, critiques the New Right in *Up From Conservatism* (1996).

Most of the historical treatments of Reagan's presidency are sharply critical. In *Dutch* (1999) Edmund Morris, Reagan's authorized biographer, produces an idiosyncratic but useful portrait of the president. Gary Wills's *Reagan's America: Innocents at Home* (1987) is the classic treatment. Lou Cannon's *President Reagan: The Role of a Lifetime* (1991) stresses theatricality in Reagan's presidency. Mark Hertsgaard's *On Bended Knee* (1988) castigates the press for glorifying Reagan. Haynes Johnson provides an overview of the country in *Sleepwalking Through History* (1991). Sidney Blumenthal and Thomas Edsall compile a series of essays on Reagan's presidency in *The Reagan Legacy* (1988).

Charles Murray outlines the major economic theories of the Reagan administration in *Losing Ground* (1984). William Greider takes the Reagan economists to task in *The Educa-*

tion of David Stockman and Other Americans (1982). Martin Carnoy's *A New Social Contract* (1983) is a socialist critique of Reagan's policies. Lester Thurow's *Zero-Sum Society* (1980) is also valuable for understanding the economics of the 1980s.

E. J. Dionne's *Why Americans Hate Politics* (1991) captures the political mood of the 1984 campaign and the dilemma faced by the Democratic Party. Peter Goldman and Tony Fuller's *The Quest for the Presidency, 1984* (1985) recounts the strategies and actions of the two campaigners. Jack Germond and Jules Witcover express cynicism over Reagan's campaign of images in *Wake Us When It's Over* (1985).

Richard Melanson argues in *Reconstructing Consensus* (1991) that the overarching foreign policy goal of the Reagan administration was to rebuild the Cold War consensus that was destroyed during the Vietnam War. In *Buildup* (1992), Daniel Wirls stresses the importance of domestic politics in Reagan's foreign policy. Strobe Talbott surveys the escalation of the arms race in *Deadly Gambit* (1984). Seweryn Bialer and Michael Mandelbaum address the emerging détente between the superpowers in *Gorbachev's Russia and American Foreign Policy* (1988).

Broad introductions to Reagan's Central American policies include Walter LaFeber's *Inevitable Revolutions* (1984) and Kenneth Coleman and George Herring's *The Central American Crisis* (1985). Robert Pastor surveys America's relations with Nicaragua in *Condemned to Repetition* (1987). The Nicaraguan operation fed directly into the Iran-contra scandal, which is covered by Jane Hunter et al. in *The Iran-Contra Connection* (1987). Bob Woodward reviews Reagan's secret operations in *Veil: The Secret Wars of the CIA* (1987).

James Steward's *Den of Thieves* is an account of the shady dealings in the financial markets during the 1980s. Connie Bruck's *The Predators' Ball* (1988) details the world of the junk bond traders. Allan Murray's *Showdown at Gucci Gulch* (1987) explains the influence such financiers had on government during the decade. Nicolaus Mills's *Culture in an Age of Money* (1990) criticizes the influence of corporations and wealth on American culture during the 1980s. Barbara Ehrenreich studies the insecurities over wealth and status that preoccupied much of the middle class in her *Fear of Falling* (1989). Kevin Phillips attacks the growth of economic inequality in the 1980s in *The Politics of Rich and Poor* (1990). Thomas Edsall explains the political motivations for attacking the poor in *The New Politics of Inequality* (1984). Leslie Dunbar analyzes the impact of Reagan's economic policies on minorities in *Minority Report* (1984), while William Julius Wilson's *The Truly Disadvantaged* (1987) studies the effects of Reaganomics in the inner cities. The war on welfare is exposed in Michael Katz's *The Undeserving Poor* (1989).

James C. Mohr's *Abortion in America* (1978) is a good one-volume history of the abortion debate. Leslie Reagan reconstructs the situation for women before *Roe* v. *Wade* in *When Abortion Was a Crime* (1997). Rosalind Petchesky explains the philosophical and legal conflicts surrounding abortion in *Abortion and Women's Choice* (1990). The definitive discussion of the political campaign over abortion is found in Kristin Luker's *Abortion and the Politics of Motherhood* (1985). Works on gay rights range from broad surveys such as Eric Marcus's *Making History: The Struggle for Gay and Lesbian Equal Rights* (1992), to studies of specific issues, such as Randy Shilts's coverage of the early AIDS epidemic, *And the Band Played On* (1987).

David Reimers's *Still the Golden Door* (1985) is a good starting point for material on immigration. Thomas Espenshade's *The Fourth Wave* (1985) describes the "New Asian" immigrants in California, while James Cockcroft's *Outlaws in the Promised Land* (1986) looks at the immigration experience of Hispanics. Peter Brimelow's *Alien Nation* (1995) offers a pessimistic analysis of the new wave of immigration.

Competing Voices | Debating the Environment

Ecodefence: A Field Guide to Monkeywrenching

Government plans to reduce the amount of roadless acreage in the American wilderness prompted environmental activist Dave Foreman to form, in 1980, a new grassroots environmental movement, EarthFirst! Placing the protection of the environment above economic demands or human progress, Foreman advocated "monkeywrenching"—the destruction of any property used to violate nature. His book *Ecodefence*, published in 1987, served as a guidebook for other radical environmentalists.

███ . . . Only one hundred and fifty years ago, the Great Plains were a vast, waving sea of grass stretching from the Chihuahuan Desert of Mexico to the boreal forest of Canada, from the oak-hickory forests of the Ozarks to the Rocky Mountains. Bison blanketed the plains—it has been estimated that 60 million of the huge, shaggy beasts moved across the grass. Great herds of pronghorn and elk also filled this Pleistocene landscape. Packs of wolves and numerous grizzly bears followed the immense herds. . . .

In the space of a few generations we have laid waste to paradise. The tall grass prairie has been transformed into a corn factory where wildlife means the exotic pheasant. The short grass prairie is a grid of carefully fenced cow pastures and wheat fields. . . .

Nonetheless, wildness and natural diversity remain. There are a few scattered grasslands ungrazed, stretches of free-flowing river undammed and undiverted, thousand-year-old forests, Eastern woodlands growing back to forest and reclaiming past roads, grizzlies and wolves and lions and wolverines and bighorn and moose roaming the backcountry; hundreds of square miles that have never known the imprint of a tire, the bit of a drill, the rip of a 'dozer, the cut of a saw, the smell of gasoline.

These are the places that hold North America together, that contain the genetic information of life, that represent sanity in a whirlwind of madness. . . .

Many of the projects that will destroy roadless areas are economically marginal. It is costly for the Forest Service, BLM, timber companies, oil companies, mining companies and others to scratch out the "resources" in these last wild areas. It is expensive to maintain the necessary infrastructure of roads for the exploitation of wild lands. The cost of repairs, the hassle, the delay, the down-time may just be too much for the bureaucrats and exploiters to accept if there is a widely dispersed, unorganized, *strategic* movement of resistance across the land.

It is time for women and men, individually and in small groups, to act heroically and admittedly illegally in defense of the wild, to put a monkey wrench into the gears of the machine destroying natural diversity. This strategic monkey wrenching can be safe, it can be easy, it can be fun, and—most importantly—it can be effective in stopping timber cutting, road building, overgrazing, oil & gas exploration, mining, dam building, powerline construction, offroad-vehicle use, trapping, ski area development and other forms of destruction of the wilderness, as well as cancerous suburban sprawl. . . .

John Muir said that if it ever came to a war between the races, he would side with the bears. That day has arrived.

Industry and the Environment: Toward a New Philosophy

The rising memberships of such movements as EarthFirst! caught the attention of industrialists such as G. M. Keller, chairman of the board and chief executive officer of the Chevron Corporation. In his speech, "Industry and the Environment," delivered to the California Manufacturers Association in October 1987, Keller emphasized the progress industry had made in the previous twenty years with respect to the environment and pointed to ways industry continued to promote a better, cleaner planet.

. . . Today, we are in a very real sense, a society of "environmentalists." We all want clean water and pure air and wilderness and wildlife. I don't know anyone who's *against* these things. Most people in industry . . . like most people in general . . . place a high value on a wholesome environment. . . .

In the past, as I've said, we've tended to let society . . . in the form of the regulators . . . tell us when some aspect of our operations has become a matter of public concern. At that point, we fix it. But *at that point*, the corrective action is apt to be disruptive and very costly . . . not only in terms of the actual dollars, but in terms of lost credibility as well.

I wonder if an objective analysis might not reveal many opportunities where companies could spend less . . . long term . . . and gain *more* . . . in terms of credibility and community standing . . . by correcting operational problems *before* they become compliance problems.

. . . By applying our research efforts to improving our manufacturing processes now . . . we can head off all sorts of environmental headaches tomorrow . . . and sharpen our competitive edge at the same time. . . .

Having said that, I want to add some important qualifiers. I am not willing to concede that the environmental activists are the legitimate representatives of the public interest in all matters touching on the environment.

For instance, there are some people for whom a love of the works of nature seems to engender a corresponding hatred of the works of man. . . .

To people with that viewpoint, *mankind* is the intruder . . . not merely the source of pollution . . . but pollution itself.

Those people need to realize that human technology . . . and the products of our industry . . . are what stand between us and the hostile elements . . . between us and constant hunger . . . between us and the ravages of disease and predation.

In fact, it is only due to the tremendous progress we've achieved . . . our liberation from the harshest imperatives of nature . . . that we finally have the luxury to look up from the business of our own survival . . . and attend to the needs of the other species on the planet.

I'm not sure what solutions we'll find to deal with all our environmental problems . . . but I'm sure of this: they will be provided by industry . . . they will be the products of technology.

The 1970s served as the decade of environmental legislation as people across the country demanded something be done to protect the nation's land and natural resources. Passage of legislation such as the Clean Air Act and the Endangered Species Act, along with the creation of the Environmental Protection Agency, indicated Americans' desire to improve their quality of life and the viability of their planet. A united conservation front, focused on the elimination of pollution and the protection of wild lands, held firm until the late 1970s when a struggling economy forced many people to question the financial costs of the new environmental regulations. By the beginning of the 1980s, business leaders had joined forces with conservatives to create a powerful coalition calling for a rollback of environmental protection.

The Reagan administration reflected the backlash against strict government control of natural resources and pollution. Business leaders like Keller found a sympathetic ear in the administration for their argument that tight enforcement of environmental laws increased prices, cost jobs, and damaged America's ability to compete in a global marketplace. As a result, Reagan moved aggressively to relax environmental quality standards, reduce the size and power of environmental regulatory bodies, and appoint pro-business agents, such as James Watt, to lead executive departments.

Mobilized by the administration's posture, a minority of environmental activists adopted a new, more radical approach. Some enthusiasts, including Foreman, claimed that traditional groups were not aggressive enough in their defense of the environment. Often resorting to "ecotage," Foreman's EarthFirst! advocated a total ban on any construction that intruded on wilderness areas. It was not only their uncompromising agenda, but their tactics, that distinguished the radicals from mainstream environmental groups. Radical environmentalists took inspiration from Edward Abbey's *The Monkey Wrench Gang* (1975), whose main characters blew up everything from billboards to bulldozers in an attempt to stop the spread of industrial progress in the Southwest. The real "monkeywrenchers" of the 1980s chained themselves to trees, formed human barricades around bulldozers, and spiked trunks marked for cutting. Ironically, these activities pushed industrialists closer to the more moderate environmentalists, opening lines of communication and negotiation.

Questions for Analysis

1. What do you think Foreman means when he says of the wilderness, "These are the places that hold North America together"?

2. Why does Foreman believe "monkeywrenching" will save the environment? Under what circumstances (if any) is the use of "admittedly illegal" acts justifiable?

3. Why does Keller believe industrialists should be more concerned about their companies' impact on the environment?

4. Considering industry's track record, can Keller be trusted or is he just a mouthpiece for the oil companies? Explain.

5. How does each man view the relationship between technology and the environment?

6. In your opinion, is Keller's or Foreman's strategy more likely to solve the environmental problems of the late twentieth century?

32

America After the Cold War, 1988–2000

On January 7, 1999, a cold, drizzly day in Washington, Chief Justice of the United States William Rehnquist, dressed in gold-striped black robes, entered the majestic nineteenth-century Senate chamber. The room was hushed, the galleries packed, and the hundred senators seated at rapt attention as the sergeant at arms opened the proceedings. "All persons are commanded to keep silence, on pain of imprisonment, while the House of Representatives is exhibiting to the Senate of the United States articles of impeachment against William Jefferson Clinton."

It was a historic event: the first impeachment trial of an elected U.S. president and only the second such trial in history. The House of Representatives had forwarded two charges against Clinton, the first two-term Democratic president since Franklin Roosevelt. The charges alleged that he had lied under oath and obstructed justice in an effort to hide his affair with Monica Lewinski, a twenty-two-year-old former White House intern. Under the Constitution, if two-thirds of the Senate, or sixty-seven senators, voted for conviction on either of the two articles of impeachment, Clinton would be removed from office and Vice President Al Gore sworn in to replace him.

After days of listening to Republican prosecutors from the House and to the president's defense lawyers, the senators closed the doors, turned off the television cameras, and deliberated. At the end of the fourth day of closed-door meetings, the doors opened and curious onlookers packed the galleries and filled the aisles to hear the verdict. "Senators, how say you? Is the respondent, William Jefferson Clinton, guilty or not guilty?" Rehnquist asked after a clerk read the first charge of perjury. As the clerk called the senators' names one by one, each stood to announce his or her verdict. Ten Republicans joined a united Democratic Party in declaring the president "not guilty," making the final count 45–55. On the obstruction of justice charge, five GOP senators crossed over, resulting in a 50–50 vote. Clinton "hereby is acquitted of the charges," the chief justice proclaimed.

A subdued Clinton emerged from the Oval Office two hours later to apologize to the American people: "I want to say again to the American people how profoundly sorry I am for what I said and did to trigger these events and the great burden they have imposed on the Congress and the American people." The president could take solace, however, from the fact that neither of the two articles of impeachment attracted even a simple majority of senators' votes, and both fell far short of the two-thirds majority needed to convict and expel him.

The trial opened a window onto the conflicting social currents of post–Cold War America. With the country's mortal enemy, the Soviet Union, dissolved, Americans in the 1990s were able to refocus their attention on domestic issues, and politicians responded by experimenting with new political techniques and agendas. The shifting political winds caught President George Bush off guard and allowed the Democrat Bill Clinton to capture the White House in 1992. Partisan divisions, which often had been kept in check by fear of a common enemy, intensified during the decade as Republicans gained a firm foothold in the Congress and the Democrats controlled the presidency. No longer consumed by the global struggle against communism, American politicians felt they had the luxury to spend thirteen months debating the private life of a public official. The explosion of new media outlets, especially the Internet and twenty-four-hour news channels, fed the public a steady diet of salacious details. The American people, however, turned out to be more interested in the new prosperity generated by a booming stock market than in the president's sexual adventures. Still, the trial increased public cynicism about Washington and provided ammunition for the restless antigovernment groups that had sprung up during the decade.

▮ How did the end of the Cold War influence American attitudes toward government?

▮ How did U.S. actions toward Iraq and Yugoslavia reflect Americans' view of their national interests?

▮ What was the "information society," and how did it affect the economy?

▮ How did partisan divisions shape American politics during the decade?

▮ What social tensions characterized the decade, and how were they expressed?

This chapter will address these questions.

Chronology

1983	*Time* names PC "Machine of the Year"
1988	Bush elected president
1989	U.S. troops invade Panama
	Tiananmen Square demonstration in China
1990	Soviet regimes topple in Eastern Europe
	Berlin Wall comes down
1991	Soviet Union dissolves; Gorbachev resigns
	Gulf War
	Thomas–Hill controversy
	Civil war in Yugoslavia
1992	Clinton elected president
	Los Angeles riots
1993	Failure of Clinton health plan
	World Trade Center bombing
1994	Beginning of Whitewater investigation
	NAFTA and GATT
	Mandela elected president of South Africa
1995	Republican government shutdown
	O. J. Simpson acquitted of murder
	Oklahoma City bombing
1996	Welfare Reform Act
	Clinton reelected
	California voters pass Proposition 209
1998	Clinton impeached
	U.S. embassies in Kenya and Tanzania bombed
1999	NATO bombs Kosovo
	Clinton acquitted
	40–60 million people worldwide on the Internet
	Columbine High School shootings

The Post–Cold War Experiment, 1988–1992

When he assumed the reins of power from Ronald Reagan in 1989, George Bush confronted a world transformed by the dissolution of the Soviet Union and the end of the Cold War. The threat of a superpower conflict receded, but Iraq's Saddam Hussein reminded Americans that the post–Cold War world was not devoid of danger. While President Bush successfully rallied world opinion and American military might in the Gulf War, establishing U.S. leadership in the post–Cold War world, he failed to exercise similar leadership in confronting a host of problems at home. In 1992 the voters rejected Bush in favor of former Arkansas governor Bill Clinton, who understood that after a generation of fighting communism, Americans were turning inward.

The Search for Reagan's Successor

The Iran-contra affair had removed some of the luster from Reagan's star, but his conservative views remained popular with most Republicans who faced the difficult task of choosing a candidate who would continue his policies. The logical choice was George Bush, who had served as Reagan's loyal vice president for the previous eight years. Bush, however, was not conservative enough for many party members, who rallied around two formidable primary opponents: televangelist Pat Robertson and Kansas senator Robert Dole. After a slow start, Bush gathered both endorsements from elected officials and votes in securing the nomination.

The son of a wealthy New England family, Bush had relocated to Texas, where he used family connections to make millions in the booming oil business and entered politics as a Goldwater Republican. During the 1970s, as conservatives were regaining a foothold in the party, Bush served in a number of appointive posts, including director of the CIA. However, when he campaigned for the presidency in 1980, it was as a moderate; at one point, he dismissed Reagan's recovery plan as "voodoo economics." He then spent the next eight years defending those same policies, often selling them to a skeptical Congress.

In his acceptance speech at the Republican convention in July 1988, Bush tried to energize the party's conservative faithful by promising to continue the fight against terrorism abroad and big government at home. The centerpiece of the speech was a dramatic and carefully scripted promise not to raise taxes. "Read my lips," he said. "No new taxes." The vice president also appealed to moderates by emphasizing his support for education and the environment. In a move that puzzled observers, and many of his closest advisers, Bush picked the untested and lightly regarded Dan Quayle, a conservative senator from Indiana, as his running mate.

The Democrats had a difficult time finding a nominee to challenge Bush. The party's front-runner, Colorado senator Gary Hart, quit the race after reporters disclosed that he was having an extramarital affair. Michael Dukakis, the Greek-American governor of Massachusetts, moved to fill the void created by Hart's absence. Dukakis and Hart shared a belief that the Democratic Party had moved too far to the left since the 1960s. Dukakis warned that the party should "break with the past." During the primaries, Dukakis bragged about his success in creating jobs and lowering taxes in his home state, the so-called "Massachusetts miracle." He promised "good jobs at good wages," clean air, child care, and increased federal support for education, but he never suggested how the additional spending would affect the deficit.

Dukakis faced a spirited challenge from African-American civil rights leader Jesse Jackson, who appealed to the party's traditional liberal base. Trying to weave together "a quilt" of mutual interests among working-class whites and blacks, Jackson called for increased government spending for social programs to help the poor and working class. He combined old-fashioned liberalism with a powerful social message. Traveling to the poorest inner-city neighborhoods, he told children to stay in school, to shun drugs, to vote, to respect themselves and one another, and to stop making mothers out of unwed teenage girls.

Jackson won some important primaries, but in the end, Dukakis's moderate message and well-oiled organization won more. Nominated at the Democratic convention in August, Dukakis tried to skirt the sensitive social issues that had divided the party since the 1960s by declaring that the campaign was about "competence, not ideology." To underscore his new centrist message, he chose conservative Texas senator Lloyd Bentsen as his running mate.

The fall contest between Dukakis and Bush degenerated into one of the most negative campaigns in modern times. The Bush campaign concentrated on convincing the public that Dukakis was soft on crime, unpatriotically weak on defense, and an enemy of family values. The Republicans also exploited racial tensions. Bush's most effective advertisement told voters about Willie Horton, an African-American who had raped a white woman while on weekend leave from a Massachusetts prison while Dukakis was governor.

Dukakis failed to respond to the Republican attacks and by late October, Gallup reported a "stunning turnaround" in the polls. On election day, Bush became the first sitting vice president since Martin Van Buren in 1836 to be elected directly to the presidency. He won 53.4 percent of the popular vote and carried forty states with 426 electoral votes. Dukakis won only ten states and the District of Columbia for a total of 111 electoral votes and 45.6 percent of the popular vote. (One Dukakis elector in West Virginia voted for Democratic vice-presidential nominee Lloyd Bentsen.) The Democrats, however, managed to increase their margins in Congress, where they held an 89-vote advantage in the House and 56 of 100 seats in the Senate (see map).

1989: "The Year of Miracles"

In 1989, as Bush was settling into office, Lech Walesa, a Polish shipyard electrician, led the Solidarity trade union movement in a series of strikes that crippled Poland's Soviet-controlled government. Reformist Soviet leader Gorbachev refused to use the military to quell the uprising, and he instructed the puppet regime to negotiate with the reformers. The result was an agreement to hold free elections in 1990—the first free elections in Poland in sixty-eight years. The seed of revolution spread rapidly from Poland to other Soviet bloc countries. In Hungary, reformers adopted a new constitution, called for elections, and disbanded the Communist Party. In

The Election of 1988 As vice president under Reagan, George Bush promised to continue the peace and prosperity he helped to create. At the same time he attacked his opponent, Massachusetts Governor Michael Dukakis, for releasing prisoners on furloughs, which left them free to commit greater crimes.

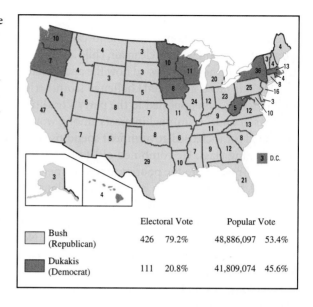

	Electoral Vote		Popular Vote	
Bush (Republican)	426	79.2%	48,886,097	53.4%
Dukakis (Democrat)	111	20.8%	41,809,074	45.6%

Czechoslovakia, playwright and populist Vaclav Havel helped orchestrate a "velvet revolution" that resulted in the resignation of the Soviet-installed regime and free elections that carried Havel to the presidency. The most dramatic events were occurring in East Germany. On November 9, the Communist Party announced that residents of East Berlin were free to leave the country, rendering the Berlin Wall, the ultimate symbol of Cold War division, irrelevant. Jubilant Germans hung a banner on the wall—"Stalin Is Dead, Europe lives"—then dismantled the barrier piece by piece.

The revolutionary fervor was not confined to communist regimes in Eastern Europe but soon swept into Soviet Union itself. The Baltic states—Estonia, Latvia, and Lithuania—had lived under Soviet rule since 1939 when Stalin seized control as part of the Nazi–Soviet pact (see page 1014). In December 1989, the Lithuanian Communist Party formally broke ties with the Soviet Union. The following year, Lithuania and Latvia declared their independence. Meanwhile, in March 1989, the Soviet Union had held its first free elections since 1917. Voters turned hundreds of party officials out of office.

All of these changes were too much for party hard-liners in the Soviet hierarchy, who staged a coup in August 1991. With Gorbachev held under house arrest, a defiant Boris Yeltsin, the newly elected chairman of the Russian parliament, rallied protesters and faced down the powerful Russian army. Gorbachev survived the failed coup, but Yeltsin emerged as the most potent force for reform. By the end of the year, Russia proclaimed its independence from Soviet control and, along with Ukraine and Byelorussia (now Belarus), formed the Commonwealth of Independent States. On Christmas Day 1991, a weary Gorbachev resigned as president of the Union of Soviet Socialist Republics that had ceased to exist.

Throughout the year, the United States played the role of a cheering but cautious spectator. Bush and his Secretary of State James A. Baker III, a fellow Texan, watched

Fall of the Berlin Wall A symbolic reminder of the division between East and West Berlin came crashing down in November 1989. As Berliners from both sides of the divide celebrated, people poured freely through the opening for the first time in decades. *(Wide World Photos, Inc.)*

from the sidelines as the startling events in Europe and the Soviet Union unfolded. The United States found itself in an awkward position: since the beginning of the Cold War, it had provided rhetorical support for pro-democracy movements in the Soviet bloc, but at the moment when the democracy movements were succeeding, U.S. leaders offered only tepid praise. The reason? The administration did not want to undermine relations with Gorbachev by appearing to exploit his troubles. Moreover, U.S. policymakers feared instability in the region. Who would control the powerful Soviet nuclear arsenal if the nation fragmented into a number of small, independent republics? "Whatever the course, however long the process took, and whatever its outcome," Bush later reflected, "I wanted to see stable, and above all peaceful, change."

The unraveling of the Soviet Union offered an opportunity to continue the progress in arms control that began in the final years of the Reagan administration. In 1989 Bush announced that it was time to "move beyond containment" by integrating the Soviet Union into "the community of nations." The following year, NATO and the Warsaw Pact (see page 1064) agreed to the biggest weapons cut in history. The accord on conventional forces in Europe slashed Warsaw Pact weapons by more than 50 percent and NATO's by 10 percent. With the Soviet threat diminished, the Pentagon announced the largest U.S. troop cut in Europe since 1948, with an initial pullback of forty thousand personnel. Bush and Gorbachev signed agreements to open trade, expand cultural exchanges, and reduce chemical weapons. The two leaders signed the START I treaty, which cut their strategic nuclear forces in half—an agreement unimaginable just a few years earlier. Two years later, Bush and Yeltsin came to terms on a START II agreement that called for further cuts and for the elimination of deadly multiple warhead (MIRV) intercontinental missiles by the year 2003. The Cold War was over.

The New World Order

President Bush declared that the end of the Cold War heralded a "New World Order" in which the United States was the only superpower, the rule of law must govern relations between nations, and the powerful must protect the weak. In some ways, the optimism seemed justified. In a globe no longer dominated by Cold War confrontations, the prospect for resolving local disputes brightened. In South Africa, U.S.-imposed economic sanctions pressured newly elected president Frederik W. de Klerk to dismantle apartheid, by which whites had dominated the black majority for forty-two years. Along with lifting the government's ban on anti-apartheid organizations, de Klerk freed African National Conference deputy president Nelson Mandela, seventy-one, who was serving the twenty-seventh year of a life prison term. A symbol of resistance to apartheid, Mandela showed that imprisonment had not tempered his commitment to black majority rule. "Power! Power! Africa is ours!" he chanted in his first public appearance following his release. In April 1994, Mandela easily won election as South Africa's first black president.

In Latin America, the end of the Cold War coincided with the demise of a number of authoritarian regimes. In Chile, General Augusto Pinochet, the last military dictator in South America (see page 1186), turned over power to elected President Patricio Aylwin. In Brazil, Fernando Collor de Mello took office as the first directly elected president since a 1964 military coup. In Haiti, a leftist Roman Catholic priest, Father Jean-Bertrand Aristide, swept that nation's first fully free democratic election for president. Elsewhere in Latin America, shaky experiments in democracy showed signs of growing stability. In Nicaragua, newspaper publisher Violeta Barrios de Chamorro defeated Marxist president Daniel Ortega in a peaceful election, ending a decade of leftist Sandinista rule. In El Salvador, the moderate government and opposition leaders signed a peace treaty early in 1992.

With the threat of Soviet influence in the region diminished, the Bush administration focused its attention on international drug sales, which the president referred to as "the gravest domestic threat facing our nation today." Though many nations were implicated in the drug trade, the administration identified Panamanian dictator General Manuel Noriega as the worst outlaw. During the 1980s, American officials ignored Noriega's notorious cocaine trading because he was a CIA informer viewed as an ally in the larger battle to prevent communist infiltration. With that threat removed, American officials decided to move against him, cutting off aid and freezing Panamanian assets in the United States. When Noriega nullified the results of free elections in Panama, Bush urged the Panamanian people to overthrow him. The revolt failed to materialize, and soon after, when soldiers loyal to Noriega killed an American marine, Bush launched Operation Just Cause. On December 20, 1989, more than twenty-two thousand U.S. troops, backed by gunships and fighter planes, invaded Panama in the largest military operation since the Vietnam War. After two days of intense fighting, Noriega's resistance crumbled, and he sought asylum at the Vatican's diplomatic mission in Panama City. On January 3, 1990, he surrendered and was flown to Florida, where he faced trial for drug-related crimes and became the first former or current head of state to be convicted by an American jury.

The end of the Cold War also improved relations in the Middle East. No longer fearing Soviet influence in the region, and less concerned about offending its ally Israel, the United States applied pressure on both Palestinian head Yasir Arafat and Israeli leader Yitzhak Rabin to work toward stability. Secretary Baker engaged in a new round of shuttle diplomacy, traveling to the Mideast eight times in 1991 to arrange negotiations in 1992. After more than a year of secret discussions, Arafat and Rabin traveled to Washington in September 1993 to sign a declaration of principles that allowed for eventual Palestinian self-rule in the Gaza Strip and the West Bank.

Only China seemed to buck the trend toward greater openness in the post–Cold War era. Bush, who had served briefly as ambassador to China under Nixon, came to office confident that he understood the Chinese leadership and could help promote closer economic ties while also encouraging the aging Chinese leadership to enact democratic reforms. His plan suffered a stunning setback in the spring of 1989 when the Chinese army brutally crushed a pro-democracy demonstration in Beijing's Tiananmen Square, killing an estimated four to eight hundred young men and women. A wave of repression, arrests, and public executions followed. The assault, covered extensively by American television, outraged the public and exposed an underlying tension in America's attitude toward the post–Cold War world: Should the United States emphasize its moral leadership by taking action against nations that failed to live up to American standards of human rights, or should it restrict itself to more practical questions of national security?

An unusual coalition of liberals and conservatives wanted the administration to punish China for its repression by imposing economic sanctions and denying it special trading privileges that promoted economic relations. Many business groups warned that sanctions would be counterproductive since they would alienate China and so limit American influence, and allow Europeans to capture the lucrative and expanding Chinese market. Bush waffled on the question. Three days after the massacre, he suspended military sales to China and declared that normal relations could not be established until Chinese leaders "recognize the validity of the pro-democracy movement." Within weeks, however, he sent his national security adviser to China and began a gradual move toward normal relations.

War with Iraq

On August 2, 1990, elite Iraqi army troops smashed across the border of Kuwait and roared down a six-lane superhighway toward Kuwait City eighty miles away. Iraqi leader Saddam Hussein, who had just ended a bloody eight-year war with neighboring Iran, justified the invasion by claiming that Kuwait had been illegally stolen from Iraq by the British in the 1920s. The justification masked a more pressing concern, however. Hussein had nearly bankrupted his country in his war with Iran and now needed Kuwait's huge oil reserves to pay the bills.

President Bush saw the invasion as a direct challenge to U.S. leadership in the post–Cold War world. "This must be reversed," he announced after learning of the attack. His advisers spelled out how the invasion threatened American interests in the region: it would give the unpredictable Hussein control over vast quantities of valuable Kuwaiti oil reserves. Hussein could use the oil revenue to develop nuclear weapons to intimidate American allies in the region, especially Israel and Saudi Arabia. Over the next few months, in an impressive display of international diplomacy, Bush rallied world opinion against "Saddam." The United Nations Security Council passed resolutions to impose economic sanctions against Iraq in an effort to force it out of Kuwait. In November, after Hussein showed no signs of retreat, the Security Council authorized the use of force for the first time since the Korean War, giving Hussein a deadline of January 15, 1991, to pull out of Kuwait or face military action.

While rallying international opinion against Iraq, Bush confronted the difficult task of convincing the American people to go to war to expel Hussein from Kuwait. The administration faced an uphill battle. Polls showed that a majority of Americans opposed intervention; most wanted to continue to rely on economic sanctions

The Gulf War   Beginning with a six-week air war in January 1991, Allied forces attacked targets across Iraq and then sent in ground troops under the leadership of General H. Norman Schwarzkopf. Within three days of the ground assault's commencement, Iraqi soldiers were in full retreat or surrender. The war resulted in the dismembering of the Iraqi army, the liberation of Kuwait and the fleeing of Kurdish refugees toward Turkey and Iran.

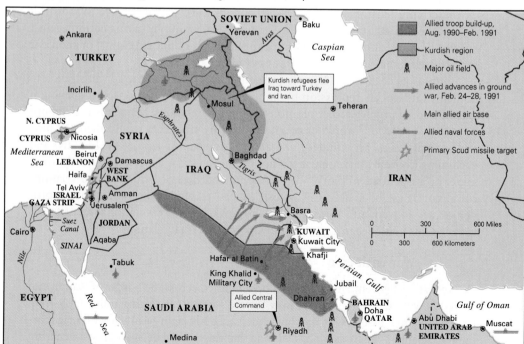

even if they failed to prod the Iraqis out of Kuwait. In January, as the deadline for military action approached, the Senate and the House passed a resolution authorizing the use of military force (see Competing Voices, page 1297). Armed with congressional approval and bolstered by strong international support, the president started the war on January 16 with a massive and sustained air assault. On February 23, the Allies under the command of U.S. General H. Norman Schwarzkopf, launched a ground offensive that forced Iraqi forces out of Kuwait in less than one hundred hours. Only 140 U.S. troops died in the battle, while the Iraqi death toll topped 100,000. On February 27, coalition forces liberated Kuwait and the president called off the attack, leaving a vanquished but defiant Saddam Hussein in power (see map).

Problems on the Home Front

Ironically, Bush's success in the Gulf War may have contributed to his political problems at home, which had begun soon after he took office. With the Cold War over, and with no clear foreign threat to distract them, Americans focused more attention on a stagnant economy. "We did not realize how much we had been leaning on the Berlin Wall until we tore it down," conceded one White House aide. While

Impact of War After Iraq's invasion of Kuwait on August 2, 1990, President Bush deployed more than 400,000 troops to Saudi Arabia in an attempt to force Iraq's withdrawal from its neighbor. Each American soldier sent to the Gulf left behind family and friends, as was the case with Army Specialist Hollie Vallance, seen here saying goodbye to her husband and seven-week-old daughter. (© *Allen Horne, Courtesy of the Columbus Ledger, Columbus, Georgia.*)

the president scored high marks for his adroit handling of the international scene, he never articulated a clear domestic agenda.

After only a few weeks in office, he angered voters and enraged conservatives by disavowing his "no new taxes" pledge. "I've started going into the numbers, finally," Bush said referring to the federal deficit, "and they're enormous." In 1990 Bush agreed to a deficit reduction compromise with Congressional Democrats that included $133 billion in new taxes. Reversing the Reagan era tax policies, the new legislation increased the top bracket from 27 percent to 31 percent, removed some exemptions used by high-income people, and increased "sin taxes" on cigarettes and alcohol. Most observers agreed with the decision to raise taxes, but few were convinced that Bush learned of the need to do so only after the election. The *New York Post*'s front page bellowed the reaction: READ MY LIPS: I LIED.

The deficit package failed to stem the fiscal hemorrhaging. The federal deficit continued its upward spiral to $290 billion in 1992, with forecasters predicting it would rise to $331 billion in 1993. The government was spending $200 billion per year—15 percent of all spending—to pay interest on the debt. The added spending weighed down the rest of the economy, which after seven booming years began to sputter. While the GNP increased at an anemic 2.2 percent, unemployment crept upward, housing starts dropped, and consumer confidence hit new lows. By 1992, Bush's approval rating sagged to 34 percent, with fewer than 20 percent of the public approving his handling of the economy. The public clamored for the president to take decisive action to revive the ailing economy, but Bush and his advisers decided to take a hands-off approach. "I don't think it's the end of the world even if we have a recession," said Treasury Secretary Nicholas Brady. "We'll pull out of it again. No big deal."

Polls showed that Americans wanted more government involvement not only in economic matters but also in issues ranging from education to health care, but the president's hands were tied by the huge budget deficit left over from the Reagan years. Bush did sign one meaningful piece of legislation—the Americans with Disabilities Act (1990), which prohibited discrimination against the 40 million Americans who suffered from mental or physical disabilities.

Bush's handling of environmental issues underscored the difficult task he faced in trying to hold together a political coalition of moderates and conservatives during tough economic times. During the 1988 campaign, Bush broke with Reagan's harsh approach to the environment, promising to be "the environmental president" who would champion tough new regulations to protect clean water and air and preserve public lands. Once in office, however, the president retreated when conservatives within the administration, led by Vice President Quayle, complained that new environmental initiatives would undermine American business competitiveness.

The debate sharpened in March 1989 when the giant oil tanker *Exxon Valdez* ran aground in Prince William Sound, Alaska, spilling 10.8 million gallons of crude oil, spoiling the pristine coastline and killing wildlife. Environmentalists called for an end to Alaskan oil drilling, but Bush disagreed, saying the oil production was essential to meet the nation's energy needs. In the Pacific Northwest, environmentalists clashed with loggers and timber companies over whether to preserve the delicate ecosystems of old-growth forest and their endangered inhabitant—the northern spotted owl. Once again Bush sided with business interests, saying that jobs and profits were a higher priority than preserving the environment. In 1992 the president attended a UN-sponsored "Earth Summit" in Rio de Janeiro, Brazil, but he refused to sign a sweeping but nonbinding resolution that would have pledged the nation's support for biodiversity. Environmentalists achieved a minor victory in 1990 when Bush signed a moderately progressive Clean Air Act, which forced gradual cutbacks on emissions from cars and power plants.

The abortion issue also complicated Bush's delicate political balancing act. In 1989 a divided Supreme Court upheld a Missouri law that restricted abortion (*Webster* v. *Reproductive Health Services*). The law banned public facilities from performing abortions that were not necessary to save the mother's life, and the Court's decision seemed a step toward outlawing all abortions. Justice Harry Blackmun, who had written the original decision in *Roe* v. *Wade* sanctioning abortion, dissented: "The signs are evident and very ominous, and a chill wind blows." The decision, which encouraged other states to pass more restrictions on abortion, enraged many moderate Republicans. Polls showed a widening political gender gap, as many women, including many Republicans, feared that more Republican judicial appointments could tip the Court's balance away from abortion rights. The justices calmed fears somewhat in 1992 when they struck down a Pennsylvania law restricting abortion because the law placed "undue burden" on women. More important, the majority stated they were reluctant to overturn *Roe*, saying the effort would cause "profound and unnecessary damage to the Court's legitimacy, and to the nation's commitment to the rule of law." That 5–4 decision, however, continued to underscore the precarious legal position of abortion rights.

Bush unintentionally widened the gender gap when he replaced the retiring liberal justice Thurgood Marshall, the only African-American on the Court, with Clarence Thomas, a black conservative federal judge who had once served as head of Reagan's Equal Employment Opportunity Commission (EEOC) but was considered an undistinguished jurist. Civil rights and liberal groups howled in protest, but the nomination seemed certain until University of Oklahoma law professor Anita Hill stepped forward to charge that Thomas had sexually harassed her when he was her boss at the EEOC. Thomas denounced the televised Senate confirmation hearings as "a high-tech lynching for uppity blacks who in any way deign to think for themselves." Although many wavering senators believed Hill's testimony and voted against Thomas, his nomination survived by a 52–48 vote—the narrowest margin for a Supreme Court nominee in the twentieth century. But the public debate over Hill's charges raised awareness about sexual harassment in the workplace. The affair also alienated many moderate women who were outraged by the way many senators dismissed and mocked Hill, and angered by the administration's unwavering support for Thomas.

The serious social problems that plagued the nation, and the president's lack of leadership, came into sharp focus when riots tore through Los Angeles in April 1992. The riots commenced after a mostly white jury in a Los Angeles suburb acquitted four white police officers accused of savagely beating an African-American motorist, Rodney King, after stopping him for a traffic violation. The jury arrived at the verdict despite the existence of a videotape showing the officers delivering numerous blows to a seemingly defenseless King. Shortly after the verdicts were announced, African-Americans in South Central Los Angeles erupted in the deadliest urban riot in over a century. By the time it ended three days later, fifty-eight people lay dead, over eight hundred buildings had been destroyed, and thousands more damaged or looted. The president's initial response was to blame the riots on failed liberal social programs from the 1960s. When that explanation failed to convince people or reassure the nation, Bush traveled to the riot area and promised more federal aid. But for many people, the response was too little, too late.

The 1992 Presidential Campaign

Already politically vulnerable because of the struggling economy and sinking job approval, Bush had to fend off a revolt of angry conservatives, who rallied around former Reagan speech writer Patrick Buchanan in the Republican primaries. Politically weaker than in 1988, Bush also faced a more formidable Democratic challenger in Arkansas governor Bill Clinton. Born in 1946 in Hope, Arkansas, Clinton attended Georgetown University and went to Oxford on a Rhodes scholarship before returning to graduate from the Yale law school. In 1978, at the age of thirty-two, he won election as governor of Arkansas. A party moderate, Clinton appealed to fellow baby boomers by casting himself as a "new Democrat" who understood the concerns of the struggling middle class. Campaigning as a cultural conservative, he professed his support for capital punishment and promised to "end welfare as we know it," to make the streets safer and the schools better, and to provide "basic health care to all Americans." For traditional Democrats he offered a message of economic populism, promising to raise taxes on the wealthy and fight to preserve popular social programs.

A charismatic personality and spellbinding speaker, Clinton emerged as the front-runner from a crowded pack of Democratic contenders. The road to the nomination, however, was strewn with questions about marital infidelity and draft dodging. His often evasive and unconvincing answers led to questions about whether Clinton possessed the strength of character to be a good president. The lingering doubts did not prevent him from winning the nomination earlier than any Democrat in more than two decades. At the party's convention in New York City, Clinton underscored the "new Democrat" theme by choosing fellow baby-boom southerner Al Gore, a senator from Tennessee, as his running mate. "There's a little Bubba in both of us," Clinton joked.

The fall race was complicated by the presence of an unpredictable third-party candidate, Texas billionaire Ross Perot. With a down-to-earth manner and a history of remarkable success in business, Perot tapped into public discontent with government and Washington by promising to balance the budget and cut the deficit. His position on most other issues remained a mystery, but by July he was leading both Clinton and Bush in the polls when he abruptly decided to leave the race. He returned just as unexpectedly in October, with only one month left, largely in the role of spoiler.

While Perot was on sabbatical from the campaign, Clinton moved to secure his followers and take the lead in the polls by focusing attention on the economy. He promised to "focus like a laser beam" on economic issues. A sign hanging in his campaign office summed up the Democratic strategy: "It's the economy, stupid." Clinton also proved an effective and unconventional campaigner, chatting with young voters on MTV, taking calls on the popular *Larry King Live* show, and playing the saxophone and discussing public policy with late-night talk show host Arsenio Hall. While Clinton climbed in the polls, Bush floundered. His greatest successes had been in dealing with Iraq and the Russians, but with the Cold War fading out of mind, the public showed little interest in foreign policy and instead directed its anger at the administration for the sluggish economy.

Voters rewarded Clinton on election night, giving him 43 percent of the popular vote, compared with 37.4 percent for Bush. Clinton's margin in the electoral college was far more decisive. He won thirty-one states and 370 electoral votes. The public registered its disenchantment with both parties by giving Perot a bigger share of the vote—18.9 percent—than any third-party candidate since Teddy Roosevelt scored 27.4 percent in 1912. The Democrats retained control of both houses of Congress. Voters sent six women to the Senate and forty-eight to the House of Representatives. Observers triumphantly called 1992 "the year of the woman" (see map).

Clinton Playing His Saxophone   Though a Yale Law School graduate and a Rhodes scholar, presidential nominee Bill Clinton was also a member of the baby boom generation, growing up listening to Elvis Presley and learning to play the saxophone. Working to increase his popularity with younger voters, Clinton appeared on MTV and on the *Arsenio Hall* show, where he sat in with the band for a rendition of "Heartbreak Hotel." *(Wide World Photos, Inc.)*

The Election of 1992

Despite George Bush's victory in Operation Desert Storm, the stagnant economy and his broken pledge not to raise taxes made him vulnerable to attacks by Democrat Bill Clinton who pledged to work for national health care, welfare reform, and a stronger economy. Dissatisfaction with Bush even spilled over into the third party of H. Ross Perot who did not win any electoral votes in November, but who did gain 18.9 percent of the popular vote—the largest third party showing since the Bull Moose Party in 1912.

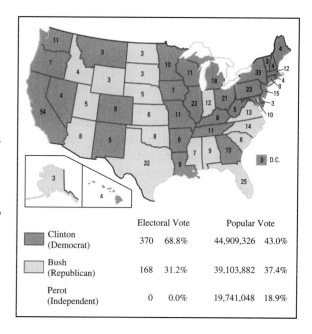

		Electoral Vote		Popular Vote	
■	Clinton (Democrat)	370	68.8%	44,909,326	43.0%
■	Bush (Republican)	168	31.2%	39,103,882	37.4%
■	Perot (Independent)	0	0.0%	19,741,048	18.9%

★ The Clinton Administration, 1992–2000

William Jefferson Clinton, the first president born after World War II, came to office promising to experiment with policies to jump-start the economy and use government power to develop solutions to pressing social problems. Despite a number of legislative victories, he failed to fulfill many of his campaign promises, and Republicans molded public disillusion into a powerful political weapon to gain control of both houses of Congress in the 1994 congressional elections. A chastened Clinton responded by moving to the center, co-opting many Republican themes and trouncing his opponent in the 1996 presidential race. While hoping to focus most of his attention on domestic issues, Clinton faced the difficult task of readjusting American foreign policy for the post–Cold War era. An impeachment trial that grew out of a sordid affair with a White House intern tarnished Clinton's final years in office.

The Clinton Agenda

As the first Democrat to occupy the White House in twelve years, Clinton set a new tone for his administration by calling for "a government that looks like America." True to his word, he appointed a number of women and minorities to top administration posts, including the first woman attorney general, Janet Reno. Ron Brown, an African-American and former head of the Democratic Party, served as secretary of commerce. Reflecting the growing political prominence of Hispanic voters, the president appointed Henry Cisneros, the mayor of San Antonio, Texas, as head of Housing and Urban Development (HUD), and Federico Pena to run the Department of Transportation.

In February, Clinton fulfilled his promise to "focus like a laser beam" on the economy by submitting an ambitious economic plan to Congress calling for a combination of spending cuts and tax increases to reduce the deficit. Both liberals and conservatives took aim at the plan. Liberals objected because it contained only one ambitious new social program—a national service corps by which college students could pay off federal education loans through community work. Conservatives opposed the tax hikes, which raised the top rate from 31 to 36 percent. After months of haggling, most Democrats fell in line with the president's proposal, and it passed the House by a one-vote margin. In an ominous warning of partisan confrontations to come, not a single House Republican voted for the Clinton program. It passed the Senate by a more comfortable margin.

Even before he submitted his economic package to Congress, Clinton created a political firestorm by proposing to lift the long-standing ban on homosexuals in the military. During the campaign Clinton had lobbied aggressively for gay votes, and once in office he moved on a number of fronts to open opportunities for homosexuals. He ended the federal policy of treating gays as security risks and invited gay activists to the White House for the first time. But his proposal to end discrimination in the military infuriated the Pentagon and aroused conservative opposition. Months of acrimonious public debate forced Clinton to retreat and agree to an unworkable "don't ask, don't tell" policy that angered both gay rights groups and conservatives. The debate over gays in the military was a political disaster for the new administration: it distracted public attention from Clinton's economic program and allowed conservatives to typecast the president as a social liberal, while the outcome disillusioned many of Clinton's liberal supporters.

After passage of his economic program, Clinton concentrated his energies on passing a complex health care proposal. In 1993 more than 37 million Americans lacked medical insurance, and millions more feared losing coverage. While coverage remained spotty, costs continued to escalate. From 1980 to 1992, Medicare and Medicaid payments jumped from $48 billion to $196 billion, consuming 14 percent of the federal budget. Shortly after the election, the president asked the First Lady, Hillary Rodham Clinton, an accomplished lawyer with liberal leanings, to set up a health care task force. In October 1993, the administration unveiled its ambitious plan, which would guarantee Americans medical coverage and an array of preventive services. The plan proposed to limit Medicare and Medicaid payments, cap premiums, and foster competition among providers. The proposal, however, was dead on arrival on Capitol Hill, the victim of its own complexity and intense partisan wrangling.

More bad news followed the failure of the health care proposal: Congress asked a special prosecutor to investigate whether the Clintons had been involved in financial wrongdoing stemming from a bad land deal in which they invested in the 1970s. The investigation into the "Whitewater" development venture in northern Arkansas focused on whether the Clintons had received favorable treatment and been forgiven loans after the failure of the project. Around the same time, new reports surfaced that Arkansas state troopers procured women for Clinton when he was governor. Together the questions over the land deal and the reports of womanizing tapped into larger public doubts about the president's character. By 1994, the news media featured more stories on Whitewater than on all facets of Clinton's domestic agenda combined.

Moving to the Center

The failure of the health reform package, controversy over the measure to allow gays in the military, and the drumbeat of charges over Whitewater eroded public support for the Clinton presidency. After two years in office, Clinton had the lowest poll ratings of any president since Watergate. Energized Republicans, led by Georgia firebrand Newt Gingrich of the House, pounced on the helpless Democrats in the 1994 midterm elections. All three hundred Republican congressional candidates signed a ten-point "Contract with America," a political wish list polished by consultants and tested in focus groups, pledging to trim government waste, cap welfare payments, raise military spending, and lower taxes. On election day, Republicans made major gains, seizing control of both houses for the first time in forty years and defeating thirty-five incumbent Democrats. "We got our butts kicked," said the chairman of the Democratic National Committee.

Clinton responded to the Republican triumph by moving to the center, co-opting Republican themes. By acting independently of both Republicans and Democrats, Clinton planned to occupy the high middle ground of American politics. Clinton's adviser Dick Morris called the strategy "triangulation." Clinton's first move was to accept the Republican goal of balancing the budget in ten years or less. "The era of Big Government is over," he announced in Reaganesque language. The president embraced other conservative proposals as well, including a crime bill that aimed at putting a hundred thousand new police on the streets and stipulated mandatory sentences for criminals convicted three times of felonies.

It was welfare reform, though, that was at the center of Clinton's new strategy. True to the terms of their "Contract with America," congressional Republicans passed the Personal Responsibility and Work Opportunity Reconciliation Act. Clinton objected to the original legislation, but later signed a bill that maintained its central features. The 1996 welfare reform bill eliminated the federal guarantee of welfare as an entitlement, replacing it with a program that collapsed nearly forty federal programs, including AFDC, into five block grants to the states, giving the states authority to develop their own plans. The most striking provision of the new bill declared that the head of every family on assistance must work within two years or the family would lose its benefits.

While embracing Republican themes, the president also tried to stigmatize the party's leadership as extremists. Newly elected House Speaker Newt Gingrich played directly into Clinton's hands, misinterpreting the public mood: Americans wanted smaller government and lower taxes, but they did not want popular programs cut. Clinton understood the contradiction and exploited it brilliantly, promising to cut the deficit and protect middle-class social programs. As part of their assault on the "welfare state," Republicans announced plans to cut projected spending on Medicare by $270 billion over five years. Gingrich shocked senior Americans who depended on the program by stating that Medicare should "wither on the vine." At the same time that he was attacking Medicare, Gingrich was pushing a tax cut for the wealthy through Congress. When Clinton vetoed their budget and spending bills, the Republicans refused to pass the customary stopgap measures to keep the government operating. An angry public blamed the Republicans for the shutdown of "nonessential" federal facilities and services.

Winning a Second Term: The 1996 Campaign

By 1996, the president's effort to rebuild public support by usurping Republican issues of welfare reform, crime, and a balanced budget had been remarkably successful. Aided by an expanding economy and declining unemployment, Clinton watched his job approval rating soar to over 60 percent—the highest rating of his presidency. Polls showed that many voters were willing to set aside concerns about Clinton's character in favor of their satisfaction with the humming economy—and their general perception that the country was headed in the right direction.

Republicans chose Kansas senator Robert Dole to challenge Clinton in the 1996 presidential contest. Dole, a seventy-three-year-old veteran of World War II and the oldest man ever to seek the presidency, failed to excite voters. In an effort to reach out to younger voters, he chose former Buffalo Bills quarterback and ex-congressman Jack Kemp as his running mate. When all else failed, Dole tried to exploit the "character" issue in the final weeks of the campaign. Nothing seemed to work.

On election day, Clinton became the first Democrat since Franklin Roosevelt to win a second term as president. Victories in thirty states and the District of Columbia gave him 379 electoral votes, 19 more than he had won in 1992. Dole and Jack Kemp carried fourteen states, primarily in the Deep South and the mountain states of the West, with a combined 159 electoral votes. Ross Perot, the Texas billionaire who ran on the ticket of the Reform Party, finished a distant third, drawing roughly half of the 18.9 percent he had won in 1992. "They have affirmed our cause and told us to go forward," Clinton said of the voters. But the election hardly represented a clear mandate. Clinton failed to produce coattails for other Democrats as the Republicans retained control of the House and gained a few seats in the Senate.

The New Internationalism

As the first president elected after the end of the Cold War, Clinton faced a variety of new and complex questions. As the only remaining superpower, what relationship should the United States have to the rest of the world? What were America's vital interests, the ones for which the country would send troops to fight and die? What was the best way for policymakers to assert military strength overseas? How should the United States protect its economy from global influences, including its jobs, trade, and commercial interests abroad?

For all of its peril, the Cold War had provided policymakers with a framework, though often a narrow one, for interpreting world events and for calculating the national interest. The United States had a grand concept—containment—to guide its approach to the world. The Clinton administration did not attempt to articulate a new framework for U.S. foreign policy in the post–Cold War era. A piecemeal approach seemed appropriate both to Clinton, who hoped the end of the Cold War would allow him to devote most of his attention to domestic issues, and to Secretary of State Warren Christopher, a detail-oriented lawyer who distrusted grand schemes and preferred to examine problems in isolation.

Without an overarching strategy to guide it, the administration appeared to lurch from one international crisis to another. The first occurred in the Horn of Africa, the northeast region of the continent, where many nations—Ethiopia, Sudan, and Somalia—had been suffering from drought, famine, and intermittent civil war. The situation grew grave in 1992 as fighting among rival factions threatened to cut off relief supplies to Somalia, leaving millions to starve. Pushed to respond by public reaction to television pictures of emaciated children, Bush had ordered nearly thirty thousand troops to Somalia on a humanitarian mission to restore order and secure relief efforts. Initially, Operation Restore Hope succeeded, but before long the rival clans tired of the U.S. presence and began putting up resistance.

Clinton inherited a complex problem. The U.S. troops could not guarantee the flow of supplies without fighting the clans, but engaging the rival factions risked getting bogged down in a quagmire. Without seeking approval from Congress, Clinton left nearly nine thousand troops in Somalia and expanded their mission to include taking on the local clans. In October 1993, eighteen U.S. Army Rangers died in a bloody firefight with a gang of Somalis. Clinton quickly retreated, withdrawing the remaining American forces. "Gosh, I miss the Cold War," Clinton remarked after learning that American soldiers had been killed.

The administration used the threat of military force more successfully closer to home in Haiti. In 1991 a band of military leaders overthrew the elected leader, Jean-Bertrand Aristide. The Clinton administration organized an international effort to restore Aristide, applying diplomatic pressure and convincing the United Nations to impose economic sanctions. The military regime showed no interest in giving up power voluntarily until Clinton decided to flex his military muscle, threatening to use the marines to expel the junta. With American warships looming off the coast, Haiti's military leaders backed down and allowed Aristide to return to power.

While uncertain about the use of military force in the post–Cold war era, the Clinton administration made economic policy a centerpiece of its approach to the world. The president described the United States as "a big corporation competing in the global marketplace." In 1994 Clinton fought a tough legislative battle to win congressional approval of the North American Free Trade Agreement (NAFTA) negotiated during the Bush presidency. The agreement gradually abolished nearly all trade barriers between the United States, Mexico, and Canada. Opponents, led by organized labor, feared the agreement would mean the loss of high-paying jobs in the United States as businesses moved to take advantage of cheap labor in Mexico. "The sucking sound you hear is all the jobs heading south of the border," declared vanquished presidential candidate Ross Perot. Clinton argued the contrary, contending the legislation would increase prosperity for all three countries and diminish the flow of illegal immigrants from Mexico. Later that year, Clinton won another key free trade battle when the administration convinced Congress to approve the General Agreement on Tariffs and Trade (GATT), which allowed the United

States to participate in a new worldwide trade agreement that would reduce tariffs over ten years. "We have put our economic competitiveness at the heart of our foreign policy," Clinton boasted in his 1994 budget message.

While fighting for free trade in the hemisphere, the administration fought to open new markets to American goods. The president created a new agency—the National Economic Council—to coordinate domestic and foreign economic policies. In 1994 the United States made its peace with Vietnam by lifting its trade embargo and normalizing relations. American companies, which had been barred from doing business in Southeast Asia, rushed into the country. Emphasizing the importance of China as a trading partner, Clinton approved China's most-favored-nation status, which gave it the same privileges as America's closest allies, despite that nation's continued crackdown on dissent.

Russia remained a major worry for the administration. The transition from communism to capitalism left the Russian economy in shambles. A collapse in its domestic market would send shock waves around the world. To help prop up the Russian economy, the administration developed a $4.5 billion aid package to facilitate reform efforts and sustain Russia's currency, the ruble. At the same time, the administration worked closely with Russian counterparts to reduce stockpiles of nuclear weapons. The issue was especially urgent now that control of the nuclear weapons had shifted from Moscow to local commanders in the various republics. In 1994 the United States signed the U.S.-Russian-Ukraine Trilateral Statement and Annex, which led to the destruction of all nuclear weapons in Ukraine. Later that month, Yeltsin and Clinton agreed to "detarget" U.S. and Russian strategic missiles—programming them all to land in the ocean. Of course, they could be reprogrammed in minutes, but the agreement represented an important psychological milestone. There were also fewer missiles to launch, thanks to the successful implementation of the START I and II treaties negotiated by the Bush administration.

Trouble Spots: Iraq and Yugoslavia

The end of the Cold War accelerated Yugoslavia's splintering into rival ethnic factions. For most of the Cold War era, the strong leadership of Josip Broz Tito managed to balance the unstable coalition of Catholic Croatians, Eastern Orthodox Serbs, and Muslims that made up the Yugoslav nation. Tito's death in 1980, combined with the dissolution of the Soviet Union and the wave of independence fever that swept through Eastern Europe, shattered the peace. In 1991 Yugoslavia's provinces of Slovenia, Croatia, and Bosnia-Herzegovina proclaimed their independence. The move infuriated the Serb-dominated federal government in Belgrade, headed by President Slobodan Milosevic. Determined to create a "Greater Serbia," Milosevic launched military attacks against Croats and Muslims living in areas dominated by ethnic Serbs. In Bosnia-Herzegovina, Serbs shelled the capital of Sarajevo and murdered, raped, and imprisoned Muslims in a vicious campaign of "ethnic cleansing." By the end of 1992, more than 150,000 people had died.

The war produced confusion in Washington. Torn between a humanitarian desire to help and a public fearful of intervention, the administration waffled. The situation took a dramatic turn in February 1994 when a mortar shell exploded in Sarajevo's open market, killing 68 people and injuring more than 200. A few days later, the president delivered an ultimatum to the Serbs: either pull back all tanks and artillery from a 12.4-mile free zone around the city or risk assault from members of the North Atlantic Treaty Organization (NATO). Later that month, NATO planes shot down Serb jets that violated the no-fly zone. It was the first time in the alliance's history that NATO planes had seen combat. The exercise of force brought all the parties to the negotiating table in 1995. Under heavy pressure from the United States, the presidents of Bosnia, Croatia, and Serbia signed a peace agreement that solved territorial differences and brought an end to hostilities. As part of the agreement, Clinton committed American troops to Bosnia as part of a multinational force to keep the peace.

Boxed in by NATO troops in Bosnia, Milosevic turned his war machine against the province of Kosovo, where ethnic Albanians were struggling for independence. When Serb troops embarked on another campaign of "ethnic cleansing" in Kosovo, NATO tried to negotiate a peaceful settlement. The Albanian Kosovars reluctantly accepted the terms of an agreement that gave them political autonomy within Serbia. But the Serbs remained defiant, refusing to sign the treaty and stepping up their campaign against innocent civilians. In March 1999, the United States and the NATO allies decided to use force to challenge the Serbs. In May, after eighty days of intense bombardment that decimated his army and destroyed his country's fragile infrastructure, Milosevic relented to NATO demands and withdrew his forces from Kosovo.

In attempting to define American national interests in the post–Cold War world, the Clinton administration was forced to revisit the lingering threat posed by Saddam Hussein. Following the tyrant's crushing defeat at the hands of the Allies, the Bush administration assumed that opposition forces would mobilize to overthrow Hussein. Instead, the cagey leader emerged from defeat as powerful as ever, crushing potential adversaries, threatening to destabilize the region, and playing a game of cat and mouse with UN inspectors assigned to root out his secret stockpiles of chemical and nuclear weapons. When Hussein made threatening moves toward Kuwait in 1994, the Clinton administration deployed 54,000 troops and more warplanes to the Gulf. Two years later, U.S. air units struck Iraqi missile targets when Iraqi troops intensified their anti-insurgent operations in the northern part of the country.

As Hussein grew more intransigent, the U.S. position hardened. The change reflected the more hawkish views of Secretary of State Madeline Albright, who took over from the retiring Warren Christopher in 1997. The first woman to serve as the nation's top diplomat, Albright possessed a different generational mindset than the baby-boomer Clinton. Born a diplomat's daughter in Prague, Czechoslovakia, in 1937, she fled Nazi occupation with her family and spent most of World War II living in London. "Some people's historical context is Vietnam; mine is Munich," she told reporters. "For me, America truly is the indispensable nation." For Albright, Hussein seemed the reincarnation of Hitler, and she was determined not to go down the failed path of appeasement. When Hussein refused to cooperate with weapons inspectors, Albright urged the president to take dramatic action. In December 1998, the United States and Britain launched the largest bombardment of

Iraq since the end of the Gulf War, unleashing cruise missiles as well as fighters and bombers. The U.S. military declared the attack a success, but Hussein remained in power and unintimidated.

Impeachment

At the same time that he was attacking Iraq, Clinton was fighting another battle at home to keep his job as president. The year-long drama that led up to the trial in January 1999 and consumed much of the nation's attention centered on an affair between Clinton and former White House intern Monica Lewinsky. When charges surfaced, a defiant president denied having had sexual relations with "that woman." After he made the same denials in a civil case, and to a grand jury, Kenneth Starr, the special prosecutor in the case, recommended that the president be impeached and removed from office for "high crimes and misdemeanors." To support his conclusion, he delivered a steamy report to the House detailing the affair and offering eleven potential grounds for impeachment.

Clinton's attorneys raised a number of objections to the whole proceeding. Having an affair with an intern and then lying about it was wrong, they contended, but it did not rise to the level of an impeachable offense. Unlike Richard Nixon's actions in Watergate, Clinton's behavior did not represent a threat to the institutions of government. Moreover, they charged, the issue was being pushed by a highly partisan special prosecutor who seemed driven to destroy the president. House Republicans, however, were determined to press forward. After weeks of public hearings, the Judiciary Committee voted to send formal charges to the House, which in turn approved two counts—perjury and obstruction of justice—and sent them on to the Senate for trial.

In 1999 the Senate rang in the New Year by putting the president on trial. Over the next few weeks, the senators listened to often repetitive charges and countercharges by the House prosecutors, also called managers, and the White House defense team. The thirteen prosecutors, all Republicans, had to convince 67 of 100 Senators both

Lewinsky Affair After Clinton's confession of "a relationship with Ms. Lewinsky that was not appropriate" the House Judiciary Committee began its investigation of the affair. Meanwhile, the scandal set off a media frenzy as the affair became the most visible topic on news shows, the Internet, and in political cartoons. *(By permission of Mike Luckovich and Creators Syndicate.)*

that the president's offenses were criminal and that they merited his removal from office. Bill Clinton had "violated the rule of law and thereby broken his covenant with the American people," declared Henry Hyde, the chief prosecutor. When the final votes were counted, the Senate failed to muster a majority on either count and fell far short of the constitutionally mandated two-thirds needed to convict the president.

In the end, everyone came out of the affair with tarnished reputations. The president enjoyed high job approval ratings throughout the investigation, but the public gave him low marks for honesty and integrity. The GOP's pugnaciously partisan pursuit of impeachment backfired. In the 1998 congressional elections, the party not holding the White House lost seats in the House for only the second time in the century. The angry recriminations that followed led to the resignation of Republican Speaker Newt Gingrich. Republicans also appeared hypocritical when reports showed that some who condemned Clinton's behavior had checkered pasts of their own. Louisiana's Robert Livingston, for example, a harsh critic of the president's behavior whom Republicans chose to succeed Gingrich as House Speaker, resigned his seat after confessing that he had "on occasion strayed from my marriage."

 ## The New Prosperity, 1992–2000

The public supported Clinton throughout the impeachment process because it credited him for the remarkable prosperity that characterized the decade. By the mid-1990s, the widespread use of personal computers, and the rise of the World Wide Web, formed the foundation of a new social and economic experiment, as the communications revolution promised to transform American business and leisure. The *Economist* magazine asserted that the Web represents "a change even more far-reaching than the harnessing of electrical power a century ago." The information society propelled the economy to new heights as high-tech firms produced a surge on Wall Street. Ironically, the experiment in high-tech prosperity did not herald a new age of leisure: in fact, most Americans were working longer hours just to maintain their standards of living. The new prosperity did, however, fill government coffers with added tax revenues, allowing both Washington and many states to balance their budgets after years of operating in the red.

The Information Society

Scientists launched the first phase of the computer revolution in 1946 when they turned the switch to start up the mammoth Electronic Numerical Integrator And Calculator (ENIAC). The mainframe computer weighed 30 tons, filled an enormous room at the University of Pennsylvania, consumed 150,000 watts of power, and used 18,000 vacuum tubes. The machine required so much power it was rumored that when the scientists turned it on, the lights in the city of Philadelphia dimmed. Over the next twenty years, business adopted mainframe computers to handle basic tasks such as automating payroll, billing, and inventory controls.

In the 1970s, a diverse collection of tinkerers working in garages in California's San Francisco bay area were responsible for the second phase of the computing revolution—the birth of the personal computer (PC). In 1971 a small Silicon valley company called Intel created the first microprocessor, an integrated circuit that put the power of a mainframe on a single chip. The microchip was to the modern information economy what the combustion engine was to the earlier industrialization of society. In 1977 a young entrepreneur, Steve Wozniak, used the chip to assemble the first Apple I computer in his garage. His invention would become the prototype of every desktop machine.

The shift from the mainframe to the PC during the 1980s was made possible by tremendous advances in technology. For example, Intel built its Pentium microprocessor on a piece of silicon the size of a thumbnail. The overall effect of two decades of steady increases in the capacity of microprocessors was to drive down prices and put tremendous computing power in the hands of the average citizen. With a PC, individuals could enhance and speed up their performance of personal and business tasks using word processors, spreadsheets, and personal databases. In 1983 *Time* magazine, instead of naming its usual "Man of the Year," named the computer the "Machine of the Year." By the mid-1990s, more than 90 percent of all businesses in the United States relied on the personal computer for essential functions. More than one-third of families had a PC at home. In 1995, for the first time, the amount of money spent on PCs exceeded that spent on televisions.

The third phase of the computer revolution began with the birth of the Internet. Founded in the late 1960s by Defense Department scientists trying to develop a decentralized communications system that could survive a nuclear war, the Internet created a set of standards, or protocols, that enabled thousands of independent computer networks to communicate. The real explosion in Internet use took place during the early 1990s with the development of the World Wide Web, whereby almost any user with a telephone line and a modem could log on to a worldwide computer communications network. By 1999, between 40 and 60 million people worldwide were using the Internet annually, and those numbers were doubling almost every year.

The Internet empowered individuals by putting vast amounts of unfiltered information at their fingertips. In medicine, patients used the Internet to find out about new treatments, breaking the monopoly that physicians once had on medical information. In business, the sharing of electronic documents gave lower-level employees access to information previously the purview of managers. Investors could bypass stockbrokers and plan retirement benefits on-line. By allowing people to communicate effortlessly across thousands of miles, the Internet gave rise to the "virtual corporation," in which employees and managers were located in different places.

For millions of Americans, the Web helped break down cultural and geographic borders by creating virtual communities of shared interests. America Online, the largest Internet provider in the United States, saw its membership soar to over 10 million by 1999. More than three-quarters of its subscribers used anonymous chat rooms to meet people who share similar interests. People from all over the globe joined together in virtual town halls to discuss issues of mutual interest. Teenagers in San Diego could discuss music with peers in Boston and Washington; a senior citizen in Texas mourning the death of a loved one could commiserate with widows and widowers in Florida; an AIDS patient in San Francisco could share treatment ideas with doctors in New York.

"Wiring" the Classroom   The computer revolution changed how Americans did almost everything, including learn. College classrooms became "interactive," often linked to other classrooms—not to mention libraries, museums, and countless other resources—across the country and around the world. In this cyber-lecture hall, Stanford students recline on beanbag chairs with their own laptop computers while a professor guides them on a projected computer screen. (*William Mercer McLeod.*)

The technology also promised to reconfigure the consumer society, providing buyers with new options and increased power. Although mail-order catalogs had existed since the nineteenth century, a local merchant had the advantage of being the only store within driving range. Now with the Web, cyberstores were only seconds away and open for business twenty-four hours a day. "The Internet is nothing less than a revolution in commerce," gloated *Business Week*. Buyers could compare prices and products on-line. New virtual stores such as Amazon.com grabbed a foothold in the book market by allowing customers to order books from the privacy of their homes. Three years after its launch, Amazon.com had 2.25 million worldwide customers and sales that reached $350 million in 1999.

E-mail emerged as the most visible and commonly used feature of the new information society. By 1999, Americans sent 2.2 billion messages a day, compared with 293 million pieces of first-class mail. Nearly every college and university in the country provided some form of e-mail access for its faculty, staff, and students. Between 70 and 80 percent of university faculty used e-mail to communicate with their colleagues. E-mail changed the workplace, allowing employees to conduct business from the road and from home.

The information revolution raised new questions and forced Americans to confront old problems. How should government balance the right to free speech on the Web with parents' interest in limiting their children's exposure to indecent material? Religious and conservative groups pressured Congress to pass legislation that would limit access to the Web by banning indecent material. Libertarian and civil liberty groups opposed any effort to limit the free flow of information. In 1996 Congress passed, and the president signed, the Communications Decency Act, which criminalized on-line communications that were "obscene, lewd, lascivious, filthy or indecent, with intent to annoy, abuse, threaten or harass another person." The Supreme Court ruled the law an unconstitutional infringement of freedom of speech, but Congress responded by passing a less restrictive law, the Child Online Protection Act. The new legislation required all commercial Web sites—even those not in the pornography business—to use special services to protect children from material deemed "harmful to minors."

Many people also worried that the nation's reliance on computers would produce "technological segregation," aggravating the gap between the educational haves and have-nots. Households with incomes of $75,000 or above were twenty times more likely to use the Internet than those with incomes of $20,000 or less. The higher-income households were nine times more likely to own a computer. Whites were 39 percent more likely than African-Americans to have access to the Internet; 43 percent more likely than Hispanics. "The digital divide is real, it is growing, and it is very divisive to the progress of the country," warned an observer.

Wall Street Boom and the Politics of Prosperity

The surge in computer-related industry helped revive the U.S. economy during the 1990s. By the end of the decade, the gross domestic product (GDP), discounted for inflation, was growing at an annual rate of 4 percent, and unemployment had fallen to a quarter-century low of 4.7 percent. The output of goods or services per hour of work (known as productivity) had risen 2 percent, well above its historically slow annual growth trend of 1 percent since the early 1970s. All the while, inflation had fallen to less than 2 percent (see graphs).

The information revolution was the cornerstone of the new prosperity, accounting for 45 percent of industrial growth. From 1987 to 1994, the U.S. software industry grew 117 percent in real terms, while the rest of the economy grew only 17 percent. By the end of the decade, computer companies based in and around the Silicon Valley possessed a market value of $450 billion. By comparison, the auto companies and suppliers of Detroit—the cornerstone of America's previous industrial revolution—were worth about $100 billion. The U.S. software industry accounted for three-fourths of the world market, and nine of the world's ten biggest software companies were located in the United States.

The nation watched as a new generation of computer moguls made millions from new inventions and rising stock prices. When *Forbes* magazine put together its

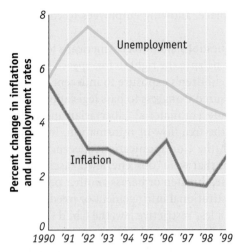

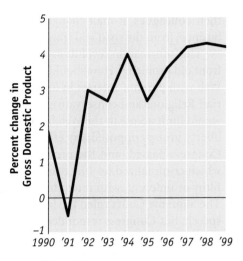

The Economic Boom of the 1990s

During the 1990s, Americans enjoyed the longest sustained period of economic growth since the end of the Second World War. Inflation remained steady, unemployment declined, and the Gross Domestic Product rose. Beginning in 1998, the government also had a rosier economic outlook as the federal budget managed a surplus. (Sources: *New York Times,* "News of the Week in Review," May 3, 1998, Copyright © 1998 by the New York Times Co. Reprinted by permission. Bureau of Labor Statistics; *Statistical Abstract of the United States, 1999; Economic Report of the President, 1999;* Bureau of Economic Analysis; Budget of the United States, 2001.)

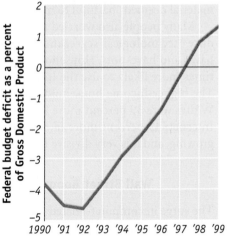

list of the four hundred richest Americans in 1990, Microsoft chief executive Bill Gates was worth $2.5 billion. By 1998, he was worth $58 billion. Much of his wealth was produced by the soaring price of Microsoft stock, which rose 38,000 percent between 1986 and 1998. By the end of the decade, high-tech industry captains held most of the places on *Fortune*'s list of wealthiest people. Of the first five, only one had not made his fortune in a computer-related field.

Wall Street was the most visible sign of the new prosperity. Between 1992 and 1998, the Dow Jones Industrial Average increased fourfold. The New York and NASDAQ stock exchanges added over $4 trillion in value—the largest single accumulation of wealth in history. With the tide rising rapidly for more than a decade, stock assets accounted for a larger share of household wealth than ever before: 24.2 percent in mid-1998. Much of the growth came about because of the creation of mutual funds—large investment groups that buy shares in a variety of stocks and bonds to limit risk. In 1980 only 6 percent of U.S. households had mutual funds accounts for stocks or bonds. By 1997, the share had leaped to 37 percent, with a colossal pool of capital approaching $5 trillion. Most of the money for mutual funds came from special retirement funds—401(k) accounts—that allowed workers to have their contributions matched by employers. By 1998, more than 25 million workers had $1 trillion invested in their 401(k) accounts.

By 1998, the combination of a healthy, growing economy, fiscal restraint, and the end of the Cold War had solved the budget crisis that had plagued Washington since the early Reagan years. In 1992 the annual deficit soared to $290 billion, an all-time high, leading politicians of both parties to warn that the United States was destined to leave its children a mountain of debt. By 1998, the federal government reported a $70 billion surplus for fiscal 1998—the first in three decades—and projected a $4.4 trillion surplus over the next fifteen years.

Most of the states, which had been financially strapped for the previous two decades, also benefited from the healthy economy. California, home of many thriving high-tech companies, projected a $4.4 billion surplus by 2000. A handful of other states—New York, Indiana, Alaska, Minnesota, North Carolina, and New Jersey—were operating more than $1 billion in the black. Unlike Washington, where spending decisions were marked by partisan wrangling, most states started spending the surpluses for tax and debt relief, education funding, infrastructure upgrades, health care, programs for children, and other projects. Education was the big winner, with average appropriations nationwide up more than 7 percent, nearly double the average rate of states' budget increases.

The 2000 Presidential Election

Prosperity provided the backdrop to the first presidential election of the new millennium. The Democrats rallied around Vice President Al Gore, who promised to sustain the Clinton-era economic growth. In August, at the party's convention in Los Angeles, Gore launched his "prosperity and progress" campaign, promising increased federal spending on health care, social security, and education. Striking a populist pose, Gore promised middle-class taxpayers that he would fight for "the people" and against "the powerful" special interests. Walking a political tightrope, Gore clung to Clinton's success while distancing himself from the president's scandals. "I stand here tonight as my own man," he told cheering delegates. As his running mate, Gore selected Joseph Lieberman, a centrist senator from Connecticut, who became the first Jewish-American nominated by a major party.

Republican leaders, eager to win back the White House, threw their support and money behind Texas Governor George W. Bush, the oldest son of the former president. After stumbling in the primaries against Vietnam War hero Senator John McCain, Bush regained his footing and captured his party's nomination. With federal coffers overflowing with revenue, Bush promised the nation "prosperity with a purpose." Calling for a "compassionate conservatism," the Republican nominee solidified his conservative base by advocating a massive tax cut while at the same time reaching out to independents with pledges to fund increased social spending for education and health care. Above all, he vowed to return honor and dignity to the White House. Ahead in the polls, and confident of victory, Bush chose the uncharismatic former defense secretary Richard Cheney as his running mate.

Bush watched his once sizeable lead in the polls evaporate through the summer and fall. For the final two months of the campaign, the two contestants remained locked in a tight race. Bush hammered away at the vice president's integrity, while Gore raised questions about Bush's stature and experience. Three presidential debates in October did little to break the logjam. Voters found Gore more knowledgeable on issues, but they felt that Bush appeared more relaxed and personable. While Gore and Bush battled each other, consumer advocate Ralph Nader, running on the Green Party platform, mocked both candidates. Nader relished the role of spoiler, threatening to siphon enough votes in key states—California, Michigan, Oregon, and Washington—to deny Gore a victory.

On election night, Gore clung to a small margin in the popular vote, but with Florida and its crucial twenty-five electoral votes too close to call, the election remained deadlocked. After a series of counts and recounts, Florida's secretary of state certified Bush the winner on November 27—more than two weeks after the election. But the campaign did not end there: Gore contested the results, claiming that many ballots remained uncounted or improperly counted, effectively disenfranchising thousands of voters. Republicans accused Gore of trying to steal the election; Democrats attacked the Republicans for thwarting the "will of the people." The nation braced for a constitutional crisis. On December 12, after weeks of legal maneuvering, a deeply divided Supreme Court ended the historic impasse. In a controversial 5–4 ruling in the case of *Bush* v. *Gore,* the justices blocked further manual recounts, which effectively named George Bush the winner. Bush became only the fourth president, and the first since 1888, to take office having lost the popular vote.

The election revealed that unprecedented prosperity had failed to mute deep social divisions in America. The public remained deeply troubled by the election outcome, the winner lacked a clear mandate, the Senate split 50–50, and Republicans held only a razor-thin majority in the House. Included among the new class of senators was New York's Hillary Rodham Clinton, who became the only first lady in history to seek and win elective office. Analysis of voting results revealed a deeply divided nation. By region, Democrats did well in urban areas; Republicans won majorities in suburban and rural areas. By race, African-Americans gave 95 percent of their votes to Gore; whites preferred Bush. By gender, women favored Democrats; men leaned toward the Republicans. Finally, by religion, regular churchgoers voted Republican; the less religious supported the Democrats.

An Age of Leisure?

Many scholars once predicted that computerization would mean more leisure for workers, since machines would be able to perform much of the work needed to fuel the economy. Instead, the computer revolution seduced Americans into working longer hours. According to some estimates, the average American in the 1990s was working 164 more hours per year than in 1970—the equivalent of an additional month. One reason for the expanded hours was that technology virtually erased the boundaries between work and leisure, allowing employers to expect workers to be accessible and productive any hour, any day.

A more compelling reason was that many people worked extra jobs to sustain their earning power. In 1979, 4.9 percent of U.S. workers reported working more than one job during the same workweek. By 1995, the percentage was up to 6.4 percent. Virtually all of this increase occurred among women, who represented nearly half of all multiple jobholders. In many families, both husband and wife were working full-time for wages. From 1969 to 1996, the proportion of married women with full-time paying jobs who had children rose from 17 to 39 percent. In households with no children, it soared from 42 to 60 percent.

Though American families were working more hours, they were not experiencing a significant increase in living standard. "To the extent that the typical American family has been able to hold its ground, the most important factor has been the large increase in the hours worked by family members," a major study of U.S. work patterns concluded in 1999. "Were it not for the extra hours of work provided by working wives, the average income of these families would have fallen in the 1990s."

Nevertheless, many people benefited from the booming economy. The poor did not get poorer in the 1990s. Their family incomes rose slightly, the number below the poverty rate fell slightly, and the average pay for low-wage jobs increased. Minorities, especially African-Americans, experienced real economic gains. In 1989, 30.8 percent of blacks qualified as poor. By 1997, 26.5 percent did. Moreover, incomes for African-American households jumped 16.8 percent, or $3,600, between 1992 and 1999—nearly three times more than incomes for the nation as a whole.

Yet while the poor were advancing by inches, the well-to-do were bounding ahead. In 1990 a corporate CEO earned 85 times as much as the average factory worker; in 1997 he or she made 324 times more. The information society's demand for educated high-tech workers contributed to the income gap. The new technology placed greater demand on people who worked with their heads, not their hands. The government classified six of every ten jobs created in the 1990s as managerial, professional, or technical. Most of the new job growth took place in industries that employed a large number of college graduates such as finance, engineering, data processing, consulting, and education. In 1990 college graduates earned 52 percent more than high school graduates; in 1997, 62 percent more.

The transition to an information economy created considerable instability in the job marketplace. The 1990s witnessed an increase in the number of workers who, although still earning, had been displaced from their former jobs. At a time of low unemployment, almost 30 percent of those employed were not in regular full-time jobs. Many worked as day laborers, held temporary jobs, or acted as independent contractors. The share of workers employed by agencies that supply temporary workers doubled between 1989 and 1997. The vast majority of these workers were married women. One estimate for 1995 placed the total number of contingent workers (part-time, temporary, and contract workers) at close to 35 million—28 percent of the civilian labor force. Despite low interest rates and strong job growth, the number of individuals filing for bankruptcy reached 1.3 million in 1998, up an astonishing 93 percent during the decade. Especially among low-income households, the desire for new consumer products outpaced income, encouraged by credit card companies that begged people to use their cards.

Social Tensions in the Nineties

The seemingly endless media coverage of the president's affair with Monica Lewinsky highlighted an important development during the decade: the explosion in the number of new media outlets. In the ravenously competitive environment, television executives often turned to sex and violence to attract audiences. The strategy raised considerable controversy, but it also sold—both at home and around the world. Few stories gripped the nation more than the sensational murder trial of former football great O. J. Simpson. His trial, and the reaction to it, underscored the deep racial division in America. While Americans worried about terrorism from abroad, the most deadly terrorists were home grown, reflecting a disturbing growth in the number of antigovernment militia groups in the nation. Americans seemed gripped by a contagion of conspiracy during the decade—much of it spread by popular culture.

Sex, Violence, and the Debate over Popular Culture

"Our culture is in warp speed," observed a media critic. "We live on novelty, with new forms, new subversions generated daily." Television led the way. The three major networks, which accounted for 90 percent of prime-time viewing in the 1970s, watched their audience share dip to 47 percent in 1998. By that time, more than 75 percent of U.S households received dozens of channels via cable or satellite dishes. The technology allowed new networks—FOX, CNN, Warner Brothers—to compete with the majors for prime-time ratings.

The scramble for viewers encouraged the networks to experiment with different themes and ideas. Comedian Ellen DeGeneres's sitcom *Ellen* featured an episode in which its central character, a lesbian, "came out" of the closet. By the end of the decade more than a half-dozen prime time shows featured gay characters, though usually in less prominent roles. Television also attempted to tackle controversial social issues, from spousal abuse to teen pregnancy. Issues featured on the evening news one week turned up the next as plots in drama series such as *NYPD Blue, The West Wing* and *The Practice.*

The most common competitive approach, however, was to lure in viewers with sex and violence. One study found that a sexual act or reference occurred every four minutes on average during prime time. Daytime television was dominated by racy talk shows on which guests openly described their sex lives and twisted family feuds. A study by the American Psychological Association concluded that the typical child, watching twenty-seven hours of TV a week, would see 8,000 murders and 100,000 acts of violence from age three to age twelve.

Many Americans reacted in horror, arguing that mass culture was responsible for producing a generation of "selfish, dishonest, sexually promiscuous, and violent" children. A 1996 poll showed two-thirds of the public believed TV shows contributed to such social problems as violence, divorce, teen pregnancy, and the decline of family values. In 1996 Congress responded to the pressure by passing the Telecommunications Reform Act. Primarily aimed at deregulation of TV, cable, and telephone services, the act required that manufacturers install parental control devices, called V-chips, into all new model televisions. Major distributors, including

Wal-Mart and Blockbuster Video, exercised their own form of censorship, refusing to stock materials they considered indecent.

A rash of school shootings in 1998 and 1999 intensified the public debate over violence on television. The most deadly attack took place in April 1999 at Columbine High School in Littleton, Colorado. During the final week of classes, two disgruntled and heavily armed students killed twelve classmates and a popular teacher, and planted thirty pipe bombs and other explosives, before taking their own lives. Polls showed that a majority of Americans held Hollywood and television executives "at least partially" to blame for the killings, claiming that they helped create a culture that made violence acceptable. Many people also found fault with the nation's lax gun laws, which allowed young people easy access to such a lethal arsenal.

Parents also worried about the appeal of new musical styles, especially hip-hop, among the young. Created by black artists on the mean streets of New York and Los Angeles, hip-hop used repetitive samples of other musical tracks as background for the rhythmic poetry of rap singers. Early rap artists dealt with issues of the urban underclass. Taking an assertively activist tone, Ice Cube attacked white racism; Ice-T sang about a cop killer; Public Enemy challenged listeners to "fight the power." By the end of the decade, however, hip-hop had gone mainstream. In 1998 rap surpassed country music as the nation's top selling format. "Hip-hop is the rebellious voice of the youth," boasted rapper Jay-Z. "It's what people want to hear."

American culture may have been controversial but it sold, both at home and around the world. During the 1990s, popular culture emerged as America's biggest export. By 1996, international sales of software and entertainment products totaled $60.2 billion, more than any other industry. The explosion in sales was spurred by the collapse of the iron curtain, rising prosperity, and the proliferation of TV sets, VCRs, stereos, personal computers, and satellite dishes. American corporations moved aggressively to tap into the new markets. The Blockbuster Video chain opened 2,000 outlets in 26 foreign countries during the decade; Tower Records operated 70 stores in 15 countries.

Race and American Justice

On June 12, 1994, police discovered the slain bodies of Nicole Brown Simpson and a friend, Ronald Goldman, at her posh Beverly Hills home. Simpson was the estranged wife of former star football player O. J. Simpson, who emerged as a prime suspect in the case. When police tried to arrest him, Simpson fled in a white Bronco in the most public police chase in history. While helicopters hovered above, broadcasting the chase into the homes of 75 million Americans, a phalanx of police cars followed Simpson as he meandered along the L.A. freeway system before finally surrendering to officials.

The ensuing televised trial, which lasted nine months, transfixed the public, breathing new life into struggling cable news shows and tabloid newspapers desperate to attract an audience. "Everyone loves a good murder," said an *Esquire* writer about what was billed as the "Trial of the Century." The prosecutors charged that Simpson murdered Nicole and Goldman, who had dropped by unexpectedly, in a jealous rage. Painting Simpson as obsessed with Nicole and prone to violence, they walked the jury through a trail of DNA evidence that they contended led directly to

Simpson. African-American defense attorney Johnnie Cochran responded by arguing that the DNA evidence was contaminated and that Simpson was framed by a racist policeman, Mark Furman. In his closing argument, Cochran played the "race card," exhorting jurors to "do the right thing" and set Simpson free as a message to the world against racism and police misconduct.

Most experts found the evidence against Simpson overwhelming. The jury of nine blacks, two whites, and one Hispanic, disagreed. After only a few hours of deliberation, they delivered a verdict of not guilty on all counts. Polls showed that blacks and whites looked at the case through race-tinted glasses. By large majorities, African-Americans believed in Simpson's innocence, convinced that the American justice system intentionally discriminated against minorities and that rogue cops such as Mark Furman often tilted the hand of justice. Their distrust of the police was so intense that even blacks who felt Simpson was guilty believed that much of the evidence was tainted. "They framed a guilty man," observed one writer. Nearly 75 percent of whites found the DNA evidence convincing, rejected the suggestion that race played a role in the investigation and prosecution, and assumed Simpson's guilt. Perhaps the American system of justice was the final victim of the trial. Blacks and whites seemed to agree on one thing: there was a different justice for those who have money and those who do not.

The racial divide exposed by the Simpson case revealed itself in the continuing controversy over affirmative action. In November 1996, California voters, by a 54–46 percent margin, passed Proposition 209, a ballot initiative that banned any preference based on race and sex in determining college admissions, contracting, and employment by the state. Men overwhelmingly supported the initiative (61 to 39 percent) while women disapproved (52 to 48 percent). Blacks and Latinos opposed it in large numbers. The ban on affirmative action had a dramatic impact on minority admissions to colleges and universities in the state. In 1998 the University of California at Berkeley reported a 57 percent drop in the number of black applicants and a 40 percent decline in the number of Hispanic high school seniors who had been accepted for admission. The University of California at Los Angeles (UCLA) experienced a 43 percent decline in admissions for African-American students and 33 percent for Hispanic-Americans.

Terrorism American Style

In the aftermath of the Gulf War, many American officials worried that Iraq would attempt to retaliate by slipping chemical or biological weapons into the United States. In 1990 the CIA warned that Iraq could use "special forces, civilian-government agents or foreign terrorists to hand-deliver biological or chemical agents clandestinely." Preparing for the possibility, Congress passed the Defense Against Weapons of Mass Destruction Act (1996), which aided local governments in planning for a possible attack. The army and marine corps created special task forces to respond to germ or gas threats, and many cities organized drills to train emergency relief workers.

While the nation braced for a possible biological or chemical attack, international terrorists used more traditional methods in their campaign of fear. In February 1993, five people died and more than one thousand were injured when a bomb exploded in New York City's World Trade Center. Federal agents traced the bombing to a group of radical Muslims in New York. The same group, it turned out, planned to blow up New York landmarks, including the UN headquarters and the George Washington Bridge. American targets outside the United States also found themselves vulnerable to attack. In 1996 a truck bomb exploded next to a military barracks in Saudi Arabia, killing nineteen U.S. servicemen. Two years later, simultaneous bombs exploded in a crowded street in Nairobi, Kenya, and 450 miles away in front of the U.S. embassy in Tanzania. The chief suspect in these bombings was an extremist Saudi millionaire, Osama bin Laden, who called on Muslims to declare war against Americans. The bombs, said *Newsweek*, offered a dramatic but simple message: "Don't forget the world's superpower still has enemies, secret, violent and determined."

Not all the terrorists were foreign extremists: alienated Americans were among the most violent and determined foes. On April 19, 1995, Gulf War veteran Timothy McVeigh parked a rented Ryder truck packed with a mixture of ammonium nitrate and fuel oil in front of the Alfred P. Murrah Federal Building in Oklahoma City. At 9:02 A.M. the bomb exploded, and the blue-orange fireball ripped through the building, collapsing all nine floors on the building's north face. The blast killed 168 people, including 19 children. The first reaction of many Americans was to blame overseas terrorists, but the worst act of domestic terrorism in American

Oklahoma City Memorial   Five years after the worst act of terrorism on American soil, the Oklahoma City Memorial was dedicated on the spot of the disaster April 19, 2000. The memorial includes a reflecting pool, a tree that survived the blast, and a museum dedicated to understanding terrorism. The most moving scene is that of the 168 empty chairs, each inscribed with the name of a victim.   *(Steve Liss/Time/Timepix.)*

history was home grown. Prosecutors in the case disclosed that McVeigh was motivated by a paranoid hatred of the U.S. government.

According to some sources, the number of militia and patriot organizations increased by 6 percent during the decade to 858 identifiable groups, including 380 that were armed with semiautomatic weapons. Although not all the groups practiced violence, most shared some variation of the view that a sinister cabal of Jews and environmentalists seek world domination, usually under the auspices of the United Nations.

Militia groups were but one manifestation of a larger culture of conspiracy. Surveys showed more than three-quarters of Americans believed President Kennedy was the victim of a massive conspiracy, not a crazed and lone gunman as a government investigation showed. Filmmaker Oliver Stone popularized the conspiracy theory in his blockbuster movie *JFK,* which speculated that Lyndon Johnson and the military backed the assassination. One of the most popular television shows of the decade, *The X-Files,* tapped into the popular fascination with imagined conspiracies. The show featured two FBI agents struggling to disentangle a vast government conspiracy involving alien/human hybridization. "The truth is out there," flashes on the screen at the beginning of each episode.

Why the proliferation of conspiracy theories? Intense public mistrust of government and the media played a role. Real conspiracies in connection with Vietnam, Watergate, and Iran-contra did little to boost public confidence and provided cynics with ample evidence that Washington was capable of deceit. The explosion in Internet use, coupled with the fragmenting of mass culture, produced an environment in which anyone could manipulate facts with no accountability to distinguish between reasoned argument and outrageous opinion. The Internet also provided virtual communities where people could find mutual support for theories about the death of Vincent Foster, the purported UN takeover of America, or other conspiratorial threats. In the end, conspiracy theories abounded because they offered simplistic and coherent explanations for complex and often incoherent events.

CONCLUSION

In 1988 George Bush won the presidency by promising to continue Reagan's conservative experiment. Following the break-up of the Soviet Union, however, Bush confronted a very different world—both at home and abroad. The public applauded the president's handling of the Gulf War, the first major foreign policy crisis of the post–Cold war era. But Bush failed to appreciate that with the nation's mortal enemy gone, Americans' interest had shifted toward solving problems closer to home. With the economy sputtering, voters in 1992 ignored Bush's foreign policy success and elected his Democratic opponent, Bill Clinton, who promised to focus like a "laser beam" on rejuvenating the economy.

Clinton came to office with high hopes and amid even higher expectations—expectations he was unable to fulfill. When Republicans scored major gains in the 1994 congressional races, capturing both houses of Congress, Clinton moved to the center, co-opting conservative themes at the same time that he demonized the Republican congressional leadership. The tactic worked: with his poll ratings rising,

Clinton scored a resounding victory against Robert Dole in the 1996 presidential campaign. Clinton may have found a successful political formula at home, but his administration struggled to develop a framework for defining and defending American global interests in the post–Cold War world. While emphasizing the importance of global trade, Clinton flexed American military muscle in Iraq, Bosnia, and Kosovo. His experiment in developing a coherent approach to the world was undermined by a highly publicized impeachment and trial that raised troubling questions about the president's character and judgment.

A buoyant economy helped keep the Clinton presidency afloat during the impeachment ordeal. A technological revolution spurred the economy to new heights during the decade. The widespread use of the World Wide Web not only served as a boon to business and consumers, it created a new generation of moguls and ignited a bull market on Wall Street. Though the new prosperity did little to address the growing gap between rich and poor, it did provide enough tax revenue to allow both federal and state governments to balance their books and pay for new social programs.

During the 1990s, Americans participated in vocal and often angry debates about public morality and race relations. The vigorous competition between the major television networks and new cable upstarts led many television executives to use sex and violence to lure viewers. The move outraged conservatives and worried parents who blamed popular culture for a variety of contemporary social problems. All television cameras were focused on the trial of African-American football hero O. J. Simpson. The public's reaction to the trial and the continuing controversy over affirmative action revealed that Americans were deeply divided about race. The decade also witnessed the emergence of a number of militia groups, which took public cynicism about government an added step by advocating the violent overthrow of the federal government.

The American experiment will confront fresh challenges and new opportunities in the twenty-first century. How will the end of the Cold War and the emergence of the global economy impact the nation's approach to the world? Will popular attitudes toward government prove capable of reconciling the demands for greater services with the traditional fear of federal power? What will it mean to be an "American" in the next century? How will society adjust to the influence of its diverse population while maintaining its sense of common identity? The answers to those questions may prove elusive, but Americans will continue their search for a better society. "The idea of the search is what holds us together," noted the historian Daniel Boorstin. "The quest is the enduring American experiment. The meaning is in the seeking."

SUGGESTED READINGS

Arthur M. Schlesinger, Jr.'s *The Disuniting of America* (1991) is a good discussion about the conflicts and tensions of 1990s American society. Robert Bellah et al. discuss the continuing presence of a national culture through the 1990s in *The Good Society* (1991). Currently, the best sources for discussion about trends in American culture and politics are periodicals—which are a useful and timely source of commentary for any period. See, for example, *The Atlantic Monthly, Business Week, Congressional Quarterly, The Economist* (London), *Fortune, Harper's Magazine, Monthly Labor Review, The New Republic, National Review, The Nation,*

The New Leader, New York Times Magazine, The Progressive, U.S. News and World Report, and *The Utne Reader.*

Bruce Buchanan's *Renewing Presidential Politics* (1996) covers the 1988 campaign. Penn Kimball's *Keep Hope Alive!* (1992) studies Jesse Jackson's Democratic challenge. Paul Taylor's *See How They Run* (1990) discusses the negative television ads of the campaign.

Extensive material has been published on the end of the Cold War. Don Oberdorfer's *From the Cold War to a New Era* (1998) is a noteworthy introduction. Thomas G. Patterson's *On Every Front* (1992) details the American response to events in Russia. Francis Fukuyama's *The End of History and the Last Man* (1992) is an early and influential discussion of the post–Cold War world. Robert Tucker and David C. Hendricksen's *The Imperial Temptation* (1992) studies the emerging debates in American foreign policy after the Cold War.

Triumph Without Victory (1992), published by *U.S. News and World Report,* is the best early history of Operation Desert Storm. Stephen R. Graubard's *Mr. Bush's War* (1992) discusses the behavior of the media during the war. Martin Yant's *Desert Mirage* (1991) is a sharply critical history of the war. Alberto Bin's *Desert Storm: A Forgotten War* (1998) discusses the dubious legacy of the conflict.

Arlene S. Skolnick's *Embattled Paradise* (1991) discusses the recession and budget crisis. Michael Meeropol's *Surrender* (1998) recounts how George Bush, and Bill Clinton after him, struggled to balance the budget. Patricia Albjerg-Graham's *SOS: Sustain Our Schools* (1992) studies the crisis in education. Alex Kotlowitz's *There Are No Children Here* (1991) is a searing depiction of urban poverty and violence in the 1990s. Roger Rosenblatt's *Life Itself* (1992) covers the abortion debate. Susan Faludi describes the growing gender gap in *Backlash* (1991).

John Hohenberg's *The Bill Clinton Story* (1994) details the 1992 Democratic campaign. Elizabeth Cook et al.'s *The Year of the Woman* (1994) studies the myths and realities about the 1992 election.

Among the several character studies of Bill Clinton, David Maraniss's *First in His Class* (1996) is the leading biography. Charles F. Allen's *The Comeback Kid* (1992) and Jim Moore's *Clinton: Young Man in a Hurry* (1992) both detail Clinton's political career.

Bob Woodward's *Agenda* (1994) is a detailed study of Clinton's first years in office. Gregory M. Herek's *Out in Force* (1996) chronicles the debate over homosexuals in the military. Jim McDougal's *Arkansas Mischief* (1998) explores the real estate dealings and partisan wrangling that led to the Whitewater scandal.

James A. Thurber's *Remaking Congress* (1995) covers the 1994 congressional elections. Newt Gingrich's *Contract with America* (1994) outlines the ambitions of the "Republican Revolution."

Michael Williams's *A History of Computing Technology* (1997) describes the development of the modern computer. In *The Politics of Cyberspace* (1997), Chris Toulouse and Timothy W. Luke explore the emerging information age. Thomas L. Friedman's *The Lexus and the Olive Tree* (1999) discusses the impact of globalization on American society. Juliet B. Schor's *The Overworked American* (1993) and *The Overspent American* (1998) both study the shrinking leisure time of Americans in the 1990s.

Popular culture in the 1990s has been exhaustively studied in popular books, though often without much historical perspective. Neal Gabler's *Life: The Movie* (1999) contains an excellent analysis of how entertainment has infiltrated and conquered reality. Lawrence M. Friedman's *The Horizontal Society* (1999) explores the democratization of modern popular culture. Richard J. Herrnstein and Charles Murray's *The Bell Curve* (1996), though still hotly debated, is emblematic of the debate over affirmative action. Richard Abanes's *American Militias: Rebellion, Racism & Religion* (1996) and Philip Lamy's *Millennium Rage* (1996) are both good introductions to the antigovernment groups of the 1990s.

Competing Voices

Congress Debates War or Peace

Voices in Favor of War with Iraq

In January 1991, President George Bush asked both the House and the Senate to approve a resolution authorizing the use of military force to drive Iraqi troops from Kuwait. The authorization, which amounted to a vote for war, divided the nation and Congress. During three days of debate, most Republicans, and a few Democrats, rose in support of the president's policy.

(Representative Robert H. Michel, R- Illinois) I speak from the prejudice of being a combat veteran of World War II. And those of our generation know from bloody experience that unchecked aggression against a small nation is a prelude to an international disaster.

Saddam Hussein today has more planes and tanks and, frankly, men under arms, than Hitler had at the time when Prime Minister Chamberlain came back from Munich with that miserable piece of paper—peace in our time. I'll never forget that replay of that movie in my life.

And I have an obligation, I guess, coming from that generation, to transmit those thoughts I had at the time to the younger generation who didn't experience what we did. Saddam Hussein not only invaded Kuwait, he occupied, terrorized, murdered civilians, systematically looted and turned a peaceful nation into a wasteland of horror. He seeks control over one of the world's vital resources, and he ultimately seeks to make himself the unchallenged anti-Western dictator of the Mideast.

Either we stop him now, and stop him permanently, or we won't stop him at all.

(Senator Orrin G. Hatch, R-Utah) Unless Saddam Hussein believes that the threat of war is real, he will not budge. I think we've learned that. The only way to avoid war, in my opinion in this particular situation, is to be prepared to go to war and to show that our resolve is for real. . . . Our actions should be decisive.

(Senator William V. Roth Jr., R-Delaware) One can only imagine what devastating consequence would fall should his dominance be allowed in the oil-rich Middle East. And this is the second reason why he must be stopped. When I speak of the danger that would result from his control of this region, I'm not talking about consequences to major oil companies—quite simply, I'm talking about jobs. I'm talking about the raw material of human endeavor.

Oil runs the economy of the world. It fuels our factories, heats our homes. Carries our products from manufacture to market. It's as basic to the economy as water is to life. And the free trade of international supplies is critical, not only for the industrial democracies, but the fragile third world nations that depend on this precious resource even more than we do.

Any attempt to disrupt these supplies will send a devastating quake to these economies, lengthening unemployment lines, boosting inflation in the industrial democracies and crushing the economies of developing countries where day to day existence depends on imported energy sources. ∎

Voices in Dissent

Leading Democrats opposed the authorization to use force, claiming that the United States should give economic sanctions more time to force Hussein to comply with the United Nations mandate to leave Kuwait.

(Senator George J. Mitchell, D-Maine) This is not a debate about whether force should ever be used. No one proposes to rule out the use of force; we cannot and should not rule it out. The question is should war be truly a last resort when all other means fail or should we start with war, before other means have been fully and fairly exhausted.

This is not a debate about American objectives in the current crisis. There is broad agreement in the Senate that Iraq must fully and unconditionally withdraw its forces from Kuwait. The issue is how best to achieve that goal. Most Americans and most members of Congress, myself included, supported the President's initial decision to deploy American forces to Saudi Arabia to deter further Iraqi aggression. We supported the President's effort in marshaling international diplomatic pressure and the most comprehensive embargo in history against Iraq.

Despite the fact that his own policy of international economic sanctions was having a significant effect upon the Iraqi economy, the President, without explanation, abandoned that approach and instead adopted a policy based first and foremost upon the use of American military force. As a result, this country has been placed on a course toward war. This has upset the balance of the President's initial policy, the balance between resources and responsibility, between interest and risk, between patience and strength. ∎

(Senator Paul D. Wellstone, D-Minnesota) I never thought that the first time I would have an opportunity to speak in this chamber the topic would be such a grave topic—life and death, whether or not to go to war, to ask America's men and women, so many of them so young, to risk life and limb, to unleash a tremendous destructive power on a foreign country and a far away people. This is the most momentous decision that any political leader would ever have to make and decide we must.

And let no one doubt that the Congress has the responsibility to make this decision. The Constitution is unambiguous on this point: Congress declares the war, not the President.

The policies that I am afraid the Administration is pursuing, the rush to war that I am afraid is so much of what is now happening in our country and the world, will not create a new order, Mr. President, it will create a new world disorder. What kind of victory will it be? What kind of victory will it be if we unleash forces of fanaticism in the Middle East and a chronically unstable region becomes even more unstable further jeopardizing Israel's security?

Some causes are worth fighting for, some causes are worth fighting for. This cause is not worth fighting for right now. We must stay the course with economic sanctions, continue the pressure, continue the squeeze, move forward on the diplomatic front and Mr. President, we must not, we must not rush to war. ∎

▌▌▌ *(Senator Edward M. Kennedy, D-Massachusetts)* I urge the Senate to vote for peace, not war. Now is not the time for war. I reject the argument that says Congress must support the President, right or wrong. We have our own responsibility to do what is right, and I believe that war today is wrong.

War is not the only option left to us in the Persian Gulf.... Sanctions and diplomacy may still achieve our objectives, and Congress has the responsibility to insure that all peaceful options are exhausted before resort to war....

Let there be no mistake about the cost of war. We have arrayed an impressive international coalition against Iraq, but when the bullets start flying, 90 percent of the casualties will be Americans. It is hardly a surprise that so many other nations are willing to fight to the last American to achieve the goals of the United Nations. It is not their sons and daughters who will do the dying....

Not a single American life should be sacrificed in a war for the price of oil. Not a single drop of American blood should be spilled because American automobiles burn too many drops of oil a mile; not a single American soldier should lose his life in the Persian Gulf because America has no energy policy worthy of the name to reduce our dependence on foreign oil. ▮

On January 12, 1991, Congress approved the resolution authorizing force in the Persian Gulf. Strong lobbying from the administration and a unified Republican Party pushed the resolution through the Senate by a narrow 52-to-47 margin, and by a more comfortable 250-to-183 margin in the House. A reporter noted that the votes "capped three days of the most intense, solemn and emotional debate seen in the Capitol in many years." The roll call marked the tenth time in history that Congress had supported sending American troops into battle. The president hailed the vote, claiming that it "unmistakably demonstrates the United States' commitment to the international demand for a complete and unconditional withdrawal of Iraq from Kuwait. This clear expression of the Congress represents the last, best chance for peace."

Despite their reservations about the war, Americans instinctively rallied around the troops once the fighting began. Unlike during coverage of Vietnam, Americans saw virtually no blood or death on their television screens. The Pentagon had imposed tough new restrictions on the press covering the war, forcing reporters to travel with escorts and exercising control over all reports from the Gulf. The victory produced an outpouring of patriotism and renewed faith in the military and its leaders that had been tarnished since Vietnam. It made heroes of military leaders, especially Norman Schwarzkopf and Colin Powell, the first African-American to serve as chairman of the Joint Chiefs of Staff. "By God, we've licked the Vietnam syndrome once and for all," Bush told a national television audience. The president reaped much of the credit for the operation. His approval rating shot to 89 percent—the highest ever recorded for a president.

Questions for Analysis

1. Why did supporters of the president's policy believe sanctions would not work?
2. What national interest did they believe was at stake in the Persian Gulf?
3. What arguments did opponents use to urge the Senate to reject the resolution?
4. How did different perceptions of national interest shape the debate over the use of force against Iraq?
5. How would you have voted?

Documents

Declaration of Independence in Congress, July 4, 1776

When, in the course of human events, it becomes necessary for one people to dissolve the political bonds which have connected them with another, and to assume, among the powers of the earth, the separate and equal station to which the laws of nature and of nature's God entitle them, a decent respect to the opinions of mankind requires that they should declare the causes which impel them to the separation.

We hold these truths to be self-evident: That all men are created equal; that they are endowed by their Creator with certain unalienable rights; that among these are life, liberty, and the pursuit of happiness; that, to secure these rights, governments are instituted among men, deriving their just powers from the consent of the governed; that whenever any form of government becomes destructive of these ends, it is the right of the people to alter or to abolish it, and to institute new government, laying its foundation on such principles, and organizing its powers in such form, as to them shall seem most likely to effect their safety and happiness. Prudence, indeed, will dictate that governments long established should not be changed for light and transient causes; and accordingly all experience hath shown that mankind are more disposed to suffer, while evils are sufferable, than to right themselves by abolishing the forms to which they are accustomed. But when a long train of abuses and usurpations, pursuing invariably the same object, evinces a design to reduce them under absolute despotism, it is their right, it is their duty, to throw off such government, and to provide new guards for their future security. Such has been the patient sufferance of these colonies; and such is now the necessity which constrains them to alter their former systems of government. The history of the present King of Great Britain is a history of repeated injuries and usurpations, all having in direct object the establishment of an absolute tyranny over these states. To prove this, let facts be submitted to a candid world.

He has refused his assent to laws, the most wholesome and necessary for the public good.

He has forbidden his governors to pass laws of immediate and pressing importance, unless suspended in their operation till his assent should be obtained; and, when so suspended, he has utterly neglected to attend to them.

He has refused to pass other laws for the accommodation of large districts of people, unless those people would relinquish the right of representation in the legislature, a right inestimable to them, and formidable to tyrants only.

He has called together legislative bodies at places unusual, uncomfortable, and distant from the depository of their public records, for the sole purpose of fatiguing them into compliance with his measures.

He has dissolved representative houses repeatedly, for opposing, with manly firmness, his invasions on the rights of the people.

He has refused for a long time, after such dissolutions, to cause others to be elected; whereby the legislative powers, incapable of annihilation, have returned to the people at large for their exercise; the state remaining, in the mean time, exposed to all the dangers of invasions from without and convulsions within.

He has endeavored to prevent the population of these states; for that purpose obstructing the laws for naturalization of foreigners; refusing to pass others to encourage their migration hither, and raising the conditions of new appropriations of lands.

He has obstructed the administration of justice, by refusing his assent to laws for establishing judiciary powers.

He has made judges dependent on his will alone, for the tenure of their offices, and the amount and payment of their salaries.

He has erected a multitude of new offices, and sent hither swarms of officers to harass our people and eat out their substance.

He has kept among us, in times of peace, standing armies, without the consent of our legislatures.

He has affected to render the military independent of, and superior to, the civil power.

He has combined with others to subject us to a jurisdiction foreign to our constitution, and unacknowledged by our laws, giving his assent to their acts of pretended legislation:

For quartering large bodies of armed troops among us;

For protecting them, by a mock trial, from punishment for any murders which they should commit on the inhabitants of these states;

For cutting off our trade with all parts of the world;

For imposing taxes on us without our consent;

For depriving us, in many cases, of the benefits of trial by jury;

For transporting us beyond seas, to be tried for pretended offenses;

For abolishing the free system of English laws in a neighboring province, establishing therein an arbitrary government, and enlarging its boundaries, so as to render it at once an example and fit instrument for introducing the same absolute rule into these colonies;

For taking away our charters, abolishing our most valuable laws, and altering fundamentally the forms of our governments;

For suspending our own legislatures, and declaring themselves invested with power to legislate for us in all cases whatsoever.

He has abdicated government here, by declaring us out of his protection and waging war against us.

He has plundered our seas, ravaged our coasts, burned our towns, and destroyed the lives of our people.

He is at this time transporting large armies of foreign mercenaries to complete the works of death, desolation, and tyranny already begun with circumstances of cruelty and perfidy scarcely paralleled in the most barbarous ages, and totally unworthy the head of a civilized nation.

He has constrained our fellow-citizens, taken captive on the high seas, to bear arms against their country, to become the executioners of their friends and brethren, or to fall themselves by their hands.

He has excited domestic insurrection among us, and has endeavored to bring on the inhabitants of our frontiers the merciless Indian savages, whose known rule of warfare is an undistinguished destruction of all ages, sexes, and conditions.

In every stage of these oppressions we have petitioned for redress in the most humble terms; our repeated petitions have been answered only by repeated injury. A prince, whose character is thus marked by every act which may define a tyrant, is unfit to be the ruler of a free people.

Nor have we been wanting in our attentions to our British brethren. We have warned them, from time to time, of attempts by their legislature to extend an unwarrantable jurisdiction over us. We have reminded them of the circumstances of our emigration and settlement here. We have appealed to their native justice and magnanimity; and we have conjured them, by the ties of our common kindred, to disavow these usurpations, which would inevitably interrupt our connections and correspondence. They, too, have been deaf to the voice of justice and of consanguinity. We must, therefore, acquiesce in the necessity which denounces our separation, and hold them, as we hold the rest of mankind, enemies in war, in peace friends.

We, therefore, the representatives of the United States of America, in General Congress assembled, appealing to the Supreme Judge of the world for the rectitude of our intentions, do, in the name and by the authority of the good people of these colonies, solemnly publish and declare, that these United Colonies are, and of right ought to be, FREE AND INDEPENDENT STATES; that they are absolved from all allegiance to the British crown, and that all political connection between them and the state of Great Britain is, and ought to be, totally dissolved; and that, as free and independent states, they have full power to levy war, conclude peace, contract alliances, establish commerce, and do all other acts and things which independent states may of right do. And for the support of this declaration, with a firm reliance on the protection of Divine Providence, we mutually pledge to each other our lives, our fortunes, and our sacred honor.

Articles of Confederation

(The text of the Articles of Confederation can be found at http://college.hmco.com.)

Constitution of the United States of America and Amendments[*]

Preamble

We the people of the United States, in order to form a more perfect union, establish justice, insure domestic tranquillity, provide for the common defense, promote the general welfare, and secure the blessings of liberty to ourselves and our posterity, do ordain and establish this Constitution for the United States of America.

Article I

Section 1   All legislative powers herein granted shall be vested in a Congress of the United States, which shall consist of a Senate and a House of Representatives.

Section 2   The House of Representatives shall be composed of members chosen every second year by the people of the several States, and the electors in each State shall have the qualifications requisite for electors of the most numerous branch of the State Legislature.

No person shall be a Representative who shall not have attained to the age of twenty-five years, and been seven years a citizen of the United States, and who shall not, when elected, be an inhabitant of that State in which he shall be chosen.

Representatives and direct taxes shall be apportioned among the several States which may be included within this Union, according to their respective numbers, *which shall be determined by adding to the whole number of free persons, including those bound to service for a term of years and excluding Indians not taxed, three-fifths of all other persons.* The actual enumeration shall be made within three years after the first meeting of the Congress of the United States,

---

[*] Passages no longer in effect are printed in italic type.

and within every subsequent term of ten years, in such manner as they shall by law direct. The number of Representatives shall not exceed one for every thirty thousand, but each State shall have at least one Representative; *and until such enumeration shall be made, the State of New Hampshire shall be entitled to choose three, Massachusetts eight, Rhode Island and Providence Plantations one, Connecticut five, New York six, New Jersey four, Pennsylvania eight, Delaware one, Maryland six, Virginia ten, North Carolina five, South Carolina five, and Georgia three.*

When vacancies happen in the representation from any State, the Executive authority thereof shall issue writs of election to fill such vacancies.

The House of Representatives shall choose their Speaker and other officers; and shall have the sole power of impeachment.

Section 3   The Senate of the United States shall be composed of two Senators from each State, *chosen by the legislature thereof,* for six years; and each Senator shall have one vote.

Immediately after they shall be assembled in consequence of the first election, they shall be divided as equally as may be into three classes. The seats of the Senators of the first class shall be vacated at the expiration of the second year, of the second class at the expiration of the fourth year, and of the third class at the expiration of the sixth year, so that one-third may be chosen every second year; *and if vacancies happen by resignation or otherwise, during the recess of the legislature of any State, the Executive thereof may make temporary appointments until the next meeting of the legislature, which shall then fill such vacancies.*

No person shall be a Senator who shall not have attained to the age of thirty years, and been nine years a citizen of the United States, and who shall not, when elected, be an inhabitant of that State for which he shall be chosen.

The Vice-President of the United States shall be President of the Senate, but shall have no vote, unless they be equally divided.

The Senate shall choose their other officers, and also a President *pro tempore,* in the absence of the Vice-President, or when he shall exercise the office of President of the United States.

The Senate shall have the sole power to try all impeachments. When sitting for that purpose, they shall be on oath or affirmation. When the President of the United States is tried, the Chief Justice shall preside: and no person shall be convicted without the concurrence of two-thirds of the members present.

Judgment in cases of impeachment shall not extend further than to removal from the office, and disqualification to hold and enjoy any office of honor, trust or profit under the United States: but the party convicted shall nevertheless be liable and subject to indictment, trial, judgment and punishment, according to law.

Section 4   The times, places and manner of holding elections for Senators and Representatives shall be prescribed in each State by the legislature thereof; but the Congress may at any time by law make or alter such regulations, except as to the places of choosing Senators.

The Congress shall assemble at least once in every year, and such meeting *shall be on the first Monday in December, unless they shall by law appoint a different day.*

Section 5   Each house shall be the judge of the elections, returns and qualifications of its own members, and a majority of each shall constitute a quorum to do business; but a smaller number may adjourn from day to day, and may be authorized to compel the attendance of absent members, in such manner, and under such penalties, as each house may provide.

Each house may determine the rules of its proceedings, punish its members for disorderly behavior, and with the concurrence of two-thirds, expel a member.

Each house shall keep a journal of its proceedings, and from time to time publish the same, excepting such parts as may in their judgment require secrecy; and the yeas and nays of the members of either house on any question shall, at the desire of one-fifth of those present, be entered on the journal.

Neither house, during the session of Congress, shall, without the consent of the other, adjourn for more than three days, nor to any other place than that in which the two houses shall be sitting.

Section 6   The Senators and Representatives shall receive a compensation for their services, to be ascertained by law and paid out of the treasury of the United States. They shall in all cases except treason, felony and breach of the peace, be privileged from arrest during their attendance at the session of their respective houses, and in going to and returning from the same; and for any speech or debate in either house, they shall not be questioned in any other place.

No Senator or Representative shall, during the time for which he was elected, be appointed to any civil office under the authority of the United States, which shall have been created, or the emoluments whereof shall have been increased, during such time; and no person holding any office under the United States shall be a member of either house during his continuance in office.

Section 7   All bills for raising revenue shall originate in the House of Representatives; but the Senate may propose or concur with amendments as on other bills.

Every bill which shall have passed the House of Representatives and the Senate, shall, before it become a law, be presented to the President of the United States; if he approve he shall sign it, but if not he shall return it with objections to that house in which it originated, who shall enter the objections at large on their journal, and proceed to reconsider it. If after such reconsideration two-thirds of that house shall agree to pass the bill, it shall be sent, together with the objections, to the other house, by which it shall likewise be reconsidered, and, if approved by two-thirds of that house, it shall become a law. But in all such cases the votes of both houses shall be determined by yeas and nays, and the names of the persons voting for and against the bill shall be entered on the journal of each house respectively. If any bill shall not be returned by the President within ten days (Sundays excepted) after it shall have been presented to him, the same shall be a law, in like manner as if he had signed it, unless the Congress by their adjournment prevent its return, in which case it shall not be a law.

Every order, resolution, or vote to which the concurrence of the Senate and House of Representatives may be necessary (except on a question of adjournment) shall be presented to the President of the United States; and before the same shall take effect, shall be approved by him, or being disapproved by him, shall be repassed by two-thirds of the Senate and House of Representatives, according to the rules and limitations prescribed in the case of a bill.

Section 8   The Congress shall have power

To lay and collect taxes, duties, imposts, and excises, to pay the debts and provide for the common defense and general welfare of the United States; but all duties, imposts and excises shall be uniform throughout the United States;

To borrow money on the credit of the United States;

To regulate commerce with foreign nations, and among the several States, and with the Indian tribes;

To establish an uniform rule of naturalization, and uniform laws on the subject of bankruptcies throughout the United States;

To coin money, regulate the value thereof, and of foreign coin, and fix the standard of weights and measures;

To provide for the punishment of counterfeiting the securities and current coin of the United States;

To establish post offices and post roads;

To promote the progress of science and useful arts by securing for limited times to authors and inventors the exclusive right to their respective writings and discoveries;

To constitute tribunals inferior to the Supreme Court;

To define and punish piracies and felonies committed on the high seas and offenses against the law of nations;

To declare war, grant letters of marque and reprisal, and make rules concerning captures on land and water;

To raise and support armies, but no appropriation of money to that use shall be for a longer term than two years;

To provide and maintain a navy;

To make rules for the government and regulation of the land and naval forces;

To provide for calling forth the militia to execute the laws of the Union, suppress insurrections, and repel invasions;

To provide for organizing, arming, and disciplining the militia, and for governing such part of them as may be employed in the service of the United States, reserving to the States respectively the appointment of the officers, and the authority of training the militia according to the discipline prescribed by Congress;

To exercise exclusive legislation in all cases whatsoever, over such district (not exceeding ten miles square) as may, by cession of particular States, and the acceptance of Congress, become the seat of government of the United States, and to exercise like authority over all places purchased by the consent of the legislature of the State, in which the same shall be, for erection of forts, magazines, arsenals, dockyards, and other needful buildings; —and

To make all laws which shall be necessary and proper for carrying into execution the foregoing powers, and all other powers vested by this Constitution in the government of the United States, or in any department or officer thereof.

Section 9   The migration or importation of such persons as any of the States now existing shall think proper to admit shall not be prohibited by the Congress prior to the year 1808; but a tax or duty may be imposed on such importation, not exceeding $10 for each person.

The privilege of the writ of habeas corpus shall not be suspended, unless when in cases of rebellion or invasion the public safety may require it.

No bill of attainder or ex post facto law shall be passed.

No capitation, or other direct, tax shall be laid, unless in proportion to the census or enumeration herein before directed to be taken.

No tax or duty shall be laid on articles exported from any State.

No preference shall be given by any regulation of commerce or revenue to the ports of one State over those of another; nor shall vessels bound to, or from, one State, be obliged to enter, clear, or pay duties in another.

No money shall be drawn from the treasury, but in consequence of appropriations made by law; and a regular statement and account of the receipts and expenditures of all public money shall be published from time to time.

No title of nobility shall be granted by the United States: and no person holding any office of profit or trust under them, shall, without the consent of the Congress, accept of any present, emolument, office, or title, of any kind whatever, from any king, prince, or foreign state.

Section 10   No State shall enter into any treaty, alliance, or confederation; grant letters of marque and reprisal; coin money; emit bills of credit; make anything but gold and silver coin a tender in payment of debts; pass any bill of attainder, ex post facto law, or law impairing the obligation of contracts, or grant any title of nobility.

No State shall, without the consent of Congress, lay any imposts or duties on imports or exports, except what may be absolutely necessary for executing its inspection laws: and the net produce of all duties and imposts, laid by any State on imports or exports, shall be for the use of the treasury of the United States; and all such laws shall be subject to the revision and control of the Congress.

No State shall, without the consent of Congress, lay any duty of tonnage, keep troops or ships of war in time of peace, enter into any agreement or compact with another State, or with a foreign power, or engage in war, unless actually invaded, or in such imminent danger as will not admit of delay.

Article II

Section 1   The executive power shall be vested in a President of the United States of America. He shall hold his office during the term of four years, and, together with the Vice-President, chosen for the same term, be elected as follows:

Each State shall appoint, in such manner as the legislature thereof may direct, a number of electors, equal to the whole number of Senators and Representatives to which the State may be entitled in the Congress; but no Senator or Representative, or person holding an office of trust or profit under the United States, shall be appointed an elector.

The electors shall meet in their respective States, and vote by ballot for two persons, of whom one at least shall not be an inhabitant of the same State with themselves. And they shall make a list of all the persons voted for, and of the number of votes for each; which list they shall sign and certify, and transmit sealed to the seat of government of the United States, directed to the President of the Senate. The President of the Senate shall, in the presence of the Senate and House of Representatives, open all the certificates, and the votes shall then be counted. The person having the greatest number of votes shall be the President, if such number be a majority of the whole number of electors appointed; and if there be more than one who have such majority, and have an equal number of votes, then the House of Representatives shall immediately choose by ballot one of them for President; and if no person have a majority, then from the five highest on the list said house shall in like manner choose the President. But in choosing the President the votes shall be taken by States, the representation from each State having one vote; a quorum for this purpose shall consist of a member or members from two-thirds of the States, and a majority of all the States shall be necessary to a choice. In every case, after the choice of the President, the person having the greatest number of votes of the electors shall be the Vice-President. But if there should remain two or more who have equal votes, the Senate shall choose from them by ballot the Vice-President.

The Congress may determine the time of choosing the electors and the day on which they shall give their votes; which day shall be the same throughout the United States.

No person except a natural-born citizen, *or a citizen of the United States at the time of the adoption of this Constitution,* shall be eligible to the office of President; neither shall any person be eligible to that office who shall not have attained to the age of thirty-five years, and been fourteen years a resident within the United States.

In cases of the removal of the President from office or of his death, resignation, or inability to discharge the powers and duties of the said office, the same shall devolve on the Vice-President, and the Congress may by law provide for the case of removal, death, resignation, or inability, both of the President and Vice-President, declaring what officer shall then act as President, and such officer shall act accordingly, until the disability be removed, or a President shall be elected.

The President shall, at stated times, receive for his services a compensation, which shall neither be increased nor diminished during the period for which he shall have been elected, and he shall not receive within that period any other emolument from the United States, or any of them.

Before he enter on the execution of his office, he shall take the following oath or affirmation:—"I do solemnly swear (or affirm) that I will faithfully execute the office of the President of the United States, and will to the best of my ability preserve, protect and defend the Constitution of the United States."

Section 2　The President shall be commander in chief of the army and navy of the United States, and of the militia of the several States, when called into the actual service of the United States; he may require the opinion, in writing, of the principal officer in each of the executive departments, upon any subject relating to the duties of their respective offices, and he shall have power to grant reprieves and pardons for offenses against the United States, except in cases of impeachment.

He shall have power, by and with the advice and consent of the Senate, to make treaties, provided two-thirds of the Senators present concur; and he shall nominate, and by and with the advice and consent of the Senate, shall appoint ambassadors, other public ministers and consuls, judges of the Supreme Court, and all other officers of the United States, whose appointments are not herein otherwise provided for, and which shall be established by law: but Congress may by law vest the appointment of such inferior officers, as they think proper, in the President alone, in the courts of law, or in the heads of departments.

The President shall have power to fill up all vacancies that may happen during the recess of the Senate, by granting commissions which shall expire at the end of their next session.

Section 3　He shall from time to time give to the Congress information of the state of the Union, and recommend to their consideration such measures as he shall judge necessary and expedient; he may, on extraordinary occasions, convene both houses, or either of them, and in case of disagreement between them, with respect to the time of adjournment, he may adjourn them to such time as he shall think proper; he shall receive ambassadors and other public ministers; he shall take care that the laws be faithfully executed, and shall commission all the officers of the United States.

Section 4　The President, Vice-President and all civil officers of the United States shall be removed from office on impeachment for, and on conviction of, treason, bribery, or other high crimes and misdemeanors.

Article III

Section 1　The judicial power of the United States shall be vested in one Supreme Court, and in such inferior courts as the Congress may from time to time ordain and establish. The judges, both of the Supreme and inferior courts, shall hold their offices during good behavior, and shall, at stated times, receive for their services a compensation which shall not be diminished during their continuance in office.

Section 2　The judicial power shall extend to all cases, in law and equity, arising under this Constitution, the laws of the United States, and treaties made, or which shall be made, under their authority;—to all cases affecting ambassadors, other public ministers and consuls;—to all cases of admiralty and maritime jurisdiction;—to controversies to which the United States shall be a party;—to controversies between two or more States;—*between a State and citizens of another State;*—between citizens of different States;—between citizens of the same State claiming lands under grants of different States, and between a State, or the citizens thereof, and foreign states, citizens or subjects.

In all cases affecting ambassadors, other public ministers and consuls, and those in which a State shall be party, the Supreme Court shall have original jurisdiction. In all the other cases before mentioned, the Supreme Court shall have appellate jurisdiction, both as to law and fact, with such exceptions, and under such regulations, as the Congress shall make.

The trial of all crimes, except in cases of impeachment, shall be by jury; and such trial shall be held in the State where said crimes shall have been committed; but when not committed within any State, the trial shall be at such place or places as the Congress may by law have directed.

Section 3　Treason against the United States shall consist only in levying war against them, or in adhering to their enemies, giving them aid and comfort. No person shall be convicted of treason unless on the testimony of two witnesses to the same overt act, or on confession in open court.

The Congress shall have power to declare the punishment of treason, but no attainder of treason shall work corruption of blood, or forfeiture except during the life of the person attainted.

Article IV

Section 1　Full faith and credit shall be given in each State to the public acts, records, and judicial proceedings of every other State. And the Congress may by general laws prescribe the manner in which such acts, records, and proceedings shall be proved, and the effect thereof.

Section 2　The citizens of each State shall be entitled to all privileges and immunities of citizens in the several States.

A person charged in any State with treason, felony, or other crime, who shall flee from justice, and be found in another State, shall on demand of the executive authority of the State from which he fled, be delivered up, to be removed to the State having jurisdiction of the crime.

No person held to service or labor in one State, under the laws thereof, escaping into another, shall, in consequence of any law or regulation therein, be discharged from such service or labor, but shall be delivered up on claim of the party to whom such service or labor may be due.

Section 3　New States may be admitted by the Congress into this Union; but no new State shall be formed or erected within the jurisdiction of any other State; nor any State be formed by the junction of two or more States, or parts of States, without the consent of the legislatures of the States concerned as well as of the Congress.

The Congress shall have power to dispose of and make all needful rules and regulations respecting the territory or other property belonging to the United States; and nothing in this Constitution shall be so construed as to prejudice any claims of the United States, or of any particular State.

Section 4   The United States shall guarantee to every State in this Union a republican form of government, and shall protect each of them against invasion; and on application of the legislature, or of the executive (when the legislature cannot be convened), against domestic violence.

Article V

The Congress, whenever two-thirds of both houses shall deem it necessary, shall propose amendments to this Constitution, or, on the application of the legislatures of two-thirds of the several States, shall call a convention for proposing amendments, which, in either case, shall be valid to all intents and purposes, as part of this Constitution, when ratified by the legislatures of three-fourths of the several States, or by conventions in three-fourths thereof, as the one or the other mode of ratification may be proposed by the Congress; provided *that no amendments which may be made prior to the year one thousand eight hundred and eight shall in any manner affect the first and fourth clauses in the ninth section of the first article;* and that no State, without its consent, shall be deprived of its equal suffrage in the Senate.

Article VI

All debts contracted and engagements entered into, before the adoption of this Constitution, shall be as valid against the United States under this Constitution, as under the Confederation.

This Constitution, and the laws of the United States which shall be made in pursuance thereof; and all treaties made, or which shall be made, under the authority of the United States, shall be the supreme law of the land; and the judges in every State shall be bound thereby, anything in the Constitution or laws of any State to the contrary notwithstanding.

The Senators and Representatives before mentioned, and the members of the several State legislatures, and all executive and judicial officers, both of the United States and of the several States, shall be bound by oath or affirmation to support this Constitution; but no religious test shall ever be required as a qualification to any office or public trust under the United States.

Article VII

The ratification of the conventions of nine States shall be sufficient for the establishment of this Constitution between the States so ratifying the same.

Done in Convention by the unanimous consent of the States present, the seventeenth day of September in the year of our Lord one thousand seven hundred and eighty-seven and of the Independence of the United States of America the twelfth. In witness whereof we have hereunto subscribed our names.

Amendments to the Constitution*

Amendment I

Congress shall make no law respecting an establishment of religion, or prohibiting the free exercise thereof; or abridging the freedom of speech, or of the press; or the right of the people peaceably to assemble, and to petition the government for a redress of grievances.

---

* The first ten Amendments (the Bill of Rights) were adopted in 1791.

Amendment II

A well-regulated militia being necessary to the security of a free State, the right of the people to keep and bear arms shall not be infringed.

Amendment III

No soldier shall, in time of peace, be quartered in any house without the consent of the owner, nor in time of war, but in a manner to be prescribed by law.

Amendment IV

The right of the people to be secure in their persons, houses, papers, and effects, against unreasonable searches and seizures, shall not be violated, and no warrants shall issue but upon probable cause, supported by oath or affirmation, and particularly describing the place to be searched, and the persons or things to be seized.

Amendment V

No person shall be held to answer for a capital, or otherwise infamous crime, unless on a presentment or indictment of a grand jury, except in cases arising in the land or naval forces, or in the militia, when in actual service in time of war or public danger; nor shall any person be subject for the same offense to be twice put in jeopardy of life or limb; nor shall be compelled in any criminal case to be a witness against himself, nor be deprived of life, liberty, or property, without due process of law; nor shall private property be taken for public use without just compensation.

Amendment VI

In all criminal prosecutions, the accused shall enjoy the right to a speedy and public trial, by an impartial jury of the State and district wherein the crime shall have been committed, which district shall have been previously ascertained by law, and to be informed of the nature and cause of the accusation; to be confronted with the witnesses against him; to have compulsory process for obtaining witnesses in his favor, and to have the assistance of counsel for his defense.

Amendment VII

In suits at common law, where the value in controversy shall exceed twenty dollars, the right of trial by jury shall be preserved, and no fact tried by a jury shall be otherwise reexamined in any court of the United States, than according to the rules of the common law.

Amendment VIII

Excessive bail shall not be required, nor excessive fines imposed, nor cruel and unusual punishments inflicted.

Amendment IX

The enumeration in the Constitution, of certain rights, shall not be construed to deny or disparage others retained by the people.

Amendment X

The powers not delegated to the United States by the Constitution, nor prohibited by it to the States, are reserved to the States respectively, or to the people.

Amendment XI

[Adopted 1798]

The judicial power of the United States shall not be construed to extend to any suit in law or equity, commenced or prosecuted against one of the United States by citizens of another State, or by citizens or subjects of any foreign state.

Amendment XII

[Adopted 1804]

The electors shall meet in their respective States, and vote by ballot for President and Vice-President, one of whom, at least, shall not be an inhabitant of the same State with themselves; they shall name in their ballots the person voted for as President, and in distinct ballots the person voted for as Vice-President, and they shall make distinct lists of all persons voted for as President, and of all persons voted for as Vice-President, and of the number of votes for each, which lists they shall sign and certify, and transmit sealed to the seat of government of the United States, directed to the President of the Senate;—the President of the Senate shall, in the presence of the Senate and House of Representatives, open all the certificates and the votes shall then be counted;—the person having the greatest number of votes for President shall be the President, if such number be a majority of the whole number of electors appointed; and if no person have such majority, then from the persons having the highest numbers not exceeding three on the list of those voted for as President, the House of Representatives shall choose immediately, by ballot, the President. But in choosing the President, the votes shall be taken by States, the representation from each State having one vote; a quorum for this purpose shall consist of a member or members from two-thirds of the States, and a majority of all the States shall be necessary to a choice. And if the House of Representatives shall not choose a President whenever the right of choice shall devolve upon them, before *the fourth day of March* next following, then the Vice-President shall act as President, as in the case of the death or other constitutional disability of the President.

The person having the greatest number of votes as Vice-President shall be the Vice-President, if such number be a majority of the whole number of electors appointed; and if no person have a majority, then from the two highest numbers on the list the Senate shall choose the Vice-President; a quorum for the purpose shall consist of two-thirds of the whole number of Senators, and a majority of the whole number shall be necessary to a choice. But no person constitutionally ineligible to the office of President shall be eligible to that of Vice-President of the United States.

Amendment XIII

[Adopted 1865]

Section 1 Neither slavery nor involuntary servitude, except as a punishment for crime whereof the party shall have been duly convicted, shall exist within the United States, or any place subject to their jurisdiction.

Section 2   Congress shall have power to enforce this article by appropriate legislation.

Amendment XIV

[Adopted 1868]

Section 1   All persons born or naturalized in the United States, and subject to the jurisdiction thereof, are citizens of the United States and of the State wherein they reside. No State shall make or enforce any law which shall abridge the privileges or immunities of citizens of the United States; nor shall any State deprive any person of life, liberty, or property, without due process of law; nor deny to any person within its jurisdiction the equal protection of the laws.

Section 2   Representatives shall be apportioned among the several States according to their respective numbers, counting the whole number of persons in each State, excluding Indians not taxed. But when the right to vote at any election for the choice of Electors for President and Vice-President of the United States, Representatives in Congress, the executive and judicial officers of a State, or the members of the legislature thereof, is denied to any of the male inhabitants of such State, being twenty-one years of age and citizens of the United States, or in any way abridged, except for participation in rebellion, or other crime, the basis of representation therein shall be reduced in the proportion which the number of such male citizens shall bear to the whole number of male citizens twenty-one years of age in such State.

Section 3   No person shall be a Senator or Representative in Congress, or Elector of President and Vice-President, or hold any office, civil or military, under the United States, or under any State, who, having previously taken an oath, as a member of Congress, or as an officer of the United States, or as a member of any State legislature, or as an executive or judicial officer of any State, to support the Constitution of the United States, shall have engaged in insurrection or rebellion against the same, or given aid or comfort to the enemies thereof. Congress may, by a vote of two-thirds of each house, remove such disability.

Section 4   The validity of the public debt of the United States, authorized by law, including debts incurred for payment of pensions and bounties for services in suppressing insurrection or rebellion, shall not be questioned. But neither the United States nor any State shall assume or pay any debt or obligation incurred in aid of insurrection or rebellion against the United States, or any claim for the loss of emancipation of any slave; but all such debts, obligations, and claims shall be held illegal and void.

Section 5   The Congress shall have power to enforce, by appropriate legislation, the provisions of this article.

Amendment XV

[Adopted 1870]

Section 1   The right of citizens of the United States to vote shall not be denied or abridged by the United States or by any State on account of race, color, or previous condition of servitude.

Section 2   The Congress shall have power to enforce this article by appropriate legislation.

Amendment XVI

[Adopted 1913]

The Congress shall have power to lay and collect taxes on incomes, from whatever source derived, without apportionment among the several States, and without regard to any census or enumeration.

Amendment XVII

[Adopted 1913]

Section 1   The Senate of the United States shall be composed of two Senators from each State, elected by the people thereof, for six years; and each Senator shall have one vote. The electors in each State shall have the qualifications requisite for electors of [voters for] the most numerous branch of the State legislatures.

Section 2   When vacancies happen in the representation of any State in the Senate, the executive authority of such State shall issue writs of election to fill such vacancies: Provided, that the Legislature of any State may empower the executive thereof to make temporary appointments until the people fill the vacancies by election as the Legislature may direct.

Section 3   This amendment shall not be so construed as to affect the election or term of any Senator chosen before it becomes valid as part of the Constitution.

Amendment XVIII

[Adopted 1919; Repealed 1933]

Section 1   After one year from the ratification of this article the manufacture, sale, or transportation of intoxicating liquors within, the importation thereof into, or the exportation thereof from the United States and all territory subject to the jurisdiction thereof, for beverage purposes, is hereby prohibited.

Section 2   The Congress and the several States shall have concurrent power to enforce this article by appropriate legislation.

Section 3   This article shall be inoperative unless it shall have been ratified as an amendment to the Constitution by the legislatures of the several States, as provided by the Constitution, within seven years from the date of the submission thereof to the States by the Congress.

Amendment XIX

[Adopted 1920]

Section 1   The right of citizens of the United States to vote shall not be denied or abridged by the United States or by any State on account of sex.

Section 2   The Congress shall have power to enforce this article by appropriate legislation.

Amendment XX

[Adopted 1933]

Section 1   The terms of the President and Vice-President shall end at noon on the 20th day of January, and the terms of Senators and Representatives at noon on the 3rd day of January, of the years in which such terms would have ended if this article had not been ratified; and the terms of their successors shall then begin.

Section 2   The Congress shall assemble at least once in every year, and such meeting shall begin at noon on the 3d day of January, unless they shall by law appoint a different day.

Section 3   If, at the time fixed for the beginning of the term of the President, the President-elect shall have died, the Vice-President–elect shall become President. If a President shall not have been chosen before the time fixed for the beginning of his term, or if the President-elect shall have failed to qualify, then the Vice-President–elect shall act as President until a President shall have qualified; and the Congress may by law provide for the case wherein neither a President-elect nor a Vice-President–elect shall have qualified, declaring who shall then act as President, or the manner in which one who is to act shall be selected, and such persons shall act accordingly until a President or Vice-President shall have qualified.

Section 4   The Congress may by law provide for the case of the death of any of the persons from whom the House of Representatives may choose a President whenever the right of choice shall have devolved upon them, and for the case of the death of any of the persons from whom the Senate may choose a Vice-President whenever the right of choice shall have devolved upon them.

Section 5   Sections 1 and 2 shall take effect on the 15th day of October following the ratification of this article.

Section 6   This article shall be inoperative unless it shall have been ratified as an amendment to the Constitution by the Legislatures of three-fourths of the several States within seven years from the date of its submission.

Amendment XXI

[Adopted 1933]

Section 1   The eighteenth article of amendment to the Constitution of the United States is hereby repealed.

Section 2   The transportation or importation into any State, Territory, or Possession of the United States for delivery or use therein of intoxicating liquors, in violation of the laws thereof, is hereby prohibited.

Section 3   This article shall be inoperative unless it shall have been ratified as an amendment to the Constitution by conventions in the several States, as provided in the Constitution, within seven years from the date of submission thereof to the States by the Congress.

Amendment XXII

[Adopted 1951]

Section 1   No person shall be elected to the office of President more than twice, and no person who has held the office of President, or acted as President, for more than two years of a term to which some other person was elected President shall be elected to the office of President more than once. But this article shall not apply to any person holding the office of President when this article was proposed by the Congress, and shall not prevent any person who may be holding the office of President, or acting as President, during the term within which this article becomes operative from holding the office of President or acting as President during the remainder of such term.

Section 2 This article shall be inoperative unless it shall have been ratified as an amendment to the Constitution by the legislatures of three-fourths of the several States within seven years from the date of its submission to the States by the Congress.

Amendment XXIII

[Adopted 1961]

Section 1 The District constituting the seat of Government of the United States shall appoint in such manner as the Congress may direct:

A number of electors of President and Vice-President equal to the whole number of Senators and Representatives in Congress to which the District would be entitled if it were a State, but in no event more than the least populous State; they shall be in addition to those appointed by the States, but they shall be considered for the purposes of the election of President and Vice-President, to be electors appointed by a State; and they shall meet in the District and perform such duties as provided by the twelfth article of amendment.

Section 2 The Congress shall have the power to enforce this article by appropriate legislation.

Amendment XXIV

[Adopted 1964]

Section 1 The right of citizens of the United States to vote in any primary or other election for President or Vice-President, for electors for President or Vice-President, or for Senator or Representative in Congress, shall not be denied or abridged by the United States or any State by reason of failure to pay any poll tax or other tax.

Section 2 The Congress shall have the power to enforce this article by appropriate legislation.

Amendment XXV

[Adopted 1967]

Section 1 In case of the removal of the President from office or of his death or resignation, the Vice-President shall become President.

Section 2 Whenever there is a vacancy in the office of the Vice-President, the President shall nominate a Vice-President who shall take office upon confirmation by a majority vote of both Houses of Congress.

Section 3 Whenever the President transmits to the President pro tempore of the Senate and the Speaker of the House of Representatives his written declaration that he is unable to discharge the powers and duties of his office, and until he transmits to them a written declaration to the contrary, such powers and duties shall be discharged by the Vice-President as Acting President.

Section 4 Whenever the Vice-President and a majority of either the principal officers of the executive departments or of such other body as Congress may by law provide, transmit to the President pro tempore of the Senate and the Speaker of the House of Representatives their written declaration that the President is unable to discharge the powers and duties of his office, the Vice-President shall immediately assume the powers and duties of the office as Acting President.

Thereafter, when the President transmits to the President pro tempore of the Senate and the Speaker of the House of Representatives his written declaration that no inability exists, he shall resume the powers and duties of his office unless the Vice-President and a majority of either the principal officers of the executive department[s] or of such other body as Congress may by law provide, transmit within four days to the President pro tempore of the Senate and the Speaker of the House of Representatives their written declaration that the President is unable to discharge the powers and duties of his office. Thereupon Congress shall decide the issue, assembling within forty-eight hours for that purpose if not in session. If the Congress, within twenty-one days after receipt of the latter written declaration, or, if Congress is not in session, within twenty-one days after Congress is required to assemble, determines by two-thirds vote of both Houses that the President is unable to discharge the powers and duties of his office, the Vice-President shall continue to discharge the same as Acting President; otherwise, the President shall resume the powers and duties of his office.

Amendment XXVI

[Adopted 1971]

Section 1   The right of citizens of the United States, who are eighteen years of age or older, to vote shall not be denied or abridged by the United States or by any State on account of age.

Section 2   The Congress shall have power to enforce this article by appropriate legislation.

Amendment XXVII

[Adopted 1992]

No law, varying the compensation for the services of the Senators and Representatives, shall take effect, until an election of Representatives shall have intervened.

A Statistical Profile of America

POPULATION OF THE UNITED STATES

Year	Number of States	Population	Percent Increase	Population Per Square Mile	Percent Urban/ Rural	Percent Male/ Female	Percent White/ Non-white	Persons Per House- hold	Median Age
1790	13	3,929,214		4.5	5.1/94.9	NA/NA	80.7/19.3	5.79	NA
1800	16	5,308,483	35.1	6.1	6.1/93.9	NA/NA	81.1/18.9	NA	NA
1810	17	7,239,881	36.4	4.3	7.3/92.7	NA/NA	81.0/19.0	NA	NA
1820	23	9,638,453	33.1	5.5	7.2/92.8	50.8/49.2	81.6/18.4	NA	16.7
1830	24	12,866,020	33.5	7.4	8.8/91.2	50.8/49.2	81.9/18.1	NA	17.2
1840	26	17,069,453	32.7	9.8	10.8/89.2	50.9/49.1	83.2/16.8	NA	17.8
1850	31	23,191,876	35.9	7.9	15.3/84.7	51.0/49.0	84.3/15.7	5.55	18.9
1860	33	31,443,321	35.6	10.6	19.8/80.2	51.2/48.8	85.6/14.4	5.28	19.4
1870	37	39,818,449	26.6	13.4	25.7/74.3	50.6/49.4	86.2/13.8	5.09	20.2
1880	38	50,155,783	26.0	16.9	28.2/71.8	50.9/49.1	86.5/13.5	5.04	20.9
1890	44	62,947,714	25.5	21.2	35.1/64.9	51.2/48.8	87.5/12.5	4.93	22.0
1900	45	75,994,575	20.7	25.6	39.6/60.4	51.1/48.9	87.9/12.1	4.76	22.9
1910	46	91,972,266	21.0	31.0	45.6/54.4	51.5/48.5	88.9/11.1	4.54	24.1
1920	48	105,710,620	14.9	35.6	51.2/48.8	51.0/49.0	89.7/10.3	4.34	25.3
1930	48	122,775,046	16.1	41.2	56.1/43.9	50.6/49.4	89.8/10.2	4.11	26.4
1940	48	131,669,275	7.2	44.2	56.5/43.5	50.2/49.8	89.8/10.2	3.67	29.0
1950	48	150,697,361	14.5	50.7	64.0/36.0	49.7/50.3	89.5/10.5	3.37	30.2
1960	50	179,323,175	18.5	50.6	69.9/30.1	49.3/50.7	88.6/11.4	3.33	29.5
1970	50	203,302,031	13.4	57.6	73.6/26.4	48.7/51.3	87.6/12.4	3.14	28.0
1980	50	226,542,199	11.4	64.1	73.7/26.3	48.6/51.4	85.9/14.1	2.75	30.0
1990	50	248,718,301	9.8	70.3	75.2/24.8	48.7/51.3	83.9/16.1	2.63	32.8
1998	50	270,299,000	8.0	76.4	NA	48.9/51.1	82.5/17.5	2.62	35.2

NA = Not available.

IMMIGRANTS TO THE UNITED STATES

Immigration Totals by Decade

Years	Number
1820–1830	151,824
1831–1840	599,125
1841–1850	1,713,251
1851–1860	2,598,214
1861–1870	2,314,824
1871–1880	2,812,191
1881–1890	5,246,613
1891–1900	3,687,546
1901–1910	8,795,386
1911–1920	5,735,811
1921–1930	4,107,209
1931–1940	528,431
1941–1950	1,035,039
1951–1960	2,515,479
1961–1970	3,321,677
1971–1980	4,493,314
1981–1990	7,338,062
1991–1998	7,605,068
Total	64,599,082

THE AMERICAN WORKER

Year	Total Number of Workers	Males as Percent of Total Workers	Females as Percent of Total Workers	Married Women as Percent of Female Workers	FemaleWorkers as Percent of Female Population	Percent of Labor Force Unemployed
1870	12,506,000	85	15	NA	NA	NA
1880	17,392,000	85	15	NA	NA	NA
1890	23,318,000	83	17	14	19	4 (1894 = 18)
1900	29,073,000	82	18	15	21	5
1910	38,167,000	79	21	25	25	6
1920	41,614,000	79	21	23	24	5 (1921 = 12)
1930	48,830,000	78	22	29	25	9 (1933 = 25)
1940	53,011,000	76	24	36	27	15 (1944 = 1)
1950	62,208,000	72	28	52	31	5.3
1960	69,628,000	67	33	55	38	5.5
1970	82,771,000	62	38	59	43	4.9
1980	106,940,000	58	42	55	52	7.1
1990	125,840,000	55	45	54	58	5.6
1998	137,673,000	54	46	53	60	4.5

NA = Not available.

THE AMERICAN ECONOMY

Year	Gross National Product (GNP) and Gross Domestic Product (GDP)[a] (in $ billions)	Steel Production (in tons)	Corn Production (millions of bushels)	Automobiles Registered	New Housing Starts	Foreign Trade (in $ millions) Exports	Imports
1790	NA	NA	NA	NA	NA	20	23
1800	NA	NA	NA	NA	NA	71	91
1810	NA	NA	NA	NA	NA	67	85
1820	NA	NA	NA	NA	NA	70	74
1830	NA	NA	NA	NA	NA	74	71
1840	NA	NA	NA	NA	NA	132	107
1850	NA	NA	592[d]	NA	NA	152	178
1860	NA	13,000	839[e]	NA	NA	400	362
1870	7.4[b]	77,000	1,125	NA	NA	451	462
1880	11.2[c]	1,397,000	1,707	NA	NA	853	761
1890	13.1	4,779,000	1,650	NA	328,000	910	823
1900	18.7	11,227,000	2,662	8,000	189,000	1,499	930
1910	35.3	28,330,000	2,853	458,300	387,000 (1918 = 118,000)	1,919	1,646
1920	91.5	46,183,000	3,071	8,131,500	247,000 (1925 = 937,000)	8,664	5,784
1930	90.7	44,591,000	2,080	23,034,700	330,000 (1933 = 93,000)	4,013	3,500
1940	100.0	66,983,000	2,457	27,465,800	603,000 (1944 = 142,000)	4,030	7,433
1950	286.5	96,836,000	3,075	40,339,000	1,952,000	9,997	8,954
1960	506.5	99,282,000	4,314	61,682,300	1,365,000	19,659	15,093
1970	1,016.0	131,514,000	4,200	89,279,800	1,434,000	42,681	40,356
1980	2,819.5	111,835,000	6,600	121,601,000	1,292,000	220,626	244,871
1990	5,764.9	98,906,000	7,933	143,550,000	1,193,000	394,030	485,453
1998	8,511.0	107,600,000	9,761	129,749,000[f]	1,617,000	682,100	911,900

[a]In December 1991 the Bureau of Economic Analysis of the U.S. government began featuring Gross Domestic Product rather than Gross National Product as the primary measure of U.S. production. [b]Figure is average for 1869–1878. [c]Figure is average for 1879–1888. [d]Figure for 1849. [e]Figure for 1859. [f]Figure for 1997. NA = Not available.

Presidential Elections

Year	Number of States	Candidates	Parties	Popular Vote	% of Popular Vote	Electoral Vote	% Voter Participation[a]
1789	10	**George Washington**	No party			69	
		John Adams	designations			34	
		Other candidates				35	
1792	15	**George Washington**	No party			132	
		John Adams	designations			77	
		George Clinton				50	
		Other candidates				5	
1796	16	**John Adams**	Federalist			71	
		Thomas Jefferson	Democratic-Republican			68	
		Thomas Pinckney	Federalist			59	
		Aaron Burr	Democratic-Republican			30	
		Other candidates				48	
1800	16	**Thomas Jefferson**	Democratic-Republican			73	
		Aaron Burr	Democratic-Republican			73	
		John Adams	Federalist			65	
		Charles C. Pinckney	Federalist			64	
		John Jay	Federalist			1	
1804	17	**Thomas Jefferson**	Democratic-Republican			162	
		Charles C. Pinckney	Federalist			14	
1808	17	**James Madison**	Democratic-Republican			122	
		Charles C. Pinckney	Federalist			47	
		George Clinton	Democratic-Republican			6	
1812	18	**James Madison**	Democratic-Republican			128	
		De Witt Clinton	Federalist			89	
1816	19	**James Monroe**	Democratic-Republican			183	
		Rufus King	Federalist			34	
1820	24	**James Monroe**	Democratic-Republican			231	
		John Quincy Adams	Independent Republican			1	

PRESIDENTIAL ELECTIONS (*Continued*)

Year	Number of States	Candidates	Parties	Popular Vote	% of Popular Vote	Electoral Vote	% Voter Participation[b]
1824	24	**John Quincy Adams**	Democratic-Republican	108,740	30.5	84	26.9
		Andrew Jackson	Democratic-Republican	153,544	43.1	99	
		Henry Clay	Democratic-Republican	47,136	13.2	37	
		William H. Crawford	Democratic-Republican	46,618	13.1	41	
1828	24	**Andrew Jackson**	Democratic	647,286	56.0	178	57.6
		John Quincy Adams	National Republican	508,064	44.0	83	
1832	24	**Andrew Jackson**	Democratic	701,780	54.2	219	55.4
		Henry Clay	National Republican	484,205	37.4	49	
		Other candidates		107,988	8.0	18	
1836	26	**Martin Van Buren**	Democratic	764,176	50.8	170	57.8
		William H. Harrison	Whig	550,816	36.6	73	
		Hugh L. White	Whig	146,107	9.7	26	
1840	26	**William H. Harrison**	Whig	1,274,624	53.1	234	80.2
		Martin Van Buren	Democratic	1,127,781	46.9	60	
1844	26	**James K. Polk**	Democratic	1,338,464	49.6	170	78.9
		Henry Clay	Whig	1,300,097	48.1	105	
		James G. Birney	Liberty	62,300	2.3		
1848	30	**Zachary Taylor**	Whig	1,360,967	47.4	163	72.7
		Lewis Cass	Democratic	1,222,342	42.5	127	
		Martin Van Buren	Free Soil	291,263	10.1		
1852	31	**Franklin Pierce**	Democratic	1,601,117	50.9	254	69.6
		Winfield Scott	Whig	1,385,453	44.1	42	
		John P. Hale	Free-Soil	155,825	5.0		
1856	31	**James Buchanan**	Democratic	1,832,955	45.3	174	78.9
		John C. Frémont	Republican	1,339,932	33.1	114	
		Millard Fillmore	American	871,731	21.6	8	
1860	33	**Abraham Lincoln**	Republican	1,865,593	39.8	180	81.2
		Stephen A. Douglas	Democratic	1,382,713	29.5	12	
		John C. Breckinridge	Democratic	848,356	18.1	72	
		John Bell	Constitutional Union	592,906	12.6	39	
1864	36	**Abraham Lincoln**	Republican	2,206,938	55.0	212	73.8
		George B. McClellan	Democratic	1,803,787	45.0	21	
1868	37	**Ulysses S. Grant**	Republican	3,013,421	52.7	214	78.1
		Horatio Seymour	Democratic	2,706,829	47.3	80	

PRESIDENTIAL ELECTIONS (*Continued*)

Year	Number of States	Candidates	Parties	Popular Vote	% of Popular Vote	Electoral Vote	% Voter Participation[b]
1872	37	**Ulysses S. Grant**	Republican	3,596,745	55.6	286	71.3
		Horace Greeley	Democratic	2,843,446	43.9	[b]	
1876	38	**Rutherford B. Hayes**	Republican	4,036,572	48.0	185	81.8
		Samuel J. Tilden	Democratic	4,284,020	51.0	184	
1880	38	**James A. Garfield**	Republican	4,453,295	48.5	214	79.4
		Winfield S. Hancock	Democratic	4,414,082	48.1	155	
		James B. Weaver	Greenback-Labor	308,578	3.4		
1884	38	**Grover Cleveland**	Democratic	4,879,507	48.5	219	77.5
		James G. Blaine	Republican	4,850,293	48.2	182	
		Benjamin F. Butler	Greenback-Labor	175,370	1.8		
		John P. St. John	Prohibition	150,369	1.5		
1888	38	**Benjamin Harrison**	Republican	5,447,129	47.9	233	79.3
		Grover Cleveland	Democratic	5,537,857	48.6	168	
		Clinton B. Fisk	Prohibition	249,506	2.2		
		Anson J. Streeter	Union Labor	146,935	1.3		
1892	44	**Grover Cleveland**	Democratic	5,555,426	46.1	277	74.7
		Benjamin Harrison	Republican	5,182,690	43.0	145	
		James B. Weaver	People's	1,029,846	8.5	22	
		John Bidwell	Prohibition	264,133	2.2		
1896	45	**William McKinley**	Republican	7,102,246	51.1	271	79.3
		William J. Bryan	Democratic	6,492,559	47.7	176	
1900	45	**William McKinley**	Republican	7,218,491	51.7	292	73.2
		William J. Bryan	Democratic; Populist	6,356,734	45.5	155	
		John C. Wooley	Prohibition	208,914	1.5		
1904	45	**Theodore Roosevelt**	Republican	7,628,461	57.4	336	65.2
		Alton B. Parker	Democratic	5,084,223	37.6	140	
		Eugene V. Debs	Socialist	402,283	3.0		
		Silas C. Swallow	Prohibition	258,536	1.9		
1908	46	**William H. Taft**	Republican	7,675,320	51.6	321	65.4
		William J. Bryan	Democratic	6,412,294	43.1	162	
		Eugene V. Debs	Socialist	420,793	2.8		
		Eugene W. Chafin	Prohibition	253,840	1.7		
1912	48	**Woodrow Wilson**	Democratic	6,296,547	41.9	435	58.8
		Theodore Roosevelt	Progressive	4,118,571	27.4	88	
		William H. Taft	Republican	3,486,720	23.2	8	
		Eugene V. Debs	Socialist	900,672	6.0		
		Eugene W. Chafin	Prohibition	206,275	1.4		
1916	48	**Woodrow Wilson**	Democratic	9,127,695	49.4	277	61.6
		Charles E. Hughes	Republican	8,533,507	46.2	254	

PRESIDENTIAL ELECTIONS (Continued)

Year	Number of States	Candidates	Parties	Popular Vote	% of Popular Vote	Electoral Vote	% Voter Participation[b]
		A. L. Benson	Socialist	585,113	3.2		
		J. Frank Hanly	Prohibition	220,506	1.2		
1920	48	**Warren G. Harding**	Republican	16,143,407	60.4	404	49.2
		James M. Cox	Democratic	9,130,328	34.2	127	
		Eugene V. Debs	Socialist	919,799	3.4		
		P. P. Christensen	Farmer-Labor	265,411	1.0		
1924	48	**Calvin Coolidge**	Republican	15,718,211	54.0	382	48.9
		John W. Davis	Democratic	8,385,283	28.8	136	
		Robert M. La Follette	Progressive	4,831,289	16.6	13	
1928	48	**Herbert C. Hoover**	Republican	21,391,993	58.2	444	56.9
		Alfred E. Smith	Democratic	15,016,169	40.9	87	
1932	48	**Franklin D. Roosevelt**	Democratic	22,809,638	57.4	472	56.9
		Herbert C. Hoover	Republican	15,758,901	39.7	59	
		Norman Thomas	Socialist	881,951	2.2		
1936	48	**Franklin D. Roosevelt**	Democratic	27,752,869	60.8	523	61.0
		Alfred M. Landon	Republican	16,674,665	36.5	8	
		William Lemke	Union	882,479	1.9		
1940	48	**Franklin D. Roosevelt**	Democratic	27,307,819	54.8	449	62.5
		Wendell L. Wilkie	Republican	22,321,018	44.8	82	
1944	48	**Franklin D. Roosevelt**	Democratic	25,606,585	53.5	432	55.9
		Thomas E. Dewey	Republican	22,014,745	46.0	99	
1948	48	**Harry S Truman**	Democratic	24,179,345	49.6	303	53.0
		Thomas E. Dewey	Republican	21,991,291	45.1	189	
		J. Strom Thurmond	States' Rights	1,176,125	2.4	39	
		Henry A. Wallace	Progressive	1,157,326	2.4		
1952	48	**Dwight D. Eisenhower**	Republican	33,936,234	55.1	442	63.3
		Adlai E. Stevenson	Democratic	27,314,992	44.4	89	
1956	48	**Dwight D. Eisenhower**	Republican	35,590,472	57.6	457	60.6
		Adlai E. Stevenson	Democratic	26,022,752	42.1	73	
1960	50	**John F. Kennedy**	Democratic	34,226,731	49.7	303	62.8
		Richard M. Nixon	Republican	34,108,157	49.5	219	
1964	50	**Lyndon B. Johnson**	Democratic	43,129,566	61.1	486	61.7
		Barry M. Goldwater	Republican	27,178,188	38.5	52	
1968	50	**Richard M. Nixon**	Republican	31,785,480	43.4	301	60.6
		Hubert H. Humphrey	Democratic	31,275,166	42.7	191	
		George C. Wallace	American Independent	9,906,473	13.5	46	
1972	50	**Richard M. Nixon**	Republican	47,169,911	60.7	520	55.2
		George S. McGovern	Democratic	29,170,383	37.5	17	
		John G. Schmitz	American	1,099,482	1.4		

PRESIDENTIAL ELECTIONS (Continued)

Year	Number of States	Candidates	Parties	Popular Vote	% of Popular Vote	Electoral Vote	% Voter Participation[b]
1976	50	**James E. Carter**	Democratic	40,830,763	50.1	297	53.5
		Gerald R. Ford	Republican	39,147,793	48.0	240	
1980	50	**Ronald W. Reagan**	Republican	43,904,153	50.7	489	52.6
		James E. Carter	Democratic	35,483,883	41.0	49	
		John B. Anderson	Independent	5,720,060	6.6	0	
		Ed Clark	Libertarian	921,299	1.1	0	
1984	50	**Ronald W. Reagan**	Republican	54,455,075	58.8	525	53.3
		Walter F. Mondale	Democratic	37,577,185	40.6	13	
1988	50	**George H. W. Bush**	Republican	48,886,097	53.4	426	50.1
		Michael S. Dukakis	Democratic	41,809,074	45.6	111[c]	
1992	50	**William J. Clinton**	Democratic	44,909,326	43.0	370	55.2
		George H. W. Bush	Republican	39,103,882	37.4	168	
		H. Ross Perot	Independent	19,741,048	18.9	0	
1996	50	**William J. Clinton**	Democratic	47,402,357	49.2	379	49.1
		Robert J. Dole	Republican	39,196,755	40.7	159	
		H. Ross Perot	Reform	8,085,402	8.4	0	
		Ralph Nader	Green	684,902	0.7	0	
2000	50	**George W. Bush**	Republican	50,456,169	48.0	271	50.7
		Albert Gore	Democratic	50,996,116	49.0	267	
		Ralph Nader	Green	2,783,728	2.7	0	

Candidates receiving less than 1 percent of the popular vote have been omitted. Thus the percentage of popular vote given for any election year may not total 100 percent. Before the passage of the Twelfth Amendment in 1804, the Electoral College voted for two presidential candidates; the runner-up became vice president. Before 1824, most presidential electors were chosen by state legislatures, not by popular vote.
[a]Percent of voting-age population casting ballots.   [b]Greeley died shortly after the election; the electors supporting him then divided their votes among minor candidates.   [c]One elector from West Virginia cast her Electoral College presidential ballot for Lloyd Bentsen, the Democratic Party's vice-presidential candidate.

Presidents and Vice Presidents

1.	President	**George Washington**	1789–1797
	Vice President	John Adams	1789–1797
2.	President	**John Adams**	1797–1801
	Vice President	Thomas Jefferson	1797–1801
3.	President	**Thomas Jefferson**	1801–1809
	Vice President	Aaron Burr	1801–1805
	Vice President	George Clinton	1805–1809
4.	President	**James Madison**	1809–1817
	Vice President	George Clinton	1809–1813
	Vice President	Elbridge Gerry	1813–1817
5.	President	**James Monroe**	1817–1825
	Vice President	Daniel Tompkins	1817–1825
6.	President	**John Quincy Adams**	1825–1829
	Vice President	John C. Calhoun	1825–1829
7.	President	**Andrew Jackson**	1829–1837
	Vice President	John C. Calhoun	1829–1833
	Vice President	Martin Van Buren	1833–1837
8.	President	**Martin Van Buren**	1837–1841
	Vice President	Richard M. Johnson	1837–1841
9.	President	**William H. Harrison**	1841
	Vice President	John Tyler	1841
10.	President	**John Tyler**	1841–1845
	Vice President	None	
11.	President	**James K. Polk**	1845–1849
	Vice President	George M. Dallas	1845–1849
12.	President	**Zachary Taylor**	1849–1850
	Vice President	Millard Fillmore	1849–1850
13.	President	**Millard Fillmore**	1850–1853
	Vice President	None	
14.	President	**Franklin Pierce**	1853–1857
	Vice President	William R. King	1853–1857
15.	President	**James Buchanan**	1857–1861
	Vice President	John C. Breckinridge	1857–1861
16.	President	**Abraham Lincoln**	1861–1865
	Vice President	Hannibal Hamlin	1861–1865
	Vice President	Andrew Johnson	1865

PRESIDENTS AND VICE PRESIDENTS (*Continued*)

17.	President	**Andrew Johnson**	1865–1869
	Vice President	None	
18.	President	**Ulysses S. Grant**	1869–1877
	Vice President	Schuyler Colfax	1869–1873
	Vice President	Henry Wilson	1873–1877
19.	President	**Rutherford B. Hayes**	1877–1881
	Vice President	William A. Wheeler	1877–1881
20.	President	**James A. Garfield**	1881
	Vice President	Chester A. Arthur	1881
21.	President	**Chester A. Arthur**	1881–1885
	Vice President	None	
22.	President	**Grover Cleveland**	1885–1889
	Vice President	Thomas A. Hendricks	1885–1889
23.	President	**Benjamin Harrison**	1889–1893
	Vice President	Levi P. Morton	1889–1893
24.	President	**Grover Cleveland**	1893–1897
	Vice President	Adlai E. Stevenson	1893–1897
25.	President	**William McKinley**	1897–1901
	Vice President	Garret A. Hobart	1897–1901
	Vice President	Theodore Roosevelt	1901
26.	President	**Theodore Roosevelt**	1901–1909
	Vice President	Charles Fairbanks	1905–1909
27.	President	**William H. Taft**	1909–1913
	Vice President	James S. Sherman	1909–1913
28.	President	**Woodrow Wilson**	1913–1921
	Vice President	Thomas R. Marshall	1913–1921
29.	President	**Warren G. Harding**	1921–1923
	Vice President	Calvin Coolidge	1921–1923
30.	President	**Calvin Coolidge**	1923–1929
	Vice President	Charles G. Dawes	1925–1929
31.	President	**Herbert C. Hoover**	1929–1933
	Vice President	Charles Curtis	1929–1933
32.	President	**Franklin D. Roosevelt**	1933–1945
	Vice President	John N. Garner	1933–1941
	Vice President	Henry A. Wallace	1941–1945
	Vice President	Harry S Truman	1945
33.	President	**Harry S Truman**	1945–1953
	Vice President	Alben W. Barkley	1949–1953
34.	President	**Dwight D. Eisenhower**	1953–1961
	Vice President	Richard M. Nixon	1953–1961

PRESIDENTS AND VICE PRESIDENTS (*Continued*)

35.	President	**John F. Kennedy**	1961–1963
	Vice President	Lyndon B. Johnson	1961–1963
36.	President	**Lyndon B. Johnson**	1963–1969
	Vice President	Hubert H. Humphrey	1965–1969
37.	President	**Richard M. Nixon**	1969–1974
	Vice President	Spiro T. Agnew	1969–1973
	Vice President	Gerald R. Ford	1973–1974
38.	President	**Gerald R. Ford**	1974–1977
	Vice President	Nelson A. Rockefeller	1974–1977
39.	President	**James E. Carter**	1977–1981
	Vice President	Walter F. Mondale	1977–1981
40.	President	**Ronald W. Reagan**	1981–1989
	Vice President	George H. W. Bush	1981–1989
41.	President	**George H. W. Bush**	1989–1993
	Vice President	J. Danforth Quayle	1989–1993
42.	President	**William J. Clinton**	1993–2001
	Vice President	Albert Gore	1993–2001
43.	President	**George W. Bush**	2001–
	Vice President	Richard Cheney	2001–

For a complete list of Presidents, Vice Presidents, and Cabinet Members, go to http://college.hmco.com.

Text Credits

pages 37–39: Samuel Eliot Morison, ed. and trans. *Journals and Other Documents on the Life and Voyages of Christopher Columbus,* Heritage, New York, 1963, pp. 151–155.

pages 79–81: Excerpts from Francis A. McNutt, *Bartholomew De Las Casas: His Life, His Apostolate, and His Writings,* G. P. Putnam's Sons, New York:, 1970, pp. 314–321. Reprinted by permission of Penguin Putnam, Inc.

page 945: Lines from "I, Too, Sing America," from *Collected Poems,* by Langston Hughes. Copyright © 1994 by the Estate of Langston Hughes. Reprinted by permission of Alfred A. Knopf, a Division of Random House, Inc.

page 1006: Excerpts from Herbert Hoover's speech of October 20, 1936, courtesy of the Hoover Presidential Library.

pages 1174–1175: Reprinted by arrangement with The Heirs to the Estate of Martin Luther King, Jr., c/o Writers House, Inc. as agent for the proprietor. Copyright © 1963 by Martin Luther King, Jr., copyright renewed 1991 by Coretta Scott King.

pages 1175–1176: Excerpts from *The Autobiography of Malcolm X* by Malcolm X with the assistance of Alex Haley. Copyright © 1964 by Alex Haley and Malcolm X. Copyright © 1965 by Alex Haley and Betty Shabazz. Reprinted by permission of Random House, Inc.

pages 1216–1217: Gloria Steinem, "What It Would Be Like If Women Win," *Time,* 31, August 1970, pp. 22 and 25. Reprinted by permission of Gloria Steinem, Consulting Editor, *Ms.* Magazine.

pages 1217–1218: Phyllis Schlafly, excerpt from *The Power of the Positive Woman* (1970), pp. 11–18. Reprinted by permission of the author.

pages 1256–1257: "Ecodefence: A Field Guide to Monkeywrenching," by Dave Foreman and Bill Haywood. *Ecodefence,* Abbzug Press, 1993, pp. 5-11. Reprinted by permission of Abbzug Press.

page 1257: G. M. Keller, Chairman of the Board and CEO of the Chevron Corporation, "Industry and the Environment" in *Vital Speeches of the Day,* No. 9, December 15, 1987, pp. 78–80. Reprinted by permission of Chevron Corporation.

Index

A. T. Stewart, 700
Abbey, Edward, 1258
Abbott, Grace, 818, 1000
Abbott, Lyman, 860
Abenaki people, 63, 105
Abilene, Kansas, 672; life in, 678
Abolitionist movement, 449–451, 475–476, 534, 535
Abolition Society of Pennsylvania, 247
Abortion: opposition to, 751, 1222, 1225, 1228, 1229, 1229(illus.); *Roe* v. *Wade* decision on, 1200, 1271; proponents of, 1228–1229, 1229(illus.); *Webster* v. *Reproductive Health Services* and, 1271
Abraham Lincoln Battalion, 1011
Abrams v. *U.S.* (1918), 906
Abyssinian Baptist Church, 628(illus.)
Abzug, Bella, 1200
Acadia: Huguenot settlers in, 46, 47; British expulsion of French from, 165–166
Acheson, Dean, 1059, 1074–1075, 1075–1076, 1084
Achille Lauro (ship), 1245
Acoma, New Mexico, 45
Acquired Immune Deficiency Syndrome (AIDS), 1230–1231
Action Comics, 992
Acts of Trade (England), 94–95, 97, 108, 130–131; enforcement of, 98; rice and, 143
Adams, Abigail, 218
Adams, Henry, 594, 694, 766, 776, 777, 789
Adams, John, 186, 191, 251, 285, 292; at Second Continental Congress, 204; Virginia resolution and, 207; form of government proposed by, 226, 227; negotiation of peace with Britain and France, 235; Constitution and, 259, 261; as vice president, 267; as president, 277–278, 288
Adams, John Quincy, 306, 312–313; Monroe Doctrine and, 316–317; as president, 373–375; support of Native Americans, 379; opposition to admission of Texas, 503
Adams, Samuel, 180, 184, 185, 186, 189
Adamson Act, 838
Adams-Onís Treaty (1819), 306, 499
Addams, Jane, 746, 804–805, 812, 818, 820, 864, 893, 953

Adding machine, invention of, 696
Addison, Joseph, 113
Adena culture, 6
Administration of Justice Act (1774) (England), 190
Adolescents, rock and roll and, 1102–1103
The Adventures of Huckleberry Finn (Twain), 642, 747
Advertising, 701–702; during World War I, 903; following World War I, 932; sexual freedom in 1920s and, 940–941; on television, 1099, 1247, 1248
Affirmative action, 1195–1197
The Affluent Society (Sandberg), 1123
Afghanistan, Soviet invasion of, 1212
Africa: West, cultures of, 1400–1600, 12–14, 13(map); Portuguese slave trade and, 25–27; World War II in, 1023, 1024(map); AIDS in, 1231. *See also* Slaves; Slave trade; *specific countries*
African-Americans: families of, 147, 459, 627; marriage of, 147, 458–459, 627; in white churches, 152, 354, 460, 468; in Continental Army, 209; following Revolutionary War, 246–248; suffrage for, 247, 368, 475, 643, 770, 823–824, 1153–1154; migration to cities, 348, 824, 902, 943, 1037–1038; churches of, 354, 468–470, 627; in northern cities, 412–413; racism against, 413–414, 642–645, 819, 838, 860, 898, 902–903, 917, 1150; education of, 432, 625, 642–643, 644, 824, 1292; coloniza-tion movement and, 447–448, 475; housing of, 458; middle-class, 468, 1195; white percep-tion as inferior, 514, 546–547, 831, 943; pro-hibition by state laws, 515; in Union army, 590–591, 591(illus.), 599; office holding by, during Reconstruction, 623–624; in southern Republican Party, 623–624; white supremacy in postwar South and, 642–645; lynchings of, 644, 645(illus.), 824, 903, 917; migration to West, 657–658; employment during 1870–1900, 714; in unions, 716, 717, 944, 1039; prohibi-tion from urban white neighborhoods, 738–739; exclusion from entertainment, 744; in baseball, 746, 936; women's associations of, 749(illus.), 750; Colored Farmers' Alliance and, 784; women's voluntary associations of,

African-Americans *(continued)*
809; during Progressive Era, 823–825; during Roosevelt's (Theodore) administration, 831; Wilson's sanctioning of discrimination against, 838; in armed forces, 860, 897–898, 1037, 1038(illus.), 1161; employment during World War I, 902; during World War I, 902–903; poverty among, following World War I, 938; employment during 1920s, 943; black identity and, 945; black nationalism among, 945; writing of, 945; during Great Depression, 973–974, 982; in sports, 992–993; New Deal and, 997–998; during Roosevelt's (Franklin) administration, 998; employment during World War II, 1037, 1039; World War II and, 1037–1039, 1038(illus.); poverty among, 1116, 1196; voter registration of, 1154, 1154(illus.); office holding by, 1195; affirmative action and, 1195–1197; AIDS among, 1231; Hispanic prejudice against, 1232–1233; Black Entertainment Television and, 1248; single mothers among, 1249; economic gains during 1989-1999, 1289; Simpson trial and, 1292. *See also* Civil rights; Freemen; Racial segregation; Racism; Slavery; Slaves; Slave trade
African Free Schools, 248
African Marine Fund, 248
African Methodist Episcopal (AME) Church, 469–470
Agee, James, 991
Agency for International Development (AID), 1138
Agnew, Spiro, 1190, 1193
Agricultural Adjustment Act (AAA), 982, 997
Agriculture: Native American, 5, 8, 9, 63; European, 1400-1600, 14–15, 15(illus.), 16, 17–19; European impact on, 31; of New World, impact on Europe, 32; in West Indies, 59–61; in colonial New England, 69–70; in Carolinas, 86–87; in colonial mid-Atlantic region, 138; in colonial Chesapeake region, 139, 142, 345; following French and Indian War, 174; in North, 295, 341–343, 415; farm women's lives and, 342, 415–416; scientific methods and crop diversification in, 342–343; farm families' houses and, 360(illus.), 361, 679; in Old Northwest Territory, 416; in South during 1820–1850, 453–454, 455(map), 456, 474–475; tenant farming in South and, 474–475, 627–629, 629(map); in California, 505–506; crop-lien system in South and, 640–641; agribusiness and, 674; technological

advances in, 674, 675(illus.); in West, 674–675; farm life in West and, 679–680; farmers' discontent during 1880-1892 and, 781–783; Alliance Movement and, 784–786; election of 1892 and, 786–788; following World War I, 936–937; subsidies during Great Depression, 982. *See also* Plantations; *specific crops*
Aguinaldo, Emilio, 864, 865
AIDS, 1230–1231
AIDS Coalition to Unleash Power (ACT UP), 1230
Aid to Families with Dependent Children (AFDC), 1235, 1276
Airplanes: *Spirit of St. Louis,* 927; B-17 bombers, 1025; in World War II, 1025; production of, women's employment in, 1037; *Enola Gay,* 1042; of Strategic Air Command, 1111; U-2 spy plane incident and, 1123; B-52s, 1183; B-1 bombers, 1240; Korean Airlines plane shot down by Soviets, 1241; terrorist attacks on, 1245
Aix-la-Chapelle, Treaty of (1748), 110
Alabama: voting rights in, 292; suffrage in, 366; secession of, 557
Alabama (ship), 576, 849
Alamance, Battle of, 153, 172, 196
Alamo, siege of, 501–502, 502(illus.)
Alaska: Seward's purchase of, 849; economy in 2000, 1287
Albany campaign, 1148
Albany Congress, 164–165
Albany Regency, 372
Albemarle Sound region, 87–88
Albright, Madeline, 1280
Alcoholic beverages: temperance movement and, 428–429, 753–754. *See also* Bars and saloons
Alcott, Louisa May, 588
Aldrich, Nelson W., 832
Alexander, Grover, 935
Alexander v. *Holmes County Board of Education* (1969), 1195
Alfred P. Murrah Federal Building bombing, 1293–1294
Alger, Horatio, 702, 703
Algonquian people, 8, 9, 46, 47, 48, 74; English relations with, 51–52
Alibamu people, 30
Alien Act (1798), 277, 278, 288
Alien Act (1918), 904
All-American Canal, 983
All-American Soapbox Derby, 992

Allen, Richard, 1240
Allen, Ethan, 153, 169, 203
Allen, Richard, 469
Allende, Salvador, 1186
Alley Gang, 740
Alliance Movement, 784–786. *See also* Populist
  Party
Allies: in World War I, 889–890, 908; in World
  War II, 1014–1015, 1023–1026, 1024(map),
  1026(illus.)
All in the Family (television show), 1202–1203,
  1248
"All Shook Up" (song), 1103
Almay, Richard, 336
Almay, William, 341
Alsop, Joseph, 1066
Alsop, Stewart, 1066
Altgeld, John Peter, 791
Altgeld, Peter, 718
Amazon.com, 1284
Amerasia magazine, 1078
American Anti-Slavery Society, 450–451, 451
American Asiatic Association, 867
American Civil Liberties Union (ACLU), 906,
  949, 965, 966
American Defense Society, 904–905
American Dictionary of the English Language,
  294
American Expeditionary Force (AEF), 908
American Family Association, 1228
American Federation of Labor (AFL), 826, 938;
  during 1886–1900, 715, 719, 724–726; during
  1933–1938, 995–996; position on women's
  employment, 999; merger with CIO, 1098
American Fur Company, 302
American Guide Series, 988
American identity: print culture and, 292–294;
  migration to western territories and, 296
American Independence Party, 1169
American Indian Movement (AIM), 1198
American Indians. *See* Native Americans; *specific
  groups*
American Medical Association (AMA), 812; op-
  position to Truman's insurance plan, 1072
The American Mercury (Mencken), 942
American Party, 544–545, 545, 546
American Philosophical Society (APS), 113, 114,
  292, 436
American Protection Association (APA), 754
American Protective League (APL), 904–905
American Psychiatric Association, 1199
American Railway Union (ARU), 791
American Revolution. *See* Revolutionary War

Americans for Democratic Action (ADA), 1068,
  1069
*American Slavery as It Is: Testimony of a Thou-
  sand Witnesses* (Grimké, Grimké, and Weld),
  451
American Society for the Promotion of Temper-
  ance, 429
American Special Forces units, 1138
American Spelling Book (Webster), 293(illus.),
  294
American Sunday School Union, 355
Americans with Disabilities Act (1990), 1270
American System, 313, 335, 373–374, 386(illus.),
  448; Jackson's attempt to dismantle, 382
American Telephone and Telegraph Company,
  696–697
American Temperance Union, 429
American Tobacco Company, 707, 830
American Tract Society, 369
America Online, 1283
Amherst, Jeffrey, 170
Amish people, 24, 223
Amsterdam, Netherlands, 48
Amusement. *See* Entertainment
Amusement parks, 744
Anabaptists, 24
Anacostia Flats, Battle of, 977
Anasazi culture, 7, 7(illus.)
Anderson, John, 1226
Anderson, Marian, 998, 999(illus.)
Anderson, Robert, 567
Andersonville, Georgia, prison at, 586
Andover Theological Seminary, 354–355
André, John, 222
Andros, Edmund, 89, 97, 98, 99
And the Band Played On (Shilts), 1230
Angelou, Maya, 1044
Anglican Church. *See* Church of England
Anglo-Dutch War: second (1665–1667), 88;
  third (1672–1674), 89
Anglo-Iranian Oil Company, 1115
Annapolis, Maryland, tea party in, 190
Annapolis Convention (1786), 260
Anthony, Susan B., 433, 434(illus.), 621–622
Antiballistic missile systems (ABMs), 1185
Anti-coolie clubs, 681
Antietam, battle at, 573(map), 577–578,
  578(illus.)
Antifederalists: form of government and,
  263, 264–265, 266; in first Congress,
  267
Antigua, 59
Anti-Imperialist League, 863–864

Antinomianism, 68

Anti-rent riots, in Hudson River valley, 153

Anti-Saloon League, 754, 814, 821–822, 906–908

Anti-Semitism, Holocaust and, 1027–1028, 1027(illus.)

Antitrust laws, 708, 781, 830, 837

Antitrust suits, against U.S. Steel, 833

Antiwar movement, 1164–1165, 1177, 1181–1182

Apache people, 305, 500, 662; Spanish attempts to convert to Catholicism, 45; resistance to white settlers, 664–665

Apalachee people, 105

Apartheid, 1240–1241, 1266

Apollo 11, 1188

Apollo Creed, 1203

Appeal . . . to the Colored Citizens (Walker), 448

Appeasement policy, toward Germany, 1010

Apple I computer, 1283

Appomattox Courthouse, Confederate surrender at, 599–600

Apprenticeship system, disruption of, 421–422

Arabic (ship), 892

Arafat, Yasir, 1267

Arapaho people, 302, 498, 662; resettlement of, 665; resistance to white settlers, 665, 666–667

Arawak people, 27

Arbella (ship), 65

Arbenz Guzman, Jacob, 1115

Architecture: skyscrapers and, 737, 932. *See also* Housing

Area Redevelopment Act, 1137

Arikara people, 666–667

Aristide, Jean-Bertrand, 1266, 1278

Arizona (ship), 1008

Arizona, entry into Union, 661

Arkansas: secession of, 568; Democratic resurgence in, 634

Arkwright, Richard, 336

Armed forces: British, in Revolutionary War, 208–211; conscription and, 223, 579–580; African-Americans in, 860, 897–898, 898, 1037, 1038(illus.), 1161; women in, 897, 910, 910(illus.), 1039; Native Americans in, 1039; racial discrimination in, Truman's attempt to end, 1068–1069; desegregation of, Korean War and, 1078; training of, 1138; buildup under Reagan, 1240; Clinton's policy toward homosexuals in, 1275. *See also* Draft; Militia; *specific forces*

Armour, Philip, 587

Arms. *See* Nuclear weapons; Weapons

Arms races, 1074; attempt to control during 1920s, 957–958; Eisenhower's attempt to end, 1112; escalation under Reagan, 1241–1242

Armstrong, Louis, 945

Armstrong, Neil, 1188

The Army Hour (radio program), 1032

Army of the Republic of Vietnam (ARVN), 1156

Arnold, Benedict, 203, 205, 211–212, 222–223

Arthur, Chester A., 772(illus.), 773, 774, 775, 776

Articles of Confederation (1781), 228–229, 255

Artisans, 332; colonial, 132–133; in cities, 349; housing of, 362; republicanism of, 392

Arts: during Renaissance, 21; museum construction and, 751; conservative war against National Endowment for the Arts and, 1227–1228. *See also specific arts*

Ashcan school, 748

Asia: beginning of American trade with, 253. *See also specific countries*

As I Lay Dying (Faulkner), 991

Assassinations: of Lincoln, 607–608; of Garfield, 776; of McKinley, 828; of Franz Ferdinand, 888; of Long, 985; of Kennedy (John), 1133–1134, 1143; of Diem, 1142; of Malcolm X, 1155; of King, 1166–1167; of Kennedy (Robert), 1167; of Allende, 1186; attempted, of Reagan, 1235–1236

Assemblies. *See* Legislatures

Assembly line, 930

Assimilation: of Native Americans, 667–669; of immigrants, public schools and, 754–756, 755(illus.); Hispanics' challenge of, 1197

Associated Press (AP), 957

Association Agreement (1774), 192, 193(illus.), 205

Astor, John Jacob, 410, 490

Astoria Hotel, 737

Aswan Dam, 1113

Atchison, David, 541

Athapaskan people, 7, 8

Atlanta, Georgia: Union burning of, 597; population growth during 1870–1900, 639; African-American employment in, 714

Atlanta Compromise, 644–645, 824

Atlanta Constitution, 639

Atlanta Rolling Mill, 714

Atlanta University, 625

Atlantic Charter (1941), 1017–1018, 1054

Atlantic Express, 661

Atomic bomb, 1042, 1043(illus.), 1047–1049

Atomic Energy Commission, 1058, 1108

Atomic power, anxiety about, 1122–1123

Attorneys, Enlightenment view of, 114

Attucks, Crispus, 186

Augustine of Hippo, St., 22

Austin, Moses, 500

Austin, Stephen, 500

Australia, in World War II, 1040

Austria, union with Germany, 1014

Automation, elimination of jobs by, 1098

Automobiles: production of, 930, 931–932, 931(illus.), 933, 1100; dating during 1920s and, 940; roads and, 1100; culture during 1945–1960 and, 1100–1101; foreign competition in market for, 1206

The Awakening (Chopin), 642

Axis powers, in World War II, 1023–1025, 1024(map)

Aylwin, Patricio, 1266

Aztec empire, 9, 10, 11(illus.), 29, 30–31; decimation by disease, 33

Babcock, Orville E., 631

Baby boom, 1094–1096, 1095(illus.); college-age population of 1960s and, 1162; money culture and, 1247

Bacall, Lauren, 1081(illus.)

Bache, Sarah Franklin, 214

Bacon, Francis, 93

Bacon, Nathaniel, 76–77, 79–81

Bacon's Rebellion, 76–77, 79–81

Bad Axe, massacre at, 381

Bailey, Josiah, 989

B-52 airplanes, 1183

Baker, James A., III, 1264–1265, 1267

Baker, Ray Stannard, 811, 912

Bakke, Allan, 1195

Bakker, Jim, 1222

Bakke v. *University of California,* 1195

Balance of trade, deficit in, 1206

Balboa, Vasco Nuñez de, 29

Baldwin, Roger, 906

Ball, George, 1141, 1156

Ballinger, Richard, 833

Baltimore (ship), 853

Baltimore, Maryland: population in 1770s, 143; during 1820–1850, 406; population in 1860, 454; odor in, 739; government of, 743

Baltimore Railroad, strike against, 774

Bankers, opposition to Bank of the United States, 384–385

Banking system, 1929 crash and, 970–971

Bank of North America (BNA), 229

Bank of the United States: First, 269, 272, 288; Second, 290–291, 313, 314, 319–321, 384–387; closing of, 970

Bankruptcies: in Panic of 1819, 314; in Panic of 1873, 633; of railroads, in 1893, 788; World War II and, 1020

Banks: failures of, Panic of 1819 and, 314; chartering of, commerce and, 339; creation of national banking system and, 587, 837; failures of, in 1893, 788; failures of, Great Depression and, 967, 970–971; Roosevelt's (Franklin) attempt to save, 979–980; savings and loan crisis and, 1237

Banks, Nathaniel P., 593

Bannaker, Benjamin, 468

Baptist Association, 248

Baptist Church, 24; in colonial Massachusetts, 68; Great Awakening and, 150, 151; following Revolutionary War, 244, 246; on abolition, 248; Second Great Awakening and, 353, 354, 355; African-American, 460, 469; southern, growth during 1965–1980, 1222

Barbados, 59; sugar cultivation and slavery in, 60–61, 145

Barbed wire, 674

Barnett, Ross, 1148–1149

Barras, Comte de, 234

Bars and saloons: in western towns, 678; immigrants and, 734; purity movement and, 753–754; prohibition and, 821–822; illegal, during Prohibition, 950, 951(illus.); gay, 1035

Barton, Bruce, 933

Baruch, Bernard, 900–901, 913

Baseball, 745–746, 745(illus.), 935–936; African-Americans in, 746, 936; gambling on, 917; during 1930s, 992

Basketball, 744

Bath, South Carolina, 88

Batista, Fulgencio, 1123

Baxter Street Dudes, 740

Bayard, Thomas F., 856

Bay of Pigs fiasco, 1139–1140

Bayonet Constitution, 855

B-1 bomber, 1240

B-17 bomber, 1025

Beard, Charles A., 808

Beard, Dewey, 654

Bear Flag Republic, 509

Bear That Catches, 654

The Beast of Berlin (movie), 903

Beat generation, 1162

Beatles, 1163

Beaufort, South Carolina, 46

Beauregard, P. G. T., 567

Bedford, Gunning, 262

Beecher, Catharine, 431, 451

Beecher, Lyman, 354, 429, 431, 435, 449, 451, 544

Beer-Wine Revenue Act (1933), 980

Beijing, China, Tiananmen Square demonstration in, 1267

Bellamy, Edward, 703, 704

Belgium: German invasion of, 1015; postwar, communism in, 1055

Belknap, Ruth, 342

Bell, Alexander Graham, 694

Bell, Daniel, 1115

Bell, John, 555, 556

Bellamy clubs, 703

Belleau Wood, battles at, 908, 909

Belle Isle, prison at, 586

Bellows, George, 748

Benedict, Ruth, 943

Benezet, Anthony, 247

Benin, early, 14

Benny, Jack, 994

Benson, Ezra T., 1107

Benton, Thomas Hart, 489, 992

Bentsen, Lloyd, 1263

Berger, Victor, 904–905

Bering Sea, closure to foreign shipping, 854

Bering Strait, ice bridge at, 5

Berkeley, John, 88–89

Berkeley, William, 76, 77

Berkman, Alexander, 925

Berle, Milton, 1099

Berlin, Irving, 1033

Berlin, Germany: division of, 1057, 1062–1063; airlift to, 1062, 1063(illus.); Soviet militancy about, 1139

Berlin Wall, 1139; fall of, 1264, 1265(illus.)

Bernard, Francis, 184

Berry, Chuck, 1103

Bessemer, invention of, 697

Beveridge, Albert, 850

Bicycling, during 1865–1910, 750

Biddle, Nicholas, 385, 386

Big Foot, 654

Big Head, Kate, 667

Big Money (Dos Passos), 991

Big Three (automakers), 933

Big Three (world leaders), 1019; at Yalta Conference, 1029–1031, 1031(illus.)

Billion Dollar Congress, 773, 780–781

Bill of Rights (1791) (United States), 268, 271

Bill of Rights (England), 98

Bin Laden, Osama, 1293

Birch, James H., 467

Birmingham, Alabama: population growth during 1870–1900, 639; civil rights movement in, 1151, 1152(illus.)

Birney, James G., 478, 508

Birth control: during 1920s, 940; Reagan's opposition to, 1228

Birth of a Nation (movie), 947

Birthrate: decline in, during 1750–1800, 352; decline in, during 1800–1820, 408–409; decline in, during 1800–1900, 748; decline in, during 1920s, 940; decline in, during Great Depression, 972; during 1945–mid-1960s, 1094–1096, 1095(illus.)

Bishop, Abraham, 378

Black, Hugo, 1148

Black Americans. *See* African-Americans

Black Ball Line, 417

Black Belt, 345, 456

Black Cat, Chief, 300

Black Codes, 467–468, 475, 477, 616

Black Coyote, 655–656

Black Death, 14

Black Elk, 656

Black Entertainment Television, 1248

Blackfoot people, 662

Black Hawk, Chief, 381

Black Kettle, 664, 665

Blackmun, Harry, 1271

Black Muslims, 1155

Black Power, 1155

Black Star Lines, 944

Black Thursday, 970

Blaine, James G., 768, 776–778, 852, 855

Blair, Francis Preston, 377

The Blast, 925

Blitzkrieg, 1014, 1015

The Blob (movie), 1122

Blockbuster Video, 1291

Bloodhound Bill, 534

Bloom, Allan, 1233

Blough, Roger, 1137

Blount, James H., 856

"Blowin' in the Wind" (song), 1163

"Blueberry Hill" (song), 1103

Board of Trade (England), 94

Boas, Franz, 942–943

Bob Jones University, 1238

Bodie, California, 679

Bodmer, Karl, 437

Boesky, Ivan, 1247

Bogart, Humphrey, 1081(illus.)

Boland Amendment (1984), 1244, 1245

Bolshevik Revolution (1917), 912, 1052

Bombing: of Vietnam, under Johnson, 1157; of Cambodia during Vietnam War, 1177, 1181–1182; of Vietnam, under Nixon, 1182–1183; of Iran, 1280–1281

Bombings: by student protesters, 1189; of U.S. Marine barracks in Lebanon, 1244–1245; of Pan Am flight over Lockerbie, Scotland, 1245; of military barracks in Saudi Arabia, 1293; of

U.S. embassies in Africa, 1293; of World Trade Center, 1293; in Oklahoma City, 1293–1294. *See also* Terrorism
Bonaparte, Joseph, 306
Bonds: to finance Civil War, 580; to finance World War I, 900; to finance World War II, 1022
Bone, Homer, 1013
Bonus Army, 977
Book of Mormon, 435
Books: sales during 1950s, 1104. *See also* Libraries
Boone, Daniel, 172, 437
Boorstin, Daniel, 1115–1116
Booth, John Wilkes, 607, 608
Booth, William, 752, 809
Bootleggers, 950
Borah, William, 1014
Borden, Gail, 418
Border ruffians, 541–542
Border States: battle for, 568–570. *See also* Delaware; Kentucky; Maryland; Missouri
Bork, Robert H., 1192–1193, 1238
Born again conversions, 1222
Bortwick, J. D., 678
Bosnia-Herzegovina, 1279
Boston, Massachusetts: trade with West Indies, 95; colonial population of, 131; wealthy families of, 132; riots against poor in, 134; minutemen's siege of, 202; growth during 1820–1850, 406; Irish immigrants in, 408; ethnic tensions during 1820–1850, 413; rescue of Anthony Burns in, 534–535; nativism in, 544; population during 1900–1915, 735; neighborhoods in, 737; fire in, 740; government of, 743; police strike in, 918
Boston Associates, 424, 454
Boston Athenaeum, 436
Boston Female Anti-Slavery Society, 451
Boston Massacre, 185–186, 187(illus.)
Boston News-Letter, 115
Boston Tea Party, 189–190
Boulder Dam, 983
Bouweries, 49
Bow, Clara, 933, 934
Bowdoin, James, 186, 254
Bowie, Jim, 501
Bowles, Chester, 1065
Boxers (Chinese society), 867
Boxing, 744, 934–935; in western towns, 678; during 1930s, 992
Boylston, Thomas, 218
Boynton, Amelia, 1150
Boy Spies of America, 904–905

Braceros, 1039
Braddock, Edward, 165
Bradford, William, 63, 64, 115
Bradley, James L., 466–467
Bradley, Joseph P., 637
Bradley, Omar, 1027
Bradley, Solomon, 590–591
Brady, Nicholas, 1270
Bragg, Braxton, 577, 594
Brandeis, Louis D., 808, 835, 838, 906
Brant, Joseph, 221, 221(illus.), 231, 258
Braun, Eva, 1031
Brazil, 1266
Breaking Away (movie), 1203
Breckinridge, John C., 555, 556
Brennan, William J., Jr., 1148
Brest-Litovsk Treaty (1918), 908
Brevisima relacion de la destruccion de las Indias (Las Casas), 38–39
Brezhnev, Leonid, 1185
Briand, Aristide, 958
Bricker, John W., 1029
Brimelow, Peter, 1233
Briscoe v. *Bank of Kentucky* (1837), 388
Britain: migration to cities from, 731; Samoa and, 856; Panama Canal and, 868; in World War I, 888, 890–891, 892, 908; control of seas during early World War I, 890; army of, in 1917, 896; appeasement policy of, 1010; in World War II, 1014, 1017–1018, 1023; Berlin airlift and, 1062; Suez affair and, 1113–1114; bombing of Iran by, 1280–1281. *See also* England
British-American Tobacco Company, 871
British East India Company, 188–189
British Guiana, boundary dispute with Venezuela, 854
Broadway Tabernacle, 356
Broidrick, Annie, 472
Brokers, 707
Brook Farm, 436, 438
Brooklyn, New York, population in 1860, 727
Brooks, Preston, 542
Brotherhood of Sleeping Car Porters, 944, 1038
Broughton, Thomas, 87(illus.)
Browder, Earl, 1084
Brown, Frederick, 526
Brown, Henry B., 644
Brown, John, 525–527, 542
Brown, Joseph E., 579
Brown, Linda, 1131–1132
Brown, Moses, 336, 341
Brown, Oliver, 1131–1132
Brown, Pat, 1156

Brown, Ron, 1274
Brown, William Hill, 293–294
Brown University, 151
Brown v. Board of Education of Topeka, Kansas (1954), 1119, 1130, 1131–1132
Brush, Charles, 698
Brussels Treaty (1948), 1062
Bryan, Charles W., 955
Bryan, William Jennings, 764–765, 793, 830, 832, 955, 959; presidential campaign of, 794, 796, 797; as secretary of state, 875, 889, 892; Scopes monkey trial and, 949, 964–965, 966
Bryce, James, 766
Bryn Mawr College, 941
Bubonic plague, 14
Buchanan, James, 514, 536, 538, 546, 551; on slavery, 549; southern secessions and, 557, 566
Buchanan, Patrick, 1230, 1243, 1272
Buchanan v. Worley, 824
Buchenwald, 1027
Bucktails, 372
Budgets. *See* Defense budget; Federal budget
Buell, Don Carlos, 575
Buffalo, 301; Plains Indians and, 663–664; railroads and, 664
Bulgaria, Soviet control of, 1057, 1064
Bulge, Battle of (1944), 1027
Bull Moose, 834, 834(illus.)
Bull Run: First Battle of (1861), 572; Second Battle of (1862), 577
Bundy, McGeorge, 1137
Bunker Hill, battle of, 202
Buntline, Ned (Edward Zane Carroll Judson), 684
Bunyan, John, 811
Bureau of Indian Affairs (BIA), 998, 1197, 1198
Bureau of Refugees, Freedmen, and Abandoned Lands. *See* Freedmen's Bureau
Burger, Warren, 1190, 1238
Burghers, 48
Burgoyne, John, 211, 212
Burke, Edmund, 193
Burleson, Albert, 904, 918
Burlington and Missouri River Railroad Company, 661
Burns, Anthony, 534–535
Burnside, Ambrose, 591, 592
Burr, Aaron, 278, 299
Burroughs, Nannie Helen, 749(illus.)
Bush, George, 1225, 1260, 1262, 1263; policy toward Soviet Union and Eastern Europe, 1264–1266; move against Noriega, 1266–1267; Gulf War and, 1267–1269, 1268(map), 1297–1299; economy under, 1269–1270; environmental policy of, 1270–1271; Supreme Court appointments of, 1271; Los Angeles riots and, 1271–1272; in election of 1992, 1272, 1273
Bush, George W., 1287–1288
Bushwhackers, 569
Business: entrepreneurs and, during 1820–1850, 421, 423; failures in Panic of 1873, 633; Harding's and Coolidge's support of, 953, 954(illus.); Hoover's views on, 954; failures during Great Depression, 971; mobilization for World War II and, 1020. *See also* Commerce; Corporations; Management, corporate; Maritime commerce; Merchants; Stores; Trusts
Business culture, 702–703
Busing, to achieve desegregation, 1195, 1196–1197
Butler, Andrew, 542
Butler, Benjamin, 622
Butler v. U. S. (1936), 982
Byelorussia (Belarus), independence of, 1264
By-employments, 137
Byrd, Harry, 1131
Byrne, David, 1232
Byrnes, James, 1047, 1051, 1057, 1057(illus.), 1059, 1068, 1090

C. Turner Joy (ship), 1157
Cabeza de Vaca, Alvar Nuñez, 30
Cable cars, 735
Cabot, John, 50
Caddell, Pat, 1222
Caddo people, 106
Cahokia culture, 6–7
Cain Ridge, Kentucky, gospel meeting at, 246
Calhoun, John C., 313, 371, 373, 418, 896; War of 1812 and, 309; on tariffs, 374; opposition to Tariff of Abominations, 382–383; Whig Party and, 388; on slavery, 478, 528–529, 532, 546–547; on Mexican territory, 507, 512
California: settlement of, 505–506; gold rush and, 516–519, 523–524, 670, 681; slavery and, 529–530; admission as state, 530, 532; agribusiness in, 674; population during 1850–1860, 675; Chinese population during 1890–1900, 681; Anglo population during 1845–1900, 683; progressive reform in, 817; crusade against Japanese immigrants in, 822–823; growth due to World War II, 1035; population growth during 1945–1960, 1101; Hispanic population during 1950s, 1117; Proposition 13 in, 1222; economy in 2000, 1287; Proposition 209 in, 1292

California, Indoors and Out (Farnham), 679
California Agricultural Labor Relations Act (1975), 1197
Californios, 505, 518; white encroachment on, 681
Callen, Michael, 1230
Calley, William L., 1161
Calvert, Cecilius, Lord Baltimore, 56, 57–58, 100
Calvert, George, Lord Baltimore, 56
Calvin, John, 23
Calvinists, 24
Cambodia, extension of Vietnam War into, 1177, 1181–1182
Cambria Iron Works, 710
Cambridge Platform, 69
Cammeyer, William H., 745
Campbell, D'Ann, 1037
Camp David Accords (1979), 1210–1211, 1211(illus.)
Camp revival meetings, 354, 355(illus.)
Canada: Cartier's exploration of, 46; French territories in, 46–48; raids in Ohio Valley from, 164; Second Continental Congress' appeals to, 203–204; American invasion of, 205; American claiming of, 235; controversy over fishing rights with Great Britain and, 854; reciprocity agreement with, 874; North American Free Trade Agreement and, 1278
Canals, 326(map), 329–332; impact of, 331–332; during 1820–1850, 419; in antebellum South, 454; Panama Canal, 845–846, 868–869; All-American Canal, 983
Canal Zone, Carter's promise to return to Panama, 1211
Canary Islands, slavery in, 26
Cane Ridge, Kentucky, open-air revival meeting at, 354
Cannibals All! Or, Slaves Without Masters (Fitzhugh), 478, 547
Cannon, Joseph, 832–833
Cape Breton Island, 50; War of Jenkins' Ear and, 110
Capone, Al "Scarface," 950
Capra, Frank, 994
Caribbean. *See* West Indies; *specific islands*
Carlos III, king of Spain, 305
Carmichael, Stokely, 1155
Carnegie, Andrew, 587, 702, 703, 705, 708, 864
Carolinas: during 1660–1685, 84–88; founding of, 85–86; rice cultivation in, 86–87; colonial economy of, 143–144. *See also* North Carolina; South Carolina
Carpetbaggers, 624
Carranza, Venustiano, 877, 878, 879

Carrizal incident, 878
Cars. *See* Automobiles
Carson, James H., 523–524
Carson, Price, Scott, 700
Carson, Rachel, 1207–1208
Carswell, G. Harrold, 1190
Carter, Jimmy, 1209–1212; in election of 1980, 1225–1226
Carteret, George, 88–89
Cartes des visite, 584
Cartier, Jacques, 46
Cartography. *See* Maps
Casa de Contratacion, 92
Casey, William, 1245
Cash register, invention of, 696
Cass, Lewis, 515, 536
Castro, Fidel, 1123, 1139
Catawba people, 8, 124, 230, 275; as loyalists, 221
Catharine of Aragon, queen of England, 24
Cather, Willa, 795
Catholic Church: Inquisition of, 21; Reformation and, 22–24; Counter-Reformation and, 23; Spanish missionaries and, 44–45; following Revolutionary War, 244; sentiment against Catholics and, 544; nativist position and, 754; schools established by, 756; Legion of Decency of, 994
Catlin, George, 437, 663
Cato's Letters, 115
Catt, Carrie Chapman, 819, 893
Cattle ranching, 672–674, 673(map)
Cattle towns, 678
Cavalry, in battle at Little Bighorn, 667
Cavelier, René-Robert, Sieur de la Salle, 48
Cayuga people, 9
Centennial Exposition, 693–694
Central America: Columbus' voyage to, 28; U.S. investment in, 872; Wilson's policy toward, 876; Reagan's policy toward, 1242–1244. *See also specific countries*
Central Intelligence Agency (CIA): establishment of, 1061; Eisenhower's expansion of role of, 1111; in Guatemala, 1115; in Iran, 1115
Central Pacific Railroad, 661
Central Powers, in World War I, 888, 908
Century of Dishonor (Jackson), 667
Chain stores, 700, 933
Chamberlain, Neville, 1014
Chambers, Margaret, 496
Chambers, Whittaker, 1079
Chamorro, Violeta, 1266
Champlain, Samuel de, 46, 47
Chancellorsville, Virginia, battle at, 592

Chandler, Lucinda, 748
Channing, William Emery, 354
Chaplin, Charlie, 933, 993
Chapman, Maria W., 451
Charge accounts, introduction of, 1096
Charity organization movement, 752–753
Charles I, king of England, 56, 57, 65, 69
Charles II, king of England, 69, 84, 85, 88, 89, 94, 97
Charles V, Holy Roman emperor, 23
Charles River Bridge Proprietors, 387
Charles River Bridge v. *Warren Bridge*, 387–388
Charleston, Oscar, 936
Charleston, South Carolina: slave rebellion in, 149, 465–466; growth during 1820–1850, 454; growth during 1940 and 1950, 1035
Charles Town, South Carolina, 77; colonial population of, 131; Cornwallis' taking of, 231. *See also* Charleston, South Carolina
Charlotte Temple (Rowson), 294
Charter of Privileges, 92
Chase, Salmon P., 580, 622; on slavery, 532, 533
Chase, Samuel, 289
Chase, Stuart, 1043
Chattanooga, Tennessee, battle at, 594
Chautauqua Literary and Scientific Circle, 752
Chavín mountain culture, 10
Cheever, John, 988
Chemical waste disposal, 1208
Cheney, Richard, 1287
Cherokee National Council, 303
Cherokee Nation v. *Georgia* (1831), 380
Cherokee people, 8, 77, 124, 302, 662; myth of creation of, 1–2; seizure of lands of, 152; in French and Indian War, 167; uprising of, 169–170; in Revolutionary War, 230, 231; adaptation to white culture, 303; resistance to removal, 380–382, 401; resettlement of, 497, 498
Chesapeake (ship), 308
Chesapeake region: early culture of, 8; colonial, life in, 58–59; tobacco and slavery in, 61–62; slavery in, 139, 141–143; colonial economy of, 139–141; migration from, 295–296. *See also* Maryland; Virginia
Chesnut, Mary, 567, 597
Chevalier, Michael, 443–444
Cheyenne people, 302, 498, 662, 666–667; resettlement of, 541, 665; resistance to white settlers, 664–665, 665, 666–667
Chiang kai-shek, 1073
Chicago, Illinois, 409, 419; population during 1860–1920, 729–730; immigrants in, 731, 733; mass transit in, 735; department stores in,

737; crowding in, 738; neighborhoods in, 738; fire in, 740; government of, 743; during depression of 1893, 789; Pullman Palace Car Company strike in, 791–792; population during 1900–1920, 814; African-American population during 1910–1920, 902; newspapers in, 934; African-American population during 1920s, 943; Democratic convention of 1968 in, 1167–1169, 1168(illus.)
Chicago Bears, 936
Chicago Eight, 1189
Chicago Tribune, report of 1948 election results in, 1070, 1070(illus.)
Chicago White Sox, 917
Chicanos. *See* Hispanics
Chickasaw people, 8, 30, 74, 77, 230, 302, 323; decimation by disease, 170; resettlement of, 497, 498; in Civil War, 570
Childbirth: western farm women and, 680. *See also* Abortion
Child labor: in textile factories, 336–337, 426; legislation of, 426; during 1870–1900, 713–714, 714(illus.); among immigrant families, 733; outlawing of, under Wilson, 838
Child Online Protection Act, 1285
Children: in medieval Europe, 15; colonial, 127; urban, disease among, 350; guidebooks on child rearing and mothering and, 351; number in families, 352; education of, 432; roles during 1820–1850, 432; African-American, 459–460, 462; slave, work of, 462; Native American, removal from families, 667–668, 668(illus.); during Great Depression, 973
Chile, 1266; *Baltimore* incident and, 853
China: European trade with, 17; American trade with, 340; trade with, 866–867; in Sino-Japanese War, 867; Taft's policy toward, 874; Japanese interest in, 875–876; in Cold War era, 1073–1074; Korean War and, 1075, 1076–1077; Eisenhower's policy toward, 1111–1112; pressure on North Vietnam to end war, 1183; détente with, 1185, 1211–1212; formal recognition of, 1210; Bush's policy toward, 1267; Clinton's policy toward, 1279. *See also* Manchuria
China Lobby, 1073
The China Syndrome (movie), 1208
Chinese Eastern Railway, 871
Chinese Exclusion Act (1882), 754
Chinese Expulsion Act (1882), 776
Chinese immigrants, 543, 657; in California, 516–517, 518; racism against, 518, 680–681; unions and, 717; legislation against, 754, 774, 776; nativist attacks on, 754

Chinook people, 340, 503

Chippewa people, taking of lands from, 257

Chivington, John M., 664

Choctaw people, 8, 74, 110, 230, 302; in French and Indian War, 167; decimation by disease, 170; resettlement of, 497, 498; in Civil War, 570

Cholera: among loyalist slaves, 221; in Philadelphia, in 1793, 350

Chopin, Kate, 642

The Christian Century, 1102

Christianity, conservative, 1221–1222

Christianity and the Social Crisis (Rauschenbusch), 808

Christianity and the Social Order (Rauschenbusch), 808

Christin, David, 1184

Christopher, Warren, 1278, 1280

Chrysler, 933

Chrysler Building, 737

Church, Benjamin, 222

Churches: new, formation during Great Awakening, 150–152; women's activities in, 353, 355–356; African-American, 354, 468–470, 627; immigrant communities and, 733–734. *See also* Clergy; Religion; *specific churches and religions*

Churchill, Winston, 910, 1014, 1019; World War II and, 1015, 1017, 1023, 1024, 1025; Atlantic Charter and, 1017–1018; at Yalta Conference, 1029–1031, 1031(illus.); Iron Curtain speech of, 1058; on European economy, 1060

Church of England, 24; Great Awakening and, 150–151; clergy of, as loyalists, 219

Church of Jesus Christ of Latter-Day Saints, 435

Cincinnati, Ohio: canals and, 331; election of 1840 in, 397(illus.); during 1820–1850, 409–410; racial tensions during 1820–1850, 413; intellectual life in, 436–437; during 1830s, 443–444; in 1843, 493(illus.); government of, 743

Cincinnati Reds, 917, 1080

Circuit riders, 244, 246

Cisneros, Henry, 1274

Cities: in medieval Europe, 19; colonial, 131–136; coastal, in early 19th century, 347; decline in intimacy of, 347–348; migration to, 347–350, 406–408, 408(illus.), 409; poverty in, 349–350, 411–412, 1116; disease in, 350; working-class housing in, 361–362, 361(illus.); growth during 1820–1850, 406–409; frontier, 409–410; wealth in, 410; lack of social order in, during 1820–1850, 414; population in 1790, 542; population in 1860, 542;

southern, rise during 1870–1900, 639; Chinese immigrants in, 680; department stores in, 700, 701, 701(illus.), 737; factories in, 710; population during 1860–1920, 727–730, 730(illus.), 732(illus.); suburbanization of, 735–737; neighborhoods in, 737–739; environment of, 739–741; political machines in, 741–743, 742(illus.), 774, 814–816; parks in, 751–752; dangers of, 761–762; defense of, 762–763; political reform during Progressive Era, 814–816; forms of government for, 815; Progressive Era mayors of, 815–816; African-American migration to, 824, 902, 943, 1037–1038; African-Americans in, 1116; Hispanics in, 1116–1117; renewal projects in, displacement of minorities by, 1117; race riots of 1960s in, 1155. *See also* Tenements; *specific cities*

Citizenship: definition by Fourteenth Amendment, 617–618; *Insular* cases and, 866

City managers, 815

"Civil Disobedience" (Thoreau), 450–451, 512

Civilian Conservation Corps (CCC), 980, 981(illus.), 997, 1028–1029

Civil rights: of free African-Americans, Black Codes and, 467–468, 475, 477, 616; Lincoln's position on, 583; Johnson's (Andrew) opposition to legislation for, 616–617; internment of Japanese-Americans during World War II and, 1033–1034, 1034(illus.); President's Committee on Civil Rights and, 1068; civil rights movement and, 1121, 1149–1156; Warren court's decisions affecting, 1148–1149; protest strategies for, 1149–1150, 1151, 1174–1175; spread of movement for, 1149–1151; Civil Rights Act of 1964 and, 1151–1153; political power and, 1153–1154; Black Power and, 1155; white backlash and, 1156; SDS and, 1163; Reagan's cuts in funding for, 1238. *See also specific rights*

Civil Rights Act (1866), 616–617

Civil Rights Act (1875), 636

Civil Rights Act (1964), 1152–1153

Civil Service Commission, 776, 1199

Civil service system: establishment of, 776; under Cleveland, 779

Civil War (1861–1865), 563–601, 573(map); creation of Confederate States of America and, 557; attempt to avert, 566; beginning of, 566–568, 568(illus.); battle for Border States and, 568–570; balance of power between North and South and, 570–571; First Battle of Bull Run and, 572; Peninsular Campaign of, 573–574; in West, 574–575; naval battles in,

Civil War (1861–1865) (continued)
575–576; Trent affair and European neutrality and, 576–577; Second Battle of Bull Run and, 577; Battle of Antietam and, 577–578, 578(illus.); raising of armies for, 579–580; financing of, 580–581; presidential leadership during, 581–583; Lincoln's position on civil liberties and, 583; camp life during, 584, 585(illus.); soldiers fighting in, 584–586, 585(illus.); economic consequences of, 586–588; women and, 588–589, 588(illus.); Emancipation proclamation and, 589–591; Battle of Gettysburg and, 591–593, 593(map); surrender of Vicksburg and, 593–594; fall of Chattanooga and, 594; approaches to warfare in, 594–596, 595(map); election of 1864 and, 596–597; Sherman's march to the sea and, 597–598; defeat of Confederacy and, 598–600, 599(illus.); music during, 604–606; aftermath of, 610–612, 611(illus.)
Civil Works Administration (CWA), 982, 1000
Claim jumpers, 518
Clark, Champ, 896
Clark, George Rogers, 231, 257
Clark, Jim, 1153
Clark, William, 737; expedition with Lewis, 299–301, 300(map)
Clausewitz, Carl von, 564
Clay, Henry, 313, 371, 373, 384, 390(illus.); War of 1812 and, 309; American System of, 313, 373–374, 382, 386(illus.), 448; in election of 1832, 385; support of Bank of the U.S., 385, 386; Whig Party and, 388; political career of, 389; on annexation of Texas, 507; compromise urged by, 531, 532–533; Lincoln's support of, 552
Clayton Anti-Trust Act (1914), 837
Clayton-Bulwer Treaty (1850), 868
Clean Air Act (1990), 1271
Clear and present danger standard, 906
Clemenceau, Georges, 911–912
Clemens, Samuel Langhorne. See Twain, Mark
Clergy: in medieval Europe, 16; of Church of England, as loyalists, 219; itinerant, 354; as leaders of intellectual communication, 435
Clermont (steamboat), 328
Cleveland, Grover, 735, 765, 773, 789, 864; environment and, 677; presidential campaigns of, 777–778, 778(illus.), 787; veto exercised by, 779; economic policy of, 788; Pullman Palace Car Company strike and, 791–792; depression politics of, 792–793; foreign policy under, 854, 856, 857
Cleveland, Ohio: canals and, 331; Johnson as mayor of, 816

Cliff dwellers, 7–8, 7(illus.)
Cliff Dwellers (Bellows), 748
Clifford, Clark, 1059, 1068, 1088, 1089–1090, 1166
Cliff Palace (Arizona), 7(illus.)
Climate, farming in West and, 679
Clinton, De Witt, 330, 371, 372
Clinton, George, 107, 119; on form of government, 264
Clinton, Henry, 211, 213–214, 222, 231, 235
Clinton, Hillary Rodham, 1275, 1288
Clinton, William Jefferson, 1273(illus.), 1290; impeachment of, 1259–1260, 1281–1282, 1281(illus.); in election of 1992, 1272, 1273; appointments made by, 1274; domestic policy of, 1275; economic policy of, 1275; character of, 1275–1276, 1281–1282; Whitewater scandal and, 1275–1276; Gingrich's attack on, 1276–1277; in election of 1996, 1277; lack of overarching foreign policy, 1277–1278; internationalism of, 1277–1279; policy toward Yugoslavia, 1279–1280; policy toward Iraq, 1280–1281
Clinton's Folly, 330
Clipper ships, 417, 417(illus.)
Clocks, production of, 335
The Closing of the American Mind (Bloom), 1233
Cloth production. See Textile production
Cloudscrapers, 737
CNN, 1248, 1290
Coal mining: in Virginia, 640(illus.); strikes and, 830, 1066; decline following World War I, 936
Cochran, Johnnie, 1292
Cody, Buffalo Bill, 684
Cohen, Richard, 1203–1204
Colden, Cadwallader, 181
Cold Harbor, Virginia, battle at, 596
Cold War: roots of, 1052–1056; Truman's policy during, 1056–1064; fall of Iron Curtain and, 1057–1059; National Security Act and, 1060–1061; Europe during, 1061(map); expansion to Asia, 1072–1078; end of, 1251, 1252(illus.), 1266
The Cold War (Lippmann), 1064
Cole, Thomas, 437
Colfax Massacre (1873), 635(illus.)
College of New Jersey, 151
College of Philadelphia, 152
College of Rhode Island, 151
Colleges and universities: Great Awakening and, 151–152; Morrill Land Grant Act and, 587, 756; black, in South, 625; for women, 748,

941; curriculum changes at, 756; enrollment during 1960s, 1162; youth culture and, 1162–1163; attempts to increase sensitivity to racial and cultural diversity, 1233; Internet and, 1284(illus.); admissions and, in California, 1292. *See also* Student protests; *specific colleges and universities*

Collier, John, 998, 1197

Collingwood, Charles, 1032

Colombia, Panama Canal and, 868–869

Colonies. *See specific colonies*

Colonization movement, 447–448, 475

Colonization Society, 447, 448

Colorado, entry into Union, 660

Colored Farmers' Alliance, 784

Colored National Labor Union (CNLU), 716

Colored Orphan Asylum, 580

Columbia Broadcasting Systems (CBS), 934

Columbian Exchange, 31

Columbia University, 152

Columbine High School, 1291

Columbus, Christopher, 27–28; Taino people described by, 37–38

Comanche people, 305, 498, 500, 662, 663; resettlement of, 665

Comets (rock group), 1103

Comic books, 1033

Coming Home (movie), 1203

Comintern, 918

Commager, Henry Steele, 1116

Commerce: European, 1400–1600, 19–20; in medieval England, 19–20; of northern colonies, 129–131; colonial cities and market towns and, 131–136; downturn following Queen Anne's War, 137–138; in Chesapeake region, 142–143; in Carolinas, 143–144; following French and Indian War, 174–175; following Revolutionary War, 252–253; Report on Manufactures and, 269–271; chartered corporations and, 339; war in Europe and, 339–340; Embargo of 1807 and, 340–341; War of 1812 and, 341; internal, in 1820–1850, 417–418; dollar diplomacy and, 871–874. *See also* Business; Economy; Maritime commerce; Mercantilism; Smuggling; Stores; Trade

Commerce and Labor Department, 830

Commercial revolution, 111

Commission form of government, 815

Committee for Industrial Organization, 996. *See also* Congress of Industrial Organization (CIO)

Committee for the First Amendment, 1081(illus.)

Committee on Public Information, 903, 926

Committee on Training Camp Activities (CTCA), 898

Committees of Correspondence, 188, 203

Committees of Observation, 192

Committees of Public Safety, 209

Committees of Safety, 192, 193

Committee to Re-elect the President (CREEP), 1192

The Common Law (Holmes), 808

Common Sense (Paine), 206–207, 226, 240–241

Commonwealth of Independent States, 1264

Communication: new forms of, 292; roads and, 325–327, 326(map); telegraph and, 418, 510–511; intellectual, clergy as leaders of, 435; innovations in, during 1865–1889, 696–697; advances in, U.S. foreign policy and, 849–850; advances in, following World War I, 933–934; e-mail and, 1284–1285. *See also* Newspapers

Communications Decency Act (1996), 1285

Communism: fear of, following World War I, 918–919; during late 1920s, 986; containment policy and, 1051, 1059–1061, 1064, 1157; in postwar Europe, 1055; in Czechoslovakia, 1060; unions and, 1068; McCarthyism and, 1082–1083, 1108–1109; ideological clash with capitalism, 1091–1092; fear of, in Guatemala, 1115; Castro's support for, 1123; Nixon's support of regimes opposing, 1185–1186; Reagan's support of regimes opposing, 1240–1241, 1243–1244; revolutions in Eastern Europe and, 1263–1265. *See also* China; Red Scares; Soviet Union

Communist Control Act (1954), 1108

Communist Information Bureau (Cominform), 1060

Communitarian societies, 435–436

Communities: African-American, 459, 460; immigrant, 732–734

Community action program (CAP), 1145

Commuter railroads, 735

Como, Perry, 1102

Compromise of 1850, 530–533, 533(map)

Compromise of 1877, 637–638, 638(map)

Compton, Arthur H., 1047

Computers, 1282–1283; adoption by corporations, 1098; education and, 1284(illus.), 1285; hours of work and, 1288

Comstock, Anthony, 753

Comstock Law (1873), 753

Comstock Lode, 519, 670, 671; towns near, 678

Concentration camps, during World War II, 1027–1028, 1027(illus.)

Concord, Massachusetts, British approach to, 193–194

Conestoga people, 171

Coney Island, 744

Confederate States of America: creation of, 557; congress of, 567; Union blockade of ports of, 570; strength of, 570–571; navy of, 575–576; conscription in, 579; army of, 584, 586; collapse of, 598–600, 599(illus.). *See also* Civil War (1861–1865); South

Confederation Congress, 228–229

Congo, early, 14

Congregational Church, 354; Great Awakening and, 151; following Revolutionary War, 244; migration and, 295

Congress: during Revolutionary War, 210, 211; limits on power of, 228; authority to tax, 229–230; Great Compromise and, 262–263; first, 267–268; Reconstruction plan of, 617–623, 650–652; impeachment of Johnson by, 622–623; Compromise of 1877 and, 637–638; settlement of West and, 660–661; Yellowstone National Park created by, 677; power of, 771; Billion Dollar, 773, 780–781; direct election of senators and, 818; support for naval buildup in, 852; entry into World War II and, 1008–1009; House Committee on Un-American Activities and, 1080; investigation of suspected communists by, 1080, 1082–1084; McCarthy's condemnation for bringing disrepute to, 1109; impeachment of Clinton and, 1281–1282; in election of 2000, 1288

Congress of Industrial Organizations (CIO), 996, 997, 1068; merger with AFL, 1098

Congress of Racial Equality (CORE), 1038–1039, 1150

Conkling, Roscoe, 768, 774, 775–776

Connally, John, 1133, 1207

Connally, Nellie, 1133

Connecticut: colonial, government of, 68; royal cancellation of charter of, 97; emancipation of slaves in, 246–247; return of loyalists to, 252; ratification of Constitution by, 265; voting rights in, 292; suffrage in, 367

Connecticut Compromise, 262–263

Connecticut Wits, 292

Conquistadores, 29–31, 42

Conscientious objectors, during World War I, 897

Conscription. *See* Draft

Conservation. *See* Environment; Environmentalism; Pollution

Conservatism: revival during 1979–1980, 1220–1222; political influence of fundamentalists and evangelists and, 1227–1228

Conspiracies, 1294

Constitution (of Confederate States of America), 557–558

Constitution (of United States), 259–266; leaders crafting, 259–260; convention to develop, 260–263; Great Compromise and, 262–263; public debate over, 263–266; ratification of, 265–266, 266(illus.); Bill of Rights and, 268, 271; prohibition of slave trade by, 456, 457; on slavery, 475; Thirteenth Amendment to, 615; Fourteenth Amendment to, 617–618, 704; Fifteenth Amendment to, 620–621; Seventeenth Amendment to, 818; Eighteenth Amendment to, 822; Nineteenth Amendment to, 908

Constitutionalist party, 227

Constitutional Revolution of 1937, 989

Constitutional societies, 272

Constitutional Union Party, 555

Constitutions (of states): suffrage and, 366–367, 367(map); on slavery, 476; of Oregon, 504; under Johnson's plan for restoration following Civil War, 614; rewriting of, to exclude black vote, 643; of California in 1879, 681. *See also* Legislatures

Constructive engagement policy, 1241

Consumer revolution, 1091–1098; baby boom and rise of mass consumption and, 1094–1096, 1095(illus.); rise of suburbs and, 1096–1097; business and employment and, 1097–1098

Consumer society: industrial revolution and, 700–702; Internet and, 1284

Consumption, New Deal and, 1001

Containment policy, 1051, 1059–1061, 1064, 1157

Continental Army, 209; food shortages and, 199–201, 219; at Valley Forge, 199–201, 212; decision to raise, 204; African-Americans in, 209; enlistment in, 212; desertion and demoralization of, 212–213; training of, 213; maturation of, 234–235; pensions promised to, 251–252

Continental Congress: First, 191–192; Second, 202–205, 228

Continental currency, 216–217, 229

Continental Navy, flag of, 203(illus.)

Contraception. *See* Birth control

Contract with America, 1276

Contras, 1244; Iran-contra affair and, 1245–1246, 1262

Convict lease system, 644

Coode, John, 100

Cook, John, 468

Coolidge, Calvin, 918, 928, 945, 953; in election of 1920, 920; on business, 932, 933; farm policy of, 937; Jr., 953; support of business, 953, 954(illus.); in election of 1924, 955, 956; decision not to run for second term, 959; foreign policy under, 959; intervention in Nicaragua, 959

Coon songs, 744

Cooper, Anthony Ashley, 85

Cooper, James Fenimore, 437

Coopers, 133(illus.)

Coral Sea, Battle of (1942), 1040

Corbett, James J., 744

Corliss engine, 694

Corn: Native American cultivation of, 5, 6, 63; European adoption of, 32; price of, 782

Cornell, Alonzo, 774

Corn Laws (England), 341

Cornwallis, Lord, 231, 233–234

Coronado, Francisco Vasquez de, 30

Corporations, 704–705; charters of, commerce and, 339; mergers of, 707, 1097–1098, 1249; public distrust of, 708, 709(illus.); profits of, during World War I, 902; lobbyists from, 1224; money culture and, 1246. *See also* Management, corporate; Trusts; *specific corporations*

Corps of Discovery, 299, 301

Corruption: in Reconstruction South, 626; under Grant, 630–632; in city government, 742–743, 742(illus.); in Harding administration, 952; under Truman, 1105

Cortés, Hernán, 29

Cortes, Isabel Tolosa, 45

Cory, Giles, 104

Cotton, 345–347; slavery and, 312, 456–458, 531; Panic of 1819 and, 314; spinning machinery for, development of, 336; cotton gin and, 346, 346(illus.), 347; export of, 347; in South during 1820–1850, 454, 455(map), 456; decline in price of, 456; gang labor and, 462; crop-lien system and, 641; child labor and, 714; price of, 782

Cotton, John, 66

Cotton gin, 346, 346(illus.), 347

Cotton mills, decline following World War I, 936

Cotton States and International Exposition, 644

Cotton Whigs, 541

Coughlin, Charles, 984

Council for Mutual Economic Assistance (COMECON), 1064

Council for New England, 63, 65

Counterculture movement, of 1960s, 1162–1163

Counter-Reformation, 23

Counties: in colonial Virginia, 56; politics of, during 1780s, 254(illus.); scope of county government and, 771

Country faction (England), 107

Coureurs des bois, 47–48

Court party (England), 106–107

Courts: in colonial Virginia, 56; in colonial Maryland, 58; establishment of, 267–268; under Jefferson, 288–291. *See also* Supreme Court

Covenant Chain, 75–76, 106, 153

Coverture, 249

Cowboys, 500; cattle drives and, 672–673, 673(map)

Cow towns, 678

Cox, Archibald, 1192

Cox, James M., 919–920, 978

Coxe, Tench, 270

Coxey, Jacob, 789

Coxey, Legal Tender, 789

Coxey's Army, 789, 790(illus.), 791

Crane, Hart, 942

Crane, Stephen, 747

Cranmer, Thomas, 24

Crawford, Joan, 933

Crawford, William, 373

Creation, fundamentalist position on, 948–949

The Creature from the Black Lagoon (movie), 1122

Credit: installment purchases and, 932; introduction of credit carand, 1096

Crédit Mobilier, 630, 775

Creek National Council, 380

Creek people, 8, 77, 105, 302, 662; decimation by disease, 170; in Revolutionary War, 230, 231; taking of lands from, 257; Jackson's campaign against, 304–305, 375, 379; land ceded by, 380; resettlement of, 497, 498

Creel, George, 903

Creoles, 44

Crèvecoeur, Michel-Guillaume Jean de, 293

Crime: newspaper reports of, 404, 413; in cities during 1820–1850, 413; in western towns, 678–679; in cities during 1865–1910, 740; organized, Prohibition and, 950; increase during 1960–1971, 1189

Critical Period, 251, 260

Crittenden, John J., 566

Crittenden Compromise, 566

Croatia, 1279

Crockett, David, 304, 501

Crockett, Susie, 680

Cromwell, Oliver, 69

Cromwell, William Nelson, 868

Cronkite, Walter, 1165

Crop-lien system, 640–641

Crops: drought-resistant, 674; fall in prices of, 674, 782–783, 782(illus.), 784, 936–937, 982. *See also* Agriculture; *specific crops*

Crosby, Bing, 994, 1033

"Cross of Gold" speech (Bryan), 794

Crown Point, fort at, 203

Crow people, 662, 666–667

Crusades, 16

Cuba: Columbus' voyage to, 27; in French and Indian War, 168; *Black Warrior* seizure by, 537; Pierce's attempt to acquire, 538; revolt against Spain, 857; McKinley's refusal to annex, 865; Platt Amendment and, 865; Roosevelt's (Theodore) policy toward, 870; revolution in, 1123; Bay of Pigs fiasco and, 1139; missile crisis and, 1139–1140. *See also* Hispanics

Culpepper, John, 77, 88

Cult Jam (rap band), 1231

Culture: North American, before European contact, 4–12, 4(map); Native American, 5–9, 301–302; Mesoamerican and South American, early, 9–12; West African, 1400–1600, 12–14, 13(map); European, 1400–1600, 14–17; effects of European contact on, 31–34; in postwar South, 641–642; urban, during 1865–1910, 743–750; of immigrants, public schools as threat to, 755–756; mass, 1104. *See also* Political culture; Popular culture; *specific aspects of culture*

Cumberland (ship), 576

cummings, e. e., 942

Currency: printing of, by colonial legislatures, 107–108; Continental, 204, 216–217, 229; printing of, to support Revolutionary War, 216–217; issued by states during Revolutionary War, 217; following Revolutionary War, 229; printing to finance Civil War, 580, 581; national, creation of, 587; greenbacks, 632–633, 772; money supply and, 772–773; gold standard and, 797–798

Currency Act (1751) (England), 107–108

Currency Act (1764) (England), 178, 187

Curry, John Steuart, 992

Curtenius, Peter, 173(illus.)

Curtiss Candy Company, 932

Custer, George, 665, 667

Cutler, Manassah, 255

Cuzco, Peru, 11, 30

Czechoslovakia: seizure by Germany, 1014; communist coup in, 1060; Soviet control of, 1064; revolution in, 1264

Dachau, 1027

Daladier, Edouard, 1014

Daley, Richard, 1167

Dallas (television show), 1246–1247

Dare, Virginia, 52

Darky shows, 744

Darnall, Eleanor, 141(illus.)

Darrow, Clarence, 795, 949, 960, 964, 966

Dartmouth, 151

Dartmouth (ship), 189

Dartmouth College v. *Woodward* (1819), 291

Darwin, Charles, 702, 948

Darwinism: fundamentalist position on, 948–949; Scopes trial and, 949, 964–966. *See also* Social Darwinism

Dating, during 1920s, 940

Datsun, 1206

Daugherty, Harry, 953

Daughters of Liberty, 184–185, 192

Daughters of the American Revolution, 998

Davenport, James, 150

Davis, David, 637

Davis, Elmer, 1032

Davis, Harry Winter, 613

Davis, Jefferson, 539, 557, 599, 600; on slavery, 533; leadership of, 582–583

Davis, John, 955

Davy Crockett (television show), 1100

Dawes, Charles G., 958; in election of 1924, 955, 956

Dawes, Henry, 669

Dawes General Allotment Act (1887), 669, 692

Dawes Plan, 958

Day, Luke, 254

The Day After (docudrama), 1242

Dayton, Ohio, 815; canals and, 331

D-Day, 1025–1026, 1026(illus.)

Dean, John, 1192

Dearborn Independent, 945

Debs, Eugene, 791, 826, 893, 904–905, 946; in election of 1912, 836

Debtors' rebellions, 253–255

Debt peonage, 629

Debts: following Revolutionary War, repayment of, 268–269; federal, during World War II, 1022; private, rise during 1950s, 1096

Declaration of Independence, 207–208, 225

Declaration of Rights, of Continental Congress, 191

Declaration of Rights and Grievances (1765), 180

Declaration of the Causes and Necessities of Taking Up Arms, 205

Declaratory Act (1766) (England), 182

Decoration Day, 641

Deere, John, 418

Deerfield, Massachusetts, 105

The Deer Hunters (movie), 1203

Defense Against Weapons of Mass Destruction Act (1996), 1292

Defense budget: during Cold War, 1074; Korean War and, 1078; New Look strategy and, 1111; under Kennedy, 1138; under Reagan, 1240

Defense Department, 1061

DeGeneres, Ellen, 1290

de Klerk, Frederik W., 1266

Delaware: establishment of, 92; slavery in, 135, 461; colonial economy of, 139; African-American voting rights in, 247; ratification of Constitution by, 265; escaped slaves in, 445, 534; in Civil War, 569. *See also* Mid-Atlantic region

Delaware people, 9, 90, 154, 275, 302; in French and Indian War, 164; decimation by disease, 170; taking of lands from, 257; land ceded by, 304; resettlement of, 497, 541

Delaware River, Washington's crossing of, 210

Delaware Valley, migration to, 125

The Deliverance (Glasgow), 642

De Lôme, Enrique Dupuy, 858, 860

De Mello, Fernando Collor, 1266

Democracy: expansion under Republican regime in South, 624–625; direct, 818; Wilson's views on, 874–875

Democracy and Education (Dewey), 808

Democratic Party: establishment of, 377; rank-and-file membership of, 378; in election of 1832, 385; workers' opposition to, 392–393; depression of 1837–1840 and, 396; on annexation of Texas, 503; in election of 1844, 507–508, 773; in election of 1848, 515, 528; slavery and, 530; in election of 1852, 536; manifest destiny and, 537; Kansas-Nebraska Act and, 540; Tammany Hall and, 544; in election of 1860, 555; coalition with Republicans during Civil War, 596; in election of 1864, 597; in election of 1868, 630; in election of 1872, 632, 768; opposition to Republican Reconstruction program, 633–635; in election of 1876, 637, 774; in election of 1896, 764–765, 795, 797(map); in election of 1880, 766, 775; divisions in, during 1877–1900, 768, 793–795; in election of 1882, 776; in election of 1884, 777, 778; in election of 1888, 779; in election of 1890, 781; in election of 1892, 786, 788; in election of 1894, 793; endorsement of women's suffrage, 820; prohibition issue and, 821; in election of 1908, 832; in election of 1912, 835, 836; in election of 1914, 838; in election of 1916, 893; Treaty of Versailles and, 915; in election of 1920, 919–920, 921(map); in election of 1924, 955–956, 956(map); in election of 1928, 959–960, 960(map); in election of 1932, 979, 980(map); in election of 1934, 984; in election of 1936, 988–989, 998; in election of 1938, 990; in election of 1940, 1016, 1016(map); in election of 1942, 1028; in election of 1944, 1029, 1030(map); division under Truman, 1068–1070; in election of 1952, 1105–1106, 1107(map); in election of 1956, 1109, 1110(map); in election of 1960, 1124–1126, 1126(map); division under Kennedy, 1138; in election of 1964, 1146, 1147(map), 1153; in election of 1966, 1156; in election of 1968, 1166, 1167–1169, 1168(illus.), 1170(map), 1189; in election of 1972, 1190–1191, 1191(map); in election of 1976, 1209, 1210(map); in election of 1980, 1225, 1226, 1226(map); in election of 1984, 1239–1240, 1239(map); in election of 1988, 1262–1263, 1264(map); in election of 1992, 1272, 1273, 1274(map); in election of 1994, 1276; in election of 1996, 1277; in election of 2000, 1287, 1288

Democratic-Republicans, 273, 286–291; opposition to Federalists, 273, 278, 288; opposition to Jay's Treaty, 274; rising strength of, 277; XYZ Affair and, 277; simplification of government under, 287–288; courts under, 288–291; on judiciary, 289; opposition to Louisiana Purchase, 298; War of 1812 and, 309, 310

Dempsey, Jack, 934–935, 936

Denmark: German invasion of, 1015; postwar, communism in, 1055

Dennis v. U. S. (1951), 1079

Department of Commerce and Labor, 830

Department of Defense, 1061

Department of Education, 1209

Department of Energy, 1209, 1237

Department of Justice, 1238

Department of the Interior, 1237

Department of Treasury, 1238

Department stores, 700, 701, 701(illus.), 737, 1246

Dependent Pension Act (1890), 781

Depressions (economic): following Revolutionary War, 252–253; Embargo of 1807 and, 308; following Panic of 1837, 395, 396, 427, 504;

Depressions (economic) *(continued)*
during 1873–1897, 711; of 1893, 788–789, 791, 792–793. *See also* Great Depression; New Deal

Deregulation, under Reagan, 1236–1237

Desertions: from Continental Army, 212–213; during Civil War, 586, 598, 599; during Vietnam War, 1161

Desert Land Act (1877), 659

De Soto, Hernando, 30

Détente, under Nixon, 1184–1185

Detroit, Michigan: immigrants in, 731, 733; Pingree as mayor of, 815–816; race riot in, 1038, 1155

Dew, Thomas R., 477, 478, 482–483; on slavery, 546–547

Dewey, George, 861

Dewey, John, 808

Dewey, Thomas E., 1029, 1068, 1069–1071

Dewson, Molly, 1001

Dias, Bartholomeu, 26

Dickinson, John, 183–184, 204–205

Diem, Ngo Dinh, 1114, 1141, 1142

Dien Bien Phu, Vietnam, 1114

Dime novels, myth of West as agrarian Eden and, 683

Diner's Club card, 1096

Dingley Tariff (1897), 797

Direct democracy, 818

Direct Tax (1798), 278

Dirksen, Everett, 1152

Discomfort index, 1205(illus.)

Discos, 1202

Discourse of Western Planting (Hakluyt), 51

Disease: Native American decimation by, 6–7, 29, 32–34, 33(illus.), 47, 124, 170, 300; Columbus' introduction of, 28; transmission to Europeans by Native Americans, 33–34; African slaves' resistance to malaria and, 87; among militiamen, 109, 110; among slaves, 221, 461; among prisoners of war, 223; in cities, 350; migration to West and, 496; among soldiers in Civil War, 586; water pollution and, 740; Panama Canal and, 846; during Spanish-American War, deaths due to, 863; venereal, education to prevent among soldiers, 898; during World War I, deaths due to, 911; conquering of, baby boom and, 1095–1096, 1096(illus.); among soldiers in Vietnam, 1161; AIDS, 1230–1231. *See also specific diseases*

Disney, Walt, 994

Disneyland, 1101, 1101(illus.)

Dissension: during Revolutionary War, 223–224; during 1920s, 939–945

District of Columbia, abolishment of slave trade in, 532

Divorce: liberalization of laws following Revolutionary War, 249; rise in rate during 1865–1910, 748; tightening of laws on, 751; rate in 1928, 940; decline in rate during Great Depression, 972

Dix, Dorothea, 431, 589

Dixiecrat Party, 1069, 1071

Dixon, Jeremiah, 89

Do and Dare (Alger), 703

Doane, William Crosswell, 741

Doctors: Enlightenment view of, 114–115; American Medical Association and, 812

Dodge, Grenville, 661

Doeg people, 76

Dole, Robert, 1262, 1277

Domestic violence, in cities during 1820–1850, 413

Dominican Republic, Roosevelt's (Theodore) policy toward, 870

Dominion of New England, 97–98

Domino, Antoine "Fats," 1103

Donaldson, Sam, 1239

Donnelly, Ignatius, 794

Donner, George, 485–488

Donner, Jacob, 485–488

Donovan, Raymond, 1236

Dorchester, Massachusetts, population during 1900–1915, 735

Dorchester Heights, battle at, 208

Dorr, Rheta Childe, 809

Dos Passos, John, 942, 946, 991

Do the Right Thing (movie), 1233

Douglas, Aaron, 945

Douglas, Michael, 1246–1247

Douglas, Stephen A., 510, 526, 536, 546; Compromise of 1850 and, 532; Kansas-Nebraska Act and, 539, 541, 552–553; Lecompton Constitution and, 549; Lincoln's campaign against, 553–554, 554(illus.), 560–562; in election of 1860, 555, 556

Douglas, William O., 1148

Douglas firs, 676

Douglass, Frederick, 448–449, 449(illus.), 464, 469, 516, 590; on Fugitive Slave Act, 535; opposition to compromise, 566; on Reconstruction, 612, 621, 625

Draft: during Revolutionary War, 223; during Civil War, 579–580; during World War I, 896–897, 899(illus.); deferments and, 897,

1161, 1164; evasion of, 897; World War II and, 1015, 1022–1023; system for, 1181

Draft Bill (1917), 925

Drake, Francis, 51, 52

Drama, Federal Theater Project and, 987, 988, 990

Drayton, William, 161–162

Dred Scott v. *Sandford* (1857), 547–549

Dreiser, Theodore, 747

Drew, Elizabeth, 1204

Drexel Institute, 756

Drinker, Elizabeth, 218

Drug use: by soldiers fighting in Vietnam War, 1161; counterculture movement of 1960s and, 1162

Drummond, William, 87–88

Dry farming techniques, 674

Duarte, José Napoleon, 1244

Du Bois, W. E. B., 645, 824–825, 902, 1037, 1176

Duer, William, 255, 269

Dukakis, Michael, 1262–1263

Duke, James Buchanan, 707

Dulles, Allen, 1111–1112

Dulles, John Foster, 1110

Dunmore, Lord, 172, 205, 219, 221

Dunmore's War, 172

Duquesne, Marquis, 154

Durant, George, 77

Dutch East India Company, 48–59, 92–93

Dutch Reformed Church, 23

Dutch West India Company, 49, 50, 92–93

Duties. *See* Tariffs; Taxes

Duty Act (1673) (England), 94

Dyer, Mary, 68

Dylan, Bob, 1162–1163

Dynamic conservatism, of Eisenhower, 1107–1109

Dynamic Sociology (Ward), 808

E. Remington and Sons, 713

Earp, Wyatt, 678

Earth Summit, 1271

Eastern Europe: Soviet seizure of, 1055, 1064; revolutions in, in 1989, 1263–1265. *See also specific countries*

Eastern Woodland cultures, 8

East Germany, 1064; revolution in, 1264

Eastland, James, 1069, 1119

Eastman, Max, 904–905

East St. Louis, race riot in, 903

Ecodefence (Foreman), 1256–1257

Ecology. *See* Environment; Environmentalism; Pollution

Economic Interpretation of the Constitution (Beard), 808

Economic Opportunity Act, 1145

Economy: colonial, 107; French and Indian War and, 173–175; following Revolutionary War, 229–230, 252–253; Embargo of 1807 and, 308; Panic of 1819 and, 313–315; Panic of 1837 and, 395–396, 427, 429, 504; of South during 1820–1850, 453–454, 455(map), 456; Panic of 1857 and, 550–551; during Civil War, 586–588; of South, Civil War and, 610–611; of North, Civil War and, 611; Panic of 1873 and, 632–633; of postwar South, 640–641; railroads' impact on, 699; Smith's ideas about, 702; Hawaiian, 855; following World War I, 929–933, 930(illus.), 931(illus.), 936–938; automobile production and, 931–932, 931(illus.); global, during 1920s, 958–959; New Deal programs to revive, 982–984; mobilization for World War II, 1019–1023, 1021(illus.); World War II and, 1043; post-World War II, 1065–1066; following World War II, 1092, 1094, 1094(illus.), 1098; under Kennedy, 1137–1138; during 1970s, 1205–1207, 1205(illus.); under Nixon, 1207; under Ford, 1209; under Carter, 1210, 1225; supply-side theory of, 1223–1224; liberal outlook on, 1228; under Reagan, 1234–1235, 1236, 1251, 1252, 1252(illus.); under Bush, 1269–1270; under Clinton, 1275, 1278–1279, 1285; during 1990s, 1285–1287, 1286(illus.). *See also* Depressions (economic); Great Depression; Gross national product (GNP); Maritime commerce; Prices; Recessions; Stock market; *specific countries*

Economy Act (1933), 980

Edict of Nantes (1598), 23

Edison, Thomas, 694, 697–698, 698(illus.)

Edison Electric Illuminating Company, 698

Edison General Electric, 697

Education: Great Awakening and, 151–152; of African-Americans, 247–248, 432, 462, 625, 642–643, 644, 824; of women during 1783–1800, 249, 250; of Native Americans, 302, 667–668, 668(illus.), 1198–1199; theological, 354–355; for missionaries, 356; of children, 432; of women during 1820–1850, 432–433; of slaves, forbidding of, 462; in post–Civil war South, 625; of women during 1865–1910, 748; of immigrants, 754–756, 755(illus.); scientific method and, 808; sexual, for U.S. soldiers, 898; teaching of Darwinism *versus* creation and, 948–949, 964–966; space

Education *(continued)*
race and, 1123–1124; of women during 1960s
and 1970s, 1200, 1201(illus.); computers and,
1284(illus.), 1285; of minorities, in Califor-
nia, 1292. *See also* Colleges and universities;
Public schools
Education Department, 1209
Edwards, Frederick T., 898
Edwards, James, 1236
Edwards, Jonathan, 150, 354
Egypt: Suez affair and, 1113–1114; in 1967 war,
1186; in Yom Kippur War, 1186; Camp David
Accords and, 1210–1211, 1211(illus.)
Eighteenth Amendment, 822
Einstein, Albert, 1042
Eisenhower, Dwight David, 1069, 1091–1092;
in World War II, 1023, 1026, 1031; as NATO
supreme commander, 1063; in election of
1952, 1105, 1106, 1112(illus.); fiscal conser-
vatism of, 1107, 1110; domestic policy of,
1107–1109; in election of 1956, 1109; foreign
policy of, 1109–1115; summit meeting with
Krushchev, 1112–1113; school desegregation
and, 1119; National Goals Commission of,
1123
Eisenhower Doctrine (1957), 1114
Elections, 370(illus.). *See also* National elections;
Political parties; Politics; Suffrage; Voting
Electricity, 930; New Deal programs and,
983–984
Electric light bulb, 697–698
Electric streetcars, 735, 736(illus.)
Electronic Numerical Integrator and Calculator
(ENIAC), 1282
Elementary and Secondary Education Act
(1965), 1147
Eliot, John, 73
Eliot, T. S., 1099
Elites: colonial, 101–102, 131–132, 140–141; def-
erence toward, 291; women's roles and, 352;
urban, housing of, 362; African-American,
468, 825. *See also* Wealth
Elizabeth I, queen of England, 24, 51, 53
Elkins Act (1903), 830
Ellen (television show), 1290
Ellington, Edward "Duke," 945
Elliot, Alfred, 1033
Ellsberg, David, 1182
Elmina, 26
El Salvador, Reagan's policy toward, 1243–1244
Elsey, George, 1088–1090
E-mail, 1284–1285
Emancipation, 246–247; abolitionist movement
and, 449–451; women's activities for, 451–452

Emancipation Proclamation (1863), 589–591
Embargo Act (1807), 308, 309(illus.)
Embargoes: during Revolutionary War, 218; of
1807, 307–308, 340–341; following War of
1812, 341
Emergency Banking Act (1933), 979
Emergency Fleet Corporation (EFC), 901
Emergency Relief Appropriation Act (ERA)
(1935), 987–988
Emerson, John, 547, 548
Emerson, Ralph Waldo: on Indian removal, 403;
transcendental philosophy of, 438; on slavery,
450–451, 533; on Civil War, 567
Empire State Building, 737, 932
Employment: putting-out system and, 19–20,
335–336, 421; of women during colonial era,
128; international commerce and, 130; colonial, 131; migration to find, 136–137; of
women during 1790–1820, 351; of women
during 1820–1840, 393; attitudes toward, 420;
during 1820–1850, 420–423; trade unions
and, 422–423; of free African-Americans, 467;
of women during Civil War, 589; of Chinese
immigrants, 681; in manufacturing, during
1860–1900, 709; working conditions in factories and, 710–711, 811; of working class,
during 1870–1900, 712; of women during
1870–1900, 712–713, 713(illus.); of African-
Americans during 1870–1900, 714; of immigrants, 733; workman's compensation and,
838; of African-Americans during World War
I, 902; of women during World War I, 902,
904(illus.); automobile production and,
931; of women following World War I, 938;
of African-Americans during 1920s, 943; of
women during Great Depression, 973; of
women during 1930s, 999–1000; of women
during World War II, 1035–1037, 1036(illus.);
of African-Americans during World War II,
1037, 1039; following World War II, 1092,
1094; in automobile industry, 1100; of
women during 1950s, 1117; of women in
1960s and 1970s, 1199, 1201; prejudice against
immigrants and, 1232, 1233; in information
society, 1288–1289. *See also* Child labor; Unemployment; Wages; *specific occupations*
Empress of China (ship), 253, 340
Enclosure Acts (England), 18, 19
Encomienda system, 42, 45
The End of Ideology (Bell), 1115
End Poverty in California (EPIC), 985
Energy: electric, 930, 983–984; OPEC oil embargo of 1973–1974 and, 1187; rising costs
during 1970s, 1205, 1210

Energy Department, 1209, 1237

Enforcement Acts (1870 and 1871), 634

Engel v. *Vitale* (1962), 1148

England: medieval, commerce of, 18–19; consolidation of, 21; Reformation in, 23–24; early 17th century migrants from, 40–41; New World colonization by, 50–53, 91(illus.); defeat of Spanish Armada, 53; navy of, 53, 208–209; relations with Native Americans, 74, 1161; trade of, 93, 94–97; King William's War and, 105; Queen Anne's War and, 105–106; settlement of Ohio Valley by, 110; in French and Indian War, 164–168; taxes to pay for French and Indian War and, 175–178; Boston Massacre and, 185–186; in battle of Bunker Hill, 202; Declaration of Independence from, 207–208; army of, 208; Spain's participation in Revolutionary War and, 230; negotiations about Northwest Territory with, 256; seizure of American ships by, 274; American trade with, 307, 308; impressment by, 307–308; War of 1812 and, 309–311; war with France, American commerce and, 339–340; demand for cotton, 347; migration to cities from, 407. *See also* Britain; Great Britain; Revolutionary War

English East India Company, 93

English-only movement, 1233

Enlightenment, 90, 111–115, 131

Enola Gay (airplane), 1042

Entertainment: public, political participation and, 370; in western towns, 678; urban, during 1865–1910, 743–744; during 1930s, 992–994; during World War II, 1032–1033; during 1945-1960, 1101, 1101(illus.). *See also specific forms of entertainment*

Entrepreneurs, during 1820–1850, 421, 423

Environment: Native American impact on, 9, 74; European deforestation and, 15; healthy, colonial population growth due to, 126; rice production and, 144; sugar production and, 144; western, impact of fur trade and settlers on, 490–491; gold rush and, 518; Native American view of, 663; hydraulic mining and, 670, 671(illus.); cattle ranching and, 673; forest depletion by lumbering and, 676–677, 676(illus.); urban, 739–741; Dust Bowl and, 975–976, 975(illus.); Great Society programs to protect, 1147; business and, 1257; during Bush administration, 1270–1271. *See also* Pollution

Environmentalism: legislation supporting, 677, 1257–1258; national parks and, 677; Roosevelt's (Theodore) support of conservation and, 831–832; Taft's policies on conservation and, 833; during 1970s, 1207–1208; monkey-wrenching and, 1256–1257; Reagan's relaxation of quality standards and, 1258

Environmental Protection Agency (EPA), 1208

Equal Employment Opportunity Commission, 1238

Equal Rights Amendment (ERA): proposed in 1923, 941–942; attempt to pass, 1200; Schlafly's opposition to, 1200–1201, 1218; Republican opposition to, 1225

Equal Rights Association, 621, 622

Equal Rights Party, 393

Equiano, Olaudah, 144, 158–159

Era of the Common Man, 410

Erie Canal, 330, 331(illus.)

Erie people, 9, 47, 74; in French and Indian War, 167

Erie Railroad, 788

Erikson, Leif, 16

Erik the Red, 16

Ervin, Sam, 1192

Escobedo v. *Illinois* (1964), 1149

Eskimo people, 16

Espionage: during World War I, 903–904; Cold War fear of, 1079–1081

Espionage Act (1917), 903–904, 905, 906, 924–925

Essay Concerning Human Understanding (Locke), 112

Essex decision, 307

Estonia: Soviet seizure of, 1055; revolution in, 1264

Ethiopia, Italian invasion of, 1010

Ethnicity: loyalists and, 220; tensions in cities during 1820–1850 and, 413–414; hope for national unity during World War I and, 903; diminishment of differences during World War II and, 1035. *See also specific groups*

Etiquette, 751

Europe: culture of, 1400–1600, 14–17; agriculture in, 1400–1600, 17–19; commerce of, 1400–1600, 19–20; nation-states of, 20–21; Renaissance in, 21–22; Reformation in, 22–24; effects of contact with, 31–34; impact of New World on, 32; colonies of, in 1650, 57(map); migrations to colonies from, 124–126, 125(map); migration to cities from, during 1865–1910, 730–731, 732(illus.); immigration quotas and, 946; Great Depression and, 971; World War II in, 1017–1018, 1023–1025, 1024(map), 1042; postwar, foreign policy toward, 1055; Marshall Plan and, 1060–1061, 1062(illus.); during Cold War,

Europe (continued)
1061(map); U.S. troop cut in, 1265–1266. See also Eastern Europe; specific countries
Evangelical Protestants, Alliance Movement and, 785–786
Evangelism: on television, 1222; political influence of, 1227–1228
Evans, Oliver, 333, 423
Evans, Priscilla, 522–523
Evans, Walker, 991
Everett, Edward, 563
Evolution. See Darwinism
Executive veto: Jackson's use of, 382, 385; Cleveland's use of, 779; Ford's use of, 1208–1209
Exodusters, 658
Expansionism: during 1820–1850, 510–511; Compromise of 1850 and, 530–533, 533(map); foreign, in 1848–1860, 537–538; during Progressive Era, 846–856; businessmen as proponents of, 850; Social Darwinism and, 850–851; during 1865–1900, 852–854, 853(map); opposition to, 863–864, 866(illus.), 884; of Mussolini, 1011; of Hitler, 1011–1012, 1014, 1015. See also Migration
Ex parte Milligan (1866), 583
Expedition Act (1903), 830
Export-Import bank (Ex-Im Bank), 1012
Exxon Valdez (ship), 1270

Facing the World (Alger), 703
Factories: development of, 333–335; in Lowell, Massachusetts, 423, 424–426; Waltham system and, 423–424; textile production in, 423–426, 426(illus.); in antebellum South, 454; in South during 1870–1900, 639; electrical power for, 698; during 1870–1900, 709–714; working conditions in, 710–711, 811; assembly line and, 930
Fads, during 1950s, 1100
Fairbanks, Douglas, 933
Fairchild, Ephraim G., 658
Fair Deal, 1072
Fair Employment Practices Committee (FEPC), 1038
Fair Oaks, battle of, 574
Fall, Albert, 952
Fallen Timbers, Battle of (1794), 275
Falwell, Jerry, 1222, 1223(illus.)
Families: West African, 1400–1600, 12; in colonial Chesapeake region, 58–59; in colonial New England, 70–71; Native American, 73; colonial, 127; African-American, 147, 459, 627; of slaves, 147; following Revolutionary War, 249–250; changing roles in, 351, 352; size of, 352; farming, houses of, 360(illus.), 361; violence in, in cities during 1820–1850, 413; in 1820–1850, 431–432; southern, 471–472, 472(illus.); of immigrants, 733; during Great Depression, 972–973; traditional family values and, 1227. See also Children; Marriage
Family Assistance Plan (FAP), 1188
Famine: in medieval Europe, 14; in Ireland, 407, 543
Farmer, James, 1150
Farmers' Alliances, 781, 784–786. See also Populist Party
Farming. See Agriculture
Farm Security Administration, 998
Farnham, Eliza, 496, 679
Farragut, David G., 575
Farrell, James T., 991
Father Knows Best (television show), 1099
Faubus, Orville, 1119
Faulkner, William, 991
Federal budget: during 1877–1900, 771; growth under Wilson, 838; World War II and, 1043; deficits in, 1252, 1252(illus.), 1270, 1287; Clinton's intention to balance, 1276; Republicans' refusal to pass stopgap budgetary measures under Clinton, 1277; surplus in, 1287. See also Defense budget
Federal Bureau of Investigation, 919
Federal Communication Commission (FCC), 1237
Federal debt, during World War II, 1022
Federal Deposit Insurance Corporation (FDIC), 980
Federal Election Campaign Act (1974), 1204
Federal Emergency Relief Administration (FERA), 981
Federal Employee Loyalty Program (1947), 1079
Federal Farm Loan Act, 838
Federal Government. See also Congress; Presidents; Supreme Court
Federal government: settlement of West and, 659–661; limited, Bellamy's and George's acceptance of, 704; regulation of trusts by, 708; during 1877–1900, 770–771; Cleveland's view of, 779; progressive view of, 813, 814; Roosevelt's (Theodore) views on strength of, 834–835; growth under Wilson, 838; public attitude toward, 838–839, 953, 1203–1204, 1223, 1270; New Deal and size and scope of, 1001; World War II's effect on size and scope of, 1042–1043; Nixon's New Federalism and, 1188; lobbyists and, 1224; Reagan's efforts to

shrink scope of, 1236–1237; militia and patriot organization hatred of, 1294
Federal Highway Act (1916), 838
Federal Home Loan Bank Act, 976
Federal Housing Administration, 1097, 1117
The Federalist, 264
Federalists, 259, 277, 366, 371; form of government and, 263, 264, 265–266; Democratic-Republican opposition to, 273, 278, 288; on judiciary, 288–289; opposition to Louisiana Purchase, 298–299; War of 1812 and, 310
Federal Music Project, 987
Federal Reserve Act (1913), 837
Federal Reserve System, 970
Federal Security Agency, 1108
Federal Theater Project, 987, 988, 990
Federal Trade Commission (FTC), 837, 953
Federal Writers Project, 988
Federated Department Stores, 1246
Fell, Margaret, 90
Female Moral Reform Society, 429
The Feminine Mystique (Friedan), 1199
Feminism. *See* Women's liberation movement; Women's rights movement
Feminization of poverty, 1202, 1249
Fendall, Josias, 100
Ferdinand II (of Aragon), king of Spain, 21, 27, 28
Ferguson, Patrick, 232, 233
Ferraro, Geraldine, 1239
Fessenden, William Pitt, 616
Fetterman, William J., 665
Fields, W. C., 993
Fifteenth Amendment, 620–621
Fifty-Four Forty or Fight, 507
Filene's, 700
Filibusters, 537–538
Filipinos: racism against, 863; United Farm Workers' organization of, 1198(illus.). *See also* Philippines
Fillmore, Millard, 546; as president, 532; on slavery, 534
Films. *See* Movies
Findley, William, 378
Finland, postwar, communism in, 1055
Finney, Charles Grandison, 356, 428, 449
Firearms. *See* Arms races; Nuclear weapons; Weapons
Fire-eaters, 554–555
Fires: in forests, 676; in cities, 740; at Triangle Shirtwaist Company, 811
Fireside Chats (Franklin Roosevelt), 979, 994, 1005–1006
First Boston Corporation, 1247

First International American Conference (1889), 852–853
First Party System, 366, 398
First Reconstruction Act (1867), 618, 619, 619(map)
Fish, Hamilton, 849
Fisher, George, 468
Fishing: rising employment in, 137; controversy over fishing rights with Great Britain and, 854
Fishing Creek, battle at, 233
Fisk University, 625
Fitness craze, during 1960s and 1970s, 1202
Fitzgerald, F. Scott, 942
Fitzhugh, George, 477–478, 547
Five-and-ten-cent stores, 700
Five Civilized Tribes, 497, 570
Five-Power Treaty, 958
Flappers, 939
Fletcher v. *Peck* (1810), 291
Flexible response defense strategy, 1138
Florida: Spanish conquer of, 30; Spanish loss of, 168; return to Spain, 235; United States annexation of eastern part of, 306; ceded by Spain, 499; admission as state, 508, 530; secession of, 557; population growth during 1945–1960, 1101
Flour mill, of Evans, 333, 334(illus.)
Flu. *See* Influenza
Flying Fortress, 1025
Flying saucers, 1122–1123
Food: of New World, European adoption of, 32; colonial agriculture and, 138; shortage of, faced by Continental Army, 199–201, 219; tin cans for preservation of, 418, 696; shortage of, during Civil War, 584; drop in prices for, 711. *See also* Agriculture; Famine; *specific foods*
Food Administration, 899–900
Food Stamps, 1235
Football, 744–745, 936; television and, 1100
Foraker Act (1900), 865–866
Forbes, Charles R., 952
Force Act (1808), 308
Force Act (1833), 384
Forced labor, in California, 505
Ford, 933
Ford, Gerald R., 1193, 1208, 1209
Ford, Henry, 930, 933, 937, 945
Foreign aid: under Kennedy, 1138; to Russia, 1279
Foreign investment: in Latin America, 958–959; following World War II, 1098
Foreign Miners Tax, 681
Foreign policy: during 1865–1889, 848–849; dollar diplomacy and, 871–874; of containment,

Foreign policy (continued)
1051, 1059–1061, 1064, 1157; toward postwar Europe, 1055; Vietnam War's effect on, 1184. See also Expansionism; specific presidents and countries

Foreman, Dave, 1256–1257

Forest Reserve Act (1891), 677

Forests, of Northwest, depletion of, 676–677, 676(illus.)

Formosa, U.S. agreement with Nationalists and, 1111

Forrestal, James V., 1056, 1064

Fort Caroline, Florida, 46

Fort Christina, 49–50

Fort Donelson, 574

Fort Duquesne, 164, 165, 168

Forten, Charlotte, 590

Fort George, 135, 181

Fort Henry, 574

Fort James, 99

Fort Laramie, Treaty of (1851), 664, 665

Fort Mandan, 300

Fort McIntosh, Treaty of (1785), 257

Fort Michilimackinac, 170

Fort Nassau, 49

Fort Necessity, 164

Fort Pitt, 168

Fort Schuyler, 211–212

Fort Stanwix, Treaty of (1784), 257

Fort Sumter, attack on, 566–568, 568(illus.)

Fort Ticonderoga, 203, 211, 212

Fort Wayne, Treaty of (1809), 304

Fort William, 99

Fort William Henry, 167

Fort Wilson riot, 219

Forty-niners, 516

Foster, Vincent, 1294

"The Foundation of the Labor Movement" (Phillips), 715

Fourier, Charles, 436

Fourierism, 436

Four-Minute Men, 903

Four-Power Treaty, 958

Fourteen Points, 911–913

Fourteenth Amendment, 617–618, 704

Fourteenth Street School, 991

Fowler, Mark, 1237

Fox, George, 90

FOX network, 1290

Fox people, 381; resettlement of, 497, 541

Frame of Government (1681), 90

France: consolidation of, 21; Reformation in, 23; empire of, 46–48, 154, 168; relations with Native Americans, 74; King William's War and,
105; Queen Anne's War and, 105–106; migrants from, in lower Mississippi River basin, 110, 111(illus.); War of Jenkins' Ear and, 110; French and Indian War and, 164–168; alliance with American independence movement, 213–214, 235; Louisiana Purchase and, 298–299; American trade with, 307, 308; war with England, American commerce and, 339–340; Civil War and, 571; in World War I, 888, 908; Versailles Treaty terms and, 912; appeasement policy of, 1010; in World War II, 1014, 1025–1026, 1026(illus.); German invasion of, 1015; surrender to Germany, 1015; postwar, communism in, 1055; Indochina and, 1074, 1114; Suez affair and, 1113–1114

Francis I, king of Italy, 46

Franck, James, 1048

Franham, Eliza, 504

Frankenstein (movie), 993

Frankfurter, Felix, 810(illus.), 901, 946

Franklin, Benjamin, 112–113, 113(illus.), 164, 171, 206, 251, 703; on population growth, 124, 126; on taxes, 179; appointment as postmaster general, 205; Virginia resolution and, 207; as liaison with French during Revolutionary War, 213; negotiation of peace with Britain and France, 235

Franz Ferdinand, archduke of Austro-Hungarian Empire, 888

Frasson, Martha, 1201(illus.)

Frazier, E. Franklin, 943

Fredericksburg, Virginia, battle at, 592

Freed, Alan, 1103

Freedmen's Bureau, 613; conflict between Johnson and Congress over, 616; education and, 625

Freedmen's organizations, 469

Freedom: emancipation of slaves and, 246–247, 449–452, 589–591; purchase by slaves, 466–467; meaning of, 626–627

Freedom Riders, 1150

Freedom's Journal, 448

Freeman, Elizabeth Mumbet, 247(illus.)

Freemen, 466–470; Underground Railroad and, 464; abduction of, 467, 534; employment of, 467; Black Codes and, 467–468, 475, 477, 616; slave ownership by, 468. See also African-Americans

Freeport Doctrine (1858), 554

Free silver cause, 793–794

Free-soil movement, 514

Free-Soil Party, 514–515, 545; in election of 1848, 515–516, 528; slavery and, 530; in election of 1852, 536

Free Speech (newspaper), 824
Free Speech Movement (FSM), 1163
Free-staters, in Kansas, 543(illus.)
The Freewheelin' Bob Dylan (album), 1162–1163
Frelinghuysen, Theodore, 150
Frémont, John C., 491, 508–509, 546, 596–597
French and Indian War (1754–1763), 164–168;
   onset of, 164–166; global spread of, 166–168;
   results of, 166(map); impact on colonists,
   173–175; British taxes to pay for, 175–178
French Canadians, as loyalists, 220
French Prairie, Oregon, 504
French Revolution: American neutrality and,
   273, 274; American support for, 307
Freston, Tom, 1248
Freud, Sigmund, 940
Frick, Henry Clay, 790
Friedan, Betty, 1199
Friedman, Milton, 1207
Frontier: poverty on, 344; housing on, 361(illus.);
   disappearance of, 684–685, 850. *See also* West
Fruitlands, 436
Fuchida, Mitsuo, 1008
Fuchs, Klaus, 1079
Fuel Administration, 899, 900
Fugitive Slave Act (1793), 475
Fugitive Slave Act (1850), 532, 534–535,
   535(illus.)
Fulbright, J. W., 1164
Fuller, Elizabeth, 342
Fuller, Margaret, 439
Fulton, Robert, 328
Fundamental Constitutions of Carolina (Locke),
   86
Fundamentalism, 1222; during 1920s, 948–950;
   political influence of, 1227–1228
Furman, Mark, 1292
Fur trade, 46–48, 110; conflicts over, 47; English,
   52; Native Americans and, 52, 74, 302, 490;
   King William's War and, 105; merchants and,
   490

Gabriel, Peter, 1232
Gadsden, Christopher, 180
Gadsden, James, 539
Gadsden Purchase (1853), 539
Gage, Thomas, 193–194, 202
Galbraith, John Kenneth, 970, 1116, 1123
Galilei, Galileo, 22
Gallatin, Albert, 325, 327
Galloping Ghost, 936
Galloway, Joseph, 191
Gallup, George, 1118

Galveston, Texas, tidal wave in, 815
Gama, Vasco da, 26
Gambling: in western towns, 678; on baseball,
   917
Gang labor, 462
Gannett, Deborah Sampson, 351
Gardoqui, Diego de, 257
Garfield, Harry, 900
Garfield, James A., 623, 773, 774–776; assassina-
   tion of, 776
Garland, Hamlin, 658, 683, 785
Garrett, Thomas, 445–446, 464
Garrison, William Lloyd, 450, 451, 514–515, 534,
   535(illus.)
Garvey, Marcus, 943–945, 944(illus.)
Gaspée (ship), 187–188
Gates, Bill, 1286
Gates, Horatio, 212, 232–233, 251
Gates, Thomas, 54
Gay Men's Health Center, 1230
Gay rights movement, 1199, 1229–1230
Gays. *See* Homosexuals
Gazette of the United States, 277
Gehrig, Lou, 935
General Agreement on Tariffs and Trade
   (GATT), 1278–1279
General Amnesty Act (1872), 635
General Electric, 710
General Federation of Women's Clubs, 749
General Mills, 932
General Motors, 933, 996–997, 1098
The General Motors Family (radio program), 934
General Telephone and Electronics, 1189
*The General Theory of Employment, Interest, and
   Money* (Keynes), 990
General Trades' Union, 394(illus.)
Genêt, Edmond, 273
Geneva Accords (1954), 1114
Genius of Universal Emancipation, 450
Gentlemen's Agreement, 823
George I, king of England, 106
George II, king of England, 106, 109, 144
George III, king of England, 176, 190, 205, 213,
   235
George, Henry, 674, 677, 704, 752
Georgia: migration to, 126; colonial economy
   of, 144; constitution of, 226; slavery in, 248;
   ratification of Constitution by, 265; Indian
   removal and, 380–381; secession of, 557;
   Democratic resurgence in, 634; African-
   Americans in, during Progressive Era, 824
German Democratic Republic. *See* East
   Germany
German Reformed Church, 23

Germany: Reformation in, 22–23; migration to colonies from, 126; immigrants from, as loyalists, 220; migration to cities from, 348, 408, 731; migration from, during 1840s and 1850s, 542–544; schools established by immigrants from, 756; Samoa and, 856, 863; in World War I, 888–892, 908, 909, 910; submarine warfare of, during World War I, 890–892, 894, 1023; proposal for military alliance with Mexico, 895; army of, in 1917, 896; anti-German sentiment during World War I and, 905–906; Versailles Treaty terms and, 912–913; reparations following World War I and, 913, 958; migration from, during 1920–1928, 946; economy of, during 1920s, 958; National Socialist Party of, 1010; expansionism of, 1011–1012, 1014, 1015; nonaggression pact with Russia, 1014; submarine warfare of, during World War II, 1018; army of, in World War II, 1023; in World War II, 1023–1025, 1024(map), 1042; Allied conquer of, 1027; surrender of, 1031; reparations following World War II and, 1056–1057; western sector of, 1061. *See also* East Germany

Gettysburg, Battle of (1863), 563, 591–593, 593(map)

Gettysburg Address (Lincoln), 563–564

Ghana Empire, 13–14

Ghent, Treaty of (1814), 311

Ghost Dance, 653, 655

Giap, General, 1159

Gibbons v. *Ogden* (1824), 329

GI Bill (1944), 1095

Gibson, Dana, 750

Gibson, Josh, 993

Gibson Girl, 750

Gideon v. *Wainwright* (1963), 1149

Gilbert, Humphrey, 51

The Gilded Age (Twain and Dudley), 765

Gilman, Charlotte Perkins, 827

Gimbel's, 700

Gingrich, Newt, 1276–1277, 1282

Ginsberg, Allen, 1162

Girard, Stephen, 339–340

GIs, 1022

Glasgow, Ellen, 642

Glasnost, 1242

Glass-Steagall Banking Act (1932), 976, 980

Glazer, Nathan, 1224

Gleason, Jackie, 1099

Glendive, Montana, 679

Glidden, Joseph F., 674

Globalization, of American culture, 957

Glorious Revolution (1688–1689), 98–99; legislatures following, 100–102

"God Bless America" (song), 1033

Godfrey, Arthur, 1099

Godkin, E. L., 777

Gold: California gold rush and, 516–519, 523–524, 670, 681; prospecting for in Native American territory, 665–667; discovery in West, migration spurred by, 670

Goldberg, Arthur, 1148

Gold Digger (movie), 993, 993(illus.)

Golden Hill riots, 185–186

Golden Hind (ship), 51

Goldman, Emma, 827, 919, 925, 926

Goldman, Ronald, 1291

Gold Standard Act (1900), 797–798

Goldwater, Barry, 1146, 1224

Goldwyn, Samuel, 1100

Gompers, Samuel, 719, 724–725, 726, 796, 837, 864, 901, 938

Gone With the Wind (Mitchell), 992

Gonorrhea, sex education to prevent among troops, 898

Goodman, Benny, 994

Good Neighbor policy, 1012

Gorbachev, Mikhail, 1242, 1263, 1264, 1266

Gordon, Thomas, 113

Gore, Al, 1259, 1272, 1287, 1288

Gore, Thomas, 976

Gore-McLemore resolutions, 891–892

Las Gorras Blancas, 683

Gospel of success, 703–704

"The Gospel of Wealth" (Carnegie), 703

Gould, Jay, 587, 630

Government: of colonial Virginia, 55–56; of colonial Maryland, 58; of Massachusetts Bay, 66; of colonial Connecticut, 68; in colonial New England, 69; of colonial Pennsylvania, 90, 92; under William and Mary, 98; representative, 99; form proposed by Adams, 226, 227; Antifederalist proposal for form of, 263, 264–265, 266; Federalist proposal for form of, 263, 264, 265–266; simplification under Jefferson, 287–288. *See also* Congress; Constitution; Federal government; Legislatures; Local government; Office holding; Regulation; State government; Taxes

Government Act (1774) (England), 190

Gracia Real de Santa Teresa de Mose, 149

Graduation Act (1854), 493

Grady, Henry, 639

Graham, Billy, 1102

Grain elevator operators, farmers' conflict with, 783

Grain reaper, invention of, 418
Grand Army of the Republic (GAR), 768
Grand Banks, 46
Grandfather clauses, 643
Grand Old Party (GOP), 767. *See also* Republican Party
Grand Union, 700
Grange, Harold Edward "Red," 936
Granges, 783
Graniteville, Georgia, cotton mill in, 454
Grant, Ulysses S., 622, 849; in Civil War, 574–575, 593–596, 595(map), 599–600; as president, 630–633, 771
The Grapes of Wrath (Steinbeck), 991
Grasshoppers, farming in West and, 679–680
Gray, Robert, 340
Grayson, William, 547
Great Atlantic and Pacific Tea Company (A&P), 700, 933
Great Awakening, 147, 149–152; Second, 246, 353–356
Great Basin, 657
Great Britain: Civil War and, 571; American Civil War and, 576–577; disputes with, stemming from Civil War, 849; controversy over fishing rights with, 854; migration from, 946. *See also* Britain; England; Scotland
Great Depression, 967, 968–977, 1007; stock market crash and, 970–971; economic hardships of, 971–976, 973(illus.); Hoover's attempts to manage, 976–977; social realism and social escape during, 991–992; entertainment during, 992–994; radio during, 994–995. *See also* New Deal
Great League of Peace, 9
Great Migration, 65
Great Pacificator, 531
Great Plains: migration to, 657; Native American people of, 662–664, 662(illus.); drought in, during Great Depression, 974–976, 975(illus.)
Great Railway Strike (1877), 716–717, 789–790
Great Society, 1146–1148, 1156–1157, 1236
The Great Train Robbery (movie), 685
Great War for Empire. *See* French and Indian War
Great White Fleet, 871, 872(illus.)
Great World Exposition, 678
Greece: migration from, 946; communist insurgency in, 1059; U.S. aid to, 1059
Greeley, Horace, 504, 596, 631, 632
Green, William, 938
Greenback Party, 769, 772
Greenbacks, 772; to finance Civil War, 580, 581; Grant's policy toward, 632–633

Green Berets, 1138
Greene, Catherine, 215, 346
Greene, Nathanael, 233
The Green Hornet (radio program), 994
Greenland, 16
Green Mountain Boys, 153, 169, 203, 257
Green Party, 1288
Greenville, Treaty of (1795), 275
Greer (ship), 1018
Gregg, William, 454
Gregory, Thomas W., 904, 905
Grenada, Reagan's invasion of, 1244
Grenville, George, 176–177, 178
Gresham, Walter Q., 852, 856
Grimké, Angelina, 451, 478, 515
Grimké, Sarah, 451, 478, 515
Griswold, Roger, 278
Griswold v. *Connecticut* (1965), 1148
Gross domestic product (GDP), during 1990s, 1285
Gross national product (GNP): during World War I, 901–902; following World War I, 929; following World War II, 1092, 1094(illus.), 1100; automobile industry and, 1100
Guadalcanal, 1041
Guadaloupe, 168
Guadalupe Hidalgo, Treaty of (1848), 510
Guam, 1041
Guantanamo Bay, U.S. lease on, 865
Guatemala, nationalist uprising in, 1115
Guerrilla warfare: Filipino, 864–865; in Vietnam, 1141; in El Salvador, 1243; in Nicaragua, 1244
Guilford Court House, battle at, 233
Guinn v. *United States* (1915), 823–824
Guiteau, Charles, 776
Gullah dialect, 147
Gullah Jack, 465–466
Gunfights, in western towns, 678–679
Gwyn, Julia, 594

Habeas corpus, presidential suspension of, 583, 634
Haig, Alexander, 1240
Haiti: Wilson's policy toward, 876; Bush's policy toward, 1266; Clinton's policy toward, 1278
Hakluyt, Richard, 51
Haldeman, H. R., 1193
Haley, Bill, 1103
Half-Breeds, 768, 776
Halfway Covenant, 69
Halifax, Nova Scotia, 203; founding of, 165
Hall, E. K., 937

Hall, Fayer, 82–83
Hall, John, 334, 335
Hamer, Fannie Lou, 1153
Hamilton, Alexander, 121, 122, 212, 270(illus.);
on return of loyalists, 252; Constitution and,
259, 260, 261; on form of government, 264; as
treasurer, 267, 268–271; Report on Manufac-
tures of, 269–271, 272, 332; Madison's oppo-
sition to, 271–272; Whiskey Rebellion and,
276, 283, 284; opposition to Burr, 278; duel
with Burr, 299
Hamilton, Lee, 1184
Hamiltonians, 271–272
Hammon, Jupiter, 248
Hammond, James Henry, 477–478
Hammond, John H., 467
Hampton Institute, 626(illus.), 644
Hancock, John, 183, 189
Hancock, Winfield Scott, 596, 775
Hanging Rock, battle at, 232, 233
Hanna, Mark, 795, 796, 828
Hanson, Ole, 918
Happiness in Marriage (Sanger), 940
Hardey, John, 678
Hardin, John Wesley, 678
Harding, Warren G., 919, 920, 952; support of
business, 953, 954(illus.); foreign policy un-
der, 957–959
Hard Labor, Treaty of, 171
"A Hard Rain's Gonna Fall" (song), 1163
Harlem, New York, African-American culture in,
945
Harper, William, 477–478
Harpers Ferry, Virginia, Brown's raid on, 526,
529(illus.)
Harrington, Michael, 1144–1145, 1188
Harriot, Thomas, 8
Harrisburg, Pennsylvania, canals and, 331
Harris, Joel Chandler, 641
Harrison, Benjamin, 773, 780, 864; expansion-
ism under, 852–854
Harrison, William H., Jr., 639
Harrison, William Henry, 303, 304, 310; in elec-
tion of 1840, 397–398; as president, 772, 788
Harris, Townshend, 537
Hartford, Connecticut, 68
Hartford Convention, 310
Hart, Gary, 1239, 1262
Hart, Nancy, 215(illus.)
Harwit, Martin, 1049
Hastie, William, 998
Hastings, Lansford, 486, 509
Hat Act (1732) (England), 109
Hatch, Orrin G., 1297

Hauptmann, Bruno, trial of, 994–995
Havana, Cuba, 43
Havel, Vaclav, 1264
Havemeyer, Henry O., 707
Hawaiian Islands: reciprocal trade agreement
with, 854–855; conflict over sugar trade with,
854–856; debate over annexation of, 856; an-
nexation of, 863
Hawkins, John, 51
Hawkins, Sam, 445
Hawthorne, Nathaniel, 439
Hay, John, 863, 867, 868–869
Hayes, Lucy, 774
Hayes, Rutherford B., 637, 773, 774
Hayes Valley gang, 740
Haymarket Square riot, 717–719, 718(illus.)
Haynsworth, Clement, 1190
Hay-Pauncefote Treaty (1901), 868
Haywood, William (Big Bill), 826
A Hazard of New Fortune (Howells), 747
Head Start program, 1145
Headwright system, 55
Health care, Clinton's attempt to reform, 1275
Health craze, during 1970s, 1202
Health insurance, Truman's proposal for, 1072
Hearst, William Randolph, 746, 857
"Heartbreak Hotel" (song), 1103
Heller, Walter, 1145
Hellman, Lillian, 1081
Helper, Hinton, 478, 483–484
Hemingway, Ernest, 942
Hemp, in South during 1820–1850, 453
Hemphill, Gina, 1219
Henderson, Leon, 1021
Henderson, Richard, 172
Henri, Robert, 748
Henry IV, king of France, 23
Henry VII, king of England, 21, 50
Henry VIII, king of England, 23–24
Henry, Patrick, 179, 180(illus.), 188, 191, 193;
Constitution and, 261; on form of govern-
ment, 264
Henry the Navigator, prince of Portugal, 26
Hepburn Railroad Regulation Act (1906), 831
Herberg, Will, 1102
Herran, Thomas, 868–869
Hessian mercenaries, in Revolutionary War, 208,
210, 223
Hester Street (Luks), 748
Hiawatha, 9
Hidalgo, Miguel, 306
Hidatsa people, 302
Higginson, Thomas Wentworth, 527, 534
High Plains, 657

Highways. *See* Roads

Hill, Anita, 1271

Hill, Benjamin H., 650–651

Hill, Evan, 1118

Hill, James J., 789

Hillsborough, Lord, 184

Hindenburg (blimp), 995

Hindenburg, Paul von, 910

Hip-hop music, 1291

Hirohito, emperor of Japan, 1042

Hiroshima, Japan, bombing of, 1042, 1043(illus.)

Hispanics: white taking of land of, 681–682; railroads' impact on, 682; attempts to preserve control of their societies, 682–683; as miners, 682(illus.); population during 1920s, 938; discrimination against, during World War II, 1039; in cities, 1116–1117; challenge to assimilation, 1197, 1198(illus.); population during 1960s and 1970s, 1197; suffrage for, 1197, 1198(illus.); United Farm Workers' organization of, 1197; AIDS among, 1231; population during 1980s, 1231, 1232(map); prejudice against, 1232–1233; education of, 1292. *See also specific groups*

Hispaniola: slavery in, 26; Columbus' voyage to, 27, 28. *See also* Haiti; Santo Domingo

Hiss, Alger, 1079, 1081

Hitchcock, Gilbert, 915

Hitler, Adolf, 1009, 1010; expansionism of, 1011–1012, 1014, 1015; D-Day attack and, 1025; concentration camps and, 1027–1028, 1027(illus.); death of, 1031

Hoar, George, 864

Hobart, Garret A., 795

Hobbes, Thomas, 14

Ho Chi Minh, 1074, 1114, 1141

Ho Chi Minh trail, 1156, 1159

Hohokam culture, 7

Holding companies, 707

Holland. *See* Netherlands

Holland Land Company, 295, 344

Holler, Martin, 1248

Hollywood Ten, 1080, 1081(illus.)

Holmes, Oliver Wendell, Jr., 808, 906, 924–925, 926

Holocaust, 1027–1028, 1027(illus.)

Holy Roman Empire, 23

Homelessness: Panic of 1819 and, 314; during depression of 1893, 789; during Great Depression, 972, 977; during 1980s, 1249, 1250(illus.)

Homemakers, 1037

Home Owners Loan Corporation (HOLC), 984

Homespun, 185

Homestead Act (1862), 587, 658–661

Homestead Act (1863), 551

Homestead Grays, 993

Homosexuals: World War II and, 1035; gay rights movement and, 1199, 1229–1230; Clinton's policy toward, 1275; television portrayal of, 1290

Hone, Philip, 389–390, 396

Honeyman, John, 222

The Honeymooners (television show), 1099

Hood, John Bell, 597–598

Hooke, Joseph, 586

Hooker, Joseph, 592

Hooker, Thomas, 68

Hoover, Herbert, 920; as Food Administration head, 899–900; views on business, 954; in election of 1928, 959, 960; attempts to manage Great Depression, 976–977; criticism of New Deal, 1006; on World War II, 1022

Hoover, J. Edgar, 919, 944–945, 1078

Hoover Dam, 983

Hoovervilles, 977

Hope, Bob, 994

Hopedale, 436

Hopewell culture, 6

Hopi people, 691; resistance to Spanish, 45

Hopkins, Harry, 987, 1000, 1031

Hopkins, Samuel, 354

Hopper, Edward, 991

Horizontal integration, 705, 706(illus.)

Hornsby, Roger, 935

Horse-drawn omnibuses, 734–735

Horse railways, 735

Horses: Plains Indians and, 663; manure in cities and, 739

Horseshoe Bend, battle at, 304

Horton, Willie, 1263

Hospital for the Sick Poor, 114

Hotels, 737

"Hound Dog" (song), 1103

House Committee on Un-American Activities (HUAC), 1080

House of Burgesses, 55

House of Representatives: Taft's attempt to reform, 832–833. *See also* Congress

Housing: in colonial Chesapeake region, 59; of African-Americans, 146–147, 360–361, 360(illus.), 458; of slaves, 146–147, 360–361, 360(illus.); of farm families, 360(illus.), 361, 679; of urban working people, 361–362, 361(illus.), 738; on frontier, 361(illus.); of affluent urban families, 362, 410, 737; of artisans, 362; of middle-class people in cities, 410, 737–738; of southern planters, 470–471;

Housing *(continued)*
balloon-frame houses and, 735–736; of urban poor, 738; demand for, following World War I, 932; New Deal loans for, 984; boom in home ownership following World War II and, 1097; prohibition on sales to minorities, 1117. *See also* Tenements
Houston, Sam, 502, 503
Howard University, 625
Howe, Elias, 411
Howells, William Dean, 747
Howe, Richard, 209
Howe, William, 202, 209, 210, 211, 235
Howl (Ginsberg), 1162
Hudson, Henry, 48–59
Hudson, Rock, 1231
Hudson River, travel on, 329
Hudson River School, 438(illus.)
Hudson River valley, anti-rent riots in, 153
Hudson's Bay Company, 490, 503, 504
Huerta, Victoriano, 876, 877
Hughes, Charles Evans, 817, 893, 957–958
Hughes, Langston, 945
Hughes, Sarah T., 1134
Huguenots, 23; in Acadia, 46, 47; migration to colonies, 126; in Georgia, 144
Hull, Cordell, 1012
Hull, William, 310
Hull House, 804–805
Humphrey, George, 1107
Humphrey, Hubert, 1068, 1069, 1072, 1187; in election of 1964, 1146; in election of 1968, 1166, 1167, 1168, 1169
Humphrey, Richard Manning, 784(illus.)
Humphrey, William, 953
Hungary: Soviet control of, 1057; Soviet invasion of, 1113; revolution in, 1263
Hunley (submarine), 575
Hunter, Robert, 711
Hunter/gatherer peoples, early, 6, 9
Huronia, 47
Huron people, 9, 47, 74, 106; in French and Indian War, 167
Hussein, Saddam, 1267, 1268, 1269, 1280, 1281
Hutcheson, "Big Bill," 996
Hutchinson, Anne, 67–68, 67(illus.)
Hutchinson, Thomas, 180, 181, 189, 219
Hyde, Henry, 1282
Hydraulic mining, 670, 671(illus.)
Hydroelectric power, Tennessee Valley Authority and, 983–984
Hydrogen bomb, 1074

Ice Age, migrations into Western Hemisphere during, 4–5
Ice Cube, 1291
Iceland, 16
Ice-T, 1291
Ickes, Harold, 981
"I have a dream" speech (King), 1151–1152
"I'll Be Home for Christmas" (song), 1033
"I'll Be Seeing You" (song), 1033
Illinois, suffrage in, 292, 366
Illinois people, 74, 111(illus.)
Illiteracy, television and, 1104
Illness. *See* Disease; *specific diseases*
I'll Take My Stand, 992
Illustrators, myth of the West and, 685
Immigrants: Jewish, in New York, 727; communities of, 732–734; employment of, 733; families of, 733; newspapers for, 747; nativist position on, 751–752, 754; education of, 754–756, 755(illus.); attempts to discourage from voting, 770; during 1920s, 946; population of, 1231; cultural impact of, 1231–1232; prejudice against, 1232–1233. *See also specific groups*
Immigration: of Huguenots to Acadia, 46; from Germany, to colonies, 126; from Germany, to cities, 348, 408; from Ireland, 407–408, 543, 544; from China, 516–517, 518, 543; from Germany, during 1840s and 1850s, 542–544; Chinese, suspension of, 681; progressive efforts to limit, 822–823; of European refugees during World War II, U.S. resistance to, 1028
Immigration Reform and Control Act (IRCA) (1986), 1233
Immigration Restriction League, 754
Imminent danger standard, 906
Impeachment: of Johnson, 622–623, 771; of Clinton, 1259–1260, 1281–1282, 1281(illus.)
The Impending Crisis of the South (Helper), 478, 483–484
Impressment, 307–308
Inca (Quechua) people, 9, 11–12, 30
Income distribution: New Deal and, 1001; disparate, among African-Americans, 1195–1197; disparate, during 1980s, 1248–1249; disparate, during 1990s, 1289. *See also* Elites; Poverty; Social classes; Wealth; *specific social classes*
Income taxes. *See* Taxes
Indentured servants, 40–41; in Chesapeake region, 58, 139; declining number of, 62, 76, 246; colonial, 128, 139
Independence, Missouri, 494

Independent Treasury Act (1837), 396
Indiana: suffrage in, 292, 366; economy in 2000, 1287
Indian Intercourse Act (1790), 274–275, 302
Indian Removal Act (1830), 380, 381
Indian Reorganization Act (1934), 998–999
Indian Rights Association, 667
Indians. *See* Native Americans; *specific groups*
Indian Territory, resettlement to, 497–498
Indigo: production in Carolinas, 143, 174; task system of labor and, 461–462
Individualism, in 1820–1850, 427–428
Indochina: Japanese invasion of, 1018; French contol in, 1074. *See also* Vietnam; Vietnam War
Indulgences, Reformation and, 22–24
Industrial revolution: inventions and, 696–698; railroads and, 698–700, 699(map); consumer society and, 700–702, 701(illus.); business culture and, 702–703; gospel of success and, 703–704; corporate management and, 704–705; industrial integration and, 705–707, 706(illus.); regulation of trusts and, 707–709, 709(illus.); factory system and, 709–711; social mobility and, 711–712; working people and, 712–714, 713(illus.), 714(illus.); unionism and, 715–717, 719; Knights of Labor and, 717–719
Industrial Workers of the World (IWW), 825, 826–827, 904–905
Industry: in cities, 348; in South during 1870–1900, 639–640; stimulation by World War II, 1035. *See also* Factories; *specific industries*
"Industry and the Environment" (Keller), 1257
Inflation: following World War I, 917–918; concern about, during World War II, 1021; following World War II, 1065, 1094; during 1960s, 1205; under Nixon, 1207; under Carter, 1210; during 1980s, 1250. *See also* Prices
The Influence of Sea Power upon History (Mahan), 852
Influenza: during World War I, deaths due to, 911; epidemic during 1918-1919, 916, 916(illus.)
Information society, 1282–1285; employment in, 1288–1289
Infrastructure: rebuilding of, in post–Civil War South, 625–626. *See also specific components of infrastructure*
Ingersoll, Jared, 181
Inheritance: gender and, 249; partible, shrinkage of farms due to, 342

In His Steps (Sheldon), 808
Inquisition, 21
Insecticides, 1208
Installment purchases, 932
Insular cases, 866
Intel, 1283
Intellectual life: elite institutions promoting during 1820–1850, 436; urban, during 1865–1910, 751–752; consensus and, 1115–1116
Intelligence testing, by U.S. Army, 898
Inter-American Conference (1936), 1012
Interchangeable parts, factories and, 333–335
Intercontinental ballistic missiles (ICBMs), 1138, 1185
Interest groups, in Progressive Era, 812–813
Interim Committee, 1047
Interior Department, 1237
Intermediate Nuclear Forces Treaty (INF), 1241, 1242
Internal Revenue Act (1862), 580
Internal Security Act (1950), 1080
International Business Machines (IBM), 1098, 1189
International Harvester Corporation, 710, 830
International Ladies' Garment Workers Union (ILGWU), 810, 995
International Telephone and Telegraph (ITT), 957, 958
International Workingmen's Association, 715
Internet, 1283–1285
Interstate Commerce Act (1887), 708
Interstate Commerce Commission, 953, 1148
Interstate Highway Act (1956), 1100
Intolerable Acts, 190
Inuit people, 16
Inventions, 694, 696–698; patents and, 333, 696; industrial revolution and, 696–698. *See also* Technological innovations
Iowa, admission as state, 530
Iowa people, resettlement of, 541
IQ testing, by U.S. Army, 898
Iran: nationalist uprising in, 1115; aid to, 1186; hostage crisis in, 1212, 1245; Iran-contra affair and, 1245–1246, 1262
Iraq: Gulf War and, 1267–1269, 1268(map), 1297–1299; Clinton's policy toward, 1280–1281
Ireland: migration to cities from, 407–408, 731; migration during 1840–1863, 543, 544; migration from, 946
Iron Act (1750) (England), 109
Ironclad ships, in Civil War, 575–576
Iron foundry, 173(illus.)

Iron industry, in South during 1870–1900, 639
Iroquois Confederacy, 164
Iroquois people, 9, 74, 90, 258; Hudson's contact with, 49; Covenant Chain and, 75–76, 106, 153; in King William's War, 105; in French and Indian War, 164, 165; as loyalists, 221; in Revolutionary War, 231; taking of lands from, 257
Irreconcilables, 913
Irving, Washington, 437
Isabella of Castile, queen of Spain, 21, 27, 28
Isolationism, limitations imposed on Roosevelt (Franklin) by, 1012–1013, 1017–1018
Israel: independence of, 1064; invasion of Sinai Peninsula, 1113; 1967 war and, 1186, 1187; in Yom Kippur War, 1186; Camp David Accords and, 1210–1211, 1211(illus.); attack on Lebanon, 1244
Italy: migration from, 731, 946; in World War I, 908; invasion of Ethiopia, 1010; expansionism of, 1011; battle for, 1024; postwar, communism in, 1055
Itinerant laborers, in western settlements, 416
Itinerant preachers, 354
Iwo Jima, 1041

J. Edgar Thompson Steel Works, 705
Jackson, Andrew, 306, 376(illus.), 596; battles with Native Americans, 304–305; in War of 1812, 311; inauguration of, 363–364; in election of 1824, 373; presidential campaign of, 375–376; as president, 376–387, 402–403, 476; cabinet of, 377; opposition to Bank of the United States, 384–387; in election of 1832, 385; on Indian removal, 402–403; on slavery, 476; offer to purchase northern Texas, 503
Jackson, Helen Hunt, 667
Jackson, Jesse, 1239, 1263
Jackson, Jimmie Lee, 1153
Jackson, Kenneth, 736, 738
Jackson, "Shoeless" Joe, 917
Jackson, Thomas "Stonewall," 572, 574
Jacksonville, Florida, 46
Jacob Fries's Rebellion (1799), 278
Jacobites, 125
Jacobs, Harriet, 463
Jagger, Mick, 1163
"Jailhouse Rock" (song), 1103
Jails: during Revolutionary War, 223. See also Prisons
James I, king of England, 53, 55
James II, king of England, 97–98
James, Duke of York and Albany, 88, 89, 92

James, William, 806–807, 864
James Town (Virginia), establishment of, 54–55
Japan: commercial treaty with, 537; in Sino-Japanese War, 867; interest in Manchuria, 870–871, 1010; control over Korea, 871; Taft's policy toward, 874; interest in China, 875–876; Treaty of Versailles and, 912; in World War II, 1018–1019, 1040–1041, 1041(map), 1042, 1043(illus.), 1047–1049; U.S. occupation of, 1073; automobiles produced by, 1206
Japanese-Americans: schools established by, 756; California's crusade against, 822–823; internment during World War II, 1033–1034, 1034(illus.)
Jarvis, Howard, 1222
Jaworski, Leon, 1193
Jay, John, 251, 365; negotiation of peace with Britain and France, 235; negotiations about Northwest Territory, 256, 257; Constitution and, 259; on form of government, 264; Jay's Treaty and, 274
Jayhawkers, 569
Jay's Treaty, 274
Jay-Z, 1291
Jefferson, Thomas, 188, 292, 782; at Second Continental Congress, 204, 205; Virginia resolution and, 207; Declaration of Independence and, 207–208; on religious freedom, 244; land ordinances drafted by, 255; Constitution and, 261; as secretary of state, 267; opposition to political parties, 276, 277; as vice president, 277; as president, 278, 285–286, 288–291, 298, 299, 300, 306–308; Whiskey Rebellion and, 283–284; inaugural address of, 285–286; on significance of land for settlement, 298; Lewis and Clark expedition and, 299–301; on Native American relations, 302; on tariffs, 374; on slavery, 447, 448, 475
Jeffersonians. See Democratic-Republicans
Jenkins, Robert, 109–110
Jerome, Chauncey, 335
Jewel Tea, 700
Jewett, Helen, 404–405, 429
Jewish Daily Forward, 747
Jews: expulsion from Spain, 21; migration to colonies, 126; following Revolutionary War, 244; immigrant, in New York, 727, 738; migration to cities, 731; Holocaust and, 1027–1028, 1027(illus.)
JFK (movie), 1294
Jiang Jeshi, 1073
Jim Crow laws, 643–644

Job Corps, 1145, 1188
Joffre, Joseph, 908
John I, king of Portugal, 21
John Birch Society, 1163–1164
"Johnny B. Goode" (song), 1103
Johns Hopkins University, 756
Johnson, Andrew, 596, 608; restoration under, 614–615, 615(illus.); Congress' opposition to, 616–617; impeachment of, 622–623, 771
Johnson, Anthony, 61
Johnson, Hiram W., 817, 914, 920
Johnson, Lady Bird, 1147
Johnson, Lyndon Baines, 1073, 1125, 1134, 1144(illus.), 1294; foreign policy of, 1114; War on Poverty of, 1143–1145; in election of 1964, 1146, 1147(map); Great Society and, 1146–1148, 1156–1157; Supreme Court during administration of, 1148–1149; civil rights and, 1152–1154; Vietnam War and, 1156–1160, 1165–1166; decision not to run for reelection, 1166
Johnson, Rafer, 1219
Johnson, Spencer, 468
Johnson, Tom, 816
Johnson, Walter, 935
Johnson-Reed Immigration Act (1924), 946
Johnston, Albert Sidney, 574–575
Johnston, Joseph E., 572, 574, 598, 600
Johnston Bill (1769), 172
Joint Chiefs of Staff, establishment of, 1061
Joint Committee of Fifteen on reconstruction, 616
Joint Electoral Commission, 637
Jones, Absalom, 248, 468–469
Jones, Samuel, 816
Jordan, in 1967 war, 1186
Jordan Marsh, 700
Joseph, Chief, 691
Journalists, muckrakers, 811
Judiciary Act (1789), 267, 289, 290
Judiciary Act (1801), 288
Judson, Edward Zane Carroll, 684
The Jungle (Sinclair), 812, 831
Jungle Warfare School, 1138
Justice Department, 1238

Kalb, Johann Baron de, 213
Kansas: Lecompton Constitution and, 549; Exodusters in, 658; entry into Union, 660; cattle ranching and growth of, 672
Kansas-Nebraska Act (1854), 538–541; Lincoln's opposition to, 552–553
Kansas Territory, 498

Kaugman, Irving, 1079–1080
KDKA, 934
Kearney, Belle, 819
Kearny (ship), 1018
Kearny, Stephen, 510
Keating, Charles, 1237
Keating-Owen Act, 838
Keayne, Robert, 66
Keller, G. M., 1257
Kelley, Abby, 451
Kelley, Florence, 809–810, 818
Kelley, Oliver Hudson, 783
Kellogg, Frank, 958
Kellogg-Briand Pact (1928), 958
Kemp, Jack, 1277
Kemp-Roth tax bill, 1223–1224
Kendall, Amos, 377
Kennan, George Frost, 1050–1051, 1059, 1060, 1090, 1164, 1241
Kennebec River, 53
Kennedy, Anthony, 1238
Kennedy, Caroline, 1137
Kennedy, Edward M., 1210, 1225, 1299
Kennedy, Jacqueline, 1133, 1134, 1136(illus.), 1137
Kennedy, John, 1137
Kennedy, John F., 1073, 1136(illus.), 1187, 1294; foreign policy of, 1114, 1138; illnesses of, 1124; in election of 1960, 1124–1126, 1125(illus.); assassination of, 1133–1134, 1143; domestic policy of, 1136–1138; Bay of Pigs fiasco and, 1139; Berlin and, 1139; summit meeting with Khrushchev, 1139; Cuban missile crisis and, 1139–1140; Soviet Union and, 1139–1140; Vietnam and, 1141–1142; Supreme Court during administration of, 1148; civil rights and, 1149–1152
Kennedy, Joseph P., 1124
Kennedy, Robert F., 1137, 1150, 1166, 1167; Cuban missile crisis and, 1140
Kent State University shooting, 1177, 1189, 1190
Kentucky: suffrage in, 366; in Civil War, 569
Kentucky Resolution (1798), 278
Kerouac, Jack, 1162
Kerr, Clark, 1163
Kerry, John, 1161
Keynes, John Maynard, 990
Khmer Rouge, 1181
Khomeini, Ayatollah, 1212
Khrushchev, Nikita, 1091–1092, 1112; summit meeting with Eisenhower, 1112–1113; U-2 spy plane incident and, 1123; summit meeting with Kennedy, 1139; Cuban missile crisis and, 1139–1140

Kickapoo people, resettlement of, 541

Kidd, William, 130

Kieft, Willem, 49

King, Charles E., 584

King, Martin Luther, Jr., 512, 1120, 1121, 1150, 1176; philosophy of, 1120; "Letter from Birmingham Jail" of, 1151, 1174–1175; "I have a dream" speech of, 1151–1152; on Vietnam War, 1164; change in philosophy of, 1166; assassination of, 1166–1167

King, Rufus, 315, 316

King, Rodney, 1271–1272

King George's War. *See* War of Jenkins's Ear (1740–1748)

King Philip (Metacomet), 74–75, 75(illus.)

Kin groups, African-American, 459

Kingsbury, F. J., 762–763

King's College, 152

King's Mountain, Battle of, 233, 234(illus.)

King William's War, 105

Kinsey, Alfred, 1117–1118

Kiowa people, 498, 662, 663; resettlement of, 665

Kirby-Smith, Edmund, 577, 600

Kirkpatrick, Jeanne, 1240

Kissinger, Henry, 1178, 1180, 1180(illus.), 1183, 1184, 1185, 1186–1187

Kitchen debate, 1091–1092

Klehr, Harvey, 1081

Knickerbocker Club, 745

Knights of Labor, 717–719, 724, 726

Know-Nothings, 544–545, 545

Knox, Henry: Constitution and, 259, 262; as secretary of war, 267

Knox, John, 23

Knox, Lucy, 215, 249

Knox, Philander C., 871

Knute Rockne, All American (movie), 1234

Koerner, William H. D., 685

Koop, C. Everett, 1230

Korea: Japanese control over, 871; Japanese annexation of, 874; prejudice against immigrants from, 1232–1233

Korean War, 1074–1078, 1076(map); Truman's conflict with MacArthur and, 1077; consequences of, 1077–1078; Eisenhower's promotion of cease-fire in, 1111

Korematsu v. *U. S.* (1944), 1033

Kosciuszko, Thaddeus, 213

Kosovo, 1280

Koster and Bial Theatre, 744

Kramer, Larry, 1230

Kristallnacht, 1027

Kristol, Irving, 1224

Kroc, Ray, 1101

Krock, Arthur, 984

Kroger, 700

Ku Klux Klan (KKK), 634, 1120–1121, 1153; revival of, 917, 947; activities of, 947–948, 948(illus.); debate over condemnation of, 955; growth during Great Depression, 974

Ku Klux Klan Act (1871), 634

Kurile Islands, 1030

Kuwait, Gulf War and, 1267–1269, 1268(map), 1297–1299

Labor: during World War I, 901–903; inequity between management and, 937; legislation governing, 937. *See also* Employment; Strikes; Unemployment; Unions; Wages; Workers

Labor-Management Relations Act (1947), 1067

Laconia (ship), 895

Ladies Association of Philadelphia, 214, 249

Lafayette, Marquis de, 213, 448

Laffer, Arthur, 1223

La Follette, Robert, Jr., 1082

La Follette, Robert M., 814, 816–817, 817(illus.), 832, 887, 893, 895, 913; in election of 1924, 956

Laissez-faire doctrine, 702

Lake Champlain, battle of (1814), 310

Lakota people, resistance to white settlers, 665

Lancaster Turnpike, 327

Land acquisition: headwright system for, 55; sales in West and, 255–256; settlement of western territories and, 298; Land Act of 1820 and, 312, 492; speculators and, in Old Northwest, 344; migration and availability of land and, 416; decline in price and, 456; in West, 492–493; in Texas, 500; free land proposal and, 550–551; Southern Homestead Act and, 620; speculation and, in West, 658, 659, 674–675; Homestead Act of 1862 and, 658–661

Land Act (1796), 298

Land Act (1801), 298

Land Act (1820), 312, 492

Land and Labor Clubs, 704

Land banks, 107, 108

Land-grant colleges, 587, 756

Land grants, to railroads, 699, 699(map)

Landon, Alfred M., 988

Land Ordinances, 255, 277

Land ownership: in medieval England, 18–19; in colonial Massachusetts, 66; in colonial New England, 69, 70, 71(map), 136, 137; in Carolinas, 86; in colonial Pennsylvania, 90; colonial conflicts over, 152–154, 169–172; Jefferson's ordinances for, 255; significance of, 298; individual, attempt to convert Native Americans to, 669; Native Americans' attitude toward, 669, 691–692; white taking of Hispanics' lands and, 681–682. *See also* Land acquisition

Lane Theological Seminary, 354, 449

Lange, Dorothea, 992

Language: Native American, early, 6; foreign-language newspapers and, 747; cleansing of, during World War I, 906; English-only movement and, 1233

Lansing, Robert, 892, 912

Lansing-Ishii Agreement, 876

Larcom, Lucy, 425

Las Casas, Bartholomé de, 38–39

Last-arrow pageants, 669

Late Great Planet Earth (Lindsey), 1208

Latin America: Monroe Doctrine and, 317; U.S. exports to, 850; U.S. presence in, during 1895–1945, 872–873, 873(map); Wilson's policy toward, 876; economy of, during 1920s, 958–959; Good Neighbor policy toward, 1012; postwar relations with, 1063–1064; at end of Cold War, 1266. *See also* Central America; South America; *specific countries*

Latrobe, Benjamin, 368

Latvia: Soviet seizure of, 1055; revolution in, 1264

Laud, William, 65

Lauren and Hardy, 993

Laurens, Henry, 183, 212

Laurens, John, 212

Law enforcement, in cities during 1820–1850, 414

Lawrence, Amos, 541

Lawrence, Jacob, 991

Lawrence, Kansas, 541, 542

Laws: during Renaissance, 22; to force colonial economic subordination, 175–178; anti-Tory, 252; regulating child labor, 426; affecting railroads, 538–541, 830, 831, 838; antitrust, 708, 781, 830, 837; social, during Progressive Era, 818; expanding government power, 830. *See also* Courts; Supreme Court; *specific laws*

Laws, Divine, Morall, and Martiall (1612), 54

Lawyers, Enlightenment view of, 114

Leach, Robin, 1246–1247

League of Nations, 913–915, 920, 1010

League of Women Voters (LWV), 941

Lear, Norman, 1202, 1228, 1248

Leary, Timothy, 1162

Lease, Mary Elizabeth, 785, 786, 794

Leatherstocking Tales (Cooper), 437

Leave It to Beaver (television show), 1099

Leaves of Grass (Whitman), 439

Lebanon: Israeli attack on, 1244; bombing of U.S. Marine barracks in, 1244–1245

Lecompton Constitution (1855), 549–550

Lee, G. W. C., 599(illus.)

Lee, Ivy, 932

Lee, Mother Ann, 435

Lee, Richard Henry, 188

Lee, Robert E., 599(illus.); in Civil War, 526, 574, 577, 586, 591–592, 598; surrender of Confederacy and, 599–600; statue of, 641

Lee, Spike, 1233

Legal Tender Act (1862), 580

Leggett, William, 393

Legion of Decency, 994

Legislation. *See* Courts; Laws; Supreme Court; *specific laws*

Legislatures: first in North America, 55; in colonial Maryland, 58; of colonial Massachusetts, 66; colonial, royal attempts to control, 97–98; Glorious Revolution and, 100–102; colonial, printing of currency by, 107–108; of colonial Pennsylvania, 118; of states, 226, 227–228; unicameral, 226. *See also* Congress

Lemnitzer, Lyman L., 1141

Lend-Lease program, 1017

Lenin, V. I., 912, 1052; western leaders' contempt for, 1054

Lenni Lenape people. *See* Delaware people

Leonard, Daniel, 239, 241

Leopard (ship), 307–308

Lesbians. *See* Homosexuals

"Letter from Birmingham Jail" (King), 1151, 1174–1175

Letters from a Farmer in Pennsylvania (Dickinson), 183–184

Letters from an American Farmer (Crèvecoeur), 293

Let Us Now Praise Famous Men (Evans), 991

Leuchtenburg, Walter, 1098

Leveraged buyouts, 1246

Lever Food and Fuel Control Act (1917), 899

Levitt, William, 1097

Lewinsky, Monica, 1259, 1281, 1281(illus.), 1290

Lewis, John L., 995–996, 1022, 1066

Lewis, Meriwether, expedition with Clark, 299–301, 300(map)

Lewis, Sinclair, 942

Lexington, Kentucky, intellectual life in, 436–437

Lexington, Massachusetts, battle at, 194

Leyte Gulf, Battle of (1944), 1041

Liberal Republicans, opposition to Grant, 631–632

Liberals. *See* Progressive Party; Progressivism

The Liberator, 450
Liberia, colonization movement and, 447
Libertarians, 1163–1164
Liberty (ship), 183
Liberty Bonds, 900
Liberty Party, 478, 508, 513–514
Libraries, 113, 114, 436; construction of, 751; Red Scare and, 1080
Library Company, 113
Library of Congress, 1204
Libya, U.S. attack on, 1245
Lieberman, Joseph, 1287
Life expectancy: in medieval Europe, 14; in colonial Chesapeake region, 58–59; in colonial New England, 70; of Native Americans, 1198
Life in America series, 988
Life Is Worth Living (television show), 1102
Life magazine, 991, 1036, 1100, 1117, 1118
Life of Washington (Weems), 293
Lifestyles of the Rich and Famous (television show), 1246–1247
Lifetime (television network), 1248
Light in August (Faulkner), 991
Liliuokalani, queen of Hawaii, 855–856, 855(illus.)
Lincoln, Abraham, 545–546; early life and political career of, 494, 551–552; on slavery, 526; *on Dred Scott* decision, 549; opposition to popular sovereignty, 552–553; campaign against Douglas for Senate, 553–554, 554(illus.), 560–562; in election of 1860, 555–556, 556(map); inauguration of, 558, 567; on equality of races, 560; Gettysburg Address of, 563–564; approach to slavery issue, 566; leadership of, 581–582, 582(illus.); on civil liberties, 583; Emancipation Proclamation of, 589–591; in election of 1864, 596–597; negotiation of Confederate surrender and, 598–599; assassination of, 607–608; conciliatory plan for South following Civil War, 612–614. *See also* Civil War (1861–1865)
Lincoln, Benjamin, 231
Lincoln, Mary, 607, 608
Lincoln Savings, 1237
Lindbergh, Charles, 927–928, 994–995, 1017–1018
Lindsay, John, 1189
Lindsey, Hal, 1208
Lippmann, Walter, 913, 939, 940, 983, 1064, 1071
Lisa Lisa (rap band), 1231
Lisler, Jacob, 99–100
Literacy rate, during 1920s, 934
Literacy tests, to exclude black vote, 643

Literature: during Renaissance, 22; African-American, 248, 945; guidebooks on child rearing and mothering, 351; during 1820–1850, 437, 438–439; abolitionist, by women authors, 452; by women authors, 452, 642; of New South, 641–642; during 1865–1910, 747–748; muckrakers and, 811–812, 815; during 1920s, 942–943; Federal Writers Project and, 988; disenchantment with World War I in, 1012–1013. *See also specific forms of literature*
Lithuania: Soviet seizure of, 1055; revolution in, 1264
Little, Malcolm (Malcolm X), 1155
Little Bighorn, battle at, 666–667
Little Richard, 1103
Little Rock, Arkansas, school desegregation in, 1119
Little Steel, 997
Little Turtle, 275
Livingston, Robert, 1282
Livingston, Robert R., 298, 328
Lloyd, Henry Demarest, 708
Lloyd George, David, 912
Loan Offices, 217
Loans: to Allies in World War I, 890. *See also* Debts
Lobbyists, 1224
Local government: political machines and, 741–743, 742(illus.); scope of, 771; city manager form of, 815; commission form of, 815
Locke, Alaine, 945
Locke, John, 32, 85–86, 98–99, 112, 113
Locofos, 393
Lodge, Henry Cabot, 850–851, 864, 1113, 1124; opposition to Treaty of Versailles, 913–914, 915
Lodge Corollary, 873
London, England: medieval, 19; trade with West Indies, 96(illus.); bombing of, 1015
The Lonely Crowd (Riesman), 1104
The Lone Ranger (radio program), 994
Long, Breckinridge, 1028
Long, Huey, 985, 1007
Long, John D., 848
Long, Stephen, 491
Long Island, Battle of, 209
Long Island, New York, 49
Long Knives, 231
Long Telegram, 1050–1051, 1090
Looking Backward (Bellamy), 703
Looking Out for #1 (book), 1202
Look magazine, 991, 1100
Lopez, Narciso, 537

Los Angeles, California: Hispanic population during 1850–1880, 683; population growth during 1870–1920, 730; suburbs of, 930(illus.); population during 1900–1930, 932; Hispanic population in 1920s, 938; growth due to World War II, 1035; suburbs of, growth following World War II, 1097; race riot in Watts section of, 1155; Olympic Games in, 1219–1220; immigrant population in 1990, 1231; 1992 riots in, 1271–1272

Los Angeles County, Hispanic population during 1950s, 1117

Los Lobos (rap band), 1231

Lost Generation, 942

Loudoun, Lord, 166, 167, 168

Louis XI, king of France, 21

Louis XVI, 273; king of France, 213

Louis, Joe, 992

Louisbourg: War of Jenkins' Ear and, 110; cost of expedition against, 135; British capture of, 168

Louisiana: French claim to, 48; French settlers in, 111(illus.); boundaries of, 306; secession of, 557

Louisiana Territory, 297–299; Lewis and Clark expedition to, 299–301, 300(map); purchase of, 491

Love Canal, New York, 1208

Lovejoy, Elijah P., 476, 552

Lowden, Frank O., 920

Lowell, Francis Cabot, 424

Lowell, Massachusetts, manufacturing in, 423, 424–426

The Lowell Offering, 425

Lower strata: colonial, 133–134; loyalists among, 220. *See also* Poverty; Workers

Lower Three Counties, 92

Loyalists: migrations of, 204; patriot battles with, 205; in British army, 208; sources of, 219–220; motivation of, 220; slaves as, 220–221; Native Americans as, 221, 221(illus.); patriots' treatment of, 221–222; condemnation of rebellion by, 239, 241; exiled, wish to return home, 252

Loyal Nine, 179–180

LSD, 1162

Luce, Henry, 1073

Luftwaffe, 1015

Luks, George, 748

Lumbering, 676–677, 676(illus.); in South during 1870–1900, 639; decline following World War I, 936

Lusitania (ship), German sinking of, 890–891, 891(illus.)

Lutheran Church, 23, 126

Luther, Martin, 22–23

Luther, Seth, 425, 426

Luxembourg, German invasion of, 1015

Lynchings: of African-Americans, 644, 645(illus.), 824, 903, 917, 974; of German-Americans during World War I, 905–906

Lynd, Helen, 936, 942, 991

Lynd, Robert, 936, 942, 991

Lynn, Massachusetts, putting out system in, 336–337

Lyon, Matthew, 278–279

McAdoo, William Gibbs, 900, 919, 955, 959

MacArthur, Douglas, 977, 1040, 1041; Japanese occupation under, 1073; in Korean War, 1075–1076; Truman's conflict with, 1077

McCain, John, 1287

McCarthy, Eugene, 1166

McCarthy, Joseph, 1051, 1066, 1082–1084, 1083(illus.), 1108–1109, 1124

McClellan, George, 573–574, 577–578, 591, 597

McCord, James, 1192

McCormick, Cyrus Hall, 418

McCormick reaper works, Haymarket Square riot and, 717–719, 718(illus.)

McCoy, Joseph G., 672

McCulloch v. *Maryland* (1819), 290, 314, 319–321

McDonald, John A., 631

McDonald's, 1101

McDowell, Irvin, 572

McFarlane, Robert, 1245, 1246

McGill, William J., 1178

McGovern, George, 1182, 1190, 1191

McGurn, "Machine Gun" Jack, 950

Machiavelli, Niccolo, 22

Machinists, republicanism of, 392

McKinley, William, 765, 793; presidential campaign of, 795, 796, 797; as president, 797–798; assassination of, 828; Spanish-American War and, 858–859, 883–884; refusal to annex Cuba, 865

McKinley Tariff, 780, 787

McKinley Tariff Act (1890), 855

McNamara, Robert, 1158, 1160

Macon's Bill No. 2 (1810), 308

McPherson, Aimee Semple, 949–950

Macune, Charles W., 784, 785

McVeigh, Timothy, 1293–1294

Macy's, 700, 701, 701(illus.), 737

Maddox (ship), 1157

Maddox, Robert, 1049

Madeira, slavery in, 26

Madero, Francisco, 876

Madison, James, 254, 290, 298; Constitution and, 259, 260–261; on form of government, 264; Bill of Rights and, 268; opposition to Hamilton, 271–272; opposition to political parties, 276; as president, 308–309, 371; Monroe Doctrine and, 316–317

Mad magazine, 1122

Madman Theory, 1181

Magazines: photojournalism and, 991–992; for women, 992; impact of television on, 1100; specialized, 1104, 1248; atomic energy fears and, 1122. *See also specific magazines*

Maginot Line, 1014

Mahan, Alfred Thayer, 852, 885

Mail-order catalogs, 700–701

Maine: Viking voyages to, 16; statehood of, 316

Maine (ship), 852, 858, 859(illus.), 860

Main Street (Lewis), 942

Maize. *See* Corn

Malaria, Panama Canal and, 846

Malcolm, John, 190

Malcolm X, 1155, 1175–1176

Malinche, Ala, 29

Mallory, Stephen R., 575

Management, corporate, 704–705, 932–933; scientific management and, 710, 933; inequity between workers and, 937

Manassas Junction, Virginia, 572

Manchuria: Russian and Japanese interests in, 870–871, 1010; Taft's policy toward, 874

Mandan people, 300–301, 302, 490

Mandela, Nelson, 1266

Manhattan, New York: purchase of, 49; population during 1900–1915, 735

Manhattan Project, 1042, 1047, 1048, 1049

Manifest destiny, 489, 537

Mann, Horace, 432

The Man Nobody Knows (Barton), 933

Manpower Retraining Bill, 1137

Manufactories, 420–421; development of, 336–337. *See also* Factories

Manufacturing. *See* Factories; Industry; Workers

Manumission, 447

Mao Zedong (Mao Tse-tung), 1073

Mapplethorpe, Robert, 1227–1228

Maps, of Waldseemüller, 28

Marbury, William, 289–290

Marbury v. *Madison* (1803), 289–290

The March of Time (radio program), 995

March on Washington (1963), 1151–1152

Marcos, Ferdinand, 1186

Marcy, William L., 537

Marion, Francis, 233

Maritime commerce: of medieval Europe, 16, 18; difficulty of travel during mid-1700s and, 124; impressment and, 307–308; in 1820–1850, 416–417; of California, 505. *See also* Smuggling

Market towns, colonial, 131–136

Mark I computer, 1098

Marriage: in medieval Europe, 15; between Spaniards and Native Americans, 45; colonial, 58–59, 126, 127, 128; African-American, 147, 458–459, 627; of slaves, 147; arranged, decline in, 249; women's demand for equal treatment in, 249; changing roles in, 351–352; polygamous, among Mormons, 435; complex, among Oneidans, 436; basis on companionship and shared interest, 940; during Great Depression, 972; age at, following World War II, 1095. *See also* Divorce; Families; Women

Marsh, Reginald, 991

Marshall, George C., 1059, 1060, 1064, 1073

Marshall, James, 516

Marshall, John, 285, 289, 290(illus.), 319, 321, 329, 380–381; judicial review and, 289–290, 291; Burr's trial and, 299

Marshall, Thurgood, 1131, 1271

Marshall Field's, 737

Marshall Plan, 1060–1061, 1062(illus.)

Martha Washington Societies, 429

Martial law, imposition during Civil War, 583

Martinique, 168

Martin, Joseph J., 1077

Martin, Luther, 261–262

Marx Brothers, 993

Mary I, queen of England, 24

Mary II, queen of England, 98, 99, 104

Maryland: colonial, 56–58; revolt in, 100; migration to, 124; economy of, colonial, 139; constitution of, 227; signing of Articles of Confederation, 229; manumission of slaves in, 248; ratification of Constitution by, 265; suffrage in, 367; runaway slaves in, 445; escaped slaves in, 534; in Civil War, 569. *See also* Chesapeake region

Mary Noble, Backstage Wife (radio program), 994

Mary Stuart, Queen of Scots, 53

Masaryk, Jan, 1060

M*A*S*H* (movie), 1203

Mason, Charles, 89

Mason, James M., 577

Mason, John Y., 538

Massachusetts: colonial, dissension in, 67–69; royal revocation of charter of, 97; voting rights in, 99; economy in, colonial, 107; Writs of Assistance and, 176; Coercive Acts and, 190; constitution of, 227–228; slavery in, 246; Shays's Rebellion in, 253–254; ratification of Constitution by, 265

Massachusetts Bay, 64–66

Massachusetts Bay Company, 65

Massachusetts Provincial Congress, 222

Massasoit, 63, 64

Mass culture, of 1950s, 1104

Mass transit, impact on cities, 734–737

Masterson, Bat, 678

Mathematical Principles of Natural Philosophy (Newton), 112

Mather, Cotton, 73, 98

Matrilinealism, West African, 12

Matsu, Chinese shelling of, 1111

Matthews, H. Freeman, 1051

Matthews, Mark, 821

Matusow, Alan, 1148

The Maxwell House Hour (radio program), 934

Maya people, 9, 10

Mayflower (ship), 63

Mayflower Compact, 63

Maysville Road bill, 382

Meade, George G., 592

Meat, cattle ranching and, 672–674

Meat Inspection Act, 831

Meatpacking industry, 705

Mechanicsville, battle at, 574

Me Decade, 1202

Mediation Commission, 901

Medicaid, 1146, 1148, 1188, 1235, 1275

Medical care: for mentally ill people, in 1820–1850, 431; during Civil War, 586. *See also* Doctors

Medicare, 1146, 1148, 1188, 1228, 1249, 1275, 1276

Medicine Lodge Creek, Treaty of (1867), 665

Mee, Charles L., Jr., 1049

Mellon, Andrew, 954, 977

Melville, Herman, 439

Memminger, Christopher, 581

Memphis, Tennessee: race riot in, 617; water pollution in, 740

Men: colonial, 127; migration from New England, 342; roles during 1790–1820, 351; suffrage for, 366–369, 367(map), 372; roles during 1820–1850, 431; slave, work of, 462; paternalism toward slaves and wives, 471–472; of South, Civil War and, 610; in African-American families, 627; in farm households, 680

Mencken, Henry Louis, 739, 942, 948, 960, 984, 1221–1222

Menéndez, Francisco, 149

Menéndez de Avilés, Pedro, 46

Mennonites, 24, 126, 223

Mentally ill people, treatment of, in 1820–1850, 431

Mercantilism, 93–94

Merchants: medieval, 19, 20(illus.); alliance with monarchs, 21; in medieval Europe, 21; colonial, royal protection of, 98; following French and Indian War, 175

Mercury Theater, 995

Meredith, James, 1148–1149

Mergers, 707; money culture and, 1246

Merrimack (ironclad ship), 576

Mesoamerica, early cultures of, 9–10

Messenger magazine, 944

Mestizos, 43

Metacomet, 74–75, 75(illus.)

Metacomet's War, 75

Methodist Church, 437; Great Awakening and, 151–152; following Revolutionary War, 244, 246; on abolition, 248; Second Great Awakening and, 353, 354, 355; African-Americans in, 460, 469

Mexican-Americans: during World War I, 903; following World War I, 938; during Great Depression, 974. *See also* Hispanics

Mexican-American War, 509–510, 511(map), 552; enthusiasm for, 510–511; opposition to, 512

Mexican Revolution, 499; Wilson's policy toward, 876–879

Mexico, 499–503; early culture of, 6, 10; Aztec empire of, 9, 10, 11(illus.), 29, 30–31, 33; uprising against royalist rule in, 306; white settlement of, 499–501; American rebellion in Texas and, 501–503; immigrants from, 657; Lodge Corollary and, 873; German proposal for military alliance with, 895; North American Free Trade Agreement and, 1278

Mexico City, 10, 43

Miami, Florida, population during 1920–1930, 932

Miami people, 275, 302; in French and Indian War, 164; taking of lands from, 258

Miami Sound Machine (rap band), 1231–1232

Michel, Robert H., 1297

Michelangelo, 21

Micmac people, 46, 47, 74

Microprocessors, 1283

Microsoft, 1286

Mid-Atlantic region: colonial economy of, 138–139, 174. *See also* Delaware; New Jersey; New York; Pennsylvania

Middle Ages, in Europe, 14–17

Middle class: emergence in early 19th-century cities, 347; in cities, 349, 349(illus.), 410–411, 737–738; women's roles and, 352; office holding by, 368; African-American, 468, 1195; women's attempts to civilize western towns, 679; reaction to new urban culture, 751–753; during Progressive Era, 812–813; alcohol use during Prohibition, 950; as beneficiary of Johnson's Great Society programs, 1148; shrinkage during 1980s, 1249; women of: in cities, 410–411; sentimental novels enjoyed by, 437

Middle East: U.S. Cold War policy in, 1064; Nixon's policy toward, 1186–1187; energy prices and, 1187, 1205; terrorism in, 1244–1245; Bush's policy toward, 1267. *See also* Organization of Petroleum Exporting Countries (OPEC); *specific countries*

Middle passage, 144, 158–159

Middletown: A Study in American Culture (Lynd and Lynd), 942

Middling colonists, 161–162; in cities and market towns, 132–133; loyalists among, 220

Midway, Battle of (1942), 1040

Midway Islands: annexation of, 848; in World War II, 1040

Midwives, slaves as, 463

Migrants, from farms, in cities, 730

Migration: earliest, into Western Hemisphere, 4–5; to Massachusetts Bay, 65; French, to lower Mississippi River basin, 110, 111(illus.); European, to colonies, 124–126, 125(map); to find employment, 136–137; to colonial Pennsylvania, 138; of loyalists, 204; population growth due to, 295; after Revolutionary War, 297(map); following War of 1812, 311–312; canals and, 332; from New England, 342; to Old Northwest, 343–344; to cities during 1790–1820, 347–350; to cities during 1820–1850, 406–408, 408(illus.), 409; availability of land and, 416; of planters and slaves during 1820–1850, 456; westward, difficulty of, 485–488, 494–497, 497(illus.), 522–523; to West, forces fueling, 489–490, 491–494; westward, forces feeding, 489–490, 491–494; transportation and, 493; to California, 516–517, 518; to Kansas, 541; American nativism and, 542–545; to West during 1862–1900, sources of, 657–658; to West, encouragement of, 658; Homestead Act of 1862 and, 658–661; railroads and, 661; to West, mining as impetus for, 670; to cities during 1860–1920, 730–731, 732(illus.); from Dust Bowl,

975–976; during World War II, breakdown of regional differences due to, 1034–1035; automobile and, 1101; of homosexuals to San Francisco, 1230. *See also* Immigration; *specific groups*

The Migration of the Negro (Lawrence), 991

Milbourne, Jacob, 100

Miles, Nelson A., 665

Military. *See* Armed forces; *specific forces*

Military contracts, during World War II, 1097

Militia: ability to endure long wars, 106; colonial, 193–194, 203; inadequacy of, 204; in Revolutionary War, 209

Militia Act (1862), 590

Militia groups, 1294

Militiamen: disease among, 105, 109, 110; battles with loyalists, 205; revolt against price increases, 218–219

Milken, Michael, 1247

Miller, Kelley, 974

Miller, Lewis, 752

Miller, Phineas, 346

Miller, William, 435

Millerites, 435

Milligan, Lambdin P., 583

Milliken v. Bradley (1974), 1196–1197

Millionaires, during 1980s, 1248

Millionaire's Club, 771

Millis, Roger, 1012

Mills, C. Wright, 1104

Mills, Florence, 945

Milosovic, Slobodan, 1279, 1280

Milwaukee, Wisconsin: immigrants in, 731; odor in, 739

The Mind of Primitive Man (Boas), 943

Mingo Creek, Pennsylvania, Whiskey Rebellion at, 275–276

Mingo people, 154

Mining: gold rush and, 516–519, 523–524; methods of, 670–671, 671(illus.); hazards of, 671; trade unionism and, 671–672; Mexican-American miners and, 682(illus.)

Mining camps: life in, 517–518, 517(illus.); violence in, 678–679

Mining companies, gold rush and, 518

Minitari people, 301

Minnesota, economy in 2000, 1287

Minnesota Farmer-Labor Party, 1068

Minuit, Pierre, 49–50

Minute Men, 904–905

Minutemen, 193–194

Miranda v. Arizona (1966), 1149

Miscegenation, 597

Miss America beauty contests, 941

Missionaries: in Spanish territories, 44–45, 305; to Native Americans, 302, 379; training of, 356; Protestant, in West, 679

Missions, Protestant, 752

Mission to Moscow (Davies), 1054

Mississippi: secession of, 557; Democratic resurgence in, 634–635; exclusion of black vote in, 643

Mississippi Freedom Democratic Party (MFDP), 1153

Mississippi River: negotiations with Spain about, 274; Union control of, 575, 594

Mississippi Valley: early culture of, 6–7; French migration to, 110

Missouri, in Civil War, 569

Missouri Compromise (1820), 315–316, 315(map), 371, 475; declared unconstitutional by Taney, 548

Mitchell, George J., 1298

Mitchell, Margaret, 992

Mitchell, Samuel, 428

Mobile, Alabama: growth during 1820–1850, 454; growth during 1940 and 1950, 1035

Mobsters, Prohibition and, 950

Moby Dick (Melville), 439

Moctezuma, 29

Model T automobiles, 930

Mohawk people, 9, 47, 75, 258; King William's War and, 105; Queen Anne's War and, 105; attempt to seize lands of, 153; as loyalists, 221; in Revolutionary War, 231

Mohawk Valley, Erie Canal in, 330, 331(illus.)

Mohican people, 11

Molasses Act (1733) (England), 83, 108, 177

Molotov, Vyacheslav, 1056

Monarchy: alliance with merchants, 21; European, consolidation by, 21

Mondale, Walter F., 1209, 1239

Monetarism, 1207

Monetary policy, under Grant, 632–633

Money. *See* Currency

Money culture, of 1980s, 1246–1247

Money supply: controversy over, 772–773; Populist position on, 785

Mongrel Tariff, 776

Monitor (ironclad ship), 576

The Monkey Wrench Gang (Abbey), 1258

Monmouth Court House, Battle of, 214

Monopoly (game), 992

Monroe, James, 312–313, 371; Monroe Doctrine and, 316–317

Monroe Doctrine, 316–317; Cleveland's invocation of, 854; Roosevelt Corollary to, 869–870; Lodge Corollary to, 873

Montagnais people, 46

Montana, entry into Union, 661

Montcalm, Louis-Joseph de, 167, 168

Monte Albán, 10

Montesquieu, Baron de, 225, 265

Montgomery, Bernard, 1023

Montgomery, Richard, 205

Montgomery, Alabama, bus boycott in, 1120–1121, 1121(illus.)

Montgomery Improvement Association (MIA), 1120, 1121

Montgomery Ward, 783

Montreal, Canada, 48; American seizure of, 205

Montserrat, 59

Moody, Dwight L., 752

Moon, Sun Myung, 1202

"Moondog's Rock and Roll Party" (song), 1103

Moon landing, 1188

Moore, John Bassett, 863

Moore's Creek Bridge, battle at, 208

Moot Club, 114

Moralists, 1163–1164

Morality, during 1920s, 939–941

Moral Majority, 1222

Moral Reform Society, 429

Moran, George "Bugsy," 950

Moravian people (Native American), 171

Moravians (religious group), 126, 223–224; in Georgia, 144

More, Thomas, 19

Morehouse University, 625

Morelos, Jose Maria, 306

Morgan, Daniel, 233

Morgan, J. Pierpont, 587, 702, 707, 792, 830

Morison, William, 121–122

Mormons, 435, 660

Morrill Land Grant Act (1862), 587, 756

Morris, Dick, 1276

Morris, Robert, 229–230, 344

Morrison, Herb, 995

Morrison, John, 710

Morse, Samuel F. B., 418, 544

Morton, Thomas, 64

Mose, 149

Moses, Robert, 1150

Mossadegha, Mohammed, 1115

Mother Earth (Goldman), 827

Mother Earth magazine, 925

Motion pictures. *See* Movies

Motley, Archibald, Jr., 945

Mott, Lucretia, 433, 451

Mound-building cultures, 6

Mountain men, 490

Mount Vernon, 362(illus.)

Mount Wollaston (Merry Mount), 64

Movies: myth of the West in, 685; first, 744; during World War I, 903; following World War I, 933–934; sexual freedom in 1920s and, 940, 941; cultural transmission by, 957; during 1930s, 993–994, 993(illus.); during World War II, 1032–1033; congressional investigation of suspected communists and, 1080; impact of television on, 1100; inspirational, 1102; atomic energy fears and, 1122; during 1960s and 1970s, 1202, 1203

Mr. X article, 1051

Ms. magazine, 1200

MTV, 1247–1248

Muckrakers, 811–812, 815

Mugwumps, 777

Muir, John, 677, 831

Mulattos, 43

Muller v. *Oregon* (1908), 808

Multicultural population, gold rush and, 518

Mumford, Lewis, 738

Munn v. *Illinois* (1877), 783

Murchison, Charles F., 780

Murder Act, 190

Murphy wagons, 494

Murray, Mrs. Robert, 210

Murrow, Edward R., 1032

Museums, construction of, 751

Music: of slaves, 460; of Civil War, 604–606; of New South, 642; sexual freedom in 1920s and, 940; African-American musicians and, 945; Federal Music Project and, 987; during World War II, 1033; rock and roll, 1102–1103; counterculture movement of 1960s and, 1162–1163; during 1960s and 1970s, 1202; of 1990s, 1291

Muskie, Edmund, 1168

Muslims: crusades against, 16; European trade with, 16–17; expulsion from Spain, 21; Serb crusade against, 1279

Mussolini, Benito, 1010, 1024; expansionism of, 1011

Mutual aid societies, 391–392; immigrants and, 734

My Lai massacre, 1161

Nabisco, 1246

Nader, Ralph, 1288

Nagasaki, Japan, bombing of, 1042

Nairobi, Kenya, bombing of U.S. embassy in, 1293

Nantes, Edict of (1598), 23

Napoleon, 306, 307; Louisiana Purchase and, 298

Narragansett people, 9, 74, 75

Narvaez, Panfilo de, 30

Nashoba, 448

Nasser, Gamel Abdel, 1113

Nast, Thomas, 632

Natchez people, 74, 110

National Advisory Commission on Civil Disorders, 1155

National Aeronautics and Space Administration (NASA), 1137

National Air Quality Standards Act, 1208

National American Woman Suffrage Association, 819, 907. *See also* League of Women Voters (LWV)

National Association for the Advancement of Colored People (NAACP), 823, 825, 903, 1119; on segregation of federal employees, 838; officer training program and, 897; Roosevelt's (Eleanor) support of, 998; membership during World War II, 1038

National Association of Colored Women (NACW), 809

National Association of Manufacturers, 812, 937

National Bank Act (1863), 587

National banking system, creation of, 587, 837

National Broadcasting Company (NBC), 934

National Civil Liberties Union, 906

National Conference of Christians and Jews, 1232–1233

National Congress of Mothers, 809

National Consumer League, 810(illus.)

National Defense Act (1916), 893

National Defense Education Act (NDEA) (1958), 1123–1124

National Economic Council, 1279

National Education Association, 812

National elections: of 1796, 277; of 1800, 278; of 1828, 363–364, 375–376; of 1824, 373; of 1832, 385; of 1836, 391; of 1840, 396–398, 397(illus.); of 1844, 507–508, 773; of 1848, 515–516, 528; of 1852, 536; of 1854, 540; of 1856, 546; of 1858, 553–554; of 1860, 555–556, 556(map); of 1864, 596–597; of 1866, 618; of 1868, 630; of 1872, 631, 768; of 1876, 637–638, 638(map), 774; of 1896, 764–765, 795–797, 796(illus.), 797(map); of 1880, 766, 775, 775(map); voter turnout during 1868–1920 and, 769–770, 770(illus.); of 1888, 773, 775(map), 779–780; of 1884, 775(map), 776–778, 778(illus.); of 1882, 776; of 1890, 781; of 1892, 785, 786–788,

787(map); of 1894, 793; voter turnout during election of 1896 and, 796–797; of 1904, 830–831; of 1908, 832; of 1912, 833–836, 837(map), 842–844; of 1914, 838; of 1916, 892–894, 894(map); of 1918, 911; of 1920, 919–920, 921(map), 934; of 1924, 955–956, 956(map); of 1928, 959–961, 960(map); of 1932, 979, 980(map); of 1934, 984; of 1936, 988–989, 998; of 1938, 990; of 1940, 1015–1016, 1016(map); of 1942, 1028; of 1944, 1029, 1030(map); of 1946, 1066; of 1948, 1068, 1069–1071, 1071(map); of 1952, 1105–1106, 1107(map), 1112(illus.); of 1956, 1109, 1110(map); of 1960, 1124–1126, 1126(map); of 1964, 1146, 1147(map); of 1966, 1156; of 1968, 1166, 1167–1170, 1168(illus.), 1170(map), 1189; of 1972, 1190–1191, 1191(map); funding methods for political campaigns and, 1204; of 1976, 1209, 1210(map); of 1980, 1225–1227, 1226(map); of 1984, 1238–1240, 1239(map); of 1988, 1262–1263, 1264(map); of 1992, 1272–1273, 1274(map); of 1994, 1276; of 1996, 1277; of 2000, 1287–1288

National Endowment for the Arts (NEA), conservative war against, 1227–1228

National Environmental Policy Act, 1208

National Federation of Settlements, 812

National Goals Commission, 1123

National Grange of the Patrons of Husbandry, 783

National Highway Traffic Safety Administration, 1237

National Housing Act (1949), 1072

National Industrial Recovery Act (NIRA), 983

Nationalism, 229, 259; Hawaiian, 855–856; black, 945; Third World, 1113–1115; Cuban, 1139. *See also* Federalists

Nationalists (Chinese), 1073, 1111

National Labor Relations Act (NLRA), 986

National Labor Relations Board (NLRB), 986

National Labor Union (NLU), 715–716

National League, 745

National Liberation Front (NLF), 1141, 1156, 1181

National Organization for Women (NOW), 1199–1200

National parks, 677, 831

National Prohibition Act, 906–908

National Recovery Administration (NRA), 983, 997, 1000

National Republican Party, 385, 388

The National Review, 1163–1164

National Road, 327, 382

National Security Act, 1060–1061

National Security Council (NSC), 1245–1246; establishment of, 1061; Memorandum 68 of, 1074

National Socialist Party. *See* Nazis

National Training School for Women and Girls, 749(illus.)

National War Labor Board (NWLB), 901, 1022

National Woman Suffrage Association (NWSA), 622

National Women's Party (NWP), 907, 941–942

National Youth Administration, 1000, 1029

Nation of Islam, 1155

Nation-states, European, 20–21

Native American Association, 544

Native American Clubs, 544

Native Americans: myths of creation of, 1–2, 4; agriculture of, 5, 8, 9, 63; ancestors of, 5; cultures of, 5–9, 301, 302; Columbus' contact with, 27–28; Spanish subjugation of, 29–31; Portuguese enslavement of, 31–32; decimation by disease, 32–33, 170; Las Casas' defense of, 38–39; Spanish view of, 42; Spanish attempts to convert to Catholicism, 44–45; knives of, 47(illus.); Dutch relations with, 49; English relations with, in Virginia, 54, 55–56; in 1650, 57(map); Pilgrims' relations with, 63–64; cultural contrasts with Europeans, 72–73; tensions between Europeans and, 73–74; conflicts with Europeans in New England, 74–76; conflicts with Europeans in South, 76–77, 79–81; Queen Anne's War and, 105–106; French and Indian War and, 164–168; uprisings of, 169–170; colonists' retaliation against, 170–171; as loyalists, 221; in Revolutionary War, 230–231; taking of lands from, 257, 258, 274–275; in Northwest Territory, 257–258; settlers' relations with, 301–305; education of, 302; fur trade and, 302, 490; white perception as savages, 302; disorientation and fragmentation of, 302–303; in Spanish territories, 305; removal of, 379–382, 381(map), 401–403; resistance to white settlers, 498, 664–667, 666(map); religion of, 653; massacres of, 653–656, 654(illus.); view of environment, 663; reservations and, 664, 665, 666(map); attempt to convert to white civilization, 667–669; attitude toward land ownership, 669, 691–692; New Deal and, 998–999; in armed forces, 1039; during World War II, 1039; red power movement of, 1197–1199; conditions faced by, in 1971, 1198–1199. *See also specific people*

Native Son (Wright), 991

Nativism, 542–545, 750–751; women's suffrage and, 819; revival during 1920s, 946

Naturalism, literary, 747

Naturalization Act, 277

Navajo people, 8, 305; Spanish attempts to convert to Catholicism, 45

Naval Act (1890), 852

Naval battles, of Civil War, 575–576

Naval Construction Act (1916), 892–893

Navies: English, 53, 208–209; Continental, flag of, 203(illus.); Union, 575, 576; Confederate, 575–576. *See also* U.S. Navy

Navigation Acts (England), 94; enforcement of, 98

Nazis, 1010; Holocaust and, 1027–1028, 1027(illus.)

Nebraska, entry into Union, 660

Nebraska Territory, 498

Negro Factories Corporation, 944

Negro League, 936

Negro World, 943

Nelson, Donald, 1020

Nelson, Lord, 307

Neolin, 170

Netherlands: New World territories of, 48–50; relations with Native Americans, 74; trade of, 92, 93–94, 95; German invasion of, 1015; postwar, communism in, 1055

Neutrality: U.S., World War I and, 888–892; American, World War II and, 1013–1015

Neutrality Act (1793), 273

Neutrality Acts (1935 and 1937), 1014–1015

Neutron bomb, 1240

Nevada, entry into Union, 660

Nevis, 59

New Amsterdam, 49, 50(illus.)

Newark, New Jersey, race riot in, 1155

Newburgh petition, 251

New Deal: banking provisions of, 979–980; relief under, 980–982, 981(illus.); economic programs of, 982–984; attacks on, 984–986, 1006; second, 986–988; end of, 990; minorities and, 997–999; women and, 1000; legacies of, 1001; dropping of programs of, 1028–1029

The New Democracy (Weyl), 814

New England: colonial, life in, 69–71; population in 1670s, 74; conflict with Native Americans in, 74–76; Dominion of, 97–98; slaves in, 135; population in 1720, 136; economy of, colonial, 136–138, 174–175; voting rights in, 292; agriculture in, 295, 341–343; migration from, 295, 342; in War of 1812, 310; family size in, 352–353. *See also* Connecticut; Maine; Massachusetts; New Hampshire; Rhode Island; Vermont

New England Anti-Slavery Society, 450, 477

New England Emigrant Aid Society, 541

New England Female Labor Reform Association of Lowell, 426

New Era Club, 750

New Federalism, 1188

Newfoundland, 50; Viking colony in, 16

New France, 46–48; settlement of, 46; fur trade in, 46–48

New Freedom, 835, 838, 842–843

New Hampshire: slavery in, 246; ratification of Constitution by, 265

New Harmony, Indiana, 436

New Haven, Connecticut, 68

New Jersey: during 1660–1685, 88–89; establishment of, 88–89; royal cancellation of charter of, 97; elite families of, 101; slaves in, 135; colonial economy of, 139; land conflicts in, 153; emancipation of slaves in, 246–247; constitution of, 251; ratification of Constitution by, 265; suffrage in, 367; progressive reform in, 817; economy in 2000, 1287. *See also* Mid-Atlantic region

New Jersey Plan, 261

New Left, 1163

New Light churches, 150–152

New Look defense strategy, 1110–1111

New Mexico: Anasazi culture of, 7, 7(illus.); Spanish colonization of, 45; admission as state, 530; entry into Union, 661; *Hispano* raids on Anglos in, 682–683

New morality, during 1920s, 939–941

New Nationalism, 834–835, 838, 842

New Netherland, 48–50

New Orleans (steamboat), 322–323

New Orleans, Battle of (1815), 311, 375

New Orleans, Louisiana: growth during 1820–1850, 454; Union attack on, 575; neighborhoods in, 738; cesspools in, 740; government of, 743

New Panama Canal Company, 868

Newport, Rhode Island, 67; colonial population of, 131; slave trade and, 135

New Right, 1163–1164, 1224, 1228; political influence of, 1227

Newspapers: colonial, 113, 115, 164; politics and, 292; political participation and, 369–370; crime stories in, 404, 413; popular opinion and, 405; African-American, 448; support of emancipation by, 450; migration routes published in, 504; enthusiasm for Mexican-American War fanned by, 510–511; southern recovery and, 639; advertising in, 701; during 1865–1910, 746–747; foreign-language, 747; muckrakers and, 811–812, 815; reporting of Cuban revolt by, 857; yellow journalism and, 857; coverage of Roosevelt's (Theodore) actions in Panama, 869; declining number of, 934; McCarthy's manipulation of, 1083; increased circulation during 1950s, 1104

New Sweden, 50

Newton, Isaac, 111–112

New York: during 1660-1685, 88; establishment of, 88; royal cancellation of charter of, 97; revolt in, 99; colonial legislature of, 119–120; slaves in, 135; colonial food production in, 138; land conflicts in, 153; constitution of, 227; emancipation of slaves in, 246–247; ratification of Constitution by, 265–266; suffrage in, 292, 367, 372; population during 1790–1820, 295; progressive reform in, 817; economy in 2000, 1287. *See also* Mid-Atlantic region

New York Call, 918

New York City: under Dutch rule, 89; revolt in, 99–100; colonial population of, 131; wealthy families of, 132; slaves in, 135; tea party in, 190; in Revolutionary War, 209–210, 210(illus.); siege of, 223; commercial district in 1792, 338(illus.); population in 1820, 348; penny press in, 369–370; during 1820–1850, 406; Corlares Hook neighborhood of, 412; police force of, 414; daily life in, during 1840s, 442–443; population in 1790, 542; nativism in, 544; riot over conscription in, 579–580; department stores in, 700, 701, 701(illus.), 737; population in 1860, 727; population growth during 1860–1920, 729; immigrants in, during 1865–1920, 731, 733; mass transit in, 734–735; neighborhoods in, 737, 738; crowding in, 738; water pollution in, 740; political machine in, 742, 742(illus.); vaudeville theaters in, 744; Central Park in, 752; population during 1900–1920, 814; African-American population during 1910–1920, 902; African-American population during 1920s, 943; suburbs of, growth following World War II, 1097; Puerto Rican population during 1950s, 1117; immigrant population in 1990, 1231

New York Daily Tribune, 504

New York Factory Commission, 818

New York Journal: reporting of Cuban revolt by, 857; publishing of De Lôme's letter by, 858

New York Society for the Suppression of Vice, 753

New York State Factory Commission, 811

New York Tribune, 631, 641

New York Weekly Journal, 115

New York Women's Trade Union League, 810

New York Working Men's Party, 392–393

New York World, 746–747; reporting of Cuban revolt by, 857

New York World's Fair, 992

Nez Percé people, 301, 662, 691

Niagara Movement, 823

Nicaragua, 1266; invasion of, 538; Panama Canal treaty with, 848; U.S. intervention in, 959; Reagan's policy toward, 1244

Nickelodeon, 1248

Nicolls, Richard, 88

Niles, Hezekiah, 320–321

Nimitz, Chester, 1040

Nine-Power Treaty, 958

Nineteenth Amendment, 908

Ninety-five theses, 22

Nipmuk people, 74

Nixon, Richard, 1091–1092, 1169, 1178, 1180, 1180(illus.); in election of 1946, 1066; in election of 1952, 1105; Checkers scandal and, 1106; foreign policy of, 1114; in election of 1960, 1124, 1125, 1126; Vietnam War and, 1177, 1180–1183, 1188; détente under, 1184–1185; visit to China, 1185; arms supply to regimes opposing Soviets, 1185–1186; Middle East policy of, 1186–1187; early life and career of, 1187; New Federalism of, 1188; social welfare under, 1188; silent majority and, 1188–1190; in election of 1972, 1191, 1191(map); Watergate crisis and, 1191–1194; tapes of private conversations of, 1192–1193; personal finances of, 1193; resignation of, 1193, 1194(illus.); personality of, 1193–1194; economic policy under, 1207; Ford's pardon of, 1208

Nobel Peace Prize, Roosevelt (Theodore) as recipient of, 871

Nobility, in medieval Europe, 15, 16

Noble Order of the Knights of Labor, 717–719, 724, 726

No-Conscription Manifesto, 925

Non-Importation Act (1806), 307

Nonimportation movements: as protest against Stamp Act, 181; as protest against Townshend Duties, 184–185, 187; during Revolutionary War, 216; under Jefferson, 307

Non-Intercourse Act (1809), 308

Norfolk, Virginia: population in 1770s, 143; burning of, 205; growth during 1940 and 1950, 1035

Noriega, Manuel, 1266–1267
The Normal Heart (Kramer), 1230
Normandy, invasion of, 1025–1026, 1026(illus.)
Norris, Frank, 747
Norris, George, 893, 895–896
Norsemen, 16
North: Revolutionary War in, 206(map), 209–213; South contrasted with, 344–345; agriculture in, 415; southern fears of industrialization in, 547; wage slavery in, 547; strength of, 570; prosperity in, during Civil War, 586–587; after Civil War, 611–612. *See also* Civil War (1861–1865); New England; Northwest Territory; Old Northwest; Union; *specific states*
North, Lord, 185, 187, 188, 190, 213, 235
North, Oliver, 1245–1246
North, Simeon, 334, 335
North America, earliest population of, 5
North American Aviation, 1037
North American Free Trade Agreement (NAFTA), 1278
North American Review, 436
North Atlantic Treaty Organization (NATO): Truman's proposal for, 1062–1063; congressional approval of, 1063; end of Cold War and, 1264; in Bosnia, 1280
North Carolina: establishment of, 88; migration to, 124; Regulators of, 153, 171–172, 196–198, 220; Revolutionary War in, 233; manumission of slaves in, 248; secession of, 568; Democratic resurgence in, 634; economy in 2000, 1287
North Dakota: immigrants in, 657; entry into Union, 660–661
Northern Pacific Railroad, 491, 788; bankruptcy of, 632
Northern Securities Company, 830
North Korea. *See* Korean War
Northrup, Solomon, 534
North Vietnam. *See* Vietnam; Vietnam War
Northwestern Alliance, 784
Northwest Ordinance (1787), 258–259, 258(map), 274
Northwest Territory, 255–258, 256(map); negotiations with Britain and Spain about, 256, 257; Native Americans in, 257–258; squatters in, 258, 296; Native American attacks on settlers in, 275; in 1820s, 492
Norway: German invasion of, 1015; postwar, communism in, 1055
Novels, 292–294; sentimental, 437; of 1820–1850, 438–439; myth of West as agrarian Eden and, 683–684; muckrakers and, 811–812, 815; during 1930s, 991, 992

Noyes, John Humphrey, 436
Nuclear power plants, 1208
Nuclear Regulatory Commission, 1237
Nuclear weapons: atomic bomb, 1042, 1043(illus.), 1047–1049; Atomic Energy Commission and, 1058; post–World War II dispute over control of, 1058; hydrogen bomb, 1074; Soviet, 1074; discussion of use in Indochina, 1114; anxiety about, 1122; Cuban missile crisis and, 1139–1140; test ban treaty with Soviets and, 1140; efforts to reduce stockpiles of, 1279
Nullification, 383–384
Nye, Gerald P., 1013
NYPD Blue (television show), 1290

Oakley, Annie, 684
Oberlin College, 432, 450
Oblinger, Uriah Wesley, 657
O'Connor, Sandra Day, 1238
The Octopus (Norris), 747
Odets, Clifford, 991
Odors, in cities during 1865–1910, 739–740
Office holding: colonial, 102; by middling people, 368; patronage under Jackson and, 377–378; by African-Americans, 1195
Office of Censorship, 1032
Office of Economic Opportunity (OEO), 1145
Office of Price Administration and Civilian Supply (OPA), 1021
Office of War Information (OWI), 1032
Oglethorpe, James, 110, 144
O'Hara, Charles, 234
Ohio, suffrage in, 366
Ohio Company, 110, 152, 255
Ohio Company of Virginia, 164
Ohio Railroad, strike against, 774
Ohio Valley: early culture of, 6; English settlement of, 110; Revolutionary War in, 231
Ohrdruf concentration camp, 1027
Oil embargo, of OPEC, in 1973–1974, 1187
Okies, 975
Okinawa, 1041
Oklahoma, entry into Union, 661
Oklahoma City bombing, 1293–1294
Oklahoma City Memorial, 1293(illus.)
Old Lights, 150–151
Old Northwest: migration to, 343–344; farming in, 416
Old Time Gospel Hour (television show), 1222
Olive Branch petition, 204–205
Oliver, Andrew, 180, 181

Oliver, Peter, 181
Oliver, Robert, 339
Olmec people, 9, 10
Olmsted, Frederick Law, 752
Olney, Richard, 791
Olson, Floyd, 985
Olympic Games: in Berlin, 992–993; in Moscow, 1212; in Los Angeles, 1219–1220
Omaha beach, attack on, 1026, 1026(illus.)
Omnibuses, horse-drawn, 734–735
Oñate, Juan de, 45
Oneidans (utopians), 436
Oneida people (Native Americans), 9, 231; King William's War and, 105; as loyalists, 221
O'Neill, Edward P., 1210
Onondaga people, 9
On the Road (Kerouac), 1162
Opechancanough, 55, 56
Open Door, Roosevelt's (Theodore) commitment to, 870
Open Door notes, 867
Open hearth, invention of, 697
Open shop, 937
Open Skies proposal, 1113
Operation Just Cause, 1267
Operation Linebacker II, 1183
Operation Menu, 1181–1182
Operation Overlord, 1026, 1026(illus.)
Operation Rescue, 1228
Operation Restore Hope, 1278
Operation Rolling Thunder, 1157
Operation TORCH, 1023
Oppenheimer, J. Robert, 1042, 1074
Order of the Star-Spangled Banner, 544
Ordinance of Nullification (1832), 383–384
Oregon, settlement of, 503–505
Oregon Societies, 504
Organization of American States (OAS), 1063
Organization of Petroleum Exporting Countries (OPEC), 1186, 1187, 1210
Organized crime, Prohibition and, 950
The Origin of Species (Darwin), 702, 948
Orlando, Vittorio, 912
Ortega, Daniel, 1266
Orville Platt, 850
Ostend Manifesto (1854), 538
O'Sullivan, John, 489
Oswald, Lee Harvey, 1134, 1143
The Other America (Harrington), 1145, 1188
Otis, James, 176
Ottawa people, 170; in French and Indian War, 164; taking of lands from, 257
Our American Cousin (play), 607
Our Country (Strong), 850

Our Country: Its Possible Future and Its Present Crisis (Strong), 751, 761–762
Owen, Robert, 436
Owen, Robert Dale, 448
Owens, Jesse, 992, 993, 1219
Ozzie and Harriet (television show), 1099

Pachakuti, 11
Pachucos, 1039
Pacific Express, 661
Pacific Railroad Act (1862), 587, 661
Pack animal trains, 325–327
Packet ships, 417
Pahlavi, Reza, shah of Iran, 1115, 1212
Paige, Satchel, 993
Paine, Thomas, 205–207, 225, 240–241, 280(illus.)
Painting: during 1820–1850, 437–438, 438(illus.); during 1865–1910, 748; African-American painters and, 945; during 1930s, 992
Paiute people, 486, 653
Paleo-Indians, 5
Palestine, partition of, 1064
Palestine Liberation Organization (PLO), 1244, 1245
Palmer, A. Mitchell, 918–919
Palmer, John M., 794
Palmerston, Henry, 577
Panama: revolt against Colombia, 869; Roosevelt's (Theodore) policy toward, 870; Carter's promise to return Canal Zone to, 1211; move against Noriega and, 1266–1267
Panama Canal, 845–846, 868–869; treaty with Nicaragua for, 848
Pan-American Highway system, 853
Panay (gunboat), 1010
Panic of 1819, 313–315, 341, 371, 456
Panic of 1837, 395–396, 427, 429, 504
Panic of 1857, 550–551
Panic of 1873, 632–633, 716
Parish, Michael, 933
Paris Peace Accords (1973), 1183–1184
Paris, Treaty of (1763), 166(map), 168, 169
Paris, Treaty of (1783), 235, 251, 252, 255
Paris, Treaty of (1898), 864
Parker, Alton B., 830
Parker, Theodore, 527
Parks: national, 677, 831; urban, construction of, 751
Parks, Rosa, 1120
Parris, Samuel, 103

Parrish, Michael, 934

Parris Island, South Carolina, 46

Patent Law (1790), 333

Patents, 696; registered by Edison, 697

Paternalism: of planters toward slaves and wives, 471–472; of employers, 937

Paterson, William, 261

Paterson, New Jersey, transformation into manufacturing entrepôt, 271

Patriot organizations, 1294

Patriots, treatment of loyalists, 221–222

Patronage: under Jackson, 377–378; under Garfield, 775–776

Patronen, 49

Patterns of Culture (Benedict), 943

Patton, George, 1024, 1026

Paul, Alice, 907

Pawnee people, 666–667

Paxton Boys, 170–171

Payne-Aldrich Tariff, 832

Peace Corps, 1138

Peace movement, in 1935, 1013

Peace of Tipitapa (1927), 959

Peale, Norman Vincent, 1102

Pearl Harbor attack, 1008, 1019

Peasant society, in medieval Europe, 14–15, 15(illus.), 16

Pemberton, John C., 593

Pena, Federico, 1274

Pendergast, Tom, 1029

Pendleton Civil Service Act (1883), 776

Peninsular Campaign, 573–574

Penn, William, 89–90, 92, 118

Penniman, Richard Wayne (Little Richard), 1103

Pennsylvania: during 1660–1685, 89–90, 92; establishment of, 89–90, 92; colonial legislature of, 118; migration to, 124; slaves in, 135; colonial food production in, 138–139; conflict over land in, 154; march against Native Americans in, 170–171; emancipation of slaves in, 246–247; return of loyalists to, 252; ratification of Constitution by, 265. *See also* Mid-Atlantic region

Pennsylvania Dutch, 126

Pennsylvania Gazette, 113, 115, 164

Pennsylvania Railroad, 700

Penny press: political participation and, 369–370; crime stories in, 404; enthusiasm for Mexican-American War fanned by, 510

Pensacola people, 105

Pensions, federal, 781

The Pentagon Papers, 1182, 1192

People for the American Way, 1228

People's Party, 786

The People the Best Government, 225–226

Pequot people, 9; conflicts with settlers, 73

Percival, John, 144

Perestroika, 1242

Perkins, Frances, 1000

Perot, Ross, 1272, 1273, 1277

Perry, Matthew C., 537

Perry, Oliver Hazard, 310

Pershing, John J., 877, 878, 897, 908

Pershing's Crusaders (movie), 903

Personal computer (PC), 1282–1283

Personal Responsibility and Work Opportunity Reconciliation Act, 1276

Perth Amboy, New Jersey, tea party in, 190

Peru, early culture of, 6, 10–12

Petroleum refining, international trade and, 850

Phalanxes, 436

Phelps, Anson, 410

Phelps, Aurora, 710

Philadelphia, Pennsylvania: settlement of, 90; in 1720, 109(illus.); colonial population of, 131; slaves in, 135; Second Continental Congress at, 202–205; Howe's attack on, 211; water system of, 350; during 1820–1850, 406; African-American population of, 412; racial tensions during 1820–1850, 413–414; police force of, 414; population in 1790, 542; nativism in, 544; population in 1860, 727; neighborhoods in, 737; cesspools in, 740; water pollution in, 740

Philadelphia and Reading Railroad, 788

Philadelphia Female Anti-Slavery Society, 451

Philadelphia Inquirer, 747

Philip II, king of Spain, 44, 53

Philippines: in French and Indian War, 168; Spanish surrender of, 861, 864; American occupation of, 863; rebellion against American occupation, 864–865; independence of, 865; American evacuation of, 1040; battle to liberate, 1041; aid to, 1186. *See also* Filipinos

Phillip, David Graham, 811

Phillips, Wendell, 621, 715

Philosophy, during Enlightenment, 112

Phips, William, 104

Phonograph, invention of, 697, 698(illus.)

Photojournalism, during 1930s, 991–992

Phyfe, Duncan, 349

Physicians, Enlightenment view of, 114–115

Pickett, George E., 592

Pierce, Franklin, 536, 546; expansionism under, 537–538

Pike, Zebulon, 301, 491

Pilgrims, 63–64

Pilgrim's Progress (Bunyan), 811

Pima people, 305
Pinchot, Gifford, 831, 833
Pinckney, Eliza Lucas, 143
Pinckney, Thomas, 274, 277
Pinckney's Treaty (1795), 305–306, 499
Pingree, Hazen, 815–816
Pinkerton National Detective Agency, 790
Pinochet, Augusto, 1186, 1266
Piracy, 130
Pitt, William, 168, 175, 176, 182, 193, 213
Pittsburgh, Pennsylvania, 169; mass transit in, 735; water pollution in, 740
Pittsburgh Crawfords, 993
Pizarro, Francisco, 30
Placer mining, 670
Plains people, 301, 662–664, 662(illus.)
Plan of Union, 164
Plantations: in Virginia, 55; in Carolinas, 87(illus.); tobacco, 145(illus.); agriculture method of, 454; life on, 470–472
Platt Amendment (1901), 865, 1012
Plessy v. *Ferguson* (1896), 644
Plumbers (Special Investigations Unit), 1192
Plymouth: settlement at, 63–64; Metacomet's attack on, 75; union with Massachusetts, 99
Pocahontas, 55
Poetry: African-American, 248; during 1920s, 942
Poindexter, John, 1246
Poland: partition of, 1014; liberation of, 1027; postwar status of, 1030; in World War II, 1042; Soviet control of, 1055, 1057, 1064; Solidarity trade union in, 1263
Police: in cities during 1820–1850, 414; of Birmingham, confrontation of civil rights demonstrators, 1151, 1152(illus.); violence at Democratic convention of 1968 and, 1167, 1168, 1168(illus.)
Poliomyelitis: Roosevelt's (Franklin) illness with, 978; conquering of, baby boom and, 1095–1096, 1096(illus.)
Political action committees (PACs), 1204, 1224
Political culture: democratization during Revolution, 228; following War of 1812, 311–316
Political Implications Committee, of University of Chicago Metallurgical Laboratory, 1048
Political machines, 741–743, 742(illus.), 774; immigrants and, 544; reform during Progressive Era, 814–816
Political parties: development of, 271–276; origins of, 276–277; move toward party system and, 277–280; First Party System and, 366, 398; opposition to, 366; recognition of role of, 366; in 1820s, 370–372; Second Party System

and, 398; Third Party System and, 546; solicitation of funds by, 1204. *See also specific parties*
Political process, print culture and, 292–294
Political reforms, of 1970s, 1204
Politics: during Renaissance, 22; Glorious Revolution and, 98–99; Franklin's entry into, 113; county, during 1780s, 254(illus.); participation in, in 1820s, 369–370; lackluster, during 1877–1900, 766–770; spoils system and, 771–772; New Deal and distribution of power and, 1001; use of television in, 1106, 1125, 1136–1137, 1252–1253, 1273, 1273(illus.)
Polk, James K.: on annexation of Texas, 507, 508(illus.); Mexican-American War and, 509–510, 512–513
Pollard, Mother, 1120
Pollock v. *Farmers Loan and Trust* (1895), 793
Poll taxes, to exclude black vote, 643
Pollution: of water, during 1865–1910, 740; regulation under Johnson, 1147
Polo, Marco, 17
Polygamy, among Mormons, 435, 660
Ponce de León, Juan, 30
Pontiac, 170
Pontiac's Rebellion, 170
Poor people. *See* Lower strata; Poverty
Poor Richard's Almanac, 113
Popé, 45
Pope, John, 577
Popular culture: myth of West as agrarian Eden and, 683–684; following World War I, 934; emphasis on sex, 940–941; during World War II, 1032–1033; during 1945–1960, 1099–1104; conservative criticism of, 1227–1228; money culture and, 1246–1247; of 1990s, 1290–1291
Popular sovereignty, 515; Calhoun's support for, 528–529; growing support for, during 1850s, 528–530; Whig Party and, 533; popular appeal of, 536; Douglas' advocacy for, 560–561
Population: Native American, early, 6; of Tenochtitlán in 1519, 10; Native American, in 1670s, 74; of North American colonies in 1700, 123; colonial growth of, 126; of colonial cities, 131; of slaves in colonial Chesapeake region, 142; of slaves, increase during 1770–1810, 248; growth following Revolutionary War, 252; growth in 1800, 295; of United States in 1800, 295; of cities in 1820, 348; growth during 1790–1820, 352; growth during 1848–1860, 542; of southern cities during 1870–1900, 639; of cities during 1860–1920, 727–730, 730(illus.), 732(illus.); of United States during 1860–1920, 728; baby boom

Population (continued)
and, 1094–1096, 1095(illus.). See also specific cities, states, and regions
Populist Party, 769, 803; in election of 1892, 785, 786–788, 787(map); in election of 1894, 793; in election of 1896, 794–795, 797(map); platform of, 801–802; White's criticism of, 802–803; progressives and, 813
Port Bill (1774) (England), 190
Porter, Bruce D., 900
Porter, Lavinia, 496
The Port Huron Statement, 1163
Portland, Oregon, growth due to World War II, 1035
Portsmouth, Rhode Island, 67
Portugal: consolidation of, 21; slave trade of, 25–27, 31–32
Potato famine, Irish migration due to, 407, 543
Potawatomi people, 302; land ceded by, 304
Potosí, Bolivia, Spanish silver mine at, 42
Potsdam, Germany, Grand Alliance meeting in, 1056–1057, 1057(illus.)
Pottinger, Hiram B., 908
Poverty: on frontier, 344; in cities, 349–350, 411–412, 738; women's roles and, 352; in South during 1820–1850, 474–475; among workers, 711; among African-Americans following World War I, 938; among African-Americans during Great Depression, 974; among African-Americans during 1950s, 1116; during 1950s, 1116–1117; war on, 1144–1145; among African-Americans during 1969–1979, 1196; among women, 1201–1202, 1249
Powderly, Terence V., 711, 717
Powell, Colin, 1299
Powell, John Wesley, 692
Powell, Louis, 1238
The Power of Positive Thinking (Peale), 1102
The Power of Sympathy (Brown), 293–294
The Power of the Positive Woman (Schlafly), 1217–1218
Powers, Gary, 1123
Powhatan, 8, 54, 55
Pownhall, Thomas, 176
The Practice (television show), 1290
Prager, Robert, 905–906
Preemption Acts (1830 and 1841), 366, 398, 492–493
Preface to Morals (Lippmann), 939
Presbyterian Church, 23; Great Awakening and, 150, 151; following Revolutionary War, 244
Presidents: as focus of political power, 771; expansion of power of, 836, 838, 1078;

Roosevelt's (Franklin) effect on presidency and, 1044; limitation of power of, 1107, 1204. See also National elections; specific presidents
President's Commission on the Assassination of President Kennedy, 1143
President's Committee on Civil Rights, 1068
Presidios: in Texas, 499, 500; in California, 505
Presley, Elvis Aaron, 1103
Prices: of tobacco, 174; during Revolutionary War, 217–219; following Revolutionary War, 249; Panic of 1819 and, 314; of cotton, 456; during Civil War, 587; of crops, fall in, 674, 782–783, 782(illus.), 784, 936–937, 982; during 1870–1900, 711; of corn, 782; of cotton, 782; of wheat, 782; following World War I, 917–918; following World War II, 1065–1066; of energy, OPEC oil embargo of 1973–1974 and, 1187; under Reagan, 1251. See also Inflation; Land acquisition
The Prince (Machiavelli), 22
Princeton University, 151
Principia (Newton), 112
Principles of Psychology (James), 806
Print culture: political process and, 292–294; optimistic portrayal of West in, 489; following World War I, 934. See also Literature; Newspapers; Novels; Penny press
Printing press, 23
Prisoners of war: during Revolutionary War, 223; during Civil War, 586; of Japanese during World War II, 1040
Prisons: in 1820–1850, 431; military, during Civil War, 586. See also Jails
Privateering, 51
Privies, odors in cities due to, 740
Proclamation Line of 1763, 166(map), 170, 177, 190; violation of, 171
Proclamation of Amnesty and Reconstruction (1863), 612
Proctor, Redfield, 858
Professional Air Traffic Controllers Organization (PATCO), 1251
Professional organizations, in Progressive Era, 812
Professional sports. See Spectator sports; specific sports
Professions: in cities, 349; women in, during 1930s, 999–1000
Profiles in Courage (Kennedy), 1124
Progress and Poverty (George), 677, 704
Progressive Party: dissolution of, 820; endorsement of women's suffrage, 820; in election of 1912, 834–835, 834(illus.); in election of 1924, 956

Progressivism, 804–840; challenge to Social Darwinism and, 806–809; women and, 809–811; muckrakers and, 811–812, 815; middle class and, 812–813; appeal of, 813–814; urban political reform and, 814–816; state political reform and, 816–819; women's suffrage and, 819–820, 907–908; prohibition and, 821–822, 906–907; immigration and, 822–823; African-American activism and, 823–825; radical reformers and, 825–827; feminism and, 827; Roosevelt (Theodore) presidency and, 827–832; Taft presidency and, 832–833; presidential campaign of 1912 and, 833–836, 837(map); Wilson presidency and, 836–839; expansion and, 846–856; opposition to Truman's hard line with Soviets and, 1067–1068

Prohibition: Progressive Era support for, 821–822; enactment of, 906–908; unintended consequences of, 950–951; end of, 980

Prohibition Party, 769

Prohibitory Act (1775) (England), 205

Promontory Point, Utah, meeting of transcontinental railroad in, 661

Propaganda: during World War I, 903; during World War II, 1032–1033

Property ownership: in medieval Europe, 15; colonial, 71, 127, 140, 146; by slaves, 146; Writs of Assistance and, 176; marriage and, 249; by women, 351–352; New Harmony, Indiana and, 436. *See also* Inheritance; Land acquisition; Land ownership

The Prophet (Tenskwatawa), 303

Proposition 209, 1292

Prospectors: gold rush and, 516; mining technique used by, 670

Prosser, Gabriel, 248, 464–465

Prostitution: in 1820–1850, 429–430; in western towns, 678; in cities, 738; purity movement and, 753; progressive crusade against, 822; venereal disease among soldiers and, 898

Protestant Association, 100

Protestant churches, recruitment during 1865–1910, 752

Protestant Episcopal Church, establishment of, 244

Protestants: Reformation and, 22–24; new denominations of, 353; Evangelical, Alliance Movement and, 785–786. *See also specific denominations*

Protests: over wages during revolutionary War, 219. *See also* Race riots; Rebellions; Revolts; Riots

Protocol of Non-Intervention, 1012

Providence, Rhode Island, 67; Metacomet's attack on, 75

Psychosexual theories, 940

PT-109 (Kennedy), 1124

Public culture, fragmentation of, 1248

Public Enemy, 1291

The Public Enemy (movie), 993

Public meetings, in 1820s, 369

Public office. *See* Office holding

Public schools: early, 432; in post–Civil war South, 625, 642–643; during 1865–1910, 754–756; desegregation of, 1119, 1195, 1196(illus.); shootings in, 1291

Public Works Administration (PWA), 980–981, 998

Pueblo people, 7–8, 30, 305, 662; Spanish missionaries and, 45

Puerto Rico: American seizure of, 861; annexation of, 861, 863; management of, 865–866; immigrants from, in cities, 1116–1117. *See also* Hispanics

Pulaski, Casimir Count, 213

Pulitzer, Joseph, 746, 857

Pullen, Frank W., 860

Pullman Car Company, 710

Pullman Palace Car Company, strike against, 791–792

Pumpkin papers, 1079

Pure Food and Drug Act (1905), 831

Puritans: in England, 24; settlement at Plymouth, 63–64; in Massachusetts, 64–65; opposition to Charles I, 69

Purity movement, 753–754

Putnam, Deborah, 215

Putting out system, 19–20, 335–336

Pyramids of the Sun and the Moon, 10

Qaddafi, Muammar, 1245

Quakers, 24, 132, 223; in colonial Massachusetts, 68; in colonial Pennsylvania, 90; Great Awakening and, 151; following Revolutionary War, 244; Second Great Awakening and, 353, 355; escaped slaves and, 534

Quartering Act (1765) (England), 178, 182, 187

Quartering Act (1774) (England), 190

Quayle, Dan, 1262

Quebec, Battle of (1759), 168

Quebec Act (1774) (England), 190

Quebec City, Canada, 48; settlement of, 46; in Queen Anne's War, 105; American attack on, 205

Queen Anne's War (1702–1713), 105–106, 134; commercial downturn following, 137–138

Queens, New York: population during 1900–1915, 735; population in 1920s, 932
Queen's College, 151
Quemoy, Chinese shelling of, 1111
Quincy, Josiah, Jr., 186
Quito, Ecuador, 43
Quiz shows, on television, 1099

R. J. Reynolds, 1246
Rabin, Yitzhak, 1267
Race riots: during 1890s and 1900s, 824; during World War I, 903; during 1919, 917; during World War II, 1037–1038
Racial segregation: of schools during Reconstruction, 625; in public facilities, 643; of Japanese-Americans, 823; of streetcars, 824; of U.S. Army, 897; of Hispanics, 903, 1039; in New Deal programs, 997; *Brown* decision and, 1119, 1130, 1131–1132; beginning of efforts to end, 1119–1120; busing to achieve desegregation and, 1195, 1196–1197
Racism: tensions in cities during 1820–1850 and, 413–414; in postwar South, 642–645; women's suffrage and, 819; Wilson's sanctioning of, 838; expansionism and, 850; against African-American soldiers, 860, 898; anti-imperialism and, 864; during World War I, 902–903; following World War I, 917; Holocaust and, 1027–1028, 1027(illus.); Freedom Riders and, 1150. *See also specific groups*
Radar, World War II naval battles and, 1025
Radical Democracy, 597
Radical Republicans: break with Lincoln, 596–597; opposition to Lincoln's plan for South, 612–613; Reconstruction and, 620–621
Radio: during 1920s, 934; Fireside Chats on, 979, 994, 1005–1006; during 1930s, 994–995; World War II coverage on, 1032; impact of television on, 1100
Radioactive fallout, 1122
Radio Corporation of America (RCA), 957
Railroad Administration, 900
Railroads: during 1820–1850, 418–420, 419(illus.); in antebellum South, 454; in West, 491; migration to West and, 493; legislation affecting, 538–541, 830, 831, 838; in 1850s, 540(map); transcontinental, Douglas' support for, 553; in North, during Civil War, 570; transcontinental, approval of, 587; in post–Civil War South, 625, 639–640; transcontinental, completion of, 661; western expansion and, 661; buffalo and, 664; lumbering and, 676; transcontinental, Chinese immigrants as

workers on, 680; impact on Hispanics, 682; refrigeration cars and, 696; industrial revolution and, 698–700, 699(map); government support of, 699; pools used to control market, 705; strikes against, 716–717, 774, 1066; commuter, 735; farmers' conflict with, 783; failures of, in 1893, 788; in China, 871; government control of, during World War I, 900; competition with trucking industry, 936
Rainbow (ship), 417
Ralegh, Walter, 51–52, 53–54
Randolph, A. Philip, 944, 1038
Randolph, Edmund, 261; as attorney general, 267
Randolph, George W., 571
Rankin, Jeanette, 896, 1009
Rankin, John, 1080
Ranson, Reverdy, Rev. and Mrs., 825(illus.)
Rap music, 1291
Rathbone, Henry, 607
Rationing, during World War II, 1021
Rauschenbusch, Walter, 808
Ray, James Earl, 1167
Reader's Digest magazine, 992
Reagan, Nancy, 1235(illus.), 1246
Reagan, Ronald Wilson, 1156, 1219, 1220, 1235(illus.), 1243(illus.), 1246; in election of 1980, 1225–1226; opposition to birth control and abortion, 1228; distancing of self from AIDS crisis, 1230–1231; early life and career of, 1234; economic policy of, 1234–1235, 1236, 1251, 1252, 1252(illus.); attempted assassination of, 1235–1236; deregulation under, 1236–1237; civil rights funding cuts under, 1238; Supreme Court appointments of, 1238; in election of 1984, 1238–1240; policy toward Soviet Union, 1240–1241; escalation of arms race under, 1241–1242; Central American policy of, 1242–1244; terrorism and, 1244–1245; Iran-Contra scandal and, 1245–1246, 1262; legacy of, 1251–1253, 1252(illus.)
Realism: literary, 747; in painting, 748; social, during 1930s, 991–992
Realpolitik, 1180
Rebellions: of debtors, 253–255; Whiskey Rebellion, 275–276; Jacob Fries's Rebellion, 278; of slaves, 478. *See also* Protests; Race riots; Revolts; Riots
Recessions: following Revolutionary War, 249; in 1834, 386; following World War I, 929; of 1937–1938, 990; during 1957-1960, 1123
Reciprocal Trade Act (RTA), 1012
Reconcentrados, 857

Reconcentration program, in Cuba, 857

Reconstruction, 607–646; Lincoln's attempt at, 610–617; Congressional plan for, 617–623, 650–652; women's suffrage and, 621–622; African-American office holding during, 623–624; failure of, 633–638

Reconstruction Finance Corporation (RFC), 976

Record of the Statesmanship and Achievements of General Winfield Scott Hancock, 775

Red Channels: The Report of Communist Influence in Radio and Television, 1080

Redeemers, 633–635

Red-lining, 1117

Red power movement, 1197–1199

Red River War (1874), 665

Red Scares: following World War I, 918–919, 938; second, 1078–1081; McCarthy and, 1082–1084, 1083(illus.)

Redwood trees, 676

Reed, Esther DeBerdt, 214

Reed, James, 485–488

Reformation, 22–24

Reform movements: during 1865–1910, 751–754. *See also* Progressivism; *specific movements*

Reform Party, 1277

Regulation: of trusts, 707–709; of grain elevators, 783; of railroads, 783; independent commissions of Progressive Era and, 818–819; deregulation under Reagan and, 1236–1237

Regulators, 152–153, 171–172, 196–197; as loyalists, 220

Rehnquist, William, 1238, 1259, 1260

Relief. *See* Social welfare

Religion: Reformation and, 22–24; in Spanish empire, 44–45; in New France, 47; religious tolerance in colonies and, 58, 90; of slaves, 147, 150, 460–461; Great Awakening and, 149–152; loyalists and, 220; following Revolutionary War, 244, 246; religious freedom following Revolutionary War and, 244; Second Great Awakening and, 353–356; during 1820–1850, 435–436; Native Americans, 653; disparities between science and, 948–949; fundamentalism and, 948–950; revival during 1945–1960, 1102; during 1960s and 1970s, 1202. *See also* Churches; Clergy; *specific religions and religious organizations*

Religious Right, 1221–1222

Renaissance, 21–22

Reno, Janet, 1274

Rensselaer, Kiliaen van, 49

Reparations: German, following World War I, 913, 958; German, following World War II, 1056–1057; from Soviet Union, 1057

Report on Manufactures (Hamilton), 269–271, 332; rejection of, 272

Report to the Nation (radio program), 1032

Representation, Constitution and, 261–263

Republican Party: Jeffersonian, 366; Van Buren, 371, 372, 373; slavery and, 526, 545; in election of 1848, 528; rise in 1850s, 545–546; in election of 1860, 555; Lincoln's leadership of, 581–582; coalition with Democrats during Civil War, 596; in election of 1864, 596, 597; in election of 1866, 618; Reconstruction and, 618, 620; southern, following Civil War, 623–626; in election of 1868, 630; in election of 1872, 631; Democratic opposition to Reconstruction program of, 633–635; abandonment of Reconstruction plan, 635–637; in election of 1876, 637; in election of 1896, 765; in election of 1880, 766; during 1877–1900, 767–768; divisions in, 768; in election of 1884, 776–778; in election of 1888, 779–780; in election of 1892, 786–787; in election of 1894, 793; endorsement of women's suffrage, 820; prohibition issue and, 821; in election of 1908, 832; in election of 1912, 833; in election of 1916, 892, 893; in election of 1918, 911; opposition to Treaty of Versailles, 913–914; in election of 1920, 920, 921(map), 952; in election of 1924, 955, 956(map); in election of 1928, 959, 960, 960(map); in election of 1932, 979, 980(map); in election of 1936, 988; in election of 1938, 990; in election of 1940, 1015–1016, 1016(map); in election of 1942, 1028; in election of 1944, 1029, 1030(map); in election of 1946, 1066; in election of 1948, 1068, 1069–1071, 1071(map); in election of 1952, 1105, 1106, 1107(map); in election of 1956, 1109, 1110(map); in election of 1960, 1124, 1125, 1126, 1126(map); in election of 1964, 1146, 1147(map); in election of 1966, 1156; in election of 1972, 1191, 1191(map), 1209, 1210(map); in election of 1980, 1225–1226, 1226(map); in election of 1984, 1238–1240, 1239(map); in election of 1988, 1262, 1263, 1264(map); in election of 1992, 1272, 1273, 1274(map); in election of 1994, 1276; in election of 1996, 1277; refusal to pass stopgap budgetary measures under Clinton, 1277; in election of 2000, 1287, 1288. *See also* Radical Republicans

Republic of China, 1073

Republic Steel, 997

Reservationists, 913

Resource Recovery Act, 1208

Restoration colonies, 84–92, 86(map). *See also* Carolinas; Delaware; New Jersey; New York; Pennsylvania

Restraining Act (1767) (England), 182

Reuben James (ship), 1018

Reuther, Walter, 1068, 1098

Revenue Act (1762) (England), 176

Revenue Act (1962), 1137

Revenue Acts (1942 and 1943), 1022

Revere, Paul, 186, 194

Revivalism, 246, 489; in 1790s to 1820s, 353–356

Revival meetings, Protestant, 752

Revolts: of slaves, 248, 464–466; Mexican, against royalist rule, 306. *See also* Protests; Race riots; Rebellions; Riots

Revolutionary War, 199–235; Continental Army in, 199–201, 209, 214–216; Second Continental Congress and, 202–205; *Common Sense* and, 205–207; in North, 206(map), 209–213; Declaration of Independence and, 207–208; British army in, 208–211; French alliance and, 213–214, 235; financial support for, 216–217; economic effects of, 217–219; loyalists during, 219–223; spies during, 222–223; prisoners of war during, 223; evaders during, 223–224; development of new government and, 224–230; in West, 224(map), 230–231; in South, 231–234, 232(map); end of, 234–235; reasons for British loss of, 235; loyalist condemnation of, 239, 241; lack of social order following, 242–243; religion following, 244, 246; debt repayment and, 268–269

Reynolds v. *Sims* (1964), 1148–1149

Rhee, Syngman, 1075

Rhett, Edmund, 616

Rhode Island: establishment of, 67; royal cancellation of charter of, 97; colonial economy in, 107; emancipation of slaves in, 246–247; ratification of Constitution by, 266

Ribault, Jean, 46

Rice: cultivation in Carolinas, 86–87, 143; effect of production on ecology, 144; slavery and, 146; in South during 1820–1850, 453; task system of labor and, 461–462

Richardson, Elliot, 1192, 1193

Richmond, Virginia: as capital of Confederacy, 568; McClellan's advance on, 573–574; ruins of, 611(illus.)

Ricos, 681

Riedesel, Baroness, 223

Riesman, David, 1104

Righteous and Harmonious Fists, 867

Rights watches, 272

Riis, Jacob, 733

Rio Treaty (1947), 1063

Riots: against poor in Boston, 134; anti-rent, in Hudson River valley, 153; Golden Hill, 185–186; over price increases during Revolutionary War, 218–219; in cities during 1820–1850, 413–414; Stonewall Inn, 1199. *See also* Protests; Race riots; Rebellions; Revolts

Risen from the Ranks (Alger), 703

The Rise of Silas Lapham (Howells), 747

Rivers, 326(map). *See also specific rivers*

Roads: during 1790–1820, 325–327, 326(map); turnpikes, 327; Jackson's opposition to building of, 382; construction under Wilson, 838; Pan-American Highway system and, 853; following World War I, 931; Interstate Highway Act and, 1100

Road to War (Millis), 1012

Roanoke, Virginia, English settlement at, 51–52, 53

The Robe (movie), 1102

Roberts, Owen, 989

Robertson, Pat, 1222, 1262

Robinson, John, 678

Robinson, Joseph G., 959

Robinson, Richard, 404, 405

Rochambeau, Comte de, 233, 234

Rochester, New York, odor in, 739

Rock and roll, 1102–1103

"Rock Around the Clock" (song), 1103

Rockefeller, John D., 587, 702, 705–707, 756, 918

Rockefeller, William, 673

Rockingham, Lord (Charles Watson-Wentworth), 181

Rockwell, Norman, 1036

Rocky (movie), 1203

Rocky Mountain Fur Company, 490

Roderique Hortalez et Compagnie, 213

Rodney, Caesar, 207

Roe v. *Wade* (1973), 1200, 1271

Rogan, "Bullet" Joe, 936

Rogers, Ginger, 993

Rogers, Will, 993

Rogers, William, 1180

Rolfe, John, 55, 61

Rolling Stones, 1163

"Roll Over Beethoven" (song), 1103

The Romance of Helen Trent (radio program), 994

Romanov, Grigory, 1241

Rommel, Erwin, 1023, 1025

Roosevelt, Eleanor, 978, 987, 998, 1000–1001, 1000(illus.)

Roosevelt, Franklin Delano, 955, 978(illus.); in election of 1920, 920; inauguration of, 967, 968; early life of, 977–978; illnesses of, 978, 1029; early political career of, 978–979; in election of 1932, 979; Fireside Chats of, 979, 994, 1005–1006; first hundred days of presidency of, 979–984; attacks on, 984–986; second New Deal of, 986–988; in election of 1936, 988–989; personality of, 988–989; attempt to reform Supreme Court, 989; African-Americans and, 998, 1038; declaration of war and, 1008; *Panay* incident and, 1010; interest in foreign affairs, 1012; in election of 1940, 1016; Lend-Lease program of, 1017; Atlantic Charter and, 1017–1018, 1054; war mobilization and, 1019–1020, 1022; World War II and, 1024, 1025, 1032; indifference to Holocaust, 1028; at Yalta Conference, 1029–1031, 1031(illus.); death of, 1031; Soviet Union and, 1054; view of postwar world, 1054. *See also* New Deal

Roosevelt, Nicholas, 322–323, 328

Roosevelt, Theodore, 673, 684, 792, 811, 828–832, 829(illus.), 872(illus.), 897, 920; on efficiency, 812; in election of 1912, 820, 834–836, 834(illus.), 842, 843–844; Japanese immigration and, 823; view of presidency, 827; early career of, 828; trusts and, 829–830; approach to labor, 830; in election of 1904, 830–831; social agenda of, 831; conservation efforts of, 831–832; attack on Taft, 833; assassination attempt against, 836; Panama Canal and, 845–846, 868–869; expansionism under, 850–851; in Spanish-American War, 858, 861, 862(illus.); attack on McKinley, 859; Roosevelt Corollary and, 869–870; Nobel Peace Prize awarded to, 871; on sinking of *Lusitania,* 891; criticism of Wilson, 892; pressure placed on Hughes by, 893

Root-Takahira agreement (1908), 871

Rosecrans, William, 594

Rose Garden strategy, 1209

Rosenberg, Ethel, 1079–1080, 1081

Rosenberg, Julius, 1079–1080, 1081

Ross, Edward A., 822

Ross, John, 303, 570

Roth, William V., Jr., 1297–1299

Rough Riders, 861, 862(illus.)

Rowe, James, 1068

Rowlandson, Mary, 75

Rowson, Susanna Haswell, 294

Royal African Company, 93

Royal Air Force (RAF), 1015, 1025

Royle, Edwin Milton, 743

Rubber, shortage of, during World War II, 1020

Ruby, Jack, 1134

Ruckelshaus, William, 1192, 1193

Ruffin, Josephine, 750

Rumania, Soviet control of, 1057

Rural Electrification Administration (REA), 984

Rush, Benjamin, 225, 250

Rush-Bagot Treaty (1817), 306

Rusk, Dean, 1137, 1140

Russia: interest in Manchuria, 870–871; in World War I, 908; nonaggression pact with Germany, 1014; in World War II, 1042; independence of, 1264; aid to, 1279. *See also* Soviet Union

Russian American Fur Company, 505

Russian Revolution (1917), 1052; World War I and, 895

Rutgers University, 151

Ruth, Babe, 935, 935(illus.), 936

Ryswick, Treaty of (1697), 105

Sacagawea, 301

Sacco, Nicola, 946

Sagadahoc, Maine, 53

St. Augustine, Florida, 46; establishment of, 42; in Queen Anne's War, 105

St. Bartholomew's Day Massacre, 23

St. Clair, Arthur, 275

St. Domingue, 105

St. Johns River, Florida, 46

St. Kitts, 59

St. Leger, Barry, 211

St. Louis (ship), 1028

St. Louis, Missouri, immigrants in, 731

St. Mary's City, Maryland, 56

St. Thomas's African Episcopal Church, 248

Saipan, 1041

Salem, Massachusetts: founding of, 65; witch trials in, 103–104, 103(illus.)

Sales clerks, women's employment as, 713

Salk, Jonas, 1095–1096, 1096(illus.)

Saloons. *See* Bars and saloons

Salvation Army, 752, 809

Salzburgers, 126; in Georgia, 144

Samoa, 863; tripartite protectorate over, 856

Samoset, 63

Samoza, Anastasio, 1244

Samuelson, Paul, 1116

San Antonio, Texas, Hispanic population in 1920s, 938

Sandberg, Carl, 1123

Sand Creek, Colorado massacre, 664–665

San Diego, California, growth due to World War II, 1035

Sandinistas, 1244

Sandwich Islands. *See* Hawaiian Islands

Sandys, Edwyn, 55

San Francisco, California: gold rush and, 517; population during 1849–1855, 675; immigrants in, 680, 731, 823; neighborhoods in, 738; growth due to World War II, 1035; homosexual population of, 1230

San Francisco Call, 746

San Francisco School Board, segregation of Japanese children by, 823

Sanger, Margaret, 940

San Jacinto (ship), 577

San Juan, Puerto Rico, 43

San Juan Hill, Roosevelt's (Theodore) charge of, 828

San Salvador (Samana Cay), 27

Santa Anna, Antonio Lopez de, 500, 501, 502–503, 510

Santa Barbara, California, Hispanic population during 1867–1873, 683

Santa Fe, New Mexico, 45

Santa Fe Railroad, 788

Santo Domingo, 43, 105; attempt to annex, 849

Saratoga, battle of, 212

Sargent, Judith, 250

Saturday Evening Post, 905, 1036, 1100

Saturday Night Fever (movie), 1202

Saudi Arabia, bombing of military barracks in, 1293

Sauk people, 381; resettlement of, 541

Savannah, Georgia: growth during 1820–1850, 454; growth during 1940–1950, 1035

Savings and loan (S&L) crisis, 1237

Scalawags, 624

Scalia, Antonin, 1238

Scandinavia: migration to cities from, 731. *See also specific countries*

Scarlet fever, water pollution and, 740

The Scarlet Letter (Hawthorne), 439

Schechter v. *U. S.* (1935), 983

Schenck, Charles, 924–925

Schenck v. *U.S.* (1919), 906, 924–925, 926

Schenectady, New York, 105

Schlafly, Phyllis, 1200–1201, 1217–1218

Schmelling, Max, 992

The School and Society (Dewey), 808

Schools. *See* Colleges and universities; Education; Public schools

Schurz, Carl, 884

Schuylkill Canal, 330

Schwarzkopf, H. Norman, 1269, 1299

Science: during Renaissance, 21–22; during Enlightenment, 111–112, 113; disparities between religion and, 948–949

Scientific inquiry, in Progressive Era, 806–808

Scientific management, 710, 933

Scopes, John Thomas, 949, 964–966

Scotland, tobacco trade with, 142

Scots: as loyalists, 220; migration to cities, 348

Scots-Irish, migration to colonies, 124–125

Scots Presbyterians, opposition to Charles I, 69

Scott, Dred, 547–549, 548(illus.)

Scott, Eliza, 548

Scott, Harriet, 548

Scott, Winfield: campaigns against Native Americans, 382; in Mexican-American War, 510, 511, 512; in election of 1852, 536; in Civil War, 569

Scottish Highlanders, in Georgia, 144

Scottsboro boys, 974

Sea Dogs, 51

Sea Islands, Georgia, 620

Sears, Roebuck, and Company, 701, 1096

Second Party System, 398

Second Treatise of Government (Locke), 113

Secoton, North Carolina, 52(illus.)

Sedition Act, 277, 278, 288

Sedition Act (1918), 904, 905

Sedition Slammers, 904–905

Segregation. *See* Racial segregation

Seigneurs, 48

Selective Service Act (1917), 899(illus.), 906–908

Selma, Alabama, voting rights campaign in, 1153–1154

Seminole people, 302; Jackson's attack on, 375; resistance to removal, 381, 403; resettlement of, 497, 498

Senate: power of, 771; direct election of senators and, 818. *See also* Congress

Senate Foreign Relations Committee, 1182

Seneca people, 9, 231; in French and Indian War, 164

Sentimentalists, 437

Separate-but-equal doctrine, 644, 1119

Separatism, of Malcolm X, 1155

Separatists, settlement at Plymouth, 63–64

Sequoyah, 303

Serbs, crusade against Muslims, 1279

Sergeant Pepper's Lonely Hearts Club Band (album), 1163

Serra, Junipero, 305

Servants. *See* Indentured servants

Service economy, criticism of, 1104

Serviceman's Readjustment Act (1944), 1095

Settlement houses, 804–805

Settlers: opposition to Bank of the United States, 384; Native American resistance to, 498, 664–667, 666(map)

Seven Pines, battle of, 574

Seventeenth Amendment, 818

Seven Years' War. *See* French and Indian War

Sewall, Arthur, 794

Seward, William Henry, 555, 608, 848–849; on slavery, 532, 533

Seward's Folly, 849

Sewing machine: change brought by, 411, 411(illus.); export of, 850

Sex discrimination: outlawing of, 1200; in workplace, 1201

Sex education, for U.S. soldiers, 898

Sexual abuse, of slave women, 147, 463

Sexual Behavior in the Human Female (Kinsey), 1118

Sexual Behavior in the Human Male (Kinsey), 1118

Sexual harassment, 1271

Sexuality: during 1920s, 940–941; during 1930s, 994; during 1950s, 1117–1118; television portrayal of, 1290. *See also* Homosexuals

The Shadow (radio program), 994

Shakers, 435

Shakespeare, William, 22

Shannessy, John, 678

Sharecropping: by African-Americans following Civil war, 627–629, 629(map). *See also* Tenant farming

Share Our Wealth plan, 985

Shawnee people, 154, 172, 230, 231, 275, 302, 662; in French and Indian War, 164; decimation by disease, 170; taking of lands from, 257; resistance against white migration, 303–304; resettlement of, 497, 541

Shays, Daniel, 254

Shaysites, 254

Shays's Rebellion, 253–254

Sheen, Fulton J., 1102

The Sheik (movie), 933

Sheldon, Charles, 808

Shepherd, Alexander R., 742–743

Sheppard-Towner Act (1921), 941

Sheridan, Robert, 468

Sherman, John, 771, 793

Sherman, Goody, 66

Sherman, Roger, 262

Sherman, William T., 665; in Civil War, 595, 597–598, 600; Reconstruction and, 620

Sherman Antitrust Act (1890), 708, 781, 830

Sherman Silver Purchase Act, 780, 792

Sherwood, William, 80

Shiloh, battle at, 575

Shilts, Randy, 1230

Shipbuilding, 340; employment in, during World War I, 902; women's employment in, during World War II, 1037

Shirley, William, 119–120

Shoemakers, 422(illus.)

Shopping malls, 1101

A Short Narrative of the Horrid Massacre in Boston (Bowdoin), 186

Shoshone people, 662

Shriver, R. Sargent, 1145

Shulz, George, 1240

Shuttle diplomacy, of Kissinger, 1186–1187

Shuttlesworth, Fred, 1150

Sicily, Allied invasion of, 1024

Sierra Club, 677, 831

Sierra redwood trees, 676

"The Significance of the Frontier in American History" (Turner), 297, 685

Silent majority, Nixon's mobilization of, 1188–1190

The Silent Scream (videotape), 1229

Silent Spring, 1207–1208

Silver: European inflation due to, 18; Spanish discovery of, 30; European extraction of, 32, 42; mining in Nevada, 519; discovery in West, migration spurred by, 670

Simmons, William J., 947

Simon, Paul, 1232

"Simpkinsville" (Stuart), 642

Simpson, Jerry, 794

Simpson, Nicole Brown, 1291

Simpson, O. J., 1290, 1291–1292

Sinatra, Frank, 994, 1102

Sinclair, Upton, 812, 831, 985

Singer, Isaac, 411

Singer Company, 850

Single tax concept, 704

Sink or Swim (Alger), 703

Sino-Japanese War, 867

Sioux people, 300, 498, 662, 666–667; resettlement of, 541; Wounded Knee massacre of, 653–656, 654(illus.); resistance to white settlers, 665–667

Sirhan, Sirhan, 1167

Sirica, John, 1192, 1193

Sister Carrie (Dreiser), 747

Sit-ins, for civil rights, 1149

Sitting Bull, 653–654, 666–667, 684

Skidmore, Thomas, 392–393

Skyscrapers, 737, 932

Slash and burn agriculture, 8

Slater, Samuel, 336, 423

Slaughterhouse Cases (1873), 636–637

Slavery: sugar production and, 26; Columbus' introduction of, 28; under Spanish, 29, 43; in West Indies, 60–61, 60(illus.); in colonial Chesapeake region, 61–62, 139, 141–143; in colonial Virginia, 76; in Carolinas, 86, 87, 143–144; colonial questioning of rightness of, 135–136; urban, in colonies, 135–136, 136(illus.); tobacco cultivation and, 145(illus.), 146; rice cultivation and, 146; cotton and, 312, 456–458, 531; Missouri Compromise and, 315–316, 315(map); Underground Railroad and, 445–446, 451, 464, 526, 534; abolitionist movement and, 449–451, 475–476, 534, 535; abduction of free African-Americans and, 467, 534; plantations and, 470, 471–472; intellectual arguments for, 477–478, 482–483; Wilmot Proviso and, 513–515; popular sovereignty and, 515, 528–530, 533, 536, 560–561; Compromise of 1850 and, 530–533, 533(map); Fugitive Slave Act of 1850 and, 534–535, 535(illus.); Republican opposition to, 545; secession of southern states and, 557; Emancipation Proclamation and, 589–591. *See also* Civil War (1861–1865)

Slaves: African, cultural impact of, 2; Native Americans as, 77; African, in colonies, 124, 144–145; rebellions of, 135, 148–149; African, in colonial Chesapeake region, 141–143; colonial conditions faced by, 144–148; communities of, in colonial North America, 145–146; West Indian, colonial, 145–146; African, culture of, 147; religion of, 147, 150, 460–461; in white churches, 150, 152; escape of, 220, 275, 464, 466, 534–535, 535(illus.); as loyalists, 220–221; emancipation of, 246–247, 449–452, 589–591; following Revolutionary War, 246–247; increase in number during 1770–1810, 248; Great Compromise and, 262–263; increase in number during 1790–1824, 296, 345; taken to frontier, 312; in Chesapeake region, 345; houses of, 360–361, 360(illus.); manumission of, 447; relocation of, 456, 457–458; marriage among, 458–459; communities of, 459, 460; families of, 459; children of, 459–460; music of, 460; disease among, 461; work of, 461–463; as midwives, 463; resistance by, 463–466; purchase of freedom, 466–467; owned by free African-Americans, 468; poor whites and, 474–475; violence toward, 476–477

Slave trade, 457(illus.); Portuguese, 25–27; in Africa, 25(illus.); sugar production and, 26, 31–32; benefits to England and its colonies, 95; middle passage and, 144, 158–159; justification of, 159–160; cotton and, 456–458; kidnapping of free African-Americans and, 467; abolishment in District of Columbus, 532

Slavs, migration to cities, 731

Slidell, John, 509, 577

Slovenia, 1279

Smallpox: Native American decimation by, 29, 33, 47, 124, 170, 300; among militiamen, 105; colonial support for inoculation against, 115; among loyalist slaves, 221; water pollution and, 740

The Smart Set (Mencken), 942

Smith, Adam, 93, 270, 702

Smith, Al, 955, 959–960

Smith, Elias, 365–366

Smith, Gerald L. K., 985

Smith, Harold D., 1021

Smith, Henry Nash, 683

Smith, Howard K., 1032

Smith, Jedediah, 490

Smith, Jesse, 952

Smith, John, 54, 63

Smith, Joseph, 435

Smith, Kate, 1033

Smith, Margaret Bayard, 364

Smith, Melancthon, 264

Smith, Richard Mayo, 751

Smith Act (1946), 1079

Smith and Wesson, 901

Smith College, 941

Smith-Connolly bill (1943), 1022

Smoking, introduction to England, 55

Smuggling: in colonial era, 82–83, 96–97, 108, 109–110, 130–131; War of Jenkins' Ear and, 109–110; Townshend Duties and, 183; French, during Revolutionary War, 213; Force Act to curtail, 308; during Embargo of 1807, 341

Snow Storm, 477

Snyder, Grace, 680

Soap operas, on radio, 994

Social classes: lessening of distinctions between, 368; following World War I, 936. *See also* Elites; Income distribution; Lower strata; Middle class; Poverty; Social structure; Wealth

Social Darwinism, 702–703; literature and, 747; progressive challenges to, 806–809; expansionism and, 850–851

Social Gospel, 808

Social intimacy, in cities, 347–348

Socialist Party, 825, 826; in election of 1912, 836; in election of 1916, 893

Socialists: prosecution during World War I, 904–905; Bolshevik Revolution and, 912

Social order: lack of, following Revolutionary War, 242–243; lacking in cities during 1820–1850, 413–414; institutions to maintain, establishment of, 414. *See also* Police

Social philosophy, progressive, 813–814

Social realism, during 1930s, 991–992

Social reform: of Enlightenment, 114; individualism and, 427–428; temperance and, 428–429, 753–754; asylums and prisons and, 429–431; family roles and education and, 431–433; women's rights and, 433–434; intellectual currents and, 434–439

Social security, 986, 1188

Social Security Act (1935), 986

Social structure: West African, 1400–1600, 12; in medieval Europe, 15; in colonial Plymouth, 64; in colonial New England, 69; in colonial cities and market towns, 131–134; in colonial Chesapeake region, 140; canals and, 332; in New England farming communities, 343; in early 19th-century coastal cities, 347; disruption of apprenticeship system and, 421–422; industrial revolution and, 711–712

Social welfare: colonial, 134; following French and Indian War, 175; during Revolutionary War, 219; during 1820s, 351; church women and, 355; mutual aid societies for, 391–392; during Civil War, 588; during depression of 1893, 789; settlement houses and, 804–805; progressive measures to provide for, 818; welfare capitalism and, 937; during Great Depression, 972, 973(illus.), 980–982, 981(illus.), 997; social security and, 986, 1188; work, under Roosevelt (Franklin), 987–988; under Eisenhower, 1108; under Kennedy, 1137–1138; Johnson's war on poverty and, 1144–1145; Johnson's Great Society and, 1146–1148; under Nixon, 1188; under Reagan, 1235, 1250; under Clinton, 1276

Society for the Propagation of the Gospel, 302, 437

Society of Friends. *See* Quakers

Sociology for the South; or, The Failure of a Free Society (Fitzhugh), 477–478, 547

Socony Mobil, 1189

Soldier cloth, 214

Soldiers: in Civil War, 584–586, 585(illus.); African-American, racism against, 860, 898; in World War I, 910, 910(illus.); in World War II, 1022; in Vietnam War, 1159(illus.), 1160–1161, 1160(illus.). *See also* Militiamen

Solidarity trade union, 1263

Somalia, 1278

Songhai (Mali), rise of, 14

Songs. *See* Music

Sonobuoys, in World War II, 1025

Sons of Liberty, 179–182, 184, 187, 220

Sorosis, 749

Soule, Pierre, 538

Souls of Black Folks (Du Bois), 824

South: colonial economy of, 174; Revolutionary War in, 231–234, 232(map); free African-Americans in, 248; Spanish claims in, 257; migration from, 296; North contrasted with, 344–345; economy during 1820–1850, 453–454, 455(map), 456; secession of states in, 556–558, 566–567, 568; economy during Civil War, 587–588; devastation by Civil War, 610–611, 611(illus.); rebuilding of infrastructure in, 625–626; industry in during 1870–1900, 639–640; crop-lien system in, 640–641; culture of, during 1870–1900, 641–642; white supremacy in, during 1870–1900, 642–645; child labor in, 714. *See also* Civil War (1861–1865); Confederate States of America; Cotton; Plantations; Reconstruction; *specific states*

South Africa, 1266; aid to, 1186; Reagan's policy toward, 1240–1241

South America: earliest population of, 5; early cultures of, 9, 10–12. *See also specific countries*

South Carolina: establishment of, 88; migration to, 125; Regulators of, 152–153, 196; constitution of, 227; Revolutionary War in, 233; slavery in, 248; ratification of Constitution by, 265; suffrage in, 367; secession of, 557

The South Carolina Exposition and Protest (Calhoun), 382–383

South Carolina Gazette, 115

South Dakota, entry into Union, 661

Southeast Asia Treaty Organization (SEATO), 1114

Southern Alliance, 784

Southern Homestead Act (1866), 620

Southern Manifesto, 1131

Southern Pacific Railroad, 539, 817

South Improvement Company, 706

South Korea. *See* Korean War

South Vietnam. *See* Vietnam; Vietnam War

Southwestern Railroad, 717

Soviet Union: revolutionary messages coming from, 912; formal recognition by United States, 1012; Lend-Lease program and, 1017–1018; in World War II, 1023–1024, 1049; domination of Eastern Europe following World War II, 1031; Kennan's Long

Soviet Union *(continued)*
Telegram and, 1050–1051; U.S. alliance with, 1054; reparations from, 1057; nuclear weapons of, 1074; decoded intelligence of, 1080–1081; Elsey's report on, 1088–1089; Eisenhower's attempt to surround strategically, 1111; Eisenhower's policy toward, 1112–1113; invasion of Hungary, 1113; *Sputnik* and, 1122; U-2 spy plane incident and, 1123; militancy about Berlin, 1139; Cuban missile crisis and, 1139–1140; pressure on North Vietnam to end war, 1183; détente with, 1185, 1211–1212; SALT talks with, 1185, 1211, 1212; Carter's policy toward, 1211–1212; invasion of Afghanistan, 1212; boycott of Los Angeles Olympic Games, 1220; Reagan's policy toward, 1240–1241, 1251, 1252(illus.); Korean Airlines plane shot down by, 1241; breakup of, 1264. *See also* Cold War; Communism; Russia

Soylent Green (movie), 1208

Space travel: space race and, 1122, 1123–1124, 1137; moon landing and, 1188

Spain: consolidation of, 21; *conquistadores* and, 29–31, 42; empire of, 29–31, 42, 44(map), 153–154, 168, 305–306, 499–503; governance of empire of, 42–45; English defeat of Armada of, 53; economic policy of, 92; Queen Anne's War and, 105–106; War of Jenkins' Ear and, 109–110; in Revolutionary War, 230; negotiations about Northwest Territory with, 257; negotiations about Mississippi River with, 274; consolidation of territorial claims of, 275; return of Louisiana to France, 298; Monroe Doctrine and, 317; refusal to give up Cuba, 538; Spanish-American War and, 857–863, 862(illus.); surrender of Philippines, 861

Spanish-American War, 857–863, 862(illus.); origins of, 857–860; McKinley's view of, 883–884; opposition to, 884

Spanish Civil War, 1011–1012

Speakeasies, 950, 951(illus.)

Specie Circular (1837), 395

Specie Resumption Act (1875), 633

The Spectator, 115

Spectator sports: during 1865–1910, 744–746; following World War I, 934–936; during 1930s, 992–993; television and, 1100. *See also specific sports*

Spending, to end depression, 990

Spies, during Revolutionary War, 222–223

Spinning, 128(illus.), 342; under putting out system, 335

Spinning machinery, development of, 336

Spinning schools, 114

The Spirit of '76 (movie), 906

Spirit of St. Louis (airplane), 927

Spirit of the Laws (Montesquieu), 225

Spirituals, 460

Spoilsmen, 630

Spoils system, 771–772

Sports. *See* Spectator sports; *specific sports*

Spotsylvania Courthouse, Virginia, battle at, 596

Sputnik, 1122

Spying. *See* Espionage

Squanto, 63

Squatters, 255; in Northwest Territory, 258, 296; Land Act of 1820 and, 312

Stagflation, 1207

Stalin, Joseph, 1019, 1049; World War II and, 1023, 1025; view of postwar world, 1025, 1030, 1054–1055; at Yalta Conference, 1029–1031, 1031(illus.); purges under, 1052; Cominform of, 1060; death of, 1112

Stallone, Sylvester, 1203

Stalwarts, 768

Stamp Act (1765) (England), 161; protests against, 178–182; repeal of, 182

Stamp Act Congress, 180

Stanbery, Henry, 623

Standard Oil Company, 705, 706(illus.), 796, 811, 871

Standard Oil of New Jersey, 830

Standard Oil Trust, 707

Standish, Miles, 64

Stanford University, 756

Stanley, William, 697

Stanton, Edwin M., 608, 622–623

Stanton, Elizabeth Cady, 433, 451, 621

Staple Act (1663) (England), 94

Stark, John, 212

Stark, Molly, 215

Starr, Ellen Gates, 804

Starr, Kenneth, 1281

Star Route Frauds, 776

Star Wars, 1242

State and Local Fiscal Assistance Act (1972), 1188

State government: regulation of trusts by, 708; scope of, 771. *See also* Constitutions (of states); Legislatures

Statehood, procedures for obtaining, 660–661

Staten Island, New York, 49

States' Rights Democratic Party, 1069, 1071

Statute of Religious Freedom (Virginia), 244

Staunton, Virginia, 815

Stay laws, 253

Steamboats, 327–329, 329(illus.); early, 322–323

Steamships, seagoing, 417

Steele, Richard, 113

Steel industry, 705, 707; inventions in, 697; strikes against, during 1937, 997

Steffens, Lincoln, 805, 811

Stegner, Wallace, 832

Stein, Gertrude, 942

Stein, Herbert, 1225

Steinbeck, John, 988, 991

Steinem, Gloria, 1216–1217

Stephens, Alexander, 557, 571, 582, 597, 598–599, 616, 632

Stephens, Uriah S., 717

Stephenson, David, 947

Stepping mill, 430(illus.)

Steuben, Baron von, 213

Stevens, John L., 855–856

Stevens, Thaddeus, 579, 613, 616, 620, 651–652

Stevenson, Adlai, 1105–1106, 1109

Sticks and Stones (Mumford), 738

Stimson, Henry L., 1019, 1047, 1049

Stirling, Kitty, 215

Stock market: Black Friday and (1893), 788; 1929 crash of, 970–971; money culture and, 1246–1247; prosperity and, 1285–1287

Stone, I. F., 1065, 1067

Stone, Lucy, 451, 621, 622

Stone, Oliver, 1246–1247, 1294

Stonewall Inn riot, 1199

Stores: chain, 700, 933; department, 700, 701, 701(illus.), 737, 1246; five-and-ten-cent, 700

Story, Joseph, 364, 387

Stowe, Harriet Beecher, 451–452, 535

Strategic Air Command (SAC), 1111

Strategic Arms Limitation Talks (SALT), 1185, 1211, 1212, 1241, 1266

Strategic Defense Initiative (SDI), 1242

Strauss, Levi, 517

Streetcars, electric, 735, 736(illus.)

Strikes: in Lowell mills, 425–426; by miners at Couer d'Alene, Idaho, 672; against railroads, 716–717, 774, 789–790; against Carnegie's steel plant, 789; against Pullman Palace Car Company, 791–792; of garment workers, 810–811; Roosevelt's (Theodore) handling of, 830; against General Motors, 996–997; during World War II, 1022; following World War II, 1066

String, George Templeton, 572

Strive and Succeed (Alger), 703

Strong, Josiah, 751, 761–762, 850

Stuart, Ruth McEnery, 642

Student Nonviolent Coordinating Committee (SNCC), 1149–1150, 1155

Student protests, 1163; antiwar movement and, 1164–1165, 1177, 1181–1182; silent majority's view of, 1189

Students for a Democratic Society (SDS), 1163

Studs Lonigan trilogy (Farrell), 991

Stuyvesant, Pieter, 50

Submarines: in Civil War, 575; during War I, 890–892, 894; during World War II, 1018, 1023

Submerged Lands Act (1953), 1108

Subscription Library Society, 114

Subsidies, agricultural, during Great Depression, 982

Subtreasuries, 785

Suburbs: development of, 735–737; growth following World War I, 932; growth following World War II, 1096–1097; uniformity *versus* individualism and, 1104; inability of minorities to move to, 1117; white flight to, 1197

Success, gospel of, 703–704

Sudbury, Massachusetts, in 1650, 71(map)

Suez Canal, Egyptian seizure of, 1113–1114

Suffolk Resolves, 191

Suffrage: colonial, 99, 102; for African-Americans, 247, 368, 475, 643, 770, 823–824, 1153–1154; for women, 251, 368–369, 621–622, 819–820, 820(illus.), 821(map), 907–908; growth of, 292; extension during 1820–1840, 366–369, 367(map); male, 366–369, 367(map), 372; for Chinese immigrants, 681

Sugar: slave trade and, 26, 31–32, 145; cultivation in West Indies, 59–61, 145; effect of production on ecology, 144; in South during 1820–1850, 453; Hawaiian, conflict over, 854–856

Sugar Act (1764) (England), 177–178

Sugar Trust, 707

Sullivan, John L., 744

Sullivan, Mark, 832

Sullivan's Island, South Carolina, 220

Summer, Donna, 1202

Sumner, Charles, 542, 612–613, 849, 864

Sumner, William Graham, 806

Sumter, Thomas, 232

The Sun Also Rises (Hemingway), 942

Sunday, Billy, 946, 949, 950

Sung, Kim Il, 1075

The Sunshine Hour (radio program), 950

Supply-side theory, 1223–1224

Supreme Court: establishment of, 267; under Jefferson, 289–290; ruling on Garrett's assistance to runaway slaves, 446; on slavery,

Supreme Court *(continued)*
547–549; undermining of protection of black rights, 636–637, 644; corporate protection provided by, 704; on income tax, 793; on African-American suffrage, 823–824; on citizenship, 866; on wartime dissension, 906; Roosevelt's (Franklin) attempt to reform, 989; on Japanese internment, 1033; racial segregation and, 1119, 1121, 1130–1132, 1195, 1196–1197; on civil rights, 1148–1149, 1238; on criminal justice, 1149; on presidential materials, 1182, 1193; Nixon's appointments to, 1190; on abortion, 1200; Reagan's appointments to, 1238; Bush appointments to, 1271. *See also specific cases*
Susquehannock people, 76
Sussex (ship), 892
Sutter, Johan Augustus, 505–506
Swann v. Charlotte-Mecklenburg Board of Education (1971), 1195
Sweden, postwar, communism in, 1055
Swift, Gustavus, 705
Swift and Company, 705, 871
Swimming, 936
Sylvis, William, 716
Syphilis: transmission to Europeans by Native Americans, 33–34; sex education to prevent among troops, 898
Syria: in 1967 war, 1186; in Yom Kippur War, 1186

Tabula rasa, 112
Taft, Robert, 1015, 1067, 1068, 1105
Taft, William Howard, 827, 832–833, 833, 937; immigration law under, 822; as governor of Philippines, 865; dollar diplomacy of, 871–874
Taft-Hartley Act (1947), 1067
Taino people, 27; decimation by disease, 32; Columbus' description of, 37–38
Taiwan, U.S. agreement with Nationalists and, 1111
Talented Tenth, 825
Talleyrand, prince, 277
Tammany Hall, 544, 742, 955; Cleveland's attacks on, 777
Taney, Roger B., 377, 385–386, 387, 446; on slavery, 548
Tanzania, bombing of U.S. embassy in, 1293
Tappan, Arthur, 450
Tappan, Lewis, 450–451
Tarbell, Ida, 811
Tariff Act (1789), 268

Tariff of Abominations (1828), 374, 376; opposition to, 382–383
Tariffs: sectional tensions over, in 1820s, 374; Jackson's opposition to, 382–384; Panic of 1857 and, 551; to finance Civil War, 580, 581; controversy over, 773; under Cleveland, 779, 792; Taft's position on, 832; reciprocity, for Latin American trade, 853
Tarleton, Sir Banastre, 233
Task system of labor, 461–462
The Tatler, 115
Taxes: on molasses, 108; for social welfare, 134; Stamp Act, 161, 178–182; to support French and Indian War, 167; Regulators' opposition to, 172; British, to pay for French and Indian War, 175–178; Townshend Duties, 182–185, 187; on tea, 187–190; to support Revolutionary War, 216; Congressional authority of levy, 229–230; attempt to ease burden of, 253–254; approved by first Congress, 269; western opposition to, 275–276; to support public schools, 432; Mexican-American War and, 512; to finance Civil War, 580, 581; for rebuilding of South, 625; to exclude black vote, 643; enactment of income tax, 793; to finance World War I, 900; progressive, 900; Mellon's position on, 954; on income, establishment of modern system of, 1022; under Kennedy, 1137–1138; under Johnson, 1144; tax revolt and, 1222–1227; under Reagan, 1235, 1236, 1251; under Bush, 1270. *See also* Tariffs
Taylor, Augustine Deodat, 736
Taylor, Frederick W., 710, 933
Taylor, Walter, 599(illus.), 600
Taylor, Zachary, 509, 510, 511, 515; as president, 516, 528, 530
Tea, tax on, 187–190
Tea Act (1773) (England), 188–189
Teachers, training of, 432–433
Tea parties, 189–190, 189(illus.)
Technological innovations: following World War I, 930; automation and, 1098; hours of work and, 1288. *See also* Industrial revolution; Inventions; *specific innovations*
Tecumseh, 303, 304(illus.), 310
Teenagers, rock and roll and, 1102–1103
Tejanos, 500–501, 502, 503
Telecommunications Reform Act (1996), 1290
Telegraph: development of, 418; during Mexican-American War, 510–511; invention of, 694, 696; foreign policy and, 849–850
Telephone: invention of, 694, 696; adoption of, 696–697, 930
Televangelists, 1222; political influence of, 1227

Television, 1091–1092; myth of the West in, 685; during 1945–1960, 1099–1100; religious programs on, 1102, 1222, 1227; debasement of American culture by, 1104; interpretation of messages viewed on, 1104; use in politics, 1106, 1125, 1136–1137, 1252–1253, 1273, 1273(illus.); coverage of Kennedy assassination, 1134; coverage of Birmingham police confrontation of civil rights demonstrators, 1151, 1152(illus.); coverage of 1968 Democratic convention, 1167; during 1960s and 1970s, 1202–1203; music, 1247–1248; during 1990s, 1290–1291; Simpson trial and, 1291–1292

Teller, Edward, 1074, 1122

Teller Amendment, 859

Temperance, 428–429, 753–754

Temples, Olmec, 10

Tenant farming: southern, during 1820–1850, 474–475; by African-Americans following Civil war, 627–629, 629(map); during Great Depression, 982. *See also* Sharecropping

The Ten Commandments (movie), 1102

Tenements, 738, 739(illus.); tenement districts in cities and, 412, 413; visiting professionals in, 810(illus.); African-Americans in, 943

Tennent, Gilbert, 150

Tennent, William, 150

Tennessee: suffrage in, 366; in Civil War, 594; Scopes trial and, 949, 964–966

Tennessee Coal and Iron Company, 833

Tennessee Valley Authority (TVA), 983–984, 997, 1108

Tennis, 936

Tenochtitlán, 10, 11(illus.), 29

Tenskwatawa (The Prophet), 303

Tenth Michigan Volunteers, 584

Tenure of Office Act (1867), 622–623

Teotihuacán, 10

Terrell, Mary Church, 809

Territories, in West, 659–660

Terrorism: during Reagan administration, 1244–1245; preparation for, 1292. *See also* Bombings; Ku Klux Klan (KKK)

Terry, Eli, 335

Terry, Randall, 1228

Tesla, Nikola, 698

Tet Offensive, 1165–1166

Texas: Mexican encouragement of American settlement in, 500; American petition for independence of, 501; battle at Alamo and, 501–502, 502(illus.); annexation of, 503, 506–509; independence granted to, 503; admission as state, 508, 530; secession of, 557; Democratic resurgence in, 634

Texas (ship), 852

Texas fever, 672

Texas longhorns, 672

Textile production: English, 18, 19–20; English woolen cloth industry and, 18, 19–20; colonial, as protest, 185; at home, 185, 332; by women during Revolutionary War, 214; development of factories for, 336–337; Embargo of 1807 and, 341; in factories, 423–426, 426(illus.); in South during 1870–1900, 639

Thames, battle of (1813), 310

Thanksgiving, first, 63

Thayer, Eli, 541

Thayer, W. M., 690

Thayer, Webster, 946

Theaters, during 1865–1910, 743–744

The Theory of Business Enterprise (Veblen), 808

A Theory of the Leisure Class (Veblen), 808

Thieu, Nguyen Van, 1183

Third Party System, 546

Thirteenth Amendment, ratification of, 615

This Is War (radio program), 1032

This Side of Paradise (Fitzgerald), 942

Tho, Le Duc, 1183

Thomas, Clarence, 1271

Thomas, Norman, 960, 1017–1018

Thomas, Seth, 335

Thomas Aquinas, St., 22

Thoreau, Henry David, 439, 450–451, 512, 527

Thornton, Mrs. William, 477

Thoughts on Government (Adams), 227

Three-fifths compromise, 263

Three Little Pigs (movie), 994

Three Mile Island, 1208

Three Rivers, Canada, 48

Tiananmen Square demonstration, 1267

Tilden, Samuel J., 637

Tillman, Ben "Pitchfork," 643, 793

Timber Culture Act (1873), 659

Timbuktu, 14

Time payment schemes, 932

"The Times They Are A-Changin'" (song), 1163

Timucua people, 46

Tin cans, 418, 696

Tin Lizzie, 930

Tipitapa (1927), Peace of, 959

Tippecanoe, battle at, 304

"Tippecanoe and Tyler Too," 398

Tito, Josip Broz, 1279

Tituba, 103

Tobacco: European adoption of, 32, 55; in West Indies, 59; production in Chesapeake region, 61–62, 142, 345; slavery and, 142, 145(illus.), 146; cultivation of, 145(illus.), 146; prices of,

Tobacco (continued)
174; production following Revolutionary War, 252; Panic of 1819 and, 314; gang labor and, 462
Tocqueville, Alexis de, 427, 453, 1207
Todd, Mary, 552
Tojo, Hideki, 1019
Toledo, Ohio, Jones as mayor of, 816
Toltec people, 9, 10, 11(illus.)
Tom Sawyer (Twain), 641
Tonkin Gulf Resolution (1964), 1157, 1182
Tontine Society, 292
Tools, Native American, early, 8
Tordesillas, Treaty of (1494), 28
Tories, 222. See also Loyalists
Torture mask, 465(illus.)
To Secure These Rights, 1068
Townsend, Francis E., 984–985
Townshend, Charles, 108, 176, 182–183
Townshend Duties, 161, 182–185; repeal of, 187
Toynbee Hall, 804
Toyota, 1206
Tracy, Benjamin F., 852
Trade: of medieval Europe, 16–17; Dutch, 92, 93–94, 95; English, 93, 94–97; colonial, with West Indies, 108–109, 129, 137–138, 174; international contact brought about by, 130; search for new partners for, 253; with England, 307, 308; with France, 307, 308; with China, 340, 866–867; during 1865–1915, 850, 851(illus.); as impetus for expansionism, 850; with Hawaiian Islands, 854–856; foreign competition and, 1206; in software and entertainment products, 1291. See also Commerce; Maritime commerce; Smuggling
Trade Acts. See Acts of Trade (England)
Trade associations, 1224
Trade fairs, 490
Trade unions. See Unions
Trading with the Enemy Act (1917), 904
Trafalgar, Battle of, 307
Trail of Tears, 381(map), 382
Transcendentalism, during 1820–1850, 438–439
Transportation: by rivers and streams, 326(map), 327; migration to West and, 493; racial segregation and, 643–644; cities during 1865–1910 and, 734–737. See also Railroads; Roads
Transylvania Company, 172
Travis, Joseph, 466
Treasury Department, 1238
Treatise on Domestic Economy (Beecher), 431
Tredegar Iron Works, 454, 569

Trenchard, John, 113
Trent affair, 576–577
Triangle Shirtwaist Company fire, 811
Trilateral Statement and Annex (1994), 1279
Tripartite Pact, 1018
Triple Entente, 888
Trist, Nicholas P., 510, 512
Trolleys, 735, 736(illus.)
Troup, George M., 380
Trucking industry, 936
Truman, Bess Wallace, 1066
Truman, Harry S, 1029, 1031, 1051, 1052; atomic bomb and, 1047–1049; foreign policy of, 1055, 1056–1064, 1088–1090; Truman Doctrine and, 1059–1060; NATO proposed by, 1062–1063; domestic policy of, 1064–1065, 1066–1069, 1072; postwar economy and, 1065–1066; early life and career of, 1066–1067; in election of 1948, 1068, 1069–1071, 1070–1071, 1070(illus.); civil rights advocacy of, 1068–1069; Fair Deal of, 1072; China and, 1073–1074; Korean War and, 1074–1076, 1076(map); conflict with MacArthur, 1077; declines to run for reelection, 1105
Truman Doctrine, 1059–1060
Trumbull, Lyman, 613
Trusts: creation of, 707; regulation of, 707–709; public dislike of, 812; Roosevelt's (Theodore) approach to, 829–830; government suits against, 833
Truth, Sojourner, 449, 451, 452(illus.), 469
Tryon, William, 153, 172
Tubman, Harriet, 449, 464
Tugwell, Rexford Guy, 967
Tunney, Gene, 934–935
Turkey: Stalin's overtures to, 1059; U.S. aid to, 1059
Turner, Frederick Jackson, 297, 684–685, 850
Turner, Henry M., 626
Turner, Nat, 466
Turner, Roscoe, 939(illus.)
Turnpikes, 327
Tuscarora people, 124, 231
Tuskegee Airmen, 1038(illus.)
Tuskegee Institute, 644
"Tutti Frutti" (song), 1103
TWA flight 847 hijacking, 1245
Twain, Mark, 641–642, 684, 765; realism and, 747
Tweed, William M., 742
Tweed Ring, 742
Twelve Years a Slave (Northrup), 534

Twenty-one Demands, 875

Two Treatises on Government (Locke), 98

Tydings, Millard, 1082–1084

Tyler, John: as president, 366, 398; in election of 1840, 397–398; on annexation of Texas, 507

Typewriter: invention of, 696; women's employment and, 713

Typhoid fever, water pollution and, 740

Typhus, among prisoners of war, 223

U. S. A. (Dos Passos), 942

Ukraine, independence of, 1264

Uncle Remus: His Songs and Sayings (Harris), 641

Uncle Tom's Cabin (Stowe), 451–452

Underground Railroad, 445–446, 451, 464, 526, 534

Underwood Tariff Act (1913), 836–837

Unemployment: Panic of 1819 and, 314; Panic of 1873 and, 633; poverty due to, during 1870–1900, 711; during depression of 1893, 789, 791; during Great Depression, 967, 972, 974; during recession of 1937–1938, 990; New Deal and, 1001; following World War II, 1065; during Korean War, 1078; among Native Americans, 1198; during 1970s, 1206(illus.)

Unidentified flying objects (UFOs), 1122–1123

Union: blockade of Confederate ports, 570; navy of, 575, 576; conscription in, 579–580; army of, 584, 590–591, 591(illus.). *See also* Civil War (1861–1865); North

Union Fire Company, 114

Union of Soviet Socialist Republics. *See* Soviet Union

Union Pacific Railroad, 630, 661, 717, 788

Union Park Gardens, 901

Union Party, 596, 988

Unions, 715–719; in 1820–1850, 422–423; in mining, 671–672; hostility to women, 712, 902; AFL, 715, 719, 724–726, 826, 938, 995–996, 999, 1098; origins of, 715–717; African-Americans and, 716, 717, 944, 1039; women in, 716, 810–811, 997; Chinese immigrants barred from, 717; Knights of Labor, 717–719, 724, 726; IWW, 825, 826–827, 904–905; legislation governing, 937; Red Scare and, 938; Mexican-Americans in, 974; during 1933–1938, 995–997, 996(illus.); CIO, 996, 997, 1068, 1098; following World War II, 1066, 1098; communism and, 1068; during 1980s, 1250–1251; Solidarity, in Poland, 1263. *See also* Strikes

Union Seminary, 468

Unitarianism, 354

United Automobile Workers (UAW), 996–997, 1068, 1098

United Confederate Veterans, 641

United Daughters of the Confederacy, 641

United Farm Workers (UFW), 1197, 1198(illus.)

United Fruit Company, 958, 1115

United Mine Workers, 995, 1022

United Nations: Yalta Conference agreement on, 1030; nuclear weapons and, 1058; Korean War and, 1075

United Negro Improvement Association (UNIA), 943, 944(illus.)

U.S. Army: African-Americans in, 860, 897–898, 1037; in Spanish-American War, 860; in 1916, 893; mobilization for World War I, 896–899; segregation of, 897; women in, 897, 910, 910(illus.); in 1940, 1022. *See also* Draft

U.S. Forest Service, 831

U.S. Navy: in 1880s, 848; buildup of, 852; women in, 897; African-Americans in, 1037

United States Chamber of Commerce, 812

United States Housing Corporation (USHC), 901

United States Steel Corporation, 707, 830, 902, 997; antitrust suit against, 833

United States v. *Cruikshank* (1876), 636–637

United States v. *Harris* (1883), 637

United States v. *Reynolds* (1878), 660

United Tailoresses Society, 393

United Textile Workers, 995

Universalists, 354

Universities. *See* Colleges and universities; *specific universities*

University of California at Berkeley, 1163

University of California at Los Angeles (UCLA), 1292

University of California Medical School at Davis, 1195

University of Chicago, 756

University of Michigan, 1164

University of Mississippi, 1148–1149

University of Pennsylvania, 113, 152

University of South Carolina, 625

Upper class. *See* Elites

Urban renewal projects, displacement of minorities by, 1117

U.S.A. (Dos Passos), 991

U.S.S.R. *See* Soviet Union

Utah: admission as state, 532; entry into Union, 661

Ute people, 662

Utopia (More), 19

Utopian societies, 435–436; socialist, 703
Utrecht, Treaty of (1713), 105

Valentino, Rudolph, 933–934
Vallance, Hollie, 1269(illus.)
Vallandigham, Clement L., 583
Valley Forge, Pennsylvania, Continental Army at, 199–201, 212
Van Buren, Martin, 371–372, 377, 507, 516; support of Jackson, 375; election as president, 391; as president, 395, 396–397
Vance, Dazzy, 935
Vandenberg, Arthur, 1015, 1043–1044, 1058, 1059, 1060, 1063, 1068
Vanderbilt, William K., 673
Vanderbilt University, 756
Vanzetti, Bartolomeo, 946
Vaqueros, 500
Vardaman, James K., 823
Vassar College, 941
Vaudeville, 743–744
V-chips, 1290
Veblen, Thorsten, 808
Venereal diseases, sex education to prevent among troops, 898
Venezuela, boundary dispute with British Guiana, 854
Venona Intercepts, 1080–1081
Vergennes, Comte de, 213
Vermont: creation of, 153; Green Mountain Boys of, 153, 169, 203, 257; establishment of, 169; constitution of, 226; abolishment of slavery in, 246; independence from New York, 257
Verrazzano, Giovanni da, 46
Versailles, Treaty of (1919), 912; controversy over ratification of, 913–915, 914(illus.)
Vertical integration, 705, 706, 706(illus.)
Vesey, Denmark, 465–466, 470
Vespucci, Amerigo, 28
Veterans Administration mortgages, 1097
Veto, executive. *See* Executive veto
Viceroys, Spanish, 42
Vicksburg, Virginia, Confederate surrender of, 593–594
Victor Emmanuel II, king of Italy, 1024
Vidal, Gore, 1001
Vietcong, 1141, 1156, 1181
Vietnam: Eisenhower's policy toward, 1114; protest against Diem government in, 1141, 1142(illus.); lifting of trade embargo and, 1279
Vietnamization policy, 1181

Vietnam War, 1156–1161, 1158(map); events leading to, 1074; American military advisors and, 1141–1142; escalation under Johnson, 1156–1158; American participation in, 1158–1160, 1159(illus.), 1160(illus.); soldiers fighting in, 1160–1161; antiwar movement and, 1164–1165, 1177, 1181–1182; Tet Offensive and, 1165–1166; under Nixon, 1177, 1180–1183; end of, 1183–1184; movies about, 1203
Vigilance committees, 556
Viking people, 16
Villa, Francisco "Pancho," 877–878, 878(illus.)
Vincennes, 231
Vincent, John, 752
Vinland, 16
Violence: domestic, in cities during 1820–1850, 413; toward slaves, 476–477; in gold mining camps, 518; in Kansas, in 1856, 542; in western towns, 678; television portrayal of, 1290; school shootings, 1291. *See also specific forms of violence*
Virginia: English claim to, 52; English settlement of, 53–56; population in mid-1600s, 56; conflict between colonists and Native Americans in, 76–77, 79–81; elite families of, 101, 102; migration to, 124; European migration to, 126; militia battles with loyalists in, 205; Revolutionary War in, 234; manumission of slaves in, 248; ratification of Constitution by, 265–266; secession of, 568; in Civil War, 570, 572, 573–574, 591–594, 595(map); Democratic resurgence in, 634. *See also* Chesapeake region
Virginia (ironclad ship), 576
Virginia Company of London, 54, 55
Virginia Company of Plymouth, 53, 62–63
Virginia Dynasty, 312
Virginia Plan, 261
Virginia resolution (1776), 207
Virginia Resolution (1798), 278
Virginia Resolves (Henry), 179
Virginius (ship), 849
The Virtues of Slavery, The Impossibility of Emancipation (Dew), 482–483
Volcker, Paul, 1210
Volstead Act, 906–908
Volunteers in Service to America (VISTA), 1145
Vorster, Balthazar, 1186
Voting: political machines and, 741; civil rights movement and, 1153–1154. *See also* Elections; National elections; Suffrage
Voting Rights Act (1965), 1154, 1195, 1197

W. B. Dinsmore ship, 417(illus.)

Wade, Benjamin, 613

Wade-Davis Bill (1863), 613

Wade-Davis Manifesto, 613

Wages: during Revolutionary War, protests over, 219; free labor and, 422; in Lowell mills, 425–426; during 1870–1900, 711; of women in 1880s, 712; reduction during depression of 1893, 791; during World War I, 901, 902; of Mexicans, 903; during Great Depression, 971, 974; during World War II, 1022, 1043; following World War II, 1092; during 1980s, 1250

Wage slavery, 547

Wagner Act, 995

Wainstock, David, 1049

Waiting for Lefty (Odets), 991

Wake Island, American claim to, 863

Walden, Or Life in the Woods (Thoreau), 439

Walden Pond, 439

Waldo, Albigense, 199

Waldseemüller, Martin, 28

Walesa, Lech, 1263

Walker, David, 448, 466, 469

Walker, William, 538

Wallace, George, 1151, 1153–1154, 1169

Wallace, Henry A., 982, 989, 1029, 1068, 1089, 1090

Wall Street. *See* Stock market

Wall Street (movie), 1246–1247

Wal-Mart, 1291

Walpole, Robert, 106–107

Walsh, Lawrence E., 1246

Walt Disney, 1246

Waltham, Massachusetts, 410; manufacturing in, 423–424

Wampanoag people, 74

Wanamaker, John, 780

Wanamaker's, 700

War bonds, during World War II, 1022

Ward, Aaron Montgomery, 700

Ward, Lester Frank, 807–808

Wards Cove v. *Atonio* (1989), 1238

Warfare: impact on colonial cities, 134–135; British *versus* colonial manner of, 167; during Revolutionary War, 211; submarine, 575, 890–892, 894, 1018, 1023; tactics of, during Civil War, 585; technology of, during Civil War, 585; Grant's strategy for, 595; radar and, in World War II, 1025; New Look defense strategy and, 1110–1111. *See also* Guerrilla warfare; *specific conflicts*

War Hawks, 309, 310, 512

War Industries Board (WIB), 900–901

War Labor Disputes Act (1943), 1022

Warner, Charles Dudley, 765

Warner Brothers, 1290

War of 1812, 309–311; road construction and, 327; commerce and, 341; Republican views and, 371

War of Jenkins's Ear (War of the Austrian Succession) (1740–1748), 109–110, 134–135, 149, 164

War of the League of Augsberg, 105

War of the Roses (1455), 21

War of the Spanish Succession. *See* Queen Anne's War

The War of the Worlds (Wells), 995

War on poverty, 1144–1145

War posters, during World War II, 1032

War Powers Act (1973), 1204

War Production Board (WPB), 1020

War Refugee Board, 1028

Warren, Earl, 1069, 1143, 1190; Supreme Court under, 1130, 1148–1149

Warren, Charles, 242

Warren, Mercy Otis, 242–243, 264–265, 293

Warren Bridge, 387

Warren Commission, 1143

Warsaw Pact, 1064, 1264

Washington, Booker T., 644, 824, 831

Washington, George, 152, 217, 594; in Ohio Valley conflict, 154; in French and Indian War, 164, 165, 168; on Coercive Acts, 190; Continental Army and, 199–201, 204, 212–213, 219, 251–252; crossing of Delaware River by, 210; spies and, 222; Constitution and, 259, 260; as president, 267, 273, 276; opposition to political parties, 276; death of, 325

Washington, Martha, 215

Washington, D. C., government of, 743

Washington, entry into Union, 661

Washington Naval Treaty, 959

Washita, battle of, 665

Watergate crisis, 1191–1194

Water pollution, during 1865–1910, 740

Water Quality Improvement Act, 1208

Waters, Ethel, 945

Watkins, Frances, 469(illus.)

Watson, Thomas, 785, 793, 794, 795

Watt, James G., 1237

Watterson, Henry, 639

Wattleton, Faye, 1228

Wayne, Anthony, 275

Wealth: colonial rise of, 122; in colonial cities and merchant towns, 131–132; changing cultural attitudes about, 134; in cities,

Wealth *(continued)*
1820–1850, 348, 410, 737; in postwar South, 641; Americans' preoccupation with, 703. *See also* Income distribution

The Wealth of Nations (Smith), 270, 702

Wea people, resettlement of, 541

Weapons: firearm production and, 334–335; of Cavalry, 666–667; in western towns, 678–679; sale to Iran, 1245–1246; in schools, 1291. *See also* Arms races; Nuclear weapons

Weasel Bear, Louise, 656

Weaver, James Baird, 786, 787

Weaving, 342. *See also* Textile production

Webster, Daniel, 291, 310, 363, 387, 418, 513; support of Bank of the U.S., 385; Whig Party and, 388; on slavery, 532, 533, 534, 535(illus.)

Webster, Noah, 293(illus.), 294

Webster v. *Reproductive Health Services* (1989), 1271

Weem, Parson, 293

Weinberger, Caspar, 1240

Weismuller, Johnny, 936

Welch, Joseph, 1109

Weld, Theodore Dwight, 449, 451

Welfare. *See* Social welfare

Welfare capitalism, 937

Welles, Gideon, 575

Welles, Orson, 988, 995

Welles, Sumner, 1056

Wells, David A., 696

Wells, H. G., 995

Wells-Barnett, Ida, 824

Wellstone, Paul D., 1298

Wentworth, Benning, 219

"We Shall Overcome" (song), 1148

West, 485–520; Revolutionary War in, 224(map), 230–231; cession of land in, 255, 256(map); settlement of, 255–259, 656–661, 660(illus.); British troops in, 256–257; Northwest Ordinance and, 258–259, 258(map); migration to, difficulty of, 485–488, 494–497, 497(illus.), 522–523; manifest destiny and, 489; forces fueling migration to, 489–490, 491–494; development of, sponsors and entrepreneurs and, 490–491; government help for development of, 491; maps and journals of, 491; trails in, 495(map); Native Americans in, 497–498; slavery in, 513–516; Civil War in, 574–575; diversity of region, 657; mining in, 670–672; life in towns of, 677–679; as agrarian Eden, myth of, 683–684; impact of World War II on, 1035. *See also* Frontier; Mexico; Northwest Territory; *specific states*

West, Mae, 994

West, Thomas, Baron De la Warr, 54–55

Western Emigration Societies, 504

Westerns, 683–684

Western Union, 696, 901

West Indies: Columbus' voyages to, 27–28; French claims in, 48; sugar and slavery in, 59–61, 60(illus.); slaves from, 87; dependencies between northern colonies and, 95–96; trade with England, 96(illus.); colonial trade with, 108–109, 129, 137–138, 174; in French and Indian War, 168; decrees closing to American ships, 253; Roosevelt Corollary to Monroe Doctrine and, 869–870; Wilson's policy toward, 876. *See also specific islands*

Westinghouse, George, 698

Westinghouse Corporation, 902

Westinghouse Electric Company, 698

Westmoreland, William, 1158–1159, 1165

Weston, Thomas, 63

The West Wing (television show), 1290

Wethersfield, Connecticut, 68

Weyerhaeuser, Frederick, 676

Weyl, Walter, 814

Weyler, Valeriano, 857, 858

Weyrich, Paul, 1227

Wheat: in Chesapeake region, 143; grain reaper and, 418; price of, 782

Wheatley, Phyllis, 248

Wheeler, Edward L., 683

Wheeling, West Virginia, 169

Whig Party: development of, 388–391; regional support for, 390–391; in election of 1840, 397–398; in election of 1844, 507, 508; opposition to Mexican-American War, 512; in election of 1848, 515; slavery and, 530; on slavery, 533; in election of 1852, 536; Kansas-Nebraska Act and, 540, 541; demise of, 545

Whiskey Rebellion, 275–276, 283–284

Whiskey Ring, 631

White, John, 52, 52(illus.), 53

White, William Allen, 795, 802–803, 813, 816, 818, 836, 956

"White Christmas" (song), 1033

White Citizens Councils, 1119, 1120–1121

White Collar (Mills), 1104

White-collar workers, during 1865–1910, 737–738

Whitefield, George, 150, 151(illus.)

Whitewater scandal, 1275–1276

Whitlock, Brand, 769

Whitman, Walt, 439

Whitney, Eli, 334–335, 346, 423

Whittier, John Greenleaf, on slavery, 533

"Whole Lotta Loving" (song), 1103

Why Johnny Can't Read, 1104
Wicker, Tom, 1168, 1187, 1203
Wild and Scenic Rivers Act (1968), 1147
Wilderness Act (1964), 1147
Wilderness Road, 172
Wild West and Congress of Rough Riders, 684
Wild West shows, 684
Wilkes, Charles, 577
Wilkes, John, 176
Wilkinson, James, 257, 299
Willamette Valley, Oregon, 504
William III, king of England, 100
William of Orange, 98, 99, 104
Williamsburg African Church, 248
Williams, Roger, 67
Williams, "Smokey Joe," 936
Williams, William Carlos, 942
Willkie, Wendell, 1015–1016
Wills, Helen, 936
Wilmot, David, 513
Wilmot Proviso (1846), 513–515, 528; Lincoln's
    support of, 552
Wilson, Charles E., 1107
Wilson, James, 218–219
Wilson, Woodrow, 817, 827–828; immigration
    law under, 822; in election of 1912, 835, 836,
    842–844; expansion of presidential power
    under, 836; views on foreign policy, 874–
    875; Far East policy of, 875–876; Central
    America and Caribbean policy of, 876;
    Mexican Revolution and, 876–879; neutrality
    and, 888–892; in election of 1916, 892–894;
    support of women's suffrage, 907; World War
    I and, 908; Fourteen Points of, 911–913; view
    of postwar world, 911–913, 1054; League of
    Nations and, 913–915; contempt for Lenin,
    1054
Wilson-Gorman Act (1894), 792–793
Windmills, in West, 674
Windsor, Connecticut, 68
Winfield, Frank, 700
Wingina, 52
The Winning of the West (Roosevelt), 684
Winthrop, Hannah, 215–216
Winthrop, John, 65, 66, 68, 127
Winthrop, John, Jr., 112
Wisconsin: admission as state, 530; progressive
    reform in, 816–817
Wisconsin Idea, 814, 817
Witchcraft, 102–104
Wobblies, 825, 826–827, 904–905
Wolcott, Marion Post, 992
Wolfe, James, 168, 169(illus.)
Wolfe, Thomas, 766

Women: in medieval Europe, 15; colonial,
    58–59, 71, 127; Native American, 73, 1039;
    slave, sexual exploitation of, 147, 463; protest
    against British taxes, 181, 184–185, 192,
    193(illus.); textile production by, 185, 214,
    332; during Revolutionary War, 200, 214–216,
    218; patriot view of, 222; following Revolu-
    tionary War, 248–251; coverture and, 249;
    education during 1783–1800, 249, 250; as
    republican virtue, 250(illus.); suffrage for,
    251, 368–369, 621–622, 819–820, 820(illus.),
    821(map), 907–908; butter and cheese pro-
    duction by, 332; in farm households, 342,
    415–416, 680; employment during 1790–1820,
    351; guidebooks on child rearing and mother-
    ing for, 351; increasing expectations for in-
    dependence and social justice, 351; number
    of children borne by, 352; church activi-
    ties of, 353, 355–356; employment during
    1820–1840, 393; unionization of, 393; middle-
    class, in cities, 410–411; putting-out system
    and, 421; employment in Lowell mills,
    424–426; temperance movement and, 429,
    753–754; roles during 1820–1850, 431; educa-
    tion during 1820–1850, 432–433; sentimental
    novels enjoyed by, 437; rights in North linked
    to women's rights under slavery, 451; emanci-
    pation activities of, 451–452; abolitionist
    literature written by, 452; slave, work of,
    462–463; paternalism of planters toward,
    471–472; migration to West and, 496–497;
    Civil War and, 588–589, 588(illus.); as army
    nurses during Civil War, 589; employment
    during Civil War, 589; African-American,
    627; New South literature written by, 642;
    attempts to civilize western towns, 679;
    unions' hostility toward, 712; employment
    during 1870–1900, 712–713, 713(illus.); in
    unions, 716, 810–811, 997; education during
    1865–1910, 748; employment in professional
    positions, 748–749; during 1865–1910,
    748–750; female-dominated institutions
    created by, 749–750, 749(illus.); Alliance
    Movement and, 785; voluntary organizations
    created by, 809–810; of Progressive Era, 818;
    in Congress, first, 896; in armed forces, 897,
    910, 910(illus.), 1039; employment during
    World War I, 902, 904(illus.); unions' hostility
    to, 902; employment following World War I,
    938; new morality of 1920s and, 939–942; in
    Ku Klux Klan, 947, 948(illus.); employment
    during Great Depression, 973; magazines for,
    992; employment during 1930s, 999–1000;
    during 1930s, 999–1001; New Deal and, 1000;

Women (*continued*)
employment during World War II, 1035–1037, 1036(illus.); employment during 1950s, 1117; during 1950s, 1117–1118, 1118(illus.); employment in 1960s and 1970s, 1199; education during 1960s and 1970s, 1200, 1201(illus.); traditional, Schlafly's defense of, 1200–1201, 1217–1218; poverty among, 1201–1202; as single parents, 1201–1202; sexual harassment of, 1271. *See also* Equal Rights Amendment (ERA); Matrilinealism; Sex discrimination

Women and Economics (Gilman), 827

Women's Christian Temperance Union (WCTU), 754, 809

Women's club movement, 749–750, 749(illus.)

Women's Convention, 749(illus.)

Women's Convention of the Black Baptist Church, 809

Women's Home Companion magazine, 1100

Women's Industrial Club, 749(illus.)

Women's liberation movement, 1199–1202, 1216–1217

Women's Loyal Union, 824

Women's National Indian Association (WNIA), 667

Women's Peace Party, 893

Women's rights movement: early, 428, 433–434; of Progressive Era, 827. *See also* Women's liberation movement

Women's Trade Union League, 809

Wood, Grant, 992

Wood, Leonard, 865, 920

Woodlands people, 6, 72–73

Woods, Rosemary, 1193

Wool Act (1699) (England), 94, 109

Woolen cloth industry: English, 18, 19–20; child labor in, 714

Woolman, John, 135

Woolworth, 700

Woolworth Building, 737

Worcester v. *Georgia* (1832), 380

Work: of slaves, 461–463. *See also* Employment; Unemployment

Work and Win (Alger), 703

Workers: in cities, 349–350, 738; itinerant, in western settlements, 416; during 1870–1900, 712–714, 713(illus.); following World War I, 937–938; replacement by machines, 1098

Workies, 392

Workingmen's parties, 391–393, 394(illus.), 395

Workman's Compensation Act, 838

Work place: home as, 185, 332. *See also* Factories

Work relations, canals and, 332

Works Progress Administration (WPA), 987–988, 987(illus.), 1000, 1028–1029

World Court, 920

World Health Organization (WHO), 1231

World Series, in 1919, 917

World Trade Center bombing, 1293

World War I: women's suffrage and, 820, 907–908; China and, 875; U.S. entry into, 886–887; American neutrality and, 888–892; election of 1916 and, 892–894, 894(map); Wilson's attempt to avoid entering, 894–896; American entry into, 895–896; U.S. Army and, 896–899; mobilization for, 899–901; financing of, 900; workers during, 901–903; handling of dissension during, 903–905; public unity during, 903–906; prohibition during, 906–907; on Western Front, 908–910, 909(map); impact of American involvement in, 910; peace negotiations following, 911–913; controversy over League of Nations and, 913–915

World War II: Pearl Harbor attack and, 1008, 1019; events leading up to, 1010–1013; American neutrality and, 1013–1015; election of 1940 and, 1015–1016, 1016(map); in Europe, 1017–1018, 1023–1025, 1024(map); in Pacific, 1018–1019, 1040–1041, 1041(map); American entry into, 1019; mobilization for, 1019–1023; D-Day and, 1025–1026; Holocaust and, 1027–1028, 1027(illus.); politics during, 1028–1029, 1030(map); Yalta Conference and, 1029–1031, 1031(illus.); propaganda and popular culture and, 1032–1033; Japanese internment during, 1033–1034; breakdown of regional differences due to, 1034–1035; women's employment during, 1035–1037, 1036(illus.); African-Americans during, 1037–1039, 1038(illus.); bombing of Japan and, 1042, 1043(illus.), 1047–1049; casualties during, 1042; legacy of, 1042–1044

World Wide Web, 1283

Wounded Knee, South Dakota, occupation by AIM members, 1198

Wounded Knee massacre, 653–656, 654(illus.)

Wozniak, Steve, 1283

Wright, Frances, 448

Wright, Orville, 697

Wright, Richard, 988, 991, 992

Wright, Wilbur, 697

Writs of Assistance, 176

Wyandot people: taking of lands from, 257; resettlement of, 497

Wyman, David, 1028

The X-Files (television show), 1294
XIT Ranch, 673
XYZ Affair, 277

Yalta Conference, 1029–1031, 1031(illus.)
Yamasee people, 77, 86, 106, 124
Yazoo Land Company, 291
Yellow Bird, 655
Yellow fever, Panama Canal and, 846
Yellow journalism, 857
Yellowstone National Park, 677, 831
Yeltsin, Boris, 1264, 1266
Yeomen, southern, 473–474, 479
Yezierska, Anzia, 727
Yom Kippur War, 1186

Yorktown (ship), 1040
Young America movement, 537
Young, Brigham, 435
Young, Charles, 897
Young Men's Moral and Literary Society, 468
Yugoslavia, Clinton's policy toward, 1279–1280
Yuppies, 1247

Zenger, John Peter, 113
Zhou Enlai, 1185
Ziegfield Follies girls, 939(illus.)
Zimmerman, Arthur, 895
Zimmerman, Robert, 1162–1163
Zoot-suiters, 1039
Zuñi people, 943

ALASKA
(U.S.)

GREENLAND
(DENMARK)

ICELAND

CANADA

60°N

IREL

UNITED STATES

40°N

PORTUGA

Azores

Midway Is.

ATLANTIC OCEAN

WESTERN
SAHARA
(MOROCCO)

M

Bermuda

Hawaiian Is.

BAHAMAS

MEXICO

DOMINICAN REP.
CUBA   Virgin Is.
JAMAICA HAITI   ST. KITTS AND NEVIS
BELIZE   Puerto Rico   ANTIGUA AND BARBUDA
HONDURAS   DOMINICA
                                   BARBADOS
GUATEMALA   ST. LUCIA   ST. VINCENT AND
EL SALVADOR NICARAGUA GRENADA   THE GRENADINES

20°N

MAURI

CAPE
VERDE   SENEGAL

GAMBIA

GUINEA-BISSAU   GUINEA

PACIFIC OCEAN

COSTA RICA

PANAMA

TRINIDAD AND TOBAGO
VENEZUELA   GUYANA

COLOMBIA

SURINAM

FR. GUIANA

SIERRA
LEONE

LIBERIA

0°

SÃO T

Equator

Galapagos Is.

ECUADOR

PERU

BRAZIL

WESTERN
SAMOA

BOLIVIA

20°S

TONGA

PARAGUAY

Easter Is.

CHILE

URUGUAY

40°S

ARGENTINA

Falkland Is.

160°W   140°W   120°W   100°W   80°W   60°W   40°W   20°W

60°S

80°S